D1422627

SUN & MOON SIGNS

JULIA AND DEREK PARKER

Photography by Monique le Luhandre
Illustrations by Danuta Mayer

Editor **Tom Fraser**
Art Editor **Ursula Dawson**
Managing Editor **Krystyna Mayer**
Managing Art Editor **Derek Coombes**
Production **Antony Heller**

This edition published in Great Britain in 1996 by
Covent Garden Books
9 Henrietta Street
London WC2E 8PS

Material in this book was previously published as 12 separate volumes, under the title of "Sun and Moon Signs Library".

A CIP catalogue record for this book is available from the British Library

ISBN 0-7513-0396-8

Printed and bound in the United States by R. R. Donnelley and Sons
Reproduced by GRB Editrice, Verona, Italy
Enlargement by Colourscan, Singapore

Contents

SUN & MOON SIGNS

ARIES

MARCH 21 – APRIL 20

INTRODUCING ARIES

ARIES, THE SIGN OF THE RAM, IS THE FIRST SIGN OF THE ZODIAC. THE SUN MOVES INTO ARIES ON OR AROUND MARCH 21, MARKING THE START OF THE ASTROLOGICAL NEW YEAR – ASTROLOGY'S NEW YEAR'S DAY.

Ariens have a psychological need to win and to stand out from the crowd, ahead of all other competition. Here is assertiveness, self-assurance, and an uncomplicated approach to life. In order to achieve their goals, Ariens will strip away everything that is unnecessary to them. Here too is lively enthusiasm and an abundance of physical energy.

Traditional groupings

As you read through this book you will come across references to the elements and the qualities, and to positive and negative, or masculine and feminine signs.

The first of these groupings, that of the elements, comprises fire, earth, air, and water signs. The second, that of the qualities, divides the Zodiac into cardinal, fixed, and mutable signs. The final grouping is made up of positive and negative, or masculine and feminine signs. Each Zodiac sign is associated with a combination of components from these groupings, all of which contribute different characteristics to it.

Arien characteristics

The Arien element is fire – a bright, crackling inner fire that is easily ignited. Ariens must do all that they possibly can to keep this fire alive, for if it vanishes, great potential is lost, enthusiasm dies, and inner fulfillment is sure to be lacking. The sign belongs to the cardinal quality, which makes Ariens outgoing in manner. It is a positive, masculine sign, and therefore its subjects are inclined to be extroverts.

The traditional color of Aries is red, although blue is sometimes suggested, and its ruling planet is the red planet, Mars. Ariens are easily roused to anger, but once they have expressed their feelings, they bear neither malice nor resentment.

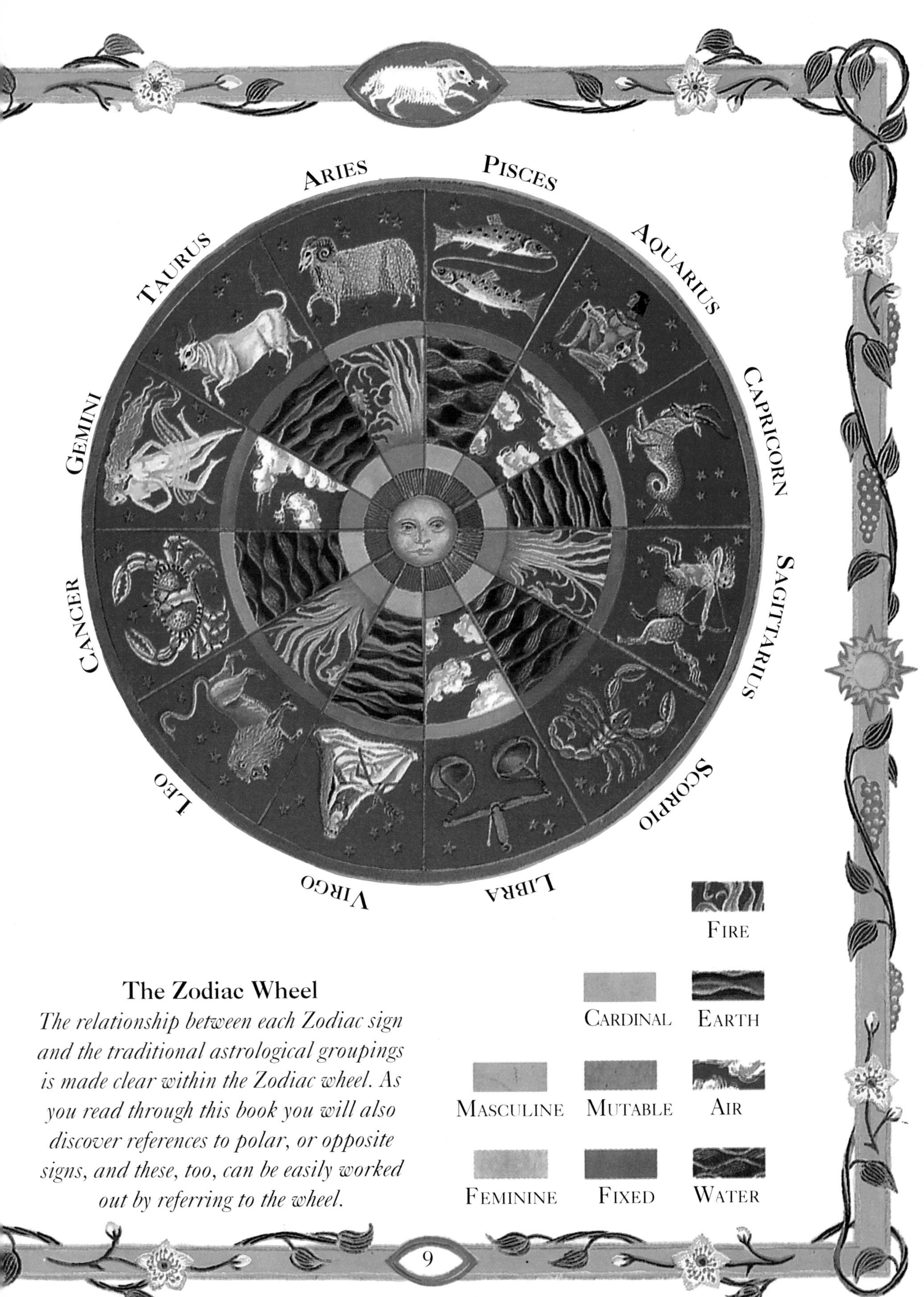

The Zodiac Wheel

The relationship between each Zodiac sign and the traditional astrological groupings is made clear within the Zodiac wheel. As you read through this book you will also discover references to polar, or opposite signs, and these, too, can be easily worked out by referring to the wheel.

ARIES
MYTHS & LEGENDS

THE ZODIAC, WHICH IS SAID TO HAVE ORIGINATED IN BABYLON AS LONG AS 2,500 YEARS AGO, IS A CIRCLE OF CONSTELLATIONS THROUGH WHICH THE SUN MOVES DURING THE COURSE OF A YEAR.

The Ram is not shown in the earliest Babylonian Zodiacs, and probably first appeared in the charts of Ancient Egyptian astronomers. It can be seen on the walls of the temple of the Egyptian Pharaoh, Ramses the Great, near the Valley of the Kings in Thebes.

The Golden Fleece
In the complicated legend of the golden ram, the Ancient Greeks continued to foster the mythical associations of the creature.

Babylonian votive ram
Since the earliest times, imagery associated with the ram has appeared in the devotional art of many different cultures.

Without elaborating upon the many characters involved, the story is basically as this: Phrixus and his sister, Helle, the children of the Boeotian King Athamas, were quietly walking in a wood one day when they met their mother, Nephele, leading a fine golden ram by the horns. She claimed that Poseidon, the god of the sea, had changed the beautiful Theophane, daughter of Bisaltes, into a ewe and himself into a ram, the better to court her. Nephele's ram was their child. She ordered Phrixus and Helle to ride him to the kingdom of Colchis, by the Black Sea,

Jason steals the Golden Fleece

This painting by Herbert Draper (1864 – 1920) shows Jason escaping from Colchis. To delay their pursuers, Medea, the daughter of the king of Colchis, who had fallen in love with Jason, threw her brother's body into the sea.

and sacrifice him to Ares, the god of war. This they did, and the ram's golden fleece was hung in the temple of Ares at Colchis, where it was guarded by a dragon that never slept.

Many years later, Jason, rightful king of Iolcus in Thessaly, could only claim his throne if he recovered the Golden Fleece. He led the Argonauts, a group of heroes, to Colchis, where, after performing a number of apparently impossible tasks, he took not only the Fleece but also Medea, daughter of the king of Colchis. In fact, if it had not been for Medea's assistance in delaying her father's pursuit, Jason could well have been unable to make his escape. Following his triumphant return, Jason mounted the throne and reigned happily ever after.

Jason's story embodies many of the qualities that are traditionally associated with Ariens: courage, an adventurous spirit, energy, and the need to triumph over adversity.

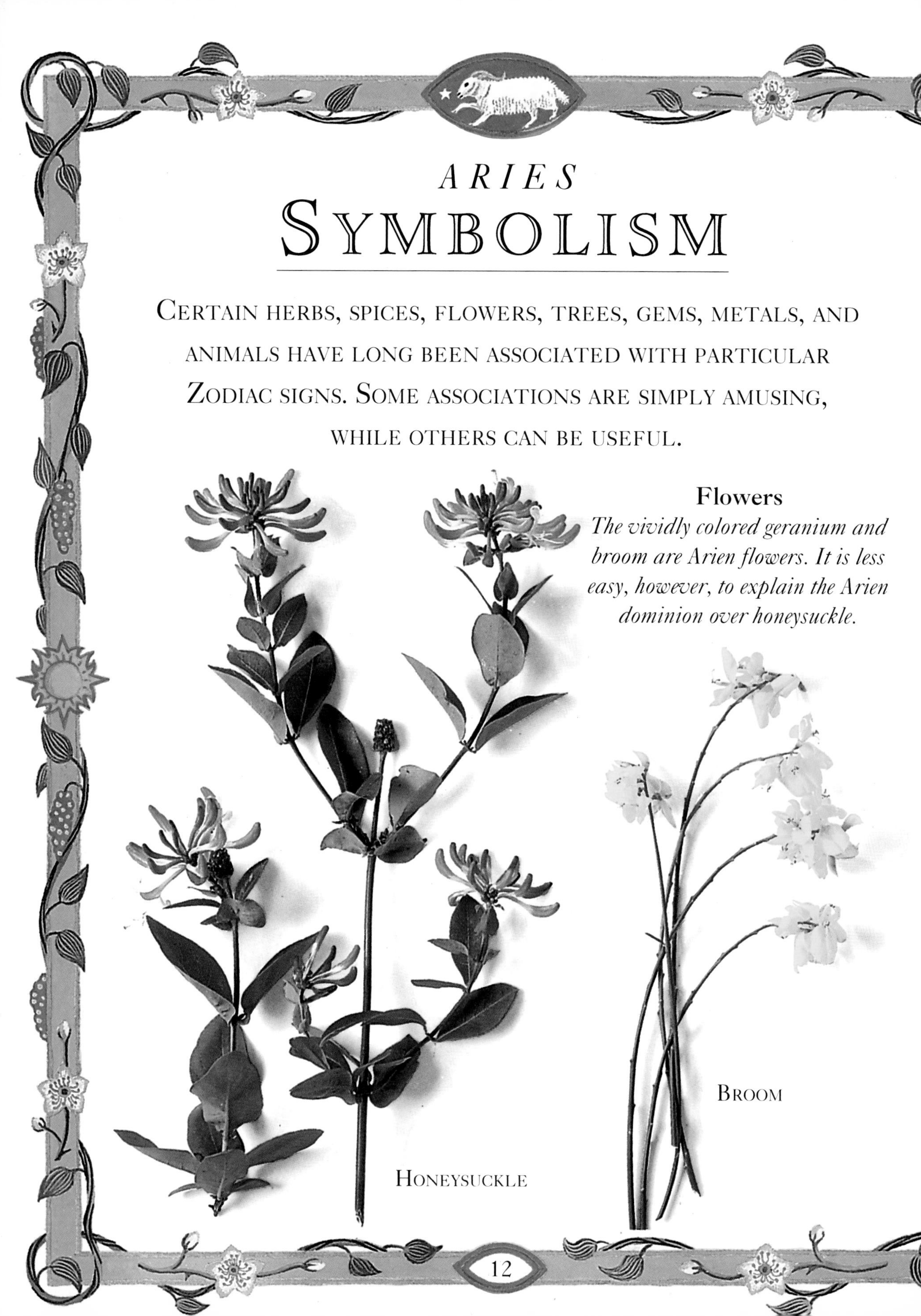

ARIES

SYMBOLISM

CERTAIN HERBS, SPICES, FLOWERS, TREES, GEMS, METALS, AND ANIMALS HAVE LONG BEEN ASSOCIATED WITH PARTICULAR ZODIAC SIGNS. SOME ASSOCIATIONS ARE SIMPLY AMUSING, WHILE OTHERS CAN BE USEFUL.

Flowers

The vividly colored geranium and broom are Arien flowers. It is less easy, however, to explain the Arien dominion over honeysuckle.

HONEYSUCKLE

BROOM

Trees

Because of their prickly nature, all thorn-bearing trees and shrubs are dominated by Aries.

Spices

Aries is a fire sign, and is therefore said to rule cayenne pepper. The same is true of mustard and tartly flavored capers.

Herbs

Peppermint, which is said to ease digestive complaints when brewed as a tea, has long been associated with Aries.

ARIES

SYMBOLISM

Metal

The Arien metal is iron. In keeping with some of this sign's characteristics, it is strong, direct, and plain.

ANTIQUE FAN WITH HORN HANDLE

LEAD TOY SHEEP

Animals

Sheep are Arien creatures, due to their association with the ram.

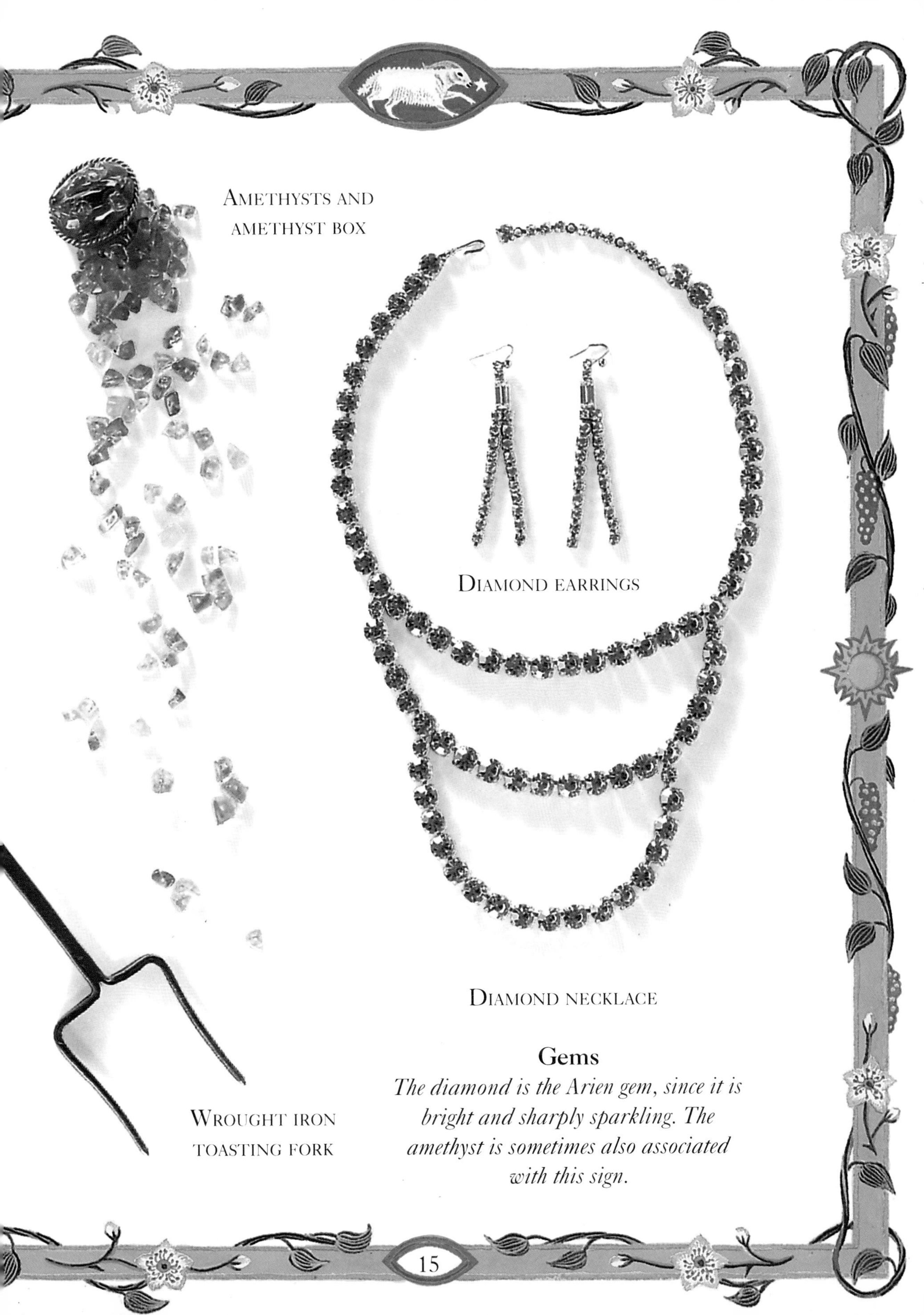

Amethysts and amethyst box

Diamond earrings

Diamond necklace

Wrought iron toasting fork

Gems

The diamond is the Arien gem, since it is bright and sharply sparkling. The amethyst is sometimes also associated with this sign.

ARIES

PROFILE

THE OVERALL PHYSICAL APPEARANCE OF THE TYPICAL ARIEN IS LIKELY TO REFLECT A SENSE OF IMMEDIACY. ARIENS ARE OFTEN IN A HURRY, AND HAVE NO TIME TO MESS AROUND WITH UNNECESSARY COMPLICATIONS.

The Arien stance is easily definable: it expresses confidence. You will be likely to stand with your feet placed well apart, distributing your weight evenly. Your gestures will probably be rather uncomplicated – just like the normally straightforward Arien approach to life.

The Arien face
The Arien glyph is often visible in the line from the eyebrows to the nose.

The body

The Arien body is, when in good condition, very wiry, giving the general impression by the very way in which it moves that it is made of elastic. It is important that you keep yourself on the lean side, since if your body becomes sluggish so will your mind, and the whole pace of your life will slow down. It is sometimes the case that an Arien will appear to be leaning forward most of the time. This pioneering approach may mean that you are forever searching for your next challenge. It may also mean that you have a tendency to jump forward in emergencies.

The face

Your hair is likely to be rather fine, or even flyaway. Male Ariens sometimes tend to lose their hair as they age – not that this need make them look any less attractive. The Arien forehead is typically broad and open, and the Arien glyph, ♈, can sometimes be seen in the line created by the eyebrows and the often prominent nose. Your eyes will no doubt betray your sense of determination; they will be clear, alert, and often quick-

The Arien stance

The Arien stance, which is very easy to recognize, is a very confident one. Your weight will be distributed very evenly.

moving. Most Ariens possess a strong and distinctive chin that often juts forward. It is unlikely that you find it difficult to break into a smile or grin.

Style

Ariens like casual clothes, uncluttered by fussy detail. At the same time, most people of this Sun sign possess the gift of always being able to look very stylish. Men look good in blazers and sweaters; women in well-matched separates. Clothes that restrict movement may, even on formal occasions, not look appropriate. Ariens can spend quite a lot of money on their wardrobes. It could be that you enjoy wearing the latest, very expensive tracksuits.

Many Ariens own a favorite item of clothing with which they will not, under any circumstances, wish to be parted. This goes against their usual reluctance to be nostalgic.

In general

Ariens are always in a hurry, taking long, determined strides at a quick pace, and often barging through doors without too much concern for others who may be in their wake. As has already been mentioned, you may lean forward when you walk, and this could lead to the development of back problems at some time in your life. You should consciously try to hold yourself more upright, making sure that you keep your head up. In all, your robust approach to life will be reflected in the way you act and dress.

ARIES
PERSONALITY

BECAUSE ARIES IS THE FIRST SIGN OF THE ZODIAC, THOSE BORN WHILE THE SUN IS TRAVELING THROUGH IT ARE NATURAL LEADERS. THEY SHOULD BE ASSERTIVE, BUT NEVER RUTHLESS, IN THEIR DEALINGS WITH OTHER PEOPLE.

Here is a Zodiac group that is positive and enthusiastic in its outlook. Ariens enjoy challenge and should always have some important goals to achieve. You probably have a high physical energy level, and it is important that you express this positively and assertively. You can do this by developing a fast-paced lifestyle that is demanding both at work and in leisure. This will satisfy your Arien psychological motivation, which is to always win and to be way out ahead of all your competitors.

At work

The straightforward Arien outlook on life is admirable: a daunting problem can be solved in a matter of minutes. In fact, those of us who allow side issues to clutter up our attitudes and opinions could take lessons from Ariens. Of course, this can lead to the one real drawback of the Arien personality. In your determination to deal with problems briskly, you may all too easily oversimplify a situation. When working on complicated projects, Ariens should have opportunities to confer with someone who can cope with the more detailed areas of the plan.

Your attitudes

Your main vice is selfishness, and no matter how well adjusted you are, or what other planets provide counter-influences, this trait can emerge. It can nearly always be traced back to the "me first" syndrome. Self-awareness, and a little forethought when dealing with other people's feelings, will help enormously in overcoming this unpleasant tendency.

Many people of this sign have a propensity to take risks. If this side of their nature is controlled and kept within certain limits, this becomes a positive adventurousness which is, of course, marvelous. If it is not, the

Mars rules Aries

Mars, the Roman god of war, represents the ruling planet of Aries. The influence of Mars, which has a strong sexual emphasis, relates to the masculine side of an Arien's nature.

individual will sometimes act in a rather hot-headed or foolhardy manner – and learn the hard way.

The overall picture

The Arien energy level, both physical and emotional, is very high. Indeed, inner fulfillment will only come when you use your body and your mind like a single well-adjusted and oiled machine. You should aim to do this during for your whole life. This is one of the signs requiring a good measure of independence. Ariens do not suffer fools gladly, and you will make quite sure that you do things in your own way. Freedom of expression is important to you.

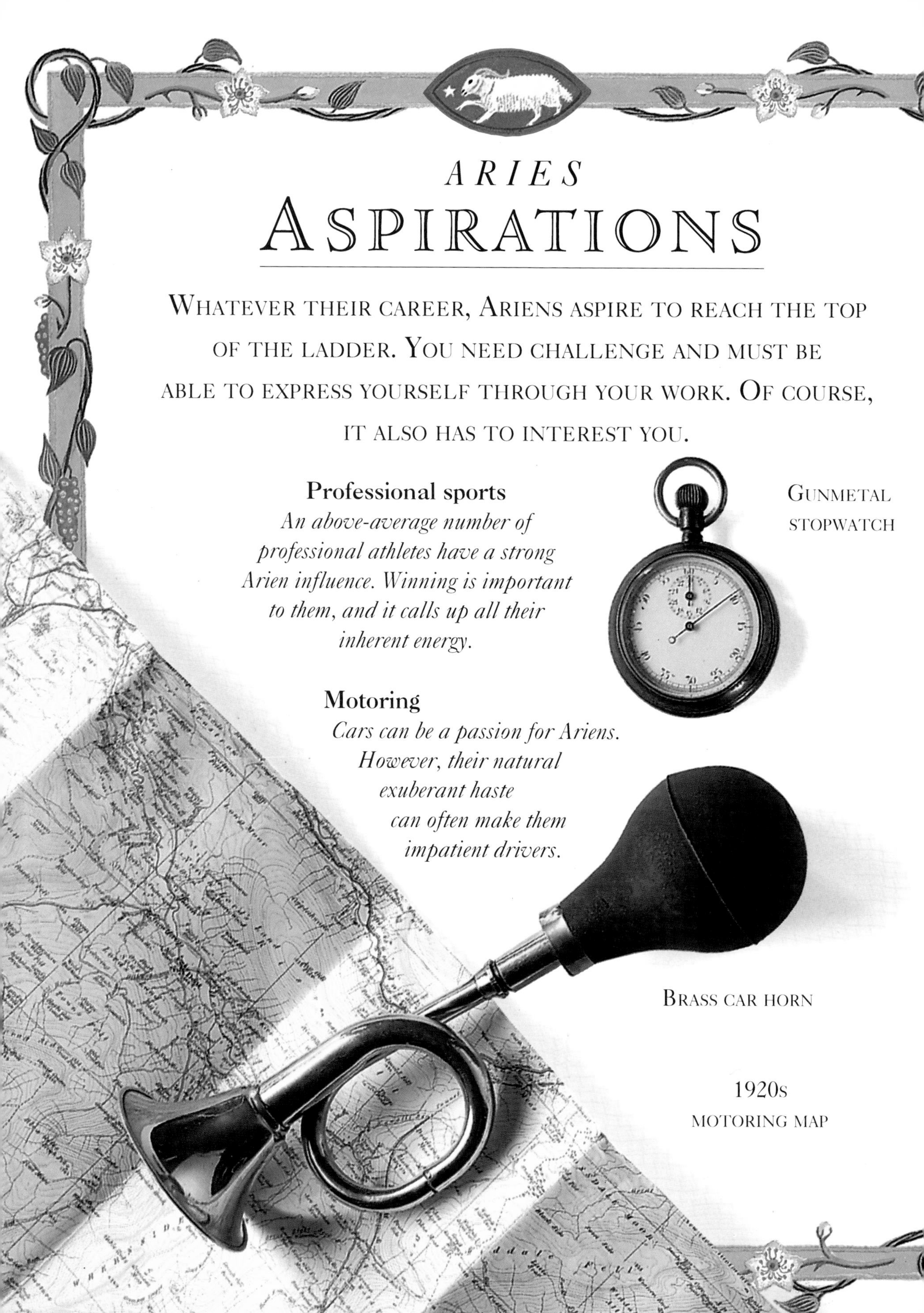

ARIES

ASPIRATIONS

WHATEVER THEIR CAREER, ARIENS ASPIRE TO REACH THE TOP OF THE LADDER. YOU NEED CHALLENGE AND MUST BE ABLE TO EXPRESS YOURSELF THROUGH YOUR WORK. OF COURSE, IT ALSO HAS TO INTEREST YOU.

Professional sports

An above-average number of professional athletes have a strong Arien influence. Winning is important to them, and it calls up all their inherent energy.

GUNMETAL STOPWATCH

Motoring

Cars can be a passion for Ariens. However, their natural exuberant haste can often make them impatient drivers.

BRASS CAR HORN

1920S MOTORING MAP

1927 CIGARETTE CARDS DEPICTING ENGINEERING

Engineering

Ariens of both sexes make good engineers and, in their spare time, are often enthusiastic amateur motor mechanics. They seem to positively enjoy getting their hands dirty.

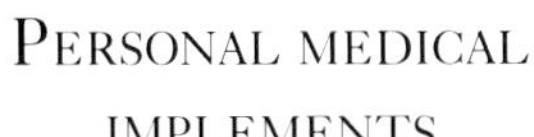

PERSONAL MEDICAL IMPLEMENTS

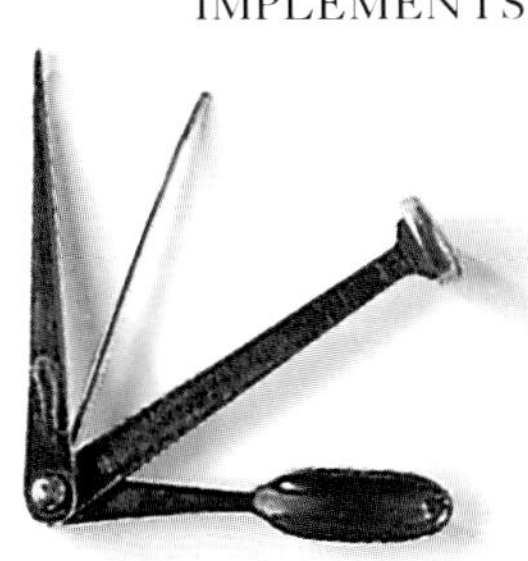

Medicine

There is a traditional link between the medical profession and this sign. Perhaps because Aries rules the head, Ariens also make good psychiatrists.

DENTAL MIRROR

Dentistry

Although Capricorn rules the teeth, Ariens are often drawn to working in the dental profession.

DENTAL PROBE

BRASS HORSE

Physical work

Arien energy is well suited to many different forms of physical activity, including farming.

ARIES

HEALTH

FOR ARIENS TO KEEP HAPPY AND HEALTHY, THEY HAVE TO BURN UP ENERGY THROUGH EXERCISE. IF YOUR WORK AND PLAY ARE PHYSICALLY DEMANDING, THEY WILL HELP YOU TO STAY IN GOOD SHAPE.

The pioneering spirit of Aries is usually motivation enough to keep you moving, but at times when life lacks challenge, even the most energetic Arien will become lazy.

Your diet

Although you may like spicy foods, these are seldom good for Ariens. You will thrive on traditional, even bland, dishes. Your diet may also benefit from being supplemented with the cell salt potassium phosphate (Kali. Phos.), which is thought to build brain cells, help prevent headaches, and alleviate depression.

Taking care

Ariens are not the most careful of Zodiac types, and you will tend to cut and burn yourself more than is common. Learn to be cautious, especially when cooking or working with sharp tools. The Arien body area is the head, and it is true to say that Ariens either suffer badly from headaches – sometimes due to minor kidney disorders – or never have any.

Ariens sometimes find it hard to modify an exercise regimen. As you get older, this could cause you to damage your body, and all of your old injuries may come back to plague you.

Italian red onions

Most strong-tasting foods, such as onions and leeks, are associated with Aries.

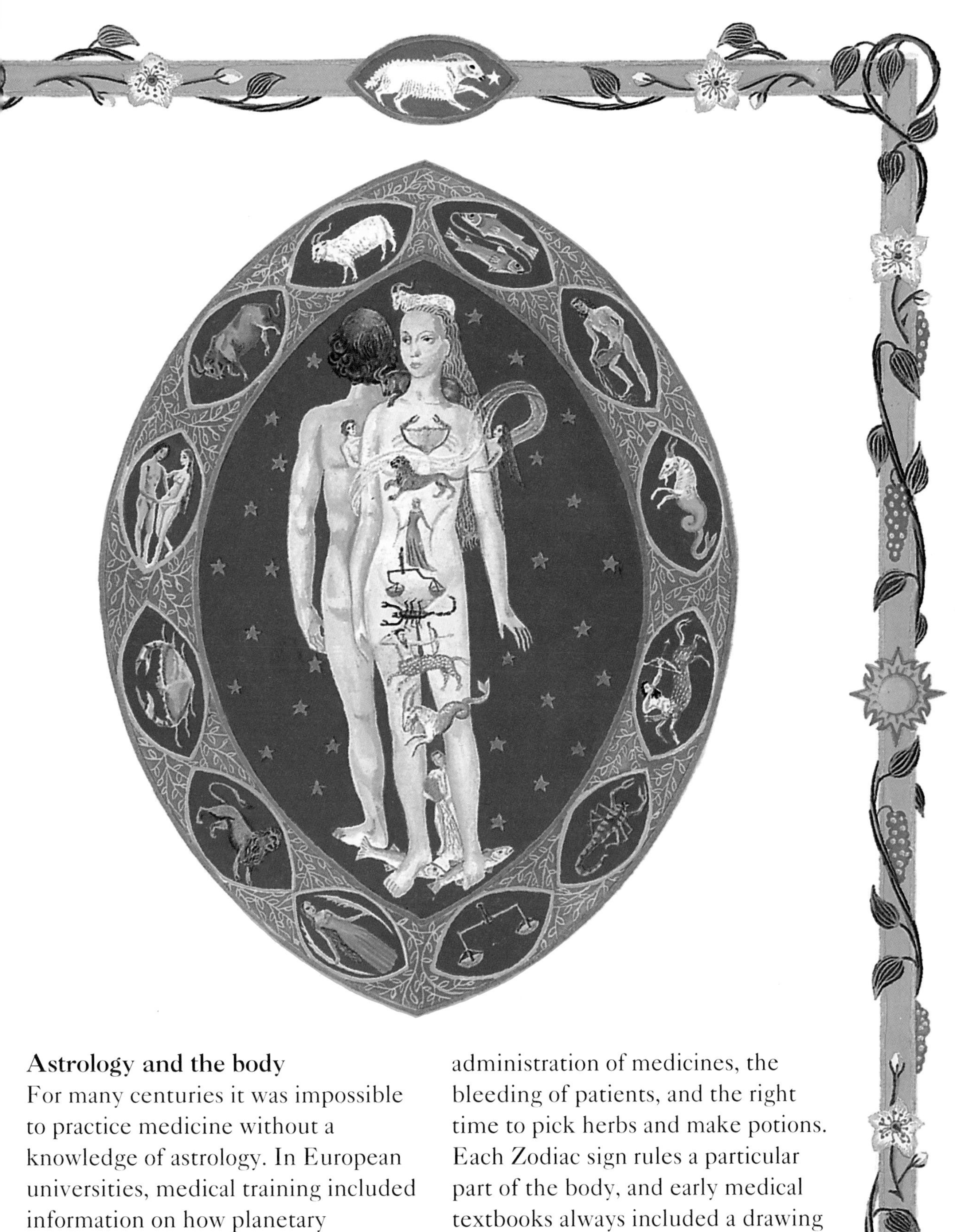

Astrology and the body

For many centuries it was impossible to practice medicine without a knowledge of astrology. In European universities, medical training included information on how planetary positions would affect the administration of medicines, the bleeding of patients, and the right time to pick herbs and make potions. Each Zodiac sign rules a particular part of the body, and early medical textbooks always included a drawing that illustrated the point.

ARIES AT
LEISURE

EACH OF THE SUN SIGNS TRADITIONALLY SUGGESTS SPARE-TIME ACTIVITIES, HOBBIES, AND VACATION SPOTS. CONSIDER SOME OF THESE SUGGESTIONS – THEY OFTEN SUIT ARIEN INTERESTS.

Travel

You will enjoy adventurous holidays, especially while you are young. Seeing the world will probably be more of a priority than comfort. Try England, Poland, France, Syria, and Israel for vacations.

POSTAGE STAMPS

VOLT-METER

Car maintenance

Ariens enjoy driving and maintaining their cars. The latter can, in fact, prove to be a lucrative hobby.

WALKING BOOTS

Horse-riding

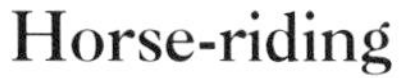

You may enjoy pony trekking and spending long days in the fresh air, whatever the weather.

HORSE'S BIT

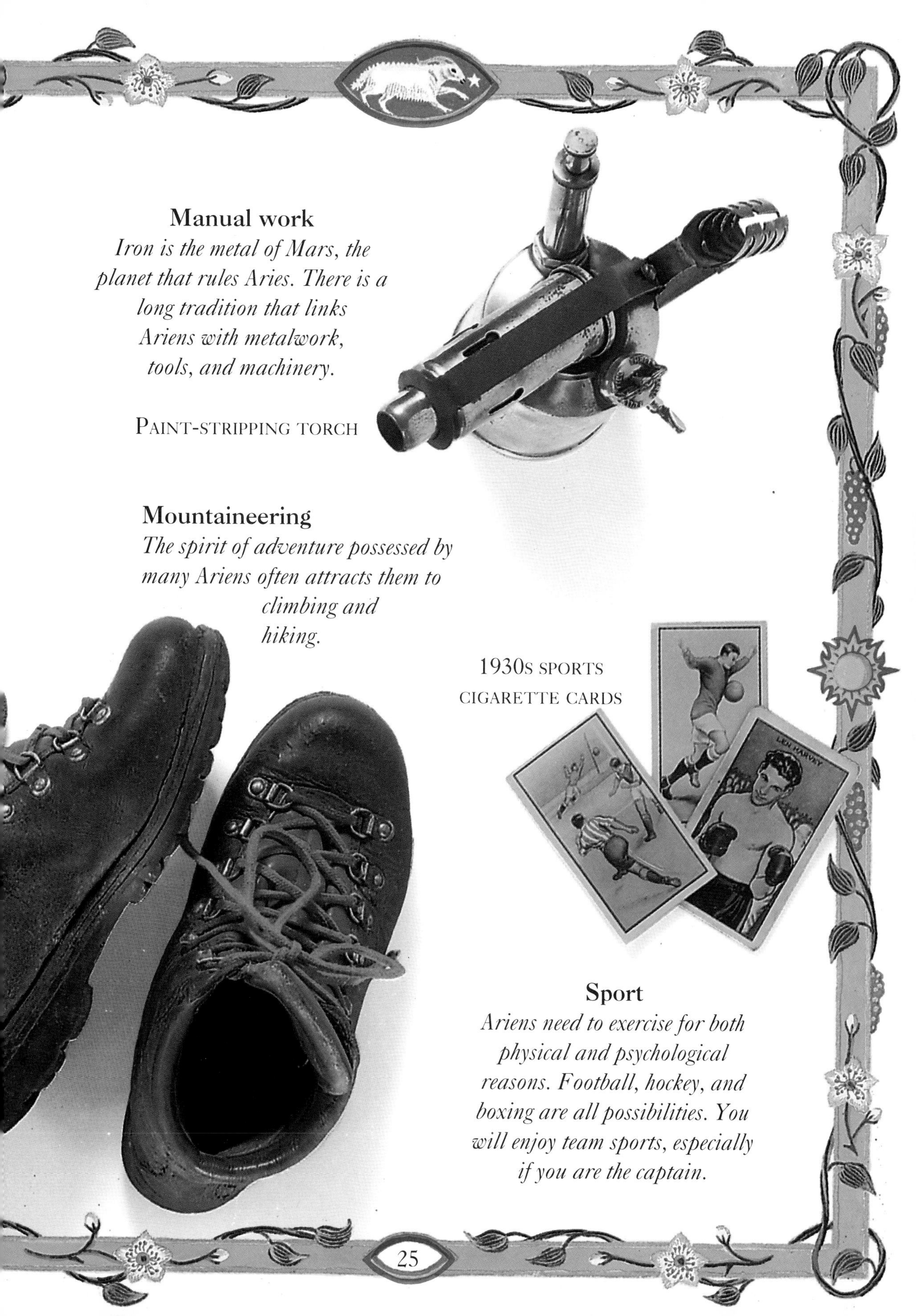

Manual work

Iron is the metal of Mars, the planet that rules Aries. There is a long tradition that links Ariens with metalwork, tools, and machinery.

PAINT-STRIPPING TORCH

Mountaineering

The spirit of adventure possessed by many Ariens often attracts them to climbing and hiking.

1930S SPORTS CIGARETTE CARDS

Sport

Ariens need to exercise for both physical and psychological reasons. Football, hockey, and boxing are all possibilities. You will enjoy team sports, especially if you are the captain.

ARIES IN LOVE

ONE OF THE MOST PASSIONATE SIGNS OF THE ZODIAC, ARIENS FALL IN AND OUT OF LOVE VERY QUICKLY. BUT A TENDENCY TO SWEEP PROSPECTIVE PARTNERS OFF THEIR FEET CAN END IN DISASTER.

You must learn to listen to your partner's needs and ensure that selfishness does not spoil this wonderful sphere of life for you.

Pleasant romantic dinners and big nights out are sure to be part of the more mature Arien approach. When they are young, however, Ariens may seek affection in the backseat of an old jalopy. All Ariens should ensure that their approach is not too gushing and fast for many people.

As a lover

Those partners on the receiving end of your admiration will no doubt find the experience both lively and enjoyable. In most cases, your enthusiasm is likely to be infectious, and the individual involved will find it both easy and pleasant to be swept up into a fastpaced, sexually rewarding experience.

Types of Arien lover

Many Ariens have a beautifully poetic streak in their expression of love. This is something that one does not automatically expect to find in those who tend to rush things. However, Ariens must be aware of the possibility that once they are in love, an uncharacteristic

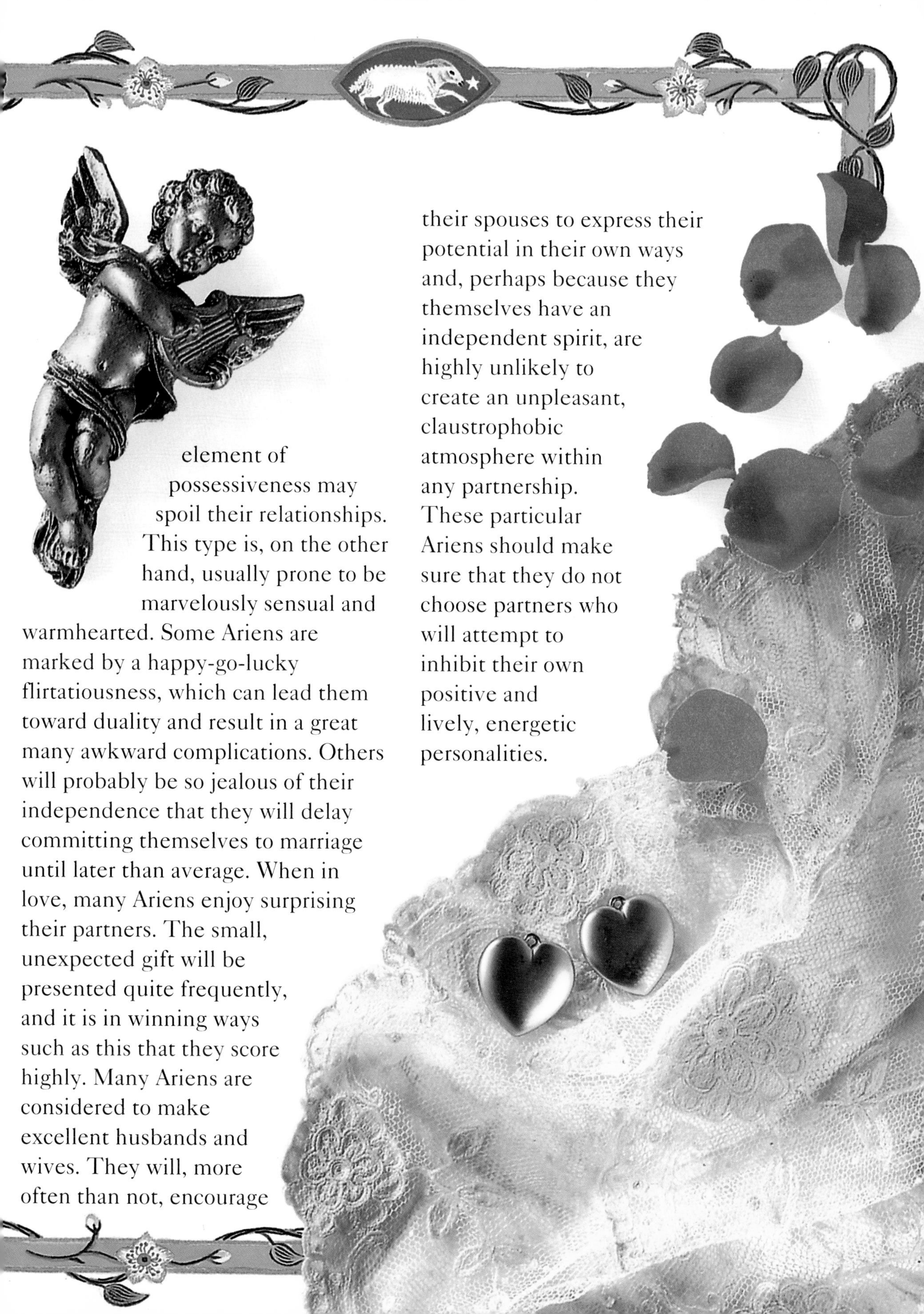

element of possessiveness may spoil their relationships. This type is, on the other hand, usually prone to be marvelously sensual and warmhearted. Some Ariens are marked by a happy-go-lucky flirtatiousness, which can lead them toward duality and result in a great many awkward complications. Others will probably be so jealous of their independence that they will delay committing themselves to marriage until later than average. When in love, many Ariens enjoy surprising their partners. The small, unexpected gift will be presented quite frequently, and it is in winning ways such as this that they score highly. Many Ariens are considered to make excellent husbands and wives. They will, more often than not, encourage their spouses to express their potential in their own ways and, perhaps because they themselves have an independent spirit, are highly unlikely to create an unpleasant, claustrophobic atmosphere within any partnership. These particular Ariens should make sure that they do not choose partners who will attempt to inhibit their own positive and lively, energetic personalities.

ARIES AT HOME

THE WARM AND WELCOMING ARIEN HOME WILL BE COMFORTABLY, SOLIDLY, AND UNFUSSILY FURNISHED. SHADES OF RED WILL ENHANCE THE FEELING OF WARMTH, AND THE BEDROOM, IN PARTICULAR, WILL HAVE A SENSUAL ATMOSPHERE.

Many Ariens will enjoy spending time on improving their home. They may, for example, replan their kitchen or garden, and then do all of the work themselves. It is in fact the process of doing the work, rather than the end result, which provides real pleasure for an Arien.

You will probably prefer living near a busy street to setting up home in a peaceful rural setting. One important thing to consider is that as an Arien you will not want to be hemmed in or feel restricted.

Candelabra
This wrought iron candelabra has been made from the Arien metal.

Furniture

Ariens tend to be rather careless, and hate anything insubstantial. You will therefore usually choose durable furniture. Furthermore, having spent time choosing pieces, you will not want to waste more time, money and energy, starting to look for new items after only a couple of years. You must, however, be rather careful that you initially take your time when deciding to buy new furniture.

Soft furnishings

Ariens like their homes to have a warm, colorful glow. You probably enjoy creating an overall atmosphere that appears pleasing and informal to all who enter it.

Ariens are not usually very adventurous when it comes to choosing wallpaper and drapes. You may well prefer plain, clear colors.

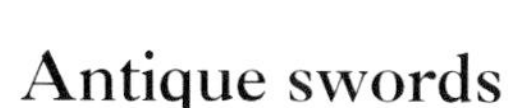

Antique swords

Mars, the planet of war, rules Aries. It is therefore hardly surprising that many Ariens decorate their homes with weapons.

Even though very young Ariens will probably choose vivid or even garish designs (for duvet covers, for instance) this tendency usually diminishes as they become older. By the time they eventually feel ready to set up their own homes a certain restraint is likely to emerge, which will make the final effect both interesting and tasteful.

Decorative objects

The decorative objects that Ariens will enjoy owning reflect certain elements of the individual's personality. Your sexual energy may well be considerable, so a reproduction of some famous erotic painting could easily end up hanging on your wall. Alternatively, a reproduction of a painting by the very famous Arien painter, Van Gogh, could find a place in the Arien home. His energetic painting of bright sunflowers sums up so much that is typical of this Sun sign.

Mars, the planet of war, rules Aries, and the Arien metal is iron. You could therefore end up possessing some weapons, such as an antique sword, or a flint-lock pistol.

Armchair and cushions

The principal Arien color is red, so there will be a good deal of it in their homes. They also like solid, functional furniture.

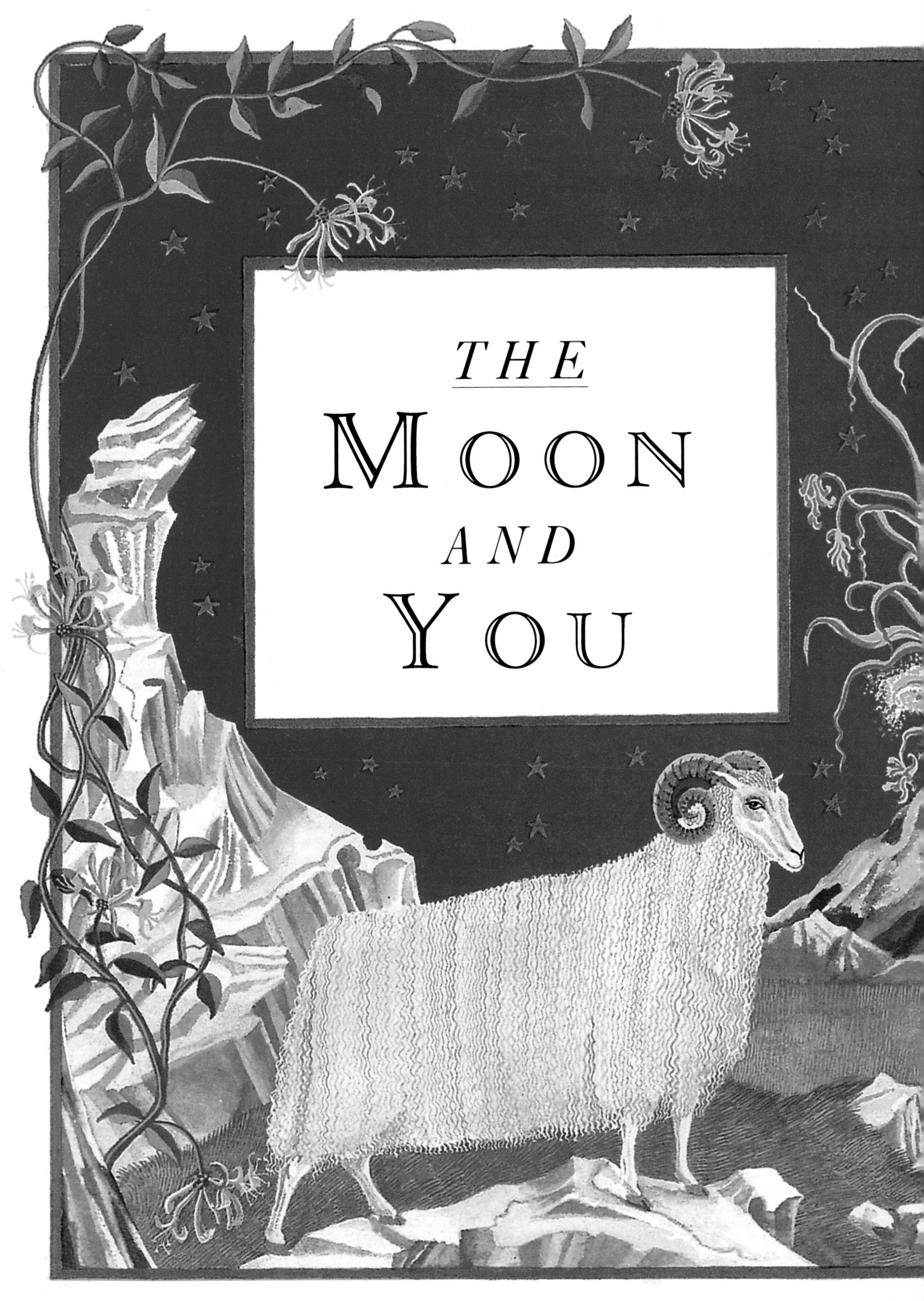
THE
MOON
AND
YOU

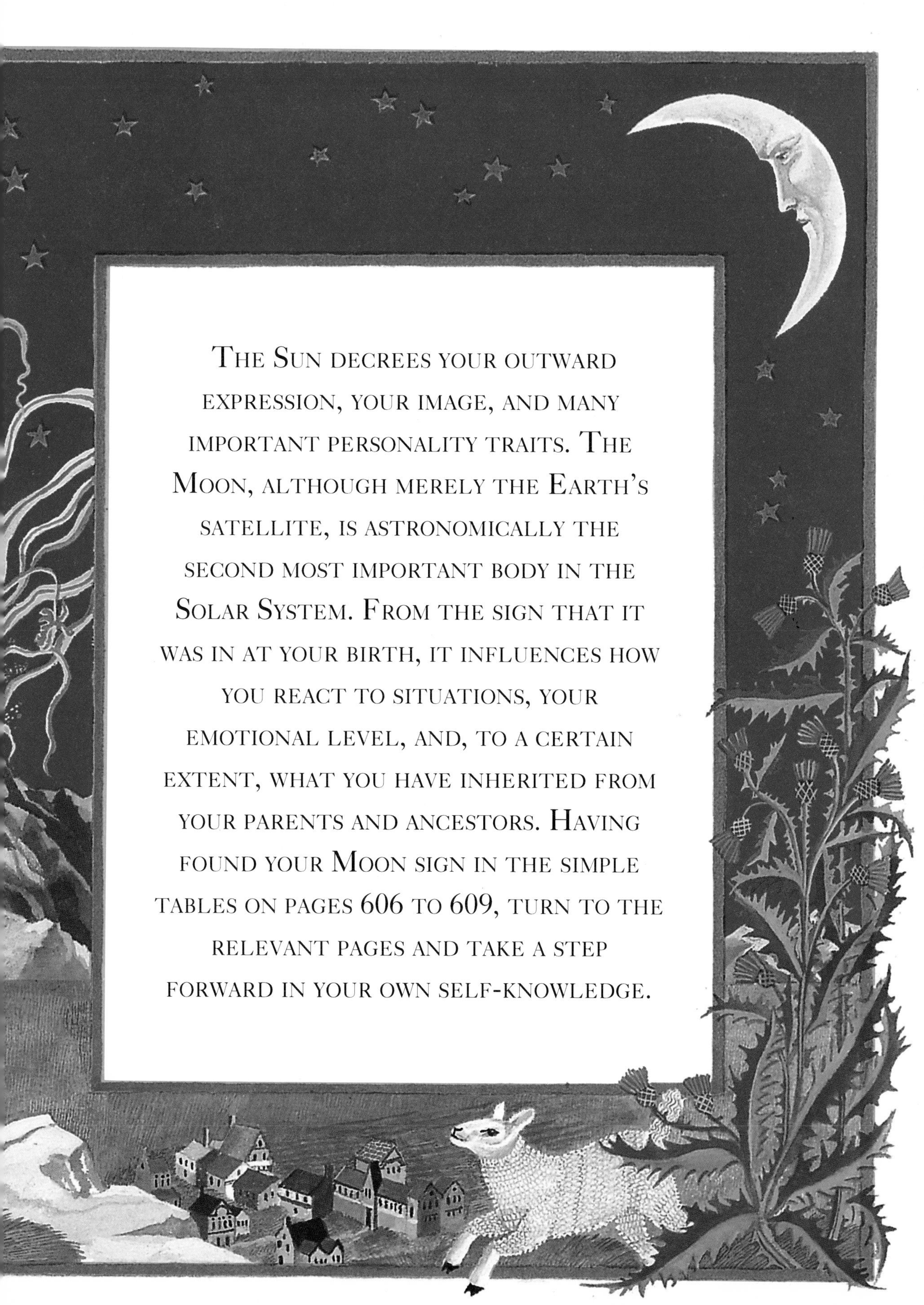

The Sun decrees your outward expression, your image, and many important personality traits. The Moon, although merely the Earth's satellite, is astronomically the second most important body in the Solar System. From the sign that it was in at your birth, it influences how you react to situations, your emotional level, and, to a certain extent, what you have inherited from your parents and ancestors. Having found your Moon sign in the simple tables on pages 606 to 609, turn to the relevant pages and take a step forward in your own self-knowledge.

THE MOON IN ARIES

WITH THE SUN AND MOON BOTH IN ARIES AT THE TIME OF YOUR BIRTH, YOU WERE BORN UNDER A NEW MOON. ARIES IS A FIRE SIGN, AND THIS ELEMENT POWERFULLY INFLUENCES YOUR PERSONALITY AND REACTIONS.

Should you study a list of your Sun sign characteristics, you will probably recognize that a great many of them apply to you. Out of a list of perhaps 20 traits of a Sun sign listed in books or magazines, most people will strongly identify with 11 or 12. For you, however, the average increases considerably because the Sun and Moon were both in Aries when you were born.

Self-expression

Your Sun sign denotes fiery, positive emotion, and so does your Arien Moon. Obviously, with such a powerful force at your disposal, you will understand that it is essential for you to express your feelings and to use your emotional energy positively. Do not bluster about or flare up unnecessarily: learn to control your emotional energy and use it calmly and constructively. Your Sun sign makes you assertive and your Moon sign emphasizes this as your main motivation. You should also be aware that you may be terribly prone to hastiness and could act prematurely.

Romance

The most serious Arien fault is selfishness and, more than for other people of your Sun sign, it could very easily mar your personal relationships. You can react to your partners in a self-centered way, putting your own interests first and ignoring their needs and suggestions. But once aware of the pitfalls of selfishness, you make a wonderful, passionate lover.

Your well-being

The effect of your Aries Moon on your health will be to increase your vulnerability to all Arien ailments. Most importantly, your inherent hastiness will incline you to be yet more accident-prone. The emotional intensity of your Moon underscores

The Moon in Aries

the likelihood of headaches. If they persist, it could be as the result of a mild kidney disorder, so arrange to have a medical checkup.

Self-control and the conscious awareness that you can overdo things are essential to your well-being.

Planning ahead

The Arien enterprising spirit will put you in good stead when it comes to finance. Ariens are extremely decisive, but due to your Arien Moon you may well react to situations without due thought. Be careful, for instance, when you invest, since mistakes can easily be made.

Parenthood

You will be a lively, energetic parent, who will encourage your children in every area of their lives. But because you are so enthusiastic about your own interests, it may be all too easy for you to make the mistake of ignoring their individual tastes.

THE MOON IN TAURUS

TAURUS IS AN EARTH SIGN, AND ITS QUALITIES ARE IN STRIKING CONTRAST TO THOSE OF YOUR FIERY ARIEN SUN SIGN. THEY WILL TEND TO MAKE YOU FAR LESS LIKELY TO EMBARK ON UNWISE PREMATURE ACTIONS.

The qualities attributed to Aries and its neighboring sign, Taurus, are totally opposite – so the fact that the Moon was in Taurus when you were born adds a very different dimension to your personality. If you are aware of these contrasting qualities, you will be able to express them without too much internal conflict.

Self-expression

Your Taurean Moon gives you an extremely useful tendency to react to situations both constructively and thoughtfully. You will not find it difficult to control a sense of urgency or hastiness, and will always want to think things through carefully.

Taurus and Aries are very much emotionally oriented signs, but you find it relatively easy to control your emotional flow and expression. At times, however, you will find it more difficult to throw off your anger than many Ariens do. Be careful that an inherent tendency toward resentment and brooding does not mar your admirably straightforward Arien approach to life.

Romance

Arien selfishness, coupled with a tendency to be possessive of your partner, can be a big stumbling block in an emotional relationship. Make sure that you use the affectionate, positive passion of your Moon to the full when responding to your partner. Allow the zest for love and sex that you obtain from your Aries Sun to color your emotional relationships.

Your well-being

Taurus rules the throat, and at the first sign of a cold, you may well lose your voice and come down with a very sore throat. Many Ariens are wiry, but your Taurean Moon could add a lot of bulk to your frame. You may find it

The Moon in Taurus

extremely difficult to resist rich, sweet food. Weight gain could be a real problem for you.

Planning ahead

The Taurean business sense often beautifully complements the Arien sense of enterprise. In fact, many people of your Sun sign are lucky enough to possess two different sources of income.

You have an extremely powerful intuitive streak when it comes to dealing with money and will take fewer risks than many Ariens. Enterprise and good business sense, along with enthusiasm and a by no means small regard for luxury, all go well together.

Parenthood

Arien enthusiasm will color your attitude to your children, but you may sometimes find yourself being over-possessive. Watch out, too, for problems with the generation gap – you can appear far more conventional to your children than you realize.

THE MOON IN GEMINI

A COMBINATION OF ARIES (A FIRE SIGN) AND GEMINI (AN AIR SIGN) WILL, WHILE INCREASING ARIEN IMPATIENCE AND RESTLESSNESS, GIVE YOU FAST RESPONSES TO SITUATIONS, A NEED FOR IMMEDIATE ACTION, AND LOTS OF BRIGHT IDEAS.

Fire and air blend well: Aries fire motivates you and colors your self-expression, while the airy Gemini Moon spurs you forward, keeps you alert, and ensures that you never waste a moment.

If your life is unrewarding, you will suffer much more than most Ariens. Avoid false starts and the temptation to give up because you are bored. If you succeed in this, you will control what amounts to your most severe problem: a pathological hatred of boredom.

Self-expression

Although Arien directness is present in your personality, it is very easy for you to get sidetracked by the versatility that derives from your Moon sign. Allow the latter tendency some expression within the confines of a few well-chosen interests, and let it support a wider dimension within your career.

You may, perhaps, not entirely trust your powerful Arien emotions. Be very careful not to suppress the expression of your feelings, nor, as you are more likely to do, simply to rationalize them out of existence.

Romance

You will possess plenty of Arien passion, and it will be clearly expressed through sex and other aspects of your emotional life. You are more than likely to be a good communicator and will respond very fairly to your partner's desires and suggestions. Most fortunately, the inherent Arien selfish streak will be considerably mitigated in you.

Your well-being

The Geminian body areas are the hands and arms, so be extra careful that the Arien tendency to be accident-prone does not lead you to cut or burn them. Your Geminian

The Moon in Gemini

Moon may provoke periods of nervous tension. This, coupled with the Arien tendency to overdo things and the need for a constant use of mental energy, could make relaxation difficult for you.

Planning ahead

In some spheres of your life, a cunning streak could combine with Arien selfishness and the desire to be first in all things. You will plan your every action and will not be averse to scheming that will put you ahead of competitors. You will certainly voice your opinions, and your dynamic force will let you lead others skillfully.

Parenthood

You will make an extremely lively parent and will find it very easy indeed to keep up with what your children are thinking, and with their various interests and crazes. In fact, it could be that you will become the trendsetter, because your Geminian Moon instills a particularly strong interest in what is new and original.

THE MOON IN CANCER

A COMBINATION OF THE FIRST ZODIAC FIRE SIGN (ARIES) AND THE FIRST WATER SIGN (CANCER) BLENDS ASSERTIVE ENTHUSIASM WITH AN INSTINCTIVE CARING, PROTECTIVE RESPONSE. IT WILL ALSO HEIGHTEN YOUR EMOTIONAL LEVEL.

The tremendously high emotional voltage of your Sun and Moon combination is a vital key to your whole personality. As the Moon traditionally rules Cancer, its effect on you is even more powerful than it is on those who have it in another sign.

Self-expression

While Aries is extroverted, Cancer tends to be introverted, and you have some of the qualities of both. But there are, of course, areas where Aries and Cancer meet. Both signs are, for instance, of the cardinal quality, and share an important and expressive outgoing nature. You are generally forthright – Aries sees to that – but the Moon is also likely to make you tender, caring, and sympathetic.

Your Moon sign will probably make you somewhat apprehensive when challenged; it will make you intuitive, which is good, but it will also make you a worrier. Couple this with a powerful Cancerian imagination, and when something troubles you, you can easily begin to feel that your world has collapsed around you.

While much about the Cancer personality is gentle and tender, there is, conversely, also a lot of toughness present, and this is very good when blended with more forthright, assertive Arien qualities.

Romance

You have the high, fiery passion of Aries plus the sensual, caring, and tender expression of love typical of Cancer. This is a pretty stunning combination, but you may find that you sometimes smother your partners with affection. Try not to be too sensitive, sentimental, or nostalgic.

Your well-being

You will work extremely hard, and could feel wound up at times; develop relaxation techniques to counter the

The Moon in Cancer

tendency. Most Ariens cope well with stress, but the Cancerian inclination to worry may stop you from taking as philosophical an attitude to problems as you otherwise might. Stress could also affect your digestion, so look carefully at your diet. It may be that you would benefit from eating far less spicy food.

Planning ahead

Your Cancerian Moon will, in general, make you marvelously – and usefully – shrewd. This is especially true when it comes to business and finance. Follow your powerful instincts, but do not let any fiery Arien enthusiasm entirely quench deep-rooted caution.

Parenthood

You will enjoy family life enormously and may be eager to have children. But even though you will be an excellent and energetic parent, when your children want to leave home, you may find it hard to let them go. Right from the start, avoid an instinctive tendency to overprotect them. While you will want to give your children a happy home, beware of trying to make it too comfortable.

THE MOON IN LEO

YOUR LIFE CAN OFTEN BE HECTIC BUT, BECAUSE YOU HAVE AN INSTINCT FOR GETTING THINGS RIGHT, YOU WILL NOT BE INCLINED TO TAKE SHORTCUTS TO ATTAIN YOUR GOALS. THIS CAUTION WILL TEMPER UNDUE HASTE OR CARELESSNESS.

You possess very powerful feelings, and will enjoy expressing them, and your opinions, forcefully and to great effect.

Self-expression

Your Arien ability and motivation to win and to lead is enhanced by Leo's instinctive organizational ability. You should, can, and must aim to go far, but without hurting others. The chances are that with this combination you are a born leader, and if you achieve inner fulfillment, others will gladly follow your example.

You may tend to react in a somewhat pompous and bossy way at times and, if accused of this, your Arien Sun will encourage you to feel embarrassed. In fact, Aries is one of the least pompous of the 12 Zodiac signs. Therefore take heed: the influence from the Moon sign is powerful, and does influence the way other people react to us.

In anyone who has an influence from Leo, there is usually an urge for some form of creative expression. Ariens often love bright, vivid colors, so you may like to paint – but you will probably not be terribly patient. Do not, therefore, concern yourself with detail. Just slap the paint on liberally and have fun, because the act of doing so can be very creative in itself.

Romance

You will make your partners feel wonderful, and be very generous with romantic and flattering gifts. Your zest for sex will encourage and help relax the shiest of partners.

When angered, you will become a real lion – if in sheep's clothing. But any resentment or brooding after you have had your say would be most uncharacteristic. Magnanimity is always present, even if you are capable of reducing a rival or an enemy to a quivering jelly.

The Moon in Leo

Your well-being

The Leo body area is the spine: look after it and exercise it. If you sit at an office desk all day, get a back-support chair. Because Leo also rules the heart, any Arien sporting activity is important, too. You do not go halfway and, with your Moon in a fire sign, you could succumb to the Arien problem of burning yourself out of both physical and emotional energy.

Planning ahead

The Arien enterprising spirit is a very necessary asset for you, since you really love luxury and expensive quality. You are often attracted to things that are well beyond your price range. If you are enterprising and creative, work hard, and make large amounts of money, you will achieve great inner fulfilment.

Parenthood

You will be a loving, if somewhat domineering, parent. If you curb the latter trait, you will be a great source of inspiration to your children, giving them every encouragement. Even when you have no alternative but to criticize them, you will do so in such a way as to encourage their efforts.

THE MOON IN VIRGO

THE ARIEN NEED FOR ACTION BLENDS WELL WITH VIRGO'S QUICK BUT CAREFUL RESPONSES TO SITUATIONS. YOU WILL BE FAR LESS LIKELY TO MAKE SILLY MISTAKES THAN OTHER PEOPLE OF YOUR SUN SIGN.

Your Moon in Virgo, which is an earth sign, gives your character a dimension that is very much in contrast to your fire sign Arien Sun.

Self-expression

While having the typical quick Arien grasp of a situation, you respond not only practically but also very analytically, seeing every loophole. Try not to become damningly critical of other people, for a very understandable tendency not to suffer fools gladly can go a bit too far at times, especially when Arien hasty action meets with Virgoan fussiness.

You are among the most practical of Ariens, being capable of either theoretical or active work, but may not be terribly patient. Take a break rather than struggling on to the point where you want to give up.

Although Ariens are certainly not celebrated for their shyness, it is just possible that in some way you have had to come to terms with a degree of reticence. Maybe it has inhibited you in just one area of your life, perhaps as the result of critical put-downs from your parents when you were young. Your Virgoan modesty could have predominated until the positive force of Aries came into its own.

Romance

Your Arien emotion is dampened by the qualities of your Moon sign. It will lead you to think sensibly before overwhelming your partner with passion. When you are annoyed you may tend to carp and nag, but you will rarely be resentful.

Your well-being

The Virgoan body area is the stomach. You need an above-average amount of fiber, and might respond well to a vegetarian diet. The Moon in Virgo can also cause a considerable buildup of tension: Many Sun sign Virgoans

The Moon in Virgo

suffer from migraines, and because Aries rules the head and makes its subjects prone to bad headaches, you could sometimes succumb to them. Find a way to counter stress; note its early symptoms, and try to distance yourself from any problem. This is vital if you are to remain productive.

Planning ahead

Ariens are generous; Virgoans, on the whole, are not. There is clearly a potential conflict between the two. If it is troublesome, then make every effort to keep the Virgoan level of your personality under control.

Parenthood

All Ariens have the capacity to enjoy parenthood, but be careful that you are not more critical toward your children than you realize. They could easily take you more seriously than you might imagine. When they do, make it up to them with some special treats to show how sorry you are.

THE MOON IN LIBRA

ARIES AND LIBRA ARE POLAR OR OPPOSITE SIGNS, WHICH MEANS THAT YOU WERE BORN AT THE TIME OF THE FULL MOON. ALWAYS GUARD AGAINST RESTLESSNESS, AND DO NOT ALLOW INDECISION TO MAR YOUR ARIEN ENTHUSIASM.

All of us, in one way or another, tend to express certain attributes of our polar, or opposite, Zodiac sign. In your case, this is Libra, which is straight across the Zodiac circle from Aries. Because the Moon happened to be in that sign when you were born, this polarity is expressed in a very interesting way: you will react to people with much greater consideration for their feelings than most people of your Sun sign.

Self-expression

You can be diplomatic and tactful, and when the going gets tough, you will recognize any negative symptoms of stress and really kick back and relax.

Having said that, most people born like you, at the time of the Full Moon, are prone to restlessness, and all too often harbor some kind of inner feeling of discontent. You must be on your guard against this. Perhaps you tend to change occupations rather too often, and therefore never manage to completely satisfy your sense of inner fulfillment. Examine your attitudes and opinions occasionally, as they may tend to be overvolatile or, conversely, stuck in a rut.

Romance

Your Libran Moon sign makes you diplomatic, far more tactful, and less hasty than most Ariens. Libra is, emotionally, not a very powerfully charged sign. It is enhanced by fiery Arien warmth, while Arien sexual passion is softened by warm affection and a beautiful expression of romance. Any selfishness is considerably mitigated in you, although you may suffer twinges of resentment from time to time.

Your well-being

The Libran body area is the kidneys, and as a result of the polar lunar influence, you may have slight kidney

The Moon in Libra

upsets. You could also suffer from many Arien headaches. No doubt you find rich, expensive, and delicious food hard to resist. If you tend to put on weight easily, keep up the exercise and sporting activities – otherwise your gourmet interests may damage your physique.

Planning ahead

Your Libran Moon sign inclines you to luxury – something many Ariens are not too obsessed about. But if you really do enjoy luxurious living, it is clear that you should exploit your enterprising qualities as much as you can. You will do well to be one of those Ariens who has two sources of income (apart from anything else, the variety will satisfy you).

Parenthood

You are an excellent parent and will be sympathetic to your children's opinions; you will not want them to be clones of yourself. A hint of Libran indecisiveness could, however, be irritating for them at times.

THE MOON IN SCORPIO

THE FIERY EMOTION OF ARIES AND THE INTENSE EMOTION OF SCORPIO BUILD POWERFUL RESOURCES ON WHICH TO DRAW DURING HARD TIMES. BE CAREFUL THAT JEALOUSY DOES NOT DESTROY YOUR ARIEN STRAIGHTFORWARDNESS.

There is a long-standing tradition that links Aries with Scorpio: both were ruled by Mars until the discovery of Pluto. After considerable discussion, Pluto was designated as the ruler of Scorpio.

Self-expression

Your resources of emotional, as well as physical, energy are considerable. You have what it takes to achieve a great deal. If you really concentrate on your objectives, you will express your potential to the full. But if you fail to do this, you are likely to suffer from an unpleasant sense of discontent.

A full, busy, rewarding life and a deep involvement in both work and spare-time activities is what you need. Stagnation is your great enemy. You have a liking for mystery, ranging from detective fiction to the occult. If you feel attracted to the latter, or think you have a psychic side to your nature, do not play around with seances or Ouija boards. Seek sound professional advice from someone who is regarded as trustworthy.

Romance

Your need for sexual fulfillment is above average. Make sure that you find a partner who is sympathetic to your demanding needs and who is as lively as you are.

Your deep and passionate emotions mean that you can respond to certain situations with a show of jealousy and, perhaps, possessiveness. Your suspicions may well be unfounded, so be careful how you express them.

Your well-being

The traditional Scorpio body area is the genitals. "Safe sex" may therefore prove to be absolutely essential for you to keep your health.

With this Sun and Moon combination, your physical energy level is very high, so exercise is

The Moon in Scorpio

terribly important to you. One of your important activities should be athletic – all kinds of swimming are excellent for you. Do not ignore your Arien competitive spirit, spiked with Scorpio emotions.

Planning ahead

As long as you control your Arien enthusiasm when faced with get-rich-quick schemes, you are usually very shrewd when dealing with money. Use your intuition to discover weaknesses and foresee problems. In general, you should invest in big companies with steady growth.

Parenthood

You will be an excellent parent, but try not to force your own interests on your children, since you may tend to dominate them. Your psychological and emotional energy is infectious. By all means let it affect your children, and be proud of their progress, but allow them to be themselves.

THE MOON IN SAGITTARIUS

YOU RESPOND TO SUGGESTIONS AND CHALLENGES IMMEDIATELY AND WITH A NATURAL ENTHUSIASM. SINCE ARIES AND SAGITTARIUS ARE FIRE SIGNS, YOU MAY HAVE TO DEVELOP YOUR STAMINA, OR YOUR PROJECTS COULD EASILY FIZZLE OUT.

You are truly blessed; an Arien Sun and a Sagittarian Moon is an extremely positive combination. With your straightforward attitude to life, you are well able to assess problems and to put them into a coherent perspective.

Self-expression

Your powerful fire element prompts you to live a full life, but it does not encourage you to cope with detail. Your boredom level is very low, and can lead you to cast aside a project or ambition just because something else seems more attractive.

You are somewhat overly optimistic, and disappointments can spread a layer of gloom over your life. Still, this should not last – soon you will be off on another venture. You do need variety in your activities, perhaps involving moving from a physically demanding project to one that exercises your brain.

Try, however, to develop consistency of effort and a little more patience. You are more versatile than most Ariens, but to avoid exhaustion, make sure that you set aside time each day for relaxation and contemplation. Some of your deepest instincts incline you to a philosophic approach to life, and to an interest in esoteric subjects such as religion.

Romance

You are a lively, passionate lover whose many delightful ways will endear you to a partner. There will, however, be an element of duality in your nature that could create some sticky situations. You should also guard against a tendency to be offhand with people.

Your well-being

The Arien body area covers the hips and thighs. Arien women with a Sagittarian Moon will tend to put on

The Moon in Sagittarius

weight in these areas quite as readily as their Sagittarian Sun sign sisters. The Sagittarian body organ is the liver. If you like rich dishes, heavy food, and red wine, you would therefore be wise to keep a hangover cure at the ready.

Take care that undue haste does not lead to you incurring long-lasting sports injuries.

Planning ahead

You are very prone to risk-taking. When you are confronted by a challenge, you will respond almost instantaneously. Be careful, since this could be foolhardy. Get-rich-quick schemes could have an almost irresistible attraction, and you may have a strong gambling streak.

Parenthood

You could scarcely be a more lively and enthusiastic parent, but because you will be so anxious for your children to progress in life, you might find it difficult to adjust to a child with a slower rate of progress than you would like. Try to be patient, and make sure that you take enough time to listen to your children attentively and sympathetically.

THE MOON IN CAPRICORN

YOUR PRACTICAL CAPRICORNIAN MOON WILL ENCOURAGE YOU TO ACHIEVE ARIEN OBJECTIVES. TO BE FIRST IS IN YOUR NATURE. CONFRONTED WITH CHALLENGES, YOUR REACTION IS AMBITIOUS: YOU ASPIRE TO REACH THE TOP.

You may take life more seriously than any other Moon sign Capricornians. This does not, however, mean that your outlook will be negative. The Moon in Capricorn gives you a marvelous, offbeat sense of humor.

Self-expression

Your Arien desire to be first will be encouraged by the Capricornian ambition to "climb every mountain." You will not only reach the top, but you could also be the first of your peer group to do so.

Oddly enough, given your Arien assertiveness and Capricornian instinct for progress, doubts will creep in from time to time when you are confronted with challenges. This is most likely if your parents were at all domineering or unsympathetic. Counter such uncertainties by recalling that you are a free agent and have what it takes to win.

Romance

Emotionally, Capricorn is a cool sign, so your Arien passion will be kept under control and carefully directed. You may find it easier to be faithful to a lover than many people of your Sun sign. You may also tend to respond well to partners who are either wealthier than you or seem to be of a superior social class. This may not always be a good thing.

Because Capricorn is an earth sign, you possess plenty of practical caution. Do not allow this to dampen your pleasure when it comes to love.

Your well-being

The Capricornian body area is the knees and shins. Capricornians are prone to stiffness in the joints, so rheumatic pains and arthritic conditions are not unknown to them. These ailments are less likely to afflict you if you exercise. If, however, you should sustain an injury while

The Moon in Capricorn

exercising, especially to your knees, go to a physical therapist at once. Otherwise long-term damage or cartilage problems may occur. Most Ariens find it easy to keep up sports and exercise regimens, and exercise is just as important for you as it is for those with different Moon signs.

Planning ahead

Caution and a practical instinct will act in your favor where financial and career matters are concerned. While, as an Arien, you will like striding forward, and perhaps taking risks, with the Moon in Capricorn you will prefer a carefully regulated pace, both in climbing the career ladder and in increasing your bank balance.

Parenthood

You will want only the best for your children. Be careful, however, about working extra hours or bringing work home in order to provide materially for your children. Make sure that you take time to enjoy their company and to have fun with them.

THE MOON IN AQUARIUS

THE MOON IN AQUARIUS IS INVENTIVE, ORIGINAL, GLAMOROUS, AND COOL, WHILE ARIES IS WARM AND PASSIONATE. BE AN INDIVIDUALIST, BUT TRY NOT TO LET YOUR AQUARIAN MOON DISTANCE YOU FROM YOUR ARIEN QUALITIES.

You are among the most inventive of Ariens and are capable of having truly original ideas. What is more, you have the enthusiasm to bring these ideas to fruition. Your potential is great and should not be ignored or suppressed.

Self-expression

Aries is a sign needing considerable independence, and Aquarius is the most independent sign in the Zodiac. It is therefore hardly surprising that you like to do things your own way and will respond very negatively to anyone who tries to boss you around or cramp your style. It is necessary for you to learn from your own mistakes, even if this means doing things the hard way.

Because Aquarius is of the fixed quality, you could well surprise others by reacting very stubbornly at times. You will also have a tendency to be unpredictable, which can often be appealing. Be careful, however, that this trait does not go hand in hand with Aquarian selfishness.

Romance

Because of your Aquarian Moon, you may tend to rationalize your emotions, or even to detach yourself from them, especially during the early stages of an emotional relationship. But there is also a very romantic side to your Aquarian Moon and an instinctive liking for glamour. These traits will inevitably color your attitudes.

An overall need for independence may mean that you put off forming a permanent relationship or marriage until quite late in life. Your sex life will, however, have the usual exuberance of Aries.

Your well-being

Aquarius rules the ankles and the circulation. You could feel the cold more than most Sun sign Ariens, and

The Moon in Aquarius

it is important that you keep your circulation in good order. If you can keep active, you should also avoid developing stiffness in the joints, to which Aquarians are prone.

Planning ahead

The Aquarian attraction to the glamorous and romantic often creates a desire for expensive, glitzy things, unusual objects for the home, and costly original clothes and perfumes. It is in these areas that Arien enthusiasm could grab you and encourage you to spend an excessive amount of money.

Parenthood

You should not find it difficult to keep up with your children's interests. At times, you may even overtake them in following fads, so you should have no problem with the generation gap. Do, however, control any tendency to be unpredictable, since children like to know where they stand.

THE MOON IN PISCES

BY COMBINING YOUR FIERY ARIEN QUALITIES WITH THE PISCEAN SENSITIVITY OF YOUR EMOTIONAL REACTIONS, YOU WILL MAKE THE MOST OF THESE VIVIDLY CONTRASTING CHARACTERISTICS.

Aries is often said to be the pioneer of the Zodiac, and Pisces the poet, so it is not surprising that you are an individual with contrasting sides to your personality.

Self-expression

Your Arien Sun gives you all the positive, forthright qualities that are associated with the sign. In fact, it could eclipse the influence of your sensitive, intuitive Moon. You may sometimes lack Arien self-confidence when confronted with a challenge. Have you a deep-rooted tendency to shy away from some situations?

Looking at this combination in another way, it is likely that you are far more caring and sympathetic than many Ariens. You will certainly spend time, energy, and money helping other people, and this could occasionally leave you feeling drained. You could well be creative, in a variety of ways. Your Piscean instinct will incline you to work behind the scenes, while your Arien Sun will want you to be in the spotlight.

Romance

Your fiery Arien emotion is combined with the emotion of Pisces, which is a water sign. This makes you a caring lover, sensitive to your partner's needs. But beware of a negative Piscean trait: deceptiveness. This is often brought on by a tendency to take the easy way out of situations.

Your well-being

The Piscean body area is the feet. You may hate the restriction of wearing shoes, especially high-heeled shoes, and going barefoot will therefore have its attractions. But remember the Arien tendency to be accident-prone, which could mean that you are easily susceptible to cut and scraped feet, bunions, or corns. You may not enjoy the rough and

The Moon in Pisces

tumble of the sports that Ariens usually like. Bearing in mind your Arien strength and vitality, however, you could well be attracted to gymnastics when you are young, and to any kind of dancing. This, and perhaps ice skating, should be particularly good for you.

Planning ahead

Enthusiasm, the inability to adopt a firm position, and a tendency to be impractical could make you fall for risky financial schemes. If, like many Ariens, you have an enterprising streak, you may need a good business partner to steady you and to keep the books. Beware of overextending yourself financially.

Parenthood

You will be sensitive to your children's needs, but may tend to worry about them too much – more, in fact, than most other Ariens. Instead of allowing your admirable Piscean imagination to invent all sorts of catastrophes that may have happened to your children, put this imagination to use in devising your own bedtime stories to enthrall them. You will not find this difficult.

SUN & MOON SIGNS

TAURUS

APRIL 21 – MAY 21

INTRODUCING TAURUS

TAURUS, THE SIGN OF THE BULL, IS THE SECOND SIGN OF THE ZODIAC. IT REPRESENTS A DESIRE FOR STABILITY IN ALL THINGS, AND AN OVERALL NEED FOR BOTH EMOTIONAL AND MATERIAL SECURITY.

Taureans like creature comforts, enjoy sweet, rich food, and are very sensual. They make marvelous lovers, but are often too possessive, and can go so far as to treat their partners as if they owned them.

Here, too, is excellent business sense. While not quick to learn, once Taureans absorb a concept, they will seldom forget it.

Traditional groupings

As you read through this book you will come across references to the elements and the qualities, and to positive and negative, or masculine and feminine signs.

The first of these groupings, that of the elements, comprises fire, earth, air, and water signs. The second, that of the qualities, divides the Zodiac into cardinal, fixed, and mutable signs. The final grouping is made up of positive and negative, or masculine and feminine signs. Each Zodiac sign is associated with a combination of components from these groupings, all of which contribute different characteristics to it.

Taurean characteristics

As the first sign of the earth element, Taurus is characteristically plodding, reliable, and predictable. Being ruled by Venus, however, it also bestows on its subjects great natural charm, and gives them the reputation of being the best-looking Zodiac group.

Taurus is a sign of the fixed quality, so stubbornness can often be present in its subjects. It is therefore very important for Taureans to learn to keep an open mind. Taurus is also, in spite of the symbolic Bull, a feminine or negative sign, which has the effect of inclining its subjects to be introverted.

The Taurean colors are those governed by the planet Venus: pastel blues, pinks, and greens.

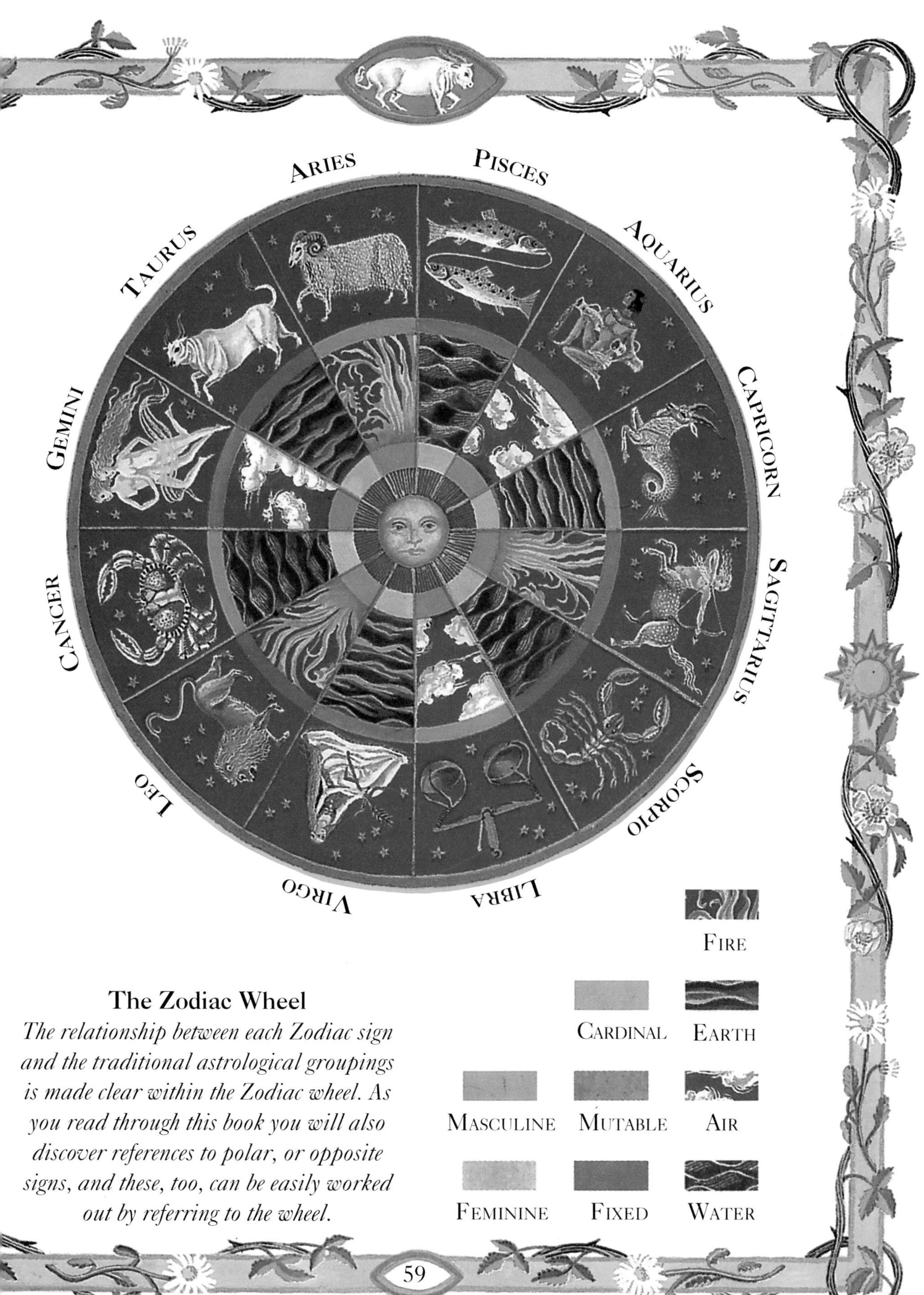

The Zodiac Wheel

The relationship between each Zodiac sign and the traditional astrological groupings is made clear within the Zodiac wheel. As you read through this book you will also discover references to polar, or opposite signs, and these, too, can be easily worked out by referring to the wheel.

TAURUS

MYTHS & LEGENDS

THE ZODIAC, WHICH IS SAID TO HAVE ORIGINATED IN BABYLON AS LONG AS 2,500 YEARS AGO, IS A CIRCLE OF CONSTELLATIONS THROUGH WHICH THE SUN MOVES DURING THE COURSE OF A YEAR.

The first myth associated with this constellation concerned the Babylonian "Bull of Heaven," Ishtar and Anu, and Gilgamesh, the great epic hero of Babylon.

Ishtar, the goddess of lechery, fell violently in love with the hero Gilgamesh. He knew, however, that she had disposed of her previous lovers in various unpleasant ways, and that she was both faithless and unreliable. Finding herself rejected, Ishtar appealed to her father, Anu, king of the gods, to create a giant Bull of Heaven that would kill Gilgamesh. This bull was Taurus.

A variety of myths

Various other bulls have been associated with the constellation. There was the white bull mentioned by the Roman poet Virgil, which was said to open "the gate of the year with his golden horns." White bulls were also sacrificed at sunset on the fifth day of the Babylonian new year festival, when the equinoctial New Moon appeared in the sign of Taurus.

Europa and the bull

Much better known than this or the Babylonian Bull of Heaven is the bull in the Greek legend of Europa.

Zeus, king of the gods, fell in love with the king of Phoenicia's extraordinarily beautiful daughter, Europa. In order to deceive her into submitting to his dubious intentions, Zeus turned himself into an incredibly handsome bull and set himself to graze among her father's herd. When Europa, who was playing by the seashore with her friends, saw Zeus as the bull, she was overcome by how majestic, yet gentle, he seemed.

The abduction

Europa approached him, and he knelt in front of her. At this, she climbed onto his back, and put a wreath of

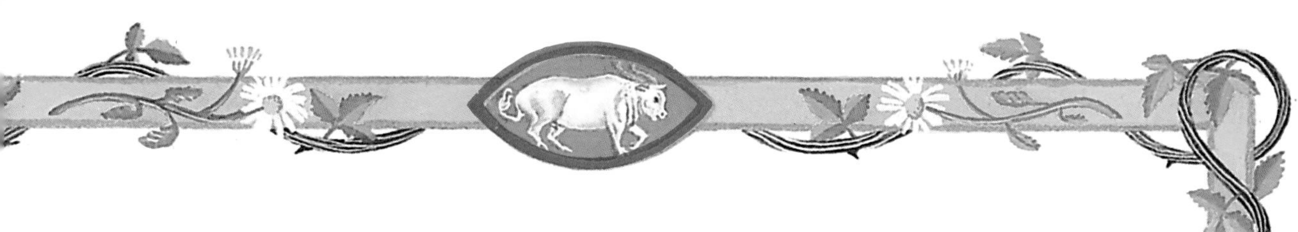

Jupiter carries off Europa

In this painting by Pierre Gobert (1662 – 1744), Europa is shown being carried off by the god Zeus, who has disguised himself as a bull.

flowers around his horns. Zeus then sprang immediately to his feet and swam across the sea to Crete. There he had his wicked way with Europa under a plane tree. (This particular tree was then granted the divine privilege of keeping its foliage through all the seasons.) Europa bore Zeus three children. Among them was Minos, who later ruled over the island after the king of Crete, Asterius, adopted all three children and invited Europa to become his wife.

Some traditions of Taurus – the sign of good looks and charm but also of possessiveness – do seem linked to that handsome bull who was really a god in disguise.

TAURUS

SYMBOLISM

CERTAIN HERBS, SPICES, FLOWERS, TREES, GEMS, METALS, AND ANIMALS HAVE LONG BEEN ASSOCIATED WITH PARTICULAR ZODIAC SIGNS. SOME ASSOCIATIONS ARE SIMPLY AMUSING, WHILE OTHERS CAN BE USEFUL.

PRIMROSES

Flowers

Taurus rules the rose, primrose, columbine, daisy, foxglove, poppy, and violet. The reasons for these attributions are lost in the mists of time.

PINK ROSES

CYPRESS

Spices

Taurus was said by ancient astrologers to rule all spices. Cloves, in particular, fall under the influence of this sign.

Trees

Taurean trees include the ash, cypress, vine, almond, fig, apple, and pear.

CINNAMON STICKS

Herbs

Spearmint is only one of the herbs traditionally linked to Taurus. Among the others, arrack was used to cure throat infections and elder root for snake bites.

SPEARMINT

CLOVES

TAURUS SYMBOLISM

UNREFINED COPPER

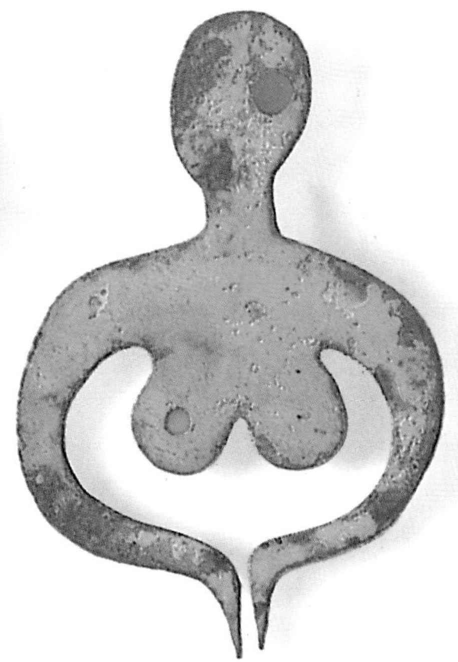

COPPER BROOCH

Metal

The Taurean metal is copper, the traditional metal of the planet Venus, which rules the sign.

TOY BULL MADE OF LEAD

Moss agate

Gems

The magnificent emerald and the moss agate are Taurean gems. Their only obvious association with the sign is through their color, green, which is a Taurean color.

Emerald brooch

Nineteenth-century bull can-opener

Spanish ceramic tile

Animals

All types of cattle fall under the domination of Taurus.

TAURUS

PROFILE

TAUREANS HAVE THE REPUTATION OF BEING THE BEST-LOOKING OF ALL 12 ZODIAC TYPES. IF THIS IS TRUE, YOU SHOULD TRY HARD TO MAINTAIN YOUR APPEARANCE. UNFORTUNATELY, THIS IS OFTEN A DIFFICULT TASK.

Taureans like to be sure that they are on firm ground, both psychologically and physically. A conventional approach appeals because they prefer established things that are secure and dependable. You are therefore likely to stand with your feet apart, your hands either in your pockets or grasping some all-important possession, for example, a handbag. You will, on the whole, be inclined to present a conventional image of yourself to those around you.

The Taurean face
Your hair is likely to be soft and curly, and may fall well onto your forehead.

The body

Taureans often have a firm, and somewhat stocky, but undeniably handsome, frame. Both men and women tend to be broad-shouldered and to have thick necks, echoing the powerful build of the animal of their sign. They are capable of having slim waists, and must constantly strive to keep themselves in good shape. Flab can, all too easily, mar their natural good looks.

The face

Taureans often have hair that falls well over their foreheads. Soft curls are quite common, and baldness is rarely seen. The forehead itself is likely to be rather low, and as you get older, you may find pronounced horizontal lines appearing there. Your eyes are probably deep-set, dark, and penetrating, but a softness is possibly

The Taurean stance

You will generally adopt a firm stance, with your feet apart, and clasping a favorite possession.

also visible. The Taurean nose is likely to be broad and rather flat, and the chin is is rarely pronounced. Any increase in your weight, and this is something that you should be wary of, may therefore lead to you developing a double chin. Your mouth is likely to reflect your purposefulness, but it can also reveal your sensitivity.

Style

Taureans will dress in a style conventional for their generation. You may therefore have to be careful that your image does not start to look dated. For women, the look tends to prettiness: pastel colors and the occasional frill or bow at the neck. The men will sometimes sport an attractively floral or pastel-colored tie, for example to relieve a formal city suit. The naturally broad shoulders of Taureans usually require a minimum of padding.

In general

The attractive, warm, and sensual speaking voice that is possessed by many Taureans often enhances their natural good looks. You may have a tendency to move rather slowly and deliberately since, although you are well aware of where you are going, and the way in which you are going to get there, you usually prefer to feel unhurried as you go about your business. Perhaps you should sometimes try speeding up a little, as this might well benefit you both mentally and physically.

TAURUS
PERSONALITY

TAURUS, THE SECOND SIGN OF THE ZODIAC, IS STEADFAST, STABLE, AND CONVENTIONAL IN OUTLOOK. IT IS IMPORTANT THAT TAUREANS DO NOT BECOME SLAVES TO A ROUTINE, OR TOO SET IN THEIR WAYS AND IMMOVABLY STUBBORN.

You are one of the most reliable of all Zodiac types and are also likely to be the most charming. People will soon come to realize that from you they will always be able to expect a warm and affectionate greeting. You have the ability to inspire confidence and will impress everyone with your genuine sincerity.

For you to be completely fulfilled, you must have both emotional and financial security. Indeed, the achievement of this often forms the basic motivation of your life.

At work

You will flourish in a steady, well-paid job, complete with the knowledge that a regular paycheck will be yours. This will enable you to plan your finances with great confidence and let you look toward the future in terms of possessions and purchases. In your case, these will no doubt include a bigger and better house, labor-saving devices to make life easy for you, handsome furniture, and a generally comfortable lifestyle.

Your attitudes

Your need for emotional security is just as strong as your delight in material possessions. There is a danger here, however, since you can unconsciously come to regard your partner as being just another possession. When this happens, the words "my wife" and "my husband" take on quite new – and not altogether pleasant – connotations. More is said on this subject elsewhere (*see pages 76 – 77*), but the tendency must be underscored. Possessiveness is by far the worst Taurean fault, and this is the most dangerous area in which it can be expressed.

Material things, for example your home and its furniture – in fact most objects a Taurean can own – may also become too important to you, just like

Venus rules Taurus

Venus, the Roman goddess of love, represents the ruling planet of Taurus and Libra. The influence of Venus extends to art and fashion, and relates to the feminine side of a Taurean's nature.

the figures in your bank balance. The trait relates, of course, to your need for security.

The overall picture

Taureans are very often passionate people with strong feelings and opinions. Luckily, you usually express your powerful emotional level in a positive way. Like the Taurean bull, however, while you may be slow to anger, once roused your rage is often considerable. Be magnanimous, and learn to reject resentfulness.

With your liking for the good life, there is a chance that you may feel a conflict between the necessity to work hard, in order to attain that prosperous, luxurious lifestyle, and a certain indulgent laziness.

TAURUS ASPIRATIONS

FOLLOWING A REGULAR ROUTINE WILL NOT WORRY YOU. YOUR ORGANIZATIONAL AND MONEY-MAKING SKILLS MAY HELP YOU TO START YOUR OWN BUSINESS. DO NOT BE AFRAID OF TAKING OCCASIONAL RISKS.

COIN BALANCE

Finance

A career in finance may suit money-loving Taureans. They will usually take great care when investing.

COINS

Arts and crafts

As an earth sign, Taurus has a strong feeling for natural materials. Taureans enjoy using wood or clay, and a variety of fabrics.

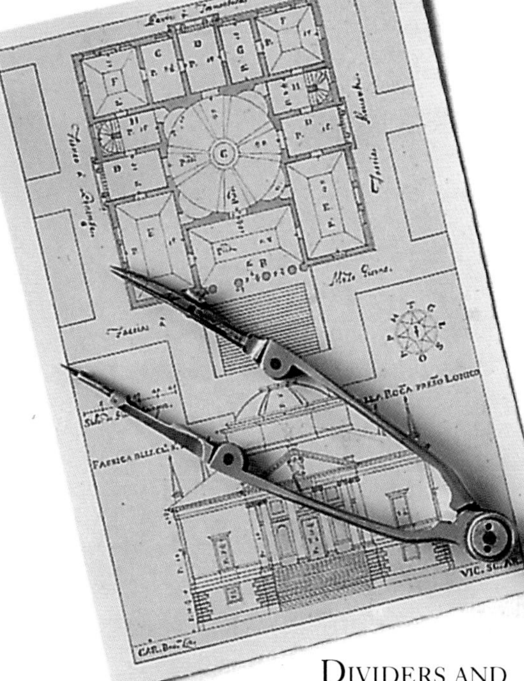

DIVIDERS AND ARCHITECTURAL PLAN

POLISH BEADWORK

Architecture

Taureans have a strong sense of balance and form. They often design buildings that have an affinity with the landscape.

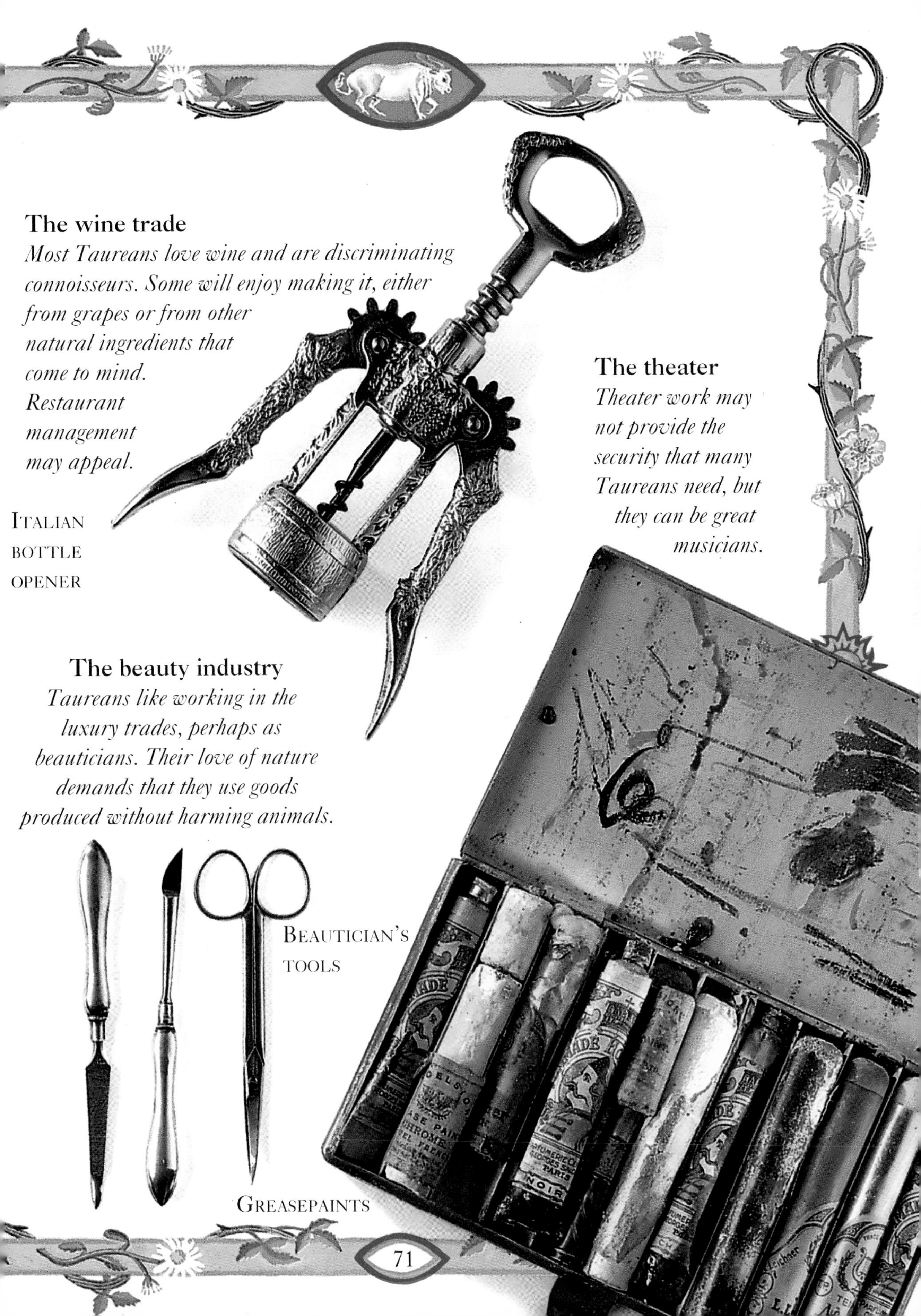

The wine trade

Most Taureans love wine and are discriminating connoisseurs. Some will enjoy making it, either from grapes or from other natural ingredients that come to mind. Restaurant management may appeal.

ITALIAN BOTTLE OPENER

The theater

Theater work may not provide the security that many Taureans need, but they can be great musicians.

The beauty industry

Taureans like working in the luxury trades, perhaps as beauticians. Their love of nature demands that they use goods produced without harming animals.

BEAUTICIAN'S TOOLS

GREASEPAINTS

TAURUS

HEALTH

BECAUSE OF THEIR LIKING FOR RICH FOOD, OFTEN COMBINED WITH A SLOW METABOLISM, MANY TAUREANS HAVE A TENDENCY TO PUT ON WEIGHT EASILY. THEIR NECKS AND THROATS ARE VULNERABLE TO INJURY OR INFECTION.

Although Taureans are generally disciplined people, they sometimes find the routine of exercise difficult to maintain.

Your diet

As a Taurean, you no doubt love your food. If you have a slow metabolism, you should therefore do what you can to speed it up, perhaps through exercise, to help you fight weight gain. You may need to supplement your diet with sodium sulfate (nat. sulph.), which helps to eliminate excess water from the body.

Taking care

It should be kept in mind that the planet Venus rules not only the sign Taurus, but also the thyroid gland. If, therefore, you are considerably overweight for no apparent reason, you should think about being tested for possible thyroid inactivity.

The Taurean body area is the throat and neck, so you should take care to sleep with a suitable pillow. You may otherwise find yourself waking up with a stiff neck.

Grapes

Among the foods traditionally associated with Taurus are grapes, cereals, berries, and beans.

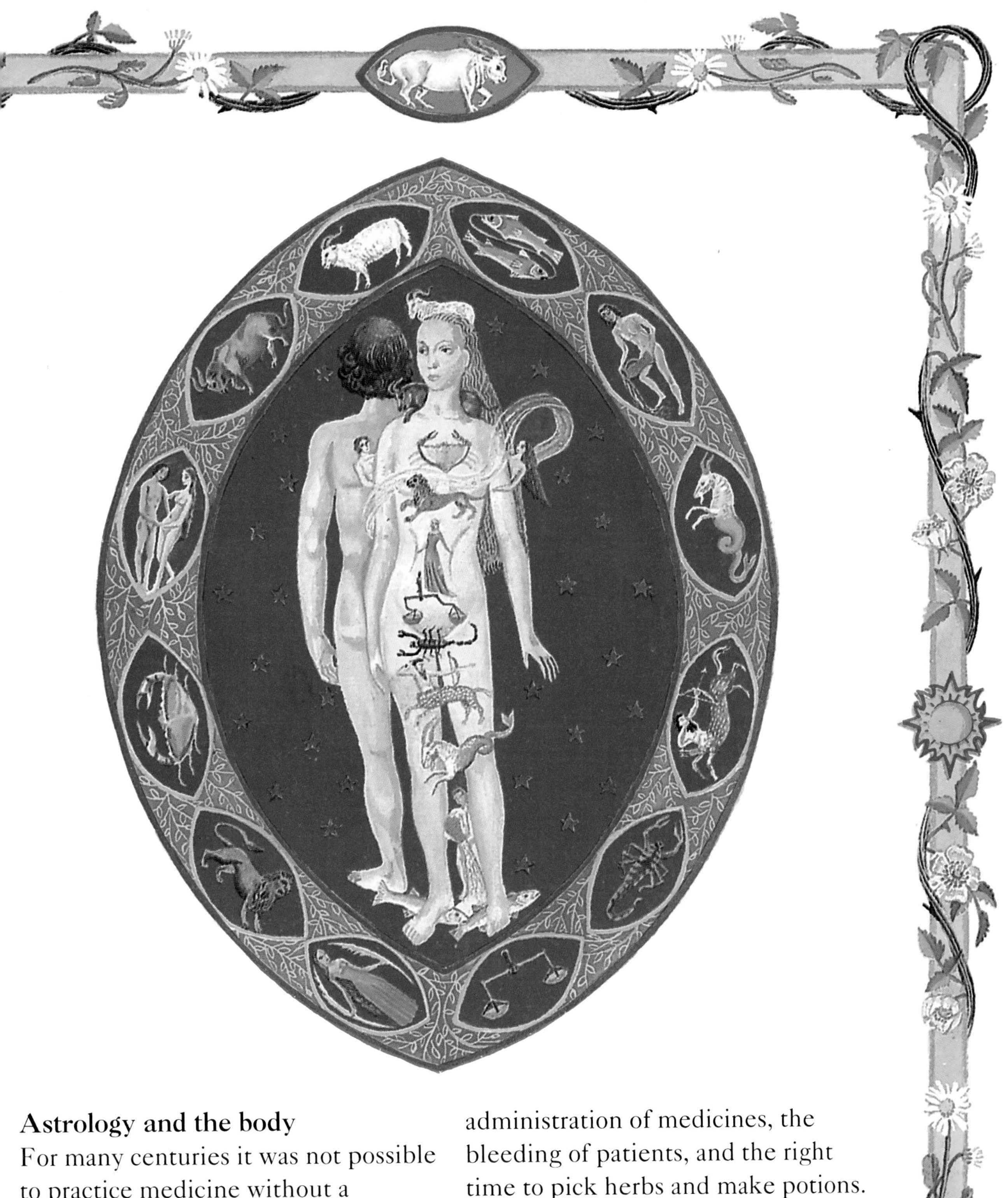

Astrology and the body

For many centuries it was not possible to practice medicine without a knowledge of astrology. In European universities, medical training included information on how planetary positions would affect the administration of medicines, the bleeding of patients, and the right time to pick herbs and make potions.

Each Zodiac sign rules a particular part of the body, and early medical textbooks always included a drawing that illustrated the point.

TAURUS AT
LEISURE

EACH OF THE SUN SIGNS TRADITIONALLY SUGGESTS SPARE-TIME ACTIVITIES. ALTHOUGH THESE HOBBIES AND VACATION SPOTS ARE ONLY SUGGESTIONS, THEY OFTEN SUIT TAUREAN INTERESTS AND TASTES.

Gardening
Taurus is an earth sign and has always been associated with gardening, especially the creation of beautiful flower gardens.

GARDENING EQUIPMENT

Comfortable hotel stays
Taureans need and enjoy their creature comforts. When you are on vacation, you no doubt like to relax in the luxury of an expensive hotel.

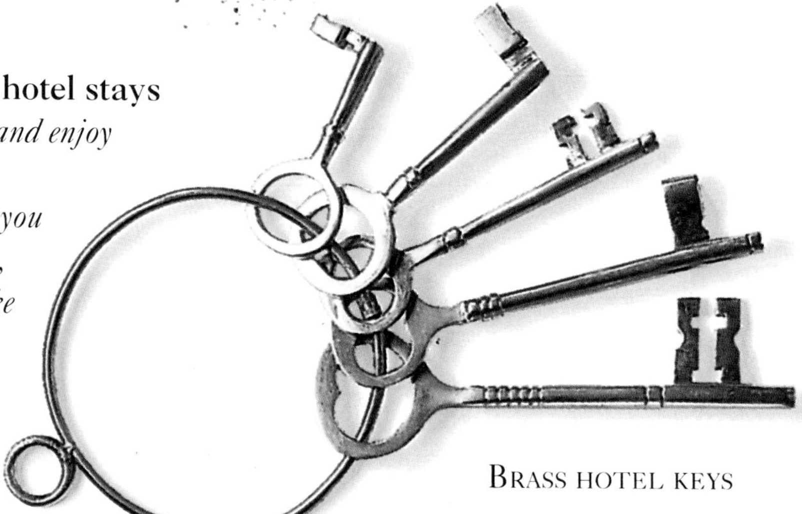

BRASS HOTEL KEYS

Embroidered handkerchief

Embroidery

Taureans are often patient, with a fondness for detail. Meticulous work such as model-making, craftwork, or embroidery will no doubt fascinate you.

Pastry cutter

Rolling pin

Cookery

Although this hobby is normally associated with Cancerians, many Taureans enjoy baking cakes and making desserts.

Postage stamps

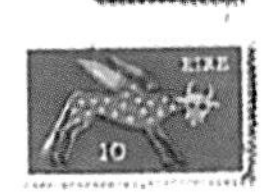

Travel

You hate uncertainty and, having found your ideal vacation destination, you are likely to return there regularly. It could be Ireland, Cyprus, the Greek islands, Iran, or Switzerland.

Bowling balls

Sport

Team sports might be fun when you are young, but these are likely to be replaced by games of skill, like bowling.

TAURUS IN LOVE

WHEN A TAUREAN IS IN LOVE, THE INFLUENCE OF VENUS RULES THE DAY. UNDER THESE CIRCUMSTANCES, YOU WILL EXPRESS YOUR VERY BEST CHARACTERISTICS IN A WAY THAT CANNOT FAIL TO IMPRESS A LOVED ONE.

You may, with your overwhelming need for emotional security, find it hard to step into the vast unknown of a new relationship. Taureans need to be very sure of their partners before making any commitment to them. The worst Taurean fault is possessiveness and, when you are in love, this tendency can be quite vehemently expressed. You may find yourself thinking: "You're mine – all mine!" Together with a tendency to cling, this may create a claustrophobic atmosphere that will put many other Sun signs off. Allowing a partner a little more freedom will be much more productive.

Taureans are very generous lovers, and your gifts may have a good investment value. Naturally, this means that you are investing in your lover's emotions, in anticipation of a long-lasting relationship; but you are also looking to the future in a more material way. If, by some misfortune, the pair of you should fall upon hard times, the gift could be sold.

As a lover

Sexually, you are likely to be an admirable lover. Every move that you make will be unhurried, and every act of love will be

beautifully paced, with consideration for your partner's needs. Joy and passion will combine to the satisfaction of you both. Without a doubt, all Taureans are capable of being exciting lovers.The best kind of Taurean lover is, of course, one who can be both protective and caring.

Types of Taurean lover

Some Taureans can be surprisingly oversensitive. Many of you are nostalgic and may tend to look to the past in a rather sentimental way. This could be a little difficult for a lively, forward-looking partner to cope with. Others of your Sun sign are prone to be more assertive; their passion is intense and fiery. They must take care not to expose a selfish streak that could mar a relationship. There are also those people who express their love in a purel Taurean way, by recognizing every one of the traits that are set out here and by learning to counter any negative possessiveness. Some of you tend to have a flirtatious side to your nature, which lightens Taurean passion. This group tends to be talkative and requires partners with active minds as well as lively bodies.

TAURUS AT HOME

COMFORT IS THE KEYNOTE OF A TAUREAN HOME, WITH TRADITION BEING THE BACKBONE OF THE FURNISHING AND DECOR. WARM PINK OR PALE BLUE COLORS MAY PREDOMINATE. ABOVE ALL, THE ATMOSPHERE WILL BE CALM AND CUSHIONED.

Taureans usually have an overall need to feel secure. A typical Taurean home will be beautiful, large and, above all, very comfortable. This may even be motivated by a conscious effort to show how comfortably placed its inhabitants are. The perfect Taurean house will have a yard, and will preferably be located in the country. If this is not possible, then a quiet suburb should suffice just as easily. When you take time to sit down and relax in your living room, you will want to feel the warmth and the security of a solid, but luxurious and very comfortable armchair.

Your choice of furniture is likely to tend toward the conventional and, if this is the case, you will probably prefer to choose styles that will not date too easily. Wildly fashionable articles are unlikely to hold much appeal for you; you will, in general, want your furniture to be easy on the eye, and very welcoming. It is likely that your furniture will be extremely pretty, perhaps containing soft, delicate shades of pink, blue, and perhaps some very pale green, which are the colors of Venus, the Taurean ruling planet.

Elegant flower display
The Taurean home is very likely to boast at least one beautiful display of flowers.

Decorative objects

Since most Taureans love flowers, there is a fair chance that you will own plenty of beautiful vases in which to put them. Taureans sometimes have a

Music stand and flute

If, like many Taureans, you play an instrument, you may give it pride of place.

collection of books on gardens or gardening. Alternatively, you might accumulate business magazines (some Taureans enjoy thinking about finance as much as gardening).

Soft furnishings

Taureans often obtain terrific pleasure from choosing new drapes and cushions. You will, more than likely, decide upon floral patterns, perhaps in a glazed cotton or shiny satin. Frills often abound in the Taurean home, and there will be a proliferation of sheers to enhance windows, or to block out any uninteresting view outside. These will, however, be kept pulled right back if you have a beautiful flower garden of which you are justifiably proud. You probably prefer thick carpets, and will use beautiful rugs not only to preserve your carpets, bur decoratively, in their own right, to enhance the look of your home.

Comfortable armchair

The floral pattern on this comfortable armchair is typically Taurean.

THE MOON AND YOU

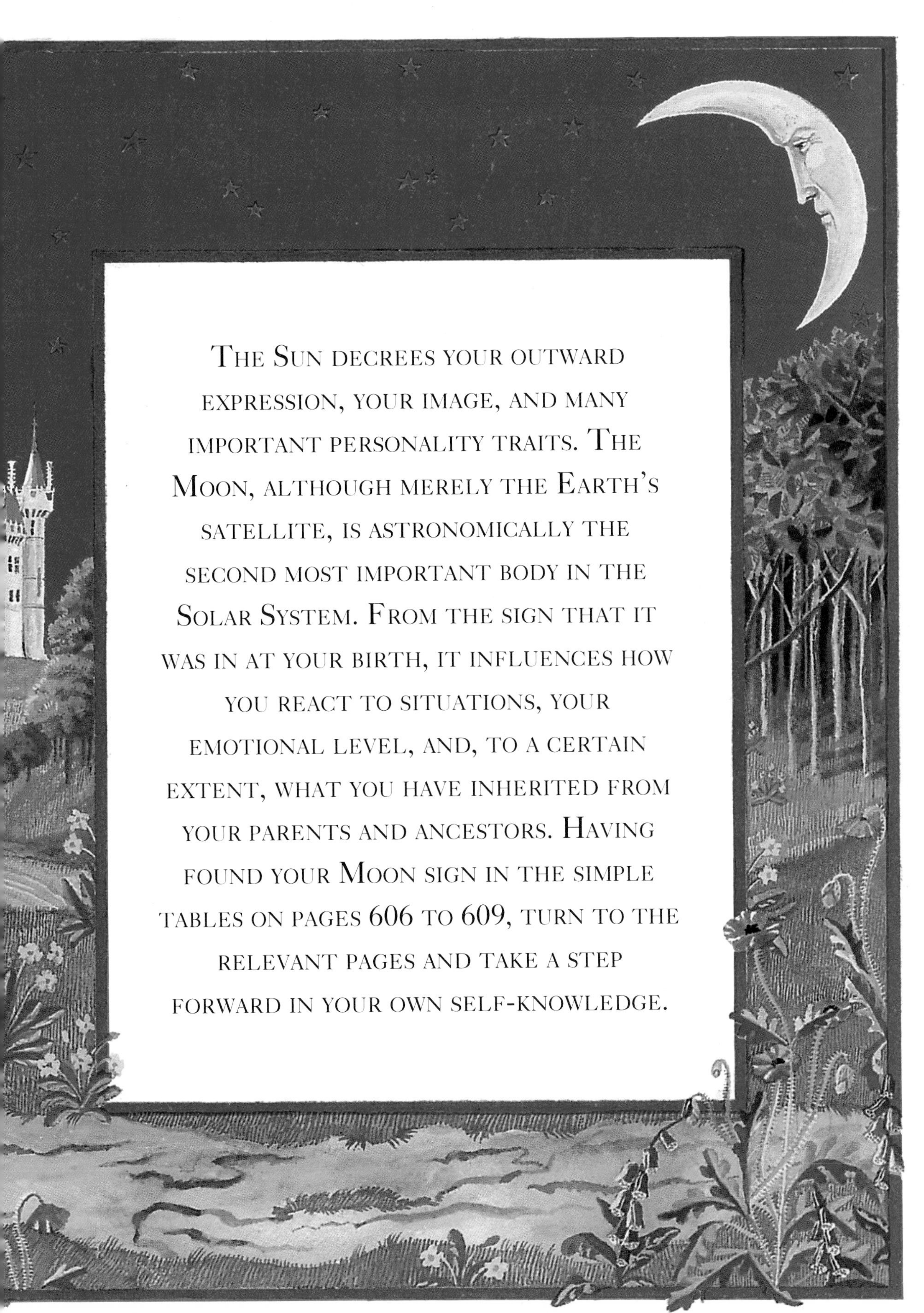

The Sun decrees your outward expression, your image, and many important personality traits. The Moon, although merely the Earth's satellite, is astronomically the second most important body in the Solar System. From the sign that it was in at your birth, it influences how you react to situations, your emotional level, and, to a certain extent, what you have inherited from your parents and ancestors. Having found your Moon sign in the simple tables on pages 606 to 609, turn to the relevant pages and take a step forward in your own self-knowledge.

THE MOON IN ARIES

ARIES IS A FIRE SIGN, SO YOUR REACTIONS TO SITUATIONS ARE ENTHUSIASTIC AND OFTEN EMOTIONAL: UNDER PRESSURE YOU COULD TAKE HASTY OR PREMATURE ACTION. MAKE AN EFFORT NOT TO SUPPRESS YOUR TAUREAN CAUTION.

Your Arien Moon enables you to respond to situations with enthusiasm and speeds up your reactions. You could occasionally act hastily, and your Moon could even allow you to take some risks.

Self-expression

Taureans are generally warm people, and because your Arien Moon also provides a highly charged emotional influence, you will have a particularly high emotional level. You will be quick to anger, and may find it a little difficult to get along with some people. But because of the speed with which the Moon works when in Aries, you can throw off anger, and dismiss any outpouring of emotion, more easily than many Taureans.

Romance

You will be a very passionate lover, and because of an element of Moon sign impatience – something that is virtually unknown to Taureans – you may tend to sweep partners off their feet. You are also less likely to succumb to Taurean possessiveness.

If you have a greater need for independence and freedom than most Taureans, do not ignore this. You most certainly have a very lively zest for love and sex which, coupled with warm Taurean sentiment and affection, plus your delightful sensuous qualities, makes you a wonderful lover.

Your well-being

The effect of an Arien Moon on your health could be to render you prone to headaches. If you suffer from them frequently, do not ignore the possibility that you may be suffering from a minor kidney problem.

You should also remember that Aries is an accident-prone sign and that, through carelessness, you may sometimes cut or burn yourself. If

The Moon in Aries

your responses to situations tend to be hurried, or you are prone to flurries of hastiness, there is a distinct possibility that you could be very vulnerable in this respect.

Planning ahead

Your Taurean business sense may be impeded by your Arien Moon. While it will encourage you to invest your money, you may do so a fraction less wisely than your Taurean Sun sign would have it. You may have a sneaking regard for quick, risky growth, and could end up learning the hard way – by losing money.

Parenthood

You will be a less conventional, and perhaps less strict, parent than with many Taureans. You will understand when your children wish to express their independence. You will also manage to sidestep the Taurean tendency to spoil them. Encourage family members to exercise plenty.

THE MOON IN TAURUS

WITH BOTH THE SUN AND THE MOON IN TAURUS AT THE TIME OF YOUR BIRTH, YOU WERE BORN AT THE TIME OF THE NEW MOON. AS AN EARTH SIGN, TAURUS POWERFULLY INFLUENCES YOUR PERSONALITY AND REACTIONS.

Should you study a list of your Sun sign characteristics, you will probably recognize that a great many of them apply to you. On average, out of a list of perhaps 20 traits of a Sun sign listed in books or magazines, most people will strongly identify with 11 or 12. In your case, however, the average increases considerably because the Sun and Moon were both in Taurus when you were born.

Self-expression

Your Sun sign makes you cautious, methodical, and not given to rushing around; your Moon sign encourages you to respond to situations in the same careful manner.

Your Taurean need for security is extremely strong, and your need for emotional security is perhaps second to none. You need a steady routine, like most people of your Sun sign, but with you it goes deeper than that. If, for instance, your schedule is unexpectedly disrupted, you will not find it easy to adjust, and your whole system could suffer.

You may fly into a rage more frequently than other Taureans, and this does not always have positive results: Try to emerge from this type of mood as quickly as you can.

Romance

You can be a wonderfully responsive Taurean lover, as long as you consciously check what may amount to a fatal flaw of being possessive. You could, without thinking, make life claustrophobic for your lover; if accused of this, you should take the rebuke seriously.

Your well-being

Healthwise, you must watch a tendency to put on weight; losing it may not be easy for you. One solution is to try to increase your metabolic rate, which may be naturally slow. For

The Moon in Taurus

instance, try walking a little more quickly and climbing stairs instead of relying on elevators.

Planning ahead

You may be something of a wizard at making money and at stretching your income much further than might seem possible. You have an excellent instinct for investment: Your cautiousness and tendency to go for steady growth ensure that you get the best possible results from your portfolio. Financial risk-taking is not something to which you are normally prone. You do, however, love luxury and creature comforts and will therefore be wise to earn as much money as you possibly can.

Parenthood

While making sure that your children have the best of everything, you may veer between being too strict and spoiling them. They may have more independent spirits than you; do not try to quell this. A show of affection will endear you to them.

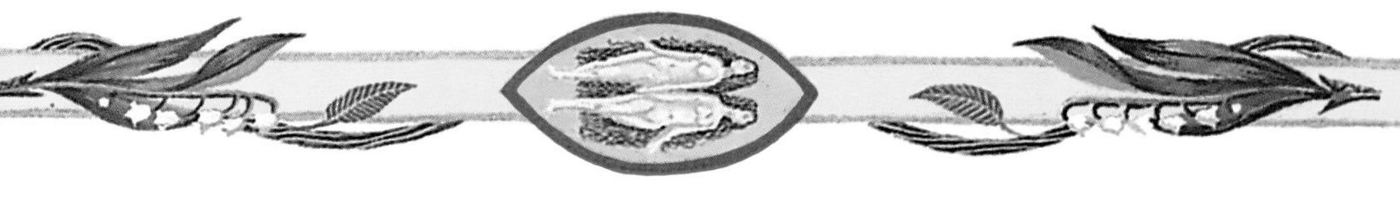

THE MOON IN GEMINI

YOUR GEMINIAN MOON PROVIDES YOU WITH UNUSUALLY RAPID RESPONSES TO SITUATIONS. SHOULD YOU SUFFER FROM RESTLESSNESS, ALLOW YOUR TAUREAN STABILITY TO CALM IT. ANY SUDDEN IDEAS COULD BE VERY ORIGINAL.

Your lighthearted Geminian Moon makes you both original and capable of conveying your ideas to other people easily. You are, no doubt, an excellent communicator, and in all kinds of situations will respond to others in an open, friendly way. You are probably more talkative than many Sun sign Taureans.

Neighboring Zodiac signs are always very different, and from Gemini the Moon gives your stable, down-to-earth Taurean character some delightfully contrasting Geminian facets.

Self-expression

Gemini is not a highly emotional sign, and your reaction to most situations may be remarkably cool and detached. It could also be well spiced with a questioning logic.

But it is likely that, having first been affected by your Geminian Moon, your Taurean qualities soon take over. When your Sun sign dominates, you do anything to get what you want, just the way you want it. In your case stubbornness, supported by verbosity, will definitely come into its own from time to time.

Romance

Your Moon sign will make you express your natural charm and affection in a delightfully flirtatious way. You will enchant and attract lovers, who will not have to wait long to know how you feel about them.

You need a certain freedom of expression in this sphere of your life. Although your Taurean possessiveness may make it difficult, you must also recognize that your partners may need some freedom, too.

Your well-being

The Geminian body area covers the arms, hands, and lungs. In your case, a sore throat could well be followed by

The Moon in Gemini

a chest cough. If the cough persists, do not ignore it, since it could develop into something more serious. Your metabolism is probably considerably faster than that of most Taureans, so a susceptibility to putting on weight could be less of a problem for you. You should enjoy exercise.

Planning ahead

You may not be quite as cautious or as interested in steady financial growth as many Taureans. From time to time you could fall for some enticing get-rich-quick scheme, with awful results. Do not always follow your first reactions to such schemes.

Parenthood

You will have fewer problems with the generation gap than is usual with Taureans, because any Geminian influence encourages one to be future-oriented. In your case it will add a certain youthfulness of outlook that will help you to respond well to the concerns, opinions, and needs of the younger generation.

THE MOON IN CANCER

WITH THE MOON IN CANCER, YOUR AFFECTIONATE QUALITIES ARE COMBINED WITH TENDER, CARING EMOTION. YOU WILL EXPRESS THIS POSITIVELY TO YOUR LOVERS AND FAMILY. BE SENSIBLE IF YOU ARE SEIZED BY AN IRRATIONAL WORRY.

Earth and water are complementary elements, and the power of your Cancerian Moon (it is strong because the Moon rules Cancer) will vie for expression with your Taurean Sun. Therefore your Taurean qualities will be very powerfully affected by protective instincts. Your need for emotional security, which is so much a part of your Taurean motivation, will also be strongly enhanced and extended toward your loved ones.

Self-expression

All Taureans are practical and have plenty of common sense. Those with the Moon in Cancer have great intuitive foresight and will instinctively know when the time is right to be determined and brave.

You will achieve much, but may be a little undisciplined in your approach to life, sometimes allowing yourself to do what your prevailing mood seems to dictate. Beware of mood swings that could hamper your progress. You have a wonderful imagination, but practical though you are, it is easy for you to succumb to worry. If your imagination takes over, you can really work yourself into a frenzy.

Your emotional resources are considerable, and you should be able to find plenty of outlets for them in all areas of your life.

Romance

You will be a romantic, perhaps even sentimental lover, capable of expressing your feelings tenderly, and you will be sensitive and responsive to your partner's needs. It may, however, be difficult for you to come to terms with the circumstances of the breakup of a relationship.

Your well-being

The chest and breasts are the Cancerian body areas, but so, to a certain extent, is the digestive system.

The Moon in Cancer

Worry is likely to cause problems in the latter area and, as a Taurean, your liking for good food and wine can exacerbate them. You can put on weight all too easily and may well have to constantly discipline yourself to a very strictly controlled diet. The best forms of exercise for you are swimming and, as has already been suggested, dance.

Planning ahead

Taurean possessiveness and the Cancerian need to hoard things work in two ways. In the first instance you can be shrewd, intuitive, and practical. But in the second, you may hoard things, and your portfolio could become cluttered with unprofitable investments. Develop an enterprising spirit that will allow you to progress.

Parenthood

As a caring parent who wants the very best for your children, do not be over-protective or possessive. This could be very difficult for you, and at times you may tend to talk about life as it was when you were a child. Try seeing the world through your children's eyes, because it will help you to avoid the generation gap.

THE MOON IN LEO

TAUREANS AND THOSE WITH THE MOON IN LEO LOVE COMFORT AND LUXURY. AS A RESULT, YOU MAY SPEND PLENTY OF MONEY IN ORDER TO ENJOY THEM. DEVELOPING YOUR NATURAL GOOD BUSINESS SENSE WILL HELP SUPPORT SUCH INDULGENCES.

Your powers of observation are enhanced by your Leo Moon, which gives you the ability to take command of almost any situation with only the briefest notice.

Self-expression

Your Taurean Sun makes you extremely reliable and full of common sense. People will take it for granted that you can cope well with any situation. In fact, they may easily tend to take advantage of these qualities – not that you will really mind. Knowing what your priorities are, you will rise above any pettiness and spend your time rewardingly.

Both Taurus and Leo are of the fixed quality, and as a result, not only can you be pretty stubborn at times, but you may also find it difficult to change your opinions.

Leo is a fiery, enthusiastic, and passionate sign, so your response to situations will be spiced with great emotion. Express your enthusiasm freely, especially in relation to your personal interests and hobbies.

Romance

When you are in love, your emotions should flow both positively and quite delightfully. You will be as lavish in expressing your feelings toward your partners as you will be in ensuring that you enjoy every possible luxury that you can, or perhaps really cannot, afford. Leos are naturally generous, and your Leo Moon makes you particularly responsive to such pleasures as beautiful, expensive evenings spent entertaining yourself and your lover.

Your well-being

The Leo body areas are the spine and back. If you have a sedentary job, get a well-designed chair to keep it in good order. The Leo organ is the heart. To benefit it, perhaps you

The Moon in Leo

should try walking or jogging regularly. Or you could work out at a pleasant, comfortable health club.

Your Taurean tendency to gain weight could be increased by the influence of Leo. If your Moon sign attracts you to exercise, it can only be a good thing.

Planning ahead

Where money is concerned, your needs are substantial. While you may be satisfied with a regular paycheck, you are unlikely to be very fulfilled by a lifestyle that does not allow you to enjoy your work and take pride in it. Think about this carefully: Money is, indeed, important, but so is your inner contentment.

Parenthood

You will work hard for your children and do a lot for them, but you must ensure that you allow them to develop in the way that they want to. Do not be overpossessive, or try to make them into clones of yourself. Provided they have one or two compelling interests, that is all they need. If you also make an effort not to be bossy, you will minimize any problems associated with the generation gap.

THE MOON IN VIRGO

WITH THE SUN AND MOON BOTH IN EARTH SIGNS, YOU ARE A VERY PRACTICAL PERSON. DO NOT LET APPREHENSIVENESS OR A LACK OF SELF-CONFIDENCE SPOIL YOUR TAUREAN ENJOYMENT OF LIFE AND ITS SENSUAL PLEASURES.

The combination of your Sun and Moon signs makes you among the most practical of Taureans. Your Moon sign is, however, not noted for self-confidence, and this may have tended to inhibit you, especially when you were a child.

Self-expression

A certain shyness may have made you very quiet when you were young. Conversely, however, you may have become nervously talkative when you felt self-conscious. Attaining a balance and allowing the inner stability of your Taurean Sun to shine through may be something you have consciously had to develop.

Both Taurus and Virgo are of the earth element – hence your strong practical qualities. At the physical level, contact with the earth may mean a lot to you. Perhaps you love gardening, or can grow beautiful indoor plants. The countryside is probably important to you, so if your career holds you to a city center, try to live near a park, or escape out of town as often as possible.

Romance

You are a good communicator and must never hold back and fail to express your real feelings. This is especially true when you are in love. Do not cramp the wonderful Taurean way in which you express yourself, or your warm, tender passion.

You may also have an uncharacteristic tendency to be overly critical of your loved ones. Bear in mind that while well-founded constructive criticism may be helpful, carping and nagging are not.

Your well-being

The Virgoan body area is the stomach and, to some extent, the nervous system. When you are worried, it may be your stomach that reacts first.

The Moon in Virgo

You definitely need a high-fiber diet, to counter the effects of Taurean indulgence in rich food. If you suffer from a buildup of tension, you could find yourself prone to migraines.

Planning ahead

Virgoans are careful with money, and for you, that carefulness works at an instinctive level. This is helpful, since Taureans can be too generous. Virgoans often find it embarrassing to be generous. You will certainly find nothing ostentatious in owning property; Taurus will balance you in this respect.

Parenthood

You may well have a natural ability to teach your children, so that by the time they go to school they will be well on the way to reading. Be proud of their efforts. As in all of your dealings, remember that you have the capacity to be far more critical than you might realize.

THE MOON IN LIBRA

AS THEY ARE BOTH RULED BY VENUS, LIBRA AND TAURUS HAVE A GREAT DEAL IN COMMON. YOUR LIBRAN MOON WILL ENCOURAGE YOU TO RESPOND VERY WELL TO EVERYTHING THAT TAUREANS FIND ATTRACTIVE.

Although Taurus is an earth sign and of the fixed quality, and Libra an air sign and of the cardinal quality, they still have much in common. Above all, they share charm.

Self-expression
You find it very easy to convey the warmth of your Taurean personality with your instinctive and strong measure of tact and diplomacy. However, just because your Libran influence makes it easy to persuade people to your way of thinking, you must not stifle your Taurean common sense. Otherwise, you may end up using people. Anyone with a strong Libran influence also tends to be indecisive. When the occasion demands it, let Taurus take control.

Romance
With the Moon in Libra, you will possess a romantic air. You will express your feelings freely and gracefully, without overwhelming your lover by too sudden an approach. Your courtship will lead gently but firmly from romance to passion.

Notorious Taurean anger is less likely to erupt openly in you than in many Sun sign Taureans. Your instincts incline you to peace at any price, and you will always try to resolve problems diplomatically.

Your well-being
The Libran body area is the kidneys, and any upsetting circumstances can cause a kidney imbalance that might lead to headaches.

The Taurean love of a relaxed lifestyle is echoed by your Moon sign – so you may need to be very strict with yourself if you start a new exercise program or a diet. It may pay for you to exercise at a good health club, where saunas and steam rooms offer both a relaxing and a sociable time. It would be best for you to avoid

The Moon in Libra

crash diets completely. Instead, very gradually teach yourself to stop eating any highly calorific foods.

Planning ahead

Compared to most Taureans, you may not have the same urge for making money. You will, however, enjoy spending it. Any spare money must therefore be invested wisely, so that as you get older, you will be able to afford more luxuries. If you are looking for extra money, selling beauty products might be a good idea. Obtain sound professional financial advice before investing your savings, but do tell your advisor about any ideas you may have. You will learn a lot in the process and grow confident about managing your own affairs.

Parenthood

You could get a little tired of your children's demands for attention, so try to arrange to have a few hours away from them each week. Always make sure that your children know where they stand with you.

THE MOON IN SCORPIO

TAURUS AND SCORPIO ARE POLAR OR OPPOSITE SIGNS, WHICH MEANS THAT YOU WERE BORN UNDER A FULL MOON. BEWARE OF RESTLESSNESS, AN UNCHARACTERISTIC TRAIT AMONG TAUREANS, AND TRY NOT TO ACT JEALOUSLY.

Each of us is, in one way or another, apt to express the attitudes of our polar, or opposite, Zodiac sign. Each sign has its partner across the horoscope; for you this is Scorpio. Furthermore, as the Moon was in Scorpio when you were born, this "polarity" (as it is known) will emerge in a very interesting way.

Self-expression

Scorpio is very highly charged with emotional and physical energy. You will therefore react strongly when you meet with a challenge. Those born under Taurus are placid enough until rage gets the better of them, but your powerful polar qualities will join forces in your personality not only when you are angry, but also when you are moved in any way.

It is very important that you try to fill your days with tasks and events that make demands on your physical energy and also provide you with psychological fulfillment. Most people born at the time of the Full Moon tend to suffer occasionally from an element of restlessness or inner discontent. In your case, you must always be on guard against this.

Romance

The chief Taurean fault, possessiveness, is related to a Scorpio weakness – jealousy. In terms of your emotional relationships, this means that while they are likely to be highly charged (and you will no doubt contribute to that), jealousy can occur. It is always a good idea to discuss problems with your partners, but do not do this if your intuition leads you to explode into anger before you are sure of your facts.

Your well-being

The Scorpio body area covers the genitals, and these, along with your Taurean throat, are vulnerable. "Safe

The Moon in Scorpio

sex" and regular testicular exams for men or gynecological visits for women are important for you.

You may easily put on weight, especially if your metabolism is on the slow side. If this is the case, try to engage in some exercise.

Planning ahead

The Taurean business sense and liking for possessions and material security marries well with similar Scorpio qualities. In your case, however, because of the Moon's influence, you also have a considerable instinct for bargains and investments. You should follow it.

Parenthood

You will work hard for your family, but you could be more strict, and more insistent on somewhat harsh discipline, than you realize. Try to be aware of this, especially when your children want to move out and start living their lives in their own ways.

THE MOON IN
SAGITTARIUS

FACED WITH A CHALLENGE, YOU WILL FIND YOURSELF RESPONDING ENTHUSIASTICALLY. USE THIS ENTHUSIASM TO YOUR ADVANTAGE, AND DO NOT SUPPRESS IT WHEN YOUR TAUREAN CAUTION STRIVES TO TAKE OVER.

Your fiery Sagittarian Moon adds many contrasting facets to your steady, more cautious, earthy Sun sign. You respond much more quickly to situations than do many people of your Taurean Sun sign.

Self-expression

Your mind is always open to challenge, once excited by an idea or a project, you will immediately want to get involved. This can be a good thing, but it can also work slightly to your disadvantage: overoptimism is a Sagittarian problem that has to be contained. Luckily, in your case, after your initial enthusiasm, your Taurean caution usually takes over.

Romance

Your intense Taurean emotions are enlivened by your Moon sign, and while, like all Taureans, you need both emotional and material security, within a relationship you also need an element of independence. This sits uneasily with your Taurean tendency to be possessive. You may well resent your partners intensely for being possessive of you, but at the same time, act just as possessively toward them. If you are accused of this, take heed. Your Sagittarian enthusiasm and passion for life will color your attitude to love just as much as they do other areas.

Your well-being

The Sagittarian body area covers the hips and thighs. Sagittarius is yet another sign that enjoys rich food, in particular hefty casseroles, but the predilection for sweet desserts is less marked than in Taureans. Taurean women with a Sagittarian influence will have a tendency to gain weight on their hips and thighs.

The Sagittarian organ is the liver, and indigestion can be a problem. Upsets in this area are common

The Moon in Sagittarius

enough after a Taurean night out, but if you also have a Sagittarian Moon? No more need be said.

Sagittarians often enjoy sports with an element of daring. Fortunately, however, your Taurean caution will let you enjoy such activities safely.

Planning ahead

A similar sneaking regard for risk-taking can emerge in your attitude toward money, where your instincts can encourage you to invest too heavily. The thought of large spoils will attract you but, in the end, you might encounter disaster. Try not to learn the hard way. Think things out before you act. In this area, always rely on your Taurean nature.

Parenthood

You will be less conservative than many Taurean parents. Your lively response to your children's questions and demands will be gladly received, and you are capable of getting really enthused by their interests. Make sure that you take time out to have fun with your children, as well as spending your hard-earned money on them. For you, the generation gap should not prove to be a problem.

THE MOON IN CAPRICORN

YOU HAVE AN AMBITIOUS STREAK AND SHOULD PURSUE YOUR ASPIRATIONS AS FAR AS YOU CAN. USE YOUR TAUREAN COMMON SENSE AND CAUTION, BUT DO NOT LET THEM CRAMP THIS VITAL URGE – IT IS YOUR PATH TO INNER FULFILLMENT.

The earth element is important to your psychological makeup: Both Taurus and Capricorn are earth signs. So when you read about Taurean practical common sense and caution, you will immediately recognize these traits in yourself.

Self-expression

Are you ambitious and aspiring, or do you fail to progress in life as much as you would like to? The latter is fine if you are managing to achieve inner fulfillment; but surely you cannot be happy with simply trundling along in the same old rut, year after year. Of course, you could experience a mixture of times when you are successful, and others when you lack self-confidence and tend to hold back.

If you feel that other people are cramping your style – or for that matter, that you are doing so yourself – remember that caution and common sense are the best building blocks, and that your Moon sign, while causing fluctuations in your responses to challenges, can also allow you to take steady strides toward bigger and better things.

Romance

Capricorn is a cool, unemotional sign, so some of your Taurean ardor will probably be stifled. Capricorn is, however, also a faithful sign, and therefore complements your Taurean qualities excellently.

One tendency of which you should be aware is a susceptibility to social climbing. This may not work well for your emotional life, whatever it does for your social position. Your heart should decide in these matters.

Your well-being

The Capricornian body area covers the knees and shins, and the bones. If you are sluggish and experience periods when you positively shun

The Moon in Capricorn

sports or other exercise, your joints could suffer. You should also make sure that you have regular dental checkups, especially if you have a Taurean sweet tooth, since Capricorn also rules the teeth.

Planning ahead

Taureans are generous, and love luxury and comfort. Capricornians are entirely the opposite. In fact, their tastes can be positively Spartan; this might cause some internal conflict that will need resolving. You should be pretty good with cash, making wise investments that show a regular, steady growth.

Parenthood

Bringing work home from the office in order to make extra money for your children's education might not be a good idea. Your concern for their material well-being may mean that they lack both affection and pleasure. Also try not to be too much of a disciplinarian; you are fair, but you may be stricter than you realize.

THE MOON IN AQUARIUS

YOUR AQUARIAN WISH TO BE UNCONVENTIONAL AND TO STAND OUT FROM A CROWD COULD CLASH WITH A TAUREAN NEED TO CONFORM. TRY TO UNDERSTAND THIS STRUGGLE; DEVELOP CREATIVE ORIGINALITY AND CHECK STUBBORNNESS.

Although they are essentially very different, Taurus and Aquarius share the same fixed quality. Stubbornness, for example, is a characteristic common to all Taureans, and in your case it is exacerbated by your Aquarian Moon.

Self-expression

It is particularly important that you recognize your potential to be stubborn. Try to remember that firmness is one thing, but a closed mind is another.

Your Aquarian Moon also lends some unusual and lively qualities to your Taurean Sun. You are, for instance, among the least conventional of a sign that tends to adhere strictly to convention. You will often surprise your friends by reacting in ways that they do not expect. This is not a bad thing, since it gives you a certain attractive sparkle. Remember that your unconventional streak can, however, make you unpredictable, and that your reactions may be inconvenient to other people.

Romance

Aquarius is not a highly emotional sign, and your Taurean passion will to some extent reflect this. However, an Aquarian enthusiasm for romance will reveal itself, to great effect, in your expression of love and sex.

You have an independent spirit and may need more freedom of expression than many Sun sign Taureans. Do not, therefore, rush into a permanent relationship or marriage. In fact, you could well have a lot to come to terms with in your love life.

Your well-being

The Aquarian body area is the ankles, so take extra care if you go skiing or skating, or decide to wear high-heeled shoes. Aquarius also rules the circulation and, while you will tend to

The Moon in Aquarius

enjoy cold, crisp weather, make sure that you keep warm; your circulation may not be too good. You could enjoy karate as a form of exercise.

Planning ahead

Financially, you may be less shrewd than many Taureans. You could be attracted to showy but not very sound investments, so be cautious, and do not gamble more than you can afford to lose. Furthermore, you are often drawn to buy interesting and unusual items for your home or wardrobe, which may be expensive and too fashionable to be wise investments.

Parenthood

It is important that your children know where they stand with you. If they do not, because you change your mind too often, you could end up causing a lot of family tension. Encouraging your children to be interested in unusual and intriguing hobbies comes easily to you.

THE MOON IN PISCES

YOU ARE SYMPATHETIC, WITH A NEED TO OFFER OTHERS A HELPING HAND. LET TAUREAN COMMON SENSE TAKE OVER, HOWEVER, BEFORE YOU GIVE TOO MUCH MONEY AWAY. YOU ARE A WONDERFUL LOVER, BUT BEWARE OF BEING TOO POSSESSIVE.

Your earth sign Taurean Sun and water sign Piscean Moon blend well. As a result, your reactions to situations are both sensitive and emotional; you respond in a very caring, sympathetic way.

Self-expression

While you are practical, your inner strength and toughness are less apparent. This is particularly true when you meet with a challenge, in that you are sometimes not as assertive or as determined as other Sun sign Taureans.

Beware of a tendency to take the easy way out of difficult situations, which could be caused by a lack of confidence. Should this be the case, think of all your past achievements and give yourself more credit.

Pisceans tend to put on rose-colored glasses at the least provocation, while Taureans usually face up to reality. A little dreaminess will not come amiss, especially when heightened by the imaginative creativity that could be an integral part of your potential.

Romance

Taurean affection and sensuality blend well with Piscean emotion, making you a wonderful lover. You should, however, beware of falling for someone too quickly, since when you meet with reality, you may come down to earth all too rapidly.

It should not be too difficult to keep Taurean possessiveness at bay, but your Piscean Moon could cause you to be deceitful in tricky situations, perhaps because you are choosing the easiest way out.

Your well-being

The Piscean body area is the feet. You may find it difficult to get shoes that fit well, or you might simply be glad to take them off and go barefoot

The Moon in Pisces

whenever possible. Like Taurus, Pisces is a sign prone to weight gain – perhaps because Pisceans get thoroughly bored when checking the calorie content of foods. Allow your gourmet tendencies their freedom, but do not fall back on junk food any more than is absolutely necessary.

Planning ahead

Kindness and sympathy, and a desire to help, may place a strain on your bank balance. Try to keep a practical outlook when someone tells you a heartrending story. Always discuss investments with an expert so that your rather impractical Piscean response to financial matters will not damage or smother your sound Taurean business sense.

Parenthood

You will make a wonderful, caring parent, who will be sensitive to your children's needs. Use your imagination not only to inspire and encourage the development of their potential, but also to help you express and develop your own. Any creative work that you do with them, for instance photography or dance classes, will be good for all of you.

SUN & MOON SIGNS

GEMINI

MAY 22 – JUNE 21

INTRODUCING GEMINI

GEMINI, THE SIGN OF THE HEAVENLY TWINS, IS THE THIRD ZODIAC SIGN. GEMINIAN SUBJECTS ARE NOTED FOR THEIR DUALITY: THEY SELDOM RESTRICT THEMSELVES TO DOING JUST ONE THING AT A TIME.

Being the first sign of the air element, Gemini bestows a light intellect. This is reflected in the fact that Geminians tend to know a little about a great range of subjects. Geminians must be aware that superficiality can lead to shallowness of character, and that restlessness may prevent them from ever managing to achieve their full potential. While recognizing that variety is essential for them, Geminians must try to develop continuity of effort if they are to achieve inner fulfillment.

Traditional groupings

As you read through this book you will come across references to the elements and the qualities, and to positive and negative, or masculine and feminine signs.

The first of these groupings, that of the elements, comprises fire, earth, air, and water signs. The second, that of the qualities, divides the Zodiac into cardinal, fixed, and mutable signs. The final grouping is made up of positive and negative, or masculine and feminine signs. Each Zodiac sign is associated with a combination of components from these groupings, all of which contribute different characteristics to it.

Geminian characteristics

The Geminian ruling planet is Mercury, which often inclines its subjects to be good communicators. Gemini is also of the mutable quality, which heightens the properties of Mercury and the intellectual approach characteristic of the sign itself.

Gemini is a positive, masculine sign, and is regarded as the most youthful of all the 12 signs of the Zodiac. Although many different colors will no doubt appeal to individual Geminians, there is, overall, a tendency for them to favor shades of yellow.

The Zodiac Wheel

The relationship between each Zodiac sign and the traditional astrological groupings is made clear within the Zodiac wheel. As you read through this book you will also discover references to polar, or opposite signs, and these, too, can be easily worked out by referring to the wheel.

GEMINI
Myths & Legends

THE ZODIAC, WHICH IS SAID TO HAVE ORIGINATED IN BABYLON AS LONG AS 2,500 YEARS AGO, IS A CIRCLE OF CONSTELLATIONS THROUGH WHICH THE SUN MOVES DURING THE COURSE OF A YEAR.

Gemini is one of only two signs whose myth has some pictorial connection with the pattern of stars that make up its constellation: it was so called because of the two bright stars it contains. The Babylonians called it the Great Twins in their Zodiac. The myth most strongly associated with the sign is that of Castor and Pollux, known as the Dioscuri, which means "the young sons of Zeus." The paternity of Castor and Pollux is in fact a complicated affair. While their mortal parents were Leda and Tyndareus, a union between Zeus, the king of the gods, disguised as a swan, and Leda confuses the issue. Leda produced two eggs. From one came Pollux and Helen; from the other, Castor and Clytemnestra. Pollux and Helen (later to be known as Helen of Troy) were said to be the children of Zeus, and therefore immortal, whereas Castor and Clytemnestra were assumed to be the mortal children of Tyndareus. It was in fact quite common for people of ancient civilizations to claim that one child from a pair of twins was

Helmet cheekpiece
A typical Roman image of one of the Dioscuri.

of divine origin. Castor and Pollux were brought up in Sparta, where they formed a very close friendship.

Among their exploits together, Castor and Pollux rescued their sister, Helen, from an abductor, Theseus, and joined Jason and the Argonauts' expedition to recover the Golden Fleece. Afterward the two boys fell in love with two sisters, Hilaeira and Phoebe, who were already betrothed at the time. When the boys carried them off, Castor was tragically killed in the ensuing brawl. Pollux, the immortal, could not bear the thought of being parted from his brother and wept over his body. Touched by the sight of such brotherly devotion, Zeus allowed Pollux to share his immortality with Castor. As a result, the twins spent half their time in the Underworld with the spirits of the dead, and half with the gods on Mount Olympus.

Great athletes when on Earth, Castor and Pollux became patrons of all athletic contests. They were also said to protect sailors, to whom they still appear during storms as the lights of St. Elmo's fire. This belief dates back to the occasion when Zeus saved the Argonauts from a violent storm that was threatening to sink their ship, the Argo: Two flames came down from the heavens and hung above the heads of the Dioscuri, signaling the end of the storm. In later times, Castor and Pollux were regarded as divine and, according to legend, were supposed to ride through the sky on two white horses, carrying dazzling spears, each with a star above his brow. During the years of Imperial Rome, Castor and Pollux were believed to descend to Earth in order to fight at the head of the Roman army whenever it did battle with its enemies.

Roman Republican coin

This coin from 210 B.C. shows Castor and Pollux riding through the heavens.

People who have a Geminian Sun sign tend to possess two distinct sides to their natures, enabling them to do two things at once. Duality is therefore very likely to constitute a strong part of your personality.

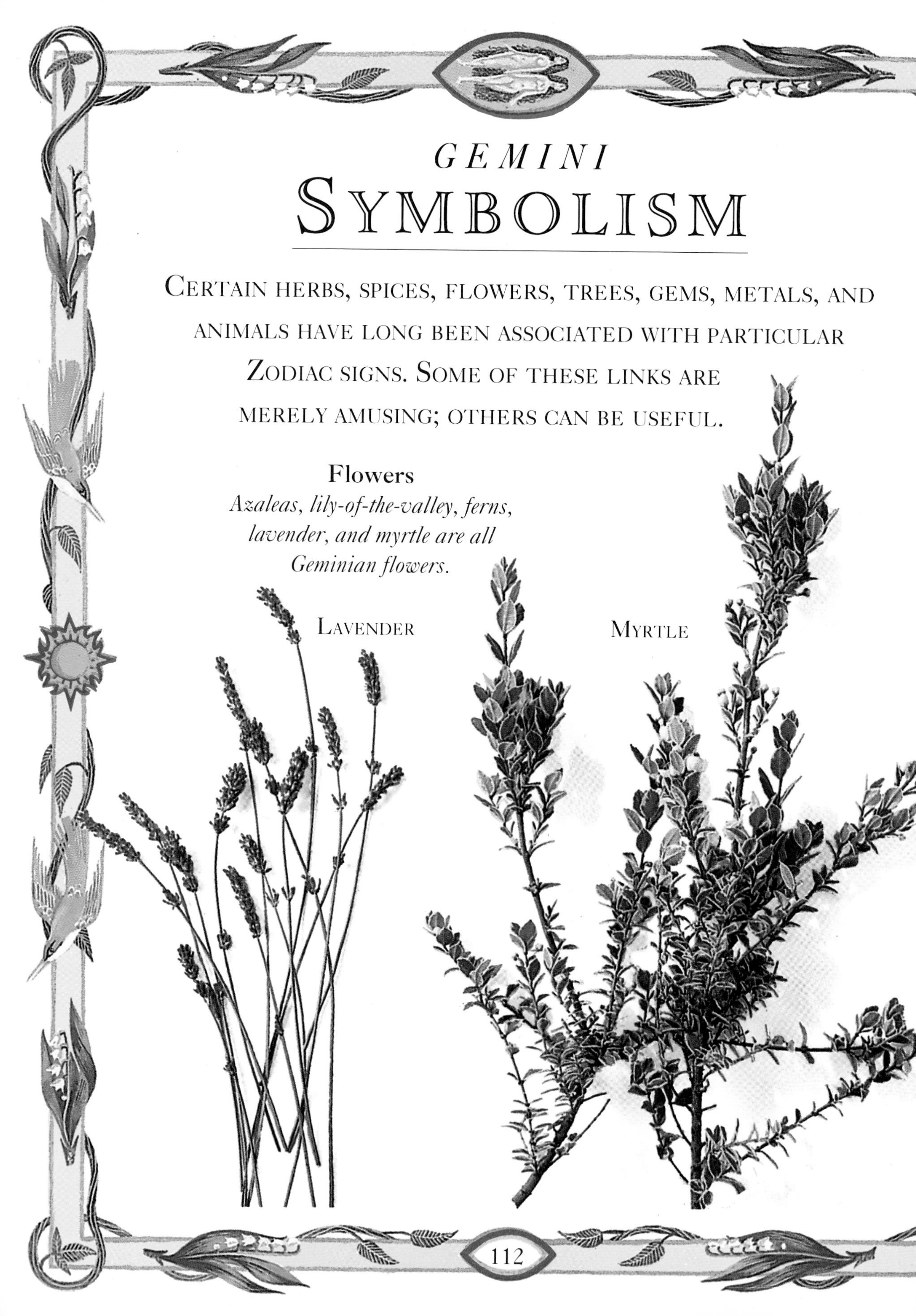

GEMINI
SYMBOLISM

CERTAIN HERBS, SPICES, FLOWERS, TREES, GEMS, METALS, AND ANIMALS HAVE LONG BEEN ASSOCIATED WITH PARTICULAR ZODIAC SIGNS. SOME OF THESE LINKS ARE MERELY AMUSING; OTHERS CAN BE USEFUL.

Flowers

Azaleas, lily-of-the-valley, ferns, lavender, and myrtle are all Geminian flowers.

LAVENDER

MYRTLE

Trees

All nut-bearing trees are ruled by Gemini, but especially the hazel and walnut.

ANISEED

CARAWAY

HAZEL

Spices

No spices are particularly associated with Gemini, but many people of this sign tend to enjoy spicy food, perhaps seasoned with aniseed or caraway.

LEMON BALM

Herbs

Lemon balm is good for curing a stitch, and arrowroot can be applied to a blister. An infusion of nettles soothes a sore throat. All of these herbs are governed by Gemini.

GEMINI SYMBOLISM

MERCURY

Metal

Mercury is both the Geminian ruling planet and, as its popular name, quicksilver, suggests, the Geminian metal.

INDIAN PARROT SPICE BOX

AGATE

Gems

Agates and emeralds are Geminian stones. But Geminians like all colors, so most glittering gems will appeal to them.

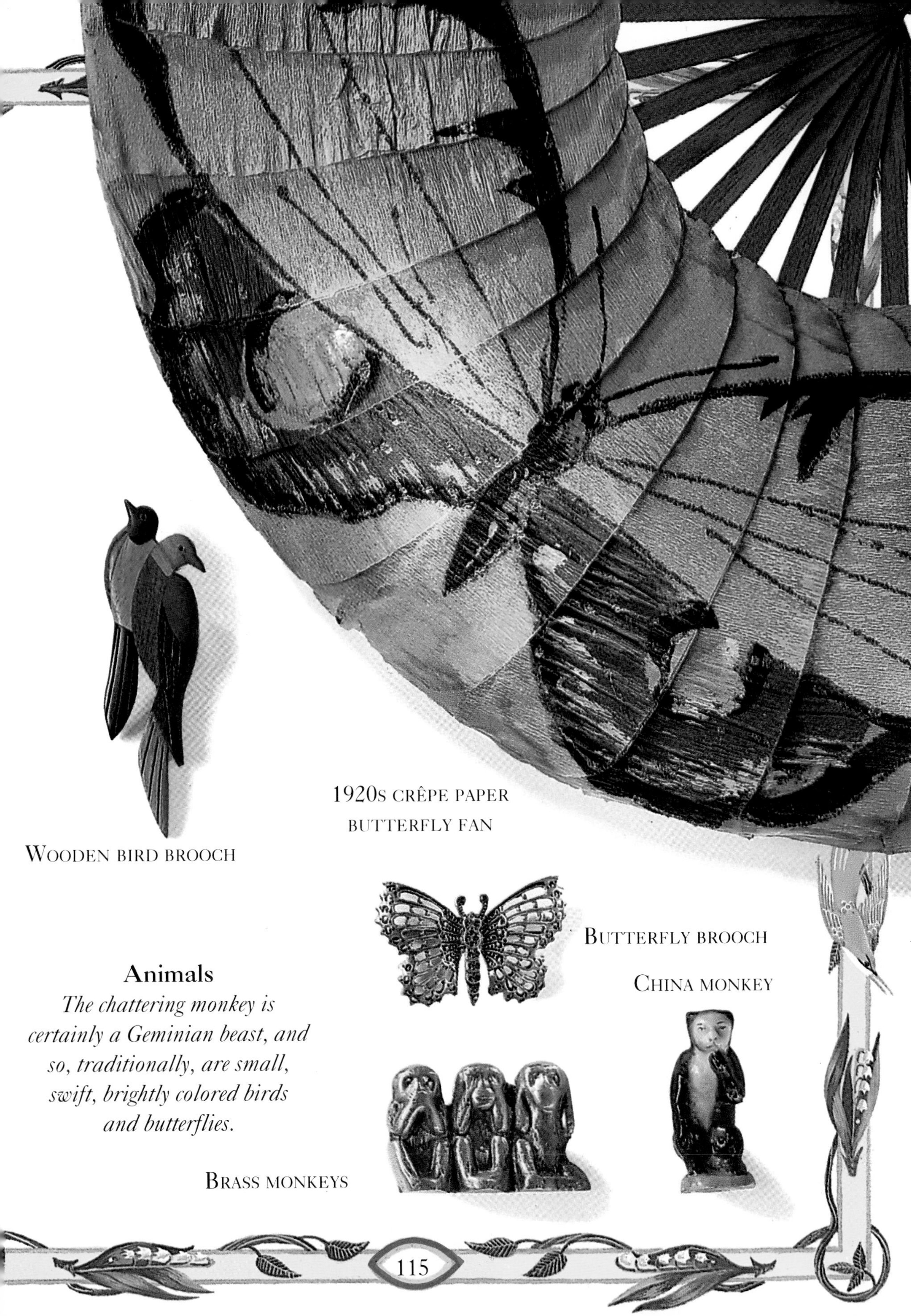

1920s CRÊPE PAPER BUTTERFLY FAN

WOODEN BIRD BROOCH

BUTTERFLY BROOCH

CHINA MONKEY

Animals

The chattering monkey is certainly a Geminian beast, and so, traditionally, are small, swift, brightly colored birds and butterflies.

BRASS MONKEYS

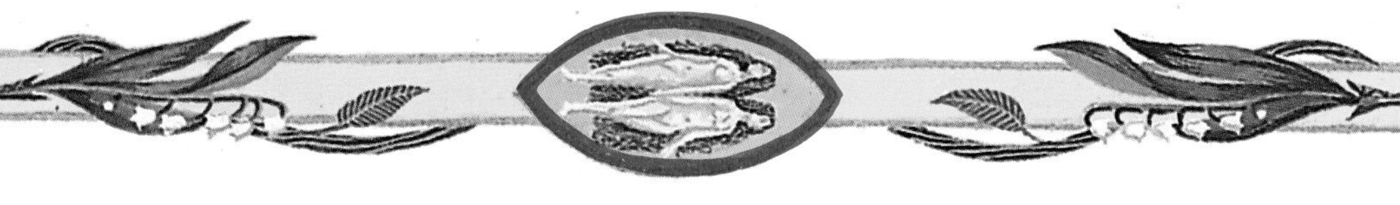

GEMINI PROFILE

THE OVERALL APPEARANCE OF A GEMINIAN IS USUALLY LIVELY, OFTEN REFLECTING RESTLESSNESS AND A KEENNESS TO BE UP TO THE MINUTE. GEMINIANS ARE OFTEN RECOGNIZED BY THEIR SPRIGHTLY, LIGHT-FOOTED WAY OF WALKING.

Geminians seem to hardly ever stand still. In a queue at a drinks party you will, for example, spend most of your time moving restlessly up and down, on and off the balls of your feet.

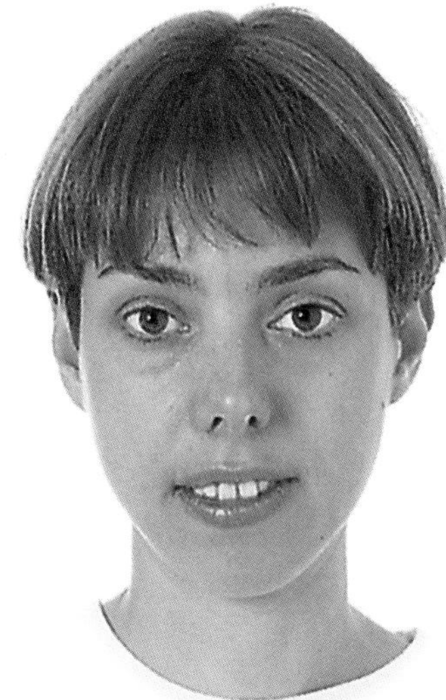

The Geminian face

You may have lively-looking features, and short, cropped hair.

The body

The Geminian body is usually long and lean. Because you have a fast metabolism, you are not inclined to put on weight; so if you are tall and slender, the chances are that you will stay that way for the whole of your life. Your arms and legs may be long, and your hands prominent and flexible. Some Geminians give the appearance of being a little bony. Geminian shoulders are not wide, and may tend to slope a little. It is very important for you to keep moving in order to burn up your high level of tense, physical Geminian energy.

The face

Many Geminians have fine hair that is cropped into an easily manageable style. Your forehead could well be rather broad, which will make you appear intelligent, and your eyes will be extremely alert, giving your whole face mobility and a bright expression. It is generally said that Geminians never stop talking, and it may well be the case with you that your lips do not seem to stop moving. You are also likely to have a particularly attractive mouth. The Geminian chin is

The Geminian stance

Many Geminians have a tendency to bob up and down on the balls of their feet whenever they have to wait for anything.

typically sharp, and sometimes pointed, which adds to the overall lively appearance.

Style

Geminians are fashionable, and like to wear the very latest styles – often favoring separates. Sometimes, through your need for variety, a "mix and match" policy may not pay off, and your appearance could become haphazard. However, with a little experience most Geminians can develop the gift of mixing separates in clever and interesting ways.

Accessories are very popular among Geminians, with trendy hats, sunglasses, belts, and fashion jewelry generally much in evidence. You may manage to accumulate quite a collection of these things. Most colors are popular among Geminians, but yellow particularly so.

In general

Even if you do not possess the typical Geminian physique, it is probable that you will still be be immediately recognizable, even from a distance, because of your distinctive way of walking: Geminians seem to positively bob up and down, as much as they move forward.

Irrespective of your nationality, you probably gesticulate with your hands and arms more than people of other Sun signs. Every movement that you make is likely to be quick, rather sudden, and sometimes even a little twitchy or jerky.

GEMINI
PERSONALITY

GEMINIANS POSSESS NIMBLE MINDS AND BODIES. THE TWINS, WHICH SYMBOLIZE THE SIGN, REPRESENT THE GEMINIAN NEED TO BE ACTIVE IN A NUMBER OF DIFFERENT FIELDS AT THE SAME TIME.

Simply because it is not in your nature, it would be wrong to urge you to do just one thing at a time. The rest of us must, however, see to it that in due course you get around to completing each project you start. This will probably subdue any restlessness and help you to achieve a sense of inner satisfaction.

At work

Geminians tend to function at a high level of nervous tension. If this is expressed positively, through work that you find rewarding, it will be burned off in a satisfactory way. On the other hand, if you are involved in repetitive work or are forced to tolerate stupidity, a great deal of stress can build up. In such cases it is very important that you find ways to ease the tension. A boring or undemanding job should be balanced with some stimulating continuing education courses. Alternatively, an exacting intellectual job should perhaps be tempered by some form of lively competitive leisure activity, such as tennis or squash.

Geminians know a little about a lot of different subjects, and are often quite rightly accused of being superficial. This could be a difficult hurdle for you to overcome, although one way might be to develop variety within the confines of a few well-chosen subjects. This will ensure that your notoriously low threshold of boredom is not reached.

Your attitudes

You possess great cunning, and because you are recognized to be the communicators of the Zodiac, you will have no difficulty in expressing ideas and opinions to anyone who cares to listen. In doing so, you will manage to change people's ideas and opinions to match your own way of thinking. This will often be accomplished very

Mercury rules Gemini

Mercury, the messenger god, represents the ruling planet of Gemini. The influence of Mercury stimulates the mind, but it can also make its subjects critical, nervous, and tense.

artfully, without people realizing that you are doing it. Be careful, however, that your native cunning does not involve duplicity.

The overall picture

It must be remembered that the Geminian mind needs continual stimulation, and the Geminian body continual movement. Both physical and mental energy must be regulated like a well-oiled machine and released at a constant level.

Geminians are usually highly motivated and can end up being great achievers, especially if they are involved in the media or sales. The influence of your ruling planet, Mercury, will help you, since Mercury is the messenger god.

GEMINI
ASPIRATIONS

IDEALLY, GEMINI WOULD LIKE TO HAVE A NEW JOB EVERY DAY. THE CHANCES ARE THAT A REGULAR ROUTINE WILL BORE YOU STIFF. IF YOU DO HAVE TO PUT UP WITH ONE, A VARIETY OF SPARE-TIME ACTIVITIES IS ESSENTIAL.

1920S OFFICE INTERCOM SYSTEM

Reception work
Geminians usually prosper in jobs related to communications. This is due to an association with the planet Mercury, which is linked with activity.

Teaching
Geminians are not known for their patience, so if they become teachers – a good choice given their excellent communications skills – they should choose to work with older children or teenagers.

PENCIL SET

1920s TELEPHONE EXTENSION

OLD BANK NOTES

International banking

The wheeling and dealing and intense activity of either international banking or a stock exchange will suit many Geminians.

Telecommunications

This type of work will suit those who are fond of communication, especially conversation.

TOOLS USED IN GRAPHIC DESIGN

MINIATURE CASH REGISTER

Media work

Many Geminians work in the media. This includes graphic design, public relations, and publicity.

Retail sales

Many Geminians have the ability to get along with anyone and to sell anything. You might enjoy the busy, lively atmosphere of a large department store.

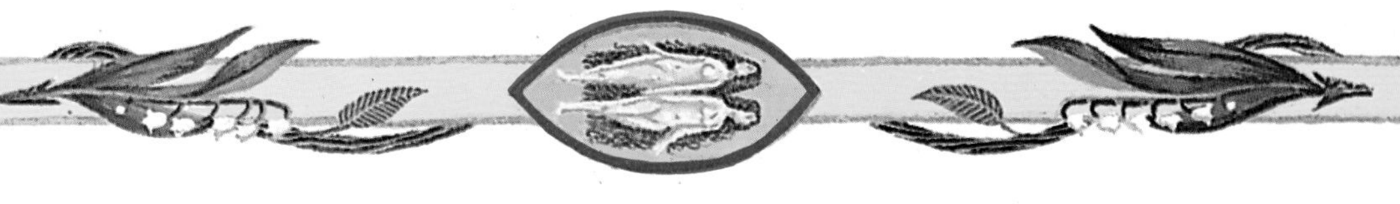

GEMINI HEALTH

GEMINI IS AN AIR SIGN, AND THIS INFLUENCES THE LUNGS. FOR GEMINIANS LIVING IN AN UNPOLLUTED ENVIRONMENT IS CRITICAL. THE ARMS AND HANDS ARE ALSO VULNERABLE.

Geminians are usually fortunate enough to have a fast metabolic rate and are unlikely to put on weight. They have the reputation of being the most youthful of all the signs, never seeming to get old.

Your diet

The Geminian diet should be light, with plenty of fresh fruit and vegetables. You may need to supplement your diet with kali muriaticum (kali. mur.), which is essential for the formation of fibron. This will help prevent bronchial congestion and swollen glands.

Taking care

Gemini rules the lungs, and there is no doubt that Geminians can suffer from bad coughs. Remember that negligence may seriously weaken your lungs. You should also try not to smoke; the habit could prove to be even more dangerous for you than it is for other people.

Gemini partly rules the shoulders and many Geminians fracture collar bones, often while participating in a sport. The Geminian hands and arms are also extremely vulnerable; you may get a lot of cuts and splinters.

Walnuts

Most nuts, and many vegetables grown above ground, are traditionally regarded as Geminian foods.

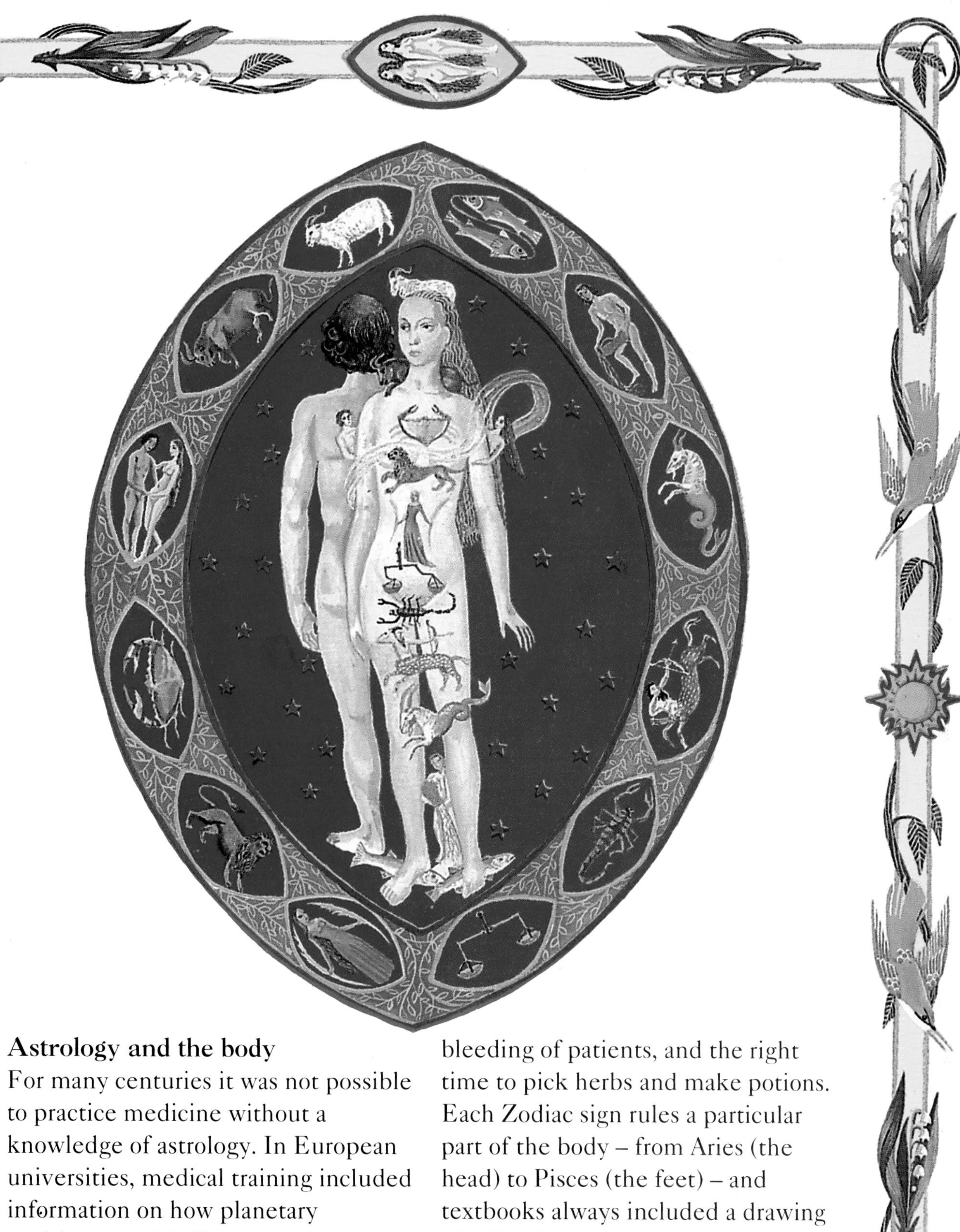

Astrology and the body

For many centuries it was not possible to practice medicine without a knowledge of astrology. In European universities, medical training included information on how planetary positions would affect the administration of medicines, the bleeding of patients, and the right time to pick herbs and make potions. Each Zodiac sign rules a particular part of the body – from Aries (the head) to Pisces (the feet) – and textbooks always included a drawing of a "Zodiac man" (or woman) that illustrated the point.

GEMINI AT LEISURE

THE SUN SIGNS TRADITIONALLY SUGGEST SPARE-TIME ACTIVITIES, HOBBIES, AND VACATION SPOTS. YOU SHOULD CONSIDER SOME OF THESE SUGGESTIONS – THEY OFTEN SUIT GEMINIAN TASTES AND INTERESTS.

Enjoying exotic food
While you may like to experiment with food and drink, you should bear in mind that a light diet usually suits Geminians best.

GARLIC PRESS

GARLIC

Amateur radio
Geminians are always trying to communicate more effectively, and you could be greatly attracted to the broad scope of ham radio.

1930S RADIO MICROPHONE

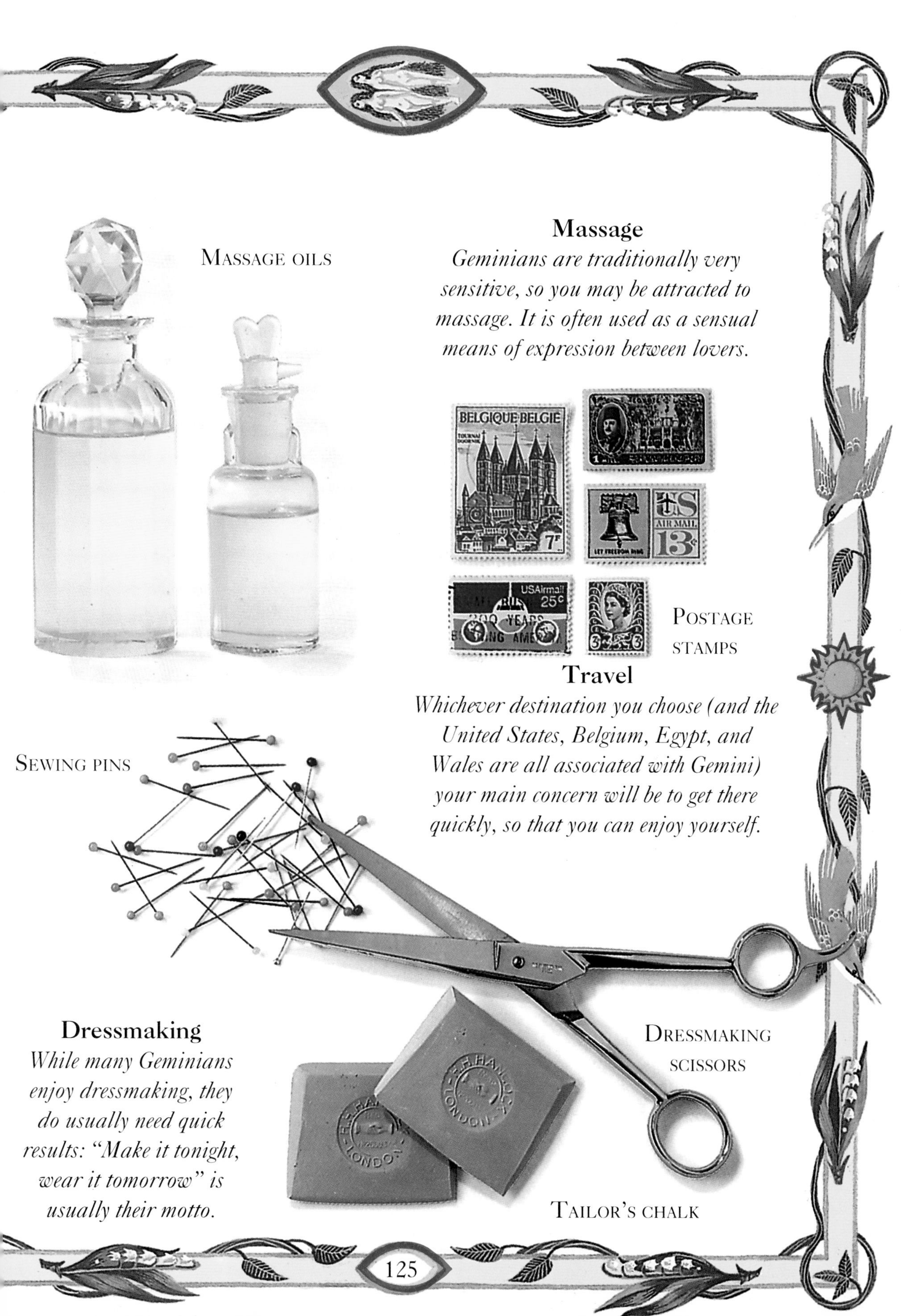

MASSAGE OILS

Massage

Geminians are traditionally very sensitive, so you may be attracted to massage. It is often used as a sensual means of expression between lovers.

POSTAGE STAMPS

Travel

Whichever destination you choose (and the United States, Belgium, Egypt, and Wales are all associated with Gemini) your main concern will be to get there quickly, so that you can enjoy yourself.

SEWING PINS

DRESSMAKING SCISSORS

Dressmaking

While many Geminians enjoy dressmaking, they do usually need quick results: "Make it tonight, wear it tomorrow" is usually their motto.

TAILOR'S CHALK

GEMINI IN LOVE

WHEN GEMINI REALIZES THAT CUPID'S DART HAS HIT HOME, A CAMPAIGN TO ATTRACT THE ATTENTION OF THE ADMIRED ONE WILL IMMEDIATELY BE LAUNCHED. WHAT IS MORE, THIS PLAN USUALLY WORKS.

You may not exactly overwhelm your lovers with passion early in an affair. However, they will no doubt enjoy themselves.

People with a Gemini Sun sign wallow in the exciting period when friendship is turning to love, and will often try to draw it out. In all Geminian relationships there are strong ties of friendship and intellectual rapport. Geminians are always happy to sing praises or indulge in a little flattery, so your lovers will always know where they stand. You will usually follow up a first flirtation with a suggestion for a date, and the occasion will never be dull or ordinary. You may decide on a rock concert or a picnic in the park.

As a lover

This sign is not as highly charged, emotionally, as some others, but Geminians enjoy a lively and very varied sex life. There is a vivacious freshness in their lovemaking, even if there is as strong a need for friendship as for passion. Despite what has been said, Geminians usually have what it takes to keep a relationship alive and flourishing. If a partner responds well to new developments and

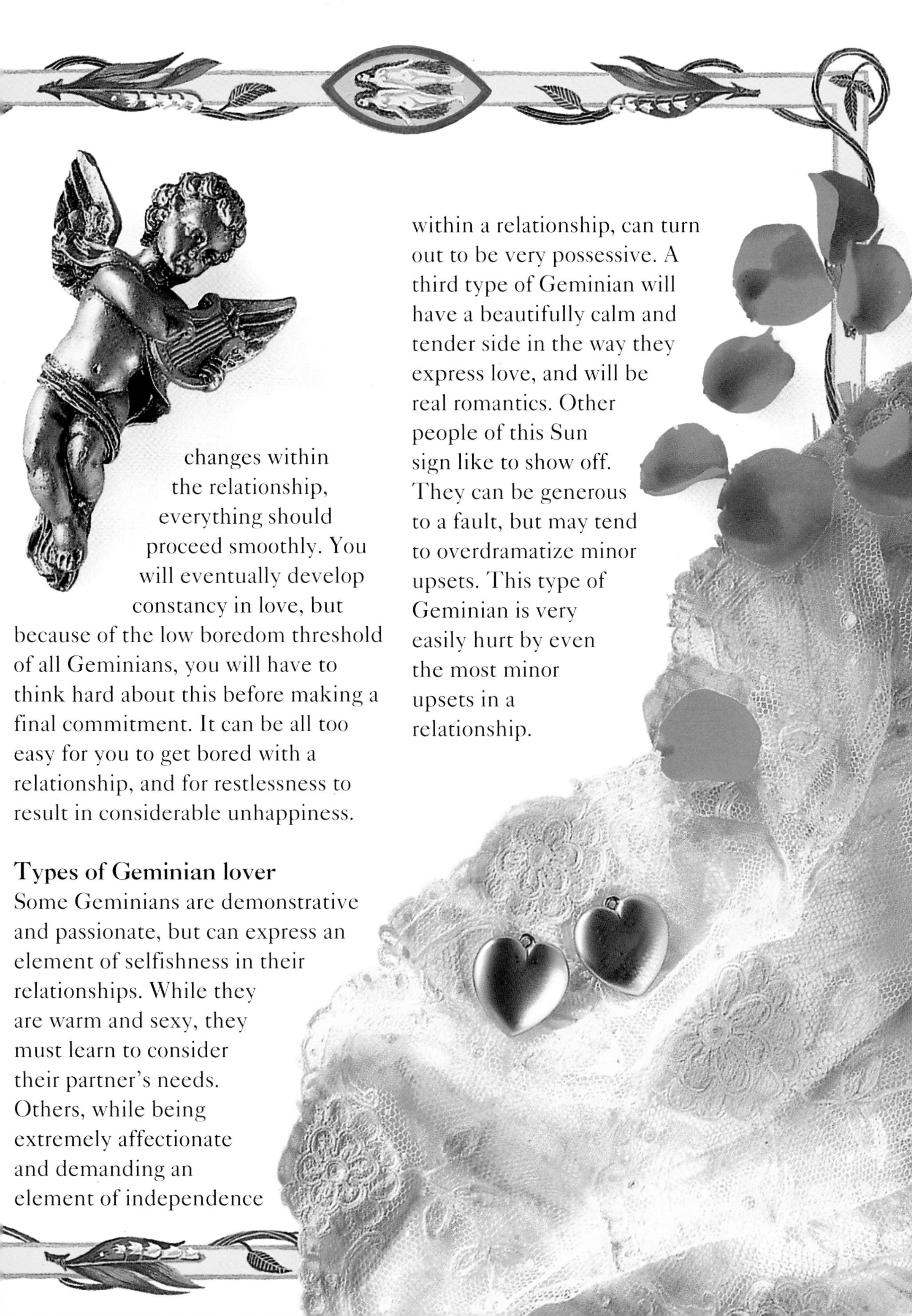

changes within the relationship, everything should proceed smoothly. You will eventually develop constancy in love, but because of the low boredom threshold of all Geminians, you will have to think hard about this before making a final commitment. It can be all too easy for you to get bored with a relationship, and for restlessness to result in considerable unhappiness.

Types of Geminian lover

Some Geminians are demonstrative and passionate, but can express an element of selfishness in their relationships. While they are warm and sexy, they must learn to consider their partner's needs. Others, while being extremely affectionate and demanding an element of independence within a relationship, can turn out to be very possessive. A third type of Geminian will have a beautifully calm and tender side in the way they express love, and will be real romantics. Other people of this Sun sign like to show off. They can be generous to a fault, but may tend to overdramatize minor upsets. This type of Geminian is very easily hurt by even the most minor upsets in a relationship.

GEMINI AT HOME

PLENTY OF LIGHT, A PLETHORA OF GADGETS, AND THE LATEST DESIGN FEATURES CHARACTERIZE THE TYPICAL GEMINIAN HOME. THE COLORS ARE BRIGHT, AND THERE IS A VARIETY OF PATTERNS IN THE WALLPAPER AND CURTAINS

Simple, uncluttered lines dominate the Geminian home, and yellow is often a favorite color choice for walls and furnishings. Glass and shiny chrome plate is popular among people of this sign, and may be combined to make a handsome dining table. As a Sun sign Geminian, you are likely to aim for an overall lightness in your decoration schemes.

Furniture

Most Geminians like to be up to date, and therefore choose the very latest styles of furniture for their homes. Your inner restlessness can, however, sometimes cause you to become dissatisfied with what you choose. After a year or two, you probably feel the need to acquire something newer and more fashionable.

Soft furnishings

You probably like to keep soft furnishings to a minimum, placing no great emphasis on heavy drapes. If you use cushions, they will be original

Workstation

A hectic workstation, with a telephone, notepads, and a fax machine, is likely to be a feature in any Geminian home.

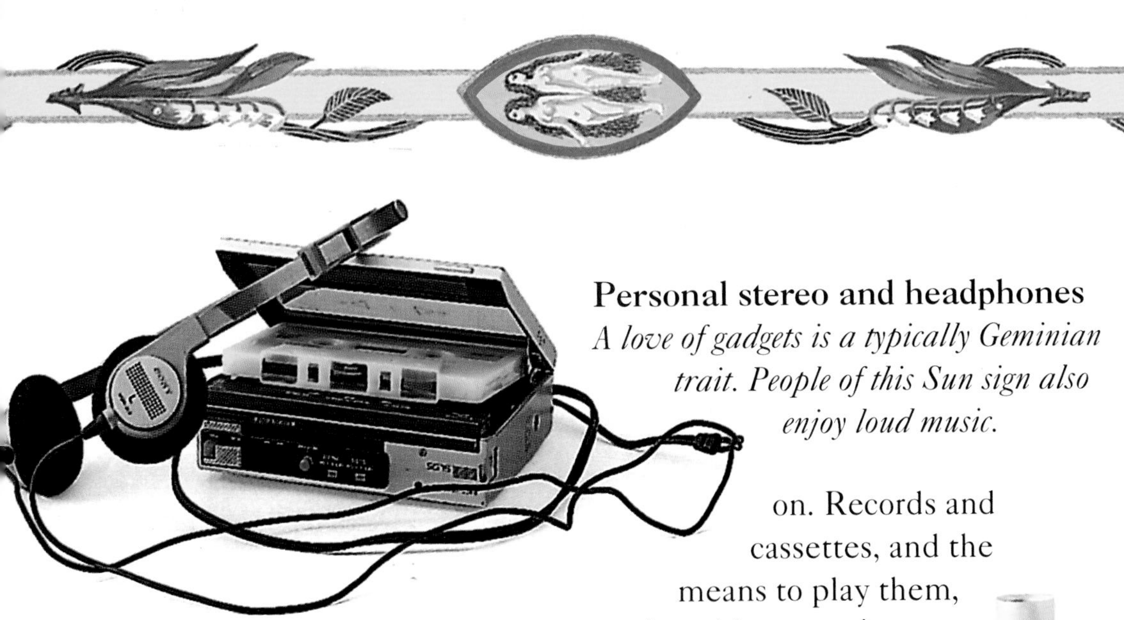

Personal stereo and headphones

A love of gadgets is a typically Geminian trait. People of this Sun sign also enjoy loud music.

in design, and somewhat unusual in style. Lightweight blinds, as an alternative to drapes, are popular among Geminians. Since Gemini is an air sign, your choice of furnishing fabrics or rugs never provokes a feeling of claustrophobia.

Decorative objects

It is in the choice of objects that Geminians usually display most of their lively personality traits. Being the arch communicators of the Zodiac, Geminians usually place their telephones in prominent positions.

You probably possess a great many magazines on an equally wide range of subjects. This underlines your Geminian versatility, and a general desire to keep up with what is going on. Records and cassettes, and the means to play them, are in evidence, as is no doubt a good video recorder and possibly a camera. Your ideal choice of painting could be something fairly enigmatic; perhaps a print of a Kandinsky, Dufy, or a Klee – unless you are lucky enough to be able to afford the real thing. A picture by one of these artists, or similarly minded lesser-known painters, will leave you with enough space to come to your own conclusions about the artist's original intentions and then, perhaps after a while, to rethink your ideas again.

Delicate, bright fabric

A Geminian home will be incomplete without some light, bright fabrics.

THE MOON *AND* YOU

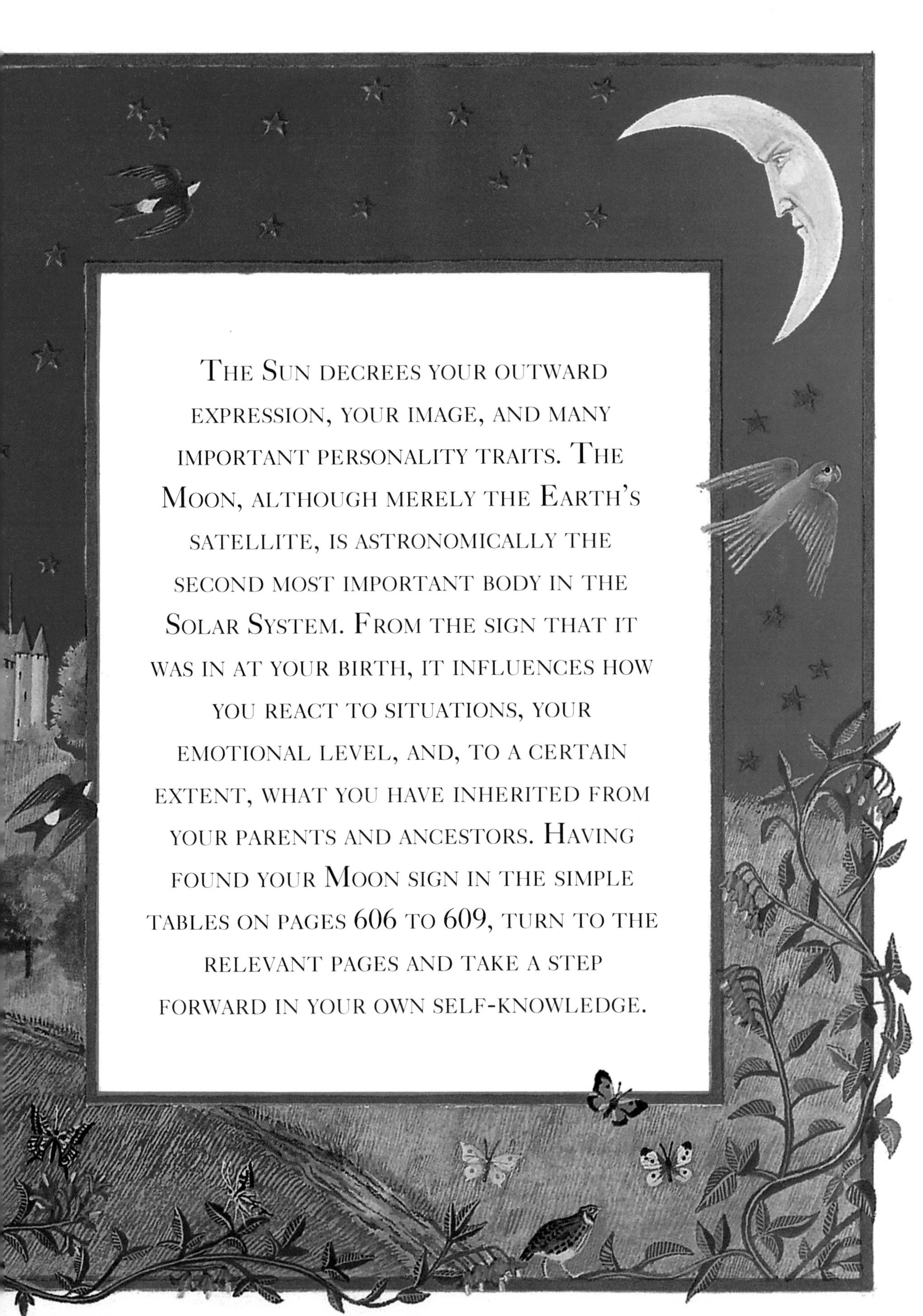

The Sun decrees your outward expression, your image, and many important personality traits. The Moon, although merely the Earth's satellite, is astronomically the second most important body in the Solar System. From the sign that it was in at your birth, it influences how you react to situations, your emotional level, and, to a certain extent, what you have inherited from your parents and ancestors. Having found your Moon sign in the simple tables on pages 606 to 609, turn to the relevant pages and take a step forward in your own self-knowledge.

THE MOON IN ARIES

YOUR ARIEN MOON WILL HEIGHTEN YOUR EMOTIONS AND ENHANCE YOUR NATURALLY RAPID GEMINIAN REACTIONS. IMPATIENCE AND RESTLESSNESS COULD LEAD YOU TO MAKE CARELESS MISTAKES ON IMPORTANT PROJECTS.

Sun sign Geminians are always alert, and your Arien Moon will speed up your already very swift reactions to situations, making you, in this respect, exceptionally Geminian. You will be extremely quick to answer back, and you always have an incisive, particularly slick response when challenged. Even more than most people of your Sun sign, you will love argument and debate.

Self-expression

You will always be in a hurry, but be careful: Undue haste could cause you problems. Also make sure that a quick response is not a selfish response.

Fire and air blend well, so your fiery Moon will help you not only to express your emotions freely, but also to feel far less anxious about them. Your characteristic Geminian versatility is often driven by a marvelous enthusiasm. But, as you know, you tend to get bored rather easily, and your Arien Moon will exacerbate this tendency. You must learn to keep it under control. Otherwise you will waste a great deal of energy on false starts.

Romance

You are more passionate than many Geminians, and tend to fall in love very quickly and easily. Although you may be familiar with the Geminian tendency to duality, this will be less characteristic of your personality. This does not mean that, over your lifetime, you are likely to have fewer partners than other Sun sign Geminians; only that a certain singularity of purpose is likely to deter you from having more than one lover at a time.

Your well-being

The Arien body area is the head, and there is a chance that you often bumped it when you were a

The Moon in Aries

youngster. This was because your instinctive hastiness, stemming from your Arien Moon, made you accident-prone. This could still be the case, and your hands and arms may get easily bruised, cut, or burned.

Planning ahead
You will not be particularly unhappy if you are presented with the opportunity to make money quickly. However, you should be careful when offered any kind of risky get-rich-quick scheme. You will probably do much better to encourage your instinct for investments that can be completely controlled.

Parenthood
You will be a very lively parent and will not find it difficult to keep up with, or indeed ahead of, your children's interests. You should have fun with your family, and they will enjoy your youthful, energetic approach toward them.

THE MOON IN TAURUS

ALLOW THE STABILITY AND INNER CALM OF YOUR TAUREAN MOON TO STEADY GEMINIAN IMPATIENCE AND RESTLESSNESS. IF YOU THINK IDEAS THROUGH CAREFULLY, YOU WILL MAKE THE MOST OF YOUR TREMENDOUS CAPABILITIES.

Your Taurean Moon will be very helpful in controlling your Geminian tendency to be a little reckless and superficial. It will stabilize your reactions and support them with a great deal of practical common sense. While it may slow down certain aspects of your behavior, it will add depth, kindness, and a warm sympathy to your dealings with other people.

Self-expression

You will be less inclined than many Geminians to talk about things that you are unsure of, and more ready to listen to others and empathize with them. Not only will you have more time for other people, but you will also be willing to use that time at a reasonable pace, without the haste and flurry of many Geminians.

Emotional and financial security may be far more important to you than you care to admit. You may need to consider this carefully when, for instance, you are choosing a career or thinking about changing your job.

Romance

It could be that your Moon sign will make you far less flirtatious and less likely to enjoy more than one partner at a time than is typical of your Sun sign. Your emotions are warmed and heightened by your Moon; you will trust them and will make an especially sensual lover. Take care, however, that you do not succumb to possessiveness, the worst Taurean fault. Some freedom is desirable for both you and your partner.

Your well-being

The Taurean body area covers the neck and throat. To a certain extent, these will be vulnerable, especially if you have been giving a speech or a lecture, or spiritedly arguing with friends. You may even lose your voice.

The Moon in Taurus

Needless to say, for you a cold will start with a sore throat. If this happens, do all you can to keep the cold from spreading to your lungs.

Planning ahead

You have a practical attitude toward finance and investment. Money is far less likely to burn a hole in your pocket than it is with most other Sun sign Geminians. You probably have a flair for selling and a strong instinct for business. You will invest wisely and, if you spurn any Geminian attraction toward quick financial growth, you will make your money work well for you.

Parenthood

You will work hard for your children, giving them a secure home, and encouraging mind-stretching interests and excursions in free time. While you are able to understand their enthusiasms and opinions, you can be quite strict at times. This is actually something that they will appreciate when they are older.

THE MOON IN GEMINI

WITH BOTH THE SUN AND THE MOON IN GEMINI AT THE TIME OF YOUR BIRTH, YOU WERE BORN AT THE TIME OF THE NEW MOON. GEMINI IS AN AIR SIGN, SO YOU ARE VERY MUCH AN "AIR" PERSON – A DOUBLE GEMINI.

Reading a list of the characteristics of your very lively Geminian Sun sign, you will probably realize that a great many of them apply to you. On average, out of 20 personality traits attributed to a sign, most people recognize 11 or 12. For you the average will be considerably higher, since both the Sun and the Moon were in Gemini when you were born.

Self-expression

Your Sun and Moon combination make you eternally youthful and an excellent communicator. You will be forever talking and voicing your opinions and will have an instinctive urge to communicate with others. Of course, being so highly motivated in this way has its complications. Do you always give yourself time to think?

Superficiality, one of the more serious Geminian faults, could be a major stumbling block for you. Counter it not by suppressing your natural versatility, but by aiming to acquire a little more knowledge about the subjects you find interesting.

You could be very mistrustful about your feelings. But make sure that you do not rationalize your emotions out of existence, or suppress them so they are never freely expressed.

Romance

Geminian duality may well have an effect upon your love life. You could end up having two partners, both of whom you love, for quite different reasons. This can obviously cause complications and, while your Geminian ability to talk yourself out of difficult situations will certainly be useful, why treat anyone unfairly?

Your well-being

The comments concerning Geminian health (*see pages 122 – 123*) particularly apply to you. In addition, you may be exceptionally vulnerable

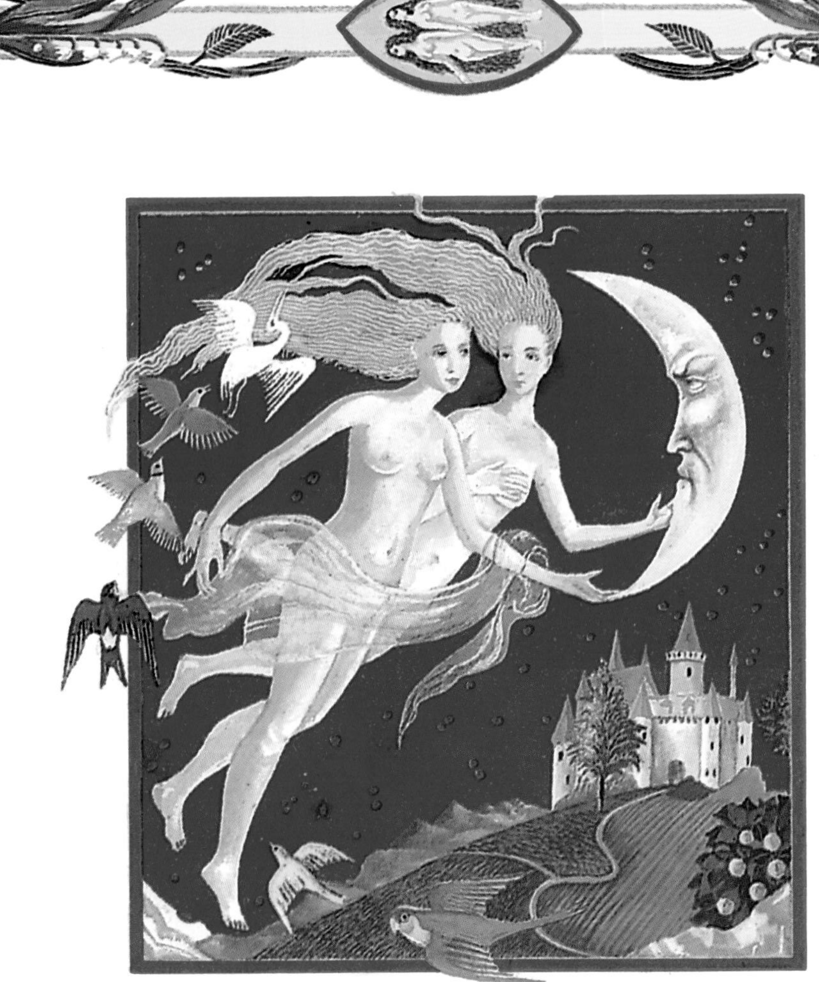

The Moon in Gemini

to anxiety and stress. It will be a very good idea for you to learn a relaxation technique such as yoga. This will help you to develop an inner calm – something that you may well need.

Planning ahead

Your attitude toward money may not be terribly sound. You will probably want to accumulate large amounts of it quickly, just so you can spend it. In fact, your general cleverness could actually lead to you being rather too clever in this area. Ensure that you do not invent money-making schemes that could end up collapsing like a house of cards.

Parenthood

You are among the most lively and forward-looking of all parents. In fact, you may even be ahead of your children's ideas and opinions. They will probably learn from you, but try to be consistent – and not too critical. As a double Gemini, both these tendencies could sometimes be a source of difficulty.

THE MOON IN CANCER

YOU HAVE A WARM, CARING QUALITY THAT IS UNCOMMON AMONG SUN SIGN GEMINIANS. BUT YOU COULD BE A COMPULSIVE, EVEN OBSESSIVE, WORRIER. TO COUNTER THIS TENDENCY, DEVELOP YOUR GEMINIAN LOGIC AND SKEPTICISM.

Because the Moon rules Cancer, its influence from that sign is very powerful. While it will affect your responses to situations, it will also have a more general effect on your personality. It is likely to make you a very caring, protective, and sympathetic person.

Self-expression

You are sensitive, and could well suffer from rapid mood swings. While you are unlikely to become quiet or morose, you will sometimes shift between feeling very positive and extroverted, and being less confident and self-expressive. Your Geminian Sun will, however, see to it that you are always able to express your emotions verbally.

You have a very powerful imagination, and should use it both positively and creatively, perhaps through writing or craftwork. But do not let your imagination work overtime in negative ways, since you are far more prone to worry than most people of your Sun sign. It is in this sphere of your life that Geminian logic must come to your aid.

Romance

Your emotional resources demand positive expression through a meaningful relationship. This will involve a partner with whom you have an excellent rapport – especially sexually. Beware of the Geminian tendency to always question your emotions. All Geminians must accept that they have a tendency to rationalize their feelings out of existence, and work against that.

Your well-being

The Cancerian body area covers the chest and the breasts, so a vulnerability to Geminian breathing problems and to bronchitis is increased. If they linger, consult your

The Moon in Cancer

doctor. The digestive system is also Cancerian: Be careful what you eat. You could suffer from digestive problems, especially when you are at all worried. Resist the instinctive tendency to worry. Counter the impulse with Geminian logic.

Planning ahead

Your intuition can help you in relation to finance. You may well have a sound business sense, and you could make a lot of money – perhaps by building a collection of unusual articles or antiques. (Do you find it difficult to throw anything away?) On the other hand if you really feel that a certain investment would be good, rely on your intuition.

Parenthood

You will be very eager to have your own home and children, and could well be somewhat overprotective toward them. Take care not to create a claustrophobic atmosphere, and be very careful not to attempt to cling to your children. Because you have a nostalgic streak, you may not be as forward-looking as most Geminians. At times, this could widen the generation gap.

THE MOON IN LEO

GEMINIANS ARE THE NATURAL COMMUNICATORS OF THE ZODIAC. COMBINE THIS QUALITY WITH LEO CREATIVITY, AND YOU COULD WELL HAVE LITERARY POTENTIAL. YOU WILL ALWAYS THINK BIG, AND HAVE A WARM HEART.

Here is a vibrant, positive combination of Gemini, an air sign, and Leo, a fire sign. Just as air fans and feeds fire, your fiery Moon sign fans and feeds the intellectual approach of your Sun sign. It allows you both more emotion than the average Geminian, and the passion with which to express it.

Self-expression

Anyone with a Leo emphasis to their personality has a creative streak, and you may well have a great urge to express yourself imaginatively and creatively, perhaps through writing or painting. You need a creative hobby of some kind, although it need not be one directly related to the fine arts.

You could tend to be more fixed in your opinions than many Geminians. This may not be altogether a bad thing; it will add stability to your character and help to mitigate any Geminian superficiality. You will tend to organize your thoughts and to consider your conclusions. Make sure that you do not become dogmatic.

Romance

You make a wonderful lover, far more passionate than many people of your Sun sign are. You will lavish not only love and affection on your partner, but also a very varied and energetic form of sexual expression.

Elegance and comfort will be as important in this sphere of your life as in every other, and you will spend a lot of money in order to ensure it for you and your partner.

Your well-being

The Leo body areas are the spine and heart, and it is very important that you sit properly, especially if you spend hours at an office desk. A well-designed chair will be especially helpful to you. Make time to regularly exercise your spine. Equally, while

The Moon in Leo

you are no more prone to heart attacks than anyone else, it is obvious that you should exercise to keep that vital organ in good working order. You are easily bored with exercise, so vary your routine as much as possible. If you jog, cover a different route each day; alternatively, a health club, with all its varied activities, should keep you happy.

Planning ahead

Because of a liking for luxury and real quality, you probably need to make a lot of money. But you also need inner fulfillment from your work; if you do not get it you will tend to flit from one job to the next, and so never have enough cash to live in the style to which you aspire. You should be fairly good at investing.

Parenthood

You will want to encourage your children, urging them to enjoy a great variety of interests. You will take them on delightful and memorable outings, for example, to museums and theaters. They will be grateful for this and will enjoy your company as much as you enjoy theirs. However, try not to boss them around too much.

THE MOON IN
VIRGO

GEMINI AND VIRGO ARE BOTH RULED BY MERCURY, SO THERE IS A NATURAL EMPATHY BETWEEN THE TWO SIGNS. YOUR MIND IS VERY SHARP AND ANALYTICAL, BUT YOU EXPRESS YOUR EMOTIONS FREELY.

Here is an example of a positive air sign (Gemini) combining with a negative earth sign (Virgo). Both signs are, however, of the mutable quality, and also share Mercury as their ruling planet.

Self-expression

You are extroverted, and a wonderful communicator. Your instincts are very practical and, although you could well be overly talkative, you will make sure of your facts before expressing your opinion. You can be extremely critical, so make an effort to express your views constructively.

Do not dither or start too many jobs at the same time. You may need to develop better organizational skills.

Romance

Virgoan modesty and a rather low emotional level, together with Geminian shyness about the expression of emotion, may lead you to mistrust your feelings and conceal them. If you lack confidence, you might benefit from counseling.

Your well-being

The Virgoan body area is the stomach, and in some cases this can become vulnerable, especially when you are worried. To overcome this, use your rational, logical approach to problems, instead of your intuition.

You need a high-fiber diet to keep your bowels in good order; many people with a strong Virgoan influence are successful on a vegetarian diet. All health foods can be beneficial to you, and you might consider investigating homeopathy and complementary medicine. With your Sun and Moon combination, you should respond very positively to them. Try to control restlessness and to develop a sense of inner peace: you will benefit from yoga or a similar discipline. If you allow tension to get

The Moon in Virgo

the better of you, there is a chance that you could become prone to migraines, which is a Virgoan ailment.

Planning ahead

Your Virgoan Moon will encourage you to be more careful with money than most Sun sign Geminians. Respond to the influence of your Moon sign, and keep a careful count of your money before you succumb to any Geminian frivolity. Mercury is the planet of trade and commerce, and you are therefore in a good position to obtain excellent returns for any outlay. Just think carefully, critically, and practically when you invest.

Parenthood

You will be an energetic, hardworking parent, but do not allow yourself to be ruled by chores. Let your children persuade you to take them out. You will argue and discuss things with them in the best possible way, so avoid nagging them.

THE MOON IN LIBRA

BOTH GEMINI AND LIBRA ARE AIR SIGNS, INCLINING THEIR SUBJECTS TO BE UNDERSTANDING AND RATIONAL. YOU MAY BE COMMUNICATIVE, BUT YOU COULD HAVE DEEP EMOTIONS THAT ARE STILL WAITING TO BE EXPRESSED.

Your Geminian intellect is spiced with Libran charm, delicacy of approach, and love of balance, harmony, and comfort.

Self-expression
You are wonderfully diplomatic in a natural, instinctive way. Social intercourse is very important to you, and you probably show an automatic interest in everyone that you meet. No doubt you have a very wide circle of friends, among whom you give the impression that you know a lot about almost everything.

Geminian logic can be weakened by Libran indecisiveness. Do not be evasive or push decisions onto other people; be self-critical and you will manage to overcome the tendency.

Romance
While Libra makes you respond immediately both to the idea of romance and to romantic situations, it may be that you tend to fall in love with love itself. In spite of a longing for romance, Libra is not really a very deeply emotional sign – and neither is Gemini. Do not let an idea be a substitute for reality.

Your well-being
You may be somewhat prone to headaches. These could relate to your kidneys – which are the Libran organ and therefore slightly vulnerable. You could, perhaps, suffer from some pain in the lumbar region of your back. This, too, may be attributable to your Libran Moon. In general make sure that you sit upright when working at a table or a desk.

Exercise will probably bore you even more than most Geminians. To keep in shape, devise a system of rewards for yourself – for example, a relaxed half hour in a sauna or steam bath, or a talk with friends at the salad bar after your workout. But be careful:

The Moon in Libra

Your Libran Moon may also give you more of a sweet tooth than most Geminians, and your waistline could suffer if you make that reward a slice of chocolate cake. The normally quick Geminian metabolism may, of course, be of some assistance here.

Planning ahead

Librans enjoy comfort and luxury. Beautiful clothes and expensive beauty products and treatments are therefore likely to cost you a lot of money. You will probably do well to take sound financial advice before investing, since you could instinctively fall for a whim that sounds good or glamorous, and end up losing in the long run.

Parenthood

You will be a kind, sympathetic parent, but might tend to bribe your children for the sake of peace and quiet. If you are too easy with them, they will soon learn to twist you around their little fingers. Use your Geminian astuteness.

THE MOON IN SCORPIO

YOUR BASIC INSTINCTS ARE VERY PASSIONATE, AND YOU ARE PARTICULARLY INTUITIVE. DO NOT ALLOW GEMINIAN LOGIC TO SUPPRESS THESE TRAITS. YOUR INQUIRING MIND MAY LEAD YOU TO BE SOMETHING OF A DETECTIVE.

A combination of Sun and Moon signs that is this dynamic is apt to make you a Geminian with a big difference. Your Scorpio Moon gives you a powerful emotional force that demands much positive expression if you are to achieve inner fulfillment.

Self-expression

If your general restlessness is not to be coupled with discontent and frustration, you must find work that is very satisfying. Go all out to achieve your aims, allowing your Geminian versatility full rein.

Unlike many Sun sign Geminians, you are not superficial; you need to get to the root of every problem.

Romance

Your emotional resources are so strong that you are unlikely to fall into the trap of letting them be dominated by your Geminian logic. Just as you need to be fulfilled in your career, so you need fulfillment in an emotional relationship. Sexual satisfaction is of above-average importance to you, and you probably demand a great deal from partners in this respect. It is important that they respond positively, perceiving your needs and being sympathetic to them. Geminians like to experiment, and this, too, is vital for you.

Your well-being

The Scorpio body area is the genitals, and regular clinical checkups in this region are always a good idea. Safe sex is another obvious precaution that both sexes should consider.

Should a mysterious illness strike you down, it may be that, contrary to the instinct of most Geminians, you are denying a problem.

Scorpios love rich food and fine wine, and while many have a wiry build, if by chance you are thick-set or have a slower metabolism than

The Moon in Scorpio

average, you could suffer from obesity and a sluggish system. Try not to get bored with exercise – perhaps taking up judo or karate would be the solution. All kinds of sports can be enjoyable if approached correctly.

Planning ahead

Your shrewdness, intelligence, and cunning, enhanced by the influence of Gemini and Scorpio, will no doubt help you to make money, so act without hesitation. Your bank balance should grow steadily, even if you occasionally go wild on a case of wine or other expensive treats.

Parenthood

As a parent, you may be stricter than you realize, and could easily overreact to any misdemeanors. On the whole, however, your Geminian Sun keeps you very youthful and in no way pedantic. You should enjoy your role as parent and have time for fun with your children.

THE MOON IN
SAGITTARIUS

AS GEMINI AND SAGITTARIUS ARE POLAR OR OPPOSITE ZODIAC SIGNS, YOU WERE BORN UNDER A FULL MOON. YOU MAY FIND IT HARD TO CONTROL AN INHERENT RESTLESSNESS. BE VERSATILE, BUT DEVELOP CONSISTENCY OF EFFORT.

Each of us is, in one way or another, liable to express certain attributes of our polar, or opposite, Zodiac signs. For Geminians, the polar sign is Sagittarius, and as the Moon was in that sign when you were born, the polarity is powerfully emphasized. A great deal of sympathy and empathy exists between Gemini and Sagittarius: both are positive, mutable signs, and are complementary air and fire signs.

Self-expression

Your Geminian communicative ability is emphasized by an instinct that will help you get your ideas across to others with tremendous enthusiasm. Your natural optimism is very infectious, and you will easily win others around to your point of view.

Your life needs challenge, but do not start looking for alternatives just for the sake of it. Sagittarius, like Gemini, gives its subjects a versatility that needs to be expressed, but to get the best effect from it, you need to always be consistent in what you do. The worst Sagittarian fault is restlessness, and those, like yourself, who are born under a Full Moon are especially prone to it.

Romance

You make the liveliest of lovers, and possess a fiery passion. You need partners who, if anything, are ahead of you in their eagerness to experiment with, and enjoy, a physical relationship. It is, however, equally important that your partners have excellent minds; otherwise, you will be unlikely to develop any true and lasting friendship with them.

Your well-being

The Sagittarian body area covers the hips and thighs, and women with this sign emphasized tend to put on weight in these areas. You may well

The Moon in Sagittarius

enjoy rather heavier food than other Sun sign Geminians, and this could make matters worse. The liver is the Sagittarian organ, so hangovers may be something of a problem for you. Like all Geminians and Sagittarians, you need plenty of variety in anything that you do, to combat boredom.

Planning ahead

It is probably true to say that while, like everyone, you generally need money, it is usually there when you want it. You may not be very interested in investments, and could well have something of a gambling streak, which you should be wary of. If you enjoy rather risky deals or gambling on the stockmarket, do not invest more money than you know you can afford to lose.

Parenthood

Your children will find your natural enthusiasm for life infectious. Bringing them up should not prove to be too much of a worry or problem, since you are so young at heart yourself. You are also a natural teacher, and will keep their minds usefully occupied. For you, the generation gap simply does not exist.

THE MOON IN CAPRICORN

GEMINI, WHICH IS AN AIR SIGN, IS NOT PARTICULARLY COMPATIBLE WITH CAPRICORN, AN EARTH SIGN. THE DIFFERENT CHARACTERISTICS THAT YOUR MOON SIGN ADDS TO YOUR PERSONALITY ARE STILL VERY INTERESTING.

Your natural instincts tell you to be practical, aspiring, and ambitious. But to develop single-minded purpose may prove difficult for a versatile Sun sign Geminian. Try to compromise where and when you can.

Self-expression

You are among the most practical members of your Sun sign group, and need a secure base upon which to build your life. Gemini is a take-charge sign, and the influence of your Moon will be to urge you on.

Aspiring with determination, you know that you will achieve the ambition on which you have set your sights. That ambition is, however, just as likely to center on a contented family with an ideal home as on some professional aspiration.

You may be a little more susceptible to worry than other Sun sign Geminians. Should this lead to bouts of despondency, let your Geminian logic and optimism take control and rationalize any problems that you are having.

Romance

Your Moon sign does not increase your ability to express your emotions freely. While you are friendly and sociable, you may tend to distance yourself from your true feelings and, in doing so, suppress them.

You need a partner who is as ambitious as you are and capable of being a good friend within any emotional relationship. Sex may not be the main reason why you want to deepen a relationship, but sexual fulfillment is as necessary for you as it is for anyone else.

Your well-being

The Capricornian body area covers the knees and shins, which are therefore vulnerable. Fortunately, Geminians like to keep moving, so

The Moon in Capricorn

Capricornian stiffness of the joints should not be too much of a problem. The teeth are also ruled by Capricorn, so regular dental checkups are of paramount importance for you.

Planning ahead

As far as finances are concerned, your instinct is to save money and to be very careful with it. But when your Geminian Sun takes over, you will feel that you want to enjoy the fruits of your hard-earned cash. Consequently, you could be faced with something of a conflict. However, you should have a skill for budgeting and investment.

Parenthood

You may give the impression that you are a strict and rigid parent, but with your Capricornian sense of humor, your children will know that this is not entirely the case. If you make sure that you have time to enjoy their company and listen to their opinions, the generation gap should not be much of a problem for you.

THE MOON IN AQUARIUS

MODERN, FORWARD-LOOKING GEMINIANS WITH A TRENDY IMAGE WILL USE AN AQUARIAN URGE FOR GLAMOUR AND ORIGINALITY TO GREAT EFFECT. DO NOT LET YOUR NEED FOR INDEPENDENCE EXCLUDE MEANINGFUL EMOTIONAL RELATIONSHIPS.

You have an extremely interesting combination of intellectually inclined signs, both of which are of the air element. You are original and very logical, if slightly unpredictable.

Self-expression

You are among the most independent of Geminians, and many of you will build a lifestyle that could well have some unique features to it.

Aquarius is a sign of the fixed quality, so you may well have to bring your Geminian Sun into play if you have a tendency to be stubborn.

While Gemini has the reputation of being the most youthful of signs, Aquarius is high on the list of the most glamorous ones. Neither sign is very emotional. There is, in fact, a rather distant quality to many Aquarians. They tend to give the impression that while you may look at and admire them, you should also keep your distance.

Romance

It is very important for both you and your partner to recognize the fact that you will always need a considerable measure of independence. Perhaps contrarily, your Moon makes you a great romantic. You will no doubt love all the trimmings of romance, for example, bouquets of flowers, wonderful candle-lit dinners, and Valentine cards. Sexual fulfillment must, for you, be colored with romance – the atmosphere has to be just right. It should not be too difficult for you to persuade your partners to go along with this.

Your well-being

The Aquarian body area covers the ankles. If you like wearing high-heeled shoes, be careful. Aquarius also rules the circulation and, while most people with this sign emphasized in their birthcharts enjoy cold weather, their circulation is not

The Moon in Aquarius

always good. Perhaps you enjoy winter sports: these will be good for you, provided that you keep warm.

Planning ahead

You may not be very good with money. Gemini likes to keep up to date, especially in image, and Aquarius is easily attracted to rather glitzy, ephemeral things. You might, for example, want to back a theater show, but no quicker way of losing money has yet been invented. Always talk potential investments over with a sound financial adviser. This will teach you how to handle your finances, and you will not have to learn the hard way.

Parenthood

You will be a typically forward-looking Geminian parent. You will sympathize with your children when they are upset, but sometimes in a too-adult way, discussing their problems when they need a cuddle.

THE MOON IN PISCES

THE AIR ELEMENT OF GEMINI CAN CLASH WITH THE EMOTIONAL CONTENT OF A PISCEAN WATER SIGN. ALLOW YOUR EMOTION TO FLOW, PERHAPS THROUGH ARTISTIC APPRECIATION OR EXPRESSION; DO NOT RATIONALIZE IT AWAY.

Although there is a clash of elements in this combination – Gemini is air and Pisces, water – both the Sun and the Moon work very well for you. On the whole, Pisces is a creative sign, and those in whose charts it is emphasized will long for some kind of creative expression.

Self-expression

You are, by nature, very versatile and probably like to have many tasks at hand at the same time. For all Geminians, developing consistency of effort and learning to finish all the tasks undertaken, is extremely important. If you do not do this, inner fulfillment will evade you.

You are likely to be very emotional. Because this trait is linked to your deepest instinctive level, you will tend to overrationalize a situation once you are aware that you are reacting emotionally to it. You will question yourself about your emotions, and may mistrust and even be inclined to suppress them. Be aware that by giving your emotions full rein, you will gain in the long run.

Romance

You make a delightful lover and are more caring of your partners – perhaps also more easily hurt, than many Geminians. Remember that Piscean and Geminian duality, plus a touch of deceit, could make for complications in your emotional life. Sexually, you enjoy variety as well as passion. But you do need to have a solid intellectual rapport and shared interests with any partners.

Your well-being

The Piscean body area is the feet, and they will be very vulnerable to blisters, corns, and cuts.

Even more than most Geminians, you are likely to worry or be apprehensive. If this is the case, let

The Moon in Pisces

your Geminian rationality take over. The best kind of exercise for you is likely to be swimming or any kind of dancing or skating.

Planning ahead

Financially, you should obtain professional advice regarding investment. As you can be a very soft touch indeed, you would be well advised not to lend money.

Parenthood

You will be a warm and loving parent, although you may sometimes have a tendency to spoil your children. You will also be very good at encouraging their interests, sometimes even getting yourself involved in things you never thought could possibly interest you. Your children will, of course, greatly appreciate this, and there is always the chance that they might even become hooked on a hobby or interest that particularly fascinates you.

The one thing that you should beware of is acting evasively toward them. It is always important for children to know exactly where they stand with their parents. In your case, the generation gap should not exist.

SUN & MOON SIGNS

CANCER

JUNE 22 – JULY 22

INTRODUCING CANCER

CANCER, THE SIGN OF THE CRAB, IS THE FOURTH SIGN OF THE ZODIAC. WHILE A CRAB CAN SOMETIMES BE CRABBY, CANCERIANS PROJECT MANY EXTREMELY POSITIVE QUALITIES THAT MIGHT BE ASSOCIATED WITH THIS CREATURE.

Similarly to the way in which a crab's hard shell protects a soft interior, Cancer's subjects develop a hard psychological shell to protect themselves and their loved ones from the rigors of life. If you challenge or threaten a Cancerian in any way, you will see this self-defensive system spring into action at once.

Traditional groupings

As you read through this book you will come across references to the elements and the qualities, and to positive and negative, or masculine and feminine signs.

The first of these groupings, that of the elements, comprises fire, earth, air, and water signs. The second, that of the qualities, divides the Zodiac into cardinal, fixed, and mutable signs. The final grouping is made up of positive and negative, or masculine and feminine signs. Each Zodiac sign is associated with a combination of components from these groupings, all of which contribute different characteristics to it.

Cancerian characteristics

Cancer is the first sign of the water element, and therefore has a very high emotional level and great intuition. Possessing an excellent memory, Cancerians sometimes recall minor injuries and slights best forgotten. As a sign of the cardinal quality, however, Cancer is outgoing toward loved ones, as well as being kind, helpful, and considerate.

The sign's ruling "planet" is the Moon. The changeability of the Moon is reflected in Cancerians: They are exceptionally prone to moodiness and sudden changes of outlook. Cancer is linked with silvery blue and smoky gray colors that reflect the colors of the Moon. It is a feminine, negative sign, which inclines its subjects toward introversion.

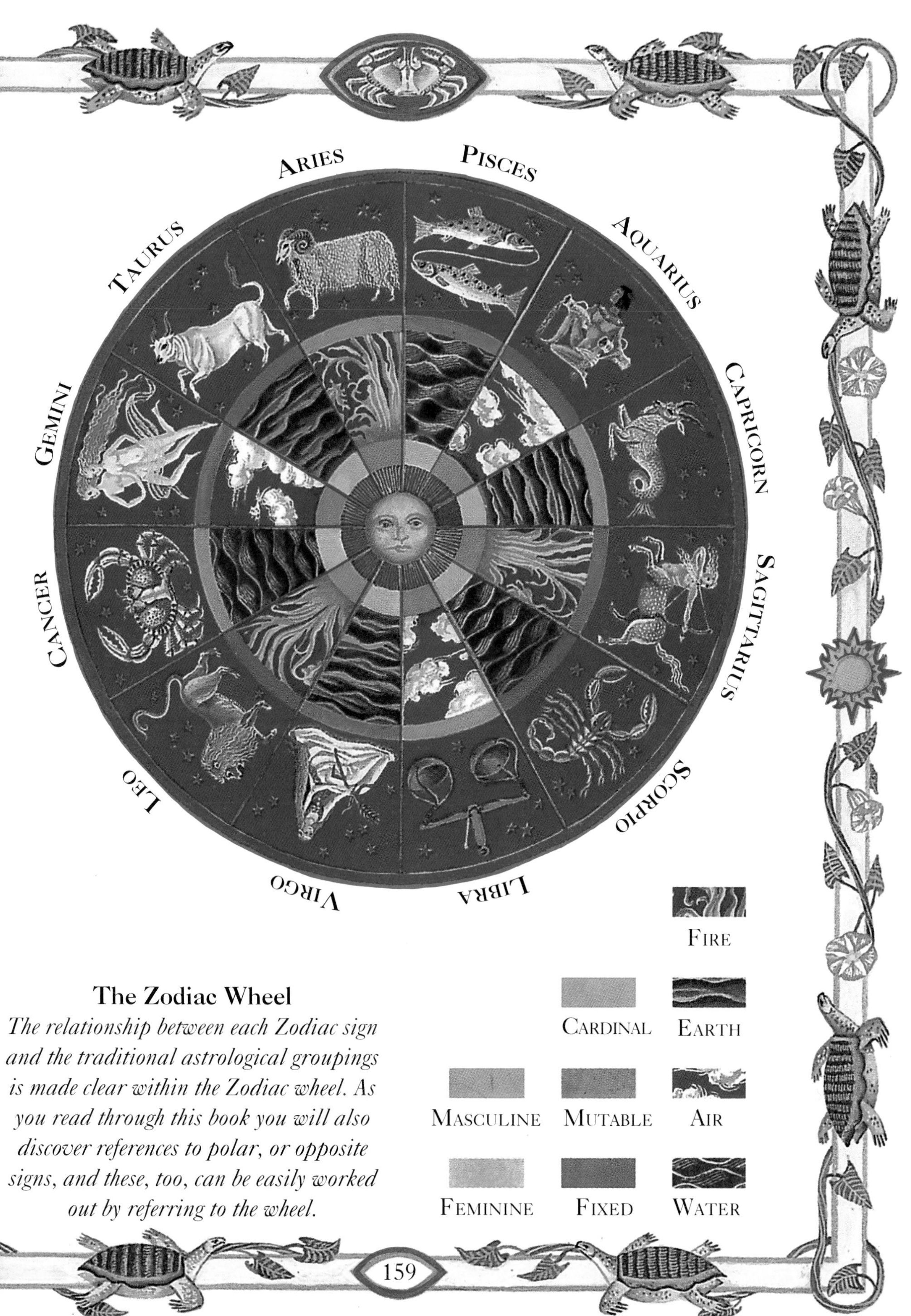

The Zodiac Wheel

The relationship between each Zodiac sign and the traditional astrological groupings is made clear within the Zodiac wheel. As you read through this book you will also discover references to polar, or opposite signs, and these, too, can be easily worked out by referring to the wheel.

CANCER

MYTHS & LEGENDS

THE ZODIAC, WHICH IS BELIEVED TO HAVE ORIGINATED IN BABYLON AS LONG AS 2,500 YEARS AGO, IS A CIRCLE OF CONSTELLATIONS THROUGH WHICH THE SUN MOVES DURING THE COURSE OF A YEAR.

The sign of Cancer probably originated in Ancient Egypt, where the constellation was first known as the sign of the Stars of the Water and later as the Two Turtles (river turtles are found in the Nile and have a hard shell, like that of a crab). In Ancient Babylon, the sign was known not only as Al. lul, a water creature – "the wicked or rebellious one" – but also as bulug, the Crab or Crayfish. Much later, the Ancient Greeks named it the Tortoise.

Hercules and the Hydra
In this fourth-century image the crab is seen assisting the Hydra.

The labors of Hercules

Of all the Zodiac signs, this constellation is perhaps the least celebrated in myth and legend. The only association that has really been made is with one of the 12 labors that the hero Hercules was made to perform by King Eurystheus, the ruler of Greece, after he had murdered his own wife and children. Having consulted the Oracle at Delphi, Hercules learned that only by showing obedience to Eurystheus could he atone for his crime. The second labor consisted of the destruction of the Hydra, a monster specially reared by the goddess Hera to fight him. It had the body of a dog, and nine snaky heads – one of which was immortal. Furthermore, its breath was so poisonous that anyone unfortunate enough to be exposed to it fell dead instantly. From its den in a marsh

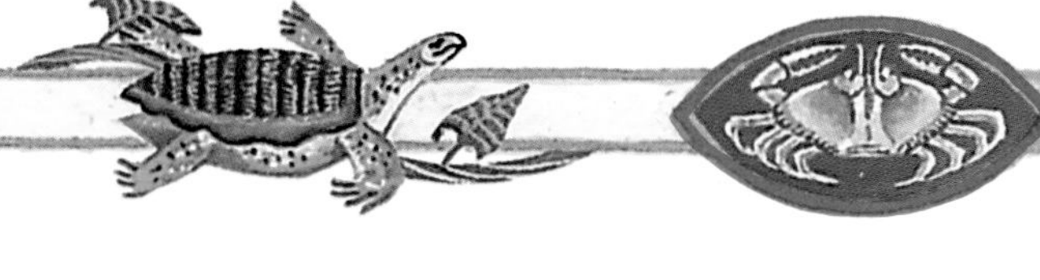

near Lerna in the Peloponnese, it would embark on great orgies of destruction and killing, devastating innumerable herds and crops.

Hercules battles the Hydra

Hercules forced the Hydra to leave its marsh by showering the beast in flaming arrows. At first his task seemed impossible; every time he struck off one of the monster's heads, two more grew in its place. Moreover, when Hercules eventually seemed to be gaining an advantage in his battle with the Hydra, Hera sent a great crab to help out, which it did by attacking the hero's foot. In the end, however, Hercules succeeded in stamping on it, disposing of it for good. Nevertheless, Hera was so grateful for the crab's assistance that she set it among the stars in a constellation of its own, which we call Cancer. Hercules went on to kill the Hydra by burning off its mortal heads with a red-hot branding iron, before slicing off its immortal head.

The characteristics of a crab can often be seen in people associated with this sign. Cancerians usually have a brittle protective shell, evident in an exterior gruffness; but this shell usually conceals a caring personality.

Egyptian mummy and coffin
This ancient wooden coffin, dating from the second century A.D., is decorated with the signs of the Zodiac.

CANCER

SYMBOLISM

CERTAIN HERBS, SPICES, FLOWERS, TREES, GEMS, METALS, AND ANIMALS HAVE LONG BEEN ASSOCIATED WITH PARTICULAR ZODIAC SIGNS. SOME ASSOCIATIONS ARE SIMPLY AMUSING, WHILE OTHERS CAN BE USEFUL.

Flowers

Plants that flower at night are connected with Cancer. Other Cancerian flowers include acanthus, honeysuckle, and white flowers such as the white rose and lily.

WHITE LILIES

WHITE ROSES

LAUREL

Trees

Cancer is said to have a special sympathy for all trees. This association is particularly strong with those trees that are rich in sap.

Herbs

Saxifrage, which calms the stomach, and purslane, good for liver ailments, are both Cancerian herbs.

SAXIFRAGE

NUTMEG

Spices

No particular spice is associated with Cancer, but coriander and nutmeg are sometimes mentioned in connection with water signs.

CORIANDER

CANCER

SYMBOLISM

Animals

The crab is, of course, associated with this sign; but so are all animals with shells or tough hides, such as the tortoise, crocodile, and armadillo.

TORTOISESHELL COMB

TORTOISESHELL BOX

FAN WITH MOTHER-OF-PEARL STICKS

CRAB

Gems

The Cancerian gem is the pearl – its luster is closely associated with the Moon, which rules Cancer.

PEARL NECKLACE

LOCKET DECORATED WITH PEARLS

Metal

Silver is the Cancerian metal. Those born under this sign often like to wear silver jewelry.

SILVER FILIGREE SPOONS

ANTIQUE SILVER PICTURE FRAME

CANCER

PROFILE

THE APPEARANCE OF TYPICAL CANCERIANS OFTEN REFLECTS THEIR HOARDING INSTINCTS. FAVORITE OLD JACKETS, OR SOME REFERENCE TO THE PAST, ARE USUALLY IN EVIDENCE. CARELESSNESS CAN SOMETIMES SPOIL THEIR IMAGE.

Many Cancerians fail to stand as straight as they should. They are often a little round-shouldered, which can tend to make them look rather fearful or apprehensive.

The body

Cancerians are generally good cooks. You may therefore tend toward being a little overweight if you are not careful about what you eat. Unless you are really keen on taking exercise you could be a little more prone to becoming flabby than many other Zodiac types.

You have a strong constitution, and will have excellent powers of resistance to illness. Many women of this sign have more than ample bosoms, which can be an asset to their powers of attraction.

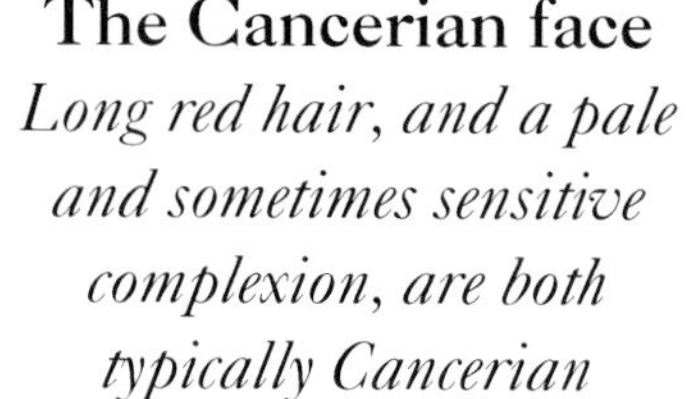

The Cancerian face

Long red hair, and a pale and sometimes sensitive complexion, are both typically Cancerian characteristics.

The face

Cancerians often have rather long hair, which can become a little untidy if it does not receive the appropriate amount of care. Red hair is very common among Cancerians. Your forehead is likely to be rather pale and pronounced, perhaps with frown lines between the eyes. The eyes themselves are usually on the small side; some Cancerians may have rather beady little eyes. Even among races with dark skin coloring, Cancerians tend to have pale skin that is rather sensitive to the sun. It is possible that scar tissue will show on

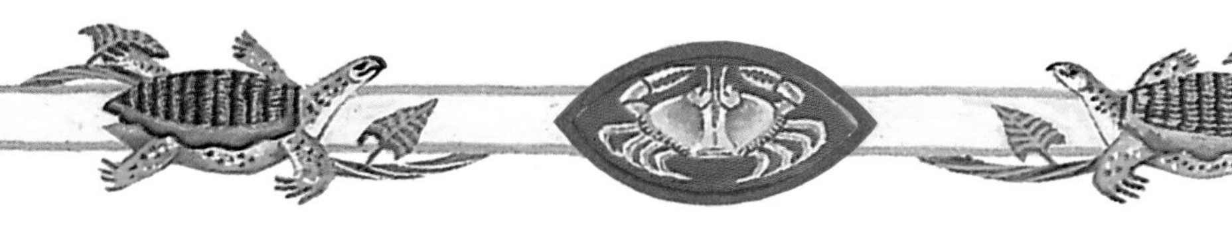

The Cancerian stance

Many Cancerians tend to hunch themselves up when they stand; this can make them look rather apprehensive.

your skin long after a wound has healed. As a Cancerian, your mouth is likely to be soft and flexible.

Style

The Cancerian style is often very distinctive. A particularly smart image is often spoiled by choosing the wrong accessories or by sheer carelessness: you may for example sometimes leave a shoulderstrap showing, or wear an untidily knotted tie. Because of this tendency you need to take great care over the way you decide to dress – more, in fact, than members of any other sign. You could have a preference for antique clothes, which can be very attractive.

You are likely to have a very good sense of color. Soft shades of blue or gray often complement the Cancerian personality. Many Cancerians also choose the fabric for their clothes extremely skillfully.

In general

Your overall appearance may be marked by a tendency to stoop, and glance furtively around you to make sure that you are not about to be challenged. As a Cancerian, you are probably also likely to pay an unusual amount of attention to the weather. In your efforts to pre-empt and cater for every type of weather condition you may sometimes appear exaggeratedly swathed in heavy layers of warm clothes and thick scarves when it is cold, but also dress extremely lightly when it is hot.

CANCER PERSONALITY

KINDNESS AND SENSITIVITY ARE DOMINANT FEATURES OF THE CANCERIAN PERSONALITY. WHILE THEY THEMSELVES ARE EASILY HURT, CANCERIANS ARE OFTEN UNAWARE THAT THEY CAN BE HARSH IN THEIR RESPONSES TO OTHERS.

The first time that someone meets you, it may be easy for them to get the wrong impression. This is because you can tend to act a little defensively toward people you do not know; you develop your own hard shell in order to protect yourself. Underneath this, however, you probably feel very vulnerable.

If others are tactful to you and take their time in getting to know you, it should not be too difficult for them to break through your defenses. When this happens, your deeply caring and understanding nature will shine through. Those who succeed in gaining your friendship will discover that you have the capacity to be a really good friend.

At work

You have a marvelously fertile imagination and should aim to use it positively and creatively under all circumstances. This applies to the way you approach your work. Only then will you be able to express your potential in the best possible way.

Your attitudes

You are probably the most tenacious of all Zodiac types, and you hang on tightly to your friends and loved ones. While you are tremendously faithful and want to do as much as possible for your family, it can be extremely difficult for you to accept the fact that your children will want to leave home and build their own lives once they grow up.

The overall picture

One of the most common character traits shared by all Cancerians, which is linked to your tenacity, is a strong tendency to hoard. You will hardly ever throw anything away – so much so that you and your home will inevitably become surrounded by clutter. If, however, you decide to

The Moon rules Cancer

The Moon, represented here by the goddess Diana, is usually shown as feminine. It encourages Cancerians to act instinctively, and influences the emotions and the digestive system.

take a serious interest either in antiques or in collecting articles that you find fascinating, this tendency will be put to good use.

By rechanneling your Cancerian hoarding instinct into a love of collecting things, you will be able to avoid having much of your space consumed by ugly heaps of newspapers, battered pots and pans, and any old junk – for example, pieces of string that are too short to be of any possible use to anyone.

Having said this, many Cancerians do have extremely good taste, and when this is fully developed, it really shows in every aspect of their lives. You are more than likely to have a great appreciation of, and sensitivity toward, everything that is beautiful.

CANCER
ASPIRATIONS

CARE-GIVING PROFESSIONS OFFER IDEAL WORK FOR CANCERIANS. YOU WILL PARTICULARLY ENJOY WORKING WITH YOUNG CHILDREN. AND SINCE YOU MAY BE THE BEST COOK IN THE ZODIAC, CATERING COULD ALSO APPEAL TO YOU.

Flight attendant
Working as a flight attendant or a courier involves a strong element of service, and you will therefore probably enjoy either profession.

MODEL JET

WHISK

SAUCEPAN

EGGS

Cooking
Cancerians are the natural cooks of the Zodiac. You may, however, be just a little temperamental when working with others in a kitchen.

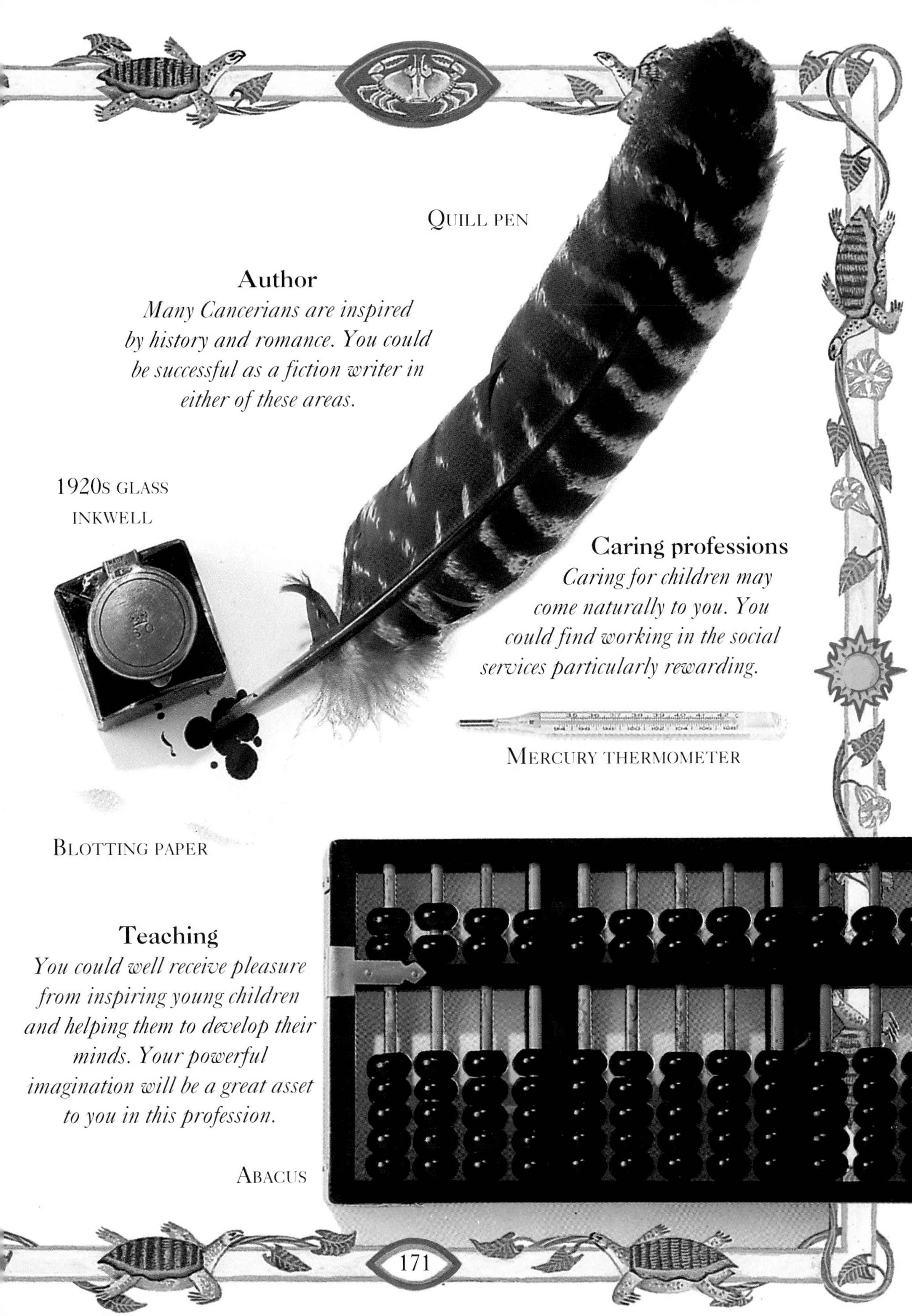

QUILL PEN

Author

Many Cancerians are inspired by history and romance. You could be successful as a fiction writer in either of these areas.

1920S GLASS INKWELL

Caring professions

Caring for children may come naturally to you. You could find working in the social services particularly rewarding.

MERCURY THERMOMETER

BLOTTING PAPER

Teaching

You could well receive pleasure from inspiring young children and helping them to develop their minds. Your powerful imagination will be a great asset to you in this profession.

ABACUS

CANCER HEALTH

THE PREVAILING ATMOSPHERE WILL HAVE A PHYSICAL, AS WELL AS AN EMOTIONAL, EFFECT ON A SENSITIVE CANCERIAN. YOUR RESPONSES TO THIS ATMOSPHERE ARE LIKELY TO BE HIGHLY INDIVIDUAL.

Sun sign Cancerians usually have somewhat pale complexions, irrespective of their background. This is not, however, a clue to how healthy or unhealthy they may be. In fact, you have a fairly strong constitution.

Your diet

As long as you beware of consuming too much cholesterol, you will benefit from a diet that includes a lot of dairy products. You may need to supplement your diet with calcium fluoride (calc. fluor.). This is considered to be important for the health of the teeth, fingernails, and bones.

Of all the 12 Zodiac signs, Cancerians are particularly prone to worrying. When you become upset, you may find yourself suffering from digestive problems.

Taking care

The traditional Cancerian body area is the breasts. Although this sign has no connection at all with breast cancer, it is sensible for all women to perform regular self-examinations. The sensitive Cancerian skin is a problem area. Protect yourself against the strong rays of the sun, as you are prone to sunburn.

Melon

Fruit and vegetables with a high water content, such as melons and pumpkins, are among the foods associated with Cancer.

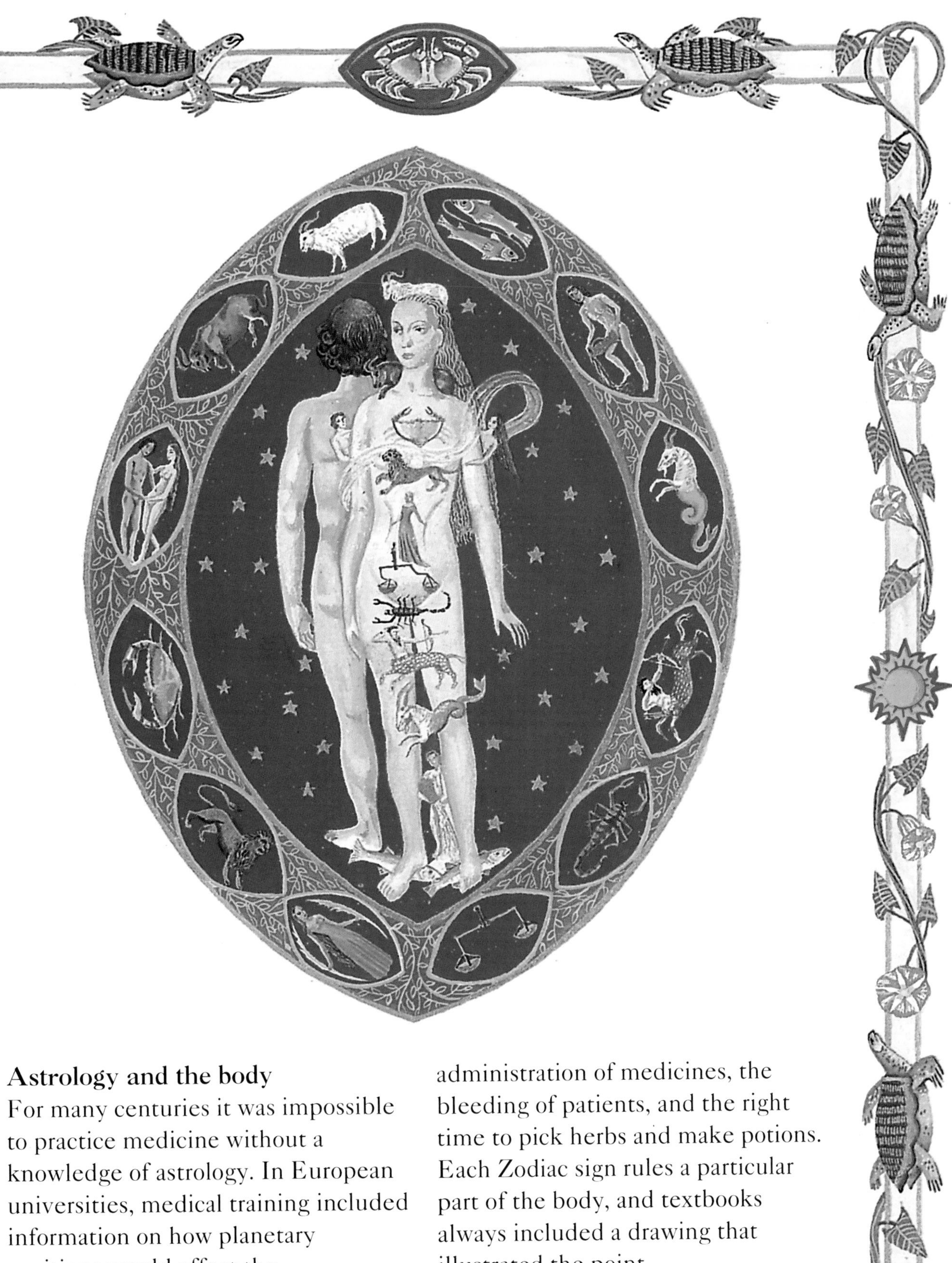

Astrology and the body

For many centuries it was impossible to practice medicine without a knowledge of astrology. In European universities, medical training included information on how planetary positions would affect the administration of medicines, the bleeding of patients, and the right time to pick herbs and make potions. Each Zodiac sign rules a particular part of the body, and textbooks always included a drawing that illustrated the point.

CANCER AT LEISURE

EACH OF THE SUN SIGNS TRADITIONALLY SUGGESTS SPARE-TIME ACTIVITIES, HOBBIES, AND VACATION SPOTS. CONSIDER SOME OF THESE SUGGESTIONS – THEY OFTEN SUIT CANCERIAN INTERESTS.

Writing

Cancerians often have fertile imaginations, and these can be expressed through creative writing.

POSTAGE STAMPS

Travel

Although a nervous traveler, you may enjoy a cruise. Your ideal location could be near a lake or the sea. Try Scotland, Holland, New Zealand, Paraguay, and North Africa as vacation destinations.

1920S FOUNTAIN PEN

Cookery

It is typical for Cancerians of either sex to find cooking for their friends and family very fulfilling.

WOODEN SPOONS FOR COOKING

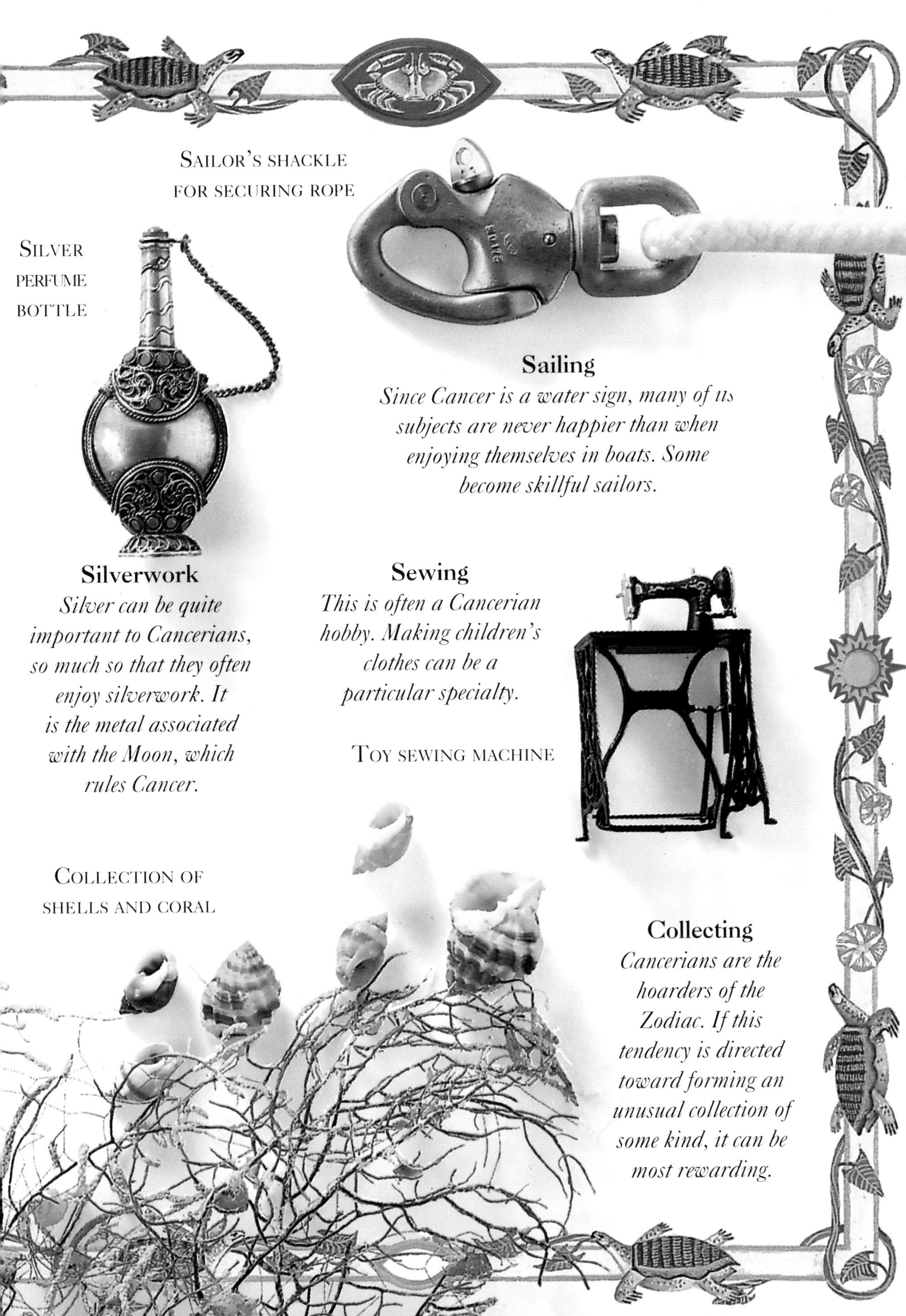

SAILOR'S SHACKLE FOR SECURING ROPE

SILVER PERFUME BOTTLE

Sailing

Since Cancer is a water sign, many of its subjects are never happier than when enjoying themselves in boats. Some become skillful sailors.

Silverwork

Silver can be quite important to Cancerians, so much so that they often enjoy silverwork. It is the metal associated with the Moon, which rules Cancer.

Sewing

This is often a Cancerian hobby. Making children's clothes can be a particular specialty.

TOY SEWING MACHINE

COLLECTION OF SHELLS AND CORAL

Collecting

Cancerians are the hoarders of the Zodiac. If this tendency is directed toward forming an unusual collection of some kind, it can be most rewarding.

CANCER IN LOVE

MANY OF THE BEST CANCERIAN QUALITIES SPRING INTO ACTION WHEN CANCER FALLS IN LOVE. THOUGH YOU ARE ROMANTIC AND PASSIONATE, YOUR REACTIONS TO BOTH THE GOOD AND BAD THINGS IN A RELATIONSHIP CAN BE EXTREME.

While Cancerian emotions find a wonderfully positive outlet when you fall in love, it is also very easy for you to express certain traits that can have a negative effect on a relationship. If, however, you are conscious of the fact that you can create a more unpleasant atmosphere for your partners than you realize, you will be able to correct yourself before anything goes drastically wrong.

You have a very powerful motivation to love, cherish, and protect your loved ones. Unless you are careful, you may end up taking this tenderness too far and create a claustrophobic atmosphere within your relationship. Many people are unable to cope with this, finding it too confining, so this tendency to limit independence or freedom of expression may sometimes come between you and your lover.

As a lover

You are likely to take your love life very seriously, and while this does not mean that you do not enjoy – indeed revel in – love and sex, it does mean that due to a strong homemaking and family-raising instinct, you may tend to look upon all relationships with this in mind.

You should be aware that many prospective partners may not be so interested in a serious commitment. You are, no doubt, a wonderful lover, since you are both sensuous and in possession of a great instinct for the kind of things that are likely to make your partners happy.

Types of Cancerian lover

When Cancerians are young, it is a good idea for them to play the field. This way, they will gain experience with the opposite sex, and later, they are experienced and mature enough to cope with a stable, long-term relationship.

The influence of other planets will produce some subtle differences from one Cancerian to the next. Some of the more clinging members of the sign will be warmly affectionate as well as passionate, but can be very possessive. Others have a wonderfully flirtatious streak, which lightens their Cancerian intensity in love; yet another group has a lot of style and elegance, and will put partners on a pedestal. Some people of this Sun sign group display a sense of modesty that often intrigues prospective partners.

CANCER AT HOME

A CANCERIAN'S DWELLING PLACE IS, ABOVE ALL, A HOME. THE LOOK OF THE ROOMS USUALLY TAKES SECOND PLACE TO CONVENIENCE, WHICH IS OFTEN THAT OF THE CHILDREN. THIS CAN LEAD TO SUPREME UNTIDINESS.

When choosing a place to live you would do well to remember that Cancerians need a degree of peace and tranquility, perhaps in the form of a beautiful view, close at hand. This does not mean that you will feel unhappy living anywhere other than the heart of the country; a tiny balcony, or a corner filled with flowers, will provide you with a quiet, calming focus. The Cancerian home will ideally be quite close to a water source such as a slow-moving river, the sea, or a lake.

Wicker sewing basket
A sewing basket, knitting, or toys may be scattered around your home.

Furniture

Cancerians love the past, and hate to throw anything away. You are likely to choose either very traditional designs or, if you can afford it, quality antique furniture. You may become so fond of articles such as favorite armchairs that you will cling to them until they eventually begin to fall to pieces.

With well-developed Cancerian taste you may, however, choose quite beautiful, extremely comfortable furniture. Since your home is likely to be so important to you, the overall effect and atmosphere may be a joy to experience.

Soft furnishings

Cancerians look to the past when deciding on drapes. Your choice may veer either toward heavy silk brocades in pale silvery gray, or pastel colors, or alternatively Victorian chintz. When

Jug and fabric
These objects reflect the Cancerian colors and metal.

choosing new drapes, make sure that they are not too heavy, and try not to create a claustrophobic atmosphere. A Cancerian will have no desire to be overlooked by neighbors, but if you happen to live near the sea or a river, you will certainly want to see it clearly. If this is the case, drapes will definitely take a back seat.

Many Cancerians enjoy creating their own cushions, perhaps using petit point or some other form of decorative needlework.

Decorative objects

The tendency to hoard can ruin the effect of the Cancerian home. It may become extremely cluttered. If, however, your tendency to hoard can be controlled, and expressed through showing off an interesting personal collection of some kind, this will obviously enhance the overall appearance of your home.

You may choose to display a painting of your children, or perhaps a seascape. If you are fortunate enough to own some silver, or perhaps some family heirlooms, these are likely to be prominently displayed. Cancerians should accept the fact that sentimentality about old things can tend to be rather counterproductive.

Armchair and doll
A comfortable, well-worn armchair may be a much-loved item in your home.

THE
MOON
AND
YOU

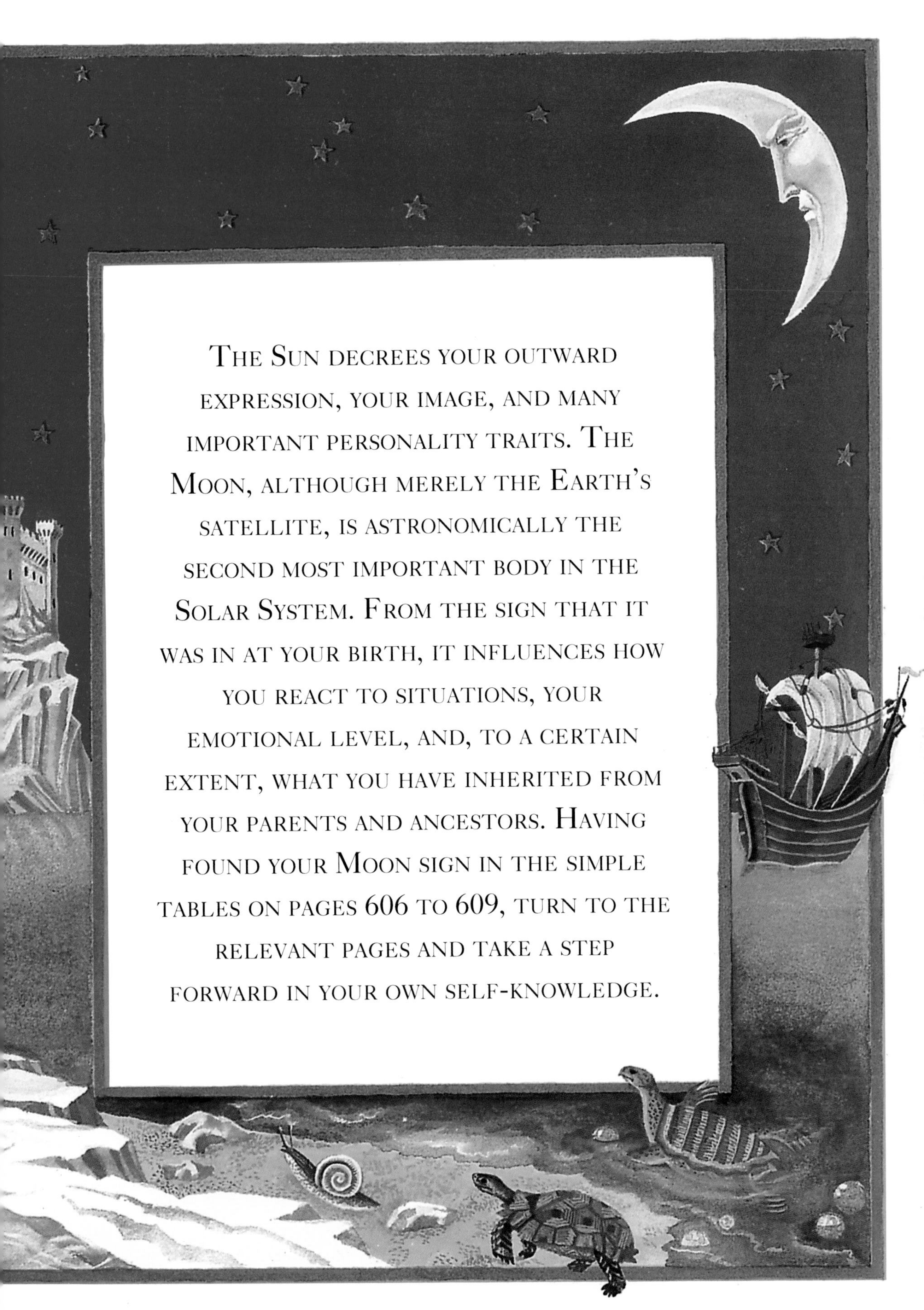

The Sun decrees your outward expression, your image, and many important personality traits. The Moon, although merely the Earth's satellite, is astronomically the second most important body in the Solar System. From the sign that it was in at your birth, it influences how you react to situations, your emotional level, and, to a certain extent, what you have inherited from your parents and ancestors. Having found your Moon sign in the simple tables on pages 606 to 609, turn to the relevant pages and take a step forward in your own self-knowledge.

THE MOON IN ARIES

JUST AS CANCER IS THE FIRST WATER SIGN, SO ARIES IS THE FIRST FIRE SIGN. BOTH SIGNS HAVE HIGH EMOTIONAL LEVELS. YOUR ARIEN MOON ADDS ENTHUSIASM TO YOUR CHARACTER, WHICH YOU ARE LIKELY TO EXPRESS AT A MOMENT'S NOTICE.

You will be eager to surge ahead with projects and to accept challenges. Cancerians are noted for being both brave and protective, and these qualities are strongly emphasized in your personality.

Self-expression

In some respects a combination of fire and water elements is not an easy one. But your fire sign Moon works positively: you will be far less apprehensive, and less introverted, than some Cancerians.

You are one of the tougher types of Cancerian and will be able to cope extremely well during demanding and strenuous periods. Perhaps your instinctively adventurous spirit will encourage you to be something of an explorer, with a penchant for visiting unusual places.

Cancerian moods, spiced with sudden emotional flare-ups, could make you a force to be reckoned with. You should try to control these impulsive outbursts; they might be more potent than you realize.

Romance

You are extremely passionate, and it is in your love life that your very high emotional level will be best expressed. However, while your Cancerian Sun makes you somewhat clinging, your Arien Moon dictates that you need an element of independence and freedom.

Your well-being

The Arien body area is the head: If you are worried, you may tend to get unpleasant headaches. These may also be due to slight kidney upsets.

Planning ahead

As well as having plenty of Cancerian shrewdness and a good business sense, you react extremely well to enterprising schemes and suggestions.

The Moon in Aries

You should, however, always think carefully before becoming involved in them, in order to avoid disappointment later.

Parenthood

A great sense of fun and a marked sentimental streak color your attitude to life – this will certainly rub off on your loved ones. Like all Cancerians, you will be eager to have children, but you will be less prone to worry about them than most people of your Sun sign. But make sure that you recognize the fact that, in due course, they will want to move away from home and live their own lives. Your Aries Moon should help you to understand this and to ensure that you do not feel life is too empty once they are gone. Try to always look to the future and to see life through your children's eyes; otherwise, your Cancerian nostalgia and sentimentality could create a generation gap.

THE MOON IN TAURUS

AS AN EARTH SIGN, YOUR TAUREAN MOON WILL STABILIZE YOUR CANCERIAN QUALITIES AND ADD A PRACTICAL INSTINCT, AS WELL AS AN APTITUDE FOR MAKING MONEY. BEWARE OF ACTING TOO POSSESSIVELY TOWARD LOVED ONES.

Earth and water signs complement each other well, and while the Moon, which rules Cancer, exerts a very powerful influence over all Cancerians it is, by tradition, well placed in Taurus. As a result you will share many of the qualities commonly attributed to Taurus.

Self-expression

It is extremely important for you to feel both materially and emotionally secure. Provided you can do this, you will flourish and be able to express many fine positive qualities.

Through Taurus, you are warm and affectionate, and will not find it difficult to combine these traits with your caring, protective Cancerian traits. But you must ensure that possessiveness, which is the worst Taurean fault, does not obscure your warmth and kindness. On another level, your Cancerian instinct toward hoarding things, together with your instinctive love of possessions, will make it difficult for you to throw anything away.

Romance

You have the capacity to love both deeply and very passionately. Cancerians are noted for the sensual expression of their emotions, and when this is combined with the warm passion of a Taurean Moon, your partners may consider themselves very fortunate indeed. You have the ability to make and maintain a long-lasting relationship.

Your well-being

The Taurean body area is the throat, so yours could be vulnerable. More importantly, if you happen to be one of those great Cancerian cooks, the likelihood is that you will specialize in making very rich desserts with lots of cream, chocolate, and liqueurs. Many Cancerians tend to put on weight

The Moon in Taurus

easily, and Taurean good looks are often endangered by their fondness for good food. In short, be careful. If you have a slow metabolism, try to speed it up a little by getting some sensible exercise.

Planning ahead

Cancerian shrewdness combines extremely well with the Taurean ability to make money. You have very valid instincts in this area. There should be no problems when you have money to invest. In fact, if you discuss your finances with professional advisers, you could end up advising them.

Parenthood

Given the Cancerian tendency to cling, and Taurean possessiveness, you should be constantly aware of the problems that can arise when you are bringing up children. Still, you have the potential to be a wonderful parent. You will be sensitive to your children's needs, giving them much love and affection.

THE MOON IN GEMINI

YOU ARE PROBABLY ABLE TO COME UP WITH PERTINENT AND WITTY COMMENTS WITH VERY LITTLE EFFORT. GEMINIAN LOGIC COMES IN HANDY WHEN YOUR CANCERIAN IMAGINATION GETS THE BETTER OF YOU.

The elements – Cancer is a water sign and Gemini, air – add a variety of interesting facets to your personality. You are quick to respond to situations and are able to act rationally under stress. Your Cancerian tendency to worry will probably be filtered by an ability to look at problems very objectively.

A powerful Cancerian trait is moodiness. Here, however, your Geminian Moon helps to steady you; it will influence your reactions and create a balance.

Self-expression

Cancerians usually have very powerful imaginations, but sometimes this potential is not quite as well developed as it should be. Your Geminian Moon will help, since it will intellectualize this area. You may have an ability for storytelling or writing, or for using your hands creatively in craftwork of all kinds. Geminians can be restless and inconsistent. Always make sure that you go on to complete every project that you begin, and counter any restlessness and inconsistency in your personality.

Romance

You may not be quite as easily overwhelmed by emotion as many people of your Sun sign. Like all of them, however, you are a genuinely caring and protective lover.

It is also very important for you to have a good tie of friendship within your relationship and to share common interests with your partner. You should consider this very carefully before deciding to deepen an emotional relationship.

Your well-being

The Geminian body area covers the arms and hands; if you are a Cancerian cook or work with metals or tools, these may be especially vulnerable.

The Moon in Gemini

The Geminian organ is the lungs. Anytime you get a cold, that settles in your chest, seek medical advice as soon as possible.

Planning ahead

Although you will probably possess Cancerian shrewdness and instinctively sound business sense, you may be attracted to get-rich-quick schemes. If this is the case, be wary of your initial reactions; they could let you down. Always take your time when making decisions of this kind.

You may have the ability to sell and will get a good price for anything you can bring yourself to part with. Cancerians are collectors and you may be attracted to gadgets of some kind, such as animated toys.

Parenthood

You are more modern in outlook, more logical, and far less clinging than most other Cancerian parents. Being less sentimental and nostalgic than many Cancerians, the generation gap should not be a problem for you.

THE MOON IN CANCER

WITH BOTH THE SUN AND THE MOON IN CANCER ON THE DAY OF YOUR BIRTH, YOU WERE BORN UNDER A NEW MOON, AND ARE KNOWN AS A DOUBLE CANCER. SINCE THE MOON RULES CANCER, YOU MAY BE VERY CANCERIAN INDEED.

Reading a list of the characteristics of your sensitive, caring Sun sign, you will probably recognize that a great many of them apply to you. On average, out of a list of 20 personality traits of any particular Sun sign, most people will identify with 11 or 12. Because the Moon was also in Cancer when you were born, for you the average increases considerably.

Self-expression

Your Sun sign makes you caring; you will like to cherish and look after people. Your Moon sign accentuates this primary motivation. You will tend to be both moody and changeable, and it is necessary that you recognize these tendencies.

It is also important for you to realize that, like the crab which is the symbol of your sign, you can easily become rather "crabby," expressing your feelings in a remarkably terse, sharp, and hurtful way.

You should find some way of positively expressing your powerful emotions. It is an excellent idea for you to have at least one compelling interest aside from your career or home and family.

Romance

You have a great deal of love to give to your partner; this is probably the most important area of emotional expression for you. But it may well be that your imagination will need to find expression. It can make you a stunning lover, capable of giving great pleasure to your partners, but it could mean that you will always be worried about them. You may find yourself either becoming jealous or thinking that the worst has happened to them.

Your well-being

As far as your health is concerned, if you read pages 172 to 173 you will probably agree that you suffer from

The Moon in Cancer

most Cancerian ailments. Many of these relate to the tendencies to worry that have been described here.

Planning ahead

You will often read that Cancerians are very shrewd in business. Because both your Sun and your Moon signs are in Cancer, you rightly conclude that you would be wise to follow your instincts in this area.

Even more than many people, you like to feel the security of a healthy bank balance, although Cancerians sometimes tend to be a little tightfisted when it comes to actually spending their money. You probably know that Cancerians are the collectors (and also the hoarders!) of the Zodiac. Any unusual articles that you care to collect may well become valuable assets in the long term.

Parenthood

You will be eager to have children and should make an excellent parent. Recognize that your children are individuals who will want to create their own lifestyles and eventually start families. If you avoid being sentimental and nostalgic, the generation gap will not be a problem.

THE MOON IN LEO

CANCER AND LEO ARE NEIGHBORING ZODIAC SIGNS AND OFFER THEIR SUBJECTS CONTRASTING CHARACTERISTICS. IF YOU HAVE AN INSTINCTIVE URGE TO BE CREATIVE, DO NOT LET ANYONE, INCLUDING YOURSELF, CRAMP YOUR STYLE.

Your Cancerian caution contrasts vividly with the nature of your Leo Moon, which is a fire sign. You will therefore respond to most things with greater enthusiasm than many Sun sign Cancerians, and you will be less apprehensive, not so prone to worry, and much better organized.

Self-expression

The Cancerian tendency toward untidiness will be considerably mitigated by your Leo Moon; it gives you a certain style and elegance that many Cancerians lack. Leo creativity blends well with the Cancerian instinct for imaginative design, and finding some form of creative expression could be of great importance to you.

The worst Leo fault is bossiness. If you are accused of this, take heed. You respond extremely quickly to other people's remarks and actions, and when this trait is combined with the Cancerian tendency to be critically aggressive, you will see how, for you, sparks might occasionally fly.

Romance

Your Leo Moon gives you very warm and passionate emotions that will be beautifully expressed toward your loved ones. Sexually, you are probably quite assertive, and perhaps more willing to take the lead than many other Sun sign Cancerians.

Because Cancerians are sensitive, you could easily be hurt if difficulties arise within a relationship. In spite of the fact that your Leo Moon makes you brave and assertive in this area, when hurt you will creep into your Cancerian shell and lick your wounds.

Your well-being

The Leo body area is the spine, and you really need to indulge in a little exercise to keep it in good condition. If you have a sedentary job, make

The Moon in Leo

sure you have a good chair that supports your spine properly.

The Leo organ is the heart: if you follow the suggestions for exercising your spine, you will automatically be strengthening your heart, too.

Planning ahead

It is very likely that, although you have a shrewd Cancerian business sense, you will enjoy luxury and real quality more than many people of your Sun sign. In order to keep your Cancerian conscience happy, it might be wise to consider quality when you go shopping – that way you will get more value for your money and thoroughly enjoy what you may consider to be slightly extravagant. Do not be afraid to think big where investment is concerned.

Parenthood

You will be a very active, positive, and encouraging parent. If you keep the negative side of your imagination under control, you will not worry unduly about your children. Try to avoid any stubborn or dogmatic reactions to their ideas and suggestions, and you will also avoid the development of a generation gap.

THE MOON IN VIRGO

CANCER AND VIRGO ARE THE TWO ZODIAC SIGNS MOST PRONE TO WORRY. CANCERIAN WORRY IS INTUITIVE AND IMAGINATIVE; VIRGOAN, MORE INTELLECTUALLY ORIENTED. TRY TO BALANCE ONE WITH THE OTHER.

Your Sun sign is of the water element, and Virgo is of the earth element. Since water and earth are complementary elements, the influences of your Sun and Moon signs generally work well together.

Self-expression

Cancer and Virgo certainly share some positive common attributes, but the signs also vie with each other to be the worst worriers of the Zodiac. Cancerian worry is emotional; Virgoan worry is illogical. But Cancerians are cautious, and Virgoans are practical. These traits will help to counter the difficulty. Try to be more logical, and bolster this with Cancerian caution.

Romance

Your Cancerian emotions may be slightly inhibited when you need to express your feelings toward lovers. Virgoans are very modest, and when someone declares their affection for you, your immediate reaction may well be to recoil a little. Try to recognize the tendency, because it could limit your delightfully sensitive, sensual, and caring qualities.

You will tend to be very critical of your partners and may nag them. If you are accused of this, take heed.

Your well-being

The Virgoan body area is the stomach; your digestive system is related to your Cancerian Sun. As a result worrying can upset your stomach. Virgoans are also prone to nervous tension and stress, which can lead to migraines. Try to develop a sense of inner calm. Perhaps a relaxation technique such as yoga will be of help to you.

Planning ahead

Your Cancerian Sun sign makes you careful with money; your Virgoan Moon sign makes you even more

The Moon in Virgo

cautious. You therefore have the ability to save wisely. Just be sure to remember to enjoy the fruits of your labors. When investing, look for slow, steady growth.

Parenthood

Although Cancerians generally make warm, caring, and protective parents, you may tend to criticize your children a little too easily. This can be far more damaging than you might realize, especially if you have energetic, exuberant children. If you criticize them too much, they will probably lose their self-confidence. In the long term, this could lead to problems, so guard against it.

Your creative imagination will stand you in good stead with your children. You are less likely than most people to have difficulty with the generation gap, since you will keep a keen and attentive eye on the values and opinions of the younger generation, encouraging lively discussions.

THE MOON IN LIBRA

IF YOUR INSTINCT TELLS YOU TO SWITCH OFF, CALM DOWN AND RELAX. BY FOLLOWING THAT INSTINCT, YOU WILL MAKE THE MOST OF YOUR FINE, DIPLOMATIC MOON IN LIBRA, AND KEEP YOURSELF IN BALANCE.

The cardinal quality is shared by both Cancer and Libra , and this gives you some very interesting personality traits.

Self-expression

No matter how busy you may be, the chances are that you will always have time for others. As a result, you may give the impression that you spend most of your time doing nothing. That is not, of course, the case. You will work hard to achieve whatever you set out to do.

You are diplomatic, and probably less likely than most Cancerians to give in to moodiness. You also have a natural instinct for beautiful things, and will want your environment and personal appearance to be pleasing.

Romance

A natural indecisiveness may make committing yourself more difficult for you than for many people. Once that commitment has been made, however, your Cancerian need for home and family life will be satisfied, and you will become a wonderful, loving partner.

You have a strong inclination toward romance, and this does a great deal to enhance both your love and sex lives. There is an air of calm and serenity about you – but this will not inhibit passionate Cancerian emotion.

Your well-being

The Libran organ is the kidneys. Recurrent headaches could indicate that you have a minor kidney disorder. On the other hand, headaches could also be the result of the Cancerian tendency to worry. Your Libran Moon will work in your favor in this area, telling you to calm down, switch off, and relax.

Bearing in mind that you could well love gourmet cooking and delicious food, and remembering that Librans

The Moon in Libra

often have a sweet tooth, there is obviously a danger that you may put on weight easily. Attend regular exercise classes at a large and friendly health club where there is the possibility of socializing after class.

Planning ahead

Cancerian financial caution could dampen a luxurious, pleasure-loving instinct bestowed on you by your Libran Moon. Look at it this way: You are clever with money, and have no lack of shrewdness, so why not give in to your love of luxury? It will make life fun and far more enjoyable, and will certainly help you relax.

Parenthood

You will probably have a more relaxed attitude about parenthood than many other Sun sign Cancerians, but you should be very careful that you do not confuse your children by being indecisive. You will always be happy to listen to your children, so in that respect there should be no difficulty with the generation gap.

THE MOON IN SCORPIO

CANCER AND SCORPIO ARE BOTH SIGNS OF THE WATER ELEMENT. YOUR MOON GIVES YOU A TERRIFIC SOURCE OF EMOTIONAL ENERGY; CHANNEL THIS WISELY, AND DO NOT RESORT TO BEING JEALOUS OR VINDICTIVE.

Because both Cancer and Scorpio are water signs, you are likely to have tremendous resources of emotional and physical energy. You must find fulfilling ways of expressing these, because inner satisfaction and psychological wholeness are of above-average importance to you.

Self-expression

Your work must satisfy you. If its demands are not enough for you and your lifestyle is equally unengaging, then develop a compelling spare-time interest. This should consume either your emotional or physical energy – or ideally, both. Cancerian tenacity and your urge to get to the bottom of every problem will blend well, whatever you do.

Romance

You have a great deal to contribute to a long-term relationship. As an extremely passionate lover, you can, however, be very demanding both sexually and in more general matters. You need an understanding partner, who is as eager as you are to live an active and full life. Should any Cancerian moods catch up with you, your partner will have to be considerate enough to understand.

The worst Scorpio fault is jealousy. If you allow your Cancerian imagination to work overtime, you could build up the most terrible tension in a relationship. Try to accept rational explanations and recognize that logic can escape you.

Your well-being

The Scorpio body area is the genitals, so regular health checks of this area are most advisable. You could be more prone to worry than is usual for Cancerians, and this could also have an effect upon your health. Remember, too, that a boring job will leave you lacking inner satisfaction.

The Moon in Scorpio

Planning ahead

You may have a really good business sense and perhaps a desire to set up and develop your own company. You are shrewd; your Cancerian Sun sees to that. But your Scorpio Moon will also stand you in excellent stead here.

Parenthood

Your Cancerian Sun makes you a good, but demanding, parent – it could be that you are considerably stricter than you may realize. You will be eager to spur your children into action, but be careful not to be too dogmatic. Encourage them, but remember that finding the appropriate kind of encouragement for each child may be difficult. Try not to push your children into following in your footsteps; they may find their own paths more rewarding. If you allow them the freedom of expression that is so necessary to young people, you will avoid problems with the generation gap.

THE MOON IN SAGITTARIUS

YOUR SAGITTARIAN INSTINCT IS FOR FREEDOM OF EXPRESSION AND INDEPENDENCE, BUT YOU ALSO VALUE CANCERIAN EMOTIONAL SECURITY AND YOUR FAMILY. LEARN TO COMPROMISE WHILE RETAINING YOUR OWN VALUES.

The combination of a Cancerian Sun and a Sagittarian Moon gives your personality some contrasting and very unusual aspects. It may even be that when you read descriptions of your Sun sign, you think some of the statements hold little or no truth at all for you.

Self-expression

You are likely to have a wider-ranging mind than other Sun sign Cancerians, incorporating qualities that differ from those normally associated with your Sun sign. While, for instance, you love and need the security of your home and family, claustrophobic feelings – brought on either by the physical layout of your home, or more psychologically, because of the pressures of family life – are something that you cannot cope with. It is important that you respond freely to the outgoing, extrovert levels of your personality. Do not let Cancerian sensitivity or inhibition cramp the open expressiveness of your Moon sign qualities.

Romance

Your attitude toward love is very positive. You will like to have fun and enjoy your relationships. Sagittarius is an emotional sign, and as a result you have abundant resources of outgoing emotion and passion.

It may be that you will take longer than many people of your Sun sign to settle into a permanent relationship. Before you do so, remember that you really need an intelligent partner, who will be equipped to stretch your mind.

Your well-being

The Sagittarian body area covers the hips and thighs. If you are a female Cancerian cook or simply love good food, you will tend to put on weight very easily around these areas. Male Cancerians can, all too easily, develop

The Moon in Sagittarius

paunches. Fortunately, you probably love many sports and participate in several. If this is not the case, try some kind of freely expressive dance. In complete contrast, horse-riding may appeal to you.

Planning ahead

A tendency to take risks can make you a little foolhardy when dealing with money. Remember, however, that Cancerians are usually shrewd and clever both in business and when dealing with cash. Try, therefore, to get the best of both your Sun sign and your Moon sign, and learn to enjoy the challenge of making money grow without letting a deep-rooted gambling instinct overpower you.

Parenthood

You will have a very positive attitude toward your children and, unlike many Cancerians, will probably not worry if they are a few minutes late getting home from school. You can inspire them, and if you allow an instinctive and very natural sense of enthusiasm full rein, you will gain their love and respect. You should have few problems with the generation gap.

THE MOON IN CAPRICORN

CANCER AND CAPRICORN ARE OPPOSITE OR POLAR ZODIAC SIGNS, SO YOU WERE BORN UNDER A FULL MOON. YOU ARE INHERENTLY PRONE TO RESTLESSNESS AND AN INNER DISCONTENT; TRY TO COUNTER ANY TENDENCY TO COMPLAIN.

You will probably be more ambitious, and aspire to greater achievements, than other Sun sign Cancerians. But because Capricorn is not particularly emotionally oriented, it may be that this ambition, which is usually so strong, will remain subdued. It is important that you do not suppress it.

Self-expression

Both Cancer and Capricorn are of the cardinal quality, and as a result, you possess the ability to use your energies freely and willingly for the benefit of others. For yourself, you have the capacity to achieve great pinnacles of happiness both at home and at work.

Be careful of one thing: You may have a tendency to grumble, especially when presented with challenges or suggestions that do not precisely fit in with your plans. This will not make you popular with other people. Be aware, too, that because you were born under a Full Moon you could tend to suffer from restlessness.

Romance

While Cancerian warmth and tenderness will color your attitude toward your partners, your first reaction when approached by a prospective lover could be slightly cool. They may well have to break through that initial chilliness, and perhaps get past the self-defensive Cancerian protective shell that could easily manifest itself if you begin to feel vulnerable or insecure. But your lover, having gained your confidence, does have someone very special, and you are more than likely to remain faithful forever.

Your well-being

The Capricornian body areas are the shins and knees. These, and your joints in general, are prone to stiffness

The Moon in Capricorn

and rheumatic pain. It is vital for you to find a form of exercise that will help you to keep mobile.

Planning ahead

One way in which the Cancerian and Capricornian "polarity" emerges is through the fact that both signs are known to be very careful with money. A little more generosity may create a more enjoyable lifestyle for you.

Your Capricornian Moon gives you a natural inclination and taste for real quality. You like to buy things that will really last – partly because you hate waste and probably loathe throwing things away. You will invest very wisely and, in general, will always aim for steady growth.

Parenthood

Avoid the tendency to distance yourself from your children. Make sure that you have fun, and that the quirky sense of humor which comes from your Capricornian Moon finds plenty of expression. By doing so, you will bridge the generation gap.

THE MOON IN AQUARIUS

TRY NOT TO BE AFRAID OF EXPRESSING YOUR UNCONVENTIONAL ORIGINALITY: IT OFFERS YOU THE CHANCE TO FIND CONSIDERABLE INNER SATISFACTION AND FULFILLMENT. AVOID DISTANCING YOURSELF FROM OTHERS.

Your air sign Aquarian Moon and water sign Cancerian Sun are not the best of bedfellows. You will, however, have some extremely interesting and unusual qualities that make you a truly fascinating person.

Self-expression

Your reactions to situations are somewhat unpredictable. On some occasions you can be sympathetic, but on others, shocked. Your Cancerian kindness and sensitivity are, however, complemented by some very humanitarian qualities. You will give both time and energy, as well as money, when and where you come across need – it will be this sense of need that instinctively motivates you. Having taken action, you will freely express your caring, protective Cancerian spirit.

Your Cancerian emotions are somewhat cooled by your Moon sign influences. You are able to rationalize your feelings and, if it becomes necessary, should be able to distance yourself from them.

Romance

At heart, you are very romantic, but it could be that an inner need for independence clashes with a desire to have your own home and family. You may be attracted to a lifestyle that is individual in some way.

A love of romance is never too far from the surface, and because of it, you are likely to enjoy love and sex in a romantic atmosphere. It should not be difficult for you to persuade your partner to go along with this. Since you have an intriguing air of glamour, and are attractive to the opposite sex, you should enjoy yourself.

Your well-being

The Aquarian body area is the ankles, and these are very vulnerable. The circulation is also governed by

The Moon in Aquarius

Aquarius, so you must be careful to take care of yourself when the weather is cold.

Planning ahead

Of all the Cancerian Sun and Moon sign combinations, yours may be the least practical when it comes to money. Of course, you have Cancerian shrewdness and business sense lurking somewhere in your personality, and you may be wasting your potential. Can you see yourself owning your own business? If you do, remember that you do not lack originality, and stand an excellent chance of finding a gap in the market.

Parenthood

As a parent, your tendency to be unpredictable, plus Cancerian changes of mood, may cause difficulties. Keeping abreast of your children's ideas and concerns will help you to come to terms with any generation gap problems.

THE MOON IN PISCES

A TENDER AND LOVING CANCERIAN, WITH THE POWERFUL, FORCE OF PISCES, HAS A TORRENT OF EMOTIONAL ENERGY. USE THAT ENERGY AND NEVER UNDERESTIMATE YOURSELF OR YOUR ABILITIES.

While the combination of two water signs will serve to integrate your instincts and self-expression successfully, you should be careful that you are not entirely swayed by your reactions to people and by the power of your emotions.

Self-expression

You will automatically follow your intuition and natural instincts. Remember, though, that because you are so very kind, helpful, and charitable, and always ready to part with time, energy, and cash, people could take advantage of you all too easily. You may consciously have to develop your protective Cancerian shell, and at times you will have to be very firm with yourself if you wish to have complete control over your life.

Your Cancerian Sun gives you inner strength and tenacity, but a very tender and ultrasensitive Piscean Moon could sometimes tend to undermine your more powerful characteristics, especially when you are moved in some way.

Romance

If you get caught up with a partner who does not allow you the freedom to develop your potential and use your vivid imagination, think again.

You need a strong partner who will encourage you in all your efforts and take some of the strain, should an area of your life fall under pressure. There is a romantic, almost poetic, side to you, which colors your expression of love and sex – your partners should really enjoy it. Be careful that you do not delude yourself when you are in love, seeing every partner as your ideal, and try not to be deceptive.

Your well-being

The Piscean body area is the feet. These could cause you a lot of trouble. On the other hand, as can be

The Moon in Pisces

the case with astrology, the reverse could be true, and your feet may be healthy and problem-free.

The Cancerian tendency to worry will certainly affect you. Make sure that this does not become irrational and that your very powerful imagination does not take over. Be guided by your intuition and control any exaggerated reactions.

Planning ahead

Your Piscean Moon may overcome your practical, cautious Cancerian qualities when it comes to dealing with money. If you are aware of this, then perhaps, over a period of time, you will learn not to be a financial soft touch. Take advice from your financial consultant, accountant, or some other professional.

Parenthood

Children are bright and, from an early age, yours may know how to handle you. It may be necessary for you to act strictly from time to time.

Try not to be too clinging and sentimental, and remember that if you do not keep up with your children's way of thinking, you may have generation gap problems.

SUN & MOON SIGNS

LEO

JULY 23 – AUGUST 23

INTRODUCING
LEO

LEO, THE SIGN OF THE LION AND KING OF BEASTS, IS THE FIFTH SIGN OF THE ZODIAC. LEOS USUALLY MANAGE TO ACQUIRE THEIR OWN INDIVIDUAL KINGDOMS OVER WHICH THEY CAN RULE SUPREME.

The Zodiac lion or lioness rules skillfully, tactfully organizing others and always expressing creativity in one form or another.

This sign is ruled by the Sun. In fact, it is almost as if the generous, bright Leo personality radiates from some inner sun. When such a forceful personality fails to shine through, one can tell that something is seriously wrong. Leos who suppress their inner glow will be unhappy and unable to fully express their potential.

Traditional groupings

As you read through this book you will come across references to the elements and the qualities, and to positive and negative, or masculine and feminine signs.

The first of these groupings, that of the elements, comprises fire, earth, air, and water signs. The second, that of the qualities, divides the Zodiac into cardinal, fixed, and mutable signs. The final grouping is made up of positive and negative, or masculine and feminine signs. Each Zodiac sign is associated with a combination of components from these groupings, all of which contribute different characteristics to it.

Leo characteristics

Leo is of the fixed quality, which means that while Leos are generally stable people, they can also be very stubborn. They work hard to curb any tendency toward being bossy or pompous, and limit their urge to overdramatize every problem.

Because Leo is a masculine, positive sign, it inclines its subjects to be extroverted. Another characteristic that makes Leos easy to identify is their enthusiasm. This is, in fact, indicative of the sign's element: fire.

Most Leos will prefer, and perhaps enjoy wearing, the opulent colors of the Sun, their ruling "planet."

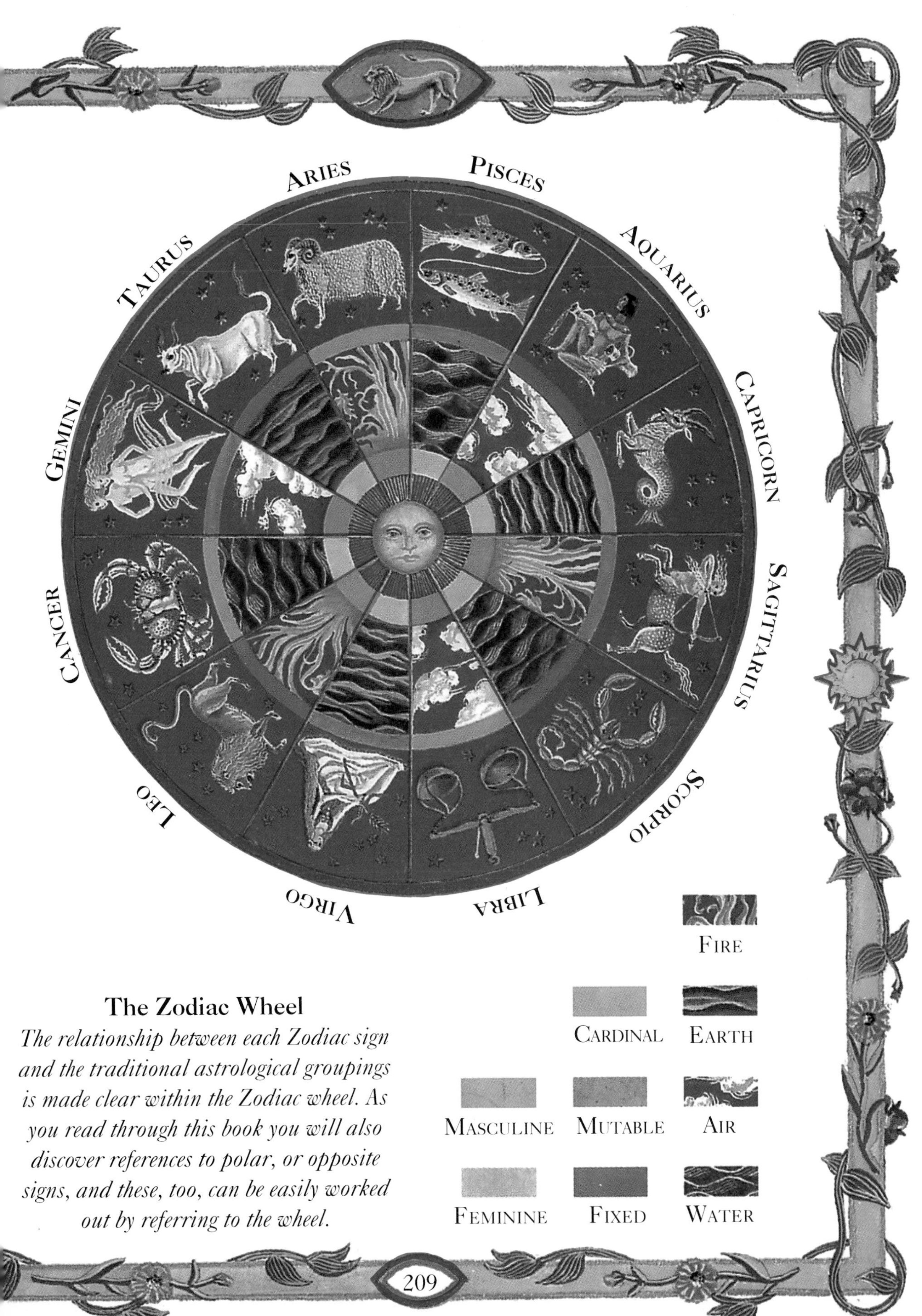

The Zodiac Wheel

The relationship between each Zodiac sign and the traditional astrological groupings is made clear within the Zodiac wheel. As you read through this book you will also discover references to polar, or opposite signs, and these, too, can be easily worked out by referring to the wheel.

LEO

MYTHS & LEGENDS

THE ZODIAC, WHICH IS BELIEVED TO HAVE ORIGINATED IN BABYLON AS LONG AS 2,500 YEARS AGO, IS A CIRCLE OF CONSTELLATIONS THROUGH WHICH THE SUN MOVES DURING THE COURSE OF A YEAR.

When the major stars of the constellation Leo are joined together, they do actually resemble a crouching beast. The ancient Babylonians called the constellation Great Dog. At least 5,000 years ago, the Egyptians gave it the name that is familiar to us today.

The Labors of Hercules

Like the Crab of Cancer, the Lion is associated with one of the 12 labors that the hero Hercules was made to perform by King Eurystheus, the ruler of Greece, as an atonement for slaughtering his own wife and children. After consulting the Oracle at Delphi, Hercules learned that only by showing obedience to King Eurystheus could he ever be forgiven for his dastardly crime.

Hercules's first labor involved killing and flaying an enormous lion, whose pelt was so tough that it could turn aside all weapons.

The Nemean lion

The lion, which lived at Nemea, in the Peloponnese, was born of Echidna the snake-woman and Typhon, a monster with a hundred eyes. The goddess Hera had sent it to wreak havoc upon the neighborhood of Nemea, the plain of which was sacred to Zeus, king of the gods.

Meeting the lion on the slopes of Mount Tretus, Hercules first shot at it with arrows (it merely yawned as they rebounded from its skin), then attacked it with his sword, and finally struck it with his club. At this point, irritated by a headache, it bit off one of Hercules's fingers.

Hercules eventually resorted to the novel idea of choking the lion to death while it was resting in its cave. On trying to skin it, however, he found that its hide resisted all knives, so that he eventually had to use its own claws – the only instruments sharp enough. Hercules subsequently

Hercules and the Nemean Lion

This Greek vase, which dates from 510 B.C., shows Hercules struggling to overcome the seemingly invincible Nemean lion.

wore the lion's impenetrable skin as armor, with the head as a helmet. The lion itself was set in effigy among the stars by Zeus.

Leo characteristics

It is, of course, virtually impossible to determine how various human qualities became associated with a particular sign of the Zodiac. It can, however, be said that those born with the Sun in Leo are extremely likely to possess the unmistakably proud demeanor of lions, and that they seem to be just as invulnerable to attack. Indeed, bravery, strong leadership, and forcefulness of personality are all definite Leo characteristics. However, when Leos find themselves troubled, they will retire to some private place in order to recover from their wounds in solitude.

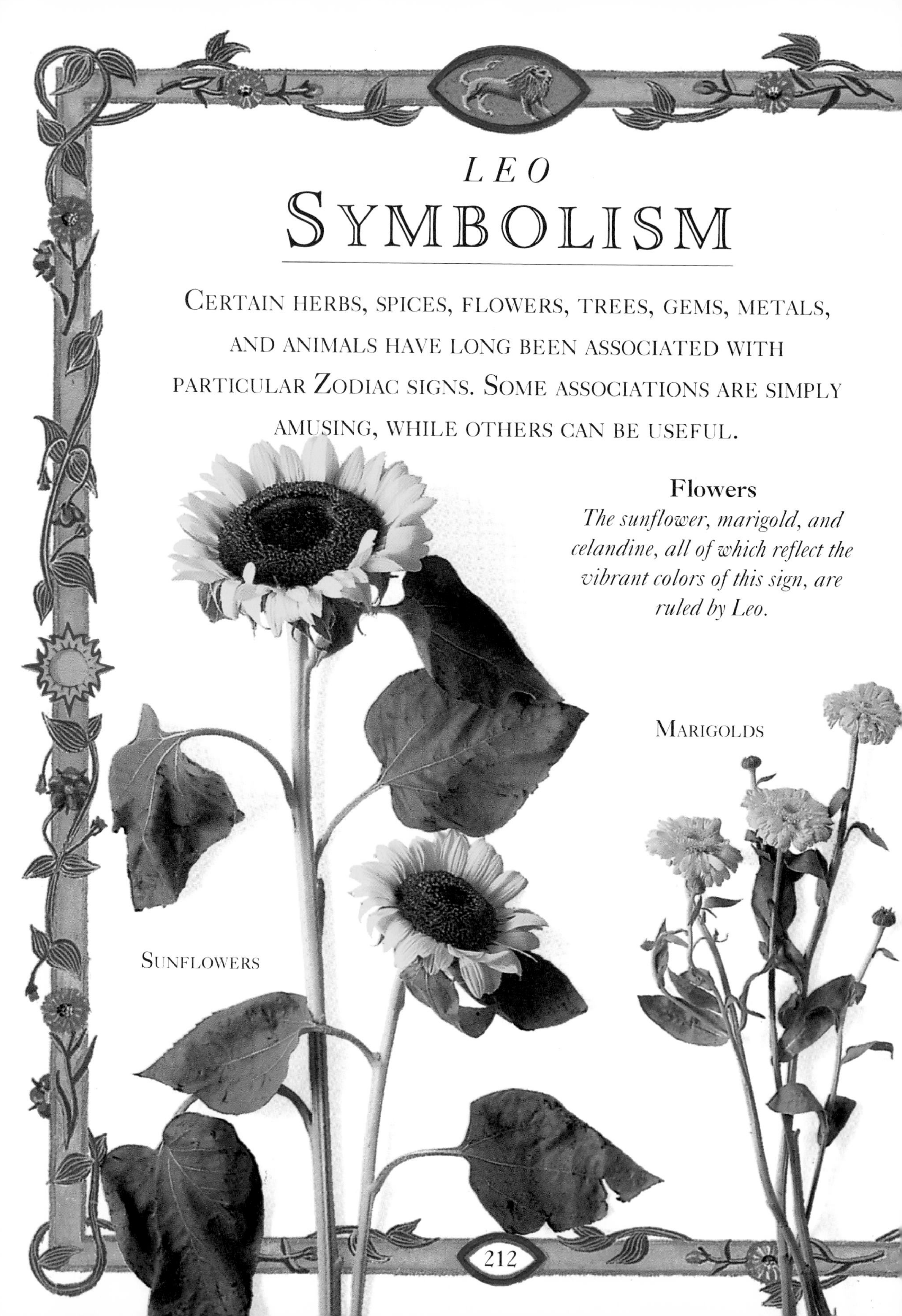

LEO SYMBOLISM

CERTAIN HERBS, SPICES, FLOWERS, TREES, GEMS, METALS, AND ANIMALS HAVE LONG BEEN ASSOCIATED WITH PARTICULAR ZODIAC SIGNS. SOME ASSOCIATIONS ARE SIMPLY AMUSING, WHILE OTHERS CAN BE USEFUL.

Flowers

The sunflower, marigold, and celandine, all of which reflect the vibrant colors of this sign, are ruled by Leo.

MARIGOLDS

SUNFLOWERS

Herbs

All herbs are believed to be ruled by Leo. This is particularly true of angelica, which "comforts the heart"; eyebright, which is good for eye ailments; and pimpernel, which alleviates toothache.

Trees

The bay, palm, and walnut are traditionally Leo trees. The same is true for the orange, lemon, and all other citrus trees.

Spices

No spices are specifically connected with Leo. As a fire sign, however, Leo surely rules pepper and mustard.

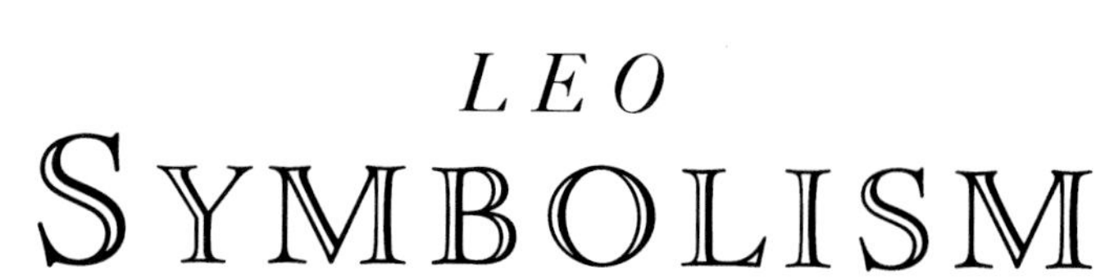

LEO
SYMBOLISM

Brass lion's-head door knocker

Animals

The lion is, naturally, the Leo animal, but all other big cats are also ruled by this sign.

Diamanté tiger brooch

Metal

Gold is the Leo metal, not only because of its association with the Sun, but also because of Leo's unquestionable taste for riches.

Wooden tiger folk carving

Gold

LEOPARD CIGARETTE LIGHTER

RUBY EARRINGS

RUBY BROOCH

TOY TIN LION

RUBY NECKLACE

Gem

The dark red, glowing ruby, the color of the Sun at dusk, is ruled by this sign.

LEO

PROFILE

THE LION'S MANE OF HAIR, THE UPRIGHT STANCE, AND A RATHER CONVENTIONAL, BUT VERY DASHING IMAGE, CHARACTERIZE THIS DRAMATIC ZODIAC SIGN. LEOS MAY SOMETIMES CONVEY AN IMAGE OF HAUGHTINESS TO OTHERS.

Sun sign Leos stand with their feet placed slightly apart and their legs held straight. They tend to make strong, meaningful gestures that are carried through in a distinctive and often dramatic way.

The Leo face

You are likely to have a noble face, with bright, clear eyes.

The body

Generally speaking, the Leo spine and back are erect, which gives people of this sign the appearance of height even if they are not tall. Leos are typically broad shouldered, and most have admirably slim waists. This can be a decided asset when fashion decrees an emphasis on that area. Leos usually move well, and should aim to keep their elegant, cat-like agility well into old age. Your feet and hands are unlikely to be large, and you will probably be small boned in comparison to members of most other Zodiac sign groups.

The face

You will hold your head high. If you leave your hair to grow long it will probably become as luxuriant and flowing as a lion's mane, although it may sometimes be equally untamable. Most Leos have clear complexions, and are likely to tan well. There is a striking nobility about the Leo forehead and face that you may well possess. Your eyes are likely to be very bright and clear, with perhaps slightly drooping eyelids, and your nose may be large and prominent. Some Leos develop a habit of occasionally looking down

The Leo stance

In keeping with their outgoing manner, Leos stand well, and are prone to making bold, meaningful gestures.

their noses at other people. You will not find it hard to break into a wide, sunny smile.

Style

Of all the Sun signs, Leo probably has the best sense of style. Since most Leos enjoy making a dramatic impact, there is often something eye-catching or spectacular about the things that they decide to wear.

Designer jeans and designer labels are very popular among Leos. However, people of this sign should make sure that they control their showiness, since too much glitter can ruin their image. Similarly, although Leos are generally inclined to buy high-quality, slightly conservative clothes, many of them will rashly spend enormous sums of money on dazzling but terribly impractical outfits that they can only wear once. Most Leos learn with experience.

People of your Sun sign usually look marvelous in the colors of the Sun, from palest lemon and pink to darkest orange, with younger people liking the brightest colors.

In general

Because the Leo body reflects the Leo psychology, it is not difficult to tell how happy a Leo is. It is obvious that a round-shouldered, stooping Leo, with eyes dimmed, is burdened with problems. On the other hand, if Leos are upright and smiling, their psychological Sun, which is so much a part of every Leo, is quite clearly shining, and all is well.

LEO
PERSONALITY

GENEROSITY AND ENTHUSIASM ARE BOTH DOMINANT LEO TRAITS. WHILE LEOS ENJOY TAKING CENTER STAGE, THEY WILL ALSO ENCOURAGE THEIR LOVED ONES AND FRIENDS TO GET THE MOST OUT OF LIFE.

Being positive and enthusiastic in outlook, Leos have a great zest for life, and if only because they put so much into it in the first place, they will get a great deal out of it. Every day has to be lived to the fullest. Inner satisfaction comes when you settle down to relax at the end of the day and realize that not only has each of your tasks been well and truly completed, but also that there is something to show for all your efforts.

At work

As a Sun sign Leo, your organizing ability is almost certain to be excellent. You can, however, sometimes express your love for organization in an extremely bossy way. This tendency to become too dominant over people must be controlled if it is not to be a source of embarrassment to your family and friends. Should you find yourself in charge of a situation (as Leos so often are), you should make sure that you hand out instructions with as much charm and warmth as you can. Bear in mind that other people thrive on receiving encouragement and praise, just as you do.

Your attitudes

Leos are known to hate pettiness of any kind. You will be very good at comprehending the overall plan and concept of a project, but will then willingly leave the smaller, fussy details to other people. Small-minded behavior and nit-picking arguments will no doubt infuriate you. When you encounter these, what might very accurately be called your "lion's roar" will be heard, and you will put the culprits in their place.

Leos usually have a well-developed sense of drama, which definitely needs to be tempered with a little restraint. At its best, however, it will provide you with a great

The Sun rules Leo

Apollo, the Greek Sun god, represents the Sun that rules over Leo. The Sun inclines its subjects to be generous, affectionate, and creative.

awareness of occasion. You will have no trouble making something special out of every get-together that you are party to, and you will really love to entertain extravagantly.

The overall picture

Firmness, determination, and decisiveness are marvelous qualities. Dogmatism and stubbornness are, however, just the opposite. You must tread very carefully in this area. Although it can be very difficult for you to develop an ability to be flexible, it will help if you consciously remember that the best rulers are those who are understanding, reasonable, and fair – especially when they are pronouncing judgment on other people.

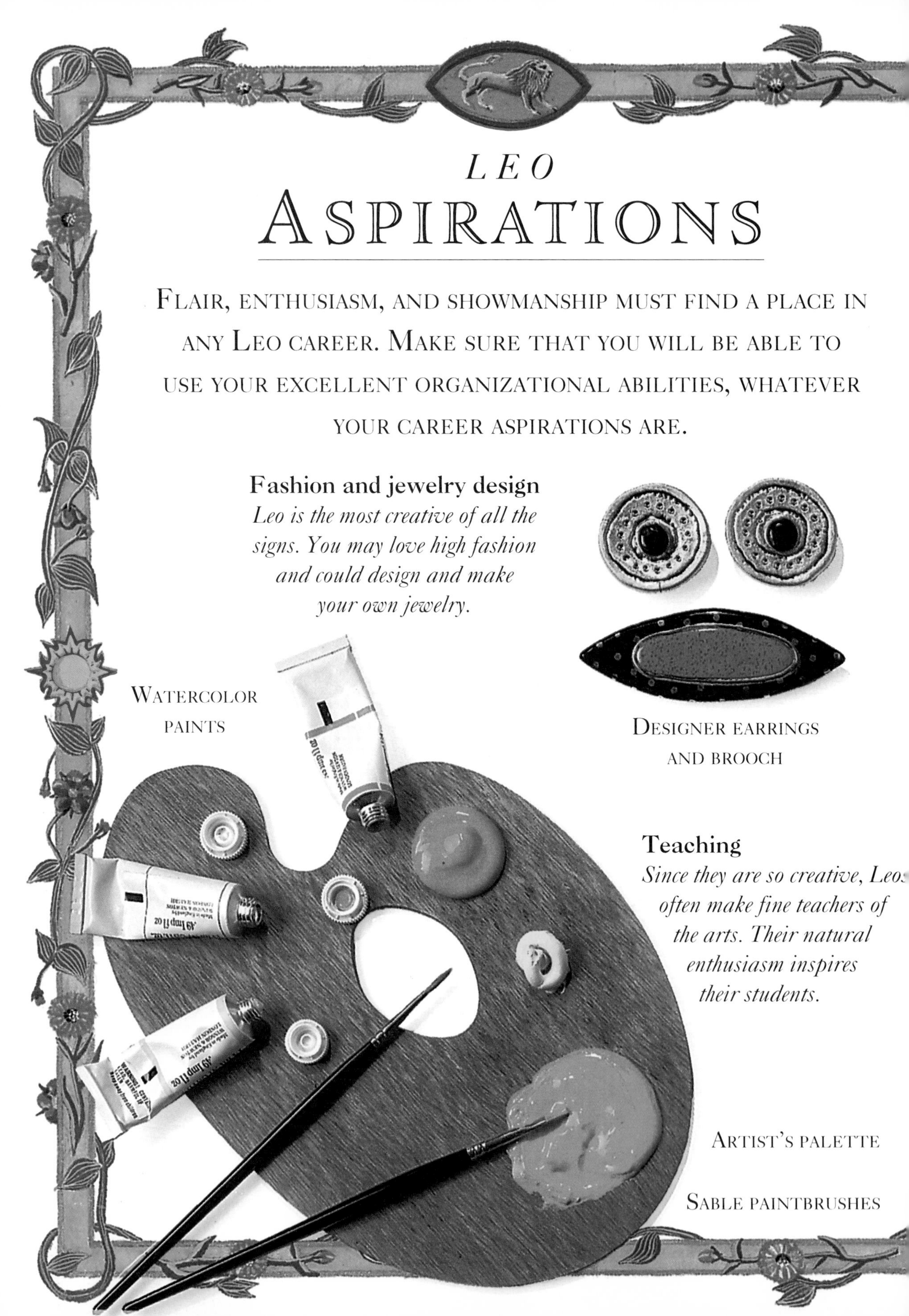

LEO

ASPIRATIONS

FLAIR, ENTHUSIASM, AND SHOWMANSHIP MUST FIND A PLACE IN ANY LEO CAREER. MAKE SURE THAT YOU WILL BE ABLE TO USE YOUR EXCELLENT ORGANIZATIONAL ABILITIES, WHATEVER YOUR CAREER ASPIRATIONS ARE.

Fashion and jewelry design
Leo is the most creative of all the signs. You may love high fashion and could design and make your own jewelry.

DESIGNER EARRINGS AND BROOCH

WATERCOLOR PAINTS

Teaching
Since they are so creative, Leos often make fine teachers of the arts. Their natural enthusiasm inspires their students.

ARTIST'S PALETTE

SABLE PAINTBRUSHES

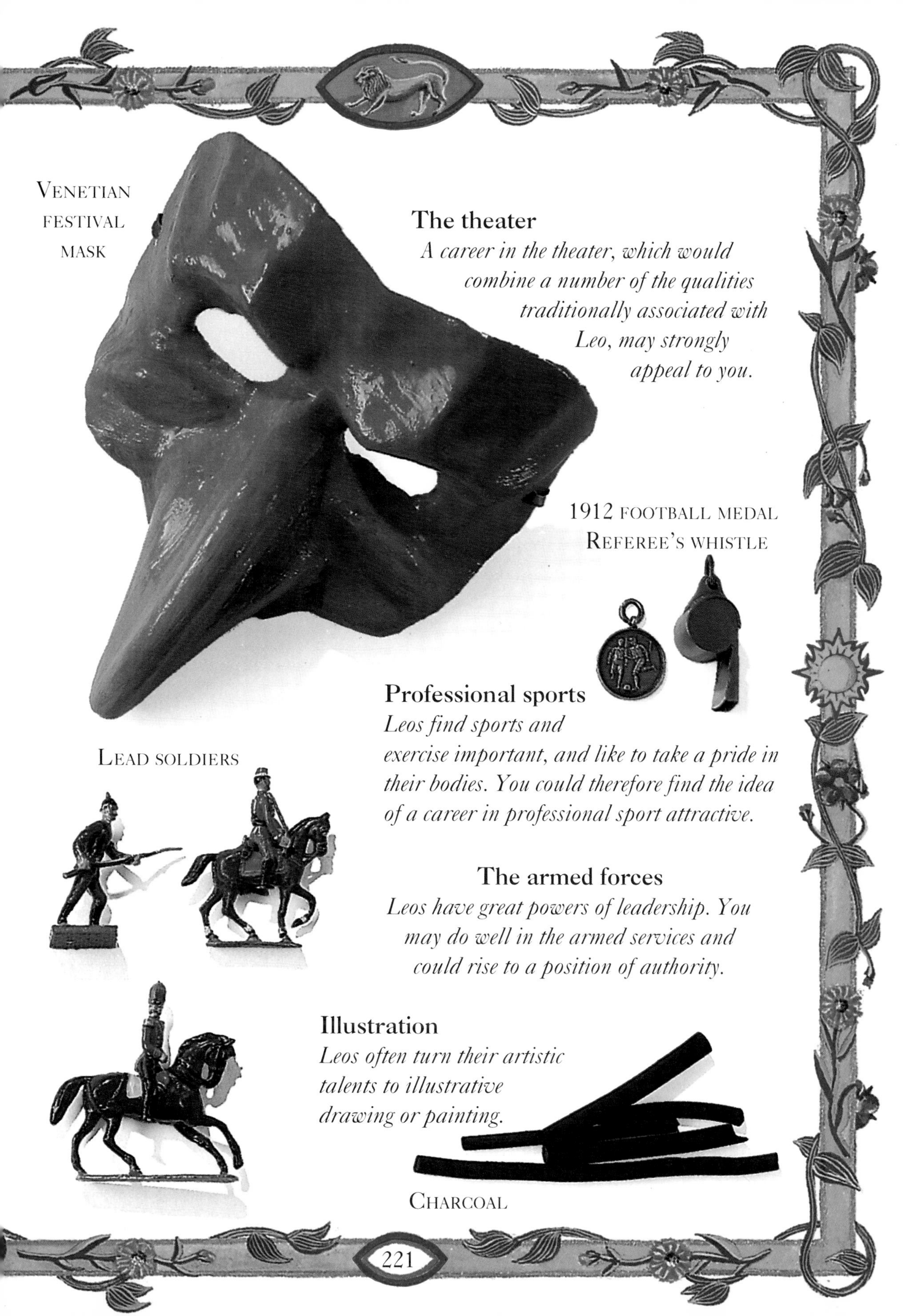

Venetian festival mask

The theater

A career in the theater, which would combine a number of the qualities traditionally associated with Leo, may strongly appeal to you.

1912 football medal
Referee's whistle

Professional sports

Leos find sports and exercise important, and like to take a pride in their bodies. You could therefore find the idea of a career in professional sport attractive.

Lead soldiers

The armed forces

Leos have great powers of leadership. You may do well in the armed services and could rise to a position of authority.

Illustration

Leos often turn their artistic talents to illustrative drawing or painting.

Charcoal

LEO
HEALTH

MORE THAN ANY OTHER ZODIAC TYPE, LEO NEEDS TO BE SOUND IN BOTH MIND AND BODY; THEY ARE UNIQUELY CONNECTED IN THIS SIGN. FOR EXAMPLE, AN INJURED BACK COULD LEAD TO DEPRESSION, OR A PRESSING PROBLEM, A HEADACHE.

The lions of the Zodiac will rapidly fall into black moods if some injury threatens to cramp their action-packed lives. You will become angry with yourself if such an injury forces you to stay away from your health club, and your irritation with an injury may far outweigh your pain or discomfort. This is because you really do not like wasting time or neglecting something you love doing. Rather fortunately for you, and perhaps for those who know you, such situations do not arise all that often.

Your diet

Mineral salts are considered to be a necessary part of the human diet. Because of modern eating habits, however, our supply of them is often unbalanced. As a Sun sign Leo you may benefit from supplementing your diet with the cell salt magnesium phosphate (mag. phos.). This is good for the heart, and helps to aid relaxation. You should also make sure that you control the amount of cholesterol you consume.

Taking care

The Leo body area is the spine and back. Chairs that offer good support are an excellent idea. So are exercises geared to strengthening the back; these will help you to avoid backache – often just a sign of stress. The Leo organ, the heart, also needs to be exercised if it is to be kept in good shape like the rest of the body.

Leos are usually strong and healthy, with mind and body at one with each other. You must be careful that you do not use up your energy – you might be forced to take a rest. Maintaining a balance is therefore of above average importance for you. Of course, you should be careful not to lose sight of the fact that when you do set aside some time to relax, you will enjoy it with all of your Leo panache.

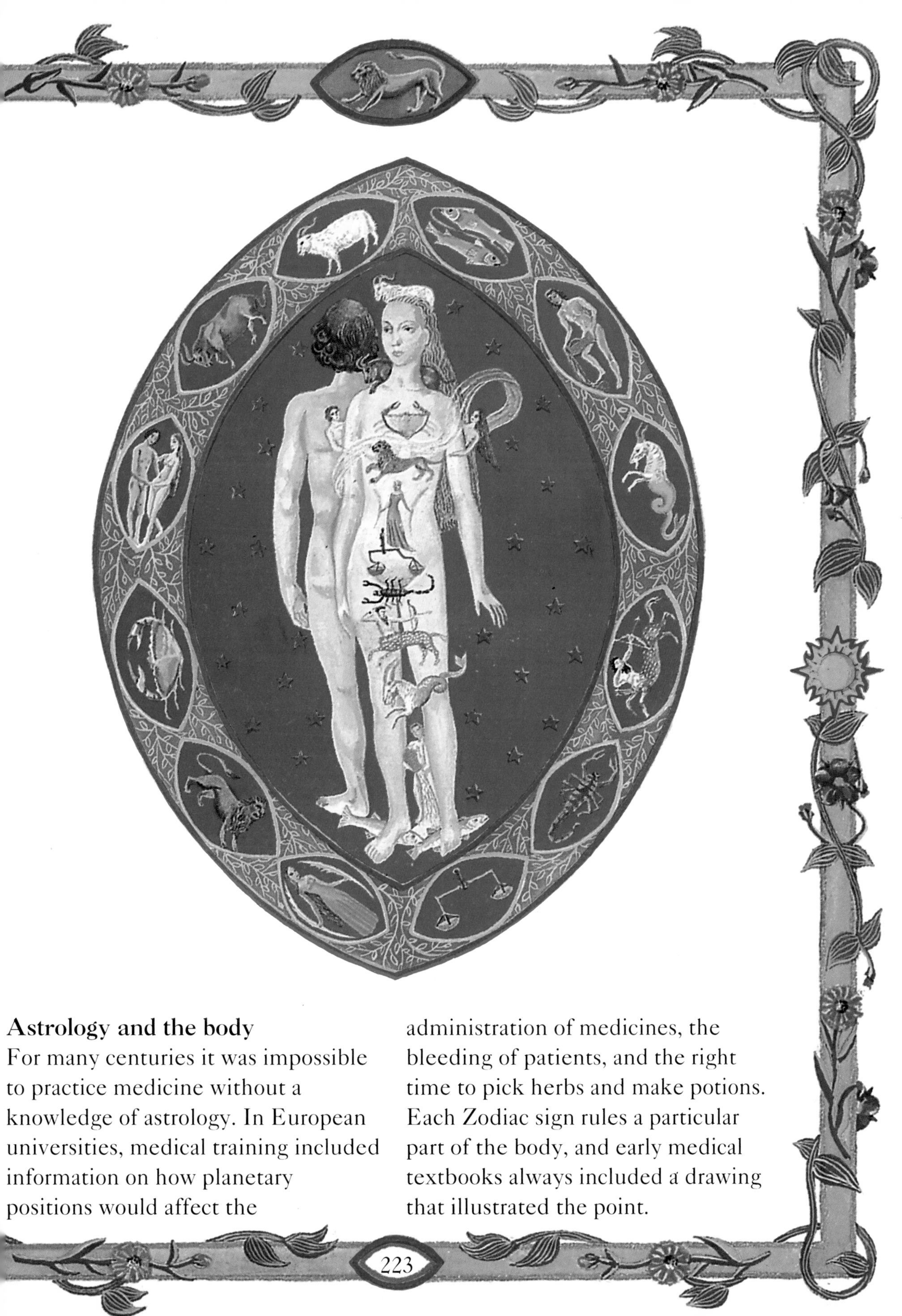

Astrology and the body

For many centuries it was impossible to practice medicine without a knowledge of astrology. In European universities, medical training included information on how planetary positions would affect the administration of medicines, the bleeding of patients, and the right time to pick herbs and make potions. Each Zodiac sign rules a particular part of the body, and early medical textbooks always included a drawing that illustrated the point.

LEO AT
LEISURE

EACH OF THE SUN SIGNS TRADITIONALLY SUGGESTS SPARE-TIME ACTIVITIES, HOBBIES, AND VACATION SPOTS. HERE ARE A FEW SUGGESTIONS THAT REFLECT LEO'S INTERESTS AND INCLINATIONS.

Astrology
Due to their eagerness to help other people make the most of their potential, Leos often make enthusiastic astrologers.

TOOLS FOR ASTROLOGICAL CALCULATIONS

Amateur theater
Leos generally enjoy amateur theater. It gives them an opportunity to express their natural dramatic flair and allows them to show off a little.

GREASEPAINTS

Plaster image of the sun

Postage stamps

Travel

Comfort, even luxury, should be the hallmark of your holiday. You would rather spend a day in a five-star hotel than a month in a tent. Italy, Iraq, the South of France, and the Alps all appeal to Leo.

The Sun

Leos love enjoying the Sun. Its light and warmth give them a sense of well-being, making them feel positive and optimistic.

Napkin and cutlery

Eating out

You no doubt have a great sense of style and occasion, and therefore only the best will be good enough for you when you choose to eat out.

LEO IN LOVE

WHEN LEO FALLS IN LOVE, THE WORLD TAKES ON A GOLDEN GLOW – BUT WHEN LEO IS REJECTED OR UNLUCKY IN LOVE, THE STORM CLOUDS GATHER. ANY WOUNDS ARE LICKED IN THE PRIVACY OF THE LAIR.

Sun sign Leos tend to put their partners on pedestals. You may be the king or queen of the Zodiac, but you will also enjoy playing consort to your partners. This means that when things go wrong, you may suffer more than most Zodiac types. Disillusion and heartbreak are common, and are sometimes followed by a loss of self-confidence that only time can heal. Unfortunately, some Leos are psychologically less developed than others and will tend to dominate a weak partner. At times this may work, if that partner is the type who needs a great deal of support, but both parties must aim to achieve a balanced relationship based upon sharing.

The generosity attributed to Leo will certainly be expressed when you are in love. The wrong partner may feel that you are showing off or trying to impress. This is not the case: with you "celebration" is the key word, and to blazes with the cost.

As a lover

The fire element of Leo burns strongly and brightly when you realize that you are in love. You will want your partner to share the sheer joy and exuberance of your

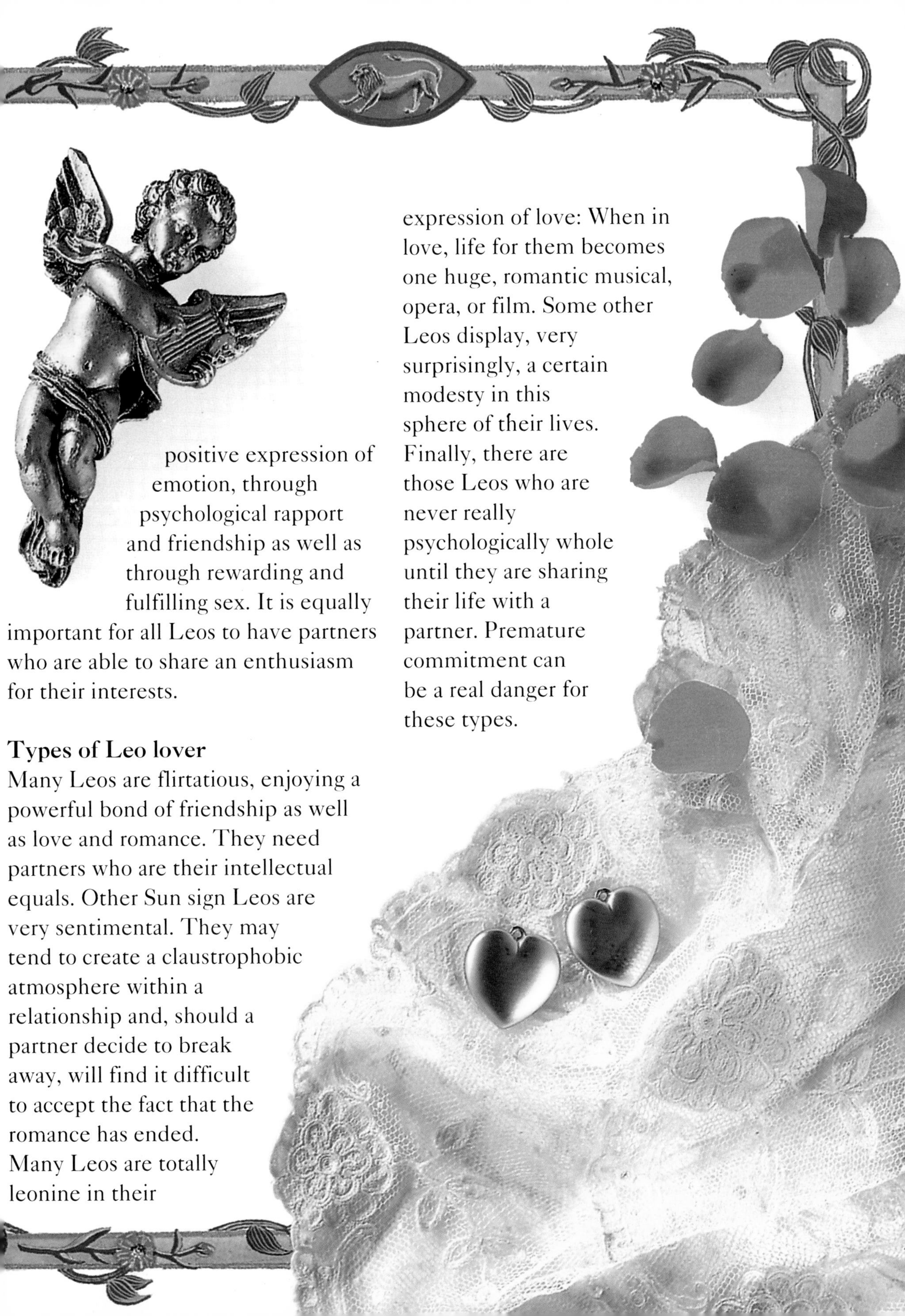

positive expression of emotion, through psychological rapport and friendship as well as through rewarding and fulfilling sex. It is equally important for all Leos to have partners who are able to share an enthusiasm for their interests.

Types of Leo lover

Many Leos are flirtatious, enjoying a powerful bond of friendship as well as love and romance. They need partners who are their intellectual equals. Other Sun sign Leos are very sentimental. They may tend to create a claustrophobic atmosphere within a relationship and, should a partner decide to break away, will find it difficult to accept the fact that the romance has ended. Many Leos are totally leonine in their expression of love: When in love, life for them becomes one huge, romantic musical, opera, or film. Some other Leos display, very surprisingly, a certain modesty in this sphere of their lives. Finally, there are those Leos who are never really psychologically whole until they are sharing their life with a partner. Premature commitment can be a real danger for these types.

LEO AT
HOME

A LEO'S WARM AND WELL-LIT HOME WILL REFLECT THE HIGHEST STANDARDS OF COMFORT. ELEGANCE, STYLE, AND BEAUTY ARE THE KEYNOTES AND, EVEN ON SLENDER MEANS, THEY WILL USUALLY BE ACHIEVED.

Wherever Sun sign Leos end up living, they always strive to make their homes very special places. You will probably spend a great deal of money on beautiful things, and on improving your home, for precisely this reason. If you have a garden, you have probably filled it with many different types of colorful flowers, and if the climate permits, attractive exotic fruits and vegetables. Your entire home is likely to have a warm and glowing atmosphere.

Classical sculpture
Leos often own a copy of an ancient sculpture.

Furniture

When it comes to choosing furniture for your home, your decisions are probably based around elegance and comfort. Leos like to relax in beautiful surroundings that are stylish, luxurious, and easy on the eye. You take great pride in your home, and will, as has already been said, spend a lot of money on it, making sure that the furniture and decor you choose is unlikely to become boring after a year or two. In this way you will avoid the disruption of the constant necessity for change. Quality is likely to be very important to you, and Leos sometimes have a marked tendency toward showiness that should be controlled. You may, for instance, overdo a room by placing too much elaborate and obviously expensive furniture together, and perhaps in inappropriate places.

Exotic wallpaper

Leo furnishings are often striking, like this wallpaper in the style of William Morris.

Soft furnishings

Texture and warm, glowing color are both important: many Leos favor rich silks and brocades, or velvet which will deepen and enhance the colors that they choose. Although you may be very much attracted to fur rugs, Leos are among the leaders in the conservation of wildlife, and are especially sympathetic toward the big cats. No self-respecting Leo would decide to own a real lion- or tiger-skin rug; it will have to be a very high-quality imitation.

Decorative objects

Only the best is good enough for Leos, whatever decorative objects they may choose. Therefore one finds ornaments in the Leo home that are as near to perfection as can be afforded, and some that may have strained the individual's purse-strings.

Your glass will be the finest crystal, and the paintings, will be beautifully framed. Leos like classical things, so a reproduction of a Greek sculpture or a miniature copy of some noble Roman emperor sitting in triumph on his horse may also make an appearance.

Colorful armchair and cushion

The golden colors of this chair and cushion reflect the colors of the sun, which are so dear to Leos.

THE
MOON
AND
YOU

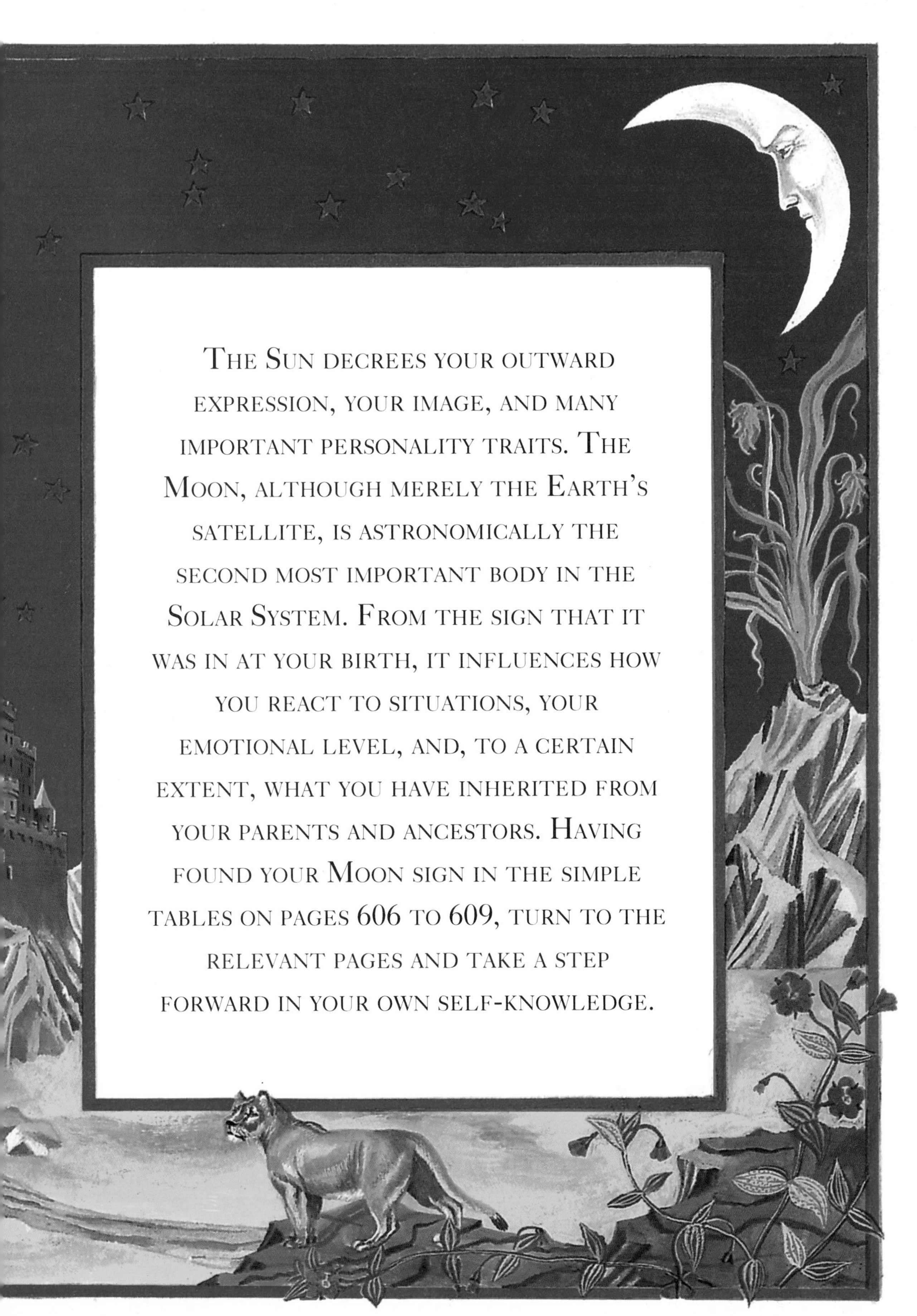

The Sun decrees your outward expression, your image, and many important personality traits. The Moon, although merely the Earth's satellite, is astronomically the second most important body in the Solar System. From the sign that it was in at your birth, it influences how you react to situations, your emotional level, and, to a certain extent, what you have inherited from your parents and ancestors. Having found your Moon sign in the simple tables on pages 606 to 609, turn to the relevant pages and take a step forward in your own self-knowledge.

THE MOON IN ARIES

A COMBINATION OF TWO FIRE SIGNS GIVES YOU A HIGH LEVEL OF PHYSICAL AND EMOTIONAL ENERGY, BUT YOU MUST LEARN TO CURB HASTINESS AND SELFISH REACTIONS TO PARTNERS. YOU ARE MORE CASUAL THAN MOST LEOS.

Basically, you are a very energetic person with a powerful motivation to win, and your Leo organizational ability will enable you to take over any critical situation at the drop of a hat.

Self-expression

You will, unfortunately, express Leo bossiness from time to time. But the lively, positive influence of your Arien Moon makes it unlikely that you will come to annoy other people too much. Your Arien Moon will also mitigate any Leo pomposity.

You should avoid being too hasty, since this could lead you into premature and ill-considered action. Learn from your past mistakes and pace yourself. You may not be too good at coping with detail; perhaps you need the help of others once you have mapped out an overall plan. You have formidable resources of energy, and could easily have a hot temper. However, neither Aries nor Leo harbors resentment, and Leo magnanimity usually emerges soon after any explosion of anger.

Romance

Your Arien Moon makes you a very passionate and lively lover, and your natural *joie de vivre* is both infectious and attractive. The worst Arien fault can be selfishness, and this trait is not at all endearing.

You are among the most highly sexed of Leos and will probably fall in love at first sight. You will expect an equally positive and immediate response from prospective partners. Remember that not everyone is as sure of their feelings as you, and try to develop patience.

Your well-being

The Arien body area is the head, and you may suffer from an above-average number of headaches. Often these

The Moon in Aries

will be caused by other people. Arien headaches may also sometimes be caused by slight kidney disorders.

You are probably somewhat accident-prone, because of hastiness and your quick reactions. Take care in dangerous circumstances.

Planning ahead

Your Arien Moon can make you somewhat impulsive financially, and you may tend to put too many eggs in one basket if you are convinced that an investment will be lucrative. A little caution is advisable, since over-enthusiasm could be your downfall.

Parenthood

You will be among the most enthusiastic and encouraging of parents, making time to enjoy your children and seeing to it that their out-of-school life is full of activity. Learn to enthuse about their projects, and you will have fun. You should have no generation gap problems.

THE MOON IN TAURUS

LEO LIKES THE BEST AND MOST EXPENSIVE OF EVERYTHING. YOUR TAUREAN MOON IS IN SYMPATHY. SINCE YOU NEED MONEY FOR ALL THOSE LUXURIES, TRY TO DEVELOP YOUR BUSINESS SENSE. MAKE AN EFFORT NOT TO BE FLASHY.

You are lucky, since in astrology the Moon is said to be "well placed" in Taurus. This means that it will exert a strong influence upon you. Your Moon sign will make you very reliable and dependable.

Self-expression

You need an above-average sense of emotional and financial security; if you have both, you will flourish.

Your Leo liking for luxury and quality will certainly be enhanced by your Taurean Moon since, after Leo, Taurus is the sign of the Zodiac most inclined toward such pleasurable things. Your Taurean Moon makes you practical and down-to-earth, and you will work hard and persistently to achieve your objectives.

Romance

Your Leo passion is enhanced by Taurean sensuality, and you are usually faithful. But you must remain aware that the worst Taurean fault, possessiveness, can very easily overcome you. Try to counter this negative trait with Leo magnanimity.

Your well-being

The Taurean body area is the throat. If your particular love is singing, you will really have to cosset it, since colds will at once settle in that area.

Very often, Taureans have a fairly slow metabolism. To prevent excessive weight gain, make sure that you exercise regularly. It is important to remember, too, that Taurus may have given you a sweet tooth, so control your intake of heavy, rich cakes and chocolates.

Planning ahead

Your luxury-loving instincts will decree that you need to earn a lot of money. Fortunately, your Moon sign endows you with a very good financial instinct, and you should follow it. You

The Moon in Taurus

will probably know intuitively when to invest and what to invest in, and will not overextend yourself in any one area.

A credit balance on your bank statement will give you much satisfaction (and proof of hard work well done); you will also be anxious to make your money work for you.

Parenthood

You will make a good parent, but will not allow your children to waste time. Both Leo and Taurus are disciplined signs, so you will be fairly strict with your offspring – at times, you may even be a little hard on them. Your children will certainly know where they stand with you: What you say is exactly what you mean. There will be no nonsense. But think carefully about this; sometimes you might just be too inflexible. Try to keep abreast of your children's opinions, and make sure that you try to move with the times. Otherwise, in spite of an excellent set of values, you may encounter great difficulties.

THE MOON IN GEMINI

YOUR LEO CREATIVITY COULD BLEND WITH YOUR GEMINIAN GIFT FOR COMMUNICATION AND MAKE YOU A WRITER. DO NOT QUESTION YOUR EMOTIONS OR TALK SO MUCH THAT THERE IS NO TIME FOR ACTION.

The fire of your Leo Sun is fanned and encouraged by your air sign Geminian Moon, which makes you respond to situations in a powerful, rational, and intellectual way. You are very quick-witted, and always ready with some clever and original remark. The Leo tendencies to formality and pomposity are unlikely to emerge in your personality.

Self-expression

You are extremely versatile and may tend to flit – perhaps too readily – from one interest or project to the next. Try to avoid superficiality and falling into the trap of leaving a clutter of unfinished tasks and abandoned hobbies in your trail.

Your Leo creativity could find expression through writing or perhaps in some glamorous craftwork – using, for instance, precious or semiprecious stones, crystals, metals, or fabrics. You do not lack enthusiasm, but may have to make a conscious effort to keep it on the boil, since boredom and that uniquely Geminian fault, restlessness, could overtake you.

Romance

You may question or rationalize your emotions, especially when you first realize that they are awakened. Make quite sure that you do not suppress your emotions altogether, since your whole personality will suffer if you do.

In love, you can be both lighthearted and passionate. When friendship embraces full, physical love, all the notes of your Leo personality will be sounded.

Your well-being

The Geminian body area covers the hands and arms, which may be particularly vulnerable to accidents; the Geminian organ is the lungs. It is absolutely vital that anyone with a Gemini emphasis who is a smoker

The Moon in Gemini

should try to limit or stop the habit. Consult your doctor right away if a cough settles on your lungs.

Planning ahead

Leos love quality goods, and need to earn as much money as possible. You may be attracted to moneymaking schemes with speedy and generous returns on capital. Be cautious: You could lose more than you gain. Take professional advice in these matters. Because you are among the most versatile of Leos, you may want to organize your life to ensure that you have two different sources of income. You could, for instance, take a hobby to professional standards and then go on to market it in some way.

Parenthood

You will probably be among the liveliest of Leo parents, since Gemini has the reputation of being the most youthful sign of the Zodiac. You will be young at heart (and probably body), and your children will appreciate the fact.

THE MOON IN CANCER

THE SUN AND MOON ARE IN THE SIGNS THAT THEY RULE, AND YOU THEREFORE HAVE A PERFECT BLEND OF POSITIVE AND NEGATIVE ELEMENTS. USE YOUR LEO SELF-EXPRESSION, AND FOLLOW YOUR CANCERIAN INTUITION AND INSTINCTS.

The Sun and Moon, the two most powerful bodies in the Solar System, work very strongly and well for you; their influences combine to give you some excellent personality traits that you should always aim to use to your full advantage.

Self-expression

Your Cancerian Moon adds a very potent intuition to your Leo Sun sign characteristics and powerful instincts that you should nurture. If you instinctively feel that you should take a certain line of action, then go ahead and do so. Your Moon sign also gives you a very powerful and vivid imagination that should be expressed creatively in some way.

By harnessing this quality, you may well produce some great work in arts and crafts. But take care that you do not let your imagination get out of hand, since you have a tendency to worry unnecessarily.

Romance

Your emotions are highly charged: The fiery, assertive, and enthusiastic emotion of Leo is joined by the more tender, sensitive emotion of the Moon in Cancer. You will not find it difficult to express your feelings to your loved ones, be they lovers, children, or a household pet. Your protective instinct is also very strong, and while you are a wonderfully exuberant and passionate lover, you may at times tend to smother your partners. Be careful, because you may create a claustrophobic atmosphere within your relationships.

Your well-being

You are far more prone to worry than most Leos. To counter any unnecessary anxiety, allow your Leo optimism plenty of free expression.

The Cancerian body area covers the chest and breasts. Women with this emphasis should examine their

The Moon in Cancer

breasts regularly – although it is important to realize that it is mere coincidence that the name of the sign is the same as that of the disease.

Planning ahead

Your Cancerian Moon gives you an instinctive business sense. You are able to invest wisely and shrewdly, although you could feel a certain amount of conflict in this area. The Leo you is very generous and enjoys spending money on pleasure and beautiful things, while your Cancerian instinct tends to make you more careful with money. A fascinating and very lucrative hobby for you could be to start an unusual collection of some kind, of objects that will increase in value over the years. This will make positive use of your Cancerian hoarding instinct.

Parenthood

You will be a very sensible and enthusiastic parent, and will encourage your children to express their own potential as fully as possible. Try not to be overprotective toward them, and allow them to leave the nest and make their own lives when they feel the need.

THE MOON IN LEO

BECAUSE BOTH THE SUN AND THE MOON WERE IN LEO ON THE DAY OF YOUR BIRTH, YOU WERE BORN UNDER A NEW MOON. LEO IS A FIRE SIGN, AND THIS ELEMENT POWERFULLY INFLUENCES YOUR PERSONALITY AND REACTIONS.

Should you study a list of your enthusiastic, optimistic, and positive Sun sign, you will realize that a great many apply to you. On average, out of a list of, say, 20 Sun sign characteristics, most people will identify with 11 or 12. For you the average increases considerably, because the Sun and Moon were both in Leo when you were born.

Self-expression

Your Sun sign makes you very positive in outlook and gives you exceptional organizing ability, plus a great deal of creative potential. Your Moon influence adds a powerful instinctive urge to express these qualities fully. Bear in mind also that since there is an additional emphasis on the fixed quality of Leo, you may sometimes be inflexible.

You will react to most situations in a very Leo way, expressing the ability to take over at a moment's notice – especially in a crisis. You can also be extremely bossy and dogmatic. Pay attention if you are accused of these unattractive characteristics.

Romance

You have a great deal of positive, fiery emotion that you express with great intensity in your relationships. Your zest for love and sex is great, but you will see to it that both you and your partner also enjoy a lifestyle highlighted by as many enjoyable events as you can (or possibly cannot) afford. Be careful not to dominate your relationships too powerfully.

Your well-being

Everything that has been said about Leo health on pages 222 to 223 really does apply to you. Make sure that you take enough exercise to keep your system, and especially your spine and heart, in good working order.
Your liking for rich living could cause

The Moon in Leo

weight gain, so keep moving. This will also help to ensure that your circulation remains good. You no doubt love sunshine and warm weather, and hate the cold. While you will probably tan well, remember to protect your skin with a powerful sun-screen cream or makeup.

Planning ahead

Because you like to do things in a refreshingly extravagant way, you will spend a lot of money, and so you need to earn plenty of it. Let your financial motto be "great oaks from little acorns grow," and get pleasure from small investments. Financial security is important to you, and although you tend to be extravagant you probably do not lack business sense.

Parenthood

Leo is the sign of parenthood and children, and you will make an excellent parent provided that you avoid being too dogmatic in your attitude. Your interest, encouragement, and enthusiasm will help build a really good relationship between you. You should try to keep abreast of your children's ideas, and you will minimize the generation gap.

THE MOON IN VIRGO

A CAUTIOUS, SOMEWHAT DAMNING INNER VOICE MAY CRITICIZE YOUR ACTIONS AND SAP YOUR SELF-CONFIDENCE. YOUR INNER LEO SUN MUST COMBAT THIS INFLUENCE TO ALLOW YOUR VIRGOAN MOON TO BE CONSTRUCTIVE AND HELPFUL.

Your earth sign Moon, while not particularly in harmony with your fire sign Sun, gives you a marvelously practical instinct that can stabilize the exuberance of your Leo Sun.

Self-expression

Your natural caution acts as a brake when you are tempted to show off or behave raucously. However, when confronted with a challenge, you sometimes feel a certain apprehension or lack of self-confidence. This is uncharacteristic for most Sun sign Leos, but it could happen in your case due to the influence of your Moon sign. If such a situation occurs, think of your achievements and allow yourself some pride.

You are very logical, with a powerful critical streak, and can cope better with detail than most Sun sign Leos. You will, however, have a tendency to be swamped by the minutiae of a project. Your Leo creativity may well find expression through gardening or craftwork involving natural materials.

Romance

Your Virgoan Moon will cool your Leo emotions and add a refreshing modesty to your personality.

Despite a passionate Leo nature, caution will be your key word in a developing relationship. Anyone who is attracted to you will be critically dissected before you make a date, and certainly before they are allowed to deepen the relationship.

Your well-being

Virgo is a sign prone to worry, and more than many Sun sign Leos, you may suffer from this. Your approach should be an analytical one; always assess your problems logically.

The Virgoan body area covers the stomach, and you may have a digestive problem that tends to recur

The Moon in Virgo

when you are under stress. You will have a great deal of nervous energy, and should this result in tension, you may be prone to migraines. If this is the case, a relaxation technique such as yoga could be of help.

Planning ahead

Your Virgoan Moon will be a vital influence when it comes to finance. Leo extravagance is less likely to affect you than other Sun sign Leos. Sometimes you will be better off than you realize; while you should not waste money, do not deny yourself things that make life enjoyable.

Parenthood

While all Sun sign Leos have fun with their children, be careful that you are not too critical of their efforts. Such criticism can lead to ebbing self-confidence in a youngster. If you respond to the younger generation's opinions and attitudes, you will not suffer from generation gap problems.

THE MOON IN LIBRA

WITH YOUR MOON IN LIBRA, YOU MAY SEEM LAZY OR DISTANT TO CASUAL OBSERVERS, BUT A LEO SUN NEEDS TO LIVE EVERY DAY TO THE FULL. YOUR MOON WILL ALSO HELP YOU TO ENJOY LIFE.

The combination of the fire element of your Sun and the air element of your Moon add some fascinating aspects to your personality.

Self-expression

You will respond to challenges with typical Leo enthusiasm. Your Libran Moon will ensure that this enthusiasm will be governed and controlled in a calm, relaxed, and diplomatic way.

With indecisiveness being the worst Libran fault, you may have uncharacteristic second thoughts, especially under pressure or in a stressful situation. At such times, use your Leo organizing ability. It will enable you to take control of your thinking processes.

Both Leos and Librans love the good life, comfort, and luxury. In this area you will experience no conflict between your Sun and Moon signs; you have the ability to sit back, relax, and simply enjoy being sociable.

Romance

You make a wonderful lover, and are, no doubt, very considerate of your partner's needs. In some respects you may not feel psychologically whole until you are settled in a permanent relationship. Be careful: in your desire to relate in depth, you may have a tendency to commit yourself prematurely. At times you could expect too much from your partner, simply because you, yourself, have so much to give.

Your well-being

The Libran body area covers the kidneys and the lumbar region of the back. Because Leo rules the spine and back, you may well be subject to pain in that area. The quality of the mattress you sleep on is important. You may also tend to get a lot of headaches, which could be due to slight kidney upset. Seek medical advice whenever necessary.

The Moon in Libra

Good food is another luxury enjoyed by both Leo and Libra; Librans tend to put on weight more easily, since many have a fairly slow metabolism. If you tend to move in a languid way and walk slowly, make an effort to speed up your metabolism through frequent exercise.

Planning ahead

Leo extravagance and love of quality will certainly eat into your finances. Since you may be bored by bookkeeping and investing, you would be wise to seek sound financial advice from an expert and to embark on a sensible saving plan.

Parenthood

Do not allow Libran indecisiveness to undermine your positive Leo qualities in your role as a parent. Your Leo Sun sign will ensure that you enjoy parenthood, and your enthusiasm for your children's interests will spur them on to greater effort. Be aware of their concerns and opinions in order to avoid the generation gap.

THE MOON IN SCORPIO

LEO QUALITIES GAIN DEPTH, INTENSITY, AND A POWERFUL, EMOTIONALLY ORIENTED DRIVING FORCE BY A SCORPIO MOON. YOU MUST BE TRULY INVOLVED IN YOUR WORK AND ENJOY A FULFILLING RELATIONSHIP.

You are likely to have very strong resources of both physical and emotional energy and, for the sake of your inner fulfillment, it is vital that your life is rewarding enough to allow them full rein.

Self-expression

You must be mentally involved in your work. If this is not the case, you will probably feel discontented and growing dissatisfaction will get the better of you.

Both Leo and Scorpio are of the fixed quality, so you may well have to consciously develop the art of being flexible. Try to keep an open mind, and take heed if someone accuses you of being dogmatic or stubborn. Be firm, but not intractable.

Romance

Possessing both the fiery emotion of Leo and the deep, intense emotion of Scorpio, you will express your feelings very fervently. You will be among the most passionate of lovers and will have a great need for a responsible partner who is as highly sexed as you are. The worst Scorpio fault is jealousy, which is not something that is usually felt by Sun sign Leos. Should you fall prey to it, try to be rational and to allow Leo magnanimity full expression.

Your well-being

The Scorpio body area is traditionally said to cover the genitals. Regular gynecological examinations are advisable for women and men should examine their testicles regularly, as good preventive measures.

While some people with a Scorpio emphasis are lean and wiry, others tend to be stocky. If you fall into the latter category you may have a slightly slow metabolism. Try to speed it up through exercise. Both Leo and Scorpio like to live life to the full, and

The Moon in Scorpio

enjoy quality food and wines. These can, of course, adversely affect your body shape. If you need to lose weight, gradually adjust your general food intake and develop a more sensibly balanced diet.

Planning ahead

You have excellent business instincts. When investing, you will probably do well by following them. Your Leo and Scorpio fondness for quality and beautiful things is likely to cost you a great deal of money. Therefore a lot of your energy should be geared to making as much money as possible.

Parenthood

You may be a strict parent. While you will enjoy being with your children, you may be a little too demanding. If you are not dogmatic, you will share a good relationship. As your children grow up, they will develop different opinions to yours, and you should try to accept them.

THE MOON IN SAGITTARIUS

YOUR SUN AND MOON SIGNS OFFER A LIVELY COMBINATION, WITH THE SAGITTARIAN MOON ADDING A CASUAL STREAK TO THE LEO SUN. YOU NEED ADVENTURE IN STUDY AND TRAVEL, AND YOU WILL COPE WITH DAUNTING CHALLENGES.

Provided that you are consciously aware of one or two negative tendencies, you should be able to make your Leo Sun and Sagittarian Moon work together for you.

Self-expression

You have great positive spirit that surfaces as soon as you are challenged in any way. When someone makes a suggestion that pleases you, you will want to encourage them. As long as you keep your enthusiasm burning bright you will ensure that, together, you will achieve every one of your goals. It is easy for you to grasp the overall picture of any situation immediately, but you should accept the fact that you are rather easily bored by detail.

You are very versatile, and for you to be really happy with this area of your personality you should have a variety of physical, mental, and creative interests. Your emotions are powerful, and it is good for you to involve yourself in a cause about which you feel strongly.

Romance

It is in the area of love and relationships that your powerful feelings can be most fully expressed. You may fall in love very quickly – perhaps even at first sight – and your love of life, enthusiasm for love and sex, and warm, affectionate nature will soon break down your prospective partner's defenses. Although you are eager for a permanent relationship, you also have a greater need for freedom of expression than most Sun sign Leos.

Your well-being

The Sagittarian body area covers the hips and thighs, where most women of this sign tend to put on weight. It is advisable for you to have a fairly light diet. The Sagittarian organ is the

The Moon in Sagittarius

liver; as a result you may suffer from hangovers rather more than most Leos if you overindulge.

Planning ahead

You may be fascinated by financial risk-taking, or even gambling. Your Leo Sun gives you extravagant tastes, so be careful. Do not risk more money than you can afford to lose, and do not be tempted by get-rich-quick schemes. You could, all too easily and all too quickly, lose a great deal of money. Always be prepared to seek sound professional advice in this area of your life.

Parenthood

Although most Leos enjoy parenthood, some tend to be rather formal in their relationships with their children. This is less likely in your case, and you will not find it difficult to enjoy their enthusiasms.

Similarly, while you will not want your children to be clones of yourself, they should not, on the whole, be bored by your own varied interests; Try to develop any creative talent that they inherit. You will be able to keep abreast of their opinions, and should suffer very few problems with the generation gap.

THE MOON IN CAPRICORN

YOU WILL BE AMBITIOUS AND WILL SUCCEED IN WHATEVER YOU PUT YOUR MIND TO. ALLOW YOUR EARTH SIGN MOON TO TELL YOU INSTINCTIVELY WHEN TO MAKE IMPORTANT MOVES, BUT DO NOT LET IT COOL YOUR WARM LEO SUN.

Your Capricornian Moon endows you with qualities that contrast strongly with those of your Leo Sun, but you should be able to blend them and make them work for you.

Self-expression

Caution and a serious, well-considered response to most situations are characteristic of you, and your Leo enthusiasm will be controlled by a practical and cool approach to important issues. But your Leo love of life will always shine through, and it is extremely likely that you have an instinctive, dry sense of humor that is more amusing than you think.

Your Capricornian Moon may have a slight dampening effect on the warmth of your Leo Sun, making you feel somewhat gloomy and depressed at times. Clouds may darken your psychological landscape until the influence of your Leo Sun takes over. Leos are generally very ambitious and like to have their own tiny kingdoms to rule. Capricornians can also be extremely ambitious and are always aspiring to rise to greater things. If all goes well, this combined attitude will help you achieve whatever you set your heart on.

Romance

Your Capricornian Moon will make you cautious in your attitude and approach to the opposite sex. Once committed, both Leos and Capricornians are usually faithful. But you may not be averse to a little social climbing, and you should curb any tendency to show off.

Your well-being

The Capricornian body area covers the knees and shins. If you suffer from stiffness of the joints, exercise may help. The teeth are also Capricorn-ruled, so make sure you

The Moon in Capricorn

have regular dental checkups. Your skin may tan less easily than that of most Leos, so wear a good sunscreen.

Planning ahead

While your Leo Sun urges you to spend and enjoy your money, your Capricornian instincts will encourage you to take a practical line and make you a wise investor. You probably have good business sense, and could do well if you start your own business. For you the most important thing is to enjoy your money. Do not waste time and energy spending it simply to impress other people. Spend it, instead, on your loved ones. Your Moon will work for you and prevent you from spending unwisely.

Parenthood

If your children ever accuse you of being pompous or a fuddy-duddy, be sure to take note. Avoid being so involved with making money for them and trying to provide everything they need, that you miss out on really knowing them.

THE MOON IN AQUARIUS

LEO AND AQUARIUS ARE POLAR OR OPPOSITE ZODIAC SIGNS, SO YOU WERE BORN UNDER A FULL MOON. YOU COULD SUFFER FROM PERIODS OF RESTLESSNESS, AND YOU MUST AVOID BEING STUBBORN. LET AQUARIAN ORIGINALITY IGNITE LEONINE CREATIVITY.

Each of us, in some way, expresses elements of our polar or opposite sign, the sign that lies across the Zodiac from our Sun sign.

For Leo, the polar sign is Aquarius, and because the Moon was in that sign when you were born, the polarity is emphasized in a most striking way.

Self-expression

You have a very independent streak and like to do things in a way that is just right for you. It may be that you have evolved a unique lifestyle that you guard jealously.

You will express your originality in a variety of ways. Perhaps you like to look a little different, or maybe your job is an unusual one. Your Leo creativity could be spiced with originality, and that will make inner fulfillment even more likely for you.

It is important that you develop flexibility; since both Leo and Aquarius are of the fixed quality, that tends to make you stubborn. Always aim to complete projects, or you will feel dissatisfied and restless. This is one effect of being born at the time of the Full Moon.

Romance

You may tend to distance yourself from prospective partners, feeling that you are not yet ready for total commitment. However, anyone with an Aquarian influence is also very romantic, and once a partner has paved the way for you, you are capable of very faithful love and a rewarding sex life – if you are given enough room to breathe, and allowed some independence.

Your well-being

The Aquarian body area covers the ankles, and you may easily twist yours. The circulation is also Aquarius-ruled, and since this is so strongly related to the heart, the Leo

The Moon in Aquarius

organ, you should make sure that your blood flows freely. You probably like cold, crisp weather more than most Leos, and may enjoy winter sports.

Planning ahead

You could be attracted to very glitzy things, such as unusual mirrors, vases, executive toys, high-fashion clothes, and jewelry. These can prove expensive and not very durable and, as a result, your finances may suffer. Try to develop a practical attitude toward money, and seek professional financial advice when you have any cash to invest.

Parenthood

You will be a lively parent, but your unpredictability may leave your children uncertain where they stand with you. You may want to test new theories by bringing them up in an unusual way. This may work well, but some children feel more secure with a strict set of rules to live by.

THE MOON IN PISCES

YOUR HIGHLY EMOTIONAL LEO FIRE SIGN IS SENSITIZED BY THE EMOTION OF YOUR WATER SIGN PISCEAN MOON. IF YOU ARE DISCIPLINED AND CHANNEL YOUR SUPERB RESOURCES, YOU WILL ACHIEVE A GREAT DEAL IN CREATIVE OR CARING WORK.

While your Sun and Moon signs suggest very different qualities, there is also great sympathy between them, which is emphasized by emotion and creative potential.

Self-expression

At times you could feel pretty unsure of yourself. It is very important for you to realize that you could deceive yourself. Do not doubt yourself, or resort to putting yourself down. Allow your Piscean Moon to be a source of inspiration and imagination; channel its force creatively. However you do this, express your abundant potential with all the Leo confidence in the world. Be bold, and you will achieve inner fulfillment.

Romance

You have a very powerful emotional energy that you may, to an extent, express toward humanitarian causes and in the relief of suffering, but it will mostly be directed toward your partner. You are capable of a really grand passion, reaching heights of happiness and the depths of despair.

There is a great dramatic sense in your attitude toward your lover – this is present in most Sun sign Leos, and in your case is made even more colorful by your Piscean Moon. You will be very sensitive to your partner's needs. Learn to be open about your own needs, since you know the things that give you pleasure, and you should not hold back.

Your well-being

The Piscean body area covers the feet. Do not hesitate to spend money on visits to the podiatrist if you have problems with your feet.

It can be difficult for those with a Piscean influence to be disciplined. When it comes to exercise and regular meals you may, for instance, simply not bother if you are alone. Try to get

The Moon in Pisces

into and stick to a regular routine; the Leo in you really needs it, if you are to express your potential fully. Any exercise that inspires you will do you good in both body and soul, and by exercising you will overcome a Piscean vulnerability to flabbiness.

Planning ahead

Being both very generous and something of a soft touch, you are probably less talented with money than many Leos. Remember, however, that some people will take advantage of you, so be firm if they ask for a loan. While you should seek financial advice before investing, you may wish to put money into building a specific collection of some kind. This will be fun and, if properly managed, it could be a good investment in itself.

Parenthood

You will be a sympathetic, enthusiastic, and encouraging parent, but do not allow your sensitive reactions to your children's needs and suggestions to get the better of you. Keep in tune with their ideas and concerns, and you will be able to bridge the generation gap.

SUN & MOON SIGNS

VIRGO

AUGUST 24 – SEPTEMBER 22

INTRODUCING
VIRGO

VIRGO, THE SIGN OF THE VIRGIN, IS THE SIXTH SIGN OF THE ZODIAC. SINCE IT IS RULED BY THE PLANET MERCURY, VIRGOANS OFTEN TEND TO BE EXCELLENT, IF SOMETIMES HYPERCRITICAL, COMMUNICATORS.

Modesty is a common Virgoan trait, and Virgoans often express themselves in a self-effacing manner. You must be careful not to underestimate your capabilities and should constantly try to build up your self-confidence. While Virgoans achieve inner satisfaction by helping and serving others, this can lead to your being imposed upon.

Virgoans tend to be practical and hardworking, but the influence of the planet Mercury can make you restless, and you may tend to do too much. You should plan your days well in advance, so that there is time for relaxation. This will also help counter stress, to which you are prone.

Traditional groupings

As you read through this book you will come across references to the elements and the qualities, and to positive and negative, or masculine and feminine signs. The first of these groupings, that of the elements, comprises fire, earth, air, and water signs. The second, that of the qualities, divides the Zodiac into cardinal, fixed, and mutable signs. The final grouping is made up of positive and negative, or masculine and feminine signs. Each Zodiac sign is associated with a combination of components from these groupings, all of which contribute different characteristics to it.

Virgoan characteristics

Virgo is a sign of the earth element, and earth is often of importance to Virgoans. You may find close contact with it to be restorative; many Virgoans are superb gardeners.

Virgo is also a sign of the mutable quality, which bestows a flexible mind and a good intellect. Because it is a negative, feminine sign, its subjects tend to be introverts. The Virgoan color is navy blue.

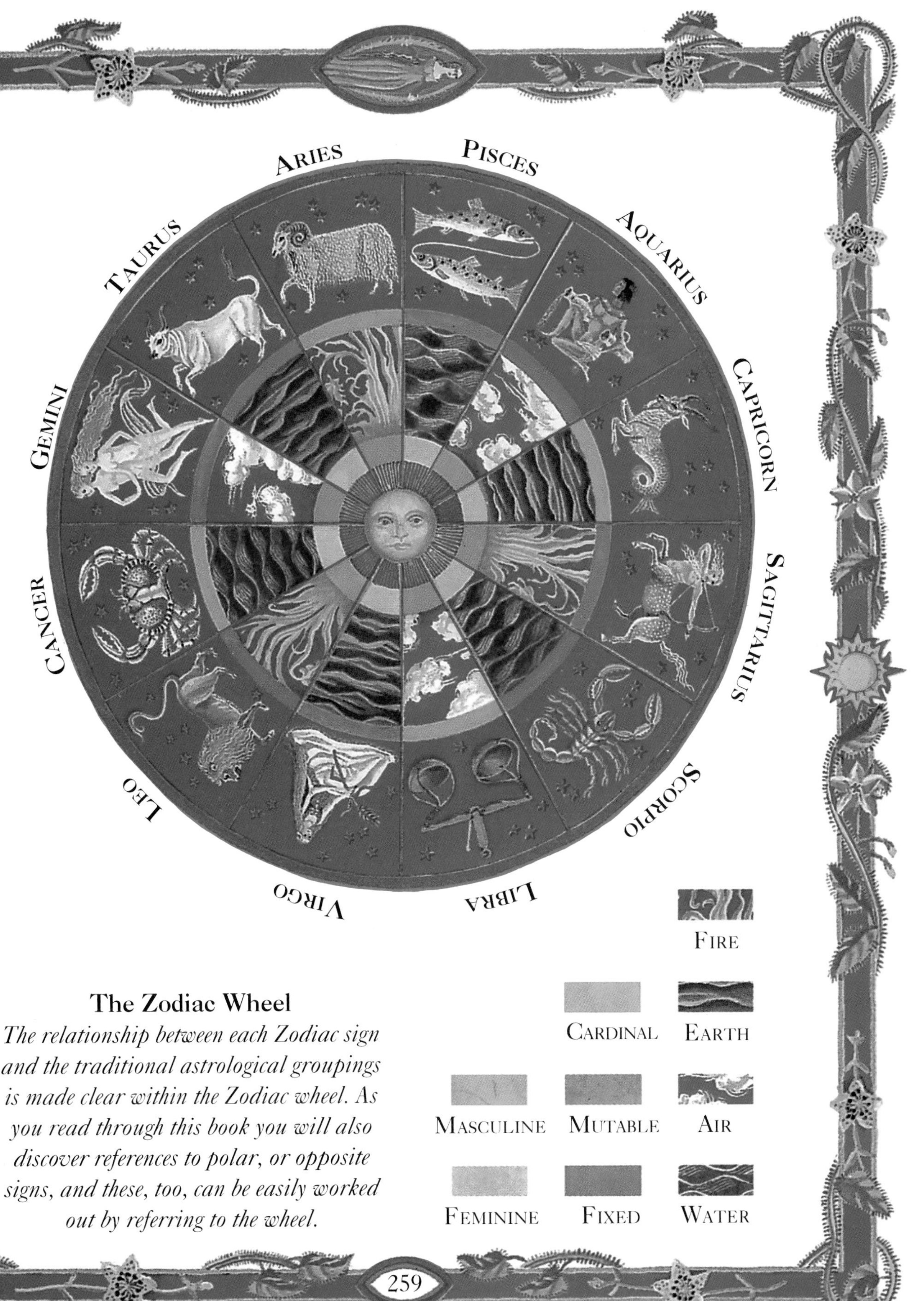

The Zodiac Wheel

The relationship between each Zodiac sign and the traditional astrological groupings is made clear within the Zodiac wheel. As you read through this book you will also discover references to polar, or opposite signs, and these, too, can be easily worked out by referring to the wheel.

MYTHS & LEGENDS

THE ZODIAC, WHICH MAY HAVE ORIGINATED IN BABYLON AS LONG AS 2,500 YEARS AGO, IS A CIRCLE OF CONSTELLATIONS THROUGH WHICH THE SUN MOVES DURING THE COURSE OF A YEAR.

The sign Virgo is thought to have been named in ancient Babylon, or perhaps Sumeria, and the original Virgin that represents the sign is considered to have been Nidaba or Shala, a grain goddess. In one ancient tablet she is described as having "a star on her head and a whip in her right hand, the thong of which stretches out over the tail of Leo." (Similarly, in an ancient Egyptian zodiac, at Esna, Virgo is shown holding Leo by the tail.) As time passed, however, the conception of a matronly goddess slowly evolved. She was gradually rendered as more youthful, and she is perceived in modern representations as being a beautiful young maiden.

Elizabeth I (1533–1603)
Those who surrounded this English queen kindly compared her to the "starry maiden."

In the first century B.C., the famous Roman writer Marcus Manilius set out an early account of astrological mythology in his *Astronomica*. He mentions two myths in relation to Virgo. In the first myth he claims that the original virgin was a young girl named Erigone, the daughter of Icarius, king of Attica and the first mortal maker of wine. Unfortunately, his gift led to Icarius's downfall: he unwisely gave some liquor to a party of shepherds, who then drunkenly murdered him. His faithful dog, Maera, took Erigone by the hem of her gown and led her to his grave, above which she hanged herself in

Ancient Map of the Heavens

This early astrological chart, Atlas Coelistis Hemisphaerium Stellatum Boreale, *dates from 1660. On it can be seen representations of each of the constellations.*

grief. Zeus, king of the gods, set Maera in the skies as the Dog-star, and Erigone as Virgo.

The starry maiden

As an alternative figure for Virgo, Manilius offers Astraea, the "starry maiden," who has long been identified with Justice and was the last of the gods to leave the Earth. Astraea lived among men in the Golden Age, but fled to heaven when mankind grew to unwisdom. The English queen Elizabeth I, also known as the Virgin Queen, was often referred to as Astraea by the sycophants who surrounded her.

It is important to remember that the earliest associations of Virgo had far more to do with beauty and kindness than with virginity and coldness. Indeed, the modern emphasis on the cool frigidity of the sign is quite ridiculous.

VIRGO SYMBOLISM

CERTAIN HERBS, SPICES, FLOWERS, TREES, GEMS, METALS, AND ANIMALS HAVE LONG BEEN ASSOCIATED WITH PARTICULAR ZODIAC SIGNS. SOME ASSOCIATIONS ARE SIMPLY AMUSING, WHILE OTHERS CAN BE USEFUL.

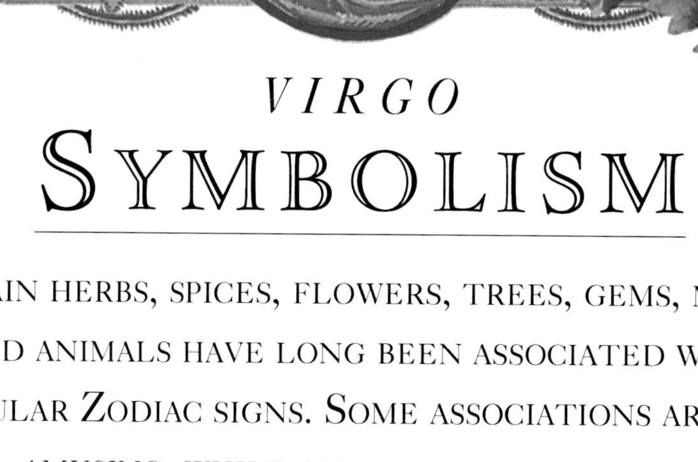

BLUE BUTTERFLY

Flowers

Red, pink, bright yellow, and bright blue flowers, particularly the cornflower, are associated with Virgo.

CORNFLOWER

Trees

Nut-bearing trees are associated with the planet Mercury, which rules Virgo.

OAK

BEECH

Spices

No spice is traditionally associated with Virgo, but cinnamon and cardamom are sometimes mentioned.

CARDAMOM

CINNAMON

Herbs

Any herb that has a red or a pink flower comes under the rulership of Virgo.

LEMON BALM

VIRGO

SYMBOLISM

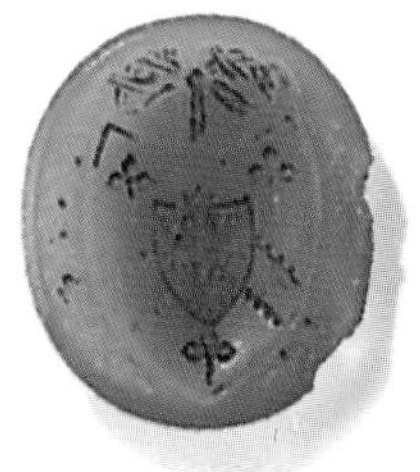

Gems

The Virgoan stone is sardonyx, which is composed of onyx, a kind of quartz, layered with sard, the yellow color of which no doubt led to the association.

SARD SEALS

Metal

As with Gemini, Mercury is a Virgoan metal. So is nickel, with its silvery white, lustrous quality.

EBONY MOUSE

NICKEL

CERAMIC RABBIT

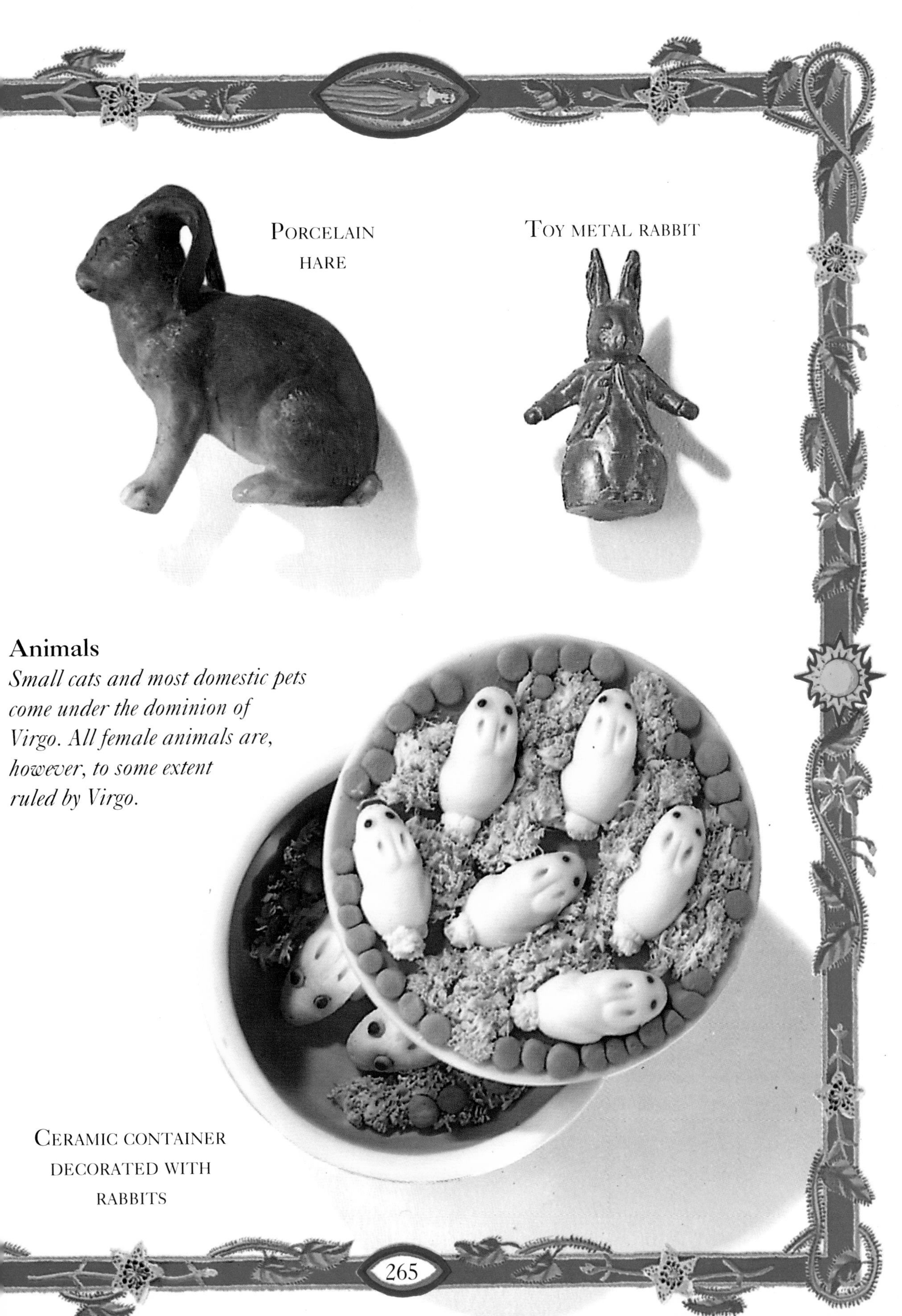

PORCELAIN HARE

TOY METAL RABBIT

Animals

Small cats and most domestic pets come under the dominion of Virgo. All female animals are, however, to some extent ruled by Virgo.

CERAMIC CONTAINER DECORATED WITH RABBITS

VIRGO
PROFILE

QUICK, SLIGHTLY JERKY MOVEMENTS OF THE HEAD AND HANDS, A VERY NEAT IMAGE, AND AN OVERALL AIR OF ACTIVITY ARE TYPICAL OF THIS ZODIAC GROUP. AS A VIRGOAN, YOU ARE ALWAYS LIKELY TO BE "ON THE GO."

Some Virgoans have a tendency to stoop. If this is the case with you, make every effort to ensure that you do not become round-shouldered. As a Virgoan, you probably keep your feet close together, and your hands clasped in front of you. While you release your hands frequently in order to gesticulate, they are usually quickly and firmly clasped again. When kept waiting, you strum your fingers impatiently. Virgoans usually have no time to waste, after all.

The Virgoan face
Virgoans often possess very quizzical expressions. You rarely miss a thing.

The body

Virgoans tend to have rather elongated bodies and limbs; their bone structures are also usually very prominent. However, because they can be very well-proportioned people, this can make them look extremely photogenic, as opposed to awkward.

The face

Your hair is likely to be well cut and cared for. In the case of many Virgoans it will also appear sleek, and people of either sex may have "widow's peaks." Virgoan eyes are usually very clear, alert, and bright, and tend to dart from side to side with curiosity – Virgoans can sometimes be a little too curious. Your nose might be rather sharp, as could your chin, and your mouth is probably quite small. You may purse your lips when you are worried. Many Virgoans have an

The Virgoan stance

Many Virgoans tend to stand with both of their feet placed close together, and their hands clasped in front of them.

extremely quizzical appearance. In fact, you might give the impression of never missing a single thing.

Style

You are likely to favor navy blue and rather dark colors, or small floral patterns that are sometimes quite brightly colored. The neat Virgoan businessman often wears a colorful floral tie, and his white collars and cuffs will stay pristine all day. Virgoan women often choose a Victorian look, and may dress in country styles, using natural fabrics.

The majority of Virgoans enjoy searching for high-quality clothes that have a long life ahead of them, as opposed to fashion items that become redundant after being worn only once.

Virgoans usually like wearing high-quality leather gloves, and beautifully made belts. However, a hat is something that you are likely to wear only for practical reasons. Overall, your image is likely to reflect Virgoan modesty, and to be extraordinarily neat, but it has a very special, alluring charm all of its own.

In general

Your bright personality is probably reflected in the quick movements that you make, and through a fast, rather bouncy walk. You sometimes tend to be rather fussy, and may be prone to flicking imaginary bits of lint from your clothes or playing with a string of beads. Due to slight nervousness, you may sometimes blink a lot.

VIRGO

PERSONALITY

VIRGOANS ARE THE WORKERS OF THE ZODIAC AND ALWAYS ENJOY WORKING FOR OTHER PEOPLE IN ONE WAY OR ANOTHER. WHILE PRACTICAL, WITH PLENTY OF COMMON SENSE, THEY ARE NOT VERY GOOD ORGANIZERS.

All Virgoans need to keep busy. In fact, many never seem to stop, and find it hard to even sit and listen to a conversation.

At work

The need to serve, or to work for other people, is a very important part of the Virgoan psychological motivation. As a direct result of this, many Sun sign Virgoans make excellent secretaries, or they may find themselves positions in which they are either helping or perhaps serving other people.

You will like to know what you have to do and when you have to do it by. It may be that your tendency to be a poor organizer stems from a certain lack of self-confidence. This, in turn, is frequently outwardly expressed through what can sometimes be a delightful, if often overplayed, modesty. You will feel, and perhaps say, that you cannot do something, and then go on to give many reasons why, and name a lot of other people who, in your opinion, could do it better. It is at times like this that friends and family are in a position to help Virgoans most. Self-effacement has charm, but it can go too far.

Your attitudes

The influence of Virgo's ruling planet, Mercury, is interesting. It is liable to make you an exceptionally good communicator, and usually pretty talkative. You are excellent at expressing your opinions, and do not need much encouragement to do so.

Mercury's influence is apt to make you very critical and could give you the ability to analyze problems in detail. As a result, Virgoans are often able to carve out successful careers for themselves in the media. However, if you feel a need to be critical in the context of personal relationships, you would be wise to exercise a little

Mercury rules Virgo

Mercury, the messenger god, represents the ruling planet of Virgo. The influence of Mercury stimulates the mind, but it can also make its subjects critical, nervous, and tense.

restraint. No one will appreciate a person who is frequently prone to nagging and criticizing their partners and friends. You do not want to obtain a reputation for being too fussy.

The overall picture

Virgoans are, for all of the reasons that have been mentioned, exceptionally prone to worry. If, however, you put yourself into a position in which you approach whatever it is that happens to be bothering you using your natural logic and analytical acumen, you will no doubt come up with some really practical answers. Making comprehensive lists of the pros and cons of a difficult situation could help you to assess and analyze it in the necessary detail.

VIRGO
ASPIRATIONS

YOU COULD EASILY BE AN EXCELLENT SECRETARY OR ASSISTANT, BUT REMEMBER THAT YOU ARE CAPABLE OF MORE THAN MERE SUBSERVIENCE. TO SATISFY YOUR NEED FOR SECURITY, YOU SHOULD MAKE YOURSELF INDISPENSABLE.

Agriculture
Because earth is the Virgoan element, working in agriculture or horticulture may come naturally to you.

MODEL TRACTOR

Library work
A career that combines serving the public and working with books could prove to be very satisfying. Similarly, you may find bookshop work appealing.

INK PAD, DATE STAMP, AND BOOKS

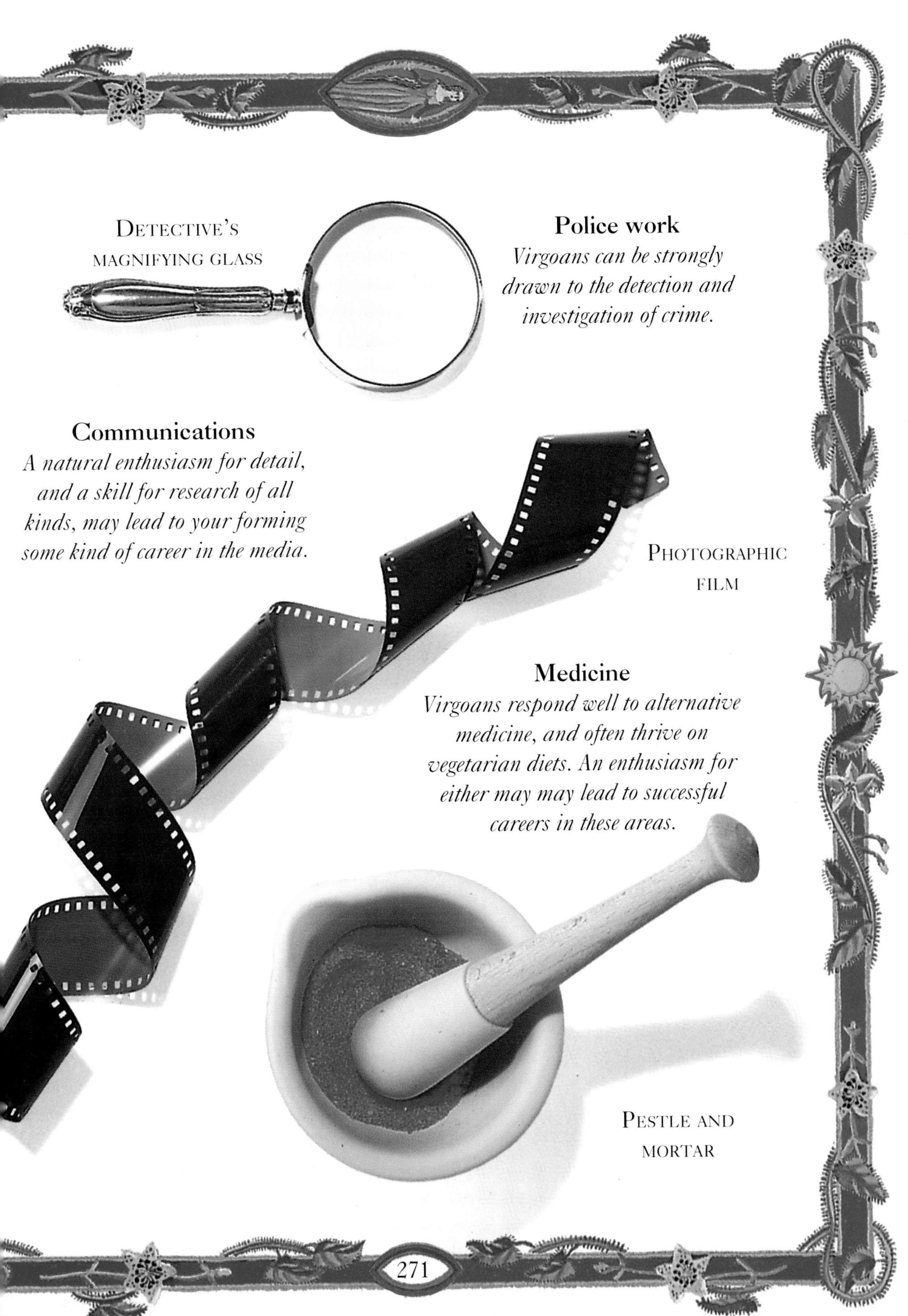

DETECTIVE'S MAGNIFYING GLASS

Police work

Virgoans can be strongly drawn to the detection and investigation of crime.

Communications

A natural enthusiasm for detail, and a skill for research of all kinds, may lead to your forming some kind of career in the media.

PHOTOGRAPHIC FILM

Medicine

Virgoans respond well to alternative medicine, and often thrive on vegetarian diets. An enthusiasm for either may may lead to successful careers in these areas.

PESTLE AND MORTAR

VIRGO HEALTH

A STEADY OUTLET FOR NERVOUS AND PHYSICAL ENERGY IS VITAL TO KEEP THE VIRGOAN SYSTEM IN GOOD ORDER. FRUSTRATION AND WORRY WILL LEAD TO PHYSICAL PROBLEMS, PLUS PSYCHOLOGICAL AND MENTAL STAGNATION.

The high level of nervous energy that most Virgoans have needs to be worked off through really satisfying work. The discipline of a relaxation technique, like yoga or meditation, can also sometimes help to calm Virgoans and get their nervous energy under control.

Your diet

Virgoans benefit from a diet that is high in fiber. It is worth noting that, before vegetarianism was fashionable, Virgoans were most inclined to it, as well as to homeopathy and complementary medical techniques.

You may benefit from the cell salt kali sulphicurum (kali. sulph.), which is said to help prevent bronchitis.

Taking care

The Virgoan body area is the stomach. Because of this many Virgoans find themselves suffering from stomach complaints when they are forced to bear strain or nervous tension. The whole nervous system is actually related to Virgo, so the fact that it is very easily upset by external influences is hardly surprising. If Virgoans become tense, there is also a good chance that they might end up succumbing to migraines.

Hazelnuts

As with Gemini, most nuts are traditionally considered to be Virgoan foodstuffs.

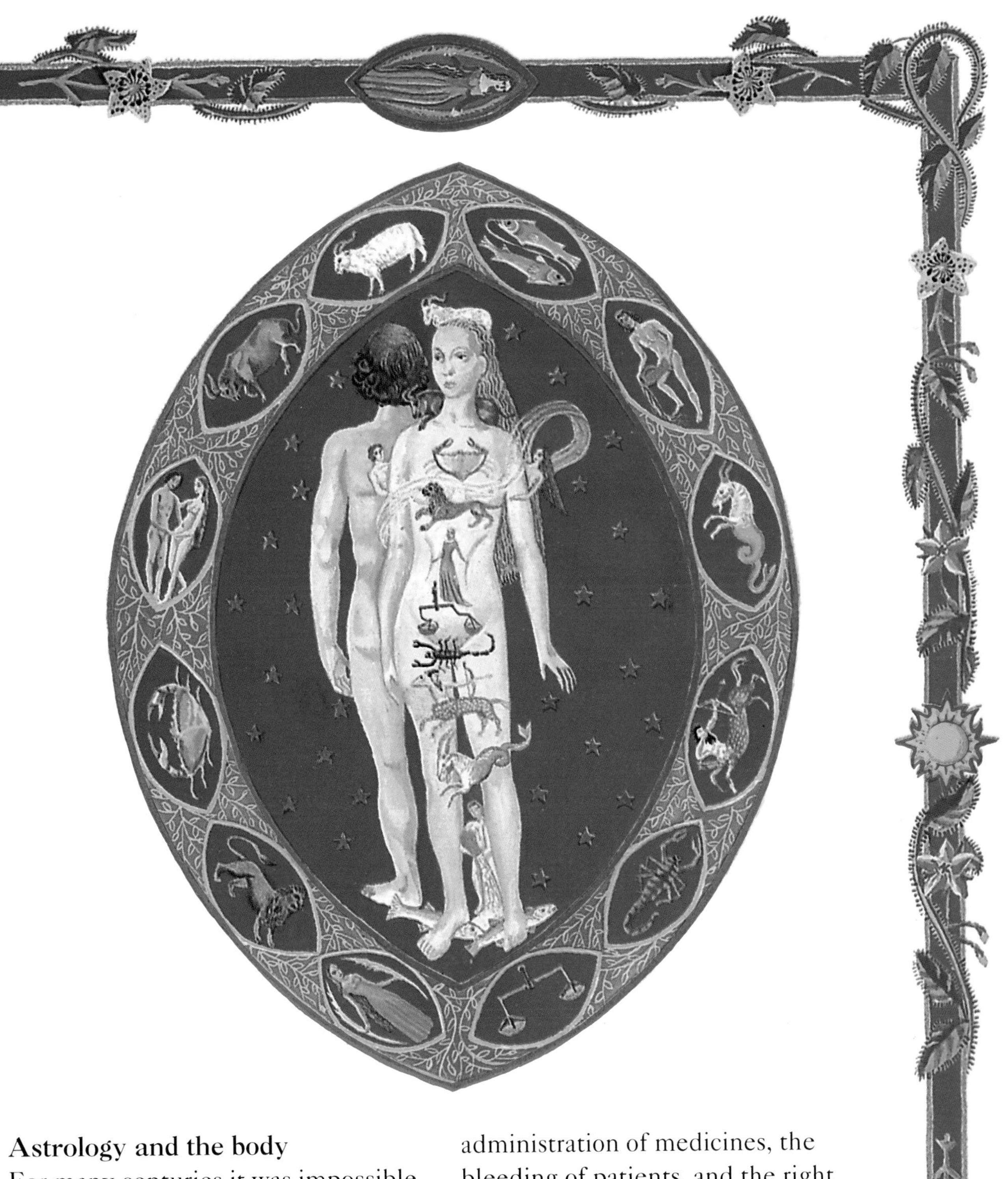

Astrology and the body

For many centuries it was impossible to practice medicine without a knowledge of astrology. In European universities, medical training included information on how planetary positions would affect the administration of medicines, the bleeding of patients, and the right time to pick herbs and make potions. Each Zodiac sign rules a particular part of the body, and early medical textbooks always included a drawing that illustrated the point.

VIRGO AT LEISURE

EACH OF THE SUN SIGNS TRADITIONALLY SUGGESTS SPARE-TIME ACTIVITIES, HOBBIES, AND VACATION SPOTS. ALTHOUGH THESE ARE ONLY SUGGESTIONS, THEY OFTEN WORK OUT WELL FOR VIRGOANS.

POSTAGE STAMPS

Sports

Outdoor sports of all kinds, like cycling or golf, will probably appeal to you.

CIGARETTE CARDS SHOWING CYCLING

Travel

As a Virgoan, you will like visiting mountainous places. A trip to Syria, Brazil, Iraq, the West Indies, or Czechoslovakia may also appeal to you.

Gardening

Virgo is an earth sign, and many Virgoans specialize in growing vegetables or small, brightly colored flowers.

GARDENING GLOVES AND PRUNING SHEARS

Pottery
You may obtain pleasure from working with natural materials, for example, clay or wool.

POTTER'S TOOLS

BOOKS AND READING GLASSES

Reading
Virgoans often like to read biographies and critical essays. Some may enjoy family sagas.

Knitting
Handicrafts that require meticulous attention to detail, such as knitting, crochet work, intricate sewing, and tailoring, are often popular with Virgoans.

WOOL AND KNITTING NEEDLES

VIRGO IN
LOVE

MODESTY AND SHYNESS, PERFECTIONISM AND A CRITICAL EYE, ARE ALL CHARACTERISTIC OF THE VERY INDIVIDUAL VIRGOAN ATTITUDE TO LOVE. VIRGOANS WILL PONDER LONG AND HARD BEFORE COMMITTING THEMSELVES TO SOMEONE.

Having such an inquiring, questioning mind, plus modesty and a certain apprehensive shyness, will tend to make loving rather tricky for many Virgoans. Their reactions will often be to question their feelings, or to try and figure out why someone finds them attractive.

The celebrated Virgoan modesty is, in fact, often a most attractive feature. If a prospective partner proceeds slowly and with care, and develops a good degree of friendship and intellectual rapport with you, there is a high chance that a rewarding bond of affection, love, and sexual fulfillment will develop. You must, however, also play a part in a relationship. Most importantly, you should not look for excuses to criticize your partner.

As a lover

In extreme cases, some Virgoans can develop a very clinical attitude to sex. They may even consider it to be "dirty" in some way. If this is the case, professional counseling should be sought. On a more positive note, because Virgoans are likely to have inquiring minds, many are extremely curious about sex from a very early age and could indulge in considerable

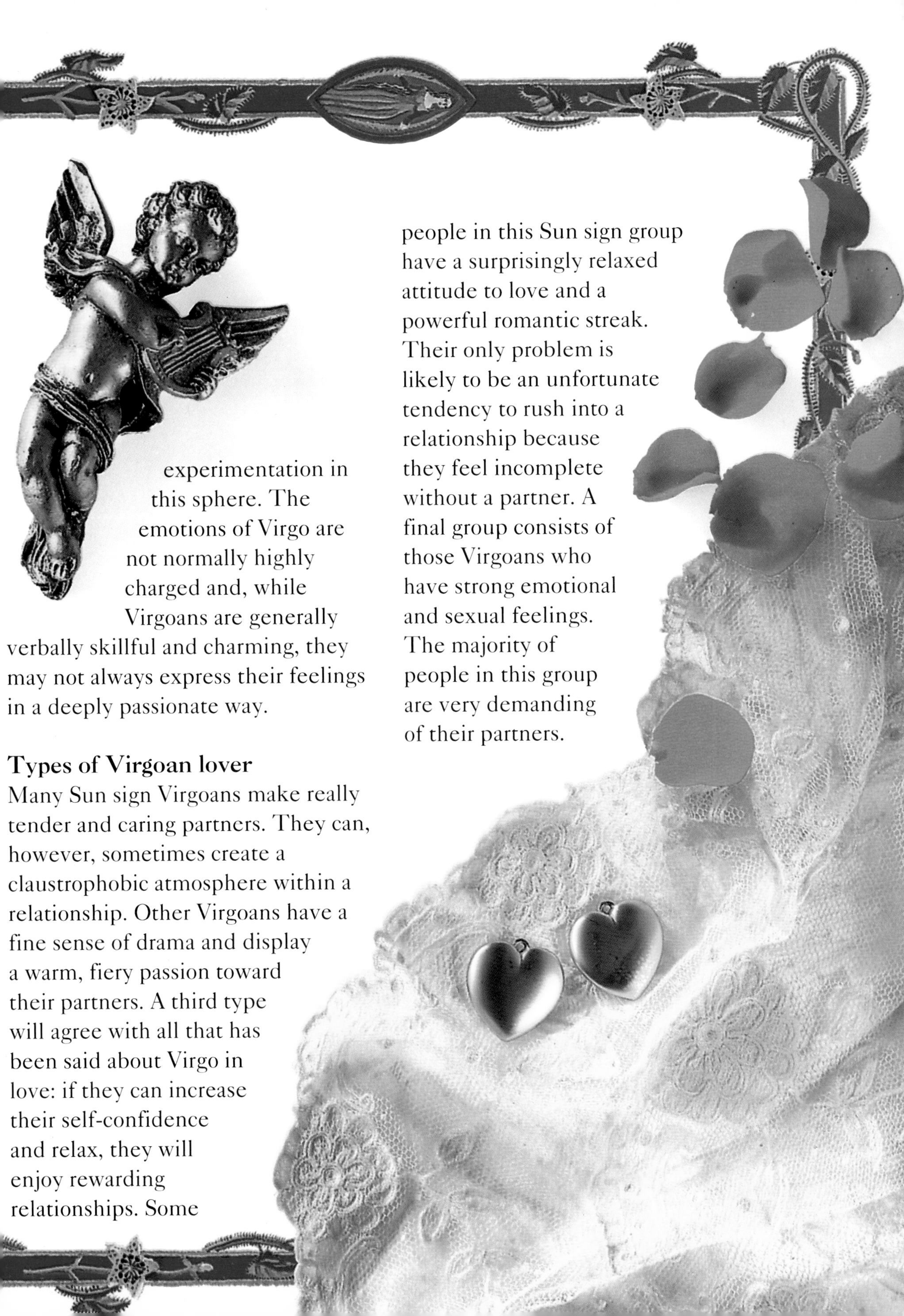

experimentation in this sphere. The emotions of Virgo are not normally highly charged and, while Virgoans are generally verbally skillful and charming, they may not always express their feelings in a deeply passionate way.

Types of Virgoan lover

Many Sun sign Virgoans make really tender and caring partners. They can, however, sometimes create a claustrophobic atmosphere within a relationship. Other Virgoans have a fine sense of drama and display a warm, fiery passion toward their partners. A third type will agree with all that has been said about Virgo in love: if they can increase their self-confidence and relax, they will enjoy rewarding relationships. Some people in this Sun sign group have a surprisingly relaxed attitude to love and a powerful romantic streak. Their only problem is likely to be an unfortunate tendency to rush into a relationship because they feel incomplete without a partner. A final group consists of those Virgoans who have strong emotional and sexual feelings. The majority of people in this group are very demanding of their partners.

VIRGO AT HOME

NEATNESS AND PERHAPS AUSTERITY CAN MAKE THE TYPICAL VIRGOAN HOME A LITTLE TOO CLINICAL FOR COMFORT. ENDEARINGLY, HOWEVER, A CLUTTER OF SMALL ORNAMENTS CAN HUMANIZE IT. THERE WILL BE PLENTY OF PLANTS.

The typical Virgoan home is pretty and neat. The colors are often very cheerful, and the rooms full of detail and clutter, as a result of your diverse and plentiful interests. If you were able to live in the ideal place of your choice, you would probably choose the country. However, as city careers are common among Virgoans, unless you feel able to face long, and often tiring, hours spent commuting you may have to make do with a home in town.

It would probably be wise for you to look at a few properties located near parks or some other form of open space whenever you are deciding where to live.

Furniture

Virgoans are usually very attracted to natural materials, so wood, particularly wood that has been treated so that its richness and natural beauty show to full advantage, is favored. This rich effect is usually enhanced by either wool or linen covers, since showy brocades or silks, and lavish or elaborate furniture, are not to the Virgoan taste. The Virgoan home

Potted plants

A selection of fascinating plants are likely to be very much in evidence in a typically Virgoan home.

sometimes has a rather ethnic look to it and, because Virgoans are practical people, durability is also very important.

You will find space in your living room for a writing desk or some kind of work table if you do not have a studio or workshop in which to relax and practice your favorite hobbies.

Soft furnishings

Checks and spots, and above all small floral patterns, are especially popular with Virgoans. It is very common to discover chintzes with a tiny flower or leaf design in either the kitchen or the living room, and the impression given is of neatness combined with a certain prettiness. This can occasionally translate into overfussiness. The cushions in a Virgoan home can sometimes be rather hard, since most Virgoans are not that keen on really relaxing. They do not always list comfort very high among their priorities.

Decorative objects

On the whole, Virgoans tend to like tiny objects and rather unusual curios, such as miniature vases, small silver boxes, and tiny, neatly framed pictures of the family. Your choice of paintings will usually be taken from schools that work in great detail. Dutch interior paintings, particularly domestic scenes, often enhance Virgoan walls. Tidiness and neatness are qualities attributed to Virgoans and, on the surface, this is true. Chaos is normally reserved for cupboards, where it cannot be seen. A sunny corner in your home, such as a windowsill, usually sports some plants that have spectacular foliage as well as flowers.

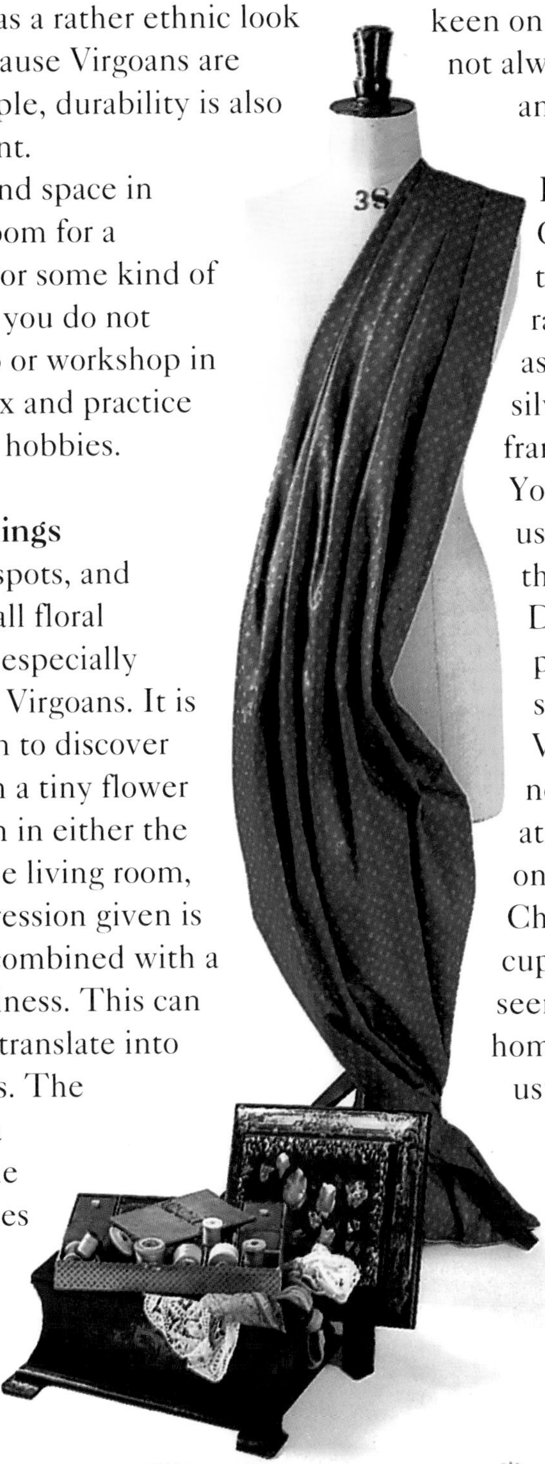

Dressmaker's dummy
Virgoans take great pride in their hobbies, and evidence of them (in this case sewing) is often visible in their homes.

THE
MOON
AND
YOU

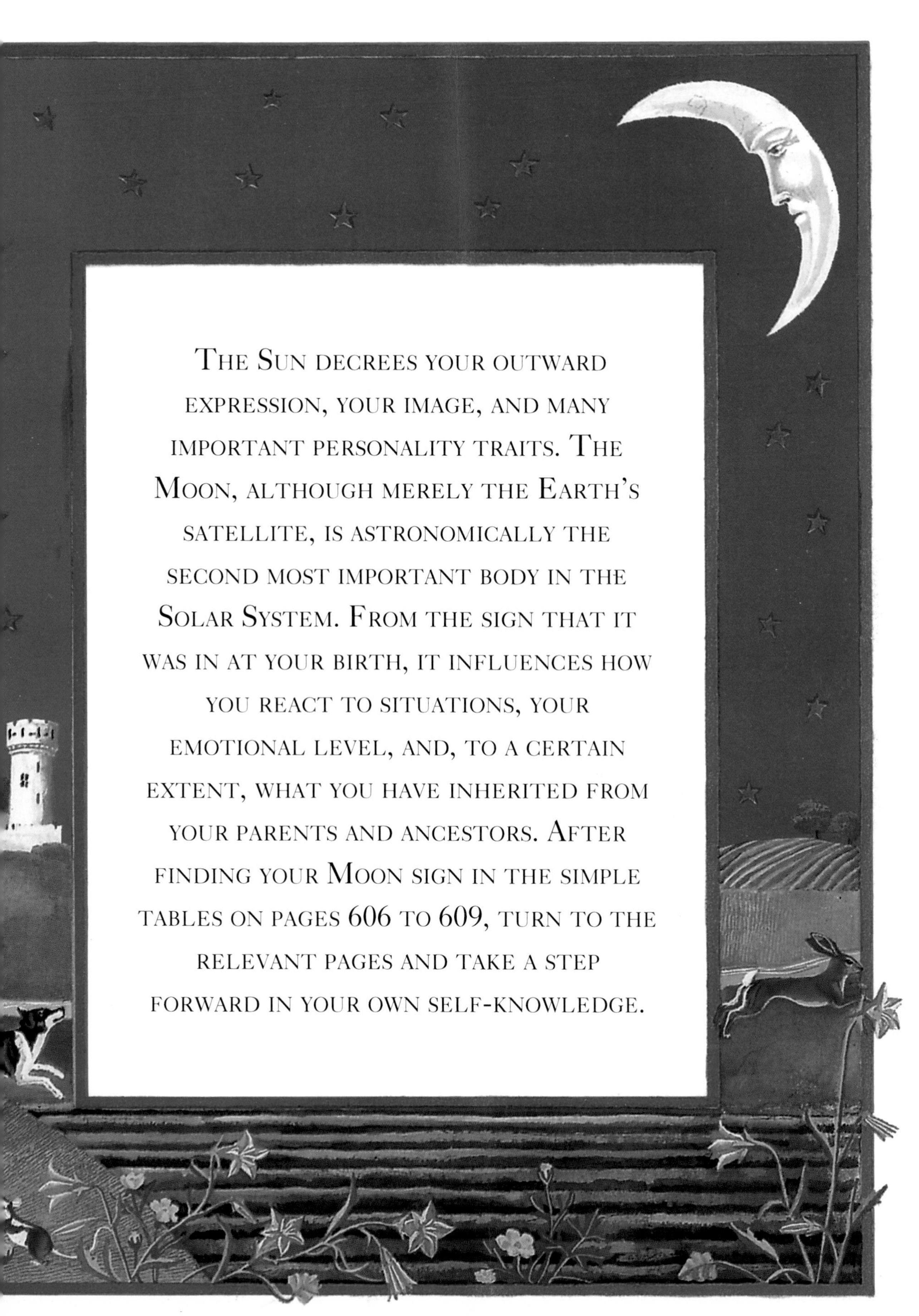

The Sun decrees your outward expression, your image, and many important personality traits. The Moon, although merely the Earth's satellite, is astronomically the second most important body in the Solar System. From the sign that it was in at your birth, it influences how you react to situations, your emotional level, and, to a certain extent, what you have inherited from your parents and ancestors. After finding your Moon sign in the simple tables on pages 606 to 609, turn to the relevant pages and take a step forward in your own self-knowledge.

THE MOON IN ARIES

YOUR ALERT AND CRITICAL VIRGOAN CHARACTERISTICS ARE SPICED WITH VERY QUICK RESPONSES TO SITUATIONS. YOU ARE EXCELLENT IN EMERGENCIES, BUT SHOULD ALWAYS BEWARE OF TAKING PREMATURE, ILL-CONSIDERED ACTION.

Your Arien Moon adds many contrasting characteristics to your practically inclined Sun. You are able to react rapidly to most situations and are good at grasping the immediate essentials of any set of circumstances.

Self-expression

You are always on the ball. There is, however, a drawback to this, since you may sometimes be impatient and too hasty. You will probably be far less cautious than many Sun sign Virgoans and should always think twice before you commit yourself.

The greatest contrast between Aries and Virgo is an emotional one. You have powerful emotional resources, and will probably be able to express them freely and rewardingly.

Romance

You have a passionate side to your nature, and characteristic Virgoan modesty will be unlikely to inhibit your approach to sex. If you manage to follow your basic intuition and impulses, you should enjoy a truly rewarding love and sex life.

When you become involved in a relationship, you may find Virgo prompting you to have second thoughts. You may ask yourself whether you are good enough for your partner. Try to ignore such doubts – they are the product of your Virgoan Sun, which will be trying to put a brake on the forthright and passionate response of your Arien Moon.

Your well-being

Ariens often suffer from headaches, and Virgoans are prone to migraine. The cause will probably be a buildup of tension, to which you will be very prone. All Virgoans have a busy lifestyle that allows little time for relaxation, and your Arien Moon chimes in with this. You need to learn how to relax, and a discipline like yoga will help. It should, however, be

The Moon in Aries

noted that headaches are sometimes the result of slight kidney disorders.

You probably have a very fast metabolic rate and will therefore be unlikely to put on excess weight.

Planning ahead

You may be far less careful with money than many people of your Sun sign. Try to control your Arien response to so-called bargains. If you are attracted to some big purchase, ask yourself if you really need it. This whole area is one that demands Virgoan caution.

Parenthood

The chances are that you will be less overtly critical of your children than many Virgoans, and this is not a bad thing. If you get really involved in their hobbies, you will develop a marvelously positive rapport with them. You should have no problems with the generation gap.

THE MOON IN TAURUS

YOUR SUN AND MOON SIGNS ARE BOTH OF THE EARTH ELEMENT, AND YOU ARE THEREFORE A PRACTICAL PERSON. ALLOW YOUR SLOW, CAREFUL RESPONSES TO SITUATIONS TO GUIDE YOU WHEN DISTURBED BY VIRGOAN TENSION AND WORRY.

Both Virgo and Taurus are earth signs, and bestow practical common sense upon their subjects. Try, however, not to be overcautious.

Self-expression

The elements of shyness or inhibition that can be a part of every Virgoan character could prompt you to develop a safe and predictable routine, which may allow little or no scope for adventure. Always aim to consider situations constructively, as challenges, taking each development step-by-step, with confident assurance. In this way you will make the most of your best qualities.

You have marvelous potential that needs to be positively expressed, perhaps through craftwork or music.

Romance

Your Taurean Moon gives you a tender and affectionate emotion that enhances your attitude to, and expression of, love. If you allow it some freedom, an instinctive sensuality, which will no doubt delight your partner, should emerge.

The worst Taurean fault is possessiveness. Virgoans are extremely rational and logical, and it is this area of your personality that you should tune into if possessiveness becomes a problem. Remember also that you can be rather critical. If you avoid carping, and allow your love room to breathe, you will enjoy a rewarding relationship.

Your well-being

The Taurean body area is the throat, and yours could be vulnerable. Always keep a remedy on hand, especially during the winter or if there is an influenza bug going around.

Your Virgoan metabolism may be somewhat slower than average, as Taureans tend to move slowly, consequently putting on weight quite

The Moon in Taurus

easily. You could also have a high regard for chocolate and most rich foods. If you are at all worried or upset, a burst of "comfort eating" may need to be resisted.

Planning ahead

You have an excellent business sense, and should be able to make good, sound investments. Taurus enjoys luxury and every creature comfort, and is very attracted to quality. On the whole, Virgo goes for economy and good value. Here, therefore, is a possible source of conflict that only you can resolve. Why not enjoy those quality luxuries, and feel no guilt?

Parenthood

You will work extremely hard in every way, but especially to give your children a good life. Make sure that you have time for fun and outings with them, and that you do not miss out on their company. You may tend to be strict and discipline them firmly. Do not overdo this, and try not to be too critical of their efforts.

THE MOON IN GEMINI

BOTH VIRGO AND GEMINI ARE RULED BY THE PLANET MERCURY, SO THERE IS GREAT EMPATHY BETWEEN THESE SIGNS. YOU HAVE A SHARP MIND, BUT DO NOT LET GEMINIAN LOGIC BE DAMAGED BY VIRGOAN CRITICISM AND NAGGING.

The planet Mercury rules over both Virgo and Gemini, and these two signs are of the mutable quality. You therefore like variety and change, and are extremely versatile.

Self-expression

Mercury is regarded as the planet of communication, so it is likely that you are an excellent communicator. You may be a good teacher, or perhaps you work in the media.

The worst Geminian faults are restlessness and superficiality. While you could juggle many tasks at the same time, remember that you will get far more inner fulfillment if you complete everything you begin.

Romance

You may tend to fight showing your true feelings. Once in love, however, your partner could well receive sackfuls of letters, postcards, poems, and the like from you. Try to relax into your relationships, and be aware that while Virgoan modesty can be charming, it should not prevent you from enjoying a rich and rewarding sex life.

It is important for you to have a high level of friendship within any emotional relationship. Seek partners who are at least your intellectual equals, and who can challenge your extremely lively mind.

Your well-being

The Geminian body areas are the arms and hands: be extra careful when using tools or when cooking. The body organ is the lungs, and it is therefore inadvisable for anyone with a Geminian influence to smoke.

You may be quite highly strung, since you have a great deal of nervous energy. This must be burned off through exercise that is both physically and mentally stimulating, for instance fast games such as

The Moon in Gemini

badminton, squash, or tennis. As a result of tension, you may suffer from migraines even more often than many Virgoans. Try to cultivate your sense of inner calm by learning some kind of relaxation technique.

Planning ahead

Mercury is the planet most closely associated with buying and selling. If you have something to sell, you will almost always contrive to get the best possible price for it. You may need to get professional advice when investing, because there is a chance that your cautious, practical Virgoan Sun could sometimes fail you.

Parenthood

You will be a very lively parent, and will not find it difficult to keep well up with, or ahead of, your children's current crazes, ideas, and opinions.

You are, however, very critical, and may tend to deflate your children by being too critical of their efforts. Be careful: such put-downs can, in the long run, be very damaging.

THE MOON IN CANCER

VIRGO AND CANCER ARE THE TWO SIGNS OF THE ZODIAC MOST PRONE TO WORRY. VIRGOAN WORRY IS INTELLECTUAL; CANCERIAN, INTUITIVE AND IMAGINATIVE. YOU SHOULD AIM TO BALANCE THESE TRAITS AGAINST EACH OTHER.

The Moon rules Cancer, and its influence over you is therefore very powerful, perhaps even to the point where you will show rather less than the average number of characteristics said to be typical of your Sun sign.

Self-expression

Your practical Virgoan Sun and extremely intuitive Moon suggest that you might possess a number of admirable virtues.

You have a very vivid and powerful imagination, which is probably highly spiced with creative potential. Try to express it whenever you can. For example, if you have a sneaking feeling that you would like to write, do not hesitate to do so.

Where your Sun and Moon signs meet all too well is in relation to anxiety. These signs seem to fight for first prize in the Zodiac where the tendency to worry is concerned. It will work at two levels, and you can fight it in two ways. The Virgoan way is to make lists of all the pros and cons of a situation; the Cancerian way is to follow your instinct and intuition.

Romance

You no doubt possess a rather high emotional level and are able to express it much more freely than many Virgoans. You also have the wonderful capacity to live a rich and fulfilling love and sex life, and the ability to contribute a great deal to a happy relationship. You must, however, recognize the fact that you can sometimes be too protective.

Your well-being

The Cancerian body area covers the chest and breasts. The sign has nothing to do with the disease of the same name, but women should, of course, check their breasts regularly. Because of your tendency to worry,

The Moon in Cancer

you may, at times, be subject to stomach (from Virgo) and digestive (from Cancer) problems. Aim for inner calm and peace, and avoid flapping about pointlessly.

You may be an excellent cook, but should watch how much you eat. You could be more prone to weight gain than most Virgoans. If your metabolism is slow, try to speed it up a little, perhaps through exercise.

Planning ahead

You will be very careful, perhaps even overly cautious with money. However, you certainly have what it takes to make money: a really shrewd and intuitive business sense, which should enable you to invest wisely.

Parenthood

You make a marvelous, caring parent, and will want to "mother" your children. Try to accept the fact that they will eventually leave home and make their own lives. It is particularly important for women with this Sun and Moon combination to develop new interests at such times. Try not to be too sentimental, recalling "the old days" too relentlessly, or the generation gap will loom large.

THE MOON IN LEO

GIVE YOUR LEO MOON ROOM TO BREATHE. IT WILL PROVIDE YOU WITH THE CONFIDENCE TO DO WHAT YOU WANT, BECAUSE IT IS RIGHT FOR YOU. DO NOT LET SHYNESS CRAMP YOUR STYLE OR INHIBIT YOU IN ANY WAY.

Your Leo Moon creates some very striking qualities that contrast strongly with those of your Virgoan Sun. Try to become more aware of them, and allow them to work for you.

Self-expression

You have greater self-confidence than many people of your Sun sign, and if you can combine this with the Virgoan ability to communicate your ideas, emotions, and opinions, you cannot fail to make excellent progress.

Should you be someone who initially seems to accept challenges and copes positively with situations, but then retreats on second thought, try to reach a better balance. Your Leo Moon is there to push you forward and boost your self-confidence.

In addition, in contrast to most Virgoans you have very good organizing ability. You do not need to be told everything that is expected of you, and you can cope well in a crisis. You may have creative potential and should try to fit time in which to express this into your busy schedule.

Romance

You have warm, fiery emotions and, because you are such a good communicator, should not find it difficult to express your feelings. You certainly have the capacity to love deeply and passionately, but must consciously dispel any typically Virgoan feelings of inferiority.

You will want to look up to your partners and do everything possible to please them, but remember that relationships should be partnerships.

Your well-being

The Leo body area is said to cover the back and spine. These are therefore vulnerable, so make sure that you take enough exercise to keep them in really good condition. Many Virgoans love walking and jogging. If you feel that this applies to you,

The Moon in Leo

remember to make sure that you walk well, with a straight back.

The Leo body organ is the heart, and this organ, like all the others, needs regular exercise. You will probably be less prone to worry than most people of your Sun sign, and this characteristic is therefore less likely to affect your health.

Planning ahead

The contrast between Leo and Virgo will emerge in your attitude toward money. Your Moon sign instinct veers toward generosity, extravagance, and quality. Your Virgoan Moon encourages a taste for simple things, of good value. Somewhere between the two is the point of balance.

You will probably invest soundly, provided your Leo Moon does not encourage you to put all your financial eggs in one basket.

Parenthood

Your natural enthusiasm will make you a lively parent. You will be less critical, and more encouraging, than most Virgoans. Take into account your children's opinions, and encourage debate among them.

THE MOON IN VIRGO

BECAUSE BOTH THE SUN AND THE MOON WERE IN VIRGO ON THE DAY OF YOUR BIRTH, YOU WERE BORN UNDER A NEW MOON. SINCE VIRGO IS AN EARTH SIGN, THIS ELEMENT POWERFULLY INFLUENCES YOUR PERSONALITY AND REACTIONS.

Should you study a list of your Sun sign characteristics, you will probably recognize that a great many of them apply to you. On average, out of a list of perhaps 20 traits of a Sun sign listed in books or magazines, most people will strongly identify with 11 or 12. In your case, however, the average increases considerably because the Sun and Moon were both in Virgo when you were born.

Self-expression

Your Sun sign will tend to make you lively and talkative, but rather cautious and, sometimes, perhaps lacking in self-confidence; your Moon sign causes you to react to challenges in the same way.

You have an alert mind, and your responses tend to be critical. Be careful that you do not get too bogged down in detail, and try consciously to develop the ability to grasp the overall concept of a suggestion or project.

Romance

Your Sun and Moon signs are not very highly charged with emotion and, when you are in love, you could well be a little apprehensive about expressing your feelings. Remember that you are good with words, and do not be afraid to say what you feel. Take your time, however, since nervousness can make you overly talkative. Do not allow yourself to be rushed into a relationship, but do not make excuses, either, in order to avoid committing yourself.

One area in which you should hold back is in being critical of your partners. Try to accept them for what they are.

Your well-being

Everything that has been said about health on pages 272 to 273 probably applies directly to you. You are possibly one of the great worriers of the world, and this could affect your

The Moon in Virgo

digestion. You probably respond very well to most homeopathic and complementary medical treatments, in particular reflexology.

Your very high nervous energy can lead to a buildup of tension. Like many Virgoans, you may therefore benefit from yoga.

Planning ahead

You will not be very adventurous when it comes to money and will spend carefully and wisely. Go for investments that show slow but steady growth. You may need professional guidance when you wish to invest or save some money.

Parenthood

You will stimulate your children's minds, but may be a little cool. They will benefit from sound explanations, but a hug is often more reassuring. Try not to be too critical. This will not be easy for you, although keeping up with your children's concerns will.

THE MOON IN LIBRA

VIRGO IS ALL ACTION, WHILE LIBRA IS MORE RELAXED. IT IS IMPORTANT FOR YOU TO KEEP YOUR PHYSICAL AND INTELLECTUAL ENERGIES IN BALANCE. A LIBRAN MOON GIVES YOU A DIPLOMATIC STREAK THAT YOU MUST NOT SUPPRESS.

Your Libran Moon lightens your personality and helps you to take a rather more relaxed attitude to life than many Virgoans.

Self-expression

When confronted by problems, you may respond with "Que sera, sera" and, while for some Zodiac types this could prove a negative or complacent reaction, for you it is actually fitting, since it allows you breathing room before your more energetic, tense nervous energy springs into action. One word of warning: you could be rather indecisive in certain situations and, to counter the tendency, should bring your marvelously logical and critical Sun sign qualities into play.

Romance

You are very romantic at heart, and should not find it too difficult to relax into emotional and sexual relationships. In fact, your response to people of the opposite sex is probably far more outgoing than that of many Sun sign Virgoans.

Be careful that you do not rush into marriage or a permanent relationship, only to find that the man or woman of your choice is terribly irritating or does not come up to your standards.

You are probably more tactful and diplomatic toward your partners than most Virgoans. Shyness and modesty will be less dominant in you, and you should have no problem enjoying a rich and fulfilling love and sex life.

Your well-being

The Libran body organ is the kidneys. Virgoan headaches and migraines, which are due to stress and tension, may be exacerbated by your Libran Sun, since there is a possibility that slight kidney upsets could also give you headaches. However, your Moon sign should help to prevent too much tension from building up.

The Moon in Libra

You may have a slower metabolism than many Sun sign Virgoans, and could enjoy rather rich food. If you are at all prone to weight gain, try to adjust your diet, and do not allow yourself to get lazy about exercise.

Planning ahead

You may well be conscience-stricken when you have been extravagant. Try not to get too concerned about such things. You may not be terribly good at handling your finances and should seek professional advice in this area, especially if you want to buy stock or are considering an investment or some form of savings plan.

Parenthood

While you will be a fine parent, it is possible that your children may not always know precisely where they stand with you. Be careful, since this can cause problems. Aim to keep a balance. Remember, too, to keep abreast of your children's opinions and concerns, in order to avoid problems with the generation gap.

THE MOON IN SCORPIO

YOU NEED TO GET TO THE BOTTOM OF ANY PROBLEM THAT YOU ENCOUNTER AND TO DELVE INTO IT IN GREAT DETAIL. YOU HAVE MORE EMOTIONAL FORCE THAN MOST VIRGOANS, AND YOU SHOULD USE THIS POSITIVELY.

The earth element of a Virgoan Sun blends well with the water element of your Scorpio Moon, for in many respects these influences have certain qualities in common.

Self-expression

You will find research compelling and should get involved in a subject into which you can delve in real depth.

You also have great determination and sense of purpose, and need to be emotionally involved with any work that you do. The inner psychological fulfillment that you will get out of this is essential to you, but you must learn to develop breadth of vision. While your flair for detail is marvelous, you may not always grasp overall concepts very well.

Romance

You need really rewarding sexual expression and fulfillment. This may not be simple, because you will be a demanding partner and, while capable of giving great sexual pleasure, you may well have special needs. Choose your partners with all the discrimination and care bestowed by your Virgoan Sun and Scorpio Moon.

The worst Scorpio fault is jealousy, and the worst Virgoan fault, that of being overly critical. Clearly, these can marry in an unfortunate way, so consciously guard against them.

Your well-being

The Scorpio body area covers the genitals. Scorpio women should make sure they have regular checkups, and men should regularly examine their testicles for irregularities. With your Sun and Moon combination, your throat may also be open to infections.

You may be very prone to Virgoan worry, as your Scorpio Moon gives you an active, fertile imagination that can sometimes prompt you to worry over nothing. This may lead to an upset

The Moon in Scorpio

stomach and minor ailments that are difficult to pin down. At such times, try to let Virgoan logic dominate.

Planning ahead

You are likely to have an instinctive business sense and a natural ability to for making money.

You will probably also have much more expensive tastes than other Virgoans, and you will need to earn a good salary in order to allow for some costly indulgences.

Parenthood

You may be a far stricter parent than you realize, but in many ways this is not a bad thing at all. You are aiming to make your childern grow up to be decent and considerate people. It may, however, be necessary for you to achieve a little more balance. Let yourself go, and allow yourself to express your enjoyment of life in your relationship with your children. In this way, you will have real fun and reduce generation gap problems.

THE MOON IN SAGITTARIUS

DO NOT UNDERESTIMATE YOUR OWN INTELLIGENCE; YOU MAY HAVE A GREAT CAPACITY FOR STUDY. BE CAREFUL THAT YOUR SAGITTARIAN MOON DOES NOT GIVE OTHERS THE IMPRESSION THAT YOU ARE UNCARING.

Both Virgo and Sagittarius offer a good intellectual capacity, and make you adaptable to changing atmospheres and conditions. Your Sagittarian Moon makes you respond optimistically to challenges and gives you a positive outlook. As a result, you should, in theory, be far less of a worrier than most Sun sign Virgoans.

Self-expression

You are always happy to become involved in the details of an argument but, because of your Sagittarian Moon, you have the breadth of vision and the ability to take in the overall situation as well. The worst Sagittarian fault happens to be restlessness; try to avoid it by developing consistency of effort.

There is an element of the "eternal student" about you. You can cope well with intellectual challenge, so it is quite important that you always have a challenging project on hand. If your work constantly taxes your brain, make sure that you spend some of your spare time involved in a physically demanding interest.

Romance

You have a fine, positive, fiery emotional force that will find its most positive expression in your love and sex life. You are unlikely to be shy or modest; your attitude to love is lively, and you have a great capacity to enjoy sexual relationships. You need partners who understand your need for an element of freedom and independence within a relationship. An even vaguely claustrophobic atmosphere will not suit you at all.

Your well-being

The Sagittarian body area covers the hips and thighs. Women who have this sign emphasized will tend to put

The Moon in Sagittarius

on weight in those areas. Only exercise and a very controlled, regular diet will help. The Sagittarian organ is the liver, and it is surprising how easy it is for you to feel unwell. Your body and mind must be kept in good running order, like a well-oiled machine. If they are not, you will suffer far more than most people.

Planning ahead

You have something of a gambling spirit, and it could well need careful control. It is related to a love of taking risks. If you are attracted to get-rich-quick schemes, always make sure that you allow your more cautious Virgoan self to have its say before embarking on them.

Parenthood

Your children will appreciate your enthusiastic responses to their suggestions, and you will not find it difficult to stimulate their minds and keep them active. They are unlikely to turn into couch potatoes, slumped in front of the television set for hours on end. If you can control any overtly critical qualities that spring from your Virgoan Sun, you ought not to experience generation gap problems.

THE MOON IN CAPRICORN

YOUR CAPRICORNIAN MOON WILL EITHER HELP YOU TO SCALE THE HEIGHTS OR HOLD YOU BACK. PRAISE YOURSELF AS OFTEN AS POSSIBLE AND YOU WILL GET TO THE TOP. FALL INTO INHIBITING SELF-CRITICISM AND YOU WILL NOT.

You are a very practical, sensible, and dependable person. Your Capricornian Moon can work for you in one of two ways. You will either respond well to challenge and be very ambitious to succeed, stepping with great agility over every difficulty that crosses your path and eventually reaching the top; or you will respond very negatively, declining to accept responsibility on the grounds that you cannot cope, or do not have the brains, the stamina, or the self-confidence. It is even possible that you may recognize both of these tendencies in yourself.

Self-expression

If you are rather timid, ask yourself whether this is due to the influence of your Virgoan Sun. The blending of the influences of your Sun and Moon is, in many ways, a great help in countering this tendency, and provides sound building blocks for your personality. You can build a reputation for reliability and common sense, and your truly practical outlook on life is enviable.

Romance

Capricorn is a cool, unemotional sign, and so is Virgo. You may therefore be inclined not to show your feelings all that readily. You will take your love and sex life very seriously, and may need to learn to relax more into your relationship if you are to experience a rewarding partnership.

Your well-being

The Capricornian body area covers the knees and shins, so if you enjoy long country hikes or jogs, you should make sure that your knees are well protected.

The skin, teeth, and bones are also Capricorn-ruled, so use good-quality, natural skin products, and do not miss out on regular dental checkups.

The Moon in Capricorn

Planning ahead

Because you are practical and cautious, you will no doubt be extremely careful with money. You probably enjoy putting carefully calculated sums aside regularly in some safe investment, for instance savings bonds or CDs.

You may also have a liking for quality, and will discreetly go for the best whenever you can. There is a chance, however, that you may not always enjoy the fruits of your labors. You should find time to relax with a few well-chosen friends, and forget about entertaining only those people that you feel obligated to.

Parenthood

You may need to modify your conventional outlook by seeking other people's opinions. Do not be too critical of your children. Always make time for them, and do not present them with logical arguments if they are upset. Give them a hug instead. Listen to their opinions, and you will avoid the generation gap.

THE MOON IN
AQUARIUS

VIRGOANS ARE PRACTICAL, AND OFTEN CONVENTIONAL. WITH AN AQUARIAN MOON YOU ARE LIKELY TO RESPOND WELL TO NEW, INVENTIVE, AND ORIGINAL IDEAS. IF YOU HAPPEN TO BE INTERESTED IN UNTRIED CONCEPTS, DO NOT DISMISS YOUR INTUITIONS.

Your Aquarian Moon and your Virgoan Sun give you an intriguing and perhaps even somewhat enigmatic personality.

Self-expression

You have a very independent streak, and will often react to situations and to the suggestions of other people in a very individual way. More than this, when it comes to helping other people, you are all kindness.

You have plenty of originality and probably a great deal of creative, artistic flair. Make sure that you have time to express this fully, as it will give you a great deal of satisfaction.

While your Virgoan Sun makes you practical and conventional, your Aquarian Moon attracts you to less conventional things. Beware of responding a little unpredictably at times; while surprising other people is great fun, unpredictability can sometimes be embarrassing.

Romance

Both Virgo and Aquarius are emotionally cool, and it may not be very easy for you to show your true feelings. However, your Aquarian Moon shines brightly for you, giving you a very romantic streak and making you a faithful lover once committed. It can also bestow a film-star glamour that is devastatingly attractive. However, like a magnet, you can distance yourself from what you attract, and may at times appear entirely out of reach. If you relax and allow your romantic side to take over, you will enjoy a very rewarding love and sex life.

Your well-being

The Aquarian body area covers the ankles. Be very careful, as they are vulnerable when you are exercising or involved in sports. The circulation is also Aquarius-ruled, so even if you enjoy bracing, cold weather, keep

The Moon in Aquarius

very warm. Your whole well-being may otherwise suffer, and you could feel uncomfortably stiff and aching.

You are less inclined to worry than many Virgoans, and the effect of worry on your health is not as bad as it can be for other Sun sign Virgoans.

Planning ahead

You are attracted to glamorous and expensive things, especially for your home and wardrobe. These will certainly eat into your finances and, while you are as practical as the next Virgoan, you could consider seeking professional financial advice.

Parenthood

Your Aquarian Moon gives you a modern outlook that your children will really appreciate. You will keep up with their ideas and should not suffer generation gap problems. You may, however, consciously need to express a little more emotional warmth from time to time.

THE MOON IN PISCES

VIRGO AND PISCES ARE POLAR OR OPPOSITE ZODIAC SIGNS, SO YOU WERE BORN UNDER A FULL MOON. RESTLESSNESS AND INNER DISCONTENT COULD BOTHER YOU. BE RATIONAL, AND DO NOT BE SWAYED BY NEGATIVE EMOTIONS.

We all commonly express certain attributes of our polar or opposite sign (the sign that is across the Zodiac circle from our Sun sign). For Virgoans, the polar sign is Pisces and, because the Sun was in that sign when you were born, the polarity is expressed in a particularly interesting way.

Self-expression

You will be very sensitive to other people's suggestions and actions, and could be more easily hurt than most Virgoans. The kindness of Virgo is powerfully emphasized in your personality; you instinctively know when help is needed, and will respond immediately.

Neither Virgo nor Pisces is basically very self-confident. You have great potential and, if there is something that you long to do or wish to study, you should give yourself the opportunity to do so. Try not to give up too quickly or easily, and develop your powers of concentration and persistence of effort.

Romance

You are among the more emotional of Virgoans, and this is good. Being practical, and not lacking in common sense, you are also able to respond to lovers in a tender, warm, and sensual way. You need to feel secure in emotional and sexual relationships; then you make a wonderful partner.

The worst Piscean fault is deceptiveness. Your Piscean Moon may also make you self-deceptive. If you remain level-headed, you will find a partner on whom you can rely.

Your well-being

The Piscean body area covers the feet, and you may have difficulty in obtaining comfortable shoes. Foot exercise sandals are very good for you, and far preferable to bare feet.

The Moon in Pisces

Your feet are particularly susceptible to blisters, cuts, and so on. Regular visits to the podiatrist are advisable.

Your Virgo and Pisces polarity increases your inclination to worry, which will, undoubtedly, affect your health. When worried, try to follow your Piscean intuition, be logical and, like most Virgoans, practical. Keep calm, perhaps by practicing a relaxation technique.

Planning ahead

You are generous and could give a great deal of money to charity. This is fine if you manage to balance the books. Do examine sob stories with a critical Virgoan eye. You have the tendency to be too soft-hearted. Do not lend money, and seek professional advice when you wish to invest.

Parenthood

You will be a kind and sympathetic parent, tending to spoil your children one moment but, perhaps, being over-critical the next. An awareness of this will help you to keep your attitude to your children in balance. Listen to their opinions and views, and you should not suffer too many problems with the generation gap.

SUN & MOON SIGNS

LIBRA

SEPTEMBER 23 – OCTOBER 23

INTRODUCING LIBRA

LIBRA, THE SIGN OF THE SCALES, IS THE SEVENTH SIGN OF THE ZODIAC. LIBRANS NEED HARMONY AND BALANCE IN THEIR LIVES. THE RULING PLANET OF THE SIGN IS VENUS, NAMED AFTER THE GODDESS OF LOVE – AND TO LIBRANS, LOVE IS ALL.

Peace is important to Librans, and they will sometimes try to obtain it at any price. Although they often have a reputation for laziness, it is generally undeserved. They usually have the motivation to work hard, but always make time to listen to others. Decision-making is hard for them as they always see both sides of a problem and tend to procrastinate.

Librans must be careful not to be overindulgent, since this may lead to weight gain that will spoil their natural good looks.

Traditional groupings

As you read through this book you will come across references to the elements and the qualities, and to positive and negative, or masculine and feminine signs.

The first of these groupings, that of the elements, comprises fire, earth, air, and water signs. The second, that of the qualities, divides the Zodiac into cardinal, fixed, and mutable signs. The final grouping is made up of positive and negative, or masculine and feminine signs. Each Zodiac sign is associated with a combination of components from these groupings, all of which contribute different characteristics to it.

Libran characteristics

Libra is a sign of the air element, and there is a certain light airiness to the Libran personality. People born under this sign are usually able to communicate with ease and are pleasantly sociable.

The sign is of the cardinal quality, which makes its subjects agreeable, outgoing, warm, and charming. It is a positive, masculine sign, and is therefore likely to incline you toward being extrovert. Venus is the sign's ruling planet, and Libran colors include pink, pale green, and different shades of blue.

The Zodiac Wheel

The relationship between each Zodiac sign and the traditional astrological groupings is made clear within the Zodiac wheel. As you read through this book you will also discover references to polar, or opposite signs, and these, too, can be easily worked out by referring to the wheel.

LIBRA
MYTHS & LEGENDS

THE ZODIAC, WHICH MAY HAVE ORIGINATED IN BABYLON AS LONG AS 2,500 YEARS AGO, IS A CIRCLE OF CONSTELLATIONS THROUGH WHICH THE SUN MOVES DURING THE COURSE OF A YEAR.

The constellation of Libra was celebrated in Babylon at least two thousand years before Christ, where it was connected to the myth of the last judgment and the weighing of souls. This is the earliest Libran association with scales. Later, the ancient Egyptians also weighed their harvest and assessed their taxes in autumn, at the time when the Babylonian judgment ceremony is believed to have taken place.

The Scorpion

In ancient times the claws of the Scorpion were recognized as occupying some of the area of the sky that is now set aside for Libra.

An ancient Babylonian name for Libra, ziba. anna, means the "horn" of a scorpion, which must actually be a reference to the creature's claws. Pictorially, these horns later developed into the scales of the balance that symbolizes Libra.

Weighing the soul

No myth is directly associated with Libra, but a single idea has been connected with the sign since at least ancient Egyptian times – that of a person's soul being weighed in the balance, after death.

The scene is shown in many illustrations in the Egyptian Book of the Dead. It features a man standing, often with his wife, beside the scales on which his heart is being weighed against a feather representing Truth. Anubis, the jackal-headed god of the dead, also known as Lord of the Mummy Wrappings, was believed to open up the roads to the afterlife for those who had died; the ancient Greeks associated him with their god, Hermes, the "Conductor of Souls." He often stands close to the scales, watching the judgment occurring. Thoth, the ibis-headed Egyptian moon-god, patron of science and literature, and of wisdom and

Judging the Dead

This scene from the Egyptian Book of the Dead, dating from 1100 B.C., shows Anubis, the jackal-headed god, and Thoth, the god of scribes, weighing a soul against Truth.

inventions, can also be seen nearby, meticulously noting down a faithful record of events.

The Bible

The conception of all the good in one's life being weighed against the sum of the evil, established by the ancient Egyptians, persisted into early Jewish culture. It is clearly reflected in the writings of what has come to be known as the Old Testament. In one passage from the Old Testament, the prophet Job asked that God "weigh him in the scales of justice," while Belshazzar was "weighed in the balance and found wanting."

Those people who are lucky enough to be born with the Sun in Libra are traditionally considered to have a particularly strong sense of justice and fairness.

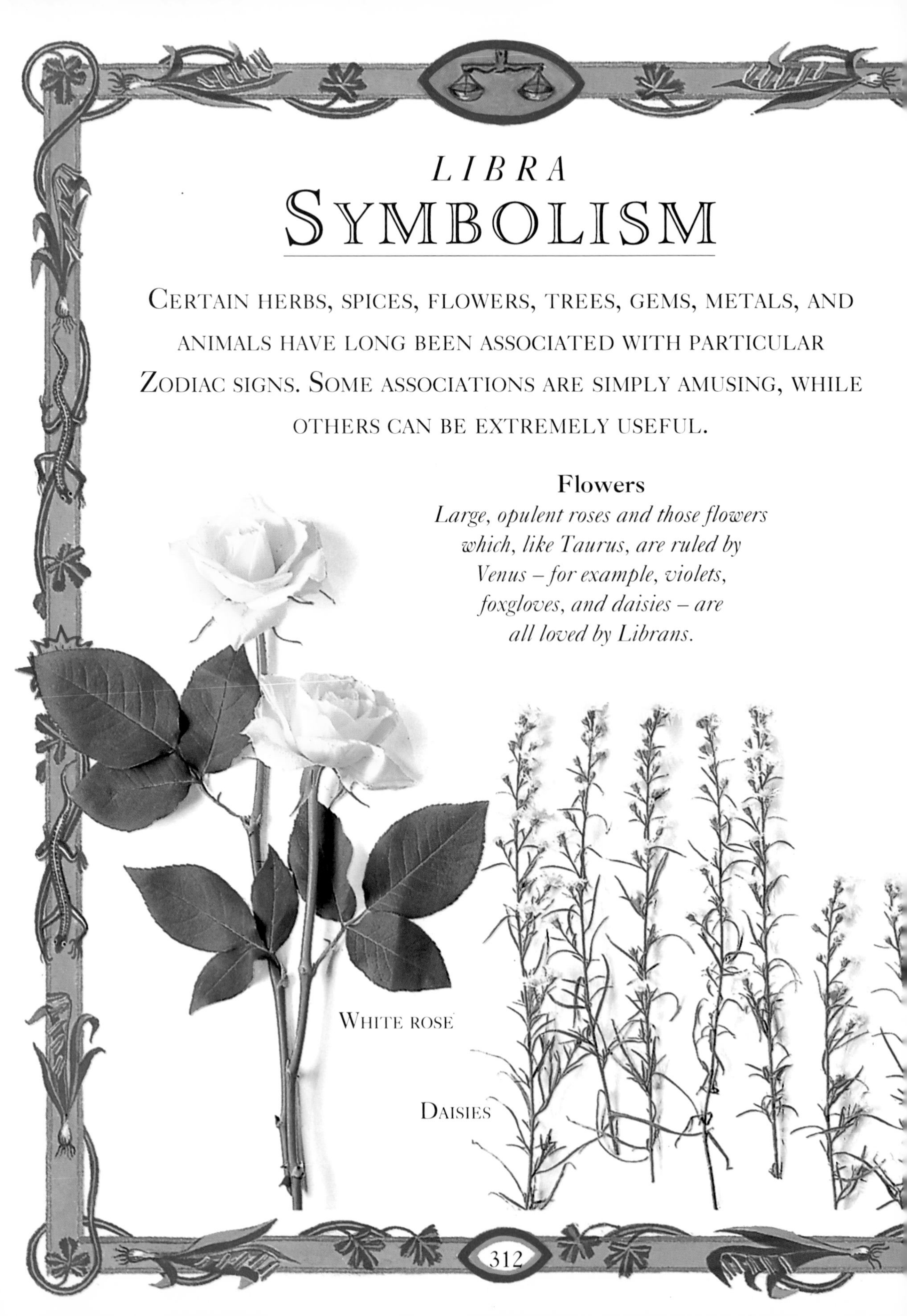

LIBRA
SYMBOLISM

CERTAIN HERBS, SPICES, FLOWERS, TREES, GEMS, METALS, AND ANIMALS HAVE LONG BEEN ASSOCIATED WITH PARTICULAR ZODIAC SIGNS. SOME ASSOCIATIONS ARE SIMPLY AMUSING, WHILE OTHERS CAN BE EXTREMELY USEFUL.

Flowers

Large, opulent roses and those flowers which, like Taurus, are ruled by Venus – for example, violets, foxgloves, and daisies – are all loved by Librans.

WHITE ROSE

DAISIES

Cypress

Trees

The ash, the cypress, all vines, and those trees governed by Taurus, which shares the same ruling planet as Libra, are Libran trees.

Sorrel

Herbs

Sorrel, which alleviates skin disorders, and figwort, which prevents blood clots, are all ruled by Libra.

Spices

No spices are particularly associated with Libra, but mace, and sometimes cloves and ginger, are generally popular among Librans.

Cloves

Ginger

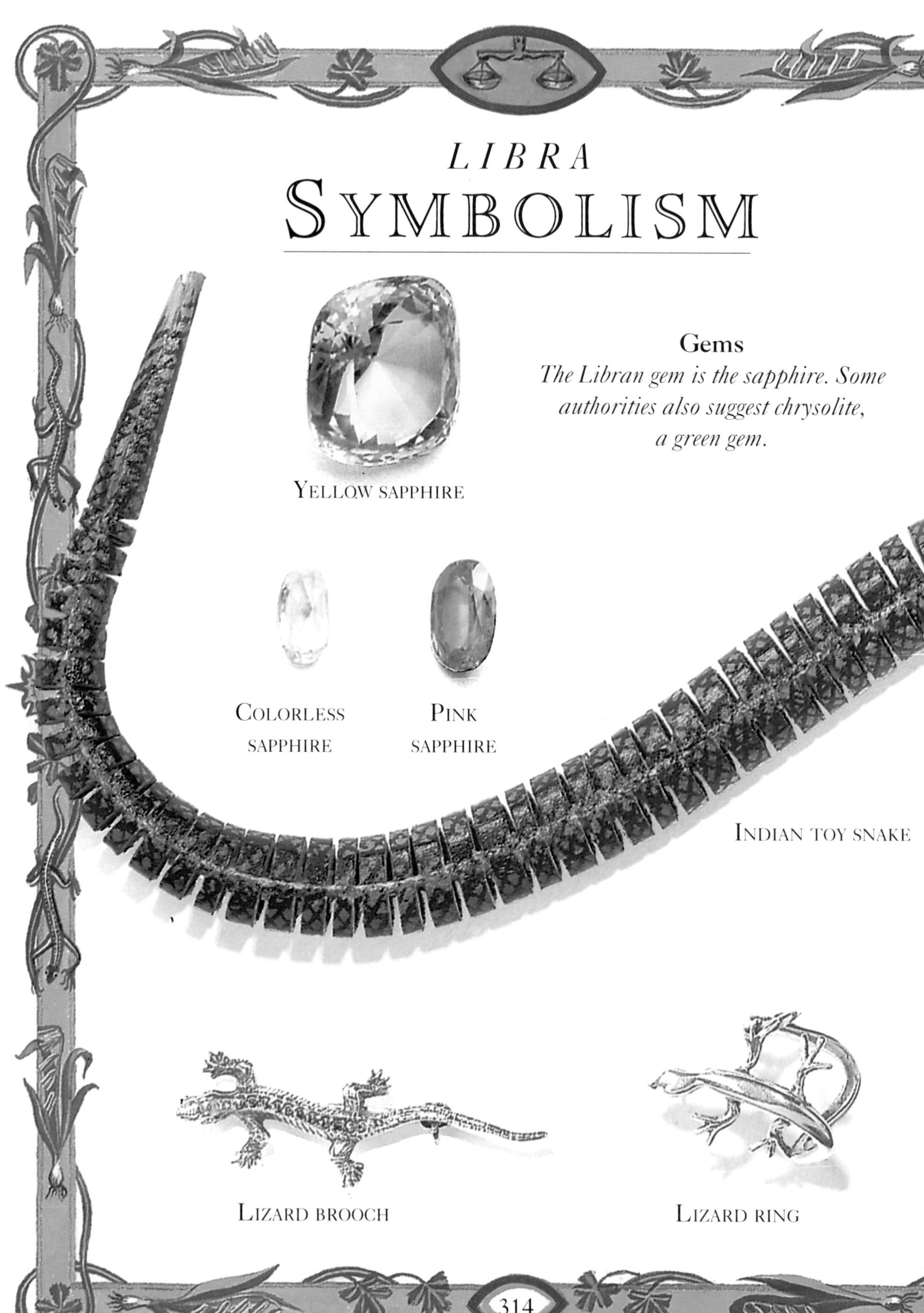

LIBRA SYMBOLISM

Gems

The Libran gem is the sapphire. Some authorities also suggest chrysolite, a green gem.

YELLOW SAPPHIRE

COLORLESS SAPPHIRE

PINK SAPPHIRE

INDIAN TOY SNAKE

LIZARD BROOCH

LIZARD RING

Metal

Copper is a Libran metal, associated, like Taurus, with Venus. Bronze, an alloy of copper and tin, is also sometimes associated with the sign.

Middle eastern copper coffee pot

Animals

Lizards and small reptiles are traditionally associated with Libra. Snakes and many small domestic animals, such as mice and hamsters, are also sometimes linked with the sign.

Silver snake brooch

LIBRA
PROFILE

THERE IS AN ATTRACTIVE SOFTNESS TO THE LIBRAN IMAGE. THE FEATURES MAY NOT BE VERY CLEAR-CUT. PEOPLE OF THIS SIGN ARE USUALLY WELL DRESSED IN THE CONTEXT OF THEIR PEER GROUP.

You might sometimes see Librans walking along, holding hands with their partners and looking affectionately at them, rather than at the road ahead. This invariably means that everything is right with their world. If, on the other hand, you see people of this sign slumping along the road, with their heads down and their hands deep in their pockets, you can assume that they lack love and affection. These signs of despondency usually mean that they are at a psychological low point.

The Libran face
Librans often appear gentle, and full of kindness and understanding.

The body

Provided you do what you can to increase your often rather slow metabolism, you will not lose your well-proportioned body and natural good looks, which contribute greatly to the enhancement of your charming personality. You may move gracefully, with a swinging gait, but are usually in no hurry. This explains your tendency to gain weight and your hesitancy in starting a diet.

The face

Libran men are inclined to have rather fine hair, and some of them are particularly prone to baldness. Your eyes are likely to show a capacity for kindness and understanding, and your nose is probably well proportioned in relation to the rest of your face. There is a tendency for the Libran chin to become less well defined with

The Libran stance

Librans often betray their uncertainty by shifting their weight from one foot to the other when in conversation.

increasing age and weight gain. You easily break into a gentle, sympathetic smile. Overall, the Libran expression often conveys a certain feyness. This usually has the effect of making the individual appear rather gentle.

Style

Librans generally have good taste in fashion. Pastel colors often suit both sexes. The women's image is rather pretty, with sexual allure, but not overt or vampish. An asymmetric line is sometimes favored, as are draped skirts. Rather light, delicate fabrics in pastel colors are often worn. These enhance the gentleness in the Libran image. Libran men, too, love to introduce a little romance into their clothes. They particularly like attractive, elaborately decorated shirts and unusual waistcoats. Hats are also very popular.

In general

The Libran stance can sometimes betray a degree of uncertainty. You may sometimes have a tendency to shift your weight from one foot to the other when you are speaking to someone. Similarly, when in conversation, you could sometimes hold your head first to one side, and then to the other. Bear in mind that people will not be slow in reading such body language.

In general, the gestures that you make tend to be quite slow, but they will always be meaningful and relatively uncomplicated.

LIBRA PERSONALITY

LIBRANS ARE BOTH KIND AND WARMLY AFFECTIONATE. THEY HAVE TIME FOR OTHER PEOPLE AND ARE NATURALLY GENEROUS. THEIR NEED TO RELATE TO OTHERS CAN, HOWEVER, SOMETIMES DRIVE THEM TO BUY FRIENDSHIP.

The Libran motivation might be summed up as a desire to keep life in balance and to relate in depth to another person.

Most Librans find loneliness almost intolerable and, until they are able to form a permanent relationship with someone, they are unlikely to be psychologically whole.

When you find yourself settled into a steady partnership, you will undergo a considerable blossoming of your Libran personality. It is, however, important for you to remember that a successful partnership is all about sharing. You must strive to keep the necessary balance and harmony that is typical of the Libran lifestyle.

At work

Librans are often lucky enough to possess the very pleasant ability to calm others and to help them unwind, giving the impression that time is no problem for them.

It is this tendency that has unfortunately given Librans in general a reputation for laziness. In fact, many of you are great achievers, who may well have reached top jobs in government, or perhaps the armed services. While Librans can sometimes be aggressive, they are also known to be peacemakers.

Your attitudes

Most Librans have the remarkably clever knack of seeing both sides of every problem. Because you understand your opponents' opinions, you may find it very difficult to draw final conclusions and come to constructive decisions. This is something that may cause you a variety of problems.

On the one hand, avoiding decisions can become so common for you that problems go away before they finally have to be faced. On the other hand, the same tendency can

Venus rules Libra

Venus, the Roman goddess of love, represents the ruling planet of both Libra and Taurus. The influence of Venus extends to art and fashion, and relates to the feminine side of a Libran's nature.

lead to immeasurable inconvenience to friends and family, who may never know quite where they stand, or what you actually plan to do and whether or not it will eventually be done.

The overall picture

While Librans are kind and do good things for others, it cannot be denied that they also enjoy receiving profuse thanks. Librans themselves are usually very forthcoming in this respect, so perhaps it is only natural that they expect the same reaction from other people. Some Zodiac types find it difficult to be even marginally gushing, but if a Libran merely receives a quiet "thank you" or, much worse, no thanks at all, resentfulness will soon set in.

LIBRA
ASPIRATIONS

YOU ARE A GREGARIOUS PERSON AND NEED COMPANY, SO WORKING IN AN OPEN-PLAN OFFICE WILL HOLD NO TERRORS. A POSITION OF AUTHORITY MAY NOT SUIT YOU; YOU COULD FIND IT TOO LONELY.

Agent
Librans have the ability to see both sides of a situation, and therefore make excellent agents in any area.

APPOINTMENT DIARY

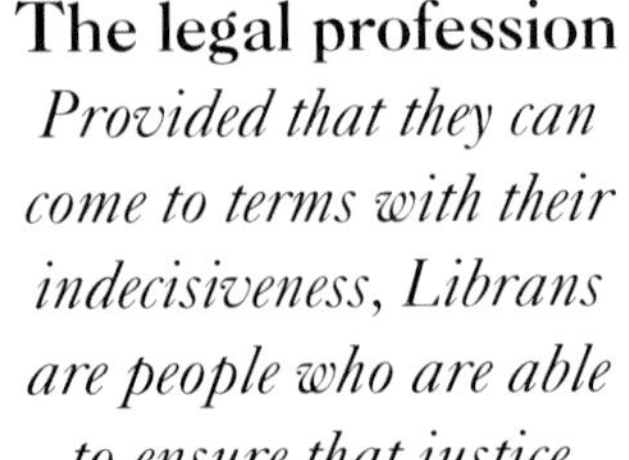

The legal profession
Provided that they can come to terms with their indecisiveness, Librans are people who are able to ensure that justice will be done.

JUDGE'S GAVEL AND BLOCK

Receptionist

Libran charm will be a considerable asset to any firm that decides to employ a person of this sign to greet its clients.

Receptionist's headphones

Makeup brushes and face powder

Diplomacy

Tact and diplomacy often come naturally to Librans. Their love of socializing helps make them natural diplomats.

The beauty trades

The Libran ruling planet, Venus, encourages Librans to make the most of their own, and other people's, looks.

Diplomat's leather case

LIBRA

HEALTH

IN ORDER FOR LIBRANS TO BE PHYSICALLY WELL, THEY NEED TO LIVE WELL-BALANCED LIVES. UPSETTING ARGUMENTS AND UNCOMFORTABLE LIVING CONDITIONS CANNOT BE TOLERATED AND MUST BE AVOIDED AT ALL COSTS.

The delicate Libran system will be thrown into disarray by almost any kind of imbalance. This will often result in both mental and physical exhaustion, leading to headaches.

Your diet

As a Sun sign Libran you may need to supplement your diet with natrum phosphate (Nat. Phos.), which reduces acidity in the stomach. It prevents and helps to dissolve gallstones, and sometimes soothes an inflamed throat.

Many Librans have a rather slow metabolism. This, coupled with a preference for rich and often sweet food, can often lead to weight gain. Regular exercise is the solution to this problem.

Red currants

Berry fruits such as red currants are strongly associated with Libra.

Taking care

The Libran body area covers the kidneys. Should a headache strike unexpectedly, and if nothing has upset you, it may be that you are suffering from a slight kidney disorder. Perhaps, as with any unexpected health problem, you would be wise to receive a medical checkup. The lumbar region of the back can be somewhat vulnerable, and people in this Sun sign group would be wise to invest in a back-rest chair if they expect to spend a lot of time sitting at an office desk.

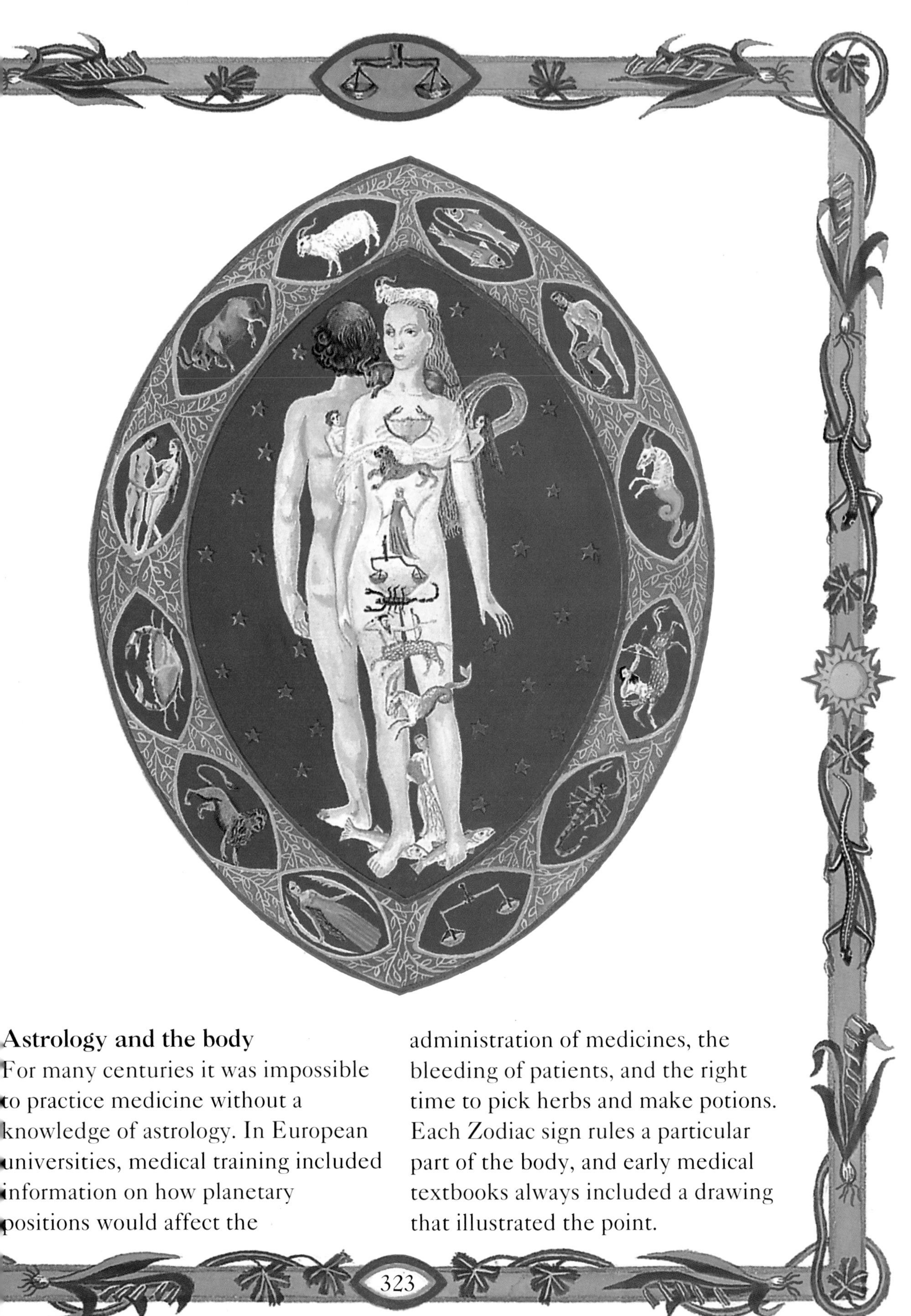

Astrology and the body

For many centuries it was impossible to practice medicine without a knowledge of astrology. In European universities, medical training included information on how planetary positions would affect the administration of medicines, the bleeding of patients, and the right time to pick herbs and make potions. Each Zodiac sign rules a particular part of the body, and early medical textbooks always included a drawing that illustrated the point.

LIBRA AT LEISURE

EACH OF THE SUN SIGNS TRADITIONALLY SUGGESTS SPARE-TIME ACTIVITIES, HOBBIES, AND VACATIONS. ALTHOUGH THESE ARE ONLY SUGGESTIONS, THEY OFTEN WORK OUT WELL, AND REFLECT LIBRAN INTERESTS.

Dressmaking

Librans who express their creativity through dressmaking may use their intuition to divine precisely the styles and colors that will be popular in the next season.

POSTAGE STAMPS

Travel

You will spend much time anticipating a month spent in Austria, Egypt, Burma, Japan, or even Tibet.

DRESSMAKING EQUIPMENT

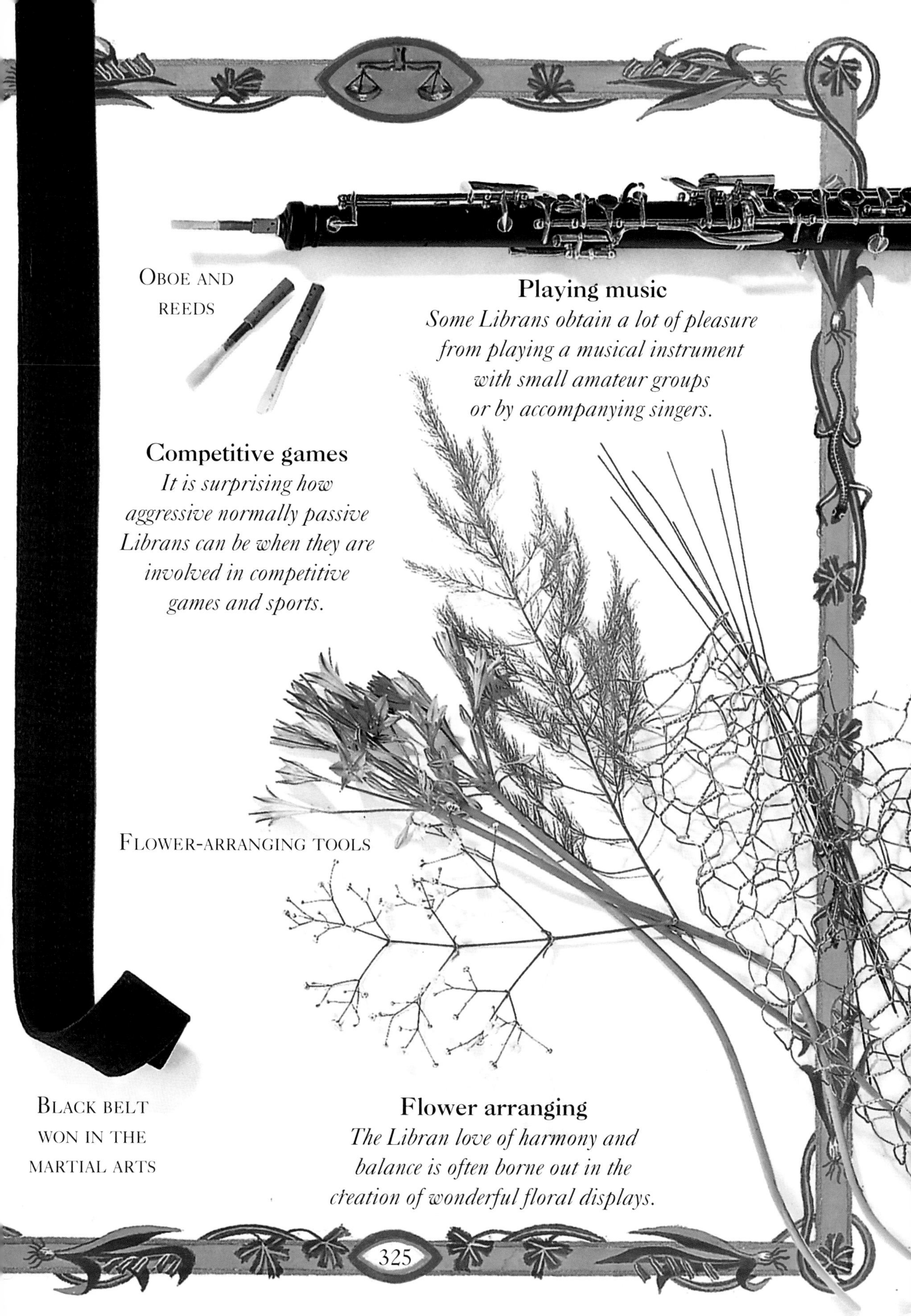

OBOE AND REEDS

Playing music

Some Librans obtain a lot of pleasure from playing a musical instrument with small amateur groups or by accompanying singers.

Competitive games

It is surprising how aggressive normally passive Librans can be when they are involved in competitive games and sports.

FLOWER-ARRANGING TOOLS

BLACK BELT WON IN THE MARTIAL ARTS

Flower arranging

The Libran love of harmony and balance is often borne out in the creation of wonderful floral displays.

LIBRA IN LOVE

FOR LIBRANS, LIFE IS AT ITS MOST BEAUTIFUL WHEN THEY FALL IN LOVE. THEY SHOULD, HOWEVER, ALWAYS REMEMBER TO STOP AND CONSIDER WHETHER THEY ARE IN LOVE WITH THEIR LOVER, OR WITH LOVE ITSELF.

The basic Libran motivation is to relate to another human being. Sharing, keeping life in balance, and living a harmonious life are all essential to you. More so than any other Zodiac type, a Libran who is alone will probably find life difficult to cope with and incomplete.

Although it might seem that a Libran's very indecisive nature could prevent commitment, this is in fact not usually the case. Librans are so eager to share and to relate that they often rush prematurely into a permanent relationship or marriage. Very often, of course, all is well, but if things go wrong, the resulting disruption to their lives can be far worse than it would be for people of any of the other Sun signs.

While in reality you are greatly in need of peace and harmony, many of you will try to pick fights with your partner just because it is so nice to kiss and make up afterward. Try not to take this too far, since such an attitude could be intensely wearing for your partners.

As a lover

It is the warmth and expression of really sincere affection that makes life with a Libran worthwhile.

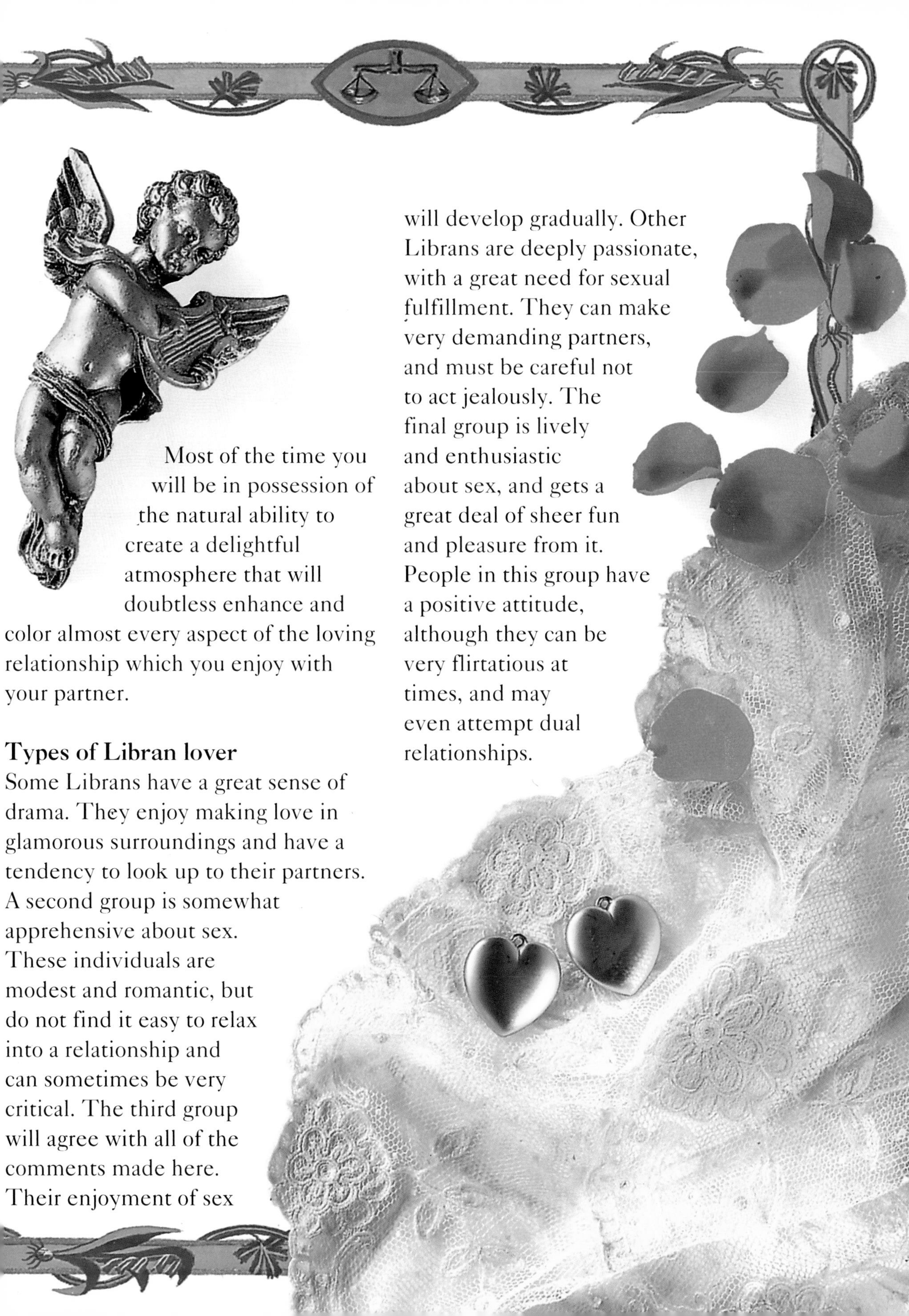

Most of the time you will be in possession of the natural ability to create a delightful atmosphere that will doubtless enhance and color almost every aspect of the loving relationship which you enjoy with your partner.

Types of Libran lover

Some Librans have a great sense of drama. They enjoy making love in glamorous surroundings and have a tendency to look up to their partners. A second group is somewhat apprehensive about sex. These individuals are modest and romantic, but do not find it easy to relax into a relationship and can sometimes be very critical. The third group will agree with all of the comments made here. Their enjoyment of sex will develop gradually. Other Librans are deeply passionate, with a great need for sexual fulfillment. They can make very demanding partners, and must be careful not to act jealously. The final group is lively and enthusiastic about sex, and gets a great deal of sheer fun and pleasure from it. People in this group have a positive attitude, although they can be very flirtatious at times, and may even attempt dual relationships.

LIBRA AT HOME

LIBRAN ROOMS ARE USUALLY HANDSOME, AND ENHANCED BY FULL, HEAVY CURTAINS AND HANGINGS, PERHAPS IN SHADES OF WARM PINK AND PALE BLUE. COMFORT IS A KEYNOTE, AND IT IS BORNE OUT BY HUGE, WELCOMING CHAIRS.

Most Librans are very adaptable people who could probably set up a happy home in just about any kind of environment. The one place that is unlikely to appeal to them is a run-down district with very obvious signs of poverty and ugliness. Librans may also experience a great deal of unhappiness if they end up living miles from their nearest neighbors. No matter how happy they may be with their partners, loneliness could be a problem.

Elegant portraits
You may choose to display some elegantly framed antique photographs

Furniture

Many Librans tend to favor traditional styles of furniture, and if some sweeping, well-balanced curves are integrated into the design, so much the better. Harsh, angular designs are not popular, since furniture like this often looks, and may even be, less than comfortable. There is no lack of elegance in the overall appearance of the home, or in individual pieces. For instance, fine legs will support occasional tables, as opposed to anything too heavy or solid. Few Librans like housework, but their sense of pride in their homes encourages them to get on with it.

Soft furnishings

Libra is a sign that positively wallows in soft furnishings. Cushions abound – they may even have been made by yourself. Curtains and drapes are of really lavish, rich velvet or lovely, printed floral satin with huge designs of roses. Austrian blinds are popular, and rugs will appear to be ankle deep. The colors are usually pastel, echoing those of Venus, the Libran ruling planet. A rich red or dark blue often makes an attractive contrast to these pale colors, and ensures that the overall effect is not too insipid.

Decorative objects

Librans are romantic, so objects that hint at love, for example heart-shaped pictures of your children, or of wedding groups, may be prominently displayed. The romantic theme often extends to your choice of paintings, and may be reflected in their soft colors or subject matter.

The emphasis that you will want to place upon stylish, cultured living will also be reflected in your paintings. A typical Libran choice might be a print of one of Gainsborough's portraits of beautiful women, an elegant painting of some flowers, or a set of prints depicting rare and exotic birds. If you actually collect prints or pictures, they will probably focus on fashion or on trades and professions from the past. A great many Librans like to collect china or porcelain figures. These need not necessarily be antiques; they could just as easily be very attractive, but relatively inexpensive, graceful modern pieces. Even if you are not directly creative (and many Librans are) you are likely to have a great love of music and a highly developed appreciation of the arts. A musical instrument, most probably of the woodwind kind, may therefore provide the focal point of a decorative scheme in your home, even if you decide to simply leave it lying around until you can persuade someone else to play it.

Cushions and curtains

The Libran home will contain plenty of cushions and curtains made from sensuous velvets and satins.

THE MOON *AND* YOU

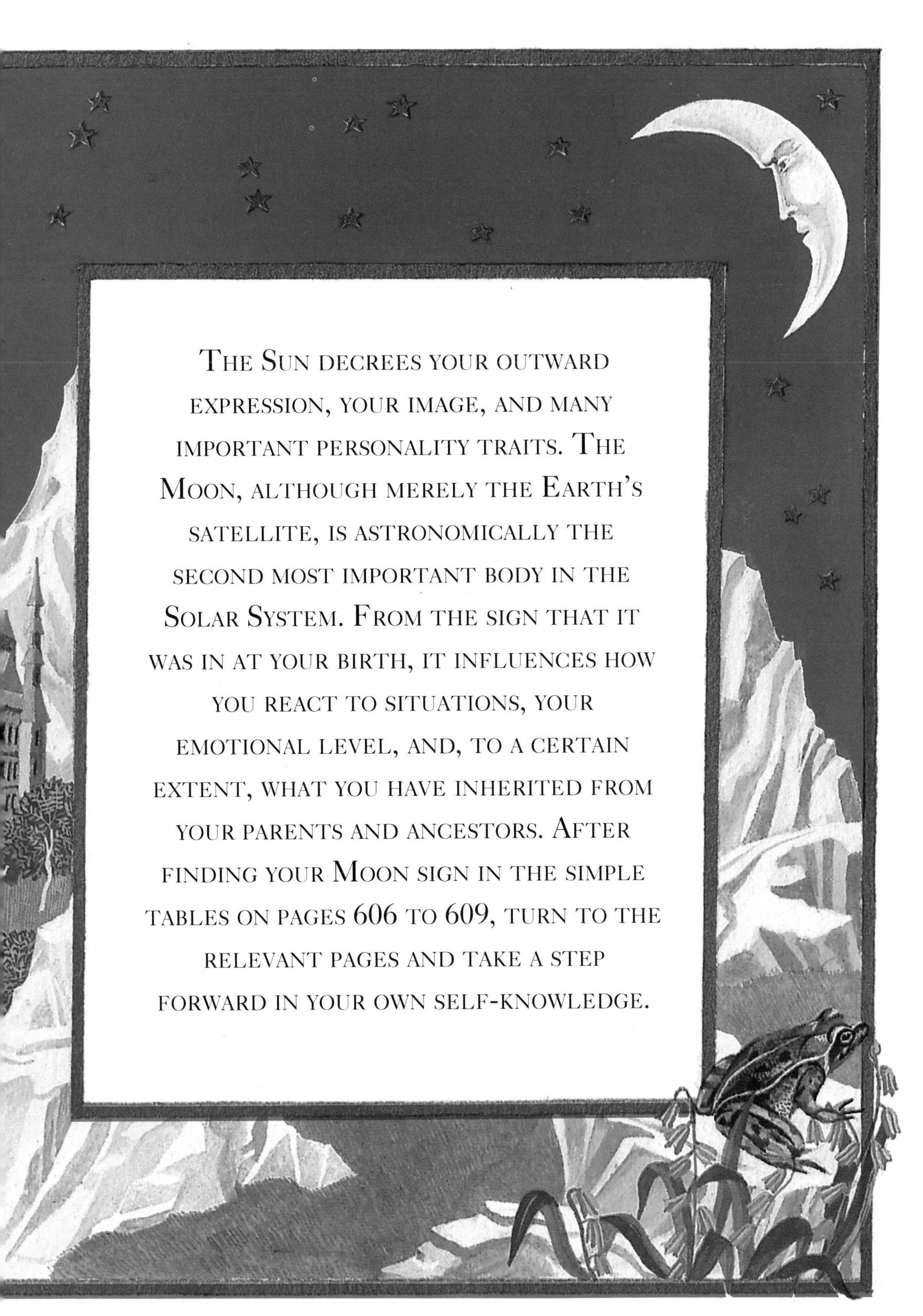

The Sun decrees your outward expression, your image, and many important personality traits. The Moon, although merely the Earth's satellite, is astronomically the second most important body in the Solar System. From the sign that it was in at your birth, it influences how you react to situations, your emotional level, and, to a certain extent, what you have inherited from your parents and ancestors. After finding your Moon sign in the simple tables on pages 606 to 609, turn to the relevant pages and take a step forward in your own self-knowledge.

THE MOON IN ARIES

LIBRA AND ARIES ARE POLAR ZODIAC SIGNS, SO YOU WERE BORN UNDER A FULL MOON. RESTLESSNESS CAN SOMETIMES BE A PROBLEM FOR YOU. WHEN YOU MEET WITH A CHALLENGE, ALLOW YOUR ARIEN MOON TO STIR YOU TO ACTION.

Each of us, in one way or another, tends to express attributes of our polar sign (the opposite sign across the Zodiac circle from our Sun sign). For Librans, this is Aries, and since the Moon was in Aries when you were born, this "polarity" is emphasized in a very interesting way.

Self-expression

The typical indecisiveness of Libra is mitigated by your Arien Moon. Provided that you consciously control the tendency to act too quickly, your first reactions will often be correct. Therefore do not change your mind, however badly you are tempted.

Romance

Your Arien Moon bestows a wealth of positive emotion, which you no doubt express freely and passionately toward your partner. You are a romantic Libran, and your tendency to rush into a relationship is heightened by your impulsive Moon.

You make a very rewarding partner, provided that you control selfishness, which is the worst Arien fault.

Your well-being

The fact that Libra and Aries are polar signs means that the relationship between the head (Aries) and the kidneys (Libra) is strongly emphasized. There are therefore two reasons why you may sometimes suffer from headaches. One may be psychologically based, while the other may be due to a mild kidney problem.

Aries is also prone to minor accidents, particularly cuts and burns. As a result you would be extremely wise to wear protective clothing whenever it is required.

Planning ahead

You have a wonderfully enterprising spirit, and provided that you do not allow your natural energy and

The Moon in Aries

enthusiasm to flag, you have what it takes to run a successful "sideline" business in addition to your main career. You will find such an interest extremely rewarding.

While you will be anxious to make your money work for you, make sure that you control impulsiveness when investing. You could, at times, get a little carried away. Remember, too, that it is not a good idea for you to put all your eggs in one basket just because of a burst of enthusiasm.

Parenthood

You respond positively and well to your children. You must, however, try very hard to be faithful to any decisions or opinions that you express. Otherwise they will be uncertain where they stand with you.

Your Arien Moon gives you the happy ability to tune into your children's ideas and interests. If you express its lively qualities toward them, you will avoid problems with the generation gap.

THE MOON IN TAURUS

LIBRA AND TAURUS ARE RULED BY THE PLANET VENUS, SO THERE IS A NATURAL SYMPATHY BETWEEN THEM. YOU LOVE COMFORT AND LUXURY, AND SHOULD USE YOUR INTUITIVE BUSINESS SENSE TO PAY FOR THEM.

You have the ability to take life as it comes and to deal easily with worries, tension, and stress, giving others the impression that you are totally laid back. In many respects, you probably are. You certainly do not lack common sense, you pace yourself well, and you are less likely to get agitated than almost any Sun and Moon combination.

Self-expression

You may consciously have to nudge yourself when a swift answer or an immediate reaction is necessary. You much prefer to work deliberately through a problem, approaching it in a step-by-step fashion.

A slight problem is that while your Libran Sun encourages you to be fond of achieving peace at any price, your Taurean Moon inclines you to a predictable routine. When combined, the two influences may manage to edge you into a rut.

Romance

You are a very romantic, emotional Libran, and your Taurean Moon adds a warm sensuality and underlying passion to your personality that should be beautifully expressed toward your partners. You do, however, need a secure relationship; if you do not know where you stand with your partner you will not function well.

The worst Taurean fault is possessiveness. If this is combined with a Libran tendency to be slightly resentful, it could sometimes mar this vital area of your life. Let your Libran qualities give your partner the chance to breathe freely, and you will achieve a very rewarding life together.

Your well-being

The Taurean body area is the throat. With the onset of a cold, you could lose your voice and will certainly get a sore throat. A worse problem may be a slow metabolism and a love of rich

The Moon in Taurus

food. Try to regulate your eating habits and to discover some form of exercise that you enjoy.

Planning ahead

You should have excellent intuition where money is concerned, and will probably be able to watch the figures in your bank book grow steadily and satisfactorily. However, the luxuries that you enjoy so much will be expensive. Go all out for a regular pay check, and invest when you can. Use your great intuition in these matters.

Parenthood

Do not let Libran indecision and Taurean possessiveness encroach on your relationship with your children. You will work hard for them, but you could be rather conservative in your attitude to their opinions and concerns. Make a conscious effort to understand their problems and you will avoid the generation gap. You will certainly give your children a good, secure background and will be kind and thoughtful. You must, however, remember to have fun, too.

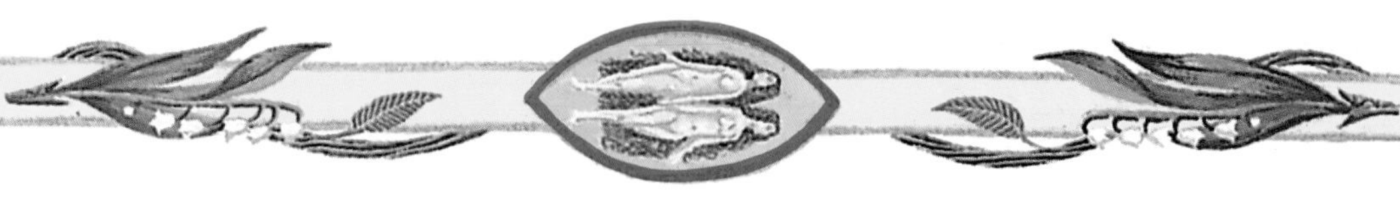

THE MOON IN GEMINI

BOTH LIBRA AND GEMINI ARE AIR SIGNS, SO IN ADDITION TO BEING SYMPATHETIC AND CHARMING, YOU ARE A GOOD COMMUNICATOR. BE CAREFUL, HOWEVER, THAT YOU DO NOT SUPPRESS YOUR DEEPER EMOTIONS.

The air element forms a large part of your personality. You have a lightness about you; a certain breezy but logical approach to problems. When challenged, you will always have flip, off-the-cuff verbal responses on hand.

Self-expression

You find conversation and social intercourse even more rewarding and entertaining than most Sun sign Librans and may well make a real hobby of entertaining your friends.

To prevent Geminian restlessness, try to develop a compelling and rewarding interest. Take care that you do not simply glide over the surface of important problems because you do not wish to get too involved.

Romance

Your love of romance will be very well expressed verbally, and to a certain extent you need a high level of friendship within an emotional relationship. While you are as romantic as any Libran, you may not be able to allow your deepest feelings to flow as freely as would be ideal.

Aim for partners who will be intellectually challenging to live with, so that your extremely lively mind will be kept active.

Your well-being

The Geminian body area covers the arms and hands, and yours may be somewhat vulnerable to accidents. The Geminian organ is the lungs, and anyone with this sign emphasized should try not to smoke.

Usually, Moon sign Geminians tend to be restless, but you should suffer less than most in this respect because of your Libran Sun. You may well enjoy exercise more than most Sun sign Librans, and this could take the form of tennis, badminton, or some other fast game. Because you

The Moon in Gemini

probably have a higher metabolic rate than many Librans, and may not have the typical taste for sweet food, you are less likely to incur excessive weight gain.

Planning ahead

As far as coping with money is concerned, you may not be terribly practical. You love luxury and are generous, but money could very easily burn a hole in your pocket, and you may be attracted to get-rich-quick schemes. Take professional financial advice in this area, and make sure that you never lay out more money than you can afford to lose.

Parenthood

You have a modern outlook, of which your children will no doubt thoroughly approve. Keeping up with their opinions and concerns will therefore be no problem for you. Provided you are firm and decisive, so that your children know where they stand, you will have no problems with the generation gap.

THE MOON IN CANCER

YOU ARE VERY GOOD AT LISTENING TO PEOPLE, BUT COULD THROW YOUR SYSTEM OUT OF BALANCE BY TAKING ON OTHERS' BURDENS. WATCH OUT FOR STRESS, AND BE AWARE THAT YOU MAY BENEFIT FROM PHYSICAL EXERCISE.

Both Libra and Cancer are of the cardinal quality, which means that you have the ability to sympathize and empathize with others, and will give of yourself to help and comfort them. Your instinct is to protect and care for your family and friends, and you do more than your fair share to help people feel good. Do not burn yourself out, emotionally or intellectually.

Self-expression
In spite of having a great deal of inner strength, you can be very easily hurt. Although you can be extremely kind, you can sometimes express yourself rather sharply, and say things that insult others. Be aware of this. It would be a pity to let such a negative trait mar your finer qualities.

You are probably very prone to worry – far more, in fact, than most Librans. You do, however, have very powerful instincts, and can use them to counter this problem. If you feel that you should take a certain line of action, go ahead and do so.

Romance
You are a wonderfully romantic and sensual lover, and should enjoy a rich and fulfilling sex life. Try, however, not to be overprotective of your partners. You may well create a rather claustrophobic atmosphere, which some people will find hard to cope with. Whether you are a man or a woman, you may occasionally tend to "mother" your partners.

Your well-being
The Cancerian body area covers the chest and breasts. Although there is no connection between this sign and the disease of the same name, regular checkups are always a good idea.

The Cancerian tendency to worry may have a negative effect on your health. Your food could tend to

The Moon in Cancer

disagree with you when you are worried. If you can keep this negative emotion under control, your digestion will be far less likely to suffer.

Planning ahead

Like all people of your Sun sign, you like luxury and creature comforts, but you are less extravagant than many Librans and have a natural instinct to be careful with money. You also have a shrewd business sense that will work well for you whether you have your own business or have merely collected a little spare money that you want to invest.

Parenthood

You make a wonderfully caring parent and will enjoy bringing up your children, although their natural exuberance and energy may tend to deflate you at times.

If you make a conscious effort to be decisive, and do your best to avoid sentimentality or dwelling on the past, you will have few problems with the generation gap. You must try not to get too upset when your children leave home to build their own lives. Rather than moping, take the opportunity to become involved in some new interests.

THE MOON IN LEO

YOU LIKE EVERYTHING THAT IS EXPENSIVE. YOU ARE ALSO WARM, SYMPATHETIC, BIG-HEARTED, AND GENEROUS, BUT IF YOU ACT ON YOUR IMAGINATIVE IDEAS WITHOUT SERIOUSLY COUNTING THE COST, YOU COULD GET INTO TROUBLE.

The combination of Libra and Leo is a good one. It makes your outlook very positive and optimistic. Much more so than many of your Sun sign compatriots, you will "think big" and be magnanimous.

Self-expression

Anyone with an emphasis on Leo has creative potential and, while this is not always expressed through the fine arts, it is nevertheless present. It is important to your sense of inner fulfillment that some form of creativity play a part in your life.

You are an excellent organizer and can readily take over in a crisis. You should enjoy work that gives you the chance to show off a little and, if Libran diplomacy is combined with Leo warmth, you can probably cope well with people and their problems.

Your Leo Moon gives you a sense of drama, but be careful not to overstep the mark. Do not make a dramatic scene over something trivial that displeases or upsets you. Calm authority is more effective.

Romance

You have a wealth of positive emotion to express toward your partners, and you want to feel proud of them.

Beware of the tendency to fall in love with love. You can be very easily hurt and, when you are, you will retire to a private lair to lick your wounds.

Your well-being

The Leo body area covers the spine and back. You must therefore make sure that you always sit correctly. A support chair is advisable for desk workers, and back-strengthening exercises are good for anyone with this emphasis.

The Leo organ is the heart, and it must be kept well toned. Therefore take regular exercise; dancing is excellent if you hate the thought of

The Moon in Leo

sports or health clubs.

Both Libra and Leo like to live the good life. This all too often means lots of rich food and, in turn, a weight problem. Try to ration the sauces and elaborate desserts.

Planning ahead

You are more than likely to be both very generous and very extravagant. It should therefore come as no surprise for you to realize that you will consequently need to earn a lot of money in order to support such habits. Quality is also important to you, so at least the things that you buy will last a long time. You could tend to over invest at times, and you may benefit from professional advice.

Parenthood

You will probably be an enthusiastic and very encouraging parent, and will be constantly delighted with your children's efforts. Spurred on by your encouragement, they will want to do even more to please you.

Be careful that you do not to change your mind too often, once you have told your children something. It is extremely important for them to know where they stand with you.

THE MOON IN VIRGO

YOUR MOON SIGN CAN CAUSE YOU TO BE MORE SPONTANEOUSLY AND HARSHLY CRITICAL OF OTHERS THAN YOU MAY REALIZE. WHILE IT MAKES YOU PRACTICAL, IT CAN ALSO MAR SOME FINE LIBRAN QUALITIES.

You may express your Libran loving-kindness very well, but you will, under some circumstances, also respond in a very critical manner. Perhaps you should try to be a little more tactful and diplomatic.

Self-expression

Your Virgoan Moon certainly gives you a lot more energy than many Sun sign Librans, and you are unlikely to waste much time.

Your initial reaction to a difficult situation may be to worry about it. Very soon, however, your attitude will take a turn toward being much more relaxed and philosophical.

You can use your Virgoan Moon to help you overcome Libran indecision. You could, for instance, analyze problems by making comprehensive lists of their positive and negative aspects, and then considering them in as detached, logical, and unemotional fashion as you are able.

Romance

Although you will certainly work very hard for your partners, and give them excellent backup, you may not find it easy to unlock your emotions and really relax. Although you are as romantic as anyone of your Sun sign, it may not be easy for you to enjoy love and sex wholeheartedly. Be very careful not to overcriticize your partner or to nag.

Your well-being

The Virgoan body area is the stomach, and it is possible that this reacts very quickly to the least worry or concern. You probably need a high-fiber diet.

Many people with this combination of signs have a fast metabolism; in these cases the tendency to put on weight is minimized. If you do move rather slowly, be careful not to eat too much heavy food. Conversely, if you are working very hard, try to make sure that you have a well-balanced

The Moon in Virgo

diet, and do not eat too much junk food. Aim for a fairly light diet that contains salads and fresh fruit.

Like many people with a Virgoan emphasis, you may be a vegetarian. If this is the case, make certain that your vitamin intake is adequate.

Planning ahead

You love your Libran luxuries, but will not waste money and will generally have enough for your needs. Making investments could, however, be rather boring for you, so keep them simple and take professional advice if you wish to invest a large sum of cash.

Parenthood

As a parent you are kind and generous, but you must watch a tendency to sometimes speak to your children rather harshly.

You are a good communicator and find it easy to get your ideas across. Listen to your children, and you will avoid generation gap problems.

THE MOON IN LIBRA

BOTH THE SUN AND THE MOON WERE IN LIBRA AT THE TIME OF YOUR BIRTH, AND YOU WERE THEREFORE BORN UNDER A NEW MOON. YOU HAVE MANY LIBRAN CHARACTERISTICS AND RESPOND TO MOST SITUATIONS IN A BALANCED AND HARMONIOUS WAY.

Should you read a list of the characteristics of your Libran Sun sign, you will probably realize that a great many of them apply to you. On average, out of a list of around 20 personality traits attributed to a sign, most people accept 11 or 12. For you the average will be much higher, since both the Sun and the Moon were in Libra when you were born.

Self-expression
You need to lead a well-balanced, harmonious life, and find quarrels very upsetting.

You always respond to situations by first considering the other people involved, and never give priority to your own considerations or opinions. This can make you very indecisive and, at times, you may well avoid a commitment simply by mulling over a situation for so long that a decision becomes unnecessary. You are very diplomatic, and respond kindly and affectionately to people around you. They will love you for your natural charm and delightful personality.

Romance
Your need to relate to another person is instinctive and runs very deep. You will be psychologically whole only when settled in a permanent relationship or marriage. It is in this area that Libran indecision can totally desert you, and you can very easily rush prematurely into a relationship just because you feel that you need one badly. A degree of objectivity could well save a lot of heartache.

Your well-being
Everything that has been said about Libran health on pages 322 – 323 will probably apply to you. You must keep your whole system balanced with steady exercise, and should refrain from overindulgence in food or drink. Your thoughts and emotions must

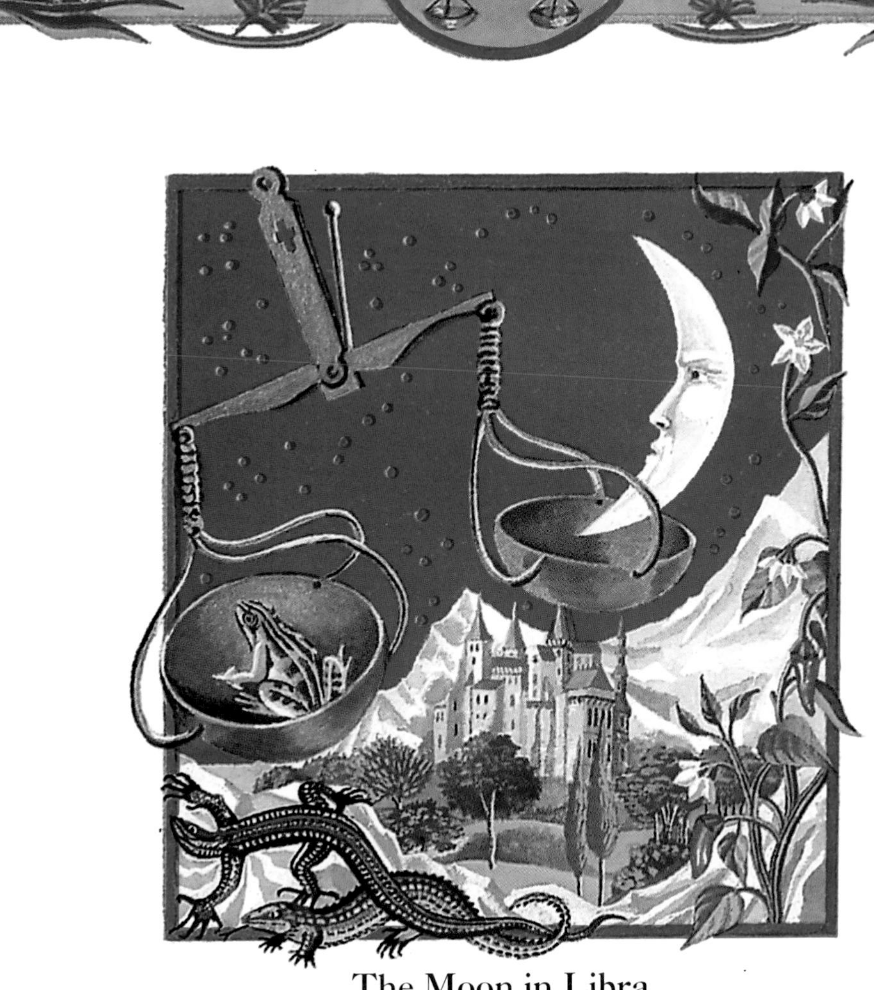

The Moon in Libra

remain at one, and you should try to avoid arguments. Learn to have your say calmly and effectively.

Planning ahead

Your creature comforts are important to you, and you will spend a lot of money on them.

You are inclined to be naturally generous and may not be terribly practical when it comes to handling money. You will probably do well to consult a professional adviser if you have money to invest.

Parenthood

You will enjoy a warm, affectionate rapport with your children and will be very kind to them. Force yourself to be decisive, and do not spoil your children for the sake of peace and quiet. They need a constructive framework and fair discipline. If you make sure that your children know where they stand with you, you will be an excellent parent.

As long as you remain interested in your children's ideas and concerns, you will bridge the generation gap.

THE MOON IN SCORPIO

YOU RESPOND TO MOST SITUATIONS WITH GREATER EMOTIONAL FERVOR AND INTENSITY THAN MANY LIBRANS, AND YOU HAVE IT IN YOU TO TAKE STRONG, DECISIVE ACTION. DO NOT SUPPRESS THIS QUALITY; LISTEN TO YOUR INTUITION.

Your Scorpio Moon gives you more determination and a stronger sense of purpose than many Sun sign Librans. You have a powerfully inquiring mind and, when challenged, strong forces immediately come into play in order to help you combat opposition.

Self-expression

Your opponents will get as good, or better, as they give, but it is important that you do not later backtrack and overapologize to them. This can upset the status quo, and lead to disruption and even quarrels, which your Libran Sun sign positively hates.

You must also aim to be emotionally involved in your work. An "ordinary" job, or drifting from one job to the next in an aimless fashion, will not do at all. Go all out for what you want to do, and do not let Libran hesitancy or indecision bog you down. You have powerful reserves of emotional energy and the ability to express them very positively through your chosen career or some other compelling interest.

Romance

You will be a demanding partner, but one who contributes greatly to a relationship. Like all Librans, you are a romantic, but you are far more passionate and highly sexed than many people of your Sun sign.

The worst Scorpio fault is jealousy. Be very careful, as you could become a victim of this very negative emotional expression.

Your well-being

The Scorpio body area is the genitals, and both men and women should pay attention to the health of that area.

You may have a tendency to bottle up your problems. When worried, make sure that you unburden yourself to a sympathetic friend.

The Moon in Scorpio

Planning ahead

Your Scorpio Moon is beneficial to you when it comes to dealing with money. It is likely to make you a shrewd and clever investor.

Anyone with a strong Scorpio influence will, however, want to both get a lot out of life and put a lot into it. This usually means resorting to heavy spending. Therefore look for savings schemes that make your money grow and work for you. You are clever enough not to make many mistakes, even if you do not take professional advice, but you may well need to curb extravagance.

Parenthood

You will have strong views about bringing up your children, but your more placid, Libran qualities could persuade you to spoil them.

Make sure that you keep up with your children's opinions and concerns. Otherwise you may encounter problems with the generation gap.

THE MOON IN SAGITTARIUS

YOU ARE EASYGOING AND HAVE MUCH INTELLECTUAL POTENTIAL. TO MAKE IT WORK FOR YOU, YOU SHOULD KEEP MOVING, BOTH PHYSICALLY AND MENTALLY. DO NOT IMMEDIATELY BRUSH ASIDE OTHER PEOPLE'S SUGGESTIONS.

The two elements of your Sun and Moon signs, air and fire, respectively, will work to your benefit. You will always have a very positive and philosophical outlook on life, and will not, on the whole, be plagued by worry or tension.

Self-expression

You like to be challenged and, upon encountering difficult situations or problems, you are always optimistic about their outcome. Your Moon sign gives you a very natural, instinctive optimism that harmonizes extremely well with your Libran qualities, but be careful not to be too laid back.

You may have a natural flair for study and could actually need this particular kind of challenge.

Romance

You have very lively and fiery emotions, and are capable of a marvelously exuberant enjoyment of love and sex. You may not always take this sphere of your life very seriously and, unlike many people of your Sun sign, you will have a strong need for independence within a relationship. As a result, you will be far less likely to rush into a commitment, in spite of all your buoyant enthusiasm. You also have something of a roving eye, and should remember that this is not necessarily a very good thing, especially in relation to love.

Your well-being

The Sagittarian body areas are the hips and thighs, and women with this sign emphasized may put on weight easily in these areas. You need more exercise than most Librans, and will perhaps enjoy the challenge of keeping fit. Maintain a steady exercise routine.

The Sagittarian organ is the liver, and anyone with a Libra and Sagittarius combination will enjoy

The Moon in Sagittarius

their food. Therefore be careful, since you are no doubt very prone to overeating and hangovers.

Planning ahead

Your Sagittarian Moon gives you a powerful gambling instinct, so beware of casinos and racetracks.

You may also be very attracted to investments that make promises of high returns on your capital. Control your enthusiasm, or you could well lose out. The same applies when a get-rich-quick scheme is put to you. Develop skepticism and always seek professional advice.

You are very generous, but should remember that it is better to give someone a few dollars than to lend them a lot, since the chances are that you will not see your money again.

Parenthood

Your Sagittarian Moon will make it easy for you to encourage your children in all their interests and studies. You will enjoy their company, and there will be an element of fun in your relationship. You will not find it difficult to keep up with your children's views and opinions, and will thus avoid the generation gap.

THE MOON IN CAPRICORN

YOU HAVE AN INNER DESIRE TO REACH THE TOP, BOTH SOCIALLY AND IN YOUR CAREER. TRY NOT TO SHOW OFF. ALLOW YOUR PRACTICAL, EARTHY MOON SIGN INSTINCTS TO STEADY YOU AND KEEP YOUR PERSONALITY IN BALANCE.

Both Libra and Capricorn are of the cardinal quality and, as a result, you may use your energies to encourage others. You will respond practically to their problems, and will cope extremely well in emergencies.

Self-expression

You may take life more seriously than many Librans. Some of the time you will feel positive and optimistic; at other times you may succumb to negative feelings.

You are probably very ambitious and a hard worker, even if you give the impression of being relaxed. You will pack a lot into the working day and, with persistence of effort, will achieve a great deal.

Romance

Libra is a warm, romantic sign, while Capricorn is rather unemotional and cool. You cope well with solitude; better, in fact, than most Librans. When you share your life with a partner, you may need to spend some time alone.

Once committed to a partner you will be faithful, but may be a little grudging in expressing your affections. Allow your Libran Sun to counter this tendency, and relax.

Your well-being

The Capricornian body area covers the knees and shins, which are therefore vulnerable.

The skin and teeth are also ruled by Capricorn. Your skin may be more sensitive to the sun than most people's, so wear a protective cream in summer. Do not neglect your regular dental checkups, either.

You may be less attracted to sweet food than many Librans and will therefore be less prone to weight gain. A tendency to incur stiffness of the joints means that you will probably benefit from exercise.

The Moon in Capricorn

Planning ahead

You are likely to be more careful when it comes to handling money than many Librans, and will no doubt tend to opt for quality in what you buy. You may spend a lot of money on impressing other people, perhaps by entertaining them lavishly.

Social climbing may be something of a hobby with you. This is fine, but it could cost you dearly and will not always have the desired effect. You will invest wisely and probably have a sensible attitude to finance in general. Concentrate on maintaining steady growth from sound, even unadventurous, investments.

Parenthood

Although you are in many ways warm and affectionate, there will be periods when you may not have time for your children. You could find it difficult to keep up with their ideas, perhaps because you are rather conventional in outlook. Try to counter this tendency, or it could well cause generation gap problems.

THE MOON IN

AQUARIUS

BOTH LIBRA AND AQUARIUS ARE AIR SIGNS. TOGETHER THEY GIVE YOU ORIGINALITY AND CHARM. YOU MAY, HOWEVER, NEED TO DEVELOP A MORE PRACTICAL AND SERIOUS APPROACH TO SOME SPHERES OF LIFE.

There is a delightful friendly and lighthearted area of your personality that immediately rises to the surface whenever you come into contact with other people.

Self-expression

Your manner is open and positive, and you are very gregarious. More than most Librans, you possess an independent streak which ensures that you do things in your own way. You have a great deal of individuality, which may be expressed creatively.

Surprisingly, you could sometimes react to situations rather stubbornly and can be very unpredictable. Try to control these tendencies, for while they can be amusing, they can also cause disruption and annoyance.

Romance

Libra and Aquarius are the two signs with the greatest inclination for real romance. Your Aquarian Moon will contribute glamour, but will also cool the emotions. You are attractive to the opposite sex, but may tend to keep people at a distance. In doing so, you will be expressing Aquarian independence, but also acting against your Libran need to relate. You need a partner who understands these areas of your personality, and who will encourage you to express your emotions freely.

Your well-being

The Aquarian body area is the ankles. You may find yourself turning your ankle all too often, which will cause you considerable discomfort.

Aquarius also rules the circulation, and you may well feel the cold very badly. Conversely, you may suffer when it is hot. Exercise is necessary to keep your circulation in good order. You could get bored with many forms of it, but should enjoy tennis, dance, or winter sports. You could

The Moon in Aquarius

participate in a variety of physical activities, changing them according to the different seasons.

Planning ahead

You have an eye for beautiful things and may end up spending a lot of money on them. Do, however, choose carefully. Many things increase in value and therefore make good investments; others lose their value. Because you are attracted to the unusual and glamorous, you could invest your funds unwisely. Always obtain financial advice when you have money to put aside, and try to save regularly.

Parenthood

You should not suffer from the generation gap as your children grow up, because you are always attracted to the new. Do, however, make a solid effort to curb unpredictability, since it is vital that your children know where they stand in relation to you.

THE MOON IN PISCES

YOUR RESPONSE TO DIFFICULT SITUATIONS MAY BE TO TAKE THE PATH OF LEAST RESISTANCE. DOING SO COULD, HOWEVER, HURT OTHERS FAR MORE THAN YOU REALIZE, THEREBY UPSETTING YOUR PRIZED HARMONIOUS LIFESTYLE.

The combination of your Sun and Moon signs makes you an extremely kind, gentle, and magnanimous person.

Self-expression

Without hesitating, you will offer help as soon as you see that it is needed and will often inconvenience yourself in order to do so. You must try to distance yourself from emotional and psychological involvement in such cases, while at the same time retaining your sympathetic and understanding rapport.

You may need to develop a sense of purpose and greater determination if you have an inclination to drift. The real reason for this tendency may be a certain lack of self-confidence.

Romance

You have a high emotional level that you will be able to express in your relationships. You will make a wonderfully caring partner, but may become a far too willing slave. Remember that partnership is about sharing. Keep your balance, and try to develop a relationship with someone who will be strong enough to lean on, but who will also recognize your talents, encourage your efforts, and help you to organize your life.

Your well-being

The Piscean body area is the feet. Your feet are therefore vulnerable to blisters, corns, and other ailments.

You are also sensitive to prevailing atmospheres. Bad ones could cause stomach upsets, as will worry, to which you may be more susceptible than many Sun sign Librans.

Planning ahead

You really are a soft touch where money is concerned. You need someone to control your finances with a rod of iron; otherwise you may end

The Moon in Pisces

up being too generous. There are, however, certain things that you can do for yourself. You can take part in a savings plan in which the contributions are taken out of your paycheck. You would be wise never to lend money and should try not to give too much of it away.

Your artistic and creative potential could well prove to be exceptionally lucrative. You should, however, concentrate on producing the raw product, and leave the difficult and specialized task of balancing the books to someone who is much more proficient at it than you.

Parenthood

As a parent, you may tend to spoil your children badly when they are young. This could be partly to buy yourself peace and quiet. Be decisive, and do not keep changing your mind when your children need direction from you. It is important for them to know where they stand with you.

You will not find it too difficult to enjoy your children's interests, and as a result you should not incur problems with the generation gap. However, never let your children twist you around their little fingers, as they will certainly try to do.

SUN & MOON SIGNS

SCORPIO

OCTOBER 24 – NOVEMBER 22

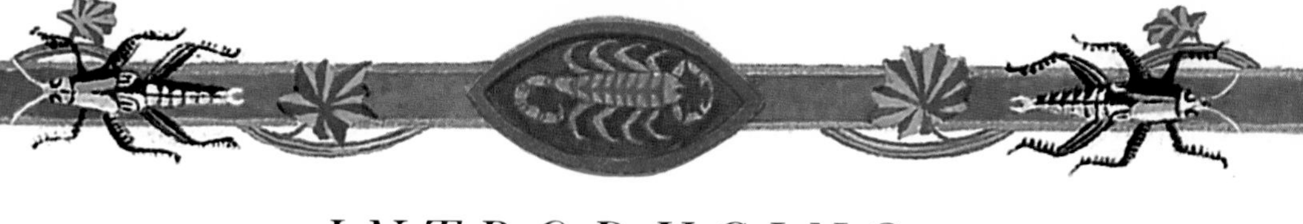

INTRODUCING SCORPIO

SCORPIO, THE EIGHTH SIGN OF THE ZODIAC, IS A SIGN OF THE WATER ELEMENT. IT BESTOWS ON ITS SUBJECTS DEEP, PENETRATING, AND INTENSE PERSONALITIES, AND GIVES THEM GREAT RESOURCES OF EMOTIONAL AND PHYSICAL ENERGY.

The qualities of Scorpio must be channeled positively to prevent jealousy and resentfulness from leading to inner dissatisfaction that can badly mar its subjects' characters.

Scorpio has the reputation for being the sexiest of the 12 Zodiac signs. Like most popular astrological beliefs, this is often unjustified. Scorpios need sexual fulfillment, but their energy can be expressed in many other ways.

Pluto, the sign's ruling planet, underlines a characteristic sense of purpose. For Scorpios to be psychologically fulfilled, every single day must have its own full and demanding schedule.

Traditional groupings

As you read through this book you will come across references to the elements and the qualities, and to positive and negative, or masculine and feminine signs. The first grouping, the elements, comprises fire, earth, air, and water signs. The second, the qualities, divides the Zodiac into cardinal, fixed, and mutable signs. The final grouping consists of positive and negative, or masculine and feminine signs. Each Zodiac sign is associated with a combination of components from these groupings, all of which add different characteristics to it.

Scorpio characteristics

The sign is of the fixed quality, which indicates stubbornness – something of a contradiction in terms when one thinks of the ebb and flow of water, the Scorpio element. The sign is also feminine and negative, which signifies introversion. There is a traditional association between Scorpio and dramatic deep shades of red and maroon.

Scorpios often have incisive minds, and sometimes a great desire to get to the bottom of every problem.

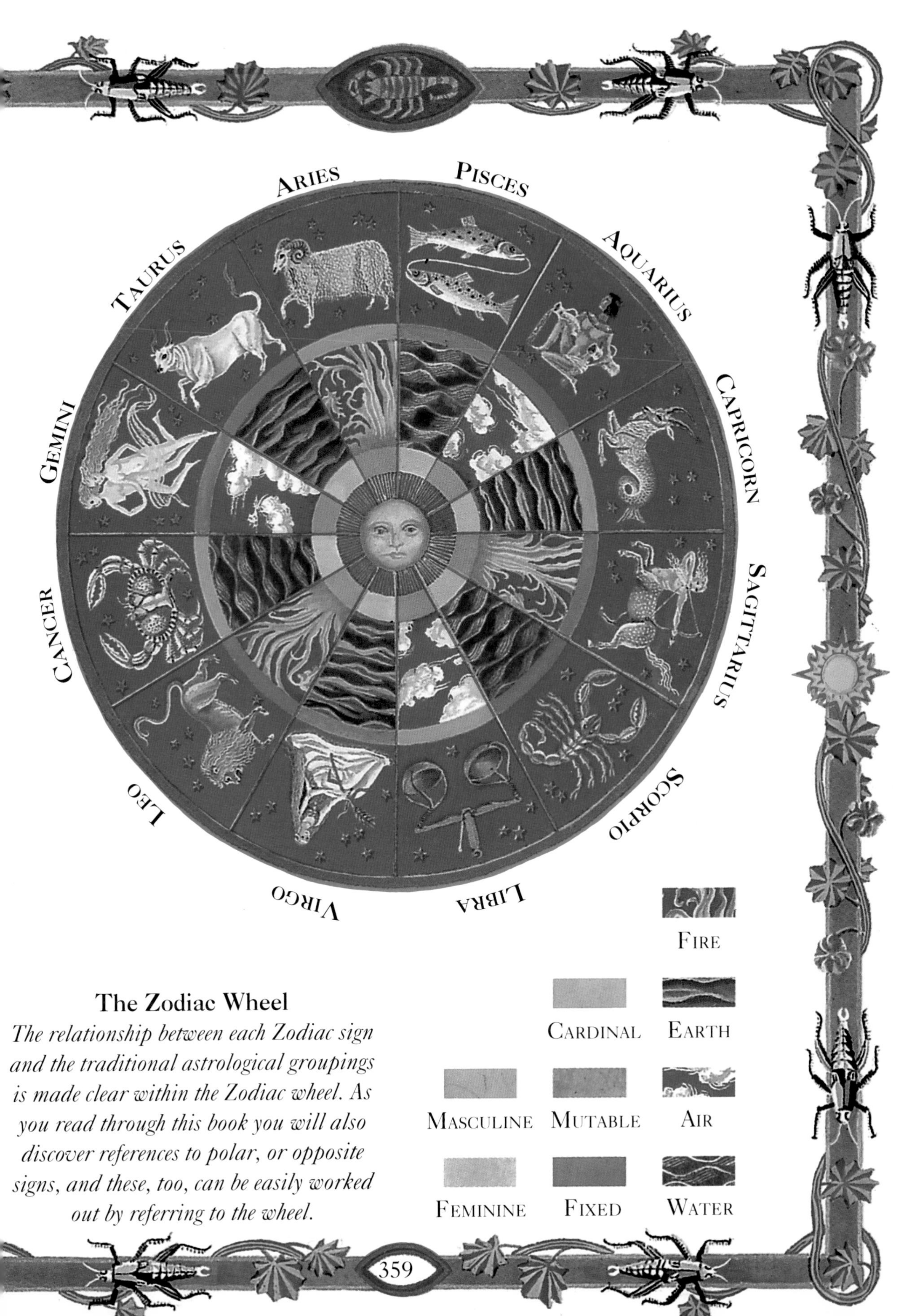

The Zodiac Wheel

The relationship between each Zodiac sign and the traditional astrological groupings is made clear within the Zodiac wheel. As you read through this book you will also discover references to polar, or opposite signs, and these, too, can be easily worked out by referring to the wheel.

SCORPIO

MYTHS & LEGENDS

THE ZODIAC, WHICH IS SAID TO HAVE ORIGINATED IN BABYLON AS LONG AS 2,500 YEARS AGO, IS A CIRCLE OF CONSTELLATIONS THROUGH WHICH THE SUN MOVES DURING THE COURSE OF A YEAR.

Fairly often, it takes a very great leap of the imagination to see any definite likeness between the "shape" of some constellations and the 12 different Zodiac symbols that have come to be associated with them. A case does, perhaps, exist for saying that the constellation of Scorpio has a tail that resembles a scorpion's. In the case of Scorpio, however, the obscure link between its Zodiac symbol and the pattern in the stars that constitutes the Scorpio constellation is quite hard to explain.

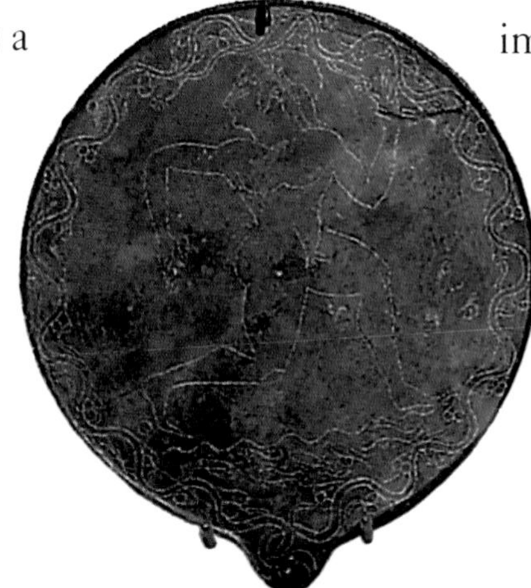

Orion the hunter

This image, cut into the back of an Etruscan mirror, shows Orion crossing the sea.

Evidence suggests that the Scorpio symbol initially had no link with a constellation. A scorpion-man, apparently not based on any group of stars, appears as a fully developed image on many Babylonian boundary stones. On the majority of these boundary stones, he is depicted with a scorpion's tail, and drawing a bow, as though he were a combination of the figures for Scorpio and Sagittarius, the Archer. This scorpion figure appeared in Babylon at least 1,000 years before he finally took his place in the Egyptian Zodiacs that were created in the ancient cities of Denderah and Esna, as the image we know today.

Orion and Eos

Manilius, the Roman writer who, in the first century B.C. set down several astrological myths, suggested that the original scorpion was connected with Orion. A Greek giant (it was said that his stature was so great that he could walk on the bottom of the sea without getting his head wet), hunter, and the handsomest man alive, he was by no means impervious to female charms.

When the dawn-goddess Eos, an inveterate collector of handsome young men, invited him to bed, he happily accepted the invitation. But Orion bragged of the conquest and also boasted that he was so great a hunter that he would exterminate all of the wild beasts.

The God Apollo, responsible for guarding herds, therefore persuaded Gaia, the Earth goddess, to send a giant scorpion with impenetrable armor to sting him to death.

The goddess Artemis

This gold plaque, dating from the seventh century B.C., shows Artemis in her role as goddess of the animals.

Artemis's mistake

Some variations of this myth say that it succeeded, others that Orion tried to escape by swimming out to sea, only to be accidentally shot by Artemis, the goddess of the hunt and Apollo's sister. Artemis, who, unsurprisingly, was very attracted to Orion, actually fired her arrow in an attempt to kill the scorpion that was molesting him. Being a magnificent shot, she struck the black head that she saw bobbing in the water with her first arrow. Tragically, however, her target turned out to be Orion's head, rather than the scorpion, and the hunter died instantly.

According to this latter version of the story, the grief-stricken Artemis then placed Orion as a constellation among the stars, where he is eternally pursued by the giant scorpion. The constellation of Orion, incidentally, sets in the sky just as the constellation of Scorpio rises.

SCORPIO
SYMBOLISM

CERTAIN HERBS, SPICES, FLOWERS, TREES, GEMS, METALS, AND ANIMALS HAVE LONG BEEN ASSOCIATED WITH PARTICULAR ZODIAC SIGNS. SOME ASSOCIATIONS ARE SIMPLY AMUSING, WHILE OTHERS CAN BE USEFUL.

WILD THISTLE

Flowers

Those flowers ruled by Aries, like the spiky thistle, and most dark red flowers, such as some geraniums, are governed by Scorpio.

GERANIUMS

Trees

The blackthorn has always been associated with Scorpio, but so are all bushy trees, such as the hawthorn, and trees that are used for hedging, like the macrocarpa.

HAWTHORN

Spices

No spices are specifically linked with Scorpio, but red or hot spices such as cayenne pepper, paprika, and chili are sometimes associated with the sign.

PAPRIKA

Herbs

Scorpio rules the same herbs as Aries, such as peppermint. It is most strongly associated with herbs that have very dark red flowers. These include figwort, which quells itching, and dovesfoot, which is good for colic and for expelling kidney stones.

PEPPERMINT

CHILI

SCORPIO
SYMBOLISM

Scorpion

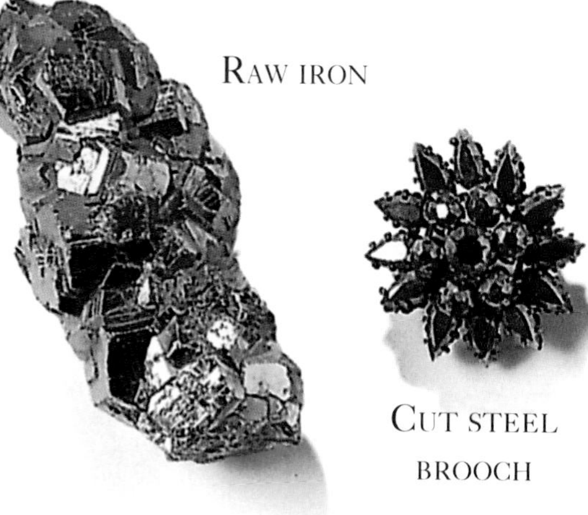

Raw iron

Cut steel brooch

Steel double-ax brooch

Jamesi scarab

West African scarab

Steel bracelet

Metal

The Scorpio metal is traditionally said to be either steel or iron.

Amber jewelry

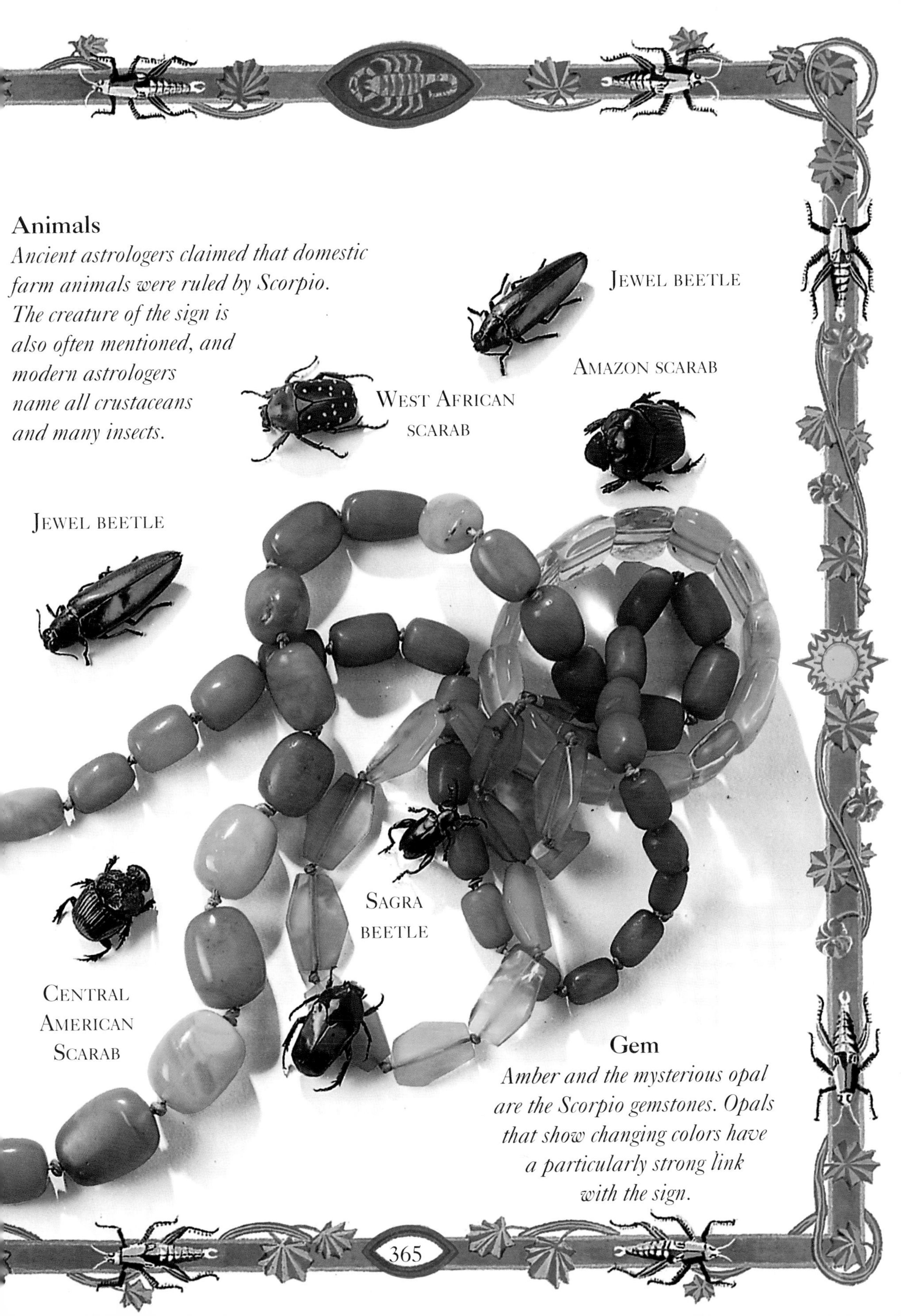

Animals

Ancient astrologers claimed that domestic farm animals were ruled by Scorpio. The creature of the sign is also often mentioned, and modern astrologers name all crustaceans and many insects.

Gem

Amber and the mysterious opal are the Scorpio gemstones. Opals that show changing colors have a particularly strong link with the sign.

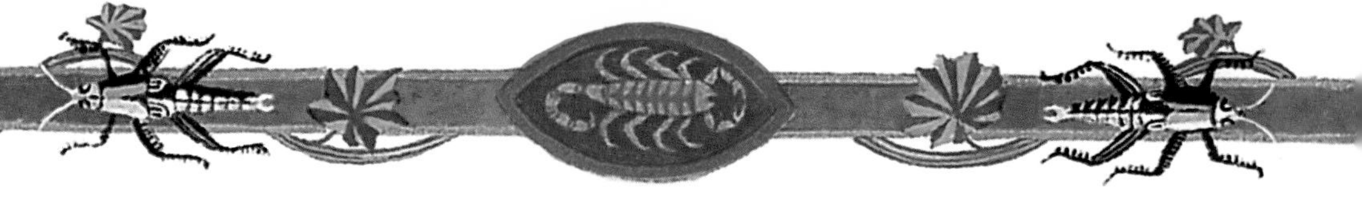

SCORPIO PROFILE

THE INTENSITY OF THE SCORPIO PERSONALITY IS USUALLY VISIBLE IN THE INDIVIDUAL'S APPEARANCE AND EXPRESSION. SHARP-EYED, THEY DO NOT MISS A THING, AND ARE THE NATURAL DETECTIVES OF THE ZODIAC.

Your determination is usually evident in your stance. You stand with your head jutting forward in a sleuth-like manner, as though you are peering through some fascinating keyhole.

The Scorpio face
An obvious characteristic of the Scorpio face is an intent and piercing gaze.

The body

There are two distinct Scorpio body types. The first is heavy, giving the impression of a certain world-weariness, as if the individual has been around for a long time, and enjoyed every minute of it. The other is very lean and wiry, probably as a result of slogging it out in a health club, and burning up all that Scorpio energy. In general, Scorpios are rarely above medium height, and some can be rather short. Female Scorpios can become very buxom if they gain weight, but they rarely lose their figures or become any less active. They tend to swing their hips as they walk.

The face

A typical Scorpio has a fairly large forehead, and deep-set, piercing eyes. Comparisons are often drawn with the eagle, a bird that is connected with this sign. The chin is usually well formed, unless the individual is overweight, and the mouth is often extremely sensual and full lipped. A typical Scorpio will have somewhat large ears, high cheek-bones, a full neck, and a wide, strong jaw. Many Scorpios have strong, but often rather coarse hair.

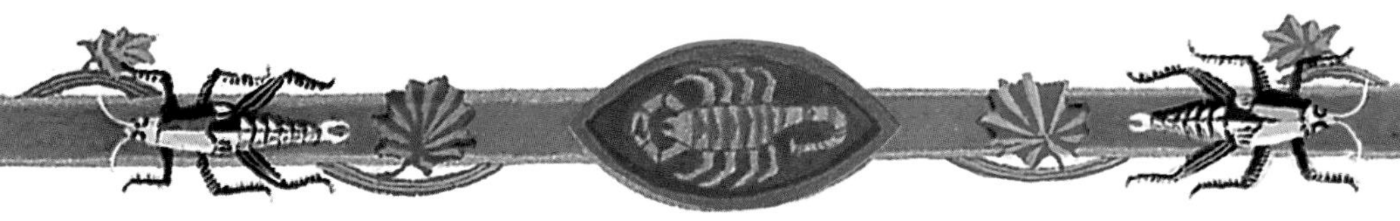

The Scorpio stance

You probably possess a determined stance that has your head jutting forward as if peering through a keyhole.

Style

Leather and the color black are popular among Scorpios, even when they are not particularly fashionable. You will probably favor an image that enhances sexiness, and if this is not overdone it works well. Many Scorpios like wearing tight jeans, leather trousers, and severely plunging necklines; not everyone is suited to each of these.

The texture of your clothing may be very important to you. Scorpios usually like the smoothness of satin and pure silk. Velvet is also popular. Any sharp, or remotely coarse material, such as wool, will probably hold no appeal for you.

On formal occasions Scorpios usually look extremely smart in somewhat severe clothes. You will not submerge your personality by dressing conventionally. All that has to be done is for you to study how to make fashion work for you. You will instinctively want to exploit your own personal image as far as you possibly can, and there is no reason why you should not do so.

In general

Many Zodiac types consciously or unconsciously tend to aspire to the image of their sign, and in Scorpios this can be very much the case. This can be amusing, but it may also be overdone at times. Sun sign Scorpios like a sense of mystery, and in extreme cases the women can be femmes fatales. Keep a sense of humor and all will be well.

SCORPIO PERSONALITY

YOU ARE LIKELY TO HAVE A STRIKING, INTENSE PERSONALITY, AND THE POTENTIAL TO BE A GREAT ACHIEVER. IF, HOWEVER, THIS POTENTIAL IS NOT FULLY EXPRESSED, YOU CAN BECOME NEGATIVE IN OUTLOOK.

Having a strong, passionate belief in whatever you do will lead to a full expression of the remarkable resources of both physical and emotional energy that you possess, which are characteristic of all Scorpios.

At work

It must be said that Scorpios with no clear objective in life, who are uninvolved in their work or in any other activity worthwhile for them, can be difficult, uncooperative, stubborn, and impervious to reason. In all, they will be a complete pain to the people around them.

It is worth remembering that while Pluto, Scorpio's ruling planet, can enable its subjects to overcome obstacles, it can also encourage a host of negative tendencies, for instance slyness, cruelty, and an urge to be somewhat overly critical. These negative characteristics, which can sometimes constitute a fairly considerable force, may make Scorpios illogically jealous of other people's achievements, especially their partners'. It may even come to the point where they will start to act in an underhanded and vindictive fashion, even scheming toward their rivals' downfall, and often giving way to outbursts of unpleasant, illogical rage when others offer help or advice.

Your attitudes

When all is well with you, however, you will know exactly what it is that you want to do in life, and will certainly see to it that whatever this is gets done. When it is properly fulfilled, this powerful and demanding motivation will lead to your finding that vital sense of inner satisfaction upon which so much of life can rest. The urge to move ambitiously forward will then follow from it, encouraging you to better and greater achievements. You will no

Pluto rules Scorpio

Pluto, god of the underworld, represents the ruling planet of Scorpio. The influence of Pluto can encourage its subjects to overcome obstacles, but may also make them critical, cruel, and secretive.

doubt value your friends highly and are likely to strive very hard in order to make your relationships work.

The overall picture

Scorpios tend to fling themselves straight into projects, whether these involve starting a business venture or embarking on demanding intellectual study. You will probably work very hard on any project for some time and achieve many of the goals that you set for yourself. Then, for no apparent reason, you will give up the whole venture and start again from the bottom of another hill.

Having said all of this, for the most part, Scorpios enjoy life, living it to the full and encouraging their friends and loved ones to do the same.

SCORPIO ASPIRATIONS

YOU ARE HAPPY DOING HARD WORK, PERHAPS INVOLVING DETAILED RESEARCH, BUT NEED TO BE REALLY INVOLVED WITH THE TASK AT HAND. A GOOD BUSINESS SENSE SHOULD HELP YOU MAKE MONEY, AND YOU WILL ENJOY ORGANIZATIONAL WORK.

BOTTLE STOPPERS AND CORKS

The wine trade

The Scorpio love of food and wine means that you could obtain a great deal of satisfaction from working in the wine trade.

POLICEMAN'S HANDCUFFS AND NIGHTSTICK

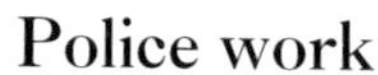

Police work

A career on the police force, especially as a detective, could prove to be an excellent choice for you. Scorpios will love searching for the facts of a crime.

1930s MINING AND ENGINEERING CIGARETTE CARDS

RIFLE BULLETS

Mining and engineering

Many Scorpios enjoy examining the Earth's resources. An interest in ecology often persuades them to discover positive ways of exploiting them.

The armed forces

Scorpio is a water sign, and many of its subjects join the navy. The army may, however, also prove attractive. Many famous generals share a Scorpio Sun sign.

CLAY PIGGY BANK AND BANK NOTES

Banking

A fascination for making money and seeing it grow can lead to careers in banking and the stock exchange.

SCORPIO HEALTH

THE SCORPIO BODY AREA IS THE GENITALS, AND IT IS THIS RELATIONSHIP THAT HAS GIVEN THE SIGN ITS OFTEN UNJUSTIFIED REPUTATION FOR OVERT SEXINESS. MANY OTHER FACTORS SHAPE THE SCORPIO CHARACTER.

Scorpio can, in a number of ways, be considered the most powerful sign of the Zodiac. Its subjects are often fortunate enough to possess tremendous resources of both physical and emotional energy. In order for you to be both psychologically whole and in the best physical shape, you must be prepared to shape your life in such a way that both of these areas manage to find some form of positive expression.

Tomatoes
The foods ruled by Aries, like tomatoes, are also associated with Scorpio.

Your diet

For most Scorpios, food is something that has to be enjoyed. You may, for instance, like a lot of rich food and wine, and dieting may prove to be difficult. You might benefit from supplementing your diet with the cell salt kali muriaticum (Kali. Mur.).

Taking care

When lacking any real objective in life, or suffering from a lack of physical exercise, a Sun sign Scorpio will become discontented, depressed, and unwell. Brooding on the situation is only likely to make matters worse. All Scorpios must realize that they need demanding projects in life, of both an intellectual and physical nature. You require goals toward which you can aim and direct your abundance of energy, and if all is well you will achieve them.

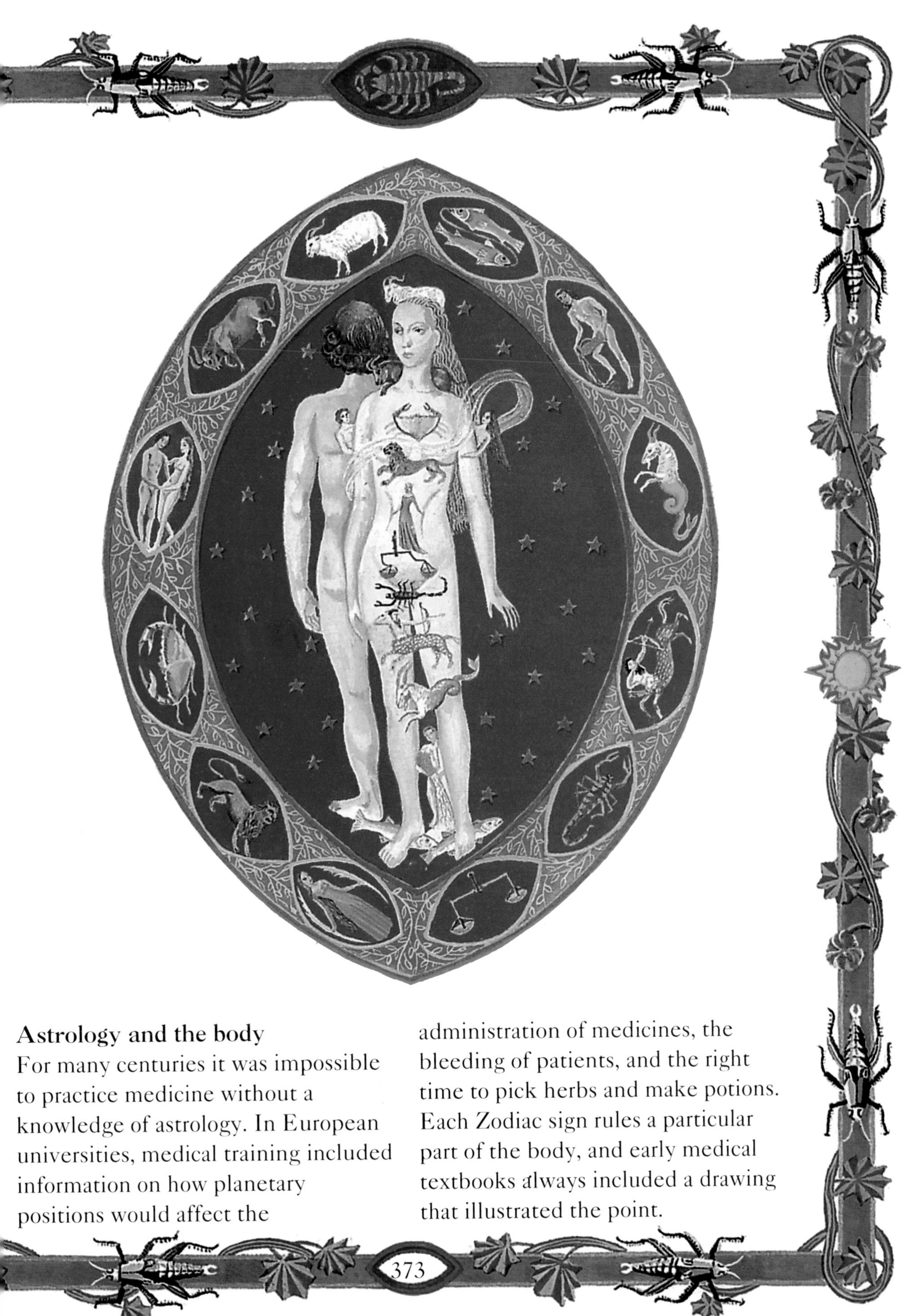

Astrology and the body

For many centuries it was impossible to practice medicine without a knowledge of astrology. In European universities, medical training included information on how planetary positions would affect the administration of medicines, the bleeding of patients, and the right time to pick herbs and make potions. Each Zodiac sign rules a particular part of the body, and early medical textbooks always included a drawing that illustrated the point.

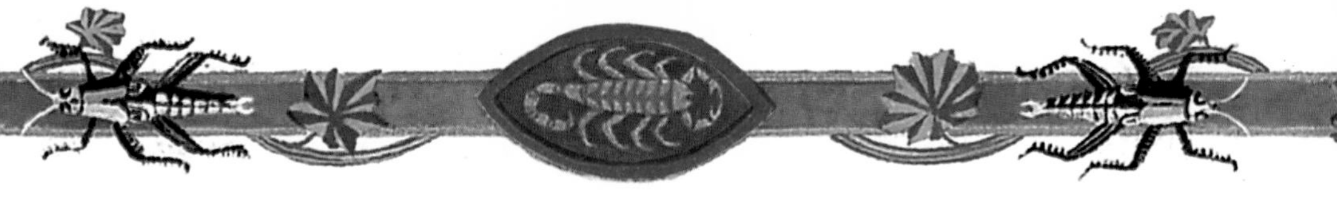

Scorpio at
Leisure

Each of the Sun signs traditionally suggests spare-time activities, hobbies, and vacation spots. Although these are only suggestions, they reflect Scorpio's tastes and interests.

Postage stamps

Motor racing

The speed and great risk involved in fast motor-cycling and driving can prove compulsive for many Scorpios.

Travel

You will enjoy visiting exotic locations such as Morocco, Syria, and Uruguay. Bavaria and Norway may have appeal.

1930s cycle racing cards

Trout-fishing fly

Fishing

Water sign Scorpios often love sitting on a riverbank with a fishing rod.

1920s magnifying glass

Detective fiction

With their inquiring minds, Scorpios will enjoy unraveling the plot of a good detective novel.

Sailing

The fact that Scorpio is a water sign could mean that you are drawn to all kinds of aquatic sports, including sailing.

SAILOR'S KNOT

HOTEL BELL

Hotel holidays

Scorpios enjoy life, so the luxury and comfort of expensive hotels with excellent facilities may well appeal to you.

Beach holidays

A beach holiday will offer you the opportunity for water sports, such as scuba diving, which are usually enjoyed by Scorpios.

RED ROSE

SEASHELLS AND SAND

Seduction

Scorpios take their love and sex lives very seriously, but there is no doubt that seduction can become a hobby for some of you.

SCORPIO IN LOVE

THE PASSIONATE EMOTION OF SCORPIO IS AT ITS MOST POTENT IN LOVE AND IN SEXUAL RELATIONSHIPS. THE NEED FOR SEXUAL FULFILLMENT IS IMPORTANT FOR THIS ZODIAC TYPE, BUT MANY ASTROLOGICAL WRITERS TEND TO OVERSTATE IT.

You may find it difficult to unburden yourself by talking things through with a sympathetic friend, let alone your partner. Therapy may provide a solution.

Scorpios have a great capacity for true love and are therefore able to contribute much to the success of a long-term relationship. The worst Scorpio fault is jealousy, and if this occurs, it can really spoil your happiness. Being aware of this tendency can help to counter it.

As a lover

Despite the traditional emphasis on Scorpio sexuality, it is wrong to think that all members of this sign are always on the rampage, moving from one conquest to the next.

Much of a Scorpio's abundant resources of emotional and physical energy are oriented toward their sex life. However, once you have found a responsive mate, with an equal level of need, fulfillment is not hard to find. Your sexual needs will take their place in a balanced life.

Types of Scorpio lover

Scorpios are capable of expressing desire in one of at least five different ways. One group takes a

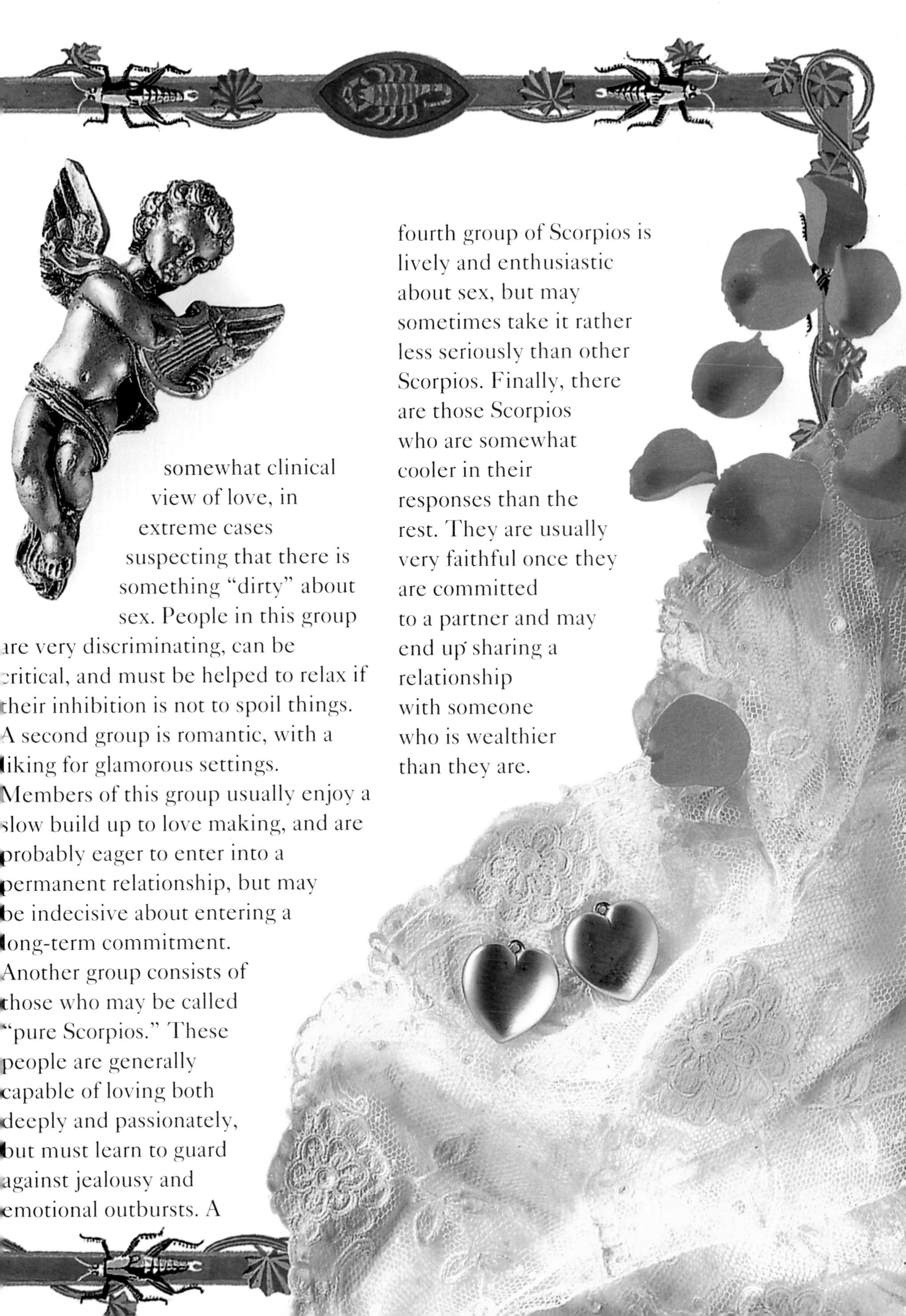

somewhat clinical view of love, in extreme cases suspecting that there is something "dirty" about sex. People in this group are very discriminating, can be critical, and must be helped to relax if their inhibition is not to spoil things. A second group is romantic, with a liking for glamorous settings. Members of this group usually enjoy a slow build up to love making, and are probably eager to enter into a permanent relationship, but may be indecisive about entering a long-term commitment. Another group consists of those who may be called "pure Scorpios." These people are generally capable of loving both deeply and passionately, but must learn to guard against jealousy and emotional outbursts. A fourth group of Scorpios is lively and enthusiastic about sex, but may sometimes take it rather less seriously than other Scorpios. Finally, there are those Scorpios who are somewhat cooler in their responses than the rest. They are usually very faithful once they are committed to a partner and may end up sharing a relationship with someone who is wealthier than they are.

SCORPIO AT HOME

SCORPIO ROOMS CAN BE ALMOST TOO COMFORTABLE. THEY MAY HAVE A SEDUCTIVE AIR THAT WILL BE ACHIEVED THROUGH DARK COLORS AND SUBDUED LIGHTING. THIS CHARACTERISTIC MAY APPLY TO ALL THE ROOMS IN YOUR HOME.

Your ideal home would be placed on the edge of an idyllic lake. However, you will probably have to compromise over this, so some form of water garden, or perhaps a well, might provide a pleasant alternative. You are also likely to feel very much at home in the city. One important factor to consider might be the need for privacy that many Scorpios have. A private study could be the answer.

Furniture

There is a certain slickness in the furniture Scorpios choose and, most often, it will be covered in leather; black is popular. Comfort is important, so while settees may be bold in appearance, they will actually be soft and seductive.

You will spend a great deal of money on furnishings, and are unlikely to take risks when choosing items that will have to be lived with for a long period of time. A classic Barcelona chair is very popular, combining as it does style, tradition, and a smart, expensive elegance. Scorpios are very image conscious in their choice of furniture as well as their clothes.

Stuffed alligator
An article like this will enhance the overall air of mystery that many Scorpios are attracted to.

Soft furnishings

The Scorpio color is basically deep crimson, which is the color of Pluto, the Scorpio ruling planet, and the overall effect of your furnishings can tend to be rather dark. It will, however, be very rich, and there will be no lack of

cushions to enhance comfort. These will often match the upholstery itself or be printed in an exotic pattern such as paisley. Dark shades of heavy satin can be popular, because texture is often important for Scorpios. Rugs will have a heavy pile, and curtains will be well lined and contribute to a somewhat seductive atmosphere.

Wine and grapes
The richnes of dark red grapes and wine boldly reflects the intensely seductive Scorpio image.

Decorative objects

A visitor's eye will be drawn very quickly to the decorative objects that you choose. They will be very striking and will make definite statements. Your choice of paintings will be dramatic and colorful; Gauguin is often a popular choice because of his sensual colors and subject matter. You may also like surreal and imaginative paintings, or energetic and aggressive works. Young Scorpios could favor posters of hard rock bands. A bowl of luscious fruit, and perhaps some splendid wine may be in evidence – they will blend beautifully with the appearance of the overall scheme. Something in metal, such as a pot or an antique weapon, could also be present, or perhaps some decorative colored glass.

The lighting in your home is probably rather subdued. A spotlight may be used to enhance one of your favorite objects, such as vases, or an unusual antique that is dear to you.

Barcelona chair
Combining style, tradition, and expensive elegance with the texture of leather, this chair is a clear choice for the Scorpio home.

THE
MOON
AND
YOU

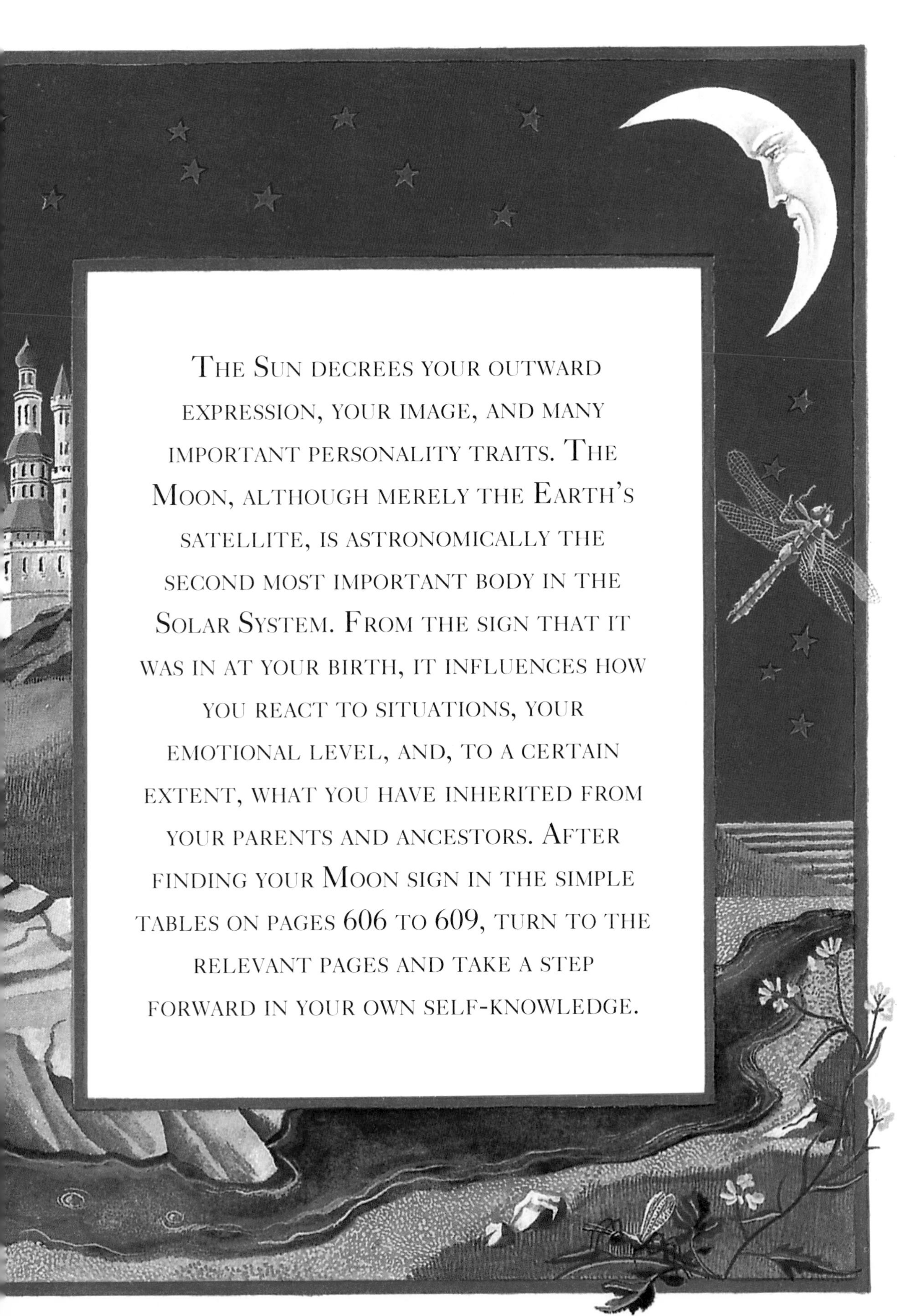

The Sun decrees your outward expression, your image, and many important personality traits. The Moon, although merely the Earth's satellite, is astronomically the second most important body in the Solar System. From the sign that it was in at your birth, it influences how you react to situations, your emotional level, and, to a certain extent, what you have inherited from your parents and ancestors. After finding your Moon sign in the simple tables on pages 606 to 609, turn to the relevant pages and take a step forward in your own self-knowledge.

THE MOON IN ARIES

THE FIERY EMOTIONAL ENERGY OF YOUR ARIEN MOON IS BACKED UP BY THE INTENSE ENERGY OF SCORPIO. YOU NEED BOTH PHYSICAL AND PSYCHOLOGICAL FULFILLMENT IN LIFE, AND SHOULD NEVER ALLOW YOURSELF TO STAGNATE.

Scorpio and Aries are both very powerful Zodiac signs, bestowing on their subjects a high level of emotional and physical energy. Your Scorpio intensity is heightened by your Arien sense of immediacy and instinct to be first.

Self-expression

With this Sun and Moon combination you will not be prepared to allow opponents to get the better of you. Inner fulfillment is essential to you, and your way of achieving it is to fill every day with work. Avoid time-filling jobs, or a career in which you have no real interest but pursue solely for money. If you have a job that is dull, make sure that your leisure hours are challenging and lively.

Romance

You have a high emotional level, and are very passionate. This passion will find its best expression within your relationships. You will possess a somewhat less smoldering intensity than many Sun sign Scorpios and will approach love and sex with an uncomplicated enthusiasm.

The worst Arien fault is selfishness. If anyone accuses you of this, listen to them, as they will probably be right.

Because of a tendency to act prematurely, you may feel inclined to deepen an emotional relationship too early. When this appears likely to happen, allow the critical faculties of your Scorpio Sun extra expression.

Your well-being

The Arien body area is the head, and you may therefore suffer from headaches, perhaps because of the way other people are acting. On the other hand, they may sometimes stem from slight kidney upsets. Because Aries promotes hastiness, you might be rather accident-prone and could often incur minor cuts and bruises.

The Moon in Aries

Planning ahead

Your Scorpio business sense is spiced with the Arien spirit of enterprise. Should you start a business venture, you will find it not only enjoyable, but also probably very financially rewarding. You are shrewd and capable with money, but may need to stop and think twice before investing, since you could be a little too enthusiastic about schemes that seem solid, but may in fact be hollow. If you give yourself time to think, your Scorpio shrewdness will come into its own and you will manage to avoid coming to grief.

Parenthood

You will make an energetic and lively parent and will expect a lot from your children. You will discipline them in a positive way and will not find it difficult to keep up with their concerns and opinions. This should avoid any problems with the generation gap.

THE MOON IN TAURUS

SCORPIO AND TAURUS ARE POLAR ZODIAC SIGNS, SO YOU WERE BORN UNDER A FULL MOON. AVOID RESTLESSNESS BY ALLOWING YOUR PRACTICAL MOON SIGN TO STEADY YOUR POWERFUL EMOTIONS AND CONTROL JEALOUSY.

Everyone, in one way or another, expresses elements of their polar or opposite sign: the sign that lies across the Zodiac circle from their Sun sign. For Scorpios, this is Taurus and, as the Moon was in that sign when you were born, this polarity is emphasized in an interesting way.

Self-expression

The Moon is, traditionally, "well placed" in Taurus. This means that its psychological effect on you is somewhat above average.

In order for you to develop your full potential and live life in a satisfying and rewarding way, you need great emotional and financial security. When you have it, you flourish and are capable of great achievements. Without it, your lifestyle suffers.

Even more than many Sun sign Scorpios, you must always have an objective in view and should carve your way toward it constructively.

Romance

Both Scorpio and Taurus are of the fixed quality and, as a result, you can be rather stubborn. Taurus, like Scorpio, is a passionate sign. It will therefore increase the smoldering intensity that your Sun sign gives you.

You will express your feelings in a warm and affectionate way, and are capable of giving great sexual enjoyment. However, the worst Taurean fault is possessiveness and, if this is ignited by Scorpio jealousy, you could well have problems. Be aware that these negative emotions could spoil your relationships.

Your need for emotional security could cause you to create something of a claustophobic atmosphere, which some partners might resent.

Your well-being

The Taurean body area covers the neck and throat. Colds will almost certainly settle in that area, so take

The Moon in Taurus

care of it, especially in winter. Taurus likes good food, and so does Scorpio. Living it up can therefore mean considerable weight gain, unless you have a high metabolic rate. Moderation and exercise will help.

Planning ahead

You will be good with money and have a great instinct for investment. Therefore your bank balance and portfolio of stocks, however small, will grow to your satisfaction. However, you certainly love luxury and will therefore also spend freely. You will probably be able to cope with your finances without professional advice.

Parenthood

You are conventional and may be somewhat conservative in outlook. Be careful: your children could accuse you of being old-fashioned. You will work hard for them, but might be stricter than you realize. If you try to keep up with all their concerns, you should have few problems with the generation gap.

THE MOON IN GEMINI

YOU ARE MORE LOGICAL AND LESS INTUITIVE THAN MANY SCORPIOS. IT IS PROBABLE THAT YOU CAN USEFULLY RATIONALIZE YOUR EMOTIONS AND INTELLECTUALIZE ANY DEEP-ROOTED PSYCHOLOGICAL PROBLEMS OR WORRIES.

The combination of two very different signs makes for a dynamic influence on your character. Gemini is an air sign and is intellectually oriented; it therefore adds a lightness and inquisitiveness to your Scorpio Sun, which makes you intense and pushes you to get to the root of every problem.

Self-expression

When challenged in any way, you will at once respond with lively, searching questions. You will be very skeptical of every theory put to you.

It may be that you are attracted to the media, and all kinds of research could well fascinate you. You are an excellent communicator, and this can be of advantage not only in your career, but also on a personal level.

When moved, you will probably try to rationalize your emotion. By all means go in for self-analysis, but remember that in the process you can rationalize away a lot of pleasure. Like many Sun sign Scorpios, you may tend to bottle up your problems. You should not, however, suffer badly from this tendency, due to the communicative nature of your Geminian Moon.

Romance

In addition to expressing Scorpio passion and achieving sexual fulfillment, you also find it very rewarding to enjoy a high level of intellectual rapport and friendship within an emotional relationship.

It is particularly good for you to have a partner who is at least your intellectual equal, if not considerably ahead of you in this area.

Your well-being

Scorpios tend to go whole hog, liking a lot of everything. If you smoke, you will probably smoke heavily, and this is inadvisable given that the Gemini

The Moon in Gemini

organ is the lungs. You have quite a high level of nervous energy, and should aim to burn that and your Scorpio physical energy positively, in sports or through demanding exercise.

Planning ahead

You may be somewhat less skillful with money than many Sun sign Scorpios. You have a natural selling ability and are capable of organizing profitable deals. Are you, however, perhaps a little too easily attracted to get-rich-quick schemes that, in the long run, turn into get-poor-quickly disasters? When tempted, remember to ask questions.

Parenthood

You probably find it easy to keep up with your children and enjoy discussing their opinions. At times, you could even be ahead of them and may surprise them with your knowledge of current trends. You should have few problems with the generation gap, especially if you maintain your acidic sense of humor.

THE MOON IN CANCER

YOUR CANCERIAN MOON INCREASES YOUR SENSITIVE AWARENESS OF OTHERS' NEEDS. YOU HAVE A PROTECTIVE INSTINCT AND GREAT EMOTIONAL ENERGY. CHANNEL THESE POSITIVELY, AND BEWARE OF IRRATIONAL WORRY.

Because Scorpio and Cancer are both water signs, the level of your emotional energy is very high. You should always be sure that you have positive and demanding ways of expressing it. You are a powerhouse of strong feeling and, for your psychological comfort, must be intensely involved in work that you find totally rewarding.

Self-expression

Your Cancerian Moon is likely to make you very intuitive, and you have an active imagination that you should make every effort to express creatively. If this does not happen, you will worry irrationally and could spend too much time waiting for the worst to happen. Also try to recognize the fact that, perhaps as the result of your sensitivity to atmospheres and other people's reactions, you may sometimes be prone to bouts of moodiness. Aim to keep your outlook positive, and endeavor to be more optimistic than you may naturally be inclined to feel.

Romance

You are a wonderfully sensual and highly sexed lover, good at assessing your partner's needs. You are also demanding and need a partner who is not only active but also sympathetic. Watch out, though, for a tendency to "mother" your partners. This can create a rather claustrophobic atmosphere, which more freedom-loving partners may resent.

Your well-being

The Cancerian body area covers the breasts and chest. While there is absolutely no connection between this sign and the disease that bears the same name, Cancerian women should be as diligent as all their sisters in regularly examining their breasts. To some extent the digestive system

The Moon in Cancer

is also Cancer-ruled and, when you are worried, you could find your stomach giving you trouble. Cancerians and Scorpios enjoy their food, which will not help. You may need strenuous exercise to keep any flab at bay.

Planning ahead

There is a fair chance that you could be something of a financial wizard. You possess Cancerian shrewdness, with the additional business acumen that springs from your Scorpio Sun. This gives you the capacity to make a lot of money, provided that you do not give in to the Scorpio tendency to suddenly stop what you are doing and begin a new project.

Parenthood

You will enjoy the responsibilities of family life and may well be eager to have your own home and children.

You will be pretty strict with your children, which is fine. Do, however, allow them the freedom to express themselves. Avoid being sentimental and harking back to the past, when you were a child. If you get involved in your children's interests, you will bridge the generation gap.

THE MOON IN LEO

YOU ARE INTENSE, AND YOUR SCORPIO ENERGY IS SPICED WITH A POWERFUL CREATIVE INSTINCT THAT YOU SHOULD EXPRESS AS FREELY AS YOU CAN. BE AWARE, HOWEVER, THAT YOU ARE PRONE TO STUBBORNNESS.

Your Scorpio personality is exaggerated by the fiery emotion and energy of your Leo Moon. You have a great deal of inner strength and determination, and marvelous organizing ability. However, you should be very careful not to become autocratic and domineering.

Self-expression

Your Scorpio passion and powerful motivation are enhanced by your instinct to do your very best and to develop every hobby and interest, as well as your career, to the highest standard. The result is that you are probably very good at everything you do. You are one of the world's workers and will like to fill every day with useful activity.

Both Scorpio and Leo are signs that are highly charged with emotion, and Leo emotion is warm, fiery, and enthusiastic. It will make you look at life in a positive, optimistic way.

Romance

Your lovemaking has style, elegance, and more than a hint of glamour, and you will see to it that your partners enjoy life as much as you do, both in and out of bed.

Both Scorpio and Leo are of the fixed quality, which means that you can be very stubborn at times. Make an effort to reassess your opinions from time to time, and never mind admitting your mistakes.

The worst Leo fault is bossiness, so be careful that this unpleasant trait does not mar your relationships.

Your well-being

The Leo body area is the spine and back, so you need exercise to keep these in good working order. A back-support chair is also an excellent idea if you work long hours at a desk.

The Leo organ is the heart, and this needs regular exercise. You may find exercise rather boring, so aim to

The Moon in Leo

find a good health club, or perhaps dance or movement classes, where some of your dramatic qualities can find creative expression.

Scorpio and Leo could encourage you to have an all-too-rich diet. Try to keep this in check; otherwise you may well put on weight.

Planning ahead

You need to earn a lot of money to cater to what are probably expensive tastes. Your financial flair and potential for success should, however, enable you to do this. You will enjoy keeping an eye on your bank statements and seeing your money grow and will usually invest wisely, but resist any tendency to put too many financial eggs in one basket.

Parenthood

You will enjoy your children, but could sometimes seem rather pompous to them, and perhaps conventional. Try to see life through their eyes, and you will avoid problems with the generation gap. If you use your lively, enthusiastic Moon qualities and are encouraging rather than critical, you will certainly win your children's love and respect.

THE MOON IN VIRGO

YOUR VIRGOAN MOON WILL ENSURE THAT YOU WILL NOT BE SATISFIED UNTIL YOU HAVE GOTTEN TO THE ROOT OF EVERY PROBLEM. BE CAREFUL, SINCE YOU COULD BECOME OBSESSIVE, AND TRY NOT TO GET TOO BOGGED DOWN IN DETAIL.

Your water sign Sun and earth sign Moon combine well and share several complementary characteristics. Scorpio enjoys mystery and getting to the root of problems; your Virgoan Moon will encourage you to analyze them.

Self-expression

You are among the natural sleuths of the Zodiac and will therefore enjoy any kind of research. Be careful, however, that in examining the minutiae of a problem you do not miss seeing the overall pattern, and try to develop breadth of vision.

You have a great deal of common sense and a very practical approach to life. However, you must keep a tendency to worry under control.

Romance

The influence of Virgo is unlikely to be highly charged, emotionally. Some of your Scorpio passion will therefore be moderated by your Moon sign. You will work hard to make your relationships work, possibly rather gradually overcoming any Virgoan timidity in your response to sex. As your tension eases and your Scorpio Sun takes over, you will find yourself enjoying an ever-increasing richness in this sphere of your life.

Your well-being

The Virgoan organ is the stomach, and you may suffer from stomach disorders when you are worried. You need a high-fiber diet.

A Virgoan influence brings with it a great deal of nervous energy. This can sometimes lead to a buildup of stress and tension, which may result in migraines. Try to relax. Outdoor exercise may help you, and so will talking things over with a friend. A relaxation technique such as yoga may prove to be useful, as will walking, cycling, and jogging.

The Moon in Virgo

Planning ahead

You may be far less of a big spender than many Scorpios, and will probably be good at balancing the books. There is even a chance that you could feel slightly guilty whenever you are extravagant. Do your best to ensure that you do not, and enjoy yourself. In particular, make sure that you do not hesitate when it comes to spending money on a favorite hobby, and go wild on good fabric, materials, tools, and machines. If you are at all apprehensive about how to invest your money, seek financial advice.

Parenthood

Be careful not to be too critical of your children's efforts. You could deflate them far more than you realize.

Scorpios are usually fairly strict, but always retain the capacity for fun. If you listen to your children's opinions, you will encounter very few problems with the generation gap.

THE MOON IN LIBRA

YOU SOMETIMES APPEAR A LITTLE LAZY BECAUSE YOUR LIBRAN MOON ENCOURAGES YOU TO RELAX AND STUDY EVERY ASPECT OF A PROBLEM. YOU ARE MORE CONSIDERATE OF OTHER PEOPLE THAN MANY SUN SIGN SCORPIOS.

The charm of your Libran Moon softens the powerful intensity of your Scorpio personality, and you always respond warmly and sympathetically to other people.

Self-expression

It may be that you are rather slower to come to decisions than many Scorpios, because your immediate reaction is to hesitate; you usually want to think at least twice before committing yourself.

You are tactful and diplomatic, especially when put on the spot in a bad situation, and you can produce the right answer at the right time. The influence of your Libran Moon will encourage you to always have time for other people.

Romance

You are among the more romantic of Scorpios, and enjoy the relaxed development of a relationship almost as much as a passionate scene. You will be considerate of your partners and will understand their needs.

A serious Libran fault is resentment, and you must guard against a tendency to cling to past differences or minor misdemeanors that your partner may have made.

Your well-being

The Libran body area is the lumbar region of the back. If you are prone to back pain, consider purchasing a back-support chair. The Libran organ is the kidneys and, as the result of a slight imbalance in that area, you may suffer from headaches.

Unless you are a quick-moving, wiry Scorpio type, your Moon sign may give you a rather slow metabolism. This can mean that with a Libran emphasis on good, rich, and sometimes sweet food, you may put on weight all too easily. Vigorous exercise will help, but you will

The Moon in Libra

probably find that physical activity will need to be accompanied by another, perhaps philosophical, element. Yoga, tai chi, and tantra are worth considering.

Planning ahead

You are more generous than the average person, and the immediate attraction of expensive clothes or fine items for the home may prove so tempting that your excellent Scorpio financial good sense could suffer. It might be advisable for you to seek professional advice when investing. Regular, steadily growing savings plans are good for you.

Parenthood

You will alternate between being a strict parent and a bit of a softy. Make certain that your children know where they stand with you, and you will develop an affectionate rapport. If you keep up with their ideas and always try to be aware of their problems, you will avoid difficulties with the generation gap.

THE MOON IN SCORPIO

WITH BOTH THE SUN AND THE MOON IN SCORPIO ON THE DAY OF YOUR BIRTH, YOU WERE BORN UNDER A NEW MOON. SINCE SCORPIO IS A WATER SIGN, THIS ELEMENT IS IMPORTANT, AND YOU WILL HAVE MANY SCORPIO CHARACTERISTICS.

Should you read a list of the characteristics of your Scorpio Sun sign, you will probably realize that a great many of them apply to you. On average, out of a list of, say, 20 personality traits of any particular Sun sign, most people will identify with 11 or 12. However, because the Moon was also in Scorpio when you were born, for you the average increases considerably.

Self-expression

You will react to most situations with a keen incisiveness, getting to the root of a matter and thrashing out every detail in the most searching way.

It is essential for all Scorpios to be emotionally involved in their work, but for you this is even more the case.

Romance

You are highly sexed and very passionate, and it is as important for you to share a rewarding relationship with someone as it is to have a satisfying job. You will contribute a great deal toward the success of your relationship, but must be aware that you are a very demanding partner. You need to share your life with someone who both realizes and understands this.

You would also do well to remember that you can sometimes be extremely susceptible to jealousy, and that this tendency can often cause problems between you and your lover.

Your well-being

As far as your health is concerned, you stand a good chance of being particularly vulnerable to Scorpio ailments (*see pages 372 – 373*). Bear in mind that Sun sign Scorpios can go hog-wild, and this applies to you more than to most people of your Sun sign. Try to keep your food intake in balance, and aim for a certain amount of moderation.

The Moon in Scorpio

You will probably enjoy all kinds of winter sports, and perhaps serious team games. It is more than likely that you will want to become very involved in whatever sport you decide to take up, and that you will be capable of great dedication to it.

Planning ahead

You should have considerable financial flair and plenty of intuition when it comes to investment. You may find a career in big business or banking rewarding. Be careful to spread your investments – while you are very capable of making a lot of money, do not overinvest.

Parenthood

You will be very anxious for your children to make good progress, and may consequently tend to push them a little too hard, and be rather strict with them. Try to make a conscious effort to be sympathetic toward their ideas and problems.

THE MOON IN SAGITTARIUS

YOUR SAGITTARIAN MOON MODERATES THE INTENSE SIDE OF YOUR PERSONALITY. YOU CAN GRASP AN OVERALL SITUATION FAR MORE EASILY THAN MOST SCORPIOS AND ARE NOT AS OBSESSED WITH DETAIL.

The qualities attributed to Scorpio and Sagittarius are very different. As a result you have some contrasting facets to your personality. You possess natural optimism and enthusiasm, which surfaces as soon as a project is given to you, or whenever you meet with a challenge.

Self-expression

Many Scorpios are properly described as "deep." Such a description is less applicable to you, and you do not find it difficult to be open and frank.

Your capacity to enjoy life, especially when you are confronted by challenge, is wonderful. You will hate the thought of wasting time even more than others of your Sun sign.

Romance

As well as burning Scorpio passion, you have a fiery liveliness in your expression of love and sex. You will probably enjoy many relationships during the course of your life and, once you are committed to a partner, you will still need a certain amount of freedom of expression.

Be careful that Scorpio jealousy does not complicate your life. Despite your instinct for independence, you will not be very happy if your partner shows signs of being even mildly flirtatious. Remember that you are sometimes capable of similar behavior, and relent a little.

Your well-being

Scorpios usually love rich and often expensive food. Sagittarians are not averse to it, either, and also love good wines and beers. The Sagittarian organ is the liver, so that in your case excesses of wining and dining may easily cause problems.

The Sagittarian body area covers the hips and thighs, and women with this sign emphasized have a tendency to put on weight in that area.

The Moon in Sagittarius

Moderation does not come naturally to either Scorpio or Sagittarius; both types find it very boring. Self-discipline is therefore important. On the plus side, Sagittarians usually like energetic exercise, so you should not find it too difficult to get involved in an appealing exercise regimen.

Planning ahead

Although you will, no doubt, have the Scorpio ability to make money, you may enjoy gambling, and could find risky financial schemes attractive. Be careful, since you could lose a lot of hard-earned money in this way. You may do well as an investor, as long as you do not take undue risks. Be aware of the extremes to which you may succumb, and maintain a balanced outlook.

Parenthood

You will be among the most lively and positive of Scorpio parents. You have the ability to share a lot of fun with your children and will encourage them in their efforts, both intellectual and physical. You will not find it too hard to understand your children's problems, and the generation gap should hold no terrors for you.

THE MOON IN CAPRICORN

YOUR OBJECTIVES ARE IMPORTANT TO YOU, AND YOU WILL SEIZE EVERY OPPORTUNITY TO ACHIEVE YOUR GOALS. DO NOT MISS OUT ON THE LIGHTER SIDE OF LIFE OR ALLOW YOUR AMBITION TO INTERFERE WITH YOUR RELATIONSHIPS.

The water element of your Scorpio Sun and the earth element of your Capricornian Moon blend well, giving you the potential to be among the most successful of Scorpio Sun and Moon combinations.

Self-expression

You take life very seriously, but have an unusual and very offbeat sense of humor that emerges naturally and often very unexpectedly.

Your objectives and ambitions are very important to you, and you get a great deal of fulfillment from pursuing them, but you should take care that you do not miss out on enjoying life – you may veer toward becoming a workaholic. Try to avoid bringing too much work home from the office.

Romance

Your powerful Scorpio emotions are calmed by your Capricornian Moon. Your reactions to situations are logical and practical, and you are rather less likely to be emotionally moved than many Scorpios. Sometimes, you may even give the impression that you are slightly aloof.

Your approach to your love and sex life is less passionate than that of many Scorpios, and you are likely to be very faithful once committed.

Your well-being

The Capricornian body area covers the knees and shins, and yours are therefore more vulnerable than other people's. It is essential that you keep moving, because people with an emphasis on Capricorn are prone to stiffness of the joints, and rheumatic and arthritic pain.

It is unlikely that you will have a weight problem, since your Capricornian Moon has probably given you a rather lean frame, and you are possibly less attracted to heavy, rich food than is the case with many

The Moon in Capricorn

Scorpios. The teeth are also ruled by Capricorn, so be careful not to neglect to have regular dental checkups.

Planning ahead

You are, or have the potential to be, something of a financial wizard. Capricornians are often good at business, as are Scorpios. If you are self-employed, you should be able to build up your business extremely well, provided you pace its development. The same applies if you have cash to invest.

Parenthood

Perhaps you need to reassess your attitude to your children, since you may be far stricter than you realize. Most children thrive when they have a secure structure to their lives, but try to avoid damaging put-downs. Also make sure that you have time to enjoy their company as opposed to just working hard to ensure that they have all the material needs of life. Consciously tune in to their opinions and concerns. Otherwise you might experience generation gap problems.

THE MOON IN AQUARIUS

STUBBORNNESS CAN BE A PROBLEM FOR YOU, BUT YOU ARE ABLE TO DETACH YOURSELF RATIONALLY FROM DIFFICULTIES AND TO BE VERY OBJECTIVE IN ASSESSING THEM. LOOK AHEAD AND TRY TO KEEP AN OPEN MIND.

Your Aquarian Moon enables you to approach problems in an unusual way. Your reaction to situations is usually logical, and you can detach yourself from your emotions and see any difficulties from various angles, quickly focusing on each before reaching practical and often unique conclusions.

Self-expression

Lateral thinking comes naturally to you, and colleagues and friends often have cause to be very grateful for your originality. Because both Scorpio and Aquarius are of the fixed quality, you may tend to be very stubborn at times. Be aware of this tendency; otherwise you may be accused of being willfully obstinate.

Romance

Life may not be particularly easy when you are beginning to solidify a personal relationship. You are a passionate Scorpio, but may, early on in a relationship, send out signals warning people to keep their distance.

You need sexual fulfillment as much as, or perhaps more than, anyone else. However, your independence will be important to you, and you must try to find partners who will not resent this need. You may delay a long-term commitment or marriage, which is no bad thing: take your time if you feel that you should.

Your well-being

The ankles are the Aquarian body area, and yours are likely to be vulnerable, especially if you enjoy wearing some types of fashionable shoes. The circulation is also Aquarius-ruled, so take care that you look after yours. Obviously, all exercise regimens and sporting activities are a help, and you shoul find time for them. Scorpios usual enjoy swimming and other water

The Moon in Aquarius

sports, but you may also be attracted to winter sports and could be particularly good at them.

Planning ahead

While Sun sign Scorpios are usually very smart about money, your originality may sometimes get the better of you, and you could end up committing yourself without due thought to some exciting but not very practical scheme that catches your imagination. Financial loss may follow. Aim for conventionality where finance is concerned. Express your originality in other ways, for example in your image or in creative work.

Parenthood

Although you will initially respond well to your children's more extreme ideas and suggestions, you may end up backtracking. Try to avoid this. Make a conscious effort to see life through their eyes and you will not be troubled by the generation gap.

THE MOON IN PISCES

YOUR POWERFUL SCORPIO CHARACTERISTICS ARE SOFTENED BY THE TENDER EMOTION OF YOUR PISCEAN MOON. YOU ARE KIND AND MORE SENSITIVE THAN MANY SCORPIOS, BUT THIS WILL NOT PREVENT YOU FROM TAKING ASSERTIVE ACTION WHEN NECESSARY.

Both Scorpio and Pisces belong to the water element and, as a result, there is a very natural sympathy between the two signs.

Self-expression

You have extremely powerful instincts and intuition, and should follow these. You also have an active imagination, and this, too, can work positively for you. However, if your imagination is operating negatively, you are capable of supposing that all sorts of things have gone wrong when, in fact, they probably have not. Try to avoid this by finding rewarding ways of expressing your imagination.

It may be that you have psychic ability. If you have premonitions or if strange things seem to happen to you from time to time, do not be worried. If, however, you want to develop your psychic powers, get special training from a psychic society of some kind. You have a powerful emotional level and may often be swayed by your emotions. This need not be a negative trait, as long as you listen to your intuition, which will guide you in the direction that you should take.

Romance

You will get much pleasure from your love and sex life, and can give a great deal of yourself to your partners. However, you can be easily hurt and, if this occurs, it may be because you have not faced up to reality.

Your well-being

The Piscean body area covers the feet. Yours are vulnerable, and you probably find it difficult to get really comfortable shoes.

Many people with a Piscean emphasis tend to put on weight relatively easily, and Scorpios love good food. It is better for you to discipline your eating habits than to go on a crash diet.

The Moon in Pisces

Planning ahead

Although your Scorpio Sun gives you a good basic financial sense, your Piscean Moon succeeds in removing rather a lot of it. You have such a sensitivity to suffering, and identify so strongly with it, that you may be over-generous to charities. It could be that you also tend to lend money far too freely. Avoid this whenever possible, and remember that it is usually much better to give a few dollars to someone than to loan them money.

You should probably take financial advice when you are thinking of investing. Should you want to start a business, it is advisable for you to work with a partner, unless you feel that you really can control your Moon in Pisces weak approach to finance.

Parenthood

You are likely to have a great understanding of human nature, and it could well be of enormous help to you in your relationship with your children. You will sometimes be very strict with them, and at others times may tend to spoil them. If you manage to succeed in keeping these two extremes in balance, you will be a splendid parent.

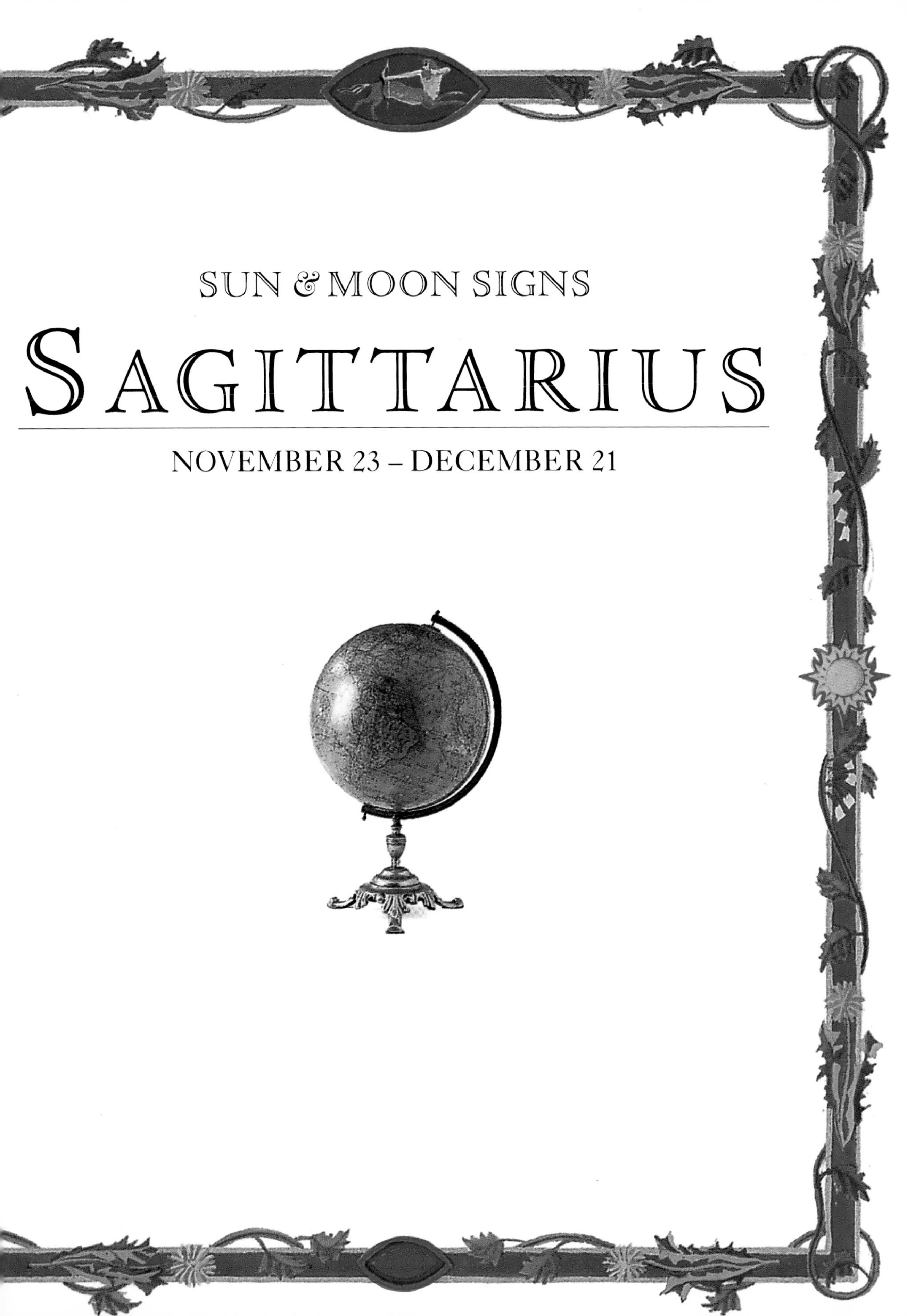

SUN & MOON SIGNS

SAGITTARIUS

NOVEMBER 23 – DECEMBER 21

INTRODUCING SAGITTARIUS

SAGITTARIUS, THE SIGN OF THE CENTAUR, THE ARCHER WHO IS HALF MAN AND HALF BEAST, IS THE NINTH SIGN OF THE ZODIAC. YOU NEED DEMANDING PHYSICAL OR INTELLECTUAL EXERCISE IN ORDER TO FULFILL YOUR POTENTIAL.

Being a Sagittarian, you should guard against restlessness, and develop a sense of purpose. This will ensure that you possess the continuity of effort required for a full expression of your potential, and thus your psychological fulfillment.

You are likely to be one of the explorers and travelers of the Zodiac – both in mind and in body. You are willing to take risks, but must control a gambling spirit that can occasionally get out of hand.

Traditional groupings

As you read through this book you will come across references to the elements and the qualities, and to positive and negative, or masculine and feminine signs.

The first of these groupings, that of the elements, comprises fire, earth, air, and water signs. The second, that of the qualities, divides the Zodiac into cardinal, fixed, and mutable signs. The final grouping is made up of positive and negative, or masculine and feminine signs. Each Zodiac sign is associated with a combination of components from these groupings, all of which contribute different characteristics to it.

Sagittarian characteristics

Being a sign of the fire element, Sagittarius bestows great natural enthusiasm upon its subjects. This often extends to a fondness for demanding physical or intellectual exercise. Since Sagittarius is also a positive, masculine sign, you are liable to be one of the optimistic extroverts of the Zodiac. Being of the mutable quality, Sagittarius is a "dual" sign, and its subjects are therefore versatile.

The ruling planet of Sagittarius is Jupiter, the giant of the Solar System, and a great god in Roman mythology. The Sagittarian colors are rich purples and dark blues.

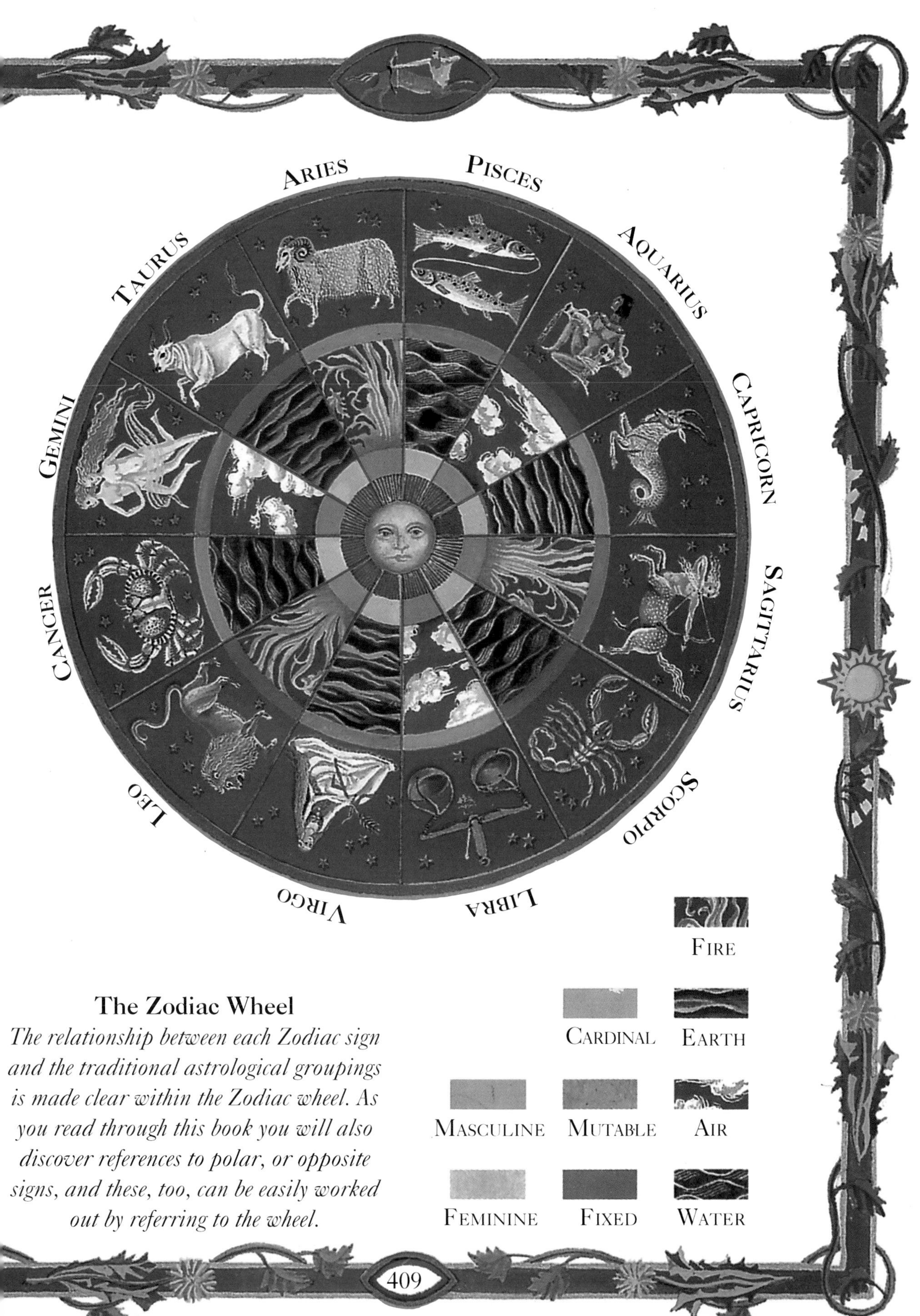

The Zodiac Wheel

The relationship between each Zodiac sign and the traditional astrological groupings is made clear within the Zodiac wheel. As you read through this book you will also discover references to polar, or opposite signs, and these, too, can be easily worked out by referring to the wheel.

SAGITTARIUS
MYTHS & LEGENDS

THE ZODIAC, WHICH IS BELIEVED TO HAVE ORIGINATED IN BABYLON AS LONG AS 2,500 YEARS AGO, IS A CIRCLE OF CONSTELLATIONS THROUGH WHICH THE SUN MOVES DURING THE COURSE OF A YEAR.

The constellation of Sagittarius first seems to have been identified and named in Babylon. The symbolic centaur with his bow began to appear in ancient Egypt much later than the time when he was carved on Babylonian boundary stones. The origin of the sign is, however, shrouded in considerable mystery, and there is no myth firmly associated with it.

Ancient Greece and Rome

In ancient Greece, Sagittarius seems to have been a satyr: in particular, one called Crotus, who lived on Mount Helicon with his foster sisters, the Muses. The satyrs were attendants of the god Dionysus; they had goats' legs and the tails of horses, and were much given to riotous living. In those days, Sagittarius had only two legs.

Later on, Manilius, the Roman writer who in the first century B.C. set down several astrological myths, and the great astronomer Hipparchus saw him as a four-footed centaur. The centaurs, who were also attendants of Dionysus, lived in Thessaly. Their heads and torsos were human, but the rest of their bodies were those of horses. It seems likely that the legend of the centaurs arose around a tribe of cow herders who lived in Thessaly. Indeed, the name "centaurs" can be translated as "those who round up bulls." Like the American cowboys, the Thessalonian herders rode on horseback when they were attending to their livestock.

In general, centaurs were thought to revel in cruelty and to indulge frequently in bouts of frenzied lechery and drunkenness.

Chiron the centaur

Some astrologers like to insist that the original Sagittarius was a centaur named Chiron, who seems to have had nothing in common with the

Achilles and Chiron, the Centaur

This late-Roman image shows Chiron schooling Achilles in the art of riding. Chiron was responsible not only for the education of Achilles, but also that of another great hero, Jason.

ordinary centaurs except his body. Although the centaur was generally considered to be a barbarous beast, his human association made Chiron kindly, learned, and a good friend to many gods and heroes.

Tutor of Jason and Achilles

Skilled in many arts, including that of prophesy, Chiron taught such famous heroes as Jason, who captured the Golden Fleece, and Achilles, who was killed by a fatal arrowshot to his legendary vulnerable heel during the capture of Troy. Chiron fed the young Achilles on a diet that consisted of the entrails of lions and the marrow bones of bears in order to give the boy courage, and taught him the valuable arts of riding, healing, hunting, and playing the pipes.

Chiron was an immortal but, after being accidentally injured by one of the hero Hercules's deadly poisoned arrows, he was in such profound pain, and was so afraid that his wound would never again heal, that he gave away the gift of his immortality to the suffering Prometheus, father of all the arts and sciences.

Zeus, the king of the gods, wanted so fine a creature as Chiron to be remembered. He therefore decided to set him in the sky as a constellation, bearing the same arrow that Hercules had used to defend Prometheus.

SAGITTARIUS
SYMBOLISM

CERTAIN HERBS, SPICES, FLOWERS, TREES, GEMS, METALS, AND ANIMALS HAVE LONG BEEN ASSOCIATED WITH PARTICULAR ZODIAC SIGNS. SOME ASSOCIATIONS ARE SIMPLY AMUSING, WHILE OTHERS CAN BE USEFUL.

Flowers

Dandelions, lime-flowers, carnations, and pinks are all flowers traditionally associated with Sagittarius.

DANDELION FLOWER

DANDELION SEED

CARNATIONS

Trees

Sagittarian trees include the oak, birch, lime, mulberry, chestnut, and ash.

Birch

Oak

Herbs

Lemon balm is a Sagittarian herb. A syrup made from it, with sugar added, was once kept in every house to relieve a weak stomach and general sickness.

Lemon balm

Spices

No spices are particularly associated with Sagittarius, but allspice is sometimes mentioned in connection with this sign.

Allspice

SAGITTARIUS SYMBOLISM

GUN DOG BROOCH

DEER BROOCH

BRONZE STAG'S HEAD

INDIAN HORSE SPICE BOX

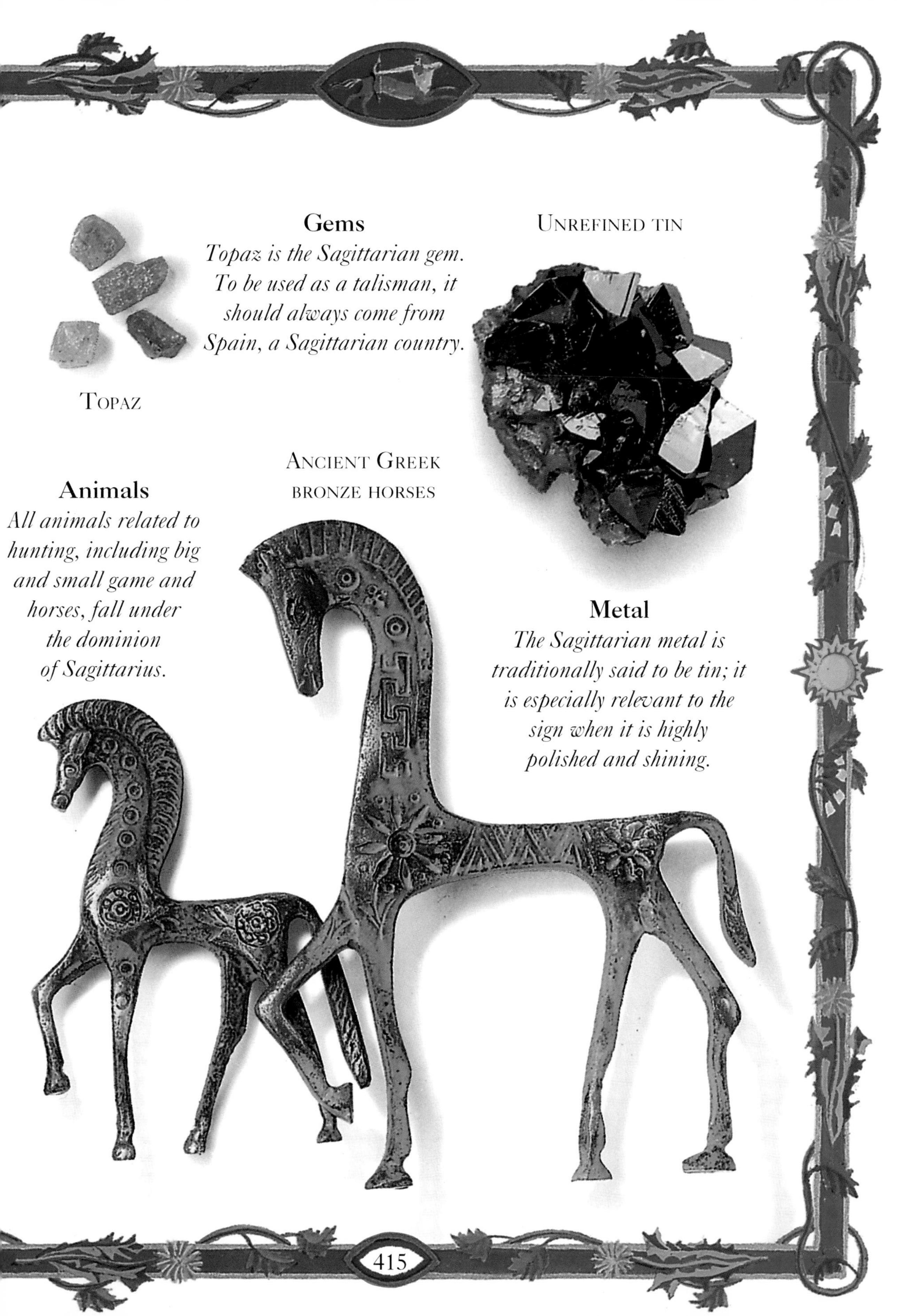

Gems

Topaz is the Sagittarian gem. To be used as a talisman, it should always come from Spain, a Sagittarian country.

TOPAZ

UNREFINED TIN

Animals

All animals related to hunting, including big and small game and horses, fall under the dominion of Sagittarius.

ANCIENT GREEK BRONZE HORSES

Metal

The Sagittarian metal is traditionally said to be tin; it is especially relevant to the sign when it is highly polished and shining.

SAGITTARIUS PROFILE

HAPPY-GO-LUCKY SAGITTARIANS GIVE THE IMPRESSION THAT THEY HAVE NOT A CARE IN THE WORLD. THEY ARE ALWAYS READY TO OFFER A FRIENDLY SMILE AND A WORD OF ENCOURAGEMENT TO LESS POSITIVE PEOPLE.

You are likely to possess a very firm stance, with your feet apart and your hands on your hips. You probably hold your head high, seeming to peer toward some distant horizon.

The Sagittarian face
Wavy hair and, in men, a beard are typical of the Sagittarian face.

The body

The Sagittarian body is often somewhat thick-set, and usually very muscular. It is, perhaps, a body designed less for office work than for sports and physical activity. There have been many great Sagittarian dancers and basketball players.

Your legs are likely to be long. The Sagittarian hips and thighs are particularly strong, but sometimes a bit too prominent, much to the annoyance of many women of the sign. If you spend all of your time following intellectual pursuits, you may develop a rather round-shouldered stoop.

The face

A number of distinctive features characterize the Sagittarian face. Your hair could be wavy and thick, and perhaps a little difficult to control. A broad, open forehead is likely to enhance your generally optimistic expression, and your eyes will probably be set wide apart, beneath straight eyebrows. Your lips are likely to be firm, and will easily break into a relaxed smile.

Style

Sagittarians often tend to cling to a "student" image, and may sport a college ring long after they are well

The Sagittarian stance
A firm stance, with feet spread wide apart, hands placed on hips, and head held high, is typically Sagittarian.

stablished in the world. You are very ikely to hate wearing formal clothes nd, whenever possible, will dress as asually as you possibly can. Polo-eck sweaters are very popular among agittarian men and women.

Clothing that permits ease of novement is advisable for you. It is, n fact, extremely important for your lothing to be comfortable, since nything restrictive will leave you eeling intolerably claustrophobic. erhaps your clothes will be in royal lue or purple, which are favorite agittarian colors.

n general

agittarians are not too concerned bout their appearance; their outlook n life usually leads them to oncentrate on other, more interesting hings. Even those who are fashion-ninded like to choose a number of garments at one session, so that they an then forget about clothes and get n with their lives. Similarly, you will o doubt want to be able to put on our clothes first thing in the norning, and then not have to worry about them again until the evening. You may be perfectly happy wearing comfortable jogging clothes or track-suits most of the time, and they can sometimes be quite fashionable.

The independent Sagittarian spirit does not encourage conformity. You should therefore be careful if you decide to bend the rules when, for instance, deciding what clothes to wear for work.

SAGITTARIUS PERSONALITY

SAGITTARIANS ARE AT THEIR BEST WHEN CHALLENGED. YOUR POSITIVE MIND WILL ALLOW YOU TO GRASP THE OVERALL STRUCTURE OF A SITUATION AND ASSESS THE BEST WAY OF SOLVING A PROBLEM, WHATEVER THE DIFFICULTIES.

People of your Sun sign sometimes seem to possess the secret of eternal youth and may appear to be perpetual students. If you are asked what you are planning for the coming months, you will almost certainly mention some study group, class, or series of lectures that you are planning to attend. If you are not the kind of person to become involved in intellectual pursuits, you will be eager to talk about the new health club that you have just joined.

At work

The duality of Sagittarius makes for an interesting influence, since it accentuates versatility. Many people of your Sun sign are likely to enjoy two quite separate occupations, or at least a rather considerable amount of variety within one.

You are often at your best expressing a number of varied talents. You may complete a task and then turn to something that puts a very different set of demands on other skill that you might have.

Your attitudes

Sagittarians usually need to be stimulated both mentally and physically. There are, however, certain types of Sagittarian who are attracted almost exclusively to either physical or mental activities.

There are the bookish types who do not care for anything resembling physical exercise, and there are the sports fiends who enjoy participating in intense team sports, even when they are well past their prime. Both types of Sagittarian may tend to hang on to their youth.

Most Sagittarians obtain a great deal of pleasure from traveling and, if it is not possible for you to do so, you will probably turn to travel books and videos as an alternative. You may have a flair for languages, and could

Jupiter rules Sagittarius

Jupiter, the Roman god of philosophy and languages, represents the Sagittarian ruling planet. It can make its subjects optimistic and loyal, but sometimes conceited.

do far worse than to invest some of your time and money in refining this particular skill.

The overall picture

Sagittarian enthusiasm is usually boundless and infectious, and it is often expressed through risk-taking, often of a physical nature. You must be careful to ensure that such risks are always extremely carefully calculated. You may also enjoy taking a small gamble from time to time, and some Sagittarians may even be unlucky enough to find the idea thoroughly irresistible. If such a tendency is not controlled, it can cause problems for weaker-minded Sagittarians.

SAGITTARIUS ASPIRATIONS

YOU WILL BE HAPPIEST IN A CAREER THAT CAN BE PLANNED IN ADVANCE. PREDICTABILITY DOES NOT HAVE OTHER APPEAL, HOWEVER, AND YOU MUST BE FREE TO DO THINGS IN YOUR OWN WAY. IT IS EXCELLENT IF YOUR WORK INVOLVES TRAVEL.

Veterinarians

A love for animals, especially horses and dogs, is a powerful Sagittarian trait. It encourages many Sagittarians to become dedicated veterinarians and trainers.

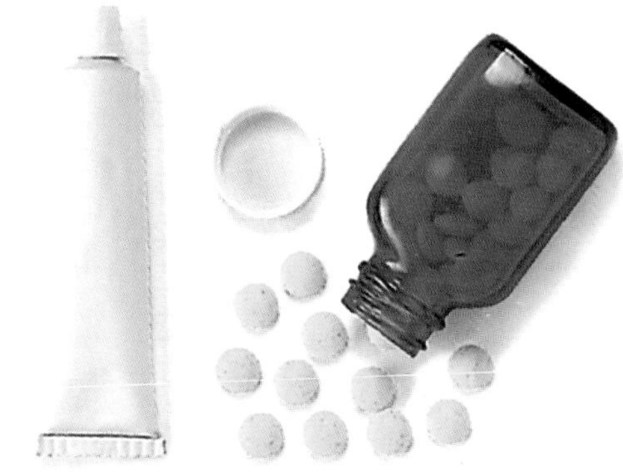

VETERINARY MEDICINES

Teaching

The centaur, which symbolizes this sign, was at one time the symbol of education. Many Sagittarians occupy teaching posts, often specializing in languages.

BLACKBOARD AND CHALK

MODEL JET LINER

The travel industry

Sagittarians enjoy traveling and like to broaden their horizons both intellectually and physically. They therefore make excellent couriers and guides.

The law

Because most Sagittarians enjoy argument and debate, and usually have no difficulty in expressing their opinions, they make excellent attorneys.

HARDBACK BOOKS

Publishing

To expand their own knowledge, and to encourage others to do the same, is a powerful Sagittarian motivation. Many people of this Sun sign are therefore attracted to publishing.

LEGAL DOCUMENTS

SAGITTARIUS HEALTH

YOUR DUAL SAGITTARIAN NATURE INCLINES YOU TO BE PHYSICALLY ACTIVE, AS WELL AS STUDIOUS AND INTELLECTUAL. IDEALLY, YOU SHOULD AIM TO KEEP THESE CHARACTERISTICS IN BALANCE.

Sagittarians need to exploit their physical and intellectual energy. They have excellent resources of both, and it is a great pity if they are not fully developed. Because your outlook is generally positive and enthusiastic, you respond well when you are challenged.

Your diet

The Sagittarian body area is traditionally said to cover the hips and thighs, and because a fairly rich, somewhat heavy diet is preferred by people of this sign, weight gain can sometimes be a problem for them.

You are likely to benefit from the cell salt Kali Muriaticum (Kali Mur.), which may help prevent bronchial congestion and swollen glands.

Taking care

The Sagittarian body organ is the liver. You should therefore make an effort to learn what does and does not agree with you, and find out exactly what your food and drink limits are. It is therefore a good idea for you to always have supply of hangover remedies in the medicine cabinet; you might even develop one of your own. Restlessness can be a problem for Sagittarians. You may find it hard to really relax; a complete change of occupation usually works well in these cases.

Asparagus
Onions, asparagus, and tomatoes are all foods linked to this sign.

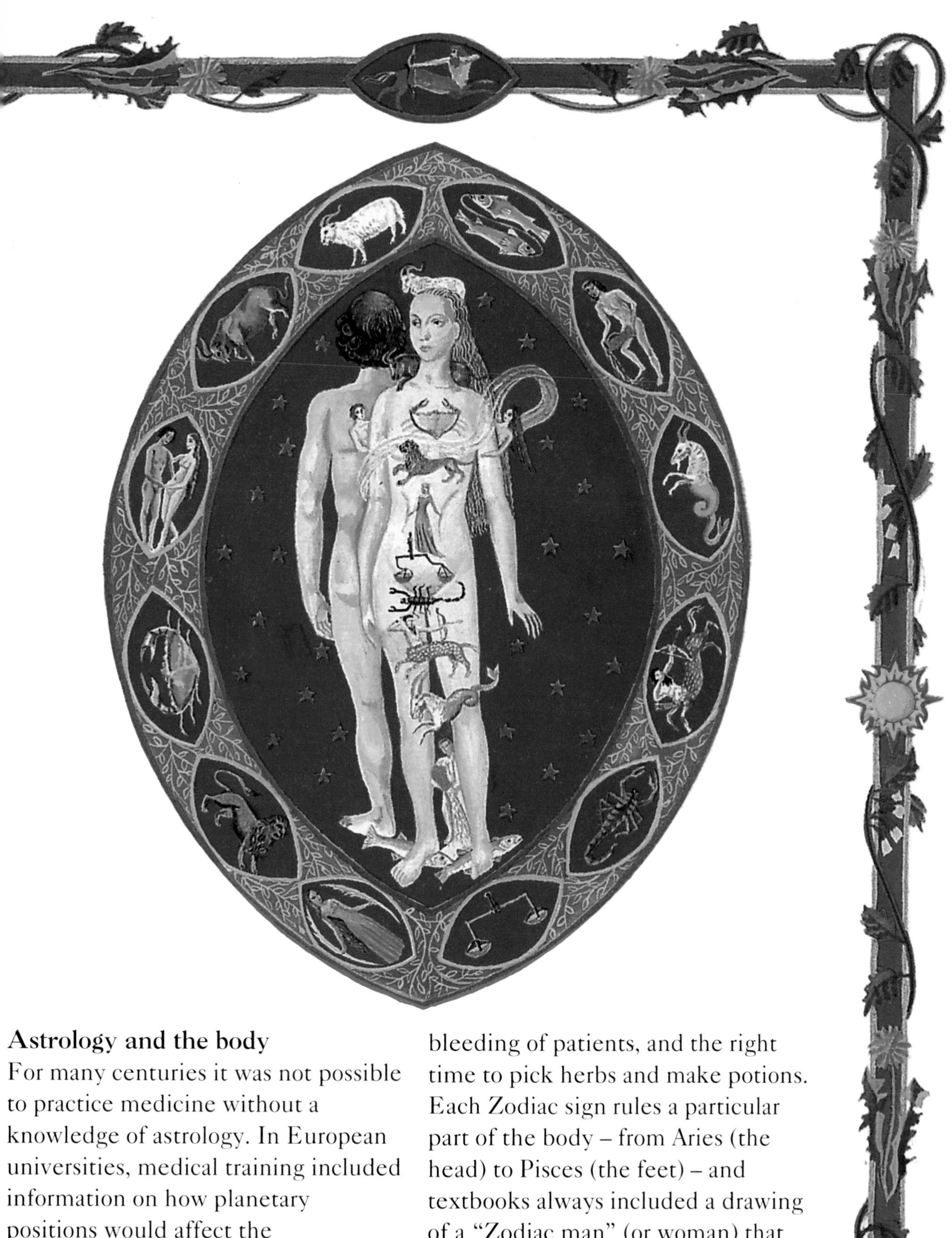

Astrology and the body

For many centuries it was not possible to practice medicine without a knowledge of astrology. In European universities, medical training included information on how planetary positions would affect the administration of medicines, the bleeding of patients, and the right time to pick herbs and make potions. Each Zodiac sign rules a particular part of the body – from Aries (the head) to Pisces (the feet) – and textbooks always included a drawing of a "Zodiac man" (or woman) that illustrated the point.

SAGITTARIUS AT LEISURE

EACH OF THE SUN SIGNS TRADITIONALLY SUGGESTS SPARE-TIME ACTIVITIES, HOBBIES, AND VACATION SPOTS. ALTHOUGH THESE ARE ONLY SUGGESTIONS, THEY OFTEN WORK OUT WELL FOR SAGITTARIANS.

POSTAGE STAMPS

Travel

Hungary, Australia, and Spain are among the countries ruled by Sagittarius. Spain is a big favorite for Sagittarian vacations.

Reading

Sagittarians are eternal students who love to study – especially foreign languages. You will therefore enjoy reading.

BOOKS

INDIAN SHAWL

ARROWS AND QUIVER

Hunting curios

As the hunters of the Zodiac, Sagittarians often enjoy searching for bargains and for unusual or exotic articles.

Archery

The mortal half of the centaur that represents Sagittarius is an archer. Sagittarians who become interested in archery are often exceptionally good at it.

MODEL PORSCHE COUPE

Driving

With their fondness for travel, Sagittarians like to be constantly on the move, and usually make excellent drivers.

SAGITTARIUS IN LOVE

TRADITIONALLY, SAGITTARIANS ARE THE HUNTERS OF THE ZODIAC. IN LOVE, AS IN OTHER AREAS OF THEIR LIVES, THE CHALLENGE OF THE CHASE IS ALL-ENGROSSING, AND MAY EVEN BE MORE EXCITING THAN THE CAPTURE.

The Sagittarian love of challenge can be ignited if the object of your affection plays hard to get. This may be very exciting for you.

As a lover

A Sagittarian's natural enthusiasm for love and sex is very infectious, and it is not difficult for people of your Sun sign to attract partners. Your need for your own space, and for a relationship without even a hint of claustrophobia, is very important. You really cannot bear to feel restricted, and your partners must realize this and allow you a measure of independence if the relationship is to last.

Once they have tamed their coltish attitudes, Sagittarians make very rewarding partners because of their love of life, optimism, and ability to encourage partners to pursue their own interests.

Types of Sagittarian lover

The influence of other planets encourages every Zodiac type to express love in one of five different ways, and it is usually fairly easy to recognize the group to which you belong. Some Sagittarians are really romantic, and go for affairs with all the memorable trimmings. They either rush into

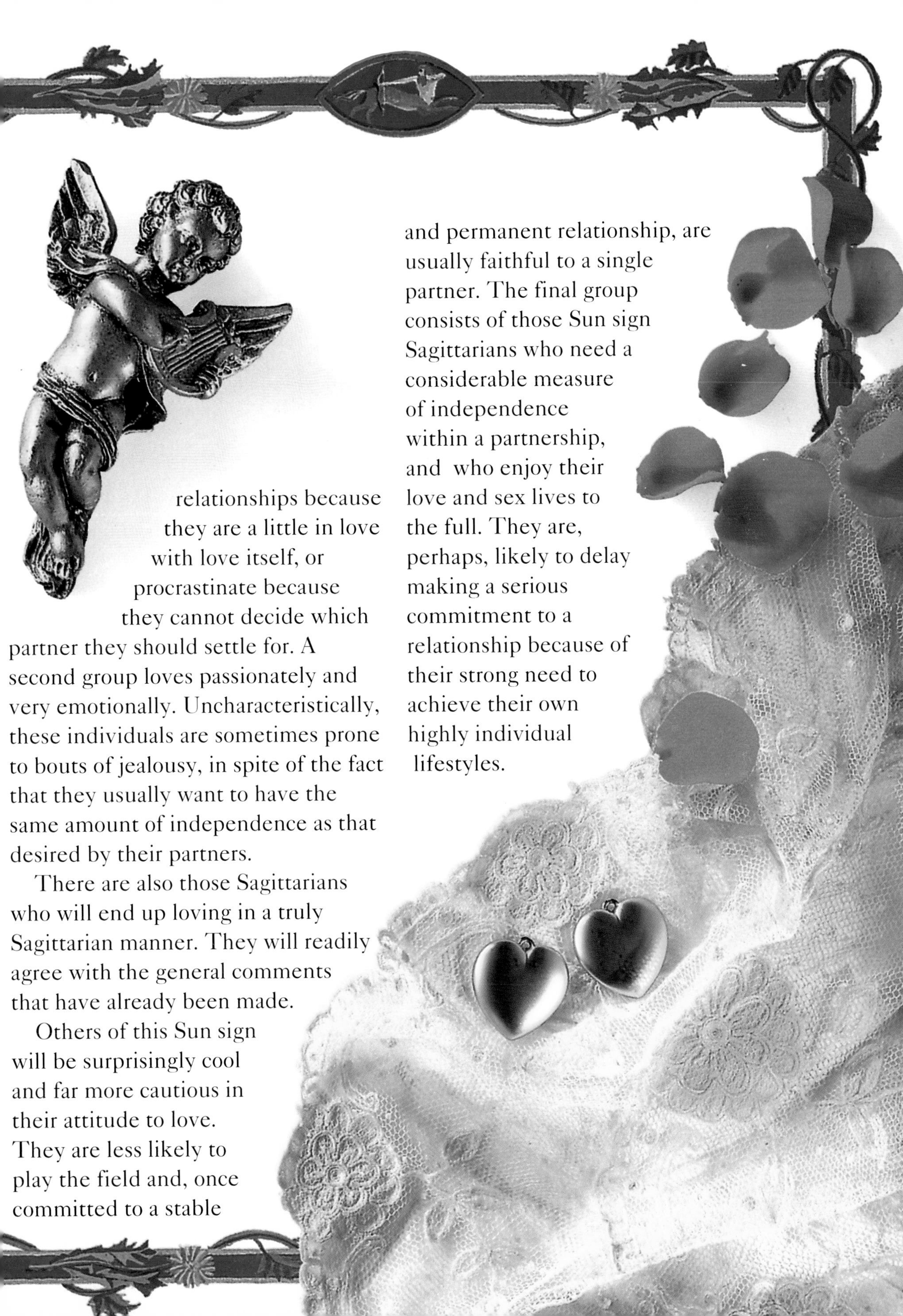

relationships because they are a little in love with love itself, or procrastinate because they cannot decide which partner they should settle for. A second group loves passionately and very emotionally. Uncharacteristically, these individuals are sometimes prone to bouts of jealousy, in spite of the fact that they usually want to have the same amount of independence as that desired by their partners.

There are also those Sagittarians who will end up loving in a truly Sagittarian manner. They will readily agree with the general comments that have already been made.

Others of this Sun sign will be surprisingly cool and far more cautious in their attitude to love. They are less likely to play the field and, once committed to a stable and permanent relationship, are usually faithful to a single partner. The final group consists of those Sun sign Sagittarians who need a considerable measure of independence within a partnership, and who enjoy their love and sex lives to the full. They are, perhaps, likely to delay making a serious commitment to a relationship because of their strong need to achieve their own highly individual lifestyles.

SAGITTARIUS AT HOME

ANY SAGITTARIAN HOME WILL FEEL VERY ROOMY, PERHAPS BECAUSE OF A CLEVER USE OF MIRRORS. THIS IS JUST AS WELL, BECAUSE FURNITURE, BOOKS, ORNAMENTS, AND CHINA WILL OCCUPY EVERY SPARE CORNER.

The Sagittarian home is usually marked by a definite tendency to steer clear of anything that might result in a rather claustrophobic atmosphere. Large windows, and spacious, open-plan living are therefore given substantial priority.

Globe of the world
A love of travel is often reflected in the Sagittarian choice of objects or pictures.

Furniture

You are one of the hunters of the Zodiac, and probably love to visit street markets and antique shops in search of bargains that suit your taste and practical needs. Sagittarians usually choose furniture that is not particularly adventurous, but that is built to last. While you like to be reasonably comfortable, space for bookshelves, or simply piles of books, and places to keep the articles of sports equipment that are so much a part of the Sagittarian lifestyle are just as important, or perhaps even more so.

Soft furnishings

The cushions in your home may appear somewhat crumpled and well used, but they will invite people to sit down. Many items, such as oriental rugs, will have originated overseas, and the fabric for the curtains will sometimes have a rather unusual design. Sagittarians often favor the strong, energetic, perennial designs of William Morris, which reflect Sagittarian energy and a liking for warm color. Dark blue and purple are popular, and those of this

Books

An interesting selection of books may reflect the fact that their owner is something of a perpetual student.

sign usually like the yellows, reds, and golds of the fire element that influences their personalities.

Decorative objects

Because most Sagittarians have lively minds, the decorative items that enhance your home, and certainly the overall effect, will often arouse interest and intellectual discussion among those who come to visit. The pictures that you choose are often open landscapes, since Sagittarians cannot bear anything claustrophobic.

There will almost certainly be interesting, rather than purely beautiful, travel souvenirs. Many Sagittarians enjoy playing the guitar, and one may be given an honored place in your home.

Guitar, rug, and chest

Sagittarian homes may display a guitar; a Spanish influence may also be evident.

Either books or sporting trophies, or perhaps even both, may be present, depending on whether you are a bookish or an athletic type of Sagittarian. There may also be a fair variety of objects scattered around your home that represent your own religious faith, such as a crucifix or some kind of icon.

Tidiness is not a characteristic that one would immediately associate with a Sagittarian home; you are very likely to position the objects in it quite indiscriminately, and then to shuffle them around continually.

THE
MOON
AND
YOU

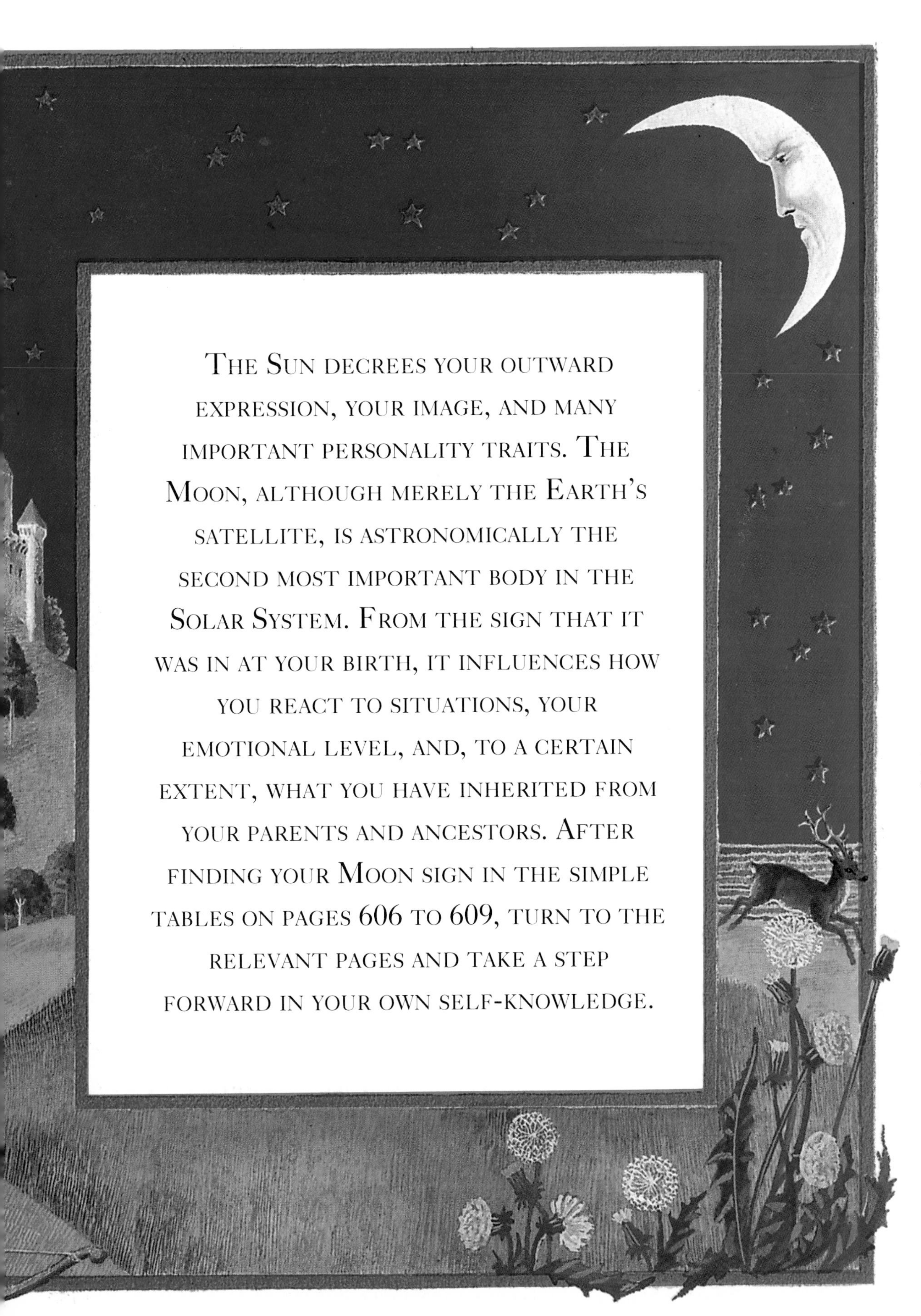

The Sun decrees your outward expression, your image, and many important personality traits. The Moon, although merely the Earth's satellite, is astronomically the second most important body in the Solar System. From the sign that it was in at your birth, it influences how you react to situations, your emotional level, and, to a certain extent, what you have inherited from your parents and ancestors. After finding your Moon sign in the simple tables on pages 606 to 609, turn to the relevant pages and take a step forward in your own self-knowledge.

THE MOON IN ARIES

BOTH THE SUN AND THE MOON WERE IN FIRE SIGNS AT THE TIME OF YOUR BIRTH. IT IS THEREFORE LIKELY THAT YOU HAVE AN ENTHUSIASTIC AND OPTIMISTIC OUTLOOK ON LIFE, AND IMMEDIATE REACTIONS TO SITUATIONS.

Some aspects of your character may have been tempered by a number of strong influences in your birth chart. Otherwise you are likely to be a lively, extroverted person.

Self-expression

You are always ready to accept daunting challenges at a moment's notice. In fact, you often throw yourself in at the deep end, without thinking about the consequences.

Perhaps even more than most Sagittarians, you have breadth of vision and the ability to grasp the essentials of a situation. But having done so, the details may defeat you; therefore either make sure that you leave them to someone else, or discipline yourself to cope with them.

Romance

Your fiery enthusiasm for love and sex should ensure that you obtain a lot of pleasure out of this sphere of your life. You may not always take your relationships too seriously, since your passion has a lighthearted air.

Be aware that the worst Arien fault is selfishness, and that you may sometimes react to your lovers in a somewhat selfish way. You certainly need a partner who can match your abundant Sagittarian and Arien emotional and physical energy, and sheer enjoyment of love and sex.

Your well-being

The Arien body area is the head, and you could be rather prone to headaches. Perhaps these are due to your frustration at other people's incompetence or their slowness to respond to you. Alternatively, you may suffer from a slight kidney problem. If your headaches persist, get a medical checkup.

Anyone with an Arien influence may, because of a tendency to be too hasty, be somewhat accident-prone.

The Moon in Aries

Minor cuts and burns, even fender benders, can easily occur. An awareness of this tendency will help you to combat it. You are pretty energetic, physically, and should have a fairly fast metabolism.

Planning ahead

Sagittarians love a gamble, and with an Arien Moon this tendency is exacerbated. While you could well enjoy investment, your enterprising spirit may be marred by this gambling streak. Therefore resist seductive schemes that may well be far less rewarding than they sound, and take professional advice in this sphere.

Parenthood

You make an excellent parent and will be as young at heart as your children, encouraging them greatly in all their interests. You should have few generation gap problems. In fact, the reverse may be true; you might have to remind yourself of your age.

THE MOON IN TAURUS

YOUR TAUREAN MOON STABILIZES YOUR FIERY CHARACTERISTICS, ESPECIALLY WHEN YOU ARE CONFRONTED BY CHALLENGES. IT ALSO HELPS TO CURB UNNECCESSARY RISK-TAKING AND A TENDENCY TO BE BLINDLY OPTIMISTIC.

The Moon is, according to traditional astrology, "well placed" in Taurus. As a result, its influence on you is rather stronger than it is on other Sagittarians.

Self-expression

Like Sagittarius, Taurus is an earth sign. It prevents you from taking premature action, and instills caution, common sense, and even a good measure of patience – not a quality that one naturally associates with Sun sign Sagittarians. Your response to most situations is not to get immediately involved. You will give yourself time to assess a situation before allowing your natural verve and enthusiasm, springing from your Sagittarian Sun sign, to emerge.

Romance

You have the warm affection usually associated with Taurus, and it is this that will first emerge when you develop an emotional relationship. Your Taurean Moon adds a great deal of natural charm to your personality, while removing nothing of the sexiness of your Sagittarian Sun.

Bear in mind that the worst Taurean fault is possessiveness. As a Sagittarian with an instinctive love of freedom, you detest this unacceptable trait, but your Moon can edge you toward it. Recognize the fact, and watch for the signs.

Your well-being

The Taurean body area is the throat, and you probably find that colds start there. You may also have trouble with your tonsils.

Those with a Taurean emphasis tend to put on weight easily, often because they have a sweet tooth. Sagittarians like rich, hearty food, so you may need to keep a constant calorie check if you want to retain your good figure. Do not let the

The Moon in Taurus

relaxed attitude of your Taurean Moon get the better of you where exercise is concerned. Sagittarians must never stagnate.

Planning ahead

You are cautious and have good business sense. As a result you can cope with money far better than many Sun sign Sagittarians. Even if you do succumb to your Sagittarian gambling instinct, the chances are that you will not fritter away more money than you can afford to lose.

Parenthood

As a parent, you no doubt get things just about right, and will discipline your children in precisely the right way, so that they know exactly where they stand with you.

The power of your Sagittarian Sun makes you an optimistic and very encouraging parent, and your children thrive on your constructive comments and warm affection. You do not find it difficult to keep up with their ideas and are unlikely to incur problems with the generation gap.

THE MOON IN GEMINI

SAGITTARIUS AND GEMINI ARE POLAR OR OPPOSITE ZODIAC SIGNS, SO YOU WERE BORN UNDER A FULL MOON. RESTLESSNESS IS A GEMINIAN CHARACTERISTIC, AND YOU SHOULD TRY TO FIGHT IT. BE VERSATILE, BUT DEVELOP CONSISTENCY OF EFFORT.

Each of us is, in one way or another, likely to express the attributes of our polar, or opposite, Zodiac sign. Each sign has its partner across the horoscope; for Sagittarians, this is Gemini and, because the Moon was in Gemini when you were born, this polarity is emphasized in an interesting and powerful way.

Self-expression

Sagittarius and Gemini are both mutable signs, which means that you are flexible and intellectual in character, and have a versatile mind. These signs are also traditionally dual in nature, and you may therefore have a tendency to do more than one thing at a time. This is probably very natural to you, and it is something that you should not try to curb. You must, however, work to avoid superficiality, which may also result from your dual nature. Always make a special effort to complete everything that you undertake. Also remember that restlessness is the worst fault of both Gemini and Sagittarius. This characteristic is further emphasized in people born under a Full Moon.

Romance

You have all the passion of your Sagittarian Sun to express in your love and sex life, added to which your Geminian Moon will make you very flirtatious. Some duality can obviously find a place in this area of your life, and it is worth remembering that you could encounter problems if you do not keep these tendencies under control. Even more than most Sagittarians, you require a good level of intellectual rapport with a lover.

Your well-being

Gemini rules the arms and hands, so yours may be vulnerable to injury. It also rules the lungs, so you could be susceptible to bronchitis and should

The Moon in Gemini

beware of a cough that will not go away. If you smoke, break the habit as soon as possible.

Your Geminian Moon gives you a great deal of nervous energy, which must be positively expressed through lively physical exercise.

Planning ahead

You should probably always seek professional advice when you have money to invest. Your Sagittarian gambling spirit may combine with a Geminian liking for get-rich-quick schemes and, as a result, you could end up losing far more money than you are really able to afford.

Parenthood

As a parent, you may even be ahead of your children in relation to the most modern trends.

It is, however, possible that a tendency to be inconsistent may damage your relationship. Make sure that your children always know where they stand with you. In this way you should avoid the generation gap.

THE MOON IN CANCER

YOU REALLY NEED INDEPENDENCE, FREEDOM OF EXPRESSION, AND EMOTIONAL SECURITY. YOUR URGE FOR THESE IS INSTINCTIVE AND POWERFUL. YOU ARE PROTECTIVE TOWARD THOSE YOU LOVE, AND VALUE SOLIDARITY.

The combination of Sagittarius, a fire sign, and Cancer, a water sign, makes for some contrasting characteristics that you should use to full advantage. Because the Moon rules Cancer, the influence of your Moon sign is very powerful.

Self-expression

You are much more sensitive than many Sagittarians, and can be more easily hurt, too. You are also prone to changes of mood. While you will have plenty of Sagittarian optimism and enthusiasm, your immediate reaction to any situation will be cautious. You have an instinctive self-defensive system that immediately springs into action when you are challenged.

Romance

You express love very sensually and have many desirable qualities that should enable you to maintain a stable, yet exciting, relationship. Your emotional level is very high, for you have all the powerful, fiery emotion of Sagittarius, which will spur you into passionate expression of love and sex. You also have the more tender emotion of Cancer, which should enable you to tune into your partner's needs on all levels.

You are probably less happy-go-lucky in your relationships than many Sun sign Sagittarians, but should be careful not to let Cancerian moodiness and a tendency to react very sharply mar so much that is positive.

Your well-being

The Cancerian body area covers the breasts and, although Cancerians are no more likely to contract cancer than anyone else, Sagittarian women should obviously make the usual regular checks.

Sagittarians are among the people who are least likely to worry when confronted with problems, whereas

The Moon in Cancer

Cancerians are among those most prone to it. The positive areas of your personality should enable you to deal with worry, although your digestion may sometimes trouble you under difficult circumstances.

Cancerians are usually good and enthusiastic cooks, and Sagittarians like tasty, rich food. If you are overweight, you may not be getting enough exercise.

Planning ahead

You are very lucky where finance is concerned. Your Sagittarian gambling spirit is mitigated by a shrewd and instinctive business sense, stemming from your Moon sign. If you are investing, follow your intuition; when you are in doubt, you would be wise to seek professional advice.

Parenthood

You are probably a far more caring and protective parent than most Sagittarians. Do not take this too far, though, and allow your enthusiasm to encourage your children. If you are not too sentimental, and manage to keep abreast of your children's thoughts and ideas, you will have few problems with the generation gap.

THE MOON IN LEO

YOUR LEO MOON PROMPTS A WELL-ORGANIZED, RATHER FORMAL APPROACH TO MOST SITUATIONS. YOUR ACCEPTANCE OF CHALLENGE IS ENCOURAGED BY AN ABILITY TO TAKE COMMAND, BUT YOU MUST TAKE CARE TO AVOID BEING BOSSY.

Your Sun and Moon signs are both of the fire element, so you have great natural enthusiasm and optimism, and an extremely positive outlook on life.

Self-expression

You may tend to be marginally more conventional than most Sun sign Sagittarians, but this only serves to make you naturally elegant and gives you a powerful instinct for real quality. Your Sun sign, on the other hand, endows you with a good mind, and you may have very considerable creative potential.

You are able to cope well with people and very possibly have excellent organizing ability. Generally speaking, your Sagittarian Sun prevents you from becoming pompous or bossy, but should you be accused of these traits, take note. You are extremely magnanimous, and never harbor a grudge.

Romance

You are a very passionate and demonstrative lover, and probably have a stylish approach to a prospective partner. You will create an expensive, romantic atmosphere, and will do everything in your power to make life happy, enjoyable, and even blissful for your lovers.

You will be a very supportive partner and, because loyalty is important to you, once you are committed you have less of a roving eye than many Sagittarians.

Your well-being

The Leo body area covers the back and spine. You will do well to remember this, and to gear part of your exercise schedule toward that area. If you have to spend a lot of time sitting at an office desk, consider getting a back-support chair. The Leo organ is the heart, and it too must be kept in good condition.

The Moon in Leo

Most Sun sign Sagittarians not only need, but also enjoy, physical exercise. Keeping fit through sports and exercise should therefore be no real problem for you. Your Leo Moon may attract you to all kinds of dance, and this is something that you should consider as an alternative to health clubs or participating in team sports.

Planning ahead

You need to earn a lot of money in order to enjoy a comfortable lifestyle; you have big ideas and may well be very extravagant. But you are not without financial flair and can be good with investments, provided that you remember to control your Sagittarian gambling spirit and the tendency to put too many eggs in one basket. Aim to have one or two really sound, secure savings plans.

Parenthood

You are a very encouraging and enthusiastic parent, and your children will thrive on your positive, lively comments on their interests. At times your children may see you as slightly pompous, but if you keep a sense of humor you should not have many problems with the generation gap.

THE MOON IN VIRGO

DO NOT HESITATE WHEN CONFRONTED BY TRICKY SITUATIONS; YOU HAVE A TENDENCY TO UNDERESTIMATE YOURSELF. GUARD AGAINST TENSION AND RESTLESSNESS. YOU ARE A GOOD COMMUNICATOR AND CAN COPE WELL WITH DETAIL.

Both Sagittarius and Virgo are mutable signs and, as a result, you have a flexible mind and great intellectual capacity.

Self-expression

While most Sagittarians find detail boring and difficult to deal with, you respond differently. You react well to it and may look at details even before looking for a broad overview.

You are critical and analytical in your approach to problems, and will probably express your Sagittarian versatility within the broad confines of one or two large subjects. Your ability to get your ideas across to other people is excellent, since you communicate fluently.

Romance

Your Sagittarian passion is somewhat moderated by your Virgoan Moon, which may inhibit you in the area of love and sex. An instinctive modesty can make you feel a little inferior in this field. In fact, you have much to offer, so try not to put yourself down.

A serious Virgoan fault is to nag and to criticize partners, often for no good reason. Your Sagittarian Sun sign will loathe this tendency and help you to bite your tongue if you find yourself beginning to complain.

Your well-being

The Virgoan body area is the stomach and, while Sagittarius is not prone to worry, Virgo certainly is. Interestingly, your stomach may react before your mind. You need a high-fiber diet and will perhaps incline to vegetarianism, to which Virgoans tend to be particularly attracted.

You have a great deal of nervous, tense energy, and periods of stress can wreak havoc with you. A calming, centering discipline such as yoga could well be of considerable benefit to you. Also think about sports and

The Moon in Virgo

exercise regimens, which could include pursuits such as walking, rambling, cycling, and gardening.

Planning ahead

You are more careful with your finances than most Sagittarians, and find it fairly easy to save money and to avoid unnecessary extravagance. Your ability to cope with detail may incline you to keep careful accounts and to watch the stock market. Do, however, guard against your Sagittarian gambling spirit, and be self-critical if it seems likely to run away with you. This will be the time to seek professional advice.

Parenthood

All your Sagittarian enthusiasm will color your attitude to your children. However, that Virgoan critical response may be far harsher in your children's eyes than it seems to you. Keep up with their concerns, and you will avoid the generation gap.

THE MOON IN LIBRA

YOUR REACTION TO ALMOST ANY SITUATION IS LIKELY TO BE VERY CALM. ALWAYS MAKE SURE THAT YOU EXPRESS YOUR SPLENDID SAGITTARIAN POTENTIAL, AND NEVER ALLOW YOUR MIND AND BODY TO STAGNATE.

The fire of your Sagittarian Sun and the air of your Libran Moon blend well. You have a warm-hearted and attractive personality, and respond well to people, showing sympathy and understanding.

Self-expression

Because of their characteristic haste, Sagittarians sometimes tend to lack tact. This is not so in your case; your Libran Moon helps you to control the tendency and, in many ways, makes you a diplomat.

When confronted with challenging situations, your immediate response may well be less assertive and positive than that of many Sun sign Sagittarians. However, once you have drawn your conclusions, your Sagittarian Sun sign usually points you in the right direction.

There is an easygoing side to your nature, and you could give the impression that you cannot be rushed. You may need to persuade yourself to be a little more self-disciplined and better organized if you are to make the best of your potential.

Romance

You are probably rather more romantic than many Sagittarians, and enjoy setting a glamorous scene in which to make love. Once committed, you make a wonderful partner. You will always be fair and listen to your lover's ideas.

Your well-being

The Libran organ is the kidneys and, if you are at all prone to headaches, there could be a minor problem with them. Very often those with a Libran influence get totally bored with exercise and just give up. Aim to avoid this, because Sagittarians have a lot of physical energy to burn, and lethargy does not suit them. Your Libran Moon may encourage you to

The Moon in Libra

eat too much sweet food, and you could well suffer from excessive weight gain as a result. Even the balance by becoming a member of a good health club with a variety of exercise programs.

Planning ahead

You are very generous and may not be terribly sensible with money. Both your Sagittarian gambling streak and your Libran Moon's sympathy for a hard-luck story may be a source of money problems. Do not overinvest in one area, do not lend money, and do not gamble more than you can afford to lose. Always aim to get professional advice in this area.

Parenthood

While you are a very enthusiastic and kind parent, you are capable of spoiling your children. Remember that indecisiveness on your part makes it difficult for them to know where they stand. If you keep up with their ideas, you will have few difficulties with the generation gap.

THE MOON IN SCORPIO

YOUR SAGITTARIAN BREADTH OF VISION IS ENHANCED BY A NATURAL ABILITY TO DELVE DEEPLY INTO PROBLEMS. THIS DERIVES FROM YOUR MOON SIGN. YOU HAVE AN INTENSE, FIERY PASSION, BUT YOU SHOULD CURB ANY TENDENCY TO JEALOUSY.

Sagittarius and Scorpio are both charged with a great deal of physical and emotional energy. Sagittarians express this in a lively, positive way, while Scorpios tend to be deeply penetrating, incisive, and generally very intuitive.

Self-expression

You obviously have extremely powerful resources on which to draw, and striking potential. You have breadth of vision and the ability to deal with any aspect of a challenge or problematic situation. Your powers of endurance, under both difficult physical conditions and intellectually demanding ones, are second to none. With all of this in mind, it is obvious that you need to be totally committed to your objectives in life, and that your reach must always exceed your grasp. If you are unfulfilled and life seems empty, few Sagittarians will suffer more than you.

Romance

Your passion for a full life is second only to your expression of love and sex. In this area you are very enthusiastic and, while you contribute a great deal to the success of a permanent emotional relationship, you are also very demanding, and need an extremely energetic and passionate partner.

The worst Scorpio fault is jealousy – something that your Sagittarian Sun sign will deplore. You may find yourself reacting negatively to a partner's mildly flirtatious behavior, while you yourself enjoy an element of freedom within a relationship.

Your well-being

The Scorpio body area covers the genitals; anyone, whatever their Sun sign, should get regular checkups in that area. But it is your emotional and physical energy that has the strongest influence on your general health and

The Moon in Scorpio

well-being. Aim to get regular exercise; all kinds of water sports should suit you.

Planning ahead

You could be very clever with money, provided that you allow your instinctive business sense and intuition to express themselves. Financial risk-taking could attract you, and you may end up taking an unwise plunge. At such times, the Scorpion is wiser than the Centaur.

Parenthood

While you are always enthusiastic and encouraging, you could be a somewhat demanding parent. Children like a well-structured life, which gives them a sense of security. Be careful not to overdo this, however, or to allow tradition and discipline to interfere with the sheer enjoyment of your children's company. Encourage their interests and ideas, and keep abreast of them in order to avoid the generation gap.

THE MOON IN
SAGITTARIUS

BECAUSE BOTH THE SUN AND THE MOON WERE IN SAGITTARIUS AT THE TIME OF YOUR BIRTH, YOU WERE BORN UNDER A NEW MOON. SAGITTARIUS IS A FIRE SIGN, SO THIS ELEMENT INFLUENCES YOUR PERSONALITY AND REACTIONS.

Should you study a list of your Sun sign characteristics, you will probably recognize that a great many of them apply to you. Out of a list of perhaps 20 traits of a Sun sign listed in books or magazines, most people will strongly identify with 11 or 12. For you, however, the average increases considerably because the Sun and Moon were both in Sagittarius when you were born.

Self-expression

Not only do you have the attributes of your Sun sign, but you also respond to situations in the same manner. When someone suggests an idea to you, your natural enthusiasm ignites, and you are eager to get involved.

You probably do not worry too much about possible pitfalls or problems, regarding them as something to be dealt with when you come to them. But it is important that you keep your initial enthusiasm on the boil, because if you do not, you could easily succumb to the most serious Sagittarian fault: restlessness. You are capable of enormous versatility, but must learn to be selective and to develop a degree of consistency. You have a high level of intellectual and physical energy, and neither must be allowed to stagnate.

Romance

You are passionate and will enjoy love and sex with a youthful exuberance. You must have a full love and sex life, and need a partner who is intellectually very stimulating.

Fidelity may not come naturally to you, and your partners must learn that you need a good measure of freedom in this sphere of your life.

Your well-being

If you turn to pages 422 to 423, you will read about Sagittarian health and well-being. As you are a "double

The Moon in Sagittarius

Sagittarian," those comments will most definitely apply to you.

Be careful not to overindulge in heavy food. You are prone to weight gain, and unwanted flesh is likely to gather around your hips and thighs – especially if you are a woman. Good workouts and some of the more daring sports are excellent for you.

Planning ahead

Your Sagittarian gambling instinct could get the better of you from time to time, and you may be strongly attracted to get-rich-quick schemes. You must be careful to curb these enthusiasms and to always get professional financial advice when you have some money to invest, no matter how convincing a deal may seem at the time.

Parenthood

You are among the most enthusiastic of parents and will always encourage your children to make the most of their potential. You probably try to see to it that they fill their days as completely as you do. You do not find it difficult to keep up with their ideas and should not incur problems with the generation gap.

THE MOON IN CAPRICORN

YOU HAVE A GREAT DEAL OF POTENTIAL AND ARE ALWAYS VERY EAGER TO GET INVOLVED IN AMBITIOUS SCHEMES. YOUR EARTHY CAPRICORNIAN MOON ADDS PRACTICALITY TO YOUR CHARACTER – AND PERHAPS A TENDENCY TO GRUMBLE.

There are some striking contrasts between Sagittarius and Capricorn and, as a result, you possess a multifaceted personality, with a great deal of potential that can be expressed in a variety of ways.

Self-expression

Your Sagittarian Sun sign gives you fiery enthusiasm and a positive outlook on life. On the other hand, the earth element of your Moon sign makes you instinctively cautious and far less likely to take risks than are many Sagittarians.

You are very ambitious and, when presented with a challenging situation, will at once be able to foresee the end result. You will then begin to plan your moves constructively toward that goal.

Sagittarians are, on the whole, good communicators, and you will certainly let it be known if you are being impeded by some form of inefficiency. Should you be accused of grumbling too much, which is usually very uncharacteristic of Sagittarians, you must take note.

Romance

You are less gushing in expressing your emotions than many people of your Sun sign, and could tend to hold back a little in the initial stages of a relationship. This does not mean that you cannot enjoy a truly rewarding and fulfilling love and sex life.

You could be more faithful, and have less of a roving eye, than other Sagittarians, and may take a while to commit yourself to a relationship.

Your well-being

The Capricornian body area covers the knees and shins. Yours will be vulnerable, especially if you engage in a lot of sporting activities. Treatment can save a great deal of pain and prevent serious problems.

The Moon in Capricorn

The teeth, skin, and bones are also in Capricorn's domain, so beware of stiffness in the joints, and keep moving. Do not neglect regular dental checkups, and wear a protective cream when the sun is strong.

You may have a rapid metabolism; if so, weight gain is unlikely to be a problem for you.

Planning ahead

Anyone with a Capricornian influence is usually careful, and often good with money. You like to see it grow, so your Sagittarian gambling streak is probably kept under control. You only take financial risks if you are sure you can afford to lose the money involved.

Parenthood

Your sense of humor is a great asset to you as a parent, but you could, surprisingly for a Sagittarian, react a little coolly to some of your children's suggestions and ideas. If you enjoy the challenge of keeping up with them, you will manage to leap across the generation gap.

THE MOON IN AQUARIUS

SAGITTARIUS AND AQUARIUS ARE BOTH SIGNS THAT REQUIRE INDEPENDENCE. TRY NOT TO ALLOW A TENDENCY TO RESPOND COOLLY AND DISTANTLY TO OTHER PEOPLE SPOIL YOUR WONDERFUL SAGITTARIAN APPROACH TO LOVE.

The fire element of Sagittarius and the air element of Aquarius blend well, not only making you the individualist of your Sun sign peers, but also putting you among those who greatly need independence and freedom of expression.

Self-expression

You may well have built a lifestyle that has certain individual features. You are a warm-hearted and very friendly person, but definitely need both physical and psychological space. Pettiness, unnecessary detail, and people who nag are not for you.

Romance

The Moon in Aquarius adds a certain glitz and glamour to your personality, but you may also respond coolly and distantly when first approached by prospective partners. You need a good period of friendship and intellectual rapport before the lively passion of your Sagittarian Sun can be fully expressed. Your love and sex life is probably rewarding, but you must cater to your need for independence. You may postpone a full commitment until you find a partner who sees this and is willing to allow you space.

Your well-being

The Aquarian body area covers the ankles, and yours are vulnerable. The circulation is also ruled by Aquarius and, if you like crisp, cold weather, you must try to keep warm.

You may enjoy skiing, skating, or dancing. In any case, you should get involved in some form of exercise. You thrive on a light diet, even if you like the heavier foods often favored by your Sun sign.

Planning ahead

You may find it quite difficult to save money regularly. You are probably attracted to fashionable clothes and

The Moon in Aquarius

fine and unusual things for the home. You could go all out for some apparently excellent savings plan and invest heavily in it, only to find that it runs into difficulty.

It may be well worth your while to seek professional financial advice when you have some money to invest. Best of all, you should seriously consider taking part in some option where a certain proportion of your regular paycheck is invested at the source before you can squander it. Remember, your Sagittarian gambling spirit is very much attracted to exciting but risky schemes.

Parenthood

You are an extremely lively parent and do not find it difficult to know what your children are thinking. If you keep up with their ideas, you should have few problems with the generation gap. Aim to display warm affection toward your children, and avoid unpredictable responses.

THE MOON IN PISCES

SAGITTARIUS AND PISCES ARE DUAL SIGNS OF THE ZODIAC, AND YOU ARE THEREFORE VERY VERSATILE. HOWEVER, YOU DO NEED TO DEVELOP CONSISTENCY OF EFFORT, AND MUST BE DISCIPLINED IF YOU ARE TO DEVELOP TO YOUR FULL POTENTIAL.

Sagittarius and Pisces are both mutable signs, and their combination makes you very flexible and easygoing. In addition, both are dual signs. Pisces is represented by two fishes swimming in opposite directions, Sagittarius by a creature who is both man and horse. These symbols represent a high degree of versatility, with enviable potential, but suggest a similarly high degree of restlessness.

Self-expression

While it is very important for you to have a variety of very different interests, you should also develop staying power and complete any project that you start, if it is to give you inner satisfaction.

Your response to challenges is complex. At first, you probably feel somewhat hesitant and lacking in confidence, but then you may decide on a line of action. Finally you will, for no apparent reason, do precisely the opposite, which may turn out to be a mistake. Your Sun sign gives you an excellent, sharp intellect and a rich imagination, possibly adding creative potential. Be firm with yourself, and exploit these qualities.

Romance

You are caring, loving, and passionate, but need a strong partner who will bring out the best in you and ignite your Sagittarian enthusiasm. You are capable of giving much to a lover, and should enjoy a rich and rewarding love and sex life.

The worst Piscean fault is deceitfulness; do not lie to yourself, especially when considering your lovers' attitudes to you.

Your well-being

The Piscean body area is the feet, and you may find it difficult to obtain comfortable shoes. You could easily

The Moon in Pisces

fall back on eating too heavily, and may be prone to putting on weight unless you are actively involved in some form of sports, for example, dancing or skating.

Planning ahead

You are sometimes left wondering where your money has gone. The answer is that you have spent it on frivolous things. You may need help from a stronger, more down-to-earth partner or a friendly bank officer in working out a sensible budget. If you have some spare money, make sure that you get financial advice before investing it. You should neither lend money, nor give so readily to charity that you get yourself into trouble.

Parenthood

You are probably a very warm and caring parent, who may well spoil your children. Take disciplinary measures when you must, even if you do not enjoy being strict, since this will help give your children a more secure background. You will always listen to your children's problems, so they will know where they stand with you. There should be no problems with the generation gap.

SUN & MOON SIGNS

CAPRICORN

DECEMBER 22 – JANUARY 20

INTRODUCING CAPRICORN

CAPRICORN, WHO IS TRADITIONALLY REPRESENTED AS THE HALF-GOAT, HALF-FISH FIGURE, IS THE TENTH SIGN OF THE ZODIAC. SUN SIGN CAPRICORNIANS GENERALLY HAVE RATHER COMPLEX CHARACTERS.

There are two distinct types of Capricornian. One type will be ambitious and enterprising, while the other will never find the motivation to move forward in life and will spend a great deal of time complaining about the real or imagined obstacles that hold them back. Even the most famous and successful Capricornian may have a tendency to grumble, and all people of this sign can feel that they are forced to carry undeserved burdens. A fondness for solitude is another Capricornian characteristic.

Traditional groupings

As you read through this book you will come across references to the elements and the qualities, and to positive and negative, or masculine and feminine signs.

The first of these groupings, that of the elements, comprises fire, earth, air, and water signs. The second, that of the qualities, divides the Zodiac into cardinal, fixed, and mutable signs. The final grouping is made up of positive and negative, or masculine and feminine signs. Each Zodiac sign is associated with a combination of components from these groupings, all of which contribute different characteristics to it.

Capricornian characteristics

Capricorn belongs to the earth element, and its subjects often have a great deal of practical common sense. It is of the cardinal quality, which may make you outgoing. However, as a negative, feminine sign Capricorn also inclines its subjects to introversion. All of these characteristics find expression in the Capricorn personality. Saturn, your ruling planet, also guides your destiny, and "saturnine" is an adjective that often applies to you. Capricornians generally prefer subdued colors such as gray or dark green.

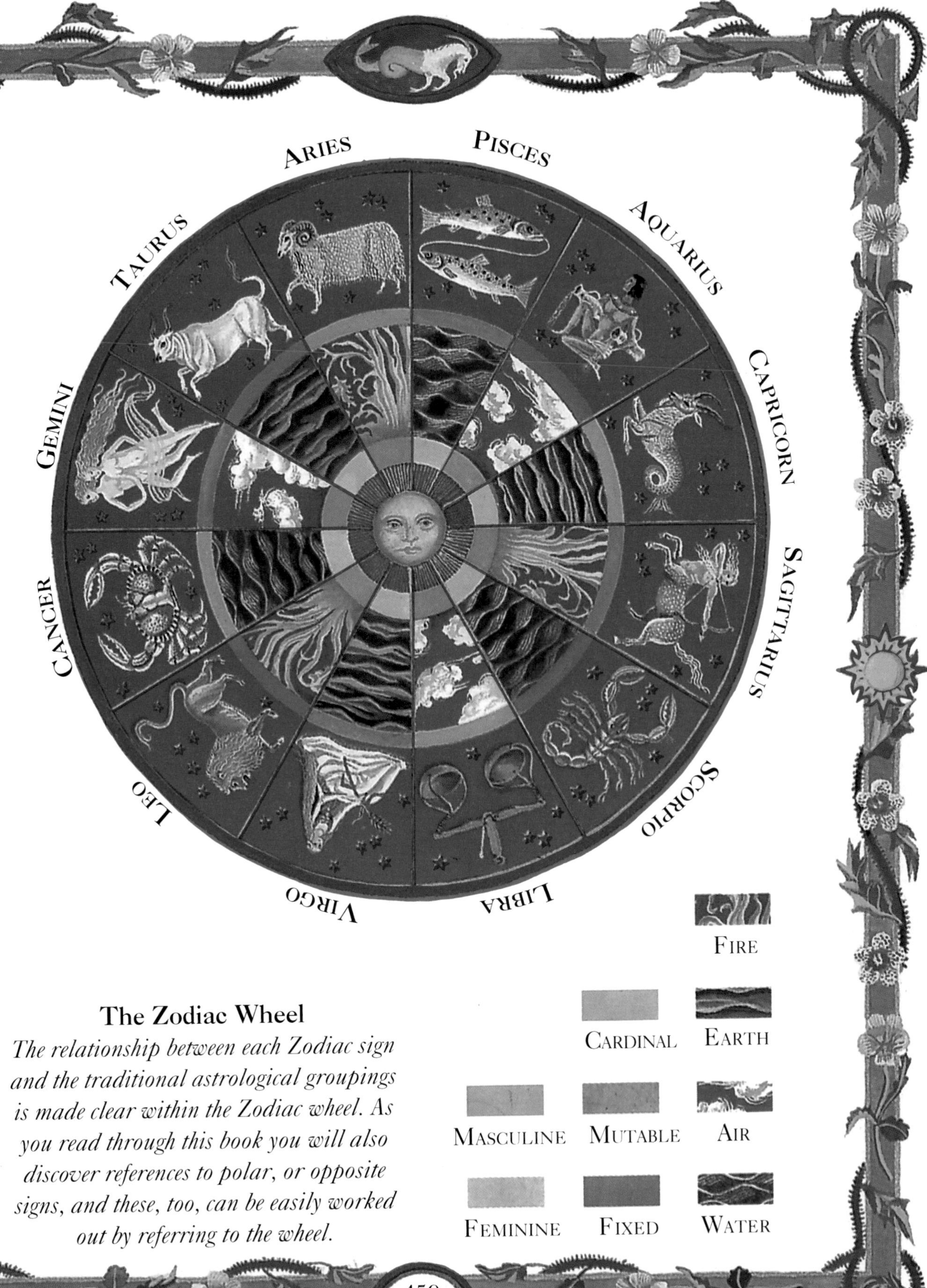

The Zodiac Wheel

The relationship between each Zodiac sign and the traditional astrological groupings is made clear within the Zodiac wheel. As you read through this book you will also discover references to polar, or opposite signs, and these, too, can be easily worked out by referring to the wheel.

CAPRICORN
MYTHS & LEGENDS

THE ZODIAC, WHICH IS BELIEVED TO HAVE ORIGINATED IN BABYLON AS LONG AS 2,500 YEARS AGO, IS A CIRCLE OF CONSTELLATIONS THROUGH WHICH THE SUN MOVES DURING THE COURSE OF A YEAR.

Many Zodiacal figures were first carved on Babylonian boundary stones. This is where Capricorn makes his first appearance, as the Goat-Fish. He is shown as Ea, a man walking in a great fish-shaped cloak, with the fish head over his head and the cloak trailing into a tail. One of his Babylonian titles was "antelope of the subterranean ocean." He was said to rise from the waters during the day in order to tutor man in the arts of civilization and to return to the depths at night.

Ea's name means "House of the Water," and perhaps this indicates the significance that was placed upon him in a country where water was such a precious commodity. He had the role of god of knowledge and presided over the work done by men. Because of this, he was devoutly worshiped by many different types of craftsmen.

Pan pipes
This bronze statuette of Pan and the syrinx dates from 430 B.C.

Later myths

The later mythological associations of Capricorn are obscure and difficult to follow. There is a distant association with Pan, no doubt because although he had a human torso and arms, other parts of his body consisted of the legs, ears, and horns of a goat. He was the son of Hermes, the messenger of the gods, but his mother's name is uncertain. According to some sources it was Callisto, but others sometimes mention Penelope.

Pan and Syrinx

Pan is perhaps best remembered as the being who was responsible for inventing the panpipes; he called them syrinx in honor of a nymph who was turned into a reed to escape his amorous attentions.

Pan loved mountains, caves, and lonely places, and it was while frisking with nymphs in one such desolate place that he gave chase to Syrinx. Just as he was about to capture her, she called out for help to her father, Ladon the river god. At her request, Ladon turned her into a reed and Pan was foiled. To console himself, Pan cut down a clump of reeds and made some pipes. The music that Pan was able to produce on his syrinx was apparently so sweet that on one occasion he challenged Apollo, the god of music and the personification of beauty, to a musical competition.

Panic fear

The feeling of loneliness that can afflict people traveling on their own through wild or inhospitable terrain was sometimes attributed to the presence of Pan. Any fear that seemed unattributable to an obvious cause has come to be known as "panic fear" – or panic for short.

The music of Pan

The image on this dish, which dates from 1515, shows Pan playing his syrinx to a couple of shepherds.

Although it does at first seem to be an extremely slender association, astrologers throughout the ages have attempted to play up with the Capricornian qualities that can be related to the goat.

The domestic animal is, for instance, often tethered in one small space, while for the wild mountain goat the mountains and hills seem to be as accessible as they once were to the god Pan himself.

Many Sun sign Capricornians have a fondness and perhaps even a real need for solitude.

CAPRICORN SYMBOLISM

CERTAIN HERBS, SPICES, FLOWERS, TREES, GEMS, METALS, AND ANIMALS HAVE LONG BEEN ASSOCIATED WITH PARTICULAR ZODIAC SIGNS. SOME ASSOCIATIONS ARE SIMPLY AMUSING, WHILE OTHERS CAN BE GENUINELY USEFUL.

Pansies and ivy
Pansies and ivy are two of the decorative plants said to be ruled by Capricorn.

PANSIES

IVY

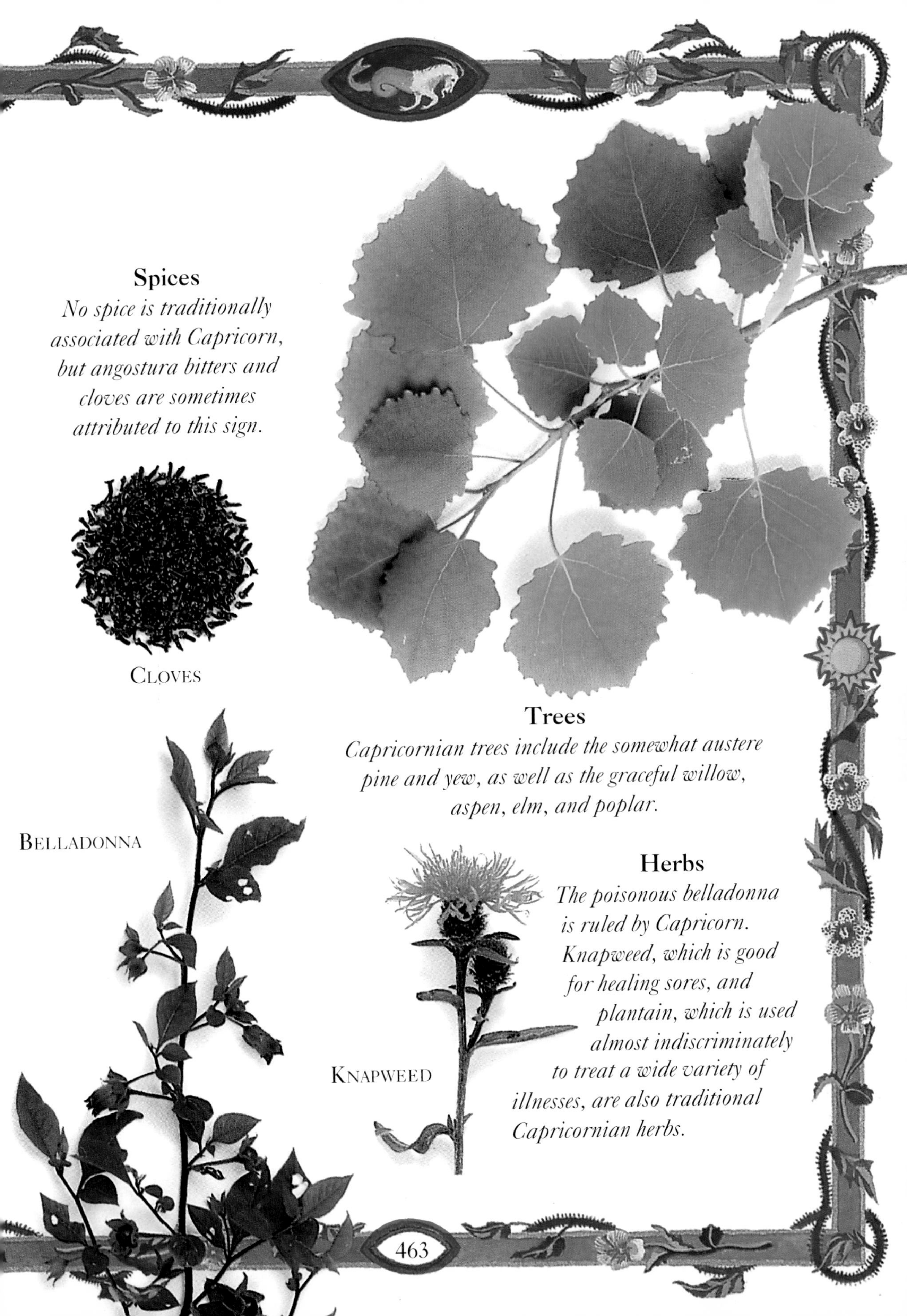

Spices

No spice is traditionally associated with Capricorn, but angostura bitters and cloves are sometimes attributed to this sign.

CLOVES

Trees

Capricornian trees include the somewhat austere pine and yew, as well as the graceful willow, aspen, elm, and poplar.

BELLADONNA

Herbs

The poisonous belladonna is ruled by Capricorn. Knapweed, which is good for healing sores, and plantain, which is used almost indiscriminately to treat a wide variety of illnesses, are also traditional Capricornian herbs.

KNAPWEED

CAPRICORN
SYMBOLISM

Metal

The traditional metal of the sign is lead, no doubt because of its gray color. When Capricornians choose jewelry, however, they often show a preference for silver items.

LEAD ORE

LEAD PENCILS

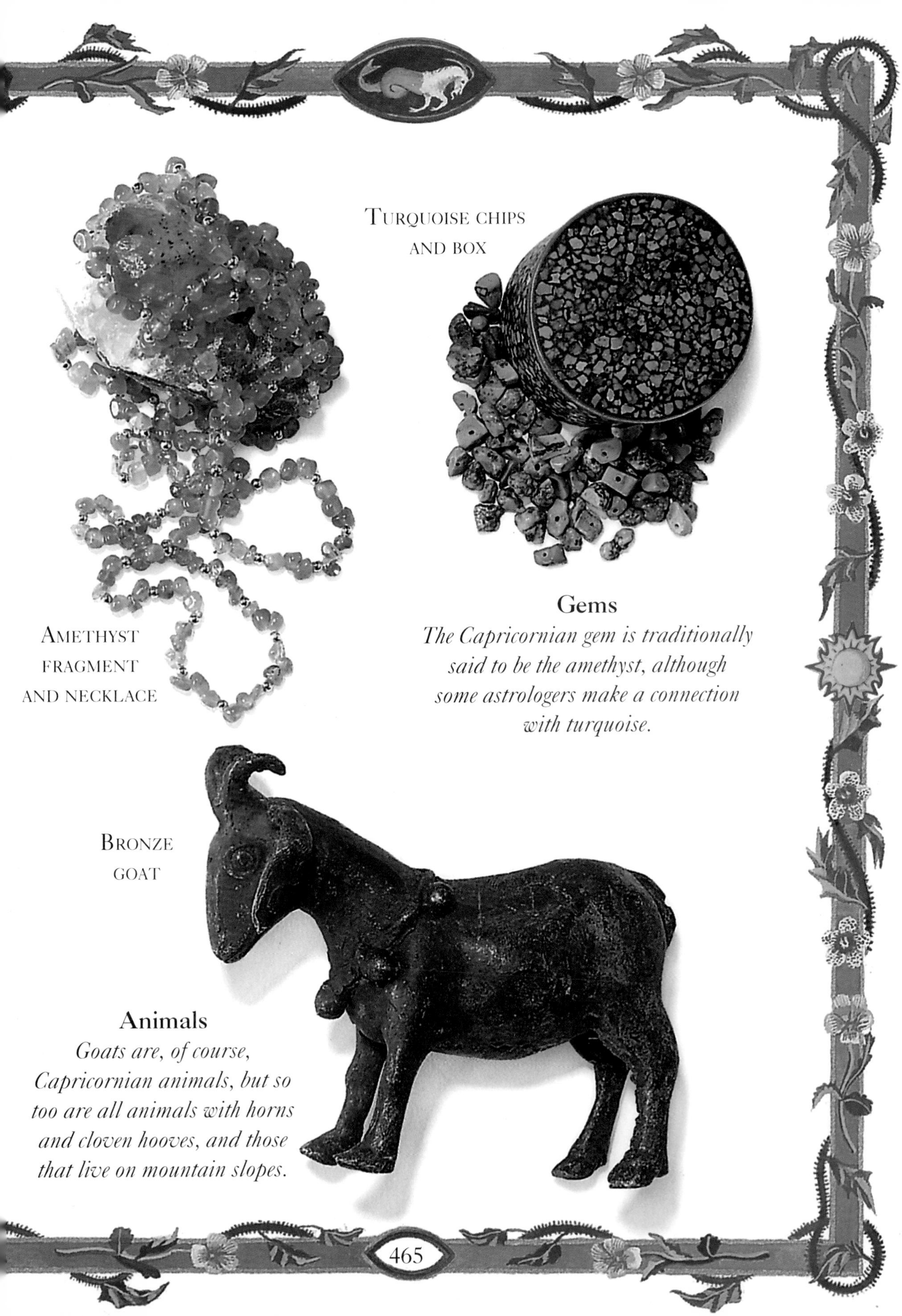

TURQUOISE CHIPS AND BOX

AMETHYST FRAGMENT AND NECKLACE

Gems

The Capricornian gem is traditionally said to be the amethyst, although some astrologers make a connection with turquoise.

BRONZE GOAT

Animals

Goats are, of course, Capricornian animals, but so too are all animals with horns and cloven hooves, and those that live on mountain slopes.

CAPRICORN PROFILE

YOUR OVERALL LOOK WILL BE CONVENTIONAL WITHIN YOUR OWN PEER GROUP. CAPRICORNIANS USUALLY WALK QUICKLY, TAKING LONG STRIDES. THEY HOLD THEIR HEADS EITHER UP OR DOWN, ACCORDING TO THEIR PREVAILING MOOD.

Many Capricornians are tall, and they may have a tendency to stoop, sometimes with their knees bent. However, when they are feeling positive they will stand erect and tall, and may occasionally appear to look down on the rest of the world.

The body

As Capricorn rules the bones, the skeletal frame is likely to be strong, with rather obvious bony wrists, elbows, and knees. A large number of Capricornians are tall and thin, with a fairly gaunt appearance. Another type of Capricornian will have a slim build, but will often be on the short side. Members of this second group can tend to have rather bony knees.

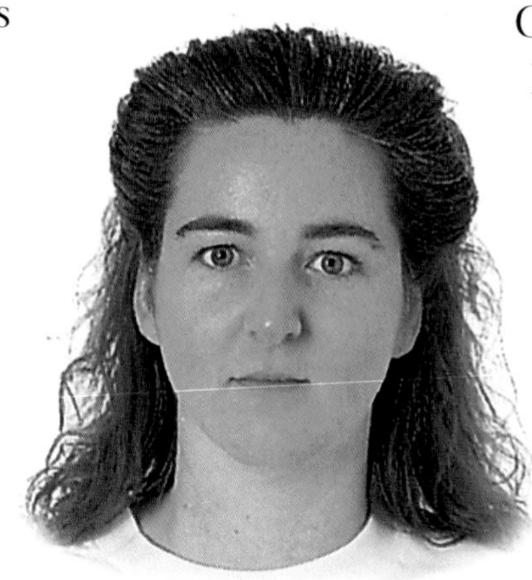

The Capricornian face
A high forehead and a direct gaze characterize the Capricorn face.

Capricornian legs are likely to be long and slim and, in the case of many women, extremely beautiful. They will quite rightly be shown to their best advantage, for example, swathed in black hosiery.

The face

Capricornians often have rather heavy hair, which tends to be sleekly styled and cut. The forehead can be high, and the eyes show directness; they are steady, although perhaps downcast. The nose is often emphasized by lines joining its sides to the corners of the mouth, which are usually turned down when the individual smiles. The chin can sometimes be fairly sharp. The shape of the entire face – the temples,

The Capricornian stance

Capricornians are often tall, perhaps with a tendency to stoop. When feeling positive they will, however, stand tall and proud.

nose, cheekbones, jaw, and chin – may reflect the rather prominent Capricornian bone structure.

Style

The Capricornian image is conventional: both men and women look marvelous in well-cut, chic suits and dark colors. A "little black dress," perhaps adorned by dramatic jewelry, is a particular favorite with women. Stylishness is the rule, even with casual clothes. Quality is important, too, and you are likely to favor designer labels. Exaggerated fashion will not appeal to you; classic clothes will.

In general

Capricornians do not like to stand out in a crowd. A reserved, quiet image is far more acceptable. Because you like to impress, but will be reluctant to make too strong a statement, you will often choose to wear high-quality, formal clothes. With experience, you will discover ways in which a dramatic but restrained look can be achieved by the addition of subtle and interesting jewelry or accessories. Capricornians tend to be attracted to high-quality belts, handbags, and briefcases. You may also have a preference for traditional fragrances, as opposed to more overpowering modern scents.

Clothes made from natural fibers such as cotton and wool, perhaps in shades of pale gray and dark green, are likely to flatter you.

CAPRICORN
PERSONALITY

CAPRICORNIANS SHOULD SET THEIR SIGHTS HIGH AND ASPIRE TO GREAT THINGS. MANY ARE TRUE ACHIEVERS, BUT OTHERS TEND TO GRUMBLE OVER THE OBSTACLES THAT PREVENT THEM FROM BEING SUCCESSFUL.

Many fine and noble qualities, for example prudence, caution, circumspection, and practical common sense, are shared by members of this Sun sign group. However, unlike the other Zodiac signs, this one produces two very contrasting types.

The symbol of the sign is a goat with a fish's tail, and this fact is significant. The fish's tail represents a powerful psychological factor in the Capricornian makeup that can curb ambition, produce a negative response to other people's suggestions, and generally spoil things not only for the Capricornian, but for others as well.

At work

You may sometimes take on a gloomy attitude because you feel that much of your success at work depends on your being thoroughly reliable in what you do, so that you must stick to a regular routine. This could make you feel perennially depressed. You will no doubt place great value upon retaining a sense of security, and are unlikely to take extravagant risks.

Your attitudes

Your depressing inner voice will all too often make itself felt when you try to be at all daring, or want to do something just for the fun of it. Try not to let it hold you back.

There is, however, another, fun-loving side to the Capricornian goat. Many people of this sign seem to manage metaphorically to slough off the fish's tail and become all goat – in fact, a giddy goat who simply will not have anything to do with the wet-blanket, depressive attitude expressed by some Capricornians. They will have fun, love life, and thoroughly enjoy the process of achieving the ambitious objectives that they decide to set themselves. These latter Capricornians are able to take care of themselves very well.

Saturn rules Capricorn

Saturn, originally an agricultural god, represents the Capricornian ruling planet. It can make its subjects practical and cautious, but also selfish and narrow-minded.

They are highly motivated people who will attempt to reach for the sky, and may well go so far as to touch it.

The overall picture

You should try to recognize which type of Capricorn you resemble most closely. Remember, however, that yours is one sign, not two; you may seem to be a placid valley goat, happily tethered to a restricting pole, but you can escape and play the giddy goat. You might lack confidence, but this should not be allowed to hold you back. Even the most successful person is, of course, entitled to grumble from time to time, but you should be aware of how this tendency affects you and those around you, and try not to succumb to it too often.

CAPRICORN ASPIRATIONS

YOUR NEED FOR SECURITY CAN CONFLICT WITH AMBITION, AND YOU MAY NOT LIKE TAKING CHANCES. A FONDNESS FOR ROUTINE MAKES YOU A VALUABLE EMPLOYEE, AND YOU MAY HAVE WHAT IT TAKES TO COPE WITH A TOP JOB.

The building trade

In the same way that Capricornians are excellent at "building" their lives, you may find inner satisfaction from working in the building trades.

TROWEL AND CEMENT

Property management

Managing the land is an attractive profession for Capricornians. You will enjoy working on site as much as in an office.

MINIATURE GLOBE

Teaching

The dry Capricornian sense of humor will be an asset to you if you decide to become a teacher. You may specialize in geography.

Documents and wax seal

Civil service

A need for security and the chance to make gradual progress, plus the possibility of involvement with those in power, attracts Capricornians to civil service.

Plans and spirit level

Applicator for dental cement

Dentistry

The powerful astrological tradition linking Capricorn with the skeletal system could draw you to the dental profession.

CAPRICORN HEALTH

CAPRICORNIANS ARE OFTEN TOO CONCERNED WITH WORLDLY MATTERS AND CARRY HEAVY BURDENS OF RESPONSIBILITY; YOU MAY TEND TO NEGLECT YOUR PHYSICAL WELL-BEING AND COULD AGE MORE QUICKLY THAN YOU SHOULD.

The Capricornian body area covers the knees and shins, but the skin, bones, and teeth are also ruled by this sign. It is important for all Sun sign Capricornians, both young and old, to keep moving. An excessively static life may result in stiffness of the joints, and rheumatism and even arthritis could eventually set in.

Your diet

Most Capricornians have a rather fast metabolism, so weight gain is less likely to be a problem for you than other Zodiac types. You might benefit from adding the cell salt calcium phosphate (calc. phos.) to your diet. As the principal salt contained in the bone structure, it may be of particular importance to you.

Taking care

Many Capricornians are interested in sports, and some may be great athletes. You could find that knee injuries will affect you more frequently than they do people of other signs. Make sure that you get medical attention for even the slightest trouble; more severe problems may develop if you are at all negligent in this area.

Even if regular dental checkups appear to be little more than an unnecessary expense, they are especially desirable for Capricornians. You might feel justifiably proud when the dentist congratulates you on your high level of oral hygiene, but you should not take this as an excuse to stop making regular visits.

As a Capricornian you may well possess unusually beautiful, fine skin, and that too could need some extra-special care. It may be ultrasensitive, in which case it would be advisable for you to use a high-factor protective cream in very strong sun to prevent redness, blotchiness, or something more serious from developing.

Astrology and the body

For many centuries it was not possible to practice medicine without a knowledge of astrology. In European universities, medical training included information on how planetary positions would affect the administration of medicines, the bleeding of patients, and the right time to pick herbs and make potions. Each Zodiac sign rules a particular part of the body – from Aries (the head) to Pisces (the feet) – and textbooks always included a drawing of a "Zodiac man" (or woman) that illustrated the point.

CAPRICORN AT
LEISURE

EACH OF THE SUN SIGNS TRADITIONALLY SUGGESTS SPARE-TIME ACTIVITIES, HOBBIES, AND VACATION SPOTS. ALTHOUGH THESE ARE ONLY SUGGESTIONS, THEY OFTEN WORK OUT WELL FOR CAPRICORNIANS.

Going to the races
A day at the races involves dressing up and mixing with the "right" people, and therefore gives satisfaction to ambitious Capricornians.

BINOCULARS

MODEL SPINNING WHEEL

Weaving
The creation of fabrics from natural materials may prove attractive to creative Capricornians.

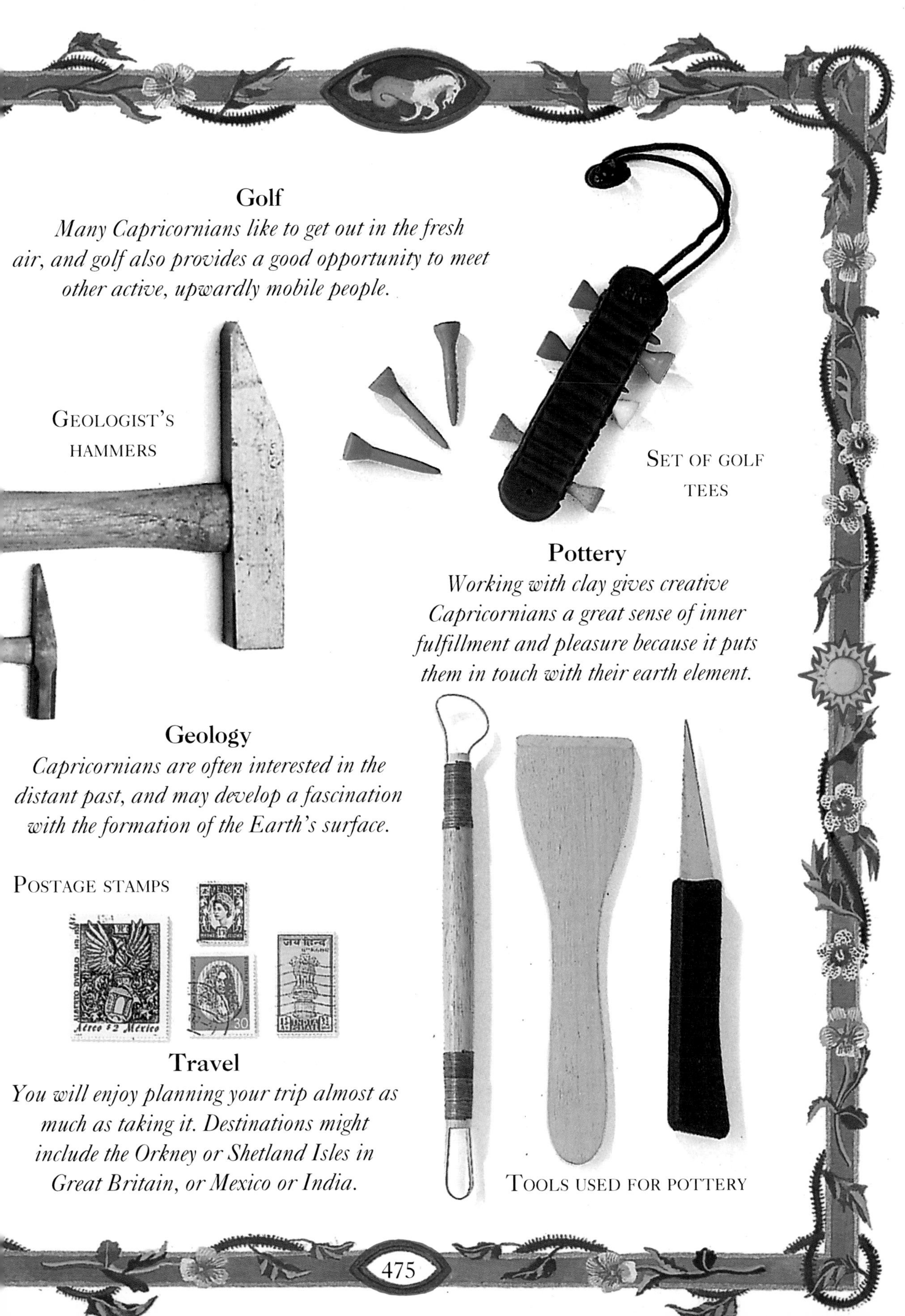

Golf

Many Capricornians like to get out in the fresh air, and golf also provides a good opportunity to meet other active, upwardly mobile people.

Geologist's hammers

Set of golf tees

Pottery

Working with clay gives creative Capricornians a great sense of inner fulfillment and pleasure because it puts them in touch with their earth element.

Geology

Capricornians are often interested in the distant past, and may develop a fascination with the formation of the Earth's surface.

Postage stamps

Tools used for pottery

Travel

You will enjoy planning your trip almost as much as taking it. Destinations might include the Orkney or Shetland Isles in Great Britain, or Mexico or India.

CAPRICORN IN LOVE

CAPRICORNIANS USUALLY KEEP THEIR EMOTIONS UNDER CONTROL AND CAN BE PEOPLE OF FEW WORDS. WHAT THEY DO SAY, HOWEVER, THEY USUALLY MEAN. TO ACHIEVE FULFILLING LOVE LIVES, THEY SOMETIMES NEED TO LEARN HOW TO RELAX.

Very possibly, it may take some time for you to realize you are in love. Once you fall for someone, however, your commitment will be deep. Your natural caution encourages you to make quite sure of your ground before committing yourself, or even before declaring your love. You may fear the thought of rejection, and it is likely to hurt you much more than it would most other Zodiac types.

As a lover

You can be very reserved indeed in the way that you express your feelings towards others,and may even take this to the point where you give the distinct impression of being rather cold and distant. This characteristic is most likely to emerge if you had a repressive or overly disciplined childhood. But with the right partner, all Capricornians will blossom and show their fun-loving characteristics. Your tendency always to do the right and proper thing will help to ensure your fidelity once you are committed to a permanent relationship. When this occurs, a strong urge to protect and look after your partner and, in due course, your children, will probably develop in you. If, however, you are

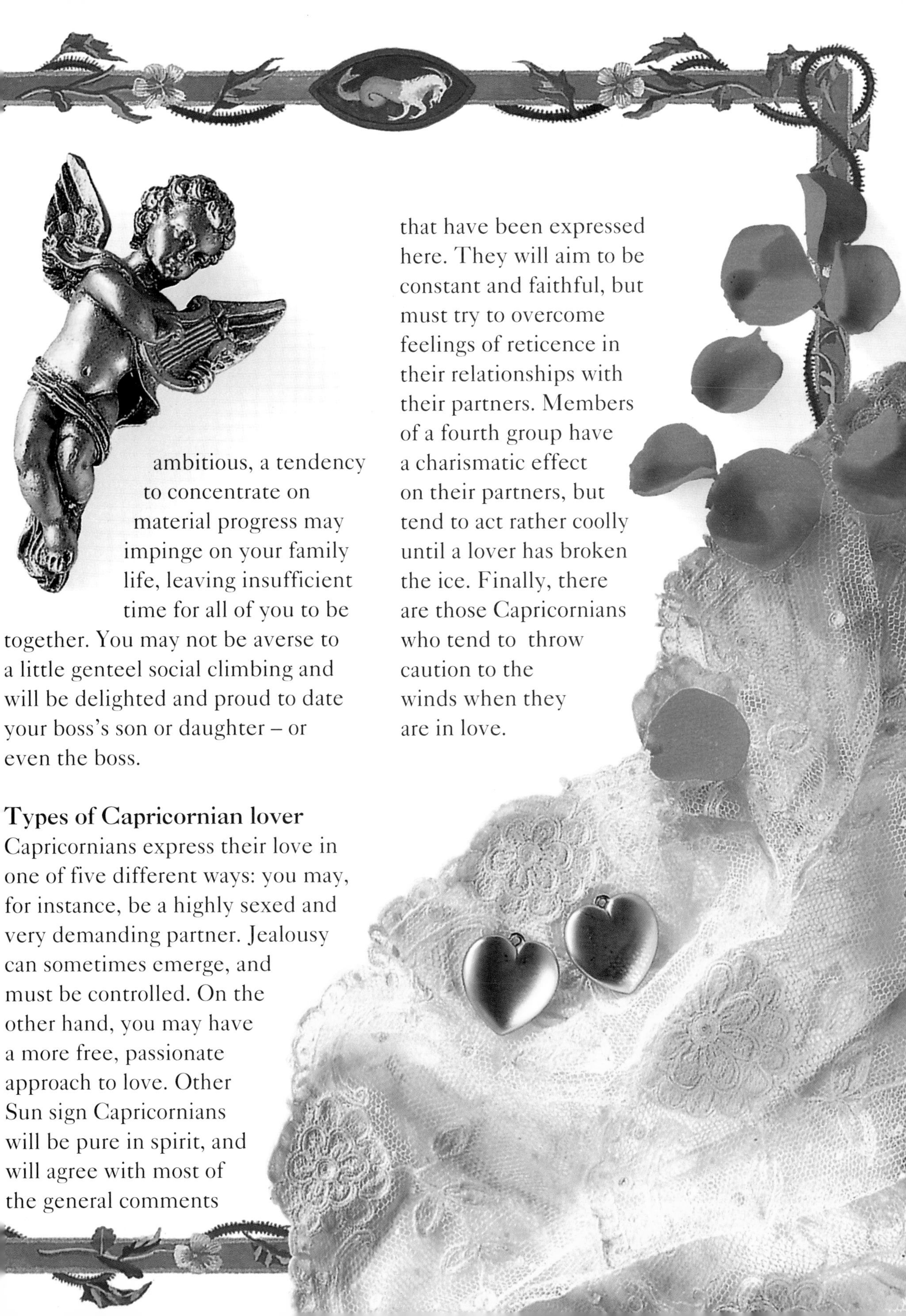

ambitious, a tendency to concentrate on material progress may impinge on your family life, leaving insufficient time for all of you to be together. You may not be averse to a little genteel social climbing and will be delighted and proud to date your boss's son or daughter – or even the boss.

Types of Capricornian lover

Capricornians express their love in one of five different ways: you may, for instance, be a highly sexed and very demanding partner. Jealousy can sometimes emerge, and must be controlled. On the other hand, you may have a more free, passionate approach to love. Other Sun sign Capricornians will be pure in spirit, and will agree with most of the general comments that have been expressed here. They will aim to be constant and faithful, but must try to overcome feelings of reticence in their relationships with their partners. Members of a fourth group have a charismatic effect on their partners, but tend to act rather coolly until a lover has broken the ice. Finally, there are those Capricornians who tend to throw caution to the winds when they are in love.

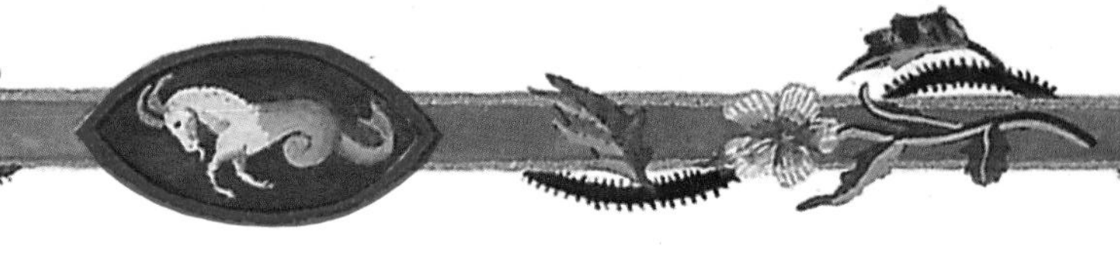

CAPRICORN AT HOME

DEPENDING ON WHAT TYPE OF CAPRICORNIAN YOU ARE, YOUR HOME WILL EITHER BE FURNISHED AND DESIGNED CHIEFLY TO IMPRESS OR EXTREMELY SPARTAN. YOU WILL PROCLAIM YOUR TRUE PERSONALITY THROUGH THE STYLE YOU CHOOSE.

Many Capricornians move from one residence to the next with unusual frequency. This is generally due to the fact that as they gradually make their way up the social ladder they want their homes to match their newfound status accordingly.

China coffee set

Articles made from china or fine porcelain are likely to be proudly displayed.

Furniture

Financially conscious Capricornians are highly unlikely to throw money away on trendy or impractical flippancies. This holds particularly true when it comes to their choice of furniture.

Your taste is possibly rather conventional, so you will choose traditional styles and, if you can afford them, antiques that are made in a traditional fashion. To obtain them you will often search at auction houses rather than large department stores. You are probably attracted to beautiful, good-quality, wood, either polished or left in its natural state. One thing that might well be worth bearing in mind is the Capricornian tendency to want to impress other people. This could end up governing your choice and, as a result, comfort may be sacrificed in a search for the correct type of appearance.

Soft furnishings

You will usually keep soft furnishings to a minimum. Curtains and drapes will be well shaped and cut, and perhaps made of natural materials such as linen. Pure silk may be another favorite with you. Your

preference for natural materials is due to the influence of the earth element of your sign. The overall effect of the Capricornian home is elegant, tasteful, and without doubt expensive-looking, even if the individual is poor. A certain severity can, however, also be present.

Decorative objects

Any inherited articles will be proudly displayed, especially if they are silver, and family portraits will be placed in prominent positions.

A tendency to show off objects on stands is common. Capricornians are often attracted to unusual rocks or shells. You may have a piece of amethyst, the Capricornian stone, glinting away on a windowsill. A restrained flower arrangement containing a few carefully placed blooms may also have a place in your home. China or pieces of porcelain will often be carefully displayed.

Gingham cloth
Materials with a subdued pattern often characterize the Capricornian home.

Elegant armchair
Settees and easy chairs may be covered in natural materials, such as wool, and are likely to be rather hard.

THE MOON AND YOU

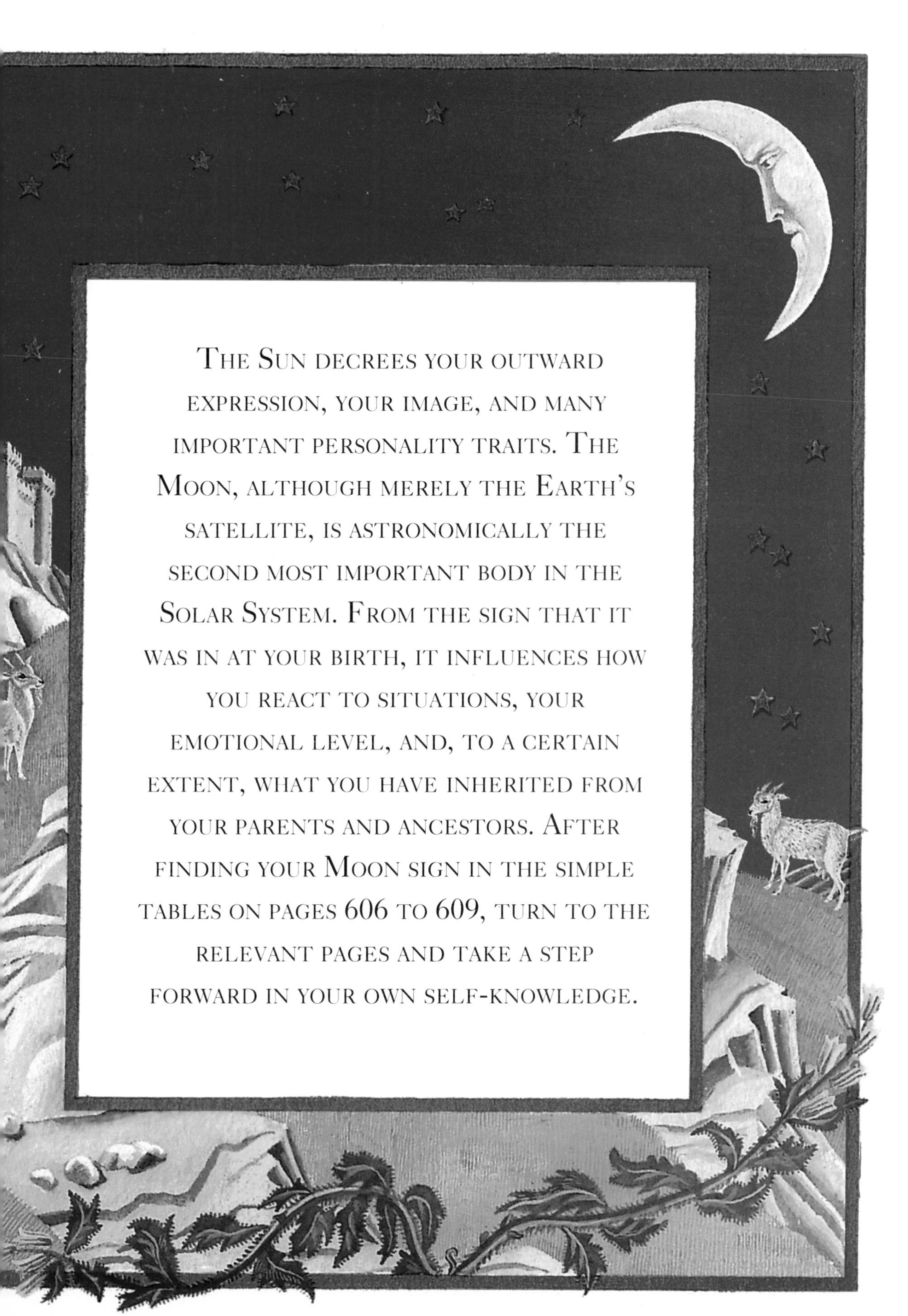

The Sun decrees your outward expression, your image, and many important personality traits. The Moon, although merely the Earth's satellite, is astronomically the second most important body in the Solar System. From the sign that it was in at your birth, it influences how you react to situations, your emotional level, and, to a certain extent, what you have inherited from your parents and ancestors. After finding your Moon sign in the simple tables on pages 606 to 609, turn to the relevant pages and take a step forward in your own self-knowledge.

THE MOON IN
ARIES

YOUR ASSERTIVE ARIEN MOON PROVIDES YOU WITH A POSITIVE AND ENTHUSIASTIC RESPONSE TO AMBITIOUS CAPRICORNIAN OBJECTIVES AND SCHEMES. IT HELPS QUELL ANY TENDENCY TO TAKE YOURSELF AND LIFE TOO SERIOUSLY.

You respond to most situations with a positive, lively enthusiasm that adds a sparkle to your practical, earthy Capricornian qualities. Your powerful motivation to be aspiring and ambitious is supported by an instinctive urge to win.

Self-expression

You have the potential to be a truly high achiever. Very few situations frighten you, and you are in an excellent position to overcome any inhibiting feelings. The emotional energy of your Arien Moon is very potent. Express it by getting involved in work that you find really rewarding.

Romance

You are among the most passionate of Capricornians, and may fall in love more quickly, and express yourself less cautiously, than many people of your Sun sign. Your partners will appreciate your positive approach to this sphere of your life. Allow your passion plenty of free expression, and do not hesitate to sweep your lovers off their feet. The worst Arien fault is selfishness, and you should be aware that it may lead to problems.

Your well-being

The Arien body area is the head, and you may consequently be rather prone to headaches. These are probably stress-related, so perhaps you would benefit from a relaxation technique such as yoga. Otherwise, there is a relationship between headaches and the kidneys, and it is possible that yours could be slightly out of balance.

Ariens are hasty and prone to minor accidents. As a Sun sign Capricornian you have enough caution and patience to overcome this tendency, but you could sometimes become uncharacteristically careless. You usually cope very well with quite vigorous sports and exercise.

The Moon in Aries

Planning ahead

In true Capricornian style, you are probably careful with money and smart with investments. Your Arien Moon gives you an enterprising spirit that encourages you to start money-making schemes.

People with an Arien emphasis commonly have two sources of income; you may well fall successfully into this category. You are probably more generous than many Sun sign Capricornians, and your immediate response to any form of need is to take direct action, often by donating some money.

Parenthood

All Capricornians like to have some time to themselves, perhaps for reading or listening to music. Make sure that you have enough of this spare time. You should not find it difficult to keep up with your children's ideas, so the generation gap will pose few problems for you.

THE MOON IN TAURUS

YOUR SUN AND MOON ARE BOTH IN EARTH SIGNS. YOUR TAUREAN MOON COMPLEMENTS YOUR CAPRICORNIAN SUN, AND ADDS A WARM AND AFFECTIONATE RESPONSE TO THE HIGHLY PRACTICAL, MORE CAUTIOUS ASPECTS OF YOUR CHARACTER.

You are among the most practical and cautious of all Sun and Moon sign combinations. Your gift is for the steady, sound development of your talents and abilities, and for solid material growth.

Self-expression

It is worth remembering that there is a lively, almost flighty side to Capricorn. If, however, you are too concerned with your career and family, and with finding a way to ensure that your children have everything they need, your livelier qualities could be somewhat subdued.

The Moon is traditionally "well placed" in Taurus. This means that its influence on you is rather stronger than on many people. Among other traits, it emphasizes an attraction to the good life and pleasure-seeking. You should allow yourself to respond positively to this, since it will let you enjoy the fruits of your labors.

Romance

Your Taurean Moon encourages your instinctive need for emotional and material security. You need a stable, permanent relationship and a reliable partner with whom you can stride forward through life.

You are a warm and sensual lover, and should enjoy a rich and rewarding love and sex life. Do, however, remember that possessiveness is the worst Taurean fault, and that you could well be too overbearing toward a lover, perhaps creating a rather claustrophobic atmosphere.

Your well-being

The Taurean body area covers the neck and throat, and you should therefore take care of it.

Those with a Taurean emphasis are often somewhat lazy when it comes to exercise and can have a rather slow metabolism. This is not usually the case with Capricornians. If you are

The Moon in Taurus

prone to weight gain, you may need to make exercise a regular part of your no doubt well-planned life. You may also have quite a sweet tooth and a preference for rich foods. The calories, and the pounds, could have an effect on your figure.

Planning ahead

You have the capacity to be very good with money. You may even have chosen a career in banking or insurance. In any case, you will certainly make your money work for you. You will not want to take financial risks of any kind and will devote a great deal of care and thought to avoiding them.

Parenthood

While you are ambitious for your children and respond warmly to them, you may be very conventional and rather strict. Try hard to make a conscious effort to remain aware of their changing problems and concerns. Otherwise the generation gap is likely to yawn wide.

THE MOON IN GEMINI

YOUR ASPIRING, AMBITIOUS QUALITIES ARE LIGHTENED BY YOUR GEMINIAN MOON, WHICH MAKES YOU VERSATILE AND SOMETIMES GIVES YOU A TENDENCY TO DITHER IN DAUNTING SITUATIONS. YOU HAVE A GREAT SENSE OF HUMOR.

The earth element of your Capricornian Sun sign, and the air element of your Geminian Moon sign, suggest that you have many interesting facets to your personality.

Self-expression

You have a lighthearted, but intellectual, response to challenges, being both inquisitive and skeptical. You are extremely lively in debate and are happy to play devil's advocate just to get your point made.

You are less single-minded than most Capricornians, and a natural versatility, a disposition to do more than one thing at a time, makes you interesting company. You probably know a little about a great many things and may be the typical collector of useless trifles.

Being a good communicator, working in some branch of the media would probably be most fulfilling for you. If you manage to guard against superficiality, you can certainly put the excellent qualities of your Geminian Moon to good use.

Romance

You may take your love life rather less seriously than many Capricornians, and can, at times, be quite flighty and flirtatious. You particularly enjoy the friendship stage of a new relationship, and friendship and intellectual rapport are essential in the long term. Your sex life may be both lively and experimental, and you should take this into account when forming a relationship. Bear in mind the Geminian tendency to duality; it can cause complications.

Your well-being

The Geminian body area covers the arms and hands, and these are therefore likely to be vulnerable. Make sure you find a hobby that encourages you to use your fingers

The Moon in Gemini

energetically; this should help avoid developing any Capricornian stiffness of the joints.

You will probably enjoy fast-moving and intellectually demanding exercise. Your low boredom threshold may, however, prove a problem when it comes to this area of your life, so endeavor to persevere.

Planning ahead

You could be less successful in organizing your financial affairs than many of your Capricornian brothers and sisters. Indeed, you may be among the few Capricornian Sun and Moon combinations who should seek financial advice when they have money to invest.

Parenthood

You keep up with your children's ideas and may sometimes even be ahead of them. Beware that you do not respond to your children too critically. Logic is admirable, but a hug and some real enthusiasm are also reassuring and encouraging.

THE MOON IN CANCER

CAPRICORN AND CANCER ARE OPPOSITE OR POLAR ZODIAC SIGNS, WHICH MEANS THAT YOU WERE BORN UNDER A FULL MOON. YOU MAY BE RATHER PRONE TO RESTLESSNESS, BUT HAVE A WARM, EMOTIONAL RESPONSE TO OTHER PEOPLE.

Each of us is, in one way or another, likely to express the attitudes of our polar, or opposite, Zodiac sign. Every sign has its partner across the horoscope; for you this is Cancer and, since the Moon was in that sign when you were born, the polarity is strongly emphasized. As the Moon also rules Cancer, its influence on you is extremely potent.

Self-expression

The influence of your Moon sign encourages you to respond warmly and sensitively to other people, but it may also mean that you have a defensive system that springs into action whenever you are challenged. It is possible that you are not particularly self-confident.

Romance

You are far more emotional than many Sun sign Capricornians and are prepared to give a great deal of yourself in a relationship. Being a very responsive lover, you will instinctively know how to please your partner sexually. You should be aware, however, that your desire to create a warm and secure environment could make it somewhat claustrophobic.

You are a natural worrier and this, plus a very powerful imagination, means that you can work yourself up into a positive frenzy if, for instance, your partner is simply late arriving home. You would be best advised to direct your imagination creatively.

Your well-being

The Cancerian body area covers the chest and breasts. There is no connection between the name of this sign and that of the disease but, as always, it is desirable for women to examine their breasts regularly.

The tendency to worry can affect your digestion, and your food could upset you when you are worried.

The Moon in Cancer

Restlessness could also affect your health. A relaxation technique like yoga may offset the tendency.

Planning ahead

As well as being a practical Capricornian, you have an instinctive shrewdness that comes from your Cancerian Moon. You are good at making your money work for you and should follow your instincts, especially when you are planning to make an investment.

You may sometimes feel that you are less well off than is the case. You will do well to review your financial situation from time to time, just to reassure yourself that you can, in fact, allow yourself to enjoy the fruits of your labors more wholeheartedly than you at first thought.

Parenthood

You make a wonderfully caring parent. You may, however, tend to resent it when your children decide to leave home; you should take up some new and demanding interest that will fill the gap. Make a conscious effort to keep up with your children's opinions and concerns, in order to avoid difficulties with the generation gap.

THE MOON IN
LEO

ALLOW THE WARMTH OF YOUR FIERY LEO MOON TO COLOR YOUR PERSONALITY AND REACTIONS, AND TO INCREASE YOUR ORGANIZATIONAL ABILITY. BE VERY CAREFUL, HOWEVER, THAT YOU DO NOT LAPSE INTO POMPOSITY AND BOSSINESS.

The fire of your Moon sign adds warmth and an optimistic enthusiasm to your response to challenges. Your instinctive organizational ability readily springs into action and, in most situations, you probably end up well in control.

Self-expression
When taking matters into your own hands, as you almost invariably do, remember to smile and charm people, so that you can achieve your objectives without being accused of undue autocracy.

Most people with a Leo emphasis have creative potential. Music, acting, wood carving, or painting could all appeal to you.

Romance
Leo and Capricorn have a fine sense of style and are not averse to showing off. This quality will certainly be in the forefront when you fall in love. Avoid bossiness at all times and, if you are accused of it, take the allegation seriously. It could detract from a relationship that would otherwise be good fun.

Your well-being
The Leo body area covers the spine and back, and you should exercise regularly to keep your spine supple. If you spend a great deal of time behind a desk, get a back-support chair.

The Leo organ is the heart, and it must be kept well exercised if it is to serve you long and well. You probably enjoy the usual Capricornian outdoor sports, like hiking and jogging, but may also be attracted to something that is a little more aesthetic, such as dancing or skating.

Planning ahead
Although in many ways Capricorn and Leo are very unlike each other, they have at least one thing in common:

The Moon in Leo

they both love and really appreciate true quality, and have somewhat expensive tastes.

There is a difference between them even here, however. Leos usually spend on quality simply because they get such a kick out of doing so, while Capricornians often spend money on impressing other people, particularly those who may be useful to them. One way or the other, you will undoubtedly end up spending a great deal of money. If your Sun sign makes you feel somewhat guilty about this, bear in mind that you generally invest wisely and are sensible about saving. You will probably not need to get professional financial advice when you have money to invest.

Parenthood

You have what it takes to be a marvelous parent, as long as you do not allow a distance to yawn between you and your children. Follow your instinct and express warm enthusiasm; encourage your children when they show you the results of their latest efforts. If you keep up with their opinions and concerns, you will avoid the generation gap.

THE MOON IN VIRGO

ALWAYS ALLOW THE AMBITIOUS, ASPIRING CAPRICORNIAN ELEMENTS OF YOUR PERSONALITY FREE EXPRESSION, AND TRY NOT TO BE HELD BACK BY INTUITIVE FEELINGS OF INFERIORITY. YOU MAY BE A WORRIER, BUT YOU WILL ALSO BE A GOOD COMMUNICATOR.

Both Capricorn and Virgo are earth signs and, as a result, you are extremely practical, with an above-average amount of straightforward, basic common sense.

Self-expression

You approach problems in a rational, logical way, although you may become rather nervous and lack self-confidence when challenged or confronted with tricky situations. If this happens, try to develop a little more Capricornian coolness.

You have a sharp and analytical mind, and are marvelous at assessing problems in detail. In doing so, do not ignore the overall pattern. Develop breadth of vision; it will be of great advantage to you.

You may be rather shy, and to cover this tend to assume a chilly, aloof air. If you were strictly brought up, it may be that you were put down by your parents once or twice too often, and that this has inhibited you a little more than it might have with other people. No doubt you have what it takes to rationalize such a background, and to deal with any problem that may have arisen as a result of it.

Romance

While you are a naturally adept communicator, you may not find it very easy to talk about your emotions. Do not be too modest. Try to relax and let your relationship develop.

Virgoans can be very critical, and you should beware of nagging your partners too much.

Your well-being

The Virgoan body area is the stomach. You really need a high-fiber diet, and could be attracted to vegetarianism. You are probably exceptionally susceptible to worry, and this will definitely affect your stomach.

The Moon in Virgo

Because you have a great deal of nervous energy, you may be prone to stress and tension, and could find it difficult to sit still, let alone really relax. A study of yoga or some other relaxation technique will go a long way toward conquering the problem.

Planning ahead

You are usually careful and very practical with money. You may, in fact, be somewhat too cautious and go for such safe investments that your money might not be working as hard for you as it could. Study various investment programs; your critical nature will ensure that you will benefit a great deal by doing so.

Parenthood

While you are fair in dealing with your children, you could respond to them more critically than you realize, which could damage their self-confidence. Encourage them; they may be just as ambitious as you are.

THE MOON IN LIBRA

YOUR LIBRAN MOON MAKES YOU VERY DIPLOMATIC, AND YOU HAVE THE ABILITY TO CHARM OTHERS. YOU RESPOND WELL TO AN ENJOYABLE SOCIAL LIFE, BUT MAY SOMETIMES SUCCUMB TO SNOBBISH SOCIAL CLIMBING.

Your Sun sign and your Moon sign are both cardinal signs, and as a result you are outgoing. You can develop excellent sympathy, even empathy, with other people.

Self-expression

When you are confronted by tricky situations, your initial response may be rather hesitant. Your Capricornian determination then takes over, letting you know where you stand and what you should do.

You live a full and busy life but, because you always find time for other people, especially if they are in trouble, you can give the impression that you are at best laid-back and, at worst, lazy. The latter is certainly not true, and neither, really, is the former.

Romance

You will probably not feel psychologically whole until you have contrived a satisfying and permanent partnership for yourself. You really do need that all-important rapport with another person who is close to you. But you also need space and time to yourself. When choosing a partner, it is important to keep this in mind.

You are among the more romantic of Sun sign Capricornians and will enjoy the most memorable, and often expensive and luxurious, occasions with your lovers.

Your well-being

The Libran body area is the kidneys, and if you suffer from constant headaches, it might be worth getting a checkup in case you have a slight kidney disorder. The lumbar region of the back is also Libra-ruled. If you suffer from pain in this region, get a back-support chair or follow a series of back-oriented exercises.

You could be less enthusiastic about exercise than most Sun sign Capricornians. Since you may also

The Moon in Libra

enjoy rich, sweet food, you could be vulnerable to weight gain. You need to exercise in a place where there is a pleasant social life – for example, in a friendly health club or gym.

Planning ahead

You are probably among the least careful of Capricornians where money is concerned. You may not waste it, but will like to own beautiful things.

Capricorn will rule at times when you have money to invest. If, however, you know that you tend not to save too determinedly, you would probably be wise to seek independent professional financial advice.

Parenthood

You will be a kind parent, as responsive to your children's needs as to everyone else's. Do not, however, let Libran indecision come between you and your children. Help them to aspire; your encouragement will pay off in the long run. Because you are always fair and attentive, you should leap across the generation gap.

THE MOON IN SCORPIO

YOU POSSESS A POWERFUL SOURCE OF EMOTIONAL ENERGY THAT INCREASES YOUR CAPRICORNIAN DETERMINATION TO SUCCEED IN ALL OF YOUR OBJECTIVES. BEWARE, HOWEVER, OF DEVELOPING OBSESSIVE TENDENCIES.

The earth element of your Capricornian Sun and the water element of your Scorpio Moon blend well. You should be able to get the best out of both of these influences.

Self-expression

You have intense emotional and physical energy that springs into action the moment you are challenged. Combined with Capricornian determination and ambition, this gives you the potential to be extremely successful.

It is important for you to be emotionally involved in your work. If you are merely working at some boring job in order to make money, your motivation and energies will stagnate. Try some self-analysis if you feel any danger signals, and make changes if necessary.

Be careful not to be too ruthless with your colleagues. You would be wise to remember the old saying: do not tread on people on the way up, since you may well encounter them again on the way down.

Romance

Your powerful emotions make you a passionate lover who needs a rich and fulfilling love and sex life. You will be a demanding partner and will need an enthusiastic lover.

The worst Scorpio fault is jealousy, and it might be that you occasionally succumb to this useless, negative emotion. Listen to rational explanations from your partner.

Your well-being

The Scorpio body area covers the genitals. Men with this Sun and Moon combination should regularly examine their testicles for irregularities, and women should have cervical smears.

Scorpios usually enjoy living it up, which means eating rich food and drinking fine wine. As a result, you

The Moon in Scorpio

may have a tendency to put on excess weight. If you have to diet, you will probably not find it easy; on reaching your ideal weight, you may rush off for a celebratory banquet. You may enjoy the discipline and steady routine of a regular sports interest.

Planning ahead

You should cope well with money and may have a considerable flair for making it. Your Sun and Moon sign combination suggests that you are good in business, and that you could build a successful business of your own. You should have no problems when you have money to invest.

Parenthood

You have the capacity to enjoy parenthood, but could be so involved with your career that you may have less time for your children than is wise. Listen to your children, and always encourage them in their ambitions and interests.

THE MOON IN SAGITTARIUS

SAGITTARIAN BREADTH OF VISION AND ABILITY TO ACCEPT CHALLENGE WORKS WELL WITH YOUR STRONG CAPRICORNIAN AMBITION. YOUR CAPRICORNIAN SENSE OF HUMOR IS FUELED BY YOUR SAGITTARIAN MOON.

The influence of your Sagittarian Moon adds some remarkably varied qualities to your personality. By expressing them you should be able to achieve a great deal.

Self-expression

Your Moon sign gives you a natural optimism, but there could be conflict here, for Sun sign Capricornians can sometimes be pessimistic and gloomy. If you tend to swing between one mood and another, try to allow Capricornian common sense and ambition to override gloom and doom.

You have a good mind and a good intellect. Do not let them stagnate; it is important for you to have an intellectual challenge of some kind, perhaps a language.

Romance

Sagittarius is a warm, loving, and emotional sign. You will not find it difficult to express these qualities. You are passionate and will want to enjoy a rich and rewarding love and sex life. Perhaps you do not take this sphere of your life as seriously as do others of your Sun sign, but the chances are that you get a lot more fun out of it. You need a measure of freedom within a relationship and should bear this in mind when considering a permanent liaison.

The worst Sagittarian fault is restlessness. Try not to take this out on your partner, or to allow that ever-so-slightly roving eye to cause too many problems.

Your well-being

The Sagittarian body area covers the hips and thighs, and women with this sign emphasized are prone to putting on weight around this area. Special exercises will help and should encourage good muscle tone. A diet of lighter food than you may like is also advisable.

The Moon in Sagittarius

The Sagittarian organ is the liver and, because it is common for people of that sign to enjoy rich, meaty foods, heavy desserts, wine, and beer, it might be wise to keep some hangover cures handy. Keep generally active with energy-consuming interests and you will thrive.

Planning ahead

Although you are practical to a fault and sensible with money, you may have a deeply ingrained gambling instinct. You are likely to enjoy the occasional financial risk, and this may take the form of a bet on a big race or some marginally unsavory stock purchase. For the most part, you can easily control this tendency. When making important financial decisions, seek the advice of an expert.

Parenthood

You will be a lively and enthusiastic parent, eager to stimulate your children's minds and to encourage their efforts. Be ambitious for them without being too heavy-handed. You should have few problems with the generation gap and will find coping with older children somewhat easier than understanding toddlers.

THE MOON IN CAPRICORN

BECAUSE BOTH THE SUN AND THE MOON WERE IN CAPRICORN AT THE TIME OF YOUR BIRTH, YOU WERE BORN UNDER A NEW MOON. THEREFORE THE EARTH ELEMENT POWERFULLY EMPHASIZES YOUR PERSONALITY AND REACTIONS.

When you read a list of the characteristics of your practical, aspiring Sun sign, you will probably recognize that a great many of them apply to you. On average, out of a list of perhaps 20 personality traits of a Sun sign, most people will identify with 11 or 12. For you, the average increases considerably, as both the Sun and the Moon were in Capricorn when you were born.

Self-expression

The influence of your Moon sign encourages you to appreciate ambitious schemes and daunting projects, which you will usually want to accept as soon as they are put to you. You may, however, tend to swing between positive, ambitious thinking and a negative, self-doubting attitude.

No doubt you have the marvelous, offbeat sense of humor that is so characteristic of Capricorn, and it will surface very spontaneously. But you are not beyond slumping into a grumbling mood and complaining that nothing is right with your world. Try to allow the positive side of your personality to dominate.

Romance

You may not express your emotions very freely. This is probably due to your natural Capricornian caution and your self-protective instinct.

Once committed, you are very faithful and will enjoy a rich, rewarding love and sex life. You will be ambitious for your partner's progress in life, but it is possible that you may have slightly old-fashioned or conventional ideas as to how your relationship should develop.

Your well-being

The pages dedicated to health and well-being (*pages 472 to 473*) are especially relevant to you, as your vulnerabilities are extremely

The Moon in Capricorn

Capricornian. You could be even more prone to rheumatic pain and arthritis than most Sun sign Capricornians.

Planning ahead

You will not be averse to making an effort to impress important people. On the whole, however, you will use your money well, although you may sometimes think you are less well off than you actually are. Make an effort to follow your naturally cautious instinct when investing, and you will not go far wrong.

Parenthood

You will want to do a lot for your children and will work hard to this end. However, because you are always busy, you may not spend as much time with them as you should, and they may feel that you are a rather distant parent.

You will be conventional in your attitude and could be rather strict. This is all right, provided that you make an effort to understand your children's concerns and problems, and thus avoid the generation gap.

THE MOON IN AQUARIUS

YOU MAY NEED TO BE INDEPENDENT, BUT TRY TO AVOID GAINING A REPUTATION FOR BEING COOL AND DISTANT. WHILE YOU ARE ATTRACTED TO THE UNCONVENTIONAL, YOU WILL ALWAYS WANT TO DO WHAT IS CONSIDERED ACCEPTABLE.

Aquarius and Capricorn are neighboring Zodiac signs and, until the discovery of Uranus in the eighteenth century, the planet Saturn ruled them both. They therefore have a certain amount in common, but in some respects they could not be more different. Your Capricornian Sun, for instance, inclines you toward conventionality in outlook and manner, while your Aquarian Moon sometimes makes you respond to situations in an unconventional way.

Self-expression

Both Capricorn and Aquarius share the tendency not to show emotion very freely. While you have a dynamic, magnetic personality that is very attractive to the opposite sex, you may instinctively send out vibes telling admirers that, while they may certainly admire you, they should also keep their distance. In spite of this, you have a romantic streak that is quite wonderful once ignited. Another aspect of your attitude to romance is that you may put off deepening an emotional relationship, or certainly committing yourself to marriage, for longer than most people. This is probably because you enjoy your independence so much.

Your well-being

The Aquarian body area covers the ankles, which are vulnerable. You may well enjoy wearing fashion shoes and could easily twist your ankle. The circulation is also Aquarius-ruled, and yours may not be too brisk, so make sure you wear several layers of light clothes in cold weather.

You will like various forms of exercise, particularly if they are an outlet for your creative flair; all kinds of dance, or perhaps skating, will probably suit you. Exercise will aid your circulation and is excellent for preventing Capricornian stiffness and

The Moon in Aquarius

rheumatic pain. Aim to keep your diet on the light side. Many Capricornians favor the great classical dishes of the world; you probably do best on poultry, fish, and a salads.

Planning ahead

You will spend money more freely than most Capricornians and may well be attracted to exciting, but perhaps not very sound, investment schemes. You must aim to be careful and should not gamble any more than you can afford to lose. In all situations, allow your Capricornian common sense to rule the day.

Parenthood

You will make a lively and well-informed parent. You should not find the generation gap to be a problem, provided that the strict, conventional Capricornian side of your personality balances your unconventional Moon sign. Bear in mind that children like to know where they stand.

THE MOON IN PISCES

YOUR PISCEAN MOON HEIGHTENS YOUR EMOTIONAL LEVEL, AND WARMS AND SENSITIZES YOUR REACTIONS. YOU MAY, HOWEVER, NEED TO CONSCIOUSLY BUILD SELF-CONFIDENCE. DO NOT SMOTHER YOUR CAPRICORNIAN AMBITION.

Your earth sign Sun and water sign Moon combine well. As a Capricornian, you are practical and cautious, but you will respond sensitively to situations and should not find it difficult to show tender emotion. You may not, however, be very self-confident and could have to make a conscious effort to allow your positive, aspiring, and ambitious Capricornian qualities full expression.

Self-expression

Because you are sensitive, there is a chance that you may have suffered more deeply than most people from parental put-downs. This could have made you fearful of taking firm steps onward and upward. Make an effort to develop your ambitions and to summon up the inner strength to achieve them.

You are a warm, kind person, who could do especially well in a career in the caring professions.

Romance

You respond warmly and lovingly to partners and are capable of a truly rewarding love and sex life. The worst Piscean fault is deceptiveness. As a Capricornian you will loathe this characteristic and should therefore be able to combat it successfully.

When you fall in love, you may have a tendency to see your partner through rose-colored glasses. Consciously allow your Capricornian qualities full expression, especially when considering a long-term commitment. Never slip into the bad habit of telling white lies in order not to hurt your partner since, in the long run, the implications could be ghastly.

Your well-being

The Piscean body area covers the feet, and yours are vulnerable. You may well enjoy going barefoot, but be careful: you are more vulnerable than most people to foot infections.

The Moon in Pisces

Pisceans tend to put on weight rather easily, usually because of a reliance on junk food. Capricornians are often lean, or perhaps even gaunt. If you do have a slow metabolism, you will need to keep a careful check on your diet. Exercise such as dancing, swimming, and downhill or cross-country skiing will help a lot.

Planning ahead

Pisceans are generally not too good at handling money, and your immediate reaction to financial problems may well be one of utter confusion. Do not make sudden decisions if you have money to invest, and be careful not to fall for get-rich-quick schemes. Let your Capricornian gift for finance overrule any Piscean impracticality.

Parenthood

You will be a good parent, who will sensitively and intuitively understand your children's needs. If you follow your Piscean instincts when dealing with your children, they will always work well, and you will have very few problems with the generation gap. Always remember to express warmth and tenderness to children, as well as Capricornian forthrightness.

SUN & MOON SIGNS

AQUARIUS

JANUARY 21 – FEBRUARY 18

INTRODUCING AQUARIUS

AQUARIUS, THE SIGN OF THE WATER BEARER, IS THE ELEVENTH SIGN OF THE ZODIAC. AQUARIANS ARE THE MOST ENIGMATIC OF ALL ZODIAC TYPES, AND ALSO THE MOST INDIVIDUAL AND INDEPENDENT.

People of this Sun sign have a powerful desire for a lifestyle that is in some way unique. They are often so devoted to it, and so intent on achieving independence, that it is somewhat difficult for them to commit themselves to permanent relationships. At the very least, such a relationship can come rather late in an Aquarian's life.

Traditional groupings

As you read through this book you will come across references to the elements and the qualities, and to positive and negative, or masculine and feminine signs.

The first of these groupings, that of the elements, comprises fire, earth, air, and water signs. The second, that of the qualities, divides the Zodiac into cardinal, fixed, and mutable signs. The final grouping is made up of positive and negative, or masculine and feminine signs. Each Zodiac sign is associated with a combination of components from these groupings, all of which contribute different characteristics to it.

Aquarian characteristics

People of this sign tend to be intellectual and, since the sign is of the fixed quality, you may also be surprisingly stubborn.

Uranus is your ruling planet, and many Aquarians are trendsetters, the leaders of their generation. Perhaps because of the fixed quality of your Sun sign, you can sometimes become a little too set in the opinions that you may have formed when you were young and may consequently lag behind current thought.

Since it is a positive, masculine sign, Aquarius inclines its subjects toward extroversion.

The Aquarian colors are traditionally considered to be electric blue and turquoise.

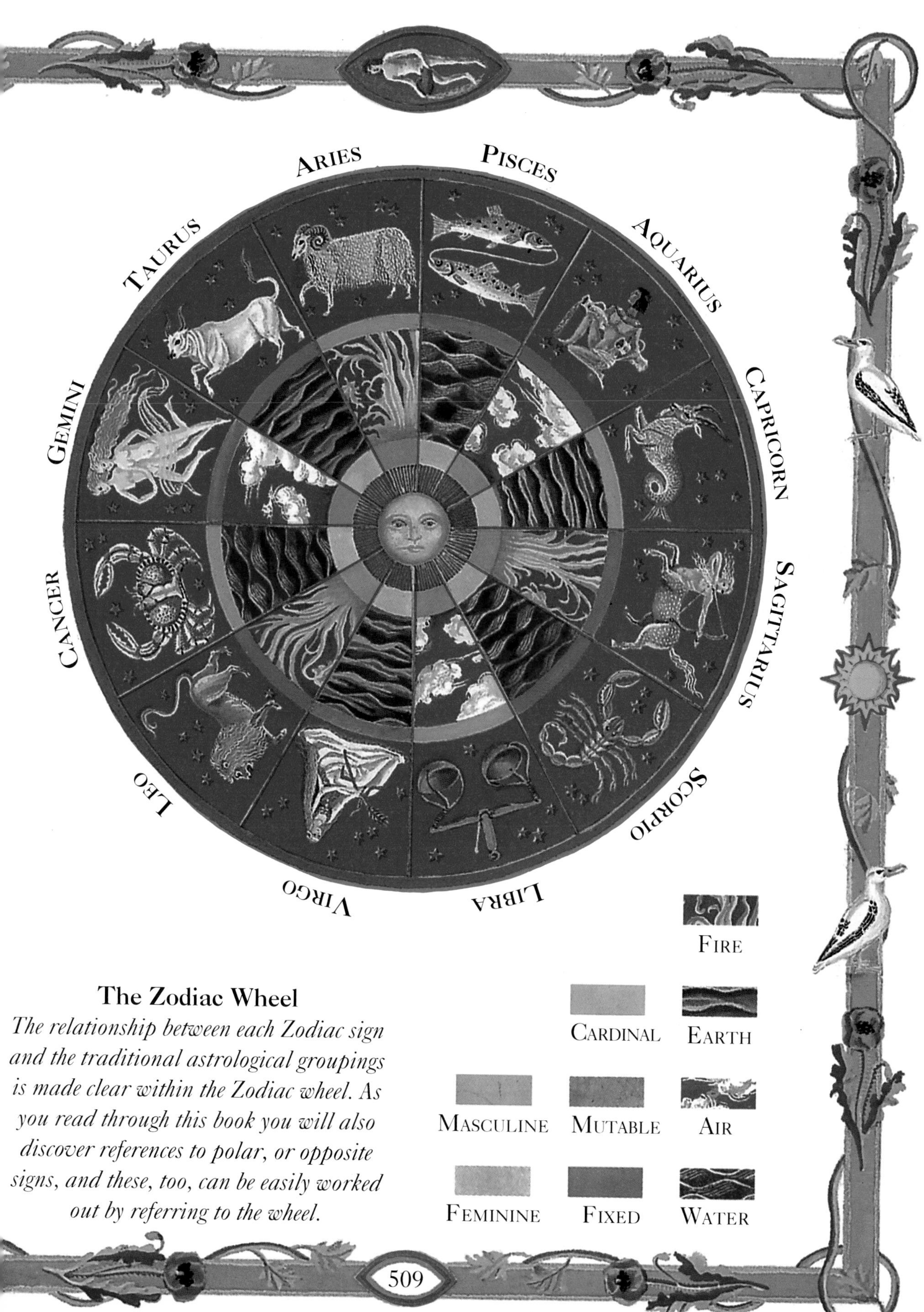

The Zodiac Wheel

The relationship between each Zodiac sign and the traditional astrological groupings is made clear within the Zodiac wheel. As you read through this book you will also discover references to polar, or opposite signs, and these, too, can be easily worked out by referring to the wheel.

AQUARIUS

MYTHS & LEGENDS

THE ZODIAC, WHICH IS RECOGNIZED TO HAVE ORIGINATED IN BABYLON POSSIBLY AS MANY AS 2,500 YEARS AGO, IS A CIRCLE OF CONSTELLATIONS THROUGH WHICH THE SUN MOVES DURING THE COURSE OF A YEAR.

Was Aquarius originally male or female? The Babylonian name for Aquarius, gu. la, has been translated as meaning both a goddess of childbirth and healing, and "constellation of the great man." The latter is thought to refer to the giant Enkidu, described in the ancient epic of Gilgamesh as a man who grew up in the desert among the wild beasts, who became his friends. He devoted his time to protecting the animals and is often shown watering an ox.

The god of fresh water

In ancient Babylon there was also a god of fresh water called Ea, known as "the god with streams," or "house of the water," who was said to dwell in the city of Eridu on the Persian Gulf. He was normally depicted with water streaming from his arms and hands, but is sometimes shown holding a pot. This seems to be a more likely Aquarian figure.

Later, the ancient Egyptians pictorially associated the constellation of Aquarius with the god Hapi, who watered the ground from two jars held in his arms and was a symbol of the River Nile.

Zeus and Ganymede

Manilius, the Roman writer who, in the first century B.C. set down several astrological myths, firmly suggests that the original Aquarian was Ganymede, the son of Tros, king of Troy. He refers to the earliest Greek myths, in which Ganymede appears to be recognized as the deity responsible for showering the earth with the heavens' rain.

The popular myth of Ganymede describes him as the most beautiful boy alive and goes on to relate how Zeus, king of the gods, fell in love with him. Turning himself into an eagle, Zeus carried the boy off to be his cup-bearer, who would pour wine,

Worshipping Ea

The Babylonian water god, Ea, whose name means "house of the water," seems a likely candidate for one of the earliest characters to prefigure Aquarius.

not water, for the gods from a golden bowl. When King Tros quite understandably protested, Zeus sent him two fine horses as compensation, and explained that his son would now be an immortal, exempt from the pains of old age.

The symbol of Ganymede

Although in the Middle Ages Ganymede became renowned as the symbol of homosexual love, during the Renaissance his flight to heaven came to symbolize the soul's ascent to the absolute.

The Age of Aquarius

One modern myth might be said to be the Age of Aquarius, which was made notorious through the radical 1960s musical *Hair*.

Every 2,500 years the Earth passes through a sign of the Zodiac, and these periods are known as ages. The Age of Aquarius may have started a century ago, or it may not begin for another century – opinions differ. One thing that can, however, be said with certainty is that few signs so frequently confer such romantic good looks on their subjects.

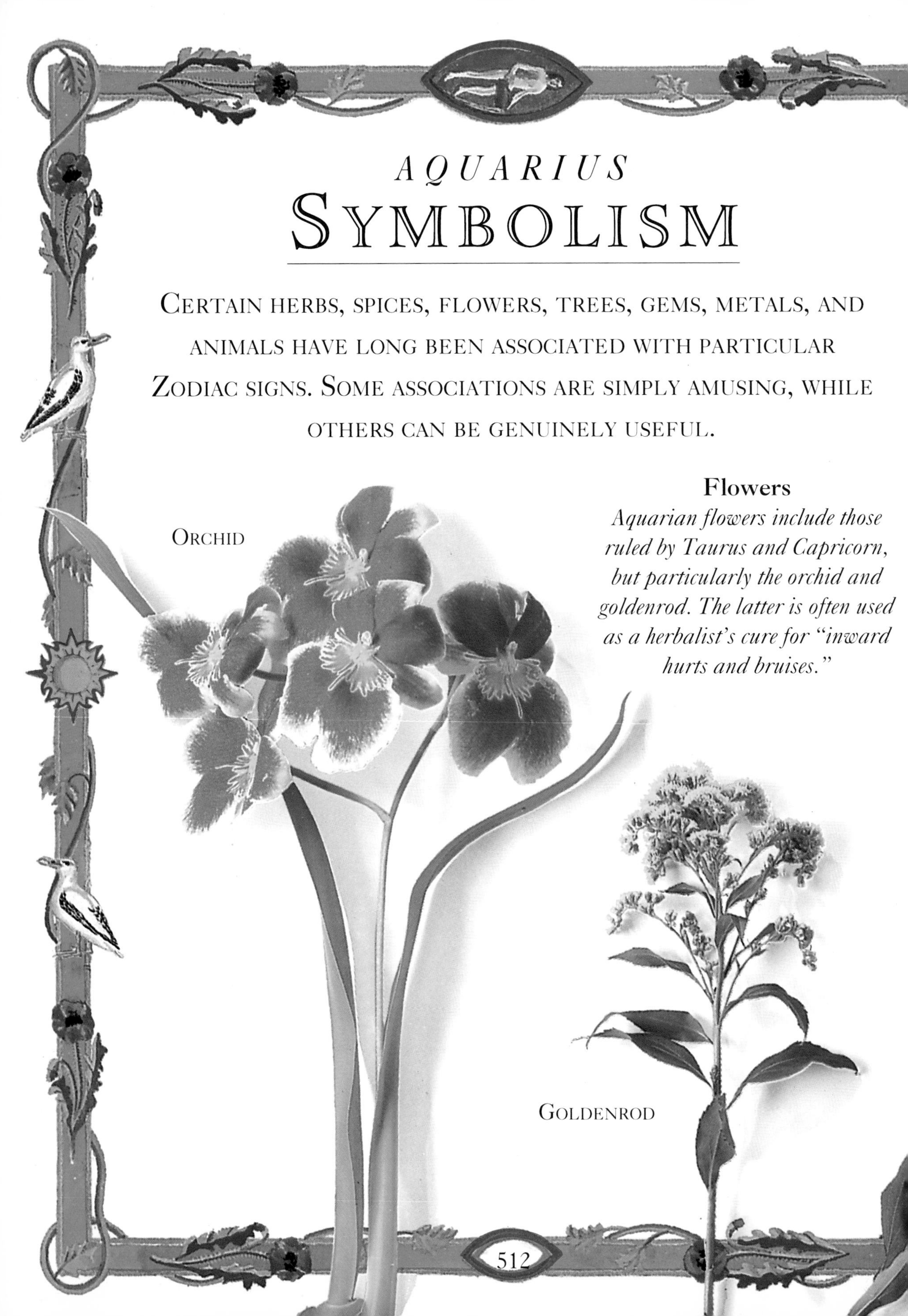

Aquarius
Symbolism

CERTAIN HERBS, SPICES, FLOWERS, TREES, GEMS, METALS, AND ANIMALS HAVE LONG BEEN ASSOCIATED WITH PARTICULAR ZODIAC SIGNS. SOME ASSOCIATIONS ARE SIMPLY AMUSING, WHILE OTHERS CAN BE GENUINELY USEFUL.

Flowers

Aquarian flowers include those ruled by Taurus and Capricorn, but particularly the orchid and goldenrod. The latter is often used as a herbalist's cure for "inward hurts and bruises."

ORCHID

GOLDENROD

Elder

Trees

Most fruit trees, such as the pear and the peach, are said to be ruled by Aquarius.

Pear Tree

Spices

No spice is particularly associated with Aquarius, but cinnamon, which is used to flavor apples and other fruit, and pepper are sometimes mentioned.

Herbs

Taurean herbs are, for the most part, also ruled by Aquarius. This is particularly true of common sorrel, which helps counter inflammations, and elder.

Pepper

Cinnamon

AQUARIUS SYMBOLISM

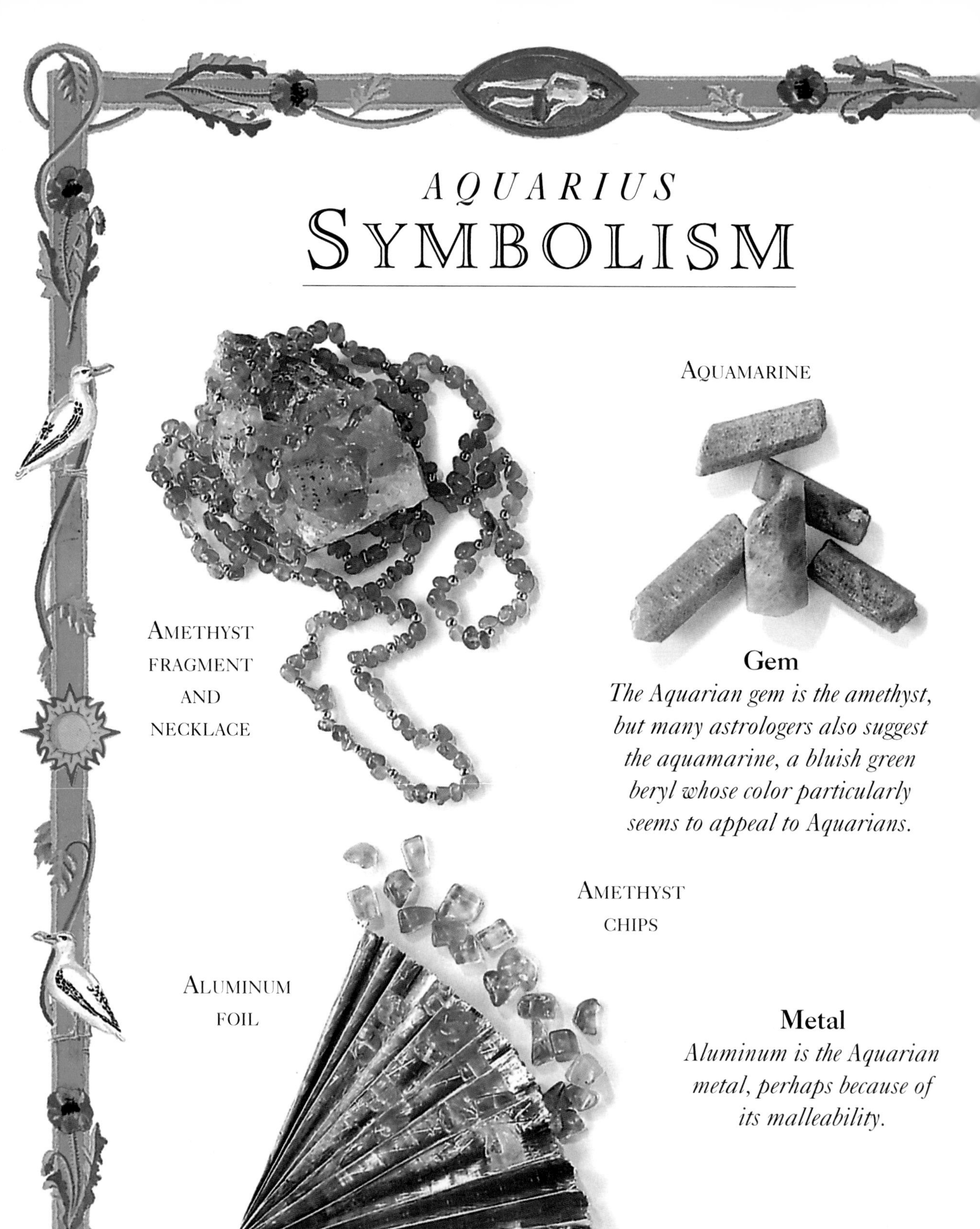

Gem

The Aquarian gem is the amethyst, but many astrologers also suggest the aquamarine, a bluish green beryl whose color particularly seems to appeal to Aquarians.

Metal

Aluminum is the Aquarian metal, perhaps because of its malleability.

Animals

Large, far-flying birds, especially those that migrate over great distances, are ruled by Aquarius.

EAGLE FEATHERS

GOOSE FEATHERS

LEAD ALBATROSS

AQUARIUS PROFILE

DUE TO THE FACT THAT AQUARIANS ARE SO INDIVIDUALISTIC, IT IS VERY DIFFICULT TO GENERALIZE ABOUT THEM. THEY ARE USUALLY FAIRLY LANKY AND, ON THE WHOLE, TEND TO HOLD THEMSELVES WELL WHEN STANDING OR WALKING.

The Aquarian stance is usually very correct. You may use your hands to gesture in an elegant, somewhat superior way, and you hold your head high, in order to make the most of your height.

The Aquarian face
Fine, neatly styled hair and pale eyes characterize the Aquarian face.

The body

Perhaps because Aquarius is an air sign, the Aquarian body gives an overall impression of lightness, even if you are overweight. Many Aquarians are rather lanky, although their bones are usually fairly well covered by flesh. You no doubt have an upright, erect carriage, with a long back and narrow waist.

Aquarian shoulders tend to be square and broad, and the body joints are prominent. Your ankles will be trim and elegant, with a high calf, and your arms and hands are perhaps longer than most people's. There is probably a certain fineness to your bone structure; your features are likely to have a chiseled appearance, as opposed to the more rounded features of, for instance, Librans and Taureans, both of which are ruled by Venus. In fact, curves are very unlikely to play a large part in the make-up of an Aquarian body. It will instead be based upon lines and geometric masses.

The face

Your hair is probably fine, well cared for, and carefully styled, and your forehead is likely to be broad and open. Aquarian eyes are typically pale

The Aquarian stance

A very correct and upright stance is characteristic of many Aquarians. They may appear to possess a certain dignity.

and may have slightly drooping lids. There is a chance that your nose may be a little on the large side, perhaps even a shade imperious; a well-shaped mouth, ready to offer a friendly smile, is also a typical Aquarian characteristic. Your chin may add dignity to your whole face.

Style

Aquarian style is very up to the minute, although some of you may cling to a look that you decided suited you years ago. This is because Aquarians become less adaptable as they age and feel most at home in the initial style that they feel defines them. You may go all out to shock, or use your originality to make a very interesting statement. Pale turquoise or "Aquarian blue" is really your color, and smooth fabrics with satin or silky textures, as opposed to rough ones, will probably suit you best.

In general

Because its subjects are so individualistic, it is very difficult to generalize about this sign. Aquarians usually carry themselves well, giving the impression that they are somewhat superior or even noble.

There is a certain wildness about some Aquarians. This can manifest itself in the the way they dress – they may, for instance, find some small way in which to bend the rules of a particular dress code. Other Aquarians are, however, impeccably neat and rather conventional.

AQUARIUS

PERSONALITY

AQUARIANS ARE THE INDIVIDUALISTS OF THE ZODIAC. YOU CAN BE INVENTIVE AND UNIQUE, BUT ALSO STUBBORN AND, AT TIMES, UNPREDICTABLE; YOU ARE FRIENDLY, KIND, AND HUMANITARIAN, BUT ALSO VERY PRIVATE.

The only thing two Aquarians will agree upon when reading a list of characteristics of their Sun sign is that they share none of them. This is chiefly because Aquarians are the individualists of the Zodiac and, either consciously or unconsciously, they like to make this known. Because of a perverse streak, they will enjoy being as different from their Sun sign brothers and sisters as they are from other people. Nevertheless, they do share certain characteristics.

At work

Your ideal career will include a good deal of human contact. Because of your happy, kind, and caring attitude, you might make an excellent social worker. Furthermore, you will not find it hard to distance yourself from suffering and will be of real assistance in difficult situations. A large number of Aquarians seem to veer toward careers that are based in the sciences. You may be involved in the development of communication techniques, or in some other field where a degree of inventiveness and originality is needed.

From time to time, real brilliance can emerge from members of this sign, and anyone close to such individuals should be careful not to write them off as harmless eccentrics.

Your attitudes

It is very difficult to talk of "knowing" an Aquarian; while people of this sign make very good, kind, and helpful friends, it usually becomes clear that because they are so private no one really knows very much about them. If they are questioned (which will seem like prying to many Aquarians) they will very kindly but firmly ease their way out of providing an answer, and put the inquisitors firmly in their place without them even noticing it.

Uranus rules Aquarius

Uranus, a rather unattractive mythical figure, represents the Aquarian ruling planet. It can make its subjects original, versatile, and independent, but also perverse and rebellious.

You will occupy your spare time in a variety of ways, perhaps by going to lectures, rehearsing with a local drama group, or even working on a local charity committee.

The overall picture

There is a tendency among Sun sign Aquarians to be forward-looking when they are young, but to become rather set in their opinions as they get older. It can be very difficult to encourage them to reassess their outlook.

Aquarians are inventive and should develop their potential originality, since they can be very creative. The need to have a distinctly individual lifestyle, as well as overall independence, is likely to provide a great motivation in your life.

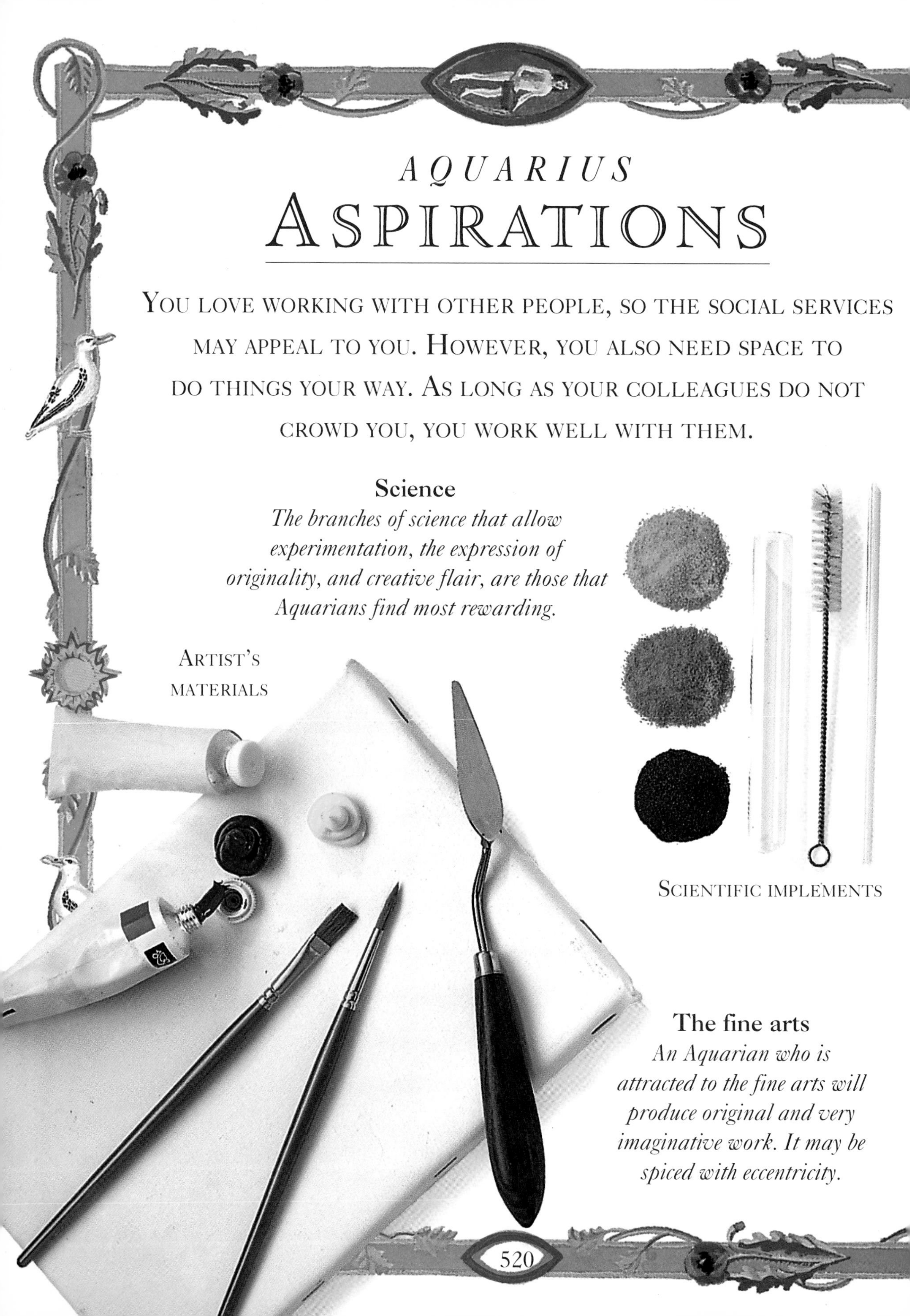

AQUARIUS
ASPIRATIONS

YOU LOVE WORKING WITH OTHER PEOPLE, SO THE SOCIAL SERVICES MAY APPEAL TO YOU. HOWEVER, YOU ALSO NEED SPACE TO DO THINGS YOUR WAY. AS LONG AS YOUR COLLEAGUES DO NOT CROWD YOU, YOU WORK WELL WITH THEM.

Science

The branches of science that allow experimentation, the expression of originality, and creative flair, are those that Aquarians find most rewarding.

SCIENTIFIC IMPLEMENTS

ARTIST'S MATERIALS

The fine arts

An Aquarian who is attracted to the fine arts will produce original and very imaginative work. It may be spiced with eccentricity.

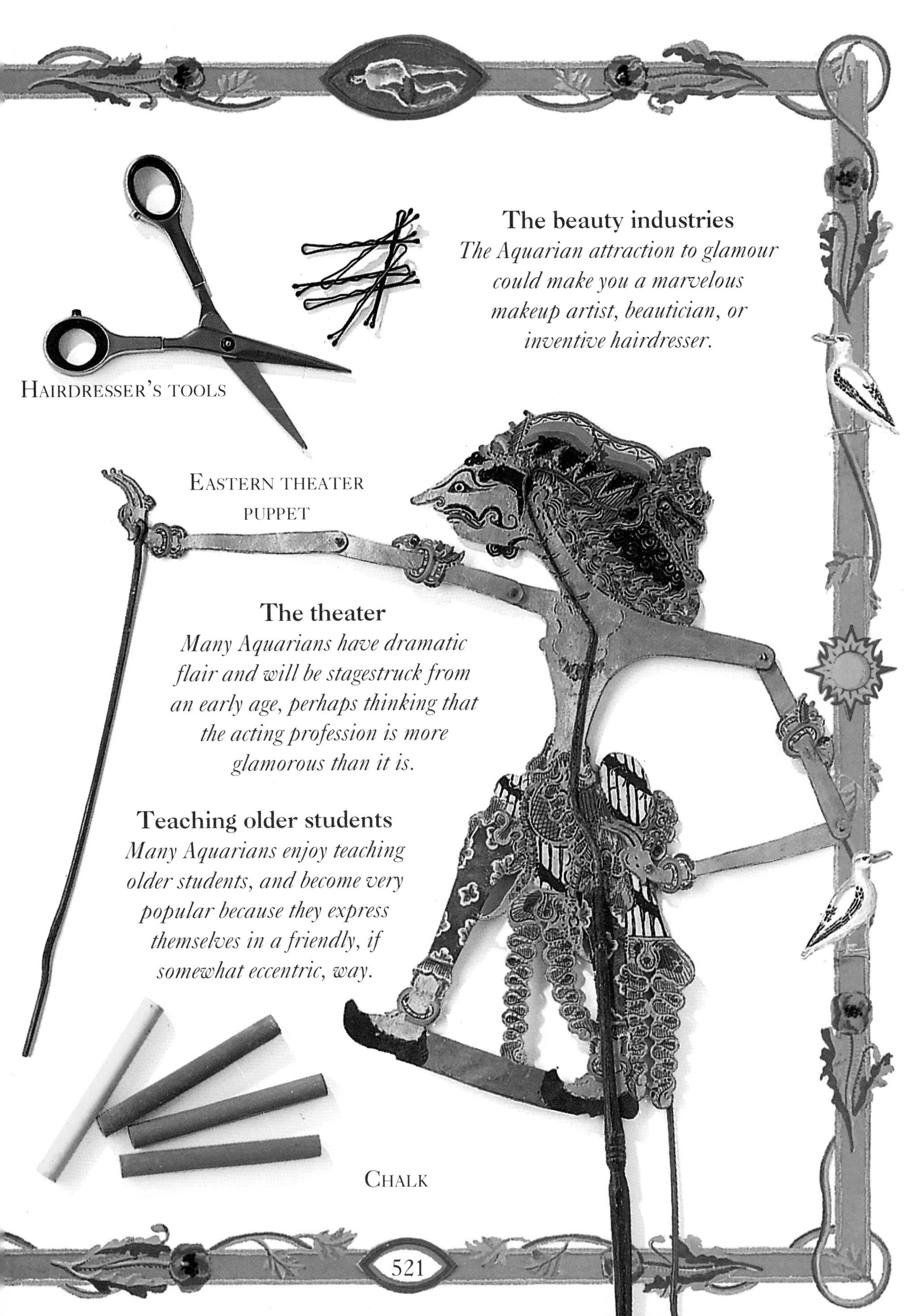

The beauty industries

The Aquarian attraction to glamour could make you a marvelous makeup artist, beautician, or inventive hairdresser.

The theater

Many Aquarians have dramatic flair and will be stagestruck from an early age, perhaps thinking that the acting profession is more glamorous than it is.

Teaching older students

Many Aquarians enjoy teaching older students, and become very popular because they express themselves in a friendly, if somewhat eccentric, way.

AQUARIUS HEALTH

AQUARIANS TEND TO SUFFER FROM STIFFNESS OF THE JOINTS, WHICH CAN LEAD TO ARTHRITIS. IT IS THEREFORE ESSENTIAL THAT YOU SHOULD KEEP MOVING AND GET IMMEDIATE TREATMENT FOR ANY SPORTS INJURIES.

While the ankles are the traditional Aquarian body area, and they are certainly vulnerable, another tradition suggests that joint pains can be a problem. Most Aquarians like keeping active, and it is important that they do so.

Your diet

Natrum muriaticum in its crude form is simple salt, and you may benefit from including it in your diet. Remember, however, that a balanced diet should give you all the salt you need. Do not oversalt your food.

Taking care

The circulation is Aquarian-ruled, and you may enjoy cold, crisp weather, but make sure that you keep warm.

Because Aquarians need a lifestyle that is unique to their own rather special needs, they tend to become ill if something conflicts with this urge. Should you find yourself falling ill without quite understanding why, or if you seem to be catching every minor infection that is going around, you should take a close look at your lifestyle – unease about this could be lowering your resistance.

Apples
Foods that preserve well, such as apples and citrus fruits, are traditionally ruled by Aquarius.

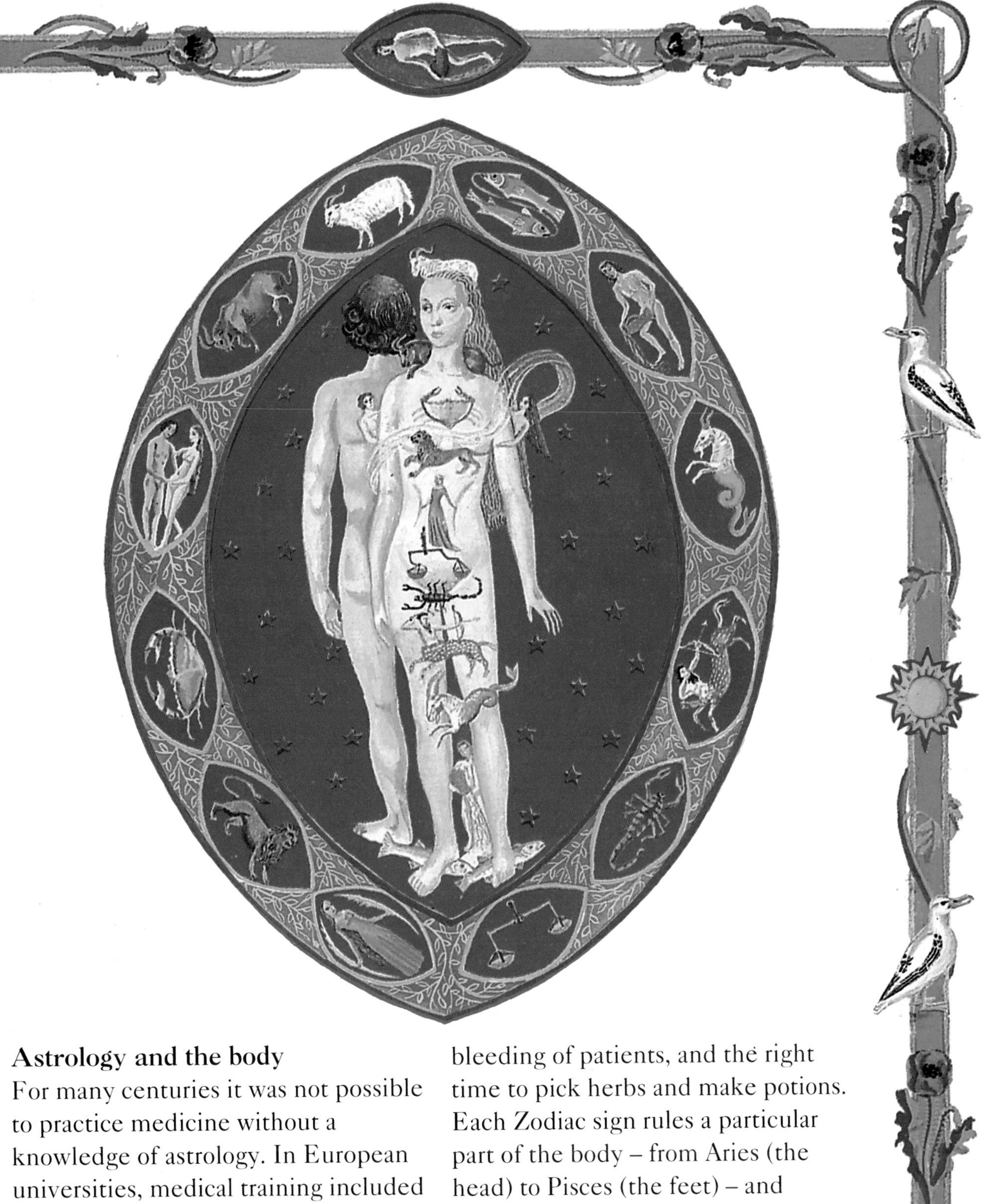

Astrology and the body

For many centuries it was not possible to practice medicine without a knowledge of astrology. In European universities, medical training included information on how planetary positions would affect the administration of medicines, the bleeding of patients, and the right time to pick herbs and make potions. Each Zodiac sign rules a particular part of the body – from Aries (the head) to Pisces (the feet) – and textbooks always included a drawing of a "Zodiac man" (or woman) that illustrated the point.

AQUARIUS AT LEISURE

EACH OF THE SUN SIGNS TRADITIONALLY SUGGESTS SPARE-TIME ACTIVITIES, HOBBIES, AND VACATION SPOTS. ALTHOUGH THESE ARE ONLY SUGGESTIONS, THEY OFTEN WORK OUT WELL FOR AQUARIANS.

Archaeology

An attraction to the deep past often encourages Aquarians to become archaeologists. This profession enables them to combine inspiration with practical research.

ANCIENT COLUMBIAN ARTEFACTS

Ballooning

Aquarius is an air sign, and its subjects love unpolluted fresh air. The idea of taking off in a balloon or glider could therefore be extremely attractive to them.

CIGARETTE CARDS SHOWING BALLOONING

MODEL OF 1930S BENTLEY

Collecting old cars

Many Aquarians are attracted to unusual hobbies, and some of them enjoy the challenge of restoring and driving old cars.

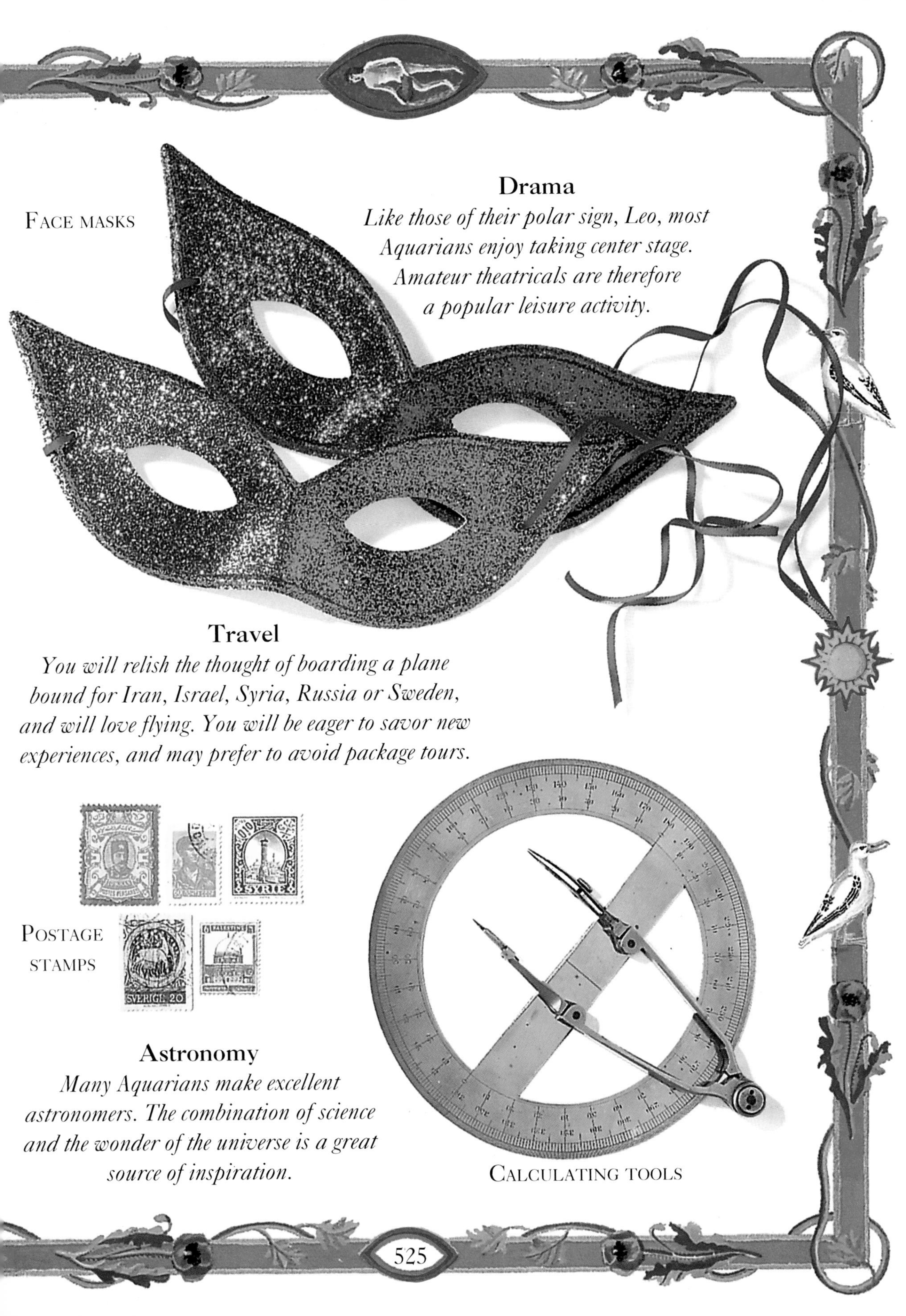

Drama

Like those of their polar sign, Leo, most Aquarians enjoy taking center stage. Amateur theatricals are therefore a popular leisure activity.

Face masks

Travel

You will relish the thought of boarding a plane bound for Iran, Israel, Syria, Russia or Sweden, and will love flying. You will be eager to savor new experiences, and may prefer to avoid package tours.

Postage stamps

Astronomy

Many Aquarians make excellent astronomers. The combination of science and the wonder of the universe is a great source of inspiration.

Calculating tools

AQUARIUS IN LOVE

AQUARIANS ARE KNOWN TO BE ROMANTIC BUT CAUTIOUS. THEY CAN BE COOL, GLAMOROUS, AND ATTRACTIVE, WITH MAGNETIC PERSONALITIES. THE ACT OF FALLING IN LOVE IS AN ESPECIALLY MEANINGFUL EXPERIENCE FOR AN AQUARIAN.

When Aquarians fall in love they are, perhaps more than any other Zodiac type, confronted with some very specific problems.

Unless you are very young you will be intent on building a lifestyle that is in some way unique, which you will be reluctant to disturb. This relates to your need for privacy, and to the fiery independent streak that persuades you to live your life in your own particular way.

Partnership clearly signifies that a great deal of change will occur in one's life; in your case, this might mean a measure of sacrifice. This can sometimes be a rather heavy burden for Aquarians, and it is the reason why many of them frequently put off marriage or forming a permanent relationship until quite late in their lives. Very often this is not a bad thing, since it can prevent a series of relationship breakdowns and a lot of unenviable heartache.

As a lover

Enjoyment of love and sex is extremely unlikely to be a problem for you. Even so, you will always be inclined to put a distance between yourself and your partners. You will, of course, want to

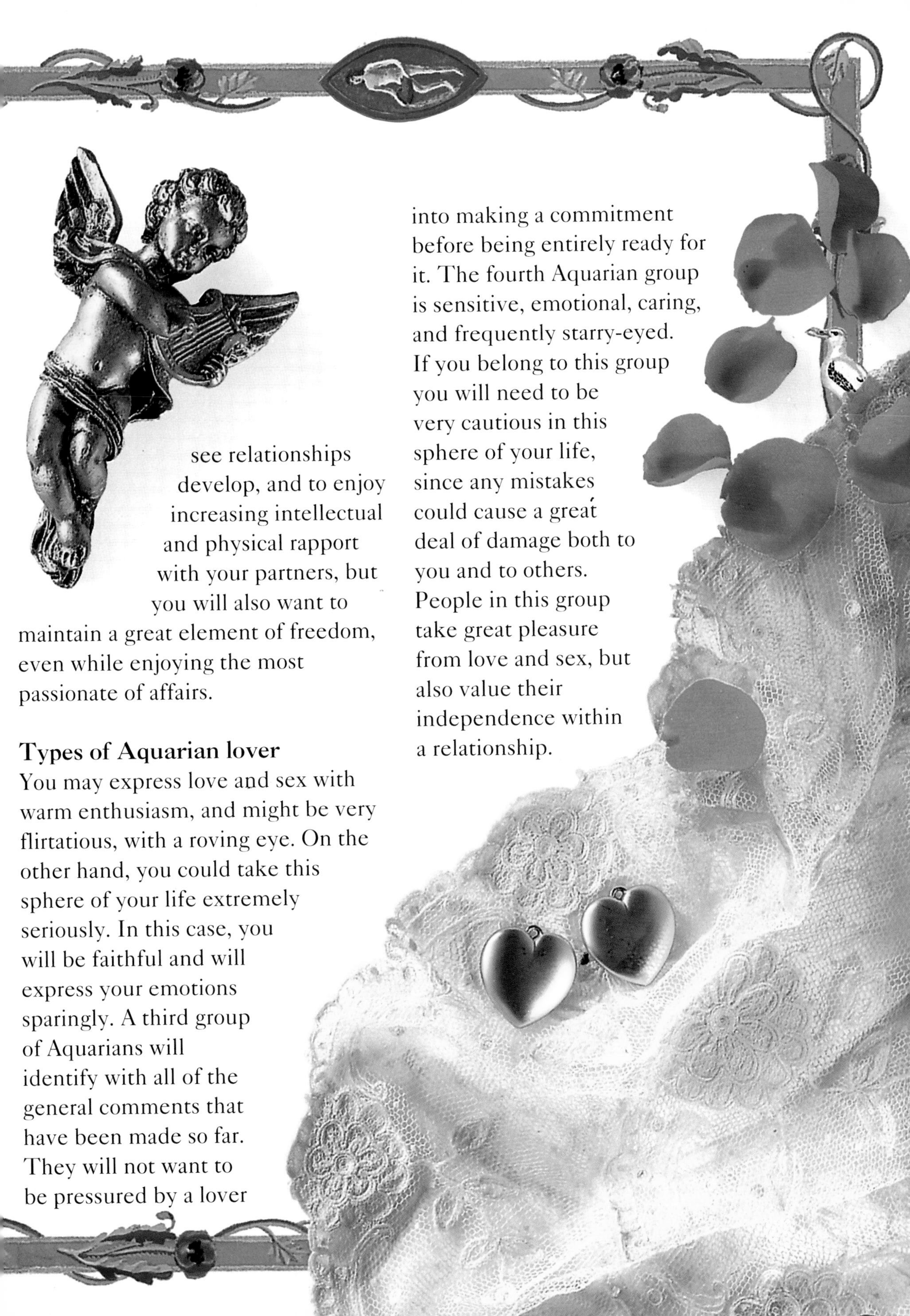

see relationships develop, and to enjoy increasing intellectual and physical rapport with your partners, but you will also want to maintain a great element of freedom, even while enjoying the most passionate of affairs.

Types of Aquarian lover

You may express love and sex with warm enthusiasm, and might be very flirtatious, with a roving eye. On the other hand, you could take this sphere of your life extremely seriously. In this case, you will be faithful and will express your emotions sparingly. A third group of Aquarians will identify with all of the general comments that have been made so far. They will not want to be pressured by a lover into making a commitment before being entirely ready for it. The fourth Aquarian group is sensitive, emotional, caring, and frequently starry-eyed. If you belong to this group you will need to be very cautious in this sphere of your life, since any mistakes could cause a great deal of damage both to you and to others. People in this group take great pleasure from love and sex, but also value their independence within a relationship.

AQUARIUS AT HOME

AQUARIAN INDIVIDUALITY WILL PROCLAIM ITSELF IN YOUR HOME. DO NOT, HOWEVER, FURNISH IT SO TRENDILY THAT IT WILL LOOK DATED IN A FEW YEARS. YOU MAY POSSESS A TALENT FOR CREATING ORIGINAL LIGHTING EFFECTS.

Most Aquarians are quite capable of organizing their lives to meet with the requirements of any particular environment. They are therefore equally at home living in either the country or a big city. Even if their dwelling place is quite small, they will make it feel spacious.

Furniture

Aquarians need a feeling of space, so there will probably be as little furniture as possible in your home. The pieces that you choose are often somewhat clinical in design and usually very modern. If they are not modern items, they will probably have originated in the 1920s or 1930s, when slickness of line and a minimum of decoration were preferred.

Since Aquarius is an air sign, heaviness and too much solidity in furniture is not usually favored. Therefore glass dining tables or

Unique ornaments

Any ornaments in an Aquarian home are likely to be unusual, perhaps because of the owner's interest in the past.

occasional tables are likely to be in evidence. It is, however, surprising how comfortable an insubstantial, angular Aquarian chair can be.

Soft furnishings

While soft furnishings do not usually abound in the Aquarian home, they most certainly add a considerable, possibly Hollywood-style, glamour to it. Aquarians love shiny fabrics, so taffetas and silks are popular among them. Transparent net curtains, or attractive blinds, pulled over only when the sunlight becomes uncomfortable, may also be apparent.

White is a very popular choice for plain walls, and it is sometimes the color used for leather furniture. It is often combined with shiny chrome, which forms the basic structure of tables and chairs. Generally, Aquarians prefer plain or striped fabrics to elaborate patterns.

Decorative objects

All kinds of glass will probably have honored places in your home. You will favor tinted vases, pieces of crystal, and Lalique or other sophisticated glass ornaments. The paintings that you are likely to prefer will be abstract and intellectually demanding, and therefore unlikely to bore you, even after many years.

Since Aquarians are often attracted to the deep past and the distant future, fossils or antiquities may have a place in a well-displayed collection. Nearly all Aquarians love mirrors; they have an unfortunate reputation for being a little vain.

Display of frosted glass fruit

Trendy and glamorous are two words frequently used to describe the Aquarian home. Glass of all kinds is very popular.

THE MOON AND YOU

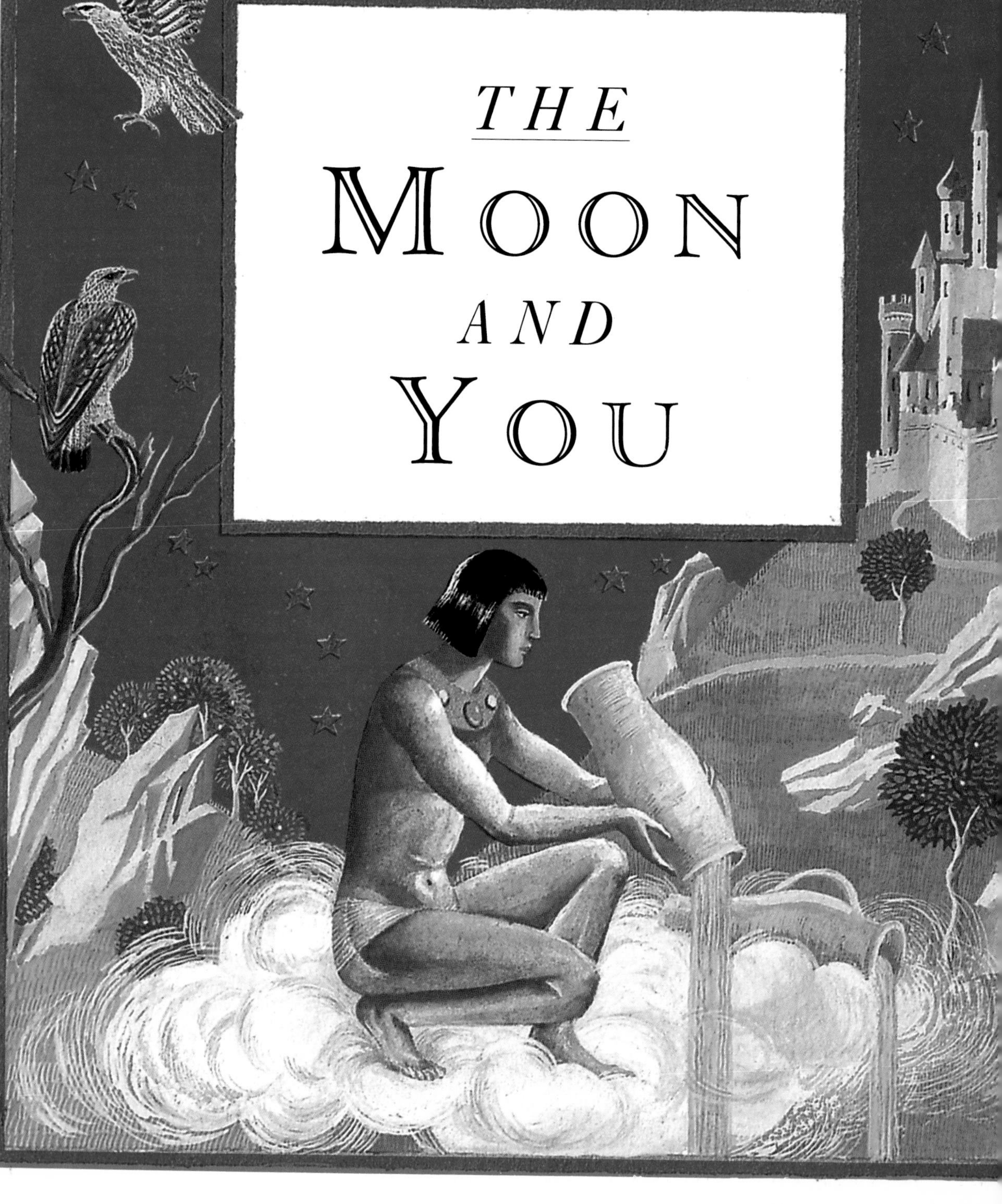

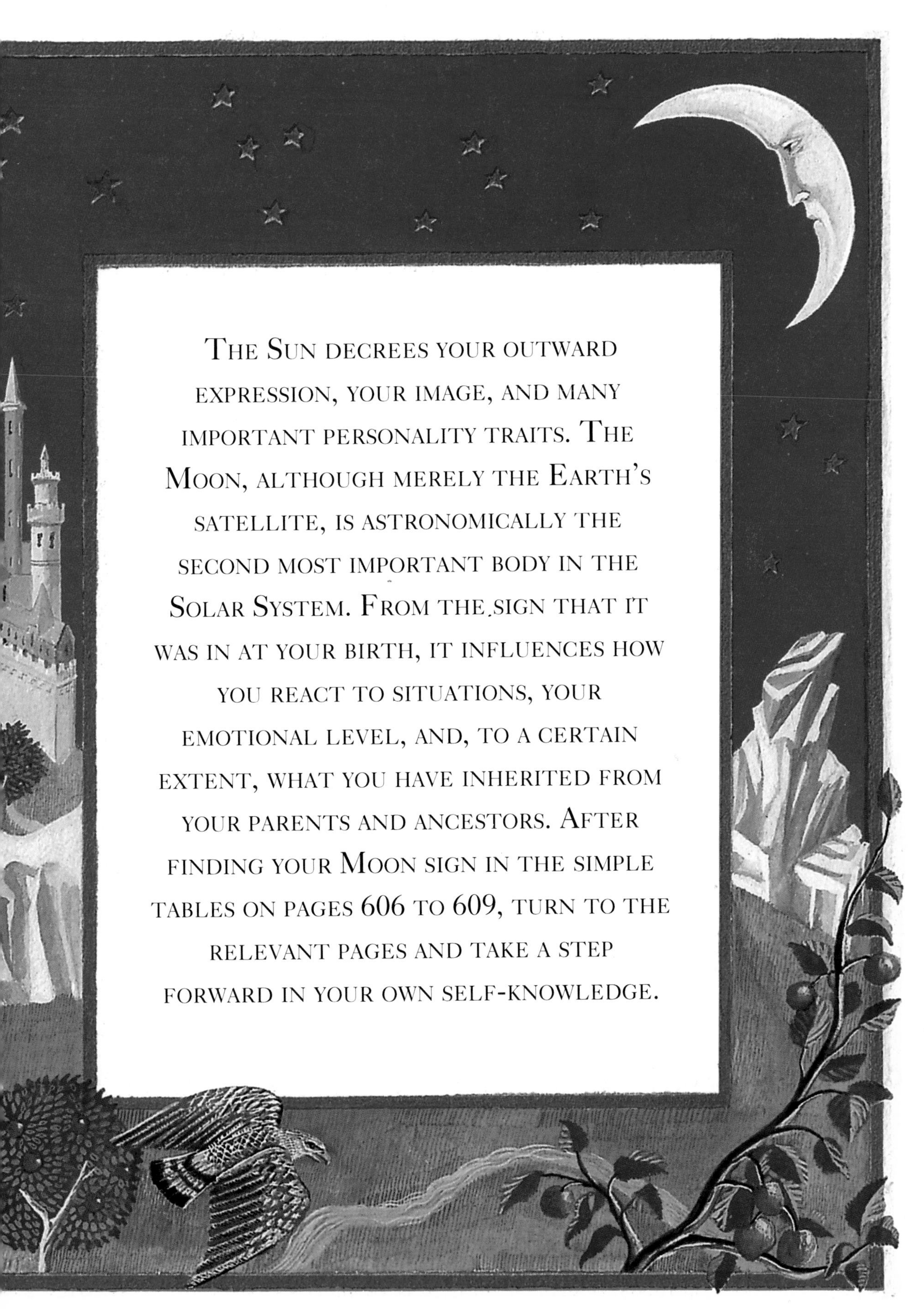

THE SUN DECREES YOUR OUTWARD EXPRESSION, YOUR IMAGE, AND MANY IMPORTANT PERSONALITY TRAITS. THE MOON, ALTHOUGH MERELY THE EARTH'S SATELLITE, IS ASTRONOMICALLY THE SECOND MOST IMPORTANT BODY IN THE SOLAR SYSTEM. FROM THE SIGN THAT IT WAS IN AT YOUR BIRTH, IT INFLUENCES HOW YOU REACT TO SITUATIONS, YOUR EMOTIONAL LEVEL, AND, TO A CERTAIN EXTENT, WHAT YOU HAVE INHERITED FROM YOUR PARENTS AND ANCESTORS. AFTER FINDING YOUR MOON SIGN IN THE SIMPLE TABLES ON PAGES 606 TO 609, TURN TO THE RELEVANT PAGES AND TAKE A STEP FORWARD IN YOUR OWN SELF-KNOWLEDGE.

THE MOON IN ARIES

YOUR AQUARIAN NEED FOR INDEPENDENCE IS HEIGHTENED BY YOUR ARIEN MOON. YOU ARE ALSO LIKELY TO BE A VERY WARM, PASSIONATE PERSON, WHO WILL EXPRESS EMOTION MORE FREELY THAN MANY OTHER SUN SIGN AQUARIANS.

The elements of Aquarius and Aries, air and fire, blend well and, as a result, you respond to most situations with warm enthusiasm. You thrive on challenge, and always want to be well ahead of your rivals.

Self-expression

Your Aquarian Sun gives you originality, which is complemented by a straightforward, uncomplicated approach to life. You are not inhibited by side issues or petty details.

In spite of your natural Aquarian friendliness, you should be aware that your rapid responses may upset other people. It could be that you organize them too sharply, hinting at incompetence on their part. Try to be considerate as well as competent.

Romance

You are among the warmest, and most passionate and highly sexed, of Sun sign Aquarians. Your Moon sign contributes a wealth of emotion to your personality and also gives you the ability to express it positively.

Aquarius and Aries are both very high on the list of Zodiac people who need independence and freedom of expression, and your partners must recognize this. When contemplating a permanent relationship, make sure you discuss this part of your character thoroughly with your partner.

Your well-being

The Arien body area is the head, and when you are subjected to tension or stress, you may incur headaches. If there is no apparent reason for these, it could be that they stem from a slight kidney imbalance, so get a medical checkup.

An Arien Moon always tends to make one impulsive and hasty. As a result, you could be slightly accident-prone. Make an effort to develop a more cautious approach.

The Moon in Aries

You enjoy sports and most forms of exercise, and should have a fast metabolism. You will therefore probably burn up calories quickly.

Planning ahead

Your originality and flair may well be expressed through enterprise; you may have two sources of income. You could invest impulsively and be attracted to unsound schemes. Keep your Aquarian cool when investing, and seek professional advice.

Parenthood

You are probably a lively parent and much of your instinctive, warm enthusiasm is likely to surface quite naturally in your children's company.

Because you are rather modern in outlook and enjoy keeping in touch with current trends, it is very unlikely that you will end up falling victim to the generation gap. In fact, the situation could even arise where your children may find it difficult to keep up with you.

THE MOON IN TAURUS

YOUR TAUREAN MOON MAKES YOU WARM AND AFFECTIONATE IN YOUR RESPONSES TO OTHERS AND GIVES YOU AN INSTINCTIVE BUSINESS SENSE. HOWEVER, SINCE BOTH AQUARIUS AND TAURUS ARE FIXED SIGNS, BEWARE OF BEING TOO STUBBORN.

The characteristics of these two signs are very different, and your immediate responses to situations could consequently be somewhat out of step with your general attitude toward life.

Self-expression

Your Moon gives you considerable stability, and a great need for emotional and financial security. Furthermore, while Aquarius is known for its unconventionality, Taurus has a liking for tradition and a mistrust of change.

Your Moon will encourage and help you to express your originality. It is very likely that you have creative flair of some kind, perhaps for music or singing, and you may want to develop this along traditional, conventional lines. Your Taurean creativity should help you to express your natural Aquarian flair and originality in a very satisfying way.

Romance

The contrast between a need for emotional security and an equal need for freedom of expression will be most marked in the area of your personal relationships. You will place some contrasting demands on your partners. Almost inevitably, you will have to make some sacrifices and compromises, and your lovers must be aware of your different needs.

Your well-being

The Taurean body area is the throat, and it is likely that when you get a cold it will start with a sore throat and end in a cough that is hard to lose.

Most people with a Taurean emphasis enjoy rich, sweet food, and you may therefore be prone to weight gain. Much depends on your metabolism. If it is slow, make sure that you exercise regularly. Also bear in mind that there is a relationship between your Taurean Moon and the

The Moon in Taurus

thyroid gland. If you eat very lightly but still find that you put on weight, get a medical checkup.

Planning ahead

There is a chance that you could be very adept at handling money. You may spend freely on your possessions, and therefore need to earn a good, regular salary.

You have a naturally good business sense and, with Aquarian flair, could do extremely well running a business of your own.

Parenthood

You probably express warm affection toward your children, but may have a tendency to be strict one moment and favor a freer style of parenthood the next. Bear in mind that your children should always know where they stand with you.

Aquarius will help you keep up to date with your children's ideas. However, your Taurean instinct for not breaking the rules may not endear you to them. Make sure that you always aim for compromise.

THE MOON IN GEMINI

YOUR AQUARIAN ORIGINALITY AND QUICK MIND BLEND VERY WELL WITH YOUR SPEEDY GEMINIAN RESPONSES AND COMMUNICATIVE ABILITY. YOU MUST BEWARE OF BEING TOO TRENDY IN YOUR IMAGE AND OUTLOOK, AND SHOULD NOT SUPPRESS YOUR EMOTIONS.

Both Aquarius and Gemini are air signs, and this element emphasizes an intellectual approach to life. You are therefore more than likely to be in possession of distinctive ideas, logic, and originality.

Self-expression

You should be able to muster your various qualities without much difficulty, although actually realizing your plans may not always be easy; you may enjoy theorizing more than taking practical action.

You probably have a very low boredom threshold, and your inherent versatility will encourage you to learn a little about a great many things. You would do better to study a few well-chosen subjects in depth.

Romance

Neither Aquarius nor Gemini is noted for being able to express their emotions very freely, and this may inhibit you. You always need a high level of friendship and intellectual rapport with a lover.

Your well-being

The Geminian body area covers the arms and hands, and they are therefore vulnerable. In addition, Aquarians are somewhat prone to arthritis, so it is a good idea for you to have at least one hobby that will keep your hands and fingers very active.

The Geminian organ is the lungs, and bronchitis could trouble you. Seek medical advice if a cough hangs on for more than a few days.

The worst Geminian fault is restlessness, which can impair achievement and sometimes lead to a buildup of tension. A calming discipline such as meditation or yoga will be most helpful.

You probably have a fast metabolism. If you do not, you may need to take regular exercise to fight

The Moon in Gemini

the flab. Fast games such as basketball, badminton, squash, and tennis are excellent for you, and you should also aim to keep your diet as light and as healthy as possible.

Planning ahead

You probably have the ability to sell ice in Alaska and will certainly strike a good deal when, for instance, you want to sell your car. But be careful: you may not be as clever as you think when you have money to invest. Seek professional financial advice and take it. If possible, favor a savings scheme to which contributions are extracted from your paycheck at the source.

Parenthood

You make a tremendously lively parent, challenging your children's opinions and keeping up with them. The generation gap will therefore never be a problem for you. You could sometimes appear a little distant to your children. Bear in mind that logic is a good thing, but a warmhearted hug is also very necessary at times.

THE MOON IN CANCER

YOUR AQUARIAN ORIGINALITY SHOULD WORK WELL, AND PERHAPS CREATIVELY, WITH CANCERIAN IMAGINATION AND INTUITION. IT WOULD BE A GOOD IDEA FOR YOU TO ENDEAVOR TO CURB ANY UNPREDICTABILITY AND SUDDEN CHANGES OF MOOD.

Your Aquarian Sun and Cancerian Moon bestow some very contrasting characteristics. They can make you a unique, interesting, extremely individualistic, and rather complex character.

Self-expression

You are probably among the most individual of Aquarians. No doubt you respond to most situations in a sensitive and emotional manner, and it is in this respect that Cancer and Aquarius meet most happily.

Aquarians give help generously where it is needed, and do so simply because the need is apparent. They are cool, logical, and rational, rather than emotional. Your Cancerian Moon allows you to be emotionally moved by the plight of others.

At a first meeting, you may give the impression of friendliness tempered by a certain degree of coolness. As acquaintance ripens into friendship, others will recognize that in some ways you can be quite a softy. But you never lose the ability to snap back when a sharp answer is required.

Romance

In emotional relationships, you may have experienced conflict. On the one hand you have a very deep-rooted longing for a home and family, while on the other there is an Aquarian insistence on retaining your own individual lifestyle.

You respond marvelously to partners and are capable of a really rich and rewarding sex life. Take care, however, that you do not create a claustrophobic atmosphere.

Your well-being

The Cancerian body area covers the chest and breasts. Although there is absolutely no connection between this sign and the disease that bears the same name, it is perhaps

The Moon in Cancer

particularly important for women with the Moon in Cancer to check their breasts regularly just in case there are any problems.

Cancerians are very prone to worry, and Aquarians are detrimentally affected by stress and tension. You may therefore suffer from headaches or even migraines. Learn to relax – yoga and other techniques might well help you to do this.

Planning ahead

You are among those Aquarians who cope very well with money, provided that you allow a naturally shrewd and clever business instinct free expression. Aim to invest in well-established companies and schemes.

Parenthood

As a protective, caring parent, you may sometimes worry unduly about your offspring. At the same time, your modern Aquarian spirit encourages them to be as independent as you are. Be understanding when they decide that it is time to leave home. As long as you curb a tendency to go on about how things were when you were young, the generation gap should not prove to be a problem.

THE MOON IN LEO

AQUARIUS AND LEO ARE POLAR OR OPPOSITE SIGNS, WHICH MEANS THAT YOU WERE BORN UNDER A FULL MOON. RESTLESSNESS MAY BE A PROBLEM, AND YOU MUST AVOID BEING STUBBORN. LET LEO CREATIVITY BLEND WITH AQUARIAN ORIGINALITY.

We all express some of the characteristics of our polar sign (the sign opposite ours across the Zodiac circle). For Aquarians, this is Leo and, because the Moon was in that sign when you were born, this polarity is strikingly emphasized.

Self-expression

You are a good organizer who is able to take over any situation at a moment's notice. However, you should be careful not to appear bossy. At times, you may seem a little distant and unapproachable.

You may have creative potential, which could be expressed through painting, acting, or maybe fashion designing. Your inventiveness could lean toward a scientific expression.

Romance

You will express your feelings with passion and with all the fire of your Leo Moon. Both in and out of bed, you will make a rewarding partner. As with all Aquarians, you need a good measure of independence, but you will also want to look up to your partners and be a power behind the throne, as well as sharing it.

Beware of a tendency to dominate your lover; anyone with a Leo emphasis can fall into this trap. Keeping a balance is essential.

Your well-being

The Aquarius and Leo polarity is at its strongest in health matters. Aquarius rules the circulation, which is, of course, driven by the heart – the Leo organ. The two influences combine most potently and call for your special attention. Exercising your heart will assist your circulation, and you must keep moving to avoid any buildup of arthritic conditions in your joints. The spine and back are Leo body areas, and they also need exercise. If you have to spend long

The Moon in Leo

hours sitting at a desk, you may benefit greatly from using an ergonomic chair.

You may like rich food but provided that you keep moving, you will burn up any unwanted calories.

Planning ahead

Aquarians are glamorous, and Leos like the best and the most expensive things. To meet these needs, you will need to earn a relatively high salary. Your Leo Moon may well also give you quite a clever flair for investment, perhaps in well-established companies making quality goods. If you ever need financial advice, you will seek it from the most knowledgeable expert you can find.

Parenthood

Leo is a sign traditionally related to parenthood, and you should get great pleasure from your children, always encouraging them to greater achievements. Always express loving, warm enthusiasm, especially when they show you their efforts. Be rational and forward-looking, and discipline your children positively. You should have no problems with the generation gap.

THE MOON IN VIRGO

YOUR VIRGOAN MOON GIVES YOU EXCELLENT DOWN-TO-EARTH QUALITIES. DO NOT LET ANY INHIBITING OR REPRESSIVE FEELINGS SUPPRESS THE DEVELOPMENT OF ORIGINAL IDEAS AND UNCONVENTIONAL SELF-EXPRESSION.

Your cool and rational Aquarian Sun combines with the natural common sense and logic of your Virgoan Moon. You are therefore able to look at every aspect of a problem in a critical, analytical way.

Self-expression

You are both original and practical, and should express those qualities fully. They are a source of excellent potential, perhaps for some unique form of craftwork.

You sometimes have a tendency to nitpick, and this can cause you to lose sight of the overall pattern of a situation. Only when your Aquarian Sun takes over are you be able to see the problem in a broader way.

Romance

Your modesty may sometimes cramp your style where love and sex are concerned. However, if you manage to relax into your relationships, you will manage to achieve a really rewarding and ultimately fulfilling love and sex life.

Your well-being

The Virgoan body area is traditionally said to cover the stomach, and you may benefit from a high-fiber diet. Like many people with a Virgoan influence, you could also respond well to vegetarianism. You may sometimes be rather prone to worry, and this could end up affecting your health, via your stomach.

Stress, tension, and a degree of restlessness can lead to migraine if you do not learn to relax. A discipline such as yoga could be of help.

Planning ahead

You will no doubt be as profoundly attracted to glamour as all Aquarians are. However, if you indulge in an excessive amount of glamorous purchases, you could end up feeling

The Moon in Virgo

very guilty. This is far less likely to be the case if the things that you buy actually have a practical purpose of some sort and, even better, if they are made of natural materials.

You may sometimes be inclined to think that you are rather less well-off financially than is in fact the case. While you are generally quite good at managing your financial affairs, you would probably be wise to seek independent professional advice when you want to start saving, or if you find yourself in possession of a substantial amount of money that you wish to invest.

Parenthood

You could be far more critical of your children than you realize. Be careful, since this could sap their confidence.

Your Aquarian Sun will no doubt enable you to keep abreast of your children's ideas. Make sure that you also provide them with adequate warmth and affection.

THE MOON IN LIBRA

YOUR LIBRAN MOON HELPS YOU TO EXPRESS YOUR THOUGHTS FREELY AND WITH ORIGINALITY. YOU ARE SOCIABLE, BUT YOU MAY NEED TO DEVELOP A MORE SERIOUS, PRACTICAL APPROACH TO SOME SPHERES OF YOUR LIFE.

Both Aquarius and Libra are air signs, so they blend very well. As a result, you are among the friendliest, most sympathetic, understanding, and diplomatic of all Aquarian Sun and Moon sign combinations.

Self-expression

Your Libran Moon gives you the instinctive ability to see all sides of a problem and to follow another person's argument sympathetically. Understandably, this characteristic can sometimes make you indecisive, and others may occasionally find it annoying because they do not know exactly where they stand with you. It may be worth trying to develop a more down-to-earth attitude.

Romance

Your Libran Moon brings out the real romance that is always lurking somewhere in the Aquarian spirit. You enjoy setting a scene for love. You will, however, react to your partners in one of two distinct ways. On the one hand, you may feel that you are incomplete as a person when you are not sharing an emotional relationship, and may rush into partnerships. On the other hand, because of your Aquarian independent streak, it is possible that you keep your distance even when a good opportunity arises. You are, of course, capable of building a rewarding and loving relationship with someone who understands you.

Your well-being

The lumbar region of the back is ruled by Libra. If you have a job that involves spending long hours at a desk, you should consider getting a back-support chair.

The Libran organ is the kidneys, and you may suffer from headaches as a result of either a buildup of stress or a slight kidney disorder. If your metabolic rate is unusually slow, you

The Moon in Libra

are quite likely to end up putting on excess weight, so it may prove wise for you to indulge in some regular exercise. You might, for example, consider skiing or working out at a friendly health club.

Planning ahead

You probably love luxury and may well have expensive tastes. Never be tempted to lend money, since you are likely to be a soft touch for unscrupulous people, and take professional advice before buying stock or starting a savings scheme. Enjoy your money, but keep a firm check on how you spend it.

Parenthood

You may have a tendency to bribe your children for a bit of peace and quiet. This is a bad idea in the long run. Be decisive, and try to be firm, so that your children know exactly where they stand with you. You will be able to keep up with their concerns and should have few problems with the generation gap.

THE MOON IN SCORPIO

YOU HAVE A POWERFUL EMOTIONAL FORCE WITH WHICH YOU MAY HAVE FOUND IT HARD TO COME TO TERMS. STUBBORNNESS COULD SOMETIMES CAUSE PROBLEMS FOR YOU. ALWAYS AIM TO BE OBJECTIVE AND TO KEEP AN OPEN MIND.

Both Aquarius and Scorpio are fixed signs, which may make you somewhat stubborn and increase your determination in life. This will help you in difficult or stressful times.

Self-expression

You are a typically free, independent Aquarian spirit, but also have all the depth and intensity of a Scorpion Moon and the need to live a really fulfilling life.

You will only be really happy in a career that gives you psychological satisfaction and burns up your great resources of emotional and physical energy. If you do not have such a career, you could stagnate.

Romance

Your powerful source of emotional energy is quite different from your Aquarian qualities. More than any other Aquarian Sun and Moon combination, you need a rich and rewarding love and sex life. You are passionate and sexually demanding, and therefore require an exuberant and responsive partner. Bearing in mind your Aquarian Sun, you also need to feel free and independent.

The worst Scorpio fault is jealousy – your Aquarian self will hate it if you allow this negative emotion to surface.

Your well-being

The Scorpio body area covers the genitals. Male Scorpios should therefore regularly examine their testicles for irregularities, while women should have cervical smears.

Scorpios enjoy living it up. They are, in many ways, the party people of the Zodiac. Too much rich food and quality wine can therefore result in excessive weight gain among people of this sign. If this is the case with you, make a disciplined and gradual change in your eating habits, however boring you may find this. In theory,

The Moon in Scorpio

you should enjoy sports and exercise. However, unless you are an enthusiast for one particular kind of exercise or team game, you may need variety – water sports, speed skating, and karate should suit you.

Planning ahead

You have a shrewd business sense, and possess what it takes to make a lot of money. This will be useful, since you could well spend money liberally. When investing you may benefit from professional advice, but tell your adviser what your instincts suggest – they could be right.

Parenthood

You could sometimes appear quirky to your children. You may be conventional one moment, and all for a modern outlook the next. Try to let your children know where they stand with you. If you fully express your Aquarian traits, you will have no problems with the generation gap.

THE MOON IN
SAGITTARIUS

AQUARIUS AND SAGITTARIUS ARE BOTH SIGNS THAT NEED SPACE AND INDEPENDENCE. ALLOW THE WARMTH OF YOUR MOON SIGN ADEQUATE FREEDOM OF EXPRESSION. THIS WILL MELT THE COOL DETACHMENT OF AQUARIUS.

The air element of your Aquarian Sun and the fire element of your Sagittarian Moon blend well, making you a very enthusiastic, optimistic person. You no doubt respond with a sense of immediacy and intensity when challenged or faced with a demanding situation.

Self-expression

You are likely to have a positive outlook on life, and will be a free spirit with a wide-ranging mind and breadth of vision. You may, however, cope badly with detail, which might be best left to others.

There is an element of the eternal student about you. You are likely to need an element of intellectual challenge in order to thrive, and should always have some interest that encourages the positive expression of this quality. Although you are a versatile person, you should make sure that you do not spread your interests too thin, since this could easily encourage you toward inconsistency of effort.

Romance

You have a marvelous source of very positive emotion and probably do not find it difficult to express your feelings. You make a very lively partner, and love and sex are a joy to you. You need a partner who is capable of recognizing your powerful need for freedom and independence, since anything smacking of claustrophobia in a relationship will be fatal to its happiness.

Your well-being

The Sagittarian body area covers the hips and thighs. Sagittarian women in particular often put on weight in this area. To make matters worse, you may have a liking for heavy foods. You should try to lean toward the more typical Aquarian diet of salads,

The Moon in Sagittarius

fish, and poultry. You clearly need a good deal of exercise and will probably enjoy one or more sports.

The Sagittarian organ is the liver, which may well be disturbed by the heavy food mentioned already. You may like taking risks, but should make sure that every one of them is carefully calculated.

Planning ahead

You have something of a gambling spirit and could be excited by moneymaking schemes that sound rewarding but may not be secure. If therefore you cannot resist a gamble, make quite sure that you do not invest more money than you can afford to lose. Take professional advice before investing; you may make mistakes here from too much optimism.

Parenthood

You are probably progressive and modern in outlook; rational and logical but, at the same time, able to show warmth and tenderness toward your children, especially when they are upset. You will encourage all their efforts and will contribute much to their education. The generation gap will not be a problem for you.

THE MOON IN CAPRICORN

YOU NO DOUBT HAVE WHAT IT TAKES IN ORDER TO REACH THE TOP, BUT YOUR AMBITIOUS CAPRICORNIAN MOON MAY TEND TO MAKE YOU A LONER. YOU COULD EXPERIENCE CONFLICT BETWEEN CONVENTIONAL AND ECCENTRIC BEHAVIOR.

Before the planet Uranus was discovered in the eighteenth century, Saturn ruled both Aquarius and Capricorn. There are therefore some interesting links between these signs, but also some vivid contrasts.

Self-expression

You will initially respond to situations in a very matter-of-fact, practical way, and will be very cautious. Subsequently, however, your more extrovert Aquarian personality is likely to come into its own. In this way, you will possess a secure basis from which to express yourself.

Capricorn is known for being very conventional, whereas Aquarius is renowned for being unconventional, and likes to surprise and sometimes shock people. You must find a compromise if you are to achieve a balance, and get the best out of both instincts without causing problems to other people. If you are particularly ambitious, you are likely to lead a very rewarding life and achieve the successful career that you desire.

Romance

Neither Aquarius nor Capricorn is a very emotional sign. You may consciously need to relax into a relationship in order to enjoy a really rich and rewarding love and sex life.

Your Aquarian Sun makes you glamorous and attractive to the opposite sex, but your Capricornian Sun may be an inhibiting factor. Even before a romance begins, you may tell yourself that it is doubtful whether you have found a suitable partner.

Your well-being

The Capricornian body area covers the knees and shins, which are therefore vulnerable. It is important for you to keep moving, and to keep exercising, since anyone with a Capricorn emphasis is particularly

The Moon in Capricorn

susceptible to rheumatic pain and stiffness of the joints. The skin and teeth, as well as the bones, are also Capricorn-ruled.

Perhaps you are fairly lean, with a fast metabolism, and therefore have no weight problem. If this is not the case, you may need to take some regular exercise.

Planning ahead

Your instinctive caution will stand you in good stead, preventing you from frittering money away. You will want the feeling of security that regular savings bring. Although you probably do not need to take financial advice, you should seek it, if only to confirm how good your own ideas are.

Parenthood

You may appear rather cool and distant to your children. While you are kind and friendly, you should make a conscious effort to reassure them in a warm and loving way when they are upset. Be progressive, and you will avoid the generation gap.

THE MOON IN AQUARIUS

BOTH THE SUN AND THE MOON WERE IN AQUARIUS AT THE TIME OF YOUR BIRTH, SO YOU WERE BORN UNDER A NEW MOON. BECAUSE AQUARIUS IS AN AIR SIGN, THIS ELEMENT POWERFULLY INFLUENCES YOUR PERSONALITY AND REACTIONS.

Should you study a list of your Sun sign characteristics, you will probably recognize that a great many of them apply to you. On average, out of a list of perhaps 20 traits of a Sun sign listed in books or magazines, most people will strongly identify with 11 or 12. In your case, however, the average increases considerably because the Sun and Moon were both in Aquarius when you were born.

Self-expression

You are perhaps among the most independent and self-contained of all Zodiac Sun and Moon sign combinations. Kind and friendly almost to a fault, you have a unique and individual lifestyle that you have developed over the years and may still be refining. You need psychological space but, since you are a very private person, you also need privacy. Even friends who truly love you may not really know you. You are not concerned with other people's private lives, and expect them not to be concerned with yours.

Romance

Your expression of love no doubt fits the general descriptions on pages 526 to 527. You should study the comments on the different ways in which your Sun sign expresses love and affection, since these variations will add a considerable dimension to your attitudes to love and sex. You have an almost magnetic appeal, but your instinctive reaction to lovers is to let them admire you, but to make them keep their distance.

Your well-being

Because the Sun and the Moon were both in Aquarius at the time you were born, your ankles (the Aquarian body area) are particularly vulnerable. There is also a chance that your circulation may not be very good. In

The Moon in Aquarius

cold weather you should keep warm by wearing several layers of light clothing rather than one heavy sweater. In addition, you should take special care of your spine and back. If you stick to a light diet, you should not incur excessive weight gain.

Planning ahead

In coping with finance you will express originality and flair. This may not be such a good thing, because neither of these traits is necessarily effective when it comes to increasing your bank balance. Always seek professional financial advice.

Parenthood

While you should experience few problems with the generation gap, you may not be sufficiently reassuring, warm, and loving toward your children. This can leave them feeling a little insecure. Remember that they may need stricter discipline than you think is necessary.

THE MOON IN PISCES

IN DIFFERENT WAYS, BOTH AQUARIUS AND PISCES ENCOURAGE HUMANITARIAN, CHARITABLE WORK. YOUR INSTINCT TO HELP OTHERS IS VERY POWERFUL, BUT DO NOT LET IT GOVERN YOUR AQUARIAN DETACHMENT AND OBJECTIVITY.

The qualities attributed to these signs are very different, making you a multifaceted person. Contrary to your Sun sign character, the influence of your Piscean Moon gives you powerful emotion that readily surfaces, and which you can express in a variety of ways.

Self-expression

You are extremely kind, friendly, and helpful – your Aquarian Sun sees to that. However, since Aquarius is humanitarian and Pisces is charitable, you can sometimes be swept up into making considerable sacrifices in order to help others in need.

You have a great deal of creative potential and must express it in a fulfilling manner.

Romance

You are more sensual and expressive in love and sex than many Aquarians. No doubt you fall in and out of love very easily, since it is not hard for you to identify with that romantic streak that so often lies deeply buried in the Aquarian personality. However, you still need Aquarian space, and an element of independence within your relationships. Equally, you need a strong partner who will encourage you in all your efforts and help to develop your self-confidence.

Deceptiveness is by far the worst Piscean fault. Do not resort to it, especially if you think it will provide an easy way out of a tricky situation. Furthermore, do not be self-deceptive when you fall in love.

Your well-being

The Piscean body area covers the feet, and yours will therefore be vulnerable to all kinds of injury. You will find exercise sandals attractive and comfortable. Pisceans tend to put on weight rather more easily than Aquarians, and you could rely too

The Moon in Pisces

heavily on junk food, or simply may not bother to eat sensibly. This can be disastrous both for your well-being and for your figure.

You will enjoy rather unusual forms of exercise and sport. Modern free-form dance, roller or ice skating, and sequence swimming are all likely to appeal to you.

Planning ahead

Money probably slips through your fingers. You may give away much more than you can afford, which is wonderfully noble, but can cause problems when you are unable to pay the rent. If you have a regular job, try to find a savings plan to which contributions are paid out of your income. Otherwise, you should always seek sound professional advice.

Parenthood

You will be a rational, sensitive, and caring parent, but must try to curb Aquarian unpredictability, since sudden changes of mind and mood do not go over well with children. You will always be prepared to give your children a hug when things go wrong and should have no problems with the generation gap.

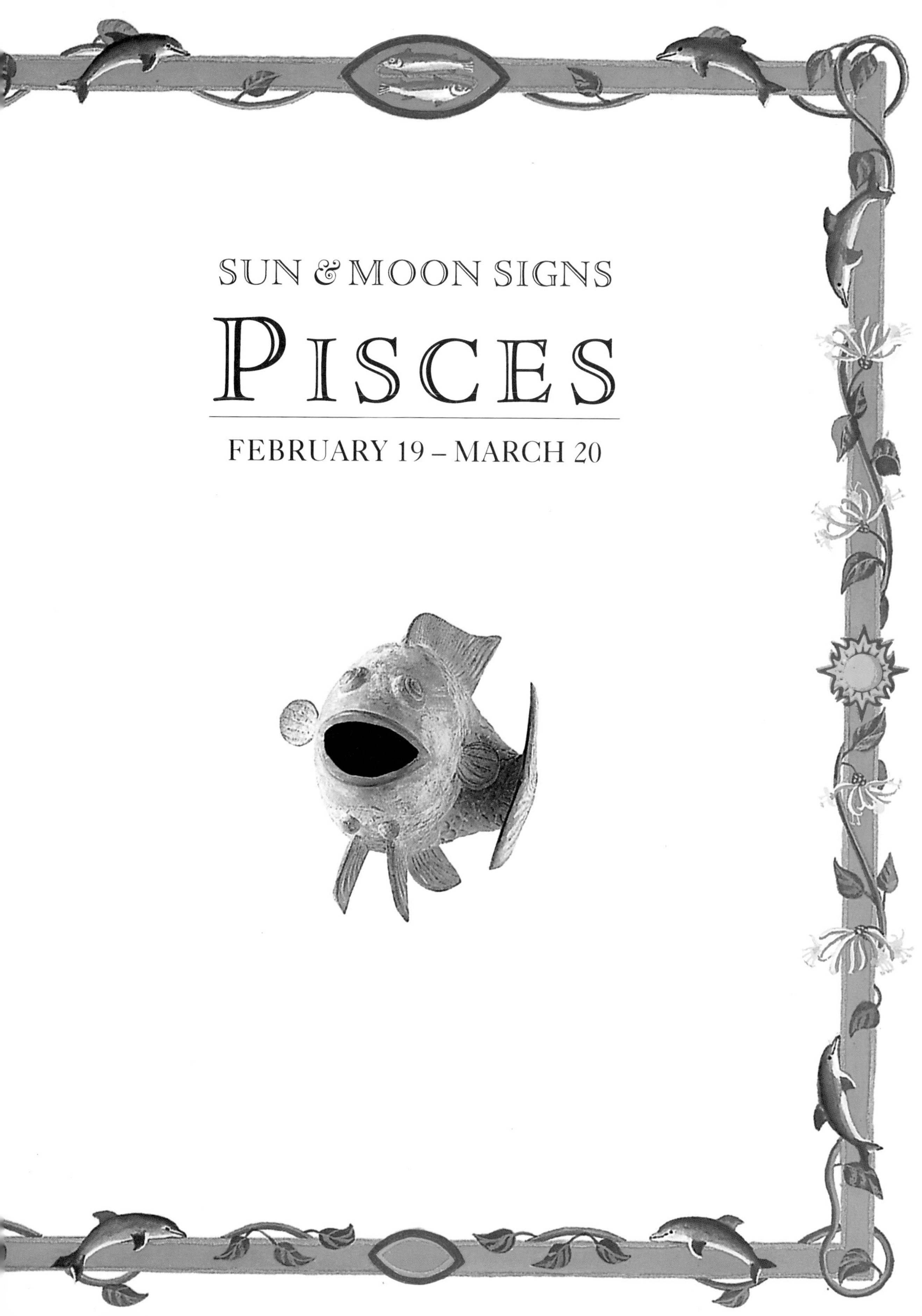

SUN & MOON SIGNS

PISCES

FEBRUARY 19 – MARCH 20

INTRODUCING PISCES

PISCES, THE SIGN OF THE TWO FISHES, IS THE TWELFTH SIGN OF THE ZODIAC. THE PISCEAN CHARACTER IS MARKED BY A NATURAL QUIRKINESS, AND THIS IS SYMBOLIZED BY THE FISH SWIMMING IN OPPOSITE DIRECTIONS.

The two fishes that symbolize this sign are connected by a cord held in their mouths and are always portrayed swimming in opposite directions. They suggest a strong characteristic of the Piscean personality: Pisceans often decide on one line of action, and then take precisely the opposite course. Not surprisingly, this may impede your progress through life.

Traditional groupings

As you read through this book you will come across references to the elements and the qualities, and to positive and negative, or masculine and feminine signs.

The first of these groupings, that of the elements, comprises fire, earth, air, and water signs. The second, that of the qualities, divides the Zodiac into cardinal, fixed, and mutable signs. The final grouping is made up of positive and negative, or masculine and feminine signs. Each Zodiac sign is associated with a combination of components from these groupings, all of which contribute different characteristics to it.

Piscean characteristics

The water element is a powerful source of emotion and, because Pisces is of the mutable quality, you are likely to be flexible in your views. You are full of marvelous creative potential, but may sometimes doubt yourself. If you lack self-confidence, you will need continual support and encouragement in order to develop and fulfill your promise.

Neptune, the god of the sea, is the Piscean ruling planet. Although you are probably very kind, Neptune's influence can persuade you to seek easy ways out of difficult situations. All too often this involves deceit. The sign is negative and feminine, so Pisceans tend to be introverts.

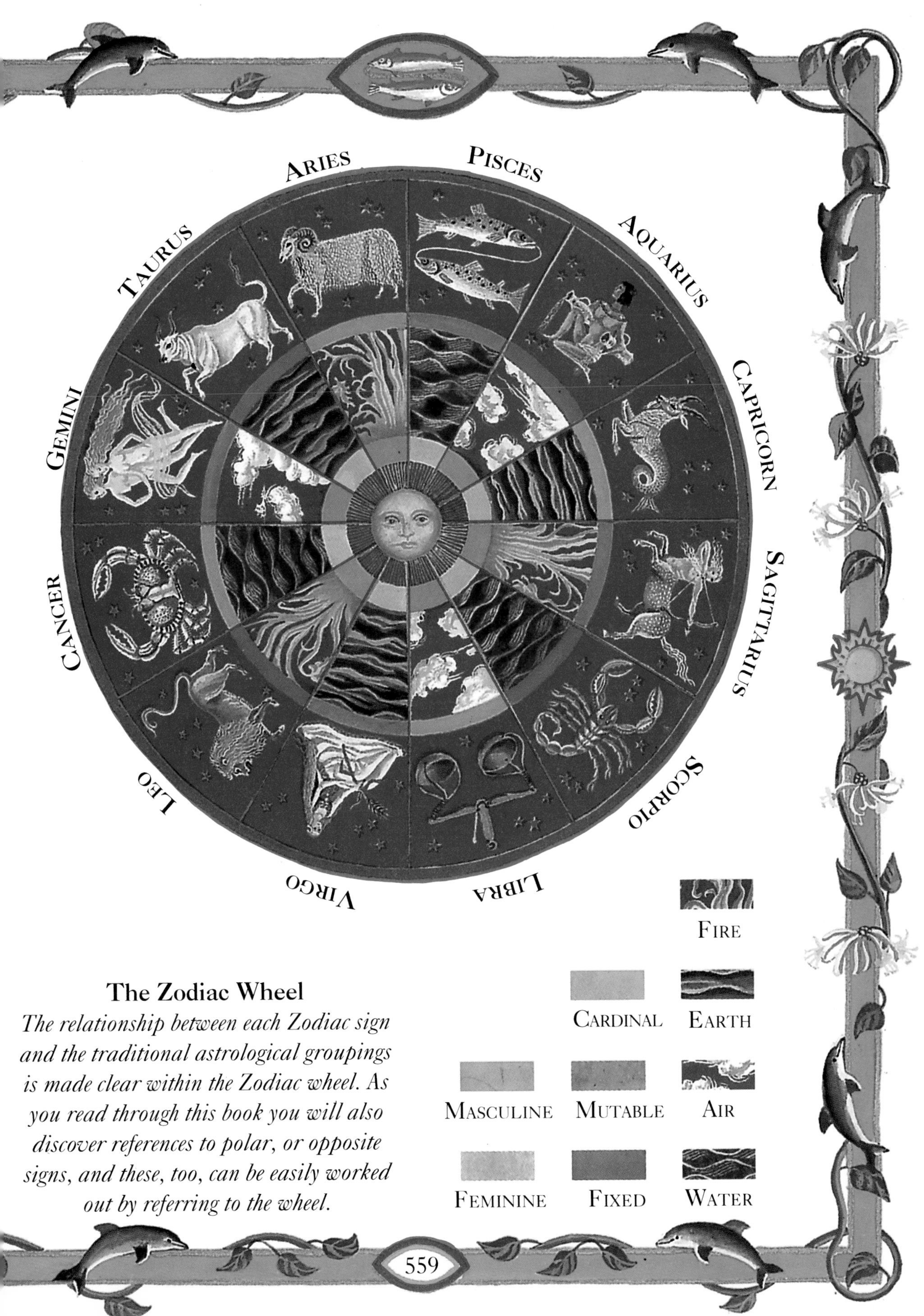

The Zodiac Wheel

The relationship between each Zodiac sign and the traditional astrological groupings is made clear within the Zodiac wheel. As you read through this book you will also discover references to polar, or opposite signs, and these, too, can be easily worked out by referring to the wheel.

PISCES

MYTHS & LEGENDS

THE ZODIAC, WHICH IS BELIEVED TO HAVE ORIGINATED IN ANCIENT BABYLON AS LONG AS 2,500 YEARS AGO, IS A CIRCLE OF CONSTELLATIONS THROUGH WHICH THE SUN MOVES DURING THE COURSE OF A YEAR.

The ancient Babylonian name for this constellation was *kun*, meaning "the tails." This title referred to the tails of the two fishes that were associated with the goddesses Anunitum and Simmah, who once represented the rivers Tigris and Euphrates. The great Roman writer Manilius, who set down a number of astrological myths, gives us a stronger link with the sign of Pisces. It actually derives from the earlier literature of the Greek writer Hyginus, who wrote one of the first works on mythology.

Typhon
Made in the sixth century B.C., this terracotta figure shows the monster Typhon.

Venus and Cupid

Hyginus's story involved Venus and Cupid, who were the Roman versions of the Greek Aphrodite and Eros. The former was the goddess of love, who was said to preside over a love that bonded all living creatures, and to inspire all of Nature's creations. The latter was her son by her husband, the graceless and ugly god Vulcan. Cupid was originally conceived as the god who was responsible for harnessing the different elements of the universe, allowing life to develop. Clearly there is a link between the role of Cupid and that of his mother. From these abstract origins, he came to be seen as an immortal child with the ambition to infect both mortals and the gods with the virus of love. Cupid is often shown firing arrows from a bow.

Venus and her son Cupid
This representation of Venus, the goddess of love, and her son Cupid was created in the 1500s by Agnolo Bronzini.

These arrows were invested with the power to stir great passion in the hearts of all those that they struck.

Typhon the monster

Far removed from the notions of love and beauty associated with Cupid and his mother was Typhon, the youngest child of Mother Earth and the largest monster ever born.

From the thighs downward he was nothing but coiled serpents, and his arms, which were said to span a hundred leagues in any direction, ended in countless serpents' heads. As his name suggests (it is the root of the word *typhoon)*, Typhon was said to be responsible for any unusually strong winds.

Venus and Cupid are transformed

According to the myth, Venus and Cupid were strolling along the banks of the Euphrates one day when they were confronted by an enraged Typhon. In order to evade him they immediately turned themselves into fish, and swam off rapidly in opposite directions. To commemorate the event, Zeus, king of the gods, placed the constellation now known as Pisces in the heavens.

The two fishes

Even today, the fishes used to represent the sign face in different directions, although they are connected by a single golden cord. This perfectly indicates the perversity that is such a powerful characteristic of Sun sign Pisceans. They will almost inevitably argue strongly for one course of action only to eventually decide to take precisely the opposite course.

PISCES SYMBOLISM

CERTAIN HERBS, SPICES, FLOWERS, TREES, GEMS, METALS, AND ANIMALS HAVE LONG BEEN ASSOCIATED WITH PARTICULAR ZODIAC SIGNS. SOME ASSOCIATIONS ARE SIMPLY AMUSING, WHILE OTHERS CAN BE GENUINELY USEFUL.

PINKS

Plants

Dandelions, lime-flowers, mosses, lichens, waterlilies, and pinks – in fact most plants that grow in Piscean colors – are all associated with this Sun sign.

MOSS

Trees

The lime, birch, mulberry, chestnut, ash, oak, birch, and all trees that grow near water are ruled by Pisces.

Herbs

Herbs ruled by Cancer and Sagittarius come under the influence of Pisces. They include sage and saxifrage.

Spices

No spice is particularly associated with Pisces, but coriander and cinnamon are sometimes mentioned.

PISCES
SYMBOLISM

FISH MOULD

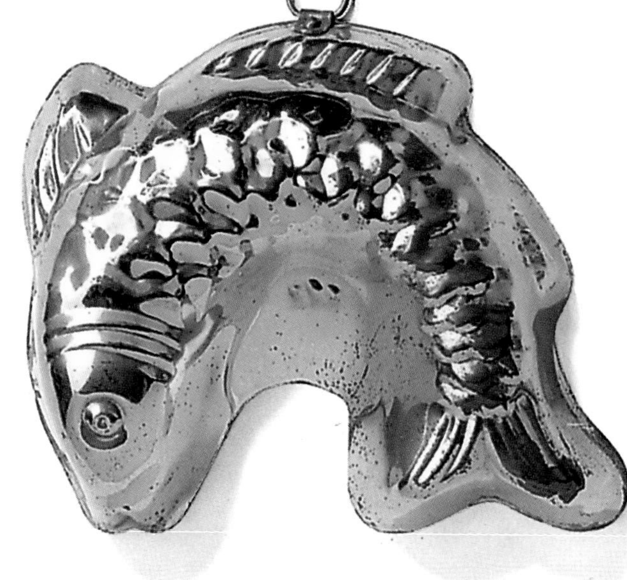

Gem

The Piscean gem is traditionally said to be the colorless moonstone. Magical properties are often attributed to it.

MOONSTONE

PLATINUM NUGGET

Metal

The Piscean metal is platinum, but traditional astrology also mentions tin and titanium, which emit the entire color range of the spectrum and are therefore well suited to Piscean taste.

PLATINUM GRAINS

Fish printer's block

Dolphin earrings

Animals

All fishes are, of course, Piscean animals, and so are all mammals – for instance, dolphins, whales, and porpoises – that live near or in the water.

Wooden fish ornament

PISCES
PROFILE

PISCEANS OFTEN SEEM TO WALK AROUND IN A DREAM, FAR AWAY FROM THE BUSTLE OF EVERYDAY LIFE. BECAUSE THEY CAN BE FORGETFUL AND MAY HAVE THEIR MINDS ON HIGHER THINGS, THEY HAVE A TENDENCY TO DRESS CARELESSLY.

Many Pisceans stand with their feet crossed, like a fish's tail. This distinctive stance is often noticeable at social gatherings or at cocktail parties.

The body

It is not difficult to recognize Pisceans who have an undisciplined and unhealthy approach to life. They will tend to look overweight, and have flabby, shapeless bodies and rather dull eyes. However, Pisceans who decide to dedicate themselves to some grueling physical activity like skating or dancing will appear to be fitness itself, even if they possess typically pale Piscean complexions. Piscean creative potential and inspiration will be likely to keep them practicing at the barre long after many other people would have decided to give up.

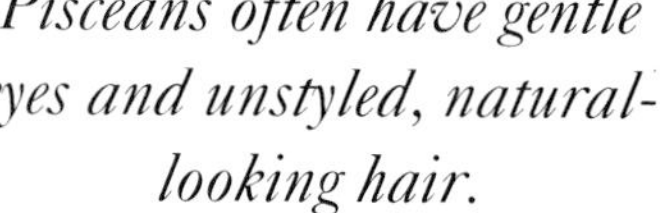

The Piscean face
Pisceans often have gentle eyes and unstyled, natural-looking hair.

The face

Pisceans will either style their hair heavily, or lean in quite the opposite direction and leave it in its natural state. You will tend to frown if you are worried or confused. The eyes are a dominant feature in many Pisceans and will probably appear to be gentle, perhaps showing a capacity to be very emotional. A dominant feature is very often a drooping line at the corner of the eye. Your nose is likely to be well shaped and from small to medium in size; some Pisceans tend to have noticeably high bridges to their noses.

The Piscean stance

Pisceans frequently stand with both feet crossed, forming the distinctive shape of a fish's tail.

Style

The Piscean image is romantic. Many Piscean men love to own velvet jackets, while Piscean women can look stunning whether they are dressed in a Paris creation or simply have a length of fabric pinned around them. Unless career commitments force you to dress conventionally, you will probably have an extremely original image and may like wearing unusual antique clothes. You are unlikely to become too great a slave of fashion, unless some aspect of your life demands it.

You will look your best wearing soft fabrics such as wool, and you may veer toward an ethnic look.

Your feet are very likely to betray the fact that you are a Piscean. Perhaps without even realizing it, you could have a tendency to wear rather broken down, well-worn shoes.

In general

A softness and gentleness, an eagerness to sympathize, is very apparent on first meeting a typical Piscean. There is nothing pushy about these people. They will always listen to others with interest, and their eyes reflect the emotions of the people they are conversing with. As has been said, the eyes are nearly always a very dominant Piscean feature. Piscean women will probably not take long to discover that they can use their eyes to their advantage. Many will develop a range of subtle expressions and inflections.

PISCES

PERSONALITY

PISCEANS ARE SAID TO BE THE POETS OF THE ZODIAC. WHILE NOT ALL OF THEM WILL SPEND HOURS PENNING VERSES TO THEIR LOVERS, MANY DO SEEM TO SHARE THE INSPIRATION ASSOCIATED WITH THIS ART.

Words such as unworldliness, dreaminess, and inspiration are all frequently used to describe head-in-the-clouds Pisceans; but so are charity, kindness, and helpfulness. You probably have a great willingness to ease other people's burdens.

Many Pisceans find it difficult to face up to reality. While you may have an ability to identify with suffering and often actually the means to do something about it, you may also have a tendency to retreat into your own little world. You could be a recluse.

At work

It should come as no surprise to find that the characteristics mentioned above may influence your choice of career. You would do best to find work that offers plenty of variety, and that does not force you to labor through the same hours every day. A predictable job might provide you with a sense of security, but it could prove to be stifling. Well-defined regulations or guidelines may provide you with a useful sense of direction, and you should have no problems in following them. Try to study and learn from the way that your superiors handle authority and manage to cope with decision making.

Your attitudes

Many Pisceans need peace and quiet. This can mean the quiet of the cloister or, ironically, it can cause you to disconnect yourself from the everyday world by blasting loud music into your ears through a personal stereo. Either way, you will probably find the experience restorative.

The overall picture

The symbolism of the sign is opposite and represents a true Piscean problem. Just as the two fishes of Pisces swim in opposite directions, Pisceans will often fail to

Neptune rules Pisces

Neptune, the Roman god of the sea, represents the Piscean ruling planet. It can make its subjects idealistic, imaginative, and sensitive, but also careless, indecisive, and deceitful.

act in their own best interests. It may be that a certain lack of self-confidence often prompts you to decide on one line of action – and to then do just the opposite. Unfortunately, you may find this happening just when you are attempting to act particularly positively and assertively. You must be careful not to rely on excuses in order to avoid starting new projects. If, for example, you say that you have no time to start something new, you are probably actually falling victim to a lack of self-confidence – whether or not there is an element of truth in your excuse. You must make an effort to harness your complete potential.

PISCES

ASPIRATIONS

IT IS POSSIBLE THAT YOU DO BETTER WORKING BEHIND THE SCENES THAN OCCUPYING A HIGH-PROFILE POSITION. IF YOU LEARN TO INTERPRET YOUR IMAGINATION PRACTICALLY, IT WILL BE A VALUABLE ASSET TO YOU.

Painting

Many Pisceans are very creative, and the work they can produce as painters may be both beautiful and imaginative. They should not underestimate their potential.

WATERCOLOR PAINTS AND BRUSHES

PRISON OFFICER'S KEYS

Prison work

If you work in the prison service you will be very sympathetic to your charges. The ability to listen to problems is a great asset in this profession.

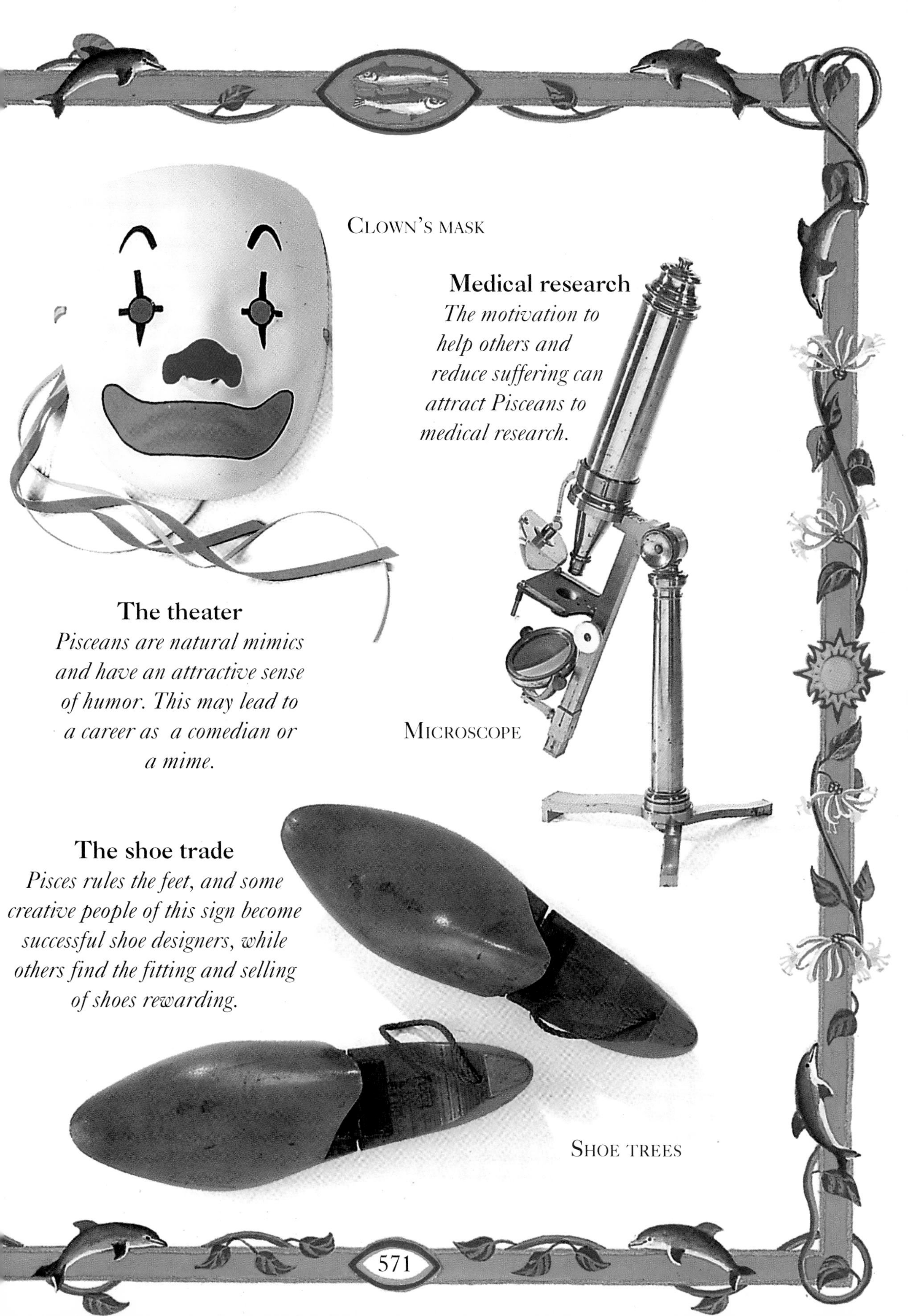

CLOWN'S MASK

Medical research

The motivation to help others and reduce suffering can attract Pisceans to medical research.

The theater

Pisceans are natural mimics and have an attractive sense of humor. This may lead to a career as a comedian or a mime.

MICROSCOPE

The shoe trade

Pisces rules the feet, and some creative people of this sign become successful shoe designers, while others find the fitting and selling of shoes rewarding.

SHOE TREES

PISCES
HEALTH

PISCEANS TEND TO BE UNDISCIPLINED, AND YOU MAY SOMETIMES NEGLECT YOUR HEALTH AND GENERAL WELL-BEING. YOU WOULD THEREFORE BE WISE TO NOTE THE FOLLOWING SUGGESTIONS AND WARNINGS.

The feet are ruled by Pisces, so people of this sign often have problems with this area of their bodies. Exercise sandals are the ideal footwear for them. More serious than problem feet may be your inclination to fall back on forms of escapist behavior, such as drug-taking and excessive drinking. This is because you often have difficulties facing up to reality, as well as a self-deceptive attitude that encourages you to take any easy way out of a problem situation. Sun sign Pisceans should recognize their vulnerability and call upon other, stronger areas of their personality to counter it. The Piscean system often tends to be sensitive, so other people's reactions or bad attitudes can have an adverse physical effect on you.

Your diet

You may benefit from supplementing your diet with Ferrum phosphate (ferr. phos.), which is a combination of iron and oxygen that enriches the blood and soothes inflammation.

Taking care

Interestingly, many Sun sign Pisceans do not respond well to medically prescribed drugs – an allergy to antibiotics is common. Alternative medicine could be the solution to this problem in some cases.

Cucumber
Cucumbers and melons are among the foods traditionally linked with Pisces.

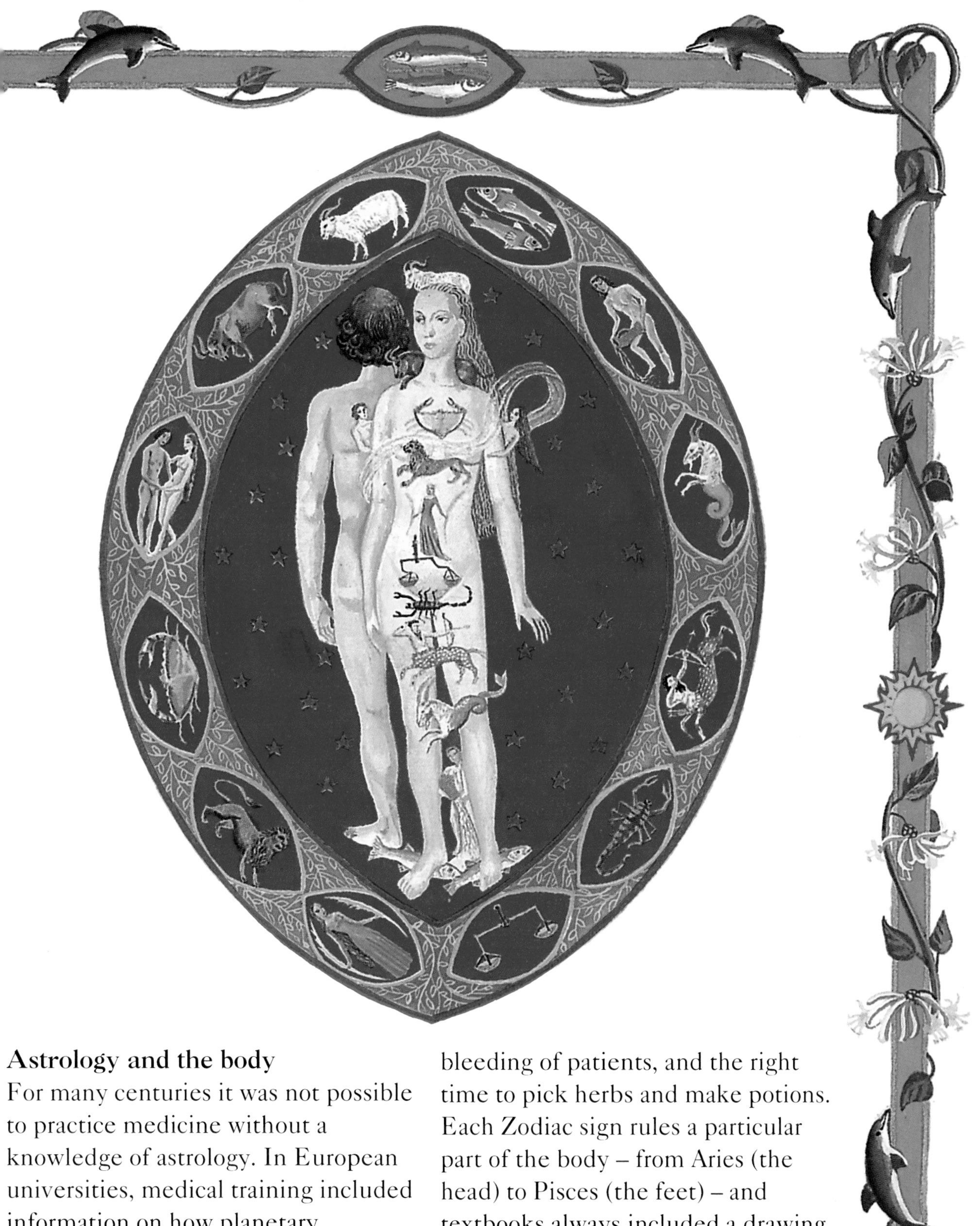

Astrology and the body

For many centuries it was not possible to practice medicine without a knowledge of astrology. In European universities, medical training included information on how planetary positions would affect the administration of medicines, the bleeding of patients, and the right time to pick herbs and make potions. Each Zodiac sign rules a particular part of the body – from Aries (the head) to Pisces (the feet) – and textbooks always included a drawing of a "Zodiac man" (or woman) that illustrated the point.

PISCES AT LEISURE

EACH OF THE SUN SIGNS TRADITIONALLY SUGGESTS SPARE-TIME ACTIVITIES, HOBBIES, AND EVEN VACATION SPOTS. ALTHOUGH THESE ARE ONLY SUGGESTIONS, THEY OFTEN WORK OUT WELL FOR PISCEANS.

POSTAGE STAMPS

Travel

You will enjoy wandering aimlessly on one of the small Mediterranean islands or in the Sahara. Portugal and Scandinavia may also be favorite destinations. You will be eager to try local food, but should watch your digestion.

Flying

The idea of "getting away from it all" is restorative to Pisceans. They will become excited at the thought of taking off in an airplane to enjoy vacations.

1916 AVIATOR'S MAPS

Dance

Lyrical dance movement can provide a non-competitive, steady, rhythmical, and therefore rewarding form of self-expression for Pisceans.

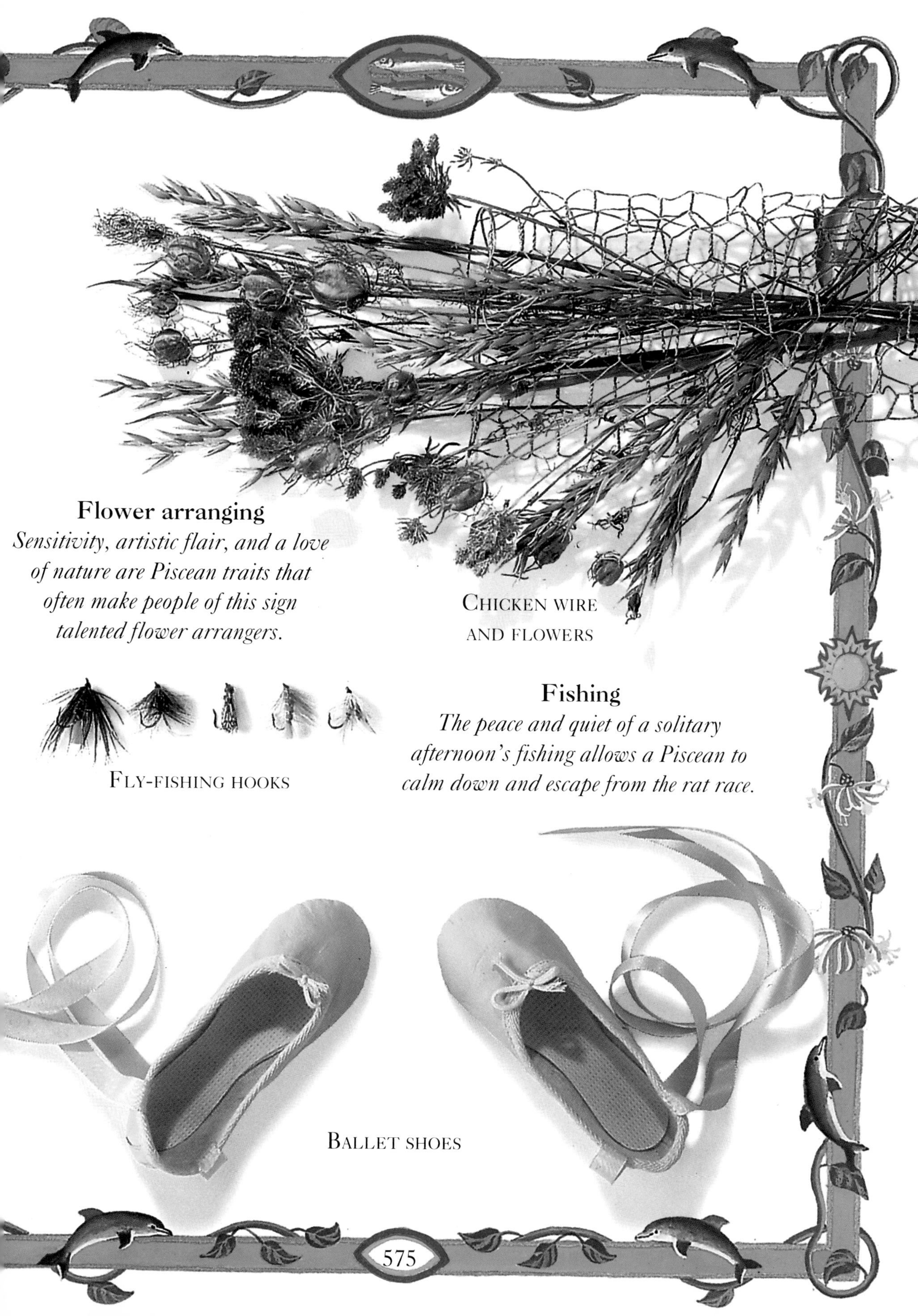

CHICKEN WIRE AND FLOWERS

Flower arranging

Sensitivity, artistic flair, and a love of nature are Piscean traits that often make people of this sign talented flower arrangers.

FLY-FISHING HOOKS

Fishing

The peace and quiet of a solitary afternoon's fishing allows a Piscean to calm down and escape from the rat race.

BALLET SHOES

PISCES IN LOVE

PISCEANS GIVE A GREAT DEAL OF THEMSELVES TO THEIR LOVERS. THIS CAN EITHER BE MARVELOUS FOR BOTH PEOPLE INVOLVED, OR IT CAN MEAN THAT THE PISCEAN WILL SACRIFICE TOO MUCH AND BECOME A DOORMAT

Many Sun sign Pisceans have a tendency to view the world through rose-colored glasses when they are in love. They often delude themselves. You may have to develop a much thicker skin than you naturally possess, and make sure that you are not taken in by a combination of flattery and good looks. Your tendency to idealize your prospective partner may sometimes cause you to either ignore or conveniently overlook the true picture.

Deceptiveness, the main Piscean fault, can surface in another way: because Pisceans hate to hurt others, they may sometimes tell white lies in order to take the easy way out of a difficult situation.

As a lover

Pisceans give a great deal of themselves to their lovers. This can either be marvelous for both people involved, or it can mean that the Piscean will sacrifice too much and become a doormat. They also often instinctively know what their partners are feeling and thinking. This is a useful, if sometimes embarrassing, asset. You are capable of sharing and maintaining an extremely rewarding,

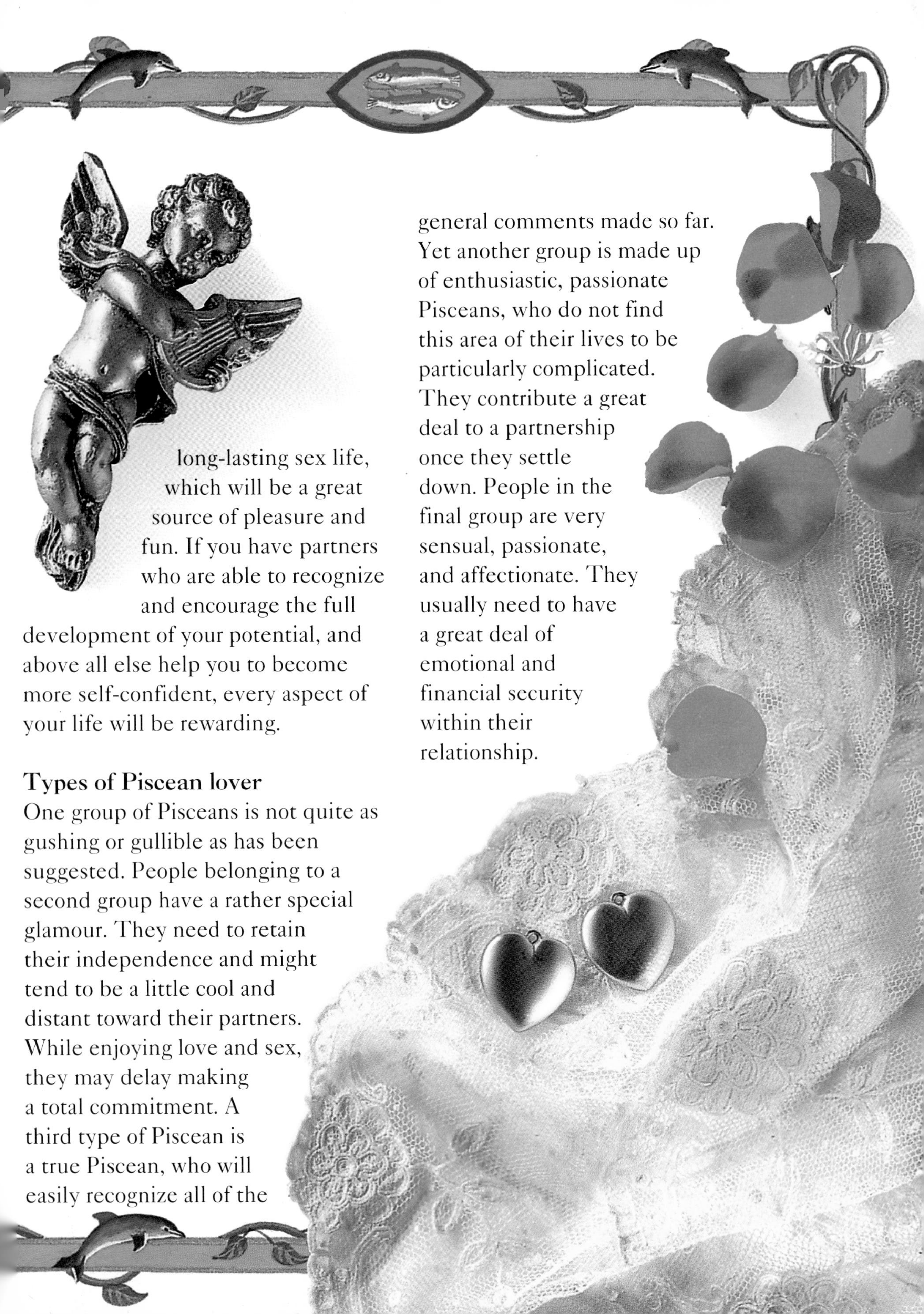

long-lasting sex life, which will be a great source of pleasure and fun. If you have partners who are able to recognize and encourage the full development of your potential, and above all else help you to become more self-confident, every aspect of your life will be rewarding.

Types of Piscean lover

One group of Pisceans is not quite as gushing or gullible as has been suggested. People belonging to a second group have a rather special glamour. They need to retain their independence and might tend to be a little cool and distant toward their partners. While enjoying love and sex, they may delay making a total commitment. A third type of Piscean is a true Piscean, who will easily recognize all of the general comments made so far. Yet another group is made up of enthusiastic, passionate Pisceans, who do not find this area of their lives to be particularly complicated. They contribute a great deal to a partnership once they settle down. People in the final group are very sensual, passionate, and affectionate. They usually need to have a great deal of emotional and financial security within their relationship.

PISCES AT HOME

YOU LIKE YOUR HOME TO BE A HAVEN OF PEACE AND TRANQUILLITY. PALE BLUE OR GREEN SOFT FURNISHINGS WILL REFLECT YOUR QUIET GOOD TASTE, AND A TROPICAL FISH AQUARIUM MAY ADD TO THE OVERALL RELAXED ATMOSPHERE.

The majority of Pisceans like to live near a source of water, ideally in a coastal area. If this is not possible they may design their own small haven of peace and tranquillity in even the most run-down or unappealing type of area. While doing so they may become heavily involved with the local community, and perhaps lend their enthusiastic support to various charitable groups or conservationist organizations.

Bronze vase
A vase or jug in the shape of a fish is not uncommon.

A Piscean home is always guaranteed to be a most interesting place to visit.

Furniture
Comfortable furniture is essential, but because Pisceans tend to be artistic and creative, the appearance of pieces is also important. If you are short of money, the look of your secondhand furniture may be enhanced by imaginative repairs and repainting. Settees and beds are generally jumbo-sized and very soft. You use them to retreat into your own blissfully private, imaginative world. Scrubbed pine is popular for kitchen and dining tables, and you may own a large china

Subtly patterned cushions
Pretty designs and soft colors will feature heavily in any Piscean decorative scheme.

cabinet or cupboard which will be full to the brim not only with cups and plates, but all types of clutter.

Soft furnishings

Piscean invention and imaginative creativity are expressed in the creation of unusual cushions and small items of furniture that enhance more important pieces. Patchwork, screen printing, and sculpting all find their place in the Piscean home.

The curtains and drapes will be either chintzy and floral, or rather shimmery, giving a waterlike appearance. Moiré silk in pale pastel shades of green, blue, or sometimes silvery gray, often features in the Piscean decorative scheme. Floor coverings are generally heavily textured or thick-piled, with Greek flokati rugs being special favorites.

Decorative items

Any paintings that you choose probably have a romantic air, and those that are psychologically restorative and calming are usually preferred. Lighting comes from shaded lamps placed in discreet corners. There may be an aquarium in your home; this will serve as both a container for extoic tropical fish and a purely decorative feature. Pisceans are often good at flower arranging, and dried flowers and bowls of potpourri may be prominently displayed around your home.

Lamp and books
Generous lampshades and piles of books typify the Piscean home.

THE
MOON
AND
YOU

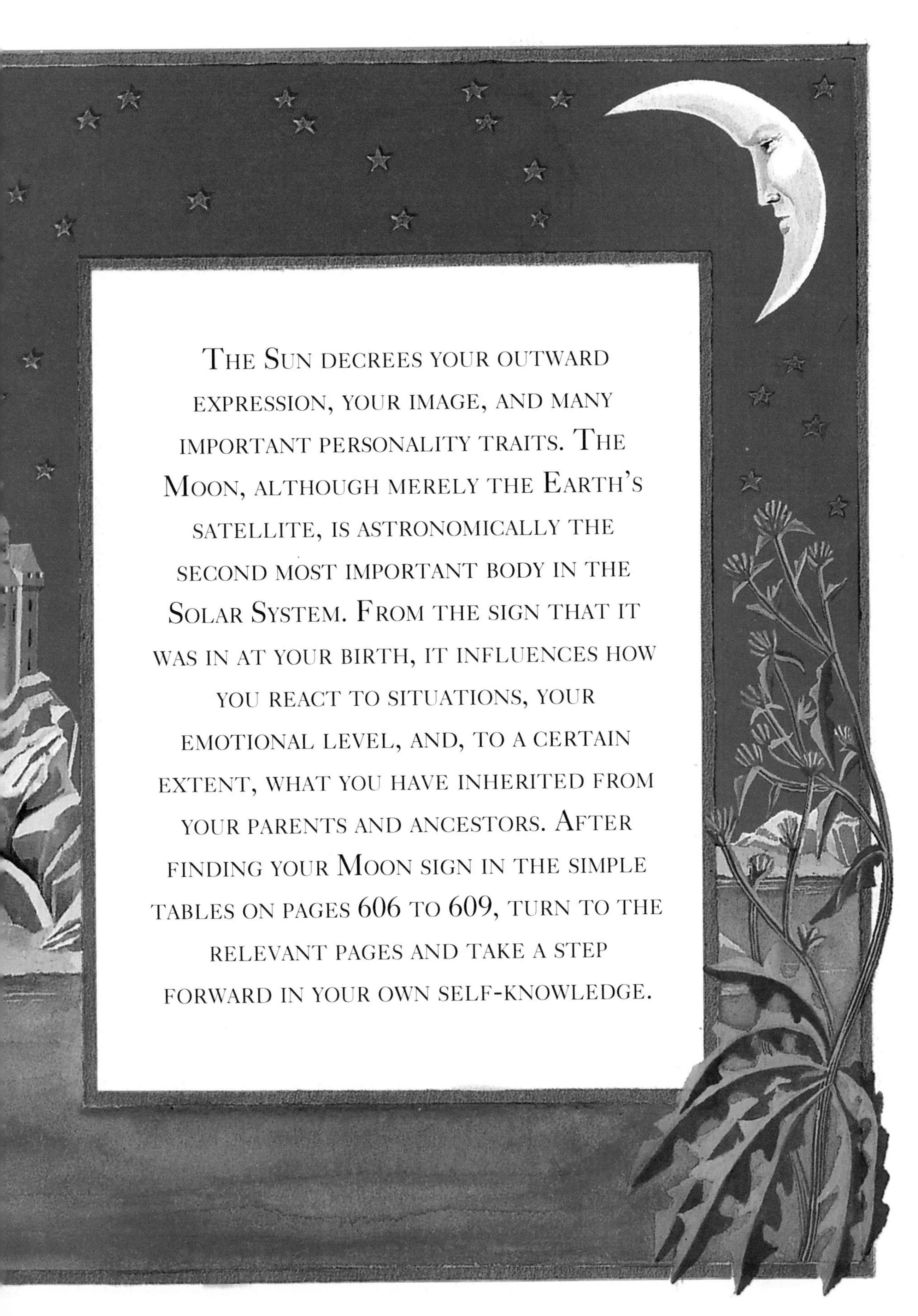

The Sun decrees your outward expression, your image, and many important personality traits. The Moon, although merely the Earth's satellite, is astronomically the second most important body in the Solar System. From the sign that it was in at your birth, it influences how you react to situations, your emotional level, and, to a certain extent, what you have inherited from your parents and ancestors. After finding your Moon sign in the simple tables on pages 606 to 609, turn to the relevant pages and take a step forward in your own self-knowledge.

THE MOON IN ARIES

YOUR FIERY, EMOTIONAL, AND LIVELY MOON LENDS A STRONG POSITIVE FORCE TO YOUR PISCEAN PERSONALITY. DO NOT BE AFRAID TO EXPRESS THIS FREELY. IT ADDS STRENGTH AND ASSERTIVENESS TO YOUR RESPONSES.

While Aries is strong, positive, and assertive, Pisces is gentle, tender, and not at all pushy. The influence of your fiery Moon gives you a powerful source of physical and emotional energy.

Self-expression

You initially respond boldly to challenges, but could later have second thoughts that eat away at your self-confidence and cause you to backtrack. Aim to move forward steadily, and to allow the gentler, more conscientious elements of your Piscean Sun to be stimulated by the strong forces of your Arien Moon.

Romance

You possess both the fiery, expressive emotion of Aries and the deep, intense emotion that derives from Pisces. In addition to these qualities you are passionate and are likely to fall in and out of love very quickly.

Your Arien Moon probably makes you more resistant to being upset than most Pisceans, and you have the ability to detach yourself once you realize that an affair is over. You have what it takes to enjoy a rewarding, fulfilling relationship, although the worst Arien fault, selfishness, could surface at times.

Your well-being

The Arien body area is the head, and you could suffer from more than an average number of headaches. These are probably the result of worry and tension. There can be a link between headaches and slight kidney disorders, so it is worth getting a medical checkup if they persist.

Like many people with an Arien emphasis, you are usually in a hurry. Because of this, you could be somewhat accident-prone; consciously take care, particularly when working with sharp tools or hot dishes.

The Moon in Aries

Although you probably enjoy sports and exercise, you do need to watch your diet. You may not worry much about it, and Piscean haste could encourage you to consume an excessive amount of junk food.

Planning ahead

You may well have an enterprising spirit that could supply you with a useful second income. However, seek financial advice when you have money to invest. Otherwise you may make serious mistakes. These will be the result of combining soft-hearted Piscean traits with those of an over-enthusiastic Arien.

Parenthood

You will be a sympathetic parent and will be anxious to see your children make progress. You will not find it difficult to keep up with their ideas. Try not to continually change your mind, or your children will not know where they stand with you.

THE MOON IN TAURUS

YOUR PISCEAN KINDNESS AND SYMPATHY DO NOT ALWAYS WORK TO YOUR COMPLETE ADVANTAGE. LISTEN TO YOUR SENSIBLE AND PRACTICAL TAUREAN MOON, AND MAKE AN EFFORT TO CURB POSSESSIVE REACTIONS.

The water element of your Piscean Sun and the earth element of your Taurean Moon blend well. You are far more reliable and stable than many Sun sign Pisceans.

Self-expression

The Moon is traditionally well placed in Taurus, which means that its influence on you is particularly strong. It gives you backbone and acts as a marvelous anchor to your personality, calming what can sometimes be a turbulent spirit.

When challenged, you face up to reality with great practicality. You can be very firm and decisive, and should always follow your most deep-rooted instincts and intuition.

Both Pisces and Taurus have considerable creative potential, and Taurus is particularly appreciative of beauty. If you enjoy embroidery, pottery, craftwork, and music, you should develop these interests.

Romance

It is very important for you to have a secure background. Material security does not always interest Pisceans, but your Taurean Moon puts an emphasis on both it and emotional security.

You will relax into and enjoy a relationship with a partner who you feel you can trust. You are a powerful source of affection and sexuality, being sensual and passionate. When you feel secure, these qualities do much to enhance your relationship.

The worst Taurean fault is possessiveness, and you will sometimes try to own your partners. Be aware that they may need some independence within a relationship.

Your well-being

The Taurean body area is traditionally said to cover the throat and neck. Your colds are likely to begin with a very sore throat and end with a cough. Make sure that you

The Moon in Taurus

keep the appropriate medicines on hand so that you can relieve any discomfort as soon as possible.

Taurus loves rich and often sweet food, so you may have a tendency to gain weight, especially since Pisceans can suffer from a similar difficulty. Discipline yourself into a reasonable diet and a regular exercise routine.

Planning ahead

You have an above-average capacity to cope with finance; it is far better than that of most Pisceans. If you do seek financial advice, you will be surprised at how close your own ideas are to those of your adviser. You will probably want to own your own home as early in life as possible.

Parenthood

You will be stricter with your children than most Pisceans and will discipline them sensibly. They will know where they stand with you, but you may have to make a conscious effort to understand their problems if you are to avoid the generation gap.

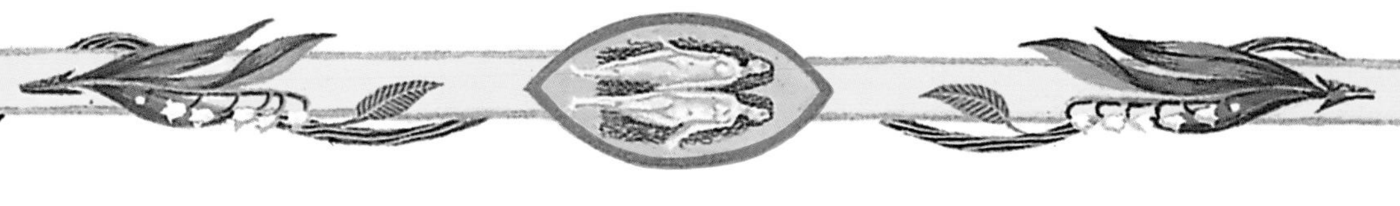

THE MOON IN GEMINI

YOUR MOON HELPS YOU TO RATIONALIZE YOUR POWERFUL PISCEAN EMOTIONS. PISCES AND GEMINI ARE BOTH DUAL SIGNS, WHICH MEANS THAT YOU ARE NATURALLY VERSATILE. YOU MUST CURB SUPERFICIALITY AND BE CONSISTENT.

The chances are that you will be a free-thinker with a flexible, open mind. This is largely because Pisces and Gemini are both mutable signs. You are also extremely versatile, enjoying a great variety of interests, and finding it easy to converse with many different kinds of people on a wide range of subjects.

Self-expression

You are a marvelous communicator and are able to get your ideas across very easily. It is, however, entirely possible that you may alter your opinions at a moment's notice.

You respond to proposals with a flurry of words, showing great enthusiasm if you like what is put to you and producing a variety of hastily invented excuses if you do not. Because of your Piscean Sun, you may lack self-confidence and could try to cover the fact by being nervously talkative. Try to take your time, and remember that a few well-chosen sentences can make a far better impression than a tumble of words.

Romance

You are probably unlikely to be completely overwhelmed by your emotions. You may rationalize your feelings, especially when you first fall in love. Try not to restrain your emotions. A certain measure of skepticism from your Geminian Moon is valuable, but do not let it smother the heart's affections. Bear in mind, too, that friendship and a good measure of intellectual rapport are as essential for you in a long-term relationship as a good sex life.

Your well-being

The Geminian body area covers the arms and hands. Yours are therefore vulnerable, perhaps to minor accidents. The Geminian organ is the lungs. Do not allow a cough to hang

The Moon in Gemini

on for more than a few days before resorting to prescribed antibiotics. Anyone with a Geminian emphasis should not smoke.

Restlessness can affect your health, but a relaxation discipline could help counter this. If your metabolism is fast, you will be less likely than most Pisceans to suffer from weight gain.

Planning ahead

Pisceans are often not particularly adept at finance, and money tends to burn holes in Geminian pockets. Resist sob-stories from those who wish to borrow your money, and get financial advice, especially before leaping into get-rich-quick schemes.

Parenthood

You will be both a loving and a very lively parent: youthful and alert, and with few generation gap problems. You may need to be a little more strict than you are if your children are to know precisely where they stand with you. Remember that they need a sense of security.

THE MOON IN CANCER

BOTH PISCES AND CANCER ARE SIGNS OF THE WATER ELEMENT, SO YOUR EMOTIONS, INTUITION, AND IMAGINATION ARE HIGHLY REFINED. YOU MUST TRY TO CHANNEL THEM IN A CONSTRUCTIVE AND POSITIVE WAY.

With Pisces and Cancer both being water signs, you have some very powerful, emotionally oriented forces within your personality. The Moon rules Cancer and is at its strongest and most influential from that sign. It will have a deep effect on your personality.

Self-expression

You have considerable strength and determination; when you are challenged in any way, an immediate and powerful self-defensive system springs into action. You respond strongly, either kindly and sympathetically or sharply, according to your opinions and the way you feel.

Both Pisces and Cancer enhance your powers of imagination, and you should always try to express your creativity, perhaps inventively. If you do not, your imagination may work overtime in a negative way. Your instincts and emotions are very powerful. If you feel that you should take a particular line of action, you will probably be right to do so. But always calm yourself down before doing anything important.

Romance

You will be a very passionate, sensual lover and will make a wonderful partner in a long-term relationship or marriage. You know how to please your lover both in and out of bed, and will not find it difficult to achieve sexual fulfillment. Make sure that you do not nag your partner, and remember that in expressing your love, it can be all too easy for you to create a claustrophobic atmosphere.

Your well-being

The Cancerian body area covers the breasts and chest. It is therefore advisable for Cancerian women to be particularly diligent in examining their breasts regularly, although there

The Moon in Cancer

is, of course, no connection between the Zodiac sign Cancer and the disease with the same name.

You enjoy good food and may well be prone to weight gain. Try to discipline yourself into getting regular exercise, perhaps swimming.

Planning ahead

Those with a Cancerian emphasis have a very shrewd business sense and are talented at making the most of what money they have. You will have some good ideas about what to do with your money, but your Piscean Sun may detract from them, and you could be overly generous to charity. Seek professional advice when you have money to invest.

Parenthood

You will be among the most sensitive and caring of all Piscean Sun and Moon sign parents, and will stimulate your children's imagination and encourage their efforts. You will be strict enough to discipline your children as and when necessary, but warm and comforting when they are distressed. Make sure that you do not get too sentimental; this could lead to problems with the generation gap.

THE MOON IN LEO

YOU HAVE MARVELOUS POTENTIAL, CAN RESPOND POSITIVELY TO MOST SITUATIONS, AND ARE PROBABLY BETTER ORGANIZED THAN MOST PISCEANS. AT TIMES, YOU MAY BE PRETTY BOSSY – BUT THAT CAN BE USEFUL TO A SENSITIVE PISCEAN.

There are some very vivid contrasts between the qualities of Pisces and Leo, but this is still a stunning combination. It makes you a fascinating individual with exciting, dynamic potential.

Self-expression

Your fiery Moon contributes a wonderfully positive enthusiasm when you are challenged. No doubt you are far more self-assured than many people of your Sun sign, and certainly much better organized. You could also be more self-confident and, at times, perhaps rather bossy.

Pisces and Leo are probably the two Zodiac signs with the most creative potential. Pisceans often do not have the confidence to develop this quality, but your Leo Moon will help you to overcome your inhibitions. Always aim to achieve the highest standard and to make a dramatic impact, whatever you do.

Romance

Like Pisces, Leo is a very emotional sign. You express your passion with great feeling and are a very ardent lover. You make a caring partner, but probably fall in love often and suffer heartbreak just as much as, if not more than, other Pisceans.

You are very sensitive and, when hurt, will instinctively creep into your lair and lick your wounds in private. It is probable that you will want to look up to and admire your partner. You will always be a splendid power behind a throne, but you also need to share it. Avoid any inclination to dominate your partner.

Your well-being

The Leo body area covers the back and spine, and yours may be vulnerable. If you work at a desk you might benefit from an ergonomic chair. Exercise will also keep the back and spine in good order.

The Moon in Leo

The Leo organ is the heart, and it also needs exercise. Work out at a health club, or find some form of exercise that expresses your sense of drama and creative talent.

Planning ahead

Unlike most Pisceans, you enjoy doing things in style and spend freely on luxuries. Since you are also generous by nature, you will need to earn a relatively high salary.

You will probably be inclined to invest in fairly safe, well-established companies making quality products. Make sure that you get your decisions confirmed by a professional financial adviser before you invest large sums of money.

Parenthood

Leo is a sign that is traditionally related to parenthood. You will make an enthusiastic parent, always ready to praise and encourage your children.

While you should not suffer from too many generation gap problems, you should try to allow your children to develop their own interests, and refrain from forcing your ideas upon them. Do not expect them to achieve goals that have always eluded you.

THE MOON IN VIRGO

PISCES AND VIRGO ARE POLAR OR OPPOSITE ZODIAC SIGNS, WHICH MEANS THAT YOU WERE BORN UNDER A FULL MOON. INNER DISCONTENT AND RESTLESSNESS MAY BOTHER YOU, BUT DO NOT BE WEIGHED DOWN BY BAD FEELINGS.

We all have a tendency to express the attitudes of our polar, or opposite, Zodiac sign. Every sign has its partner across the horoscope; for you this is Virgo, and since the Moon was in this sign when you were born, the polarity is expressed in a very interesting way.

Self-expression

Virgo is an earth sign, and this element blends well with the water element of Pisces, making you practical and rational. You are an excellent communicator, and enjoy a good, lively discussion or argument.

It is possible that you may not be very self-confident, and a certain shyness can inhibit you. You are very good at covering this up, perhaps by being overly talkative, but your lack of self-confidence is very deeply rooted. When asked to organize something, or when an opportunity for promotion occurs, you may well not be willing to accept it. It is entirely possible that you are seriously underestimating your abilities.

Romance

Lack of confidence could also emerge when someone makes a romantic approach to you. You have a delightful natural modesty, but do not let it inhibit you to the extent where you lose the opportunity for what might be a rewarding relationship.

Also bear in mind that the worst Virgoan fault is to be overcritical. Beware of a tendency to nag your partner; it could be devastating.

Your well-being

The Virgoan body area covers the stomach, and since those with a Virgoan influence are very prone to worry, the physical effects usually center around an upset stomach, pains, and cramps. You need a high-fiber diet, and may be sympathetic to

The Moon in Virgo

vegetarianism. Perhaps you are less prone to weight gain than many Pisceans. This could be because you have a high metabolism and therefore a lot of nervous energy to burn. Exercising will alleviate restlessness and encourage sleep. You will favor outdoor sporting activities.

Planning ahead

You are careful with money, and may be too worried about losing it to take any undue risks. You would be wise to go for safe investments with steady growth and to obtain financial advice when you have money to invest.

Parenthood

You will be sensitive and caring with your children, but may tend to be hypercritical. Help them to develop their imaginations and creative abilities by expressing your own. It should not be hard for you to keep up with your children's ideas and thus avoid the generation gap.

THE MOON IN LIBRA

PISCES AND LIBRA ARE GENTLE SIGNS. YOU COULD FEIGN A VERY CALM ATTITUDE WHEN MAKING DECISIONS. TRY TO MAKE AN EFFORT TO DEVELOP A MORE PRACTICAL APPROACH TO LIFE, OR YOU MAY NOT FEEL FULFILLED.

The effect of both Pisces and Libra can be to make their subjects charming, friendly, kind, and very sympathetic. You show gentle understanding when challenged or confronted, but may not be eager to make essential snap decisions.

Self-expression

You should consciously try to be more forthright and assertive, and perhaps also more rational and constructively self-critical.

You are diplomatic and always have time for other people, especially if they are upset or in trouble. You have the knack of relaxing them and making them feel much better.

Your Sun and Moon sign combination does not give you a great deal of inner strength, although it is perfectly possible that the influence of other planets within the Solar System have strengthened your psychological muscle.

Romance

You are probably extremely romantic and have a tendency to fall in love with love itself. You may well not feel psychologically whole until you are sharing an emotional relationship.

You are very attractive to the opposite sex, and capable of enjoying a highly rewarding love and sex life.

Your well-being

The lumbar region of the back is ruled by Libra, and you may therefore benefit from an ergonomic chair. The Libran organ is the kidneys, and it is possible that you suffer from an above-average number of headaches. Pressure from other people may provoke these but, if this is not the case, it will be well worth getting a checkup, just in case you have a slight problem with your kidneys.

You probably loathe exercise, but may put on weight if you avoid it completely. Try to be disciplined

The Moon in Libra

about this and about what you eat. Do remember that too much smoking, drinking, or any kind of negative escapism is not good for you. Also note that you can react very badly to many drugs.

Planning ahead

You enjoy your creature comforts, so much of the money that you make probably slips too easily through your fingers. It would be wise for you to follow a savings plan in which a regular payment is deducted from your salary. You are also so generous that some people may seek to take advantage of you. Seek professional advice in all money matters.

Parenthood

You will be a very easygoing parent, and your children will discover that they can manipulate you. They will appreciate your tremendous kindness and sympathy, but remember that children also benefit from a certain amount of discipline. The generation gap should not prove to be a problem.

THE MOON IN SCORPIO

BOTH PISCES AND SCORPIO ARE SIGNS OF THE WATER ELEMENT, WHICH WILL HEIGHTEN YOUR ALREADY ABUNDANT PISCEAN EMOTIONS. LET DETERMINATION OVERCOME INHIBITION AND ANY LACK OF SELF-CONFIDENCE. SUPPRESS JEALOUSY.

Scorpio is, in many respects, the strongest of the 12 Zodiac signs. Since it is of the water element, its influence blends well with that of your Sun sign.

Self-expression
In addition to your Piscean qualities, you have further inner strength, and considerable resilience and determination when faced with a challenge or a demanding situation. These qualities encourage you to overcome any Piscean reticence, shyness, or lack of self-confidence.

You need to be emotionally involved with your work. While you enjoy making money, it is still more important for you to obtain inner satisfaction from your job.

Romance
You are highly sexed and very passionate. You need an energetic partner who can match your passion, who will challenge you and keep you stimulated. The worst Scorpio fault is jealousy, and you may sometimes succumb to it. Bear in mind that you could create a somewhat claustrophobic atmosphere within your relationship.

Your well-being
The Scorpio body area covers the genitals. Male Scorpios should therefore regularly examine their testicles for malformations, and women should have cervical smears.

Those with a Scorpio emphasis love good food and wine, and are therefore likely to gain weight. Moderation is the best solution to this problem.

Planning ahead
You will probably cope well with money; much better, in fact, than many Sun sign Pisceans. You may have a certain financial flair, but could tend to put too many eggs in a single

The Moon in Scorpio

basket. If you feel that this tendency is likely to affect you, you should go for safe savings plans and, if you are feeling adventurous, seek professional financial advice.

Although many Scorpio types manage to do well in their own businesses, they sometimes get rather bored, make an attempt to organize a change, and finally end up going too far. In the end they are faced with no real choice but to start again at the very bottom.

Parenthood

While Pisces is likely to make you a kind and easygoing parent, your Scorpio Moon encourages you to be much stricter. This is fine, since it enables you to give your children a good, secure background. You will, however, probably have to make a conscious effort to learn about your children's concerns and problems if you are to avoid running into the many problems associated with the generation gap.

THE MOON IN
SAGITTARIUS

BEFORE NEPTUNE WAS DISCOVERED, THE PLANET JUPITER RULED BOTH SAGITTARIUS AND PISCES. THERE IS THEREFORE A NATURAL SYMPATHY BETWEEN THEM, WHICH IS HEIGHTENED BY THE FACT THAT THEY ARE DUAL AND MUTABLE SIGNS.

Many Sagittarians respond to challenges in a lively, optimistic, and enthusiastic way. In fact they thrive on them and derive a great deal of excitement from them.

Self-expression

Although you are very good at grasping the overall view of any situation, you could find the details terribly boring. You have a tremendous zest for life and enjoy action more than many Pisceans. Your outlook is philosophical, and you have an admirable mind that should always be engaged in study of some kind, perhaps of a foreign language.

Romance

You have the positive, fiery emotion of Sagittarius, as well as the more sensitive emotion of Pisces. They combine well when it comes to love and sex. You could well have something of a roving eye, and will certainly get a lot of fun out of this sphere of your life. You tend to fall in and out of love rather often, but will take a broken heart in your stride and readily accept the challenge of finding someone new.

Once you have settled down, other factors come into play, and you will get great satisfaction from a rewarding love and sex life with a partner who is also a good friend.

Your well-being

The Sagittarian body area covers the hips and thighs, and women with this sign emphasized are more than likely to put on weight in those areas. The Sagittarian organ is the liver, and hangovers are often common, so keep a remedy on hand.

A preference for rather heavy dishes and good wine and beer can mean a buildup of weight, so follow your Sagittarian Moon and keep up with sports. Riding is traditionally a

The Moon in Sagittarius

Sagittarian form of exercise. Restlessness is the worst Sagittarian fault. You should try to curb it, or it will lead to stress and tension because of feelings of unfulfillment. Alternating from physical to mental interests and vice versa provides an excellent antidote.

Planning ahead

It is important for you to seek financial advice when you want to start an investment or savings plan. Being a Piscean soft touch is one thing, but having a Sagittarian inclination to take a gamble is quite another. You could fall very easily for get-rich-quick schemes. If you must place a bet, never stake more money than you can easily afford to lose.

Parenthood

You will be an enthusiastic parent and will be extremely eager to encourage your children to stimulate their minds. In addition to this, you will have a great deal of fun with them, and should have almost no difficulty in keeping up with their ideas. The specter of the generation gap should therefore hold no real terrors for you.

THE MOON IN CAPRICORN

YOU HAVE HIGH ASPIRATIONS, BUT YOUR SENSITIVE PISCEAN SUN SIGN COULD INHIBIT PROGRESS. BE SELF-CONFIDENT AND AMBITIOUS, AND FOLLOW YOUR INSTINCTS. THEY MAY WELL BE MORE PRACTICALLY FOUNDED THAN YOU REALIZE.

The elements of water, for Pisces, and earth, for Capricorn, blend well and give you some very positive common sense.

Self-expression

When challenged, you could be somewhat overcautious. This is fine for a Sun sign Piscean, provided that your natural caution does not sap your self-confidence. To avoid this, set yourself ambitious but attainable objectives, and make sure that you continually aspire to meet every one of them.

There is another side to the Capricornian influence, which could cause you to grumble or to take a negative view of life. Try not to let this tendency get the better of you.

Romance

Your Capricornian Moon prevents you from being gullible in your love life, and you are less likely than many Pisceans to don rose-colored spectacles when falling in love. Capricorn is not a sign that bestows a high emotional level; Pisces, on the other hand, gives you a capacity to express emotion forcefully towards a partner. You are probably very faithful and eager to see your partner progress in life. Possibly more than most people, you need security within your relationship. You will work really hard for this and do everything in your power to make it work. Do not allow feelings of inferiority to creep into your attitude.

Your well-being

The Capricornian body area covers the knees and shins, as well as the bones, teeth, and skin. It is important for you to get exercise to keep you moving. Jogging, aerobics, or even walking will ensure that you keep rheumatic pains and stiffness of the joints, especially in the knees, at bay.

The Moon in Capricorn

Your skin could be rather sensitive, whatever your race, and it is best to protect it from the sun. You should also have regular dental checkups.

Most people with a Capricornian influence are not heavy eaters. Provided that your Piscean influence does not make you lazy, you should have no problems with your weight.

Planning ahead

You probably cope fairly well with money, although you may have a tendency to think that you are less well-off than you really are. You must get value for your money, so seek financial advice when investing.

Parenthood

You will be a kind, understanding parent and will discipline your children fairly whenever it is necessary. Be careful to avoid undue criticism or put-downs, and allow your tender Sun sign qualities plenty of expression. If you listen to your children, you will leap across the generation gap.

THE MOON IN AQUARIUS

YOU ARE ALL EMOTION, BUT THE COOL DETACHMENT OF AQUARIUS WHICH COLORS YOUR REACTIONS MAY MAKE YOU APPEAR A LITTLE BRITTLE. YOUR SENSITIVE, CHARITABLE PISCEAN WARMTH USUALLY EMERGES WHEN PEOPLE GET TO KNOW YOU.

The tender warmth of Pisces is contrasted in a very vivid and exciting way against the cool glamour and originality of Aquarius. When challenged, you find it easy to distance yourself from a problem and to respond logically.

Self-expression

You may sometimes give the impression of being cool and distant. However, once people get to know you, they discover a very different person. Aquarius is known for general friendliness and kind, humanitarian qualities, and Pisces for charity. You will therefore give a great deal of yourself to people in need.

Romance

You are a very caring, loving, and tender partner with a high emotional level. While you are extremely attractive to the opposite sex, you may distance yourself when you feel that a prospective lover is pressing you too fast. You have a very independent streak that may well influence your whole lifestyle. Perhaps you have built a life that is in some way unique. If this is the case, do not allow yourself to be pressured into changing it. Aim to achieve a rewarding love and sex life with partners who recognize your strong need for independence.

Your well-being

The Aquarian body area covers the ankles. Because Pisces rules the feet, and since your ankles are vulnerable due to your Moon sign's influence, you need to make sure that you always buy comfortable footwear.

The circulation is also ruled by Aquarius but, while you may feel the cold fairly easily, you also enjoy cold, clear winter weather. Make sure that you keep warm by wearing several layers of light clothing.

The Moon in Aquarius

It is advisable for you to try to get aesthetic satisfaction from exercise, so that your mind, body, and spirit will be at one. You also need to keep moving because of possible circulation problems. You could well be a natural iceskater, skier, or synchronized swimmer.

Planning ahead

Coping with money may not be very easy for you – unless other planets within the Solar System contribute a positive influence to this sphere. You may spend heavily on glamorous items. Always seek professional advice before investing.

Parenthood

Your attitude toward your children may be unconventional. You have plenty of ideas about bringing them up; make sure they always know where they stand. You look to the future, so the generation gap should not trouble you.

THE MOON IN
PISCES

BECAUSE THE SUN AND THE MOON WERE BOTH IN PISCES AT THE MOMENT OF YOUR BIRTH, YOU WERE BORN UNDER A FULL MOON. SINCE PISCES IS A WATER SIGN, THIS ELEMENT POWERFULLY INFLUENCES YOUR PERSONALITY AND REACTIONS.

When you read a list of the characteristics of your sensitive and emotional Sun sign, you will probably recognize that many of them apply to you. On average, out of a list of perhaps 20 personality traits attached to a Sun sign, most people identify with 11 or 12. For you the average increases greatly, since the Sun and the Moon were both in Pisces when you were born.

Self-expression

Your Sun sign makes you highly imaginative and gives you some very powerful emotions; because the Moon was also in Pisces when you were born, you will sometimes react very emotionally to situations.

Far more than most Sun sign Pisceans, you will be inclined to decide on one line of action, and then do the opposite. As a result of this, you may cause yourself a considerable amount of worry and confusion.

Romance

You will give a great deal of yourself to your lovers and readily make sacrifices for them. Think about this, and make sure that you do not compromise too often.

You want a good, stable relationship and a partner who will encourage and support you, spurring you on to express your potential. You are a very sensual lover, and will enjoy a rich and rewarding sex life with your partner. It is possible that you fall in love too easily, and you could well deceive yourself about your lovers' qualities, ignoring their faults and foibles. Be cautious in this sphere.

Your well-being

The comments made on pages 572 to 573 about Piscean health and well-being really do apply to you. You can hardly escape having problem feet and must recognize their great vulnerability. Only go barefoot in the

The Moon in Pisces

house; otherwise you will pick up foot infections very easily. Also watch your eating habits. Many Pisceans are prone to weight gain, and this tendency will probably affect you more than most. Although you may not be enthusiastic about the idea, you should discipline yourself in the way that you eat, and make sure that you take regular exercise.

Planning ahead

In regard to money, the less you have to do with balancing your books the better. This may be something that a partner should take care of. If you have money to invest, then get professional advice. If you have a regular income, embark on a savings plan in which contributions can be deducted at the source.

Parenthood

You may find disciplining your children rather difficult, and you could spoil them. For their sakes, and your own peace of mind, work on disciplining them when they start to grow up. Because you have an instinctive understanding of human nature, you should have no problems with the generation gap.

MOON CHARTS

THE FOLLOWING TABLES WILL ENABLE YOU TO DISCOVER YOUR MOON SIGN. THEN, BY REFERRING TO THE PRECEDING PAGES, YOU WILL BE ABLE TO INVESTIGATE ITS QUALITIES, AND SEE HOW THEY WORK WITH YOUR SUN SIGN.

By referring to the charts on pages 607, 608, and 609 locate the Zodiacal glyph for the month of the year in which you were born. Using the Moon table on this page, find the number opposite the day you were born that month. Then, starting from the glyph you found first, count off that number using the list of Zodiacal glyphs (below, right). You may have to count to Pisces and continue with Aries. For example, if you were born on May 21, 1991, first you need to find the Moon sign on the chart on page 609. Look down the chart to May; the glyph is Sagittarius (♐). Then consult the Moon table for the 21st. It tells you to add nine glyphs. Starting from Sagittarius, count down nine, and you find your Moon sign is Virgo (♍).

MOON TABLE

DAYS OF THE MONTH AND NUMBER OF SIGNS THAT SHOULD BE ADDED

DAY	ADD	DAY	ADD	DAY	ADD	DAY	ADD
1	0	9	4	17	7	25	11
2	1	10	4	18	8	26	11
3	1	11	5	19	8	27	12
4	1	12	5	20	9	28	12
5	2	13	5	21	9	29	1
6	2	14	6	22	10	30	1
7	3	15	6	23	10	31	2
8	3	16	7	24	10		

ZODIACAL GLYPHS

♈	Aries
♉	Taurus
♊	Gemini
♋	Cancer
♌	Leo
♍	Virgo
♎	Libra
♏	Scorpio
♐	Sagittarius
♑	Capricorn
♒	Aquarius
♓	Pisces

	1923	1924	1925	1926	1927	1928	1929	1930	1931	1932	1933	1934	1935
JAN	♊	♏	♈	♌	♐	♈	♍	♑	♉	♎	♓	♋	♏
FEB	♌	♐	♉	♍	♑	♊	♏	♓	♋	♐	♈	♌	♑
MAR	♌	♑	♉	♍	♒	♋	♏	♓	♋	♐	♉	♍	♑
APR	♎	♓	♋	♏	♈	♍	♑	♉	♍	♒	♊	♎	♓
MAY	♏	♈	♌	♐	♉	♎	♒	♊	♎	♓	♋	♐	♈
JUN	♑	♉	♍	♒	♋	♏	♓	♌	♐	♉	♍	♑	♊
JUL	♒	♋	♏	♓	♌	♐	♈	♍	♑	♊	♎	♓	♋
AUG	♈	♌	♐	♉	♍	♒	♊	♏	♓	♋	♐	♈	♌
SEP	♉	♎	♒	♋	♏	♓	♌	♐	♈	♍	♑	♊	♎
OCT	♊	♏	♓	♌	♐	♉	♍	♑	♉	♎	♓	♋	♏
NOV	♌	♑	♉	♍	♑	♊	♏	♓	♋	♐	♈	♌	♑
DEC	♍	♒	♊	♎	♓	♌	♐	♈	♌	♑	♉	♍	♒

	1936	1937	1938	1939	1940	1941	1942	1943	1944	1945	1946	1947	1948
JAN	♈	♌	♑	♉	♍	♒	♊	♎	♓	♌	♐	♈	♍
FEB	♉	♎	♒	♊	♏	♈	♌	♐	♉	♍	♑	♊	♎
MAR	♊	♎	♒	♋	♐	♈	♌	♐	♉	♎	♒	♊	♏
APR	♌	♐	♈	♌	♑	♉	♎	♒	♋	♏	♓	♌	♑
MAY	♍	♑	♉	♎	♒	♊	♏	♓	♌	♐	♉	♍	♒
JUN	♎	♒	♋	♏	♈	♌	♑	♉	♎	♒	♊	♏	♓
JUL	♏	♈	♌	♑	♉	♍	♒	♊	♏	♓	♌	♐	♈
AUG	♑	♉	♎	♒	♋	♏	♈	♌	♐	♉	♍	♑	♊
SEP	♓	♋	♏	♈	♌	♑	♉	♍	♒	♋	♏	♓	♌
OCT	♈	♌	♑	♉	♎	♒	♊	♎	♓	♌	♐	♈	♍
NOV	♊	♎	♒	♊	♏	♈	♌	♐	♉	♍	♑	♊	♏
DEC	♋	♏	♓	♌	♑	♉	♍	♑	♊	♎	♒	♋	♐

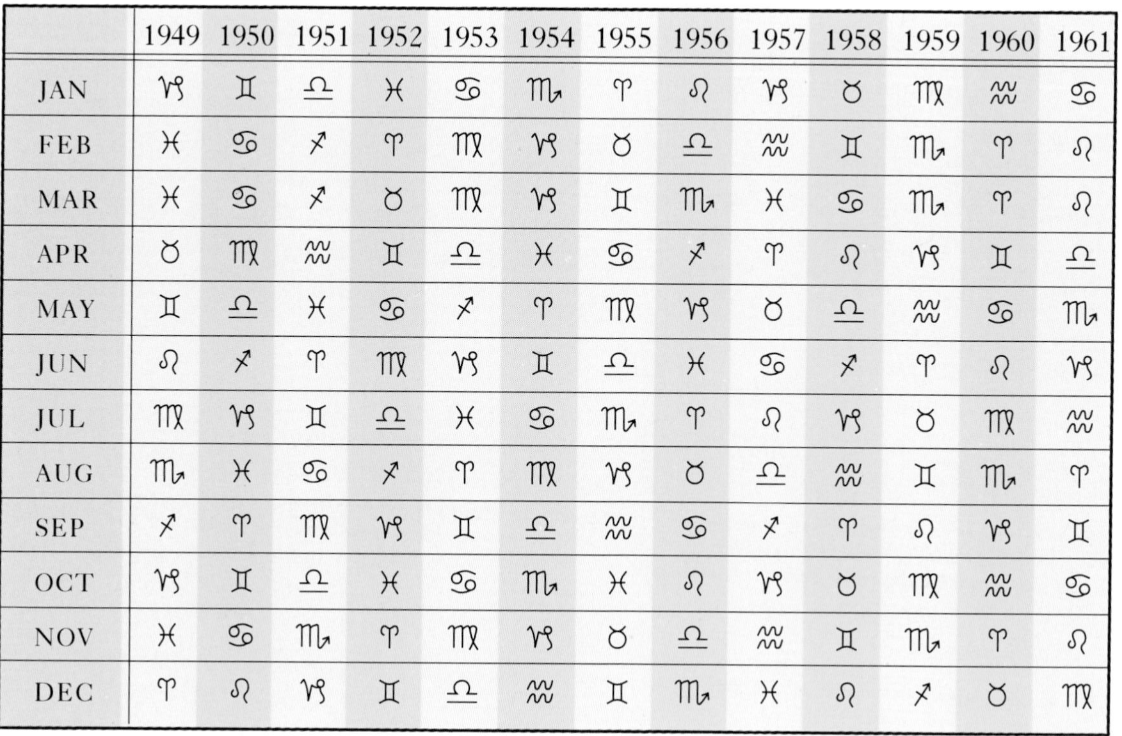

	1949	1950	1951	1952	1953	1954	1955	1956	1957	1958	1959	1960	1961
JAN	♑	♊	♎	♓	♋	♏	♈	♌	♑	♉	♍	♒	♋
FEB	♓	♋	♐	♈	♍	♑	♉	♎	♒	♊	♏	♈	♌
MAR	♓	♋	♐	♉	♍	♑	♊	♏	♓	♋	♏	♈	♌
APR	♉	♍	♒	♊	♎	♓	♋	♐	♈	♌	♑	♊	♎
MAY	♊	♎	♓	♋	♐	♈	♍	♑	♉	♎	♒	♋	♏
JUN	♌	♐	♈	♍	♑	♊	♎	♓	♋	♐	♈	♌	♑
JUL	♍	♑	♊	♎	♓	♋	♏	♈	♌	♑	♉	♍	♒
AUG	♏	♓	♋	♐	♈	♍	♑	♉	♎	♒	♊	♏	♈
SEP	♐	♈	♍	♑	♊	♎	♒	♋	♐	♈	♌	♑	♊
OCT	♑	♊	♎	♓	♋	♏	♓	♌	♑	♉	♍	♒	♋
NOV	♓	♋	♏	♈	♍	♑	♉	♎	♒	♊	♏	♈	♌
DEC	♈	♌	♑	♊	♎	♒	♊	♏	♓	♌	♐	♉	♍

	1962	1963	1964	1965	1966	1967	1968	1969	1970	1971	1972	1973	1974
JAN	♏	♓	♌	♐	♈	♍	♑	♊	♎	♒	♋	♐	♈
FEB	♐	♉	♍	♒	♊	♏	♓	♋	♏	♈	♍	♑	♉
MAR	♐	♉	♎	♒	♊	♏	♈	♌	♐	♉	♍	♑	♊
APR	♒	♋	♏	♈	♌	♑	♉	♍	♒	♊	♏	♓	♋
MAY	♓	♌	♐	♉	♍	♒	♊	♎	♓	♋	♐	♈	♍
JUN	♉	♎	♒	♊	♏	♓	♌	♐	♉	♍	♑	♊	♎
JUL	♊	♏	♓	♌	♐	♈	♍	♑	♊	♎	♓	♋	♐
AUG	♌	♐	♉	♎	♒	♊	♏	♓	♋	♏	♈	♍	♑
SEP	♍	♒	♋	♏	♓	♋	♐	♉	♍	♑	♊	♎	♓
OCT	♏	♓	♌	♐	♈	♍	♒	♊	♎	♒	♋	♐	♈
NOV	♐	♉	♎	♒	♊	♎	♓	♋	♐	♈	♍	♑	♉
DEC	♑	♊	♏	♓	♋	♐	♈	♌	♑	♉	♎	♒	♊

	1975	1976	1977	1978	1979	1980	1981	1982	1983	1984	1985	1986	1987
JAN	♌	♑	♉	♍	♒	♊	♏	♓	♌	♐	♉	♍	♑
FEB	♎	♒	♋	♏	♈	♌	♐	♉	♍	♒	♊	♎	♓
MAR	♎	♓	♋	♏	♈	♍	♑	♉	♎	♒	♊	♏	♓
APR	♐	♈	♍	♑	♊	♎	♒	♋	♏	♈	♌	♑	♉
MAY	♑	♉	♎	♒	♋	♏	♓	♌	♐	♉	♍	♒	♊
JUN	♓	♋	♐	♈	♌	♑	♉	♎	♒	♊	♏	♓	♌
JUL	♈	♌	♑	♉	♍	♒	♋	♏	♓	♌	♐	♉	♍
AUG	♉	♎	♓	♋	♏	♈	♌	♐	♈	♎	♒	♊	♎
SEP	♋	♐	♈	♌	♐	♊	♎	♒	♊	♏	♓	♌	♐
OCT	♌	♑	♉	♍	♒	♋	♏	♓	♋	♐	♉	♍	♑
NOV	♎	♓	♋	♏	♓	♌	♐	♉	♍	♒	♊	♎	♓
DEC	♏	♈	♌	♐	♉	♍	♑	♊	♎	♓	♋	♐	♈

	1988	1989	1990	1991	1992	1993	1994	1995	1996	1997	1998	1999	2000
JAN	♊	♎	♒	♋	♏	♈	♌	♑	♉	♎	♒	♊	♏
FEB	♋	♐	♈	♍	♑	♉	♎	♒	♋	♏	♈	♌	♐
MAR	♌	♐	♉	♍	♒	♊	♎	♓	♋	♏	♈	♌	♑
APR	♍	♒	♊	♏	♓	♋	♐	♈	♍	♑	♊	♎	♓
MAY	♏	♓	♌	♐	♈	♍	♑	♉	♎	♒	♋	♏	♈
JUN	♐	♉	♍	♑	♊	♎	♓	♋	♐	♈	♌	♑	♉
JUL	♑	♊	♎	♒	♋	♐	♈	♌	♑	♉	♎	♒	♋
AUG	♓	♌	♐	♈	♍	♑	♉	♎	♓	♋	♏	♓	♌
SEP	♉	♍	♑	♊	♏	♓	♋	♏	♈	♌	♑	♉	♎
OCT	♊	♎	♒	♋	♐	♈	♌	♑	♉	♎	♒	♊	♏
NOV	♌	♐	♈	♍	♑	♉	♎	♒	♋	♏	♈	♌	♑
DEC	♍	♑	♉	♎	♒	♋	♏	♈	♌	♐	♉	♍	♒

THE SOLAR SYSTEM

THE STARS, OTHER THAN THE SUN, PLAY NO PART IN THE SCIENCE OF ASTROLOGY. ASTROLOGERS USE ONLY THE BODIES IN THE SOLAR SYSTEM, EXCLUDING THE EARTH, TO CALCULATE HOW OUR LIVES AND PERSONALITIES CHANGE.

Pluto
Pluto takes 246 years to travel around the Sun. It affects our unconscious instincts and urges, gives us strength in difficulty, and may emphasize any inherent cruel streak.

Neptune
Neptune stays in each sign for 14 years. At best it makes us sensitive and imaginative; at worst it encourages deceit and carelessness, making us worry.

Uranus
The influence of Uranus can make us friendly, kind, eccentric, inventive, and unpredictable.

Saturn
In ancient times, Saturn was the most distant known planet. Its influence can limit our ambition and make us either overly cautious (but practical), or reliable and self-disciplined.

PLUTO

NEPTUNE

URANUS

SATURN

Jupiter

Jupiter encourages expansion, optimism, generosity, and breadth of vision. It can, however, also make us wasteful, extravagant, and conceited.

Mars

Much associated with energy, anger, violence, selfishness, and a strong sex drive, Mars also encourages decisiveness and leadership.

Earth

Every planet contributes to the environment of the Solar System, and a person born on Venus would no doubt be influenced by our own planet in some way.

The Moon

Although it is a satellite of the Earth, the Moon is known in astrology as a planet. It lies about 240,000 miles from the Earth and, astrologically, is second in importance only to the Sun.

THE MOON

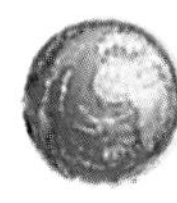

MARS

The Sun

The Sun, the only star used by astrologers, influences the way we present ourselves to the world – our image or personality; the face we show to other people.

Venus

The planet of love and partnership, Venus can emphasize all our best personal qualities. It may also encourage us to be lazy, impractical, and too dependent on other people.

Mercury

The planet closest to the Sun affects our intellect. It can make us inquisitive, versatile, argumentative, perceptive, and clever, but perhaps inconsistent, cynical, and sarcastic.

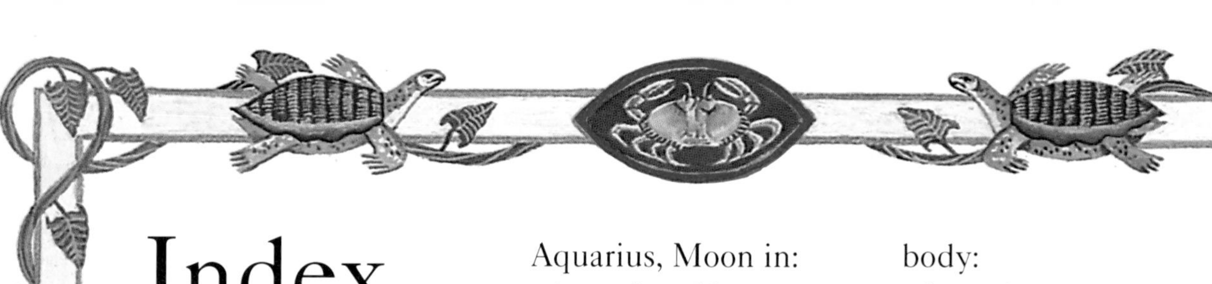

Index

A

B

C

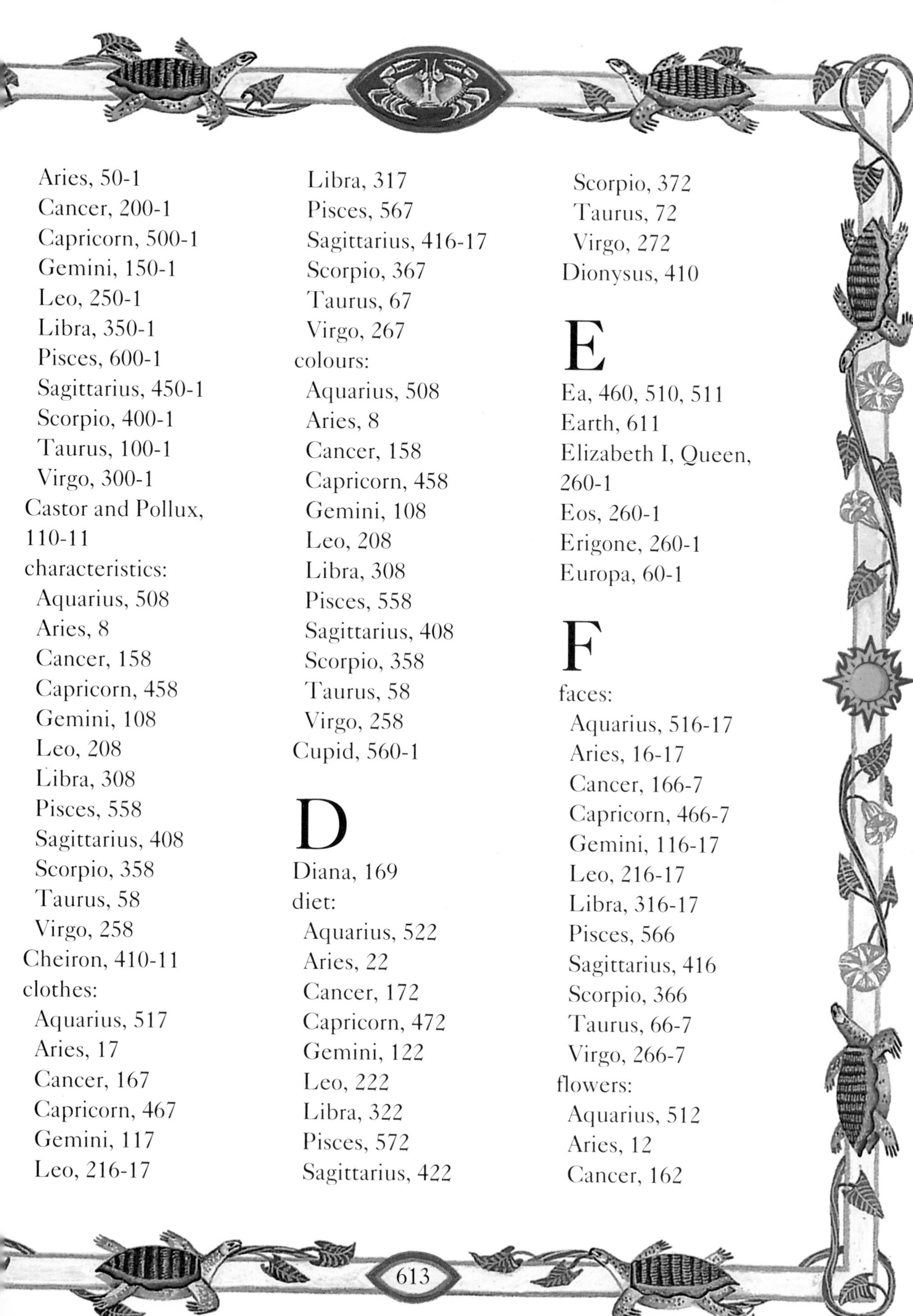

D

E

F

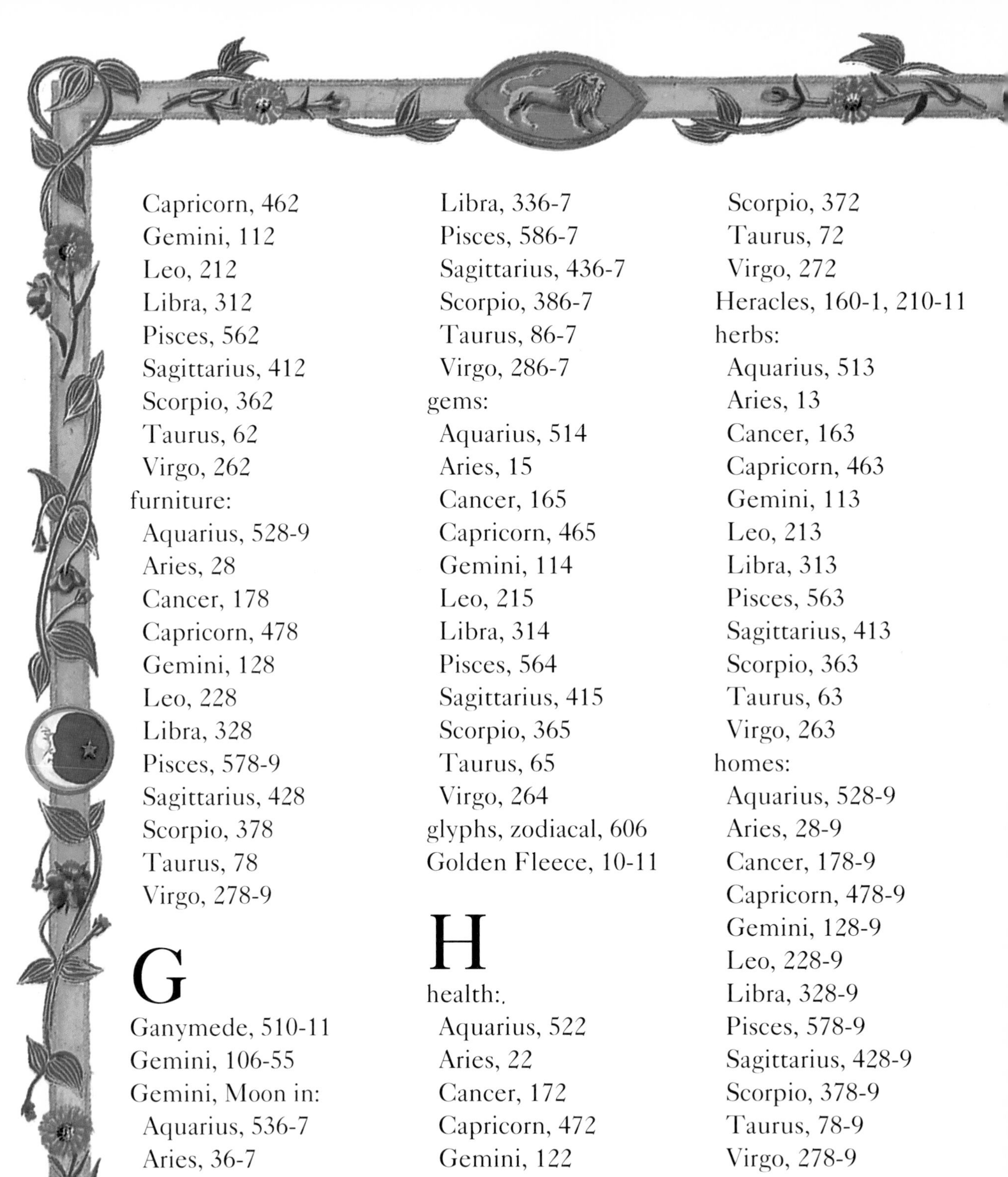

G

H

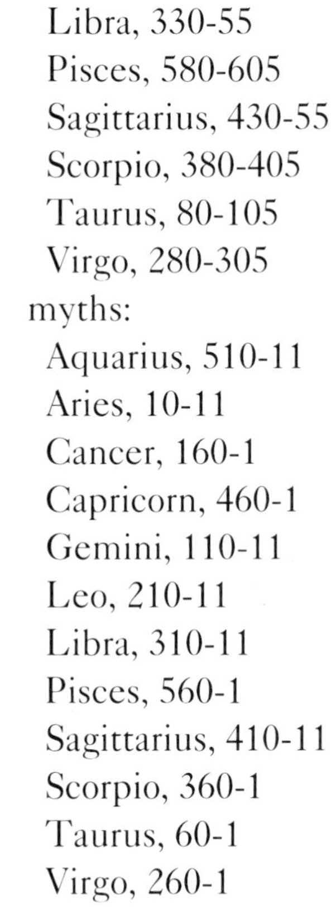

N

O

P

S

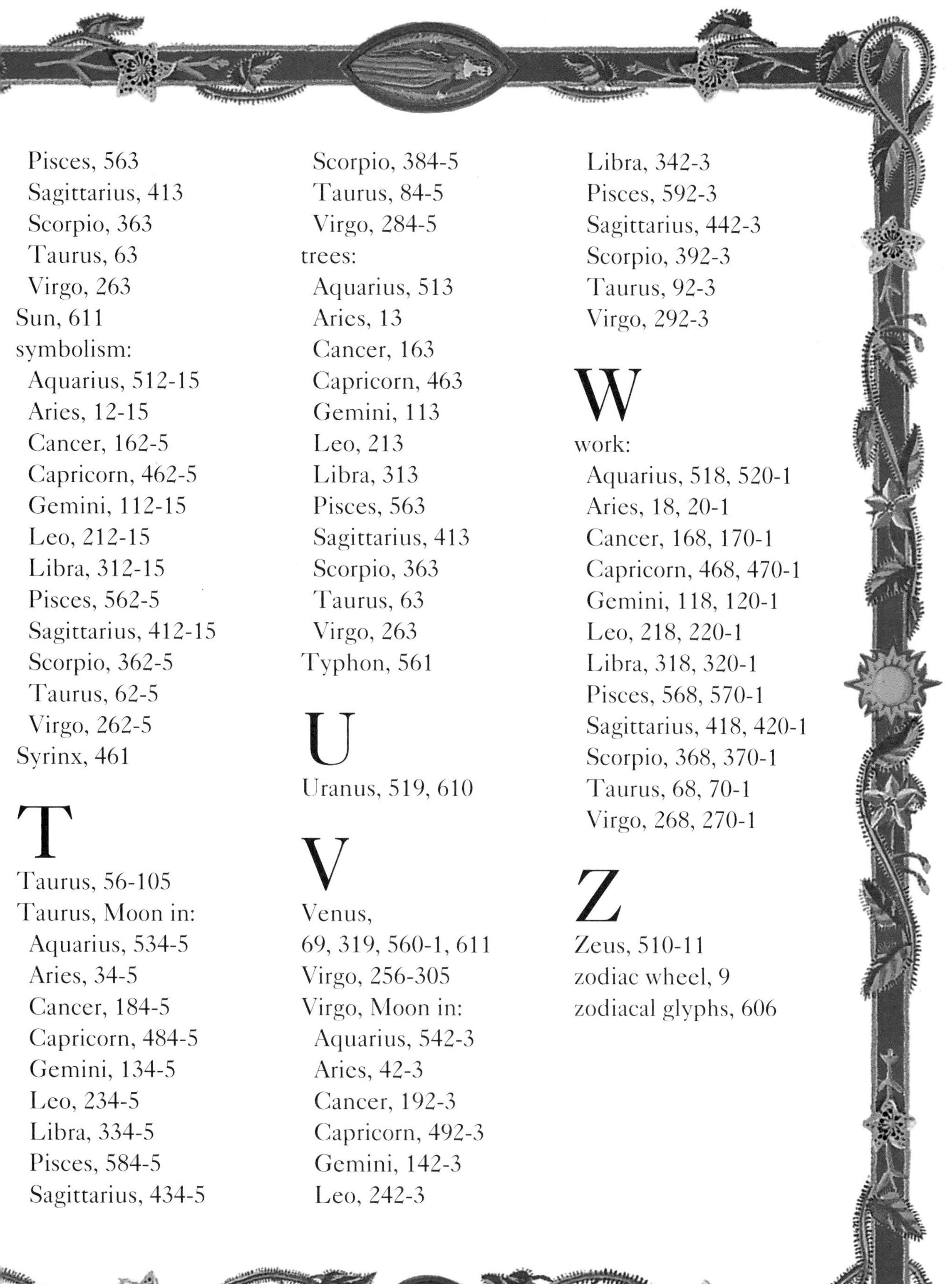

T

U

V

W

Z

ACKNOWLEDGMENTS

ARIES
Photography p 10 British Museum, London/Bridgeman Art Library, London; p 11 Bradford Art Galleries and Museums/Bridgeman Art Library, London; p 16 Tim Ridley. Stylist pp 28-29 Lucy Elworthy.

TAURUS
Photography p 61 by courtesy of the Board of Trustees of the Victoria and Albert Museum/Bridgeman Art Library, London; p 66 Tim Ridley. Stylist pp 78-79 Lucy Elworthy.

GEMINI
Photography p 110 Museum of Antiquities, Newcastle Upon Tyne/Bridgeman Art Library, London; p 111 Ronald Sheridan/Ancient Art and Architecture Collection; p 116 Tim Ridley. Stylist pp 128-129 Lucy Elworthy.

CANCER
Photography p 160 Ronald Sheridan/Ancient Art and Architecture Library; p 161 ©Michael Holford/British Museum; p 166 Tim Ridley. Stylist pp 178-179 Lucy Elworthy.

LEO
Photography p 211 © Michael Holford/British Museum; p 216 Tim Ridley. Stylist pp 228-229 Lucy Elworthy.

VIRGO
Photography p 260 ET Archive/British Museum; p 261 CM Dixon; p 266 Tim Ridley. Stylist pp 278-279 Lucy Elworthy.

LIBRA
Photography p 311 © Michael Holford/British Museum; p 316 Tim Ridley. Stylist pp 328-329 Lucy Elworthy.

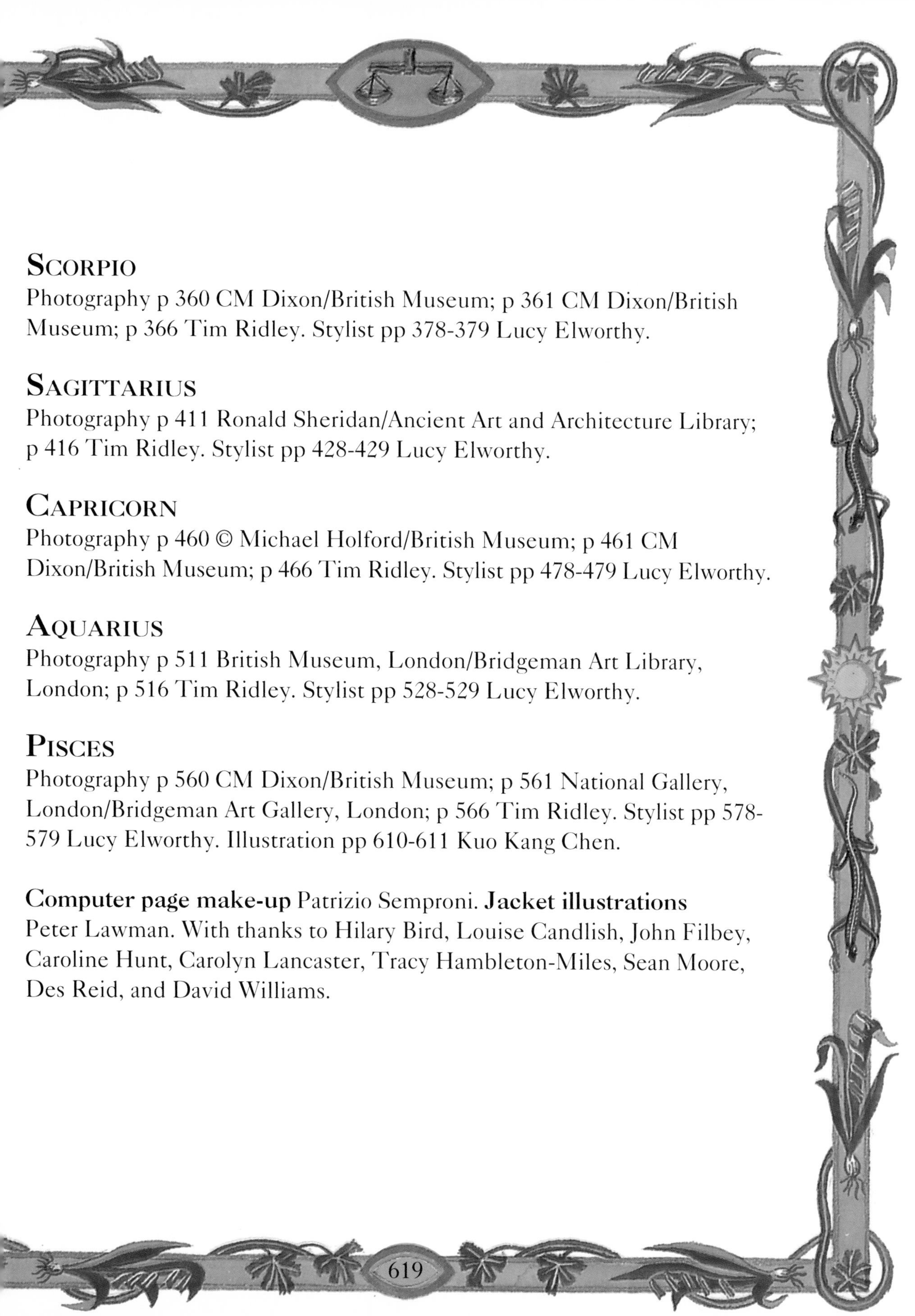

Scorpio

Photography p 360 CM Dixon/British Museum; p 361 CM Dixon/British Museum; p 366 Tim Ridley. Stylist pp 378-379 Lucy Elworthy.

Sagittarius

Photography p 411 Ronald Sheridan/Ancient Art and Architecture Library; p 416 Tim Ridley. Stylist pp 428-429 Lucy Elworthy.

Capricorn

Photography p 460 © Michael Holford/British Museum; p 461 CM Dixon/British Museum; p 466 Tim Ridley. Stylist pp 478-479 Lucy Elworthy.

Aquarius

Photography p 511 British Museum, London/Bridgeman Art Library, London; p 516 Tim Ridley. Stylist pp 528-529 Lucy Elworthy.

Pisces

Photography p 560 CM Dixon/British Museum; p 561 National Gallery, London/Bridgeman Art Gallery, London; p 566 Tim Ridley. Stylist pp 578-579 Lucy Elworthy. Illustration pp 610-611 Kuo Kang Chen.

Computer page make-up Patrizio Semproni. **Jacket illustrations** Peter Lawman. With thanks to Hilary Bird, Louise Candlish, John Filbey, Caroline Hunt, Carolyn Lancaster, Tracy Hambleton-Miles, Sean Moore, Des Reid, and David Williams.

Notes

Notes

Notes

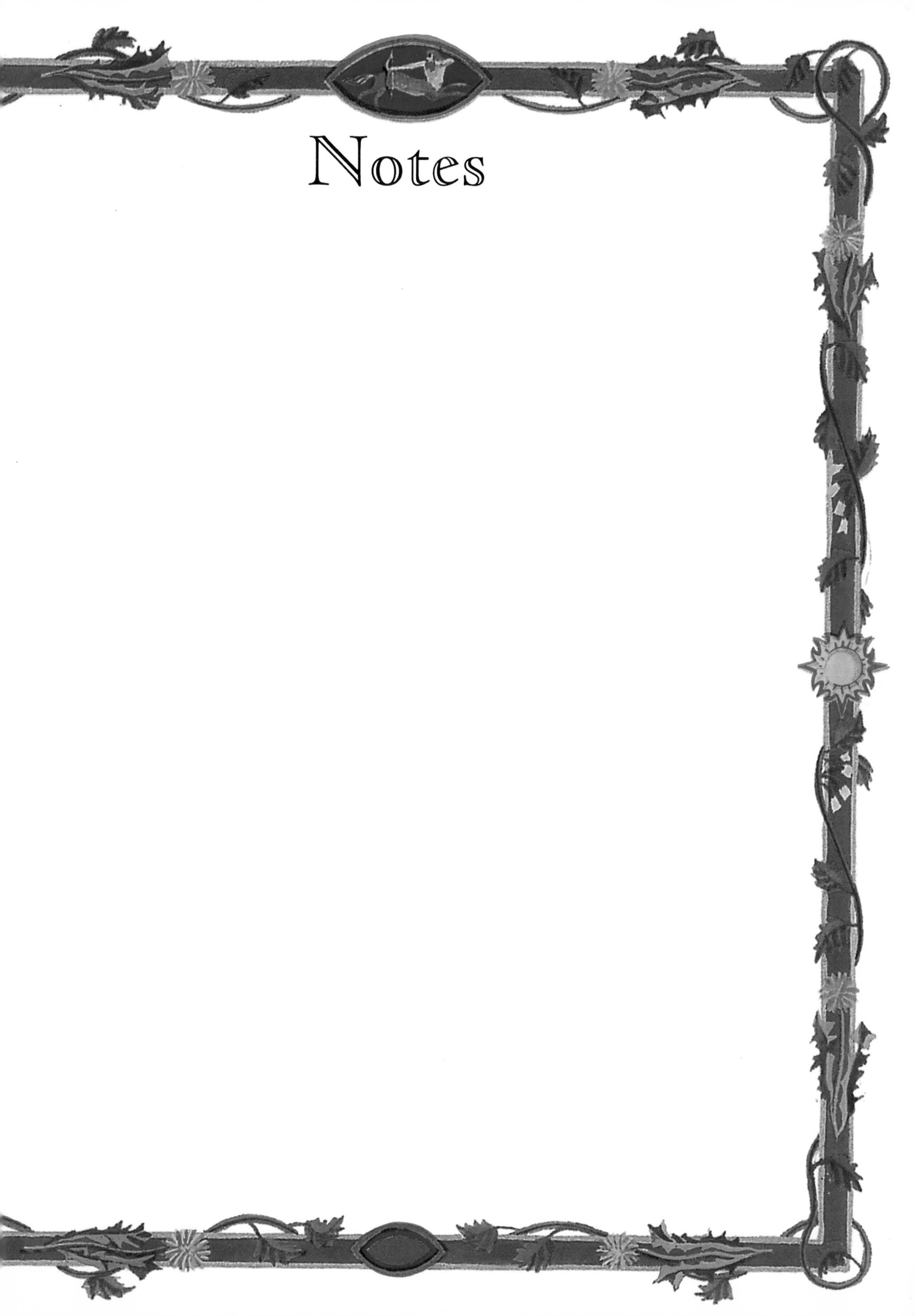

Notes

Manufacturers and Consultants

using space in this issue. For Classified List of Products and Services see page 6. For the cards of Consulting Engineers, see pages 25-49.

For the largest available directory of consultants in the municipal field listing their specialties see pages 25-49.

Classified List of Products and Services

Numbers appearing after names refer to advertising pages in this book. All the products listed on the next 19 pages are made or sold by the manufacturers advertising in this book. Not all these products are described in the advertisements. If you turn to an ad and do not find there some product under which the manufacturer is listed here, write the manufacturer for literature. This index is published as an aid to the reader, but the publishers assume no responsibility for errors or omissions.

Abrasive Wheels Diamond
Felker Mfg. Co., 118-121
Accountants and Auditors
(see Directory of Consultants, 25-49)
Accounting and Adding Machines
National Cash Register Co., 1047-1050
Remington Rand, Inc., 1051-1054
Underwood Corp., 1055-1058
Accounting and Billing Machines
National Cash Register Co., 1047-1050
Remington Rand, Inc., 1051-1054
Underwood Corp., 1055-1058
Activated Alum
Olin Mathieson Chemical Corp., 410, 411; 1038, 1039
Activated Carbon
Graver Water Conditioning Co., 402, 403
Adaptors
Hays Mfg. Co., 436
Aerators
John Bean Division, 971; 1009
Chicago Pump Co., 523
Dorr-Oliver, Inc., 466-469
General Filter Co., 400, 401
Graver Water Conditioning Co., 402, 403
Layne & Bowler, Inc., 344-347
Pacific Flush-Tank Co., 519-522
Permutit Co., 416, 417
Power Implement Division, 1004
Aerial Surveys
Abrams Aerial Survey Corp., 54
Aero Service Corp., 55
Air Compressors
Allis-Chalmers Mfg. Co., 285-288
De Laval Steam Turbine Co., 313-316
Schramm, Inc., 218-221
Air Compressors, Portable
Jaeger Machine Co., 158-161
Schramm, Inc., 218-221
Air Compressors, Self-Propelled
Schramm, Inc., 218-221
Air Conditioning Equipment
John Bean Division, 971; 1009
General Electric Co., 398, 399; 791-794
Graybar Electric Co., 830
Westinghouse Electric Corp., 821-824
Air Diffusion Equipment
Pacific Flush-Tank Co., 519-522
Air-Gas Torches
Hauck Mfg. Co., 138-141
Air Placement Equipment
Air Placement Equip. Co., 68
Airport & Airway Cables
Collyer Insulated Wire Co., 851
General Electric Co., 398, 399; 791-794
Graybar Electric Co., 830
Airport & Airway Lighting
B & B Engineering Corp., 976, 977
Crouse-Hinds Co., 878-881
Graybar Electric Co., 830
Holophane Co., Inc. 795-798
Line Material Co., 803-806
Revere Electric Mfg. Co., 814-817
Street Lighting Equip. Corp., 834
Time-O-Matic, Inc., 895
Wallace & Tiernan Inc., 378-381
Westinghouse Electic Corp., 821-824
Airport Crash Trucks
Maxim Motors Co., 980, 981
Airport Lighting Circuit Controls
South Bend Current Controller Co., Inc. 833
Airport Runway Control Joint Cutters
Felker Mfg. Co., 118-121
Airport Runway Drag Brooms
Kennedy's Van Brush Mfg. Co., 173-176
Mid-Western Industries, Inc., 133-136
Work Bulls Div., Massey-Harris-Ferguson, 213-216
Airport Runway Grades
(see Road Graders)
Airport Runway Joint Cleaning Machines
G. & H. Tennant Co., 130-132; 957
Airport Runway Marking
Kelly-Creswell Co., 963-966
Prismo Safety Corp., 944-947
Wald Industries, Inc., 948, 949
Airport Runway Paving Equip.
Aeroil Products Co., Inc., 69-72
Byerlyte Corp., 146, 147
Heltzel Steel Form & Iron Co., 117
Littleford Bros., 169-172
Pressite Keystone Engr. Prod. Co., 189-192
White Mfg. Co., 230-233
Airport Runway Paving Material
Servicised Products Corp., 201-204
Airport Sweepers
Detroit Harvester Co., 157
Ernest Holmes Co., 142-145
Little Giant Products Co., 177-180
Work Bulls Div., Massey-Harris-Ferguson, 213-216
Airport Taxiway & Runway Lighting
Line Material Co., 803-806
Revere Electric Mfg. Co., 814-817
Airport Trench Grates
Dravo Corp., 168, 551
Algaecides
Inertol Co., Inc., 473
Modern Swimming Pool Co., 1035
Alum-Ammonium & Potassium
General Chemical Div., 234; 430
Aluminum Gratings & Treads
Dravo Corp., 168; 551
Aluminum Markers
Lake Shore Markers, Inc., 952, 953
Michaels Art Bronze Co., Inc., 862-864; 1060
Aluminum Stencils
Sargent-Sowell, Inc., 939-942
Aluminum, Street & Highway Signs
National Safety Engineers, 935-938
Aluminum Sulfate
General Chemical Div., 234; 430
Modern Swimming Pool Co., 1035
Ammonia Control Apparatus
Fischer & Porter Co., 317-320
Wallace & Tiernan Inc., 378-381
Anhydrous Ammonia
Olin Mathieson Chemical Corp., 410, 411; 1038, 1039
Anhydrous Bisulfite of Soda
General Chemical Div., 234; 430
Appraisals, Tax
J. M. Cleminshaw Co., 50, 51
Cole - Layer - Trumble Company, 52, 53
Aqua Ammonia
General Chemical Div., 234; 430
Olin Mathieson Chemical Corp., 410, 411; 1038, 1039
Armored Vests
Federal Laboratories, Inc., 988
Asbestos Cement
Philip Carey Mfg. Co., 92
Asbestos Products
Barrett Div., Allied Chemical & Dye Corp., 269
Byerlyte Corp., 146, 147
Johns-Manville, 406, 407; 536, 537
Asphalt
Barrett Div., Allied Chemical & Dye Corp., 269
Byerlyte Corp., 146, 147
Presstite Keystone Engineering Products Co., 189-192
Asphalt Curb Pavers
E. D. Etnyre & Co., 106-109
Asphalt Cutting & Sawing
Felker Mfg. Co., 118-121
Asphalt Emulsion
Byerlyte Corp., 146, 147
Asphalt Emulsion Sprayers
(see Distributors, Asphalt, Oil, etc.)
Asphalt Mixers, Portable
Gruendler Crusher & Pulverizer Co., 470
White Mfg. Co., 230-233
Asphalt Planking
Byerlyte Corp., 146, 147
Philip Carey Mfg. Co., 92
Presstite Keystone Engineering Products Co., 189-192
Servicised Products Corp., 201-204
Asphalt Plant Burners
Hauck Mfg. Co., 138-141
Asphalt Plants
Allied Steel & Tractor Products, Inc., 77
Barber-Greene Co., 73-76
F. D. Cummer & Son Co., 137
White Mfg. Co., 230-233
Asphalt Plants & Equipment
R. D. Cole Mfg. Co., 305-308
White Mfg. Co., 230-233
Wylie Mfg. Co., 235-238
Asphalt Surface Heaters
Hauck Mfg. Co., 138-141
Littleford Bros., 169-172
White Mfg. Co., 230-233
Asphalt Tools
Aeroil Products Co., Inc., 69-72
Clarksville Foundry & Machine Works, 373
Littleford Bros., Inc., 169-172
Athletic Field Lighting Circuit Controls
South Bend Current Controller Co., Inc., 833
Augers, Earth, Post Hole
J. H. Holan Corp., 831
Tel-E-Lect Products, Inc., 835
Work Bulls Div., Massey-Harris-Ferguson, 213-216
Augers, Sewer & Pipe
Flexible, Inc., 476-470
O'Brien Mfg. Co., 515-518
Roto-Rooter Corp., 565
W. H. Stewart, Inc., 506-509
Auto License Plates & Tags
Grimm Stamp & Badge Co., 906-909
National Safety Engineers, 935-938
Sargent-Sowell, Inc., 939-942
Aviation Beacon Flashers
(see Airport & Airway Lighting)
Aviation Floodlights
(see Floodlights)

Backfill Blades
Arps Corp., 64-67
Work Bulls Div., Massey-Harris-Ferguson, 213-216
Backfill Tampers
Homelite Division, 263-267
Mid-Western Industries, Inc., 133-136
Schramm, Inc., 218-221
Backfillers
Austin-Western Co., 78-81
Mid-Western Industries, Inc., 133-136
Work Bulls Div., Massey-Harris-Ferguson, 213-216
Backhoes
Badger Machine Co., 87-90

The purpose of the MUNICIPAL INDEX

is to help city officials purchase the equipment, materials and services for the construction, operation and maintenance of municipal activities.

Manufacturers and Consultants

are listed alphabetically on page 3 to 5.

Advertisers are indexed

by the products they sell right here in these 19 pages of the Classified List of Products and Services.

Advertising catalogs

appear in four major sections with an index of advertisers' names in front of each.

Modern Swimming Pool Co., Inc., 1035
Permutit Co., 416, 417

Clarifiers, Oil Separating
Hardinge Co., Inc., 556

Classified Plastic Street Markers
Lyle Signs, Inc., 923-926

Clay Pipe
American Vitrified Products Co., 465

Clay Pipe & Fittings
Robinson Clay Product Co., 563

Cleaners, Steam
Aeroil Products Co., Inc., 69-72

Cleaning Compounds
John Bean Division, 971; 1009
Columbia - Southern Chemical Corp., 382

Cleaning Equipment
Aeroil Products Co., Inc., 69-72

Cloths for Uniforms
Franklin Worsted Co., 989
Metcalf Bros. & Co., 990

Coal Handling Machinery, Truck Bodies, Conveyors
Barber-Greene Co., 73-76
Baughman Mfg. Co., 86
Ernest Holmes Co., 142-145
Frank G. Hough Co., 113-116
Littleford Bros., 169-172
LoDal, Inc., 162-165

Coatings, Corrosion Resistant
Hamilton Kent Mfg. Co., 555

Cocks, Curb and Corporation
Haydenville Co., 434
Hays Manufacturing Co., 436
A. Y. McDonald Mfg. Co., 352-355

Coin Bags, Boxes, Stackers & Trays
Abbott Coin Counter Co., Inc., 875

Coin Changers
Johnson Fare Box Co., 870, 871

Coin Counting & Packaging Machines
Abbott Coin Counter Co., Inc., 875
Brandt Automatic Cashier Co., 861

Coin Counters
Brandt Automatic Cashier Co., 861
Johnson Fare Box Co., 870, 871

Coin Paying & Changing Machines
Abbott Coin Counter Co., Inc., 875
Brandt Automatic Cashier Co., 861

Coin Sorters
Abbott Coin Counter Co., Inc., 875
Johnson Fare Box Co., 870, 871

Coin Sorting & Counting Machines
Abbott Coin Counter Co., Inc., 875
Brandt Automatic Cashier Co., 861

Coin Wrappers
Abbott Coin Counter Co., Inc., 875
Brandt Automatic Cashier Co., 861
Johnson Fare Box Co., 870, 871

Cold Forged Steel Unions
Rockwood Sprinkler Co., 984, 985

Combustion (CO_2) Indicater & Recorder
Permutit Co., 416, 417

Comminutors
Chicago Pump Co., 523

Communication Receivers, Police & Fire
Industrial Radio Corp., 992

Communications Systems
General Electric Co., 398, 399; 791-794
Graybar Electric Co., Inc., 830
Industrial Radio Corp., 992

Community Buildings
Wesley Bintz, 1031

Compost Innoculum, Aerobac
Reliance Chemicals Corp., 562

Compressors, Air Rotary
Roots-Connersville Blower, 564

Compressors, Centrifugal
Roots-Connersville Blower, 564

Compressors, Gas
Roots-Connersville Blower, 564

Compressors (see Air Compressors)

Compressors, Spiraxial
Roots-Connersville Blower, 564

Concrete Breakers
Sargent-Sowell. Inc., 939-942
Schramm, Inc., 218-221

The products sold by our advertisers

to municipalities are listed here with the names of the advertisers and their page numbers under each product. There are over 1000 product headings and 2,800 listings.

Concrete Chippers
G. H. Tennant Co., 130-132; 957

Concrete Curing
Byerlyte Corp., 146, 147
Columbia - Southern Chemical Corp., 382
Presstite Keystone Engineering Products Co., 189-192
Servicised Products Corp., 201-204

Concrete Cutters (or Saws)
Felker Mfg. Co., 118-121
Tri-Line Co., 252, 253

Concrete Cutting Blades
Tri-Line Co., 252, 253

Concrete Cutting Machines
Tri-Line Co., 252, 253

Concrete Cutting & Sawing
Clipper Mfg. Co., 240, 241
Felker Mfg. Co., 118-121

Concrete Grinders
White Mfg. Co., 230-233

Concrete Grouting Equipment
Air Placement Equipment Co., 68

Concrete Gunning
Air Placement Equip. Co., 68

Concrete Heaters
Aeroil Products Co., Inc., 69-72
Hauck Mfg. Co., 138-141
Littleford Bros., 169-172

Concrete Lamp Posts
(see Street Light Posts, Concrete)

Concrete & Masonry Restoration Equipment
Air Placement Equip. Co., 68

Concrete Mixers
Air Placement Equip. Co., 68
Jaeger Machine Co., 158-161

Concrete Pipe
American Vitrified Products Co., 465
Lock Joint Pipe Co., 341-343; 558

Concrete Trowelers
White Mfg. Co., 230-233

Concrete Vibrators
Homelite Division, 263-267
Schramm, Inc., 218-221
White Mfg. Co., 230-233

Condensers, Electrical
Allis-Chalmers Mfg. Co., 285-288
General Electric Co., 398, 399; 791-794
Moloney Electric Co., 852
Westinghouse Electric Corp., 821-824

Condensers, Steam
Allis-Chalmers Mfg. Co., 285-288
Westinghouse Electric Corp., 821-824

Conduit Rods & Accessories
(see Sewer Rods & Accessories)

Construction Signs, Road & Highway
National Safety Engineers, 935-938

Consulting Engineers
(see pages 25-49)

Contraction Joint Cutters
Felker Mfg. Co., 118-121

Contraction Joint Sealers
Clipper Mfg. Co., 240, 241

Contractor's Measuring Wheels
Rolatape, Inc., 260

Contractors' Pumps
(see Pumps, Contractors')

Control Joint Cutters
Felker Mfg. Co., 118-121

Control Panels
Permutit Co., 416, 417

Controls, Communication
Industrial Radio Corp., 992

Controls for Lighting of Streets, Airports, Athletic Fields, Etc.
General Electric Co., 398, 399; 791-794
Line Material Co., 803-806
South Bend Current Controller Co., 833

Westinghouse Electric Corp., 821-824

Controls, Heating & Air Conditioning
General Electric Co., 398, 399; 791-794

Controls, Pressure
Fischer & Porter Co., 317-320
General Electric Co., 398, 399; 791-794
Water Level Controls Div., Healy-Ruff Co., 438

Controls, Tank & Pump
Bailey Meter Co., 480
Fischer & Porter Co., 317-320
General Electric Co., 398, 399; 791-794
Golden-Anderson Valve Specialty Co., 437
Water Level Controls Div., Healy-Ruff Co., 438

Controls, Traffic Signal, Electric
(see Traffic Signal Controls)

Controllers, Rate
Bailey Meter Co., 480
Fischer & Porter Co., 317-320
Permutit Co., 416, 417
Simplex Valve & Meter Co., 422, 423

Conveyors, Belt
Barber-Greene Co., 73-76
Baughman Mfg. Co., 86
Bosworth Mfg. Co., 328
Heltzel Steel Form & Iron Co., 117
Wickwire Spencer Steel Div., 1018

Conveyors, Bucket
Barber-Greene Co., 73-76
Bosworth Mfg. Co., 328
Chain Belt Co., 105
Littleford Bros., 169-172

Conveyors, Chain & Spiral
Baughman Mfg. Co., 86
Chain Belt Co., 105
Wickwire Spencer Steel Div., 1018

Conveyors, Drag Chain
Bosworth Mfg. Co., 328

Conveyors, Portable
Bosworth Mfg. Co., 328

Conveyors, Screen
F. D. Cummer & Son Co., 137

Conveyors, Stationary
Bosworth Mfg. Co., 328

Coppersetters and Copperhorns
Ford Meter Box Co., Inc., 329-332

Copper Pipe (see Pipe, Copper)

Copper Sulphate
General Chemical Div., 234; 430
Tennessee Corp., 276; 304; 325; 567

Copper Water Tube
American Brass Co., 538, 539
Revere Copper & Brass, Inc., 445

Corporation Stops
Haydenville Co., 434
Hays Mfg. Co., 436

Counters, Traffic
Denominator Co., Inc., 956

Couplings
Chain Belt Co., 105
Hays Mfg. Co., 436
Philadelphia Gear Works, 444
Smith-Blair, Inc., 374-377

Couplings, Pipe
(see Pipe Couplings)

Covers, Shuredry
Fulton Bag & Cotton Mills, 991

Covers, Sprinkling Filter & Tank
Lord & Burnham Corp., 559

Crack Filling Equipment
(see Filling Equipment for Cracks & Joints)

Cranes, Hydraulic, Mobile, Truck & Tractor
Garwood Industries, Inc., 242, 243; 532, 533

Following these classified listings

come the condensed catalog advertising to which these listings refer by page numbers. The advertisements are arranged in four groups: Street construction and maintenance equipment; water works equipment; sewers, sewage treatment equipment, refuse collection and disposal; public safety and service equipment.

Fischer & Porter Co., 317-320
Simplex Valve & Meter Co., 422, 423
Gauges, Volume & Pressure, Gas
Bailey Meter Co., 480
Fischer & Porter Co., 317-320
Gears
Clarksville Foundry & Machine Works, 373
De Laval Steam Turbine Co., 313-316
Philadelphia Gear Works, 444
Glass Beads
Flex-O-Lite Mfg. Corp., 915-918
Glass Enclosures
Lord & Burnham Corp., 559
Glassware & Globes for Street Lighting
(see Street Light Globes)
Golf Course Equipment
John Bean Division, 971; 1009
Lake Shore Markers, 952, 953
Littleford Bros., 169-172
Worthington Mower Co., 995-998
Goosenecks, Copper
Hays Mfg. Co., 436
A. Y. McDonald Mfg. Co., 352-355
Graders, Road (see Road Graders)
Grandstands and Portable Stands
American Bridge Div., 1011
Leavitt Products Co., 1016, 1017
Pittsburgh-Des Moines Steel Co., 418, 419; 544, 545
Grass Seed
O. M. Scott & Sons Co., 1046
Grates, Incinerator
American Engineering Co., 568
Grating, Aluminum
Dravo Corp., 168; 551
Grating, Steel
Blaw-Knox Co., 82-85
Dravo Corp., 168; 551
Grating, Steel, Platform, Sidewalk & Subway
Dravo Corp., 168; 551
Irving Subway Grating Co., Inc., 257
Gravel Plants
(see Sand & Gravel Plants)
Greenhouses
Lord & Burnham Corp., 559
Grinders, Concrete
White Mfg. Co., 230-233
Guard Railings
(see Highway Guard)
Gunite
Pressure Concrete Co., 420, 421
Gutter Drainage Covers
Irving Subway Grating Co., Inc., 257
Neenah Foundry Co., 259
Gutter Forms
Blaw-Knox Co., 82-85
Heltzel Steel Form & Iron Co., 117

Hanger Floodlights
(see Floodlights)
Hangers
Pressure Concrete Co., 420, 421
Harrows, Spike & Disc
Tractor & Implement Div., Ford Motor Co., 209-212
Heaters, Asphalt, Pitch, Tar Kettle, Tool, Etc.
Aeroil Products Co., Inc., 69-72
Hauck Mfg. Co., 138-141
Littleford Bros., 169-172
Rosco Mfg. Co., 197-200
White Mfg. Co., 230-233
Heating Wagons, Oil & Tar
Aeroil Products Co., Inc., 69-72
Hauck Mfg. Co., 138-141
Littleford Bros., 169-172
Rosco Mfg. Co., 197-200
Hickory
Otto Gerdau Co., 122-125
Sargent-Sowell, Inc., 939-942
Highway Guard
Anchor Post Products, Inc., 1019
Bethlehem Steel Co., 326, 327; 485
Highway Lighting
(see Street Lighting)
Highway Lighting Refractors
(see Refractors)
Highway Markers
(see Traffic Signs & Signals)
Highway Reflecting Signals
(see Reflector Signals & Signs)
Hoisting Machinery
Jaeger Machine Co., 158-161
Hose, Fire (see Fire Hose)
Hose Reels
Schramm, Inc., 218-221

After the red pages

you will find the municipal trends and Who's Who in equipment and supplies with forewords on how to select the equipment particularly suited to your needs.

Stedt Hydraulic Crane Co., 546, 547; 1118, 1119
House Numbers
Lake Shore Markers, Inc., 952, 953
Miro-Flex Co., 931-934
Municipal Street Sign Co., Inc., 910
Sargent-Sowell, Inc., 939-942
Hydrants, Fire
Eddy Valve Co., 272, 273
Iowa Valve Co., 274, 275
The Kennedy Valve Mfg. Co., 337-340
Ludlow Valve Mfg. Co., Inc., 348-351
M & H Valve & Fittings Co., 357-360
Traverse City Iron Works, 450
R. D. Wood Co., 387-390
Hydraulic Hoists
Gar Wood Industries, Inc., 242, 243; 532, 533
Heil Company, 488-491
Hydrants, Yard
The Kennedy Valve Mfg. Co., 337-340
M & H Valve & Fittings Co., 357-360
Hypochlorinators
Fischer & Porter Co., 317-320
Modern Swimming Pool Co., Inc., 1035
National Pool Equip. Co., 1036, 1037
Wallace & Tiernan Inc., 378-381
Hypochlorite of Lime
(see Calcium Hypochloride)

Ice Control Equipment
Baughman Mfg. Co., 86
Identification Tags, Numbered
Grimm Stamp & Badge Co., 906-909
Sargent-Sowell, Inc., 939-942
Illumination Service
Holophane Co., Inc., 795-798
Incinerator Buckets
Blaw-Knox Co., 82-85
Hayward Co., 534, 535
Stedt Hydraulic Crane Co., 546, 547; 1118, 1119
Incinerator Grates
American Engineering Co., 568
Incinerator Refractories
Carborundum Co., 501
Incinerators
American Incinerator Corp., 528, 529
Combustion Engineering Inc., 461-464
M. H. Detrick Co., 550
Dravo Corp., 168; 551
Illinois Stoker Co., 557
Morse Boulger Destructor Co., 502-505
Nichols Eng. & Research Corp., 510-513
Pittsburgh-Des Moines Steel Co., 418, 419; 544, 545
Plibrico, Inc., 561
Incinerators, Trash (For Parks, Beaches, Etc.)
Cyclone Fence Dept., 148; 395; 1012, 1013
Indicator Posts
M & H Valve & Fittings Co., 357-360
Traverse City Iron Works, 450
Industrial Sweepers, Yard
Detroit Harvester Co., 157
Ernest Holmes Co., 142-145
Wayne Mfg. Co., 226-229
Work Bulls Div., Massey-Harris-Ferguson, 213-216

Industrial Tractors (see Tractors)
Industrial Waste Incinerators
(see Incinerator)
Insecticides
Gulf Oil Corp., 1010
Insect Control
General Chemical Div., 234; 430
Instruments & Laboratory Equipment
Industrial Radio Corp., 992
Instruments for Land Measuring
Rolatape, Inc., 260
Instruments for Measuring CO_2 in Flue Gases
Permutit Co., 416, 417
Instruments for Weighing Motor Trucks & Buses
Loadometer Corp., 958
Insulation
Barrett Div., Allied Chemical & Dye Corp., 269
Philip Carey Mfg. Co., 92
Celotex Corp., 91
M. H. Detrick Co., 550
Ion Exchange Resins
Permutit Co., 416, 417

Joint Cleaning Machines
G. H. Tennant Co., 130-132; 957
Jointing Compounds
Byerlyte Corp., 146, 147
Philip Carey Mfg. Co., 92
Modern Swimming Pool Co., Inc., 1035
Presstite Keystone Engineering Products Co., 189-192
Robinson Clay Products Co., 563
Servicised Products Corp., 201-204
Joint Cutters, Control & Contraction
Clipper Mfg. Co., 240, 241
Felker Mfg. Co., 118-121
Joint Cutting Machines
Clipper Mfg. Co., 240, 241
Tri-Line Co., 252, 253
Joint Expansion
U. S. Rubber Co., 1121
Joint Filler
Barrett Div., Allied Chemical & Dye Corp., 269
Byerlyte Corp., 146, 147
Philip Carey Mfg. Co., 92
Heltzel Steel Form & Iron Co., 117
Inertol Co., Inc., 473
Modern Swimming Pool Co., Inc., 1035
Presstite Keystone Engineering Products Co., 189-192
Servicised Products Corp., 201-204
Joint Sealers, Pressure
Clipper Mfg. Co., 240, 241
Joint Sealing Compound
Radiator Specialty Co., 959-962

Kerosene Burners
Aeroil Products Co., Inc., 69-72
Hauck Mfg. Co., 138-141
Littleford Bros., Inc., 169-172
White Mfg. Co., 230-233
Kettles for Asphalt & Tar Heating
Aeroil Products Co., Inc., 69-72
Clipper Mfg. Co., 240, 241
Hauck Mfg. Co., 138-141
Littleford Bros., 169-172
Rosco Mfg. Co., 197-200
Standard Steel Works, 205-208
White Mfg. Co., 230-233

Ladders, Aerial, Fire Dept.
J. H. Holan Corp., 831
Peter Pirsch & Sons Co., 993
Ladders, Ground, Fire Dept., Wood & Aluminum
Peter Pirsch & Sons Co., 993

Meters, Oil
Badger Meter Mfg. Co., 293-296
Buffalo Meter Co., 356
Fischer & Porter Co., 317-320
Neptune Meter Co., 369-372
Simplex Valve & Meter Co., 422, 423
Worthington-Gamon Meter Div., 391-394

Meters, Parking
(see Parking Meters)

Meters, Portable Test
Badger Meter Mfg. Co., 293-296
Fischer & Porter Co., 317-320
General Electric Co., 398, 399; 791-794
Graybar Electric Co., Inc., 830
Hersey Mfg. Company, 404, 405
Neptune Meter Co., 369-372
Sparling Meter Co., 447
Westinghouse Electric Corp., 821-824

Meters, Positive Displacement
Roots-Connersville Blower, 564

Meters, Sewage
Bailey Meter Co., 480
Fischer & Porter Co., 317-320
Simplex Valve & Meter Co., 422, 423

Meters, Sewage Gas
Fischer & Porter Co., 317-320

Meters, Venturi Type
Bailey Meter Co., 480
Simplex Valve & Meter Co., 422, 423

Meters, Water
Badger Meter Mfg. Co., 293-296
Buffalo Meter Co., 356
Fischer & Porter Co., 317-320
Hersey Mfg. Company, 404, 405
Neptune Meter Co., 369-372
Well Machinery & Supply Co., Inc., 383-386
Worthington-Gamon Meter Div., 391-394

Meters, Water (Electrically Operated)
Fischer & Porter Co., 317-320
Sparling Meter Co., 447

Meters, Water Main-Line
Fischer & Porter Co., 317-320
Hersey Mfg. Company, 404, 405
Sparling Meter Co., 447
Worthington-Gamon Meter Div., 391-394

Meters, Weir
Bailey Meter Co., 480
Fischer & Porter Co., 317-320
Simplex Valve & Meter Co., 422, 423

Microfilming Machines & Service
Remington Rand, Inc., 1051-1054

Mixing Equipment
Dorr-Oliver, Inc., 466-469

Moldboard Shift
Rivinius, Inc., 250, 251

Motor Truck Trailers
(see Trailers)

Motor Trucks
Ingersoll - Kalamazoo Division, 497-500
Sicard Industries, Inc., 110-112; 566

Motorized Graders
Austin-Western Co., 78-81
LeTourneau - Westinghouse Co., 58-63
M. B. Corp., 246, 247; 560; 967

Motors, Electric
(see Electric Generators and Motors)

Motors, Gasoline
(see Engine, Gas)

Movable Bases
Lyle Signs, Inc., 923-926
Traffic & Street Sign Co., 954, 955

Mowers
John Deere Industrial Division, 101-104
Devere Co., 999
Eclipse Lawn Mower Co., 1000
General Playground Equipment, Inc., 1025
Gravely Tractors, Inc., 1001
Hal-Gan Products, Inc., 1002
Locke Power Lawn Mowers, 1003
Power Development Co., Inc., 1005
Power Implement Division, 1004
O. M. Scott & Sons Co., 1046
Servis Equipment Co., 1006
Wood Brothers Mfg. Co., 1007
Work Bulls Div., Massey-Harris-Ferguson, 213-216

Worthington Mower Co., 995-998
Yazoo Mfg. Co., 1008

Municipal & Contractors Supplies
Sargent-Sowell, Inc., 939-942

Municipal Incinerators
Plibrico, Inc., 561

Non-Return Valves
Golden-Anderson Valve Specialty Co., 437

Nozzles, Fog (see Fog Nozzles)

Nozzles, Sprinkling Filters
Pacific Flush-Tank Co., 519-522

Nozzles, Waterfog, Fogfoam
Rockwood Sprinkler Co., 984, 985

Odor Control
(see Taste & Odor Control)

Office Furniture
Cramer Posture Chair Co., 1059

Office Supplies
Remington Rand, Inc., 1051-1054
Underwood Corp., 1055-1058

Oil Burners
Aeroil Products Co., Inc., 69-72
General Electric Co., 398, 399; 791-794
Hauck Mfg. Co., 138-141
Littleford Bros., 169-172
Standard Steel Works, 205-208
White Mfg. Co., 230-233

Oil Meters
(see Meters, Oil)

Oils, Road
Barrett Div., Allied Chemical & Dye Corp., 269
Byerlyte Corp., 146, 147

One-Way Tiller
Tractor & Implement Div., Ford Motor Co., 209-212

Orifice Meters
Bailey Meter Co., 480
Fischer & Porter Co., 317-320

Ornamental Lighting Units
American Concrete Corp., 825
Elreco Corp., 828
General Electric Co., 398, 399; 791-794
Graybar Electric Co., Inc., 830
Ryther-Purdy Lumber Co., 832
Union Metal Mfg. Co., 818-820; 896
Westinghouse Electric Corp., 821-824

Outdoor Lighting
(see Street Lighting)

Paint Burners
Aeroil Products Co., Inc., 69-72

Paint, Traffic (see Traffic Paint)

Paints
Barrett Div., Allied Chemical & Dye Corp., 269
Inertol Co., Inc., 473
M. B. Corp., 246, 247; 560; 967
Prismo Safety Corp., 944, 947
Wald Industries, Inc., 948, 949

Paints, Acid & Chemical Resistant
Barrett Div., Allied Chemical & Dye Corp., 269
Inertol Co., Inc., 473

Paints, Metal Protection
Barrett Div., Allied Chemical & Dye Corp., 269
Byerlyte Corp., 146, 147
Philip Carey Mfg. Co., 92
Inertol Co., Inc., 473

Paints, Swimming Pool
Inertol Co., Inc., 473
Modern Swimming Pool Co., Inc., 1035
National Pool Equip. Co., 1036, 1037

Palmyra Stalks
Detroit Harvester Co., 157

Otto Gerdau Co., 122-125
Sargent-Sowell, Inc., 939-942

Park Benches (see Benches)

Park Developments
Wesley Bintz, 1031
Ingersoll - Kalamazoo Division, 497-500

Park Swings
American Playground Device Co., 1026-1029
General Playground Equipment, Inc., 1025
Trojan Playground Equipment Mfg. Co., 1030

Parking Barriers
Parking Corp. of America, 968, 969
Western Railroad Supply Co., 972-975

Parking Control
Karpark Corp., 853-856
Lyle Signs, Inc., 923-926
Magee-Hale Park-O-Meter Co., 857-860
Michaels Art Bronze Co., Inc., 862-864; 1060
Municipal Street Sign Co., Inc., 910
National Safety Engineers, 935-938
Parking Corp. of America, 968, 969
M. H. Rhodes, Inc., 865-868

Parking Lot Gates
Parking Corp. of America, 968, 969

Parking Meters
Dual Parking Meter Co., 869
Duncan Parking Meter Corp., 874
Karpark Corp., 853-856
Magee-Hale Park-O-Meter Co., 857-860
Michaels Art Bronze Co., Inc., 862-864; 1060
Parkit-Lockit Co., 872, 873
Red Ball Parking Meters, 876
M. H. Rhodes, Inc., 865-868

Parking Meter Coin Sorting, Counting, Packaging Equipment
Abbott Coin Counter Co., Inc., 875
Brandt Automatic Cashier Co., 861

Parking Restriction Signs
(see Traffic Signs)

Parking Systems, Automatic
Parking Corp. of America, 968, 969

Parkway Cables
General Electric Co., 398, 399; 791-794
Graybar Electric Co., Inc., 830

Partitions & Enclosures, Wire
Anchor Post Products, Inc., 1019
Colorado Fuel & Iron Corp., 1018
Cyclone Fence Dept., 148; 395; 1012, 1013
Page Fence Assn., 1021
Wickwire Spencer Steel Div., 1018

Patching Equipment
Barber-Greene Co., 73-76

Patching Materials for Streets
Barrett Div., Allied Chemical & Dye Corp., 269
Byerlyte Corp., 146, 147

Pavement Breakers
Allied Steel & Tractor Products, Inc., 77
Homelite Division, 263-267
Mid-Western Industries, Inc., 133-136
Schramm, Inc., 218-221

Pressure Regulators
Bailey Meter Co., 480
Fischer & Porter Co., 317-320
Vapor Recovery Systems Co., 471
Protection Devices for Crossing & Bridges
Western Railroad Supply Co., 972-975
Pumps, Air
Roots-Connersville Blower, 564
Pumps, Bilge
Chicago Pump Co., 523
Layne & Bowler, Inc., 344-347
Pumps, Boiler Feed
Allis-Chalmers Mfg. Co., 285-288
Chicago Pump Co., 523
De Laval Steam Turbine Co., 313-316
Fairbanks, Morse & Co., 530, 531
Pumps, Booster
Allis-Chalmers Mfg. Co., 285-288
De Laval Steam Turbine Co., 313-316
Fairbanks, Morse & Co., 530, 531
Layne & Bowler, Inc., 344-347
Pumps, Centrifugal
Allis-Chalmers Mfg. Co., 285-288
Chicago Pump Co., 523
De Laval Steam Turbine Co., 313-316
Fairbanks, Morse & Co., 530, 531
Homelite Division, 263-267
Jaeger Machine Co., 158-161
Layne & Bowler, Inc., 344-347
A. Y. McDonald Mfg. Co, 352-355
Marlow Pumps, 361-364
Roots-Connersville Blower, 564
Pumps, Chemical
Allis-Chalmers Mfg. Co., 285-288
Dorr-Oliver, Inc., 466-469
Fischer & Porter Co., 317-320
Layne & Bowler, Inc., 344-347
Pumps, Circulating
Allis-Chalmers Mfg. Co., 285-288
Chicago Pump Co., 523
De Laval Steam Turbine Co., 313-316
Fairbanks, Morse & Co., 530, 531
Layne & Bowler, Inc., 344-347
Pumps, Condensation, Drainage, House
Allis-Chalmers Mfg. Co., 285-288
Chicago Pump Co., 523
De Laval Steam Turbine Co., 313-316
Fairbanks, Morse & Co., 530, 531
Layne & Bowler, Inc., 344-347
Pumps, Contractors'
Fairbanks, Morse & Co., 530, 531
Homelite Division, 263-267
Marlow Pumps, 361-364
Pumps, Deep Well
Fairbanks, Morse & Co., 530, 531
Layne & Bowler, Inc., 344-347
Pumps, Diaphragm
Dorr-Oliver, Inc., 466-469
Fischer & Porter Co., 317-320
Hardinge Co., 556
Jaeger Machine Co., 158-161
Marlow Pumps, 361-364
Pumps, Fire
Allis-Chalmers Mfg. Co., 285-288
John Bean Division, 971; 1009
Chicago Pump Co., 523
De Laval Steam Turbine Co., 313-316
Fairbanks, Morse & Co., 530, 531
Homelite Division, 263-267
Jaeger Machine Co., 158-161
Layne & Bowler, 344-347
Marlow Pumps, 361-364
Pumps, Fuel Oil
De Laval Steam Turbine Co., 313-316
Layne & Bowler, Inc., 344-347
Pumps, Gasoline & Oil
Allis-Chalmers Mfg. Co., 285-288
De Laval Steam Turbine Co., 313-316
Fairbanks, Morse & Co., 530, 531
Homelite Division, 263-267
Layne & Bowler, Inc., 344-347
A. Y. McDonald Mfg. Co., 352-355
Marlow Pumps, 361-364
Pumps, Geared to Steam Turbines
Allis-Chalmers Mfg. Co., 285-288
De Laval Steam Turbine Co., 313-316
Layne & Bowler, Inc., 344-347
Pumps, High Pressure for Snow Plows, etc.
Wausau Iron Works, Inc., 261
Pumps, Irrigation
Allis-Chalmers Mfg. Co., 285-288
Homelite Division, 263-267

Marlow Pumps, 361-364
Pumps, Jetting
Marlow Pumps, 361-364
Pumps, Metering
Roots-Connersville Blower, 564
Pumps, Plunger
Marlow Pumps, 361-364
Pumps, Portable
Allis-Chalmers Mfg. Co., 285-288
Fairbanks, Morse & Co., 530, 531
Homelite Division, 263-267
Jaeger Machine Co., 158-161
Marlow Pumps, 361-364
Pumps, Rotary
Roots-Connersville Blower, 564
Pumps, Sand & Other Materials
Allis-Chalmers Mfg. Co., 285-288
Dorr-Oliver, Inc., 466-469
Pumps, Screw
Allis-Chalmers Mfg. Co., 285-288
Chicago Pump Co., 523
De Laval Steam Turbine Co., 313-316
Layne & Bowler, Inc., 344-347
Pumps, Sewage
Allis-Chalmers Mfg. Co., 285-288
John Bean Division, 971; 1009
Blackburn-Smith Mfg. Co., Inc., 496
Chicago Pump Co., 523
De Laval Steam Turbine Co., 313-316
Dorr-Oliver, Inc., 466-469
Fairbanks, Morse & Co., 530, 531
Jaeger Machine Co., 158-161
Marlow Pumps, 361-364
Pumps, Sludge
Allis-Chalmers Mfg. Co., 285-288
Chicago Pump Co., 523
Dorr-Oliver, Inc., 466-469
Jaeger Machine Co., 158-161
Marlow Pumps, 361-364
Pumps, Spray
John Bean Division, 971; 1009
Gravely Tractors, Inc., 1001
Pumps, Suction & Force
Jaeger Machine Co., 158-161
Pumps, Sump
Allis-Chalmers Mfg. Co., 285-288
John Bean Division, 971; 1009
Chicago Pump Co., 523
De Laval Steam Turbine Co., 313-316
Fairbanks, Morse & Co., 530, 531
Layne & Bowler, Inc., 344-347
Pumps, Swimming Pool
General Playground Equip. Co., 1025
Modern Swimming Pool Co., Inc., 1035
Pumps, Tar & Asphalt
Aeroil Products Co., Inc., 69-72
E. D. Etnyre & Co., 106-109
Hauck Mfg. Co., 138-141
Littleford Bros., 169-172
Rosco Mfg. Co., 197-200
Pumps, Turbine
Layne & Bowler, Inc., 344-347
Pumps, Vacuum
Allis-Chalmers Mfg. Co., 285-288
Chicago Pump Co., 523
Roots-Connersville Blower, 564
Punched-Card Accounting Machines
Remington Rand, Inc., 1051-1054
Underwood Corp., 1055-1058
Putting Green Mowers
(see Mowers)

Radio Communications Equipment
General Electric Co., 398, 399; 791-794
Industrial Radio Corp., 992
Westinghouse Electric Corp., 821-824
Radio Equipment for Police Use
(see Police Radio Equipment)
Rail Filler
Philip Carey Mfg. Co., 92
Railings, Highway & Bridge
(see Highway Guard)
Railing (Pipe or Ornamental)4
Clarksville Foundry & Machine Works, 373
Modern Swimming Pool Co., Inc., 1035
Railroad Crossing Pavement
Barrett Div., Allied Chemical & Dye Corp., 269
Philip Carey Mfg. Co., 92
Railway Equip. & Supplies
Western Railroad & Supply Co., 972-975
Rate Controllers
Fischer & Porter Co., 317-320
Sparling Meter Co., 447
Real Estate Assessment Equalization
J. M. Cleminshaw Co., 50, 51
Cole-Layer-Trumble Co., 52, 53
Rear-Mounted Scoop
Tractor & Implement Div., Ford Motor Co., 209-212
Recorders, Electrical
B & B Engineering Corp., 976, 977
Bailey Meter Co., 480
Fischer & Porter Co., 317-320
General Electric Co., 398, 399; 791-794
Permutit Co., 416, 417
Simplex Valve & Meter Co., 422, 423
Sparling Meter Co., 447
Wallace & Tiernan Inc., 378-381
Westinghouse Electric Corp., 821-824
Recorders, Pneumatic
Simplex Valve & Meter Co., 422, 423
Recorders, Pressure
Bailey Meter Co., 480
Fischer & Porter Co., 317-320
Recorders, Temperature
Bailey Meter Co., 480
Reflective Glass Beads
Cataphote Corp., 911-914
Flex-O-Lite Mfg. Corp., 915-918
Reflective Liquid for Painting or Spraying Hazards (Codit Brand)
Minnesota Mining & Mfg. Co., 927-930
Reflective Sign Materials
Cataphote Corp., 911-914
Flex-O-Lite Mfg. Corp., 915-918
Grote Mfg. Co., Inc., 919-922
M. B. Corp., 246, 247; 560; 967
Minnesota Mining & Mfg. Co., 927-930
Municipal Street Sign Co., Inc., 910
Prismo Safety Corp., 944-947
Wald Industries, Inc., 948, 949
Reflective Traffic Paints
Cataphote Corp., 911-914
Prismo Safety Corp., 944-947
Sargent-Sowell, Inc., 939-942
Reflector Buttons
Cataphote Corp., 911-914
Lyle Signs, Inc., 923-926
Municipal Street Sign Co., 910
Sargent-Sowell, Inc., 939-942
Reflector Signals & Signs
B & B Engineering Corp., 976, 977
Cataphote Corp., 911-914
Flex-O-Lite Mfg. Corp., 915-918
General Tire & Rubber Co., 950, 951
Grimm Stamp & Badge Co., 906-909
Grote Mfg. Co., Inc., 919-922
Lake Shore Markers, Inc., 952, 953
Lyle Signs, Inc., 923-926
Marbelite Co., Inc., 877
Minnesota Mining & Mfg. Co., 927-930
Miro-Flex Co., 931-934

Graybar Electric Co., Inc., 830
Marbelite Co., 877
Sargent-Sowell, Inc., 939-942
Westinghouse Electric Co., 821-824
Stops, Curb, Corporation & Gas
Haydenville Co., 434
Hays Mfg. Co., 436
A. Y. McDonald Mfg. Co., 352-355
Storage Batteries
B & B Engineering Corp., 976, 977
Electric Storage Battery Co., 987
Straight Edges, Aluminum, Steel
Cleveland Formgrader Co., 166, 167
Street Castings
(see Castings, Street & Sewer)
Street Cleaners' Carts
W. E. Grace Mfg. Co., 239
Sargent-Sowell, Inc., 939-942
Street Cleaning Apparatus
(see Street Sweepers, Street, Flushers, etc.)
Street Drags & Scrapers
(see Road Scrapers)
Street Flushers & Sprinklers
E. D. Etnyre & Co., 106-109
Heil Company, 488-491
Municipal Supply Co., 181-184
Rosco Mfg. Co., 197-200
Sicard Industries, Inc., 110-112; 566
Standard Steel Works, 205-208
Street Light Posts, Concrete
American Concrete Corp., 825
General Electric Co., 398, 399; 791-794
Graybar Electric Co., Inc., 830
Street Light Posts, Metal
Elreco Corp., 828
General Electric Co., 398, 399; 791-794
Graybar Electric Co., Inc., 830
Hubbard & Co., 799-802
Millerbernd Mfg. Co., 810-813
Pfaff & Kendall, 826, 827
Revere Electric Mfg. Co., 814-817
Union Metal Mfg. Co., 818-820; 896
Street Light Posts, Wood Ornamental
Ryther-Purdy Lumber Co., 832
Street Lighting Cable
Anaconda Wire & Cable Co., 849
Collyer Insulated Wire Co., 851
General Electric Co., 398, 399; 791-794
Graybar Electric Co., Inc., 830
Street Lighting Brackets & Mast Arms
Kerrigan Iron Works, Inc., 258; 807-809
Line Material Co., 803-806
Street Lighting Current Regulators
General Electric Co., 398, 399; 791-794
Moloney Electric Co., 852
Street Lighting Engineering Service
General Electric Co., 398, 399; 791-794
Holophane Co., Inc., 795-798
Line Material Co., 803-806
Westinghouse Electric Corp., 821-824
Street Lighting Globes
General Electric Co., 398, 399; 791-794
Graybar Electric Co., Inc., 830
Line Material Co., 803-806
Westinghouse Electric Corp., 821-824
Wheeler Reflector Co., 836
Street Lighting Lamps
Line Material Co., 803-806
Westinghouse Electric Corp., 821-824
Street Lighting Luminaires
Line Material Co., 803-806
Revere Electric Mfg. Co., 814-817
Westinghouse Electric Corp., 821-824
Wheeler Reflector Co., 836
Street Lighting Refractors
General Electric Co., 398, 399; 791-794
Holophane Co., Inc., 795-798
Line Material Co., 803-806
Westinghouse Electric Corp., 821-824
Street Lighting Standards
American Concrete Corp., 825
Elreco Corp., 828
Hubbard & Co., 799-802
Millerbernd Mfg. Co., 810-813
Revere Electric Mfg. Co., 814-817
Ryther-Purdy Lumber Co., 832
Smith-Blair, Inc., 374-377
Street Lighting Equipment Corp., 834
Union Metal Mfg. Co., 818-820; 896
Street Lighting Systems
General Electric Co., 398, 399; 791-794
Graybar Electric Co., Inc., 830
Line Material Co., 803-806
Westinghouse Electric Corp., 821-824
Street Lighting Transformers
Line Material Co., 803-806
Revere Electric Mfg. Co., 814-817
Street Lighting Units
General Electric Co., 398, 399; 791-794
Line Material Co., 803-806
Revere Electric Mfg. Co., 814-817
Westinghouse Electric Corp., 821-824
Street Marking, Reflective Materials
Flex-O-Lite Mfg. Corp., 915-918
J. W. Neff Laboratories, Inc., 970
Street Marking Paint
(see Traffic Paint)
Street Measuring
Rolatape, Inc., 260
Sargent-Sowell, Inc., 939-942
Street Resurfacing
A. Reed Wilson Co., 262
Street Signs
(see Signs, Street, Road, Safety)
Street Sign Brackets
Cataphote Corp., 911-914
Grimm Stamp & Badge Co., 906-909
Lake Shore Markers, Inc., 952, 953
Lyle Signs, Inc., 923-926
Municipal Street Sign Co., Inc., 910
National Safety Engineers, 935-938
Sargent-Sowell, Inc., 939-942
Street Sign Frames
Municipal Street Sign Co., Inc., 910
Street Sprinklers
(see Street Flushers)
Street and Road Sweepers
Austin-Western Co., 78-81
Detroit Harvester Co., 157
Ernest Holmes Co., 142-145
Little Giant Products, Inc., 177-180
M. B. Corp., 246, 247; 560; 967
Mobil-Sweeper, 255
Municipal Supply Co., 181-184
Schramm, Inc., 218-221
Shawnee Mfg. Co., Inc., 222-225
G. H. Tennant Co., 130-132; 957
Wayne Mfg. Co., 226-229
Street & Road Sweeping Brooms
Detroit Harvester Co., 157
W. E. Grace Mfg. Co., 239
Gravely Tractors, Inc., 1001
Kennedy's Van Brush Mfg. Co., 173-176
Littleford Bros., 169-172
Little Giant Products, Inc., 177-180
Mid-Western Industries, Inc., 133-136
Municipal Supply Co., 181-184
Rosco Mfg. Co., 197-200
Shawnee Mfg. Co., Inc., 222-225
Standard Steel Works, 205-208
Street Sweeper Fibre (see Fibre)
Street Sweepers
Kennedy's Van Brush Mfg. Co., 173-176
Street Sweepers, Pick-Up
Ernest Holmes Co., 142-145
Mobile Sweeper Div., 255
Municipal Supply Co., 181-184
Wayne Mfg. Co., 226-229
Work Bulls Div., Massey-Harris-Ferguson, 213-216
Stripers for Street & Highway Marking
Kelly-Creswell Co., 963-966
Striping, Reflective for Streets & Highways
Minnesota Mining & Mfg. Co., 927-930
Sargent-Sowell, Inc., 939-942
Subgraders, Precision
Blaw-Knox Co., 82-85
Surge Tanks
Koven Fabricators, Inc., 440
Sulkies, Riding
Gravely Tractors. Inc., 1001
Power Implement Division, 1004
Sulphate of Alumina
Olin Mathieson Chemical Corp., 410, 411; 1038, 1039
Surface Heaters for Repairing Street Pavements
(see Asphalt Surface Heaters)
Surge Tanks
Hammond Iron Works, 432
Surveying Instruments (Levels, Transits, Theodolites & Accessories)
Wild-Heerbrugg Instruments, Inc., 56
Suspended Arches & Walls
M. H. Detrick Co., 550
Sweepers, Curb & Gutter
G. H. Tennant Co., 130-132; 957
Work Bulls Div., Massey-Harris-Ferguson, 213-216
Sweepers, Road & Street
Detroit Harvester Co., 157
Little Giant Products Co., 177-180
G. H. Tennant Co., 130-132; 957
Work Bulls Div., Massey-Harris-Ferguson, 213-216
Swimming Pool Cleaners
American Playground Device Co., 1026-1029
Cardinal Pools, Inc., 1033
General Playground Equip. Co., 1025
Modern Swimming Pool Co., Inc., 1038
National Pool Equip. Co., 1036, 1037
Roberts Filter Mfg. Co., 1042
Swimquip, Inc., 1043
Swimming Pool Construction & Maintenance Equipment
Air Placement Equipment Co., 68
Swimming Pool Covers
Modern Swimming Pool Co., Inc., 1035
National Pool Equip. Co., 1036, 1037
Swimming Pool Design & Consultation
Wesley Bintz, 1031
Cardinal Pools, Inc., 1033
Modern Swimming Pool Co., Inc., 1035
Pressure Concrete Co., 420-421
Swimming Pool Enclosures, Glass
Lord & Burnham Corp, 559
Swimming Pool Equipment
Cardinal Pools, Inc., 1033
Fischer & Porter Co., 317-320
General Filter Co., 400, 401
General Playground Equipment Inc., 1025
Graver Water Conditioning Co., 402, 403
Modern Swimming Pool Co., Inc., 1035
National Pool Equip. Co, 1036, 1037
Permutit Co., 416, 417
Swimquip, Inc., 1043
Swimming Pool Filters & Sterilization
Bowser, Inc., 1032
Cardinal Pools, Inc., 1033
Columbia - Southern Chemical Corp., 382
Fischer & Porter Co., 317-320
General Filter Co., 400, 401
Graver Water Conditioning Co., 402, 403
Layne & Bowler, Inc., 344-347
Olin Mathieson Chemical Corp., 410, 411; 1038, 1039
Modern Swimming Pool Co., Inc., 1035
National Pool Equip. Co., 1036, 1037
Permutit Co., 416, 417
Roberts Filter Mfg. Co., 1042
Swimquip, Inc., 1043
Wallace & Tiernan Inc., 378-381
Swimming Pool Filtration
(see Filtration Plant Equipment)
Swimming Pool Lighting
Cardinal Pools, Inc., 1033
Crouse-Hinds Co., 878-881
General Electric Co., 398, 399; 791-794
Modern Swimming Pool Co., Inc., 1035
National Pool Equip. Co., 1036, 1037
Westinghouse Electric Corp., 821-824

General Electric Co.. 398, 399; 791-794
Graybar Electric Co., Inc., 830
Marbelite Co., Inc., 877
Sargent-Sowell, Inc., 939-942
Southern Signals, Inc., 889-894
Traffic Signal Poles
Crouse-Hinds Co., 878-881
Elreco Corp., 828
Marbelite Co., Inc., 877
Southern Signals, Inc., 889-894
Union Metal Mfg. Co., 818-820; 896
Traffic Signal Pulsators
Southern Signals, Inc., 889-894
Traffic Signal Reflectors
Cataphote Corp., 911-914
Crouse-Hinds Co., 878-881
Graybar Electric Co., Inc., 830
Grote Mfg. Co., Inc., 919-922
Southern Signals, Inc., 889-894
Traffic Signal Standards
American Concrete Corp., 825
Crouse-Hinds Co., 878-881
Eagle Signal Corp., 882-884
Elreco Corp., 828
General Electric Co., 398, 399; 791-794
Graybar Electric Co., Inc., 830
Hubbard & Co., 799-802
Marbelite Co., Inc., 877
Pfaff & Kendall, 826, 827
Southern Signals, Inc., 889-894
Traffic & Street Sign Co., 954, 955
Union Metal Mfg. Co., 818-820; 896
Traffic Signal Systems
Automatic Signal Div., 837-840
Electronic Protection, Inc., 885-888
Southern Signals, Inc., 889-894
Traffic Signs & Signals
B & B Engineering Corp., 976, 977
Cataphote Corp., 911-914
Crouse-Hinds Co., 878-881
Eagle Signal Corp., 882-884
Eastern Metal of Elmira, Inc., 901-904
Electronic Protection, Inc., 885-888
Flex-O-Lite Mfg. Corp., 915-918
General Electric Co., 398, 399; 791-794
General Tire & Rubber Co., 950, 951
Graybar Electric Co., Inc., 830
Grimm Stamp & Badge Co., 906-909
Grote Mfg. Co., Inc., 919-922
Lyle Signs, Inc., 923-926
Marbelite Co., 877
Miro-Flex Co., 931-934
Municipal Street Sign Co., Inc., 910
National Safety Engineers, 935-938
Portable Traffic Signals, Inc., 897-900
Prismo Safety Corp., 944-947
Radiator Specialty Co., 959-962
Sargent-Sowell, Inc., 939-942
Smith-Blair, Inc., 374-377
Southern Signals, Inc., 889-894
Time-O-Matic, Inc., 895
Traffic & Street Sign Co., 954, 955
Wald Industries, Inc., 948, 949
Trailers
Aeroil Products Co., Inc., 69-72
John Deere Industrial Division, 101-104
Hyde Corp., 492-495
Littleford Bros., 169-172
M. B. Corp., 246, 247; 560; 967
Trailgraders
Cleveland Formgrader Co., 166, 167
Traps, Sediment & Drip
Vapor Recovery Systems Co., 471
Transformers
(see Electric Transformers)
Transformers, Distribution
Line Material Co., 803-806
Transmissions, Winch & Digger Drive
Tel-E-Lect Products, Inc., 835
Trash Cans (see Cans)
Trash Baskets
Cyclone Fence Dept., 148; 395; 1012, 1013
Treads, Aluminum
Dravo Corp., 168; 551
Treads, Safety
Dravo Corp., 168; 551
Servicised Products Corp., 201-204
Treads, Stairway
Irving Subway Grating Co., Inc., 257
Tree Guards
Cyclone Fence Dept., 148; 395; 1012, 1013
Irving Subway Grating Co., Inc., 257
Tree Sprayers
John Bean Division, 971; 1009
Gravely Tractors, Inc., 1001
Trench Diggers
Arps Corp., 64-67
Badger Machine Co., 87-90
Barber-Greene Co., 73-76
Gar Wood Industries, Inc., 242, 243; 532, 533
Mid-Western Industries, Inc., 133-136
Pippin Construction Equipment, Inc., 248, 249
Schramm, Inc., 218-221
Shawnee Mfg. Co., Inc., 222-225
Sherman Products, Inc., 172 ABCD
Work Bulls Div., Massey-Harris-Ferguson, 213-216
Trench Rollers
Blaw-Knox Co., 82-85
Trowelers, Concrete
White Mfg. Co., 230-233
Truck Bodies
Blaw-Knox Co., 82-85
Gar Wood Industries, Inc., 242, 243; 532, 533
Hyde Corp., 492-495
Hydro-E-Z Pack Div., 481-484
Ingersoll - Kalamazoo Division, 497-500
Truck Flares (see Flares)
Truck Mixers & Agitators
Blaw-Knox Co., 82-85
Truck Sweepers
Little Giant Products Co., 177-180
Truck Tractors (see Tractors)
Trucks & Carts, Garbage
(see Garbage Trucks & Carts)
Trucks, Motor (see Motor Trucks)
Tubes & Tubing (Copper & Brass)
American Brass Co., 538, 539
Revere Copper & Brass, Inc., 445
Turbine Sewer Cleaners
Ace Pipe Cleaning, Inc., 524, 525
American Pipe Cleaning Co., 453-456
National Power Rodding Corp., 540, 541
Turbines, Hydraulic
Allis-Chalmers Mfg. Co., 285-288
De Laval Steam Turbine Co., 313-316
Turbines, Steam
Allis-Chalmers Mfg. Co., 285-288
De Laval Steam Turbine Co., 313-316
General Electric Co., 398, 399; 791-794
Westinghouse Electric Corp., 821-824
Turntables, Truck
Blaw-Knox Co., 82-85
Typewriters
Remington Rand, Inc., 1051-1054
Underwood Corp., 1055-1058
Underbody Grader & Ice Planer
Wausau Iron Works, Inc., 261
Uniform Fabrics
Franklin Worsted Co., 989
Metcalf Brothers & Co., Inc., 990
Unloaders, Hopper Car
Barber-Greene Co., 73-76
Utility Blades
Arps Corp., 64-67
Utility Bodies
J. H. Holan Corp., 831
Vacuum Cleaners, Swimming Pool
Modern Swimming Pool Co., Inc., 1035
National Pool Equip. Co., 1036, 1037
Swimquip, Inc., 1043
Valve Boxes & Housings
Alabama Pipe Co., 277-280
Buffalo Pipe & Foundry Co., 281-284
Chapman Valve Mfg. Co., 300-303
Clarksville Foundry & Machine Works, 373
The Kennedy Valve Mfg. Co., 337-340
Ludlow Valve Mfg. Co., Inc., 348-351
M & H Valve & Fittings, 357-360
R. D. Wood Co., 387-390
Valve Control
Chapman Valve Mfg. Co., 300-303
Fischer & Porter Co., 317-320
Golden-Anderson Valve Specialty Co., 437
The Kennedy Valve Mfg. Co., 337-340
Ludlow Valve Mfg. Co., Inc., 348-351
Permutit Co., 416, 417
Philadelphia Gear Works, 444
Simplex Valve & Meter Co., 422, 423
Valve Operating Mechanisms, Electric
Chapman Valve Mfg. Co., 300-303
Philadelphia Gear Works, 444
Valve Operating Mechanisms, Portable
Philadelphia Gear Works, 444
Valve Operating Mechanisms, Truck Mounted
Philadelphia Gear Works, 444
Valves, Air
DeZurik Shower Co., 1115
Fischer & Porter Co., 317-320
Golden-Anderson Valve Specialty Co., 437
Ludlow Valve Mfg. Co., Inc., 348-351
Simplex Valve & Meter Co., 422, 423
Valves, Altitude
Golden-Anderson Valve Specialty Co., 437
Valves, Backpressure Check
Vapor Recovery Systems Co., 471
Valves, Backwater, Sewer, Water Mixing
Kennedy Valve Mfg. Co., 337-340
Valves, Ball Type, Bronze, Stainless, Brass, Barstock
Rockwood Sprinkler Co., 984, 985
Valves, Check
Chapman Valve Mfg. Co., 300-303
Eddy Valve Co., 272, 273
Golden-Anderson Valve Specialty Co., 437
Iowa Valve Co., 274, 275
Kennedy Valve Mfg. Co., 337-340
Ludlow Valve Mfg. Co., Inc., 348-351
M & H Valve & Fittings Co., 357-360
Traverse City Iron Works, 450
Valves, Compounding
Neptune Meter Co., 369-372
Valves, Cone
Chapman Valve Mfg. Co., 300-303
Golden-Anderson Valve Specialty Co., 437
Valves, Electrically Operated
Chapman Valve Mfg. Co., 300-303
DeZurik Shower Co., 1115
Eddy Valve Co., 272, 273
General Electric Co., 398, 399; 791-794
Golden-Anderson Valve Specialty Co., 437
Iowa Valve Co., 274, 275
Kennedy Valve Mfg. Co., 337-340
Ludlow Valve Mfg. Co., Inc., 348-351
M & H Valve & Fittings Co., 357-360
Permutit Co., 416, 417
Philadelphia Gear Works, 444
Valves, Engine Stop
Golden-Anderson Valve Specialty Co., 437
Valves, Flap
Chapman Valve Mfg. Co., 300-303
Eddy Valve Co., 272, 273
Filer & Stowell Co., 552
Iowa Valve Co., 274, 275
Ludlow Valve Mfg. Co., Inc., 348-351
M & H Valve & Fittings Co., 357-360
Neenah Foundry Co., 259
Traverse City Iron Works, 450
Valves, Float
Golden-Anderson Valve Specialty Co., 437
Ludlow Valve Mfg. Co., Inc., 348-351
Valves, Gate & Indicator Posts
Chapman Valve Mfg. Co., 300-303
DeZurik Shower Co., 1115
Eddy Valve Co., 272, 273
Filer & Stowell Co., 552

THESE POST CARDS ARE FOR YOUR CANVENIENCE IN SECURING CATALOGS OR QUOTATIONS

I should like to receive catalogs and price lists on the following products:

....

....

....

....

....

....

Name ....

Title ....

....

City .... **State** ....

57

I should like to receive catalogs and price lists on the following products:

....

....

....

....

....

....

Name ....

Title ....

....

City .... **State** ....

57

I should like to receive catalogs and price lists as listed below:

Name of manufacturer ....

....

.... **Page of ad** .....

Name of manufacturer ....

....

.... **Page of ad** .....

I should also like further information on:

....

....

Name ....

Title ....

....

City .... **State** ....

57

I should like to receive catalogs and price lists as listed below:

Name of manufacturer ....

....

.... **Page of ad** .....

Name of manufacturer ....

....

.... **Page of ad** .....

I should also like further information on:

....

....

Name ....

Title ....

....

City .... **State** ....

57

Postage Will be Paid by Addressee

No Postage Stamp Necessary If mailed in the United States

BUSINESS REPLY CARD

FIRST CLASS PERMIT No. 281, Sec. 34.9, P. L. & R., NEW YORK, N. Y.

The Municipal Index,

470 Fourth Avenue,

New York 16, N Y.

Postage Will be Pa[illegible] by Addresse[illegible]

No Postage Stamp Necessary If mailed in the United States

BUSINESS REPLY CARD

FIRST CLASS PERMIT No. 281, Sec. 34.9, P. L. & R., NEW YORK, N. Y.

The Municipal Index,

470 Fourth Avenue,

New York 16, N. Y.

Postage Will be Paid by Addressee

No Postage Stamp Necessary If mailed in the United States

BUSINESS REPLY CARD

FIRST CLASS PERMIT No. 281, Sec. 34.9, P. L. & R., NEW YORK, N. Y.

The Municipal Index,

470 Fourth Avenue,

New York 16, N. Y.

Postage Will be Paid by Addressee

No Postage Stamp Necessary If mailed in the United States

BUSINESS REPLY CARD

FIRST CLASS PERMIT No. 281, Sec. 34.9, P. L. & R., NEW YORK, N. Y.

The Municipal Index,

470 Fourth Avenue,

New York 16, N. Y.

PLEASE NOTE THAT NO POSTAGE STAMPS ARE NECESSARY FOR MAILING

THE MUNICIPAL INDEX DIRECTORY OF CONSULTANTS

These cards are arranged by states and cities—for alphabetical listing see index to advertisers starting on page 3

CHAS. W. COLE & SON

Engineers — Architects

Municipal — Industrial — Commercial
Water Supply—Sewerage—
Sewage Treatment

220 W. LaSalle St. So. Bend, Ind.
Phone 4-0127

PATZIG TESTING LABORATORIES

Inspection Service

Chemical and Physical Testing of Paving and Building Materials, Metals, Fuel, Oils, Water, Etc.

2215 Ingersoll Ave. Des Moines, Ia.

DOANE APPRAISAL SERVICE

Over 35 Years of Appraisal Service

Property Tax Equalization Appraisals — Municipal County Personal Prop.

328 Main, P. O. Box 379
Ames, Iowa

STANLEY ENGINEERING CO.

Consulting Engineers

327 S. La Salle St. Chicago 4, Ill. — Hershey Bldg. Muscatine, Ia.

HOWARD R. GREEN CO.

40th YEAR

Consulting Engineers

Municipal and Industrial Water Supply and Treatment; Sewerage and Disposal
Airports, Paving, Bridges, Industrial Structures

Bever Building Cedar Rapids, Iowa

Servis, Van Doren & Hazard

Engineers

Structures, Buildings, Foundations, Sewerage, Water Supply, Streets, Highways, Airports, Flood Control, Drainage, Power Plants, Electrical Distribution.

2910 Topeka Boulevard, Topeka 4, Kansas
Phone 4-6603

BROWN ENGINEERING COMPANY

Consulting Engineers

K. P. Building Des Moines 9, Iowa

HOWARD K. BELL

Consulting Engineers

G. S. Bell C. G. Gaither J. K. Latham
J. W. Finney, Jr., Assoc.

Water Works Sewage Treatment
Water Purification Sewerage
Swimming Pools Refuse Disposal
Industrial Wastes

533 S. Limestone St. Lexington, Ky.

HAVENS AND EMERSON

W. L. Havens
J. W. Avery
F. S. Palocsay

A. A. Burger
H. H. Moseley
E. S. Ordway

F. C. Tolles, *Consultant*

Water, Sewerage, Garbage, Industrial Wastes, Valuations—Laboratories

Leader Bldg.
Cleveland 14, Ohio

Woolworth Bldg.
New York 7, N. Y.

ALDEN E. STILSON & ASSOCIATES, LIMITED

Consulting Engineers

Water Supply — Sewerage — Waste Disposal — Bridges — Highways — Studies — Surveys — Industrial Buildings — Reports

245 North High Street, Columbus, Ohio

ARTHUR E. ROWE & ASSOCIATES

Municipal Buildings, Swimming Pools, Parking Facilities, Incinerators, Stadia, etc.

3125 Prospect Ave., Cleveland 15, Ohio

UHLMANN ASSOCIATES

J. M. Brundage
Carl E. Kuck

H. E. Bonhan
Nye Grant

Consulting Engineers

Sewage and Industrial Waste Treatment
Water Supply and Purification

4954 N. High St. Columbus 14, Ohio

BURGESS & NIPLE

Civil and Sanitary Engineers

Philip Burgess
Chester A. Niple
Ben K. Bare
Clayton C. Bull

Raymond Fuller
B. F. Hatch
Tahlman Krumm
R. E. Peters

Robert Wolfe

Design—Construction—Reports—
Planning—Valuations—Rates—
Supervision—Laboratory

WATER & SEWAGE CONSULTANTS

2015 West Fifth Ave. Columbus 12, Ohio

W. L. BARROWS & ASSOCIATES

Consulting Engineers

Mechanical — Civil — Electrical —
Hydraulic
Industrial & Municipal
Betterment & Improvements

1169 Reibold Bldg., Dayton 2, O.

THE JENNINGS-LAWRENCE CO.

Civil & Municipal Engineers

Water Supply—Treatment—Distribution
Sewerage—Sewage Treatment—Paving
Drainage—Dams—Surveys—Mapping
Reports—Plans—Supervision

1392 King Ave. Columbus 12, Ohio

COLE, LAYER, TRUMBLE COMPANY

Revaluations—Appraisals

MUNICIPAL and COUNTY
TAX REVALUATIONS

Descriptive Material Upon Request

11 West Monument Ave.,
Dayton 2, Ohio

Gannett Fleming Corddry and Carpenter, Inc.

Engineers

Dams, Water Works, Sewage, Industrial Wastes & Garbage Disposal, Highways, Bridges & Airports, Traffic & Parking. Appraisals, Investigations and Reports

HARRISBURG, PA.

Branch Offices:
Pittsburgh, Pa. **Philadelphia, Pa.**
Daytona Beach, Fla.

ALBRIGHT & FRIEL, INC.

Consulting Engineers

Water, Sewage and Industrial Waste Problems, Airfields, Refuse Incinerators & Power Plants. Industrial Building. City Planning, Laboratory, Reports, Valuations.

3 Penn Center Plaza Philadelphia 2

GLACE AND GLACE

Consulting Sanitary Engineers

Sewerage, Sewage and Industrial Wastes Treatment
Design, Construction and Supervision of Operation
Laboratory Service

Front at Boas St. Harrisburg, Pa.

C. C. COLLINGS & CO., Inc.

Financial Consultants

Specialists in Direct Obligation, Revenue & Municipal Authority Financing

Fidelity-Philadelphia Trust Bldg.
Philadephia (9), Penna.

HILL AND HILL

Engineers

Sewage and Waste Disposal, Water Supply and Filtration, Dams, Reservoirs, Tunnels, Airports and Topographic Survey

Home Office:
8 Gibson St. **North East, Pa.**

FRIDY-GAUKER-TRUSCOTT & FRIDY

Architects & Engineers

Water Supply & Treatment, Sewers & Waste Disposal, Incineration, Roads, Airports, Power & Lighting, Schools, Private & Municipal Buildings.

REPORTS, PLANS, SUPERVISION

1321 Arch St., Philadelphia 7, Pa.

AERO SERVICE CORPORATION

Oldest Flying Corporation in the World
Founded 1919

EXPERIENCE COUNTS: Dependable Photo Maps, Topographic Maps, Tax Maps.

HEADQUARTERS: 210 E. Courtland St., PHILADELPHIA 20. **OFFICES:** 1401 S. Detroit St., TULSA; 120 N. Fourth Ave., DULUTH; 34 Richard St., SALT LAKE CITY 10; 68 Post St., SAN FRANCISCO

GEORGE A. GIESEKE

Consulting Engineers

Municipal Engineering Problems
Surveying—Housing Development
Water Supply—Industrial Wastes
Sewerage—Refuse Incineration
Design—Supervision of Construction

3705 N. Broad St. **Philadelphia 40, Pa.**

The Kuljian Corporation

engineers • consultants
construction supervision

Designs • Surveys • Planning

POWER PLANTS, AIRPORTS and AIRPORT FACILITIES, HIGHWAYS, EXPRESSWAYS, WATER and SEWAGE WORKS, FLOOD CONTROL, IRRIGATION, INDUSTRIAL PLANTS

1200 North Broad Street, Philadelphia 21, Pa.

MORRIS KNOWLES, INC.

Engineers

Water Supply and Purification, Sewerage and Sewage Disposal Valuations, Laboratory, City Planning.

1312 Park Bldg. Pittsburgh 22, Pa.

AMERICAN AIR SURVEYS, INC.

Tax Maps—Aerial Photos & Mosaics
Topographic Maps—Planimetric Maps—Plan & Profile

907 Penn Ave., Pittsburgh 22, Pa.
Phone Express 1-3969

BROCHURE
ON REQUEST

GILBERT ASSOCIATES, INC.

Engineers and Consultants

Water Supply and Purification
Sewage, Industrial Waste, Chemical Laboratory

NEW YORK — READING, PA. — WASHINGTON

THE CHESTER ENGINEERS

**Water Supply and Purification
Sewage and Industrial Waste Treatment—Power Plant—Incineration—Gas Systems
Valuations—Rates—Management
Laboratory—City Planning**

601 Sulsmon St., Pittsburgh 12, Pa.

MICHAEL BAKER, JR., INC.

The Baker Engineers

Civil Engineers—Planners—Surveyors—Municipal Engineers—Airport Design—Sewage Disposal Systems—Water Works Design and Operation—Consulting Services—Surveys and Maps

Home Office—Rochester, Pa.
Branch Office—Jackson, Miss.

AIR POLLUTION CONSULTANTS

Community Surveys

Dust—Fly Ash—Smoke—Fumes—Odors

HEMEON ASSOCIATES

121 Meyran Ave., Pittsburgh 13, Pa.

DAMON & FOSTER

Consulting Civil Engineers and Surveyors

Water Supply, Sewerage, Sewage Disposal, Surveys, Land Subdivision, City and Town Planning, Reports, Design, Supervision

Sharon Hill Pennsylvania

JACK AMMANN

AERIAL MAPS—Indispensable aids to cities, counties, states and consulting engineers.

PHOTOGRAMMERIC ENGINEERS, INC.
Broadway at Tenth San Antonio 5, Texas

BRANCH OFFICES:

Manhasset, N. Y.— 200 Plandome Rd.
Atlanta, Ga.— 685 W. Peachtree St., N.E.
Houston, Tex— 1354 Chantilly St.
Chicago, Ill.— 5144 North Avers St.
Dener, Colo.—995 Flower St.
Seattle (Mercer I.), Wash.— 4035 85th Ave. S.E.
Kingsburg, Calif.— 2490 18th Ave.
Tripoli, Libya and Perth, Australia, Nueva Rosita, Coahuila, Mexico

WHIPP and HARRISON

Consulting Engineers and Land Surveyors

Bridges, Buildings, Sub-Divisions Boundary Survey, Quantity Surveying, Construction Surveying

3214 W. Broadway, Hopewell, Va.
Telephone 2019

Air Survey Corporation

Photogrammetric Engineering

Precise Topographic and Planimetric Maps
Tax Maps and Atlas Sheets
Controlled Photo Maps
Route and Location Surveys
Field Surveys
Aerial Photography

1101 LEE HIGHWAY, ARLINGTON 9, VA.

WILEY & WILSON

Consulting Engineers

Municipal Planning, Water Supply, Sewerage, Sewage and Waste Treatment, Incinerators, Streets and Pavements, Airports, Light and Power Plants. Reports-Plans-Supervision.

620 Court St., Lynchburg, Va.
711 West Main St., Richmond 20, Va.

L. B. GRIFFITH

Consulting Engineer

Research, Reports and Designs on Sewage and Industrial Waste Treatment

22 S. Edison St. Arlington 4, Va.

Lublin, McGaughy & Assoc.

Architects and Consulting Engineers

Water supply, sewage disposal, airports, streets, improvements, municipal planning, buildings, recreational facilities, reports and appraisals.

220 W. Freemason St., Norfolk 10, Va.
1001 Connecticut Ave., Washington, D. C.

OLIVER COMSTOCK

Consultant, Organization and Procedures
Experienced in City Management and Business Management

Surveys and Reports at Local, State and Federal Levels

1117 Princess Anne Lane
Falls Church, Virginia

Gellert, Griffin, Williams & Associates

Consulting Engineers

N. Henry Gellert, *executive partner*
DeWitt C. Griffin, *exec. sec'y partner*
Wayne C. Harrigan, *partner*
Paul A. Williams *partner*

Lyon Building • Seattle 4, Wash.
MAin 1080

THE J. M. CLEMINSHAW CO.

1601 Brookpark Road
Cleveland 9, Ohio

Standard Municipal and County Practice requires the EQUITABLE distribution of local governmental costs according to the EQUITABLE value of taxable property. This is the duty of the assessor. The assessor cannot perform this duty without property and valuation facts. It is manifestly impossible for an assessor, in the usual time allowed and with the usual annual budgeted funds, to measure, describe, price and record all taxable property and at the same time perform all other duties of office. This is obviously a job for the expert disinterested appraiser specializing in this class of service.

The J. M. Cleminshaw Co. has devoted over thirty-four years to helping the assessor achieve tax equalization of real, personal and public utility properties, as expertly and fairly as humanly possible. The experience of over one hundred-fifty appraisers in the revaluation of two hundred ninety towns, cities and counties in twenty-six states is available to you at a cost that is extremely low in comparison with the benefits received.

Regional Managers or Partners are readily reached in New England, New Jersey, Ohio and Iowa. Our brochure and descriptive literature is available on request.

Your inquiry is cordially invited.

COLE · LAYER · TRUMBLE COMPANY

Branch Offices

207 Investment Bldg., Pittsburgh 22, Pennsylvania
329 Coddington Bldg. Charlotte, North Carolina
84 Peachtree Street, N. W., Atlanta 3, Georgia
415 Congress St., Portland 3, Maine
172 Clinton Ave., New Rochelle, New York

Revaluation Programs now in progress conducted by the Cole·Layer·Trumble Company

Franklin County, (Columbus) Ohio
Montgomery County, (Dayton) Ohio
Pickaway County, (Circleville) Ohio
Mercer County, (Celina) Ohio
Hardin County, (Kenton) Ohio
Fairfield County, Lancaster) Ohio
Delaware County, (Delaware) Ohio
Preble County, (Eaton) Ohio
Butler County, (Hamilton) Ohio
Beaver County, (Beaver) Pennsylvania
Lycoming County, (Williamsport) Pennsylvania
Blair County, (Hollidaysburg) Pennsylvania
Cambria County, (Ebensburg) Pennsylvania
Schuylkill County, (Pottsville) Pennsylvania
City of Kalamazoo, Michigan
City of Battle Creek, Michigan
City of Presque Isle, Maine
Town of Skowhegan, Maine
Town of Darien, Connecticut
Town of Smithfield, Rhode Island
Town of Natick, Massachusetts
Township of Livingston, New Jersey

Further information concerning our service will be sent upon request

COLE · LAYER · TRUMBLE COMPANY

How to speed engineering plans and development in your city

CITY GROWTH CALLS FOR NEW PROJECTS like water mains, sanitary sewers, drainage systems. AERO maps can speed planning on these and many important projects.

RECONNAISSANCE PHOTOS from speeding AERO planes aid planning for industrial sites, housing, location of new streets, by-passes, parks, playgrounds.

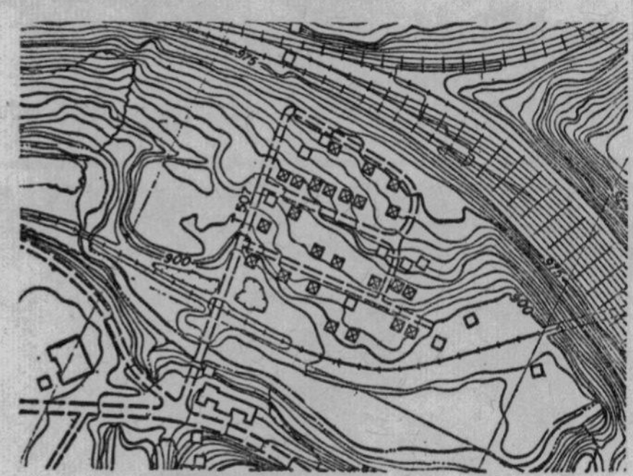

AERO TOPOGRAPHIC MAPS at 5 ft. contour interval provide precise, detailed data for engineering planning . . . help advance construction starting dates.

CITIES OF ALL SIZES throughout the U. S. have been mapped by AERO, pioneer and leader in aerial surveys.

Save time, money and manpower. AERO's trained pilots, field surveymen and photogrammetrists do the whole mapping job — leave your own busy staff free for other work. Get the facts on economical, up-to-date maps for your city. And ask about AERO tax mapping, now!

AERO SERVICE CORPORATION

Philadelphia 20, Pa.

Oldest Flying Corporation in the World

PRECISE AERIAL MOSAICS • TOPOGRAPHIC MAPS • PLANIMETRIC MAPS • RELIEF MODELS

WILD® HEERBRUGG

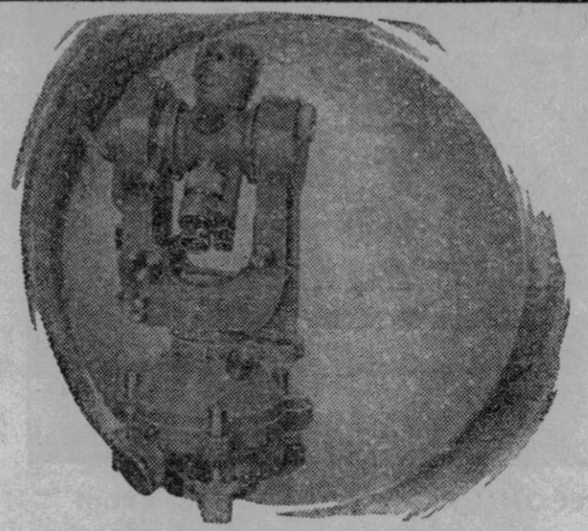

WILD T-2 UNIVERSAL THEODOLITE

From any point of view . . . here is the WILD instrument for precision, speed, convenience, versatility and ease of operation!

- Reading on both circles direct to 1 second
- Rapid optical plummet centering
- Large fatigue-free field of view
- Complete range of accessories

WILD T-3 PRECISION THEODOLITE

A WILD instrument designed for highest accuracy, time-saving conveniences, and a remarkable work potential.

The Wild T-3 Precision Theodolite is the supreme instrument in its class . . . for accuracy . . . versatility . . . and for its proved reliability in virtually all conditions of weather and climate.

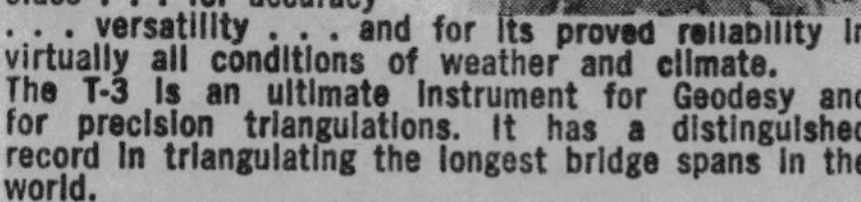

The T-3 is an ultimate instrument for Geodesy and for precision triangulations. It has a distinguished record in triangulating the longest bridge spans in the world.

NOTABLE FEATURES OF THE WILD T-3

- Performs triangulations of the first and second order.
- Circle reading direct to 0.2 seconds.
- Telescope magnification 24x, 30x, 40x.
- No eccentricity error.
- Ideal for ultra-precise measurements in industry and laboratory.

WILD T-16 OPTICAL TRANSIT

The T-16 embodies many brilliant new concepts. They add up to a degree of optical and mechanical precision, as well as versatility, that you'll find impossible to duplicate with any other instrument at this price.

NOTABLE FEATURES OF THE WILD T-16

- Direct scale reading to 1 minute; safe interpolation to 20 seconds.
- Azimuth and vertical scales seen simultaneously and read directly.
- Built-in repeating clamp for setting on zero. Eliminates lower plate motions.
- New optical plumb with upright image to speed setting up.
- Optional accessories include battery box providing illumination for scales, level vials and telescope reticle.
- Excellent for mining, highway and land surveying.

PRICE: $700 F.O.B. Port Washington, N. Y. Tripods extra.

WILD N-III PRECISION LEVEL

Speed and ease of set-up and operation, yes! *And with no compromise in absolute accuracy, versatility and dependability under all conditions.* Here, literally, is the standard of the world in precision levels.

THREE MODELS FOR EVERY REQUIREMENT

STANDARD METRIC AT $560. Reading direct to .1 mm, estimation to .01 mm. Use with Wild precision Invar Rods.

SPECIAL INDUSTRIAL AT $687. Reading direct to .001 inch. Use with Wild Stainless Steel Rods 3' and 6' long.

SPECIAL ENGINEER AT $595. Reading direct to .0005 ft., esimation to .0001. Use with standard leveling rods. All models have tilting screw, coincidence level and built-in optical micrometer.

Write for booklets . . . and use the Wild Heerbrugg advisory services without obligation.

WILD HEERBRUGG INSTRUMENTS, inc.

Main at Covert Streets · Port Washington, N.Y. POrt Washington 7-4843

SALES · FULL FACTORY SERVICES

Street Construction and Maintenance Equipment

LeTourneau-WESTINGHOUSE Company

PEORIA, ILLINOIS

Adams grader with scarifier opens-up material too hard for blade to cut . . . easily rips up sheet asphalt, old gravel, stone, or blacktop surfaces, heavy clay, shale, and hard-pan. Strong, fast cutting, V-type scarifier (straight-type on "220") has quick-change, removable teeth with replaceable points, 1¼" steel plate drawbars.

Smoother Streets at ower cost

with Adams graders

You can make your budget go farther; keep streets, alley, school-yards and parks in better condition when you equip with modern Adams graders. Adams gives you bonus working speeds . . . wider range of effective combinations of power and speed to push bigger, heavier loads . . . make deeper cuts faster . . . to provide more accurate finished grades than do ordinary graders. You'll do more work . . . do it better . . . finish it faster . . . keep your constituents happier . . . *all* at lower tax-dollar cost per project.

All four 80 to 150 hp Adams models provide 15 speeds—8 forward, 4 reverse, 3 optional creeper gears—so your grader can work, maneuver, and travel at fastest, most productive rate. Creeper gears permit full-power operation at speeds as low as 32' per minute . . . give extra "muscle" for ripping-up old asphalt or gravel surfaces. These low-low gear ratios sup-

Mixing blacktop and oil-mix in streets, parking lots and yard areas is *fast* with Adams' power and speed . . . is *easy* with high-arch front axle, enclosed gears, clean-rolling mold board.

General street maintenance is handled quickly . . . thoroughfares are smoother, street-cleaning easier, tax-payers happier . . . when Adams helps you complete more projects each week.

LeTourneau-WESTINGHOUSE Company

PEORIA, ILLINOIS

ply precisely-controlled power for working thru broken pavement, rocks and roots, for fine grading, working close against forms or curbs, and for maneuvering in close quarters.

Adams graders also reduce non-productive time. High reverse speeds, to 13.7 mph, provide fast back-up on one-way work, speed up shuttle turns in close quarters. High travel speeds—to 26 mph—save time on job-to-job moves and between garage and job for a longer productive day's work.

The sixth and smallest grader in the Adams line is the 60 hp Model 220. It works at 10 full-power speeds . . . leads its class with 5 forward, 1 reverse, 4 optional creepers. "220" is a medium-duty grader (15,500 lb.) and gives you all the power and speed you want for street and alley maintenance and general grading. It is a top producer in its class, gives you efficient service at low initial cost.

At the top of the Adams line is the new "POWER-*Flow* 660", a big 190 hp diesel with *torque-converter* drive. This machine gives you multiplied work-power . . . provides infinite number of power-speed combinations within 4 speed-ranges forward and 4 reverse. This super heavy-duty grader provides extra push-power to start heavy loads fast . . . to blade steadily against varying loads . . . to absorb hard shock-loads . . . to eliminate engine lugging . . . to make operation simpler and easier.

Throughout the entire line (6 machines) Adams' work power is backed by rugged tandem drive . . . all-welded, one piece, high-arch, wishbone frame . . . husky front-end . . . welded, short-coupled blade mechanism.

SEE FOR YOURSELF how Adams' big capacity for hard work can save tax-dollars and speed municipal projects. Call us or write for an Adams grader demonstration.

On heavy-dirt work, such as ditching, new street-grading, spreading fill, Adams' wider range of speed-power combinations gets work done at fastest, most-productive rate.

Bank-sloping is easy with an Adams. All blade positions you normally need are controlled entirely from cab . . . from horizontal to vertical in less than a minute. Optional power-shift adjusts moldboard, right or left in 10 seconds, on-the-go, without physical effort . . . reaches out, works around poles and other obstructions . . . reduces maneuvering time.

You have a low-cost, snow-removal machine in an Adams grader. Grader blade clears streets quickly. Hydraulically controlled, V-type 9' wide snowplow and 12' wing attachment clears suburban and outlying thoroughfares. Plow has high-lift curvature . . . busts drifts. Rotary snowplow also available.

For odd-jobs, backfilling, setting culverts, rooting-out rocks, and casting piled-up dirt and debris, optional bulldozer comes in handy. Blade is 8' wide, 35" high . . . hydraulic power raises, applies down pressure. Comfortable, stand-up-height cab is optional on all six Adams models.

Adams, POWER-*Flow*—Trademark

LeTourneau-WESTINGHOUSE Company

PEORIA, ILLINOIS

Cut truck-loading costs

TraveLoader speeds handling of aggregates, dirt, topsoil, snow, oil-mix

Adams TraveLoader loads 600 to 1200 cu. yds. per hour into trucks, from windrow, stockpile or bank . . . handles many loading jobs quickly . . . keeps your truck fleet working steadily . . . speeds completion of city projects.

TraveLoader picks-up surplus material on construction projects . . . handles sand, gravel, stone, and oil-mix on resurfacing jobs. It digs and loads black dirt for landscaping . . . clears snow-clogged streets . . . loads cinders for ice control . . . speeds all sorts of loading for other construction and repair work . . . travels garage to project, and job-to-job at 26.7 mph.

Fast-loading TraveLoader works within one traffic-lane . . . loads to rear . . . does not tie-up passing vehicles. To cut truck-spotting time, it can also be equipped with cross-conveyor, for loading trucks on either side.

Machine loads all kinds of loose or non-packed materials from windrows, stockpiles, or bank. It works much faster than a front-end loader . . . moves ever-forward as it loads, without turns, or other non-productive lost motion. It drives forward at 25′ to 167′ per minute . . . gathers-up material from 8′ width. Trough-type conveyor loads trucks quickly. Discharge height is adjustable. Machine is powered by either 55 hp gasoline or 60 hp diesel engine . . . unit weighs 16,700 lbs. with normal optional equipment.

Check the ways TraveLoader can speed your truck-loading . . . reduce construction and maintenance costs for your city. Write or phone your local distributor for facts and figures.

Adams—Trademark

Making clean, 8′ wide pick-up, TraveLoader follows grader, loads surplus material windrowed on side of street, without interference to passing traffic.

TraveLoader digs and loads gravel, sand, topsoil, and other non-packed materials from natural bank, without prior preparation. Moves job-to-job at 26.7 mph.

Clearing snow from busy city streets, TraveLoader heaps trucks in 20 to 30 seconds . . . loads up to 1200 cu. yds. per hour in one traffic lane.

LeTourneau-WESTINGHOUSE Company

PEORIA, ILLINOIS

Handyman dirt-mover

Model D Tournapull

With one or more 1-man D Tournapulls, your Sanitation, Street, Park, Water, and Engineering Depts. can handle a wide variety of handyman dirtmoving jobs. You'll save time and tax-money on landfill method of refuse and garbage disposal . . . on any load-haul-and-spread earthmoving for construction and maintenance.

Handyman "D" with scraper moves dirt, grades, dozes, hauls material, plows snow, and does many other chores. 9 yd. rig self-loads or can be push-loaded . . . 2 "D's" can push-load each other. Scraper can be shovel, conveyor, or hopper loaded thru open top. Tournapull travels via streets, alleys or cross-country where a truck cannot go, spreads its load accurately on-the-run. Self-propelled, 138 hp machine works economically on big or small assignments. It's only 8′ wide, and within 9-ton axle-weight limits. "D" is faster, more maneuverable than any tractor-scraper combination. When current job is done, "D" *runs* to the next project . . . at speeds to 29.5 mph.

Handyman "D" levels, packs refuse and spreads dirt cover on sanitary landfills, helps eliminate odor and vermin. Electric-controlled dozer-blade comes in handy for clearing, leveling and backfilling. Rig travels over streets, alleys, curbs, sidewalks, tracks, etc. without damage to footing or tires.

As work needs change, you can readily convert prime mover to pull interchangeable trail-units . . . assure steady, efficient use of manpower and equipment the year around. Extra trail units—rear-dump, lift-and-carry crane, flat-bed—cost only about ¼ the price of original Tournapull scraper combination.

You'll like the way self-loading "D" can work alone, or with other equipment . . . its go-anywhere mobility . . . its versatility as handyman or production dirt-mover. Taxpayers will like the speed at which projects are completed . . . you'll like the lower cost per job assignment.

Why not call or write your local distributor?

Tournapull—Trademark Reg. U.S. Pat. Off.

LeTourneau-WESTINGHOUSE Company

PEORIA, ILLINOIS

On sanitary landfill, rubber-tired Tournatractor excavates pits, stock-piles material for cover, dozes and compacts refuse, blankets each day's collection of rubbish with earth, grades and compacts cover and topsoil for landscaping or redevelopment.

Goes anywhere over city-streets . . . rubber-tired Tournatractor

Big, low-pressure tires give work-and-run Tournatractor exclusive advantages in speed and mobility you cannot match with crawler-tractors. Its high speeds forward and reverse help you complete more work . . . handle more jobs faster . . . eliminate time-consuming, expensive, hand-labor operations.

Typically, your 208 hp, 17 mph Tournatractor might spend its day this way: Travel to dump, 4 mi. (16 min.) . . . maintain sanitary landfill (3 hrs.) . . . move to sewer job 2 mi. (8 min.) . . . back-fill and compact 60′ trench (15 min.) . . . drive to street project, 3 mi. (12 min.) . . . take time-out for lunch . . . loosen and pile-up broken pavement (1 hr.) . . . rip-up 1000′ of old asphalt surface (2.5 hrs.) . . . move to zoo parking-lot, 1 mi. (4 min.) . . . spread truck-hauled gravel (25 min.) . . . return to garage, 2 mi. (8 min.) . . . park for the night . . . equip for snow-emergency (30 min.) . . . plow snow (6 hrs.) . . . equip for next day and park.

208 hp Tournatractor handles many jobs in a single day . . . moves across town, thru traffic . . . gives tractor service to projects where crawlers are impractical . . . speeds job completion and cuts hand-labor costs.

Because it drives job-to-job under its own power, rubber-tired Tournatractor eliminates need for flat-bed and crew . . . you have no delays for loading and unloading. Rig starts to job on a moment's notice, drives up to 17 mph in traffic, thru steets, alleys, or cross-country . . . goes over curbs, sidewalks, driveways, tracks, etc. without damage to pavement or tires, which are 5½′ high, nearly 2′ wide.

Tournatractor's drawbar power and speed also pay-off on scraper push-loading. And for other jobs: rig pulls scrapers, sheepsfoot rollers . . . hauls wagons and other equipment between jobs. Tournatractor's dependable electrical system also is source of electricity for hand tools or emergency power.

Consider what faster job-to-job moves, wider versatility, lower hand-labor costs, and instant availability of Tournatractor can mean to *your* city. Get all the facts. Write for name and address of your local distributor.

Tournatractor—Trademark Reg. U.S. Pat. Off. G-1242-MU

LOW COST, VERSATILE TRENCHER HANDLES BIG YARDAGE JOBS

Now every municipality can afford to own one or more of these top capacity trenching machines and get big trencher performance on all municipal jobs. Arps Trench Hogs are low-priced and economical to operate because they mount right on standard wheel tractors.

TRENCH HOG ADVANTAGES

★ VERSATILITY TO MATCH ANY JOB
Choice of three boom lengths providing digging depths of 3½′, 5½′ and 7′. Quick-change cutters furnished in 6″ to 20″ widths. Special cutters make fast work of rocky or frozen ground. Heavy duty power sprocket increases torque by 18% for exceptionally tough digging conditions.

★ FAST, STEADY OPERATION
Seven digging speeds allow operator to fit digging rate to the job. Trench Hog can dig as much as 800′ per hour. Complete mobility of unit means greater maneuverability on the job —less travel time between work sites. The Trench Hog can go wherever a tractor can.

★ ACCURATE, PRECISE CONTROL
Digging depth is hydraulically controlled for greater precision. Independent speed control for each wheel assures positive regulation for either straight line trenching or digging on a curve.

★ REAL TRENCHING ECONOMY
Low initial cost—much less than comparable capacity machines having their own traveling mechanisms. One-man operation and transportation means additional savings over digging with hand labor.

★ RUGGED, QUALITY CONSTRUCTION
Top-grade components, including anti-friction bearings, overstrain safety features, heat-treated parts at all points of greatest wear. Thoroughly engineered to take all digging strains on the toughest trenching jobs. Thousands of Arps Trench Hogs now in operation all over the world.

TRENCHERS • HALF-TRACKS
BULLDOZERS • UTILITY BLADES

Low Cost, Big Capacity Bulldozer

Put this economical, rugged bulldozer to work backfilling, spreading aggregates during street construction, snowplowing sidewalks, spreading and removing topsoil, grading, terracing, controlling soil erosion, landscaping, spreading fertilizer, stockpiling material, plus many other applications. Blades supplied in 4′, 5′ and 6′ lengths to meet every need. "Close-quarters" mobility enables bulldozer speed and economy to be utilized instead of costly hand labor. One-man operation further reduces overall expense.

Performance Features

Positive Blade Down Pressure
Real blade bite for tough, packed, or partially frozen ground. Double-acting hydraulic control with improved high pressure control valve assures precise blade handling—enables the blade to be held at any desired height. Down pressure great enough to lift front end of tractor off the ground.

Wide Range of Blade Positions
Five angular blade adjustments. May be used as a bulldozer or an angledozer. Cutting pitch adjustable to three positions. Depth gauge attached to ram instantly shows operator where cutting edge is in relation to wheel level.

Quick, Easy Installation
Simple frame construction and hydraulic control keeps installation time to a bare minimum. Subframe and blade can be removed from tractor in seconds.

High Lift With Ample Clearance
When traveling through ditches, down steep banks—over any type of obstruction, blade can be raised 18″ off ground to prevent "hanging up." This versatile feature speeds up dirt and snow moving operations.

Rugged, Long-Life Construction
Frame is fabricated from heavy bar stock with strong but lightweight tubular subframe. Blade is ⅜″ reinforced plate, 19″ high with ⅜″ x 4″ cutting edge, reversible and sharpened on both sides.

OPTIONAL EQUIPMENT

SIDE PLATES WITH SKID SHOES
Move 3 to 5 times as much dirt using side plates with adustable skid shoes—assure 100% production with each pass. Blade will not gouge too deep to stall tractor; dirt stays within width of blade; super-smooth surfacing job results.

SNOW PLOW ACCESSORIES
SPILLPLATE for 6′ dozer blades keeps snow from spilling over top. Spring Kit tips and raises blade to clear obstructions; adjustable Mushroom Skid Shoes prevent blade from cutting into unfrozen ground.

SCARIFIER ATTACHMENT to rip up very hard ground and simplify dirt moving.

SPECIFICATIONS

FRAME: Heavy bar stock construction, bolted to implement mounting pads of tractor; tubular subframe.

BLADE CONTROL: Dual action; two-way hydraulic control.

BLADE CONSTRUCTION:: ⅜″ reinforced plate, 19″ high; 4′, 5′ and 6′ lengths.

CUTTING EDGE: ⅜″ x 4″, reversible and sharpened on both edges.

APPROXIMATE SHIPPING WEIGHTS:

Blades—4 ft.	191 lbs.	
5 ft.	229 lbs.	
6 ft.	263 lbs.	
Frame with Hydraulic Controls		210 lbs.
Side Plates with Skid Shoes		69 lbs.
Spill Plate		52 lbs.
Spring Kit		32 lbs.
Mushroom Skid Shoes		18 lbs.

TRENCHERS • HALF-TRACKS
BULLDOZERS • UTILITY BLADES

Arps half-tracks provide as much as 440% greater traction at a fraction of the cost of a crawler tractor.

Handy Year 'Round Tool

Any 3-point hitch tractor, through the 3-plow class, can be equipped with the Arps Utility Blade for ditching, terracing, grading, landscaping, backfilling, land leveling, road building, snow removal and dozens of other jobs where this handy, versatile tool will save time and money over costly hand labor. Blade is 72" wide for man-sized dirtmoving performance. Tilts up or down 35°—has five positions. Nine angular positions forward and three in reverse. Offsets to right or left with eight blade adjustments. Rotates full 360°—reversing feature provides backfill operation. Gauge wheel assures precise finishing.

Utility Blade Advantages

Strong, Tubular Frame Construction
Built to take all the strains and stresses imposed by continuous use and tough, hard-to-work soils. Tubular construction is heavy duty, yet weight-saving. Cutter bar is high carbon steel—reversible for maximum life.

Blade Tilts, Offsets, Angles, Reverses
Tilt of 35°, plus ditching point means positive penetration even in hard, packed ground. Blade can be offset 15" to left or right to get outside of either rear wheel. Reverses in seconds with choice of three angular positions. Nine angular positions forward—maximum 45°. For easy travel, blade lifts as high as 36" depending upon make of tractor.

Blade Adjustments Without Wrench
All blade adjustments for both forward and backward movement extremely simple to make—not even a wrench required. One man alone can easily make adjustments.

Adjustable Gauge Wheel Assures Precise Cuts
This optional equipment is controlled from rear of the tractor seat. With the handy gauge wheel depth of the cut can be controlled to the fraction of an inch. Especially needed for landscaping.

Ripper Attachment
Easily attached scarifier for ripping hard or frozen soils, sod, blacktop and similar tough material. Seven hard-surfaced ripper teeth have three depth positions—3½", 5½" and 7". Teeth fold up out of the way when backfilling in reverse. Relative position of teeth to cutting edge of blade leaves ground perfectly leveled and pulverized.

Specifications

Moldboard length	72"
height	17"
Cutter bar 5/16 x 5 High carbon (reversible)	
Frame Heavy duty tubular	

Weights	
Utility Blade	460 lbs.
Gauge Wheel	50 lbs.
Ditching Point	16 lbs.
Side Plates (pr.)	31 lbs.
Skid Shoes (pr.)	18 lbs.
Ripper Attachment	273 lbs.

AIR PLACEMENT EQUIPMENT COMPANY

1005A West 24th Street, Kansas City 8, Missouri

Manufacturers of Advanced Design Concrete Gunning
Mixing • Grouting • Sandblasting Equipment

AIRPLACO®

GUNNING EQUIPMENT

MAKES BUDGET DOLLARS GO FURTHER

For any kind of concrete restoration or maintenance job.

The AIRPLACO gunning rig (illustrated) consists of a BONDACTOR or NUCRETOR, a MIX-ELVATOR and a SAND LOADER combined into one compact portable unit.

Public Works Officials Use AIRPLACO Equipment For:

- Swimming pool construction
- Curb, street, road, sidewalk repair
- Restoration of bridges, ditches, dams, reservoirs, culverts, retaining walls.
- Storm and sanitary sewer repairs.
- Wet & dry sandblasting
- Playground and park maintenance

FREE CATALOG

Write today for illustrated catalog, packed with application ideas, helpful information and additional details.

A Complete Line of Gunning Equipment in a Range of Sizes

BONDACTOR MODEL 750—½ to ¾ cu. yd. per hour with 75 or 125 CFM Compressor.

BONDACTOR MODEL 1250S—½ to 1¼ cu. yd. per hour with 105 or 125 CFM compressor.

BONDACTOR MODEL 1250L—1 to 2½ cu. yd. per hour with 210 CFM compressor.

NUCRETOR MODEL 1500S—up to 3½ cu. yd. per hour with 250 CFM compressor and 1¼" placement hose or up to 5 cu. yd. per hour with 315 CFM compressor and 1½" hose.

NUCRETOR MODEL 1500L—up to 7 cu. yd. per hour with 365 CFM compressor and 1⅝" placement hose.

MIX-ELVATOR MODEL 405—up to 12 cu. yd. per hour capacity: proportioning range from 1:3 to 1:7.

Also available are water pressure systems, sandblasting machines, pressure grouting machines and sand loaders.

AEROIL PRODUCTS COMPANY, INC.

69 Wesley Street, Dept. M6 • South Hackensack, New Jersey

"Quality Guaranteed Since 1917"

BRANCHES: CHICAGO AND LOS ANGELES

EQUIPMENT FOR ROOFING, CONSTRUCTION, ROADS AND INDUSTRY

Aeroil

THE COMPLETE LINE OF MELTING KETTLES FOR ROAD MAINTENANCE WORK

economical . . . efficient
TUBE AND BOTTOM-FIRED KETTLES

Save on initial cost with Aeroil modern production manufacturing techniques. Save on operating costs with proven "wrap-around heat flow" design that instantly spreads 2000°F. direct heat!

An increasing number of road departments find the Aeroil patented immersion tube-fired kettles ideally suited to their type of work.

- Choice of types and capacities from 80 to 500 gallons.
- Choice of liquefied petroleum (bottled) gas or oil firing.
- Choice of pneumatic tires, skids, hard rubber or steel wheels.

Bottom Fired KEB Type

HEET-MASTER JUMBO TUBE TYPE KETTLE

500 GAL. CAPACITY FOR ROAD STREET & HIGHWAY WORK

The modern, immersion tube heated road repair kettle saves time, money and labor. Produces hot stuff in half the time required by bottom fired units. Can be equipped with hand or power spray attachments, barrel hoist, etc. Equipped to burn kerosene or Liquefied Petroleum Gas. Entire heating unit can be removed for cleaning. Sizes 80 to 500 gallons.

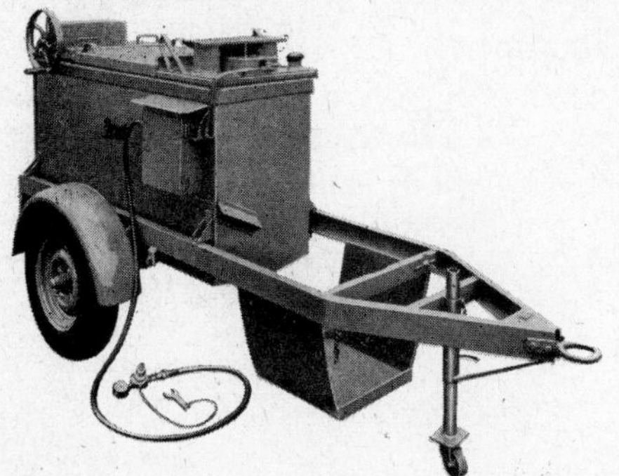

HEET-MASTER® DVP KETTLES FOR RUBBERIZED ASPHALT

Highway, turnpike, road and airport users benefit substantially from the working simplicity and economical operation of the Heet-Master DVP Kettles. They deliver *controlled, uniform, indirect* heat to rubberized asphalts, preserving *all* essential elastic qualities.

Thermostatically controlled liquefied petroleum gas firing insures clean, efficient performance. Models from 50 to 120 gallon capacities.

Write for useful product literature.

ALL AEROIL PRODUCTS ARE GUARANTEED

AEROIL PRODUCTS COMPANY, INC.

69 Wesley Street · Dept. M6 · South Hackensack, N. J.

double-duty COMBINATION TOOL AND ASPHALT HEATER

One compact unit cuts equipment investment, hauling and labor in half! This kettle heats 10 to 15 paving tools and up to 45 gallons of asphalt binder *at the same time.*

Used extensively by townships, parks and Works Departments when larger and more numerous pieces would be impractical. Mounted on automotive type running gear for smooth trailing behind light trucks.

EFFICIENT, POSITIVE-ACTION BITUMINOUS SPRAYERS AND SPRAY ATTACHMENTS

Cut-Back and Emulsion Sprayers

One man can easily disperse all types of free flowing liquids as well as heavier materials. Cut-back Sprayer is equipped with heating unit. For departments that require a sprayer for emulsions only, the Aeroil emulsion sprayer (without flue and burner unit) is recommended.

Both types come in 120 and 200 gallon capacities.

Road Oil Distributors

This versatile sprayer is engineered to handle every kind of liquid bituminous material from light road oils, cut-backs and emulsions to heavy penetration asphalt. Centralized controls permit simplified operation of fixed recirculating & floating spray bar and one or more hand sprays. Fast, easy to fill and drain. 400, 500, and 600 gallon capacities.

Mobile Utility Sprayer

A completely self-contained mobile unit that rapidly, economically sprays all light liquids directly from delivery drum. Invaluable for efficient insect and mosquito control as well as road maintenance.

Power Spray Attachment

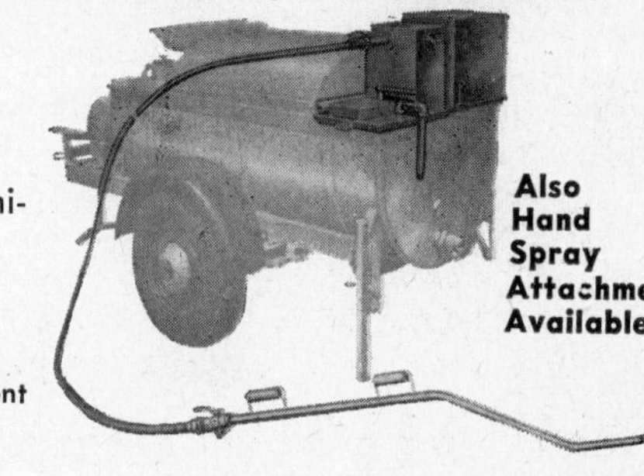

Also Hand Spray Attachments Available

Converts heating kettles to highly practical bituminous applicators!

Check these important features:

- Driven by air-cooled 1½ hp gasoline engine.
- 40 GPM at normal operation.
- Built-in pressure relief valve for continuous and intermittent spraying.
- Protective, detachable metal housing.

AEROIL PRODUCTS COMPANY, INC.

69 Wesley Street · Dept. M6 · South Hackensack, N. J.

Lead Melting Furnaces and Compound Pots

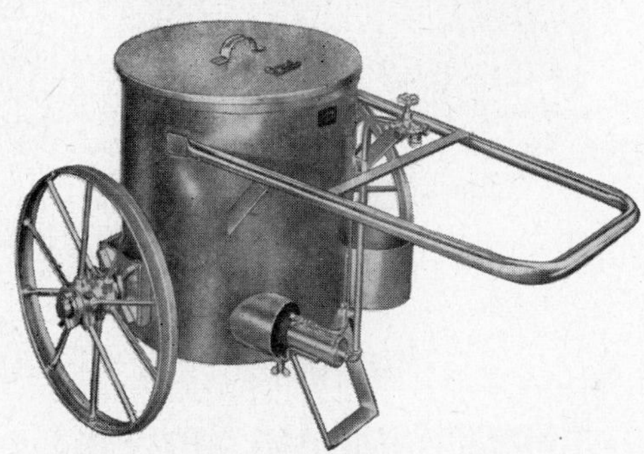

Used to melt lead or heat sewer and electrical pipe compounds as well as somastic compound and other hard-to-melt coatings.

- Choice of liquefied petroleum gas or oil firing.
- Oil burner can be used as portable torch.
- Sizes from 10 to 50 gallons and 50 to 150 pound melt capacities.

Pouring Pots and Pavers Tools

A wide assortment of round and oblong pots with specially designed spouts for general purpose and specific pouring. Used for fixing cracks in pavement, expansion joints and other repairs. Suitable for waterproofing.

Full line of pavers tools includes tampers, smoothers, rakes, sandals.

Patrol and Maintenance Heater

Practical "one man" unit for road patrol, expansion joint filling, small patch work, pipeline coating and similar repair work. Removable torch can be used for all thawing, melting, drying and heating purposes.

Low fuel consumption — only 1 gallon of kerosene per hour. Built for heavy-duty service.

Burners and Torches

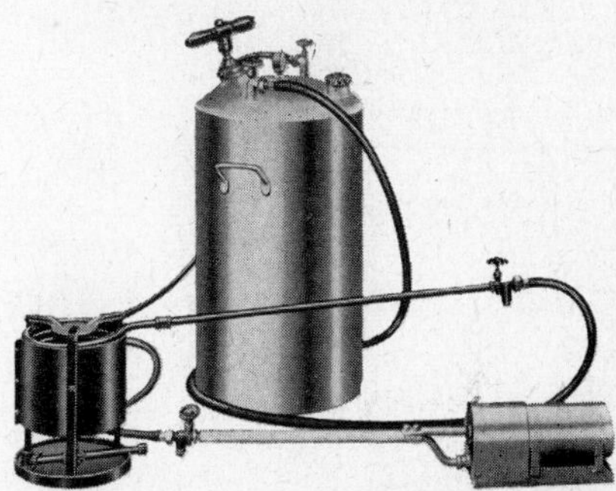

Heavy-duty units heat, thaw and melt effectively with easily-controlled 2000° F. flame. Also used to fire melting kettles, in pre-heating and forging, and for scores of maintenance and construction purposes.

- **SAFE**—Individually factory tested.
- **ECONOMICAL**—Burns low cost kerosene or light furnace oil.
- **LONG-LIFE**—Rugged welded steel construction.
- **3 CHOICES**—Burner Outfit (upright burner plus tank). Torch Outfit (torch plus tank). Comb. Outfit.

Write for useful product literature.

ALL AEROIL PRODUCTS ARE GUARANTEED

AEROIL PRODUCTS COMPANY, INC.

69 Wesley Street, Dept. M6 • South Hackensack, N. J.

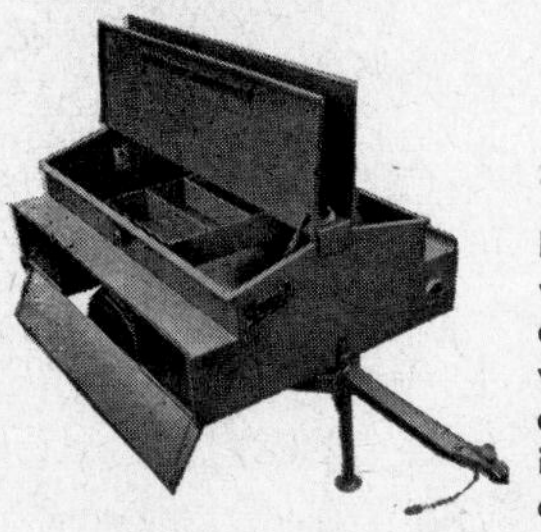

Tool-Master® Tool Trailers

Rugged tamper and weather proof units that offer spacious storage and work areas. Used wherever complete tool mobility, protection and control are needed. Available in 6 and 8 foot models, mounted on automotive trailing gear. Other type trailers built to specifications.

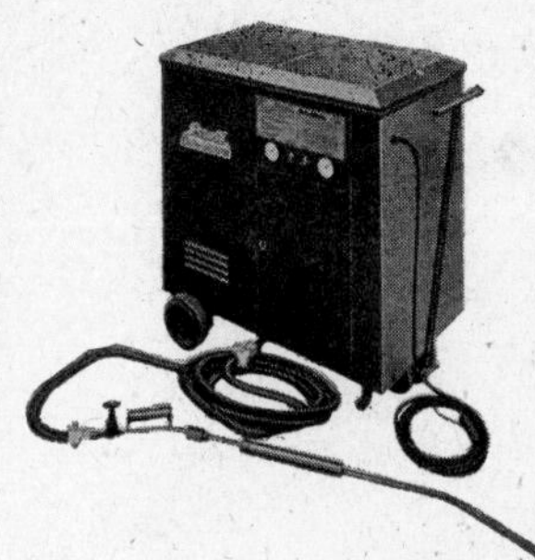

Steam Cleaners

Clean most stubborn grime faster with steam. Entire operation can be learned in minutes. Choice of portable and stationary models in a variety of sizes are capable of developing 100 pounds of steam pressure in 90 seconds. Modern design features assure quiet, trouble-free service.

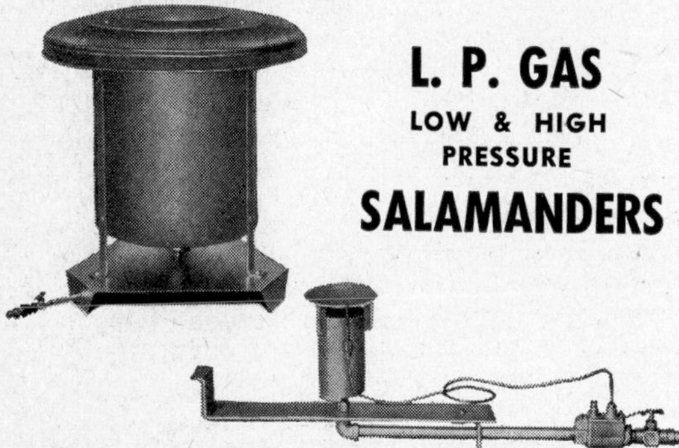

L. P. GAS
LOW & HIGH PRESSURE
SALAMANDERS

We are featuring the very latest and finest of Gas Salamanders with B. T. U. Ratings up to 120,000. All accessories are available . . . INCLUDING SAFETY P. O. L. Connections and COMPLETE AUTOMATIC CUT OFF VALVES. All burn with clear blue flame . . . perfect combustion. Salamanders priced at large discounts for quantity. Now you can buy an AEROIL in the popular price range. L. P. G. Thawing.

Portable Compressed Air Sprayer

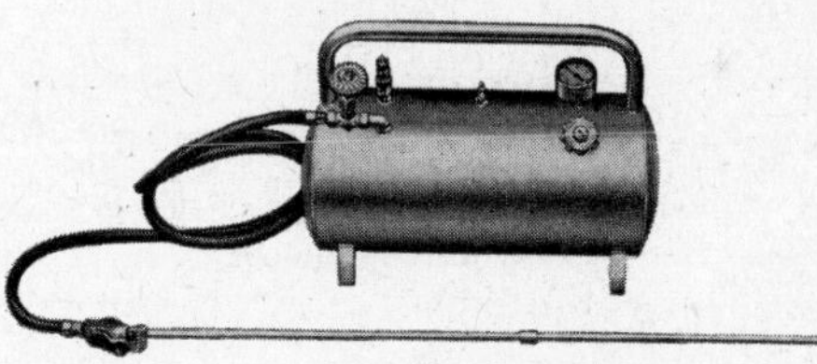

Particularly suitable for dispensing volatile liquid solutions. Used "on-the-job" to remove dirt, grease, paint from engines, trucks, airplanes and similar heavy equipment. No moving parts assures maintenance-free long-life! Simple to operate. . . ends hand pumping. Available in 3 gallon tank capacity with 8 foot hose and 6 gallon tank capacity with 12 foot hose.

Sprayer and Burner Outfits

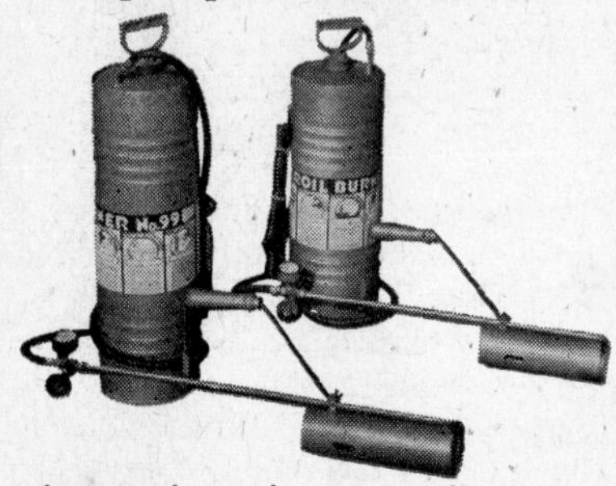

Permanently destroys every known weed with intense 2000° F. flame. Also used to sterilize soil, disinfect, exterminate, cremate and for many other jobs in parks, playgrounds, roads, etc. Aeroil Sprayer Attachment converts unit to a handy high pressure sprayer perfect for disinfectants, insecticides, whitewash and similar liquids. Comes in 4 and 5 gallon tank capacities.

Parts Washers and Cleaning Equipment

For every automotive maintenance need, Aeroil makes a complete line of Metal Parts Washers, Vapor Degreasers, Hot and Cold Dip Tanks and Rinse Tanks. All equipment has been performance-proven by cities and towns throughout the country!

Write for useful product literature.

ALL AEROIL PRODUCTS ARE GUARANTEED

Barber-Greene LOADERS

MODEL 543 BUCKET LOADER

The Model 543 Bucket Loader handles aggregate from stockpile to truck in one fast-moving stream. Pneumatic tires give fast travel between jobs at speeds to 15 m.p.h. Hydraulically controlled swivel conveyor trims load. Power hydraulic boom hoist. Dual transmission. Easily converted for loading coal, snow, or leaves.

Capacities to 3 cu. yds. per min.

MODEL 544 SNOW LOADER

The Model 544 Snow Loader is a conversion of the Model 543. It gives low-cost, high-speed snow removal. Trimmer conveyor allows operation in one traffic lane by loading over truck cab. Also loads over the side of even the longest, highest trucks. Ideal for coal loading, and easily converted for aggregate or leaf loading. Cab optional extra.

Capacities to 11 cu. yds. per min.

MODEL 82-A BUCKET LOADER

The crawler-mounted Model 82-A Bucket Loader gives sure-footed operation even on soft or uneven ground. Loads trucks from stockpile or bank, and also does topsoil stripping and low-cost scalping and screening. As with all Barber-Greene Loaders, controls are within easy reach, and no special operator is required. Gravity and vibrating screens available.

Capacity to 3 cu. yds. per min.

MODEL 550 WINDROW LOADER

The Model 550 Windrow Loader, designed with a realistic capacity, will easily keep ahead of all the trucks that will normally be available. Outstanding advantages include lower cost, greater travel speed from job to job, real maneuverability, and simple operation. Feeder automatically lifts to prevent overload, automatically returns to normal position. Loads earth, snow, and leaves.

Capacities to 4 cu. yds. per min. loading earth and similar materials, and to 6 cu. yds. per min. loading snow.

For full information, write Barber-Greene Company, Aurora, Illinois, U.S.A.

Barber-Greene

Barber-Greene

MODEL 845 CONTINUOUS PLANT

The Model 845 Plant offers a unique combination of unexcelled portability and the ability to meet any mix specification. Mixer and two-bin gradation unit are combined on one chassis, with auxiliary two-bin gradation unit optional where three or four aggregate control is required. Full range of balanced plant components available for all mixing requirements.

Capacity ranges from 60 to 90 T.P.H.

MODEL 840-B CONTINUOUS PLANT

The Model 840-B gives all the advantages of the high capacity plants, including gradation control after drying. Like all Barber-Greene plants, these are highly portable, easily erected, and inherently automatic. Wide range of components available, including dryer, gradation unit, dust collector, fines feeder, and wide range of cold feeders.

Capacity ranges from 20 to more than 50 T.P.H.

Barber-Greene CONVEYORS

MODEL 375 TRANSFER-CONVEYOR

The Model 375 Transfer-Conveyor is economical because it was engineered for the short job. Special drive, pulleys, and take-up are mounted on a five-inch channel frame to provide a low-cost, short permanent conveyor. Horsepower is limited to that required for the job to be done. Units are easily selected right from the catalog.

Lengths from 8′ to 44′. Capacities to 300 T.P.H.

MODEL 363 PORTABLE CONVEYOR

Long, short, light, and heavy-duty portable conveyors and car unloaders are all available to cut your costs . . . simplify and speed your operations in handling all bulk materials. The Model 363 Portable Conveyor and Model 358 Car Unloader team shown here is practically automatic after being started. Pneumatic tires give real portability.

Portable conveyors available in lengths to 60′, with capacities to 430 T.P.H. Unloaders available with capacities to 150 T.P.H.

For full information, write Barber-Greene Company, Aurora, Illinois, U.S.A.

Barber-Greene

Barber-Greene DITCHERS

MODEL 705-B DITCHER

The Model 705-B Runabout Ditcher, with its 15 m.p.h. road speed, is specifically designed for scattered jobs. Its exclusive vertical boom digs right up to obstructions, leaves no ramp at end of ditch. Hydra-Crowd gives finger-tip control of crowding speed independent of bucket line speed. Fluid coupling provides constant cushion of oil to eliminate shock loads.

Depths to 48″. Widths to 10½″.

MODEL 44-C DITCHER

The crawler-mounted Model 44-C Ditcher gives top performance in even the toughest digging conditions. Wide range of widths and depths gives unusual versatility. Fast milling action digs through toughest materials. New curved teeth last three to five times longer, never need sharpening. Automatic overload release. Exclusive vertical boom.

Depths to 8′3″. Widths to 24″.

MODEL 711 DITCHER

The mobility and easy operation of the Model 711 Ditcher set a new high in cost-saving potential. It is mounted on a 4-wheel drive Dodge Power Wagon with travel speeds to 45 m.p.h. Hydra-Crowd simplifies operation and assures maximum crowding speed for each digging condition. May be operated from ground or cab with equal ease.

Depths to 5′. Widths to 18″.

MODEL 702 DITCHER

The new Model 702 Ditcher has made hand digging uneconomical, even on the smallest job. Designed and built to "take it," it does much work that normally would tie up heavier, more expensive, less portable equipment. It is easily towed from job to job by a light truck, or even a passenger car. Narrow cutting widths allow digging a trench just wide enough to suit the job.

Depths to 40″. Widths to 5″.

For full information, write Barber-Greene Company, Aurora, Illinois, U.S.A.

Barber-Greene BG

ALLIED STEEL & TRACTOR PRODUCTS, INC.

7835 Broadway • Cleveland 5, Ohio

REBUILD WORN TRACTOR SHOES

With Bulldog Grip Lugs

Bulldog Tractor Grip-Lugs can rebuild the grouser shoes of track-laying or crawler type equipment—at a fraction of the cost of new replacement parts. Equipment can be "re-lugged" without dismantling—saving hours of valuable down-time and labor.

Grip-Lugs are easily welded to the worn shoe. Made of special work-hardening steel, they become tougher and harder with use—usually out-wear the original grouser.

Supplied in 5 sizes to fit any track-laying or crawler type equipment. Write for catalog M-1.

CUT REPLACEMENT TOOTH COSTS UP TO 65%

With Bulldog Replaceable Digger Teeth

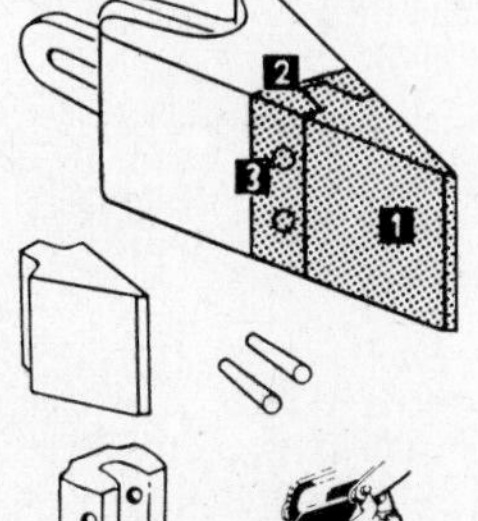

Revolutionary New Design has just three parts

1 Easy Change Replaceable Tooth changed with a hammer and punch. Has reversible bevel point. Made of highest quality alloy steel, heat treated to outwear all other teeth.

2 Universal Weld - On Adapter uses old tooth as a base. Same adapter fits on several different types of equipment Easily welded on worn teeth.

3 Positive Lock Pin gives a tight fit to the replaceable tooth and is easily removed for replacement.

Sizes to Fit All Popular Makes of

Shovel Dippers
Back Hoe Buckets
Dragline Buckets
Clamshell Buckets
Loader Buckets

Write for catalog M-2

REPAIR WORN TRUCK BEDS, SCRAPERS AND CHUTES

With Tuf-a-brase Alloy Wear Resisting Plate

A tough, long wearing plate of special alloy steel for repairing truck and trailer beds, chutes, scoops, bang boards and other equipment subject to abrasive wear and shock. In stock sizes of 4′, 5′, 6′ widths x 4′, 6′, 8′, 10′, 12′ and 20′ lengths. Thickness range from 3/16″ to 1½″. Write for catalog M-4.

PNEUMATIC TOOLS FOR PAVING BREAKING, ROCK DRILLING AND DIGGING

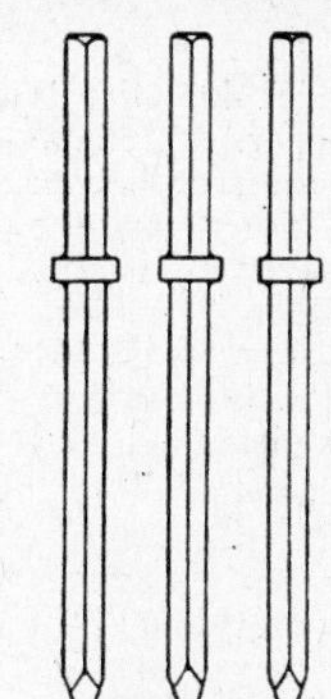

Complete line of Bulldog Pneumatic Tools includes chisels, chisel bits, moil points, asphalt cutters, clay spades, frost wedges and dirt tampers. Forged from special alloy steel, heat treated for durability. Complete range of sizes. Write for catalog M-3.

Territories Open for Agents and Dealers

AUSTIN-WESTERN WORKS

Construction Equipment Division *Baldwin-Lima-Hamilton Corporation*

Aurora, Illinois, U. S. A.

DISTRIBUTORS IN PRINCIPAL CITIES

MODEL 60 MOTOR SWEEPER

Newest in the Austin-Western line of equipment "Built to Outperform" is the Model 60 Motor Sweeper designed and engineered to meet the most exacting large capacity sweeping requirements.

A completely new 4-plus cubic yard hopper capacity motor sweeper, the Model 60 incorporates all the time-tested features of the popular Model 40 Motor Sweeper.

Front steer results in maximum versatility, as well as complete all-around visibility for fast, safe operation.

The Model 60 can be equipped with either right-hand and/or left-hand Gutter Broom. Brooms are oscillating, eliminating any danger of damage when bumping the curb or any other obstruction, and are provided with a parallel lift arrangement which maintains correct and constant pitch of the brush wire during its entire life.

Maximum work capacity is assured with an 8 foot 2 inch sweeping width when using a single Gutter Broom and a 10 foot 10 inch sweeping width when using double Gutter Brooms.

The large 4-plus cubic yard capactiy hopper is of rugged all-welded construction, and there is a separate hydraulic control for opening and closing the clam doors.

The Model 60 Motor Sweeper, equipped with a six-cylinder gasoline engine and a four-speed transmission, has a road speed range of from 3.8 mph in first gear to 20.9 mph in fourth gear.

A Leaf Broom attachment is also available for speeding up the work of collecting heavy accumulations of leaves. Concave in shape and design, it can be very quickly attached or detached as needed.

MODEL 40 MOTOR SWEEPER

The Model 40 has through the years developed a reputation second to none for fast, low-cost sweeping.

With its 3-wheel design, front steer, rear dump and 2 cubic yard capacity hopper, the Model 40 is the answer to many sweeping requirements.

Structural strength of the Model 40 is unequalled. The main frame incorporates the hopper, water tank, transmission, and engine supports in one all-welded unit. The best of materials have been used throughout the Sweeper with the skill born of years of research.

There is no conveyor in the Model 40. Dirt is thrown directly into the 2-yard hopper. A unique and simple arrangement which uses the rear broom as a gate enables the hopper to be closed and the load transported to any location desired. The rear broom is mounted close to the rear wheels, enabling the Model 40 to sweep closer to parked cars, safety islands, street corners, and obstructions than any sweeper in the world—and to do a cleaner, better job of sweeping.

The Model 40 can be equipped with either right-hand or left-hand Gutter Brooms, or both together. Brooms are oscillating, eliminating any danger of damage when bumping the curb or any other obstruction, and are provided with a parallel lift attachment which maintains correct and constant pitch of the brush wire during its entire life.

Driving mechanism is simple, positive and trouble-free. The Model 40 (with the exception of the chains driving the two rear wheels) is driven throughout by propeller shafts and gears. A four-speed transmission with all constant-mesh gears adds an extra low speed for sweeping under extremely adverse conditions and at the same time allows a higher speed for transporting the Sweeper.

A Leaf Broom attachment simplifies and speeds up the work of collecting heavy accumulations of leaves. It is simple in design, sturdy in construction and can be very quickly attached.

AUSTIN-WESTERN WORKS

Construction Equipment Division *Baldwin-Lima-Hamilton Corporation*

Aurora, Illinois, U. S. A.

DISTRIBUTORS IN PRINCIPAL CITIES

"99-L" POWER GRADER WITH SCARIFIER ATTACHMENT

POWER GRADERS

No motor grader without All-Wheel Drive and All-Wheel Steer can possibly equal the all-around performance of a 88-C Super "88", "99-L" or Super "99". All-Wheel Drive puts every pound of weight on a driving wheel, contributing 100% to traction, and delivering maximum power at the blade. With the unequalled maneuverability of All-Wheel Steer these graders can work in places where ordinary graders cannot go.

"99" POWER GRADERS

All-Wheel Drive and Steer, plus features never before combined in any power grader give these machines superb earth-moving ability. The High-Lift Blade slopes banks up to 90° and the blade can be changed from any conventional operating position to any bank cutting angle without the operator leaving the platform. The "99's" provide unequalled blade reach. From a normal operating position the blade can be extended to 89½ inches beyond the rear tire. By using All-Wheel Steer to offset the rear truck it is possible for the blade to reach 10 feet, 1½ inches beyond the rear tireline, a figure not approached by any other grader. The blade of these graders can be set at any grading angle; positioned to cut flat-bottomed ditches of any width; or completely reversed, without removing scarifier teeth.

All adjustments, including steering, are made by smooth, fast, positive hydraulic controls.

An unrivaled line of attachments is available for the "99-L" and Super "99"—versatile tools for those extra jobs which mean extra profits. "V" Plow, Snow Wing, Scarifier, Bulldozer, Roller, Plainsman Elevating Grader—each one doubly effective due to All-Wheel Drive and Steer.

"88" POWER GRADERS

Outstanding in its class, the "88" series, including the "88-L" and the Super "88," include the unusual and exclusive features of the heavier "99's." Work of all types, from routine grading to operations impossible for any grader without All-Wheel Drive and All-Wheel Steer are easily within reach of an "88."

A wide variety of attachments is also available for the "88-L" and the Super "88"—scarifier, "V" plow, snow wing, and bulldozer—each one far more efficient due to the exclusive combination of All-Wheel Drive and All-Wheel Steer.

SUPER "88" TANDEM POWER GRADER WITH 6-WHEEL DRIVE AND 6-WHEEL STEER.

AUSTIN-WESTERN WORKS

Construction Equipment Division *Baldwin-Lima-Hamilton Corporation*

Aurora, Illinois, U. S. A.

DISTRIBUTORS IN PRINCIPAL CITIES

3-WHEEL ROLLERS

The Austin-Western 3-Wheel Rollers are conspicuous for their fine design, construction, and long trouble-free life of economical service.

To attain the ultimate in roller performance, Austin-Western uses full length side plates of heavy steel, between which is firmly anchored all of the operating mechanism. Multiple crossties and a heavy cast saddle at the front end prevent flexing of the frame. This type of construction, along with a low center of gravity, avoids sway and bounce and provides for safety.

All gears are of alloy steel, machine cut and heat-treated. The shafts are of alloy steel, heat-treated, hardened, ground, and with splined connections and antifriction bearings.

Smooth, accurate control is provided through hydraulic power.

Overhead hatches and side ports are provided for easy accessibility. The openings are adequate for making all adjustments or removing clutches, gears or shafts.

A smooth running, accurately balanced, industrial type engine provides ample power for even the most difficult work and, where traction is available, steep grades are no problem.

In these Rollers the combination of better balance, less vibration, rugged construction and dependable power make for a long life of smooth, accurate performance with minimum operating cost.

They are available in the following sizes: 8-11, 10-12 and 12-14 ton.

TANDEM ROLLERS

Tandem Rollers of Austin-Western design are the finest in a series of models which began over 35 years ago. While built for general rolling use, these Tandems include a number of important improvements and refinements designed to provide exceptionally smooth and steady performance on precision jobs.

To maintain true alignment for precision rolling, the welded main frame of heavy box-type construction, is stoutly reinforced, to provide secure anchorage, for all members. A welded, large capacity sprinkler tank, forming a part of the frame, and forward supporting plates, also welded, provide additional rigidity with high resistance to flexing. Adequate openings for convenient servicing are provided.

Both the compression and steering or guide rolls are made of heavy steel plate, well reinforced.

To secure perfect balance, engine and transmission are mounted slightly off-center, counteracting the weight of the final drive.

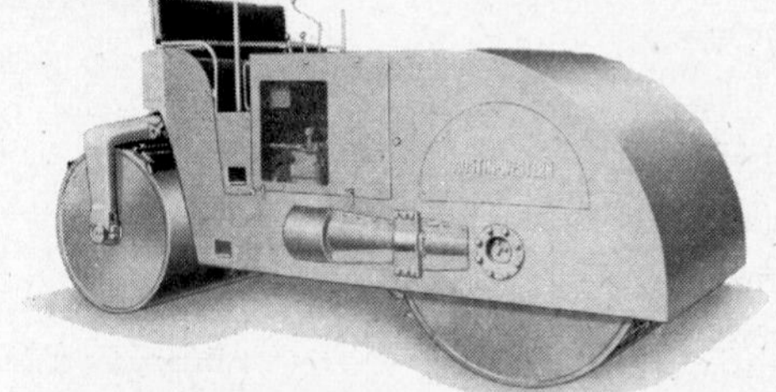

These Rollers are built so that frame overhang does not interfere with rolling close to obstructions, and there is sufficient ground clearance for rolling close to high curbs.

Uniform weight distribution and a low center of gravity eliminate side sway.

Effortless, smooth hydraulic power is used for steering.

The Austin-Western Variable Weight Tandem Rollers are made in 5-8, 8-12 and 10-14 ton sizes.

PORTABLE TANDEM ROLLER

Completing the Austin-Western Roller line is the new 3½—6 Ton Portable Tandem Roller, designed and engineered for complete versatility—the perfect Roller for a wide range of jobs such as rolling paving mats, surfacing driveways, parking lots, street and highway patching, and preparing subgrades.

Weight distribution on the compression roll varies from 60 percent dry to 70 percent fully ballasted, resulting in greater compaction for heavier jobs.

Simple and compact throughout, this Portable Tandem Roller affords excellent operator visibility.

AUSTIN-WESTERN WORKS

Construction Equipment Division *Baldwin-Lima-Hamilton Corporation*

Aurora, Illinois, U. S. A.

DISTRIBUTORS IN PRINCIPAL CITIES

THE INDOOR-OUTDOOR CRANE OF MANY USES

The tractor-mounted, All-Wheel Drive and All-Wheel Steer Hydraulic Crane with its pickup, carrying, and placement capabilities combines the best features of crawler, truck and erection cranes with those of industrial shop cranes. All movements of the boom are actuated by fast, smooth, positive hydraulic power.

Steering, too, is done hydraulically—front wheels power-booster steered, while the rear axle has a straight hydraulic, lever-actuated steering control—affording the shortest possible turning radius of 15 feet.

This tractor crane can be equipped with either a gasoline or diesel engine and has a full reverse six-speed transmission with torque converter. A three-speed transmission is optional.

The telescopic boom can be raised from the horizontal to an approximate 66° angle or to any intermediate point, and is continuously rotatable through a full 360°. Two or more movements of the boom and cable are possible while the tractor is in motion. The angle of the boom is quickly and easily changed while operating under load.

The crane can lift and transport its maximum load any distance, through low-clearance doors, and then, with the boom extended, the hook can be raised 24 feet or lowered 30 feet below ground level.

Manual boom extensions in 6, 8, 10, 12, 14 and 17 foot lengths are available as optional equipment, affording a maximum horizontal reach of 35 feet.

Special attachments include a lift fork, maintenance platform, orange peel bucket, clamshell bucket and an electric magnet.

TRUCK-MOUNTED MODEL

For added working capacities, hydraulic outriggers, hydraulic or mechanical winches, front and rear mounted carrying platform, snow plow and bulldozer are also available.

It weighs approximately 18,000 pounds, and traveling speeds range from 1.88 mph in low to approximately 20.56 mph in high at full engine throttle.

The Austin-Western Hydraulic Crane can be mounted on any truck meeting the minimum chassis requirements, and proves particularly advantageous for long-distance, high-speed runs on the job or from job to job.

Complete hydraulic operations include: continuous 360° turntable rotation, extension and retraction of the boom, raising and lowering of the cable and boom elevation.

Outriggers are added to prevent frame distortion, as well as to insure sufficient stability.

BLAW-KNOX COMPANY

CONSTRUCTION EQUIPMENT DIVISION

MATTOON, ILLINOIS

BRANCH OFFICES

New York, 405 Lexington Ave. Philadelphia, 931 Suburban Station Building Pittsburgh, Blaw-Knox Bldg. Birmingham, Brown-Marx Bldg. Chicago, Peoples Gas Bldg. Washington, D. C., 209 Wire Bldg. San Francisco, 681 Market St. Export Cable Address: BLAWKNOX, Mattoonill, U.S.A., Mattoon, Ill.

BLAW-KNOX CONSTRUCTION EQUIPMENT INCLUDES

Clamshell Buckets — Aggregate Batching Plants — Bulk Cement Plants — Truck Mixer Loading Plants — Hi-Boy Trukmixers — Central Mixing Plants — Steel Curb and Gutter Forms — Steel Road Forms — Precision Subgraders — Concrete Paving Spreaders — Finishing Machines — Concrete Buckets — Steel Forms for General Construction — Concrete Pavers — Asphaltic Concrete Pavers — Road Wideners — Base Pavers — Trench Rollers

BLAW-KNOX BATCHING PLANTS

For Storing and Measuring Coarse Aggregates and Cement

Blaw-Knox offers a complete line of self-cleaning steel batching plants for aggregate storage or fast accurate batching, and a complete line of plants for handling and batching bulk cement. Capacities of aggregate plants range from 100 to 400 tons. Two, three or four compartment styles are available. Bulk cement plants of 200 to 600 bbl. sizes are available with combination arrangements to multiply these capacities. The portability and flexibility of Blaw-Knox batching plants make them especially adaptable to municipal requirements. Bulletin 2488 gives full information.

BLAW-KNOX CLAMSHELL BUCKETS

for incinerator service

The economical operation of an incinerator plant is materially influenced by efficient and dependable bucket operation in lifting the collected refuse into the furnace. The Blaw-Knox lever arm type bucket is preferred for incinerator service because it handles larger average loads and averages more trips per minute, allowing trucks to dump as soon as they reach the plant. Simple design, with built-in weight distribution, results in longer life and lower maintenance. Blaw-Knox modern type buckets are especially designed for the characteristic requirements of incinerator operation. Full details, including structural and operating advantages of Blaw-Knox two-line lever arm buckets, are given in Bulletin 2350, which also includes a typical bucket and tine-type grapple specification for your guidance.

for digging and material handling

For any type of municipal digging or material handling job, the careful selection of the correct type and weight of bucket and consideration of service requirements will result in the greatest possible tonnage from crane equipment. Blaw-Knox Clamshell Buckets permit a higher ratio between bucket performance and payload because they are designed for maximum yardage, easier and faster work, and reduced all-over maintenance costs. Blaw-Knox buckets are available in the type, size and weight, and with the proper accessories, to fit every requirement. Catalog 2472-E gives complete information.

BLAW-KNOX ROAD WIDENERS lay concrete *without forms*, asphaltic concrete and all kinds of aggregate

Blaw-Knox Model 95 Road Widener spreading crushed stone. Note one-man operation and perfect visibility.

No forms required for laying concrete! The strike-off gate distributes the concrete over the desired strip, the vibrator "sets-up" the concrete, and the trailing shoe neatly shapes it.

Economical widening jobs are assured with time and labor saving Blaw-Knox Wideners. They handle concrete without forms, asphaltic concrete, stone, slag, gravel, soil cement or crusher-run aggregate at lowest possible costs. Speedy, efficient operation builds earth shoulders at the rate of 200 tons per hour . . . spreads and finishes concrete up to 1½ miles per day. On one ten-mile concrete strip, six feet wide, a Blaw-Knox Road Widener **saved over $10,000!** It's a heavy-duty money-saver, for spreading from 2′ to 10′ widths. Special attachment can be ordered for reducing the minimum width to 18″.

BLAW-KNOX BASE PAVERS cut *weeks* off schedule time

Base course paving is fast, accurate and economical with this high tonnage producer. You can spread stone, slag, gravel, soil cement or crusher-run aggregates to depths up to 20″ and widths up to 16′ in one pass, with no segregation of material, and at a rate up to 400 tons per hour. There's plenty of traction and power to push your trucks, yet flotation for the softest surfaces. Oscillating action of the V-type screed "knits" material into the voids for accurately level and smooth base courses. Operating costs are low. Hand dressing behind the unit is reduced to the minimum. Blaw-Knox Base Pavers are available in two models to meet every base pavement requirement.

Model P-150 Base Paver spreading crusher-run material, from 5″ to dust, to a depth of 9″ and 14′ width. Note how fines are carried to the extreme edges. There is no segregation.

BLAW-KNOX STEEL CURB and GUTTER FORMS

The Complete Steel Form System for Curbs, Curb and Gutters, Sidewalks, Integral Concrete Curbs, Gutters

The modern and cost saving method for every sidewalk and curb job, large or small! Blaw-Knox Steel Curb and Gutter Forms do a better job while saving time and reducing labor costs. They are easy to set, strip and handle. They eliminate the building of expensive wood forms, especially on curves, and require a minimum of hand finishing. A Blaw-Knox Form set-up is available for every type of work. For full information on the complete form system and detailed "how-to-use" instructions, ask for Bulletin 2259R.

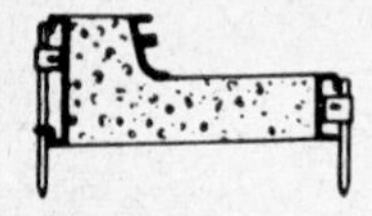
CURB AND GUTTER FORMS with common type face forms when joints are 5 or 10 feet feet apart

CURB AND GUTTER FORMS with common type face forms when joints are not 5 or 10 feet apart

CURB AND GUTTER FORMS with special type face forms when joints are 5 or 10 feet apart

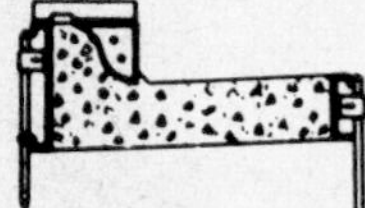
CURB AND GUTTER FORMS with special type face forms when joints are not 5 or 10 feet apart

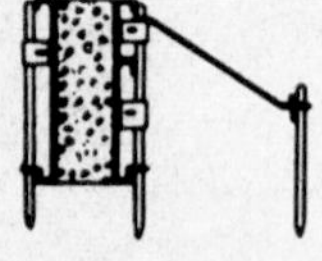
CURB FORMS—Vertical back and face

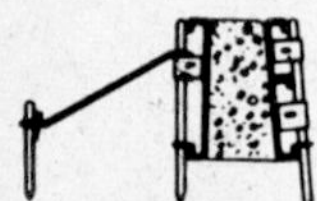
CURB FORMS—Vertical back with battered face

CURB FORMS — Battered exposed face

INTEGRAL CURB FORMS

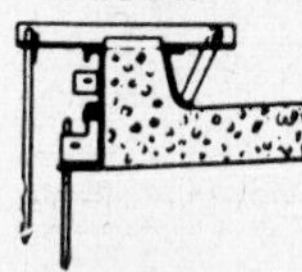
INTEGRAL CURB FORMS

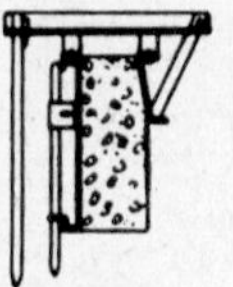
INTEGRAL CURB FORMS

INTEGRAL CURB FORMS

FLEXIBLE RADIUS FORMS—For curved work of variable radius

FLEXIBLE RADIUS FACE FORMS—For use with fixed radius back and gutter forms

FIXED RADIUS FORMS—For curved work when same radius is repeated.

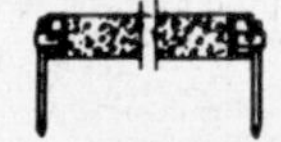
SIDEWALK FORMS—For any width or thickness of sidewalk

SPECIAL CURB FORMS — Designed and engineered to meet non-standard conditions

BLAW-KNOX *Electroforged* STEEL GRATING

for Sidewalks · Sidewalk Doors · Stairways · Tree Guards · Subway Gratings · Catwalks · Flooring Platforms · HUNDREDS OF OTHER USES

Blaw-Knox Steel Grating is *electroforged* into one piece for high strength and permanence. Twisted cross bar construction provides safe, sure footing and is easy to protect against corrosion. Paint reaches the entire surface. Absence of crevices or acute angles prevents accumulation of dirt. Maximum open area admits light and air. Easily adapted to many uses. Blaw-Knox Electroforged Steel Grating is ideal for all grating and open floor requirements. Send for Bulletin 2365; also ask for information about Blaw-Knox *Electroforged* Steel Stair Treads.

FOR HIGH PRODUCTION BITUMINOUS PAVING the BLAW-KNOX PAVER FINISHER Model PF-90

The Blaw-Knox Bituminous Paver Finisher Model PF-90 has demonstrated conclusively the superiority of wheel mounting for laying bituminous paving on any type of big production job. Its rubber-tired mounting gives you twice the speed with half the maintenance cost of a crawler-mounted unit. Fast paving at up to 52 feet per minute, speedy returns for restarts at up to 7.4 miles per hour and quick, easy maneuvering allow you to make fast work of every paving job. By eliminating 500 to 600 parts characteristic of crawlers and by reducing vibration that causes wear and tear on the paver you will have half the maintenance of ordinary bituminous pavers. You get this speed and low maintenance without sacrificing ability to meet the most rigid city or state paving specifications. It also has the traction to handle boxcar size trucks on tough grades.

NEW BLAW-KNOX BLACK TOP PAVER MODEL PF-45

Requires Low Investment

Now, *for little more than half the cost* of a big paver, you can get the new, small, lightweight Blaw-Knox Model PF-45 Black Top Paver for highest quality bituminous pavement work. Similar in design and construction to the big Blaw-Knox Model PF-90 Paver Finisher, the Model PF-45 Black Top Paver is the first machine of its kind that is designed specifically for smaller paving jobs such as city streets, parking areas, sidewalks, park roadways, alleys, and driveways. It is completely self-propelled and has the speed, power, maneuverability, versatility and low operating cost that have never before been put into a black top paver requiring so low an investment.

The combination of a 4-ton hopper, self-power, speed and maneuverability allows this PF-45 to make easy work of paving a school playground where trucks can't maneuver.

BAUGHMAN MANUFACTURING COMPANY

157 Shipman Road
Jerseyville, Illinois

Complete line of
ICE CONTROL SPREADING EQUIPMENT

Sand & Cinder Spreader (Model K5-SC)

Available in 4 drives! Combination of P. T. O. or Auxiliary Engine with Hydraulic or Mechanical Operation. Two-speed chain and sprocket drive for chemical or large volume spreading. Adaptable to year-round use: ice control in winter, chip spreading and oil blotting rest of year.

HYDRAULIC SPREAD-MOBILE

Features exclusive "Center-Spred" design for spreading under all 4 wheels, improving driver visibility . . . complete cab operated controls for width and amount of spread . . . baffle arrangement for safe spreading in presence of passing cars or pedestrians.

Tailgate Spreaders

A choice of models, with such features as metering valve control of volume . . . hydraulic or auxiliary engine drives for spread patterns up to 30′ wide . . . self-leveling body mounting for upright spread position. Handy controls for width and amount of spread.

Super Spreader

Forward or reverse spreading. Mechanical or Hydraulic Drive. Any material to ½″ dia. Fits any dump body. Hard-metal criss-cross tread provides even application.

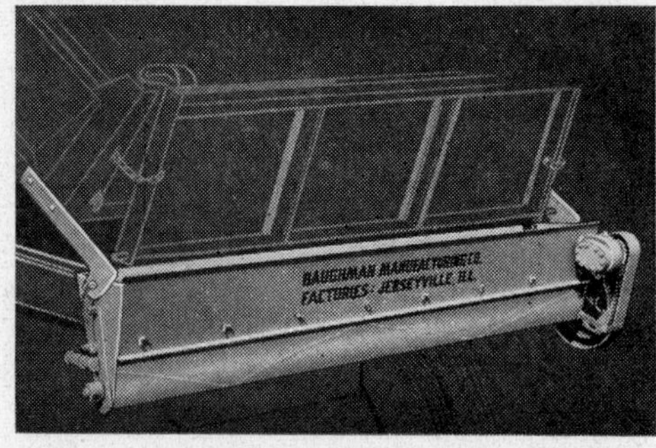

Pull Type Spreader

Traction operation. 360° spread pattern. Adjustable valve for quantity control.

WRITE for new ICE CONTROL BULLETIN A-408

BADGER MACHINE CO.

HOPTO HYDRAULIC DIGGER • SHOVEL • CRANE • LOADER

1124 West Fifth St., Winona, Minnesota

TRUCK MOUNTED

MODEL 360-57-90 HOPTO

A completely hydraulic ⅜-½ yard unit with 360° swing. Cab turns with boom. Unit has fast cycle, 20′ digging depth and 15′-6″ loading height with backhoe on a 25′ radius and 16′-9″ loading height at a 27′ radius when equipped with a shovel bucket. The 360-57-90 features a triple tandem pump with a split valve bank assuring full power at all times. Safety relief valves and cushioning valves throughout the hydraulic system protect the machine from over-loading. Equipped with individually controlled hydraulic outriggers.

In travel position boom is carried next to half-cab so as not to obstruct driver's visibility. Note compactness of unit which meets all legal height and width requirements.

TRUCK MOUNTED
MODEL 200 DTM-57-72 HOPTO

Unit mounts on any 2-ton or larger truck, has 200° swing, 13½′ digging depth and loading height of 11½′ with backhoe on 10½′ radius; 11′ dumping height of shovel bucket at 13′ radius. Backhoe and shovel buckets are interchangeable, have replaceable H & L teeth and are available in a wide variety of widths and sizes for this and all models shown. Equipped with triple tandem pump and split hydraulic system with safety relief valves and cushioning valves throughout the hydraulic system.

Note hydraulic outriggers, operator's unrestricted visibility and clearance of shovel bucket over truck. Backhoe also has ample clearance for loading in highest truck.

Exclusive bucket tilt feature permits tilting of bucket a full 180°. Digs straight-sided, square - cornered holes.

MODEL 185 SPR

This is an integral self-powered self-propelled backhoe on rubber featuring "over-the-road" mobility and fast "job-to-job" mobility. Swivel seat enables operator to move machine ahead with little lost time. Model 185 SPR has the same specifications as above listed truck model.

MODEL 190 SPC
HOPTO

The Model 190 SPC is a low cost Crawler Mounted Backhoe with a 190° continuous swing. Both backhoe and shovel buckets are available in widths up to 30" wide. 8½' tracks provide a low bearing pressure for "off-the-road-operation." Swivel seat enables operator to move machine ahead with little lost time. Cycling time and ease of operation are the same as that of all models of the HOPTO.

MODEL 80 CTM HOPTO

HOPTO uses the power you already have. Mountings available for most popular makes of track-type tractors; does not interfere with the operation of the tractor or front-end equipment. Has 180° continuous swing, 10' digging depth, approximately 10' loading height and 180° bucket tilt. Individually operated hydraulic outriggers stabilize and hold machine even under adverse digging conditions. There are no cables, drums, sheaves, chains, belts, or clutches on this or any other model of the HOPTO. Make the tractor which has been "written off" a useful tool with the addition of a HOPTO.

MODEL 80 RTM HOPTO

The Model 80 RTM HOPTO is a quarter yard unit designed for mounting on any standard make wheel-type tractor. Unit is powered from the power take-off of the tractor. Hydraulic outriggers and boom retract so as to not interfere with normal front-end operations. Has 11′ digging depth, approximately 10′ loading height, 180° continuous swing and 180° tilt of bucket. Unit shown is mounted on an International Harvester Tractor and has HOPTO's power-crowding front-end loader for material handling and back filling of trenches, etc.

MODEL 180
PTO OPERATED **HOPTO**

A light weight but sturdy quarter-yard unit in a trailer model. Available for operation from power take-off or in self-powered model. Digs 11′ deep and has ample loading height for large trucks. Has a lifting capacity of one ton or more, depending on type and weight of tractor with which used. Trails well at speeds up to 25 miles per hour. Backhoe and shovel buckets are interchangeable. Has 180° continuous swing and 180° tilt of bucket. Recommended as a utility unit or for trenching and material handling.

BADGER ALSO MANUFACTURES A COMPLETE LINE OF CONTINUOUS TRENCHERS

BADGER MACHINE CO.

1112 WEST FIFTH ST. • WINONA, MINNESOTA

SUBSIDIARY:

NORTHEASTERN HOPTO CO., INC.
RUSSELL ROAD, ROUTE 20, WESTFIELD, MASS.

THE CELOTEX CORPORATION

Chicago, Illinois

TOP PERFORMANCE

proved on many of the nation's biggest jobs!

FLEXCELL

REG. U. S. PAT. OFF.

BITUMINOUS FIBER EXPANSION JOINT FILLER

FLEXCELL Expansion Joint Filler is a premoulded fiber product of cellular nature, impregnated throughout with a durable asphaltic compound. It is used between slabs of concrete in highways, runways, floors, or any large area where normal expansion and contraction must be compensated.

1—**Fiber**—The base of Flexcell Joint Filler is made from long, tough, springy cane fiber.

2—**Impregnation**—From 35 to 50 per cent by weight of asphaltic compound is introduced into the fibers by the Flexcell process.

3—**Compressibility**—Flexcell is compressible to 50 per cent of its original thickness under a pressure ranging between 300 to 600 lbs. per square inch.

4—**Resiliency**—Tests show that Flexcell, after compression to 50 per cent, returns to more than 70 per cent of its original thickness.

5—**Non-Extrusion**—Flexcell is non-extruding because the air chambers retained within the board permit it to be compressed without being displaced.

6—**Bonding Properties**—The rough surface of Flexcell permits the concrete to grip and hold firmly to the Flexcell filler, thus providing a tight joint and anchoring it in position.

7—**Ease of Handling**—Easily handled at all temperatures. Does not become hard or brittle in cold weather, nor soft and sticky in hot weather.

8—**Durability**—Flexcell in use over a period of 20 years has shown that light, heat, moisture, freezing, and thawing have no harmful effects.

SIZES, THICKNESSES

Flexcell Expansion Joint is available in ¼", ⅜", ½", ¾" and 1" thicknesses. Standard sheet size is 36" x 10'. Other sheet sizes available.

SUGGESTED SPACING AND THICKNESS OF EXPANSION JOINTS

When expansion joints are placed at intervals of..	10 to 20 ft.	20 to 30 ft.	30 to 50 ft.	50 to 70 ft.	70 to 100 ft.
Suggested thickness of joint filler	¼ in.	⅜ in.	½ in.	¾ in.	1 in.

SHORT FORM SPECIFICATION

Joint Filler: Premoulded cane fiber uniformly impregnated with between 35% and 50% durable asphaltic compound by weight. Sample when compressed to 50% of original thickness under a pressure ranging between 300 to 600 lbs. per sq. in. and released, shall show at least 70% recovery within one hour, and shall not extrude more than ⅛".

FLEXCELL JOINT FILLER COMPLIES WITH:

American Association of State Highway Officials Standard Specification M 153-52, Type III.

Federal Specifications HH-F-341a, Type I, Class B.

American Society for Testing Materials Standard Specifications for preformed Expansion Joint Fillers for Concrete D544-52T, Type III.

U. S. Navy Dept., Bureau of Yards and Docks Spec. 4 Yd, Item 1-10.

State Highway Department Specifications for Bituminous Fiber Expansion Joint for Use on State and Federal Aid Projects.

NEVER DOES THIS

When solid asphalt type joint yields to pressure, it extrudes and the joint bulges

ALWAYS LIKE THIS

Flexcell Expansion Joint Filler never extrudes. It gives under pressure and springs back into position

THE PHILIP *Carey* MFG. COMPANY

General Offices, Cincinnati 15, Ohio

Elastite Highway Products

Careylastic Sealing Compound is a mixture of rubbers, asphalts and plasticizers which retains its plastic and elastic properties at summer and winter temperatures.

When hot-poured into an expansion joint, Careylastic Sealing Compound bonds to the sides of the joint and effectively seals the joint against infiltration of water and incompressible materials. Careylastic requires no maintenance and is packaged in 50 lb. multiple wall strippable bags or nine 50 lb. cakes per steel drum.

Careylastic meets Federal Specification SS-F-336a, superseded by SS-S-164, A.S.T.M. D1190-52T.

Asphalt Expansion Joint, the original preformed expansion joint, is composed of two sheets of asphalt-saturated felt with an intermediate layer of heavy plastic-asphalt compound. Elastite Asphalt Expansion Joint can be installed in concrete walks, streets, roads and bridges. It is easy to apply and economical to maintain.

Asphalt Expansion Joint is made in a wide variety of thicknesses, in any width up to 36 inches. Lengths of 5 feet and 10 feet are standard, but special lengths and shapes can be made to requirements. Asphalt Expansion Joint meets state specifications and Federal Specifications AASHO M-33-48, ASTM D-994-53.

Fiber Expansion Joint is a fibrous material produced by saturating fiber board with a durable asphaltic compound. It is rigid enough for handling in the field, yet can be compressed to 50% of its original thickness.

Fiber Expansion Joint is furnished in ¼″, ⅜″, ½″, ¾″ and 1″ thicknesses, and in any size up to 3′ x 12′6″. When properly designed and installed, this material is an economical, nonextruding joint filler.

Fiber Expansion Joint meets state specifications and Federal Specifications HH-F-341a, type 1, class B. It also meets specifications AASHO M-153-54 (type 3) and ASTM D-544-52T (type 3).

Filler Asphalts are used for filling joints and cracks in roads, streets and highways. Standard Specification materials are carried in stock.

Jet Fuel Resistant Careylastic Sealing Compound is a mixture of rubbers, tars, plasticizers and fillers capable of retaining its plastic and elastic properties at both summer and winter temperatures.

This compound is used to seal joints in concrete paving for airfields and other areas where jet fuel comes in contact with the paving. Applied hot, it bonds to the sides of the joint and effectively seals the joint through periods of structural expansion and contraction.

J.F.R. Careylastic is packaged in multiple wall strippable paper bags with instructions printed on the bag. Each bag contains 50 pounds. This compound complies with Interim Federal Specification SS-S-00167.

Asphalt Plank is a dense, hard, tough composition of asphalt, fiber and mineral. The conveniently sized planks are formed under great pressure.

Carey developed Asphalt Plank as a wearing surface for bridges and as a protective course over membrane waterproofing. It is readily applied over wood, concrete or steel. When applied over a good base, Asphalt Plank provides a durable paving surface for heavy traffic.

Asphalt Plank is furnished in thicknesses from ½″ to 2″, in convenient widths up to 12″, and in standard lengths of 3′ and 6′. It is also furnished with 1 pound per square foot of ½″ trap rock impressed into the wearing surface for skid resistance. This type of plank is available from 1″ to 2″ thick, 12″ x 24″ size.

Asphalt Plank meets various state specifications, AASHO Specification M-46-38, ASTM Specification D-517-40, D-517-50 and AREA Specification 29-2-8, Sec. 16.

It is in use on many famous bridges, including the nationally known New York Triborough and Chicago La Salle Street Bridges.

Information, specifications, samples and prices will be sent on request.

ow CLEANLINESS
is automatic with

WASTE RECEPTACLES

with non-rusting stainless steel feet

↑ BENNETT SELF-CLOSING WASTE RECEPTACLE

BENNETT
DROP-IN
WASTE
RECEPTACLE
↓

Design
Pat.
Pending

See the inside story of Bennett Waste Receptacles plus the complete line of models.

THE BENNETT MANUFACTURING COMPANY

ALDEN, N. Y.

ONLY  RECEPTACLES

Everybody is automatically a member of your cleaning department by conveniently placing Bennett Bilt Waste Receptacles to invite their use.

Phosphate treated metal and baked enamel finish provide neat appearance and increase corrosion resistance.

Non-rusting stainless steel feet eliminate corrosion and rust marks.

Extra heavy gauge steel and all welded construction. Reinforced corners.

Positive closing doors repel insects, rodents and also reduce fire hazard.

Catalog Number	Size of Base	Body Height	Overall Height	Approximate Shipping Weight	Inner Containers Furnished as Standard
19-L	9″ x 9″	4″	10″	7 lbs.	Gal. Inner Can with 12 Waxed Paper Bags
112-L	11½″ x 11½″	27½″	34½″	28½ lbs.	1 Galv. Inner Can
125	11½″ x 11½″	19″	26″	19 lbs.	12 Waxed Paper Bags
125-L	11½″ x 11½″	19″	26″	27 lbs.	1 Galv. Inner Can
142	11½″ x 11½″	34″	41″	26 lbs.	1 Hvy. Osnaberg Bag
142-L	11½″ x 11½″	34″	41″	33 lbs.	1 Galv. Inner Can
130	16″ x 16″	26″	36″	33 lbs.	1 Hvy. Osnaberg Bag
130-L	16″ x 16″	26″	36″	43 lbs.	1 Galv. Inner Can
140 (Heavy)	16″ x 16″	31″	41″	40½ lbs.	1 Hvy. Osnaberg Bag
140-L (Heavy)	16″ x 16″	31″	41″	52½ lbs.	1 Galv. Inner Can
148 (Heavy)	22″ x 22″	37″	49″	77½ lbs.	1 Hvy. Osnaberg Bag
148-L (Heavy)	22″ x 22″	37″	49″	100 lbs.	1 Galv. Inner Can

Standard Colors: Green, Gray or White

NOTE: Model numbers with L are supplied with Galvanized Liners instead of bags. Models 140 and 148 are ideal for outdoor use. Specially designed, light weight shipping cartons protect receptacle and reduce freight costs. Specifications Subject to Change Without Notice.

Both doors may be opened independently.

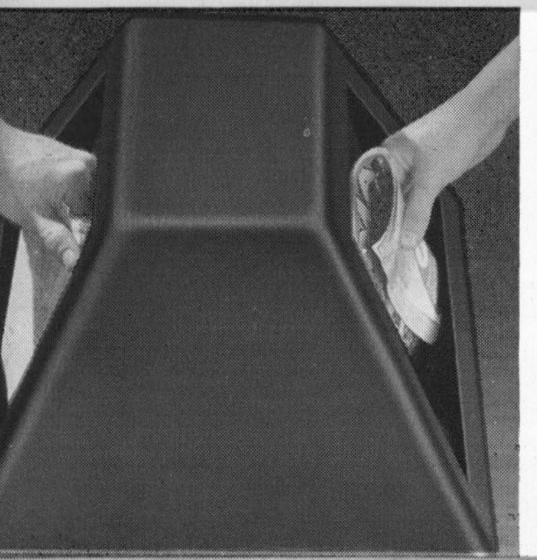

Doors stay closed eliminating the necessity of placing these receptacles on level floors or sidewalks.

Osnaberg bags and galvanized liners ar[e] quickly removed when filled with waste. Fu[ll] swing, unobstructed open top permits easie[r] removing and replacing inside containers.

THE BENNETT MANUFACTURING COMPANY, Alden, N. Y

Give You All These Features

Sturdy design to withstand continuous, hard everyday use is a direct result of over 50 years' experience in metal fabrication.

A few of the many features that make Bennett Bilt Waste Receptacles a natural "buy" are pointed out in the illustration at the right. Quality and every consideration for hard usage are self-evident both inside and outside of these receptacles.

WHEREVER PEOPLE CONGREGATE THERE IS A PLACE FOR

WASTE RECEPTACLES

WRITE FOR CATALOG

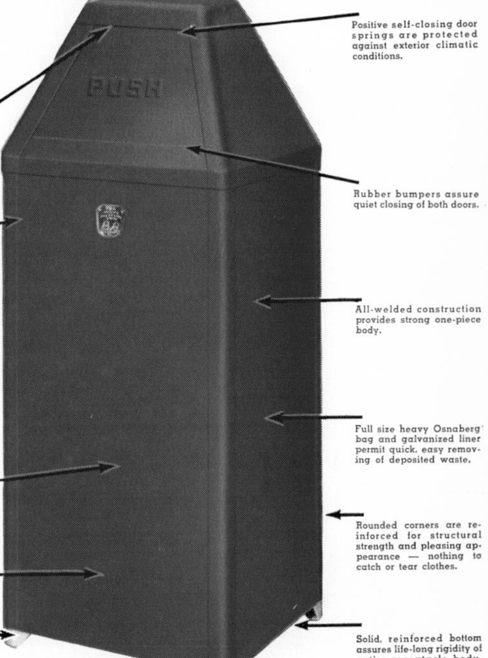

Self-closing door spring mechanism assures positive closed doors when not in use and permits easy opening of independent doors with fingertip pressure.

Welded and ground joints with rounded corners provide smooth appearance.

Available in WHITE, GRAY, GREEN.

Other colors available on request.

Acid resisting baked enamel finish for permanent protection of metal OUTDOORS and INDOORS. Phosphate treatment of steel provides corrosion resistance.

Extra heavy gage steel used throughout assures heavy-duty service.

Four stainless steel feet on all models prevent rust marks on floors and sidewalks.

Positive self-closing door springs are protected against exterior climatic conditions.

Rubber bumpers assure quiet closing of both doors.

All-welded construction provides strong one-piece body.

Full size heavy Osnaberg bag and galvanized liner permit quick, easy removing of deposited waste.

Rounded corners are reinforced for structural strength and pleasing appearance — nothing to catch or tear clothes.

Solid, reinforced bottom assures life-long rigidity of entire receptacle body.

AVAILABLE STENCILS FOR SLOGANS

No. 142 or No. 142-L Receptacle
- Help Keep Our School Clean

No. 130 or No. 130-L Receptacle
- Help Keep Our Plant Clean
- Help Keep Our Shop Clean
- Help Keep Our School Clean
- Help Keep Your Plaza Clean
- Paper Only
- Refuse

No. 140 or No. 140-L Receptacle
- Help Keep Our Streets Clean
- Help Keep Our City Clean
- Help Keep Our Plant Clean
- Help Keep Your Campus Clean
- Help Keep Our Campus Clean
- Help Keep Our School Clean
- Help Keep Our Shop Clean
- Help Keep Our Park Clean
- Help Keep Your Village Clean
- Help Keep Your Plaza Clean
- Paper Only
- Refuse

No. 148 or No. 148-L Receptacle
- Please Deposit Paper in Container
- Help Keep Our Borough Clean
- Help Keep Our City Clean
- Help Keep Our Streets Clean
- Help Keep Your Campus Clean
- Help Keep Our Campus Clean
- Help Keep Our Shop Clean
- Help Keep Your Village Clean
- Help Keep Our Plant Clean
- Help Keep Our Park Clean
- Help Keep Your Plaza Clean
- Paper Only
- Refuse

In Offices

In Washrooms

CUSTOM METAL CRAFTSMEN SINCE 1906

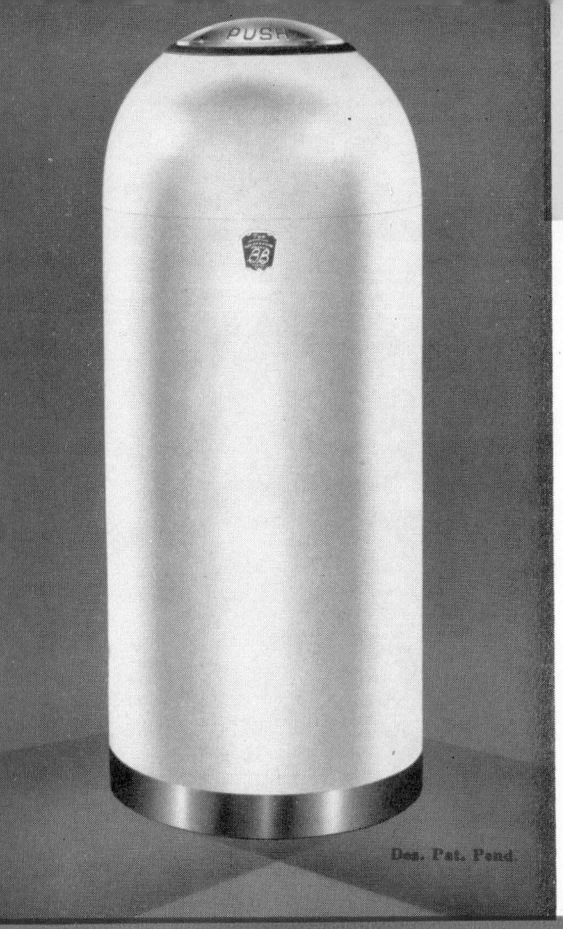

BENNETT

DROP-IN
WASTE RECEPTACLES

BENNETT CLOSED DROP-IN WASTE RECEPTACLES wi self-closing chromium plated "Tip-Top" door has unusual gentle, silent spring action for all around accessibility. Th modern design eliminates stopping or standing in line throw away litter. White baked-on enamel finish wi wrap around stainless steel base provides a harmonio combination of beauty. Rubber gasket around top ope ing finishes off the smart appearance. Extra heavy du steel is chemically treated for corrosion resistance. Ide for outdoor as well as indoor locations. Complete wi galvanized liner for fast emptying. BENNETT OPE DROP-IN WASTE RECEPTACLES leave both hands fre nothing to open, for fast depositing. Just drop pap towels, cups and other waste in top. Complete with g vanized liner. Closed Drop-in Model 36 — Height 36 Diameter 15″; Approximate Shipping Weight 25 lb Open Drop-in Model 35 — Height 35″; Diameter 15 Approximate Shipping Weight 24 lbs. Write for Catal and Prices.

paper towel and tissue paper dispensers

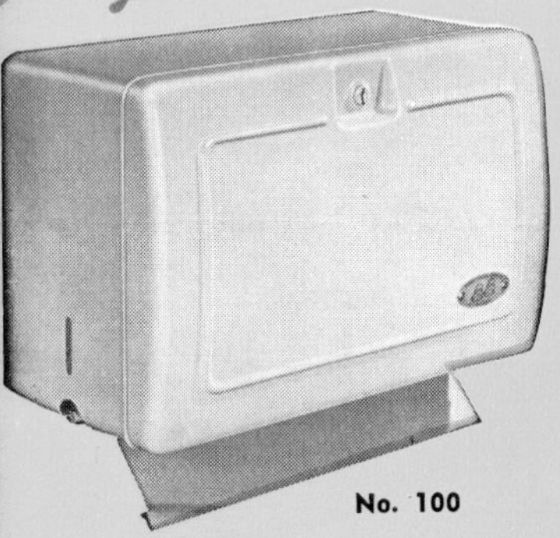

No. 100

No. 100 Enameled Junior Single-fold Towel Dispenser

No. 200 Chrome Junior Single-fold Towel Dispenser

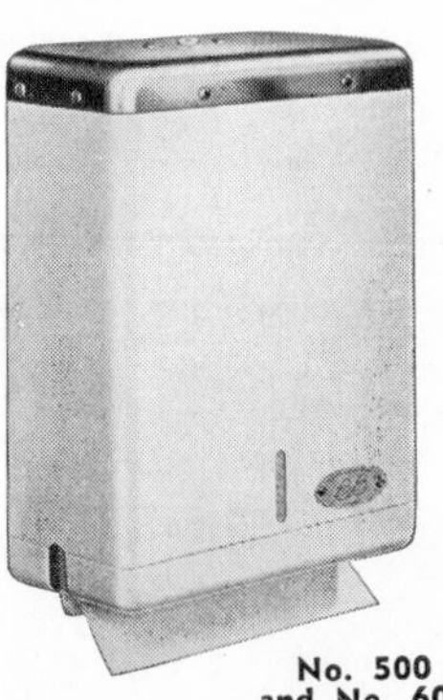

No. 500 and No. 600

No. 300 Chrome Double-fold Towel Dispenser

No. 400 Enameled Double-fold Towel Dispenser

No. 500 and 600 Single and Double-fold Toilet Tissue Dispensers

No. 300

No. 200

The many fine features built into Bennett Dispensers prove that nothing has been overlooked from the standpoint of quality, convenience and value. The paper is automatically fed by gravity through the bottom slot at the exact angle to eliminate binding, cross-feeding and inaccessability of towels. Side or front slots permit checking towel or tissue supply at a glance.

Model	Width	Depth	Height	Finish
100	12¼″	6½″	7¾″	Baked White Enamel
200	12¼″	6½″	7¾″	Chrome Plated
300	10¾″	3¾″	14¾″	Chrome Plated
400	10¾″	3¾″	14¾″	Baked White Enamel
500	5⅜″	2⅞″	7¾″	*Stainless Steel Tops with Baked White Enamel Bodies
600	5⅜″	2¼″	7¾″	

*Stainless steel tops withstand discoloring caused by burning cigarettes.

No. 400

THE BENNETT MANUFACTURING CO., ALDEN, N. Y.

and OH the COST to the taxpayer...

and the snow will go on . . . all winter . . . so where does that leave the Highway Official? . . . with heavy traffic? . . . on several hundred miles of icy roads?

It leaves him in control of the situation if he uses

CAYUGA ROCK SALT

Cayuga Rock Salt:

MELTS THE SNOW AND ICE
THE AIR THEN EVAPORATES IT
THE ROADS ARE THEN DRY AND SAFE

is so SMALL...

cayuga rock salt company

Phone: Lansing 4-4221 • Myers, N.Y.

it is mined deep in the earth and is actually harder than many types of rock

it is gritty enough to provide good traction on icy roads

it actually melts the ice while providing traction (water evaporates leaving the road dry)

it is economical to buy

it is very easy to use, spreads evenly

THAT'S HOW CAYUGA ROCK SALT

gives you

SAFE — UNINTERRUPTED — ECONOMICAL

Use of your roads

ALL WINTER  **EVERY WINTER**

cayuga rock salt company

Phone: Lansing 4-4221 • Myers, N.Y.

HOW FAR CAN $1.00 GO in controlling ICE and SNOW?

These days Highway Officials are perhaps more cost conscious than at any other time in history. With the phenomenal increase of traffic on one hand and growing demand for optimum road conditions the year 'round, on the other, the road program in this country accounts for an appreciable share of every tax dollar spent. By using Cayuga Rock Salt for Ice and Snow Control, an official is assured of safe highways through the winter season and also getting maximum value for every dollar. Check your Cayuga Rock Salt Distributor listed on page 100.

CAYUGA ROCK SALT . . . . . .

Distributors

CAYUGA SALT SALES
Div. of Highway Materials Co., Inc.
Groton, N. Y.
Phone 154 and 307

CAYUGA SALT SALES
Branch Office and Warehouse:
Robinson & Dickson Sts.
Newburgh, N. Y.
Phone 2034

CAYUGA SALT SALES
Branch Office and Warehouse:
172 Saratoga St.
Cohoes, N. Y.
Phone Cohoes Cedar 7-7211

THE CHEMICAL CORP., INC.
Main Office: 54 Waltham Ave.
Springfield 23, Mass.
Phone Springfield Republic 9-5601

THE CHEMICAL CORP., INC.
Office: 80 Boylston St.
Boston, Mass.
Phone LIberty 2-7171
Warehouse: Natick, Mass.

THE CHEMICAL CORP., INC.
Branch Office and Warehouse:
P. O. Box 466
Pittsfield, Mass.
Phone 2-0718

THE CHEMICAL CORP., INC.
Branch Office and Warehouse:
91 Fessenden St.
S. Portland, Maine
Phone 2-4261

E. J. FEDIGAN, INC.
Office: Anderson & Isabella Sts.
Warehouse: B&O RR Warehouse Bldg.
North Side, Pittsburgh 12, Pa.
Phone Pittsburgh Cedar 1-6767

HARVEY SALT CO., INC.
415 Guilford Ave.
Baltimore 2, Md.
Phone Saratoga 7-5030

NORTHRUP EQUIPMENT CO.
Parkersburg, W. Va.
Phone Parkersburg 8-6331

SALT SERVICE, INC.
Creighton & Jefferson Sts.
Philadelphia 31, Pa.
Phone TRinity 8-0972

CHAS. SCHAEFER & SON OF N. J., INC.
P. O. Box 236
Elizabeth 3, N. J.
Phone Elizabeth 2-7010
Warehouse: Magie Ave. & Harding Rd.
Townley, N. J.

CHAS. SCHAEFER & SON, INC.
69-50 Austin Ave.
Forest Hills 75, N. Y.
Phone Boulevard 3-0045

SOUTHERN SALT CO., INC.
222 W. Main St.
Norfolk 14, Va.
Phone Madison 2-4638

THE WATKINS SALT CO., INC
Watkins Glen, N. Y.
Phone 13

YOUNGSTOWN ICE CO.
1505 Logan Ave.
Youngstown 4, Ohio
Phone Riverside 3-4101

JOHN DEERE

Municipal TRACTORS AND EQUIPMENT

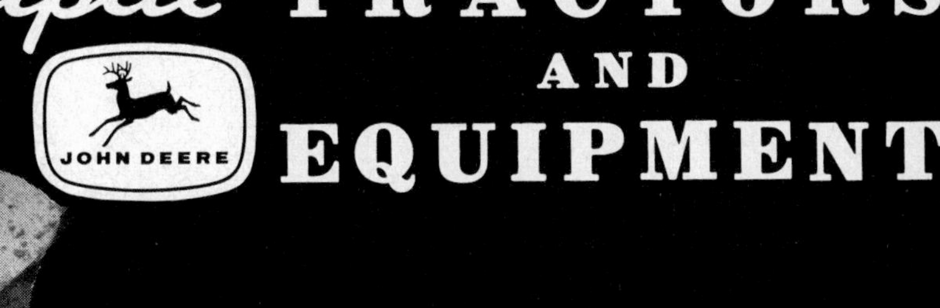

Crawler and Wheel-Type Mobile Units
for Cutting Costs on all Types of Work

JOHN DEERE
INDUSTRIAL DIVISION
Moline, Illinois

JOHN DEERE Gives You Low-Cost POWER Aplenty for These and Your Other Important Jobs

LOADING

Heavy-duty front-end loaders with rear-end scarifiers make fast work of materials-handling jobs. Available for John Deere 30-h.p. Crawler and Wheel-Type tractors. Rugged, compact mobile units. Highly maneuverable. Choice of bucket sizes. Attachments include crane, backfill blade, fork lifts, snow blade, street broom. Overhead loader available for Crawler.

DOZING—BACKFILLING

Inside- and outside-mounted, hydraulically controlled bulldozers team up with the high-torque John Deere Crawler to handle wide variety of work. Direction reverser (optional) saves up to one hour each day on the job. Tractor can be equipped with 3-point hitch for rear-mounted hydraulically controlled tools. Keep both ends busy!

SANITARY LANDFILLS

Economical, efficient equipment for building landfills, compacting and covering refuse. Three combinations—crawler with wheel-type scraper, crawler-loader, and crawler-bulldozer—all available in the big John Deere-Allied line at a cost within reach of the smallest communities.

NATIONWIDE SALES and SERVICE

JOHN DEERE
INDUSTRIAL DIVISION
Moline, Illinois

JOHN DEERE

TRENCHING

You will find just the equipment you are looking for in the John Deere-Allied line. Initial cost will please you but wait until you experience the low operating and maintenance costs! Deep-digging, highly maneuverable backhoes and power-operated trenching units for Crawler or Wheel-Type tractors.

CUTTER-BAR MOWING

Easy-to-handle, center-mounted, heavy-duty cutter-bar mowers for John Deere 30 h.p. or 21 h.p. Utility Tractors handle this important work at typically low cost. Units are low-built for extra stability on the slopes. Touch-o-matic hydraulic control governs cutting height at any position up to vertical. Safety release feature regular.

GANG MOWING

Fast, low-cost mowing in parks, golf courses, cemeteries, etc. Close-coupled units work close to fences, shrubs, and trees; easy to handle in tight places. Self-transporting—gangs raised and lowered by Touch-o-matic hydraulic control. Can be used on finest lawns without damage to turf. Five-speed transmission and foot throttle available.

SWEEPING

One-way, power-driven rotary broom for John Deere Utility Tractor sweeps 4- or 5-foot path. Simple. Durable. Ideal for all types of pavement including bituminous. Does a fast, clean job of snow removal. Long-life, high-quality bearings. Choice of palmyra or steel-filled brush. Sprinkler attachment.

. . . See Next Page for Branch Listing 

JOHN DEERE
INDUSTRIAL DIVISION
Moline, Illinois

Some New John Deere Features *(Optional at extra cost)*

Time-Saving DIRECTION REVERSER

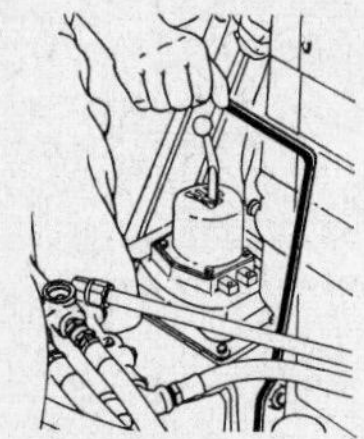

Lets you move forward or backward at same speed —no time wasted shifting transmission gears. Investigate — you can save as much as an hour a day in travel time. Available for John Deere "420" Crawler and Utility tractors.

Time-Saving FOOT THROTTLE

Increases engine speed and ground travel speed up to 25 per cent—makes possible speeds up to 17 mph on highway. Helpful when maneuvering in close quarters. Inexpensive. Easy to attach to tractor. Available for "420" Crawler and Utility tractors.

Heavy-Duty 3-POINT HITCH

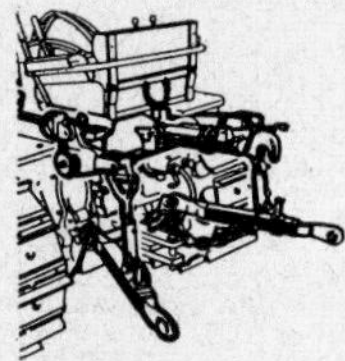

Enables you to use both ends of your crawler tractor. Change rear-mounted tools in minutes, raise and lower them hydraulically. Heavy - duty constuction. Leveling adjustments made without leaving tractor seat. Optional for John Deere Crawlers.

Time-Saving 5-SPEED TRANSMISSION

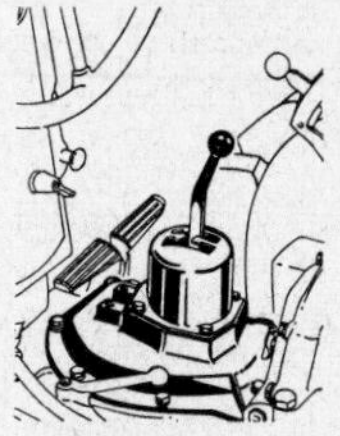

Provides an extra speed forward for increased versatility in many operations. On mowing work of all kinds, on long hauls, and on such work as finished blading and landscaping, the 5 - speed transmission quickly repays its small extra cost.

Branch Offices JOHN DEERE INDUSTRIAL DIVISION

United States:

Baltimore, Maryland, 2524 Kirk Ave.

Chamblee (Atlanta), Georgia

Columbus, Ohio, 1573 Olentangy River Road

Dallas, Texas, 10650 Hines Blvd.

Indianapolis, Indiana, 1025 W. Washington St.

Kansas City, Mo., 3210 E. 85th St.

Lansing, Michigan, 735 E. Michigan Ave.

Minneapolis, Minn., 800 Washington Ave. N

Moline, Illinois, 400 19th St.

Omaha, Nebraska, 912 Howard St.

Portland, Oregon, 215 S. E. Morrison St.

Salt Lake City, Utah, 1841 W. 1700 South

San Francisco, Calif., 651 Brannan St.

St. Louis, Mo., 2212-20 N. Bway.

Syracuse, N. Y., Midler-Court Industrial Park

Canada:

Calgary, Alberta, 201 Tenth Ave. E.

Hamilton, Ontario, Box 355

Regina, Saskatchewan, 7th Ave. and Broad St.

Winnipeg, Manitoba, 1500 Notre Dame Ave.

Mexico:

Mexico City, D.F., JOHN DEERE C.A.

Overseas:

Moline, Illinois, JOHN DEERE C.A.

CURB, GUTTER and SIDEWALK FORMS

Speed Up Your Construction Program with "Fast Delivery" from REX

Avoid waiting weeks for curb and gutter forms . . . eliminate the high cost of short-lived plywood forms . . . order from CHAIN Belt where two modern production lines guarantee fast delivery.

From CHAIN Belt, in addition to fast delivery, you get the most modern designed forms available today. Whatever your specifications or particular forming requirements might be, you can answer them better and faster with the complete Rex line.

CURB and GUTTER FORMS for constructing combined curbs and gutters from 4″ to 14″ high, from 18″ to 42″ wide. Face forms designed for straight, single radius or double radius work; battered or non-battered.

FLEXIBLE FORMS from 4″ to 24″ high. For inside or outside radius or serpentine construction. The only flexible form that is truly hinged.

SIDEWALK FORMS 3″ to 6″ depth for widths from 18″ to 8′0″.

HI-CURB FORMS

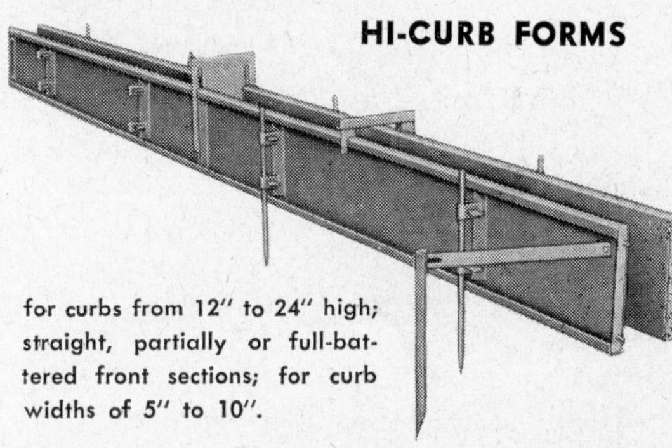

for curbs from 12″ to 24″ high; straight, partially or full-battered front sections; for curb widths of 5″ to 10″.

All necessary auxiliary equipment such as stakes, division plates, overhead hangers, staking braces, etc., are also included in the Rex (R)Form product line. Write for helpful new literature on complete line.

CHAIN Belt Company
4640 W. Greenfield Ave., Milwaukee 1, Wisc.

E. D. ETNYRE & CO.

Main office and plant, Oregon, Ill.

New automatic curb-paver eliminates curb forms...lays 4-6 feet per minute

Here is the newest advance in street- and road-building economy, offered by the makers of famous Etnyre "Black-Topper" Bituminous Distributors. The new self-propelled Etnyre Heavy-Duty Automatic Curb-Paver lays, compacts, and finishes straight or curved bituminous curbs in one fast, easy trip. The machine weighs 750 lb, requires no rails, is easily maneuverable. The two men who operate it need no special training.

Compaction is equal to that of a 12- to 15-ton roll. Every foot of curb is "ironed" by the engine-exhaust-heated Etnyre curbing mold for exceptionally smooth, weatherproof finish. Mold also blast-cleans and preheats paving surface ahead of machine. Exclusive offset lays curbing at very edge of pavement. Standard or special molds are available to your specifications. Molds easily interchangeable. Write, wire, or phone for details.

E. D. ETNYRE & CO.

Main office and plant, Oregon, Ill.

ETNYRE "Sanitary" STREET FLUSHERS

SUPERLINER MODEL—REAR ENGINE DRIVE—A streamlined, modern street flusher regularly furnished with 3 nozzles, 600 gpm pump, Hercules QXC5 engine, 800- to 3000-gallon tank, hydraulic controls, and globe valves.

Hundreds of cities all over the globe find Etnyre Street Flushers the complete answer to street sanitation problems. Knife-edge, high-pressure streams of water force all dust and waste to the gutter and on into the sewer. Streets up to 42′ wide can be cleansed from curb to curb in ONE trip—reducing bacterial count by 65%! And the flushing goes on irrespective of parked cars. The result is clean, fresh, attractive streets which make taxpayers and city officials proud and happy.

When not used for flushing streets, Etnyres are kept at work cleaning sewers, sprinkling dusty surfaces (race tracks, etc.), pumping out flooded basements, spraying trees, watering shrubbery, and fighting fires.

Etnyre Flushers are available in three models, four styles, front or rear engine drive. Mounted on truck, semi-trailer, or 4-wheel trailer—special mountings quoted upon request. Write, wire, or phone for specifications and prices on "The machine of a dozen uses."

E. D. ETNYRE & CO.

Main office and plant, Oregon, Ill.

ETNYRE "Black-Topper" DISTRIBUTORS For economy, accuracy, dependability

You need look no further for the very best bituminous distributor . . . on all counts! Pioneer in its field, the Etnyre "Black-Topper" has kept ahead of the parade for decades by leading the development of every major operating feature. Highway and street engineers, plus the majority of contractors, swear by the Etnyre for greater accuracy, reliability of operation, and economical performance over extremely long life.

Today you can get a "Black-Topper" almost custom-built for your requirements. Tank sizes range from 650 to 3000 gallons. Both medium and full heating systems are available. You can choose between low- and high-pressure heating systems, front or rear engine mounting, different makes of engines, and Full Circulating or Turn-Up Folding types of spray bars.

In all cases, you get Etnyre's compact, patented circulating system, exclusive "Vacu-Flo" cleaning system, triple-lap coverage, double-welded tank construction, pressure-relieving manhole cover, and dozens of other superior advantages. Write, wire, or phone for your free copy of "Foto-Facts" which gives you the complete Etnyre story.

E. D. ETNYRE & CO.

Main office and plant, Oregon, Ill.

ETNYRE MAINTENANCE UNITS

Companion to the Etnyre "Black-Topper" is this moneysaving maintenance unit, Model "MU." With it you can handle all maintenance and construction work where the size of the job does not warrant the use of a regular size distributor. Field experience has proved its dependable, economical, and efficient performance.

Operating crew members have found this unit to be ruggedly built, with the lowest possible center of gravity for fast highway speeds. Convenient, easy-to-operate controls expedite filling, circulating in tank, heating, spraying through bar, transferring, handspraying, and gravity draw-off.

Models are available with 400- or 600-gallon tanks, mounted on a four-wheel trailer or on a skid for truck mounting. You have your choice of engines, pumps, and types of spray bars. Heating system is complete with generating burners, 6" return flues, fuel tank, and fuel pump. The compact circulating system is designed for complete drainage, easy cleaning, simplified operation. Complete details are available in Data Bulletin No. 352—see your nearby Etnyre dealer or write us for your copy.

Our smallest snow blower . . . the BB series with 36 H.P. Wisconsin engine, Twin-Disc clutch and gear reduction, and final chain drive. There are no V belts to slip in this unit. Mounts on most tractors and loaders. Available—4'4" for sidewalk narrow gauge tractors and 6'6" for most other tractors. Push-frame is pivoted on rear axle and counterbalanced. Hydraulic or manual telescopic and rotating chute. Weight 2000 lbs. Capacity—approximately 5 tons per minute—Factory approved by leading tractor manufacturers.

THE BM...
SECOND IN SIZE...

also a detachable type snow blower with 95 H.P. Chrysler or International engine

Ideal for installation on large front end loaders and crawlers. Uses the same principle of chewing the snow before feeding it to the impeller. 8′6″ wide x 36″ high. Installed or dismantled in minutes. Telescopic and rotating hydraulic chute. Weight 4000 lbs. Capacity—Approximately 10 tons of snow per minute.

The BB and BM detachable type blowers are sold thru tractor and front end loader dealers. Inquiries invited.

SICARD INDUSTRIES INC. **SICARD** 753 WEST MAIN ST., WATERTOWN, N.Y.

THE SICARD SNOW MASTER JUNIOR

The Sicard Snow Master Junior; a compact and powerful blower designed principally for municipalities. Check these features: Chassis: All-wheel-traction, short 100" wheel-base, short turning radius, Chrysler engine with fluid drive. Blower: dual augers, large turbine for blowing, telescopic rotating chute for loading, powerful Buda auxiliary engine. Approx. weight 12,500 lbs. Capacity 15 tons of snow per minute.

SICARD SNOW MASTER

This unit is recognized as the standard of performance wherever in use throughout the world. The U.S.A.A.F. have recently ordered another 139 of these blowers to add to their growing fleet. Powered to your needs . . . to undertake any snow removal job, 200 to 350 H.P. and over. Weight 25,000 lbs. or more. Minimum width 8 ft. Capacity 22 to 60 tons per minute.

PAYLOADER®

TRACTOR SHOVELS

PAYLOADER®

MANUFACTURED BY

THE FRANK G. HOUGH CO. LIBERTYVILLE, ILL.

955 Sunnyside Ave., Libertyville, Ill., U.S.A.

SUBSIDIARY—INTERNATIONAL HARVESTER COMPANY

FOR

All Season

SERVICE

PAYLOADER® TRACTOR-SHOVELS

model HU

Four-wheel Drive
Rear-wheel Power-steer
Hydraulic Load-shock-absorber
Planetary Final Drives
Power-shift Transmission
Power-transfer Differentials
Four-wheel Power Brakes
Gas. or Diesel Power

Hough pioneered the first 4-wheel drive tractor-shovel in 1948, and is proud to present this model HU, the smallest of a great new series of four-wheel drive "PAYLOADER" Models. It features the all-new Hough bucket action that provides 40 degrees of bucket tip-back at ground level, tremendous pry-out bucket-loading action and greatly increased safety, balance and stability characteristics. Many versatile attachments available, including back-hoe, "V," blade and rotary snow plows, pick-up street sweeper and Drott 4-in-1 bucket.

SPECIFICATIONS

Bucket Capacity, Payload	1-1/3 cu. yd.
Bucket Capacity, Struck	1 cu. yd.
Bucket Width	78″
Lifting Capacity at 0-mph	8,000 Lbs.
Carry Capacity at 4-mph	4,000 Lbs.
Maximum Dumping Height	8′0″
Engine hp., Stripped, Diesel	84
Gasoline	84
(No. Speeds) — Range, mph,	
Forward	(3)0-17.5
Reverse	(3)0-22.6
Weight, approx. lbs., Diesel	14,200
Gasoline	13,920

model HH

Four-wheel Drive
Rear-wheel Power-steer
Hydraulic Load-shock-absorber
Planetary Final Drives
Power-shift Transmission
Power-transfer Differentials
Four-wheel Power Brakes
Gas. or Diesel Power

A new "PAYLOADER" with many improvements that give greater yardage output, greater usefulness, greater safety and easier operation. Has the all-new Hough bucket action with 40 degree tip-back at ground level and tremendous pry-out bucket-loading action. Like the smaller model HU, this model HH, though new, is thoroughly proven by months of proving ground testing and operation. The same wide range of extra attachments as shown for the Model HU.

SPECIFICATIONS

Bucket Capacity, Payload	1¾ cu. yd.
Bucket Capacity, Struck	1-1/3 cu. yd.
Bucket Width	84″
Lifting Capacity at 0-mph	11,000 Lbs.
Carry Capacity at 4-mph	5,500 Lbs.
Maximum Dumping Height	9′0″
Engine hp., Stripped, Diesel	92
Gasoline	100
(No. Speeds) — Range, mph,	
Forward	(3)0-19
Reverse	(3)0-24
Weight, approx. lbs., Diesel	15,700
Gasoline	15,300

— THE COMPLETE PROVEN LINE

model HO

Four-wheel Drive
Power-shift Transmission
Planetary Final Drives
Power-transfer Differentials
Rear-wheel Power-steer
Four-wheel Power Brakes
Gas. or Diesel Power

The model HO is the largest of the great new four-wheel drive "PAYLOADER" models. It has all the new advanced features built into the Models HU and HH including power-shift transmission — the finest, fastest transmissions ever put into tractor-shovels. The foot clutch is eliminated. All shifts are made by finger-tip action. Any shift can be made at full throttle, without stopping. The same wide choice of extra attachments as listed for the Model HU.

SPECIFICATIONS

Bucket Capacity, Payload	2¼ cu. yd.
Bucket Capacity, Struck	1¾ cu. yd.
Bucket Width	90″
Lifting Capacity at 0-mph	15,000 Lbs.
Carry Capacity at 4-mph	7,500 Lbs.
Maximum Dumping Height	10′0″
Engine hp., Stripped, Diesel	122
Gasoline	125
(No. Speeds) — Range, mph,	
Forward	(3)0-24
Reverse	(3)0-24
Weight, approx. lbs., Diesel	23,200
Gasoline	22,250

model HF

Rear-wheel Drive
Front-wheel Steer
Four-speed Full-reversing Transmission
Torque-converter Drive

This is one of the most popular sizes of "PAYLOADER" tractor-shovels, for city use. Its rear-wheel drive enables it to dig and grade as well as load trucks, carry and stockpile. Gets to the job fast at speeds up to 19.5 mph — has four reverse speeds up to 28 mph, plus torque-converter. The same basic machine is available with extra high lift and called the model HFH. It can dump over truck and bin edges 11½ ft. high.

SPECIFICATIONS

Bucket Capacity, Payload	1 cu. yd.
Bucket Capacity, Struck	¾ cu. yd.
Bucket Width	60″
Lifting Capacity at 0-mph	6,500 Lbs.
Carry Capacity at 4-mph	3,000 Lbs.
†Maximum Dumping Height	7′11″
Engine hp., Stripped, Gasoline	66.5
(No. Speeds) — Range, mph,	
Forward	(4)0-19.5
Reverse	(4)0-28.7
Weight, approx. lbs., Gasoline	10,750

†Also available as the model HFH with 10½ foot dumping height.

PAYLOADER® FRONT-WHEEL DRIVE TYPES

model HA

Front-wheel Drive
Rear-wheel Steering
Full-reversing Transmission
Gas. or Diesel Power
Torque Converter
Hydraulic Load-shock-absorber

This front-wheel driven "PAYLOADER" is an improved version of the model that has been proven and endorsed by thousands of owners in all kinds of industries. It is fast, maneuverable and versatile for handling loose materials indoors and outdoors — can go in and out of boxcars to load or unload them.

SPECIFICATIONS

Bucket Capacity, Payload	18 cu. ft.
Bucket Capacity, Struck	14 cu. ft.
Bucket Width	48″
Lifting Capacity at 0-mph	3,000 Lbs.
Carry Capacity at 4-mph	2,000 Lbs.
Maximum Dumping Height	5′2½″
Engine hp., Stripped, Diesel	38
Gasoline	33
(No. Speeds) — Range, mph,	
Forward	(2)0- 6.3
Reverse	(2)0-10.
Weight, approx. lbs., Diesel	5,285
Gasoline	5,050

model HAH

Front-wheel Drive
Rear-wheel Power-steer
Power-transfer Differentials
Torque Converter
Hydraulic Load-shock-absorber

This machine is especially designed for stockpile work, with rear-wheel power-steer for fast maneuverability, and a high lift to load trucks and elevated hoppers . . . has compact, rugged construction to meet the demands of the most rigorous bulk-material handling work . . . can work indoors, or outdoors on unpaved ground.

SPECIFICATIONS

Bucket Capacity, Payload	1 cu. yd.
Bucket Capacity, Struck	¾ cu. yd.
Bucket Width	72″
Lifting Capacity at 0-mph	4,000 Lbs.
Carry Capacity at 4-mph	3,000 Lbs.
Maximum Dumping Height	7′10″
Engine hp., Stripped, Gasoline	51
(No. Speeds) — Range, mph,	
Forward	(4)0-17
Reverse	(4)0-29
Weight, approx. lbs., Gasoline	9,600

Attachments for PAYLOADER® tractor-shovels

HYDRAULIC BACK-HOE

V-TYPE SNOW PLOW

PICK-UP STREET SWEEPER

ROTARY SNOW PLOW

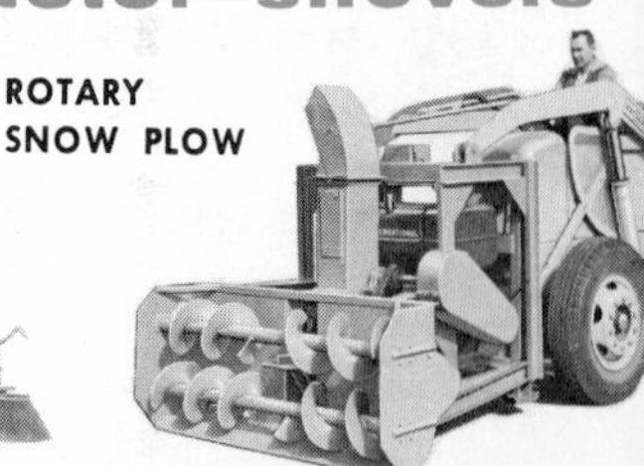

ALSO: One-way trip-blade snow plow; crane hook; lift fork; snow bucket; Drott 4-in-one bucket; operator cab; bucket teeth; scarifier

Form No. 319

Litho in U.S.A.

HELTZEL STEEL FORM & IRON CO.

Warren, Ohio, U.S.A.

CURB & GUTTER FORMS HAVE 3 INTERCHANGEABLE FACE FORMS

Heltzel BUILDS IT BETTER

CURB FORMS AND ACCESSORIES
●
COMBINED CURB & GUTTER
●
SIDEWALK FORMS
●
RIGID RADIUS FORMS
●
FLEXIBLE FORMS
●
SPECIAL FORMS
●

Heltzel steel forms augmented by various improvements through the years are the most rigid, advanced equipment obtainable. Your consideration of the many varied applications of these steel forms is respectfully invited. Write for Bulletin L-20.

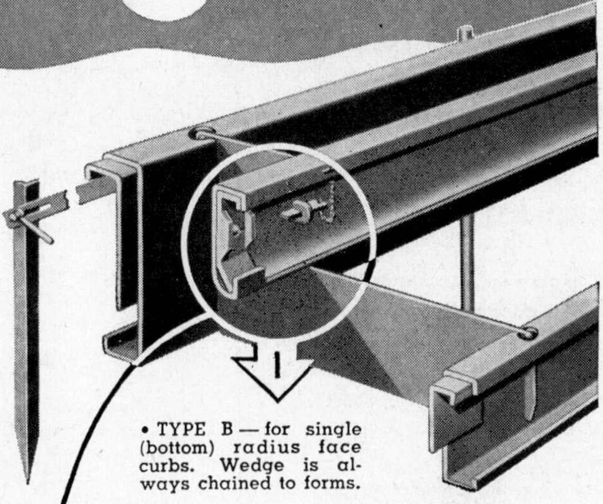

• TYPE B — for single (bottom) radius face curbs. Wedge is always chained to forms.

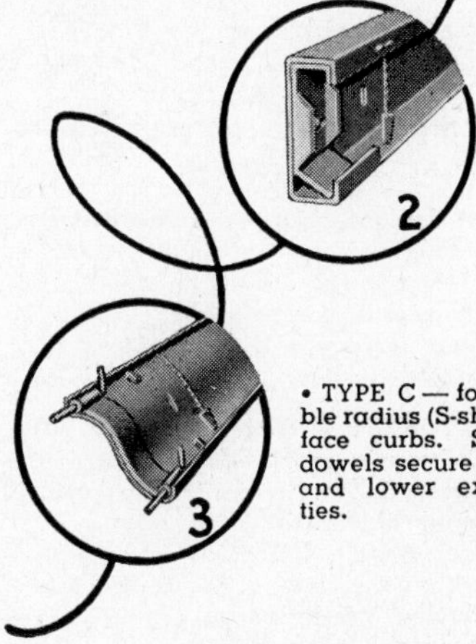

• TYPE A — for straight face curbs (no radii). Slide lock is rigid, positive.

• TYPE C — for double radius (S-shaped) face curbs. Sliding dowels secure upper and lower extremities.

● Heltzel supplies forms for any required curb and gutter shape. Special engineering makes details of every job easier to work. Heltzel's is the only flexible form with three alternate methods of support — (1) Full-depth division plates, (2) Skeleton division plates and (3) Overhead hangers. Ideal for use where specifications prohibit use of dummy or full-depth joints. Both battered and non-battered face plates are available.

HELTZEL STEEL FORMS

THE HELTZEL STEEL FORM AND IRON COMPANY
WARREN, OHIO

FELKER MANUFACTURING CO.

World's Largest Manufacturer of Diamond Abrasive Cut-Off Wheels and Equipment

TORRANCE, CALIF.

Dealers in all important areas. 24 hour diamond blade service wherever you are!

FELKER DI-MET CONCRETE CUTTERS AND SEGMENTED DIAMOND BLADES

Chosen by Municipalities Nation-wide!

SAWS BOTH CONCRETE AND ASPHALT PAVING

The result of years of experience in the field, Felker Concrete Cutters combine maximum speed, maneuverability, ease of operation and overall dependability. Machines are abundantly powered—of value not only in handling all operations encountered, but insuring superior diamond wheel life!

Models are available covering the complete range of asphalt and cement-concrete operations, from low cost machines to multi-bladed production models.

Use These Felker Concrete Cutters For:

cutting control joints, trenches, floors, curbs, sidewalks, ramps; for making traffic signal installations; laying or repairing pipe lines, telephone and electric lines under pavement; taking core samples; for scoring and grooving; for cutting off and slitting terra cotta, transite and concrete pipe, for maintaining bridges, tunnels, tubes, etc.

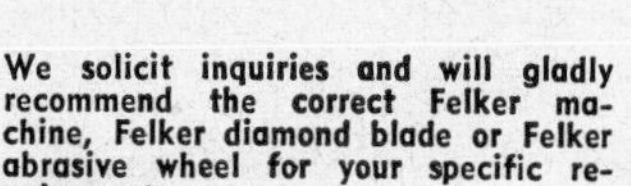

We solicit inquiries and will gladly recommend the correct Felker machine, Felker diamond blade or Felker abrasive wheel for your specific requirements.

Felker Model 100 Concrete Cutter

FELKER MODEL 100 CONCRETE CUTTER

Low cost machine for all patchwork and light cutting

Built to meet budget prices, this low-cost machine is built to the same high quality standards found in all Felker models. Ideal for all common concrete cutting jobs. Unusual maneuverability is due to light weight and excellent balance without sacrificing strength and rigidity.

7.5 H.P. WISCONSIN ENGINE: Powered by a full 7.5 h.p. Wisconsin gasoline engine. Equipped with Blade-Saver Collars which greatly prolong life of diamond blades. Uses 8″ through 12″ blades on double-end spindle for easy right or left-hand operation. Blade raises hydraulically and is gradually lowered with hydraulic retardant. Lightweight alloy frame is of sturdy, webbed construction. Rigid four wheel mounting maintains horizontal frame position and vertical alignment of blade even when traversing uneven surfaces, prevents blade damage from cramping or binding. Hinged 12″ blade guard raises, exposing blade for close-up work and can be reversed for right or left-hand use without disturbing water supply. Adjustable handles provide maximum operator convenience.

BLADE-SAVER COLLARS ON ALL FELKER MACHINES

Felker Blade-Saver Collars

The new Blade-Saver Collars give **extra** blade life by insuring positive coolant distribution! Here's how: A high speed rotating blade builds up an air blanket next to its surface. Directing water **through** this blanket is only partially effective. Blade-Savers do it the easy way—eject the water **under** the air blanket from the hub itself. Water velocity is rapidly increased by centrifugal force, washing down each blade side and flushing **deep into the cut!** With Blade-Savers, it's **goodbye** to unwanted sludge!

FELKER MODEL 200 CONCRETE CUTTER

A heavy duty model that features plenty of power for deep cutting, yet is so well balanced and so maneuverable, it handles like a light-weight! Here is an **all-purpose machine** that includes all the proven features resulting from 30 years' experience in diamond blade manufacture and concrete cutting!

POWERFUL 13.5 WISCONSIN ENGINE—Husky 13.5 h.p. Wisconsin gasoline engine provides an abundance of power and maintains full diamond wheel speed and efficiency at all cutting depths. Uses economical 10" and 12" blades, cutting to maximum depths of 2¾" and 3¾" respectively. Can also use 14" blades.

Adjustable graduated stop sets blade at desired cutting depth. Reversible hinged blade guard can be quickly changed for right or left hand operation. Front half lifts to expose blade for close-up jobs **without disturbing the water supply.** Spindle is double-end, blade mounts on either side. Water connection is provided and water is pressurized by coolant pump. An instant-acting shut-off valve conserves water when machine is not actually cutting.

EQUIPPED WITH EXCLUSIVE BLADE-SAVER COLLARS to insure positive coolant distribution over the blade and deep into the cut. Blade-Savers flush out sludge, keep rims cool and clean, prolong life of diamond blades!

POWER DRIVE removes manual effort on straight-away cuts, lengthens blade life as much as 100%. Speed is completely variable from 0 to 12' per minute.

HYDRAULICALLY CONTROLLED—Blade is lifted out of cut by foot-operated hydraulic jack. Finger-tip release of hydraulic retardant valve gently eases blade down; insures a smooth uniform entrance into concrete.

EASY TO MANEUVER precision balanced, Model 200 can be easily tilted on front or back wheels, insuring utmost maneuverability on the job and easy loading. Newly designed light-weight alloy frame is heavily reinforced and webbed for maximum strength. Rigid suspension of all wheels overcomes binding by maintaining vertical position of diamond blade when traversing uneven surfaces. Equipped with guide pointers on both front and rear for aligning blade to desired cutting path.

ACCESSORIES — Model 200 comes equipped with power drive and auxiliary coolant pump assembly or these may be purchased as accessories and field installed later, if desired. Self starter, generator and battery must be specified on original order.

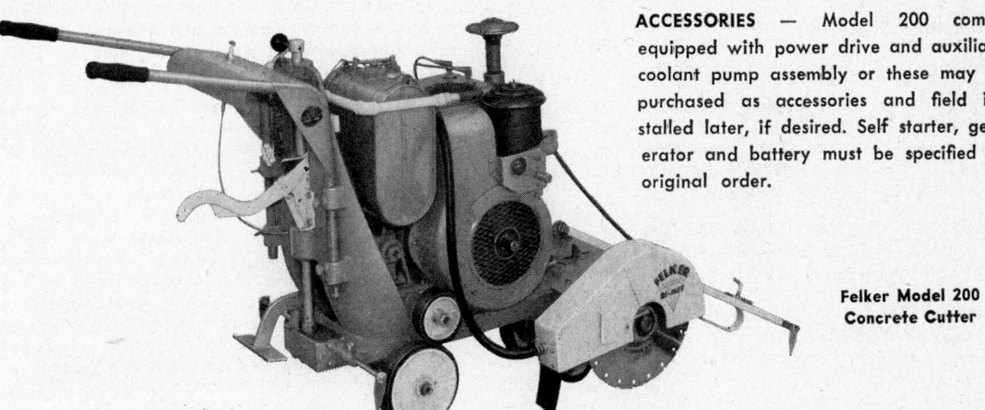

Felker Model 200 Concrete Cutter

FELKER HEAVY-DUTY MODELS 254 AND 364 CONCRETE CUTTERS

HEAVY DUTY WISCONSIN ENGINES keep blade speeds constant under heaviest cuts and with maximum blade sizes.

Model 254, 25 hp.—Model 364, 36 hp.

MORE POWER TO THE SPINDLE cog type timing-belt drive to diamond blade eliminates belt slippage, insures positive drive and puts the power where it's needed . . . at the spindle!

BLADE-SAVER COLLARS insure utmost diamond blade life.

NEW OPTIONAL HYDRAULIC POWER DRIVE no slippage to drive wheels, stepless speed control to 20′ per minute.

Handles blade diameters from 8" to 18". Cuts to 6¾" maximum.

PERFECT BALANCE—Despite size, power and weight one operator can maneuver either the 254 or 364 by tilting on front or rear wheels . . . turns in its own length, spins out of corners, lines up easier without back-breaking effort, greatly simplifies loading and unloading.

POWER DRIVE CUTS LABOR—Standard equipment on Models 254 and 364; takes the work out of heavy cutting, produces more footage per day, increases blade life. Speed range completely varaible. Hydraulic type drive available as optional equipment.

DOUBLE END SPINDLE mounts blade for either right or left hand cutting. Blade guard is reversible for use on either side, is hinged to expose front half of blade without disturbing water supply. 14″ blade guard standard, 18″ guard available.

HYDRAULIC CONTROLS—Blade lifts from cut by means of hydraulic jack, is smoothly and gradually eased into cut with hydraulic retardant control.

PUMP INSTANTLY ENGAGED—No belts to shift, no inconvenient delays to start or stop the pump. Instant acting push-pull clutch on pump pressurizes coolant when supplied from a tank, shut-off valve saves water when not in use. Special pump by-pass provided when connected to pressurized source.

RIGID 4 WHEEL MOUNTING enables machine to climb obstacles or pass over chuck holes without cramping blade in cut. Keeps blade in vertical alignment on any surface.

SELF STARTER, GENERATOR AND BATTERY included as standard equipment.

OTHER FEATURES—Blade depth adjustment; guide pointers front and rear; extendable handles which provide maximum leverage for easy maneuvering yet can be telescoped when not in use.

The "254" pivots on front or rear wheels for greatest handling ease!

FELKER MASONRY SAW

Felker Masonry Saw

Built for **life-time** duty! Easy to operate—easy to maintain—ideal for one-man set-ups. Cuts all types of masonry materials . . . wet or dry. Removable Spindle Quill insures new-saw performance without time-consuming repairs. No bearings to remove, no spindle damage to risk, simply slip out the old quill, insert a replacement right on the job! **BLADE-SAVER COLLARS** add **more cuts per blade.** Unit is driven by a powerful new G.E. "Tri-clad" motor weighing only 15 lbs. Provides a full 1.5 h.p. for deep, fast cuts through tough masonry materials. Reduction in motor weight means easier portability, quicker set-ups, faster knock-downs. "Mistake-proof" electrical connection permits fool-proof operation on either 110 or 220 volts, a.c. eliminates errors by always insuring the correct lead-line plug in the right connector. No motor rewiring is necessary.

FELKER SEGMENTED TYPE DIAMOND BLADES

By far the preferred blade for all concrete and masonry sawing, the result of over 30 years intensive diamond abrasive wheel research and engineering development! Metal bonded diamond sections are permanently brazed to the rigid, all-steel cores resulting in a blade that cuts smoothly and swiftly through concrete, granite, marble, clay products and all masonry materials. Felker Segmented Type Diamond Blades far outlast other wheels, maintain full diameter and rim speed throughout life. All metal construction eliminates breakage hazards. Sizes from 6" to 24" in diameter, with arbor holes to fit all standard machines and cut-off saws.

Felker Segmented Type Diamond Abrasive Wheel

SPECIFICATION CHART

Blade Number	Recommended application
FCW-101	For hard, dense, well cured concrete
FCW-103	For maximum life in hard, dense, well cured concrete
FCB-303	For asphalt and soft aggregate green concrete
FCG-201	For 8 to 36 hour green and extra hard abrasive concrete
FCG-204	For maximum life in green and extra hard abrasive concrete

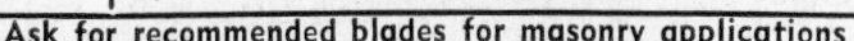
Ask for recommended blades for masonry applications

Dry Cutting, Wet Cutting, Break-Resistant

FELKER ABRASIVE WHEELS

Felker provides a complete selection of abrasive wheels for wet cutting, dry cutting, and in break-resistant types. Wide selection insures your **exact** choice for maximum cutting speed, longest overall life and lowest cost per cut!

FELKER CORE DRILLS

Electroplated, Standard, Segmented types

Felker diamond abrasive core drills do many drilling jobs quicker and more accurately! They produce long, smooth, unbroken test cores in concrete; drill holes in concrete, marble, granite, glass, etc., for mounting any type of equipment; drill through brick and concrete walls for pipelines and conduits; make round, clean holes in tile for plumbing connections without chipping or patching. Available in a wide range of sizes from ½" to 2½" O.D. in fractional steps, other sizes available on order.

Descriptive circulars are available on all Felker products. Write for yours today!

FELKER MANUFACTURING CO.
Torrance, California

THE OTTO GERDAU CO.

ESTABLISHED 1872

82 Wall Street, New York 5, N. Y.

Importers and Exporters

AFRICAN BASS FIBRES

•

INDIA PALMYRA STALKS

•

MOUNTAIN HICKORY SPLINTS

Fresh, resilient fibres and wire, for all types of rotary sweeper brooms.

THE OTTO GERDAU CO.

GUTTER BROOM STEEL WIRE

•

SNOWSWEEPER RATTAN

•

SPLIT BAMBOO

OFFICES: **ENGLAND - INDIA - FRANCE - HONGKONG - JAPAN - MEXICO**
INDONESIA - SIAM - GERMANY

M.B. Corp. broom—equipped with Gerdau broom fibres

Leaves of a palm tree in India—the origin of Palmyra Stalks

High quality broom fibres last longer

The longer mileage you obtain from fresh broom fibres means less time-taking refilling of the broom core and valuable man-hours available for other purposes. The use of fresh, high-quality fibres in your mechanical sweeper is sound economy these days.

Packed and ready for the U.S.A.

GERDAU Broom Fibres are available in all sizes and types....We hope the information on the following pages will be helpful to you in selecting your requirements.

INDIA PALMYRA STALKS

This is the most popular of the sweeping fibres. It is coarse in texture, tough wearing, and excellent for rough sweeping. It is modestly priced, and easy to work. When wet, it becomes exceptionally pliable for fast and firm insertion into the core. During the war it was widely used by both the Army and Navy for sweeping airfields. Palmyra Stalks are imported from the southernmost regions of India, and come packed in burlap-covered bales of 112 pounds net.

AFRICAN CALABAR BASS

This material is generally acknowledged to be the most durable of the rotary sweeper fibres, giving longest sweeping mileage. Calabar Bass comes from British West Africa. It is wire-like and tough, therefore particularly suited for use on rough stone streets, brick and cobble construction. On ordinary pavements it gives much extra wearing quality. Calabar Bass does not readily absorb water, so bristles do not become soft on wet streets, but remain stiff, tough sweepers.

GERDAU Broom Fibres are available to fit all makes of sweepers.

Gerdau broom fibres are used on the street sweepers of the City of New York—where they give excellent service under stress of metropolitan traffic.

HICKORY FIBRE

Hickory Fibre, a product of the mountain regions of North Carolina, is regularly used by many municipalities. Its application is generally the same as Palmyra Stalks, and it is also moderately priced. We furnish hickory cut from a choice grade of logs. Widths are either 1/4″ or 1/8″, as desired.

GUTTER-BROOM STEEL WIRE

We can furnish your needs in the best quality lead-tempered steel wire and usually maintain stocks in almost every size. The most popular specifications are:

.032 x .094 x 26″ (heavy)
.020 x .080 x 26″ (light)

SNOWSWEEPER RATTAN

Genuine snowsweeper rattan is available, its supremacy more firmly established than ever, since no satisfactory substitute was found during the war. Orders should be placed well in advance of the winter season to allow ample time for shipment from Indonesia.

You can assure yourself of good broom fibres all the time by joining the many municipalities which use Gerdau fibres year after year with complete satisfaction.

All types—all sizes—
Samples on request.

Chicago

GOOD ROADS MACHINERY CORPORATION

Minerva, Ohio

SCAVENGER, LEAF COLLECTOR AND LEAF LOADER

SCAVENGER

The low-cost method of eliminating all types of debris and rubbish including bottles cans, papers, cartons, leaves, twigs, of almost any size, wet or dry, on highways, streets, alleys, parks, picnic and recreation grounds, golf courses, cemeteries or wherever refuse is carelessly scattered or blown by wind. New "Catch Basin Cleaner" attachment permits Scavenger to be used for year around catch basin cleaning . . . large diameter hose won't clog . . . does the job in minutes.

LEAF COLLECTOR

Inhales and pulverizes wet or dry leaves and turns them into a rich compost in one operation. Compacts loads, eliminating frequent trips for dumping. The intake hose is flexible and maneuvers easily into driveways, under and around corners and catch basins, under cross-walks and other "hard-to-reach" places.

In both units the hydraulic system is independently operated making "hook-up" and dumping a matter of seconds. Their large sized litter carriers have tremendous capacity and smooth interiors, free of obstructions, assuring clean-dumping of full load. Both units can be towed by any prime mover: truck, tractor or jeep.

LEAF LOADER

Trailer mounted, it hitches to any dump truck. It is equipped with a rigid intake snout which permits automatic pick-up in a 30" path, and is interchangeable with a flexible rubber intake for hand operation. The Leaf Loader is an economical unit designed for use by small cities, parks, golf courses, etc.

GOOD ROADS MACHINERY CORPORATION

Minerva, Ohio

CHAMPION SPREADERS

FOR SLEET AND ICE CONTROL
5 MODELS GOOD ROADS JETS

- **JET ACE**—Gasoline Motor Driven, Twin Spinner, Electric Cab Controls.
- **JET KING**—Gasoline Motor Driven, Twin Spinner, Cable Cab Controls.
- **JET QUEEN**—Gasoline Motor Driven, Single Spinner, Cable Cab Controls
- **JET JACK**—Power Take-Off Driven, Single Spinner, Cable Cab Controls.
- **JET HYDRAULIC**—Full Hydraulic operation on conveyor and spinners with cab controls.

Designed for fast action, maneuverability and wide coverage during icing conditions. Also used for seal-coating and aggregate spreading.

THE CHAMPION HANDY

8-9-10-11-12-13 Foot

Spreads sand, aggregate and other materials. Has automatic transmission for moving forward or backward without shifting or de-clutching gears. Flexible "keyboard" permits oversized particles to work through, eliminating streaks and delay in spreading operations.

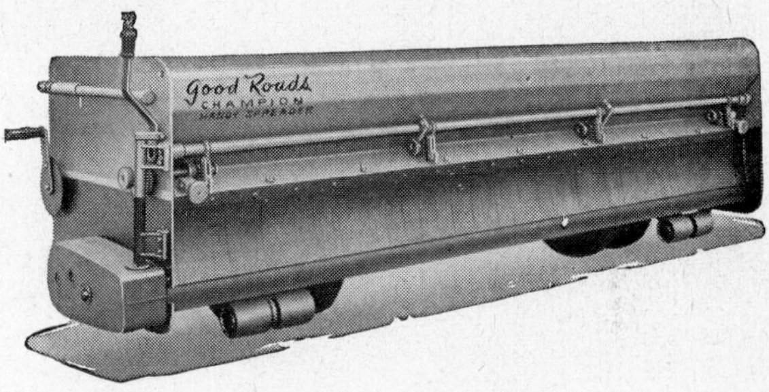

Optional Equipment: Agitator, Safety Platform, Block Off Plates, etc.

THE ODELL SPREADER

Hitches to any standard dump or semi-dump in a few seconds without special attachments. Spreads hot or cold mix asphalt, bank-run gravel, coarse or fine slag and limestone, cinders and practically any kind of base material. Accurate spread control from feather edge to 8 inches deep, and from any width up to 10 feet.

GOOD ROADS MACHINERY CORPORATION

Minerva, Ohio

CHAMPION SNOW PLOWS

"TRAILMAKER"—600 Series

"No Cables — Full Power Hydraulic Wing

The 600 series is designed for tough going in deep snow, bucking drifts, opening blockades or widening cuts. Wings are hydraulically controlled from cab—An ideal unit for heavier trucks.

"TRAILMAKER"

500 Series

Excellent for moderately deep snow on highways, cemeteries, estates and industrial plants. Used on 1½ and 2 ton trucks—has tremendous capacity at high or low speeds with minimum tractive effort.

Model 51—LEVELING WING

(Full Hydraulic Power)

Wing with complete hydraulic control from cab, for front or rear of moldboard in vertical and horizontal directions. Companion unit to "V" type or one-way snow plows. Standard 10, 11 or 12-foot lengths, or custom-built to specifications.

GOOD ROADS MACHINERY CORPORATION

Minerva, Ohio

CHAMPION SNOW PLOWS

SNO-CHASER

This One Way Plow, has the speed and capacity to make it ideal for highways—features 3 plowing angles and adjustable vertical pitch, and is flexible to conform to highway contours. Available in light tractor to 10-ton trucks.

SNO-DOZER

This Reversible Blade Plow is a favorite for municipal, industrial, airport and private use, because of easy operation in small and congested areas. Blade adjusts to 5 different plowing angles. Available in sizes for light tractors to 10-ton trucks.

Both models are equipped with the "Good Roads" patented safety trip device for protection of truck and driver.

GOOD ROADS SAFETY BLADE TRIP

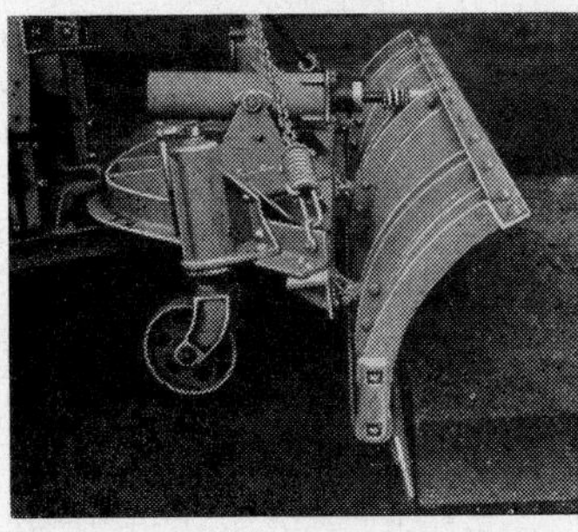

Plow strikes 8" obstruction at full speed . . . springs compress in cylinders and top of blade tilts forward to absorb shock.

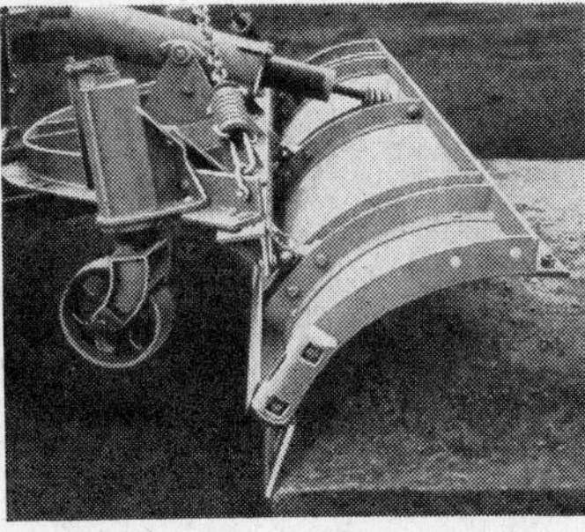

Blade continues forward and rides upward, carrying plow over obstruction with impact negligible to truck or operator.

Still moving at original speed, blade snaps back to plowing position with no damage to machine or operator and without spilling load.

G. H. TENNANT COMPANY

765 North Lilac Drive · Minneapolis 22, Minnesota

Compact sweeper cuts hand sweeping costs 30% to 60%

This husky compact sweeper—the Tennant model "80"—is exclusively designed to do many jobs that can't be handled by larger sweepers. It brings *low-cost mechanization* to such jobs as sweeping parking lots, ramps, garages, sidewalks, bridges—even congested downtown areas.

Its compact size and unusual maneuverability permit easy cleaning of these problem areas. The Model "80" cleans a 54 in. path (with sidebrush) . . . has automotive-type steering that makes it ideal for sharp-angle turns and sweeping around parked cars. Sweeper is only 56 in. wide; works easily in traffic.

Sweeps extra-clean—does a cleaner job than is possible with larger sweepers. Picks up dirt, dust, paper, loose sand and other usual soilage common to downtown areas. A 21″ sidebrush sweeps flush with curb—pushes litter into path of 42 in. main broom. At the same time, a powerful vacuum system sucks in dust and lighter dirt. No need for a water spray.

Saves labor—usually saves 30% to 60% in hand sweeping costs; can do the work of 3 to 12 men; sweeps 2 or more curb miles per hour. EXCLUSIVE features: instant reverse; no gears to shift; 5-minute brush change; extra long-life construction.

WORKS IN TIGHT AREAS. Rear-wheel, cam-and-lever steering provides excellent maneuverability; permits sweeping between cars and in other congested areas.

DUMPS HYDRAULICALLY. At the touch of a lever, twin hydraulic cylinders raise dirt hopper, dump load in 8 seconds. "Floating" hopper holds up to 800 lbs.

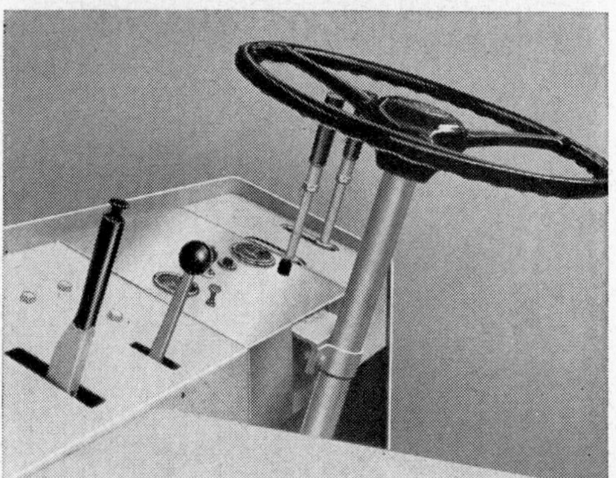

HAS SAFE, HANDY CONTROLS all within easy reach of operator. Instant forward-reverse—no gears to shift. Convenient knob accurately adjusts brush height.

PERMITS 5-MINUTE BRUSH CHANGE. Door provides easy access to brush compartment. Removal of two bolts is all it takes to replace the 42" main brush.

FEATURES

Extra-Clean Sweeping: Tennant Model 80 has powerful brush-plus-vacuum. High volume vacuum fan draws dust from enclosed brush compartment into bag . . . fast-revolving brush flips heavy litter into dirt hopper.

Rugged Construction: Designed for years of dependable service. Has $3/16''$ steel plate frame; steel gussets at major load points. Heavy ⅝" roller chain and husky bevel gear drive. All moving parts 100% protected from grit.

Power Dumping: Operator just pushes lever on dash. Twin hydraulic cylinders tilt and dump dirt hopper in one fast operation. Complete cycle takes only about 20 seconds.

High Maneuverability: Rear-wheel, Ross cam-and-lever steering—plus sweeper's compact design—means you sweep easily in tight, congested areas. Turning radius is only 64".

Safe, Easy Operation: All controls in front of operator and within easy reach. No gears to shift—one pedal regulates forward-reverse travel . . . the other controls speed. Operator has full view of path ahead.

Durable Brush: Tubular, one-piece brush can be changed in 5 minutes. Rugged, dependable unit—yet it's light weight. No brush strips to refill . . . no supplementary parts to wear out, because entire brush is disposable.

PRINCIPAL OFFICES

Arlington, Va.
Atlanta, Ga.
Buffalo, N. Y.
Cambridge, Mass.
Charlotte, N. C.
Chicago, Ill.
Cleveland, Ohio
Dallas, Texas
Detroit, Mich.
Ft. Wayne, Ind.
Greensboro, N. C.
Houston, Texas
Los Angeles, Calif.
Milwaukee, Wis.
Minneapolis, Minn.
Newark, N. J.
Philadelphia, Pa.
Pittsburgh, Pa.
St. Louis, Mo.
San Francisco, Calif.
Seattle, Wash.

CANADA

Montreal, Quebec
Toronto, Ontario

G. H. TENNANT COMPANY

765 North Lilac Drive · Minneapolis 22, Minnesota

Model G-25

Joint Cleaning and Concrete Routing Machine

- Cleans pavement joints, winding cracks for resealing. Helps assure good bond.
- Chips off worn concrete; leaves ideal bonding surface for retopping.
- Many other uses—levels bumps, smooths rough spots, removes extruded seal, etc.

CLEANING CONCRETE transverse joint for resealing. Machine rapidly removes old seal and refaces joint sidewalls; assures a good bonding surface.

CHIPPING OFF CONCRETE from badly spalled bridge deck (1½″ depth reached in two passes). Machine cut 7 days off estimated removal time.

On joint resealing jobs, it instantly pulverizes and routs out old seal, pebbles and dirt from joints *and winding cracks.* Cleans and refaces sidewalls at the same time. Helps assure tight-bonding surface and longer seal life. Cutters can be easily spaced to fit any joint (⅜″ to 4″ wide). It also eliminates hand spudding around joint shoulders by quickly shaving off extruded seal.

For surface removal work, this 25 hp machine can, for example, chip off ½″ of 4000-lb. test concrete from a 150 sq. ft. area in one hour. Provides excellent bonding surface for new topping. Its 1600 rpm cutting head covers a 4″ path . . . leaves aggregate at base of cut tightly imbedded . . . gives an even, uniform cut without deep gouges. Coverage data on request.

JOINT CLEANING cutter head revolves at 1600 rpm. Has 6 heat-treated alloy steel cutters (4″ or 4¾″ diam.); powerful v-belt drive.

AT AIRPORTS LIKE THIS the G-25 often cleans up to 15,000 feet of runway joints per day. Covers 6,000 feet or more on highways.

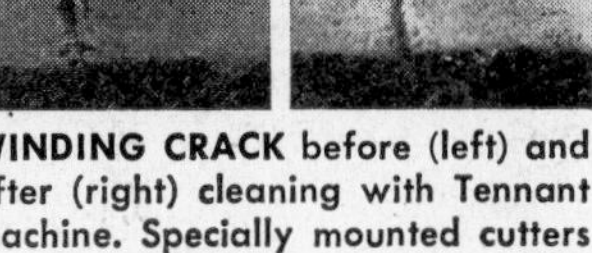

WINDING CRACK before (left) and after (right) cleaning with Tennant machine. Specially mounted cutters are free to follow irregular path.

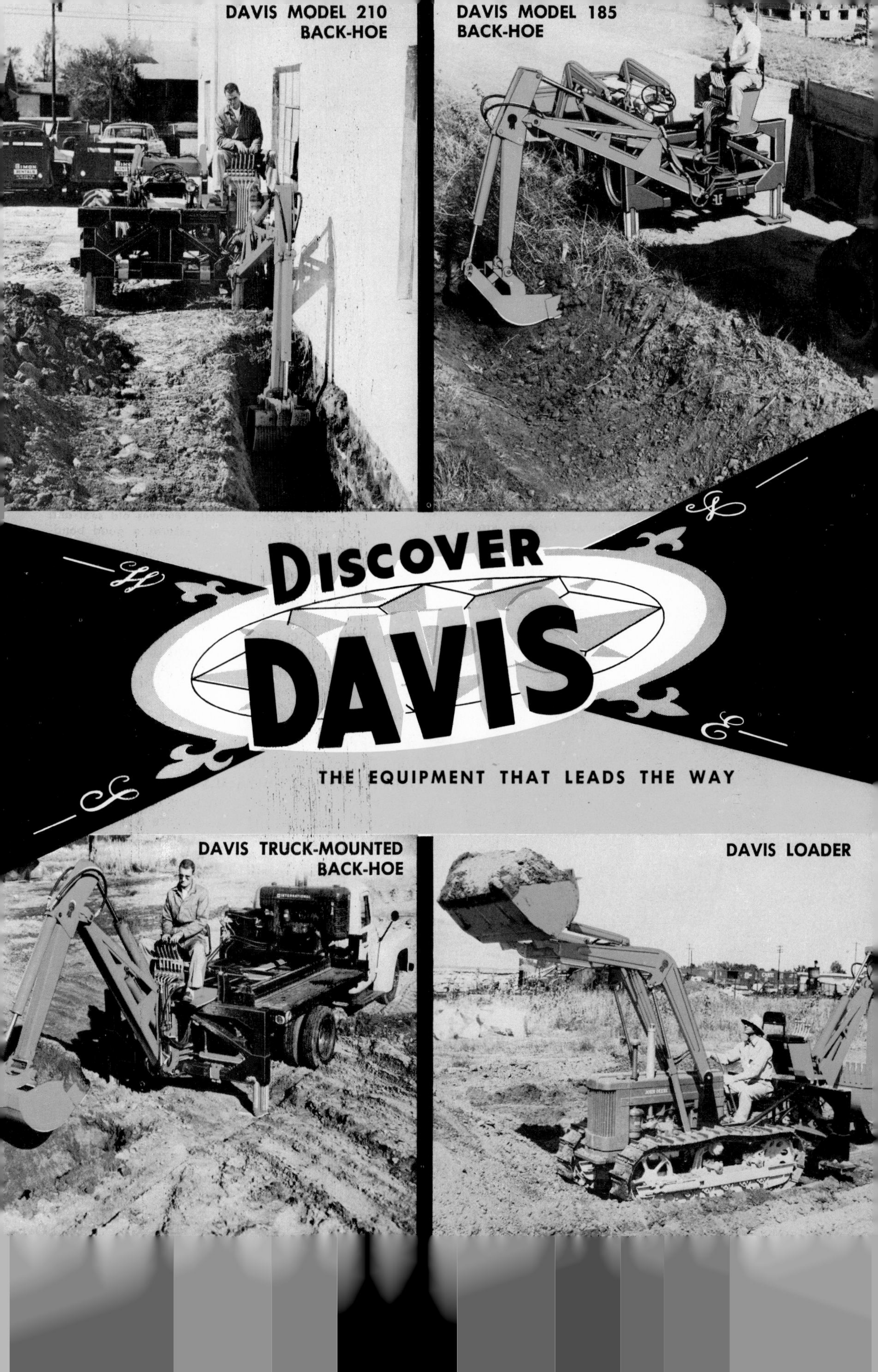
DAVIS MODEL 210
BACK-HOE
DAVIS MODEL 185
BACK-HOE
DISCOVER
DAVIS
THE EQUIPMENT THAT LEADS THE WAY
DAVIS TRUCK-MOUNTED
BACK-HOE
DAVIS LOADER

Any way you go . .

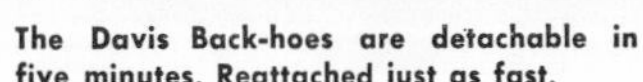

The Davis Back-hoes are detachable in five minutes. Reattached just as fast.

The Davis 210 mounted on the side for flush digging alongside a wall.

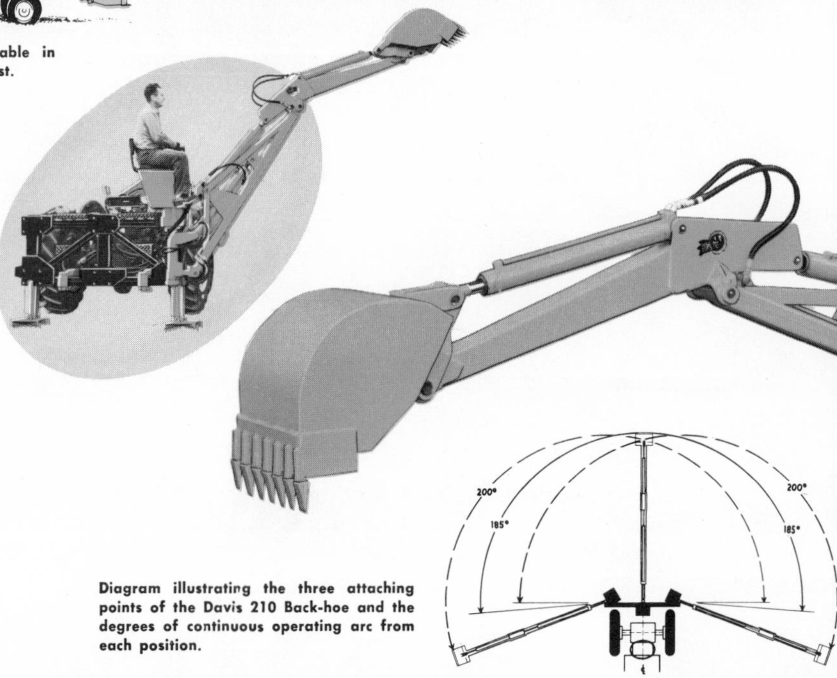

Diagram illustrating the three attaching points of the Davis 210 Back-hoe and the degrees of continuous operating arc from each position.

DAVIS *the world's most wanted* BACK-HOE

NOW AVAILABLE WITH FLUSH DIGGING AND 200° CONTINUOUS OPERATING ARC 7,000 POUNDS BREAKAWAY POWER

Davis Back-hoes are now available in two great models – the popular 185 and the new 210. This revolutionary model offers an engineering achievement desired by all – but accomplished only by Davis... an **exclusive hydraulic rotary boom swing cylinder** capable of giving a smooth, **continuous 200° cushioned operating arc** without ever changing a pin... plus three interchangeable mounting points on the frame so you can switch from center to side for flush digging alongside buildings, fences, and other places which formerly had to be dug by hand. Both models have **7,000 pounds of breakaway power** – nearly twice as much as other makes, some of which require two crowd cylinders. New comfort design includes an adjustable seat and extended foot rests. Larger hydraulic tubing eliminates excessive back pressure. And Davis is still priced lower than ordinary back-hoes.

Both the Davis 210 and the 185 will dig 13' deep and have wide dumping range for putting the spoils all to one side.

AVAILABLE FOR ALL

Both models will dig at right angles permiting you to work where conventional units can stretch out. Cab is optional.

Snow bucket is 74" wide, has one-cub yard capacity.

MID-WESTERN INDUSTRIES, INCORPORATED

ı'll make more profit with  

Crane attachment has adjustable boom.

Scarifier attachment fits on pivot points of bucket. Floats free when not in use.

DAVIS LOADER

HAS NEW FEATURES FOR MORE RUGGED WORK

The Davis Loader is already the possessor of more "firsts" than any other loader. Its streamlined, step-in design has been so popular that others have been forced to copy it, but none have been able to match it in quality, performance, and versatility. It **affords maximum clearance** — no obstructions to mar visibility and maneuverability. It has **maximum strength** for less down time and longer life with box-frame construction, new heavier-duty pump drive and pump mounting. The valve is equipped with **hardened steel sleeves** that last longer and require less maintenance. It is the only loader that has an **oil filter** as standard equipment. The rams are second to none with the shafts flame hardened, ground and finished in hardened chrome to prevent rusting and denting. Compare it feature for feature, pound for pound . . . you get more for your money in a Davis.

Landscape bucket is 66″ wide.

MAKES OF TRACTORS

Fork lift attachment has two adjustable tines and a 1,000-pound capacity.

Dozer attachment has 62″ hydraulically controlled blade.

Utility bucket is 60″ wide. Ideal for light-weight aggregates, etc.

1009 SOUTH WEST STREET — WICHITA, KANSAS

THE DAVIS TRUCK-MOUNTED BACK-HOE

Low silhouette in the transport position.

Being lowered to the digging position hydraulically in one minute.

Completely detached in five minutes.

LOW-COST, COMPLETELY DETACHABLE

Both the popular Davis Model 185 and the revolutionary Model 210 Back-hoes are available as low-cost, truck-mounted units which can be completely removed from the truck in less than five minutes.

The basic back-hoe fits onto a truck-attaching kit that is adaptable to any one-ton or larger flat-bed truck without modifying the truck bed. This kit is equipped with retractable runners which are actuated by a hydraulic ram so that the unit can be loaded or unloaded from the truck hydraulically.

In the transport position it folds into a compact, rigid unit with the weight centered directly over the truck axle. Lowered to the digging position, accomplished in one minute, the stabilizer feet absorb the stress from digging merely using the truck as a counter balance.

The hydraulic system is powered by any one of a number of suitable industrial gasoline engines.

The unit can be completely removed from the truck, engine and all, in less than five minutes. Two telescoping legs fold down at the front, and along with the two stabilizer feet, form a rigid support for the entire unit. This frees the truck so it can move out for other work, and, of course, the back-hoe remains in position for quick attaching whenever the truck moves back in.

This is another example of Davis versatility. Get complete information from your dealer or write for specific literature and name of dealer.

MID-WESTERN INDUSTRIES, INC.
1009 SOUTH WEST STREET WICHITA 15, KANSAS

THE F. D. CUMMER & SON CO.
2110 EAST 21st STREET CLEVELAND 15, OHIO

Cummer Asphalt Plants Are Designed for High Production at Low Operating Cost

Cummer PORTABLE Asphalt Plant: 50-70 tons per hour guaranteed capacity (see *Note* below). Mixers—2,000-2,500 lbs. Hot Bins—25 tons. Truly portable, these plants may be assembled in as few as 12 hours, then disassembled for quick transportation to another location.

Cummer STATIONARY Asphalt Plant: 80-140 tons per hour guaranteed capacity (see *Note* below). Mixers—4,000-6,000 lbs. Hot Bins—60-90 tons. Combustion in *all* Cummer Plants is by means of either gas or oil using high pressure steam or low pressure air as the atomizing agent.

Cummer SEMI-PORTABLE Asphalt Plant: 70-100 tons per hour guaranteed capacity (see *Note* below). Mixers—4,000 lbs. Hot Bins—60 tons.

Note: Guaranteed capacity is based on 5% initial water content dried to within ½ of 1% and heated to 350°-400°F. Cummer Asphalt Plants complete with all motors and starter switches. Each drive equipped with individual motor or gear motor. Shafting, sprockets, chains and belt drives eliminated. *New Cummer Live Roller Path and Horizontal Tangential Chain and Sprocket Drive step up production, lower operating costs. *Optional equipment includes dust collecting system which discharges reclaimed dust into hot elevator—steam jacketed valves, piping and fittings—Cummer-G. E. Timers, etc. *Cummer Plants are "batch" type for perfectly controlled mix throughout.

NEW, FULLY-ILLUSTRATED CUMMER CATALOG SENT ON REQUEST

HAUCK MANUFACTURING COMPANY

Oil Burning Construction and Maintenance Equipment

Established 1900

112-122 Tenth Street, Brooklyn 15, N. Y.

4657 W. Harrison St., Chicago 44, Ill. — 625 Third St., San Francisco 7, Calif.

HAUCK BURNERS FOR HEATING • MELTING • THAWING

Oil Burning

FIRE-GUNS—with automatic safety pressure check; sturdy, lightweight. Deliver large, smokeless, powerful 2000° F. torch flame. Provide quick, intense, portable heat for any maintenance, repair or thawing job. Burn kerosene, coal oil, range oil or light furnace oil; can be furnished for gasoline. Complete outfit includes heavy steel fuel tank, brass hand pump, pressure gauge, oil resisting hose, coil burner with valve and snap-on web shoulder strap. Two popular sizes. Fully guaranteed. Bulletin 1045B.

TORCH FLAME BURNER OUTFITS—Hand pump type, provide heavy duty, clean flame power for one man operation. Deliver large, controlled, powerful flame. Complete, portable, efficient. 8 sizes. Same outfits also in single or double burner types mounted on roller bearing wheels, as shown at right. Have handle bars and hose racks. Bulletin 1066.

ROAD OIL DISTRIBUTOR BURNERS—Fit all standard size firing tubes on road oil distributors. Heavy, seamless steel removable coil oil burner for steady, uninterrupted service. Can also be furnished for L-P gas. Bulletin 1052 and 1094.

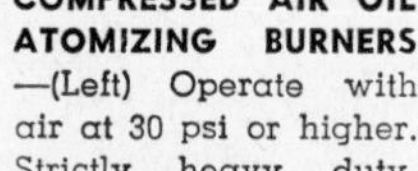

COMPRESSED AIR OIL ATOMIZING BURNERS—(Left) Operate with air at 30 psi or higher. Strictly heavy duty. Provide fast controlled heat to 2700° F. flame temperature. No preheating required. Bulletin 1055A.

Gas Burning

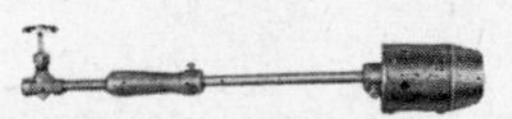

PORTABLE GAS TORCH — hand type for L-P gas pressure from 15 to 30 psi but no compressed air. Clean, steady, smokeless, easily adjustable flame. Bulletin 1078.

PORTABLE GAS TORCH — burn L-P gas, for heavy duty heating at temperature to 2200° F. Flame adjustable over wide range. Best operating range 25 psi. No compressed air needed. With straight or bent handle. Bulletin 1078.

HIGH PRESSURE GAS-AIR TORCHES — with "Retain-a-Flame" burner nozzles; burn any fuel without compressed air; produce 2200° F. flame; high max. firing rate with low heat turndown. Bulletin 1043C.

HIGH PRESSURE AIR-GAS TORCHES — with "Retain-a-Flame" burner nozzles; burn any gas fuel with compressed air; for high temperature applications with low pressure gas. Bulletin 1043C.

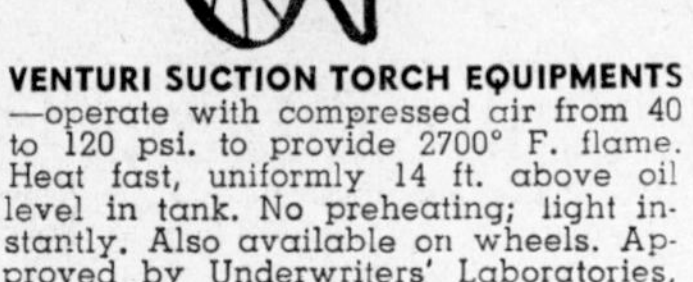

VENTURI SUCTION TORCH EQUIPMENTS—operate with compressed air from 40 to 120 psi. to provide 2700° F. flame. Heat fast, uniformly 14 ft. above oil level in tank. No preheating; light instantly. Also available on wheels. Approved by Underwriters' Laboratories, Inc. Bulletin 1056.

TORCH OUTFIT FOR STARTING PULVERIZED COAL FIRES—burns oil, operates with compressed air at 40 psi or more. Produce long, strong, voluminous 2700° F. flame, without clogging or carbonizing torch. Outfit mounted on all steel truck. Bulletin 1074.

MELTING KETTLES

For Tar • Asphalt • Pitch • Bituminous Enamels and Compounds

BOTTOM FIRED KETTLES for street and highway maintenance, pipe lines, paving, roofing, waterproofing, etc. Burn kerosene; can be furnished for L-P gas. Fast melting; low cost operation. Easy trailing on pneumatic or rubber tired or steel wheels. 55, 80, 115, 165 and 230 gal. capacities. Bulletin 1053B.

BARREL HOIST consisting of davit, ½ ton differential chain block and barrel tongs. One man can load full barrel of asphalt with little effort. Bulletin 1058C.

"SPEED-MASTER" KETTLES—with fire-box steel internal firing tube heating system. Burn kerosene or L-P gas. Rugged chassis frame assures fast, safe mobility. Stack flues insulated; new faster melting and draw-off. Standard sizes—55, 80, 115, 165, 230 and 330 gal. for trailer models; 40, 55, 80, 115 and 165 gal. for skid models. Bulletin 1058C.

BOTTOM FIRED SKID KETTLES for paving and pipe line work. Rugged yet lightweight. Easily loaded on truck; easy to carry. Heated by improved torch type oil burner or can be furnished for L-P gas. Kettle mounted on rugged legs. Torch is detachable for heating and thawing work. Bulletin 1054B.

POWER SPRAY ATTACHMENT (right) for distributing hot bitumen under pressure for patching and treating roads. Equipment includes 1½ hp air cooled gasoline engine with twin disc clutch, rotary gear pump, hose, valves and fittings and spray bar with removable circular spray tip. Kettles can also be provided with hand spray attachment. Bulletin 1058C.

PAVING TOOL HEATERS

For heating tampers, smoothers, shovels in bituminous pavement construction and street repair work. Heat 16 or more tools in 5 minutes. Available with or without binder cement kettle. 3 improved type kerosene torch burners fire ino tool heating chamber. Heater mounted on pneumatic tires for easy trailing. Also available with L-P gas burners. Bulletin 1062.

ASPHALT SURFACE HEATERS

With hood which folds back over handle for easy trailing. Heavy gauge steel hood has base plate and air space between. Fuel tanks and burners easily removable for other service. Made with heating pans of 2'x4', 3'x5' and 4'x6'. Bulletin 1062.

ASPHALT PLANT BURNERS

Consist of fully equipped low pressure oil burner with steel jacketed refractory ignition cone and mounting position support; can be furnished as high pressure atomizing oil burners; also as low pressure combination oil and gas burners or straight gas burners.

LEAD MELTING FURNACES

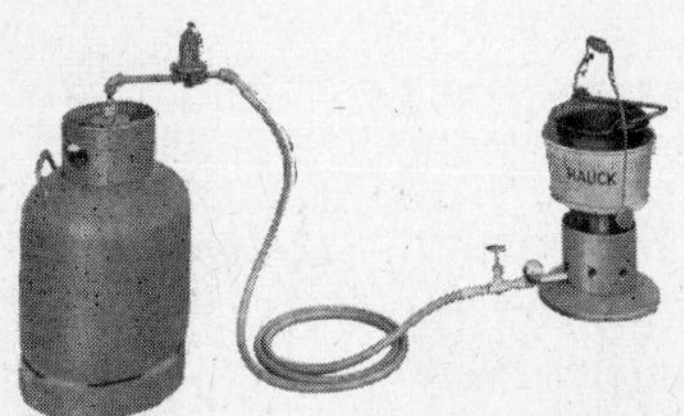

RED DOT MELTING FURNACE melts 50 lbs. lead or babbitt in 9 minutes. Burns L-P gas. A single valve regulates flame for any desired temperature. Overall furnace height with handle raised only 20". No pumping; no priming; no carbon; no overheating. Bulletin 1084.

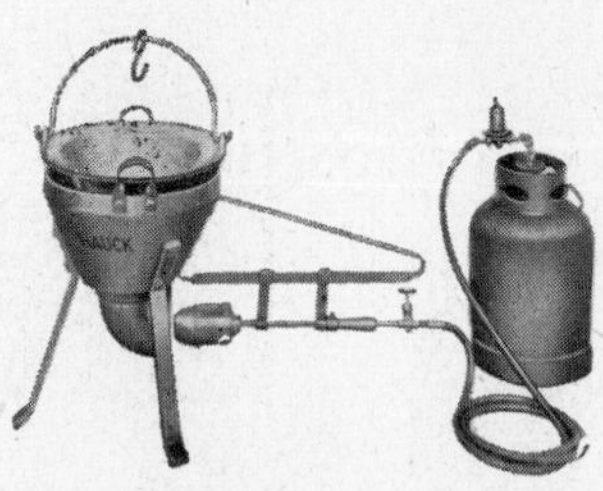

COMBINATION FURNACE ON LEGS and portable L-P gas torch. Melts pot of 200 lbs. of lead or babbitt to pouring temperature in 10 minutes. Bulletin 1084.

COMBINATION FURNACE ON WHEELS easy to move by one man as job progresses. Burns L-P gas. Burner easily regulated to provide heat as required. Rugged steel furnace and frame. Bulletin 1084.

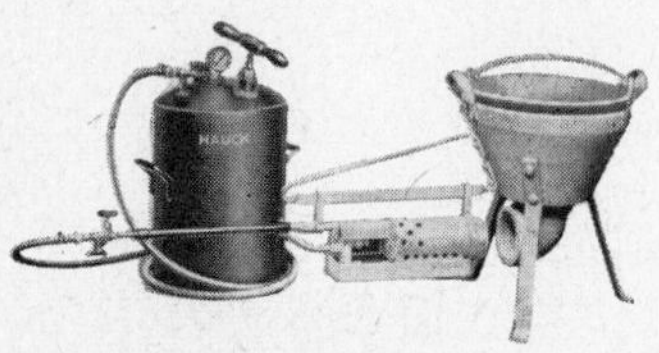

COMBINATION FURNACE ON LEGS and portable oil burning torch. Fast melting—no stops for feeding or cleaning fires; smokeless, clean. No air compressor needed. Improved torch type burner instantly removable for other heating jobs. Bulletin 1076.

COMBINATION FURNACE ON WHEELS — burns oil. Provides extra speed and convenience in melting lead for pipe laying jobs. One man moves furnace from job to job. Burner equipment removable for many other operations. Bulletin 1076.

COMPOUND MELTING FURNACES

for Mineralead, Bondo, Leadite, Ric-Wil, Puro-Seal, GK, Sewer Seal, KNR, Duro Seal, Haymanite, Wedgetite, JC60, Hydro-tite, etc.

FURNACE, wheel type, (agitator optional on 25 gal. model) insures uniform, faster melting and avoiding localized heating. Oil fired by hand pump type torch burner equipment, which is removable for other heating uses. Steel melting pot removable; capacities — 8, 15 and 25 gal. Bulletin 1075.

FURNACE, wheel type; (agitator optional). Burns L-P gas with internal jet burner and adjustable heat input. Quick melting without overheating. Steel melting pot removable; capacities—10, 15 and 25 gal. Bulletin 1077.

JACKETED FURNACE for rubberized joint sealers; melts 16 gal. to pouring temperature in one hour. Uses cylinder oil for heat transfer. Burns L-P gas with internal jet burner; infinite heat control. Has rotary ring agitator. Bulletin 1081A.

STEAM THAWERS

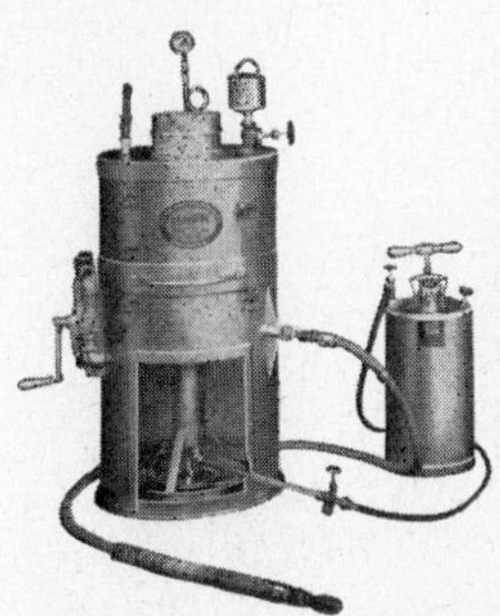

SUPERHEATED STEAM THAWERS supply steam in 1 minute after lighted burner is placed under boiler. Thaw frozen hydrants, culverts, sewers, gas and water pipes, mains, etc. Cut through ice in a few seconds. Flash coil generator produces steam at uniform pressure. Oil torch burner equipment provides powerful heat input. Thawer available with injector pump (as shown) or without pump. Bulletin 1066.

"FIRE ENGINE" THAWER supplies superheated steam 15 seconds after lighting burner; burns acetylene at 15 lbs. operating pressure. No hand pumping. Readily clamped to fire apparatus. Steam capacity — 6 qt. Bulletin 1066.

STEAM THAWER generates steam at 10 lbs. in 10 minutes. Burns gasoline. 3 gal. generator operates steadily 40 minutes ¾ full of water. Burner tank—1½ gal. capacity. Bulletin 1066.

STEAM GENERATOR

Multiple purpose unit for thawing and cleaning. Cover up shows accessibility of generator. Specially designed coil burner for fuel oils, gasoline; can be furnished for L-P gas. Low pressure unit develops 4 BHP of steam per hour at 15 psi and 220° F. steam temperature. High pressure unit develops 6 BHP of steam per hour at 75 psi and 320° F. steam temperature. Water storage capacity—28 gal. Generator easily removable. Burner and fuel tank stored in front end of chassis. Bulletin 1071.

WATER HEATERS

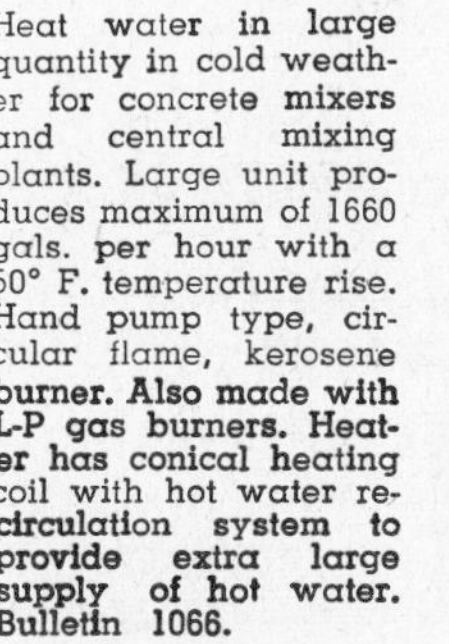

Heat water in large quantity in cold weather for concrete mixers and central mixing plants. Large unit produces maximum of 1660 gals. per hour with a 50° F. temperature rise. Hand pump type, circular flame, kerosene burner. Also made with L-P gas burners. Heater has conical heating coil with hot water recirculation system to provide extra large supply of hot water. Bulletin 1066.

PORTABLE THAWING TUBES FOR HOPPER CARS

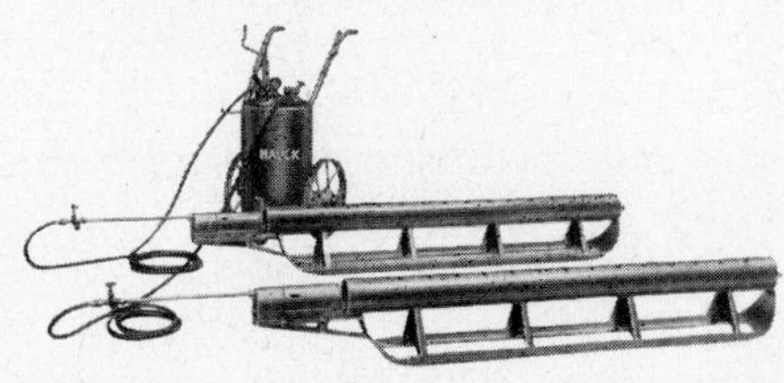

For speedy thawing of frozen coal or sand hopper cars. Burn kerosene or light furnace oil with compressed air type venturi suction torch burners or hand pump type torch flame burners (shown). Heat instantly regulated; intense, powerful, smokeless flames. No installation expense. Bulletin 1063D.

SALAMANDERS

L-P GAS SALAMANDER for heavy duty, clean safe heating; sizes—150,000 and 225,000 Btu per Hour. Heavy gauge steel shell fired by internal jet gas burner noted for heating power and fuel economy. Available in low and high pressure gas types. Bulletin 1091.

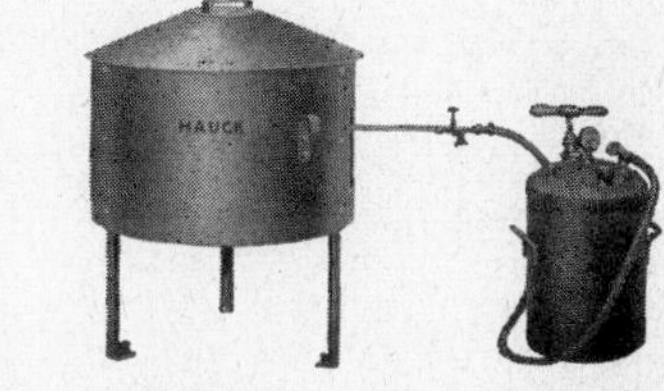

OIL BURNING SALAMANDER heats approx. 1200 sq. ft. floor space with average ceiling height; larger size —1900 sq. ft. Available in double units operating from one fuel tank. Fired by circular flame kerosene burner. Bulletin 1066.

ERNEST HOLMES COMPANY

CHATTANOOGA 7, TENN.

All lifting and shoveling movements of bucket hydraulically operated by driver from truck cab.

Driver-Operated Unit REDUCES COST on many of TODAY'S JOBS

SAVINGS in LABOR and EQUIPMENT MORE than PAY for LOADER . . .

Trucks equipped with HOLMES-OWEN LOADERS are substantially reducing the cost of many varied types of operations performed by States, Counties, Townships and Municipalities. Some of the more important of these jobs are: Maintenance of streets, parks, airports and other public properties. Removal of debris, broken pavement, and hard deposits of wash-in dirt that settle on city streets. Collecting of trash, leaves, and dumpings of street sweepers. Handling of sand, dirt, ashes, and even snow. These are but a few of the many jobs that are today being handled at lower cost with a Loader.

The use of a hydraulically operated Truck Loader speeds up loading and hauling, thereby assuring faster, more efficient work. It saves time, labor and equipment by permitting the truck driver to do light digging, grading, cleaning-up and loading, without additional man power or the use of more costly equipment. A truck with such versatile operations has many practical uses that lowers job cost and saves users thousands of dollars annually.

The HOLMES-OWEN LOADER can be installed on most 1½ to 2 ton trucks with any standard type dump body, and is available with either the standard or Forward-Tipping Bucket. The Loader lifts from ½ to 2/3 yards of material depending upon type of bucket used. Loads average dump body in approximately 4 minutes.

SAVES up to 50% on Street Maintenance

The Loader when used with a mobile truck-towed repaver, makes a most efficient street repair unit. Broken pavement, dirt, etc., can then be picked-up by the Loader or hand shoveled into the loader bucket thereby eliminating the necessity of extra handling in shoveling dirt to the street and then into the truck. Such a unit greatly expedites work, reduces interference to traffic and lowers the cost of some jobs as much as 50%.

VERSATILE ONE-MAN USE reduces cost of removing dirt, debris, etc., from streets.

The Loader when equipped with a hydraulically operated Forward - Tipping Bucket can be used for either loading other trucks or for work as an independent unit handling its own light digging, loading and hauling.

NEW TYPE BUCKET lowers Cost of Material Handling

The new Forward-Tipping Bucket substantially lowers the cost of material handling by assuring faster, more efficient loading and hauling. With this type loader bucket, the truck driver can quickly load any number of trucks then pick up his own load for hauling and dumping. All digging and loading operations are activated from controls located on the steering column. The entire loader is hydraulically operated with the bucket being powered by two double acting cylinders which can be rotated in any position up to 120 degrees.

MECHANICAL FEATURES:

DUAL HYDRAULIC CYLINDERS mounted on each arm accurately control all movement of bucket. The hydraulic system is a precision unit with heavy tubing and high pressure hose to develop adequate pressure for efficient operation on all types of work.

ELBOW ACTION—The Lifting Arms are built in two sections to give each movement of bucket flexibility of elbow action.

RUGGED CONSTRUCTION — Built with heavy subframe securely anchored at four points with bracing and reinforcement to support bucket and arms. The entire loader is of sturdy construction with ample strength at all points to assure long and dependable service.

Write TODAY for Details —

ERNEST HOLMES CO.

2505 East 43rd Street

CHATTANOOGA 7, TENNESSEE

ERNEST HOLMES COMPANY

CHATTANOOGA 7, TENN.

HOLMES has UNEQUALED RECORD of PERFORMANCE in WRECKER FIELD

HOLMES 460 MODEL

The principles of wrecker construction developed by HOLMES during the past 42 years have established Holmes' leadership in the Wrecker field. HOLMES is today the world's most widely used wrecker because its unequaled performance assures Fast, Flexible and positive action on *any* terrain and under *every* possible working condition. The Holmes features which make possible such efficient operation are the results of many years of engineering progress in the development of equipment to meet the requirements of every type service. The fact is, few products have ever been so TRIED, TESTED and APPROVED by so many, under such entirely different circumstances.

HOLMES Power Operated Wreckers are designed to LIFT or PULL from either side through double swinging booms. Outrigger legs transfer all strain from truck frame to ground thus assuring safety when making direct lifts from deep ditches and up mountain sides.

The HOLMES Double Boom type wrecker can be set-up quickly and easily on the open road with minimum interference to or from passing traffic. Recoveries are then made without obstructing the flow of traffic, or endangering either life or property.

The Towing Equipment provided with all Holmes Models is made to be quickly attached to either front or rear end of any model car or truck. It is easy to hook-up and when attached and secured permits disabled vehicle to be towed with speed and safety.

HOLMES offers WIDE CHOICE of Models for USE in PUBLIC SAFETY

HOLMES 470 MODEL

460 MODEL—6 TON WRECKER (Shown on opposite page) For light pick-up and towing of all cars. Fast, Flexible, easy to maneuver in city traffic. Rated capacity 3 tons per boom. Recommended for use on truck of 1 to 2 ton capacity.

HOLMES 525 MODEL

470 MODEL—8 TON WRECKER Handles all cars and light trucks. Fast, Versatile, especially suited for work in congested areas and on winding ramps. Rated capacity 4 tons per boom. Recommended for use on truck of 1 to 2 ton capacity.

525 MODEL—12 TON WRECKER An all purpose unit. Handles all cars and average trucks. Has long range of operation and is capable of handling wide variety of work. Rated capacity 6 tons per boom. Recommended for use on truck of 1½ to 2½ ton capacity.

HOLMES 650 MODEL

650 MODEL—20 TON WRECKER Built for Heavy Duty work yet fast and flexible enough to be economically used on light cars and trucks. Rated capacity 10 tons per boom. Recommended for use on truck of 23,000 lbs. gross vehicle weight.

850 MODEL—30 TON WRECKER Built for handling all large trucks, buses, trailers, etc., that are too big and heavy for the average wrecker. Rated capacity 15 tons per boom. Recommended for use on trucks of 30,000 lbs. gross vehicle weight.

HOLMES 850 MODEL

Write for Model Specifications, prices (low as $395.00), and name of local Distributor.

ERNEST HOLMES COMPANY
Chattanooga 7, Tennessee

World's First Manufacturer of Asphalt

Since 1894 . . . Products for Paving . . . Waterproofing and Maintenance

Central Plant Locations Insure Service

for information inquire

BYERLYTE CORPORATION

2302 West 3rd St. **Cleveland 13, Ohio**

CYCLONE FENCE DEPARTMENT

AMERICAN STEEL AND WIRE DIVISION
UNITED STATES STEEL CORPORATION

General Offices: Waukegan, Illinois

FACTORIES—Waukegan, Ill.; Newark, N. J.; Fort Worth, Texas; Greensburg, Ind.; DeKalb, Ill.; Oakland, Calif.

UNITED STATES STEEL

CYCLONE SAFEGUARD CHAIN LINK FENCE

U•S•S Cyclone Safeguard Fence is a practical, trim-appearing fence for school yards, playgrounds, cemeteries, airports and similar municipal property. It is a safe fencing for areas in which children are likely to play, because no barbed wire is used in its construction. Cyclone Safeguard has become almost a standard specification for schools, playgrounds and parks; prevents anyone engaged in play from inadvertently running into the path of traffic on adjacent streets or highways.

Cyclone Safeguard Fence can be installed in any height desired from three feet up with gates to match. It also comes in three different weights of wire, No. 6, No. 9 or No. 11 gauge, woven in a two-inch mesh. It can be installed with or without a top rail.

Posts are spaced in line of fence not farther apart than 10-foot centers. Line posts for fence four feet or lower are set 24 inches in concrete base; terminal posts are set 30 inches in concrete base. In fence five feet high and over, all posts are set 36 inches in concrete base.

Like all Cyclone Fence, Safeguard is made of special-analysis steel, galvanized *after weaving* with a heavy coating of zinc. It offers the protection you need over an exceptionally long period of wear-life.

ONLY UNITED STATES STEEL CORPORATION MANUFACTURES CYCLONE FENCE. ACCEPT NO SUBSTITUTE. Remember—no job is too large—no job is too small for Cyclone.

HUBER-WARCO COMPANY

MARION, OHIO

GENERAL AND HEAVY DUTY MOTOR GRADERS

TORQUE CONVERTER MOTOR GRADERS

The combination of torque converter and full power-shift transmission on Huber-Warco graders permits shifting under full load with no loss of power. No foot clutch is required.

A tail shaft governor automatically adjusts engine RPM to meet load conditions, maintaining any predetermined working speed.

Hydraulically cab-controlled blade movement—90° either side with no manual adjustments. Power sliding moldboard is standard equipment.

6-D (102 H.P.) *6-D2 (125 H.P.)*
7-D (140 H.P.) *7-D2 (150 H.P.)*
5D-190 (195 H.P.)

STANDARD TRANSMISSION MOTOR GRADERS

Complete hydraulic cab-controlled movement of the blade from 90° elevation on one side to 90° on the other, eliminates any manual adjustment.

Huber-Warco motor graders are diesel powered and have mechanical steering with a hydraulic booster. Controls are located for ease of operation.

Other features include: extra clearance under high-arched front axle and 360° blade rotation without removing scarifier teeth. Power sliding moldboard is optional.

4D-75 (75 H.P.)
4D-85 (100 H.P.)
4D-115 (123 H.P.)

HUBER-WARCO COMPANY

MARION, OHIO, U. S. A.

Road Machinery

CABLE ADDRESS: HUBARCO

ROAD ROLLERS • MOTOR GRADERS • MAINTAINERS • GRINDERS

MODEL M-52 MAINTAINER
AN ALL-PURPOSE, YEAR-'ROUND PERFORMER

The Huber-Warco Maintainer, powered by a 45½ H. P. gasoline engine, has plenty of reserve power and strength for the toughest jobs.

A torque converter reduces shock loads and wheel slippage. The unit picks up and carries loads smoother and faster. The engine won't stall—regardless of grade.

With a weight of 6250 lbs. (7205 lbs. with calcium chloride in the tires), there is enough weight for all maintenance jobs. A power sliding moldboard is standard equipment.

Hydraulically controlled attachments convert the machine for service as a bulldozer, broom, side dozer, lift-loader, snow plow, patch roller, berm leveler or mower.

Owners credit Huber-Warco's blade pushing design for a THIRD MORE WORK than conventional pulled blades would produce in its weight class.

HUBER-WARCO COMPANY

MARION, OHIO, U. S. A.

Road Machinery

CABLE ADDRESS: HUBARCO

ROAD ROLLERS • MOTOR GRADERS • MAINTAINERS • GRINDERS

VARIABLE WEIGHT TANDEM ROLLERS

With Torque Converter and 2-Speed Transmission

5-8 • 8-10 • 8-12 • 10-14 TON

Combination of a torque converter and two-speed transmission gives all the well-known advantages of a torque converter PLUS more economical operation, fast steering at even extremely slow roller speeds and reduced strain on parts.

Other major features include a tail shaft governor, full hydraulic steering, two independent brake systems, completely adjustable guide roll assembly, and choice of diesel or gasoline power.

(Also available is a 3-5 ton tandem with torque converter. For easy movement from job to job, this model can be equipped with a towing attachment or retractable wheel attachment.)

General Purpose • Finishing • Variable Weight
3-WHEEL ROLLERS with Torque Converter

10 TON • 12 TON • 14 TON
10-12 TON • 12-14 TON

All Huber-Warco 3-wheel rollers feature both a torque converter and two-speed transmission. This combination yields all converter benefits . . . and more economical operation, longer parts life, and fast steering at all roller speeds.

Other outstanding features — tail shaft governor, 3-point "live" suspension of subframe to cushion shocks, two brake systems, completely adjustable guide roll assembly, money-saving removable tire design on cast rolls.

HUBER-WARCO COMPANY

MARION, OHIO, U. S. A.

Road Machinery

CABLE ADDRESS: HUBARCO

ROAD ROLLERS • MOTOR GRADERS • MAINTAINERS • GRINDERS

EAMAN-GUNNISON Safety front-end air control

Bituminous DISTRIBUTORS with full circulating Swing-Bar

UP

DOWN

180° TURN

LEFT

RIGHT

180° TURN

Patented hinges permit full circulation with end sections extended; automatically confine circulation to center section when swung back. Air control gives instant flow to nozzles or complete shutoff in a split second—eliminating "lean" spots when starting and "fat" spots from drip when stopping. Spray bar position instantly adjusted to desired position by means of front-mounted, finger-tip controls.

ront-end control—Operator, safely out of e way of fumes and vapors, has complete ew of his work; can instantly communicate ith the driver.

. . Or, complete ONE-MAN operation ith air-operated controls dash-mounted in the uck cab.

DISTRIBUTORS
Condensed Specifications

Engine: Continental PF-162, 42.8 hp @ 2,400 rpm.

Pumps: Viking EQ 250 gpm. Viking EM, 375 gpm, optional at added cost.

Tank Capacities: Truck-mounted, eliptical; 800, 1,000, 1,250, 1,500, 1,750, 2,000 US gal. Trailer-mounted, eliptical; 1,500, 1,750, 2,000, 2,500, 3,000, 3,250, 3,500, 4,000 US gal.

Insulation: 1-in cross-corrugated air cell asbestos, **non-settling.** Covered with No. 20 gauge cold-rolled sheet.

Heating: 2 pairs, 7-in dia flues, up to 1,250 gal; 8-in dia flues, 1,500 to 4,000 gal. Low-pressure, high-pressure, or butane burners available. Tank contents are pump-circulated to prevent "hot spots", and thus prevent coking.

Spray Bars: Front-controlled. Gunnison **Air-type** 12-ft (four 3-ft, individually controlled sections, two swing-back); or Gunnison **No-drip,** hydraulically controlled, full-circulating with reverse suction; 9 ft with swing back end sections.

Standard Equipment: 1-in x 20-ft hand hose spray; hand spray bar; 3-in x 15-ft metal loading hose; tank car cock, vented; tank car coupling; tachometer and charts; pump-over valve; thermometer; running boards. Mounted on customer's truck without charge at Baraboo, Wisconsin.

For complete information write

Seaman-Gunnison Corporation

Dept. MI—2763 S. 27th St., Milwaukee 15, Wis.

Gunnison HYDRO-JET FLUSHERS

Streamlined truck and semi-trailer units—Sizes fro 1,000 to 2,000 gal, full-skirted to running board level, wit beaver tail body and fully enclosed pumping unit. Prop erly directed jet *cleans* as it flushes. Continental F-622 or Ford Model 223 six-cylinder engine. Centrifugal pum with bronze rotor and steel shaft, 650 gpm. Hose outle for emergency use in fire fighting. Each jet is separatel controlled from the truck cab.

Model WM flushers—Trailer-mounted: 800, 1,000, and 1,200 gal capacity. Truck-mounted: sizes 1,000 to 2,000 gal. Front-mounted pump, 350 gpm. Wisconsin Model VE-4, 4-cylinder, air-cooled engine. Three adjustable brass nozzles on truck-mounted tanks; two flusher nozzles and two sprinkler nozzles on trailer-mounted.

Water distributors for accurate, pressure-regulated control of water application to secure optimum moisture content in soil-cement processing; calcium chloride, lime, sand clay, and other stabilizations. Truck or trailer mounting, tanks from 800 to 3,000 gal capacity. Wisconsin VE-4 or VG-4, 4-cylinder, air-cooled engine.

For complete specifications on Gunnison street flushers, write Form GF-56. Address Seaman-Gunnison Corporation, 2763 S. 27th Dept. G, Milwaukee 15, Wis.

Duo-Grader—A multi-purpose, self-propelled grader, ditcher and land leveler. Hydraulic steering, front and rear. 180° turning. Right or left offset for ditching or sloping. International "450" prime mover.

SEAMAN-GUNNISON
2763 South 27th Street
Milwaukee 15, Wisconsin

DETROIT HARVESTER CO.

IMPLEMENT DIVISION

P. O. Box 231, Zanesville, Ohio

DETROIT SWEEPERS

25 MINUTES TO REMOVE OR RE-INSTALL

CONSTRUCTION: Frame of rigid structural steel. Heavy duty transmission with precision steel alloy gears running on heavy duty roller and ball bearings. Palmyra brush quickly demountable and reversible for even wear. Brush fully adjustable to compensate for various sweeping conditions.

CAPACITY: Six foot model sweeps path 5 feet wide. Five foot model sweeps path 4 feet wide. Both will handle snow up to 10″ deep. Six foot model sweeps over 20,000 sq. yds. per hour with tractor speed of 8 MPH.

OPERATION: Sweeping operation fully visible and controlled from driver's position. Broom pressure adjustable with balance spring. Brush elevation from driver's seat.

MODELS: Five and six foot units immediately available for FORD, FERGUSON, ALLIS-CHALMERS, CASE and CLARK tractors. Other models available upon submission of specifications. Approximate shipping weight 1000 lbs.

BRUSH REFILLS AND REPAIR PARTS AVAILABLE FOR ALL MODELS.

HIGHWAY CLEANING AND MAINTENANCE

SNOW REMOVAL

THE JAEGER MACHINE COMPANY

703 Dublin Avenue, Columbus 16, Ohio

DISTRIBUTORS IN 153 CITIES OF THE UNITED STATES AND CANADA

Two 80 lb. breakers, powered by a Jaeger "125" Roto Air-Plus, cutting and breaking a 7" course of paving brick topped with asphalt, averaged 400 linear ft. of 3 ft. wide trench (1200 sq. ft.) each 8 hours with an average fuel consumption of only 1½ gallons per hour.

FIRST FULLY EFFICIENT ROTARY COMPRESSORS

Roto Air-Plus® Compressors have all the advantages of rotary design—fewer moving parts, less weight, vibrationless operation and cooler air temperatures—plus the exclusive Jaeger advantages of lower operating speeds and simplified precision controls. Because they produce equal air volume at slower speeds, Jaeger rotary compressors have the lowest fuel consumption and longest life of any rotary on the market today.

The Roto "125" (illustrated right) is typical. Upon demand this model will instantly produce any volume up to 125 cfm at 100 psi (sufficient capacity to run two heavy duty pavement breakers or operate a 5 h.p. Ka-Mo drill at full efficiency) with a full load speed of only 1700 rpm. Air flow is direct and continuous and precisely regulated to consumption. Simplified precision controls positively prevent over-run and resultant racing of the engine. A half-turn of a regulator lever starts and stops compressor without unhooking and rehooking linkage.

Jaeger Roto Air-Plus "125": 125 cfm at constantly maintained 100 psi. A-frame tow bar with spring loaded eye and retractable pneumatic tired dolly wheel are standard. Tool boxes large enough for a full set of tools.

Jaeger Roto Air-Plus "250": 250 cfm at constantly maintained 100 psi. Two-wheel trailer mounting. Gasoline or diesel power.

Roto Air-Plus Compressors available in 125 to 600 cfm capacities

Jaeger rotary compressors are available in 125 to 600 cfm capacities to meet a wide range of air requirements. All models have wrap-around bumpers, fuel tanks with 8-hours capacity, radiator shutters adjustable to weather, and tube finned multi-pass oil coolers that insure cool operation in ambient temperatures exceeding 100°. Discharge air temperatures are at least 100° F. cooler than in the best 2-stage reciprocating compressors. In cold weather, an automatic valve positively insures by-passing oil to compressor to eliminate "dry starts."

Jaeger Reciprocating Air-Plus "75": 75 cfm at 100 psi. Compressor is light, perfectly balanced for easy trailing. Timken bearing wheels, springs and rigid frame.

Light, portable Jaeger "75" reciprocating compressor

Instead of the usual 60 cfm capacity, the Jaeger "new standard" "75" 2-stage vertical air-cooled compressor provides 75 cfm at 100 pounds pressure—ample air to power a heavy duty pavement breaker, a heavy sheeting driver, or 3 tampers at full efficiency. You'll get more work from the same tools or put more tools to work and average 1/3 more production with an Air-Plus "75."

SPECIFICATIONS • JAEGER AIR-PLUS COMPRESSORS

	Model "75"	Model "125"	Model "250"		Model "365"	Model "600"
COMPRESSOR TYPE	Reciprocating	2-Stage Oil-Cooled Rotary				
Actual Air Delivery, Cfm	75	125	250		365	600
Normal Pressure, Psi	100	100	100		100	100
Full Load Speed, Rpm	1500	1700	1700		1700	1650
Idle Speed, Rpm	—	800-900	800-900		800-900	800-900
Oil System Capacity, Gals.	1	7	13		20½	30
ENGINE TYPE	Continental F-140	Continental F-226	Cont. B-427	GM Diesel Model 3-71	GM Diesel Model 4-71	GM Diesel Model 6-71
Water Capacity, Gals.	5	21	13	13	12.½	14
Oil Capacity, Qts.	5	6	7	11	17	20
Fuel Tank Capacity, Gals.	17	20	38	38	47	85
Electric Starting System	6 volts	12 volts	12 volts	12 volts	12 volts	12 volts
DIMENSIONS						
Length, Less Draw Bar	118¾"*	99"	122⅝"	115½"	132"	156"
Width	56"	61"	70½"	74"	72"	72"
Height, With Muffler	54¼"	63½"	78½"	84"	84¾"	91"
Height, Skid Mounted	50"	51½"	63"	70½"	72"	80"
WEIGHT, 2 pneumatic, dry	1925 lbs.	3000 lbs.	4250 lbs.	5050 lbs.	6900 lbs.**	8615 lbs.**

* Includes Draw Bar
**4-Wheel Pneumatic

"SURE-PRIME" PORTABLE PUMPS

1½" to 10" Self-Priming Centrifugals
Capacities—4,000 to 240,000 gph

1½" and 2" Aluminum Pumps

Long life, low maintenance gasoline and diesel-engine-driven pumps. Fast and sure to prime because of their dual priming action. Hold that prime indefinitely. Big shells, non-clog impellers, streamlined passages, over-size heat treated shafts, and patented Jaeger "Lubri-Seal" shaft seal assure dependability.

Aluminum "Bantam"—1½" Size. Weighs only 52 pounds. Capacity—5200 gph. (With 2" suction—5,700 gph.). Recognized as the lightweight champion for manhole pumping, cleaning swimming pools, draining basements after fires, and other "carry around" service. Larger Model 2PAF, also aluminum, weighs 105 pounds, pumps 9,000 gph. Two men carry it easily.

2" to 10" Portables—Two and four wheel models on cushion rubber, pneumatic or steel tires. All models feature replaceable liner plates which need only to be renewed after long service to make the pumps as good as new. On all 4" to 10" heavy duty models an extra and massive bearing gives additional support to the shaft.

3" Heavy Duty

Model	Capacity	Model	Capacity
2XP	7,000 gph	4P	40,000 gph
2PN	10,000 gph	6P	90,000 gph
3XP	15,000 gph	8P	125,000 gph
3P	20,000 gph	10P	228,000 gph
4XP	30,000 gph	10PD	240,000 gph

Pressure Pumps, 2" to 8" sizes, pressures up to 275 lb.

Also, electric-motor-driven pumps—1½ to 10-inch sizes—¾ to 40 horsepower.

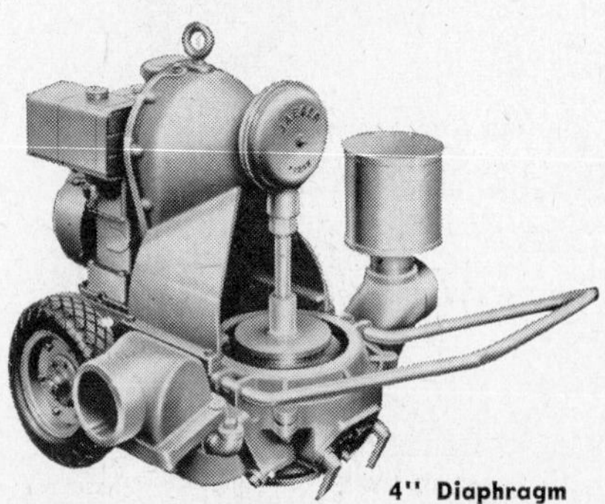

4" Diaphragm

Diaphragm Pumps—3" and 4" suction and discharge. Recommended for pumping sludge, mud, septic tanks, seepage, small trenches. Capacities: 3", 3000 gph.; 4", 6000 gph. at 10" suction lift.

Exclusive spring-bottom bowl that is shock-absorbing and self-cleaning is a major improvement over similar pumps. Light-weight, free-swinging check valves, surge chamber and quick changing diaphragm are other features. 3" model weighs less than 150 lbs.

Self-Priming pumps are available in sizes from 1½" to 10" for the wide variety of municipal uses.

"SPEEDLINE" PORTABLE CONCRETE MIXERS

Speed King 3½-S

3½ Cubic Foot Tilting Mixer—A "half-bag" mixer that trails easily behind lightest automobile or truck. Spots easily alongside material piles, because there are no feet or legs on discharge or loading sides. Towpole telescopes. Wheelers get barrows in and away without jockeying. Easily turns out 35 cubic yards of concrete per day. Gasoline engine or electric motor powered. (Built by SPEED KING Manufacturing Co., Division of The Jaeger Machine Company.)

3½-S "Auto-Loader"

3½ Cubic Foot "Auto-Loader" Mixer—Fastest "half-bag" mixer made. Its wide-mouthed hopper loads while a batch is mixing. When that batch is discharged, open the hopper and in goes the next—shaken in quickly without pounding or scraping. No waiting between batches—and 12 to 15 more cubic yards of concrete per day as a result. Mixing drum is famous Jaeger "Dual-Mix" that gives the batch a criss-crossing re-mixing action. Gasoline engine or electric motor powered. Easily mixes up to 50 cu. yds. per day.

11-S "Speedline" Mixer with Skip-Shaker Loader. Typical of Jaeger 6, 11 and 16 cu. ft. mixers.

6, 11 and 16 Cubic Foot "Skip-Shaker Loaders"—Two- and four-wheel mixers that tow fast and stably on automotive type wheels and pneumatic tires, and maneuver at the job easily. Loading skips descend to take materials while a batch mixes, then rise and shake their loads into the drum, fast and clean. Mixing drums are "Dual Mix" design—give the batch a constant criss-cross re-mixing action. Drums turn on chilled iron carwheel-type rollers—each roller supported by two Timken roller bearings. Drum tracks are heavy steel, integrally welded and accurately machined. Accurate-metering water tanks are standard equipment.

LODAL, INC.

Hydraulic Truck Loaders • Fluid Drive Sweepers • Truck Self Loaders • Sno Plows
Norway, Michigan

the most *Versatile* machine your city can buy!

LoDaL

MULTI-PURPOSE
HYDRAULIC TRUCK LOADER

3000 lb Capacity

Loads One Truck or Many!

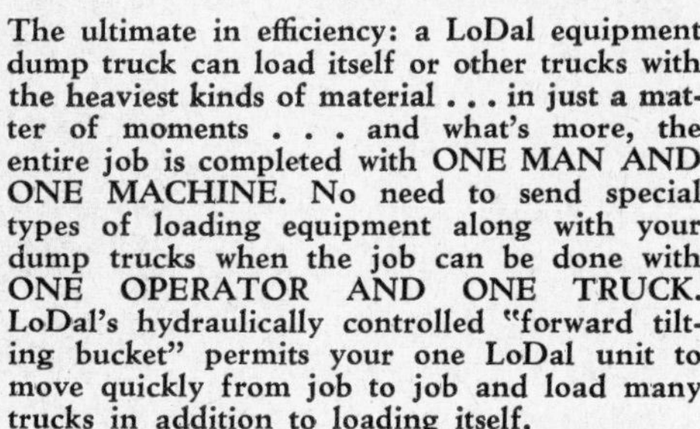

The ultimate in efficiency: a LoDal equipment dump truck can load itself or other trucks with the heaviest kinds of material . . . in just a matter of moments . . . and what's more, the entire job is completed with ONE MAN AND ONE MACHINE. No need to send special types of loading equipment along with your dump trucks when the job can be done with ONE OPERATOR AND ONE TRUCK. LoDal's hydraulically controlled "forward tilting bucket" permits your one LoDal unit to move quickly from job to job and load many trucks in addition to loading itself.

You will find LoDal's versatility hard to beat for construction cleanup or removing debris from construction sites. The true efficiency of LoDal will prove itself again and again in the wide variety of municipal applications. Many municipalities throughout the United States have found LoDal worth its price alone for removing rainstorm debris on major streets and intersections, for here is a unit which saves maneuvering and permits easy freedom of movement of the unit when working in restricted areas.

DOES MANY JOBS—WITH JUST YOUR TRUCK

Add the *refuse lip* to your standard LoDaL bucket—and you have a "low lift height" rubbish collection unit. Bucket rubbish lip can be added or removed—in just a matter of moments.

LoDaL

LOADS 5 YDS. OF SAND OR GRAVEL – 3 MINUTES

The truck itself being used to self-load sand from a natural pit. LoDaL speed—and truck power—give loading speeds equal to heavy duty tractor loaders.

Heavy timbers to handle? LoDaL unit being used to lift telephone poles—or other heavy timbers. 3,000 pound capacity makes a highly mobile unit.

For all types of maintenance work

LoDaL hydraulic truck loaders are rugged machines engineered to fit most makes of dump trucks. With a LoDaL, your truck becomes a complete working unit: one that can *load, haul* and *dump* . . . with one man and one machine. For municipal operations it is a very flexible unit . . . you can use it as a bucket loader . . . a snow plow . . . or a rubbish collector. All with simple change-over.

As a bucket loader, LoDaL can compete with front end tractor loaders costing many times as much. Load sand or gravel . . . 4 to 5 yards . . . in as little as 3 minutes. Powerful . . . smooth . . . speedy lifting action . . . with 3,000 pound capacity.

Operator controlled, 5/8 cubic yard "hydraulic" forward tilting bucket can be used for self loading . . . or for loading other trucks as well. The "direct thrust" principle permits the LoDaL to safely absorb all the thrust your truck can give. Sturdy main beam and wide spread frame mounting, assure full distribution of stress throughout the truck frame.

LoDaL units are in daily use in cities throughout the country . . . for such jobs as loading sand or gravel, street repairs, sweeper pickup, snow removal, rubbish collection, leaf loading, coal handling, cinder removal . . . and many other daily tasks.

THE MOST ECONOMICAL MACHINE YOUR CITY CAN BUY

The basic LoDaL and the dump body all metal sideboard extensions installed on a conventional dump body, afford a high speed . . . low cost snow removal unit. Users report that *one man* operating a LoDaL can move as much snow as a tractor loader and 3 to 4 dump trucks. With the LoDaL "Sideboards", one truck load is equal to 3 or 4 ordinary trucks . . . plus the speed and capacity of the LoDaL bucket with its two-yard snow capacity.

The LoDaL can be quickly converted from a bucket loader to a snow plow. The high-speed hydraulic lift of the twin loader booms permits raising the plow to any desired position. The plow can always be lifted high enough to clear the snow bank, and thus permits turning or backing in tight areas. Plow can be lifted to a traveling position back on the dump body for complete travel safety.

City after city is finding LoDaL's year-round utility to be the most efficient, economical and versatile answer to their problems. Why buy 5 machines when one LoDaL, with attachments will do the job.

Write, Wire or Phone:

"DOLLAR FOR DOLLAR YOUR BEST BUY"

THE CLEVELAND FORMGRADER CO.

MILLS ROAD DEPT. M AVON, OHIO

ALL STEEL BULL FLOAT

A piece of equipment to smooth irregularities from surface after finishing machines have been used and before concrete has set.

Specifications
Channel formed from steel sheet, cross braced for stiffness, with vertical adjustment for alignment. Plow handles furnished with vertical and width adjustments so that float can be adjusted to individual operators requirements. Available in widths of 8", 10" and 12", lengths of 10, 12, 14 and 16 ft.

FORM AND STAKE PULLER

The ideal tool to pull forms and stakes without damage. Designed to lift straight up so as to eliminate the possibility of damage to pavement.

Specifications
Reinforced oak handle, steel frame. 12" cast rubber wheels or 4.00x12 pneumatic tire wheels. Both have roller bearings for ease of handling.

PULL BROOMS

For use when the specifications call for concrete pavement to be "broom finished". Brooms are of two types, 2 row Bass fibre or 3 row Bassine fibre—24" long with fibres 4½" long. Available with adjustable aluminum or malleable holders and either aluminum or steel handles. Handle lengths from 12 to 16 ft.

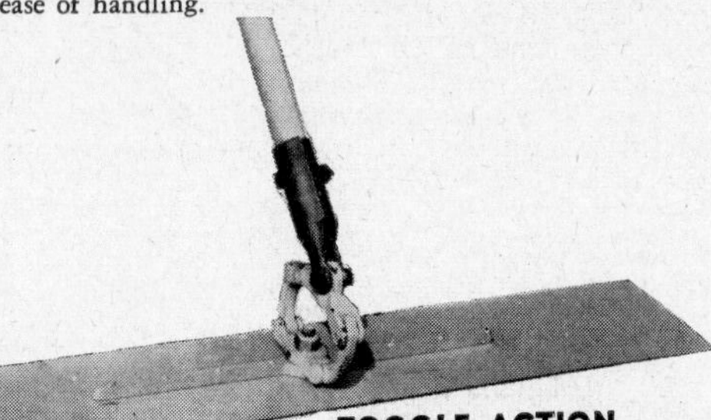

TOGGLE ACTION FLOATS AND TROWELS

Excellent tools for concrete finishing.

Specifications
Floats have beveled edges—Trowels are flat. Both have double action floating obtained through means of toggle type attachments on handle. Available in 16 ga. steel, 6" width, 18, 24 or 36" lengths with 6 ft. handles (larger handles available).

STEEL HAND FLOATS

A pan type float for finishing concrete.

Specifications
16 ga. steel, 6" wide with a 1" turned up flange. Lengths of 4, 5 or 6 ft. with 12 ft. rigid steel handles cross-braced and reinforced (larger handles available).

LUTES

All steel, ideal for cutting down high spots. Available in 4, 6 and 10 ft. blade lengths with handles 7, 12, 14 or 16 ft. long. Weight of 10 ft. Lute with 12 ft. handle is 27½ lbs.

POWEROLL

For black top and patching work on driveways, sidewalks and parking lots, etc. The Poweroll is extremely maneuverable and ideal for rolling those "hard to get at" places. A simplified transmission makes this an easy to use, versatile piece of equipment.

Specifiications
Equipped with 3 HP air cooled 4 cycle gasoline engine, forward and reverse transmission and foot brake. The main drum is 3/16" plate 34" diameter, 3 ft. wide and the steering drum is 14" ODx20" wide. The gross weight is ½ ton.

THE CLEVELAND FORMGRADER CO.

MILLS ROAD DEPT. M AVON, OHIO

FORM TAMPER

For tamping the earth under the forms to prevent form settlement.

Saves time and money and does away with time consuming and inefficient hand tamping. Meets State specifications. Ideal for street, highway and turnpike construction.

Tamps and oils forms at same time. Powered by a Briggs & Stratton 3 HP engine. Available in two models, standard and opposite hand. Each machine adjustable to several size forms (specify height and width of form when ordering.)

In just a few hours a man can tamp and oil forms for a day's run. Result: a smoother more accurate concrete surface at lower cost in less time.

ALUMINUM OR STEEL STRAIGHT EDGES

Precision engineered for outstanding accuracy

Aluminum, light weight, reduces fatigue, affords quick accurate checking. Available with a 10 ft. blade and 12′-14′- or 16-ft. handles and with either round or flat bottom blades.

STEEL—Made of special steel formed to meet requirements of unusual strength—accurate, light weight. Standard size is a 10 ft. blade with a 12 ft. seamless steel tube handle. Also available with 12, 14, 16 ft. blades and 14 or 16 ft. handles.

A complete line of paving equipment: Formgraders for digging the form trench—Subgrade Scrapers—Concrete Strike-Offs—Stake and Form Pullers—Finishing Bridges—Bull Floats—Trowels—Lutes—Pull Brooms—Trailgraders.

JUNIOR TRAILGRADER

A machine that finishes the subgrade to exact contour just before the concrete is placed. Adjustable draw bars or cables are furnished for pulling. Ideal for use where a grader is needed to do the job and yet the equipment should be light and easy to handle.

Specifications

Frame made of heavy H column giving strength and rigidity. Adjustable vertically to 16″. Can be extended 2 ft. Blades are of high carbon steel, heat treated, single edge. Cutting blades are mounted with bolts through slotted holes thus allowing for setting to crown. Wheels are extra heavy with deep flanges and are run on oversize axles. Grease reservoirs in each wheel assure ample lubrication. Weight of machine varies according to size from 1200 lbs. to 1850 lbs. Available in combination road widths from 10 ft. to 22 ft.

SUBGRADE SCRATCH TEMPLATE

For accurately and quickly checking your subgrade. Of Steel construction—moves backward and forward on forms in vertical position. Mounted on flanged wheels. Adjustable vertically. Pins spaced 6″ from center to center and are adjustable vertically so as to conform to the required cross section of the subgrade.

Available in a standard and heavy duty model. Standard Scratch Template weighs approximately 20 lbs. per lineal foot. Heavy Duty Scratch Template 53 lbs. per lineal foot.

DRAVO CORPORATON

National Distributor for Tri-Lok Grating

Sales Representatives in Principal Cities

Dravo Building, Pittsburgh 22, Pennsylvania

Tri-Forged Welded Rectangular Grating

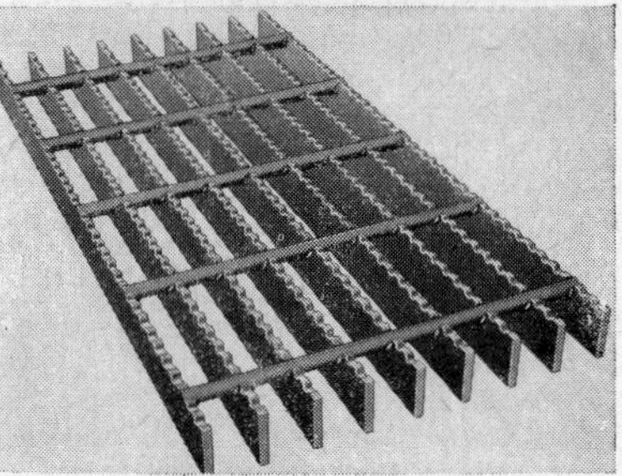

Tri-Forged Welded Serrated Grating

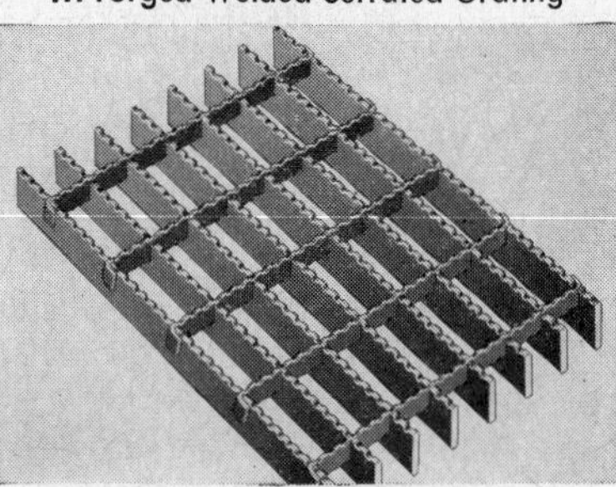

Tri-Lok Interlocked Serrated Grating

Tri-Lok Interlocked Super-Safety Grating

Tri-Forged and Tri-Lok

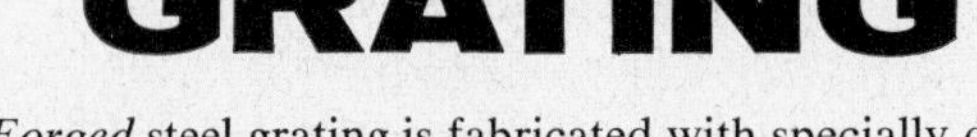

Tri-Forged steel grating is fabricated with specially designed double triangular-shaped cross bars forge-welded to the bearing bars to form one-piece construction.

Tri-Lok steel grating is mechanically interlocked under 1600-ton pressure which forces straight cross bars into alternating "J" slots in the bearing bars. The resulting triple twist lock insures rigid construction.

Tri-Forged grating and stair treads are available in steel and stainless steel only. Tri-Lok grating and treads can also be manufactured from a variety of other metals—such as aluminum alloy, stainless steel, brass, bronze, alloy steel, etc.

For further information on Tri-Forged or Tri-Lok products, write to Dravo Corporation, Dravo Building, Pittsburgh 22, Pennsylvania.

Ideally suited for:

- **Boiler room walkways**
- **Bridge sidewalks**
- **Open grid flooring**
- **Gallery floors**
- **Loading platforms**
- **Sidewalk doors over transformer vaults**
- **Stair treads**

CORPORATION

Blast furnace blowers • boiler and power plants • bridge sub-structures • cab conditioners • docks and unloaders • dredging • fabricated piping foundations • gantry and floating cranes • gas and oil pumping stations • locks and dams • ore and coal bridges • process equipment • pumphouses and intakes • river sand and gravel • sintering plants • slopes, shafts, tunnels • space heaters • steel grating • towboats, barges, river transportation

LITTLEFORD BROS., INC.

441 East Pearl St. Cincinnati, Ohio

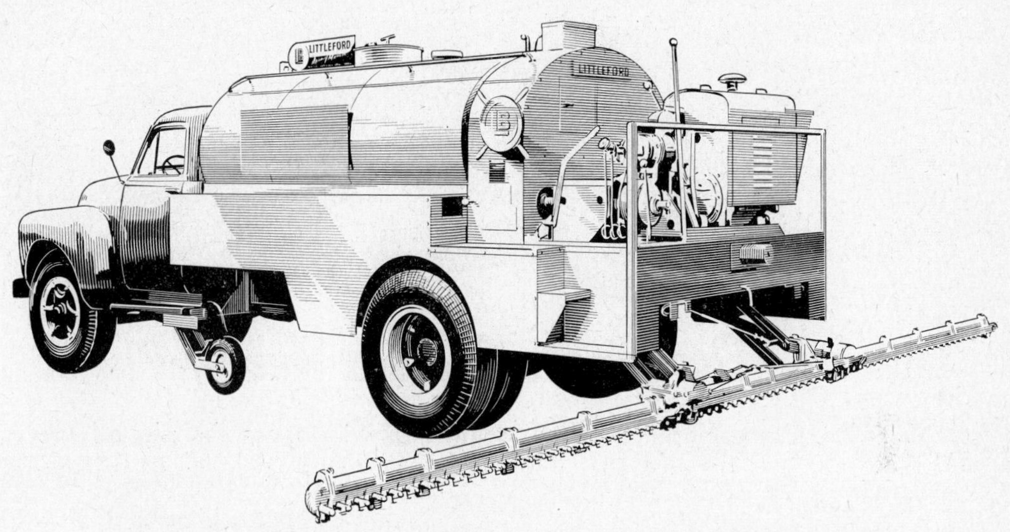

Spray Master Bituminous Distributor

The Spray Master bituminous distributor—with full circulating mechanically operated spray bar—offers a combination of exclusive deluxe Littleford engineered features that make it the most economical and easy to operate pressure distributor on the market. This statement is amply supported by reports from our many satisfied distributor customers.

Spray bar raised and folded for traveling

Here are a few of the features that account for this wide acceptance:

Multi-pass continuous heat flue system at no extra cost on sizes 800 through 1200 gallon. Most economical heat system, puts more heat in the material in the tank; the exhaust temperature is by actual test lower than any other unit.

•

Patented damper preheats pump, main valve and piping. It's faster: saves at least thirty minutes a day. Safer: allows you to preheat with burner even when flues are exposed or when tank is empty.

•

Air-cooled flue liner . . . patented single valve controls all operations . . . 4" Viking pump . . . right angle drive . . . 4-speed transmission . . . 2-section full area spray bar . . . complete coverage . . . no dripping or streaking . . . exclusive hydraulic operated bar lift.

•

Sizes range from 800 to 2000 gal. truck mounted, and 1250 to 4000 gal. frameless semi-trailer mounted. Whatever that municipal job, from a patch to a new roadway, the Spray Master can do it better and for less. Ask for Bulletin 14.

Littleford-Clarkmoore Surface Heater-Planer

The Littleford-Clarkmoore Heater-Planer planes the road surface so smooth you can lay the surface course directly on it . . . thus reducing the amount of new asphalt required, and thereby introducing a whole new technique in street and highway maintenance.

In many instances the planed streets can be used immediately and indefinitely without adding asphalt and without surface treating. In all cases the planed material can be re-used. Conservative estimates indicate the new heater-planer will save a minimum of 63¢ a square yard on black-top maintenance. Bulletin 18.

Surface irregularities **quickly planed off by the powerful combined heating-planing action.**

Windrowed material **left behind for easy pick-up by front end loader . . . for re-use.**

Kwik-Steam Generator Delivers steam in 2 minutes from a cold start. Cuts fuel consumption and labor costs. Year-round operation. Sizes 20 to 165 bhp. Bulletin 22.

Littleford Bituminous Distributor With full circulating mechanically operated spray bar. Patented engineering features built into Littleford distributors save an hour a day. 800 to 2000 gallon tank capacty. Write for bulletin 30.

Portable Tandem Rollers 3 models: 2-3 tons, 3-5 tons and 4-6 tons, all equipped to give variable compaction. No separate trailer required to transport roller. Easily hitched to towing truck. Bulletins 20, 24 and 32.

2-way Road Broom Sweeps right or left. Has exclusive wear-reducing hydraulic lift that raises, lowers and adjusts the heavy duty brush. Power and traction driven models. Write for bulletin 19.

Tar and Asphalt Kettle The 84HD, with its patented double heat circulation system, delivers more "hot stuff" faster, at lower cost and with greater safety. Hand spray and motor attachments. Bulletin 1.

Utility Spray Tank Perfect for muncipality work: for small application jobs, for hand spraying and for crack and joint filling. Truck mounted and trailer types. Write for bulletin 5.

LITTLEFORD

Surface Heater-Planer Heats *and* planes a path 81" wide in one continuous operation. May be used as surface heater without planing action. Bulletin 18.

Bituminous Supply Tank Hauls hot bituminous materials. Single and tandem axle models, 2,000 gallons up to maximum allowable weight. Bulletin 25.

True-Lay Paver-Spreader The only paver-spreader that gives compaction. A 60% heavier unit designed to put more weight on the mat. Bulletin 33.

160 Roller Portable tandem roller with full-time power steering, hydraulic conversion, maximum compaction and stability, 19.5 hp air-cooled engine. Bulletin 32.

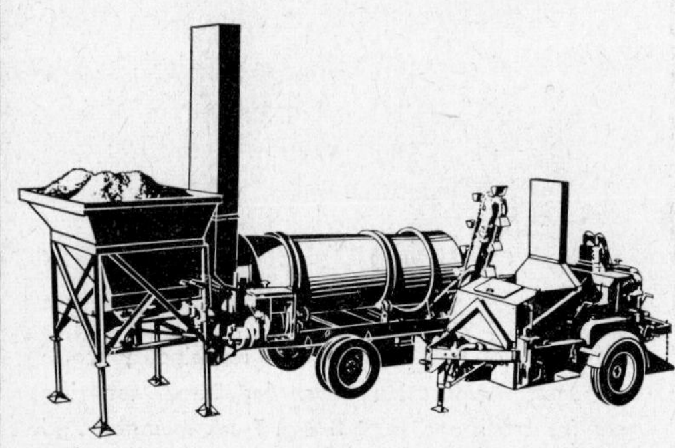

Small Portable Asphalt Plant, consisting of dual feeder bin (left), Trail-O-Dryer (middle) and Trail-O-Patcher (right). Operation of the Littleford Dryer-Patcher combination is simple and practically automatic.

Trail-O-Dryer produces 15 to 25 tons of hot, dry aggregate per hour. It will boost your Trail-O-Patcher output 200% and may be used with other types of bituminous mixers, too. Write for bulletin 36.

Trail-O-Patcher Portable bituminous mixer produces hot or cold bituminous concrete right on the job. Two models available. Write for bulletins 35 and 29.

world's most complete line of completely engineered black top equipment

Economical Excavating For Municipalities
SHERMAN
A Ford Tractor with a Sherman Backhoe has more flexibility than any other equipment on the construction site today. It can be used on any number of jobs: trenching for footings, service lines, sewers and drains—digging holes for tanks and catch basins—and dozens of other jobs.
There are two big reasons why more Shermans are in use than any other make: First, greater digging production and, second, better service because factory-trained mechanics and parts are available at Ford Tractor Dealers.
Sherman
PRODUCTS, INC.
ROYAL OAK, MICHIGAN
POWER DIGGERS*• FRONT END LOADERS • FORK LIFTS
esigned, Engineered and Manufactured jointly by Sherman Products, Inc., Royal Oak, Michigan. Wain-Roy Corporation, Hubbardston, Mass.
©1956 Sherman Products, Inc.

Sherman MAJOR POWER DIGGER
FOR FAST, POWERFUL DIGGING ACTION

Here at last is a heavy-duty backhoe unit engineered especially for the Fordson Major Tractor. The Sherman Major Power Digger takes advantage of the economy and dependability of this rugged, diesel tractor. Result: A tractor-digger combination that can't be equalled for low-cost, high-production excavating.

SPECIFICATIONS:

Sherman Major features include heavy steel plate construction, large diameter hinge pins, replaceable hardened steel bushings, heavy-duty steel castings, newly designed dipstick, boom, cylinders, bucket, sub-frame assembly and twin crowd cylinders for balanced power to permit efficient digging through any soil.

Loading height........................8′ 8″

Reach behind rear axle at grade........18′ 3″

Digging reach (at grade from center line of swing axis).............15′

Reach below grade...................12′ 6″

Swing arc...........................180°

Operating pressure...............1500 P.S.I.

Pump volume at optimum engine rpm (1500)...........17.5 G.P.M.

The operator of the Sherman owned by the city of Dearborn, Michigan says: "We couldn't do the jobs we are doing with any other machine. We've got to have the power and strength the Sherman Major offers to dig as hard and as deep as we do."

THE *Sherman* FRONT-END LOADER*

FOR FORDSON MAJOR TRACTORS

a balanced combination of REACH, STABILITY, CAPACITY, LOADING HEIGHT

The Sherman Front End Loader is designed especially for the Fordson Major Tractor. Built to handle the heaviest loading jobs, it features a design principle that transmits the load to the rear wheels for greater traction and maximum performance. The Sherman Front End Loader gives greater load, lift and breakaway capacities than any comparable machine. It offers dumping height and reach equalled by none and adds many exclusive design features that make it rugged, easy to install and easy to operate.

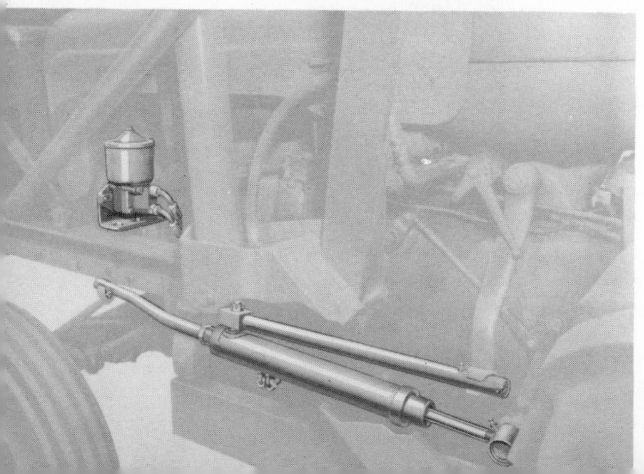

SHERMAN POWER STEERING

Sherman Hydraulic Power Steering does the work *and* absorbs shocks that normally transmit through the steering mechanism to the wheel. The unit consists of a hydraulic servo valve and cylinder connected to the conventional steering mechanism and actuated by the steering arm. Hydraulic power is supplied by a self-contained pump and reservoir unit that is driven by a V-belt from the generator pulley.

*Manufactured for Sherman Products, Inc., by Johnson Hydraulic Equipment Company, Minneapolis, Minnesota

Handle Materials over Rough Terrain with a

The Sherman Fork Lift converts the Ford Tractor into a rugged, useful lift truck that travels over *any type of terrain—paved or unpaved.* Pays for itself in the paving it saves! Keeps paying for itself in more efficient materials handling! The Sherman lifts 4,000 pounds as high as ten feet (can be modified to twelve feet) and travels at top tractor speed. A complete line of quick-change attachments handles a variety of materials.

SHERMAN COMBINATION TRANSMISSION

Supplies extra gears *between, above and below* standard to give more economy or more power when needed.

SHERMAN REVERSING TRANSMISSION

The auxiliary Sherman Reversing Transmission provides five gear speeds in either direction with quick shifting from forward to reverse.

Form No. SP 637

*Manufactured exclusively for us by K-D Mfg. Co., Cleburne, Texa

KENNEDY'S

VAN BRUSH MANUFACTURING CO., INC.

327 Southwest Blvd. Since 1928 Kansas City 8, Missouri

ROAD CONTRACTORS HEADQUARTERS FOR BRUSHES—BROOMS, DRAG LEVELERS, ETC.

ROAD BUILDERS–CONTRACTORS–ENGINEERS
HIGHWAY COMMISSIONS—WE'RE READY TO HELP
IN THE *$50,000,000,000* PLUS ROAD PROGRAM

OUR WAREHOUSES ARE BULGING WITH ROTARY BROOM SWEEPER CORES—STEEL WIRE AND FIBRE DRAG BROOM LEVELERS—PUSH BROOMS, COCOA MATS, etc.

IMMEDIATE SERVICE—WE SHIP WORLD WIDE

YOU CAN BUY DIRECT AND SAVE FROM THE MAKERS OF

ROTARY SWEEPER BROOM CORES

OF THE POPULAR MAKES THAT FIT THE TYPES LISTED. ALL LENGTHS

ANNOUNCING!!

A NEW TYPE SERVICE FOR THOSE WHO WANT TO SAVE MONEY

BUY CORE ONLY — WITHOUT FIBRES — READY TO FILL

SAVE $$ ON FREIGHT—IMMEDIATE SHIPMENT

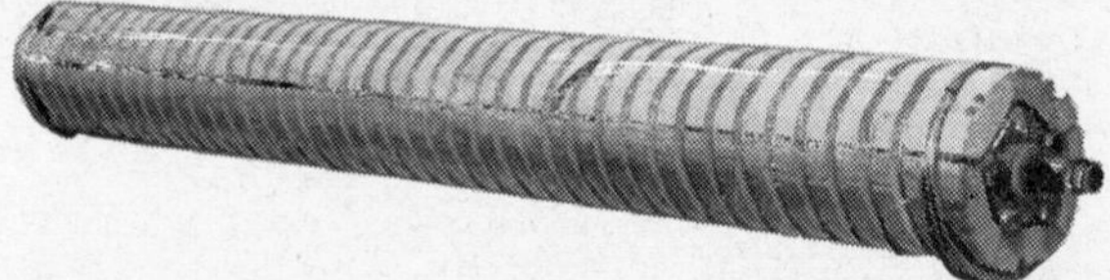

NO FILLING
NO CRATING
with or without cable

NOTE: Unfilled Cores—Burlap Wrapped—Not crated. Subject to Low Freight Rate.

- DETROIT-HARVESTER
- FORDSON
- GRACE (3 types)
- HOUGH
- HUBER
- LITTLEFORD
- LITTLE-GIANT
- LULL
- MELI (M-B) BLUMBERG
- ROSCO
- SPEARSWELL

and many others

REPAIR PARTS FOR BROOMS LISTED

HUBS—WOOD SLATS—STEEL SHAFTING—STEEL CABLE, ETC.

CORES ALSO FURNISHED WITH SPRING STEEL WIRES

CALIBAR BASS—INDIA PALMYRA OR HICKORY FIBRES

SEE OUR OTHER ADS

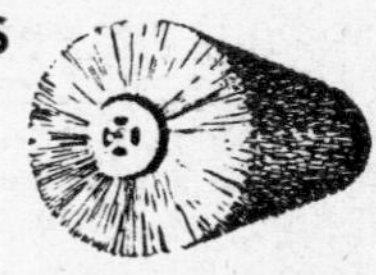

LET US DO YOUR DIRTY WORK

WE'RE SPECIALISTS IN REPAIRING — REBUILDING — REFILLING ANY MAKE, SIZE OR TYPE OF (WOOD) BROOM CORES

NEED **SPECIAL** ROTARY BROOM **BRUSHES** SEND US YOUR SPECIFICATIONS

LET OUR ENGINEERING SPECIALISTS BE OF SERVICE

TRADE MARK REG.

PECKERWOOD

KENNEDY'S

VAN BRUSH MFG. CO. INC.

327 SOUTHWEST BLVD., KANSAS CITY 8, MISSOURI

Contractor's Headquarters Since 1928

NEW! NEW! NEW!

ROAD BUILDERS – CONTRACTORS!!

WHY USE STREET PUSH BROOMS — DO IT CHEAPER

FIBRE DRAG BROOM LEVELERS

NOW IN STOCK

USE OUR FIBRE DRAG FOR THAT PARTICULAR FINE JOB!

THE LARGE PECKERWOOD HEAVY DUTY FIBRE DRAG

Six (6) Inches Wide and ANY LENGTH TO 12 FEET

TWICE THE WIDTH OF STREET PUSH BROOM YES—MADE C-O-N-T-I-N-U-O-U-S IN LENGTH

MADE WITH

CALIBAR BASS or PALM FIBRE

Weight 4 lbs. Foot
6" Trim

IN STOCK LENGTHS

4- 6- 8- and 10-FOOT

OR NAME YOURS

ILLUSTRATION OF 10 FOOT LENGTH

NO FRAME TO BUY
IT'S FRAMELESS
ASSEMBLE YOUR OWN
in minutes with 2 x 4's or angle iron
or we furnish assembled
ALL PRICES SUBJECT TO CHANGE

BIG ILLUSTRATION ASSEMBLED

DOUBLE DUTY DRAGS

ONLY $3.00 running foot

DOUBLE DUTY WITH 4 SIX FOOT LENGTHS HINGED IN CENTER — DRAG DOUBLE THE WIDTH. WT. APPROX. 102 LBS.

THE SMALL PECKERWOOD SINGLE FIBRE DRAG

MADE
THREE (3") INCHES WIDE, 15 INCHES LONG WITH 2 BOLTS, 9½" CENTERS
WEIGHT APPROX. 3 LBS. EA.

THESE MADE WITH
CALIBAR BASS or PALM FIBRE
6" Trim

ILLUSTRATION OF UNIT 15" LENGTH

NOW $2.25 ea.

CHEAPER THAN STREET PUSH BROOMS

OUR FIBRE DRAG FITS STANDARD FRAME

NOW AVAILABLE IN C-O-N-T-I-N-U-O-U-S LENGTHS

TO 12 FEET LONG

ONLY $2.10 PER FOOT

Weight 2 1/3 lb. ea.

Illustration of Continuous Length

NOTE—ALSO FURNISHED WITH STEEL WIRES

**NOW IN STOCK
COCOA MATS for
BITUMINOUS ROLLERS
STREET BROOMS—PAINT & VARNISH BRUSHES**

MOUNT EITHER DRAG BEHIND MOULD BOARD BLADE

SEE OUR OTHER ADS FOR ROTARY BROOM CORES—STEEL WIRE DRAGS, ETC.

TRADE MARK REG.

Home of the Peckerwood Brushes—Brooms

—FLAT STEEL WIRE—

ROAD BUILDERS, IT'S SENSATIONAL!!

PECKERWOOD

STEEL WIRE DRAG BROOM LEVELERS

DRAG ROADS THE MODERN WAY WITH HIGHWAY COMMISSION APPROVED BROOMS

IT'S A TOUGHIE AND A BULLDOZER FOR PUNISHMENT

BOTH OUR DRAGS DID THE JOB IN THE KOREAN WAR—GOVERNMENT APPROVED

THE BIG PECKERWOOD STEEL WIRE

WITH FLAT STEEL SPRING WIRES
SIX INCHES WIDE

NOT STAPLE SET
TRIPLE (3) WIRES OUT
EACH HOLE 5½" OUT

—YES—
6 INCHES WIDE
AND MADE
C-O-N-T-I-N-U-O-U-S
IN LENGTH TO
12 FEET LONG

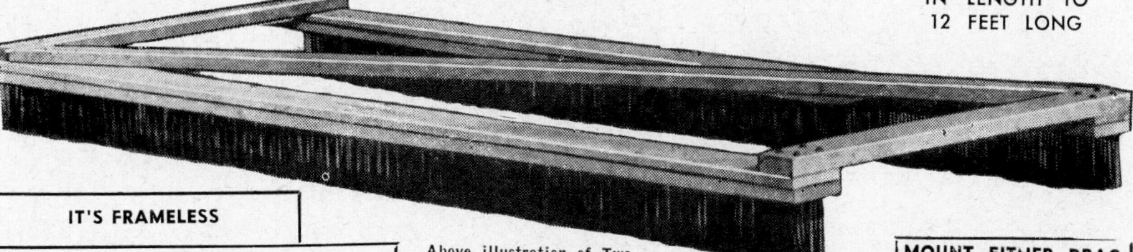

IT'S FRAMELESS

NO EXPENSIVE FRAME TO BUY

Assemble in any Shape wanted. x's, z's, y's, etc. with 2 x 4's or angle iron.

Above illustration of Two 10 foot sections, Assembled, and Single 10 Foot below.

ONLY $3.50 per foot

All prices subject to change

ORDER LENGTH WANTED
ASSEMBLE YOUR OWN

MOUNT EITHER DRAG BEHIND MOULD BOARD

Extra Heavy Duty Type—Weight Approx. 5½ pounds per foot. Kiln Dried Hard Wood.

YES! MADE IN CONTINUOUS LENGTHS TO 12 FEET

in stock lengths
6', 7', 8', 9', 10' and 12'

THE LITTLE PECKERWOOD STEEL WIRE

$2.50 ea.

SINGLE STEEL FLAT WIRE DRAG
3¼ INCHES WIDE
SAME AS STREET BROOM

Heavy Duty Type Double (2) wires out, each hole 4½ out.

Weight approx. 4 lbs. each

—3 INCHES WIDE

—15 INCHES LONG WITH 2 BOLTS, 9½" CENTERS

YES! BOTH FIT THE STANDARD FRAME

THE LITTLE PECKERWOOD NOW MADE IN

C-O-N-T-I-N-U-O-U-S LENGTHS TO
12 FEET LONG—NAME YOUR LENGTH

$2.25 per foot

NOT STAPLE SET
THIS FITS THE STANDARD 3 WIDE FRAME
THE LITTLE PECKERWOOD
NOW AVAILABLE IN C-O-N-T-I-N-U-O-U-S LENGTHS TO 12 FT

SEE OUR OTHER ADS FURNISHED WITH **FIBRE**

THESE ALSO FURNISHED IN THE ASSEMBLED BIG OR SMALL
DOUBLE DUTY DRAGS

DOUBLE LENGTHS ASSEMBLED
DOUBLE WEIGHT
DOUBLE HINGED IN CENTER

ROAD CONTRACTORS HEADQUARTERS FOR BRUSHES—BROOMS

KENNEDY'S

VAN BRUSH MANUFACTURING CO., INC.

327 SOUTHWEST BLVD. SINCE 1928 KANSAS CITY 8, MISSOURI

LITTLE GIANT PRODUCTS, INC.

1530-1550 N. ADAMS STREET, PEORIA, ILLINOIS

LITTLE GIANT FM-C

FRONT-MOUNTED SWEEPER

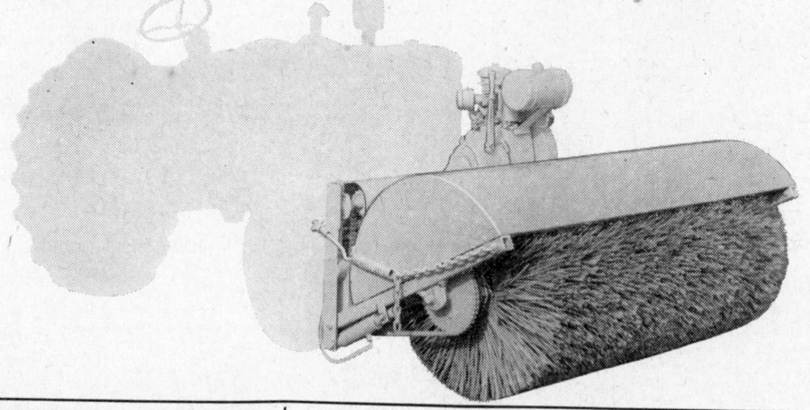

BRIEF SPECIFICATIONS

Boom of 2½" extra heavy pipe ruggedly reinforced. *Hood* of 16 gauge steel, covers entire brush. *Brush* has tough, Palmyra fibre bristles; mounted in self-aligning, pre-sealed ball bearings; revolves at 150 RPM. *Power* is an 8 HP (at 2400 RPM) air-cooled engine. *Drive* is through cold-rolled shafts, No. 60 roller chains and steel sprockets. *Lift control* is hydraulic, using system of prime mover or optional hand pump. *Adjustments:* brush tilts up or down 6°, angles left or right 30°. *Optional equipment:* sprinkler system; mounting kit; hand hydraulic pump; front deflector; steel-bristled broom; parking stand. *Dimensions:* Height 51"; brush diameter 31".

Choice of brushes:	4'	5'	6'	7'	8'
Sweeping path at 30° angle	3'1"	4'1"	5'1"	6'1"	7'1"
Width	4'10"	5'10"	6'10"	7'10"	8'10"
Weight	480	510	540	570	600

For use with *any* truck, jeep or tractor!

A simple set of mounting brackets and a FM-C Sweeper converts any truck, Jeep or tractor into an efficient, low-cost sweeping unit in *minutes*. No complicated and time-consuming hook-up to PTO or crankshaft is required.

An independent 8 HP engine, mounted on sweeper frame, rotates the brush at any desired speed regardless of speed of prime mover. Brush adjusts for wear; angles 30° left or right for windrowing trash or snow; tilts at either end.

Sweeper assembly can be attached or detached instantly by pulling one pin and disconnecting a quick-detachable hydraulic coupling.

The low-cost FM-C offers fast, efficient sweeping with minimum operating expense.

For information, see your Little Giant distributor or write direct — now!

LITTLE GIANT ROAD BIRD

TOW-TYPE SWEEPER

BRIEF SPECIFICATIONS

Frame is of 4″ structural steel channel. *Boom* is of 2½″ extra heavy pipe ruggedly reinforced. *Hood*, of 16 gauge steel, covers entire broom. *Brush* has tough Palmyra fibre bristles; revolves at 150 RPM; mounted in self-aligning, pre-sealed ball bearings. *Tongue* 60″ long is 2″ pipe. *Wheels*, mounted on tapered roller bearings, have 5.50 x 16, 4 ply tires. *Power* is an 8 HP (at 2400 RPM) air-cooled engine. *Drive* is through cold-rolled shafts, No. 60 roller chains and steel sprockets. *Optional equipment:* sprinkler system; front deflector; electric starter; steel-bristled brush. *Dimensions:* Height 51″; brush diameter 31″; length 132″; tread (rear axle) 60″; wheelbase 100″; turning radius 110″.

Choice of brushes:	4′	5′	6′	7′	8′
Sweeping path at 30° angle	3′1″	4′1″	5′1″	6′1″	7′1″
Width	4′10″	5′10″	6′10″	7′10″	8′10″
Weight	1010#	1130#	1250#	1370#	1490#

For a cleaner sweep at lowest cost, it's the Little Giant Road Bird! The tough Palmyra fibre-bristled brush, driven by its own independent 8 HP engine, sweeps dirt, trash, rock, gravel, snow or other material from any surface in one pass. Flexible construction absorbs sweeping shocks to reduce maintenance costs and prolong sweeper life. Less pulling power is required because dead-weight is reduced to a minimum. A short wheel base permits turns in tight quarters.

There are no gear boxes, power-take-offs, transmissions, belts or pulleys to wear or cause trouble. Brush adjusts for wear and sweeping need.

BUY 1 . . . GET 2

Buy one Road Bird and one set of FM-C mounting brackets and you get (1) a Road Bird tow-type sweeper and (2) a FM-C front-mounted sweeper for use with **any** truck, tractor or prime mover. Remove one pin and the entire brush assembly with its own engine can be detached for mounting on any available prime mover!

Get the facts on the Road Bird from your Little Giant distributor or write direct!

LITTLE GIANT HY-PORT

TOW-TYPE SWEEPER

With plenty of power for heavy-duty sweeping, the Hy-Port is light enough to be towed by any truck, Jeep or tractor. Big 15 HP air-cooled engine rotates the brush at 150 RPM, through a positive drive arrangement that eliminates transmissions, belts, pulleys, and gear boxes. Road shocks are absorbed into the flexible construction for longer, trouble-free service.

Streets, parking lots, roads, shoulders, parks, new surfacing, runways, can be kept clear of dirt, trash, rock, gravel and snow. Short turning ability permits use on narrow streets and areaways.

Broom angles up to 30° left or right and tilts up to 6° at either end. Lift control is regulated by rugged hand hydraulic pump.

The Hy-Port was developed originally for military installations; its superior performance gained rapid acceptance by commercial, industrial and governmental agencies. Powerful, light and easy to operate, the Hy-Port offers all-'round sweeping ability.

BRIEF SPECIFICATIONS

Frame is of 4" structural steel channel. *Boom* is of 2½" extra heavy pipe, ruggedly reinforced. *Hood,* of 16 gauge steel, covers entire broom. *Brush* has tough Palmyra fibre bristles; revolves at 150 RPM; mounted in self-aligning, pre-sealed ball bearings. *Tongue,* 60" long, is of 2" pipe. *Wheels,* mounted on tapered roller bearings, have 5.50 x 16, 4-ply tires. *Power* is a 15 HP, 4 cylinder, air-cooled engine (at 1600 RPM). *Drive* is through cold-rolled shafts, No. 60 roller chains and steel sprockets —no gear boxes, transmissions, belts or pulleys. *Adjustments:* brush angles to 30° left or right; tilts up or down 6°. *Optional equipment:* sprinkler system; front deflector; electric starter; steel bristled brush.
Dimensions: Height 51"; brush diameter 31"; length 132"; tread, rear axle, 60"; wheelbase 100"; turning radius 110".

Choice of brushes,	4'	5'	6'	7'	8'
Sweeping path at 30° angle	3'1"	4'1"	5'1"	6'1"	7'1"
Width	4'10"	5'10"	6'10"	7'10"	8'10"
Weight	1210#	1330#	1450#	1570#	1690#

Your nearby Little Giant distributor has complete information . . . or write direct!

LITTLE GIANT PRODUCTS, INC.

1530-1550 N. ADAMS STREET, PEORIA, ILLINOIS

LITTLE GIANT SP-C

SELF-PROPELLED SWEEPER

BRIEF SPECIFICATIONS

Prime Mover
Power: 48 HP industrial water-cooled engine, completely enclosed.
Transmission: automotive-type, 4-speed; PTO
Clutch: 10" heavy-duty, spring-loaded automotive-type
Axle-driving: Spicer-Jeep 48" tread
Steering Gear: Automotive-type
Brakes: Two wheel hydraulic
Wheels: Unsprung. Front wheels drive; rear wheels steer.
Tires: Four 5.50 x 16, 4-ply implement tread.
Turning Radius: 11'
Dimensions: Height 4'3"; width 5'8"; tread-front 4'; rear 5'; wheelbase 5'.
Weight (Approx.) 2200#.

Sweeper
Power: 8 HP (at 2400 RPM) air-cooled engine.
Drive: No. 60 roller chains, driving steel sprockets, mounted on cold-rolled shafts.
Boom: 2½" extra-heavy pipe, reinforced.
Hood: 16 ga. steel; covers entire brush.
Brush: Tough Palmyra fibre bristles.
Speed: 150 RPM at 2400 RPM engine speed.
Lift Control: Hydraulic; lift 7".
Adjustments: Angles 30° left or right; tilts 6° up or down.
Optional Equipment: Sprinkler system; front deflector; electric starter; steel-bristled brush.
Dimensions: Height 4'3"; length (overall) 11'6"; brush diameter 31".

Choice of brushes:	4'	5'	6'	7'	8'
Sweeping path at 30° angle	3'1"	4'1"	5'1"	6'1"	7'1"
Width overall	4'10"	5'10"	6'10"	7'10"	8'10"
Wgt. (Approx. #)	480	510	540	570	600
Weight (complete unit) (approx. #)	2680	2710	2740	2770	2800

The SP-C is a powerful prime mover, teamed with a proven sweeper, to form a self-propelled sweeping unit with unlimited versatility.

The brush is rotated by an 8 HP engine at any desired speed regardless of speed of prime mover. Brush adjusts for wear; angles 30° to left or right for windrowing trash or snow. Just one pin need be removed and a hydraulic hose uncoupled to detach the entire sweeping assembly, freeing the prime mover for use as a utility tractor.

The prime mover, powered by a water-cooled industrial engine, with automotive clutch and four speed transmission has speeds up to 40 MPH. Weight is concentrated on front wheels for traction while sweeping; automotive-type steering is through rear wheels. Non-stop turns can be made on narrow streets.

The fast, economical SP-C has countless applications in commercial and industrial fields and with governmental agencies. The SP-C can save money for you—as a prime mover . . . as a sweeper!

See for yourself . . . phone your nearby Little Giant distributor . . . or write direct to Little Giant!

Cleaning and Maintaining the World's Streets for 37 Years

MODEL "E" PICK-UP STREET SWEEPER

Ideal for small towns and cities up to 50,000 population. Extremely maneuverable, easy to operate. Built for long life, low maintenance. Average operating cost is only 50c per mile. Tops in operator comfort and visibility. Write for detailed catalog.

Special Features

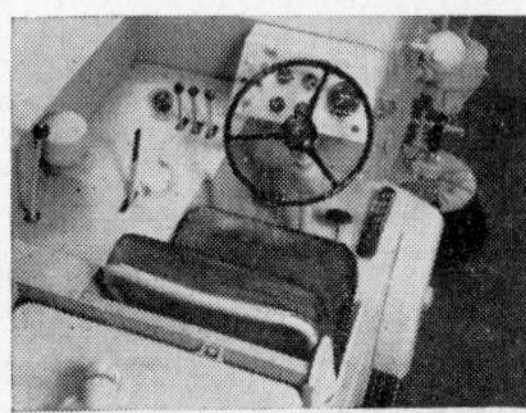

EASE OF CONTROL and OPERATOR COMFORT

Minimum of controls, all in easy reach. Operator has direct view of curb line without bending. Full-floating, spring-mounted, Naugahyde covered seat increases operator efficiency.

SIMPLE MAINTENANCE

All major operating parts are concentrated for ease of maintenance and lubrication. Top quality components assure long, trouble-free life.

GENERAL SPECIFICATIONS

Width of Sweep. 6 feet.

Brooms. 30″ dia. gutter broom, wire filled. 34″ dia. x 48″ long pick-up broom, Palmyra Stalk filled. Individual hydraulic power lifts.

Hopper. 2 cubic yard capacity.

Water Tank and Spray. 160 gal. capacity. Atomized water sprays full width of brooms.

Speeds. 4 speeds forward, max. 13 m.p.h.; 1 reverse speed.

Engine. 4 cyl. heavy duty Continental. Develops 37 B.H.P. at 1700 R.P.M.

EXTRA EQUIPMENT

Metal Cab. Open or closed.

Broom Filling Machine. For filling pick-up broom.

Leaf Rake Attachment.

MUNICIPAL SUPPLY COMPANY
2510 S. MAIN STREET, SOUTH BEND 23, INDIANA, U. S. A.
EXPORT OFFICE: 44 WHITEHALL ST., NEW YORK, N. Y.

Cleaning and Maintaining the World's Streets for 37 Years

SOUTH BEND STREET FLUSHER

Semi-Streamlined Styling

Gives streamlined effect at moderate price. Air, hydraulic, or electrically operated nozzle controls.

SOUTH BEND STREET FLUSHER

Conventional Styling

Pump may be mounted as shown or in rear. Installation may be made on either a conventional or C.O.E. type truck cab and chassis. Budget priced.

GENERAL SPECIFICATIONS

Tank. Elliptical. Heavy 3/16" steel plate electrically welded. 800 gallon to 3000 gallon capacity.

Tank Mounting. Electrically welded to longitudinal steel supports.

Engine. 6 cyl. Continental Model F-226. 65 B.H.P. at 2400 R.P.M.

Pump. Centrifugal, single stage. Max. pressure 125 pounds. Max. cap. 700 G.P.M.

Piping. Wrought steel, leakproof couplings.

Nozzles. Exclusive design. Delivers fan shaped streams of water at any desired angle.

Controls. Installed in cab. Hydraulic, air, or electric vacuum operation.

Gauges. Tank capacity and pressure gauges in cab.

Filling Hose. 15′, 2½″ double jacket, cotton covered, rubber lined.

EXTRA EQUIPMENT

Sprinkler Attachment. Two horizontal sprinkler heads will sprinkle a strip up to 50 feet wide. Independent controls for cab.

Booster Pump for Fire Fighting. Boosts pressure from tank or hydrant. Shoots 1″ stream 92′ high.

Filling and Pumping Attachment. Piping, valves, primer and 20 foot suction hose for filling tanks, pumping cisterns, flooded basements, etc.

Fire Hose Connection. Special valve enables connection with hose coupling, hose and nozzle for blowing out clogged sewers, fire fighting, cleaning sidewalks, etc.

Equipment for Salt Water. All pipe and fittings galvanized. Corrosion resistant tank.

MUNICIPAL SUPPLY COMPANY

2510 S. MAIN STREET, SOUTH BEND 23, INDIANA, U.S.A.

EXPORT OFFICE: 44 WHITEHALL ST., NEW YORK, N.Y.

Cleaning and Maintaining the World's Streets for 37 Years

MODEL "L" BITUMINOUS DISTRIBUTOR

SPECIFICATIONS

Tank. Elliptical. Grade "A" steel. Electrically welded. 1½" Rock Wool insulation.

Capacities. 800 to 2100 gallons, truck mounted. 1500 to 3000 gallons, semi-trailer mounted.

Heating System. Four 8" heating flues, 2-pass circulation.

Burners. Low pressure, torch or propane type.

Spray Bars. Full circulating or suck-back.

Engine. 4-cylinder Continental F-162. 33 B.H.P. at 1500 R.P.M.

Transmission. 4 forward speeds, 1 reverse speed.

Pump. Capacity 375 G.P.M. at 375 R.P.M. Self-draining.

2100 gallon tank illustrated

For fully controlled application of asphalt, tar emulsion, or road oil . . . 1/10 gallon to 3 gallons per square yard. Triple spray pattern insures full coverage 2 feet to 24 feet in width. Features self-draining pump that eliminates costly starting delays. Volume production permits early deliveries and highest quality at lowest cost. Send for detailed information.

MODEL "A" MAINTENANCE DISTRIBUTOR

Designed to do maintenance and repair work economically. Available truck mounted or trailer mounted. Budget priced. Send for literature.

SPECIFICATIONS

Tank. Elliptical. Grade "A" steel, electrically welded. Insulation extra.

Capacities. 400 to 600 gal., trailer mounted. 600 to 1200 gal., truck mounted.

Heating System. 4—6" heating flues, torch or propane burners.

Spray Bar. 4' to 12' lengths. Full circulating spray bar extra.

Engine. Wisconsin Model AHH. 8 H.P., 2 and 4 cyl. engines available.

Pump. Rotary Viking. 100 G.P.M. capacity.

MUNICIPAL SUPPLY COMPANY

2510 S. MAIN STREET, SOUTH BEND 23, INDIANA, U. S. A.

EXPORT OFFICE: 44 WHITEHALL ST., NEW YORK, N. Y.

FILTER SAND SPECIFICATIONS are carefully laid. The Effective Size and Uniformity Coefficients used by Consulting Engineers and also recommended by the American Water Works Association are the result of long years of research and experience.

The Northern Gravel Company is equipped to give you prompt shipment whether it be one bag or many carloads, exact to specification. Filter sand can be furnished with any effective size between .35 MM and 1.20 MM.

The new Northeast Station in the City of Detroit (above), recently completed, is one of the major projects included in the water department's expansion program. The Northern Gravel Company furnished 120 carloads of filtering materials for the 48 rapid sand filters incorporated in this plant.

NORTHERN GRAVEL COMPANY

P.O. Box 307 MUSCATINE, IOWA Phone 4261

CHEMICAL QUALITY of the filter sand is also important. It must be hard, not smooth and free of soluble particles. This requires perfect washing, and grading facilities. We have every modern device for washing, drying, screening and testing.

FILTER GRAVEL supporting the Filter Sand Bed must be, in turn, properly graded to sizes calculated to support the Filter Sand, and be relatively hard, round and resistant to solution.

The South District Filtration Plant of the city of Chicago, pictured above, is the largest in the world. Northern Gravel Company furnished them 422 carloads with clocklike regularity, enabling installation continuously and economically.

NORTHERN GRAVEL COMPANY

P.O. Box 307 MUSCATINE, IOWA Phone 4261

RAPID SAND FILTER

99% of the Water Purification and Water Softening plants in the United States, and Canada, complete the process by passing the water through "Rapid Sand Filters."

Since the sand does the final filtering, it is obviously the heart of the filtering plant. Most careful selection is made of the elements of the plant, the pretreatment, the controls, the underdrains, the wash troughs, and so, the heart of the plant deserves the best available filtering sand and gravel.

Sand performs its function as a filtering medium through its ability to hold back the coagulum or precipitate containing the suspended and colloidal impurities to be removed.

PERFECTION OF OPERATION

Thus the part that filter sand plays in a Rapid Sand Filter plant is of vital importance. This is the exact reason we have placed such emphasis on the perfection of every operation here at the vast plant of the Northern Gravel Company.

Northern Gravel has no equal in facilities and our reserves of both sand and gravel are inexhaustible. Northern Gravel Company has been in business over 40 years. We guarantee uniformity of products and our records enable us to duplicate your requirements on short notice. Our location is central and we have commodity rates in every direction.

Please write us for further information.

NORTHERN GRAVEL COMPANY

P.O. Box 307 MUSCATINE, IOWA Phone 4261

PRESSTITE-KEYSTONE

PAVING PRODUCTS

PRESSTITE-KEYSTONE PAVING PRODUCTS

KAPCO TONGUE AND GROOVE JOINT

This non-extruding joint absorbs warping action of the slab, eliminates dangers of tilting and spalling. Note use of stake pins.

DESCRIPTION:

A keyed joint for construction and load transfer units, for all concrete structures and pavements. Consists of strips of mastic board ⅛″ thick, with outside liners of asphalt saturated heavy kraft, preformed to provide tongue and groove design of maximum efficiency.

GENERAL CHARACTERISTICS:

Rigid. Resists deforming forces of concrete placement. *Economical.* Strength well beyond job-need, at fraction the cost of steel. *Durable, Non-Rusting.* Exceedingly weatherproof. Readily absorbs expansion of slab, without extruding. *Water-Proof.* Absorbs no more than 8% water when tested according to A.A.S.H.O. Standard Method T-42-49.

Kapco Tongue & Groove Joint is especially suitable for lane-at-a-time highway construction. May be used for either longitudinal center strip or transverse contraction joint.

SIZES:

Furnished in standard lengths of 10′-1″ to provide for overlap. Punchings are on 2′-6″ centers for ½″ dowel, on 24″ centers for stakes. Packaged in durable weatherproof carton.

SPECIFICATIONS:

This product is generally an alternate to specifications wherever state specifies keyed type joint.

NEW TONGUE & GROOVE JOINT FOR AIRPORTS

New trapezoid dimensions, designed primarily for airport construction where slabs range from 14″ to 20″ thick are also available as follows: 1¼″ deep, 4½″ wide at base and 3½″ wide at top.

PRESSTITE-KEYSTONE PAVING JOINTS

PRESSTITE-KEYSTONE PAVING JOINTS

KAPCO PREMOULDED ASPHALT EXPANSION JOINT

Kapco Premoulded Asphalt Joint is completely waterproof because of its asphalt and lamination construction.

DESCRIPTION:
Composed of asphalt fibre and mineral filler, premoulded into sheets with asphalt impregnated liners on outside surfaces.

GENERAL CHARACTERISTICS:
Entirely waterproof because of its asphalt and lamination construction.

SIZES:
Available in ¼", ⅜", ½", ¾" and 1" thicknesses, 36" wide. Standard lengths: 5' to 10', though available in any desired length. Also available punched for dowels.

SPECIFICATIONS:
Meets Specs. A.A.S.H.O. M-33-48; U.S. Navy Dept. 4-Y-D, Paragraph 1-10, Part 3 and Navy Spec. 13-Y-C, Paragraph 2-12, Part 2; A.S.T.M. Spec. D-994-53. Also meets specs. for U.S. Engineers, Federal Works Agency and the Bureau of Public Roads.

KAPCO FIBRE EXPANSION JOINT

DESCRIPTION:
Fabricated from top grade fibres and treated with special impregnation of the finest waterproof asphalt.

GENERAL CHARACTERISTICS:
High degree of resiliency, light in weight, very durable and easy to handle. Does not get brittle in winter or tacky in summer.

SIZES:
Standard slab sizes of 48" x 10', in thicknesses of ¼", ⅜", ½", ¾" and 1". Also available in 11' and 12' lengths.

SPECIFICATIONS:
Meets all Standard Specs. of State Highway Depts. Complies with A.A.S.H.O. Spec. M-59-49; M-153-52, Type III; M-153-54, Type III; Federal Specs. HH-F-341a, Type I, Class B and U.S. Navy BY&D. Spec. 4YD, Paragraph 1-10, Part 2, also A.S.T.M. D-544-49. Type V; A.S.T.M. D-544-52, Type III. Approved by U.S. Engineers, Civil Aeronautics Authority, Bureau of Public Roads and Federal Works Agency.

KAPCORK® NON-EXTRUDING EXPANSION JOINT

DESCRIPTION:
Consists of pre-formed strips of cork granule base in a watertight bituminous binder.

GENERAL CHARACTERISTICS:
Resilient. Recovers up to 80% of original thickness after three 50% compressions. *Non-Extruding.* Will not extrude more than 0.25 inch on free side when other three sides are restrained and product is compressed to 50% of original thickness. *Moisture-Resistant.* Will not absorb more than 8% by volume.

SIZES:
Comes in slab size of 10' long, 36" wide in ¼", ⅜", ½", ¾" and 1" thicknesses.

SPECIFICATIONS:
Meets requirements of A.A.S.H.O. Spec. M-153-52, Type III; A.S.T.M. Spec. D-544-49, Type V; A.S.T.M. Spec. D-544-52T, Type III; Federal Spec. HH-F-341a, Type I, Class B and U.S. Navy BY & D Spec. 4YD Paragraph 1-10, Part 2.

KAPCO DUMMY JOINT

DESCRIPTION:
Widely accepted for longitudinal or transverse contraction joints of the "Plane of Weakness" type.

GENERAL CHARACTERISTICS:
Is rigid, non-brittle (won't crack or shatter) and waterproof because of its mastic core.

SIZES:
Available in ⅛", 3/16" and ¼" thicknesses, in any job-specified lengths or widths.

SPECIFICATIONS:
Whenever a state specifies a joint of the longitudinal and/or transverse contraction type.

Installing channels are available in standard 10' or 11' lengths, complete with handles.

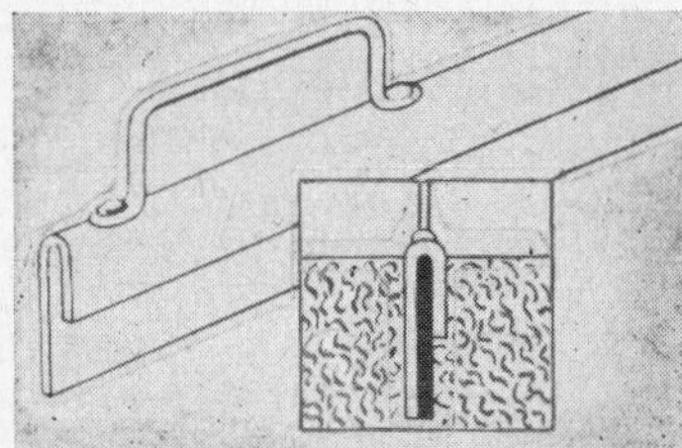

PRESSTITE-KEYSTONE PAVING JOINT SEALERS

PRESSTITE NO. 99

Cold-applied #99 is jet-blast, jet-heat and jet-fuel resistant.

Airfield Paving Sealer (Cold Applied)

DESCRIPTION:
A cold-applied sealer of two-component type for use on all sawed or formed joints on jet airfields.

GENERAL CHARACTERISTICS:
Easy to apply and economical to use, No. 99 bonds at low temperatures, won't slump at high ones. It is *(1) Jet-Blast Resistant.* Resists the high engine thrusts developed by today's jets. *(2) Jet-Heat Resistant.* Withstands super-elevated temperatures of sustained jet engine blast at 1500°-1600° without being melted out. *(3) Jet-Fuel Resistant.* Unaffected by direct exposure to fuel under actual service conditions.

PACKAGE:
60 lb. unit, including proper proportions of dry and liquid components.

SPECIFICATIONS: Complies with Federal Spec. SS-S-170, 23 May 1955; Dept. of the Navy, Bureau of Yards and Docks, Spec. No. 46 Ya, Dec. 1952, as amended by Addendum No. 2, April, 1955.

KAPCO JET AIRPORT SEALER

JET-FUEL RESISTANT SEALING COMPOUND (Hot Pour)

DESCRIPTION:
Non-asphaltic hot-poured rubberized sealer for horizontal joints.

GENERAL CHARACTERISTICS:
Durable, plasticized rubber; *Resilient,* resistant to repeated cycles of expansion and contraction; *Jet-Fuel Resistant,* unaffected by jet fuels, and other petroleum derivatives.

PACKAGE:
Handy five gallon steel container, plastic lined for easy removal of contents.

SPECIFICATIONS:
Complies with Federal Specs. SS-S-00167 (GSA-FSS).

PRESSTITE NO. 67

PAVING JOINT SEALER (Cold Applied)
(Supersedes No. 77)

DESCRIPTION:
Rubber base, single-component, ready-to-use sealing compound.

GENERAL CHARACTERISTICS:
No heating or proportioning; can be applied at low temperatures; high flexibility and resiliency factors. Will not cold flow at high temperatures; withstands heavy impact, high-speed traffic.

PACKAGE:
55 gal. open head steel drums.

SPECIFICATIONS:
Meets adhesion and bond of Federal Spec. SS-S-159 for new and maintenance sealing of pavements. Also flow requirements after evaporation of solvents.

KAPCO RUBBER-ASPHALT

JOINT SEALING COMPOUND (Hot Pour)

DESCRIPTION:
Hot pour type sealer for concrete joints. For use on roads, airport runways and aprons, sidewalks, industrial floors, etc.

GENERAL CHARACTERISTICS:
Water-tight. Won't crack or break bond. Eliminates "pumping" of joints. *Weather-Resistant.* Blend of rubber and high-quality asphalt enable it to remain flexible and resilient at all temperatures. *Resilient.* Has the needed "stretchiness" for the give-and-take of repeated contraction and expansion cycles. Compresses readily at high temperatures, extends smoothly at low temperatures.

PACKAGE:
Available in waterproof multi-wall paper bag with special plastic liner. Approx. 50-lbs. per bag.

SPECIFICATIONS:
Meets Fed. Specs. SS-S-164 (Superseding Fed. Spec. SS-F-336a).

PRESSTITE-KEYSTONE SEWER JOINT SEALERS

PRESSTITE-KEYSTONE SEWER JOINT SEALERS

PRESSTITE 3-STEP SEWER SEALING SYSTEM

1 PRESSTITE PRIMER

DESCRIPTION:
Hard based asphalt priming paint.

GENERAL CHARACTERISTICS:
Dries to form hard film which improves bond between pipe and joint sealing compound.

PACKAGE:
Available in 5 and 55 gal. drums.

2 PRESSTITE ROPAX®

DESCRIPTION:
Non-porous, adhesive packing. Fibrous core impregnated with blend of selected asphalts.

GENERAL CHARACTERISTICS:
Low susceptibility to temperature change, very adhesive.

PACKAGE:
In ⅜", ½", ¾", 1" and 1¼" dia., on convenient spools.

3 PRESSTITE KALKTITE®

DESCRIPTION:
Cold-applied, internal-setting asphaltic cement.

GENERAL CHARACTERISTICS:
Will set up even under water. Tough, flexible—permits normal sewer line settlement and some alignment deflection during backfilling, without breaking bond.

OTHER CONSTRUCTION PRODUCTS

- **Kapco Concrete Curing Compound**
- **Kapco Air Entraining Agent**
- **Presstite Coal-Tar Base Ready Mix Sewer Joint Compound**

PRESSTITE-KEYSTONE
ENGINEERING PRODUCTS
COMPANY

A DIVISION OF AMERICAN-MARIETTA COMPANY
3772 CHOUTEAU AVENUE, ST. LOUIS 10, MISSOURI

UNITED *Swing Top* WASTE RECEPTACLES

Deliver...... Longer Lasting Service Better Sanitary Efficiency More for Your Money

No. 150 No. 150 W — No. 130 — No. 115 — No. 112 — No. 110

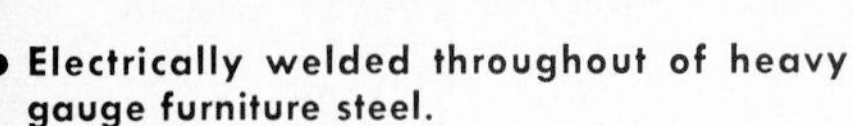

- Electrically welded throughout of heavy gauge furniture steel.
- Two independently-operating scientifically counter-balanced silent doors. No springs to go out of order.
- Tops gabled for strength. Mounted on two concealed hinges which hold top open when swung back. No interfering chains.
- Inner container easily removable.
- Bonderized. Heavy enamel finish baked on at high temperature.
- Colors: Olive Green, Hammertone Green, Gray, White. Inner containers furnished.

Dimension Chart

CATALOG NUMBER	SIZE OF BASE INCHES	BODY HEIGHT INCHES	OVERALL HEIGHT INCHES	SHIP WEIGHT LBS.	INNER CONTAINER FURNISHED AS STANDARD	CAPACITY GALLONS
135	$6\frac{3}{4}$ x $9\frac{3}{4}$	11	11	8	1 Galv. Container	
13	$9\frac{3}{4}$ x $9\frac{3}{4}$	11	11	11	1 Galv. Container	
110	$11\frac{1}{2}$ x $11\frac{1}{2}$	18	$24\frac{3}{4}$	20	2 Paper Bags	
110	$11\frac{1}{2}$ x $11\frac{1}{2}$	18	$24\frac{3}{4}$	24	1 Galv. Container	$9\frac{1}{2}$
112	$11\frac{1}{2}$ x $11\frac{1}{2}$	28	$34\frac{1}{2}$	31	1 Galv. Container	18
115	$11\frac{1}{2}$ x $11\frac{1}{2}$	35	$41\frac{3}{4}$	36	1 Galv. Container	23
115	$11\frac{1}{2}$ x $11\frac{1}{2}$	35	$41\frac{3}{4}$	28	1 Burlap Bag	
130	16 x 16	27	$35\frac{1}{2}$	39	1 Burlap Bag	
130	16 x 16	27	$35\frac{1}{2}$	47	1 Galv. Container	27
150	21 x 21	35	46	74	1 Burlap Bag	
150	21 x 21	35	46	86	1 Galv. Container	65
•150W	21 x 21	35	46	74	1 Burlap Bag	
•150W	21 x 21	35	46	86	1 Galv. Container	

•Finished With Special Outdoor Paint

All United Swing-Top Receptacles are furnished with heavy gauge stainless steel feet.

And Where Appearance Counts - It Tops Them All

UNITED ROUND TOP RECEPTACLE

- For Appearance
- Ease of Maintenance
- Sanitation
- Durability

APPEARANCE... Best-looking waste receptacle of its kind ever made.

ONE-PIECE CONSTRUCTION... Outer shell electrically welded throughout of heavy gauge furniture steel. Stainless steel base protects floors and finish of receptacle.

BONDERIZED... for corrosion resistance.

SELF-CLOSING STAINLESS STEEL DOOR... Dependable action.

SANITARY WHITE heavy enamel finish baked on at high temperature. Also, Coke Red, Hammertone Green, Gray and Special Colors.

DURABILITY... Like other United receptacles it will set records for long service.

FEATHERWEIGHT LIGHTNESS... Finger-tips easily lift outer shell to expose **GALVANIZED STEEL** corrosion-resistant inner container with handle. Will not leak under normal usage.

Style #R1536
Height 36"
Diameter 15"
Gal. Capacity 15½
Shipping Wt. 28 lbs.

Note: Also Available in
Style #R1530
Height 30"
Diameter 15"
Gal. Capacity 12½
Shipping Wt. 25 lbs.

UNITED SANITARY NAPKIN DISPOSAL UNITS

Models #13 and #135 answer all sanitary needs for the ladies' lavatory.

Eliminate clogged drains, promote cleanliness and more hygienic conditions wherever used.

No. 13—Closed view

No. 135—Closed view

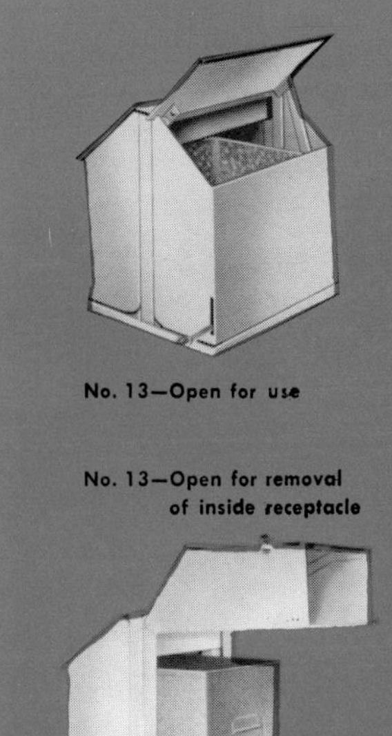

No. 13—Open for use

No. 13—Open for removal of inside receptacle

FOOT PEDAL ACTION makes napkin disposal easy. Doors close automatically... keep the receptacle almost airtight and eliminate offensive odor. Two individually operating doors on No. 13 permit use under a partition to service adjacent booths at one time.

LEAKPROOF INNER CONTAINER is made of galvanized steel. Removes easily when hinged front of receptacle is swung back.

AMPLE CAPACITY for all normal needs. Bonderized. Made of heavy-gauge cold-rolled furniture steel with a baked-on enamel finish in Olive Green, Hammertone Green, Gray or White.

UNITED METAL CABINET CORP.

14th and Laurel Streets
Pottsville, Pa. • MArket 2-7715

IN ST. LOUIS...EVERYONE AGREES THAT UNITED DOES THE JOB BEST!

Leading firms feature and sell UNITED.

IN ST. LOUIS cleanliness is automatic with United's model 150 Waste Receptacle.

Public Works officials all over the country have learned that budget dollars go much further when they use United waste receptacles. Hundreds of users all over the country find that United waste receptacles are the complete answer to their sanitation problems. For the best and the most popular waste receptacles . . . just check UNITED, the world's largest selling line of waste receptacles.

Above: Mr. J. J. Standford of City Janitor Supply is showing Mr. Hoppius (right) of the Department of Streets and Sewers the functional features of the model 150.

Right: More than 200 UNITED self-closing waste receptacles are now in use on major intersections in the City of St. Louis. Looking on, left to right, are St. Louis Street Cleaning Superintendent Ray Hoppius and salesman Charles F. Weilert of the Industrial Soap and Janitor Supply Co., St. Louis.

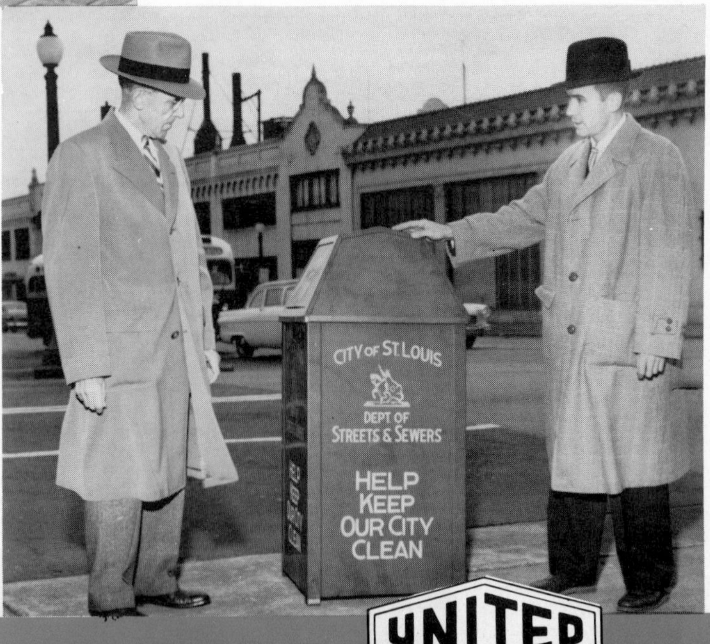

UNITED

UNITED METAL CABINET CORP.

ROSCO MANUFACTURING CO.

3118 Snelling Ave., Minneapolis 6, Minn.

CAPACITIES
800 U. S. GAL.
AND UP

Model RQE distributor with Type G full-circulating spraybar folded, ready for travel

Apply Bitumen the Modern Way

Rosco is the only Distributor designed for the application of bitumen through PRESSURE METERING. This exclusive design eliminates the inaccuracies of pump metering. With engine speed remaining constant, Rosco's Pressure Metering Master Valve goes to work for you, automatically maintaining a specified pressure at the spraybar. This modern method guarantees accuracy of application.

Rosco Distributors Can Have Front or Rear Mounting of Engine and Pump *with the Same Application Controls*

All normal operations with the ORIGINAL patented single valve control directing flow of material — starting spray — quick cut-off at nozzle through reverse suction—circulate—load—transfer—clean-out and pressure control.

ORIGINAL patented 4 section folding spraybar with vertical lift and shift—horizontal bar pivot for safety — 2 types — MODEL H conventional plain bar with sump and rising stem nozzles.

MODEL G full circulating horizontally and folded — spraybar valves lock in folded sections — obstruction-free spraybar line—spraybar feed through main and return circulating line—always hot—no cold spots—Other features, sump type suction—tell-tale loading gauge—safety manhole cover—roomy elevated rear operator's platform.

INSTANT CUT-OFF IS ASSURED THROUGH REVERSE SUCTION WITH EITHER G OR H BAR.

Model RRE Distributor has engine, pump and valve with auxiliaries and application controls mounted complete at the rear. Illustration at the left shows full circulating 12′ Spraybar in folded position, ready for travel. Model RRE has identical functional operations of other Rosco Distributors with Pressure Metering. Application pressure is constantly maintained automatically. All Rosco full circulating Spraybars are equipped with Vee-Jet nozzles, developed after many years of experimentation in design to obtain the best all around performance in relation to the elimination of streaking, nozzle clogging and reduction of atomizing. These features of Rosco Distributors are specifically designed to handle all your Street or Road jobs at the lowest possible cost.

Inquire About Rosco Distributors for Trailer Mounting—Data and Specifications Gladly Furnished

SEND FOR 6-PAGE BULLETIN

ROSCO STREET FLUSHER

Streamlined

MODEL MTA

1200-1600-2000 GALLON CAPACITIES

ROSCO ENGINEERED TO PROVIDE EXTREMELY HIGH PRESSURE STREAMS OF WATER FOR THOROUGH CLEANING OF PAVED SURFACES

Utmost safety and control for one man operation. An exclusive Rosco design, a single lever control valve is mounted on the truck dash together with flusher engine choke, ignition and starter switch for complete flusher nozzle and engine control. Rosco advanced designing offers greater values.

Lower operating costs. By designing to the power application required, Rosco is able to use a smaller engine and maintain greater nozzle pressure than normally offered on similar application. Whether you need 3 or 4 flushing nozzles, you'll get 60 lbs. pressure at each.

MODIFIED MODELS AVAILABLE

Designed to mount directly on a wide range of truck manufacturers normal WB chassis having single rear axle—two speed axle recommended

A Modern, Efficient Machine for Flushing and Other Water Application

ROSCO 2-WHEEL FLUSHER

MODEL MFR

CAPACITY 1000 GALLONS

Sprinkling—Flushing—Fire Fighting—Power Pumping—Independent Power Unit—

- **LOADS** From hydrant through ell connection at top rear of tank or through manhole without using pump.
- **PUMPS** From outside source of supply using a suction hose and engine exhaust type pump primer.
- **DISCHARGES** For transfer to another outside source or for one or more $1^1/_2$" or other hose lines.

Write for Specification 550-B

Model MFR (2) for truck mounting as shown below.

Send for 6 page Bulletin

CALCIUM CHLORIDE APPLICATOR

MODEL MCC

Designed for dissolving and application of Calcium Chloride in solution. For truck mounting in 1000 to 2000 gallons. Standard with 500 GPM front mounted pumping unit. 12'4 section folding safety bar.

ROSCO MAINTENANCE UNIT

MODEL RMT

High Speed Saves Time, Money

Rear Mounted Pump and Engine

Front Mounted Heaters

CAPACITY 400-500-600 GALS.

This low cost heating and spraying unit is ideal for high-speed maintenance work on highways or street improvement and maintenance programs. Also widely used for driveways, parking areas, airports, bridges and for secondary construction.

Designed to load, transfer, circulate and spray. Handles all types of bitumen through 4 to 8' spraybar or handspray attachment. An economical unit offering a wide variety of auxiliary equipment for every user's requirement.

• Check these features:

• Pumping unit at tank rear entirely removed from excess heat and fire hazard • Complete protection of pump provided by screen at its suction intake • Spraybar or hand spray pressure regulated by single lever control • Automatic by-pass relief prevents stalled pump on spray shut-off • Suction line provided with sump for complete drainage of tank • Gravity draw-off connection from tank for filling hand pots • Transfer material from one outside source to another • Load tank through pump from drums or supply tank • Drain pump and pipe lines without draining tank • Circulate material in tank while heating • Spray from tank through hand spray • Spray from tank through spraybar.

Write for Specifications 545-B

ROSCO MAINTENANCE DISTRIBUTOR

Truck Mounted Type

MODEL RHU

CAPACITY 800-1000 U. S. GALS.

Does a Lot of Jobs For a Little Investment

Cities and Towns with limited budgets will find Model RHU the perfect answer to their street or road maintenance and repair problems. This general purpose unit will handle all types of bituminous materials. Built for complete and economical use, it will do a lot of jobs too expensive to handle with a larger Distributor.

• Check these features: LOAD • TRANSFER • SPRAY • HANDSPRAY • CIRCULATE • SUCK-BACK • CLEANOUT • GRAVITY DRAW-OFF •

Model RHU is designed for mounting on trucks of 1½ ton or more capacity of approximately 72" from back of cab to center rear axle. A quick-detachable, non-folding stationary spraybar is standard equipment in lengths governed by pump capacity. The two burners, engine and the pump are all compactly mounted at the rear.

Convenient operating control levers are within easy reach of the operators side platform-indicator plates at sprayline valves. MODEL RHU IS DESIGNED TO MAINTAIN A CONSTANT SPRAYLINE PRESSURE THROUGH USE OF A BY-PASS VALVE TO THE TANK. Rosco's special designed square return bend double flues increase the rate of heating and concentrate more of the heat within the tank.

MODEL RHU FITS THE JOB AND THE BUDGET • Write for Specifications 555B

ROSCO SELF-PROPELLED ROLLER MODEL SR-9-0

Multiple speeds forward and reverse. Nine wheel pneumatic tired. Power hydraulic steering—self energizing brakes. Short turning radius with maximum visibility for close operations.

Pull-type pneumatic tired compaction rollers also available in 9 or 13 wheel sizes.

ROSCO STREET CLEANER MODEL MBC

Settles Dust As It Cleans

Specially designed for maintaining sanitary streets in city and town. There's nothing like it on the market . . . for sweeping . . . sprinkling . . . flushing . . . sewer cleaning . . . tree spraying . . . fire fighting . . . a 310 gallon tank furnishes water. For one man operation—tows easily behind a tractor, truck or car.

A full width water blanket spray in front of brush dissipates obnoxious dust ordinarily associated with dry sweeping. Palmyra 7 ft. brush sweeps right or left at 15 and 30 degrees.

Nozzles at the rear provide 40 lbs. pressure for washing and will adjust to sprinkle 25 ft. wide area. Brush life lengthened by constant wetting through auxiliary piping.

ROSCO ROAD SWEEPER MODEL B7

A heavy duty, highly efficient unit for preparing bituminous bases, and for all surface cleaning or road maintenance requirements.

Speed of towing does not affect the operation of this power-driven brush. It has a swivel turn table broom support and a safe, roomy operators platform with controls within easy reach.

TORCH HEATER

Unit built in four standard sizes — Equipped with air pump—gauge—air and fuel valve as shown.

ASPHALT KETTLES

Portable units that give quick, uniform heat with two-pass heating system — rugged construction guarantees safety of operation.

Flue type single shell in sizes 110, 165, 220 gallon — single axle wheel type or stationary.

Other Products: QUICK COUPLERS. POWER PUMPING UNITS. WHEEL TACHOMETERS.

WRITE FOR LITERATURE FULLY DESCRIBING ANY ROSCO UNIT

SERVICISED PRODUCTS CORPORATION

6051 W. 65th Street, Chicago 38, Illinois

A Complete Line of JOINT SEALING and CONCRETE CURING COMPOUNDS

SEALING COMPOUNDS

HOT POURED *Para-Plastic*®

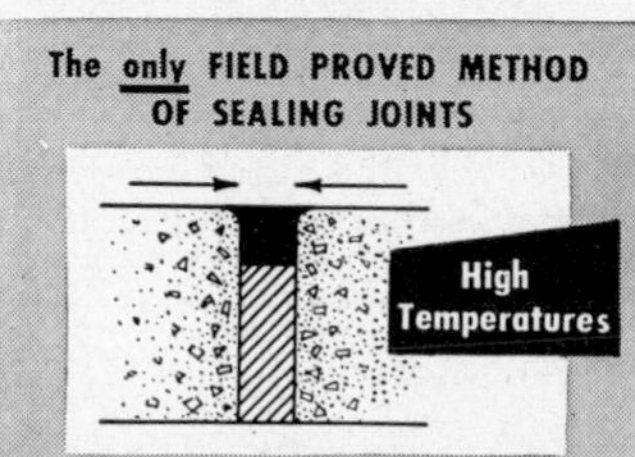

Summer temperatures do not affect Para-Plastic sealing efficiency

Para-Plastic remains plastic—maintains bond at 0° F.

Para-Plastic is the orginal rubberized asphalt joint sealing compound that when melted and poured, forms a resilient, adhesive and watertight seal of the joint opening which is unaffected by temperature extremes from summer heat to subzero. Designed essentially for the sealing of horizontal joints in highway and airfield paving, warehouse floors, etc., it prevents infiltration of water or other foreign substances during concrete contraction. Should not be used as a waterstop when hydrostatic pressure is present.

Recommendations and technical advice on joint sealing problems are available from our engineers.

Para-Plastic JF For Airports

Hot-poured Para-Plastic JF has all the resilience, adhesive and cohesive qualities of the original Para-Plastic, is unaffected by temperature extremes and has the additional quality of being impervious to jet fuel used by aircraft and other petroleum solvents. It is widely specified and used for sealing of joints in airfield runways, taxiways and aprons used by jet propelled aircraft.

Cold Applied "Zero-Lastic"® JF—A two-component jet fuel resistant material having sealing characteristics similar to the hot-poured Para-Plastic JF.

ZERO-LASTIC® Cold Applied JOINT SEALING COMPOUND

A cold-applied ready-mixed rubberized asphalt sealing compound designed for sealing expansion, contraction, and dummy joints to prevent infiltration of water and foreign material in concrete pavement of highways, airports, and other public and private projects. Cold-applied sealing compound is suitable for use in new construction as well as maintenance.

CONCRETE CURING COMPOUNDS

Servicised offers a complete line of curing compounds to meet every requirement. Each of the types listed below meet Federal, AASHO and ASTM specifications.

WHITE PIGMENTED

White Pigmented—Code 2803

Produces a membrane capable of reflecting heat to reduce concrete temperatures approximately 15° F.

White Pigmented—Code 2803-M

Identical to Code 2803 but containing a higher percentage of solids.

CLEAR

Servicised Clear Compounds are available in Wax-Resin as well as Resin base types. They are usually supplied with a fugitive dye which helps in securing proper coverage and disappears shortly after application.

Wax-Resin Base—Code 2801—for mass concrete, pavements, runways, etc., where no further treatment is required.

Resin Base—Code 2802—recommended for pavement slabs, bridge floors, etc. where large areas are exposed. Dries rapidly.

Resin Base—Code 2802-S—recommended for floors on which asphalt, rubber or linoleum floors are to be laid. Dries rapidly, permits early application of adhesives or paint.

KORK-PAK® non-extruding Expansion Joint Filler used in Airfield pavement construction.

SERVICISED PREMOLDED JOINT FILLER

KORK-PAK*

is a premolded expansion joint developed by Servicised Products Corporation, which is composed of granulated cork and fibrous material bound together with asphalt and formed between two sheets of asphalt saturated paper.

Advantages

1. It is non-extruding.
2. Recovers more than 80% of original thickness after compression.
3. Low moisture absorption.
4. Readily handled without breakage.
5. Least expensive non-extruding type.

*T.M. reg.

ASPHALT

is the earliest type developed, consisting of a composition of asphalt, vegetable fiber and a small percentage of finely divided mineral filler, formed between two sheets of asphalt saturated paper, which increases strength and rigidity and improves handling.

Advantages

1. Forms an easily compressible cushion.
2. Is highly waterproof.
3. Low in cost.

CORK

is composed of granulated cork and synthetic resin binder molded under heat and pressure to form a flexible, waterproof filler.

Advantages

1. It is light in color.
2. Can be compressed without extrusion.
3. Recovers approx. 95% of original thickness after compression.

SELF-EXPANDING CORK

is similar in composition to the regular cork expansion joint but is specially treated to enable it to expand as much as 50% beyond original thickness.

Advantages

1. Will keep joint space filled under contraction which opens space to more than original size.
2. Fully compressible.
3. Non-extruding and resilient.

SPONGE RUBBER CEMENTONE®

— a composition of high quality blown sponge rubber, cement gray in color to blend with the concrete in appearance.

Advantages

1. Highly compressible.
2. Fully resilient.

TONGUE and GROOVE JOINT

- 1/8" Thickness—asphalt composition.
- Provides quick, low cost tongue and groove joints for keyed slab construction.
- Rigid . . . easy to handle and install.
- Waterproof . . . durable . . . non-extruding.
- Made of high grade asphalt mastic core formed between sheets of heavy asphalt saturated paper.

Widely used in street and highway work and for industrial and commercial floor construction, for longitudinal and transverse joint keying Servicised Tongue and Groove Joint offers a low cost, easily installed method of forming keyed joints. Our long experience in the manufacture of all types of bituminous products for the construction industry assures you of highest quality and rigid adherence to specifications.

Servicised Tongue and Groove Joint is made in standard widths for slabs from 5" to 14" in thickness. Standard construction practice calls for the tongue and groove joint to be recessed ½" below the slab surface. For example, for a 6" slab, a 5½" Servicised Tongue and Groove Joint should be ordered. This will allow for ½" depth of Servicised Para-Plastic poured joint sealing material.

Standard punching is 2'6" on centers for ½" dowel bars and 24" on centers for stake pins. Stake pins 18 gauge channel type, 15 inches long which assure a perfect fit and elimination of any slipping or displacement, can be furnished.

When required, Servicised Tongue and Groove Joint can be supplied without punching.

SERVICISED AIR ENTRAINING AGENT

Servicised Air Entraining Agent is a liquid and can be added to gauge water or introduced into the mix. A relatively small quantity produces maximum air dispersion, yet it is not so critical as to create wide fluctuations in the amount of entrained air should slight variations in the amount used occur. It will not settle out in storage or gum the dispenser, and its action is not jeopardized by the presence of calcium chloride. Servicised Air Entraining Agent meets all standard specifications, comes ready to use, and requires no additional ingredients or treatment before using. Write for circular.

RUBBER WATERSTOP

The development, design and production of Servicised Rubber Waterstop has kept pace with the increasing demands created by accelerated construction of dams, water works, sewage treatment plants, hydro-electric installations, or any type of construction where hydro-static water pressure is involved.

Servicised engineers and technicians have worked closely with specifying authorities in the development of adaptations, improved types and new materials in the effort to produce better waterstop materials and designs.

CENTER BULB TYPE

A 9" Hollow Bulb Type embedded in concrete with an expansion joint. The Hollow Bulb Type is frequently specified where a high degree of expansion and contraction is expected.

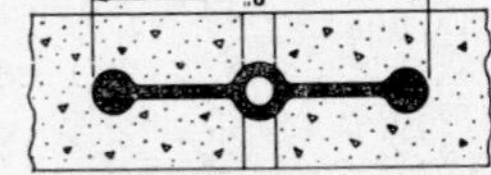

FLAT DUMBBELL TYPE

A 6" Flat Dumbbell Type embedded in concrete with a construction joint. The Dumbbell Type is generally used where little concrete movement is expected.

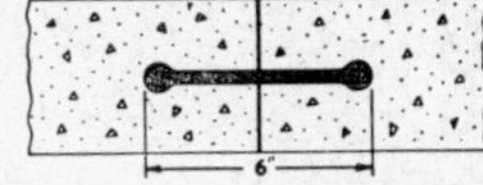

SPLIT DUMBBELL TYPE
Eliminates Split Bulkheading

FASTER, EASIER INSTALLATION

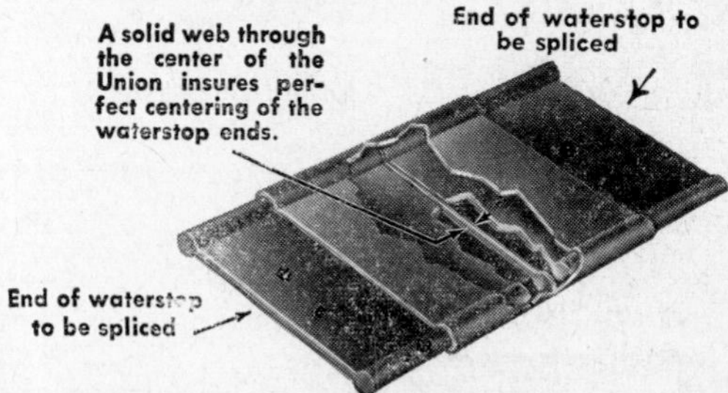

Made from the same stock and meeting the same specifications as standard Flat Dumbbell type, except that one-half of the width is split so that it may be fastened to the inside of the bulkhead in such a manner as to form a "T". After the section has been poured and bulkhead stripped, divided sections are fastened together by stapling.

WATERSTOP UNION

The Servicised Rubber Union with rubber cement provides a fast, simple method of field splicing. The Union is hollow and is made from rubber meeting the same specifications as the waterstop. It is 3/32" thick, 4" long and is available for splicing 6" and 9" Flat Dumbbell and Center Bulb Type Servicised Waterstops.

SERVICISED VERTISEAL

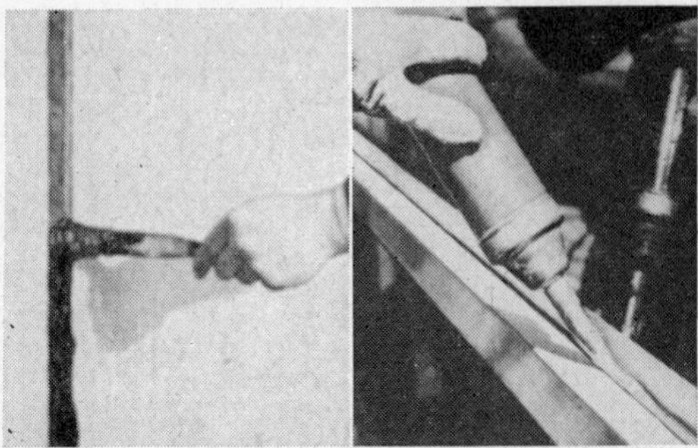

VERTISEAL is applied by troweling into the joint or with a caulking gun. Pouring grade consistency is merely poured into horizontal joints from a suitable container after being thoroughly mixed.

- **Forms a self-vulcanizing, cured rubber seal**
- **Maintains bond from 0° F to 250° F.**
- **No cold flow after cure**
- **Two colors . . . BLACK . . . WHITE**

Servicised VERTISEAL is an extremely efficient and versatile cold-applied joint sealing and caulking or glazing compound. It is weather and time proof, and may be used on concrete, metal, glass, masonry, or any combination of these materials. Properly installed, it sets up into a tough, resilient, self-vulcanizing rubber seal. VERTISEAL is available in two consistencies—troweling and gun grade for vertical and sloping applications, and pouring grade for horizontal joints. VERTISEAL is especially recommended for vertical joints because it eliminates all possibility of cold flow from the joint. It is impervious to petroleum derivatives, most common acids, fats, alkalis and high temperature liquids.

PARABOUND

Additive for Pavement

Parabound Tar-Rubber Blend is meeting Corps of Engineers interim specifications for tar-rubber pavement on runways, aprons and taxiways in airport and air field construction.

Parabound Asphalt Rubber is rubberized asphalt compound made by adding oils and asphalt to unvulcanized rubber. It is ideally suited for mixing in asphaltic pavement.

Complete details on the use of either type of Parabound additive will be furnished on request.

PREMOLDED *Para-Plastic* PRODUCTS

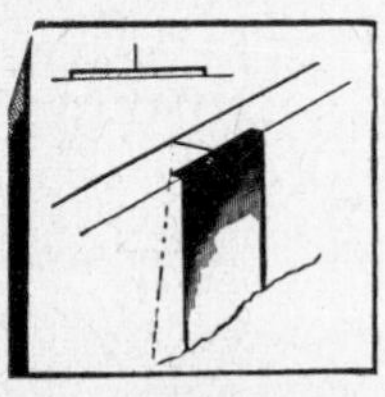

Para-Lateral Strip

Designed for sealing back-filled vertical construction joints in retaining walls, tunnels, foundations, etc., against seepage to exposed side. Para-Plastic facing of rigid Mastic backing assures permanent adhesion to concrete.

Molded Para-Plastic

Bituminous rubber sealing compound in molded form for sealing keyed construction joints in vertical and horizontal surfaces. Maintains bond from 0 to 180° F.

Servicised Premolded Para-Plastic and Rubber Waterstop has wide application in sewage treatment and water filtration plants.

SERVICISED PRODUCTS CORPORATION

6051 W. 65th Street, Chicago 38, Illinois

STANDARD STEEL WORKS, INC.

North Kansas City, Mo.

BITUMINOUS PRESSURE DISTRIBUTOR

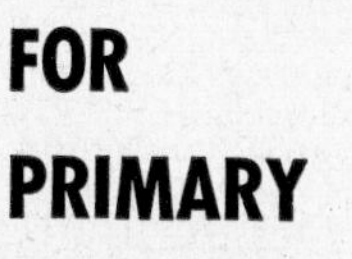

FOR PRIMARY BLACKTOP

"IT'S THE SPRAY-BAR THAT COUNTS"

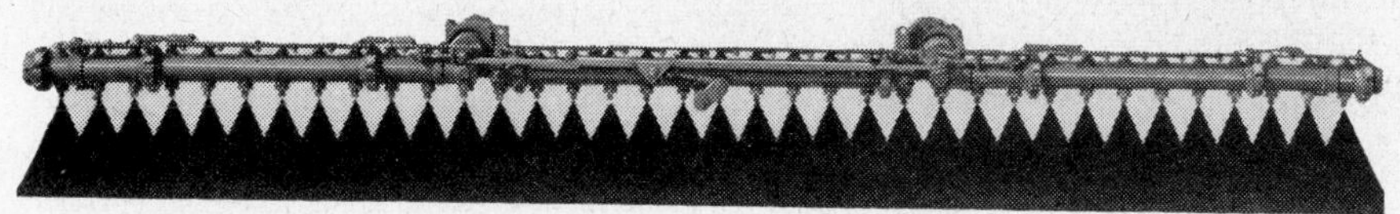

The Standard Steel Works Miracle Spray-Bar is the basic reason why this unit can maintain uniform temperature and pressure hour after hour, thereby holding down costs on all primary blacktop applications.

Check these advantages on the Standard Steel Works Model 424 Pressure Distributor:

1. Full circulation on the new mechanically operated Spray Bar with individual nozzle cut off.
2. Accurate application at lower cost per gallon means higher profit—No delays—No test runs—No warm up.
3. Satisfied operator eliminates costly labor turn over.

The Standard Steel Works Full Circulating Bar in comprehensive tests produced even pressure along the entire 24′ length. Temperature gauges on each end of the bar showed exactly the same temperature — absolutely no temperature drop in the Full Circulating Spray Bar.

STANDARD STEEL WORKS, INC.

North Kansas City, Mo.

MODEL "SJ" DISTRIBUTOR

For SECONDARY JOBS and GENERAL MAINTENANCE

This unit is complete in every respect—it has its own heating, pumping, and power unit—it can handle spray bars up to 12′ in length with pump output of 50 G.P.M. to 100 G.P.M. Two powerful burners pour heat through two 5″ return bend fire tubes provide hot materials quickly and steadily. Dual lever controls all pumping operations.

Full circulating, gang operated or standard spray bars available. Model SJ, with its low center of gravity, can be trailed or carried on a truck up to 40 miles per hour. 600, 800 and 1000 gallon capacity, either trailer or truck mounted.

TAR-KETTLES—FOR LOW COST PATCHING

This heavy-duty highway kettle, shown at right, is available in sizes from 80 to 325 gallons and on rubber tires or steel wheels.

Its "floating" vat will not warp. Coilless burners (standard equipment) are easily cleaned, need fewer replacements. Heavy-duty springs and fenders—removable vat—one-piece rain-tight lid—even heat circulation—all are time tested features.

Accessories such as hand spray, warming hood, barrel hoist, etc., are always available.

STANDARD STEEL WORKS, INC.

North Kansas City, Mo.

CONSTRUCTION BROOMS

ENGINE and TRACTION DRIVEN

The Standard Steel Works Construction Broom and Maintenance Sweeper incorporates a pulling principle which eliminates broom chatter, excessive wear, thereby providing a definite saving in broom replacement costs—lower cost sweeping per mile.

Quick and easy adjustment to road crown, no tools needed. Two-way pitch—right or left up to 30°. Height adjustment of broom is provided by quick-acting screw type lift. All bearings are permanently dust sealed and oversized for long life. Broom-end bearings are self-aligning. Engine-driven model is powered by a powerful Wisconsin VE-4 Engine through hand-operated clutch.

AGGREGATE SPREADER

The Standard Steel Spreader is a complete piece of equipment in itself, using the truck only for movement on the road and as a supply source.

Levers at each end provide quick adjustment for tapered spread. Simple roller chain transmission provides easy operation and lowest maintenance cost.

Closing off a portion of the opening between feed roller and shutter bar narrows the strip surfaced as desired. This unit comes in three lengths: 8′-10′-12′—and with capacities from 1.2 to 1.8 cubic yards.

STANDARD STEEL WORKS, INC.

North Kansas City, Mo.

MODEL 55–1½ to 2½ Ton TANDEM ROLLER

was designed to provide two important advantages:

(1) Adequate compaction for patch rolling requirements and

(2) Ideal roll dimensions for smoothing and finishing work combines steel and water ballast. Steel ballast is removable in 70# sections providing a wide choice of compaction ranges.

• The maximum weight with all ballast is 4600#. Shipping weight is 3600#. Speed—from 1.75 MPH to 3.5 MPH.

PROVIDES PRECISION ROLLING TO CURB

The Model 55 will roll to within 2 inches of wall or building on driver's side and to 4½ inches on opposite side. Eight inch ground clearance provides flush rolling adjacent to curbings. Automotive steering makes easy driving. Upholstered seat, safety seat rail, speed control, throttle and foot brake are of motor-car type—and water valve is in easy reach of operator. Low cost Model 55-T Transport Trailer also available.

STANDARD STEEL STREET FLUSHERS

It takes a powerful flush to sweep dirt and dust into gutters and sewers. Mere wetting of streets is not enough. Standard Steel equipment is built to supply a full 50 pounds pressure on each nozzle.

They carry a heavy load—reloading is quickly accomplished—ease of operating this type flusher is well known to every city using Standard Steel Flushers.

Embodying every new mechanical feature, styled for beauty, they reflect the progressive spirit of any city. For Complete Details, Write for Catalog.

How 180 Ford Tractors cut maintenance costs on Indiana highways

Three years ago the State Highway Department of Indiana switched from single-purpose equipment to multi-purpose Ford Tractors and Industrial Equipment for maintenance work. The result has been better and more economical maintenance of Indiana's 12,000-mile highway system. These Indiana officials explain why:

"We've cut our mowing costs in half!" reports Virgil W. Smith, Chairman, Indiana State Highway Commission

"Like most states, we find that mowing is our most expensive operation. Hilly terrain in sections of Indiana adds to our mowing costs. Since we put Ford Tractors and Rotary Cutters on the job we've cut mowing costs in half . . . actually found that Ford Rotary Cutters outmow conventional sickle-bar types by 3 to 1!"

"Operator training is no longer needed," says Al Magenheimer, Personnel Director

"Ford Tractors are so easy to operate that we've eliminated operator training. We've also greatly reduced our maintenance accident rate, even with an increase in highway traffic. With a Ford and Rotary Cutter, the operator is completely off the highway when he makes his first cut."

"We have many sources for emergency parts," explains Harold Mason, Superintendent of Equipment

"Each of our 36 sub-district garages has 5 Ford Tractors, 4 Rotary Cutters, 5 Industrial Loaders, 1 Post Hole Digger and 2 Rear Blades. With this equipment our Ford Tractors are never idle. They mow in the summer, load snow-and-ice-control materials in the winter, dig guard-rail post holes, and grade berm any time. Parts and service availability couldn't be better."

Turn the page and find out more

FORD TRACTORS AND

...for low-cost production

600 SERIES

You can choose from 5 advanced models . . . with or without built-in hydraulic system . . . either 4- or 5-speed transmission . . . with or without PTO . . . either high-cleat or non-skid "button" tread rear tires. You pay only for the features you need! All 5 models deliver 29 horsepower at the drawbar.

You see more **FORDS**

INDUSTRIAL EQUIPMENT

on over a hundred jobs!

800 SERIES

For those jobs where stepped-up lugging ability is needed, 800 Series Ford Tractors deliver 40 drawbar horsepower and more than 4500 pounds of drawbar pull. The 172-cubic-inch engine, 5-speed transmission and 10-inch clutch are designed for extra power. Available with or without hydraulic system and PTO.

...because they save more money

Low-cost tractors and attachments

designed for each other

Here's an outstanding new family of power-matched packages
5 tractors (34 to 52 hp) and 20 easily interchangeable attachments.

42 hp

Work Bull Model 303
is shown with a fork lift attachment mounted on lifting arms of 500 loader. Switch to other attachme can be completed by one man — without special tools, in only 5 to 15 minutes. Powerful, but economi to-operate 208-cu. in. gasoline engine is standard, b diesel engine is optional at extra cost.

M·H·F WORK BULLS

Low in initial cost... high in year-round versatility!

Low-cost Work Bulls give you ideal power and equipment selectivity... the right combination of tractor and power-matched attachments to dig, doze, load and lift... trench, grade and backfill... mow grass, plow snow or lay flexible pipe and cable ... haul or skid.

52 hp

Work Bull Model 404
develops high-torque pulling and pushing power . . . delivers maximum engine power through rugged precision-built, 5- speed transmission. Model shown has 5/8-yd loader bucket with scarifier and rear-mounted hydraulic backhoe. It mounts broom, utility boom, fork lift and blades on same arms used for loader bucket. Note clean lines for outstanding visibility. Gas or diesel engine. Road speeds to 15 mph.

34 hp

Work Bull Model 202
is a small but surprisingly powerful and versatile low silhouette tractor. In addition to attachments previou mentioned and side-mounted mower, shown, it's also available with — rotary or reel mowers, rotary trencher, post hole digger, grader blade or pipe and cable layer. Versatility plus low price tag makes it a ideal unit for both large and small communities.

You get a single source, one responsibility for sales and serv

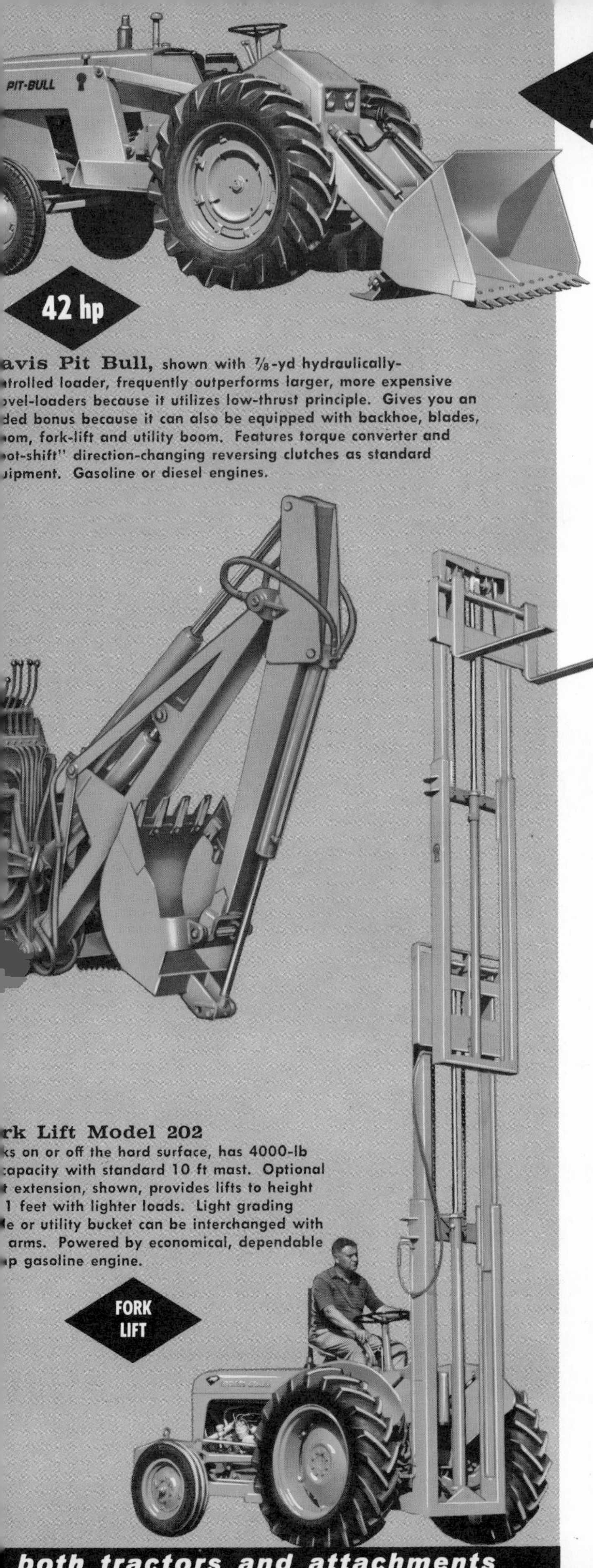

Look at this wide choice of power-matched attachments!

LOADERS
9 or 11 cu. ft., 5/8 or 7/8 yd.

BACKHOES
12 to 36 in. buckets, dig to 12½ feet

MOWERS
Reel, rotary or side-mounted

FORK LIFTS
2000 and 4000-lb. capacities

BLADES
Bull dozer, angle dozer or rear-mounted blades

BROOMS OR SWEEPERS
5 and 8-ft. widths

POST HOLE DIGGERS

ROTARY TRENCHERS

PIPE AND CABLE LAYERS

SNOW PLOWS

UTILITY BOOMS

SCARIFIERS

HAULING HITCHES

M·H·F WORK BULLS

Division of Massey-Harris-Ferguson, Inc.
12-L Quality Avenue, Racine, Wisconsin

M·H·F WORK BULLS

pay off as . . .

primary equipment

Work Bull Model 303 with backhoe digs to depth of 12½ feet. Front-end loader does backfilling or loading.

Using same arms required for loader, 404 with Utility Boom handles material on or off the hard surface.

With side-mounted mower, 202 t highway shoulders. Cutter ba hydraulically raised or lowered.

back-up machines

Model 202 with hydraulically controlled backhoe has exceptional visibility, quick and sure speed. Stabilizers are adjusted from control panel.

Model 202 with rotary trencher digs to depth of 5 feet . . . economically handles assignments too small for single-purpose rigs.

With both angle dozer and Model 303 performs jobs too for hand work, too small for nary equipment.

utility or clean-up tools

With 8-ft wide broom, Model 404 sweeps debris and dust from streets in summer, mounts plow to clear snow in winter.

Model 202 with rear-mounted grader blade maintains haul roads; finish-grades fill areas, parks and municipal lots.

Complementing larger equipn 202 with auger puts in bell or holes — perpendicularly — reg less of working slope.

M·H·F WORK BULLS

Division of Massey-Harris-Ferguson, Inc.

12-L QUALITY AVENUE, RACINE, WISCONSIN

THE FLINK COMPANY
STREATOR, ILLINOIS

Teamed for Complete Snow and Ice Control

BAKER *Flink* SNOW PLOWS

With Automatic Trip BLADE PROTECTION
Famous Baker "Safety Trip Bladed" Plows with "Roll Action" moldboards are specialized for high speed snow removal on highways and airport runways. Safety trip blades (sectional) lets plow pass over expansion joints and other immovable objects in the road without danger to plow or truck. Write for data—Catalog No. 110, no obligation.

Reversible and one-way plows . . . hydraulic power lift controls to meet your specifications . . . available in either underframes or front push models.

Flink SPREADERS

Model SS Spreader Low cost, pull-type for ice, dust control and seal coating. Spreads all granular materials.

"Even - Seal" Spreader for seal and cover coat spreading. Eliminates hand shoveling. Fits all dump trucks.

LMC Hopper Spreader for heavy duty ice control operations. New drive design cuts maintenance costs to absolute minimum. Write for Flink Spreader Catalogs.

SCHRAMM, INC.

MANUFACTURERS OF AIR COMPRESSORS

880 East Virginia Ave., West Chester, Pennsylvania

REPRESENTATIVES AND DISTRIBUTORS IN ALL PRINCIPAL CITIES

SCHRAMM STANDARD PNEUMATRACTOR

Self-propelled 125 cfm air compressor operating three-gang tamper.

The Pneumatractor drives right to the job and along with the job as it progresses. Produces 125 cfm of compressed air for the operation of paving breakers, tampers, diggers, sump pumps, rock drills and all types of tools. It can also be fitted with a snow plow or rotary brush. The cost of the Pneumatractor is low; lower than some two wheel mounted (that have to be pulled) 125 cfm compressors.

SWEEPS DUST, SNOW OR LIGHT DIRT. Standard Pneumatractor with Rotary Sweeper is equipped with 84″ rotary brush. Rotation of brush is independent of the speed of the Pneumatractor.

SCHRAMM, INC.

MANUFACTURERS OF AIR COMPRESSORS

880 East Virginia Ave., West Chester, Pennsylvania

REPRESENTATIVES AND DISTRIBUTORS IN ALL PRINCIPAL CITIES

SCHRAMM HEAVY PNEUMATRACTOR with Backhoe, digging trench (loader frame with backfill blade also mounted).

Schramm Heavy Pneumatractor uses the same 125 cfm engine compressor unit—with the same ability to operate pneumatic tools—mounted with a heavy industrial type rear axle and transmission, and a frame on which can be mounted a front end loader, backhoe, bulldozer blade, snow plow, sweeper, hoist and other accessory equipment.

HEAVY PNEUMATRACTOR WITH ONE YARD BUCKET. Because of the crowding ability this bucket will load a full cubic yard, lift 4000 pounds and load it in a dump truck.

BULLDOZER BLADE.—7′ long and 23″ high, mounted on Schramm Heavy Pneumatractor, may be used angled or straight—can also be tilted for gutter and shoulder grading.

SCHRAMM, INC.

MANUFACTURERS OF AIR COMPRESSORS

880 East Virginia Ave., West Chester, Pennsylvania

REPRESENTATIVES AND DISTRIBUTORS IN ALL PRINCIPAL CITIES

SCHRAMM PNEUMAPOWER 125

Shortest, lightest, narrowest, 125 cfm engine driven compressor.

Mounts on truck, behind the cab, with plenty of room for men and equipment. Use it to power two paving breakers or sheeting drivers, three backfill tampers or one three-gang tamper, three diggers or any other tools required by the water, sewer or street department. Also available two wheel spring-mounted.

SCHRAMM PNEUMAPOWER MODEL 75

Lowest cost compressor for hand-held tools

Model 75 will handle any of the tools used by the street, sewer and water departments. You actually get 75 cfm at 100 pounds gauge pressure, just right for operating paving breakers, diggers, tampers, rock drills and sump pumps. Balanced reciprocating parts, vibrationless operation, pressure lubrication make for long operation without maintenance. Also available skid mounted.

SCHRAMM, INC.

MANUFACTURERS OF AIR COMPRESSORS

880 East Virginia Ave., West Chester, Pennsylvania

REPRESENTATIVES AND DISTRIBUTORS IN ALL PRINCIPAL CITIES

Sump Pump handles sludge and raw sewage

SCHRAMM SUMP PUMP OPERATES FROM ANY AIR COMPRESSOR

The Schramm Sump Pump is an essential tool for every municipal water, sewer and street department. It is useful in removing water from trenches, cellars, manholes, catch basins, disposal tanks or wherever water is not wanted. It operates from a Schramm 75 or larger compressor.

MANUFACTURERS OF AIR COMPRESSORS

880 EAST VIRGINIA AVENUE

Pumps 400 gallons per minute against 10 foot head

SHAWNEE "LOADMASTER"

For the really big jobs, this extra duty industrial type loader with 2/3 yard bucket lifts approximately 3500 pounds to 9 feet dumping height. Main cylinders are 3 inch, double acting. Twin bucket cylinders are 2½ inch, double acting.

SHAWNEE "CHIEF"

The biggest of the backhoes digs 15 feet deep; provides tremendous digging force with push-pull cylinders operating synchronously. Six spool control panel enables use of any or all controls at one time. Rugged, welded box frame construction—chrome plated rods and polished cases.

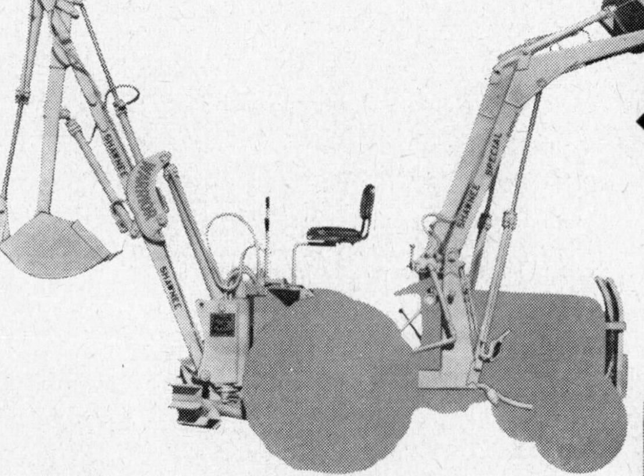

SHAWNEE "SPECIAL"
Heavy Duty

Built to stand rough, hard usage . . . the "Special" lifts 2000 pounds to 9 feet dumping height. Down pressure enables handling of tough, hard packaged materials. Double acting cylinders with chromium plated rods.

SHAWNEE "WARRIOR"

With push-pull power. Digs 12 feet deep. Three 120° quadrants of operation, changeable from operator's position, totaling 170° range. Hydraulic stabilizers align the tractor quickly for plumb digging.

SHAWNEE MODEL "62"

Designed for lighter digging needs, the "62" is exceptionally well built—smooth and fast in operation. Digs 7½ feet deep.

NATIONWIDE SALES AND SERVICE

SHAWNEE MANUFACTURING COMPANY, INC.
1947AP TOPEKA AVENUE TOPEKA, KANSAS

ATTACHMENTS LOADER

Adding to the versatility of Shawnee Loaders are these low cost attachments which are interchangeable with the bucket on both the "Special" and the "Loadmaster". Easy to mount or remove.

SNOW and UTILITY BUCKET

STREET BROOM

MANURE FORK

ANGLE DOZER

CRANE ATTACHMENT

FORK LIFT

BULLDOZER

NATIONWIDE SALES AND SERVICE

SHAWNEE MANUFACTURING COMPANY, INC.
1947AP TOPEKA AVENUE · TOPEKA, KANSAS

LOW PRICED EARTH MOVING TOOLS

SHAWNEE SCRAPER

Ideal for excavations—the Scraper has a 66 inch hydraulically operated blade that extends beyond widest point of tractor and makes possible digging to unlimited depth. 5/8 yard capacity.

SHAWNEE HYDRO-CLAM

Grave digging tool that digs square cornered holes with flat bottoms. Tremendous power to dig through hard, frozen ground. Ideal for spot excavations.

SHAWNEE REAR BLADES

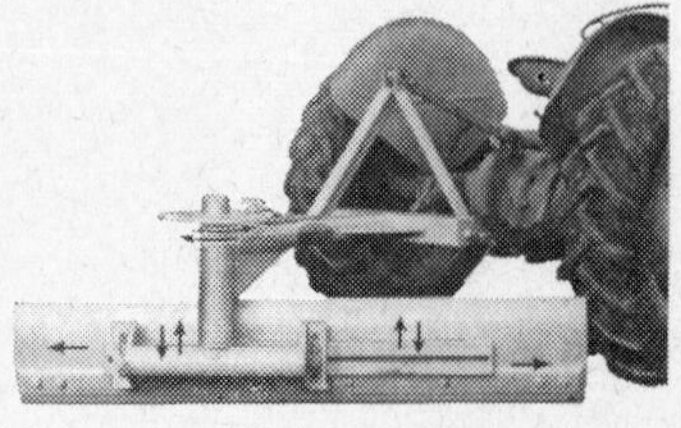

MODEL 200

All positions from driver's seat. Blade can be tilted or extended right or left manually and is instantly reversible. Ideal for "V" ditches.

MODEL 150

Offers greatest number of adjustments at low cost. Various tilt positions. Fits all 3-point linkage.

MODEL 100

Lowest priced blade. Manually adjusted to 9 positions, plus reversible. Efficient operation at greatest economy.

SALES AND SERVICE SHAWNEE COAST TO COAST

NATIONWIDE SALES AND SERVICE

SHAWNEE MANUFACTURING COMPANY, INC.

1947AP TOPEKA AVENUE TOPEKA, KANSAS

WAYNE MANUFACTURING COMPANY

1223 E. Lexington Ave. Pomona, Calif.

Eastern Division: 472 U.S. Highway No. 1, Newark 5, N. J.

World's largest producer of power sweepers for cities and industry.

Engineered to Outlast — Powered to Outperform All Others!

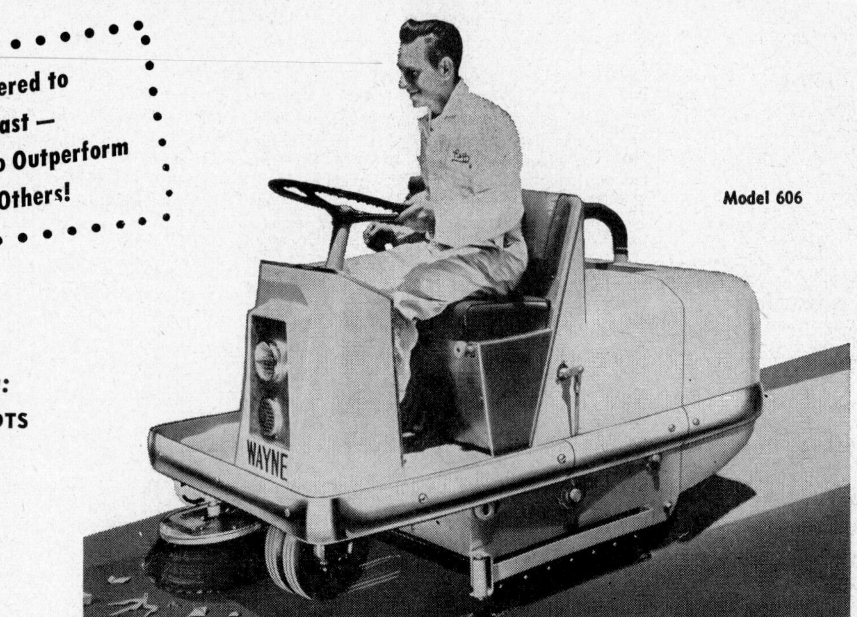

Model 606

For Sweeping:

PARKING LOTS
GARAGES
SHOPS
PARKS
WALKS
ALLEYS

NEW WAYNE SETS NEW STANDARDS IN SWEEPING!

Forget old ideas about power sweepers! These new Waynes are completely different . . . ruggedly built for the heaviest kind of work, day in and day out . . . built to last for years and years with a minimum of service and maintenance. They're designed with engineering principles never before found in power sweepers except giant street sweepers, also built by Wayne.

ONLY WAYNE HAS ALL THESE IMPORTANT STANDARD FEATURES!

—"Filter-Vac" Control—NO DUST BAG TO EMPTY.

—Power Dumping while operator is seated.

—Extra power—Model 606 has about twice the horsepower of any other sweeper.

—Larger hoppers mean more hours of sweeping.

—Faster sweeping—over 100,000 sq. feet per hour in open areas with Model 606.

—Power-Flex lift action enables Wayne to pick up large, bulky objects.

—Automotive-type steering.

—Vacuum attachments available.

—4 models. A size for every job. All available with LP GAS powered engines; also with VACUUM hose attachment if desired. Electric model also available.

Write for descriptive literature or demonstration.

NEW WAYNE POWER SWEEPERS FULLY INCORPORATE PROVED ENGINEERING PRINCIPLES OF WAYNE STREET SWEEPERS

4 NEW SWEEPER MODELS TO MEET YOUR SWEEPING NEEDS

	606	605	503	502
General:	Fully self-contained 48-inch power sweeper with steering wheel, hydraulic hopper unloading, 3 speed transmission, differential, operator protective shield guard, standard color yellow and grey.	Fully self-contained 36-inch power sweeper with steering wheel, hydraulic hopper unloading, 3 speed transmission, differential, operator protective shield guard, standard color yellow and grey.	Fully self-contained 36-inch power sweeper, walker type with rider attachment (optional), mechanical hopper unloading, standard color yellow and grey.	Fully self-contained 24-inch power sweeper, walker type with rider attachment (optional), mechanical hopper unloading, standard color yellow and grey.
Dimensions:	Length—82" Width—58" with side broom Height—49" w/o muffler	Length—82" Width—46" with side broom Height—48" w/o muffler	Length — 72" without rider Width—46½" with side broom Height—45"	Length — 72" without rider Width — 34½" with side broom Height—45"
Weight:	Approx. 1600 lbs. Shipping weight 1835 lbs.	Approx. 1325 lbs. Shipping weight 1560 lbs.	Approx. 555 lbs. Shipping weight 650 lbs.	Approx. 505 lbs. Shipping weight 550 lbs.
Sweeping Path:	48" without side broom 60" with 1 side broom 72" with 2 side brooms	36" without side broom 48" with 1 side broom 60" with 2 side brooms	36" without side broom 46" with 1 side broom 56" with 2 side brooms	24" without side broom 34" with 1 side broom 44" with 2 side brooms
Area Coverage:	110,000 sq. ft. per hr.	90,000 sq. ft. per hr.	45,000 sq. ft. per hr.	30,000 sq. ft. per hr.
"Filter-Vac" Dust Control:	High velocity fan deposits fine dust in main dirt hopper.	High velocity fan deposits fine dust in main dirt hopper.	High velocity fan deposits fine dust in main dirt hopper.	High velocity fan deposits fine dust in main dirt hopper.
Capacity:	All steel, 15 cu. ft. hopper with hydraulic unloading.	All steel, 10.5 cu. ft. hopper with hydraulic unloading.	All steel, 6.5 cu. ft. hopper with mechanical unloading.	All steel, 4.5 cu. ft. with mechanical unloading.
Side Broom:	Swivel action. Rugged worm gear drive.	Swivel action. Rugged worm gear drive.	Swivel Action. Rugged worm gear drive.	Swivel Action. Rugged worm gear drive.
Engine:	14.6 h.p. Wisconsin Model TFD Twin Cylinder, Stelite valves, self-starter, generator, battery, signal horn, lights, Protectoseal gas tank.	8.2 h.p. Wisconsin Model AEND, Stelite valves, self-starter, generator, battery, signal horn, lights, Protectoseal gas tank.	6.2 h.p. Wisconsin Model AKND, Stelite valves, manual starting (electric optional), Protectoseal gas tank.	6.2 h.p. Wisconsin Model AKND, Stelite valves, manual starting, (electric optional), Protectoseal gas tank.
Pick-up Broom:	16 fibre and wire strip brushes with 3½ inch trim, dual mounted in 8 steel holders. Free floating, self-aligning ball bearing brushholders. Pressure adjustment and engaging controls.	16 fibre and wire strip brushes with 3½ inch trim, dual mounted in 8 steel holders. Free floating, self-aligning ball bearing brush holders. Pressure adjustment and engaging controls.	12 fibre and wire strip brushes with 3½ inch trim, dual mounted in 6 steel holders. Free floating, self-aligning ball bearing brush holders. Pressure adjustment and engaging controls.	12 fibre and wire strip brushes with 3½ inch trim, dual mounted in 6 steel holders. Free floating, self-aligning ball bearing brush holders. Pressure adjustment and engaging controls.

WHITE MANUFACTURING COMPANY

1235 West Beardsley Avenue, Elkhart, 25, Indiana

PRODUCTS SOLD THROUGH EXCLUSIVE DISTRIBUTORS IN ALL STATES

Export Office: 50 Church St., New York 7, N. Y.

Established in 1920

White Manufacturing Company Products

Asphalt Plants
Burners, Kerosene
Coal Screens
Dryers, Material
Grinders, Concrete
Heaters, Surface
Heaters, Paving Tool
Kettles, Asphalt and Tar
Lead Melters
Mixers, Pug Mill
Pavement Repair Trucks
Sprayers, Asphalt
Torches, Kerosene
Trowelers, Concrete
Vibrators, Concrete

CATALOG SENT ON REQUEST

These White Complete Asphalt Plants Are Suited For All Moderate Paving Programs

Almost any type of bituminous pavement can be producd economically and effectively with a White Stationary Asphalt Plant. Asphalt, brick, or concrete can be patched or resurfaced. Complete new pavement can be laid.

These plants are especially suited for moderate size cities; or for suburbs of large cities to avoid long hauls. Any city can thus afford to pave or maintain its own streets, with city forces; to do the work whenever needed, in Summer or Winter, avoiding delays when large plants are shut down.

They are excellent for medium contract work, to pave or repair streets and highways, railway crossings, driveways, alleys, parking lots. They produce material to match any bituminous surface for immediate hot application, or for deferred laying. Operating cost, including labor, overhead, deferred charges, bitumen and aggregate, averages about $5.00 per ton at the plant. Only 2 men are required to operate plant.

Model L-12 has capacity up to 20 tons per hour; Model L-25, up to 30 tons per hour.

Plants contain internally oil fired rotating dryer; twin axle pug mill batch mixer; multiple deck vibrating screen; divided hot aggregate bin; asphalt heating kettle; weigh scales; dust collector; air controls; cold elevator with plate feeder; compressor; enclosed hot elevator; gasoline or diesel engine or electric motors.

These complete asphalt plants are well designed for simplicity in operation, low maintenance expense, and components synchronized. Minimum cost for setting up or moving.

Picture above left shows Model L-25; below, Model L-12 owned by a city for extensive maintenance.

White Models L-8 and L-10 Asphalt Plants

Prices Surprisingly Moderate

These are the most complete small asphalt plants for street, highway, airport, and general pavement maintenance. They are widely used by contractors in paving driveways, alleys, sidewalks, industrial floors, parking lots. Are particularly valuable for State Highway Departments repairing sheet asphalt city streets on through routes.

They must not be compared with small patching units producing cold or low temperature material. White plants match nearly any formula for high grade hot aggregate.

Can be operated in seasons when large plants are closed. Are so economical that hot mix can be made for about $4.50 per ton at the plant, including labor, overhead, material.

Capacities of genuine hot mix: Model L-8 up to 15 tons per hour, Model L-10 up to 20 tons. Capacity can be increased on cool mixes for deferred laying. Only 2 men needed for full operation of plant.

Full size dryer drum: Model L-8 36" x 10', Model L-10 46" x 10'. Batch type pug mixer, L-8 850#, L-10 1000#. Pivoted loading elevator; accurate volumetric measurement; air control; bitumen heating kettle; folding stack; oil burners; engine or electric power. Supplied for portable use on 6 pneumatic tires, or for stationary placement.

Upper picture is portable plant with cold elevator extended. Machine ready to run when delivered. Lower picture shows stationary mounting, with White reciprocating feeder.

White Kerosene Torches

These heavy-duty kerosene torches are widely used wherever clean, hot, voluminous flame is desired. They are sturdy, to give long life in all types of heating and melting service. Produce 1500° to 1800° F., in long clean flame. NOTE: Amount of heat is not determined by length of flame but by volume of fuel burned with complete vaporization. Model C-1 3-gal., below, is only hand torch burning entire fuel supply vertically or horizontally.

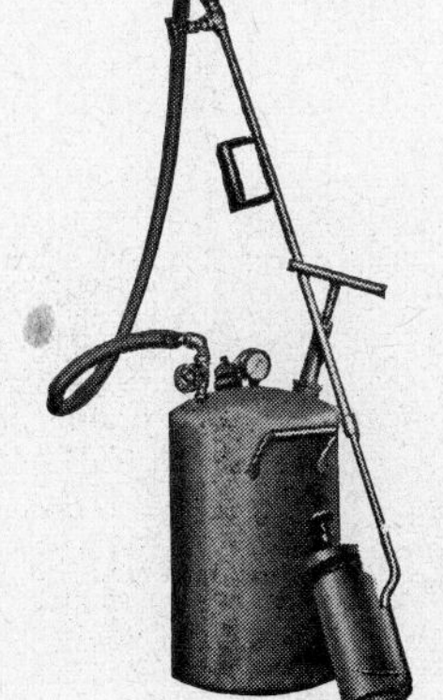

Hose connected torches, at left, made with 5, 15, 20 gal. heavy steel tanks. Also with 2 burners. Round pot burner for boilers.

White Heating Kettles Have Fire-Proof Tops

White asphalt and tar heating kettles are used all over the world, giving excellent service and long life.

The FIRE-PROOF top, an exclusive feature, excludes rain water which causes foaming and fires. Hinged tops supplied, if requested, such as for roofing work.

Used for pavement repairs, filling cracks, joints, penetration patching, painting curbs. Cut-back and other inflammable material can be heated with full safety.

Front View, showing 2 burners, Fire-Proof top

Model F-4 with engine driven spray pump

Model F-3 with hand spray

Kettles shown here are typical of the sturdy design of all White kettles. All have oil burners (propane burners available); detachable fuel tank, pneumatic tires, roller bearings, asbestos insulated fenders; double heat circulation; non-collapsible steady rest; overflow and gas release at rear, far from burners to reduce fire hazard.

White kettles made in 5 sizes: 1, 2, 3, 4, and 6 barrel capacity, or 80, 115, 165, 225, 325 gallons. Orders should include direct reading dial thermometer. All can be equipped with hand spray pump. Three larger sizes can have engine driven spray outfit, barrel hoist, warming hood for extra barrel. Spray pumps save material.

Model F-10 is most successful oil jacketed kettle for heating elastic crack and joint filler. Capacity 120 gallons of "dope," 60 gallons heat transfer oil. Hand agitator. Non-explosive.

Self-Heating Smoothing Iron

A handy tool for single patching jobs, such as utility cuts. Standard 45-lb. iron. 3-gallon torch is detachable, for many uses.

Tool Heater—Tar Kettle Unit

A combination fire wagon and bitumen heating kettle. Heats tampers, smoothers, rakes, shovels and A.C. for painting joints. Made in 2 sizes, 65 and 115 gal. capacity. Sliding damper under kettle prevents overheating bitumen while having full heat on tools. 2 oil burners. Pneumatic tires. Asbestos insulated fire box and fenders.

Concrete Vibrators With Many Exclusive Features

White concrete vibrators offer many improved features which provide more satisfactory operation, longer life, less maintenance cost. Many years of strenuous duty, all over the world, prove their reliability.

Dependable Flexible Drive. All sections are interchangeable, in 7′ and 12′ multiples. No special sections are required. Each casing has ball bearing connector. Each alloy steel core has slip joint which does not separate in service. It prevents stretching and overheating. No limit to length of drive.

Reliable Vibrating Heads. Also interchangeable. Can be applied to any drive section. Heads can be opened for repairs. Rotor mounted on double row bearings. Head diameters: 1½″, 2″, 2⅜″, 3″.

High Grade Power Units. Gasoline engines, 5.6 and 6¾ hp., with speed increasing countershaft; 2 hp. direct-connected. Electric motors, 2 hp. universal light weight motors, 110 volt, any cycle AC or DC; 1½ hp. heavy duty 220/440 volt, 50 and 60 cycle, 3 phase. Standard engines and motors can be serviced nearly anywhere.

Concrete Grinders. Speed reducing heads to hold grinding wheels, can be attached to any drive section.

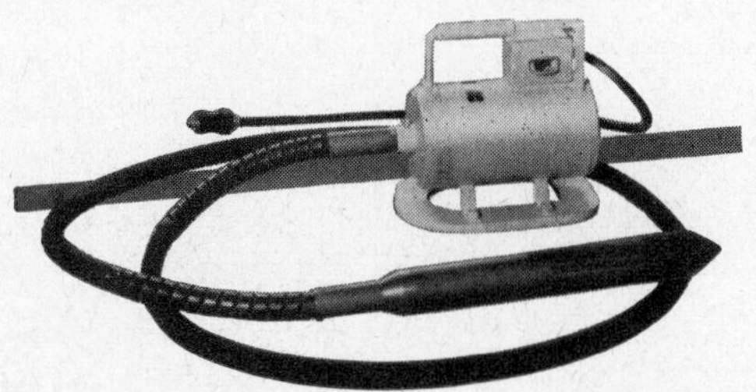

PICTURES: At left, light weight electric operated White vibrator. Top, popular Models M-12 and M-13, 5.6 and 6.7 hp., as mounted on wheeled chassis. Center, light high-speed Model M-9, 2½ hp. engine, swivel base.

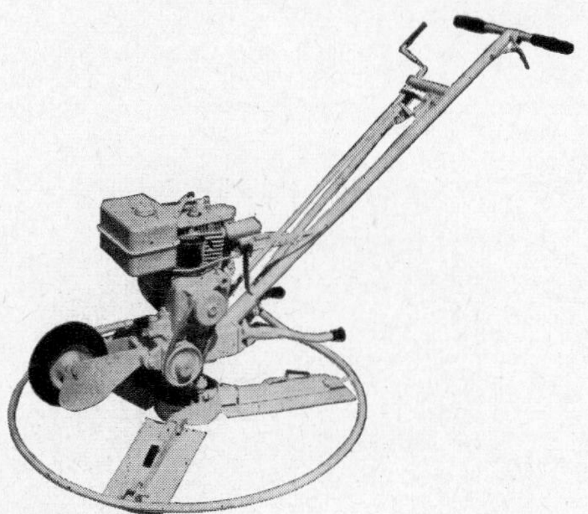

White Cement Troweler

HERE, for the first time is a ONE-MAN troweler. Note the retractable WHEEL, and folding steady rest! No extra man needed to move.

And, ring stops turning when operator removes hand from throttle! Engine idles, clutch releases, ring stops. No more running away!

No wrench needed to drop ring and remove blades. Blades slip on and off to square driving shafts. Blades are reversible, giving double life.

Model T-1 has 36″ ring, 3 blades, 2½ hp. engine.
Model T-2 has 48″ ring, 3 blades, 6 hp. engine.
Model T-3, 28″ stationary, no wheel ring.

Ring, blades, control column, and engine are quickly disassembled, to put into car trunk.

GENERAL CHEMICAL DIVISION

ALLIED CHEMICAL & DYE CORPORATION

40 Rector Street, New York 6, N. Y.

Offices: Albany • Atlanta • Baltimore • Birmingham • Boston • Bridgeport • Buffalo • Charlotte • Chicago • Cleveland Denver • Detroit • Greenville (Miss.) • Houston • Jacksonville • Kalamazoo • Los Angeles • Milwaukee Minneapolis • New York • Philadephia • Pittsburgh • Providence • San Francisco • Seattle • St. Louis • Yakima (Wash.)

In Canada: The Nichols Chemical Company, Limited • Montreal • Toronto • Vancouver

---

For Chemical Control of Weeds, Brush, and Insects

2,4-D WEED KILLERS

For control of ragweed and other annual and perennial broad-leaf weeds. Developed especially for low-gallonage application, equally effective in high-volume equipment.

UROX*

Highly potent new herbicide for long-lasting control. Kills a wide variety of plants. Provides long-lasting soil sterilization . . . one dose gives full season control. Applied in granular form . . . no dilution required.

2,4-D AND 2,4,5-T BRUSH KILLERS

Effective control of poison ivy, ash, osage orange, choke cherry, mesquite, brambles and many other woody plants. Excellent for use along right-of-ways, fence rows, storage yards, etc.

GENITE® EM-923

A single application of this miticide gives excellent control of mites on elms.

ELM TREE SPRAY

Special formulation for the control of Elm Bark Beetles. An efficient, economical means of checking the spread of Dutch Elm Disease.

*General Chemical Trade-Mark

FOR FLY AND MOSQUITO CONTROL

- 20% Lindane Emulsifiable Concentrate
- 50% Dieldrin Spray Powder
- Dieldrin EM-1½ Emulsifiable Concentrate (1½ pounds Dieldrin per gallon)
- Technical DDT for use in preparing 5% and other oil solutions
- DDT EM-2 Emulsifiable Concentrate

WYLIE MANUFACTURING CO., INC.

OKLAHOMA CITY, OKLA.

The Complete Mobile Asphalt Repair Unit (Model PM-215)

Single unit mixes, heats and makes hot patches

The answer to costly paving repair maintenance

The Model PM-215 Patchmobile is a compact mobile asphalt repair unit, designed and built to produce hot asphalt materials equal in quality to mixes of large stationary plants. It is complete with rotary dryer, asphalt kettle, engine-driven asphalt pump with spray attachment, pugmill and volumetric asphalt-metering system. The PM-215 is available with either kerosene or propane heating system.

Patchmobile's exclusive one-unit design minimizes traffic hazards, and means less equipment in the maintenance of roads and streets. It is popular among contractors when used as a central stationary plant, either on skids or standard mounting. The PM-215 is ideal for producing asphalt material used in building up shoulders on highways, bridge approaches, and railroad crossings and for maintenance of asphalt surfaces in general.

Specifications

CAPACITY: 6-8 tons hot mix per hour depending on moisture content and type of aggregate.
MATERIALS: Aggregate ¾" minus. **ASPHALTS:** Asphalt cement, cutback asphalts and emulsions.
DIMENSIONS: Length—156", Width—72", Height 84".
WEIGHT: 3990 lbs.
ASPHALT SUPPLY: 165-gallon capacity built-in tank.
DRUM COMPARTMENT: For warming 55-gallon drums of asphalt.
BATCHING HOPPER: Discharges aggregate directly into pugmill.
VOLUMETRIC MEASURING SYSTEM: Adds accurately measured amount of hot asphalt from pump into pugmill.
MATERIAL ELEVATOR: (Optional) For charging dryer from stockpile when machine is used as a stationary unit.
DRYER: Rotary tube type.
ENGINE: Air-cooled gasoline engine.
TOOL HEATING COMPARTMENT: Door in firebox for heating asphalt tools.
HEATING SYSTEMS: Following types optional: (a) Vaporizing kerosene burners. (b) Low-pressure oil burners. (c) Liquid gas (propane) burners.
PUGMILL: 5 cu. ft. capacity.
ASPHALT PUMP: Power-driven rotary gear type.
SPRAY BAR: For sealing and tack coating.
TOWING HITCH: With adjustable screw—jack for leveling machine on inclines—For raising and lowering front of machine to control flow of aggregate through dryer.

MODEL PM-215 PATCHMOBILE

WYLIE MANUFACTURING CO., INC.

OKLAHOMA CITY, OKLA.

MODEL 1520
Roadmaster
Asphalt Plant

The completely mobile, self-contained asphalt plant

Ready to operate in minutes — 20 ton hourly capacity

The mobile asphalt plant that has everything!!! This 20 ton per hour unit is a complete self-contained machine featuring a 400 gallon asphalt tank, 12′ rotary dryer with forced draft, twin-shaft pugmill with reciprocating feeder, dual low-pressure burners for both dryer and asphalt tank, positive pressure blower, cyclone type dust collector, and fully automatic aggregate batching and asphalt metering cycle.

The "1520" Roadmaster is the answer to the small as well as large municipality's asphalt problem, being especially designed as a mobile unit for fast moving and quick set-up time at the jobsite. It is available on six pneumatic tired wheels and level load axles, as shown above, for moving from one location to another, or can be used as a central plant. The Roadmaster is also furnished on steel skids, less running gear, for strictly stationary operation at the material yard.

MODEL 1520 ROADMASTER

WYLIE MANUFACTURING CO., INC.

OKLAHOMA CITY, OKLA.

MODEL 1520 ROADMASTER

The completely mobile asphalt plant

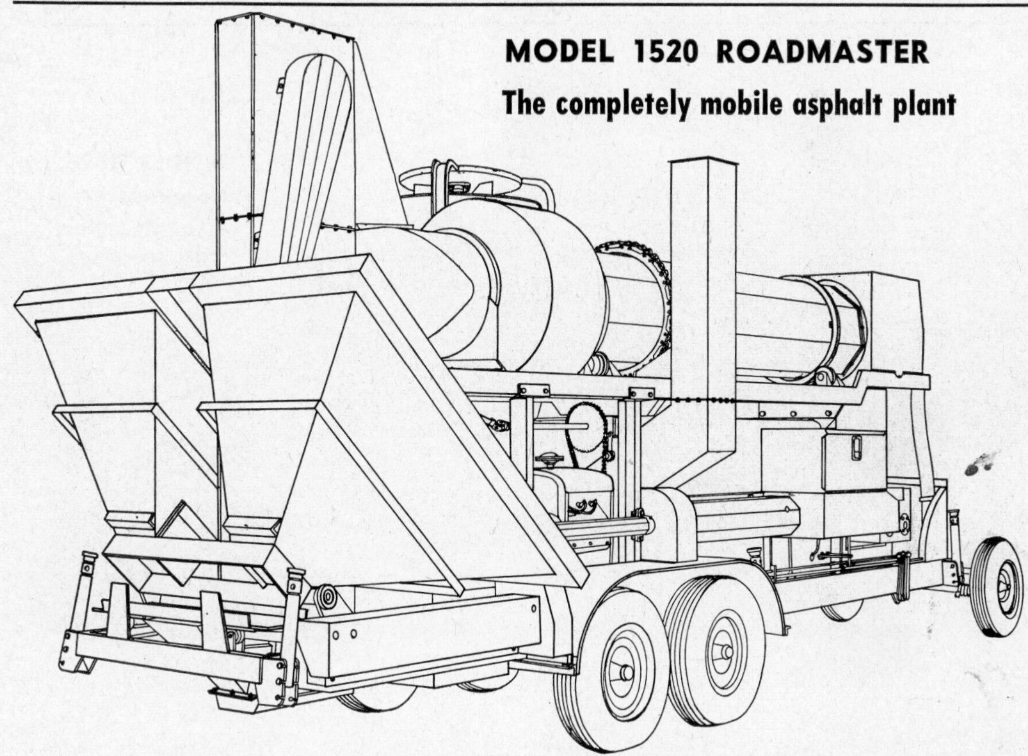

SPECIFICATIONS

CAPACITY: 20 tons hot mix asphalt per hour depending on moisture content and type of aggregate.
ASPHALT TANK: 400 gallons capacity—Under fired and with heat tubes. Provided with charging opening for lowering drums of paving asphalt into tank. Heats any type asphalt. Equipped with asphalt thermometer.
PUGMILL: 7 cu ft. twin-shaft, continuous type, equipped with individual replaceable mixing blades and liners. Equipped with screw operated discharge gate. Pugmill shafts are gear driven by spur and bevel gears and pinions totally enclosed in oil bath.
DRYER: 24" diameter, 144" length of dryer drum and charging chamber. Mounted on six 4" ball bearing trunnion rollers. Aggregate charged into dryer charging chamber by material bucket elevator. Dryer has forced draft induced by a 20" heavy-duty blower fan.
WEIGHING BATCHER: Equipped with scale beam weighing mechanism which releases aggregate into pugmill when weight of aggregate in hopper reaches weight set on scale beam. Asphalt is automatically added simultaneously as aggregate enters pugmill.
ASPHALT MEASURING SYSTEM: Equipped with indicator so exact amount of asphalt required for each batch can be pre-set and sprayed into pugmill under pressure. A Viking rotary gear pump forces hot asphalt alternately into two adjustable stroke measuring cylinders, controlled by a 4-way valve operated by aggregate batching mechanism.
MATERIAL ELEVATOR: Bucket type—25 tons per hour capacity—Bottom take ups—With charging boot.
HOPPERS & FEEDERS: Consisting of two 1 cu. yd. hoppers. Each hopper equipped with proportioning gate to regulate flow of material to twin reciprocating feeder plates.
HEATING SYSTEM: Four low-pressure oil burners. (Two each for heating and drying aggregate in dryer and asphalt in tank.) Compressed air for vaporizing fuel supplied by a Roots-Connersville blower with built-in fuel pump.
DUST COLLECTOR: Special designed cyclone type, which collects abrasive dust before exhaust air from dryer passes through built-in blower fan. Equipped with dust injector for returning part of dust to batching hopper.
BURNER FUEL TANK: 65 gallon capacity. Fuel pumped to burners through fuel pump on blower.
ASPHALT PUMP: Viking rotary pump, engine driven through Twin-Disc clutch.
STABILIZERS: Six adjustable screw-type stabilizers for stationary operation.
BEARINGS: Heavy duty ball bearings throughout drive system.
INSTRUMENT PANEL: Contains engine hourmeter, aggregate and asphalt dial thermometers, and fuel pressure gauge, all located on panel in front of machine operator.
WHEELS & AXLES: Truck type wheels—15" front wheels mounted on 6.70-15 6-ply tires—16" rear tandem wheels mounted on 7.50-16 10-ply tires. Front and rear axles equipped with load leveling springs which maintain greater stability than conventional leaf springs. (Electric brakes OPTIONAL at extra cost.)
POWER UNIT: Model VF-4 Wisconsin 4 cyl., 4 cycle, V-type air-cooled, 25 H.P. gasoline engine, with clutch reduction, oil bath air cleaner, fuel pump and engine housing. With 6 gallon fuel tank. Equipped with 6-volt electrical system and starter.
CHASSIS FRAME: All electric welded, rigidly braced and reinforced.
DIMENSIONS: Length: 24' 5" with towing tongue and material hoppers in raised position. Width: 7' 6". Height: 10' 7". (By removing top section of elevator, height can be reduced to 9' 5" for shipping.)
WEIGHT: Approximately 11,400 lbs.

WYLIE MANUFACTURING CO., INC.

OKLAHOMA CITY, OKLA.

For heating and remixing stockpiled asphalt patch material

A completely self-contained pugmill and material heater

The Model 30-R Heat-A-Mix is a tailgate mixer for heating and remixing stockpiled asphalt patch material. This unit is also used to reactivate unworkable blade-mixed, windrowed material to any desired temperature, and to produce asphalt material using any type of asphalt and aggregate. With its forward and reverse transmission, it is possible to retain the material in the pugmill until properly mixed and heated.

The Heat-A-Mix is attached to the dump truck by means of mounting hooks, and can be quickly and easily removed. With the transfer legs the machine may be transferred from one truck to another without the use of a crane or hoist.

Specifications

CAPACITY: Output up to 8 tons per hour.

DIMENSIONS: Length, 79"; Height, 28". (Overall height to top of charging hopper, 63"; depth, 22".)

WEIGHT: 1100 lbs.—Shipping weight 1290 lbs.

PUGMILL: 48" long x 13" diameter.

HEATING SYSTEM: High-pressure propane or kerosene heating system.

ENGINE: Air-cooled gasoline engine.

TRANSMISSION: Forward and reverse transmission, with control lever at discharge end of machine.

MOUNTING: Unit attached to truck by means of hooks over tailgate.

TRANSFER KIT: Four removable and adjustable legs for transferring unit from truck to truck on the road without use of crane or hoist.

FIREBOX: Insulated combustion chamber, lined with heavy fire-plate heat deflectors.

HOT MATERIAL PAN: Constructed of heavy-gauge steel, hinged to raise when not in use or traveling. In raised position material drops through open back of pan directly onto road surface.

MODEL 30-R HEAT-A-MIX

W. E. GRACE MFG. CO.

6009 S. Lamar St., Dallas, Texas

ASPHALT CONSTRUCTION AND MAINTENANCE EQUIPMENT

Rapidspray 600 Gallon Maintenance Distributor — for Patching or Construction — Truck or Trailer Mounted

Spreaders for Cover Stone on Seal or Surface Treatment

3 Models of Road Sweepers — Axle Driven, Engine Driven, and Tractor Mounted. Also Power Driven Brush Filling Machines

Sheepsfoot Rollers — Single or Double Drum in 2 Weights and 3 Foot Styles

Pneumatic Rollers — Self Powered, with Open Body for Sand Ballast, or 1,000 Gallon Water Tank Equipped for Sprinkling

Drag Brooms for Maintenance and Construction of Sealed Surfaces

Spreaders for Hot or Cold Asphaltic Concrete

Circulating Heaters for Tank Cars of Asphalt, or for Storage Tanks. Also Asphalt Pumps and Stationary Heaters for Storage Tanks

Street Cleaners' Carts, Roller Bearings, Rubber Tired. Also Concrete Carts

Drawn Type Pneumatic Rollers 7 to 50 Tons

WRITE TODAY FOR DETAILED INFORMATION AND NAME OF NEAREST DEALER

CLIPPER MANUFACTURING COMPANY

GENERAL OFFICES AND FACTORY

2800 Warwick, Kansas City 8, Mo.

BRANCH OFFICES IN PRINCIPAL CITIES THROUGHOUT U.S.A.

SPECIALISTS in CONCRETE SAWING *and* HOT *or* COLD SEALING *for* . . . .

- **STREET REPAIR** MAINTENANCE and CONSTRUCTION

CITY — STATE — COUNTY

- **CONTRACTION JOINT SEALING** HIGHWAYS — AIRFIELDS
- **PATCHING**
- **TRENCHING**
- **DRIVEWAYS - SIDEWALKS**
- **CONCRETE FLOORS**

There's A CLIPPER CONCRETE SAW For EVERY JOB— 14.6, 25 and 36 H. P. Also available in electric models. Clipper Concrete Saws are SIMPLE — RUGGED — DEPENDABLE. LOWEST COST PER FOOT OVER ANY OTHER METHOD!

CP-400 COLD APPLIED Joint Sealer. Seals up to 2 miles of joints per day under controlled pressure. A low cost unit of many uses.

AC-40 HOT POUR Joint Sealer. Combines melting and sealing. Now seal up to 1250 feet per hour with any hot pour sealing compound.

WRITE—WIRE—PHONE FOR **FREE JOB DEMONSTRATION**

• A Clipper Factory Trained Representative is always on call to demonstrate and help you select the right Clipper Concrete Saw and Hot or Cold Contraction Joint Sealer for your job. For any CITY, COUNTY, STATE Asphalt or Concrete Sawing Job — There's a Clipper Model for the Fastest Sawing . . . At the Lowest Cost . . . With the Greatest Footage per Blade over any saw or blade available. Call Clipper Today for Immediate Shipment — or Service

MR. CLIPPER

427X

Clipper
"SAILS RIGHT THRU"
CONCRETE SAWING... BLADES
BEST for...
All SAWS
Any AGGREGATE
Every JOB!
• YOU NAME IT...
The Saw-The Job-The Aggregate
...Clipper will name the Best Blade to guarantee you the FASTEST CUT... at the LOWEST COST...with the GREATEST EASE—Anytime—Anywhere
FREE—A Factory Trained Representative will demonstrate a Clipper Concrete Saw right on your job, with Diamond or Green-Con Abrasive Blades and recommend the best Blade for your Job. You can see for yourself new speed and economy you never thought possible. Only Clipper, with its 20 years of experience, has facilities for research and development which offers the widest range of Blades for every concrete sawing need.
DIAMOND
GREEN-CON
DIAMOND
• WIRE—WRITE—PHONE your Clipper Factory Trained Representative for SAME DAY SHIPMENT on Clipper Superior Blades, or for blade recommendations for any materials. He can also arrange for your FREE TRIAL of a New 2 H.P. CLIPPER SUPER MASONRY SAW, the Greatest High-Production Masonry Saw ever built!
Clipper MANUFACTURING CO. • Phone VIctor 2-3113 • 2800 Warwick • Kansas City 8, Mo.
ALBANY Phone 8-0338
ATLANTA MUrray 8-4229
AUSTIN, TEX. GReenwood 6-6555
BIRMINGHAM, ALA. ALpine 2-8240
BOSTON HAncock 6-0512
BUFFALO VIctoria 7707
CHARLOTTE, N. C. FRanklin 6-0257
CHICAGO SUperior 7-1351
CINCINNATI CHerry 1-5720
CLEVELAND CHerry 1-7080
DALLAS PRospect 3491
DAVENPORT Phone 6-2342
DENVER ALpine 5-6790
DETROIT WOodward 1-7117
HARTFORD CHapel 7-5768
HOUSTON CApitol 5-6616
INDIANAPOLIS WAlnut 3-8947
LOS ANGELES MUtual 4589
MILWAUKEE BRoadway 3-5362
MINNEAPOLIS FEderal 3-7629
NEWARK MArket 3-6952
NEW ORLEANS MAgnolia 5497
NEW YORK MUrray Hill 7-8460
OKLAHOMA CITY JAckson 4-1647
PHILADELPHIA EVergreen 2-2962
PITTSBURGH EVerglade 1-6200
SAN FRANCISCO UNderhill 3-4324
ST. LOUIS MIssion 5-5530
WASHINGTON, D. C. REpublic 7-3087
MR. CLIPPER
FACTORIES IN ENGLAND, FRANCE, GERMANY, ITALY.
528X

GAR WOOD INDUSTRIES, INC.

Customer Service Dept., Wayne, Michigan

TRUCK EQUIPMENT PRODUCTS: Hoists, Dump Bodies, Refuse Collection Bodies, Frate-Gates, Winches, Cranes, Pole Derricks, Snowplow Controls

FRATE - GATES — Newest and most advanced gates on the market. Models and capacities to fit any truck. Also a Frate-Gate for pick-up trucks.

Request literature Form W-175

"DUMP-IT" CONVERSION HOISTS — Smooth, trouble-free operation. A complete line to meet the needs of municipalities.

Request literature Form W-176

America's newest, most advanced line of truck equipment

Two famous names in hydraulic hoists—Gar Wood and St. Paul—now identify today's most modern line of truck equipment. Over 88 years of combined engineering know-how and manufacturing skill are reflected in this advanced line.

Sales and service are available from one world-wide organization of leading truck equipment distributors . . . experienced in application, qualified to analyze your equipment requirements.

Before you specify *any* truck equipment, get all the facts about today's most advanced line. See your nearest Gar Wood-St. Paul distributor or write direct to Customer Service Dept., Gar Wood Industries, Inc., Wayne, Michigan.

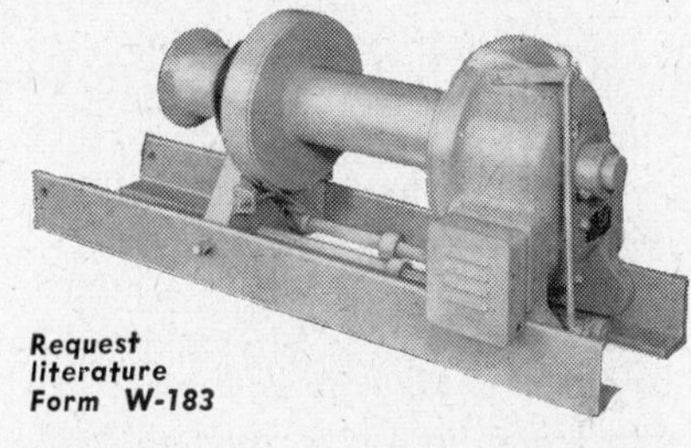

Request literature Form W-183

TRUCK WINCHES—Dependable and safe. All types and sizes with capacities from 7,000 to 100,000 pounds.

Request literature Form W-187

"DUMP-O-MATIC" HOISTS — Lightweight, low-cost twin cylinder hydraulic hoists for pick-up trucks.

Request literature Form WC-202R

TRUCK CRANES — Space-saving cranes that let you load and haul with one truck. Available in capacity from 2,000 to 24,000 lbs.

KLAUER MANUFACTURING CO.

Dubuque, Iowa

SnoGo is the fatest known method of loading snow, filling the largest truck in 10 to 20 seconds. Owing to the force with which **SnoGo** handles the snow, it compacts so that the truck has greater capacity.

It pays to put a **SnoGo** to work on your city streets. Don't just push the snow against the curb, thus building snow banks to delay traffic and hamper parking. Remove the snow completely. **SnoGo** will throw the snow into a parkway or load it directly into a truck.

SnoGo, a rotary type of snow remover, is furnished for mounting on heavy trucks of all-wheel-drive type of suitable speed range. The mechanism is operated by a separate 165-hp. engine. The blades, which operate on the principle of an auger, force the snow back into a revolving blade, much like a fan, which tosses the snow outward through a spout. This action removes the snow right down to the surface. The **SnoGo** is built for continuous operation and has a snow discharge directional chute hydraulically operated by the driver in the cab. It permits the direction of snow displacement to be changed while the equipment is in motion.

Note the economy of this method of snow removal on airports or country highways, since the snow is tossed into the fields where it can do no harm. Since the snow is removed some two hundred feet from the highway or airport runway, no bank is left to trap drifting snow, and no snow is piled up in the ditch to block drainage.

SnoGo Model TU is for mounting on heavy-duty four-wheel drive trucks, **Model MTR** for mounting on medium-duty four-wheel drive trucks, and **Model LTR** for mounting on the special Marmon-Herrington Ford V-8.

Model TU-3 has a cutting width of 101 5/8 inches. The equipment carries three 18-inch-diameter augers driven by roller chain in an oil-tight housing. A shear pin device is provided in the driving flange of the drive sprocket at the rear of the snow hood. The auger and fan drives also are fitted with individual shear pin safety devices, which are accessible for replacement, and protect the units against damage when fouled by unusual substances or by incorrect operation.

Model TU SnoGo for mounting on heavy-duty all-wheel-drive trucks

Model LTR with truck loading chute

The end shoes and center shoes of **Model TU-3 SnoGo** are equipped with bolted-on alloy wear plates, easily replaceable. The rear shoes are adjustable to control contact with the road surface. A high-carbon steel replaceable scraper blade is used. Shafts are steel, heat treated and ground. All shafts and rotating parts are journaled in ball or roller bearings.

The attaching frame is of unit construction with a straight vertical lift. The hydraulic power-lift gear with full cab control incorporates a stabilizer to maintain a level position of the equipment in relation to the road. The snowstream directional control (hydraulically operated) instantly adjusts to discharge to either side and at any angle of discharge through an arc of 160 degrees. Two hand control levers for the hydraulic control in the cab are convenient for either the driver or his assistant. The hydraulic system is fitted with a high efficiency rotor type pump, and copper tubing with high-pressure hose (where flexibility is required) is used.

The power plant is a Climax R-165 valve-in-head 6-cylinder engine, 6⅛-inch bore, 7-inch stroke, 1237.53 cu. in. displacement, 880 ft. lb. maximum torque; developing in excess of 200 horsepower at 1300 rpm, ledge mounting; and full pressure lubrication throughout. A heavy-duty, over-center type clutch is used and the take-off transmission drive is by multiple roller chain running in an oil-tight welded steel case. Adjustment is provided for correct tension. The drive to the rotary units is by two double universal joint assemblies with intermediate ball-bearing mountings.

Model LTR SnoGo combines all features of the larger models with ample capacity and the smaller capital investment offered for the smaller budgets, and is ideal for fleet operation. This model, when equipped with truck loading mechanism, provides an economical, fast and efficient method of loading snow.

Model MTR on fwd SnoGo special chassis Model "KS"

M. B. CORPORATION

FORMERLY MEILI-BLUMBERG CORP.

New Holstein, Wisc.

SWEEPERS

M-B produces a complete line of tractor-mounted, truck-mounted and pull type sweepers for municipal use. In the pull type, both engine drive and traction drive are available.

Tractor Mounted—Shafts turn on anti-friction bearings and all moving parts are fully protected. Easily installed and removed. Hydraulically controlled. Sweeps 5′-6′ path. Broom can be disengaged while travelling. Fibre or wire brush available.

Pull Type—Sweeps 30° to right or left. Main frame of 5″ tubular steel. Features a 96″ x 30″ brush on self-aligning, anti-friction bearings. Exclusive spring balance permits brush to float over uneven surfaces. Hydraulic controls.

Truck Mounted—Quickly attaches to any truck with adjustable undercarriage. Two-way sweeping action controlled from cab. Sweeper broom is independently powered, has 8-ft. fibre or steel brush.

SNOW REMOVAL: Keeps your tractor working all year around. Keeps streets, roads, parking areas and ice skating ponds clear of snow.

GENERAL SWEEPING: Keeps roads and streets clean and safe. Ideal for sweeping leaves. Brush may be raised 8″ to clear obstructions.

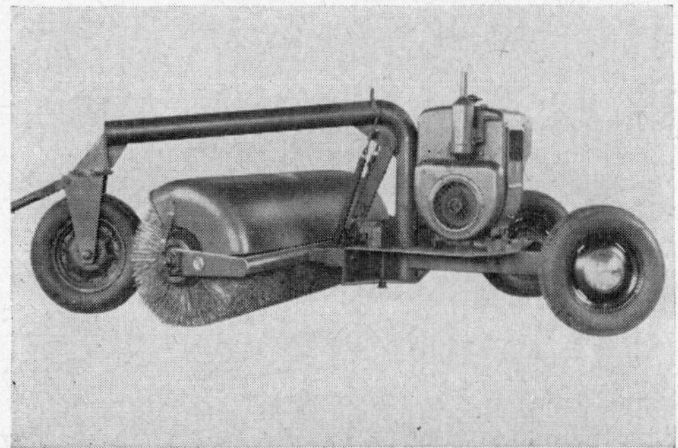

PULL TYPE ENGINE DRIVEN: Engine is 4-cylinder, 4 cycle, 16-18 HP, governor controlled with built-in heavy duty clutch. Full dust protection on intake and crankcase.

PULL TYPE TRACTION DRIVE: Maximum utility at minimum investment. Brush rotates through a drive from the rear wheels. Two-speed transmission fully enclosed in oil bath.

TRACTOR SWEEPERS BUILT FOR

FORD • CASE • FERGUSON • OLIVER • INTERNATIONAL HARVESTER • JOHN DEERE ALLIS-CHALMERS • WILLYS JEEP

TRUCK LOADER

Self-Loading Bucket
Fast, One-Man Operation

Here's a new truck loader with a unique, self-loading bucket—unlike any other loader. Now one man with an M-B Truck Loader can quickly and efficiently handle dozens of year 'round municipal and county jobs.

The powerful jaw action of the self-unloading bucket eliminates ramming of the truck into a stockpile for a full bucket. There are no shock loads on the truck, its frame or the loader mechanism. Small piles can be picked up easily without the need for additional men to sweep or shovel into the bucket . . . there's no "chasing" of material down the street.

An M-B Truck Loader can take care of sweeper pile pick-up, removing excess spoil, leaf pick-up, sand and gravel operations, snow removal, street and highway maintenance and similar jobs. All loading, hauling and dumping are accomplished by the one unit.

OUTSTANDING FEATURES

- Full hydraulic power throughout entire cycle.
- Eliminates truck shock loads.
- Material may be dumped anywhere in the truck body for even load distribution.
- High carbon steel boom arms provide maximum strength and minimum weight.
- Fits almost all types of trucks—unit width is kept within legal restrictions.
- Heavy duty ½-yd. bucket—larger capacites available for special jobs.
- Enthusiastic user approval.

The JAW Makes the Difference!

In loading position the bucket is placed on the ground before the material to be loaded. The jaw swings down and reaches out to meet ground level approximately 13″ forward of the lower bucket lip. Two double-acting hydraulic cylinders smoothly complete the closing cycle by pulling in and holding a "full bite" load in the bucket. The loading action is accomplished entirely by the bucket alone, without using the truck as a tractor.

PIPPIN CONSTRUCTION EQUIPMENT, INC.

White River Junction, Vermont

Pippin "*Model 195*"

THE ALL NEW EXCAVATOR

DIGS 13 FEET DEEP
SWINGS FULL 180°
LOADS 9 FEET HIGH

RUGGEDLY ATTACHED
EASILY REMOVED
MORE POWER & SPEED

The new PIPPIN Model 195 is the result of many months of intensive research and development, followed by over six months of rigid field testing. It is outstanding in every way: operator's comfort and visibility, stability in every direction even when digging to full 13 feet at 90°, eye appeal with 90% of the hydraulics concealed, and perfect balance with the PIPPIN Loader without danger of tractor breakage. The Model 195 is as versatile as always with a wide variety of attachments for many jobs.

Pippin MODEL 125 LOADER

an Ideal Combination with the Pippin Excavator

STRONGEST, BOX WELDMENT CONSTRUCTION
1¼" DIAMETER ALLOY STEEL PINS THROUGHOUT
32 REPLACEABLE HARDENED STEEL BUSHINGS

The PIPPIN Loader is especially designed as a companion unit for use with the PIPPIN Excavator. A rigid combination subframe accommodates both units thereby relieving the tractor of harmful stresses. Your satisfaction is assured because time and expense have not been spared in building this quality product, and it has been thoroughly tested. It has all the features you want; cylinders are precision honed, all pins are 1¼" diameter alloy steel, every wear point has a replaceable hardened bushing of bearing steel. Both the Excavator and Loader are quickly and easily removed from the tractor. The PIPPIN Loader will do what any loader can do—plus lasting longer with less maintenance.

RIVINIUS, INC.

EUREKA, ILLINOIS

RIVINIUS SNOW LOADER

Blower-type loader fits on moldboard of any "Cat" No. 12 or No. 112 Motor Grader. Blade still changes angle. No windrowing . . . snow and ice is bladed from street and blown into truck in one operation. Blower compacts snow 25% to 50% to increase truck load. Operator visibility is fully retained.

BLOWER: 6-bladed, 42" diameter

DRIVE: Auxiliary gasoline engine

SPEED: 380 r.p.m.

Will load three tons of snow in one minute, fifteen seconds.

WEIGHT (approx.): 2000 lbs.

For "Caterpillar" Motor Graders...

RIVINIUS SNOW WING BLOWER

Operates on snow wing of "Cat" No. 12 or No. 112 Motor Grader. Horizontal discharge blows snow and ice a distance of 90 feet, clearing highway shoulder. No open drive . . . no frozen mechanism . . . no power loss.

BLOWER: 4-bladed, 54" diameter
DRIVE: Power Takeoff Hydraulic
SPEED: 650 r.pm
MATERIAL: Welded steel plate
WEIGHT: (approx.) 1200 lbs.

FOR COMPLETE INFORMATION SEE YOUR CATERPILLAR DEALER, OR WRITE:

RIVINIUS, INC. • EUREKA, ILLINOIS

9 REASONS WHY *Tri-Line* CONCRETE CUTTERS OFFER FASTER • MORE ECONOMICAL SAWING

FOR: Contractors • State and County Highway Departments • City Street Departments • Utilities • Industries • Airports

1. Exclusive three-wheel undercarriage prevents tilting, eliminates blade bind and excessive wear.
2. Direct-acting hydraulic control permits quick, effortless depth-of-cut adjustments.
3. Maximum maneuverability afforded by tricycle design. Turns within its own length without jockeying.
4. Sturdy construction means less vibration, less blade wear. A full 700 pounds of ruggedness.
5. Thirty-gallon tank provides water when supply is inconvenient. Can be attached to hydrant if desired.
6. Vital engine parts protected from blade spray. No shut-downs due to engine "drownings".
7. Abundant power from 13 hp., two-cylinder Wisconsin air-cooled engine for full-depth, full-speed cutting.
8. Double-ended arbor permits cutting on either side of the machine . . . in places normally inaccessible.
9. 16" Semi-pneumatic rear wheels for easier operation

TRI-LINE Concrete Cutters save labor costs in highway repair, industrial floor cutting and airport contraction joint sawing.

Wedge-type cut eliminates spalling and settling in highway repair and underground services.

Floor cutting in industry for machine installation.

Cutting contraction joints on new aiprort construction.

ACTUAL TESTS SHOW *Tri-Line* BLADES OUTPERFORM OTHER BLADES

Tests run in our own laboratory simulating actual concrete sawing conditions plus constant "in-the-field" performance has proven Tri-Line's longer cutting life! These special double-bonded diamond cutting edges produce fast, clean cuts with rapid cooling and cleaning of material being cut. For greater economy per lineal foot of cutting, specify Tri-Line blades.

Tri-Line supplies concrete cutting blades for all makes of machines . . .

Whatever make of concrete saw you are now using, you can get Tri-Line blades for increased economy in cutting. Tri-Line's double-bonded diamond grit-edged blades are slotted for faster cooling . . . for more efficient clearing of sludge from cut. Send us arbor hole size, make of machine and quantity of blades you need. Then you'll find out for yourself about Tri-Line quality in actual use.

Write for a FREE demonstration in your area!

Send for FREE Illustrated brochure which gives complete specifications and construction details, and the name of our nearest representative . . . without obligation.

Tri-Line CONCRETE CUTTERS

Manufactured by

TRI-LINE COMPANY • 931 Carroll St. • Racine, Wis.

MOBIL SWEEPER®

Division of The Conveyor Co., 3260 E. Slauson Avenue, Los Angeles 58, California

DEALERS IN PRINCIPAL CITIES

WE'VE CUT STREET SWEEPING COSTS

...in municipalities like yours!

As much as 50% savings are reported by municipalities on their street sweeping costs since purchasing a Mobil Sweeper. Here's how Mobil Sweeper can save money for your community—

A Proven Design—Mobil Sweeper is used by city, county, state and Federal road divisions.

Cleaner Sweeping—Longer draught arms on the rear pickup broom assure clean sweeps even in deep dips and depressions.

More Sweeping Miles from the Gutter Broom—The decreased-arc type broom-segments used retain their flipping action longer and save on replacement.

Less Dead-Heading Time—Mobil Sweeper is fastest to and from sweeping area—travels up to 55 m.p.h.

Easy to Operate—Any driver who operates a truck can operate a Mobil Sweeper, saving expensive training.

Easy to Maneuver—Same maneuverability around parked cars as other high capacity sweepers *but* with less tail swing.

Large Dirt Hopper—It fills to capacity every time—a point to check when figuring capacity of any sweeper. The proven squeegee type dirt conveyor handles objects up to 11", permitting operators to go over such objects, not around them.

Fewer Stops are Required—Mobil Sweeper has a 200-gallon water tank that needs refilling less often.

Lower Maintenance—You save because this fine sweeper utilizes International Harvester valve-in-head engine, transmission, front axle and 2½-ton rear axle. Your present maintenance system can care for this sweeper.

Safest Sweeper Built—Has low overall height (87" from ground to top of cab). The Fiber Glass cab with safety glass windshield (both standard equipment) protects driver from weather and low-hanging branches. This saves thousands of dollars for tree trimming. Four-wheel hydraulic brakes mean sure stops. You can't beat four-wheel stability. Write for complete Mobil Sweeper literature.

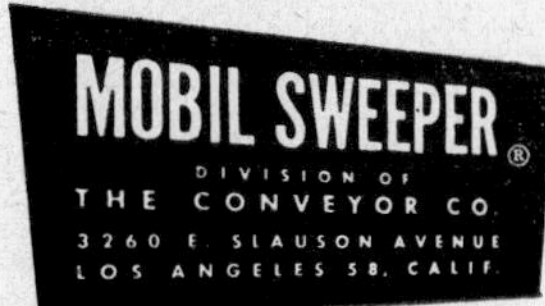

CONSTRUCTION CASTINGS
for
Highway • Municipal • Building
Industrial • Communication
Public Works • Airport
Utilities • Transportation
Patterns for 15,000 different Gray Iron
Castings used on Construction Projects.
Write for our 135-page
Catalog "R," Second Edition
NEENAH FOUNDRY CO.
NEENAH, WISCONSIN
Chicago Office
5445 North Neva Avenue, Chicago 31, Illinois

ROLATAPE, INC.

1741 Fourteenth St., P.O. Box 1190, Santa Monica, Calif.

Manufacturers of Measuring Wheels — Send now for detailed information and prices

---

FOR EVERY MEASURING NEED . . . *FROM 19-INCHES TO 19-MILES . . .*

Rolatape Measuring Wheels make Measuring Easier & Faster

TRAFFIC MODEL 200

Rolatape will save time with **Safety** on all traffic accident investigation measurements, position of vehicles, skid marks, braking distance, general dimensions of streets and intersections.

Rolatape Traffic Model measures and records feet and inches as you walk. Gives accurate total at all times. Line to line, line to curb, curb to curb, also skid marks, straight or curved—accurately and easily taken. Carrying case included.

"Should be included in every Traffic Investigation Kit."

MODEL 200

A compact measuring wheel registers feet and inches

HAS 101 USES outdoors and indoors

The Model 200 is the result of years of development and field testing under all conditions. Can be operated on most surfaces to be encountered anywhere. Traction is provided by two Neoprene tires which are precision ground and specially designed to retain their calibrated accuracy even after many miles of hard usage.

Measures wall to wall as simply as line to line. Total distance is recorded in feet and inches by a built-in totalizer and the recessed scale on circumference. Clearly audible click every two feet permits a running count. Knob permits presetting for a desired distance. Loud bell tone indicates the 100-foot mark. Weights 2¾ lbs., yet withstands hard use.

CARRYING CASE INCLUDED

MODEL 400

FOR LONGER DISTANCES . . . ROUGHER SURFACES . . . 4-FOOT CIRCUMFERENCE . . .

is a favorite for road and construction work, utilities, water and sewage departments. This advanced design, lightweight precision calibrated wheel for accurately measuring distances up to 100,000 feet or almost 19 miles. Registers in feet, but can be counted in 2" or finer, by inspection. Face of counter is in plain view at all times to provide second-by-second measurement of distance travelled. Convenient stand permits data logging without loss of position. Wide tire provides positive traction. Can be operated safely from car window at slow speeds.

Can be had in equipment orange or instrument black.

MODEL 600

FOR CROSS-COUNTRY MEASURING . . . ROUGH TERRAIN . . . 6-FOOT CIRCUMFERENCE

Largest model in the Rolatape line, Model 600, can be used for estimating or plotting extremely long line or conduit distances where very rough terrain poses particular traction problems. Six foot circumference wheel measures up to 100,000 feet or almost 19 miles. Face of counter is in plain view at all times to provide second-by-second measurement of distance travelled. Designed primarily for foot operation in surveying, location of points, map checking, etc. over long distances and rough terrain.

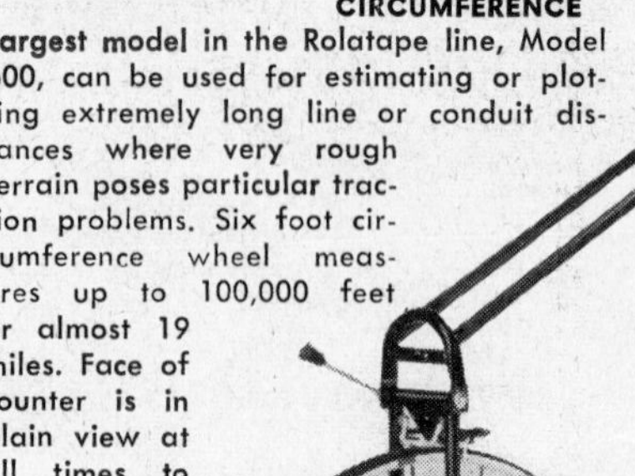

NOW—A universal Rear Mount Hitch For Rolatape #600 Permits its use with Car, Jeep, or Tractor.

Can be had in equipment orange or instrument black.

WAUSAU IRON WORKS, INC.

Pioneer Snow Plow Builders

Wausau, Wis.

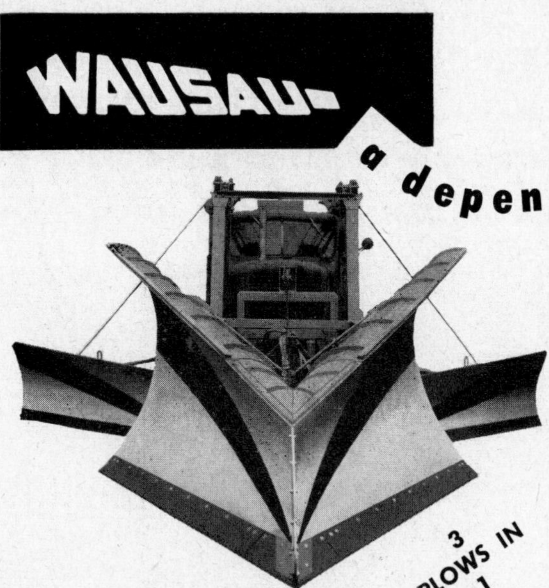

a dependable name in . . .

★ SNOW PLOWS
★ MATERIAL SPREADERS
★ ICE PLANERS

The new WAUSAU 3-Way Plow is the first major snow plow improvement in years . . . gives you three snow plows for one investment. It is the new approach to snow removal where plowing with the wind is desirable and discharge to either the right or left is necessary . . . plus the insurance of a Vee. Cab controlled power hydraulics allow operator to position the plow to a one-way left discharge, a one-way right discharge, or a Vee. Another WAUSAU innovation is power controlled deflector to shape the moldboard to suit the snow conditions.

TRUCK PATROL-ICE PLANER

For year 'round maintenance . . . for roads, streets, airports, the WAUSAU Truck Patrol-Ice Planer maintains, cuts and grades all types of gravel and dirt roads, eliminates ruts, holes and washboards. For winter operation it planes, breaks and removes ice and hard-packed snow hazards from highways, streets and airports . . . truly a versatile year 'round maintenance unit that maintains roads, streets and airports at speeds fom 6 to 20 miles per hour. Full power hydraulic control from the cab permits operator to reverse, tilt and rotate the working blade to the best operating position for all conditions. For performance, versatility, dependability, low maintenance and operational cost the WAUSAU Truck Patrol-Ice Planer is the answer.

WAUSAU MATERIAL SPREADERS

The WAUSAU Model RT-1 Material Spreader is the result of a three-year development program to design a full power hydraulic speader which would handle all ice control materials with a minimum of maintenance cost and down-time. To eliminate the troublesome conveyor, a hydraulically controlled ejector plate within the spreader box propels the entire mass of material forward to the point of discharge as required. Simple and positive speed settings for both feed auger and spinner allow exact control of the amount of material and width of spread. Check these features, You will find them all in no other material spreader: • Positive ejection, • Self-cleaning body, • exact control of spinner speeds, • One man cab control, • Low loading height and low center of gravity, • WAUSAU rugged construction.

Write for complete details **- WAUSAU SNOW PLOWS - WAUSAU SPREADERS**

SOLD and SERVICED By LEADING EQUIPMENT DISTRIBUTORS

A. REED WILSON COMPANY

1320 McGee Street, Kansas City 6, Missouri

REPRESENTED BY:

Municipal Services Inc.
1 Jackson Street
Worcester 8, Mass.
PLeasant 4-6542

Rudolph "Rudy" Blick
Albee Building
1426 G Street, N.W.,
Washington 5, D.C.
REpublic 7-2271

Riner Corporation
8 So. Michigan Blvd.
Chicago 3, Illinois
FRanklin 2-3305

Ray Cooksey
635 West Morgan
Rialto, California

NO TRAFFIC TIE-UP

FAST
SAFE
ECONOMICAL
PRACTICAL
PATENTED

when you resurface streets using the WB

*"MANHOLE ADAPTER"**

Traffic can be moving normally only four hours after completion of the project. Masonry does not have to be rebuilt. This easy-to-install, safe, economical, patented adapter ring does the job in a fraction of the time required by other methods. . . .

You need ALL the startling facts. Mail blueprints of your standard manhole ring and cover, and tell us the elevation or amount of resurfacing material to be used.

* Registered U. S. Patent Office

SEND FOR NEW BROCHURE

HOMELITE

a division of Textron Inc.

Carryable *Pumps, Generators, Chain Saws and Blowers*

Port Chester, New York

HOMELITE CHAIN SAWS

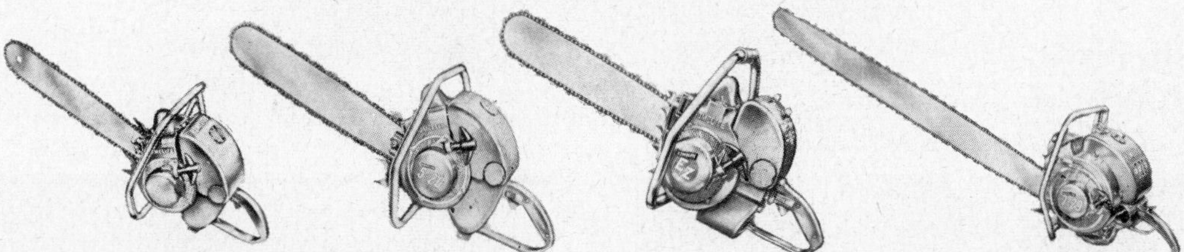

MODEL 17 . . . an all purpose saw that brings down trees up to 4 feet in diameter. 3½ horsepower, 20 pounds. Attachments for complete versatility.

MODEL EZ . . . lightest, most powerful direct drive chain saw ever developed. Only 19 pounds, full 5 horsepower. Brings down trees 3 feet in diameter.

MODEL 5-20 . . . all the versatility of the 17 with added power. 5 full horsepower—20 pounds. Brings down trees up to 6 feet in diameter.

MODEL 7-29 . . . the most powerful one man chain saw you can own. 7 full horsepower, 29 pounds. Cuts down trees up to 10 feet in diameter.

Homelite gasoline-engine-driven chain saws are precision built for every chain saw job—from production cutting to harvesting a woodlot. They pack more power into less weight than any other chain saws available. With perfectly balanced construction, they're easy to handle in any terrain . . . and you can depend on fast starts, smooth performance in any climate.

Homelite Chain Saws make every type of cut from all angles and positions—left, right, up, down, and upside down.

These attachments give HOMELITE CHAIN SAWS Complete Versatility

Clearing Attachment—makes your 17 or 5-20 Saw a fast-cutting clearing tool. With this clearing bar you can plunge cut tough saplings and small trees up to 8 inches in diameter without bending or stooping.

Brush-Cutter—converts your Homelite 17 or 5-20 into an easy-to-operate power brush saw in minutes. Clears land of brush or dense undergrowth six times faster than hand methods.

Plunge Cut Bows—14 and 18 inch—for pulp production cutting. Won't bind in any cut . . . gives lowest stump in felling . . . eliminates lifting while bucking sticks. Available for Homelite 17, 5-20 and 7-29 saws.

HOMELITE Alternating Current GENERATORS

115 Volt 60 Cycle Single Phase Gasoline Engine Driven

You can speed work and save money . . . day and night . . . with these Homelite Carryable Generators. They operate powerful flood lights plus cost-cutting AC and Standard Universal power tools. Small, compact and light in weight, they're easy to get to the job. And they're highly dependable on the job. A Homelite starts quickly in any temperature. Air cooled engine can't freeze or overheat. Not affected by rain, snow, ice or dust. Has large overload capacity and automatic voltage control for varying load conditions.

Model 35A115
1500 Watts, 115 Volt 60 cycle AC.
Weight—90 pounds

Model 24A115
2500 Watts
115 volt, 60 cycle AC
Weight—135 pounds

HOMELITE Dual-Voltage A. C. GENERATORS

115-230 Volt 60 Cycle 1 Phase Alternating Current Gasoline Engine Driven

Model 24A115/230 2500 Watts
Weight—137 pounds

Homelite Dual-Voltage Generators have a dual output of both 115 and 230 volt alternating current. They will operate both 115 volt and 230 volt electric tools or equipment . . . provide emergency power for communications and essential equipment when normal power fails.

Model 32A115/230 5000 Watts
Weight—228 pounds

HOMELITE Dual-Purpose High-Cycle GENERATORS

Model 24HY
Capacity—
2500 watts
Weight—135 lbs.

Homelite's Dual-Purpose High-Cycle Generator has a dual output of 230 volt, 180 cycle, 3-phase alternating current and 110 volt, direct current. With one generator you can operate lighter weight, more efficient, high-cycle tools as well as standard, universal power tools and floodlights. Small, compact, and lightweight, this generator is easily and quickly put into operation anywhere it is needed.

HOMELITE High-Cycle Concrete Vibrator

- *Simple, rugged construction*
- *Can be handled by one man*
- *Long service life, low maintenance costs*
- *Faster placement of concrete*

One man can place concrete faster, easier, and more profitably than ever before with a Homelite high-cycle electric concrete vibrator. The Homelite high-cycle generator stays on ground out from under foot and away from pouring operation. No special scaffolds or cradles needed. You can handle 30-40 cubic yards of 2-inch slump concrete per hour with this vibrator. Tough kink-proof hose cannot be injured by bending . . . rugged, high cycle motor built into vibrator head will give long profitable service at lowest maintenance cost.

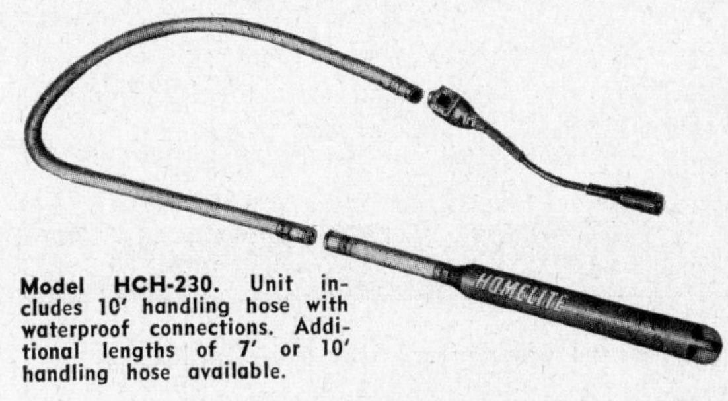

Model HCH-230. Unit includes 10′ handling hose with waterproof connections. Additional lengths of 7′ or 10′ handling hose available.

---

115 Volt AC-DC Concrete Vibrator

In addition to the high-cycle vibrator, Homelite also has a 115 volt AC-DC vibrator for working concrete in small forms, re-inforced concrete columns, and in other "tight spots." Weighing only 32 pounds complete, it can be carried and used anywhere by one man. It will operate from either a standard 115 volt "house" current or from a low cost Homelite carryable generator.

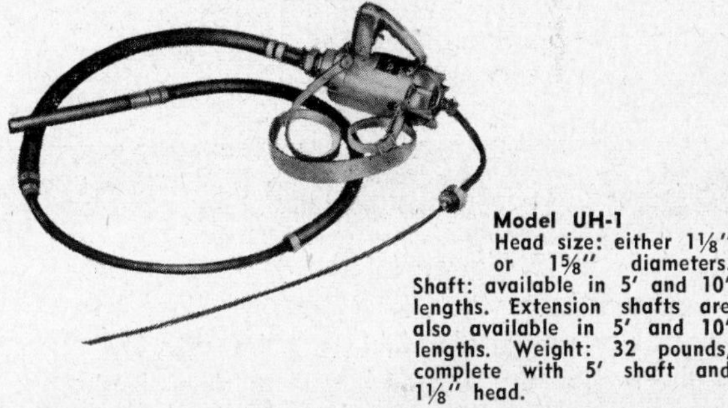

Model UH-1
Head size: either 1⅛″ or 1⅝″ diameters. Shaft: available in 5′ and 10′ lengths. Extension shafts are also available in 5′ and 10′ lengths. Weight: 32 pounds, complete with 5′ shaft and 1⅛″ head.

BOSCH (Germany) High-Cycle ELECTRIC TOOLS

These tools, imported from Germany and sold exclusively by Homelite in the United States, are real cost-cutters on any job. They combine low initial cost with low operating cost. Lightweight and simple in design, they give performance equal to bulky, expensive compressed air equipment. Operation is by high-cycle power from a Homelite dual purpose generator.

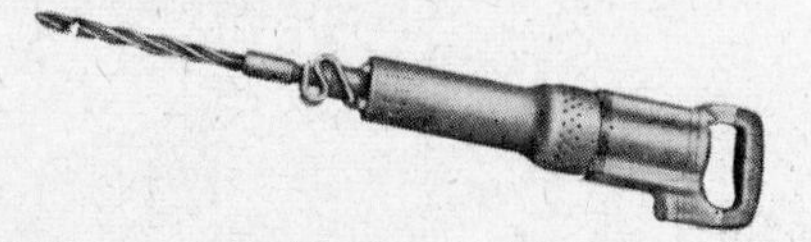

Rock Drill—equipped with pressure blower. Weights: Drill—65 pounds. Blower—20 pounds.

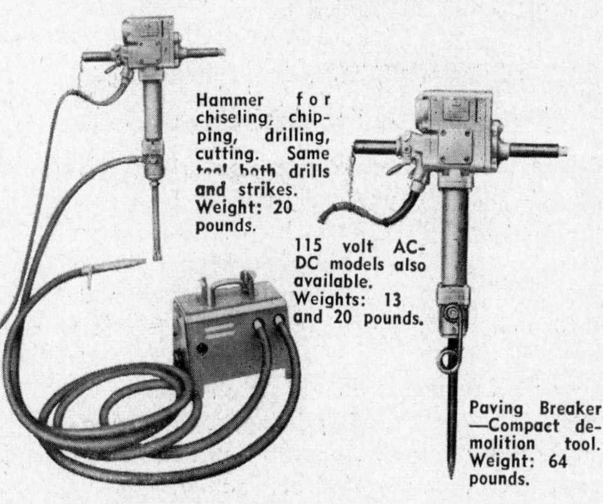

Hammer for chiseling, chipping, drilling, cutting. Same tool both drills and strikes. Weight: 20 pounds.

115 volt AC-DC models also available. Weights: 13 and 20 pounds.

Paving Breaker—Compact demolition tool. Weight: 64 pounds.

HOMELITE Floodlights

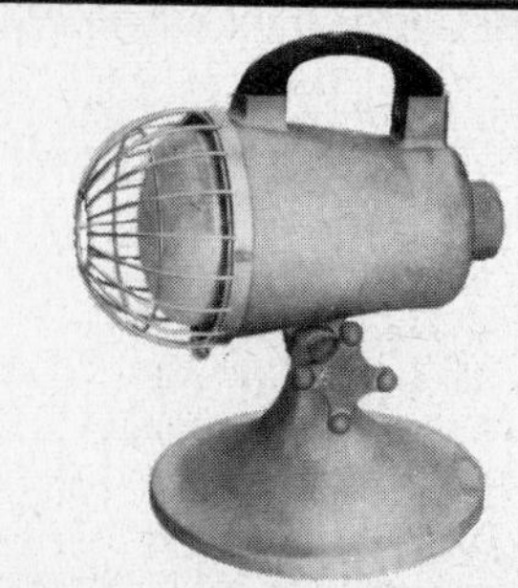

Homelite cast aluminum floodlights answer the demand for lightweight, sealed-beam floodlights which are low in cost and built for tough service in any weather. *Twistlock* connector fastens cable tightly to floodlight during use. One twist disconnects for storage or transportation . . . never any tangle of cable around light. Both 300 or 500 watt models available.

HOMELITE High-Cycle Electric CHAIN SAW

Operates on power from Homelite Dual-Purpose Generator. Weighing only 17 pounds, this saw is ideal for aerial cutting in trees as well as for felling, bucking and clearing. Cuts extremely fast. Simple to operate. Requires only a minimum of maintenance.

HOMELITE Carryable BLOWER

The HOMELITE Blower (Model 20B) may be used as either a blower or an exhaust fan. An 8-inch non-collapsible duct may be attached at the suction opening and used to draw bad air or noxious gases from a tank or manhole. The duct can then be attached at the discharge opening to blow fresh air into the tank or manhole. Lightweight and compact, this unit can easily be carried to any location.

DIAPHRAGM PUMP

This new 3 inch gasoline-engine-driven diaphragm pump is specifically designed for continuous heavy duty work. It will dewater an area at a 5000 gph clip, then keep right on going to handle seepage in the thickest mud, muck and sand. And it gets to the job fast over the roughest terrain—weighs only 120 pounds. Operates 6 hours on one gallon of fuel . . . fast, automatic priming . . . non-clogging construction . . . operates efficiently and economically in any kind of weather.

Model 20DP3-1 Diaphragm Pump. Suction 3". Discharge 3". Automatic priming—primes dry up to 15'. Weight (complete with built-in engine): 120 pounds. Capacity: 5000 gallons per hour.

HOMELITE Carryable PUMPS GASOLINE ENGINE DRIVEN

Self-Priming Centrifugal Pumps

Homelite pumps are fast-action pumps . . . pumps that one man can pick up, carry, and put into operation quickly and easily, any place. Quick starting in any temperature, a Homelite gives you the fastest possible self-priming. Has a guaranteed 28 foot suction lift and large on-the-job capacity. Keeps seepage automatically at strainer level. Handles water thick with mud and sand without lubrication problems and is rainproof, dustproof, foolproof.

Model 20S1½
Suction 1½"—Discharge 1½"
Capacity: 5500 gals. per hr.
Weight: 45 pounds

Model 23S2
Suction 2"—Discharge 2"
Capacity: 10,000 gals. per hr.
Weight: 85 pounds

Model 24S3
Suction 3"—Discharge 3"
Capacity: 15,000 gals. per hr.
Weight: 95 pounds

Variable Speed Pump

Model 36S2
This quiet, Homelite pump is ideal for work at night or in residential areas. Its hushed operation, even at full throttle (2650 rpm, no load), is still more impressive when throttled down to 1500 rpm. Suction: 2". Discharge: 2". Capacity: 9000 gallons per hour. Weight: 87 pounds.

Pressure Pump

Model 24S3-1P
Use this new Homelite pump for any job that requires dependable, high-volume, pressure pumping. Capacity: 55 gallons per minute at 70 psi . . . 205 gpm at open discharge. Suction 3". Weight: 107 pounds.

HOMELITE FIELD SERVICE

Homelite sales and service factory branches are located throughout the country. Before you even buy a Homelite unit, this field service works for you. Homelite representatives are always handy and ready to show by actual demonstration on your job exactly what a Homelite can do for you. Then, after you become a Homelite user, these men—service men as well as salesmen—are always available, ready and willing, to keep your Homelites running at top performance at all times and with the least possible trouble to you. To get quick Homelite action, write, wire or phone our factory or your nearest Homelite representative.

HOMELITE • Port Chester, New York
A Division of Textron American, Inc.

BRANCH OFFICES

California: Fresno, Los Angeles, Sacramento, and San Francisco
Colorado: Denver
Connecticut: Byram and Hartford
Florida: Jacksonville
Georgia: Atlanta
Illinois: Bloomington, Chicago (Stone Park)
Indiana: Indianapolis
Louisiana: New Orleans (Metairie) and Shreveport (Bossier City)
Maine: Orono
Maryland: Baltimore
Massachusetts: Boston (Allston)
Michigan: Detroit, Grand Rapids and Saginaw
Minnesota: St. Paul
Mississippi: Jackson
Missouri: Kansas City and St. Louis
Nebraska: Omaha
New Jersey: North Arlington and Woodbridge
New York: Albany, Buffalo, New York (North Arlington, N. J.), Port Chester, Rochester, Syracuse, and West Hempstead
North Carolina: Charlotte
Ohio: Cincinnati, Cleveland and Toledo
Oklahoma: Oklahoma City
Oregon: Portland
Pennsylvania: Altoona, Erie, Harrisburg, Hazelton, Malvern, Philadelphia and Pittsburgh
South Carolina: Columbia
Tennessee: Memphis and Knoxville
Texas: Dallas, Houston, Lufkin, Silsbee and Tyler
Utah: North Salt Lake City
Vermont: Brandon
Virginia: Arlington, Richmond and Roanoke
Washington: Seattle, Spokane and Tacoma
Washington, D. C.: (Arlington, Va.)
West Virginia: Charleston
Wisconsin: Milwaukee

Water Works Equipment

BARRETT DIVISION

ALLIED CHEMICAL & DYE CORPORATION

40 Rector Street, New York 6, N. Y.

COAL-TAR ENAMELS and COATINGS

PRODUCTS. Barrett Waterworks Enamel, a coal-tar base enamel for coating and lining steel waterlines; Barrett Pipeline Enamels, Barrett AA Enamel, Barrett Millwrap Enamel, Barrett 34 Yb Enamel, Barrett Hotline Enamel—all used for gas, oil or other transmission lines; Barrett Eternium* Paint for exposed metal work; Barrett Industrial Coating for heavy duty or more corrosive conditions; Barrett C.A.-50 Cold Coating; Barrett 34 Yb Cold Coating for metal septic tanks and for exposure to salt water spray conditions; Coal-Tar Saturated Asbestos Pipeline Felt (Plain, Perforated or Glass Reinforced) for auxiliary pipeline coating or wrapping; Barrett Sewer Joint Compound and Cold Application Service Materials.

TECHNICAL LITERATURE AND REFERENCE MANUALS

Technical literature and descriptive bulletins on Barrett Protective Coatings are available free to municipal engineers, water department officials and others. Let us know your problem and we will send you the appropriate literature.

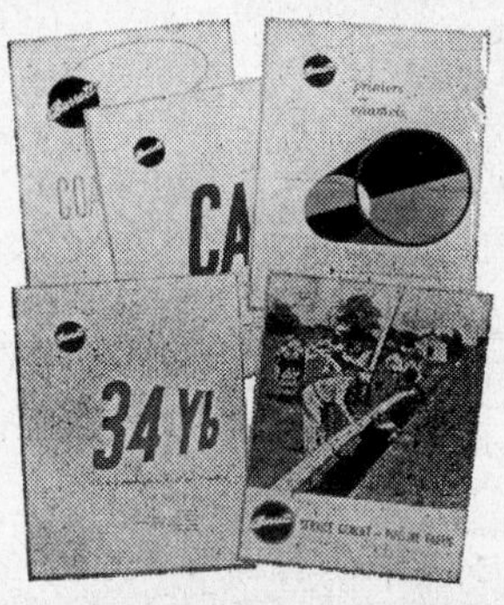

Barrett Protective Coatings protect 25-mile length of new 56-66-inch Bull Run water pipeline, Portland, Oregon.

10 ADVANTAGES OF BARRETT WATERWORKS ENAMEL

1. Meets every requirement of the American Water Works Association's Standard Specifications for Coal-tar Enamel Protective Coatings for Steel Water Pipe.

2. Prevents tuberculation and incrustation of interiors.

3. Protects pipeline exterior against corrosion, permitting use of thin-wall, lighter weight steel pipe.

4. High dielectric properties.

5. Impermeable to moisture, non-absorptive, non-porous.

6. High ductility and flexibility, low friction drag.

7. Unusual tenacity, high cohesive forces assure firm bond at the interfaces.

8. Meets every pipe-coating need . . . under all types of climatic conditions and topography.

9. Available through applicators all over the country.

10. Barrett engineering and technical service available without obligation.

*Reg. U. S. Pat. Off.

CLOW CAST

FITTINGS • VALVES •

FOR UNDERGROUND LINES

Mechanical Joint

...manufactured to current ASA, AWWA, and Federal Specifications, for underground water and gas service. Complete line of fittings and accessories meets all requirements. Sizes 3″ through 24″.

Bell and Spigot

... wherever calked joints are desired. Manufactured to current specifications with a complete line of fittings—both ASA short body, and AWWA long pattern. Sizes 3″ through 24″.

Roll-On Joint

... for water and sewage under pressure. Rubber-sealed joint, used with mechanical joint or all bell calking fittings. Cast to Federal Specifications. Sizes 3 through 24 inches.

EVERYTHING FOR THE

BIRMINGHAM PLANT

Sales offices

BIRMINGHAM 2, ALA.
CHICAGO 80, ILLINOIS
CLEVELAND 14, OHIO
COLUMBUS 12, OHIO
DALLAS 6, TEXAS
DES MOINES 10, IA.
DETROIT, 2, MICH.
HOUSTON 6, TEXAS
JACKSONVILLE BEACH, FLA.
KANSAS CITY 5, MO.
MINNEAPOLIS 2, MINN.
NASHVILLE 12, TENN.
NEW YORK 6, N. Y.
OSHKOSH, WIS.
PITTSBURGH 28, PA.
RIPON, WIS.
ST. LOUIS 24, MO.
SOUTH BEND 1, IND.

Catalog on request

EDDY VALVE COMPANY

A Subsidiary of James B. Clow & Sons, Inc.

WATERFORD, NEW YORK

---

you can rely on EDDY
to supply all your needs!

EDDY VALVES and HYDRANTS

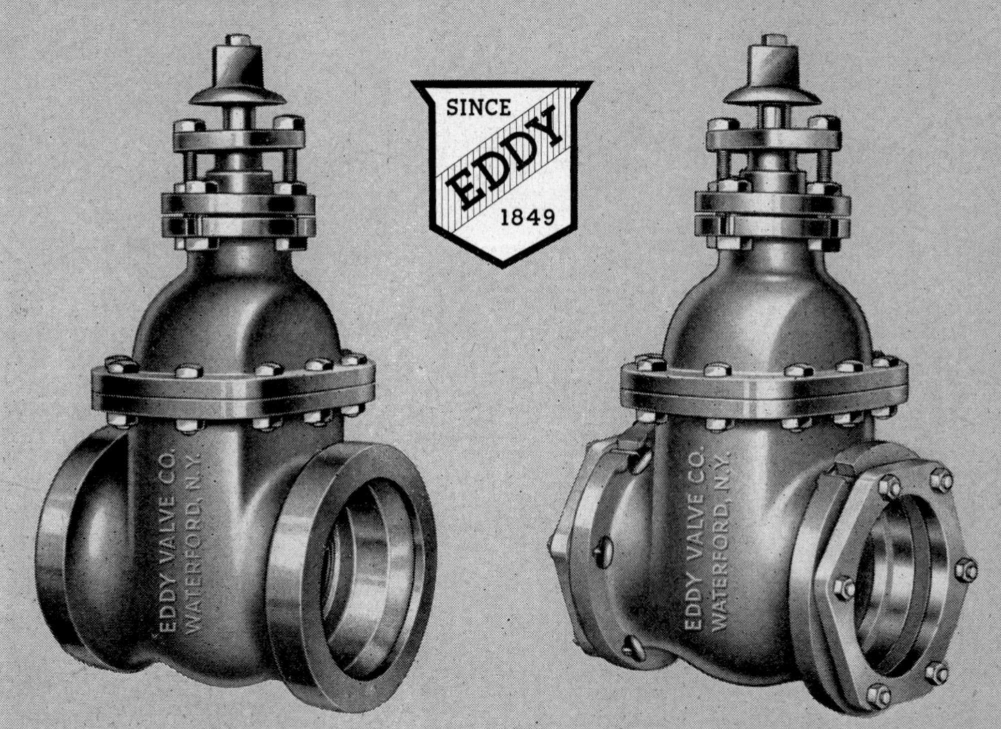

AWWA (UNDERGROUND) VALVES

Everything in AWWA valves for underground use in your waterworks system is quickly available from Eddy—gate valves; cutting-in valves and sleeves; tapping valves and sleeves. And, remember, Eddy's more than 100 years' dependable operation is your assurance of service far into the future.

EDDY VALVE COMPANY

A Subsidiary of James B. Clow & Sons, Inc.

WATERFORD, NEW YORK

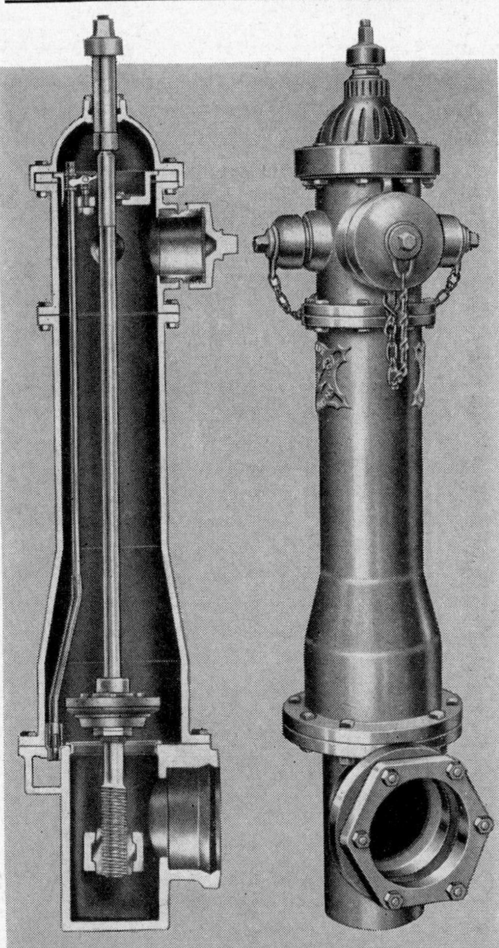

WHATEVER you need . . . call on Eddy. A large selection of valves furnished for special application.

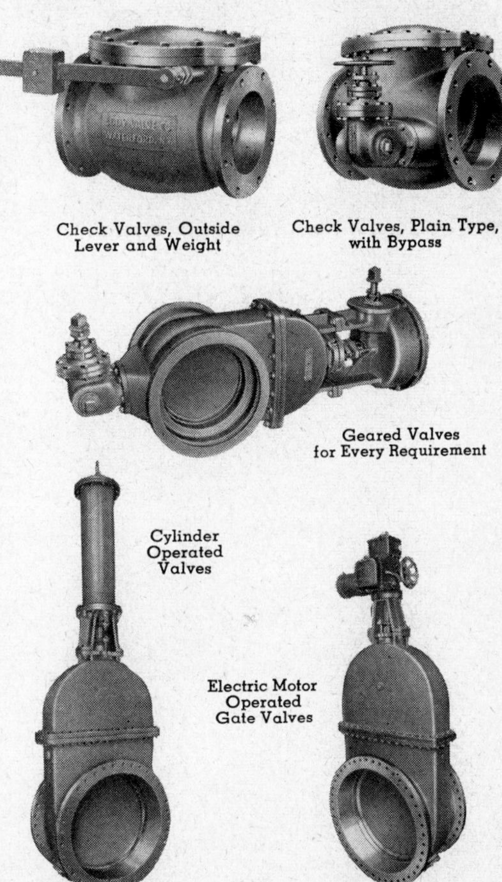

Check Valves, Outside Lever and Weight

Check Valves, Plain Type, with Bypass

Geared Valves for Every Requirement

Cylinder Operated Valves

Electric Motor Operated Gate Valves

AWWA EDDY BRONZE-MOUNTED HYDRANTS

EDDY Bronze-Mounted HYDRANTS open smoothly with the pressure and close without water hammer. One man can easily remove all operating mechanism for inspection and repair. Positive drip action automatically drains the standpipe, safeguarding against freeze-ups. Stem held in place below hydrant valve means that there is no water loss due to a bent stem.

Send today for full data on the complete line of Eddy Valves, Hydrants, and other waterworks' necessities. No obligation.

EDDY VALVE COMPANY

A Subsidiary of James B. Clow & Sons, Inc.

WATERFORD, NEW YORK

IOWA VALVE COMPANY

OSKALOOSA, IOWA

A subsidiary of James B. Clow & Sons, Inc.

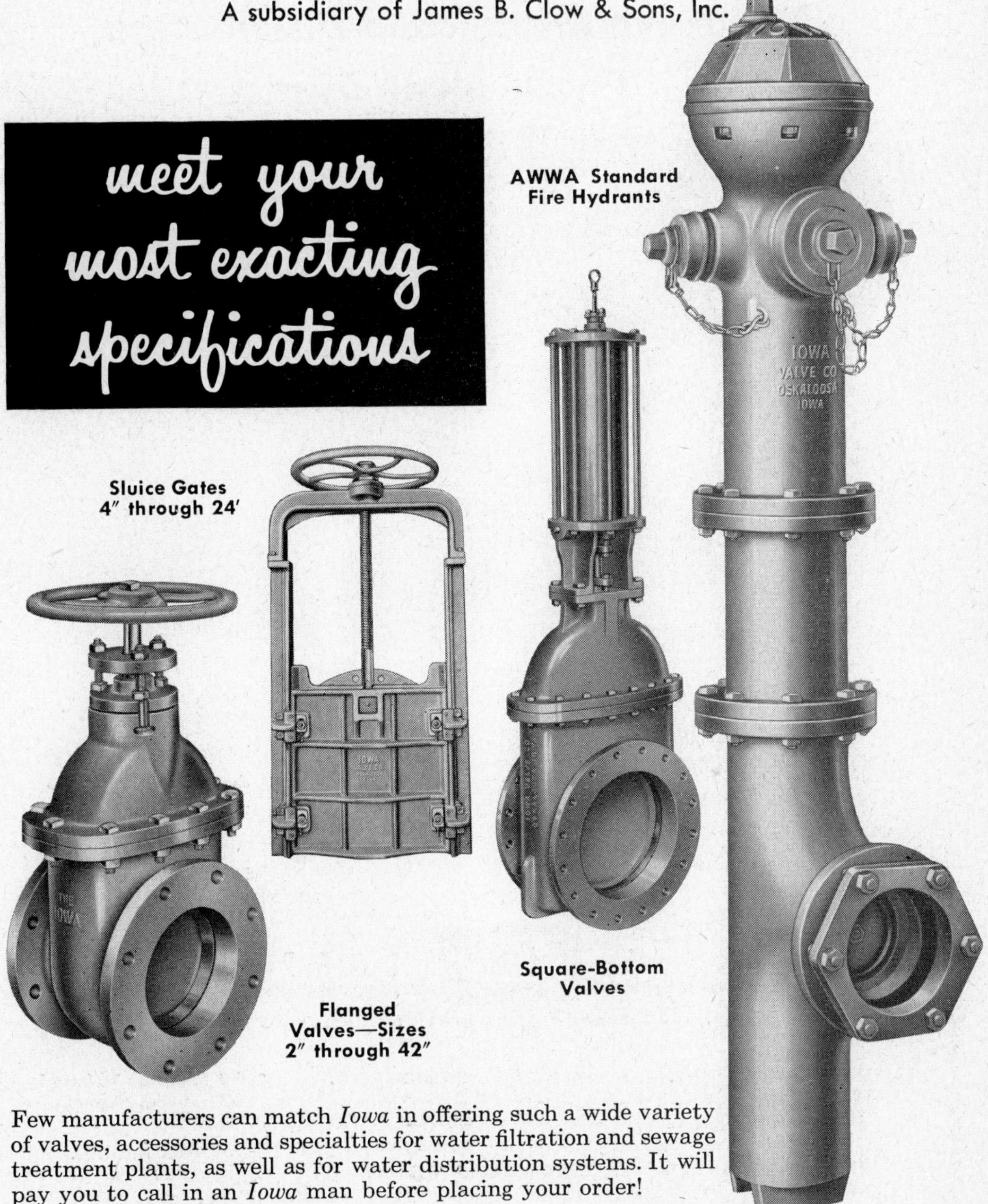

IOWA VALVE COMPANY

Oskaloosa, Iowa

TO BETTER SERVE YOU—

We Have Established Distribution Points Near By—

To better serve the many Ferri-Floc users throughout the country, we have appointed distributors at strategic points to better serve this ever expanding market. We are proud of these outstanding distributors. Their service is at your disposal. Contact your nearest distributor for faster, more efficient delivery and service on Ferri-Floc.

Free Booklet—

Let us send you without charge a 38-page booklet that deals specifically with all phases of coagulation. Send card to—

TENNESSEE  **CORPORATION**

617-629 Grant Building, Atlanta, Georgia

BARTLETT CHEMICALS, INC.
1460 South Peters Street
New Orleans, La.

•

BENLO CHEMICALS
1907-25 South 89th St.
Milwaukee, Wis.

•

FASEY & BESTHOFF, INC.
325 Spring Street
New York, N. Y.

THE HERBERT CHEMICALS CO.
Vine St. and Murray Road
Cincinnati, Ohio

•

LYON CHEMICALS, INC.
2305 Hampden Avenue
St. Paul, Minn.

•

THOMPSON-HEYWARD CHEMICALS, INC.
121 W. Pershing Road
Chicago, Ill.

29th & Southwest Boulevard
Kansas City, Missouri

36 North Guthrie St.
Tulsa, Okla.

5 Carr Street
St. Louis, Missouri

2600 Crockett St.
Houston, Texas

ALABAMA PIPE COMPANY

General Offices — General Sales Office

P. O. BOX 791 Anniston, Alabama PHONE, ADAMS 6-7601

Cast Iron Super-DeLavaud, Centrifugally Cast in Metal Molds in 18 Foot Lengths

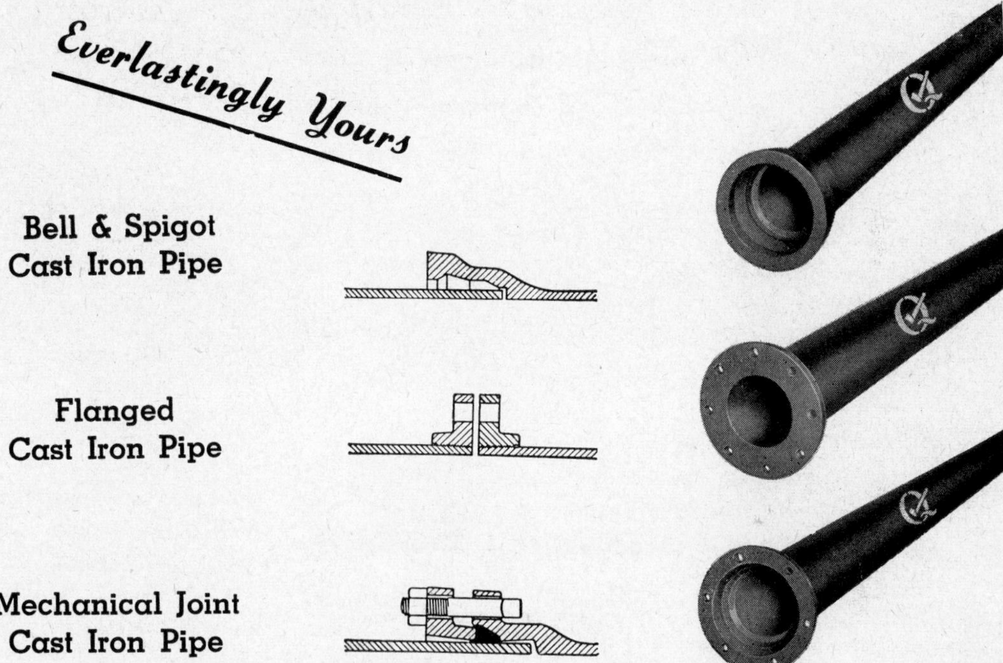

There are many cities in the United States and other countries with records of a century or more of cast iron pipe service. "APCO" cast iron water and gas main is available in sizes 3" through 24" diameters.

For further information, write for our catalogues or contact our nearest sales office.

Cast Iron fittings and special castings for every use. Cast Iron Service, Roadway, Valve and Meter Boxes, Manhole Frames & Covers and Special Municipal Castings.

SERVICE BOX

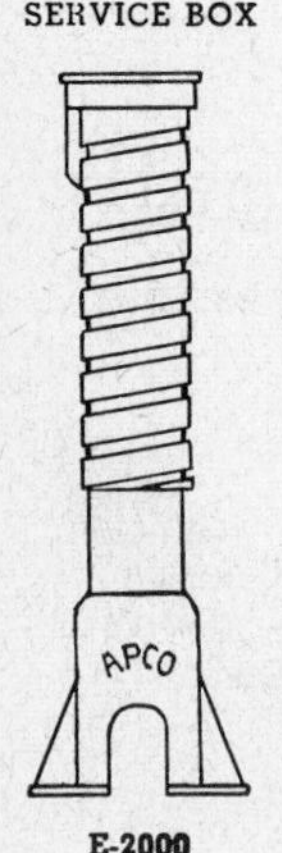

E-2000

Service Boxes

With 2½" or 3" Shaft

For ½" to 1½" Stop Cocks. Enlarged bases for 2" Stop Cocks. We also manufacture a complete line of special Service Boxes required by various cities.

SQUARE HEAD LOCK BOX

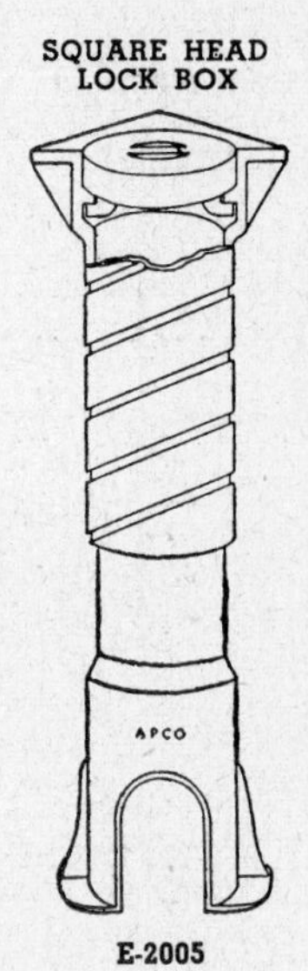

E-2005

FLANGE BASE ROADWAY BOX

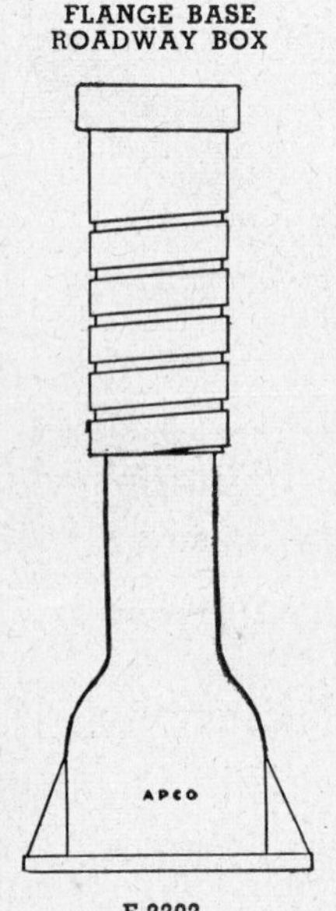

E-2202

Roadway Boxes

With 4¼" Shaft

For 1" to 3" Valves in various trench depths.

We also offer our Square Head Roadway Boxes and special patterns if required.

OPEN BASE ROADWAY BOX

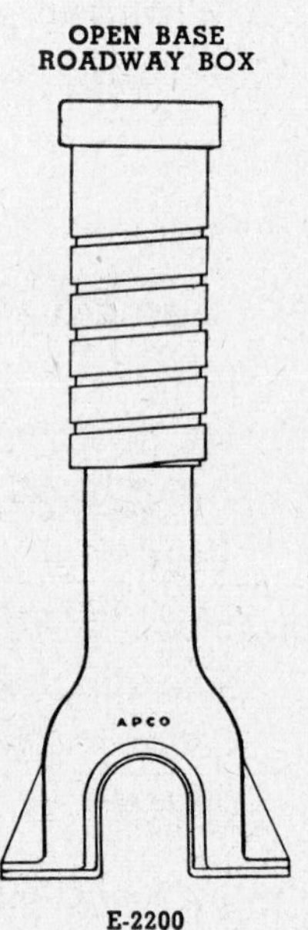

E-2200

WRITE FOR BULLETIN 2000

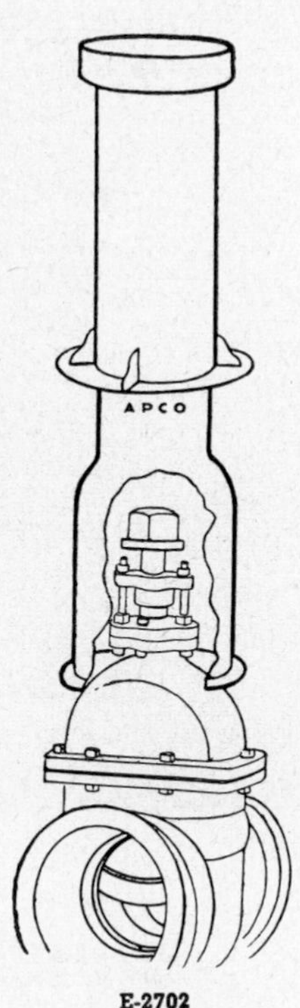

E-2702

Valve Boxes

With 5¼" Shaft

For 3" to 20" valves in various trench depths.

Two-piece slip type boxes E-2702 very popular for sizes up to 10".

Three-piece screw type boxes E-3002 with separate bases for 3" to 20" valves.

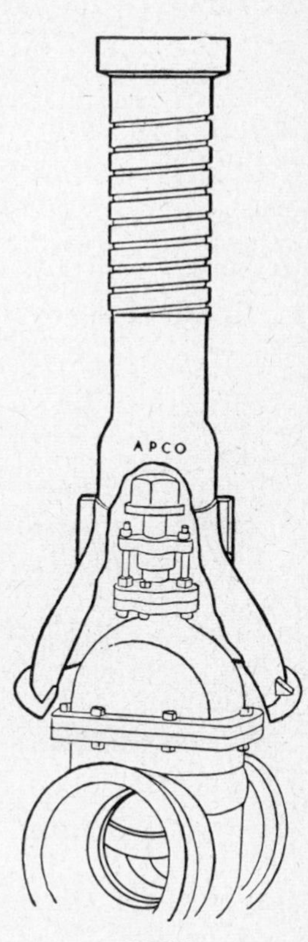

E-3002

APCO Manhole Frames and Covers

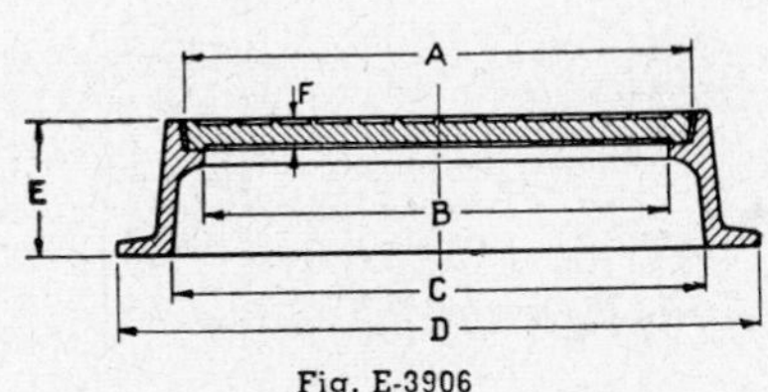

Fig. E-3906

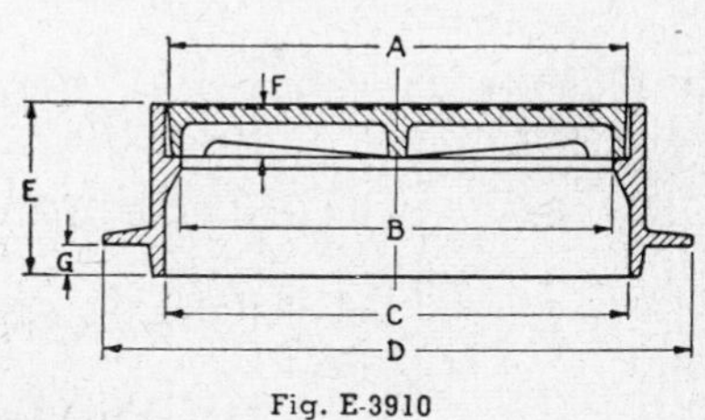

Fig. E-3910

We have many designs of Manhole Frames and covers to meet the requirements of various cities.

WRITE FOR BULLETIN 2000

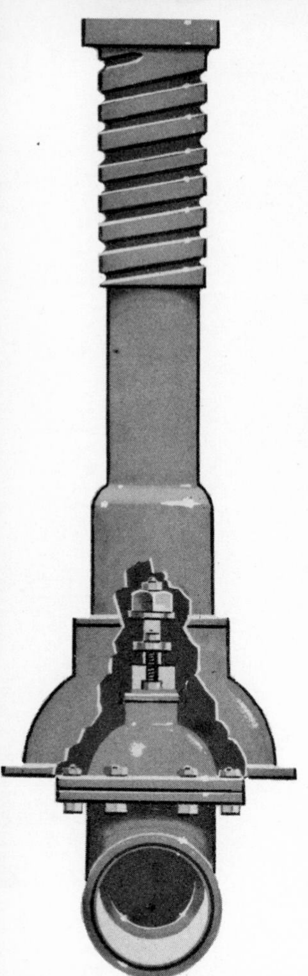

THREE-PIECE SCREW TYPE ADJUSTABLE VALVE BOXES

"Buffalo" three-piece valve boxes are the result of many years experience in the water and gas field. "Buffalo" boxes are heavy and rugged in construction — designed for life-time service under modern traffic conditions. These late model "Buffalo" boxes are interchangeable with earlier "Buffalo" models.

5¼-Inch Shaft

Size	Extension
AAA	17 in. stationary length
AA	1 ft. 10 in. to 2 ft. 4 in.
A	2 ft. 4 in. to 3 ft. 4 in.
B	3 ft. to 4 ft.
C	3 ft. 6 in. to 4 ft. 6 in.
CC	4 ft. to 5 ft.
D	3 ft. 6 in. to 5 ft. 6 in.
E	4 ft. to 6 ft.
F	5 ft. to 7 ft.
G	6 ft. to 8 ft.

7-Inch Shaft

Size	Extension
II	1 ft. 9 in. to 2 ft. 3 in.
I	2 ft. 3 in. to 3 ft. 3 in.
J	2 ft. 9 in. to 3 ft. 9 in.
K	3 ft. 3 in. to 4 ft. 3 in.
L	3 ft. 3 in. to 5 ft.
M	5 ft. to 6 ft.
O	6 ft. to 7 ft.
P	6 ft. to 8 ft.

VALVE BOX BASES

1. No. 4 round base, for 4-inch valves or smaller. Inside diameter at bottom, 10⅞ inches; height, 8 inches. Makes valve box 3 inches shorter than No. 6.
2. No. 6 round base, for 8-inch round valves or smaller. This is the standard size used in quoting lengths and prices. Diameter inside at bottom, 14⅜ inches; height, 11 inches. Unless otherwise specified, No. 6 will be shipped on all orders.
3. No. 160 oval base, for 16-inch valves or smaller. Bottom diameter inside, 21x12½ inches; height, 9½ inches. Makes valve box 1½ inches shorter than No. 6.

1.

2.

3.

EXTENSIONS

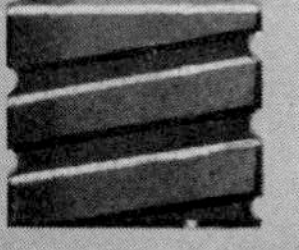

These sturdy extensions for screw-type boxes come in either 5¼ inch or 7 inch shaft—increasing the length of either size by 14 inches.

5¼ in. shaft—No. 58

7 in. shaft—No. 71

RODS AND RINGS

Rods and Guide Rings for any length 2½ or 3 inch box shaft and combination 18" and 27" keys are available. We will be happy to make any special rods upon request.

EXTENSION SERVICE BOXES

FOR WATER OR GAS

2½-Inch Shaft

Size	Extension
89-A	1 ft. to 1 ft. 8 in.
90-B	1 ft. 6 in. to 2 ft. 2 in.
91-C	1 ft. 9 in. to 2 ft. 9 in.
92-C	2 ft. to 3 ft. 2 in.
92-D	2 ft. to 3 ft. 6 in.
93-D	3 ft. to 4 ft.
93-E	3 ft. to 4 ft. 6 in.
94-D	3 ft. 6 in. to 4 ft. 9 in.
94-E	3 ft. 6 in. to 5 ft.
95-E	4 ft. to 5 ft. 6 in.
100-E	4 ft. 6 in. to 6 ft.
100-F	4 ft. 6 in. to 6 ft. 6 in.
95-G	4 ft. to 7 ft.
100-G	4 ft. 6 in. to 7 ft. 6 in.

3-Inch Shaft

Size No.	Extension
0	Stationary length 10 in.
1	1 ft. 1 in. to 1 ft. 9½ in.
1½	1 ft. 6 in. to 2 ft. 4 in.
2	2 ft. to 3 ft. 3 in.
3	2 ft. 8 in. to 4 ft.
4	2 ft. 10 in. to 4 ft. 10 in.
5	3 ft. 6 in. to 5 ft. 6 in.
7	4 ft. to 6 ft.

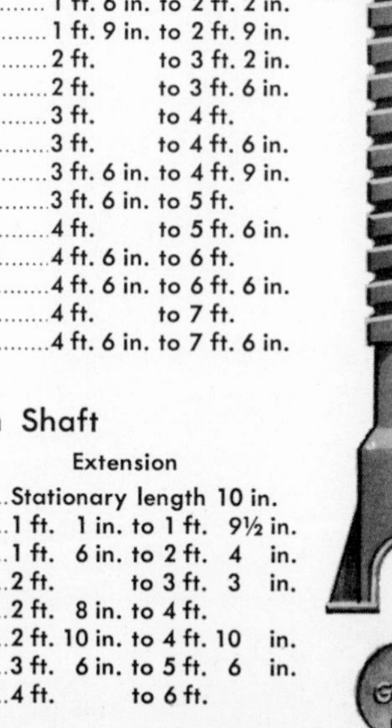

TWO-PIECE ADJUSTABLE VALVE BOXES

Our two-piece sliding type valve boxes — designed to cover the stuffing boxes of valves — are rapidly becoming the favorite two-piece boxes of water and gas companies throughout the country.

The two-piece screw-type boxes — extra heavily constructed — have the same adjustment features as our three-piece boxes — but are designed to cover stuffing boxes of small valves — rather than the larger valves accommodated by our three-piece boxes.

Heavy water covers — cast with "gas" or "water" are included with either of above boxes.

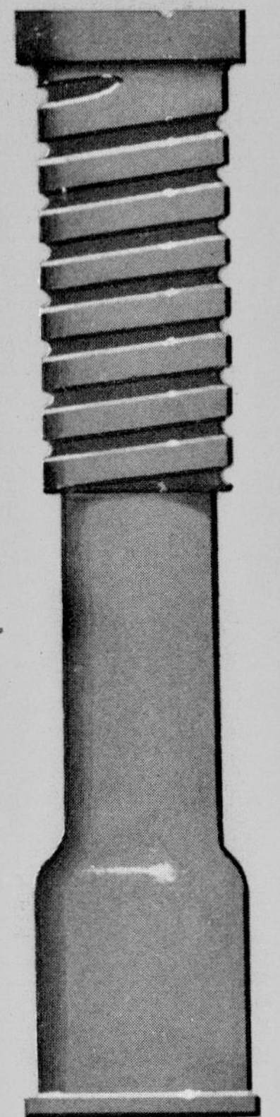

SLIDING TYPE

5¼ - Inch Shaft

Size	Extension
5562-S	2 ft. to 3 ft.
5564-S	3 ft. to 4 ft.
5662-S	2 ft. 6 in. to 4 ft.
5664-S	3 ft. to 5 ft.
5666-S	4 ft. to 6 ft.
5668-S	5 ft. to 7 ft.

SCREW TYPE

5¼ - Inch Shaft

Size	Extension
20	2 ft. to 3 ft.
21	3 ft. to 4 ft.
22	3 ft. to 5 ft.
23	4 ft. to 6 ft.
24	5 ft. to 7 ft.
25	6 ft. to 8 ft.

ROADWAY BOXES

These boxes are made to cover valves up to 3" in size — and are extra heavy for use on streets and highways under heavy traffic conditions. Either round or square tops —with the bottom made to fit either over valve or around pipe.

ROUND HEAD

4¼-Inch Shaft With Open Base

Size	Extension
140 Q	1 ft. 6 in. to 2 ft.
141 Q	1 ft. 10 in. to 2 ft. 4 in.
142 Q	2 ft. 3 in. to 2 ft. 10 in.
142 R	2 ft. 3 in. to 3 ft. 6 in.
143 R	2 ft. 10 in. to 4 ft.
144 R	3 ft. 3 in. to 4 ft. 6 in.
145 R	3 ft. 10 in. to 5 ft.

4¼-Inch Shaft With Flange Base

Size	Extension
41 Q	1 ft. 10 in. to 2 ft. 4 in.
42 Q	2 ft. 3 in. to 2 ft. 10 in.
42 R	2 ft. 3 in. to 3 ft. 6 in.
43 R	2 ft. 10 in. to 4 ft.
44 R	3 ft. 3 in. to 4 ft. 6 in.
45 R	3 ft. 10 in. to 5 ft.

EXTENSION PIECE FOR ROADWAY BOXES

These extensions — with standard 4¼" shaft—will increase the length of either type roadway box by 18 inches. Item No. 49.

SQUARE HEAD

4¼-Inch Shaft With Open Base

Size	Extension
137	12 inches stationary
138	16 inches stationary
140 U	1 ft. 6 in. to 2 ft. 1 in.
141 S	1 ft. 10 in. to 2 ft. 7 in.
142 S	2 ft. 1 in. to 2 ft. 11 in.
142 T	2 ft. 5 in. to 3 ft. 6 in.
144 T	3 ft. 5 in. to 4 ft. 6 in.
145 T	4 ft. 1 in. to 5 ft. 1 in.

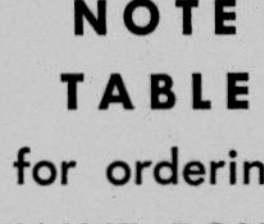

NOTE TABLE for ordering VALVE BOXES on page 4

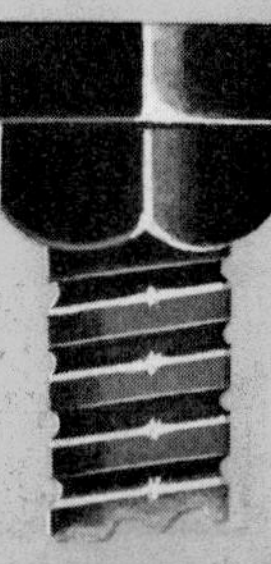

THE SQUARE HEADS on these boxes are extremely heavy and sturdy.

MANHOLE FRAMES AND COVERS

Sturdy, heavily constructed manhole frames and covers that will stand any traffic. Several sizes available — or sizes to meet your specifications will be fabricated on short notice.

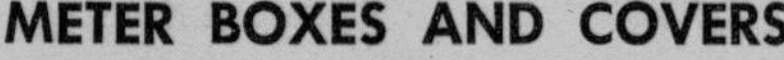

METER BOXES AND COVERS

These meter boxes — made for either gas or water — with the name of the supplier cast into the top — are available in several sizes. Special boxes will be made to order.

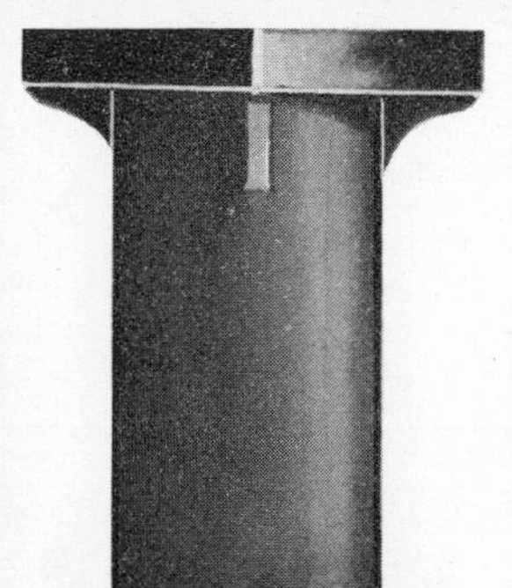

GAS DRIP BOXES

Gas Drip Boxes in diameters from 4⅞″ to 13″ and in several lengths are available in either round or square top styles. "Buffalo" made gas drip boxes are now standard equipment on the distribution lines of the largest gas companies in the United States.

EXTRA HEAVY SLIDING TYPE TOP

Available in 2½″ shaft size, these 24½ inch boxes have been designed to meet the demand for a service box to stand extra heavy traffic conditions.

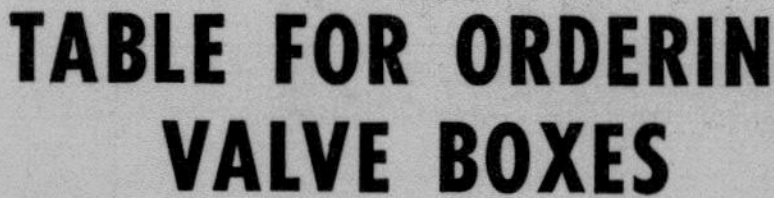

TABLE FOR ORDERING VALVE BOXES

Three-Piece Adjustable Valve Box Screw or Sliding Type, 5¼″ Shaft

PLUG HEAD SERVICE BOXES

These 2½″ shaft measurement boxes — with square head and deep set plug cover — are available in the same lengths as those shown on page 2.

SIZE OF ALVE	BOTTOM OF BASE TO BOTTOM OF TRENCH	NO. OF BASE USED	3′ TRENCH	3′ 6″ TRENCH	4′ TRENCH	4′ 6″ TRENCH	5′ TRENCH	5′ 6″ TRENCH	6′ TRENCH	6′ 6″ TRENCH	TR
3	8	4	A	B	C	CC	D	E	F	F	
4	12½	4	A	A	B	C	CC	D	E	F	
6	15	6	AA	A	A	B	C	CC	D	E	
8	19	6	AA	A	A	B	B	C	CC	D	
10	24	6		AA	A	A	B	B	C	CC	
12	31	160			AAA	A	A	B	B	C	
14	36½	160				AA	A	A	B	B	
16	41½	160					AA	AA	A	B	

BUFFALO PIPE & FOUNDRY CORP.

BOX 55—STATION B DE. 6764 BUFFALO, N. Y.

Public Works Equipment

Concurrent with the rise of America's great cities was the rapid expansion of American industry. These two closely interdependent forces gave impetus to each other as they forged mutual destinies. In 1847 the firm that was to be Allis-Chalmers operated a small factory in Milwaukee. Much of its earliest work was for the city . . . and as the years passed and the company grew, for other cities. Today Allis-Chalmers operates 14 plants in the U.S. employing 40,000 workers . . . offering over a thousand major products to large and small communities.

Today Allis-Chalmers can supply a major percentage of the equipment needed for sewage plants, water works, municipal power plants, street and highway construction, and other public works. See the three following pages for further information on A-C equipment.

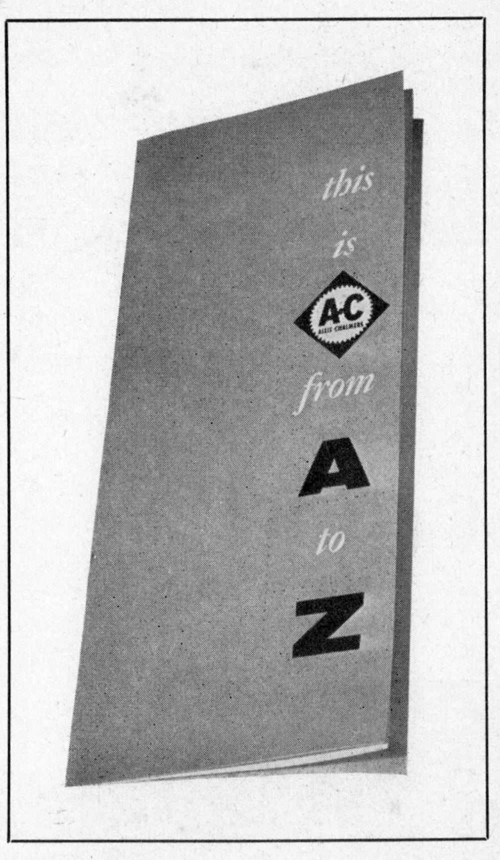

FREE LITERATURE

Bulletin 25B6057 is a directory of Allis-Chalmers products and engineering literature. Listing the complete line of A-C equipment, this handy booklet is a valuable reference aid. It will simplify the problem of obtaining literature on any Allis-Chalmers equipment you may need. Send for your free copy . . . Allis Chalmers Mfg. Co., Milwaukee 1, Wis., or to any of the sales offices listed below.

ALLIS-CHALMERS SALES OFFICES

ALA., Birmingham; **ARIZ.,** Phoenix; **CALIF.,** Los Angeles, San Diego, San Francisco; **COLO.,** Denver; **CONN.,** Hartford, New Haven; **D.C.,** Washington; **FLA.,** Jacksonville, Miami, Tampa; **GA.,** Atlanta; **ILL.,** Chicago, Peoria, Rockford; **IND.,** Indianapolis, Evansville; **IOWA,** Davenport; **KAN.,** Wichita; **KY.,** Louisville; **LA.,** New Orlans, Shreveport; **ME.,** Augusta; **MD.,** Baltimore; **MASS.,** Boston; **MICH.,** Detroit, Grand Rapids, Jackson; **MINN.,** Duluth, Minneapolis; **MO.,** Kansas City, St. Louis; **NEB.,** Omaha; **N. J.,** Newark; **N. Y.,** Buffalo, New York, Rochester, Syracuse; **N. C.,** Charlotte; **OHIO,** Akron, Cincinnati, Cleveland, Columbus, Toledo, Youngstown; **OKL.,** Oklahoma City, Tulsa; **ORE.,** Portland; **PA.,** Philadelphia, Pittsburgh, Wilkes-Barre, York; **R. I.,** Providence; **TENN.,** Chattanooga, Knoxville, Memphis; **TEX.,** Amarillo, Beaumont, Corpus Christi, Dallas, El Paso, Fort Worth, Houston, San Antonio; **UTAH,** Salt Lake; **VA.,** Richmond; **WASH.,** Seattle; **W. V.,** Charleston; **WISC.,** Appleton, Milwaukee; **CANADA,** Montreal, Toronto, Winnipeg, Calgary, Vancouver.

A-3912

ALLIS-CHALMERS A-C

Complete Pumping Units

The record of Allis-Chalmers in building centrifugal pumps speaks for itself. Of thousands built, no A-C centrifugal pump has ever failed to meet its guaranteed efficiency. This means that when you specify *Allis-Chalmers* you are getting exactly what you intended to buy . . . exactly what you need.

Hundreds of cities . . . large and small . . . are already profiting from the efficiencies of Allis-Chalmers pumps. The range of types and capacities of A-C pumps will meet the needs of any city. There are special pumps for water supply, fire protection, sewage, and drainage. Sizes range from small compact units handling only a few gpm to huge 72-inch pumps capable of handling three hundred thousand gpm.

Also worth while remembering is that you can get the entire pumping unit from Allis-Chalmers . . . for this company builds motors of every type, for operating every size of pump. You can also get the proper A-C starter for controlling the motor. A-3913

Left: Low lift pump room, South District Filtration Plant, Chicago. Allis-Chalmers pumps, installed in 1945, are rated 69,500 gpm and 34,750 gpm.

Below: Allis-Chalmers pumps and motors installed in a Gulf Coast municipal pumping station.

ALLIS-CHALMERS A-C

Generators

Allis-Chalmers engine type synchronous generators are built in a wide range of standard ratings from 25 to 10,000 kva for standard speeds from 100 to 600 rpm. They are used with all types of relatively low speed prime movers. Allis-Chalmers generator experience extends back over sixty years. Continued electrical and mechanical improvements, together with constant testing and experimenting, have resulted in generators that are reliable in operation, compactly built and with characteristics to suit the driving unit.

Voltage Regulators

Rocking-Contact voltage regulators are used on generators of all ratings. They have immediate response with little movement or friction, and are sensitive to small voltage changes. When a voltage change is required, the *Rocking Contact* sector moves to cut resistance in or out of the field circuit to bring voltage to normal. There are no sliding or vibrating contacts to replace or cause trouble.

Centrifugal Blowers

Allis-Chalmers builds centrifugal blowers in a wide range of ratings. Two of the most important applications of blowers in public works are sewage aeration and furnishing scavenging air for diesel engines. A scavenging blower is shown on the left. Below is shown one of three 100,000 cfm blowers for sewage aeration in the city of Chicago.

A-3914

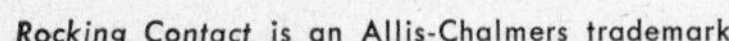

Rocking Contact is an Allis-Chalmers trademark.

For Distribution of Electric Power

Allis-Chalmers 4160 volt switchgear units in municipal power plant in Colorado.

Three 3333 kva oil-sealed inert gas equipped Allis-Chalmers power transformers installed in Missouri.

Allis-Chalmers can supply a major percentage of all power generation, and electrical control and distribution equipment for public works. Included in the power generation line are steam turbine generator units, surface condensers, condenser and boiler feed pumps, water conditioning service and equipment.

The range of electrical products includes all types and sizes of motors from 1 hp to 24,000 hp and up, and starters or control to suit every application.

Allis-Chalmers indoor and outdoor high and low voltage switchgear provides maximum protection and flexible control of power distribution circuits. All units are metal enclosed, factory built, so they need only be bolted in place and lines connected. Switchboards are custom built to fill your needs.

A-C builds a complete line of power and distribution transformers. Most sizes can be cooled with either oil or *Chlorextol* non-inflammable liquid, or they can be of the air-cooled type.

Load center, single circuit and multi-circuit unit substations are built in standard ratings to meet every application. They are completely factory built and can be installed adjacent to equipment being served.

A-3915

Chlorextol is an Allis-Chalmers trademark.

Right: Rear view of 3000 kva, 4160-2400 volt unit substation with both incoming line section and distribution feeder section consisting of metal-clad switchgear.

The world's largest individual pipe plant

Aerial view of American Cast Iron Pipe Company's extensive facilities and part of the grounds.

From its location in the industrial Southeast, readily accessible to excellent truck and rail transportation facilities, the American Cast Iron Pipe Company is prepared to serve completely and economically.

The wide range of sizes centrifugally cast by the American Cast Iron Pipe Company — from 2″ through 48″ — assures that American can furnish exactly the pipe and fittings your job requires. Let American's long-experienced staff of skilled engineers, metallurgists and craftsmen help you solve your next pipe installation problem.

Service...

has been the guiding principle at the American Cast Iron Pipe Company for over fifty years. Because both the company and its product have been proved by time, municipalities and industries of all types now depend on American when efficient, economical service is required.

In Industry...

paper, chemical, steel, petroleum and many other types of plants are served by installations of American Cast Iron Pipe and fittings. Industrial piping experts are at *your* service when you specify "American."

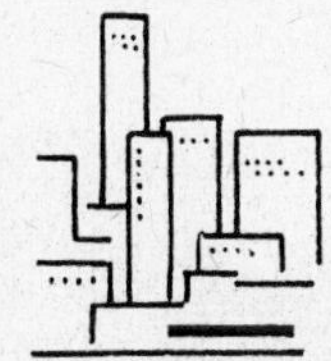

In Municipalities...

installations of American Cast Iron Pipe now serve utilities, both public and private, throughout the world. Both large and small jobs receive the same attentive, skilled service.

American Cast Iron Pipe Company

American Roll-On Joint Pipe

The Roll-On joint developed by the American Cast Iron Pipe Company is now accepted as a standardized joint by the Federal Government. It is offered as an alternate for other types of joints and is included as Type II in Federal Specification WW-P-421a. Proved by service for over 17 years, American Roll-On Joint combines the advantages of a positive, rubber-under-compression, bottle-tight seal, with the proven durability and strength of cast iron pipe.

American 48″ Roll-On Joint Pipe installed for water service at Corpus Christi, Texas.

IN A WIDE RANGE OF SIZES

2″ through 48″, American Roll-On Joint pipe is economical in both installation cost as well as material cost. Specify American Roll-On joint pipe for bottle-tight joints and performance plus . . . at low cost.

QUICK AND EASY TO ASSEMBLE

MATERIALS

ROLL ON GASKET

PLACE IN POSITION

ATTACH ASSEMBLY TOOL

CALK AND SEAL

SALES OFFICES

BIRMINGHAM	LOS ANGELES	CLEVELAND
CHICAGO	MINNEAPOLIS	PITTSBURGH
DALLAS	NEW YORK	DENVER
KANSAS CITY	SAN FRANCISCO	ORLANDO

BIRMINGHAM 2, ALABAMA

6 basic styles in 15 sizes ⅝″ to 12″ meet specifications of A.W.W.A. for every type of water service

Shown here are representative Badger water meters available for any community or industrial water measuring job.

Sizeable savings result from standardizing on Badger meters. Because of the easy interchange of parts, users can count on lower stock inventories. Minimum repair time and less parts cost help keep meters in service earning more dollars for your community.

OIL ENCLOSED TRAIN METER
(Three gear type)

Badger Models A-10T and SC-10T with oil-enclosed gear train, are available in sizes ⅝″ to 1¼″ inclusive. The oil-enclosed gear train is mounted directly on the chamber, providing positive alignment of all working parts. Precision machining assures extreme sensitiveness and positive accuracy at all rates of flow. Model A-10T frostproof meter, is designed for cold climates or where insurance against freezing is necessary. Model SC-10T is a split case type for warmer climates or where there is no danger of freezing. Write for complete information and prices.

OIL ENCLOSED TRAIN METER
(Four gear type)

Badger Models A-SOT and SC-SOT are equipped with built-in gear trains, operating in oil. This construction assures easy access to all working parts and assures low maintenance cost. The A-SOT model is designed for cold climates where provision against freezing is necessary. The SC-SOT model is designed for warmer climates. Available in sizes ⅝″ to 1¼″ inclusive. Write for complete information and prices.

BADGER METERS MEASURE THE WATER OF THE WORLD

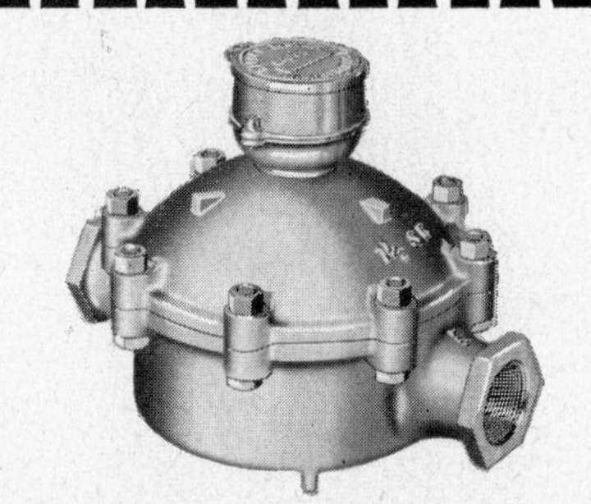

OIL ENCLOSED TRAIN

Heavy duty disc meter

The Badger Heavy-Duty Model SC-SOT disc meter is available in sizes 1½″ to 4″ inclusive. It embodies all of the advance features found in smaller Badger disc meters. Oil-enclosed gear trains, unit assembly, and precision machining assure trouble free performance wherever used. Write for complete information and prices.

OIL ENCLOSED TRAIN

Turbine (current) meter

The Badger Turbine meter is designed for exceptional heavy service such as railroad standpipe, hydraulic elevators and water supply mains, where it is desired to measure large volumes of water with very little loss of line pressure. Although built to handle heavy services, it is surprisingly accurate on small flows. Badger Turbines are available in sizes 2″ to 12″ inclusive. Write for complete information and prices.

OIL ENCLOSED TRAIN

Compound meter

The Badger Compound Meter will accurately measure all flows (minimum to capacity of meter.). This is accomplished by a small disc meter and large turbine meter in a common housing with their action properly synchronized by a compounding valve. Meter is operated by volume flow rather than pressure differentials — so positive in its action that no appreciable loss of accuracy is noted even at the cross-over point. When disc meter is in operation, the turbine meter is inactive and vice versa. Badger Compounds are available in sizes 2″ through 10″; they are designed for services supplying office buildings, hotels, manufacturing plants, etc. Write for complete information and prices.

BADGER METERS MEASURE THE WATER OF THE WORLD

Badger Meter Testers are available in four sizes to test 2-4-6-8 meters of all types and makes at one time . . . a complete test laboratory— everything furnished.

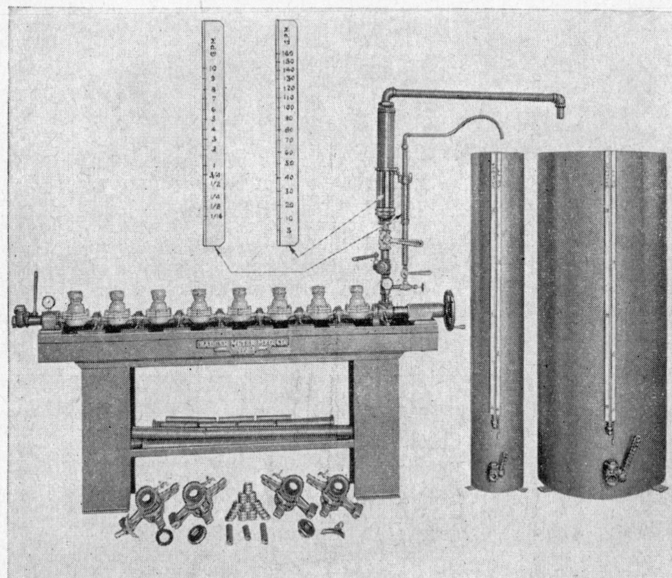

Includes:

- All adaptors, supports, adjusting cradles, spacer pieces — to test ⅝ through 2″ meters up to the capacity of the machine.
- Ten gallon and one hundred gallon tank — each accurately calibrated in gallons, cubic feet or in the metric system.
- Visible rate of flow indicators (2) for testing 1/16 to 10 gpm: and 5 to 160 gpm.
- Test bench has meter supports locked into bench to prevent buckling of meters while testing.
- Meter supports slide into any desired position — equipped with pet cocks to release all air and set meter test hands to zero before testing.
- Bed (five inches deep) has anti-splash feature — particularly useful in testing larger sizes of meters.

Testing on Badger Multiple Testers not only saves time and labor cost, but reduces the quantity of water used during operation

The Badger Meter Test Machine equips you to get maximum performance from accurate calibration. A *must* for revealing any lost revenue from inaccurate meters. The two visible rate-of-flow controllers, for example, greatly simplify this operation. The precision-machined, tapered, non-corrosive metal plungers are designed to be self-flushing and remain *permanently* accurate. Write for complete information and prices.

BADGER METERS MEASURE THE WATER OF THE WORLD

CHICAGO BRIDGE & IRON COMPANY

Atlanta 3............2104 Healey Bldg.
Birmingham 1........1568 North 50th St.
Boston 10.....1023—201 Devonshire St.
Chicago 4.........2470 McCormick Bldg.
Cleveland 14.........2239 Midland Bldg.
Detroit 26..........1537 Lafayette Bldg.
Houston 2..........2117 C & I Life Bldg.
New York 6..........3392—165 Broadway
Philadelphia 3.1634-1700 Walnut St. Bldg.
Pittsburgh 19..........3226 Alcoa Bldg.
Salt Lake City 4...523 W. 17th South St.
San Francisco 4......1539—200 Bush St.
Seattle 1 ...... 1323 Henry Bldg.
South Pasadena......712 Fair Oaks Ave.
Tulsa 3...............1608 Hunt Bldg.

Plants at: Chicago, Ill.; Salt Lake City, Utah; Greenville, Pa.; and Birmingham, Ala.
In Canada: HORTON STEEL WORKS, Limited, Fort Erie, Ontario

ELEVATED STEEL WATER TANKS

Elevated steel tanks are used to provide gravity water pressure in municipal and industrial water distribution systems. In small systems, the tank is used to supply water directly, the tank being refilled intermittently by pumping. In large systems, the tank rides on the distribution mains, supplying the increased flow of water needed at peak demand periods, and permitting a more constant rate of pumping. The tank is elevated above the ground to a height sufficient to give an adequate minimum pressure.

Elevated tanks operate on the gravity principle and therefore are dependable. With elevated storage, pumping facilities in large systems are most efficient when they are operated at a uniform rate. In small systems, the pumps can be operated intermittently at greater efficiency. By pumping during off-peak electric load periods, lower power rates are sometimes available. Maintenance costs for an elevated tank are low, as regular painting inside and outside keeps the steel in good condition.

100,000-gallon elevated Watersphere, 103 ft. to bottom at South Houston, Texas. The riser pipe, ladder and overflow are located inside the supporting column.

2,000,000-gallon radial-cone elevated water tank at Decatur, Ala. It is 90 ft. to bottom and has a range in head of 35 ft.

WATERSPHERE and WATERSPHEROID

The Horton Watersphere® and Waterspheroid are modern elevated water tanks supported by single columns. The columns are flared at the bottom into a relatively large base which rests on a concrete foundation and is fastened to it by anchor bolts. The simplicity of design give the structures a striking and pleasing appearance. Their smooth surfaces also make them easy to paint.

Waterspheres have been built in capacities of 25,000 to 250,000 gallons; Waterspheroids from 250,000 to 500,000 gallons. Intermediate sizes or higher structures are built to special designs.

RADIAL-CONE TANKS

The Horton® radial-cone bottom design enables us to build elevated tanks of large capacity with a low range in head between the upper and lower water levels. Many tanks of this design have been built with capacities of from one to two million gallons with a range in head of only 25 feet. The radial-cone design can also be used economically where a range of 30 to 50 feet is permissible.

It can be built with or without a balcony. A table of standard capacities appears on the next page.

An ellipsoidal-bottom tank with ellipsoidal roof at Levelland, Tex. It is 87 ft. to the bottom and has a capacity of 400,000 gallons.

ELLIPSOIDAL-BOTTOM TANKS

Horton ellipsoidal-bottom tanks are built in standard capacities as shown in the table at the top of next column. This design of tank has a relatively large diameter and shallow depth, giving it pleasing proportions, and reducing the variation in pressure as water is used from the tank. The riser for ellipsoidal-bottom tanks, which is usually from three to six feet in diameter, is welded directly to the bottom of the tank. There is no expansion joint to require inspection or packing. The larger risers are usually installed in northern climates where there is danger of freezing.

RADIAL-CONE BOTTOM ELEVATED TANK SIZES

Capacity in U.S. Gals.	Diam. of Tank	Range in Head	Capacity in U.S. Gals.	Diam. of Tank	Depth of Tank
500,000	60'-4"	25'	1,500,000	96'-0"	30'
750,000	74'-3"	25'	1,500,000	88'-0"	35'
750,000	67'-6"	30'	2,000,000	102'-0"	35'
1,000,000	86'-0"	25'	2,000,000	112'-0"	30'
1,000,000	78'-0"	30'	2,500,000	114'-0"	35'
1,000,000	71'-6"	35'	3,000,000	126'-0"	35'
1,500,000	104'-0"	25'	3,000,000	117'-0"	40'

WELDED ELLIPSOIDAL-BOTTOM ELEVATED TANKS

Capacity in U. S. Gals.	Tank Dimensions: Diam. of Tank	Range in Head	Vertical Height of Shell
15,000	15' 6"	11' 0"	7' 0"
20,000	15' 6"	14' 9"	10' 3"
25,000	18' 0"	14' 0'	9' 0"
30,000	18' 0"	16' 6"	11' 0'
40,000	20' 0"	18' 0"	12' 0"
50,000	22' 0"	19' 0"	11' 0"
60,000	24' 0"	19' 0"	11' 0"
75,000	26' 0"	21' 0"	11' 0"
100,000	28' 0"	24' 0"	14' 0"
125,000	30' 0"	25' 6"	15' 0"
150,000	32' 0"	27' 6"	15' 0"
200,000	36' 0"	29' 6"	15' 0"
250,000	40' 0'	29' 0"	15' 0"
300,000	43' 0	30' 0"	15' 6"
400,000	46' 0"	35' 0"	19' 0"
400,000	50' 0'	30' 0"	13' 0"
500,000	50' 0"	37' 6"	19' 0"
500,000	56' 0"	30' 0"	11' 4"

WASH-WATER TANKS

Elevated tanks are widely used at filtration plants for washing filter beds. They are built in ellipsoidal-bottom or radial-cone design, depending on the capacity and head desired.

Operating and investment costs are materially reduced by using an elevated tank. The tank can be filled between washings by a small pump. Furthermore, periodical heavy drafts from the distribution system or source are eliminated. Tanks for wash water can be varied in design to suit the architectural treatment of the filter plant buildings by changing the roof, bottom, or tower design.

40,000-gallon ellipsoidal-bottom elevated tank, 37-ft. to bottom, at Lynden, Washington.

A welded flat-bottom steel reservoir with a capacity of 500,000 gallons. It is 60 ft. in diam. by 24 ft. high.

STEEL RESERVOIRS

Steel reservoirs are used to provide gravity pressure where natural elevations are available. In other instances they are installed to provide storage facilities for large quantities of water at ground level.

Steel will not crack and develop leaks due to uneven settlement. The tank may be built of riveted or welded construction, and the size varied to suit local requirements. Maintenance costs are low, for regular painting inside and outside will keep the steel in good condition.

In some instances it is desirable to use a standpipe type of reservoir. When these reservoirs are located in a residential district, they may be given special architectural treatment.

This ornamental welded steel standpipe at Clearwater, Florida, has a capacity of 1,000,000 gallons. It is 43 ft. in diam. by 95 ft. high.

ELEVATED HORTONSPHEROIDS

The Hortonspheroidal elevated tank is spheroidal in shape and is supported on two rings of cylindrical columns. We also build spheroidal tanks with one ring of cylindrical columns and a large central riser.

HORTONSPHEROIDAL ELEVATED TANK SIZES

CAPACITY IN U. S. GALLONS	DIAMETER OF TANK	RANGE AT HEAD
1,000,000	87'6"	25'
1,000,000	81'0"	30'
1,500,000	92'0"	35'
2,000,000	106'0"	35'
2,500,000	117'0"	35'
3,000,000	120'0"	40'

2,500,000-gallon Hortonspheroidal elevated water tank, 68 ft. to bottom at Cincinnati, Ohio.

STEEL PIPE

We are equipped to build welded steel pipe, 60 in. in diameter or larger, for water intakes and transmission lines. We have facilities at all of our plants for assembling sections that can be shipped complete and fabricating plates for larger sizes to be field-erected.

STEEL PLATE WORK

We build self-supporting steel smokestacks, tanks and hoppers for coal or chemicals, and other special types of heavy steel plate work.

INFORMATION

We have facilities at all four of our strategically located plants to pickle and paint fabricated steel work by the Horton Process.

We will be pleased to discuss the advantages of various designs, or submit estimating figures to waterworks engineers or municipal officials. Write or call our nearest office. For special structures, other than elevated tanks of standard capacity, please submit design drawings and specifications whenever possible.

CHICAGO BRIDGE & IRON COMPANY

THE CHAPMAN VALVE MANUFACTURING COMPANY

Cable Address "VALVE", Indian Orchard

General Office and Works Indian Orchard, Mass.

BRANCH OFFICES

Atlanta, Ga.
New York, N. Y.
Chicago, Ill.
Cleveland, Ohio
Detroit, Ohio
Tulsa, Okla.
Boston, Mass.
San Francisco, Calif.
St. Louis, Mo.
Syracuse, N. Y.
Philadelphia, Pa.
Los Angeles, Calif.
Pittsburgh, Pa.
Houston, Tex.

CHAPMAN VALVES AND SLUICE GATES FOR WATERWORKS and SEWERAGE A COMPLETE SERVICE FOR ALL USES AND PRESSURES

One of the largest and oldest manufacturers of gate valves in the United States, The Chapman Valve Manufacturing Company is thoroughly equipped for the manufacture of valves, sluice and shear gates, indicator posts, hydrants, floorstands, as well as electric and hydraulic operating mechanisms. Where variations from standard designs are required, Chapman engineers stand ready to submit specially designed products to meet unusual service conditions.

LIST 61 IRON BODY, BRONZE MOUNTED, DOUBLE DISC GATE VALVES BELL OR HUB END

This valve is built in strict accordance with American Water Works Association specifications. Prices and Dimensions will be sent on application.

Fig. 273

IRON BODY, BRONZE MOUNTED GATE VALVES, FLANGE, SCREW OR BELL END

Fig. 70 Stationary Spindle, Screw End

Fig. 73 Rising Spindle Flange End

SOLID WEDGE TYPE LIST 25

DOUBLE DISC PARALLEL SEAT TYPE, LIST 59½

Sizes 2 to 12 inch
175 lbs. water pressure

Sizes 14 to 24 inch
150 lbs. water pressure

Sizes 30 to 36 inch
120 lbs. water pressure

WRITE FOR CATALOG 63A FOR PRICES AND DIMENSIONS

Fig. 263 Rising Spindle Flange End

CHAPMAN TILTING DISC TYPE CHECK VALVES

PROVIDES MINIMUM WEAR OF MOVING PARTS, CLOSING WITHOUT SLAM, ABSOLUTE TIGHTNESS, AND REDUCED LOSS OF HEAD OVER CONVENTIONAL TYPE CHECKS

The Chapman Tilting Disc Check Valve consists essentially of a cylindrical housing, within which is pivoted a circular disc. The pivots are located just above the center of the disc, and offset from the plane of the body seat. This design gives a bell-crank action to the movement of the disc, allowing the disc to clear the seat as it revolves. The seat is of the circular bevel type and the disc drops out of contact without rubbing.

The illustration represents a vertical section through the center line of the valve. A B C D shows the valve seat and X O Y is the angle of the seat bevel. A E and C F are normals to X O and Y O respectively, meeting at G. From an inspection of the diagram, it will be seen that if the disc is pivoted around a point to the left of A E, every part of the edge of the disc between A and B will lift freely out of contact with the seat in the body. Similarly, every part between C and D will lift freely if the pivot is located to the right of C F. Hence if the pivot is confined within the angle F G A, every part of the disc edge will rotate freely out of contact with the seat in the body.

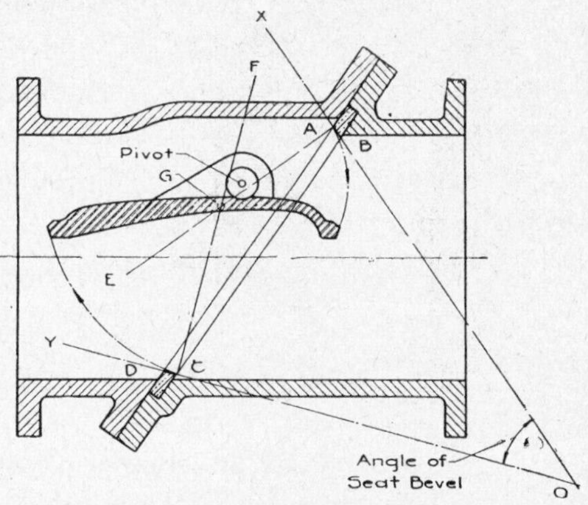

Thus the disc seat lifts away from the body seat when opening and drops into contact when closing, with no sliding or wearing of the seats. There is a small clearance at the pivots so that the disc when closed makes contact only with the seat in the body and is entirely free at the pivots, making the valve "drop-tight."

There's less wear on seating surfaces, pivot pins and bearings with the cushioned closing action in a Chapman Tilting Disc Check Valve. No fatiguing flutter. No vibration of pipe lines or adjacent structure—nor danger of opening pipe joints or rupturing pipe lines. Just a quick and quiet closure that cuts maintenance costs.

And what's more, the balanced streamlined discs in Chapman Tilting Disc Check Valves ride smoothly on the stream—reduce head losses 65 to 80% over conventional swing type checks. You'll want to know more about this maintenance-saving, more efficient check valve. Write today for engineering data, Bulletin #30-A.

LOW PRESSURE IRON BODY GATE VALVES INSIDE OR OUTSIDE SCREW

LIST 35-X SOLID WEDGE TYPE

50 lbs. working water pressure

100 lbs. test

LIST 58½ DOUBLE DISC TYPE

Sizes 10 to 30 inch

50 lbs. working water pressure

100 lbs. test

Sizes 36 to 72 inch

35 lbs. working pressure

70 lbs. test

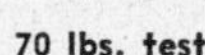

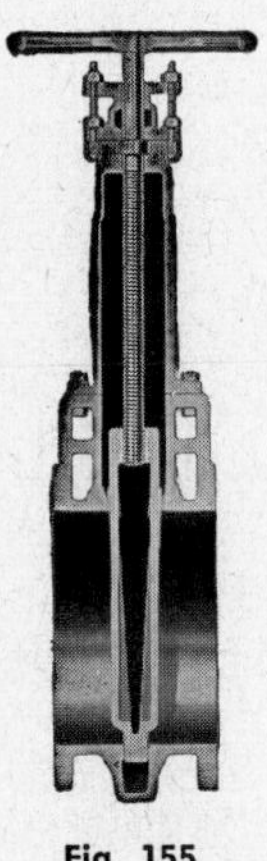

Fig. 155 With Inside Screw

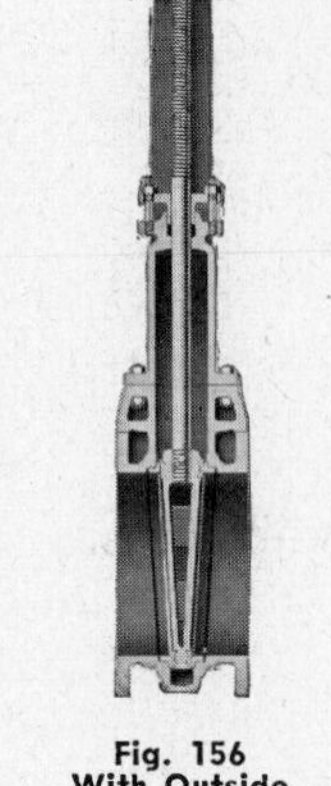

Fig. 156 With Outside Screw

These valves are designed for low pressure water, steam, gas and air. They are made with iron bodies and caps, bolted joints, iron wheels, bronze spindles, bronze faced or all iron plugs, bronze or solid seats, all iron or bronze mounted.

DIMENSIONS AND PRICES ON APPLICATION

Fig. 254C

BEAMED WATERWAY GATE VALVES

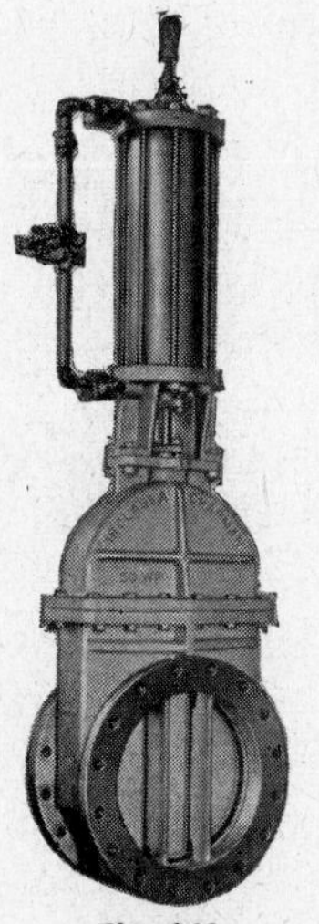

Fig. 940

These valves are especially designed for use under throttling conditions, such as "Wash Water Valves" in filtration plants.

Bronze faced beams located in a vertical position in the downstream port of the valve body, and bronze strips in the downstream disc form a bearing contact and prevent uneven wear of seats.

Can be furnished in all sizes of Class AA, A, B and C gate valves, with any desired method of operation.

Fig. 470
Rising spindle sluice gate

CHAPMAN SLUICE GATES

Are available in all standard sizes, circular and rectangular. Many special sizes can be supplied from patterns developed during a long period of manufacture. All parts of standardized gates and operating mechanisms are interchangeable and replacements can be installed in the field.

NO. 25 BULLETIN GIVES COMPLETE DETAILS AND SPECIFICATIONS AND IS AVAILABLE UPON REQUEST

CHAPMAN CONE VALVES

Cone Valves, because of low head loss, ease of operation, and automatic control, are particularly well adapted for service as: check valves in pump discharge lines, control valves for altitude tanks, liquid level control valves, pressure reducing valves, and stop valves.

Chapman Cone Valves are of the plug type, with circular opening of full pipe diameter through the valve. This insures that the loss of head through the valve will be no greater than through an equivalent diameter piece of pipe.

These valves may be operated manually, electrically, or by hydraulic cylinder. We supply the electrically and hydraulically-operated valves with suitable control valves for automatic action.

VALVE OPERATING MECHANISMS

Chapman Valves and Sluice Gates can be equipped for operation by hand wheel, by hand-operated floorstand (with or without gearing), by hydraulic cylinder, or by the Chapman Motor Unit. Complete data on operating mechanisms will be furnished on request.

Chapman Motor Units for electrical Push-Button Control of Valves and sluice gates

THE CHAPMAN VALVE MANUFACTURING COMPANY

INDIAN ORCHARD, MASS.

R. D. COLE MANUFACTURING COMPANY

Established 1854  *103 Years Experience*

Newnan, Georgia

A pioneer in the field of metal plate construction, with more than a century of experience. Complete facilities for designing, fabricating and erecting tanks, vessels and processing equipment from Carbon and Stainless Steel, Aluminum and Alloys.

●

1,500,000 Gallon "Cole Colonial" Design

Elevated tanks, when required in capacities from one million to two million gallons, can be attractively designed in the "Cole Colonial" pattern, as indicated in the above photograph of a very beautiful and imposing structure recently completed for the City of Greensboro, North Carolina. Tanks of this character are impressive and monumental in appearance. They not only provide the facilities necessary, but add materially to the skyline of the city.

Fabricators of Carbon and Stainless Steel, Aluminum and Alloys.

MUNICIPAL

The "Cole Ovaloid" is one of the more outstanding types used for municipal service in capacities from 300,000 to 750,000 gallons. These tanks are provided on structural or tubular towers. They are neat in appearance, require minimum service per gallon of storage, thus limiting maintenance. They contain the stored water in a shallow depth, which maintains an almost constant pumping head. Very desirable structure for general municipal service.

Cole "Ovaloid"

COLE SPHERICAL

Cole Spherical tanks on tubular towers combine sound engineering with pleasing design. Modern, streamlined. Base of structure is designed to occupy a minimum of ground space. Further information on Cole Ovaloid, Colonial or Spherical tanks may be obtained by writing for our publication—"Tank Talks."

INDUSTRIAL

For industrial service, including fire protection, we supply tanks in capacities from 5,000 to 2,000,000 gallons—in designs ranging from standard elevated tanks with hemispherical self-supporting bottom, to the modern type of ground-level reservoir shown above.

•

We will be glad to give full information as to the application of these tanks, or submit estimating figures to municipal officials.

COMPUTER-MEASUREMENTS CORPORATION

Utilities Instruments Division

5528 Vineland Ave., North Holywood, California

Still the same, famous Detectron electronic locating instruments

A new name . . . yes. But, now under the Computer-Measurements Corporation banner, famous Detectron Pipe Detectors and other instruments, long a standard among utilities companies, municipalities, etc., will be even superior to those furnished in the past.

Formerly operated as a division of The Detectron Corporation, this newly formed corporation is already in full scale operation in our ultra-new, modern design factory. An extensive product improvement program is already in progress under the new management. An enlarged engineering staff, expanded manufacturing facilities and improved production techniques coupled with a rigid quality control system are your positive assurance of the finest in electronic locating instruments. The same capable manufacturers' representatives in all major industrial areas of the U.S. and Canada are at your service.

SEE INSIDE CATALOG PAGES

Detectron "505" THE SUPERIOR PIPE DETECTOR

***Instantaneous Battery Testing**

Found ONLY on the "505" PIPE DETECTOR

Now . . . you can have positive assurance of maximum battery function at all times while detecting, tracing and estimating the depth and location of buried pipe, cable, and conduit. No more "in-the-field" battery failure or poor operation. Just flick the switch on either transmitter or receiver and get an immediate reading of battery condition.

The Detectron line, although widely copied, has never been equalled or surpassed! Unlike others, the DETECTRON "505" Pipe Detectors are original creations developed in their entirety by electronic engineers with many years of experience in the building and maintenance of underground detection equipment.

Clearing ahead of ditcher

In determining the exact location and depth of hidden pipes, valves, services, stubs, manhole covers, communication cables and other metallic objects, the DETECTRON "505" does a truly outstanding job. Its constant accuracy is due, in part, to the newly developed simplified electronic circuit with single knob, locked-in tuning, the elimination of many unnecessary parts, the aluminum case with static-repulsing shielded loops, unit construction and less dramatic but nonetheless valuable differences.

Results! No broken pipes!

The DETECTRON "505" is no "crystal ball"—there's no guess work about the serious business of knowing the exact location of buried pipelines or cables. Damage, either direct or indirect, is both dangerous and expensive. Broken lines disrupt service and often constitute a serious hazard to life and property. Since yours is a problem of "To know—or not to know . . ."—it is far better, and much cheaper, to be absolutely sure of their exact location. And the "505" provides that extra security you need.

Exclusive Detectron "505" *Features*

ALUMINUM CASE

Detectron engineers were the first to prove the value of the metal case. They found that in spite of added costs and many technical construction problems, the lightweight, rust-and-corrosion resisting aluminum case had many apparent as well as hidden advantages over steel or steel-over-wood cases. The "505" aluminum case with its artistic instrument panels is durably finished in brilliant red Duco enamel. The rust-proof feature alone makes the aluminum-plus-Duco case of the "505" doubly acceptable for all types of field work in any weather or ground conditions.

SHIELDED LOOPS

Detectron's exclusive shielding of circuit and loop aids in minimizing static from nearby high tension wires or neon signs which would otherwise distort or nullify the signal. Thus the "505" has new effectiveness and greater accuracy under the most grueling operating conditions.

UNIT CONSTRUCTION

As illustrated, both transmitter and receiver are "unit-built" for added economy. Heretofore accidental damage to a set made it necessary to practically rebuild the entire instrument. Now the "505" if damaged, requires only the replacement of the damaged unit—a panel, a base, an individual part—at a new low in economy.

HANDLES

The newly developed E-Z-grip fatigue-lessening aluminum connecting handle, with its instant acting built-in drop handle, contains the famous Detectron "snap-in" locks. No gadgets to fumble with, no wing nuts to loosen!

LIFETIME GUARANTEE

Your DETECTRON "505" is unconditionally guaranteed for the life of the instrument if used and cared for according to the terms of the written guarantee which accompanies each instrument.

Highest quality parts, finest construction and a better engineered instrument plus direct factory service when necessary are your assurance of the maximum operating satisfaction with a minimum of lost time or expense.

SPECIFICATIONS

UNIT: Transmitter, Receiver, Headphones, Mounting Handle and Direct Connection Lead.

SIZE: 9½"x12½"x6" (clamped together). Handle, 34" long.

WEIGHT: Transmitter, 4 lbs.; Receiver, 5 lbs.; Handle, 1½ lbs.

BATTERIES: 3 size "D" flashlight cells; 2 Eveready #467 "B" or equivalent.

TUBES: 3 1U4, 1 3V4, 1 1U5, 1 1R5 miniature type radio tubes.

FINISH: Anodized Aluminum Case and panels finished in baked red enamel.

Detectron "505-C"

COMBINATION PIPE AND LEAK DETECTOR

A complete dual-purpose instrument for detecting, tracing and depth estimation of buried pipes and for checking those pipes for leaks. The 505-C is a versatile, sensitive instrument which is indispensable to many pipeline operations. Newly designed, it uses the latest electronic tubes and features a specially constructed vibration pickup that assures maximum sensitivity. Constructed for rugged field use, it features an aluminum case and uses standard batteries.

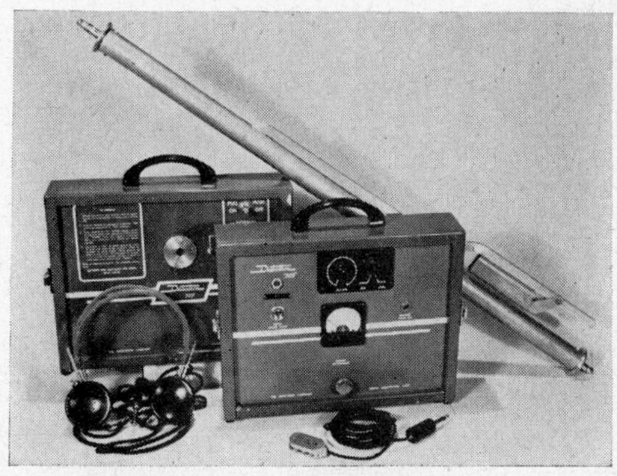

COMPUTER-MEASUREMENTS CORPORATION

Utilities Instruments Division

5528 Vineland Ave., North Holywood, California

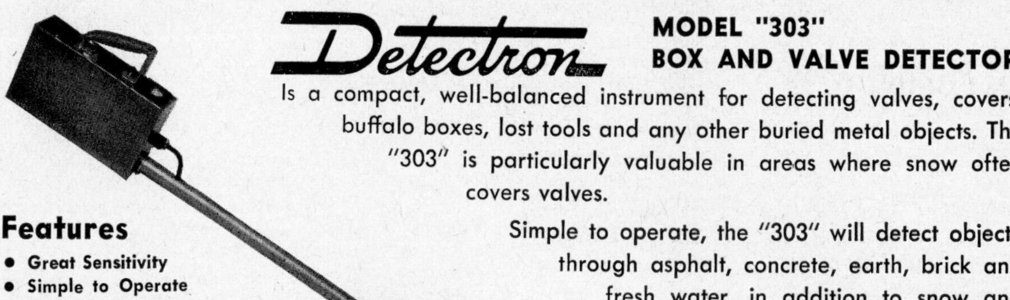

MODEL "303"
BOX AND VALVE DETECTOR

Is a compact, well-balanced instrument for detecting valves, covers, buffalo boxes, lost tools and any other buried metal objects. The "303" is particularly valuable in areas where snow often covers valves.

Simple to operate, the "303" will detect objects through asphalt, concrete, earth, brick and fresh water, in addition to snow and ice. Write today for complete details on DETECTRON "505" and "303."

Features

- **Great Sensitivity**
- **Simple to Operate**
- **Two-Part Guarantee**
- **Hi-Impedance Phones**
- **Low Cost Operation**
- **Signal Intensity Meter**
- **Light Weight (only 7 lbs.)**

GUARANTEE

1 **PARTS AND MATERIALS: The Model 303 is guaranteed for ONE YEAR against defects in workmanship and materials. This guarantee covers all parts which are not covered by guarantees of individual manufacturers.**

2 **PERFORMANCE: If, within 30 days from the date of purchase ANY competitive instrument is proved superior for detecting buried valves, covers, buffalo-boxes, etc., return the instrument and your money will be refunded.**

MODEL "LD-22"
LEAK DETECTOR

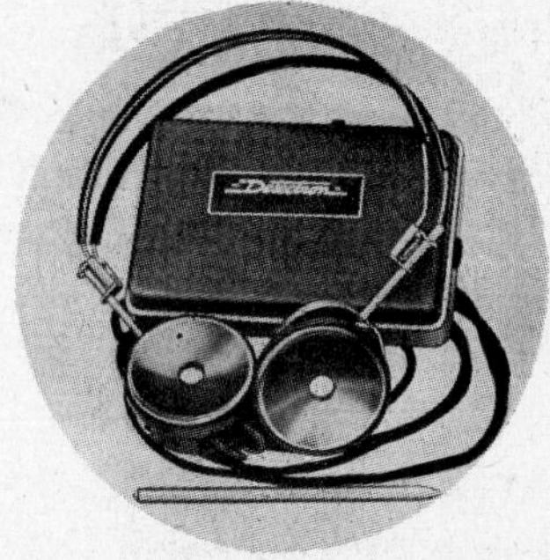

A light weight (2 pounds) compact instrument designed for rapid detection of leaks, the LD-22 is excellent for detecting costly and wasteful leaks in buried pipelines. Fundamentally a sound detector, the LD-22 amplifies the slight noise the fluid in the pipe makes as it leaks out. No calculations are necessary. The detector is very simple to use and it operates on low cost batteries. Simply listen for the maximum-signal in the headphones, to localize the leaks. Guaranteed one year against defects in workmanship and materials.

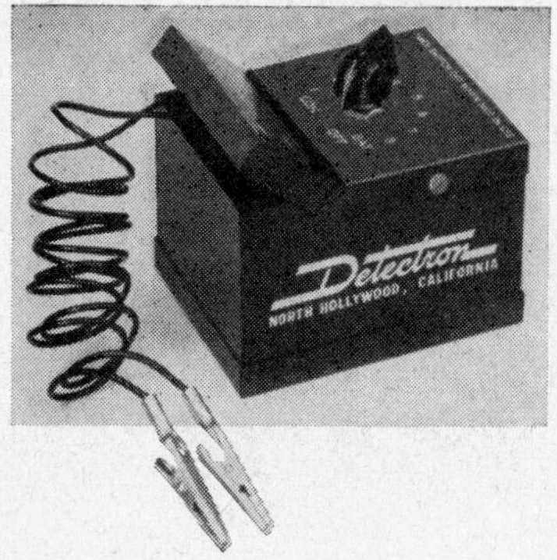

Detectron

MODEL T-8
AUTOMATIC
SHUT OFF TESTER

Completely automatic. This new thermomagnetic Valve Tester has been designed to test the B-60 and other thermomagnetic devices including thermocouples and thermopiles without guesswork and without shutting down the appliance. Operates as a continuity tester to trace wiring of appliances also switches that open and close. Eight switch positions. Tester may be left attached to appliance to supply current until permanent repairs can be made. Weighs only 1 lb. Very economical price.

DE LAVAL STEAM TURBINE COMPANY

Main Office and Works, 863 Nottingham Way, Trenton 2, New Jersey

DISTRICT OFFICES, SALES OFFICES AND FOREIGN REPRESENTATIVES

Atlanta, Ga. • Billings, Mont. • Boston, Mass. • Buffalo, N. Y. • Charlotte, N. C. • Chicago, Ill. • Cincinnati, Ohio • Cleveland, Ohio • Denver, Colo. • Detroit, Mich. • El Paso, Texas • Glen Falls, N. Y. • Houston, Texas • Indianapolis, Ind. • Kansas City, Mo. • Los Angeles, Calif. • Minneapolis, Minn. • New Haven, Conn. • New Orleans, La. • New York, N. Y. • Philadelphia, Pa. • Pittsburgh, Pa. • Salt Lake City, Utah • San Francisco, Calif. • Seattle, Wash. • St. Louis, Mo. • Tucson, Arizona • Tulsa, Okla. • Washington, D. C. • Canada: Calgary, Alberta • Edmonton, Alberta • Montreal, Quebec • Toronto, Ontario • Vancouver, B. C. • Mexico: Mexico, D. F. • Guatemala: Guatemala City • El Salvador: San Salvador • Honduras: San Pedro Sula • Nicaragua: Managua • Costa Rica: San Jose • Republic of Panama: Panama • Colombia: Bogota, Cali • Brazil: Rio De Janeiro • Sao Paulo • Ecuador: Guayaquil • Uruguay: Montevideo • Argentina: Buenos Aires • Chile: Santiago • Venezuela: Caracas • Puerto Rico: San Juan • Cuba: Havana • Dominican Republic: Ciudad Trujillo • Haiti: Port-Au-Prince • Jamaica, B.W.I.: Kingston • Trinidad, B.W.I.: San Fernando • Hawaii, Honolulu • Philippine Islands: Manila • Israel: Tel Aviv • Formosa • Spain: Madrid

water works pumps

These four De Laval pumping units, having a total capacity of 36 mgd, are installed in the Chester Municipal Water Authority new intake and Filtration Plant at Oxford, Penna.

Centrifugal pumps for water works service were introduced in the United States by the De Laval Steam Turbine Co. in the year 1901. Since that time De Laval alone has installed water works pumps having a total capacity of well over 20,000,000,000 gallons daily or more than enough to supply all the water requirements of the entire population of the United States.

From the beginning De Laval centrifugal pumps have been characterized by high sustained efficiency, accessibility, ease of maintenance, high head per stage and trouble-free operation.

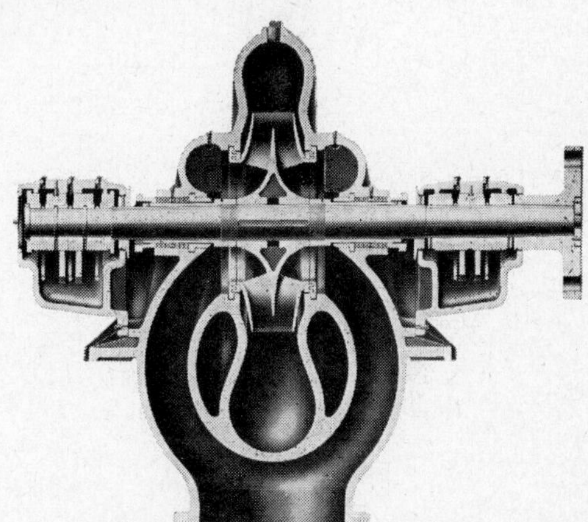

Note De Laval Labyrinth wearing rings at running joints between impeller and casing

sewage pumps

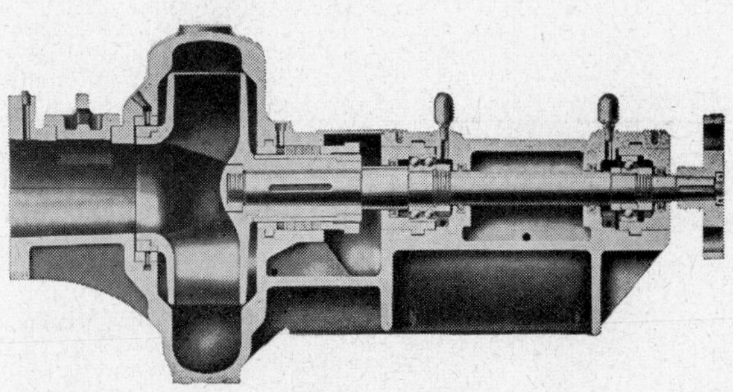

Capacity to 20,000 gpm. heads to 100 feet.

clogless pumps

De Laval clogless pumps are designed to meet the exacting requirements of sewage service. The passages are free and open to avoid clogging. Interior parts can be easily reached without disturbing piping connections. All parts are built on an interchangeable basis to permit easy replacement when necessary to overcome the effect of wear inevitably encountered in a pump handling water filled with grit and trash.

mixed flow pumps

The Mixed Flow pump is particularly well suited for handling large capacities at low heads. Operating at relatively high speeds, it permits a lower cost installation than would be possible with a conventional radial flow centrifugal pump. Because of its widely spaced impeller vanes, the mixed flow pump is also well suited for handling fluids carrying solids. Sizes 12″ to 42″; 3000 gpm at 10 foot head to 45,000 gpm. at 45 foot head.

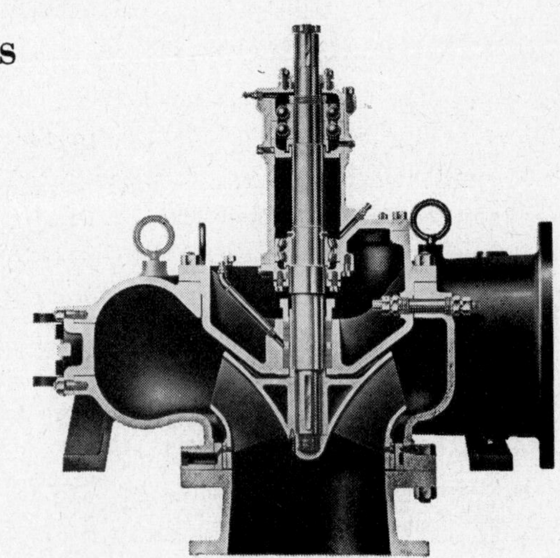

turbine generators

De Laval turbine generator unit

De Laval turbine generators are designed in units up to 11,500 kw capacity and for operation under all steam conditions including the high pressures and temperatures employed in the most advanced practice.

Engineers of the De Laval Steam Turbine Co. will be glad to submit complete cost figures for any municipality planning upon adding to its generating facilities.

mechanical drive turbines

For more than fifty years, De Laval turbine-driven pumps have demonstrated the advantages and economies of turbine drives. With steam turbine drive, speed can be readily varied to meet changes and demand, operation is independent of electrical disturbances and, in the larger sizes economy is unexcelled. Single stage turbines, 5 to 2000 hp multi-stage turbines to 25,000 hp.

De Laval turbine driven waterworks pump

5 Chlorinators

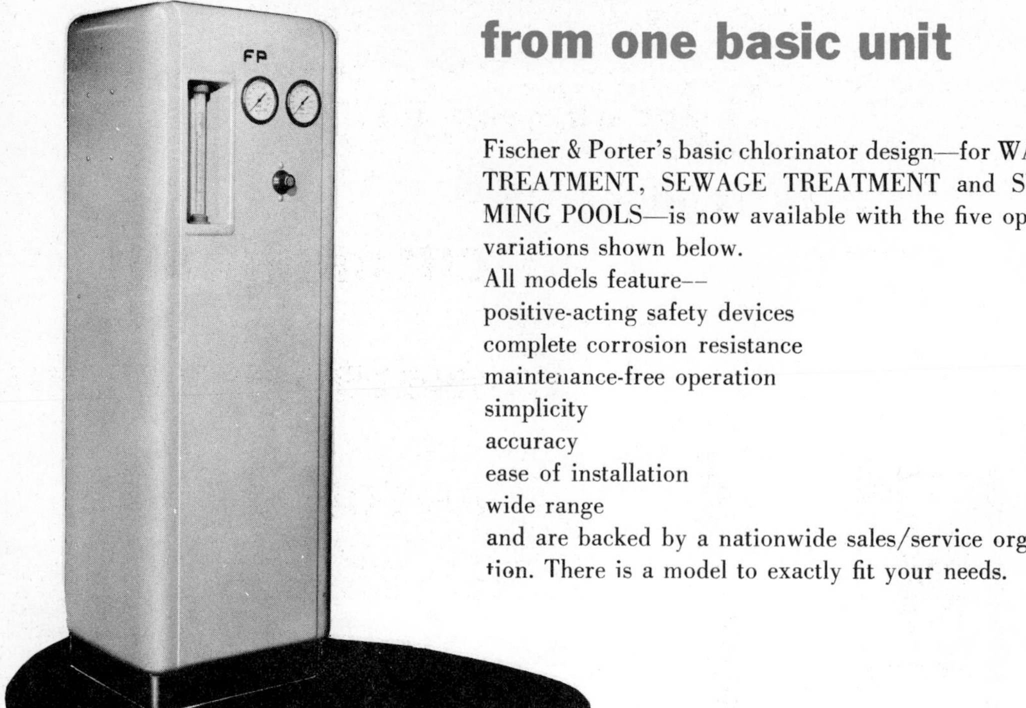

from one basic unit

Fischer & Porter's basic chlorinator design—for WATER TREATMENT, SEWAGE TREATMENT and SWIMMING POOLS—is now available with the five optional variations shown below.

All models feature—
positive-acting safety devices
complete corrosion resistance
maintenance-free operation
simplicity
accuracy
ease of installation
wide range
and are backed by a nationwide sales/service organization. There is a model to exactly fit your needs.

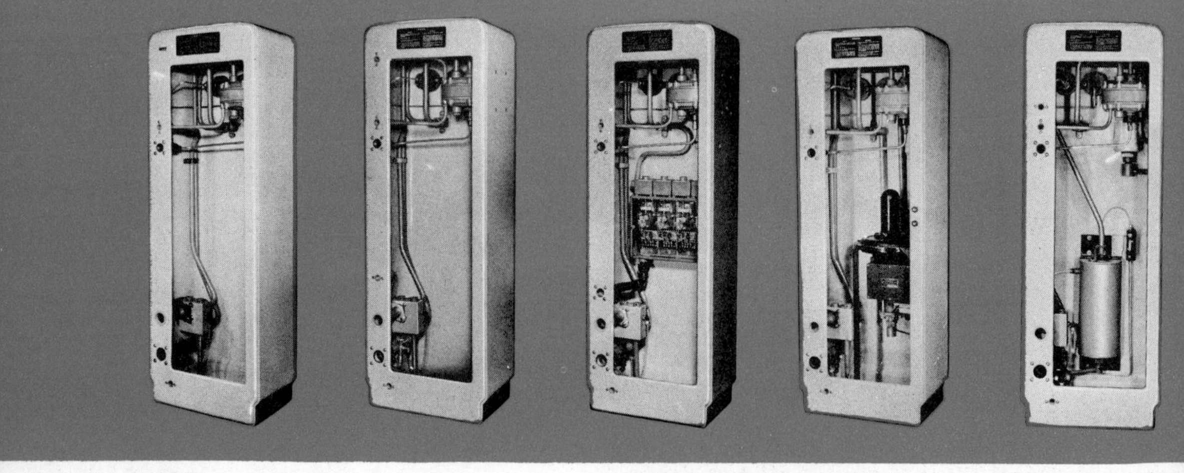

1 2 3 4 5

1 Manual operated 1050-A Chlorinator—Model C-1410

2 Automatic proportioning 1050-A Chlorinator—Model C-1420

3 Multiple rate 1050-A Chlorinator —Model C-1444

4 Remote set 1050-A Chlorinator—Model C-1455

5 Fluo 1950-A Chlorinator—Model F-1410
(For simultaneous fluoridation and chlorination)

Other Corrosion Resistant Chlorination Equipment

Fig. 1052-A High Capacity Chlorinator 8000 PPD max. (Also available with alarm system.)

Fig. 1054 Portable Chlorinator

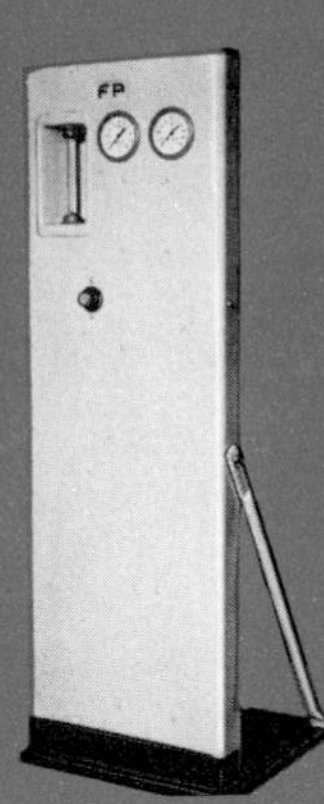

Fig. 1053-A Swimming Pool Chlorinator

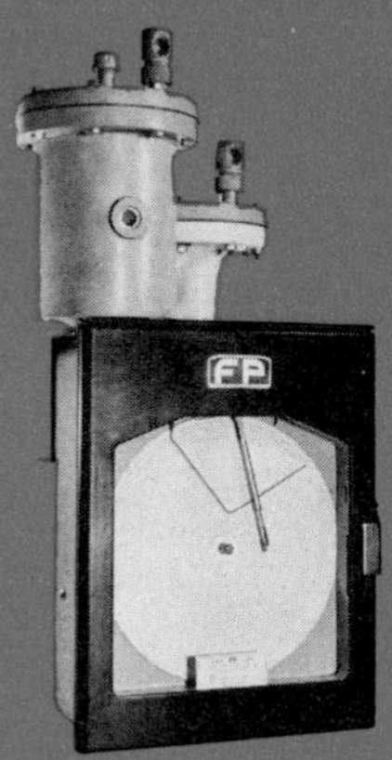

F&P Chlorine Flow Indicating Recorder

Water Purification

For measurement of filter water and wash water flow rates, F&P supplies a wide variety of flow meters and transmitters. The filter table console (below, left) contains all controls for operating a filter system.

The miniature instrument panel (below, right) houses indicators, recorders, totalizers, controllers and alarm systems for temperature, pressure, flow, liquid level and other variables.

Mercury Manometer for differential pressure measurement (Venturi and orifices)

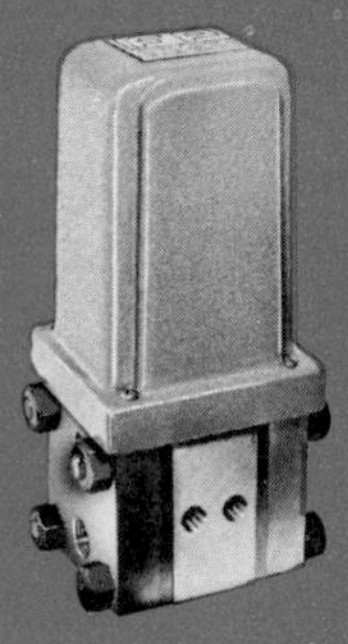

The new F&P force-balance transmitter converts differential pressure to pneumatic signals.

FISCHER & PORTER

DATA REDUCTION AND AUTOMATION

New system monitors at a central location any number of widely separated pumping stations, filter plants and reservoirs by continuously scanning such variables as water level, flow rates, valve positions, pressures, water consumption. Data is recorded on central log sheet, on punched cards or punched tape for control, statistical or accounting purposes. Advantages are: elimination of man-hours—immediate detection of trouble—avoidance of washouts, closed streets, detours.

The F&P Centralized Data Logging System is a means of automatically translating pneumatic and electrical measurements to a digital (number) form for automatic control, computing or cost accounting. It can be used in an existing as well as a proposed water plant, and is the modern way of handling a number of continually changing operating measurements. Provisions can be made for positive supervisory control of the remote stations.

- Relieves operating supervisors of the burden of manually logging, collating and interpreting operating information.
- Increases efficiency through faster, more accurate reporting of works and operating conditions.
- Alarms abnormal conditions occurring at any time.
- Reduces confusion when information appears rapidly or from many points.
- Provides an automatic, permanent log independent of operating personnel.
- Stores data for subsequent use.

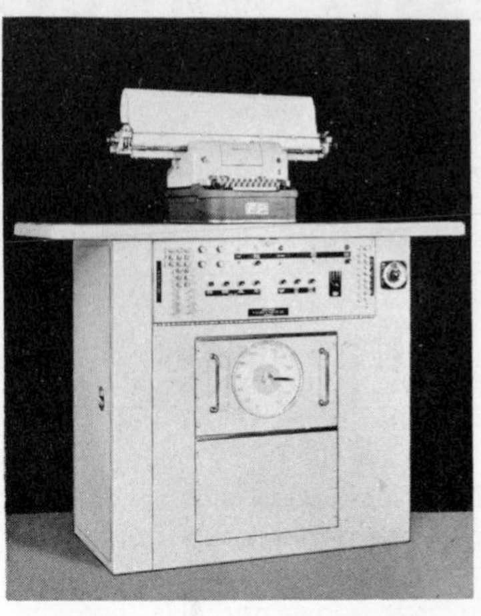

The F&P Automatic Logger presents data in typewritten form at hourly or other pre-set intervals.

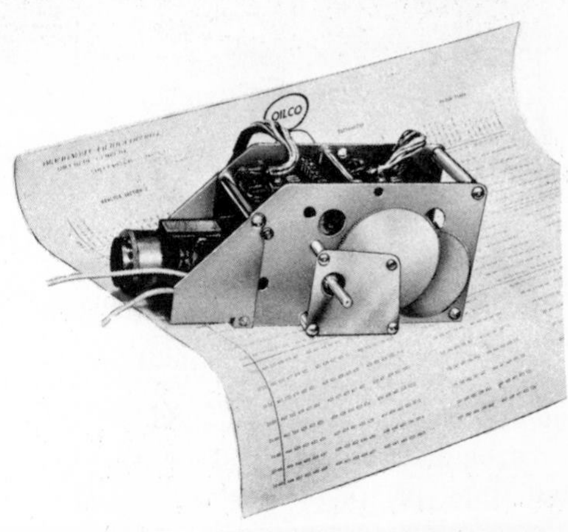

The Digi-Coder is an electromechanical device that converts shaft position to any digital code.

FISCHER & PORTER CO.

850 WARMINSTER ROAD HATBORO, PENNA.

Write for Free Literature and Information on Any of the Products Described.

SALES ENGINEERING OFFICES, U.S.A.

ALBANY, N.Y.
ATLANTA, Ga.
BALTIMORE, Md.
BIRMINGHAM, Ala.
BOSTON, Mass.
BUFFALO, N.Y.
CHARLESTON, W. Va.
CHARLOTTE, N.C.
CHICAGO, Ill.
CINCINNATI, Ohio
CLEVELAND, Ohio
DALLAS, Texas
DENVER, Colo.
DETROIT, Mich.
HOUSTON, Texas
JACKSONVILLE, Fla.
KANSAS CITY, Mo.
KNOXVILLE, Tenn.
LOS ANGELES, Calif.
MEMPHIS, Tenn.
MILWAUKEE. Wis.
MINN.-ST.PAUL, Minn.
NEW ORLEANS, La.
NEW YORK, N.Y.
OAKLAND, Calif.
PHILADELPHIA, Pa.
PITTSBURGH, Pa.
RICHMOND, Va.
ST. LOUIS, Mo.
SALT LAKE CITY, Utah
SEATTLE, Wash.
TULSA, Okla.
WASHINGTON, D.C.
WILMINGTON, Del.

DRESSER MANUFACTURING DIVISION

One of the Dresser Industries

Bradford, Pennsylvania

SALES OFFICES: NEW YORK CHICAGO HOUSTON SOUTH SAN FRANCISCO

In Texas: 1121 Rothwell St., Houston

In Canada: Dresser Manufacturing Co. Ltd., Toronto, Ontario and Calgary, Alberta

Time-Tested Solutions for Piping Problems

Dresser-Coupled steel mains deliver water cheaper by reducing installation costs, eliminating leakage and maintenance. These couplings also simplify installation of gallery piping. Their flexibility prevents strains on valve bodies and gives permanently tight joints under conditions of pulsation and vibration. They save time in cleaning and servicing valves, pumps and other units. Wherever pipe is joined—Dresser Couplings offer advantages.

PROBLEM AT MEDFORD, ORE.—This 20" line involved many creek, canal and railroad crossings—grades up to 55%. Lighter weight steel pipe plus flexible Dresser Couplings solved these problems.

PROBLEM AT HAMILTON, ONT.—Seven miles of line up to 48" were needed fast to supply 10 mgd to meet demands of the city's rapid expansion. To speed installation and assure permanently tight joints, a Dresser-Coupled steel line was specified with confidence.

PROBLEM AT OAKLAND, CALIF.—Morris Pumps are hooked up with flexible Dresser Couplings in sewage disposal plant operated by East Bay Municipal Utility District. Dresser Couplings permit easy dismantling, prevent strains on pump casings.

PROBLEM AT RICHMOND, VA.—Complicated, close-quarter piping in No. 2 Purification Plant was simplified by Dresser Couplings. No exact pipe fitting was required. Pipe movement is absorbed without leakage.

See following pages for data on Dresser Couplings and Complete Line of Repair Clamps and Sleeves

Dresser Style 38 Couplings are available for plain-end steel, cast iron or other pipe. Sizes from ³⁄₈" I.D. to 72" O.D. and larger.

Important advantages of coupled steel lines

Besides the obvious value of quicker installation, a Dresser-coupled steel line gives you the full, lifelong advantage of glass-smooth modern pipe linings. There can be no damage to the lining because no heat is used at the joint and there is no need for men to enter the pipe. Also, the shatterproof nature of steel pipe gives you an extra safety margin.

The *modern* water line is a *coupled steel* water line.

Partial list of cities using Dresser-coupled steel lines

BOSTON, MASS.
JERSEY CITY, N. J.
NEW YORK, N. Y.
WASHINGTON, D. C.
SAVANNAH, GA.
CLEVELAND, OHIO
DETROIT, MICH.
CHICAGO, ILL.
KANSAS CITY, MO.
DENVER, COLO.
SPOKANE, WASH.
PORTLAND, ORE.

DRESSER STEEL COUPLING Style 38

Proved on half a million miles of pipe, the Dresser Coupling is ruggedly dependable under the toughest operating conditions. Specially compounded rubber gaskets form a permanently "Flexible-Tight" joint which harmlessly absorbs vibration, expansion, contraction and other earth movement.

The flexibility of Dresser Couplings also permits laying curves with straight pipe —another time and money saver.

Many municipalities install pipelines with their own crews because Dressers make the work so simple. The only joining tool needed is a wrench.

Installation Procedure

1. Place a follower, then a gasket, over each pipe-end.

2. Stab middle ring over the laid pipe-end.

3. Stab other pipe-end into middle ring.

4. Move up gaskets and followers to middle ring.

5. Insert bolts and tighten nuts finger tight.

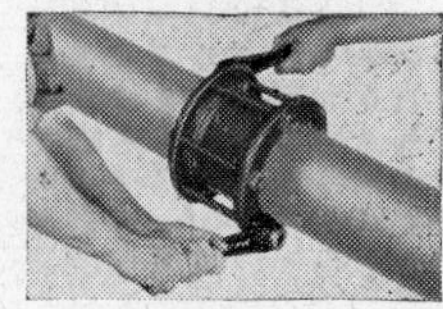

6. Draw up nuts with a Dresser ratchet wrench.

Average installation time: 2 man-minutes per bolt

DRESSER ADJUSTABLE BELL-JOINT CLAMP

Style 60

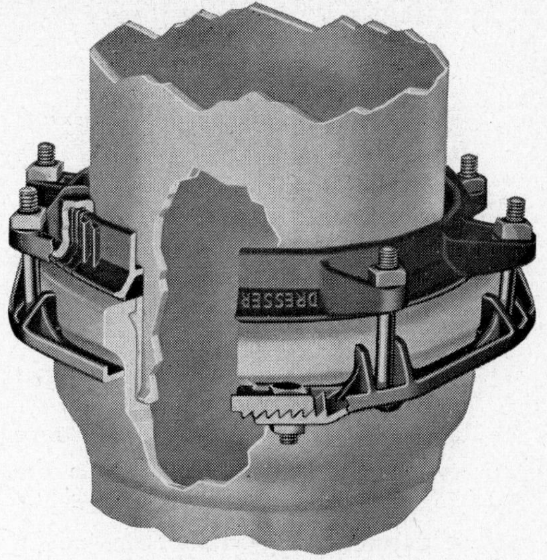

Dresser Style 60 Bell-Joint Clamps are available in sizes ranging from 3" to 60" CIP.

Designed for true adjustability, the Dresser Bell-Joint Clamp provides a positive, tight fit, even on off-size pipe. Both bell ring and spigot ring are fully adjustable.

The Style 60 Clamp makes a permanent repair and is cheaper in the long run than recaulking because you only dig once to repair a leaking joint if you use a Dresser Clamp.

The dependability of the Style 60 has been proved in literally thousands of installations under railroad tracks and highways, on bridges and in swampy country where operating conditions are particularly difficult. Their outstandingly successful performance in these "tough spots" is their best recommendation for use on all bell-joint repairs and in leakage reduction programs.

FOR BROKEN OR CRACKED BELLS

Dresser Bell-Pack Sleeve, Style 126, completely encloses damaged bell or leaking mechanical joint, makes a permanent repair. Strongly made, but lighter in weight and lower in cost than most comparable products. Easy to install.

DRESSER *Hydrepair** CLAMPS

Style 179

To repair asbestos-cement and cast-iron pipe

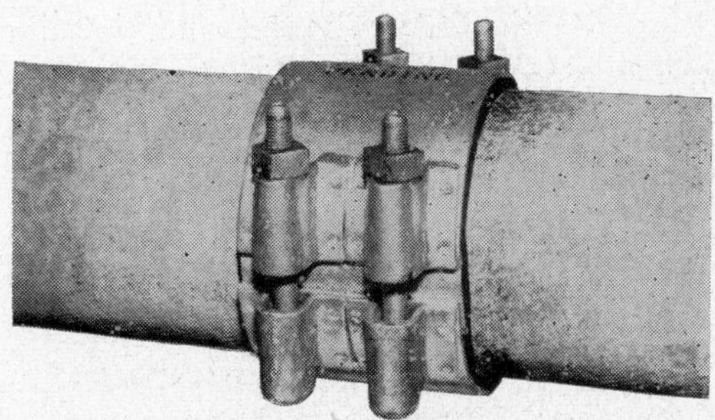

Style 179 Dresser Hydrepair Clamp

Featuring a "wrap-around" gasket seal, this lightweight, low-cost, galvanized clamp repairs breaks and holes quickly, permanently. Repairs either rough barrel or machined ends of asbestos-cement pipe, and all classes of CIP.

Unique adjustability enables it to fit virtually all diameters within a nominal pipe size range. Only one size clamp need be stocked for each nominal pipe size in service. Complete clamp boxed with step-by-step instructions—easy to store, easy to use.

*Hydrepair is a trademark of Dresser Manufacturing Division

DRESSER "ADJUSTABLE" REPAIR SLEEVE

Style 82

This low-cost, factory-assembled sleeve repairs breaks, splits and holes in the straight run of cast iron pipe—quickly, easily, permanently—without service interruption. It is highly adjustable to pipe diameters. Also ideal as a tapping sleeve. Sizes 4", 6", 8" CIP. Mueller taps.

DRESSER CAST SPLIT SLEEVE

Style 57C

Leaks, breaks and splits up to 8" in the run of cast iron pipe are permanently repaired by this sleeve. Each sleeve is tested with 60-pound air pressure and 500-pound hydrostatic pressure before shipment. Sizes 2" to 12" CIP.

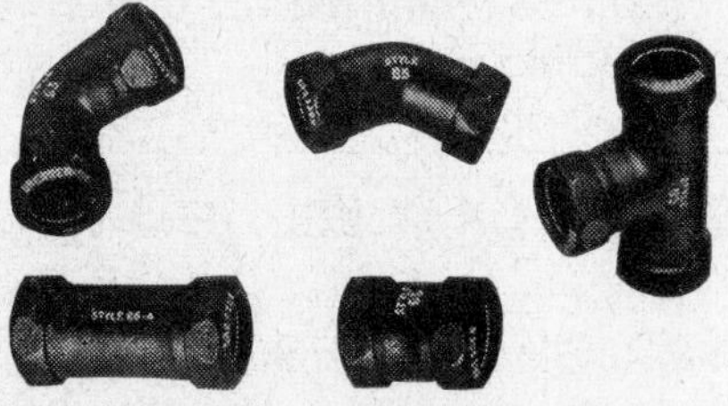

DRESSER "NO THREAD" FITTINGS

Style 65

These handy fittings speed and simplify the joining of small piping in IPS sizes ⅜" to 2". No threading to weaken pipe walls. No exact pipe fitting. Simply stab over plain pipe ends and tighten end nuts with a wrench. Style 90 (steel) for underground work and Style 88 (brass) for copper tubing sizes are also available. All standard shapes.

DRESSER SERVICE SADDLE

Style 91

New Dresser Service Saddles provide maximum economy, ease in making service connections. Body of rugged malleable iron construction, resilient Dresser gasket cemented in place. High tensile flat steel straps conform to pipe, prevent cutting, crushing. Available with AWWA Corporation or IPS Thread taps. Galvanized or plastic coated. Fits steel, cast iron and asbestos cement pipe, 2" to 12".

Catalogs and further information on request, or consult your Dresser Sales Engineer

WE ARE BASIC PRODUCERS

We mine Copper, Iron, Manganese and Zinc and are basic producers of their chemical derivatives. Our technical know-how and basic position in these minerals is your assurance of exacting quality control, strict uniform consistency and a plentiful supply.

ferri-floc
FERRIC SULPHATE

FERRI-FLOC

FERRI-FLOC, the economical all-purpose coagulant. Effective floc formation. Taste and odor control. Softening. Turbidity removal.

SULFUR-DIOXIDE

SULFUR DIOXIDE is effectively used in water treatment to remove objectionable odors remaining after purification.

SULFUR DIOXIDE
HIGHEST QUALITY
SO_2

COPPER SULFATE

COPPER SULFATE will control about 90% of the micro-organisms normally encountered in water treatment plants more economically than any other chemical.

FREE LITERATURE! — Send card or letter to Tennessee Corporation, Grant Building, Atlanta, Georgia.

TENNESSEE  CORPORATION

617-629 Grant Building, Atlanta, Ga.

BETHLEHEM STEEL COMPANY

GENERAL OFFICES: BETHLEHEM, PA.

SALES OFFICES:

Akron, Albany, Atlanta, Baltimore, Boston, Buffalo, Chicago, Cincinnati, Cleveland, Columbus, Dallas, Dayton, Detroit, Greensboro, N. C., Houston, Indianapolis, Jacksonville, Johnstown, Pa., Milwaukee, New Haven, New Orleans, New York, Philadelphia, Pittsburgh, Providence, Richmond, Springfield, Mass., St. Louis, St. Paul, Syracuse, Toledo, Tulsa, Washington, Wilkes-Barre, York

On the Pacific Coast Bethlehem products are sold by Bethlehem Pacific Coast Steel Corporation.
Sales Offices: Los Angeles, Phoenix, San Francisco, Portland, Seattle, Spokane.
Export Distributor: Bethlehem Steel Export Corporation, New York

Tar-Enameled Steel Pipe

Your Best Bet for Water Mains

Here are six good reasons for using Bethlehem Tar-Enameled Steel Pipe:

1. BEAM STRENGTH—Steel pipe has ample beam strength to span washouts that would cause the collapse of other types of pipe.

4. LEAKPROOF JOINTS — You get a tight line whether you choose flexible mechanical couplings, welding or riveting.

2. CORROSION - RESISTANCE Modern coal-tar enamel coatings and linings are virtually impervious to corrosion and incrustation, assure high flow-coefficients year after year.

5. RESILIENCE—Steel pipe combines resilience with strength—it "gives" under loadings and soil movements that would cause failure in more rigid types of pipe.

3. SHOCK - RESISTANCE Bethlehem Steel Pipe can withstand at least three times the calculated maximum allowable working pressure before bursting.

6. 40-FT LENGTHS—Only 132 joints per mile, compared to 300 or more for other types of pipe. Bethlehem Steel Pipe is available from 18 in. ID to the largest sizes permitted by carriers.

Bethlehem Tar-Enameled Steel Pipe is excellent for large-size sewage lines. See our advertisement under "Sewers and Sewage Treatment Equipment."

TESTED FOR STRENGTH—*Every length* of Bethlehem Steel Pipe is hydrostatically tested in accordance with AWWA requirements, ordinarily to 200 pct of the working pressure.

THEORETICAL INTERNAL PRESSURES OF STEEL PIPE

	1/4 in.			5/16 in.			3/8 in.			7/16 in.			1/2 in.		
INSIDE DIAM INCHES	EST SHIP WT LB/FT	MAX WRK PRESS PSI	MIN BURST PRESS PSI	EST SHIP WT LB/FT	MAX WRK PRESS PSI	MIN BURST PRESS PSI	EST SHIP WT LB/FT	MAX WRK PRESS PSI	MIN BURST PRESS PSI	EST SHIP WT LB/FT	MAX WRK PRESS PSI	MIN BURST PRESS PSI	EST SHIP WT LB/FT	MAX WRK PRESS PSI	MIN BURST PRESS PSI
18	50	445	1390	62	555	1735	75	665	2080	88	775	2430	101	890	2780
20	55	400	1250	69	500	1560	83	600	1875	97	700	2180	111	800	2500
22	61	365	1135	76	465	1420	91	550	1700	107	640	1985	122	730	2270
24	67	335	1040	83	420	1300	100	505	1560	116	585	1820	133	665	2080
30	83	270	835	104	340	1040	125	405	1250	145	475	1455	166	535	1670
36	104	225	695	128	280	870	154	340	1040	179	395	1210	204	445	1390
42	116	195	595	144	240	745	173	285	890	202	335	1040	231	380	1190
48	132	170	520	165	210	650	198	250	780	231	290	910	264	330	1040
54				186	190	580	223	225	695	260	260	810	297	295	925
60				207	170	525	248	200	625	289	235	730	330	265	835
72							306	170	520	355	195	605	405	220	695
84							346	145	450	403	170	520	460	190	595
96										464	145	455	524	165	520
108													*605	150	465
120													*656	135	415

The recommended minimum wall thickness is approximately the pipe diameter divided by 165. Pipe having this diameter-thickness ratio, when backfilled and properly tamped, will withstand any depth of cover.

For buried pipe, the recommended minimum thicknesses are shown immediately to the right of the heavy black line.

*Under certain conditions stiffeners may be required to reduce deflections.

$P = \frac{t \times Ts}{r}$ | P = internal pressure, psi | t = thickness, in. | Ts = allowable unit stress = 60% x 27,000 (yield point) = 16,000 psi | r = radius of pipe, in.

Based on use of ASTM A-283, Grade B Steel, 50,000 psi min. ultimate tensile strength.

BOSWORTH MANUFACTURING CO.

MILLS ROAD DEPT. M AVON, OHIO

Speed Material Handling with **Bosworth Conveyors**

BIN-VEYOR

The Bin-Veyor depicted here is a special unit developed for stationary applications such as floor to floor, railroad car to bin, floor to hopper, etc., and will handle such items as concrete aggregate and mixed concrete, packages, hundred pound grain sacks, bulk sand, etc. Bin-Veyors can be furnished in any length up to 30 feet. They have been giving trouble free and long life performance to foundries, grain elevators, potteries, concrete block plants and countless other industries. These units are often times operated in tandem with a Moto-Trimmer. Standard synthetic rubber or Neoprene belts can be furnished in plain or cleated surfaces.

CONVEYALL

For handling boxes, cartons, etc., also furnished with sides for conveying sand, gravel or any bulk material from 300 mesh to 2" x 8" egg size coal. Variable discharge elevations and portability make BOSWORTH Conveyall ideal for use in builders supply yards, foundries, coal yards, etc. They are applicable to most conveying operations.

Please write us for complete information

MOTO-TRIMMER

Portable conveyor for all types material handling. Made in three standard models its light weight and sturdy construction makes BOSWORTH conveyors a "must" for any industry. The thousands of units in use bear out the statement "they pay for themselves."

BUCKET-L-VATOR

Vertical, centrifugal discharge type, spaced bucket, belt type elevator. Rated at 25 TPH based on material weighing 50 lbs. per cubic foot. It will handle any dry, free flowing material up to 2" maximum lumps. Like all BOSWORTH equipment it is correctly engineered and customer tested.

THE FORD METER BOX COMPANY, INC.

Setting and Testing Equipment for Water Meters

1000 MANCHESTER AVENUE WABASH, INDIANA, U. S. A.

These pages give but a brief listing of the most complete line of equipment for making better meter settings for all conditions and for testing meters in shops of every size. Catalog No. 56 gives the complete story and is available on request.

WATER METER INSTALLATIONS

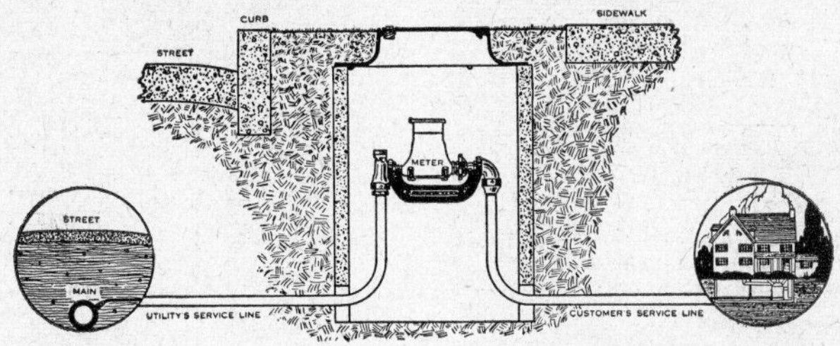

Upon the correct installation of a water meter depends to a large extent the satisfaction and service it renders the utility and the favorable impression it makes on the customer. So it behooves every water works in putting in its meters to follow the rules of good practice as outlined in our catalog which will be sent on request. A water meter in a service line should be well protected and as easily available for reading and changing as is economically practicable. A properly installed curb meter is at the logical point for metering, being at the beginning of customer's service. Meter reading and changing are independent of the customer's presence or whims. Meters can ordinarily be read much faster. In cold climates where outside settings must be deep, large and consequently expensive, economy sometimes dictates basement settings. Heavy and enduring snows can make reading of outside meters slow and difficult, or piping and other conditions can favor inside settings. Location of water meters is a separate problem for each water utility, even for each service, and deserves careful consideration.

BASEMENT METER SETTINGS

The majority of basement meters can best be set in vertical piping. The Ford Copperhorn and Kornerhorn are ideal for such settings, putting the meter in the correct position and providing other important advantages. The Copperhorn is best for new services, The Kornerhorn for installing in existing piping.

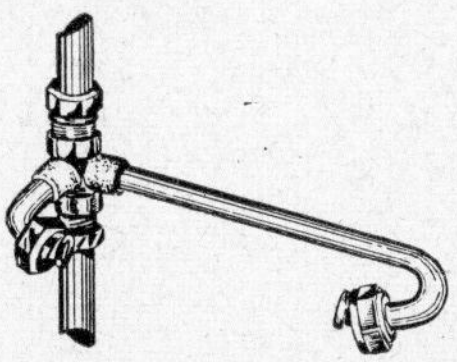

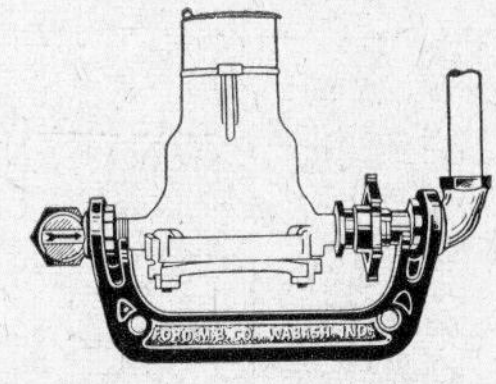

Meters should be set in basement or utility rooms when the winter climate is so severe that a safe curb setting must be large and expensive, or difficult of access because of deep snow. Meters set inside should be in as clean, protected and available a location as possible, safe from freezing and mechanical damage. They should be from one to three feet above the floor, set level with the dial up. The Ford Yoke, Copperhorn, Kornerhorn, and Linesetter offer real advantages for inside settings. They provide a permanent physical support and electrical bond for the service piping. Meters can be changed without disconnecting or disturbing customer's plumbing and without danger of starting leaks. Easy, trouble-free meter changes result in better-cared-for meters which are more accurate and earn more for the utility.

OUTSIDE METER SETTINGS FOR ALL CLIMATES

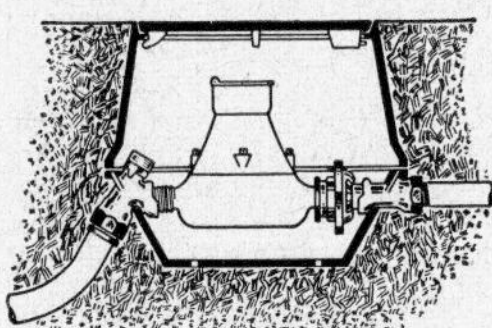

For shallow services where frost protection is not a problem the lower type Yokebox provides protection for meter and pedestrian, keeps meter clean and easy to read, and permits easy meter changing without physically disconnecting or disturbing service line.

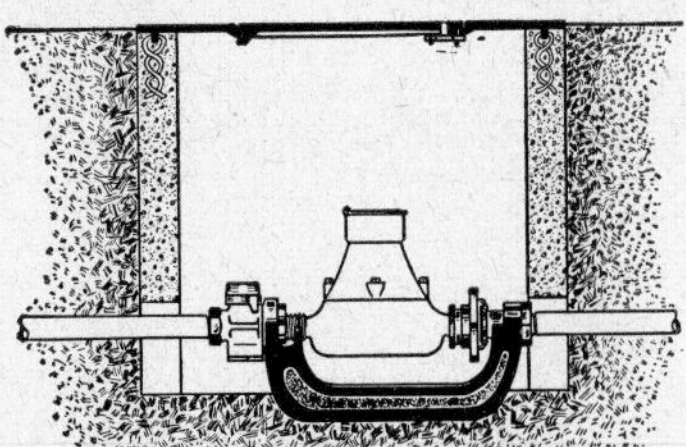

The Ironcrete Box can be made from 12″ to 24″ in depth and is well adapted to a rather wide variety of conditions. The Straight Line Yoke puts the meter in line with the service, assuring easy and trouble-free meter changes.

Where the service line from main to meter is deeper than from meter to house, the Angle Yoke makes a very satisfactory setting. In this picture the copper service line is bent up into the Yoke valve and the iron pipe at the outlet is horizontal. An 18″ deep Ironcrete Box completes the setting.

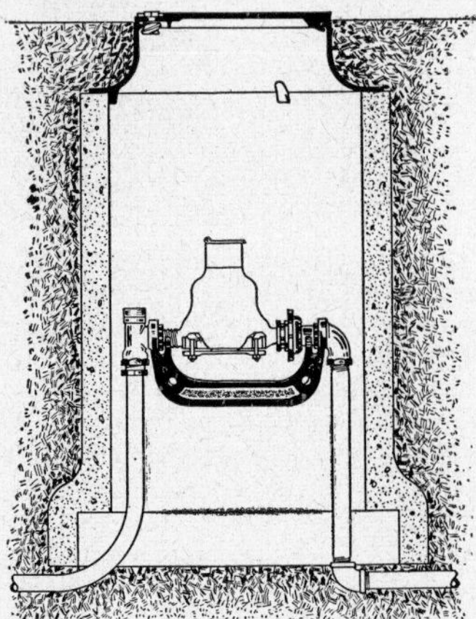

This setting is made up of a 15″ I. D. bell-end vitrified tile 24″ long, a No. 31 Type C Cover and a Riser Yoke. The distance from the surface to the meter spud is 20″.

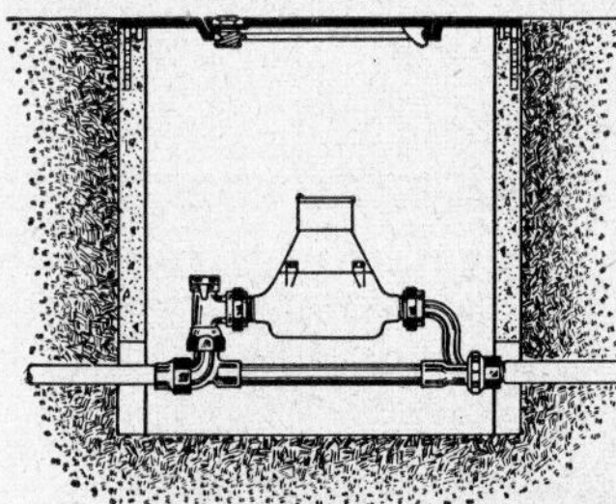

In this setting the service and the Ironcrete box are 3″ deeper than above, and the meter is raised that far in the box by the Linesetter. The bar of the Linesetter holds the service line in proper spacing and alignment even with the meter out.

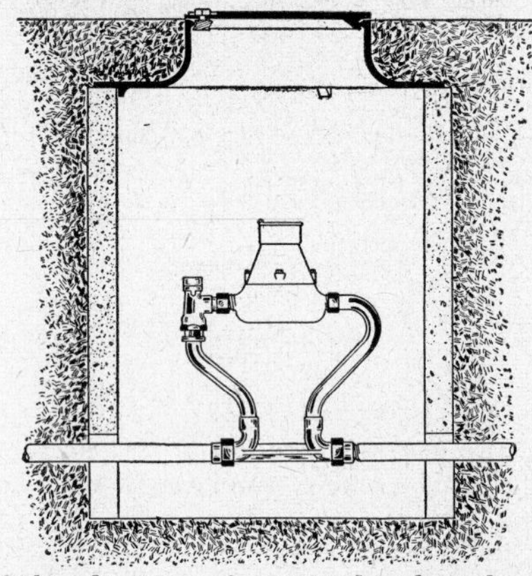

One of the advantages of concrete barrels is the ease of making notches in them. This 18″ barrel is notched about 4″ and has a No. 32 Type C Cover. The meter is raised 9″ by the Coppersetter.

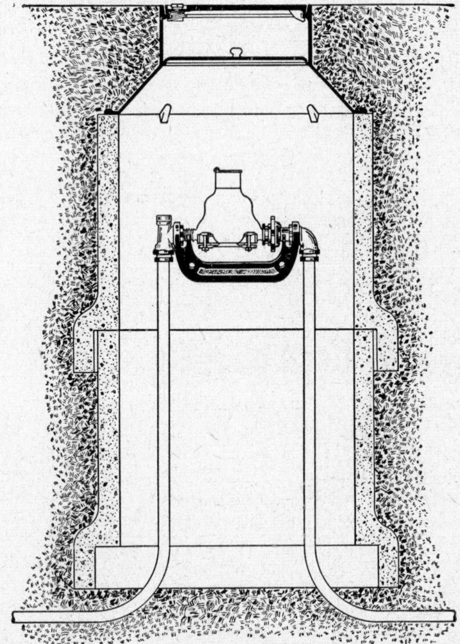

With increasing depth of services, riser pipes become longer and the many advantages of Ford Yokes become more obvious. In this setting the service is 54″ deep and two lengths of 20″ I. D. vitrified tile, bell ends down, are topped by a No. 3 Wabash Cover.

METER BOX COVERS

Ford meter box covers are made in dozens of types and sizes for meter box barrels ranging in diameter from 15" to 36", for rectangular meter pits, and for Ironcrete meter boxes. All have Lifter Worm Locks.

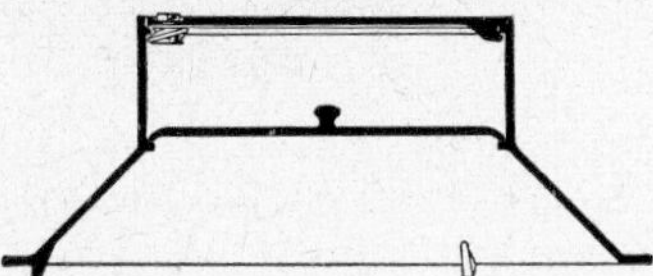

Wabash Double-lid covers provide a dead-air space in the neck to insulate against heat loss to the atmosphere. The extra depth of the cover and sloping sides also help to make Wabash covers the best meter protection available.

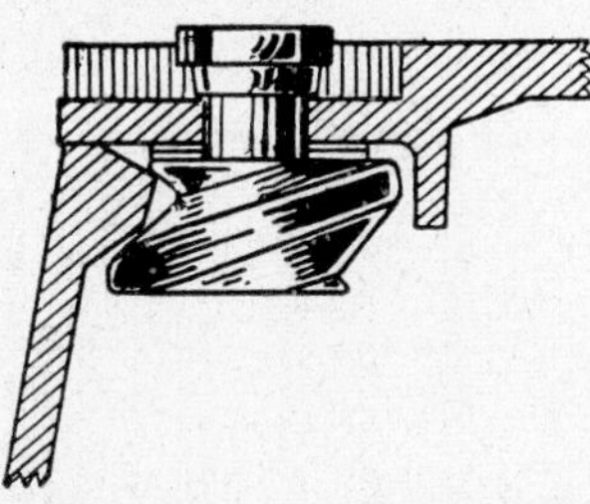

The distinguishing feature of all Ford meter box covers is the Lifter Worm Lock. Not only does it lock the lid firmly and safely in place but the action of unlocking raises the lid with a powerful screw-jack action, breaking the seal of ice or dirt. The key also automatically attaches to the bolt head so that it can be used as a lifting handle.

THE FORD RESETTER

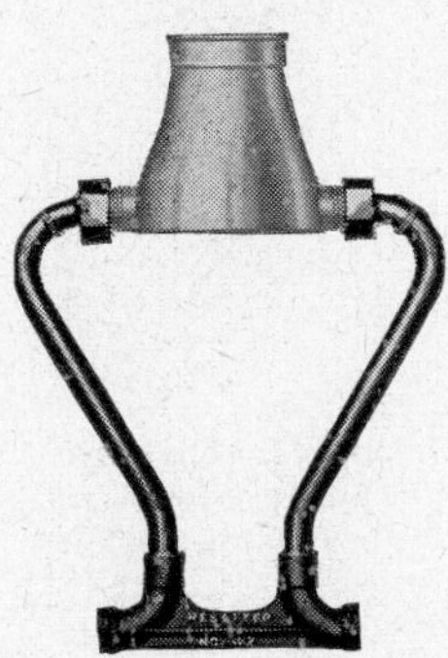

Many water meters in pits are set too low, bewteen ordinary meter couplings in straight runs of piping. Such meters are frequently covered with dirt or water, are hard to read and even harder to change. . . . The Resetter, all brass and copper, can be connected between the old couplings and the meter then set in the raised position. Resetters are made from 6" to 36" in height, both with and without valves.

FORD YOKES

Ford Yokes are made in a variety of types for all kinds of meter pits. They have been perfected and proved during forty years of service and millions are in use. Our catalog with the complete Ford Yoke story will be sent on request.

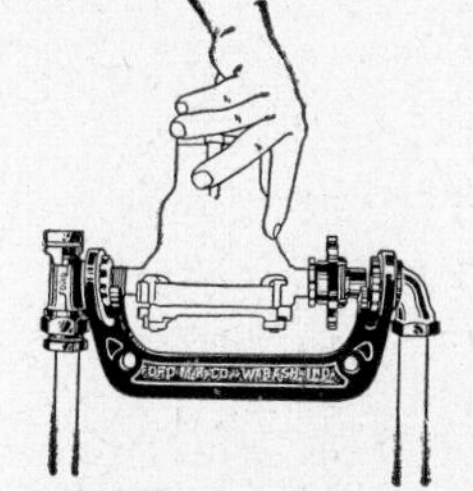

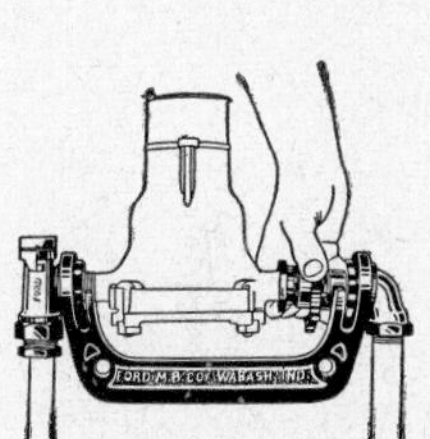

With Ford Yokes, meter changes are quick, easy and trouble-free. Service piping is not disturbed. Turning Expansion Connection handwheel makes or unmakes compression joints. No wrench is required in meter box.

RINGSTYLE VALVES AND COUPLINGS

The inclusion of a meter coupling nut with a service valve saves space and material and offers other valuable advantages. The nut on a Ringstyle valve is held behind the flange by a strong bronze ring.

Ringstyle valves are made in angle and straight line types and in sizes from ⅝" thru 1". Samples are available to any water works.

FORMS FOR CONCRETE BARRELS

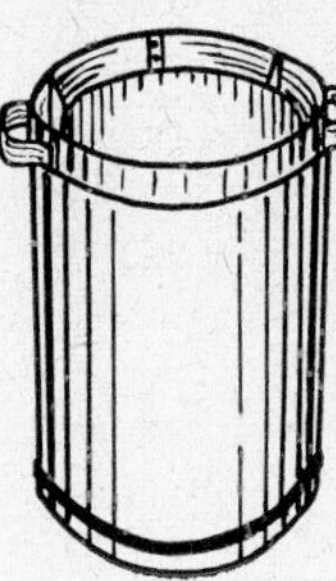

The use of Fiberforms for making concrete meter box barrels requires but a small initial investment. Thus, for small quantities, there are worthwhile savings. For large quantities required in a limited time there may be savings also, as many Fiberforms can be filled at one time. Fiberforms are made in diameters of 15", 18", 20" and 24" and in lengths from 15" to 24".

FORD METER TESTING EQUIPMENT

Complete catalog gives information on test benches and calibrated tanks for all sizes of meter shops, as well as useful accessories. Write for your copy.

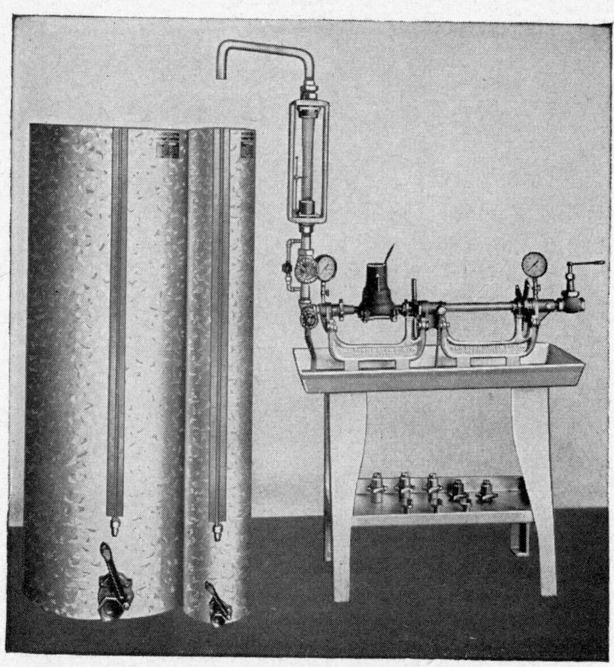

A two-unit Standard Test Bench with Testerate Indicator and Nos. 1 and 4 Calibrated Tanks provide convenience and accuracy for the small meter shop. Similar benches are made for holding up to eight meters.

The Clearvue Test Dial offers real advantages in series testing. It magnifies the motion of the test hand so that accurate tests can be made with one cubic foot or ten gallons. The dial plate is of transparent plastic and the hand has a friction drive so that it can be quickly adjusted to zero before a test is started.

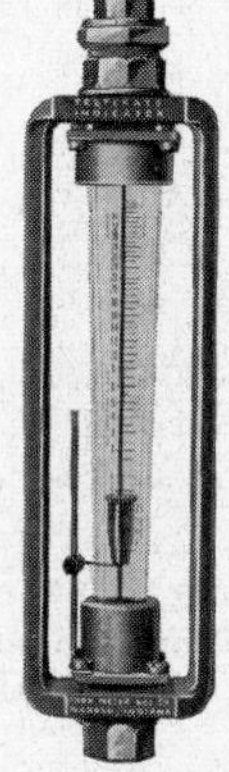

The Testerate Indicator shows clearly, quickly and accurately rates of flow in meter testing. It gives valuable information in any meter shop.

A 12-unit Indianapolis Type Test Bench with electric control in use in the water department at Akron, Ohio. Provides maximum efficiency in testing large numbers of 5/8″ meters.

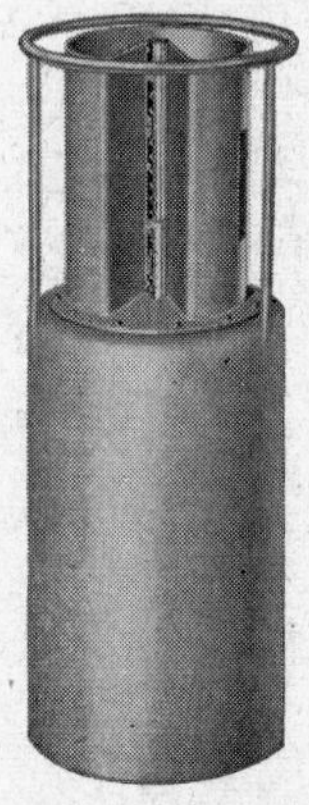

Portable Meter Testing Tanks are made for tests of one cubic foot or ten gallons and are accurate without being levelled. Useful for proving meter accuracy to doubting customers.

GREENLEE TOOL CO.

DIVISION OF GREENLEE BROS. & CO. 

1714 COLUMBIA AVE., ROCKFORD, ILL.

No. 790 Greenlee Hydraulic Pipe Pusher with Power Pump pushing pipe under roadway.

Two No. 795 Greenlee Pushers on the job pushing large concrete drainage duct 70 feet under several railroad tracks.

FAST, ECONOMICAL WAY TO INSTALL UNDERGROUND PIPE

quickly push pipe under streets, tracks, walks, lawns with Greenlee Hydraulic Pusher

Save hours of time . . . leave paving, sidewalks, lawns and tracks undisturbed . . . with this quick, low-cost way of installing underground pipe for gas, water, sewers, and electrical cables.

With a GREENLEE Hydraulic Pipe Pusher *one or two men* can quickly push pipe, drainage duct and concrete sewer pipe . . . either manually or with the GREENLEE Hydraulic Power Pump as shown in upper photo at left. No extensive trenching necessary, as short ground opening accommodates the Pusher. Eliminates tearing up, tunneling, backfilling, tamping, repaving . . . saves inconvenience to yourself, property owners, and the public.

Cut costs greatly, speed jobs . . . put this timesaving equipment to work in your city. See how it can pay for itself on the first few jobs.

TWO MODELS TO FIT YOUR EXACT NEEDS

Whether it's pipe, drainage ducts, or concrete sewer pipe you are installing, there's a GREENLEE Pusher for the job.

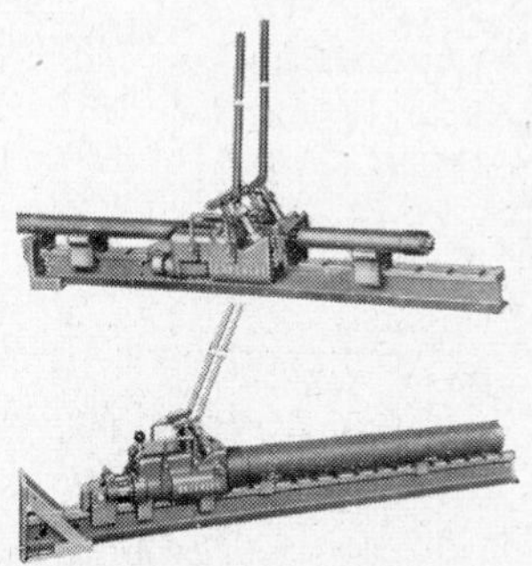

No. 790 For pushing ¾″ to 4″ pipe. Six operating speeds for varying soil conditions—with pushing pressure ranging from 6,500 to 40,000 pounds.

No. 795 For pipe larger than 4″, drainage ducts and concrete sewer pipe. Six operating speeds — 25,000 to 150,000 pounds pushing pressure.

FREE CATALOG DESCRIBING HYDRAULIC PIPE PUSHERS AND OTHER GREENLEE TIMESAVING TOOLS FOR ELECTRICAL AND CONSTRUCTION WORK

Well illustrated 12-page book gives complete data on GREENLEE Pipe Pushers and Power Pumps. Also describes GREENLEE Hydraulic Pipe Benders that let one man quickly make accurate bends in pipe up to 5″, conduit, tubing, bus-bars. Other tools shown include tubing benders, plumbers' bit sets, electricians' auger bits, cable pullers, joist borers, knockout punches and cutters, and many more. Write for your free copy today . . . ask for Catalog No. 35-E. Greenlee Tool Co., 1714 Columbia Avenue, Rockford, Illinois.

GREENLEE TOOL CO.

DIVISION OF GREENLEE BROS. & CO. 

1714 COLUMBIA AVE., ROCKFORD, ILL.

EASY, FAST METHOD OF BENDING PIPE, CONDUIT, TUBING, BUS-BARS

make smooth, accurate bends in a few minutes with a portable Greenlee Hydraulic Bender

Save time, cut costs on piping and conduit installations with a GREENLEE Bender. One-man operated, compact, portable. Makes smooth, accurate bends in just a few minutes by pumping handle. Can also be operated with a GREENLEE Power Pump for fast production jobs. No kinking or damage to pipe or conduit.

Newest of GREENLEE Benders is the No. 880 *lightweight* Hydraulic Bender, illustrated at right, for bending pipe and conduit of ½″ to 2″ sizes. Easily carried and operated by one man. Pipe supports are designed to serve also as rollers for easy moving of the unit.

Makes a full 90° bend with one stroke of the ram.

Light, but strong, aluminum alloy is used for many parts for big savings in weight with no sacrifice in strength. Separate two-speed hydraulic hand pump with special speed coupling on the hose and pump for simplified handling, quick setup.

No. 880 Hydraulic Bender

Other advanced features include new design of the bending ram so that it will also fit GREENLEE thin-wall conduit, tubing, and bus bar bending attachments. Designed for easy hand operation, the No. 880 can also be teamed with a GREENLEE Power Pump.

NO. 770 HYDRAULIC BENDER FOR 1¼″ - 3″ PIPE AND CONDUIT

Designed for bending conduit and pipe from 1¼″ to 3″ size, has a maximum piston pressure of 25 tons for fast, easy bending. The No. 770 Bender with regular equipment is designed to make bends in 1¼″, 1½″, 2″, 2½″, and 3″ conduit or pipe, without the use of heat or filler. Extra attachments available for bending ½″, ¾″, and 1″ sizes.

NO. 775 HYDRAULIC BENDER FOR PIPE AND CONDUIT UP TO 5″

Similar in design and construction to the No. 770 Bender, but of larger size, heavier weight, and greater hydraulic power. This GREENLEE Bender, especially designed to bend larger size conduit and pipe, has a maximum pressure of 40 tons and will easily make smooth bends in cold conduit and pipe. Accurately bends 3″, 3½″, 4″, and 5″ sizes. Extra shoes and supports are available for this machine, making it possible to bend 8 sizes of pipe from 1¼″ to 5″.

GREENLEE TOOL CO.

DIVISION OF GREENLEE BROS. & CO. 

1714 COLUMBIA AVE., ROCKFORD, ILL.

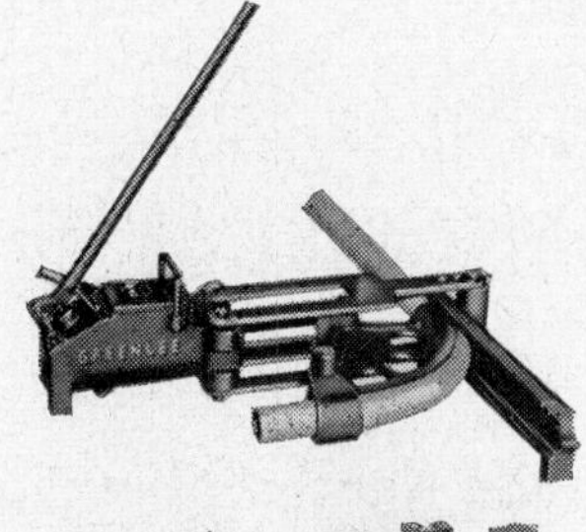

NOS. 770-T and 775-T THIN-WALL HYDRAULIC CONDUIT BENDERS

Consists of the Greenlee No. 770 or 775 Power Unit with attachments designed to make a full 90° bend quickly with one forward movement of the ram. The regular attachment for this machine, which will bend $\frac{3}{4}$", 1", $1\frac{1}{4}$", $1\frac{1}{2}$", and 2" thin-wall conduit, can easily and quickly be applied to the No. 770 or 775 Power Unit.

NOS. 770-BB and 775-BB HYDRAULIC BUS BAR BENDERS

For making accurate bus bar bends in a wide range of sizes. Consists of either the No. 770 or 775 Power Unit fitted with a Greenlee bus bar bending attachment. Regular "U" bends, 90° bends, or offsets are easily made.

NO. 785-BE POWER BENDER

A powerful portable bender for heavier bending assignments. Develops 100 tons of ram pressure to bend rigid conduit or standard pipe in $1\frac{1}{4}$" to 5" diameters, and is rugged enough to bend 5" extra-heavy or double extra-heavy material with ease. 20" stroke permits 90° bends in one setting. Can be driven by either an electric or gasoline motor.

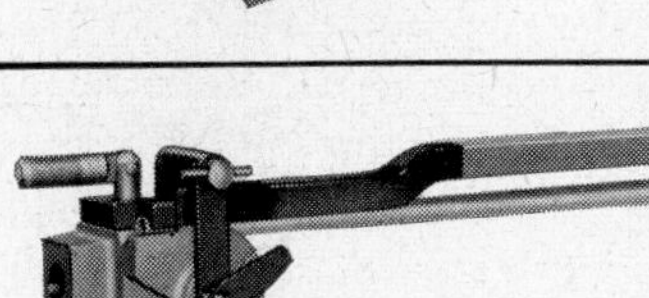

HAND BENDERS FOR TUBING, CONDUIT

Swiftly produce accurate small-radius bends (up to 180°) in conduit, pipe, and tubing. No flattening or kinks. Greenlee Hand Benders are especially designed to form neat bends to fit sharp corners, nooks, and other close quarters. Eliminates need for many manufactured bends and fittings. Various sizes and models for pipe, conduit, and steel, copper, brass, and aluminum tubing.

POWER PUMPS FOR HYDRAULIC BENDERS, PIPE PUSHERS, AND OTHER HYDRAULIC TOOLS

NO. 798-CO

NO. 798-GM

NO. 798-CO

Powerful, portable, lightweight. Operates at 10,000 psi intermittent pressure, 6,000 psi continuous pressure. $\frac{1}{2}$-hp, 115-volt a-c — d-c universal motor. (Also available with $\frac{1}{2}$-hp, 110-volt constant-speed motor.)

NO. 798-GM

Same as 798-CO above, but with $1\frac{1}{2}$-hp gasoline engine for use on jobs where electrical power is not available.

NO. 797-E

Double-piston, single-valve type developing up to 10,000 psi. Usually supplied with 2-hp, 60-cycle, 3-phase motor.

NO. 797-G

Same as No. 797-E above, but with $4\frac{1}{2}$-hp gasoline engine. Rubber-wheeled undercarriage also available.

NO. 797-E

NO. 797-G

WRITE FOR FREE CATALOG 35-E with complete data. Greenlee Tool Co., Rockford, Ill.

GREENLEE TOOL CO.

DIVISION OF GREENLEE BROS. & CO.  1714 COLUMBIA AVE., ROCKFORD, ILL.

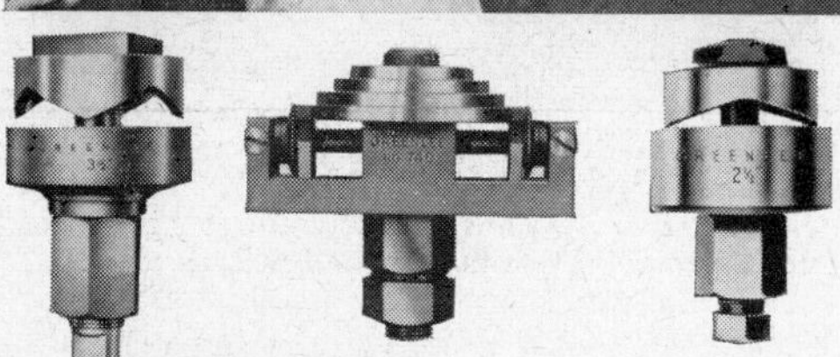

ACCURATE, CLEAN OPENINGS FOR CONDUIT MADE IN 1½ MINUTES OR LESS...

with Greenlee Knockout Punches

Speed the installation of conduit, reflectors in metal street signs, and other jobs with GREENLEE Knockout Punches and Cutters. Eliminate drilling and filing to enlarge holes. Do the job with these GREENLEE tools that cut smooth holes up to 4½″ for conduit in sizes ranging from ½″ to 4″. Do the job neater, faster, easier, this way. Turn with an ordinary wrench, or for faster, practically effortless operation use the GREENLEE Hydraulic Knockout Punch Driver. Delivers over 11 tons of ram pressure . . . cuts holes in 10-guage metal with ease.

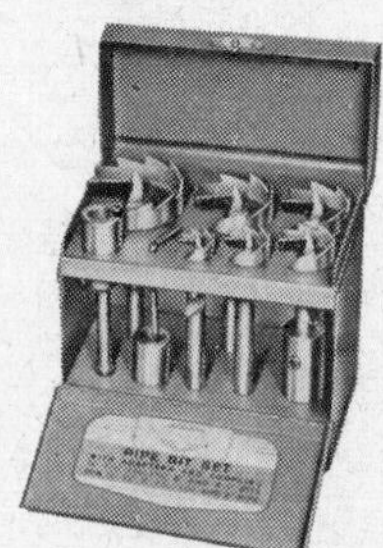

PLUMBER'S BIT SET FOR BORING PIPE-SIZE HOLES IN WOOD

Set of six fast-cutting bits designed especially for boring holes in wood for pipe and conduit. Furnished in a sturdy metal carrying case with convenient handle. Bits are sized to make holes for these sizes of pipe: ½″, ¾″, 1″, 1¼″, 1½″, 2″. Bits are designed for use in portable electric drills, but an adapter is also provided for use with standard auger bit braces.

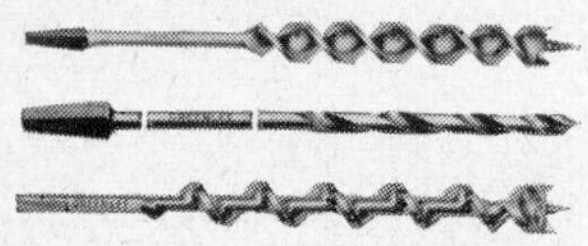

GREENLEE BORING TOOLS FOR BRACES AND ELECTRIC DRILLS

For quickly making clean, smooth openings, the GREENLEE line of high-quality boring tools includes Solid-Center Auger Bits; Electricians' Auger Bits; Expansive Bits; Electric-Drill Bits; Bell Hangers' Drills; Bit Extensions; Car Bits; and others.

SAVE TIME, CUT COSTS ON ELECTRICAL, PIPING, AND PLUMBING INSTALLATIONS WITH GREENLEE TOOLS . . . WRITE FOR CATALOG 35-E WITH COMPLETE DETAILS

GREENLEE timesaving tools are specifically engineered to save time on the job, make possible valuable savings in both work and materials. In many instances owners report that GREENLEE tools more than pay for themselves on the first few jobs. Get the new GREENLEE catalog now and see how you too can reduce costs with these tools . . . and get your jobs done better, faster. Greenlee Tool Co., 1714 Columbia Ave., Rockford, Illinois

KENNEDY VALVE MFG. CO.

Elmira, New York

SALES OFFICES

New York Philadelphia Chicago San Francisco Seattle Los Angeles

Export Office: 67 Wall St., New York 5, N. Y.

WAREHOUSES

New York Chicago San Francisco Atlanta

KENNEDY "SAFETOP" FIRE HYDRANTS

Fig. 1280
Kennedy
"SAFETOP"
Fire Hydrant

Distinguishing feature is the Safety Breakable Section. This section is fully as strong as the standpipe and stem of any hydrant, but in the event of a smashing impact it breaks cleanly apart when properly installed. Thus, damage is strictly localized to inexpensive parts. Numerous demonstrations and service tests with vehicles have proven the clean breaking of the "Safetop" hydrant with greatly reduced chances of injury to occupants.

The Safety Breakable Section consists of a standpipe breaking ring and a stem coupling both located a few inches above the ground level.

If broken, these parts may be renewed with the hydrant back in service within a half hour. Repair parts cost only about $10.00 and installation is made without excavating and without shutting off water service.

Collision repair parts are furnished compactly boxed for convenience and storage. The repair can be made by one man with a few commonly used tools.

• SPECIAL FEATURES •

Simple, positive operation — centrally located straight line mechanism without levers, pins or other complications.

Minimum Friction loss — carefully proportioned elbow without depressions or pockets; inlet valve with net area greater than nominal size of hydrant; nozzles have bell entrances and carefully shaped interiors.

Extra-large standpipe — 7" diameter for 4" size; 8½" diameter for 5" and 6" sizes; smooth and free from obstructions.

Flood-proof — inlet valve closes in the direction of pressure from the main; therefore, the water pressure alone keeps the valve tightly closed in case of accidental breakage of the standpipe.

Frost-proof — double, positive-acting drain valve automatically opens when the inlet valve is closed, keeping the standpipe free from water.

Leak-proof, durable valves and gaskets — G. R. S. synthetic rubber inlet valve, best quality leather-faced double drain valve, special composition gaskets.

Convenience of adjustment — all operating parts readily accessible without excavation; hydrant readily altered for change of grade without shutting off the water pressure.

Protected from theft or tampering — all adjustable parts fully enclosed within the cover; nozzles screwed and pinned in standpipe.

Best material — vital parts made of hard bronze; bronze stuffing box and gland nuts and rust-proofed studs; standpipe exceptionally heavy for resistance to impacts and tested to 300 lbs. hydrostatic pressure.

Write for Bulletin 105

Fig. 1080
Kennedy
STANDARD
Fire Hydrant
Fig. 56

KENNEDY STANDARD FIRE HYDRANTS

This design is a one-piece fire hydrant with the same cover assembly, operating mechanism, inlet and drain valves as in the "SAFETOP" Fire Hydrant. The same special features are incorporated into its design and manufacture as those listed under the "SAFETOP".

Many hundreds of thousands of these hydrants are in use all over the country. They have the same sturdy construction, simple positive operation and attractive appearance as the "SAFETOP" Fire Hydrant but they do not have the safety breakable section since the standpipe and stem are each in one piece.

KENNEDY VALVE MFG. CO.

Elmira, New York

Fig. 56

Fig. 571

KENNEDY A.W.W.A. VALVES

Kennedy A.W.W.A. valves are designed for use in water works systems. They conform to specifications of the American Water Works Association and in several particulars these valves exceed these A.W.W.A. standard requirements of strength and refinements of design.

While the A.W.W.A. specifications cover only bell end and flanged non-rising stem valves, the Kennedy line of A.W.W.A. Standard Gate Valves includes outside-screw-and-yoke valves, as shown on the opposite page, with various types of end connections listed at the bottom of both pages.

Kennedy A.W.W.A. valves are made in sizes of 2" through 48" and are designed for water working pressures of from 50 through 150 lbs. They may be furnished for manual, gear, electric motor or hydraulic cylinder control. Valves can be supplied to operate horizontally, upright or at an angle.

Special feature is the hook-and-wedge-type disc mechanism consisting of two wedges and two hooks actuated by stops cast in the valve body. In closing, the parallel discs and seat faces move so closely upon each other that foreign matter is scraped off. At the instant of closing, the discs are exactly opposite their ports and are forced by the wedges against their seats. In opening, the action is reversed. The discs are released by the first stem movement while further stem movement completes the operation with an ease not obtainable with other types of valves. Either disc may be toward the pressure. Large size valves for horizontal operation have discs equipped with rollers traveling on tracks to reduce friction and have scrapers to keep these tracks clean.

O-RING SEALS

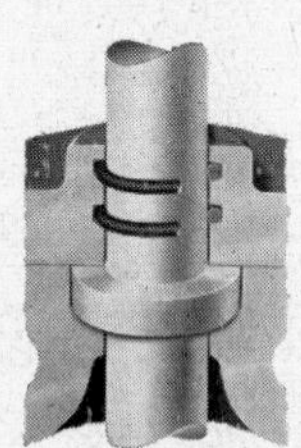

Kennedy A.W.W.A. valves may be furnished with O-Ring Seals. These are assembled into the stuffing box which forms the top thrust bearing for the stem collar. The top O-Ring is the dirt seal and the lower O-Ring is the pressure seal eliminating any need of further adjustment. O-Rings provide an excellent seal, preventing any binding of the stem and resulting in very easy valve operation.

Special feature of Kennedy O-Ring construction is that the O-Ring packing lies above the collar and therefore, permits repacking of the valve while under pressure.

A.W.W.A. Non-Rising Stem Gate Valves for installation in Water Distribution Systems, Pumping Stations and Water Treatment Plants are available with a variety of pipe connections. Valves can be furnished with pipe connections as identified below or in combinations of these pipe connections.

TYPES OF CONNECTIONS	Figure Numbers
Bell Ends	56
Mechanical Joint Ends	571
Asbestos Cement Pipe Ends	—
Ring-Tite Ends	573
Universal Ends	562
Flanged Ends	561
Spigot Ends	570
One end bell and one end flanged	563
One end bell and one end spigot	560
One end ring-tite and one end flanged	579

These valves will be furnished with conventional stuffing boxes, packing and gland unless otherwise specified. If valves are required with O-Ring Seals, the suffix "X" will be added to the figure number to properly identify this construction.

KENNEDY VALVE MFG. CO.

Elmira, New York

KENNEDY A.W.W.A. VALVES

Fig. 566

CONSTRUCTION

DISCS are of Kennedy Higher-Strength Cast Iron with Bronze Facings. Deep ribs assure ample strength in resisting distortion. In sizes 14" and larger, discs are provided with wedge contact surfaces of Kennedy Standard Bronze. In the 3" size, the entire disc assembly is Kennedy Standard Bronze.

WEDGES are Kennedy Standard Manganese Bronze. They have the same angle on both sides and are interchangeable.

HOOKS are of Kennedy Higher-Strength Cast Iron, extremely heavy. They are retained in place by ribs in the back of each disc.

STEMS of 24" and smaller valves are Kennedy Standard Manganese Bronze of 60,000 lbs. per sq. in. tensile strength. In sizes 30" and larger, Kennedy Higher-Strength Manganese Bronze of 80,000 lbs. per sq. in. tensile strength is used.

STEM NUT is Kennedy Standard Bronze with ample thread contact.

BONNETS. In sizes 14" and larger, the bonnet thrust bearing recess and stem hole are bronze bushed and body-to-bonnet flanges are positioned by dowel pins.

STUFFING BOX is Kennedy Higher-Strength Cast Iron and is bronze bushed on 14" and larger valves.

GLANDS on 12" and smaller valves are of Kennedy Standard Bronze and the gland follower is of Kennedy Higher-Strength Cast Iron. In larger sizes the gland is of Kennedy Higher-Strength Cast Iron and is bronze bushed.

In non-rising stem valves the gland is secured by three or more bolts and in outside-screw-and-yoke valves the glands have two bolts. Gland adjusting nuts are bronze.

TESTING. Each valve is tested at 300 lbs. per sq. in. hydrostatic pressure and at the rated Working Water Pressure.

PAINTING. Two coatings of asphalt varnish are applied both inside and outside to ferrous parts of these valves.

Fig. 565

While the A.W.W.A. Specifications cover only bell end and flanged end non-rising stem gate valves in the size range of 3" through 48", these Kennedy Outside-Screw-and-Yoke Gate Valves conform with these A.W.W.A. detailed specifications. These valves can be furnished in sizes 3" through 48" and with a variety of pipe connections as shown in the following table:

TYPES OF CONNECTIONS	Figure Numbers
Bell Ends	565
Mechanical Joint Ends	581
Asbestos Cement Pipe Ends	—
Ring-Tite Ends	583
Universal Ends	567
Flanged Ends	566
Spigot Ends	590
One end bell and one end flanged	568
One end bell and one end spigot	580
One end ring-tite and one end flanged	584

KENNEDY VALVE MFG. CO.

Elmira, New York

• Other KENNEDY Products •

125-Pound IRON-BODY WEDGE GATE VALVES

Iron-Body Bronze-Mounted or All-Iron

INSIDE SCREW NON-RISING STEM

Bronze-mounted valves recommended for steam, oil, water or gas lines.

All-Iron for handling fluids that attack bronze parts. Fig. 058 is Bronze - Mounted, Bronze Stem. Fig. 083 is All-Iron, Steel Stem.

Fig. 058

OUTSIDE-SCREW-AND-YOKE

Bronze-mounted valves recommended for steam, water, oil or gas lines.

All-Iron for handling fiuids that attack bronze parts. Fig. 0611 is Bronze - Mounted, Bronze Stem. Fig. 086 is All-Iron, Steel Stem.

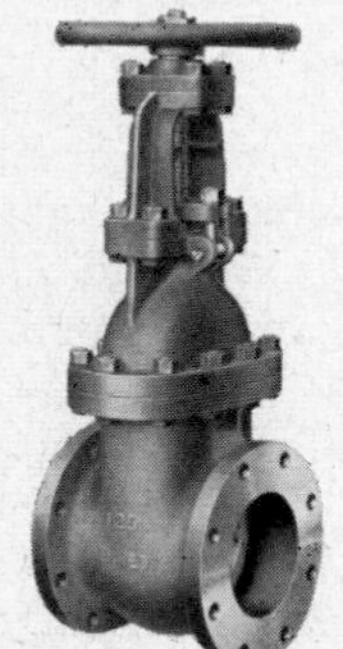

Fig. 0611

KENNEDY - PENNIE Back-Water and Sewer-Gas Valve

Fig. 55

Iron-Body Bronze-Mounted with counterbalanced disc. Bell and Spigot ends. A positive-acting seal against back water, sewer gas and vermin in waste pipes.

UNDERWRITER'S-APPROVED "National Standard" Valves and Indicator Posts

Fig. 70

Fig. 54 Assembly of Fig. 70 Bell End valve and Fig. 541 Indicator Post with Fig. 543 Operating Wrench.

At left, Fig. 70 with Bell Ends. Valves furnished with Screwed, Flanged or Mechanical Joint Ends.

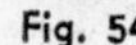

Fig. 54

HYDRAULIC CONTROLS

Fig 611FTR

Recommended for the following conditions:

On valves located in places of difficult access; on valves where speedy opening or closing is desired; in installations comprising a large number of valves which are to be frequently operated; on extra-large valves for easy operation.

ELECTRICAL CONTROLS

Recommended for the following conditions:

On large valves requiring considerable time and labor to open or close manually; on emergency valves or valves which must be speedily opened or closed; on valves in hard - to - reach locations; on valves with controls at two or more points; on valves in large installations and requiring frequent operation.

Fig. 611G

LOCK JOINT PIPE COMPANY

East Orange, New Jersey

Sales Offices: Chicago, Ill. • Columbia, S. C. • Denver, Col.
Detroit, Mich. • Hartford, Conn. • Kansas City, Mo.

on a Lock Joint "Foundation"

City planners and engineers are taking a long, hard look at everything connected with water supply — the most serious problem affecting the city's future growth. That's why so many cities, all over the world, have selected Lock Joint Pressure Pipe's greater security, more dependable performance, longer life. They know that their plans for meeting future water supply requirements must include pipes whose high carrying capacity will be as great scores of years from now as they are today.

In addition to a solid foundation for the water supply system of the future, Lock Joint Pressure Pipe offers important economies — low first cost, economical installation, low pumping costs and negligible maintenance charges.

LOCK JOINT PIPE CO.

East Orange, N. J.

***Sales Offices:* Chicago, Ill.; Columbia, S. C.; Denver, Col.; Detroit, Mich.; Hartford, Conn.; Kansas City, Mo.**

LOCK JOINT PIPE COMPANY specializes in the manufacture of reinforced concrete pressure pipe in diameters ranging from 16" to 150" and upward for any pressure common to water works practice. This pipe is available in such a wide variety of designs that it is possible to select one which will be ideally suited both in performance and in economy to the individual requirements of any pipeline project. The basic designs are:

REINFORCED CONCRETE PRESSURE PIPE—In diameters from 24" upward, and designed for pipelines whose maximum working pressure is less than 100' of head.

REINFORCED CONCRETE CYLINDER PIPE—A heavy duty pipe produced in diameters from 24" upward and designed for any pressure common to water works practice.

PRESTRESSED CONCRETE CYLINDER PIPE—A lighter weight pipe, exceptionally resistant to external loading. Available in diameters from 16" to 48" and designed for any pressure common to water works practice.

PRESTRESSED CONCRETE EMBEDDED CYLINDER PIPE—An extremely rugged pressure pipe recommended for pipelines of large diameter and high operating head.

REINFORCED CONCRETE SUBAQUEOUS PIPE—A heavy walled pipe with a special joint harness for subaqueous installation. Produced in diameters from 24" upward, this pipe may be constructed with or without the steel cylinder, according to pressure requirements.

All five types of pipe, starting at a stipulated minimum design, may be engineered to meet individual specification for pressure and backload. Incorporated in all designs is an ample safety factor for water hammer based on conservative allowance for surge pressures to which the individual pipeline may be subjected. All basic designs of Lock Joint Pressure Pipe may be made to the specifications approved by the American Water Works Association for the manufacture of reinforced concrete pressure pipe.

The Lock Joint Rubber and Steel Joint is an integral part of every type of Lock Joint Pressure Pipe. This joint, sealed by a rubber gasket is completely watertight and amply flexible to provide for expansion or contraction due to temperature changes, to accommodate ground settlement and to resist shocks and vibration.

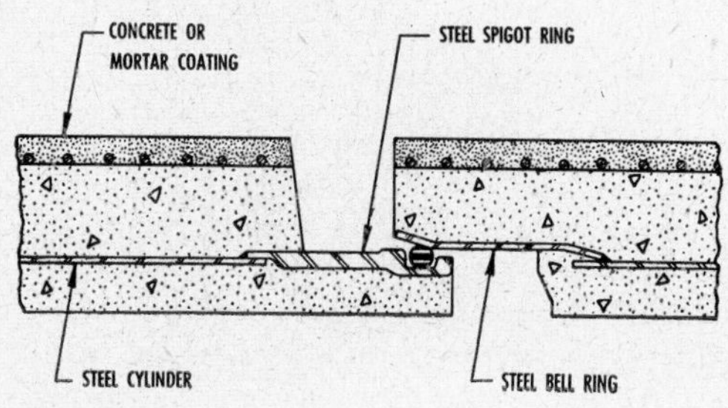

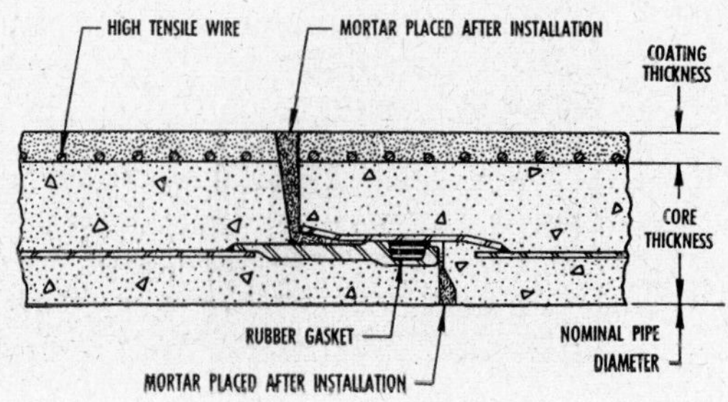

WATER
YOUR PLANTS
AND WATCH
THEM GROW!
Today, water is as basic to industrial development as it always has been to agriculture. Since thriving industry is essential to the growth and prosperity of the community, a water supply system capable of sustaining a high rate of industrial expansion is a prime concern of the community.
Such a system requires that the water supply and distribution pipelines be as efficient and indestructible as is economically possible. In pipelines 16 inches in diameter and larger, this can best be realized with LOCK JOINT CONCRETE PRESSURE PIPE.
This pipe retains its initial high carrying capacity throughout an exceptionally long life, is low in initial cost, and requires very little, if any, maintenance. More important still, its record for unfailing, trouble-free service is unexcelled
LOCK JOINT PIPE COMPANY
East Orange, New Jersey
Sales Offices: Chicago, Ill. • Columbia, S. C. • Denver, Col. • Detroit, Mich. • Hartford, Conn. • Kansas City, Mo.
Pressure • Water • Sewer • REINFORCED CONCRETE PIPE • Culvert • Subaqueous

A complete service from exploration to installation of Layne equipment in Layne-drilled wells.

Cities, large and small—not only in this country, but the wide world over—have found that by putting all of their water eggs in the Layne basket they have attained highest efficiency, lowest operating cost and an absolute minimum of maintenance and upkeep cost.

Layne service is unique in its completeness. Through Layne associate companies, Layne service is available anywhere to users large and small. Layne service means individual responsibility from preliminary surveys through every phase of development, including the design, manufacture and installation of required well screens, large diameter well casing and vertical turbine pumping equipment, all for each particular installation. Expert supervision is provided during construction work and assistance given in placing the completed system in service.

The various associate companies are located throughout the United States and in Canada, Mexico and many foreign countries. Each company has its own trained and experienced personnel, thoroughly familiar with ground water and pumping conditions peculiar to its territory. They offer, without any obligation, an advisory service to all present and prospective users of ground water. This service coordinates with and supplements services of water works superintendents and consulting engineers.

Upon inquiry, complete information will be supplied on the construction of a new well water system of any size, the reconditioning of old wells, the supplying and installation of Layne Vertical Turbine Pumps from 40 gallons to 20,000 gallons per minute—or the installation of a complete water treatment unit. Complete catalogs, bulletins and descriptive literature will be supplied without cost or obligation. Your inquiry may be made to your nearest Layne Associate Company or direct to

LAYNE
& BOWLER, INC.
MEMPHIS
General Offices and Factory
Memphis 8, Tennessee, U.S.A.

Gravel Wall Wells

The most efficient way to secure water from underground formations is with a Layne Gravel Wall Well. Here are just four important reasons why:

1. Effective retention of native sands without movement into the gravel envelope during maximum pumping demands
2. Greatly increased specific capacity, resulting in decreased pumping head and reduced pumping cost
3. Prevention of mineral and other deposits upon the screen which tend to close the openings and bring about decreased production, greater pumping head and resultant increased pumping costs, and
4. Very low inflow and entrance velocity, making for permanence.

For severe conditions, or when there is any possibility of contamination from surface waters, Layne Cemented Wells afford the ultimate in safety (purity of supply) and durability (longevity). All space about the well casing is completely filled from bottom to top with pure cement slurry. This effectively seals off and preserves the original source of supply.

The illustration shows how it is possible to under-ream (enlarge) the water-bearing formation and finish a large diameter gravel wall well. The cross sectional area of the under-reamed portion of the well is considerably larger than that of the casing set in the bore hole. This type well when constructed properly produces a phenomenal quantity of sand-free water.

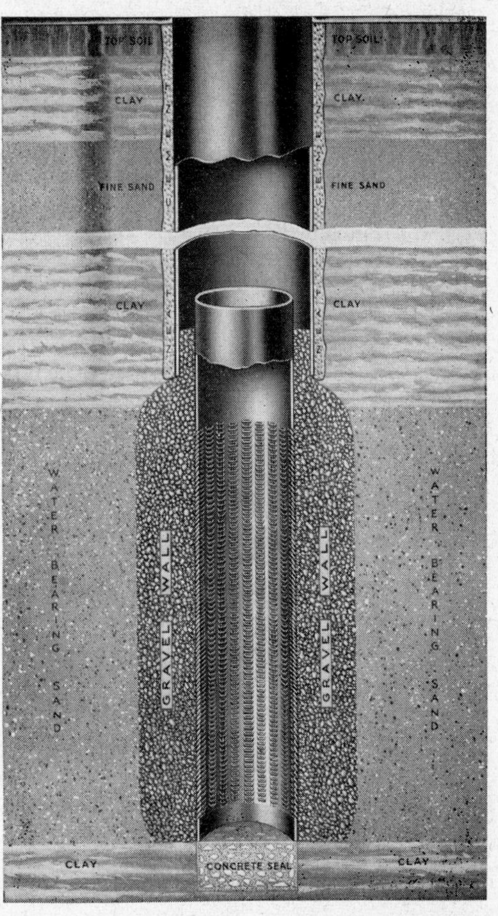

APPROVED FIRE UNDERWRITERS' PUMPS

Special Drive Head for approved Fire Underwriters' Pumps, using vertical hollow shaft, direct connected electric motors. Photograph shows complete set of Underwriter approved fittings which may be furnished with drive head at additional cost. These special heads are available for various sizes and capacities of Fire Underwriters' pumps, as covered by specifications of Fire Underwriters' Laboratories, Incorporated, and all carry the Underwriters' label.

Fire Underwriters' Pumps are furnished in short coupled types for pumping from reservoirs, tanks, or other sources of supply involving low lifts. They also are available for pumping from wells.

SHUTTER-TYPE GRAVEL SCREENS

Designed and Manufactured for Layne Gravel Wall Wells

Layne Shutter Screen is designed for installation in Layne Gravel Wall Wells only. It is not used in tubular or other type wells nor is it sold indiscriminately for installation by drillers or others who do not have the knowledge and experience necessary for the reclamation of ground water by means of properly constructed gravel wall wells.

Welded pipe or tubing is used for manufacturing Layne Shutter Screen. No wire, bars, supports or gadgets are used —nothing to become loose or get out of adjustment. The openings are made without loss of material and are arched to increase the strength of the screen.

No well is better than the screen set in the water-bearing sands. It must permit free entrance of water, yet exclude the sand. Selection of the proper type, size and quantity of screen is one of the most important phases of ground water development. Nearly all well screens are designed for use in tubular wells only, and if used in gravel wall wells, results are usually disappointing.

A study of the illustrations on this page will bring conviction that this is a different screen, one that is the result of approaching a problem from an unconventional angle, developing an idea and then proving it with actual field construction throughout a period of years. For example, Layne Shutter Screen is made by using a plain cylinder or tube and die punching a series of openings or slots without removing even a trace of material. All openings are uniform in length and width. The metal at each opening is pushed outward and slightly upward. Thus the louvers form an arch which strengthens the cylinder and protects the openings.

For Unusual Conditions

The screen is the most important part of a gravel wall well. Upon it largely depend both performance and permanence—the difference between success and failure. No well can be better than the screen set in the water-bearing formation. Water frequently is corrosive and attacks ordinary well screens. For such conditions Layne Shutter Screens can be furnished in Silicon-Manganese (Everdur) Bronze, Stainless Steel and Monel Metal, depending upon requirements of the individual installation.

The precision machining of Layne Shutter-Type Gravel Screens is evident in the cutaway photograph at top. Screens are manufactured in 4" to 48" diameters and 5' lengths which are welded together to form 10', 15' and 20' field lengths. Joints are prepared for field welding (lower photo) as screen is placed in well. Screw-coupled connections can be furnished also.

Vertical Turbine Pumps

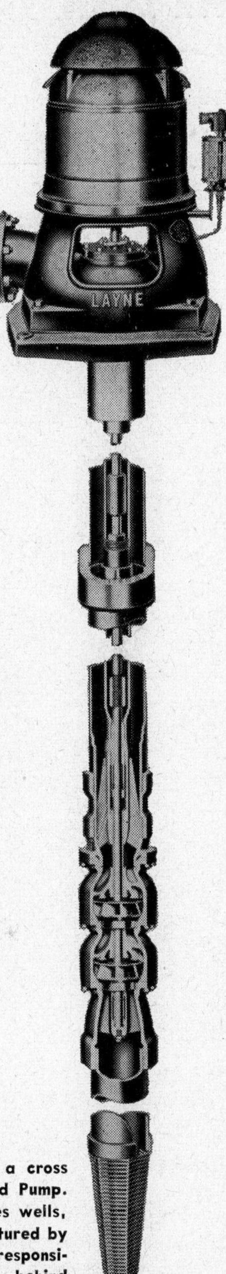

They are designed and built to perform specific jobs. Years of Layne experience in underground water development are backed by a performance test of each Layne pump before it is shipped to the job. Ability to meet the specific needs of a specific job is checked and re-checked by actual test before it is shipped into the field.

Bowls

Standard bowls are semi-steel with zincless, phosphor gear bronze, enclosed impellers mounted on oversize stainless steel shafts. Each bowl or stage is fitted with plastic bronze bearing and removable wear ring.

Discharge Column

Column pipe is full weight. No casing or thin pipe is supplied on Layne pumps. Connections are either flanged type or heavy cast semi-steel couplings. Column sections are made in lengths of 10 or 20 feet. An aligning spider is installed in each joint. Shafting is highest grade steel bought under rigid specifications for quality, straightness and roundness. Shaft couplings are made from solid shaft stock. Shaft bearings are plastic bronze and threaded on the outside to serve as couplings for the shaft tubing. The entire line shaft operates in a continuous extra heavy steel tubing which not only protects the shafting but also provides for thorough and positive lubrication of its entire length.

Pump Heads

Head assemblies are arranged for drive by any standard make of hollow shaft or solid shaft motor, by direct connected vertical steam turbine, by belt or right angle gear for engine drive, or with special heads for combination motor-engine drive.

Water Lubricated Pumps

Layne Pumps are furnished for water lubrication if preferred. Capacities and types are the same as the standard Layne oil lubricated pumps. Line shaft bearings are Goodrich Cutless rubber mounted in hollow spider hubs at each column joint. That portion of the line shaft coming in contact with the rubber bearing is covered with a non-corrosive sleeve.

For further information catalogs, etc., address

LAYNE
& BOWLER, INC.
MEMPHIS
General Offices and Factory
Memphis 8, Tennessee, U.S.A.

The illustration at the right shows a cross section view of a Layne Oil Lubricated Pump. No other concern in the world furnishes wells, screens casings and pumps, all manufactured by one organization. There is no divided responsibility. The Layne organization stands behind every pump and is always available if and when service is needed.

ASSOCIATE COMPANIES

- Layne-Arkansas Co. Stuttgart, Arkansas
- Layne-Atlantic Co. Norfolk, Va.
- Layne-Central Co. Memphis, Tennessee
- International Water Corp. Pittsburgh, Pa.
- International Water Supply, Ltd. London, Ont.
- Layne-Louisiana Co. Lake Charles, La.
- Louisiana Well Co. Monroe, La.
- Layne-Minnesota Co. Minneapolis, Minn.
- Layne-New York Co., Inc. Linden, N. J.
- Layne-Northern Co. Mishawaka, Ind.
- Layne-Northwest Co. Milwaukee, Wis.
- Layne-Ohio Co. Columbus, Ohio
- Layne-Pacific, Inc. Seattle, Wash.
- Layne Pumps, Inc. Lubbock, Tex.
- Layne Texas Co. Houston, Tex.
- Layne-Western Co. Kansas City, Mo.
- Layne Irrigation Co. Kearney, Neb.

THE LUDLOW VALVE MANUFACTURING CO., INC.

TROY, N. Y.

(LUDLOW) Ludlow and Rensselaer Valves and Hydrants (RENSSELAER)

Canadian Ludlow Valve Mfg. Co., Ltd., Montreal

(LUDLOW)

List 90-0

A. W. W. A.

FIRE HYDRANTS

1. **LESS OPERATING TORQUE!** New, non-binding upper and lower "O" rings trap lubricant . . . assure positive watertight seal . . . require no servicing.
2. **POP-OFF SLEEVE COUPLING** releases hydrant head from stem in event of traffic damage.
3. **GROUND LINE FLANGE** eliminates digging.
4. **90,000 TENSILE STRENGTH** Rolled Everdur threaded stem section completely eliminates stem failure.
5. **NO FLOODING.** Closed hydrant remains locked — even in event of traffic accident.
6. **NO FREEZING.** Positive drip action, at extreme bottom, assures complete drainage.

ASK FOR THE BULLETINS

Mechanical Joint End

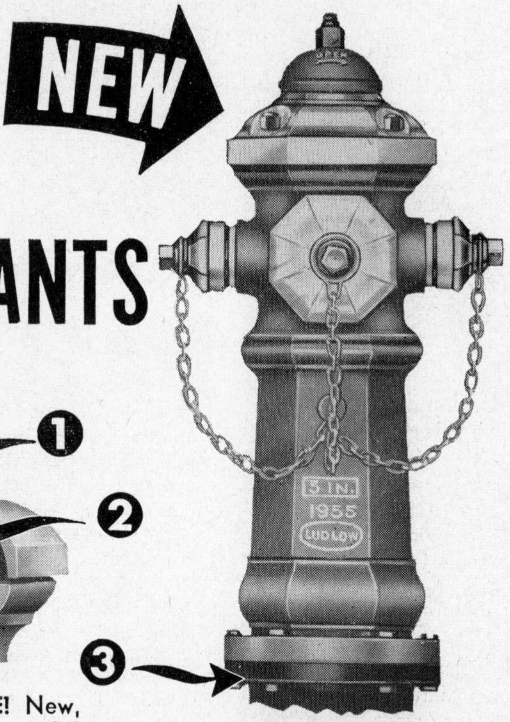

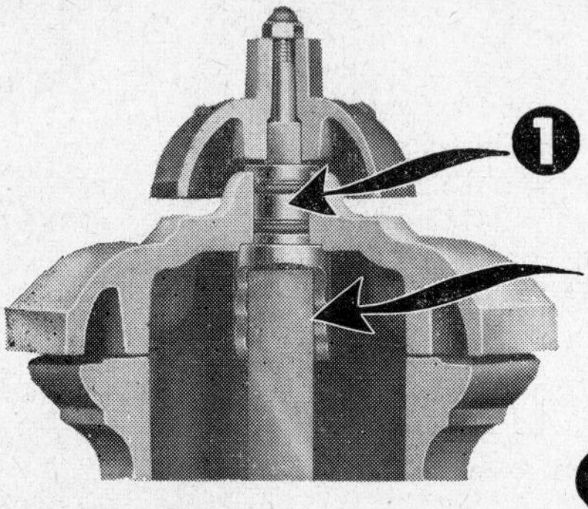

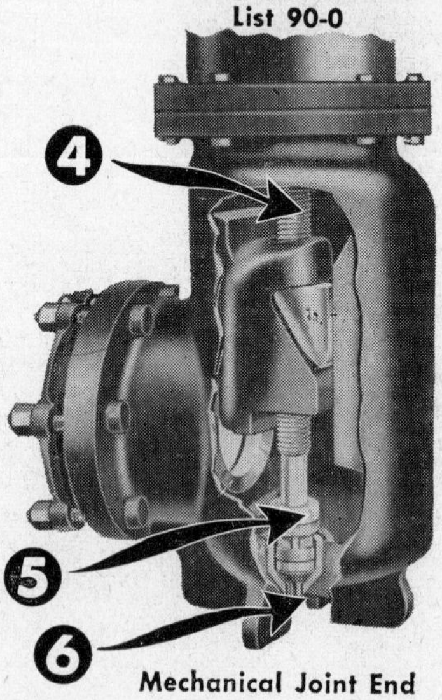

THE LUDLOW VALVE MANUFACTURING CO., INC.

TROY, N. Y.

Ludlow and Rensselaer Valves and Hydrants
Canadian Ludlow Valve Mfg. Co., Ltd., Montreal

Hub Ends with "O" Ring Stuffing Box.

A.W.W.A.

DOUBLE DISC PARALLEL SEAT

GATE VALVES

- SIMPLICITY OF DESIGN provides for greater ease of operation, maintenance and installation.
- SUPERIOR MATERIALS and PRECISION MACHINING assure longer, trouble-free service life, eliminating need for costly repairs.
- EASY OPENING and CLOSING mean smoother operation, less wear and tear.
- NO GRINDING WEAR on gates and case rings makes for greater efficiency of operation.
- PARALLEL SEAT construction provides wiping action, removing foreign matter from seats when closing.
- GATE and WEDGE MECHANISM complete in four rugged parts.
- PRECISION CUT MODIFIED ACME TREADS ON STEM.
- WITHSTANDS PRESSURE from either side of gates.
- TIGHT SEATING assured by Micro Finished seats.
- EACH VALVE INDIVIDUALLY INSPECTED and HYDROSTATICALLY TESTED in accordance with A. W. W. A. Specifications.

Mechanical Joint Ends Available with Conventional or "O" Ring Stuffing Box.

Bevel Gear, Gear Cover, By-Pass and Position Indicator. (Available with Hub, Flanged or Mechanical Joint Ends)

ASK FOR THE BULLETINS

THE LUDLOW VALVE MANUFACTURING CO., INC.

TROY, N. Y.

Ludlow and Rensselaer Valves and Hydrants
Canadian Ludlow Valve Mfg. Co., Ltd., Montreal

GATE VALVES

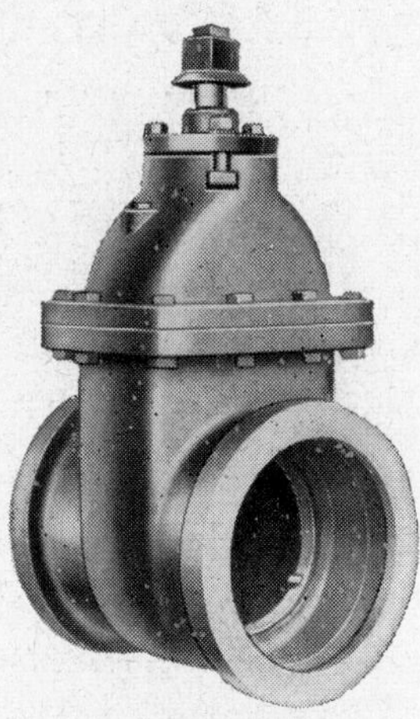

DOUBLE DISC: In closing these valves, gates are WEDGED tight, the moment they reach closing point opposite seats. In opening, the wedge is positively and mechanically released by very first turn of valve stem, loosening BOTH gates. Additional turns lift loosened gate to full open position. Thus Rensselaer wedge-action means easy closing and opening, minimizes frictional wear on gate and seat rings. Simple, rugged construction. Types include both non-rising stem and outside screw and yoke valves, and may be furnished with hub, flange, screw or other connections and combinations when specified.

SQUARE BOTTOM: The pioneer valve supporting the downstream gate in THREE places at EVERY point in its travel. Constant 3-point support eliminates tendency of downstream gate to tilt into downstream port opening when partly open, and scar the face of gate and seat rings. During entire operation, stainless steel tracks hold gate free of seat ring, until near closing point — then tracks taper, allowing contact. Recommended for main line valves, emergency shut-off, frequent operation, throttling service, vertical pipe lines.

ASK FOR THE BULLETINS

THE LUDLOW VALVE MANUFACTURING CO., INC.

TROY, N. Y.

Ludlow and Rensselaer Valves and Hydrants
Canadian Ludlow Valve Mfg. Co., Ltd., Montreal

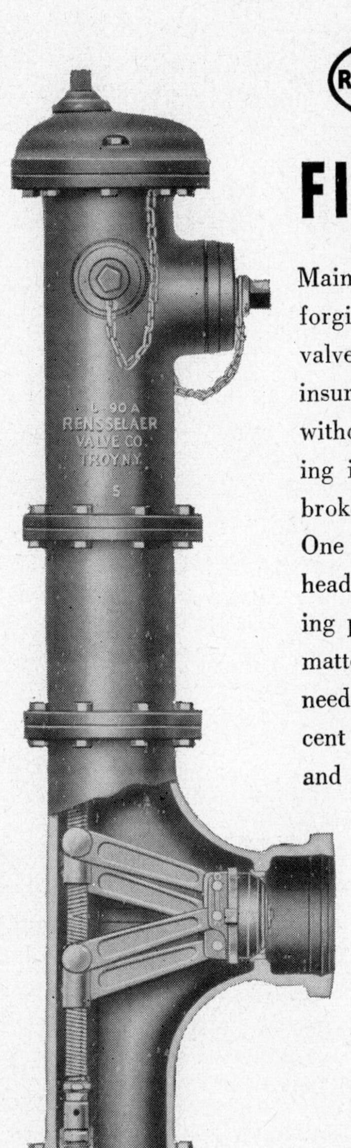

RENSSELAER **COREY**

FIRE HYDRANTS

Main valve mechanically locked shut by steel forgings bearing against case. Special rubber valve seats will not scar or leak. Solid bronze insures long life of vital parts. Drains fast, without clogging. No water hammer. No flooding if barrel is broken. No digging to renew broken barrel, thanks to flange at ground line. One man, just by opening valve and removing head, can easily take out and replace all working parts of the Rensselaer Fire Hydrant in a matter of minutes. No special tools or hoist needed. Thousands in satisfactory service. Recent developments include the "O" Ring Seal and Ring-Tite joints.

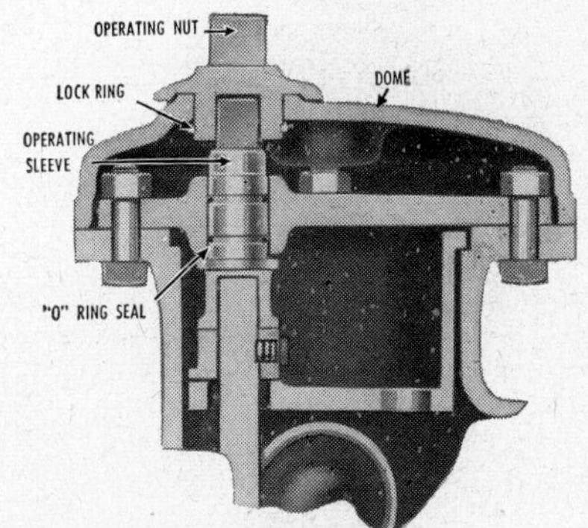

Hydrant Head with "O"-Ring Seal

ASK FOR THE BULLETINS

A. Y. McDONALD MFG. CO.

DUBUQUE, IOWA

over a century of dependable service

E-4701—Corporation Stop with straight coupling nut Inlet is Standard A.W.W.A. thread. Outlet is for copper service pipe same size as stop except ⅝ inch size which is for ¾ inch copper tubing. Sizes—½, ⅝, ¾, 1, 1¼, 1½ and 2 inches.

E-3123—Corporation Stop with eighth bend union coupling. Inlet is standard A.W.W.A. thread. Outlet end threaded to fit Mueller machine. Tapped inside to be installed with male screw plug. Can be furnished with quarter bend or straight coupling when desired. Sizes—½, ⅝, ¾, 1, 1¼, 1½ and 2 inches.

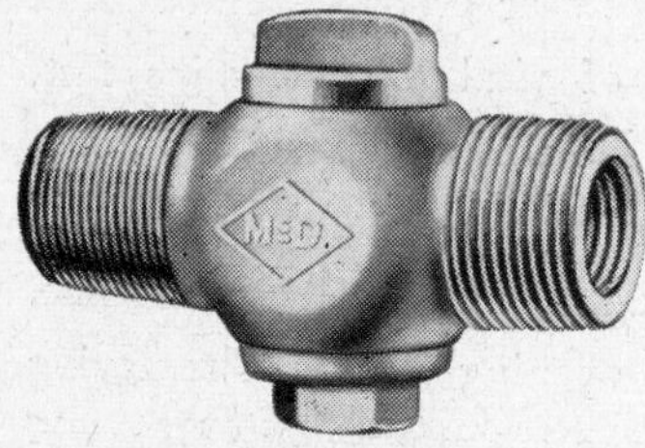

E-3121—Corporation Stop without Coupling. Inlet is standard A.W.W.A. thread. Outlet end increasing iron pipe thread. Outlet end has inside screw plug thread. Sizes: ½, ⅝, ¾, 1, 1¼, 1½, 2 inches.

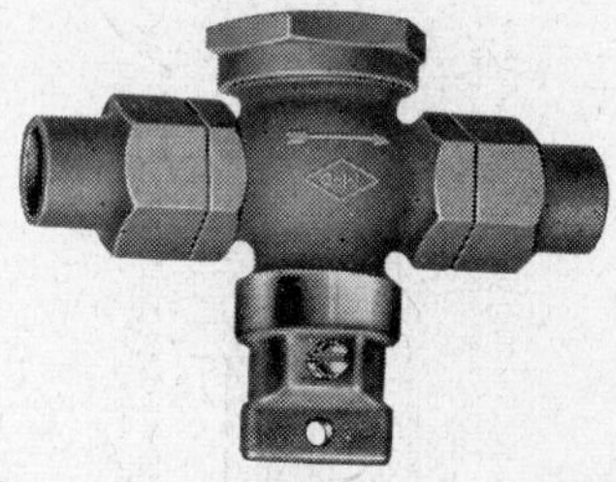

E-4713—Combined Cap and Tee Handle Inverted Key Curb Stop—Copper to Copper—Round Way. Sizes: ½, ¾, 1, 1¼, 1½, and 2.

E-3061—Combined Cap and Tee Handle Inverted Key Curb Stop. Round way. For iron pipe. Also available in stop and drain pattern. Sizes—½, ⅝, ¾, 1, 1¼, 1½ and 2 inches.

E-4717—Minneapolis Pattern. Combined cap and tee handle inverted key curb stop. Both ends copper pipe couplings. Round way. Also available in stop and drain pattern. Sizes—½, ¾, 1, 1¼, 1½ and 2 inches.

For McDonald's complete line of Brass Goods, write for Catalog.

A. Y. McDONALD MFG. CO.

DUBUQUE, IOWA

WATERWORKS BRASS GOODS

McDonald Diamond Line Waterworks, brass goods and specialities have earned a nation-wide reputation for highest quality. 101 years' manufacturing experience coupled with topmost engineering skill and a desire to constantly produce a better product are behind each item. For the complete line of McDonald Waterworks Goods consult the McDonald Catalog or write.

E-2931—Solid Tee Handle Stop for iron pipe. Round way. Also available in stop and drain pattern. Sizes—½, ⅝, ¾, 1, 1¼, 1½ and 2 inches.

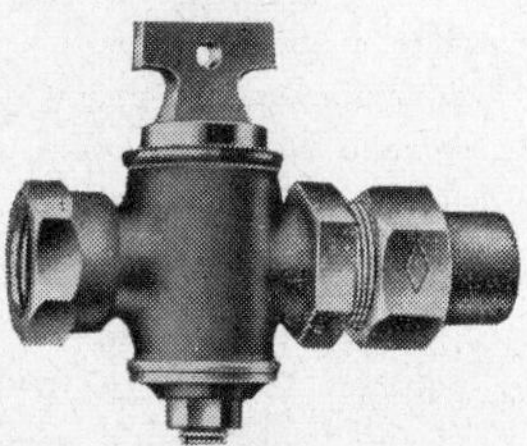

E-4721—Stop. Inlet end has copper pipe coupling. Outlet has inside iron pipe thread. Also available in stop and drain pattern. Sizes—½, ¾, 1, 1¼, 1½ and 2 inches.

E-4711—Inverted Key Curb Stop. Copper to inside iron pipe. Also available in stop and drain pattern. Sizes: ½, ¾, 1, 1¼, 1½, 2.

E-4753—Copper service pipe fitting. Copper to outside iron pipe. Sizes: ½", ¾", 1", 1¼", 1½", 2". Also available in same sizes—copper to female iron pipe and copper to copper.

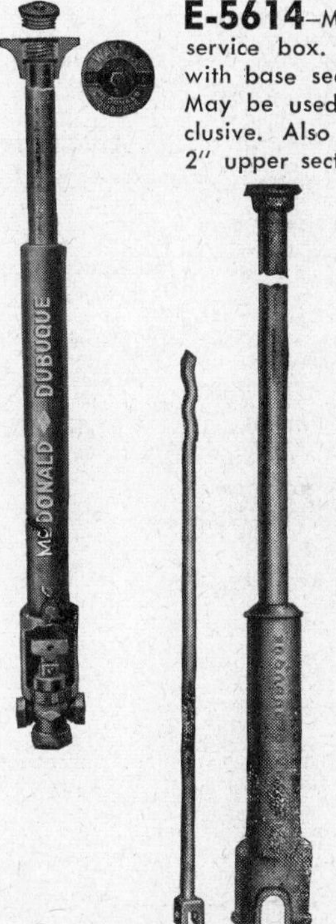

E-5614—Minneapolis pattern base service box. Has 1¼" upper section with base section tapped 1½" or 2". May be used for stops ½" to 1" inclusive. Also available with 1½" or 2" upper section. Length 2 ft. to 8 ft.

E-5601—"Arch" pattern service box with stationary rod. Has 1" upper section. For use with ½" to 1" stops inclusive. For stops larger than 1" specify E-5603. Lengths 2 ft. to 8 ft.

For McDonald's Complete Line of Brass Goods, write for Catalog.

A. Y. McDONALD MFG. CO.
DUBUQUE, IOWA

Closed coupled Centrifugal Pumps

High quality McDonald construction features assure long life and dependable performance. Close coupled design, with pump impeller mounted directly on the motor shaft, eliminates coupling and assures correct alignment. Impeller, wear rings, shaft sleeve, water seal ring and gland are of bronze. A cast iron volute is carefully designed and machined for correct hydraulic relation. High efficiency throughout the range of the pump is assured. Motors are 2-pole, 3-phase, drip-proof, and built to NEMA dimensions.

Figure 7620

Moderate pressure, centrifugal pumps, sizes 1¼, 1½ and 2 inch, embrace an operating range from 160 ft. max. to 30 ft. min. Capacities to 300 gals./min. Motors 1 to 10 HP. Pressure to 65 P.S.I. with normal suction lift.

Figure 7520

High pressure centrifugal with ideal operating range varying from 265 ft. down to 75 ft. of head. Capacities to 950 gals./min. Sizes from 1½ inch to 4 inch flanged with 2 to 60 HP motors. Pressures up to 100 P.S.I. with normal suction lift.

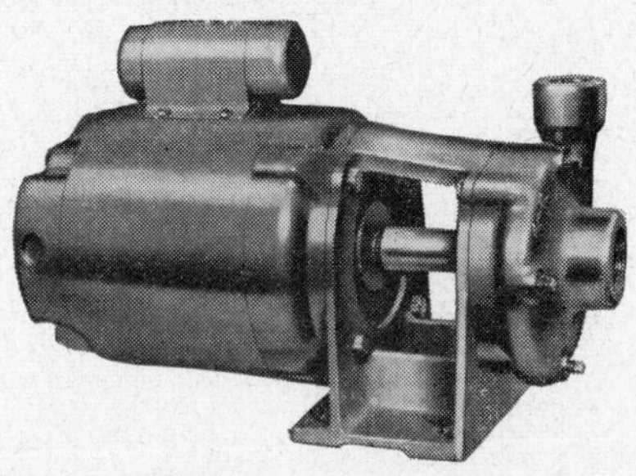

Figure 7720

Fractional horsepower, close-coupled centrifugal pumps. ¼ or 1/3 HP—¾ inch discharge 1 inch suction tapped. ½-¾ or 1 HP—1 inch discharge 1¼ inch suction tapped. Capacities 10 to 70 gallons per minute. Total heads 20 to 85 feet. Excellent small units for booster or general service; ideal for air conditioning.

For McDonald's Complete Line of Pumps, write for Bulletins.

A. Y. McDONALD MFG. CO.
DUBUQUE, IOWA

BUFFALO METER CO.

2900 Main Street, Buffalo 14, N. Y.

REPRESENTATIVES IN ALL LEADING TRADE CENTERS

Specialists in the Manufacture of Disc-Type Water Meters

AMERICAN (Bronze Casing)

Established in 1892, the Buffalo Meter Company has been dedicated from its beginning to the manufacture of water meters of simple design which would provide accuracy and long-lived service at moderate cost. The disc meter was developed to best meet the requirements, in preference to the oscillating, rotary, current or reciprocating types.

Since that time, Buffalo Meter's engineering and development work has been concentrated on further improving the accuracy and simplifying the design of its disc-type meters.

As a result, Buffalo Meter Co. now manufactures a line of AMERICAN (**bronze casing**) and NIAGARA (**galvanized iron casing**) Meters which offer more exclusive features than meters of any other make.

These special AMERICAN features are:

1. *SIMPLICITY*

In American and Niagara Meters Simplicity of construction means fewer moving parts and simplified repair problems. Moderate initial cost and minimum maintenance requirements make Buffalo Meters the most economical you can buy.

2. *UNSURPASSED INTERCHANGEABILITY*

American and Niagara Meters contain exactly the same works in the solid-casing and frost-bottom types. It's not "interchangeability" of expensive unit assemblies, but a **full interchangeability of parts, piece for piece**—an outstanding AMERICAN feature.

3. *PATENTED FROST BOTTOM*

The patented, pre-tested frost bottom in American Meters prevents costly damage. If the meter freezes, the bottom casting breaks, relieving pressure and allowing all working parts to separate.

Not dependent on flange bolts.

Damage is limited to the frost bottom, which can be replaced in a few minutes.

4. *GEAR TRAIN: FROST-SEPARABLE, CORROSION-RESISTING, DIRT-PROOF*

When the frost bottom of an American Meter breaks, the gears and other interior parts separate and move with the ice to avoid damage. Only Buffalo-made meters afford complete frost protection to all working parts in both water-lubricated and oil-enclosed gear train models.

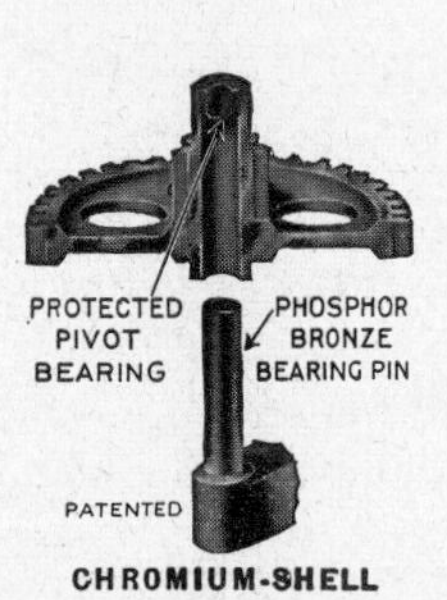

CHROMIUM-SHELL

Bronze gears and pinions coated with chromium, giving surface harder than steel and proof against corrosion from any chemicals found in drinking water. Bearings enclosed against dirt by patented pivot mounting illustrated. Simplest gear train preferred by most waterworks.

OIL-ENCLOSED

Used where open gear train would be clogged by accumulations inside meter, or where very hard or corrosive water is measured with bronze-casing meter. Direct mounting on measuring chamber insures perfect alignment. Can be easily inspected or repaired.

5. *EASE OF ASSEMBLY*

Because of their simplicity of construction, American Meters can be taken apart and put together more quickly than meters of more complicated design. This time-saving feature cuts down repair-shop work; reduces maintenance costs; simplifies storage of replacement parts.

Write for complete information on Buffalo AMERICAN Water Meters in new catalog

NIAGARA

Same as American except for the Galvanized Iron Casing

Used especially in 2" to 6" sizes

M&H VALVE and FITTINGS COMPANY

Anniston, Alabama

Telephone ADams 7-3521

GATE VALVE
HUB ENDS

M&H A.W.W.A. GATE VALVES

Iron Body, bronze mounted, or all iron gate valves furnished in the double disc parallel seat or solid wedge types with non-rising stem, or outside screw and yoke. Supplied to fit any standardized pipe connections. Classes A & B for low pressure services; A.W.W.A. Class C, and Class 250 for higher pressures. Cast iron used meets A.S.T.M. Specification A-126, Class B, 31,000 psi tensile strength; bronze meets A.S.T.M. Specification B-62, 30,000 psi tensile strength. Stems, nuts and spreaders are manganese bronze, A.S.T.M. Specification B-132, 60,000 psi tensile strength. Further details on page 360.

GATE VALVE
MECHANICAL JOINT

M&H A.W.W.A. HYDRANTS

Conform to latest A.W.W.A. specifications. Simple, rugged design minimizes maintenance costs.

1. Dry Top—Operating threads protected from action of water. No rust, corrosion or freezing.
2. Easy Lubrication of operating nut, threads and packing through lubricating hole in top of operating nut.
3. Revolving Head, enabling outlets to be faced in any direction.
4. Addition of Steamer Nozzle, without digging up hydrant or requiring complete new barrel.
5. Lengthening of Hydrant without digging up or requiring complete new barrel.
6. Double Lead Gaskets on Bronze Valve seat to give double guarantee against leakage.
7. Removal of Bronze Seat, along with any other working parts, through the barrel or standpipe without digging up Hydrant.
8. Double Drain Valves, absolutely positive, insuring quick and complete draining.
9. Lugs on Bell of Hydrant Shoe for strapping to the water main if desired.
10. Compression Type (valve opens against pressure and closes with pressure). The water pressure keeps the valve tight under all conditions, even when broken off above ground.

LEFT: STANDARD MODEL HYDRANT.

RIGHT: TRAFFIC MODEL HYDRANT.

M&H SPECIAL MODEL HYDRANTS

In case of collision, Traffic Model is easily repaired with special breakable bolts and coupling and without shutting off water. Special Flush Type Hydrant sets even with ground surface and offers no obstruction to traffic. Recommended for airport runways and industrial plants.

SHORT BODY FITTINGS

Lighter weight due to shorter length reduces cost of material and labor. Socket and spigot dimensions, and metal thickness, conforms to A. W. W. A. class "D." Approved by Underwriters and Factory Mutuals.

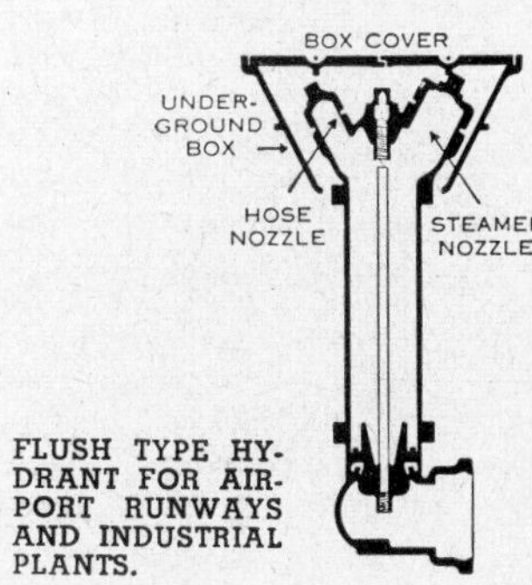

FLUSH TYPE HYDRANT FOR AIRPORT RUNWAYS AND INDUSTRIAL PLANTS.

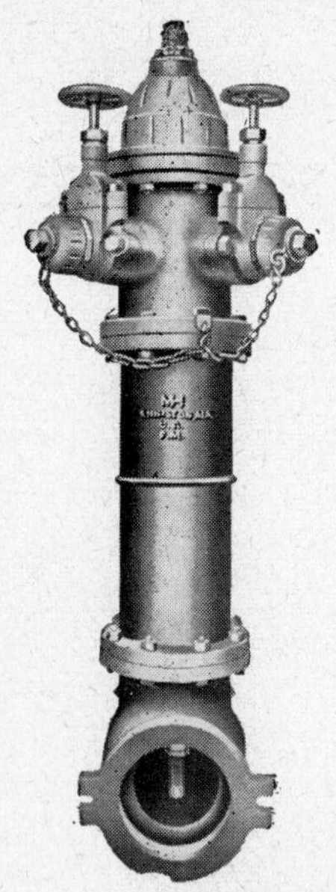

LEFT: MILL YARD HYDRANT
INDEPENDENT HOSE
GATE VALVES

RISING STEM
GATE VALVE

Underwriters and Factory Mutual Listed and Approved

RIGHT: ADJUSTABLE
INDICATOR POST

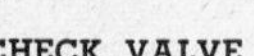

CHECK VALVE

M&H HYDRANTS, VALVES, ETC., FOR FIRE PROTECTION

M&H makes a complete line of valves, hydrants, indicator posts and underground pipe fittings for fire protection water systems. All of these M&H products are approved and listed by the National Board of Fire Underwriters of Chicago and by the Associated Factory Mutuals of Boston for use in underground water mains in connection with fire protection equipment such as automatic sprinklers, open sprinklers and standpipe. All castings therefore are marked "UA—FM."

Outstanding features are simplicity of design, rugged construction and highest quality material and workmanship.

M&H TAPPING VALVES AND SLEEVES

The M&H Tapping Valves shown below are for use with any standard tapping machine and can be furnished for use with or without post indicator. Tapping sleeve is made with hub or mechanical joints, and with flanged connection to valve.

POST INDICATOR
GATE VALVE

POST INDICATOR VALVE

Designed for installation in underground pipe line leading to automatic sprinkler system. Special flange on bonnet of valve fits flange on base of indicator post. Valves are double disc parallel seat type, fully bronze mounted. They are equally tight with pressure on either side of the gate. May be ordered valve only, or complete with indicator post.

TAPPING VALVE
AND SLEEVE

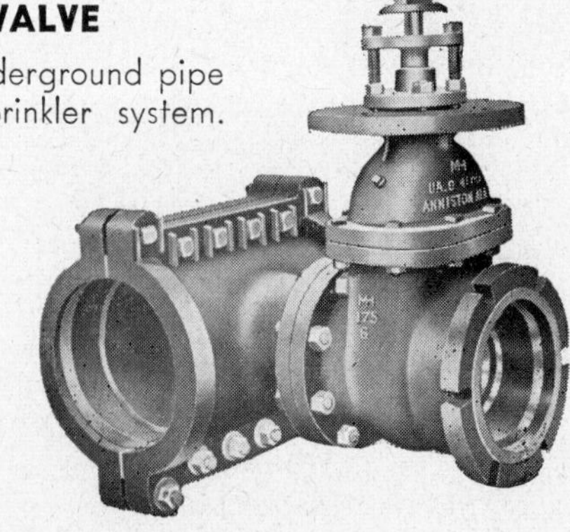

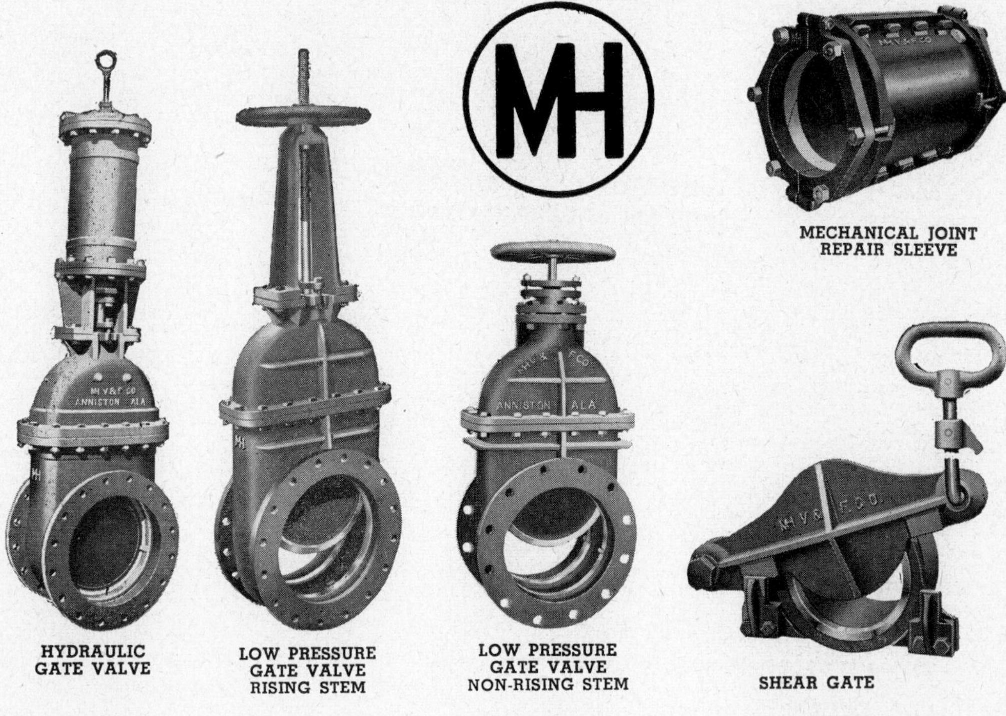

MECHANICAL JOINT REPAIR SLEEVE

HYDRAULIC GATE VALVE

LOW PRESSURE GATE VALVE RISING STEM

LOW PRESSURE GATE VALVE NON-RISING STEM

SHEAR GATE

M&H SPECIAL TYPE VALVES AND OTHER PRODUCTS USED IN SEWAGE TREATMENT

M&H FLAP VALVE

Hydraulically and electrically operated M&H Valves are used in sewage treatment plants, water works, filter plants, etc., to save time and labor since these valves can be operated by remote control for quick, easy closing or opening. They are also used as emergency valves to admit higher water pressures into the mains in case of fire. They are dependable in operation.

M&H Square Bottom Gate Valves may be installed for throttling purposes, or in a vertical pipe line. Recommended for intake towers or at the foot of dams; for pressure regulation in centrifugal pump discharge lines; for regulation of flow in feed line, and for flow regulation where there is unbalanced pressure against gates. See page 360.

MUD VALVE

M&H Flap Valves and Shear Gates are iron body, bronze mounted, used in Filtration and Sewage Disposal Plants.

M&H Mud Valves are used principally in Filter Plants, Settling Basins, Drains, Blowoffs in sumps or irrigation projects.

TRADEMARK

The letters M&H are the sign of quality on Valves, Hydrants and Pipe Line accessories. High quality materials, simplicity of design and expert workmanship have established for M&H enviable reputation for dependable service in the water works and sewage fields and for industrial uses. M&H products are modern in design, with many exclusive M&H features, and are furnished to fit standard type pipe connection such as hub, spigot, mechanical joint, ring-tite, flanged, screwed, Universal, cement asbestos, and combinations of above.

CLASS 250 GATE VALVE

FEATURES OF M&H GATE VALVES

M&H Valves are furnished stuffing box type, with gland-follower and packing material at top of stem, or valves can be furnished if desired with rubber O-Ring seals instead of conventional stuffing box design.

In opening valve, discs move laterally away from seats BEFORE upward motion starts. In closing, the lateral motion wedges the discs against the seats AFTER downward motion stops. Thus M&H valves operate easily, with minimum friction and without dragging the gate discs across the body rings.

Upon request, detailed information will be furnished on gearing; by-passes; double square bottom; rollers, tracks and scrapers; hydraulic and motor operation; indicators; clean-outs; chain wheels; floor stands; extension stems, etc.

SQUARE BOTTOM GATE VALVE

M&H PRODUCTS FOR FILTRATION PLANTS

Many M&H Valves are widely used in water works filter plants. Our square bottom double-disc gate valves are designed to prevent the downstream gate from tilting into the downstream port opening and cut or damage its seat and gate rings by chatter or vibration. This valve is used to regulate the flow of water in the feed line to filter bed, to regulate the flow of water in the discharge line of centrifugal pumps, or from a reservoir where there is unbalanced pressure against the gates. Engineers are finding greater use and need for these valves almost daily.

SPRING AND LEVER SWING CHECK VALVE

OTHER M&H PRODUCTS INCLUDE—

- FLOOR STANDS
- EXTENSION STEMS
- VALVE BOXES
- B & S FITTINGS
- MOTOR OPERATED VALVES
- CUTTING-IN TEES
- WEIGHTED-LEVER SWING CHECK VALVES
- FLANGE AND FLARE FITTINGS
- WALL CASTINGS
- FLANGED FITTINGS

AND MANY OTHERS

RISING STEM GATE VALVE

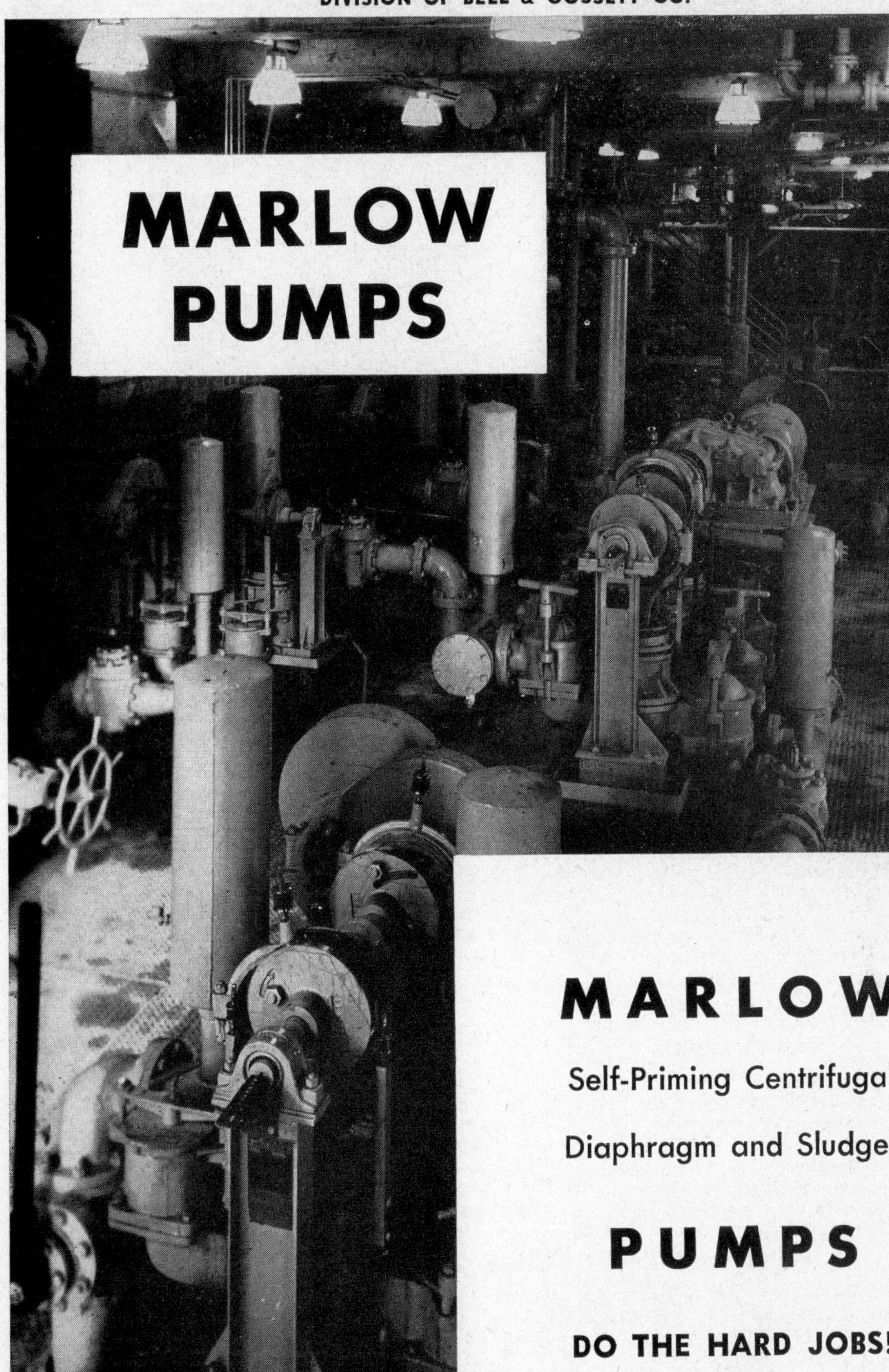
MARLOW
PUMPS

MARLOW HIGH-PRESSURE PLUNGER SLUDGE PUMPS

The famous MARLOW plunger sludge pumps are made in four sizes, as shown in the specifications below, and in two types, PE and RPE. They are best known for removing sludge from settling tank hoppers and transferring material from digestion tanks to storage units and sludge beds. Bulky debris and nearly solid wastes are handled in stride. When you write us, we will on request send you a list of 400 typical municipal installations in 39 states. Communications to our Engineering Department will receive prompt and careful attention.

MARLOW "PE" Simplex Sludge Pump

DETAILED SPECIFICATIONS

(Larger and Smaller sizes available)

	Simplex	Duplex	Triplex	Quadruplex
Number of Plungers	1	2	3	4
Standard Displacement in U. S. gallons per hour	3,150	6,300	9,450	12,600
Maximum Displacement in U. S. gallons per hour	4,200	8,400	12,600	16,800
Maximum Suction Lift	20 ft.	20 ft.	20 ft.	20 ft.
Maximum Discharge Head*	80 ft.	80 ft.	80 ft.	Special
Air Chambers, size and number	1—8"x30"	2—8"x30"	2—8"x30"	2—8"x30"
H.P. of Electric Motor recommended (see note below)	3	5	7½	10
Size Pipe Connections (standard flange)	4"	4"	6"	6"
Net Weight	1,230 lbs.	2,400 lbs.	3,400 lbs.	4,600 lbs.
Dimension Prints:				
"PE" with built-in gearing, V-belt drive	PE-81W	PE-82W	PE-83W	PE-84W
"RPE" with gear motor and roller chain drive	RPE-71W	RPE-72-W		

* Discharge head up to 130 feet may be obtained by using motor of greater horsepower.

Note: Ample power. The electric motors recommended in detailed specifications, can be relied on to give trouble-free service under severe conditions. Smaller motors can be used, but with excessive moisture in pump rooms, occasional blockage in line, and possibility the necessity for a long run to empty a tank, may seriously overload a motor which is too small. A few dollars saved on the original cost by using a motor which may burn out is expensive economy.

RECOMMENDED OUTLINE SPECIFICATIONS

Contractor shall furnish and install where shown on plans (Quantity) Marlow Type "PE" ("RPE") Simplex (Duplex, Triplex) Plunger Sludge Pump(s) with (cast iron-bronze) plunger(s) with ball valves not less than 5⅛" diameter, with shear pin on each eccentric and not less than 11 positions for shear pin device, each position fitted with hardened steel bushings, each eccentric lubricated by sight-feed oiler, flanges on each side of eccentric, each plunger to have not less than 5 rings of ¾" square packing, with roller bearings on main drive shaft, with "PE" V-belt drive. ("RPE" roller chain drive) properly guarded, each pump driven by and including a .... HP motor .... phase .... cycle .... volt of the squirrel cage induction type. Pump as manufactured by Marlow Pumps of Midland Park, N. J.

MARLOW SELF-PRIMING CENTRIFUGALS

4M AGC Rating

1½-Inch Suction and Discharge

1½-INCH 5,500 GPH, SMALLEST OF NUMEROUS MARLOW CENTRIFUGALS RANGING TO 240,000 GPH

It's the diffuser instead of a wasteful recirculation device that makes MARLOW self priming centrifugal pumps outstandingly efficient and virtually clog-proof. They are built in performance sizes to fit municipal requirements for portables up to 240,000 gallons per hour. At right are principal specifications covering four popular municipal models. . . . The 1½A1 shown almost runs itself hour after hour delivering 92 gpm, primes automatically on suction lift to 25 feet. . . . 2A1 with only one moving part pumps 26,000 gallons on one gallon of gasoline. It's designed for dewatering, filling swimming pools, and work in cemeteries; trash laden water is no problem. . . . 2B3 is trouble-free, adaptable, two-man portable, automatic. . . . 3B1 is our smallest sized 3-inch for rapid discharge and portability. . . . This is a glimpse of the MARLOW line of centrifugals, reliable, simple, portable, every pump guaranteed. For further details, get in touch with your Marlow distributor or with the Marlow factory.

SPECIFICATIONS

Model	1½A1	2A1	2B3	3B1
Max. solid handled, inches	⅜	⅜	½	¾
Body Material	Aluminum	Aluminum	Aluminum	Aluminum
Net weight, pounds	53	55	111	119
Height with Engine, inches	16½	16½	21	21
Length with Engine, inches	19½	19½	22½	24¼
Width wtih Engine, inches	14	14	20	20½
Suction and Discharge	1½	2	2	3
Gallons per Hour	5,500	7,000	10,000	18,000
Engine Horsepower	1.5	1.9	4.2	5.7

"MARLOW MUD HOG" for DIRTY WORK

3- and 4-INCH SINGLE SIZES

For pumping water, sewage, sluice, sand and trash laden liquids, use Marlow Mud Hog diaphragm pumps. The first "Marlow Mud Hog" ever made has been in service since 1924. Specially clog - proof. All parts are "heavier than necessary." Pumps either a trickle or full capacity at each stroke. Thousands are in daily use.

SPECIFICATIONS
Entire Unit (Pump and Engine)

Model Numbers	202A & 302A	303 & 304	403 & 404
Connections, Size	2 & 3 inch	3-inch	4-inch
AGC Rating, 10 Ft. Lift (Gals. per Hour)	3,120	3,500	6,000
AGC Rating, 20 Ft. Lift (Gals. per Hour)		1,500	3,000
Suction Lift		Guaranteed 20 Feet	
Size of Diaphragm	No. 3	No. 3	No. 4
Operating Strokes per Minute	60	60	60
Mounting	Wheels	Base or Wheels (Pneumatic or Steel)	
Net Weight	280 Lbs.	670 Lbs.	735 Lbs.
Export Gross Weight	465 Lbs.	900 Lbs.	970 Lbs.
Cubic Feet Boxed	27	40	45
Height of Unit, Inches	30½	36	36
Length of Unit, Inches	45½	62	62
Width of Unit, Inches	29½	32	37

Write for information on the New Marlow "LIGHTWEIGHT" MUD HOGS

Unqualified Guarantee:

Marlow Pumps are guaranteed to meet all standard performance ratings. They are made of quality materials, by skilled workmen, in a modern factory, and all parts are guaranteed to be perfect. Should any part prove defective within one year, it will be replaced without argument and without charge.

MARLOW PUMPS

Division of BELL & GOSSETT Company

MIDLAND PARK, NEW JERSEY
MORTON GROVE, ILLINOIS
LONGVIEW, TEXAS

Marlow Pumps
MIDLAND PARK, N.J.

WATER MAINS CLEANED BY NATIONAL:

Lower operating costs

Without clean water mains unnecessarily large pipes and pumps often must be employed with correspondingly high fixed and high operating costs. Frequently, the savings in pumping charges alone are sufficient to repay the entire cost of cleaning, within the first year or two.

Increase capacity

Since water mains assumed to be in perfect or fair condition are often operating at but a fraction of maximum capacity due to tuberculation, incrustation and sediment, cleaning should always be considered as an inexpensive alternate to laying new pipe or installing booster pumps, when an increase in capacity is called for.

Roughness and accumulations can, and frequently do, reduce the capacity of a water main 50% or even more. For example, tuberculation may reduce the carrying capacity of a 48″ pipe to the capacity equivalent to that of a pipe smaller than 40″ while reducing the Hazen & Williams Coefficient "C" from 130 to 60.

Increase pressure

The most immediate and noticeable result of water main cleaning is the increased pressure. One Virginia town reported that cleaning reduced loss of head from 3 ft. per thousand feet to 3 inches per thousand and raised the value of the Williams & Hazen Coefficient from 70 to 135!

Reduce fire hazard

Increased pressures and increased rates of flow, made possible by water main cleaning, often make possible lower insurance rates and reduced fire losses. These savings are worthwhile, even if not shown in Water Department budgets.

Please customers

Industrial and domestic consumers appreciate an adequate supply of pure water at satisfactory pressures. Only with clean mains can the consumer be assured of the utmost in service at the lowest possible cost for pipe investment, pump investment and pump operation—all of which must be included in water or tax rates.

Before cleaning

The tubercules in this pipe were approximately 1½" high. The coefficient before cleaning was approximately 96, indicating a carrying capacity of about 74% of normal.

After cleaning

Notice the clean smooth pipe interior. The coefficient rose from 96 to 130, indicating a carrying capacity close to 100%. The entire pipe line, some 7,000 ft. in length, was cleaned in one day.

SPECIALISTS IN WATER MAIN CLEANING SINCE 1906

Since 1906 The National Water Main Cleaning Co. has specialized in cleaning water mains exclusively and through the development of methods and machines has made water main cleaning accepted standard practice throughout the continents of North and South America.

The highly specialized equipment employed by The National Water Main Cleaning Co. today includes: walkie-talkie radio systems for maintaining constant communication between the point of operation and control valves or pumping stations, electronic locators for tracing underground pipe, electronic valve and valve box locators, high capacity pumps for dewatering, trailer-mounted booster pumps for stepping-up pressure, pipe cutting machines and a tremendous variety of cleaning devices developed to meet the requirements of varying pipe sizes, conditions and layouts.

WALKIE-TALKIE EMPLOYED BY NATIONAL WATER MAIN CLEANING CO.

Even more important than adequate equipment is the experience necessary to cope with all conditions and situations. In water main cleaning no single plan of procedure can be adopted as a standard method. The nature of the obstruction, varying pipe sizes, unusual pipe layouts, the condition of the pipe, the character of the water—all make each cleaning assignment an individual problem calling for specialized experience, skill and equipment.

With this extensive background NATIONAL has developed an integrated coordination of engineering, shop facilities and field experience which enable the organization to handle any job efficiently, quickly and economically with but little interruption in service, with a minimum of supplementary labor costs and without undue trouble or commotion. The results are guaranteed.

Ask for a water flow survey

An engineer of The National Water Main Cleaning Co. will be glad to check the condition of your water mains, recommend the required treatment and estimate the cost of National Water Main Cleaning service.

DON'T LET THIS HAPPEN TO YOUR SYSTEM

'Out of Sight—Out of Mind' can be a mighty expensive philosophy in any water distribution system. The unretouched photographs shown below clearly proves this point. Resultant higher pumping cost with reduced pressure and carrying capacity make it costly to tolerate such conditions. That's why the savings effected in reduced pumping costs frequently pay for the low cost of NATIONAL Water Main Cleaning.

Don't let this happen to your system—call NATIONAL today.

These are actual unretouched photographs of water mains before cleaning by NATIONAL.

NATIONAL KNOW-HOW PAYS!

*National knows how to work **quickly*** reducing supplementary labor costs and service interruptions.

National knows how to clean the difficult jobs, including hard incrustations, unusual obstructions and pipes of unusually large or small diameter.

National knows how to clean long runs with a minimum number of pipe entries.

National knows how to avoid trouble, such as can occur from improper provision for drainage of flush water from large mains or from the use of excessive pressures.

National knows how to clean so thoroughly that restoration of 95% of the original pipe capacity is guaranteed.

National Know-How comes from over 40 years of experience cleaning water mains.

Write or call today for information and prices.

NEPTUNE METER COMPANY

Main Office: 19 West 50th Street, New York 20, N. Y.

FACTORY: 22-42 Jackson Ave., Long Island City 1, N. Y.

BRANCH OFFICES

Atlanta 18, Ga.
200 Permalume Place, N.W.
Boston 16, Mass.....250 Stuart St.
Chicago 24, Ill..4048 W. Taylor St.
Dallas 7, Tex.........315 Cole St.
Denver 17, Colo.....1700 - 15th St.
Los Angeles 22, Cal.
5540 E. Harbor St.
Louisville 17, Ky..320 Eastern Pkwy.
No. Kansas City 16, Mo.25 W. 15th St.
Portland 9, Ore...1238 N.W. Glisan St.
San Francisco—Bay Area
101 Rollins Rd., Millbrae, Cal.
Philadelphia 2, Pa...1420-26 S. Penn Sq.
Philadelphia Meter Co.

NEPTUNE METERS, LTD. Main Office and Factory: 1430 LAKESHORE ROAD, TORONTO 14, ONTARIO
Offices: Calgary, Halifax, Montreal, St. Johns, Vancouver, Winnipeg.

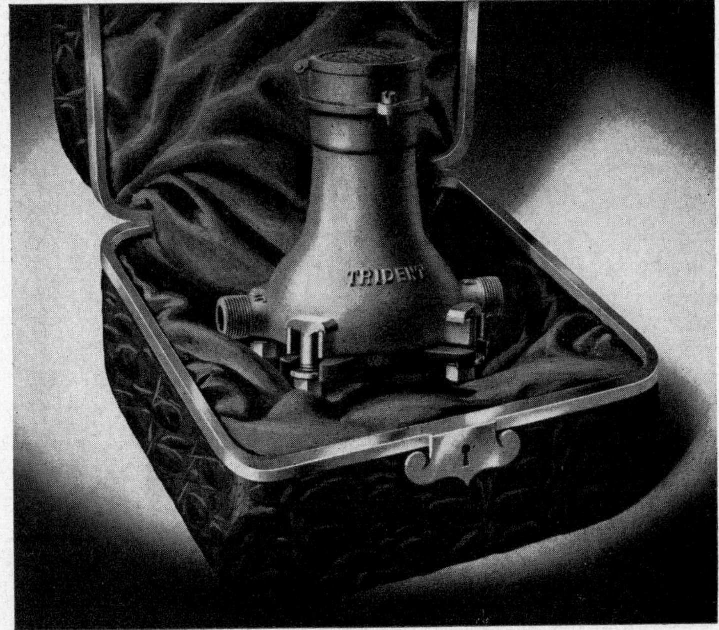

TRIDENT WATER METERS

. . . Job Tested Ten Million Times

For over 50 years, more Trident meters have been purchased than any other make. Most of these . . . even the oldest . . . are still in faithful service . . . still running accurately. This long serviceable life means lower amortization, obsolescence and replacement costs.

Trident meters have long led the field in design improvements, and today are the finest, most modern meters available. Every improvement has been made to fit all older Tridents. This is one of Trident's biggest advantages.

A planned schedule of testing and repair with Trident meters gives you a continuous program of meter modernization . . . at far less cost than scrap-and-replace methods. Repairs take less time, too, aided by Trident's extreme simplicity. A moderate stock of only the *latest* parts services *all* your Tridents. You waste no time searching or waiting for parts for old meters. Trident parts are *always* available. Your repair men have no obsolete models to learn. If they can repair one Trident, they can repair all . . . efficiently, economically.

Trident's 50-year record is your assurance that the Trident meters you buy today will be assets for your community for years and years to come.

TRIDENT METERS FOR DOMESTIC SERVICES

in Cold or Warm Climates

Trident meters combine fine-instrument construction with the inherent high accuracy achieved only in disc-type, positive displacement water meters. Accurate at all rates of flow within normal test flow limits and remarkably sensitive to small flows.

Trident Frost-Proof Meter embodies the original frost-proof meter feature. If the water freezes and expands, the cast iron bottom cap breaks, relieving the working parts from strain. The bottom cap can be replaced at very nominal cost. For warm climates, the Trident Split-Case Meter is recommended.

Among exclusive features for long accurate life are: Gear train is fully oil-enclosed, including the stuffing box, to isolate vital parts from abrasives, turbulence, corrosive elements, and to provide permanent lubrication. Anti-friction thrust roller absorbs disc thrust, making the Trident virtually immune to disc breakage. Heat-proof, hard rubber bushings in gear train and register are interchangeable. Sand ring keeps abrasive material out of working parts. Materials are corrosion-resistant, with special materials for unusual corrosion problems.

Easy to service and repair . . . makes big savings in meter costs over the years. Register has no screws. Chamber is snap-joint. Disc is in three parts, easy to adjust. Guide pins, slots, etc., assist in assembling meter properly.

TRIDENT FROST-PROOF METERS

Size In's	Wt. Lbs.	Lgth. In's	Wdth. In's	Ht. In's	Base to Center of Pipe	*Del U.S. Gal. Min.
5/8	10 3/4	7 1/2	5 1/2	8 3/4	1 3/4	20
5/8 x 3/4	11 1/2	7 1/2	5 1/2	8 3/4	1 3/4	20
3/4	15	9	6	8 3/4	1 3/4	30
1	26	10 3/4	9 3/8	9 1/2	2	50
1 x 1 1/4	26	10 3/4	9 3/8	9 1/2	2	50

TRIDENT SPLIT-CASE METERS

Size In's	Wt. Lbs.	Lgth. In's	Wdth. In's	Ht. In's	Base to Center of Pipe	*Del U.S. Gal. Min.
5/8	9	7 1/2	5	7 3/4	1	20
5/8 x 3/4	9 1/2	7 1/2	5	7 3/4	1	20
3/4	12	9	5 5/8	8 1/8	1 3/16	30
1	20	10 3/4	7 1/2	8 3/4	1 5/8	50
1 x 1 1/4	20	10 3/4	7 1/2	8 3/4	1 5/8	50

STYLE 3 TRIDENTS FOR MEDIUM RATES OF FLOW

A disc-piston meter for commercial and other installations requiring medium rates of flow larger than household consumption, but not great volumes. Also excellent for "battery" settings where preferred for metering wide flow ranges. In addition to sensitivity on low flows inherent in disc meters, it has the Trident oil-enclosed gear train, heat-proof removable bushings in register and gear train, interchangeable parts and other Trident features which give it sustained accuracy and low maintenance cost. On 1½" and 2" sizes, a "delivery adjustment" can be regulated in relation to line pressure to prevent racing. These two sizes of Style 3 Meters do the work of any compound meter of equivalent size and, being simpler, they do it with less cost for maintenance and repair.

TRIDENT STYLE 3 METERS

Size In's	Wt. Lbs.	Lgth. In's	Wdth. In's	Ht. In's	Base to Center of Pipe	*Del. U.S. Gal. Min.
1½ Scr.	36	12⅝	10	10⅝	2⅜	100
1½ Flge.	40	13	10	10⅝	2⅜	100
2 Scr.	58	15¼	12 3/16	11¾	3¼	160
2 Flge.	61	17	12 3/16	11¾	3¼	160
3 Flge.	105	24	16 3/16	17⅞	3⅞	300
4 Flge.	257	29¼	22 7/16	20⅝	4¾	500
6 Flge.	589	36¾	29	25⅜	5⅞	1000

CREST METERS FOR BULK WATER DELIVERIES

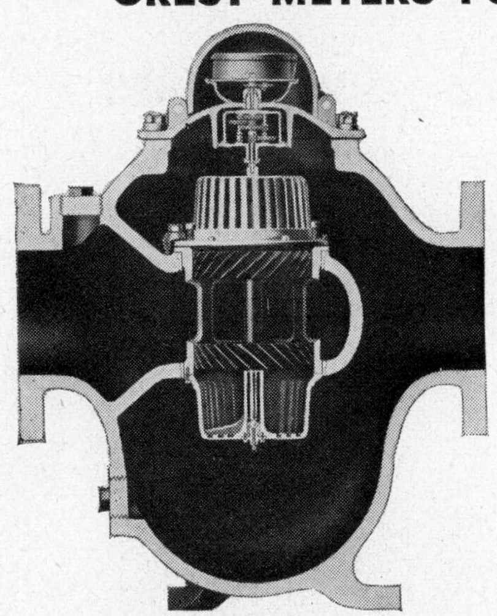

For "bulk" water deliveries at periodic or continuous high rates of flow—i.e., where mains deliver water to adjacent townships; hydraulic elevators, cranes, pile-jetting apparatus, etc., the Crest Meter is recommended. Of the velocity type, a turbine is rotated by the water at a speed directly proportional to rate of flow. Among features is the hollow hard-rubber turbine revolving on agate bearing, resulting in minimum friction, maximum sensitivity, sustained accuracy. Standard Trident register and gear train features. All parts interchangeable.

TRIDENT CREST METERS

Size In's	Wt. Lbs.	Lgth. In's	Wdth. In's	Ht. In's	Base to Center of Pipe	*Del. U.S. Gal. Min.
1½ Scr.	65	12¾	8½	16¼	6⅜	100
1½ Flge.	65	13	8½	16¼	6⅜	100
2 Scr.	83	15½	8⅞	16¾	6⅞	170
2 Flge.	85	17	8⅞	16¾	6⅞	170
3 Flge.	250	24	13⅝	27¼	13¼	400
4 Flge.	260	24	13⅝	27¼	13¼	700
6 Flge.	300	24	14⅝	28¾	14¾	1600
8 Flge.	500	26¾	17½	30¼	15¾	2800
10 Flge.	800	30	26¾	29¼	13⅞	4400
12 Flge.	1200	36	30½	34⅞	16½	6400
16 Flge.	1950	42	36½	40⅞	19¾	12400

*Am. Wt. Wks. Asso. & New Eng. Wt. Wks. Asso. Std. Specifications

COMPOUND METERS FOR WIDE WORKING RANGES

Use this Compound Meter for services with a maximum demand beyond the range of equivalent disc meters—yet with the probability of occasional small rates of flow. Accurate over a wide working range. Measures high rates of flow through a Trident Crest Meter unit and small flows, which cannot be recorded accurately by the Crest, through a Trident Disc Meter unit. In addition to the standard Trident features of both these meters, a specially constructed valve automatically directs the water to the proper unit, depending on rate of flow. Single cast iron casing. All parts interchangeable.

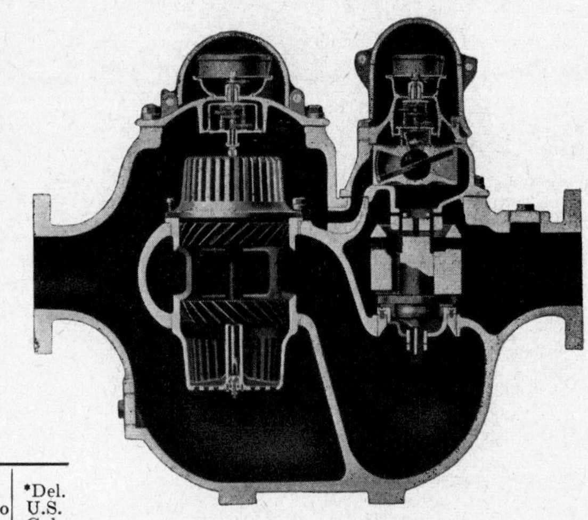

TRIDENT COMPOUND METERS

Size In's	Wt. Lbs.	Lgth. In's	Wdth. In's	Ht. In's	Base to Center of Pipe	*Del. U.S. Gal. Min.
3	460	33	13¾	27⅛	13¼	320
4	475	33	13¾	27⅛	13¼	500
6	685	36½	14⅝	28⅝	14¾	1000
8	970	42	17½	29⅞	15¾	1600
10	1500	45 7/16	20⅝	29⅛	13⅞	2300

PROTECTUS METERS FOR FIRE SERVICE LINES

Designed for fire line use where both high and low flows occur, and loss of head is an important factor. Meets such requirements with (a) accuracy on all flows and (b) low loss of head plus reliability of operation, satisfying both Water Works officials and Underwriters. Measures low flows through a Trident Disc Meter unit. Large flows are measured proportionally by a **Trident Crest unit.** Water-way is clear, unobstructed. Both units have standard Trident features which insure accuracy, long life and low maintenance cost.

TRIDENT PROTECTUS METERS

Size In's	Wt. Lbs.	Lgth. In's Incl. Incr.	Wdth. In's	Ht. In's	Base to Center of Pipe	*Del. U.S. Gal. Min.
3	700	64⅜	22¾	21½	8	400
4	900	67	24	24⅜	8	700
6	1600	83⅞	29	27½	10	1600
8	2250	89¾	32¾	30⅞	11¾	2800
10	3400	98⅛	38½	37⅜	14⅜	4375

*Am. Wt. Wks. Asso. & New Eng. Wt. Wks. Asso. Std. Specifications

NEPTUNE METER COMPANY, NEW YORK 20, N. Y.

See Page 369 for Branch Offices and Factories

CLARKSVILLE FOUNDRY & MACHINE WORKS

Clarksville, Tennessee

MUNICIPAL CASTINGS

CLARKSVILLE NON-LOCKING OVAL METER BOX (Center lift top optional) **Special** lettering—Water Meter. Name of City, etc., as desired.

TYPE C ROUND METER BOX (with or without lock)

SUPREME TYPE G RECTANGULAR METER BOX

Also available: **TYPES F, EF, M&M** and **A** Round Meter Boxes and **TYPE F FROST PROOF** Meter Box Rims with Double Lid Covers.

METER BOXES AND COVERS

STREET AND SEWER CASTINGS

MANHOLE RING AND COVER—BOTTOM FLANGE TYPE, in 13 sizes (**TOP FLANGE TYPE** also available, in 7 sizes)

CAST IRON CATCH BASIN—CLARKSVILLE TYPE—4 pieces (Also **PADUCAH TYPE,** straight and curved)

DRAINAGE OR INLET GRATE with FRAME—BOTTOM FLANGE TYPE, in 14 sizes (**TOP FLANGE TYPE** also available in 7 sizes)

OTHER PRODUCTS:

- Valve Boxes
- Curb Boxes
- Asphalt Smoothers
- Tampers, Earth and Concrete
- Machine Parts, Gears
- Plumbing Specialties
- Railings (Pipe and Ornamental)

Write for Illustrated booklets

SMITH-BLAIR, INC.

Main Office and Factory — **SOUTH SAN FRANCISCO, CALIFORNIA • (P. O. BOX 666)**

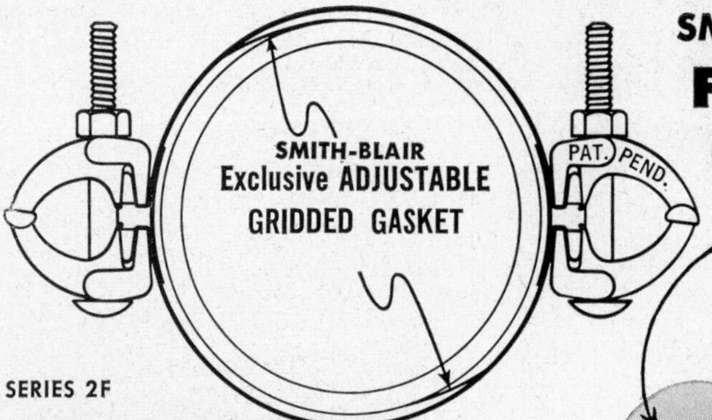

SMITH-BLAIR
Exclusive ADJUSTABLE
GRIDDED GASKET

PAT. PEND.

SERIES 2F

SMITH-BLAIR
FULL CIRCLE CLAMP COUPLING

STRAIGHT PULL FLOATING BOLTS . . . are free from all bending!

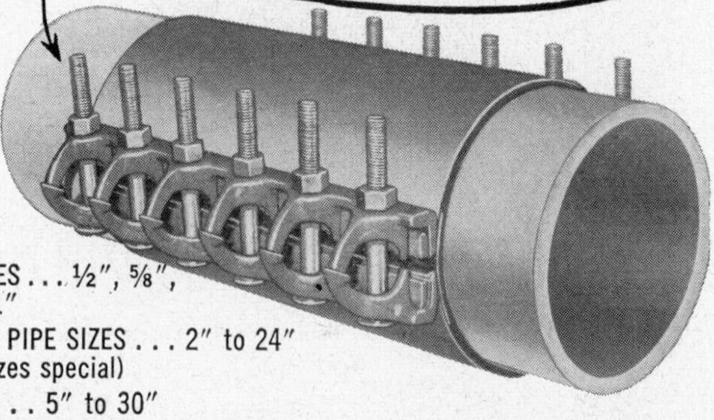

For Repairing AWKWARD BREAKS in Asbestos-Cement or Cast Iron Pipe by INCREASED HOLDING POWER

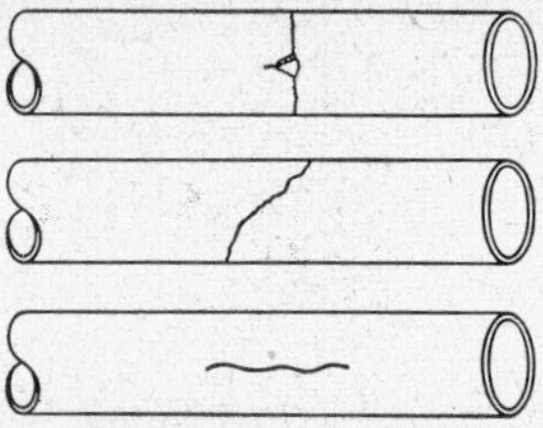

- BOLT SIZES . . . ½", ⅝", ¾" and 1"
- NOMINAL PIPE SIZES . . . 2" to 24" (larger sizes special)
- WIDTHS . . . 5" to 30"
- COPPER OR STAINLESS STEEL BANDS

EASILY INSTALLED UNDER PRESSURE

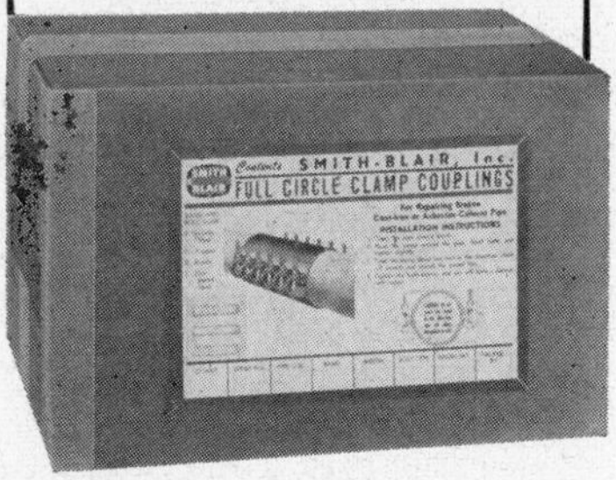

INDIVIDUALLY PACKAGED

and labeled at the factory. Complete and ready for shipping, storing or installing.

MATCHING GASKETS ARE AN INTEGRAL PART OF EACH FULL CIRCLE CLAMP COUPLING

The bonded-in gaskets are matched so that their tapered ends properly overlap. The sealing effect on this overlap comes from the squeezing action of the flexible heavy metal band. Uniformity of sealing action under every square inch of the rubber gasket is an extremely desirable and advantageous feature of this clamp. The special molded rubber gasket has a pre-formed and molded-in copper-armor tongue which accomplishes the full-circle closure. The interior surface of the gasket is thoroughly gridded. The gridding not only obtains a more thorough grip on the pipe, but also dykes off the flow for more thorough control.

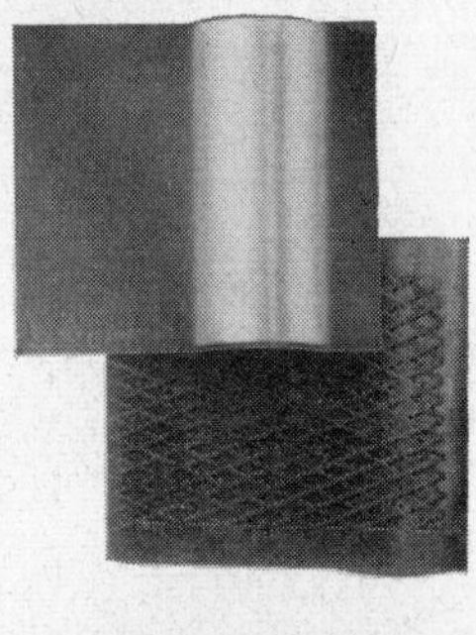

TAPER ENDS OVERLAP FOR FREE ADJUSTMENT TO PIPE O.D. VARIATIONS.

Main Office & Factory: **P. O. Box 666 • SOUTH SAN FRANCISCO, CALIFORNIA**

Branches: **South Gate, California • Greensburg, Pennsylvania**

STOCKING JOBBERS IN PRINCIPAL CITIES

SB-218A

TAPER-SEAL SERVICE CLAMP

IRON or BRONZE

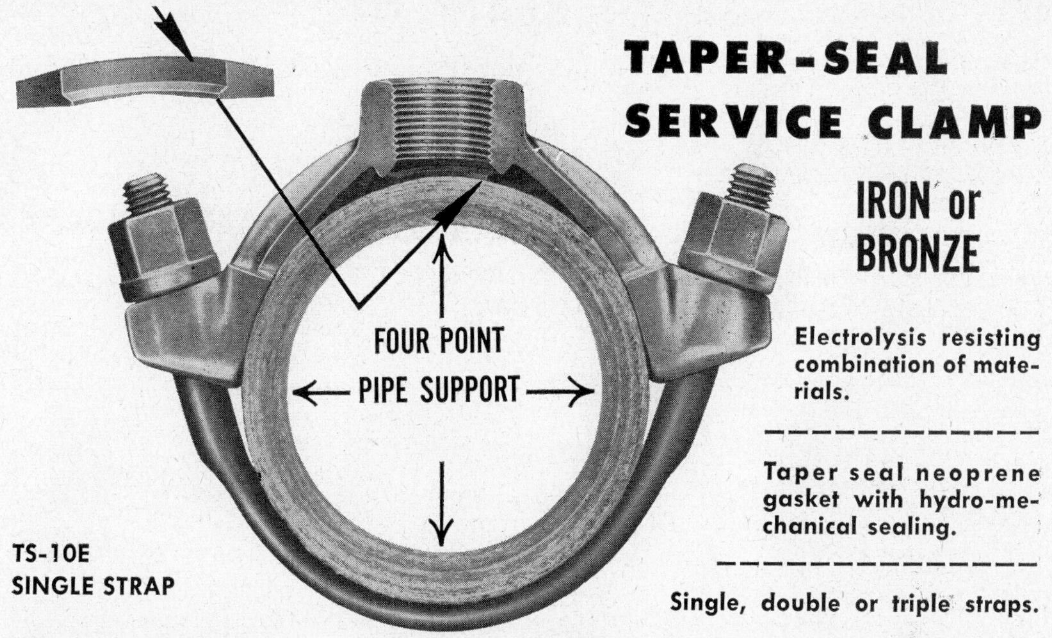

TS-10E
SINGLE STRAP

Electrolysis resisting combination of materials.

Taper seal neoprene gasket with hydro-mechanical sealing.

Single, double or triple straps.

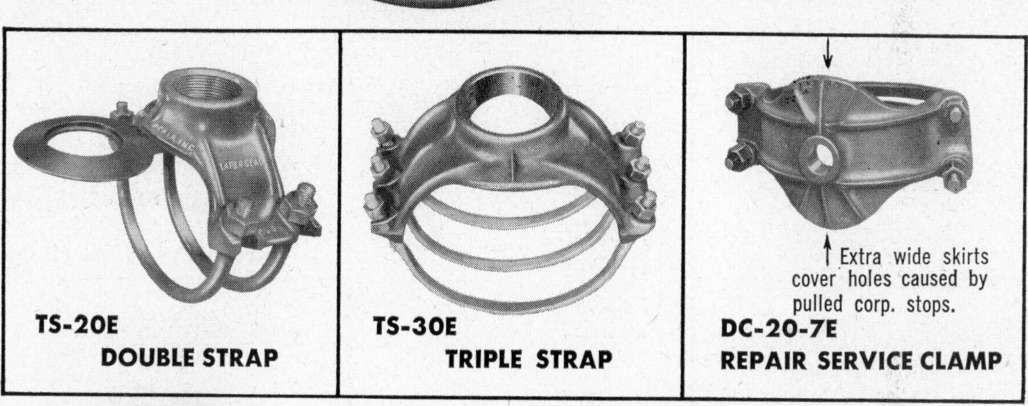

TS-20E
DOUBLE STRAP

TS-30E
TRIPLE STRAP

Extra wide skirts cover holes caused by pulled corp. stops.

DC-20-7E
REPAIR SERVICE CLAMP

- WRAP-AROUND PRINCIPLE CONFORMS TO SHAPE OF PIPE
- MINIMUM OF STRAP TIGHTENING REQUIRED
- HYDRO-MECHANICAL SEALING PRINCIPLE
- LOW COST—SIMPLE INSTALLATION
- SIZES . . . 1-5/16" O.D. to 24" O.D. Tap size ½" to 4"

WRITE FOR FREE CATALOG *and other information.*

SMITH BLAIR INC.

Main Office & Factory: P. O. Box 666 • SOUTH SAN FRANCISCO, CALIFORNIA
Branches: South Gate, California • Greensburg, Pennsylvania
STOCKING JOBBERS IN PRINCIPAL CITIES

SB-218B

SMITH-BLAIR FABRICATED FLEXIBLE COUPLINGS
Large diameters, all sizes and lengths.

SMITH-BLAIR FLEXIBLE C.I. COUPLINGS
For cast iron and asbestos-cement pipe.

SMITH-BLAIR FLEXIBLE STEEL COUPLINGS
For steel pipe.

SMITH-BLAIR FLEXIBLE REDUCING COUPLINGS
For all types of pipe.

. . . ALWAYS SPECIFY
SMITH-BLAIR
WHEN ORDERING
WATER-WORKS FITTINGS

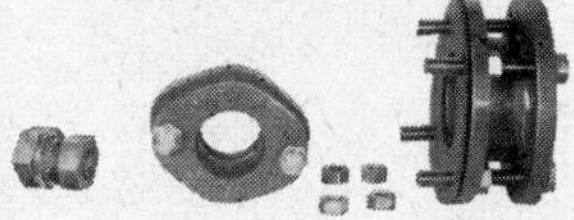

SMITH-BLAIR FLEXIBLE METER COUPLINGS & FLANGE ADAPTER COUPLINGS

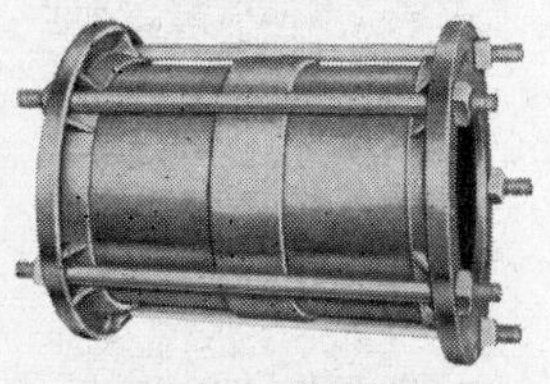

SMITH-BLAIR FLEXIBLE CUT-IN COUPLINGS
For repairing broken bells and collars.

SMITH-BLAIR MISCELLANEOUS SPECIAL FLEXIBLE FITTINGS
For asbestos-cement pipe (on order).

SMITH-BLAIR PIPE REPAIR LUGS
For making your own pipe repair clamps.

SMITH-BLAIR FLEXIBLE TEE COUPLINGS

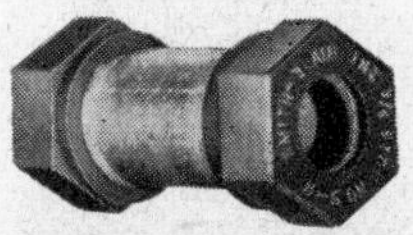

SMITH-BLAIR SERVICE COUPLINGS
For connecting small diameter pipe.

Main Office & Factory: **P. O. Box 666 • SOUTH SAN FRANCISCO, CALIFORNIA**
Branches: **South Gate, California • Greensburg, Pennsylvania**
STOCKING JOBBERS IN PRINCIPAL CITIES SB-218C.

Patented

SMITH-BLAIR FAST ACTION CLAMPS
For repairing broken cast iron or asbestos-cement pipe.

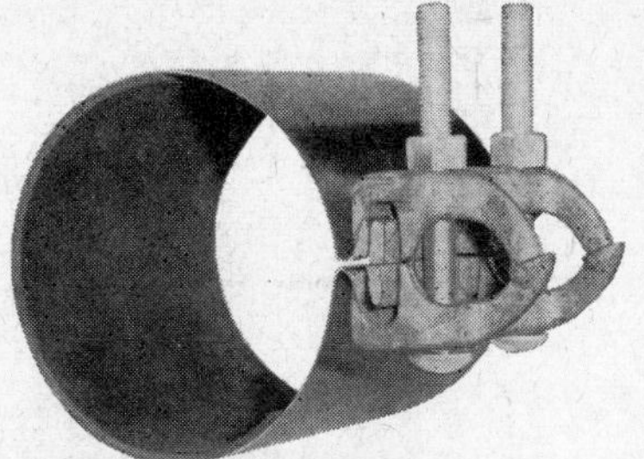

SMITH-BLAIR
PIPE REPAIR CLAMPS

... ALWAYS SPECIFY
SMITH-BLAIR
WHEN ORDERING
WATER-WORKS
FITTINGS

Patented

SMITH-BLAIR
WATER LOCK RINGS

SMITH-BLAIR CAP COUPLINGS
For all types and sizes of pipes.

SMITH-BLAIR
SIMPLEX FLANGE ADAPTERS
For connecting asbestos-cement pipe to flanged fittings.

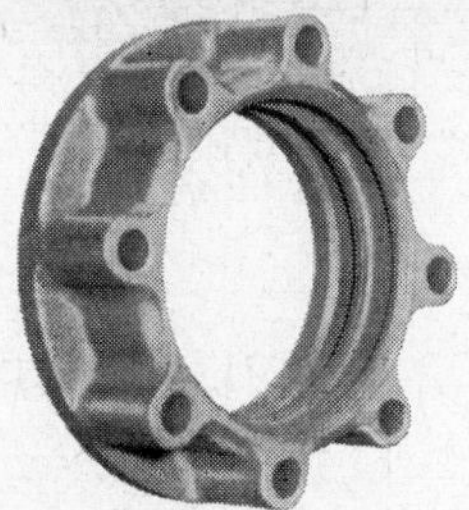

SMITH-BLAIR
RING-TITE FLANGE ADAPTERS
For connecting J-M Ring-Tite pipe to flanged fittings.

SMITH-BLAIR C.I. TEES
Plain end and flanged outlets. Sizes 4" to 12" inclusive. Also steel fabrications in all types and sizes.

SMITH-BLAIR, Inc., with its many years of experience in the manufacturing of water-works fittings and the designing of special fittings, welcomes your request for special pipeline fittings. The illustrations shown on the preceding pages are typical examples of Smith-Blair answers to pipeline problems. The Smith-Blair engineering staff will be pleased to offer its recommendations to you without obligation. Just write to Engineering Department, Smith-Blair, Inc., P. O. Box 666, South San Francisco, California. State your specific problem, listing pipe sizes, type of pipe, and other pertinent information.

***WRITE FOR FREE CATALOG** and other information.*

SMITH BLAIR INC.

Main Office & Factory: **P. O. Box 666 • SOUTH SAN FRANCISCO, CALIFORNIA**
Branches: **South Gate, California • Greensburg, Pennsylvania**
STOCKING JOBBERS IN PRINCIPAL CITIES

SB-218D

WALLACE & TIERNAN INCORPORATED

25 Main St., Belleville 9, N. J.

CHLORINATORS for Water Treatment Sewage & Waste Treatment Swimming Pools

V-NOTCH CHLORINATORS

Series A-711, A-712

Feed rates: 25 to 2,000 lbs per 24 hours.

Type: V-notch variable orifice, vacuum, solution feed type. Unit is completely corrosion resistant and has an attractive fiber-glass cabinet.

Control of Feed Rates: Manual, intermittent, automatic proportional, or program control. Feed range is 10 to 1 on Series A-711; 20 to 1 on Series A-712.

Shipping Weight with remote injector: 150 lbs.

Dimensions: Width 27"; depth 16-11/16"; Height 62".

For complete information write for Catalog Files #25.100, and 25.110.

A-703 MANUAL CONTROL CHLORINATOR

Feed Rates: 5 to 500 lbs. per 24 hrs. and 10 to 1000 lbs. per 24 hrs. Feed range of 100 to 1 without replacing meters.

Type: Visible Vacuum Solution Feed with dual orifice meters.

Control of Feed Rates: Manual control. Feed control knob and dual scale select 10 to 1 or 100 to 1 range.

Shipping Weight with Standard Accessories: 550 lbs.

Dimensions (overall): Width 20"; Depth 31" (36" with injector mounted); Height 68".

For complete information write for Catalog File #10.200.

V-NOTCH CHLORINATORS

Feed Rates: 30 to 8000 lbs. per 24 hrs.

Type: Visible Vacuum Solution Feed, with pneumatic operation of critical control parts.

Control of Feed Rates: Manual, intermittent, automatic proportional, or program control.

Shipping weight with Standard Accessories: 830 lbs.

Dimensions (overall): Width 42"; Depth 25"; Height 72".

For complete information write for Catalog File #10.160.

WALLACE & TIERNAN INCORPORATED

25 Main St., Belleville 9, N. J.

Hypochlorinator

HYPOCHLORINATOR

Feed Rates: 1.9 to 68 gals. per 24 hrs. (Max. of 5 lbs. chlorine per 24 hrs. using 1% hypochlorite solution)
Type: Electrically operated diaphragm type solution pump. Resistant to corrosion from hypochlorite.
Control of Feed Rates: Manual or intermittent control (other models available for automatic proportional control)
Shipping Weight with Standard Accessories: 100 lbs.
Dimensions (overall): Width 15 5/16"; Depth 10⅞" Height 15".
For complete information write for TP-30C-4.

Residual Recorder

CHLORINE RESIDUAL RECORDER

The W & T Chlorine Residual Recorder automatically records on a 24 hour circular chart either free or total chlorine residual. With this amperometric Recorder installed, a plant obtains a continuous, permanent record of its chlorination efficiency. For convenience, remote residual indicators, recorders or alarms may be used with the Recorder, being installed wherever desired throughout the plant. For complete information write for Catalog File #50.250.

WT SILACTOR

The WT Silactor (pronounced Sill -actor) provides a system for the continuous production of activated silica with chlorine. Raw materials—chlorine and sodium silicate—are withdrawn directly from their own containers without handling or dilution. All chlorine used in the WT Silactor is available for the normal functions of chlorine, such as killing bacteria and algae, or the oxidation of iron, manganese and other oxidizable material. For complete information write for Catalog File #60.110.

W T Silactor

METHODS OF CHLORINATOR CONTROL

In addition to chlorinators, Wallace & Tiernan also manufactures a complete selection of equipment for chlorinator control. Whether it is intermittent, automatic proportional, rate or program control, accessory equipment by W&T can make the installation complete.

W & T SERVICE

A complete line of chlorinators and chemical feeders assures you that there is always W&T Equipment to fit your water, sewage, waste or pool treatment problem. W&T's nationwide service staff, always on call, is prepared to furnish advice on the selection of proper equipment and to furnish prompt service on all W&T machines.

WALLACE & TIERNAN INCORPORATED

25 Main St., Belleville 9, N. J.

DRY CHEMICAL FEEDERS

W&T's complete line of dry chemical feeders provides a model for every job, whether the requirements call for weigh belt gravimetric feeders, loss-of-weight gravimetric feeders, or volumetric feeders. Standard accessories include W&T Dust Collectors, dissolving chambers, and extension hoppers.

A-552 VOLUMETRIC FEEDER

Screw Type feeder which controls all dry chemicals with an accuracy of ± 4%.

Hopper agitation prevents caking or arching.

Solution tanks and overhead hoppers available.

For complete information write for TP-35-C.

A-635 FLUORIDATORS

Screw type-feeder available as either volumetric or gravimetric model.

Gravimetric Model:

Loss of weight feed control and recording.

Accuracy ± 1%.

Volumetric Model:

Optional loss of weight recording—independent of the feed control mechanism.

For complete information write for TP-4-M & TP-5-M.

MOF & MOI VOLUMETRIC FEEDERS

An oscillating feed spout with a free wheeling feed roll or orifice plate (depending on chemical) provides a continuous smooth chemical discharge.

Accuracy of ± 5%.

Overhead loading or storage can be provided.

For complete information write for TP-39-M.

ELECTRO RUST-PROOFING CORP. (N.J.)

30 Main Street, Belleville 9, N. J.

PREVENTIVE MAINTENANCE WITH CATHODIC PROTECTION REDUCES COSTS

At this water plant, both the elevated tank and the underwater clarifier equipment are kept corrosion free by ERP cathodic protection.

E.R.P. cathodic protection systems are designed and installed to meet the requirements of each individual job and can—as proved by thousands of installations — successfully control rust and corrosion.

Electro Rust-Proofing Corporation furnishes a complete service of design, installation and service for the application of cathodic protection to either new or old steel water storage tanks, deep well pumps, clarifier and flocculator mechanisms in water and sewage treatment plants. For the protection of pipe lines and other buried structures in contact with soil, services are available for survey, design and supervision of installation.

Technical representatives are available in most areas and inquiries will be given prompt attention.

NOTE: Under certain conditions, galvanic anodes may be employed and the rectifier eliminated or a combination of the two may be used —for example— electrolytic bowl anodes and galvanic riser anode—all depending upon particular job requirements.

Insulators
Electrolytic Bowl Anodes
Electrolytic Riser Anode
Cations
Anions
Electrons
Lead wire to Anodes
Ground
Rectifier
A. C. power

TYPICAL WATER STORAGE TANK APPLICATION OF CATHODIC PROTECTION

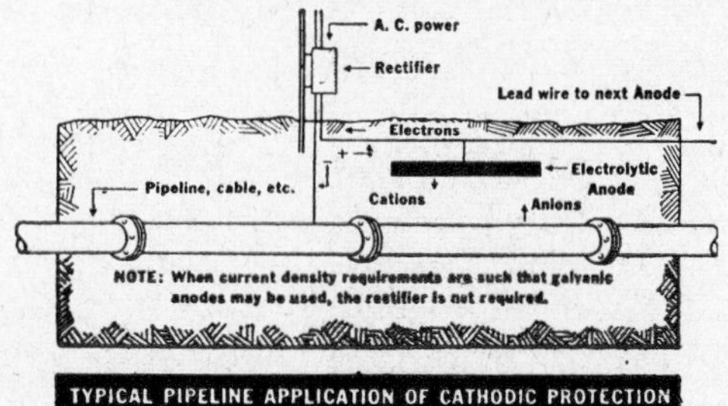

TYPICAL PIPELINE APPLICATION OF CATHODIC PROTECTION

PRECISION ACCURACY

CALMET'S oscillating piston is semi-floating, perfectly balanced . . . a meter that accurately measures the various flows even down to the smallest drip.

MAXIMUM REVENUE

Because CALMET accurately registers every drop . . . because it gives years of service without replacement . . . because it requires a bare minimum of low-cost maintenance, CALMET assures you of every revenue dollar.

EXTREME LONG LIFE

CALMET'S slow-moving oscillating piston and gear train ratio of 256-to-1 assures long-life and less wear on precision parts. Simple design assures years of service with a minimum of attention.

LOW UPKEEP

CALMETS are easy to take apart, easy to repair. The split case design permits quick removal of working parts for cleaning or inspection without breaking the line connection.

Manufactured by

WELL MACHINERY AND SUPPLY CO., INC.

1629 MAIN STREET FORT WORTH, TEXAS

• *These CALMET features assure you satisfaction*

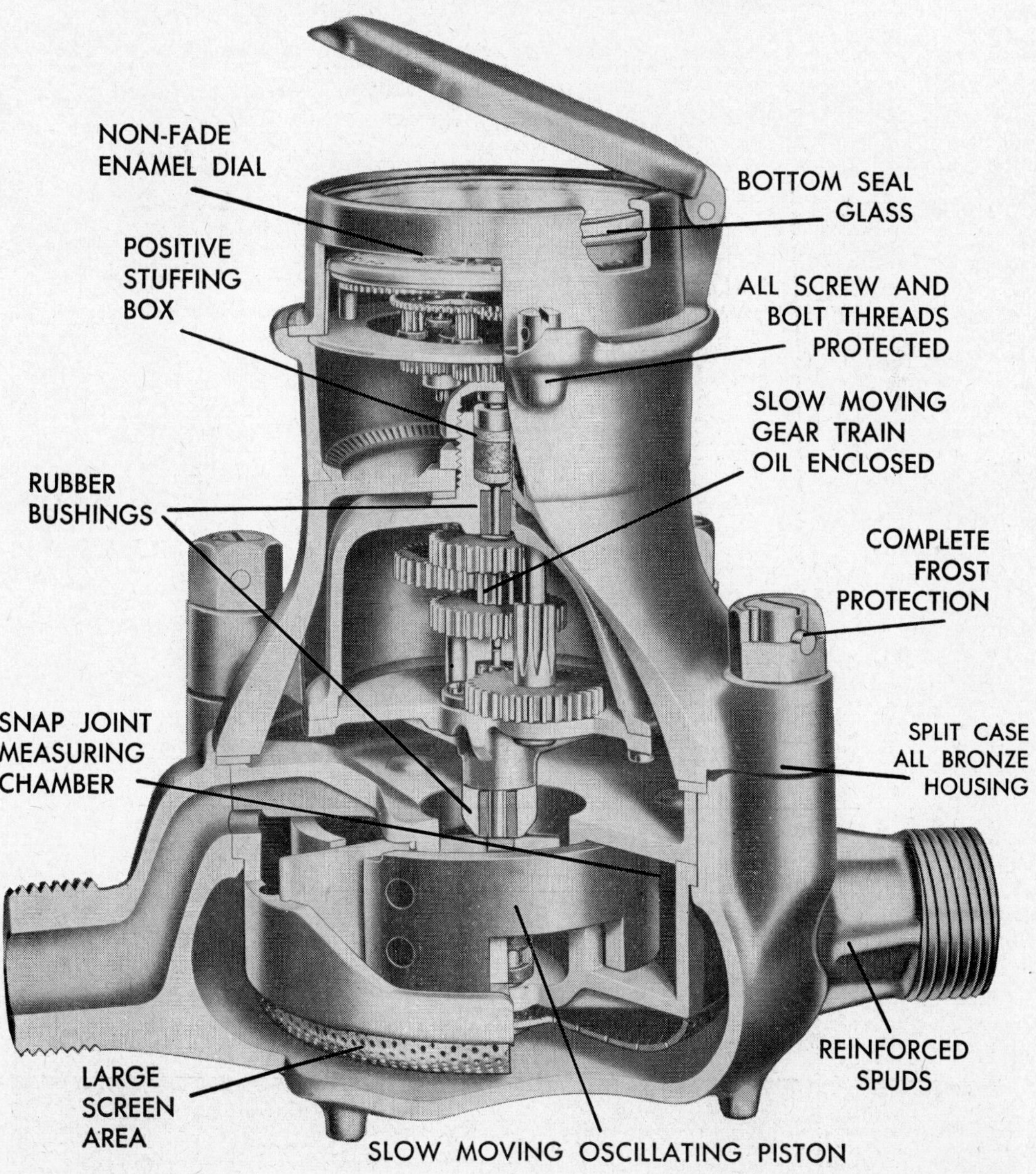

ONLY CALMET HAS AN *ALL BRONZE FROST PROTECTED SPLIT CASE

*The CALMET case is poured from high grade corrosion resisting bronze. The casing wall is reinforced where it supports the heavy bolt lugs on both upper and lower main case, and heavy ribs reinforce spuds.

CALMET WATER METER

PRICE SCHEDULE "A"

Effective MARCH 10, 1955

Size		Model	Length Inches	Weight Each Pounds	List Price (Subject to Discount)
5/8" x 1/2"	L/C	AA	7½	10½	33.00
5/8" x 1/2"	W/C	AA	7½	10½	34.50
5/8" x 3/4"	L/C	AB	7½	10¾	33.00
5/8" x 3/4"	W/C	AB	7½	10¾	35.25
3/4" x 3/4"	L/C	AC	7½	11	39.00
3/4" x 3/4"	W/C	AC	7½	11	41.25
3/4"	L/C	BC	9	11½	48.00
3/4"	W/C	BC	9	11½	50.25
1"	L/C	BD	10¾	25½	72.00
1"	W/C	BD	10¾	25½	75.25
1" x 1¼"	L/C	BE	10¾	26	78.00
1" x 1¼"	W/C	BE	10¾	26	82.50
1½"	L/C	*BFS	13	40	138.00
1½"	W/C	*BFS	13	40	142.50
1½"	W/F	BF	13	40	142.50
2"	L/C	*BGS	17	60	204.00
2"	W/C	*BGS	17	60	216.00
2"	W/F	BG	17	60	216.00

*Spud Type — Internal Threads

NET EXTRAS

Fog-Tite Registers .... }
Double Lids .... } Available at Extra Cost

Prices subject to change without notice.

F.O.B. POINT

Fort Worth, Texas, with full freight allowed on shipments of 150 lbs. or more (12-5/8" meters make freight allowed shipment).

WRITE FOR FREE CATALOG

See every part and exclusive feature of the precision built CALMET Water Meter, faithfully pictured and described in our handsome catalog. All sizes of CALMET METERS are shown with full specifications.

Manufactured by

WELL MACHINERY AND SUPPLY CO., INC.

1629 MAIN STREET FORT WORTH, TEXAS

R. D. WOOD COMPANY

Philadelphia, Pa.

Manufacturers of

Cast Iron Pipe, Fittings, Fire Hydrants, Valves

WORKS: Florence, N. J.

"SAND - SPUN"

Cast Iron Pressure Pipe
Bell and Spigot—Mechanical Joint

"SAND - SPUN" is the trademark name for R. D. WOOD COMPANY cast iron pressure pipe, cast centrifugally in sand-lined molds. After placing the sand-lined mold horizontally in a centrifugal casting machine, and while the mold is revolving, the required quantity of molten metal is introduced. The centrifugal motion forces the molten iron onto the wall of the sand-lined mold, thus forming the pipe.

Following one of the most important clauses of the American Water Works Association specifications, the pipe is allowed to remain in the sand-lined mold until all color of heat has disappeared, eliminating all casting strains.

"SAND-SPUN" cast iron pipe is similar in structure to pipe cast in vertical sand-lined molds, which was the standard practice for many years, except the centrifugal force eliminates all gas pockets, blow holes and inclusions, resulting in a pipe of superior quality with greater flexibility, more homogeneous and denser in structure. The pipe is concentric and of uniform metal thickness throughout.

SPECIFICATIONS FURNISHED ON REQUEST

THIS 6-INCH PIPE, 16 FEET 6 INCHES LONG, SHOWED A DEFLECTION OF 3⅛-INCH BEFORE BREAKING, DEMONSTRATING THE ELASTICITY, STRENGTH AND TOUGHNESS OF "SAND-SPUN" CAST IRON PIPE, "CAST AND CURED IN THE SAND"

GATE VALVES

Reliability is the big important consideration in the choice of gate valves for water works. Because of their inaccessibility under ground, repairs always are laborious, expensive, and a source of annoyance to operators and consumers. Interruptions of service are fire hazards as well as perils to health.

"Wood" Gate Valves are especially designed for severe underground service, and can be counted on to do what is expected of them. They are simple in design, rugged in construction, fully bronze mounted, and suitable for working pressures up to 175 pounds.

The taper-seat type, double disc assures tightness and ease of operation. There are no pockets to fill up with sediment and scale that might cause the valves to jam.

"Wood" Gate Valves conform to the specifications of the American Water Works Association. They are made of **thoroughly seasoned** castings, are inspected rigidly, and fully tested to 300 pounds hydrostatic pressure.

Operation: **In closing,** the gates first are lowered from the bonnet into position opposite the valve openings, before the spreading action begins. The center, or "hub," of the spreader then forms a point of contact with the discs on each side of the trunnions, where the discs are reinforced. The pressure is distributed equally from the center, allowing exact adjustment of the discs to the brass seats without distortion, resulting in all-round tightness. Both discs are equally tight against pressure from either side of the valve.

In opening, the spreader first moves upward and away from the discs, allowing them to **move free of the seats before lifting them** into the bonnet.

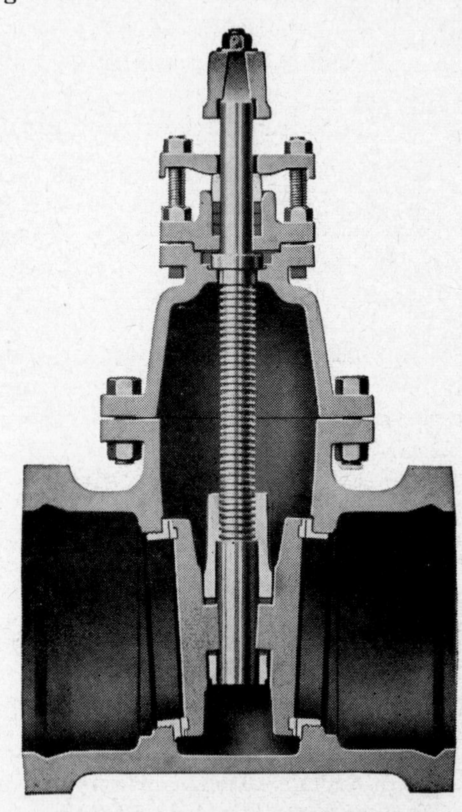

"WOOD" GATE VALVE—SECTIONAL VIEW

"Wood" Gate Valves are furnished either with bell or flanged ends, or for connection to any standard-type joint, including mechanical joint.

MATHEWS FIRE HYDRANTS

Mathews Hydrants have been the leader for more than a half century—over 500,000 of them are in use.

New and unique features make the Mathews Modernized Hydrant more desirable than ever: simplified in design; greater protection throughout against rust; greater shock-resisting strength of the barrel and protection case; the swivel flange that permits taking off the nozzle section before lifting out the barrel, thus making this operation easier.

The **swivel flange** permits the facing of nozzles in any direction quickly without removing the bolts or disturbing the barrel. The **shield-operating** nut prevents rain and sleet from seeping down and freezing around the operating nut.

The Mathews Modernized Hydrant can be adjusted to changed grades, either increasing or decreasing the length, without disturbing the elbow or protection case and without excavating the hydrant.

With all these improvements, the Mathews Modernized Hydrant is interchangeable with old installations.

As a result of more traffic accidents, an increasing number of hydrants are being broken. On this point alone, the Mathews saves large sums for the municipalties which have them.

A broken Mathews cannot leak, and it can be replaced easily in a few minutes without digging or breaking the pavement.

Avoid having to dig up streets and break pavements to replace broken hydrants. Install Mathews.

Hydrants can be equipped with pipe connections other than bell, including standardized mechanical joint.

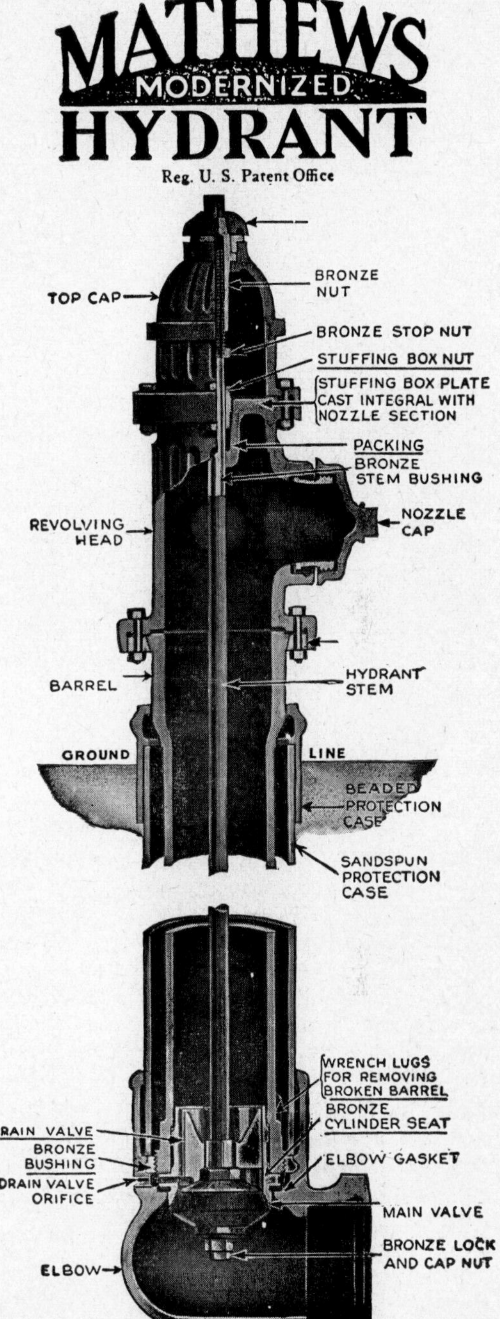

The leader for more than half a century
More than 500,000
in use throughout the world
SEND FOR A DESCRIPTIVE CIRCULAR

BIRD'S-EYE VIEW OF WORKS AT FLORENCE, N. J.

FITTINGS

Bell and Spigot or flanged fittings made to American Water Works Association or A.S.A. specifications.

Mechanical joint fittings.

Special castings.

CUTTING-IN TEES

A special fitting, especially designed for use in cutting in on a main line. This tee eliminates the use of a sleeve, and necessitates but two joints.

PRODUCTS

"Mathews" Fire Hydrants

"Mathews" Flange Barrel Fire Hydrants

"R.D. Wood" Fire Hydrants

Gate Valves

Valve Boxes

Indicator Posts

Floor Stands

"Sand-Spun" (Centrifugal) Cast Iron Pipe

Mechanical Joint Sand-Spun Cast Iron Pipe

Standard Fittings

Reduced Fittings

Cutting-in-Specials

Gray Iron Castings

Hydraulic Machinery

Hydraulic Operating Valves

Automatic Gas Producers

WORTHINGTON-GAMON *WATCH DOG* DISC WATER METER

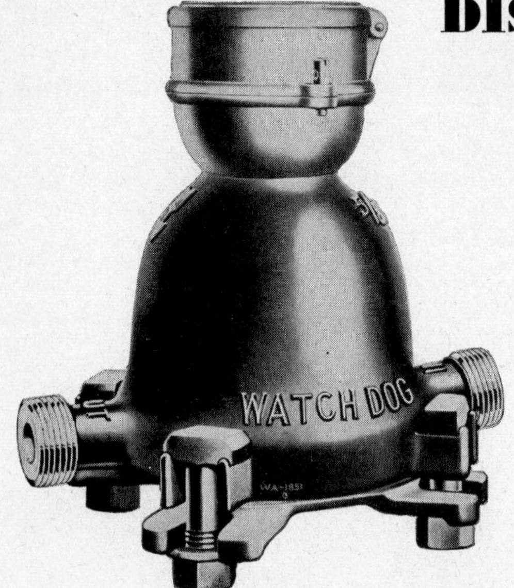

WATCH DOG Meters are available with

GEAR TRAINS—OPEN OR ENCLOSED
DISCS—REINFORCED OR WITH THRUST ROLLER
REGISTERS—CIRCULAR or STRAIGHT READING
DIALS—CUBIC FEET or GALLONS

FROST-PROOF MODEL
Sizes ⅝", ¾" and 1"

The Frost-Proof Model WATCH DOG Disc Meter, designed for regions having freezing temperatures, is furnished with a bottom cap designed to break when the water in the meter freezes. Bronze bolts engage the main casing and the bottom cap through slotted lugs permitting easy removal when replacement is necessary. The washers and hexagonal nuts are of brass. The close-grained cast iron bottom cap is completely lined, insuring an entirely non-ferrous meter interior.

Like all WATCH DOG meters, this Frost-Proof Model has numerous features which make for continuous operation and reduced maintenance costs, such as:

Main casing of bronze, with high copper content.
Leakproof stuffing box.
Gear train—open or enclosed—so designed as to be easily removed along with chamber and disc without disturbing register box or stuffing box.
Disc chamber in two sections held together without screws—for easy disassembly.
Disc with thrust roller or metal reinforcement. All parts are interchangeable.
Register—circular or straight reading type, with dials indicating cubic feet, U.S. gallons, Imperial gallons or metric measure—all parts of non-corroding materials.

Write for Bulletin M-975-B41

WORTHINGTON-GAMON *WATCH DOG* DISC WATER METER

SPLIT CASE MODEL
Sizes ⅝", ¾" and 1"

The Split Case Model WATCH DOG Disc Meter is especially adapted for use in temperate and warm climates, where the meter is not subject to freezing conditions. The main casing consists of an upper and a lower half case of bronze, with connection spuds in the lower case. The upper case (main casing cover) and the lower case (main casing) are held securely together by bronze bolts which, when removed, give access to the internal mechanism. These cases are accurately machined and closely fitted to insure perfect alignment.

Write for Bulletin M-975-B40

For rates of flow of 50 gallons or less, use WATCH DOG *FROST-PROOF* DISC METER or WATCH DOG *SPLIT-CASE* DISC METER in sizes ⅝", ¾" or 1"

WORTHINGTON-GAMON *WATCH DOG*
DISC WATER METER

STYLE 3
Sizes 1½" and 2"

Style 3 WATCH DOG Disc Water Meter, sizes 1½" and 2", supplements the line of smaller WATCH DOG Meters used for water supply. This larger model split case meter is especially adapted for ease of maintenance while in service, as it may be repaired without disconnecting it from the piping. As in the smaller models, the main casing consists of an upper and a lower half case of bronze, with the connection spuds in the lower case. The inlet and outlet can be furnished with either oval flanges or hexagonal ends with internal pipe threads. Upper and lower cases are held securely together by bronze bolts which, when removed, give access to the internal mechanism.

Ask for Bulletin M-975-B42

For rates of flow greater than 50 gpm, use
WATCH DOG *STYLE 3* DISC METER
in sizes 1½" and 2"
WATCH DOG *HEAVY DUTY* DISC METER
in sizes 3" and 4"
WATCH DOG *COMPOUND* METER
in sizes 2", 3", 4", 6" and 8"
WORTHINGTON-GAMON *TURBINE* METER
in sizes 2", 3", 4", 6" and 8"

WORTHINGTON-GAMON *WATCH DOG*
DISC WATER METER

HEAVY DUTY TYPE
Sizes 3" and 4"

The *Heavy Duty* WATCH DOG Disc Water Meters are designed for large services such as hotels, apartment buildings, mercantile establishments, large office buildings, manufacturing plants, etc., where the demand is too high for *Style 3* Meter. The main casing is similar to that of the Split Case Meter described on the preceding page. Upper and lower cases are held securely together by means of bolts and nuts which, when removed, give access to the internal mechanism. As in all WATCH DOG Meters, the bronze composition has a high copper content and is particularly adapted for waterworks service under all conditions.

Write for Bulletin M-975-B34B

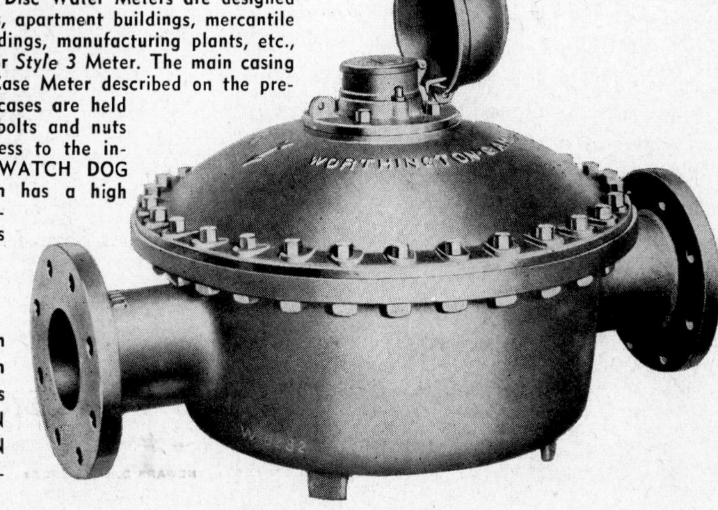

All WATCH DOG meters conform to the standards and perform well within the test specifications adopted by the AMERICAN WATER WORKS ASSOCIATION and the NEW ENGLAND WATER WORKS ASSOCIATION.

WORTHINGTON-GAMON *WATCH DOG* COMPOUND WATER METER

Sizes 2", 3", 4", 6" and 8"

The WATCH DOG Compound Meter consists of a standard WATCH DOG *positive displacement disc* meter and a standard WATCH DOG *current* meter, in combination with an automatic compounding valve, for which we hold exclusive patents, all complete in a single casing.

The purpose of this arrangement is to provide a measuring device for recording accurately the entire range of flows through large service pipes from the smallest stream to full demand.

When the rate of flow is beyond the capacity of the *disc* meter, the changeover valve causes the *current* meter to register. When flow decreases, the reverse action takes place.

Write for Bulletin M-975-B44

WORTHINGTON-GAMON *MODEL IH* TURBINE WATER METER

Sizes 2", 3", 4", 6", 8"

The Worthington-Gamon Turbine Meter is a development of the well-known Worthington Turbine Pump. This meter is of the current or velocity type, designed to handle large volumes of water at a minimum loss of pressure. The design permits easy cleaning and repair, and includes an integral strainer which is accessible without disturbing the moving parts. There are no large-contact wearing surfaces, and the moving parts are not subject to breakage due to water hammer.

Write for Bulletin M-975-B43A

WORTHINGTON-GAMON METER DIVISION

Worthington Corporation

296 SOUTH STREET NEWARK 5, NEW JERSEY

CYCLONE FENCE DEPARTMENT

AMERICAN STEEL AND WIRE DIVISION
UNITED STATES STEEL CORPORATION

General Offices: Waukegan, Illinois

FACTORIES—Waukegan, Ill.; Newark, N. J.; Fort Worth, Texas; Greensburg, Ind.; DeKalb, Ill.; Oakland, Calif.

UNITED STATES STEEL

CYCLONE INVINCIBLE CHAIN LINK FENCE

U·S·S Cyclone Invincible Fence is an almost impenetrable barrier and enclosure for use around reservoirs, power plants, and similar municipal projects where intruders *must* be kept out. It has proved itself to be one of the most effective and economical means of property and personal protection.

This fence also has been used effectively for years by school officials for enclosing athletic fields; by private enterprises for insuring paid attendance at race tracks, baseball and football fields and other outdoor sport arenas, and by municipal and state officials for enclosing fair grounds, swimming pools and other public properties.

The fabric is heavy No. 6 or No. 9 wire; line posts are H-column steel posts, and the corner posts are three-inch steel pipe. The upper arms, which may extend either in, out, or straight up, as desired, carry three strands of barbed wire which render this fence practically impassable except at regular authorized entrances.

Unless it is erected properly, the best fence cannot give you good service. Cyclone Erection Crews or Erection Supervisors see that every Cyclone Fence is erected to definite and specific standards of excellence. Coupled with the long-lasting qualities built into Cyclone Fence, these standards assure you the best possible service from Cyclone.

ONLY UNITED STATES STEEL CORPORATION MANUFACTURES CYCLONE FENCE.

ACCEPT NO SUBSTITUTE.

**No job is too large —
No job is too small for Cyclone.**

COOK WELL STRAINER CO.

6330 Glenway Ave. • Cincinnati 11, Ohio

WELL STRAINERS

WIRE-WOUND AND TUBE

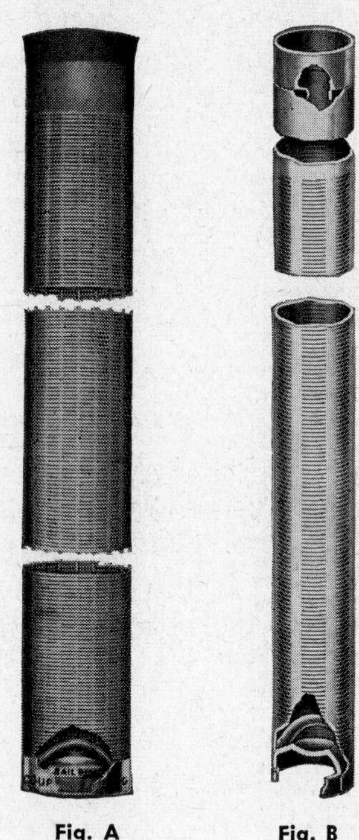

Fig. A Fig. B

EXCLUSIVE FEATURES: COOK designed the first strainer in 1882 with a V-shaped self-cleaning slot. This arrangement of slotting is found in all COOK strainers and eliminates the possibility of clogging. This is of great importance where development involves the removal of fine and coarse sand. In a straight slot, or a drilled or punched opening, small particles of sand and fine gravel find a place to lodge and automatically valve-off a large portion of the waterway.

FLEXIBILITY: Many years of experience have proven that in order to furnish strainers, for wells from 2″ to 40″ diameter, for fine and coarse gravel, for shallow and deep wells, materials of different sizes are absolutely necessary. The COOK line is flexible enough to take care of any of these conditions. Strainers can be furnished with slots as fine as .006″ or as coarse as .25″. For the larger wells and for severe conditions heavier material can be provided to give added strength for supporting pipe or unusual pressures and deep wells.

CAPACITY: This is directly relative to inlet area—COOK strainers can be furnished with an inlet area equal to that of any other type. In considering the maximum area we must keep in mind that strength and wearing qualities are equally important.

CONSTRUCTION:

Wire-Wound (Fig. A): In this design the bars which form the internal support are placed in the winding machine, and as the bar section revolves each bar is notched. Special shaped wire is placed in the notch and securely caulked. This arrangement gives you a continuous slot.

Tube (Fig. B): Made from special, hard-drawn, seamless brass tubing, straight and round. The slots, being cut from within the tube, are larger inside than outside. Any particle that may enter a slot will pass through without choking it since there is no interference placed in its way.

ADVANTAGES: The design of the COOK well strainer permits the most direct and unobstructed water way from the water bearing formation into the well. The V-shaped slot strainer allows for maximum development which is accomplished by the removal of silt, alluvium, clay and fine sand from around the outside of the strainer, thus providing a natural filter of coarser and more uniform sand and gravel.

Exposing the V-shaped slot directly to the water bearing formation permits the water to flow into the well with a minimum friction

loss. This results in decreased draw-down and lower pumping costs. A reduction of a few feet in the total pumping head effects a saving in power sufficient to pay for the initial cost of the strainer in one to two years time.

Eliminating sand from the pump is another money saving feature obtained by using the COOK well strainer—75% of the wear on the average pump is due to the abrasive action of sand that it must handle.

The reduction in pumping costs alone justi-

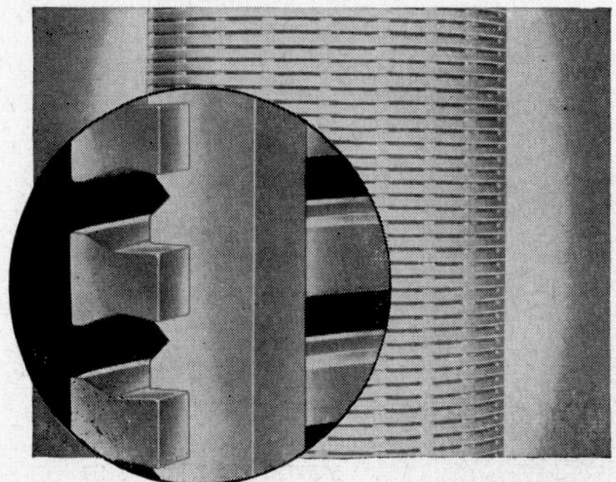

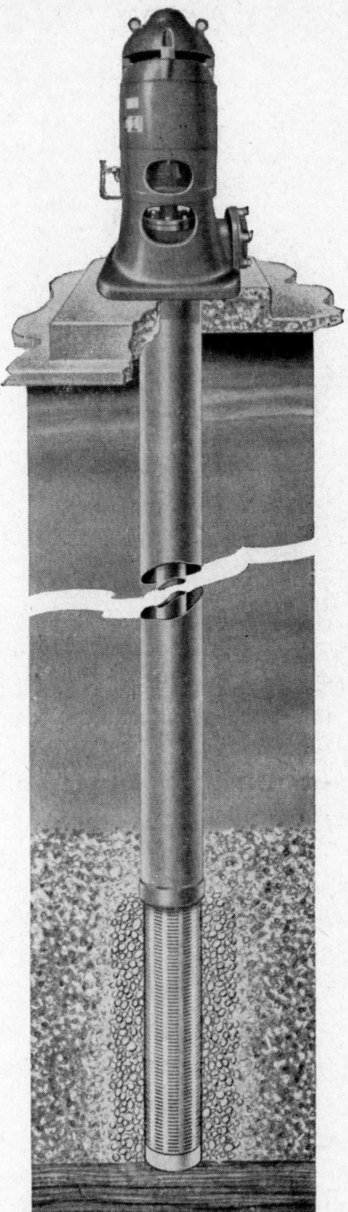

fies the investment in a COOK well strainer, but in addition to this the COOK strainer insures the maximum life from both the well and pumping equipment. Since 1882 the COOK well strainer has made a reputation for itself for the many years of service that it gives—25 years service is very common with COOK strainers. For complete information write for catalog or call HU: 1-8800.

ELECTRIC EQUIPMENT

FOR WATER AND SEWAGE-TREATMENT PLANTS

MOTORS

HIGH-SPEED SYNCHRONOUS MOTORS

General Electric can supply all of the many types of motors used in water and sewage plants, with various types of enclosures and mountings. The majority of applications require the use of the simple, rugged, squirrel-cage induction motor. Initial costs and maintenance costs for this motor are low, and the necessary starting equipment is simple and comparatively inexpensive.

The unity-power-factor synchronous motor is ideally suited for water works requiring large drives, because of its high efficiency, good power factor, and low cost in the larger sizes.

The wound-rotor induction motor is used extensively for adjustable-speed drives and occasionally for starting duty where there is a stringent limitation on kva inrush.

*Reg. trade-mark of General Electric Co.

GROUPED CONTROL

General Electric now offers two types of low-voltage grouped control equipment, both of which provide the ease of operation and maintenance associated with centrally located control.

Cabinetrol* units, specially engineered to your requirements and shipped ready for lead connections—saving hours of installation time — are recommended where special equipment is involved.

Motor control centers, made up of standard components, are now available at low cost for centralized control of conventional equipment. Assembled to your specifications, these centers accommodate NEMA Size 1 to 7 starter units and are available in three types of construction: NEMA Types A, B, and C.

CABINETROL MOTOR CONTROL UNIT

DOUBLE-ENDED LOAD-CENTER UNIT SUBSTATION

UNIT SUBSTATIONS

Unit substations, either indoor or outdoor, are used in water and sewage plants to transform and make available to utilization circuits the power required for plant operating machinery. Each substation is factory designed and co-ordinated as a packaged unit which can be quickly and easily installed. Simple bus connection of the co-ordinated units means improved reliability; metal enclosure of all current-carrying parts makes for improved safety.

MEDIUM-VOLTAGE CONTROL

Limitamp* control provides complete control and protection for 2300- to 4600-volt synchronous, wound-rotor, and induction motors up to 3000 hp. Employing current-limiting fuses that limit current and minimize damage under fault conditions, Limitamp controllers provide interrupting capacity of 150,000 kva at 2300 volts and 250,000 kva at 4600 volts. Enclosed in cabinets of modern design, Limitamp controllers contribute to the appearance of any electric installation.

*Reg. trade-mark of General Electric Co.

SWITCHGEAR

Metal-enclosed switchgear is used for either distribution power switching or motor starting and control. Since all breaker elements are removable for servicing and for interchange, a high degree of service reliability is maintained.

CABLE AND PANELBOARDS

General Electric can furnish all types of cable and small circuit-breaker panelboards required in water and sewage plants for lighting and low-capacity distribution circuits.

Whatever your requirements, an engineer at a near-by General Electric office will be glad to help you select the equipment you need. Or address Section 640-461, General Electric Co., Schenectady 5, N. Y.

Progress Is Our Most Important Product

GENERAL ELECTRIC

GFC
BETTER WATER

Layne

GRAVER WATER CONDITIONING CO.

DIVISION OF GRAVER TANK & MFG. CO., INC.

216 West 14th Street, New York 11, N. Y.

District Offices: Chicago, Ill.; Cincinnati, Ohio; Cleveland, Ohio; Detroit, Mich.; Houston, Texas; Philadelphia, Pa.

ENGINEERING REPRESENTATIVES IN ALL PRINCIPAL CITIES.

GRAVER

EQUIPMENT FOR CONVENTIONAL CONDITIONING PLANTS

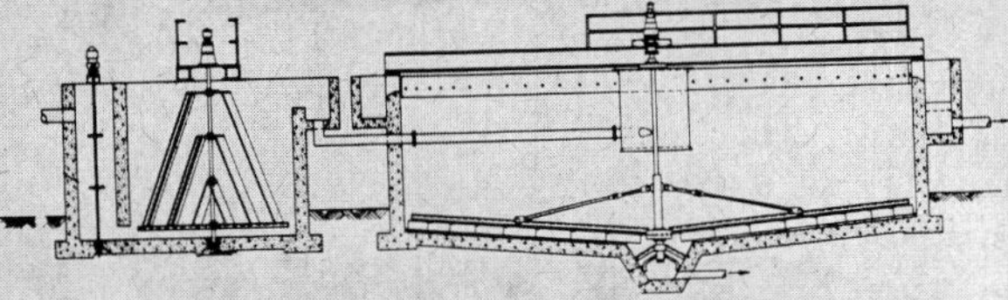

Flash Mixers—provide rapid and thorough mixing with minimum power.
Spirol-Mix Flocculators—eliminates short-circuiting and assures rapid floc formation.
Roto-Rake Sedimentation Basins—Round, square or rectangular basins with sludge removal by revolving or chain-type scrapers over entire bottom.

WATER STORAGE TANKS

Graver designs and manufactures a complete line of water storage tanks — standpipes, steel reservoirs, and elevated storage tanks — backed by almost 100 years of steel vessel construction experience.

INTEGRATED REACTIVATOR TREATMENT PLANTS

A complete, functionally integrated treatment plant for the smaller community including Reactivator, filters, chemical feeders, piping and all accessories.

IRON REMOVAL PLANTS

Graver's seven different methods of iron removal utilizing aeration, clarification in the Graver Reactivator, filtration and ion exchange, are designed to meet all possible requirements.

ZEOLITE SOFTENERS

Graver zeolite softeners are available in a complete range of sizes and types with either manual, semi-automatic or fully automatic controls. Features include low initial cost — simplicity of operation.

REACTIVATORS FOR SOFTENING AND CLARIFYING

The Graver Reactivator®, a high-rate, upflow, solids-contact unit performs in one compartment tank all the functions of coagulation, flocculation, sedimentation and sludge removal—provides important advantages of rapid treatment, small space requirements. Its surgeability design lessens carryover danger.

offers... a complete line of water treatment and storage equipment

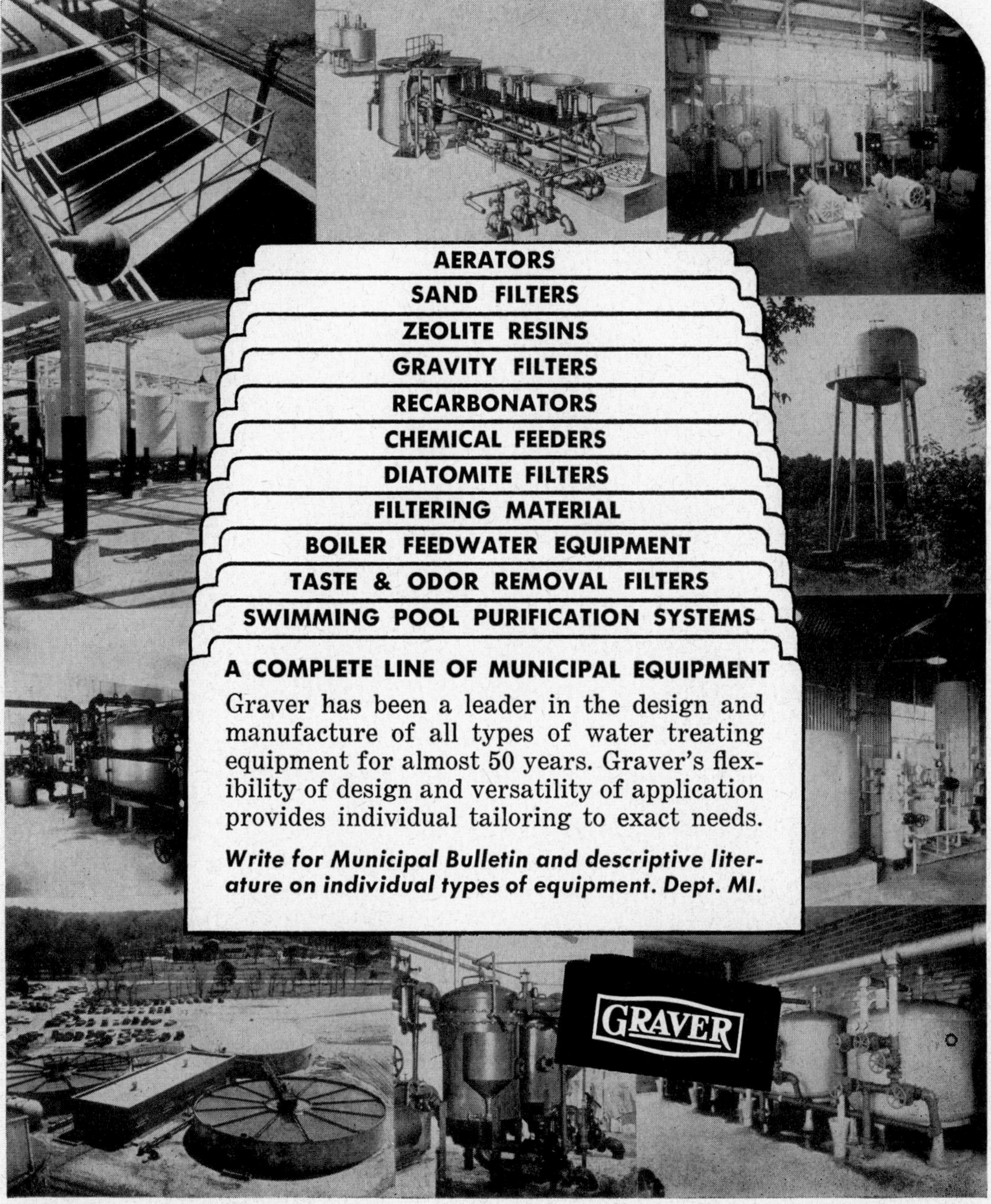

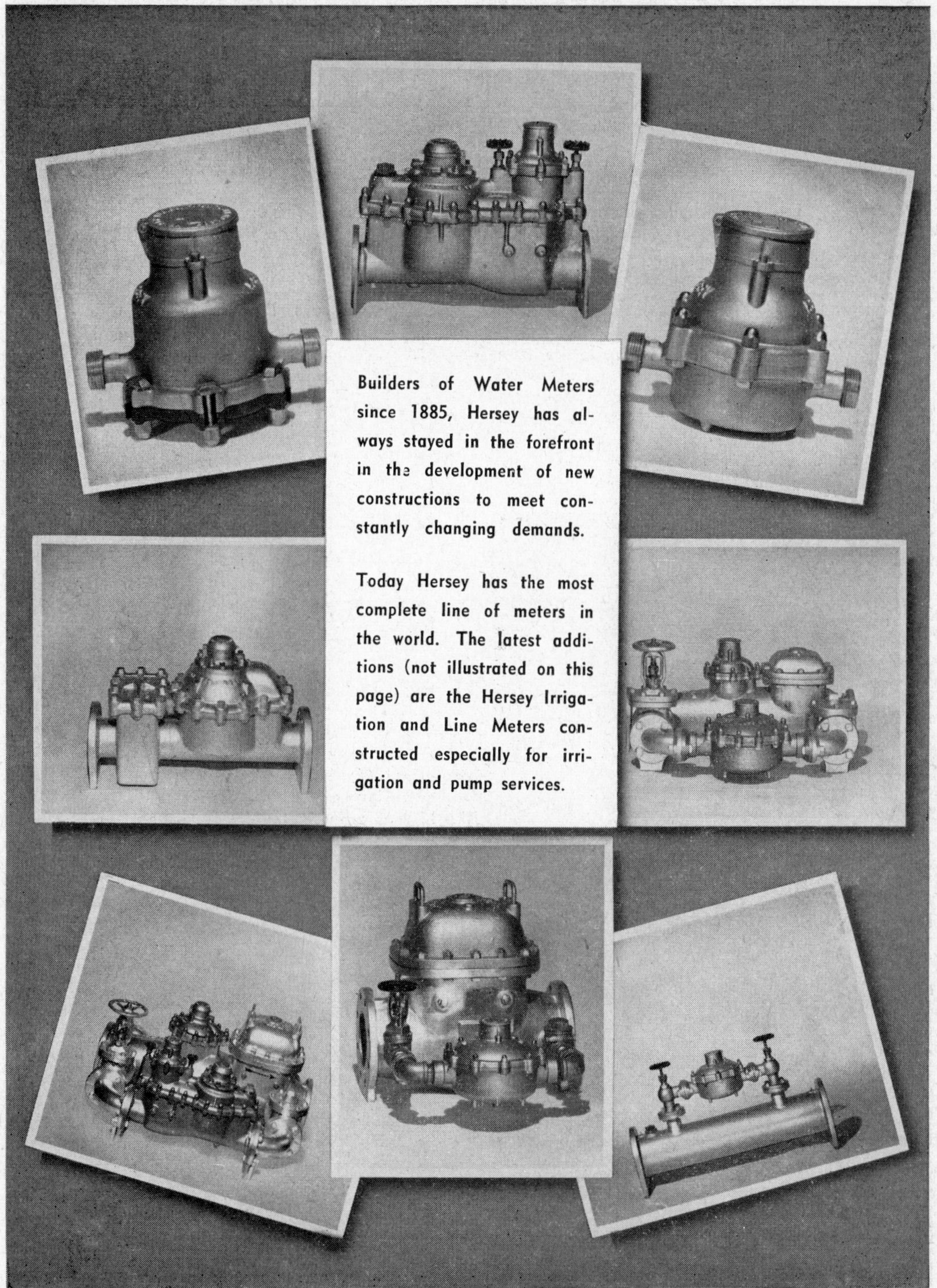

Shown above are some of the many types of Water Meters produced by Hersey.

JOHNS-MANVILLE

Executive Offices: 22 East 40th St., New York 16, N. Y.

OFFICES IN LARGE CITIES

TRANSITE® PRESSURE PIPE

Assures Dependable Service Through the Years
At Lower Cost to the Taxpayer

Engineers and city officials alike face much the same problem in pipe selection. It is twofold: (1) How to make sure the community gets many long years of trouble-free performance from its pressure mains, and (2) How to do this as economically as possible by choosing pipe for durability plus savings.

Transite Pressure Pipe is solving this problem in hundreds of municipalities and water districts from coast to coast. It maintains clean pure water from pumping station to consumer, helps assure high pressure needed for fire protection, at lower cost to taxpayers.

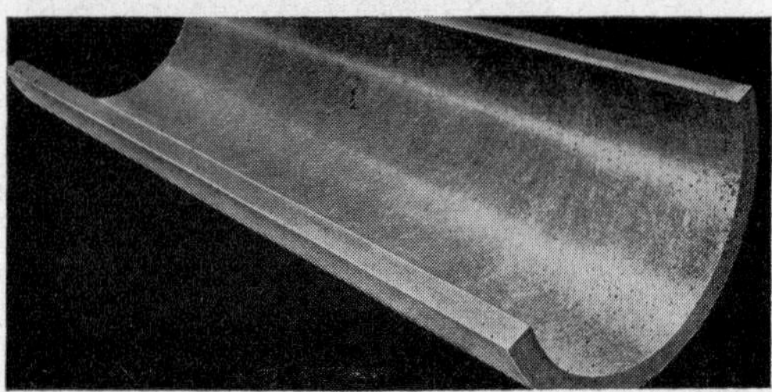

A section of Transite Pressure Pipe, showing the smooth interior that helps assure and maintain lower pumping costs.

Transite Pressure Pipe's long service life is due to its asbestos-cement structure and to Johns-Manville's manufacturing "know-how".

Long Life

Made of asbestos-cement, tough, durable and strong, Transite Pipe cannot rust, is immune to electrolysis and resists corrosion, thus assuring the dependable long life that makes a water main material a sound community investment.

Economic Service

Transite's smooth interior surface stays smooth. (Its flow coefficient is C = 140.) It cannot tuberculate. Since deposits from this form of interior corrosion cannot build up, its flow capacity stays high to keep community pumping costs low. The fact that Transite is immune to tuberculation often permits the selection of smaller pipe sizes to handle the required volume and, of even greater importance, the water system can be designed without allowing for future flow reduction.

Wide Acceptance

Savings in installed cost, its permanent high flow capacity, tight, flexible joints and long life have earned for Transite Pressure Pipe the universal acceptance it now enjoys in thousands of municipal water systems and government and industrial installations throughout the country.

Classes and Sizes

Transite Pressure Pipe is furnished in three pressure classes: Class 100, Class 150 and Class 200 for maximum working pressures of 100, 150 and 200 psi respectively. All are made in standard 13-ft. lengths in 4, 6, 8, 10, 12, 14 and 16-inch diameters.

TRANSITE PRESSURE PIPE and the RING-TITE® COUPLING

Save Assembly Time Every Step of the Way

The Transite Ring-Tite method is the last word in efficient, economical assembly of asbestos-cement pipe. It consists of Transite Pressure Pipe joined by the Transite Ring-Tite Coupling made of the same tough durable material as the pipe itself.

This method offers many automatic features. It gives to municipal water systems the ultimate in locked-in tightness and a completed pipe line that assures the utmost in full, free flow of water under pressure.

Tight, Flexible Joints

The Ring-Tite Coupling speeds and simplifies joint assembly. Workmen simply smooth rubber sealing rings into grooves, lubricate the pipe end, and pull pipe and coupling together. Shoulders on the pipe itself position the ends in the joint automatically. The result is a joint with positive seal, yet remarkably flexible. Rings cannot blow out, and the automatic separation of the pipes within the coupling helps to relieve line stresses in service.

Low Installed Cost

The community benefits at the very outset with Transite Pressure Pipe and the Ring-Tite Coupling since both handling and assembly are so simple that crews can install as fast as the trench is opened. Installation can go forward at a rapid pace, even in bad weather and under difficult temperature and terrain conditions.

With the Ring-Tite Coupling, rings are simply, speedily "smoothed" into grooves in the Transite sleeve. This spots them easily and accurately in exact position, ready for assembly.

Transite Pressure Pipe with the Ring-Tite Coupling is so quickly and surely assembled that the speed of laying is often limited only to the speed of opening the trench. Note in photograph how installation follows digger closely.

The Ring-Tite method saves time and money by joining Transite Pressure Pipe directly to fittings, valves and hydrants embodying the Ring-Tite design . . . no special tools needed, no poured joints.

Transite Pressure pipe and Ring-Tite Couplings are listed by Underwriters' Laboratories, Inc. and both Transite Pressure Pipe and the coupling sleeve are made to meet standard AWWA specifications.

KEASBEY & MATTISON COMPANY

Ambler, Pennsylvania

JOB AFTER JOB in every part of the country PROVES K&M ASBESTOS-CEMENT PRESSURE PIPE is the economical water pipe

Sabine Pass, Texas, Jefferson County Fresh Water District #1. K&M Pressure Pipe replaces more than 10 miles of metallic pipe corroded through by extreme saline soil conditions. K&M Pipe is non-corroding.

Tacoma, Washington. The Lakewood Water District installed 13 miles of long-lasting K&M Pressure Pipe for new water-system spur. K&M Pressure Pipe is strong . . . effectively resists vibration.

Stanhope, New Jersey. Installation of K&M Pressure Pipe for Brookwood Estates. More and more new water systems use K&M Pipe . . . it's non-tuberculating, has long life.

South Hadley Falls, Massachusetts. This illustration shows K&M Asbestos-Cement Pressure Pipe being laid in the hard, rock-filled soil of New England.

Yardley, Pennsylvania, installation for the Yardley Water & Power Company. The use of the new "Fluid-Tite" Couplings permitted installation under adverse ground conditions.

Lake Almanor, California, uses K&M Pressure Pipe for new housing development water system. In this rough country great savings are made on installation with K&M Pipe. It's light in weight, needs no heavy machinery or skilled labor for installation.

K&M PRESSURE PIPE

is made of strong, durable, lightweight asbestos-cement. Therefore, it is non-tuberculating, non-corroding, non-electrolytic . . . and its smooth bore stays smooth. By specifying K&M Asbestos-Cement Pressure Pipe you save money at every stage—transporting, handling, installing, maintaining.

Meets all specifications • K&M Asbestos-Cement Pressure Pipe and "Fluid-Tite" Couplings are approved by Underwriters' Laboratories, Inc., and K&M Pressure Pipe conforms with A.W.W.A. Specification C 400-53T, A.S.T.M. Specification C 296-55, and U.S. Federal Specification SS-P351-a.

Complete information available on request.

NO CUMBERSOME COUPLING PULLER NEEDED with K&M Pipe and "Fluid-Tite" Couplings. For larger sizes, only a lightweight puller is necessary.

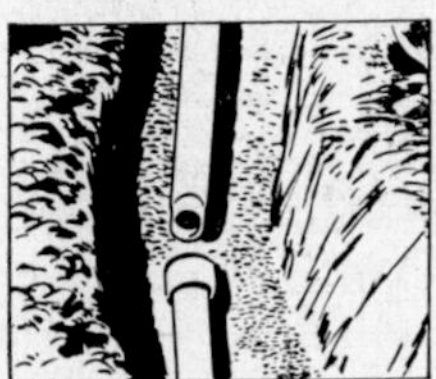

5° CURVE PERMITTED AT EACH JOINT with K&M "Fluid-Tite" Couplings. Greater freedom in laying lines, high resistance to vibration.

HERE'S THE EXCLUSIVE, K&M "FLUID-TITE"® COUPLING* THAT MAKES INSTALLATION EASY EVEN WITH UNSKILLED LABOR

One . . . lubricate rubber rings.

Two . . . insert pipe. That's all!

A permanent, watertight seal—quickly, automatically.

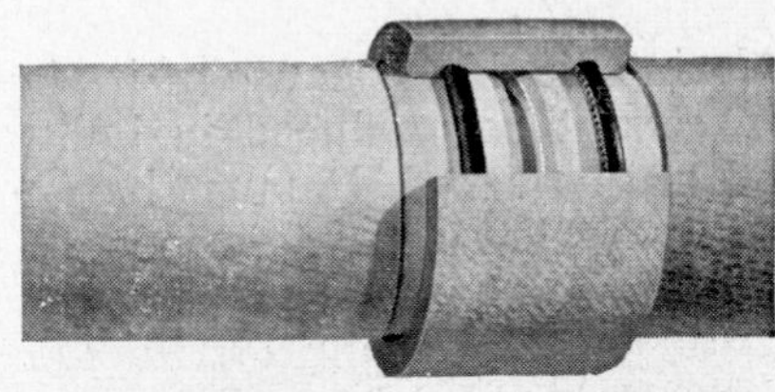

A

B

THE HOLES IN THE RINGS ARE THE SECRET.

A Rubber rings are easily compressed, tapered edges ease pipe insertion.

B Water pressure expands rings . . . the higher the pressure, the tighter the seal.

*PATENT APPLIED FOR

OLIN MATHIESON CHEMICAL CORPORATION
INDUSTRIAL CHEMICALS DIVISION

Baltimore 3, Md.

BRANCH OFFICES

Atlanta 2, Georgia • Buffalo 3, N. Y. • Charlotte 2, N. C. • Chicago 11, Ill. • Cincinnati 2, Ohio
Houston 2, Tex. • Montreal, Can. • New Orleans 12, La. • New York 22, N. Y. • Pasadena 8, Calif.
Philadelphia 7, Pa. • Providence 3, R. I. • St. Louis 2, Mo.

CHLORINE DIOXIDE IN TREATMENT OF POTABLE WATER

FOR MANY YEARS America has enjoyed the safest water in the world, thanks to the combined efforts of health authorities, water works officials and manufacturers of treating chemicals and equipment. Yet certain objectionable tastes and odors have persistently defied elimination by nearly all known purification methods.

Now, however, amazing results in the removal of objectionable tastes and odors are produced by the use of chlorine dioxide, ClO_2. This powerful new reagent, possessing 2½ times the oxidizing capacity of chlorine, is formed by the chemical reaction of chlorine and Mathieson Sodium Chlorite. The technique of applying chlorine dioxide, now in successful use in scores of communities in the United States and Canada, was developed by the Olin Mathieson technical staff.

Chlorine dioxide, because of its instability, cannot be produced in bulk and stored until wanted. It must be generated in very low concentrations at the point of use, and consumed immediately. This was not feasible until sodium chlorite, $NaClO_2$, was made available by Olin Mathieson some years ago. Sodium chlorite is very soluble in water, and stable both in the dry state and in solution. It is intermediate in properties between hypochlorite and chlorate, and the pure material contains 157 per cent available chlorine. The commercial product is flaked, very soluble in water, and contains approximately 79% sodium chlorite.

For water treatment, the most practical method for generating chlorine dioxide consists in feeding a chlorine solution from a standard gas chlorinator and a sodium chlorite solution into a chlorine dioxide generator. The two solutions then pass through this mixing chamber to complete the reaction. The chlorine dioxide solution thus formed is usually introduced into the water after filtration. Normal procedure combines pre-treatment with chlorine for disinfection and post-treatment with chlorine dioxide to destroy taste and odor. For plants treating a relatively small gallonage of water, chlorine dioxide may also be generated by the inter-reaction of solutions of sodium chlorite, hypochlorite and an acid.

Generating Chlorine Dioxide Solution
In this large installation, chlorine solution from the chlorinators and chlorite solution pumped from tank at left, are fed into chlorine dioxide generators on rear wall at upper left and upper right.

Water works officials in communities troubled with taste and odor problems are invited to investigate the new Mathieson Chlorine Dioxide technique.

HTH — A HIGH TEST CALCIUM HYPOCHLORITE

During the last score of years, the dry chlorine carrier has become an increasingly important factor in many phases of water purification practice. The reason for this trend is not difficult to find —with the development of HTH there became available for the first time a stable, readily soluble, high test chlorine carrier in dry form. While liquid chlorine will no doubt continue to be the chief source of supply for large scale chlorinating operations, HTH solves many a treating problem where difficulties of transportation, handling, and application make liquid chlorine either impractical or uneconomic. Simple equipment now available for proportioning feed of hypochlorite solutions prepared from HTH has widened the range of usefulness for this product where continuous chlorination of water supplies is required.

For smaller communities, and wherever low first cost is an important factor, the possibilities of safeguarding water supplies with HTH in this way should be given careful consideration. Moreover, at both large and small water works, HTH completely satisfies the requirements for a reliable emergency or stand-by source of chlorine.

HTH is a true calcium hypochlorite in which the active element exists as Ca $(OCl)_2$. With an available chlorine concentration of at least 70%, it has excellent stability and maintains its concentration even after months of storage at summer temperatures. The active ingredient in HTH goes into solution rapidly and completely.

The cans of HTH Granular and HTH Tablets, packed in cases, are particularly convenient for hypochlorination of pipe lines, isolated water supplies and at locations where transportation of the chlorine product is a troublesome problem. For continuous or emergency hypochlorination of water supplies, the 100-lb. lithographed drum is an economical package.

Note: Read about HTH Tablets and HTH Tablet Hypochlorinator on page 1039.

The handbook, "Hypochlorination of Water", contains a complete discussion of water treatment problems commonly encountered and suggests modern methods for their solution. Among the subjects discussed are: Safeguarding smaller water supplies; Combating algae and slime growths; Conditioning filters, sterilizing filter sand; Disinfecting new reservoirs, basins, tanks; Sterilizing water mains following construction and repair; Feeding hypochlorite — selection of proper equipment; Insuring safety in emergencies. Reference tables summarize ordinary and emergency conditions, how to do it with an tell you what to do and eye to economy as well as results. A copy will gladly be sent you upon request.

HTH Granular and HTH Tablets are both available in lithographed drums containing 100 lbs. net.

SULPHATE OF ALUMINA
ACTIVATED ALUM BRAND
see page 1039

PALMER FILTER EQUIPMENT CO.

P.O. Box 1696 • Ph: 4-3901 • Erie, Pa.

Why Have Dirty Filters That Look Like The One Shown Below?

Install Palmer Filter Bed Agitators And Have Clean Filters At All Times Like This.

Only a clean filter can operate at peak efficiency—operators can now compensate for turbidity changes—algae growth and seasonal variations by the controlled operation of agitators.

PALMER FILTER EQUIPMENT COMPANY

P.O. Box 1696 • Ph: 4-3901 • Erie, Pa.

Palmer Filter Bed Agitators

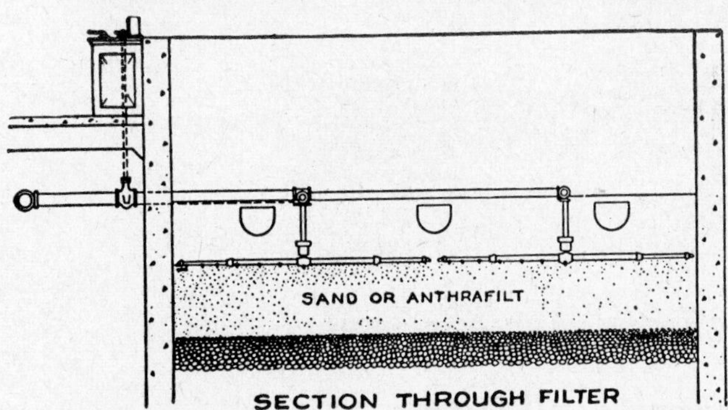

SECTION THROUGH FILTER

PALMER FILTER BED AGITATOR

The Palmer Filter Bed Agitator is a simple and inexpensive device that is being incorporated in new and existing plants to increase the filtration capacity and eliminate mud balls.

ENGINEERING FACTS

CONSTRUCTION—The Palmer Filter Bed Agitator is constructed of brass and bronze throughout. Nozzles can be removed easily from the agitator arm.

SIZES—Palmer Agitators are adaptable to any size or type of filter. Available in lengths up to 18′.

WATER REQUIRED—The Palmer Agitator operates with low volume at high velocity. Usually, a delivery of ½ g.p.m. per square foot of filter bed is ample.

PRESSURE REQUIRED—40 lbs. and upwards.

R.P.M.—The speed of the Agitator varies from seven to eighteen r.p.m.

SIMPLICITY—Simple to install, easily observed and inspected.

THE Palmer Agitator consists of a horizontal bronze arm suspended just above the surface of the Anthrafilt or sand. The agitator arm contains jet nozzles through which water is forced at extremely high velocity. The jets are pointed downward to penetrate the sand before the wash water is turned on. This penetration breaks up the surface of the sand bed while the agitator revolves slowly, propelled by the velocity of the water through the jets. Thus, the media is in a fluid condition and free from encrusted deposits when the wash water is turned on. When the wash water reaches the level of the agitator arm, the tremendous velocity of the jets causes violent turbulence while the upper strata of the sand or Anthrafilt is expanded. The Palmer Agitator remains in action until shortly before stopping the filter wash.

TECHNICAL ADVANTAGES

- 1—Requires an average of 40% less wash water
- 2—Completely eliminates mud balls
- 3—Eliminates cracking or shrinking of the beds
- 4—Produces "new" filter media after short period of normal operation
- 5—Turns out purer, better tasting water
- 6—Low installation cost
- 7—Low operating cost
- 8—More water through the filters
- 9—Less "time out" washing filters

The Palmer Filter Bed Agitator is covered by U. S. Patents 2309166 and 2309917.

HERE ARE JUST A FEW WHO ORIGINALLY TRIED AGITATORS THEN COMPLETED THEIR PLANTS & BUY FOR NEW ADDITIONS.

DETROIT, MICH.	WASHINGTON, D. C.
BALTIMORE, OHIO	AEC, HANFORD, WASH.
PHILADELPHIA, PA.	KANSAS CITY, KAN.
CLEVELAND, OHIO	SPARTANBURG, S. CAR.
DENVER, COLO.	DALLAS, TEXAS
MIAMI, FLA.	OKLAHOMA CITY, OKLA.
BUFFALO, N. Y.	AKRON, OHIO

REPEAT SALES ARE THE BEST PROOF OF PERFORMANCE.

ANTHRACITE EQUIPMENT CORP.

241 Old River Rd., Wilkes Barre, Pa.

ANTHRAFILT

the modern, all-purpose filtering medium that creates greater efficiency for filters of all types.

ANTHRAFILT HAS THESE CHARACTERISTICS:

Made from a selected Pennsylvania anthracite of minimum ash, carefully cleaned, screened and sized, Anthrafilt is used as a mechanical aggregate in place of sand and gravel. Anthrafilt increases capacity and lowers maintenance costs in existing filtration plants. In new filtration plants, Anthrafilt makes possible lower investment and building costs as well. The entire filter bed can be made up of Anthrafilt in various sizes, or Anthrafilt may be used as the top layer over the usual bed of gravel. It has these qualities:

IRREGULAR SHAPE—The varied angular surfaces of the Anthrafilt particles result in a greater entrapping area and in greater porosity. This makes possible a more rapid rate of filtration without any loss in effectiveness. In back washing, the angular grains are more thoroughly agitated so that Anthrafilt beds are cleaned more quickly and easily.

VARYING DENSITY—The variable densities of Anthrafilt particles result in less classification after back washing. Among other things, this allows the entire depth of the filter bed to be active in operation.

LIGHT WEIGHT—Weights run about 53 pounds per cubic foot for Anthrafilt compared with 100 pounds for sand. This greater bulk means less tonnage is needed per filter bed . . . saves on freight and handling. The light weight of the particles also makes for easier expansion and cleaning.

HIGHLY STABLE—Anthrafilt is insoluble in acids or alkalis—produces silica-free water in hot-process water softening. It also successfully removes lime, iron and manganese salts without acquiring a permanent coating if filters are properly managed.

8 reasons why

ANTHRAFILT gives longer runs, higher rates, and lower wash-water consumption in new or old installations:

1. *High Filtration Rate*—Rates up to 200 mgad are obtainable with Anthrafilt without sacrifice of effluent quality. The accepted average rate with sand is 125 mgad.

2. *Longer Filter Runs*—The large, irregular Anthrafilt particles allow less clogging with algae or other fibrous substances and at the same time the angular surfaces provide greater entrapping areas for removal of turbidity and bacteria.

3. *Low Wash-Water Costs*—The less frequent washing that results from longer filter runs, plus the low degree of packing after back washing cut the usual wash-water requirements at least in half.

4. *No Cementing with Lime, Manganese or Iron*—Lime will coat on Anthrafilt, but this coating readily flakes off if filters are properly operated. Manganese and iron salts precipitated on Anthrafilt by the lime treatment are easily removed by back washing.

5. *High Degree of Expansion*—50% expansion is obtained with half the back wash velocity required for sand.

6. *Coarse Sizes Can Be Used*—Irregular shape and natural filtration characteristics permit the use of much larger sizes with equal results.

7. *Gravel Beds Stay Flat*—No ridging or mounding and less cracking and pulling away from sidewalls during operation.

8. *Low First Cost*—Lighter weight per unit of volume balances the price differential between Anthrafilt and sand, and saves on freight and handling charges. Attrition losses amount to less than 0.25% per year.

ANTHRAFILT

Trade Mark Reg. U. S. Pat. Off.

For further information, test samples, and quotations write to:

PALMER FILTER EQUIPMENT CO.
820 East 8th St., Erie, Pa.

Representing

ANTHRACITE EQUIPMENT CORPORATION
241 Old River Rd., Wilkes-Barre, Pa.

PERMUTIT®

330 West 42nd Street, New York 36, N. Y. • Tel: LOngacre 3-4930

WATER CONDITIONING • Equipment • Resins • Experience

SALES OFFICES

Boston 16, Mass., 404 Statler Bldg.
Charlotte 3, N. C., 831 E. Morehead St.
Chattanooga 2, Tenn., 517 Hamilton National Bank Building
Chicago 5, Ill., 407 S. Dearborn St.
Cincinnati 2, Ohio, 617 Vine St.
Cleveland 15, Ohio, 1836 Euclid Ave.
Decatur, Ill., 250 North Water St.
Detroit 1, Mich., 2111 Woodward Ave.
Houston 4, Texas, 4101 San Jacinto
Jacksonville 4, Fla., 115 Park St.
Kansas City 8, Mo., 2201 Grand Ave.
Los Angeles, Calif., 302-B S. Brand Blvd., Glendale 4, Cal.
Minneapolis 3, Minn., 1111 Nicollet
Philadelphia 3, Pa., 34 S. 17th St.
Pittsburgh 22, Pa., 708 Empire Bldg.
Ridgewood, N. J., 10 Wilsey Sq.
Rochester 18, N. Y., 375 Glen Ellyn Way
St. Louis 8, Mo., 3903 Olive St.
San Francisco 5, Cal., 55 New Montgomery St.
Washington 4, D. C., 918 F. St., N. W.
Canada: Toronto 1, Ont., Permutit Company of Canada, Ltd., 207 Queen's Quay

Zeolite water softeners completely remove hardness to prevent scale. **Dealkalizing:** Using both sodium and hydrogen regenerants gives water of any desired alkalinity.

Spiractor® softens and reduces alkalinity. Recommended for clear, hard water. Compact . . . takes only 8 minutes! There is no sludge.

Vertical Precipitator clarifies and softens water, reduces color, taste, odor, silica, iron, manganese. Removes suspended solids from large volumes of water at low cost.

Horizontal Precipitator: Same action as vertical Precipitator. Can be built into old settling basins at low cost—doubling capacity.

Chemical feeders feed coagulants and chemicals to Precipitators, detention tanks, etc. Wet or dry types, pressure or gravity, constant or proportionating.

Gravity filters remove fine traces of suspended solids: *Monocrete®* underdrains speed construction, cut costs. Also operating tables, rate controllers, gauges.

Pressure filters save on pumping, deliver effluent under pressure. Sand or Anthrafilt media for regular requirements. Neutralite filters control pH. *Carbo-Dur®* removes taste, odor.

Control cubicles centralize operation of water-conditioning systems. Provide semi-automatic or full automatic systems that backwash, regenerate, rinse and return units to service.

How Permutit solves your problem

Here's how Permutit works with you and your consultants to solve your problem:

Complete analysis and study of the problem by Permutit's experts in water conditioning provide data on several methods of treatment. Best process is selected on basis of initial vs. operating costs, balanced against quality of effluent desired.

Complete proposal by Permutit engineers covers type, size, and capacity of equipment along with price and performance guarantees.

Manufacturing—After the proposal is accepted, Permutit designs the entire project, schedules assembly and shipping. Critical parts, ion exchange resins, control panels are all made in Permutit Plants. (No other U. S. firm makes all these components.)

Test runs—Where required, Permutit checks the installation, supervises start-up and initial operation, trains permanent operating personnel.

For further information look up the Permutit office in your city or write to The Permutit Company, Dept. MI-57, 330 West 42nd St., New York 36, N. Y.

PERMUTIT®
WATER CONDITIONING
Equipment • Resins • Experience

PITTSBURGH-DES MOINES STEEL COMPANY

Plants at PITTSBURGH, DES MOINES, SANTA CLARA, FRESNO, and CADIZ, SPAIN

Sales Offices at:

PITTSBURGH (25), ... 3460 Neville Island
NEWARK (2), ... 245 Industrial Office Bldg.
CHICAGO (3), . 1264 First National Bank Bldg.
EL MONTE, CAL. . . . . P. O. Box 2068
DES MOINES (8), ... 961 Tuttle Street
DALLAS (1), ... 1265 Praetorian Bldg.
SEATTLE, ... 568 Lane Street
SANTA CLARA, CAL., ... 667 Alviso Road
MADRID, SPAIN, ... Diego DeLeon, 60

Elevated steel tanks
Standpipes
Steel reservoirs
Surge tanks

Pipe lines
Penstocks
Oil tanks
Pressure gasholders

Highway bridges
Airplane hangars
Steel bins
Steel grandstands

Water treating plants
General waterworks construction
Radio towers

CAPACITIES AND SIZES OF STANDARD ELEVATED STEEL TANKS

In these compact but complete tables, data are furnished on the various types of elevated steel tanks, and on steel reservoirs. For full information as to the application of these tanks, for designs, for specifications, or for estimates, write—without obligation to our nearest office.

Double Ellipsoidal

TABLE I—DOUBLE ELLIPSOIDAL TANKS

Capacity U.S. Gallons	Tank Dimensions					Balcony Width	Number of Columns	Radial Bevel of Columns	Tower Height H
	D	V	B	C	T				
25,000	18'0"	14'4⅜"	4'9"	6'0¼"	3'7⅛"	24"	4	1:12	see note**
30,000	18'0"	17'0"	4'9"	8'7¾"	3'7¼"	"	"	"	
40,000	20'0"	18'6⅝"	5'2⅜"	9'4¼"	4'0"	"	"	"	"
50,000	22'0"	19'2½"	5'11"	8'10¾"	4'4¾"	"	"	"	"
50,000	24'0"	16'8⅛"	6'4⅛"	5'6⅜"	4'9⅝"	"	"	"	"
60,000	24'0"	19'7½"	6'4⅛"	8'5¾"	4'9⅝"	"	"	"	"
75,000	26'0"	21'2⅛"	6'10½"	9'1¼"	5'2⅜"	"	"	"	"
100,000	28'0"	23'8¾"	8'7"	9'6½"	5'7¼"	"	"	"	"
100,000	30'0"	21'0⅞"	8'11"	6'1⅞"	6'0"	"	"	"	"
150,000	32'0"	27'4"	9'4¼"	11'7"	6'4¾"	"	"	"	"
150,000	34'0"	24'9¾"	9'10½"	8'1⅝"	6'9⅝"	"	"	"	"
200,000	36'0"	29'4½"	10'6⅛"	11'8"	7'2⅜"	"	"	"	"
250,000	38'0"	33'0"	11'3⅜"	14'3¾"	7'4⅞"	30"	6	1:20	"
250,000	40'0"	30'10½"	11'10½"	8'6"	10'6"	"	"	"	"
300,000	44'0"	30'9"	13'0½"	7'11⅞"	9'8⅝"	"	"	"	"
400,000	48'0"	34'3⅜"	14'7"	11'0"	8'8⅜"	"	"	"	"
500,000	50'0"	39'0⅞"	15'6⅝"	15'5⅝"	8'0⅝"	"	8	"	"
500,000	55'0"	29'11"	12'0"	10'11"	7'0"	"	"	Vertical*	"
600,000	50'0"	45'10½"	15'6⅝"	22'3¼"	8'0⅝"	"	"	1:20	"
750,000	60'0"	41'7⅝"	18'0"	11'10⅝"	11'9"	"	"	Vertical*	"
750,000	65'0"	37'0⅜"	20'1⅞"	6'5"	10'5½"	"	"	"	"
1,000,000	65'0"	47'1¼"	20'1⅞"	16'5⅞"	10'5½"	"	10	"	"
1,000,000	70'0"	42'6½"	23'0"	10'9½"	8'9"	"	"	"	"
1,000,000	75'0"	35'0"	20'6"	8'o"	6'0"	"	"	"	"
1,250,000	70'0"	51'2¾"	23'0"	19'5¾"	8'9"	"	12	"	"
1,500,000	70'0"	59'10⅞"	23'0"	28'1⅞"	8'9"	"	"	"	"

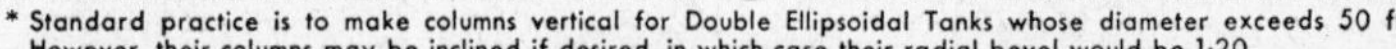

* Standard practice is to make columns vertical for Double Ellipsoidal Tanks whose diameter exceeds 50 ft. However, their columns may be inclined if desired, in which case their radial bevel would be 1:20.
** Standard tower heights (H) are as follows: — Up to 50 ft. in even 2 ft. intervals, from 50 ft. to 100 ft. in even 5 ft. intervals, and over 100 ft. in even 10 ft. intervals.
Most common standard tower heights are 75 ft. and 100 ft.

TABLE II—HEMISPHERICAL BOTTOM TANKS

Capacity in U.S. Gallons	Tank Dimensions				No.** of Columns	Balcony Width	TOWER HEIGHT H
	D	V	B	C*			
25,000	15'0"	19'10½"	5'4"	14' 6½"	4	18"	AS REQUIRED
30,000	15'0"	23' 8¼"	5'4"	18' 4¼"	4	18"	
40,000	17'0"	24'11¼"	6'8"	18' 3¼"	4	24"	
50,000	19'0"	25' 6"	8'0"	17' 6"	4	24"	
60,000	19'0"	30' 3⅛"	8'0"	22' 3⅛"	4	24"	
75,000	21'0"	30' 6¼"	8'0"	22' 6¼"	4	24"	
100,000	24'0"	30'11¾"	8'6"	22' 5¾"	4	24"	

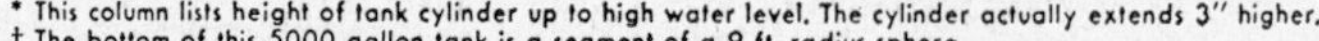

* This column lists height of tank cylinder up to high water level. The cylinder actually extends 3" higher.
† The bottom of this 5000 gallon tank is a segment of a 9 ft. radius sphere.
** Radial bevel of columns of 4 column towers is 1-11/16:12; of 6 column towers 1:10.

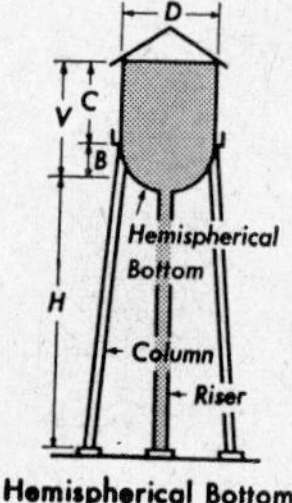

Hemispherical Bottom

TABLE III—STEEL RESERVOIRS

Capacity in U. S. Gallons	Diameter	Height
50,000	20′	21′ 6″
60,000	22′	21′ 6″
75,000	24′	22′ 6″
100,000	26′	25′ 6″
150,000	30′	28′ 9″
200,000	34′	29′ 9″
250,000	38′	29′ 9″
300,000	42′	29′ 3″
400,000	46′	32′ 6″
500,000	50′	34′ 6″
750,000	60′	35′ 9″
1,000,000	70′	35′ 0″
1,500,000	80′	40′ 3″
2,000,000	95′	38′ 3″
2,500,000	110′	35′ 6″
3,000,000	120′	35′ 9″
4,000,000	130′	40′ 9″

TABLE IV—RADIAL CONE BOTTOM TANKS

CAPACITY U.S. GALLONS	TANK DIMENSIONS D	V	NUMBER OF COLUMNS	TOWER HEIGHT H
300,000	53′ 0″	20′ 0″	8	As Required
500,000	60′ 0″	25′ 0″	"	" "
750,000	73′ 0″	25′ 0″	"	" "
750,000	67′ 0″	30′ 0″	"	" "
1,000,000	85′ 0″	25′ 0″	10	" "
1,000,000	77′ 0″	30′ 0″	"	" "
1,000,000	71′ 0″	35′ 0″	"	" "
1,250,000	95′ 0″	25′ 0″	12	" "
1,250,000	87′ 0″	30′ 0″	"	" "
1,250,000	80′ 0″	35′ 0″	"	" "
1,250,000	74′ 0″	40′ 0″	"	" "
1,500,000	103′ 6″	25′ 0″	"	" "
1,500,000	95′ 0″	30′ 0″	"	" "
1,500,000	88′ 0″	35′ 0″	"	" "
1,500,000	81′ 6″	40′ 0″	"	" "
2,000,000	108′ 6″	30′ 0″	16	" "
2,000,000	101′ 0″	35′ 0″	"	" "
2,000,000	94′ 0″	40′ 0″	"	" "
2,500,000	121′ 6″	30′ 0″	"	" "
2,500,000	112′ 0″	35′ 0″	"	" "
2,500,000	105′ 0″	40′ 0″	"	" "
3,000,000	123′ 6″	35′ 0″	20	" "

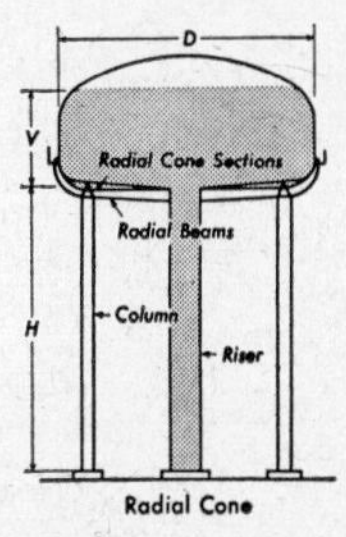

SIMPLEX VALVE & METER COMPANY

Reliable equipment for accurate measurement and control

Dept. MI-56, 7 E. Orange St., Lancaster, Pa.

VENTURI TUBES

WRITE FOR CATALOG 004

For accurate measurement of hot or cold water, gases, sewage, sludge or trade wastes under wide ranges of pressures. Flanged, bell, or spigot ends in any size or design . . . cast-iron, cast steel or steel plate, bronze, or combinations.

ELLIPTICAL VENTURI TUBES

WRITE FOR BROCHURE

Developed specifically for accurate measurement of low velocity sewage, sludge or heavily laden trade wastes—flowing under low pressure conditions. Flat top prevents air binding! Flat invert is self-scouring!

PARABOLIC FLUMES

WRITE FOR BULLETIN 800

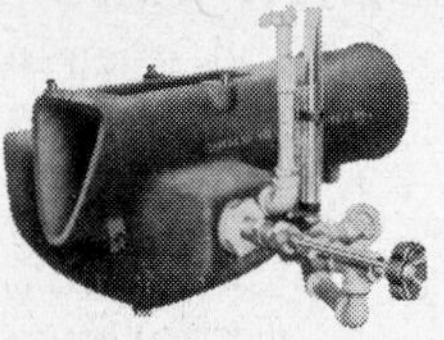

Specially designed to measure sewage, sludge, and trade wastes under low heads or open flow. Can be used for indicating, or with meter to record and totalize. Simple to install. Full 20 to 1 flow range. Flanged, bell or spigot inlet in 6″ to 36″ standard pipe sizes.

PITOT EQUIPMENT

WRITE FOR BULLETIN 1300

Leaks and line breaks are quickly located with Simplex pitot rods, manometers and recorders. Light-weight, compact design makes them truly portable. Invaluable for overall survey of your distribution system's efficiency.

FILTER GAUGES

WRITE FOR BULLETIN 1000

Indicate and/or record essential data on rate of flow, loss of head, sand expansion, water level, etc. Attractive units with easy to read dials. Floor stand mounting—or Operating Tables for convenient centralized control.

CONTROLLED CLOSING VALVE

WRITE FOR BROCHURE

Prevents surge and water hammer damage when filling larger size pipe lines. Controls speed of line closure, vents air and, if necessary, discharges water to prevent damage. Admits air to protect against pipe collapse from line breaks.

SIMPLEX VALVE & METER COMPANY

SIMPLEX FLOW METERS

TYPE MO METERS

Most accurate inferential type instrument for water, sewage, sludge, industrial liquors. Indicates, records, totalizes. Measures within ±2% over ranges up to 20 to 1. Easy-to-read, evenly-spaced rectangular chart. Wall, floor stand, or panel mountings.

WRITE FOR BULLETIN 500

REMOTE TRANSMISSION

PNEUMATIC — New Simplex Laminair® is fast and accurate. Permits centralizing instruments in main control panel away from primary devices.

ELECTRIC — New Simplex Orthoflow® transmits data over in-plant circuits and leased telephone channels. Accuracy within ±2% for ranges up to 20 to 1.

WRITE FOR BROCHURE

TYPE H METERS

Mercury-float type indicating, recording and totalizing unit. Gives ±2% accuracy at any point for flow ranges up to 13 to 1. Evenly spaced scales make accurate readings easy. Wall, panel, or floor stand mounting.

WRITE FOR BULLETIN 402

FLOW RATE CONTROLLERS

SLUDGE CONTROLLERS—Accurately control flow of sewage, sludge, trade wastes. Most accurate primary device, a Simplex Venturi Tube, has a special throat section of flexible rubber—measures as it controls! Motor-driven clamp adjusts throat . . . keeps flow at control point. Viscous flows contact no moving parts.

WRITE FOR BROCHURE

TYPE S FLOW CONTROLLERS

Keep flow constant despite changes in head of filter effluent or wash water. Control within ±3% over 5 to 1 range. Exclusive balanced guillotine valves quickly respond to slightest change. Standard sizes from 3″ to 24″.

WRITE FOR CATALOG 004

SIMPLEX AIR RELEASE & INLET VALVES

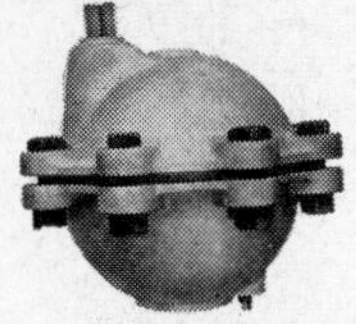

AIR RELEASE VALVES

Vent air accumulations to eliminate binding at high points, increase pumping efficiency. Simple, rugged 1″ and 2″ sizes for up to 250 psi. Special valves available for up to 800 psi.

WRITE FOR BULLETIN 1204

AIR INLET VALVES

Prevent collapse of thin-walled pipes from sudden pressure drops in gravity lines. Simple, reliable float control quickly admits air to break vacuum. Available in 4″ to 10″ sizes.

WRITE FOR BULLETIN 1202

COMBINATION INLET-RELEASE VALVE

One compact unit with a 2″ connection does work of two separate valves! High discharge and inlet capacities. Invaluable for venting large quantities of air when filling systems.

WRITE FOR BULLETIN 1205

RELATED SIMPLEX® EQUIPMENT

- FLOW REGULATORS
- INSERT-TYPE VENTURI TUBES
- LARGE DIAL GAUGES
- SPECIAL VALVES
- TAILOR-MADE MEASUREMENT & CONTROL EQUIPMENT

SIMPLEX VALVE & METER COMPANY

SPARKLER MANUFACTURING CO.

Mundelein, Ill.

MUNICIPAL WATER SUPPLY FILTERS

Mundelein, Ill. ***Service Representatives in principal cities***

Outstanding advantages of the Sparkler SCJ Diatomite water filter for municipal water supply plants.

The highest quality pure crystal clear water is obtained with the Sparkler SCJ Diatomite filter. The high percentage of bacteria and organic material removed with diatomite filtering reduces the required chlorination.

FIRST COST

The Sparkler SCJ Filter can be installed for about ½ the cost of a sand filter of equal capacity.

FLOOR SPACE

Only about 1/6 the floor space is required for a Sparkler SCJ filter as compared with a sand filter of equal capacity. A sand filter occupying a floor area 20 x 20 ft. can be replaced with a Sparkler SCJ filter that requires only 9 x 6 ft. And the housing and piping system on the SCJ filter is much simpler.

ECONOMY IN OPERATION

The Volume of backwash water required to flush out a sand filter is many times that used in the same capacity Sparkler SCJ filter. The Sparkler SCJ filter of 400 sq. ft. capacity can be cleaned with the wash off jet spray and the residue flushed out in 5 minutes with the use of only 1000 gallons of water. A fresh coating of diatomite can be precoated on the filter plates and the unit back in operation within a 15 minute cleaning cycle period.

With a sand filter the incident of mud balls, channeling, and bacteria adhering to the sand, presents a problem that requires special treatment of the sand bed. None of this trouble is occasioned with a diatomite filter, as all residue is disposed of completely in flushing the filter cake off the plates.

The Sparkler SCJ diatomite filter readily removes 80% to 100% of bacteria, depending on the type of bacteria and the grade of diatomite used, in addition to all suspended matter, either colloidal or solid. Thus, the required chlorination after filtration is comparatively low compared with sand filtration.

Diatomite filtration does not affect the pH of the water. Constant quality of the water passing through a Sparkler SCJ filter is maintained regardless of the pH.

In engineering a Sparkler SCJ filter installation, it is advisable to install two or more filter units to insure filtered water during unusual demands, or due to heavy increase in turbidity, as well as maintaining a constant water supply during cleaning cycles.

For intermittent operation, when water requirements are low, a recirculating holding pump is used to maintain the diatomite cake in standard position for resumption of filtering at any time, without the loss of efficiency and quality of filtering.

When required, complete accessory equipment can be included in engineering a municipal water supply system.

AS A PORTABLE FILTER

The SCJ model is readily adaptable to portable application by mounting the desired size of filter with accessory equipment, such as pump, debris catcher, chlorinator, slurry feeder, gasoline or electric motor, all on a movable base. This portable filter unit may be a life-saver in the event of disaster, such as flood, fire, or earthquake. Hundreds of Sparkler portable water filter units using diatomaceous filter aid are used by the U. S. Government in Pacific operations.

SPARKLER MODEL SCJ available in capacities up to 5,000,000 gallons per 24 hour operation.

Architect's and Engineer's Specifications for Sparkler Recirculation Systems

DIATOMITE FILTERS

TANKS

The tanks shall be mild steel Heli-arc welded and the joints ground smooth. They shall be horizontal with dished heads and be tested for pressures 50% in excess of a 60 PSI working pressure. A removable head shall be provided for easy access to filter elements, and a sight glass shall be provided and so placed that a portion of the filter elements can be observed during filtration and cleaning. The tank shall be suitably rubber coated to prevent rust and corrosion and given an exterior coating of high grade paint. The tank shall be provided with a pressure gauge and an air vent at the highest point of the tank.

OPERATION

The filter shall be cleaned by a combination of backwash and jet spray action. The valves supplied shall be the quick opening type, and the filter manufacturer shall supply the necessary pipe, valves and fittings for the filter's operation. No dissimilar metals which might cause electrolitic action shall be used.

FILTER ELEMENTS

Filter elements shall consist of disc-shaped plates mounted in a vertical position on a hollow center shaft. They shall be constructed of perforated stainless steel, covered with orlon cloth. The orlon cloth shall be stitched at the outer edge with orlon thread and a sealing material applied to prevent by-pass. The center shaft shall be plastic, or rubber coated steel.

FEEDER

(a) The diatomite feeder tank shall be Pittchem lined mild steel. It shall have a dish bottom and be provided with a drain. It shall have sufficient capacity to hold the amount of slurry used in 24 hours under normal conditions.

(b) The feeder tank shall be provided with a slow speed agitator under (100 RPM) to keep the filter aid in suspension.

(c) Mounted on the feeder tank shall be a positive displacement piston-type pump with variable feed.

PRECOAT

Use either a funnel mounted on filter inlet elbow or a hydraulic ejector mounted on feeder tank.

SPARKLER SCJ FILTER CAPACITIES

Model	Filter Area Sq. Ft.	Pipe Conn. Inches	Approx. Floor Area (Feet)	Gallons Per Day* 1 GPM/Ft. 2	2 GPM/Ft. 2
Model SCJ-24-9	50	4	5 x 3	72,000	144,000
Model SCJ-24-17	100	4	6½ x 3	144,000	288,000
Model SCJ-33-18	200	6	8½ x 5	288,000	576,000
Model SCJ-40-19	300	8	9 x 6	432,000	864,000
Model SCJ-40-25	400	8	9 x 6	576,000	1,152,000
Model SCJ-64-24	1000	12	9 x 17	1,440,000	2,880,000
Model SCJ-96-21	2000	16	13 x 23	2,880,000	5,760,000

(*) Lower or higher flow rates (GPM/Ft. 2) may be used when advantageous to the problem involved.
Write for plans and prices on your requirements. Our filtration engineer will give personal service to your filtering problems.

YARDLEY PLASTICS COMPANY

142 Parsons Ave., Columbus, Ohio

IN CANADA, DAYMOND CO., LTD., CHATHAM, ONT.

NEW Yardley *ClearStream*

For Municipal Water Systems

Now you can *safely* design a flexible pipe distribution system to meet the pressure conditions in your community. No more doubts—no more experimenting.

ClearStream PressuRated Pipe is built to withstand the working pressures shown for the various types. It is now made for three pressure ratings—75 lb., 100 lb. and 125 lb. in sizes ½ through 2″. For your protection and easy identification, the pressure rating is continuously stamped on every length, in every size.

Yardley ClearStream PressuRated Pipe is top-quality—100% virgin Polyethylene. Guaranteed against rot, rust or electrolytic corrosion. And like all Yardley ClearStream Pipe it handles and installs faster, easier, because it weighs ⅛ as must as steel; requires fewer fittings; cuts installation costs up to 60%; delivers 25% greater volume for the same head loss.

Complete line of necessary plastic fittings available.

Other YARDLEY *ClearStream Pipe*

M-22 — Twin-du-it, 2 pipes in 1 for Jet Pumps
M-21 — Sub-du-it, with built-in suspension cable for submersible pumps
M-2 — The quality flexible pipe for every cold water use

EMSCO SCREEN PIPE COMPANY

Ricks Road, Houston, Texas

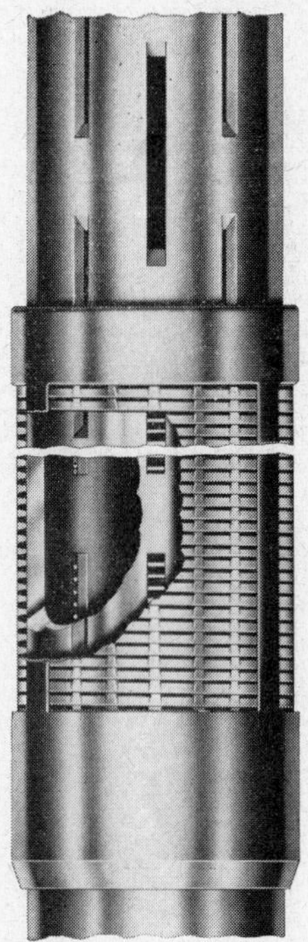

Vertically Slotted
Wire Wrapped Screen

EMSCO SLOTTED...

A SUPERIOR WATER WELL SCREEN furnished in a full range of slot gauges

With Emsco, the manufacture of slotted screen pipe is serious business. Our shop is equipped with machines designed especially for this purpose . . . machines that produce high quality slotted screen pipe, with slots ranging from .010 to .100 or larger if required.

We're proud of our facilities for producing this full range of slotted pipe. We're proud, also, of the record established by Emsco Slotted Pipe in wells all over the world. It retains 80% to 85% of the original collapse strength of the pipe . . . it may be spudded or rotated reasonably without damage . . . may be easily cut and pulled . . . and its V-shaped slots provide maximum drainage with minimum clogging. It's furnished, of course, in all popular sizes of pipe, to length as specified.

Emsco also manufactures "Vertical Slotted" Wire Wrapped Screen, with slotted openings that stay open longer, provide more drainage area per foot and retain 25% more strength than pipe with drilled holes with equal area. Also available: Emsco Drilled Holes with Wire Wrap.

For full information on Emsco "Slotted" and "Wire Wrapped" Screen Pipe, write for a copy of our latest literature and price lists.

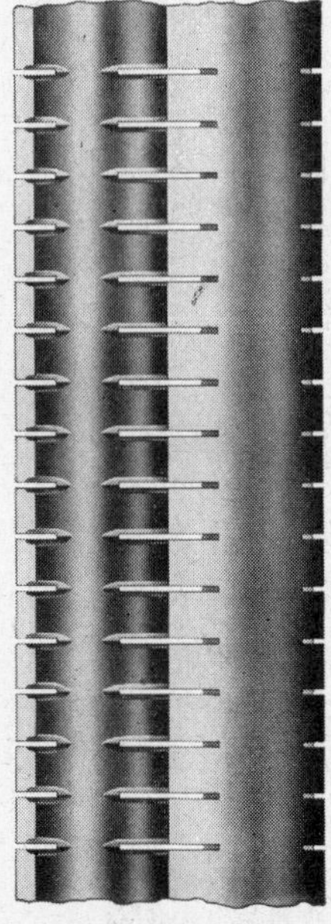

Slotted Screen

EMSCO
SCREEN PIPE COMPANY

RICKS ROAD Phone CApitol 7-6346 HOUSTON, TEXAS
Export Representative:
Val R. Wittich, Inc., 30 Rockefeller Plaza, New York 20, N. Y.

GENERAL CHEMICAL DIVISION

ALLIED CHEMICAL & DYE CORPORATION

40 Rector Street, New York 6, N. Y.

Offices: Albany • Atlanta • Baltimore • Birmingham • Boston • Bridgeport • Buffalo • Charlotte • Chicago • Cleveland Denver • Detroit • Greenville (Miss.) • Houston • Jacksonville • Kalamazoo • Los Angeles • Milwaukee Minneapolis • New York • Philadephia • Pittsburgh • Providence • San Francisco • Seattle • St. Louis • Yakima (Wash.)

In Canada: The Nichols Chemical Company, Limited • Montreal • Toronto • Vancouver

---

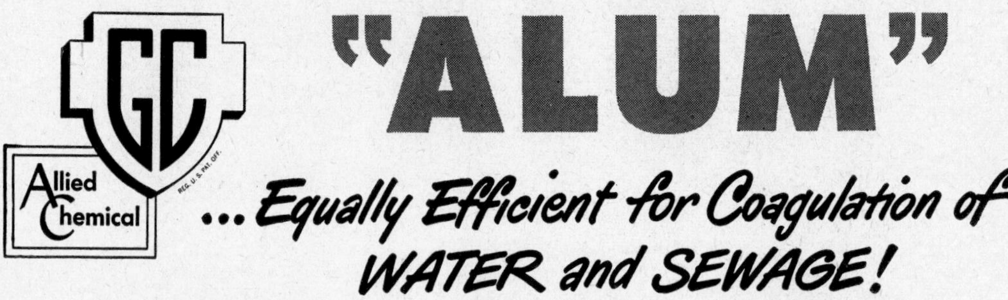

FOR WATER WORKS

1. Produces crystal clear water.
2. Gives better floc formation.
3. Promotes better settling and longer filter runs.
4. Aids in reduction of tastes and odors.
5. Has no chlorine demand.
6. Is a *low cost* coagulant.
7. Superior in tests against other coagulants.
8. High in quality. Its constant uniformity can be depended upon.

FOR SEWAGE PLANTS

1. Clean, easy to handle.
2. Dry feeds well or dissolves readily for solution feeding.
3. Simple application. Requires only low cost feeding apparatus and minimum attention.
4. Clear, colorless effluents are possible.
5. Sludge digests readily.
6. Treated digested sludge dries quickly with minimum of odor.
7. Chlorine consumption is cut due to lower demand of clarified sewage.
8. Economical to use.

Other General Chemical Products for Treatment of Water & Sewage

For FLUORIDATION
SODIUM FLUORIDE
SODIUM SILICOFLUORIDE
HYDROFLUORIC ACID

COAGULATION
Ammonium Alum
Potassium (Potash) Alum
Sodium Silicate

DECHLORINATION
Sodium Sulfite
Sodium Bisulfite, Anhy.
Sodium Thiosulfate

BOILER WATER
Sodium Sulfate, Anhy.
Disodium Phosphate, Anhy.
Trisodium Phosphate
Tetrasodium Pyrophosphate
Sodium Tripolyphosphate
Sodium Silicate
Sulfuric Acid

CORROSION CONTROL
Sodium Silicate

FOR OTHER USES:
Glauber's Salt, Crystal
Aqua Ammonia
Hydrochloric Acid (Muriatic)

THE HAYDENVILLE COMPANY

Haydenville, Mass.

WATER WORKS BRASS GOODS

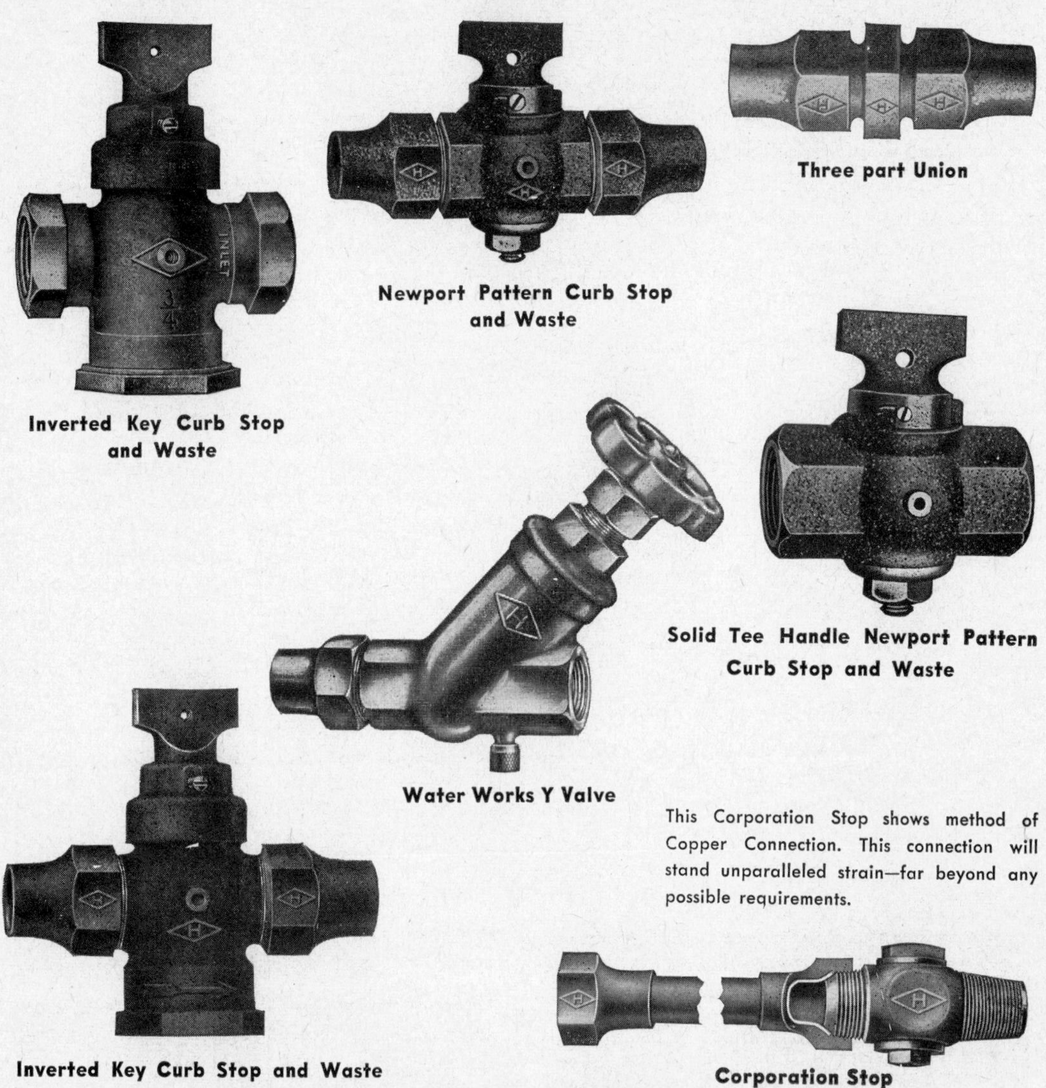

Inverted Key Curb Stop and Waste

Newport Pattern Curb Stop and Waste

Three part Union

Solid Tee Handle Newport Pattern Curb Stop and Waste

Water Works Y Valve

Inverted Key Curb Stop and Waste

This Corporation Stop shows method of Copper Connection. This connection will stand unparalleled strain—far beyond any possible requirements.

Corporation Stop

As a manufacturer of high grade brass goods for 110 years, THE HAYDENVILLE COMPANY welcomes your inquiries and seeks the opportunity to supply your requirements.

WRITE FOR OUR COMPLETE CATALOG

CENTRILINE CORPORATION

A subsidiary of Raymond Concrete Pile Co.

140 CEDAR STREET, NEW YORK 6, N. Y.

Branch Offices in Principal Cities of the United States and Latin America

CEMENT MORTAR LININGS FOR PIPE IN PLACE

For Pipelines 4 Inches to 144 Inches in Diameter

WHAT IS CENTRILINING

A mechanically controlled process for centrifugally cement-mortar lining pipe lines in place.

HOW IT WORKS

For pipe sizes 16 Inches and over in diameter.

After the pipe is thoroughly cleaned, the cement mortar is either pumped or transported by a self driven buggy to the lining machine where it is thrown by centrifugal force at uniformly high velocity against the inside walls of the pipe. The thickness of the lining is determined by the lining machine's rate of speed through the pipe. Mechanical trowels smooth the lining to an even finish.

The Centriline Process conforms in every respect with American Water Works Association Specification C-602-54T.

For pipe sizes 4 inches to 15 inches in diameter the Tate method of lining is used.

After the pipe is thoroughly cleaned, mortar is fed into the open end of the pipe in-place and pressed on to the pipe wall by a tapered cable-drawn mandrel.

WHAT IT DOES

- **Permanently establishes highest hydraulic capacity.**
- **Prevents all leakage.**
- **Permanently stops corrosion and tuberculation.**

• • •

A 12-page Illustrated Booklet on the Centriline Process Will Be Sent Upon Request

BEFORE CENTRILINING

The encrustment of tubercles in this 48″ pipe almost halved the effective flow, before it was Centrilined.

THE CENTRILINE MACHINE

From mobile mixing stations, cement-mortar is fed into the Centriline machine, which throws it to the pipe walls and trowels it to a smooth finish.

AFTER CENTRILINING

Carrying capacity was increased 77% in this 40-year-old pipe—12% better than when it was first installed.

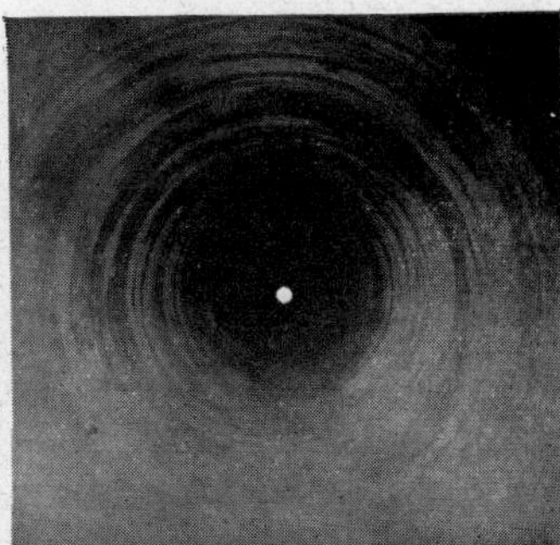

HAYS MANUFACTURING COMPANY

12th and Liberty Streets, Erie, Pennsylvania

HAYS® WATER SERVICE PRODUCTS

CORPORATION STOP
DUO-STOP CORPORATION STOP and SADDLE COMBINED
MAIN DRILLING MACHINE
ROUNDWAY CURB STOP and DRAIN
INVERTED PLUG CURB STOP
EXTENSION SERVICE BOX
MODEL B TAPPING MACHINE
MALE ELBOW
"Y" TYPE TWO BRANCH
MALE ADAPTOR
"Y" TYPE THREE BRANCH
UNION

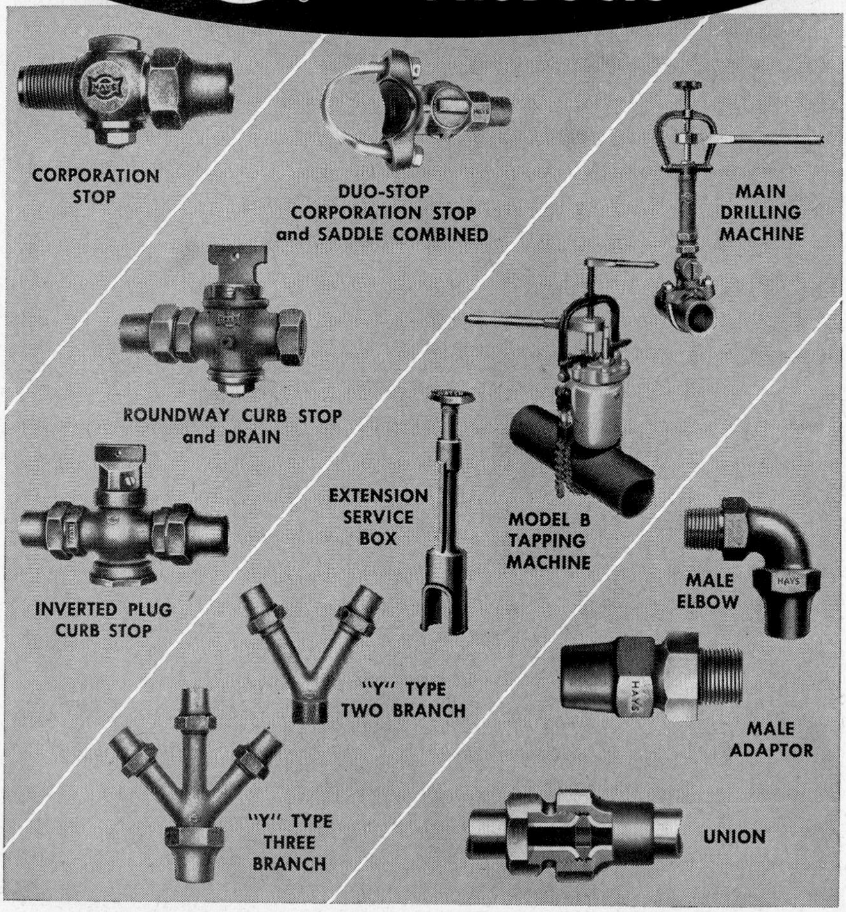

It Pays to Buy Hays . . . The items shown above are only a few of the HAYS complete line of water service products.

Over 80 years of manufacturing experience . . . interchangeable with those of other manufacturers . . . corporation stops can be installed with any standard tapping machine.

Send for HAYS complete catalog.

Join the A. W. W. A. HAYS is one of the eleven Charter Members of the Manufacturers Section of the American Water Works Association.

HAYS®

WATER WORKS PRODUCTS
HAYS MANUFACTURING CO.
ERIE, PA.

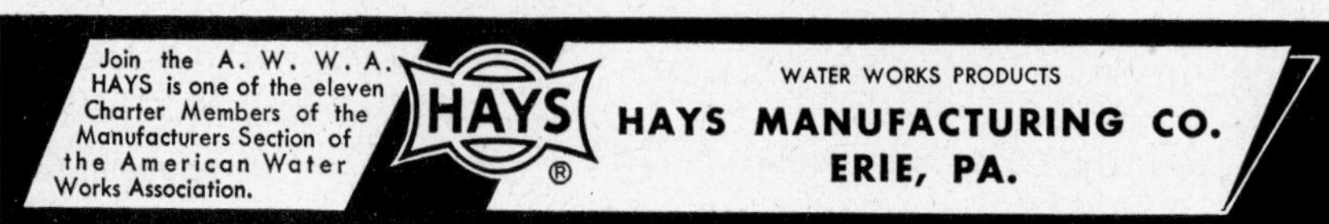

GOLDEN-ANDERSON VALVE SPECIALTY COMPANY

1232 Ridge Avenue • Pittsburgh 33, Pa.

Designers and Manufacturers of VALVES FOR AUTOMATION

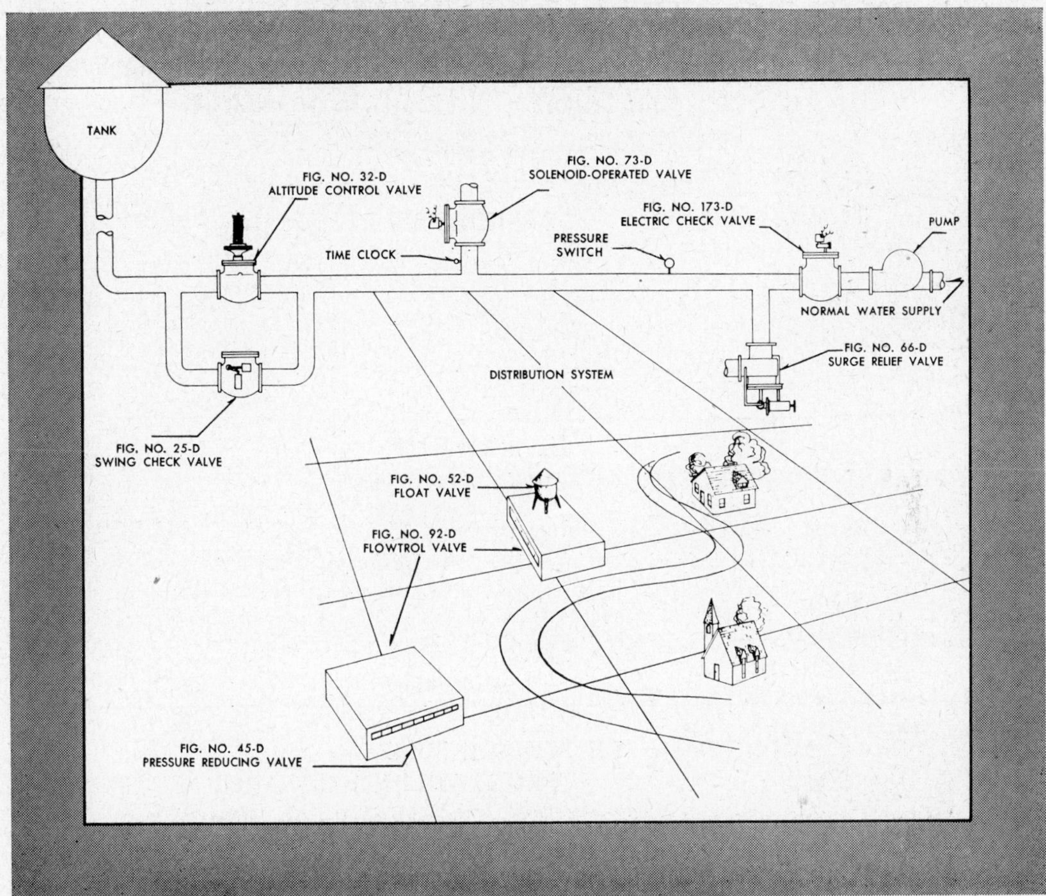

GOLDEN-ANDERSON *Cushioned* VALVES

Give Dependable, Low-Maintenance Service in

MUNICIPAL WATER WORKS SYSTEMS

G-A Electric Double-Cushioned CHECK VALVE —(Bulletin W-10)

G-A SOLENOID-OPERATED VALVE—(Bulletin W-7)

G-A ALTITUDE CONTROL VALVE—(Bulletin W-4)

G-A SWING CHECK VALVE—(Bulletin W-1)

G-A PRESSURE REDUCING VALVE—(Bulletin W-3)

G-A SURGE RELIEF VALVE—(Bulletin W-2)

G-A COLD WATER FLOAT VALVE—(Bulletin (W-5)

G-A FLOWTROL VALVE—(Bulletin W-8-A)

HEALY-RUFF COMPANY

833 Hampden Avenue Tel. Midway 6-2701
St. Paul 14, Minnesota

Condensed Roto-Trol Data

WRITE FOR COMPLETE BULLETINS WHICH CONTAIN FULL DESCRIPTIONS, ENGINEERING DATA, MECHANICAL AND ELECTRICAL SPECIFICATIONS

TYPE A

ROTO-TROLS FOR ELEVATED TANKS, STANDPIPES, RESERVOIRS—BULLETIN R-4

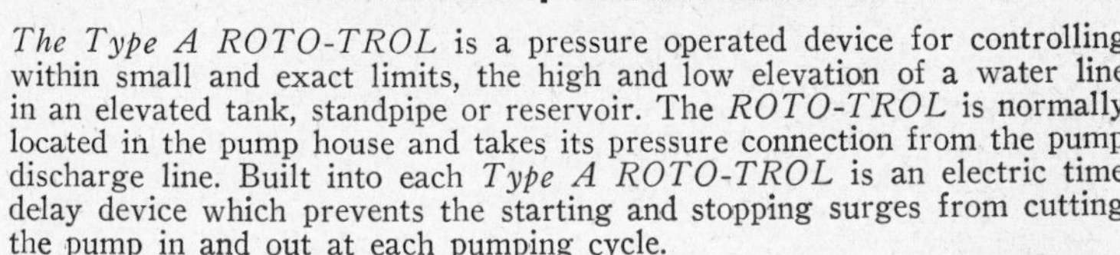

The Type A ROTO-TROL is a pressure operated device for controlling within small and exact limits, the high and low elevation of a water line in an elevated tank, standpipe or reservoir. The *ROTO-TROL* is normally located in the pump house and takes its pressure connection from the pump discharge line. Built into each *Type A ROTO-TROL* is an electric time delay device which prevents the starting and stopping surges from cutting the pump in and out at each pumping cycle.

ROTO-TROLS FOR "CLOSED SYSTEMS" "BOOSTER SYSTEMS"—BULLETIN R-4

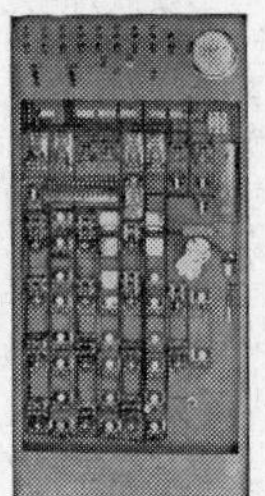

The Type A ROTO-TROL is also furnished in cubicle mounting for the automatic operation of several pumps either through straight sequence or through a programming action of the pumps to maintain given pressures in either a "Closed System" or to act as a Booster Pump Controller.These units come equipped with synchronous motor time delay.

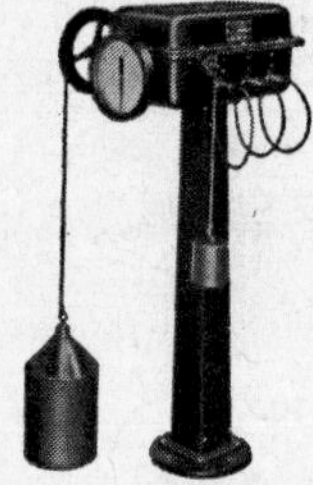

ROTO-TROLS FOR SEWAGE PUMPS—PROGRAMMING CONTROL BULLETIN 940

Bulletin 940 ROTO-TROL is a float control operating two to ten pumps which are pumping into or out of a wet well. Each pump can have several starting and stopping positions, thus the *940* provides programming control. The *940 ROTO-TROL'S* standard equipment consists of cast iron cabinet, mercury switches, pedestal, transfer plugs for manually alternating the sequence of operation of the pumps, depth indicator, stainless steel tape, and ceramic float.

PRESSURE OPERATED SUMP CONTROL BULLETIN RS-3

The RS-3 ROTO-TROL is a pressure operated sewage pump control for starting and stopping one or more pumps discharging out of a wet well. The RS-3 ROTO-TROL has built into it a time delay device which keeps the last pump operating until the end of the compression pipe is clear. This gives assurance that the compression pipe will never become waterlogged.

KOVEN FABRICATORS, INC.

Tel. NEW YORK
WORTH 4-7395

90 East Dickerson St., Dover, N. J.

Tel. DOVER, N. J.
FOXCROFT 6-0400

ADVANTAGES OF KOVEN BUILT RESERVOIRS

FULL RESPONSIBILITY

From the time design drawings are approved until the final inspection is made Koven assumes full responsibility for every phase of fabrication as well as tank erection. Only when the finished tank has been rigidly checked for quality and workmanship is the job considered complete.

EXPERIENCE, FACILITIES, "KNOW-HOW"

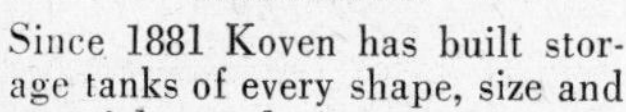

Since 1881 Koven has built storage tanks of every shape, size and design in any commercial metal, in any gauge—standard or special. Tanks are built to rigid Koven, API or AWWA standards.

PROTECTION AGAINST CORROSION

When buying a reservoir it is important to consider installation of some method of preventing corrosion of the water tank interior. The electrolytic (cathodic) method is recommended by the AWWA as being entirely satisfactory when properly installed and maintained. Koven can provide the complete service, when desired, at extra cost.

To prolong the life of your reservoir, we recommend shot-grit blasting or pickling of the plates before painting, followed by shop painting of a prime coat on both sides of the plates. In the field two finish coats are given to both the inside and outside of the completed reservoir. Lead paint is recommended, as specified by AWWA, to give the best service.

FULLY GUARANTEED

Koven steel reservoirs are fully guaranteed against all defects in design, material and workmanship—your assurance of dependable, trouble-free operation.

Send for Bulletin No. 555.

ALL THE ADVANTAGES OF KOVEN STEEL CONSTRUCTION

Koven steel reservoirs offer many advantages in design and construction. They cost considerably less than any other type of construction. Their light weight—1/8 that of masonry—is another important cost advantage when the construction location is difficult to reach.

Koven reservoirs can be erected at any time of the year without affecting the quality of the finished job. The steel plate construction assures uniform, pre-determined strength as well as the most permanently water tight construction.

Koven steel reservoirs last a lifetime. They are not affected by frost. A coat of paint every few years not only protects the reservoir but also keeps it permanently new and clean in appearance.

REPRESENTATIVE SIZES

Nominal Capacities	Reservoirs	Actual Capacities	Standpipes	Actual Capacities
50,000	20′ x 23′	54,000	16′ x 35′	52,000
100,000	26′ x 26′	103,000	20′ x 45′	106,000
150,000	30′ x 30′	159,000	22′ x 55′	156,000
200,000	35′ x 30′	216,000	26′ x 55′	219,000
250,000	35′ x 35′	252,000	25′ x 70′	257,000
300,000	40′ x 32′	301,000	30′ x 60′	318,000
400,000	50′ x 30′	441,000	32′ x 70′	432,000
500,000	50′ x 35′	515,000	35′ x 72′	520,000
750,000	60′ x 36′	763,000	40′ x 80′	753,000
1,000,000	60′ x 48′	1,017,000	50′ x 75′	1,104,000
1,500,000	70′ x 54′	1,557,000	57′ x 80′	1,530,000
2,000,000	80′ x 54′	2,034,000		
2,500,000	92′ x 52′	2,591,000		

ENGINEERING & SALES DEPT., DOVER, N. J.
MEMBER OF STEEL PLATE FABRICATORS ASSN.

Koven FABRICATORS, INC. a division of L. O. KOVEN & BRO., Inc.

90 EAST DICKERSON ST., DOVER, N. J. PLANTS: JERSEY CITY, N. J. • DOVER, N. J. • TRENTON, N. J.

L·O·F GLASS FIBERS COMPANY

TOLEDO 1, OHIO

Low-cost DURATAPE guards pipeline joints, slashes application time in the field

Now save up to 37% on pipeline joint wrapping with L·O·F Glass Fibers' Duratape wrap. Duratape costs less to buy . . . less to apply . . . provides better protection for steel gas- and water-pipelines.

Glass-mat-reinforced Duratape combines high dielectric strength with excellent resistance to corrosive elements. Properly applied, it bonds very tightly for long-lasting protection.

Application is fast and easy: 1. Wrap preheated, pliable Duratape strips around joints and fittings; 2. Flash-seal lightly with a butane torch, after wrapping.

And for complete pipeline protection, specify Blue Flag glass fibers pipe wrap and Duramat outer wrap on your mill-wrapped pipe. For more information, write Department 24-7.

L·O·F GLASS FIBERS COMPANY, TOLEDO 1, OHIO

Duratape applies easily, securely: preheat strips; hand-wrap; flash-seal with torch after application. No other tools or fasteners are needed.

WATER STORAGE TANKS all types . . . all sizes

- **Over half a century experience in tank fabrication of all kinds**
- **Shop Fabricated and Field Erected**

ELEVATED WATER TANK
75,000 Gallon capacity

GROUND LEVEL TANK
2,500,000 gallon capacity

STANDPIPE
125,000 gallon capacity

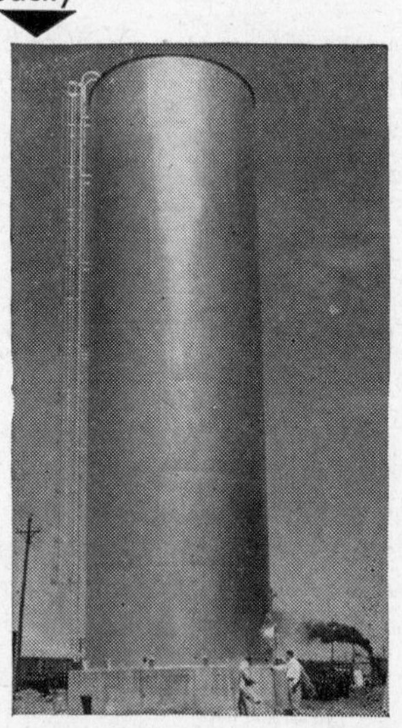

with EVERY NOOTER TANK

you benefit from:

- Deliveries You Can Depend On. Work scheduling is an important aspect of Nooter fabrication . . . dependable delivery dates are a basic policy with Nooter.
- Competitive Prices. Solid prices backed up by sound money saving techniques, resulting from 59 years of tank-fabrication.

NOOTER CORP. **1407 S. SECOND ST.** **ST. LOUIS, MO.**

PHILADELPHIA GEAR WORKS

Manufacturers of Gears, Speed Reducers, Valve Control Equipment and Couplings

Erie Avenue, and "G" Street • Philadelphia 34, Pa.

BRANCH SALES OFFICES AND DISTRIBUTORS IN PRINCIPAL CITIES

LIMITORQUE MOTOR-OPERATED VALVE CONTROLS

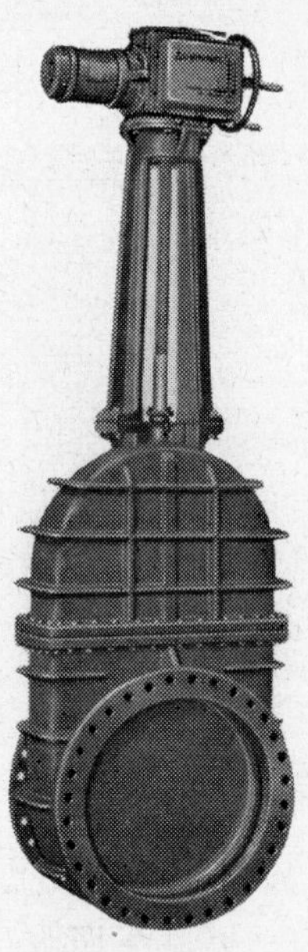

Type "SM" LimiTorque Motor-Operated Valve Control on 36" gate valve.

WIDE RANGE OF APPLICATION

LimiTorque Control is an efficient, extremely compact, automatic, mechanically-actuated device for opening and closing operations of globe, gate, butterfly and rotary plug valves, sluice gates and many other applications in Water Works, Hydro-Electric Plants, Gas Manufacturing Plants, Sewage Treatment Plants, etc.

Opening and closing stops are predetermined to suit the application. Operation can be effected by manual, push-button or automatic control.

LimiTorque may be fitted to any make valve up to 120" diameter, in almost any position or location—indoors or out. It is readily adapted to existing equipment, and it utilizes any available power source: electricity, oil, gas, water, air, etc.

PROTECTS VALVE PARTS

The word "LimiTorque" means that the Torque Limit Switch mechanism actually limits the torque that may be applied to the valve operating parts. This eliminates any possibility of breakage or jamming and assures against improper valve seating . Regardless of the nature or location of the obstruction, LimiTorque immediately shuts off the operating power.

DEPENDABLE

The LimiTorque, with all its remarkable sensitivity, is a very simple mechanism, containing as few parts as possible to operate a valve. For emergency service where handwheel operation is necessary LimiTorque will close valves 3 to 4 times faster than other types of valve operators. A hand declutching lever disengages the power operated stem nut gearing and permits manual operation without rotation of the electric motor shaft. LimiTorque can always be declutched for handwheel operation regardless of weather or electrical conditions.

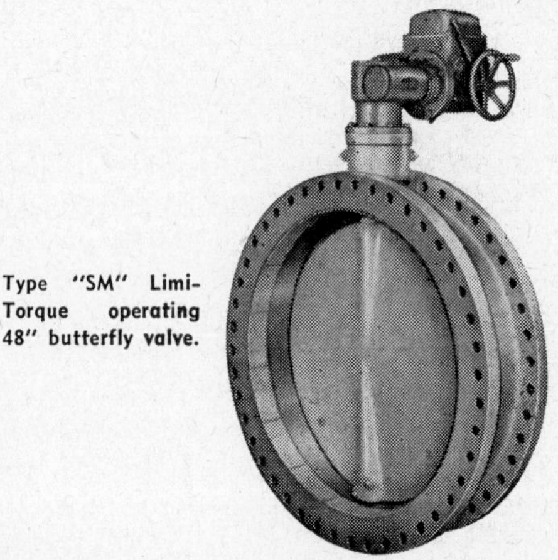

Type "SM" LimiTorque operating 48" butterfly valve.

LIMITORQUE FLOOR STANDS

For installations where it is not advisable to attach the control unit directly to the valve yoke, Floor Stand Controls can be supplied.

CATALOG—Catalog L-560 illustrating and describing all types of LimiTorque Controls will be sent upon request.

REVERE COPPER and BRASS INCORPORATED

EXECUTIVE OFFICES

230 Park Avenue, New York 17, N. Y.

DIVISION OFFICES AND MILLS

Baltimore Division, Baltimore, Md.
Pacific Coast Division, Los Angeles, Calif.
Dallas Division, Chicago, Ill.
Rome Division, Rome, N. Y.
New Bedford Division, New Bedford, Mass.
Michigan Division, Detroit, Mich.

DISTRICT SALES OFFICES

Atlanta	Cincinnati	Dayton	Houston	Milwaukee	Philadelphia	St. Louis
Boston	Cleveland	Grand Rapids	Indianapolis	Minneapolis	Pittsburgh	San Francisco
Buffalo	Dallas	Hartford	Miami	New York	Providence	Seattle

REVERE COPPER WATER TUBE FOR UNDERGROUND SERVICES

Revere Copper Water Tube (Type K, Soft Temper) is ideally suited for underground water service lines because it is non-corrosive with most waters, flexible, and easily connected with either solder or compression fittings. It meets government and A.S.T.M. Specifications for underground use. It is available in 15 sizes from ¼″ to 6″. Sizes up through 1½″ come in handy long coils, so that in many cases one continuous length can be used from the street main to the meter inside a building. All sizes come in straight lengths of 12′ and 20′. Working pressures of 400 psi for hard and 250 psi for soft temper tube provide an ample factor of safety in all water supply applications.

COSTS LESS PER YEAR OF SERVICE

The permanently smooth interior of Revere Copper Water Tube permits full and unrestricted flow for a lifetime of continuous service. Due to the long life of copper and the painstaking care with which Revere Tube is made, this tube guards against leaks, rusty water, inadequate flow, and faulty circulation. Being flexible, this tube both compensates for main "travel" and eliminates the need for special goosenecks. It can be bent to pass around rocks and other obstructions. Fittings used are of the solder or compression type, which in addition to being strong and permanently tight are quick and economical to install. The total result of these advantages of long life and economical installation is that Revere Copper Water Tube costs less per year of service.

Revere Copper Water Tube Heating Coils for

SEWAGE DIGESTER TANKS

Revere Copper Water Tube, Type K, has proved its ability to give durable service as heating coils in sewage digester tanks. Revere will be glad to give you information about existing installations or provide technical data and assistance in connection with new installations.

Herculoy for

SEWAGE DISPOSAL EQUIPMENT

Herculoy is a copper silicon alloy having a resistance to corrosion similar to that of copper and a strength equal to that of mild steel. Furthermore, it is readily welded by all commercial methods. This combination of properties makes Herculoy particularly suited for sewage screens, sluice gates, swing gates, aprons, weirs, baffle brackets, hoppers, filter parts, bolts and nuts. Its use is particularly recommended for parts embedded in concrete or located in inaccessible places. Herculoy is also ideally suited for parts which are subject to alternate immersion in sewage and exposure to the atmosphere.

YOU CAN BE SURE OF QUALITY

Revere Copper Water Tube is stamped at regular intervals with the Revere name and type. These are more than identification marks—they are your assurance of smooth interiors, full wall thickness, and the close dimensional tolerances so essential for tight soldered joints.

* * * * *

For detailed information about Revere Copper Water Tube and Herculoy, address REVERE COPPER and BRASS INCORPORATED, 230 Park Avenue, New York 17, N. Y., or any Division or District Sales Office.

M. B. SKINNER CO.

Repair Clamps and Saddles for Steel and Cast Iron Pipe

South Bend, Ind.

Established 1898

SKINNER-SEAL EMERGENCY PIPE CLAMP

For stopping leaks in water mains or pipe lines — instantly, permanently. The standard pipe repair the world over. Makes a tremendous saving over the old method of repairing leaks, as one man can apply it in ten minutes' time. Made of malleable iron; hinged along one side, with electro-plated steel bolts on the other. Bolt nuts always accessible from above. A gasket completes the clamp. Comes in both cast iron main and steel pipe sizes. Write for discount, and **complete** list of sizes.

Size	½"	¾"	1"	1¼"	1½"	2"	3"	4"	4" C. I.	6" or C.I.	8" or C.I.	10" or C.I	12" or C.I.
Wgt.	1¼	1½	1¾	2⅝	3	3¾	5¾	9⅛	10⅞	16⅛	30½	51	61¼

SKINNER-SEAL PIPE LINE CLAMP

The same principle as an Emergency Pipe Clamp, but about double the length. Especially valuable on splits, or cases of extended corrosion. Like the Emergency Pipe Clamp, it is made of malleable iron, is hinged along one side and provided with electro-plated tightening bolts. Tremendously rugged and strong. Economical in first cost and in installation because one man can apply it quickly and easily. An absolutely permanent repair. Write for discount.

Size	¾"	1"	1¼"	1½"	2"	3"	4"	4" C.I.	6"	6" C.I
Wgt.	2⅞	3¼	4¼	4¼	8⅜	16¼	18⅜	20⅜	34	33⅜

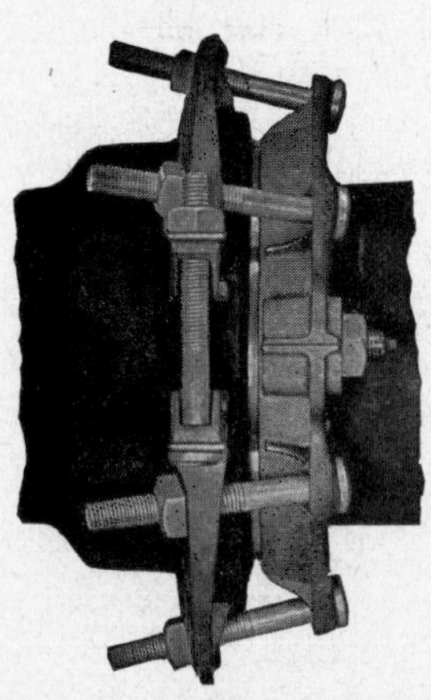

SKINNER-SEAL BELL JOINT CLAMP

For stopping bell and spigot leaks permanently, under pressure. The only clamp with the following features: (1) The large soft gasket is completely SEALED —by Monel band at top, by hard gasket tip at rear. (2) Clamp is equipped with patented distortion-proof anchor ring, (3) is completely adjustable to all variations in both pipe and bell sizes, (4) is made of malleable iron and equipped with ¾" electro-plated steel bolts. Net prices. Write for complete schedule.

Size	3"	4"	6"	8"	10"	12"	16"	20"	24"
Wgt.	20½	23	27	33½	37½	41½	61	95	109

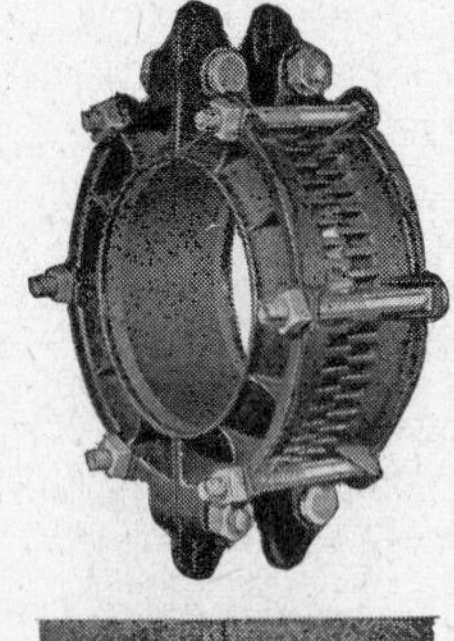

SKINNER-SEAL SPLIT COUPLING CLAMP

For repairing clean breaks in cast iron pipe. Two malleable iron rings with intermeshing fingers, drawn together by heavy steel bolts, compress a double-taper soft gasket over the break and permanently shut off the leak. Gasket is completely sealed by Monel band at top and by hard gasket tips at the sides. Applied in 10 minutes. Self-adjusting fit. Write for discount.

Cross Section

Size	2"	3"	4"	6"	8"	10"	12"
Wgt.	28	34	36	44	53	59	67

SKINNER-SEAL SERVICE SADDLE

Write for Discount

Size	2"	2½"- 2C.I.	3"	3"	3" C.I.	3" C.I.	4"	4"	4" C.I.
Tap	½"-1¼"	½"-1½"	½"-1¼"	1½, 2"	½"-1¼"	1½", 2"	½"-1¼"	1½", 2"	½"-1¼"
Wgt.	3⅝	4¼	5⅜	6⅛	5⅜	6¼	5¾	7	6½
Size	4" C.I.	6"	6" C.I.	8"	8" C.I.	10"	10" C.I.	12"	12" C.I.
Tap	1½", 2"	½"-2½"	½"-2"	½"-2"	½"-2"	½"-2"	½"-2"	½"-2"	½"-2"
Wgt.	7⅜	13½	14½	24	23½	26	26	30¾	30¾

WRITE FOR CATALOG SHOWING OTHER CLAMPS AND SADDLES, AND DRILLING EQUIPMENT

SPARLING METER COMPANY, INC.

225 N. Temple City Blvd., El Monte, Calif.

Atlanta 3 66 Luckie St. N. W.
Chicago 4 220 So. State St.
Cincinnati 2 626 Broadway
Dallas 1 505 No. Ervay St.
Kansas City 6, Mo. 6 E. Eleventh St.
Los Angeles 54 945 No. Main St.
Roselle, N. J. 650 First Ave. West
San Francisco 24 85 Industrial St.
Seattle 99 904A Elliott West
Toronto, Can. 207 Queens Quay West
Romford, England 248 London Rd.

The complete line of metering equipment!

Sparling equipment is famous for the variety of water metering problems it can handle. Whether it's a river or a few gpm in a 6-inch line, there's a Sparling meter to perform the service.

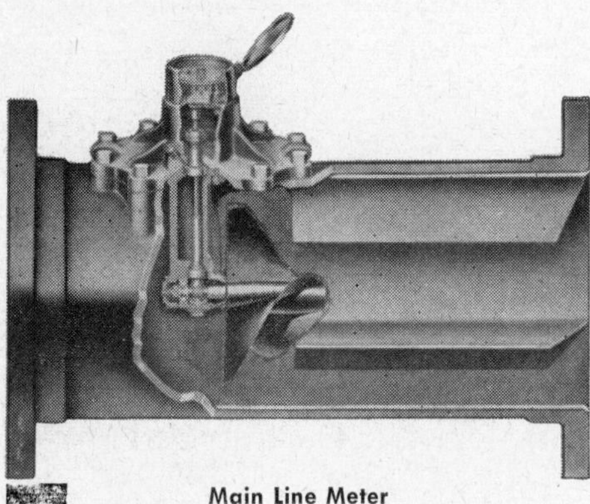

Main Line Meter

The Sparling Main Line meter is typical . . . installed as easily as a length of pipe, it gives you Direct Action Totalization actuated by the flow in the pipe without further instrumentation. Negligible loss of head pressure is characteristic of Sparling meter performance. Little maintenance is required and long life is assured!

Every Sparling Main Line meter is triple-tested in the appropriate line against the outflow from a volumetric tank.

When properly installed, accuracy within rated range is guaranteed within two per cent. (Ask for Bulletin 313)

Broad Gauge Compound Meter

Other Sparling Equipment

- Compound meters with an effective range of 125-1
- Indicator-Totalizer Recording Instruments
- Open-Flow meters
- Metering equipment for sewage treatment, open flow, or Parshall flume and weir recording equipment
- Auto-metered controls for chemical feed equipment

MI

COAST-TO-COAST SERVICE!

W. A. TAYLOR & COMPANY

418 Rodgers Forge Rd., Baltimore 4, Md.

Manufacturers of equipment and reagents for all types of colorimetric analysis

Portable sets with Color Standards that are guaranteed against fading are available from your chemical supply or laboratory equipment dealer. Many Taylor comparators operate in three simple steps — mix sample, compare with standard, read result direct. Others require only one or two additional steps. Write for free handbook, "Modern pH and Chlorine Control", giving theory and application of pH and chlorine control—illustrates and describes over 40 pieces of Taylor apparatus.

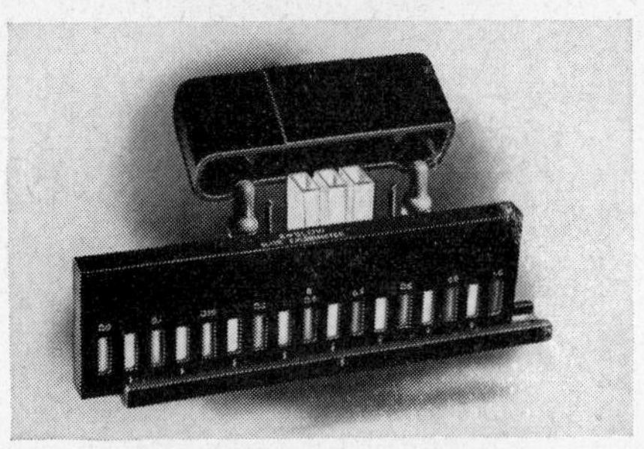

1200 TAYLOR ENSLOW SLIDE CHLORIMETER—Determines pH and free or residual chlorine content of water, sewage, industrial wastes, etc., simply and accurately. Adapted to OTA test. Chlorimeter includes base with 3 molded Lucite cells, color standard slide, pipettes and reagents.

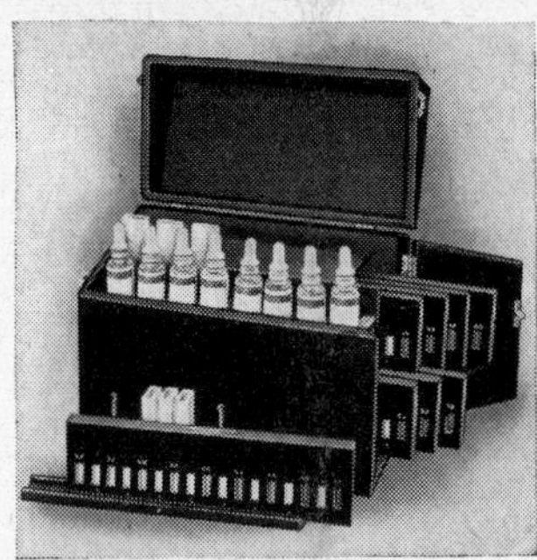

Models L-3 to L-8 COMBINATION pH and CHLORINE COMPARATOR—For control of both pH and chlorine where sample is relatively clear and colorless. Includes carrying case containing reagents, indicators, Taylor-Enslow Slide Chlorimeter and from 2 to 7 pH slides of your choice (depending on set size).

1236 MIDGET SWIM POOL TESTER—For pH and chlorine. A compact pool tester which combines rugged durability and extreme ease of operation. Held in one hand while operator makes a determination. Kit includes comparator block, Lucite cell, two indicators and pipettes. Plastic carrying case also available.

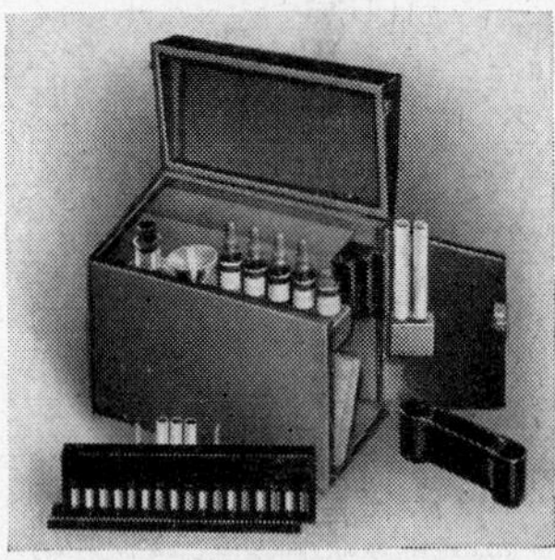

1101 BOILER WATER COMPARATOR—For pH and phosphate determinations. Two models available: "P" for phosphates only, and "W" for both pH and phosphates. Both models available for either low or high phosphates. Includes carrying case containing reagents, indicators and slides.

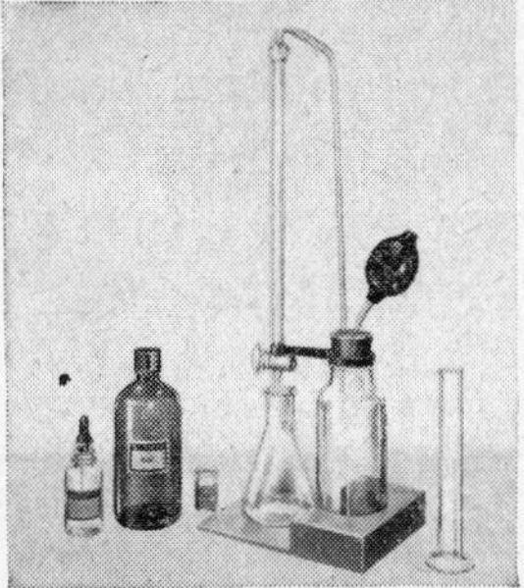

1123 TOTAL HARDNESS SET—Complete outfit. Includes all necessary reagents, accessories and instructions for accurate determination that's as simple as an alkalinity titration. Superior to soap method both in accuracy and speed. Equal in accuracy to the time consuming soda reagent method.

1300 WATER ANALYZER—Determines pH, chlorine, fluoride, color, total iron, aluminum, etc., quickly and easily. Outfit includes analyzer and one color standard slide. 18 other slides available.

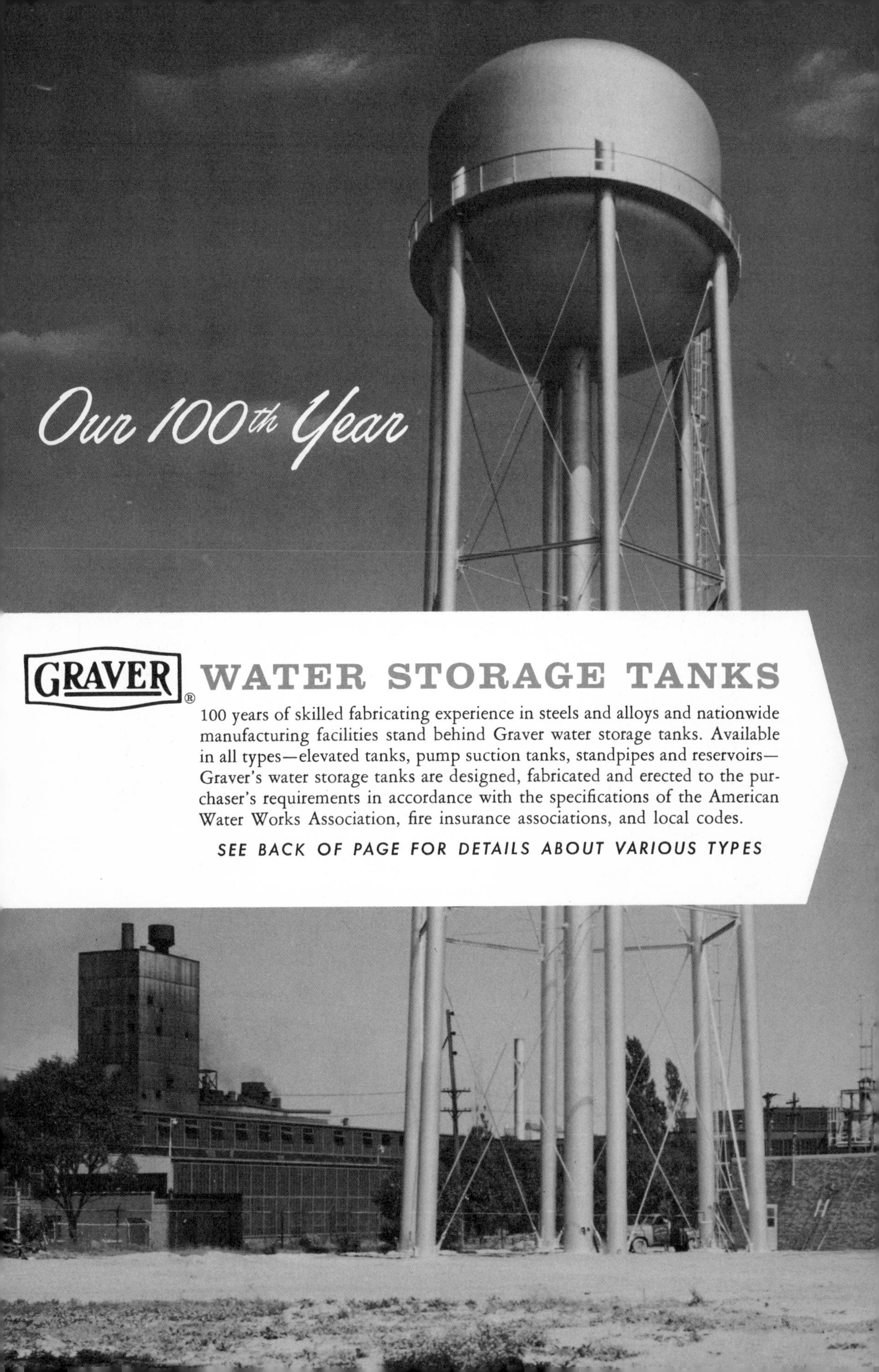

Our 100th Year

WATER STORAGE TANKS

100 years of skilled fabricating experience in steels and alloys and nationwide manufacturing facilities stand behind Graver water storage tanks. Available in all types—elevated tanks, pump suction tanks, standpipes and reservoirs—Graver's water storage tanks are designed, fabricated and erected to the purchaser's requirements in accordance with the specifications of the American Water Works Association, fire insurance associations, and local codes.

SEE BACK OF PAGE FOR DETAILS ABOUT VARIOUS TYPES

GRAVER ELEVATED WATER TANKS

Graver elevated water tanks are expertly fabricated from carbon steel, stainless steel or aluminum at Graver plants across the country and are erected on the site by experienced Graver crews to the highest welding standards.

The selection of one of the standard sizes shown in the table offers the advantage of lowest cost and quick deliveries. Should one of the standard sizes not be suitable, special designs by Graver's engineers is a regular service.

Capacity Gallons	Diameter	Head Range	Number of Columns
25,000	18′ 0″	13′ 9″	4
30,000	18′ 0″	16′ 6″	4
40,000	20′ 0″	17′ 10″	4
50,000	22′ 0″	19′ 0″	4
60,000	24′ 0″	19′ 0″	4
75,000	26′ 0″	21′ 0″	4
100,000	28′ 0″	23′ 9″	4
125,000	30′ 0″	25′ 9″	4
150,000	32′ 0″	27′ 11″	6
200,000	36′ 0″	29′ 11″	6
250,000	40′ 0″	29′ 2″	6
300,000	44′ 0″	30′ 0″	6
400,000	50′ 0″	30′ 0″	8
500,000	52′ 0″	35′ 0″	8
500,000	55′ 0″	30′ 0″	8
600,000	55′ 0″	40′ 0″	8
600,000	61′ 0″	35′ 0″	8
750,000	61′ 0″	40′ 0″	8
750,000	65′ 0″	35′ 0″	8

Graver is an approved fabricator of pump suction tanks under the Factory Mutual Fire Insurance Companies specifications. All standard sizes shown in the table have ¼″ bottoms, $^{13}/_{16}$″ self-supporting roofs and shells of thickness such that stress does not exceed 15,000 psi.

Rated Capacity Gallons	Actual Capacity Liquid Depth = Height—6″	Diameter	Height
100,000	100,470	27′ 0″	23′ 11½″
150,000	150,120	28′ 6″	31′ 11½″
200,000	200,730	33′ 0″	31′ 10½″
250,000	250,340	37′ 0″	31′ 7½″
300,000	300,550	42′ 0″	29′ 6″

GRAVER PUMP SUCTION TANKS

GRAVER STANDPIPES AND RESERVOIRS

Water supply storage tanks whose height exceeds the diameter are referred to as standpipes. When the diameter exceeds the height, they are called reservoirs. Standpipes normally provide static head to the water distribution system; reservoirs usually are intended for storage and reserve supplies. For both types of water tanks, there can be no standard sizes offered. Since the size and form depend upon local conditions and individual requirements, standpipes and reservoirs must be designed in accordance with the special needs of the users and the characteristics of the site.

Building for the Future on 100 Years of Craftsmanship in Steels and Alloys

GRAVER TANK & MFG. CO., INC.

GRAVER® 1857-1957

EAST CHICAGO, INDIANA • NEW YORK • PHILADELPHIA • EDGE MOOR, DELAWARE
PITTSBURGH • DETROIT • CHICAGO • TULSA • SAND SPRINGS, OKLAHOMA
HOUSTON • LOS ANGELES • FONTANA, CALIFORNIA • SAN FRANCISCO

THE TOLEDO PIPE THREADING MACHINE CO.

Toledo 4, Ohio

TOLEDO POWER DRIVE

For Operating Sluice Gates

Save man hours—reduce costs—with a Toledo Universal Power Drive for operating sluice gates, street valves and similar jobs. It's portable . . . weighs only 165 lbs. . . . steel or rubber-tired wheels . . . operates from light socket on 115 volts . . . or can be furnished for 230 volts. Easily controlled. Rugged ½ H.P. reversible motor. Safety device for overload.

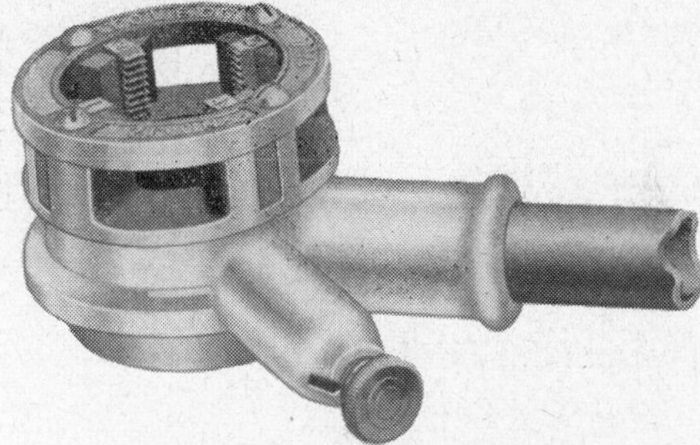

TOLEDO SMALL RATCHET PIPE THREADERS

These small, compact, easy cutting drop-head tools are ideal for bench work and close corner jobs. Instant die change . . . dies are easily reground. Sizes ⅛″ to 2″.

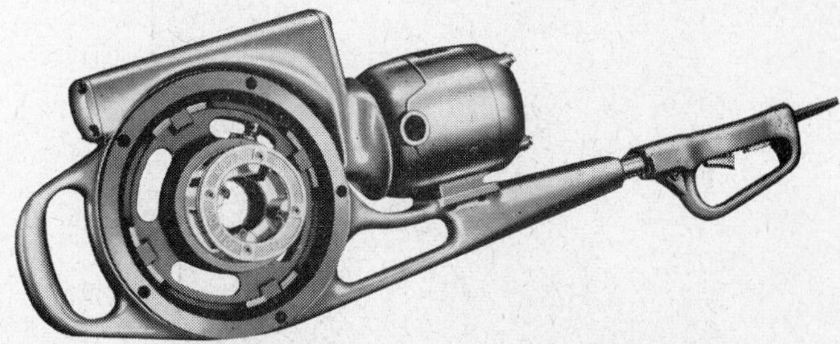

TOLEDO No. 68 SUPER MODEL PORTABLE POWER DRIVE

A 33 lb. power drive—carry it anywhere. Threads, cranks, pulls, lifts—versatile and powerful. Write for complete information.

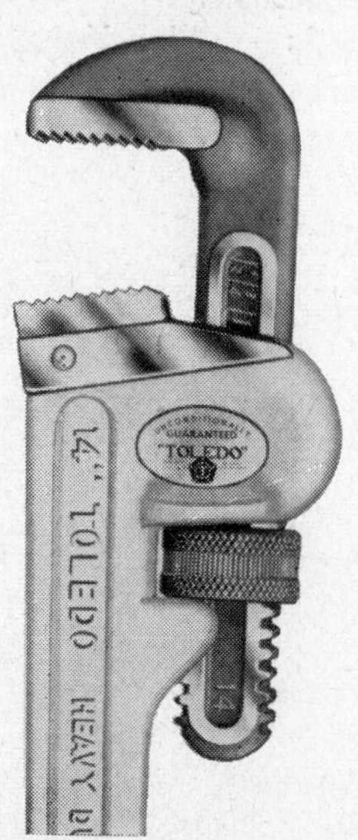

HEAVY DUTY PIPE WRENCHES

Unconditionally guaranteed. Built for hard, rugged service. Sizes 6″ to 48″.

TRAVERSE CITY IRON WORKS

Traverse City, Michigan

P. O. Box 348 Phone 3785

UNDERWRITERS' LABORATORIES
and
FACTORY MUTUAL
approved

FIRE HYDRANTS
INDICATOR VALVES
INDICATOR POSTS
O.S. & Y. VALVES
CHECK VALVES
(Bell—Mechanical—or flanged ends on above Hydrants & Valves)

Bell End Fittings with lugs for clamping

Mechanical Joint fittings
Flange & Bell Pieces
Flange & Spigot Pieces

AMERICAN WATER WORKS
ASSOCIATION SPECIFICATION

FIRE HYDRANTS
AND
GATE VALVES
(Bell—Mechanical—or flanged with conventional or O-Ring packing)

Bell & Spigot, Flanged & Mechanical Joint fittings

Special Pipe and Fittings, Valves and Accessories
for
Water and Sewage Treatment Plants
including

Floor Stands **Flap Valves**
Shear Gates **Mud Valves**
Telescopic Valves

Mechanical Joint Indicator Valve

Indicator Post

Mechanical Joint Gate Valve

For additional information write for our catalog No. 16.

Sewers, Sewage Treatment and Refuse Collection and Disposal Equipment

Kitchen Food Waste Disposers

A frank statement by American Pipe Cleaning Co. about the cost of keeping sewer and water pipe lines free of obstruction

A simple appraisal of your present policy and methods (you can do it in less than 5 min.) will tell you whether it is more economical to "do it yourself" or to employ an outside contractor specializing in this work.

TO BEGIN, ASK YOURSELF THESE QUESTIONS →

BEFORE CLEANING SEWERS ASK YOURSELF THESE QUESTIONS:

1. *Do I have regular and trained personnel with sufficient experience in cleaning operations?* *answer*____________

2. *Do I have enough equipment and, of the right type?* *answer*____________

3. *Do my workers have sufficient time allotted to them to handle a cleaning and maintenance program?* *answer*____________

If you have answered "yes" to all the questions on the preceding page your municipality is one of the select 4% whose facilities for cleaning and maintaining sewer and water lines are adequate.

If, however, you must answer "no" to one or more of these questions, read this advertisement and learn how you will benefit from the services offered by the American Pipe Cleaning Company.

APCO cleans sanitary sewers, storm sewers and water mains for municipalities of all sizes, either undertaking the entire operation, or supplementing the basic program already being used by the community. This supplementary service is ideal for those who have answered "no" to any one of the questions on the opposite page.

On the other hand, if your answer to at least two questions is "no," your municipality is not properly prepared to handle your own maintenance or emergency pipe cleaning. Your municipality would save money by using APCO for all, or at least a major part of the cleaning required.

A 22-Year History

Many municipalities find it too costly to own and maintain their own equipment or to support the force of skilled labor necessary for consistently satisfactory sewer and pipe cleaning maintenance. For this reason, the American Pipe Cleaning Co., pioneers in the field of municipal sewer cleaning without digging, was organized in 1936. By combining cleaning techniques, learned through those 20 years, with the newest types of mechanized equipment, APCO has developed a large organization, equipped to handle any municipal pipe cleaning job, no matter what the size pipe, length of line, or degree of obstruction.

Every municipality is aware that clogging of sewer and water mains can result in costly damages. In municipal sanitary sewers, clogging from roots, sand and various disposal wastes can cause extensive property damage when basement sewers "back up." Frequently sand will get into treatment plant grit chambers when sewers are not properly cleaned, and manhole cover "blow ups" may occur, due to sewer gases. Clogged, slow-flowing sewer lines carry disease, too, a threat to the health of any community.

And an important fact sometimes overlooked is if the old sewers are not cleaned before sewer extensions are made, debris will soon be washed into the new sewers.

Clogged storm sewers can be troublesome, too, often causing pavement heaving and flooded streets. Equally important are clean full capacity water pipes to insure proper water pressure for adequate fire protection. Full pressure helps to maintain the purity of the water, too.

How long has it been since your sewers have really been looked at? You may be confronted with some of the problems outlined above, as a result of pipe line congestion. American Pipe Cleaning Company, with its 20-year history of expert sewer and pipe cleaning and maintenance, can advise you reliably.

What Does APCO Do?

First, experienced engineers make a survey of your facilities, considering the age and size of your system, complaints, history of repairs and maintenance. Then a block by block study can be carried out to determine the nature and degree of the restriction in the lines. This enables APCO engineers to draw up a full scale plan based on **complete** knowledge of the facts. Finally if requested, American Pipe Cleaning will prepare a complete proposal which includes: (1) outline of the areas requiring immediate cleaning by APCO. (2) plan of areas that need attention in the future. (3) recommendations for future maintenance. (4) a review of your equipment and its suitability for carrying out a maintenance program.

Once the actual cleaning job is contracted for, all debris, such as roots, sand, lime, etc., is removed by automatic bucketing machines, pipes are scraped with specially designed rotating blades, then brushed and flushed to remove every trace of obstruction. Debris is hauled away in Company trucks. All the work is done without digging, using flexible rodding and bucketing equipment of the latest design.

In addition, American Pipe Cleaning Co. provides a consulting maintenance program to inspect sewer lines at intervals, cleaning those where pending trouble is evident.

Organization and Equipment

American Pipe Cleaning Company has over 45 pieces of equipment including trucks, pumps, winches, conveyors, automatic rodders, flushing tools and loaders. Equipment varies in size to fit pipes from 1½" to 72" in diameter. Equipment is driven by power plants ranging up to 80 h.p. to provide the right power needed for the particular line to be cleaned. Whatever labor force is required is furnished by American Pipe Cleaning Company, including experienced foremen and expertly trained workmen to perform the entire cleaning job in record time without disruption of normal municipal activities.

Powerful and Efficient Equipment to Meet and Handle Situations Illustrated as Just Routine.

OK CHAMPION
SINCE 1897

the inventor and pioneer manufacturer of power sewer cleaning machines and accessories

This tremendous root mass was removed with an 8.3 H.P. Model C8-AEN OK Champion Power Sewer Cleaner.

KEEP YOUR MEN OUT OF THE MANHOLE!

OK CHAMPION pole suspended guide wheel fits any model OK CHAMPION power sewer cleaner

"SET-UP-TIME" REDUCED TO A FEW MINUTES—The simplicity of positioning this pole suspended guide wheel of rugged modern design, results in a definite savings in labor cost and speeds up your sewer cleaning program. Now, all the work can be done from the street level, eliminating the dangers to men working in manholes. Belt driven models designed to allow transportation of suspended guide wheel without removing from sewer cleaner.

OK CHAMPION ALL PURPOSE WINDLASS — is the answer for smaller communities with a limited budget and with their smaller populations their cleaning requirements are smaller.

MOTORIZE — your all purpose windlass. If you already have or are considering the purchase of an OK CHAMPION ALL PURPOSE WINDLASS do away with the drudgery of hand cranking.

OK CHAMPION EXPANSION SEWER BUCKETS

OK CHAMPION expanding sewer buckets are constructed of heavy 3/8" steel jaws and 8 Ga. steel bodies. The jaws are opened with the forward pull. This motion also expands the bucket 10% for pick-up. This same action is utilized to facilitate the dumping of the bucket at the street level. The retrieving action closes the jaws and contracts the body to prevent it from becoming hung up in the sewer line.

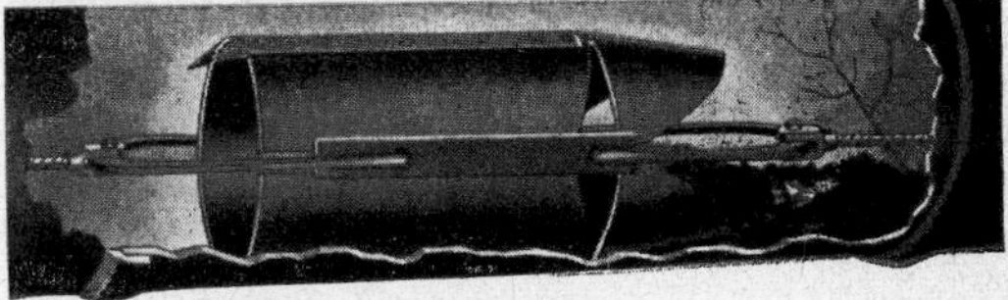

CHAMPION CORPORATION, HAMMOND, INDIANA

COMBUSTION ENGINEERING, INC.

New York 16, 200 Madison Avenue   Chicago 22, 1319 North Branch Street
Los Angeles 14, 510 West Sixth Street
Other offices in principal cities

C-E RAYMOND FLASH DRYING & INCINERATION SYSTEMS

For Sewage Sludge Disposal

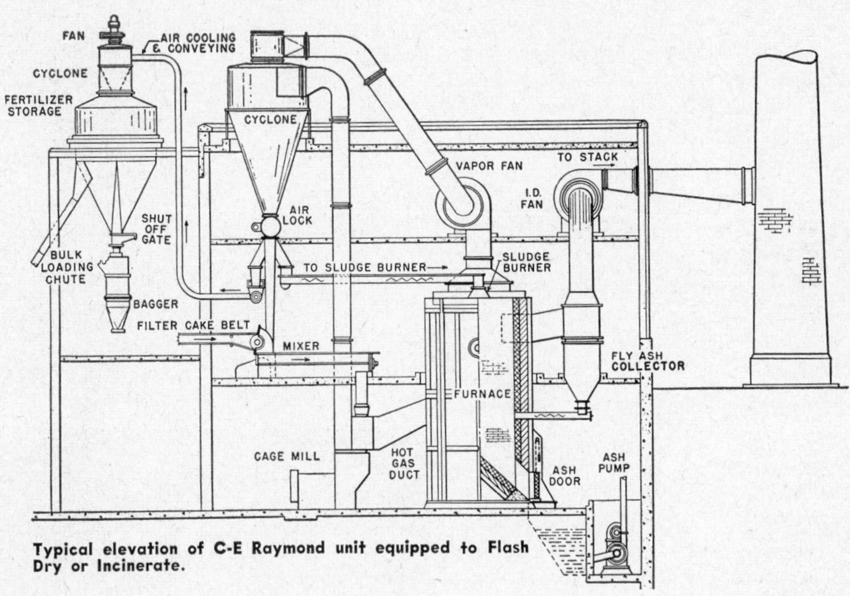

Typical elevation of C-E Raymond unit equipped to Flash Dry or Incinerate.

SEWAGE SLUDGE

The C-E Raymond Flash Drying System provides the complete answer to your sludge disposal problem. It incinerates, it flash dries, it deodorizes. It can perform these functions separately or in any combination, controllably, accurately and economically. Its service-proved flexibility and dependability are evidenced by the fact that the capacity of C-E Raymond Systems installed or on order exceed by 50% the combined capacity of all other systems that use heat for the disposal of sludge. These C-E Raymond Systems serve an equivalent population of more than 21,000,000 people. Such widespread acceptance is based on the many advantages that the flash drying system offers communities of all sizes.

FLEXIBILITY

Most of the systems in service which, at the will of the operator, can incinerate or dry to produce fertilizer are C-E Raymond Systems. When used to incinerate, the C-E Raymond System reduces sludge to a fine ash, free from clinker and unburned material. When combined with the high temperature deodorization system, all objectionable odors are eliminated. This allows considerably more latitude in choosing a plant location.

Where sewage sludge is not contaminated or toxic, the C-E Raymond Flash Drying System can economically convert it into a salable soil conditioner. Today, dried sludge has a value which

See Following 3 Pages

ranges between $5.00 and $33.00 per ton. By using such a disposal method the problem of ash handling encountered with incineration is completely eliminated. Ash removal can be a costly item since approximately 50% of the dry solids of digested sludge remain as ash.

The C-E Raymond Flash Drying System is the only system that combines these two best methods of sewage sludge disposal—flash drying and incineration—in a single unit that can perform either function alternately or concurrently.

DESIGN

The furnace of the C-E Flash Drying System is not complicated by the use of multiple, sprung, refractory arches. It has only one roof arch which is of the suspended type. Using this construction, each piece of arch tile is individually hung from steel supports located above and outside the furnace. No group of arch bricks is dependent on any other group for support and consequently arch failure or collapse is virtually impossible. Because this single furnace arch is independently supported from the outside, it is not subjected to the compression stresses of expansion and contraction.

MAINTENANCE

The sturdy construction of the Raymond System and the elimination of multiple, sprung arches makes it unnecessary to maintain constant furnace temperatures in order to prevent refractory failure. As a consequence, the unit is ideally suited for quick start-ups and shut-downs. Accordingly it eliminates the labor, fuel and power costs otherwise required for standby operation. Maintenance costs of the arch and fire brick are negligible.

Houston, Texas uses two large C-E Raymond Flash Drying Units.

Bethlehem, Pennsylvania uses a C-E Flash Drying and Incineration System.

Schenectady, New York and Wyomissing Valley, Pennsylvania both dry sludge using C-E Systems.

C-E RAYMOND FLASH DRYING & INCINERATION SYSTEMS

DETAIL OF TYPICAL ARCH CONSTRUCTION

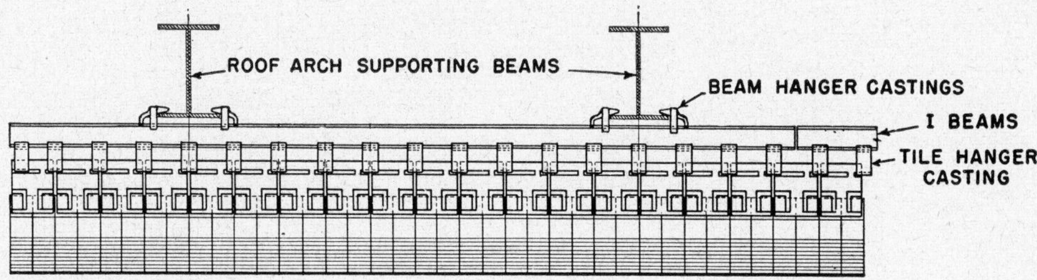

Sectional Side Elevation

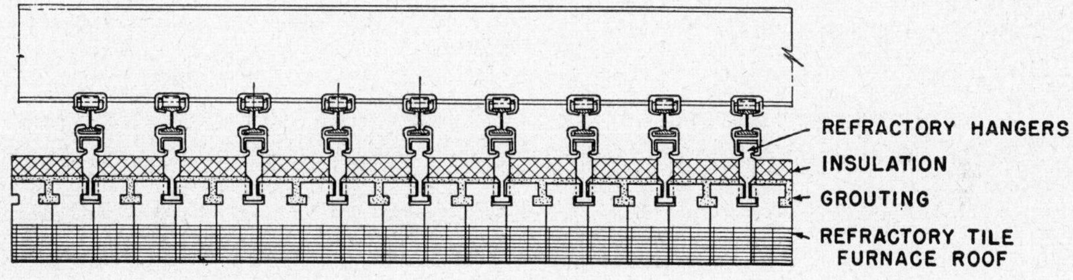

Front Elevation

Cross section of roof arch. This construction prevents arch failure and allows rapid start-ups and shut-downs—virtually eliminating stand-by labor, power and fuel.

EXPERIENCE

A major reason for the success and widespread acceptance of C-E Raymond Systems is the exceptional background of experience represented in their design and manufacture. This is the result of the Company's long identification with the field of drying through its Raymond Division and with the processes of combustion and heat transfer through its background in the fields of fuel burning and steam generation. The services of C-E specialists are available to assist you in finding the best solution to your sludge disposal problems.

WATER TREATMENT PLANTS

C-E Raymond Flash Drying Systems are now available in certain sizes to reclaim lime used in water treatment operations. Requiring little space, and ideally suited for intermittent operation, these units assure the plant of a reliable lime supply and at the same time, virtually eliminate all sludge disposal problems.

More complete information is available upon request.

C-E RAYMOND FLASH DRYING SYSTEMS PRODUCING FERTILIZER

CITY	TYPE	UNITS	SIZE #H_2O/Hr. per unit	CAPACITY Tons Fertilizer Per Year
Baltimore, Md.	Act. Dig.	3	6,140	29,800
Battle Creek, Mich.	Pri. Dig.	1	2,370	2,550
Birmingham, Ala.	Pri. Dig.	1	12,000	13,452
Chicago, Ill.				
Calumet	Act.	3	6,667	15,850
Southwest	Act.	8	21,000	148,500
Southwest Ext.	Act.	6	21,000	49,500
*Edgewater, N. J.	Pri. Dig.	1	795	150
Fond du Lac, Wis.	Pri. Dig.	1	2,350	1,300
*Galveston, Texas	Act.	1	6,260	2,775
Houston, Tex.	Act.	2	12,000	30,400
Lansing, Mich.	Act. Dig. & Garbage	1	6,667	6,780
Los Angeles, Cal.	Act. Dig.	4	22,500	79,500
Louisville, Ky.	Pri. Dig. Elu.	2	9,200	15,728
San Diego, Cal.				
#1 Plant	Pri. Dig.	1	3,500	7,500
#2 Plant	Pri. Dig.	1	5,000	13,200
San Francisco, Cal.	Pri. Dig.	3	6,250	36,400
Schenectady, N. Y.	Pri. Dig.	1	3,370	2,970
Sheboygan, Wis.	Pri. Dig.	1	3,040	3,060
Stamford, Conn.	Pri. Dig.	1	3,330	1,780
*Washington, D. C.	Pri. Dig. now / Act. Dig. later	3	12,000	65,500
Wyomissing, Pa.	Pri. Dig.	1	2,218	848

C-E RAYMOND FLASH DRYING & INCINERATION SYSTEMS

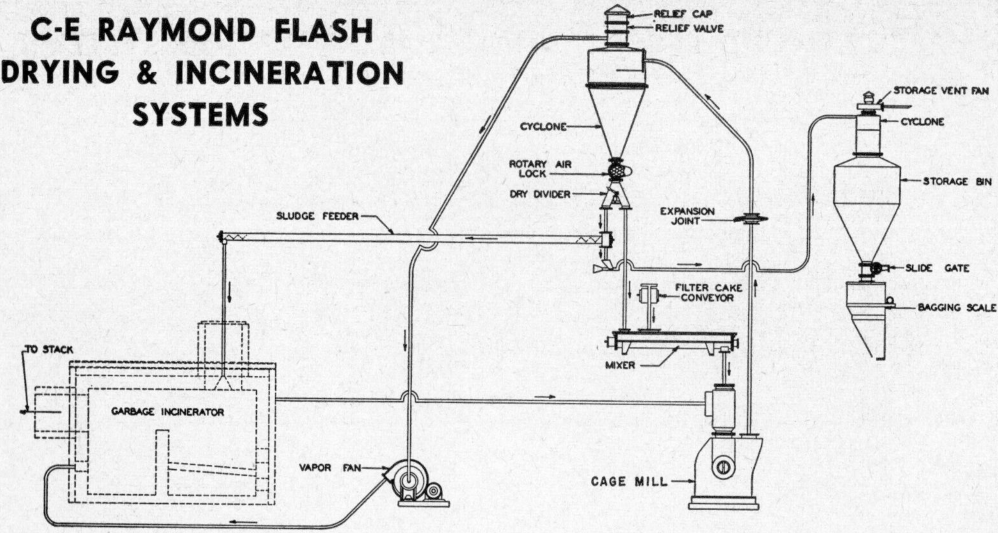

C-E Raymond System with refuse incinerator. This is one of the most economical methods available for sludge disposal.

REPRESENTATIVE LIST OF C-E RAYMOND INCINERATION SYSTEMS

CITY	EQUIVALENT POPULATION
Bethlehem, Pa.	100,000
Buffalo, New York	625,000
Camden, New Jersey	350,000
Cuyahoga Falls, Ohio	22,500
Duluth, Minnesota	125,000
Miami, Florida	283,000
Neenah-Menasha, Wis.	100,000
New Rochelle, N. Y.	80,000
Pittsburgh, Pa.	1,400,000
Springfield, Mass.	190,000
Waterbury, Conn.	100,000

Hyperion Plant at Los Angeles, Cal. with Dryer Building in foreground.

C-E Raymond System with refuse incinerator at Fond du Lac, Wisconsin

San Francisco uses three C-E Raymond units.

AMVIT* JOINTED CLAY PIPE gains wide acceptance, more than 60 major installations completed in 1955

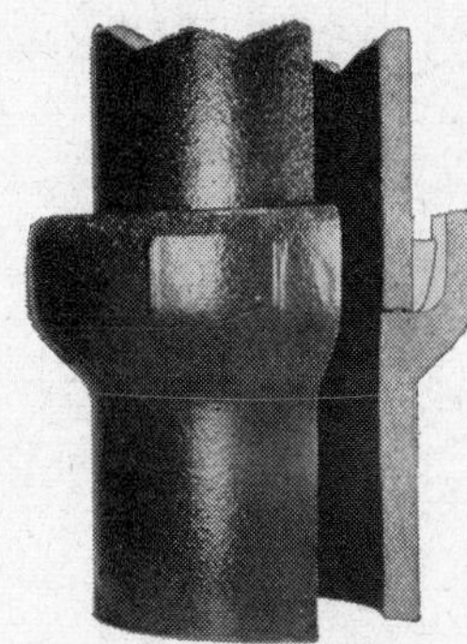

Never before has a new product gained such wide acceptance and usage in such a short period of time.

In the first year since Amvit Jointed Clay Pipe was introduced more than 60 major installations have been completed with outstanding results. Such pioneer cities as Dayton, Ohio, Camden, New Jersey, Ostego, Michigan, Victor, New York, have installed their second and third Amvit Jointed sanitary lines

Prevents Infiltration

Field tests from these installations show that ground water infiltration can be controlled and prevented—thus reducing pumping and treatment plant costs. Amvit is a compression type joint on the ball and socket principle. Nothing can enter the line after it is complete

Quick Installation Saves Labor

Since no other material such as caulking, joint compound, hot-pots or ladles are needed to make the Amvit Joint, installation is quick and easy. The joint is on the pipe delivered to the job ready to use. Savings with Amvit Jointed Clay Pipe mean *lower cost of pipe in place* when the line must meet a rigid test.

Amvit Jointed Clay Pipe, in sizes 4" through 24", together with all fittings is available for immediate delivery in the Northeast and Central States.

For more information, write or call American Vitrified Products Company, National City Bank Building, Cleveland, Ohio, or our office nearest you.

Indiana

New Jersey

Michigan

Wisconsin

Illinois

*T M. Registered Patents Pending

MANUFACTURERS of: Clay pipe, flue liners, clay liner plates and concrete pipe.

Plants Across the Nation...Brazil, Indiana • Chicago, Illinois • Cleveland, Ohio • Crawfordsville, Indiana • Detroit, Michigan • East Liverpool, Ohio Fenton, Michigan • Grand Ledge, Michigan • Lisbon, Ohio • Los Angeles, California • Milwaukee, Wisconsin • South Bend, Indiana • Uhrichsville, Ohio

DORR-OLIVER
Incorporated
Barry Place, Stamford, Conn.

DORR-OLIVER Equipment and Methods

DORRCO BAR SCREEN

Dorrco Bar Screens are mechanically cleaned units designed to eliminate the manual labor in smaller plants or do a reliable job in the large multiple unit installations. Two types are available: the simple Type VN for shallower channels, which consists of a revolving rake mounted on a horizontal motor driven shaft and engaging a curved bar rack; and the automatic Type S for deeper channels. This consists of a moving rake mounted on a frame pivoted from a top suspension shaft, which causes the rake to descend in a path ahead of the bars and then engage the rake bars on the ascending or raking operation.

Both types can be equipped with the Dorrco Bar Screen Float Control which saves wear on the unit.

A Dorr Detritor installation

DORRCO VACUATOR

The Dorrco Vacuator was developed primarily for the removal of oils, grease, scum and light solids from sewage and trade wastes. It makes a three product separation consisting of (a) grease and scum (b) an improved effluent for subsequent treatment and (c) a sludge containing substantial quantities of grit. It is usually used ahead of primary sedimentation.

The Vacuator consists of a cylindrical container with a dome roof in which a constant vacuum is maintained. Feed enters the tank through a central, subsurface draft tube; and the floating solids are removed from the liquid surface into a trough from which they are continuously discharged to a sump. Effluent overflows a peripheral channel to a sealed chamber and any settled solids are raked to a sludge outlet.

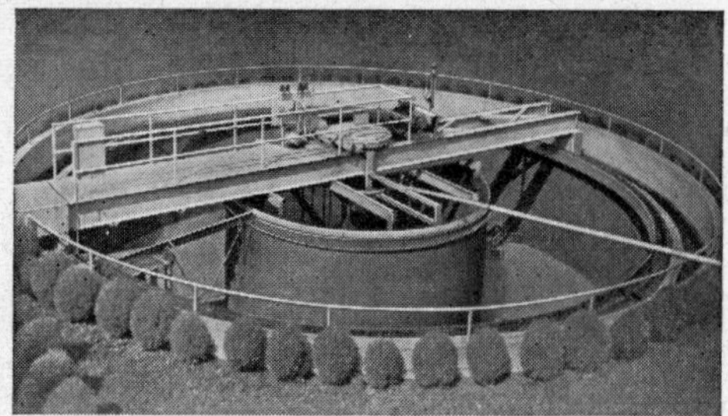

A Dorrco Aerator-Clarifier installation.

DORR DETRITOR

The Dorr Detritor is a continuous, mechanically operated grit chamber. It produces a substantially grit-free liquid and a clean, well washed and drained grit. The washed grit may be used for sand beds, walkways, fill, etc.

Sewage enters the Detritor uniformly through training deflectors along one side of a square tank and after depositing its load of grit overflows a weir along the side directly opposite. A revolving mechanism rakes the deposited solids radially outward into a chute which discharges them into the adjacent, grit washing channel. A reciprocating raking mechanism moves the grit up the sloping bottom of the channel washing and draining it and then depositing it into a receptacle. The grit washing mechanism may be located separately from the collecting tank at an elevation suitable for discharge of grit into trucks, etc.

Dorrco Vacuator at Santa Maria, Calif.

DORRCO AERATOR-CLARIFIER

The Dorrco Aerator-Clarifier is a compact, combination unit designed for the preaeration and clarification of sewage and trade wastes. The aeration chamber consists of a steel shell suspended in the Clarifier with air supplied through fixed diffuser tubes in the chamber. After the aeration period, feed enters the Clarifier through a central opening in the floor of the Aerator.

for Modern Sewage Treatment

DORR CLARIFIERS

Dorr Clarifiers are continuous, mechanically cleaned sedimentation units for removing settleable solids from sewage and compacting these solids in a thickened sludge. Designed for either round or square tanks, the Dorr Clarifier mechanism consists of rotating rakes which plow settled solids inward to a central discharge hopper. Round units, in 10 to 200 ft. dia., are fed through a central feed well with the effluent overflowing a peripheral weir. Square units, in sizes of 20 to 200 ft. square, may be fed either at the center or along one side if cross flow is used. Either type can be provided with continuous skimmers which sweep scum from the surface of the tank and remove it through a separate outlet.

Close-up of Dorrco Monorake

DORRCO DISTRIBUTORS

Dorrco Distributors are of the rotary self-propelled type capable of handling dosing rates of from 350 to 24,000 gallons/square yard. They may be supplied with either two or four arms, each arm having either one or two compartments, depending upon the total dosing rate and flow variation. In larger sizes fabricated steel arms with flat rectangular section reduce hydraulic losses and eliminate the awkwardness of standard circular piping.

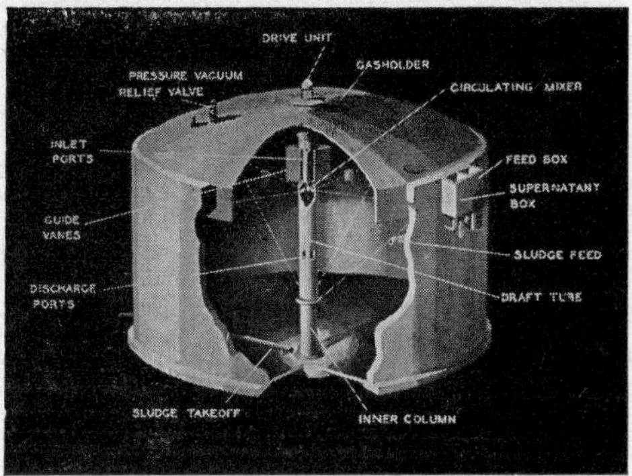

The Dorr Type MA Digester

Interior view of Dorr S-7 Clarifier

DORRCO MONORAKE

This unit is available for rectangular tanks up to 80 ft. wide and any desired length. Balanced raking mechanisms are supported and operated from a carriage traveling on longitudinal rails. The rakes sweep settled solids to one or more sludge discharge ports. Skimming can also be provided. The Monorake may also be combined with Flocculators.

A high-rate Dorrco Distributor installation

DORR TYPE MA DIGESTER

The Dorr Type MA Digester provides for the first time the advantages of gas storage and intensive mixing in a single unit. Gas storage, as provided by the movable steel dome top, insures a constant flow of gas to boilers and other gas burning equipment at a constant pressure. The propeller type mixer operating in a vertical draft tube reduces or eliminates scum formation, mixes indigestible scum with sludge for removal and insures uniform temperatures.

SPIRAL HEAT EXCHANGER

Consisting of two concentric spiral passageways through which sludge and hot water flow counter-currently, the Spiral Heat Exchanger combined with a standard hot water boiler offers a new and improved means of externally heating digestion tanks equipped with mechanical mixing devices.

The Dorr Multdigestion System

THE OLIVER SEWAGE SLUDGE DEWATERER

The Oliver Sewage Sludge Dewaterer is a dependable vacuum filter designed to remove water from sludges produced in municipal and industrial waste treatment plants. Corrosion resistant, rugged construction insures long life and reliable service. Installation and operation are extremely simple, and power requirements are kept to a minimum. Units are available in a wide range of sizes to solve any sludge dewatering problem.

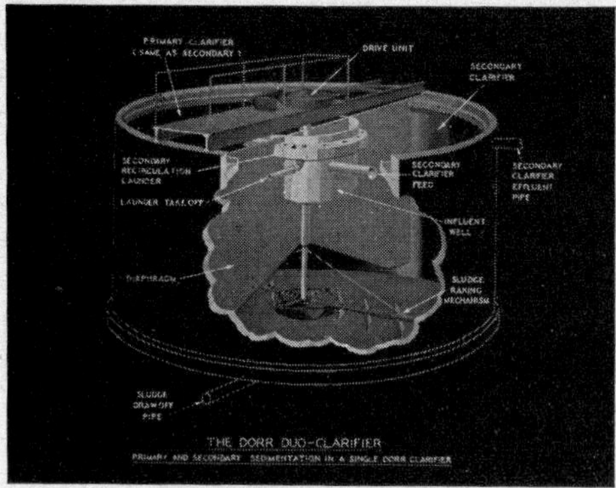

The Dorr Duo-Clarifier

DORRCO DUO-FILTER

The Dorrco Duo-Filter consists of a trickling filter, subdivided into a circular central section for primary filtration and an outer annular section for secondary filtration. Both sections are dosed by a single, four-arm Dorrco Distributor, the two short arms of which serve the inner section, the long arms serving the outer.

DORR MULTDIGESTION SYSTEM

The Dorr Multdigestion System carries out the essential phases of digestion in two stages, employing separate primary and secondary tanks. It is suitable for both medium and large sized plants.

The heated and covered primary digester compartment is at all times filled with mechanically mixed, homogeneous sludge. Raw sludge enters the primary where about 85% of the digestion takes place. The sludge is transferred automatically from the primary to the secondary compartment at the rate of feed. No overflow liquor is drawn off from the primary.

The secondary compartment is essentially for sludge and gas storage. The contents of this secondary compartment are in a quiescent state, stratified into two layers. The upper layer is a well settled, supernatant liquor suitable for return to process. The lower layer is a well thickened sludge that may be drawn off at a minimum water content.

The Oliver Sewage Sludge Dewaterer

DORR DUO-CLARIFIER

The Dorr Duo-Clarifier consists of a standard Dorr Clarifier separated into two equal sedimentation compartments by a vertical, diametrically placed dividing wall. Each of the two compartments functions as a separate unit—thus providing primary and secondary clarification in a single tank.

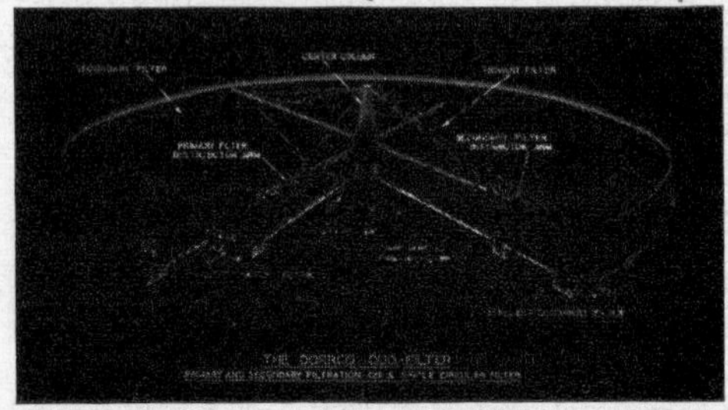

The Dorrco Duo-Filter

A Currie Claraetor installation

CURRIE CLARAETOR

The Currie Claraetor is a self-contained, low cost unit for the clarification and aeration of sewage in the activated sludge process. Clarification takes place in a centrally located compartment which may be either round or square. Aeration occurs in an annular compartment located between the outer tank wall and the clarification compartment. It is especially suitable for small activated sludge plants.

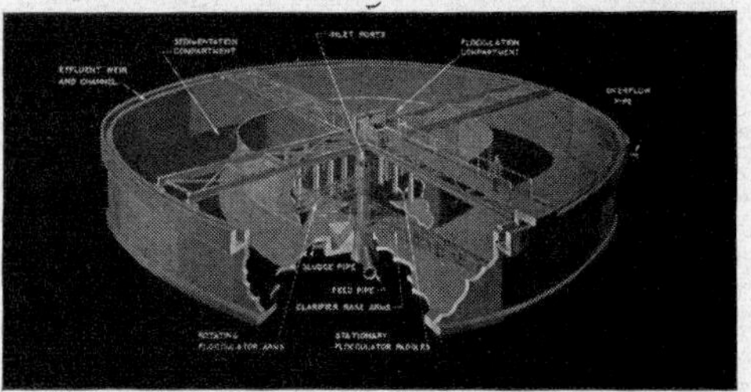

The Dorrco Clariflocculator

DORRCO CLARIFLOCCULATOR

This unit is a combined Dorrco Flocculator and Dorr Clarifier in a single tank. Flocculation takes place in the inner circular compartment; clarification in the outer annular compartment. Feed enters centrally, overflow is taken off peripherally and thickened sludge is discharged from the bottom as in standard Clarifier practice. The high solids removals possible with this unit are due to first, the transfer of well formed flocs from the flocculation to the clarification compartment without disintegration and second, the rapid sedimentation of these flocs that takes place in the clarification compartment.

A Dorr Clarigester installation

DORR CLARIGESTER

The Dorr Clarigester is essentially a mechanical two story tank for small sewage treatment plants. The top compartment contains a clarifier mechanism and in the lower compartment a digester mechanism provides separate sludge digestion under controlled conditions. Transfer of sludge from settling to digestion compartment is automatic and requires no sludge pump, and supernatant withdrawal is controlled by the operator. The Clarifier can be provided with an automatic skimmer and the Digester can be heated in colder climates. This is an ideal unit for primary treatment of sewage from 500 to 5000 persons.

The Complete Line of Dorr-Oliver Equipment for Sewage Treatment

Dorrco Bar Screen
Dorrco Fine Screen
Dorrco Sulzer Disintegrator
Dorr Detritor®
Dorrco Vacuator®
Dorrco Aerator-Clarifier
Dorrco Flocculator®
Dorr Clarifier
Dorrco Monorake®
Dorrco Sludge Pump
Dorrco Distributor
Dorr Thickener
Dorr Digester
Dorr Multdigestion® System
Dorrco Densludge Digestion System
Spiral Heat Exchanger
Dorr Duo-Clarifier
Dorrco Duo-Filter
Dorrco Clariflocculator®
Dorr Clarigester®
Currie Claraetor
Oliver Sewage Sludge Dewaterer

DORR-OLIVER Incorporated
Barry Place, Stamford, Conn.

Stamford, Connecticut Barry Place	Chicago 54, Illinois 942 Merchandise Mart	Virginia, Minn. 204½ Chestnut Ave.	Los Angeles 14, Calif. 811 West 7th Street
New York 16, New York 99 Park Avenue	Cleveland 15, Ohio 1032 Midland Building	Denver, Colorado P.O. Box 149 (Englewood)	Oakland, California 2900 Glascock Street
Atlanta, Georgia 900 Peachtree Street N.E.	St. Paul 4, Minnesota 2631 University Avenue	Dallas 30, Texas 6115 Berkshire Lane	Seattle 1, Washington 3104 Smith Tower

RESEARCH AND TESTING LABORATORIES: OAKLAND, CALIF., WESTPORT, CONN.

GRUENDLER CRUSHER & PULVERIZER CO.

St. Louis 6, Mo.

WHY NOT DOWNTOWN TOO?

Eliminate *All* Food Waste Collection...

Domestic Food Wastes Disposal Units do part of the job. . . . Now the Gruendler Heavy Duty Food Waste Shredder for Hotels, Hospitals and Restaurants makes possible a 100% city-wide elimination of garbage nuisance and expense.

Reduce Food Wastes to a Free Flowing Pulp

Improves Sanitation at points of Mass Feeding Where Most Needed

ADVANTAGES OF THE GRUENDLER SHREDDER

1. Fool-proof operation with automatic water control.
2. Silverware salvage trap.
3. Handles wax paper cartons without difficulty . . . will not be damaged by accidental introduction of crockery, glass ware or bottle caps. Has tramp metal catcher.
4. Pre-rinse available for units installed in dish scraping tables.

Municipal Garbage Grinder

GRUENDLER

also builds . . .

SEWAGE, GARBAGE and REFUSE DISPOSAL UNITS for MUNICIPAL PLANTS.

WRITE FOR BULLETIN SG10

Typical Sewage Shredder and Bar-Screen (City of Cortland, N. Y.)

Also manufacturers of Wood-Hogs, Coal Crushers, Rubbish Shredders, Lime Breakers, Rock & Gravel Crushing and Screening Machinery.

THE VAPOR RECOVERY SYSTEMS CO.

COMPTON, CALIFORNIA

"Varec" SEWAGE GAS CONTROL EQUIPMENT

Available from Authorized Sewage Equip ment Agents throughout U.S. and Canada

Cable Address: VAREC COMPTON CALIF. (USA. All Codes)

FIGURE NO. 5800C
"VAREC" Pressure Relief and Vacuum Breaker Valve with Flame Arrester

Installed on digesters and gas holder domes, it affords emergency pressure and vacuum relief and prevents flame entrance from atmospheric disturbances. Equipped with telescopic flame arresting element for easy inspection and maintenance. Aluminum construction. Sizes 2" to 10".

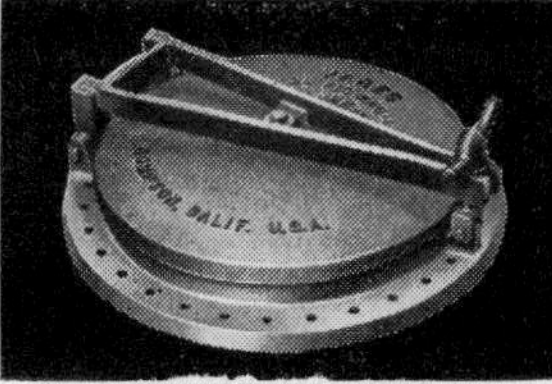

FIGURE NO. 220A
"VAREC" Manhole Cover

Installed on digester and gas holder domes, it affords quick and easy access. Nonsparking. Gastight. Sizes—18", 20", 24", 30".

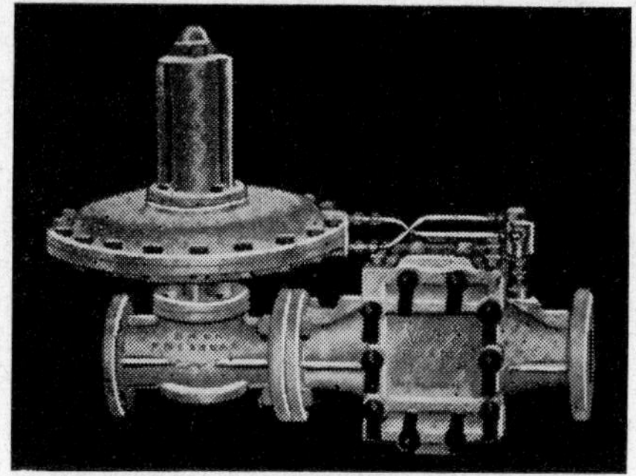

FIGURE NO. 440
"VAREC" Pressure Relief and Flame Trap Assembly

Maintains a predetermined back pressure, passing surplus gas to Burner. Consists of diaphragm-operated regulator, flame trap and thermal shut-off valve. Patented telescopic flame trap element simplifies inspection and maintenance. Aluminum and stainless steel construction. Sizes 2" to 8".

FIGURE NO. 450
"VAREC" Flame Trap Assembly

Installed in all gas lines supplying gas utilization equipment. Consists of flame trap and thermal shutoff valve. Aluminum and stainless steel construction. Sizes 2" to 8".

"VAREC" Waste Gas Burner→

Installed wherever disposal of surplus gas is a problem. Adjustable air intake. Outside pilot valve adjustment. With or without pedestal. Sizes 2", 3", 4", 6".

FIG. NO. 236

FIGURE NO. 216A
"VAREC" Manometer

Single or triple tube. Open or push-button control. Aluminum housing. Bronze fittings. Pyrex glass. Sizes 10", 15", 20".

FIGURE NO. 52A
"VAREC" Flame Check

Flame check for small gas lines. Union type fitting. Aluminum construction. Sizes ½" to 2".

FIGURE NO. 386 & 387
"VAREC" Sensitive Pressure Regulator—Single Port

Maintains upstream or downstream pressure to within 0.5" of water of predetermined pressure. Aluminum body, stainless steel trim. Sizes 2" to 8".

FIGURE NO. 211A
"VAREC" BACK Pressure Check Valve

For installation in low pressure gas lines to prevent back flow. Non-chattering, non-pulsating. Non - sparking. Sizes 2" to 8".

FIGURE NO. 187
"VAREC" Supersensitive Pressure Regulator—Double Port

Maintains upstream or downstream pressure to within 0.2" of water of predetermined pressure. Aluminum body, stainless steel trim. Sizes ½" to 6".

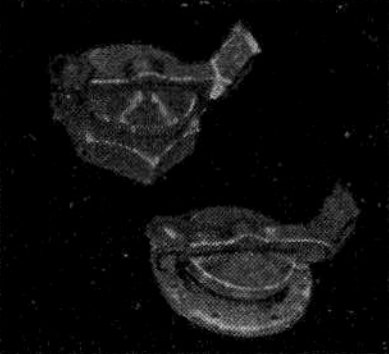

FIGURE NOS. 48 & 42A
"VAREC" Sampling Hatch Covers

For use on digester domes. Self closing, gastight, sparkproof. Flanged or screwed connections. Sizes 4" to 10".

FIGURE NO. 232D
"VAREC" Sediment Trap and Condensate Drip Trap Assembly

Cast iron construction. Stainless steel trim. Hand operated or automatic. Sizes 2" and 2½".

EXPANDING SEWER MACHINE CO.

Complete Sewer Cleaning Equipment

108 East Walnut Street, Nappanee, Indiana

Relieve Unsanitary Conditions With

Expanding Root Cutter and Sewer Cleaner

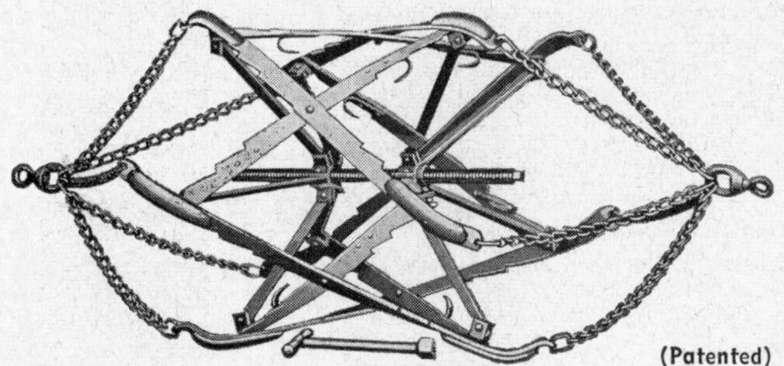

(Patented)

Works on a Lazy Tong Principle

It can be expanded and contracted to fit any sewer within the limits of the three sizes in which it is made in thirty seconds by placing Tee wrench or either end of the 1-inch screw, fitted with left and right hand threads, which turns through two brass spiders connected to the blades by ten radius rods, holding the blades in position.

Spring Steel Blades

The 10 cutting blades are constructed of ¼-inch x 1½-inch *Spring Steel;* heat treated with both edges notched and sharpened like a hay knife; assembled with 10 Bronze hinge joints.

The 10 shoes or runners guide the machine over the irregular joints.

Cleaner Completely Contracted

The Many Outstanding Features

Which have been incorporated in the Expanding Root Cutter and Sewer Cleaner make it possible to do the most thorough job of sewer cleaning with less cost.

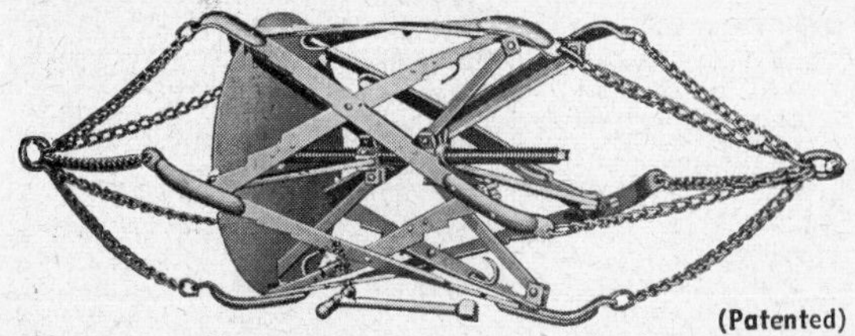

(Patented)

14" Disc in Position Forming a Bucket, Ready for Work—Requiring No Bolts or Screws

1. Effective in either direction the machine is pulled.
2. The roots are severed by five sets of double knives which operate in V-shape formation like the blades of a pair of scissors.
3. Forty feet of cutting edge, twenty feet of which is notched like a hay knife.
4. Roots are cut at an angle or bias.
5. Ten steel claws that catch the severed root-masses.
6. Four removable sediment discs which can be placed in either end, forming four sizes of buckets.
7. Only one machine required for the entire sewer system.
8. No additional cost for hose or water.
9. A great time, labor and money saver.

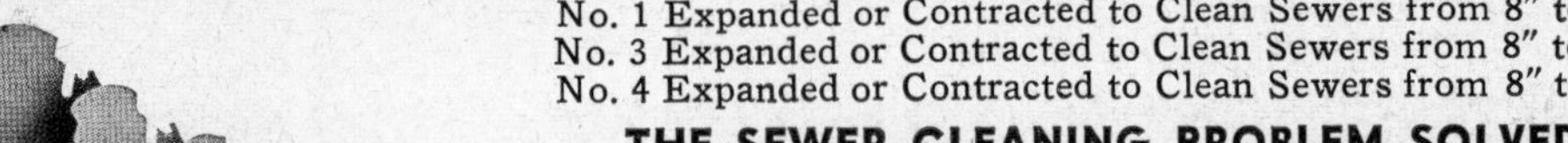

No. 1 Expanded or Contracted to Clean Sewers from 8" to 30".
No. 3 Expanded or Contracted to Clean Sewers from 8" to 24".
No. 4 Expanded or Contracted to Clean Sewers from 8" to 15".

17½" 14" 11" 9"

Write for descriptive catalog and prices of Complete Sewer Cleaning Equipment.

THE SEWER CLEANING PROBLEM SOLVED!

The best equipment we ever used. We cleaned 4,500 feet of 15-inch sewer at an expense of only $95.00

Commercial and residential routes make up the majority of work done by a sanitation department. So, it makes good sense to buy the type body that can handle both jobs best. PAK-MOR's proven features make it the ONE refuse body that can do both jobs equally well. PAK-MOR's large unlimited loading area allows quick loading — without flattening or folding bulky objects, just throw them in, Direct Compaction of Paker Plate does the rest. At heavy stops, material can be thrown directly into PAK-MOR's barrel — a real advantage over limited hopper space and numerous packing cycles. PAK-MOR speeds up pickup-time, enables you to make more stops — more quickly and cover routes faster.

FINGER STAYS (TOP OF BARREL) PROVIDE POSITIVE RETENTION OF LOAD.

Direct Compaction of Packer Plate traveling full length of barrel breaks down load and packs it densely under 50,000 pounds of pressure. Finger Stays provide Positive Retention to hold load in barrel and prevent fall back into loading area. Reason why PAK-MOR picks up heavier loads faster and goes farther on every route. PAK-MOR's heavier loads allow you to spend more time on the pickup route and less time traveling to and from the dump.

Because of PAK-MOR's few moving parts, all accessible, maintenance and lubrication are handled quickly and easily.
Ask for a PAK-MOR demonstration before you buy. There's a PAK-MOR Distributor in your area who can show you how PAK-MOR can do a better job for you.

PAK-MOR'S DIRECT COMPACTIONS PACKS HEAVIER LOADS.

LOOP 13 & ROOSEVELT AVE. POST OFFICE BOX 6147 WA 3-4317 SAN ANTONIO, TEXAS
EXPORT DIVISION — TIFCO INTER-AMERICA CORP. P. O. BOX 13361 HOUSTON, TEXAS

WHETHER YOU USE . . .

Sanitary Landfill or Incineration

PAK-MOR'S *designed to do a better job!*

PAK-MOR overcomes the problems of inclement weather and uneven terrain at the landfill and low overhead clearance at the incinerator because PAK-MOR does not have to tilt its body to unload. Just back right in — open the back doors and start the Packer Plate as in a normal packing cycle and the PAK-MOR completely unloads.

There's no picking a level spot to overcome excessive shift of gravity as in tilt-type bodies and there is no worry of capsizing. No extreme weight is pivoted on the rear wheels — and no back and forth jogging is necessary in the unloading operation.

At incinerators, if you can back in, you can unload with a PAK-MOR — because overhead clearance is no problem.

For overall operating efficiency — on the route or at the dump — PAK-MOR's definite advantages can save you time and money.

Ask for a PAK-MOR demonstration — so you can observe these proven features in operation on your own job. There's a PAK-MOR Distributor in your area who can show you how PAK-MOR can do a better job for you.

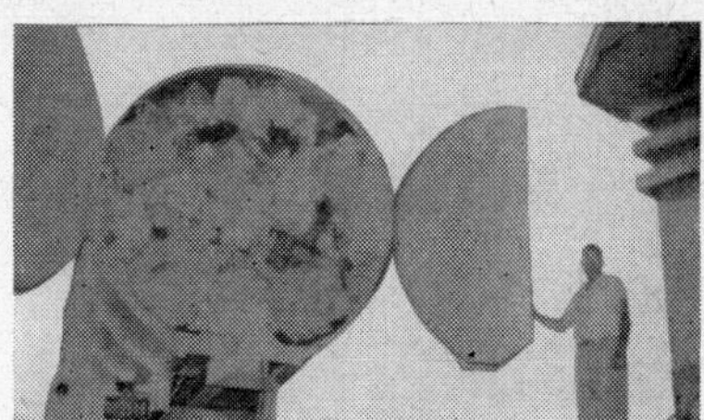

JUST BACK RIGHT IN AT INCINERATOR.

PAK-MOR UNLOADS QUICKLY AND CLEANLY.

LOOP 13 & ROOSEVELT AVE. POST OFFICE BOX 6147 WA 3-4317 SAN ANTONIO, TEXAS
EXPORT DIVISION — TIFCO INTER-AMERICA CORP. P. O. BOX 13361 HOUSTON, TEXAS

FLEXIBLE INC.

3786 Durango Ave., Los Angeles 34, Calif.

BRANCHES AT DALLAS, TEXAS AND LIMA, OHIO

Power Bucket Machine!

Another "FLEXIBLE" *Original*

10 MODELS
9 to 25 H.P.

- Automatic Bucket Dumper
- Automatic Level Wind
- Automatic Cable Tension Control
- Safety Belt Booster
- New Overnite Level Wind
- Surface-Hung Manhole Rollers

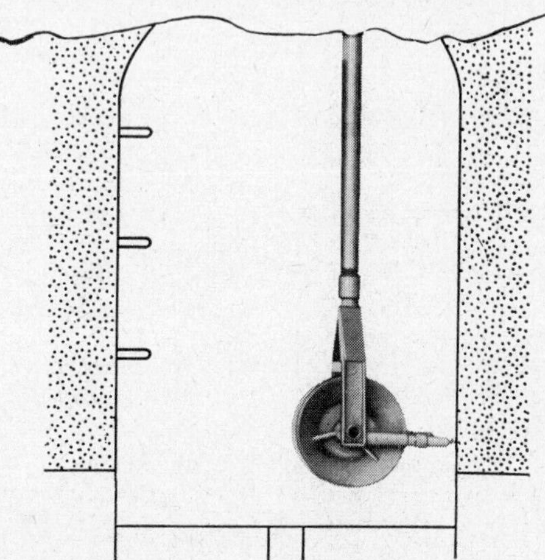

For Removal of Sand, Gravel, Grease or Heavy Roots, Only "Buckets" can do the Job!

FLEXIBLE MANUFACTURERS PIPE-CLEANING EQUIPMENT ONLY

NOW! A FULLY AUTOMATIC Sewer Rodding Machine

For Greater Cleaning Economy and Worker Safety

"FLEXIBLE"

- IT PUSHES
- IT PULLS
- IT ROTATES

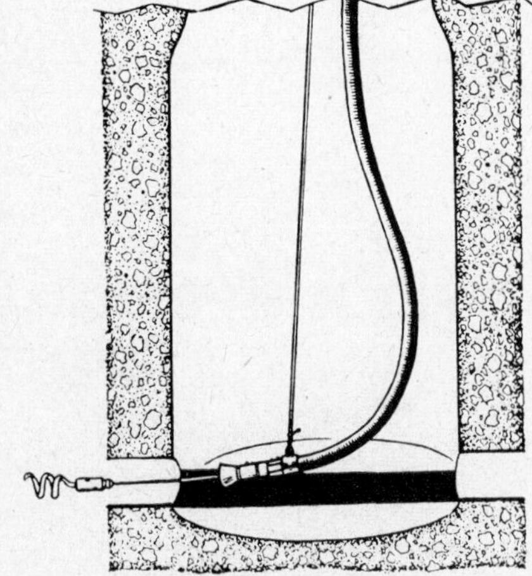

STREET LEVEL OPERATION

It Cleans from 4″ to 12″ Pipe.

It Carries up to 900 Feet of Rod.

It Rods up to 3,000 Feet Per Day.

Can Be Set at Any Angle.

One Man Operation.

Positive Dual Chain Drive.

FLEXIBLE MANUFACTURERS PIPE-CLEANING EQUIPMENT ONLY

STREET-SURFACE SEWER-CLEANING

Originated by "Flexible" 25 YEARS AGO is UNIVERSAL PRACTICE Today!

"FLEXIBLES" TOOK THE HARD WORK OUT OF CLEANING SEWERS BY ORIGINATING:

• Flexicrome Rods & Couplings • Street Surface Hand or Power Turning • Corkscrews, Augers, Porcupines • Root Saws, Hole Openers, Sand Cups, Reels, and many other tools and accessories which are now—

STANDARD CITY EQUIPMENT

The "Flexible" POWER DRIVE

5 times F-A-S-T-E-R than Hand Turning

Exclusive Advantages

- SAFETY CLUTCH CONTROL LEVER
- 4 CYCLE BRIGGS & STRATTON ENGINE
- HANDY OPEN TOOL BOX
- EASY TO PUSH AND MANEUVER
- RIGHT OR LEFT TURN

FLEXICROME RODS

(The Original Steel Sewer Rod)

A "Flexible" exclusive developed by metallurgists after years of trial and error experiments.

They Last Longer!

"FLEXIBLE" GRoovED COUPLINGS

They wear longer and couple in half the time!

It it's GRoovED it's Flexible
If it's Flexible it's GRoovED.

FLEXIBLE MANUFACTURERS PIPE-CLEANING EQUIPMENT ONLY

NOW *YOU* CAN CLEAN YOUR OWN MAINS!

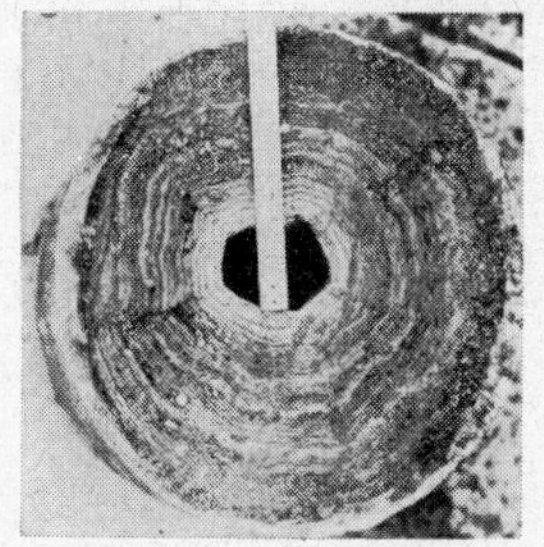

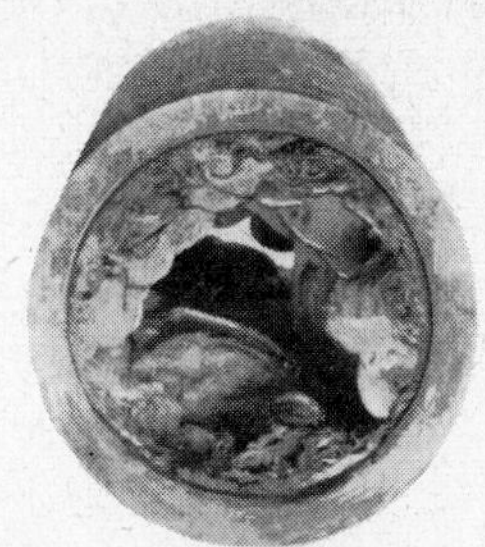

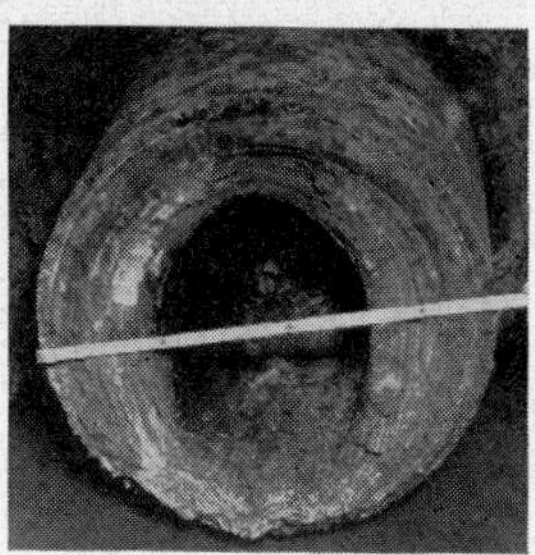

It's Easy . . . It's Fast . . . It's Economical . . . It's Sure!

FOR LONG LINES . . .
Use the **PRESSURE LINE SCRAPER**

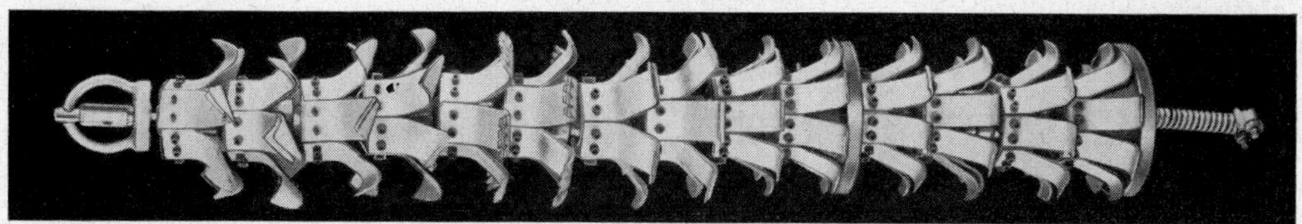

FOR SHORT LINES and HARD DEPOSITS . . .
or into the "T" . . . Use the Revolving **CHAIN HEAD AUGER**

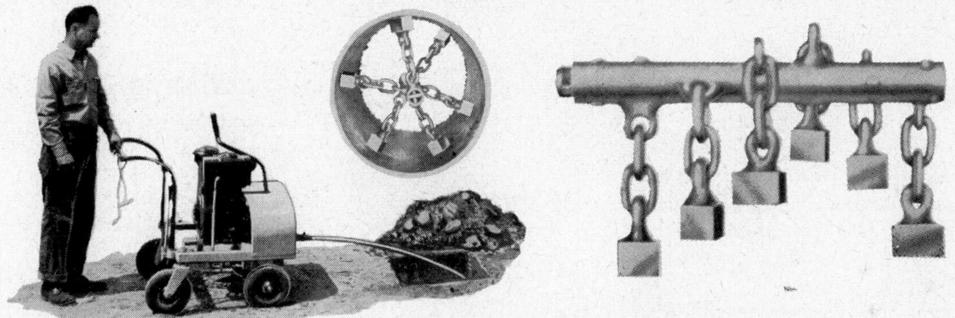

FLEXIBLE MANUFACTURERS PIPE-CLEANING EQUIPMENT ONLY

BAILEY METER COMPANY

1035 Ivanhoe Road
Cleveland 10, Ohio

BRANCHES IN 24 PRINCIPAL CITIES

PRODUCTS—ARMORTUBE Cable, Basin and Reservoir level gages, Blower control, Butterfly valve operators, Chemical feed controllers, Elevated tank level control, Filter operating panels, Incinerator and Sludge dryer controls, Loss of head gages, Main meter panels, pH Recorders, Rack differential gages, Rate controllers, Sand expansion gages, Sewage, Sludge and Subnatant flow meters, Telemetering systems, Temperature and Pressure Recorders, Vacuum filter control, Weir and Flume meters.

BAILEY FILTER OPERATING PANELS

Shown are two of the standard Bailey steel panels for rapid sand filter operation. Each panel features: inclined operating surface for optimum readability of the instruments and efficient operation of all hand control stations; sturdy, all-welded construction by use of 3/16-inch steel plate; attractive contour; any desired color; furnished complete with factory installed instruments, tubing and wiring.

BAILEY RATE CONTROLLERS

The Bailey Rate Control system is designed to meet the specific requirements of each application. It operates at peak efficiency on either filter backwash, filter effluent, or filter surface sand wash systems. This is possible since the Bailey Rate Control system can be used with Venturi tubes, flow tubes, flow nozzles or orifices plates. This standard package also provides a selection of meter differentials from 12.5 inches to 1200 inches of water.

BAILEY FLUME AND WEIR METERS

These simple self-cleaning meters indicate, record and integrate sewage or water flows. Standard packages are available for both indoor and outdoor installation.

Complete flexibility of installation can be provided by using the Bailey Telemetering system. (See BAILEY TRANSMISSION SYSTEMS).

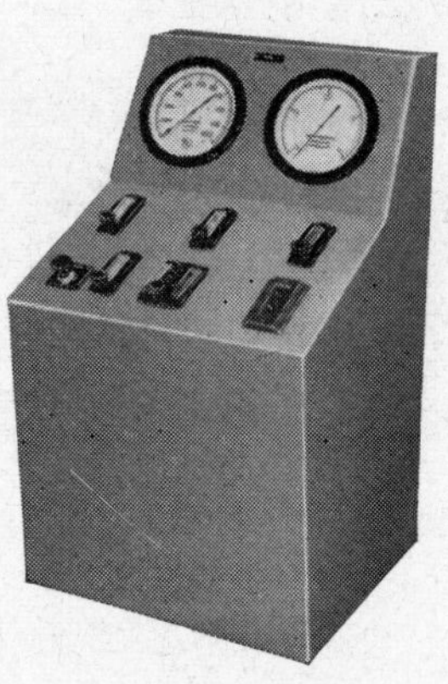

Standard Bailey Panels for Filter Operation

BAILEY TRANSMISSION SYSTEMS

Bailey Transmission systems are available for both short and long-distance telemetering and control. The short-distance systems can be either pneumatic, electrical, or a combination of both. Particular plant conditions, economics and preference will dictate the transmission medium used.

For long-distance transmission, the electrical system provides a selection of either AC or DC circuits. Up to 100 functions (metered quantities and control) can be transmitted on a single-pair telephone line.

BAILEY BOILER AND INCINERATOR CONTROLS

Standard Bailey instruments and controls are available for boilers, incinerators, flash dryers, etc. These can be furnished as package units, completely engineered. The complete system includes a Bailey panel with all instruments and controllers factory mounted, tubed and wired.

BAILEY SMOKE DENSITY RECORDER

Density of smoke from stacks is recorded on a 12-inch diameter, 24-hour chart. It tells operators when corrections are to be made for reduction of smoke and the results of those corrections.

Controls for smoke correction may be actuated by the Recorders. Signals and alarms may also be turned on.

Hydro E-Z PACK

garbage and refuse bodies

HYDRO E-Z PACK

faster refuse collection
improved sanitation
powerful compaction
handles all refuse
greater capacity
lower operating costs

Hydro E-Z PACK

HYDRO E-Z PACK DIVISION

HERCULES GALION PRODUCTS, INC. • GALION, OHIO

for efficient, sanitary and economical refuse collection,

select . . . Hydro E-Z PACK

Hydro E-Z PACKS can cut your refuse collection costs! Efficient operation, faster collections, actual load-crushing compaction, greater refuse capacity, fewer trips to the dump, lower first cost, reduced truck operating expense, lowest possible maintenance cost, fewer crew man-hours per ton of refuse handled—all these add up to a sharp reduction in over-all collection costs!

You'll find that the Hydro E-Z PACK will out-perform any other type of refuse collection body. A demonstration on your routes will convince you!

LOOK AT THESE FEATURES!

TIME-SAVING ROUTE COVERAGE — Large side loading openings permit fast, efficient loading from both sides at once. Loading area holds 40 to 50 pick-ups—packer moves refuse back out of the way between stops to eliminate lost time. Large refuse capacity means fewer trips to the dump—more time on the route.

IMPROVED SANITATION—Hydro E-Z PACK body is watertight. Effective seals and special quick-opening clamping devices on rear door prevent dripping of filthy water on streets. Liquids collect in large, easily-drained sump at front of body. Enclosed loading area prevents scattering of refuse by wind.

MAXIMUM SAFETY — Loaders work where truck driver can see them—driver controls packer from truck cab. Curbside loading in congested areas or heavy traffic keeps loaders out of the street—out of danger! Hydro E-Z PACK has no moving chains or whirling metal fingers. What's more, refuse is enclosed during compaction—there's no danger from flying glass or other shattered objects. And, the truck can't up-end while unloading —no front-end counterweights or hold-down chains are needed.

QUIET OPERATION — No continuous rattle of chains, rumble of grinding mechanism or hydraulic whine. Hydro E-Z PACKS pack only once every 40 to 50 pick-ups—pack quietly, quickly and efficiently without noisy racing of truck engine.

LOW MAINTENANCE COSTS — Simple 2-part packing mechanism operates intermittently—requires minimum maintenance. There are no continuously operating hydraulic motors and pumps to require frequent expensive repairs—no chains to break or cables to stretch. And, intermittent packing means truck engine and transmission maintenance costs are lower, too. Hydro E-Z PACK has no complicated interlocked sequencing controls requiring constant adjustment and repair.

LOW OPERATING COSTS—Fewer trips to the dump and intermittent compaction reduce fuel, oil and truck maintenance costs. Also, Hydro E-Z PACKS handle all refuse materials—eliminate costly doubling back on routes with open trucks to pick up bulky items often passed up by conventional packers. Hydro E-Z PACKS require fewer crew man-hours per ton of refuse collected.

HANDLE ANY ROUTE—Hydro E-Z PACK will take all kinds of refuse, from ashes to bulky crates and furniture—there's no need to match trucks to routes. Large loading openings permit hauling of any material the crew can load. Top loading doors also allow overhead loading, when desired. Compact design, short over-all length and versatile loading arrangements give the Hydro E-Z PACK an advantage over other units in congested areas and narrow alleys.

USE ANY DISPOSAL METHOD — Because it dumps by pushing its load out the rear, the Hydro E-Z PACK is ideal for use in incinerator buildings with low clearance and at the edge of land-fill trenches. The body does not lift to unload — there's no danger of up-ending or dumping accidents. And, true hydraulic compaction dries out the load—crushes bulky objects—increases incinerator and land-fill efficiency.

MINIMUM CAPITAL INVESTMENT—Square shape and compact design of the Hydro E-Z PACK uses all available space to best advantage—permits mounting on shorter truck. Lighter weight due to elimination of heavy complicated mechanisms decreases truck capacity requirements. Lower cost of body and truck mean lower initial cost—less depreciation.

POWERFUL DIRECT HYDRAULIC COMPACTION

. . . greater refuse capacity

. . . fast, complete unloading!

HERE'S PROOF!

A heavily-reinforced sliding packer, powered by a single multi-stage telescopic cylinder applies up to 82,500 pounds of crushing force to compact the Hydro E-Z PACK'S load into a dense mass, free of voids.

The packer plate lifts the load as it moves back, packs it tightly at the rear—then moves forward quickly, ready for another load.

Compaction pressures become progressively greater as the body fills—an exclusive feature provided only by Hydro E-Z PACK'S multi-stage cylinder.

BEFORE — The Hydro E-Z PACK handles bulky objects like this heavy steel washing machine with ease.

AFTER — Hydro E-Z PACK'S tremendous compaction forces have crushed this washing machine almost beyond recognition.

Release the tailgate, operate the packer and the Hydro E-Z PACK'S tightly packed load dumps quickly, completely, safely!

Hydro E-Z PACKS

speed collection schedules—

CUT LABOR AND TRUCK OPERATING COSTS!

In a recent direct comparison test, a 16 yd. Hydro E-Z PACK was pitted against a 16 yd. rear-loading hydraulic packer. The test was run over the same route, on succeeding weeks, using the same crews. Look at the results!

here's an example...

TEST 1—HYDRO E-Z PACK
RESIDENTIAL AREA 350 STOPS

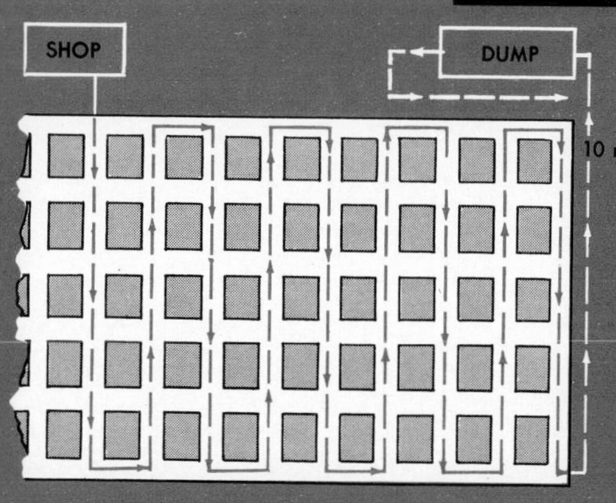

Hydro E-Z PACK started at 7:00 A.M., handled 350 pick-ups in 1 load, then made a trip to the dump to unload and was back ready to start a new route at noon!

TEST 2—OTHER PACKER
RESIDENTIAL AREA 350 STOPS

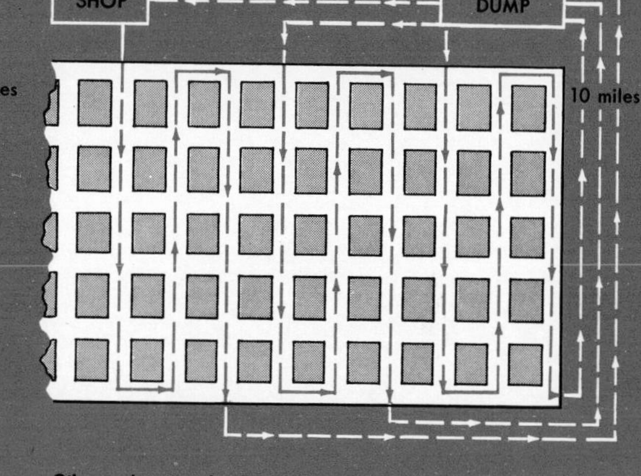

Other packer started at 7:00 A.M., handled 350 pick-ups in 3 loads, made a total of 3 trips to the dump to unload and was not finished until 4:30 P.M.—too late to start a new route.

In this actual test, the Hydro E-Z PACK . . .

- covered the same route in 4 hours less time!
- saved 40 miles of route-to-dump travel!
- cut collection time almost in half!

Can you afford to pass up savings like these?

practical . . . dependable . . .

FULL HYDRAULIC OPERATION

. . . only 2 working parts!

The Hydro E-Z PACK'S full hydraulic compaction mechanism features simplicity, dependability and powerful direct hydraulic action.

The system consists of two basic parts. A high volume roller bearing pump, driven through a transmission power take-off provides hydraulic pressure. The packer is operated by a powerful, double-acting multi-stage telescopic cylinder. Packer action is controlled by a simple 4-way spool valve designed for long life and trouble-free operation. Packer slides on special, lubricated, fully enclosed guide blocks.

All hydraulic components are time-tested and dependable . . . are readily accessible . . . can be serviced, when required, without unloading the body.

There are no complicated automatic controls, hydraulic motors, chain drives or winches—no group of several hydraulic cylinders to maintain. The Hydro E-Z PACK is easy to service. . . will be at work on your routes when you need it!

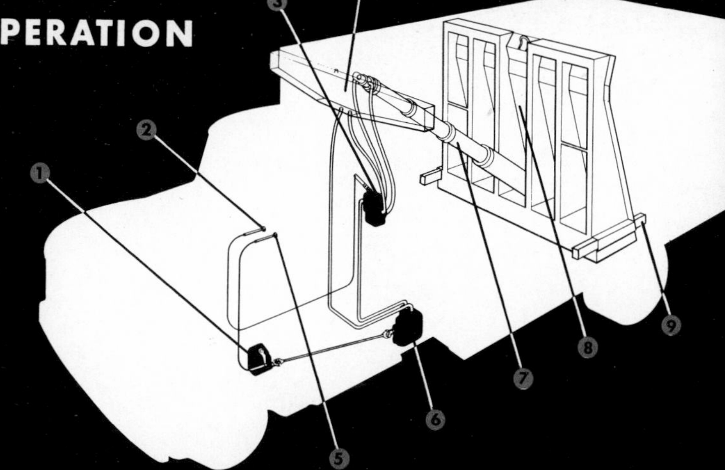

1 PTO
2 Packer control
3 Packer valve
4 Oil reservoir
5 PTO control
6 Pump
7 Multi-stage cylinder
8 Packer
9 Guide blocks

FEATURES

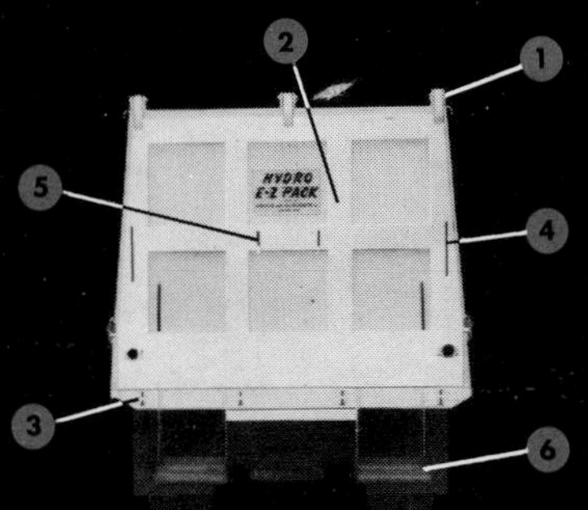

1 rugged offset fabricated hinges
2 box-frame reinforced tailgate
3 quick-opening clamps
4 grab rails
5 basket hooks
6 adjustable steps

7 signal pushbutton
8 box frame reinforced body structure
9 top loading door
10 upper loading door—swings back and locks
11 center loading door—swings back and locks

12 lower loading door—drops down
13 oil reservoir
14 grab rail
15 large capacity sump
16 sump drain
17 folding side step

CONDENSED SPECIFICATIONS

BODY LENGTH	BODY CAPACITY*	OVER-ALL LENGTH A	INSIDE WIDTH	OVER-ALL WIDTH	OVER-ALL HEIGHT B	DOOR OPENING C	OIL CAPACITY
14 ft.	16¾ cu. yd.	168 in.	80¼ in.	95½ in.	117½ in.	36 in.	33 gal.
16 ft.	20 cu. yd.	192 in.	80¼ in.	95½ in.	117½ in.	36 in.	33 gal.

BODY LENGTH	BODY LIQUID CAPACITY	CYLINDERS STAGES	CYLINDERS LENGTH	BODY WEIGHT	CHASSIS REQUIRED	CAB-TO-AXLE CA	PACKING PRESSURE†
14 ft.	830 gal.	8-7-6-5 in.	113 in.	6300 lb.	1½ to 2 ton	102 in.	82,500 lbs.
16 ft.	946 gal.	8-7-6-5-4 in.	136 in.	6600 lb.	2 ton	120 in.	82,500 lbs.

*Platen face to tailgate. †Maximum

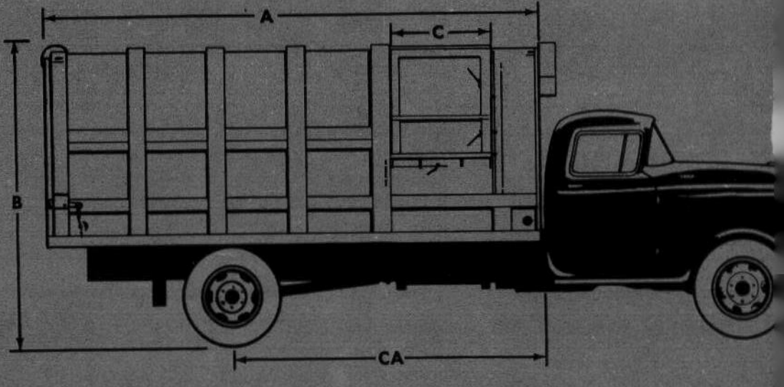

Standard Equipment

DRIVE MECHANISM — Power take-off; drive shaft, 1¼ in. with 2 heavy duty universal joints; high volume roller bearing gear-type pump; multi-stage telescopic cylinder with special chevron packers and dirt wiper seals; 4-way spool-type valve.

CONTROLS — Cab-mounted remote cable controls for power take-off and packer valve.

DOORS—2 sliding top loading doors; 2 hinged upper side loading doors open to rear and lock; 2 center side loading doors, open to rear and lock; 2 lower side loading doors, swing down; spring-loaded latches on all side doors. One-piece top-hinged tailgate; quick-opening clamps; special one-piece rubber seal across bottom and 60 in. up sides.

BODY— Floor sheets, tailgate and packer face 10 ga. hi-tensile steel; upper side sheets 12 ga. hi-tensile steel; lower side sheets 3/16 in. hi-tensile steel; all box frame bracing 10 ga. hi-tensile steel. Watertight to 14 in. above floor line.

SUMP—Forward-mounted sump; 2 lever-operated sump drains; Entire lower portion of body watertight, total capacity approximately 830 to 950 gal., depending on body length.

SILLS—Tapered sill spacers to provide liquid drainage forward into sump. Length to suit body length.

STEPS — Folding roll-over steps with "Grip-Strut" treads on both sides of body below loading openings. No springs or catches required.

REAR STEPS—2 tailgate-mounted rear steps, adjustable height, with grab handles.

LIGHTS—ICC lights, reflectors.

SIGNALS—2 push button signals at rear, 1 each side, operate truck horn to signal driver.

PAINT—Rust-resistant gray non-sanding prime coat.

Optional Equipment

LIGHTS—Turn signals, price upon application.

PAINT—High gloss white enamel finish over gray non-sanding prime coat standard. Any color combination or special paint work priced upon application.

MOUNTING—Factory mounting available.

HYDRO E-Z PACK DIVISION

HERCULES GALION PRODUCTS, INC. • GALION, OHIO

Litho in U. S. A. 6/56 LL-3509

BETHLEHEM STEEL COMPANY

GENERAL OFFICES: BETHLEHEM, PA.

SALES OFFICES:

Akron	Columbus	Milwaukee	St. Louis
Albany	Dallas	New Haven	St. Paul
Atlanta	Dayton	New Orleans	Syracuse
Baltimore	Detroit	New York	Toledo
Boston	Greensboro, N. C.	Philadelphia	Tulsa
Buffalo	Houston	Pittsburgh	Washington
Chicago	Indianapolis	Providence	Wilkes-Barre
Cincinnati	Jacksonville	Richmond	York
Cleveland	Johnstown, Pa.	Springfield, Mass.	

On the Pacific Coast Bethlehem products are sold by Bethlehem Pacific Coast Steel Corporation. *Sales Offices:* Los Angeles, Phoenix, San Francisco, Portland, Seattle, Spokane. *Export Distributor:* Bethlehem Steel Export Corporation, New York

BETHLEHEM TAR-ENAMELED SEWER PIPE

RESISTS CORROSION. Modern coal-tar enamel coatings and linings effectively resist corrosion caused by hydrogen sulphide, carbon dioxide and other sewage gases.

LEAKPROOF JOINTS. Steel pipe gives you the tightest line possible whether you use mechanical couplings or welds. And 40-ft. pipe lengths mean far fewer joints per mile.

RESILIENT. In addition to its strength, Bethlehem Steel Pipe is resilient. This characteristic enables it to "give" slightly when subjected to soil movements, impact, and surface vibrations.

ECONOMY. Bethlehem Tar-Enameled Sewer Pipe is economically installed, and once in the ground it assures you of years of excellent service. Available in 40-ft lengths and in all diameters from 18 in. ID to the largest permitted by common carriers.

We invite your inquiries. Kindly call on the Bethlehem sales office nearest you.

PAK-MOR Trailers . . .
Streamline Operations

At Large Generation
And In Concentrated Pickups

(Official Photograph U. S. Navy)

RAMP-TYPE OPERATION

PAK-MOR Trailers overcome increased handling costs encountered where separate facilities have to be used to handle refuse at large generation points.

Due to flexibility of design PAK-MOR Trailers can almost always work with present systems to effect drastically lower operating costs.

Where container systems are used with PAK-MOR, many containers travel to the dump at one time — giving faster service to each container as it is dumped on the spot (by a special hoist), or taken to a centrally located ramp area and dumped into the PAK-MOR Trailer — using same hoist trucks and no special equipment. Either way, more containers are serviced in a shorter period of time at less operational costs.

At supermarkets, community centers or at industrial sites . . . your route pickup trucks, with limited capacity, are relieved and these areas are serviced quickly and efficiently.

It will pay you to investigate the practicality of PAK-MOR Trailers in your operations. PAK-MOR Trailers can be modified to meet the requirements of your particular problem.

HOIST-TYPE OPERATION

LOOP 13 & ROOSEVELT AVE. POST OFFICE BOX 6147 WA 3-4317 SAN ANTONIO, TEXAS
EXPORT DIVISION — TIFCO INTER-AMERICA CORP P. O. BOX 13361 HOUSTON, TEXAS

Reduce Operation Costs

In Transfer And Long-Haul Operations

PAK-MOR Trailers answer the growing demands of how you can give increased service while staying within your budget's limits and how can the longer and longer haul to the dump be overcome.

By the use of a centrally located Transfer Station and PAK-MOR Trailers, tremendous savings can be realized.

Increased service can be rendered to each section of a city without having to increase the number of route pickup trucks and crews.

(Official Photograph U. S. Navy)

MANY LOADS MAKE ONE LOAD

LOOP 13 & ROOSEVELT AVE. POST OFFICE BOX 6147 WA 3-4317 SAN ANTONIO, TEXAS
EXPORT DIVISION — TIFCO INTER-AMERICA CORP. P. O. BOX 13361 HOUSTON, TEXAS

TRANSFER STATION

Route truck operational expenses will be reduced as route service is efficiently increased because of the elimination of the long haul and the costly expense for pickup crews to remain on a standby basis until trucks return from the dump. More time is spent in refuse collection by route trucks and less time is spent making long hauls.

With each PAK-MOR Trailer that is unloaded at the dump your operating costs are reduced because with PAK-MOR Trailers many route truck loads comprise one PAK-MOR Trailer load. PAK-MOR Trailers are designed to make economic refuse handling a standard practice! Write for further details.

THE HEIL CO.

DEPT. 4557
3045 W. MONTANA ST., MILWAUKEE 1, WIS.
Factories: Milwaukee, Wis.—Hillside, N. J.—Lancaster, Pa
Heil Sales Offices: New York, Lancaster, Pa., Union, N. J., Atlanta, Cleveland, Milwaukee, Chicago, Kansas City, Denver, Dallas, Los Angeles, Seattle

HEIL BODIES AND HOISTS...

HEIL BODIES

A wide variety of sizes and types fit any truck, cut costs on dozens of different jobs. All Heil Bodies have these important money-saving features: *Light-weight* design to permit hauling greater pay load, save gas and tires by making fewer trips—*Easy installation* because Heil dump units are mounted above the frame. They fit any truck chassis regardless of tire size. *Long service life* with "no-sag" construction. Subframe cross members and long members are interlocked and welded into a single assembly, which is welded integrally with the body for extra strength under load.

HEIL HYDRAULIC HOISTS

From the light-weight but rugged Heil Telescopic Hoist to the Model 2426 Light Duty Twin Arm Hoist, there's a Heil Hoist assembly to meet every dumping need and save money. Trouble-free operation assures faster dumping, shorter cycle time. On the twin arm hoist, the simple toggle principle of the linkage eliminates troublesome parts to reduce maintenance. Arm assembly is made of heavy structural steel welded to extra heavy reinforced tubing for the strength necessary to raise and hold loads dependably. Hoist frame takes all stresses imposed by action of the hoist without transferring any stress to the truck frame. Long-lasting hydraulic Perma-Pump hardened gears operate between wear plates which can be reversed when worn or easily replaced.

HEILOADER ELEVATING TAILGATES

Two models permit loading and unloading of heavy, bulky articles weighing up to 2 tons! Both platform and ramp-type styles are available in 2000-lb. and 4000-lb. capacity models to meet every weight and size requirement. Can be mounted on any truck, including trailers and semi-trailers. With the Heiloader, one man replaces two or three for loading and unloading heavy articles, and gets the job done in less than half the time. The smooth, effortless power of the single hydraulic cylinder does all the work . . . lowering and raising the platform . . . automatically opening and closing it as a tailgate. Savings in time and labor alone will pay for your Heiloaders in a short time.

DEPT. 4557
3045 W. MONTANA ST., MILWAUKEE 1, WIS.
Factories: Milwaukee, Wis.—Hillside, N. J.—Lancaster, Pa.
Heil Sales Offices: New York, Lancaster, Pa., Union, N. J., Atlanta, Cleveland, Milwaukee, Chicago, Kansas City, Denver, Dallas, Los Angeles, Seattle

THE ALL-NEW COLECTOMATIC

Here is the simplest, safest and easiest-to-operate-and-service collection unit you ever saw! The new Heil Colectomatic is unexcelled for the simplified design that reduces maintenance costs, for the easy service accessibility that saves time and money, for the big capacity that cuts down on the number of trips to the dump. Its quiet operation, odor-free collection, safety features for personnel, and neat, trim appearance are some of the other plus features that make the Heil Colectomatic the "most wanted" enclosed refuse unit on the market.

THE FIRST SANITARY REFUSE COLLECTION UNIT EVER DESIGNED BY YOU . . . THE USER

Here is a garbage and refuse collection unit which *YOU*, Mr. User, created! In a two-year survey conducted among city sanitation employees, supervisors, inspectors and private operators, we asked *"If you could design a new refuse collection unit, what improvements would you make over your present equipment?"*

The answers and suggestions you gave us have been built into the new Heil Colectomatic to make this truly the design that will do more for *you*, based on *your* experience and job requirements!

MORE COLECTOMATIC FEATURES THAT SPEED THE JOB . . . CUT COSTS

- Short overall length and low height for greater maneuverability.
- Completely sealed body keeps garbage and liquids out of sight and smell.
- Balanced weight distribution. More tailgate weight rests on truck longitudinals.
- Low, wide loading sill for faster, more comfortable loading. Plenty of elbow room for two men to load the hopper at the same time.
- Push buttons at rear to signal driver when pick-up is completed.
- Fits any standard truck chassis, cab-over-engine or conventional models.

Refuse and Garbage Collection Units...

GREATER SERVICE ACCESSIBILITY . . . LOWER MAINTENANCE

Simply open the sectional panels on either side of the tailgate and the entire packing mechanism is there before you, within easy reach from a standing position! The 4-way single-spool valve controlling the packing jacks is mounted on the underbody hoist frame for greater accessibility. Simplified design of the entire operating mechanism cuts down the number of component parts to maintain. There are *only three hydraulic jacks* for loading, packing and dumping. "Bulldozer" type packing plate eliminates the need for troublesome retainer plates. There is no continuous operation to cause unproductive wear of the loading mechanism. Colectomatics need load and pack only when the hopper is full . . . usually after three or four pick-ups are made.

ALL-AUTOMATIC PACKING

A flick of one lever starts the automatic "bulldozer" packing cycle . . . closes the safety door, "dozes" the load out of the hopper and packs it into the body, retains it there, then opens the safety door for the next load, all in an average time of 22 seconds! Only one single-spool 4-way valve is used to actuate the packing mechanism as well as raise and lower the tailgate.

Jamming of the packing mechanism is a remote possibility because the Colectomatic has no chains or retainer plate to catch or wedge material. However, if anything should stick between hopper and packer plate, it can be quickly and easily removed. Just trip a small lever to drop the hinged hopper away from the packing plate, then another touch of the operating lever resumes the packing cycle.

BIG CAPACITY SMART APPEARANCE

Big capacity in a refuse collection unit is a must to save gas, tires and time with fewer trips to the dump. The interior of the Colectomatic is completely unobstructed to hold more. Body floor is flat . . . there are no wheel housings or ramps to take up space or obstruct the free flow of material into the front of the body. The "bulldozing" action of the packer plate exerts tremendous compaction pressure against the material to compress more pounds into each cubic yard.

The Colectomatic's attractive appearance and trim body lines have definite eye appeal and advertise your modern sanitation methods to citizens and visitors alike.

STOPPAGE CONTROL SAVES TIME, PREVENTS DAMAGE

In all mechanical packing-type units stoppages frequently occur when refuse wedges between the packer plate or chain flights and the hopper. Refuse rarely sticks in the COLECTOMATIC because of its clean design. However, should this situation occur, the hinged hopper can be released to drop away from the packing plate, freeing the jammed refuse. A touch of the operating lever again starts the packing cycle. No cost-consuming time is wasted eliminating jams.

THREE CONVENIENT SIZES AVAILABLE

The same excellent operating features are found in all three—the 13-cu-yd, the 16-cu-yd and the 20-cu-yd COLECTOMATIC. Get the complete story by writing:

Dept. 4557, THE HEIL CO., Milwaukee 1, Wisconsin

HYDE CORPORATION

Truck Trailer and Body Manufacturers

Factory
CLEBURNE, TEXAS

General Offices
FORT WORTH, TEXAS

HYDEPAK REFUSE COLLECTION BODY

HYDEPAK is the simplest, most economical refuse collection body to operate.

SIMPLICITY of operation is made possible through automatic, push-button controls on *each side* of the loading chamber, which start, stop or reverse the packing cycle.

CAPACITY of HydePak is *equal* to higher priced packers of the same cubic yardage—and *above* those packers in the same price range. *High Compaction* allows HydePak to carry the most weight per cubic yard of capacity, making fewer trips to the dump yard necessary.

OPERATION facilities of HydePak allow quickest loading with more work time saved. Front loading, easily reached from both sides of the body, saves on manpower and is large enough to handle any type of refuse. *Rear Unloading* deposits the load into a highly compressed pile or directly into a sanitary fill or incinerator hopper.

MAINTENANCE of HydePak is lowest because there are fewer working parts in the automatic hydraulic system and the fact that most HydePak parts are standard automotive items, easily replaceable anywhere. As rugged as HydePak is—construction is of lightweight materials, allowing for greater gas and oil savings. Also, smaller, popular priced trucks may be used.

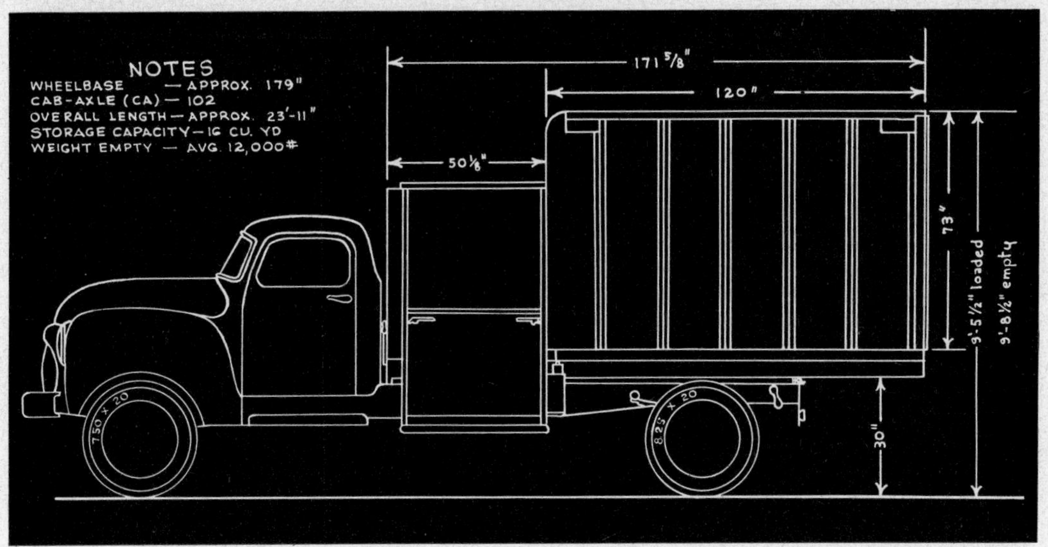

1957 HYDEPAK SPECIFICATIONS

	Model 1316 13 Yds. (16 Yds. Including Loading Space)	*Model 1619 16 Yds. (19 Yds. Including Loading Space)*	*Model 2023 20 Yds. (23 Yds. Including Loading Space)*	*Model 2427 24 Yds. (27 Yds. Including Loading Space)*
Weight	6000 lbs.	6600 lbs.	7100 lbs.	7600
Length of Body	14'2"	14'2"	16'2"	18'2"
Width of Body	7'11"	7'11"	7'11"	7'11"
Required CA Dimension	102"	102"	120"	138"
Dumping Angle	39 degrees	39 degrees	39 degrees	39 degrees
Taper of Body	2"	2"	2"	2"
Loading Compartment	41½x72x49½	41½x72x49½	41½x72x49½	41½x72x49½
Loading Comp. Capacity	3 cu.yds.	3 cu.yds.	3 cu.yds.	3 cu.yds.
Loading Ht. Above Frame	25"	25"	25"	25"
Top of Frame to Top of Body	71"	81"	81"	81"
Packing Cylinder Diameter	6¼"	6¼"	6¼"	6¼"
Packing Cylinder Stroke	48"	48"	48"	48"
Total Compression Force	36,216	36,216	36,216	36,216
Packing Ram Area	25.4 sq.ft.	25.4 sq.ft.	25.4 Sq.Ft.	25.4 Sq.Ft.
Hoisting Cylinder Diam.	4½" (2)	4½" (2)	4½" (2)	4½" (2)
Hoisting Cylinder Stroke	26"	26"	26"	26"

RECOMMENDED TRUCK REQUIREMENTS

Chassis Type	Std. or Cab Fwd.	Std. or Cab Fwd.	Std. or Cab Fwd.	Std. or Cab Fwd.
Chassis Size	2 ton Std.	2 ton Hvy Duty	2½ to 3 ton	3 ton
G.V.W. Min.	16,000	18,000	21,000	25,000
Approx. Wheel Base	172"	172"	196"	214"
Required CA (minimum)	102"	102"	120"-126"	138"

HYDE CORPORATION

Truck Trailer and Body Manufacturers

Factory
CLEBURNE, TEXAS

General Offices
FORT WORTH, TEXAS

HYDEPAK Rated 'Best' by Users

The men who know, sanitary engineers, city managers and refuse collection companies, rate HydePak tops in its field.

The proof is in their letters to the Hyde Corporation—and in their re-orders of additional HydePak units.

These are just a few excerpts from unsolicited letters addressed to the Hyde Corporation and are on file at the Fort Worth office. (Names on request.)

". . . We wish to state that they (HydePak bodies) have performed far beyond our expectations."

". . . We have the route built up now to where we need to trade it (another mechanical packer) for a HydePak to handle the increased business."

". . . We are only using six men now on our entire operation in River Oaks (with our HydePaks) and very little overtime."

". . . Operating expense has been so low on our HydePaks compared with other types of bodies we were using. Gas and oil consumption is about 15% under the mechanical bodies of the same age and capacity."

". . . Confirming our conversation, we are today forwarding our order to you for our second HydePak Refuse Packer, Model #1619."

". . . When we took delivery of our first HydePak in April, we let one man go, and still packed up Monday and Tuesday's route on Monday, the first day we operated the truck."

". . . Our mechanic likes the simplicity of your packer and the fact it has so few working parts and so little maintenance."

". . . You may use our city as a reference if you care to. We have operated other kinds of packers and believe we know what we are talking about when we say that your packer is the finest piece of equipment this city has ever purchased."

COMPETITIVE TESTS PROVE HYDEPAK'S SUPERIOR OPERATION

These unsolicited testimonials offer further proof, then, that in city after city, in competitive tests, tests, HydePak makes *more* pick-ups *faster*—while original cost is *lowest*. And with HIGH COMPACTION, it can carry the most weight per cubic yard of capacity, allowing for fewer trips to the dump yard.

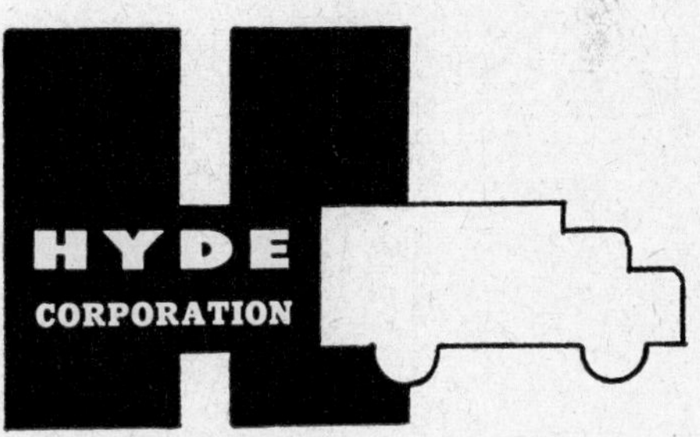

It will pay *you* to check on the HydePak . . . available in 13 yd., 16 yd., 20 yd., and 24 yd. capacities. Low in price . . . in quality and service . . . and in capacities . . . HydePak has never been surpassed!

BLACKBURN-SMITH MFG. CO.

65 Garden Street, Hoboken, N. J.

Telephone: OLdfield 9-4425 N. Y. Telephone: BArclay 7-0600

BLACKBURN-SMITH

PNEUMATIC SEWAGE EJECTORS

The Modern, Efficient Way to Lift Sewage

30 to 500 gpm single and twin units for discharge heads up to 150 ft.

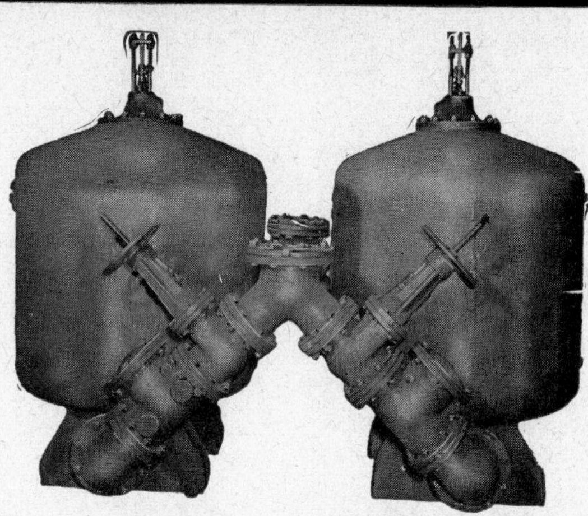

Duplex Sewage Ejector, showing inlet piping.

Blackburn-Smith Pneumatic Sewage Ejectors have ended screen and pump cleaning in hundreds of sewage booster stations. For over 60 years, Blackburn-Smith Ejectors have proved their economy, efficiency, and reliability under all conditions.

Blackburn-Smith Ejectors are preferred by engineers because

- ★ **They are more sanitary, less messy than other types of ejectors or pumps.**
- ★ **No complicated piping.**
- ★ **No place for collection of solids within pots.**
- ★ **No worry over operation in water with all-pneumatic system.**

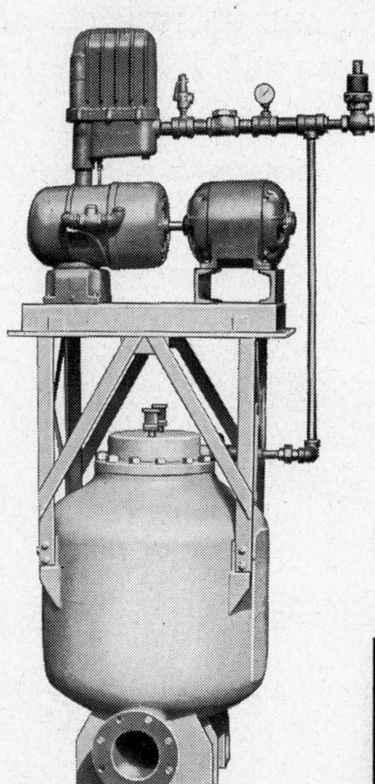

Compact ejector system having motor compressor assembly and all controls in one "packaged" unit.

Exclusive Blackburn-Smith Features

Only the Blackburn-Smith Pneumatic Ejector System, with or without air receivers, offers the following choice of controls:

1—Float and electric float switch;
2—Float and pneumatically controlled snap-action valve;
3—Electrode controls.

Catalog S-50 gives full details.
Send for it now.

INGERSOLL KALAMAZOO DIVISION

BORG-WARNER CORPORATION

1808 N. Pitcher St. Kalamazoo, Michigan

SAVES DOLLARS...MAKES SENSE

in handling rubbish and garbage

Reduces collection costs...

A single Load Lugger equipped truck easily serves dozens of Load Lugger containers spotted at strategic points in city commercial and industrial areas—does the work of several conventional trucks —saves man-power—reduces equipment investment and maintenance. Versatility—the ability to efficiently perform work in addition to refuse collection and disposal—are *plus* benefits you get with The LOAD LUGGER System.

The LOAD LUGGER System ➡

Keeps your city's "back yard" premises neat, clean and sanitary —as this typical example shows . . .

Refuse stored in cardboard cartons is an ever-present fire hazard and presents an untidy appearance.

before LOAD LUGGER

Refuse litters alleys and areaways, blows about, invites rats and flies, takes up needed parking space, obstructs alley traffic.

Load Lugger containers minimize fire and health hazards, promote pride in community cleanliness.

after LOAD LUGGER

No litter, no rats, no flies, no odor. Alleys are clean and unobstructed. A single Load Lugger container serves several establishments is easy to charge and conserves space.

The LOAD LUGGER System . . .

At sewage treatment plants Load Lugger simplifies removal of grit.

Load Lugger picks up full container, leaves empties to be filled. Containers are mounted on dollies and moved on rails to and from hoppers.

Load Lugger containers placed under grit chamber hoppers receive the grit as it is raked from the bottom of the chamber. The necessity for leaving a truck standing under the hopper is eliminated. In addition, the Load Lugger equipped truck is free to perform other work.

For park maintenance and street repair work, Load Lugger's unique versatility comes in handy.

Only Load Lugger has an unobstructed flat deck which can be used to transport equipment and materials. Sand, gravel, wet concrete, broken pavement etc. can be handled in Load Lugger containers. One Load Lugger equipped truck can serve several widely scattered jobs.

Load Lugger can be used as a flat-bed truck as the need arises.

Exposed garbage attracts flies and rats, causes obnoxious odors, creates a highly unsanitary condition.

Unsightly refuse takes up valuable space, creates a fire hazard and is inaccessible for easy removal.

Load Lugger container replaces unsightly garbage cans and old oil drums. Wet garbage can't leak out.

Load Lugger container keeps area clean and free of litter, provides additional parking space.

efficient ... economical ... versatile ...

Load Lugger about to pull full container from beneath hopper after which empties will be positioned for filling.

Container load of grit is dumped into road fill area. Load Lugger containers are leak-proof and dump clean.

Load Lugger takes away container full of broken pavement, leaves an empty to be filled by street crew.

Reprocessed paving materials drop from crusher direct to Load Lugger containers. Re-handling is eliminated.

Use these LOAD LUGGER FEATURES as your standard of Comparison

SIMPLE, RUGGED DESIGN

Only two double-acting cylinders, a hydraulic pump and a hydraulic valve do the whole job. There's no complicated mechanism to lubricate or keep aligned. Fewer parts mean less deadweight, lower operating cost, minimum maintenance.

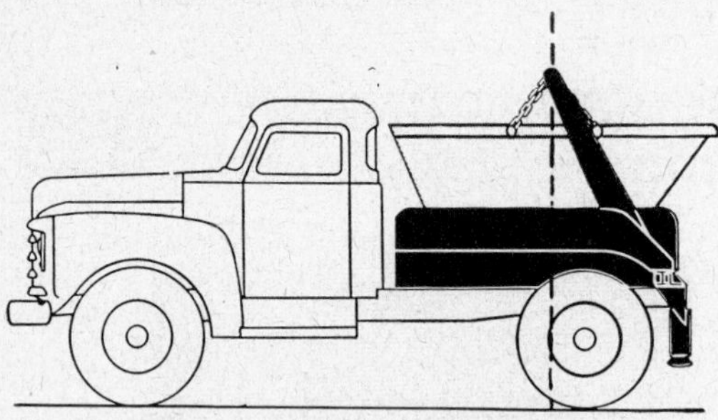

ENGINEERED WEIGHT DISTRIBUTION

Center of gravity of container load is carried *forward of truck's rear axle.* The result is good roadability, easier driving, longer tire life, less wear and tear on differential and rear axles.

SAFE OPERATION

Hoist mechanism has two *double-acting* cylinders. Should truck engine fail, hoist arms and container will not drop. *Four-point* suspension of container and location of chain lugs *above* container's center of gravity keep it in constant *safe* balance.

PATENTED FULLY-ENCLOSED LEAK-PROOF STEEL CONTAINERS

Have tight-fitting, rubber-sealed doors, are verminproof, fly-proof and prevent odors. *Only Load Lugger containers can be charged from waist-high level.* Load Lugger containers are the tilt-type and dump easily and cleanly.

MAXIMUM EFFICIENCY

Load Lugger's simple design and engineered weight distribution permit the use of a smaller, lower cost, shorter wheelbase truck chassis and smaller, less expensive tires than other equipment of comparable load-carrying capacity.

WIDE RANGE OF SIZES

Eleven Load Lugger models, capacities 4500 to 18,000 pounds and four enclosed, sealed-door containers provide a choice to suit your particular needs. Load Lugger's engineers and refuse disposal experts will be glad to survey your community and recommend the Load Lugger equipment which will do the job most efficiently and economically.

Ingersoll KALAMAZOO DIV.
BORG-WARNER CORPORATION
1957 North Pitcher Street, Kalamazoo, Michigan
Telephone Fireside 5-3501
EXPORT SALES: BORG-WARNER INTERNATIONAL CORP., CHICAGO

CARBORUNDUM

Registered Trade Mark

Dept. M157, Refractories Division, Perth Amboy, N. J.

SOLVE WATER FILTRATION, SEWAGE TREATMENT AND INCINERATOR PROBLEMS!

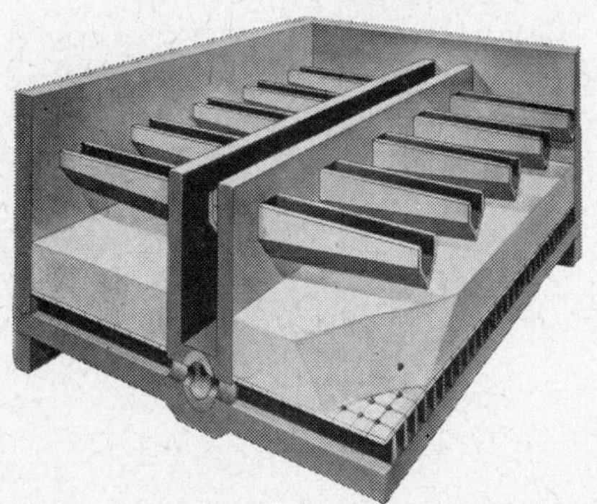

FOR WATER FILTRATION—ALOXITE® aluminum oxide porous filter bottoms are usually rated as the "lowest installed cost" system. ALOXITE bottoms are also more efficient and cheaper to maintain than a graded gravel system. That's because with an ALOXITE bottom, only one filter medium is required—there's no gravel . . . no upset beds . . . no cost of rebuilding.

FOR INCINERATOR PROBLEMS—SUPER REFRACTORIES BY CARBORUNDUM on stoking doors, sidewalls and charging holes resist mechanical wear better, show less cracking, and do not cut away. Because they last longer, repairs are rare and you have much less downtime.

FOR SEWAGE TREATMENT—ALOXITE aluminum oxide plates and tubes provide uniform diffusion of *small* bubbles because they are a porous ceramic material. They are chemically inert, strong and rugged—and for all forms of sewage aeration, more ALOXITE plates and tubes have been used than any other make.

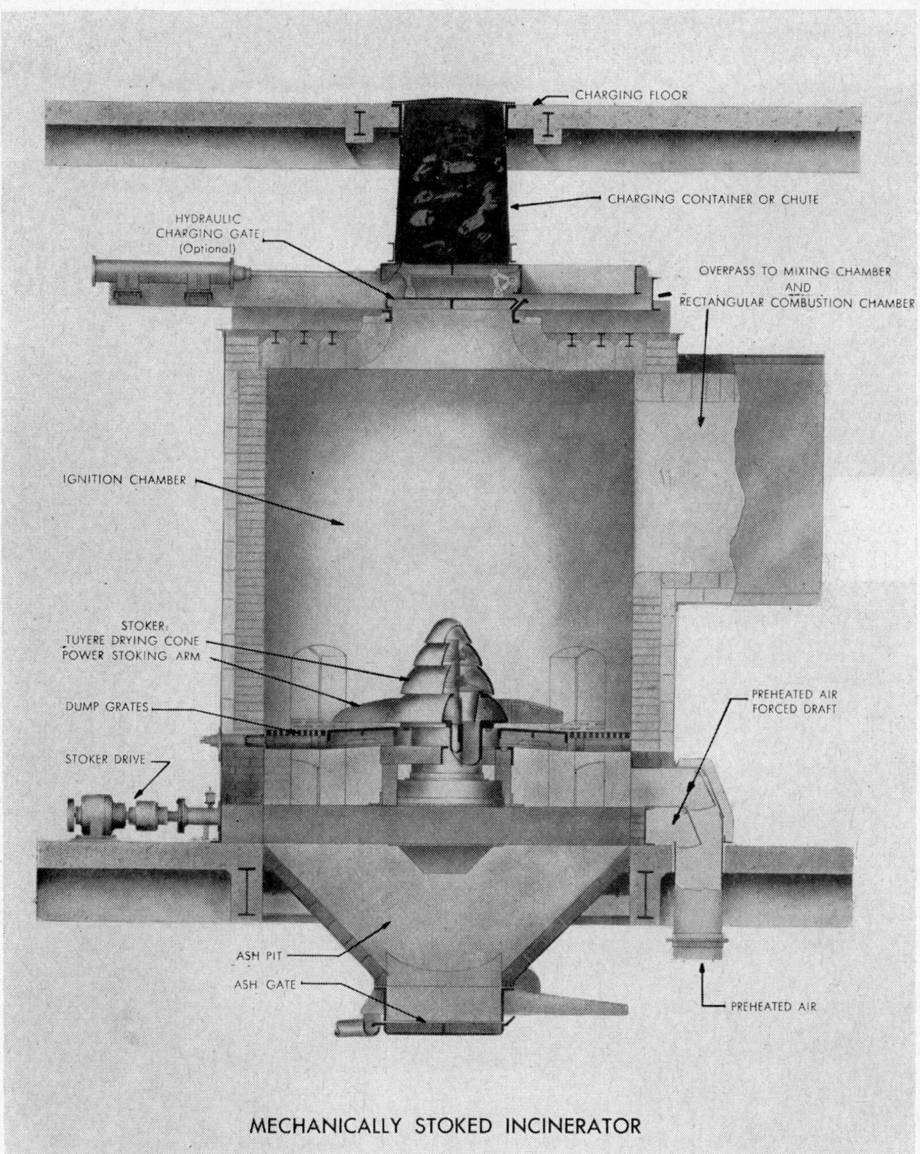

Morse Boulger Mechanically stoked incinerator, the Morbostoker Unit for handling garbage and rubbish.

MORSE BOULGER MORBOSTOKER UNIT

The circular mechanically stoked incinerator, here exemplified in the extremely rugged Morbostoker is the most modern of incinerators. The Morbostoker performs excellently in many communities all over the U.S. These communities range in population upwards from 12,000. Morbostoker performance is a guide post of the incinerator industry.

Morse Boulger Multiple Hearth Furnace for dehydration on incineration of sewage sludge and industrial wastes.

MORSE BOULGER MULTIPLE HEARTH FURNACE

The multiple hearth furnace has been well known for many years in the metallurgical and other industrial fields. In the past 20 years this has become the standard sewage sludge incinerator and drier. Multiple hearth furnaces can be built in sizes suitable for any community. Our company will be glad to discuss waste disposal problems of any kind whether they involve combinations of city refuse, sewage sludge and industrial waste, or any one alone.

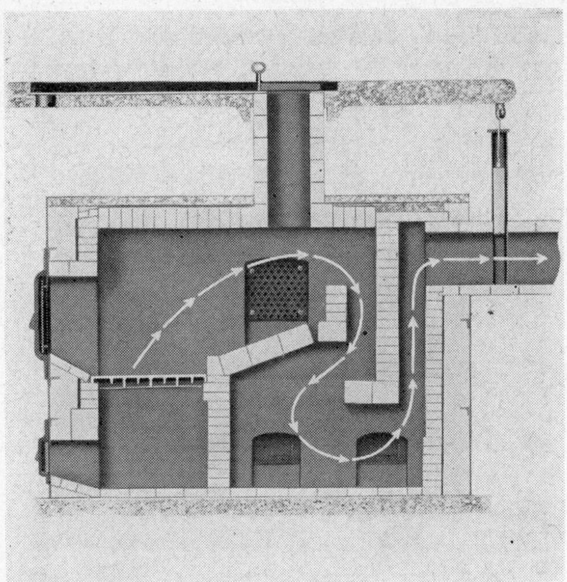

Type A Incinerator; suitable for wide variation in wet-dry combinations.

TYPE A INCINERATOR

While the "A" type unit is designed primarily as an industrial incinerator, it has found its place in municipal incineration in small communities where the use of mechanically stoked incinerators would be impractical and uneconomical. Units of this type ably serve small communities incinerating today's refuse with their widely varying wet-dry combination.

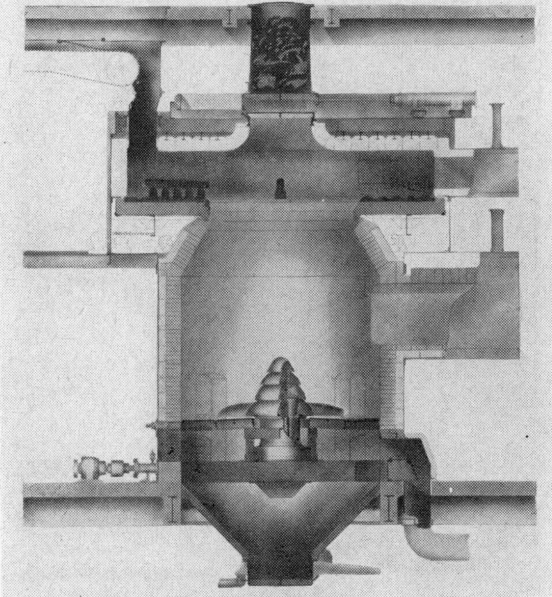

Morse Boulger combination single hearth sludge drier and Morbo-stoker mechanically stoked incinerator for handling both the refuse and dried sludge.

COMBINATION SINGLE HEARTH DRIER AND MECHANICALLY STOKED INCINERATOR

The Morse Boulger Combination Sludge-Refuse Incinerator is ideal for the smaller community which has to dispose of both sewage sludge and municipal refuse.

This unit consists of a mechanically stoked refuse incinerator combined with a top rotation sludge drying hearth. Rabble arms move the dried sludge off the hearth and discharge it into the refuse unit where it is burned with the refuse. A single combustion chamber serves both the drying hearth and the burning chamber. This unique Morse Boulger design results in a compact plant that is economical in first cost as well as in operation.

STEWART SEWER MACHINES & RODS

202 Kratz Ave. **W. H. STEWART, INC.** Syracuse 8, N. Y.

sectional steel rod kits

Here is a practical, compact emergency kit for opening stoppages and removing roots

1 Rod Guide
1 Rod Guide Holder
1 Turning Handle
1 Ratchet Handle
1 Pickup Tool
1 2″ Cork Screw, Round Stock
1 Cork Screw 4″ Sq. Stock
1 Cork Screw 6″ Sq. Stock
1 Cork Screw 8″ Sq. Stock
105 (315 Feet) 3 ft. Screw Rods
1 Rod Reel Holding Frame
1 Rod Reel Stand

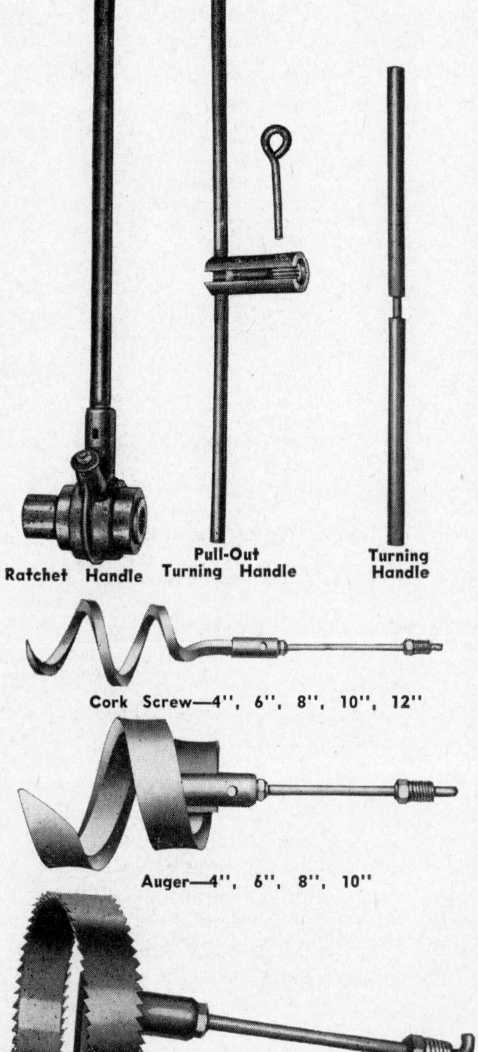

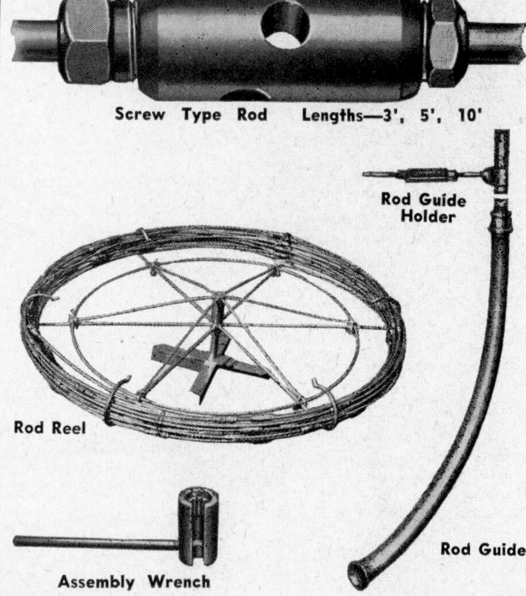

- Clutch and Throttle Controls Within Easy Reach of Operator
- 2 or 3 H.P. Briggs and Stratton or Lauson Engines
- Recoil Starters
- Enclosed 6-1 Reduction Unit
- Three Wheel Mounting
- Sturdy Frames
- Two Way Rotation
- Chuck for Attaching Rods

STEWART SEWER MACHINES & RODS

202 Kratz Ave. **W. H. STEWART, INC.** Syracuse 8, N. Y.

one unit does the work of two

ONE UNIT DOES ALL THE WORK

One man controls the forward and backward pull of buckets or cutters.

Equipped with a safety automatic clutch—to safeguard equipment in case of an overload.

This single unit, double drum machine operates entirely over one opening—no hand signaling—no confusion.

Two set ups are shown—one with return cable on the street—the second with the return cable in the line.

9 HP 13 HP 21 HP
AIR COOLED ENGINES

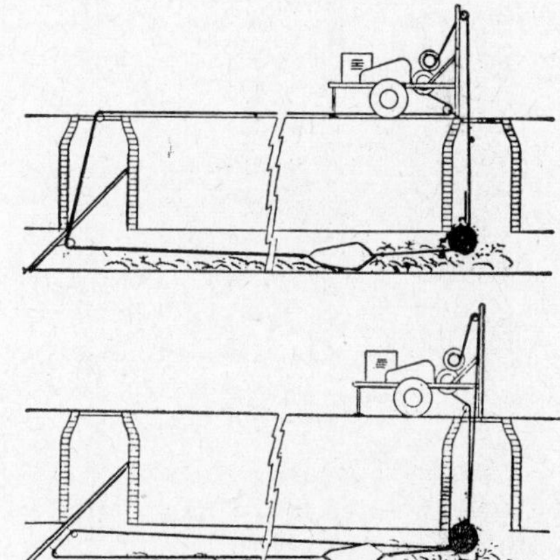

2, 3 and 4-Wheel Suspensions

---

multiple unit machines

9 HP 13 HP 21 HP
AIR COOLED ENGINES
2, 3 and 4-Wheel Suspensions

sewer drag tools

stewart root cutter—#9

Constructed with five double cutting edges on top and five double cutting edges on the bottom. The lower knives are rigid, the top knives are controlled by spring tension. 4″ to 15″.

stewart welded root cutter—#9X

Another type for easier, more efficient cutting. Diagonal strips are welded onto oval shape frame. End attachments for pulling forward and backwards.

stewart welded root cutter—#9A

Five cutting edges scarifies and cuts roots or deposits from inner diameter of pipe. A powerful, rigidly constructed tool, with or without sand damper. 4″ to 24″.

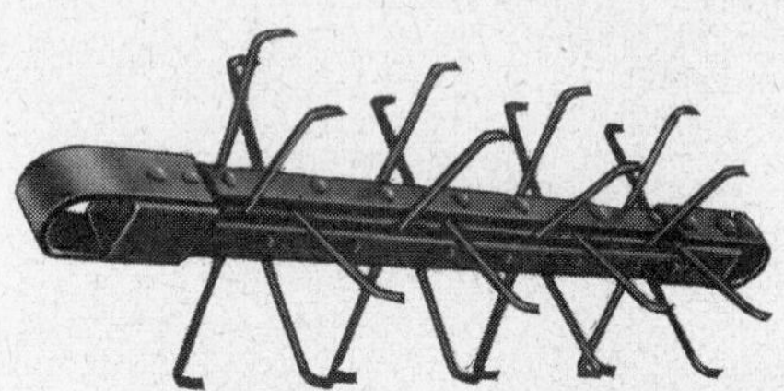

porcupine scraper

Constructed with spring steel cutting teeth. The spring tension is great enough to create a tremendous digging power. 6″ to 48″.

guard cage bucket

The Guard Cage prevents injury to uneven joints and also prevents the bucket from hanging. 6″ to 36″.

clam shell bucket

Cuts through obstruction with ease due to clam shell construction that forms a sharp cutting edge. 6″ to 24″ and larger.

stewart wood sectional sewer rods

No. 10 Jumbo Sewer Rod
1½" x 1⅜" Octagon
LENGTHS—2', 2½', 3', 3½' and 4'

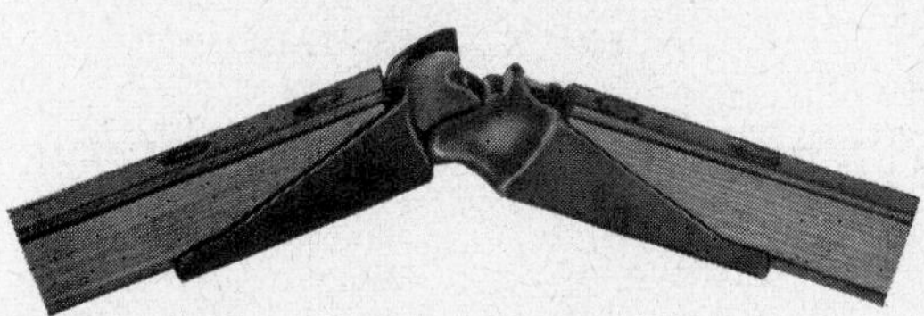

No. 1 Sewer and Conduit Rod
1⅛" x ⅞" Square
LENGTHS—2', 2½', 3', 3½' and 4'

No. 5 Round
Two diameter sizes, ⅞" and 1⅛"
LENGTHS—2', 2½', 3', 3½' and 4'

hand operated windlasses regular and multiplied power

stewart safety frame

Reels and Unreels Steel Snakes

Constructed to hold ½", ¾" and 1¼" tapes. One man operation—SAFE, PRACTICAL and FAST—equipped with or without tapes.

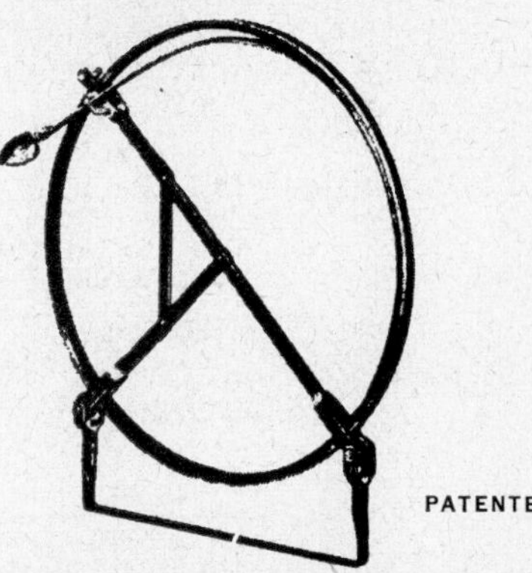

PATENTED

self-propelling nozzles

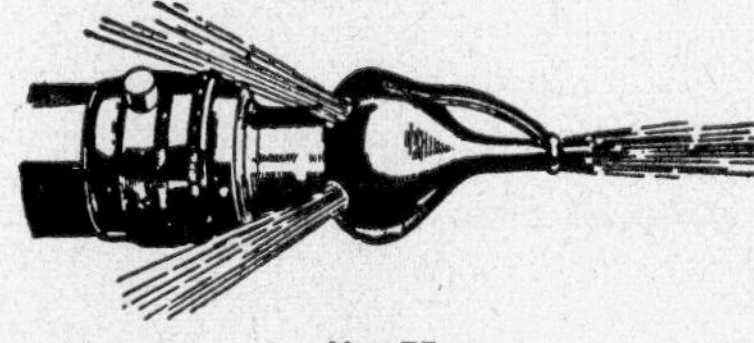

No. 77

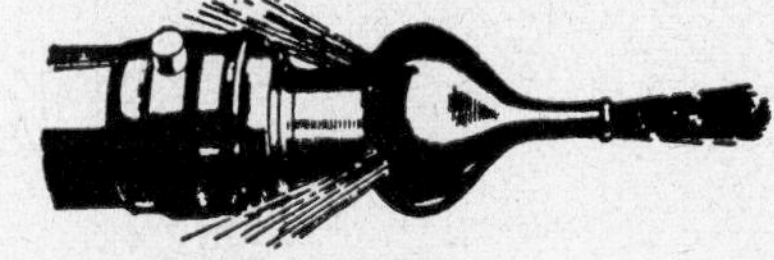

No. 7

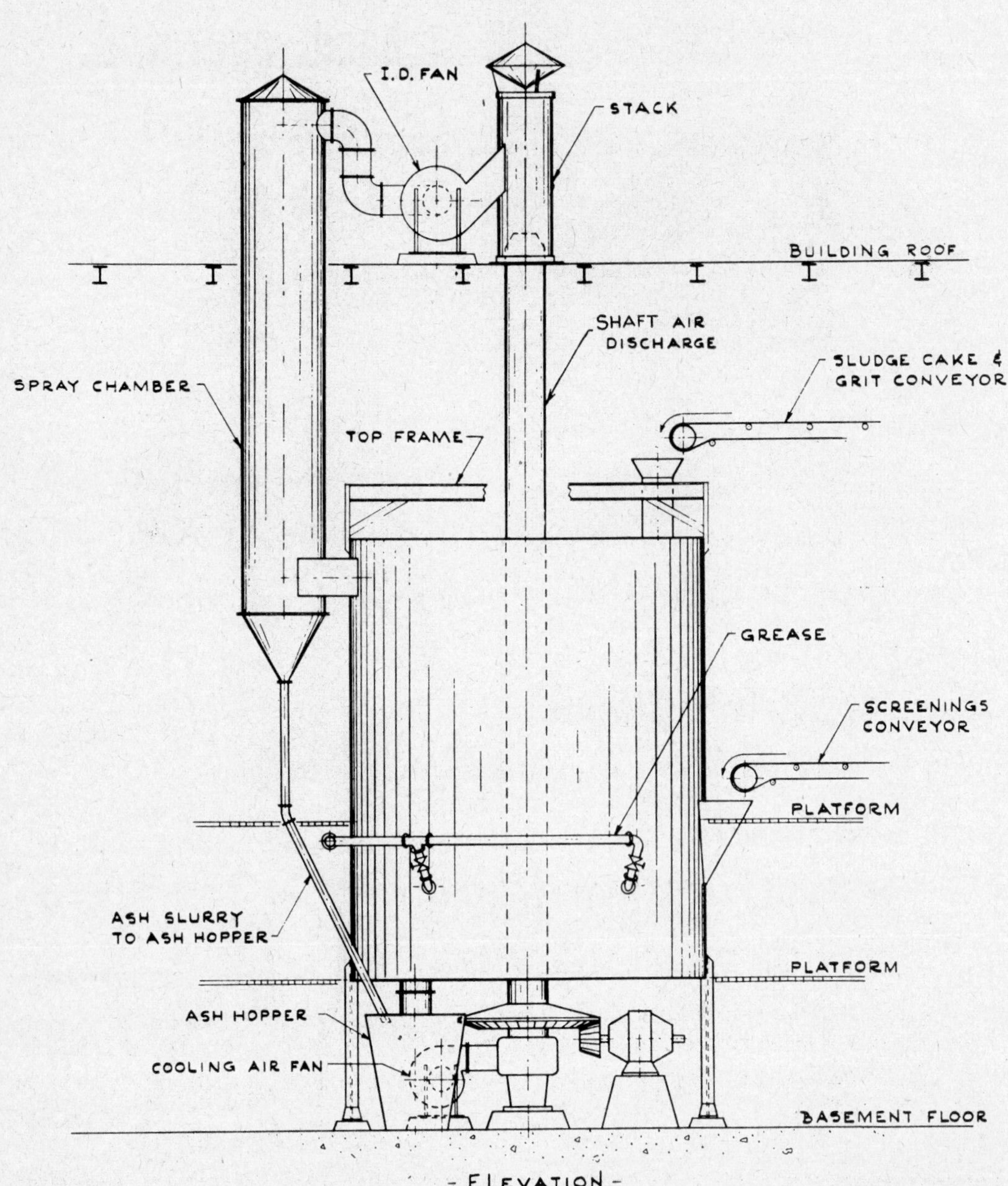

- ELEVATION -

NICHOLS HERRESHOFF MULTIPLE HEARTH
SLUDGE, GRIT, SCREENINGS & GREASE FURNACE

NICHOLS ENGINEERING & RESEARCH CORP.

Waste Disposal Engineers

70 Pine St., New York 5, N. Y.

1637 N. Illinois St., Indianapolis 2, Ind. **1477 Sherbrooke St. W., Montreal 25, Canada**

NICHOLS HERRESHOFF Multiple Hearth furnaces

BURN: Grits, Grease, Skimmings, Screenings, Sludge

.. For burning all the solids removed from sewage, or drying the sludge–the Herreshoff way is the *Simplest* .. *Cleanest* .. *Most economical* of ALL heat disposal methods

Clean? Ask the neighbors of these plants in West New York, N. J., and Bridgeport, Conn. Both recent installations, these Nichols Herreshoff equipped plants are operating successfully and inobtrusively, adjacent to large housing facilities.

West New York, N. J. sewage treatment plant

Bridgeport West, Conn., sewage treatment plant

More than 21,000 tons of NICHOLS MONOHEARTH daily incinerator capacity in operation or contracted for

Worcester, Mass., 450 tons daily capacity

Milwaukee, Wis., 300 tons daily capacity

Miami, Fla., 900 tons daily capacity

Kewaskum, Wis., Vertical Monohearth. 24 tons daily capacity

CHICAGO BRIDGE & IRON COMPANY

Atlanta 3..............2104 Healey Bldg.
Birmingham 1........1568 North 50th St.
Boston 10......1023—201 Devonshire St.
Chicago 4..........2470 McCormick Bldg.
Cleveland 14........2239 Midland Bldg.
Detroit 26..........1537 Lafayette Bldg.
Houston 2..........2117 C & I Life Bldg.
New York 6..........3392—165 Broadway
Philadelphia 3.1634-1700 Walnut St. Bldg.
Pittsburgh 19..........3226 Alcoa Bldg.
Salt Lake City 4...523 W. 17th South St.
San Francisco 4......1539—200 Bush St.
Seattle 1............1323 Henry Bldg.
South Pasadena........712 Fair Oaks Ave.
Tulsa 3................1608 Hunt Bldg.

Plants at: Chicago, Ill.; Salt Lake City, Utah; Greenville, Pa.; and Birmingham, Ala.
In Canada: HORTON STEEL WORKS, Limited, Fort Erie, Ontario

DISPOSAL PLANT EQUIPMENT

The utilization of gas produced in sewage digesters to provide power and heat at disposal plants is becoming more common as new plants are built or old ones modernized. It is advantageous to collect digester gas and store it to provide a continuous supply when production is low. The Hortonsphere® is widely used for this purpose. It is a compact unit, easily operated and maintained. The Hortonsphere is built for pressures up to 75 lbs. per sq. in. and up to 80 ft. in diameter.

When facilities to store gas at low pressure are satisfactory, lift type holders are used. They are built in standard capacities of 250,000 cu. ft. and larger.

Public utilities also use Hortonspheres and lift type holders in municipal gas distribution systems.

300,000-cu. ft. lift type holder for storing gas at the sewage disposal plant

53-ft. 6-in. diam. Hortonsphere used to store sewage gas at Akron, Ohio

The lift type holder is usually located near the plant while the Hortonsphere is often used in outlying sections of the system, to provide a reserve supply of gas that can be fed into the mains to keep the pressures constant.

Information, estimating prices, or quotations on both types of gas holders will be furnished without obligation.

36-ft. diam. Hortonsphere used to store gas at 35 lbs. per sq. in. pressure at Ann Arbor, Mich.

ELEVATED TANKS AT SEWAGE DISPOSAL PLANTS

As in the case of municipal or industrial water distribution systems, elevated tanks are often used to provide gravity water pressure for general service at sewage disposal plants. Such systems may also supply sprinklers for gardens and landscaping surrounding the plant buildings.

60,000-gallon ellipsoidal - bottom elevated tank. It is 75 ft. to the bottom

It's new! It's *completely different!*

IT CLEANS SEWERS BETTER!

The improved . . .

CABLE-TYPE POWER RODDER

Cleans sewers up to 500 feet in length

•

All-power operation

•

Minimum street occupancy

•

Completely self-contained and portable

O'BRIEN MANUFACTURING CORPORATION

5662 Northwest Highway • Chicago 30, Illinois

SEE NEXT THREE PAGES

THE SPEEDY WAY

O'Brien sewerking®

TO CLEAN SEWERS

THE SPEEDY WAY **O'Brien Sewerking®** TO CLEAN SEWERS

CABLE-TYPE POWER RODDER

—does the most effective cleaning job in less time—no manual labor!

Blocked sewers, whether from tree roots, sand or foreign objects, are opened up quickly with an O'BRIEN SEWERKING. The secret is this is a machine engineered to use continuous, heavy steel cable, to reach the obstruction. This is a great advance over the use of solid rods—which often break, take time to connect and later disconnect; and are difficult to use when the sewer obstruction is at a long distance, with corners or bends to get around. SEWERKING cable-type power rodding eliminates these difficulties.

Here's how you SAVE with SEWERKING cable-type power rodding . . .

The strong, 1″ flexible cable, is started from the storage drum; then fed through the OB Power Transmission, illustrated below. A cutting tool is attached to the forward end of the cable. With the transmission shift lever in "forward" and the engine in gear, the cable is projected into the sewer—rotated at proper speed to clear the obstruction. Power does the entire job—feeds the cable, rotates it for cutting, retrieves the cable and recoils it in the drum! Fast—efficient—at a tremendous saving in manpower and time!

Only the O'BRIEN SEWERKING has the OB Power Transmission*

This important engineering development makes possible the control and precise feeding of heavy cable, by power, into the sewer. The horizontal lever (at left) *locks* the threaded cable to the two gears at top. The vertical lever (at right) provides quick shift control—forward, neutral or reverse. The improved OB Power Transmission is built for heavy duty, dependability, and full utilization of power to drive the cable.

*Patent applied for

O'BRIEN SEWERKING FEATURES AND SPECIFICATIONS

1. **LONG DISTANCE**—500′ of sewer can be cleaned from one manhole, entirely by power.
2. **VARIABLE SPEED** — Cable rotated from 75 to 225 RPMs to cut properly.
3. **THROWOUT CLUTCH**—Shift lever to engage or disengage power.
4. **HEAVY DUTY ALL-STEEL CHASSIS**—Two wheel trailer with hitch for car or truck. Special jack support to raise or lower front end to desired height.
5. **LARGE, WATERPROOF TOOL BOX**—Also open tool box for extras and manhole guide.
6. **BRIGGS AND STRATTON ENGINE**—Easily serviced locally.
7. **DURABLE PAINT** — Municipal orange color—for lasting protection.

OB ROD ADAPTER available for use of solid rods when desired.

PRECISION BUILT—HEAVY DUTY CONSTRUCTION—FOR YEARS OF DEPENDABLE SERVICE

THE SPEEDY WAY O'Brien sewerking® TO CLEAN SEWERS

TO CLEAN SEWERS

O'Brien Sewerking

THE SPEEDY WAY

A COMPLETE LINE . . .
O'BRIEN Sewerking ACCESSORIES

There are especially designed cutting tools for the O'BRIEN SEWERKING cable, to cut away any obstruction encountered.

Also available, solid rods, cable, couplings and other sewer cleaning tools not illustrated.

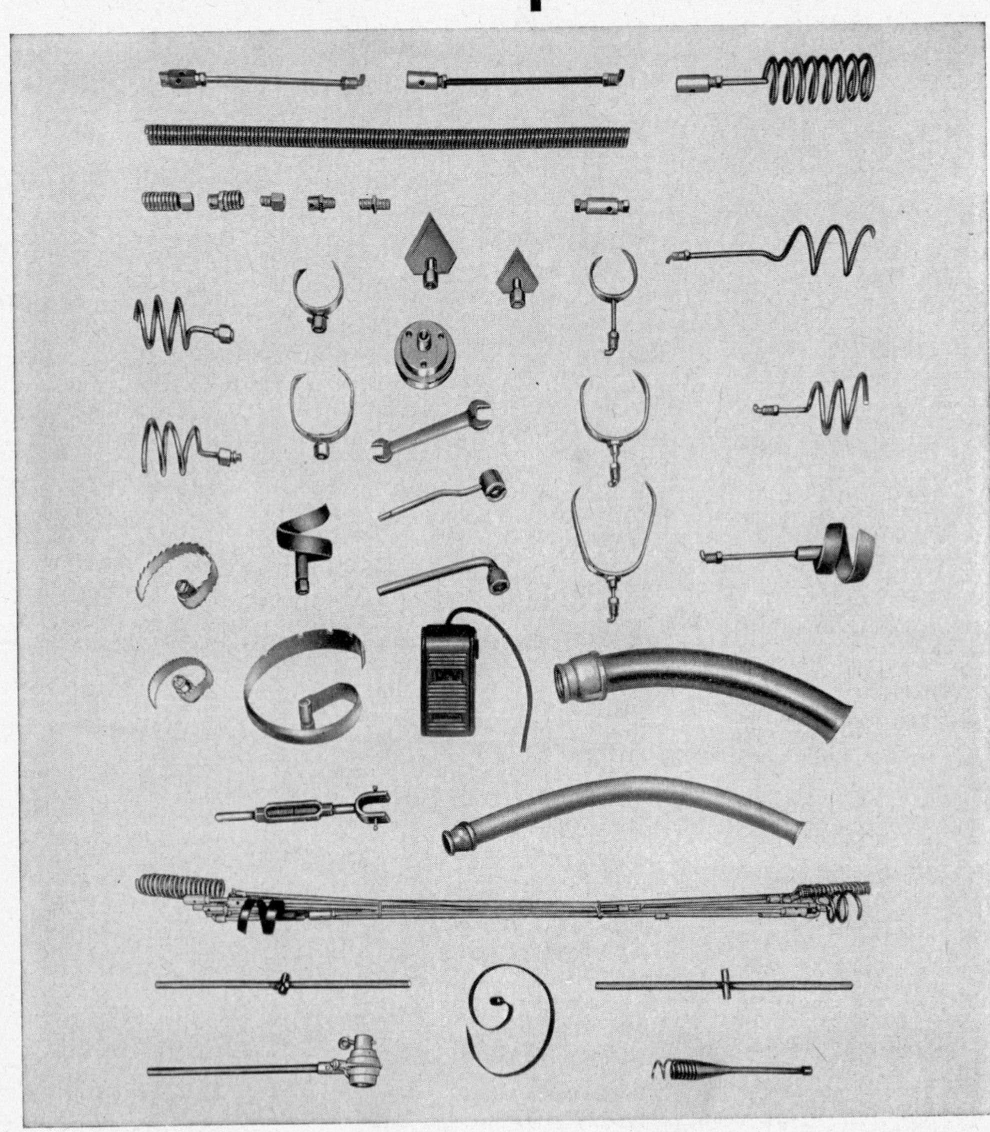

FREE!
Illustrated
SEWERKING Literature
WRITE TODAY!

Now Available—O'BRIEN power rodding service. Includes men and equipment. Allowance toward purchase of equipment later. Have the information in your file when emergencies develop—or for a preventive program.

O'BRIEN MANUFACTURING CORPORATION
5662 Northwest Highway • Chicago 30, Illinois

PACIFIC FLUSH TANK COMPANY

Designers and Manufacturers of Sewage and Sewage Treatment Equipment Exclusively Since 1893

4241 Ravenswood Ave., Chicago 13, Ill.

Port Chester, N. Y. — San Mateo, Calif. — Denver — Charlotte, N. C. — Jacksonville

PRODUCTS

Floating Cover Digesters
Pearth Gas Recirculation System
Universal Prefabricated Roofing
Supernatant Selectors and Gauges
Digester Heaters and Heat Exchangers
Sludge Gas Control Equipments
Rotary Distributors
Twin Tank Controls
Alternating Siphons
Sewage Siphons
Sprinkling Filter Nozzles
Flush-Tank Siphons and Regulators
Kraus Interchange Process
Aeration Equipment

P.F.T. FLOATING COVER DIGESTERS

For effectively controlling and accelerating the action in digestion tanks, eliminating odors and collecting

gas for heating and power purposes. Used in two stage processes as well as in single tanks.

Available in all sizes, Floating Covers are adaptable to the smallest and largest plants. Shown here are 10 circular covers (100′ diameter) at San Francisco. Also shown is a 20′ cover at Postville, Iowa. Send for Catalog 332.

P.F.T. PEARTH GAS RECIRCULATION SYSTEM

Rate of digestion is increased and scum accumulations are eliminated by means of this simple and effective system of recirculating gas in sludge digestion tanks. With this system there are no moving parts in the digestion tank contents and the problem of clogging is eliminated. The system is available either as an integral part or an attachment to the standard P.F.T. Floating Cover. Also available for use with fixed concrete covered tanks. Bulletin No. 332.

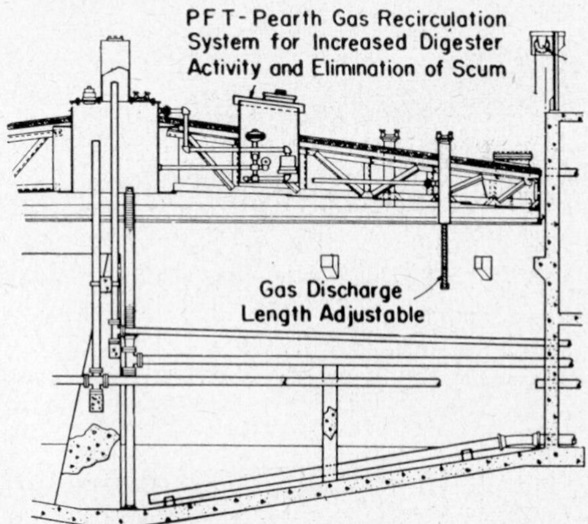

P.F.T. LIQUID LEVEL GAUGE

For accurately indicating the position of the Floating Cover in the digestion tank, this Liquid Level Gauge is calibrated in feet and inches. Both high level and low level alarm horn and indicator lights are available, mounted in a single compact case. This unit provides complete operating control and a record of the contents of the digester from within the control building. Bulletin No. 236.

P.F.T. UNIVERSAL PREFABRICATED ROOFING

Pictured here is an installation of P.F.T.—Universal Prefabricated Roofing on a digester floating cover at Woodstock, Ill. The metal-clad, fiber-glas sections are formed to fit standard sizes of P.F.T. Floating Covers. Insulation is sealed in each section to resist moisture. Top surface may be supplied in pebble grain 18 gage aluminum. Underside is of corrugated steel and is hot dipped galvanized to resist corrosion. No composition roofing or field painting required on any surface. Completed roofing will support 7 men on the outer section of the greatest unsupported span. Catalog 332.

P.F.T. SUPERNATANT LIQUOR SELECTOR

This simple equipment assures the withdrawal of the best supernatant liquor at a slow, continuous rate from the digestion tank, regardless of its location. Increases effective capacity of tanks and decreases amount of supernatant piping required. Bulletin No. 443.

P.F.T. SUPERNATANT LIQUOR GAUGE

The rate of withdrawal of supernatant is properly controlled by the use of the P.F.T. Supernatant Gauge, Sight Glass and Sampler with the Supernatant Selector. Bulletin No. 443.

P.F.T. DIGESTER HEATER AND HEAT EXCHANGER

Does away with constantly decreasing heat transfer, reduces the labor of cleaning inaccessible coils and minimizes operating interruptions. Provides continuous operation and more efficient heat transfer by heating raw sludge and/or material from the digestion tank within the unit.

P.F.T. Digester Heaters are available for burning sludge gas. Burners and controls are available for using oil as a supplemental fuel or for using oil exclusively. The units above are Model 750 Digester Heaters arranged for burning sludge gas with supplementary natural gas. Firing for temperature of sludge in digester is manually controlled. Circulation of sludge from digester is automatic and intermittent. Control of building heating temperature is automatic.

Output is 750,000 b.t.u. for sludge heating plus 375,000 b.t.u. for building heating. Note P.F.T. Pressure Gauges, Flame Traps, and Pressure Relief Check Valve in background.

Also shown is a P.F.T. Model 629 Heat Exchanger. In this unit gas engine jacket water or hot water from other sources is circulated through tubes within which are smaller tubes through which sludge from the digester or added raw sludge is circulated. Ask for Bulletin 235.

P.F.T. GAS SAFETY EQUIPMENT

P.F.T. offers complete equipment for safely utilizing gas generated in the sludge digestion tanks. The fire and explosion hazards have been eliminated. These units, in part, are briefly described below.

P.F.T. PRESSURE RELIEF WASTE GAS FLAME TRAPS

Pressure Relief Waste Gas Flame Traps have found wide favor for eliminating the explosion hazard from digestion tank gases. Provide adequate protection without water seals. Minimize pressure loss. Bulletin No. 321.

P.F.T. FLAME TRAPS

Flame Traps protect against explosion hazards, but do not have the pressure relief feature. Bulletin No. 321.

P.F.T. WASTE GAS BURNERS

Consist of burner pot fitted with fire baffles. Has adjustable pilot. Bulletin No. 321.

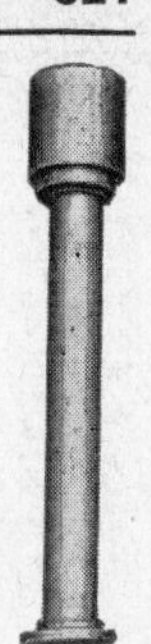

P.F.T. CONDENSATE DRIP TRAP

Condensate can safely be removed from sewage gas lines without danger of gas leakage through the use of P.F.T. Drip Trap at the lowest points in the line. Bulletin No. 321.

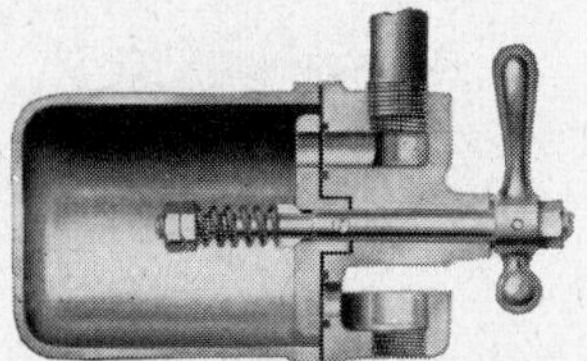

P.F.T. PRESSURE INDICATING GAUGES

Provide readily visible readings on gas pressure in digester, service line and waste. Bulletin No. 321.

P.F.T. ROTARY DISTRIBUTORS

Featuring the P.F.T. Spreader Jet, unique bearing arrangement and positive mercury seal. "Double Flow" types employing vented "humps" or shunts on two of the four distributor arms provide maximum range of flow while operating under minimum differential of head.

In many cases where loadings tend to exceed the capacity of P.F.T. Rotary Distributors, higher rates of application may be a solution to the problem. In such cases existing units may be replaced with larger units to handle more gallons daily. A recently designed spreader jet has a removable orifice and deflector. Unit is designed to prevent clogging.

166′ 0″ diameter P.F.T. Rotary Distributor at Stockton, Calif., has "cantilever" supported 14″ dia. arms, easy to clean spreader jets, handles 12.0 m.g.d.

To handle increased flows twenty 165' P.F.T. Rotary Distributors at Dayton, Ohio, are now being converted to larger rotary units incorporating latest design of center column.

P.F.T. SPRINKLING FILTERS

The ideal method of secondary treatment of sewage. Separate and common field types. P.F.T. supplies all equipment necessary except piping for laterals and risers in bed. Complete data in Catalog No. 130. Deflector Nozzles for Fixed Nozzle Filters. Bulletin No. 312.

P.F.T. TWIN TANK CONTROLS AND SIPHONS

Twin Tank Controls for efficient, automatic dosing of sprinkling filter beds. Siphons for dosing rotary distributors. Twin Tank Controls, Bulletin No. 130; Standard Sewage Siphons, Bulletin No. 125; Sand Filter Siphons, Bulletin No. 224; Flush-Tank Siphons, Bulletin No. 222; Flush-Tank Regulators and Dosing Counters, Bulletin No. 103.

P.F.T. "CONTROLLED" ACTIVATED SLUDGE PROCESS

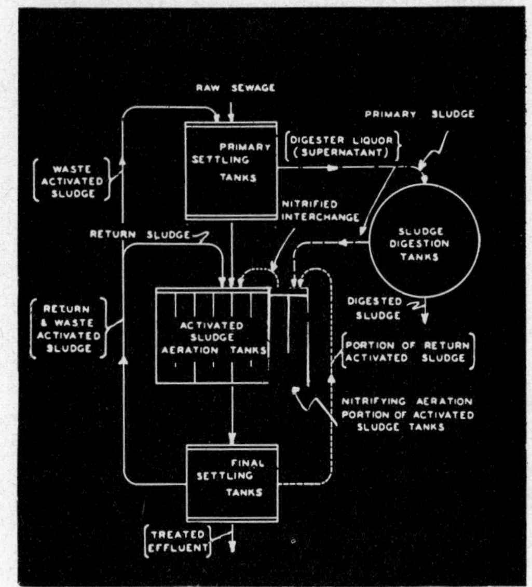

Kraus Interchange Process —

A process of aerating waste activated sludge, utilizing the digester supernatant liquor to produce highly nitrified solids that: (1) During *normal* loads, produce sludge that settles more readily to provide greater purification. (2) During *peak* loads, provide a reserve of highly nitrified active solids which balance the increased load of organic matter. A truly "controlled" activated sludge process.

Kraus Distributed Air Process —

A new method of introducing air into aeration tanks. Combined with the Kraus Interchange Process, it provides: (1) Greater stability of activated sludge treatment, (2) More efficient treatment of shock loads, (3) More efficient use of aeration tank capacity, (4) Lowered power requirements for air.

•

Complete details are available on request.

waste treatment equipment exclusively since 1893

PACIFIC FLUSH TANK COMPANY

4241 Ravenswood Avenue
Chicago 13, Illinois

SWING DIFFUSER UNITS with PRECISION TUBES

For continuous, Wide Band Aeration. Most economical and provide highest aeration capacity of any system. Individual tubes easily cleaned without taking tank out of service. Over 300 installations.

AERATOR-CLARIFIER UNITS

Equipment specifically developed for small communities and industrial plants. Serve population equivalents from 100 to 5,000. No highly trained operator necessary. Over 230 installations.

For Effective, Economical
WASTE and SEWAGE TREATMENT
Specify . . .

CHICAGO SEWAGE EQUIPMENT

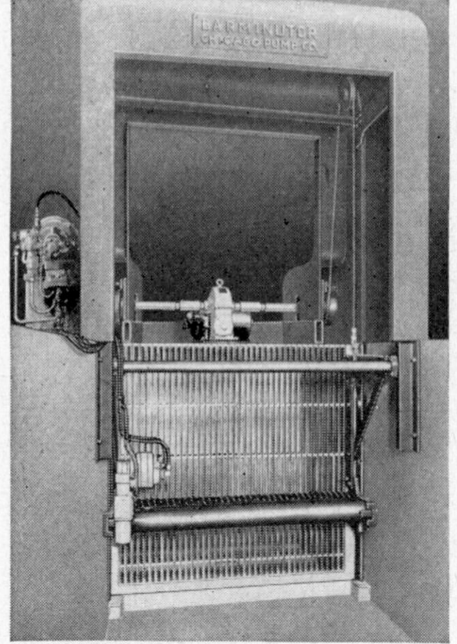

BARMINUTOR® SCREENING AND COMMINUTING MACHINES

Bring advantages of Comminutor Machines to sewage treatment plants, pumping stations, and out-fall sewers requiring higher sewage flows or rectangular channels. Over 3,500 comminution installations.

FLUSH-KLEEN® Sewage EJECTORS

The *only* truly clog-proof pump for handling raw sewage. Automatically backwashes strainer. Keeps solids from basin and pumps—water only handled by impeller. Never clogs. Over 12,000 in service in municipalities, buildings and on ships.

SCRU-PELLER® SLUDGE PUMPS

Pumping action chops all coarse and stringy material into small pieces to prevent clogging and jamming. 8,000 in use.

CHICAGO PUMP COMPANY

Subsidiary of Food Machinery and Chemical Corporation

SEWAGE EQUIPMENT DIVISION

622 DIVERSEY PARKWAY • CHICAGO 14, ILLINOIS

Flush Kleen ®, Scru-Peller ®, Plunger, Horizontal and Vertical Non-Clogs Water Seal Pumping Units, Samplers . . . Swing Diffusers, Stationary Diffusers, Mechanical Aerators, Combination Aerator-Clarifiers, Barminutor ®, Comminutors.

SEWER PIPE CLEANING

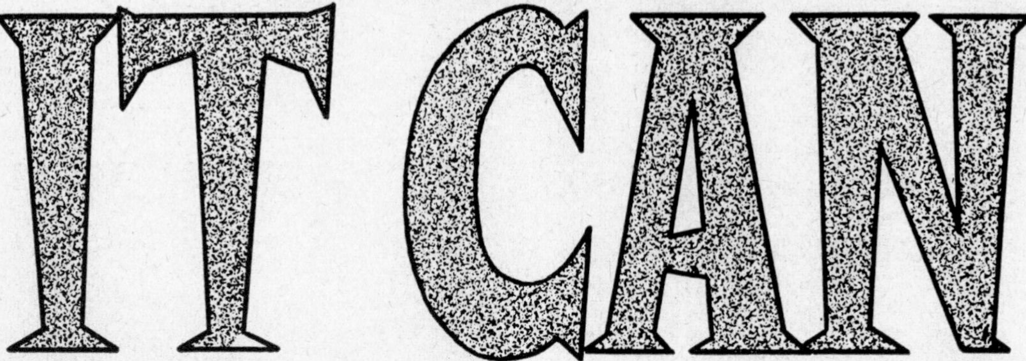

QUICKLY, EASILY, AT LESS COST

NEW PATENTED EQUIPMENT INSURES SUCCESS

Specially designed mobile, truck-mounted equipment has revolutionized the pipe cleaning industry. This new machinery, coupled with new cleaning methods and backed by thoroughly trained crews form a team fully capable of solving any pipe cleaning problem.

TRAINED PERSONNEL MAKES IT WORK FOR YOU

Supervisors, crews, engineers . . . all trained in the new Ace method mean more speed, more efficiency of the job . . . resulting in lower costs plus maximum rehabilitation of the lines.

THE AMERICAN BRASS COMPANY

Waterbury 20, Conn.

ANACONDA METALS FOR SEWAGE

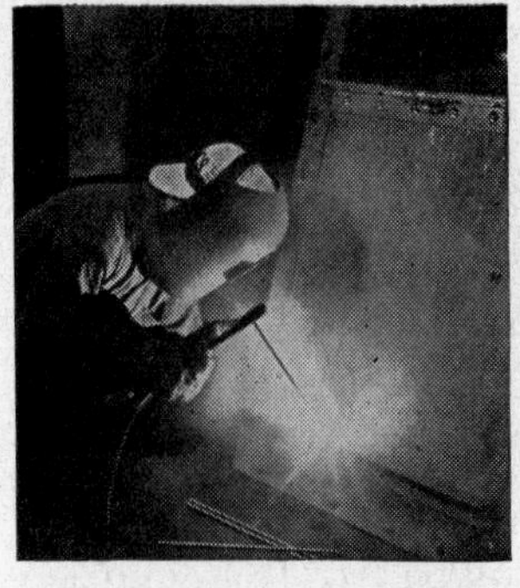

Everdur is easy to weld. Here an Everdur angle is being welded to Everdur plate in fabricating one of the 64 slide gates installed in the Northeast Sewage Plant, Philadelphia, Pa.

Anaconda Metals manufactured by The American Brass Company are finding increasing use as materials for sewage treatment and water works equipment.

SEWAGE TREATMENT EQUIPMENT

Since 1927 Everdur* Metal, the original copper-silicon alloy group, has been used successfully for sewage equipment, where its unusual physical and chemical properties have earned it an enviable reputation for long-lived, economical service under severely corrosive operating conditions. These high-strength, highly corrosion-resistant alloys have replaced heavy, cumbersome, cast equipment, such as stop and sluice gates, weirs and brackets, with lightweight wrought equipment assembled by welded construction. These lightweight assemblies not only require less power to operate, but because of the exceptional corrosion-resistant properties of Everdur, outlast cast, rustable gates and other equipment, and are less apt to become inoperable.

Everdur is also used for electrical conduit, both Rigid and E.M.T., in galleries and other locations where corrosive fumes or liquids are present. Everdur Electrical Conduit is manufactured under Factory Inspection and Label Service Procedure by Underwriters' Laboratories, Inc.

Everdur Alloys are also in wide use for manhole steps and anchor bolts, and in a number of treatment plants for rotary fine screens of both the slotted-plate and wedge-wire types.

Other Anaconda products used extensively in sewage treatment equipment are 85 Red Brass, S.P.S. Pipe, Copper Water Tubes (Types K and L), various copper alloys in the form of rods, bars and shapes. The table opposite briefly summarizes Anaconda Products suitable for sewage treatment equipment.

* Reg. U. S. Pat. Off.

SERVICE	FORM	MATERIAL
Pump galleries, over tanks, screen rooms, etc.	Rigid conduit & E.M.T.	Everdur-1015
Coarse bar screen enclosures	Sheet	Everdur-1010
Grit chamber proportional weir	Sheet	Everdur-1010
Weirs and brackets in sedimentation tanks	Sheet	Everdur-1010
Gates	Sheet Rod Angles Channels	Everdur-1010 Everdur-1010 Everdur-1010 Everdur-1010
Air lines for aeration tanks	Pipe and Tube	85 Red Brass & Copper
Meter and control lines	Tube	Copper
Sampling tubes for digesters	Tube	Copper
Heating coils for digesters	Tube	Copper
Hangers and fittings for heating coils	Rod	Everdur-1010 and-1015
Sludge gas lines	Pipe	85 Red Brass
Rotary fine screens	Rod Bars Channels Wire Plate	Everdur-1010 Everdur-1010 Everdur-1010 Everdur-1010 Everdur-1010
Valve and gate stems	Rod	Tobin Bronze*-452 Leaded Naval Brass-612 Everdur-1012 or -1014 Manganese Bronze-937
Vacuum filters	Wire Screws Bolts Nuts Strip	Everdur-1010 Everdur-1015 Everdur-1015 Everdur-1015 Everdur-1010
Studs, bolts and nuts	Rod	Tobin Bronze-452 Naval Brass-450 Everdur-1010 or -1015
Guides, seats, sealing strips	Bars Shapes Strips	Naval Brass-450 Manganese Bronze-937 Everdur-1010
Manhole steps and anchors	Rods	Everdur-1015

THE AMERICAN BRASS COMPANY

Waterbury 20, Conn.

TREATMENT AND WATER WORKS EQUIPMENT

WATER SUPPLY AND DISTRIBUTION EQUIPMENT

Everdur Metal has been used for more than 30 years for reservoir, water-treatment, and distribution equipment such as screen frames and screens in surface reservoir outlets; large-diameter, cylindrical well screens, which are usually made of punched or milled plates or from special-shape wire and rods, and assembled by welding, or swaging, for handling underground waters; spillway fittings; flash board supports; valve stems and fittings; guides; seats; and sealing strips. Everdur has also been used in large quantities in the form of solid and stranded wire, U-bolts, nuts, clips and saddles for the making, assembling and laying of articulated concrete mattresses for revetments for flood control in the Mississippi River.

Anaconda 85 Red Brass Pipe and Anaconda Type K Copper Water Tube are building-code materials for service lines from mains to household and building plumbing connections in many cities in the United States and Canada.

The following table gives a brief summary of Anaconda Products in use in Water Works projects.

SERVICE	FORM	MATERIAL
Reservoir outlet screens	Wire mesh	Everdur-1010
Screen frames	Bar	Phosphorized Copper—103; Everdur-1010
Well screens	Plate, Tube; Special-Shape wire; Rod	85 Red Brass; Everdur-1010
Filter distribution lines	Pipe	85 Red Brass
Winding wire for vacuum filter	Wire	Copper; Phosphor Bronze-361; Everdur-1015
Vacuum filter piping	Pipe; Tube	85 Red Brass; Copper
Vacuum filter vat	Sheet	Copper; Everdur-1010
Service lines	Pipe; Tube	85 Red Brass; Copper
Valve and gate stems	Rod	Tobin Bronze-452; Leaded Naval Brass-612; Everdur-1012 or-1014; Manganese Bronze-937
Studs, bolts and nuts	Rod	Tobin Bronze-452; Naval Brass-450; Everdur-1010 and-1015
Guides, seats, sealing strips	Bars; Shapes; Strips	Naval Brass-450; Manganese Bronze-937; Everdur-1010

In addition to welded construction, mechanical bonds are readily made with Everdur. In this "Cook" Wire-Wound Well Screen Strainer, keystone-shaped Everdur wire is mechanically bonded to the longitudinal bars. Everdur provides excellent resistance to a wide variety of corrosive ground waters.

Engineering Service

The engineering staff of the Technical Department of The American Brass Company is always available to public works or consulting engineers for consultation on proper selection of materials for equipment to be exposed to corrosive elements, or which must withstand unusual physical conditions, or undergo special fabricating operations. This service is offered without cost. Anaconda Publication E-11 discusses the use of Everdur for sewage treatment and water works equipment. This and other Anaconda publications will be forwarded upon request. Write:

The American Brass Company
Waterbury 20, Connecticut

Modern Municipal Incin-

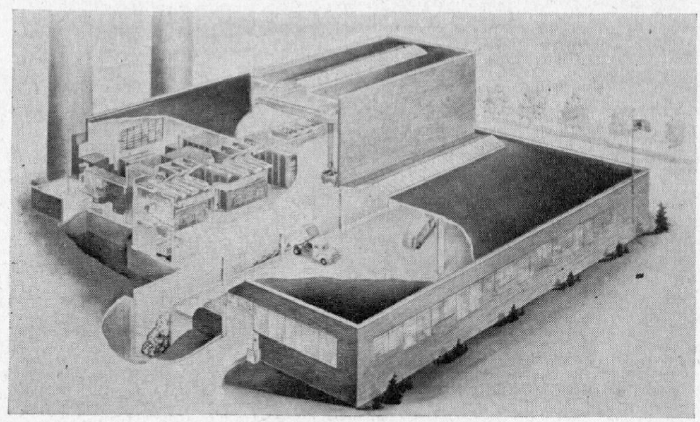

Cutaway view of a modern municipal incinerator plant . . . *BY AMERICAN* . . . having four rectangular furnaces each with a capacity of 180 tons or a total of 720 tons per day for the plant.

Hundreds of cities, counties and groups of smaller communities are turning to "the modern way" of disposing of rubbish, garbage and other waste materials. . . MUNICIPAL INCINERATION.

The American Incinerator Corporation has pioneered in the engineering development of plants of all sizes for the sanitary, safe and efficient handling of the waste disposal problem for many such municipalities, and for similar large industrial requirements.

To Architects, Engineers, Public Officials, Purchasing Officers, Contractors, Builders, and to other responsible officials, American offers the assistance of a large staff of design and combustion engineers and specialists in planning and designing all types of incinerator equipment.

For 30 years, American has specialized exclusively in the design, manufacture and erection of thousands of successful incinerator installations, and has originated or adapted many features for labor saving, safety, economy and air pollution control. Key features pioneered by American include:

1. Mechanical stoking grates.
2. Crane, hydraulic ram and other mechanical feeding or charging devices.
3. Electronically-controlled combustion regulation.
4. Smoke alarms and fume burners.
5. Specially designed precipitators for fly-ash elimination.
6. Mechanical ash collecting and removal methods.

Let American assist you in solving your incinerator problems. Write for our new Municipal brochure "Incinerama" describing modern incineration attained by American cities of varying sizes. Or have your Engineers or Consulting Architects & Engineers ask for special assistance in garbage or waste analysis, capacity determination, appropriation estimates, custom-tailored design characteristics or other helps in planning a waste disposal program for your community. These services are available to you WITHOUT COST OR ANY OBLIGATION.

The accompanying illustrations depict typical "Modern Municipal Incineration" . . . a cutaway view of a complete 720 ton per day plant; materials handling in charging and ash removal; combustion chambers, and fume. fly-ash and smoke elimination equipment; and actual photographs of selected types of charging, stoking and control equipment — *BY AMERICAN!*

THE AMERICAN INCINERATOR CORPORATION

Member of the Air Pollution Control Association

eration . . . by American!

Cross-sectional view of the same plant showing functional operating characteristics.

Crane bin charging from storage bin to hoppers, at the National Institute of Health, Bethesda, Maryland . . . *BY AMERICAN.*

Features illustrated above:

1. Materials Handling Cycle:
   - (a) Large storage bin prevents unloading delays.
   - (b) Crane bin feeding of hoppers having mechanical charging gates.
   - (c) Inclined mechanically operated stoking grates.
   - (d) Mechanical ash removal gates.
2. Combustion Handling Cycle:
   - (a) Primary chamber charged to the rear prevents "snuff-out" by succeeding charges.
   - (b) Secondary chamber with auxiliary burners for smoke and fume elimination.
   - (c) Large settling and subsidence chambers with wet spray system for fly ash removal.

Modern hydraulically operated super heavy duty guillotine type cast iron stoking doors equipped with specially-designed sliding observation openings, at the Youngstown, Ohio Municipal Plant . . . *BY AMERICAN.*

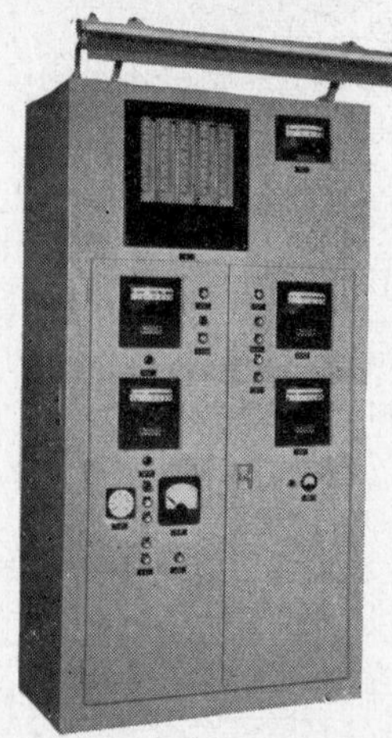

One of the Control panels of electronic and automatic control equipment at the Medill Avenue Municipal Incinerator Plant of the City of Chicago . . . *BY AMERICAN.*

AMERICAN INCINERATOR CORPORATION

"The Greatest Name in Incineration"

5710 E. NEVADA, DETROIT 34, MICHIGAN **TELEPHONE: FOREST 6-2810**

Municipal—Industrial—Institutional—Commercial—Residential

FAIRBANKS, MORSE & CO.
600 SOUTH MICHIGAN AVENUE
DEPT. MIX **CHICAGO 5, ILLINOIS**

For Pumps and Engines . . .

FAIRBANKS-MORSE

Fairbanks-Morse has served the power generation, water supply and sewage disposal needs of the municipalities, large and small, everywhere, for well over a half century. The long record of reliable and efficient performance of Fairbanks-Morse products in municipal power stations and pumping plants is due in a measure to the planned interrelation of their design. One manufacturer builds the driving and the driven member, designs them for one another, and accepts the responsibility for their good service. Fairbanks, Morse & Co., Dept. MIX, 600 South Michigan Ave., Chicago 5, Illinois.

Diesels to 3500 hp. for high demand power generation.

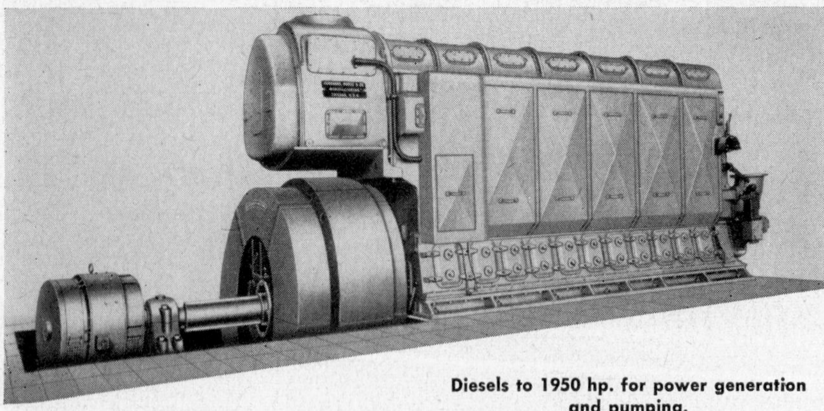

Diesels to 1950 hp. for power generation and pumping.

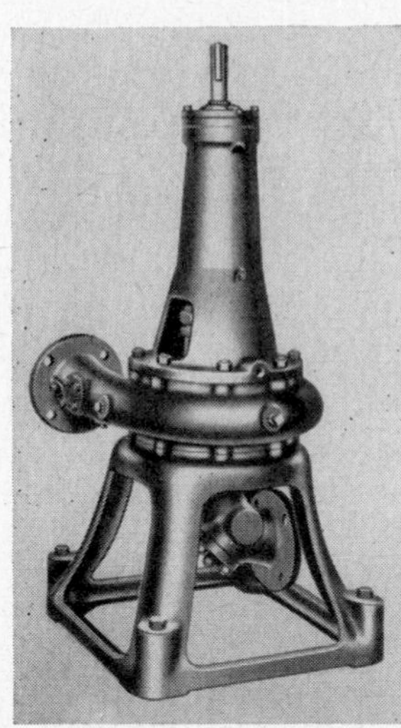

Bladeless pumps for primary sewage handling.

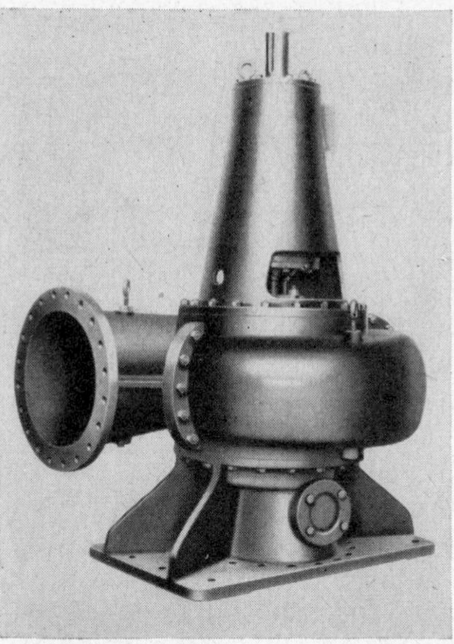

"Angleflow" pumps for large-capacity sewage plants.

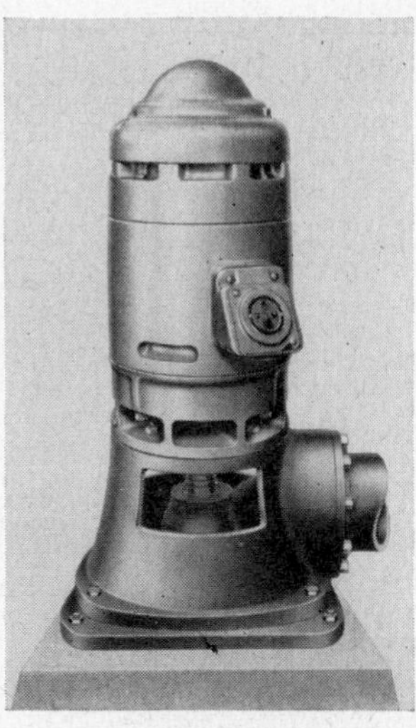

Pomona turbine pumps for deep-well water supply.

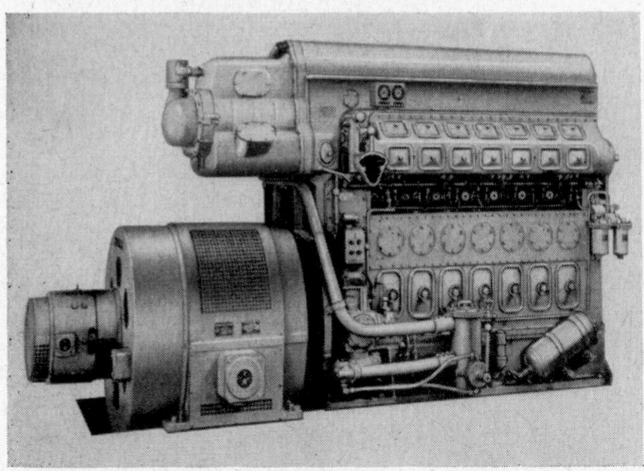

Diesels to 750 hp. for pumping and emergency stand-by service.

Centrifugal pumps for water supply and fire protection.

FAIRBANKS-MORSE

a name worth remembering when you want the BEST

PUMPS • SCALES • DIESEL LOCOMOTIVES AND ENGINES • ELECTRICAL MACHINERY • RAIL CARS
HOME WATER SERVICE EQUIPMENT • MOWERS • MAGNETOS

GAR WOOD INDUSTRIES, INC.

Customer Service Dept., Wayne, Michigan

CONSTRUCTION MACHINERY PRODUCTS: Ditchers, Excavators, Fine-graders, Spreaders, Hi-Way Wideners, Tractor Equipment

DITCHERS

Through the years, Gar Wood-Buckeye ditchers have earned an enviable reputation for digging more ditch per dollar. Today's advanced models deliver this same outstanding performance and low-cost, dependable service.

In the Gar Wood-Buckeye line you'll find a complete range of sizes and types. And, to fit them exactly to your municipality's specifications, you'll find the greatest selection of factory options of any line on the market! Contact your Gar Wood-Buckeye dealer or write direct to Customer Service Dept., Gar Wood Industries, Inc., Wayne, Michigan.

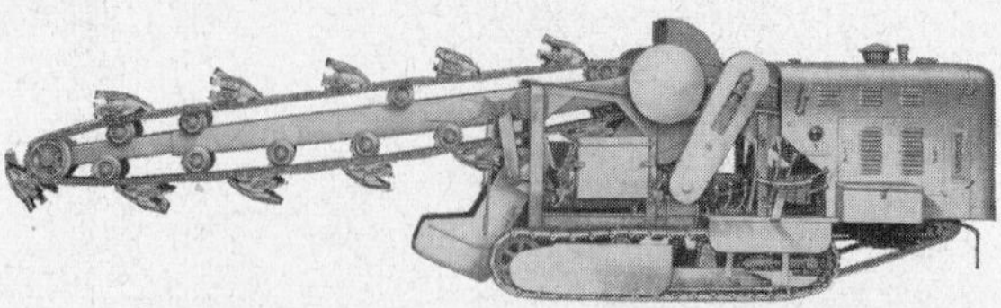

MODEL 407—Easiest machine to operate on the market! Live hydraulic boom hoist . . . push-button conveyor control . . . fast, positive steering add up to more digging time, higher production. Compact, highly maneuverable machine. Digs 8 feet deep; 17, 19, 22 or 24 inches wide. And, it's on crawlers to dig service ditch on time!

MODEL 305—Most advanced wheel-type ditcher available! Features live hydraulic wheel hoist for fast, accurate positioning of digging wheel . . . hydraulic conveyor drive with forward and reverse speeds to handle any conveyor need . . . track-type crawlers that last longer, cost less to maintain, and enable you to dig regardless of conditions. Digs 5 feet, 6 inches deep; from 12 to 24 inches wide in 2 inch increments.

GarWood

EXCAVATORS

The many outstanding advantages of the series 75 excavators reflect Gar Wood's specialization in ¾ yard machines. Power actuated drum clutches . . . direct gear drive or optional fluid coupling . . . direct manual controls . . . positive, independent chain crowd . . . worm driven boom hoist . . . power steering . . . independent travel while swinging . . . fast, easy convertibility. Complete range of front attachments available for conversion. See your Gar Wood dealer or write direct to Customer Service Dept., Gar Wood Industries, Inc., Wayne, Mich.

GAR WOOD INDUSTRIES, INC.

Customer Service Dept., Wayne, Michigan

TRUCK EQUIPMENT PRODUCTS: Hoists, Dump Bodies, Refuse Collection Bodies, Frate-Gates, Winches, Cranes, Pole Derricks, Snowplow Controls

THE HAYWARD COMPANY

50 Church St., New York 7, N. Y.

Rehandling and Digging Buckets • Cable Take-Up Reels • Grapples

Hayward Incinerator Bucket and Grapple

Wherever municipal incinerators are operated there is the problem of getting the collected refuse into the furnace. The usual method is the pit-and-crane, by which a clam shell bucket or grapple, operating from an overhead crane, moves the refuse from the collection pit to the furnace hopper. The Hayward E-14 Clam Shell Bucket (shown at the left) and the Hayward Grapple (at the right) are specially designed for this service. For very bulky refuse the grapple is preferred. The bucket is equipped with manganese corner pieces which prevent damage to the bucket when hitting the concrete walls. The grapple is equipped with manganese steel tines of a type which can be readily removed for replacement when damaged or worn.

Hayward E-14 bucket about to release load in the new incinerator in the residential section of prosperous Brookline, Mass.

E-15 **Hayward Coal and Coke Clam Shell Bucket,** the pioneer in this field, built to handle a pound of coal per pound of bucket weight—1400 pounds up.

E-16 **Hayward Clam Shell Bucket** for rehandling sand, gravel, crushed stone, etc.; ½ cubic yard up. Designed and built for continuous heavy service.

K-6 **Hayward Digging Clam Shell Bucket** is designed for heavy excavation service of all kinds. Sizes ⅜ cubic yard up.

Electric Motor Hayward Bucket is the perfected modern self-powered hook-on type bucket for either A.C. or D.C. Sizes 7½ cubic feet upward.

Hayward Catch-Basin Bucket

In every City and Town throughout the country, the problem of cleaning Sewer Catch-Basins has to be met. These settling basins fill with the street's drainage and at frequent intervals this material has to be removed to keep the sewers in proper working order.

Many methods have been used in the past but nothing has worked out so successfully as the specially designed Hayward Bucket, known as the Catch-Basin type, which may be operated by most any type of machine equipped with a double drum power hoist. In cases where speed is not essential, hand power hoists may be employed.

These husky little buckets are built along the same general lines as the larger sizes of Hayward Orange Peel Buckets. The materials used in their construction are best suited to withstand wear and hold down up-keep costs and their design is so simple that there is practically nothing to get out of order. When replacements of worn parts do become necessary, they can be easily and inexpensively made.

Question from 1953
"The American City Quiz"

QUESTION

1. *How many catch-basins should a crew be able to clean in a year if it uses a dump truck carrying an "orange-peel" bucket?*

ANSWER

1. Roland N. Barton, Commissioner of Service, Cleveland Heights, Ohio, finds that his crews can clean 3,500 catch-basins per year using a 2½-ton White dump truck equipped with a Hayward orange-peel bucket powered by a power take-off from the truck.

In addition to Catch-Basin Buckets, we build small Orange Peel and Clam Shell Buckets for cleaning out traps and septic tanks and tar and pitch from settling tanks.

Our engineers have had many years' practical experience along these lines and will gladly help solve your problems.

With a Hayward orange peel bucket and a truck, the City of Scranton, Pa. cleans 25 catch basins a day in hillside terrain where rains wash sand and gravel from dirt streets into the basins. Irvington, N. J., cleans 30 catch basins a day during the three fall months (the leaf season) with a Hayward orange peel bucket on a 4-yard truck body with an operator and helper.

JOHNS-MANVILLE

Executive Offices: 22 East 40th St., New York 16, N. Y.

OFFICES IN LARGE CITIES

TRANSITE® BUILDING SEWER PIPE

The Modern Asbestos-Cement Pipe For Efficient Disposal of Sewage From Building to Street Sewers and Septic Tanks

Transite Building Sewer Pipe was designed by Johns-Manville especially for conveying sewage from house to street sewer or septic tank. Its tough, dense asbestos-cement composition provides great strength, durability and corrosion-resistance. Its high flow capacity and quick flushing action result from its smooth interior, extra long 10-ft. lengths, and the design of the Ring-Tite® Coupling.

ENGINEERED TO KEEP ROOTS OUT

Transite Building Sewer Pipe is engineered to forestall line clogging by tree roots, perhaps the largest single problem in domestic waste disposal. It is designed to give year after year service without blocking of flow and the resulting backup of sewage into the house thereby endangering health and comfort.

TIGHT JOINTS

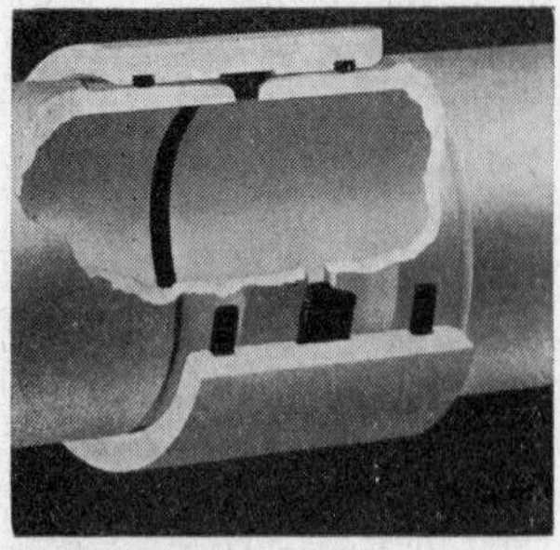

A cross-sectional view of the Ring-Tite Coupling after joint has been made. Note how rubber rings are compressed in grooves, providing a tight, positive seal.

The Ring-Tite Coupling for Transite Building Sewer Pipe combines greater efficiency with greater ease of installation. The joint formed is tight and lasting to provide for uninterrupted flow of sewage. And it is also flexible to protect against flexural stresses building up in the line. The Ring-Tite Coupling also speeds assembly—requires no tools, rubber rings are pre-positioned at the factory, ready for assembly, and pipe ends are automatically locked within the coupling.

LONG LENGTHS

Transite Building Sewer Pipe is available in 4", 5" and 6" sizes and in long 10-ft. as well as 5-ft. lengths. These long lengths speed and simplify installation because fewer joints are needed and pipe is easier to lay to grade accurately. The resulting long uninterrupted runs eliminate pockets or dips in the line where sewage might accumulate, helping to keep the line free flowing. They go under sidewalks more easily, minimizing disturbance to property.

COMPLETE LINE OF FITTINGS AND ADAPTORS

A variety of Transite fittings and adaptors is available for making changes of direction or connections to other pipe. All Transite Fittings employ the Ring-Tite assembly feature.

CHECK LIST OF ADVANTAGES

- **Corrosion-resistant** — Transite is non-metallic, cannot rust or rot
- **Strong**—reinforced by its millions of tough, strong asbestos fibres
- **High Flow Capacity** — Pipe has unusually smooth interior surface
- **Protection against Infiltration**—with tighter joints and fewer of them
- **Protection from Ground Pollution** — and resulting health hazards
- **Easy to Handle** — one man can carry standard 10-foot length
- **Easily connected to other pipes**—with Transite adaptors
- **A Full Line of Fittings**—

JOHNS-MANVILLE

Executive Offices: 22 East 40th St., New York 16, N. Y.

OFFICES IN LARGE CITIES

TRANSITE® SEWER PIPE

Provides Tighter, More Economical Sewerage Systems

The engineer, the contractor, the taxpayer — all benefit when Transite Pipe is used for sewer lines. They will find a combination of qualities in performance-proved Transite Sewer Pipe that will fit their individual needs. This holds true whether the local conditions call for (a) tight joints to protect against root growth and infiltration of ground water or (b) the strength and flow characteristics that mean definite savings in the design stage, during trenching and installation, and in operation as well.

Reduces infiltration . . . keeps out roots The combination of the Ring-Tite® Coupling and Transite Sewer Pipe makes a tight line that can be counted on to stay tight in service. This is why a Transite system reduces infiltration to a minimum, keeps it low year after year. This year-after-year tightness also means positive protection against tree roots entering the sewer line causing service disruption and continual maintenance problems.

High carrying capacity Transite Sewer Pipe's flow coefficient (n-0.010 derived from the Manning formula) indicates an unusually high flow capacity. Because of this, substantial savings are often effected either through designing for smaller diameter pipe, or designing for flatter grades with the shallower trenches such slopes permit. Economies like these are made possible by Transite's smooth interior and long 13-foot lengths.

Speeds installation Work goes ahead faster all along the line because of Transite's longer lengths, light weight, ease of assembly and tight, quickly-made joints with the simple, efficient Ring-Tite Coupling. Easy-to-assemble Transite fittings with Ring-Tite assembly are also available for quick, economical installation.

Lower maintenance Made of asbestos-cement, Transite Sewer Pipe is tough and strong. Its maintained strength, smooth interior and tight, resilient Ring-Tite joints make for a pipeline that stays sound and tight, resulting in minimum maintenance costs.

KEASBEY & MATTISON COMPANY

Ambler, Pennsylvania

For true economy in any gravity sewer system, look for savings all down the line—from planning, through installation, to operation and maintenance. For this "multiconomy" specify Keasbey & Mattison Sewer Pipe with K&M "Fluid-Tite" Couplings.

K&M Asbestos-Cement Sewer Pipe is made of mineral asbestos fibers and age-hardening portland cement and therefore is non-metallic, non-corroding, and non-electrolytic. It is strong, light in weight, easy to handle. Its smooth bore *remains* smooth—low-friction Manning factor of n=0.010.

The "Fluid-Tite" Coupling simplifies installation, and with it infiltration and root entrance are virtually impossible. Therefore . . .

YOU SAVE IN PLANNING—flatter grades, smaller-diameter pipe, fewer lift stations, higher-level filtration plants.

YOU SAVE IN INSTALLATION—No stopping for unfavorable weather or ground conditions; Fewer workers needed; Rapid installation even with unskilled labor; No machinery required except for largest sizes; Permanent watertight joints—immediately and simply; Economical transportation and handling.

YOU SAVE IN OPERATION—Infiltration and root entrance practically impossible; Permanently smooth bore maintains full flow capacity; Fewer inspections and cleanings; Vibration absorbed by the rings in the coupling.

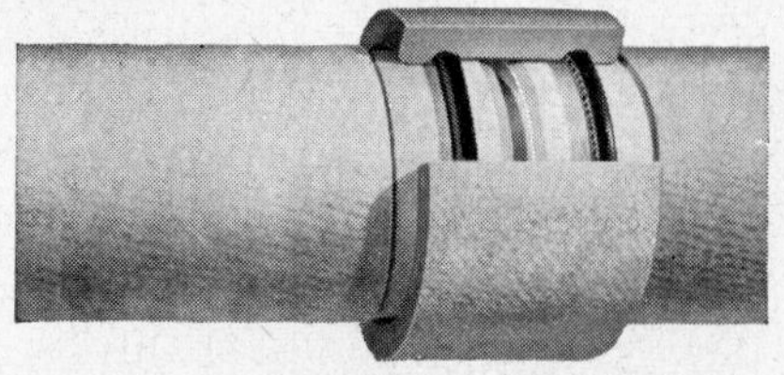

THE EXCLUSIVE K&M "Fluid-Tite"® COUPLING* WHICH PREVENTS INFILTRATION

Two simple steps for permanent, watertight joints which allow 5° deflection in each 13-foot length:

One—lubricate rubber rings.

Two—slide pipe in. That's all!

Infiltration Test

Here, K&M "Fluid-Tite" Coupling and rings undergo external water-pressure test of 25 psi (equivalent of 58-foot head, which far exceeds field conditions) with no pressure inside the pipe. No infiltration, even under this exacting test!

AND FOR HOUSE-TO-SEWER USE...

K&M Asbestos-Cement Building Sewer Pipe

The same advantages offered by K&M Sewer Pipe and "Fluid-Tite" Couplings are available to homeowners and builders in K&M Asbestos-Cement Building Sewer Pipe. All couplings and fittings required for cut-in to sewer lines are offered by K&M for quick, simple installation. Write for details.

KEASBEY & MATTISON

COMPANY • AMBLER • PENNSYLVANIA

See the K&M advertisement elsewhere in this book describing K&M Asbestos-Cement Pressure Pipe.

*PATENT APPLIED FOR

NELSON . . . . . NELSON

MODEL 200 TRACTOR SHOVEL

2 YARD *PLUS* CAPACITY

The newest piece of equipment to roll off the Nelson assembly line is this modern, 19,000 lb. tractor shovel. . . . It boasts an Allison torqmatic, full-reversing transmission, 3 speeds forward or reverse, either gas or Diesel engine, 4-wheel drive, planetary axle and underslung arms for full operator safety. . . . The Model 200 will lift 13,000 lbs., has a maximum dumping height of 9 ft. 6 in. and will dig to a depth of 12 inches. The Model 200 completes its cycle of raising, dumping and lowering in under 17 seconds. . . . Travel speeds are 28.3 M.P.H. in forward, 27.4 in reverse

NELSON R-11 SNOW LOADER

20 cu. yds. per min. with the R-11. Steel-toothed blades feed loose snow or hard-packed ice with equal ease. . . . It's easily maneuverable and operates efficiently without let-up.

NELSON P-11B BUCKET LOADER

4 cu. yds. per min. with the P-11B. Hydraulic swivel discharge conveyor turns full 180°, adjustable discharge from 11′5″ to 14′2″ reaches over 11′. No waste time—allows multiple truck loading.

LOADING EQUIPMENT

The Nelson manufacturing skill and know-how has been gained over a 40 year period—time enough to establish the company as a leader in the loading fields. . . . The coming years will see many more improvements to meet loading needs.

CATCH BASIN CLEANER

The Nelson Catch Basin Cleaner is strong and sturdy—heavily built for long years of troublefree operation at maximum efficiency. . . . You get hydraulic bucket action with a power controlled boom for raising and swinging. . . . All operations can be performed simultaneously. . . . The entire digging, swinging and loading cycle caan be completed in 30 seconds with all operating controls centralized in the cab. . . . Unit can be mounted in less than one hour!

HYDRAULIC BUCKETS AVAILABLE

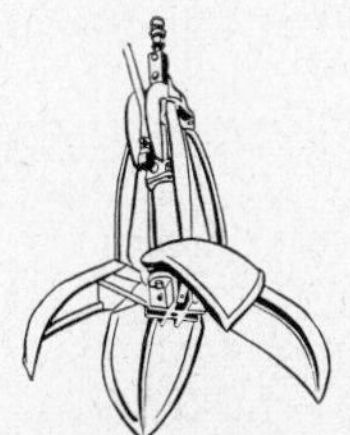

ORANGE PEEL BUCKET

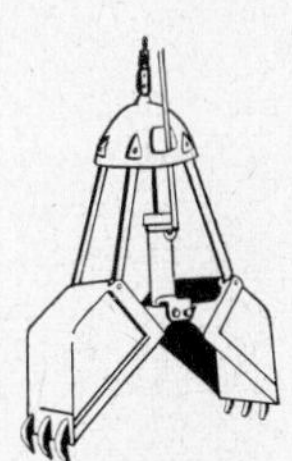

CLAMSHELL BUCKET

N. P. NELSON IRON WORKS, INCORPORATED

CLIFTON, NEW JERSEY

40 YEARS EXPERIENCE IN THE MANUFACTURE OF LOADING AND CONSTRUCTION EQUIPMENT

PITTSBURGH-DES MOINES STEEL COMPANY

Plants at PITTSBURGH, DES MOINES, SANTA CLARA, FRESNO, and CADIZ, SPAIN

Sales Offices at:

PITTSBURGH (25), ... 3460 Neville Island
NEWARK (2), ... 245 Industrial Office Bldg.
CHICAGO (3), . 1264 First National Bank Bldg.
EL MONTE, CAL. . . . . P.O. Box 2068
DES MOINES (8), ... 961 Tuttle Street
DALLAS (1), ... 1265 Praetorian Bldg.
SEATTLE, ... 568 Lane Street
SANTA CLARA, CAL., ... 667 Alviso Road
MADRID, SPAIN, ... Diego DeLeon, 60

Builders of *The "Pittsburgh-Des Moines" Incinerator*

High efficiency in the incineration of sludge and refuse, with excellent operating economy, is achieved without smoke or other nuisance by Pittsburgh-Des Moines *High Temperature* Incineration Plants. Correct in design, practical in arrangement and built to withstand intensive service, these plants are guaranteed to deliver satisfactory performance.

Pittsburgh-Des Moines Incineration Plants feature the following advantages, in plants of every size from 15 tons per day to those with capacities to serve the largest municipalities:

Baltimore, Md. Daily capacity 800 tons

Mechanical Stoking Mechanism—an important new Pittsburgh-Des Moines advantage, applicable to new or existing P-DM and other rectangular furnaces. The system provides mechanical stoking of refuse over the grates from charging end to front of chamber, preventing large clinker formation and maintaining uniform burning conditions with a minimum of attention from control operator. Capacity of incinerator plant is greatly increased, manhours and labor are reduced, high furnace temperatures are maintained and refractory life materially lengthened. Full details on application.

Dual Hearth—sloping toward front of furnace in each unit. Sludge and refuse are charged on upper portion (the drying

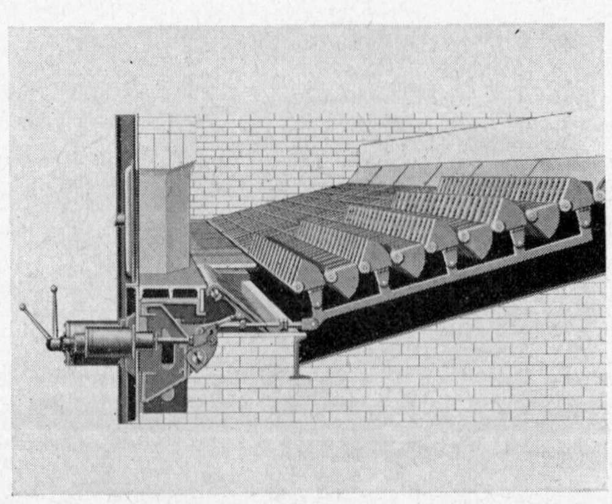

Cross-section of furnace, showing hydraulic stoker linkage

Multiple-cell furnace, showing mechanical stoking controls

hearth), and material is conveyed mechanically or manually down to the lower burning hearth as it dries out.

Large Combustion Chamber—at rear of furnace into which burning gases from the fire are discharged after passing over drying hearth. Combustion is completed in this chamber, after which gases pass inert and odorless up the stack.

Forced Air Blast—(may be preheated) applied directly under burning hearth, increases intensity of fire.

Independent Cleaning and Charging of Cells. Any cell may be charged or cleaned without interfering with normal operation of the others.

Economy of Operation—Charging, stoking and removal of ash are accomplished with a minimum of manpower. Highly insulated furnaces and combustion chambers contain heat of combustion, utilize it for drying fresh charges, and keep outside room temperature normal.

Stamford, Conn. Daily capacity 225 tons

For information regarding the capacity of plant your community should have, and its cost, write to our nearest office—and ask for a copy of our latest "Modern Refuse Incineration" Bulletin. P-D M maintains an advisory service at the free disposal of interested municipal authorities or civic groups. No obligation whatever is involved in receiving from our expert representatives all possible information on refuse disposal by incineration. Your inquiries are cordially invited.

Fond du Lac, Wisc. Daily capacity 90 tons

Little Falls, N. Y. Daily capacity 30 tons

STEDT HYDRAULIC CRANE CO.

Originators and Manufacturers of Stetco Catch Basin Cleaner

93 Cordaville Road, Ashland, Mass.

THE ORIGINAL AND FULLY HYDRAULIC

STETCO CATCH BASIN CLEANER

((PATENTS PENDING)

AND HIAB CRANE

Pat. in U.S. & Canada

Above is Stetco equipment mounted on a large truck at work in Brookline, Mass.

1. STETCO double action Buckets are built heavy and designed to really dig in hard, dry material.
2. Clean your catch basins with One Man — loading his own or other trucks.
3. Dual controls permit full operation from either side of truck.
4. Your truck is available for its regular work when not being used as a crane truck or for cleaning catch basins. (The bucket can be attached or detached in seconds after initial installation). **Also see pages 1118, 1119**

5. STETCO bucket equipment can be installed on any HIAB crane already in service.

6. Can also be adapted for use on other truck or tractor mounted cranes and back hoes.

7. Remove two opposite blades and the bucket becomes an efficient hydraulic tong for loading brush, branches, logs, pipes, etc.

8. All parts of both Crane and Bucket equipment are made of highest quality materials. Low initial cost — Low operating costs.

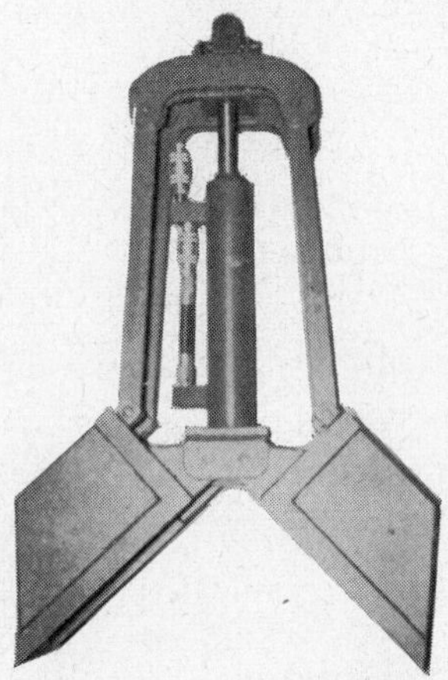

12" x 17" Clam Shell Bucket
Capacity—2 Cubic Feet

SPECIFICATIONS

Operation—Hydraulic—Double or Single Action; Bucket Diameter Closed—15 inches; Bucket Diameter Open—36 inches; Capacity—1 1/3 Cubic Feet; Weight of Bucket—250 pounds, approx.; Height of Bucket 49½ inches closed—45 inches open; Material—Cast Steel. 13½ inch and 18 inch diameter buckets also available, as well as 12 inches x 17 inches and 1/3 Cubic Yard Clamshell Buckets. Special sizes available on order.

All bushings and pins are hardened and interchangeable and held in place by lock rings.

SERVICE

In addition to regular dealer service we offer complete repair or rebuilding facilities for re-tipping blades, installing new pins and bushings, etc., at nominal cost to the user. All parts are readily available from stock.

TRADE MARK

Write today for full details and complete descriptive literature.

STEDT HYDRAULIC CRANE CO.

93 Cordaville Road Ashland, Mass.

TRinity 2-2030

TURBINE SEWER MACHINE CO.

DIVISION OF CHAS. H. STEHLING CO.

1303 North 4th STREET Milwaukee 12, Wis., U. S. A.

Telephone—Broadway 1-2011

SEWER CLEANING EQUIPMENT SPECIALISTS

CHECK THE EXPERTS!

Learn Why
ENGINEERS and MUNICIPAL
OFFICIALS everywhere
agree:

The standard for FASTER—BETTER—SAFER Sewer Cleaning Equipment for all conditions is

Turbine

HYDRAULIC STIFF LEGS

TURCO MAXI-POWER "TWIN" UNITS
CONTROLLED POWER TO REMOVE ANY STOPPAGE

SURFACE HUNG GUIDE JACK

Surface Hung Guide Jack Features:

- ★ All Steel Construction.
- ★ Any Size Bucket Contact Arc.
- ★ Street-level Bucket Dumping.
- ★ Adjustable for all Manholes.
- ★ Simply, Easily Installed.

See Back-Cover Pages 1122, 1123

PROVEN ACCESSORIES (Partial List)

CLAM-EXPANDING BUCKETS — TYPE BEC

For the removal of sand deposits 6″-22″ inclusive

SELF-PROPELLING STOPPAGE-BUSTERS

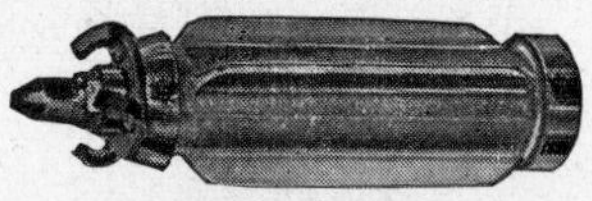

FERRET TURBINE

Excellent!
Universally Used.
2-Models Each.

GO-GETTER NOZZLE GK
Also
TYPE GG WITHOUT KNIVES

TURCO SEWER FLUSHERS

Flush sluggish lines with pressured water. Can be used as plugs. 4″ to 30″.

TURCO HERCULES SEWER BRUSHES

A real Sewer Brush! *Replaceable Bristles.*

WRITE FOR THIS CATALOG →

CONTAINS PICTURES 6" TO 36" SPECIFICATIONS AND ENGINEERING DATA

See Back-Cover Pages 1122, 1123

M. H. DETRICK COMPANY

Engineered Heat Enclosures for all Types of Units

111 W. Washington Street—Chicago 2, Illinois

PITTSBURGH, 22	NEW YORK, 7	PHILADELPHIA, 3
1620 Oliver Bldg.	50 Church St.	1616 Walnut St. Bldg.

And Other Principal Cities

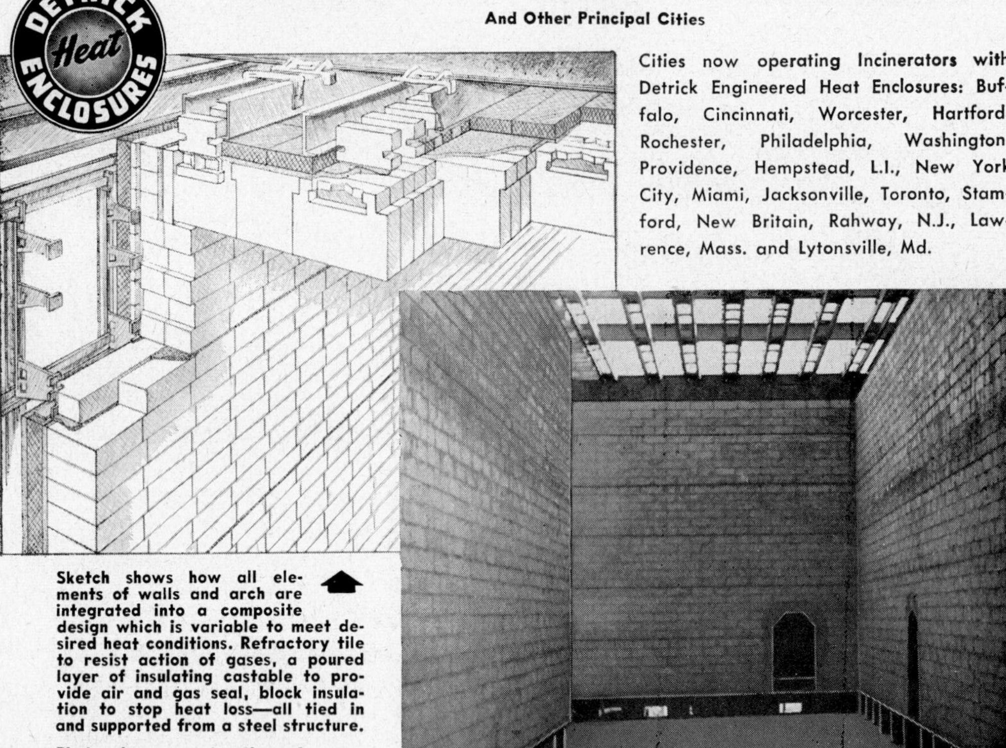

Cities now operating Incinerators with Detrick Engineered Heat Enclosures: Buffalo, Cincinnati, Worcester, Hartford, Rochester, Philadelphia, Washington, Providence, Hempstead, L.I., New York City, Miami, Jacksonville, Toronto, Stamford, New Britain, Rahway, N.J., Lawrence, Mass. and Lytonsville, Md.

Sketch shows how all elements of walls and arch are integrated into a composite design which is variable to meet desired heat conditions. Refractory tile to resist action of gases, a poured layer of insulating castable to provide air and gas seal, block insulation to stop heat loss—all tied in and supported from a steel structure.

Photo shows construction of supported walls. Arch will be hung on steelwork above.

For more than 40 years the Detrick organization has been concentrating on the development of heat enclosures. It has contributed to the development of furnaces for all types of industry including: oil, steel, copper, glass, chemical, utilities and municipalities. Wherever there are heat enclosures Detrick is rendering outstanding service.

Detrick provides all the engineering of the heat enclosure and supplies supervision of construction which assures satisfactory performance of the enclosure.

Here are some of the advantages of Detrick engineered heat enclosures for Incinerators.

1. ECONOMICAL, on the basis of initial cost, longer life and lower maintenance.
2. SUSPENDED Construction provides completely integrated walls and arches including insulation, refractory and supporting structure.
3. ADAPTABLE. It is applicable to any type of incinerator unit regardless of variations in capacity, method of charging or flue arrangement.

To learn more about the Detrick organization and its service, send for special booklet entitled INCINERATOR ENCLOSURES. It illustrates the modern trend in Municipal Incinerator Design.

DRAVO CORPORATON

Incinerators

Dravo Building, Pittsburgh 22, Pennsylvania

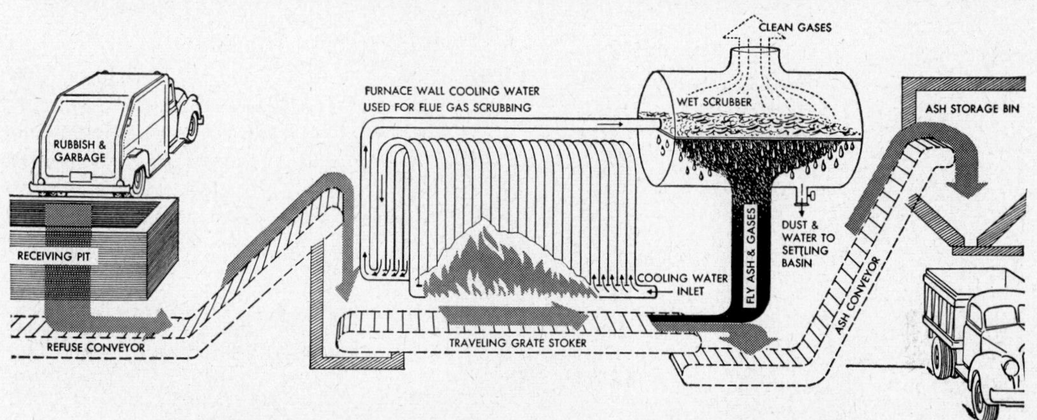

DRAVO INCINERATORS

. . . for ECONOMICAL refuse disposal

The Dravo Incinerator is a complete package unit, adaptable to various contours and sizes of plots. Since there is no need for overhead cranes, runways or heavily reinforced construction, Dravo Incinerators do not require expensive buildings, and can often be installed in existing structures.

The unique design of Dravo Incinerators makes for low first cost and low operating cost.

Scientifically designed to provide continuous, controlled combustion of all burnable refuse regardless of moisture content, Dravo Incinerators produce no smoke, no odor and fly ash discharge from the plant is well below code requirements.

Here are some of the Dravo Incinerator features that assure economy and efficiency:

CONTINUOUS FLOW—The controlled, automatic movement of rubbish and garbage from receiving pits through the furnace permits controlled and positive combustion of all burnable refuse.

WATER-WALL FURNACE—Water tube construction of furnace walls minimizes use of expensive refractories—reduces first cost and lowers maintenance. No secondary combustion chambers needed.

AUTOMATIC CONTROLS—Furnace temperature, cooling water flow, refuse handling system, etc. are all under automatic control. Operating personnel kept to minimum and clean, smokeless operation maintained.

COMPLETE UNIT—The Dravo Incinerator is a complete package—delivered, installed, ready to use.

Write for Bulletin No. 1506 for more information on Dravo Incinerators, or, if you wish, one of our engineers will be happy to discuss your community's particular problem. Address DRAVO CORPORATION, DRAVO BUILDING, PITTSBURGH 22, PENNSYLVANIA.

C O R P O R A T I O N

Blast furnace blowers • boiler and power plants • bridge sub-structures • cab conditioners • docks and unloaders dredging • fabricated piping • foundations • gantry and floating cranes • gas and oil pumping stations • locks and dams • ore and coal bridges • process equipment • pumphouses and intakes • river sand and gravel • sintering plants • slopes, shafts, tunnels • space heaters • steel grating • towboats, barges, river transportation

THE FILER & STOWELL COMPANY

147 East Becher Street, Milwaukee, Wisconsin

Sluice Gates

The Filer & Stowell Company manufactures a Sluice Gate for every kind of service, in a wide range of types and sizes, for filtration and water softening plants, pumping stations and sewage treatment plants. A Filer & Stowell Sluice Gate always gives dependable service because it is accurately machined for true alignment and smooth trouble-free operation under all conditions.

This Company has amply proportioned its Sluice Gates to meet all normal conditions, however, if your requirements do not come within the standard sluice gate range, our engineering department will be glad to work with you and make recommendations on any special installation. However, many specials (so called) have already been developed and can be used without increase in price.

Operating Mechanisms

Sluice Gates may be operated by manual, hydraulic or electric power. For gates with non-rising stems (self-contained) the operating mechanisms are made a part of the sluice gate units. For gates with rising stems, the operating mechanisms are placed in convenient locations and connected to the sluice gates by means of extension stems.

Specifications

Specification for Standardized Sluice Gates for all kinds of service and in all sizes can be obtained by simply writing for your copy of our Bulletin No. 753.

Floorstands

Filer & Stowell Floorstands are of sturdy design and arranged for complete lubrication. Working parts are completely enclosed for protection against the weather. All gears have machine-cut teeth and are smooth-running.

Geared floorstands can be furnished with stem covers, position indicators, and one or two cranks.

Motor-Operated Floorstands

Motor-operated floorstands are desirable for the frequent operation of sluice gates, also for large gates which require considerable time to open or close with manual operation.

Operation of the floorstands may be controlled at the stand, or at a central control station, or automatically. The motor-operated floorstands are completely wired and assembled ready for operation. In case of power failure, provision is made for hand operation. Electrical controls can be mounted on the floorstand or furnished for mounting at a remote location.

Gate Valve

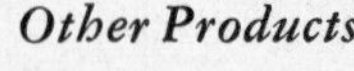

Other Products

Gate Valves Flap Valves
Hydraulic Cylinders

The demand for Filer & Stowell quality products is ever increasing because engineers and plant superintendents know that quality products mean long life, reliable service and minimum maintenance. The Filer & Stowell Company has aided many municipalities in better serving their communities by designing and building dependable water control equipment.

Flap Valve

FINE ORGANICS

211 E. 19th Street, New York, N. Y. GRamercy 5-1030

OUTSTANDING CHEMICALS FROM: **FINE ORGANICS**
FOR MUNICIPAL SANITATION

FOAMWILT CIFON

FINE ORGANICS CIFON

An emulsifiable solution of Orthodichlorobenzene used by sewage disposal plants for the control of odor . . . in the grit bar . . . sedimentation tank and effluent. It also lowers chlorine requirements. It is extremely useful for controlling odors in the forming of sanitary landfill as well as incinerators. Many municipalities, both large and small are satisfied repeat users.

FINE ORGANICS FOAMWILT

The foam control chemical that has excelled in every comparison test conducted by actual users. Foam is brought under control in plants using the activated sludge method quickly and economically, by using only 0.5 to 1 ppm. Material has uniform viscosity over a long range of temperatures (0°F to 110°F) Clear and even flow at all temperatures. Method of application is simple and insures good travel and knockdown. FOAMWILT does not affect activated sludge, and has been proven by cities, towns, and villages who are steady users.

FINE ORGANICS ARODON

A scientifically formulated chemical for control of odor by the "spray method" ARODON forms a curtain of mist, which prevents the odor from travelling. Particularly applicable where the material from individual cesspools is brought into a sewage disposal plant by tank truck for processing.

Complete technical data, prices and characteristics on all FINE ORGANICS products are available on request. Write or call today:

IN PLANNING SEWERS AND DRAINS

Specify TYLOX

flexible rubber PIPE JOINTS

AND GET MORE FOR YOUR SEWER BOND DOLLAR

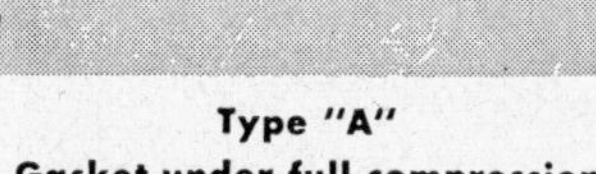

Type "A"
Gasket under full compression

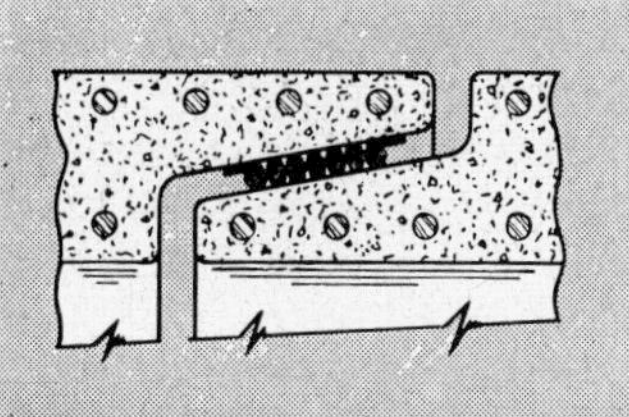

Type "B"
Gasket under full compression

The sections on the left show how Tylox Rubber Gaskets "pack" the joints of tongue-and-groove or bell-and-spigot pipe, under *compression,* to form a flexible, yet mechanically tight seal. Sewerage and drainage lines thus jointed with Tylox Gaskets give more efficient, more economical service and cost less to build because:

YOU CAN LAY MORE PIPE PER DAY—Tylox not only eliminates tedious mortaring, calking, collaring and "pouring" operations, but other costly pipe-laying delays as well . . . For instance, Tylox may be properly installed in wet trenches, and its *flexibility* — which compensates for angularities in the line — permits immediate backfilling . . . even use of straight pipe "on radius."

TYLOX NEVER DETERIORATES — Non-corroding, non-crumbling Tylox Joints don't have to be "dug up" for repairs. Made of rubber compounded specially to resist sewage and industrial waste acids, alkalies or abrasives, Tylox *stays* flexible and tight, reducing sewerage and drainage maintenance to bare minimums by keeping roots and sediment out of the pipe "for the life of the line."

TYLOX PREVENTS INFILTRATION — *Compression-tight* Tylox joints reduce sewage treatment costs by keeping ground water *out* of the line. As a result, less power is required at the treatment plant, and portions of plant capacity are conserved to help meet future sewerage and drainage expansion.

Consider these Tylox cost-saving advantages, and help your community get the most for its sewerage and drainage dollar by insisting on Tylox specifications for your local pipe jobs. For complete Tylox information, data and illustrated case histories of Tylox installations, write to:

HAMILTON KENT MANUFACTURING COMPANY
427 W. Grant St. Kent, Ohio Tel. ORchard 3-9555

HARDINGE COMPANY, INCORPORATED

Main Office and Works, 240 Arch St., York, Pennsylvania

SAN FRANCISCO · SALT LAKE CITY · HOUSTON · HIBBING · CHICAGO · NEW YORK · TORONTO

CIRCULAR CLARIFIERS

Hardinge Circular Clarifiers are available in sizes up to 200′ diameter, either center-column or beam supported for steel, concrete, wood or tile tanks. Sludge scrapers remove settled solids rapidly through central underflow discharge. Bulletin 35-D-28.

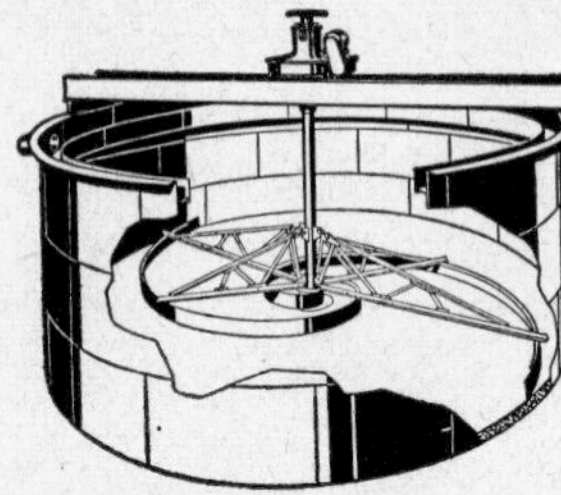

THICKENERS

For removal of fine suspended solids from supply water, waste water and sewage. "Auto-Raise" mechanism prevents scraper breakage. Bulletin 31-E-28.

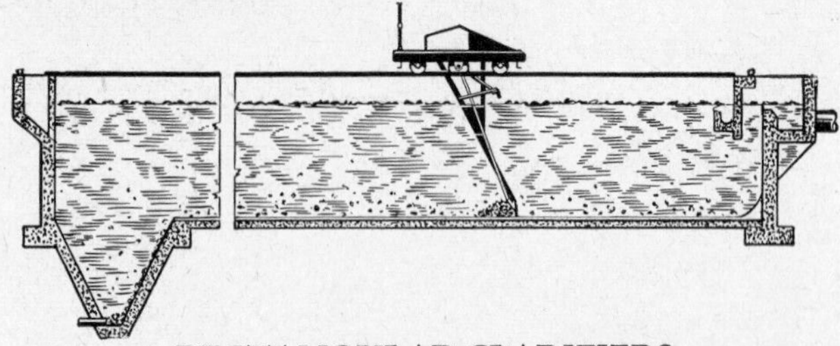

RECTANGULAR CLARIFIERS

Especially suited for limited spaces or where sludge delivery is desired at one end of the tank. A traveling scraper and skimmer carriage removes settled solids from the tank bottom and scum from the top. Bulletin 35-D-28.

AUTOMATIC BACKWASH SAND FILTERS

For high removal of non-settling or slow settling suspended matter. Self-cleaning sand bed. No shut-down necessary for backwashing. Traveling backwash mechanism. Bulletin 46-A-28.

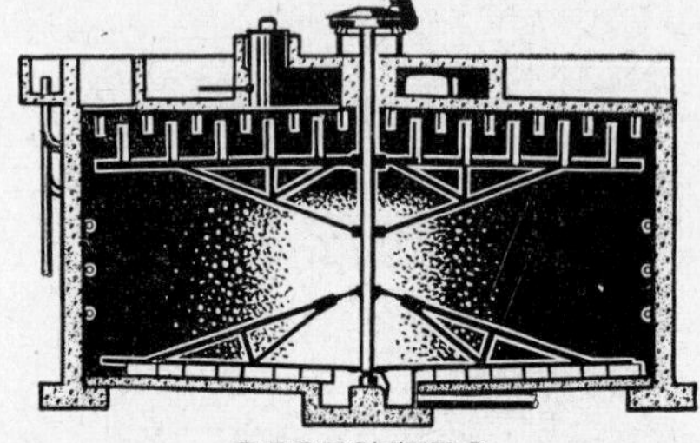

DIGESTERS

Sludge scrapers and scum breaker arms prevent scum accumulation, insure uniform gas production. Emit a dense digested sludge. Bulletin 35-D-28.

FLOCCULATING UNITS

Slowly rotating paddles on vertical shafts bring the small flocs into contact to form larger masses and hasten precipitation. Bulletin 35-D-28.

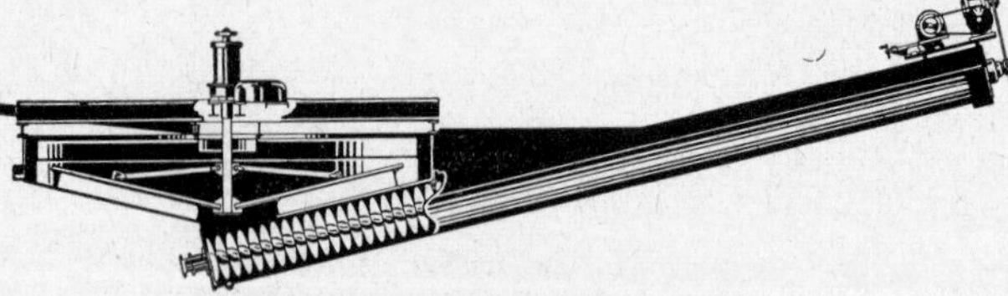

HYDRO CLASSIFIERS

A large-volume classifier for rapid separation of coarse and fine suspended solids. Frequently used for by-product recovery from waste water. Bulletin 39-B-28.

LOCK JOINT PIPE COMPANY

P.O. Box 269, East Orange, N. J.

SEWER & CULVERT PIPE PLANTS

Hartford, Conn.—P.O. Box 21 West Hartford 7, Conn. Tel. Hartford 9-2688

Kenilworth, N. J. — P.O. Box 245 Kenilworth, N. J. Tel. Roselle 4-6300

Wichita, Kan. — P.O. Box 434, Wichita, Kan. Tel. Wichita 5-8834

Denver, Colo.—535 Cooper Building, Denver 2, Colo. Tel. Tabor 1643

Chicago, Ill.—6601 W. 66th Pl., Chicago 38, Ill. Tel. Portsmouth 6630

Kansas City, Mo.—13th & Gentry Sts., No. Kansas City, Mo. Tel. Norclay 4545

Cheyenne, Wyo. — P.O. Box 524 Cheyenne, Wyo.

Lock Joint Pipe Co. of Puerto Rico, P.O. Box 152, Hato Rey, Puerto Rico. Also Ponce, Puerto Rico

North Haven, Conn.—P.O. Box 273, North Haven, Conn. Tel. Spruce 7-1418

St. Louis, Mo.—700 Marshall Ave., Valley Park, Mo. Tel. Valley Pk. 158

Rock Island, Ill.—31st Ave., Rock Isl. Tel. Rock Island 1493

Oklahoma City, Okla.—P.O. Box 2, Oklahoma City, Okla.

Tulsa, Okla.—P.O. Box 2231, Tulsa, Okla.

Beloit, Wisc.—P.O. Box 110, Beloit, Wisc.

PLAIN AND REINFORCED CONCRETE SEWER PIPE

Concrete Pipe for sewers, storm drains and culverts has been recognized for many years by leading sanitary and highway engineers as the most economical construction based on safety, long life, high carrying capacity, low first cost and ready availability.

Careful control of manufacturing operations by men long experienced in the business assures the following high qualities in Lock Joint's finished product:

1. STRENGTH TO WITHSTAND HEAVY BACKLOADS—Rich mixes of concrete, careful selection of aggregates, with density assured by machine tamping or vibration.
2. TIGHT JOINTS—Accurate moulds produce snug fitting joints, requiring a minimum of joint material and labor to be tight against infiltration or leakage.
3. HIGH CARRYING CAPACITY—Dense concrete provides enduring smooth surfaces for maximum flow.
4. AVAILABILITY — Eleven permanent plants throughout the country provide prompt delivery. On large contracts, temporary plants can be erected locally for greater economy.
5. ECONOMY — As the oldest manufacturer of concrete pipe, long years of experience have resulted in low production costs.

BELL JOINT

Mortar or Joint Compound

Inside dia.

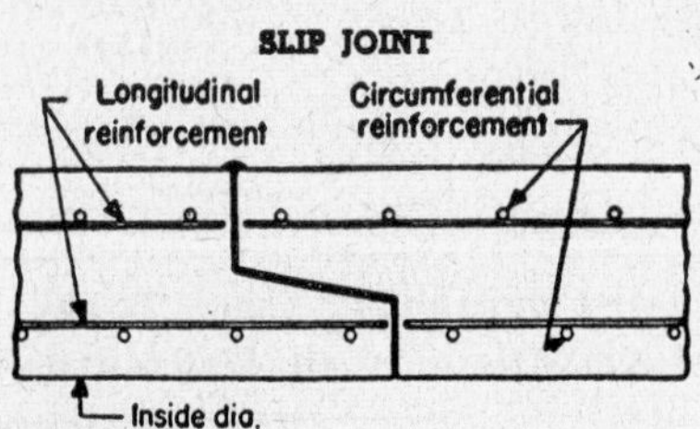

Lock Joint Concrete Pipe is furnished in sizes from 6 in. to 120-in. diameter in standard lengths of 3, 4 or 5 ft. Certain types and sizes of pipes can be supplied in lengths up to 16 ft. Pipes are either Plain or Reinforced according to size and loading requirements.

The latest development in the sewer and culvert pipe field advanced by Lock Joint Pipe Co. is the Roller Suspension Type Pipe. This pipe is produced by a method which, without adding to the weight or wall thickness, materially increases the strength of the pipe and its resistance to abrasion. This type pipe is made in 8' lengths, and its joint ends are precision made. This last factor makes the pipe ideally suited for use with the Lock Joint Riblock Gasket for maximum insurance against ground water infiltration.

The types of joints illustrated below are available in Lock Joint sewer and culvert pipe according to size and class of service.

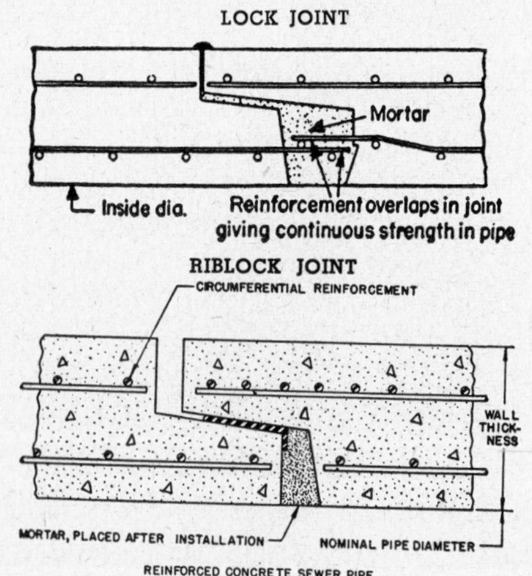

REINFORCED CONCRETE SEWER PIPE "RIBLOCK" RUBBER GASKET SEAL

LORD & BURNHAM

DIVISION BURNHAM CORPORATION

Des Plaines, Ill. | Irvington, N. Y. | St. Catharines, Ont.

LORD & BURNHAM GLASS ENCLOSURES

For Sewage Treatment Plants

The Latest in Aluminum and Steel Construction for Sludge Beds, Sprinkling Filters, Tanks and Wherever Glass Enclosures Are Needed

Five glass covered sludge drying beds, each 40 ft. wide by 125 ft. long, containing 25,000 square feet of bed area, for the City of Taunton, Mass. Fay, Spofford & Thorndike, Engineers; Gil Wyner Co., Inc., General Contractors; Glass Covers by Lord & Burnham.

Lord & Burnham Glass Enclosures .....

Increase Operating Efficiency
Hide Sludge From View
Speed Up Sludge Drying
Control Offensive Odors
Prevent Breeding of Insects
Reduce Sludge Bed Area

We invite engineers to make full use of our long experience and Engineering Service whenever sewage treatment plants are under consideration. The latest data is available on maintenance-free aluminum construction. Walter Kelsey is always on call for consultation on any glass enclosure project.

ENGINEERS' SERVICE SHEETS

You will find our Engineering Service Sheets of immeasurable value when designing and specifying glass enclosures. All sizes are detailed with recommendations for most economical coverage.

A single unit glass cover as used by smaller communities.

LORD & BURNHAM PRODUCTS: GLASS ENCLOSURES of every description; Sludge Drying Beds, Sprinkling Filters, Skimming Tank Enclosures. Greenhouses, Conservatories, etc. Send for Literature

M. B. CORPORATION

FORMERLY MEILI-BLUMBERG CORP.

New Holstein, Wisc.

PACKER

GARBAGE BODY

check these money saving features

- Low cost body
- Low cost, widely used truck chassis
- Simple design reduces maintenance repairs and servicing
- Fast, safe, easy loading and packing
- More load capacity because of complete compaction
- Low cost per mile of operation
- Less manpower than conventional methods of collection

• packs more refuse per cubic yard

• lowest body cost • lowest truck cost

M-B Packers handle full 12-14-16-20-24 cubic yards of compacted refuse.

You get the most for your money with an M-B. • M-B Packers are easy and safe to load from either side. • M-B takes less men per truck than other methods of collection. • M-B handles large wooden crates and boxes through its rear doors—material that would ordinarily be left by other bodies. • M-B Packers have racks on top to handle bed springs, mattresses and other odd-shaped refuse. • M-B Packer plate completely compacts 2 cubic yards of loose garbage at a cycle. • M-B unloads itself by ejecting load out the rear—fast and safely—without danger of upending. • M-B mounts on popular, low-cost, light weight trucks. • You can use the M-B Packer as a general purpose truck when you desire.

PLIBRICO COMPANY

1834 Kingsbury St. · Chicago 14, Ill.

SALES OFFICES

ALABAMA Birmingham
CALIFORNIA El Cerrito (San Francisco), Huntington Park (Los Angeles)
COLORADO Denver
CONNECTICUT Bridgeport, Hartford
FLORIDA Miami, Pensacola, Winter Haven
GEORGIA Atlanta, Columbus
INDIANA Fort Wayne, Indianapolis
IOWA Davenport, Des Moines
KANSAS Kansas City
KENTUCKY Louisville
LOUISIANA New Orleans, Shreveport
MAINE Portland
MARYLAND Baltimore
MASS. Andover, Cambridge, Springfield
MICHIGAN Detroit, Grand Rapids
MINNESOTA Minneapolis, St. Paul
MISSOURI St. Louis
NEBRASKA Omaha
NEW JERSEY Newark, TRENTON
NEW YORK Albany, Buffalo, Long Island City, NEW YORK CITY, Syracuse
N. CAROLINA Charlotte
OHIO Akron, Cincinnati, Cleveland, Columbus, Dayton, Toledo
OKLAHOMA Oklahoma City, Tulsa
OREGON Portland
PENNSYLVANIA Easton, Harrisburg, Philadelphia, Pittsburgh
RHODE ISLAND Providence
SOUTH CAROLINA Columbia
TENNESSEE Chattanooga, Knoxville, Memphis, Nashville
TEXAS Dallas, Ft. Worth, Houston
UTAH Salt Lake City
VERMONT Essex Junction
VIRGINIA Roanoke
WASHINGTON Seattle, Spokane, Tacoma
WEST VIRGINIA Charleston
WISCONSIN Madison, Milwaukee

CUT INCINERATOR PLANT SIZE . . . WITHOUT CUTTING CAPACITY!

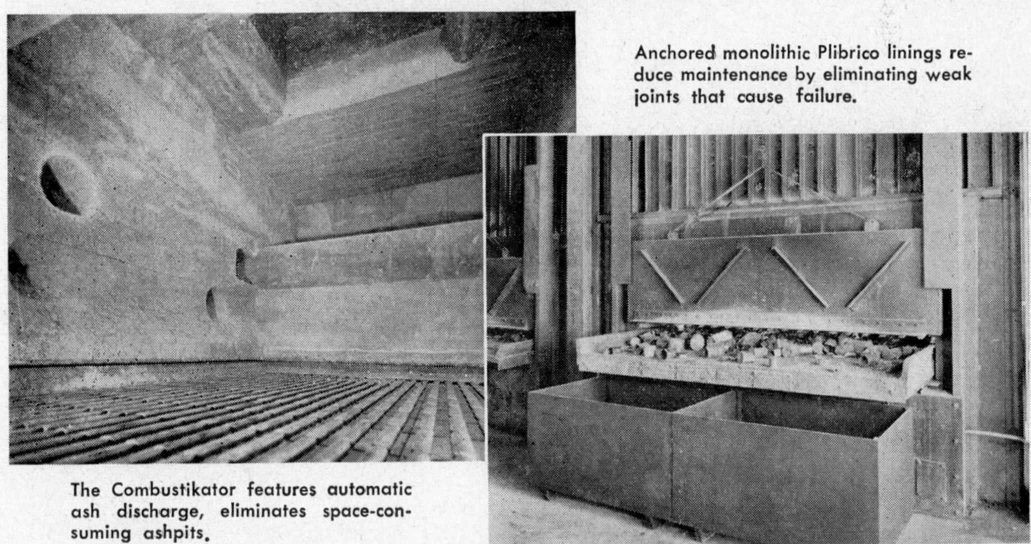

Anchored monolithic Plibrico linings reduce maintenance by eliminating weak joints that cause failure.

The Combustikator features automatic ash discharge, eliminates space-consuming ashpits.

A Plibrico Incinerator with the new Combustikator Stoker costs less to build . . . operate . . . maintain

You can cut the size of your incinerator building by a full story . . . and save accordingly . . . when you specify a Plibrico Incinerator equipped with the effective new Combustikator stoker. Tried and proven at Skokie, Ill., this stoker provides automatic ash discharge, eliminating the need for costly, space-consuming ashpits . . . hence the full story saved. Additional savings can be realized on the cost of the incinerator itself, the amount varying with the type of ash handling system you prefer.

Operational savings can be effected through reduced manpower, for in addition to automatic ash discharge, the Combustikator has a stoker surface that's self-cleaning.

From the maintenance standpoint, the anchored monolithic lining of a Plibrico Incinerator is more durable than ordinary fire brick construction. It's the joints that cause trouble and needless expense, and a Plibrico lining doesn't have those countless joints.

Plibrico designs incinerators for municipalities of all sizes. Discuss your needs with us or with your local Plibrico distributor. Find out more about the advantages above, and many others as well. To effect the greatest savings, do it before your finalize your plans.

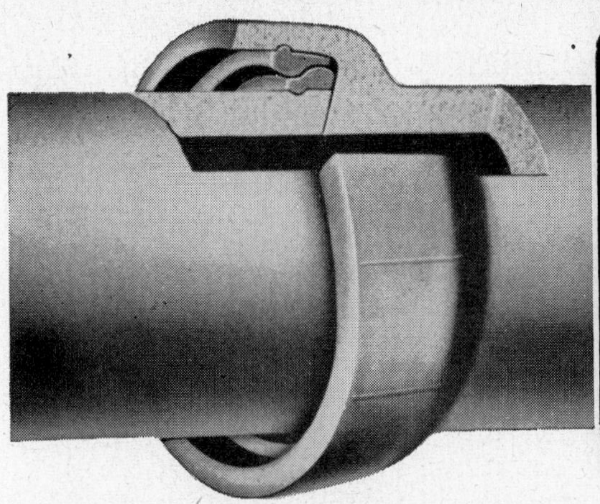

Wedge-Lock* CLAY PIPE by ROBINSON

PLASTISOL JOINTS SNAP TOGETHER!

Wet or dry . . . hot or cold . . . roots or mud—Wedge-Lock, available in 4, 6, 8, 10 and 12 inch diameters with matching fittings, goes in fast and easy. Lubricated with Wedge-Lock Adhesive, its double-ball Plastisol joints "snap home" distinctly—stay in continuous compression. Inspection shows immediately when joints are completed. The smooth curves are self-cleaning during assembly—there is no straight taper to lock foreign material in the joint. And Plastisol does not sag away from the pipe when exposed to heat or sunlight. It's far superior to other jointing materials in chemical resistance, solvent action, and weather exposure. **Request literature from The Robinson Clay Product Co., Akron 9, Ohio.**

*T.M. Reg. App. For. Patents Pending.

Just paint the Plastisol jointing surfaces with Wedge-Lock Adhesive . . .

And push home. Wedge-Lock snaps distinctly into place. You can backfill immediately.

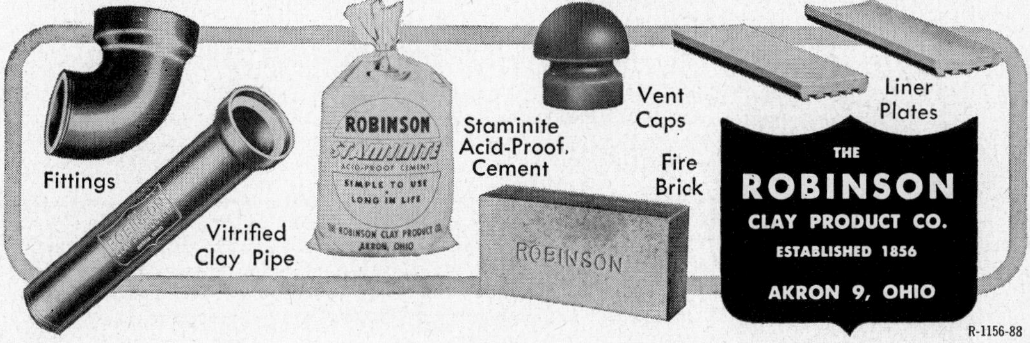

R-1156-88

ROOTS-CONNERSVILLE BLOWER

A DIVISION OF DRESSER INDUSTRIES, INC.

156 Cherry Avenue, Connersville, Indiana

Sales Offices: BIRMINGHAM · BOSTON · BUFFALO · CHATTANOOGA · CHICAGO CLEVELAND · DALLAS · DENVER · DETROIT · HOUSTON · JOHNSON CITY, TENN. KANSAS CITY, MO. · LOS ANGELES · NEW ORLEANS · NEW YORK · PHILADELPHIA PHOENIX · PITTSBURGH · PORTLAND · ST. LOUIS · SALT LAKE CITY · SAN FRANCISCO TORONTO, ONT. · TULSA · WASHINGTON

CENTRIFUGAL BLOWERS

Built in standard single-stage units or in multistage units designed to meet specific conditions.

Capacities from 2,000 cfm to 100,000 cfm or more, at highest practical pressures. Send for details in Bulletin 120-B-14.

ROTARY POSITIVE BLOWERS

Capacities range from 5 cfm to 50,000 cfm. All R-C Blowers work equally well under suction or pressure or both. Detailed information on small sizes in Bulletin AF-154; on larger sizes in Bulletin RB-154.

ROTARY POSITIVE GAS PUMPS

Capacities from 5 cfm to 50,000 cfm, at moderate pressures in small sizes; up to 15 lbs. differential in larger units. Accurate volume control. Details in Bulletin 31-B-17 for small sizes; in 32-33-B-13 for larger sizes.

INERT GAS GENERATORS

Stationary or portable units, in capacities from 1,000 cfh to 100,000 cfh. Driven by gas or oil engines or electric motors. Exceptionally economical, with minimum of attention. Request details in Bulletin IGG-155.

POSITIVE DISPLACEMENT METERS

Long time accuracy maintained, with capacities from 4,000 cfh to 1,000,000 cfh. Small space requirements, low installation cost and little maintenance. Can be fitted with standard instruments. Details in Bulletin M-152.

ASK FOR DETAILED INFORMATION—Send for bulletins on any desired equipment, or consult with our sales offices or factory for assistance on any problem of handling gas or air. Our 100 years of experience assures dependable engineering and performance.

ROTO-ROOTER CORPORATION

Manufacturers of Sewer & Drain Cleaning Equipment

301 University Ave., Des Moines 14, Iowa

IF IT'S SEWER CLEANING PRODUCTION YOU ARE AFTER ROTO-ROD IS THE ANSWER

The Roto-Rod will *clean* 8"-10"-12" sanitary sewers in a fraction of the time required with motorized bucketing equipment. The Roto-Rod works on much the same principle as the nationally known Roto-Rooter machine, except a high quality solid steel rod 1000' long is used in place of coiled cable. Sharp blades revolving at high speed, cut roots, grease, scale, sludge and other debris. Rod is in one continuous length—no nuts to tighten—no screws to set—no couplings to bother you. Measuring meter eliminates "blind" rodding, shows exact amount of rod in the line at all times.

The Roto-Rod is powered by 10 h.p. gasoline engine complete with electric starter.

A 20 PAGE ILLUSTRATED BOOKLET YOURS FOR THE ASKING. WRITE ROTO-ROOTER CORP. DES MOINES 14, IOWA

Cleans Sanitary sewers of: Roots mud sludge

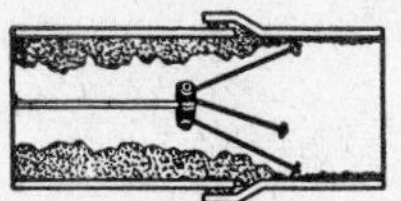

Cleans water mains of hard encrustations

Rods storm sewers makes quick opening

Rods, cleans and threads underground cable ducts

MUNICIPAL AND INDUSTRIAL SEWER CLEANING SERVICE

If you are not interested in buying equipment, the following firms equipped with Roto-Rod offer a complete municipal & industrial sewer and drain cleaning service in the areas shown —no equipment to buy—no help to hire. These firms are in position to give you prompt, efficient service.

MIDDLE ATLANTIC

J. J. BAUER
1911 S. Salina St.
Syracuse, New York

ROTO-ROOTER SERVICE, INC.
P.O. Box 56
Mahopac, New York

ROTO-ROOTER SERVICE
1547 Hertel Ave.
Buffalo, New York

WESTCHESTER ROTO-ROOTER CO.
38 William St.
Mt. Vernon, New York

GUSTAFSON SUPPLY CO.
26 Lincoln St.
Worcester, Massachusetts

O. E. BRUWELHEIDE
7214 Fleury Way
Pittsburgh, Pennsylvania

GEORGE V. ESSLINGER, JR.
408 Marion St.
Clarks Summit, Pennsylvania

EAST NORTH CENTRAL

J. C. KULLBERG
1315 15th Ave.
Rockford, Illinois

GEORGE C. GRAVES
3714 Lake Ave.
Fort Wayne, Indiana

JOHN W. FISCHER
P.O. Box 934
Terre Haute, Indiana

DOETSCH BROS., INC.
3675 East Vernor Highway
Detroit, Michigan

SANITATION ENGINEERING SERVICE
204 N. Elmwood Ave.
Traverse City, Michigan

ALLIED ROTO-ROOTER SERVICE
1801 W. 5th St.
Columbus, Ohio

A. K. PIERCE
1034 Glendale Ave.
Columbus, Ohio

WEST NORTH CENTRAL

ROTO-ROOTER SERVICE
200 E. 4th Ave.
Denver, Colorado

ROTO-ROOTER CORPORATION
301 University Ave.
Des Moines, Iowa

V. N. JACKSON
610 Morgan
Keokuk, Iowa

C. R. ALEXANDER
1652 S. Washington
Wichita, Kansas

ROTO-ROOTER SEWER SERVICE
1819 Nicollet Ave.
Minneapolis, Minnesota

ROTO-ROOTER SEWER SERVICE
534 Selby Ave.
St. Paul, Minnesota

WARD'S ROTO-ROOTER SERVICE
5016 Belmead Rd.
Kansas City, Missouri

WEST SOUTH CENTRAL

ROTO-ROOTER SERVICE
2023 Westheimer
Houston, Texas

BAKER BROS.
2533 No. Henderson
Dallas, Texas

ROTO-ROOTER SERVICE
P.O. Box 4688
Baton Rouge, Louisiana

HOLLEY & COMPANY, INC.
1886 Lamar
Memphis, Tennessee

PACIFIC

ROTO-ROOTER SERVICE
4137 Carrington
Oakland, California

ROTO-ROOTER SERVICE & PLBG. CO.
318 So. Fresno St.
Los Angeles, California

GEORGE EDWARDS
3047 Harvard Ave.
Fresno, California

ROTO-ROOTER SERVICE
260 Vine St.
San Jose, California

MASTER FLUSHER

Freshly cleaned streets are the mark of a proud community

This high velocity, four-jet street flusher really pounds the pavement clean from curb to curb. And yet, it requires less water for a given area because of the high pressure maintained at the jets. It can also be used for sprinkling, sewer cleaning, fire fighting, spraying of shrubs, trees, dumps, and embankments. Hoses are quickly connected for coverage beyond reach of the nozzles. In the snow belt States, the Sicard Master Flusher can be mounted on a heavier four-wheel-traction truck permitting the installation of a grader and plow for snow removal operations, and 12 month use of the combination unit. Capacities up to 2800 gallons. Write for folder and specifications.

SICARD INDUSTRIES INC.

753 WEST MAIN ST., WATERTOWN, N.Y.

TO THE CONSULTING ENGINEER

Don't Limit Your New Water Or Sewage Plant To One Coagulant—

Suitable feeding equipment is available that is adaptable to all coagulants. Our engineers would be happy to consult with you and advise suitable feeders that will accommodate all types of coagulants.

FERRI-FLOC (Ferric Sulfate) is a highly efficient coagulant for all types of water. This has been found true in all sections of the country under varying conditions. Much thought should be given toward incorporating in new plant designs, suitable feeding equipment that will accommodate not just one, but all coagulants.

Let us send you without charge, our 38 page booklet describing fully the use and application of FERRI-FLOC that will be helpful in solving your feeding equipment problems.

TENNESSEE TC CORPORATION

617-29 Grant Building, Atlanta, Georgia

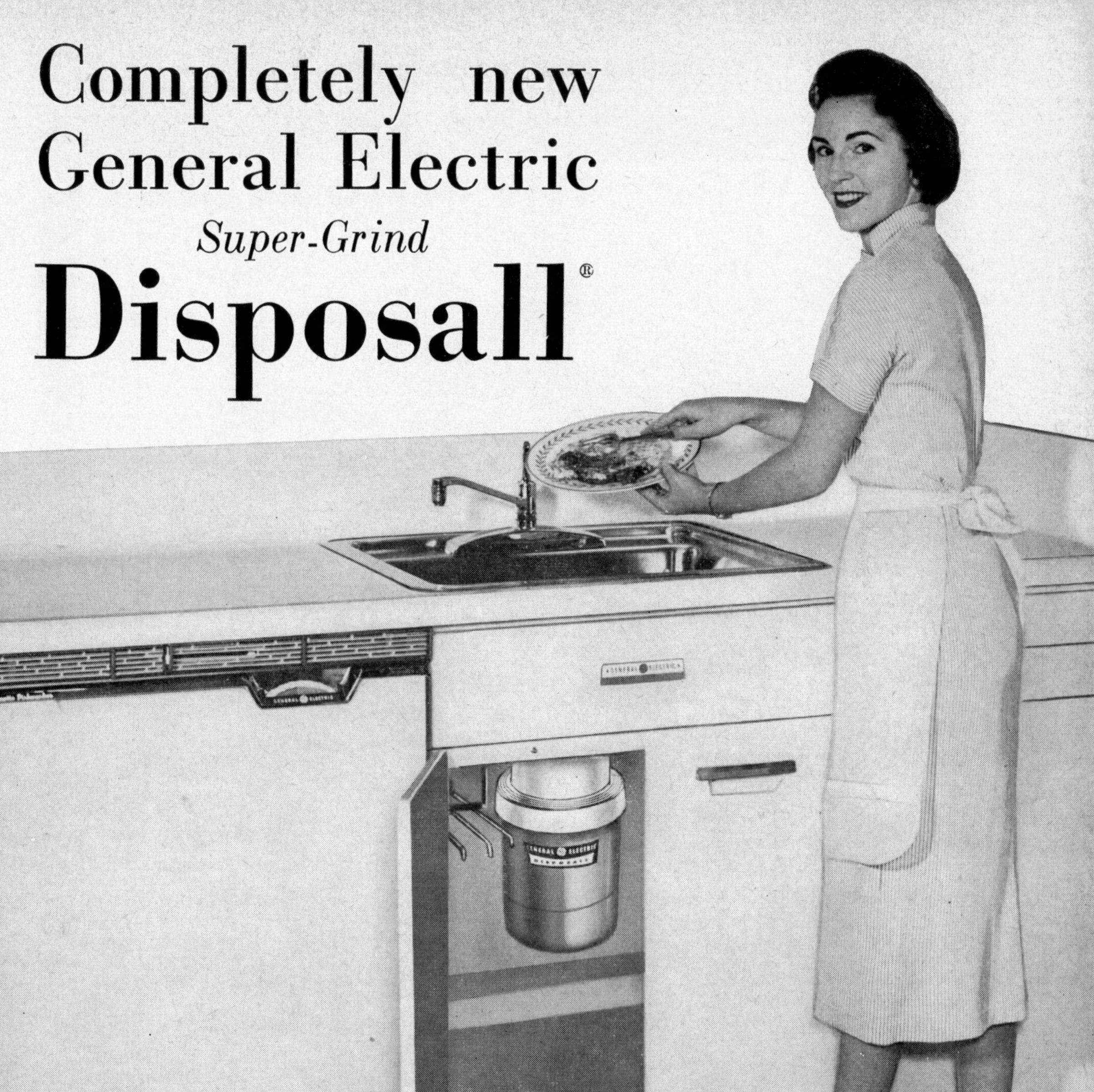

Rated superior in tests against 15 other leading brands

In 1956, United States Testing Company, Incorporated, conducted a series of laboratory tests comparing two 1957 General Electric Disposalls with 15 other leading competitive brands then on the market.

According to their reports, General Electric Disposalls *"are superior to all of the competitive units"* . . . in that "the G-E units will grind a larger variety of items faster and with a finer texture of discharge."

*United States Testing Company Report E-14013 dated June 29, 1956.

Gets rid of food waste

Custom model FA-60

Safety Twistop control eliminates expense of separate wall switch installation. Keeps food waste in, and unwanted objects out.

When the General Electric Disposall is installed, all you see in your sink is the beautiful, stainless steel cover in your present sink opening. Disposall hangs under the sink out of sight and out of the way.

Your Disposall is suspended in rubber where it connects to the sink. This rubber "shock absorber" cuts down noise and vibration.

Handy dishwasher drain connection. A plug punches out to accommodate the drain line from a General Electric Dishwasher, saving the cost of a second trap.

Super-strong shredding mechanism is made of a new type, jet-plane stainless steel alloy . . . one of the toughest of metals. Never requires resharpening.

5 reasons why the General

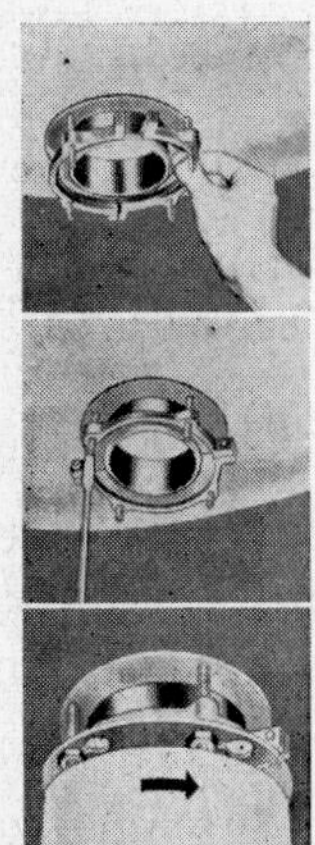

1. Simplified sink flange assembly. Mounts quickly in the sink for easy hanging of Disposall. After the sink flange is installed, the gasket and clamping ring are added. Then both halves of the support ring are placed over the ridge of the sink flange. The support halves fasten together with the two screws provided. When its four mounting studs are tightened, the Disposall is ready to hang.

2. Quick "Key-Hole" mounting. Just lift and turn Disposall, then have both hands free. The lightweight Disposall can easily be lifted so the hex nuts can pass through the large openings in the mounting ring. When the unit is turned all the way to the right and the four hex nuts are tightened, the sink mounting is complete.

before it becomes garbage

Constant permanent lubrication. Your Disposall never requires oiling for the life of the unit. Operates smoothly, efficiently without any attention on your part.

Movable drain outlet can be rotated 360° for easy installation—reduces cost of installation, too.

New 1/3 horsepower General Electric motor is designed to give maximum power and performance at minimum cost.

Food waste from Disposalls can be handled by any adequate sewage system — municipal sewage plant, septic tank or even cesspool. The added load from a Disposall has about the same effect as adding one more person to the average household.

De luxe model FC-40

Continuous feed type. Top serves as sink stopper, permits water drainage, or serves as Disposall cover when the unit operates.

Electric Disposall® is easy to install

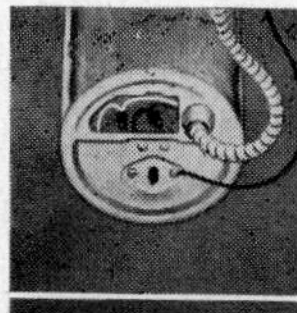

3. Simplified wiring. Spacious junction box plus convenient prestripped leads are provided for quick, easy wiring of both models. (FC-40 requires wall switch.)

4. Simplified plumbing. Handy 1½″ tailpiece supplied with every unit to fit standard plumbing fixtures. Provision is made in the upper housing for dishwasher drain connection. This eliminates the cost of a second drain trap for the dishwasher. The Disposall can be rotated in either direction to make drain connections quicker, simpler, easier.

5. Simplified special installations. Optional fittings are available to install the Disposall in double-bowl sinks, with existing high-wall drains, offset drains and with many other special problems.

How the SUPER-GRIND Disposall® helps your community

1. **Happy home owners, builders, developers**
Once the convenience of using a Disposall is discovered, home owners and renters wonder how they ever did without. Easy to install in new or remodeled homes. Developers report it is increasingly difficult to sell or rent unless a garbage disposer is installed—and survey after survey has shown home makers' preference for General Electric appliances.

2. **Elimination of smelly garbage**
Eliminates the unpleasant tasks of messing with foul-smelling garbage—storing, wrapping, storing again, and cleaning up after the garbage is gone. Eliminates a source of food for disease-carrying vermin. A Disposall is designed to help give you maximum sanitation for modern living.

3. **Reduction of flies and rats**
Studies of community-wide installation of Disposalls in one town showed an almost total absence of flies and rats. This report is based not only on observation but on statistics compiled from actual count by a State Board of Health.

4. **Reduction of contagious diseases**
And surveys made at the time a town installed Disposalls on a community-wide scale show that contagious diseases—especially those known to be carried by flies—were greatly reduced. Included in this reduction was the reduction of polio. (Of course, these facts are no assurance that polio or any other disease has been eliminated by the adoption of Disposalls, since diseases spread in many ways. The trend in the case of one town, however, was considered significant.) For further information write General Electric Company, Dishwasher and Disposall Department, Appliance Park, Louisville, Kentucky.

What is the "DETROIT PLAN" for a garbage-free city?

Briefly, it is a plan for eventually disposing of all vermin attracting, disease spreading food waste at the point where it originates...homes, restaurants, food processing plants. It is a plan to end, once and for all, need for messy, costly garbage collection trucks and dumps.

HEART OF THE PLAN is a city ordinance which went into effect January 1, 1956, requiring installation of food waste grinders of approved makes to dispose of garbage through the sewage system on all new construction, or of installation of other "on-the-site disposal" equipment (primarily approved incinerators).

CHOICE OF THE MAKE OF GRINDER AND INSTALLER IS LEFT TO THE INDIVIDUAL, THUS SAFEGUARDING FREE ENTERPRISE AND LOCAL BUSINESS.

Eventually, it is hoped to require similar disposal systems in all existing construction.

BASIC POINTS TO BE INCLUDED IN GARBAGE GRINDER ORDINANCE

1. That it should apply to all dwelling units and other structures where food waste originates or accumulates, including vegetable or animal matter or a combination thereof.
2. That the grinder should operate electrically with water flowing into the grinder and through the sink drain.
3. That the grinder shall discharge wastes at a reasonably uniform rate, in fluid form which will readily flow through an approved trap, drain line or soil line. That the grinder shall be of such construction that at least 40% of all material discharged from it will pass through a No. 8 sieve, and at least 65% will pass through a No. 3 sieve, and 100% will pass through a ½ inch screen.
4. That the grinder shall be self-scouring.
5. That it shall be free from electrical or mechanical hazards.
6. That the make of grinder shall be approved by the (Public Works or other appropriate Department).
7. That selection of make of grinder, and person to install it shall be at the selection of the individual, provided that the grinder and the installer have been approved by the appropriate city department.
8. That the entire installation shall comply in all particulars with provisions of the plumbing and electrical code of the city.

A copy of the Detroit Ordinance will be sent to you on request by Waste King Corporation, Los Angeles 58, California.

How did it originate and what were steps for putting it into operation?

As in other cities, civic minded leaders in Detroit were aware of the menace and cost of antiquated methods of garbage disposal. The "Detroit Committee for a Garbage-Free City" was formed and included public officials, representatives of the Property Owners Association, Public Utilities, the FHA and other finance interests. The cooperation of plumbing contractors and garbage grinder manufacturers was requested *and quickly obtained.*

- Outdated municipal plumbing and electrical codes were checked and revised to make installation of garbage grinders simpler.
- An advertising and educational campaign was launched to acquaint people, both potential builders and present owners, with the advantage of garbage grinders. Manufacturers were encouraged to promote disposers in Detroit. For the general campaign, support was obtained from plumbing contractors and other groups.
- FHA and other financing was arranged.
- Various makes of garbage grinders were checked and placed on approved list by city authorities.
- A city ordinance requiring disposers (or equivalent facilities) in new construction was drafted, and after public hearings, was passed.

WASTE KING CORPORATION WILL GLADLY FURNISH ADDITIONAL INFORMATION, AND COOPERATE WITH YOU TO HELP MAKE YOUR CITY GARBAGE-FREE, TOO.

WASTE KING CORPORATION
3300 E. 50th Street, Los Angeles 58, Calif.
America's Largest Producer of Garbage Disposers

YOUNGSTOWN KITCHENS DIVISION

OF AMERICAN-STANDARD

WARREN, OHIO

Does garbage in streets and yards brand your city

OLD-FASHIONED?

Garbage is a costly nuisance—everyone knows that. But, in progressive cities across the nation, officials are *doing* something about this age-old health hazard.

Many are encouraging citizens to install food waste disposers; some even have made it a law! These officials are ridding their cities of a serious health problem, while saving public funds, too!

Mr. City Official, are you standing idle while progress bypasses *your* city? Are you not obligated to promote the safety and welfare of your city? You owe your citizens:

CLEAN AIR

No more smoke, fumes, and foul odors from burning garbage!

CLEAN ALLEYS

No more smelly breeding grounds for rats, vermin, and stray animals!

CLEAN STREETS

No more ugly, dirty garbage cans lined for pickup along pleasant residential streets!

LOWER COSTS

No more tax money wasted on endless rounds of garbage collections!

YOUNGSTOWN KITCHENS DIVISION

OF AMERICAN-STANDARD

WARREN, OHIO

For best results, insist that Food Waste Disposers feature:

FLEXIBILITY: Youngstown Kitchens Food Waste Disposers install easily in any modern sink with a 3½- to 4-inch opening. Installation is quick, easy, water-tight.

SELF-CLEANSING: Water action and rotation of the shredder automatically keep the Youngstown Kitchens Food Waste Disposer clean and odor-free.

FOUR-WAY ACTION: The Youngstown Kitchens Food Waste Disposer files, mills, cuts, and clips wastes to just the right size for best drain action, easier treatment. Removable, reversible cutter blades double disposer life.

QUIET POWER: Powerful ⅓-hp motor is permanently lubricated and sealed in the Youngstown Kitchens Food Waste Disposer. The entire unit floats quietly on vibration-free mountings.

AUTOMATIC OVERLOAD PROTECTION: Protects the Youngstown Kitchens Food Waste Disposer and house wiring.

SAFETY-TESTED: The Youngstown Kitchens Food Waste Disposer is listed by Underwriters' Laboratories, Inc., and approved by Good Housekeeping, McCall's magazine, and The Canadian Standards Association.

WARRANTY: Youngstown Kitchens Food Waste Disposers carry a full one-year labor warranty, plus a 5-year parts warranty. Disposer has rust-resistant, stainless-steel interior grinding chamber.

CONTINUOUS FEED: By eliminating starting and stopping between loads, the Youngstown Kitchens Food Waste Disposer saves time, reduces possibility of jamming.

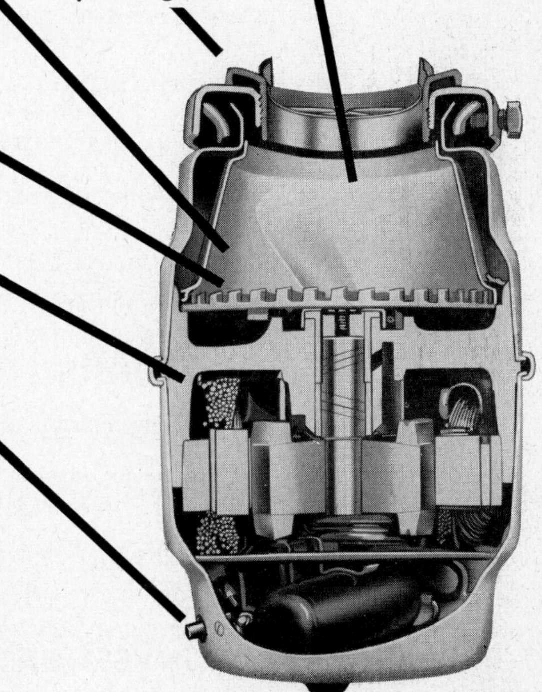

Municipal Index Maps and City Lists

In this section of the MUNICIPAL INDEX there will be found, in addition to the maps listed below, individual lists by states of all places in the United States credited by Census authorities with a population of 1,000 or more.

What the Symbols Mean

LETTERS AND FIGURES IN TABLES ON FOLLOWING PAGES give the key to the location of each place on its map. The index reference gives the location of the city or town on the state map. The name is found within the square formed by the two lines of latitude and the two lines of longitude which enclose each of the index reference coordinates — i.e., the marginal letters and numbers.

CAPITAL LETTERS indicate the name of the capital city of each state.

URBAN AND RURAL POPULATION BY SIZE OF PLACE

Based on 1950 Census figures supplied by the Bureau of the Census.

Size of Place	Number of Places	Population	Per Cent of Total Population of United States
1,000,000 or more	5	17,404,450	11.5
500,000 to 1,000,000	13	9,186,945	6.1
250,000 to 500,000	23	8,241,560	5.5
100,000 to 250,000	65	9,478,662	6.3
50,000 to 100,000	126	8,930,823	5.9
25,000 to 50,000	252	8,807,721	5.8
10,000 to 25,000	778	11,866,505	7.9
5,000 to 10,000	1,176	8,138,596	5.4
2,500 to 5,000	1,846	6,490,406	4.3
Under 2,500 in urbanized areas	457	577,992	0.4
Unincorporated parts of urbanized areas	....	7,344,026	4.9
Total urban territory	....	96,467,686	64.0
Total rural territory	....	54,229,675	36.0
Total population of the United States in 1950	....	150,697,361	100.0

Nearly two-thirds of the continental United States population of 150,697,361 enumerated in the 1950 Census, namely 96,467,686 or 64.0 per cent resided in urban territory. The remainder of the population, 54,229,675 or 36.0 per cent, resided in rural territory.

Almost three-fourths of the urban population of 96,467,686, namely 69,249,148 or 71.8 per cent, was concentrated in 157 urbanized areas defined about central cities of 50,000 or more population, while the remainder, 27,218,538 or 28.2 per cent, resided in other urban places of 2,500 or more population located outside the 157 urbanized areas.

The population of the 157 urbanized areas, 69,249,148, was 46.0 per cent of the country's total population of 150,697,361, while the remainder of the urban population residing outside the urbanized areas, 27,218,538, represented 18.1 per cent of the total population.

Within the 157 urbanized areas, 48,377,240, or 69.9 per cent of their combined population of 69,249,148, resided in the central cities, while 20,871,908, or 30.1 per cent of the urbanized areas' total, resided in the urban-fringe areas of the central cities.

The population of 48,377,240 in the central cities of the 157 urbanized areas represented 32.1 per cent of the national population of 150,697,361, while the population of 20,871,908 in the urban-fringe areas represented 13.9 per cent of the national total.

URBAN AND RURAL POPULATION OF STATES: 1950

STATE	Total	Urban	Rural	% Urban
U. S. Total	150,697,361	96,467,686	54,229,675	64.0
Alabama	3,061,743	1,340,937	1,720,806	43.8
Arizona	749,587	416,000	333,587	55.5
Arkansas	1,909,511	630,591	1,278,920	33.0
California	10,586,223	8,539,420	2,046,803	80.7
Colorado	1,325,089	831,318	493,771	62.7
Connecticut	2,007,280	1,558,642	448,638	77.6
Delaware	318,085	199,122	118,963	62.6
Dist. of Columbia	802,178	802,178	....	100.0
Florida	2,771,305	1,813,890	957,415	65.5
Georgia	3,444,578	1,559,447	1,885,131	45.3
Idaho	588,637	252,549	336,088	42.9
Illinois	8,712,176	6,759,271	1,952,905	77.6
Indiana	3,934,224	2,357,196	1,577,028	59.9
Iowa	2,621,073	1,250,938	1,370,135	47.7
Kansas	1,905,299	993,220	912,079	52.1
Kentucky	2,944,806	1,084,070	1,860,736	36.8
Louisana	2,683,516	1,471,696	1,211,820	54.8
Maine	913,774	472,000	441,774	51.7
Maryland	2,343,001	1,615,902	727,099	69.0
Massachusetts	4,690,514	3,959,239	731,275	84.4
Michigan	6,371,766	4,503,084	1,868,682	70.7
Minnesota	2,982,483	1,624,914	1,357,569	54.5
Mississippi	2,178,914	607,162	1,571,752	27.9
Missouri	3,954,653	2,432,715	1,521,938	61.5
Montana	591,024	258,034	332,990	43.7
Nebraska	1,325,510	621,905	703,605	46.9
Nevada	160,083	91,625	68,458	57.2
New Hampshire	533,242	306,806	226,436	57.5
New Jersey	4,835,329	4,186,207	649,122	86.6
New Mexico	681,187	341,889	339,298	50.2
New York	14,830,192	12,682,446	2,147,746	85.5
North Carolina	4,061,929	1,368,101	2,693,828	33.7
North Dakota	619,636	164,817	454,819	26.6
Ohio	7,946,627	5,578,274	2,368,353	70.2
Oklahoma	2,233,351	1,139,481	1,093,870	51.0
Oregon	1,521,341	819,318	702,023	53.9
Pennsylvania	10,498,012	7,403,036	3,094,976	70.5
Rhode Island	791,896	667,212	124,684	84.3
South Carolina	2,117,027	777,921	1,339,106	36.7
South Dakota	652,740	216,710	436,030	33.2
Tennessee	3,291,718	1,452,602	1,839,116	44.1
Texas	7,711,194	4,838,060	2,873,134	62.7
Utah	688,862	449,855	239,007	65.3
Vermont	377,747	137,612	240,135	36.4
Virginia	3,318,680	1,560,115	1,758,565	47.0
Washington	2,378,963	1,503,166	875,797	63.2
West Virginia	2,005,552	694,487	1,311,065	34.6
Wisconsin	3,434,575	1,987,888	1,446,687	57.9
Wyoming	290,529	144,618	145,911	49.8

POPULATION ESTIMATES

CONTINENT OR COUNTRY	Est. Population
Africa	190,000,000
Asia	1,301,000,000
Australia	7,579,358
Canada	14,009,429
Europe	551,000,000
South America	109,500,000
United States	150,697,361
World	2,200,000,000

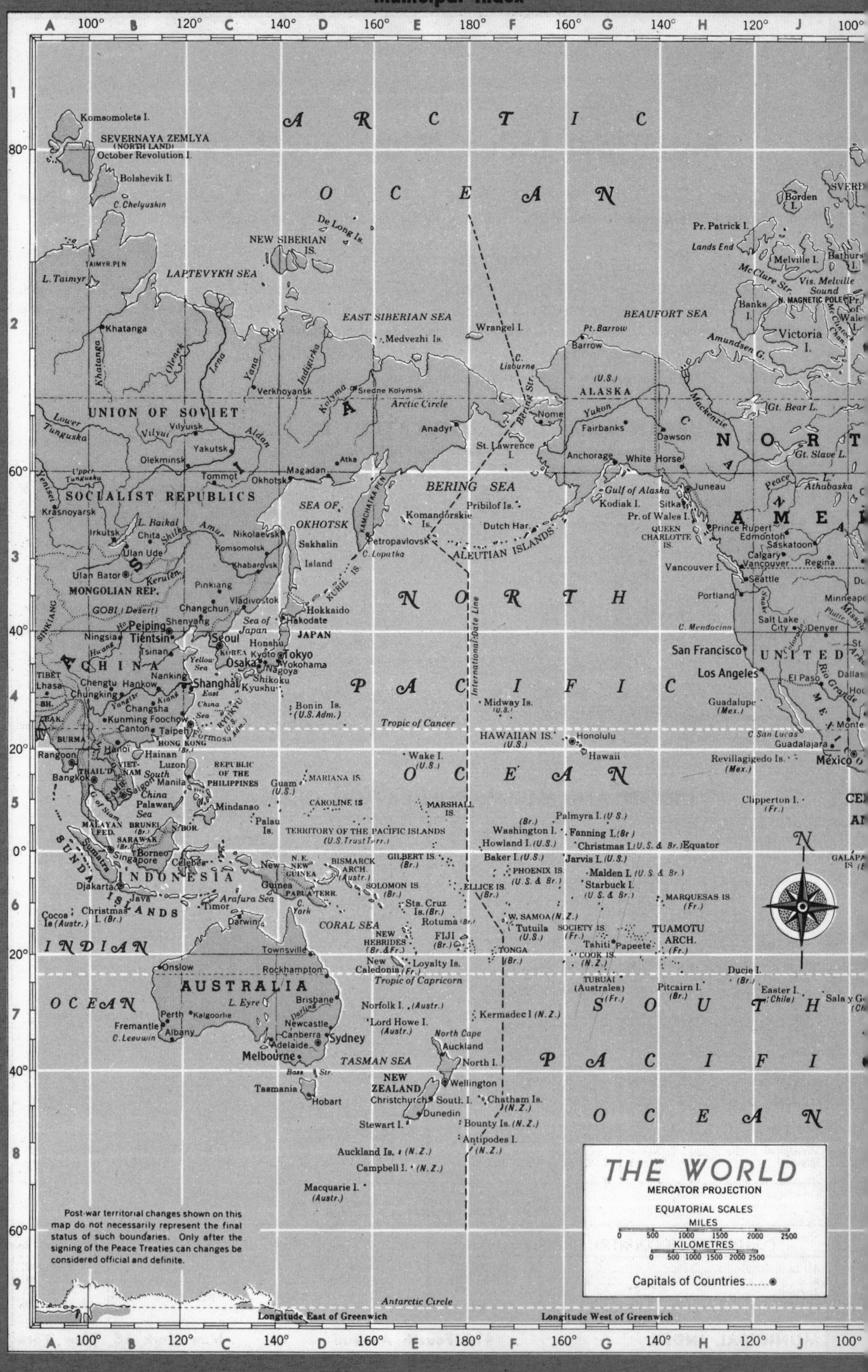
THE WORLD
MERCATOR PROJECTION
EQUATORIAL SCALES
MILES
0 500 1000 1500 2000 2500
KILOMETRES
0 500 1000 1500 2000 2500
Capitals of Countries
Post-war territorial changes shown on this map do not necessarily represent the final status of such boundaries. Only after the signing of the Peace Treaties can changes be considered official and definite.
Longitude East of Greenwich
Longitude West of Greenwich
ARCTIC OCEAN
NORTH PACIFIC OCEAN
SOUTH PACIFIC OCEAN
INDIAN OCEAN
UNION OF SOVIET SOCIALIST REPUBLICS
CHINA
MONGOLIAN REP.
JAPAN
AUSTRALIA
NEW ZEALAND
INDONESIA
REPUBLIC OF THE PHILIPPINES
ALASKA
Komsomolets I.
SEVERNAYA ZEMLYA (NORTH LAND)
October Revolution I.
Bolshevik I.
C. Chelyuskin
NEW SIBERIAN IS.
De Long Is.
LAPTEVYKH SEA
EAST SIBERIAN SEA
BEAUFORT SEA
BERING SEA
SEA OF OKHOTSK
Sea of Japan
East China Sea
CORAL SEA
TASMAN SEA
Arafura Sea
Wrangel I.
Medvezhi Is.
Khatanga
Verkhoyansk
Sredne Kolymsk
Arctic Circle
Anadyr
Yakutsk
Olekminsk
Magadan
Okhotsk
Krasnoyarsk
Irkutsk
L. Baikal
Chita
Ulan Ude
Ulan Bator
Nikolaevsk
Komsomolsk
Khabarovsk
Vladivostok
Sakhalin Island
Petropavlovsk
KURIL IS.
ALEUTIAN ISLANDS
Komandorskie Is.
Dutch Har.
Pribilof Is.
St. Lawrence I.
Nome
Fairbanks
Anchorage
Gulf of Alaska
Kodiak I.
Juneau
Sitka
White Horse
Dawson
Pt. Barrow
Barrow
Bering Str.
Hokkaido
Hakodate
Honshu
Tokyo
Yokohama
Kyoto
Osaka
Nagoya
Shikoku
Kyushu
Seoul
KOREA
Peiping
Tientsin
Shenyang
Changchun
Ningsia
Tsinan
Nanking
Shanghai
Hankow
Chengtu
Chungking
Changsha
Kunming
Foochow
Canton
Taipeh
Formosa
HONG KONG
Hainan
Hanoi
Lhasa
TIBET
SINKIANG
GOBI (Desert)
BURMA
Rangoon
Bangkok
THAIL'D
Saigon
Luzon
Manila
Mindanao
South China Sea
Palawan
BRUNEI
SARAWAK
Borneo
Celebes
Singapore
Sumatra
Java
Djakarta
Timor
SUNDA ISLANDS
MALAYAN FED.
Christmas I. (Br.)
Cocos Is (Austr.)
Darwin
Townsville
Rockhampton
Brisbane
Onslow
L. Eyre
Perth
Kalgoorlie
Fremantle
Albany
C. Leeuwin
Newcastle
Sydney
Canberra
Adelaide
Melbourne
Bass Str.
Tasmania
Hobart
Auckland
North I.
Wellington
South I.
Christchurch
Dunedin
Stewart I.
Chatham Is. (N.Z.)
Bounty Is. (N.Z.)
Antipodes I. (N.Z.)
Auckland Is. (N.Z.)
Campbell I. (N.Z.)
Macquarie I. (Austr.)
Norfolk I. (Austr.)
Lord Howe I. (Austr.)
Kermadec I (N.Z.)
New Guinea
NEW GUINEA (Austr.)
PAPUA TERR.
BISMARCK ARCH. (Austr.)
SOLOMON IS. (Br.)
Sta. Cruz Is. (Br.)
NEW HEBRIDES (Br. & Fr.)
New Caledonia (Fr.)
Loyalty Is.
FIJI (Br.)
Rotuma (Br.)
TONGA (Br.)
W. SAMOA (N.Z.)
Tutuila (U.S.)
ELLICE IS. (Br.)
GILBERT IS. (Br.)
PHOENIX IS. (U.S. & Br.)
MARSHALL IS.
CAROLINE IS.
MARIANA IS.
Guam (U.S.)
Palau Is.
TERRITORY OF THE PACIFIC ISLANDS (U.S. Trust Terr.)
Wake I. (U.S.)
Bonin Is. (U.S. Adm.)
RYUKYU (U.S. Adm.)
Midway Is. (U.S.)
HAWAIIAN IS. (U.S.)
Honolulu
Hawaii
Tropic of Cancer
Tropic of Capricorn
International Date Line
Antarctic Circle
Palmyra I. (U.S.)
Washington I. (Br.)
Fanning I. (Br.)
Howland I. (U.S.)
Christmas I. (U.S. & Br.)
Equator
Baker I. (U.S.)
Jarvis I. (U.S.)
Malden I. (U.S. & Br.)
Starbuck I. (U.S. & Br.)
MARQUESAS IS. (Fr.)
SOCIETY IS. (Fr.)
Tahiti
Papeete
TUAMOTU ARCH. (Fr.)
COOK IS. (N.Z.)
TUBUAI (Australes) (Fr.)
Pitcairn I. (Br.)
Ducie I. (Br.)
Easter I. (Chile)
Sala y Gomez
Clipperton I. (Fr.)
Revillagigedo Is. (Mex.)
Guadalupe (Mex.)
C. San Lucas
Guadalajara
Mexico
El Paso
Rio Grande
Los Angeles
San Francisco
C. Mendocino
Salt Lake City
Denver
Portland
Seattle
Vancouver I.
Vancouver
Calgary
Edmonton
Saskatoon
Regina
Prince Rupert
QUEEN CHARLOTTE IS.
Pr. of Wales I.
Gt. Slave L.
Gt. Bear L.
Athabaska L.
Victoria I.
Banks I.
Melville I.
Pr. Patrick I.
Lands End
Borden I.
McClure Str.
Vis. Melville Sound
N. MAGNETIC POLE
Amundsen G.
Mackenzie
Yukon
Lower Tunguska
Upper Tunguska
Yenisei
Khatanga
Olenek
Lena
Yana
Indigirka
Kolyma
Aldan
Vilyui
Amur
Shilka
Kerulen
Hwang Ho
Yangtze
G. of Siam
Peace
Snake
Platte
Colorado

80° L 60° M 40° N 20° O 0° P 20° R 40° S 60° T 80° U
LINCOLN SEA
PEARY LAND
KING FREDERIK VIII LAND
FRANZ JOSEF LAND (FRIDTJOF NANSEN LAND)
Graham Bell I.
Vilchek I.
SVALBARD (SPITSBERGEN) (Nor.)
N. E. Land
W. Spitsbergen
Edge I.
Ellesmere Island
Kane Basin
Etah
GREENLAND (Den.)
Thule
GREENLAND SEA
BARENTS SEA
Bear I. (Nor.)
NOVAYA ZEMLYA
Baffin Bay
Upernivik
KARA SEA
Baffin Island
Disko I.
Godhavn
Davis Strait
Scoresby Sd.
Jan Mayen (Nor.)
Nordkapp
Murmansk
Vaigach
Kolguev
Dudinka
Igarka
Foxe Basin
Arctic Circle
KING CHRISTIAN IX LD.
Str. of Denmark
FREDERIK VI COAST
Angmagssalik
ICELAND
Reykjavik
Lofoten
NORWEGIAN SEA
Kirovsk
White Sea
Arkhangelsk
Salekhard
Berezovo
Godthaab
Frederikshaab
Hudson Str.
C. Chidley
Julianehaab
C. Farewell
Faeroe Is. (Den.)
Shetland Is.
Orkney Is.
Hebrides
GREAT BRITAIN
NORWAY
SWEDEN
FINLAND
G. of Bothnia
Helsinki
Oslo
Stockholm
Tallin
Leningrad
L. Onega
L. Ladoga
Kotlas
Dvina
Pechora
UNION OF SOVIET SOCIALIST REPUBLICS
Kirov
Molotov
Tobolsk
Tomsk
Kalinin
Riga
Moskva
Sverdlovsk
Chelyabinsk
Omsk
Novosibirsk
LABRADOR
Hopedale
North Sea
Glasgow
DENMARK
Baltic Sea
Gdansk
Kaunas
Minsk
Gorki
Ufa
Magnitogorsk
IRELAND
Birmingham
London
NETH.
Berlin
GERMANY
Warszawa
POLAND
Voronezh
Saratov
Kuibyshev
Semipalatinsk
Str. of Belle Isle
NEWFOUNDLAND
Moosonee
Quebec
G. of St. Lawrence
St. John's
C. Race
St. Pierre & Miquelon (Fr.)
Montreal
Ottawa
Halifax
Eng. Chan.
BELG.
Bonn
Praha
CZECHO.
Wien
AUST.
Budapest
HUN.
Kiev
Kharkov
Stalingrad
Rostov
Volga
Ural
Akmolinsk
Irtish
L. Balkhash
Paris
FRANCE
SWITZ.
Bay of Biscay
Milano
Beograd
YUGO.
RUM.
Bucuresti
BULG.
Odessa
Astrakhan
Caspian Sea
L. Aral
Syr
Amu
Tihwa
Cleveland
Boston
NORTH
New York
Philadelphia
C. Finisterre
Marseille
Madrid
Barcelona
PORTUGAL
SPAIN
Roma
ITALY
Sardegna
Sicilia
Istanbul
Black Sea
Tbilisi
Baku
Tashkent
Samarkand
Mary
SINKIANG
Lisboa
AZORES (Port.)
C. S. Vicente
Gibraltar (Br.)
Str. of Gibraltar
GREECE
Athenai
Ankara
TURKEY
Tehran
IRAN
Kabul
AFGHANISTAN
KASH. & JAM.
TIBET
C. Hatteras
Bermuda (Br.)
Madeira (Port.)
Rabat
Alger
Tunis
MEDITERRANEAN SEA
Krete
Cyprus
SYRIA
LEB.
ISR.
Bagdad
IRAQ
Basra
Savannah
ATLANTIC
Marrakech
MOROCCO
Sidi Ifni
TUNISIA
Tripoli
Bengasi
Alexandria
JOR.
KUWAIT
Persian G.
PAKISTAN
Lahore
Delhi
New Delhi
NEPAL
Ganges
Indus
Orleans
CANARY IS. (Sp.)
ALGERIA (Fr.)
LIBYA
Cairo
Asyut
EGYPT
Suez Canal
SAUDI ARABIA
Riyadh
Karachi
Miami
BAHAMA IS. (Br.)
Tropic of Cancer
Villa Cisneros
SP. W. AFRICA
SAHARA
Gat
Nile
Red Sea
Mecca
Masqat
OMAN
Ahmadabad
INDIA
Calcutta
WEST INDIES
CUBA
DOM. REP.
HAITI
Hispaniola
PUERTO RICO (U.S.)
C. Blanco
Bilma
FRENCH WEST AFRICA
ARABIAN SEA
Bombay
Bay of Bengal
OCEAN
LESSER ANTILLES
St. Louis
Tombouctou
CAPE VERDE IS. (Port.)
Dakar
Bathurst
AFRICA
Khartoum
SUDAN
YEMEN
ADEN (Br.)
Aden
Gulf of Aden
Socotra (Br.)
Hyderabad
GOA (Port.)
Madras
Caribbean Sea
Curaçao (Neth.)
Trinidad
PORT. GUINEA
Bamako
Niger
TOGO
NIGERIA
FR. EQUAT. AFRICA
FR. SOM.
Berbera
BR. SOM.
Laccadive Is. (India)
Panama
Caracas
VENEZUELA
Georgetown
Paramaribo
Freetown
SIERRA LEONE (Br.)
GOLD COAST
Lagos
Addis Ababa
ETHIOPIA
C. Comorin
Colombo
CEYLON
Bogota
COLOMBIA
BR. G.
SUR.
Cayenne
FR. GUIANA
Monrovia
LIBERIA
Abidjan
Accra
Gulf of Guinea
CAMEROON
Yaounde
Congo
UGANDA
KENYA
SOM. I.D.
Mogadiscio
Maldive Is. (Br.)
Quito
ECUADOR
Equator
Belém (Pará)
Amazon
Manaus
SP. GUINEA
BELGIAN
Chisimaio
Fortaleza (Ceará)
C. de São Roque
Natal
Recife (Pernambuco)
Brazzaville
Leopoldville
Cabinda (Port.)
L. Victoria
Nairobi
Mombasa
ZANZIBAR
Dar es Salaam
L. Tanganyika
TANGANYIKA TERR.
SEYCHELLES (Br.)
Chagos Arch. (Br.)
SOUTH
BRAZIL
Madeira
Tapajós
Xingu
Tocantins
São Francisco
PERU
Ascension (Br.)
Loanda
CONGO
Elisabethville
Is. Comores
Lima
Callao
AMERICA
Salvador (Bahia)
Benguela
Nova Lisboa
L. Nyasa
Moçambique
INDIAN
Arequipa
La Paz
BOLIVIA
Cuiabá
Belo Horizonte
St. Helena (Br.)
ANGOLA (Port.)
FED. OF RHO. & NYA.
Lusaka
Salisbury
MOZAMBIQUE
Mozambique Chan.
MADAGASCAR (Fr.)
Tananarive
Rodrigues
Mauritius (Br.)
Réunion (Fr.)
Tacna
Arica
Sucre
Iquique
PARAGUAY
Paraná
S. Paulo
Santos
Rio de Janeiro
S. W. AFRICA
Windhoek
Walvis Bay
BECH. PROT.
Pretoria
Johannesburg
Antofagasta
Asunción
Tropic of Capricorn
Lourenço Marques
C. Ste. Marie
Ambrosio
Tucumán
Coquimbo
Córdoba
Pto. Alegre
UNION OF SOUTH AFRICA
Orange
Durban
Valparaiso
Santiago
Rosario
URUGUAY
Montevideo
ATLANTIC
Capetown
Port Elizabeth
C. of Good Hope
Concepción
Talca
R. de la Plata
Eva Perón
Buenos Aires
Tristan da Cunha (Br.)
Amsterdam I. (Fr.)
St. Paul I. (Fr.)
Valdivia
Pto. Montt
Bahia Blanca
Gough I. (Br.)
Rawson
OCEAN
Crozet Is. (Fr.)
Pr. Edward Is. (S. Afr.)
ARGENTINA
Sta. Cruz
FALKLAND IS. (Br.)
Port Stanley
Kerguelen (Fr.)
Punta Arenas
Magellan Str.
Tierra del Fuego
C. Horn
S. Georgia (Br.)
Bouvet I. (Nor.)
McDonald I.
Heard I. (Austr.)
SCOTIA SEA
SOUTH SANDWICH IS. (Br.)
Drake Passage
SOUTH ORKNEY IS. (Br.)
S. Shetland Is.
PALMER ARCH.
SEA
Antarctic Circle
Longitude West of Greenwich
Longitude East of Greenwich
Copyright by C. S. HAMMOND & CO., N.Y.
95124

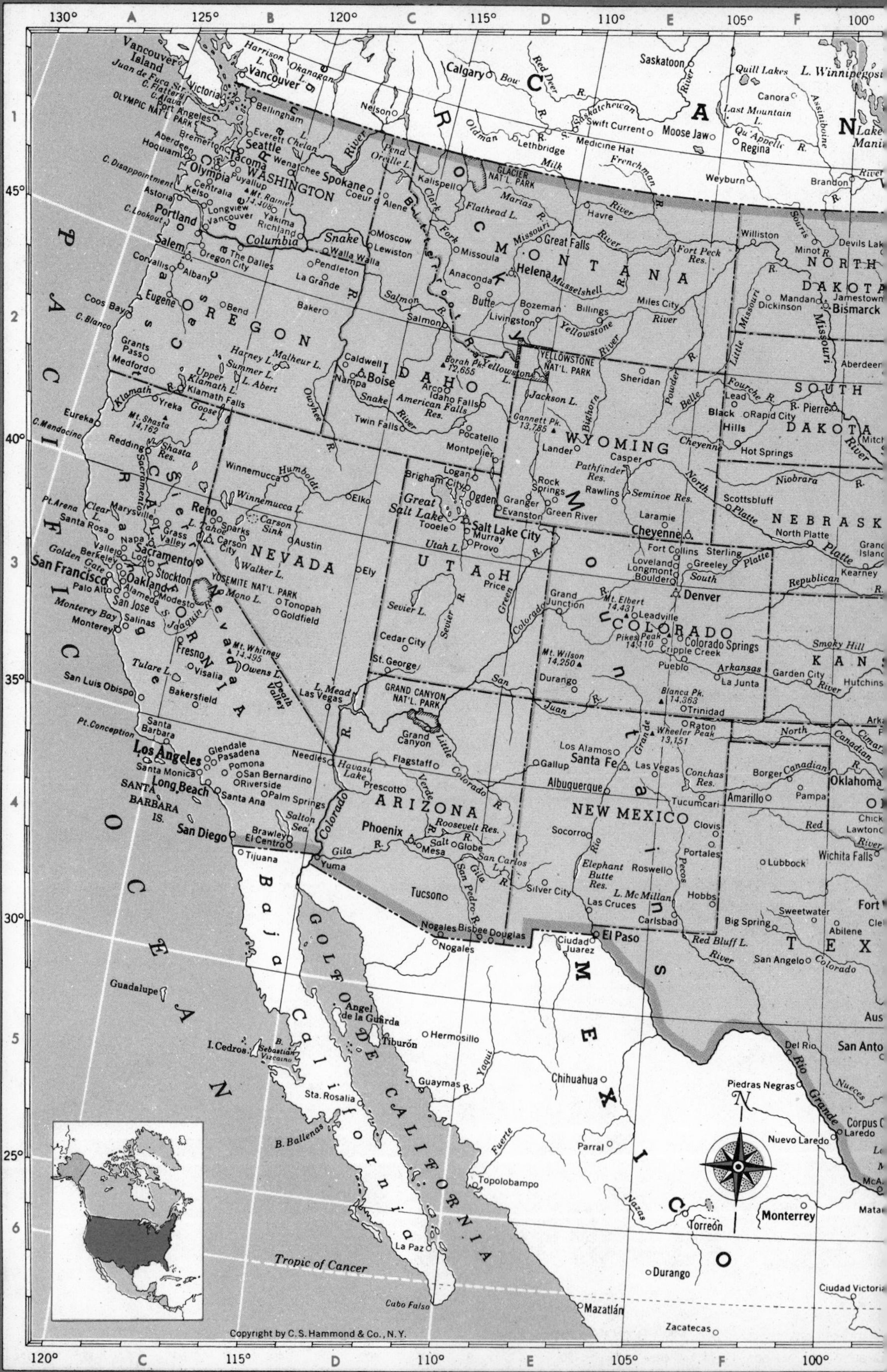

130° A 125° B 120° C 115° D 110° E 105° F 100°

PACIFIC OCEAN

CANADA: Vancouver Island, Victoria, Vancouver, Harrison L., Okanagan L., Nelson, Calgary, Bow, Red Deer R., Saskatoon, Saskatchewan R., Swift Current, Moose Jaw, Regina, Quill Lakes, L. Winnipegosis, Canora, Last Mountain L., Qu'Appelle R., Assiniboine, Lethbridge, Oldman, Medicine Hat, Frenchman, Weyburn, Brandon, Lake Manitoba

WASHINGTON: Juan de Fuca Str., C. Flattery, C. Alava, Port Angeles, OLYMPIC NAT'L PARK, Bellingham, Everett, Chelan L., Bremerton, Seattle, Tacoma, Wenatchee, Spokane, Aberdeen, Hoquiam, Olympia, Puyallup, Mt. Rainier 14,408, Centralia, Kelso, Longview, Vancouver, Yakima, Richland, Walla Walla, Snake, Columbia, Pend Oreille L., Coeur d'Alene, C. Disappointment

OREGON: Astoria, C. Lookout, Portland, Salem, The Dalles, Oregon City, Corvallis, Albany, Pendleton, La Grande, Eugene, Bend, Baker, Coos Bay, C. Blanco, Grants Pass, Medford, Harney L., Malheur L., Summer L., Upper Klamath L., L. Abert, Klamath Falls, Goose L.

IDAHO: Moscow, Lewiston, Salmon, Caldwell, Boise, Nampa, Borah Pk. 12,655, Arco, Idaho Falls, American Falls Res., Twin Falls, Pocatello, Montpelier, Owyhee

MONTANA: GLACIER NAT'L. PARK, Kalispell, Flathead L., Clark Fork, Missoula, Marias R., Milk, Havre, Great Falls, Missouri, Fort Peck Res., Helena, Anaconda, Butte, Bozeman, Livingston, Billings, Musselshell, Miles City, Yellowstone, ROCKY MOUNTAINS, Bitterroot R.

WYOMING: YELLOWSTONE NAT'L. PARK, Jackson L., Gannett Pk. 13,785, Sheridan, Bighorn, Powder, Belle Fourche R., Lander, Casper, Pathfinder Res., Rock Springs, Rawlins, Seminoe Res., Granger, Evanston, Green River, Laramie, Cheyenne, North Platte

NORTH DAKOTA: Williston, Minot, Devils Lake, Mandan, Dickinson, Bismarck, Jamestown, Souris

SOUTH DAKOTA: Aberdeen, Lead, Rapid City, Black Hills, Pierre, Hot Springs, Cheyenne R., Mitchell

NEBRASKA: Niobrara R., Scottsbluff, North Platte, Platte, Grand Island, Kearney, Republican

CALIFORNIA: Eureka, C. Mendocino, Yreka, Mt. Shasta 14,162, Redding, Shasta Res., Sacramento, Pt. Arena, Clear L., Marysville, Santa Rosa, Napa, Grass Valley, Vallejo, Berkeley, Golden Gate, San Francisco, Oakland, Alameda, Palo Alto, San Jose, Stockton, Lodi, Modesto, Monterey Bay, Monterey, Salinas, San Joaquin, YOSEMITE NAT'L. PARK, Mono L., Fresno, Visalia, Mt. Whitney 14,495, Owens L., Tulare L., Death Valley, San Luis Obispo, Bakersfield, Santa Barbara, Pt. Conception, Los Angeles, Glendale, Pasadena, Pomona, San Bernardino, Riverside, Santa Monica, Long Beach, Santa Ana, Palm Springs, SANTA BARBARA IS., San Diego, Salton Sea, Brawley, El Centro, Needles, Sierra Nevada

NEVADA: Winnemucca, Humboldt, Winnemucca L., Elko, Reno, Carson Sink, Sparks, L. Tahoe, Carson City, Austin, Walker L., Ely, Tonopah, Goldfield, L. Mead, Las Vegas

UTAH: Logan, Brigham City, Ogden, Great Salt Lake, Tooele, Salt Lake City, Murray, Provo, Utah L., Price, Green, Sevier L., Sevier R., Cedar City, St. George

COLORADO: Sterling, Fort Collins, Loveland, Longmont, Greeley, Boulder, Denver, South Platte, Grand Junction, Mt. Elbert 14,431, Leadville, Pikes Peak 14,110, Colorado Springs, Cripple Creek, Mt. Wilson 14,250, Pueblo, Arkansas, La Junta, Durango, Blanca Pk. 14,363, Trinidad

KANSAS: Smoky Hill, Garden City, Hutchinson

ARIZONA: GRAND CANYON NAT'L. PARK, Grand Canyon, Little Colorado R., Flagstaff, Havasu Lake, Prescott, Verde R., Roosevelt Res., Phoenix, Salt R., Mesa, Globe, San Carlos L., Gila, Yuma, Tucson, San Pedro R., Nogales, Bisbee, Douglas

NEW MEXICO: Raton, Wheeler Peak 13,151, Los Alamos, Santa Fe, Gallup, Las Vegas, Conchas Res., Albuquerque, Tucumcari, Socorro, Rio Grande, Clovis, Portales, Roswell, Pecos, Elephant Butte Res., Silver City, L. McMillan, Las Cruces, Carlsbad, Hobbs, San Juan

TEXAS / OKLAHOMA: Amarillo, Pampa, Borger, Canadian, Oklahoma City, Red River, Lawton, Wichita Falls, Lubbock, Big Spring, Sweetwater, Abilene, Fort Worth, El Paso, Red Bluff L., San Angelo, Colorado, Austin, San Antonio, Del Rio, Nueces, Corpus Christi, Laredo, Cimarron

MEXICO: Tijuana, Baja California, Guadalupe, I. Cedros, B. Sebastian Vizcaino, Angel de la Guarda, Tiburón, Hermosillo, Guaymas, Yaqui R., GOLFO DE CALIFORNIA, Sta. Rosalia, B. Ballenas, Fuerte, Topolobampo, La Paz, Cabo Falso, Tropic of Cancer, Ciudad Juarez, Chihuahua, Parral, Nazas, Torreon, Durango, Mazatlán, Zacatecas, Piedras Negras, Nuevo Laredo, Monterrey, Ciudad Victoria, Rio Grande

120° C 115° D 110° E 105° F 100°

UNITED STATES

POLYCONIC PROJECTION

SCALE OF MILES

0 50 100 200 300 400

SCALE OF KILOMETRES

0 100 200 300 400

Capitals of Countries

State Capitals

International Boundaries

Longitude 95° West of H Greenwich 90° J 85° K 80° L 75° 25124

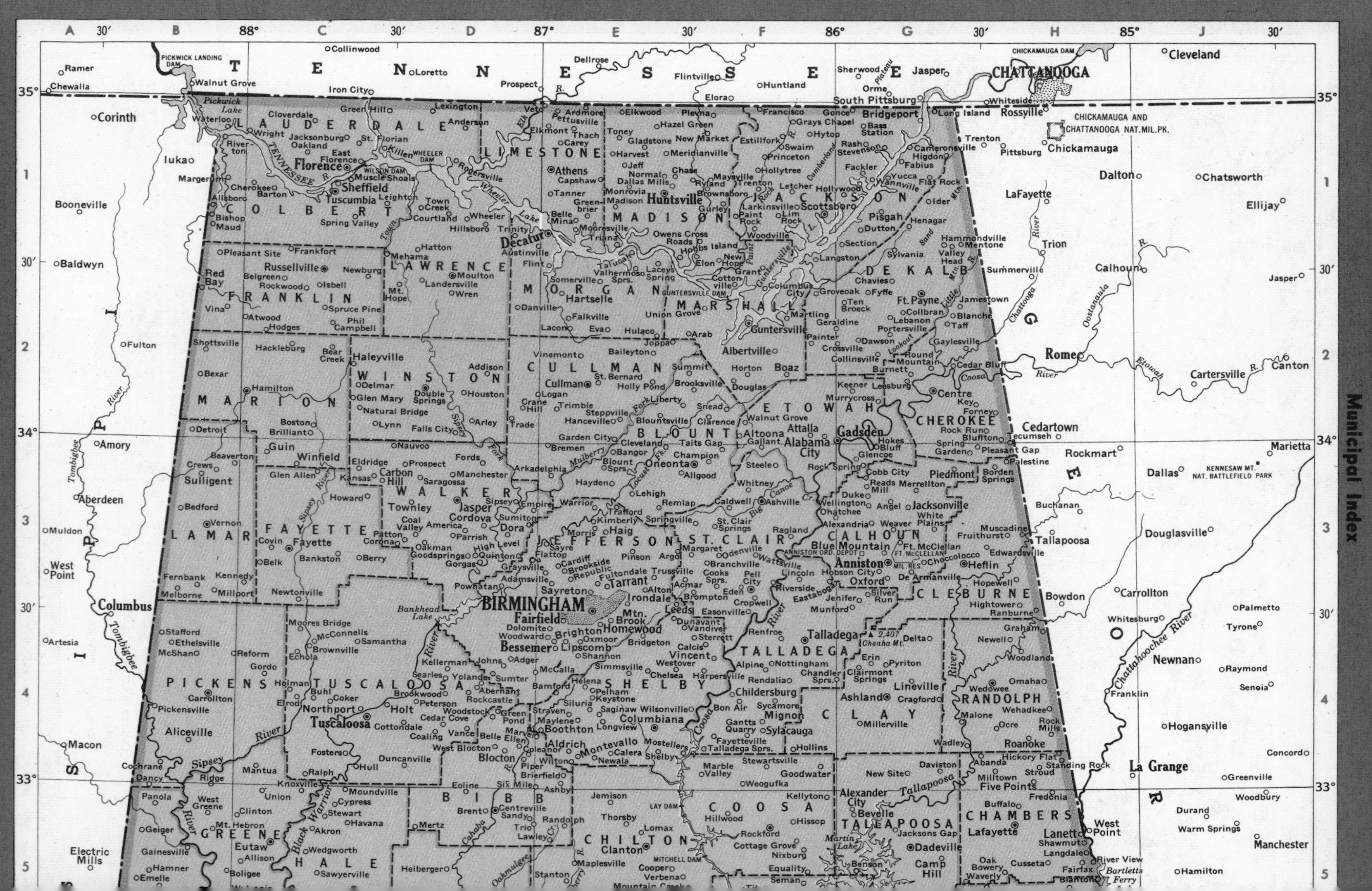
TENNESSEE
GEORGIA
MISSISSIPPI
CHATTANOOGA
Chickamauga
CHICKAMAUGA AND CHATTANOOGA NAT. MIL. PK.
CHICKAMAUGA DAM
PICKWICK LANDING DAM
Cleveland
Dalton
Chatsworth
Ellijay
Jasper
Canton
Cartersville
Marietta
KENNESAW MT. NAT. BATTLEFIELD PARK
Dallas
Douglasville
Calhoun
Rome
Cedartown
Rockmart
Tallapoosa
Bowdon
Carrollton
Newnan
La Grange
West Point
Hogansville
Manchester
LaFayette
Trion
Summerville
Rossville
Corinth
Iuka
Booneville
Baldwyn
Fulton
Amory
Aberdeen
Columbus
West Point
Macon
Tombigbee
Tennessee R.
Coosa River
Chattahoochee River
Etowah R.
Oostanaula
Black Warrior River
Tallapoosa R.
LAUDERDALE
LIMESTONE
MADISON
JACKSON
DE KALB
COLBERT
LAWRENCE
MORGAN
MARSHALL
FRANKLIN
CULLMAN
BLOUNT
ETOWAH
CHEROKEE
MARION
WINSTON
WALKER
ST. CLAIR
CALHOUN
CLEBURNE
LAMAR
FAYETTE
JEFFERSON
TALLADEGA
CLAY
RANDOLPH
PICKENS
TUSCALOOSA
SHELBY
COOSA
TALLAPOOSA
CHAMBERS
BIBB
CHILTON
GREENE
HALE
Florence
Sheffield
Tuscumbia
Muscle Shoals
Athens
Huntsville
Decatur
Scottsboro
Ft. Payne
Guntersville
Albertville
Boaz
Cullman
Gadsden
Attalla
Alabama City
Anniston
Oxford
Jacksonville
Talladega
Sylacauga
BIRMINGHAM
Bessemer
Fairfield
Tuscaloosa
Northport
Jasper
Hamilton
Russellville
Fayette
Vernon
Clanton
Columbiana
Alexander City
Dadeville
Lafayette
Lanett
Eutaw
Carrollton
Centre
Heflin
Ashland
Wedowee
Oneonta
Leeds
Homewood
Wheeler Lake
Pickwick Lake
Martin Lake
Bankhead Lake
WHEELER DAM
WILSON DAM
GUNTERSVILLE DAM
LAY DAM
MITCHELL DAM
Cheaha Mt.

ALABAMA
SCALE OF MILES
0 5 10 20 30 40
State Capitals
County Seats
Copyright by C. S. Hammond & Co., N. Y.
GULF OF MEXICO
FLORIDA
MISSISSIPPI
MONTGOMERY
MOBILE
PENSACOLA
COLUMBUS
Dothan
SUMTER
AUTAUGA
MACON
RUSSELL
MARENGO
DALLAS
LOWNDES
MONTGOMERY
BULLOCK
BARBOUR
CHOCTAW
WILCOX
BUTLER
CRENSHAW
PIKE
CLARKE
MONROE
CONECUH
COFFEE
DALE
HENRY
WASHINGTON
ESCAMBIA
COVINGTON
GENEVA
HOUSTON
MOBILE
BALDWIN
MOBILE BAY
Longitude West of Greenwich
0581

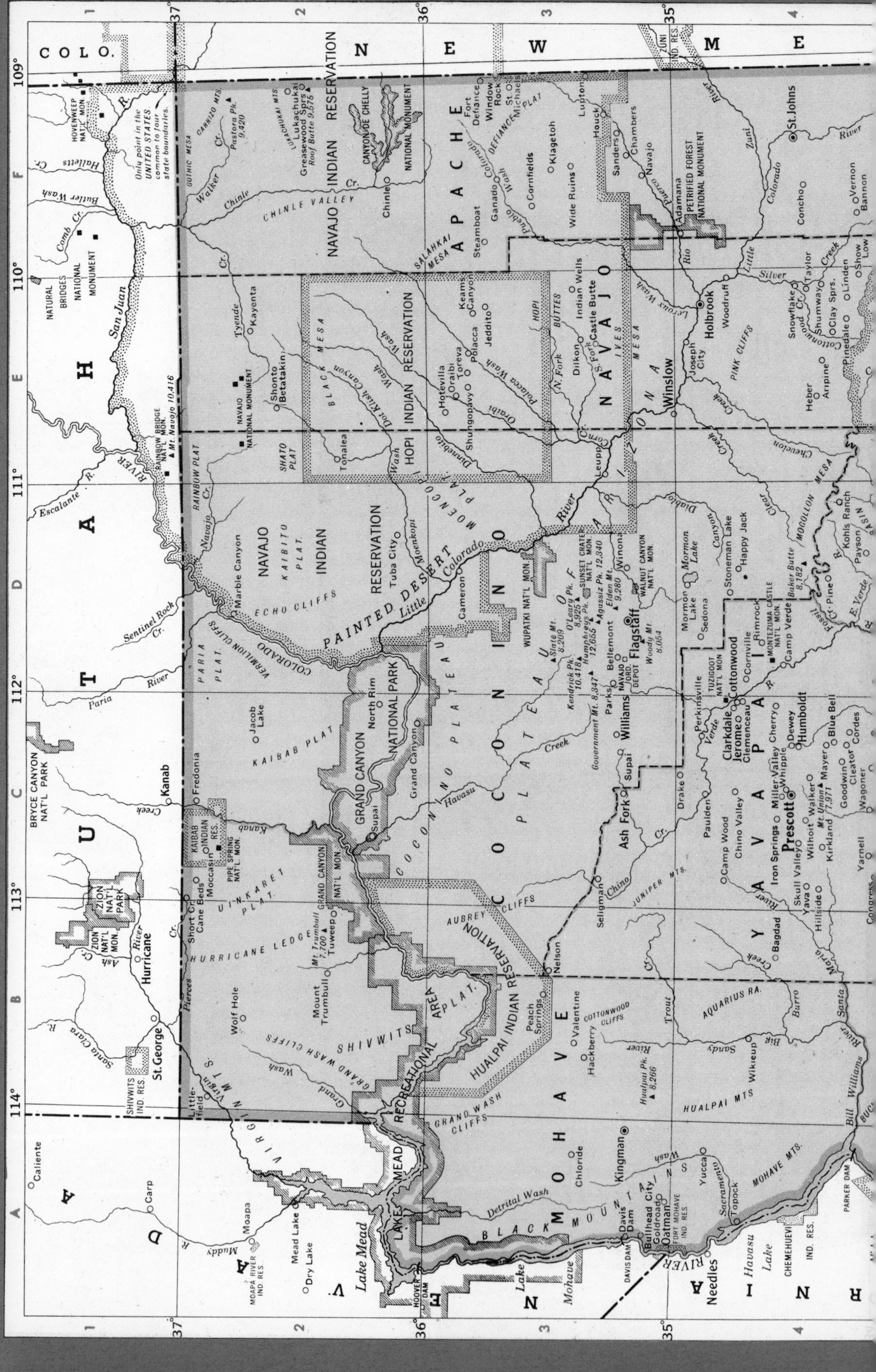

UTAH
COLO.
NEW MEXICO
ARIZONA
NEVADA
CALIF.

NAVAJO INDIAN RESERVATION
HOPI INDIAN RESERVATION
HUALPAI INDIAN RESERVATION
KAIBAB INDIAN RES.
SHIVWITS IND. RES.
MOAPA RIVER IND. RES.
FORT MOHAVE IND. RES.
CHEMEHUEVI IND. RES.
ZUNI IND. RES.

GRAND CANYON NATIONAL PARK
GRAND CANYON NAT'L MON.
ZION NAT'L PARK
ZION NAT'L MON.
BRYCE CANYON NAT'L PARK
NATURAL BRIDGES NATIONAL MONUMENT
HOVENWEEP NAT'L MON.
RAINBOW BRIDGE NAT'L MON.
NAVAJO NATIONAL MONUMENT
CANYON DE CHELLY NATIONAL MONUMENT
PETRIFIED FOREST NATIONAL MONUMENT
WUPATKI NAT'L MON.
SUNSET CRATER NAT'L MON.
WALNUT CANYON NAT'L MON.
TUZIGOOT NAT'L MON.
MONTEZUMA CASTLE NAT'L MON.
PIPE SPRING NAT'L MON.
LAKE MEAD RECREATIONAL AREA

Only point in the UNITED STATES common to four state boundaries.

COCONINO
MOHAVE
YAVAPAI
APACHE
NAVAJO
COCONINO PLATEAU
PAINTED DESERT
MOENCOPI PLAT.
KAIBAB PLAT.
KAIBITO PLAT.
PARIA PLAT.
UINKARET PLAT.
SHIVWITS PLAT.
ECHO CLIFFS
VERMILION CLIFFS
AUBREY CLIFFS
GRAND WASH CLIFFS
HURRICANE LEDGE
BLACK MESA
MOGOLLON MESA
PINK CLIFFS
HUALPAI MTS
AQUARIUS RA.
JUNIPER MTS.
BLACK MOUNTAINS
MOHAVE MTS.
CHINLE VALLEY

Flagstaff
Williams
Winslow
Holbrook
Prescott
Kingman
Needles
St. George
Kanab
Hurricane
Fredonia
Tuba City
Cameron
Ash Fork
Seligman
Cottonwood
Clarkdale
Jerome
St. Johns
Chinle
Ganado
Kayenta
Leupp
Sedona
Oatman
Bullhead City
Lake Mead
Lake Mohave
Lake Havasu

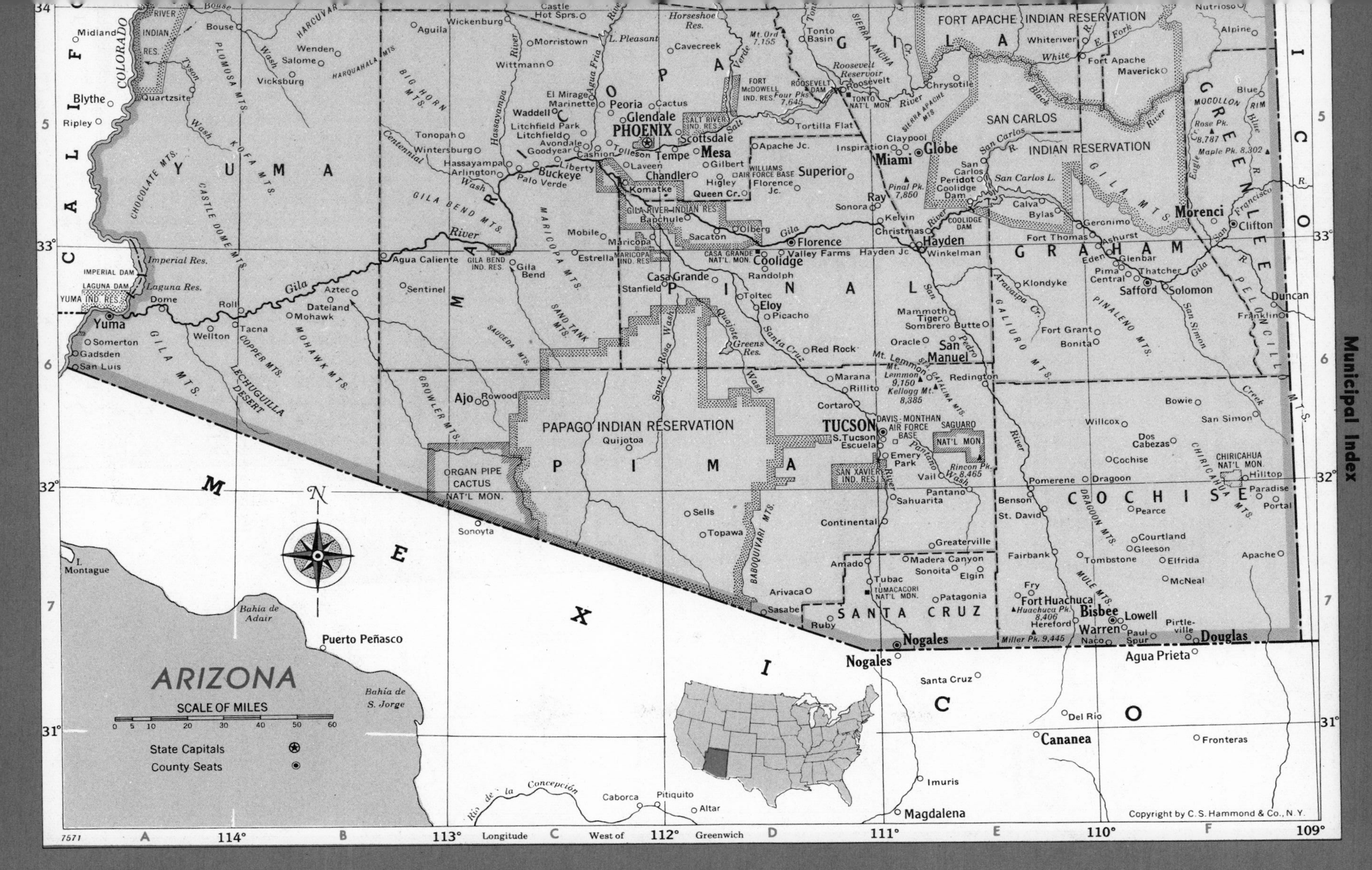
ARIZONA
SCALE OF MILES
0 5 10 20 30 40 50 60
State Capitals
County Seats
YUMA
MARICOPA
PINAL
PIMA
GILA
GRAHAM
GREENLEE
COCHISE
SANTA CRUZ
PAPAGO INDIAN RESERVATION
FORT APACHE INDIAN RESERVATION
SAN CARLOS INDIAN RESERVATION
CALIF
MEXICO
PHOENIX
TUCSON
Yuma
Nogales
Douglas
Bisbee
Globe
Florence
Safford
Clifton
Longitude West of Greenwich
Copyright by C.S. Hammond & Co., N.Y.
7571

ARKANSAS

SCALE OF MILES

0 5 10 20 30 40

State Capitals

County Seats

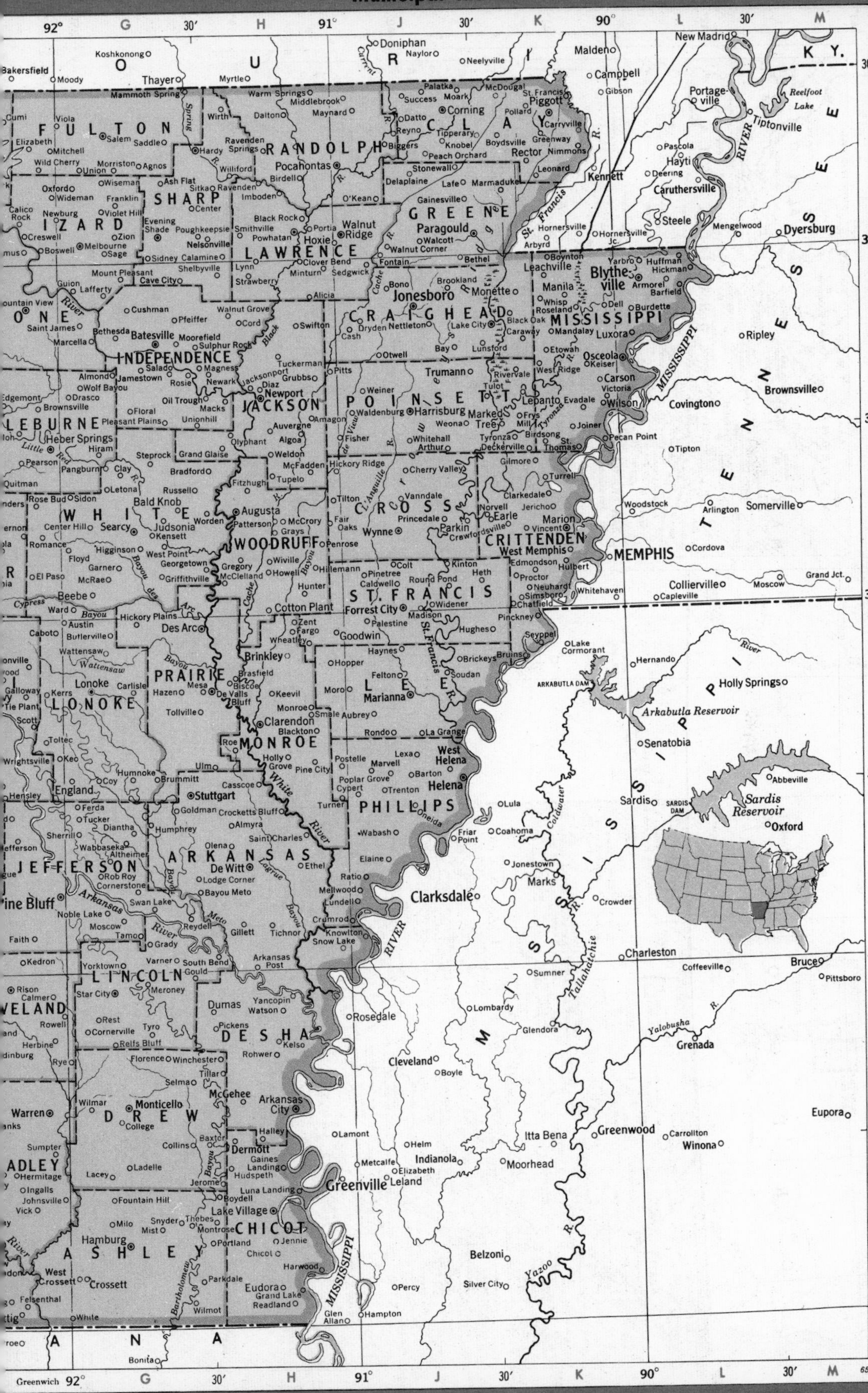

92° G 30′ H 91° J 30′ K 90° L 30′ M
FULTON
SHARP
IZARD
RANDOLPH
LAWRENCE
CLAY
GREENE
CRAIGHEAD
MISSISSIPPI
INDEPENDENCE
JACKSON
POINSETT
CROSS
CRITTENDEN
WHITE
WOODRUFF
ST. FRANCIS
PRAIRIE
LONOKE
LEE
MONROE
PHILLIPS
ARKANSAS
JEFFERSON
LINCOLN
DESHA
DREW
CHICOT
ASHLEY
KY.
TENNESSEE
MISSISSIPPI
MEMPHIS
Blytheville
Jonesboro
Paragould
Pine Bluff
Stuttgart
Greenville
Clarksdale
Helena
West Helena
Forrest City
Newport
Batesville
Searcy
Osceola
Dyersburg
Caruthersville
Greenwood
Grenada
Oxford
Holly Springs
Senatobia
Arkabutla Reservoir
Sardis Reservoir
Reelfoot Lake
Tiptonville
New Madrid
Kennett
Marianna
Wynne
Harrisburg
Trumann
Lake Village
Monticello
McGehee
Dumas
Crossett
Hamburg
De Witt
Lonoke
Brinkley
Clarendon
Des Arc
Augusta
Pocahontas
Walnut Ridge
Piggott
Corning
Rector
Cleveland
Indianola
Leland
Belzoni
Charleston
Winona
Eupora
Ripley
Covington
Brownsville
Somerville
Collierville
Greenwich 92° G 30′ H 91° J 30′ K 90° L 30′ M
36° 35° 34° 33°
1 2 3 4 5 6 7
6591

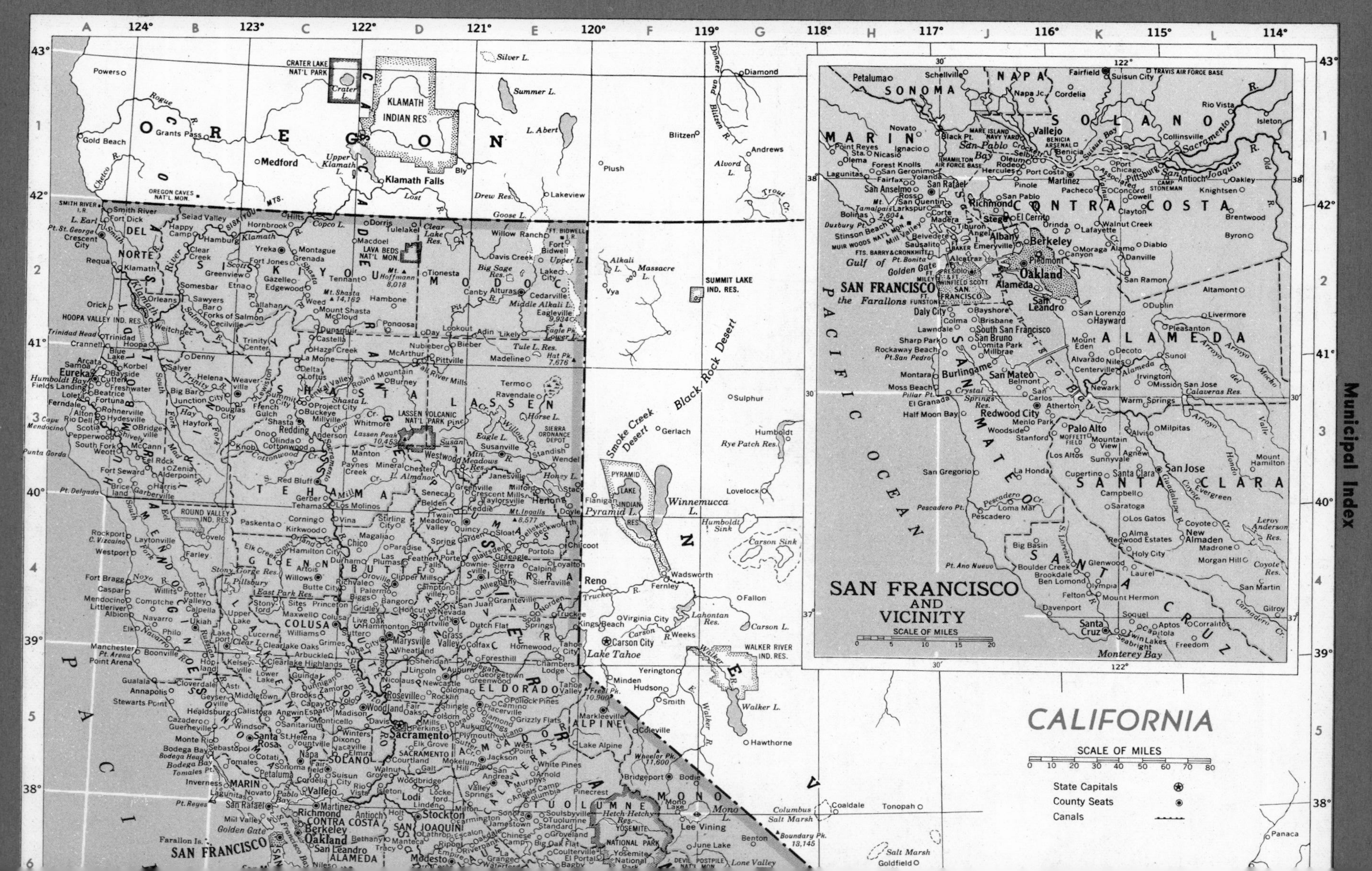
CALIFORNIA
SCALE OF MILES
0 10 20 30 40 50 60 70 80
State Capitals
County Seats
Canals
SAN FRANCISCO AND VICINITY
SCALE OF MILES
0 5 10 15 20
PACIFIC OCEAN
OREGON
NEVADA
KLAMATH INDIAN RES
CRATER LAKE NAT'L PARK
LAVA BEDS NAT'L MON.
LASSEN VOLCANIC NAT'L PARK
SUMMIT LAKE IND. RES.
WALKER RIVER IND. RES.
ROUND VALLEY IND. RES.
HOOPA VALLEY IND. RES.
OREGON CAVES NAT'L MON.
Black Rock Desert
Smoke Creek Desert
Medford
Klamath Falls
Reno
Carson City
Lake Tahoe
Sacramento
San Francisco
Oakland
San Jose
Stockton
Eureka
Redding
Chico
Santa Rosa

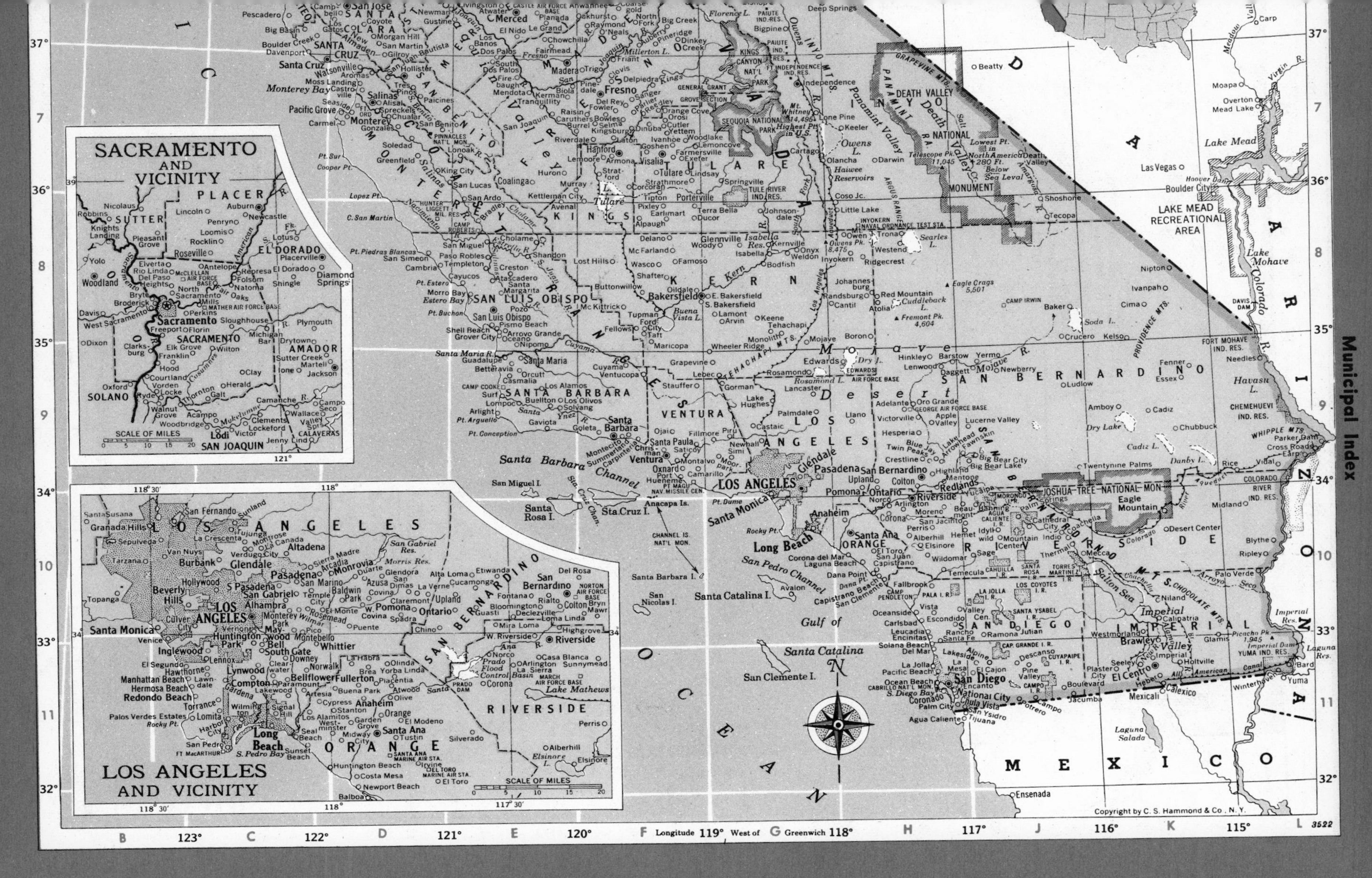
SACRAMENTO AND VICINITY
LOS ANGELES AND VICINITY
DEATH VALLEY NATIONAL MONUMENT
JOSHUA TREE NATIONAL MON.
LAKE MEAD RECREATIONAL AREA
SEQUOIA NATIONAL PARK
KINGS CANYON NAT'L PARK
SAN BERNARDINO
LOS ANGELES
SANTA BARBARA
VENTURA
KERN
TULARE
KINGS
MONTEREY
SAN LUIS OBISPO
SAN BENITO
Mojave Desert
RIVERSIDE
ORANGE
SAN DIEGO
IMPERIAL
ARIZONA
MEXICO
Santa Barbara Channel
San Pedro Channel
Gulf of Santa Catalina
Santa Catalina I.
San Clemente I.
San Nicolas I.
Santa Rosa I.
Sta. Cruz I.
Salton Sea
Lake Mead
Colorado R.
SCALE OF MILES
Copyright by C. S. Hammond & Co., N. Y.
Longitude 119° West of Greenwich 118°
3522

COLORADO
SCALE OF MILES
State Capitals
County Seats
Canals
MOFFAT
ROUTT
JACKSON
RIO BLANCO
GRAND
GARFIELD
EAGLE
SUMMIT
MESA
PITKIN
LAKE
DELTA
GUNNISON
CHAFFEE
MONTROSE
OURAY
SAN MIGUEL
SAGUACHE
HINSDALE
DOLORES
SAN JUAN
MINERAL
RIO GRANDE
ALAMOSA
MONTEZUMA
LA PLATA
ARCHULETA
CONEJOS
Craig
Meeker
Steamboat Springs
Walden
Glenwood Springs
Grand Junction
Delta
Montrose
Gunnison
Leadville
Salida
Ouray
Silverton
Durango
Cortez
Alamosa
Del Norte
Saguache
Pagosa Springs
Telluride
Lake City
Creede
DINOSAUR NAT'L MON.
COLORADO NAT'L MON.
BLACK CANYON OF THE GUNNISON NAT'L MON.
MESA VERDE NAT'L PK.
YUCCA HOUSE NAT'L MON.
HOVENWEEP NAT'L MON.
GREAT SAND DUNES NAT'L MON.
UTE MOUNTAIN INDIAN RES.
SOUTHERN UTE IND. RES.
NAVAJO INDIAN RESERVATION
JICARILLA IND. RES.
Only point in the UNITED STATES common to four state boundaries.
Copyright by C. S. Hammond & Co., N. Y.
Longitude 106° West of

CONNECTICUT
SCALE OF MILES
0
5
10
15
State Capitals
Court Houses
45′
A
30′
B
15′
C
73°
D
42°
41°
1
2
3
4
Longitude
West
of
Mt. Frissell 2,380
Bear Mountain 2,355
Gridley Mtn.
Riga L.
Taconic
Twin Lakes
Toni Mtn.
Ashley Falls
Canaan
East Canaan
Benedict Pd.
Ball Mt.
Haystack Mt.
Doolittle Pond
Blackberry River
Canaan Mtn.
Wangum Lake
West Hartland
East Hartland
North Granby
Barkhamsted Res.
Salisbury
Lakeville
Wononskopomuc Lake
Millerton
Norfolk
Dutton Mtn.
Colebrook
Robertsville
Riverton
West Granby
Falls Village
Hallenbeck R.
Wononpakook Pond
Lime Rock
Indian Mtn.
Dennis Hill
Mad River
Barkhamsted
Indian Pond
Titus Mt.
Cream Hill
Mudge Pond
Highland Lake
Winchester Center
Winsted
Pleasant Valley
East Branch Res.
Sharon Valley
Sharon
North Canton
Simsbury
West Cornwall
Burrville
Burr Reservoir
New Hartford
Shepherd Pd.
Pine Meadow
West Simsbury
Canton Center
Red Mtn.
Tyler Pd.
Cornwall
West Goshen
Goshen
Mohawk Mtn.
Ellsworth Hill
Cornwall Bridge
West Torrington
Dog Pd.
Bakersville
Nepaug Res.
Weatogue
Canton
Collinsville
Avon
Millbrook
LITCHFIELD
Torrington
Harwinton
North Kent
Flanders
Milton
East Litchfield
Burlington
West Avon
Unionville
Kent Furnace
Warren
East Kent
Litchfield
Kent
S. Spectacle Pd.
N. Spectacle Pd.
Bantam
Campville
Farmington Sta.
Lake Waramaug
Woodville
Bantam Lake
East Morris
Northfield
New Preston
Lakeside
Morris
South Kent
Romford
Thomaston
Terryville
Bristol
Forestville
Plainville
Pequabuck
Plymouth
Gaylordsville
Bear Hill
Marble Dale
Washington Depot
Long Meadow Pond
Reynolds Bridge
Washington
Bethlehem
Shuttle Meadow Res.
Northville
Hancock
Greystone
Boardmans Bridge
Watertown
Wolcott
Southington
Judds Bridge
Oakville
Waterville
Wattle Pond
Sherman
Pawling
Whaley Lake
New Milford
Hotchkissville
Minortown
Plantsville
Waterbury
Marion
Milldale
Roxbury Station
Roxbury
Still River
North Woodbury
Quassapaug Pond
Waterbury Reservoir
Bridgewater
Woodbury
Roxbury Falls
Middlebury
Union City
West Cheshire
Prospect
South Meriden
Candlewood Lake
Brookfield
Cheshire
Yalesville
South Britain
Southbury
Naugatuck
Ball Pond
Boyd Corners Reservoir
New Fairfield
Brookfield Center
Southford
Titicus Mt.
East Lake
Brookfield Junction
Brooksvale
West Branch Reservoir
Carmel
Bog Brook Res.
Hawleyville
Berkshire Jc.
Sandy Hook
HOUSATONIC
Oxford
Beacon Falls
East Branch Reservoir
Brewster
Newtown
Bethany
Mahopac Lake
Danbury
Lake Zoar
Seymour
Mt. Carmel
Northford
Mill Plain
Croton Falls Reservoir
Peach Lake
Bethel
Stevenson
North Haven
Hamden
Botsford
Ansonia
Woodbridge
Highwood
Montowese
Whitney Lake
Whitneyville
West Redding
Redding Ridge
Monroe
Titicus Reservoir
Muscoot Res.
Stepney
Shelton
Derby
Topstone
Redding
NEW HAVEN
Golden's Bridge
Ridgefield
Stepney Depot
Huntington
Allingtown
Cross River Reservoir
Florida
Cooper
Branchville
Long Hill
Orange
Tyler City
West Haven
Branford
Short Beach
East Haven
Croton Lake
FAIRFIELD
Georgetown
Easton
Trumbull
Nichols
Oronoque
North Wilton
Cannondale
Aspetuck
Woodmont
Oyster River Pt.
Morgan Pt.
Branford Harbor
Mt. Kisco
Weston
Milford
Devon
Hurlbutt
Wilton
Stratford
Pond Pt.
Byram Lake
South Wilton
Greenfield Hill
BRIDGEPORT
Wildermere Beach
High Ridge
Long Ridge
Cranbury
Milford Pt.
New Canaan
Winnipauk
Westport
Fairfield
Long Beach
Stratford Pt.
Pleasantville
North Stamford
Southport
Greens Farms
Kensico Res.
Talmadge Hill
Saugatuck
Pine Creek Pt.
Norwalk
Round Hill
Springdale
West Norwalk
East Norwalk
Sherwood Pt.
South Norwalk
Rye Pd.
Darien
Rowayton
Cockenoe I.
Glenbrook
Noroton Hts.
Wilson Point
Noroton
Norwalk Is.
Mianus
Stamford
White Plains
Glenville
Cos Cob
Riverside
Old Greenwich
Long Neck Pt.
Westcott Cove
Greenwich
Shippan Pt.
Greenwich Pt.
Port Chester
Byram
Byram Pt.
Mamaroneck
Housatonic River
Naugatuck River
Croton River
Fishkill Creek
Wassaic Creek
Webatuck Creek
Ten Mile River
Titicus Br.
Saugatuck River
Norwalk River
Silvermine R.
Mianus River
Byram R.
Farmington R.
Salmon Brook
Still River
Shepaug River
Pomperaug R.
Quinnipiac
Mill River
Eight Mile Brook
Farm River
Pequabuck R.
MASSACHUSETTS
NEW YORK
HARTFORD
NEW HAVEN
LONG ISLAND

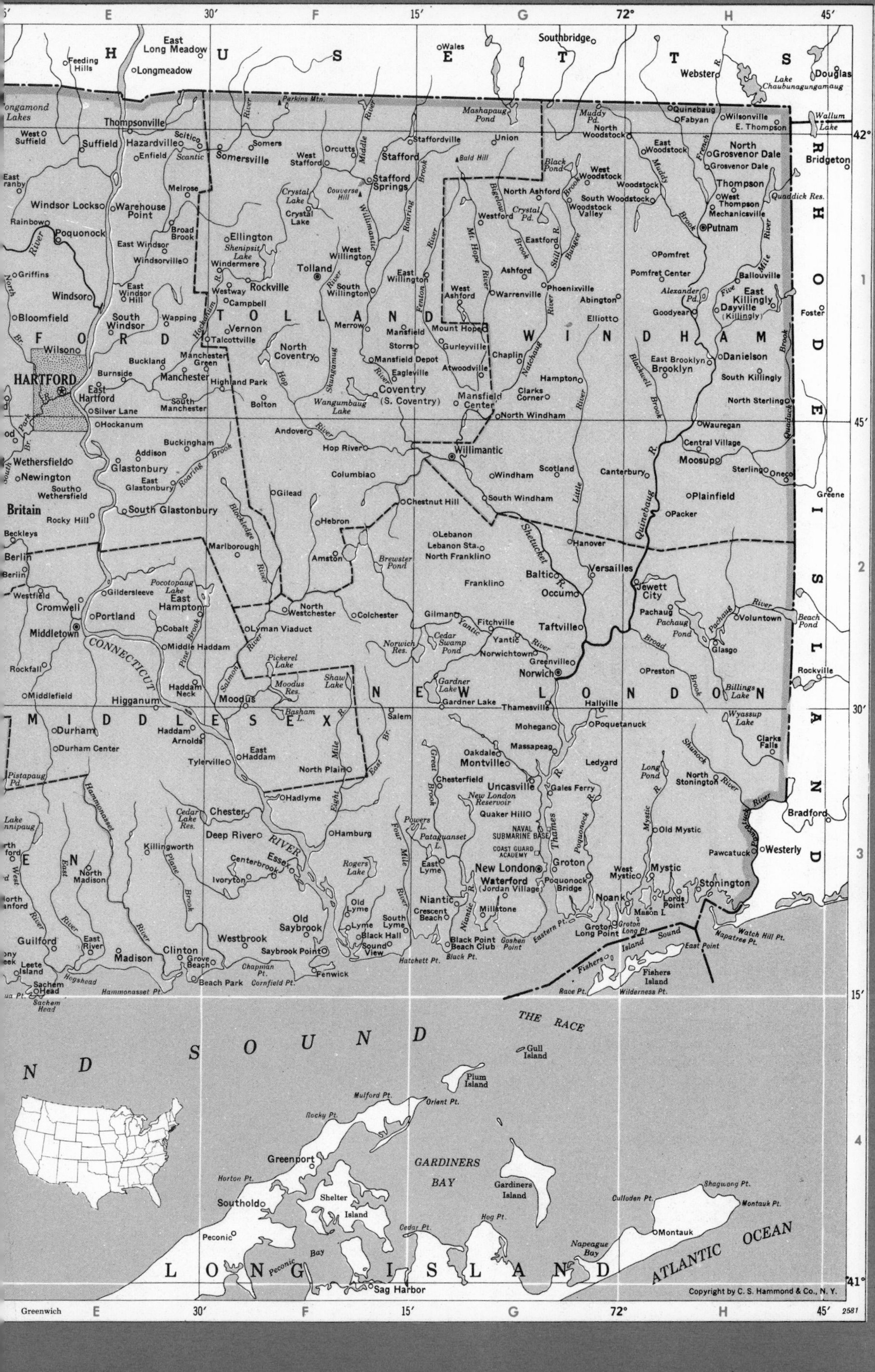

E 30′ F 15′ G 72° H 45′

MASSACHUSETTS
East Long Meadow
Feeding Hills
Longmeadow
Wales
Southbridge
Webster
Douglas
Lake Chaubunagungamaug
Parkins Mtn.
Mashapaug Pond
Muddy Pd.
Quinebaug
Fabyan
Wilsonville
E. Thompson
Wallum Lake
Thompsonville
Congamond Lakes
West Suffield
Suffield
Hazardville
Scitico
Somers
Somersville
Enfield
Scantic
Orcutts
West Stafford
Stafford
Staffordville
Union
Bald Hill
North Woodstock
East Woodstock
North Grosvenor Dale
Grosvenor Dale
Bridgeton
Melrose
Crystal Lake
Couverse Hill
Stafford Springs
Black Pond
West Woodstock
Woodstock
North Ashford
South Woodstock
Woodstock Valley
Thompson
West Thompson
Mechanicsville
Quaddick Res.
Windsor Locks
Warehouse Point
Crystal Pd.
Westford
Putnam
Rainbow
Poquonock
Broad Brook
East Windsor
Ellington
Shenipsit Lake
Windsorville
Windermere
Eastford
West Willington
Tolland
Pomfret
Griffins
East Windsor Hill
Westway
Rockville
Campbell
South Willington
East Willington
Ashford
West Ashford
Warrenville
Phoenixville
Abington
Pomfret Center
Alexander Pd.
Ballouville
Five Mile River
East Killingly
Dayville (Killingly)
Goodyear
Foster
Windsor
Bloomfield
South Windsor
Wapping
Vernon
Talcottville
TOLLAND
Merrow
Mansfield
Mount Hope
Storrs
Gurleyville
Elliott
WINDHAM
HARTFORD
Wilson
North Coventry
Manchester Green
Buckland
Manchester
Burnside
East Hartford
Highland Park
Mansfield Depot
Eagleville
Atwoodville
Chaplin
Hampton
Danielson
East Brooklyn
Brooklyn
South Killingly
Silver Lane
South Manchester
Bolton
Coventry (S. Coventry)
Wangumbaug Lake
Mansfield Center
Clarks Corner
North Sterling
Hockanum
North Windham
Andover
Buckingham
Addison
Hop River
Willimantic
Wauregan
Central Village
Moosup
Wethersfield
Newington
South Wethersfield
Glastonbury
East Glastonbury
Columbia
Windham
Scotland
Canterbury
Sterling
Oneco
Gilead
South Windham
Plainfield
Greene
Britain
South Glastonbury
Rocky Hill
Chestnut Hill
Hebron
Packer
Beckleys
Berlin
Marlborough
Amston
Lebanon
Lebanon Sta.
North Franklin
Brewster Pond
Hanover
Versailles
Westfield
Gildersleeve
Pocotopaug Lake
East Hampton
Franklin
Baltic
Occum
Jewett City
Cromwell
Portland
Cobalt
North Westchester
Colchester
Gilman
Fitchville
Pachaug
Pachaug Pond
Voluntown
Beach Pond
Middletown
Middle Haddam
Lyman Viaduct
Yantic
Norwich Res.
Cedar Swamp Pond
Taftville
Norwichtown
Greenville
Glasgo
Rockfall
CONNECTICUT RIVER
Pickerel Lake
Haddam Neck
Moodus Res.
Shaw Lake
Norwich
Preston
Rockville
Middlefield
Higganum
Moodus
Basham L.
Gardner Lake
Thamesville
Hallville
Billings Lake
MIDDLESEX
NEW LONDON
Durham
Haddam
Arnolds
Salem
Mohegan
Poquetanuck
Wyassup Lake
Durham Center
East Haddam
Massapeag
Clarks Falls
Tylerville
Oakdale
Montville
Ledyard
Long Pond
North Plain
Pistapaug Pd.
Chesterfield
Uncasville
Gales Ferry
North Stonington
Hadlyme
New London Reservoir
Quaker Hill
Bradford
Lake Quonnipaug
Cedar Lake Res.
Chester
Powers L.
Naval Submarine Base
Deep River
Hamburg
Pataguanset L.
Coast Guard Academy
Old Mystic
Killingworth
Essex
East Lyme
Groton
Westerly
Pawcatuck
Centerbrook
Rogers Lake
New London
West Mystic
Mystic
North Madison
Ivoryton
Waterford (Jordan Village)
Poquonock Bridge
Stonington
Niantic
Noank
Mason I.
Lords Point
Old Lyme
Crescent Beach
Millstone
Guilford
East River
Old Saybrook
Lyme
South Lyme
Groton Long Point
Watch Hill Pt.
Napatree Pt.
Clinton
Westbrook
Black Hall
Black Point Beach Club
Goshen Point
Eastern Pt.
East Point
Madison
Grove Beach
Saybrook Point
Sound View
Fishers Island Sound
Leete Island
Chapman Pt.
Hatchett Pt.
Black Pt.
Fishers Island
Sachem Head
Hogshead
Beach Park
Cornfield Pt.
Fenwick
Hammonasset Pt.
Race Pt.
Wilderness Pt.
THE RACE
LONG ISLAND SOUND
Gull Island
Plum Island
Mulford Pt.
Orient Pt.
Rocky Pt.
Greenport
GARDINERS BAY
Gardiners Island
Horton Pt.
Shelter Island
Southold
Culloden Pt.
Shagwong Pt.
Montauk Pt.
Cedar Pt.
Hog Pt.
Montauk
Peconic
Peconic Bay
Napeague Bay
ATLANTIC OCEAN
LONG ISLAND
Sag Harbor
RHODE ISLAND

Greenwich E 30′ F 15′ G 72° H 45′ 2581

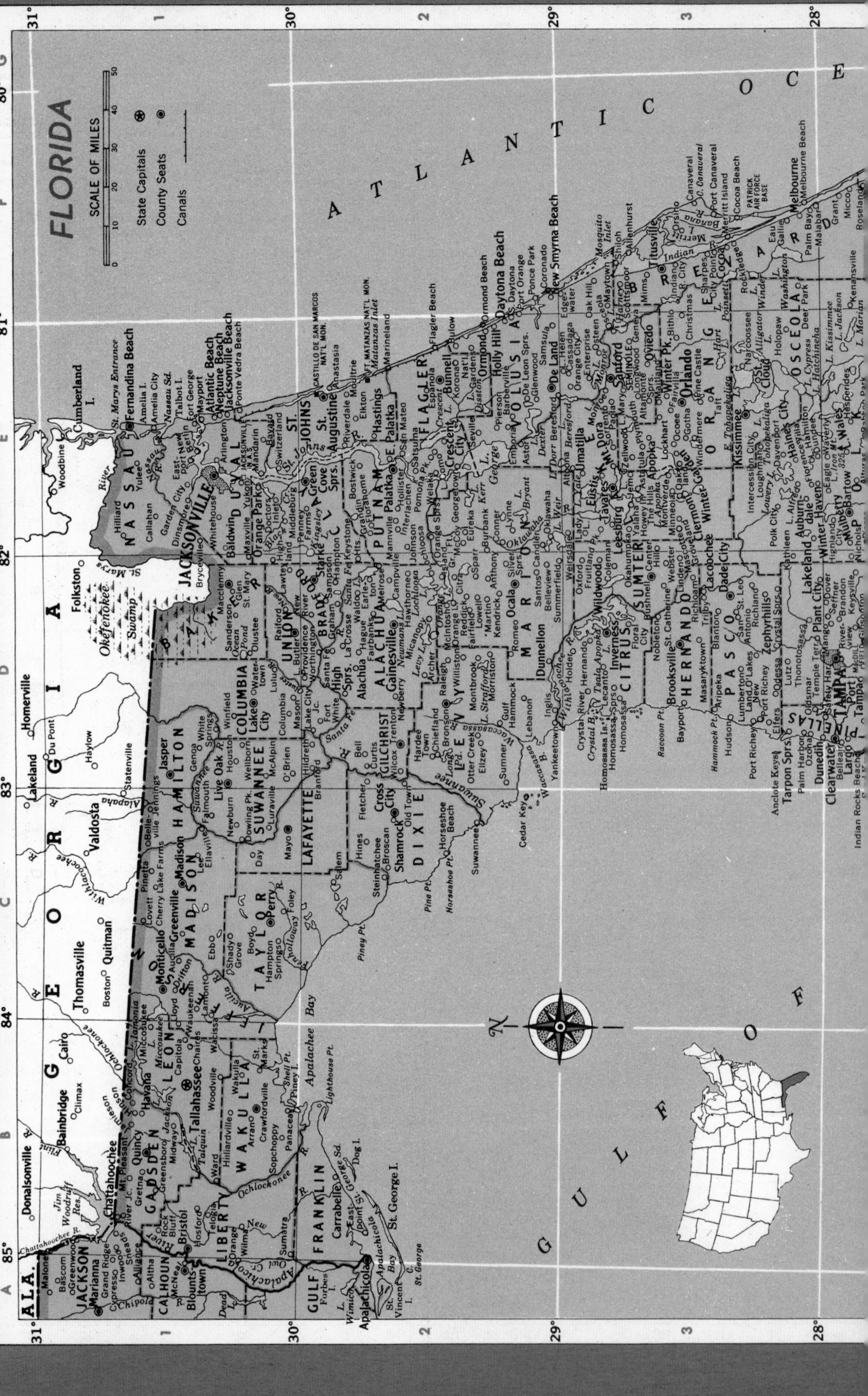

FLORIDA

SCALE OF MILES

0 10 20 30 40 50

State Capitals

County Seats

Canals

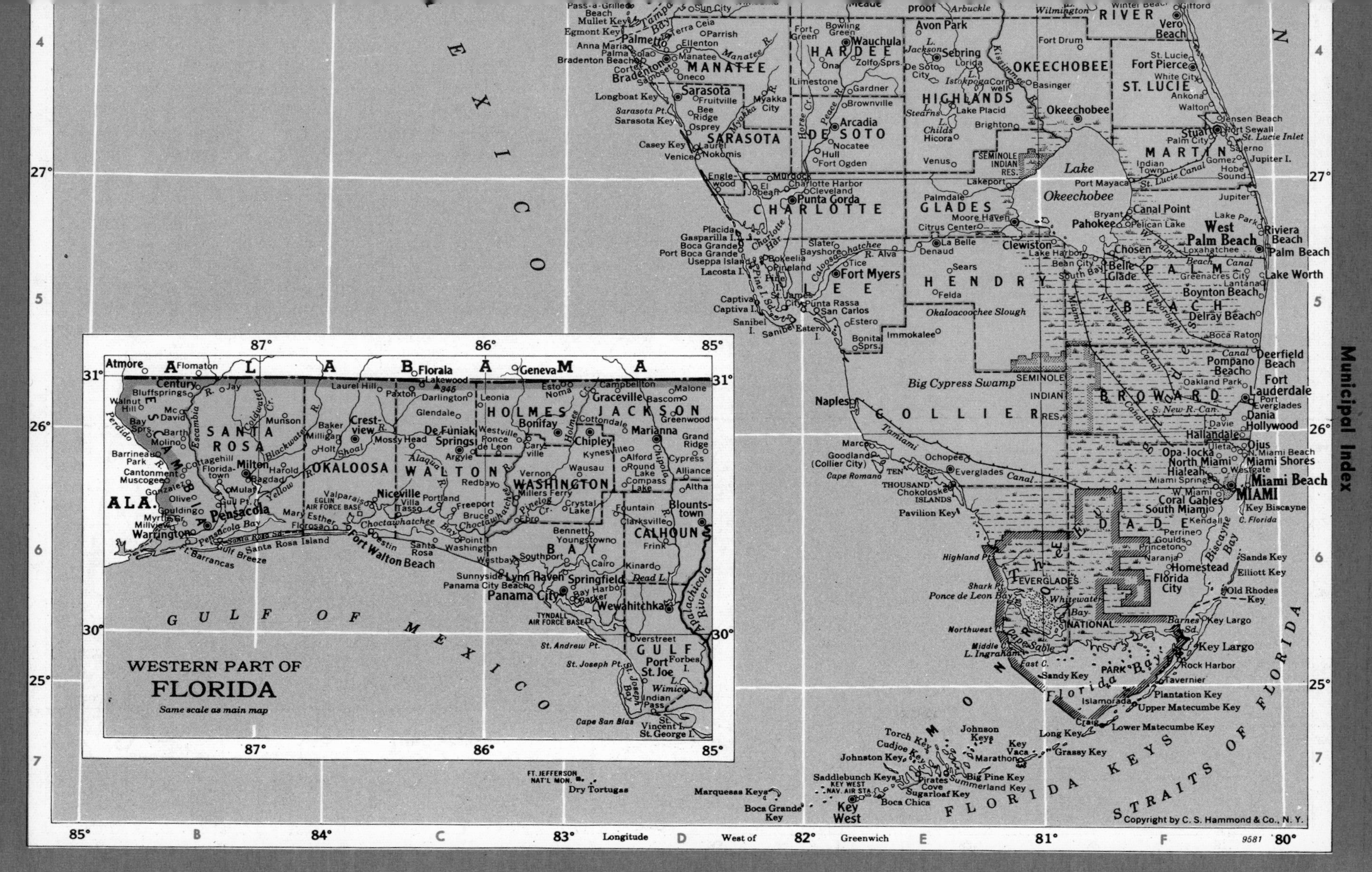
WESTERN PART OF
FLORIDA
Same scale as main map
GULF OF MEXICO
ALABAMA
ALA.
ESCAMBIA
SANTA ROSA
OKALOOSA
WALTON
HOLMES
WASHINGTON
JACKSON
CALHOUN
BAY
GULF
Pensacola
Fort Walton Beach
Panama City
Marianna
MEXICO
MANATEE
SARASOTA
HARDEE
DE SOTO
CHARLOTTE
LEE
HIGHLANDS
GLADES
HENDRY
COLLIER
OKEECHOBEE
ST. LUCIE
MARTIN
PALM BEACH
BROWARD
DADE
MONROE
Lake Okeechobee
Big Cypress Swamp
Okaloacoochee Slough
EVERGLADES NATIONAL PARK
Florida Bay
Sarasota
Fort Myers
Punta Gorda
Naples
Fort Pierce
West Palm Beach
Fort Lauderdale
Hollywood
Miami Beach
MIAMI
Coral Gables
Homestead
Key Largo
Key West
Dry Tortugas
Marquesas Keys
FLORIDA KEYS
STRAITS OF FLORIDA
Copyright by C. S. Hammond & Co., N. Y.
85° B 84° C 83° Longitude D West of 82° Greenwich E 81° F 80°
9581

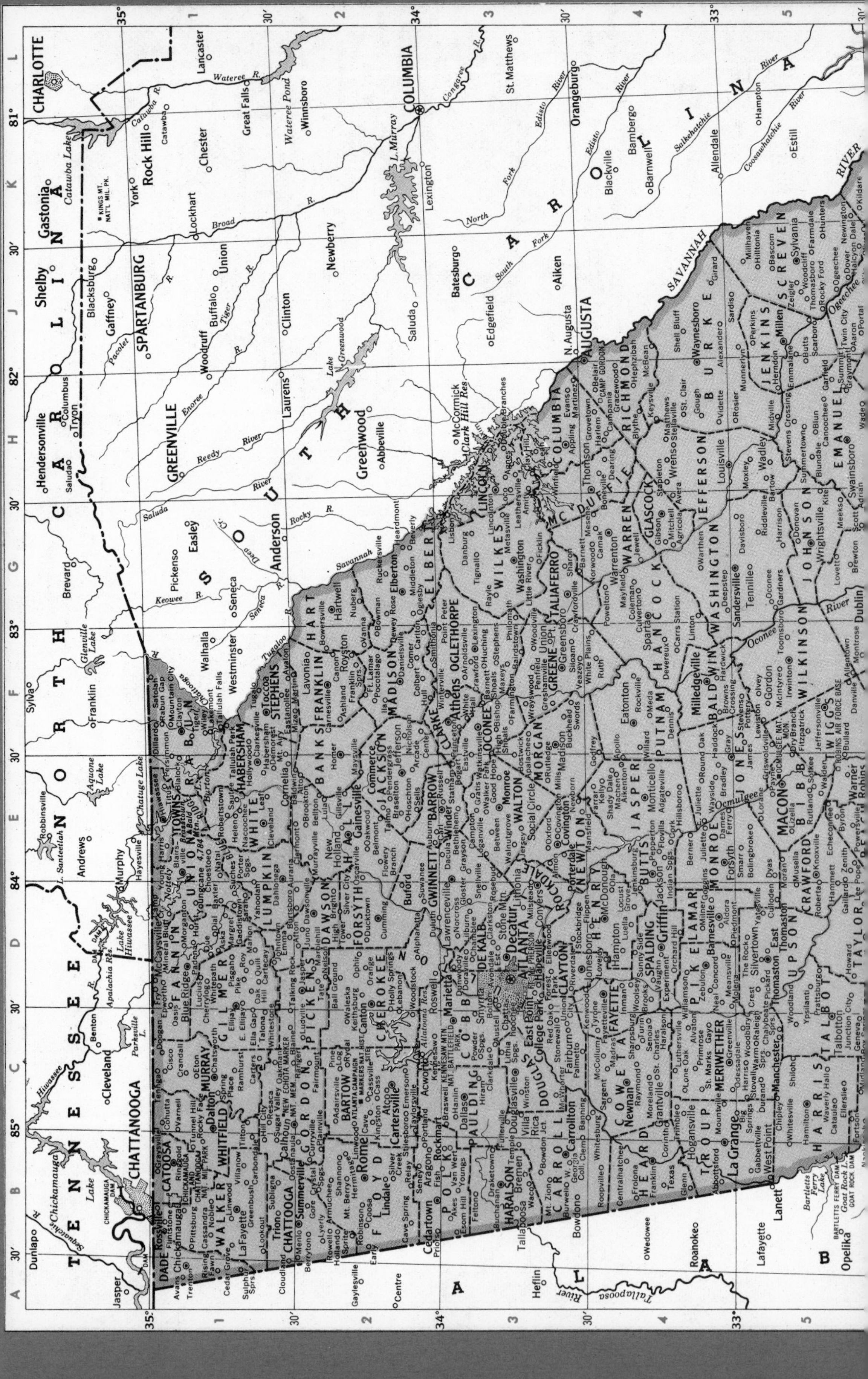

GEORGIA

SCALE OF MILES

0 5 10 20 30 40

State Capitals

County Seats

Copyright by C. S. Hammond & Co., N. Y.

9581

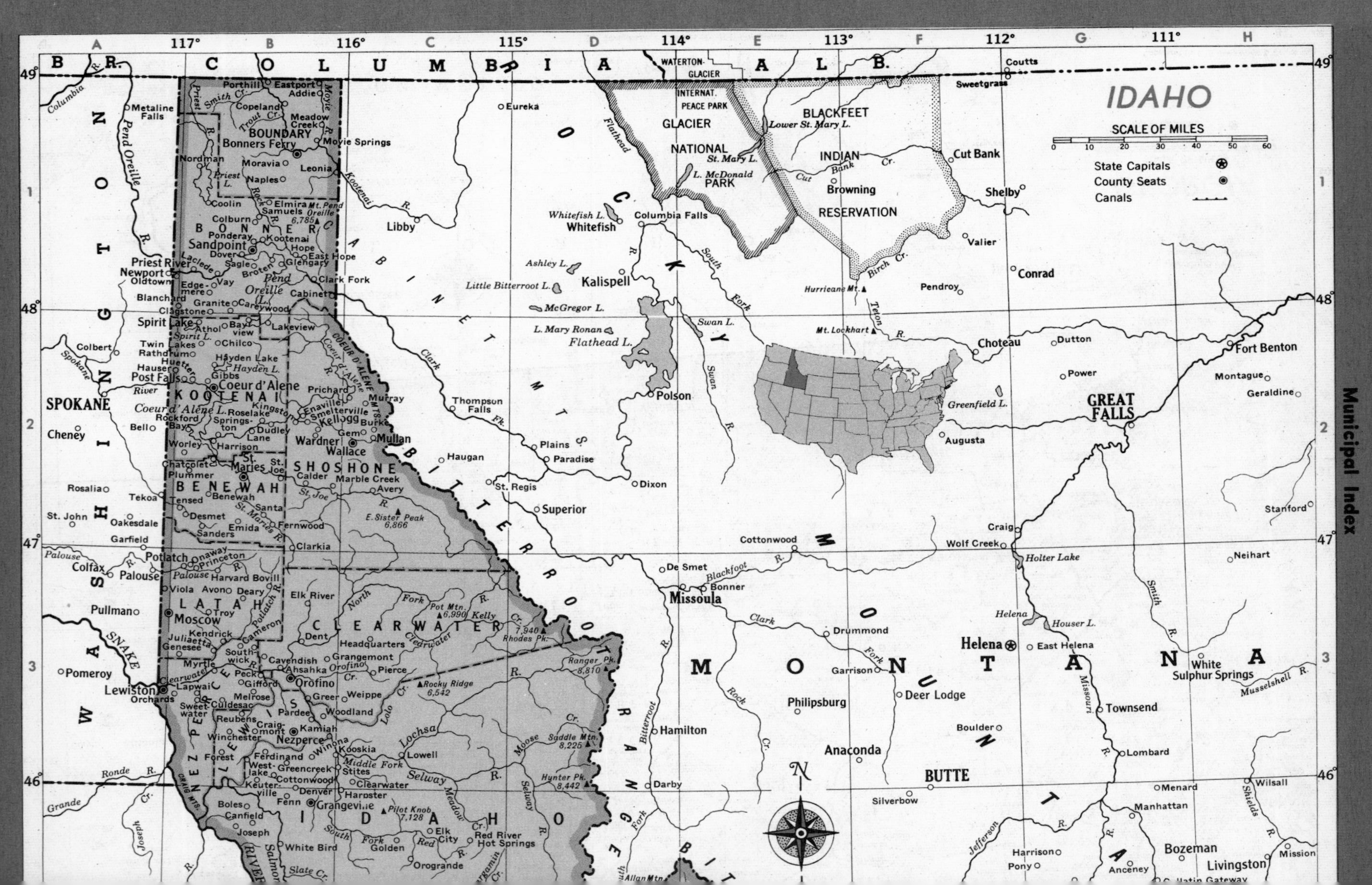
IDAHO
SCALE OF MILES
0 10 20 30 40 50 60
State Capitals
County Seats
Canals
B. R. COLUMBIA
ALB.
MONTANA
WASHINGTON
IDAHO
ROCKY MTS.
BITTERROOT RANGE
CABINET MTS.
COEUR D'ALENE MTS.
BLACKFEET INDIAN RESERVATION
GLACIER NATIONAL PARK
WATERTON-GLACIER INTERNAT. PEACE PARK
BOUNDARY
BONNER
KOOTENAI
SHOSHONE
BENEWAH
LATAH
CLEARWATER
NEZ PERCE
LEWIS
SPOKANE
GREAT FALLS
BUTTE
Helena
Missoula
Kalispell
Whitefish
Polson
Bozeman
Livingston
Anaconda
Philipsburg
Deer Lodge
Hamilton
Townsend
White Sulphur Springs
Fort Benton
Shelby
Cut Bank
Conrad
Choteau
Browning
Columbia Falls
Libby
Eureka
Thompson Falls
Superior
Sandpoint
Bonners Ferry
Coeur d'Alene
Kellogg
Wallace
St. Maries
Moscow
Lewiston
Orofino
Grangeville
Nezperce
Pullman
Colfax
Cheney
Priest River
Newport
Palouse
Pomeroy
Salmon
Snake
Pend Oreille
Kootenai
Clark Fork
Missouri
Flathead L.
Coeur d'Alene L.
49°
48°
47°
46°
117°
116°
115°
114°
113°
112°
111°

BOUNDARY · FREMONT · CLARK · LEMHI · CUSTER · BUTTE · JEFFERSON · MADISON · TETON · BONNEVILLE · BINGHAM · CARIBOU · BEAR LAKE · FRANKLIN · ONEIDA · POWER · BANNOCK · CASSIA · MINIDOKA · BLAINE · LINCOLN · JEROME · GOODING · TWIN FALLS · CAMAS · ELMORE · OWYHEE · ADA · BOISE · VALLEY · ADAMS · WASHINGTON · PAYETTE · GEM · CANYON · IDAHO

Longitude West of Greenwich

CHICAGO AND VICINITY
SCALE OF MILES
LAKE MICHIGAN
L. MICHIGAN
CHICAGO
Evanston
Waukegan
Joliet
Aurora
Elgin
Rockford
Freeport
Dixon
Sterling
Peoria
Galesburg
Kankakee
Bloomington
Champaign
Urbana
Danville
Quincy
Moline
Rock Island
Davenport
Clinton
Dubuque
Keokuk
Burlington
Muscatine
IOWA
WISCONSIN
INDIANA
GARY
Mississippi
Des Moines
Illinois R.
Kankakee R.
Vermilion R.
Rock R.
Fox R.
JO DAVIESS
STEPHENSON
WINNEBAGO
BOONE
MC HENRY
LAKE
CARROLL
OGLE
DE KALB
KANE
DU PAGE
COOK
WHITESIDE
LEE
BUREAU
LA SALLE
KENDALL
GRUNDY
WILL
KANKAKEE
ROCK ISLAND
HENRY
MERCER
KNOX
STARK
MARSHALL
PUTNAM
PEORIA
WOODFORD
LIVINGSTON
IROQUOIS
FORD
HENDERSON
WARREN
FULTON
TAZEWELL
MC LEAN
DE WITT
CHAMPAIGN
VERMILION
HANCOCK
MC DONOUGH
SCHUYLER
MASON
LOGAN
MENARD
ADAMS
BROWN
CASS
PIATT
MACON
88°
89°
90°
91°
92°
42°
41°
40°

ILLINOIS
SCALE OF MILES
0 5 10 20 30 40
State Capitals
County Seats
Canals
Longitude West 90° of Greenwich
Copyright by C. S. Hammond & Co., N. Y.
8581
ST. LOUIS
EVANSVILLE
Terre Haute
Vincennes
Paducah
Cairo
Jefferson City
Cape Girardeau
Mississippi
Missouri
Ohio
Wabash
MADISON
ST. CLAIR
MO.

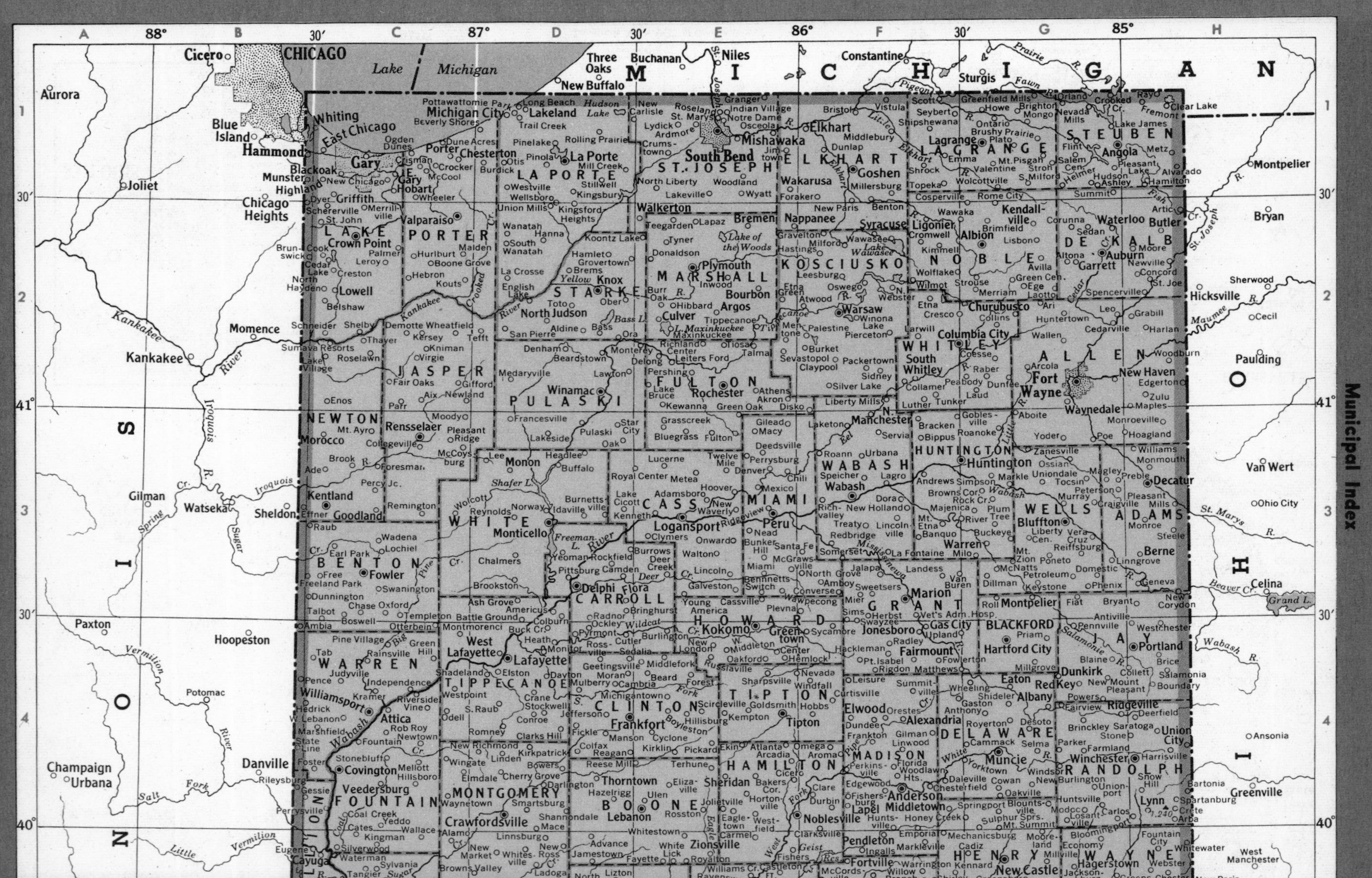
MICHIGAN
OHIO
ILLINOIS
Lake Michigan
CHICAGO
STEUBEN
LAGRANGE
ELKHART
ST. JOSEPH
LA PORTE
PORTER
LAKE
DE KALB
NOBLE
KOSCIUSKO
MARSHALL
STARKE
JASPER
NEWTON
ALLEN
WHITLEY
FULTON
PULASKI
WHITE
BENTON
WARREN
TIPPECANOE
CARROLL
CASS
MIAMI
WABASH
HUNTINGTON
WELLS
ADAMS
GRANT
HOWARD
CLINTON
BOONE
MONTGOMERY
FOUNTAIN
TIPTON
HAMILTON
MADISON
DELAWARE
BLACKFORD
JAY
RANDOLPH
HENRY
WAYNE
Fort Wayne
South Bend
Gary
Hammond
Lafayette
Kokomo
Muncie
Anderson
Marion
Logansport
Elkhart
Michigan City

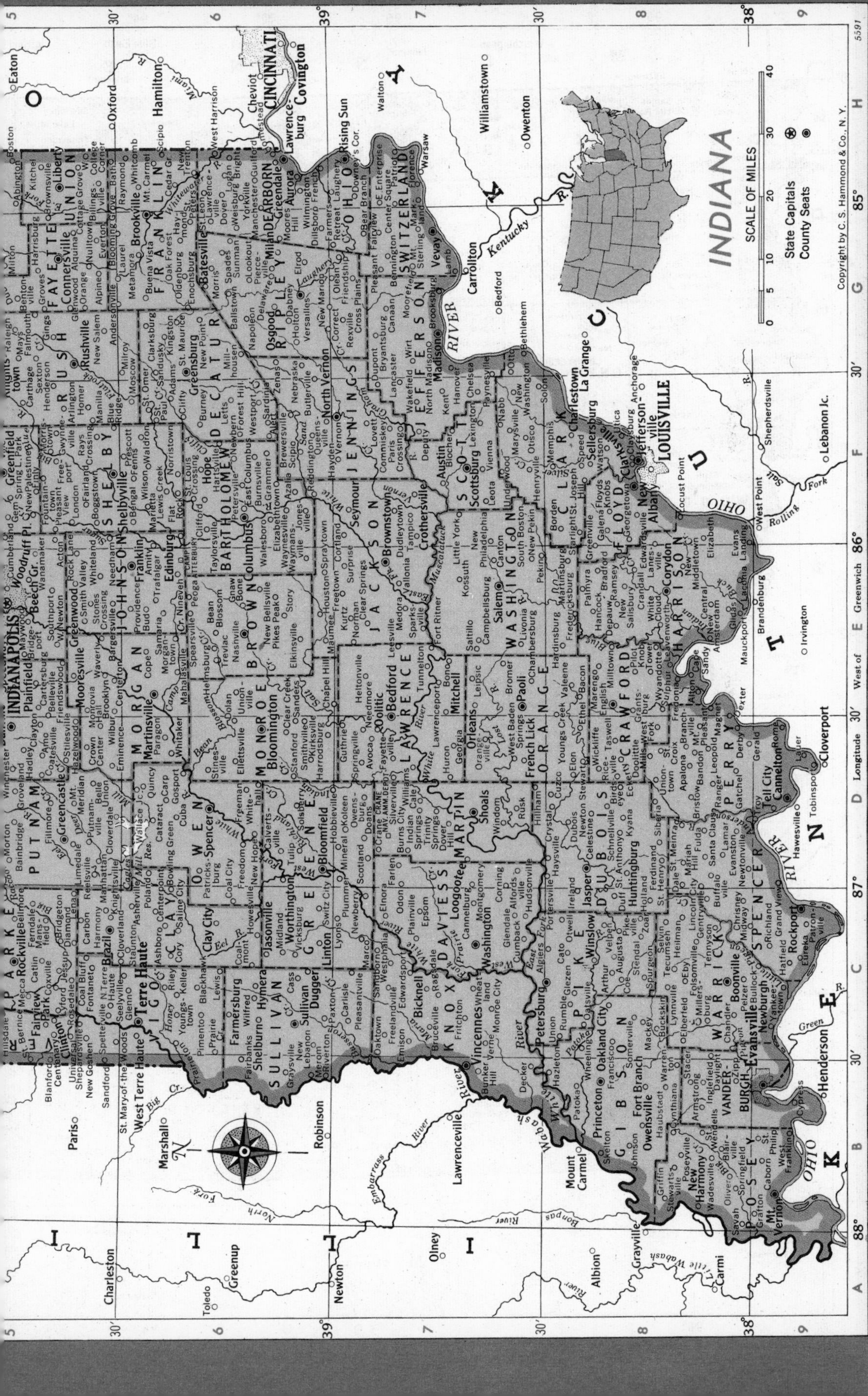

INDIANA

SCALE OF MILES

0 5 10 20 30 40

State Capitals

County Seats

Longitude West of Greenwich

5591

30′
A
96°
B
30′
C
95°
D
30′
E
94°
F
M I N N E
Worthington
Fairmont
Blue Earth
Albert L
Jackson
Hills
Ellsworth
Bricelyn
Tuttle L.
S. DAK.
N E B R A S K A
LYON
OSCEOLA
DICKINSON
EMMET
KOSSUTH
WINNEBAGO
SIOUX
O'BRIEN
CLAY
PALO ALTO
HANCOCK
PLYMOUTH
CHEROKEE
BUENA VISTA
POCAHONTAS
HUMBOLDT
WRIGHT
WOODBURY
IDA
SAC
CALHOUN
WEBSTER
HAMILTON
MONONA
CRAWFORD
CARROLL
GREENE
BOONE
STO
HARRISON
SHELBY
AUDUBON
GUTHRIE
DALLAS
POLK
POTTAWATTAMIE
CASS
ADAIR
MADISON
WARRE
MILLS
MONTGOMERY
ADAMS
UNION
CLARKE
FREMONT
PAGE
TAYLOR
RINGGOLD
DECATUR
Granite
Larchwood
Lester
Rock Rapids
Little Rock
Edna
Alvord
Inwood
Canton
Beloit
Doon
George
Ocheyedan Mound 1,675
Allendorf
Harris
Sibley
Ocheyedan
Ashton
Melvin
Lake Park
Spirit L.
Orleans
Superior
Montgomery
The Inn
Spirit Lake
Okoboji
W. Okoboji
Arnolds Park
Milford
Terril
Huntington
Estherville
Dolliver
Armstrong
Gruver
Maple Hill
Wallingford
Ringsted
Gerled
Ledyard
Swea City
Lakota
Rake
Scarville
Buffalo Cen.
Thompson
Lake Mills
Leland
Forest City
Fertile
Rock Valley
Matlock
Hull
Perkins
Boyden
Sioux Center
Hospers
Hawarden
Orange City
Ireton
Alton
Granville
Maurice
Chatsworth
Sheldon
Sanborn
Hartley
Archer
Moneta
Primghar
Paullina
Gaza
Sutherland
Calumet
Fostoria
Langdon
Everly
Trumbull L.
Spencer
Dickens
Royal
Gillett Grove
Rossie
Greenville
Webb
Cornell
Peterson
Palo Alto L.
Graettinger
Osgood
Medium Lake
Lost Island L.
Ruthven
Emmetsburg
Cylinder
Ayrshire
Rodman
Curlew
Mallard
West Bend
Lone Rock
Titonka
Bancroft
Fenton
Burt
Algona
Sexton
Wesley
Whittemore
St. Benedict
Irvington
Lu Verne
Woden
Crystal Lake
Hayfield
Miller
Eagle L.
Britt
Ventura
Garner
Corwith
Klemme
Kanawha
Goodell
Craig
Struble
Akron
Seney
Oyens
Brunsville
Remsen
Le Mars
Westfield
Merrill
Hinton
James
Kingsley
Larrabee
Marcus
Cleghorn
Meriden
Cherokee
Aurelia
Quimby
Washta
Linn Grove
Sioux Rapids
Marathon
Rembrandt
Albert City
Truesdale
Alta
Storm L.
Storm Lake
Lakeside
Sulphur Sprs.
Newell
Laurens
Plover
Havelock
Ware
Rolfe
Pocahontas
Gilmore City
Varina
Palmer
Fonda
Ottosen
Bode
Livermore
Renwick
Bradgate
Hardy
Rutland
Humboldt
Dakota City
Pioneer
Thor
Belmond
Holmes
Rowan
Clarion
Goldfield
Galt
Eagle Grove
Dows
Woolstock
Sioux City
Pierson
Lawton
Moville
Correctionville
Sergeant Bluff
Bronson
Dakota City
Anthon
Cushing
Luton
Climbing Hill
Salix
Oto
Sloan
Hornick
Smithland
Danbury
Holstein
Galva
Ida Grove
Arthur
Battle Creek
Nemaha
Schaller
Early
Sac City
Lytton
Odebolt
Lake View
Wall Lake
Carnarvon
Ulmer
Auburn
Herring
Pomeroy
Knoke
Manson
Jolley
Knierim
Lavinia
Richards
Rockwell City
Somers
Sherwood
Yetter
Rinard
Farnhamville
Lake City
Lohrville
Clare
Barnum
Fort Dodge
Badger
Vincent
Tara
Duncombe
Clay Works
Otho
Coalville
Kalo
Moorland
Callender
Lehigh
Burnside
Gowrie
Harcourt
Lanyon
Dayton
Stratford
Williams
Blairsburg
Webster City
Kamrar
Jewell
Ellsworth
Stanhope
Randall
Rodney
Grant Center
Mapleton
Whiting
Ticonic
Castana
Ute
Onawa
Turin
Soldier
Blencoe
Moorhead
Kiron
Schleswig
Ricketts
Deloit
Charter Oak
Westside
Vail
Denison
Arion
Dow City
Buck Grove
Aspinwall
Manilla
Astor
Boyer
Breda
Arcadia
Lidderdale
Maple River
Carroll
Glidden
Halbur
Roselle
Willey
Templeton
Manning
Dedham
Coon Rapids
Lanesboro
Churdan
Adaza
Paton
Dana
Ralston
Farlin
Grand Jc.
Jefferson
Scranton
Carrollton
Rippey
Cooper
Jamaica
Boxholm
Pilot Mound
Fraser
Boone
Jordan
Beaver
Ogden
Moingona
Berkley
Luther
Madrid
Angus
Story City
Roland
Gilbert
Ontario
Ames
Kelley
Huxley
Slater
Sheldahl
Lyons
Oakland
Tekamah
Pisgah
Little Sioux
River Sioux
Orson
Dunlap
Woodbine
Mondamin
Magnolia
Panama
Logan
Modale
California
Missouri Valley
Persia
Yorkshire
Defiance
Earling
Botna
Irwin
Kirkman
Westphalia
Harlan
Portsmouth
Tennant
Corley
Elk Horn
Shelby
Gray
Ross
Audubon
Hamlin
Kimballton
Exira
Brayton
Bayard
Bagley
Herndon
Dawson
Yale
Panora
Guthrie Cen.
Monteith
Glendon
Casey
Menlo
Perry
Bouton
Woodward
Minburn
Moran
Granger
Dallas Cen.
Linden
Adel
Redfield
Dale
Dexter
De Soto
Van Meter
West Des Moines
Herrold
Grimes
Johnston
Urbandale
Waukee
Clive
Windsor Hts.
Clover Hills
Commerce
Fort Des Moines
Polk City
Elkhart
Ankeny
Carney
Saylor
Blair
Arlington
Fremont
OMAHA
Carter Lake
Papillion
Loveland
Honey Creek
Neola
Minden
Avoca
Walnut
Crescent
Underwood
Bentley
Hancock
Weston
McClelland
Oakland
Council Bluffs
Carson
Treynor
Macedonia
Marne
Anita
Wiota
Atlantic
Lewis
Cumberland
Massena
Griswold
Greenfield
Fontanelle
Bridgewater
Orient
Stanzel
Adair
Stuart
Earlham
Cumming
Norwalk
Summerset
Spring Hill
Churchville
Bevington
Martensdale
Patterson
Winterset
Wick
Indianola
St. Charles
St Marys
Peru
E. Peru
Truro
Macksburg
Liberty Cen
New Virginia
Ashland
Plattsmouth
Mineola
Henderson
Silver City
Glenwood
Hastings
Pacific Jc.
Malvern
Emerson
Strahan
Tabor
Elliott
Grant
Stennett
Morton Mills
Red Oak
Stanton
Villisca
Coburg
Mt. Etna
Nevinville
Carl
Carbon
Quincy
Prescott
Corning
Brooks
Nodaway
Summit Lake
Creston
Lorimor
Cromwell
Talmage
Afton
Thayer
Kent
Arispe
Shannon City
Liberty
Jamison
Murray
Osceola
Woodburn
Hopeville
Leslie
Weeping Water
Union
Nebraska City
Dunbar
Bartlett
Randolph
Imogene
Thurman
McPaul
Anderson
Percival
Sidney
Farragut
Riverton
Payne
Hamburg
Essex
Hepburn
Shenandoah
Yorktown
Page
Clarinda
Coin
College Sprs.
Northboro
Blanchard
Sharpsburg
Gravity
New Market
Shambaugh
Bedford
Clearfield
Conway
Lenox
Blockton
Braddyville
Athelstan
Knowlton
Tingley
Ellston
Beaconsfield
Diagonal
Benton
Kellerton
Mount Ayr
Maloy
Delphos
Redding
Weldon
Van Wert
Le Roy
Grand River
Garden Grove
Decatur
Leon
Woodland
Davis City
Lamoni
Pleasanton
Talmage
Tecumseh
Grant City
Maryville
Cainsville
Bethany
Albany
Princet
M I S S
Rock River
Big Sioux
Floyd
Little Sioux River
Boyer
Raccoon
Des Moines
Nishnabotna
West Nishnabotna
East
Nodaway
Thompson
Grand
Platte
Elkhorn
MISSOURI RIVER
Platte River
Fork
1
2
3
4
5
6
7
8
30′
43°
42°
41°
N
Longitude West of

IOWA
SCALE OF MILES
0 5 10 20 30 40
State Capitals
County Seats
MITCHELL
HOWARD
WINNESHIEK
ALLAMAKEE
FLOYD
CHICKASAW
FAYETTE
CLAYTON
BUTLER
BREMER
BLACK HAWK
BUCHANAN
DELAWARE
DUBUQUE
GRUNDY
MARSHALL
TAMA
BENTON
LINN
JONES
JACKSON
CLINTON
CEDAR
SCOTT
MUSCATINE
JOHNSON
IOWA
POWESHIEK
JASPER
MAHASKA
KEOKUK
WASHINGTON
LOUISA
MARION
MONROE
WAPELLO
JEFFERSON
HENRY
DES MOINES
APPANOOSE
DAVIS
VAN BUREN
LEE
CEDAR RAPIDS
DAVENPORT
Dubuque
Waterloo
Iowa City
Ottumwa
Burlington
Keokuk
Clinton
Muscatine
Fort Madison
Mason City
Marshalltown
Rock Island
Moline
Galesburg
MISSISSIPPI
RIVER
W I S.
I L L I N O I S
M I S S O U R I
M I N N E S O T A
Copyright by C.S.HAMMOND & CO.,N.Y.
7581

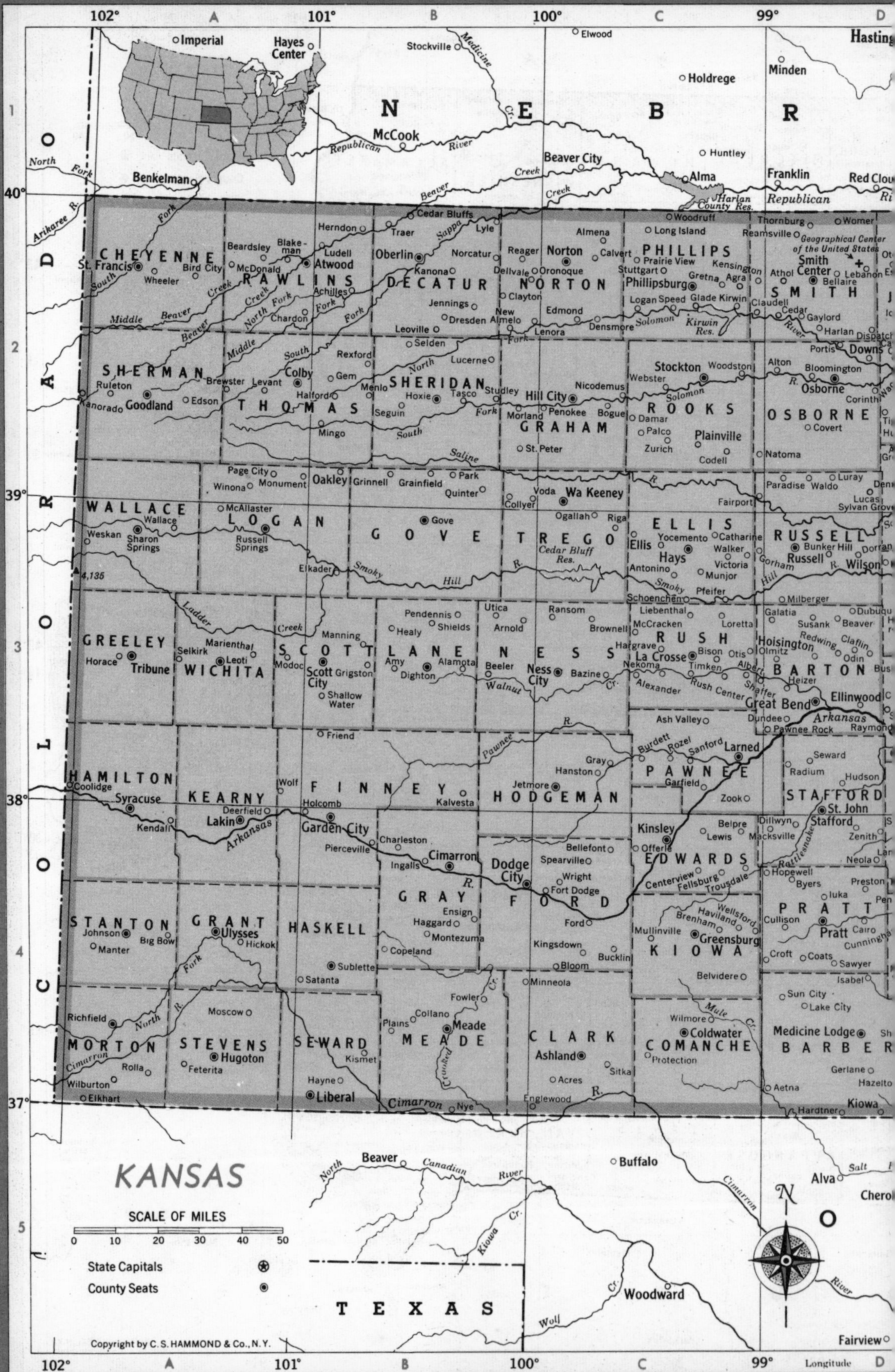

KANSAS

SCALE OF MILES

0 10 20 30 40 50

State Capitals

County Seats

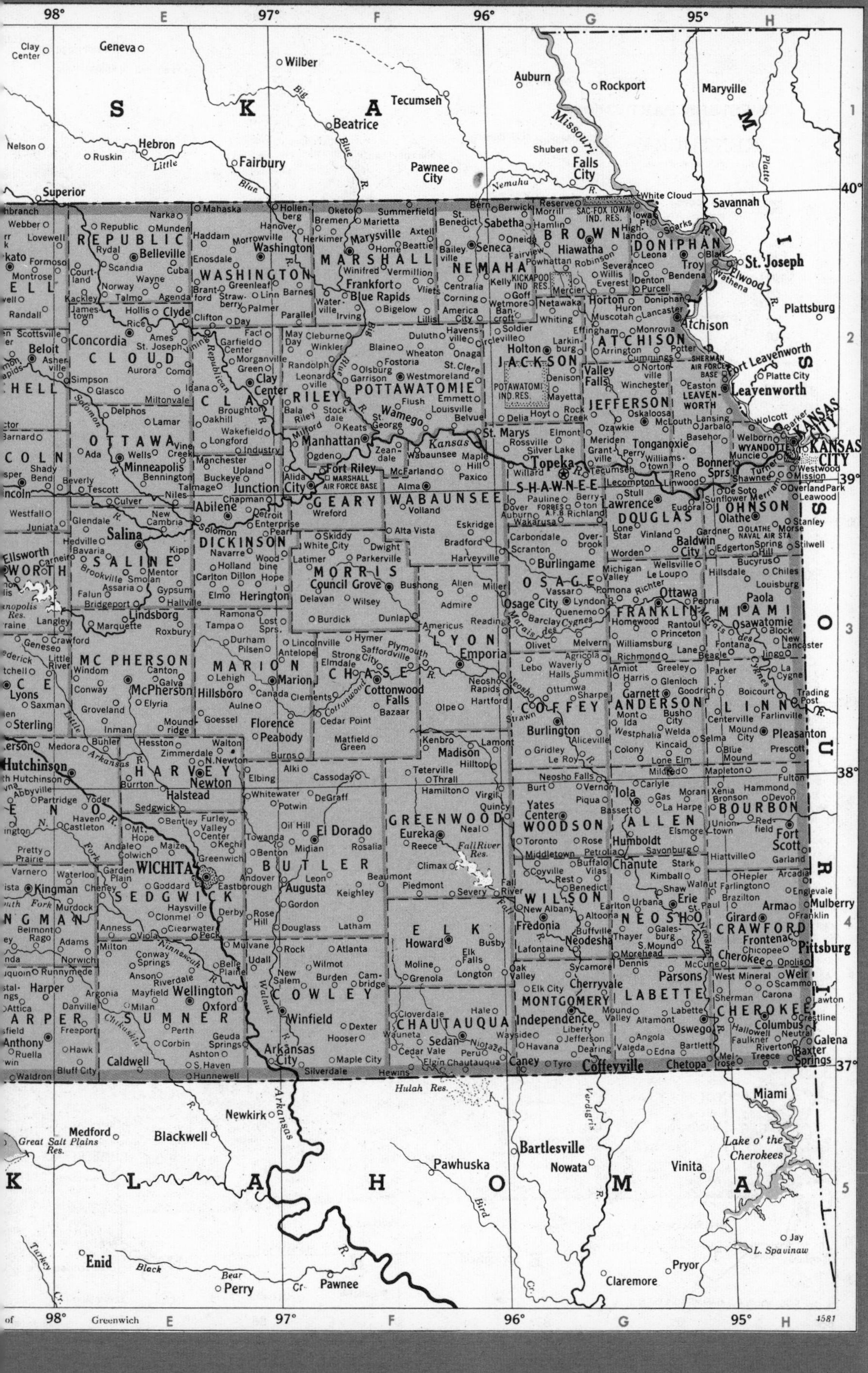

98° E 97° F 96° G 95° H

NEBRASKA

MISSOURI

KANSAS

REPUBLIC · WASHINGTON · MARSHALL · NEMAHA · BROWN · DONIPHAN · CLOUD · CLAY · RILEY · POTTAWATOMIE · JACKSON · ATCHISON · JEFFERSON · LEAVENWORTH · OTTAWA · GEARY · WABAUNSEE · SHAWNEE · WYANDOTTE · DICKINSON · SALINE · MORRIS · OSAGE · DOUGLAS · JOHNSON · MC PHERSON · MARION · CHASE · LYON · FRANKLIN · MIAMI · COFFEY · ANDERSON · LINN · HARVEY · BUTLER · GREENWOOD · WOODSON · ALLEN · BOURBON · SEDGWICK · ELK · WILSON · NEOSHO · CRAWFORD · SUMNER · COWLEY · CHAUTAUQUA · MONTGOMERY · LABETTE · CHEROKEE

OKLAHOMA

of 98° Greenwich E 97° F 96° G 95° H

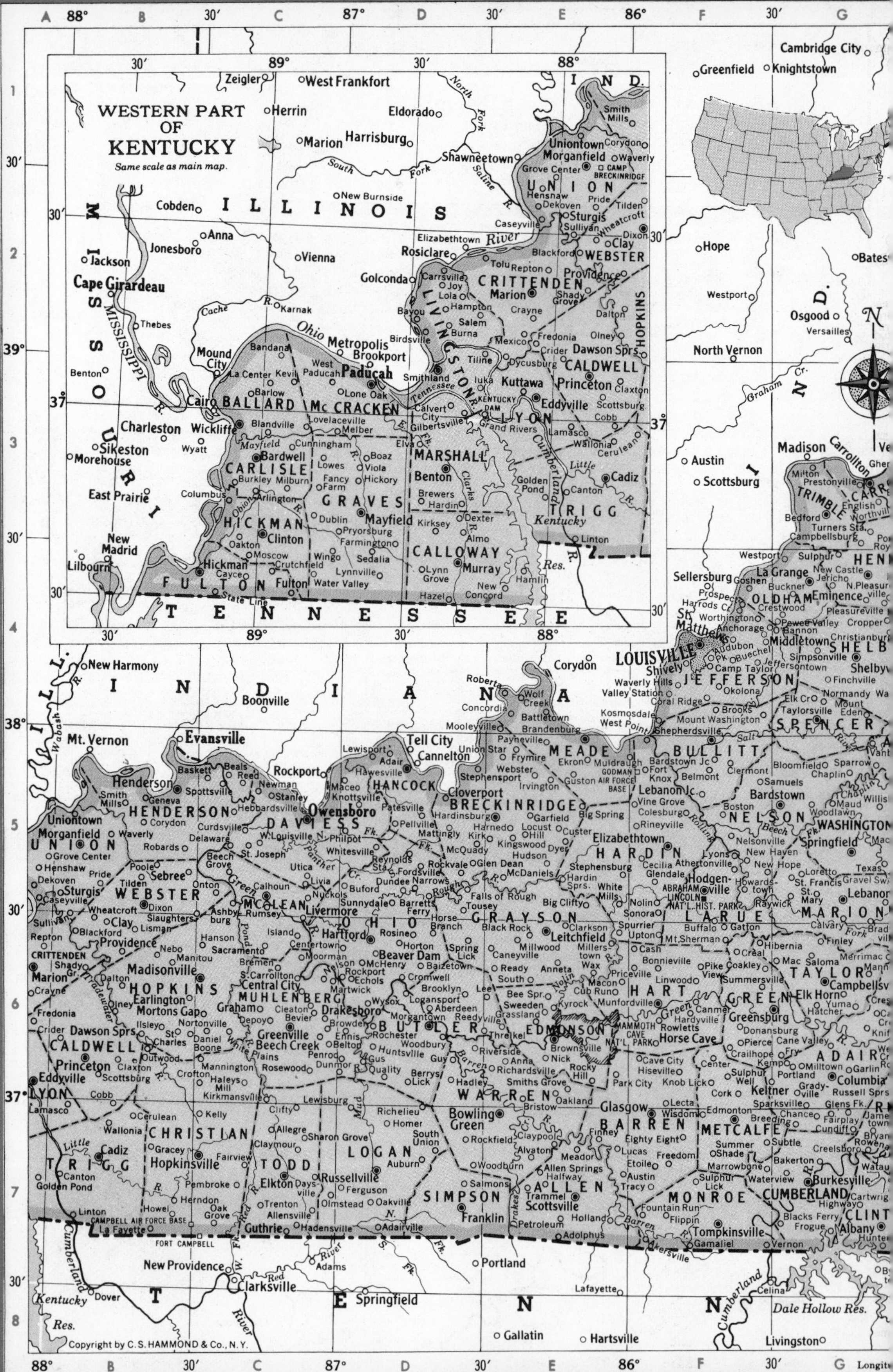

WESTERN PART OF KENTUCKY

Same scale as main map.

KENTUCKY

SCALE OF MILES

0 5 10 20 30 40

State Capitals

County Seats

LOUISIANA
SCALE OF MILES
0 5 10 20 30 40
State Capitals
Canals
Parish Seats
ARKANSAS
TEXAS
MISSISSIPPI
GULF OF MEXICO
CADDO
BOSSIER
WEBSTER
CLAIBORNE
UNION
MOREHOUSE
WEST CARROLL
EAST CARROLL
LINCOLN
OUACHITA
RICHLAND
MADISON
BIENVILLE
JACKSON
CALDWELL
FRANKLIN
TENSAS
DE SOTO
RED RIVER
WINN
NATCHITOCHES
SABINE
GRANT
LA SALLE
CATAHOULA
CONCORDIA
VERNON
RAPIDES
AVOYELLES
BEAUREGARD
ALLEN
EVANGELINE
ST. LANDRY
POINTE COUPEE
WEST FELICIANA
WEST BATON ROUGE
CALCASIEU
JEFFERSON DAVIS
ACADIA
LAFAYETTE
ST. MARTIN
IBERVILLE
CAMERON
VERMILION
IBERIA
ST. MARY
SHREVEPORT
Bossier City
Minden
Homer
Ruston
Monroe
Farmerville
Bastrop
Natchitoches
Many
Winnfield
Alexandria
Pineville
Colfax
Leesville
De Ridder
Oberlin
Oakdale
Ville Platte
Opelousas
Marksville
Lafayette
Crowley
Jennings
Lake Charles
Sulphur
Abbeville
New Iberia
Franklin
Morgan City
Cameron
Vidalia
Natchez
Beaumont
Orange
Port Arthur
Port Neches
Sabine Lake
Calcasieu Lake
White L.
Grand Lake
Vermilion Bay
West Cote Blanche Bay
Atchafalaya Bay
Marsh Island
Pecan Island
Red River
Sabine R.
Neches River
Ouachita R.
Black L.
Caddo L.
Toledo Bend
Catahoula L.
Lake Iatt
94° 93° 92° 30′
33° 32° 31° 30°
B C D E F G H
1 2 3 4 5 6 7 8

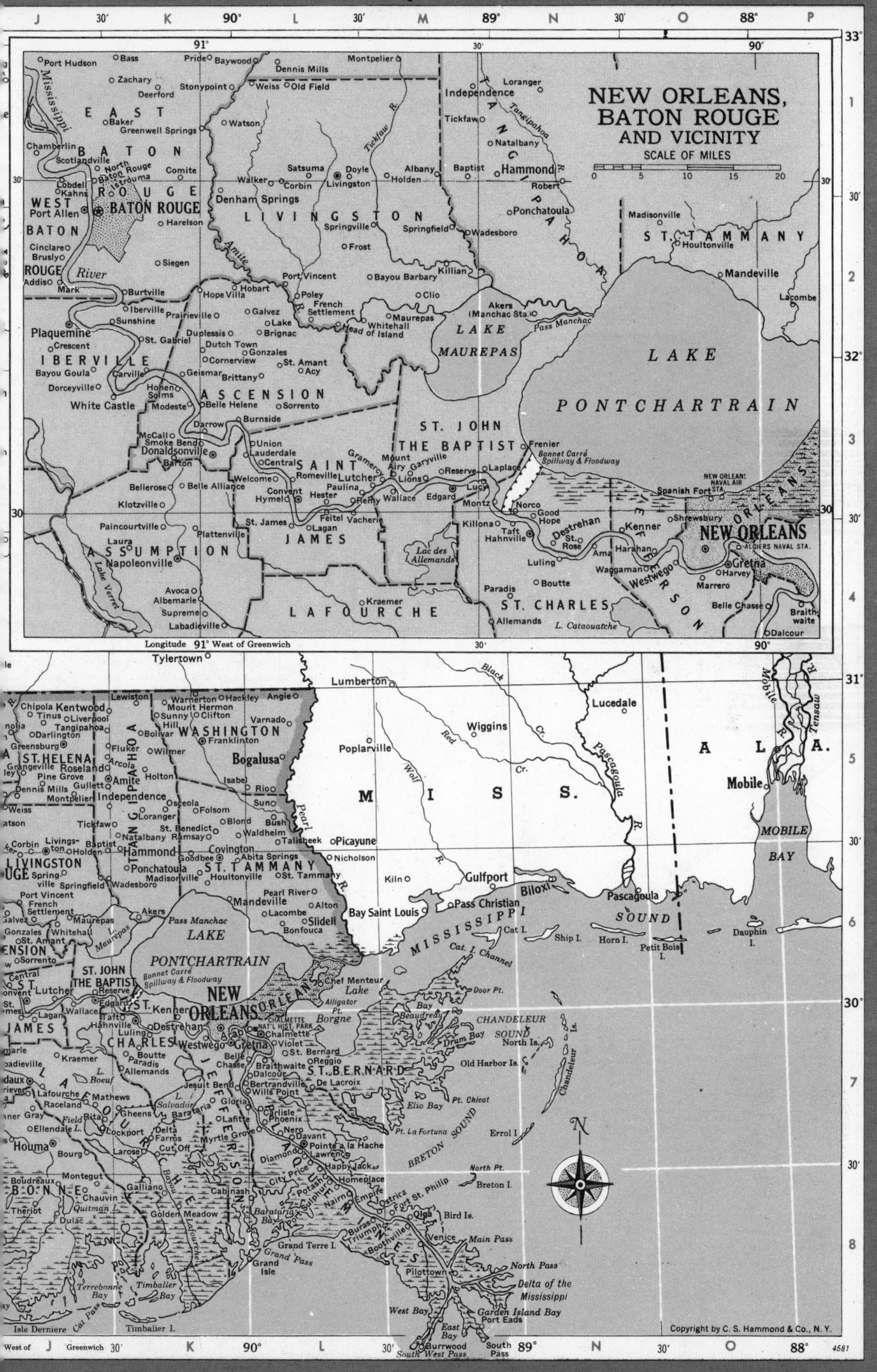
NEW ORLEANS, BATON ROUGE AND VICINITY
SCALE OF MILES
0 5 10 15 20
Longitude 91° West of Greenwich
EAST BATON ROUGE
WEST BATON ROUGE
BATON ROUGE
LIVINGSTON
TANGIPAHOA
ST. TAMMANY
IBERVILLE
ASCENSION
ST. JOHN THE BAPTIST
SAINT JAMES
ASSUMPTION
LAFOURCHE
ST. CHARLES
JEFFERSON
LAKE MAUREPAS
LAKE PONTCHARTRAIN
Bonnet Carré Spillway & Floodway
NEW ORLEANS NAVAL AIR STA.
ALGIERS NAVAL STA.
NEW ORLEANS
Lac des Allemands
L. Cataouatche
Port Hudson
Bass
Zachary
Deerford
Baker
Greenwell Springs
Chamberlin
Scotlandville
North Baton Rouge
Istrouma
Comite
Lobdell
Kahns
Port Allen
Harelson
Cinclare
Brusly
Addis
Mark
Siegen
Burtville
Iberville
Sunshine
Plaquemine
Crescent
St. Gabriel
Carville
Bayou Goula
Dorceyville
White Castle
Hohen Solms
Modeste
Belle Helene
Sorrento
Darrow
Burnside
McCall
Smoke Bend
Donaldsonville
Barton
Union
Lauderdale
Central
Welcome
Romeville
Lutcher
Gramercy
Mount Airy
Garyville
Lions
Reserve
Laplace
Frenier
Bellerose
Belle Alliance
Convent
Hymel
Hester
Paulina
Remy
Wallace
Edgard
Lucy
Montz
Norco
Good Hope
Klotzville
Paincourtville
Plattenville
St. James
Lagan
Feitel
Vacherie
Killona
Taft
Hahnville
Destrehan
St. Rose
Ama
Kenner
Harahan
Shrewsbury
Gretna
Harvey
Marrero
Westwego
Waggaman
Luling
Boutte
Paradis
Allemands
Belle Chasse
Braithwaite
Dalcour
Laura
Napoleonville
Avoca
Albemarle
Supreme
Labadieville
Kraemer
Pride
Baywood
Stonypoint
Weiss
Old Field
Dennis Mills
Montpelier
Watson
Walker
Corbin
Satsuma
Doyle
Livingston
Albany
Holden
Denham Springs
Springville
Springfield
Frost
Port Vincent
Poley
French Settlement
Bayou Barbary
Killian
Clio
Maurepas
Whitehall
Head of Island
Hobart
Hope Villa
Galvez
Lake
Brignac
Prairieville
Duplessis
Dutch Town
Gonzales
Cornerview
St. Amant
Acy
Geismar
Brittany
Loranger
Independence
Tickfaw
Natalbany
Baptist
Hammond
Robert
Ponchatoula
Wadesboro
Akers
(Manchac Sta.)
Pass Manchac
Madisonville
Houltonville
Mandeville
Lacombe
Spanish Fort
Mississippi
Amite R.
Tickfaw R.
Tangipahoa R.
River
Tylertown
Lumberton
Lucedale
Wiggins
Poplarville
Picayune
Nicholson
Kiln
Gulfport
Biloxi
Pascagoula
Pass Christian
Bay Saint Louis
Mobile
MOBILE BAY
MISS.
ALA.
MISSISSIPPI SOUND
Cat I.
Ship I.
Horn I.
Petit Bois I.
Dauphin I.
Cat. I. Channel
Chef Menteur
Lake Borgne
CHANDELEUR SOUND
Chandeleur Is.
North Is.
Old Harbor Is.
Door Pt.
Drum Bay
Pt. Chicot
Elio Bay
Pt. La Fortuna
BRETON SOUND
Errol I.
North Pt.
Breton I.
Main Pass
North Pass
Delta of the Mississippi
Garden Island Bay
Port Eads
East Bay
West Bay
Burrwood
South Pass
South West Pass
Pilottown
Venice
Boothville
Buras
Triumph
Empire
Ostrica
Fort St. Philip
Olga
Bird Is.
Nairn
Potash
Port Sulphur
Homeplace
Happy Jack
City Price
Diamond
Lawrence
Pointe a la Hache
Davant
Nero
Phoenix
Carlisle
Wills Point
Bertrandville
De Lacroix
Dalcour
Braithwaite
Reggio
St. Bernard
ST. BERNARD
Violet
Chalmette
CHALMETTE NAT'L HIST. PARK
Arabi
Jesuit Bend
Gloria
Barataria
Lafitte
Myrtle Grove
Barataria Bay
Grand Terre I.
Grand Pass
Grand Isle
Timbalier Bay
Timbalier I.
Terrebonne Bay
Cat Pass
Isle Derniere
Golden Meadow
Cabinash
Galliano
Cut Off
Larose
Delta Farms
Lockport
Gheens
Raceland
Mathews
Lafourche
Field L.
Rita
Ellendale L.
Gray
Houma
Bourg
Montegut
Boudreaux
Chauvin
Theriot
Dulac
Quitman L.
Kentwood
Chipola
Tinus
Liverpool
Tangipahoa
Darlington
Greensburg
ST. HELENA
Grangeville
Roseland
Pine Grove
Amite
Gullett
Montpelier
Fluker
Arcola
Wilmer
Holton
Bolivar
Lewiston
Warnerton
Hackley
Angie
Mount Hermon
Sunny Hill
Clifton
Varnado
WASHINGTON
Franklinton
Bogalusa
Isabel
Rio
Sun
Osceola
Folsom
Blond
Bush
St. Benedict
Ramsay
Waldheim
Talisheek
Covington
Goodbee
Abita Springs
Pearl River
Alton
Slidell
Bonfouca
Lacombe
Pearl R.
Wolf R.
Red Cr.
Black Cr.
Pascagoula R.
Mobile R.
Tensaw R.
L. Salvador
Bayou Lafourche
L. Boeuf
Copyright by C. S. Hammond & Co., N. Y.
4581
West of Greenwich
J K L M N O P
30′ 90° 30′ 89° 30′ 88°
33° 30′ 32° 30′ 31° 30′ 30° 30′
1 2 3 4 5 6 7 8

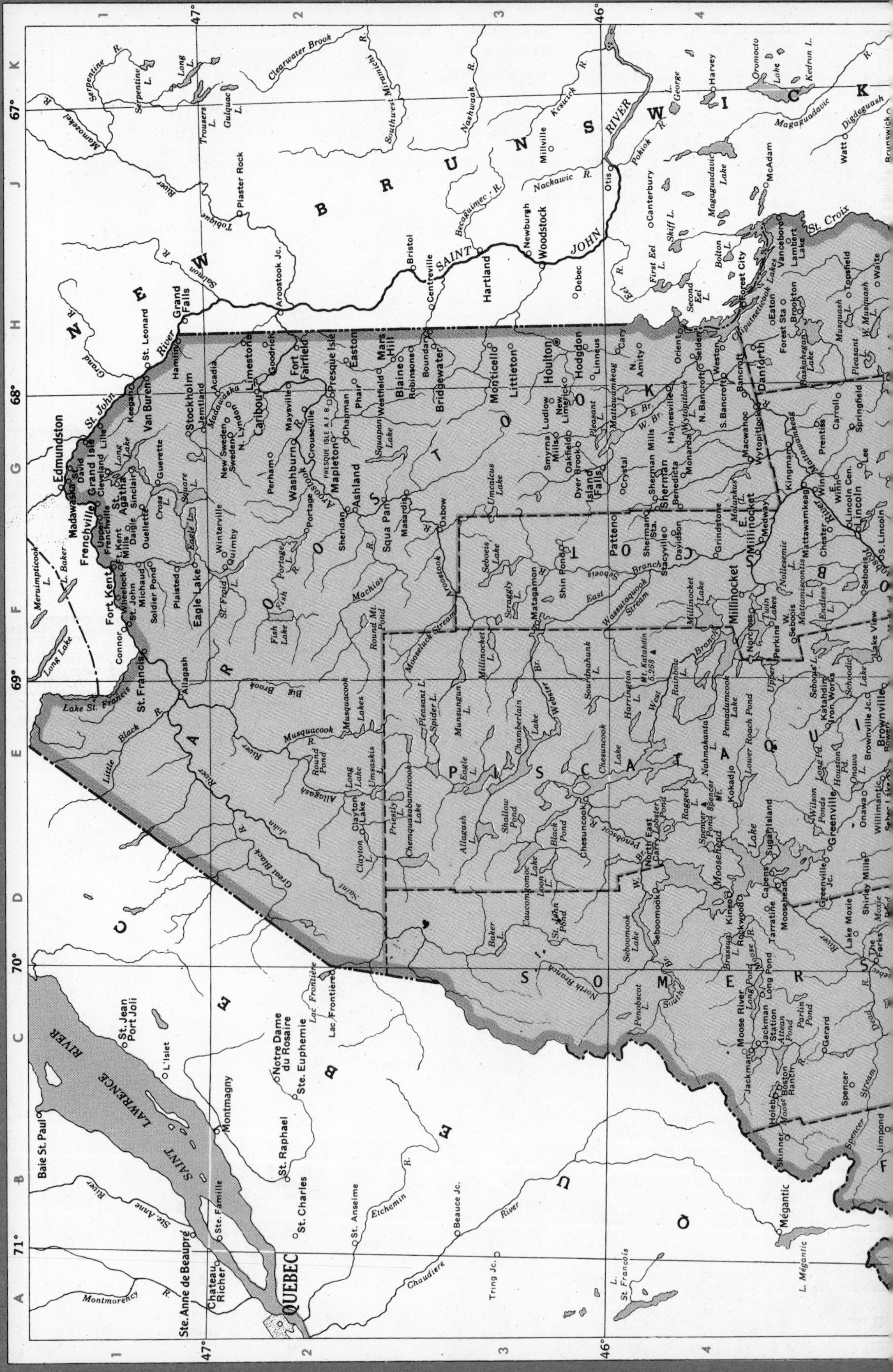
NEW BRUNSWICK
AROOSTOOK
PISCATAQUIS
SOMERSET
PENOBSCOT
QUEBEC
SAINT LAWRENCE RIVER
SAINT JOHN RIVER
Edmundston
Madawaska
Frenchville
Fort Kent
St. Francis
Allagash
Van Buren
Grand Falls
Grand Isle
Caribou
Presque Isle
Fort Fairfield
Mars Hill
Limestone
Washburn
Mapleton
Ashland
Houlton
Hodgdon
Littleton
Monticello
Bridgewater
Patten
Sherman
Island Falls
Millinocket
E. Millinocket
Danforth
Lincoln
Greenville
Moosehead Lake
Brownville
Jackman
Moose River
Mégantic
Woodstock
Hartland
Stockholm
Eagle Lake
Squa Pan
Oxbow
Chesuncook
Rockwood
Ste. Anne de Beaupré
Chateau Richer
St. Jean Port Joli
Montmagny
St. Raphael
St. Charles
Baie St. Paul
Lac Frontière
Mt. Katahdin 5,268

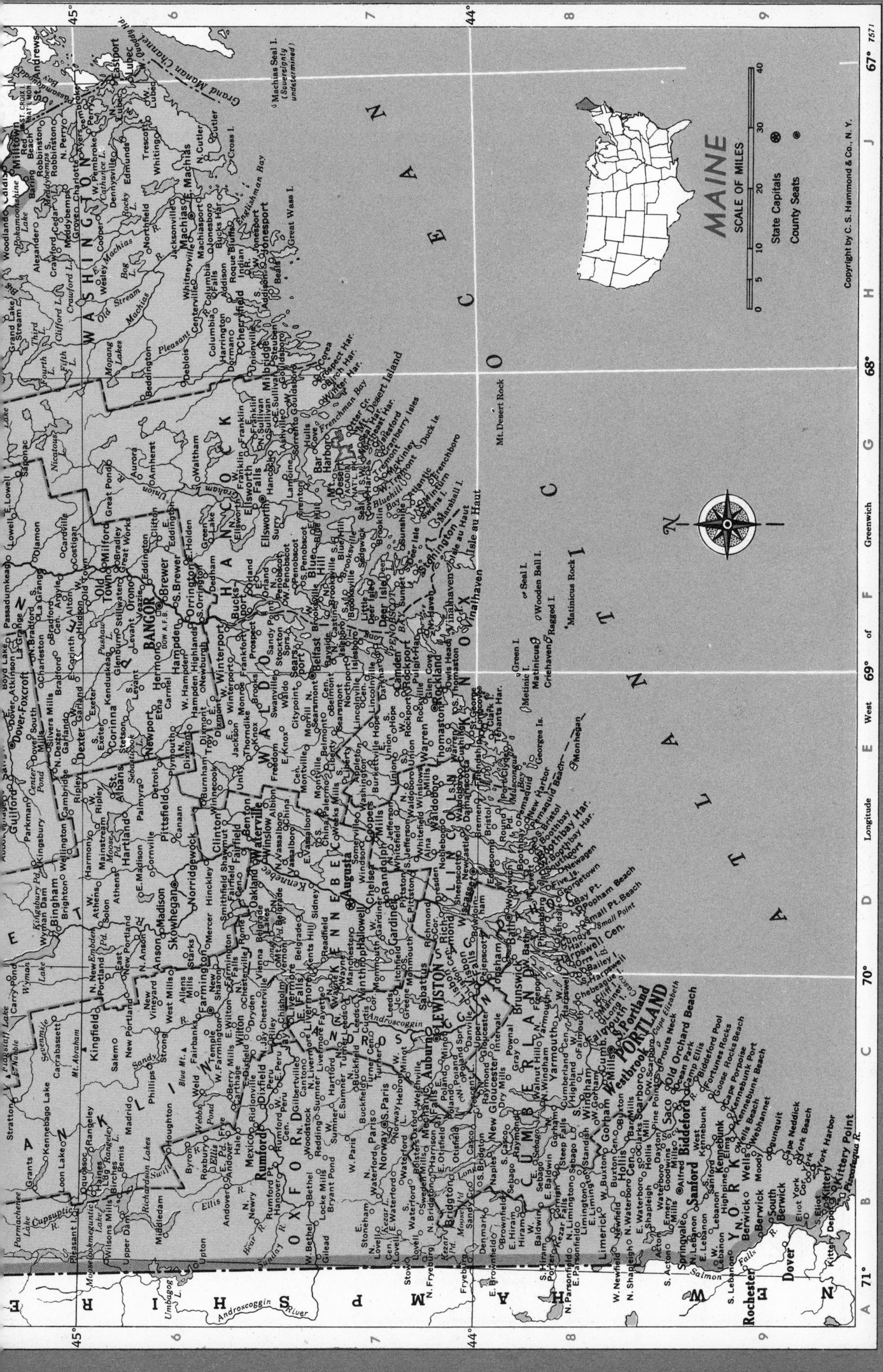

MAINE

SCALE OF MILES

0 5 10 20 30 40

State Capitals

County Seats

Copyright by C. S. Hammond & Co., N. Y.

Longitude West of Greenwich

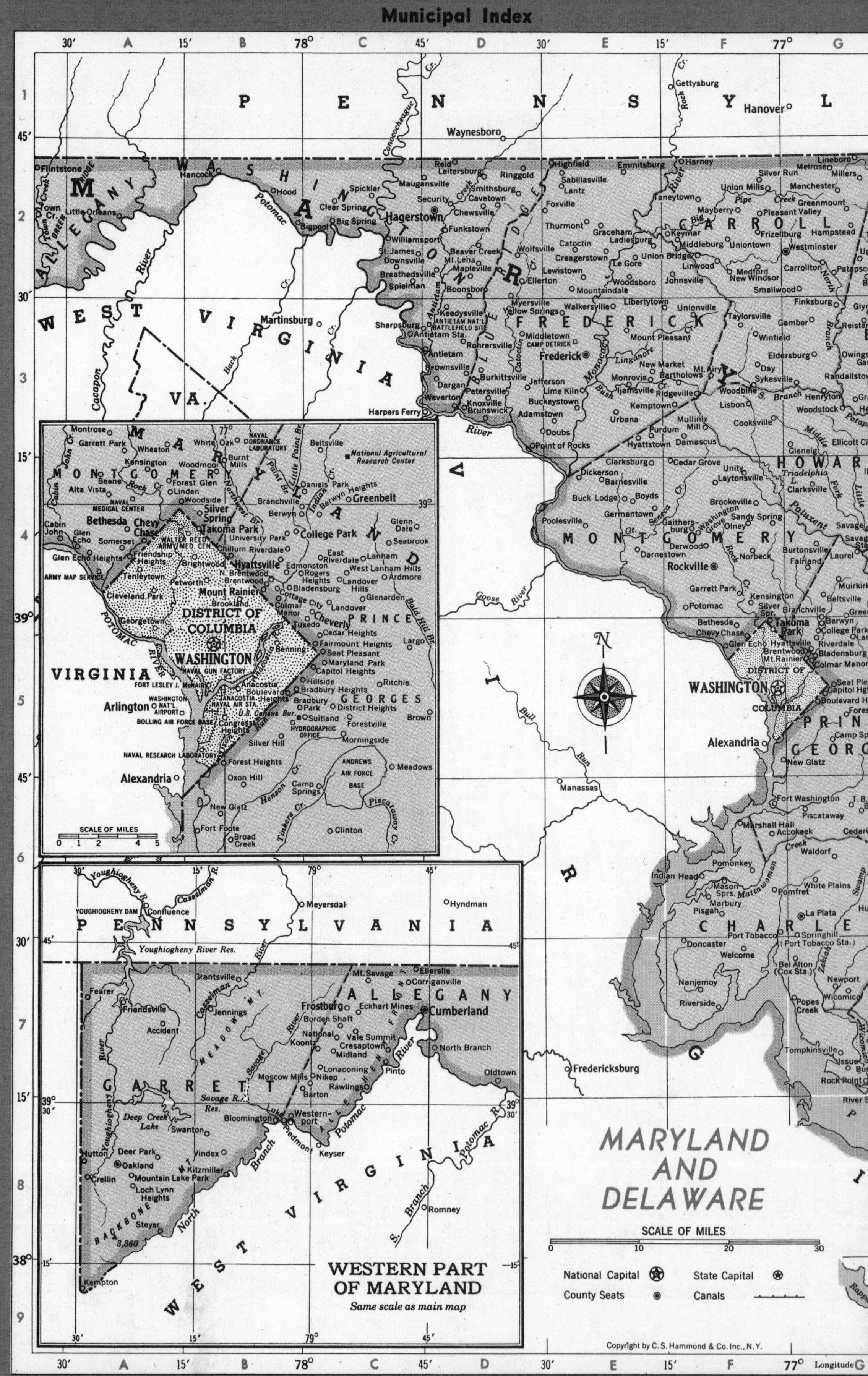
MARYLAND
AND
DELAWARE
SCALE OF MILES
National Capital
State Capital
County Seats
Canals
WESTERN PART
OF MARYLAND
Same scale as main map
DISTRICT OF
COLUMBIA
WASHINGTON
Copyright by C. S. Hammond & Co. Inc., N. Y.

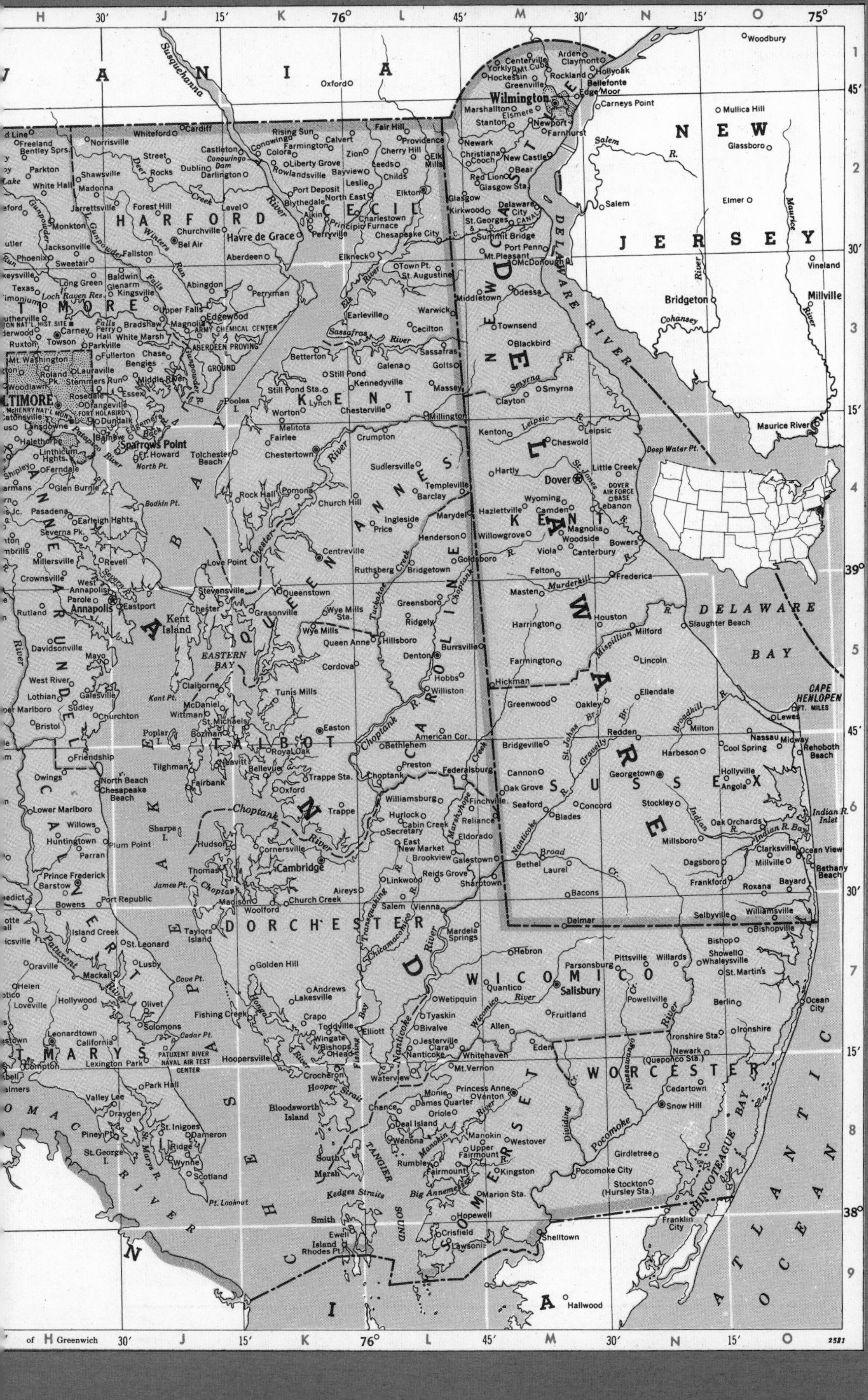

PENNSYLVANIA

NEW JERSEY

DELAWARE

MARYLAND

VIRGINIA

CHESAPEAKE BAY

DELAWARE BAY

ATLANTIC OCEAN

of Greenwich

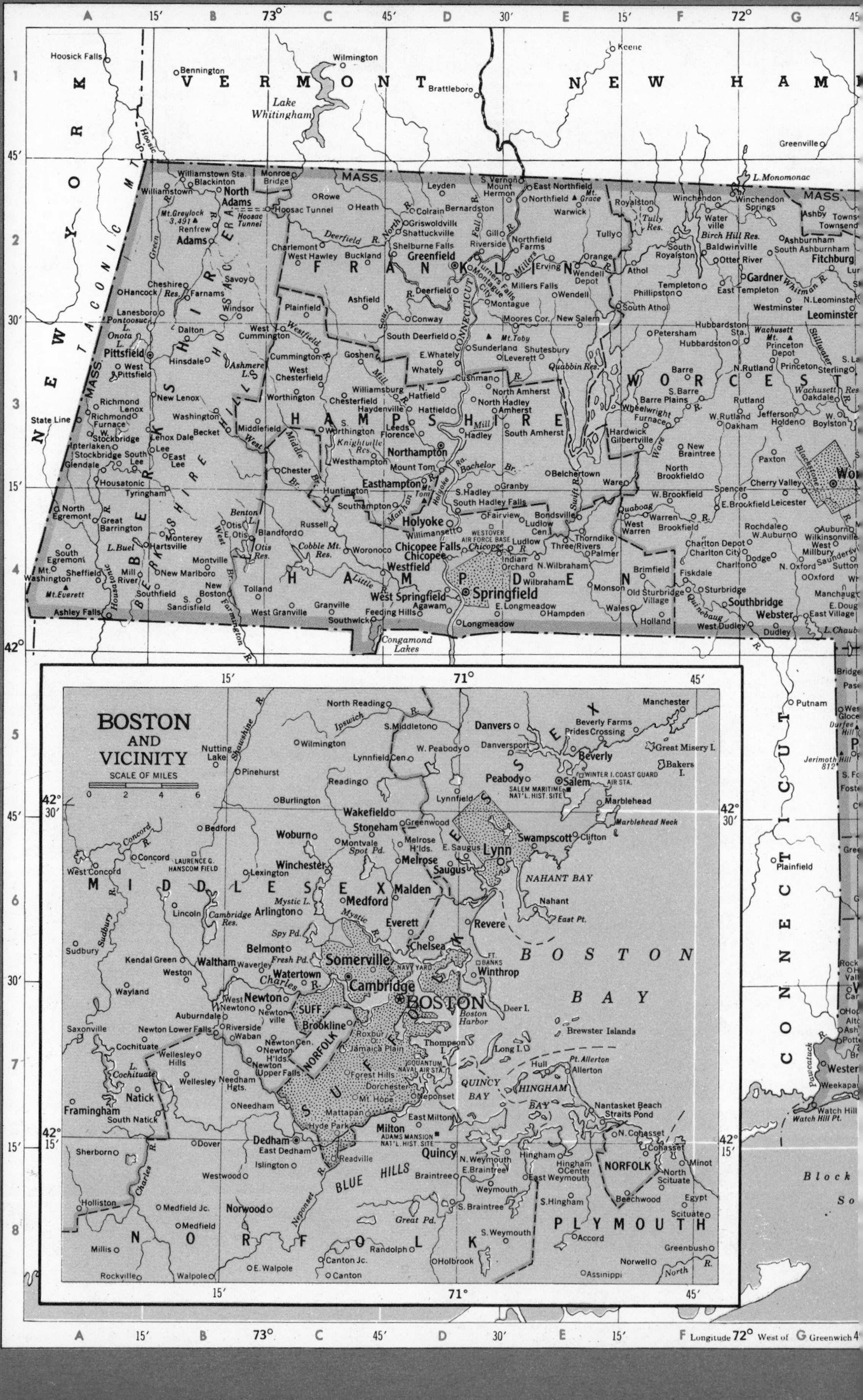

A 15′ B 73° C 45′ D 30′ E 15′ F 72° G 45′

1 2 3 4 5 6 7 8

45′ 30′ 15′ 42°

VERMONT NEW HAMPSHIRE NEW YORK MASS. CONNECTICUT

TACONIC MT. HOOSAC RANGE BERKSHIRE HILLS

BERKSHIRE FRANKLIN HAMPSHIRE HAMPDEN WORCESTER

Hoosick Falls, Bennington, Wilmington, Lake Whitingham, Brattleboro, Keene, Greenville, L. Monomonac

Williamstown Sta., Blackinton, Williamstown, North Adams, Mt. Greylock 3,491, Renfrew, Adams, Hoosac Tunnel, Monroe Bridge, Rowe, Heath, Leyden, Colrain, Bernardston, Griswoldville, Shattuckville, S. Vernon, Mount Hermon, East Northfield, Northfield, Mt. Grace, Warwick, Royalston, Tully Res., Tully, Winchendon, Winchendon Springs, Ashby, Townsend, Water ville, Birch Hill Res., Baldwinville, Ashburnham, South Ashburnham, Fitchburg

Charlemont, West Hawley, Buckland, Deerfield R., Shelburne Falls, Greenfield, Gill, Riverside, Northfield Farms, Turners Falls, Montague City, Millers R., Erving, Wendell Depot, Orange, Athol, South Royalston, Otter River, Gardner, Templeton, Phillipston, East Templeton, Westminster, Leominster, N. Leominster

Cheshire, Cheshire Res., Savoy, Hancock, Farnams, Windsor, Ashfield, Deerfield, Conway, Millers Falls, Montague, Wendell, South Athol, Lanesboro, Pontoosuc L., Onota L., Dalton, Pittsfield, West Pittsfield, Hinsdale, Plainfield, West Cummington, Cummington, Westfield R., Goshen, South Deerfield, Moores Cor., New Salem, Mt. Toby, Sunderland, Shutesbury, Leverett, Quabbin Res., Petersham, Hubbardston Sta., Hubbardston, Wachusett Mt., Princeton Depot, Princeton, Sterling

West Chesterfield, Ashmere L., E. Whately, Whately, Cushman, North Amherst, North Hadley, Amherst, Barre, S. Barre, Barre Plains, N. Rutland, Rutland, Wachusett Res., Oakdale, Richmond, Lenox, Richmond Furnace, New Lenox, Washington, Worthington, Chesterfield, Williamsburg, N. Hatfield, Haydenville, Hatfield, Mill R., Hadley, South Amherst, Wheelwright, Furnace, Hardwick, Gilbertville, W. Rutland, Jefferson, Oakham, Holden, W. Boylston

State Line, W. Stockbridge, Lenox Dale, Becket, Middlefield, S. Worthington, Leeds, Florence, Interlaken, Stockbridge, South Lee, Lee, East Lee, Glendale, Knightville Res., Northampton, Westhampton, Mount Tom, Bachelor Br., New Braintree, Paxton, Blackstone R., Worcester

Housatonic, Tyringham, Chester, Easthampton, Mt. Tom, Huntington, Southampton, Holyoke, Manhan R., S. Hadley, Granby, South Hadley Falls, Belchertown, Ware, North Brookfield, Spencer, Cherry Valley, W. Brookfield, E. Brookfield, Leicester

North Egremont, Great Barrington, Monterey, Hartsville, Benton L., Otis, E. Otis, Otis Res., Russell, Blandford, Fairview, Westover Air Force Base, Bondsville, Ludlow Cen., Quaboag R., Warren, West Warren, Brookfield, Rochdale, W. Auburn, Auburn, Wilkinsonville

South Egremont, L. Buel, Montville, Cobble Mt. Res., Woronoco, Chicopee Falls, Chicopee, Willimansett, Ludlow, Thorndike, Three Rivers, Palmer, Charlton Depot, Charlton City, Dodge, West Millbury, Saundersville, Sutton, Mt. Washington, Sheffield, Mill River, New Marlboro, Westfield, Indian Orchard, N. Wilbraham, Brimfield, Fiskdale, Charlton, N. Oxford, Oxford

Mt. Everett, Southfield, New Boston, S. Sandisfield, Tolland, Little R., Wilbraham, Monson, Old Sturbridge Village, Sturbridge, Southbridge, Manchaug, West Springfield, Springfield, Agawam, E. Longmeadow, Wales, Granville, West Granville, Feeding Hills, Hampden, Holland, Webster, East Douglas, East Village, Ashley Falls, Southwick, Longmeadow, Dudley, Quinebaug R., West Dudley, L. Chaubunagungamaug, Congamond Lakes, Farmington R., Housatonic R.

Putnam, Jerimoth Hill 812, Plainfield, Pawcatuck R., Westerly, Weekapaug, Watch Hill, Watch Hill Pt., Block Island Sound

BOSTON AND VICINITY

SCALE OF MILES 0 2 4 6

15′ 71° 45′ 42° 30′ 42° 15′

MIDDLESEX ESSEX SUFFOLK NORFOLK PLYMOUTH BOSTON BAY

North Reading, Ipswich R., S. Middleton, Danvers, Manchester, Beverly Farms, Prides Crossing, Wilmington, Nutting Lake, Shawsheen R., Lynnfield Cen., W. Peabody, Danversport, Beverly, Great Misery I., Bakers I., Pinehurst, Reading, Peabody, Salem, Winter I. Coast Guard Air Sta., Salem Maritime Nat'l. Hist. Site, Burlington, Lynnfield, Marblehead, Wakefield, Marblehead Neck

Bedford, Concord R., Woburn, Stoneham, Greenwood, Montvale, Spot Pd., Melrose H'lds., Swampscott, Clifton, Concord, Laurence G. Hanscom Field, Winchester, Melrose, E. Saugus, Lynn, West Concord, Lexington, Saugus, Nahant Bay, Malden, Mystic L., Medford, Nahant, Lincoln, Cambridge Res., Arlington, Mystic R., Everett, East Pt., Spy Pd., Revere, Sudbury, Sudbury R., Belmont, Chelsea, Ft. Banks, Kendal Green, Waltham, Waverley, Fresh Pd., Somerville, Navy Yard, Winthrop, Weston, Watertown, Charles R., Cambridge, Wayland, West Newton, Newton, Boston, Boston Harbor, Deer I.

Auburndale, Newtonville, Saxonville, Newton Lower Falls, Riverside, Waban, Brookline, Roxbury, Brewster Islands, Cochituate, Newton Cen., Jamaica Plain, Thompson I., Long I., Wellesley Hills, Newton H'lds., Squantum Naval Air Sta., Hull, Pt. Allerton, Allerton, L. Cochituate, Newton Upper Falls, Forest Hills, Wellesley, Needham Hgts., Dorchester, Quincy Bay, Hingham Bay, Natick, Mt. Hope, Neponset, Framingham, Needham, Mattapan, East Milton, Nantasket Beach, Straits Pond, South Natick, Hyde Park, Milton, Adams Mansion Nat'l. Hist. Site, N. Cohasset, Dedham, East Dedham, Quincy, Hingham, Hingham Center, Cohasset, Sherborn, Dover, Readville, N. Weymouth, Minot, Islington, E. Braintree, Norfolk, North Scituate, Westwood, Blue Hills, Braintree, Weymouth, East Weymouth, Holliston, Medfield Jc., Neponset R., S. Braintree, S. Hingham, Beechwood, Egypt, Norwood, Medfield, Great Pd., Scituate, S. Weymouth, Accord, Millis, Randolph, Greenbush, Canton Jc., Holbrook, Norwell, North R., Rockville, Walpole, E. Walpole, Canton, Assinippi

A 15′ B 73° C 45′ D 30′ E 15′ F Longitude 72° West of G Greenwich

MASSACHUSETTS AND RHODE ISLAND

SCALE OF MILES

0 5 10 20

State Capitals ⊛ Canals

County Seats ◉

7581

MICHIGAN

SCALE OF MILES
0 10 20 30 40 50

State Capitals
County Seats
Canals

Same scale as main map

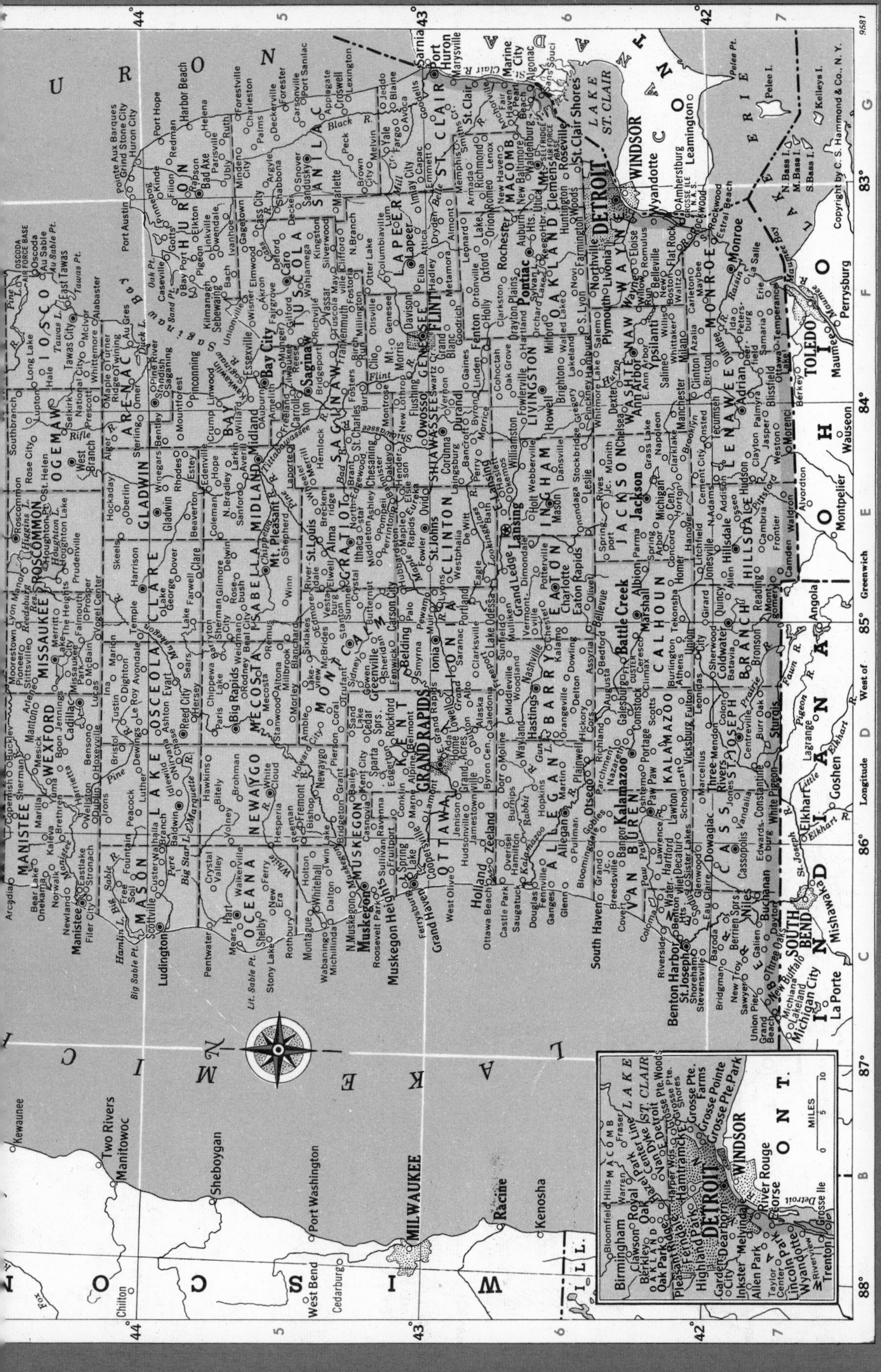

LAKE HURON
Saginaw Bay
LAKE MICHIGAN
LAKE ST. CLAIR
LAKE ERIE
ONT.
WISCONSIN
ILL.
INDIANA
OHIO

MANISTEE, WEXFORD, MISSAUKEE, ROSCOMMON, OGEMAW, IOSCO, MASON, LAKE, OSCEOLA, CLARE, GLADWIN, ARENAC, OCEANA, NEWAYGO, MECOSTA, ISABELLA, MIDLAND, BAY, HURON, MUSKEGON, MONTCALM, GRATIOT, SAGINAW, TUSCOLA, SANILAC, OTTAWA, KENT, IONIA, CLINTON, SHIAWASSEE, GENESEE, LAPEER, ST. CLAIR, ALLEGAN, BARRY, EATON, INGHAM, LIVINGSTON, OAKLAND, MACOMB, VAN BUREN, KALAMAZOO, CALHOUN, JACKSON, WASHTENAW, WAYNE, CASS, ST. JOSEPH, BRANCH, HILLSDALE, LENAWEE, MONROE

Grand Rapids, Lansing, Flint, Saginaw, Bay City, Pontiac, Detroit, Windsor, Toledo, Kalamazoo, Battle Creek, Jackson, Ann Arbor, Muskegon, Milwaukee, Racine, Kenosha, South Bend, Port Huron

Longitude West of Greenwich

Copyright by C. S. Hammond & Co., N. Y.

9581

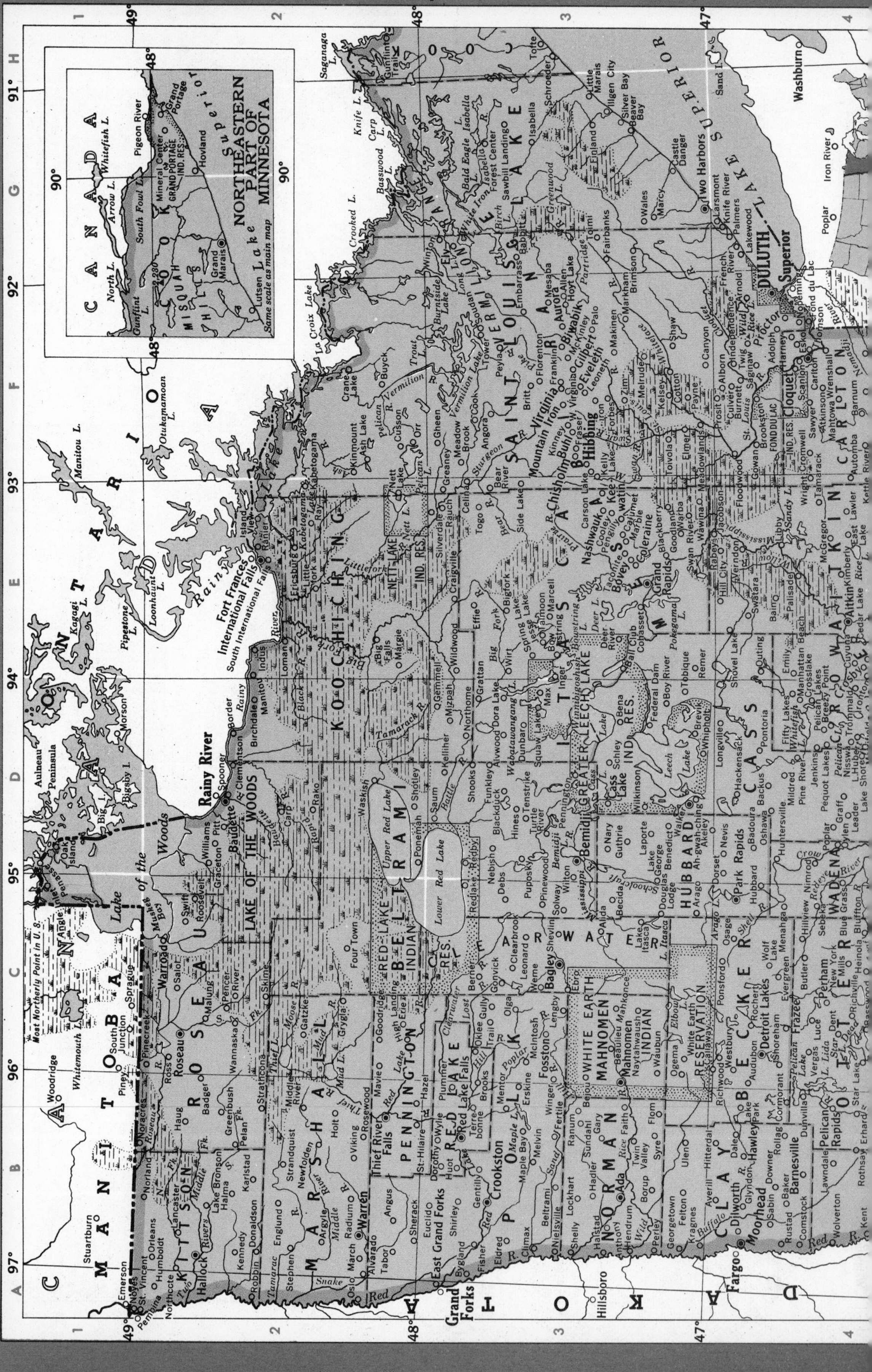
NORTHEASTERN PART OF MINNESOTA
Same scale as main map
CANADA
MANITOBA
ONTARIO
Lake of the Woods
Most Northerly Point in U.S.
KITTSON
ROSEAU
LAKE OF THE WOODS
KOOCHICHING
MARSHALL
PENNINGTON
RED LAKE
BELTRAMI
RED LAKE INDIAN RES.
Upper Red Lake
Lower Red Lake
POLK
CLEARWATER
NORMAN
MAHNOMEN
WHITE EARTH INDIAN RESERVATION
CLAY
BECKER
HUBBARD
CASS
ITASCA
SAINT LOUIS
LAKE
COOK
CARLTON
AITKIN
CROW WING
WADENA
OTTER TAIL
LAKE SUPERIOR
DULUTH
Superior
Fargo
Moorhead
Grand Forks
East Grand Forks
Crookston
Bemidji
Hibbing
Virginia
International Falls
Fort Frances
Rainy River
NORTH DAKOTA

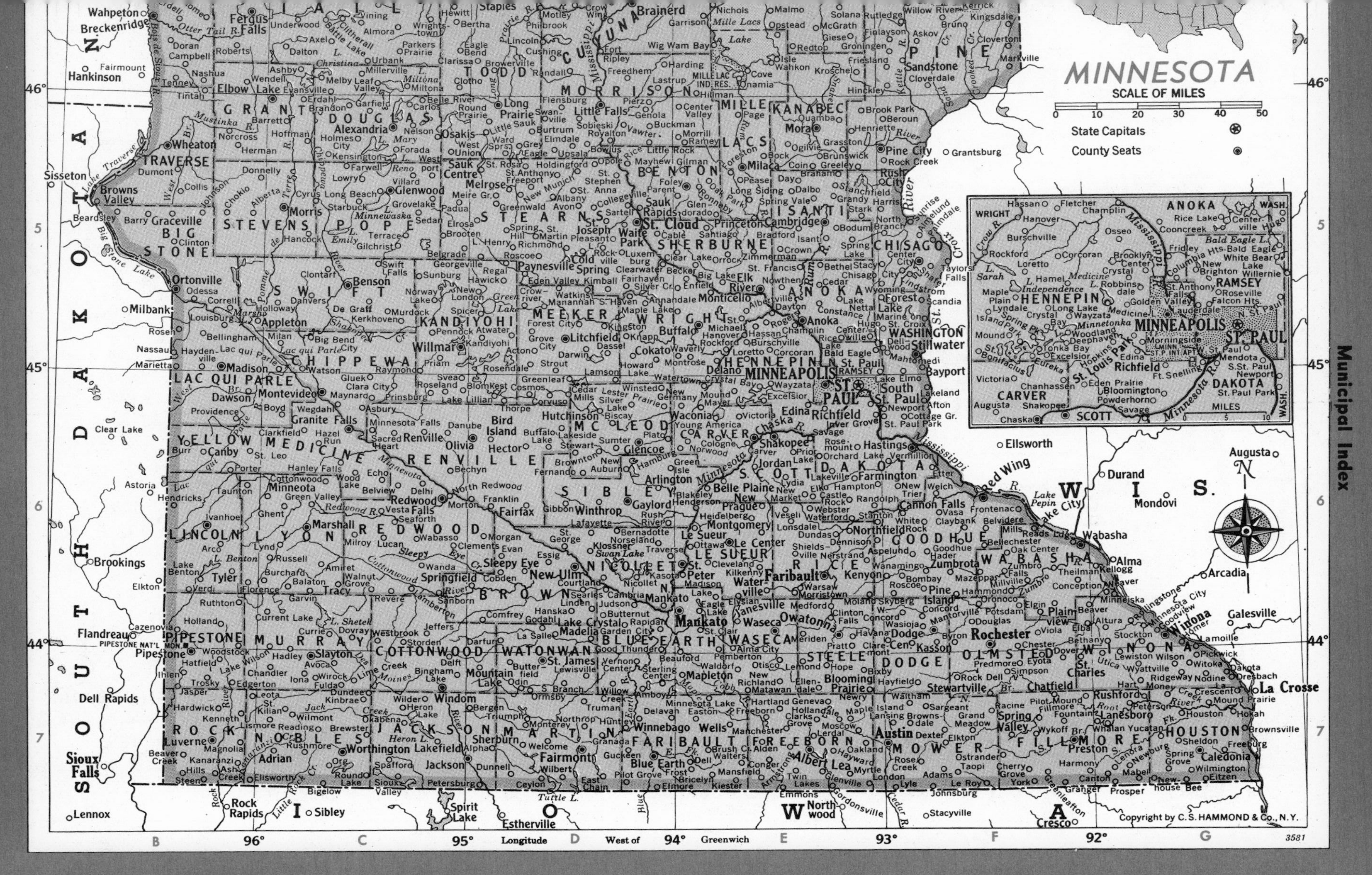
MINNESOTA
SCALE OF MILES
0 10 20 30 40 50
State Capitals
County Seats
Longitude West of Greenwich
Copyright by C. S. HAMMOND & Co., N. Y.
3581
MINNEAPOLIS
ST. PAUL
NORTH DAKOTA
SOUTH DAKOTA
IOWA
WIS.
Mississippi R.
Lake Pepin
Mille Lacs Lake
Big Stone Lake
Lake Traverse
Minnesota R.
St. Croix R.
Rochester
St. Cloud
Mankato
Winona
La Crosse
Brainerd

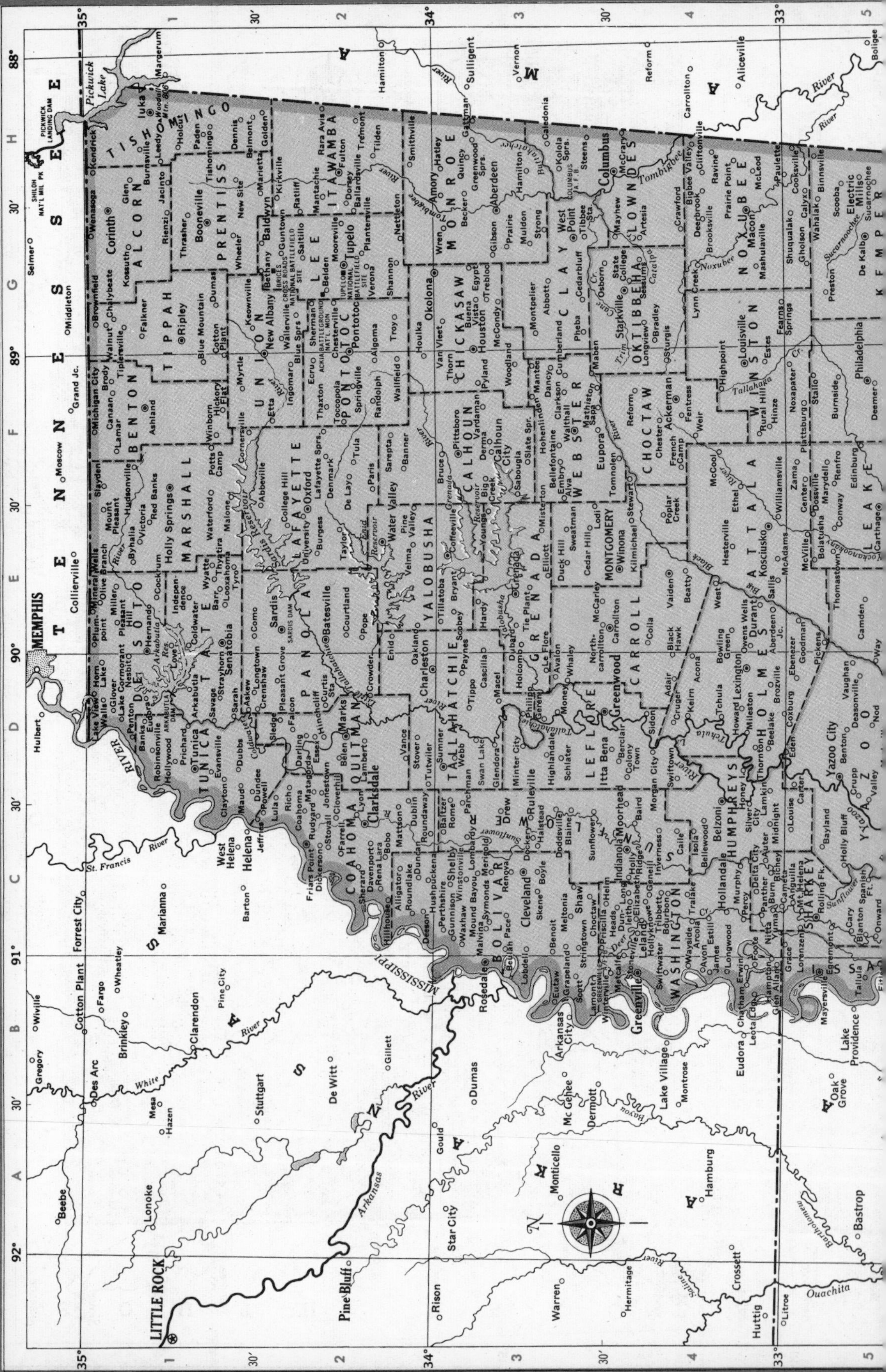

MEMPHIS
LITTLE ROCK
TENNESSEE
ARKANSAS
MISSISSIPPI
TISHOMINGO
ALCORN
TIPPAH
BENTON
MARSHALL
DE SOTO
TUNICA
TATE
PANOLA
LAFAYETTE
UNION
PONTOTOC
LEE
ITAWAMBA
PRENTISS
MONROE
CHICKASAW
CALHOUN
YALOBUSHA
QUITMAN
COAHOMA
TALLAHATCHIE
GRENADA
WEBSTER
CLAY
LOWNDES
OKTIBBEHA
CHOCTAW
MONTGOMERY
CARROLL
LEFLORE
BOLIVAR
SUNFLOWER
WASHINGTON
HUMPHREYS
HOLMES
ATTALA
WINSTON
NOXUBEE
KEMPER
LEAKE
SHARKEY
YAZOO
Corinth
Tupelo
Columbus
Oxford
Clarksdale
Greenville
Greenwood
Cleveland
Grenada
Starkville
Pine Bluff
Helena
West Helena
Forrest City
Yazoo City
Kosciusko
Philadelphia
Louisville
Lake Providence
Mississippi River
Arkansas River
White River
St. Francis River
Ouachita
Pickwick Lake
PICKWICK LANDING DAM
SHILOH NAT'L MIL PK

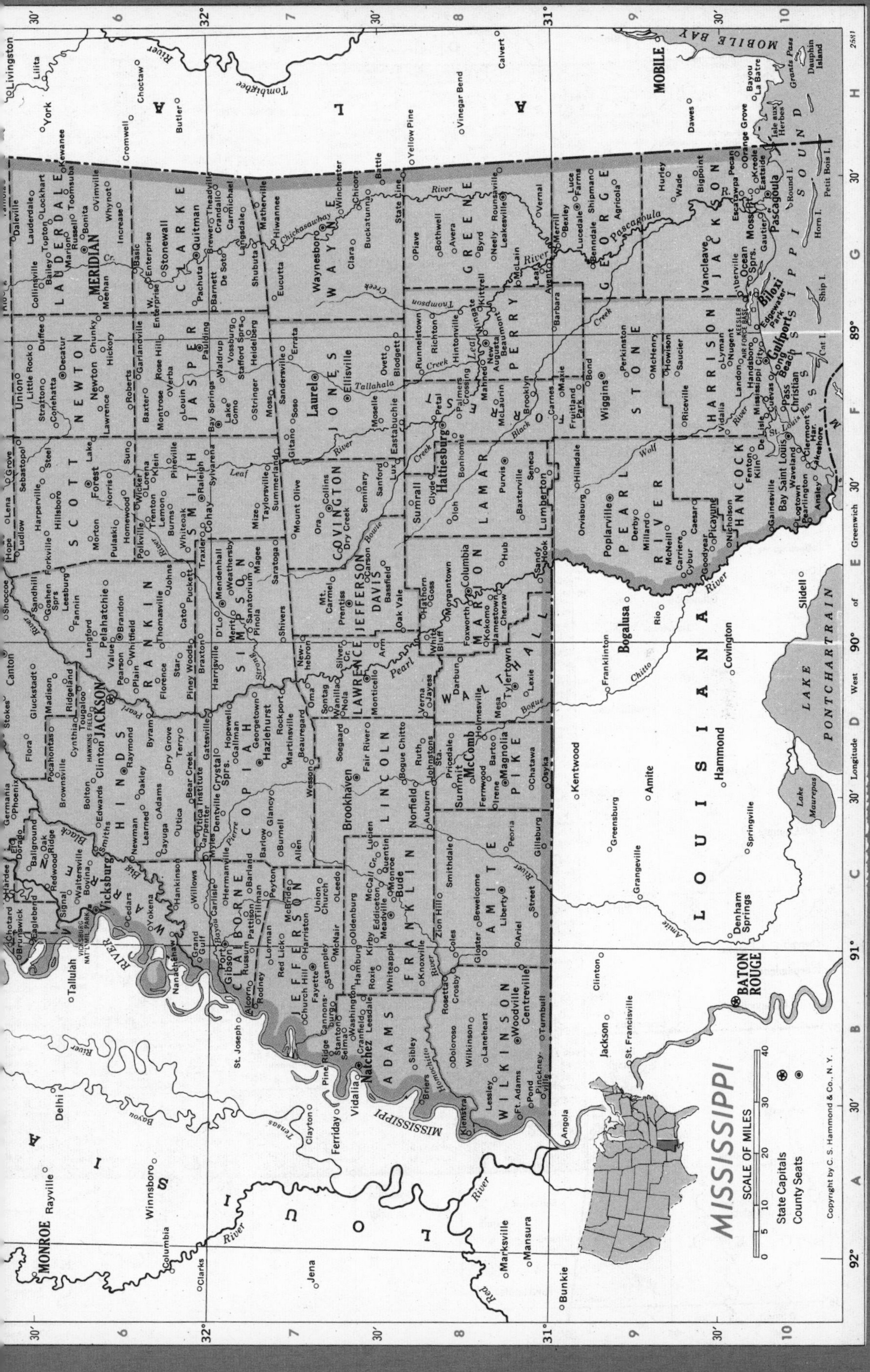

MISSISSIPPI

SCALE OF MILES

0 5 10 20 30 40

State Capitals

County Seats

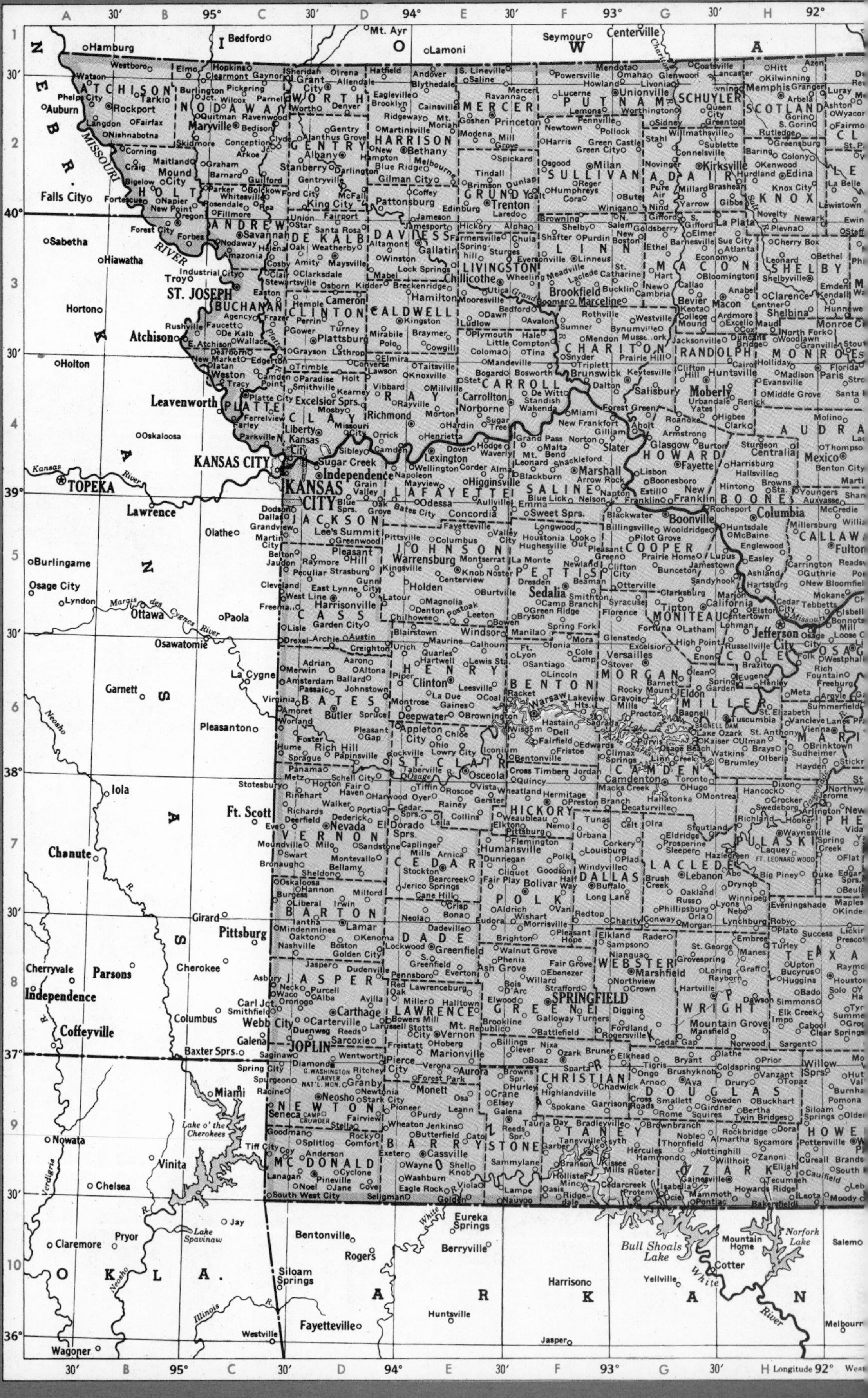

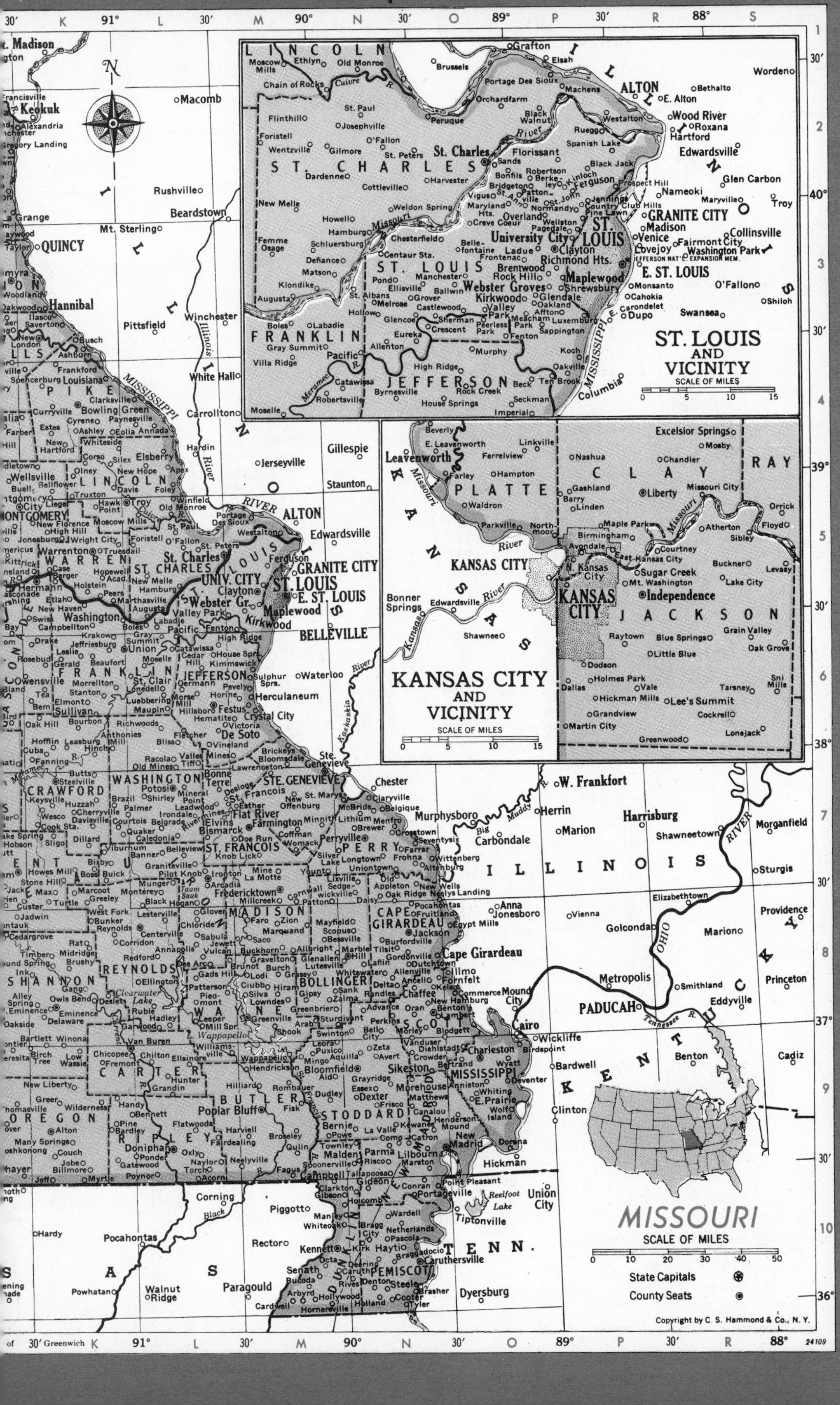

ST. LOUIS AND VICINITY

SCALE OF MILES

0 5 10 15

KANSAS CITY AND VICINITY

SCALE OF MILES

0 5 10 15

MISSOURI

SCALE OF MILES

0 10 20 30 40 50

State Capitals ⊛

County Seats ◉

24109

MONTANA

SCALE OF MILES

0 10 20 40 60 80

State Capitals ⊛

County Seats ◉

Longitude

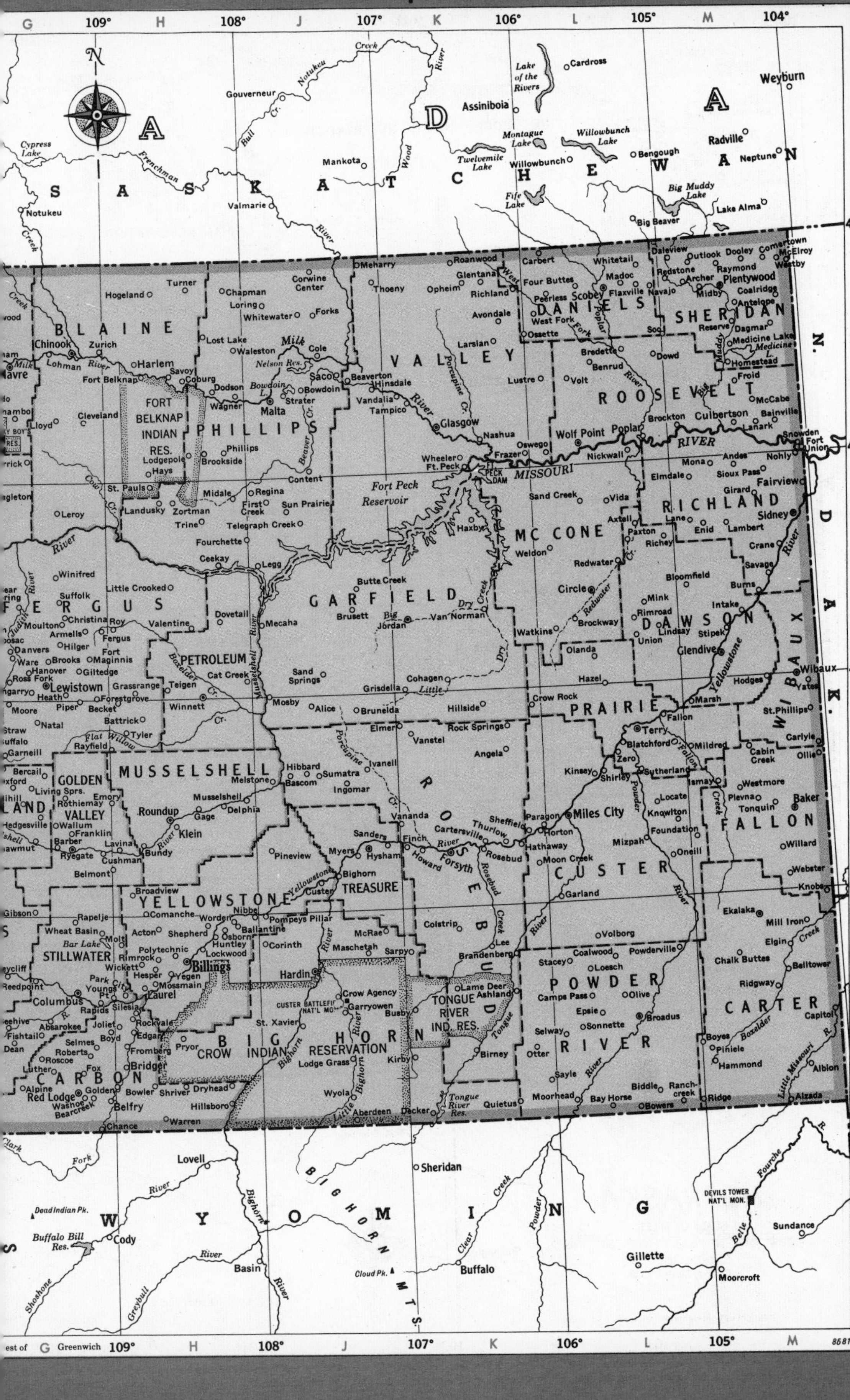

G 109° H 108° J 107° K 106° L 105° M 104°

S A S K A T C H E W A N
Weyburn
Cardross
Lake of the Rivers
Assiniboia
Gouverneur
Cypress Lake
Frenchman
Mankota
Montague Lake
Willowbunch Lake
Twelvemile Lake
Willowbunch
Bengough
Radville
Neptune
Big Muddy Lake
Fife Lake
Notukeu
Valmarie
Lake Alma
Big Beaver

BLAINE
Turner
Hogeland
Chinook
Zurich
Harlem
Lohman
Fort Belknap
Havre
Cleveland
Lloyd
Leroy
FORT BELKNAP INDIAN RES.
Lodgepole
Hays
St. Pauls
Landusky
Zortman

PHILLIPS
Chapman
Loring
Whitewater
Corwine Center
Forks
Lost Lake
Waleston
Nelson Res.
Cole
Savoy
Coburg
Dodson
Bowdoin
Saco
Wagner
Malta
Strater
Phillips
Brookside
Midale
Regina
First Creek
Sun Prairie
Content
Trine
Telegraph Creek
Fourchette
Ceekay
Legg

VALLEY
Meharry
Thoeny
Opheim
Roanwood
Glentana
Richland
Avondale
Larslan
Beaverton
Hinsdale
Vandalia
Tampico
Glasgow
Nashua
Lustre
Frazer
Oswego
Wheeler
Ft. Peck
Fort Peck Reservoir

DANIELS
Carbert
Four Buttes
Whitetail
Madoc
Scobey
Flaxville
Peerless
West Fork
Ossette

SHERIDAN
Daleview
Outlook
Dooley
Comertown
McElroy
Westby
Redstone
Raymond
Archer
Plentywood
Navajo
Midby
Coalridge
Antelope
Reserve
Dagmar
Medicine Lake
Homestead
Froid

ROOSEVELT
Bredette
Benrud
Dowd
Volt
McCabe
Brockton
Culbertson
Bainville
Lanark
Wolf Point
Poplar
Snowden
Fort Union
Nickwall

RICHLAND
Mona
Andes
Nohly
Elmdale
Sioux Pass
Fairview
Girard
Sidney
Lane
Enid
Lambert
Crane
Savage

MC CONE
Sand Creek
Vida
Axtell
Paxton
Richey
Haxby
Weldon
Redwater
Circle
Brockway
Watkins

GARFIELD
Butte Creek
Brusett
Jordan
Van Norman
Sand Springs
Cohagen
Grisdella
Alice
Brunelda
Hillside
Mosby

FERGUS
Winifred
Suffolk
Little Crooked
Moulton
Christina
Roy
Armells
Fergus
Danvers
Hilger
Ware
Brooks
Fort Maginnis
Hanover
Giltedge
Ross Fork
Lewistown
Heath
Forestgrove
Moore
Piper
Becket
Natal
Battrick
Tyler
Rayfield

PETROLEUM
Dovetail
Valentine
Mecaha
Cat Creek
Grassrange
Teigen
Winnett

DAWSON
Bloomfield
Mink
Rimroad
Lindsay
Union
Burns
Intake
Stipek
Glendive

WIBAUX
Wibaux
Hodges
Yates
Marsh

PRAIRIE
Olanda
Hazel
Crow Rock
Fallon
Terry
Blatchford
Mildred
Zero
Kinsey
Shirley
Sutherland
Ismay

MUSSELSHELL
Elmer
Rock Springs
Vanstel
Angela
Hibbard
Ivanell
Melstone
Bascom
Sumatra
Ingomar
Musselshell
Delphia
Roundup
Gage
Klein
Bundy

GOLDEN VALLEY
Bercail
Oxford
Living Sprs.
Rothiemay
Emory
Wallum
Franklin
Barber
Lavina
Ryegate
Cushman
Belmont

ROSEBUD
Vananda
Sanders
Myers
Hysham
Finch
Cartersville
Thurlow
Sheffield
Forsyth
Howard
Rosebud
Colstrip
Lee
Brandenberg
Lame Deer
Ashland
TONGUE RIVER IND. RES.
Birney

CUSTER
Paragon
Miles City
Horton
Hathaway
Moon Creek
Locate
Knowlton
Foundation
Mizpah
Oneill
Garland
Volborg

FALLON
St. Phillips
Carlyle
Cabin Creek
Ollie
Westmore
Plevna
Tonquin
Baker
Willard
Webster
Knobs

TREASURE
Bighorn
Custer
Pineview

YELLOWSTONE
Broadview
Comanche
Worden
Nibbe
Pompeys Pillar
Ballantine
Shepherd
Acton
Huntley
Osborn
Lockwood
Corinth
Billings
Mossmain
Laurel

STILLWATER
Gibson
Rapelje
Wheat Basin
Molt
Bar Lake
Polytechnic
Rimrock
Wickett
Hesper
Park City
Youngs Pt.
Columbus
Reedpoint
Rapids
Silesia

BIG HORN
McRae
Maschetah
Sarpy
Hardin
Custer Battlefield Nat'l Mon.
Crow Agency
Garryowen
Busby
St. Xavier
CROW INDIAN RESERVATION
Pryor
Lodge Grass
Kirby
Wyola
Aberdeen
Decker
Dryhead
Hillsboro
Warren

CARBON
Rockvale
Edgar
Joliet
Boyd
Absarokee
Fishtail
Dean
Selmes
Roberts
Roscoe
Fromberg
Bridger
Luther
Fox
Alpine
Golden
Red Lodge
Washoe
Bearcreek
Bowler
Shriver
Belfry
Chance

POWDER RIVER
Coalwood
Powderville
Stacey
Loesch
Camps Pass
Olive
Epsie
Broadus
Sonnette
Selway
Otter
Sayle
Moorhead
Bay Horse
Biddle
Ranchcreek
Bowers
Quietus
Tongue River Res.

CARTER
Ekalaka
Mill Iron
Elgin
Chalk Buttes
Belltower
Ridgway
Capitol
Boyes
Piniele
Hammond
Albion
Ridge
Alzada

N. DAKOTA

W Y O M I N G
Lovell
Sheridan
Dead Indian Pk.
Cody
Buffalo Bill Res.
Basin
BIGHORN MTS.
Cloud Pk.
Buffalo
Gillette
Devils Tower Nat'l Mon.
Sundance
Moorcroft

1 2 3 4 5 6
49° 48° 47° 46° 45°

West of Greenwich
8581

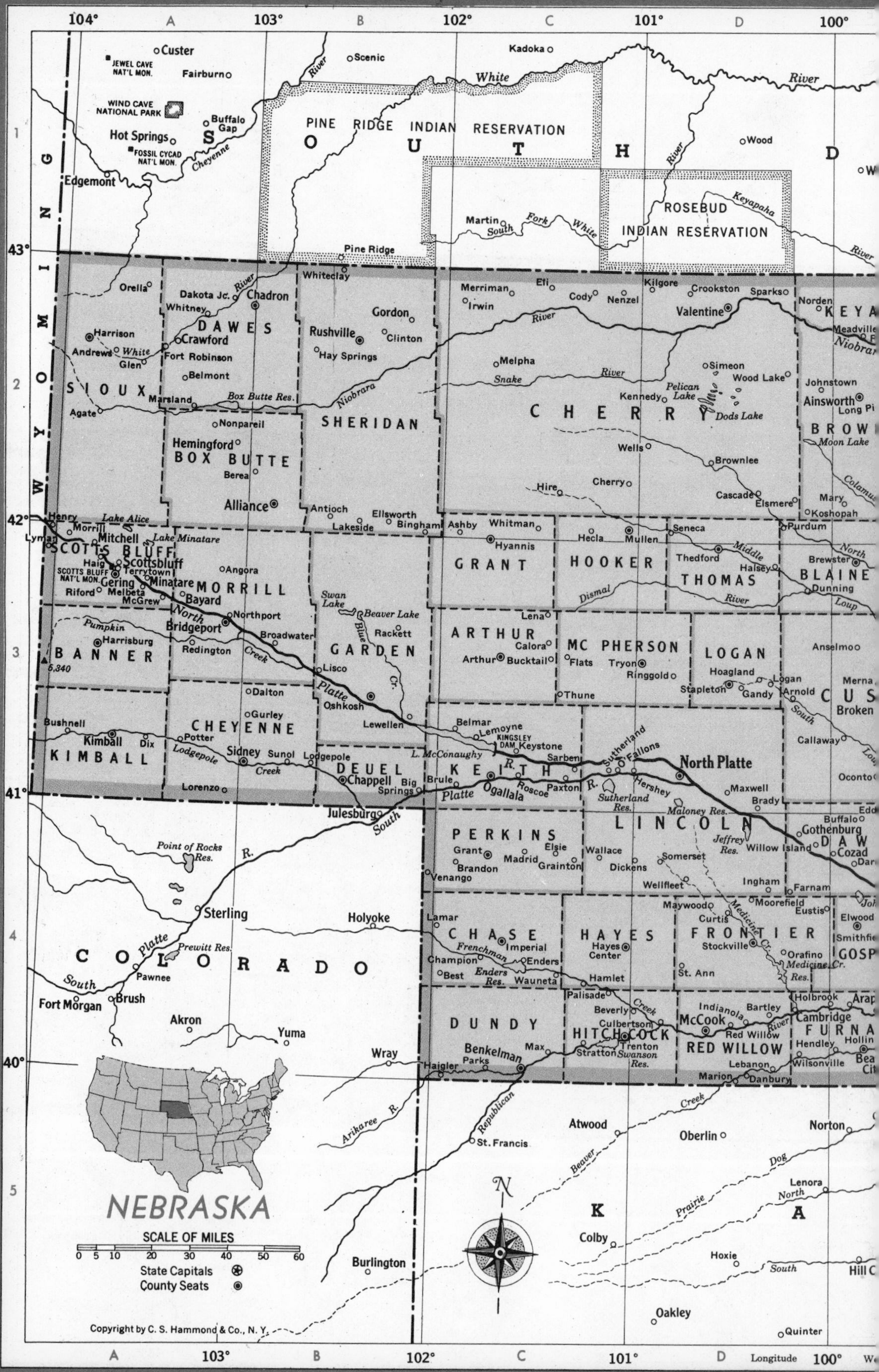

NEBRASKA

SCALE OF MILES

0 5 10 20 30 40 50 60

State Capitals

County Seats

E
99°
F
98°
G
97°
H
96°
J
Chamberlain
White Lake
Red Lake
Plankinton
Platte Lake
Mitchell
Alexandria
Stickney
West
Salem
East
Fork
Colton
River
Luverne
M I N N.
Worthington
Jackson
SIOUX FALLS
James
Fork
1
A K O T A
Platte
Armour
Parker
Vermillion
Rock Rapids
Sibley
Canton
Rock
Sheldon
Hartley
Spencer
Fort
Randall
Reservoir
Burke
Lake Andes
Tripp
Olivet
Scotland
Centerville
Sioux
Primghar
Hawarden
Orange City
43°
MISSOURI
Tyndall
Volin
Big
Jamison
Anoka
Gross
Naper
BOYD
Butte
Spencer
Bristow
Monowi
Lynch
Springfield
Yankton
Santee
Saint Helena
Vermillion
Le Mars
Cherokee
Dustin
River
Verdel
R.
Niobrara
Crofton
Wynot
Fordyce
Maskell
Elk Point
Merrill
Floyd
Storm Lake
Redbird
Dorsey
Star
KNOX
Center
Hartington
Obert
Newcastle
Ponca
Mariaville
Newport
Stuart
Verdigre
Bloomfield
CEDAR
DIXON
SIOUX CITY
South Sioux City
Bassett
HOLT
Atkinson
Walnut
Winnetoon
Bazile Mills
Wausa
Coleridge
Martinsburg
Waterbury
Goodwin
Correctionville
2
Middlebranch
Venus
Creighton
Magnet
Laurel
Allen
Jackson
Dakota City
Emmet
O'Neill
Elkhorn
Page
McLean
Belden
Randolph
Dixon
Hubbard
IDAKOTA
Ida Grove
Inman
Brunswick
Plainview
Osmond
Sholes
Concord
Nacora
Homer
WINNEBAGO IND. RES.
Orchard
Royal
Foster
Carroll
Wakefield
Emerson
Winnebago
Ewing
Rose
Amelia
Chambers
ANTELOPE
PIERCE
Pierce
Wayne
WAYNE
Thurston
THURSTON
OMAHA IND. RES.
Clearwater
Neligh
Winside
Pender
Walthill
Macy
Onawa
Ute
Hadar
Hoskins
Oakdale
River
Norfolk
Altona
Bancroft
Rosalie
Tilden
Pilger
Wisner
Decatur
42°
Denison
Elgin
Meadow Gr.
Battle Creek
Beemer
Lyons
GARFIELD
WHEELER
MADISON
Enola
Stanton
STANTON
CUMING
BURT
Manilla
Bartlett
Raeville
Petersburg
West Point
Oakland
Loup
River
Burwell
Cedar
Ericson
Madison
Craig
Tekamah
Loretto
Newman Gr.
Clarkson
Dodge
Crowell
Uehling
Logan
Harlan
Loup
Taylor
BOONE
Lindsay
Creston
Leigh
Howells
Snyder
Herman
Sargent
Elyria
Spalding
Albion
Bradish
Cornlea
Humphrey
Scribner
Winslow
Missouri Valley
Primrose
Boone
Tarnov
Hooper
Fontanelle
River
Ord
GREELEY
St. Edward
PLATTE
COLFAX
DODGE
Blair
Avoca
3
VALLEY
Greeley
Platte Center
Nickerson
WASHINGTON
Kennard
Comstock
Horace
Cedar Rapids
Brayton
Belgrade
Monroe
Schuyler
Rogers
North Bend
Ames
Arlington
Ft. Calhoun
Minden
North Loup
Scotia
Genoa
Columbus
Fremont
Washington
Arcadia
Wolbach
NANCE
Duncan
Richland
Morse Bluff
Cedar Bluffs
Valley
Bennington
Westerville
Cotesfield
Fullerton
Silver Creek
Octavia
Linwood
Leshara
Waterloo
Elkhorn
OMAHA
COUNCIL BLUFFS
Cushing
Elba
Loup
Bellwood
Abie
Prague
Colon
Yutan
DOUGLAS
Ansley
Loup City
Ashton
Farwell (Posen)
St. Paul
Palmer
Clarks
POLK
David City
Bruno
BUTLER
Malmo
SAUNDERS
Mead
Millard
Ralston
Mason City
SHERMAN
Litchfield
HOWARD
MERRICK
Osceola
Shelby
Rising City
Garrison
Brainard
Weston
Wahoo
Ithaca
Chalco
Gretna
Papillion
Bellevue
Rockville
Dannebrog
Archer
Stromsburg
Surprise
Touhy
Wann
SARPY
Fort Crook
Hastings
Hazard
Boelus
Central City
Loma
Swedeburg
Memphis
Springfield
St. Libory
Hordville
Polk
Ulysses
Dwight
Valparaiso
Ceresco
Ashland
Plattsmouth
41°
Sweetwater
Cairo
Chapman
Benedict
Gresham
Bee
Raymond
Greenwood
Louisville
Mynard
Pleasanton
St. Michael
Ovina
Grand Island
Marquette
Arborville
Thayer
Stapleharst
Garland
Davey
Waverly
Murdock
Manley
Murray
Miller
Poole
Ravenna
Phillips
Hampton
YORK
Waco
Utica
Tamora
Seward
Malcolm
CASS
Weeping Water
Shenandoah
BUFFALO
HALL
Murphy
Bradshaw
York
SEWARD
Alvo
Elmwood
Nehawka
Amherst
Alda
Wood River
Aurora
Charleston
Goehner
Pleasant Dale
West Lincoln
Walton
Eagle
Avoca
Union
Sidney
Riverdale
Shelton
Giltner
HAMILTON
Henderson
Beaver Crossing
Milford
Denton
LINCOLN
Otoe
Nebraska City
Elm Creek
Kearney
Gibbon
Doniphan
Stockham
Lushton
McCool Jc.
Cordova
LANCASTER
Palmyra
Unadilla
Payne
Odessa
Denman
Prosser
Trumbull
Eldorado
Fairmont
Exeter
Dorchester
Roca
Bennet
Hickman
Syracuse
OTOE
Dunbar
Paul
Hamburg
PLATTE
Newark
Lowell
Hayland
Hansen
Hastings
Harvard
Sutton
Grafton
Burress
Friend
Crete
Kramer
Sprague
Panama
Douglas
Talmage
Lorton
HELPS
KEARNEY
Kenesaw
Juniata
Inland
Saronville
Pleasant Hill
Hallam
Firth
Burr
Cook
Brock
Julian
Peru
4
Heartwell
Norman
ADAMS
Glenvil
Clay Cen.
Verona
FILLMORE
Geneva
SALINE
Cortland
Sterling
Adams
St. Mary
Johnson
Auburn
Brownville
Loomis
Axtell
Minden
Holstein
Roseland
Spring Ranch
CLAY
Milligan
Tobias
Wilber
Clatonia
Tecumseh
Graf
Funk
Keene
Ayr
Fairfield
Martland
Strang
De Witt
Blue
Pickrell
Vesta
Rohrs
NEMAHA
Atlanta
Wilcox
Pauline
Deweese
Edgar
Ong
Shickley
Ohiowa
Western
Swanton
GAGE
Crab Orchard
JOHNSON
Howe
Nemaha
Ragan
Hildreth
Upland
Campbell
Bladen
Blue Hill
Rosemont
Lawrence
Angus
Sedan
Oak
Davenport
Bruning
Carleton
Belvidere
Daykin
Alexandria
Plymouth
JEFFERSON
Beatrice
HOMESTEAD NAT'L MON.
Filley
Virginia
Elk Creek
Lewiston
Steinauer
Shubert
Stella
Barada
Mascot
Huntley
Macon
FRANKLIN
WEBSTER
NUCKOLLS
Hebron
Powell
Harbine
Ellis
Holmesville
Table Rock
RICHARDSON
Verdon
ARLAN
Orleans
Alma
Franklin
Riverton
Cowles
Red Cloud
Guide Rock
Mt. Clare
Nelson
Nora
Ruskin
Deshler
Gilead
Gladstone
Jansen
Fairbury
Blue Springs
Wymore
Burchard
Pawnee City
Humboldt
Dawson
Falls City
Rulo
THAYER
Endicott
Diller
Odell
Liberty
PAWNEE
Salem
Preston
Cadams
Superior
Chester
Reynolds
Steele City
Barneston
DuBois
40°
Republican City
Naponee
Bloomington
Inavale
Bostwick
Hardy
Byron
Hubbell
Lanham
Sabetha
Harlan County Res.
Little Blue
R.
Hiawatha
Belleville
Marysville
Seneca
Burr Oak
Republican
Mankato
Cuba
Washington
Frankfort
Delaware
Phillipsburg
Smith Cen.
Irving
Solomon
Whiting
Clifton
5
N
S
Downs
Concordia
A
S
Holton
Stockton
Solomon
Osborne
Beloit
Solomon
Clay Cen.
Westmoreland
Valley Falls
Miltonvale
River
River
River
Barnard
Manhattan
River
Minneapolis
KANSAS
RIVER
Luray
Lincoln
Junction City
Alma
TOPEKA
E
Greenwich
99°
F
98°
G
97°
H
96°
J
7581

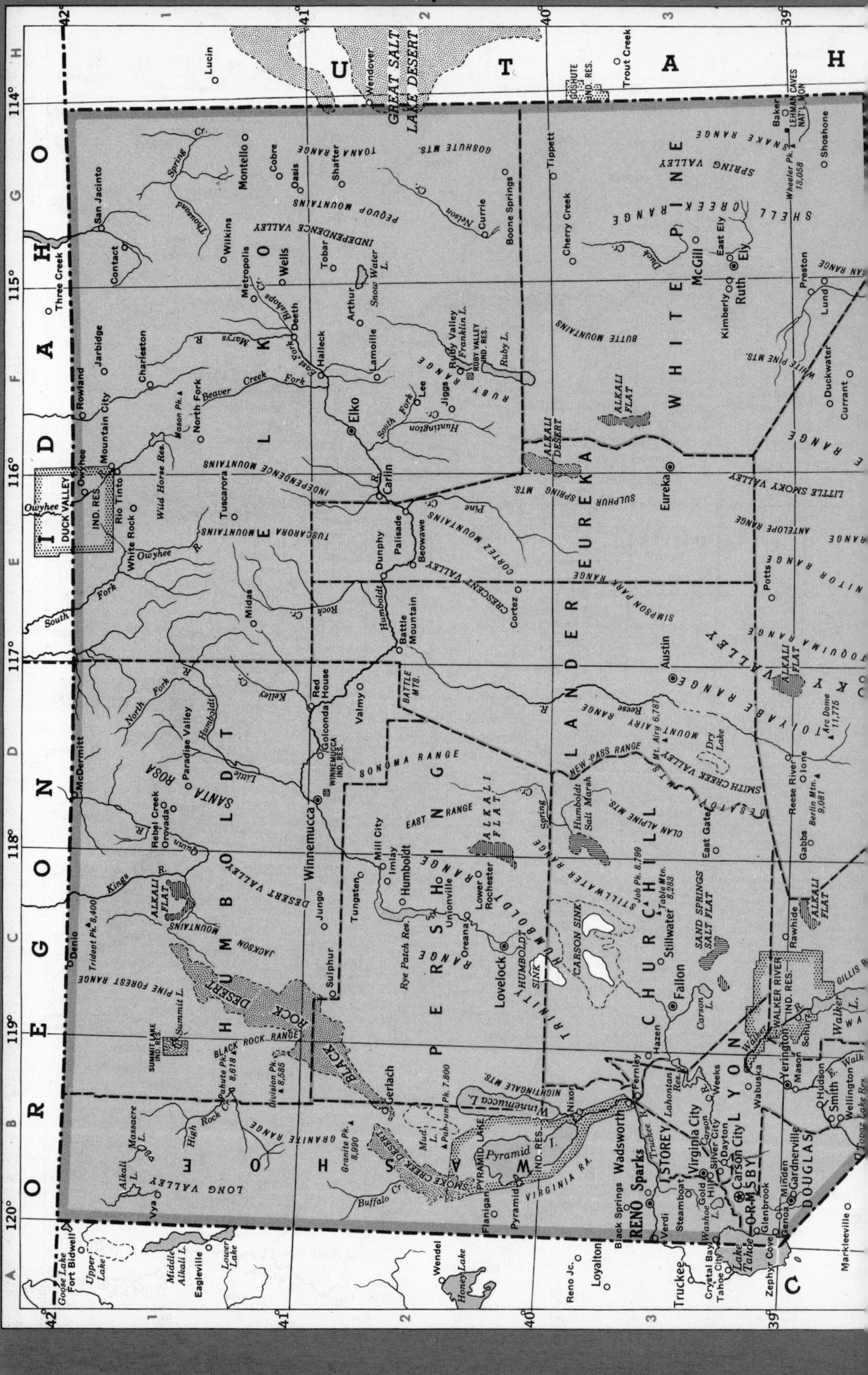

OREGON
IDAHO
UTAH
C

HUMBOLDT
ELKO
WHITE PINE
EUREKA
LANDER
PERSHING
CHURCHILL
WASHOE
STOREY
LYON
ORMSBY
DOUGLAS

GREAT SALT LAKE DESERT
BLACK ROCK DESERT
SMOKE CREEK DESERT
CARSON SINK
HUMBOLDT SINK
ALKALI DESERT
ALKALI FLAT
SAND SPRINGS SALT FLAT
Humboldt Salt Marsh

PINE FOREST RANGE
BLACK ROCK RANGE
JACKSON MOUNTAINS
GRANITE RANGE
LONG VALLEY
DESERT VALLEY
SANTA ROSA
INDEPENDENCE MOUNTAINS
INDEPENDENCE VALLEY
TUSCARORA MOUNTAINS
PEQUOP MOUNTAINS
TOANA RANGE
GOSHUTE MTS.
RUBY RANGE
BUTTE MOUNTAINS
SNAKE RANGE
SPRING VALLEY
SHELL CREEK RANGE
WHITE PINE MTS.
SULPHUR SPRING MTS.
CORTEZ MOUNTAINS
CRESCENT VALLEY
SIMPSON PARK RANGE
LITTLE SMOKY VALLEY
ANTELOPE RANGE
TOQUIMA RANGE
TOIYABE RANGE
SMITH CREEK VALLEY
DESATOYA MTS.
CLAN ALPINE MTS.
NEW PASS RANGE
STILLWATER RANGE
SONOMA RANGE
EAST RANGE
HUMBOLDT RANGE
TRINITY RANGE
NIGHTINGALE MTS.
VIRGINIA RA.
BATTLE MTS.

Trident Pk. 8,400
Pahute Pk. 8,618
Division Pk. 8,585
Granite Pk. 8,990
Pah-rum Pk. 7,800
Mason Pk.
Wheeler Pk. 13,058
Job Pk. 8,799
Table Mtn. 8,283
Mt. Airy 6,787
Arc Dome 11,775
Berlin Mtn. 9,081

Humboldt R.
Owyhee R.
South Fork
Marys R.
Beaver Creek
Thousand Spring Cr.
Bishops Cr.
Rock Cr.
Kelley Cr.
Reese R.
Quinn R.
Kings R.
Carson R.
Walker R.
Truckee R.
Buffalo Cr.

Pyramid L.
Winnemucca L.
Mud L.
Rye Patch Res.
Lahontan Res.
Carson L.
Walker L.
Lake Tahoe
Ruby L.
Franklin L.
Snow Water L.
Wild Horse Res.
Summit L.
Massacre L.
Alkali L.
Upper Lake
Middle Alkali L.
Lower Lake
Goose Lake
Honey Lake
Topaz Lake Res.
Dry Lake

DUCK VALLEY IND. RES.
SUMMIT LAKE IND. RES.
PYRAMID LAKE IND. RES.
WINNEMUCCA IND. RES.
RUBY VALLEY IND. RES.
GOSHUTE IND. RES.
WALKER RIVER IND. RES.
LEHMAN CAVES NAT'L MON.

Denio, McDermitt, Orovada, Rebel Creek, Paradise Valley, Winnemucca, Golconda, Red House, Valmy, Jungo, Sulphur, Gerlach, Vya, Mill City, Imlay, Humboldt, Tungsten, Unionville, Oreana, Lower Rochester, Lovelock, Battle Mountain, Midas, Tuscarora, White Rock, Rio Tinto, Mountain City, Owyhee, Rowland, Jarbidge, Charleston, North Fork, Contact, San Jacinto, Three Creek, Wilkins, Metropolis, Wells, Deeth, Halleck, Elko, Lamoille, Arthur, Tobar, Montello, Cobre, Oasis, Shafter, Currie, Boone Springs, Lee, Jiggs, Ruby Valley, Carlin, Palisade, Beowawe, Dunphy, Cortez, Wendover, Lucin, Trout Creek, Tippett, Cherry Creek, McGill, East Ely, Ely, Ruth, Kimberly, Preston, Lund, Baker, Shoshone, Duckwater, Currant, Eureka, Austin, Potts, Ione, Reese River, Gabbs, East Gate, Rawhide, Stillwater, Fallon, Hazen, Fernley, Nixon, Wadsworth, Sparks, Reno, Verdi, Black Springs, Pyramid, Flanigan, Steamboat, Virginia City, Gold Hill, Silver City, Dayton, Carson City, Washoe, Glenbrook, Genoa, Minden, Gardnerville, Wabuska, Weeks, Yerington, Mason, Schurz, Hudson, Smith, Wellington, Fort Bidwell, Eagleville, Wendel, Reno Jc., Loyalton, Truckee, Crystal Bay, Tahoe City, Zephyr Cove, Markleeville

42°, 41°, 40°, 39°
114°, 115°, 116°, 117°, 118°, 119°, 120°
A, B, C, D, E, F, G, H
1, 2, 3

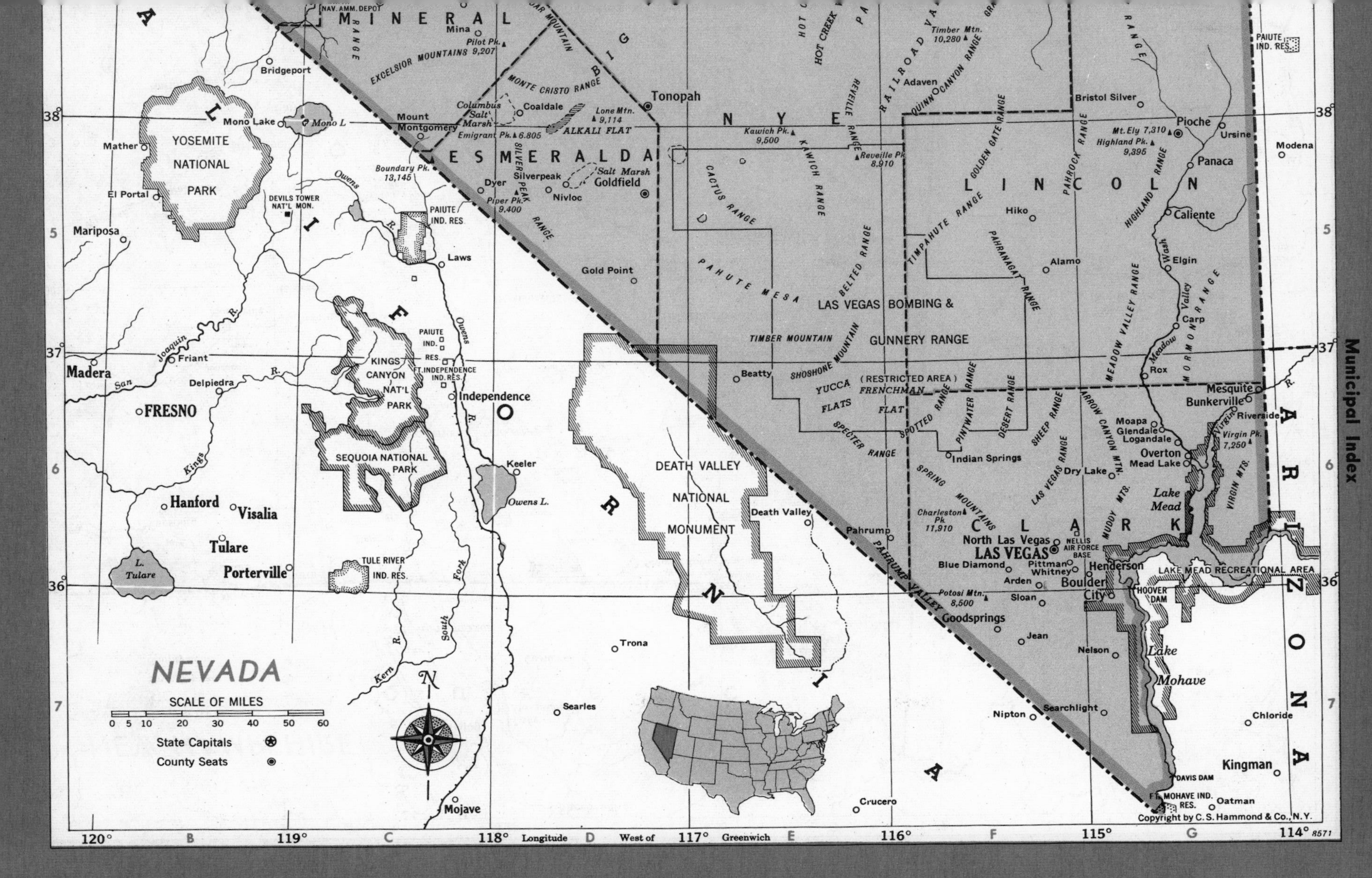
NEVADA
SCALE OF MILES
0 5 10 20 30 40 50 60
State Capitals
County Seats
Copyright by C.S. Hammond & Co., N.Y.
8571
West of Greenwich Longitude
ARIZONA
CALIFORNIA
MINERAL
ESMERALDA
NYE
LINCOLN
CLARK
LAS VEGAS BOMBING & GUNNERY RANGE
(RESTRICTED AREA)
DEATH VALLEY NATIONAL MONUMENT
YOSEMITE NATIONAL PARK
KINGS CANYON NAT'L PARK
SEQUOIA NATIONAL PARK
DEVILS TOWER NAT'L MON.
LAKE MEAD RECREATIONAL AREA
HOOVER DAM
DAVIS DAM
Lake Mead
Lake Mohave
Owens L.
L. Tulare
Mono L.
PAIUTE IND. RES.
TULE RIVER IND. RES.
FT. INDEPENDENCE IND. RES.
FT. MOHAVE IND. RES.
NELLIS AIR FORCE BASE
NAV. AMM. DEPOT
Tonopah
Goldfield
Pioche
Panaca
Caliente
Ursine
Modena
Elgin
Carp
Rox
Mesquite
Bunkerville
Riverside
Moapa
Glendale
Logandale
Overton
Mead Lake
Dry Lake
Indian Springs
North Las Vegas
LAS VEGAS
Henderson
Boulder City
Pittman
Whitney
Arden
Blue Diamond
Sloan
Jean
Goodsprings
Nelson
Searchlight
Nipton
Pahrump
Beatty
Alamo
Hiko
Bristol Silver
Adaven
Gold Point
Silverpeak
Nivloc
Dyer
Coaldale
Mina
Mount Montgomery
Death Valley
Kingman
Oatman
Chloride
Crucero
Trona
Searles
Mojave
Keeler
Independence
Laws
Bridgeport
Mono Lake
Mather
El Portal
Mariposa
Madera
FRESNO
Friant
Delpiedra
Hanford
Visalia
Tulare
Porterville
Mt. Ely 7,310
Highland Pk. 9,395
Virgin Pk. 7,250
Charleston Pk. 11,910
Potosi Mtn. 8,500
Reveille Pk. 8,910
Kawich Pk. 9,500
Timber Mtn. 10,280
Lone Mtn. 9,114
Emigrant Pk. 6,805
Piper Pk. 9,400
Boundary Pk. 13,145
Pilot Pk.
EXCELSIOR MOUNTAINS 9,207
MORMON RANGE
HIGHLAND RANGE
MEADOW VALLEY RANGE
PAHROCK RANGE
VIRGIN MTS.
MUDDY MTS.
ARROW CANYON MTN.
SHEEP RANGE
LAS VEGAS RANGE
DESERT RANGE
PINTWATER RANGE
SPOTTED RANGE
SPECTER RANGE
SPRING MOUNTAINS
PAHRUMP VALLEY
PAHRANAGAT RANGE
GOLDEN GATE RANGE
TIMPAHUTE RANGE
QUINN CANYON RANGE
RAILROAD VALLEY
REVEILLE RANGE
KAWICH RANGE
BELTED RANGE
CACTUS RANGE
PAHUTE MESA
TIMBER MOUNTAIN
SHOSHONE MOUNTAIN
YUCCA FLATS
FRENCHMAN FLAT
HOT CREEK
MONTE CRISTO RANGE
ALKALI FLAT
SILVER PEAK RANGE
Salt Marsh
Columbus Salt Marsh
Meadow Valley Wash
Virgin R.
Owens R.
San Joaquin R.
Kings R.
Kern R.
South Fork

NEW HAMPSHIRE

SCALE OF MILES
0 5 10 15 20 25

State Capitals
County Seats

CANADA
QUEBEC
MAINE
COOS
WHITE MTS.
VERMONT

Sherbrooke, Magog, Lake Magog, Lake Memphremagog, Lake Massawippi, Coaticook, Stanstead, Derby Line, Derby, Salem Pd., Newport, Orleans, Barton, Crystal L., Clyde R., Willoughby Lake, Seymour L., Island Pond, Norton Pd., Beecher Falls, West Stewartstown, Stewartstown, Colebrook, Paquette, Canaan, North Stratford, Stratford, Maidstone L., Guildhall, Groveton, Northumberland, Lancaster, Dalton, Whitefield, Gilman, Concord, St. Johnsbury, Lyndonville, West Burke, Passumpsic, Moose, Danville, Mollys Falls Res., L. Groton, Wells River, Woodsville, Swiftwater, Bath, Lisbon, Monroe, North Monroe, Littleton, Sugar Hill, Landaff, Easton, Bethlehem, Maplewood, Franconia, Apthorp, Twin Mountain, Carroll, Jefferson, Meadows, Coos Jc., Grange, Randolph, Gorham, Berlin, Berlin Mills, Cascade, Shelburne, Milan, West Milan, Dummer, Crystal, Stark, Percy, Errol, Wentworth Location, Dixville Notch, Pittsburg, Back L., L. Francis, First Connecticut Lake, Second Lake, Third L., Perry Stream, Indian Stream, Halls Stream, Magalloway Mtn. 3,360, Dixville Pk. 3,482, Rice Mtn. 3,370, Blue Mtn. 3,723, Long Mtn. 3,340, Mt. Cabot 4,200, Hutchins Mtn. 3,710, Mt. Starr King 3,913, Mt. Waumbek 4,005, Nash Stream, Upper Ammonoosuc R., Mohawk R., Androscoggin River, Connecticut River, Ammonoosuc, Wild Ammonoosuc R.

Mt. Madison 5,363, Mt. Adams 5,798, Mt. Jefferson 5,715, Mt. Washington 6,288, Mt. Monroe 5,385, N. Carter Mtn. 4,565, Carter Dome 4,860, Pinkham Notch, Crawford House, Fabyan House, Bretton Woods, Mt. Tom, Mt. Willey, Crawford Notch, Twin Mtn. 4,769, N. Twin Mtn. 4,926, Mt. Lafayette 5,249, Mt. Lincoln 5,108, Franconia Notch, Profile Mtn. 4,070, Kinsman Mtn. 4,363, Mt. Liberty 4,460, Mt. Bond, Mt. Hancock 4,430, Mt. Carrigain 4,647, Kinsman Notch, PRESIDENTIAL RANGE, Willey House, Bartlett, Glen, Jackson, Intervale, Kearsarge, Chatham, North Chatham, South Chatham, North Conway, Saco R., Ellis R., Lincoln, Benton, North Haverhill, East Haverhill, Pike

Stratton, Kennebago L., Kennebago Lake, Rangeley, Rangeley Lake, Mooselookmeguntic Lake, Richardson Lakes, Cupsuptic R., Parmachenee L., Aziscohos Lake, Umbagog L., Phillips, Sandy R., Strong, Wilton, Swift River, Mexico, Rumford, Dixfield, Livermore Falls, Ellis Pd., Andover, Ellis R., Bear R., Bethel, Gilead, West Paris, Paris, South Paris, Norway, Oxford, Mechanic Falls, Thompson Lake, Lewiston, Auburn, Bridgton, Kezar L., Kezar Pd.

North Troy, Missisquoi River, Richford, Abercorn, Montgomery Cen., Enosburg Falls, L. Carmi, Black R., Barton R., Caspian L., Wolcott, Hardwick, Morrisville, Hyde Park, Johnson, Lamoille River, Stowe, Waterbury, Winooski River, Montpelier, Plainfield, Barre, Websterville, Graniteville, Northfield, Dog R., Mad R., Waits R., Wells R.

45° 30' 72° 71°

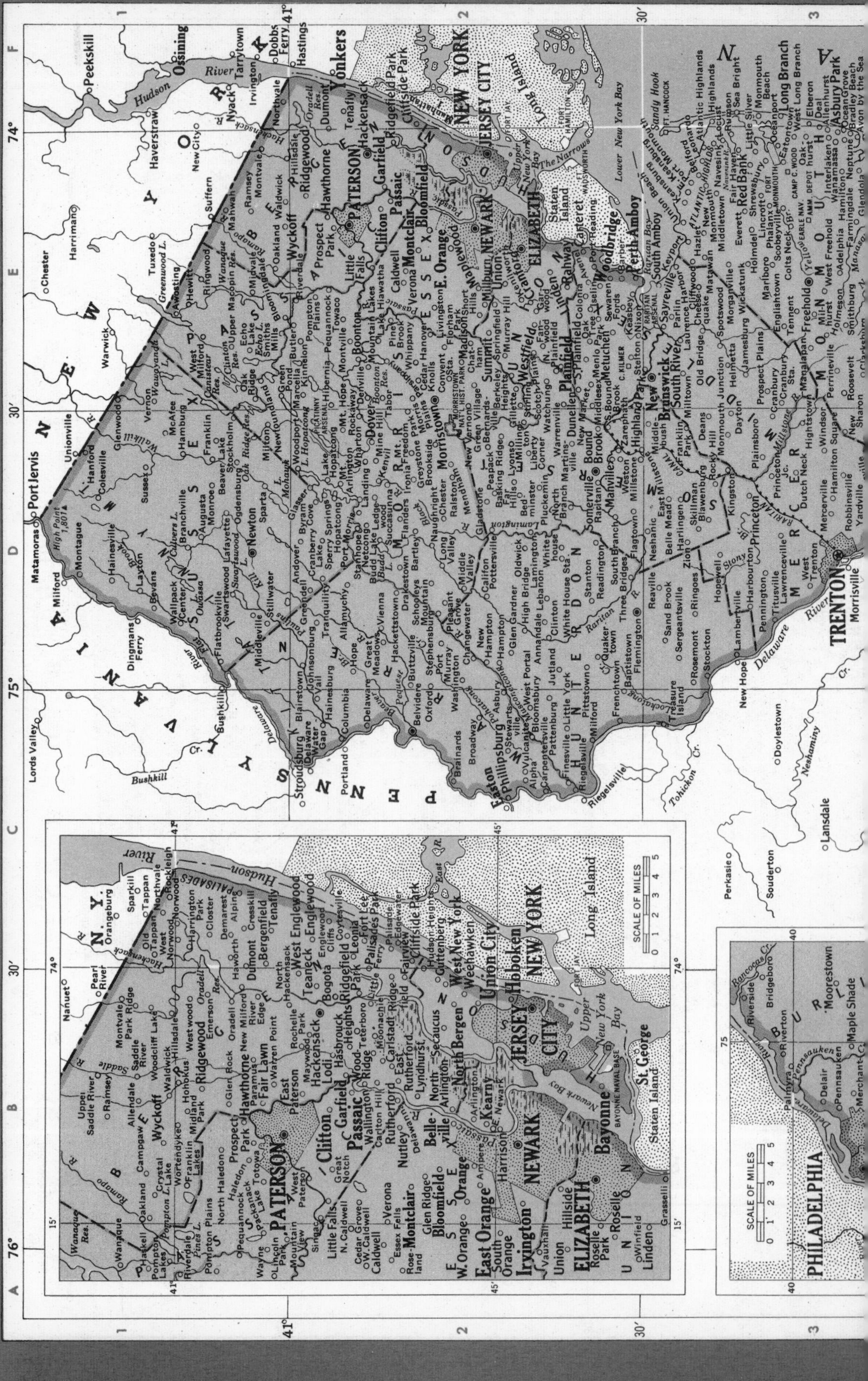
NEW YORK
PENNSYLVANIA
NEW YORK CITY
JERSEY CITY
NEWARK
ELIZABETH
PATERSON
TRENTON
PHILADELPHIA
Yonkers
Long Island
Staten Island
Perth Amboy
New Brunswick
Plainfield
Morristown
Dover
Newton
Port Jervis
Phillipsburg
Flemington
Princeton
Somerville
Woodbridge
Red Bank
Long Branch
Asbury Park
Freehold
Hudson River
Delaware River
Raritan R.
Upper New York Bay
Lower New York Bay
Sandy Hook
N. Y.
JERSEY CITY
Hoboken
Bayonne
Kearny
Union City
Irvington
East Orange
Montclair
Bloomfield
Passaic
Clifton
Hackensack
Ridgewood
St. George
SCALE OF MILES

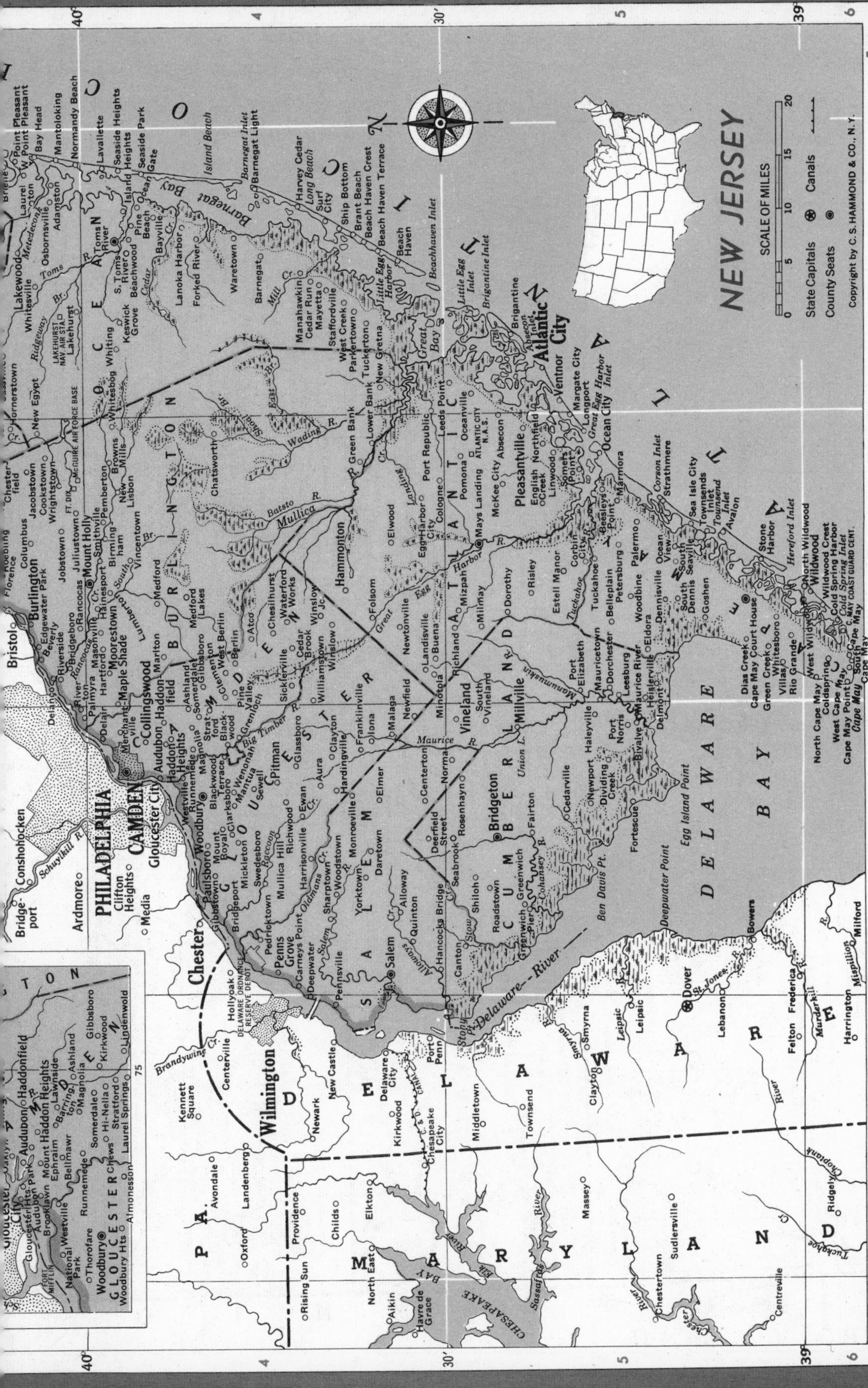

NEW JERSEY

SCALE OF MILES

0 5 10 15 20

State Capitals ⊛ Canals

County Seats ◉

Longitude 75° West of Greenwich

6581

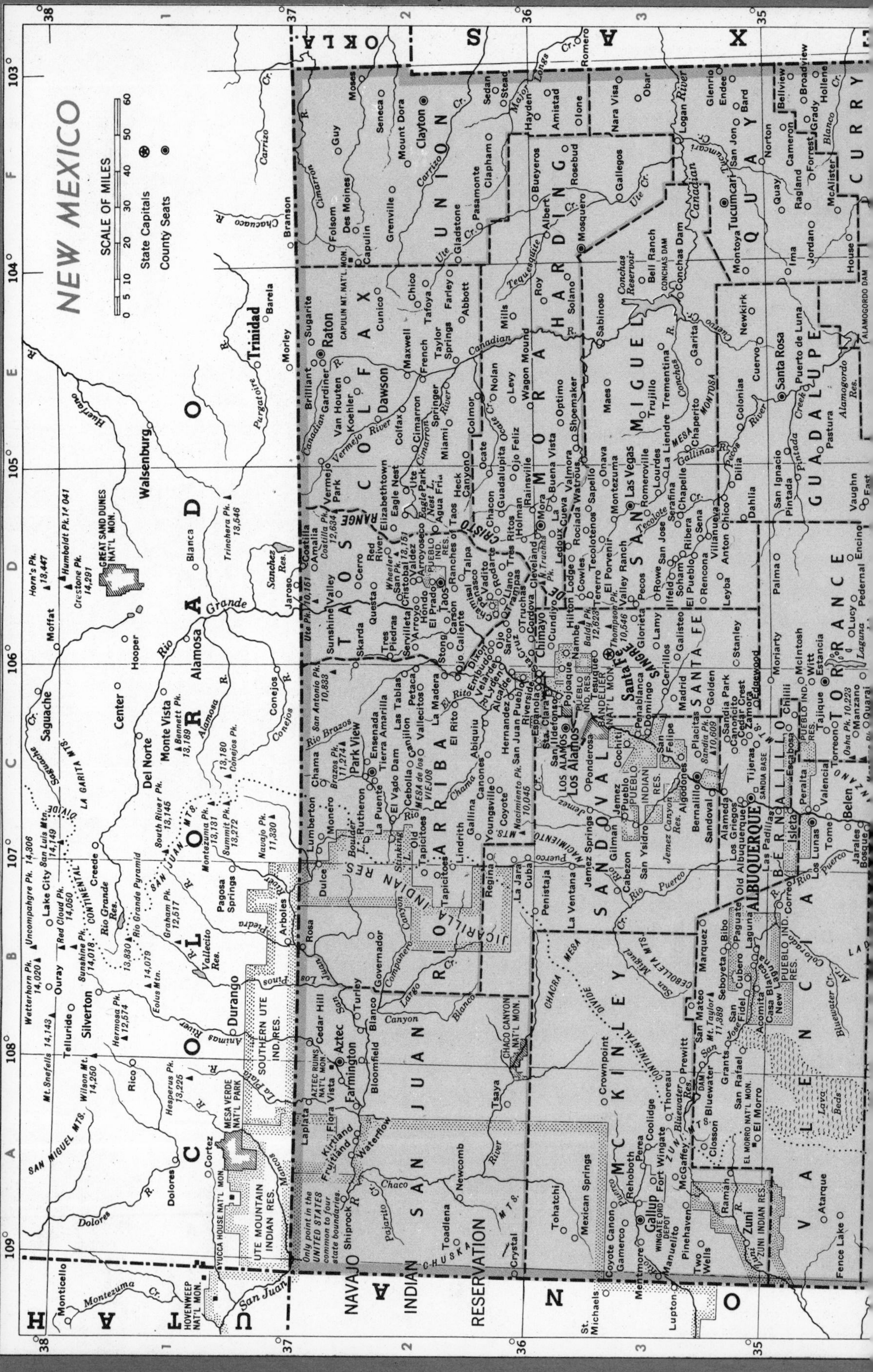

NEW MEXICO

SCALE OF MILES

0 5 10 20 30 40 50 60

State Capitals

County Seats

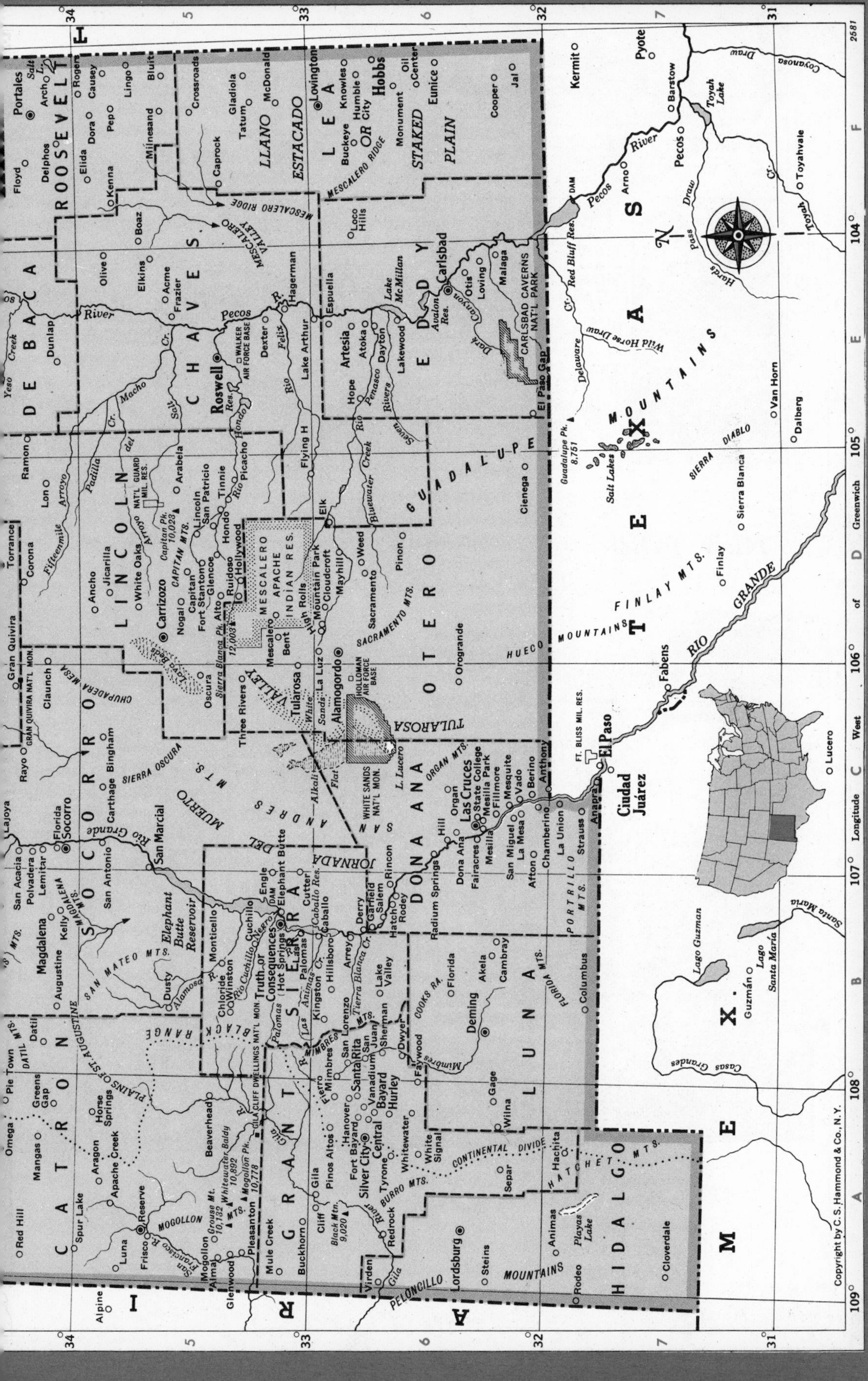
ROOSEVELT
DE BACA
CHAVES
LINCOLN
TORRANCE
SOCORRO
CATRON
SIERRA
OTERO
LEA
EDDY
DONA ANA
LUNA
GRANT
HIDALGO
TEXAS
MEXICO
ARIZONA
Portales
Floyd
Delphos
Elida
Kenna
Dora
Causey
Rogers
Pep
Lingo
Bluitt
Milnesand
Crossroads
Caprock
Gladiola
Tatum
McDonald
Lovington
Knowles
Humble City
Hobbs
Buckeye
Monument
Oil Center
Eunice
Cooper
Jal
Kermit
Pyote
Barstow
Pecos
Toyahvale
Toyah Lake
Loco Hills
Carlsbad
Otis
Loving
Malaga
Lake McMillan
Artesia
Atoka
Dayton
Lakewood
Hope
Espuella
Hagerman
Dexter
Lake Arthur
Roswell
Walker Air Force Base
Elkins
Boaz
Olive
Acme
Frazier
Dunlap
Ramon
Lon
Corona
Jicarilla
Ancho
White Oaks
Carrizozo
Nogal
Capitan
Fort Stanton
Lincoln
San Patricio
Tinnie
Hondo
Picacho
Arabela
Glencoe
Ruidoso
Hollywood
Alto
Mescalero Apache Indian Res.
Mescalero
Bent
High Rolls
Mountain Park
Cloudcroft
Mayhill
Weed
Sacramento
Pinon
Elk
Flying H
Gran Quivira
Claunch
Oscura
Three Rivers
Tularosa
La Luz
Alamogordo
Holloman Air Force Base
Orogrande
White Sands Nat'l Mon.
Rayo
Bingham
Carthage
Florida
Socorro
Lajoya
San Acacia
Polvadera
Lemitar
San Antonio
San Marcial
Elephant Butte Reservoir
Magdalena
Kelly
Augustine
Datil
Pie Town
Omega
Greens Gap
Horse Springs
Aragon
Apache Creek
Mangas
Red Hill
Spur Lake
Luna
Reserve
Frisco
Beaverhead
Engle
Elephant Butte
Cutter
Caballo
Derry
Garfield
Salem
Rincon
Hatch
Rodey
Radium Springs
Hill
Dona Ana
Organ
Las Cruces
State College
Mesilla Park
Fillmore
Mesilla
Fairacres
Mesquite
Vado
Berino
Anthony
San Miguel
La Mesa
Chamberino
La Union
Afton
Strauss
Anapra
El Paso
Ciudad Juárez
Fabens
Cienega
Dalberg
Van Horn
Sierra Blanca
Finlay
Lucero
Monticello
Cuchillo
Chloride
Winston
Truth or Consequences (Hot Springs)
Las Palomas
Hillsboro
Kingston
Arrey
Lake Valley
San Lorenzo
Santa Rita
San Juan
Sherman
Dwyer
Faywood
Florida
Akela
Cambray
Deming
Columbus
Gage
Wilna
Hachita
Separ
Mimbres
Fierro
Hanover
Vanadium
Bayard
Hurley
Fort Bayard
Central
Silver City
Pinos Altos
Tyrone
Whitewater
White Signal
Gila
Cliff
Buckhorn
Mule Creek
Redrock
Virden
Lordsburg
Steins
Animas
Playas Lake
Rodeo
Cloverdale
Glenwood
Alma
Mogollon
Pleasanton
Alpine
Guzmán
Lago Guzman
Lago Santa Maria
LLANO ESTACADO
STAKED PLAIN
MESCALERO RIDGE
GUADALUPE MOUNTAINS
SACRAMENTO MTS.
SAN ANDRES MTS.
JORNADA DEL MUERTO
SIERRA OSCURA
CHUPADERA MESA
SAN MATEO MTS.
BLACK RANGE
MOGOLLON MTS.
PLAINS OF ST. AUGUSTINE
CONTINENTAL DIVIDE
BURRO MTS.
COOKS RA.
FLORIDA MTS.
PORTRILLO MTS.
HATCHET MTS.
PELONCILLO MOUNTAINS
HUECO MOUNTAINS
FINLAY MTS.
SIERRA DIABLO
TULAROSA
RIO GRANDE
Pecos River
Red Bluff Res.
Carlsbad Caverns Nat'l Park
El Paso Gap
Guadalupe Pk. 8,751
Salt Lakes
Sierra Blanca Pk. 12,003
Capitan Pk. 10,023
Whitewater Baldy 10,892
Mogollon Pk. 10,778
Black Mtn. 9,020
Ft. Bliss Mil. Res.
Longitude West of Greenwich
Copyright by C. S. Hammond & Co., N. Y.
2581

Southeastern Part of New York

Same scale as main map

NEW YORK

SCALE OF MILES

0 5 10 20 30 40

State Capitals ⊛ Canals

County Seats ◉

LAKE ONTARIO

LAKE ERIE

ATLANTIC OCEAN

LONG ISLAND SOUND

PENNSYLVANIA

ONT.

CONN.

PA.

Longitude 77° West of Greenwich

A 30′ B 79° C 30′ D 78° E 30′ F 77° G

42° 30′ 43° 30′ 44° 30′ 41° 30′

4581

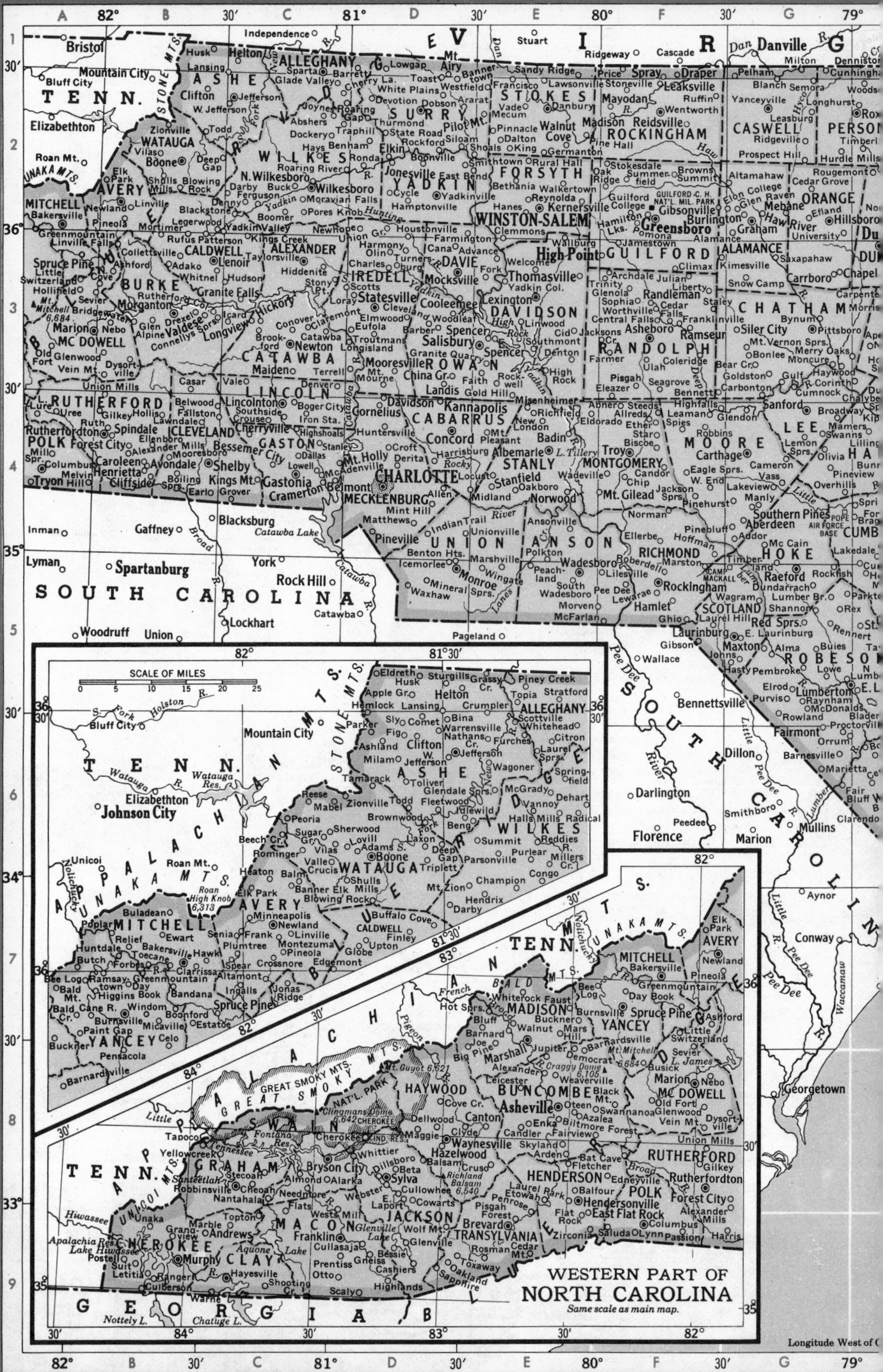
WESTERN PART OF
NORTH CAROLINA
Same scale as main map.
SCALE OF MILES
0 5 10 15 20 25
Longitude West of G
TENN.
VIRGINIA
SOUTH CAROLINA
GEORGIA
APPALACHIAN MTS.
BLUE RIDGE
UNAKA MTS.
STONE MTS.
GREAT SMOKY MTS.
NAT'L. PARK
ALLEGHANY
ASHE
SURRY
STOKES
ROCKINGHAM
CASWELL
PERSON
WATAUGA
WILKES
YADKIN
FORSYTH
GUILFORD
ALAMANCE
ORANGE
AVERY
MITCHELL
CALDWELL
ALEXANDER
IREDELL
DAVIE
DAVIDSON
RANDOLPH
CHATHAM
BURKE
MC DOWELL
CATAWBA
ROWAN
LINCOLN
RUTHERFORD
POLK
CLEVELAND
GASTON
MECKLENBURG
CABARRUS
STANLY
MONTGOMERY
MOORE
LEE
UNION
ANSON
RICHMOND
HOKE
SCOTLAND
ROBESON
YANCEY
MADISON
BUNCOMBE
HAYWOOD
SWAIN
GRAHAM
JACKSON
HENDERSON
TRANSYLVANIA
MACON
CLAY
CHEROKEE
CHARLOTTE
WINSTON-SALEM
Greensboro
High Point
Asheville
Danville
Bristol
Spartanburg
Rock Hill
Florence
Johnson City

NORTH CAROLINA

ATLANTIC OCEAN

PAMLICO SOUND

ALBEMARLE SOUND

ONSLOW BAY

RALEIGH BAY

SCALE OF MILES

0 10 20 30 40 50

State Capitals

County Seats

Canals

B 104° C 30' D 103° E 30' F 102° G 30' H 101° J 30'

1 2 3 4 5 6 7 8

49° 30' 48° 30' 47° 30' 46°

S A S K A T C H E W A N · C A N · M A

Oxbow · Estevan · Carnduff · Melita · Deloraine

Westby · Colgan · Ambrose · Fortuna · Crosby · Kermit · Noonan · Alkabo · Stady · D I V I D E

Portal · Northgate · Columbus · Larson · Stampede · Lignite · Flaxton · Woburn · Bowbells · Coteau · B U R K E

Sherwood · Antler · Loraine · Mohall · Norma · Tolley · Niobe · Kenmare · Kenaston · Greene · Grano · Coulee · Donnybrook · R E N V I L L E · Souris R. · Des Lacs River · Sevenmile Cr.

Kuroki · Westhope · Roth · Landa · Souris · Carbury · Lake Metigoshe · Bottineau · Dunning · Maxbass · Eckman · Truro · Hurd · Lansford · Forfar · Glenburn · Newburg · Russell · Gardena · Kramer · Deep · Upham · B O T T I N E A · Deep R.

Grenora · Hanks · Zahl · Appam · Corinth · Alamo · Wildrose · Hamlet · McGregor · Battleview · Powers Lake · Marmon · Bonetraill · Temple · Tioga · Epping · Ray · Wheelock · Spring Brook · Williston · Trenton · Buford · W I L L I A M S · Little Muddy Cr. · Missouri River

Lundsvalley · Lostwood · White Earth · Manitou · Ross · Stanley · Blaisdell · Palermo · Belden · Shell Cr. · Charlson · Keene · Newtown · Parshall · Plaza · Wabek · M O U N T R A I L · White Earth R. · Little Knife R. · VERENDRYE NAT. MON.

Aurelia · Carpio · Hartland · Tagus · Foxholm · Berthold · Lonetree · Burlington · Des Lacs · Minot · Logan · Sawyer · Surrey · Makoti · Ryder · Douglas · W A R D · Wolseth · Egg Cr.

Deering · Rising · North Lake · Buffalo Lodge Lake · Granville · Denbigh · Norwich · M C H E N R Y · Simcoe · Verendrye · Karlsruhe · Velva · Rangeley · Voltaire · Bergen · Balfour · Kongsberg · Ruso · Butte · Strawberry Lake · Long Lake · Crooked Lake · Bantry · Towner · Kief · Anamoose · Norfolk · Guthrie

Cartwright · Fairview · East Fairview · Dore · Charbonneau · Alexander · Rawson · Arnegard · Watford City · Sidney · M C K E N Z I E · Cherry Cr. · Searing · Banks · Little Missouri · THEODORE ROOSEVELT NAT'L MEM. PARK (NORTH UNIT) · Yellowstone R.

FORT BERTHOLD INDIAN RESERVATION · Raub · Roseglen · Blackwater · Elbowoods · Emmet · Garrison · Maxo · Benedict · M C L E A N · Coleharbor · Turtle L. · Turtle Lake · Riverdale · GARRISON DAM · Pick City · Big Bend · Underwood · Mercer · Falkirk · Garrison Reservoir

S H E R I D A N · McClusky · Pickardville · Denhoff · Alta

Skaar · Oakdale · Grassy Butte · Killdeer · Dunn Center · Werner · Halliday · Dodge · Spring Cr. · Fayette · Manning · D U N N · Willmen · Marshall · New Hradec

Goldenvalley · Zap · Beulah · Hazen · Stanton · M E R C E R · Knife River · MISSOURI

Fort Clark · Hensler · Washburn · Sanger · Wilton · Center · Hannover · Otter Creek · Price · O L I V E R · Still · Regan · Baldwin

Trotters · Beaver Creek · THEODORE ROOSEVELT NAT'L MEM. PARK (ELKHORN RANCH SITE) · Fairfield · Gorham · Green R. · G O L D E N · B I L L I N G S · THEODORE ROOSEVELT NAT'L MEM. PARK (SOUTH UNIT) · Wibaux · Beach · Chama · Sentinel Butte · Medora · Fryburg · Belfield · V A L L E Y · Sentinel Butte · Golva

Dickinson · Zenith · South Heart · Lehigh · Dickinson Res. · Taylor · Gladstone · Richardton · Antelope · S T A R K · Schefield · Lefor · Heart R.

Hebron · Bluegrass · Rosebud · Youngtown · Harmon · New Salem · Judson · Glen Ullin · Sims · Almont · Muddy Cr. · Mandan · Sweetbriar · M O R T O N · Heart Butte · Heart Butte Res. · Schmidt · St. Anthony · Huff · Fort Rice · Livona

B U R L E I G H · Bismarck · McKenzie · Menoken · Apple Creek · Moffit

Black Butte 3,468 · Amidon · S L O P E · De Sart · Pierce · Marmarth · Bad Lands · Little Missouri River

New England · Havelock · H E T T I N G E R · Regent · Mott · Burt · Watrous · Thirtymile Creek

Clark Buttes · G R A N T · Elgin · New Leipzig · Odessa · Heil · Carson · Leith · Lark · Flasher · Fallon · Raleigh · Brisbane · Timmer · Breien · Freda · Cannonball · Cedar Creek · Bentley

Ives · Rhame · Griffin · Bowman · Buffalo Springs · Scranton · Gascoyne · B O W M A N · Haley

Whetstone Buttes · Reeder · Bucyrus · A D A M S · Hettinger · Haynes · Petrel · Lemmon

Solen · Cannon Ball · Shields · Porcupine Cr. · Fort Yates · Selfridge · S I O U X · STANDING ROCK · E M M O N S · Emmonsburg · Strasburg · Westfield

McIntosh · INDIAN RESERVATION · McLaughlin · Oak Creek · North Fork · South Fork · Grand River · S O U T H

Longitude

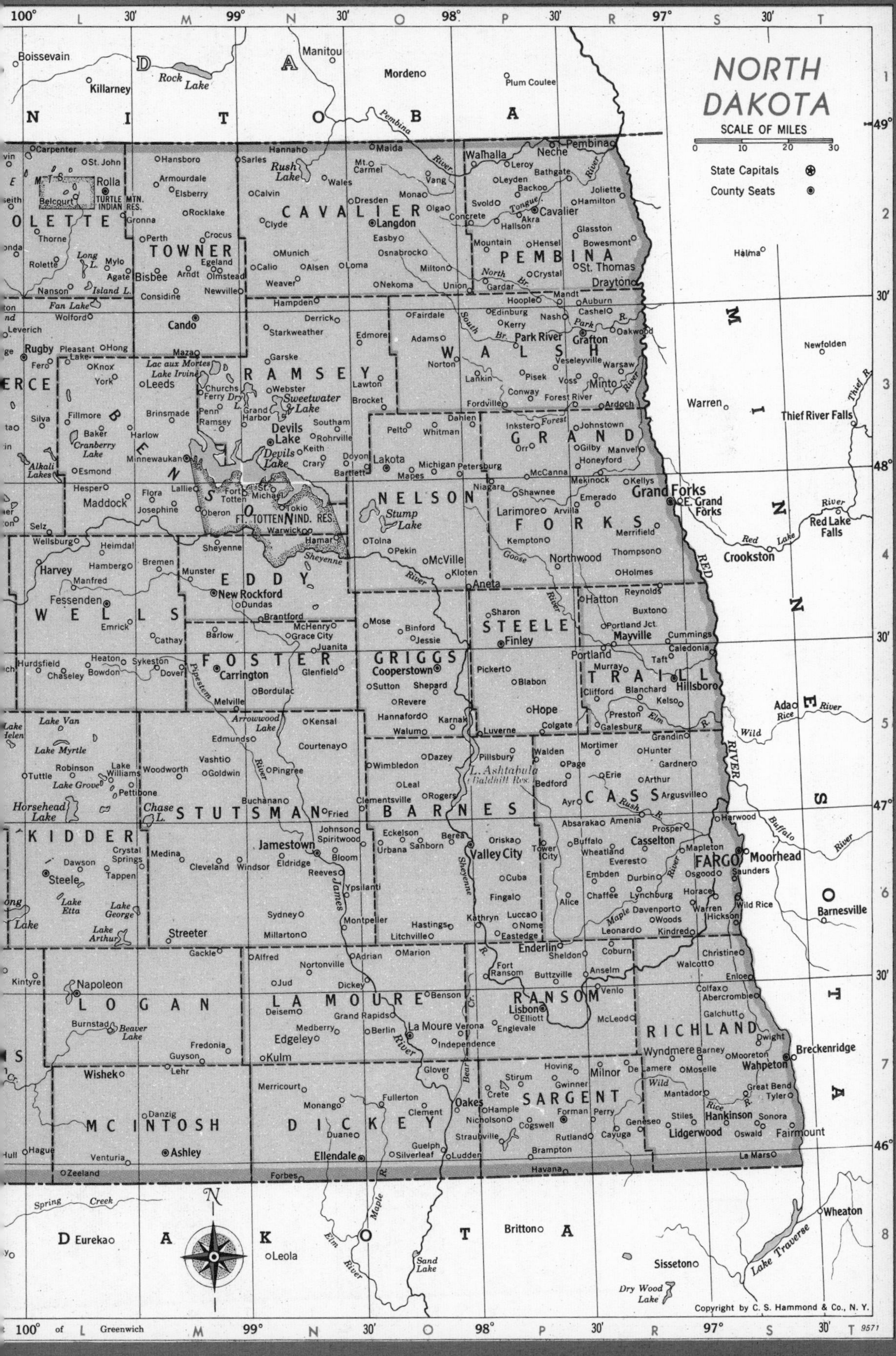

NORTH DAKOTA

SCALE OF MILES

0 10 20 30

State Capitals

County Seats

100° L 30' M 99° N 30' O 98° P 30' R 97° S 30' T

1 2 3 4 5 6 7 8

49° 30' 48° 30' 47° 30' 46°

MANITOBA

Boissevain, Killarney, Rock Lake, Manitou, Mordeno, Plum Coulee, Pembina River

PEMBINA

Pembina, Walhalla, Neche, Leroy, Bathgate, Leyden, Backoo, Joliette, Svold, Tongue, Hamilton, Cavalier, Concrete, Akra, Hallson, Glasston, Mountain, Hensel, Bowesmont, North Br., Crystal, St. Thomas, Gardar, Drayton

CAVALIER

Hannah, Maida, Sarles, Rush Lake, Mt. Carmel, Wales, Vang, Calvin, Dresden, Mona, Olga, Langdon, Clyde, Easby, Osnabrock, Munich, Milton, Calio, Alsen, Loma, Weaver, Nekoma, Union

TOWNER

Hansboro, Armourdale, Elsberry, Rocklake, Perth, Crocus, Egeland, Bisbee, Arndt, Olmstead, Considine, Newville, Cando

ROLETTE

Carpenter, St. John, Rolla, Belcourt, Turtle Mtn. Indian Res., Gronna, Thorne, Long L., Mylo, Rolette, Agate, Nanson, Island L.

WALSH

Hampden, Fairdale, Edinburg, Kerry, Auburn, Cashel, Nash, Park R., Park River, Grafton, Oakwood, Adams, South Br., Norton, Veseleyville, Warsaw, Lankin, Pisek, Voss, Minto, Conway, Forest River, Fordville, Ardoch

RAMSEY

Derrick, Starkweather, Edmore, Garske, Lawton, Webster, Sweetwater Lake, Brocket, Churchs Ferry, Dry L., Grand Harbor, Penn, Ramsey, Devils Lake, Southam, Rohrville, Keith, Crary, Doyon, Bartlett

BENSON

Maza, Lac aux Mortes, Lake Irvine, Knox, York, Leeds, Brinsmade, Harlow, Minnewaukan, Fillmore, Baker, Cranberry Lake, Alkali Lakes, Esmond, Hesper, Maddock, Flora, Lallie, Josephine, Fort Totten, St. Michael, Tokio, Oberon, Ft. Totten Ind. Res., Warwick

PIERCE

Wolford, Leverich, Rugby, Pleasant Lake, Hong, Fero, Silva, Fan Lake

GRAND FORKS

Inkster, Forest, Johnstown, Orr, Gilby, Manvel, Honeyford, McCanna, Niagara, Mekinock, Kellys, Grand Forks, Shawnee, Emerado, Larimore, Arvilla, Merrifield, Kempton, Goose, Northwood, Thompson, Holmes, Reynolds

NELSON

Pelto, Dahlen, Whitman, Lakota, Michigan, Petersburg, Mapes, Stump Lake, Tolna, Pekin, McVille, Kloten, Aneta

EDDY

Hamar, Sheyenne, Munster, New Rockford, Dundas

WELLS

Wellsburg, Heimdal, Harvey, Hamberg, Bremen, Manfred, Fessenden, Emrick, Cathay, Hurdsfield, Heaton, Sykeston, Chaseley, Bowdon, Dover

FOSTER

Brantford, McHenry, Barlow, Grace City, Juanita, Carrington, Glenfield, Pipestem, Bordulac, Melville

GRIGGS

Mose, Binford, Jessie, Cooperstown, Sutton, Shepard, Revere, Hannaford, Karnak, Walum

STEELE

Sharon, Finley, Pickert, Blabon, Hope, Colgate, Luverne

TRAILL

Hatton, Buxton, Portland Jct., Mayville, Cummings, Portland, Caledonia, Taft, Murray, Hillsboro, Clifford, Blanchard, Kelso, Preston, Elm, Galesburg

CASS

Grandin, Walden, Mortimer, Hunter, Page, Gardner, Erie, Arthur, Bedford, Ayr, Argusville, Rush R., Absaraka, Amenia, Harwood, Prosper, Casselton, Mapleton, Tower City, Buffalo, Wheatland, Everest, Fargo, Embden, Durbin, Osgood, Horace, Chaffee, Lynchburg, Alice, Maple, Davenport, Woods, Leonard, Kindred, Warren, Hickson

BARNES

Dazey, Pillsbury, L. Ashtabula (Baldhill Res.), Wimbledon, Leal, Rogers, Clementsville, Eckelson, Berea, Oriska, Urbana, Sanborn, Valley City, Cuba, Fingal, Kathryn, Lucca, Nome, Eastedge, Hastings, Litchville

STUTSMAN

Edmunds, Arrowwood Lake, Kensal, Courtenay, Vashti, Woodworth, Goldwin, Pingree, Buchanan, Chase L., Fried, Johnson, Spiritwood, Medina, Jamestown, Bloom, Cleveland, Windsor, Eldridge, Reeves, Ypsilanti, James, Sydney, Montpelier, Streeter, Millarton

KIDDER

Lake Van, Lake Myrtle, Robinson, Lake Williams, Tuttle, Lake Grove, Pettibone, Horsehead Lake, Crystal Springs, Dawson, Steele, Tappen, Lake Etta, Lake George, Lake Arthur

RANSOM

Enderlin, Sheldon, Coburn, Fort Ransom, Buttzville, Anselm, Venlo, Lisbon, Elliott, Englevale, McLeod

RICHLAND

Christine, Walcott, Enloe, Colfax, Abercrombie, Galchutt, Dwight, Wyndmere, Barney, Mooreton, Lamere, Moselle, Wahpeton, Wild Rice, Mantador, Great Bend, Tyler, Hankinson, Stiles, Sonora, Lidgerwood, Oswald, Fairmount, La Mars

LOGAN

Gackle, Kintyre, Napoleon, Burnstad, Beaver Lake, Fredonia, Guyson, Lehr

LA MOURE

Alfred, Adrian, Marion, Nortonville, Jud, Dickey, Benson, Deisem, Grand Rapids, Medberry, Berlin, La Moure, Verona, Edgeley, Independence, Kulm

SARGENT

Hoving, Milnor, Stirum, Gwinner, Crete, Hample, Nicholson, Forman, Perry, Geneseo, Cogswell, Rutland, Cayuga, Brampton, Havana

DICKEY

Glover, Merricourt, Fullerton, Monango, Clement, Oakes, Straubville, Duane, Guelph, Ellendale, Silverleaf, Ludden, Forbes, Bear Cr.

McINTOSH

Wishek, Danzig, Hague, Venturia, Ashley, Zeeland

MINNESOTA

Halma, Newfolden, Thief R., Warren, Thief River Falls, Grand Forks, E. Grand Forks, River, Red Lake Falls, Red Lake, Crookston, Red River, Ada, Rice, Wild Rice River, Buffalo River, Moorhead, Saunders, Barnesville, Breckenridge, Wheaton, Lake Traverse

SOUTH DAKOTA

Spring Creek, Eureka, Leola, Maple R., Elm River, Sand Lake, Britton, Sisseton, Dry Wood Lake

100° of Greenwich L M 99° N 30' O 98° P 30' R 97° S 30' T 9571

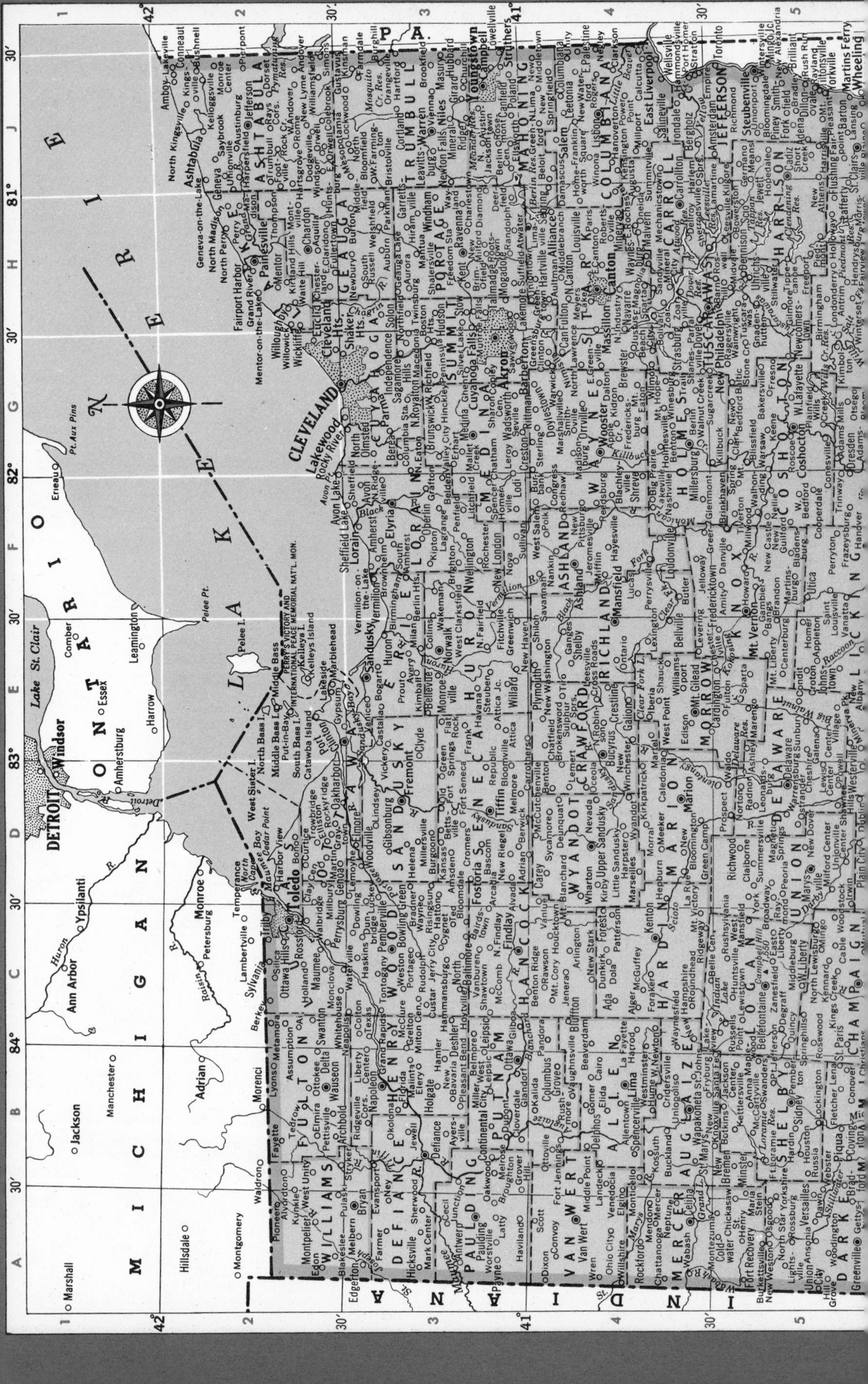

MICHIGAN
ONTARIO
LAKE ERIE
PA.
INDIANA
DETROIT
Windsor
CLEVELAND
Toledo
Akron
Youngstown
Canton
Lake St. Clair

OHIO
SCALE OF MILES
State Capitals
County Seats
West of Greenwich
CLEVELAND
LAKE ERIE
CINCINNATI
Columbus
Copyright by C. S. HAMMOND & Co., N. Y.
3564

A
30′
B
100°
C
30′
D
99°
E
30′
F
98°
G
37°
1
30′
2
36°
3
30′
4
35°
5
30′
6
34°
7
8
K
A
N
T
E
X
A
S
E
X
Englewood
Willard
Kiowa
Waldron
Caldw
Manchester
Gibbon
Renfrow
Forgan
Mocane
Knowles
Gate
Turpin
North
Beaver
Canadian
Buffalo
Rosston
Lookout
Farry
Tegarden
Capron
Salt
Burlington
Amorita
Byron
Sand Creek
Wakita
Cimarron
Selman
Edith
Freedom
Fairvalley
Alva
Driftwood
Ingersoll
Great Salt Plains Res.
Medford
HARPER
WOODS
Cherokee
ALFALFA
GRA
Boyd
BEAVER
Laverne
Clear Lake
Avard
Hopeton
Lambert
Yewed
Hawley
Jeffe
Balko
Elmwood
Kiowa
Cr.
R.
Dacoma
Nash
Pondcreek
May
Dunlap
Logan
Waynoka
Jet
Salt
Gray
Ft. Supply
Ft. Supply Res.
River
Carmen
Helena
Hillsdale
Kremlin
Chaney
Belva
Aline
Goltry
Perryton
Follett
Catesby
Woodward
Curtis
Quinlan
Carrier
North Enid
Bre
Tangier
Mooreland
Cleo Springs
Lahoma
ENID
Fargo
Cr.
WOODWARD
Cedardale
Sherman
Ringwood
Orienta
Meno
GARFI
Wolf
Gage
MAJOR
VANCE AIR FORCE BASE
Fairmont
Drummond
Covin
Lipscomb
Shattuck
ELLIS
Sharon
Fairview
Waukomis
Goodwin
Mutual
Chester
Isabella
Douglas
Richmond
Ames
Bison
Higgins
Arnett
Harmon
Vici
Cestos
Seiling
Canton Res.
Longdale
Homestead
Turkey
Marsha
Okeene
Lenora
Taloga
Southard
Hennessey
Camargo
Canton
DEWEY
Carlton
Canadian
Grand
Peek
Eagle City
Loyal
Dover
Canadian
River
Webb
Oakwood
North
BLAINE
Hitchcock
KINGFISHER
River
Durham
Leedey
Putnam
Crawford
Rhea
Aledo
Watonga
Omega
Kingfisher
Fay
Cashion
Miami
Washita
Moorewood
Thomas
Okarche
R.
ROGER MILLS
CUSTER
Greenfield
Canadian
Strong City
Butler
Custer
Piedmont
Reydon
Geary
Cheyenne
Herring
Hammon
Arapaho
Calumet
Concho
Richland
Clinton
Indianapolis
CANADIAN
Fort Reno
Carpenter
Stafford
Hydro
Bridgeport
El Reno
Banner
Yukon
Bethan
Grimes
Berlin
Weatherford
Hinton
Wheeler
Sweetwater
Foss
OKLAHOM
Coltexo
Elk City
Canute
Corn
Bessie
Mayfield
Burns Flat
Colony
Union
Mus
Sayre
Doxey
WASHITA
Lookeba
Cogar
BECKHAM
Eakly
Binger
Minco
Tuttle
Dill City
Cordell
McLean
Shamrock
Texola
Erick
Carter
Port
Albert
Newcas
Elk
Cloud Chief
Alfalfa
Gracemont
North
Sentinel
Pocasset
Delhi
Rocky
CADDO
Amber
Ft Cobb
Washita
Willow
Cambridge
Gotebo
Mountain View
Carnegie
Verden
Chickasha
Brinkman
Fork
Cr.
Hobart
Komalty
Anadarko
Tabler
Jester
Granite
Lone Wolf
GRADY
Reed
Steckero
Norge
Clarendon
GREER
Cement
Ninnekah
Vinson
Mangum
L. Altus
Lugert
KIOWA
Apache
Alex
Wellington
Coopertono
Cyril
Bradley
Salt
Fork
Hester
Saddle Mountain
Roosevelt
Shrewder
Blair
Wichita Mts.
Mt. Scott
Fletcher
Acme
Dodsonville
Russell
Red
Cold Springs
Meers
L. Lawtonka
Elgin
Sterling
Rush Springs
HARMON
East Duke
Martha
Medicine Park
FORT SILL MIL. RES.
Gould
Duke
Mountain Park
Fort Sill
Cox City
Hollis
McQueen
Altus
Headrick
COMANCHE
Prairie
Dog
Town
Louis
JACKSON
Snyder
Cache
Marlow
Bray
Indiahoma
Fork
Olustee
Humphreys
LAWTON
Wildhorse
Manitou
Geronimo
Duncan
Cla
Eldorado
Elmer
Tipton
Hess
Faxon
Beaver
STEPHEN
Childress
Frederick
Chattanooga
Empire City
Santa Fe
Ve
Cache
Odell
Walters
North
Acme
TILLMAN
Pease
Quanah
Hollister
COTTON
Comanche
Loveland
Loco
R.
Chillicothe
Temple
Addington
Mud
Davidson
Cr.
Grandfield
Hastings
Devol
Waurika
Ring
Pease
R.
Vernon
Red
River
Randlett
JEFFERSO
Burkburnett
Sugden
Matador
Electra
Byers
R.
Ryan
Grady
Crowell
Oscar
Beaver
Cr.
Iowa Park
Wichita
Terral
Fleetwo
Wichita Falls
103°
30′
102°
30′
101°
30′
100
37°
COLORADO
Elkhart
KANSAS
Englewood
Black Mesa 4,978
Regnier
NEW MEXICO
Tyrone
Forgan
Mocane
Knowles
Kenton
Cimarron
River
Pony
Cr.
Hooker
Baker
Turpin
Canadian
Gate
Rosston
Gulf
Beaver
River
Keyes
Cr.
North
Mexhoma
Wheeless
Boise City
Eva
TEXAS
Optima
Adams
Laver
CIMARRON
BEAVER
Guymon
Boyd
Clear Lake
Hardesty
Cr.
North
Canadian
Elmwood
Felt
Griggs
River
Goodwell
Balko
Logan
Kiowa
Texhoma
Gray
Kerrick
Hitchland
TEXAS
103°
30′
102°
30′
101°
30′
100
A
30′
B
100°
C
30′
D
99°
E
30′
F
Longitude 98° West of
G
Gre

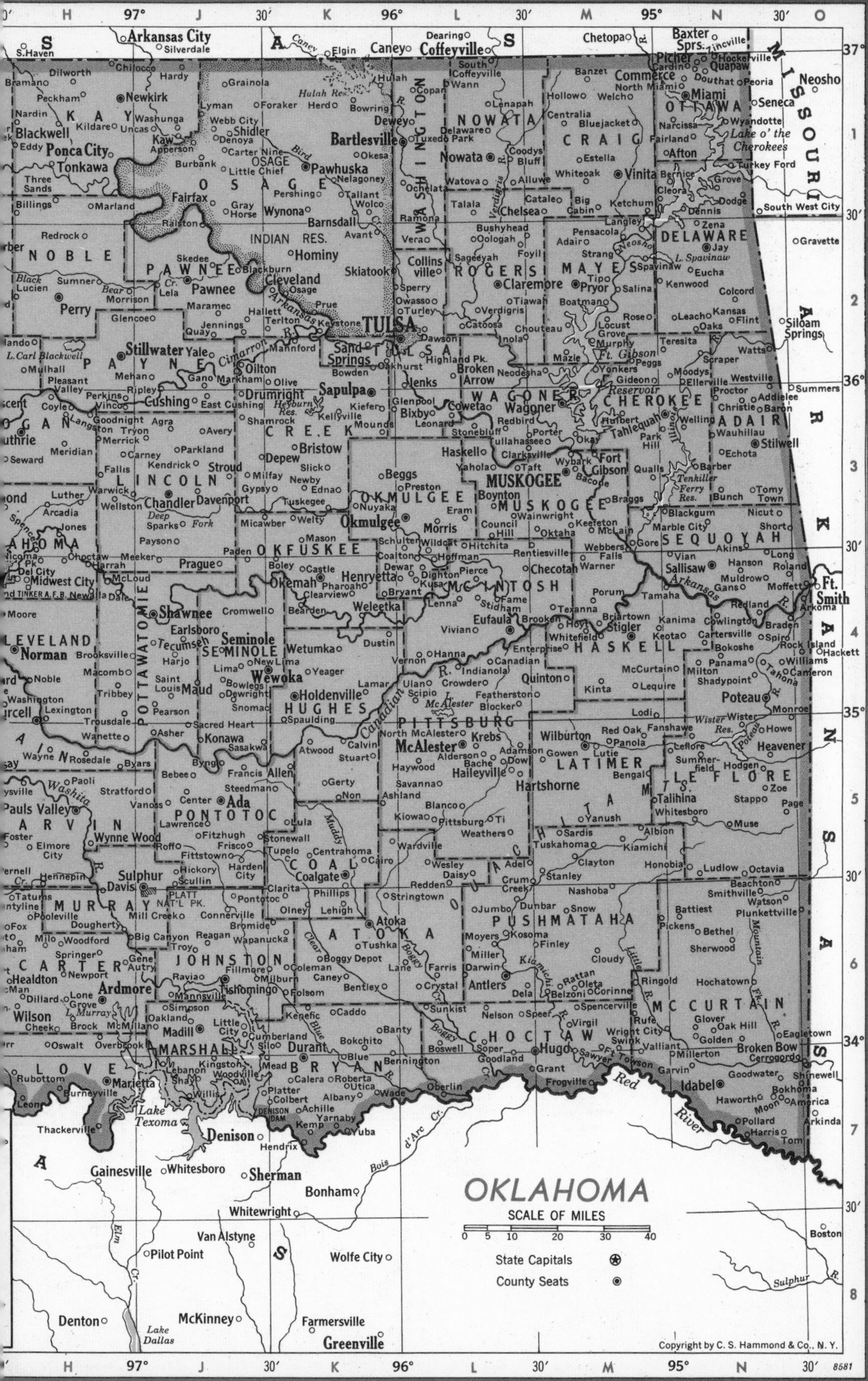

OKLAHOMA

SCALE OF MILES

0 5 10 20 30 40

State Capitals

County Seats

8581

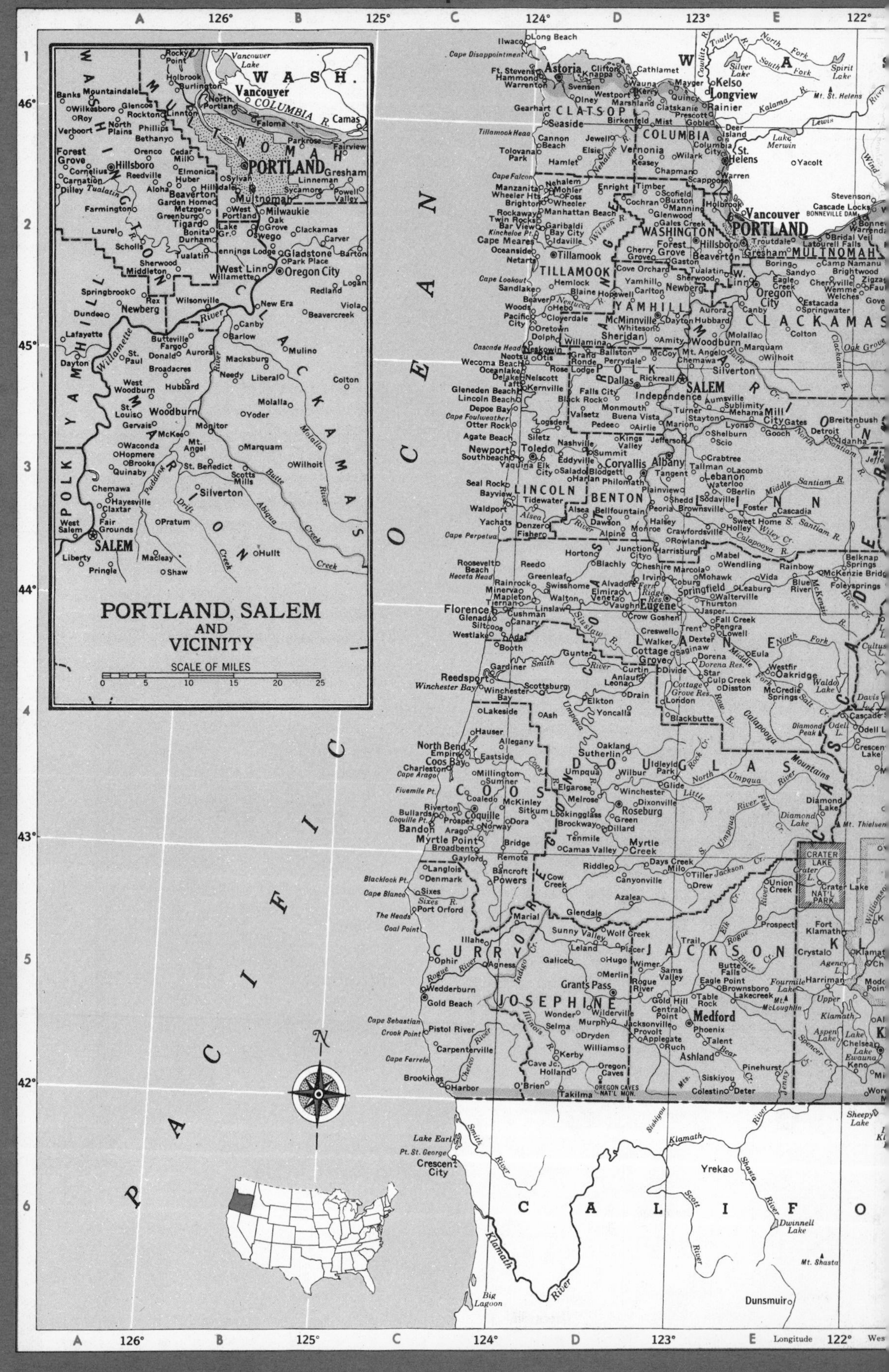

A
126°
B
125°
C
124°
D
123°
E
122°
1
46°
2
45°
3
44°
4
43°
5
42°
6
Longitude
West
PORTLAND, SALEM
AND
VICINITY
SCALE OF MILES
0
5
10
15
20
25
WASH.
Vancouver
Vancouver Lake
COLUMBIA R.
Camas
MULTNOMAH
PORTLAND
Gresham
Hillsboro
Forest Grove
Beaverton
Tigard
Milwaukie
Oswego
Lake Gr.
Gladstone
Oregon City
West Linn
Willamette
Tualatin
Sherwood
Newberg
Wilsonville
New Era
Canby
Barlow
Aurora
Donald
Butteville
St. Paul
Woodburn
Hubbard
Molalla
Mulino
Yoder
Marquam
Monitor
Mt. Angel
St. Benedict
Scotts Mills
Silverton
Gervais
St. Louis
Chemawa
Hayesville
Claxtar
Fair Grounds
West Salem
SALEM
Liberty
Pringle
Macleay
Shaw
Pratum
Hullt
Wilhoit
Colton
Liberal
Needy
Macksburg
Dayton
Lafayette
Dundee
Springbrook
Rex
Middleton
Scholls
Laurel
Farmington
Banks
Mountaindale
Wilkesboro
Glencoe
Rockton
Roy
North Plains
Verboort
Phillips
Bethany
Cornelius
Carnation
Dilley
Reedville
Aloha
Elmonica
Huber
Orenco
Cedar Mill
Garden Home
Metzger
Greenburg
Bonita
Durham
Clackamas
Carver
Barton
Park Place
Redland
Logan
Viola
Beavercreek
YAMHILL
POLK
MARION
CLACKAMAS
WASHINGTON
P A C I F I C   O C E A N
WASHINGTON
Long Beach
Ilwaco
Cape Disappointment
Astoria
Ft. Stevens
Hammond
Warrenton
Cathlamet
Kelso
Longview
Rainier
Mt. St. Helens
Gearhart
Seaside
CLATSOP
COLUMBIA
Cannon Beach
Tolovana Park
Vernonia
St. Helens
Scappoose
Yacolt
Vancouver
PORTLAND
Tillamook Head
Cape Falcon
Manzanita
Nehalem
Wheeler
Rockaway
Garibaldi
Bay City
Cape Meares
Oceanside
Netarts
Tillamook
TILLAMOOK
Cape Lookout
Sandlake
Hebo
Cloverdale
Pacific City
Cascade Head
Neskowin
Otis
Wecoma Beach
Oceanlake
Delake
Nelscott
Taft
Kernville
Gleneden Beach
Lincoln Beach
Depoe Bay
Cape Foulweather
Otter Rock
Agate Beach
Newport
Toledo
Siletz
LINCOLN
Seal Rock
Waldport
Yachats
Cape Perpetua
YAMHILL
McMinnville
Sheridan
Willamina
Grand Ronde
POLK
Dallas
Independence
Monmouth
Falls City
SALEM
Silverton
Woodburn
MARION
CLACKAMAS
Oregon City
Canby
Molalla
Stayton
Mill City
Detroit
Albany
Corvallis
BENTON
Philomath
Lebanon
Sweet Home
Brownsville
Harrisburg
Junction City
Eugene
Springfield
Cottage Grove
Creswell
Florence
Mapleton
Heceta Head
Oakridge
Westfir
Reedsport
Gardiner
Winchester Bay
Scottsburg
Drain
Yoncalla
Elkton
North Bend
Coos Bay
Empire
Charleston
Cape Arago
COOS
Coquille
Myrtle Point
Bandon
Roseburg
Sutherlin
Oakland
DOUGLAS
Glide
Winchester
Myrtle Creek
Riddle
Canyonville
Glendale
Port Orford
Cape Blanco
Powers
Gold Beach
Wedderburn
CURRY
Agness
Pistol River
Brookings
Harbor
Cape Sebastian
Cape Ferrelo
JOSEPHINE
Grants Pass
Cave Jct.
Kerby
O'Brien
Takilma
OREGON CAVES NAT'L MON.
JACKSON
Medford
Ashland
Jacksonville
Central Point
Eagle Point
Butte Falls
Rogue River
Gold Hill
Talent
Phoenix
Siskiyou
Colestin
CRATER LAKE NAT'L PARK
Crater Lake
Diamond Lake
Fort Klamath
Harriman
Klamath
Lake Earl
Pt. St. George
Crescent City
Smith River
Klamath River
Big Lagoon
Yreka
Scott River
Shasta River
Dwinnell Lake
Mt. Shasta
Dunsmuir
Sheepy Lake
C A L I F O

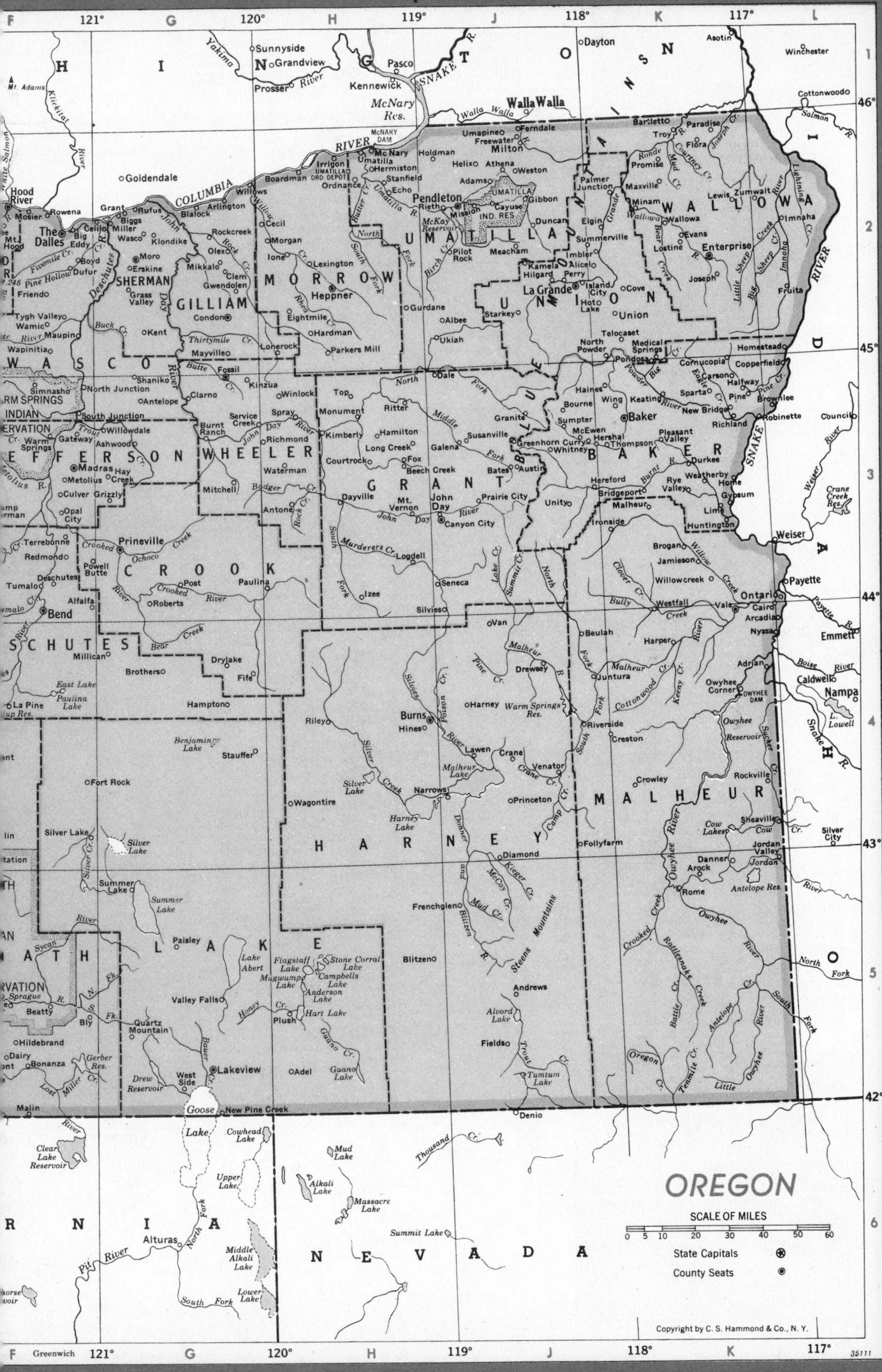

OREGON

SCALE OF MILES

0 5 10 20 30 40 50 60

State Capitals ⊛

County Seats ◉

35111

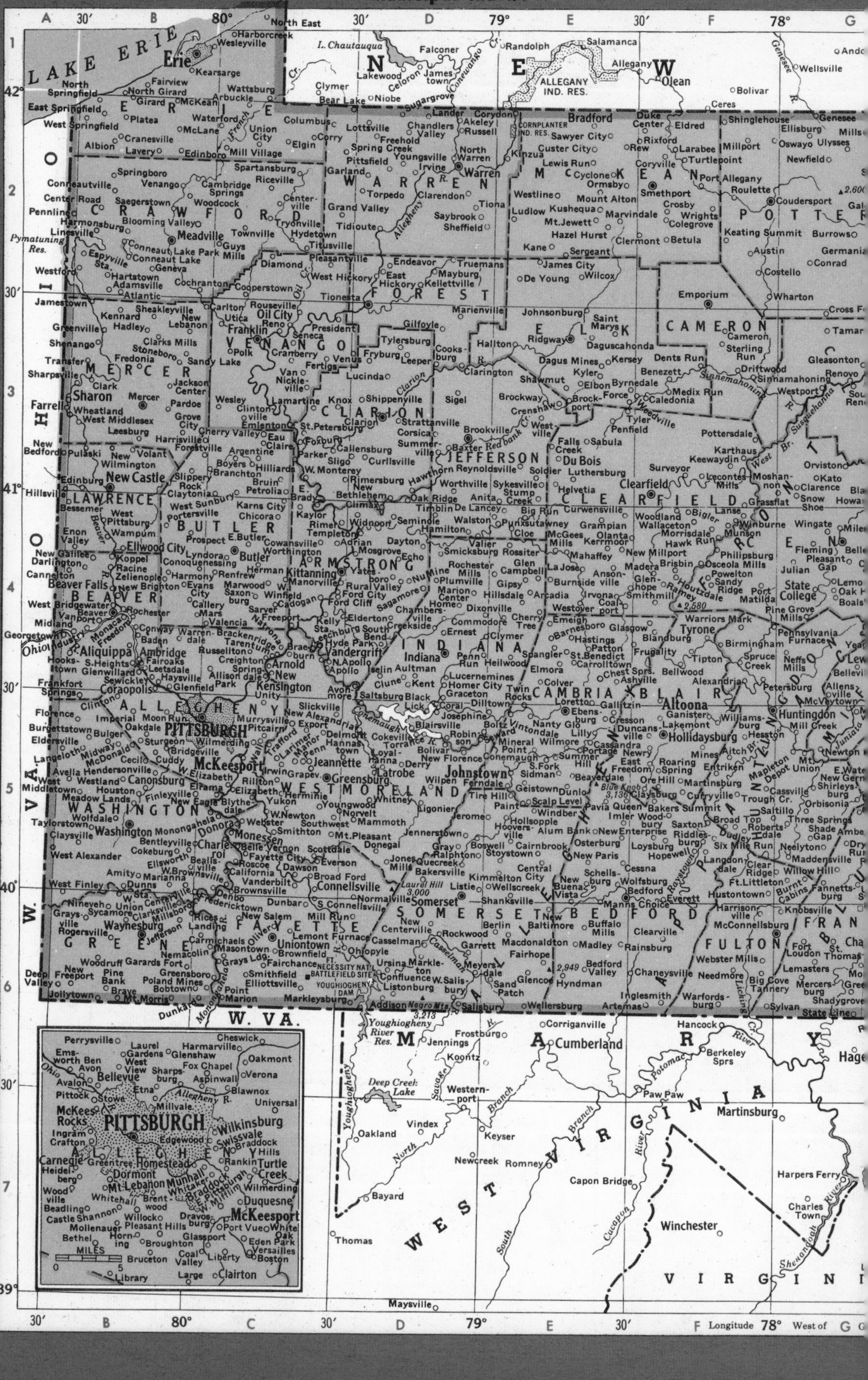

LAKE ERIE

NEW YORK

OHIO

W. VA.

MARYLAND

WEST VIRGINIA

VIRGINIA

ERIE · CRAWFORD · WARREN · MC KEAN · POTTER · FOREST · VENANGO · MERCER · CAMERON · ELK · CLARION · JEFFERSON · CLEARFIELD · LAWRENCE · BUTLER · ARMSTRONG · BEAVER · INDIANA · CAMBRIA · BLAIR · ALLEGHENY · WESTMORELAND · WASHINGTON · HUNTINGDON · FAYETTE · SOMERSET · BEDFORD · FULTON · GREENE

Erie · Meadville · Warren · Smethport · Coudersport · Oil City · Franklin · Sharon · New Castle · Butler · Kittanning · Clarion · Brookville · Du Bois · Clearfield · Indiana · Johnstown · Altoona · Hollidaysburg · Huntingdon · Pittsburgh · McKeesport · Greensburg · Washington · Uniontown · Connellsville · Somerset · Bedford · Waynesburg · Cumberland · Martinsburg · Winchester

PITTSBURGH

MILES

0 5

Longitude 78° West of G

PENNSYLVANIA

SCALE OF MILES

0 5 10 20 30 40

State Capitals

County Seats

Canals

55111

SOUTH CAROLINA

SCALE OF MILES

0 5 10 20 30 40

State Capitals

County Seats

Canals

Longitude West of

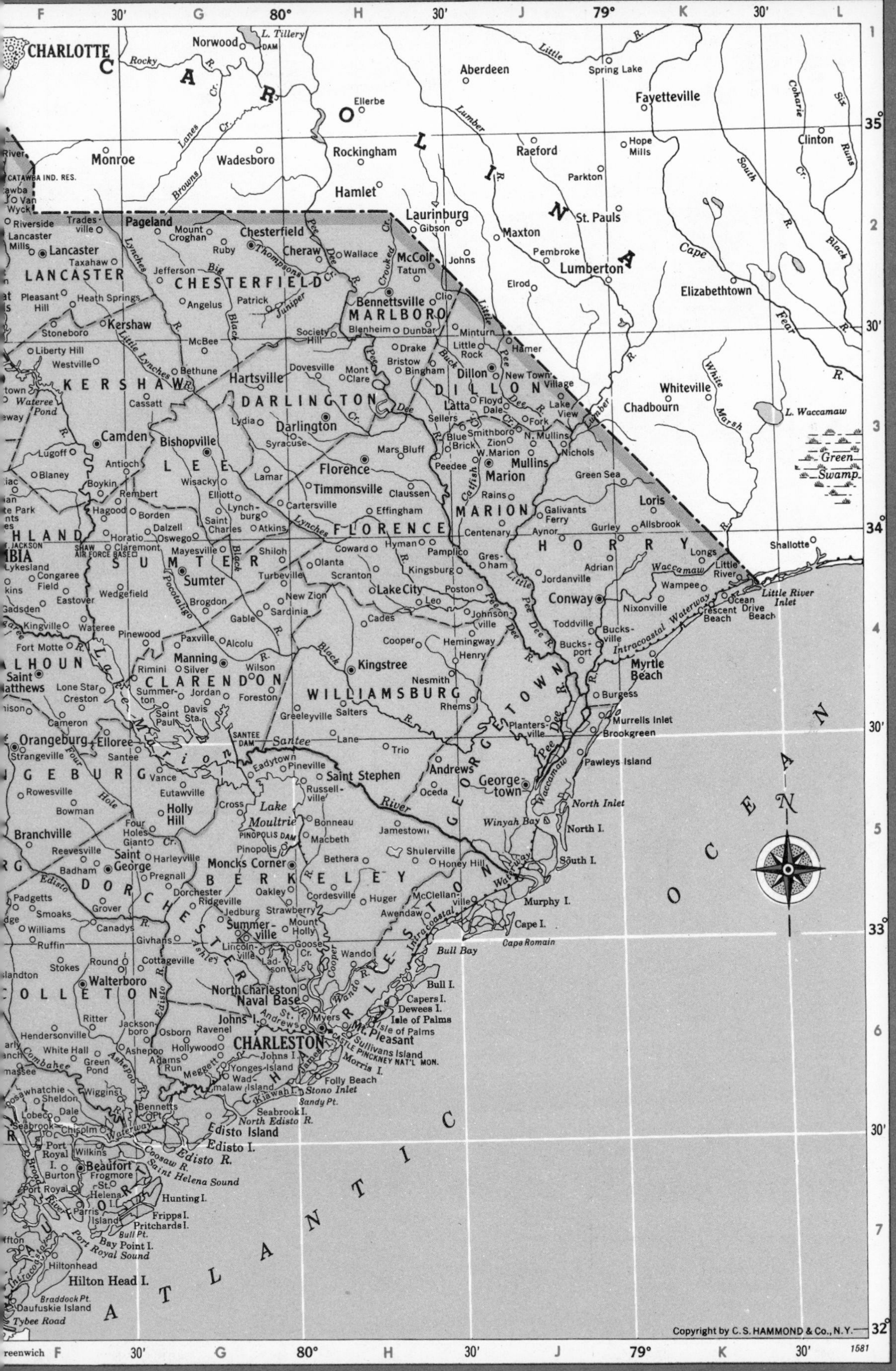

F 30′ G 80° H 30′ J 79° K 30′ L

NORTH CAROLINA

Charlotte, Norwood, L. Tillery Dam, Aberdeen, Spring Lake, Fayetteville, Ellerbe, Monroe, Wadesboro, Rockingham, Raeford, Hope Mills, Clinton, Parkton, Hamlet, Catawba Ind. Res., Laurinburg, Gibson, St. Pauls, Maxton, Pembroke, Lumberton, Elrod, Elizabethtown, Johns, Whiteville, Chadbourn, L. Waccamaw, Green Swamp, Shallotte

Rocky R., Lanes Cr., Browns Cr., Little R., Lumber R., South R., Coharie Cr., Six Runs, Black R., Cape Fear R., White Marsh

SOUTH CAROLINA

LANCASTER, CHESTERFIELD, MARLBORO, KERSHAW, DARLINGTON, DILLON, LEE, FLORENCE, MARION, HORRY, SUMTER, CLARENDON, WILLIAMSBURG, GEORGETOWN, CALHOUN, ORANGEBURG, BERKELEY, DORCHESTER, COLLETON, CHARLESTON, BEAUFORT

Riverside, Lancaster Mills, Lancaster, Trades-ville, Pageland, Mount Croghan, Chesterfield, Ruby, Cheraw, Wallace, McColl, Tatum, Taxahaw, Jefferson, Pleasant Hill, Heath Springs, Angelus, Patrick, Bennettsville, Clio, Kershaw, Stoneboro, McBee, Society Hill, Blenheim, Dunbar, Minturn, Hamer, Liberty Hill, Westville, Bethune, Drake, Little Rock, Bristow, Bingham, Dovesville, Mont Clare, Dillon, New Town, Lake View, Hartsville, Cassatt, Wateree Pond, Latta, Floyd Dale, Fork, Sellers, Lydia, Darlington, Syracuse, Camden, Bishopville, Mars Bluff, Blue Brick, Smithboro, Zion, N. Mullins, Nichols, Lugoff, W. Marion, Mullins, Antioch, Florence, Peedee, Marion, Blaney, Boykin, Lamar, Wisacky, Timmonsville, Claussen, Green Sea, Loris, Rembert, Elliott, Rains, Cartersville, Galivants Ferry, Hagood, Borden, Lynchburg, Effingham, Saint Charles, Atkins, Allsbrook, Dalzell, Horatio, Oswego, Centenary, Aynor, Gurley, Claremont, Shaw Air Force Base, Mayesville, Shiloh, Coward, Hyman, Pamplico, Longs, Gresham, Adrian, Little River, Lykesland, Olanta, Kingsburg, Jordanville, Waccamaw, Congaree Field, Sumter, Turbeville, Scranton, Wampee, Eastover, Wedgefield, Brogdon, New Zion, Lake City, Leo, Poston, Conway, Nixonville, Ocean Drive Beach, Little River Inlet, Gadsden, Kingville, Sardinia, Johnson-ville, Crescent Beach, Gable, Wateree, Pinewood, Cades, Toddville, Bucksville, Fort Motte, Paxville, Alcolu, Cooper, Hemingway, Bucksport, Manning, Silver, Henry, Myrtle Beach, Saint Matthews, Rimini, Wilson, Kingstree, Nesmith, Lone Star, Creston, Summerton, Jordan, Foreston, Rhems, Burgess, Saint Paul, Davis Sta., Greeleyville, Salters, Murrells Inlet, Cameron, Planters-ville, Brookgreen, Orangeburg, Elloree, Santee Dam, Lane, Trio, Strangeville, Santee, Eadytown, Pineville, Pawleys Island, Vance, Saint Stephen, Andrews, Rowesville, Eutawville, Russellville, Georgetown, Oceda, Bowman, Holly Hill, Cross, Lake Moultrie, North Inlet, Branchville, Four Holes, Giant, Bonneau, Jamestown, Winyah Bay, North I., Reevesville, Pinopolis Dam, Macbeth, Shulerville, Pinopolis, Bethera, Honey Hill, South I., Badham, Saint George, Harleyville, Moncks Corner, Pregnall, Padgetts, Dorchester, Oakley, Cordesville, Huger, McClellanville, Murphy I., Ridgeville, Smoaks, Grover, Jedburg, Strawberry, Awendaw, Cape I., Williams, Canadys, Summerville, Mount Holly, Ruffin, Givhans, Lincolnville, Goose Cr., Wando, Cape Romain, Bull Bay, Stokes, Round, Cottageville, Ladson, Walterboro, Bull I., North Charleston, Naval Base, Capers I., Dewees I., Ritter, Jacksonboro, Johns I., Myers, Isle of Palms, Hendersonville, Ravenel, Osborn, Charleston, Mt. Pleasant, White Hall, Green Pond, Ashepoo, Hollywood, Sullivans Island, Castle Pinckney Nat'l. Mon., Adams Run, Meggett, Yonges Island, Morris I., Wadmalaw Island, Folly Beach, Stono Inlet, Sandy Pt., Wiggins, Sheldon, Dale, Bennetts Pt., Kiawah I., Seabrook I., North Edisto R., Lobeco, Seabrook, Chisolm, Edisto Island, Edisto I., Port Royal I., Wilkins, Burton, Beaufort, Frogmore, Saint Helena Sound, Port Royal, St. Helena I., Hunting I., Parris Island, Fripps I., Pritchards I., Bull Pt., Bay Point I., Port Royal Sound, Hiltonhead, Hilton Head I., Braddock Pt., Daufuskie Island, Tybee Road

Lynches R., Little Lynches R., Big Black Cr., Thompsons Cr., Juniper Cr., Crooked Cr., Pee Dee R., Little Pee Dee R., Buck Cr., Catfish Cr., Black R., Pocotaligo R., Wateree R., Congaree R., Santee R., Lake Marion, Four Hole Sw., Edisto R., Ashley R., Cooper R., Wando R., Stono R., Combahee R., Ashepoo R., Coosaw R., Broad R., Intracoastal Waterway, Waccamaw R.

ATLANTIC OCEAN

N

1 2 3 4 5 6 7 — 35° 30′ 34° 30′ 33° 30′ 32°

Greenwich F 30′ G 80° H 30′ J 79° K 30′

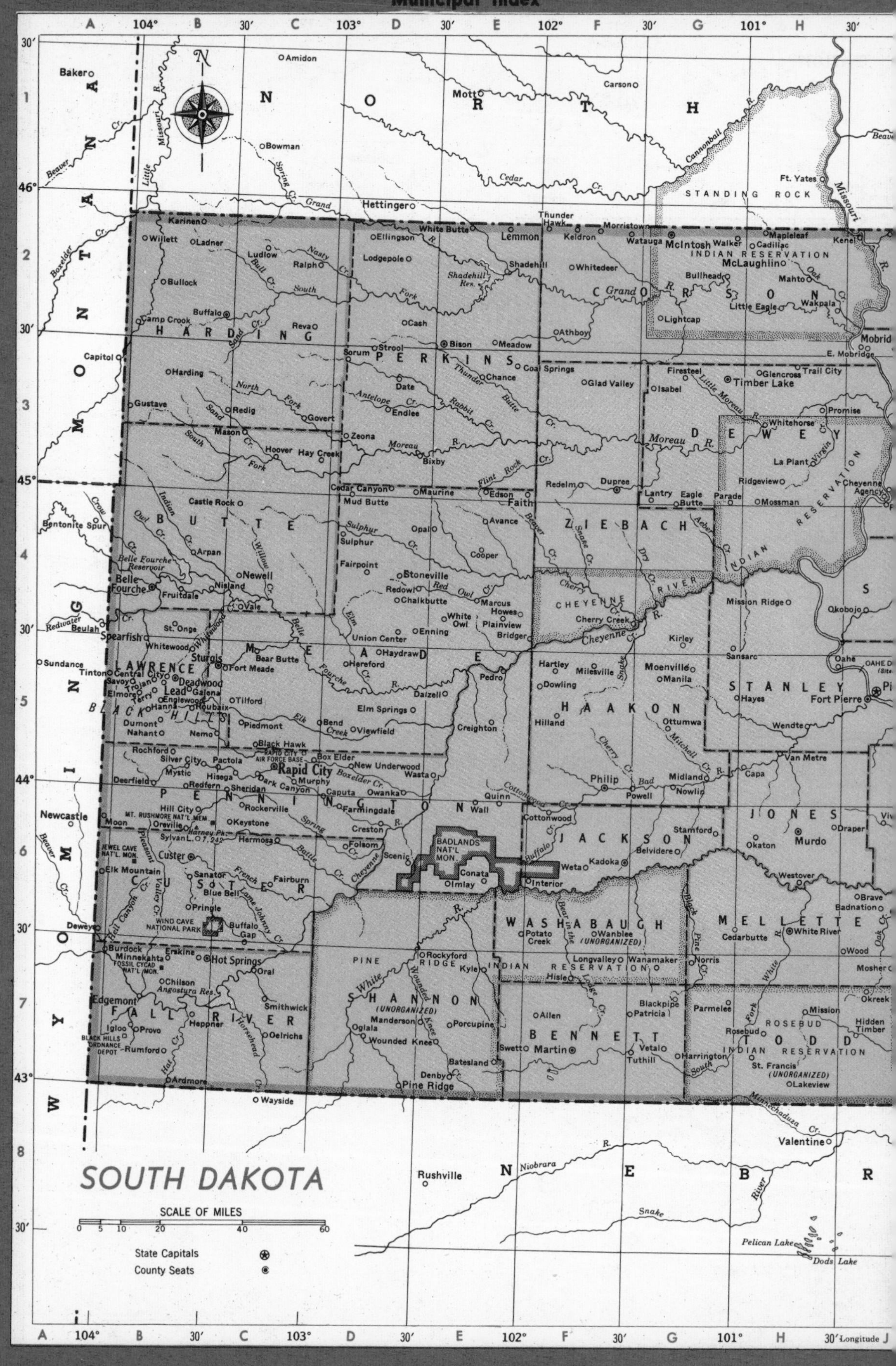
SOUTH DAKOTA
SCALE OF MILES
0 5 10 20 40 60
State Capitals
County Seats
NORTH DAKOTA
MONTANA
WYOMING
NEBRASKA
HARDING
PERKINS
CORSON
BUTTE
ZIEBACH
DEWEY
MEADE
LAWRENCE
PENNINGTON
CUSTER
FALL RIVER
SHANNON
(UNORGANIZED)
WASHABAUGH
(UNORGANIZED)
BENNETT
JACKSON
HAAKON
STANLEY
JONES
MELLETTE
TODD
(UNORGANIZED)
STANDING ROCK
INDIAN RESERVATION
CHEYENNE RIVER
INDIAN RESERVATION
PINE RIDGE
INDIAN RESERVATION
ROSEBUD
INDIAN RESERVATION
BADLANDS NAT'L MON.
WIND CAVE NATIONAL PARK
JEWEL CAVE NAT'L. MON.
FOSSIL CYCAD NAT'L MON.
MT. RUSHMORE NAT'L MEM.
BLACK HILLS ORDNANCE DEPOT
RAPID CITY AIR FORCE BASE
BLACK HILLS
Harney Pk. 7,242
Amidon
Baker
Bowman
Mott
Carson
Hettinger
Ft. Yates
Karinen
Willett
Ladner
Ludlow
Ralph
Bullock
Buffalo
Camp Crook
Reva
Capitol
Harding
Gustave
Redig
Govert
Mason
Hoover
Hay Creek
Ellingson
White Butte
Lemmon
Thunder Hawk
Morristown
Keldron
Watauga
McIntosh
Walker
Mapleleaf
Cadillac
Kenel
McLaughlin
Bullhead
Mahto
Little Eagle
Wakpala
Lightcap
Lodgepole
Shadehill
Whitedeer
Cash
Bison
Meadow
Athboy
Mobridge
E. Mobridge
Sorum
Strool
Chance
Coal Springs
Glad Valley
Firesteel
Isabel
Timber Lake
Glencross
Trail City
Date
Endlee
Promise
Whitehorse
Zeona
Bixby
La Plant
Ridgeview
Cheyenne Agency
Mossman
Parade
Eagle Butte
Lantry
Redelm
Dupree
Cedar Canyon
Maurine
Edson
Faith
Mud Butte
Castle Rock
Avance
Opal
Sulphur
Cooper
Fairpoint
Arpan
Newell
Belle Fourche
Nisland
Fruitdale
Vale
Stoneville
Redowl
Chalkbutte
Marcus
Howes
Plainview
White Owl
Enning
Bridger
Cherry Creek
Mission Ridge
Okobojo
Kirley
Sansarc
Oahe
Beulah
St. Onge
Spearfish
Whitewood
Sturgis
Fort Meade
Bear Butte
Union Center
Haydraw
Hereford
Sundance
Tinton
Central City
Savoy
Trojan
Deadwood
Lead
Galena
Elmore
Terry
Englewood
Roubaix
Hanna
Dumont
Nahant
Nemo
Tilford
Piedmont
Bend
Viewfield
Elm Springs
Dalzell
Pedro
Creighton
Hartley
Milesville
Dowling
Hilland
Moenville
Manila
Ottumwa
Hayes
Fort Pierre
Wendte
Rochford
Silver City
Pactola
Black Hawk
Box Elder
Rapid City
New Underwood
Wasta
Mystic
Hisega
Murphy
Deerfield
Redfern
Sheridan
Dark Canyon
Caputa
Owanka
Hill City
Rockerville
Farmingdale
Keystone
Quinn
Wall
Philip
Powell
Midland
Nowlin
Capa
Van Metre
Newcastle
Moon
Oreville
Sylvan L.
Hermosa
Creston
Folsom
Scenic
Cottonwood
Stamford
Belvidere
Okaton
Murdo
Draper
Custer
Elk Mountain
Sanator
Blue Bell
Fairburn
Conata
Imlay
Interior
Weta
Kadoka
Westover
Brave
Badnation
Pringle
Buffalo Gap
Dewey
Potato Creek
Wanblee
Cedarbutte
White River
Wood
Burdock
Minnekahta
Erskine
Hot Springs
Oral
Rockyford
Kyle
Longvalley
Wanamaker
Norris
Hisle
Mosher
Chilson
Angostura Res.
Edgemont
Smithwick
Heppner
Igloo
Provo
Rumford
Oelrichs
Manderson
Oglala
Wounded Knee
Porcupine
Allen
Batesland
Swett
Martin
Blackpipe
Patricia
Parmelee
Mission
Okreek
Hidden Timber
Rosebud
Vetal
Tuthill
Harrington
St. Francis
Lakeview
Ardmore
Denby
Pine Ridge
Wayside
Valentine
Rushville
Pelican Lake
Dods Lake
Missouri R.
Little Missouri R.
Grand R.
Moreau R.
Cheyenne R.
White R.
Bad R.
Belle Fourche R.
Cannonball R.
Cedar Cr.
Niobrara R.
Snake
Minnechaduza Cr.
Shadehill Res.
Belle Fourche Reservoir
Longitude
104° 30' 103° 30' 102° 30' 101° 30'
46° 45° 44° 43°

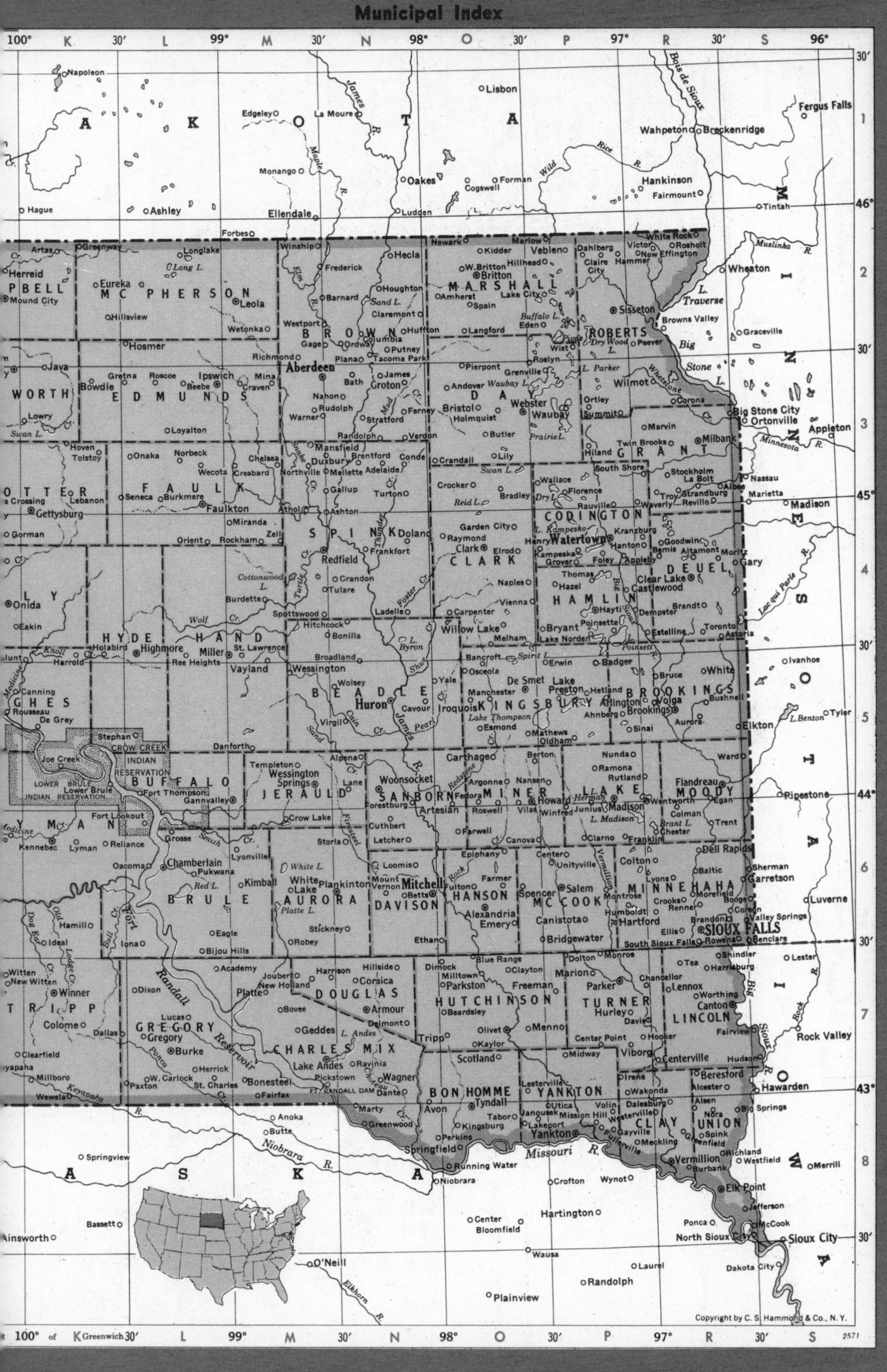

100°
K
30′
L
99°
M
30′
N
98°
O
30′
P
97°
R
30′
S
96°
Napoleon
Lisbon
Fergus Falls
Edgeley
La Moure
James R.
Bois de Sioux
A
K
O
T
A
Wahpeton
Breckenridge
Maple R.
Rice R.
Monango
Oakes
Cogswell
Forman
Wild
Hankinson
Fairmount
Hague
Ashley
Ellendale
Ludden
Tintah
46°
Forbes
Artas
Greenway
Longlake
Winship
Hecla
Newark
Kidder
Marlow
Veblen
Dahlberg
Victor
White Rock
Rosholt
New Effington
Muslinka R.
Herreid
Long L.
Frederick
W. Britton
Britton
Hillhead
Claire City
Hammer
Wheaton
PBELL
Eureka
MC PHERSON
Leola
Houghton
MARSHALL
Lake City
Mound City
Elm R.
Barnard
Amherst
Spain
L. Traverse
Sand L.
Sisseton
Hillsview
Claremont
Buffalo L.
Browns Valley
Wetonka
Westport
BROWN
Huffton
Langford
Eden
ROBERTS
Graceville
Hosmer
Gage
Ordway
Columbia
Putney
Piyas
Wist
Dry Wood L.
Peever
Big
Richmond
Tacoma Park
Roslyn
30′
Java
Aberdeen
Plana
Pierpont
Grenville
L. Parker
Whetstone
Stone
Gretna
Roscoe
Ipswich
Mina
James
Bath
Groton
Waubay L.
Wilmot
L.
WORTH
Bowdle
EDMUNDS
Beebe
Craven
Andover
DAY
Webster
Mud
Nahon
Bristol
Ortley
Corona
Lowry
Rudolph
Holmquist
Waubay
Summit
Big Stone City
Warner
Stratford
Ferney
Ortonville
Marvin
Appleton
Swan L.
Loyalton
Randolph
Verdon
Butler
Prairie L.
Twin Brooks
Milbank
Hoven
Mansfield
Lily
Hiland
GRANT
Minnesota R.
Tolstoy
Onaka
Norbeck
Chelsea
Duxbury
Brentford
Conde
Crandall
Snake
Wecota
Cresbard
Northville
Mellette
Adelaide
Swan L.
South Shore
Stockholm
OTTER
La Bolt
Albee
Nassau
Lebanon
FAULK
Gallup
Turton
Crocker
Wallace
Florence
Strandburg
45°
Crossing
Seneca
Burkmere
Faulkton
Reid L.
Bradley
Dry L.
Troy
Marietta
Gettysburg
Athol
Ashton
Rauville
Waverly
Revillo
Madison
Miranda
Garden City
CODINGTON
Gorman
Orient
Rockham
Zell
SPINK
Doland
Raymond
L. Kampeska
Henry
Watertown
Kranzburg
Goodwin
Frankfort
Clark
Hanton
Bemis
Altamont
Moritz
Redfield
Elrod
Kampeska
Gary
CLARK
Grover
Foley
Appleby
DEUEL
Cottonwood L.
Grandon
Thomas
Clear Lake
Naples
Hazel
Castlewood
Tulare
Big Sioux
Onida
Burdette
Vienna
HAMLIN
Lac qui Parle R.
Brandt
Ladelle
Foster Cr.
Carpenter
Hayti
Dempster
Eakin
Wolf Cr.
Spottswood
Bryant
Poinsette
Toronto
Hitchcock
Willow Lake
Estelline
Astoria
HYDE
HAND
Bonilla
L. Byron
Melham
Lake Norden
30′
Holabird
Highmore
Miller
St. Lawrence
Bancroft
Spirit L.
Erwin
Badger
Poinsett
Ivanhoe
Knoll
Harrold
Ree Heights
Broadland
Osceola
Bruce
White
Vayland
Wessington
Shue
De Smet
Lake Preston
Hetland
Yale
BROOKINGS
Canning
Wolsey
Manchester
Arlington
Volga
Bushnell
BEADLE
KINGSBURY
GHES
Huron
Cavour
Iroquois
Ahnberg
Brookings
Rousseau
De Grey
Virgil
Lake Thompson
Aurora
Elkton
L. Benton
Tyler
Cain
Esmond
Sinai
Sand
Cr.
James
Pearl
Stephan
CROW CREEK INDIAN RESERVATION
Mathews
Oldham
Danforth
Carthage
Berton
Nunda
Ward
Joe Creek
Alpena
Ramona
Templeton
Wessington Springs
LOWER BRULE INDIAN RESERVATION
Lower Brule
BUFFALO
Fort Thompson
JERAULD
Lane
Woonsocket
Redstone
Argonne
Nansen
Rutland
Flandreau
Pipestone
Gannvalley
SANBORN
MINER
LAKE
MOODY
44°
Forestburg
Fedora
Howard
Herman
Madison
Wentworth
Egan
Artesian
Roswell
Vilas
Winfred
Junius
L. Madison
Colman
Fort Lookout
Crow Lake
Firesteel
Brant L.
Trent
Medicine
Cuthbert
Farwell
Chester
Kennebec
Lyman
Reliance
Grosse
Smith Cr.
Storla
Letcher
Canova
Clarno
Franklin
Dell Rapids
Lyonville
Epiphany
Center
Oacoma
Chamberlain
Pukwana
White L.
Loomis
Unityville
Colton
Baltic
Sherman
Red L.
Kimball
White Lake
Plankinton
Mount Vernon
Mitchell
Rock
Farmer
Salem
Lyons
Garretson
BRULE
AURORA
Betts
Fulton
HANSON
Spencer
MC COOK
Montrose
MINNEHAHA
Morefield
Dog Ear Cr.
Old
DAVISON
Vermillion
Crooks
Renner
Booge
Luverne
Fort
Platte L.
Alexandria
Humboldt
Corson
Hamill
Emery
Canistota
Hartford
Brandon
Valley Springs
Bull Cr.
Stickney
Ellis
SIOUX FALLS
Ideal
Lodge Cr.
Eagle
Ethan
Bridgewater
Iona
Robey
South Sioux Falls
Rowena
Renclare
30′
Bijou Hills
Blue Range
Dolton
Monroe
Shindler
Lester
Academy
Harrison
Hillside
Dimock
Clayton
Tea
Witten
Joubert
Marion
Chancellor
Harrisburg
New Witten
Corsica
Milltown
Freeman
Parker
Lennox
Winner
Dixon
New Holland
Parkston
Worthing
Randall
Platte
DOUGLAS
HUTCHINSON
TURNER
Canton
TRIPP
Bovee
Armour
Beardsley
Hurley
LINCOLN
Rock
7
Colome
Lucas
Delmont
Davis
GREGORY
Geddes
L. Andes
Tripp
Olivet
Menno
Fairview
Rock Valley
Dallas
Gregory
Reservoir
Center Point
Hooker
Clearfield
Burke
CHARLES MIX
Kaylor
Midway
Viborg
Ponca
Scotland
Centerville
Hudson
Wayapaha
Herrick
Lake Andes
Ravinia
Beresford
Millboro
W. Carlock
Choteau
Wagner
Lesterville
Irene
Paxton
St. Charles
Bonesteel
Pickstown
Alcester
Hawarden
Keyapaha
FT. RANDALL DAM
Dante
BON HOMME
YANKTON
Wakonda
Wewela
Fairfax
Tyndall
Utica
Volin
Dalesburg
Big Springs
43°
Marty
Avon
Janousek
Mission Hill
Westerville
CLAY
UNION
Anoka
Greenwood
Tabor
Lakeport
Alsen
Kingsburg
Gayville
Nora
Butte
Perkins
Yankton
Fullerville
Meckling
Spink
Springview
Niobrara R.
Springfield
Missouri R.
Glenfield
Richland
Westfield
Vermillion
Burbank
Merrill
8
A
S
K
A
Running Water
Niobrara
Crofton
Wynot
Elk Point
Jefferson
Bassett
Center
Bloomfield
Hartington
Ponca
McCook
Ainsworth
North Sioux City
Sioux City
30′
Wausa
O'Neill
Laurel
Dakota City
Randolph
Elkhorn R.
Plainview
M
I
N
N
E
S
O
T
A
I
O
W
A
1
2
3
4
5
6
Copyright by C. S. Hammond & Co., N. Y.
100° of Greenwich
K
30′
L
99°
M
30′
N
98°
O
30′
P
97°
R
30′
S
2571

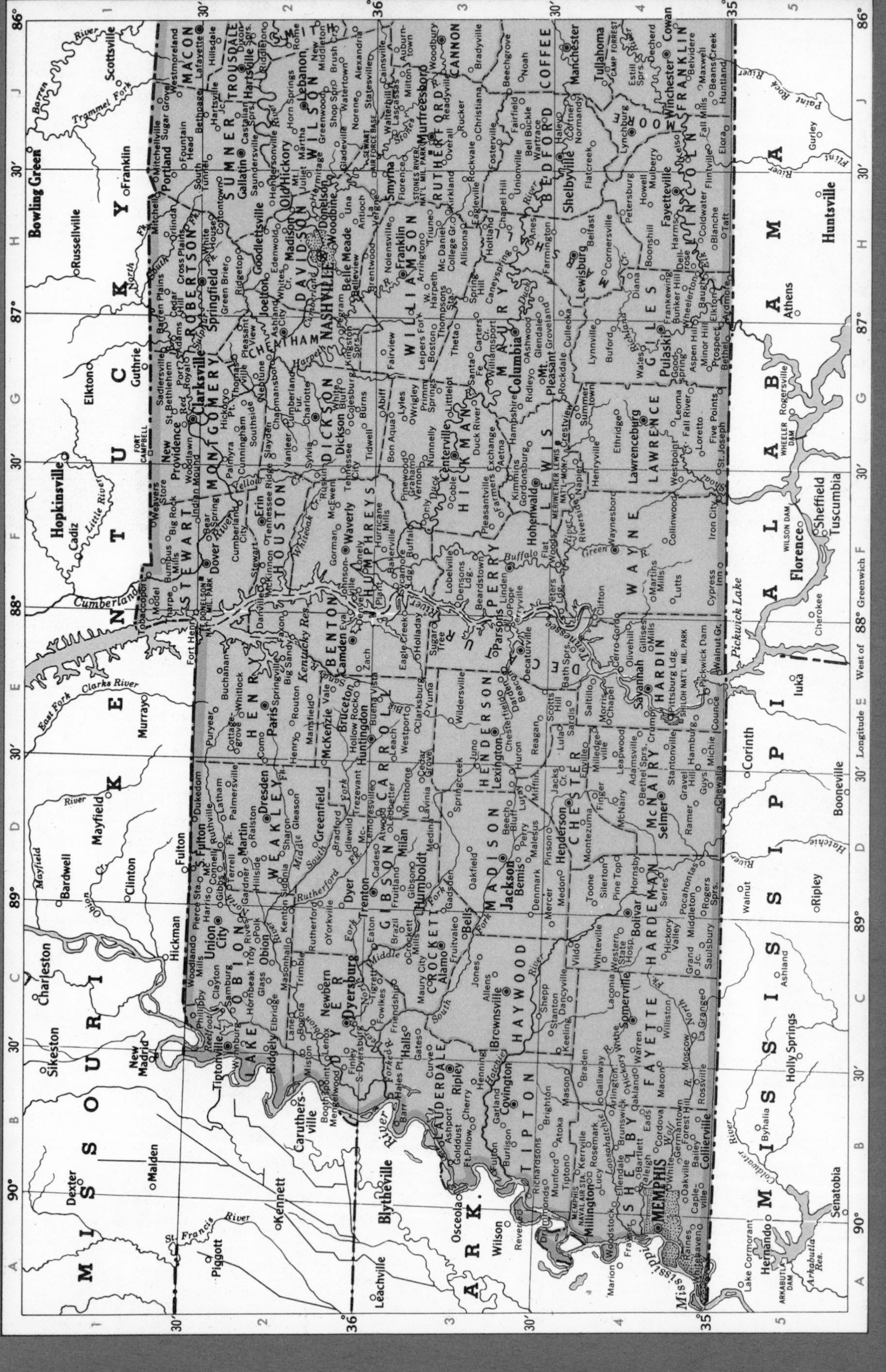
KENTUCKY
MISSOURI
ARK.
MISSISSIPPI
ALABAMA
LAKE
OBION
WEAKLEY
HENRY
STEWART
MONTGOMERY
ROBERTSON
SUMNER
MACON
TROUSDALE
SMITH
WILSON
DAVIDSON
CHEATHAM
DICKSON
HOUSTON
HUMPHREYS
BENTON
CARROLL
GIBSON
DYER
LAUDERDALE
CROCKETT
HAYWOOD
TIPTON
SHELBY
FAYETTE
HARDEMAN
MADISON
HENDERSON
CHESTER
McNAIRY
HARDIN
DECATUR
PERRY
HICKMAN
LEWIS
WAYNE
LAWRENCE
GILES
MAURY
WILLIAMSON
RUTHERFORD
CANNON
COFFEE
BEDFORD
MARSHALL
LINCOLN
FRANKLIN
MOORE
Memphis
Nashville
Jackson
Clarksville
Murfreesboro
Columbia
Dyersburg
Paris
Union City
Huntsville
Florence
Bowling Green
Hopkinsville
Blytheville
Kentucky Res.
Pickwick Lake
Mississippi
Cumberland
Tennessee
Longitude West of Greenwich

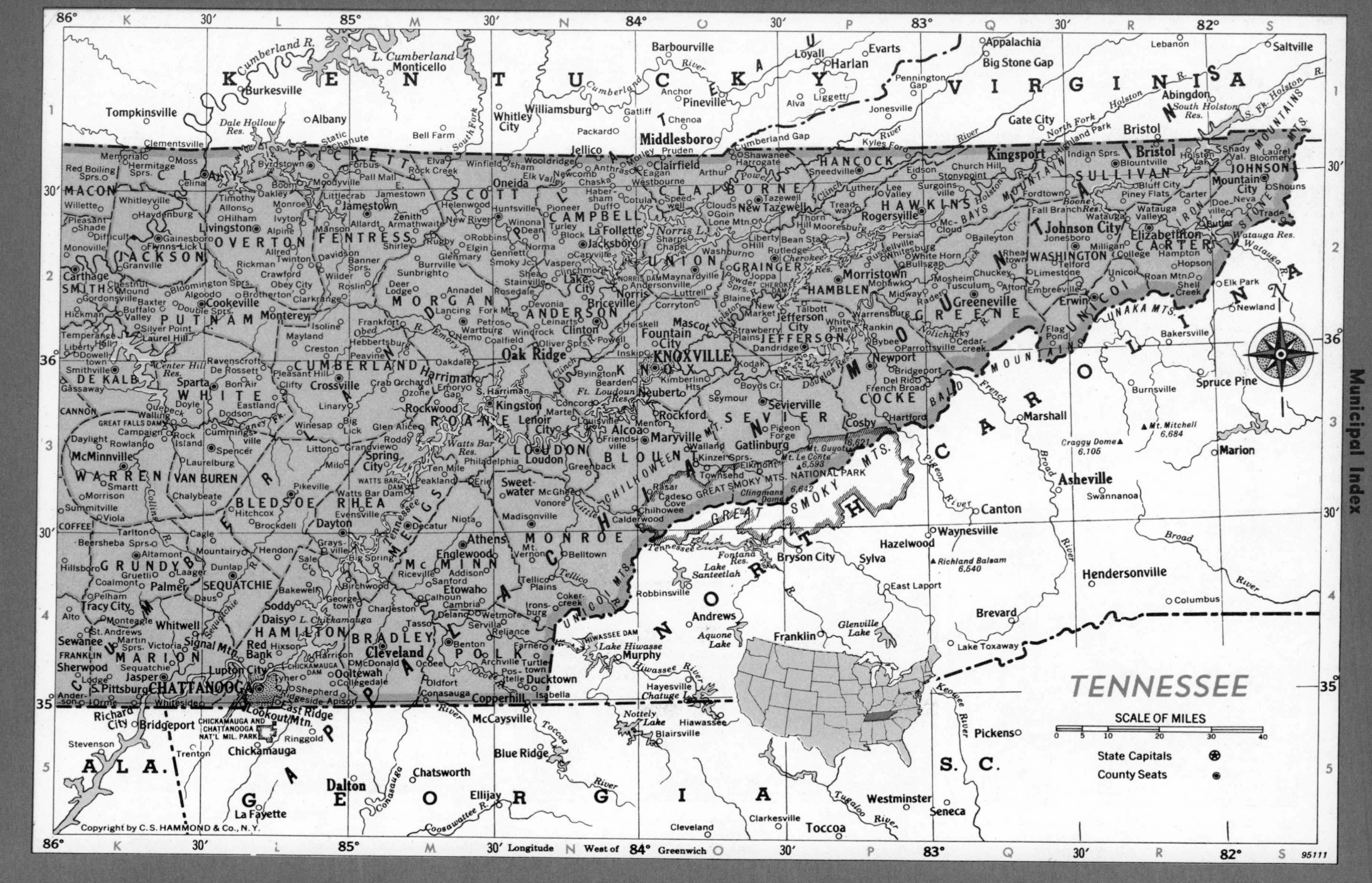
TENNESSEE
SCALE OF MILES
0 5 10 20 30 40
State Capitals
County Seats
KENTUCKY
VIRGINIA
NORTH CAROLINA
GEORGIA
ALA.
S.C.
GREAT SMOKY MTS. NATIONAL PARK
KNOXVILLE
CHATTANOOGA
Bristol
Kingsport
Johnson City
Elizabethton
Greeneville
Morristown
Oak Ridge
Maryville
Gatlinburg
Sevierville
Cleveland
Athens
Crossville
Cookeville
Asheville
Middlesboro
Longitude West of 84° Greenwich
Copyright by C.S. HAMMOND & Co., N.Y.
95111

Galveston Bay
Trinity Bay
HOUSTON
Pasadena
Baytown
Texas City
Galveston
BRAZORIA
GALVESTON
FORT BEND
CHAMBERS
FORT WORTH
DALLAS
TARRANT
ROCKWALL
KAUFMAN
COLLIN
JOHNSON
Amarillo
Lubbock
Wichita Falls
Abilene
San Angelo
Midland
Odessa
Big Spring
Waco
Tyler
Texarkana
Sherman
Denison
Lawton
Ardmore
Red

GULF OF MEXICO
TEXAS
SCALE OF MILES
0 20 40 60 80 100
State Capitals
County Seats
Copyright by C. S. HAMMOND & Co., N.Y.
MEXICO
WESTERN PART OF TEXAS
Same scale as main map
Longitude 98° West of Greenwich 97°

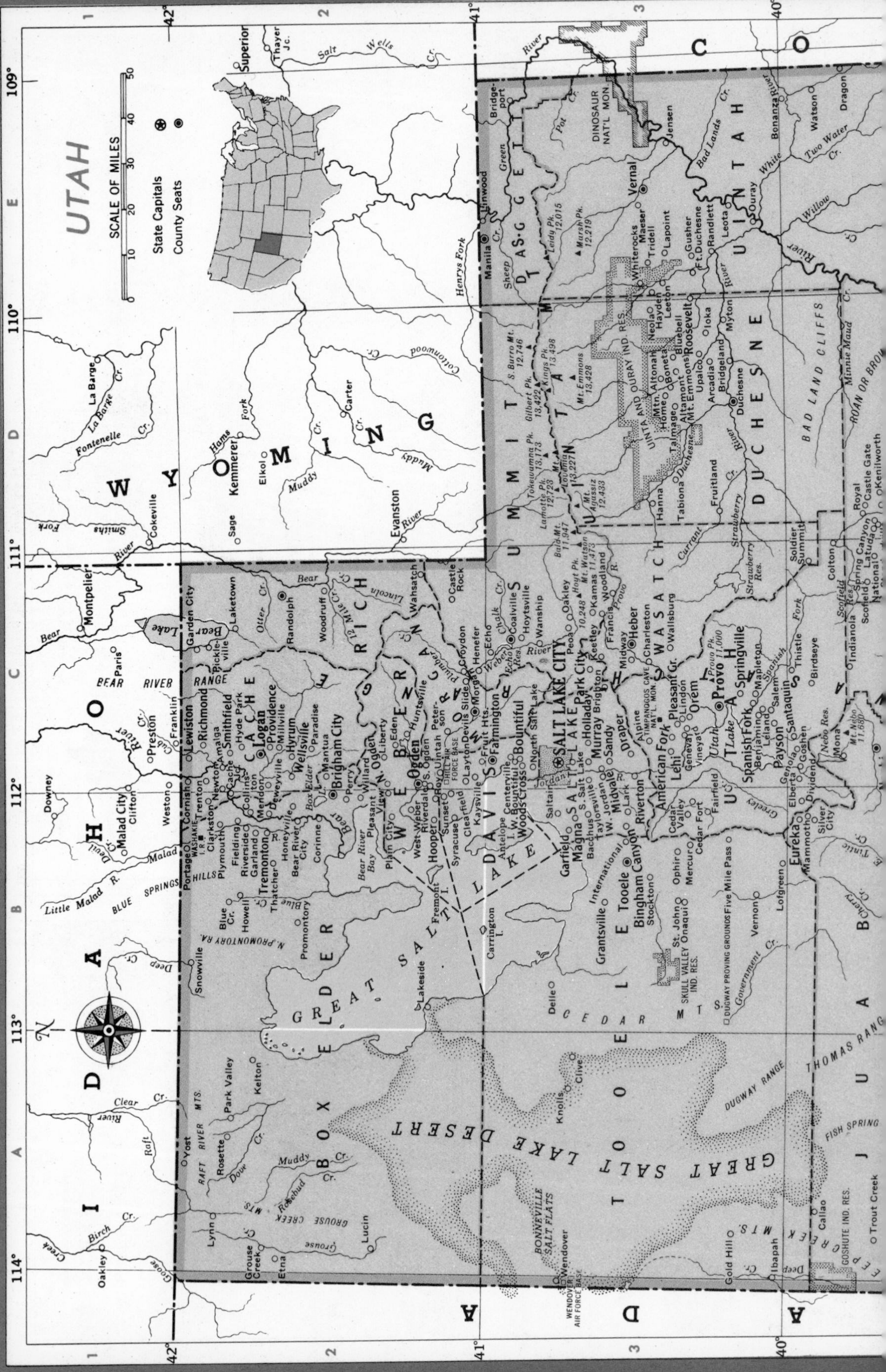

UTAH

SCALE OF MILES

0 10 20 30 40 50

State Capitals

County Seats

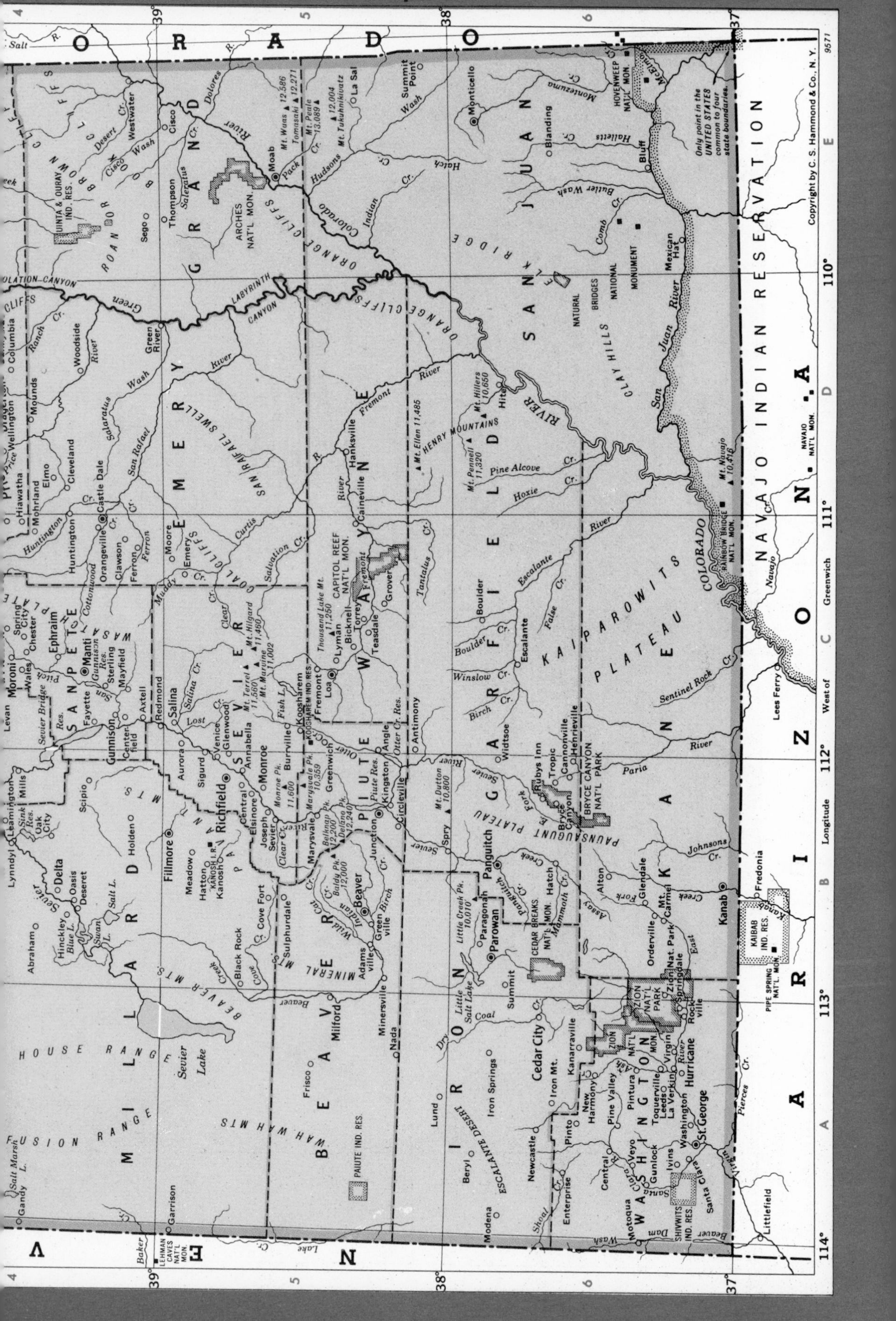

C O L O R A D O
A R I Z O N A
N E V A D A
M I L L A R D
J U A B
S A N P E T E
E M E R Y
G R A N D
S E V I E R
W A Y N E
P I U T E
B E A V E R
G A R F I E L D
S A N   J U A N
I R O N
K A N E
W A S H I N G T O N
N A V A J O   I N D I A N   R E S E R V A T I O N
Moab
Monticello
Blanding
Bluff
Mexican Hat
La Sal
Summit Point
Cisco
Westwater
Thompson
Sego
Green River
Woodside
Wellington
Price
Mounds
Columbia
Cleveland
Elmo
Hiawatha
Mohrland
Huntington
Castle Dale
Orangeville
Clawson
Ferron
Moore
Emery
Hanksville
Caineville
Fremont
Loa
Lyman
Bicknell
Torrey
Teasdale
Grover
Koosharem
Burrville
Antimony
Angle
Kingston
Circleville
Junction
Marysvale
Greenwich
Hite
Boulder
Escalante
Cannonville
Henrieville
Tropic
Rubys Inn
Widtsoe
Panguitch
Hatch
Spry
Alton
Glendale
Orderville
Mt. Carmel
Kanab
Fredonia
Lees Ferry
Moroni
Wales
Ephraim
Spring City
Chester
Manti
Sterling
Mayfield
Fayette
Gunnison
Centerfield
Axtell
Levan
Redmond
Salina
Aurora
Sigurd
Venice
Glenwood
Annabella
Central
Richfield
Monroe
Elsinore
Joseph
Sevier
Fillmore
Holden
Scipio
Mills
Leamington
Lynndyl
Oak City
Delta
Oasis
Deseret
Hinckley
Abraham
Meadow
Hatton
Kanosh
Cove Fort
Sulphurdale
Black Rock
Beaver
Greenville
Adamsville
Minersville
Milford
Frisco
Nada
Garrison
Gandy
Parowan
Paragonah
Summit
Cedar City
Kanarraville
Iron Mt.
Iron Springs
Lund
Beryl
Modena
Newcastle
Pinto
New Harmony
Pine Valley
Pintura
Toquerville
Leeds
La Verkin
Hurricane
Virgin
Rockville
Springdale
Zion
Central
Veyo
Gunlock
Motoqua
Enterprise
Ivins
Santa Clara
Washington
St. George
Littlefield
Mt. Waas 12,586
Tomasaki 12,271
Mt. Peale 13,089
12,004
Mt. Tukuhnikivatz
Mt. Ellen 11,485
Mt. Pennell 11,320
Mt. Hillers 10,650
Mt. Navajo 10,416
Thousand Lake Mt. 11,250
Mt. Terrel 11,560
Mt. Hilgard 11,460
Mt. Marvine 11,002
Monroe Pk. 11,600
Marysvale Pk. 10,359
Belknap Pk. 12,200
Delano Pk. 12,240
Baldy Pk. 12,000
Mt. Dutton 10,800
Little Creek Pk. 10,010
ARCHES NAT'L MON.
CAPITOL REEF NAT'L MON.
NATURAL BRIDGES NATIONAL MONUMENT
HOVENWEEP NAT'L MON.
RAINBOW BRIDGE NAT'L MON.
NAVAJO NAT'L MON.
BRYCE CANYON NAT'L PARK
CEDAR BREAKS NAT'L MON.
ZION NAT'L PARK
ZION NAT'L MON.
PIPE SPRING NAT'L MON.
LEHMAN CAVES NAT'L MON.
KAIBAB IND. RES.
SHIVWITS IND. RES.
PAIUTE IND. RES.
KOSHAREM IND. RES.
UINTA & OURAY IND. RES.
KAIPAROWITS PLATEAU
PAUNSAUGUNT PLATEAU
WASATCH PLATEAU
SAN RAFAEL SWELL
HENRY MOUNTAINS
ELK RIDGE
CLAY HILLS
ORANGE CLIFFS
BOOK CLIFFS
ROAN CLIFFS
BROWN CLIFFS
LABYRINTH CANYON
DESOLATION CANYON
MINERAL MT.
BEAVER MTS.
WAH WAH MTS.
HOUSE RANGE
CONFUSION RANGE
ESCALANTE DESERT
Sevier Lake
COLORADO RIVER
San Juan River
Green River
Dolores River
Fremont River
Escalante River
Paria River
Sevier River
Only point in the UNITED STATES common to four state boundaries.
Longitude West of Greenwich
Copyright by C. S. Hammond & Co., N. Y.
9571

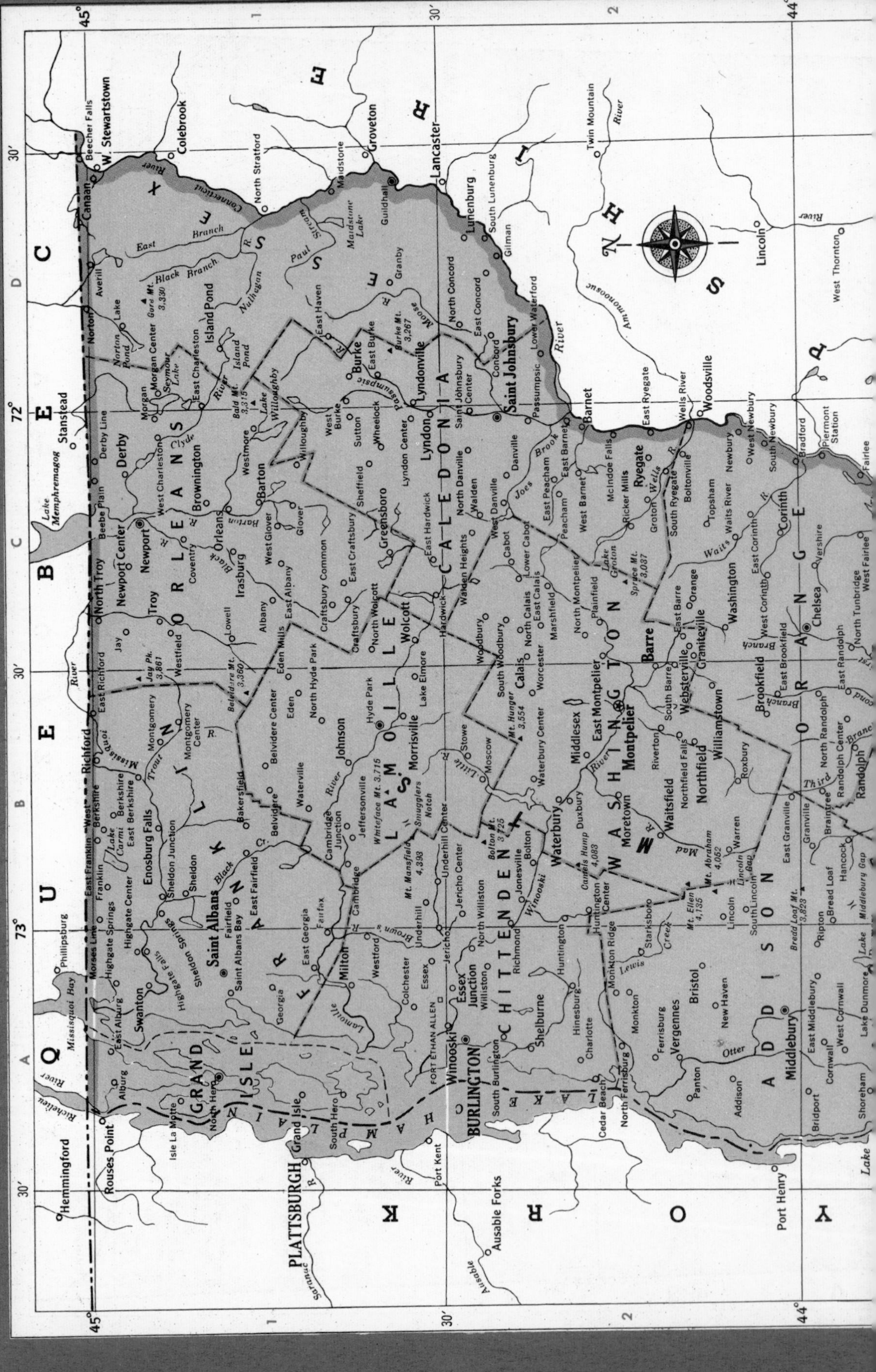
QUEBEC
NEW HAMPSHIRE
NEW YORK
ORLEANS
ESSEX
CALEDONIA
LAMOILLE
FRANKLIN
GRAND ISLE
CHITTENDEN
WASHINGTON
ORANGE
ADDISON
LAKE CHAMPLAIN
Lake Memphremagog
Missisquoi Bay
Connecticut River
Saint Albans
Burlington
Montpelier
Barre
Saint Johnsbury
Newport
Middlebury
Plattsburgh
Rouses Point
Swanton
Enosburg Falls
Richford
North Troy
Derby
Island Pond
Lyndonville
Lancaster
Woodsville
Morrisville
Stowe
Waterbury
Winooski
Essex Junction
Vergennes
Bristol
Northfield
Randolph
Bradford
Mt. Mansfield 4,393
Camels Hump 4,083
Jay Pk. 3,861
Whiteface Mt. 3,715
Mt. Ellen 4,135
Mt. Abraham 4,052
Bread Loaf Mt. 3,823
Burke Mt. 3,267
Bald Mt. 3,315
Gore Mt. 3,330
Spruce Mt. 3,037
Mt. Hunger 3,554
Bolton Mt. 3,725
Belvidere Mt. 3,360
45°
44°
73°
72°
30'

VERMONT

SCALE OF MILES

0 5 10 20

State Capitals

County Seats

Canals

6522

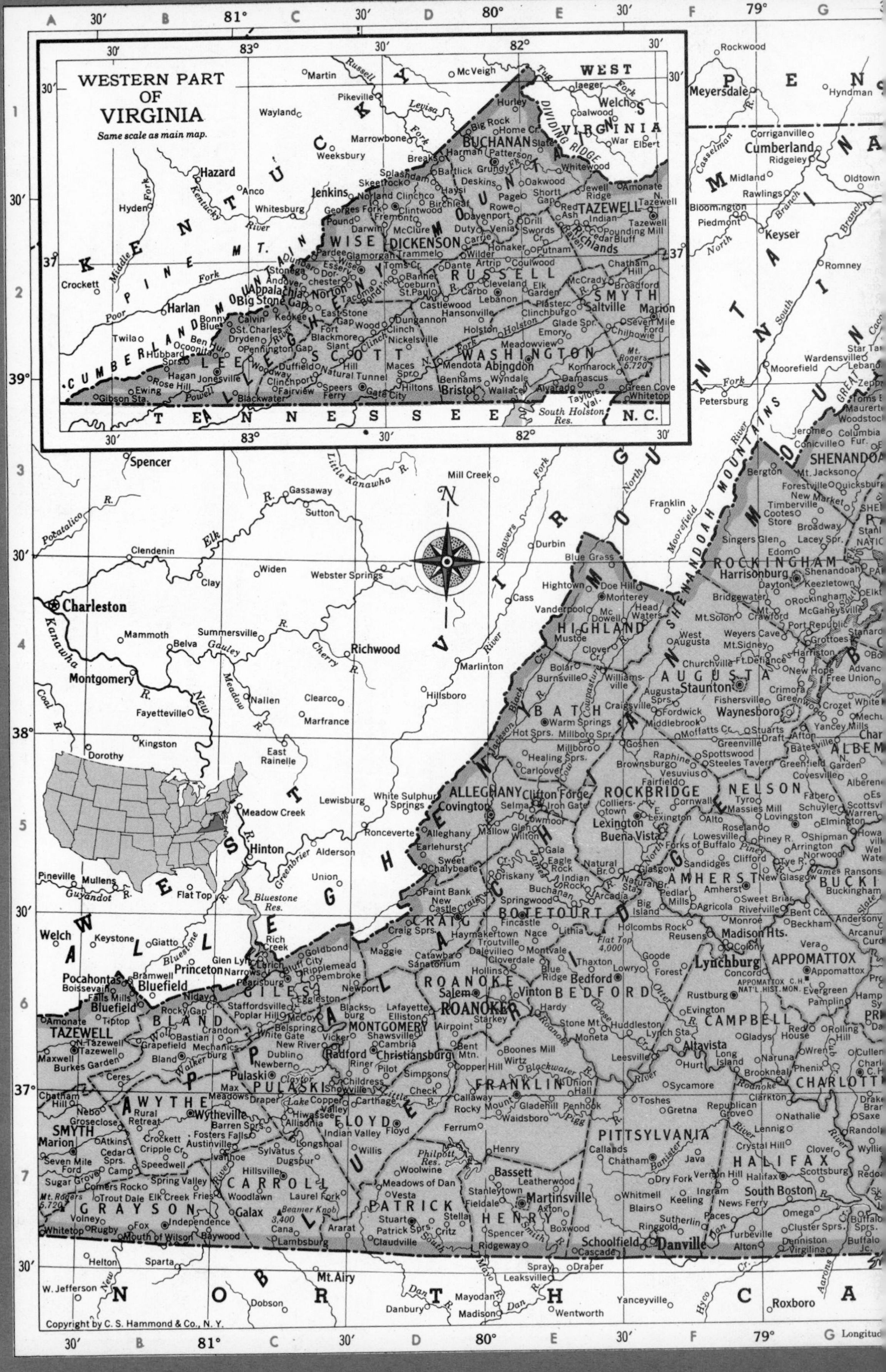

WESTERN PART OF VIRGINIA

Same scale as main map.

VIRGINIA

SCALE OF MILES

0 5 10 20 30 40

National Capital

State Capitals

County Seats

Canals

65124

WASHINGTON
SCALE OF MILES
0 5 10 20 30 40
State Capitals
County Seats
Copyright by C.S. HAMMOND & Co., N.Y.
SEATTLE
Seattle
Tacoma
Olympia
Spokane
Everett
Bellingham
Bremerton
Vancouver
PORTLAND
Aberdeen
Hoquiam
Port Angeles
Port Townsend
Victoria
Vancouver I.
Strait of Juan de Fuca
PACIFIC OCEAN
CLALLAM
JEFFERSON
GRAYS HARBOR
MASON
THURSTON
PACIFIC
WAHKIAKUM
COWLITZ
LEWIS
PIERCE
KING
SNOHOMISH
SKAGIT
WHATCOM
SAN JUAN
ISLAND
KITSAP
CLARK
SKAMANIA
OLYMPIC NATIONAL PARK
MT. RAINIER NAT'L. PK.
Mt. Rainier 14,408
Mt. St. Helens 9,677
Mt. Adams 12,307
Mt. Baker 10,750
Mt. Olympus 7,954
COAST RANGE
CASCADE RANGE
Columbia R.
BRITISH COLUMBIA
OREGON
Longitude
124° 123° 122° 121°
49° 48° 47° 46°

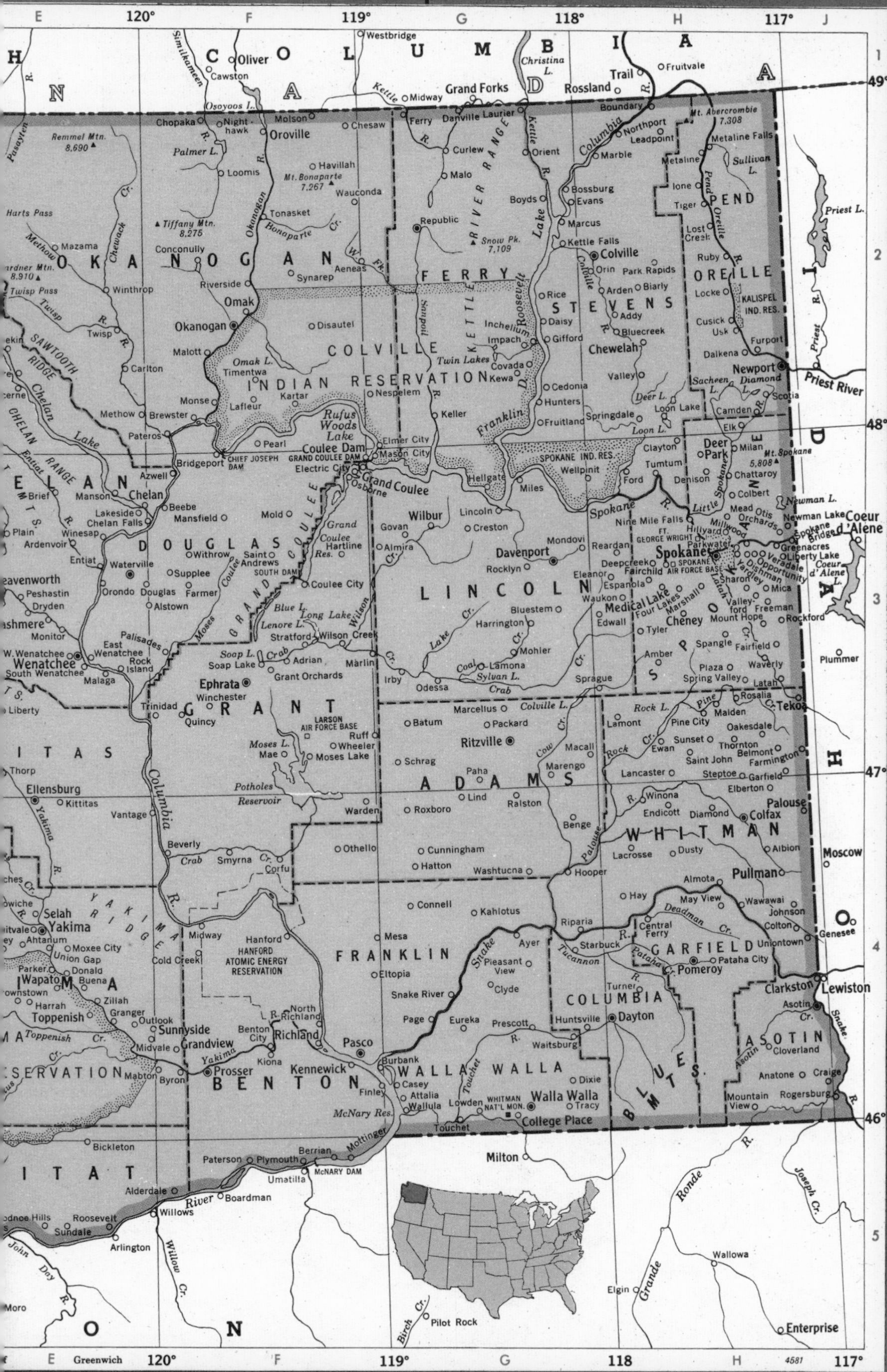

E 120° F 119° G 118° H 117° J

C O L U M B I A
Westbridge
Oliver
Cawston
Similkameen R.
Osoyoos L.
Kettle R.
Midway
Grand Forks
Christina L.
Rossland
Trail
Fruitvale
Columbia R.
49°

Chopaka
Nighthawk
Molson
Oroville
Chesaw
Ferry
Danville
Laurier
Boundary
Mt. Abercrombie 7,308
Northport
Leadpoint
Metaline Falls
Metaline
Sullivan L.
Remmel Mtn. 8,690
Palmer L.
Loomis
Havillah
Mt. Bonaparte 7,267
Wauconda
Curlew
Malo
Orient
Marble
Bossburg
Evans
Boyds
Ione
Tiger
Pend Oreille R.
Priest L.
Harts Pass
Tiffany Mtn. 8,275
Tonasket
Bonaparte Cr.
Republic
Kettle River Range
Snow Pk. 7,109
Marcus
Kettle Falls
Lost Creek
Mazama
Methow R.
Chewack Cr.
Conconully
Aeneas
Colville
Orin
Park Rapids
Ruby
Gardner Mtn. 8,910
O K A N O G A N
Synarep
F E R R Y
Riverside
Twisp Pass
Winthrop
Omak
Rice
Arden
Biarly
Locke
P E N D O R E I L L E
S T E V E N S
Kalispel Ind. Res.
Okanogan
Disautel
Daisy
Inchelium
Addy
Cusick
Usk
Twisp
Sanpoil R.
Gifford
Bluecreek
Furport
Sawtooth Ridge
Malott
C O L V I L L E
Impach
Chewelah
Dalkena
Carlton
Omak L.
Timentwa
Twin Lakes
Covada
Kewa
Newport
Priest River
I N D I A N R E S E R V A T I O N
Valley
Sacheen L.
Diamond L.
Kartar
Nespelem
Cedonia
Monse
Lafleur
Hunters
Deer L.
Scotia
Chelan Lake
Methow
Brewster
Rufus Woods Lake
Keller
Springdale
Loon Lake
Camden
Pateros
Fruitland
Franklin D. Roosevelt Lake
Loon L.
Elk
48°
Chief Joseph Dam
Pearl
Coulee Dam
Elmer City
Clayton
Deer Park
Milan
Mt. Spokane 5,808
Bridgeport
Grand Coulee Dam
Mason City
Spokane Ind. Res.
Tumtum
Electric City
Wellpinit
Azwell
Grand Coulee
Osborne
Hellgate
Miles
Ford
Denison
Chattaroy
Chelan Range
Chelan
Beebe
Colbert
Newman L.
Brief
Manson
Lakeside
Mansfield
Mold
Wilbur
Lincoln
Nine Mile Falls
Mead
Otis Orchards
Newman Lake
Coeur d'Alene
Chelan Falls
Govan
Creston
Ft. George Wright
Hillyard
Millwood
Spokane Bridge
Plain
Winesap
Grand Coulee
Hartline
Mondovi
Reardan
Parkwater
Greenacres
Ardenvoir
D O U G L A S
Almira
Davenport
Spokane
Veradale
Liberty Lake
Entiat
Withrow
Saint Andrews
Deepcreek
Spokane Air Force Base
Opportunity
Coeur d'Alene L.
Waterville
South Dam
Rocklyn
Fairchild
Dishman
Leavenworth
Supplee
Coulee City
Eleanor
Espanola
Yardley
Sharon
Mica
Peshastin
Orondo
Douglas
Farmer
L I N C O L N
Waukon
Medical Lake
Four Lakes
Marshall
Valleyford
Freeman
Dryden
Alstown
Blue L.
Bluestem
Edwall
Cheney
Mount Hope
Rockford
Cashmere
Lenore L.
Long Lake
Harrington
Tyler
Monitor
Palisades
Stratford
Wilson Creek
Spangle
Fairfield
W. Wenatchee
East Wenatchee
Soap L.
Adrian
Mohler
Amber
Plummer
Wenatchee
Rock Island
Soap Lake
Marlin
Lamona
S P O K A N E
Waverly
South Wenatchee
Grant Orchards
Sylvan L.
Plaza
Malaga
Ephrata
Irby
Odessa
Crab Cr.
Sprague
Spring Valley
Latah
Winchester
Marcellus
Colville L.
Rosalia
Liberty
Trinidad
G R A N T
Rock L.
Tekoa
Quincy
Larson Air Force Base
Batum
Packard
Lamont
Pine City
Malden
Ruff
Oakesdale
Wheeler
Ritzville
Sunset
Thornton
Moses L.
Moses Lake
Macall
Ewan
Belmont
Mae
Schrag
Saint John
Farmington
Thorp
Columbia R.
Paha
Marengo
Lancaster
Steptoe
Garfield
47°
Ellensburg
Potholes Reservoir
A D A M S
Elberton
Kittitas
Lind
Ralston
Winona
Palouse
Vantage
Warden
Roxboro
Endicott
Diamond
Colfax
Benge
W H I T M A N
Beverly
Othello
Cunningham
Lacrosse
Dusty
Albion
Moscow
Smyrna
Corfu
Hatton
Washtucna
Hooper
Pullman
Almota
Yakima Ridge
Connell
Hay
May View
Wawawai
Selah
Kahlotus
Johnson
Yakima
Riparia
Central Ferry
Colton
Genesee
Ahtanum
Midway
Hanford
Mesa
Ayer
Starbuck
Uniontown
Moxee City
Hanford Atomic Energy Reservation
F R A N K L I N
Pleasant View
Tucannon
G A R F I E L D
Union Gap
Cold Creek
Pataha City
Parker
Donald
Eltopia
Pomeroy
Wapato
Buena
Clyde
Turner
Clarkston
Lewiston
Harrah
Zillah
Snake River
C O L U M B I A
Asotin
Toppenish
Granger
North Richland
Page
Eureka
Prescott
Huntsville
Dayton
Outlook
Sunnyside
Benton City
Richland
Waitsburg
Grandview
Pasco
A S O T I N
Midvale
Kiona
Burbank
Cloverland
Mabton
Byron
Prosser
Kennewick
W A L L A W A L L A
Dixie
Anatone
Craige
B E N T O N
Finley
Casey
Blue Mts.
Attalia
Whitman Nat'l Mon.
Walla Walla
Mountain View
Rogersburg
Wallula
Lowden
Tracy
McNary Res.
Touchet
College Place
46°
Bickleton
Berrian
Mottinger
Milton
Paterson
Plymouth
Umatilla
McNary Dam
Ronde R.
Joseph Cr.
Alderdale
River
Boardman
Willows
Goodnoe Hills
Roosevelt
Sundale
Arlington
Willow Cr.
Wallowa
John Day R.
Grande
Elgin
Moro
Birch Cr.
Pilot Rock
O N
Enterprise

E Greenwich 120° F 119° G 118 H 4581 117°

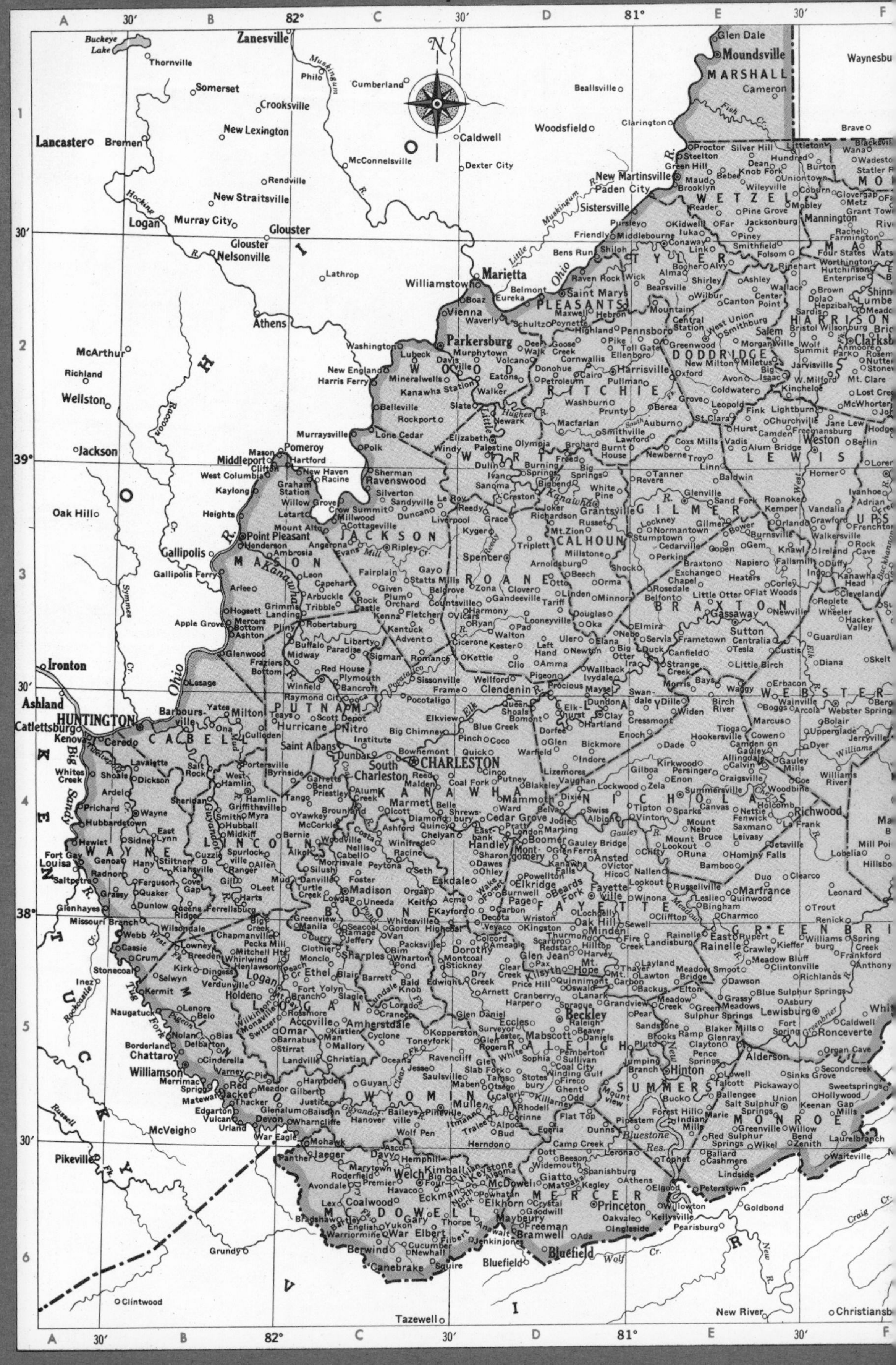
A
30′
B
82°
C
30′
D
81°
E
30′
F
1
2
3
4
5
6
30′
39°
30′
38°
30′
N
OHIO
KENTUCKY
VIRGINIA
Buckeye Lake
Zanesville
Thornville
Somerset
Crooksville
New Lexington
Lancaster
Bremen
Philo
Cumberland
Caldwell
Dexter City
McConnelsville
Rendville
New Straitsville
Logan
Murray City
Glouster
Nelsonville
Lathrop
Athens
McArthur
Richland
Wellston
Jackson
Oak Hill
Gallipolis
Gallipolis Ferry
Ironton
Ashland
Catlettsburg
HUNTINGTON
Kenova
Louisa
Fort Gay
Pikeville
McVeigh
Grundy
Clintwood
Tazewell
Bluefield
New River
Christiansburg
Beallsville
Woodsfield
Clarington
Glen Dale
Moundsville
MARSHALL
Cameron
Waynesburg
Brave
New Martinsville
Paden City
Sistersville
WETZEL
TYLER
Middlebourne
Marietta
Williamstown
Belmont
Saint Marys
PLEASANTS
Parkersburg
Vienna
WOOD
RITCHIE
Harrisville
Pennsboro
DODDRIDGE
HARRISON
Clarksburg
Salem
West Union
Weston
LEWIS
Point Pleasant
MASON
JACKSON
Ripley
Ravenswood
Spencer
ROANE
WIRT
Elizabeth
CALHOUN
Grantsville
GILMER
Glenville
BRAXTON
Sutton
Gassaway
WEBSTER
Webster Springs
Milton
CABELL
PUTNAM
Winfield
Hurricane
Nitro
Saint Albans
South Charleston
CHARLESTON
KANAWHA
Clendenin
CLAY
Clay
NICHOLAS
Summersville
Richwood
WAYNE
Wayne
LINCOLN
Hamlin
BOONE
Madison
Montgomery
FAYETTE
Fayetteville
Oak Hill
GREENBRIER
Lewisburg
Ronceverte
Rainelle
LOGAN
Logan
MINGO
Williamson
Matewan
WYOMING
Mullens
Pineville
RALEIGH
Beckley
SUMMERS
Hinton
MONROE
Union
MERCER
Princeton
Athens
Bluefield
McDOWELL
Welch
Gary
Kimball
Keystone
Northfork
War
Iaeger
Ohio R.
Kanawha R.
Muskingum R.
Hocking R.
Raccoon Cr.
Symmes Cr.
Big Sandy R.
Tug Fork
Guyandot R.
Elk R.
Gauley R.
New R.
Greenbrier R.
Bluestone Res.
Little Kanawha R.
Coal R.
Wolf Cr.
Russell Fk.

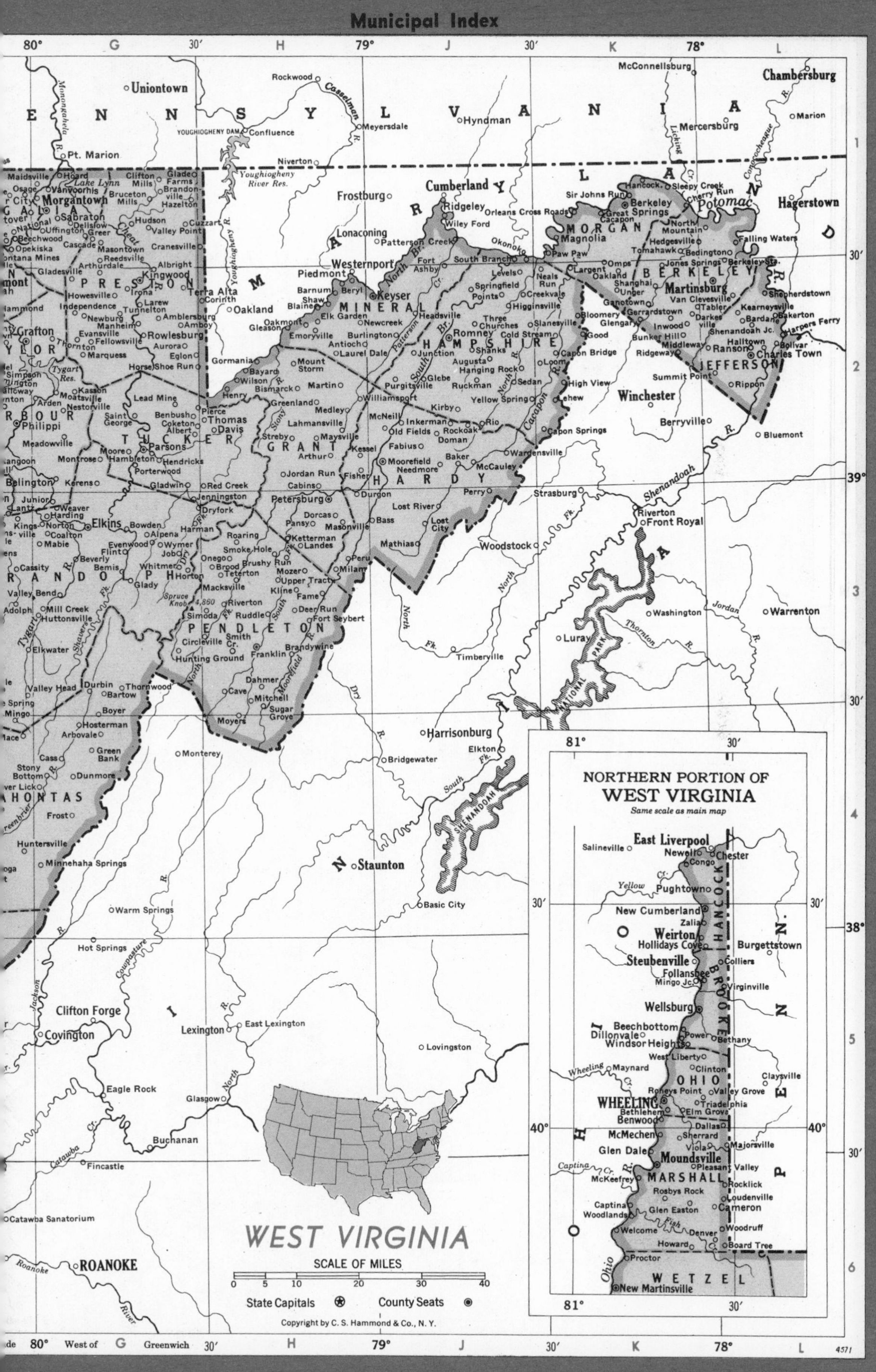

WEST VIRGINIA
SCALE OF MILES
0 5 10 20 30 40
State Capitals
County Seats
NORTHERN PORTION OF WEST VIRGINIA
Same scale as main map
PENNSYLVANIA
MARYLAND
VIRGINIA
OHIO
MINERAL
HAMPSHIRE
MORGAN
BERKELEY
JEFFERSON
PRESTON
TUCKER
GRANT
HARDY
PENDLETON
RANDOLPH
HANCOCK
BROOKE
MARSHALL
WETZEL
Morgantown
Cumberland
Hagerstown
Martinsburg
Winchester
Charles Town
Keyser
Romney
Elkins
Petersburg
Franklin
Harrisonburg
Staunton
Clifton Forge
Covington
Lexington
ROANOKE
Wheeling
Moundsville
Weirton
Steubenville
Wellsburg
East Liverpool
New Martinsville
Copyright by C. S. Hammond & Co., N. Y.
West of Greenwich
4571

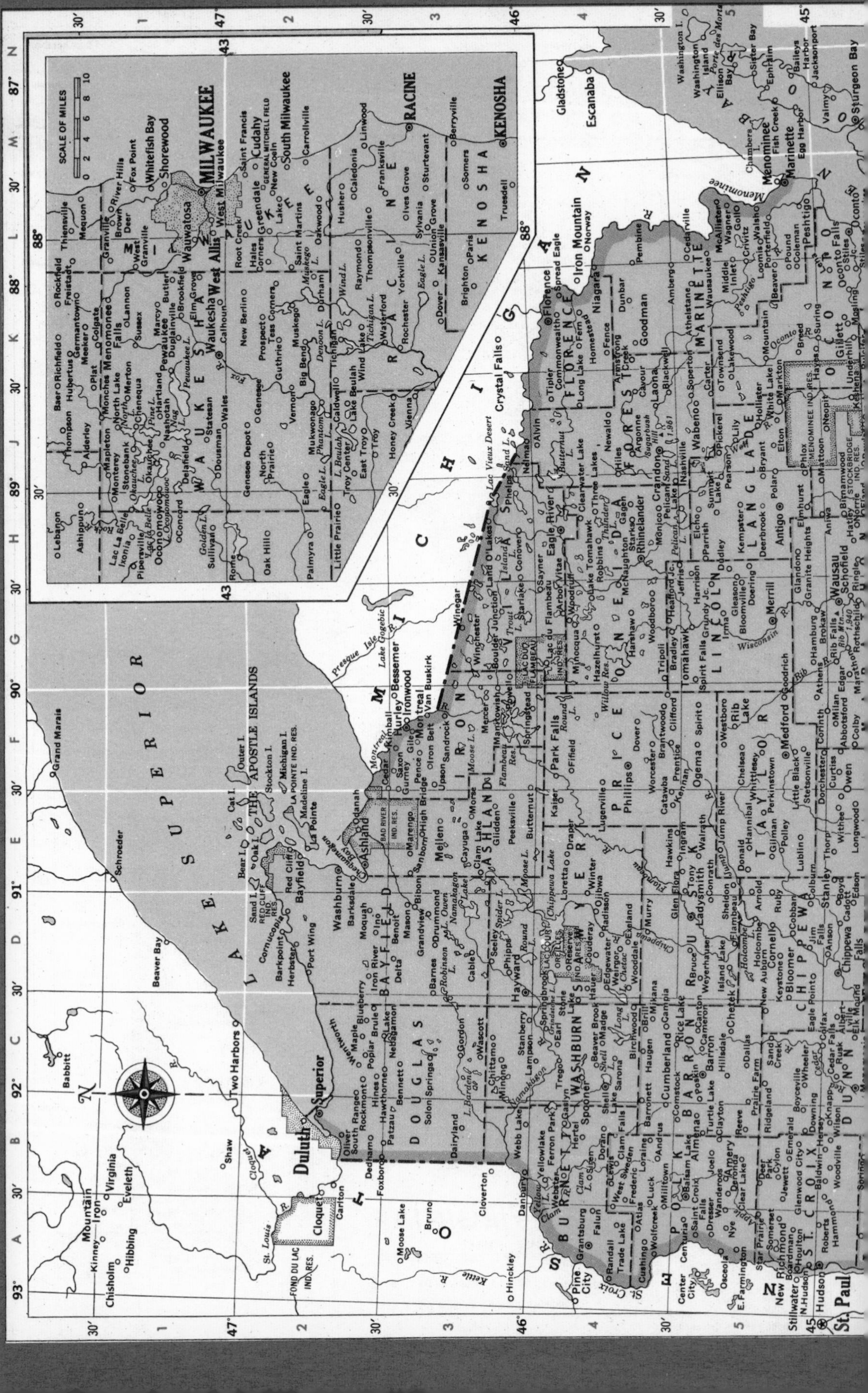

LAKE SUPERIOR

THE APOSTLE ISLANDS

MICHIGAN

WISCONSIN

SCALE OF MILES
0 2 4 6 8 10

MILWAUKEE

RACINE

KENOSHA

WAUKESHA

DOUGLAS · BAYFIELD · ASHLAND · IRON · VILAS · FLORENCE · FOREST · ONEIDA · PRICE · SAWYER · WASHBURN · BURNETT · POLK · BARRON · RUSK · TAYLOR · LINCOLN · LANGLADE · MARINETTE · OCONTO · MARATHON · CHIPPEWA · DUNN · ST. CROIX · MENOMINEE IND. RES.

WISCONSIN

SCALE OF MILES

0 5 10 20 30 40

State Capitals

County Seats

Canals

A
111°
B
110°
C
109°
D
108°
E
M O N T
45°
44°
43°
42°
41°
1
2
3
4
Electric Pk. 11,155
Gardiner
Cooke
Chance
Warren
Abers
Yellowstone Park
Index Pk. 11,738
Elk Basin
Frannie
Deaver
Cowley
Kane
Parkman
Ranchester
Dayton
Gray Pk. 10,300
Tower Falls
Badger Basin
Clark
Hebgen Res.
Mt. Washburn 10,346
Mt. Holmes 10,300
Canyon
Lamar R.
Clark Fork
Painter
Garland
Powell
Lovell
Byron
Tongue
BIGHORN
YELLOWSTONE
W. Yellowstone
Ralston
Shoshone R.
Hunt Mtn. 10,151
Fishing Bridge
Lake Outlet
NATIONAL
PARK
Big Springs
Old Faithful
Thumb
Yellowstone Lake
Shoshone L.
Lewis L.
Heart L.
Eagle Pk. 11,360
MADISON PLATEAU
ABSAROKA RANGE
Pahaska
North Fork
Buffalo Bill Res.
BUFFALO BILL DAM
Cody
SHOSHONE CAVERN NAT'L MON.
Wapiti
BIG HORN
Bighorn
Emblem
Burlington
Greybull
Shell
Shell Cr.
Otto
Basin
Cloud Pk. 13,16
PARK
Fortress Mtn. 12,073
BIGHORN BASIN
Manderson
Hyattville
Valley
South Fork
Greybull
Fifteen Mile Cr.
Nowood
Needle Mtn. 12,190
Pitchfork
Meeteetse
Hazelton Pk
Lamont
Sunshine
Wood R.
Dickie
Gooseberry
Worland
Ten Slee
GRAND TETON
Jackson Lake
Moran
TETON RANGE
CONTINENTAL DIVIDE
Mt. Burwell 11,738
Mt. Crosby 12,435
WASHAKIE
Felt
Tetonia
Driggs
Buffalo Fork
Elk
Table Pk. 11,101
NAT'L PARK
Jenny Lake
Grand Teton Pk. 13,766
Moose
Grovont
Kelly
Mt. Leidy 10,317
Diamond G Ranch
Grass Creek
Winchester
No Water
Hamilton Dome
Gebo
Kirby
Anchor
Lucerne
Bigtrails
North Fork
Owl Cr.
Victor
Gros Ventre
HOT SPRINGS
Thermopolis
E. Thermopolis
TETON
Du Noir R.
North Fork
Duncan
OWL CREEK MTS.
Wilson
Jackson
Snake
BACON RIDGE
Dubois
Jackson Pk. 10,707
Boysen
Boysen Res.
Badger Cr.
Green River Mtn. 10,175
WIND RIVER
Muddy
Fivemile Cr.
Dry Cr.
Hoback
Doubletop Pk. 11,715
Burris
Crowheart
Bonneville
Lost Cabin
Alpine
Bondurant
Bull Lake Res.
Pilot Butte Res.
Pavillion
Morton
Kinnear
Badwater
Lysite
Shoshoni
Moneta
Hoback Pk. 10,864
Gannett Pk. 13,785
Kendall
New Fork Lks.
Fremont Pk. 13,730
FREMONT
Poison
Hila
Etna
Deadman Mtn. 10,365
WIND RIVER IND. RES.
Fort Washakie
Ethete
Riverton
Waltma
Freedom
Willow L.
Fremont L.
Saint Stephens
Muskrat Cr.
Thayne
Bedford
Merna
Horse Cr.
Cora
Wind River
Arapahoe
Turnerville
Auburn
Grover
Daniel
Pinedale
Mt. Bonneville 12,530
Hudson
Lander
Popo Agie R.
Erva
Afton
Halfway
Boulder Lake
Boulder
SUBLETTE
East Fork
WYOMING RANGE
SALT RIVER RANGE
Greys R.
Fairview
Smoot
Salt R.
Middle Piney Cr.
Marbleton
Big Sandy
Little Popo Agie
Beaver Cr.
RATTLE
GRANITE MTS.
Wyoming Pk. 11,363
Atlantic Pk. 12,734
Sweetwater
Mt. Thompson 9,748
South Piney Cr.
Big Piney
Atlantic City
South Pass City
Split Rock
Geneva
Mt. Isabel 10,154
Smiths Fork
Fontenelle
ANTELOPE HILLS
GREEN MTS.
Calpet
Green
Continental Pk.
St. Marys Pk.
Big Sandy Res.
La Barge
La Barge Cr.
Eden Reservoir
Lamont
Border
Bairoil
Camp Ferris
LINCOLN
Farson
Little Sandy
Pegram
Cokeville
Slate Cr.
Sandy
Eden
Fontenelle
GREAT DIVIDE BASIN
Bear R.
Green
SWEETWATER
Nugget
Fossil
Hams
Frontier
Kemmerer
Superior
South Superior
Rawlins
Sage
Winton
Diamondville
Opal
Fork
Dines
Elkol
Blazon
Green River
Point of Rocks
Reliance
Gunn
Bitter Cr.
Thayer Junction
Wamsutter
Brilliant
Muddy
BEAR RIVER DIVIDE
Blacks Fork
Granger
Rock Springs
Bitter Creek
Church Buttes
Carter
Quealy
CA
Green River
ASPEN MTS.
Salt Wells Cr.
Albert
UINTA
Evanston
Fort Bridger
Lyman
Le Roy
Urie
Aspentunnel
Piedmont
Mountainview
Knight
Altamont
Robertson
Cottonwood Cr.
Savery Cr.
Tul
Lonetree
McKinnon
Baggs
Dixon
Savery
Manila
Battle
UTAH
Bridgeport
C O
IDAHO
Longi

WYOMING

SCALE OF MILES
0 10 20 40

State Capitals
County Seats

F 106° G 105° H 104° J 103°

45° 44° 43° 42° 41°

1 2 3 4

CANADA

Decker, Quietus, Moorhead, Alzada, Colony, Bentonite Spur, Passaic, Rockypoint, Wyarno, Sheridan, Leiter, Spotted Horse, Recluse, Weston, Stroner, New Haven, Seely, Hulett, Alva, Aladdin, Ulm, Clearmont, Arvada, Banner, Wild Cat, Oshoto, Devils Tower Nat'l Mon., Devils Tower, Beulah, Ucross, Kearney, Croton, Carlile, Saddlestring, Echeta, Sundance, Keyhole Res., Buffalo, Oriva, Gillette, Rozet, Moorcroft, Moskee, Inyan Kara Mtn. 6,313, Thornton, Upton, Buckhorn, Horton, Four Corners, Osage, Savageton, Lawver, Newcastle, Mayoworth, Clareton, Kaycee, Sussex, Clifton, Pine Tree, Teckla, Turnercrest, Midwest, Columbine, Edgerton, Ross, Dull Center, Bill, Leverett, Bright, Bear Creek, Lance Creek, Hat Creek, Powder River, Natrona, Casper Air Force Base, Mills, Evansville, Glenrock, Orpha, Whitman, Kirtley, Casper, Parkerton, Careyhurst, Lost Springs, Manville, Lusk, Goose Egg, Douglas, Shawnee, Keeline, Jireh, Node, Freeland, Orin, McKinley, Van Tassell, Boxelder, Alcova, Alcova Res., Flattop, Glendo, Jay Em, Pathfinder Reservoir, Little Medicine, Esterbrook, Cassa, Wendover, Sunrise, Hartville, Guernsey, Guernsey Res., Marshall, Laramie Pk., Fletcher Park, Leo, Muddy, Shirley, Dwyer, Fort Laramie, Lingle, Fort Laramie Nat'l Mon., Uva, Garrett, Seminoe Res., Torrington, Wheatland, Rockeagle, Huntley, Veteran, Yoder, Elmo, Como, Hanna, Medicine Bow, Wheatland Res., Slater, Rock River, Kyle, Chugwater, Hawk Springs, Walcott, Elk Mountain, Lookout, Cooper L., McFadden, Lagrange, Underwood, Bosler, Arlington, Iron Mountain, Little Bear, Meriden, Saratoga, Horse Creek, Albin, Centennial, Divide, Ryan Park, Lindbergh, Laramie, Federal, Riverside, Encampment, Hillsdale, Pine Bluffs, Albany, Burns, Egbert, Holmes, Buford, Francis E. Warren Air Force Base, Cheyenne, Arcola, Jelm, Tie Siding, Granite Canon, Speer, Carpenter, Foxpark, Hereford

SHERIDAN, JOHNSON, CAMPBELL, CROOK, WESTON, NIOBRARA, CONVERSE, NATRONA, PLATTE, GOSHEN, LARAMIE, ALBANY, CARBON

BEAR LODGE MTS., CASPER RA., HAYSTACK RA., SHIRLEY BASIN, SHIRLEY MTS., LARAMIE RANGE, MEDICINE BOW RANGE, SIERRA MADRE, DIVIDE

Powder R., Lit. Powder R., Little Missouri R., Belle Fourche R., Clear Cr., Crazy Woman Cr., Rawhide Cr., Caballo Cr., North Fork, Red Fork, Dry Fork, Black Thunder Cr., Little Thunder Cr., Lodgepole Cr., Porcupine Cr., Cheyenne R., South Fork, Antelope Cr., Dry Fork, Willow Cr., Lance Cr., Lightning Cr., Old Woman Cr., Spider Cr., Beaver Cr., N. Platte R., Bow R., Muddy Cr., Horseshoe Cr., Laramie R., Rawhide Cr., Medicine Bow R., Sybille Cr., Chugwater Cr., Horse Cr., Bear Cr., Lodgepole Cr., Crow Cr., Little Laramie R., Encampment R., Pass Cr.

COLORADO

Spearfish, Sturgis, Trojan, Lead, Deadwood, Elk Cr., Boxelder Cr., Silver City, Rapid City, Keystone, Spring Cr., Custer, Pleasant Valley, S. DAK., Pringle, Wind Cave Nat'l Park, Dewey, Minnekahta, Buffalo Gap, Hot Springs, Fossil Cycad Nat'l Mon., Edgemont, Cheyenne River, Hat Cr., Chadron, Harrison, White R., Crawford, Niobrara R., Hemingford, NEBR., L. Alice, L. Minatare, Lyman, Scottsbluff, Scotts Bluff Nat'l Mon., Gering, North Platte R., Bridgeport, Harrisburg

Columbine, Cowdrey, Buckeye, Carr, Grover

Copyright by C. S. Hammond & Co., N. Y.

7° West of Greenwich F 106° G 105° H 104° J

8571

A 150° B 140° C 130° D 120° E 110° F 100° G

ALASKA
BEAUFORT SEA
Banks Island
Melville I.
Viscount Melville Sd.
Victoria Island
DISTRICT OF FRANKLIN
Amundsen Gulf
Prince Albert Sd.
Coronation Gulf
Queen Maud Gulf
Boothia Pen.
King William I.
Prince of Wales I.
NORTH MAGNETIC POLE
Resolute Bay
Cambridge Bay
Coppermine
Bathurst Inlet (Burnside Har.)
Perry River
Peterson
Arctic Circle

Yukon R.
Fairbanks
Fort Yukon
Circle
Tanana R.
Porcupine R.
Copper R.
Forty Mile
Dawson
Stewart River
Mayo Landing
Ft. Selkirk
Mt. St. Elias 18,008
Mt. Logan 19,850
Mt. Fairweather 15,300
Kluane L.
Laberge
White Horse
L. Teslin
Watson Lake
Skagway
Juneau
Sitka
Baranof I.
Chichagof I.
Wrangell
Ketchikan
Prince of Wales I.
Portland Canal
Stewart
Dixon Entr.
Prince Rupert
Queen Charlotte Is.
Hecate Str.
Queen Charlotte Sd.
C. Scott
YUKON

Mackenzie Bay
Aklavik
Reindeer Depot
Tuktoyaktuk
Kittigazuit
Ft. McPherson
Arctic Red River
Peel R.
Stanton
Anderson R.
Paulatuk
Ft. Good Hope
Norman Wells
Ft. Norman
Ft. Franklin
Great Bear Lake
Wrigley
Ft. Simpson
Liard R.
Ft. Liard
Trout L.
Great Slave Lake
Lac la Martre
Rae
Yellowknife
Port Radium
Sawmill Bay
Hottah L.
Ft. Providence
Hay River
Ft. Resolution
Taltson River
Snowdrift
Reliance
L. Eileen
Ft. Smith
DISTRICT OF MACKENZIE
NORTHWEST TERRITORIES
Thelon R.
Dubawnt L.
Baker Lake
Baker L.
Yathkyed L.
Chesterfield
Kazan R.
Padlei
Kasba L.
Nueltin Lake
Nueltin L.
L. Garry
Back R.
DISTRICT OF KEEWATIN
Nunnuk

BRITISH COLUMBIA
ROCKY MOUNTAINS
Fort Nelson
Churchill Pk. 10,500
Finlay R.
Peace R.
Ft. St. John
Dawson Cr.
Hazelton
Terrace
Kitimat
Skeena
Smithers
Babine L.
Burns Lake
Francois L.
Vanderhoof
Prince George
Quesnel
Quesnel L.
Williams Lake
Mt. Robson 12,972
Mt. Waddington 13,260
Lillooet
Fraser R.
Kamloops
Shuswap L.
Revelstoke
Vernon
Kelowna
Okanagan L.
Merritt
Hope
Chilliwack
North Vancouver
Vancouver
New Westminster
Vancouver I.
Courtenay
Nanaimo
Victoria
Str. of Juan de Fuca
C. Flattery
Kaslo
Cranbrook
Nelson
Trail
Rossland
Fernie
Kootenay L.
GLACIER NAT'L PK.
YOHO NAT'L PK.
KOOTENAY NAT'L PK.
PACIFIC OCEAN

ALBERTA
Ft. Vermilion
Hay R.
Peace River
Grouard Mission
Spirit River
Hythe
Grande Prairie
Smoky R.
Lesser Slave L.
Athabaska
Wabiskaw R.
Ft. Fitzgerald
WOOD BUFFALO NATIONAL PARK
L. Claire
Ft. Chipewyan
L. Athabaska
Uranium City
Fond-du-Lac R.
MacKay
McMurray
Lac la Biche
St. Paul
Beaver R.
Ft. Saskatchewan
ELK ISLAND NAT'L PK.
Edmonton
Edson
JASPER NAT'L PK.
Jasper
Mt. Alberta 11,874
Rocky Mountain House
Wetaskiwin
Leduc
Vegreville
Vermilion
Wainwright
Camrose
Lacombe
Stettler
Red Deer
Didsbury
Lake Louise
BANFF PARK
Banff
Calgary
Hanna
Drumheller
High River
Bow R.
Coleman
Ft. Macleod
Medicine Hat
Lethbridge
Raymond
Pincher Creek
Cardston
WATERTON GLACIER INTERNATIONAL PEACE PARK

SASKATCHEWAN
Wollaston L.
Cree L.
Reindeer L.
Brochet
Lynn Lake
Southern Indian L.
Churchill R.
Granville L.
L. la Ronge
Big River
PRINCE ALBERT NATIONAL PARK
St. Walburg
Prince Albert
Shellbrook
North Battleford
Battleford
Rosthern
Melfort
Tisdale
Humboldt
Biggar
Rosetown
Saskatoon
Watrous
Kindersley
Eston
Wynyard
Kamsack
Yorkton
Melville
Swift Current
Maple Creek
Shaunavon
Indian Head
Regina
Moose Jaw
Moosomin
Weyburn
Radville
Estevan
Saskatchewan R.

MANITOBA
Flin Flon
Sherridon
Snow Lake
The Pas
L. Winnipegosis
Swan River
Winnipegosis
Dauphin
RIDING MOUNTAIN NAT'L PK.
L. Winnipeg
Norway House
Berens River
Berens R.
Riverton
L. Manitoba
Portage la Prairie
Selkirk
Brandon
Souris
Winnipeg
St. Boniface
Carman
Emerson
Morden
Killarney
Boissevain
Deloraine
Red Lake
Kenora
L. of the Woods
Rainy River
Fort Frances
Port Nelson
Amery
Nelson R.
Hayes R.
Gods L.
Island L.
Sandy L.
Seal R.
C. Churchill
Churchill
Herchmer

WASH.
Seattle
Portland
Columbia R.
Spokane
IDA.
MONT.
Shelby
Milk R.
N. DAK.
Bismarck
Fargo
Yellowstone R.
S. DAK.
Pierre
Missouri R.
Dakota R.
Niobrara R.
NEBR.
IOWA
MINN.
Minneapolis
Duluth
UNITED STATES

Inset:
82° 80°
MICH.
Sandusky
Lake Huron
Walkerton
Alliston
Newmarket
Mt. Forest
Shelburne
Aurora
Bowmanville
Cobourg
Wingham
Palmerston
Orangeville
Weston
Port Hope
Goderich
Clinton
Listowel
Fergus
Brampton
Oshawa
TORONTO
Seaforth
Waterloo
Guelph
Mimico
L. Ontario
Kitchener
Preston
Stratford
Galt
Dundas
St. Catharines
St. Mary's
Brantford
Hamilton
Niagara Falls
Niagara Falls
Woodstock
Port Huron
Strathroy
Welland
Sarnia
Petrolia
London
Ingersoll
Buffalo
Wallaceburg
St. Thomas
Simcoe
Dunnville
Walkerville
Aylmer
Port Dover
Welland Can.
Port Colborne
DETROIT
Dresden
L. St. Clair
N.Y.
Windsor
Ridgetown
Long Pt.
Sandwich
Chatham
Tilbury
Amherstburg
Essex
Leamington
Kingsville
Pt. Pelee
LAKE ERIE
Erie
MILES 0 20 40
43°

120° E 110° F 100° G

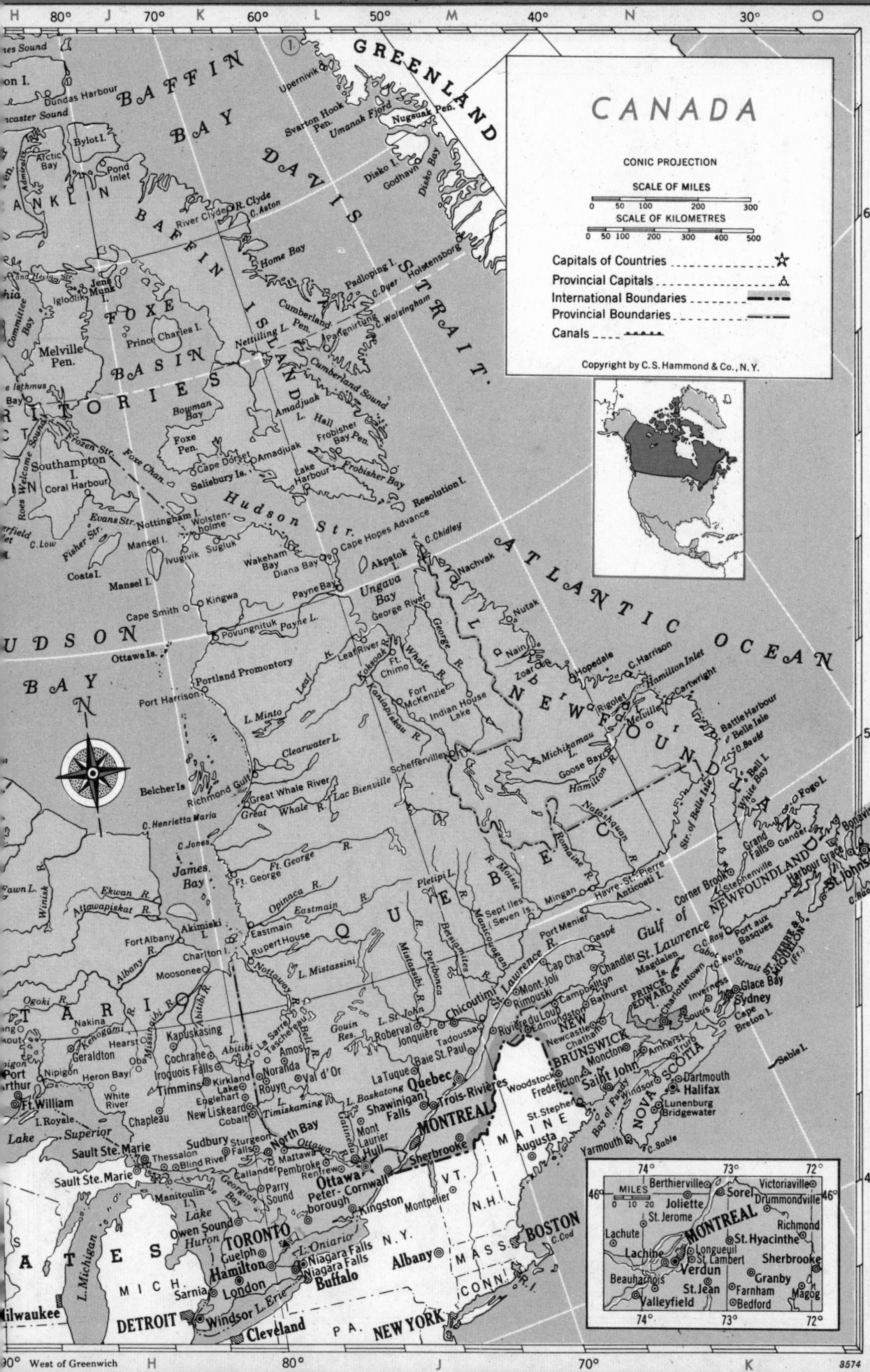

CANADA

CONIC PROJECTION

SCALE OF MILES

0 50 100 200 300

SCALE OF KILOMETRES

0 50 100 200 300 400 500

Capitals of Countries
Provincial Capitals
International Boundaries
Provincial Boundaries
Canals

West of Greenwich

ALASKA

POLYCONIC PROJECTION

SCALE OF MILES

0 50 100 150 200 250

SCALE OF KILOMETRES

0 50 100 150 200 250

Capitals ⊛

Same scale as main map

8544

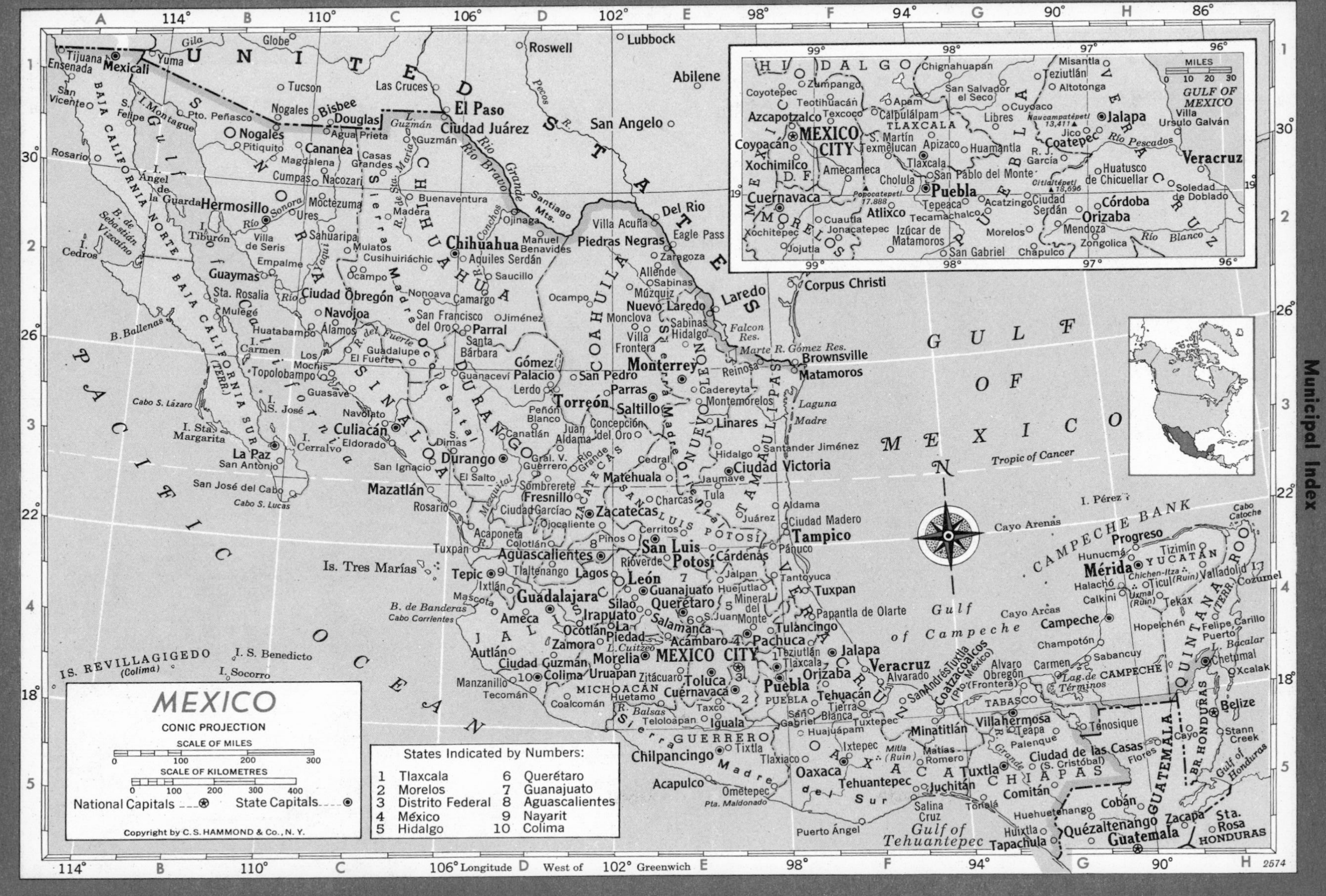
MEXICO
CONIC PROJECTION
SCALE OF MILES
0 100 200 300
SCALE OF KILOMETRES
0 100 200 300 400
National Capitals
State Capitals
Copyright by C. S. HAMMOND & Co., N. Y.
States Indicated by Numbers:
1 Tlaxcala
2 Morelos
3 Distrito Federal
4 México
5 Hidalgo
6 Querétaro
7 Guanajuato
8 Aguascalientes
9 Nayarit
10 Colima
UNITED STATES
GULF OF MEXICO
PACIFIC OCEAN
Gulf of California
Gulf of Campeche
Gulf of Tehuantepec
CAMPECHE BANK
Tropic of Cancer
GUATEMALA
BR. HONDURAS
HONDURAS
Longitude West of Greenwich
2574

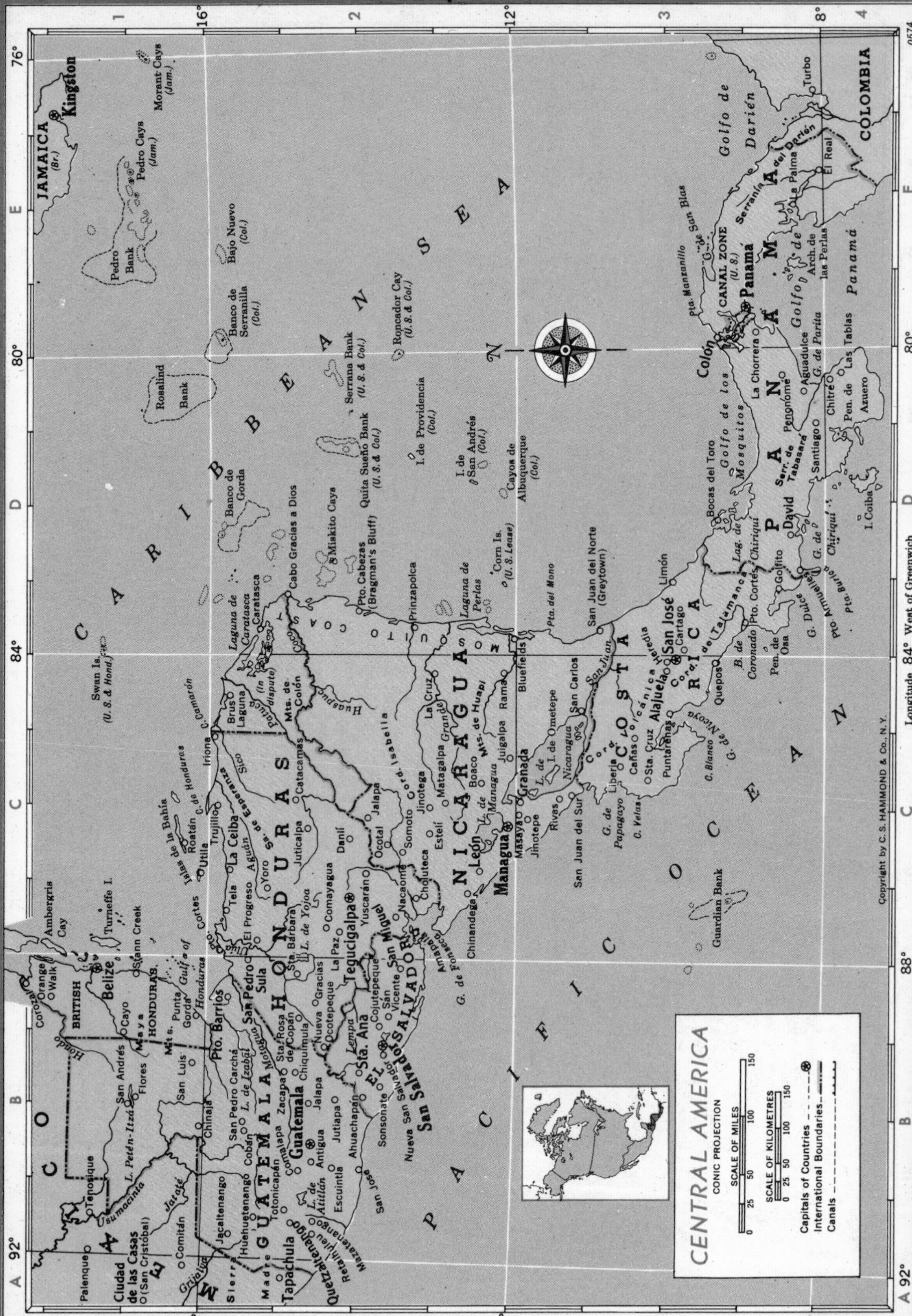

CENTRAL AMERICA
CONIC PROJECTION

SCALE OF MILES
0 25 50 100 150

SCALE OF KILOMETRES
0 25 50 100 150

Capitals of Countries
International Boundaries
Canals

Longitude 84° West of Greenwich

WEST INDIES

CONIC PROJECTION

SCALE OF MILES: 0 50 100 200

SCALE OF KILOMETRES: 0 50 100 200 300

Capitals ⊛

Copyright by C. S. HAMMOND & Co., N. Y.

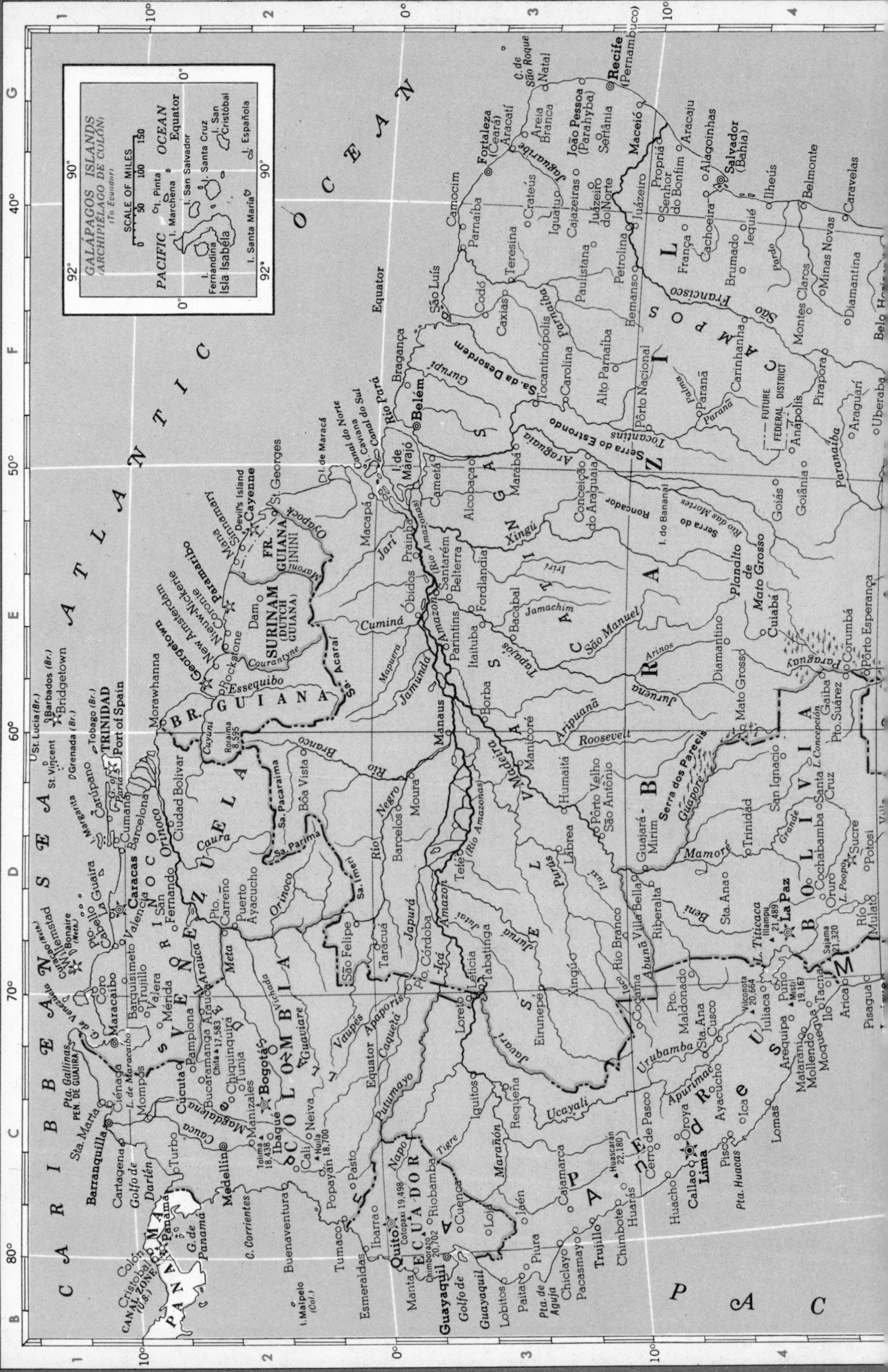

CARIBBEAN SEA
ATLANTIC OCEAN
PACIFIC
GALÁPAGOS ISLANDS (ARCHIPIÉLAGO DE COLÓN) (To Ecuador)
SCALE OF MILES 0 50 100 150
PACIFIC OCEAN Equator
I. Pinta
I. Marchena
I. San Salvador
I. Santa Cruz
I. San Cristóbal
I. Española
I. Santa María
I. Fernandina
Isla Isabela
92° 90°
PANAMA
Colón
Cristobal
CANAL ZONE (U.S.)
Panamá
G. de Panamá
Golfo de Darién
Cartagena
Barranquilla
Sta. Marta
Ciénaga
Pta. Gallinas
PEN. DE GUAJIRA
G. de Venezuela
Maracaibo
L. de Maracaibo
Mompós
Cúcuta
Bucaramanga
Pamplona
Chiquinquirá
Tunja
Bogotá
Chita 17,583
Medellín
Manizales
Ibagué
Neiva
Cali
Popayán
Pasto
Tolima 18,438
Huila 18,700
Turbo
C. Corrientes
Buenaventura
I. Malpelo (Col.)
COLOMBIA
LLANOS
Cauca
Magdalena
Meta
Vichada
Guaviare
Vaupés
Apaporis
Caquetá
Putumayo
Tumaco
Esmeraldas
Ibarra
Quito
Cotopaxi 19,498
Chimborazo 20,702
Riobamba
Cuenca
Loja
Manta
Guayaquil
Golfo de Guayaquil
ECUADOR
Napo
Tigre
Marañón
Curaçao (Neth.)
Willemstad
Bonaire (Neth.)
Coro
Barquisimeto
Trujillo
Valera
Mérida
Arauca
Pto. Cabello
La Guaira
Caracas
Valencia
San Fernando
I. Margarita
Carúpano
Cumaná
Barcelona
Ciudad Bolivar
Caura
Orinoco
Pto. Carreño
Puerto Ayacucho
VENEZUELA
Sa. Pacaraima
Sa. Parima
Sa. Imeri
Bôa Vista
Roraima 8,595
Cuyuni
Morawhanna
Georgetown
New Amsterdam
Rockstone
Essequibo
BR. GUIANA
Sa. Acaraí
St. Lucia (Br.)
St. Vincent
Grenada (Br.)
Barbados (Br.)
Bridgetown
Tobago (Br.)
TRINIDAD
Port of Spain
G. of Paria
Nieuw-Nickerie
Coronie
Paramaribo
Courantyne
SURINAM (DUTCH GUIANA)
Dam
Maroni
Mana
Sinnamary
Devil's Island
Cayenne
FR. GUIANA
ININI
Oyapock
St. Georges
I. de Maracá
Canal do Norte
I. Caviana
Canal do Sul
Rio Pará
Macapá
I. de Marajó
Belém
Bragança
Equator
Jari
Prainha
Santarém
Óbidos
Belterra
Fordlândia
Cuminá
Mapuera
Jamundá
Amazon
Rio Amazonas
Parintins
Itaituba
Manaus
Borba
Manicoré
Madeira
Humaitá
Pôrto Velho
São Antônio
Rio Negro
Rio Branco
Moura
Barcelos
Tefé
Rio Amazonas
Purús
Lábrea
Ituxi
Juruá
Jutaí
Japurá
Pto. Córdoba
Taracuá
São Felipe
Içá
Leticia
Tabatinga
Loreto
Iquitos
Requena
Ucayali
Javari
Eirunepé
Xingú
Rio Branco
Iaco
Abunã
Villa Bella
Riberalta
Cocama
Pto. Maldonado
Beni
Mamoré
Guajará-Mirim
Serra dos Parecis
Guaporé
Aripuanã
Roosevelt
Juruena
Arinos
Tapajós
Bacabal
Jamachim
São Manuel
Diamantino
Cuiabá
Mato Grosso
Planalto de Mato Grosso
Serra do Rio das Mortes
Roncador
I. do Bananal
Araguaia
Conceição do Araguaia
Xingú
Iriri
Alcobaça
Cametá
Marabá
Tocantins
Serra do Estrondo
Gurupi
Sa. da Desordem
Tocantinópolis
Carolina
Alto Parnaíba
Pôrto Nacional
Paranã
Palma
FUTURE FEDERAL DISTRICT
Anápolis
Goiás
Goiânia
Paranaíba
Araguari
Uberaba
Pirapora
Carinhanha
Montes Claros
Minas Novas
Diamantina
Belo Horizonte
São Luís
Codó
Caxias
Teresina
Parnaíba
Camocim
Fortaleza (Ceará)
Aracatí
Jaguaribe
Crateús
Iguatu
Cajazeiras
Juàzeiro do Norte
Paulistana
Petrolina
Remanso
Juàzeiro
São Francisco
Areia Branca
C. de São Roque
Natal
João Pessoa (Parahyba)
Sertânia
Recife (Pernambuco)
Maceió
Propriá
Aracaju
Senhor do Bonfim
Alagoinhas
Salvador (Bahia)
Cachoeira
França
Brumado
Jequié
Ilhéus
Belmonte
Caravelas
Pardo
SELVAS
CAATINGAS
BRAZIL
CAMPOS
Corumbá
Pôrto Esperança
Paraguay
Gaiba
Pto. Suárez
Mato Grosso
Santa Cruz
San Ignacio
L. Concepción
Trinidad
Grande
Cochabamba
Sucre
Potosí
Oruro
L. Poopó
Sta. Ana
La Paz
Illimani 21,489
Sajama 21,320
L. Titicaca
Río Mulato
BOLIVIA
Arica
Pisagua
Tacna
Ilo
Moquegua
Mollendo
Matarani
Arequipa
Misti 19,167
Puno
Juliaca
Vilcanota 20,664
Cusco
Sta. Ana
Urubamba
Apurímac
Ayacucho
Ica
Lomas
Oroya
Cerro de Pasco
Lima
Callao
Pisco
Pta. Huacas
Huacho
Huascarán 22,180
Huarás
Chimbote
Trujillo
Pacasmayo
Chiclayo
Pta. de Aguja
Paita
Piura
Lobitos
Cajamarca
Jaén
ANDES
PERU
B C D E F G
1 2 3 4
10° 0° 10°
80° 70° 60° 50° 40°

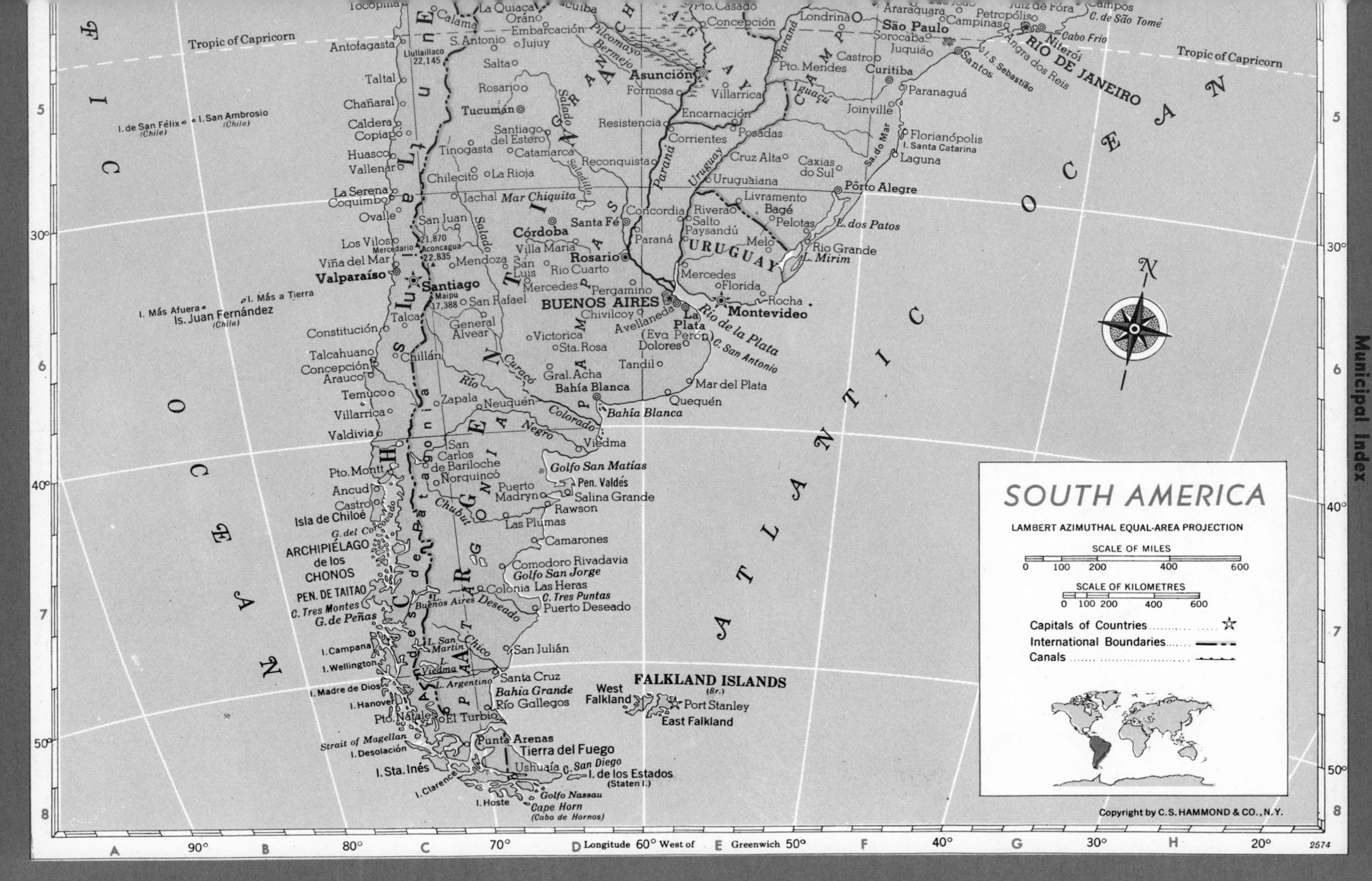
SOUTH AMERICA
LAMBERT AZIMUTHAL EQUAL-AREA PROJECTION
SCALE OF MILES
0 100 200 400 600
SCALE OF KILOMETRES
0 100 200 400 600
Capitals of Countries
International Boundaries
Canals
Copyright by C. S. HAMMOND & CO., N.Y.
2574
ATLANTIC OCEAN
PACIFIC OCEAN
ARGENTINA
CHILE
PATAGONIA
PAMPA
URUGUAY
PARAGUAY
BUENOS AIRES
Montevideo
Santiago
Valparaíso
Asunción
RIO DE JANEIRO
São Paulo
Curitiba
Pôrto Alegre
Córdoba
Rosario
Santa Fé
Mendoza
Tucumán
Bahía Blanca
Mar del Plata
La Plata
Río de la Plata
Concepción
Valdivia
Pto. Montt
Isla de Chiloé
ARCHIPIÉLAGO de los CHONOS
PEN. DE TAITAO
Golfo San Matías
Golfo San Jorge
Comodoro Rivadavia
FALKLAND ISLANDS
(Br.)
West Falkland
East Falkland
Port Stanley
Strait of Magellan
Punta Arenas
Tierra del Fuego
Ushuaía
I. de los Estados
(Staten I.)
Cape Horn
(Cabo de Hornos)
Is. Juan Fernández
(Chile)
I. de San Félix
I. San Ambrosio
Tropic of Capricorn
Longitude 60° West of Greenwich

40° A 30° B 20° C 10° D 0° E 10° F

70° Jan Mayen (Nor.)

Nord Kap, Breidha Fjördhur, Hunaflói, Reykjavik, ICELAND, Akureyri, Langanes, Mt. Hekla, Seydhisfjördhur, Hornafjördhur, Arctic Circle

Senja, Vesterålen, Lofoten, Vestfjorden

ATLANTIC OCEAN

Faeroe Is. (Dan.), Thorshavn, Trondheimsfjorden, Namsos, Kristiansund, Ålesund, Trondheim, Östersund, Sundsvall, Shetland Is., Lerwick, Sognefjord, Lillehammer, Bergen, Hardangerfjord, Söderhamn, Falun, Rockall, Orkney Is., Pentland Firth, Kirkwall, Haugesund, Oslo, Drammen, Uppsala, Hebrides, The Minch, Moray Firth, Stavanger, Fredrikstad, Larvik, Karlstad, Västerås, NORWAY, SWEDEN, Inverness, SCOTLAND, Aberdeen, Arendal, Halden, Vänern, Örebro, Norrköping, BRITISH ISLES, Glasgow, Dundee, GREAT BRITAIN, Lindesnes, Kristiansand, Skagerrak, Göteborg, Vättern, Linköping, NO. IRELAND, Donegal Bay, North Chan., Edinburgh, NORTH SEA, Borås, Jönköping, Visby, IRELAND, Belfast, I. of Man, Aalborg, Kattegat, DENMARK, Dundalk, Galway, Carlisle, Newcastle, Århus, Hälsingborg, Öland, Limerick (Luimneach), Dublin, Manchester, IRISH SEA, Leeds, Esbjerg, Copenhagen, Lund, Karlskrona, Waterford, Liverpool, Hull, Odense, Malmö, BALTIC, Cork, Cobh, C. Clear, St. George's Chan., WALES, Sheffield, The Wash, Flensburg, Bornholm, Helgoland, Frisian Is., Lübeck, Kiel, Stralsund, Słupsk, Amsterdam, The Hague, NETHERLANDS, Bremen, Hamburg, Rostock, Kołobrzeg, ENGLAND, Birmingham, Swansea, Cardiff, LONDON, Utrecht, EAST, Szczecin (Stettin), Bydgoszcz, Bristol, Plymouth, Southampton, Portsmouth, Rotterdam, Antwerp, Münster, Weser, Hannover, Elbe, BERLIN, Poznań, Lands End, Brunswick, Magdeburg, Oder, POLAND, English Channel, Boulogne, Calais, Ghent, Essen, Dortmund, GERMANY, Warta, Cherbourg, Le Havre, BELGIUM, Brussels, Düsseldorf, Kassel, Halle, Leipzig, Dresden, Wrocław (Breslau), I. d'Ouessant (Ushant I.), Channel Is. (Br.), Lille, Liège, Aachen, Cologne, Erfurt, Rouen, Amiens, Bonn, Wiesbaden, Chemnitz, Częstochowa, Brest, LUX., Mainz, Frankfurt, Plauen, Zabrze, Rennes, Seine, Marne, Versailles, Reims, Saarbrücken, Mannheim, Prague (Praha), Ostrava, Belle Isle, St. Nazaire, Angers, Loire, Orléans, PARIS, Nancy, Karlsruhe, Nuremberg, Regensburg, Plzeň, Olomouc, CZECHOSLOVAKIA, Strasbourg, Stuttgart, Danube, Brno, Nantes, Tours, Augsburg, Bay of Biscay, La Rochelle, I. d'Oléron, FRANCE, Mulhouse, Dijon, Freiburg, Munich, Linz, VIENNA (Wien), Bratislava, Basel, Zürich, Constance, LIECHTENSTEIN, Innsbruck, Salzburg, Limoges, Vichy, Lausanne, Bern, SWITZERLAND, AUSTRIA, Graz, Győr, HUNGARY, Sopron, El Ferrol, la Coruña, C. Finisterre, Gijón, Santander, San Sebastián, Biarritz, Bordeaux, Clermont-Ferrand, Lyon, Geneva, L. Geneva, Mt. Blanc, Alps, Maribor, Balaton, Oviedo, Dordogne, St.-Etienne, Grenoble, Bolzano, Trento, Venice (Venezia), Ljubljana, Pécs, Vigo, Miño, Bilbao, Garonne, Bayonne, Montauban, Rhône, Turin (Torino), Milan, Brescia, Verona, Padua, Trieste, Zagreb, Drava, Oporto (Porto), Braga, León, Valladolid, Pyrenees, Toulouse, Nîmes, Genoa, Parma, Po, Ferrara, Rijeka (Fiume), Burgos, Ebro, Modena, Bologna, Banja Luka, YUGOSLAVIA, Coimbra, PORTUGAL, Douro, Salamanca, Duero, Saragossa, ANDORRA, Montpellier, Nice, MONACO, Marseille, La Spezia, Florence (Firenze), SAN MARINO, Ancona, Zadar (Zara), Sarajevo, Sa. de Guadarrama, G. of Lions, Toulon, Leghorn (Livorno), Lisbon (Lisboa), Tejo, MADRID, SPAIN, Siena, Perugia, Split, Mostar, ADRIATIC SEA, Setubal, Tagus (Tajo), Barcelona, Corsica (Corse), Elba, Tiber, ITALY, Dubrovnik, Guadiana, Toledo, Tarragona, Ajaccio, ROME, Cetinje, Shkodër, Evora, Badajoz, VATICAN CITY, C. St. Vincent, Sierra Morena, Albacete, Valencia, Balearic Is., Sassari, Terranova, Foggia, Vesuvius, Bari, Córdoba, Minorca, Sardinia (Sardegna), Guadalquivir, Palma, Majorca (Mallorca), Naples (Napoli), Taranto, Murcia, Ibiza, Brindisi, G. of Cadiz, Seville, Lorca, Alicante, Str. of Gibraltar, Cádiz, Jerez, Granada, Sa. Nevada, Iglesias, TYRRHENIAN SEA, G. of Taranto, Cartagena, Cagliari, Catanzaro, Tangier, GIBRALTAR (Br.), Málaga, Almería, MEDITERRANEAN, Ceuta (Sp.), Algiers (Alger), Philippeville, Palermo, Messina, Reggio, IONIAN SEA, Port-Lyautey, Oran, Bizerte, C. Bon, Etna, Casablanca, Rabat, Melilla (Sp.), Constantine, Bône, Sicily (Sicilia), Catania, MOROCCO, Meknès, Fez, ALGERIA, TUNISIA, Tunis, Pantelleria, Syracuse, Marrakech (Morocco), Sousse, Biskra, Malta (Br.), Valletta

60° 50° 40° 3 4 5

Longitude West D of Greenwich 0° Longitude East E of Greenwich 10° F

EUROPE
LAMBERT AZIMUTHAL EQUAL-AREA PROJECTION
SCALE OF MILES
0 100 200 300 400 500
SCALE OF KILOMETRES
0 100 200 300 400 500
Capitals of Countries
International Boundaries
Canals
Copyright by C.S. HAMMOND & CO., N.Y.
7586
BARENTS SEA
White Sea
BLACK SEA
CASPIAN SEA
Sea of Azov
UNION OF SOVIET SOCIALIST REPUBLICS
RUSSIAN SOVIET FEDERATED SOCIALIST REPUBLIC
UKRAINIAN S.S.R.
WHITE RUSSIAN S.S.R.
LATVIAN S.S.R.
LITHUANIAN S.S.R.
ESTONIAN S.S.R.
MOLDAVIAN S.S.R.
GEORGIAN S.S.R.
ARMENIAN S.S.R.
AZERBAIDZHAN S.S.R.
ROMANIA
BULGARIA
GREECE
TURKEY
FINLAND
Caucasus
Ural
KOLA PEN.
KANIN PEN.
CRIMEAN PEN.
Kolguev I.
Cheshskaya Bay
Mezen Bay
North Cape
L. Inari
L. Oulu
L. Onega
L. Ladoga
L. Ilmen
L. Peipus
Rybinsk Res.
Tsimlyansk Res.
Gulf of Finland
G. of Riga
Kara-Bogaz-Gol
Sea of Marmara
Bosporus
Dardanelles
Iron Gate
Salekhard (Obdorsk)
Berezovo
Khanty-Mansiisk
Surgut
Ob
Irtish
Tobolsk
Tobol
Tyumen
Kurgan
Vorkuta
Naryan Mar
Pechora
Usa
Vadsö
Pechenga (Petsamo)
Murmansk
Kirovsk
Kandalaksha
Mezen
Ust Tsilma
Archangel
Northern Dvina
Onega
Kem
Tornio
Oulu
Vaasa
Kuopio
Joensuu
Sortavala
Petrozavodsk
Tampere
Helsinki (Helsingfors)
Vyborg
Kotka
LENINGRAD
Cherepovets
Vologda
Nyandoma
Kotlas
Veliki Ustyug
Syktyvkar
Kirov (Vyatka)
Kotelnich
Izhevsk
Sarapul
Berezniki
Kama
Molotov (Perm)
Krasnouralsk
Nizhni Tagil
Kirovgrad
Sverdlovsk
Zlatoust
Chelyabinsk
Troitsk
Magnitogorsk
Kustanai
Ufa
Belaya
Tallinn (Revel)
Narva
Kingisepp
Tartu
Pärnu
Pskov
Cēsis
Riga
Rezekne
Jelgava
Panevežys
Šiauliai
Bigosovo
Daugavpils
Velikie Luki
Kaunas
Vilna
Kaliningrad
Vitebsk
Smolensk
Minsk
Negoreloye
Grodno
Stolbtsy
Białystok
Pinsk
Brest
Bug
Lublin
Kalinin (Tver)
Shcherbakov
Yaroslavl
Kostroma
Ivanovo
Balakhna
Dzerzhinsk
Gorki (Nizhni Novgorod)
Volga
Kazan
MOSCOW (Moskva)
Orekhovo-Zuevo
Serpukhov
Oka
Kaluga
Tula
Ryazan
Michurinsk
Tambov
Penza
Ulyanovsk
Kuibyshev (Samara)
Chkalov (Orenburg)
Aktyubinsk
Uralsk
Temir
Chelkar
Emba
Saratov
Engels
Bryansk
Orel
Kursk
Voronezh
Gomel
Dnepr
Kiev
Rovno
Zhitomir
Kharkov
Poltava
Kremenchug
Dneprodzerzhinsk
Donets
Millerovo
Voroshilovgrad (Lugansk)
Kramatorsk
Stalingrad
Guriev
Shepetovka
Przemyśl
Lvov
Vinnitsa
Kirovograd
Dnepropetrovsk
Zaporozhe
Stalino
Shakhty
Makeevka
Taganrog
Rostov
Don
Astrakhan
Stanislav
Dnestr
Chernovtsy
Mukachevo
Krivoi Rog
Nikolaev
Dnieper
Zhdanov
Stepnoi
Fort Shevchenko
Satu Mare
Debrecen
Oradea
Cluj
Roman
Iaşi
Kishinev
Bendery
Tiraspol
Kherson
Odessa
Belgorod Dnestrovski
Krasnodar
Armavir
Novorossisk
Maikop
Pyatigorsk
Kislovodsk
Grozny
Makhachkala
Arad
Timişoara
Sibiu
Oraşul Stalin (Braşov)
Brăila
Galati
Sulina
Simferopol
Sevastopol
Kerch
Yalta
Tuapse
Sochi
Klukhori
Elbrus
Ordzhonikidze
Krasnovodsk
Ploesti
Bucharest
Craiova
Constanţa
Danube
Sukhumi
Kutaisi
Tbilisi
Baku
Batumi
Leninakan
Erivan
Nakhichevan
Araxes
Dzhulfa
Pleven
Ruse
Varna
Sofia
Sliven
Burgas
Plovdiv
Stara Zagora
Skopje
Edirne (Adrianople)
ISTANBUL (Constantinople)
Sinop
Samsun
Trabzon
Erzurum
Bitola
Salonika
Kavalla
Tekirdağ
Üsküdar (Skutari)
Ereğli
Kizilirmak
Sivas
Bursa
Ankara (Angora)
Eskişehir
Kayseri
Maraş
Larisa
Vólos
Trikkala
Lamia
Chalcis
Athens
Piraeus
Corinth
Patras
Kalamai
Matapan
Lesbos
Chios
Samos
Euboea
Manisa
İzmir (Smyrna)
Afyon Karahisar
Konya
Adana (Seyhan)
Tarsus
Mersin (İçel)
Antalya
Antakya
Aleppo
Nicosia
El Ladhiqiya
Larnaca
Cyprus (Br.)
Rhodes
Crete
Canea
Candia
AEGEAN SEA
30°
40°
50°
60°
70°
80°

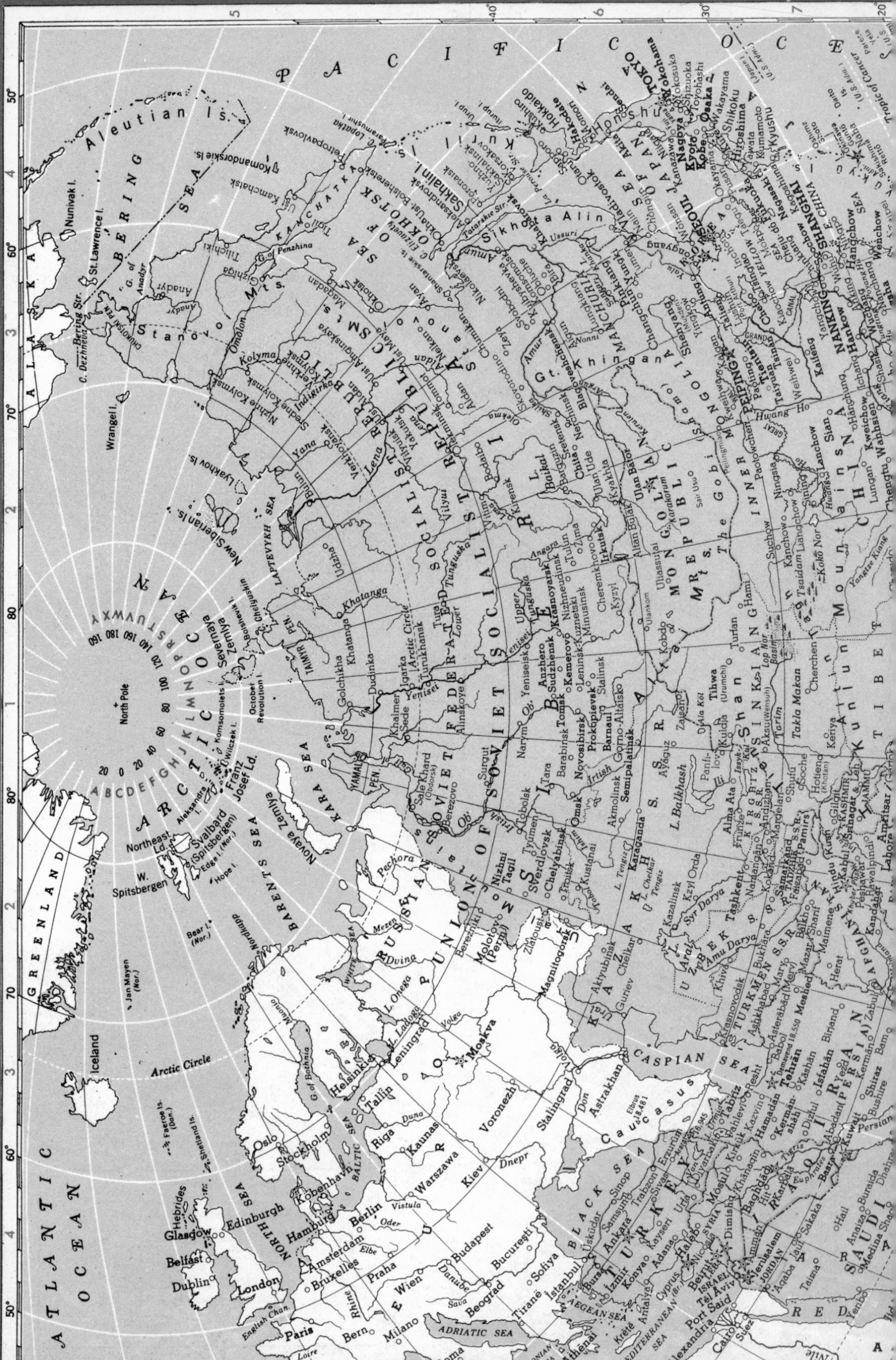

ATLANTIC OCEAN
ARCTIC OCEAN
PACIFIC OCEAN
North Pole
Arctic Circle
UNION OF SOVIET SOCIALIST REPUBLICS
RUSSIAN SOVIET FEDERATED SOCIALIST REPUBLIC
KAZAKH S.S.R.
MONGOLIAN PEOPLE'S REPUBLIC
MANCHURIA
INNER MONGOLIA
CHINA
JAPAN
TIBET
TURKEY
IRAN (PERSIA)
IRAQ
SAUDI ARABIA
AFGHANISTAN
GREENLAND
ALASKA
BERING SEA
SEA OF OKHOTSK
SEA OF JAPAN
YELLOW SEA
BARENTS SEA
KARA SEA
LAPTEVYKH SEA
NORTH SEA
BALTIC SEA
BLACK SEA
CASPIAN SEA
MEDITERRANEAN SEA
ADRIATIC SEA
AEGEAN SEA
RED SEA
Aleutian Is.
Kurile Is.
Sakhalin I.
Kamchatka
New Siberian Is.
Severnaya Zemlya
Franz Josef Ld.
Novaya Zemlya
Svalbard (Spitsbergen)
Iceland
Moskva
Leningrad
London
Paris
Berlin
Tokyo
Shanghai
Peiping
Nanking

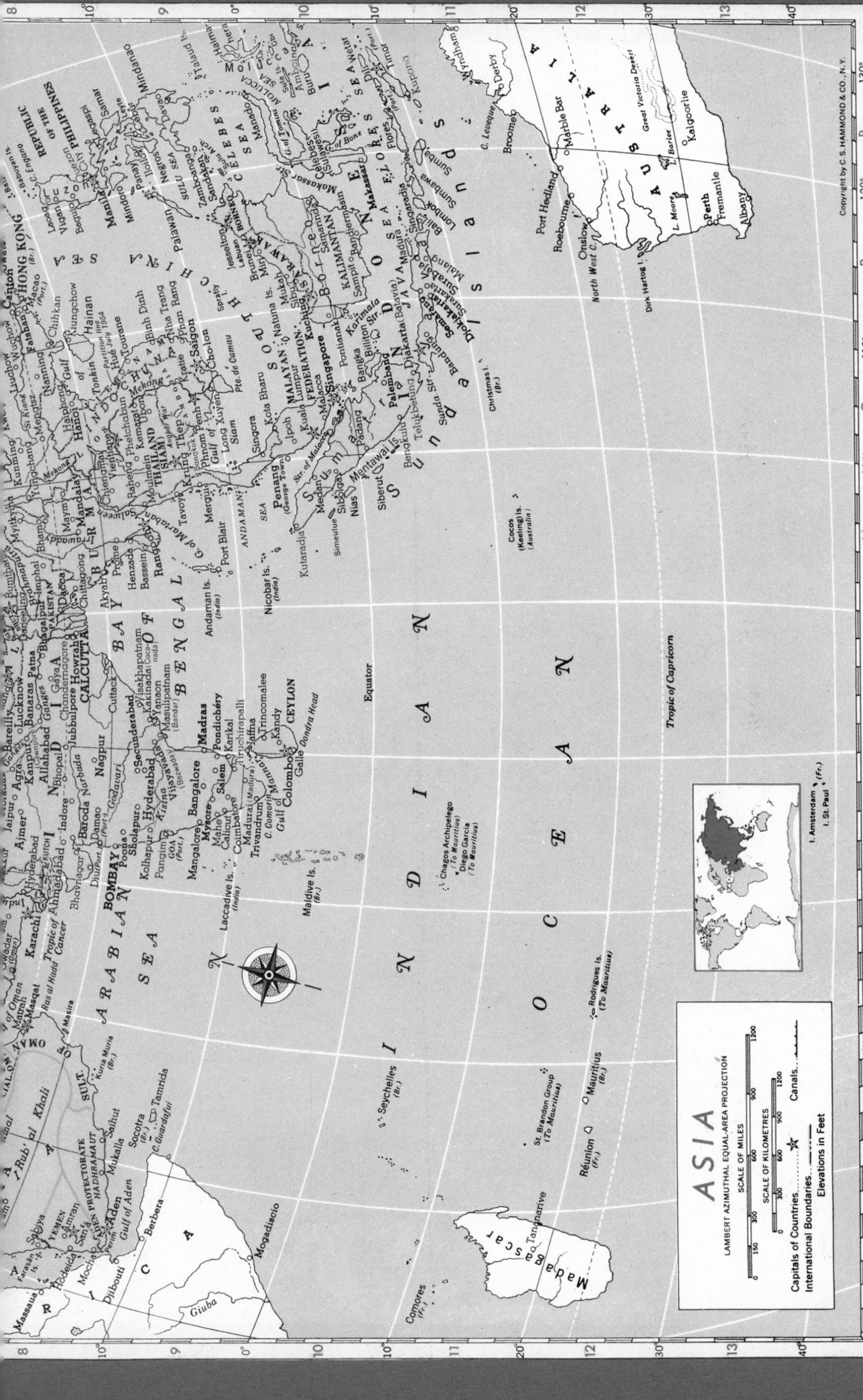

ASIA

LAMBERT AZIMUTHAL EQUAL-AREA PROJECTION

SCALE OF MILES

0 150 300 600 900 1200

SCALE OF KILOMETRES

0 300 600 900 1200

Capitals of Countries ☆

Canals

International Boundaries

Elevations in Feet

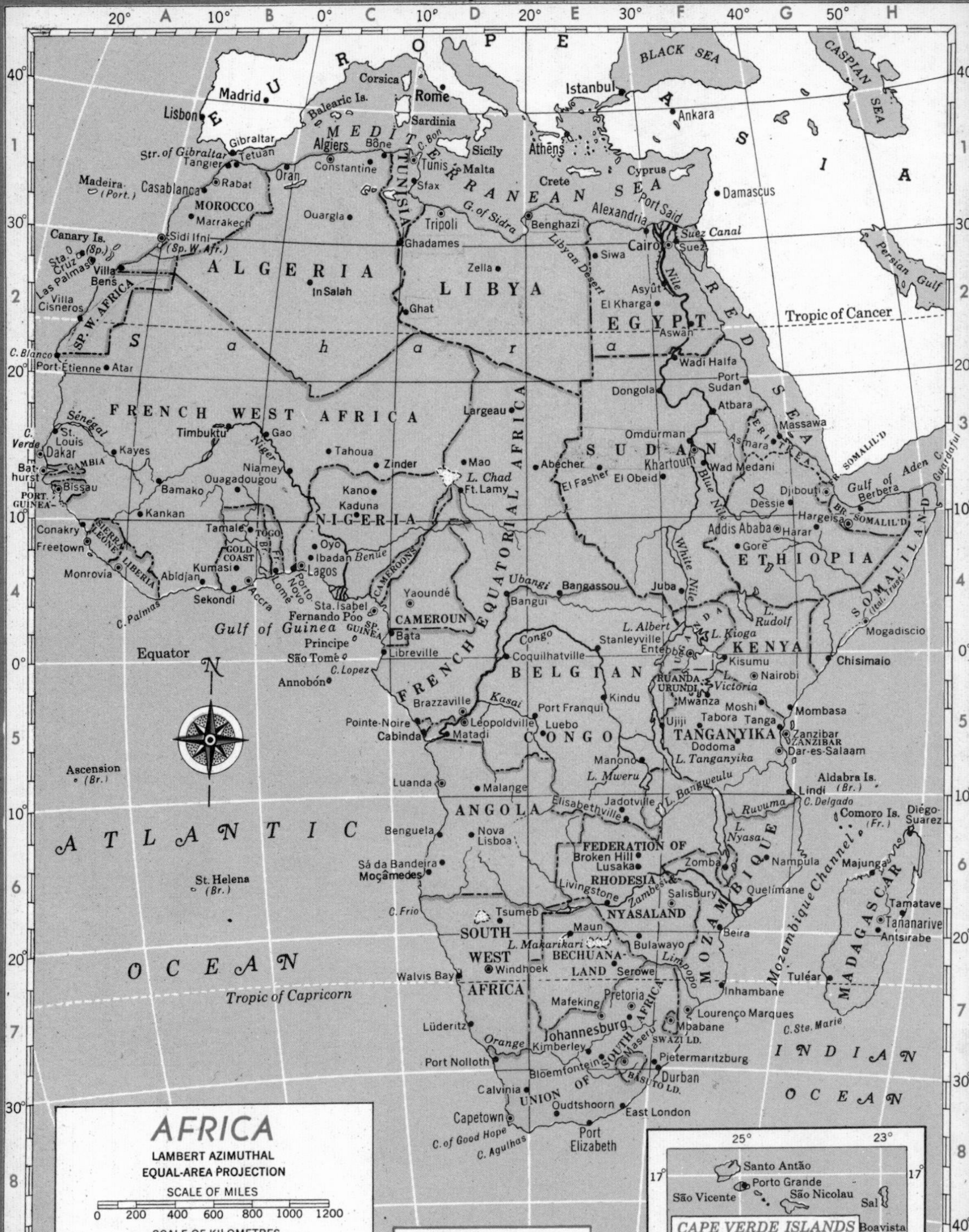

AFRICA

LAMBERT AZIMUTHAL
EQUAL-AREA PROJECTION

SCALE OF MILES
0 200 400 600 800 1000 1200

SCALE OF KILOMETRES
0 400 800 1200

Capitals
International Boundaries
Canals

CAPE VERDE ISLANDS
(Ilhas do Cabo Verde)
(PORTUGUESE)
SCALE OF MILES
0 50 100

Long. West of Greenwich 20° A 10° B 0° C 10° D 20° E 30° F 40° G Long. 50° East H of 60° Greenwich

7511

CITIES AND TOWNS IN THE UNITED STATES

of 1000 or more inhabitants (1950 Census figures)

The index reference gives the location of the city or town on the state map. The name is found within the square formed by the two lines of latitude and the two lines of longitude which enclose each of the index reference coordinates — i.e., the marginal letters and numbers.

△Population figure for an entire township, district or minor civil division. ‡Not shown on map. Index refers to the county in which place is located.

ALABAMA

Name & Index *Pop.*

Abbeville (H7) 2,162
Adamsville (D3) 1,531
Albertville (F2) 5,397
Aldrich (E4) 1,000
Alexander City (G5) 6,430
Aliceville (B4) 3,170
Andalusia (E8) 9,162
Anniston (G3) 31,066
Arab (E2) 1,592
Ashford (H8) 1,400
Ashland (G4) 1,593
Athens (E1) 6,309
Atmore (C8) 5,720
Attalla (F2) 7,537
Auburn (H5) 12,939
Austinville (D1) 1,110
Bay Minette (C9) 3,732
Bayou la Batre (B10) 2,196
Bessemer (D4) 28,445
Birmingham (D3) 326,037
Birmingham (urban area) 438,726
Blocton (D4) 1,500
Boaz (F2) 3,078
Brantley (F7) 1,102
Brent (D5) 1,100
Brewton (D8) 5,146
Bridgeport (G1) 2,386
Brighton (E4) 1,689
Brundidge (G7) 2,605
Calera (E4) 1,361
Camp Hill (G5) 1,296
Carbon Hill (D3) 2,179
Centre (G2) 1,672
Centreville (D5) 1,160
Chickasaw (B9) 4,920
Childersburg (F4) 4,023
Citronelle (B8) 1,350
Clanton (E5) 4,640
Clayton (G7) 1,583
Collinsville (G2) 1,023
Columbiana (E4) 1,761
Cordova (D3) 3,156
Cullman (E2) 7,523
Dadeville (G5) 2,354
Dallas Mills (E1) 2,200
Daphne (C9) 1,041
Decatur (D1) 19,974
Demopolis (C6) 5,004
Dolomite (D4) 4,500
Dothan (H8) 21,584
East Brewton (E8) 2,173
Elba (F8) 2,936
Enterprise (G8) 7,288
Eufaula (H7) 6,906
Eutaw (C5) 2,348
Evergreen (E8) 3,454
Fairfax (H5) 2,717
Fairfield (E3) 13,177
Fairhope (C10) 3,354
Fayette (C3) 3,707
Flomaton (D8) 1,036
Florala (F8) 2,713
Florence (C1) 23,879
Foley (C10) 1,301
Fort Deposit (E7) 1,358
Fort Payne (G2) 6,226
Frisco City (D8) 1,068
Fultondale (E3) 1,304
Gadsden (G2) 55,725
Geneva (G8) 3,579
Georgiana (E7) 1,596
Glencoe (G3) 1,466
Good Water (F4) 1,227
Goodsprings (D3) 1,000
Greensboro (C5) 2,217
Greenville (E7) 6,781
Grove Hill (C7) 1,443
Guin (C3) 1,137
Guntersville (F2) 5,253
Haleyville (C2) 3,331
Hamilton (C2) 1,623
Hartford (G8) 1,655
Hartselle (E2) 3,429
Headland (H8) 2,091
Heflin (G3) 1,982
Hokes Bluff (G3) 1,158
Holt (D4) 2,400
Homewood (E4) 12,866
Huntsville (E1) 16,437
Irondale (E3) 1,876
Jackson (C8) 3,072
Jacksonville (G3) 4,751
Jasper (D3) 8,589
Jefferron (C6) 3,200
Kimberly (E3) 1,100
Lafayette (H5) 2,353
Lanett (H5) 7,434
Langdale (H5) 2,721
Leeds (E3) 3,306
Leighton (D1) 1,080
Linden (C6) 1,363
Lineville (G4) 1,548
Lipscomb (E4) 2,550
Livingston (B5) 1,681
Loxley (C9) 1,000
Luverne (F7) 2,221
Margaret (F3) 1,144
Marion (D5) 2,822
Marvel (D4) 1,238
Mignon (F4) 3,053
Mobile (B9) 129,009
Mobile (urban area) 180,892
Monroeville (D7) 2,772
Montevallo (E4) 2,150
MONTGOMERY (F6) 106,525
Montgomery (urban area) 108,034
Moulton (D2) 1,384
Mount Vernon (B8) 2,300
Mountain Brook (E4) 8,359
Mulga ‡(D3) 1,743
Muscle Shoals (C1) 1,937
New Brockton (G8) 1,055
Normal (E1) 1,400
Northport (C4) 3,885
Oakman (D3) 1,022
Oneonta (E3) 2,802
Opelika (H5) 12,295
Opp (F8) 5,240
Oxford (G3) 1,697
Ozark (G8) 5,238
Pell City (F3) 1,189
Pepperell (H5) 1,166
Phenix City (H6) 23,305
Piedmont G3) 4,498
Pleasant Grove ‡(E3) 1,802
Prattville (E6) 4,385
Prichard (B9) 19,014
Ragland (F3) 1,008
Red Bay (B2) 1,805
Reform (G4) 1,141
River View (H5) 1,322
Roanoke (H4) 5,392
Robertsdale (C9) 1,128
Russellville (C2) 6,012
Samson (F8) 2,204
Satsuma (B9) 1,592
Scottsboro (F1) 4,731
Selma (E6) 22,840
Shawmut (H5) 3,266
Sheffield (C1) 10,767
Siluria (E4) 2,850
Sipsey (D3) 1,000
Slocomb (G8) 1,219
Sulligent (B3) 1,209
Sumiton (D3) 1,334
Sylacauga (F4) 9,606
Talladega (F4) 13,134
Tallassee (G5) 4,225
Tarrant (E3) 7,571
Thomaston (C6) 1,027
Thomasville (C7) 2,425
Troy (G7) 8,555
Trussville (E3) 1,575
Tuscaloosa (C4) 46,396
Tuscumbia (C1) 6,734
Tuskegee (G6) 6,712
Tuskagee Inst. (G6) 2,642
Union Springs (G6) 3,232
Uniontown (D6) 1,798
Vincent (F4) 1,240
Warrior (E3) 1,384
West Blocton (D4) 1,280
Wetumpka (F5) 3,813
Winfield (C3) 2,180
York (B6) 1,774

ARIZONA

Name & Index *Pop.*

Ajo (C6) 5,817
Avondale (C5) 2,505
Benson (E7) 1,440
Bisbee (F7) 3,801
Buckeye (C5) 1,932
Casa Grande (D6) 4,181
Chandler (D5) 3,799
Clarkdale (C4) 1,609
Claypool (E5) 1,200
Clifton (F5) 3,466
Coolidge (D6) 4,306
Cottonwood (D4) 1,326
Douglas (F7) 9,442
Eloy (D6) 3,580
Flagstaff (D3) 6,771
Florence (D5) 1,776
Gilbert (D5) 1,114
Glendale (C5) 8,179
Globe (E5) 6,419
Goodyear (C5) 1,254
Grand Canyon (C2) 1,001
Hayden (E5) 1,494
Holbrook (E4) 2,336
Jerome (C4) 1,233
Kingman (A3) 3,342
Lowell (F7) 1,136
McNary (F4) 1,902
Mesa (D5) 16,790
Miami (E5) 4,329
Miller Valley (C4) 2,953
Morenci (F5) 6,541
Nogales (E7) 6,153
Parker (A4) 1,201
PHOENIX (C5) 106,818
Phoenix (urban area) 214,335
Pirtleville (F7) 1,246
Prescott (C4) 6,764
Ray (E5) 2,000
Safford (F6) 3,756
St. Johns (F4) 1,469
Scottsdale (D5) 2,032
Somerton (A6) 1,825
Sonora (D5) 1,821
South Tucson (D6) 2,364
Superior (D5) 4,500
Tempe (D5) 7,684
Thatcher (F6) 1,284
Tolleson (C5) 3,042
Tucson (D6) 45,454
Warren (F7) 2,610
Wickenburg (C5) 1,736
Willcox (F6) 1,266
Williams (C3) 2,152
Winslow (E3) 6,518
Yuma (A6) 9,145

ARKANSAS

Alma (B3) 1,228
Arkadelphia (D5) 6,819
Arkansas City (H6) 1,018
Ashdown (B6) 2,738
Atkins (E3) 1,291
Augusta (H3) 2,317
Bald Knob (G3) 2,022
Batesville (G2) 6,414
Bauxite (F4) 2,459
Bearden (E6) 1,300
Beebe (G3) 1,192
Benton (E4) 6,277
Bentonville (B1) 2,942
Berryville (C1) 1,753
Blytheville (L2) 16,234
Booneville (C3) 2,433
Brinkley (H4) 4,173
Cabot (F4) 1,147
Camden (E6) 11,372
Carlisle (G4) 1,396
Clarendon (H4) 2,547
Clarksville (D3) 4,343
Conway (F3) 8,610
Corning (J1) 2,045
Cotter (E1) 1,089
Cotton Plant (H3) 1,838
Crossett (F7) 4,619
Cullendale (E7) 3,225
Dardanelle (D3) 1,772
De Queen (B5) 3,015
De Witt (H5) 2,843
Dermott (H7) 3,601
Des Arc (G4) 1,612
Dierks (B5) 1,253
Dumas (H6) 2,512
Earle (K3) 2,375
El Dorado (E7) 23,076
England (G4) 2,136
Eudora (H7) 3,072
Eureka Spgs. (C1) 1,958
Fayetteville (B1) 17,071
Fordyce (F6) 3,754
Forrest City (J3) 7,607
Fort Smith (B3) 47,942
Fort Smith (urban area) 55,947
Gould (G6) 1,076
Greenwood (B3) 1,634
Gurdon (D6) 2,390
Hamburg (G7) 2,655
Harrisburg (J2) 1,498
Harrison (D1) 5,542
Hazen (G4) 1,270
Heber Springs (G2) 2,109
Helena (J4) 11,236
Hope (C6) 8,605
Hot Springs Nat'l Park (D4) 29,307
Hoxie (H1) 1,855
Hughes (J4) 1,686
Huntsville (C1) 1,010
Huttig (F7) 1,038
Jacksonville (F4) 2,474
Jonesboro (J2) 16,310
Judsonia (G3) 1,122
Junction City (E7) 1,013
Lake Village (H7) 2,484
Leachville (K2) 1,230
Lepanto (K2) 1,683
Lewisville (C7) 1,237
LITTLE ROCK (F4) 102,213
Little Rock-North LittleRock (urban area) 150,758
Lonoke (G4) 1,556
Luxora (K2) 1,302
Magnolia (D7) 6,918
Malvern (E5) 8,072
Manila (K2) 1,729
Marianna (J4) 4,530
Marked Tree (K2) 2,878
Marrhall (E2) 1,189
Marvell (J4) 1,121
McCrory (H3) 1,115
McGehee (H6) 3,854
Mena (B4) 4,445
Monette (K2) 1,114
Monticello (G6) 4,501
Morrilton (E3) 5,483
Mountain Home (F1) 2,217
Mountain Pine (D4) 1,155
Mountain View (F2) 1,043
Murfreesboro (C5) 1,079
Nashville (C6) 3,548
Nettleton (J2) 1,382
Newport (H2) 6,254
No. Little Rock (F4) 44,097
No. Little Rock-Little Rock (urban area) 150,758
Osceola (K2) 5,006
Ozark (C3) 1,757
Paragould (J1) 9,668
Paris (C3) 3,731
Parkin (J3) 1,414
Piggott (K1) 2,558
Pine Bluff (F5) 37,162
Pocahontas (E1) 3,840
Prescott (D6) 3,960
Rector (K1) 1,855
Rogers (B1) 4,962
Russellville (D3) 8,166
Searcy (G3) 6,024
Sheridan (F5) 1,893
Siloam Springs (B1) 3,270
Smackover (E7) 2,495
Springdale (B1) 5,835
Stamps (D7) 2,552
Star City (G6) 1,296
Stephens (E7) 1,283
Stuttgart (H4) 7,276
Texarkana (C7) 15,875
Trumann (J2) 3,744
Tuckerman (H2) 1,253
Van Buren (B3) 6,413
Waldo (D7) 1,491
Waldron (B4) 1,292
Walnut Ridge (J1) 3,106
Warren (F6) 6,319
West Helena (J4) 6,107
West Memphis (K3) 9,112
Wilson (K2) 1,301
Wynne (J3) 4,142

CALIFORNIA

Alameda (J2) 64,430
Alamo (K2) 2,673
Albany (J2) 17,590
Alhambra (C10) 51,359
Alisal (D7) 16,714
Alta Loma (E10) 1,200
Altadena (C10) 37,500
Alturas (E2) 2,819
Alvarado (K2) 2,000
Anaheim (D11) 14,556
Anderson (C3) 1,501
Angels Camp (E5) 1,147
Antioch (L1) 11,051
Arbuckle (C4) 1,150
Arcadia (D10) 23,066
Arcata (A3) 3,729
Arlington (E11) 4,326
Armona (F7) 1,274
Arroyo Grande (E8) 1,723
Artesia (C11) 15,920
Arvin (G8) 5,007
Atascadero (E8) 3,443
Atherton (K3) 3,630
Atwater (E6) 2,856
Auburn (C8) 4,653
Avalon (G10) 1,506
Avenal (E8) 3,982
Azusa (D10) 11,042
Bakersfield (G8) 34,784
Balboa (D11) 3,000
Baldwin Park (D10) 28,000
Banning (J10) 7,034
Barstow (H9) 6,135
Bayshore (J2) 2,726
Beaumont (J10) 3,152
Bell (C11) 15,430
Bellflower (C11) 40,000
Belmont (J3) 5,567
Benicia (K1) 7,284
Berkeley (J2) 113,805
Beverly Hills (B10) 29,032
Big Bear Lake (J9) 1,434
Bishop (G6) 2,891
Bloomington (E10) 10,100
Blythe (L10) 4,089
Bolinas (H1) 1,006
Boulder Creek (J4) 1,497
Brawley (K11) 11,922
Brea (D11) 3,208
Brentwood (L2) 1,729
Brisbane (J2) 4,500
Buena Park (D11) 5,483
Burbank (C10) 78,577
Burlingame (J3) 19,886
Burney (D3) 1,513
Byron (L2) 1,117
Calexico (K11) 6,433
Calipatria (K10) 1,428
Calistoga (C5) 1,418
Campbell (K3) 10,000
Capitola (K4) 1,848
Carlsbad (H10) 4,383
Carmel (C7) 4,351
Carpinteria (F9) 2,864
Casa Blanca (E11) 1,585
Castroville (D7) 1,865
Cathedral City (J10) 2,058
Centerville (K3) 1,401
Central Valley (C3) 2,202
Ceres (D6) 2,351
Chester (D3) 1,197
Chico (D4) 12,272
Chino (D10) 5,784
Chowchilla (E6) 3,893
Chrisman (F9) 4,211

Name & Index	Pop.
Chula Vista (J11)	15,927
Claremont (D10)	6,327
Clearwater (C11)	8,586
Cloverdale (B5)	1,292
Clovis (F7)	2,766
Coachella (J10)	2,755
Coalinga (E7)	5,539
Colton (E10)	14,465
Colusa (C4)	3,031
Compton (C11)	47,991
Concord (K1)	6,953
Corcoran (F7)	3,150
Corning (C4)	2,537
Corona (E11)	10,223
Coronado (H11)	12,700
Corte Madera (J2)	1,933
Costa Mesa (D11)	11,844
Covina (D10)	3,956
Crescent City (A2)	1,706
Crockett (J1)	6,000
Cucamonga (E10)	1,255
Culver City (B10)	19,720
Cupertino (K3)	2,438
Cutler (F7)	1,768
Cutten (A3)	1,340
Cypress (D11)	1,318
Daly City (H2)	15,191
Danville (K2)	3,130
Davis (B8)	3,554
Decoto (K2)	2,830
Del Paso Hts. (B8)	15,000
Del Rosa (E10)	1,154
Delano (F8)	8,717
Dinuba (F7)	4,971
Dixon (B9)	1,714
Dos Palos (E6)	1,394
Downey (C11)	35,000
Duarte (D10)	10,000
Dunsmuir (C2)	2,256
Earlmart (F8)	2,162
East Bakersfield (G8)	38,177
El Cajon (J11)	5,600
El Centro (K11)	12,590
El Cerrito (J2)	18,011
El Monte (D10)	8,101
El Segundo (B11)	11,688
Elsinore (F11)	2,068
Emeryville (J2)	2,889
Empire (D6)	1,448
Encinitas (H10)	7,000
Escalon (E6)	1,569
Escondido (H10)	6,544
Etiwanda (E10)	1,200
Eureka (A3)	23,058
Exeter (F7)	4,078
Fair Oaks (C8)	5,000
Fairfax (H1)	4,078
Fairfield (K1)	3,118
Fallbrook (H10)	1,735
Ferndale (A3)	1,032
Fillmore (F9)	3,884
Folsom (C8)	1,690
Fontana (E10)	28,000
Fort City (F8)	4,347
Fort Bragg (B4)	3,826
Fortuna (A3)	1,762
Fowler (F7)	1,857
Freedom (L4)	2,765
Fresno (F7)	91,669
Fresno (urban area)	129,275
Fullerton (D11)	13,958
Galt (C9)	1,333
Garberville (B3)	1,350
Garden Grove (D11)	3,762
Gardena (C11)	14,405
Gilroy (L4)	4,951
Glendale (C10)	95,702
Glendora (D10)	3,988
Goleta (F9)	1,548
Gonzales (D7)	1,821
Grass Valley (D4)	5,283
Greenfield (D7)	1,309
Greenville (E3)	1,153
Gridley (D4)	3,054
Grover City (E8)	2,500
Guadalupe (E9)	2,429
Guerneville (B5)	1,250
Gustine (D6)	1,984
Half Moon Bay (H3)	1,168
Hanford (F7)	10,028
Harbor City (C11)	7,500
Hawthorne (B11)	16,316
Hayward (K2)	14,272
Healdsburg (B5)	3,258
Hemet (J10)	3,386
Hermosa Beach (B11)	11,826
Highland (H9)	8,500
Hillsborough ‡(J2)	3,552
Hollister (D7)	4,903
Hollywood (C10)	179,749
Holtville (K11)	2,472
Hopland (B5)	1,150
Hughson (E6)	1,816
Huntington Beach (D11)	5,237
Huntington Park (C10)	29,450
Imperial (K11)	1,759
Indio (J10)	5,300
Inglewood (B11)	46,185
Ione (C9)	1,071
Irvington (K3)	2,500
Isleton (L1)	1,597
Ivanhoe (F7)	1,172
Jackson (C9)	1,879
Jamestown (E6)	1,300
Kerman (E7)	1,563
King City (D7)	2,347
Kingsburg (F7)	2,310
Klamath (B2)	1,012
La Canada (C10)	8,200
La Crescenta (C10)	16,000
La Habra (D11)	4,961
La Jolla (H11)	13,000
La Mesa (H11)	10,946
La Sierra (E11)	3,802
La Verne (D10)	4,198
Lafayette (K2)	10,500
Laguna Beach (G10)	6,661
Lakeport (C4)	1,983
Lakewood (C11)	31,000
Lamont (G8)	3,571
Lancaster (G9)	3,594
Larkspur (H1)	2,905
Lawndale (C11)	31,000
Lemoore (F7)	2,153
Lennox (C11)	25,000
Lincoln (B8)	2,410
Lindsay (G7)	5,060
Live Oak (D4)	1,770
Livermore (L2)	4,364
Livingston (E6)	1,502
Lodi (C9)	13,798
Loma Linda (E10)	4,000
Lomita (C11)	10,000
Lomita Park (J2)	1,800
Lompoc (E9)	5,520
Lone Pine (H7)	1,415
Long Beach (C11)	250,767
Los Altos (K3)	11,000
Los Angeles (C10)	1,970,358
Los Angeles (urban area)	3,970,595
Los Banos (E6)	3,868
Los Gatos (K4)	4,907
Lynwood (C11)	25,823
Madera (E7)	10,497
Manhattan Beach (B11)	17,330
Manteca (D6)	3,804
Martinez (K1)	8,268
Marysville (D4)	7,826
Maywood (C10)	13,292
McCloud (C2)	1,394
McFarland (F8)	2,183
Mendocino (B4)	1,250
Mendota (E7)	1,516
Menlo Park (J3)	13,587
Mentone (H9)	3,525
Merced (E6)	15,278
Midway City (D11)	1,421
Mill Valley (H2)	7,331
Millbrae (J2)	8,972
Mira Loma (E10)	1,555
Mission San Jose (L3)	1,080
Modesto (D6)	17,389
Mojave (G8)	2,055
Monrovia (D10)	20,186
Montebello (C10)	21,735
Montecito (F9)	4,052
Monterey (D7)	16,205
Monterey Park (C10)	20,395
Montrose (C10)	8,500
Moorpark (G9)	1,146
Morgan Hill (L4)	1,627
Morro Bay (D8)	1,659
Mount Shasta (C2)	1,909
Mountain View (K3)	6,563
Napa (C5)	13,579
National City (J11)	21,199
Needles (L9)	4,051
Nevada City (D4)	2,505
New Cuyuma (F9)	1,079
Newark (K3)	1,532
Newhall (G9)	2,527
Newman (D6)	1,815
Newport Beach (D11)	12,120
Niles (K3)	1,519
Norco (E11)	1,584
N. Fork (F6)	1,453
N. Sacramento (B8)	6,029
Norwalk (C11)	6,300
Novato (H1)	3,496
Oakdale (E6)	4,064
Oakland (J2)	384,575
Oakland-San Francisco (urban area)	1,997,303
Oakley (L1)	2,892
Ocean Beach (H11)	16,600
Oceano (E8)	1,446
Oceanside (H10)	12,881
Oildale (F8)	16,615
Ojai (F9)	2,519
Ontario (D10)	22,872
Orange (D11)	10,027
Orange Cove (F7)	2,395
Orcutt (E9)	1,001
Orinda (K2)	5,000
Orland (C4)	2,067
Oroville (D4)	5,387
Oxnard (F9)	21,557
Pacific Beach (H11)	23,600
Pacific Grove (C7)	9,623
Palm Springs (J10)	7,660
Palo Alto (K3)	25,475
Palos Verdes Estates (B11)	1,963
Paradise (D4)	4,426
Paramount (C11)	10,006
Parlier (F7)	1,419
Pasadena (C10)	104,577
Paso Robles (E8)	4,835
Patterson (D6)	1,343
Perris (F11)	1,807
Petaluma (H1)	10,315
Pico (C10)	9,000
Piedmont (J2)	10,132
Pinedale (F7)	2,220
Pinole (J1)	1,147
Pismo Beach (E8)	1,425
Pittsburg (K1)	12,763
Pixley (F8)	2,000
Placentia (D11)	1,682
Placerville (C8)	3,749
Pleasanton (L2)	2,244
Pomona (D10)	35,405
Port Chicago (K1)	3,000
Port Hueneme (F9)	3,024
Porterville (F7)	6,904
Portola (E4)	2,261
Project City (C3)	1,200
Puente (D10)	3,000
Quincy (E4)	1,330
Ramona (J10)	1,158
Red Bluff (C3)	4,905
Redding (C3)	10,256
Redlands (H9)	18,429
Redondo Beach (B11)	25,226
Redwood City (J3)	25,544
Reedley (F7)	4,135
Rialto (E10)	3,156
Richmond (J1)	99,545
Ridgecrest (H8)	2,028
Rio Dell (A3)	1,862
Rio Vista (L1)	1,831
Ripon (D6)	1,550
Riverbank (E6)	2,662
Riverside (E10)	46,746
Rocklin (B8)	1,155
Rodeo (J1)	6,500
Rohnerville (B3)	1,500
Rosemead (D10)	15,230
Roseville (B8)	8,723
Ross (H1)	2,179
SACRAMENTO (B8)	137,572
Sacramento (urban area)	210,081
Saint Helena (C5)	2,297
Salinas (D7)	13,917
San Andreas (E5)	1,263
San Anselmo (H1)	9,188
San Bernardino (E10)	63,058
San Bernardino (urban area)	135,394
San Bruno (J2)	12,478
San Carlos (J3)	14,371
San Clemente (H10)	2,008
San Diego (J11)	334,387
San Diego (urban area)	413,274
San Dimas (D10)	1,840
San Fernando (C10)	12,992
San Francisco (H2)	775,357
San Francisco-Oakland (urban area)	1,997,303
San Gabriel (C10)	20,343
San Jacinto (H10)	1,778
San Jose (L3)	95,280
San Jose (urban area)	175,983
San Juan Bautista (D7)	1,031
San Juan Capistrano (H10)	1,250
San Leandro (J2)	27,542
San Lorenzo (K2)	10,570
San Luis Obispo (E8)	14,180
San Marino (D10)	11,230
San Mateo (J3)	41,782
San Pablo (J1)	14,476
San Pedro (C11)	74,000
San Rafael (J1)	13,848
San Ysidro (J11)	2,381
Sanger (F7)	6,400
Santa Ana (D11)	45,533
Santa Barbara (F9)	44,913
Santa Clara (K3)	11,702
Santa Cruz (K4)	21,970
Santa Maria (E9)	10,440
Santa Monica (B10)	71,595
Santa Paula (F9)	11,049
Santa Rosa (C5)	17,902
Saratoga (K4)	1,329
Saticoy (F9)	2,216
Sausalito (H2)	4,828
Scotia (A3)	1,017
Seal Beach (C11)	3,553
Seaside (D7)	10,226
Sebastopol (C5)	2,601
Selma (F7)	5,964
Sepulveda (B10)	4,500
Shafter (F8)	2,207
Sierra Madre (D10)	7,273
Signal Hill (C11)	4,040
Solana Beach (H11)	1,350
Soledad (D7)	2,441
Solvang (E9)	1,025
Sonoma (C5)	2,015
Sonora (E6)	2,448
Soquel (K4)	2,400
S. Bakersfield (F8)	12,120
S. Gate (C11)	51,116
S. Pasadena (C10)	16,935
S. San Francisco (J2)	19,351
Stanford (J3)	10,000
Stanton (D11)	1,762
Stockton (D6)	70,853
Stockton (urban area)	113,362
Strathmore (F7)	2,500
Sunland (C10)	5,000
Sunnyvale (K3)	9,829
Susanville (E3)	5,338
Sutter Creek (C9)	1,151
Taft (F8)	3,707
Tarzana (B10)	10,000
Tehachapi (G8)	1,685
Temple City (C10)	25,000
Topanga (B10)	3,278
Torrance (C11)	22,241
Tracy (D6)	8,410
Trona (H8)	2,450
Truckee (E4)	1,025
Tujunga (C10)	14,000
Tulare (F7)	12,445
Tulelake (D2)	1,028
Tuolumne (E6)	1,284
Turlock (D6)	6,235
Tustin (D11)	1,143
Twentynine Palms (K9)	1,022
Ukiah (B4)	6,120
Upland (D10)	9,203
Vacaville (D5)	3,169
Vallejo (J1)	26,038
Van Nuys (B10)	90,000
Venice (B11)	58,871
Ventura (F9)	16,534
Verdugo City (C10)	2,100
Victorville (H9)	3,241
Visalia (F7)	11,749
Vista (H10)	1,705
Walnut Creek (K2)	2,420
Warco (F8)	5,592
Waterford (E6)	1,777
Watsonville (D7)	11,572
Weaverville (C3)	1,800
Weed (C2)	2,739
W. Covina (D10)	4,499
W. Riverside (E10)	3,798
Westminster (D11)	3,131
Westmorland (K10)	1,213
Westwood (D3)	3,618
Whittier (D11)	23,820
Williams (C4)	1,134
Willits (B4)	2,691
Willows (C4)	3,019
Wilmar (C10)	8,000
Wilmington (C11)	30,000
Winters (D5)	1,265
Woodlake (G7)	2,525
Woodland (B8)	9,386
Yorba Linda (D11)	2,000
Yreka (C2)	3,227
Yuba City (D4)	7,861
Yucaipa (J9)	1,515

COLORADO

Name & Index	Pop.
Aguilar (K8)	1,038
Akron (N2)	1,605
Alamosa (H8)	5,354
Animas (D8)	2,500
Antonito (H8)	1,255
Arvada (J3)	2,359
Aurora (K3)	11,421
Boulder (J2)	19,999
Brighton (K3)	4,336
Brush (M2)	2,431
Burlington (P4)	2,247
Canon City (J6)	6,345
Center (G7)	2,024
Cheyenne Wells (P5)	1,154
Colorado Spgs. (K5)	45,472
Cortez (B8)	2,680
Craig (D2)	3,080
Del Norte (G7)	2,048
Delta (D5)	4,097
DENVER (K3)	415,786
Denver (urban area)	495,513
Derby (K3)	2,840
Durango (D8)	7,459
Eads (O6)	1,015
Eaton (K2)	1,276
Edgewater (J3)	2,580
Englewood (K3)	16,869
Estes Park (J2)	1,617
Fitzsimons (K3)	5,000
Florence (J6)	2,773
Fort Collins (J1)	14,937
Fort Lupton (K2)	1,907
Fort Morgan (M2)	5,315
Fowler (L6)	1,025
Fruita (B4)	1,463
Fruitvale (B4)	2,275
Glenwood Spgs. (E4)	2,412
Golden (J3)	5,238
Grand Jct. (C4)	14,504
Greeley (K2)	20,354
Gunnison (E5)	2,770
Haxtun (O1)	1,006
Holly (P6)	1,236
Holyoke (P1)	1,558
Idaho Springs (H3)	1,769
Ivywild (K5)	2,849
Jansen (K8)	1,500
Julesburg (P1)	1,951
La Junta (M7)	7,712
Lafayette (K3)	2,073
Lamar (O6)	6,829
Las Animas (N6)	3,223
Leadville (G4)	4,081
Limon (M4)	1,471
Littleton (K3)	3,378
Longmont (J2)	8,099
Louisville (J3)	1,978
Loveland (J2)	6,773
Manitou Spgs. (J5)	2,580
Meeker (D2)	1,658
Monte Vista (G7)	3,272
Montrose (D6)	4,964
Oak Creek (F2)	1,488
Ordway (M6)	1,290
Ouray (D6)	1,089
Pagosa Springs (E8)	1,379
Paonia (D5)	1,257
Pueblo (K6)	63,685
Pueblo (urban area)	73,102
Rifle (D3)	1,525
Rocky Ford (M6)	4,087
Roswell (K5)	1,029
Saguache (G6)	1,024
Salida (H6)	4,553
San Luis (J8)	1,239
Sheridan ‡(K3)	1,715
Silverton (D7)	1,375
Sopris (K8)	1,330
South Canon (J6)	1,588
Springfield (O8)	2,041
Starkville (L8)	1,000
Steamboat Spgs. (F2)	1,913
Sterling (N1)	7,534
Telluride (D7)	1,101
Trinidad (L8)	12,204
Walsenburg (K7)	5,596
Westminster (J3)	1,686
Wheat Ridge (J3)	7,000
Windsor (J2)	1,548
Wray (P2)	2,198
Yuma (O2)	1,908

CONNECTICUT

Name & Index	Pop.
Allingtown (D3)	4,800
Andover (F2)	▵1,034
Ansonia (C3)	18,706
Avon (D1)	▵3,171
Baltic (G2)	1,345
Beacon Falls (C3)	▵2,067
Berlin (E2)	▵7,470
Bethany (C3)	▵1,318
Bethel (B3)	▵5,104
Bethlehem (C2)	▵1,015
Bloomfield (E1)	▵5,746
Bolton (F1)	▵1,279
Branford (D3)	2,552
Bridgeport (C4)	158,709
Bridgeport (urban area)	237,954
Bristol (D2)	35,961
Bristol-New Britain (urban area)	122,618
Broad Brook (E1)	2,140
Brookfield (B3)	▵1,688
Brooklyn (H1)	▵2,652
Burlington (D1)	▵1,846
Byram (A4)	8,000
Canaan (B1)	1,189
Canterbury (H2)	▵1,321
Canton (D1)	▵3,613
Cheshire (D2)	▵6,295
Chester (F3)	▵1,920
Clinton (E3)	▵2,466
Colchester (F2)	1,522
Collinsville (D1)	2,078
Columbia (F2)	▵1,327
Cos Cob (A4)	6,800
Coventry (F1)	▵4,043
Cranbury (B4)	3,000
Cromwell (E2)	▵4,286
Danbury (B3)	22,067
Danielson (H1)	4,554
Darien (B4)	▵11,767
Dayville (Killingly) (H1)	1,105
Deep River (F3)	▵2,570
Derby (C3)	10,259
Durham (E3)	▵1,804
East Berlin (E2)	1,000
E. Brooklyn (H1)	1,062
E. Granby (E1)	▵1,327
E. Haddam (F3)	▵2,554
E. Hampton (E2)	▵4,000
E. Hartford (E1)	▵29,933
E. Haven (D3)	▵12,212
E. Lyme (G3)	▵3,870
E. Norwalk (B4)	5,000
E. Windsor (E1)	▵4,859
Easton (B4)	▵2,165
Ellington (F1)	▵3,099
Elmwood (D2)	6,000
Enfield (E1)	▵15,464
Essex (F3)	▵3,491
Fairfield (B4)	▵30,489
Farmington (D2)	▵7,026
Forestville (D2)	6,000
Glastonbury (E2)	▵8,818
Goodyear (H1)	1,000
Granby (D1)	▵2,693
Greenwich (A4)	▵40,835
Groton (G3)	7,036
Guilford (E3)	▵5,092
Haddam (E3)	▵2,636

Name & Index	Pop.
Hamden (D3)	▲29,715
HARTFORD (E1)	177,397
Hartford(urban area)	299,676
Harwinton (C1)	▲1,858
Hazardville (E1)	1,272
Hebron (F2)	▲1,320
Jewett City (H2)	3,702
Jordan Village (Waterford) (G3)	▲9,100
Kensington (D2)	4,700
Kent (B2)	▲1,392
Killingly (H1)	1,105
Lebanon (G2)	▲1,654
Ledyard (G3)	▲1,749
Litchfield (C2)	1,174
Madison (E3)	▲3,078
Manchester (E1)	▲34,116
Mansfield (F1)	▲10,008
Meriden (D2)	44,088
Middlebury (C2)	▲3,318
Middlefield (E2)	*1,983
Middletown (E2)	29,711
Milford (C4)	▲26,870
Milldale (D2)	1,200
Monroe (C3)	▲2,892
Montville (G3)	▲4,766
Moodus (F2)	1,400
Moosup (H2)	2,909
Mystic (H3)	2,266
Naugatuck (C3)	17,455
New Britain (E2)	73,726
New Britain-Bristol (urban area)	122,618
New Canaan (B4)	▲8,001
New Fairfield (B3)	▲1,236
New Hartford (C1)	▲2,395
New Haven (D3)	164,443
New Haven (urban area)	242,589
New London (G3)	30,551
New Milford (B2)	▲5,799
Newington (E2)	▲9,110
Niantic (G3)	1,746
Nichols (C4)	1,171
Noank (G3)	1,149
Norfolk (C1)	*1,572
Noroton (B4)	3,000
Noroton Heights (B4)	3,918
N. Branford (E3)	▲2,017
N. Grosvenor Dale (H1)	2,232
N. Guilford (E3)	1,000
N. Haven (D3)	▲9,444
N. Stonington (H3)	▲1,367
Norwalk (B4)	49,460
Norwalk-Stamford (urban area)	172,197
Norwich (G2)	23,429
Norwichtown (G2)	2,916
Oakville (C2)	5,100
Old Greenwich (A4)	5,348
Old Lyme (F3)	▲2,141
Old Saybrook (F3)	▲2,499
Orange (C3)	▲3,032
Oxford (C3)	▲2,037
Pawcatuck (H3)	5,269
Pine Orchard (D3)	5,100
Plainfield (H2)	▲8,071
Plainville (D2)	▲9,994
Plantsville (D2)	1,536
Plymouth (C2)	▲6,771
Pomfret (H1)	▲2,018
Poquonock (E1)	1,200
Poquonock Bridge (G3)	4,050
Portland (E2)	▲5,186
Preston (H2)	▲1,775
Prospect (D2)	▲1,896
Putnam (H1)	8,181
Quaker Hill (G3)	1,260
Redding (B3)	▲2,037
Ridgefield (A3)	▲4,356
Riverside (A4)	2,000
Rockfall (E2)	2,000
Rockville (F1)	8,016
Rocky Hill (E2)	▲5,108
Rowayton (B4)	3,200
Salisbury (B1)	▲3,132
Sandy Hook (B3)	1,600
Saugatuck (B4)	1,500
Seymour (C3)	▲7,832
Sharon (B1)	▲1,889
Shelton (C3)	12,694
Simsbury (D1)	▲4,822
Somers (F1)	▲2,631
S. Coventry (F1)	1,617
S. Meriden (D2)	1,600
S. Norwalk (B4)	18,000
S. Windsor (E1)	▲4,066
Southbury (C3)	▲3,828
Southington (D2)	▲13,061
Southport (B4)	3,000
Springdale (A4)	5,280
Stafford (F1)	▲6,471
Stafford Sprs. (F1)	3,396
Staffordville (G1)	1,000
Stamford (A4)	74,293
Stamford-Norwalk (urban area)	172,197
Stepney Depot (B3)	3,000
Sterling (H2)	▲1,298
Stonington (H3)	1,739
Stony Creek (E3)	1,800
Stratford (C4)	▲33,428
Suffield (E1)	▲4,895
Taftville (G2)	3,598
Terryville (C2)	6,500
Thamesville (G2)	5,518
Thomaston (C2)	▲4,896
Thompson (H1)	▲5,585
Thompsonville (E1)	9,633
Tolland (F1)	▲1,659
Torrington (C1)	27,820
Trumbull (C4)	▲8,641
Union City (C2)	5,000
Unionville (D1)	2,197
Vernon (F1)	▲10,115
Wallingford (D3)	11,994
Wapping (E1)	1,000
Warehouse Point (E1)	1,283
Washington (B2)	▲2,227
Waterbury (C2)	104,477
Waterbury (urban area)	131,442
Waterford (Jordan Village) (G3)	▲9,100
Watertown (C2)	▲10,699
Wauregan (H2)	1,002
W. Cheshire (D2)	1,000
W. Hartford (D1)	▲44,402
W. Haven (D3)	▲32,010
W. Mystic (H3)	2,362
W. Redding (B3)	1,000
W. Suffield (E1)	1,800
Westbrook (F3)	▲1,549
Westfield (E2)	1,250
Weston (B4)	▲1,988
Westport (B4)	▲11,667
Wethersfield (E2)	▲12,533
Willimantic (G2)	13,586
Wilson (E1)	3,500
Wilton (B4)	▲4,558
Windham (G2)	▲15,884
Windsor (E1)	▲11,833
Windsor Locks (E1)	▲5,221
Winnipauk (B4)	3,600
Winsted (C1)	8,781
Wolcott (D2)	▲3,553
Woodbridge (D3)	▲2,822
Woodbury (C2)	▲2,564
Woodmont (C4)	5,000
Woodstock (H1)	▲2,271
Yalesville (D3)	1,122

DELAWARE

Name & Index	Pop.
Bellefonte (N1)	1,472
Bridgeville (M6)	1,468
Claymont (N1)	5,370
Delaware City (M2)	1,363
Delmar (M7)	1,015
DOVER (M4)	6,223
Elsmere (M2)	5,314
Georgetown (N6)	1,923
Harrington (M5)	2,241
Hockessin (M1)	1,200
Hollyoak (N1)	1,450
Laurel (M6)	2,700
Lewes (O5)	2,904
Marshallton (M2)	1,600
Middletown (M3)	1,755
Milford (N5)	5,179
Milton (N5)	1,321
New Castle (M2)	5,396
Newark (M2)	6,731
Newport (M2)	1,171
Rehoboth Beach (O6)	1,794
Seaford (M6)	3,087
Selbyville (N7)	1,086
Smyrna (M3)	2,346
Wilmington (M2)	110,356
Wilmington (urban area)	186,265

FLORIDA

Name & Index	Pop.
Alachua (D2)	1,116
Apalachicola (A2)	3,222
Apopka (E3)	2,254
Arcadia (E4)	4,764
Arlington (E1)	3,200
Atlantic Beach (E1)	1,604
Auburndale (E3)	3,763
Avon Park (E4)	4,612
Babson Park (E4)	1,000
Bagdad (B6)	1,500
Baldwin (E1)	1,048
Bartow (E4)	8,694
Bay Harbor (D6)	1,676
Belle Glade (F5)	7,219
Biscayne Park ‡(F6)	2,009
Blountstown (A1)	2,118
Bonifay (C5)	2,252
Boynton Beach (F5)	2,542
Bradenton (D4)	13,604
Brandon (D4)	1,250
Bristol (B1)	1,800
Brooksville (D3)	1,818
Bunnell (E2)	1,341
Canal Point (F5)	1,022
Century (B5)	1,350
Chattahoochee (B1)	8,473
Chipley (D6)	2,959
Chosen (F5)	1,873
Clearwater (D4)	15,581
Clermont (E3)	2,168
Clewiston (E5)	2,499
Cocoa (F3)	4,245
Coral Gables (F6)	19,837
Crescent City (E2)	1,393
Crestview (C6)	5,003
Cross City (C2)	1,522
Crystal River (D3)	1,026
Dade City (D3)	3,806
Dania (F5)	4,540
Daytona Beach (F2)	30,187
De Funiak Springs (C6)	3,077
De Land (E2)	8,652
Deerfield Beach (F5)	2,088
Delray Beach (F5)	6,312
Dinsmore (E1)	1,010
Dover (D4)	1,000
Dundee (E3)	1,152
Dunedin (D3)	3,202
Dunnellon (D2)	1,110
Eagle Lake (E4)	1,060
East Palatka (E2)	1,367
Eau Gallie (F3)	1,554
El Portal ‡(F6)	1,371
Englewood (D5)	1,206
Eustis (E3)	4,005
Fairvilla (E3)	1,000
Fernandina (E1)	4,420
Florence Villa (E3)	2,500
Florida City (F6)	1,547
Floridatown (B6)	1,200
Foley (C1)	1,014
Ft. Lauderdale (F5)	36,328
Ft. Meade (E4)	2,803
Ft. Myers (E5)	13,195
Ft. Pierce (F4)	13,502
Ft. Walton (C6)	2,463
Frostproof (E4)	2,329
Gainesville (D2)	26,861
Gifford (F4)	1,459
Goulds (F6)	1,000
Graceville (D5)	1,638
Green Cove Spgs. (E2)	3,291
Greenville (C1)	1,163
Groveland (E3)	1,028
Gulfport (D4)	3,702
Haines City (E3)	5,630
Hallandale (F6)	3,886
Havana (B1)	1,634
Hawthorne (D2)	1,058
Hialeah (F6)	19,676
High Springs (D2)	2,088
Highland City (E4)	1,600
Holly Hill (E2)	3,232
Hollywood (F5)	14,351
Homestead (F6)	4,573
Immokalee (E5)	1,200
Inverness (D3)	1,471
Jacksonville (E1)	204,517
Jacksonville (urban area)	241,579
Jacksonville Beach (E1)	6,430
Jasper (D1)	2,327
Kendall (F6)	2,100
Key West (E7)	26,433
Kissimmee (E3)	4,310
Lacoochee (D3)	1,792
Lake Alfred (E3)	1,270
Lake Butler (D1)	1,040
Lake City (D1)	7,571
Lake Wales (E4)	6,821
Lake Worth (G5)	11,777
Lakeland (D3)	30,851
Largo (D4)	1,547
Leesburg (E3)	7,395
Live Oak (D1)	4,064
Lockhart (E3)	1,200
Lutz (D3)	1,800
Lynn Haven (C6)	1,787
Macclenny (D1)	1,177
Madison (C1)	3,150
Marathon (E2)	1,200
Marianna (A1)	5,845
Mayport (E1)	1,300
Melbourne (F3)	4,223
Miami (F6)	249,276
Miami (urban area)	453,004
Miami Beach (F6)	46,282
Miami Shores (F6)	5,086
Miami Springs (F6)	5,108
Milton (B6)	2,040
Mims (F3)	1,500
Monticello (C1)	2,264
Mt. Dora (E3)	3,028
Mulberry (E4)	2,024
Naples (E5)	1,465
Neptune Beach (E1)	1,767
New Port Richey (D3)	1,512
New Smyrna Beach (F2)	5,775
Niceville (C6)	2,497
Nocatee (E4)	1,200
North Miami (F6)	10,734
N. Miami Beach (F6)	2,129
Oakland Park (F5)	1,295
Ocala (D2)	11,741
Ocoee (E3)	1,370
Ojus (F6)	3,791
Okeechobee (F4)	1,849
Opa-Locka (F6)	5,271
Orange Park (E1)	1,502
Orlando (E3)	52,367
Orlando (urban area)	72,572
Ormond (E2)	3,418
Otter Creek (D2)	1,050
Oviedo (E3)	1,601
Pahokee (F5)	4,472
Palatka (E2)	9,176
Palm Beach (G5)	3,886
Palmetto (D4)	4,103
Panama City (C6)	25,814
Parrish (D4)	1,200
Pass-a-Grille Beach (D4)	1,000
Pensacola (B6)	43,479
Perrine (F6)	2,859
Perry (C1)	2,797
Pine Castle (E3)	2,000
Pinellas Park (D4)	2,924
Plant City (D3)	9,230
Pompano Beach (F5)	5,682
Ponte Vedra Beach (E1)	1,000
Port Orange (F2)	1,201
Port Saint Joe (D6)	2,752
Port Tampa (D4)	1,497
Princeton (F6)	1,300
Punta Gorda (E5)	1,915
Quincy (B1)	6,505
Riviera Beach (F5)	4,065
Rockledge (F3)	1,347
St. Augustine (E2)	13,555
St. Cloud (E3)	3,001
St. Petersburg (D4)	96,738
St. Petersburg (urban area)	113,378
Samoset (D4)	1,617
Sanford (E3)	11,935
Sarasota (D4)	18,896
Sebring (E4)	5,006
Sneads (B1)	1,074
South Bay (F5)	1,050
South Miami (F6)	4,809
Springfield (D6)	1,084
Starke (D2)	2,944
Stuart (F4)	2,912
Surfside ‡(F6)	1,852
TALLAHASSEE (B1)	27,237
Tampa (D4)	124,681
Tampa (urban area)	178,398
Tarpon Springs (D3)	4,323
Tavares (E3)	1,763
Terra Ceia (D4)	1,500
Tice (E5)	1,133
Titusville (F3)	2,604
Umatilla (E3)	1,312
Valparaiso (C6)	1,047
Vero Beach (F4)	4,746
Warrington (B6)	13,570
Watertown (D1)	1,473
Wauchula (E4)	2,872
Waverly (E4)	1,000
West Miami (F6)	4,043
W. Palm Beach (F5)	43,162
Westgate (F6)	3,303
Wewahitchka (D6)	1,289
Wildwood (D3)	2,019
Williston (D2)	1,323
Winter Garden (E3)	3,503
Winter Haven (E3)	8,605
Winter Park (E3)	8,250
Yukon (E1)	2,000
Zellwood (E3)	1,500
Zephyrhills (D3)	1,826

GEORGIA

Name & Index	Pop.
Acworth (C2)	1,466
Adel (F8)	2,776
Albany (D7)	31,155
Alma (G7)	2,588
Americus (D6)	11,389
Aragon (B2)	1,272
Arlington (C8)	1,382
Ashburn (E7)	2,918
Atco (C2)	1,443
Athens (F3)	28,180
ATLANTA (D3)	331,314
Atlanta (urban area)	502,204
Augusta (J4)	71,508
Augusta (urban area)	87,823
Austell (C3)	1,413
Avondale Estates (D3)	1,070
Bainbridge (C9)	7,562
Barnesville (D4)	4,185
Baxley (H7)	3,409
Bibb City (B5)	1,452
Blackshear (H8)	2,271
Blakely (C8)	3,234
Blue Ridge (D1)	1,718
Boston (E9)	1,035
Bowdon (B3)	1,155
Bremen (B3)	2,299
Brunswick (K8)	17,954
Buena Vista (C6)	1,428
Buford (D2)	3,812
Butler (D5)	1,182
Cairo (D9)	5,577
Calhoun (B1)	3,231
Camilla (D8)	3,745
Canton (C2)	2,716
Carrollton (C3)	7,753
Cartersville (C2)	7,270
Cedartown (B2)	9,470
Chamblee (D3)	3,445
Chatsworth (C1)	1,214
Chickamauga (B1)	1,747
Clarkesville (F1)	1,106
Clarkston (D3)	1,165
Claxton (J6)	1,923
Clayton (F1)	1,302
Cochran (F6)	3,357
College Park (C3)	14,535
Collegeboro (J6)	1,000
Colquitt (C8)	1,664
Columbus (C6)	79,611
Columbus (urban area)	118,122
Commerce (E2)	3,351
Conyers (D3)	2,003
Cordele (E7)	9,462
Cornelia (E1)	2,424
Covington (E3)	5,192
Cumming (D2)	1,264
Cuthbert (C7)	4,025
Dahlonega (D1)	2,152
Dallas (C3)	1,817
Dalton (B1)	15,968
Darien (K8)	1,380
Dawson (D7)	4,411
Decatur (D3)	21,635
Demorest (F1)	1,166
Donalsonville (C8)	2,569
Douglas (G7)	7,428
Douglasville (C3)	3,400
Dublin (G5)	10,232
East Point (C3)	21,080
East Thomaston (D5)	3,082
Eastman (F6)	3,597
Eatonton (F4)	2,749
Edison (C7)	1,247
Elberton (G2)	6,772
Ellijay (C1)	1,527
Experiment (D4)	4,265
Fairburn (C3)	1,889
Fayetteville (C4)	1,032
Fitzgerald (F7)	8,130
Folkston (H9)	1,515
Forest Park (D3)	2,653
Forsyth (E4)	3,125
Fort Gaines (C7)	1,339
Fort Valley (E5)	6,820
Gainesville (E2)	11,936
Garden City (K6)	1,557
Glennville (J7)	2,327
Gordon (F5)	1,761
Grantville (C4)	1,359
Graymont (Twin City) (H5)	1,018
Greensboro (F3)	2,688
Griffin (D4)	13,982
Hahira (F9)	1,010
Hapeville (D3)	8,560
Hardwick (F4)	3,000
Harlem (H4)	1,033
Hartwell (G2)	2,964
Hawkinsville (E6)	3,342
Hazlehurst (G7)	2,687
Hebardville (H8)	1,113
Helena (G6)	1,027
Hinesville (J7)	1,217
Hogansville (C4)	3,769
Homerville (G8)	1,787
Jackson (E4)	2,053
Jasper (D2)	1,380
Jefferson (F2)	2,040
Jesup (J7)	4,605
Jonesboro (D4)	1,741
Kingsland (J9)	1,169
La Grange (B4)	25,025
LaFayette (B1)	4,884
Lakeland (F8)	1,551
Lavonia (F2)	1,766
Lawrenceville (D3)	2,932
Lincolnton (H3)	1,315
Lindale (B2)	2,834
Lithonia (D3)	1,538
Louisville (H4)	2,231
Ludowici (J7)	1,332
Lumber City (G7)	1,232
Lumpkin (C6)	1,209
Lyons (H6)	2,799
Macon (E5)	70,252
Macon (urban area)	93,305
Madison (F3)	2,489
Manchester (C5)	4,036
Marietta (D3)	20,687
Marshallville (D6)	1,121
Martinez (H3)	2,500
McCaysville (D1)	2,067
McDonough (D4)	1,635
McRae (G6)	1,904
Meigs (D8)	1,125
Metter (H6)	2,091
Milledgeville (F4)	8,835
Millen (J5)	3,449
Milstead (D3)	1,075
Monroe (E3)	4,542
Montezuma (E6)	2,921
Monticello (E4)	1,918
Moultrie (E8)	11,639
Mount Berry (B2)	1,500
Murrayville (E2)	1,000
Nashville (F8)	3,414
New Holland (E2)	1,618
Newnan (C4)	8,218
Norcross (D3)	1,340
North Atlanta ‡(D3)	5,930
Ocilla (F7)	2,697
Oconee (G5)	1,500
Oglethorpe (D6)	1,204
Palmetto (C3)	1,257
Pearson (G8)	1,402
Pelham (D8)	4,365

Name & Index	Pop.
Pembroke (J6)	1,171
Perry (E6)	3,849
Port Wentworth (K6)	1,500
Porterdale (E3)	3,207
Quitman (E9)	4,769
Reidsville (H6)	1,266
Richland (C6)	1,571
Ringgold (B1)	1,192
Rochelle (F7)	1,097
Rockmart (C2)	3,821
Rome (B2)	29,615
Rossville (B1)	3,892
Roswell (D2)	2,123
Royston (F2)	2,039
St. Marys (J9)	1,348
St. Simons Isl. (K8)	1,706
Sandersville (G5)	4,480
Sargent (C4)	1,250
Savannah (L6)	119,638
Savannah (urban area)	128,190
Savannah Beach (L7)	1,036
Shannon (B2)	1,676
Shellman (C7)	1,090
Silvertown (D5)	3,387
Smyrna (D3)	2,005
Social Circle (E3)	1,685
Soperton (G6)	1,667
Sparta (F4)	1,954
Statenville (G9)	1,000
Statesboro (J6)	6,097
Stone Mountain (D3)	1,899
Summerville (B2)	3,973
Summit (Twin City) (H5)	1,018
Swainsboro (H5)	4,300
Sylvania (J5)	2,939
Sylvester (E7)	2,623
Talbotton (C5)	1,175
Tallapoosa (B3)	2,826
Tennille (G5)	1,713
Thomaston (D5)	6,580
Thomasville (E9)	14,424
Thomson (H4)	3,489
Thunderbolt (K6)	1,238
Tifton (F8)	6,831
Toccoa (F1)	6,781
Trion (B1)	3,028
Twin City (H5)	1,018
Unadilla (E6)	1,098
Union City (D3)	1,490
Union Point (F3)	1,724
Valdosta (K9)	20,046
Vidalia (H6)	5,819
Vienna (E6)	2,202
Villa Rica (C3)	1,703
Wadley (H5)	1,624
Warner Robins (E5)	7,986
Warrenton (G4)	1,442
Washington (G3)	3,802
Waycross (H8)	18,899
Waynesboro (J4)	4,461
West Bainbridge (C9)	3,000
West Point (B5)	4,076
Winder (E3)	4,604
Wrens (H4)	1,380
Wrightsville (G5)	1,750

IDAHO

Name & Index	Pop.
Aberdeen (F7)	1,486
Alameda (F7)	4,694
American Falls (E7)	1,874
Ashton (G5)	1,256
Blackfoot (F6)	5,180
BOISE (B6)	34,393
Bonners Ferry (B1)	1,776
Buhl (D7)	2,870
Burley (E7)	5,924
Caldwell (B6)	10,487
Coeur d'Alene (B2)	12,198
Emmett (B6)	3,067
Filer (D7)	1,425
Glenns Ferry (C7)	1,515
Gooding (D7)	3,099
Grangeville (B4)	2,544
Hailey (D6)	1,464
Homedale (A6)	1,411
Idaho Falls (F6)	19,218
Jerome (D7)	4,523
Kellogg (B2)	4,913
Kimberly (D7)	1,347
Lewiston (A3)	12,985
Maland City (F7)	2,715
McCall (C5)	1,173
Meridian (B6)	1,810
Montpelier (G7)	2,682
Moscow (B3)	10,593
Mountain Home (C6)	1,887
Mullan (C2)	2,036
Nampa (B6)	16,185
Orchards (A3)	4,494
Orofino (B3)	1,656
Parma (B6)	1,369
Payette (B5)	4,032
Pocatello (F7)	26,131
Post Falls (A2)	1,069
Potlatch (A3)	1,024
Preston (G7)	4,045
Priest River (A1)	1,592
Rexburg (G6)	4,253
Rigby (G6)	1,826
Rupert (E7)	3,098
Saint Anthony (G6)	2,695
St. Maries (B2)	2,220
Salmon (D4)	2,648
Sandpoint (B1)	4,265
Shelley (F6)	1,856
Shoshone (D7)	1,420
Soda Springs (G7)	1,329
Twin Falls (D7)	17,600
Wallace (C2)	3,140
Weiser (B5)	3,961
Wendell (D7)	1,483

ILLINOIS

Name & Index	Pop.
Abingdon (C3)	3,300
Adeline (D1)	1,135
Albion (E5)	2,287
Aledo (C2)	2,919
Algonquin (E1)	1,223
Alorton (B6)	2,547
Alsip (B2)	1,228
Altamont (E4)	1,580
Alton (A6)	32,550
Amboy (D2)	2,128
Anna (D6)	4,380
Antioch (E1)	1,307
Arcola (E4)	1,700
Argo (B2)	9,000
Arlington Hts. (A1)	8,768
Arthur (E4)	1,573
Ashland (C4)	1,039
Assumption (E4)	1,466
Astoria (C3)	1,308
Athens (D4)	1,048
Atlanta (D3)	1,331
Auburn (D4)	1,963
Aurora (E2)	50,576
Barrington (E1)	4,209
Barry (B4)	1,529
Bartonville (D3)	2,437
Batavia (E2)	5,838
Beardstown (C3)	6,080
Beckemeyer (D5)	1,045
Belleville (B6)	32,721
Bellevue ‡(D3)	1,529
Bellwood (A2)	8,746
Belvidere (E1)	9,422
Bement (E4)	1,459
Benld (D4)	2,093
Bensenville (A1)	3,754
Benton (E6)	7,848
Berkeley (A2)	1,882
Berwyn (B2)	51,280
Bethalto (B6)	2,115
Bloomington (D3)	34,163
Blue Island (B2)	17,622
Bourbonnais (F2)	1,598
Bradley (F2)	5,699
Braidwood (E2)	1,485
Breese (D5)	2,181
Bridge View (B2)	1,393
Bridgeport (F5)	2,358
Broadview (A2)	5,196
Brookview (A2)	15,472
Brooklyn (Lovejoy) (A6)	2,568
Brookport (E6)	1,119
Bunker Hill (D4)	1,238
Burnham (B2)	1,331
Bushnell (C3)	3,317
Byron (D1)	1,237
Cairo (D6)	12,123
Calumet City (B2)	15,799
Calumet Park (B2)	2,500
Cambridge (C2)	1,489
Canton (C3)	11,927
Carbondale (D6)	10,921
Carlinville (D4)	5,116
Carlyle (D5)	2,669
Carmi (E5)	5,574
Carpentersville (E1)	1,523
Carriers Mills (E6)	2,252
Carrollton (C4)	2,437
Carterville (D6)	2,716
Carthage (B3)	3,214
Casey (F4)	2,734
Caseyville (B6)	1,209
Central City (D5)	1,231
Centralia (D5)	13,863
Cerro Gordo (E4)	1,052
Champaign (E3)	39,563
Charleston (E4)	9,164
Chatsworth (E3)	1,119
Chenoa (E3)	1,452
Chester (D6)	5,389
Chicago (B2)	3,620,962
Chicago (urban area)	4,902,801
Chicago Heights (B3)	24,551
Chillicothe (D3)	2,767
Chrisman (F4)	1,071
Christopher (D6)	3,545
Cicero (B2)	67,544
Clarendon Hills (A2)	2,437
Clay City (E5)	1,103
Clinton (E3)	5,945
Coal City (E2)	2,220
Cobden (D6)	1,104
Colchester (C3)	1,551
Collinsville (B6)	11,862
Columbia (C5)	2,179
Cottage Hills (B6)	3,357
Coulterville (D5)	1,160
Crete (F2)	2,298
Creve Coeur (D3)	5,499
Crotty (Seneca) (E2)	1,435
Crystal Lake (E1)	4,832
Cuba (C3)	1,482
Dallas City (B3)	1,275
Danville (F3)	37,864
De Kalb (E2)	11,708
Decatur (E4)	66,269
Decatur (urban area)	75,148
Deerfield (F1)	3,288
Delavan (D3)	1,248
Depue (D2)	2,163
Des Plaines (A1)	14,994
Divernon (D4)	1,013
Dixmoor (B2)	1,327
Dixon (D2)	11,523
Dolton (B2)	5,558
Downers Grove (A2)	11,886
Du Quoin (D5)	7,147
Dundee (E1)	3,414
Dupo (A6)	2,239
Dwight (E2)	2,843
Earlville (E2)	1,217
E. Alton (B6)	7,290
E. Chicago Hts. (B3)	1,548
E. Dubuque (C1)	1,697
E. Dundee (Dundee) (E1)	1,466
E. Hazel Crest (B2)	1,066
E. Moline (C2)	13,913
E. Peoria (D3)	8,698
E. Saint Louis (B6)	82,295
Edwardsville (B6)	8,776
Effingham (E4)	6,892
El Paso (D3)	1,818
Eldorado (E6)	4,500
Elgin (E1)	44,223
Elmhurst (A2)	21,273
Elmwood (D3)	1,613
Elmwood Park (B2)	18,801
Erie (C2)	1,180
Eureka (D3)	2,367
Evanston (B1)	73,641
Evergreen Park (B2)	10,531
Fairbury (E3)	2,433
Fairfield (E5)	5,576
Fairmont City (B6)	2,284
Farmer City (E3)	1,752
Farmington (C3)	2,651
Flora (E5)	5,255
Flossmoor (B3)	1,804
Forest Park (B2)	14,969
Forrest (E3)	1,040
Forreston (D1)	1,048
Fox Lake (E1)	2,238
Fox River Grove (E1)	1,313
Franklin Park (A2)	8,899
Freeburg (D5)	1,661
Freeport (D1)	22,467
Fulton (C2)	2,706
Galena (C1)	4,648
Galesburg (C3)	31,425
Galva (D2)	2,886
Geneseo (C2)	4,325
Geneva (E2)	5,139
Genoa (E1)	1,690
Georgetown (F4)	3,294
Gibson City (E3)	3,029
Gillespie (D4)	4,105
Gilman (E3)	1,602
Girard (D4)	1,740
Glen Carbon (B6)	1,176
Glen Ellyn (F2)	9,524
Glencoe (F1)	6,980
Glenview (B1)	6,142
Golconda (E6)	1,066
Grafton (C5)	1,117
Grandview (D4)	1,349
Granite City (B6)	29,465
Grayslake (E1)	1,970
Grayville (E5)	2,461
Greenup (E4)	1,360
Greenville (D5)	4,069
Griggsville (C4)	1,199
Gurnee (F1)	1,097
Hamilton (B3)	1,776
Hanover (C1)	1,643
Harrisburg (E6)	10,999
Hartford (B6)	1,909
Harvard (E1)	3,464
Harvey (B2)	20,683
Havana (D3)	4,379
Hazel Crest (B2)	2,129
Henry (D2)	1,966
Herrin (E6)	9,331
Heyworth (E3)	1,072
Highland (D5)	4,283
Highland Park (F1)	16,808
Highwood (F1)	3,813
Hillsboro (D4)	4,141
Hillside (A2)	2,131
Hinsdale (A2)	8,676
Homer (F3)	1,028
Homewood (B3)	5,887
Hoopeston (F3)	5,992
Ingalls Park (F2)	6,840
Itasca (F2)	1,274
Jacksonville (C4)	20,387
Jerseyville (C4)	5,792
Johnston City (E6)	4,479
Joliet (E2)	51,601
Jonesboro (D6)	1,607
Kankakee (F2)	25,856
Keithsburg (B2)	1,006
Kenilworth (B1)	2,789
Kewanee (C2)	16,821
Kincaid (D4)	1,793
Knoxville (C3)	2,209
La Grange (A2)	12,002
La Grange Park (A2)	6,176
La Harpe (C3)	1,295
La Salle (D2)	12,083
Lacon (D2)	2,020
Ladd (D2)	1,224
Lake Bluff (F1)	2,000
Lake Forest (F1)	7,819
Lanark (D1)	1,359
Lansing (B3)	8,682
Lawrenceville (F5)	6,328
Le Roy (E3)	1,820
Lebanon (D5)	2,417
Lemont (A2)	2,757
Lena (D1)	1,227
Lewistown (C3)	2,630
Lexington (E3)	1,181
Libertyville (F1)	5,425
Lidice (E2)	3,000
Lincoln (D3)	14,362
Lincolnwood (B1)	3,072
Lisle (E2)	4,500
Litchfield (D4)	7,208
Lockport (F2)	4,955
Lombard (A2)	9,817
Lovejoy (A6)	2,568
Loves Park (E1)	5,366
Lovington (E4)	1,152
Lyons (B2)	6,120
Mackinaw (D3)	1,011
Macomb (C3)	10,592
Madison (B6)	7,963
Mahomet (E3)	1,017
Manteno (F2)	1,789
Marengo (E1)	2,726
Marion (E6)	10,459
Marissa (D5)	1,652
Markham (B2)	2,753
Maroa (E3)	1,100
Marseilles (E2)	4,514
Marshall (F4)	2,960
Martinsville (F4)	1,440
Mascoutah (D5)	3,009
Mason City (D3)	2,004
Matteson (B3)	1,211
Mattoon (E4)	17,547
Maywood (A2)	27,473
McHenry (E1)	2,080
McLeansboro (E5)	3,008
Melrose Park (A2)	13,366
Mendota (D2)	5,129
Merrionette Park (B2)	1,101
Metamora (D3)	1,368
Metropolis (E6)	6,093
Midlothian (B2)	3,216
Milan (C2)	1,737
Milford (F3)	1,648
Milledgeville (D1)	1,044
Millstadt (B6)	1,566
Milton (B6)	8,232
Minonk (D3)	1,955
Moline (C2)	37,397
Moline-Rock Island, Ill.-Davenport, Iowa (urban area)	193,733
Momence (F2)	2,644
Monmouth (C3)	10,193
Monticello (E3)	2,612
Morris (E2)	6,926
Morrison (C2)	3,531
Morrisonville (D4)	1,182
Morton (D3)	3,693
Morton Grove (B1)	3,926
Mound City (D6)	2,167
Mounds (D6)	2,001
Mt. Carmel (F5)	8,732
Mt. Carroll (D1)	1,950
Mt. Morris (D1)	2,709
Mt. Olive (D4)	2,401
Mt. Prospect (A1)	4,009
Mt. Pulaski (D3)	1,526
Mt. Sterling (C4)	2,246
Mt. Vernon (E5)	15,600
Moweaqua (E4)	1,475
Mundelein (E1)	3,189
Murphysboro (D6)	9,241
Naperville (E2)	7,013
Nashville (D5)	2,432
Nauvoo (B3)	1,242
Neoga (E4)	1,125
New Athens (D5)	1,518
New Baden (D5)	1,428
New Lenox (F2)	1,235
Newman (F4)	1,140
Newton (E5)	2,780
Niles (A1)	3,587
Nokomis (D4)	2,544
Normal (E3)	9,772
Norridge (B1)	3,428
Norris City (E6)	1,370
N. Chicago (F1)	8,628
N. Chillicothe (D3)	1,741
N. Lake (A2)	4,361
N. Pekin ‡(D3)	1,758
N. Quincy (B4)	2,985
N. Riverside (B2)	3,230
Northbrook (A1)	3,348
Northfield (B1)	1,426
Oak Forest (B2)	1,856
Oak Park (B2)	63,529
Oaklawn (B2)	8,751
Oblong (F5)	1,639
Odin (D5)	1,341
O'Fallon (B6)	3,022
Oglesby (D2)	3,922
Olney (E5)	8,612
Onarga (F3)	1,455
Oregon (D1)	3,205
Oswego (E2)	1,220
Ottawa (E2)	16,957
Palatine (E1)	4,079
Palestine (F4)	1,589
Pana (D4)	6,178
Paris (F4)	9,460
Park Forest (B3)	8,138
Park Ridge (A1)	16,602
Paxton (E3)	3,795
Pecatonica (D1)	1,438
Pekin (D3)	21,858
Peoria (urban area)	154,084
Peotone (F2)	1,395
Peru (D2)	8,653
Peoria Heights (D3)	5,425
Petersburg (D4)	2,325
Phoenix (B2)	3,606
Pickneyville (D5)	3,299
Pittsfield (C4)	3,564
Plainfield (E2)	1,764
Plano (E2)	2,154
Polo (D1)	2,242
Pontiac (E3)	8,990
Port Byron (C2)	1,050
Posen (B2)	1,795
Princeton (D2)	5,765
Princeville (D3)	1,113
Prophetstown (D2)	1,691
Quincy (B4)	41,450
Rantoul (E3)	6,387
Red Bud (D5)	1,519
Ridgway (E6)	1,148
River Forest (B2)	10,823
River Grove (A2)	4,839
Riverdale (B2)	5,840
Riverside (B2)	9,153
Riverton (D4)	1,450
Roanoke (D3)	1,358
Robbins (B2)	4,766
Robinson (F5)	6,407
Rochelle (D2)	5,449
Rock Falls (D2)	7,983
Rock Island (C2)	48,710
Rock Island-Moline, Ill.-Davenport, Iowa (urban area)	193,733
Rockdale (E2)	1,393
Rockford (D1)	92,927
Rockford (urban area)	121,723
Rockton (E1)	1,432
Roodhouse (C4)	2,368
Roselle (E1)	1,038
Roseville (C3)	1,080
Rosiclare (E6)	2,086
Rossville (F3)	1,382
Round Lake Beach ‡(E1)	1,892
Round Lake Park ‡(E1)	1,836
Roxana (B6)	1,911
Royalton (D6)	1,506
Rushville (C3)	2,682
St. Anne (F2)	1,403
St. Charles (E2)	6,709
St. Elmo (E4)	1,716
St. Francisville (F5)	1,117
Salem (E5)	6,159
Sandoval (D5)	1,531
Sandwich (E2)	3,027
Savanna (C1)	5,058
Schiller Park (A1)	1,384
Seneca (E2)	1,435
Sesser (D5)	2,086
Shawneetown (E6)	1,917
Shelbyville (E4)	4,462
Sheldon (F3)	1,114
Silvis (C2)	3,055
Skokie (B1)	14,832
S. Beloit (E1)	3,221
S. Chicago Hts. (B3)	2,129
S. Elgin (E2)	1,220
S. Holland (B2)	3,247
S. Jacksonville (C4)	1,165
S. Pekin (D3)	1,043
Sparta (D5)	3,576
Spring Valley (D2)	4,916
SPRINGFIELD (D4)	81,628
Springfield (urban area)	96,649
Staunton (D5)	4,047
Steeleville (D6)	1,353
Steger (F2)	4,358
Sterling (D2)	12,817
Stickney (B2)	3,317
Stockton (C1)	1,445
Stone Park ‡(A2)	1,414
Stonington (D4)	1,120
Streator (E2)	16,469
Sullivan (E4)	3,470
Summit (B2)	8,957
Sumner (F5)	1,170
Swansea (B6)	1,816
Sycamore (E2)	5,912
Taylorville (D4)	9,188
Thornton (B3)	1,217
Tilton (F3)	1,638
Tinley Park (B2)	2,326
Tolono (E3)	1,065
Toluca (D2)	1,419

Name & Index	Pop.
Toulon (D2)	1,173
Tremont (D3)	1,138
Trenton (D5)	1,432
Troy (B6)	1,260
Tuscola (E4)	2,960
Urbana (E3)	22,835
Vandalia (D5)	5,471
Venice (A6)	6,226
Vienna (E6)	1,085
Villa Grove (E4)	2,026
Villa Park (A2)	8,821
Virden (D4)	3,206
Virginia (C4)	1,572
Walnut (D2)	1,093
Wamac (D5)	1,429
Warren (C1)	1,378
Warsaw (B3)	2,002
Washington (D3)	4,285
Washington Park (B6)	5,840
Waterloo (C5)	2,821
Watseka (F3)	4,235
Wauconda (E1)	1,173
Waukegan (F1)	38,946
Waverly (D4)	1,330
Wenona (E2)	1,005
W. Chicago (E2)	3,973
W. City (E5)	1,081
W. Dundee (Dundee) (E1)	1,948
W. Frankfort (E6)	11,384
Westchester (A2)	4,308
Western Springs (A2)	6,364
Westmont (A2)	3,402
Westville (F3)	3,196
Wheaton (E2)	11,638
White Hall (C4)	3,082
Willow Springs (A2)	1,314
Wilmette (B1)	18,162
Wilmington (E2)	3,354
Winchester (C4)	1,591
Windsor (E4)	1,008
Winnetka (B1)	12,105
Winthrop Harbor (F1)	1,765
Witt (D4)	1,156
Wood Dale (A1)	1,857
Wood River (B6)	10,190
Woodstock (E1)	7,192
Worth (A2)	1,472
Wyoming (D2)	1,496
Zeigler (D6)	2,516
Zion (F1)	8,950

INDIANA

Name & Index	Pop.
Albany (G4)	1,846
Albion (G2)	1,341
Alexandria (F4)	5,147
Anderson (F4)	46,820
Andrews (F3)	1,083
Angola (G1)	5,081
Arcadia (E4)	1,073
Argos (E2)	1,284
Attica (C4)	3,862
Auburn (G2)	5,879
Aurora (H6)	4,780
Austin (F7)	2,906
Batesville (G6)	3,194
Bedford (E7)	12,562
Beech Grove (E5)	5,685
Berne (H3)	2,277
Bicknell (C7)	4,572
Bloomfield (D6)	2,086
Bloomington (D6)	28,163
Bluffton (G3)	6,076
Boonville (C8)	5,092
Bourbon (E2)	1,404
Brazil (C5)	8,434
Bremen (E2)	2,664
Brookston (D3)	1,014
Brookville (G6)	2,538
Brownsburg (E5)	1,578
Brownstown (F7)	1,998
Butler (H2)	1,914
Cambridge City (G5)	2,559
Cannelton (D9)	2,027
Carmel (E5)	1,009
Carthage (F5)	1,065
Cayuga (C5)	1,022
Cedar Lake (C2)	3,907
Centerville (H5)	1,386
Chandler (C8)	1,050
Charlestown (F8)	4,785
Chesterfield (F4)	1,086
Chesterton (D1)	3,175
Churubusco (G2)	1,232
Cicero (E4)	1,021
Clarksville (F8)	5,905
Clay City (C6)	1,068
Clinton (C5)	6,462
Columbia City (G2)	4,745
Columbus (E6)	18,370
Connersville (G5)	15,550
Corydon (E8)	1,944
Covington (C4)	2,235
Crane (D7)	2,000
Crawfordsville (D4)	12,851
Crothersville (F7)	1,276
Crown Point (C2)	5,839
Culver (E2)	1,563
Danville (D5)	2,802
Decatur (H3)	7,271
Delphi (D3)	2,530
Dugger (C6)	1,204
Dunkirk (G4)	3,048
Dunlap (F1)	1,154
Dyer (C1)	1,556
East Chicago (C1)	54,263
East Gary (C1)	5,635
Eaton (G4)	1,598
Edinburg (E6)	3,283
Elkhart (F1)	35,556
Elwood (F4)	11,362
Evansville (C9)	128,636
Evansville (urban area)	133,200
Fairmount (F4)	2,646
Farmersburg (C6)	1,024
Ferdinand (D8)	1,252
Flora (E3)	1,657
Fort Branch (B8)	1,944
Fort Wayne (G2)	133,607
Fort Wayne (urban area)	139,529
Fortville (F5)	1,786
Fowler (C3)	2,117
Frankfort (E4)	15,028
Franklin (E6)	7,316
Frankton (F4)	1,047
French Lick (D7)	1,946
Garrett (G2)	4,291
Gary (C1)	133,911
Gas City (F4)	3,787
Goodland (C3)	1,218
Goshen (F1)	13,003
Greencastle (D5)	6,888
Greendale (H6)	2,018
Greenfield (F5)	6,159
Greensburg (G6)	6,599
Greentown (E4)	1,160
Greenwood (E5)	3,066
Griffith (C1)	4,470
Hagerstown (G5)	1,694
Hammond (B1)	87,594
Hanover (F7)	1,060
Hartford City (G4)	7,253
Hebron (C2)	1,010
Highland (B1)	5,878
Hobart (C1)	10,244
Home Corner (Vet's Adm. Hosp.) (F3)	3,950
Hope (F6)	1,215
Huntingburg (D8)	4,056
Huntington (G3)	15,079
Hymera (C6)	1,069
INDIANAPOLIS (E5)	427,173
Indianapolis (urban area)	499,799
Ingalls (F5)	666
Jasonville (C6)	2,937
Jasper (D8)	5,215
Jeffersonville (F8)	14,685
Jonesboro (F4)	1,973
Kendallville (G2)	6,119
Kentland (C3)	1,633
Kingsford Heights (D2)	1,104
Knightstown (F5)	2,486
Knox (D2)	3,034
Kokomo (E4)	38,672
Kountz Lake (D2)	1,200
La Porte (D1)	20,414
Lafayette (D4)	35,568
Lagrange (F1)	1,892
Lakeland (D1)	2,172
Lapel (F4)	1,389
Lawrence (E5)	1,951
Lawrenceburg (H6)	4,806
Lebanon (D4)	7,631
Liberty (H5)	1,730
Ligonier (F2)	2,375
Linton (C6)	5,973
Logansport (E3)	21,031
Long Beach (D1)	1,103
Loogootee (D7)	2,424
Lowell (C2)	1,621
Lydick (E1)	1,175
Lynn (H4)	1,149
Madison (G7)	7,506
Marion (F3)	30,081
Martinsville (D6)	5,991
Merrillville (C2)	1,400
Michigan City (C1)	28,395
Middletown (F4)	1,731
Milan (G6)	1,014
Mishawaka (E1)	32,913
Mitchell (E7)	3,245
Monon (D3)	1,439
Monroeville (H3)	1,150
Montezuma (C5)	1,220
Monticello (D3)	3,467
Montpelier (G3)	1,826
Mooresville (E5)	2,264
Morocco (C3)	1,141
Mt. Vernon (B9)	6,150
Muncie (G4)	58,479
Munster (B1)	4,753
Nappanee (F2)	3,393
New Albany (F8)	29,436
New Castle (G5)	18,271
New Harmony (B8)	1,360
New Haven (H2)	2,336
Newburgh (C9)	1,324
Noblesville (F4)	6,567
N. Judson (D2)	1,705
N. Liberty (E1)	1,165
N. Manchester (F3)	3,977
N. Vernon (F6)	3,488
Notre Dame (E1)	5,000
Oakland City (C8)	3,539
Odon (C7)	1,177
Oolitic (E7)	1,125
Orleans (D7)	1,531
Osceola (E1)	1,091
Osgood (G6)	1,228
Owensville (B8)	1,110
Paoli (E7)	2,575
Pendleton (F5)	2,082
Peru (E3)	13,308
Petersburg (C7)	3,035
Plainfield (E5)	2,585
Plymouth (E2)	6,704
Porter (C1)	1,458
Portland (H4)	7,064
Poseyville (B8)	1,005
Princeton (B8)	7,673
Red Key (G4)	1,639
Remington (C3)	1,053
Rensselaer (C3)	4,072
Richmond (H5)	39,539
Rising Sun (H7)	1,930
Rochester (E2)	4,673
Rockport (C9)	2,493
Rockville (C5)	2,467
Rome City (G1)	1,303
Rushville (G5)	6,761
Russiaville (E4)	1,025
St. Bernice (C5)	1,200
St. Mary of the Woods (B6)	1,300
Salem (E7)	3,271
Schererville (C2)	1,457
Scottsburg (F7)	2,953
Sellersburg (F8)	1,664
Seymour (F7)	9,629
Shelburn (C6)	1,412
Shelbyville (F6)	11,734
Sheridan (E4)	1,965
Shirley (F5)	1,087
Shoals (D7)	1,039
South Bend (E1)	115,911
South Bend (urban area)	167,879
S. Whitley (F2)	1,299
Speed (F8)	1,000
Speedway (E5)	5,498
Spencer (D6)	2,394
Sullivan (C6)	5,423
Summitville (F4)	1,061
Syracuse (F2)	1,453
Tell City (D9)	5,735
Terre Haute (C6)	64,214
Terre Haute (urban area)	77,845
Thorntown (D4)	1,380
Tipton (E4)	5,633
Union City (H4)	3,572
Upland (F4)	1,565
Valparaiso (C2)	12,028
Veedersburg (C4)	1,719
Veterans Adm. Hospital (F3)	3,950
Vevay (G7)	1,309
Vincennes (C7)	18,831
Wabash (F3)	10,621
Wakarusa (F1)	1,143
Walkerton (E2)	2,102
Warren (G3)	1,247
Warsaw (F2)	6,625
Washington (C7)	10,987
Waterloo (G2)	1,414
West Baden Spring (D7)	1,047
W. Lafayette (D4)	11,873
W. Terre Haute (B6)	3,357
Whiting (C1)	9,669
Williamsport (C4)	1,241
Winamac (D2)	2,166
Winchester (G4)	5,467
Winona Lake (F2)	1,366
Winslow (C8)	1,322
Woodruff Place (E5)	1,557
Worthington (C6)	1,627
Yorktown (G4)	1,109
Zionsville (E5)	1,536

IOWA

Name & Index	Pop.
Ackley (G3)	1,608
Adel (E5)	1,799
Akron (A3)	1,251
Albia (H6)	4,838
Algona (E2)	5,415
Alta (C3)	1,348
Alton (A3)	1,038
Ames (F4)	22,898
Anamosa (L4)	3,910
Anita (D6)	1,112
Ankeny (F5)	1,229
Arnolds Park (C2)	1,078
Atlantic (D6)	6,480
Audubon (D5)	2,808
Avoca (C6)	1,955
Bedford (D7)	2,000
Belle Plaine (J5)	3,056
Bellevue (M4)	1,932
Belmond (F3)	2,169
Bettendorf (N5)	5,132
Bloomfield (J7)	2,688
Boone (F4)	12,164
Britt (F2)	1,908
Brooklyn (J5)	1,323
Buffalo Center (F2)	1,087
Burlington (L7)	30,613
Camanche (N5)	1,212
Carroll (D4)	6,231
Carter Lake (B6)	1,183
Cascade (L4)	1,299
Cedar Falls (H3)	14,344
Cedar Rapids (K5)	72,296
Cedar Rapids (urban area)	77,990
Centerville (H7)	7,625
Chariton (G6)	5,320
Charles City (H2)	10,309
Cherokee (B3)	7,705
Clarinda (C7)	5,086
Clarion (F3)	3,150
Clarksville (H3)	1,210
Clear Lake (G2)	4,977
Clinton (N5)	30,379
Colfax (G5)	2,279
Columbus Junction (L6)	1,123
Coon Rapids (D5)	1,676
Corning (D7)	2,104
Corydon (G7)	1,870
Council Bluffs (B6)	45,429
Cresco (J2)	3,638
Creston (E6)	8,317
Davenport (M5)	74,549
Davenport, Iowa — Rock Island, Ill.—Moline, Ill. (urban area)	193,733
De Witt (N5)	2,644
Decorah (K2)	6,060
Denison (C4)	4,554
DES MOINES (F5)	177,965
Des Moines (urban area)	198,892
Dubuque (M3)	49,671
Dunlap (B5)	1,409
Durant (M5)	1,075
Dyersville (L3)	2,416
Dysart (J4)	1,089
Eagle Grove (F3)	4,176
Eldon (J7)	1,457
Eldora (G4)	3,107
Elkader (L3)	1,584
Emmetsburg (D2)	3,760
Estherville (D2)	6,719
Evansdale (J4)	3,571
Exira (D5)	1,129
Fairfield (J6)	7,299
Fayette (K3)	1,469
Fonda (D3)	1,120
Forest City (F2)	2,766
Ft. Dodge (E3)	25,115
Ft. Madison (L7)	14,954
Garner (F2)	1,696
George (B2)	1,210
Glenwood (B6)	4,654
Gowrie (E4)	1,052
Graettinger (D2)	1,016
Grand Junction (E4)	1,036
Greene (H3)	1,347
Greenfield (D6)	2,102
Grinnell (H5)	6,828
Griswold (C6)	1,149
Grundy Center (H4)	2,135
Guthrie Center (D5)	2,042
Guttenberg (L3)	1,912
Hamburg (B7)	2,086
Hampton (G3)	4,432
Harlan (C5)	3,915
Hartley (C2)	1,611
Hawarden (A2)	2,625
Holstein (B4)	1,336
Hull (A2)	1,127
Humboldt (E3)	3,219
Ida Grove (B4)	2,202
Independence (K4)	4,865
Indianola (F6)	5,145
Iowa City (L5)	27,212
Iowa Falls (G3)	4,900
Jefferson (E4)	4,326
Jesup (J4)	1,158
Keokuk (L8)	16,144
Keosauqua (J7)	1,101
Keota (K6)	1,145
Kingsley (A3)	1,098
Knoxville (G6)	7,625
La Porte City (J4)	1,770
Lake City (D4)	2,308
Lake Mills (F2)	1,560
Lake View (C4)	1,158
Lamoni (F7)	2,196
Lansing (L2)	1,536
Laurens (D3)	1,556
Le Claire (N5)	1,124
Le Mars (A3)	5,844
Lenox (D7)	1,171
Leon (F7)	2,139
Logan (B5)	1,550
Madrid (F5)	1,829
Malvern (B7)	1,263
Manchester (L3)	3,987
Manila (C5)	1,035
Manly (G2)	1,473
Manning (C5)	1,801
Manson (D3)	1,622
Mapleton (B4)	1,857
Maquoketa (M4)	4,307
Marcus (B3)	1,263
Marengo (J5)	2,151
Marion (K4)	5,916
Marshalltown (G4)	19,821
Mason City (G2)	27,980
Mc Gregor (L2)	1,138
Milford (C2)	1,375
Missouri Valley (B5)	3,546
Monona (L2)	1,346
Monroe (G5)	1,108
Montezuma (H5)	1,460
Monticello (L4)	2,888
Mt. Ayr (E7)	1,793
Mt. Pleasant (L7)	5,843
Mt. Vernon (K5)	2,320
Muscatine (L6)	19,041
Mystic (H7)	1,233
Nashua (J3)	1,609
Nevada (G5)	3,763
New Hampton (J2)	3,323
New London (L7)	1,510
New Sharon (H6)	1,089
Newton (H5)	11,723
Nora Springs (H2)	1,257
Northwood (G2)	1,767
Oakland (C6)	1,296
Odebolt (C4)	1,279
Oelwein (K3)	7,859
Ogden (E4)	1,486
Onawa (A4)	3,498
Orange City (A2)	2,166
Osage (H2)	3,436
Osceola (F6)	3,422
Oskaloosa (H6)	11,124
Ottumwa (J6)	33,631
Panora (E5)	1,062
Parkersburg (H3)	1,300
Paulina (B3)	1,289
Pella (H6)	4,427
Perry (E5)	6,174
Pocahontas (D3)	1,949
Postville (K2)	1,343
Primghar (B2)	1,152
Red Oak (C6)	6,526
Reinbeck (H4)	1,460
Remsen (B3)	1,280
Rock Rapids (A2)	2,640
Rock Valley (A2)	1,581
Rockwell City (D4)	2,333
Sac City (C4)	3,170
Sanborn (B2)	1,337
Seymour (G7)	1,223
Sheffield (G3)	1,163
Sheldon (B2)	4,001
Shell Rock (H3)	1,013
Shenandoah (C7)	6,938
Sibley (B2)	2,559
Sidney (B7)	1,132
Sigourney (J6)	2,343
Sioux Center (A2)	1,860
Sioux City (A3)	83,991
Sioux City (urban area)	90,144
Sioux Rapids (C3)	1,010
Spencer (C2)	7,446
Spirit Lake (D2)	2,467
State Center (G5)	1,040
Storm Lake (C3)	6,954
Story City (F4)	1,545
Strawberry Point (K3)	1,247
Stuart (E6)	1,500
Summer (J3)	1,911
Tama (H5)	2,930
Tipton (L5)	2,633
Toledo (H4)	2,106
Traer (J4)	1,627
Tripoli (J3)	1,124
Urbandale (F5)	1,777
Villisca (C7)	1,838
Vinton (J4)	4,307
Wapello (L6)	1,755
Washington (K6)	5,902
Waterloo (J4)	65,198
Waterloo (urban area)	83,551
Waukon (L2)	3,158
Waverly (J3)	5,124
Webster City (F4)	7,611
Wellman (K6)	1,071
W. Burlington (L7)	1,614
W. Des Moines (F5)	5,615
W. Liberty (L5)	1,866
W. Union (K3)	2,141
What Cheer (J6)	1,119
Williamsburg (J5)	1,183
Wilton Junction (M5)	1,446
Windsor Heights (F5)	1,414
Winterset (E6)	3,570
Woodbine (B5)	1,304

KANSAS

Name & Index	Pop.
Abilene (E3)	5,775
Anthony (D4)	2,792
Arkansas City (E4)	12,903
Arma (H4)	1,334
Ashland (C4)	1,493
Atchison (G2)	12,792
Atwood (B2)	1,613
Augusta (F4)	4,483
Baldwin City (G3)	1,741
Baxter Springs (H4)	4,647
Belleville (E2)	2,858
Beloit (D2)	4,035
Blue Rapids (F2)	1,430
Bonner Springs (H2)	2,277
Burlingame (G3)	1,065
Burlington (G3)	2,304
Caldwell (E4)	2,000
Caney (G4)	2,876
Cedar Vale (F4)	1,010
Chanute (G4)	10,109

Name & Index	*Pop.*
Cherryvale (G4)	2,952
Chetopa (G4)	1,671
Cimarron (B4)	1,189
Clay Center (E2)	4,528
Clyde (E2)	1,067
Coffeyville (G4)	17,113
Colby (A2)	3,859
Coldwater (C4)	1,208
Columbus (H4)	3,490
Concordia (E2)	7,175
Council Grove (F3)	2,722
Dighton (B3)	1,246
Dodge City (B4)	11,262
Downs (D2)	1,221
El Dorado (F4)	11,037
Elkhart (A4)	1,132
Ellinwood (D3)	2,569
Ellis (C3)	2,649
Ellsworth (D3)	2,193
Elwood (H2)	1,020
Emporia (F3)	15,669
Erie (G4)	1,296
Eureka (F4)	3,958
Fairway ‡(H2)	1,816
Florence (E3)	1,009
Ft. Riley (F2)	2,531
Ft. Scott (H4)	10,335
Frankfort (F2)	1,237
Fredonia (G4)	3,257
Frontenac (H4)	1,569
Galena (H4)	4,029
Garden City (B4)	10,905
Garnett (G3)	2,693
Girard (H4)	2,426
Goodland (A2)	4,690
Great Bend (D3)	12,665
Greensburg (C4)	1,723
Halstead (E4)	1,328
Harper (D4)	1,672
Hays (C3)	8,625
Herington (E3)	3,775
Hiawatha (G2)	3,294
Hill City (C2)	1,432
Hillsboro (E3)	2,150
Hoisington (D3)	4,012
Holton (G2)	2,705
Horton (G2)	2,354
Howard (F4)	1,149
Hoxie (B2)	1,157
Hugoton (A4)	2,781
Humboldt (G4)	2,308
Hutchinson (D3)	33,575
Independence (G4)	11,335
Iola (G4)	7,094
Junction City (E2)	13,462
Kansas City (H2)	129,553
Kingman (D4)	3,200
Kinsley (C4)	2,479
Kiowa (D4)	1,561
La Crosse (C3)	1,769
Lakin (A4)	1,618
Larned (C3)	4,447
Lawrence (G3)	23,351
Leavenworth (H2)	20,579
Leawood (H3)	1,167
Leoti (A3)	1,250
Liberal (B4)	7,134
Lincoln (D2)	1,636
Lindsborg (E3)	2,383
Lyons (D3)	4,545
Madison (F3)	1,212
Manhattan (F2)	19,056
Mankato (D2)	1,462
Marion (F3)	2,050
Marysville (F2)	3,866
McPherson (E3)	8,689
Meade (B4)	1,763
Medicine Lodge (D4)	2,288
Merriam (H3)	1,649
Minneapolis (E2)	1,801
Mission (H2)	13,000
Mission Hills ‡(H2)	1,275
Mulvane (E4)	1,387
Neodesha (G4)	3,723
Ness City (C3)	1,612
Newton (E3)	11,590
Nickerson (D3)	1,013
Norton (C2)	3,060
Oakley (B2)	1,915
Oberlin (B2)	2,019
Olathe (H3)	5,593
Osage City (G3)	1,919
Osawatomie (H3)	4,347
Osborne (D2)	2,068
Oswego (G4)	1,997
Ottawa (G3)	10,081
Overland Park (H3)	10,000
Paola (H3)	3,972
Parsons (G4)	14,750
Peabody (E3)	1,194
Phillipsburg (C2)	2,589
Pittsburg (H4)	19,341
Plainville (C2)	2,082
Pleasanton (H3)	1,178
Pratt (D4)	7,523
Russell (D3)	6,483
Sabetha (G2)	2,173
St. Francis (A2)	1,892
St. John (D3)	1,735
St. Marys (G2)	1,201
Salina (E3)	26,176
Scott City (B3)	3,204
Sedan (F4)	1,640
Seneca (F2)	1,911
Smith Center (D2)	2,026
S. Hutchinson (D3)	1,045
Stafford (D4)	2,005
Sterling (D3)	2,243
Stockton (C2)	1,867
Sunflower (G3)	3,834
Syracuse (A3)	2,075
Tonganoxie (G2)	1,138
TOPEKA (G2)	78,791
Topeka (urban area)	88,100
Tribune (A3)	1,010
Turner (H2)	1,500
Ulysses (A4)	2,243
Valley Falls (G2)	1,139
Wakeeney (C2)	2,446
Wamego (F2)	1,869
Washington (E2)	1,527
Welborn (H2)	3,425
Wellington (E4)	7,747
Westwood (H2)	1,581
Wichita (E4)	168,279
Wichita (urban area)	192,009
Wilson (D3)	1,039
Winfield (F4)	10,264
Yates Center (G4)	2,178

KENTUCKY

Name & Index	*Pop.*
Albany (G7)	1,920
Alva (L7)	1,341
Ashland (M4)	31,131
Ashland, Ky.—Huntington, W. Va. (urban area)	156,136
Audubon Park (F4)	1,790
Augusta (J3)	1,599
Barbourville (K7)	2,926
Bardstown (G5)	4,154
Bardwell (C3)	1,033
Beattyville (K5)	1,042
Beaver Dam (D6)	1,349
Belfry (N5)	1,315
Bellevue (L1)	9,040
Benham (M7)	3,982
Benton (D3)	1,980
Berea (J5)	3,372
Blue Diamond (L6)	1,968
Bowling Green (D7)	18,347
Bulan (L6)	1,446
Burkesville (G7)	1,278
Cadiz (B7)	1,280
Campbellsville (G6)	3,477
Carlisle (J4)	1,524
Catlettsburg (M4)	4,750
Cave City (F6)	1,118
Cawood (L7)	1,232
Central City (C6)	4,110
Clay (B6)	1,291
Clinton (C3)	1,593
Cloverport (D5)	1,357
Columbia (G6)	2,167
Coral Ridge (F4)	3,010
Corbin (J7)	7,744
Covington (K1)	64,452
Cumberland (M6)	4,249
Cynthiana (J4)	4,847
Danville (H5)	8,686
Dawson Springs (B6)	2,374
Dayton (L1)	8,977
Drakesboro (D6)	1,102
Earlington (B6)	2,753
Eddyville (B6)	1,840
Elizabethtown (F5)	5,807
Elkhorn City (Praise) (N6)	1,349
Elkton (C7)	1,312
Elsmere (K2)	3,483
Eminence (G4)	1,462
Erlanger (K2)	3,694
Evarts (L7)	1,937
Falmouth (J3)	2,186
Flemingsburg (K4)	1,502
Florence (J2)	1,325
Fonde (K7)	1,300
Fort Knox (F5)	10,000
Fort Thomas (L1)	10,870
FRANKFORT (H4)	11,916
Franklin (D7)	4,343
Fullerton (L3)	1,501
Fulton (C4)	3,224
Georgetown (H4)	5,516
Glasgow (E6)	7,025
Grayson (M4)	1,383
Greensburg (F6)	1,032
Greenup (M3)	1,276
Greenville (C6)	2,661
Guthrie (C7)	1,253
Harlan (L7)	4,786
Harrodsburg (H5)	5,262
Hartford (D6)	1,564
Hazard (L6)	6,985
Henderson (B5)	16,837
Hickman (C4)	2,037
Highland Heights (L1)	1,569
Highsplint (L7)	1,500
Hodgenville (F5)	1,695
Hopkinsville (B7)	12,526
Horse Cave (F6)	1,545
Irvine (K5)	3,259
Jackson (L5)	1,978
Jamestown (G7)	1,064
Jeffersontown (G4)	1,246
Jenkins (M6)	6,921
Kenvir (L7)	3,250
Kitts (L7)	1,431
La Grange (G4)	1,558
Lancaster (H5)	2,402
Lawrenceburg (H4)	2,369
Lebanon (G5)	4,640
Lebanon Junction (F5)	1,243
Leitchfield (E6)	1,312
Lexington (J4)	55,534
Liberty (H6)	1,291
Livermore (C5)	1,441
London (J6)	3,426
Loneoak (D3)	1,250
Lookout (N6)	1,300
Lothair (L6)	1,313
Louellen (L7)	1,600
Louisa (M4)	2,015
Louisville (F4)	369,129
Louisville (urban area)	470,394
Loyall (L7)	1,548
Ludlow (K1)	6,374
Lynch (M7)	3,970
Madisonville (B6)	11,132
Majestic (N5)	1,140
Manchester (K6)	1,706
Marion (A6)	2,375
Martin (M5)	1,170
Mayfield (D3)	8,990
Maysville (K3)	8,632
McRoberts (M6)	2,500
McVeigh (N5)	1,292
Middlesboro (K7)	14,482
Middletown (G4)	1,500
Monticello (H7)	2,934
Morehead (L4)	3,102
Morganfield (B5)	3,257
Mortons Gap (B6)	1,081
Mount Sterling (J4)	5,294
Mount Vernon (J6)	1,106
Murray (D4)	6,035
Neon (M6)	1,055
Newport (L1)	31,044
Nicholasville (J5)	3,406
North Corbin (J7)	1,077
Okolona (F4)	1,047
Olive Hill (L4)	1,351
Owensboro (C5)	33,651
Owenton (H3)	1,249
Paducah (D3)	32,828
Paintsville (M5)	4,309
Paris (J4)	6,912
Park Hills (K1)	2,577
Parkway Village ‡(F4)	1,036
Pikeville (N6)	5,154
Pineville (K7)	3,890
Praise (N6)	1,349
Prestonsburg (M5)	3,585
Princeton (B6)	5,388
Providence (B6)	3,905
Raceland (M3)	1,001
Richmond (J5)	10,268
Russell (M3)	1,681
Russell Springs (G6)	1,125
Russellville (D7)	4,529
Salyersville (L5)	1,174
Scottsville (E7)	2,060
Sebree (B5)	1,158
Shelbyville (G4)	4,403
Shively (F4)	2,401
Somerset (J6)	7,097
So. Ft. Mitchell (K2)	3,142
So. Portsmouth (L3)	1,196
So. Shore (M3)	1,497
Southgate (L1)	1,903
Springfield (G5)	2,032
Stanford (H5)	1,861
Stearns (J7)	3,000
Sturgis (B5)	2,222
Tompkinsville (F7)	1,859
Uniontown (B5)	1,054
Van Lear (M5)	1,096
Vanceburg (L3)	1,528
Verda (L7)	1,446
Versailles (H4)	2,760
Vicco (L6)	1,008
Vine Grove (F5)	1,252
Walton (H3)	1,358
Wayland (M6)	1,807
Weeksbury (M6)	1,340
West Point (E4)	1,669
West Russell (M4)	1,200
Westwood (F4)	4,000
Wheelwright (M6)	2,037
Whitesburg (M6)	1,393
Whitley City (J7)	2,500
Wickliffe (C3)	1,019
Williamsburg (J7)	3,348
Williamstown (H3)	1,466
Wilmore (H5)	2,337
Winchester (J4)	9,226
Wooton (L6)	2,725

LOUISIANA

Name & Index	*Pop.*
Abbeville (F7)	9,338
Albany (M1)	1,000
Alexandria (E4)	34,913
Amite (K5)	2,804
Arcadia (E1)	2,241
Baldwin (H7)	1,138
Basile (E5)	1,572
Bastrop (G1)	12,769
Batchelor (G5)	1,936
BATON ROUGE (K2)	125,629
Baton Rouge (urban area)	137,108
Bernice (E1)	1,524
Berwick (H7)	2,619
Bogalusa (L5)	17,798
Bossier City (C1)	15,470
Breaux Bridge (G6)	2,492
Broussard (F6)	1,237
Bunkie (F5)	4,666
Buras (L8)	1,200
Campti (D3)	1,014
Carencro (F6)	1,587
Carville (K3)	2,200
Chalmette (L7)	1,695
Chauvin (J8)	3,500
Church Point (F6)	2,897
Clarks (F2)	1,345
Clinton (J5)	1,383
Colfax (E3)	1,651
Convent (L3)	1,200
Cotton Valley (D1)	1,188
Cottonport (F5)	1,534
Coushatta (D2)	1,788
Covington (K5)	5,133
Crowley (F6)	12,784
De Quincy (D6)	3,837
De Ridder (D5)	5,799
Delcambre (F7)	1,463
Delhi (H2)	1,861
Denham Springs (L2)	2,053
Donaldsonville (K3)	4,150
Doyline (D1)	1,170
Elizabeth (E5)	1,113
Elton (E6)	1,434
Erath (F7)	1,514
Eunice (F6)	8,184
Fairbanks (F1)	1,000
Farmerville (F1)	3,173
Ferriday (G3)	3,847
Franklin (G7)	6,144
Franklinton (K5)	2,342
Galliano (K8)	2,100
Garyville (M3)	1,850
Gibsland (E1)	1,085
Gilliam (C1)	1,579
Glenmora (E5)	1,556
Gloster (C2)	1,000
Golden Meadow (K8)	2,820
Gonzales (L2)	1,642
Goosport (D6)	8,318
Grambling (E1)	1,100
Gramercy (M4)	1,184
Grand Coteau (G6)	1,103
Grand Isle (L8)	1,190
Gretna (O4)	13,813
Gueydan (E6)	2,041
Hackberry (D7)	1,500
Hackley (K5)	1,100
Hahnville (N4)	1,475
Hammond (N1)	8,010
Harahan (O4)	3,394
Haynesville (D1)	3,040
Hodge (E2)	1,386
Homer (D1)	4,749
Houma (J7)	11,505
Independence (M1)	1,606
Iota (E6)	1,162
Iowa (D6)	1,125
Jackson (H5)	6,772
Jeanerette (G7)	4,692
Jena (F3)	1,438
Jennings (E6)	9,663
Jonesboro (E2)	3,097
Jonesville (G3)	1,954
Kaplan (F6)	4,562
Kenner (O4)	5,535
Kentwood (J5)	2,417
Kinder (E6)	2,003
Lafayette (F6)	33,541
Lake Arthur (E6)	2,849
Lake Charles (D6)	41,272
Lake Providence (H1)	4,123
Laplace (N3)	2,352
Larose (K7)	1,286
Lecompte (F4)	1,443
Leesville (D4)	4,670
Lockport (K7)	1,388
Logansport (C3)	1,270
Longleaf (E4)	1,200
Loranger (N1)	1,000
Lutcher (L3)	2,198
Mamou (F5)	2,254
Mandeville (L6)	7,368
Mansfield (C2)	4,440
Mansura (G4)	1,439
Many (C3)	1,681
Marksville (G4)	3,635
Melville (G5)	1,901
Merryville (D5)	1,383
Minden (D1)	9,787
Monroe (F1)	38,572
Morgan City (H7)	9,759
Napoleonville (K4)	1,260
Natchitoches (D3)	9,914
New Iberia (G6)	16,467
New Orleans (O4)	570,445
New Orleans (urban area)	655,822
New Roads (G5)	2,818
Newellton (H2)	1,280
Norco (N3)	2,400
Oak Grove (H1)	1,796
Oakdale (E5)	5,598
Oberlin (E5)	1,544
Olla (F3)	1,115
Opelousas (G5)	11,659
Paradis (N4)	1,500
Patterson (H7)	1,938
Pineville (F4)	6,423
Plain Dealing (C1)	1,321
Plaquemine (J2)	5,747
Pointe a la Hache (L7)	1,000
Ponchatoula (N2)	4,090
Port Allen (J2)	3,097
Port Barre (G5)	1,066
Raceland (J7)	2,025
Rayne (F6)	6,485
Rayville (G2)	3,138
Remy (L3)	1,064
Reserve (M3)	4,465
Ringgold (D2)	1,007
Roseland (J5)	1,038
Ruston (E1)	10,372
St. Joseph (H3)	1,218
St. Martinville (G6)	4,614
Scotlandville (J1)	4,368
Shreveport (C1)	127,206
Shreveport (urban area)	148,296
Simmesport (G5)	1,510
Slidell (L6)	3,464
Springfield (M2)	1,000
Springhill (D1)	3,383
Sulphur (D6)	5,996
Sunset (F6)	1,080
Supreme (K4)	1,000
Swartz (G1)	1,000
Tallulah (H2)	7,758
Thibodaux (J7)	7,730
Urania (F3)	1,004
Vacherie (L3)	4,026
Venice (M8)	1,500
Vidalia (G3)	1,641
Ville Platte (F5)	6,633
Vinton (C6)	2,597
Vivian (B1)	2,426
Washington (G5)	1,291
Water Proof (H3)	1,180
Weeks (G7)	1,499
Welsh (E6)	2,416
West Monroe (F1)	10,302
Westlake (D6)	1,871
Westwego (O4)	8,281
White Castle (J3)	1,839
Winnfield (E3)	5,629
Winnsboro (G2)	3,655
Zachary (K1)	1,542
Zwolle (C3)	1,555

MAINE

Name & Index	*Pop.*
Alfred (B9)	▲1,112
Anson (D6)	▲2,199
Ashland (G2)	▲2,370
Auburn (C7)	23,134
AUGUSTA (D7)	20,913
Bangor (F6)	31,558
Bar Harbor (G7)	▲3,864
Bath (D8)	10,644
Belfast (F7)	5,960
Belgrade (D7)	▲1,099
Benton (D6)	▲1,421
Berwick (B9)	▲2,166
Bethel (B7)	▲2,367
Biddeford (C9)	20,836
Bingham (D5)	▲1,354
Blaine (H2)	▲1,118
Blue Hill (F7)	▲1,308
Boothbay (D8)	▲1,559
Boothbay Harbor (D8)	▲2,290
Bowdoinham (D7)	▲1,039
Brewer (F6)	6,862
Bridgewater (H3)	▲1,279
Bridgton (B7)	▲2,950
Bristol (E8)	▲1,476
Brownville (E5)	▲1,964
Brownville Jct. (E5)	1,086
Brunswick (C8)	▲10,996
Bucksport (F6)	▲3,120
Buxton (C8)	▲2,009
Calais (J5)	4,589
Camden (F7)	▲3,670
Caribou (G2)	▲9,923
Chelsea (D7)	▲2,169
China (E7)	▲1,375
Chisholm (C7)	1,135
Clinton (D6)	▲1,623
Corinna (E6)	▲1,752
Cumberland Ctr. (C8)	▲2,030
Damariscotta (E7)	▲1,113
Danforth (H4)	▲1,174
Deer Isle (F7)	▲1,234
Dexter (E5)	▲4,126
Dixfield (C6)	▲2,022
Dover-Foxcroft (E5)	▲4,218
Eagle Lake (F1)	▲1,516
E. Machias (J6)	▲1,101
E. Millinocket (F4)	▲1,358
E. Pittston (D7)	1,050
Easton (H2)	▲1,664
Eastport (K6)	3,123
Eliot (B9)	▲2,509
Ellsworth (F6)	3,936
Enfield (F5)	▲1,196
Fairfield (D6)	▲5,811
Falmouth (C8)	▲4,342
Farmington (C6)	▲4,677
Fort Fairfield (H2)	▲5,791
Fort Kent (F1)	▲5,343
Freeport (C8)	▲3,280

Name & Index — *Pop.*

Frenchville (G1) ... ▲1,528
Fryeburg (A7) ... ▲1,926
Gardiner (D7) ... 6,649
Gorham (C8) ... ▲4,742
Gouldsboro (H7) ... 1,168
Grand Isle (G1) ... ▲1,230
Gray (C8) ... ▲1,631
Greenville (D5) ... ▲1,889
Guilford (E5) ... ▲1,842
Hallowell (D7) ... 3,404
Hampden (F6) ... ▲3,608
Harrison (B7) ... ▲1,026
Hartland (D6) ... ▲1,310
Hermon (F6) ... 1,728
Hodgdon (H3) ... ▲1,162
Houlton (H3) ... ▲8,377
Howland (F5) ... ▲1,441
Island Falls (G3) ... ▲1,237
Jay (C7) ... ▲3,102
Jefferson (D7) ... ▲1,215
Jonesport (H6) ... ▲1,727
Keegan (G1) ... 1,100
Kennebunk (B9) ... ▲4,273
Kennebunk Port (C9) ▲1,522
Kezar Falls (B8) ... 1,400
Kittery (B9) ... ▲8,380
Kittery Depot (B9) ... 1,220
Kittery Point (B9) ... 1,137
Lebanon (B9) ... ▲1,499
Lewiston (C7) ... 40,974
Limestone (H2) ... ▲2,427
Lincoln (G5) ... ▲4,030
Lisbon (C7) ... ▲4,318
Lisbon Falls (D7) ... 2,155
Littleton (H3) ... ▲1,001
Livermore (C7) ... ▲1,313
Livermore Falls (C7) ... ▲3,359
Lubec (K6) ... ▲2,973
Machias (J6) ... ▲2,063
Madawaska (G1) ... ▲4,900
Madison (D6) ... ▲3,639
Mapleton (G2) ... ▲1,367
Mars Hill (H2) ... ▲2,060
Mechanic Falls (C7) ... ▲2,061
Mexico (B6) ... ▲4,762
Milbridge (H6) ... ▲1,199
Milford (F6) ... ▲1,435
Millinocket (F4) ... ▲5,890
Milo (F5) ... ▲2,898
Monmouth (D7) ... ▲1,683
Monticello (H3) ... ▲1,284
Mount Desert (G7) ... ▲1,776
New Gloucester (C8) ... ▲2,628
Newcastle (D7) ... ▲1,021
Newport (E6) ... ▲2,190
Norridgewock (D6) ... ▲1,784
N. Anson (D6) ... 1,000
N. Berwick (B9) ... ▲1,655
N. Vassalboro (D7) ... 1,000
Norway (B7) ... ▲3,811
Oakfield (G3) ... ▲1,009
Oakland (D6) ... ▲2,679
Old Orchard Beach (C9) ... ▲4,707
Old Town (F6) ... 8,261
Orland (F6) ... ▲1,155
Orono (F6) ... ▲7,504
Orrington (F6) ... ▲1,895
Otter Creek (G7) ... 1,000
Oxford (C7) ... ▲1,569
Paris (B7) ... ▲4,358
Patten (F4) ... ▲1,536
Peru (C6) ... ▲1,080
Phillips (C6) ... ▲1,088
Phippsburg (D8) ... ▲1,134
Pittsfield (E6) ... ▲3,909
Pittston (D7) ... ▲1,258
Poland (C7) ... ▲1,503
Porter (B8) ... ▲1,052
Portland (C8) ... 77,634
Portland (urban area) ... 112,659
Presque Isle (H2) ... ▲9,954
Prouts Neck (C9) ... 2,000
Randolph (D7) ... ▲1,733
Rangeley (B6) ... ▲1,228
Readfield (D7) ... ▲1,022
Richmond (D7) ... ▲2,217
Ridlonville (C6) ... 2,000
Rockland (E7) ... 9,234
Rockport (F7) ... ▲1,656
Rumford (B6) ... ▲9,954
Sabattus (C7) ... 1,216
Saco (C9) ... 10,324
Saint Agatha (G1) ... ▲1,512
St. Albans (E6) ... ▲1,035
St. David (G1) ... 1,000
St. Francis (E1) ... ▲1,384
St. George (E7) ... ▲1,482
Sanford (B9) ... ▲15,177
Sangerville (E5) ... ▲1,161
Scarboro (C8) ... ▲4,600
Searsport (F7) ... ▲1,457
Shawmut (D6) ... 1,200
Sherman (G4) ... ▲1,029
Sherman Mills (G4) ... 1,030
Skowhegan (D6) ... ▲7,422
S. Berwick (B9) ... ▲2,646
S. Eliot (B4) ... 1,331
S. Paris (C7) ... 2,067
S. Portland (C8) ... 21,866
S. Windham (C8) ... 1,569
Southwest Harbor (G7) ▲1,534
Springvale (B9) ... 2,745
Standish (B8) ... ▲1,786

Name & Index — *Pop.*

Stonington (F7) ... ▲1,660
Strong (C6) ... ▲1,036
Thomaston (E7) ... ▲2,810
Topsham (D8) ... ▲2,626
Tremont (G7) ... ▲1,115
Turner (C7) ... ▲1,712
Union (E7) ... ▲1,085
Unity (E6) ... ▲1,014
Van Buren (G1) ... ▲5,094
Vassalboro (D7) ... ▲2,261
Vinalhaven (F7) ... ▲1,427
Waldoboro (E7) ... ▲2,536
Warren (E7) ... ▲1,576
Washburn (G2) ... ▲1,913
Waterboro (B8) ... ▲1,071
Waterville (E6) ... 18,287
Wells (B9) ... ▲2,321
W. Falmouth (C8) ... 1,500
W. Scarboro (C8) ... 1,500
Westbrook (C8) ... 12,284
Whitefield (D7) ... ▲1,030
Wilton (C6) ... ▲3,455
Winslow (D6) ... ▲4,413
Winterport (F6) ... ▲1,694
Winthrop (C7) ... ▲3,026
Wiscasset (D7) ... ▲1,594
Woodland (H5) ... ▲1,292
Woolwich (D8) ... ▲1,344
Yarmouth (C8) ... ▲2,669
York (B9) ... ▲2,000

MARYLAND

Aberdeen (K2) ... 2,944
Alta Vista (A4) ... 3,000
ANNAPOLIS (H5) ... 10,047
Arbutus (H3) ... 4,000
Arlington (H3) ... 71,750
Baltimore (H3) ... 949,708
Baltimore (urban area) ... 1,151,050
Bel Air (J2) ... 2,578
Berlin (O7) ... 2,001
Bethesda (A4) ... 36,000
Bladensburg (C4) ... 2,899
Boonsboro (D2) ... 1,071
Bradbury Heights (C5) 1,800
Brandywine (G6) ... 1,000
Brentwood (B4) ... 3,523
Brunswick (D3) ... 3,752
Cabin John (A4) ... 2,000
Cambridge (K6) ... 10,351
Capitol Heights (C5) ... 2,729
Carney (H3) ... 1,523
Catonsville (H3) ... 29,638
Centreville (K4) ... 1,804
Chesapeake City (L2) ... 1,154
Chester (J5) ... 1,100
Chestertown (K4) ... 3,143
Cheverly (C4) ... 3,318
Chevy Chase (A4) ... 1,971
Chillum (B4) ... 15,000
Cockeysville (H3) ... 3,000
College Park (C4) ... 11,170
Colmar Manor (B4) ... 1,732
Cottage City (B4) ... 1,249
Cresaptown (C7) ... 2,000
Crisfield (L9) ... 3,688
Cumberland (D7) ... 37,679
Damascus (F3) ... 1,000
Deal Island (L8) ... 1,200
Delmar (M7) ... 1,328
Denton (L5) ... 1,806
District Heights (C5) ... 1,735
Dundalk (J3) ... 40,182
East Riverdale (C4) ... 1,200
Easton (K5) ... 4,836
Eckhart Mines (C7) ... 2,350
Edgemere (J3) ... 6,000
Edmonston (C4) ... 1,190
Elkridge (H4) ... 3,000
Elkton (L2) ... 5,245
Ellicott City (G3) ... 1,500
Emmitsburg (E2) ... 1,261
Essex (J3) ... 35,000
Fairmount Heights (C5) 2,097
Federalsburg (L6) ... 1,878
Ferndale (H4) ... 2,500
Forest Glen (B4) ... 1,500
Forest Heights (B5) ... 1,125
Forestville (C5) ... 1,500
Ft. Howard (J4) ... 1,000
Frederick (E3) ... 18,142
Frostburg (C7) ... 6,876
Fruitland (M7) ... 1,028
Fullerton (J3) ... 2,500
Gaithersburg (F4) ... 1,755
Garrison (G3) ... 1,000
Glen Burnie (H4) ... 8,000
Grasonville (K5) ... 1,200
Greenbelt (C4) ... 7,074
Greensboro (L5) ... 1,181
Hagerstown (C2) ... 36,260
Halethorpe (H4) ... 5.000
Hanover (G4) ... 1,000
Havre de Grace (K2) ... 7,809
Highfield (E2) ... 1,000
Hillside (C5) ... 3,000
Hyattsville (B4) ... 12,308
Kensington (A4) ... 1,611
Landover (C4) ... 1,175
Landover Hills (C4) ... 1,661
Lanham (C4) ... 1,133
Lansdowne (H3) ... 7,500

Name & Index — *Pop.*

Laurel (G4) ... 4,482
Leonardtown (H7) ... 1,017
Lexington Park (J7) ... 6,000
Linden (A4) ... 1,000
Linthicum Heights (H4) 3,500
Lonaconing (C7) ... 2,289
Lutherville (H3) ... 2,800
Manchester (G2) ... 1,027
Maryland Park (C5) ... 1,500
Middle River (J3) ... 27,500
Morningside (C5) ... 1,520
Mount Airy (F3) ... 1,061
Mt. Rainier (B4) ... 10,989
Mt. Savage (C7) ... 2,094
Mt. Washington (H3) ... 4,153
N. East (L2) ... 1,517
Oakland (A8) ... 1,640
Ocean City (O7) ... 1,234
Odenton (H4) ... 1,059
Oella (G3) ... 1,500
Olney (F4) ... 1,000
Owings Mills (G3) ... 1,500
Parkville (H3) ... 6,500
Parole (H5) ... 1,032
Pasadena (H4) ... 1,500
Perry Hall (H3) ... 1,000
Pikesville (G3) ... 15,000
Piney Point (H8) ... 1,000
Pocomoke City (M8) ... 3,191
Port Deposit (K2) ... 1,139
Princess Anne (L8) ... 1,407
Randallstown (G3) ... 1,550
Reisterstown (G3) ... 1,500
Relay (H4) ... 1,000
Riverdale (B4) ... 5,530
Rockville (F4) ... 6,934
Rogers Heights (C4) ... 2,000
Roland Park (H3) ... 12,000
Rosedale (H3) ... 3,000
St. Michaels (J5) ... 1,470
Salisbury (M7) ... 15,141
Savage (G4) ... 1,238
Seabrook (C4) ... 2,500
Seat Pleasant (C5) ... 2,255
Severna Park (H4) ... 1,000
Shipley (H4) ... 1,500
Silver Hill (B5) ... 1,000
Silver Spring (B4) ... 75,000
Snow Hill (N8) ... 2,091
Sparrows Point (J4) ... 12,000
Stemmers Run (H3) ... 1,260
Suitland (C5) ... 2,500
Takoma Park (B4) ... 13,341
Taneytown (F2) ... 1,420
Thurmont (E2) ... 1,676
Tilghman (J6) ... 1,250
Timonium (H3) ... 1,300
Towson (H3) ... 11,000
Tuxedo (C5) ... 1,000
University Park (B4) ... 2,205
Waldorf (G6) ... 1,100
W. Lanham Hills (C4) ... 1,200
Western Port (B8) ... 3,431
Westminster (G2) ... 6,140
Wheaton (A3) ... 20,000
Williamsport (C2) ... 1,890
Woodlawn (H3) ... 5,000
Woodside (B4) ... 3,500

DISTRICT OF COLUMBIA

WASHINGTON, D. C. (B5) ... 802,178
Washington (urban area) ... 1,281,572

MASSACHUSETTS

Abington (L4) ... ▲7,152
Acton (J3) ... ▲3,510
Acushnet (L6) ... ▲4,401
Adams (B2) ... ▲12,034
Agawam (D4) ... ▲10,166
Amesbury (L1) ... ▲10,851
Amherst (E3) ... ▲10,856
Andover (K2) ... ▲12,437
Arlington (C6) ... ▲44,353
Ashburnham (G2) ... ▲2,603
Ashby (G2) ... ▲1,464
Ashland (J3) ... ▲3,500
Assonet (K5) ... 1,002
Athol (F2) ... ▲11,554
Attleboro (J5) ... 23,809
Attleboro Falls (J5) ... 2,500
Auburn (G4) ... ▲8,840
Auburndale (B7) ... 6,218
Avon (K4) ... ▲2,666
Ayer (H2) ... ▲5,740
Baldwinville (F2) ... 1,407
Ballard Vale (K2) ... 1,200
Barnstable (N6) ... ▲10,480
Barre (F3) ... ▲3,406
Bedford (B6) ... ▲5,234
Belchertown (E3) ... ▲4,487
Bellingham (J4) ... ▲4,100
Belmont (C6) ... ▲27,381
Berkley (K5) ... ▲1,284
Berlin (H3) ... ▲1,349
Bernardston (D2) ... ▲1,117
Beverly (E5) ... 28,884
Beverly Farms (E5) ... 2,500
Billerica (J2) ... ▲11,101
Blackstone (H4) ... ▲4,968

Name & Index — *Pop.*

Bondsville (E4) ... 1,200
BOSTON (D7) ... 801,444
Boston (urban area) ... 2,218,893
Bourne (M6) ... ▲4,720
Braintree (D8) ... ▲23,161
Bridgewater (K5) ... ▲9,512
Brimfield (F4) ... ▲1,182
Brockton (K4) ... 62,860
Brockton (urban area) 92,086
Brookfield (F4) ... ▲1,567
Brookline (C7) ... ▲57,589
Brookville (K4) ... 1,300
Buckland (C2) ... ▲1,605
Burlington (C5) ... ▲3,250
Buzzards Bay (M5) ... 1,459
Cambridge (C6) ... 120,740
Canton (C8) ... ▲7,465
Carver (M5) ... ▲1,530
Centerville (N6) ... 1,100
Charlton (F4) ... ▲3,136
Charlton City (F4) ... 1,200
Chatham (P6) ... ▲2,457
Chelmsford (J2) ... ▲9,407
Chelsea (D6) ... 38,912
Cherry Valley (G3) ... 1,300
Cheshire (B2) ... ▲2,022
Chester (C3) ... ▲1,292
Chicopee (D4) ... 49,211
Chicopee Falls (D4) ... 12,915
Clifton (E6) ... 5,000
Clinton (H3) ... ▲12,287
Cochituate (A7) ... 2,500
Cohasset (F7) ... ▲3,731
Collinsville (J2) ... 1,500
Colrain (D2) ... ▲1,546
Concord (A6) ... ▲8,623
Dalton (B3) ... ▲4,772
Danvers (D5) ... ▲15,720
Danversport (E5) ... 2,500
Dartmouth (K6) ... ▲11,115
Dedham (C7) ... ▲18,487
Deerfield (D2) ... ▲3,086
Dennis (O5) ... ▲2,499
Dennis Port (O6) ... 1,200
Dighton (K5) ... ▲2,950
Dodgeville (K5) ... 1,500
Douglas (H4) ... ▲2,624
Dover (B7) ... ▲1,722
Dracut (J2) ... ▲8,666
Dudley (G4) ... ▲5,261
Duxbury (M4) ... ▲3,167
E. Braintree (D8) ... 7,000
E. Bridgewater (L4) ... ▲4,412
E. Brookfield (G4) ... ▲1,243
E. Dedham (C8) ... 5,000
E. Douglas (G4) ... 1,846
E. Falmouth (M6) ... 1,405
E. Freetown (L5) ... 1,200
E. Longmeadow (E4) ... ▲4,881
E. Milton (D7) ... 7,500
E. Pepperell (H2) ... 2,500
E. Taunton (K5) ... 5,000
E. Templeton (G2) ... 1,200
E. Walpole (C8) ... 2,000
E. Weymouth (E8) ... 10,000
Easthampton (D3) ... ▲10,694
Easton (K4) ... ▲6,244
Edgartown (M7) ... ▲1,508
Erving (E2) ... ▲1,322
Essex (L2) ... ▲1,794
Everett (D6) ... 45,982
Fairhaven (L6) ... 12,764
Fairview (D4) ... 2,108
Fall River (K6) ... 111,963
Fall River (urban area) ... 117,881
Falmouth (M6) ... ▲8,662
Farnumsville (H4) ... 1,427
Fayville (H3) ... 1,000
Feeding Hills (D4) ... 3,500
Fisherville (H4) ... 1,167
Fitchburg (G2) ... 42,691
Florence (D3) ... 4,500
Forest Hills (C7) ... 10,000
Forge Village (H2) ... 1,115
Foxboro (J4) ... ▲7,030
Framingham (A7) ... ▲28,086
Framingham Center (J3) ... 4,500
Franklin (J4) ... ▲8.037
Gardner (G2) ... 19,581
Georgetown (L2) ... ▲2,411
Gilbertville (F3) ... 1,039
Gill (D2) ... ▲1,070
Gloucester (M2) ... 25,167
Grafton (H4) ... ▲8,281
Granby (E3) ... ▲1,861
Graniteville (J2) ... 1,000
Great Barrington (A4) ... ▲6,712
Greenfield (D2) ... ▲17,349
Greenwood (D6) ... 5,500
Groton (H2) ... ▲2,889
Groveland (L1) ... ▲2,340
Hadley (D3) ... ▲2,639
Hamilton (L2) ... ▲2,764
Hampden (E4) ... ▲1,322
Hanover (L4) ... ▲3,389
Hanson (L4) ... ▲3,264
Hardwick (F3) ... ▲2,348
Harvard (H2) ... ▲3,983
Harwich (O6) ... ▲2,649
Harwich Port (O6) ... 1,350
Hatfield (D3) ... ▲2,179

Name & Index — *Pop.*

Haverhill (K1) ... 47,280
Haydenville (C3) ... 1,009
Hingham (E8) ... ▲10,665
Hinsdale (B3) ... ▲1,560
Holbrook (D8) ... ▲4,004
Holden (G3) ... ▲5,975
Holliston (A8) ... ▲3,753
Holyoke (D4) ... 54,661
Holyoke-Springfield (urban area) ... 356,471
Hopedale (H4) ... ▲3,479
Hopkinton (J4) ... ▲3,486
Housatonic (A3) ... 1,601
Hubbardston (F3) ... ▲1,134
Hudson (H3) ... ▲8,211
Hull (E7) ... ▲3,379
Huntington (C4) ... ▲1,257
Hyannis (N6) ... 4,235
Indian Orchard (E4) ... 10,000
Ipswich (L2) ... ▲6,985
Islington (C8) ... 2,300
Kingston (M5) ... ▲3,461
Lakeville (L5) ... ▲2,066
Lancaster (H3) ... ▲3,601
Lanesboro (A2) ... ▲2,069
Lanesville (M2) ... 1,046
Lawrence (K2) ... 80,536
Lawrence (urban area) ... 111,937
Lee (B3) ... ▲4,820
Leeds (D3) ... 1,700
Leicester (G4) ... ▲6,029
Lenox (A3) ... ▲3,627
Leominster (G2) ... 24,075
Lexington (B6) ... ▲17,335
Lincoln (B6) ... ▲2,427
Littleton (H2) ... ▲2,349
Littleton Common (J2) ... 1,017
Longmeadow (D4) ... ▲6,508
Lowell (J2) ... 97,249
Lowell (urban area) ... 105,783
Ludlow (E4) ... ▲8,660
Lunenburg (H2) ... ▲3,906
Lynn (D6) ... 99,738
Lynnfield (D5) ... ▲3,927
Lynnfield Center (C5) 2,600
Malden (D6) ... 59,804
Manchester (F5) ... ▲2,868
Mansfield (J4) ... ▲7,184
Marblehead (E5) ... ▲13,765
Marion (L6) ... ▲2,250
Marlboro (H3) ... 15,756
Marshfield (M4) ... ▲3,267
Mattapoisett (L6) ... ▲2,265
Maynard (J3) ... ▲6,978
Medfield (B8) ... ▲4,549
Medford (C6) ... 66,113
Medway (J4) ... ▲3,744
Melrose (D6) ... 26,988
Melrose Highlds. (D6) ... 7,713
Mendon (H4) ... ▲1,619
Merrimac (L1) ... ▲2,804
Methuen (K2) ... ▲24,477
Middleboro (L5) ... ▲10,164
Middleton (K2) ... ▲2,916
Milford (H4) ... ▲15,442
Millbury (H4) ... ▲8,347
Millers Falls (E2) ... 1,134
Millis (A8) ... ▲2,551
Millville (H4) ... ▲1,692
Milton (D7) ... ▲22,395
Monson (E4) ... ▲6,125
Montague (E2) ... ▲7,812
Mt. Hope (C7) ... 5,000
Nahant (E6) ... ▲2,679
Nantasket Beach (E7) ... 1,900
Nantucket (O7) ... ▲3,484
Natick (A7) ... ▲19,838
Needham (B7) ... ▲16,313
Needham Hts. (B7) ... 5,500
New Bedford (K6) ... 109,185
New Bedford (urban area) ... 125,354
Newbury (L1) ... ▲1,994
Newburyport (L1) ... 14,111
Newton (C7) ... 81,994
Newton Center (C7) ... 15,214
Newton Highlands (C7) ... 11,480
Newton Lower Falls (B7) ... 1,215
Newton Upper Falls (C7) ... 3,451
Newtonville (C7) ... 13,689
Norfolk (J4) ... ▲2,704
N. Abington (L4) ... 3,906
N. Adams (B2) ... 21,567
N. Andover (K2) ... ▲8,485
N. Attleboro (J5) ... ▲12,146
N. Billerica (J2) ... 3,300
N. Brookfield (F3) ... ▲3,444
N. Chelmsford (J2) ... 3,249
N. Dighton (K5) ... 1,000
N. Easton (K4) ... 4.000
N. Grafton (H4) ... 2,000
N. Hadley (D3) ... 1,000
N. Oxford (G4) ... 1,250
N. Plymouth (L5) ... 4,000
N. Reading (C5) ... ▲4,402
N. Scituate (F8) ... 1,100
N. Uxbridge (H4) ... 2,100
N. Westport (K6) ... 3,000
Northampton (D3) ... 29,063

Name & Index	Pop.
Northboro (H3)	▲3,122
Northbridge (H4)	▲10,476
Northfield (E2)	▲2,246
Norton (K5)	▲4,401
Norwell (F8)	▲2,515
Norwood (B8)	▲16,636
Oak Bluffs (M7)	▲1,521
Ocean Grove (K6)	1,000
Onset (M6)	1,674
Orange (E2)	▲5,894
Orleans (O5)	▲1,759
Osterville (N6)	1,003
Oxford (G4)	▲5,841
Palmer (E4)	▲9,533
Paxton (G3)	▲1,066
Peabody (E5)	22,645
Pembroke (L4)	▲2,579
Pepperell (H2)	▲3,460
Pigeon Cove (M2)	1,011
Pinehurst (B5)	2,905
Pittsfield (A3)	55,348
Plainville (J4)	▲2,088
Plymouth (M5)	▲13,608
Pottersville (K6)	2,700
Princeton (G3)	▲1,032
Provincetown (O4)	▲3,795
Quincy (D7)	83,835
Randolph (D8)	▲9,982
Raynham (K5)	▲2,426
Raynham Center (K5)	1,800
Reading (C5)	▲14,006
Readville (C8)	6,000
Rehoboth (K5)	▲3,700
Revere (D6)	36,763
Rochdale (G4)	1,800
Rochester (L6)	▲1,328
Rockland (L4)	▲8,960
Rockport (M2)	▲4,231
Rowley (L2)	▲1,768
Russell (C4)	▲1,298
Rutland (G3)	▲3,056
Sagamore (M5)	1,500
Salem (E5)	41,880
Salisbury (L1)	▲2,695
Sandwich (N5)	▲2,418
Saugus (D6)	▲17,162
Saxonville (A7)	3,200
Scituate (F8)	▲5,993
Seekonk (J5)	▲6,104
Sharon (K4)	▲4,847
Shawsheen Village (K2)	2,100
Sheffield (A4)	▲2,150
Shelburne Falls (D2)	2,364
Sherborn (A8)	▲1,245
Shirley (H2)	▲4,271
Shirley Center (H2)	1,082
Shrewsbury (H3)	▲10,594
Silver Lake (L5)	2,024
Somerset (K5)	▲8,566
Somerville (C6)	102,351
S. Acton (J3)	1,200
S. Ashburnham (G2)	1,000
S. Barre (F3)	1,800
S. Braintree (D8)	5,600
S. Dartmouth (L6)	6,300
S. Deerfield (D3)	1,418
S. Easton (K4)	1,500
S. Hadley (D4)	▲10,145
S. Hadley Falls (D4)	4,000
S. Lancaster (H3)	1,462
S. Lawrence (K2)	25,000
S. Natick (A7)	1,500
S. Weymouth (E8)	8,500
S. Yarmouth (O6)	1,185
Southampton (C4)	▲1,387
Southboro (H3)	▲2,760
Southbridge (G4)	▲17,519
Southwick (C4)	▲2,850
Spencer (F3)	▲7,027
Springfield (D4)	162,399
Springfield-Holyoke (urban area)	356,471
Sterling (G3)	▲2,166
Stockbridge (A3)	▲2,311
Stoneham (C6)	▲13,229
Stoughton (K4)	▲11,146
Stow (H3)	▲1,700
Sturbridge (F4)	▲2,805
Sudbury (A6)	▲2,596
Sutton (G4)	▲3,102
Swampscott (E6)	▲11,580
Swansea (K5)	▲6,121
Taunton (K5)	40,109
Templeton (F2)	▲4,757
Tewkesbury (K2)	▲7,505
Thorndike (E4)	1,650
Three Rivers (E4)	2,359
Topsfield (L2)	▲1,412
Townsend (H2)	▲2,817
Turners Falls (D2)	5,179
Tyngsboro (J2)	▲2,059
Upton (H4)	▲2,656
Uxbridge (H4)	▲7,007
Vineyard Haven (M7)	1,864
Waban (B7)	6,000
Wakefield (C5)	▲19,633
Walpole (B8)	▲9,109
Waltham (B6)	47,187
Ware (E3)	▲7,517
Wareham (L5)	▲7,569
Warren (F4)	▲3,406
Watertown (C6)	▲37,329
Waverly (B6)	10,000
Wayland (A7)	▲4,407
Webster (G4)	▲13,194
Wellesley (B7)	▲20,549
Wellesley Hills (B7)	18,000
Wellfleet (O5)	▲1,123
Wenham (L2)	▲1,644
W. Acton (H3)	1,300
W. Boylston (G3)	▲2,570
W. Bridgewater (K4)	▲4,059
W. Brookfield (F4)	▲1,674
W. Concord (A6)	1,285
W. Hanover (L4)	1,200
W. Medway (J4)	1,625
W. Newbury (L1)	▲1,598
W. Newton (B7)	15,000
W. Peabody (D5)	1,100
W. Pittsfield (A3)	2,000
W. Springfield (D4)	▲20,438
W. Stockbridge (A3)	▲1,165
W. Upton (H4)	1,400
W. Warren (F4)	1,244
W. Yarmouth (N6)	1,355
Westboro (H3)	▲7,378
Westfield (D4)	20,962
Westford (J2)	▲4,262
Westminster (G2)	▲2,768
Weston (B6)	▲5,026
Westport (K6)	▲4,989
Westwood (B8)	▲5,837
Weymouth (D8)	▲32,690
Whitinsville (H4)	5,662
Whitman (L4)	▲8,413
Wilbraham (E4)	▲4,003
Williamsburg (C3)	▲2,056
Williamstown (B2)	▲6,194
Williamstown Station (B2)	5,000
Willimansett (D4)	9,474
Wilmington (C5)	▲7,039
Winchendon (F2)	▲6,585
Winchester (C6)	▲15,509
Winthrop (D6)	▲19,496
Woburn (C6)	20,492
Worcester (H3)	203,486
Worcester (urban area)	217,705
Wrentham (J4)	▲5,341
Yarmouth (O6)	▲3,297

MICHIGAN

Name & Index	Pop.
Adrian (F7)	19,393
Albion (E6)	10,406
Algonac (G6)	2,639
Allegan (D6)	4,801
Allen Park (B7)	12,329
Alma (E5)	8,341
Almont (F6)	1,035
Alpena (F3)	13,135
Ann Arbor (F6)	48,251
Auburn Heights (F6)	2,500
Bad Axe (G5)	2,973
Bangor (C6)	1,694
Battle Creek (D6)	48,666
Bay City (F5)	52,523
Belding (D5)	4,436
Belleville (F6)	1,722
Bellevue (E6)	1,168
Benton Harbor (C6)	18,769
Benton Heights (C6)	6,160
Berkley (B6)	17,931
Berrien Springs (C7)	1,761
Bessemer (F2)	3,509
Big Rapids (D5)	6,736
Birmingham (B6)	15,467
Blissfield (F7)	2,365
Bloomfield Hills (B6)	1,468
Boyne City (E3)	3,028
Bridgeport (F5)	1,200
Brighton (F6)	1,861
Bronson (D7)	2,106
Buchanan (C7)	5,224
Cadillac (D4)	10,425
Calumet (A1)	1,256
Capac (G5)	1,104
Carleton (F6)	1,039
Caro (F5)	3,464
Carrollton (E5)	2,000
Carson City (E5)	1,168
Caspian (G2)	1,608
Cass City (F5)	1,762
Cassopolis (C7)	1,527
Cedar Springs (D5)	1,378
Center Line (B6)	7,659
Charlevoix (D3)	2,695
Charlotte (E6)	6,606
Cheboygan (E3)	5,687
Chelsea (E6)	2,580
Chesaning (E5)	2,264
Clare (E5)	2,440
Clawson (B6)	5,196
Clinton (F6)	1,344
Clio (F5)	1,963
Coldwater (D7)	8,594
Coleman (E5)	1,024
Coloma (C6)	1,041
Colon (D7)	1,000
Comstock (D6)	8,314
Constantine (D7)	1,514
Coopersville (C5)	1,371
Corunna (E6)	2,358
Croswell (G5)	1,775
Crystal Falls (A2)	2,316
Davison (F5)	1,745
Dearborn (B7)	94,994
Decatur (C6)	1,664
Detroit (B7)	1,849,568
Detroit (urban area)	2,644,476
Dexter (F6)	1,307
Dowagiac (D6)	6,542
Drayton Plains (F6)	3,500
Dundee (F7)	1,975
Durand (E6)	3,194
East Ann Arbor (F6)	1,826
E. Detroit (B6)	21,461
E. Grand Rapids (D6)	6,403
E. Jordan (D3)	1,779
E. Lansing (E6)	20,325
E. Tawas (F4)	2,040
Eaton Rapids (E6)	3,509
Ecorse (B7)	17,948
Eloise (F6)	5,000
Escanaba (C3)	15,170
Essexville (F5)	3,167
Evart (D5)	1,578
Fair Haven (G6)	1,200
Farmington (F6)	2,325
Fenton (F6)	4,226
Ferndale (B6)	29,675
Ferrysburg (C5)	1,454
Flat Rock (F6)	1,931
Flint (F6)	163,143
Flint (urban area)	197,151
Flushing (F5)	2,226
Fowlerville (F6)	1,466
Frankenmuth (F5)	1,208
Frankfort (C4)	1,858
Fraser (B6)	1,379
Freeland (E5)	1,000
Fremont (D5)	3,056
Galesburg (D6)	1,200
Garden City (B7)	9,012
Gaylord (E3)	2,271
Gladstone (C3)	4,831
Gladwin (E5)	1,878
Grand Haven (C5)	9,536
Grand Ledge (E6)	4,506
Grand Rapids (D5)	176,515
Grand Rapids (urban area)	225,427
Grandville (D6)	2,022
Grayling (E4)	2,066
Greenville (D5)	6,668
Grosse Ile (B7)	2,500
Grosse Pointe (B7)	6,283
Grosse Pointe Farms (B6)	9,410
Grosse Pointe Park (B7)	13,075
Grosse Pointe Shores (B6)	1,032
Grosse Pointe Woods (B6)	10,381
Hamtramck (B6)	43,355
Hancock (G1)	5,223
Harbor Beach (G5)	2,349
Harbor Springs (D3)	1,626
Harper Woods (B6)	9,148
Hart (C5)	2,172
Hartford (C6)	1,838
Haslett (E6)	1,000
Hastings (D6)	6,096
Hazel Park (B6)	17,770
Highland Park (B6)	46,393
Hillsdale (E7)	7,297
Holland (C6)	15,858
Holly (F6)	2,663
Holt (E6)	6,500
Home Acres (D6)	20,000
Homer (E6)	1,301
Houghton (G1)	3,829
Howell (E6)	4,353
Hubbell (A1)	1,690
Hudson (E7)	2,773
Hudsonville (D6)	1,101
Huntington Woods (F6)	4,949
Imlay City (F5)	1,654
Inkster (B7)	16,728
Ionia (D6)	6,412
Iron Mountain (B3)	9,679
Iron River (G2)	4,048
Ironwood (F2)	11,466
Ishpeming (B2)	8,962
Ithaca (E5)	2,377
Jackson (E6)	51,088
Jonesville (E6)	1,594
Kalamazoo (D6)	57,704
Kalamazoo (urban area)	82,859
Kalkaska (D4)	1,250
Keego Harbor (F6)	7,700
Kingsford (A3)	5,038
Lake Linden (A1)	1,462
Lake Odessa (D6)	1,596
Lake Orion (F6)	2,385
L'Anse (G1)	2,376
LANSING (E6)	92,129
Lansing (urban area)	133,625
Lapeer (F5)	6,143
Laurium (A1)	3,211
Lawton (D6)	1,206
Leslie (E6)	1,543
Lincoln Park (B7)	29,310
Livonia (F6)	17,534
Lowell (D6)	2,191
Ludington (C5)	9,506
Mancelona (E4)	1,000
Manchester (E6)	1,388
Manistee (C4)	8,642
Manistique (C3)	5,086
Manton (D4)	1,085
Marcellus (D6)	1,014
Marenisco (F2)	1,300
Marine City (G6)	4,270
Marlette (G5)	1,489
Marquette (B2)	17,202
Marshall (E6)	5,777
Marysville (G6)	2,534
Mason (E6)	3,514
Melvindale (B7)	9,483
Menominee (B3)	11,151
Michigan Center (E6)	3,012
Middleville (D6)	1,047
Midland (E5)	14,285
Milan (F6)	2,768
Milford (F6)	1,924
Millington (F5)	1,043
Monroe (F7)	21,467
Montague (C5)	1,530
Morenci (E7)	1,983
Mount Clemens (G6)	17,027
Mt. Morris (F5)	2,890
Mt. Pleasant (E5)	11,393
Munising (C2)	4,339
Muskegon (C5)	48,429
Muskegon (urban area)	84,775
Muskegon Heights (C5)	18,828
Nashville (D6)	1,374
Negaunee (B2)	6,472
New Baltimore (G6)	2,043
New Buffalo (C7)	1,565
New Haven (G6)	1,082
Newaygo (D5)	1,385
Newberry (D2)	2,802
Niles (C7)	13,145
N. Muskegon (C5)	2,424
Northville (F6)	3,240
Norway (B3)	3,258
Novi (F6)	1,000
Oak Park (B6)	5,267
Onaway (E3)	1,421
Ontonagon (F1)	2,307
Oscoda (F4)	1,800
Otsego (D6)	3,990
Ovid (E5)	1,410
Owosso (E5)	15,948
Oxford (F6)	2,305
Painesdale (G1)	1,100
Parchment (D6)	1,179
Paw Paw (D6)	2,382
Pentwater (C5)	1,097
Perry (E6)	1,203
Petersburg (F7)	1,001
Petoskey (E3)	6,468
Pigeon (F5)	1,015
Pinconning (F5)	1,223
Plainwell (D6)	2,767
Pleasant Ridge (B6)	3,594
Plymouth (F6)	6,637
Pontiac (F6)	73,681
Pontiac (urban area)	91,799
Port Huron (G6)	35,725
Portage (D6)	1,677
Portland (E6)	2,807
Quincy (E7)	1,527
Ramsay (F2)	1,200
Reading (E7)	1,125
Reed City (D5)	2,241
Republic (B2)	1,092
Richmond (G6)	2,025
River Rouge (B7)	20,549
Riverview (B7)	1,432
Rochester (F6)	4,279
Rockford (D5)	1,937
Rockwood (F6)	1,044
Rogers City (F3)	3,873
Romeo (F6)	2,985
Romulus (F6)	1,300
Roosevelt Park (C5)	1,254
Roseville (G6)	15,816
Royal Oak (B6)	46,898
Saginaw (F5)	92,918
Saginaw (urban area)	105,358
Saint Charles (E5)	1,469
St. Clair (G6)	4,098
St. Clair Shores (G6)	19,823
St. Ignace (E3)	2,946
St. Johns (E6)	4,954
St. Joseph (C6)	10,223
St. Louis (E5)	3,347
Saline (F6)	1,533
Sandusky (G5)	1,819
Sault Sainte Marie (E2)	17,912
Schoolcraft (D6)	1,078
Scottville (C5)	1,142
Sebewaing (F5)	1,911
Shelby (C5)	1,500
S. Haven (C6)	5,629
S. Lyon (F6)	1,312
S. Rockwood (F7)	1,100
Sparta (D5)	2,327
Spring Lake (C5)	1,824
Stambaugh (G2)	1,969
Standish (F5)	1,186
Stanton (D5)	1,123
Stockbridge (E6)	1,098
Sturgis (D7)	7,786
Swartz Creek (F6)	1,000
Sylvan Lake (F6)	1,165
Tawas City (F4)	1,441
Taylor Center (B7)	20,000
Tecumseh (E7)	4,020
Temperance (F7)	1,062
Three Oaks (C7)	1,572
Three Rivers (D7)	6,785
Traverse City (D4)	16,974
Trenton (B7)	6,222
Union City (D6)	1,564
Utica (F6)	1,196
Van Dyke (B6)	21,000
Vassar (F5)	2,530
Vicksburg (D6)	2,171
Wahjamega (F5)	1,613
Wakefield (F2)	3,344
Walled Lake (F6)	2,788
Watervliet (C6)	1,327
Wayland (D6)	1,591
Wayne (F6)	9,409
West Branch (E4)	2,098
White Pigeon (D7)	1,113
Whitehall (C5)	1,819
Whitmore Lake (F6)	1,500
Williamston (E6)	2,051
Willow Run (F6)	11,365
Wyandotte (B7)	36,846
Yale (G5)	1,641
Ypsilanti (F6)	18,302
Zeeland (D6)	3,075
Zilwaukee (F5)	1,219

MINNESOTA

Name & Index	Pop.
Ada (B3)	2,121
Adrian (C7)	1,115
Aitkin (E4)	2,079
Albany (D5)	1,196
Albert Lea (E7)	13,545
Alexandria (C5)	6,319
Anoka (E5)	7,396
Appleton (C5)	2,256
Arlington (D6)	1,313
Aurora (F3)	1,371
Austin (F7)	23,100
Bagley (C3)	1,554
Bald Eagle (E5)	1,650
Barnesville (B4)	1,593
Bayport (F5)	2,502
Belle Plaine (E6)	1,708
Bemidji (D3)	10,001
Benson (C5)	3,398
Bird Island (D6)	1,333
Biwabik (F3)	1,245
Blooming Prairie (E7)	1,442
Blue Earth (D7)	3,843
Bovey (E3)	1,320
Brainerd (D4)	12,637
Breckenridge (B4)	3,623
Brooklyn Center (G5)	4,284
Browns Valley (B5)	1,117
Buffalo (E5)	1,914
Buhl (F3)	1,462
Caledonia (G7)	2,243
Cambridge (E5)	2,978
Canby (B6)	2,173
Cannon Falls (F6)	1,831
Cass Lake (D3)	1,936
Chaska (E6)	2,008
Chatfield (F7)	1,605
Chisholm (E3)	6,861
Clara City (C6)	1,106
Clarkfield (C6)	1,012
Cloquet (F4)	7,685
Cokato (D5)	1,403
Cold Spring (D5)	1,488
Coleraine (E3)	1,321
Columbia Heights (G5)	8,175
Crookston (B3)	7,352
Crosby (D4)	2,777
Crystal (G5)	5,713
Dawson (B6)	1,834
Deephaven (F5)	1,823
Deer River (E3)	1,033
Delano (E5)	1,386
Detroit Lakes (C4)	5,787
Dilworth (B4)	1,429
Dodge Center (F6)	1,151
Duluth (F4)	104,511
Duluth, Minn.-Superior, Wis. (urban area)	142,344
East Grand Forks (B3)	5,049
Edina (E6)	9,744
Elbow Lake (B4)	1,398
Elk River (E5)	1,399
Elmore (D7)	1,074
Ely (G3)	5,474
Eveleth (F3)	5,872
Excelsior (E6)	1,763
Fairfax (D6)	1,143
Fairmont (D7)	8,193
Falcon Heights (G5)	3,884
Faribault (E6)	16,028
Farmington (E6)	1,916
Fergus Falls (B4)	12,917
Foley (D5)	1,089
Forest Lake (F5)	1,766
Fort Snelling (G5)	1,096
Fosston (C3)	1,614
Frazee (C4)	1,021
Fridley (G5)	3,796
Fulda (C7)	1,149
Gaylord (D6)	1,229
Gilbert (F3)	2,247
Glencoe (D6)	2,801

Municipal Index

Name & Index — Pop.

Glenwood (C5) 2,666
Golden Valley (G5) 5,551
Grand Marais (G2) 1,078
Grand Rapids (E3) 6,019
Granite Falls (C6) 2,511
Hallock (A2) 1,552
Harmony (F7) 1,022
Hastings (F6) 6,560
Hawley (B4) 1,196
Hector (D6) 1,196
Henning (C4) 1,004
Hibbing (F3) 16,276
Hopkins (G5) 7,595
Hutchinson (D6) 4,690
International Falls (E2) 6,269
Island Park (F5) 1,357
Jackson (C7) 3,313
Janesville (E6) 1,287
Jordan (E6) 1,494
Kasson (F6) 1,353
Keewatin (E3) 1,807
Kenyon (E6) 1,651
La Crescent (G7) 1,229
Lake City (F6) 3,457
Lake Crystal (D6) 1,430
Lakefield (C7) 1,651
Lamberton (C6) 1,208
Lanesboro (G7) 1,100
Lauderdale (G5) 1,033
Le Center (E6) 1,314
Le Sueur (E6) 2,713
Litchfield (D5) 4,608
Little Falls (D5) 6,717
Long Prairie (D5) 2,443
Luverne (B7) 3,650
Madelia (D6) 1,790
Madison (B5) 2,303
Mahnomen (C3) 1,464
Mahtomedi (F5) 1,375
Mankato (E6) 18,809
Mapleton (E7) 1,083
Marshall (C6) 5,923
Melrose (D5) 2,106
Milaca (E5) 1,917
Minneapolis (E5) 521,718
Minneapolis-St. Paul (urban area) 977,931
Minneota (C6) 1,274
Montevideo (C6) 5,459
Montgomery (E6) 1,913
Monticello (E5) 1,231
Moorhead (B4) 14,870
Moose Lake (E4) 1,603
Mora (E5) 2,018
Morningside (G5) 1,699
Morris (C5) 3,811
Mound (E6) 2,061
Mountain Iron (F3) 1,377
Mountain Lake (D7) 1,733
Nashwauk (E3) 2,029
New Brighton (G5) 2,218
New Prague (E6) 1,915
New Ulm (D6) 9,348
Newport (F6) 1,672
North Mankato (D6) 4,788
North Saint Paul (E5) 4,248
Northfield (E6) 7,487
Olivia (C6) 2,012
Ortonville (B5) 2,577
Osakis (C5) 1,488
Osseo (G5) 1,167
Owatonna (E6) 10,191
Park Rapids (D4) 3,027
Paynesville (D5) 1,503
Pelican Rapids (B4) 1,676
Perham (C4) 1,926
Pine City (F5) 1,937
Pine Island (F6) 1,298
Pipestone (B7) 5,269
Plainview (F6) 1,524
Powderhorn (G6) 11,118
Preston (F7) 1,399
Princeton (E5) 2,108
Proctor (F4) 2,693
Red Lake Falls (B3) 1,733
Red Wing (F6) 10,645
Redwood Falls (C6) 3,813
Renville (C6) 1,323
Richfield (E6) 17,502
Robbinsdale (G5) 11,289
Rochester (F6) 29,885
Roseau (C2) 2,231
Roseville (G5) 6,437
Rush City (F5) 1,175
Rushford (G7) 1,270
St. Anthony Falls (G5) 1,406
St. Charles (F7) 1,548
St. Cloud (D5) 28,410
St. James (D7) 3,861
St. Joseph (D5) 1,246
St. Louis Park (G5) 22,644
SAINT PAUL (E6) 311,349
St. Paul-Minneapolis (urban area) 977,931
St. Paul Park (F6) 2,438
St. Peter (E6) 7,754
Sandstone (F4) 1,097
Sauk Centre (C5) 3,140
Sauk Rapids (D5) 3,410
Shakopee (E6) 3,185
Sherburn (D7) 1,221
Slayton (C7) 1,887
Sleepy Eye (D6) 3,278
Soudan (F3) 1,190
South International Falls (E2) 1,840
South St. Paul (F6) 15,909
Spring Grove (G7) 1,093
Spring Valley (F7) 2,467
Springfield (C6) 2,574
Staples (D4) 2,782
Starbuck (C5) 1,143
Stewartville (F7) 1,193
Stillwater (F5) 7,674
Thief River Falls (B2) 6,926
Tracy (C6) 3,020
Truman (D7) 1,106
Two Harbors (G3) 4,400
Tyler (B6) 1,121
Virginia (F3) 12,486
Wabasha (F6) 2,468
Waconia (E6) 1,569
Wadena (C4) 3,958
Waite Park (D5) 1,639
Walker (D3) 1,192
Warren (B2) 1,779
Warroad (C2) 1,276
Waseca (E6) 4,927
Waterville (E6) 1,627
Wayzata (E6) 1,791
Wells (E7) 2,475
W. Saint Paul (G5) 7,955
Westbrook (C6) 1,017
Wheaton (B5) 1,948
White Bear Lake (G5) 3,646
Willmar (C5) 9,410
Windon (C7) 3,165
Winnebago (D7) 2,127
Winona (G6) 25,031
Winthrop (D6) 1,251
Worthington (C7) 7,923
Zumbrota (F6) 1,686

MISSISSIPPI

Aberdeen (H3) 5,290
Ackerman (F4) 1,463
Amory (H3) 4,990
Baldwyn (G2) 1,567
Batesville (E2) 2,463
Bay Saint Louis (F10) 4,621
Bay Springs (F7) 1,302
Beaumont (G8) 1,200
Belzoni (C4) 4,071
Biloxi (G10) 37,425
Bonneville (G1) 3,295
Brandon (E6) 1,827
Brookhaven (C7) 7,801
Bruce (F3) 1,719
Bude (C8) 1,195
Calhoun City (F3) 1,319
Canton (D5) 7,048
Carthage (E5) 1,925
Centerville (B8) 2,025
Charleston (D2) 2,629
Clarksdale (D2) 16,539
Cleveland (C3) 6,747
Clinton (D6) 2,255
Collins (E7) 1,293
Columbia (E8) 6,124
Columbus (H3) 17,172
Corinth (G1) 9,785
Crosby (B8) 1,152
Crystal Springs (D7) 3,676
Decatur (F6) 1,225
D'Iberville (G10) 1,429
Drew (C3) 1,681
Durant (E4) 2,311
East Side (H10) 1,215
Edwards (C6) 1,002
Ellisville (F7) 3,579
Eupora (F3) 1,338
Fayette (B7) 1,498
Forest (F6) 2,874
Fulton (H2) 1,343
Gloster (B8) 1,467
Greenville (B4) 29,936
Greenwood (D4) 18,061
Grenada (E3) 7,388
Gulfport (F10) 22,659
Handsboro (F10) 1,275
Hattiesburg (F8) 29,474
Hazlehurst (D7) 3,397
Hernando (E1) 1,206
Hollandale (C4) 2,346
Holly Springs (E1) 3,276
Horn Lake (D1) 1,000
Houston (G3) 1,664
Indianola (C4) 4,369
Inverness (C4) 1,010
Itta Bena (D4) 1,725
Iuka (H1) 1,527
JACKSON (D6) 98,271
Jackson (urban area) 99,677
Kosciusko (E4) 6,753
Kreole (H10) 1,106
Lambert (D2) 1,023
Laurel (F7) 25,038
Leland (C4) 4,736
Lexington (D4) 3,198
Long Beach (F10) 2,703
Louisville (G4) 5,282
Lucedale (G9) 1,631
Lumberton (E8) 1,803
Macon (G4) 2,241
Magee (E7) 1,738
Magnolia (D8) 1,984
Marks (D2) 2,209
McComb (D8) 10,401
Mendenhall (E7) 1,539
Meridian (G6) 41,893
Mississippi City (F10) 2,125
Monticello (D7) 1,382
Moorhead (C4) 1,749
Morton (E6) 1,664
Moss Point (G10) 3,782
Mound Bayou (C3) 1,328
Natchez (B7) 22,740
Nettleton (G2) 1,204
New Albany (G2) 3,680
Newton (F6) 2,912
Ocean Springs (G10) 3,058
Okolona (G2) 2,167
Oxford (F2) 3,956
Pascagoula (G10) 10,805
Pass Christian (F10) 3,383
Petal (F8) 2,148
Philadelphia (F5) 4,472
Picayune (E9) 6,707
Pontotoc (G2) 1,596
Poplarville (E9) 1,852
Port Gibson (B7) 2,920
Prentiss (E7) 1,212
Pulaski (E6) 1,000
Purvis (F8) 1,270
Quitman (G6) 1,817
Raymond (D6) 1,259
Richton (G8) 1,158
Ripley (G1) 2,383
Rolling Fork (C5) 1,229
Rosedale (B3) 2,197
Ruleville (C3) 1,521
Sardis (E2) 1,913
Scott (B3) 2,000
Senatobia (E1) 2,108
Shaw (C3) 1,892
Shelby (C3) 2,148
Starkville (G4) 7,107
State College (G4) 4,000
Stoneville (C4) 1,015
Summit (D8) 1,558
Taylorsville (F7) 1,116
Tupelo (G2) 11,527
Tylertown (D8) 1,331
Union (F5) 1,559
University (E2) 1,200
Vicksburg (C6) 27,948
Water Valley (E2) 3,113
Waynesboro (G7) 3,442
Wesson (D7) 1,235
West Point (G3) 6,432
Wiggins (F9) 1,436
Winona (E4) 3,441
Woodville (B8) 1,609
Yazoo City (D5) 9,746

MISSOURI

Affton (P3) 5,000
Albany (D2) 1,850
Anderson (D9) 1,073
Appleton City (E6) 1,150
Arbor Terrace ‡(P3) 1,150
Aurora (E9) 4,153
Ava (G9) 1,611
Bel-Nor ‡(P3) 1,290
Bel-Ridge ‡(P3) 1,116
Belton (C5) 1,233
Berkeley (P2) 5,268
Bernie (M9) 1,308
Bethany (E2) 2,714
Bismarck (L7) 1,244
Bloomfield (M9) 1,382
Blue Springs (R6) 1,068
Bolivar (F7) 3,482
Bonne Terre (L7) 3,533
Boonville (G5) 6,686
Bowling Green (K4) 2,396
Branson (F9) 1,314
Breckenridge Hills ‡(P3) 4,063
Brentwood (P3) 7,504
Brookfield (F3) 5,810
Brunswick (F4) 1,653
Buffalo (F7) 1,213
Butler (D6) 3,333
Cabool (H8) 1,245
California (H5) 2,627
Camdenton (G6) 1,142
Cameron (D3) 3,570
Campbell (M9) 1,931
Canton (J2) 2,490
Cape Girardeau (O8) 21,578
Carl Junction (C8) 1,006
Carrollton (E4) 4,380
Carterville (D8) 1,552
Carthage (D8) 11,188
Caruthersville (N10) 8,614
Cassville (E9) 1,441
Centralia (H4) 2,460
Chaffee (N8) 3,134
Charlack ‡(P3) 1,528
Charleston (O9) 5,501
Chillicothe (E3) 8,694
Clarence (H3) 1,123
Clarkton (M10) 1,004
Clayton (P3) 16,035
Clinton (E6) 6,075
Columbia (H5) 31,974
Concordia (E5) 1,218
Country Club Hills (P2) 1,731
Crestwood ‡(P3) 1,645
Creve Coeur (O3) 2,040
Crystal City (M6) 3,499
Cuba (K6) 1,301
De Soto (M6) 5,357
Des Peres ‡(P3) 1,172
Desloge (M7) 1,957
Dexter (N9) 4,624
Dodson (P6) 1,500
Doniphan (L9) 1,611
East Prairie (O9) 3,033
Edina (H2) 1,607
El Dorado Springs (E7) 2,618
Eldon (G6) 2,766
Elsberry (L4) 1,565
Elvins (L7) 1,977
Esther (M7) 2,000
Excelsior Spgs. (R4) 5,888
Farmington (M7) 4,490
Fayette (G4) 3,144
Ferguson (P2) 11,573
Festus (M6) 5,199
Flat River (M7) 5,308
Flordell Hills ‡(P3) 1,214
Florissant (P2) 3,737
Fornfelt (O8) 1,539
Fredericktown (M7) 3,696
Frontenac (O3) 1,099
Fulton (J5) 10,052
Gallatin (E3) 1,634
Gashland (P5) 1,200
Gideon (N10) 1,754
Glasgow (G4) 1,440
Glendale (P3) 4,930
Granby (D9) 1,670
Grandview (P6) 1,556
Grant City (D2) 1,184
Greenfield (E8) 1,213
Hamilton (E3) 1,728
Hanley Hills ‡(P3) 2,219
Hannibal (K3) 20,444
Harrisonville (D5) 2,530
Hayti (N10) 3,302
Herculaneum (M6) 1,603
Hermann (K5) 2,523
Hickman Mills (P6) 1,325
Higginsville (E4) 3,428
Hillsdale ‡(P3) 2,902
Holden (E5) 1,765
Houston (J8) 1,277
Huntsville (H4) 1,520
Illmo (O8) 1,247
Independence (R5) 36,963
Ironton (L7) 1,148
Jackson (N8) 3,707
JEFFERSON CITY (H5) 25,099
Jennings (P2) 15,282
Joplin (D8) 38,711
Kahoka (J2) 1,847
Kansas City (P5) 456,622
Kansas City (urban area) 689,350
Kennett (M10) 8,685
King City (D2) 1,031
Kinloch (P2) 5,957
Kirksville (H2) 11,110
Kirkwood (O3) 18,640
La Grange (K2) 1,106
La Plata (H2) 1,331
Ladue (P3) 5,386
Lamar (D8) 3,233
Leadwood (L7) 1,479
Lebanon (G7) 6,808
Lee's Summit (R6) 2,554
Lexington (E4) 5,074
Liberty (R5) 4,709
Lilbourn (N9) 1,361
Louisiana (K4) 4,389
Macon (H3) 4,152
Malden (M9) 3,396
Maplewood (P3) 13,416
Marceline (F3) 3,172
Marionville (E8) 1,167
Marshall (F4) 8,850
Marshfield (G8) 1,925
Maryville (C2) 6,834
Memphis (H2) 2,035
Mexico (J4) 11,623
Milan (F2) 1,972
Moberly (G4) 13,115
Monett (E9) 4,771
Monroe City (J3) 2,093
Montgomery City (K5) 1,679
Morehouse (N9) 1,635
Mound City (B2) 1,412
Mount Vernon (E8) 2,057
Mountain Grove (H8) 3,106
Neosho (D9) 5,790
Nevada (D7) 8,009
New Franklin (G4) 1,060
New Haven (K5) 1,009
New Madrid (O9) 2,726
Norborne (E4) 1,114
Normandy (P3) 2,306
N. Kansas City (P5) 3,886
Northwoods ‡(P3) 1,602
Oakland (P3) 1,041
Odessa (E5) 1,969
Olivette ‡(P3) 1,761
Oran (N8) 1,156
Osceola (E6) 1,082
Overland (P3) 11,566
Owensville (K6) 1,946
Ozark (F8) 1,087
Pacific (N4) 1,985
Pagedale (P3) 3,866
Palmyra (J3) 2,295
Paris (J4) 1,407
Parkville (O5) 1,186
Parma (N9) 1,163
Pasadena Hills ‡(P2) 1,102
Perryville (N7) 4,591
Piedmont (L8) 1,548
Pierce City (E8) 1,156
Pine Lawn (P3) 6,425
Plattsburg (D3) 1,655
Pleasant Hill (D5) 2,200
Poplar Bluff (L9) 15,064
Portageville (N10) 2,662
Potosi (L7) 2,359
Princeton (E2) 1,506
Rich Hill (D6) 1,820
Richland (H7) 1,133
Richmond (D4) 4,299
Richmond Hts. (P3) 15,045
Robertson (P2) 1,200
Rock Hill (P3) 3,847
Rockport (B2) 1,511
Rolla (J7) 9,354
St. Ann (P3) 4,557
St. Charles (O2) 14,314
St. Clair (L6) 1,779
St. James (J6) 1,811
St. Johns (P2) 2,499
St. Joseph (C3) 78,588
St. Joseph (urban area) 79,280
St. Louis (P3) 856,796
St. Louis (urban area) 1,394,051
Ste. Genevieve (M6) 3,992
Salem (J7) 3,611
Salisbury (G4) 1,676
Sarcoxie (D8) 1,042
Savannah (C3) 2,332
Sedalia (F5) 20,354
Senath (M10) 1,528
Seneca (C9) 1,195
Seymour (G8) 1,015
Shelbina (H3) 2,113
Shrewsbury (P3) 3,382
Sikeston (N9) 11,640
Slater (G4) 2,836
Springfield (F8) 66,731
Springfield (urban area) 75,117
Stanberry (C2) 1,651
Steele (N10) 2,360
Steelville (K7) 1,157
Sugar Creek (R5) 1,858
Sullivan (K6) 3,019
Sweet Springs (F5) 1,439
Tarkio (B2) 2,221
Thayer (J9) 1,639
Tipton (G5) 1,234
Trenton (E2) 6,157
Troy (L5) 1,738
Union (L6) 2,917
Unionville (G2) 2,050
University City (P3) 39,892
Valley Park (O3) 2,956
Vandalia (J4) 2,624
Velda Village Hills ‡(P3) 1,527
Versailles (G6) 1,929
Vinita Park ‡(P3) 1,801
Warrensburg (E5) 6,857
Warrenton (K5) 1,584
Washington (K5) 6,850
Waynesville (H7) 1,010
Webb City (C8) 6,919
Webster Groves (P3) 23,390
Wellston (P3) 9,396
Wellsville (K4) 1,519
Wentzville (M2) 1,227
West Plains (J9) 4,918
Weston (C4) 1,067
Willow Springs (H9) 1,914
Windsor (E5) 2,429

MONTANA

Anaconda (C4) 11,254
Baker (M4) 1,772
Big Timber (G5) 1,679
Billings (H5) 31,834
Black Eagle (E3) 1,449
Boulder (E4) 1,017
Bozeman (F5) 11,325
Browning (C2) 1,691
Butte (D5) 33,251
Centerville (D4) 1,800
Chinook (G2) 2,307
Choteau (D3) 1,618
Columbia Falls (B2) 1,232
Columbus (G5) 1,097
Conrad (D2) 1,865
Cut Bank (D2) 3,721
Deer Lodge (D4) 3,779
Dillon (D5) 3,268
E. Helena (E4) 1,216
Forsyth (K4) 1,906
Ft. Benton (F3) 1,522
Ft. Browning (D2) 1,674
Ft. Peck (K2) 1,214
Glasgow (K2) 3,821
Glendive (M3) 5,254
Great Falls (E3) 39,214
Hamilton (B4) 2,678

Name & Index	Pop.
Hardin (J5)	2,306
Harlem (H2)	1,107
Harlowton (F4)	1,733
Havre (G2)	8,086
HELENA (E4)	17,581
Kalispell (B2)	9,737
Laurel (H5)	3,663
Lewistown (G3)	6,573
Libby (A2)	2,401
Livingston (F5)	7,683
Malta (J2)	2,095
Miles City (L4)	9,243
Missoula (C4)	22,485
Philipsburg (C4)	1,048
Plentywood (M2)	1,862
Polson (B3)	2,280
Poplar (L2)	1,169
Red Lodge (G5)	2,730
Ronan (C3)	1,251
Roundup (H4)	2,856
Scobey (L2)	1,628
Shelby (E2)	3,058
Sidney (M3)	3,987
Terry (L4)	1,191
Three Forks (E5)	1,114
Townsend (E4)	1,316
Walkerville (D4)	1,631
Warmsprings (D4)	2,000
White Sluphur Springs (E4)	1,025
Whitefish (B2)	3,268
Wolf Point (L2)	2,557

NEBRASKA

Name & Index	Pop.
Ainsworth (D2)	2,150
Albion (F3)	2,132
Alliance (A2)	7,891
Alma (E4)	1,768
Arapahoe (E4)	1,226
Ashland (H3)	1,713
Atkinson (E2)	1,372
Auburn (J4)	3,422
Aurora (F4)	2,455
Basset (E2)	1,066
Bayard (A3)	1,869
Beatrice (H4)	11,813
Bellevue (J3)	3,858
Benkelman (C4)	1,512
Blair (H3)	3,815
Bloomfield (G2)	1,455
Bridgeport (A3)	1,631
Broken Bow (E3)	3,396
Burwell (E3)	1,413
Cambridge (D4)	1,352
Central City (F3)	2,394
Chadron (B2)	4,687
Chappell (B3)	1,297
Columbus (G3)	8,884
Cozad (E4)	2,910
Crawford (A2)	1,824
Creighton (G2)	1,401
Crete (G4)	3,692
David City (G3)	2,321
Deshler (G4)	1,063
Fairbury (G4)	6,395
Falls City (J4)	6,203
Franklin (E4)	1,602
Fremont (H3)	14,762
Friend (G4)	1,148
Fullerton (F3)	1,520
Geneva (G4)	2,031
Genoa (G3)	1,026
Gering (A3)	3,842
Gibbon (F4)	1,063
Gordon (B2)	2,058
Gothenburg (D4)	2,977
Grand Island (F4)	22,682
Grant (C4)	1,091
Hartington (G2)	1,660
Hastings (F4)	20,211
Hay Springs (B2)	1,091
Hebron (G4)	2,000
Holdrege (E4)	4,381
Humboldt (J4)	1,404
Imperial (C4)	1,563
Kearney (E4)	12,115
Kimball (A3)	2,048
Lexington (E4)	5,068
LINCOLN (H4)	98,884
Lincoln (urban area)	99,500
Louisville (H3)	1,014
Loup City (E3)	1,508
Lyons (H3)	1,011
Madison (G3)	1,663
McCook (D4)	7,678
Minden (F4)	2,120
Mitchell (A3)	2,101
Nebraska City (J4)	6,872
Neligh (G2)	1,822
Newman Grove (G3)	1,004
Norfolk (G2)	11,335
North Platte (D3)	15,433
Oakland (H3)	1,456
Ogallala (C3)	3,456
Omaha (J3)	251,117
Omaha (urban area)	306,291
Oneill (F2)	3,027
Ord (F3)	2,239
Osceola (G3)	1,098
Oshkosh (B3)	1,124
Oxford (E4)	1,270
Papillion (J3)	1,034
Pawnee City (H4)	1,606
Pender (H2)	1,167
Peru (J4)	1,265
Pierce (G2)	1,167
Plainview (G2)	1,427
Plattsmouth (J3)	4,874
Ralston (J3)	1,300
Randolph (G2)	1,029
Ravenna (F4)	1,451
Red Cloud (F4)	1,744
Rushville (B2)	1,266
St. Paul (F3)	1,676
Schuyler (G3)	2,883
Scottsbluff (A3)	12,858
Seward (H4)	3,154
Shelton (F4)	1,032
Sidney (B3)	4,912
South Sioux City (H2)	5,557
Stanton (G3)	1,403
Stromsburg (G3)	1,231
Superior (G4)	3,227
Sutton (G4)	1,353
Syracuse (H4)	1,097
Tecumseh (H4)	1,930
Tekamah (H3)	1,914
Tilden (G2)	1,033
Trenton (D4)	1,239
Valentine (D2)	2,700
Valley (H3)	1,113
Wahoo (H3)	3,128
Wakefield (H2)	1,027
Wayne (G2)	3,595
Weeping Water (J4)	1,070
West Point (H3)	2,658
Wilber (G4)	1,356
Wisner (H3)	1,233
Wymore (H4)	2,258
York (G4)	6,178

NEVADA

Name & Index	Pop.
Babbitt (C4)	2,464
Boulder City (G7)	3,903
Carlin (E2)	1,203
CARSON CITY (B3)	3,082
East Ely (G3)	1,000
Elko (F2)	5,393
Ely (G3)	3,558
Fallon (C3)	2,400
Hawthorne (C4)	1,861
Henderson (G6)	3,643
Las Vegas (F6)	24,624
Lovelock (C2)	1,604
McGill (G3)	2,297
North Las Vegas (F6)	3,875
Pioche (G5)	1,392
Reno (B3)	32,497
Ruth (F3)	1,244
Sparks (B3)	8,203
Tonopah (D4)	1,375
Winnemucca (D2)	2,847
Yerington (B4)	1,157

NEW HAMPSHIRE

Name & Index	Pop.
Allenstown (D5)	△1,540
Alton (D5)	△1,189
Amherst (C6)	△1,461
Andover (C5)	△1,057
Antrim (C5)	△1,030
Ashland (C4)	△1,599
Auburn (D5)	△1,158
Barrington (E5)	△1,052
Bartlett (D3)	△1,074
Bedford (C6)	△2,176
Belmont (D5)	△1,611
Berlin (D3)	16,615
Boscawen (C5)	△1,857
Bow (C5)	△1,062
Bristol (C4)	△1,586
Campton (C4)	△1,149
Canaan (B4)	△14,065
Candia (D5)	△1,243
Cascade (D3)	1,000
Charlestown (B5)	△2,077
Claremont (B5)	12,811
Colebrook (D2)	△2,116
CONCORD (C5)	27,988
Contoocook (C5)	1,000
Conway (D4)	△4,109
Derry (D6)	△5,826
Dover (E5)	15,874
Durham (E5)	△4,770
E. Jaffrey (B6)	1,866
E. Rochester (E5)	1,100
Enfield (B4)	△1,612
Epping (D5)	△1,796
Exeter (E6)	△5,664
Farmington (D5)	△3,454
Franklin (C5)	6,552
Gilford (D4)	△1,251
Goffstown (C5)	△5,638
Gonic (E5)	1,000
Gorham (D3)	△2,639
Grasmere (D5)	1,545
Greenville (C6)	△1,280
Groveton (C2)	1,918
Hampton (E6)	△2,847
Hanover (B4)	△6,259
Haverhill (B3)	△3,357
Henniker (C5)	△1,675
Hillsboro (C5)	△2,179
Hinsdale (A6)	△1,950
Hollis (C6)	△1,196
Hooksett (D5)	△2,792
Hopkinton (C5)	△1,831
Hudson (D6)	△4,183
Jaffrey (B6)	△2,911
Keene (B6)	15,638
Kingston (D6)	△1,283
Laconia (D4)	14,745
Lakeport (C4)	3,600
Lancaster (C3)	△3,113
Lebanon (B4)	△8,495
Lincoln (C3)	△1,415
Lisbon (C3)	△2,009
Littleton (C3)	△4,817
Londonderry (D6)	△1,640
Loudon (D5)	△1,012
Manchester (C6)	82,732
Manchester (urban area)	84,768
Marleboro (B6)	△1,561
Meredith (C4)	△2,222
Merrimack (C6)	△1,908
Milford (C6)	△4,159
Milton (E5)	1,510
Nashua (C6)	34,669
New Ipswich (C6)	△1,147
New London (C5)	△1,484
Newmarket (D5)	△2,709
Newport (B5)	△5,131
Newton (E6)	△1,173
N. Conway (D3)	1,200
N. Hampton (E6)	△1,104
N. Walpole (B5)	1,000
Northfield (C5)	△1,561
Northumberland (D2)	△2,779
Ossipee (D4)	△1,412
Pelham (D6)	△1,317
Pembroke (D5)	△3,094
Penacook (C5)	3,100
Peterborough (C6)	△2,556
Pittsfield (D5)	△2,321
Plainfield (B4)	△1,011
Plaistow (D6)	△2,082
Plymouth (C4)	△3,039
Portsmouth (E5)	18,830
Raymond (D5)	△1,428
Rochester (D5)	13,776
Rye (E5)	△1,982
Rye Beach (E6)	1,000
Salem (D6)	△4,805
Salem Depot (D6)	1,637
Salmon Falls (E5)	1,290
Seabrook (E6)	△1,788
Somersworth (E5)	6,927
S. Seabrook (E6)	1,000
Sunapee (B5)	△1,108
Swanzey (B6)	△2,806
Tamworth (D4)	△1,025
Tilton (C5)	△2,085
Troy (B6)	△1,360
Wakefield (E4)	△1,267
Walpole (B5)	△2,536
Warner (C5)	△1,080
Weare (C4)	△1,345
W. Lebanon (B4)	1,737
W. Swanzey (B6)	1,400
Whitefield (C3)	△1,677
Wilton (C6)	△1,952
Winchester (B6)	△2,388
Wolfeboro (D4)	△2,581
Woodsville (B3)	1,542

NEW JERSEY

Name & Index	Pop.
Absecon (D5)	2,355
Allendale (B1)	2,409
Alpha (C2)	2,117
Ampere (B2)	10,000
Arlington (B2)	16,000
Asbury Park (F3)	17,094
Ashland (D4)	1,240
Atco (D4)	2,500
Atlantic City (E5)	61,657
Atlantic City (urban area)	105,326
Atlantic Highlands (F3)	3,083
Audubon (C4)	9,531
Audubon Park (B3)	1,859
Avenel (E2)	8,700
Avon by the Sea (F3)	1,650
Barnegat (E4)	1,150
Barrington (B3)	2,651
Basking Ridge (D2)	1,899
Bayonne (B2)	77,203
Bayville (E4)	2,000
Beach Haven (E4)	1,050
Beachwood (E4)	1,251
Belford (E3)	1,832
Belleville (E2)	32,019
Bellmawr (B3)	5,213
Belmar (E3)	4,636
Belvidere (C2)	2,406
Bergenfield (C1)	17,647
Berkeley Heights (E2)	3,460
Berlin (D4)	2,339
Bernardsville (D2)	3,956
Beverly (D3)	3,084
Blackwood (C4)	1,344
Blackwood Terrace (C4)	2,100
Bloomfield (B2)	49,307
Bloomingdale (E1)	3,251
Bogota (B2)	7,662
Boonton (E2)	7,163
Bordentown (D3)	5,497
Bound Brook (D2)	8,374
Bradley Beach (F3)	3,911
Bridgeton (C5)	18,378
Brielle (E3)	1,328
Brigantine (E5)	1,267
Brooklawn (B3)	2,262
Budd Lake (D2)	1,032
Buena (D4)	2,640
Burlington (D3)	12,051
Butler (E2)	4,050
Caldwell (E2)	6,270
Camden (C4)	124,555
Cape May (D6)	3,607
Cape May Court House (D5)	1,093
Carlstadt (B2)	5,591
Carlton Hill (B2)	1,000
Carneys Point (C4)	4,000
Carteret (E2)	13,030
Cedar Grove (A2)	7,723
Cedar Knolls (E2)	1,500
Cedarville (C5)	1,009
Chatham (E2)	7,391
Chews (B4)	1,500
Clayton (C4)	3,023
Clementon (D4)	3,191
Cliffside Park (F2)	17,116
Cliffwood (E3)	1,800
Clifton (E2)	64,511
Clinton (D2)	1,118
Closter (C1)	3,376
Collingswood (C4)	15,800
Coytesville (C2)	2,500
Cranbury (E3)	1,843
Cranford (E2)	△18,602
Cresskill (C1)	3,534
Deal (F3)	1,064
Deepwater (C4)	1,500
Delair (C4)	2,237
Delanco (D3)	2,494
Demarest (C1)	1,786
Denville (E2)	6,058
Dover (D2)	11,174
Dumont (F2)	13,013
Dunellen (D2)	6,291
East Keansburg (E3)	2,596
E. Newark (B2)	2,173
E. Orange (B2)	79,340
E. Paterson (B2)	15,386
E. Rutherford (B2)	7,438
Eatontown (E3)	3,044
Edgewater (C2)	3,952
Egg Harbor City (D4)	3,838
Elberon (E3)	1,200
Elizabeth (E2)	112,817
Elmer (C4)	1,460
Emerson (B1)	1,744
Englewood (C2)	23,145
Englishtown (E3)	1,004
Erlton (B3)	2,000
Essex Fells (A2)	1,617
Fair Haven (E3)	3,560
Fair Lawn (B1)	23,885
Fairview (C2)	8,661
Fanwood (E2)	3,228
Flemington (D2)	3,058
Florence (D3)	3,460
Florham Park (E2)	2,385
Fords (E2)	5,200
Forked River (E4)	1,000
Fort Lee (C2)	11,648
Franklin (D1)	3,864
Franklin Lakes (B1)	2,021
Franklinville (C4)	1,226
Freehold (E3)	7,550
Frenchtown (C2)	1,305
Garfield (E2)	27,550
Garwood (E2)	4,622
Gibbstown (C4)	2,546
Gillette (E2)	1,300
Glassboro (C4)	5,867
Glen Ridge (B2)	7,620
Glen Rock (B1)	7,145
Gloucester City (C4)	14,357
Gloucester Heights (B3)	1,200
Great Notch (B2)	1,000
Guttenberg (C2)	5,566
Hackensack (F2)	29,219
Hackettstown (D2)	3,894
Haddon Heights (C4)	7,287
Haddonfield (D4)	10,495
Hainesport (D4)	1,130
Haledon (B1)	6,204
Hamburg (D1)	1,305
Hamilton Square (D3)	3,500
Hammonton (D4)	8,411
Harrington Park (C1)	1,634
Harrison (B2)	13,490
Hasbrouck Heights (B2)	9,181
Haskell (A1)	3,000
Haworth (C1)	1,612
Hawthorne (E2)	14,816
High Bridge (D2)	1,854
Highland Park (E2)	9,721
Highlands (F3)	2,959
Hightstown (D3)	3,712
Hillsdale (E2)	4,127
Hillside (B2)	△21,007
Hoboken (C2)	50,676
Hohokus (B1)	2,254
Hopatcong (D2)	1,173
Hopewell (D3)	1,869
Hudson Heights (C2)	2,000
Irvington (B2)	59,201
Iselin (E2)	7,000
Jamesburg (E3)	2,307
Jersey City (F2)	299,017
Keansburg (E3)	5,559
Kearny (B2)	39,952
Kenilworth (E2)	4,922
Kenvil (D2)	1,361
Keyport (E3)	5,888
Kinnelon (E2)	1,350
Lafayette (D1)	1,100
Lake Hopatcong (D2)	5,000
Lakehurst (E3)	1,518
Lakewood (E3)	9,970
Lambertville (D3)	4,477
Landing (D2)	1,500
Landisville (D4)	1,500
Laurel Springs (B4)	1,540
Lawnside (B3)	1,566
Lawrenceville (D3)	1,056
Leonardo (E3)	1,887
Leonia (C2)	7,378
Liberty Corner (D2)	1,500
Lincoln Park (A1)	3,376
Linden (E2)	30,644
Lindenwold (B4)	3,479
Linwood (D5)	1,925
Little Falls (E2)	6,600
Little Ferry (B2)	4,955
Little Silver (F3)	2,595
Livingston (E2)	10,100
Lodi (B2)	15,392
Long Branch (F3)	23,090
Lyndhurst (B2)	△19,980
Madison (E2)	10,417
Magnolia (C4)	1,883
Mahwah (E1)	3,800
Manahawkin (E4)	1,200
Manasquan (E3)	3,178
Manville (D2)	8,597
Maple Shade (D4)	7,500
Maplewood (E2)	△25,201
Margate City (E5)	4,715
Martinsville (D2)	2,700
Masonville (D4)	1,500
Matawan (E3)	3,739
Mays Landing (D5)	1,301
Maywood (B2)	8,667
Medford (D4)	1,300
Mendham (D2)	1,724
Mercerville (D3)	5,000
Merchantville (C4)	4,183
Metuchen (E2)	9,879
Middlesex (E2)	5,943
Midland Park (B1)	5,164
Midvale (E1)	2,000
Milford (C2)	1,012
Millburn (E2)	△14,560
Milltown (E3)	3,786
Millville (C5)	16,041
Milton (D1)	1,100
Mine Hill (D2)	2,297
Montclair (E2)	43,297
Montvale (E1)	1,856
Moonachie (B2)	1,775
Moorestown (D4)	9,175
Morris Plains (D2)	2,707
Morristown (D2)	17,124
Mt. Ephraim (B3)	4,449
Mt. Holly (D4)	8,206
Mt. Hope (D2)	1,500
Mountain Lakes (E2)	2,806
Mountain View (A2)	5,000
Mountainside ‡(E2)	2,046
National Park (B3)	2,419
Navesink (E3)	1,085
Neptune (E3)	3,073
Netcong (D2)	2,284
New Brunswick (E3)	38,811
New Egypt (E3)	1,294
New Market (D2)	1,500
New Milford (B1)	6,006
New Providence ‡(E2)	3,380
New Vernon (D2)	1,100
Newark (E2)	438,776
Newfield (D4)	1,010
Newton (D1)	5,781
Nixon (E2)	2,500
N. Arlington (B2)	15,970
N. Bergen (B2)	△41,560
N. Caldwell (B2)	1,781
N. Haledon (B1)	3,550
N. Plainfield (E2)	12,766
N. Wildwood (D6)	3,158
Northfield (D5)	3,498
Northvale (F1)	1,455
Norwood (C1)	1,792
Nutley (B2)	26,992
Oak Tree (E2)	2,000
Oakhurst (E3)	2,388
Oakland (E1)	1,817
Oaklyn (B3)	4,889
Ocean City (D5)	6,040
Ocean Grove (F3)	3,806
Oceanport (E3)	7,588
Oceanville (D5)	1,500
Ogdensburg (D1)	1,169
Old Bridge (E3)	3,500
Oradell (B1)	3,665
Orange (B2)	38,037
Oxford (C2)	1,041
Packanack Lake (B1)	3,000
Palisade (C2)	3,784

Municipal Index

Name & Index	Pop.
Palisades Park (C2)	9,635
Palmyra (D4)	5,802
Paramus (B1)	6,268
Park Ridge (B1)	3,189
Parlin (E3)	2,000
Passaic (E2)	57,702
Paterson (E2)	139,336
Paulsboro (C4)	7,842
Pemberton (D4)	1,194
Pennington (D3)	1,682
Penns Grove (C4)	6,669
Pennsauken (B3)	▲22,767
Pennsville (C4)	3,500
Pequannock (E2)	2,500
Perth Amboy (E2)	41,330
Phillipsburg (C2)	18,919
Pine Hill ‡(C4)	2,546
Pitman (C4)	6,960
Plainfield (E2)	42,366
Plainsboro (D3)	1,118
Pleasantville (D5)	11,938
Point Pleasant (E3)	4,009
Point Pleasant Beach ‡(E3)	2,900
Pompton Lakes (A1)	4,654
Pompton Plains (E2)	3,500
Port Monmouth (E3)	1,767
Port Morris (D2)	1,735
Port Norris (C5)	2,050
Port Reading (E2)	3,500
Princeton (D3)	12,230
Prospect Park (E2)	5,242
Quinton (C4)	1,000
Rahway (E2)	21,290
Ramsey (E1)	4,670
Raritan (D2)	5,131
Red Bank (E3)	12,743
Ridgefield (B2)	8,312
Ridgefield Park (F2)	11,993
Ridgewood (E2)	17,481
Ringwood (E1)	1,752
River Edge (B1)	9,204
Riverdale (E2)	1,352
Riverside (D3)	7,199
Riverton (D3)	2,761
Robbinsville (D3)	2,038
Rochelle Park (B2)	4,475
Rockaway (D2)	3,812
Roebling (D3)	3,325
Roseland (A2)	2,019
Roselle (B2)	17,681
Roselle Park (A2)	11,537
Rosenhayn (C5)	1,000
Rumson (F3)	4,044
Runnemede (C4)	4,217
Rutherford (B2)	17,411
Saddle River (B1)	1,003
Salem (C4)	9,050
Sayreville (E3)	10,338
Scotch Plains (E2)	9,000
Sea Girt (E3)	1,178
Seabrook (C5)	3,000
Secaucus (B2)	9,750
Sewaren (E2)	1,800
Short Hills (E2)	7,000
Shrewsbury (E3)	1,613
Sicklerville (D4)	3,500
Skillman (D3)	3,500
Somerdale (D4)	1,417
Somers Point (D5)	2,480
Somerville (D2)	11,571
So. Amboy (E3)	8,422
So. Belmar ‡(E3)	1,294
So. Bound Brook (E2)	2,905
So. Orange (A2)	15,230
So. Plainfield (E2)	8,008
So. River (E3)	11,308
Sparta (D1)	3,300
Spotswood (E3)	2,325
Spring Lake (F3)	2,008
Spring Lake Heights ‡(E3)	1,798
Springfield (E2)	▲7,214
Stanhope (D2)	1,351
Stewartsville (C2)	1,000
Stirling (E2)	1,076
Stratford (C4)	1,356
Succasunna (D2)	1,022
Summit (E2)	17,929
Sussex (D1)	1,541
Swedesboro (C4)	2,459
Tabor (E2)	2,500
Teaneck (B2)	▲33,772
Tenafly (F2)	9,651
Titusville (D3)	2,500
Toms River (E4)	2,517
Totowa (B1)	6,045
Towaco (E2)	1,500
TRENTON (D3)	128,009
Trenton (urban area)	189,276
Tuckerton (E4)	1,332
Union (E2)	▲38,004
Union Beach (E3)	3,636
Union City (C2)	55,537
Vauxhall (A2)	7,000
Ventnor (E5)	8,185
Verona (E2)	10,921
Vineland (C5)	8,155
Waldwick (E1)	3,963
Wallington (B2)	8,910
Wanamassa (E3)	2,512
Wanaque (B1)	4,222
Warren Point (B1)	5,000
Washington (D2)	4,802

Name & Index	Pop.
Watchung (E2)	1,818
Waterford Works (D4)	1,200
Weehawken (C2)	▲14,380
Wenonah (C4)	1,511
W. Caldwell (A2)	4,666
W. Englewood (C2)	14,000
W. Long Branch (F3)	2,739
W. New York (C2)	37,683
W. Norwood (C1)	1,900
W. Orange (A2)	28,605
W. Paterson (B2)	3,931
W. Pt. Pleasant (E3)	3,000
Westfield (E2)	21,243
Weston (D2)	1,500
Westville (C4)	4,731
Westwood (B1)	6,766
Wharton (D2)	3,853
Whippany (E2)	2,100
White House Station (D2)	1,750
Wildwood (D6)	5,475
Wildwood Crest (D6)	1,772
Williamstown (D4)	2,632
Winfield (B3)	2,720
Wood-Lynne (B3)	2,776
Wood-Ridge (B2)	6,283
Woodbine (D5)	2,417
Woodbridge (E2)	▲35,758
Woodbury (C4)	10,931
Woodbury Hts. (B4)	1,373
Woodcliff Lake (B1)	1,420
Woodport (D2)	2,000
Woodstown (C4)	2,345
Wrightstown (D3)	1,199
Wyckoff (E2)	5,400
Yardville (D3)	1,600

NEW MEXICO

Name & Index	Pop.
Alameda (C3)	1,792
Alamogordo (C6)	6,783
Albuquerque (C3)	96,815
Artesia (E6)	8,244
Bayard (A6)	2,119
Belen (C4)	4,495
Bernalillo (C3)	1,922
Carlsbad (E6)	17,975
Carrizozo (D5)	1,389
Cebolla (C2)	1,000
Cedar Crest (C3)	1,000
Central (A6)	1,511
Chama (C2)	1,300
Chamberino (C6)	1,000
Chimayo (D3)	1,550
Clayton (F2)	3,515
Clovis (F4)	17,318
Dawson (E2)	1,206
Deming (B6)	5,672
Dixon (D2)	1,250
East Vaughn (D4)	1,800
El Rito (C2)	1,200
Espanola (C3)	1,446
Eunice (F6)	2,352
Farmington (A2)	3,637
Ft. Sumner (E4)	1,978
Gallup (A3)	9,133
Grants (B3)	2,251
Hagerman (E5)	1,024
Hanover (A6)	1,200
Hatch (B6)	1,064
Hobbs (F6)	13,875
Hurley (A6)	2,079
Isleta (C4)	1,400
Jal (F6)	2,047
Jarales (C4)	1,199
La Jara (B2)	2,500
Laguna (B3)	3,004
Las Cruces (C6)	12,325
Las Vegas (city) (D3)	7,494
Las Vegas (town) (D3)	6,269
Lordsburg (A6)	3,525
Los Alamos (C3)	9,934
Los Griegos (C3)	3,025
Loving (E6)	1,487
Lovington (F6)	3,134
Magdalena (B4)	1,297
Mesilla (C6)	1,264
Mesilla Park (C6)	2,000
Montezuma (D3)	1,200
Mora (D3)	1,750
Mountainair (C4)	1,418
Pecos (D3)	1,241
Portales (F4)	8,112
Questa (D2)	1,400
Ranches of Taos (D2)	1,386
Raton (E2)	8,241
Roswell (E5)	25,738
Roy (E3)	1,074
San Juan Pueblo (C2)	1,200
SANTA FE (C3)	27,998
Santa Rita (B6)	2,135
Santa Rosa (E4)	2,199
Silver City (A6)	7,022
Socorro (C4)	4,334
Springer (E2)	1,558
State College (C6)	1,200
Taos (D2)	1,815
Truth or Consequences (B5)	4,563
Tucumcari (F3)	8,419
Tularosa (C5)	1,642
Vaughn (D4)	1,356
Wagon Mound (E2)	1,120
Zuni (A3)	2,563

NEW YORK

Name & Index	Pop.
Adams (J3)	1,762
Addison (F6)	1,920
Akron (C4)	2,481
ALBANY (N5)	134,995
Albany-Troy (urban area)	290,209
Albion (D4)	4,850
Alden (C5)	1,252
Alexandria Bay (J2)	1,688
Alfred (E6)	2,053
Allegany (C6)	1,738
Altamont (M5)	1,127
Amagansett (G2)	1,000
Amenia (N7)	1,300
Amityville (E3)	6,164
Amsterdam (M5)	32,240
Andover (E6)	1,351
Angola (C5)	1,936
Arcade (D5)	1,818
Ardsley (H1)	1,744
Arlington (N7)	5,374
Athens (N6)	1,545
Atlantic Beach (D3)	2,000
Attica (D5)	2,676
Au Sable Forks (N2)	1,643
Auburn (G5)	36,722
Avon (E5)	2,412
Babylon (D2)	6,015
Bainbridge (J6)	1,505
Baldwin (B3)	22,000
Baldwinsville (H4)	4,495
Ballston Spa (N5)	4,937
Batavia (D5)	17,799
Bath (F6)	5,416
Bay Shore (E2)	9,665
Bayport (E2)	1,463
Bayville (B2)	1,981
Beacon (N7)	14,012
Bellerose (A2)	1,134
Bellmore (B2)	12,000
Bellport (F2)	1,449
Belmont (E6)	1,211
Binghamton (J6)	80,674
Binghamton (urban area)	144,570
Black River (J3)	1,062
Blasdell (C5)	3,127
Bolivar (D6)	1,490
Bolton Landing (N3)	1,200
Boonville (K4)	2,329
Boston (C5)	1,500
Branchport (F5)	1,000
Brentwood (E2)	2,803
Brewster (D1)	1,810
Briarcliff Manor ‡(D1)	2,494
Bridgeport (J4)	1,800
Brightwaters ‡(E2)	2,336
Broadalbin (M4)	1,400
Brockport (D4)	4,748
Brocton (B6)	1,380
Bronx, The (D2)	1,451,277
Bronxville (J1)	6,778
Brooklyn (C2)	2,738,175
Brownville (H3)	1,013
Buchanan (D1)	1,820
Buffalo (B5)	580,132
Buffalo (urban area)	794,747
Caledonia (E5)	1,683
Cambridge (O4)	1,692
Camden (J4)	2,407
Camillus (H4)	1,225
Canajoharie (L5)	2,761
Canandaigua (F5)	8,332
Canastota (J4)	4,458
Canisteo (E6)	2,625
Canton (K1)	4,379
Carmel (D1)	1,526
Carthage (J3)	4,420
Castile (D5)	1,072
Castleton-on-Hudson (N5)	1,751
Catskill (N6)	5,392
Cattaraugus (C6)	1,190
Cayuga Hts. ‡(G5)	1,131
Cazenovia (J5)	1,946
Cedarhurst (B3)	6,051
Celoron (B6)	1,555
Center Moriches (F2)	1,761
Central Valley (C1)	1,300
Chadwicks (K4)	2,500
Champlain (N1)	1,505
Chateaugay (N1)	1,234
Chatham (N6)	2,304
Chenango Bridge (J6)	2,500
Chester (B1)	1,215
Chittenango (J4)	1,307
Cicero (H4)	1,000
Clarence (C5)	1,018
Clayton (H2)	1,981
Clifton Springs (F4)	1,838
Clinton (K4)	1,630
Clyde (G4)	2,492
Cobleskill (L5)	3,208
Coeymans (N6)	1,250
Cohoes (N5)	21,272
Cold Spring (C1)	1,788
Cold Spring Harbor (E2)	1,500
Colonie ‡(N5)	2,068
Comstock (O4)	2,250
Constantia (H4)	1,250
Cooperstown (L5)	2,727
Corinth (N4)	3,161

Name & Index	Pop.
Corning (F6)	17,684
Cornwall (C1)	2,211
Cortland (H5)	18,152
Coxsackie (N6)	2,722
Croton Falls (D1)	1,000
Croton-on-Hudson (C1)	4,837
Cuba (D6)	1,783
Cutchogue (F2)	1,500
Dannemora (N7)	4,122
Dansville (E5)	5,253
Delhi (L6)	2,223
Depew (C5)	7,217
Deposit (K6)	2,016
Dexter (H2)	1,038
Dobbs Ferry (H1)	6,268
Dolgerville (L4)	3,204
Dundee (F5)	1,165
Dunkirk (B5)	18,007
E. Aurora (C5)	5,962
E. Greenbush (N5)	1,100
E. Hampton (G2)	1,737
E. Hills ‡(D2)	2,547
E. Islip (E2)	2,834
E. Moriches (F2)	1,500
E. Northport (E2)	3,842
E. Rochester (F4)	7,022
E. Rockaway ‡(D2)	7,970
E. Syracuse (H4)	4,766
E. Williston ‡(D2)	1,734
Eden (C5)	1,394
Ellenville (M7)	4,225
Ellicottville (C6)	1,073
Elmira (G6)	49,716
Elmira Heights (G6)	5,009
Elmont (B2)	21,125
Elmsford (J1)	3,147
Endicott (H6)	20,050
Fairport (F4)	5,267
Falconer (B6)	3,292
Farmingdale (D2)	4,492
Fayetteville (J4)	2,624
Floral Park (A2)	14,582
Florida (B1)	1,376
Flower Hill ‡(D2)	1,948
Fonda (M5)	1,026
Fort Edward (O4)	3,797
Fort Plain (L5)	2,935
Frankfort (K4)	3,844
Franklinville (D6)	2,092
Fredonia (B6)	7,095
Freeport (B3)	24,680
Frewsburg (B6)	1,383
Friendship (D6)	1,344
Fulton (H4)	13,922
Garden City (B2)	14,486
Garrison (C1)	1,600
Geneseo (E5)	2,838
Geneva (G5)	17,144
Glasco (M6)	1,300
Glen Cove (B2)	15,130
Glens Falls (N4)	19,610
Gloversville (M4)	23,634
Goshen (B1)	3,311
Gouverneur (K2)	4,916
Gowanda (B6)	3,289
Granville (O4)	2,826
Great Neck (A2)	7,759
Great Neck Estates (A2)	2,464
Great Neck Plaza (A2)	4,246
Green Island (N5)	4,016
Greene (J6)	1,628
Greenport (F1)	3,028
Greenwich (O4)	2,212
Groton (H5)	2,150
Hagaman (M5)	1,114
Hamburg (C5)	6,938
Hamilton (J5)	3,507
Hammondsport (F6)	1,190
Hampton Bays (F2)	1,269
Hancock (K7)	1,560
Hastings on Hudson (J1)	7,565
Haverstraw (C1)	5,818
Hempstead (A2)	29,135
Herkimer (L4)	9,400
Hicksville (B2)	13,000
High Falls (M7)	1,000
Highland (M7)	3,035
Highland Falls (C1)	3,930
Hillburn (C2)	1,212
Hilton (E4)	1,036
Holley (D4)	1,551
Homer (H5)	3,244
Honeoye Falls (F5)	1,460
Hoosick Falls (O5)	4,297
Hornell (E6)	15,049
Horseheads (G6)	3,606
Hudson (N6)	11,629
Hudson Falls (O4)	7,236
Huntington (E2)	9,324
Hyde Park (N7)	1,059
Ilion (K5)	9,363
Inwood (A3)	9,200
Irondequoit (E4)	▲34,417
Irvington (H1)	3,657
Island Park (B3)	2,031
Islip (E2)	5,254
Ithaca (G6)	29,257
Jamaica (D2)	100,000
Jamestown (B6)	43,354
Jamesville (H5)	1,200
Johnson City (J6)	19,249
Johnstown (M4)	10,923

Name & Index	Pop.
Jordan (H4)	1,295
Keene Valley (N2)	1,000
Keeseville (O2)	1,977
Kenmore (C5)	20,066
Kerhonkson (M7)	1,000
Kings Park (E2)	10,960
Kings Point ‡(E2)	2,445
Kingston (M7)	28,817
Lackawanna (B5)	27,658
Lake George (N4)	1,005
Lake Placid (N2)	2,999
Lake Success (A2)	1,264
Lakewood (B6)	3,013
Lancaster (C5)	8,665
Larchmont (J1)	6,330
Lawrence (A3)	4,681
Le Roy (E5)	4,721
Levittown (B2)	40,000
Lewiston (B4)	1,626
Liberty (L7)	4,658
Lima (E5)	1,147
Lindenhurst (E2)	8,644
Little Falls (L4)	9,541
Little Valley (C6)	1,287
Liverpool (H4)	2,933
Lockport (C4)	25,133
Long Beach (B3)	15,586
Long Lake (L3)	1,000
Lowville (J3)	3,671
Lynbrook (A3)	17,314
Lyon Mountain (N1)	1,053
Lyons (G4)	4,217
Malone (M1)	9,501
Malverne (A2)	8,086
Mamaroneck (J1)	15,016
Manchester (F5)	1,262
Manhattan (C2)	1,960,101
Manlius (J5)	1,742
Manorhaven ‡(D2)	1,819
Marathon (J6)	1,057
Marcellus (H5)	1,382
Marlboro (M7)	1,709
Massapequa Park‡ (D2)	2,334
Massena (L1)	13,137
Mattituck (F2)	1,089
Maybrook (B1)	1,316
Mayville (A6)	1,492
McGraw (H5)	1,197
Mechanicville (N5)	7,385
Medina (D4)	6,179
Menands ‡(N5)	2,453
Mexico (H4)	1,398
Middleburg (M5)	1,298
Middleport (C4)	1,641
Middletown (B1)	22,586
Millbrook (N7)	1,568
Millerton (O7)	1,048
Mineola (B2)	14,831
Minoa (J4)	1,008
Mohawk (L4)	3,196
Monroe (C1)	1,753
Montgomery (B1)	1,063
Monticello (L7)	4,223
Montour Falls (G6)	1,457
Moravia (H5)	1,480
Morrisville (J5)	1,250
Mt. Kisco (D1)	5,907
Mt. Morris (E5)	3,450
Mt. Vernon (H1)	71,899
Munsey Park ‡(D2)	2,048
Napanoch (M7)	1,094
Naples (F5)	1,141
New Berlin (K5)	1,178
New Hartford (K4)	1,947
New Hyde Park (A2)	7,349
New Paltz (M7)	2,285
New Rochelle (J1)	59,725
New Windsor (C1)	2,754
New York (5 Boroughs) (C2)	7,891,957
New York-Northeastern New Jersey (urban area)	12,222,963
New York Mills (K4)	3,366
Newark (G4)	10,295
Newark Valley (H6)	1,027
Newburgh (C1)	31,956
Newfane (C4)	1,578
Niagara Falls (C4)	90,872
Niagara Falls (urban area)	97,648
Norfolk (K1)	1,252
N. Chili (E4)	1,000
N. Collins (C5)	1,325
N. Pelham (H1)	5,046
N. Syracuse (H4)	3,356
N. Tarrytown (H1)	8,740
N. Tonawanda (C4)	24,731
Northport (E2)	3,859
Northville (M4)	1,114
Norwich (J5)	8,816
Norwood (L1)	1,995
Nunda (E5)	1,224
Nyack (C2)	5,889
Oakfield (D4)	1,781
Oceanside (B3)	15,000
Ogdensburg (K1)	16,166
Old Westbury (B2)	1,160
Olean (D6)	22,884
Oneida (J4)	11,325
Oneonta (K6)	13,564
Orchard Park (C5)	2,054
Oriskany (K4)	1,346
Ossining (D1)	16,098

Name & Index	Pop.
Oswego (G4)	22,647
Owego (H6)	5,350
Oxford (J6)	1,811
Oyster Bay (B2)	5,215
Painted Post (F6)	2,405
Palmyra (F4)	3,034
Patchogue (E2)	7,361
Pawling (N7)	1,430
Peekskill (D1)	17,731
Pelham ‡(H1)	1,843
Pelham Manor (H1)	5,306
Penfield (F4)	1,013
Penn Yan (F5)	5,481
Perry (D5)	4,533
Peru (N1)	1,000
Phelps (F5)	1,650
Philmont (N6)	1,792
Phoenix (H4)	1,917
Piermont (C2)	1,897
Pine Bush (B1)	1,100
Pittsford (E4)	1,668
Plandome ‡(D2)	1,102
Plattsburgh (O1)	17,738
Pleasantville (D2)	4,861
Port Byron (G4)	1,013
Port Chester (J1)	23,970
Port Dickinson ‡(J6)	2,199
Port Ewen (N7)	1,885
Port Henry (O2)	1,831
Port Jefferson (E2)	3,296
Port Jervis (A1)	9,372
Port Washington (A2)	15,000
Portville (D6)	1,151
Potsdam (K1)	7,491
Poughkeepsie (N7)	41,023
Pulaski (H3)	2,033
Queens (D2)	1,550,849
Randolph (C6)	1,455
Ravena (N6)	2,006
Red Hook (N7)	1,225
Rensselaer (N5)	10,856
Rhinebeck (N7)	1,923
Richfield Spgs. (K5)	1,534
Richmond (C3)	191,555
Ripley (A6)	1,229
Riverhead (F5)	4,251
Rochester (E4)	332,488
Rochester (urban area)	406,923
Rockville Centre (B2)	22,362
Rome (J4)	41,682
Ronkonkoma (E2)	1,334
Roosevelt (B2)	10,500
Roslyn (B2)	1,612
Rouses Point (O1)	2,001
Rye (J1)	11,721
Sackets Harbor (H3)	1,247
Sag Harbor (G2)	2,373
St. George (C3)	4,900
St. Johnsville (L5)	2,210
Salamanca (C6)	8,861
Salem (O4)	1,067
Sand Lake (O5)	1,300
Saranac Lake (M2)	6,913
Saratoga Spgs. (N4)	15,478
Saugerties (M6)	3,907
Sauquoit (K5)	1,227
Sayville (E2)	4,251
Scarsdale (J1)	13,156
Schenectady (M5)	91,785
Schenectady (urban area)	123,573
Schoharie (M5)	1,059
Schuylerville (N4)	1,314
Scotia (N5)	7,812
Scottsville (E4)	1,025
Sea Cliff (B2)	4,868
Seneca Falls (G5)	6,634
Sherburne (K5)	1,604
Sheridan (B5)	1,050
Sherrill (K4)	2,236
Shortsville (F5)	1,314
Sidney (K6)	4,815
Silver Creek (B5)	3,068
Skaneateles (H5)	2,331
Sloan (C5)	4,698
Sloatsburg (C2)	2,018
Smithtown Branch (E2)	1,424
Sodus (G4)	1,588
Solvay (H4)	7,868
S. Fallsburg (L7)	1,147
S. Glens Falls (N4)	3,645
S. Nyack ‡(C2)	3,102
Southampton (G2)	4,042
Southold (F2)	1,027
Spencerport (E4)	1,595
Spring Valley (C2)	4,500
Springville (C5)	3,322
Stamford (L6)	1,162
Stewart Manor ‡(D2)	1,879
Stillwater (N5)	1,276
Stony Point (C1)	1,438
Stottville (N6)	1,020
Suffern (C2)	4,010
Syosset (B2)	1,133
Syracuse (H4)	220,583
Syracuse (urban area)	264,610
Tarrytown (H1)	8,851
Thomaston (B2)	2,045
Ticonderoga (N3)	3,517
Tonawanda (B4)	14,617
Troy (N5)	72,311
Troy-Albany (urban area)	290,209
Trumansburg (G5)	1,479
Tuckahoe (H1)	5,991
Tupper Lake (M2)	5,441
Unadilla (K6)	1,317
Upper Nyack ‡(C2)	1,195
Utica (K4)	101,531
Utica (urban area)	117,390
Valatie (N6)	1,225
Valley Stream (A2)	26,854
Vestal (H6)	5,000
Victor (F5)	1,066
Walden (B1)	4,559
Wallkill (M7)	1,145
Walton (K6)	3,947
Wappingers Falls (N7)	3,490
Warrensburg (N3)	2,358
Warsaw (D5)	3,713
Warwick (B1)	2,674
Waterford (N5)	2,968
Waterloo (G5)	4,438
Watertown (J3)	34,350
Waterville (K5)	1,634
Watervliet (N5)	15,197
Watkins Glen (G6)	3,052
Waverly (G6)	6,037
Wayland (E5)	1,834
Webster (F4)	1,773
Weedsport (G4)	1,588
Wellsville (E6)	6,402
W. Carthage ‡(J3)	2,000
W. Haverstraw ‡(C1)	3,099
W. Hurley (M6)	1,000
W. Point (C1)	5,000
W. Sayville (E2)	1,370
Westbury (B2)	7,112
Westfield (A6)	3,663
Westhampton Beach (F2)	1,087
White Plains (J1)	43,466
Whitehall (O3)	4,457
Whitesboro (K4)	3,902
Williamson (F4)	1,520
Williamsville (C5)	4,649
Williston Park (B2)	7,505
Wingdale (N7)	1,300
Witherbee (N2)	1,388
Wolcott (G4)	1,516
Woodbourne (M7)	1,600
Woodstock (M6)	1,500
Worcester (L5)	1,000
Yaphank (E2)	1,200
Yonkers (H1)	152,798
Yorkville (K4)	3,528

NORTH CAROLINA

Name & Index	Pop.
Aberdeen (G4)	1,603
Ahoskie (L2)	3,579
Alarka (D8)	1,000
Albemarle (E4)	11,798
Alexander (E8)	1,200
Altamahaw (G2)	1,200
Andrews (C9)	1,397
Angier (H4)	1,182
Apex (H3)	1,065
Archdale (F3)	1,218
Asheboro (F3)	7,701
Asheville (E8)	53,000
Asheville (urban area)	57,658
Aulander (L2)	1,112
Ayden (L4)	2,282
Badin (E4)	2,126
Beaufort (M5)	3,212
Belhaven (M3)	2,528
Belmont (D4)	5,330
Benson (J4)	2,102
Bessemer City (C4)	3,961
Bethel (L3)	1,402
Biscoe (F4)	1,034
Black Mountain (F8)	1,174
Boger City (C4)	1,733
Boiling Springs (B4)	1,145
Boone (D6)	2,973
Brevard (E9)	3,908
Bryson City (D8)	1,499
Burgaw (J5)	1,613
Burlington (F2)	24,560
Burnsville (B7)	1,341
Canton (E8)	4,906
Caroleen (B4)	1,712
Carolina Beach (K6)	1,080
Carrboro (G3)	1,795
Carthage (F4)	1,194
Cary (H3)	1,446
Castle Hayne (K6)	1,000
Chadbourn (H6)	2,103
Chapel Hill (H3)	9,177
Charlotte (D4)	134,042
Charlotte (urban area)	140,085
Cherryville (C4)	3,492
China Grove (D3)	1,491
Clayton (J3)	2,229
Cliffside (B4)	1,388
Clinton (J5)	4,414
Coats (H4)	1,047
Columbia (N3)	1,161
Concord (D4)	16,486
Conover (C3)	1,164
Cooleemee (D3)	1,925
Cornelius (D4)	1,548
Cramerton (C4)	3,211
Dallas (C4)	2,454
Davidson (D4)	2,423
Draper (F1)	3,629
Dunn (H4)	6,316
Durham (H2)	71,311
Durham (urban area)	72,369
E. Lumberton (H5)	1,106
E. Spencer (E3)	2,444
Edenton (M2)	4,468
Elizabeth City (N2)	12,685
Elizabethtown (H5)	1,611
Elkin (D2)	2,842
Elon College (G2)	1,109
Enfield (K2)	2,361
Enka (E8)	1,792
Erwin (H4)	3,344
Fair Bluff (H6)	1,056
Fairmount (G6)	2,319
Farmville (K3)	2,942
Fayetteville (H4)	34,715
Flat Rock (F9)	1,000
Forest City (B4)	4,971
Fort Bragg (H4)	16,000
Franklin (C9)	1,975
Franklinton (J2)	1,414
Fremont (J3)	1,395
Fuquay Springs (H3)	1,992
Garner (H3)	1,180
Gaston (K1)	1,218
Gastonia (C4)	23,069
Gibsonville (F2)	1,866
Goldsboro (K4)	21,454
Granite Falls (C3)	2,286
Grantsboro (M4)	1,500
Greensboro (F2)	74,389
Greensboro, (urban area)	82,719
Greenville (L3)	16,724
Hamlet (F5)	5,061
Hanes (E2)	1,000
Harkers Island (M5)	1,244
Havelock (M5)	4,500
Haw River (G2)	1,175
Hazelwood (D8)	1,769
Henderson (J2)	10,996
Hendersonville (F8)	6,103
Henrietta (B4)	1,013
Hertford (N2)	2,096
Hickory (C3)	14,755
High Point (E3)	39,973
Hillsboro (G2)	1,329
Hollyridge (L6)	1,082
Hope Mills (H5)	1,077
Icard (C3)	1,100
Jacksonville (K5)	3,960
Jonesville (D2)	1,768
Kannapolis (D4)	28,448
Kenly (J3)	1,129
Kernersville (E2)	2,396
King (E2)	1,000
Kings Mountain (C4)	7,206
Kinston (K4)	18,336
La Grange (K4)	1,852
Lakedale (H4)	4,000
Landis (D3)	1,827
Laurinburg (F5)	7,134
Leaksville (F2)	4,045
Lenoir (C3)	7,888
Lexington (E3)	13,571
Liberty (F3)	1,342
Lillington (H4)	1,061
Lincolnton (C4)	5,423
Littleton (K2)	1,173
Longhurst (G2)	1,539
Longview (C3)	2,291
Louisburg (J2)	2,545
Lowell (C4)	2,313
Lumberton (G5)	9,186
Madison (F2)	1,789
Maiden (C3)	1,952
Marion (A3)	2,740
Mars Hill (E7)	1,404
Marshville (E4)	1,258
Maxton (G5)	1,974
Mayodan (F2)	2,246
McAdenville (D4)	1,060
Mebane (G2)	2,068
Midway Park (L5)	3,703
Mocksville (D3)	1,909
Monroe (E5)	10,140
Mooresville (D3)	7,121
Morehead City (M5)	5,144
Morganton (B3)	8,311
Mount Airy (D1)	7,192
Mt. Gilead (F4)	1,201
Mt. Holly (D4)	2,241
Mt. Olive (K4)	3,732
Mt. Pleasant (E4)	1,019
Murfreesboro (M2)	2,140
Murphy (C9)	2,433
Nashville (K3)	1,302
New Bern (L4)	15,812
Newton (C3)	6,039
N. Wilkesboro (C2)	4,379
Norwood (E4)	1,735
Oteen (E8)	1,000
Oxford (H2)	6,685
Pembroke (G5)	1,212
Pilot Mountain (D2)	1,092
Pinehurst (F4)	1,016
Pinetops (K3)	1,031
Pineville (D4)	1,373
Pittsboro (G3)	1,094
Plymouth (M3)	4,486
Pomona (F2)	1,500
Raeford (G5)	2,030
RALEIGH (H3)	65,679
Raleigh (urban area)	68,190
Ramseur (F3)	1,134
Randleman (F3)	2,066
Red Springs (G5)	2,245
Reese (C6)	1,450
Reidsville (F2)	11,708
Roanoke Rapids (K2)	8,156
Robbins (F4)	1,158
Robersonville (L3)	1,414
Rockingham (F5)	3,356
Rocky Mount (K3)	27,697
Roseboro (J5)	1,241
Rowland (G5)	1,293
Roxboro (H2)	4,321
Rural Hall (E2)	1,200
Rutherfordton (A4)	3,146
Saint Pauls (H5)	2,251
Salisbury (D3)	20,102
Sanford (G4)	10,013
Scotland Neck (L2)	2,730
Selma (J3)	2,639
Shelby (C4)	15,508
Siler City (G3)	2,501
Skyland (E8)	1,200
Smithfield (J3)	5,574
Southern Pines (G4)	4,272
Southport (J7)	1,748
Spencer (D3)	3,242
Spindale (B4)	3,891
Spray (F1)	5,542
Spring Hope (K3)	1,275
Spring Lake (H4)	3,500
Spruce Pine (C7)	2,280
Stanley (C4)	1,644
Statesville (D3)	16,901
Stony Point (C3)	1,020
Swannanoa (F8)	1,800
Sylva (D8)	1,382
Tabor City (H6)	2,033
Tarboro (K3)	8,120
Taylorsville (C3)	1,310
Thomasville (E3)	11,154
Toast (D2)	1,401
Troy (F4)	2,213
Tryon (A4)	1,985
Valdese (B3)	2,730
Wadesboro (E5)	3,408
Wake Forest (H3)	3,704
Walkertown (E2)	1,000
Wallace (J5)	1,622
Walnut Cove (E2)	1,132
Wanchese (O3)	1,000
Warrenton (J2)	1,166
Warsaw (J4)	1,598
Washington (M3)	9,698
Waynesville (E8)	5,295
Weaverville (E8)	1,111
Weldon (K2)	2,295
Wendell (J3)	1,253
Whiteville (H6)	4,238
Whitnel (B3)	1,405
Wilkesboro (C2)	1,370
Williamston (M3)	4,975
Wilmington (J6)	45,043
Wilson (K3)	23,010
Windsor (L2)	1,781
Winston-Salem (E2)	87,811
Winston-Salem, (urban area)	91,493
Yanceyville (G2)	1,391
Zebulon (J3)	1,378

NORTH DAKOTA

Name & Index	Pop.
Ashley (M7)	1,423
Beach (C6)	1,461
Belfield (D6)	1,051
Beulah (G5)	1,501
BISMARCK (J6)	18,640
Bottineau (J2)	2,268
Bowman (D7)	1,382
Cando (M3)	1,530
Carrington (M5)	2,101
Casselton (R6)	1,373
Cavalier (P2)	1,459
Cooperstown (O5)	1,189
Crosby (D2)	1.689
Devils Lake (N3)	6.427
Dickinson (F6)	7,469
Ellendale (N7)	1,759
Enderlin (P6)	1,504
Fargo (S6)	38,256
Garrison (H4)	1,890
Glen Ullin (G6)	1,324
Grafton (R3)	4,901
Grand Forks (R4)	26,836
Hankinson (S7)	1,409
Harvey (L4)	2,337
Hazen (G5)	1,230
Hebron (G6)	1,412
Hettinger (E8)	1,762
Hillsboro (S5)	1,331
Jamestown (N6)	10.697
Kenmare (G2)	1,712
La Moure (O7)	1,010
Lakota (O3)	1,032
Langdon (O2)	1,838
Larimore (P4)	1.374
Lidgerwood (R7)	1,147
Linton (K7)	1,675
Lisbon (P7)	2.031
Mandan (J6)	7,298
Mayville (R4)	1,790
Minot (H3)	22,032
Mohall (G2)	1,073
Mott (F7)	1,583
Napoleon (L6)	1,070
New England (E6)	1,117
New Rockford (N4)	2,185
Northwood (R4)	1,182
Oakes (O7)	1,774
Park River (P3)	1,692
Riverdale (H5)	2,551
Rolla (L2)	1,176
Rugby (L3)	2,907
South West Fargo (S6)	1,032
Stanley (F3)	1,486
Underwood (H5)	1,061
Valley City (P6)	6,851
Velva (J3)	1,170
Wahpeton (S7)	5,125
Walhalla (P2)	1,463
Watford City (D4)	1,371
Williston (C3)	7,378
Wishek (L7)	1,241

OHIO

Name & Index	Pop.
Ada (C4)	3,640
Addyston (B9)	1,651
Adena (J5)	1,517
Akron (G3)	274,605
Akron (urban area)	365,130
Alliance (H4)	26,161
Amherst (F3)	3,542
Amsterdam (J5)	1,048
Andover (J2)	1,102
Antwerp (A3)	1,162
Arcanum (A6)	1,530
Archbold (B2)	1,486
Arlington Hts. (C9)	1,312
Ashland (F4)	14,287
Ashtabula (J2)	23,696
Ashville (E6)	1,303
Athens (F7)	11,660
Austinburg (J2)	1,375
Avon (F3)	2,773
Avon Lake (F2)	4,342
Baltimore (E6)	1,843
Barberton (G4)	27,820
Barnesville (H6)	4,665
Barton (J5)	1,300
Batavia (B7)	1,445
Bay Village (G9)	6,917
Beachwood ‡(G3)	1,073
Bedford (J9)	9,105
Bellaire (J5)	12,573
Bellefontaine (C5)	10,232
Bellevue (E3)	6,906
Bellville (E4)	1,355
Belpre (G7)	2,451
Berea (G10)	12,051
Bergholz (J4)	1,035
Bethel (B8)	1,932
Bethesda (H5)	1,158
Bexley (E6)	12,378
Blanchester (B7)	2,109
Blue Ash (C9)	1,420
Bluffton (C4)	2,423
Bowling Green (C3)	12,005
Bradford (B5)	2,055
Bratenahl (H9)	1,240
Brecksville (H10)	2,664
Bremen (F6)	1,187
Brewster (G4)	1,618
Bridgeport (J5)	4,309
Bridgetown (B9)	1,500
Brilliant (J5)	2,066
Broadview Hts. (H10)	2,279
Brook Park (G9)	2,606
Brookfield (J3)	1,000
Brooklyn (H9)	6,317
Brookville (B6)	1,908
Bryan (A3)	6,365
Buckeye Lake (F6)	1,401
Bucyrus (E4)	10,327
Byesville (G6)	2,236
Cadiz (J5)	3,020
Caldwell (G6)	1,767
Cambridge (G5)	14,739
Camden (A6)	1,084
Campbell (J3)	12,882
Canal Fulton (H4)	1,258
Canal Winchester (E6)	1,194
Canfield (J3)	1,465
Canton (H4)	116,912
Canton (urban area)	173,215
Cardington (E5)	1,465
Carey (D4)	3,260
Carrollton (J4)	2,658
Cedarville (C6)	1,292
Celina (A4)	5,703
Chagrin Falls (J9)	3,085
Chardon (H2)	2,478
Chauncey (F7)	1,016
Chesapeake (E9)	1.285
Cheviot (B9)	9,944
Chillicothe (E7)	20,133
Cincinnati (B9)	503,998
Cincinnati (urban area)	808,021
Circleville (D6)	8,723
Cleveland (H9)	914,808
Cleveland (urban area)	1,372,274
Cleveland Hts. (J9)	59,141

Name & Index	Pop.
Cleves (B9)	1,981
Clyde (E3)	4,083
Coal Grove (E9)	2,492
Coldwater (A5)	2,217
Columbiana (J4)	3,369
COLUMBUS (E6)	375,901
Columbus (urban area)	436,257
Columbus Grove (B4)	1,936
Conneaut (J2)	10,230
Continental (B3)	1,023
Corning (F6)	1,215
Cortland (J3)	1,259
Coshocton (G5)	11,675
Covington (B5)	2,172
Crestline (E4)	4,614
Creston (G3)	1,300
Crooksville (F6)	2,960
Cuyahoga Falls (G3)	29,195
Dayton (B6)	243,872
Dayton (urban area)	343,781
Deer Park (C9)	7,241
Defiance (B3)	11,265
Delaware (E5)	11,804
Delphos (B4)	6,220
Delta (B2)	2,120
Dennison (H5)	4,432
Deshler (C3)	1,623
Dillonvale (J5)	1,407
Dover (G4)	9,852
Doylestown (G4)	1,358
Dresden (G5)	1,310
E. Canton (H4)	1,001
E. Cleveland (J9)	40,047
E. Liverpool (J4)	24,217
E. Palestine (J4)	5,195
Eastlake (J8)	7,486
Eaton (A6)	4,242
Edgerton (A3)	1,246
Elmore (D3)	1,215
Elmwood Place (B9)	4,113
Elyria (F3)	30,307
Euclid (J9)	41,396
Fairborn (B6)	7,847
Fairport Harbor (Fairport) (H2)	4,519
Fairview (G9)	9,311
Fayette (B2)	1,003
Findlay (C3)	23,845
Flushing (J5)	1,158
Forest (C4)	1,114
Forestville (C10)	1,500
Fort Recovery (A5)	1,231
Fostoria (D3)	14,351
Franklin (B6)	5,388
Fredericktown (F5)	1,467
Fremont (D3)	16,537
Galion (E4)	9,952
Gallipolis (F8)	7,871
Gambier (F5)	1,037
Garfield Hts. (J9)	21,662
Garrettsville (H3)	1,504
Gates Mills (J9)	1,056
Geauga Lake (J10)	1,300
Geneva (J2)	4,718
Genoa (D2)	1,723
Georgetown (C8)	2,200
Germantown (B6)	2,478
Gibsonburg (D3)	2,281
Girard (J3)	10,113
Glendale (C9)	2,402
Glouster (F6)	2,327
Golf Manor (C9)	3,603
Grafton (F3)	1,194
Grandview Hts. (D6)	7,659
Granville (E5)	2,653
Green Springs (E3)	1,082
Greenfield (D7)	4,862
Greenhills (B9)	3,005
Greenville (A5)	8,859
Greenwich (E3)	1,204
Grove City (D6)	2,339
Groveport (E6)	1,165
Hamilton (A7)	57,951
Hamilton (urban area)	63,021
Harrison (A9)	1,943
Hartville (H4)	1,200
Hicksville (A3)	2,629
Hillsboro (C7)	5,126
Hinckley (G3)	1,796
Holgate (B3)	1,092
Hubbard (J3)	4,560
Hudson (H3)	1,538
Huron (E3)	2,515
Independence (H9)	3,105
Indian Hill (C9)	2,090
Ironton (E8)	16,333
Jackson (E7)	6,504
Jamestown (C6)	1,345
Jefferson (J2)	1,844
Jewett (H5)	1,019
Johnstown (E5)	1,220
Kent (H3)	12,418
Kenton (C4)	8,475
Kingsville (J2)	1,000
Lakemore (H3)	2,463
Lakeside Park (E2)	1,034
Lakeville (J2)	3,432
Lakewood (G9)	68,071
Lancaster (E6)	24,180
Lansing (J5)	2,000
Leavittsburg (J3)	2,533
Lebanon (B7)	4,618
Leetonia (J4)	2,565

Name & Index	Pop.
Leipsic (C3)	1,706
Lewisburg (A6)	1,230
Lima (B4)	50,246
Lincoln Hts. (C9)	5,531
Lisbon (J4)	3,293
Lockland (C9)	5,736
Lodi (F3)	1,523
Logan (F6)	5,972
London (C6)	5,222
Lorain (F3)	51,202
Loudonville (F4)	2,523
Louisville (H4)	3,801
Loveland (D9)	2,149
Lowellville (J3)	2,227
Lyndhurst (J9)	7,359
Madeira (C9)	2,689
Madison (H2)	1,127
Malvern (H4)	1,277
Manchester (C8)	2,281
Mansfield (F4)	43,564
Mantua (H3)	1,059
Maple Heights (H9)	15,586
Mariemont (C9)	3,514
Marietta (G7)	16,006
Marion (D4)	38,817
Martins Ferry (J5)	13,220
Marysville (D5)	4,256
Mason (B7)	1,196
Massillon (H4)	29,594
Masury (J3)	2,151
Maumee (C2)	5,548
Mayfield Hts. (J9)	5,807
McArthur (F7)	1,456
McComb (C3)	1,026
McConnelsville (G6)	1,941
McDonald ‡(J3)	1,858
Mechanicsburg (C5)	1,920
Medina (G3)	5,097
Mentor (H2)	2,383
Mentor-on-the-Lake (G2)	1,413
Miamisburg (B6)	6,329
Middleburg Hts. (G10)	2,299
Middlefield (H3)	1,141
Middleport (F7)	3,446
Middletown (A6)	33,695
Milford (D9)	2,448
Millersburg (F4)	2,398
Mineral Ridge (J3)	1,750
Minerva (H4)	3,280
Mingo Junction (J5)	4,464
Minster (B5)	1,728
Mogadore (H3)	1,818
Monroeville (E3)	1,275
Montpelier (A2)	3,867
Moreland Hills ‡(H3)	1,040
Morrow (B7)	1,137
Mt. Gilead (E4)	2,351
Mt. Healthy (B9)	5,533
Mt. Sterling (D6)	1,172
Mt. Vernon (E5)	12,185
Napoleon (B3)	5,335
Navarre (H4)	1,763
Neffs (J5)	1,024
Nelsonville (F7)	4,845
New Boston (E8)	4,754
New Bremen (B5)	1,546
New Carlisle (C6)	1,640
New Concord (G6)	1,797
New Lexington (F6)	4,233
New London (F3)	2,023
New Miami (A7)	1,860
New Paris (A6)	1,046
New Philadelphia (G5)	12,948
New Richmond (B8)	1,960
New Straitsville (F6)	1,122
Newark (F5)	34,275
Newburgh Hts. (H9)	3,689
Newcomerstown (G5)	4,514
Newton Falls (J3)	4,451
Newtown (C10)	1,462
Niles (J3)	16,773
N. Baltimore (C3)	2,771
N. Canton (H4)	4,032
N. College Hill (B9)	7,921
N. Industry (H4)	1,800
N. Kingsville (J2)	1,271
N. Olmsted (G9)	6,604
N. Ridgeville (F3)	1,700
N. Royalton (H10)	3,939
Norwalk (E3)	9,775
Norwood (C9)	35,001
Oak Hill (E8)	1,615
Oakharbor (D2)	2,370
Oakwood (B6)	9,697
Oberlin (F3)	7,062
Obetz (E6)	1,049
Olmstead Falls (G9)	1,137
Orrville (G4)	5,153
Ottawa (B3)	2,962
Ottawa Hills (C2)	2,333
Oxford (A6)	6,944
Painesville (H2)	14,432
Parma (H9)	28,897
Parma Heights (G9)	3,901
Paulding (A3)	2,352
Payne (A3)	1,062
Peebles (D8)	1,498
Pemberville (C3)	1,099
Perrysburg (C2)	4,006
Piney Fork (J5)	1,660
Piqua (B5)	17,447
Plain City (D5)	1,715
Plymouth (E4)	1,510
Poland (J3)	1,652

Name & Index	Pop.
Pomeroy (G7)	3,656
Port Clinton (E2)	5,541
Portsmouth (D8)	36,798
Powhatan Point (J6)	2,135
Prospect (D5)	1,031
Randolph (H3)	1,000
Ravenna (H3)	9,857
Reading (C9)	7,836
Richwood (D5)	1,866
Ripley (C8)	1,792
Rittman (G4)	3,810
Rockford (A4)	1,112
Rocky River (G9)	11,237
Roseville (F6)	1,808
Rossford (C2)	3,963
Rossmoyne (C9)	1,660
Sabina (C7)	1,696
St. Bernard (B9)	7,066
St. Clairsville (J5)	3,040
St. Marys (B4)	6,208
St. Paris (C5)	1,422
Salem (J4)	12,754
Salineville (J4)	2,018
Sandusky (E3)	29,375
Sawyerwood (G3)	1,585
Scio (H5)	1,152
Sebring (H4)	4,045
Seven Hills ‡(G3)	1,350
Shadyside (J6)	4,433
Shaker Hts. (H9)	28,222
Sharonville (C9)	1,318
Shawnee (F6)	1,145
Sheffield (F3)	1,147
Sheffield Lake (F3)	2,381
Shelby (E4)	7,971
Shreve (F4)	1,287
Sidney (B5)	11,491
Silver Lake (G3)	1,040
Silverton (C9)	4,827
Smithfield (J5)	1,255
Solon (J9)	2,570
Somerset (F6)	1,383
S. Amherst (F3)	1,020
S. Charleston (C6)	1,452
S. Euclid (H9)	15,432
S. Lebanon (B7)	1,291
S. Zanesville (F6)	1,477
Spencerville (B4)	1,826
Springdale (B9)	1,200
Springfield (C6)	78,508
Springfield (urban area)	81,837
Steubenville (J5)	35,872
Stow (H3)	2,140
Strasburg (G4)	1,366
Strongsville (G10)	3,504
Struthers (J3)	11,941
Stryker (B3)	1,026
Swanton (C2)	1,740
Sylvania (C2)	2,433
Tallmadge (H3)	5,821
Terrace Park (D9)	1,265
Tiffin (D3)	18,952
Tiltonsville (J5)	2,202
Tipp City (B6)	3,304
Toledo (D2)	303,616
Toledo (urban area)	361,493
Toronto (J5)	7,253
Trilby (C2)	2,750
Trotwood (B6)	1,066
Troy (B5)	10,661
Twinsburg (J10)	1,200
Uhrichsville (H5)	6,614
Union City (A5)	1,622
University Hts. (J9)	11,566
Upper Arlington (D6)	9,024
Upper Sandusky (D4)	4,397
Urbana (C5)	9,335
Utica (F5)	1,510
Van Wert (A4)	10,364
Vermilion (F3)	2,214
Versailles (A5)	1,812
Wadsworth (G3)	7,966
Walbridge (C2)	1,152
Wapakoneta (B4)	5,797
Warren (J3)	49,856
Warrensville Hts. (J9)	4,126
Washington Court House (D6)	10,560
Waterville (C3)	1,110
Wauseon (B2)	3,494
Waverly (D7)	1,679
Waynesburg (H4)	1,258
Waynesville (B6)	1,016
Wellington (F3)	2,992
Wellston (F7)	5,691
Wellsville (J4)	7,854
W. Alexandria (A6)	1,183
W. Carrollton (B6)	2,876
W. Jefferson (D6)	1,647
W. Lafayette (G5)	1,346
W. Liberty (C5)	1,397
W. Milton (B6)	2,101
W. Portsmouth (D8)	2,613
W. Union (C8)	1,508
Westerville (D5)	4,112
Westlake (G9)	4,912
Wheelersburg (E8)	1,013
Whitehall (E6)	4,877
Wickliffe (J9)	5,002
Willard (E3)	4,744
Williamsburg (B7)	1,490
Willoughby (J8)	5,602
Willowick (G2)	3,677
Wilmington (C7)	7,387

Name & Index	Pop.
Windham (H3)	3,968
Wintersville (J5)	1,950
Woodlawn (C9)	1,335
Woodsfield (H6)	2,410
Woodville (D3)	1,358
Wooster (G4)	14,005
Worthington (E5)	2,141
Wright View (B6)	2,500
Wyoming (C9)	5,582
Xenia (C6)	12,877
Yellow Springs (C6)	2,896
Yorkville (J5)	1,854
Youngstown (J3)	168,330
Youngstown (urban area)	297,084
Zanesville (G6)	40,517

OKLAHOMA

Name & Index	Pop.
Ada (J5)	15,995
Afton (N1)	1,252
Allen (K5)	1,215
Altus (D5)	9,735
Alva (E1)	6,505
Anadarko (F4)	6,184
Antlers (L6)	2,506
Apache (F5)	1,190
Ardmore (H6)	17,890
Arkoma (O4)	1,691
Atoka (K6)	2,653
Barnsdall (K1)	1,708
Bartlesville (K1)	19,228
Beaver (B1)	1,495
Beggs (L3)	1,214
Bethany (G3)	5,705
Bixby (L3)	1,517
Blackwell (H1)	9,199
Blanchard (G4)	1,311
Boise City (B8)	1,902
Bristow (K3)	5,400
Broken Arrow (L2)	3,262
Broken Bow (N7)	1,838
Buffalo (C1)	1,544
Carnegie (E4)	1,719
Cement (F5)	1,076
Chandler (J3)	2,724
Checotah (M4)	2,638
Chelsea (L1)	1,437
Cherokee (F1)	2,635
Cheyenne (C3)	1,133
Chickasha (G4)	15,842
Claremore (M2)	5,494
Cleveland (K2)	2,464
Clinton (D3)	7,555
Coalgate (K5)	1,984
Colinsville (L2)	2,011
Comanche (G6)	2,083
Commerce (M1)	2,442
Cordell (E4)	2,920
Coweta (L3)	1,601
Crescent (G3)	1,341
Cushing (J3)	8,414
Davis (H5)	1,928
Del City (H4)	2,504
Dewar (L4)	1,015
Dewey (L1)	2,513
Drumright (K3)	5,028
Duncan (G5)	15,325
Durant (K6)	10,541
Edmond (G3)	6,086
El Reno (F3)	10,991
Elk City (D4)	7,962
Enid (G2)	36,017
Erick (C4)	1,579
Eufaula (L4)	2,540
Fairfax (J1)	2,017
Fairview (E2)	2,411
Ft. Gibson (M3)	1,496
Frederick (D6)	5,467
Geary (F3)	1,614
Grandfield (E6)	1,232
Granite (D5)	1,096
Guthrie (H3)	10,113
Guymon (D8)	4,718
Haileyville (L5)	1,107
Hartshorne (M5)	2,330
Haskell (L3)	1,676
Healdton (H6)	2,578
Heavener (N5)	2,103
Hennessey (G2)	1,264
Henryetta (K4)	7,987
Hinton (F4)	1,025
Hobart (E5)	5,380
Holdenville (K4)	6,192
Hollis (C5)	3,089
Hominy (K2)	2,702
Hooker (E7)	1,842
Hugo (M6)	5,984
Idabel (N7)	4,671
Jenks (L2)	1,037
Kingfisher (G3)	3,345
Konawa (J5)	2,707
Krebs (L5)	1,532
Laverne (C1)	1,269
Lawton (F5)	34,757
Lexington (H4)	1,176
Lindsay (G5)	3,201
Madill (J6)	2,791
Mangum (C5)	4,271
Marietta (H7)	1,875
Marlow (F5)	3,399
Maud (J4)	1,389
Maysville (H5)	1,294

Name & Index	Pop.
McAlester (L5)	17,878
Medford (G1)	1,305
Miami (N1)	11,801
Midwest City (H4)	10,166
Morris (L3)	1,122
Mountain View (E4)	1,009
Muskogee (M3)	37,289
Newkirk (J1)	2,201
Nichols Hills ‡(H3)	2,606
Nicoma Park (H4)	1,200
Norman (H4)	27,006
Nowata (L1)	3,965
Oilton (J2)	1,109
Okeene (F2)	1,170
Okemah (K4)	3,454
OKLAHOMA CITY (H4)	243,504
Oklahoma City (urban area)	273,424
Okmulgee (K3)	18,317
Panama (N4)	1,027
Pauls Valley (H5)	6,896
Pawhuska (K1)	5,331
Pawnee (J2)	2,861
Perry (H2)	5,137
Picher (N1)	3,951
Ponca City (H1)	20,180
Pondcreek (G1)	1,066
Poteau (N4)	4,776
Prague (J4)	1,546
Pryor (M2)	4,486
Purcell (H4)	3,546
Ringling (G6)	1,092
Rush Springs (G5)	1,402
Ryan (G6)	1,019
Sallisaw (N4)	2,885
Sand Springs (K2)	6,994
Sapulpa (K3)	13,031
Sayre (C4)	3,362
Seminole (J4)	11,863
Sentinel (D4)	1,131
Shattuck (C2)	1,692
Shawnee (J4)	22,948
Skiatook (K2)	1,734
Snyder (E5)	1,646
Spiro (N4)	1,365
Stigler (M4)	2,125
Stillwater (J2)	20,238
Stilwell (N3)	1,813
Stratford (H5)	1,065
Stroud (J3)	2,450
Sulphur (J5)	4,389
Tahlequah (M3)	4,750
Tecumseh (J4)	2,275
Temple (F6)	1,442
Texhoma (D8)	1,464
Thomas (E3)	1,171
Tipton (D6)	1,172
Tishomingo (J6)	2,325
Tonkawa (H1)	3,643
Tulsa (K2)	182,740
Tulsa (urban area)	203,968
Tuxedo Park (L1)	1,179
Velma (G6)	1,034
Veterans Village ‡(H2)	3,355
Vinita (M1)	5,518
Wagoner (M3)	4,395
Walters (F6)	2,743
Warr Acres (G3)	2,378
Watonga (F3)	3,249
Waurika (G6)	2,327
Waynoka (E1)	2,018
Weatherford (E4)	3,529
Weleetka (K4)	1,548
Wetumka (K4)	2,025
Wewoka (K4)	6,747
Wilburton (M5)	1,939
Wilson (H6)	1,832
Woodward (D2)	5,915
Wright City (M6)	1,121
Wynne Wood (H5)	2,423
Yale (J2)	1,359
Yukon (G3)	1,990

OREGON

Name & Index	Pop.
Albany (D3)	10,115
Altamont (F5)	9,419
Ashland (E5)	7,739
Astoria (D1)	12,331
Baker (K3)	9,471
Bandon (C4)	1,251
Beaverton (A2)	2,512
Bend (F3)	11,409
Brookings (C5)	1,000
Brownsville (E3)	1,175
Burns (H4)	3,093
Canby (B2)	1,671
Carlton (D2)	1,081
Central Point (D5)	1,667
Coos Bay (C4)	6,223
Coquille (C4)	3,523
Corvallis (D3)	16,207
Cottage Grove (D4)	3,536
Dallas (D3)	4,793
Drain (D4)	1,150
Elgin (K2)	1,223
Empire (C4)	2,261
Enterprise (K2)	1,718
Eugene (D3)	35,879
Florence (C4)	1,026
Forest Grove (A2)	4,343
Freewater (J2)	1,489
Garibaldi (D2)	1,249

Name & Index	Pop.
Gladstone (B2)	2,434
Grants Pass (D5)	8,116
Gresham (B2)	3,049
Hayesville (A3)	2,697
Heppner (H2)	1,648
Hermiston (H2)	3,804
Hillsboro (A2)	5,142
Hood River (F2)	3,701
Independence (D3)	1,987
Jacksonville (D5)	1,193
Jennings Lodge (B2)	3,500
John Day (J3)	1,597
Junction City (D3)	1,475
Klamath Falls (F5)	15,875
La Grande (J2)	8,635
Lake Grove (B2)	4,000
Lakeview (G5)	2,831
Lebanon (E3)	5,873
Madras (F3)	1,258
Mapleton (C3)	1,016
McMinnville (D2)	6,635
Medford (E5)	17,305
Metzger (A2)	2,000
Mill City (E3)	1,792
Milton (J2)	2,362
Milwaukie (B2)	5,253
Molalla (B3)	1,497
Monmouth (D3)	1,956
Mount Angel (B3)	1,315
Multnomah (B2)	5,000
Myrtle Creek (D4)	1,781
Myrtle Point (C4)	2,033
Newberg (A2)	3,946
Newport (C3)	3,241
North Bend (C4)	6,099
Nyssa (K4)	2,525
Oak Grove (B2)	2,000
Oakridge (E4)	1,562
Ontario (K3)	4,465
Oregon City (B2)	7,682
Oswego (B2)	3,316
Parkrose (B2)	3,800
Pendleton (J2)	11,774
Philomath (D3)	1,289
Portland (B2)	373,628
Portland (urban area)	509,120
Prineville (G3)	3,233
Rainier (E1)	1,285
Redmond (F3)	2,956
Reedsport (C4)	2,288
Rockaway (C2)	1,027
Roseburg (D4)	8,390
St. Helens (E2)	4,711
SALEM (A3)	43,140
Sandy (E2)	1,003
Seaside (D2)	3,886
Sheridan (D2)	1,922
Silverton (A3)	3,146
Springfield (E3)	10,807
Stayton (E3)	1,507
Sutherlin (D4)	2,230
Sweet Home (E3)	3,603
Sylvan (B2)	1,500
The Dalles (F2)	7,676
Tillamook (D2)	3,685
Toledo (D3)	2,323
Union (K2)	1,307
Vale (K4)	1,518
Vernonia (D2)	1,521
Wallowa (K2)	1,055
Warrenton (C1)	1,896
West Linn (B2)	2,945
West Portland (B2)	3,000
Westfir (E4)	1,200
Willamina (D2)	1,082
Woodburn (A3)	2,395

PENNSYLVANIA

Name & Index	Pop.
Adamstown (K5)	1,020
Akron (K5)	1,028
Albion (B2)	1,729
Aldan (M7)	3,430
Aliquippa (B4)	26,132
Allentown (L4)	106,756
Allentown-Bethlehem (urban area)	225,155
Allison Park (C4)	2,000
Altoona (F4)	77,177
Altoona (urban area)	86,249
Ambler (M5)	4,555
Ambridge (B4)	16,429
Andalusia (N5)	1,800
Annville (J5)	3,564
Apollo (D4)	3,015
Archbald (M2)	6,304
Ardmore (M6)	20,000
Arnold (C4)	10,263
Ashland (K4)	6,192
Ashley (L3)	5,243
Aspinwall (C6)	4,084
Athens (K2)	4,430
Atlas (K4)	3,090
Avalon (B6)	6,463
Avella (B5)	1,356
Avis (H3)	1,193
Avoca (L3)	4,040
Avonmore (C4)	1,367
Baden (B4)	3,732
Bangor (M4)	6,050
Barnesboro (E4)	3,442
Bath (M4)	1,824
Beaver (B4)	6,360

Name & Index	Pop.
Beaver Falls (B4)	17,375
Beaver Meadows (L4)	1,723
Beaverdale (E5)	2,200
Bedford (F5)	3,521
Belle Vernon (C5)	2,271
Bellefonte (G4)	5,651
Belleville (G4)	1,304
Bellevue (B6)	11,604
Bellwood (F4)	2,559
Ben Avon (B6)	2,465
Bentleyville (B5)	3,295
Berlin (E6)	1,507
Berwick (K3)	14,010
Berwyn (L5)	3,000
Bessemer (B4)	1,461
Bethel (B7)	11,324
Bethlehem (M4)	66,340
Bethlehem-Allentown (urban area)	225,155
Birdsboro (L5)	3,158
Black Lick (D4)	1,000
Blairsville (D5)	5,000
Blakely ‡(L3)	6,828
Blandburg (F4)	1,200
Blawnox (C6)	2,165
Bloomfield (New Bloomfield) (H5)	1,098
Bloomsburg (J3)	10,633
Blossburg (H2)	1,954
Bobtown (B6)	1,553
Boothwyn (L7)	4,500
Boston (C7)	1,700
Boswell (E5)	1,679
Boyertown (L5)	4,074
Brackenridge (C4)	6,178
Braddock (C7)	16,488
Braddock Hills (C7)	1,965
Bradford (E2)	17,354
Branch Dale (K4)	1,500
Brentwood (B7)	12,535
Bridgeport (M5)	5,827
Bridgeville (B5)	5,650
Bridgewater (W. Bridgewater) (B4)	1,316
Bristol (N5)	12,710
Brockway (E3)	2,650
Brookhaven (M7)	1,042
Brookville (D3)	4,274
Broomall (M6)	6,000
Broughton (B7)	2,500
Brownstown ‡(E5)	1,508
Brownsville (C5)	7,643
Bryn Mawr (M5)	12,000
Burgettstown (A5)	2,379
Burnham (H4)	2,954
Butler (C4)	23,482
Cairnbrook (E5)	1,504
California (C5)	2,831
Cambridge Spgs. (C2)	2,246
Camp Hill (H5)	5,934
Canonsburg (B5)	12,072
Canton (J2)	2,118
Carbondale (L2)	16,296
Carlisle (H5)	16,812
Carnegie (B7)	12,105
Carrolltown (E4)	1,452
Castle Shannon (B7)	5,459
Catasauqua (M4)	4,923
Catawissa (K4)	2,000
Cecil (B5)	1,200
Centerville (B6)	5,845
Central City (E5)	1,935
Centralia (K4)	1,986
Chalfant ‡(C7)	1,381
Chambersburg (G6)	17,212
Charleroi (C5)	9,872
Cheltenham (M5)	▲22,854
Chester (L7)	66,039
Cheswick (C6)	1,534
Chicora (C4)	1,172
Christiana (K6)	1,043
Churchill ‡(C7)	1,733
Clairton (C7)	19,652
Clarence (G3)	1,700
Clarion (D3)	4,409
Clarks Summit (L3)	2,940
Claysburg (F5)	1,355
Clearfield (F3)	9,357
Cleona ‡(K5)	1,483
Clifton Heights (M7)	7,549
Clymer (E4)	2,500
Coaldale (L4)	5,318
Coalport (E4)	1,052
Coatesville (L5)	13,826
Cochranton (B2)	1,092
Cokeburg (B5)	1,170
Collegeville (M5)	1,900
Collingdale (N7)	8,443
Columbia (K5)	11,993
Colver (E4)	1,708
Colwyn ‡(M7)	2,143
Conemaugh (E5)	5,000
Confluence (D6)	1,037
Conneautville (A2)	1,177
Connellsville (D5)	13,293
Conshohocken (M5)	10,922
Conway (B4)	1,570
Coopersburg (M5)	1,462
Coplay (L4)	2,994
Coraopolis (B4)	10,498
Cornwall (K5)	1,760
Corry (C2)	7,911
Coudersport (G2)	3,210
Crafton (B7)	8,066
Cresson (E5)	2,569

Name & Index	Pop.
Cressona (K4)	1,758
Crum Lynne (M7)	3,500
Cuddy (B5)	2,500
Curwensville (E4)	3,332
Dale ‡(E5)	3,310
Dallas (K3)	1,674
Dallastown (J6)	3,304
Dalton (L2)	1,109
Danville (J4)	6,994
Darby (N7)	13,154
Denbo (C6)	1,300
Denver (K5)	1,658
Derry (D5)	3,752
Dickson City (L3)	8,948
Dillsburg (J5)	1,146
Dixonville (D4)	1,050
Donora (C5)	12,186
Dormont (B7)	13,405
Downingtown (L5)	4,948
Doylestown (M5)	5,262
Dravosburg (C7)	3,786
Drexel Hill (M6)	40,000
Du Bois (E3)	11,497
Duboistown (H3)	1,140
Duke Center (F2)	1,200
Dunbar (C6)	1,363
Duncannon (H5)	1,852
Duncansville (F5)	1,391
Dunlo (E5)	2,200
Dunmore (L3)	20,305
Dupont ‡(L3)	4,107
Duquesne (C7)	17,620
Duryea (L3)	6,655
E. Brady (C3)	1,400
E. Conemaugh ‡(E5)	4,101
E. Greenville (L5)	1,945
E. Lansdowne ‡(M7)	3,527
E. Mauch Chunk ‡(L4)	3,132
E. McKeesport ‡(C5)	3,171
E. Petersburg (K5)	1,268
E. Pittsburgh (C7)	5,259
E. Stroudsburg (M4)	7,274
E. Vandergrift ‡(C4)	1,665
E. Washington ‡(B5)	2,304
Easton (M4)	35,632
Ebensburg (E5)	4,086
Eddington (N5)	2,000
Eddystone (M7)	3,014
Eden Park (C7)	1,531
Edgewood (B7)	5,292
Edgeworth ‡(B4)	1,466
Edinboro (B2)	1,567
Edwardsville ‡(L3)	6,686
Eldred (F2)	1,199
Elizabeth (C5)	2,615
Elizabethtown (J5)	5,083
Elizabethville (J5)	1,506
Elkins Park (M5)	12,000
Elkland (H1)	2,326
Ellport ‡(B4)	1,122
Ellsworth (B5)	1,670
Ellwood City (B4)	12,945
Elmora (E4)	1,850
Elrama (C5)	1,675
Elwyn (L7)	1,800
Emmaus (M4)	7,780
Emporium (F2)	3,646
Emsworth (B6)	3,128
Enola (J5)	2,500
Ephrata (K5)	7,027
Erie (B1)	130,803
Erie (urban area)	151,282
Ernest (D4)	1,170
Essington (M7)	3,700
Etna (B6)	6,750
Evans City (B4)	1,637
Evansburg (Evans City) (B4)	1,637
Everson (C5)	1,520
Exeter ‡(L3)	5,130
Export (C5)	1,690
Factoryville (L2)	1,005
Fairchance (C6)	2,091
Fairoaks (B4)	1,600
Falls Creek (E3)	1,191
Farrell (A3)	13,644
Fayette City (C5)	1,404
Ferndale (D5)	2,619
Fleetwood (L5)	2,338
Flemington (G3)	1,446
Florin (J5)	1,319
Folcroft (M7)	1,909
Folsom (M7)	2,500
Ford City (D4)	5,352
Forest City (L2)	3,122
Forest Hills ‡(C5)	6,301
Forty Fort (L3)	6,173
Fountain Hill ‡(M4)	5,456
Fox Chapel (C6)	1,721
Frackville (K4)	6,541
Franklin (C3)	10,006
Franklin ‡(E5)	1,833
Fredericktown (C6)	1,000
Freedom (B4)	3,000
Freeland (L3)	5,909
Freemansburg (M4)	1,739
Freeport (C4)	2,685
Galeton (G2)	1,646
Gallitzin (E4)	3,102
Geistown (E5)	2,148
Gettysburg (H6)	7,046
Gilberton (K4)	2,641
Girard (B2)	2,141
Girardville (K4)	3,864

Name & Index	Pop.
Glassport (C7)	8,707
Glen Lyon (K3)	3,921
Glen Olden (M7)	6,450
Glen Rock (J6)	1,477
Glenshaw (C6)	8,000
Glenside (M5)	8,000
Glenwillard (B4)	1,200
Gordon ‡(K4)	1,039
Granville (G4)	2,157
Grapeville (C5)	1,563
Grassflat (F3)	1,000
Greencastle (G6)	2,661
Greensburg (D5)	16,923
Greentree (B7)	2,818
Greenville (B3)	9,210
Grove City (B3)	7,411
Hallstead (L2)	1,445
Hamburg (L4)	3,805
Hanover (J6)	14,048
Harmarville (C6)	3,000
HARRISBURG (J5)	89,544
Harrisburg (urban area)	168,933
Harveys Lake (L3)	1,500
Hastings (E4)	1,846
Hatboro (M5)	4,788
Hatfield (M5)	1,624
Haverford (M6)	▲39,641
Havertown (M6)	22,000
Hawley (M3)	1,602
Hazleton (L4)	35,491
Heidelberg (B7)	2,250
Heilwood (E4)	1,000
Hellertown (M4)	5,435
Herminie (C5)	2,072
Hershey (J5)	4,500
High Spire (J5)	2,799
Hokendauqua (L4)	1,460
Hollidaysburg (F5)	6,483
Homer City (D4)	2,372
Homestead (B7)	10,046
Honesdale (M2)	5,662
Hooversville (E5)	1,240
Houston (B5)	1,957
Houtzdale (F4)	1,306
Hughestown ‡(L3)	1,888
Hughesville (J3)	2,095
Hummelstown (J5)	3,789
Huntingdon (G5)	7,330
Hyndman (E6)	1,322
Imperial (B5)	1,895
Indiana (D4)	11,743
Ingram (B7)	4,236
Irwin (C5)	4,228
Jeannette (C5)	16,172
Jenkintown (M5)	5,130
Jermyn (L2)	2,535
Jerome (D5)	1,960
Jersey Shore (H3)	5,595
Jessup (L3)	6,650
Jim Thorpe (L4)	2,959
Johnsonburg (E3)	4,567
Johnstown (D5)	63,232
Johnstown (urban ar.)	92,780
Kane (E2)	5,706
Kelayres (K4)	1,059
Kenhorst ‡(L5)	2,551
Kennett Square (L6)	3,699
Kingston (K3)	21,096
Kittanning (C4)	7,731
Knox (C3)	1,213
Koppel (B4)	1,137
Kulpmont (J4)	5,199
Kutztown (L4)	3,110
Lakemont (F5)	1,600
Lancaster (K5)	63,774
Lancaster (urban area)	76,087
Langeloth (A5)	1,068
Langhorne (N5)	1,579
Lansdale (M5)	9,762
Lansdowne (M7)	12,169
Lansford (L4)	7,487
Larimer (C8)	1,057
Larksville ‡(L3)	6,360
Latrobe (D5)	11,811
Laurel Gardens (B6)	1,200
Laureldale (L5)	3,585
Lebanon (K5)	28,156
Lebanon Independent ‡(K5)	2,778
Leechburg (C4)	4,042
Leetsdale (B4)	2,411
Lehighton (L4)	6,565
Lemoyne (J5)	4,605
Lester (M7)	2,100
Levittown (N5)	42,000
Lewisburg (J4)	5,268
Lewistown (G4)	13,894
Liberty (C7)	1,900
Library (B7)	2,124
Ligonier (D5)	2,160
Lilly (E5)	1,898
Linesville (A2)	1,246
Linfield (L5)	1,025
Linwood (L7)	5,000
Lititz (K5)	5,568
Littlestown (H6)	2,635
Lock Haven (H3)	11,381
Lorain ‡(E5)	1,406
Lucernemines (D4)	1,075
Luzerne (L3)	6,176
Lykens (J4)	2,735
Lyndora (B4)	4,800
Mahanoy City (K4)	10,934

Name & Index	Pop.
Malvern (L5)	1,764
Manchester (J5)	1,264
Manheim (K5)	4,246
Manor (C5)	1,230
Mansfield (J2)	2,657
Marcus Hook (L7)	3,843
Marianna (B5)	1,269
Marienville (D3)	1,000
Marietta (J5)	2,442
Marion Heights ‡(K4)	1,551
Mars (C4)	1,385
Martins Creek (M4)	1,000
Martinsburg (F5)	1,562
Marysville (H5)	2,158
Masontown (C6)	4,550
Matamoras (N3)	1,731
Mauch Chunk (L4)	2,959
Mayfield (L2)	2,373
McAdoo (L4)	4,260
McClure (H4)	1,000
McConnellsburg (F6)	1,126
McDonald (B5)	3,543
McKees Rocks (B7)	16,241
McKeesport (C7)	51,502
McSherrystown (H6)	2,510
Meadow Lands (B5)	1,059
Meadville (B2)	18,972
Mechanicsburg (H5)	6,786
Media (L7)	5,726
Mercer (B3)	2,397
Mercersburg (G6)	1,613
Merion Station (M6)	2,000
Meyersdale (E6)	3,137
Middleburg (H4)	1,283
Middletown (J5)	9,184
Midland (A4)	6,491
Mifflinburg (H4)	2,259
Mifflintown (H4)	1,013
Mildred (K3)	1,000
Milford (N3)	1,111
Mill Hall (G3)	1,677
Millersburg (J4)	2,861
Millerstown (Chicora) (C4)	1,172
Millersville (K6)	2,551
Millsboro (B6)	1,100
Millvale (B7)	7,287
Milmont Park (M7)	2,200
Milroy (G4)	1,443
Milton (J3)	8,578
Minersville (K4)	7,783
Mohnton (L5)	2,004
Monaca (B4)	7,415
Monessen (C5)	17,896
Monongahela (B5)	8,922
Montgomery (H3)	2,166
Montoursville (J3)	3,293
Montrose (L2)	2,075
Moon Run (B5)	1,143
Moosic (L3)	3,965
Morrisdale (F4)	1,000
Morrisville (N5)	6,787
Morton (M7)	1,352
Moscow (L3)	1,050
Mt. Carmel (K4)	14,222
Mt. Holly Springs (H5)	1,701
Mt. Jewett (E2)	1,415
Mt. Joy (K5)	3,006
Mt. Lebanon (B7)	▲26,604
Mt. Oliver ‡(B7)	6,646
Mt. Penn ‡(L5)	3,635
Mt. Pleasant (D5)	5,883
Mt. Union (G5)	4,690
Mt. Wolf (J5)	1,164
Mountville (K5)	1,064
Muncy (J3)	2,756
Munhall (C7)	16,437
Myerstown (K5)	3,050
Nanticoke (K3)	20,160
Nanty Glo (E5)	5,425
Narberth (M6)	5,407
Nazareth (M4)	5,830
Nemacolin (B6)	1,930
Nescopeck (K3)	1,907
New Bethlehem (D3)	1,604
New Bloomfield (H5)	1,098
New Brighton (B4)	9,535
New Castle (B3)	48,834
New Cumberland (J5)	6,204
New Eagle (B5)	2,316
New Freedom (J6)	1,271
New Holland (K5)	2,602
New Hope (N5)	1,066
New Kensington (C4)	25,146
New Oxford (H6)	1,366
New Philadelphia (K4)	2,200
New Salem (C6)	1,000
New Wilmington (B3)	1,943
Newport (H5)	1,893
Newtown (N5)	2,095
Newville (H5)	1,788
Norristown (M5)	38,126
North Apollo (D4)	1,502
N. Belle Vernon ‡(C5)	3,147
N. Braddock ‡(C7)	14,724
N. Catasauqua ‡(M4)	2,629
N. Charleroi ‡(C5)	2,554
N. East (C1)	4,247
N. Girard (B1)	1,369
N. Irwin ‡(C5)	1,076
N. Wales (M5)	2,998
N. York ‡(J5)	2,445
Northampton (M4)	9,332
Northumberland (J4)	4,207
Norwood (M7)	5,246

Name & Index	Pop.
Nu Mine (D4)	2,000
Nuremberg (K4)	1,200
Oakdale (B5)	1,572
Oakford (N5)	1,900
Oakmont (C6)	7,264
Oil City (C3)	19,581
Old Forge (L3)	9,749
Oliver (C6)	2,180
Olyphant (L3)	7,047
Orwigsburg (K4)	2,309
Osceola Mills (F4)	1,992
Oxford (K6)	3,091
Paint (E5)	1,547
Palmerton (L4)	6,646
Palmyra (J5)	5,910
Palo Alto ‡(K4)	1,767
Paoli (M5)	3,029
Parkesburg (L6)	2,611
Parkside (M7)	1,637
Patton (E4)	3,148
Paxtang ‡(J5)	1,857
Pen Argyl (M4)	3,878
Penbrook ‡(J5)	3,691
Penndel ‡(N5)	1,100
Pennsburg (M5)	1,625
Perkasie (M5)	4,358
Perrysville (B6)	1,500
Philadelphia (N6)	2,071,605
Philadelphia (urban area)	2,913,516
Philipsburg (F4)	3,988
Phoenixville (L5)	12,932
Pine Grove (K4)	2,237
Pine Grove Mills (G4)	1,200
Pitcairn (C5)	5,857
Pittock (B7)	2,600
Pittsburgh (B7)	676,806
Pittsburgh (urban area)	1,525,966
Pittston (L3)	15,012
Plains (L3)	▲12,541
Pleasant Gap (G4)	1,312
Pleasant Hills (B7)	3,808
Plymouth (K3)	13,021
Point Marion (C6)	2,197
Polk (C3)	4,004
Port Allegany (F2)	2,519
Port Carbon (K4)	3,024
Port Vue (C7)	4,756
Portage (E5)	4,371
Pottstown (L5)	22,589
Pottsville (K4)	23,640
Pringle ‡(L3)	1,727
Prospect Park (M7)	5,834
Punxsutawney (E4)	8,969
Quakertown (M5)	5,673
Quarryville (K6)	1,187
Rankin (C7)	6,941
Reading (L5)	109,320
Reading (urban area)	154,571
Red Lion (J6)	5,119
Reedsville (G4)	1,238
Reno (C3)	1,000
Renovo (G3)	3,751
Reynoldsville (D3)	3,569
Richland (K5)	1,090
Ridgway (E3)	6,244
Ridley Park (M7)	4,921
Rimersburg (D3)	1,398
Roaring Spring (F5)	2,771
Robesonia (K5)	1,590
Rochester (B4)	7,197
Rockledge ‡(M5)	2,261
Rockwood (D6)	1,237
Roscoe (C5)	1,396
Rosemont (M5)	2,000
Roseto (M4)	1,676
Rossiter (E4)	1,078
Rothsville (K5)	1,000
Rouseville (C3)	1,009
Rouzerville (G6)	1,000
Royalton (J5)	1,175
Royersford (L5)	3,862
Russellton (C4)	1,670
Sagamore (D4)	1,128
St. Clair (K4)	5,856
St. Marys (E3)	7,846
Saltsburg (D4)	1,156
Saxton (F5)	1,093
Sayre (K2)	7,735
Scalp Level (E5)	1,756
Schaefferstown (K5)	1,000
Schuylkill Haven (K4)	6,597
Scottdale (C5)	6,249
Scranton (L3)	125,536
Scranton (urban area)	235,122
Secane (M7)	1,500
Selinsgrove (J4)	3,514
Sellersville (M5)	2,373
Sewickley (B4)	5,836
Shamokin (J4)	16,879
Sharon (B3)	26,454
Sharon Hill (N7)	5,464
Sharpsburg (B6)	7,296
Sharpsville (A3)	5,414
Sheffield (D2)	2,087
Shenandoah (K4)	15,704
Shickshinny (K3)	2,156
Shillington (K5)	5,059
Shinglehouse (F2)	1,201
Shippensburg (H5)	5,722
Shoemakersville (K4)	1,066
Simpson (M2)	2,800

Name & Index	Pop.
Sinking Spring (K5)	1,982
Slatington (L4)	4,343
Slickville (C5)	1,266
Slippery Rock (B3)	2,294
Smethport (F2)	1,797
Smithfield (C6)	1,066
Smithmill (F4)	1,500
Somerset (D6)	5,936
Souderton (M5)	4,521
S. Coatesville ‡(L6)	1,996
S. Connellsville (D6)	2,610
S. Fork (E2)	2,616
S. Greensburg ‡(C5)	2,980
S. Mountain (H6)	1,300
S. Waverly (J2)	1,298
S. Williamsport (J3)	6,364
Southmont ‡(E5)	2,278
Southwest Greensburg ‡(C5)	3,144
Spangler (E4)	3,013
Speers ‡(C5)	1,089
Spring City (L5)	3,258
Spring Grove (J6)	1,238
Springdale (C4)	4,939
Springfield (M7)	8,000
State College (G4)	17,227
Steelton (J5)	12,574
Stewartstown (K6)	1,133
Stoneboro (B3)	1,294
Stowe (L5)	2,524
Stowe (B7)	▲12,210
Strasburg (K6)	1,109
Stroudsburg (M4)	6,361
Sturgeon (B5)	1,150
Sugar Notch (L3)	2,002
Summit Hill (L4)	4,294
Sunbury (J4)	15,570
Susquehanna (L2)	2,646
Swarthmore (M7)	4,825
Swissvale (C7)	16,488
Swoyersville ‡(L3)	7,795
Sykesville (E3)	1,652
Tamaqua (L4)	11,508
Tarentum (C4)	9,540
Taylor (L3)	7,176
Telford ‡(M5)	2,042
Temple (L5)	1,460
Templeton (C4)	1,000
Terre Hill (L5)	1,000
Throop (L3)	5,861
Titusville (C2)	8,923
Topton (L5)	1,572
Towanda (J2)	4,069
Tower City (J4)	2,054
Trafford (C5)	3,965
Trainer (L7)	2,001
Tremont (K4)	2,102
Trevorton (J4)	2,545
Troy (J2)	1,371
Tunkhannock (L2)	2,170
Turtle Creek (C7)	12,363
Twin Rocks (E4)	1,850
Tyrone (F4)	8,214
Union City (C2)	3,911
Uniontown (C6)	20,471
Uniontown ‡(J4)	1,280
Universal (C7)	3,200
Upland (L7)	4,081
Upper Darby (M6)	▲84,951
Valley View (J4)	1,618
Vandergrift (D4)	9,524
Vanport (B4)	2,500
Verona (C6)	4,235
Versailles (C7)	2,484
Villanova (M6)	1,500
Vintondale (E5)	1,185
Wall (C5)	1,850
Wallingford (L7)	6,000
Walnutport (L4)	1,427
Wampum (B4)	1,090
Wanamie (L3)	1,092
Warren (D2)	14,849
Warrior Run ‡(L3)	1,056
Washington (B5)	26,280
Waterford (B2)	1,195
Watsontown (J3)	2,327
Waymart (M2)	1,068
Wayne (M6)	6,000
Waynesboro (G6)	10,334
Waynesburg (B6)	5,514
Weatherly (L4)	2,622
Wellsboro (H2)	4,215
Wernersville (K5)	1,280
Wesleyville (C1)	3,411
W. Bridgewater (B4)	1,316
W. Brownsville (C5)	1,610
W. Chester (L6)	15,168
W. Conshohocken ‡(M5)	2,482
W. Easton ‡(M4)	1,368
W. Elizabeth (C5)	1,137
W. Fairview ‡(J5)	1,896
W. Grove (L6)	1,521
W. Hazleton (K4)	6,988
W. Homestead ‡(B7)	3,257
W. Lawn (K5)	2,144
W. Leechburg ‡(C4)	1,113
W. Mayfield ‡(B4)	1,768
W. Middlesex (B3)	1,217
W. Mifflin (C7)	17,985
W. Nanticoke (K3)	1,780
W. Newton (C5)	3,619
W. Pittston ‡(L3)	7,230
W. Reading ‡(L5)	5,072
W. View (B6)	7,581

Name & Index	Pop.
W. Wyoming ‡(L3)	2,863
W. York ‡(J6)	5,756
Westfield (H2)	1,357
Westland (B5)	1,025
Westmont ‡(C5)	4,410
Wheatland (B3)	1,402
Whitaker (C7)	2,149
White Haven (L3)	1,461
White Oak (C7)	6,159
Whitehall (B7)	7,342
Wiconisco (J4)	1,549
Wilcox (E2)	1,000
Wilkes-Barre (L3)	76,826
Wilkes-Barre (urban area)	270,978
Wilkinsburg (C7)	31,418
Williamsburg (F5)	1,792
Williamsport (H3)	45,047
Williamstown (J4)	2,332
Willow Grove (M5)	7,000
Wilmerding (C7)	5,325
Wilson (M4)	8,159
Windber (E5)	8,010
Windgap (M4)	1,577
Windsor (J6)	1,126
Winton (M3)	6,280
Womelsdorf (K5)	1,549
Woodland (F4)	1,000
Woodlyn (M7)	5,000
Woodville (B7)	3,775
Wormleysburg ‡(J5)	1,511
Wrightsville (J5)	2,104
Wyoming (L3)	4,511
Wyomissing (K5)	4,187
Yardley (N5)	1,916
Yatesboro (D4)	1,264
Yeadon (N7)	11,068
Yeagertown (G4)	1,.628
York (J6)	59,953
York (urban area)	78,495
Youngsville (D2)	1,944
Youngwood (D5)	2,720
Yukon (C5)	1,099
Zelienople (B4)	2,981

RHODE ISLAND

Name & Index	Pop.
Anthony (H6)	2,000
Arctic (J6)	3,000
Ashaway (G7)	1,022
Ashton (J5)	1,000
Barrington (J6)	▲8,246
Bradford (H7)	1,024
Bristol (J6)	▲12,320
Centerdale (H5)	2,500
Central Falls (J5)	23,550
Charlestown (H7)	▲1,598
Chepachet (H5)	1,200
Coventry (H6)	▲9,869
Cranston (J5)	55,060
Crompton (J6)	1,500
Davisville (H6)	1,400
East Greenwich (H6)	▲4,923
E. Providence (J5)	▲35,871
Esmond (H5)	2,000
Exeter (H6)	▲1,870
Foster (H5)	▲1,630
Georgiaville (H5)	1,247
Greenville (H5)	2,000
Harrisville (H5)	1,055
Hope Valley (H6)	1,000
Hopkinton (H7)	▲3,676
Howard (J5)	6,000
Jamestown (J6)	▲2,068
Kingston (J7)	2,156
Little Compton (K6)	▲1,556
Lonsdale (J5)	2,500
Manton (J5)	2,500
Manville (H5)	3,429
Mapleville (H5)	1,015
Middletown (J6)	▲7,382
Narragansett (J7)	▲2,288
Natick (H6)	2,000
Newport (J7)	37,564
North Scituate (H5)	1,000
N. Tiverton (K6)	4,000
Norwood (J5)	2,300
Oakland Beach (J6)	10,000
Pascoag (H5)	1,760
Pawtucket (J5)	81,436
Peace Dale (J7)	2,177
Phenix (H6)	1,500
Phillipsdale (J5)	1,500
Portsmouth (J6)	▲6,578
PROVIDENCE (H5)	248,674
Providence (urban area)	581,607
River Point (H6)	1,000
Riverside (J5)	10,000
Rumford (J5)	10,000
Saylesville (J5)	3,500
Shawomet (J6)	1,500
Slatersville (H4)	1,780
Tiverton (K6)	▲5,659
Valley Falls (J5)	2,500
Wakefield (H7)	3,047
Warren (J6)	▲8,513
Warwick (J6)	43,028
Washington (H6)	2,800
West Barrington (J5)	4,250
Westerly (G7)	▲12,380
Wickford (J6)	2,437
Woonsocket (J4)	50,211

SOUTH CAROLINA

Name & Index	Pop.
Abbeville (C3)	5,395
Aiken (D4)	7,083
Allendale (E5)	2,474
Anderson (B2)	19,770
Andrews (H5)	2,702
Arcadia (C2)	2,554
Ariail (B2)	1,098
Baldwin Mills (E2)	1,440
Bamberg (E5)	2,954
Barnwell (E5)	2,005
Batesburg (D4)	3,169
Bath (D5)	1,232
Beaufort (F7)	5,081
Belton (C2)	3,371
Belton Mills (B2)	1,500
Bennettsville (H2)	5,140
Bishopville (G3)	3,076
Blacksburg (D1)	2,056
Blackville (E5)	1,294
Branchville (F5)	1,353
Buffalo (D2)	1,580
Calhoun Falls (B3)	2,396
Camden (F3)	6,986
Cayce (E4)	3,294
Cedar Springs (D2)	1,500
Central (B2)	1,263
Charleston (G6)	70,174
Charleston (urban area)	116,441
Cheraw (H2)	4,836
Chesnee (D1)	1,051
Chester (E2)	6,893
Chesterfield (G2)	1,530
Clemson (B2)	1,204
Clifton (D2)	1,707
Clinton (D3)	7,168
Clover (E1)	3,276
COLUMBIA (F4)	86,914
Columbia (urban area)	119,747
Converse (D2)	1,200
Conway (J4)	6,073
Cowpens (D1)	1,879
Darlington (H3)	6,619
Denmark (E5)	2,814
Dents (F3)	1,000
Dillon (J3)	5,171
Drayton (D2)	1,228
Due West (C3)	1,033
Easley (B2)	6,316
Eau Claire (E3)	9,238
Edgefield (C4)	2,518
Edisto Island (G6)	2,500
Elloree (F4)	1,127
Enoree (D2)	1,045
Estill (E6)	1,659
Eureka Mills (E2)	1,990
Fairfax (E6)	1,567
Florence (H3)	22,513
Forest Acres (F3)	3,240
Fort Mill (F1)	3,204
Fountain Inn (C2)	1,325
Gaffney (D1)	8,123
Georgetown (J5)	6,004
Glendale (D2)	1,244
Gluck (B3)	1,634
Goldville (Joanna) (D3)	1,730
Graniteville (D4)	3,362
Great Falls (F2)	3,533
Greenville (C2)	58,161
Greenwood (C3)	13,806
Greer (C2)	5,050
Hampton (E6)	2,007
Hartsville (G3)	5,658
Hiltonhead (F7)	1,600
Holly Hill (G5)	1,116
Honea Path (C3)	2,840
Industrial Mills (E2)	1,868
Inman (C1)	1,514
Isle of Palms (H6)	1,379
Iva (B3)	1,164
Jamestown (H5)	1,100
Joanna (D3)	1,730
Johns Island (G6)	5,000
Johnston (D4)	1,426
Jonesville (D2)	1,345
Kershaw (G2)	1,376
Kingstree (H4)	3,621
Lake City (H4)	5,112
Lancaster (F2)	7,159
Lancaster Mills (F2)	4,313
Landrum (C1)	1,333
Langley (D4)	3,000
Latta (J3)	1,602
Laurens (C3)	8,658
Leesville (E4)	1,453
Lexington (E4)	1,081
Liberty (B2)	2,291
Lockhart (D2)	1,685
Loris (K3)	1,614
Lydia Mills (D3)	1,212
Lyman (C2)	1,365
Manning (G4)	2,775
Marietta (C1)	1,000
Marion (J3)	6,834
McColl (H2)	2,688
McCormick (C4)	1,744
Monarch Mills (D2)	2,158
Moncks Corner (G5)	1,818
Mount Pleasant (H6)	1,857
Mullins (J3)	4,916
Myrtle Beach (K4)	3,345
Newberry (D3)	7,546
Newry (B2)	1,000
Ninety Six (D3)	1,556
North Augusta (C5)	3,659
North Charleston (G6)	18,000
Orangeburg (F4)	15,322
Orr (B3)	2,625
Pacolet Mills (D2)	2,170
Pageland (G2)	1,925
Pawleys Island (J5)	2,000
Pelzer (B2)	2,692
Pendleton (B2)	1,432
Pickens (B2)	1,961
Pickens Mill (B2)	1,000
Piedmont (C2)	2,673
Ridgeland (E7)	1,078
Rock Hill (E2)	24,502
Saint Andrews (G6)	20,000
Saint George (F5)	1,938
Saint Matthews (F4)	2,351
Saint Stephen (H5)	1,341
Saluda (D4)	1,594
Seneca (A2)	3,649
Simpsonville (C2)	1,529
Slater (C1)	1,000
South Greenwood (C3)	3,712
Spartanburg (C1)	36,795
Startex (C2)	1,638
Summerton (G4)	1,419
Summerville (G5)	3,312
Sumter (G4)	20,185
Taylors (C2)	1,518
Timmonsville (H3)	2,001
Travelers Rest (C2)	1,200
Union (D2)	9,730
Varnville (E6)	1,180
Wadmalaw Island (G6)	2,500
Walhalla (A2)	3,104
Walterboro (F6)	4,616
Ware Shoals (C3)	3,032
Warrenville (D4)	1,604
Wattsville (D3)	1,649
West Columbia (E4)	4,373
Westminster (A2)	2,219
Whitmire (D3)	3,006
Whitney (D1)	1,611
Williamston (B2)	2,782
Winnsboro (E3)	3,267
Winnsboro Mills (E3)	2,936
Woodruff (D2)	3,831
York (E1)	4,181

SOUTH DAKOTA

Name & Index	Pop.
Aberdeen (M3)	21,051
Arlington (P5)	1,096
Belle Fourche (B4)	3,540
Beresford (R7)	1,686
Britton (O2)	1,430
Brookings (R5)	7,764
Canton (R7)	2,530
Centerville (R7)	1,053
Chamberlain (L6)	1,912
Clark (O4)	1,471
Clear Lake (R4)	1,105
Custer (B6)	2,017
De Smet (O5)	1,180
Deadwood (B5)	3,288
Dell Rapids (R6)	1,650
Edgemont (B7)	1,158
Elk Point (R8)	1,367
Eureka (K2)	1,576
Flandreau (R5)	2,193
Gettysburg (K3)	1,555
Gregory (L7)	1,375
Groton (N3)	1,084
Highmore (L4)	1,158
Hot Springs (C7)	5,030
Howard (P5)	1,251
Huron (N5)	12,788
Igloo (B7)	1,920
Ipswich (L3)	1,058
Lake Andes (M7)	1,851
Lead (B5)	6,422
Lemmon (E2)	2,760
Lennox (R7)	1,218
Madison (P6)	5,153
Milbank (R3)	2,982
Miller (L4)	1,916
Mitchell (N6)	12,123
Mobridge (J2)	3,753
Parker (P7)	1,148
Parkston (O7)	1,354
Pickstown (M7)	2,217
PIERRE (J5)	5,715
Pine Ridge (E7)	2,000
Platte (M7)	1,069
Rapid City (C5)	25,310
Redfield (N4)	2,655
Salem (P6)	1,119
Scotland (O7)	1,188
Sioux Falls (R6)	52,696
Sisseton (R2)	2,871
So. Sioux Falls (R6)	1,586
Spearfish (B6)	2,755
Sturgis (B5)	3,471
Tyndall (O8)	1,292
Vermillion (R8)	5,337
Wagner (N7)	1,528
Watertown (P4)	12,699
Webster (P3)	2,503
Wessington Spgs. (M5)	1,453
Winner (K7)	3,252
Woonsocket (N5)	1,051

Municipal Index

Name & Index	Pop.
Yankton (P8)	7,709

TENNESSEE

Name & Index	Pop.
Alamo (C3)	1,501
Alcoa (N3)	6,355
Ashland City (G2)	1,024
Athens (M4)	8,618
Atwood (D3)	1,000
Bearden (N3)	1,600
Belle Meade (H2)	2,831
Bells (C3)	1,225
Bemis (D3)	3,248
Berry Hill ‡(H2)	1,248
Bluff City (R2)	1,074
Bolivar (C4)	2,429
Briceville (N2)	2,500
Bristol (R1)	16,771
Brownsville (C3)	4,711
Bruceton (E2)	1,204
Camden (E2)	2,029
Carthage (K2)	1,604
Caryville (N2)	1,234
Celina (K1)	1,136
Centerville (G3)	1,532
Chattanooga (K4)	131,041
Chattanooga (urban area)	167,031
Church Hill (Q1)	1,741
Clairfield (O1)	2,000
Clarksville (G1)	16,246
Cleveland (M4)	12,605
Clinton (N2)	3,712
Collegedale (M4)	1,200
Collierville (B4)	1,153
Columbia (G3)	10,911
Cookeville (L2)	6,924
Corryton (O2)	1,275
Covington (B3)	4,379
Cowan (J4)	1,835
Crossville (L3)	2,291
Cypress Inn (F4)	1,000
Daisy (L4)	1,336
Dayton (L3)	3,191
Decherd (J4)	1,435
Dickson (G2)	3,348
Donelson (H2)	1,765
Dresden (D2)	1,509
Ducktown (N4)	1,064
Dyer (D2)	1,864
Dyersburg (C2)	10,885
East Ridge (L5)	9,645
Elizabethton (R2)	10,754
Embreeville (Q2)	1,273
Englewood (M4)	1,545
Erwin (R2)	3,387
Etowah (M4)	3,261
Fayetteville (H4)	5,447
Finley (B2)	1,000
Fountain City (O2)	15,000
Franklin (H3)	5,475
Gallatin (H2)	5,107
Gatlinburg (O3)	1,301
Gleason (D2)	1,063
Goodlettsville (H2)	1,590
Greenback (N3)	1,200
Greeneville (Q2)	8,721
Greenfield (D2)	1,706
Halls (C3)	1,808
Hampton (R2)	1,164
Harriman (M3)	6,389
Hartsville (J2)	1,130
Henderson (D4)	2,532
Hendersonville (J2)	1,000
Highland Park (R1)	3,500
Hixon (L4)	2,100
Hohenwald (F3)	1,703
Humboldt (D3)	7,426
Huntingdon (E2)	2,043
Huntsville (N2)	1,400
Inskip (N2)	5,000
Jacksboro (N2)	1,500
Jackson (D3)	30,207
Jamestown (M2)	2,115
Jasper (K4)	1,198
Jefferson City (P2)	3,633
Jellico (N1)	1,556
Joelton (H2)	2,500
Johnson City (R2)	27,864
Jonesboro (Q2)	1,126
Kingsport (Q1)	19,571
Kingston (N3)	1,627
Knoxville (O3)	124,769
Knoxville (urban area)	148,174
Kodak (O3)	1,670
La Follette (N2)	5,797
Lafayette (J1)	1,195
Lake City (N2)	1,827
Lawrenceburg (G4)	5,442
Lebanon (J2)	7,913
Lenoir City (N3)	5,159
Lewisburg (H4)	5,164
Lexington (E3)	3,566
Livingston (L2)	2,082
Lookout Mountain (L5)	1,675
Loudon (N3)	3,567
Lupton City (L4)	1,250
Madison (H2)	7,000
Madisonville (N3)	1,487
Manchester (J4)	2,341
Martin (D2)	4,082
Maryville (O3)	7,742
Mascot (O2)	2,500
McKenzie (E2)	3,774
McMinnville (K3)	7,577
Memphis (B4)	396,000
Memphis (urban area)	404,033
Milan (D3)	4,938
Millington (B4)	4,696
Monterey (L2)	2,043
Morristown (P2)	13,019
Mount Pleasant (G3)	2,931
Mountain City (S2)	1,405
Murfreesboro (J3)	13,052
NASHVILLE (H2)	174,307
Nashville (urban area)	257,898
Neubert (O3)	2,800
New Providence (G1)	1,825
New Tazewell (O2)	1,400
Newbern (C2)	1,734
Newport (P3)	3,892
Norris (N2)	1,134
Oak Ridge (N2)	30,229
Oakville (A4)	1,500
Obion (C2)	1,212
Old Hickory (H2)	10,000
Olive Springs (N2)	1,089
Oneida (N1)	1,304
Paris (E2)	8,826
Parsons (E3)	1,640
Pigeon Forge (O3)	1,500
Portland (H1)	1,660
Pulaski (G4)	5,762
Raleigh (B4)	1,100
Red Boiling Springs (K1)	1,000
Ridgely (B2)	1,504
Ripley (B3)	3,318
Roan Mountain (R2)	1,000
Rockford (O3)	1,500
Rockwood (M3)	4,272
Rogersville (P2)	2,545
Savannah (E4)	1,698
Selmer (D4)	1,759
Sevierville (P3)	1,620
Sewanee (K4)	1,407
Shady Valley (S1)	2,238
Shelbyville (H4)	9,456
Shepherd (L4)	1,000
Signal Mountain (L4)	1,786
Smithville (K3)	1,558
Smyrna (H3)	1,544
Soddy (L4)	2,157
Somerville (C4)	1,760
S. Fulton (D2)	2,119
S. Harriman (M3)	2,761
S. Pittsburg (K4)	2,573
Sparta (K3)	4,299
Spring City (M3)	1,725
Springfield (H2)	6,506
Sweetwater (N3)	4,199
Tazewell (P2)	1,000
Tiptonville (B2)	1,953
Tracy City (K4)	1,414
Trenton (D3)	3,868
Tullahoma (J4)	7,562
Tyner (L4)	1,000
Unicoi (R2)	1,500
Union City (C2)	7,665
Waverly (F2)	1,892
Waynesboro (F4)	1,147
Western State Hospital (C4)	3,000
Whitehaven (A4)	1,311
Whitwell (K4)	1,586
Winchester (J4)	3,974
Woodbury (J3)	1,000

TEXAS

Name & Index	Pop.
Abernathy (B4)	1,692
Abilene (E5)	45,570
Alamo (F11)	3,017
Alamo Hts. ‡(F8)	8,000
Albany (E5)	2,241
Alice (F10)	16,449
Almeda (J2)	1,800
Alpine (D11)	5,261
Alta Loma (K3)	1,400
Alto (J6)	1,021
Alvarado (G5)	1,656
Alvin (J3)	3,701
Amarillo (C2)	74,246
Amarillo (urban area)	74,450
Anahuac (K8)	1,284
Andrews (B5)	3,294
Angleton (J8)	3,399
Anson (E5)	2,708
Anthony (A10)	1,200
Aransas Pass (G10)	5,396
Archer City (K4)	1,901
Arlington (F2)	7,692
Asherton (E9)	2,425
Aspermont (D4)	1,062
Athens (J5)	5,194
Atlanta (K4)	3,782
AUSTIN (G7)	132,459
Austin (urban area)	135,465
Azle (E1)	1,700
Baird (E5)	1,821
Ballinger (E6)	5,302
Bandera (F8)	1,036
Bartlett (G7)	1,727
Bastrop (G7)	3,176
Bay City (H9)	9,427
Baytown (L2)	22,983
Beaumont (K7)	94,014
Beaumont (urban area)	94,050
Beeville (G9)	9,348
Bellaire (J2)	10,173
Bellville (H8)	2,112
Belton (G7)	6,246
Benavides (F10)	3,016
Bessmay (L7)	1,800
Big Lake (C6)	2,152
Big Spring (C5)	17,286
Big Wells (E9)	1,077
Bishop (G10)	2,731
Bloomington (H9)	1,500
Boerne (F8)	1,802
Boling (H8)	1,200
Bon Wier (L7)	1,200
Bonham (H4)	7,049
Borger (C2)	18,059
Bowie (G4)	4,544
Brackettville (D8)	1,858
Brady (E6)	5,944
Breckenridge (F5)	6,610
Bremond (H6)	1,141
Brenham (H7)	6,941
Bridgeport (G4)	2,049
Bronte (D6)	1,020
Brookshire (J8)	1,015
Brownfield (B4)	6,161
Brownsville (G12)	36,066
Brownwood (F6)	20,181
Bryan (H7)	18,102
Burkburnett (F3)	4,555
Burnet (F7)	2,394
Caldwell (H7)	2,109
Call (L7)	1,500
Calvert (H7)	2,548
Cameron (H7)	5,052
Canadian (D2)	2,700
Canutillo (A10)	1,326
Canyon (C3)	4,364
Carrizo Spgs. (E9)	4,316
Carrollton (G1)	1,610
Carthage (K5)	4,750
Cayuga (J6)	1,200
Cedar Bayou (L2)	1,000
Celina (H4)	1,051
Center (K6)	4,323
Charlotte (F9)	1,272
Childress (D3)	7,619
Chillicothe (E3)	1,215
Cisco (E5)	5,230
Clarendon (C3)	2,577
Clarksville (K4)	4,353
Cleburne (G5)	12,905
Cleveland (K7)	5,183
Clifton (G6)	1,837
Cockrell Hill (G2)	2,207
Coleman (E6)	6,530
College Station (H7)	7,925
Colorado City (C5)	6,774
Columbus (H8)	2,878
Comanche (F6)	3,840
Comfort (F7)	1,200
Commerce (J4)	5,889
Conroe (J7)	7,298
Coolidge (H6)	1,062
Cooper (J4)	2,350
Cooperas Cove (G6)	1,052
Corpus Christi (G10)	108,287
Corpus Christi (urban area)	122,354
Corrigan (K7)	1,417
Corsicana (H5)	1,921
Cotulla (E9)	4,418
Crane (B6)	2,154
Crockett (J6)	5,932
Crosbyton (C4)	1,879
Cross Plains (E5)	1,305
Crowell (E4)	1,912
Crystal City (E9)	7,198
Cuero (G8)	7,498
Daingerfield (K4)	1,668
Daisetta (K7)	1,764
Dalhart (B1)	5,918
Dallas (H2)	434,462
Dallas (urban area)	536,864
Dawson (H6)	1,107
Dayton (J7)	1,820
De Kalb (K4)	1,928
De Leon (F5)	2,241
Decatur (G4)	2,922
Del Rio (D8)	14,211
Denison (H4)	17,504
Denton (G4)	21,372
Denver City (B4)	1,855
Devine (E8)	1,672
D'Hanis (E8)	1,000
Diboll (K6)	2,391
Dickinson (K3)	2,704
Dilley (E9)	1,809
Dimmitt (B3)	1,461
Donna (F11)	7,171
Dublin (F5)	2,761
Dumas (C2)	6,127
Eagle Ford (G2)	4,679
Eagle Lake (H8)	2,787
Eagle Pass (D9)	7,276
Eastland (F5)	3,626
Edcouch ‡(H11)	2,925
Eden (E6)	1,993
Edinburg (F11)	12,383
Edna (H9)	3,855
El Campo (H8)	6,237
El Paso (A10)	130,485
El Paso (urban area)	136,430
Eldorado (D7)	1,663
Electra (F4)	4,970
Elgin (G7)	3,168
Elsa (G11)	3,179
Encinal (E9)	1,071
Ennis (H5)	7,815
Fabens (A10)	3,089
Fairfield (H6)	1,742
Falfurrias (F10)	6,712
Farmersville (H4)	1,955
Ferris (G2)	1,735
Flatonia (G8)	1,098
Floresville (F9)	1,949
Floydada (C3)	3,210
Forest Hill (F2)	1,519
Forney (H5)	1,425
Fort Davis (D11)	1,200
Fort Hancock (B11)	1,000
Fort Stockton (A7)	4,444
Fort Worth (E2)	278,778
Ft. Worth (urban area)	313,872
Franklin (H6)	1,209
Frankston (J5)	1,050
Fredericksburg (E7)	3,854
Freeport (J9)	6,012
Freer (F10)	2,280
Friona (B3)	1,202
Gainesville (G4)	11,246
Galena Park (J1)	7,186
Galveston (L3)	66,568
Galveston (urban area)	71,000
Ganado (H8)	1,258
Garland (H1)	10,571
Gatesville (G6)	3,856
George West (F9)	1,533
Georgetown (G7)	4,951
Giddings (H7)	2,532
Gilmer (J5)	4,096
Gladewater (K5)	5,305
Glen Rose (G5)	1,254
Goldsmith (B5)	1,200
Goldthwaite (F6)	1,566
Goliad (G9)	1,584
Gonzales (G8)	5,659
Gorman (F5)	1,317
Graham (F4)	6,742
Granbury (G5)	1,683
Grand Prairie (G2)	14,594
Grand Saline (J5)	1,810
Granger (G7)	1,637
Grapeland (J6)	1,358
Grapevine (F1)	1,824
Greenville (H4)	14,727
Greggton (K5)	2,168
Griffing Park ‡(K8)	2,096
Groesbeck (H6)	2,182
Grulla (F11)	1,013
Hale Center (C4)	1,626
Hallettsville (G8)	2,000
Haltom City (F2)	5,760
Hamilton (G6)	3,077
Hamlin (E5)	3,569
Harlingen (G11)	23,229
Haskell (E4)	3,836
Hearne (H7)	4,872
Hebbronville (F10)	4,302
Hempstead (J7)	1,395
Henderson (K5)	6,833
Henrietta (F4)	2,813
Hereford (B3)	5,207
Hico (F6)	1,212
High Island (K8)	1,000
Highland Park (G2)	11,405
Highlands (K1)	2,723
Hillcrest (H8)	2,826
Hillsboro (G5)	8,363
Hitchcock (K3)	1,105
Holiday (F4)	1,007
Hondo (E8)	4,188
Honey Grove (J4)	2,340
Honey Island (K7)	1,250
Hooks (K4)	2,319
Houston (J2)	596,163
Houston (urban area)	697,287
Hubbard (H6)	1,768
Hughes Spgs. (K5)	1,445
Hull (K7)	1,200
Humble (J7)	1,388
Huntington (K6)	1,039
Huntsville (J7)	9,820
Idalou (C4)	1,014
Iowa Park (F4)	2,110
Iraan (B7)	1,196
Irving (G2)	2,621
Italy (H5)	1,185
Itasca (G5)	1,718
Jacinto City ‡(J1)	6,856
Jacksboro (F4)	2,951
Jacksonville (J5)	8,607
Jasper (L7)	4,403
Jefferson (K5)	3,164
Jourdanton (F9)	1,481
Junction (E7)	2,471
Karnes City (G9)	2,588
Kaufman (H5)	2,714
Keene (G5)	1,200
Keltys (K6)	1,091
Kemah (K2)	1,000
Kenedy (G9)	4,234
Kennedale (F2)	1,046
Kerens (H5)	1,198
Kermit (B6)	6,912
Kerrville (E7)	7,691
Kilgore (K5)	9,638
Killeen (G6)	7,045
Kingsville (G10)	16,898
Kirbyville (K7)	1,150
Knox City (E4)	1,489
Kountze (K7)	1,651
La Feria (G11)	2,952
La Grange (G8)	2,738
La Porte (K2)	4,429
Ladonia (J4)	1,104
Lake Jackson (J9)	2,897
Lake June (H2)	1,517
Lake Worth (E2)	2,351
Lakeview ‡(K8)	3,091
Lamarque (K3)	7,359
Lamesa (C5)	10,704
Lampasas (F6)	4,869
Lancaster (G2)	2,632
Laredo (E10)	51,910
League City (K2)	1,341
Leonard (H4)	1,211
Levelland (B4)	8,264
Lewisville (G5)	1,516
Liberty (K7)	4,163
Lindale (J5)	1,105
Linden (K4)	1,744
Littlefield (B4)	6,540
Livingston (K7)	2,865
Llano (F7)	2,954
Lockhart (G8)	5,573
Lockney (C3)	1,692
Longview (K5)	24,502
Loraine (D5)	1,045
Los Fresnos (G11)	1,113
Lubbock (C4)	71,747
Lufkin (K6)	15,135
Luling (G8)	4,297
Lyford (G11)	1,473
Lytle (F8)	1,000
Madisonville (J7)	2,393
Malakoff (H5)	1,286
Marble Falls (F7)	2,044
Marfa (C12)	3,603
Marlin (H6)	7,099
Marshall (K5)	22,327
Mart (H6)	2,269
Mason (E7)	2,456
Matador (D3)	1,335
Mathis (G9)	4,050
McAllen (F11)	20,067
McCamey (B6)	3,121
McGregor (G6)	2,669
McKinney (H4)	10,560
McLean (D2)	1,439
McNair (K1)	1,313
Memphis (D3)	3,810
Menard (E7)	2,685
Mercedes (F12)	10,081
Meridian (G6)	1,146
Merkel (E5)	2,338
Mesquite (H2)	1,696
Mexia (H6)	6,627
Midland (C6)	21,713
Midlothian (G5)	1,177
Mineola (J5)	3,626
Mineral Wells (F5)	7,801
Mission (F11)	10,765
Monahans (B6)	6,311
Moody (G6)	1,084
Morton (B4)	2,274
Mt. Pleasant (K4)	6,342
Mt. Vernon (J4)	1,433
Muleshoe (B3)	2,477
Munday (E4)	2,280
Nacogdoches (J6)	12,327
Naples (K4)	1,346
Natalia (F8)	1,175
Navasota (J7)	5,188
Nederland (K8)	3,805
New Boston (K4)	2,688
New Braunfels (F8)	12,210
New London (K5)	1,800
Newgulf (J8)	1,803
Nixon (G8)	1,875
Nocona (G4)	3,022
N. Texarkana (L4)	1,328
Oak Knoll (F2)	3,930
Odem ‡(G10)	1,680
Odessa (B6)	29,495
O'Donnell (C4)	1,473
Olmos Park ‡(F8)	2,841
Olney (F4)	3,765
Olton (B3)	1,201
Orange (L7)	21,174
Orangefield (L7)	1,500
Overton (K5)	2,001
Ozona (C7)	2,885
Paducah (D4)	2,952
Palacios (H9)	2,799
Palestine (J6)	12,503
Pampa (D2)	16,583
Panhandle (C2)	1,406
Paris (J4)	21,643
Pasadena (K2)	22,483
Pear Ridge ‡(K8)	2,029
Pearland (J2)	1,250
Pearsall (E9)	4,481
Pecos (D10)	8,054
Perryton (D1)	4,417
Pharr (F11)	8,690
Phillips (C2)	4,105
Pilot Point (H4)	1,176
Pineland (L6)	1,454

Name & Index	Pop.
Pittsburg (J4)	3,142
Plainview (C3)	14,044
Plano (H4)	2,126
Pleasanton (F9)	2,913
Port Arthur (K8)	57,530
Port Arthur (urban area)	81,763
Port Isabel (G11)	2,372
Port Lavaca (H9)	5,599
Port Neches (K7)	5,448
Portland (G10)	1,292
Post (C4)	3,141
Poteet (F8)	2,487
Poth (F8)	1,089
Premont (F10)	2,619
Presidio (C12)	2,000
Quanah (E3)	4,589
Ralls (C4)	1,779
Ranger (F5)	3,989
Rankin (B6)	1,139
Raymondville (G11)	9,136
Refugio (G9)	4,666
Richardson (H1)	1,289
Richmond (J8)	2,030
Rio Grande City (F11)	3,992
Rio Hondo (G11)	1,125
Rising Star (F5)	1,289
River Oaks (E2)	7,097
Robert Lee (D5)	1,069
Robstown (G10)	7,278
Roby (D5)	1,051
Rockdale (G7)	2,321
Rockport (H9)	2,266
Rocksprings (D8)	1,436
Rockwell (H5)	1,501
Roma-Los Saenz (E11)	1,576
Roscoe (D5)	1,584
Rosebud (G6)	1,730
Rosenberg (J8)	6,210
Rotan (D5)	3,163
Round Rock (G7)	1,438
Roxton (J4)	1,000
Royse City (H4)	1,266
Rule (E4)	1,251
Runge (G9)	1,055
Rusk (J6)	6,598
Sabinal (E8)	1,974
Saint Joe (G4)	1,147
San Angelo (D6)	52,093
San Antonio (F8)	408,442
San Antonio (urban area)	447,365
San Augustine (K6)	2,510
San Benito (G12)	13,271
San Diego (F10)	4,397
San Elizario (A10)	1,200
San Juan (F11)	3,413
San Marcos (F8)	9,980
San Saba (F6)	3,400
San Ygnacio (E10)	1,800
Sanatorium (D6)	1,275
Sanderson (B7)	2,500
Sanger (G4)	1,170
Sansom Park Village ‡(E2)	1,611
Santa Anna (E6)	1,605
Saratoga (K7)	1,500
Schulenburg (H8)	2,005
Seabrook (K2)	1,800
Seagoville (H2)	1,927
Seagraves (B5)	2,101
Sealy (H8)	1,942
Seguin (G8)	9,733
Seminole (B5)	3,479
Seymour (E4)	3,779
Shamrock (D2)	3,322
Sherman (H4)	20,150
Shiner (G8)	1,778
Silsbee (K7)	3,179
Sinton (G9)	4,254
Slaton (C4)	5,036
Smeltertown (A10)	3,500
Smithville (G7)	3,379
Snyder (D5)	12,010
Somerville (H7)	1,425
Sonora (D7)	2,633
Sourlake (K7)	1,630
South Houston (J2)	4,126
Southside Place (J2)	1,436
Spearman (C1)	1,852
Spur (D4)	2,183
Stamford (E5)	5,819
Stanton (C5)	1,603
Stephenville (F5)	7,155
Stinnett (C2)	1,170
Stockdale (G8)	1,105
Stratford (C1)	1,385
Sudan (B3)	1,348
Sugar Land (J8)	2,285
Sulphur Spgs. (J4)	8,991
Sundown (B4)	1,492
Sunray (C1)	1,530
Sweeny (J8)	1,393
Sweetwater (D5)	13,619
Taft (G9)	2,978
Tahoka (C4)	2,848
Taylor (G7)	9,071
Teague (H6)	2,925
Temple (G6)	25,467
Terrell (H5)	11,544
Terrell Hills ‡(F8)	2,708
Texarkana (L4)	24,753
Texas City (K3)	16,620
Three Rivers (F9)	2,026
Throckmorton (F4)	1,320
Timpson (K6)	1,455
Tomball (J7)	1,065
Trinity (J7)	2,054
Troup (J5)	1,539
Tulia (C3)	3,222
Turkey (D3)	1,005
Tyler (J5)	38,968
University Park (H2)	24,275
Uvalde (E8)	8,674
Valley Mills (G6)	1,037
Van Alstyne (H4)	1,649
Van Horn (C11)	1,161
Velasco (J9)	2,260
Vernon (E3)	12,651
Victoria (H9)	16,126
Voth (K7)	1,200
Waco (G6)	84,706
Waco (urban area)	92,299
Waelder (G8)	1,275
Wake ‡(K4)	1,066
Wallis (H8)	1,500
Waxahachie (H5)	11,204
Weatherford (G5)	8,093
Weimar (H8)	1,663
Wellington (D3)	3,676
Weslaco (G11)	7,514
West (G6)	2,130
W. Columbia (J8)	2,100
W. University Pl. (J2)	17,074
Wharton (J8)	4,450
White Settlement (E2)	10,827
Whitesboro (H4)	1,854
Whitewright (H4)	1,372
Whitney (G6)	1,383
Wichita Falls (F4)	68,042
Wiergate (L6)	1,000
Willis (J7)	1,164
Wills Point (J5)	2,030
Wink (A6)	1,521
Winnsboro (J5)	2,512
Winters (E6)	2,676
Wolfe City (J4)	1,345
Woodsboro (G9)	1,836
Woodville (K7)	1,863
Wooster (K2)	2,500
Wortham (H6)	1,170
Wylie (H5)	1,295
Yoakum (G8)	5,231
Yorktown (G9)	2,596
Ysleta (A10)	4,782
Zapata (E11)	1,409

UTAH

Name & Index	Pop.
American Fork (C3)	5,126
Beaver (B5)	1,685
Bingham Canyon (B3)	2,569
Blanding (E6)	1,177
Bountiful (C3)	6,004
Brigham City (C2)	6,790
Cedar City (A6)	6,106
Centerville (C3)	1,262
Clearfield (B2)	4,723
Delta (B4)	1,703
Dragerton (D4)	3,453
Draper (C3)	2,000
Ephraim (C4)	1,987
Eureka (B4)	1,318
Farmington (C3)	1,468
Fillmore (B5)	1,890
Garfield (B3)	2,079
Garland (B2)	1,008
Grantsville (B3)	1,537
Gunnison (C4)	1,144
Heber (C3)	2,936
Helper (D4)	2,850
Hiawatha (D4)	1,421
Holladay (C3)	3,100
Hooper (B2)	1,243
Huntington (C4)	1,029
Hurricane (A6)	1,271
Hyrum (C2)	1,704
Kanab (B6)	1,287
Kaysville (B2)	1,898
Layton (C2)	3,456
Lehi (C3)	3,627
Lewiston (C2)	1,533
Logan (C2)	16,832
Magna (B3)	3,502
Manti (C4)	2,051
Mapleton (C3)	1,175
Midvale (B3)	3,996
Milford (A5)	1,673
Moab (E5)	1,274
Monroe (B5)	1,214
Monticello (E6)	1,172
Morgan (C2)	1,064
Moroni (C4)	1,076
Mount Pleasant (C4)	2,030
Murray (C3)	9,006
Nephi (C4)	2,990
North Ogden (C2)	1,105
Ogden (C2)	57,112
Orem (C3)	8,351
Panguitch (B6)	1,501
Park City (C3)	2,254
Parowan (B6)	1,455
Payson (C3)	3,998
Pleasant Grove (C3)	3,195
Price (D4)	6,010
Providence (C2)	1,055
Provo (C3)	28,937
Richfield (B5)	4,212
Richmond (C2)	1,091
Riverton (B3)	1,666
Roosevelt (D3)	1,628
Roy (B2)	3,723
Saint George (A6)	4,562
Salina (C5)	1,789
SALT LAKE CITY (C3)	182,121
Salt Lake City (urban area)	226,880
Sandy (C3)	2,095
Santaquin (C4)	1,214
Smithfield (C2)	2,383
South Jordan (C3)	1,048
S. Ogden (C2)	3,763
S. Salt Lake (C3)	7,704
Spanish Fork (C3)	5,230
Springville (C3)	6,475
Sunnyside (D4)	1,881
Tooele (B3)	7,269
Tremonton (B2)	1,662
Vernal (E3)	2,845
Wellsville (C2)	1,241
W. Jordan (C3)	2,107

VERMONT

Name & Index	Pop.
Barnet (D2)	△1,425
Barre (C2)	10,922
Barton (C1)	1,267
Bellows Falls (C4)	3,881
Bennington (A5)	8,002
Berkshire (B1)	△1,063
Bethel (B3)	△1,534
Brandon (A3)	△3,304
Brattleboro (C5)	△11,522
Bristol (A2)	1,308
Burke (D1)	△1,042
Burlington (A2)	33,155
Castleton (A3)	△1,748
Cavendish (B4)	△1,374
Charlotte (A2)	△1,215
Chelsea (C2)	△1,025
Colchester (A1)	△3,897
Danville (C2)	△1,312
Dorset (A4)	△1,150
E. Montpelier (B2)	△1,128
Enosburg Falls (B1)	1,289
Essex (A1)	△3,931
Essex Junction (A2)	2,741
Fair Haven (A3)	2,058
Fairfax (B1)	△1,129
Fairfield (B1)	△1,428
Ferrisburg (A2)	△1,387
Georgia (A1)	△1,055
Graniteville (C2)	1,500
Hardwick (C2)	1,696
Hartford (C3)	△5,827
Hartland (C3)	△1,559
Hinesburg (A2)	△1,120
Island Pond (D1)	1,252
Jericho (A2)	△1,135
Ludlow (B4)	1,678
Lunenburg (D2)	△1,299
Lyndon (C1)	△3,360
Lyndonville (D1)	1,506
Middlebury (A2)	3,614
Montgomery (B1)	△1,091
MONTPELIER (B2)	8,599
Morrisville (B1)	1,995
Newbury (C2)	△1,667
Newport (C1)	5,217
North Bennington (A5)	1,327
N. Troy (C1)	1,057
Northfield (B2)	2,262
Norwich (C3)	△1,532
Orleans (C1)	1,261
Pawlet (A4)	△1,156
Poultney (A3)	1,685
Pownal (A5)	△1,453
Proctor (A3)	1,813
Putney (B4)	△1,019
Randolph (B3)	2,223
Richford (B1)	1,916
Royalton (B3)	△1,331
Rutland (B3)	17,659
Saint Albans (A1)	8,552
St. Johnsbury (D2)	7,370
Shelburne (A2)	△1,365
Sheldon (B1)	△1,352
S. Burlington (A2)	△3,279
Springfield (C4)	4,940
Swanton (A1)	2,275
Thetford (C3)	△1,046
Troy (C1)	△1,786
Vergennes (A2)	1,736
Wallingford (A4)	△1,482
W. Rutland (A3)	△2,487
White River Jct. (C3)	2,365
Wilder (C3)	1,097
Williamstown (B2)	△1,600
Williston (A2)	△1,182
Windsor (C4)	3,467
Winooski (A2)	6,734
Woodstock (B3)	1,326

VIRGINIA

Name & Index	Pop.
Abingdon (E2)	4,709
Alexandria (L3)	61,787
Altavista (F6)	3,332
Amherst (F5)	1,038
Amonate (A6)	1,800
Appalachia (C2)	2,915
Appomattox (G6)	1,094
Arlington (L3)	135,449
Ashland (J5)	2,610
Bassett (E7)	3,421
Bastian (B6)	1,200
Bedford (E6)	4,061
Berryville (J2)	1,401
Big Stone Gap (C2)	5,173
Blacksburg (D6)	3,358
Blackstone (J6)	3,536
Bluefield (B6)	4,212
Boissevain (B6)	1,197
Bon Air (J5)	1,500
Bridgewater (F4)	1,537
Bristol (D3)	15,954
Buchanan (E5)	1,300
Buena Vista (F5)	5,214
Cape Charles (M6)	2,427
Cedar Bluff (E2)	1,083
Charlottesville (H4)	25,969
Chase City (H7)	2,519
Chatham (F7)	1,456
Cheriton (M6)	1,000
Chester (K6)	1,168
Chilhowie (E2)	1,022
Chincoteague (O5)	2,724
Christiansburg (D6)	2,967
Clarksville (H7)	1,035
Clifton Forge (E5)	5,795
Clincho (D1)	1,390
Clintwood (D2)	1,366
Colonial Beach (L4)	1,464
Colonial Heights (K6)	6,077
Covington (D5)	5,860
Craigsville (E4)	1,200
Crewe (H6)	2,030
Crozet (G4)	1,000
Culpeper (H4)	2,527
Damascus (E2)	1,726
Dante (D2)	2,405
Danville (F7)	35,066
Deltaville (M5)	1,000
Denbigh (L6)	1,500
Dorchester (C2)	1,129
Dublin (C6)	1,313
Dumfries (K3)	1,300
Elkton (G4)	1,361
Emporia (J7)	5,664
Esserville (C2)	1,000
Ettrick (K6)	3,030
Ewing (B2)	1,000
Exmore (N5)	1,362
Fairfax (K3)	1,946
Falls Church (K3)	7,535
Falmouth (K4)	1,176
Farmville (H6)	4,375
Fiedale (D7)	1,295
Fort Monroe (M6)	2,500
Franklin (L7)	4,670
Fredericksburg (J4)	12,158
Fries (B7)	1,442
Front Royal (H3)	8,115
Galax (C7)	5,248
Gate City (C3)	2,126
Gordonsville (H4)	1,118
Grundy (D1)	1,947
Hampton (M6)	5,966
Harrisonburg (F4)	10,810
Herndon (K3)	1,461
Highland Springs (K5)	3,171
Hilton Village (L6)	4,486
Hopewell (K6)	10,219
Hot Springs (E4)	1,500
Kenbridge (H7)	1,176
Lakeside (J5)	9,000
Lawrenceville (J7)	2,239
Leesburg (J2)	1,703
Lexington (F5)	5,976
Luray (H3)	2,731
Lynchburg (F6)	47,727
Madison Heights (F6)	2,830
Manassas (K3)	1,804
Marion (A7)	6,982
Martinsville (E7)	17,251
Mathews (M6)	1,500
Matoaca (J6)	1,027
Max Meadows (C6)	1,000
McClure (D2)	1,000
McLean (K3)	1,094
Mechanicsville (K5)	1,500
Messick (M6)	2,000
Morrison (L6)	2,357
Narrows (C6)	2,520
Newport News (M7)	42,358
Norfolk (M7)	213,513
Norfolk-Portsmouth (urban area)	351,342
Norton (C2)	4,315
Oceana (N7)	1,500
Onancock (N5)	1,353
Orange (H4)	2,571
Pearisburg (C6)	2,005
Pembroke (C6)	1,010
Pennington Gap (C2)	2,090
Petersburg (J6)	35,054
Phoebus (M6)	3,694
Pocahontas (B6)	2,410
Portlock (M7)	3,809
Portsmouth (M7)	80,039
Portsmouth-Norfolk (urban area)	351,342
Pound (C1)	1,193
Pulaski (C6)	9,202
Quantico (K3)	1,240
Radford (C6)	9,026
Richlands (E1)	4,648
RICHMOND (K5)	230,310
Richmond (urban area)	257,423
Roanoke (D6)	91,921
Roanoke (urban area)	105,883
Rockymount (E7)	1,432
St. Paul (D2)	1,014
Salem (D6)	9,962
Saltville (E2)	2,678
Sandston (K5)	3,500
Seaford (M6)	1,500
Selma (E5)	1,200
Shenandoah (G4)	1,903
Smithfield (L7)	1,180
South Boston (G7)	6,057
South Hill (H7)	2,153
South Norfolk (M7)	10,434
Staunton (F4)	19,927
Stonega (C2)	1,400
Strasburg (H3)	2,022
Suffolk (L7)	12,339
Tappahannock (K5)	1,011
Tazewell (B6)	1,347
Victoria (H6)	1,607
Vienna (K3)	2,029
Vinton (E6)	3,629
Virginia Beach (N7)	5,390
Warrenton (J3)	1,797
Warwick (L6)	39,875
Waverly (K6)	1,502
Waynesboro (F4)	12,357
West Point (L5)	1,919
Williamsburg (L6)	6,735
Winchester (H2)	13,841
Wise (C2)	1,574
Woodstock (G3)	1,816
Wytheville (C7)	5,513

WASHINGTON

Name & Index	Pop.
Aberdeen (B3)	19,653
Anacortes (C2)	6,919
Appleyard (South Wenatchee) (E3)	1,479
Arlington (C2)	1,635
Auburn (C3)	6,497
Bellevue (B2)	14,182
Bellingham (C2)	34,112
Blaine (C2)	1,693
Bothell (B1)	1,019
Bremerton (A2)	27,678
Bryn Mawr (B2)	4,781
Buckley (D3)	2,705
Burien (A2)	4,387
Burlington (C2)	2,350
Camas (C5)	4,725
Cashmere (E3)	1,768
Castle Rock (B4)	1,255
Centralia (C4)	8,657
Chehalis (C4)	5,639
Chelan (E3)	2,157
Cheney (H3)	2,797
Chewelah (H2)	1,683
Chico (A2)	1,151
Clarkston (H4)	5,617
Cle Elum (E3)	2,206
Clinton (C3)	1,623
Colfax (H4)	3,057
College Place (G4)	3,174
Colville (H2)	3,033
Cosmopolis (B4)	1,164
Davenport (G3)	1,417
Dayton (H4)	2,979
Deer Park (H3)	1,167
Des Moines (B2)	2,694
Eatonville (C4)	1,048
Edmonds (C3)	2,057
Electric City (F3)	1,484
Ellensburg (E3)	8,430
Elma (B4)	1,543
Enumclaw (D3)	2,789
Ephrata (F3)	4,589
Everett (C3)	33,849
Fairchild (H3)	10,000
Fircrest ‡(C3)	1,459
Forks (A3)	1,120
Fort Lewis (C3)	35,000
Fruitvale (E4)	3,654
Goldendale (E5)	1,907
Grand Coulee (G3)	2,741
Grandview (F4)	2,503
Granger (E4)	1,164
Greenacres (J3)	1,287
Hoquiam (A3)	11,123
Houghton (B2)	1,005
Kalama (C4)	1,121
Kelso (C4)	7,345
Kenmore (B1)	2,500
Kennewick (F4)	10,106
Kennydale (B2)	2,200
Kent (C3)	3,278
Kirkland (B2)	4,713
Lacey (C3)	1,952
Lake City (B1)	2,800
Lake Forest Park (B1)	3,500
Lake Stevens (D3)	2,586
Leavenworth (E3)	1,503
Longview (B4)	20,385
Lowell (C3)	1,754
Lynden (C2)	2,161
Manson (E3)	2,000

Municipal Index

Name & Index	Pop.
Maple Valley (C3)	1,800
Marysville (C2)	2,259
Mason City (G3)	2,606
McCleary (B3)	1,175
McLoughlin Heights (C5)	14,500
Medical Lake (H3)	4,488
Mercer Island (B2)	6,000
Millwood (H3)	1,240
Milton (C3)	1,374
Monroe (D3)	1,556
Montesano (B4)	2,328
Morton (C4)	1,140
Moses Lake (F3)	2,679
Mt. Vernon (C2)	5,230
Neah Bay (A2)	1,000
Newport (H2)	1,385
N. Richland (F4)	3,067
Oak Harbor (C2)	1,193
Odessa (G3)	1,127
Okanogan (F2)	2,013
OLYMPIA (C3)	15,819
Omak (F2)	3,791
Opportunity (H3)	10,000
Oroville (F2)	1,500
Orting (C3)	1,299
Otis Orchards (H3)	1,500
Palouse (H4)	1,036
Parkland (C3)	3,000
Parkwater (H3)	1,000
Pasco (F4)	10,288
Pinehurst (C3)	4,260
Pomeroy (H4)	1,775
Port Angeles (B2)	11,233
Port Orchard (A2)	2,320
Port Townsend (C2)	6,888
Poulsbo (A1)	1,014
Prosser (F4)	2,636
Pullman (H4)	12,022
Puyallup (C3)	10,010
Raymond (B4)	4,110
Renton (B2)	16,039
Richland (F4)	21,809
Richmond Highlands (A1)	11,081
Ritzville (G3)	2,145
Riverton Heights (B2)	3,060
Roslyn (E3)	1,537
Seahurst (A2)	2,305
Seattle (A2)	467,591
Seattle (urban area)	616,047
Sedro Woolley (C2)	3,299
Selah (E4)	2,489
Sequim (B2)	1,044
Shelton (B3)	5,045
Silverlake (C4)	1,500
Snohomish (D3)	3,094
Soap Lake (F3)	2,091
S. Bend (B4)	1,857
S. Wenatchee (E3)	1,479
Spokane (H3)	161,721
Spokane (urban area)	174,853
Steilacoom (C3)	1,233
Sumner (C3)	2,816
Sunnydale (B2)	1,296
Sunnyside (F4)	4,194
Suquamish (A1)	1,000
Tacoma (C3)	143,673
Tacoma (urban area)	166,910
Tekoa (H3)	1,189
Tillicum (C3)	3,000
Toppenish (E4)	5,265
Tumwater (B3)	2,725
Union Gap (E4)	1,766
Vancouver (C5)	41,664
Veradale (H3)	1,700
Waitsburg (G4)	1,015
Walla Walla (G4)	24,102
Wapato (E4)	3,185
Washougal (C5)	1,577
Waterville (E3)	1,013
Wenatchee (E3)	13,072
West Wenatchee (E3)	2,690
White Center (A2)	30,000
White Salmon (D5)	1,353
Wilbur (G3)	1,043
Woodland (C5)	1,292
Yakima (E4)	38,486

WEST VIRGINIA

Name & Index	Pop.
Accoville (C5)	1,400
Addison (Webster Springs) (F4)	1,313
Alderson (E5)	1,489
Anawalt (D6)	1,383
Anmoore (F2)	1,388
Ansted (D4)	1,543
Baileysville (C5)	1,127
Barboursville (B4)	1,943
Barrackville (F1)	2,500
Bartley (C6)	1,275
Bath (Berkeley Sprs.) (K1)	1,213
Beaver (Glen Hedrick) (D5)	1,484
Beckley (D5)	19,397
Belington (F2)	1,699
Belle (C4)	2,350
Benwood (K5)	3,485
Berkeley Springs (K1)	1,213
Berwind (C6)	1,354
Bethany (L5)	1,063
Bethlehem (K5)	1,146
Bluefield (D6)	21,506
Bradshaw (C6)	1,062
Bramwell (D6)	1,587
Bridgeport (F2)	2,414
Buckhannon (F3)	6,016
Cameron (L6)	1,736
Cedar Grove (D4)	1,738
Ceredo (B4)	1,399
Chapmanville (B5)	1,349
Charles Town (L2)	3,035
CHARLESTON (D4)	73,501
Charleston (urban area)	130,122
Chattaroy (B5)	1,484
Chesapeake (D4)	2,566
Chester (L4)	3,758
Clarksburg (F2)	32,014
Clendenin (D3)	1,475
Coal City (D5)	1,000
Coal Fork (D4)	1,185
Coalwood (C6)	1,310
Davis (H2)	1,271
Davy (C6)	1,650
Delbarton (B5)	1,353
Dunbar (C4)	8,032
E. Rainelle (E5)	1,695
Eccles (D5)	1,885
Eckman (C6)	1,574
Elbert (C6)	1,565
Elkhorn (D6)	1,035
Elkins (G3)	9,121
Elm Grove (K5)	8,000
Enterprise (F2)	1,200
Ethel (C5)	1,032
Fairmont (F2)	29,346
Fayetteville (D4)	1,952
Follansbee (K5)	4,435
Gary (C6)	1,600
Gassaway (E3)	1,306
Gauley Bridge (D4)	1,134
Glen Dale (K5)	1,467
Glen Jean (D5)	1,800
Glen Hedrick (Beaver) (D5)	1,484
Glen Rodgers (D5)	1,593
Glenville (E3)	1,789
Grafton (G2)	7,365
Grant Town (F1)	1,273
Granville (Mona) (G3)	1,004
Handley (D4)	1,007
Harrisville (E2)	1,387
Hemphill (C6)	2,300
Henlawson (B5)	1,750
Hinton (E5)	5,780
Huntington (A4)	86,353
Huntington, W. Va. — Ashland, Ky. (urban area)	156,136
Hurricane (C4)	1,463
Iaeger (C6)	1,271
Jeffery (C5)	2,000
Jenkinjones (D6)	1,859
Kenova (A4)	4,320
Keyser (J2)	6,347
Keystone (D6)	2,594
Kimball (C6)	1,359
Kingston (D5)	1,098
Kingwood (G2)	2,186
Kistler (C5)	1,072
Kopperston (C5)	1,112
Lewisburg (E5)	2,192
Logan (B5)	5,079
Lorado (C5)	1,087
Lumberport (F2)	1,198
Mabscott (D5)	1,665
Madison (C4)	2,025
Mallory (C5)	1,286
Mammoth (D4)	1,000
Man (C5)	1,632
Mannington (F1)	3,241
Marlinton (F4)	1,645
Marmet (C4)	2,515
Martinsburg (K2)	15,621
Marytown (C6)	1,268
Matoaka (D6)	1,003
Maybeury-Switchback (D6)	1,646
McMechen (K5)	3,518
Milton (B4)	1,552
Minden (D5)	2,200
Mona (G1)	1,004
Monongah (F2)	1,622
Montgomery (D4)	3,484
Moorefield (J2)	1,405
Morgantown (G1)	25,525
Moundsville (K6)	14,772
Mt. Clare (F2)	1,236
Mt. Hope (D5)	2,588
Mullens (D5)	3,470
Nellis (C4)	1,200
New Cumberland (K4)	2,119
New Martinsville (E1)	4,084
Newell (K4)	2,101
Nitro (C4)	3,314
Nutter Fort (F2)	2,285
Oak Hill (D4)	4,518
Oceana (C5)	1,373
Omar (C5)	1,500
Paden City (D1)	2,588
Parkersburg (D2)	40,492
Parsons (G2)	2,009
Pemberton (D5)	1,000
Pennsboro (E2)	1,753
Petersburg (H3)	1,898
Philippi (G2)	2,531
Piedmont (H2)	2,565
Pineville (C5)	1,082
Point Pleasant (B3)	4,596
Powellton (D4)	1,477
Premier (C6)	1,000
Princeton (D6)	8,279
Rachel (F1)	1,200
Raleigh (D5)	1,164
Ranson (L2)	1,436
Ravenswood (C3)	1,175
Red Jacket (B5)	1,575
Richwood (F4)	5,321
Ridgeley (J1)	1,754
Ripley (C3)	1,813
Rivesville (F1)	1,343
Romney (J2)	2,059
Ronceverte (F5)	2,301
Rowlesburg (G2)	1,299
Saint Albans (C4)	9,870
St. Marys (D2)	2,196
Salem (E2)	2,578
Seth (C4)	1,033
Shepherdstown (L2)	1,173
Shinnston (F2)	2,793
Sistersville (D1)	2,313
Smithers ‡(D4)	2,208
Sophia (D5)	1,430
S. Charleston (C4)	16,686
Spencer (D3)	2,587
Sprague (D5)	2,626
Squire (C6)	1,240
Star City (F1)	1,205
Stonewood (F2)	2,066
Summersville (E4)	1,628
Sutton (E3)	1,070
Terra Alta (H2)	1,649
Thomas (H2)	1,146
Thorpe (D6)	1,362
Vienna (D2)	6,020
War (C6)	3,992
Ward (D4)	2,055
Watson (F2)	1,200
Wayne (B4)	1,257
Webster Springs (F4)	1,313
Weirton (K5)	24,005
Welch (C6)	6,603
Wellsburg (K5)	5,787
W. Union (E2)	1,341
Weston (F2)	8,945
Westover (F1)	4,318
Wheeling (K5)	58,891
Wheeling (urban area)	106,151
White Sulphur Springs (F5)	2,643
Whitesville (C4)	1,017
Widen (E4)	1,274
Williamson (B5)	8,624
Williamstown (C2)	2,001
Windsor Heights (K5)	1,230
Winona (E4)	1,050

WISCONSIN

Name & Index	Pop.
Abbotsford (F6)	1,013
Adams (G8)	1,425
Algoma (M6)	3,384
Allouez (K7)	4,094
Alma (C7)	1,068
Altoona (C6)	1,713
Amery (B5)	1,625
Antigo (H5)	9,902
Appleton (J7)	34,010
Arcadia (D7)	1,949
Ashland (E2)	10,640
Augusta (D6)	1,458
Baldwin (B6)	1,100
Baraboo (G8)	7,264
Barron (C5)	2,355
Barton (K9)	1,039
Bayfield (E2)	1,153
Beaver Dam (J9)	11,867
Beloit (J11)	29,590
Berlin (H8)	4,693
Black River Falls (E7)	2,824
Bloomer (D5)	2,556
Boscobel (E9)	2,347
Brillion (L7)	1,390
Brodhead (G10)	2,016
Burlington (K10)	4,780
Butler (K1)	1,047
Campbellsport (K8)	1,254
Carrollville (M2)	1,240
Cedar Grove (L8)	1,010
Cedarburg (L9)	2,810
Chetek (C5)	1,585
Chilton (K7)	2,367
Chippewa Falls (D6)	11,088
Clinton (J10)	1,138
Clintonville (J6)	4,657
Colfax (C6)	1,044
Columbus (H9)	3,250
Cornell (D5)	1,944
Crandon (J4)	1,922
Cuba City (F10)	1,333
Cudahy (M2)	12,182
Cumberland (C4)	1,872
Darlington (F10)	2,174
De Pere (K7)	8,146
Delafield (J1)	2,000
Delavan (J10)	4,007
Denmark (L7)	1,012
Dodgeville (F10)	2,532
Durand (C6)	1,961
Eagle River (H4)	1,469
East Troy (J2)	1,052
Eau Claire (D6)	36,058
Edgerton (H10)	3,507
Elkhorn (J10)	2,935
Ellsworth (A6)	1,475
Elm Grove (K1)	2,000
Elroy (F8)	1,654
Evansville (H10)	2,531
Fennimore (E9)	1,696
Florence (K4)	1,400
Fond du Lac (K8)	29,936
Fort Atkinson (J10)	6,280
Fox Lake (J8)	1,153
Fox Point (M1)	2,585
Galesville (D7)	1,193
Gillett (K6)	1,410
Glidden (E3)	1,221
Goodman (K4)	1,020
Grafton (L9)	1,489
Green Bay (K6)	52,735
Greendale (L2)	2,752
Hales Corners (L2)	1,200
Hartford (K9)	4,549
Hartland (J1)	1,190
Hayward (D3)	1,577
Hillsboro (F8)	1,341
Horicon (J9)	2,664
Hortonville (J7)	1,081
Hudson (A6)	3,435
Hurley (F3)	3,034
Independence (D7)	1,088
Janesville (J10)	24,899
Jefferson (J10)	3,625
Juneau (J9)	1,444
Kaukauna (K7)	8,337
Kenosha (M3)	54,368
Kewaskum (K8)	1,183
Kewaunee (M7)	2,583
Kiel (L8)	2,129
Kimberly (K7)	3,179
Kohler (L8)	1,716
La Crosse (D8)	47,535
Ladysmith (D5)	3,924
Lake Geneva (K10)	4,300
Lakemills (H9)	2,516
Lancaster (E10)	3,266
Leona (J4)	1,113
Little Chute (K7)	4,152
Lodi (G9)	1,416
Loyal (E6)	1,104
MADISON (H9)	96,056
Madison (urban area)	109,577
Manitowoc (L7)	27,598
Maple Bluff ‡(H9)	1,361
Marinette (L5)	14,178
Marion (J6)	1,118
Markesan (J8)	1,010
Marshfield (F6)	12,394
Mauston (F8)	3,171
Mayville (K9)	3,010
Medford (F5)	2,799
Mellen (E3)	1,306
Menasha (J7)	12,385
Menomonee Falls (K1)	2,469
Menomonie (C6)	8,245
Merrill (G5)	8,951
Middleton (G9)	2,110
Milton (J10)	1,549
Milton Junction (H10)	1,104
Milwaukee (M1)	637,392
Milwaukee (urban area)	823,430
Mineral Point (F10)	2,284
Mondovi (C6)	2,285
Monona ‡(H9)	2,544
Monroe (G10)	7,037
Montello (H8)	1,069
Montreal (F3)	1,439
Mosinee (G6)	1,453
Mt. Horeb (G10)	1,716
Mukwonago (J2)	1,207
Muscoda (F9)	1,046
Muskego (K2)	1,958
Neenah (J7)	12,437
Neillsville (E6)	2,663
Nekoosa (G7)	2,352
Neopit (J6)	1,257
New Glarus (G10)	1,224
New Holstein (K8)	1,831
New Lisbon (F8)	1,482
New London (J7)	4,922
New Richmond (A5)	2,886
Niagara (K4)	2,022
N. Fond du Lac (J8)	2,291
Oconomowoc (H1)	5.345
Oconto (L6)	5,055
Cconto Falls (K6)	2,050
Okauchee (J1)	1,673
Omro (J7)	1,470
Onalaska (D8)	2,561
Oregon (H10)	1,341
Oshkosh (J8)	41,084
Osseo (D6)	1,126
Owen (F6)	1,034
Pardeeville (H8)	1,112
Park Falls (F4)	2,924
Perrigo Place (H10)	3,315
Peshtigo (L5)	2,279
Pewaukee (K1)	1,792
Phillips (E4)	1,775
Platteville (F10)	5,751
Plymouth (L8)	4,543
Port Edwards (G7)	1,336
Port Washington (L9)	4,755
Portage (G8)	7,334
Prairie du Chien (D9)	5,392
Prairie du Sac (G9)	1,402
Preble (L6)	5,092
Prescott (A6)	1,005
Princeton (H8)	1,371
Pulaski (K6)	1,210
Racine (M3)	71,193
Racine (urban area)	76,101
Randolph (H8)	1,350
Reedsburg (G8)	4,072
Rhinelander (H4)	8,774
Rice Lake (C5)	6,898
Richland Center (F9)	4,608
Ripon (J8)	5,619
River Falls (A6)	3,877
Rothschild (G6)	1,425
St. Croix Falls (A5)	1,065
Sauk City (G9)	1,755
Schofield (H6)	1,948
Seymour (K6)	1,760
Sharon (J11)	1,013
Shawano (J6)	5,894
Sheboygan (L8)	42,365
Sheboygan Falls (L8)	3,599
Shorewood (M1)	16,199
Shorewood Hills (G9)	1,594
Shullsburg (F10)	1,306
South Milwaukee (M2)	12,855
Sparta (E8)	5,893
Spooner (B4)	2,597
Spring Green (G9)	1,064
Stanley (E6)	2,014
Stevens Point (G7)	16,564
Stoughton (H10)	4,833
Sturgeon Bay (M6)	7,054
Sturtevant (M3)	1,176
Sun Prairie (H9)	2,263
Superior (city) (C2)	35,325
Superior, Wis.-Duluth, Minn. (urban area)	142,344
Thorp (E6)	1,383
Tomah (F8)	4,760
Tomahawk (G5)	3,534
Two Rivers (M7)	10,243
Union Grove (L3)	1,358
Viroqua (D8)	3,795
Walworth (J10)	1,137
Washburn (D2)	2,070
Waterford (K3)	1,100
Waterloo (J9)	1,667
Watertown (J9)	12,417
Waukesha (K1)	21,233
Waunakee (G9)	1,042
Waupaca (H7)	3,921
Waupun (J8)	6,725
Wausau (G6)	30,414
Wautoma (H7)	1,376
Wauwatosa (L1)	33,324
West Allis (L1)	42,959
West Bend (K9)	6,849
West Milwaukee (L1)	5,429
West Salem (D8)	1,376
Westby (E8)	1,491
Weyauwega (H7)	1,207
Whitefish Bay (M1)	14,665
Whitehall (D7)	1,379
Whitewater (J10)	5,101
Williams Bay (J10)	1,118
Wind Lake (K2)	1,067
Winneconne (J7)	1,078
Wisconsin Dells (G8)	1,957
Wisconsin Rapids (G7)	13,496

WYOMING

Name & Index	Pop.
Afton (B3)	1,319
Basin (E1)	1,220
Buffalo (F1)	2,674
Casper (F3)	23,673
CHEYENNE (H4)	31,935
Cody (D1)	3,872
Douglas (G3)	2,544
Evanston (B4)	3,863
Fort Washakie (C2)	1,500
Gillette (G1)	2,191
Glenrock (G3)	1,110
Green River (C4)	3,187
Greybull (E1)	2,262
Hanna (F4)	1,326
Jackson (B2)	1,244
Kemmerer (B4)	1,667
Lance Creek (H2)	2,000
Lander (C3)	3,349
Laramie (G4)	15,581
Lovell (D1)	2,508
Lusk (H3)	2,089
Midwest (F2)	2,000
Newcastle (H2)	3,395
Powell (D1)	3,804
Rawlins (E4)	7,415
Riverton (D2)	4,142
Rock Springs (C4)	10,857
Sheridan (F1)	11,500
Superior (D4)	1,580
Thermopolis (D2)	2,870
Torrington (H4)	3,247
Wheatland (H3)	2,286
Worland (E1)	4,202

Better Streets

WITH HALF the Federal Highway System's $33 billion to be spent in urban areas, and the state highway departments to administer this work, cities must be alert to prevent a rural highway design being used where urban standards are needed, in particular on points such as these:

1. *Routing into and through the city.* No one should know better than the city itself about how the streets should pass through urban areas, or how to distribute the traffic, once it enters.
2. *Asphalt or Concrete?* Local officials should have no hesitancy in stating their preference.
3. *Bridges.* Highway engineers customarily design bridges with low, graceful handrailings, suitable in rural areas with virtually no pedestrian traffic, but a hazard in cities.
4. *Drainage.* Rural highways can handle drainage situations much more casually than can cities. The city officials will have to follow through these drainage situations to avoid headaches later.
5. *Protective fencing.* Physical barriers to prevent pedestrians from crossing these limited-accessway arteries are not so mandatory in rural areas but assume great importance in cities. One should look at these new arteries as routes for missiles weighing 1½ to 3 tons each and traveling at 60 feet per second (40 mph) under far from precise control. These roadways are no place for a man or child on foot.

The Regular Street Job

When streets are planned, it goes without saying that a city is best served by building them to as good a standard as possible. At least 25 years of relatively maintenance-free service is within the capabilities of the street designer.

Concrete Streets

Concrete is strong, and probably has been penalized for its sturdiness. Streets carrying a substanial amount of heavy truck traffic will use concrete pavements 8 to 10 inches thick. In residential areas, thin slabs 4½ to 6 inches thick, laid on a good base have worked well. A great deal of money has been wasted building thicker concrete pavement unnecessarily.

Concrete using an air-entraining portland cement has provided a toughness against weathering and a resistance to scaling damage caused by salts customarily used to eliminate ice and snow during winter. However, one does not need to purchase a special cement; and air-entraining agent can be added to standard portland cement and produce the same result. In either case, the concrete will have from 3% to 6% of its total volume as entrained air at a very slight sacrifice in structural strength.

To install contraction joints in concrete pavement, the trend today is toward sawing them in the pavement after it has been laid, rather than going to the trouble of placing devices in the pavement to create planes of weakness where the joint will break.

Power saws equipped with diamond or silicon-carbide blades cut the joints neatly and inexpensively, making a groove only one eighth of the depth of the pavement. This produces a weakened plane that is narrow, easily filled and maintained, and does not interfere with the orderly construction of the street.

The same saws simplify the task of making cuts in the pavement for water and sewer repairs or other utilities. The repair crew need only score the pavement about 1 inch deep; then the pneumatic hammer can break out the opening, leaving a neat line on the surface for the maintenance crew when it replaces the concrete. Many cities now specify that all openings in concrete pavement be prepared in this way.

Expansion joints can be limited to the intersections of each block. The customary practice is to surround each intersection with expansion joint material, preferably of a non-extruding type. Both expansion and contraction joints properly should be reinforced with the customary load-transfer dowel bars carefully prepared so that one end does not bond to the concrete in which it is embedded.

Asphalt Pavements

Taken the nation over, cities use asphalt for a paving material far more often than they do any other material. The reason is that most city work is resurfacing, rather than new construction. While an existing street may have become rough, at the same time, traffic has compacted it to a firm, solid base over which an asphalt surfacing can be laid easily.

Most street officials and city engineers do not like to disturb a well-compacted base that has demonstrated its ability to carry traffic.

Another advantage that appeals to city officials is that streets can be resurfaced with a minimum of disturbance to residents and business. Since the base does not need disturbing, the asphalt paver can pass over quickly, completing its work in a few days as contrasted to possibly as much as two months for other types of surfacing.

Most will agree that a hot mix is preferable to other types of asphaltic surfacing; however, the inverted penetration or "blotter" type surfacing, nevertheless, remains the most popular by a wide margin. The chief advantage is its simplicity. The pressure distributor is the only large specialized unit required. The aggregate spreader also can be used to apply sand and salt in winter. The rollers can be used for other street maintenance work. Furthermore, the city's street sweeper can pick up extra aggregate if desired.

Hot mixes have grown sufficiently in popularity to justify the construction of small portable patching mixers that can be used for maintenance work. In the large cities, and also in cities remotely located away from asphalt producing plants, the cities themselves buy and operate their own central asphalt mixing plants. In general, the cities would prefer awarding contracts for asphalt surfacing if a project can be developed large enough to interest a contractor. Since much of the work is repair and maintenance and is hard to describe in plans and specifications, a central mixing plant operated by the city appears necessary.

Both concrete and asphalt surfaces need a good base. The simplest type is a compacted rock or gravel base.

A more permanent type of base is one that has been stabilized with soil and cement. It has the great advantage of utilizing the natural soil, eliminating much costly material handling. The cement content generally averages 7% or more of the total. The construction procedure requires the base to be compacted firmly to the sub-base so that it has good load-carrying characteristics. The base itself is hard and tough and gives an excellent account of itself when covered with an asphalt surfacing. Virtually all the pavements using soil-cement bases built in the last 20 years still are in service. The bases are not difficult to build and require only simple construction equipment.

Construction like this, however, needs to be reinforced with good curb and gutter, since the edge of the pavement is its weakest point. Today, curb-and-gutter construction has become mechanized. A small, simple paver will build the curb to good, consistent lines. Good, solid asphalt curbs also are being built today mechanically. These curbs are strong enough to develop a substantial amount of structural strength.

In certain cities with heavy bus traffic, the engineers have provided bus stopping platforms made of portland cement concrete. Since the buses are much heavier than other vehicles and since they start and stop at the same locations, they have a tendency to tear up the asphalt surfacing. The "stopping islands" eliminate this and make the bus stops more identifiable.

Street Cleaning

STREET sanitation today is feeling the stimulating effect of mechanization. One skilled man on the right mechanical sweeper can keep streets cleaner at lower cost than a half dozen men with push brooms could do in the past.

This mechanization has not eliminated the familiar "whitewing" with his hand-pushed broom, but it has changed him. Certain cities, particularly in the west, have now given him a motor scooter or three-wheeled motorcycle to increase his range of operation. A great many cities now insist that the whitewing be uniformed smartly, rather than be attired like a relief patron. Some cities supplement his work with the small sweeper with about a 10 cubic foot hopper. In one city, these sweepers have been able to do the work of three men pushing hand carts at a cost of roughly half the hand operation.

Flushers customarily precede the sweepers, directing all street debris to the gutter where it can be picked up easily. Some cities also flush the sidewalks, using a hose attachment, and a few cities add detergents to the flushing water to increase its cleaning ability.

Big Sweepers Speed Up

However, the most pronounced advance has been in the operation of the big sweepers. Today the sweepers have hoppers holding as much as four cubic yards. The sweepers have been designed to travel at truck velocities when loaded, thus permitting them to drop their load of street debris at a central point rather than in the street gutter. Little cities are making increased use of the mechanical sweeper. Today nearly half the 4,000 sweepers in operation are used in cities with populations of less than 15,000, and nearly 20% are in cities of less than 5,000.

The sweepers, however, need clear curbs to operate, so cities are enforcing and the public is accepting parking bans for limited periods of time to permit the sweepers to travel without interference. Best acceptance appears to be to a ban on parking at night. However, a number of large cities prohibit parking in the daytime and find good cooperation.

In general, streets are swept daily in the downtown areas and once or twice a month in residential areas. Sweepers can clean 20 gutter miles daily without difficulty. To help in picking up street debris, many cities now equip trucks with front-end loaders so that the truck driver can pick up and carry away the debris.

A few cities have adopted the use of a sweeper with a detachable hopper that can be picked up by a truck with a special hoist. This completely eliminates any debris on the streets.

For broom fibres, cities use either palmyra stalks, split hickory, African bass or bamboo. A few are experimenting with plastic fibres, more expensive but reportedly able to give a much longer service life. Most larger cities rewind their own brooms, however small cities with only a limited amount of streets often find it advisable to get brooms already wound. Broom winders have now been constructed that can refill a broom in minutes.

To get accurate performance, more cities are attaching recorders to the sweepers to show how long the sweeper has operated and for what period of the day.

Leaf Disposal

Leaf collection also has been mechanized. Blower units draw the leaves into large bodies, shred them to resemble earth. Local greenhouses and park departments like the leaves for use as humus. The same blowers can pick up sand and cinders from the streets and can gather paper and other debris from parks and play areas.

Other types of leaf collectors also are frequently used. Some cities use their snow blowers. Conveyor-type loaders are frequently used as well as various front-end loaders.

Anti-Littering

Most street debris can be prevented. Consequently, cities have to adopt vigorous public education programs. Parky the Cleanup Kangaroo, the Litterbug, Sanitation Sam are among the personalized devices used in this educational program.

The degree of cleanliness of a city's streets is reflected by the public's attitude. One rule is that street cleaning is good when less than 5% of the complaints on street conditions concern street-sanitation problems. The proper mechanical equipment, plus its intelligent administration, should make this goal within reach of every city.

Snow Removal—Ice Control

TO keep snow removal from being the most unpredictable of all municipal services requires prompt action, organization, and the right equipment.

For economy, snow-clearing equipment should be able to do other work so as to be useful the year round. Lacking this, it should be modestly priced, reliable, easily stored, and easily put into service.

Prompt action means to have the plows on the streets when two inches of snow have fallen, when more is expected, and when the temperature is below freezing. Ice storms, with no snow involved, require sand and salt trucks to go into service immediately.

Local experience will in the last analysis dictate how many pieces of each type of equipment are needed. Studies by the MUNICIPAL INDEX show these general practices among cities in the northern portion of the United States:

Snowfall range inches	Average inches	No. of storms needing plows	Plows	Loaders	Other
			Per 100 miles of streets		
20 or less	6	6	7	2	⅓
21-50	32	6	7	2	¾
51 or more	83	15	16	2	½

Truck-mounted plows are the backbone of any snow-fighting program. The most popular is the straight-bladed plow, mounted on a standard truck. These can be classified as one-way tripping; one-way rigid; reversible tripping; and reversible rigid. The tripping feature means that the plow has shock absorbers that permit it to ride over obstructions in the pavement hidden in the snow. The reversible feature permits the plows to throw the snow either to the right or left, at various selected angles, or to bulldoze it straight ahead.

V-plows are particularly useful in heavy snow, and will open a street in one pass, although the roadway opened will be narrow. Virtually all the big heavy-duty, four-wheel drive trucks can carry this type plow. Graders and tractors also will carry them, and certain front-end loaders can have them mounted in place of the bucket. This is helpful because the plow can be lifted above the pavement in case the operator would like to plow in two passes. About 15% of all plows are of the v-type.

In general, cities will open streets in lightly traveled areas and will clear completely arteries and downtown streets. To do this, various types of loading equipment are put into use. The tractor-mounted front-end loader is probably the most popular since it can be used for so many duties the year around. The various conveyor types, also useful in warm-weather months, have proved their value when equipped with larger snow buckets.

Cities in the heavy snow areas will use the high-capacity snow blowers that do a fast, efficient job of picking up snow without requiring it to be windrowed first. These units also can be used to pick up leaves in the fall.

Other equipment will include graders, bulldozers and tractors. A growing number of cities equip themselves with sidewalk plows.

However, plowing snow is only part of the story. Ice storms occur more frequently. In the study mentioned previously, cities surveyed experienced 10½ storms per year where icy streets were the chief problem. One city had 75 such experiences during the year.

Cities are turning in increasing numbers to the use of plain salt, expressing the opinion that it clears the pavement faster, provides better drainage, and reduces overall costs. Many use salt prior to sending out plows to keep the snow from bonding to the pavement. About 15% blend it with a phosphate to inhibit corrosion that salt is reported to cause to car underbodies. A limited number have discovered that in very cold weather they can combine salt with a small amount of calcium chloride and improve performances. The calcium chloride goes to work quickly, however, the salt persists in its action for a longer period of time.

Most of the cities using clear salt also use either sand or cinders as abrasives on certain selected streets. A few, located close to chemical plants, use clear calcium chloride without abrasives.

Weather forecasting is the most controversial portion of snow removal. If a city can get reliable advance notice of a storm it can swing into action without too much trouble. While the U. S. Weather Bureau furnishes a general weather forecast, more detailed information would be helpful. Consequently certain cities are employing private weather consultants who survey the U. S. Weather Bureau results and make specialized advance warnings. Airports also have excellent weather information that cities frequently use.

Water Supply and Treatment

WATER supply still appears troublesome, particularly in those metropolitan areas where the population is increasing and cities are hard pressed to adjust to these changing conditions. It is troublesome in the midwest and southwest where drought conditions have temporarily caused difficulties, and are stimulating more and bolder plans for water supply development. The plan to bring water from northern California to the south is one; the resourceful research aimed at reducing substantially evaporation losses in open reservoirs, now being developed in Fort Worth, Tex., is another; the wider acceptance of weather modification to increase the quantity of rainfall by the use of silver iodide and similar methods is still another.

The treatment of water has not changed greatly. It still remains fundamentally a six-step operation designed primarily to remove harmful bacteria, and secondarily, however, by no means a minor consideration, to free the water from troublesome tastes, odors, and to make it reasonably soft.

The six steps in purification are basically: chlorination; chemical addition; coagulation; settling; filtering; and finally, adjustment of the chlorine residual which is not always required. If the water is stored in untreated reservoirs, an additional pre-treatment step often is needed to remove the algae. Copper sulphate is the long-time remedial agent. At one time, water works men would simply tow a gunnysack of the sulphate behind a row boat back and forth across the reservoir. Today, however, many prefer putting the copper sulphate into solution and spraying it over the reservoir to provide quicker, more thorough algae kill.

The algae are not harmful, but they impart taste to the water, often resembling cucumber or watermelon. While the public does not mind eating either of these, it does object strenuously to their taste in water.

The first step, chlorination, has two tasks: It must kill the harmful bacteria; and it should oxidize any troublesome organic matter that imparts tastes and odors to the water. Chlorination to a free residual generally appears best for this step, with the goal of permitting a residual of 1 part per million to persist through the treatment process.

This step, however, has not been able to remove all troublesome tastes, so waterworks men customarily add activated carbon. This is a porous product free from organic matter and having a great capacity to absorb tastes and odors. There is no danger of overtreating the water since the carbon is removed on the filters.

Under certain conditions, water plants will use chlorine dioxide. This has to be produced at the plant, however, and methods of producing it are not difficult. It has a much stronger oxidizing power than chlorine itself, and often can counteract such troublesome taste producers as phenols, and other more difficult organic compounds.

Simple aeration sometimes helps, and is particularly useful when a city must use a well water containing carbon dioxide, hydrogen sulphide, iron or manganese. Aeration releases the carbon dioxide and hydrogen sulphide, and oxidizes the remainder, allowing them to be removed on the filters.

From the standpoint of chemicals, the most significant step in today's treatment has been the use of liquid alum. The larger plants find that it produces a floc more quickly and simplifies storage and handling problems. Most smaller plants, however, prefer alum or iron salts in dry form applied preferably by a gravimetric chemical feeder.

Settling tanks that receive the water and its chemical floc also are being redesigned. In the past, most felt it sufficient to provide a tank large enough to detain the water for some specified period of time, varying all the way from 1½ to 6 hours.

Today, however, designers recognize that neither the depth of the settling tank nor the time of detention is as important as the surface area exposed. The important factor is that the sediment drop away from the surface far enough so clear water can be skimmed off. Consequently the designers will permit the basin to receive water at 1000 to 1200 gallons per day per square foot of surface area.

The upflow suspended solids contact unit often produces savings over the standard settling basin. Water, mixed with coagulating chemicals, enters the lower portion of the chamber and flows upward, passing through a layer of suspended flocculent material. Such a unit requires much less space and does not require as long a detention period, but it does require closer attention by the operators.

Filters that receive the water from these basins also are undergoing change. Ever since the day that rapid sand filters were first developed, designers have been using the figure of 2 gallons per square foot per minute as the proper rate of flow through them. However, modern tests have shown clearly that they can receive water at a much greater rate successfully, so most designers now make the pipes, valves and other connections large enough to permit a flow of 50% to 100% greater than this. Thereby anticipating that as the demand for water increases, the filters can receive the greater load without impairing quality.

Most filters have surface wash arrangements to assist in cleaning. Many use finely ground anthracite coal instead of sand, and some use porous carborundum plates instead of gravel for the understrain system.

The final step is the adjustment of the chlorine residual. Good practice insists that a residual persist throughout the system and frequently the plant will blend chlorine and ammonia to produce a chloramine. While it does not have the germicidal power of free chlorine residuals, it does persist longer and gives a better indication that the water is safe. At times, the water works will add a hexametaphosphate that has the quality of overcoming corrosive tendencies in the water.

If the water is hard, it generally will be softened in a plant almost identical to one that removes sediment. However, the plant will use lime and soda ash to combine with the "hardness" and remove them in the settling tanks and on the filters. The water in general will be alkaline after passing through the softening process, so carbon dioxide must be added to correct the alkalinity. In the past, the carbon dioxide has been added by taking flue gas from a small coal or gas burner. However, more recent plants have used underwater burners that use natural gas for fuel. These burners can be adjusted precisely to the alkalinity determined by a recording instrument. Certain other plants have used dry ice as their source of carbon dioxide.

In certain smaller plants, zeolite can be used. This is a complex sodium compound which, when in contact with hard water, will exchange the calcium and magnesium hardness for sodium, thus forming sodium carbonates and sulphates that remain soluble and do not prevent the water from forming a lather.

Recently, demineralizing materials have been produced that remove the hardness in much the same way. These are hydrogen exchange compounds; in this case, the hydrogen reacts with the carbonates to form water and carbon dioxide, leaving the calcium and magnesium on the exchange material. If the hardness is in the form of sulphates, the hydrogen combines to form a weak sulphuric acid that can be removed by a deacidizer if necessary.

Fluoridation is an added treatment step, quite apart from the purification of the water itself. Long-time tests have proved that a fluoride content of 1 ppm in the water will provide a condition that reduces dental problems in children's teeth by about 60%. These were based on controlled tests in Grand Rapids, Mich., Newburgh, N. Y. and Brantford, Ontario, Canada. As result of these tests, the American Dental Association and the American Medical Association both openly endorse the use of fluorides in water to reduce tooth decay. Today more than 1400 cities and towns with a total population of over 30,000,000 now treat water in this way as a dental health measure. The larger cities include Chicago, Philadelphia, Baltimore, Washington, Pittsburgh, Cleveland, Milwaukee, San Francisco, St. Louis and Buffalo, N. Y.

Pumps also have undergone certain revisions. Today we find the close-coupled turbine pump replacing the more conventional horizontal-shafted centrifugal in many installations. It requires less floor space, and is not troubled by priming problems that the centrifugal often has to face. These pumps also can be equipped with weatherproof motors that eliminate the need for a pump house.

The so-called submersible pump has gained favor. This type of pump is powered by a waterproof motor submerged, and connected directly to it. This eliminates the long shaft required in standard wells and also does away completely with the need for a pump house. If the well column is not straight, the pump still will operate without difficulty.

Water storage also is subject to changing trends, particularly in the highly populated areas. While a town of small or moderate size will be proud of its elevated tank, metropolitan residential areas become annoyed with them. Consequently, designers may be forced to store the water in covered reservoirs on the ground, supplying them with complex automatic pumping systems to provide the same type of service that the simple and reliable elevated tank can supply.

Water pipe using mechanical joints is gaining favor, also the use of asbestos cement pipe appears increasing, however, the familiar bell-and-spigot cast iron pipe is still firmly entrenched.

The use of water is growing. The great trend toward air conditioners, the larger lot sizes with more lawn area to sprinkle, washing machines and other household devices have increased the use of water to a figure far greater than the increase in population. In the past the peak loads would be between 1½ and 2 times the average daily load. Today, in certain areas, this peak can rise to as much as 7 or 8 times the average.

Water supply is a big industry. More than 117 million people in the nation depend on public water supplies. On a volume basis the water works produce 68 million tons of marketable products each day, or more than 18 times that produced by the steel, coal, petroleum and agricultural industries combined. And this water still can be delivered to the user at a price of five to fifteen cents a ton.

Sewerage and Sewage Treatment

SEWAGE-treatment construction for the next decade ought to increase. Legislation under the new Federal Water Pollution Control Act provides a limited amount of Federal grants aimed at stimulating this work. These grants are a quiet indication that stream pollution has become a national rather than a local problem, and the Federal Government is taking a hand in correcting it.

Public Health Service records indicate that $533 million will have to be spent annually for the next ten years to correct these pollution problems.

The Federal program grants 30% of the project cost, or $250,000, whichever is smaller, to any city building a sewage treatment plant under the terms of the new act. This means that small plants will get the greatest benefit under these terms. This is helpful because the cost per capita of the small plants is substantially higher than costs of large plants.

The most troublesome part of sewage plant construction is the financing. It must be from the city's general funds. However, state-imposed limitations on bonded indebtedness frequently prevents using this method. Consequently, cities often resort to financing the plant by service charges based on the volume of sewage contributed and often on the strength of the sewage to be purified. This means that revenue bonds can be used to finance the construction, however, they customarily require a higher rate of interest than the general obligation bonds, and thus increase the overall cost of the project.

Officials in Marple Township, Pa. solved the problem of providing sewers in new subdivisions currently not served by trunk sewers by requiring the developers to install and cap the sewers, anticipating their availability for use later when trunk sewers reach the area. A court decision has upheld the ordinance.

The problem of supplying sewerage service to areas some distance from the treatment plants have been eased greatly by the introduction of automatic lift stations. Manufacturers now produce these in self-contained units, able to be installed underground so that they will not be visible. Using modern control equipment, these stations will perform with reliability resembling that of a sewer flowing by gravity.

With the growing tendency toward sanitary sewers separated from storm sewers, designers are giving greater attention to the problem of infiltration. This means that the sewer must have tight joints to prevent plain water needing no purification from entering and flowing to the treatment plant. A number of cities are showing increasing interest in asbestos-cement pipe for sewers because of this factor, and also because of its smooth interior surface that lets the sewage flow faster and carry a greater volume.

In the treatment of sewage, most plants follow the familiar pattern of screening or grinding, grit removal, sedimentation, seperate sludge digestion, and the use of trickling filters or activated sludge for further purification if necessary.

A growing number of plants will bypass the digester by simply dewatering the raw sludge on a vacuum filter. The dewatered sludge then can be sent directly to a sanitary fill where its disposal is no more troublesome than any other solid waste.

The very small plants will use hand-cleaned bar screens to remove the varied assortment of large material that comes to the plant. Plants of even moderate sizes will use either mechanically cleaned bar screens or comminutors. The bar screens frequently will be provided with grinder to shred the solids and return them to the sewage, later to be removed in the settling tanks. This is a good practical operation, with everything easily available to the operator, however, most prefer the comminutor, with its dependable ability to grind the solids into small particles without removing them from the sewage stream.

For removal of grit and other inorganic solids, many are turning to the aerated grit chambers because of their ability to remove grit in cleaner condition, and also because of the freshening of the sewage itself. In many cases this makes the subsequent treatment steps easier.

To remove the settleable solids, the traditional settling tank still remains uncontested. Although in theory, one may prefer a long narrow, shallow tank, in practice one finds round, square, or rectangular tanks being used. The square and rectangular tanks produce construction economics through their use of a common wall, when more than one tank is involved. The round tank requires less material if single unit is needed.

In few cases, plants will use a vacuum flotation unit that draws solids to the surface where they can be skimmed off, doing the work in 10 to 25 minutes, whereas the settling tank will require 2 to 3 hours. However, the simplicity of the settling tank has prevented any great growth of these vacuum units.

Some interest has been expressed in the use of fine screens instead of a settling tank. These are helpful when the sewage is of a nature that requires treatment as fast as possible to prevent further septic action.

Digestion tanks that receive the settled solids are becoming smaller, through better understanding of digestion processes. Improved methods of digester heating and recirculation of diffused digester gas and other methods all help step up the efficiency of these units. There is a growing interest in the use of digester gas as a fuel for engines providing power at the plant. With the advent of dual-fuel engines, the designers have much more flexibility of design. If the supply of digester gas drops, the engine can be switched to diesel fuel without loss of power.

A great deal of interest, particularly among small cities, has been expressed in the compact units that place a settling tank directly on the digester. These little 2-story units eliminate much piping, provide simplified operation, and also permit use of the unit as a digester in case the plant is outgrown.

Sewage requiring further treatment still is purified either by some form of trickling filters or by one of the various types of activated sludge treatment. The latter has run into headaches recently because of the tendency of the sewage to foam when agitated by the compressed air. A new type of activated sludge has been introduced recently from England called the Ames Crosta Milles Simplex system. This uses rotating paddle blades to introduce the air into the sewage. The results show that it has not been troubled by foaming, and that it produces its purifying action at favorable operating costs.

Sewage lagoons are receiving increased attention in midwest and southwest areas among municipalities of less than 1,000. The lagoon must be shallow, no more than 3 to 5 feet deep, and should provide a minimum area of about 10 acres for each 1,000 population served. Results indicate that they do an excellent job of purification at low capitalized and operating costs.

Refuse Collection and Disposal

REFUSE collection and disposal is probably changing more than other municipal services. Collection trucks are becoming models of efficiency. Odor and flyash are being eliminated from the operation of incinerators. Sanitary fills are reclaiming ground that perhaps appeared forever unusable. Investigators are still exploring the possibility of transforming refuse into a marketable fertilizer.

Modern Collectors

Cities insist on a refuse truck that is closed, watertight, and able to carry a compact load. Some of these trucks have simple bodies with a traveling bulkhead that packs the refuse, and discharges it by pushing it out the end. In general, these trucks are loaded at shoulder height. Other trucks are loaded through waist-high hoppers at the rear. Some have packing mechanisms that push the refuse into the truck by a hydraulically operated tailgate mechanism. Some have an escalator arrangement that continuously feeds the refuse into the truck. One has a rough grinding mechanism that also feeds the refuse continuously.

These trucks outperform the old open-bodied type. A 15-yard compactor-type truck can carry more refuse than a 24-yard open truck. The open truck required four men, took 2¼ hours to load, for a rate of 614 pounds per man hour, and held 214 pounds per cubic yard. The closed truck required only three men, who did the work in the same time for a work load of 1,081 pounds per man hour, and held 476 pounds per cubic yard.

Some of the larger cities are ingeniously combining the big portable containers with the trucks to simplify refuse collection in crowded areas. In these cases, they use an oversize refuse truck built so that a separate truck can bring the large container to the truck and empty its contents into the truck. In other cities, the truck itself is provided with hydraulically operated arms so that it can lift the container over the truck cab and dump into the oversize truck.

Under normal conditions, a crew will collect from 200 to 500 residences per day, depending on the size of the area, type of residence and method of working the crew. If the householder will place the refuse container at the curb, the crews can work much faster. If the home owner cannot be persuaded to do this, then an advance crew that moves the containers to the curb for the truck sometimes helps.

Collection freqency still remains at about two or three times per week in residential areas and daily in commercial or multiple-dwelling areas. Many cities finance the service by charges or rates that make the work self-supporting. These charges range from $1 to $5 per month per family, depending on the type of service provided. In commercial and industrial areas, the big containers referred to previously provide a means of cleaning up markets. The city purchases the hoisting truck and the commercial areas supply the containers.

Sanitary Fills

To dispose of the refuse, sanitary fills are the most popular. These fills require an average of one acre of land per 10,000 people served per year, for a compacted depth of 7 feet. The fill probably will settle from 10 to 25% and can be used safely after around two years. If the land is moist and the weather is warm the fills become stabilized rather quickly.

Fills have been constructed in areas close to good residences. Odors associated with the work can be expected to travel for 200 or more feet. However, the assurance that the work will be performed promptly and in a good business-like manner to reclaim marginal property and make it useful will overcome objections expressed by nearby residents.

Cities can use the "trench," "area" or "ramp" methods to build the fills. These have been discussed in detail and studies are available to officials showing how each operates.

Equipment needs are simple, consisting of a tractor with front-end loader. In general, the tractor uses track-type treads, however, rubber-tired tractors could be used. One rule states that a tractor with a 1-yard bucket will serve a population of 15,000; if it has a 2-yard bucket, it serves 20,000. Larger, to a maximum of 75,000, two tractors with 3-yard buckets will be needed.

The chief difficulty associated with sanitary fills is the need for land. As a city grows larger, its need for fill sites becomes greater and trucking costs rise. Finally a point can be reached where the added trucking costs become so great that a city would save money to operate an incinerator.

Other problems that sanitary fills encounter are that seepage generally has a high oxygen demand and may pollute streams or cause trouble to nearby well supplies. When the material decomposes, it generates gas and this can be dangerous in the basements of buildings built in the fill. Extremely cold weather also makes the work more difficult. The greatest difficulty, however, is that the operation of the fill becomes sloppy and degenerates into little more than an open dump.

Incinerators

Incinerators have the great advantage of reducing the refuse to an inert ash or residue that can be used for fill immediately and can be counted on for substantial load-carrying characteristics. They reduce the volume of refuse by about 95%.

If the incinerator is small, burning less than 50 tons per day, the designer will generally permit it to be charged directly from the floor. This is the least costly type of construction, however, the incinerator furnace must be large enough to receive its entire load in about 6 working hours while the trucks are operating. It does not allow close control over burning since the refuse must be discharged as soon as the truck arrives.

The more popular type is one that uses a storage pit, with a crane that transfers the refuse to the furnace as burning conditions dictate. With this, the collections can arrive as desired and if collections are particularly heavy, the incinerator can be operated for longer hours to dispose of the accumulated refuse.

The cylindrical furnace with rotating stoking arms has been popular. The rotating arms help the burning and the cylindrical shape permits easy access to all sides so that supplemental stoking can be provided easily.

Rectangular furnaces almost always are supplied with an inclined grate with movable sections so that the refuse can enter the upper end and proceed down the slope, reaching the bottom completely burned.

Hogs Are Out

Hog feeding as a means of disposing of garbage has undergone substantial changes. In the past it was popular because it provided a slight revenue. However, the hogs became infected with trichinosis. Later studies showed other infectious diseases that have induced many states to prohibit the practice unless the garbage is cooked thoroughly. Garbage cooking is an unwieldy operation, feasible only in large cities. Consequently, many more cities have turned to the sanitary fill or incineration.

Is there Money in It?

Composting, or other means of processing a city's wastes into a marketable fertilizer, still persists in the field of municipal sanitation. Last year a new plant was erected at McKeesport, Pa., built by private capital, receiving municipally collected garbage and refuse.

Composting is a natural process that has to work and has been working as long as nature itself. However, in the past it has run across economic roadblocks that have made it unfavorable for cities. In the first place, many such processes could handle only the organic portion of the wastes, still leaving bottles, tin cans, and the multitude of other material to be picked out by hand. Next, it involved a selling operation that does not suit itself well to municipal operation. Municipal government is organized to provide service that protects the health and welfare of the people within its limits; it is not geared to sell a product over a wide market, nor should it be.

Possibly a workmanlike arrangement between private industry can be established permitting a city to deliver its refuse to a manufacturing or composting plant operated by private capital. A city would be justified in paying a fee to dispose of its refuse at such a plant provided the operators would protect the city from damages associated with odor nuisances and health hazards, and also provided the operators would guarantee to take a fixed volume of refuse daily. The McKeesport, Pa. and Baton Rouge, La. projects will give guidance along that line. However, the many past failures call for caution.

Some cities have found revenue from the operation of their incinerators. Atlanta, Ga., produces steam as a byproduct of its incinerator operation, sells it to the local power company, and earns enough to amortize the cost of the plant. Miami, Fla., produces steam from its incinerator to heat a nearby hospital and to provide power for a nearby water pumping station. Fort Worth, Tex., has entered into a contract with a salvage group that reclaims tin cans and earns a small profit. Many cities have gained appreciably in land values by reclaiming waste land by the sanitary fill method.

Closer to Garbage Elimination

FOOD WASTE disposers are being installed at a rate of over 600,000 a year—600,000 in 1956 and 650,000 predicted for 1957.

A sound prediction, moreover, foresees sales of disposers increasing 20% each succeeding year until they reach 10% of the total market for kitchen food waste disposers.

At this rate, installations will reach a million or more a year by 1950 and a total of over 7,000,000 families supplied. That is about twice the present estimate of 3,275,000 sink type disposers being used by American homemakers today or 6½% of the nation's homes.

The big news on this page one year ago was the Detroit program of a disposer in every home. Detroit is one of 30 cities taking this stand. Dump land near the outskirts of cities is diminishing in availability. Costs of hauling and burning garbage are rising, as is also the cost of making land fill. More and more cities will join the vanguard of the 30 forward lookers.

Fears and suspicions of troubles that grinders were supposed to produce have long been dissipated. The ground garbage does not clog sewers. The slurry flows without difficulty in any sewer system that successfully carries normal sewage. The grinders add no volume of consequence to the sewage; the actual water volume added will amount to no more than 2% or 3% of the total sewage. The units are remarkably dependable. In one exhaustive test made by the Chicago Plumbing Testing Laboratory, a standard grinder was forced to operate for a year, receiving a great volume of food waste, and in addition, limestone chips, sand, and malleable iron fittings. At the end of this gruelling test, the unit was still operating satisfactorily, although somewhat slower.

Septic tanks and cesspools function without difficulty when receiving ground garbage. The grinders do introduce more solids, however, they are of a type that the bacteria thrive on. The grinders introduce organic wastes equivalent to one or two extra members of an average family.

The grinders will affect the design of treatment plants somewhat, since they will add organic pollution to the sewage. One estimate is that the strength of the sewage will increase 20% to 25% if every home is equipped with a food waste disposer. The plant will have to be furnished with more digester capacity. In some cases, plants now providing primary treatment may have to adopt a more thorough type of purification. Responsible engineers say that any plant built today should be able to receive ground garbage.

As mentioned previously, the overall municipal advantage of the grinders is great. They correct one of the most knotty sanitation problems at the source—in the home. Health authorities have branded the garbage pail as the weak link in municipal fly-control programs, and flies have been identified as proved vectors in the spread of disease.

Food waste disposers reduce the tonnage of refuse to be collected by 20% to 25% and make the disposal of the remaining refuse easier. Without the decomposable garbage in the refuse pail, collection crews can reduce the number of visits per week without endangering health or creating a nuisance.

Currently, the grinders are being installed at the rate of about 600,00 per year. The more receptive attitude of city health officials is playing a vital role in their advance along the road to better municipal sanitation.

Practical Thoughts Regarding Modern Street Lighting

by S. E. SISCO
Electrical Engineer
Ebasco Services Inc.
2 Rector Street
New York 6, New York

ALERT municipal thinking recognizes the importance of modern adequate street and highway lighting as a practical and economical public service. Records prove significant crime and accident reductions, increased business activity and enthusiastic public acceptance resulting from well planned street lighting installations and modernization programs. These advantages far outweigh financially the insignificant percentage of a municipal budget that such improvement costs.

From the municipal viewpoint, a comprehensive study of street lighting modernization needs should include:

1. Development of a program for step-by-step improvement in order of importance.
2. Classification of streets according to magnitude of night traffic and type of area.
3. Magnitude of peak-hour, night vehicular and pedestrian traffic at pertinent locations.
4. Locations of night crimes and accidents.
5. Standards for lighting intensity according to street classification.
6. Standards for type of lighting according to street classification.
7. Standards for lighting equipment according to street classification.
8. Estimates of investment and annual cost.
9. Review of plans for new and relocated streets and highways.
10. A promotional campaign to inform and sell the program to municipal officials, business interests, and citizens.

Launching a street lighting modernization program requires the active support of municipal departments; the electric utility; the newspapers; radio and television stations; business, civic and other groups which may be in a position to understand and communicate the need for lighting improvements to the citizens of the community; and the citizens themselves.

With the wholehearted cooperation of all concerned, modern street lighting can make a community a brighter, safer, and more pleasant place in which to live, work, and do business.

Turning the Thoughts Into A Municipal Street Lighting Plan

JUST how practical Mr. Sisco's "Thoughts" are will quickly be seen by any city which starts to set up a preliminary study along the lines he recommends.

The result will be a comprehensive tabulation of all the data needed for determining what to do about "your" street lighting. In fact, it will be the "development of a program for step-by-step improvement in order of importance."

very light traffic, light traffic, medium traffic, heavy, very heavy, or heaviest traffic. All that is necessary is to turn to the little tables on page 9 of your copy of the American Standard Practices of Street and Highway Lighting put out by the Illuminating Engineering Society, 1860 Broadway, New York 23, N. Y., 50 cents. Having these street classifications, the typical data for filling in the numbers, size and type of units for each street will be found in Table

	Typical Peak-Hour number at night		Year number at night		Luminaires	lumen	
	cars	*pedestrians*	*crimes*	*traffic accidents*	*number*	*size*	*type*
Main Business							
Main St.							
Front St.							
Secondary Business							
Fourth St.							
Fifth St.							
Traffic Arteries, etc.							
Industrial, etc.							
Residential							

The tabulation will consist of a listing of city streets under the left-hand column with the data indicated by the headings as shown.

With these data, all readily available to any town or city, it will be possible to determine which are the more critical streets in (a) volume of traffic and (b) crime and (c) traffic accidents.

Having the volume of cars and pedestrians at maximum night hour, it is possible to classify each street according to whether it carries

V on page 23 of the I. E. S. Code.

Except in municipalities possessing electrical engineers, two factors should be considered and acted on by the officials. One is that costs are held down by a knowledge of the subject. The second is that the new installation can be either commonplace or exceptionally attractive. Both these objectives—economy and excellence—are worth seeking. To attain them usually requires competent technical guidance.

Buying Traffic Signals

THE PURPOSE of traffic signals is to make automobile traveling simple and easy as well as safer. There does seem to be a definite trend toward the design of more complicated and expensive traffic control equipment in order to provide ever smoother and safer travel and walking.

Today's traffic authority does not ask the storekeeper to wrap up four traffic controllers and a dozen signal heads. He outlines his city's problem, and says either, "This is what I want," or "What do you prescribe?"

Running down the roster of those responsible for traffic signals in cities, one soon runs out of traffic engineers and runs into police captains, lieutenants and sergeants, city electricians, fire alarm superintendents, and others. If you haven't a traffic engineer in your city, the first thing to do is to send a dollar to the Superintendent of Documents, Washington, D. C., for a copy of the Manual on Uniform Traffic Control Devices for Streets and Highways published by the Public Roads Administration. Its over 200 pages are packed with information and instructions concerning advance engineering data required.

The Traffic Engineer of an eastern city gives some sound buying advice:

First be sure that you have a clear grasp of your traffic problem.

Aim to solve the main congestion and order equipment accordingly.

Beware of over-design that complicates the problem.

Have expansion in mind when buying.

Get acquainted with all the products and purchase the one that best suits your municipality.

Never let the lowest price govern purchase.

How to Buy Wisely

If there is no local experienced traffic authority, it is suggested that the city make use of the engineering service available from the various traffic signal manufacturers. In order for the manufacturers to supply a recommendation, certain basic information should be submitted to them.

A large map showing all or a good portion of the downtown area of the city should be submitted, and on this map should be indicated any existing signal locations and cable installations. If the project involves only one or two particular intersections, scale maps of these intersections should be supplied.

Maps should show as much detail as possible, covering such items as location of existing poles, driveways close to the intersection, etc. If signals are already in use at other intersections, the manufacturer will be interested in the type installed and the method of operation.

Furnish as much information as possible on the specific nature of the traffic. Some indication must be given as to traffic volumes on the various streets involved, and the more detailed the information supplied, the more accurate the recommendation will be. If possible, make a 12-hour count (or a peak-hour or even a 15-minute count) of traffic at each intersection, indicating hourly flow of traffic in all directions, as well as turns. Outline the relation between the proposed new intersections and any adjacent signalized intersections. Indicate any unusual grades and parking problems. Give an idea of the average speed of traffic in this locality, or specify the existing speed limit.

With the above information, the traffic signal engineers employed by most manufacturers will be able to suggest and recommend the types of control equipment best suited to control efficiently the traffic at specific locations.

How Cities Connect to the Interstate Highway System

HOW THE cities propose to connect their street grid to the National System of Interstate Highways was examined by Municipal Index for over 60 cities. The first step in every instance where it has not already been taken is to protect the business district from an inpouring of through traffic. The Modesto map shows how this will be accomplished by U. S. 99 and the State Highways 120, 110, 132, and the several connecting streets. Note the parking lots located on the rim of the business district. The map was prepared specially by Douglas J. Carmody, Traffic Engineer, City of Modesto, Calif., population 17,000.

The next step is to remove long-time, all-day commuter parking from the business district and locate it in dual parking areas, wherever possible, on either side of the loop or ring or freeway encircling the district.

How Cities Connect to the Interstate Highway System

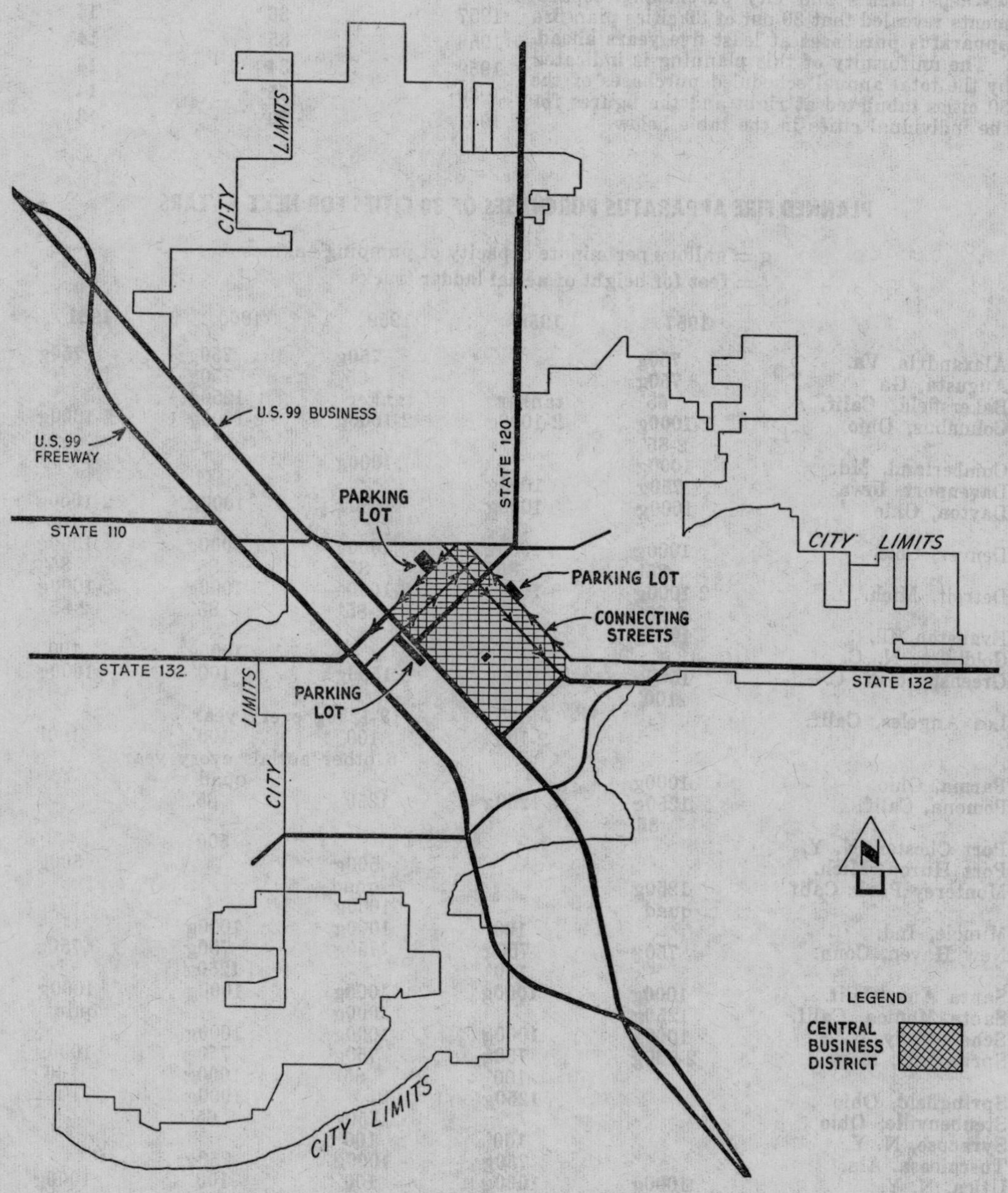

MAP showing how the City of Modesto, California, proposes to connect with the National System of Interstate Highways, prepared by Douglas J. Carmody, Traffic Engineer. Note the connecting streets around the business district and the parking lots located along these streets.

Scheduling Fire Truck Purchases

A MUNICIPAL INDEX survey among fire departments and city purchasing departments revealed that 30 out of 80 cities plan fire apparatus purchases at least five years ahead.

The uniformity of this planning is indicated by the total annual scheduled purchases of the 30 cities tabulated at right and the figures for the individual cities in the table below.

	Pumping Engines	*Aerial Trucks*
1957	36	14
1958	35	14
1959	34	14
1960	35	14
1961	29	13

PLANNED FIRE APPARATUS PURCHASES OF 30 CITIES FOR NEXT 5 YEARS

g = gallons per minute capacity of pumping engines
′ = feet for height of aerial ladder trucks

	1957	1958	1959	1960	1961
Alexandria, Va.	750g		750g	750g	750g
Augusta, Ga.	750g		65′	750g	
Bakersfield, Calif.	65′	tanker	tanker	1250g	
Columbus, Ohio	2-1000g 2-85′	2-1000g	2-1000g	2-1000g	2-1000g
Cumberland, Md.	1000g		1000g		
Davenport, Iowa	750g	1000g			
Dayton, Ohio	1000g	1000g	1000g	1000g	2-1000g 100′
Denver, Colo.	1000g 85′	1000g 85′	1000g 85′	1000g 85′	1000g 85′
Detroit, Mich.	2-1000g 2-85′	3-1000g 85′	2-1000g 2-85′	3-1000g 85′	2-1000g 2-85′
Evanston, Ill.	1000g	1000g			
Goldboro, N. C.		2-750g		1000g	100′
Greensboro, N. C.	1500g 100′	1000g quad	1500g	100′	1000g
Los Angeles, Calif.			12-1250g every year		
		2-100′	100′	100′	100′
			6 other aerials every year		
Parma, Ohio	1000g			quad	
Pomona, Calif.	1250g 85′	1250g	1250	65′	
Port Chester, N. Y.				500	
Port Huron, Mich.			500g		500g
Monterey Park, Calif.	1250g quad		quad 1000g		
Muncie, Ind.		100′	1000g	1000g	
New Haven, Conn.	750g	750g 100′	750g	750g 1250g	750g
Santa Ana, Calif.	1000g	1000g	1000g	1000g	1000g
Santa Monica, Calif.	1250g		1000g		quint
Schenectady, N. Y.	1000g	1000g	1000g	1000g	
Springfield, Mass.	2-750g	750g 100′	750g 65′	750g 1000g	1000g 100′
Springfield, Ohio		1250g		1000g	
Steubenville, Ohio			750g	65′	
Syracuse, N. Y.		100′	100′		
Tuscaloosa, Ala.		750g	1000g	750g	
Utica, N. Y.	1000g	1000g	100′	100′	1000g
Wilmington, Del.	750g	750g	750g	quad	quad
Pumping Engines	36	35	34	35	29
Aerial Trucks	14	14	14	14	13

Electronic Computers Are on the Municipal Threshold

NOT only has the essentiality of business machines to cities been explained here in many editions of Municipal Index but the repeated and varied expositions appear to have been marked and heeded. The tabulation on the following page gives the number of basic machines owned by 21 cities in 1955 compared with 1935. The increase in use of these familiar adding, bookkeeping and calculating machines rises from a mere 89% increase in Enid, Okla., to 1110% in Park Ridge, Ill.

In recent years a new type of business machine has appeared and rapidly developed, first as an invaluable aid to science, but now with even greater promise to business and government. This is as good a time as any to say "Howdy" to electronic computers and processing equipment.

A large body of literature is building up in the data processing field. Conflicting terminology has caused confusion where none should exist. It is essential that city officials stay acquainted with definitions and terms in the field in order to keep in step with technical advancements as they take place.

In addition, it is important that each city make a detailed survey and analysis of its individual needs and requirements. This is the first step toward making a profitable installation of integrated data processing equipment.

At right are the names of business machine manufacturers who are well acquainted with the municipal field. The models listed are of various sizes and capacities but they all do an enormous volume and variety of operations at tremendous speed as if conscious of their need to earn their cost through obvious savings.

Burroughs Corporation, Detroit 22, Mich., makes a desk-size computer (E101) for payroll, assessments and revaluations and utility billing.

Friden Calculating Machine Co., Inc., San Leandro, Calif., makes calculating and adding equipment which enter original data in punched paper tape and cards that can be used by the other machines which process data and compute.

International Business Machines Corp., 590 Madison Ave., New York 22, features the IBM 705 electronic data processing machine and the Type 650 computer which computes the 11,000-man payroll of the Los Angeles Department of Water and Power.

The National Cash Register Co., Dayton 9, Ohio, has developed three categories of new National business machines: specific-purpose electronic machines; original-entry machines, such as accounting machines, cash registers, and adding machines, that are linked to punched paper tape recorders; complete data processing systems including electronic computers.

Remington Rand Div., 315 Fourth Ave., New York 10, offers the famous Univac which computes and writes New York City's payroll.

Underwood Corp., One Park Ave., New York 16, offers Elecom 50 which combines into one operation the computing, analyzing, proving and reporting steps of a procedure.

Number of Conventional Office Machines Owned—1955 vs. 1935

City	Population	Adding	Bookkeeping	Calculating	Per Cent Increase
Beverly Hills, Calif.					
1955	29,032	18	1	6	200
1935	17,429	7	0	1	
Charleston, S. C.					
1955	70,000	11	3	1	115
1935	62,000	5	0	2	
Cleveland Heights, Ohio					
1955	59,141	9	3	2	100
1935	50,943	4	1	2	
Compton, Calif.					
1955	48,000	16	3	11	200
1935	13,000	6	1	3	
Enid, Okla.					
1955	36,000	13	2	2	89
1935	26,400	8	1	0	
Escanaba, Mich.					
1955	15,000	11	3	4	157
1935	15,000	7	0	0	
Fremont, Neb.					
1955	15,000	10	1	1	100
1935	11,000	4	2	0	
Hastings, Neb.					
1955	20,000	12	2	5	111
1935	15,000	6	1	2	
Manchester, N. H.					
1955	83,000	4	2	2	
1935	77,000	0	0	0	
Morgantown, W. Va.					
1955	26,000	8	1	3	300
1935	16,000	3	0	0	
Muskogee, Okla.					
1955	37,289	13	1	1	275
1935	32,026	4	0	0	
Park Ridge, Ill.					
1955	17,000	7	2	3	1110
1935	10,000	1	0	0	
Pottstown, Pa.					
1955	22,589	4	0	0	300
1935	19,430	1	0	0	
Poughkeepsie, N. Y.					
1955	41,000	25	1	3	480
1935	40,300	5	0	0	
Roswell, N. M.					
1955	26,000	8	1	2	267
1935	11,000	2	0	1	
Sanford, Fla.					
1955	11,935	7	2	2	175
1935	10,143	2	1	1	
Santa Barbara, Calif.					
1955	44,913	38	4	10	180
1935	33,613	15	2	3	
Sumter, S. C.					
1955	20,200	7			250
1935	11,800	2	0	0	
Tuscon, Ariz.					
1955	45,400	302	3	16	600
1935	32,500	4	1	2	
University City, Mo.					
1955	40,000	10	3	2	200
1935	26,000	5	0	0	
Xenia, Ohio					
1955	37,289	13	1	1	275
1935	32,026	4	0	0	

Who's Who in

Equipment and Supplies

Indexed by Products—Turn to page numbers shown for listing of manufacturers under each product

Street Construction and Maintenance Equipment

Tools for Maintenance and Repair

Water Supply, Sewage and Refuse Disposal

Electrical Generation and Distribution

Outdoor Lighting Equipment

Traffic Control Equipment

Fire Protection Equipment

Parks, Playgrounds, Swimming Pools

Public Office Equipment

Who's Who in Equipment and Supplies

Page numbers after many of the listings are references to the suppliers' catalog advertising in this issue.

Street and Airport Construction and Maintenance Equipment

ADDITIVES FOR STREETS

Colgate-Palmolive Co., 105 Hudson St., Jersey City, 2 N.J. Air entraining agents for concrete.
Dewey & Almy Chemical Co., 62 Whittemore Ave., Cambridge 40, Mass. Darex AEA, concrete air entraining agents; Darakote, anti-stripping compound for asphalt pavements; Daraweld for bonding new concrete to old.
Techkote Co., Inc., 600 Lairport St., El Segundo, Calif. Durair, air-entraining agents. Vinsol-resin type meeting A.S.T.M. Designation C 260-52T, Federal Spec. SS-C192a and Corps of Engrs. Spec. CRD-C13-49. Dispenser 3 to 30 ounces; Air Meter ¼ cu. ft.
U. S. Rubber Co., Naugatuck Chemical Div., Naugatuck, Conn. Surfa-Sealz thermoplastic rubber compound used as an additive for asphalt and tar products; Surfa-Aero-Sealz, a jet-fuel resistant rubber for airfield surfacing.

AIR COMPRESSORS
(See page 751)

ASPHALT PLANK
(See Bridge Plank Flooring)

ASPHALT PLANTS AND EQUIPMENT

Allied Steel & Tractor Products, Inc., 7835 Broadway, Cleveland 5, Ohio. Wear resistant conveyor buckets made on order from special steels. See page 77.
Barber-Greene Co., 400 N. Highland Ave., Aurora, Ill. Asphalt finishers, mixing plants. See pages 73-76.
Blaw-Knox Co., 30 Charleston Ave., Mattoon, Ill. Bituminous paver finisher operates at speeds of from 15 fpm to 54 fpm, rubber tired. See pages 82-85.
The F. D. Cummer & Son Co., 1827 E. 18th St., Cleveland 14, Ohio. Four sizes up to 1,200 tons per day; dryers 40 to 180 tph; electric batch timers. Complete plants or any individual units. See page 137.
White Mfg. Co., 1227 W. Beardsley Ave., Elkhart, Ind. Asphalt plants, portable and stationary; mixers, pugmill. See pages 230-233.
Wylie Mfg. Co., Inc., P. O. Box 7086, Oklahoma City 12, Okla. Patchmobile for producing bituminous patch material, and Roadmaster for producing hot bituminous paving material. See pages 235-238.
Cartwright Industries, P. O. Box 3251 S. Highlands Sta., Birmingham 5, Ala. "Pavette" hitches behind maintenance truck and sprays bituminous tack coat to repair spot.
Cleaver-Brooks Co., 326 E. Keefe Ave., Milwaukee 12, Wis. Tank car heaters, bituminous boosters, high temperature oil boosters. Automatic, self-contained steam boilers.
Hetherington & Berner, Inc., 731 Kentucky Ave., Indianapolis 7, Ind. Asphalt plants. Moto-Paver for mixing and laying mixed-in-place material.
Iowa Manufacturing Co., 916 16th St., Cedar Rapids, Iowa. Portable and stationary Batch Type and Volumetric types, driers, pugmills.
K. E. McConnaughay, 424 Columbia St., Lafayette, Ind. Model HTD multi-plug asphalt patch mixer. Emulsified asphalt plants.
Madsen Works, Division of Baldwin-Lima-Hamilton Corp., La Mirada, Calif. Asphalt paving plants, oil-mix plants, counter-flow dryers, asphalt tanks, roadpug travel-mix plants, twin-shaft pugmill mixers.
Pioneer Engineering Works Inc., 3200 Como Ave., Minneapolis 14, Minn. Asphalt and gravel plants, bituminous pavers.
Posey Iron Works, Inc., formerly Lancaster Iron Works, Inc., Iroquois Div., South & Prince Sts., Lancaster, Pa. Pugmill mixers, all sizes; aggregate dryers; complete asphalt paving plants; steam-heated and specially designed direct fired asphalt storage tanks; steam jacketed asphalt pumps, pipe and fittings; asphalt pairing tools.
The Simplicity System Co., Chattanooga, Tenn. Hot or cold asphalt mix plants.
Universal Engr. Corp., 620 C Ave., N.W., Cedar Rapids, Ia. Sub. of Pettibone-Mulliken. Portable and stationary, rock, gravel and lime crushing, screening and loading plants. Washing and asphalt plants.

BACKFILL TAMPERS
(See Pavement Breakers, Tampers)

BACKHOES, HYDRAULIC

The Frank G. Hough Co., 955 Sunnyside Ave., Libertyville, Ill. Backhoe attachment for "Payloader" tractor-shovels. width. See pages 248, 249.
Mid-Western Industries, Inc., 1009 S. West St., Wichita, Kans. Model "185" Back-Hoe digs 13' deep, dumping height of 7'6". See pages 133-136.
Pippin Construction Eqpt. Co., Inc., White River Jct., Vt. Pippin Excavator, hydraulic backhoe and shovel for rubber tired and crawler tractors. Digs over 10' deep, loads trucks to 9'. 14 bucket sizes from 8½" to 38" See pages 113-116.
Shawnee Mfg. Co., Inc., 1947 N. Topeka, Topeka, Kans. Shawnee Scout backhoe, 14' reach, 12' digging depth, 12" to 24" widths. Shawnee Chief backhoe, 20' plus reach, reach below grade 15', effective digging to 14'. Shawnee Hydro-Clam digs 8½' deep to 36" wide. See pages 222-225.
Sherman Products, Inc., 3200 W. 14 Mile Rd., Royal Oak, Mich. The Sherman power digger, an all-hydraulic backhoe for mounting on rubber-tired tractors. Shovel widths from 12 to 36". Digs 10' below grade, up to 45 cu. yds. per hour capacity. See pages 172 ABCD.
Bucyrus-Erie Co., 1046 Monroe Ave., S. Milwaukee, Wis. All hydraulic truck-mounted 5-ton Hydrocrane—available as Hydrohoe, and 10-ton Hydrocrane.
Energy Farm Eqpt. Co., Monticello, Ia. Hydraulic truck-mounted backhoe for loading and digging, digs up to 11' deep.

BATCHERS

Blaw-Knox Co., 30 Charleston Ave., Mattoon, Ill. Batcher plant for storing and measuring sand and coarse aggregate. See pages 82-85.
The Conveyor Co., 3260 E. Slauson Ave., Los Angeles 58, Calif. Wet or dry Batch Plants—automatic or manual control with self-contained bulk cement silo. Four compartment aggregate bins and material elevators. See page 255.
Heltzel Steel Form & Iron Co., Warren, Ohio. See page 117.
Erie Strayer Co., 612 Geist Rd., Erie, Pa. Weighing batchers for sand, gravel and cement.
Gar-Bro Mfg. Co., 2415 E. Washington Blvd., Los Angeles 21, Calif. Unit batching.
The C. S. Johnson Co., Box 71, Champaign, Ill. Portable and stationary batchers for cement, sand, aggregate and water in sizes from wheelbarrow batching scales for small mixers to full automatic plants for largest dams.
Shovel Supply Co., P. O. Box 1369 Dallas, Texas. Batchers.

BINS, SAND AND GRAVEL

Blaw-Knox Co., 30 Charleston Ave., Mattoon, Ill. See pages 82-85.
The Conveyor Co., 3260 E. Slauson Ave., Los Angeles 58, Calif. All sizes and capacities. See page 225.
Heltzel Steel Form & Iron Co., Warren, Ohio. See page 117.
Butler Bin Co., Waukesha, Wis.
Erie Strayer Co., 612 Geist Rd., Erie, Pa. Steel bins for sand, gravel and cement.
The C. S. Johnson Co., Box 71, Champaign, Ill. Roadbuilder's bins and batchers.
Pioneer Steel Fabricators, Inc., Minneapolis 13, Minn. Heavy duty steel bins for aggregates, 21, 28, 33, 38 to 100 yds., single or double compartments: bin gates and legs.
Shovel Supply Co. P.O. Box 1369, Dallas, Texas. Bins.
Virginia Bridge Co., U. S. Steel Subsidiary, Roanoke 9, Va. Steel storage bins.

BITUMINOUS DISTRIBUTORS

Bituminous pressure distributors may be truck-mounted units carrying 800-2,000 gallons, with spray bar up to 24 feet. Or they may be semi-trailer mounted with capacities ranging from 1,200 to 3,000 gallons. They use a 375-gpm pump.

E. D. Etnyre & Co., 200 Jefferson St., Oregon, Ill. Bituminous distributors (asphalts, tars, emulsions and road oils), 650-5000 gal. capacity with Etnyre 400 gpm. Asphalt pump—24' full circulating spray bar, insulated with 2" asbestos block or fibre glass. See pages 106-109.
Littleford Bros., Inc., 457 E. Pearl St., Cincinnati 2, Ohio. Bituminous distributors with full circulating spray bar up to 24 ft. for spraying asphalt and tar. See pages 169-172.
Municipal Supply Co., 2508 S. Main St., South Bend 23, Ind. Bituminous distributor, sturdy construction, simple operation, applies any material in any width up to 24 ft. and any quantity from 1/10th to 3 gal. per sq. yd. See pages 181-184.
Rosco Mfg. Co., 3118 Snelling Ave., Minneapolis 6, Minn. Bituminous distributors for truck or trailer mountings. See pages 197-200.
Seaman-Gunnison Corp., 201 Lynn Ave., Baraboo, Wis. Swing bar distributors, 800 to 3,000 gal. See pages 153-156.
Standard Steel Works, 16th and Howell, North Kansas City 16, Mo. Distributors for all types of asphalt construction jobs. See pages 205-208.
Cartwright Industries, P. O. Box 3251 S. Highlands Sta., Birmingham 5, Ala. Bituminous distributors 600 gal. and up for spraying asphalt, tar, road oils and emulsions.

BITUMINOUS MAINTENANCE UNITS

Street departments use maintenance distributors to apply bituminous material to a freshly cleaned street surface. This is immediately covered with mineral aggregate. The distributors may be trailer-mounted units with a 12-foot spray bar and extensions in 2-foot multiples, capable of doing crack-filling, patching, resurfacing parking lots and to a limited extent building new roadway. Facilities are usually available for the attachment of a hose and manually operated spray for patch work and miscellaneous work. The maintenance distributor is built in capacities up to 1,000 gallon for truck mounting, is normally designated as such by the fact that it has a maximum of 100 gpm asphalt pump and a maximum of a 15 hp. engine. In most cases, the spray bar length on these is limited to approximately 10 feet because the smaller engine and pump will not service a longer spray bar. For small work, one can use 2-wheel trailer units with a maximum capacity of 600 gallons and with a spray bar whose maximum width is 12 feet.

E. D. Etnyre & Co., 200 Jefferson St., Oregon, Ill. 400- or 600-gallon bituminous maintenance units mounted on 4-wheel trailer or on a skid for truck mounting. See pages 106-109.
W. E. Grace Mfg. Co., 6009 S. Lamar St., Dallas, Texas. 600-gal. maintenance distributor, truck and trailer mounted. See page 239.
Littleford Bros., Inc., 457 E. Pearl St., Cincinnati 2, Ohio. 400 and 600 gal. maintenance unit with 10-ft. wide circulating spray bar, 100 gal. pump. See pages 169-172.
Municipal Supply Co., 2508 S. Main St., South Bend 23, Ind. Bituminous maintenance units apply all grades of material through spray bar or hand spray. See pages 181-184.
Rosco Mfg Co., 3118 Snelling Ave., Minneapolis 6, Minn. Maintenance unit handles all types of bitumen through 4 to 8" spray bar or hand spray attachment; capacity 400-500-600 gals. See pages 197-200.
Standard Steel Works, 16th & Howell, North Kansas City 16, Mo. Maintenance unit for repairs and secondary construction; spray bars up to 12' in length with pump output of 50 gpm to 100 gpm. See pages 205-208.
American Steel Works, 1211 W. 27th St., Kansas City, Mo. All purpose pressure maintenance units.

BITIMINOUS MATERIALS

Barrett Div., Allied Chemical & Dye Corp., 40 Rector St., New York 6, N. Y. "Tarvia" Bituminous Gel. Tarvia road tar, Tarvia-Lithic bituminous concrete. See page 269.
Byerlyte Corp., 2302 W. 3rd St., Cleveland 13, Ohio. For all types of highway construction; road oils, cutbacks, emulsions; brick filler, crack filler. See pages 146, 147.
American Bitumuls & Asphalt Co., Executive Offices, 200 Bush St., San Francisco 4, Calif. Bitumuls emulsified asphalt for street construction and maintenance.
Berry Asphalt Co. of Arkansas, 141 W. Jackson Blvd., Chicago 4, Ill. All grades of rubberized asphalts for paving and roofing-increased adhesion.
Bitucote Products Co., 1337 Kings Highway, St. Louis, Mo. Bitucote emusified asphalt for new or resurfacing street pavement.
Koppers Company, Inc., Tar Products Div., 1450 Koppers Bldg., Pittsburgh 19, Pa. Coal tar road paving and cold patching material.
W. R. Meadows, Inc., 4 Kimball St., Elgin, Ill. Paving, cutback, emulsified asphalt; poured asphalt crack filler, plant mix for cold patch, road oils; asphalt plank, subgrade papers and sewer joint compounds.
Reilly Tar & Chemical Corp., 11 S. Meridian St., Indianapolis 4, Ind. Bituvia road tar, Plastuvia crack and joint filler, coal tar enamel, pipe coatings.
Rubarite, Incorporated, 1702 Philtower Bldg., Tulsa, Okla. Rubarite rubberizing agent that gives flexibility and greater adhesion to asphalt paving mixes.
Standard Oil Co. (Indiana), 910 S. Michigan Ave., Chicago 80, Ill.
The Texas Co., Asphalt Sales Div., 135 E. 42nd St., New York 17, N. Y. Asphalt, asphaltic cements, cutback asphalts and slow-curing asphaltic oils for heavy-duty paving, low-cost asphalt surfacing, and maintenance of streets, roads and airports.

BITUMINOUS MIXERS

Barber-Greene Co., 400 N. Highland Ave., Aurora, Ill. Continuous and batch-type mixing plants for all asphalt mixes. Complete line includes mixers, gradation units, dryers, dust collectors, cold feeders, and other accessories for every capacity from 20 to over 200 T.P.H. See pages 73-76.
The F. D. Cummer & Son Co., 1827 E. 18th St., Cleveland 14, Ohio. From 2,000 lb. to 8,000 lb. capacity bituminous mixers. Steam jacketed, sturdily constructed. See page 137.
White Mfg. Co., 1227 W. Beardsley Ave., Elkhart, Ind. Bituminous pugmill mixers made in one and two axle types. See pages 230-233.
Wylie Mfg. Co., Inc., P. O. Box 7086, Oklahoma City 12, Okla. Patchmobile for producing bituminous patch material; Roadmaster for producing hot bituminous paving material, and Heat-A-Mix tailgate unit for reclaiming stockpile asphalt material. See pages 235-238.

Cartwright Industries, P. O. Box 3251 S. Highlands Sta., Birmingham 5, Ala. Portable bituminous mixer.

Construction Machinery Co., Box 120, Waterloo, Ia. Hoe-type plaster, mortars, and bituminous (cold patch) mixers.

Hetherington & Berner, Inc., 731 Kentucky Ave., Indianapolis 7, Ind. Travel plants, central mix plants and patch mixers.

Kwik-Mix Co., 235 W. Grand Ave., Port Washington, Wis. Portable bituminous mixer for jobs where the aggregates are usually mixed at atmospheric temperatures and the bituminous cement does not have to be heated above 170 degrees, sizes 10 and 14 cu. ft.

K. E. McConnaughay, 424 Columbia St., Lafayette, Ind. Model HTD multi-plug bituminous patch mixers.

Madsen Works, Division of Baldwin-Lima-Hamilton Corp. La Mirada, Calif. Madsen Road Pug mixer for bituminous and stabilized base.

Pettibone Wood Manufacturing Co., Box 620, 6900 Tujunga Ave., North Hollywood, Calif. 2 models—Preparizer: Scarifies and pulverizes pavements. Roadmixers in four models: 42-S, 48-S, 54-S and 54-A, up to 350 tons per hour. Speedmixers in three models.

Posey Iron Works, Inc., formerly Lancaster Iron Works Inc., Iroquois Div., South & Prince Sts., Lancaster, Pa. Twin shaft pugmill mixers.

Seaman-Andwall Corp., 305 N. 25th St., Milwaukee 8, Wis. Seaman self-propelled Trav-L-Plants and Pulvi-Mixers. 7' mixing width.

BITUMINOUS TOOLS AND EQUIPMENT

Aeroil Products Company, Inc., 50 Wesley St., South Hackensack, N. J. Tar and asphalt melting kettles. Sprayers. Mobile spray tank. Oil and gas heaters. Tool heaters. Tool trailers. Pots, dippers, ladles, buckets. Cut-back and emulsion sprayers. See pages 69-72.

E. D. Etnyre & Co., 200 Jefferson St., Oregon, Ill. Bituminous maintenance units (asphalts, tars, emulsions, and road oils). See pages 106-109.

W. E. Grace Mfg. Co., 6009 S. Lamar St., Dallas, Texas. Circulating heaters for tank cars of asphalt. Asphalt pumps and stationary heaters for storage tanks. Barrel heating kettles. Drag brooms for maintenance of sealed surfaces. See page 239.

Hauck Mfg., Co., 124-136 Tenth St., Brooklyn 15, N. Y. Straight flame burners, combination lead melting furnace and torch, super-heated steam thawers, heaters for concrete mixers, water heaters, salamanders, asphalt melting kettles, tool and cement heaters, surface heaters, patrol kettle for gas and oil. See pages 138-141.

Littleford Bros., Inc., 457 E. Pearl St., Cincinnati 2, Ohio. "Tankar" steam heater; tar and asphalt kettles; road brooms; utility spray tanks; supply tank for bituminous material Heater-planers. Trail-o-Patchers, portable asphalt mixer; asphalt tools and accessories. True-Lay paver-spreader, cut-back and emulsion sprayers. See pages 169-172.

Rosco Mfg. Co., 3118 Snelling Ave., Minneapolis 6, Minn. Asphalt kettles, street and road oilers, street flushers, sweepers. See pages 197-200.

Standard Steel Works, 16th and Howell, North Kansas City 16, Mo. Tar kettles for patch work; traction and engine driven construction brooms, and asphalt tools and buckets and tandem patch rollers. See pages 205-208.

White Mfg. Co., 1227 W. Beardsley Ave., Elkhart, Ind. Burners, kerosene; drivers, material; heaters, concrete mixers, kettles, asphalt and tar heating; pavement, asphalt repair trucks; sprayers, asphalt; torches, kerosene. See pages 230-233.

American Steel Works, 1211 W. 27th St., Kansas City, Mo. Asphalt, tar and pitch heaters; heating kettles; asphalt tool heater, surface heater; heating kettles for pipe line coating; relay and supply tanks; hand and power pump spray trailer unit.

Asphalt Highway Surface Heater Co., 9153 Beachy Ave., Pacoima, Calif. Surface heaters.

Wm. Bros Boiler & Mfg. Co., 1057 Tenth Ave., S.E., Minneapolis 14, Minn. Portable circulating heaters (retort type for asphalt and road oils).

Camm Manufacturing, 1425 First St., San Fernando, Calif. Surfa-Slick, self-heating, asphalt surfacing irons; P.L.G. paver, Lute-O-Rade; a magnesium tool for asphalt leveling which is also a full rake equipped with carbon steel teeth.

Essick Mfg. Co., 1950 Santa Fe Ave., Los Angeles 21, Calif. Emulsion sprayers.

Hetherington & Berner, Inc., 731 Kentucky Ave., Indianapolis 7, Ind. Moto-Patcher, mobile mixing unit, for mixing bituminous patching materials.

Salem Tool Co., S. Ellsworth Ave., Salem, Ohio. Pressed steel melting, dipping and pouring kettles and ladles.

Scheu Products Co., 272 Stowell St., Upland, Calif. Hy-Lo salamanders, 160,000 B.T.U. capacity, oil-burning return stack type. Hy-Lo "Hotshot" forced air portable heater, 300,000 P.T.U. capacity.

Tarrant Mfg. Co., 27-29 Jumel St., Saratoga Springs, N.Y. Sprayers—power operated for tars, emulsions, cutbacks; pouring pots, buckets, and dippers for tar and asphalt. Dryer for sand, stone and gravel. Gas fired barrel heaters.

BLADES, GRADER, DOZER, ETC.

The Colorado Fuel and Iron Corp., Continental Oil Bldg., Denver, Colorado. Bulldozer, scraper and motor grader blades. See page 1018.

Ford Motor Co., Tractor & Implement Div., 2500 E. Maple Rd., Birmingham, Mich. Light industrial tractor with hydraulically controlled grading and dozing blades. See pages 209-212.

LeTourneau-Westinghouse Co., 2301 N. Adams St., Peoria, Ill. Blades for scrapers; bulldozer, motor graders. See pages 58-63.

Mid-Western Industries, Inc., 1009 S. West St., Wichita, Kans. See pages 133-136.

Brighton Steel Co., Stormville, N. Y. Grader and bulldozer blades meeting American Standard Highway specifications.

Bucyrus Blades, Inc., Beal Ave., Bucyrus, Ohio. High carbon, manganese steel blades and cutting edges.

Energy Farm Equipment Co., Monticello, Iowa. Bulldozer and grader blades.

Ottawa Steel Div., L. A. Young Spring & Wire Corp., Ottawa 60, Kansas. Bulldozer and angle-dozer blades as attachments for hydraulic front end tractor loaders.

The Rocklin Mfg. Co., Grand Ave. at Jenning St., Sioux City 2, Iowa. Center mount grader blades, and also rear scraper and leveling blades.

Shovel Supply Co., P. O. Box 1369, Dallas, Texas. Blades for graders, scrapers, bulldozers and trail-builders.

Shunk Mfg. Co., Bucyrus, Ohio. Blades; scarifier teeth, bucket lips.

BRIDGE PLANK FLOORING

The Philip Carey Mfg. Co., Lockland, Cincinnati 15, Ohio. Complete line of asphalt plank and mineral-surfaced bridge flooring. See page 92.

Irving Subway Grating Co. Inc., 5046 27th St., Long Island City 1, N.Y.; P.O. Box 333 Bayshore Sta., Oakland 23, Calif. Bridge decking, catwalks, platforms and stair steps of grating. See page 257.

Johns-Manville, 22 E. 40th St., New York 16, N. Y. Mineral-surfaced and smooth-surfaced asphalt bridge plank. See pages 406, 407; 536, 537.

Presstite-Keystone Engineering Products Company, Div. American Marietta Co., 3772 Chouteau Ave., St. Louis 10, Mo. Kapco asphalt coated membrane board—prevents moisture destruction. See pages 189-192.

Klemp Metal Corp., 6601 So. Melvina Ave., Chicago 38, Ill. Open steel bridge decking; Hexteel heavy duty surface armor for bridge flooring.

Servicised Products Corp., 6051 W. 65th St., Chicago 38, Ill. Standard and mineral surfaced asphalt planking. See pages 201-204.

Koppers Company, Inc., Wood Preserving Div., 1450 Koppers Bldg., Pittsburgh 19, Pa. Pressure-creosoted lumber.

W. R. Meadows, Inc., 4 Kimball St., Elgin Ill. Complete line asphalt plank for bridge and industrial flooring; also mineral-surfaced asphalt plank.

United Steel Fabricators Inc., 333 Gasche St., Wooster, Ohio. Corrugated steel structural plate bridge flooring for use with bituminous surfaces.

BROOMS DRAG

W. E. Grace Mfg. Co., 6009 S. Lamar St., Dallas, Texas. Drag brooms for maintenance and construction of sealed surfaces. See page 239.

Van Brush Mfg. Co., Inc., 327 Southwest Blvd., Kansas City 8, Mo. Fibre and flat steel wire drag levelers, 3" or 6" wide, and any length up to 12-ft. Stock items. See pages 173-176.

American Push Broom & Brush Co., 114 Fern St., San Francisco, Calif. Drag brooms for spreading gravel and heavy sweeping.

Flour City Brush Co., 1501 Fourth Ave., So., Minneapolis 4, Minn. Flat steel wire drag brooms for surface maintenance.

Henke Mfg. Corp., Janesville, Ia. Bituminous drag brooms for surface maintenance.

BROOM REFILLING, FIBRES, WIRE

Otto Gerdau Co., 82 Wall St., New York 5, N. Y. Filler materials for rotary sweeper brooms; fresh fibres of all types—African calabar, bass, palmyra stalks, split bamboo, hickory splints, gutter broom wire; snow-sweeper rattan. See pages 122-125.

W. E. Grace Mfg. Co., 6000 S. Lamar St., Dallas, Texas. Wire broom fibres. See page 239.

Industrial Broom Refilling Service, 3942 E. Nine Mile Rd., Hazel Park, Mich. Any rotary power brooms in the field refilled in 24 hours. See page 256.

M-B Corporation, Box 260, New Holstein, Wis. Palmyra stalks and steel wire for refilling of fibre or steel brooms. Also refilling service. See pages 246, 247; 560; 967.

Mobil-Sweeper Div. of The Conveyor Co., 3260 E. Slauson Ave., Los Angeles 58, Calif. Gutter brooms, steel pickup brooms, fibre for streetsweepers. See page 255.

Van Brush Mfg. Co., Inc., 327 Southwest Blvd., Kansas City 8, Mo. Specialists in refilling road sweeping broom cores, also gutter brooms, with palmyra, calabar bass and hickory fibres, plastics and flat steel wires. Rebuild wrecked or damaged cores, 48 hour service. See pages 173-176.

American Push Broom & Brush Co., 114 Fern St., San Francisco, Calif. Palmyra stalks in 26, 22 and 18" lengths. Hickory fibre in 26" lengths. Gutter broom wire.

Brooklyn Fibre Broom Co., Inc., 47 Dinsmore Pl., Brooklyn 8, N. Y. Refill power sweeper cores—calabar, palmyra stalks, rattan fibres. All kinds of fibres for refilling rotary sweeper brooms.

Flour City Brush Co., 1501 Fourth Ave., So., Minneapolis 4, Minn. Palmyra stalks, African bass, split hickory and flat steel wire for refilling street sweeper brooms and gutter booms.

Johnson Steel & Wire Co., Inc., P.O. Box 1211, Worcester 1, Mass. Roadmaster street sweeper wire in 100 and 200 lb. boxes.

Tuffibre Co., 17 Kearney St., E. Orange, N. J. Refill broom fibre for street sweeping machines. Palmyra stalks, hickory fibre, Sherbo and Calabar African bass, and gutter broom wire.

BRUSHES

W. E. Grace Mfg. Co., 6000 S. Lamar St., Dallas, Texas. Rotary brushes. See page 239.

Gravely Tractors, Inc., Box 78, Dunbar, W. Va. Power-driven brush for general cleaning or snow removal, 38" wide. Available in either fine or coarse fibres; angle or straight position. See page 1001.

M-B Corporation, Box 260, New Holstein, Wis. Tractor mounted or pull type brooms or Palmyra fibre or steel wire for general sweeping or snow removal. Also brush refilling service. See pages 246, 247; 560; 967.

Standard Steel Works, 16th and Howell, North Kansas City 16, Mo. Engine driven and traction driven, two way brooms. See pages 205-208.

Van Brush Mfg. Co., Inc., 327 Southwest Blvd., Kansas City 8, Mo. Street push brooms, garage brushes, floor brushes, concrete brushes, paint and varnish brushes, car and truck washing brushes, and complete janitor supply items. Peckerwood steel wire, also fibre drag levelers, 3" and 6" wide and any length to 12-ft. See pages 173-176.

American Push Broom & Brush Co., 114 Fern St., San Francisco, Calif. Drag brooms for spreading gravel and heavy sweeping. Street and road brooms. Specialty brooms.

Brooklyn Fibre Broom Co., Inc., 47 Dinsmore Pl., Brooklyn 8, N. Y. Institutional and firefighting Perfex Fibre Brooms.

Flour City Brush Co., 1501 Fourth Ave., So., Minneapolis 4, Minn. Complete line of brushes for all industries and institutions.

The Fuller Brush Co., 3586 Main St., Hartford 15, Conn. Cleaning equipment for public buildings.

Harper Brush Works, Fairfield, Ia. Heavy duty hand push brooms.

J. I. Holcomb Mfg. Co., Holcomb & Thomas Sts., Indianapolis, Ind. Floor, wall, and street brushes.

Milwaukee Dustless Brush Co., 534 N. 22nd St., Milwaukee 3, Wis. Street brushes, heavy duty, bassine; all other types of floor brushes and push brooms; Speed-Wash fountain brushes for washing trucks and buses.

BUCKETS

Blaw-Knox Co., 300 Sixth Ave., Pittsburgh, Pa. Digging bucket in a complete range of sizes. See pages 82-85.

The Hayward Co., Dept. S, 50 Church St., New York 7, N. Y. Clamshell, orange peel, electric motor buckets. See pages 534, 535.

Heltzel Steel Form & Iron Co., Warren, Ohio. Concrete buckets—½ yd. to 3 yd. capacity. See page 117.

American Manganese Steel Div., American Brake Shoe Co., 388 E. 14th St., Chicago Heights, Ill. Dipper buckets, back hoe, elevator buckets, scraper-buckets. Hard-facing welding rods.

Bucyrus-Erie Co., 1046 Monroe Ave., S. Milwaukee, Wis. Buckets for power draglines.

Drake-Williams-Mount Co., 23rd and Hickory, Omaha, Nebr. "Omaha" dragline bucket in four types, sizes from ⅜-yd. to 4-yd. inclusive. Larger sizes available on special order.

Electric Steel Foundry Co., 2141 N. W. 25th Ave., Portland 10, Oreg. Dragline, dipper, hoe, orange-peel, clamshell buckets. Dozer-rooter blades and end bits, points and adapters, chain. Miscellaneous bucket, rigging.

Gar-Bro Mfg. Co., 2415 E. Washington Blvd., Los Angeles 21, Calif. Concrete buckets.

George Haiss Mfg. Co., Subsidiary of Pettibone-Mulliken Corp., 350 Fifth Ave., New York 1, N. Y. Hi-Power clamshell excavating, rehandling, coal handling, snow removal.

Henke Mfg. Co., Janesville, Ia. Concrete handling buckets. Available in three sizes.

Insley Mfg. Corp., Box 167, Indianapolis 6, Ind. Concrete buckets.

The C. S. Johnson Co., Box 71, Champaign, Ill. Clamshell buckets in three types. 10 sizes, ⅜ to 3 yd. capacity. Concrete buckets in three types, sizes ½ to 8 yd. capacity.

The Owen Bucket Co., 6030 Breakwater Ave., Cleveland, Ohio. Buckets: clamshell, incinerator, excavator, ditch, and trench; grapples for rock and scrap.

Page Engineering Co., Clearing Post Office, Chicago 38, Ill. Diesel walking dragline, 4 to 20 yd. capacity. Automatic dragline buckets ⅝ to 40 yd. capacity.

Schield Bantam Co., 200 Park St., Waverly, Ia. Dragline, clamshell, 20, 25 and 30 in. trench hoe (others on special order), ⅜ yd. shovel, ½ yd. material handling bucket, all for truck-mounted, crawler-mounted and self-propelled Bantam.

Williams Bucket Division, The Wellman Engineering Co., 7004 Central Ave., Cleveland 14, Ohio. Clamshell and dragline buckets.

BUILDINGS, PREFABRICATED

(See page 786)

BULLDOZERS

Bulldozers are front-end attachments made for specific models of crawler and rubber tired tractors as well as motor graders. They are used for pioneering, land clearing, and leveling, road building and maintenance, short distance earth moving, rough excavating and snow removal. They have also found much popularity in refuse sanitary fill work and coal stockpiling. Most manufacturers of bulldozers also make angledozers, sometimes called trail, grade or road builders. In addition to the straight-forward bulldozing position, angledozers have hight and left side casting positions, (blade at right angles to the center line of tractor). Where a considerable amount of sidecasting work is to be done, angledozers should be used. Consider blade length, height to which the blade can be lifted, number of inches the blade can be dropped as well as whether a free floating cable control or positive pressure blade giving smoother grade is needed.

Austin-Western Works, Baldwin-Lima-Hamilton Corp., Aurora, Ill. Bulldozer attachment for all-wheel drive, all-wheel steel Model 99-L Super 99, 88-L and Super 88, graders, hydraulic controlled. Can be used for angledozing. See pages 78-81.

The Heil Co., 3042 W. Montana, Milwaukee 1, Wis. Hydraulic bulldozer for Oliver tractors; 79-103 in. blade, 10-13 in. drop, 47-61 in. lift; trailbuilders—98-153 in. blade, 49-69 in. lift, 12-24 in. drop. Cable-dozers: Bulldozer blade for I-H Trac Tractors 76-120 in. blade, 50-65 in. lift; trailbuilders—98-153 in. blade, 49-69 in. lift, 12-24 in. drop. See pages 488-491.
LeTourneau-Westinghouse Co., 2301 N. Adams St., Peoria, Ill. Bulldozer attachments for tractors, Tournapulls, motor graders (down pressure optional). See pages 58-63.
Mid-Westen Industries, Inc., 1009 S. West St., Wichita, Kans. Bulldozer 62 in. blades. See pages 133-136.
Pippin Construction Eqpt. Co., Inc., White River Jct., Vt. Bulldozers for most popular makes of tractors. See pages 248, 249.
Shawnee Manufacturing Co., Inc., 1947 N. Topeka Ave., Topeka, Kans. Shawnee bulldozer, double acting hydraulic cylinder for up and down pressures, 5'6" blade. See pages 222-225.
Caterpillar Tractor Co., Peoria, Ill. 23 models of straight, angling, and U-shaped bulldozer blades, cable and hydraulic control.
The Oliver Corp., 400 W. Madison St., Chicago 6, Ill. Bulldozers for Oliver Tractors.

CATCH BASIN CLEANERS

The positive type of small orange peel or clam shell buckets have proved to be the most efficient and practical answer to cleaning catch basins and sumps because they have great power for opening as well as closing. This equipment can be installed on most any size truck for self loading or loading into other trucks. When not being used for cleaning catch basins, the bucket is detached, making equipment available as a crane truck or for regular work.

The Hayward Co., Dept. 6, 50 Church St., New York 7, N. Y. Orange-peel bucket especially for cleaning catch basins. See pages 534, 535.
N. P. Nelson Iron Works, Inc., 850 Bloomfield Ave., Clifton, N. J. Self-powered, truck mounted, with hydraulic orange peel and clamshell buckets. See pages 542, 543.
Pippin Construction Eqpt. Co., Inc., White River Jct., Vt. Hydraulic catch basin attachment quickly mounts on Excavator. Cleans basins rapidly and loads directly into truck. See pages 248, 249.
Stedt Hydraulic Crane Co., 93 Cordaville Rd., Ashland, Mass. Fully hydraulic Stetco catch basin cleaner and Hiab crane with bucket for truck mounting. See pages 546, 547; 1118, 1119.
The Elgin Corp., 231 S. LaSalle St., Chicago, Ill.
The Gorman-Rupp Co., Mansfield, Ohio. Odorless Sanitary septic tank cleaners for cisterns, vaults, septic tanks by agitation and pumping into truck tank.
Netco Div., Clark-Wilcox Co., 118 Western Ave., Boston 34, Mass., Netco catch-basin cleaners with (1) orange peel bucket which operates in 16-inch opening; (2) clamshell for rectangular frames as small as 13½ x 19".
Silent Hoist & Crane Co., 842 63rd St., Brooklyn 20, N. Y. Power-operated cranes (self-propelled) and equipped with orange-peel bucket for catch basin duty.

CHEMICALS FOR STREETS

Cayuga Rock Salt Co., Inc., Myers, N. Y. Rock salt. See pages 97-100.
Columbia-Southern Chemical Corp., 1 Gateway Center, Pittsburgh 22, Pa. Calcium chloride for dustlaying and skid proofing. Also for base stabilization, ice control and concrete admixture. Furnished in 100-pound moisture-proof paper bags. See page 382.
Calgon Co., Div. of Hagan Chemicals & Controls, Inc., Box 1346, Pittsburgh 30, Pa. Banox rust inhibitor for de-icing salt.
The Dow Chemical Co., Midland, Mich. Dowflake calcium chloride flake 77-80% and Peladow calcium chloride pellets 94-97% for use in road base stabilization, control of ice on highways and control of dust on gravel or crushed stone roads.
International Salt Co., Scranton Life Bldg., Scranton, Pa. Sterling Rock Salt for ice control and road stabilization.
Michigan Chemical Corp., St. Louis, Mich. Liquid calcium-magnesium chloride, Common salt (sodium chloride).
Morton Salt Co., Industrial Div., 120 So. LaSalle St., Chicago 3, Ill. Morton rock salt for road stabilization.
Solvay Process Div., Allied Chemical & Dye Corp., 61 Broadway, New York 6, N. Y. Calcium chloride.
Wyandotte Chemicals Corp., Michigan Alkali Div., Wyandotte, Mich. Calcium chloride for dust laying, de-icing and skidproofing; concrete construction; solution for filling tractor tires; shipped as liquid, flake, or pellets.

CLOTHES, WORKMEN'S
(See Firemen's Clothing)

COMPACTORS, VIBRATORY

Jackson Vibrators, Inc., 1947 Ludington Ave., Ludington, Mich. Side form vibrator for mounting on any finisher. Vibratory paving tube, heavy-duty highway paving vibrator. Vibratory compactor for consolidating granular soils and crushed material and for highway patching. Multiple vibratory compactor for base and macadam.

CONCRETE CARTS, WHEELBARROWS

Gar-Bro Mfg., Co., 2415 E. Washington Blvd., Los Angeles 21, Calif. Concrete carts and wheelbarrows.
Insley Mfg. Corp., Box 167, Indianapolis 6, Ind. Concrete handling equipment, carts, hoppers.
Lansing Co., P. O. Box 750, Lansing, Mich. Wheelbarrows.
Maxon Construction Co., Inc., Manufacturing Div., 131 N. Ludlow St., Dayton 2, Ohio. Dumpcrete bodies for hauling of air-entrained concrete.
Whiteman Mfg. Co., 13020 Pierce St., Pacoima, Calif. Powered wheelbarrows.

CONCRETE CURING MATERIALS

Fulton Bag & Cotton Mills, P.O. Box 198, New Orleans 3, La. Mats for curing concrete. See page 991.
Minnesota Mining and Mfg. Co., 900 Fouquier Ave., St. Paul 6, Minn. "Scotch" Brand masking tape, wind and moisture resistant tape, for joining strips of concrete curing blankets. See pages 927-930.
Presstite-Keystone Engineering Products Co., Div. American Marietta Co., 3772 Chouteau Ave., St. Louis 10, Mo. Kapco concrete curing compound for maximum water retention. A membranous film that withstands high vapor pressure. Meets Federal and State specifications. See pages 189-192.
Servicised Products Corp., 6051 W. 65th St., Chicago 38, Ill. Wax resin base, all resin base and white pigmented curing compounds. See pages 201-204.
Aluminum Industries, Inc., Permite Curing Compound Division, 3670 Werk Road, Cincinnati 11, Ohio. Permite membrane concrete curing compounds; clear and white pigmented; for horizontal and vertical surfaces above and below the ground.
Dewey & Almy Chemical Co., 62 Whittemore Ave., Cambridge 40, Mass. Daraseal, concrete curing compound.
Hunt Process Co., Inc., 7012 Stanford Ave., Los Angeles 1, Calif., and P. O. Box 420, Ridgeland, Mass.
Master-Builders Co., Cleveland 3, Ohio. 21 products for concrete and mortar treatment—including concrete floor hardeners, curing compounds, patching and resurfacing products, protective coating and finishers.
W. R. Meadows, Inc., 4 Kimball St., Elgin Ill. Sealtight concrete curing compound, a membrane type furnished in both resin base and wax base; also white pigmented concrete curing compound.
Techkote Co., Inc., 600 Lairport St., El Segundo, Calif. Four types: black, clear, pigmented (white and gray) and resin base. Membrane forming concrete curing compound.
Truscon Laboratories, Caniff and G. T. R. R., Detroit 11, Mich.

CONCRETE FINISHERS

Blaw-Knox Co., 30 Charleston Ave., Mattoon, Ill. See pages 82-85.
The Jaeger Machine Co., 702 Dublin Ave., Columbus 16, Ohio. Concrete finishers. See pages 158-161.
Flexible Road Joint Machine Co., Warren, Ohio.
General Road Machines, Inc., Niles, Ohio. Compacting transverse screed finisher, portable and non-portable longitudinal finisher.

Koehring Co., 3025 W. Concordia Ave., Milwaukee 16, Wis. Longitudinal finisher produces accurate surfaces fast.
Master Vibrator Co., 149 Stanley Ave., Dayton 1, Ohio. Master vibrator finishing screeds strike-off accurately and compact in one easy operation. Also troweling machines.
Stow Mfg. Co., Binghamton, N. Y. 2-hp. concrete vibrating screed, finishing machines and rotary trowels.
Whiteman Mfg. Co., 13020 Pierce St., Pacoima, Calif. Whiteman concrete paving screeding machines.

CONCRETE FINISHERS, TROWELERS

The Cleveland Formgrader Co., Mills Road, Avon, Ohio. Long handled floats or trowels, double action type for finishing concrete. See pages 166, 167.
White Mfg. Co., 1227 W. Beardsley Ave., Elkart, Ind. One-man machines, with retractable wheel; reversible blades; safety control stops ring and blades; immediate tilt adjustment. See pages 230-233.
Mall Tool Co., Div. of Remington Arms Co., Inc., 25000 S. Western Ave., Park Forest, Ill. 2 and 4 cycle gasoline engine trowels. Electric and pneumatic trowels. 26", 36" or 45" rings.
Master Vibrator Co., 149 Stanley Ave., Dayton 1, Ohio. Turn-A-Trowel—gasoline engine and electric power models. Also 24" Midget Power Trowel.
Stow Mfg. Co., Binghamton, N. Y. 2.2, 2½ and 6.2 h.p. gasoline engine Roto-Trowels; 1½ h.p. electric Roto-Trowel.

CONCRETE MACHINERY, MISCELLANEOUS

Aeroil Products Co., Inc., 50 Wesley St., South Hackensack, N. J. Water heater. Concrete heater. Sprayers for concrete curing solutions. See pages 69-72.
Air Placement Equipment Company, 1005A West 24th Street, Kansas City, Mo. Manufacturers of Airplaco concrete gunning equipment, including the Bondactor, Nucretor, and Mix-Elvator. See page 68.
Chain Belt Co., 4640 W. Greenfield Ave., Milwaukee 1, Wis. Pumpcrete (concrete pump)—15 to 65 cu. yd. per hour capacity. See page 105.
The Conveyor Co., 3260 E. Slauson Ave., Los Angeles 58, Calif. Bulk cement plants, complete—automatic batching plants, belt conveyors, bucket conveyors, portable and stationary wet or dry batchers. Remote control and automatic weighing scales. See page 255.
Heltzel Steel Form and Iron Co., Warren, Ohio. Portable and semi-portable bulk cement plants, aggregate measuring plants, bulk cement unloaders, concrete proportion plants, concrete buckets, finishing tools for concrete roads, belt conveyors, chutes, scales. See page 117.
G. H. Tennant Co., 701 N. Highway 100, Minneapolis, Minn. Joint-cleaning and grooving machines for cleaning pavement joints and irregular cracks: grooving and scoring concrete surfaces; and leveling humps. See pages 130-132; 957.
White Mfg. Co., 1227 Beardsley Ave., Elkart, Ind. Concrete grinders and concrete trowels. See pages 230-233.
General Road Machines, Inc., Niles, Ohio. Curb-building machine (integral curb); automatic concrete curing machine and hand-type concrete curing rig.
The C. S. Johnson Co., Box 71, Champaign, Ill. Cement handling equipment; complete bulk cement plants; concentric batchers, for multiple material and cement.
Koehring Co., 3025 W. Concordia Ave., Milwaukee 16, Wis. The Mud-Jack for restoring subgrades and raising concrete.
Mixermobile Distributors, Inc., 8027 N.E. Killingsworth St., Portland 20, Oreg. Towermobile self-propelled portable hoisting unit; 35-ft. tower plus 10-ft. tower extension. Additional 16 ft. tower extensions available.
Prehy Company, 420 Lexington Ave., New York 17, N. Y. Pneumatic concrete and aggregate mix placing equipment.
Tarrant Mfg. Co., 27-29 Jumel St., Saratoga Springs, N. Y. Dryer for sand, stone and gravel.
Thor Power Tool Co., 181 N. State St., Aurora, Ill. Thor pneumatic concrete surfacing grinders for finishing, polishing on concrete, marble, granite and other hard materials.
True Gun-All Equipment Corp., Midstate Bldg., Tulsa, Okla. A wet-mix machine for pneumatically applying concrete and cementitious materials.

CONCRETE MIXERS

Portable sizes of 3½ to 16 cubic feet. The 3½-cubic foot models are available as tilters or non-tilters, and the larger models are non-tilters.

Air Placement Equipment Company, 1005A West 24th Street, Kansas City, Mo. Manufacturers of the portable Mix-Elvator, the automatic continuous dry mixer. See page 68.
Chain Belt Co., 4640 W. Greenfield Ave., Milwaukee 1, Wis. Rex concrete mixers, 3½ to 16 cu. ft. sizes; Rex Moto-Mixers (truck mixers), 3½, 4½, 5½, 6½ and 7½ yd. capacities: Rex mortar and plaster mixers, 2, 4 and 6 cu. ft. capacity. See page 105.
The Jaeger Machine Co., 702 Dublin Ave., Columbus 16, Ohio. Concrete mixers, portable sizes 3½ cu. ft., 6 ft., 11 ft., and 16 ft. See pages 158-161.
C. H. & E. Manufacturing Co., 3810 N. Palmer St., Milwaukee 12, Wis. Plaster-mortar mixer, batch type, 3½ cu. ft. capacity. Mortar mixer, continuous trough type, 7 cu. ft. capacity.
Construction Machinery Co., Box 120, Waterloo, Ia. Concrete mixers, in all sizes up to 3 yd. capacity; Transcrete, truck mixers, 3½ to 7 yd. capacities.
Cook Bros. Eqpt. Co., 3334 San Fernando Rd., Los Angeles 65, Calif. Challenge concrete mixers.
Energy Farm Equipment Co., Monticello, Iowa. Sealed gear utility mixer, 3½ cu. ft. capacity.
Erie Strayer Co., 612 Geist Rd., Erie, Pa. Central mixing plants, truck mixer plants, bulk cement plants, and portable concrete mixing plants.
Essick Mfg. Co., 1950 Santa Fe Ave., Los Angeles 21, Calif. Tilter, 3½, 6, and 9 cu. ft.
Koehring Co., 3025 W. Concordia Ave., Milwaukee 16, Wis. Concrete mixers, tilt and non-tilt types up to 4 cu. yds. and pavers.
Kwik-Mix Co., 235 W. Grand Ave., Port Washington, Wis. From ½ to 3 bag size, 2 and 4 wheel models, side or end discharge, tilting and non-tilting types, water measuring tank. Also power wheelbarrows with interchangeable attachments; 10 and 15 cu. ft. hopper body, 1500 and 2000 lb. flat-bed, ½ and ¾ ton fork lift or 5 ft. scraper blade.
Mixermobile Distributors, Inc., 8027 N. E. Killingsworth St., Portland 20, Oreg. Self-propelled Mixermobiles, portable, central and elevating plants, 2 cu. yd. capacity. 35 ft. Std. tower with additional 10 ft. tower sections available. Mixes up to 50 cu. yd. per hour. See paegs 00-00.
Muller Machinery Co. Inc., 248 Whitman Ave., Metuchen, N. J. Concrete and mortar mixers.
Worthington Corp., Concrete Machinery Dept., Plainfield, N. J. Truck and portable mixers.

CONCRETE PAVERS
(See Pavers)

CONCRETE PAVING VIBRATORS
(See Compactors, Vibratory)

CONCRETE VIBRATORS

White Mfg. Co., 1227 W. Beardsley Ave., Elkhart, Ind. Gasoline and electric vibrators and grinders. See page 230-233.
Chicago Pneumatic Tool Co., 6 East 44th Street, New York 17, N. Y. Concrete vibrators.
Complete Machinery & Equipment Co., Inc., 36-40 Eleventh St., Long Island City 6, N. Y. Portable electric, gas or air driven vibrators.
Jackson Vibrators, Inc., 1947 Ludington Ave., Ludington Mich. Internal type concrete vibrators; flexible-shaft driven gas-engine or electric motor driven models. Electric heavy-duty internal vibrator (Model VS-4) for mass concrete.
Mall Tool Co., Div. of Remington Arms Co., Inc., 25000 S. Western Ave., Park Forest, Ill. Concrete vibrators, gasoline, electric and pneumatic models.
Marvel Equipment Corp., 215 Eagle St., Brooklyn 22, N. Y. Gasoline and electric concrete vibrators, generators, grinders.

Master Vibrator Co., 149 Stanley Ave., Dayton 1, Ohio. Vibrators.

Roeth Vibrator, Inc., 9229 Chestnut St., Franklin Park, Ill. Light weight portable vibrator.

Shovel Supply Co., P.O. Box 1369, Dallas, Texas. Multiple concrete pavement vibrators.

Stow Mfg., Co., Binghamton, N. Y. 2 hp electric and gas concrete vibrators and vibrating screeds.

Syntron Co., 431 Lexington Ave., Homer City, Pa. Two models external concrete form vibrators, three models flexible shaft concrete vibrators.

Thor Power Tool Co., 181 N. State St., Aurora, Ill. Thor electric and pneumatic concrete vibrators, for heavy duty work, ball and roller bearing construction.

Viber Co., Dept. 12, Burbank, Calif. Line of electric, pneumatic and gasoline engine internal vibrators. Also electric and pneumatic external vibrators.

CONVEYORS, SCREENS

Air Placement Equipment Company, 1005A West 24th Street, Kansas City, Mo. Manufacturers of the portable Mix-Elvator, the automatic continuous dry mixer. See page 68.

Barber-Greene Co., 400 N. Highland Ave., Aurora, Ill. Permanent and portable belt conveyors; bucket loaders; ditcher: windrow loaders. See pages 73-76.

Baughman Mfg. Co., Inc., 157 Shipman Rd., Jerseyville 1, Ill. Troughed-belt conveyors, standard and special built-to-order for mass or bulk handling of all materials. Chain and flight conveyors, portable and stationary. All electric-motor or gas-engine powered. Also portable or stationary screw conveyors for all non-abrasive materials that become fluid in motion. See page 86.

The Conveyor Co., 3260 E. Slauson Ave., Los Angeles 58, Calif. Engineered to your specifications. See page 255.

Eagle Crusher Co., Inc., 900 Harding Way East, Galion, Ohio. Belt conveyors and revolving screens.

The Fairfield Engineering Co., 342 Chicago Ave., Marion, Ohio. Light, heavy duty or power moved troughed belt conveyors, power moved belt car unloader and all-aluminum utility conveyors for handling sand, gravel, cinders, etc.

A. B. Farquhar, Div., The Oliver Corp., 221 Duke St., York, Pa. Permanent or portable belt conveyors for sand, gravel, coal, coke.

Fuller Co., Fuller Bldg., Catassauqua, Pa, The Airveyor, pneumatic conveyor, for handling pebble lime, alum, and soda ash in water filtration plants.

George Haiss Mfg. Co., Inc., Subsidiary of Pettibone-Mulliken Corp., 350 Fifth Ave., New York, N. Y. Belt-type car unloader and portable trough conveyor for coal, sand, gravel.

The Jeffrey Mfg. Co., 970 N. 4th St., Columbus 16, Ohio. Conveyors, screens, feeders.

Kolman Mfg. Co., W. 12th St. Rd., Sioux Falls, S. Dak. Portable and stationary belt conveyors, vibrating screens.

Nordberg Mfg. Co., 3073 S. Chase Ave., Milwaukee 1, Wis. Symons vibrating bar and rod grizzlies, rod deck screens, horizontal and "V" screens for scalping, sizing, wet or dry screening or dewatering of sand, gravel or crushed stone.

Pioneer Engineering Works, Inc., 3200 Como Ave., Minneapolis 14, Minn. Conveyors and conveyor-trucks, screens vibrating, revolving and buzzer.

Stephens-Adamson Mfg. Co., 275 Ridgeway Ave., Aurora, Ill. Belt conveyors in widths of 12 to 60". "Zipper" enclosed-belt conveyor elevator.

CRANES

(See Power Cranes and Shovels)

CRUSHERS

Municipalities owning quarries, gravel pits, stone and gravel plants making concrete aggregates with crushers, often use jaw, impact breakers or gyratory crushers for breaking the large stone and cone, gyratory secondary crushers, roll crushers, hammermills or ring crushers, for producing the finer sizes. Crushers may be portable or stationary. Portable plants are available in various combinations. The crushers are furnished in conjunction with a screen and conveyor to deliver the crushed stone to a loading bin or truck. To determine the correct type and size of crusher to be purchased, specify the size of stone to be reduced, the desired size of the product and the capacity per hour or per day.

Allied Steel & Tractor Products, Inc., 7835 Broadway, Cleveland 5, Ohio. Repair parts for gyratory jaw, roll crushers and hammermills. See page 77.

Allis-Chalmers Mfg. Co., 866 S. 70th St., Milwaukee 1, Wis. Jaw crusher, 4 x 6 to 60 x 84 in. receiving openings; capacities ¼ to 630 tph. Primary gyratory crushers 8 to 60 in. openings; 30 to 3000 tph. Fine gyratory crushers 22 to 84 in. head diameter, 10 to 1000 tph. Double roll crushers from 9 to 42 in. diameter x 9 to 16 in. width. Hammermills from 18 in. diameter x 9 in. wide to 42 in. diameter x 48 in. wide Vibrating screens and washers. See pages 285-288.

Gruendler Crusher & Pulverizer Co., 2915 N. Market St., St. Louis 6, Mo. Portable, semi-portable and stationary plants, feeders, bins, screens, conveyors. Jaw crushers—10 x 16 to 30 x 42 in. size, 40-200 tph, 2½-6 in. product. Roll crushers 18, 24, 30, 40, 56 in. diameter. Hammermills up to 36 in. feeder, 5-50 tph. See page 470.

Eagle Crusher Co., Inc., 900 Harding Way East, Galion, Ohio. Jaw crushers—gravel, truck, tractor, trailer, portable, roadside mountings. Jaw opening 10 x 16 to 20 x 36 in., 2½ to 150 tph capacity, ½ to 5 in. product. Impact breaker and pulverizer—12 x 16 in., 18 x 36 in. opening, 1/16-4 in. product, 7-300 tph.

Iowa Manufacturing Co., 916 16th St., Cedar Rapids, Ia. Jaw crushers, 6 x 12 to 42 x 48 in. opening, 2 to 500 tph. Roll crushers 16 x 16 to 55 x 30 in., ¼ to 2½ in. product, 15 to 210 tph.

Nordberg Mfg. Co., 3073 S. Chase Ave., Milwaukee 1, Wis. Nordberg gyratory crushers for primary crushing, 30 to 72 in. feed opening, 3500 tph limestone, rock or stone. Symons cone crushers, stationary or portable, for secondary and third stage crushing, 22 in. to 7 ft. diameter head.

Pioneer Engineering Works, Inc., 3200 Como Ave., Minneapolis 14, Minn. 10 x 16 to 42 x 48 in. jaw opening, ¾—12 in. product, 5-1000 tph. Roll crusher, —24 x 16 to 54 x 24 in. diameter, ¼ to 4 in. product, 13-515 tph. Feeders, conveyors, screens, dehydrators. Portable washing and gravel plants.

Smith Engineering Works, 532 E. Capitol Dr., Milwaukee, Wis. Telsmith equipment—jaw crushers, gyratory breakers, gyrasphere, intercone and roll type secondary crushers. Vibrating screens, super-scrubbers, washing screens, sand classifiers, feeders, and portable plants.

Universal Engr. Corp., 620 C Ave., N.W., Cedar Rapids, Ia., Sub. Pettibone-Mulliken Corp. Jaw crushers: 10 x 16 to 44 x 48 inch opening, ¾ to 12 inch product, 5-1000 tph. Roll crushers: 18 x 16 to 54 x 24 inch sizes, ¼ to 4 inch product, 14-380 tph. TwinDual roll crushers: 24, 30 and 40 inch ¼-2 inch product, 40 to 263 tph. Hammermills: 16 x 20 to 41 x 36 inch opening, 7-180 tph. Impact Masters: 32 x 40 to 57 x 60 inch opening. 2½ Minus to 4 inch minus product, 150 to 750 tph complete portable and stationary aggregate plants.

CURB EQUIPMENT

E. D. Etnyre & Co., 200 Jefferson St., Oregon, Ill. Self-propelled curb-paver lays, compacts, and finishes bituminous curbs in one trip. See pages 106-109.

Dotmar Industries, 502 Hanselman Bldg., Kalamazoo, Mich. Dotmar self-powered curb and gutter paver lays five lineal feet per minute minimum.

E. L. Hardin Associates, Inc., Salisbury, N. C. Stephens-Canfield automatic curber lays 1800 ft. of finished curb a day without forms. Smith-Field automatic integral curb and gutter machine lays up to 1,000 ft. per day without forms.

DITCHERS

(See Trenching Machines)

DUST CONTROL EQUIPMENT

Gulf Oil Corp., 1822 Gulf Bldg., Pittsburgh 30, Pa. Gulf Sani-Soil-Set for dust control. See page 1010.

Complete Machinery & Equipment Co., Inc., 36-40 Eleventh St., Long Island City 6, N. Y. Manufacturers of Kadco dust control systems.

Johnson-March Corp., 1724 Chestnut St., Philadelphia 3, Pa. Chemicals and equipment for dust control.

Techkote Co., Inc., 600 Lairport St., El Segundo, Calif. Concrete floor hardener and dustproofing compound.

Wheelabrator Corporation, Byrkit Ave., Mishawaka, Indiana. Dust and fume control equipment.

ENGINES, INTERNAL COMBUSTION

(See page 774)

EXPANSION JOINTS

(See Paving Joints and Compound)

FIBRES, BROOM

(See Broom Refilling, Fibres, Wire)

FORMS

Forms for bridges, culverts, curbs, combined curb and gutter, foundations, sewers, sidewalk, tunnels, walls, special purposes.

Blaw-Knox Co., 30 Charleston Ave., Mattoon, Ill. Steel forms for streets and sidewalks, curb and gutter. See pages 82-85.

Chicago Bridge & Iron Co., 322 So. Michigan Ave., Chicago 4, Ill. Movable steel forms for tunnels, conduits, culverts and dam. See pages 297-299; 514.

Heltzel Steel Form and Iron Co. Warren, Ohio. Highway, airport, curb, combined curb and gutter and sidewalk forms. See page 117.

Armco Drainage & Metal Products, Inc., 5896 Curtis St., Middletown, Ohio. Steel sheeting for trenches, bulkheads, cofferdams, cutoff walls and aprons. Flange and interlocking. Steel liner plates for tunnels, caissons, conduits, and underpasses.

Atlas Steel Construction Co., 20 Vesey St., New York 7, N. Y. Concrete forms of all types, plate work, large tanks.

Economy Forms Corp., P. O. Box 128, Des Moines 13, Ia. Steel forms for concrete tanks, culverts, sewage and water treatment plants.

General Road Machines, Inc., Niles, Ohio. Road, street, airport, sidewalk, curb and combination curb and gutter forms.

Irvington Form & Tank Corp., 20 Vesey St., New York 7, N. Y. Atlas Speed and Atlas Compo steel forms for sewage disposal and water filtration plants, sewers, manholes, circular tanks, buildings, etc.

GRADERS, CONSTRUCTION AND MAINTENANCE

The modern motor grader is capable of doing a wide variety of jobs including ditching, bank cutting, scarifying, moving windrows, heavy and surface maintenance, blading oil mix and plowing snow. In selecting graders, give careful thought to the amount and kind of work you want to do and how quickly it must be done. Then purchase a grader with sufficient weight, strength and horsepower to do the job. Cities with a limited amount of grading should consider the attachments available for the machine. Graders are available in several sizes best indicated by horsepower ratings. For a large program of heavy construction work, machines of 190 hp to 140 hp can well be considered. Next come the graders of about 115 hp, which are also capable of heavy grading and scarifying. For medium grading and general maintenance consider the 75 hp graders. For occasional light construction, but primarily for maintenance, machines of 50 hp can prove satisfactory. Graders of lesser horsepower generally should be used on surface maintenance only. Blades for mounting under truck bodies and other nonself-propelled models are also listed below. It should be noted that weight in these cases is not indicative of the type grading they can perform.

Allis-Chalmers Mfg. Co., Tractor Div., 886 S. 70th St., Milwaukee 1, Wis. Model Forty-Five, 23,800 lb., 120 brake hp. diesel extra heavy-duty model: Cab, scarifier, bulldozer blade, V-type snow plow and wings, attachments. Model D gasoline or diesel for light grading and maintenance, 8,800 lb., 50 bhp. Cabs, rear-mounted hydraulic loader, scarifier, shoulder maintainer, windrow eliminator, snow plows. See pages 285-288.

Austin-Western Works, Baldwin-Lima-Hamilton Corp., Aurora, Ill. All-wheel drive and all-wheel steer power graders (4 and 6-wheel) for all types of grading, bank sloping, scarifying, and oil mix. Extra-heavy, heavy, medium, and light-duty models. Attachments include bulldozer, V-type snow plows and wings, rotary type snow plows, elevating grader, rear mounted roller and loader. See pages 78-81.

The Cleveland Formgrader Co., Mills Road, Avon, Ohio. Cleveland heavy duty Trail Grader for finishing the subgrade to exact contour just before the concrete is placed. See pages 166, 167.

Good Roads Machinery Corp., Minerva, Ohio. Underbody type, truck-mounted graders and center plows; full power hydraulic; cab controlled. See pages 126-129.

The Huber-Warco Co., 202 N. Greenwood St., Marion, Ohio. Five models of diesel powered, torque converter and power shift transmission graders 102 to 195 hp; three models of diesel powered standard transmission graders 75 to 125 hp; maintainer, 45 hp., gas or diesel, with 8 attachments. See pages 149-152.

LeTourneau-Westinghouse Co., 2301 N. Adams St., Peoria, Ill. Diesel engine graders No. 660 POWER-Flow torque converter model 190 hp., standard transmission model 150 hp., both are extra-heavy-duty with weight up to 30,000 lb. No. 550-123 hp. heavy-duty model to 27,000 lb.; No. 440-104 hp. to 24,500 lb.; No. 330-80 hp. to 24,000 lb.; No. 220-60 hp. to 16,000 lb. Also pull-type graders. See pages 58-63.

M-B Corporation, Box 260, New Holstein, Wis. For Case, Minneapolis-Moline wheel tractors for maintaining and light construction; 7,100 lb. overall weight, 4,340 lb. blade pressure. See pages 246, 247; 560; 967.

Servis Equipment Co., 1000 Singleton Blvd., Dallas, Texas. Servis lift-type blade and angledozers. Also whirlwind terracers, lift and pull types. See page 1006.

Wausau Iron Works, Wausau, Wis. Truck graders, underbody type. See page 261.

The Burch Corp., Crestline, Ohio. Under-truck and drawn type road maintainers.

Caterpillar Tractor Co., Peoria 8, Ill. Diesel motor graders in three sizes.

Danuser Machine Co., Fulton, Mo. Blade, 6 or 8 ft., for grading, ditching, snow-removal, backfilling.

Energy Farm Equipment Co., Monticello, Iowa. Husky No. 22 and No. 33 "all purpose" road graders and maintainers; the hydraulic Husky; Husky No. 11 terracer, grader and ditcher.

The Four Wheel Drive Auto Co., Clintonville, Wis. Four Wheel drive truck with road maintainer for grading, ditch construction, shoulder maintenance.

The Galion Iron Works and Mfg. Co., 1954 South St., Galion, Ohio. Eight models of graders and maintainers.

The Gledhill Road Machinery Co., 57 S. Lera Rd., Galion Ohio. Truck or tractor drawn graders for berm cutting, light ditching and patrol work. 4 models. Also rear strike-off blade for shoulder maintenance.

Gradall Div., The Warner & Swazey Co., Cleveland 3, Ohio. Multi-purpose Gradall, earth moving and construction machine.

Hasselbalch & Sons, 1112 Capitol Ave., Omaha 2, Nebraska. Shoulder finishers and sloping attachments for motor graders.

Pneu-Hydro Road Machinery Co., Cadillac Mich. Underbody mounted grader.

Pettibone New York Corp., Div. Pettibone-Mulliken Corp., Rome, N. Y. Graders.

GRATING, SIDEWALK AND BRIDGE

Blaw-Knox Co., 300 Sixth Ave., Pittsburgh, Pa., Electroforged steel grating for sidewalks, flooring, subway gratings, platforms, doors. See pages 82-85.

Dravo Corp., Machinery Div., Dravo Bldg., Pittsburgh 22, Pa. Tri-Lock interlocked and Tri-Forged welded grating and stair treads. See pages 168; 551.

Irving Subway Grating Co., Inc., 5009 27th St., Long Island City 1, N. Y.; P.O. Box 333 Bayshore Sta., Oakland 23, Calif. Bridge decking, sidewalks, catwalks and stair steps. See page 257.

Kerrigan Iron Works, Inc., 1033 Herman St., Nashville, Tenn. Weldforged steel gratings, sidewalks, bridges, in 24" or 36" width panels; three types of stair treads. See pages 258; 807-809.

Neenah Foundry Co., 505 Winneconne Ave., Neenah, Wis. Sidewalks, gutter and trench plates, driveways and ramps; bridge and building drains, pressure manhole covers. See page 259.

Klemp Metal Corp., 6601 South Melvina Ave., Chicago 38, Ill. Bridge decking, open steel grating for sidewalks, catwalks and walkways.

Hendrick Mfg. Co., 40 Dundaff St., Carbondale, Pa. Perforated metal grilles, Mitco Interlocked steel gratings.

JOINTS

(See Paving Joints and Compounds)

LOADERS, CONVEYOR TYPE

Conveyor-type loaders generally fall into two classes—the bucket type and belt type. The bucket type loaders are designed primarily to load out of stockpiles such material as sand, gravel, slag, crushed stone, cinders, etc. Belt type loaders generally have a paddle-type feeder with flights or screws feeding material to the paddles, which deposit the material on a conveyor belt for loading into trucks. These machines are mounted on rubber tires and are especially suitable for loading from windrows. Municipalities have many uses for self-propelled loaders in picking up and loading into trucks surplus material from street and alley grades which has been windrowed by a motor grader, and for loading windrowed snow for busy streets. In purchasing a conveyor-type loader consider the type material to be loaded, capacity of the loader, unloading height, method of feed and maneuverability.

Barber-Greene Co., 400 N. Highland Ave., Aurora, Ill. Portable belt conveyors, 150-430 tph capacity, 18, 24 and 30 in. belts for all bulk products. Mechanical or gravity feeder accessories. Crawler or pneumatic tired bucket loaders. Spiral feed, ½-3 cu. yd per min. capacity, 9-11 ft. discharge height. Window loaders. See pages 73-76.

Bosworth Mfg. Co., Mills Road, Avon, Ohio. Conveying equipment for loading and unloading bins and trucks. Models that will handle up to 75 tons per hour. See page 328.

Le Tourneau-Westinghouse Co., 2301 N. Adams St., Peoria, Ill. Self-propelled (to 25 mph) self-feeding Traveloader, paddletype feeder places material on 30 in. trough-type belt. Loads sand, gravel, slag, cinders, crushed stone from stockpiles; dirt, sod, scarified blacktop, oil-mix patch material from windrows. Up to 10 cu. yds. per min. or 20 cu. yd. snow. See pages 58-63.

N. P. Nelson Iron Works, Inc., 850 Bloomfield Ave., Clifton, N. J. Bucket loaders, crawler and rubber tired mounting. Capacities up to 10 ton per minute. See pages 542, 543.

Athey Products Corp., 5631 W. 65th St., Chicago 38, Ill. Two models.

Eagle Crusher Co., Inc., 900 Harding Way East, Galion, Ohio. Truck-mounted bucket loaders.

Pettibone-Mulliken Corp., 4700 W. Division St., Chicago 51, Ill. Speed loader.

Pneu-Hydro Road Machinery Co., Cadillac, Mich. Pneu-Hydro Sno-Loder-Conveyor type.

LOADERS, FRONT END

The front-end loader is a piece of equipment to be installed on a wheel type or track type tractor for the purpose of loading dirt or material. Some may be used for digging, pushing dirt or backfilling. Many loaders are manufactured by loader manufacturers to be adapted to various makes of tractors. Others are designed and built by tractor companies to be sold as integral units with their tractors.

Which loader or loader-equipped tractor to choose for the many municipal operations calls for a study of literature and specifications. A number of manufacturers valuing your business provide this specific information. The difficulties of making a choice are indicated by the numerous types and capacities offered. Will they handle loose material only? Will they dig hard ground? Will they backfill? How high a truck will they load? Do they load overhead or to the front only? How fast is the loading cycle? Will they clear land and do sanitary landfill work? What capacity loader is needed? Should the tractor be wheel type or crawler type? These are only a few of the problems to be analyzed. Factors to consider are mounting, horsepower, weight, bucket capacity and dumping clearance. The best thing a loader prospect can do is set up his own specifications—how many trucks does he want to operate? size and capacity of trucks? length of haul (time)? Then go to loader manufacturer to help him figure it out. An idle loader is both too big and too expensive and an idle truck means the loader is too small or too inexpensive.

Below will be found a wide selection of loaders and tractors with loaders to facilitate your choosing a suitable unit. Turn then to the advertising pages of the MUNICIPAL INDEX elaborating the specification and performance data. The catalog information is prepared especially for municipal officials and is often sufficient to reach a decision as to choice.

Allis-Chalmers Mfg. Co., 886 S. 70th St., Milwaukee 1, Wis. Four tractor shovels with standard buckets of 1¼, 2¼, 3 and 4 cu. yds. Light materials buckets, rock buckets, bulldozer blades, lift forks; rock forks and trench hoe attachments. See pages 285-288.

The Frank G. Hough Co., 955 Sunnyside Ave., Libertyville, Ill. "Payloader" tractor-shovels, 18 cu. ft. front wheel drive unit; 1 cu. yd. rear wheel drive unit. 1⅛, 1¾ and 2¼ cu. yd. four-wheel drive. Backfill blade, back-hoe, crane hook, fork lift, plows; pick-up sweeper, land-clearing rake bucket teeth, and snow bucket. See pages 113-116.

Ernest Holmes Co., 2505 E. 43rd St., Chattanooga, Tenn. Holmes-Owen loader. See pages 142-145.

Ford Motor Co., Tractor & Implement Div., 2500 E. Maple Rd., Birmingham, Mich. Tractor mounted industrial loader, lifts 1,000 lb., dumping height 8½'. See pages 209-212.

The Huber-Warco Co., 202 N. Greenwood St., Marion, Ohio. Lift-Loader attachment that converts Huber maintainer to a ⅜ cu. yd. material handler. Lifts 1,700 lb. lb. 9½ ft. high. See pages 149-152.

The Jaeger Machine Co., 703 Dublin Ave., Columbus 16, Ohio. "Load-Plus" tractor loader with 1 cu. yd. bucket capacity, static load capacity 5,000 lb. Torque converter, front wheel drive, rear axle power steering with 8' 2" dumping clearance at 24" reach and turns 14' radius. See pages 158-161.

LoDal Inc., Norway, Mich. Hydraulic truck loader—¾ cu. yd. non-tilt bucket, ½ cu. yd. hydraulic tilt bucket. 1,500 or 3,000 lb. lift. See pages 162-165.

Mid-Western Industries, Inc., 1009 S. West St., Wichita, Kans. Model "500" Heavy Industrial Loader with ¾ yd. capacity. Model "101" with 9 cu. ft. capacity and "102" with 11 cu. ft. capacity. See pages 133-136.

Pippin Construction Eqpt. Co., Inc., White River Jct., Vt. Hydraulic front end loaders for most popular tractors. See pages 248, 249.

Schramm, Inc., West Chester, Pa. PNEUMATRACTOR, a front end loader, a snow plow, a backfill blade, a backhoe and an air compressor. See pages 218-221.

Shawnee Mfg. Co., Inc., 1947 N. Topeka Ave., Topeka, Kansas. Special loader for Ford, Ferguson, Oliver, Allis-Chalmers, International Harvester and John Deere tractor, 11 cu. ft. bucket, 9' dump, 2,000 lb. lift. Loadmaster for Fordson Major Diesel and Case tractors, ⅝ yd., 9' dump, 3,500 lb. lift, double acting cylinders. See pages 222-225.

Sherman Products, Inc., 3200 West 14 Mile Rd., Royal Oak, Michigan. The Sherman Front End Loader mounted on Fordson Major Diesel Tractor, hydraulically operated, models AJ-20 and AJ-25, 2,000 and 2,500 lbs. lifting capacities, 3,500 and 4,500 breakaway capacities, 12'10" lifting height. Also a Fork-lift, rear mounted, lifts 4,000 lbs. to a height of 10 ft. See pages 172ABCD.

American Tractor Corp., 800 Ft. Wayne St., Churubusco, Ind. Terraload'r.

Baker-Raulang Co., Sub. of Otis Elevator Co., 1250 W. 80th St., Cleveland 2, Ohio. "Shoveloader" lifts 1,500 lbs. to 9½' high. ¾ cu. yd. buckets.

Bucyrus-Erie Co., 1046 Monroe Ave., S. Milwaukee, Wis. Model H-3 Hydroshovel with 60" wide reversible dipper.

J. I. Case Co., 700 State St., Racine, Wis. Powerloaders, wheel type, gasoline and diesel power; 3 models.

Caterpillar Tractor Co., Peoria, Ill. Three sizes of Traxcavators, from 1 to 2¼ cu. yd. bucket capacity.

Contractors Machinery Co., Inc., Clinton St., Batavia, N. Y. Trojan Loadster, rubber tired unit in three models.

Drott Mfg. Corp., 3126 So. 27th St., Milwaukee 15, Wis. Drott Skid-Shovel.

Energy Farm Eqpt. Co., Monticello, Ia. Hydraulic heavy-duty loaders with lifting capacities up to 5,700 lbs. for all Row Crop type tractors. Heavy-duty loaders for Ford and Ford-Ferguson tractors, 2 ton capacity, 9½' lift.

International Harvester Co., Chiacgo 1, Ill. McCormick U-34A loader for International 300 and 350 Utility tractors. Manual or hydraulic tilt bucket, 2,000 lb breakaway, 1,350 lb lift to 10 ft. Utilizes tractor's Hydra-Touch system.

Mixermobile Distributors, Inc., 8027 N. E. Killingsworth St., Portland 20, Oreg. Scoopmobile front-end loader with ¾ cu. yd. bucket lifts 4,000 lb. 8, 9, 10 ft. Models with or without cable lift design. Up to 2 cu. yd. buckets. Concrete hopper, lift fork, crane boom, backfiller blade and rotary broom attachments. See pages 00-00.

Napco Industries, Inc., 834 N. 7th St., Minneapolis, Minn. Transo loader, capacities 12 cu. ft., 1 and 1½ cu. yds.

Ottawa Steel Div., L. A. Young Spring & Wire Corp., Ottawa 60, Kans. Hydraulic front-end loader models.

Pettibone-Mulliken Corp., 4700 W. Division St., Chicago 51, Ill. Speedball, front end loader, capacity 1 to 2½ cu. yds.

Ray-Lind Mfg. Co., Iron River, Mich. Eight models of loaders in standard fold over cab and elevating mast models.

Reese Engineering Co., 7517 E. Rush St., El Monte, Calif. Loader attachment for tractors.

Service Supply Corp., Mfg. Div., 3600 N. 20th St., Philadelphia 32, Pa. Lodover—front or rear dump tractor mounted loader.

Tractomotive Corp., Deerfield, Ill. Tracto-shovel and tracto-loader.

Ulrich Products Corp., Roanoke, Ill. Front end hydraulic loader.

Wagner Iron Works, 1905 S. 1st St., Milwaukee 1, Wis. Wagner WM-4 loaders for Industrial wheel type tractors, Wagner W30 Backhoe, Wagner W20 Rear Fork Lift, and W10 Scarifier.

LOADERS, LEAF

Good Roads Machinery Corp., Minerva, Ohio. Leaf collector, scavenger and leaf loader. See pages 126-129.

LoDal, Inc., Norway, Mich. Truck self loaders with grappling type bucket. Compresses leaves and dumps into truck body; also can be used as materials loader. Attachments available. See pages 162-165.

American Structural Steel & Tank Co., 21050 W. 8 Mile Road, Detroit 19, Mich. American vacuum leaf loaders for removing wet or dry leaves and litter from streets and parkways by suction.

M. A. Elliotte, P. O. Box 930, Pontiac, Mich. Leaf loaders.

The Gledhill Road Machinery Co., 57 S. Lera Rd., Galion, Ohio. "Sucker-Upper" Elliotte vacuum leaf loader.

Wm. W. Meyer & Sons, Inc., 8311 Niles Center Rd., Skokie, Ill. Leaf loaders.

Tarrant Mfg. Co., 27-29 Jumel St., Saratoga Springs, N. Y. Tarco Gutter-Vac for use as a vacuum leaf collector and for sucking up gutter litter within 24" of the street curb.

LOADERS, SNOW

(See Snow Loaders and Blowers)

PAVEMENT BREAKERS, TAMPERS

Allied Steel & Tractor Products, Inc., 7835 Broadway, Cleveland 5, Ohio. Paving breaker accessory tools, moil points, chisel bits, asphalt cutters, concrete busters, pipe drivers, clay spades, tampers, rock bits. See page 77.

The Cleveland Formgrader Co., Mills Road, Avon, Ohio. Cleveland Form Tamper for compacting earth under forms. See pages 166, 167.

Schramm, Inc., West Chester, Pa. Hand held rock drills, paving breakers, trench diggers, clay spades and backfill tampers; wagon drills towing type and self-propelled, self-powered. See pages 218-221.

Athey Products Corp., 5631 W. 65th St., Chicago 38, Ill. PB-3 portable breaker teams with Athey 7-11 Force-Feed Loader to load and reduce to specific aggregate size scarified windrowed black-top material. Portable.

Barco Mfg. Co., 500 Hough St., Barrington, Ill. Portable gasoline hammers, paving breakers, rock drills, backfill tampers. The Barco Vibra-Tamp portable gasoline tamper for compaction of granular base materials and bituminous surfaces.

Brunner & Lay, Inc., 9300 King St., Franklin Park, Ill.; also 150 Leslie St., Dallas, Texas; also 2425 E. 37th St., Los Angeles, Calif. Paving breaker accessory tools: moil points and chisel bits, asphalt cutters and concrete busters, pipe drivers, clay spades, tampers, rock bits.

Chicago Pneumatic Tool Co., 6 East 44th St., New York, 17, N. Y. Chippers, scalers, tampers, spades.

Cleco Div. of Reed Roller Bit Co., P. O. 2119, Houston, Texas. Cleco pneumatic pavement breakers. Air operated backfill tampers; full power stroke gives faster compaction and deeper penetration. Moil points and steels for paving breakers.

The Cleveland Trencher Co., 20100 Saint Clair Ave., Cleveland 17, Ohio. Combination backfilling and mechanical tamping machines.

Cuterete Mfg. Corp., 9530 East Rush St., El Monte, Calif. Dy-namic concrete breaker with asphalt cutter and tamping heads.

Gardner-Denver Co., 100 Williamson St., Quincy, Ill.

Gunderson-Taylor Machinery Co., 1237 Shoshone St., Denver 4, Colo. Gunderson-Taylor Triplex backfill tamper uses 105 cfm air.

Ingersoll-Rand Co., 11 Broadway, New York 4, N. Y.

Joy Mfg. Co., Henry W. Oliver Bldg., Pittsburgh 22, Pa. Paving breakers, rock drills, wagon drills, and pneumatic tools.

Le Roi Division, Westinghouse Air Brake Co., 1706 S. 68th St., Milwaukee 14, Wis. Le Roi-Cleveland paving breakers, rock drills, and clay spades.

Novo Pump and Engine Co., Lansing 5, Mich.

Ottawa Steel Div., L. A. Young Spring & Wire Corp., Ottawa, Kans. Self-propelled concrete breaker and backfill tamper. Hydraulically operated by one man. A small portable pile driver with 400 or 600 lb. hammer.

Master Vibrator Co., 149 Stanley Ave., Dayton 1, Ohio. Gasoline or electric tampers.

R. P. B. Corp., 2751 E. 11th St., Los Angeles 23, Calif. The Mighty Midget pneumatic pavement breaker, backfill tampers.

Syntron Co., 431 Lexington Ave., Homer City, Pa. Self-contained, portable gasoline hammers for breaking, digging, cutting, tamping; portable electric hammers, and drills.

Thor Power Tool Co., 181 N. State St., Aurora, Ill. Thor 30, 60, 70, 80 lb. class paving breakers and accessories. Also Thor standard or heavy duty backfill tampers. Available in 3-tamper combination with supporting frame.

Vulcan Tool Mfg. Co. 41 Liberty St., Quincy 69, Mass. Pavement breaking tools, rock drill steels, detachable bit rods and clay digging tools for use with compressed air and gasoline driven hammers.

Worthington Corp., Portable Compressor & Air Tool Div., Holyoke, Mass. Pavement breakers, rock drills, air tools, clay and trench diggers, tampers, rock hammers and portable compressors.

PAVERS

Barber-Greene Co., 400 N. Highland Ave., Aurora, Ill. Asphalt finishing machines. Asphalt mixing plants for new construction, resurfacing and maintenance. See pages 73-76.

Blaw-Knox Co., 30 Charleston Ave., Mattoon, Ill. Base pavers for spreading stone, slag, gravel, soil cement or crusher-run aggregates. Road wideners for laying concrete without forms. See pages 82-85.

Chain Belt Co., 4640 W. Greenfield Ave., Milwaukee 1, Wis. Rex concrete Road Pavers, 34 cu ft. capacity concrete, double drum. See page 105.

The Burch Corp., Crestline, Ohio. Resurfacing and paving machines; road wideners; bituminous pavers.

Cartwright Industries, P. O. Box 3251 South Highlands Sta., Birmingham 5, Ala. "Pavette" for blacktop maintenance.

Dotmar Industries, 502 Hanselman Bldg., Kalamazoo, Mich. Paves separate curbs, combination curbs and gutters, highway strip widening, highway median strip and sidewalk paving up to 6′ overall widths.

Koehring Co., 3025 W. Concordia Ave., Milwaukee 16, Wis. 34-E Twinbatch and 16-E Twinbatch with rubber tire mounting. Mud-Jack for restoring subgrades and raising structures to original level.

PAVING JOINT CLEANERS

G. H. Tennant Co., 701 N. Highway 100, Minneapolis, Minn. Machines for cleaning pavement and runway joints. Cutting head of hardened alloy steel, 2 standard sizes. Semi self-propelled. Air cooled 25 hp. engine. See pages 130-132; 957.

PAVING JOINTS AND SEALING COMPOUNDS

Expansion joints, to permit volume changes in concrete pavements, and contraction (weakened plane) joints to control random cracking require sealing to prevent infiltration of moisture, leakage or filling up with incompressible dirt. Hot and cold applied rubber-asphalt compounds are the preferred types of non-cracking, high-bond sealers.

Premolded fillers are used beneath the sealing compounds. They are composed of asphalt formed between asphalt saturated paper, fiber joint consisting of cork and asphalt or asphalt saturated fiberboard, and other types such as cork, self-expanding cork, and sponge rubber. Also listed below are manufacturers of other paving joints and sealing compounds.

Bethlehem Steel Co., Bethlehem, Pa. The Bethlehem Dowel Unit, a transverse joint support, for concrete highways and airport paving reduces load-transfer problems caused by heavy wheel loads. See pages 326, 327; 485.

Byerlyte Corp., 2302 W. 3rd St., Cleveland 13, Ohio. Paving joints and compounds, expansion joints. See pages 146, 147.

The Philip Carey Mfg. Co., Lockland, Cincinnati 15, Ohio. Highway expansion joint. Also Careylastic, a poured joint compound. See page 92.

The Celotex Corp., 120 S. LaSalle St., Chicago 3, Ill. Flexcell—resilient, non-extruding expansion joint filler. See page 91.

Clipper Mfg. Co., 2813 Warwick, Kansas City 8, Mo. Joint sealer for properly melting sealing compound and for its correct application. See pages 240, 241.

Johns-Manville, 22 E. 40th St., New York 16, N. Y. Felt-sided asphalt expansion joint for concrete runways, streets, highways. See pages 406, 407; 536, 537.

Presstite-Keystone Engineering Products Co., Div. American Marietta Co., 3772 Chouteau Ave., St. Louis 10, Mo. Kapco fiberglas expansion joint, composed of non-rotting inorganic glass fibers meeting Federal and State specifications. Kapco fiber and asphalt expansion joints. Kapco Mastic board tongue & groove joint for center strip and transverse contraction joints, dummy joints, Kapco 336A rubberized asphalt joint sealing compound, sewer joint compounds. See pages 189-192.

Servicised Products Corp., 6051 W. 65th St., Chicago 38, Ill. Premolded asphalt, cork and asphalt, sponge rubber, and cork expansion joint fillers. Hot-poured Para-Plastic joint sealing compound. See pages 201-204.

Flexible Road Joint Machine Co., Warren, Ohio. Complete line of expansion joint holders and contraction joint materials and joint installing machines.

Flinkote Co., 4126 R. C. A. Bldg., New York 20, N. Y. Flintseal (hot poured joint sealing compound). Flinkote CPS (cold poured joint sealing compound). Flintar (coal tar emulsion oil resistant surface sealer). Flintbinder A-2 (rubber-asphalt flexible pavement binder).

Koppers Company, Inc., Tar Products Div., 1450 Koppers Bldg., Pittsburgh 19, Pa. Joint sealing compound.

Laclede Steel Co., Arcade Bldg., St. Louis 1, Mo. Expansion-contraction dowel assemblies and spacers.

W. R. Meadows, Inc., 4 Kimball St., Elgin, Ill. A complete line of expansion joints including asphalt, fibre, corkfill expansion joint as well as sponge-rubber and self-expanding cork, tongue and groove center strip, hardboard, dummy joint and base plate for all expansion joints. Seal-tight rubber-asphalt joint sealing compound and plain asphaltic types of joint sealers. Also Durajoint Polyvinylchloride waterstop.

Techkote Co., Inc., 600 Lairport St., El Segundo, Calif. Three types: 2-component, cold-applied, internal setup mastic filler; single-component, ready-to-use, cold-applied rubber sealer; liquid rubber, cold-applied filler mixed with a setting agent.

U. S. Rubber Co., Naugatuck Chemical Div., Naugatuck, Conn. Joint-Sealz for sealing joints in concrete pavements. Aero-Sealz jet-fuel resistant, joint-sealing material for airfields.

PIPE FOR DRAINAGE

Alabama Pipe Co., Anniston, Ala. Apco soil pipe and fittings and threaded drainage pipe vent, revent and stringer fittings. See pages 277-280.

American Cast Iron Pipe Co., 2930 16th St., N., Birmingham 2, Ala. See pages 289-292.

James B. Clow & Sons, Inc., P. O. Box 6600-A, 201-299 N. Talman Ave., Chicago 80, Ill. Cast-iron pipe and fittings. See pages 270-275.

The Robinson Clay Product Co., 65 W. State St., Akron 9, Ohio. Vitrified clay channel pipe; perforated pipe. See page 563.

R. D. Wood Co., Philadelphia 5, Pa. Cast iron pipe. See pages 387-390.

Alco Products, Inc., Schenectady 5, N. Y. Electric welded steel pipe, 20″ diameter and up.

Armco Drainage & Metal Products, Inc., 5896 Curtis St., Middletown, Ohio. Corrugated metal pipe 6-in. to 15-ft. diameter for drainage and subdrainage.

The Bowerston Shale Co., P. O. Box 17, Bowerston, Ohio. Perforated plain end pipe for airport and highway drainage. Drain tile and sewer pipe.

McWane Cast Iron Pipe Co., 1201 Vanderbilt Rd., Birmingham 2, Ala. Cast iron. See pages 000-000.

United States Pipe and Foundry Co., 3300 First Ave., N., Birmingham, Ala. Cast iron pipe and fittings.

United Steel Fabricators, Inc., 333 Gasche St., Wooster, Ohio. Corrugated metal, riveted, pipe and pipe arches. Sectional plate pipe, pipe arches, and arches.

Universal Concrete Pipe Co., 101 E. Ontario St., Chicago 11, Illinois. Culvert, sewer, flat base and lo-hed pipe.

POWER CRANES AND SHOVELS

Suppose you want a machine to dig and load sand, gravel, or rock into trucks, to handle the setting of pipe, steel, pouring concrete, unloading cars and storing material; or an excavator to dig roadside ditches or to build excavations. If these operations are not simultaneous or continuous, the ideal method would be to buy one machine which would handle all these chores. Of course, if the operations ARE simultaneous, it will be necessary to buy all three separate machines to accomplish the entire job.

When you buy a power crane, however, you have the base for all the machines needed to handle these chores. Different attachments convert this basic machine for crane, dragline, shovel, trenchhoe, clamshell, pile driving and skull-cracker work, making it a versatile all-purpose tool.

What size type of power or boom machine to buy? In most cities, mobility of machines is an all-important factor. Jobs such as street repairs, sewer repairs, new water line laying and street building require that the machine move to scattered spots about the city. Traveling over concrete streets, asphalt, or compacted dirt roads without damage to the surface, the truck-mounted machine can move quickly to any spot to handle these jobs. No extra hauling equipment is necessary to complete these moves, meaning a saving in both time and expense to the municipality.

Crawler-type machines are best suited for jobs where extra flotation and traction are required to handle excavating or lifting chores under adverse ground conditions. Greater stability gives the crawler-mounted machine an advantage in heavy-duty digging. Whereas the truck-mounted crane-shovels require the operation of two men, a truck driver and a crane operator, the self-propelled crawler-mounted and wheel-mounted machine require only one man.

For the reasons given above, it is important that the buyer study the type of job or jobs which his equipment must handle before purchasing a power crane-shovel. Concerning cost on various machines of this type, first cost rises at the rate of at least $5,000 per ¼ cubic yard capacity from 3/10 cubic yards to the ½ and ¾ yard machines. Where there is a large volume of digging it should be borne in mind that the cost per yard of material moved decreases as the machine size increases.

For municipal work there are numerous sizes running from 3/10 to 3 cubic yards and larger. Hourly output in cubic yards of "good common earth" range from 70 to 400 by shovel and 55 to 265 by dragline. As for cranes the rated lifting capacities range from 5 to 75 tons or more.

Whatever size you decide you need, scan the following which lists the various manufacturers of this type equipment and the types and sizes made by each.

Austin-Western Works, Baldwin-Lima-Hamilton Corp., Aurora, Ill. Hydraulic, self-propelled crane, gas or diesel. Continuous 360 degree boom rotation, 2250 lb. capacity at 24-ft. radius, 10,000 lb. capacity at 10 ft. radius. See pages 78-81.

Badger Machine Co., 1124 Fifth St., Winona, Minn. "Hopto" TM truck cranes and backhoes for 1½ ton or larger truck. See pages 87-90.

Gar Wood Industries, Inc., 36253 Michigan Ave., Wayne, Mich. Convertible power shovel ¾ yd. standard and heavy duty. Crawler or truck mounted. Boring and bell attachment available. See pages 242, 243; 532, 533.

The Frank G. Hough Co., 955 Sunnyside Ave., Libertyville, Ill. "Payloader" tractor-shovels. Front, rear and four-wheel drive units. Torque converter and hydraulic breakout bucket standard equipment. Back hoe, sweeper, snow plow and other attachments available. See pages 113-116.

LeTourneau-Westinghouse Co., 2301 N. Adams St., Peoria, Ill. One man operated mobile, sideboom and job cranes of 10, 20, 30 or more tons. See pages 58-63.

Pippin Construction Eqpt. Co., Inc., White River Jct., Vt. Digging and loading attachment for Ferguson, Ford, John Deere, International, Cockshutt, David Brown, Oliver, Case, Massey Harris, Trojan, Terratrac, and Schramm tractors. See pages 248, 249.

Sherman Products, Inc., 3200 W. 14 Mile Rd., Royal Oak, Mich. The Sherman power digger, an all-hydraulic back hoe for mounting on rubber-tired tractors. Shovel widths from 12 to 36 in. Digs 10 ft. below grade, up to 45 cu. yds. per hour capacity. See pages 172 ABCD.

Stedt Hydraulic Crane Co., 93 Cordaville Rd., Ashland, Mass. Hiab hydraulic truck crane lifts 1,125 lbs. with boom extended. See pages 546, 547; 1118, 1119.

American Hoist & Derrick, 57 S. Roberts St., St. Paul, Minn. American 100-200-300-700 series crawler and rubber mounted cranes and excavators ½ yd. to 2 yd. capacity.

Baldwin-Lima-Hamilton Corp., Construction Equipment Div., Lima, Ohio. Lima shovels, cranes, draglines, pull shovels, ½ to 6 cu. yds. crawler or rubber mounted (certain types). Austin-Western crushing equipment.

Bay City Shovels, Inc., 2611 Center Ave., Bay City, Mich. ½ to 1½ yd. crane-shovel. Crawler and pneumatic tire cranes, shovels, draglines and hoes.

Bucyrus-Erie Co., 1046 Monroe Ave., S. Milwaukee, Wis. Shovels ⅜ to 4 cu. yd., lifting cranes, transit cranes 15 & 25 ton, all-hydraulic truck mounted 5-ton Hydrocrane—available as Hydrohoe, and 10-ton Hydrocrane.

Clark Equipment Co., Construction Machinery Div., 599 Pipestone Rd., Benton Harbor, Mich. Michigan Tractor shovels, 15 cu. ft.—2¾ cu. yd. Tractor dozers. Excavator-cranes—truck and crawler mounted; ⅜-¾ cu. yd.

The Cleveland Trencher Co., 20100 Saint Clair Ave., Cleveland 17, Ohio. Model 80 and 80-W tamper, backfiller, side crane.

Gradall Division, The Warner & Swasey Co., 5701 Carnegie Ave., Cleveland 3, Ohio. Gradall, multi-purpose earth moving and construction machine.

The Hanson Clutch & Machinery Co., Tiffin, Ohio. Three models: ⅜, ½ and ¾ cu. yd., yard and dock cranes of 3 and 5 ton capacities.

Harnischfeger Corp., 4400 W. National Ave., Milwaukee, Wis. P&H truck crawler shovels, P&H truck cranes.

Hughes-Keenan Corp., 1934 Smith St., Delaware, Ohio. Model V Roustabout motive crane lifts up to 20,000 lb.

Hyster Co., 2902-63 N. E. Clackamas St., Portland 8, Oregon. Self-propelled, rubber mounted crane, 6,000 lbs. and 10,000 lbs. capacity.

Insley Manufacturing Corp., Box 167, Indianapolis 6, Ind. Power shovels, cranes, draglines and hoes.

Koehring Co., 3025 W. Concordia Ave., Milwaukee 16, Wis. Crawler and rubber tire mounted excavators; ½ to 3 cu. yd. dipper capacity; lift capacity up to 95 tons.

Link-Belt Speeder Corp., 1201 Sixth St., S.W., Cedar Rapids, Ia. A complete line of crawler, truck and wheel mounted shovel-cranes.

Marion Power Shovel Co., Marion, Ohio. Shovels, cranes, crawler and rubber mounted.

Pettibone-Mulliken Corp., 4700 W. Division St., Chicago 51, Ill. Speed swing yard crane; tractor-shovels.

Quick-Way Truck Shovel Co., P. O. Box 1800, Denver 1, Colo. Truck mounted—3/10, 4/10, 5/10 and 6/10 cu. yd. and 3¼, 8½, 10½ and 12½ ton crane capacities.

Schield Bantam Co., 220 Park St., Waverly, Ia. Bantam truck-mounted crawler-mounted and self-propelled power cranes and shovels—3/8 cu. yd., 5-6-7 ton capacity.

Service Supply Corp., Mfg. Div., 3600 N. 20th St., Philadelphia 32, Pa. S & L mobile crane, 5 ton.

The Superior Equipment Co., Bucyrus, Ohio. Side boom, erection booms, swing cranes, blade and bucket backfillers mounted on crawler tractor.

The Thew Shovel Co., Lorain, Ohio. Shovels, draglines, clamshells and hoes.

Ulrich Manufacturing Co., Roanoke, Ill. Ulrich No. 2 tractor shovel for Caterpillar non-oscillating D2 tractors. Ulrich D4-H tractor shovel for Caterpillar non-oscillating D4 tractors.

Unit Crane & Shovel Corp., 6411 W. Burnham St., Milwaukee 14, Wis. Truck cranes.

PROTECTIVE COATINGS

(See Protective Coatings—
Water Supply, Traffic Control and Parks)

PUMPS, PORTABLE

Chain Belt Co., 4640 W. Greenfield Ave., Milwaukee 1, Wis. Water pumps 4,000 to 90,000 gals. per hour. See page 105.

Homelite, Port Chester, N. Y. Self-priming centrifugal pumps, lightweight gasoline engine driven units, sizes 1½', 2" and 3". See pages 263-267.

The Jaeger Machine Co., 702 Dublin Ave., Columbus 16, Ohio. Portable pumps, automatic-priming, centrifugal, 3,000 to 240,000 gph sizes 1½ to 10". See pages 158-161.

Marlow Pumps, Box 200, Midland Park, N. J. Self-priming centrifugal pumps up to 240,000 gph; Mud Hog diaphragm pump for heavy, dirty pumping, plunger sludge pumps for sewage. See pages 361-364.

Schramm, Inc., West Chester, Pa. Pneumatic sump pump, maximum capacity 375 g.p.m. will pump water, sludge and raw sewage. See pages 218-221.

American-Marsh Pumps, Inc., 205 Capital Ave., N.E., Battle Creek, Mich. Portable pumps.

Barnes Mfg. Co., Mansfield, Ohio. Self-priming centrifugal pumps; 8,000 to 100,000 gals. per hour.

C. H. & E. Manufacturing Co., 3810 N. Palmer St., Milwaukee 12, Wis. Diaphragm pumps, single and double 2, 3 and 4" sizes. Self-priming centrifugal, gasoline and electric, 1½ to 8". Sewage and trash pumps 3 to 6".

Ralph B. Carter Co., 196 Atlantic Ave., Hackensack, N. J. Humdinger contractor's self-priming, centrifugal pumps, 1½" to 8", gasoline or electric driven; single and double diaphragm pumps; plunger; plunger sludge pumps; fire-fighting pumps.

Chicago Pneumatic Tool Co., 6 East 44th Street, New York 17, N. Y. Portable sludge and sump pumps.

Cleco Div. of Reed Roller Bit Co., P. O. Box 2119, Houston, Texas. Air operated centrifugal sump pump, 340 gpm against 10 ft. head, 124 gpm against 70 ft. head.

Complete Machinery & Equipment Co., Inc., 36-40 Eleventh St., Long Island City 6, N. Y. Wellpoint pumps and "Complete" wellpoint systems, high-pressure jetting pumps. Also self-priming centrifugals 1½-10" and diaphragm pumps. Also trash pumps.

Construction Machinery Co., Box 120, Waterloo, Ia. Self-priming centrifugal pumps to 10 in., power diaphragm. Also portable fire fighters.

The Deming Co., 15 Broadway, Salem, Ohio. Portable centrifugal pumps.

The Gorman-Rupp Co., Mansfield, Ohio. Complete centrifugal line. Trash-type sump pumps. G-R lightweight pump for dewatering.

Griffin Equipment Corp., 880 E. 141st St., New York 54, N. Y. Pumps.

Hale Fire Pump Co., 749 Spring Mill Ave., Conshohocken, Pa. For fire fighting and dewatering.

Hetherington & Berner, Inc., 731 Kentucky Ave., Indianapolis 7, Ind. Sand and gravel pumps and accessories.

Novo Pump & Engine Co., Lansing 5, Mich. Diaphragm and pressure pumps.

John W. Stang Corp., 8221 Atlantic Ave., P. O. Box 631, Bell, Calif. Centrifugal pumps.

Sterling Machinery Corp., 1950 Santa Fe Ave., Los Angeles 21, Calif. Self-priming centrifugal.

Worthington Corp., Harrison, N. J. Portable self-priming centrifugal pumps.

RADIO

(See page 786)

REFUSE COLLECTION

(See Refuse Trucks, page 766)

REFUSE RECEPTACLES

(See Waste Receptacles)

REINFORCING, WELDED WIRE

Welded wire fabric is produced from cold-drawn steel wire and used for reinforcement for concrete pavement, floors, walls, pipe in the construction of airports, buildings, conduits and reservoirs. It is a prefabricated square or rectangular reinforcement that can be placed quickly from sheets or rolls in continuous strips.

Bethlehem Steel Co., Bethlehem, Pa. Bethlehem concrete reinforcing bars, round and deformed, of new billet steel. Bethlehem wire rope is available in all the sizes, types and constructions needed for power shovels, cranes, draglines. See pages 326, 327; 485.

The Colorado Fuel and Iron Corp., Continental Oil Bldg., Denver, Colo. Welded wire fabric for reinforcing runways and streets. 7-wire galvanized twisted for applications where A.S.T.M. specifications must be met; also general purpose steel strand for lighter applications, See page 1018.

Continental Steel Corp., 1150 So. Main St., Kokomo, Ind. Welded wire reinforcing fabric. See page 1020.

Wickwire Spencer Steel, Div. The Colorado Fuel & Iron Corp., 361 Delaware Ave., Buffalo 2, N. Y. Wickwire rope for elevators, cranes, dragline shovels. See page 1018.

American Steel & Wire Div., U. S. Steel, 970 Rockefeller Bldg., Cleveland 13, Ohio.

Keystone Steel & Wire Co., Peoria 7, Ill.

Laclede Steel Co., Arcade Bldg., St. Louis 1, Mo.

Northwestern Steel & Wire Co., Sterling, Ill.

Pittsburgh Steel Products Division of Pittsburgh Steel Co., Grant Bldg., Box 118, Pittsburgh 30, Pa. Welded wire reinforcing.

Sheffield Steel, Division, Armco Steel Corporation, Sheffield Sta., Kansas City 25, Mo.; Houston, Texas; Tulsa, Okla. Welded wire fabric.

Truscon Steel Division, Republic Steel Corp., Youngstown 1, Ohio. Welded wire fabric.

ROAD BROOMS AND SWEEPERS

Detroit Harvester Co., Implement Div., P. O. Box 231, Zanesville, Ohio. Tractor drawn sweepers for highway cleaning and maintenance, snow removal; 5' and 6' models. See page 157.

W. E. Grace Mfg. Co., 6000 S. Lamar St., Dallas, Texas. Tractor drawn open type 2-way axle driven or motor driven sweeper cleans 80 in. swath. Front-end models sweep 53 in. path. 150 gal. water tank and spray attachment, blower attachment. See page 239.

Littleford Bros., Inc., 457 E. Pearl St., Cincinnati 2, Ohio. Tractor or truck drawn open-type models; No. 108—2-way engine-driven broom for sweeping roads before applying bituminals, for dirt and light snow removal, 7 or 8 ft. brush, sprinkler or blower attachments; No. 118—for wet or dry sweeping and flushing. See pages 169-172.

Little Giant Products, Inc., 1530 N. E. Adams St., Peoria, Ill. Self-propelled sweeper 6'-8' brush. Engine driven tow sweepers Hy-Port and Road Bird 6'-8' brush. Front mounted sweeper 4'-8' brush. See pages 177-180.

M-B Corporation, Box 260, New Holstein, Wis. Complete line of truck mounted and tractor mounted sweepers including both one way and two way sweeping, powered from P.T.O., engine or hydraulic pump and motor. Pull type sweepers also. Tractor type for all popular make tractors. See pages 246, 247; 560; 967.

Rosco Mfg. Co., 3118 Snelling Ave., Minneapolis 6, Minn. Tractor or truck drawn type street cleaner sweeps 8 ft. path to right or left, 310 gal. water tank. For wet or dry street sweeping, flushing, sprinkling, tree spraying, emergency fire fighting, sewer cleaning. Model MBC street cleaner, Model B7 road broom. See pages 197-200.

Standard Steel Works, North Kansas City 16, Mo. Engine driven and traction driven, two-way brooms. See pages 205-208.

Van Brush Mfg. Co., Inc., 327 Southwest Blvd., Kansas City 8, Mo. Special broom cores to your specifications. 15 of the most popular wood type broom cores, all in stock. Specialists in rebuilding, repairing, refilling all makes, types and sizes, 48 hour service. See pages 173-176.

Henke Mfg. Corp., Janesville, Ia. Tractor or truck drawn open type street cleaning or bituminous road construction broom. Available in 7 ft., 8 ft. and 10 ft. models. Furnished as optional equipment with spraybar and flusher.

ROAD WIDENERS

(See Pavers)

ROLLERS, ROAD

Rollers differ in type and in size. Basically, there are five types of rollers: tandem, 3-wheel, pneumatic, sheepsfoot, and grid. Grid rollers are used for primary compaction, and for bituminous pavement salvage. Sheepsfoot rollers are used for primary compaction or where compaction is difficult. Rubber-tired or pneumatic rollers are used for primary and some surface compaction. Three-wheel rollers are used for subbase materials, earth fills and in rolling top material. The tandem roller is a finishing tool, for finished surface compaction.

Rollers are available in a wide range of weights. Tamping rollers are used singly, in two's or in tandem depending on the degree of compaction needed. Three-wheel and tandem rollers are often available in weights variable by the addition of water or sand ballast. The ½-ton tandem roller is used for parks, lawns, tennis courts, ball parks, and often supplements heavier rollers on bituminous work. These small sizes are available as attachments for small utility tractors. For patching, maintenance of parking areas and runways, ½, 1, 1½ and 2-3, 3-5 ton sizes are suitable. The variable-weight tandem roller of 5-8, 8-10½, 8-12 and 10-14 tons are able to do all of the rolling in any city, county or state. Models are available up to 21 tons.

In purchasing a roller consider the kinds of rolling to be done, the amount of compaction needed to do this rolling, volume of work and speed of progress desired. Specifications giving this information: type roller, weight of roller, lbs. compression per square or lineal inch, width of roll, rolling speed, turning radius, traveling speed or means of transportation.

Austin-Western Works, Baldwin-Lima-Hamilton Corp., Aurora, Ill. Variable weight Tandem Rollers, 5-8, 8-12 and 10-14 ton sizes. 3-Wheeled Rollers, 5-7, 6-8, 7-10, 8-11, 10-12 and 12-14 ton sizes. This complete line of rollers (Tandem and 3-Wheeled) is available with Torque Converter Drive, which controls power automatically, increases the life of power unit and clutch, cushions the reversing action, and provides an infinite number of speeds. Modern industrial engines (gas or diesel and either two- or four-speed transmissions optional) furnish a smooth flow of steady power. Effortless, hydraulic power is used for steering. See pages 78-81.

W. E. Grace Manufacturing Co., 6009 S. Lamar St., Dallas, Tex. Self-propelled pneumatic roller has 10-14 tires with 66-93 in. rolling width. Body capacity 75-110 cu. ft., 1,000 gal. water tank available. Sheepsfoot tamping roller, 95-136 ft. per drum, pressure 180-765 psi full. See page 239.

The Huber-Warco Co., 202 N. Greenwood St., Marion, Ohio. Three wheel rollers, 10-14 ton sizes, 6'7" to 7' rolling width, 301-479 lb. compression. Variable-weight tandem rollers—3-5, 5-8, 8-10, 8-12, 10-14 ton sizes, 97-326 lb. compression, 8'2" to 4½' rolling width. See pages 149-152.

Littleford Bros., Inc., 457 E. Pearl St., Cincinnati 2, Ohio. Trail-O-Roller, portable 2-3 ton tandem unit for patching and maintenance, 75-160 psi compaction. Vari-Packer, 4-6 ton portable, hydraulic steering, for construction and maintenance compaction, 100-170 lb. Model 160—3 to 5 ton portable tandem roller with finger-tip controlled power steering and hydraulic powered trailing conversion. See pages 169-172.

Rosco Mfg. Co., 3118 Snelling Ave., Minneapolis 6, Minn. Rosco compaction rollers in 9 or 13 wheel models with special 7.50-15 smooth tread pneumatic tires. See pages 197-200.

Standard Steel Works, North Kansas City 16, Mo. Model 55-1½ to 2½ ton tandem roller for small hot-mix jobs and patching. See pages 205-208.

Acme Iron Works, Cubebra at Expressway, San Antonio, Texas. Tandem 5-8 ton, 8-10 ton variable-weight Ingram roller, 50 in. rolling width, water ballast. Ingram 3-wheel rollers in 5, 6, 8, 10, 12 ton sizes, variable weight.

Acme Road Machinery Co., Frankfort, N. Y. Tandem rollers, 4-10 ton sizes roll 62 in. path, 133-278 lb. compression. 5-10 ton pony rollers, 48-64 in. roller, 219-389 lb. compression. 3-wheel models 5-15 ton sizes, 48 in. roller, 350-437 lb. compression.

American Steel Works, 1211 W. 27th St., Kansas City, Mo. Sheepsfoot and pneumatic tire tamping rollers.

Wm. Bros Boiler & Mfg. Co., 1057 Tenth Ave., S.E., Minneapolis 14, Minn. Self-propelled pneumatic tired rollers.

The Buffalo-Springfield Roller Div., Koehring Co., 1210 Kenton St., Springfield, Ohio. Tandem Rollers: 3-5 ton, standard duty 5-8, 6-9, 8-10, 8-12 10-14 ton, heavy duty 5-8, 6-9, 8-14, 10-16 ton. Three-axle tandem rollers: 13-20 ton. Variable weight 3-wheel rollers: 10-14 12-15 ton. Four-wheel segmented Kompactor: 15 tons.

C. H. & E. Manufacturing Co., 3810 N. Palmer St., Milwaukee 12, Wis. 2-ton variable-weight tandem roller for patching, light road work, rolls 34 in. path; 3-4 ton for sub-grade compaction, parking lots, general utility municipal work. 130-165 psi. Trailer available.

Clyde Iron Works, Inc., Duluth 1, Minn. Model 21 for walks, patching, lawns, parking areas: 2000-2565 lb., 47-67 lb. compression, 32" width.

John R. Cook, P. O. Box 597, Augusta, Ga. Pneumatic-tired ditch roller for compacting backfill. Can be attached to any Caterpillar patrol grader.

Essick Mfg. Co., 1950 Santa Fe Ave., Los Angeles 21, Calif. 1½ to 2, 2-3, 5-8 ton variable-weight tandem rollers. 60-215 lbs. psi, 30-50 in. width. Trailers available. Also vibrating rollers: 28" hand-guided, self-propelled, 32" tandem, 54" tow model.

The Galion Iron Works & Mfg. Co., 1954 South St., Galion, Ohio. Portable and variable weight tandem models 3-20 ton. Trench rollers; 3-wheel rollers, 6-15 ton.

Hyster Co. 2902-63 N.E. Clackamas St., Portland 8, Oreg. Hyster Grid roller, 32 in. width, each drum. For salvaging bituminous pavement, embankment compaction and crushing pit-run material. Total weight 30,000 lbs.

Iowa Manufacturing Co., 916 16th St., Cedar Rapids, Ia. The Compactor, vibrating pneumatic tired rollers.

Pfahler Mfg. Co., Galion, Ohio. Ken-Roll roller, 1 to 3 ton general purpose roller. Compression roll (water ballast) sprinkler tank has 93 gal. capacity.

Seaman-Andwall Corp., 417 N. 25th St., Milwaukee 1, Wis. Rollers; portable, self-propelled, steel, pneumatic. Portable 2-3 ton and 7-10 ton tandem rollers.

Shovel Supply Co., P. O. Box 1369, Dallas, Texas. Portable and tandem, sheepsfoot, tamping, rubber tired: pulled type and self-propelled.

Southwest Welding & Mfg. Co., 3201 West Mission Rd., Alhambra, Calif. Compaction rollers—pneumatic tired mounted in individual weight box—5 to 100 ton capacity. Heavy duty sheepsfoot tamping rollers, 5 x 5 drum, 16,000 to 30,000 lb. weight empty. Light duty sheepsfoot tamping rollers, 40 in. x 4 ft. drum. Solid or removable type feet.

W. Whitney Stueck, Inc., Old Saybrook, Conn. Power rollers: standard model 800-1,200 lb.; all-purpose model 375-1,400 lb.

Tampo Manufacturing Co., 1146 West Laurel St., San Antonio, Tex. Sheepsfoot tamping rollers. 6 models. Towed pneumatic rollers. Self propelled pneumatic tired roller 72". Road broom, towed traction type.

SCRAPERS, ROAD

Used where materials must be moved over distances longer than bulldozer hauls. Drawn by either track-type or wheel-type tractor, depending on terrain and haul distance, scrapers have the ability to dig in-place materials, haul at highest possible speed and spread evenly over a fill or spoil area. Scrapers are available in self-powered or models drawn by separate industrial tractors.

Allis-Chalmers Mfg. Co., 886 S. 70th St., Milwaukee, Wis. Hydraulically operated, rubber-tired, 4 yd.; cable-operated, 6, 8 and 15 yd.; self-propelled, 11 and 15 yds.; self-propelled wagons, (bottom dump), 17 yds., rear dump, 11 yds. See pages 285-288.

The Cleveland Formgrader Co., Mills Road, Avon, Ohio. Subgrade scraper in adjustable widths of 9 to 12 ft., 15 to 20 ft., 18 to 22 ft. Also scratch template for checking subgrade. See pages 166, 167.

LeTourneau-Westinghouse Co., 2301 N. Adams St., Peoria, Ill. Self-propelled Tournapulls, 25, 18, and 9 yd. sizes; tractor drawn cable scrapers, 31, 19, 16, and 10.5 yd. sizes; rear dumps 35, 22, and 11 ton sizes; bottom dumps 18 ton size. See pages 58-63.

Caterpillar Tractor Co., Peoria, Ill. Eight models of scrapers, up to 27 cu. yd. heaped capacity, cable control, open bowl.

Euclid Div., General Motors Corp., 1361 Chardon Rd., Cleveland 17, Ohio. S-7 scraper, 143 hp.; 7 yd. scraper.

The Gledhill Road Machinery Co., 57 S. Lera Rd., Galion, Ohio. Earth moving 1 yd. and 2 yd., two-wheel drawn hydraulically operated.

Root Spring Scraper Co., 545 W. North St., Kalamazoo, Mich. Underbody scraper for street, alley, parking lot maintenance, snow and ice removal.

Southwest Welding & Mfg. Co., 3201 W. Mission Rd., Alhambra, Calif. Road scrapers.

Woolridge Mfg. Div., Of Continental Copper & Steel Industries, Inc., Sunnyvale, Calif. Self-propelled scrapers, self-propelled hauling wagons, tractor-drawn scrapers, cable rippers, cable power control units.

SHOVELS

(See Power Cranes and Shovels)

SNOW LOADERS AND BLOWERS

Snow loaders, designed primarily for this purpose, include the conveyor and the blower types and both will load wet or dry snow. Most conveyor types can be used to load sand, cinders, etc., out of stockpiles for ice control and load other materials during summer months. The blower types have adjustable chutes so that the snow either can be loaded into a truck or can be blown into an adjacent field. This makes it particularly useful for airport snow work. Small snow-throwers also have been developed for use on sidewalks, parking and shipping areas.

Barber-Greene Co., 400 N. Highland Ave., Aurora, Ill. Snow loaders. See pages 73-76.

Gravely Tractors, Inc., Box 78, Dunbar, W. Va. Snow blower for 5 hp tractor unit. May be used with Gravely steering sulky. See page 1001.

The Frank G. Hough Co., 955 Sunnyside Ave., Libertyville, Ill. "Payloader" tractor shovels for loading trucks with snow and other materials. V and One-way plow and rotary plow attachments available. See pages 113-116.

Klauer Manufacturing Co., Dubuque, Ia. Snogo, snow-loaders and rotary plows. See pages 244-245.

LeTourneau-Westinghouse Co., 2301 N. Adams St., Peoria, Ill. Self-propelled, self-feed belt type TraveLoader for snow and other materials. See pages 58-63.

LoDal, Inc., Norway, Mich. Truck self loaders for mounting on truck chassis. Overhead discharge with bucket capacity of 1½ and 2 yd. Cab controlled, loading time 2 min. See pages 162-165.

Mid-Western Industries, Inc., 1009 S. West St., Wichita, Kans. See pages 133-136.

N. P. Nelson Iron Works, Inc., 850 Bloomfield Ave., Clifton, N. J. Snow Loaders, rubber tired mounting: 12 and 20 cu. yd. per min. capacities. Also handle sand, snow, gravel, coal cinders, leaves, without changeover or special attachments. Capacity 3 cu. yd. per min. heavy material, 9-11 ft. discharge heights. See pages 542, 543.

Rivinius, Inc., Eureka, Ill. Rivinius hydraulically-driven Snow Loader, attachment for Caterpillar motor grader. See pages 250, 251.

Shawnee Mfg. Co., Inc., 1947 N. Topeka Ave., Topeka, Kans. Shawnee Special heavy-duty loader for snow removal. See pages 222-225.

Sicard Industries, Inc., Watertown 1, N. Y. Snow blower for clearing airports, highways, city streets, and loading trucks. See pages 110-112; 566.

George Haiss Mfg. Co., Subsidiary of Pettibone-Mulliken Corp., 350 Fifth Ave., New York 1, N. Y. Bucket loaders, snow and coal loaders.

The Maxim Silencer Co., 84 Homestead Ave., Hartford 1, Conn. Maxim Snow Throwers 4.6 to 8 hp. for municipal sidewalk, and comparable use.

Pioneer Gen-E-Motor Corp., 5841 M West Dickens Ave., Chicago 39, Ill. Sno-mover for sidewalks and driveways.

Pneu-Hydro Road Machinery Co., Cadillac, Mich. Sno-loaders, snow plow lifts and cylinders.

Sensation Mower, Inc., Ralston, Nebr. Sno-Blo with 3½ hp. self-propelled engine for paths and crosswalks. Also push type Sno-Blo, 2½ hp.

Ulrich Manufacturing Co., Roanoke, Ill. The Ulrich snow blower for Caterpillar No. 12 and No. 112 motor graders equipped with snow wings.

SNOW PLOWS

Most popular in snow removal work is the truck-mounted displacement plow, one-way type, which will push the snow to the side of the truck. Heavy, tractor, motor-grader or truck mounted V-plows find use where snow is heavy. For really difficult work cities can use special, heavy duty, 4-wheel drive trucks with V-plows and wing plows, with underbody blades and spreaders that apply abrasives.

Small tractors equipped with snow plow blades have been found very useful for sidewalk snow removal. Moldboard glaze applied to plowing surface prevents snow from adhering to metal and reduces friction.

Austin-Western Works, Baldwin-Lima-Hamilton Corp., Aurora, Ill. Giant "V" type snow plows and wings, and rotary type snow plows as attachments for all-wheel drive and all-wheel steer power graders. See pages 78-81.

The Colorado Fuel and Iron Corp., Continental Oil Bldg., Denver, Colo. Dozer, scraper, grader and snow plow blades See page 1018.

Flink Co., Streator, Ill. Snow plows for trucks. See page 217.

Ford Motor Co., Tractor & Implement Div., 2500 E. Maple Rd., Birmingham, Mich. Tractor mounted adjustable blade plows. See pages 209-212.

Good Roads Machinery Corp., Minerva, Ohio. From sidewalk to 12-ton sizes. See pages 126-129.

Gravely Tractors, Inc., Box 78, Dunbar, W. Va., 48" blade-type snow plow attachment. May be used with Gravely Steering Sulky. See page 1001.

LeTourneau-Westinghouse Co., 2301 N. Adams St., Peoria, Ill. V-plows, rotary-type wings and rotary snow plows for Adams motor graders. See pages 58-63.

LoDal, Inc., Norway, Mich. Reversible and one-way plows for use in conjunction with LoDal Truck self-loader. See pages 162-165.

Schramm, Inc., West Chester, Pa. PNEUMATRACTOR, a front end loader, a snow plow, a backfill blade, a backhoe and an air compressor. See pages 218-221.

Wausau Iron Works, Inc., Wausau, Wis. Complete line of snow plows for trucks, graders, wheel-tractors. Hydra clutch pump and Jarp Pum Pac for lifting snow plows. See page 261.

Brighton Steel Co., Stormville, N. Y. Snow plow blades.

Wm. Bros. Boiler & Mfg. Co., 1057 Tenth Ave., S.E., Minneapolis 14, Minn. 36 hp and 200-300 hp rotary snow plows for tractors and trucks. Push type snow plows for trucks and automobiles, 3½ and 6½ hp sidewalk rotary snow plows.

The Burch Corp., Crestline, Oho. Ross snow plows; under truck blades; spreaders for ice control.

Frink Snow Plows, Inc., Clayton, N. Y. Snow plows.

The Galion Iron Works & Mfg. Co., 1954 South St., Galion, Ohio. Snow plow, and wing for Galion motor graders.
The Gledhill Road Machinery Co., 57 S. Lera Rd., Galion, Ohio. Twenty-six models. "V" type, taper-blade and straight-blade types, one-way, reversible type, automatic safety blade trip, hydraulically controlled.
Henke Mfg. Co., Janesville, Ia. "V" type and straight-blade snow plows.
The Jarp Corp., Wausau, Wis. Snow plows for 1 to 4 ton trucks, hydraulic equipment including Jarp Pum Pac and Hydra-Clutch, Norgahn snow plow specialties.
Monarch Road Machinery Co., 1331 Michigan St., N.E., Grand Rapids 3, Mich. Hydraulic power controls.
The Norgahn Co., 406 Eleventh Ave., South, Wausau, Wis. Snow plow specialties—distributed by the Jarp Corp., Wausau, Wis. Moldboard glaze (Beeswax coatting for snow plow moldboards). Wingslide compound (heavy grease resists water and sludging for any exposed metal to metal surface). Special low cold test hydraulic fluid for snow plows.
The Prime-Mover Co., Muscatine, Ia. Snow plow attachment.
The Rocklin Mfg. Co., Grand Ave. at Jennings, Sioux City 7, Iowa. Vee-type snow plow fits most loaders and the rear of tractors for mounting to the 3-point hitch.
Root Spring Scraper Co., 545 W. North St., Kalamazoo, Mich. 41 models of one-way tripping and V-type Sno-Plows.
Walter Motor Truck Co., 1001-19 Irving Ave., Ridgewood 27, L. I., N. Y. Snow fighters.

SNOW REMOVAL—SPECIAL

Gravely Tractors, Inc., Box 78, Dunbar, W. Va. Power-driven snow blower moves any snow from ½ in. to 4 or 5 ft. drifts to either the left or right at any angle. Power-driven brush for snow removal, 38 in. wide; 48 in. wide snow plow. See page 1001.
Brighton Steel Co., Stormville, N. Y. Snow fence with spruce pickets ½ in. thick, 4 ft. high. Snow fence posts of rail steel.
Denning Mfg. Co., Box 1396, Joliet, Ill. Snow fence.
Northfield Iron Co., P. O. Box 30-H, Northfield, Minn. Blizzard-Buster all-steel snow fence.
Tarrant Mfg. Co., 27-29 Jumel St., Saratoga Springs, N. Y. Stainless steel "Scotchman" chemical spreader for ice and snow control.

SPREADERS, AGGREGATE AND ABRASIVES

Spreaders apply fine and coarse aggregate to streets in asphalt seal coating work. They apply abrasives or salt in winter ice control work. These can be small units attached to a dump truck, small utility truck or they can be large, self-contained, truck-mounted equipment. Some do the spreading by a spinner with adjustable baffles controlling the width of spread. Some discharge from a specially designed, trailer mounted trough.

Baughman Mfg. Co., Inc., 157 Shipman Rd., Jerseyville 1, Ill. Cab controlled, self-unloading bodies for spreading cinders, sand, salt and abrasives for ice control. Pull-type spreaders, traction powered, spread in full 360 degree circle under wheels of truck. Hydraulic or chain driven cinder cracker for dump bodies, handle up to ½" rock for skid-proofing winter highways. Three types of endgate spreaders. See page 86.
Flink Co., Streator, Ill. Spreaders for ice control, dust control. See page 217.
Gar Wood Industries, Inc., 36253 Michigan Ave., Wayne, Mich. Spreaders for sand, gravel, slag, etc. adjustable width. See pages 242, 243; 532, 533.
Good Roads Machinery Corp., Minerva, Ohio. Truck mounted and towed-type spreader and complete line to meet every need. See pages 126-129.
W. E. Grace Mfg. Co., 6000 S. Lamar St., Dallas, Texas. For cover stone and for hot or cold asphaltic concrete. See page 239.
The Jaeger Machine Co., 702 Dublin Ave., Columbus 16, Ohio. Self-propelled, handles all types of aggregates and stones including slow-curing emulsions. See pages 158-161.
Standard Steel Works, 16th and Howell, North Kansas City 16, Mo. Gravel spreaders. See pages 205-208.
Wausau Iron Works, Wausau, Wis. Sand and material spreaders for ice control. See page 261.
Brighton Steel Co., Stormville, N. Y. Sand spreaders.
The Burch Corp., Crestline, Ohio. Sanders for tail gate mountings. Truck body spinner type spreaders. Pull type bituminous spreader. Calcium, salt, sand and cinder spreaders. Spreaders for dust control.
Cartwright Industries, P. O. Box 3251 S. Highlands Sta., Birmingham 5, Ala. "Sealcoater" applies bituminous materials and covers the bitumen with aggregate and rolls the aggregate in one operation.
Central Engr. Co., Inc., 4429 W. State St., Milwaukee 8, Wis. Hydraulic tail gate, spreaders for ice control and seal coating.
Construction Equip. Div., Blaw-Knox Co., Mattoon, Ill. Bituminous spreaders.
M. A. Elliotte, P. O. Box 930, Pontiac, Mich. Salt spreaders.
The Fairfield Engineering Co., 842 Chicago Ave., Marion, Ohio. Material spreader for snow and ice control.
Flexible Road Joint Machine Co., Warren, Ohio. Concrete spreaders.
The Gledhill Road Machinery Co., 57 S. Lera Rd., Galion, Ohio. Spreader for ice control. Spreads salt, cinders, calcium chloride, chips.
Highway Equipment Co., Inc., 626 D Ave., N.W., Cedar Rapids, Ia. Sand, salt, and cinder spreaders for all-purpose spreading; material or aggregate spreaders; model as bituminous concrete and aggregate spreader; lime and fertilizer spreaders.
Seaman-Andwall Corp., 417 N. 25th St., Milwaukee 1, Wis. Cement and materials spreaders. "Posi-Feed" Model HY-4 tailgate spreader for ice control.
Swenson Spreader & Mfg. Co., Lindenwood, Ill. Self-feeding, cab controlled material spreaders to fit any dump body.
Tarrant Mfg. Co., 27-29 Jumel St., Saratoga Springs, N. Y. "Scotchman" chemical spreader using bagged or bulk chemicals from any truck.

STREET FLUSHERS

E. D. Etnyre & Co., 200 Jefferson St., Oregon, Ill. Sanitary street flushers. Full or medium stream 800 to 4,000 gallon capacity. Truck or trailer mounted. See pages 106-109.
Municipal Supply Co., 2508 S. Main St., South Bend 23, Ind. "Big 6" street flusher, suitable for truck or semi-trailer mounting, 8 sizes, 800 to 3,000 gallons, can clean 42 foot width. See pages 181-184.
Rosco Mfg. Co., 3118 Snelling Ave., Minneapolis 6, Minn. Truck mounted 1200-1600-2100 gallons capacity. Also 1000 gallons for tractor towing. See pages 197-200.
Seaman-Gunnison Corp., 201 Lynn Ave., Baraboo, Wis. Trailer or truck-mounted flushers. See pages 153-156.
Sicard Industries, Inc., Watertown 1, N. Y. Sicard street flushers, high-speed filling, four jets, for street cleaning, sprinkling or pumping. See pages 110-112; 566.
Standard Steel Works, 16th and Howell, North Kansas City 16, Mo. Street flushers, truck mounted and trailer type. See pages 205-208.
City Tank Corp., 53-09 97th Pl., Corona 68, Long Island, N. Y. Street flushers.

STREET GUTTER CLEANERS

Tarrant Mfg. Co., 27-29 Jumel St., Saratoga Springs, N. Y. Tarco Gutter-Vac for sucking up gutter litter within 24" of the street curb and for use as a vacuum leaf collector.

STREET SWEEPERS

Street sweepers vary from small units with 42-inch main brooms and 54-inch total swath to large 4 cubic yard hopper machines. The small sweepers work well where light sweeping is done in highly congested, confined areas, such as business districts. Newest units have hydraulic-dump hoppers. Most large machines of the pick-up type have been designed to travel at over 15 mph with the hopper full, thus allowing them to carry loads to the final disposal point or a central dumping point, thereby eliminating the rehandling of debris. One pick-up sweeper is available with detachable hopper. Cities, particularly those with a limited budget, use the open street broom type sweepers to clear away debris before applying bituminous materials and for light snow removal. These sweepers are used for regular cleaning of streets and in some cases, where a fogging nozzle is attached, to force debris into a windrow, which is later swept into piles for front-end loader pick-up. Sweepers have a sprinkler system installed for dust control which lengthens the life of the fibre brush due to the action of the water in keeping the brush soaked. The larger machines have been used successfully to pick up excess rock chips in street seal coating work. When purchasing a sweeper, consider uses of the machine, hopper capacity, speeds at which the machine sweeps and travels to and from the dump, width of swath, maneuverability and available attachments. In buying, prices should be compared on the basis of equipment included in the list price. For example, some companies regard headlight, taillights, horn, hydraulic lift, hand throttle and silent muffler as "extras."

Austin-Western Works, Baldwin-Lima-Hamilton Corp., Aurora, Ill. Model "40" motor sweeper—front steer pick up and carry type with 2 cu. yd. hopper. Model "60" motor sweeper—front steer pickup and carry type with 4 cu. yd. hopper. Leaf broom attachment and streamlined cab available as extras. Dual controls NOT required for double gutter broom operation. See pages 78-81.

Mobil-Sweeper Div. of The Conveyor Co., 3260 E. Slauson Ave., Los Angeles 58, Calif. Mobil-Sweeper, self-propelled pickup type. Single gutter broom model cleans 7 ft. 3 in. path. Standard enclosed cab. 2 2/3 cu. yd. hopper, 200 gal. water tank for control of dust. Double gutter broom models available. See page 255.

Municipal Supply Co., 2508 S. Main St., South Bend 23, Ind. Gutter-Snipe, pick-up sweeper cleans 6 ft. path, 2 cu. yd. hopper capacity, self-propelled. 160 gal. water tank for sprayer type dust eliminator. 1¾ to 7 mph sweeping speeds. See pages 181-184.

Shawnee Mfg. Co., Inc., 1947 N. Topeka Ave., Topeka, Kans. Rotary broom. See pages 222-225.

G. H. Tennant Co., 701 N. Highway 100, Minneapolis, Minn. Model 75 sweeps 48" path. Has ratchet dump hopper. Vacuum dust control; automotive steering; gas powered. For removing dirt, dust, loose sand and other light litter from gutters, walks, alleys, parking lots and other relatively smooth areas. Also LP-gas and electric models. See pages 130-132; 957.

Van Brush Mfg. Co., Inc., 327 Southwest Blvd., Kansas City 8, Mo. Rotary and power sweeper broom cores of the popular makes, also gutter brooms; over 15 types in stock. Specialists in rebuilding, repairing all makes, sizes and types, 48 hour service. Rebuilt cores in stock, old cores taken in trade. See pages 173-176.

Wayne Manufacturing Co., 1201 E. Lexington St., Pomona, Calif. Self-propelled pick up sweeper with hopper capacities of 3 and 4 cu. yds. See pages 226-229.

The Elgin Corp., 231 So. LaSalle St., Chicago 4, Ill. Elgin Street King—pick-up sweeper, 8-10 ft. path, 4 cu. yds. capacity, 250-gal. water tank, sweeps up to 10 m.p.h. Dual controls, power steering, cab, leaf piler available as optional equipment. Model Elgin Street King-D (3 cu. yds. capacity) has detachable dirt hopper, eliminating rehandling of sweepings.

M. A. Elliotte, P. O. Box 930, Pontiac, Mich. The Street Master, towed by a truck into which it loads, sweeps a 10' swath.

Modern Power Sweeper Co., 738 N. McKeever Ave., Azusa, Calif. 27", 36" and 48" sweep medium duty models with gutter brush. Also heavy duty riding type 36" and 48" sweep models with self starter engines.

Wilshire Power Sweeper Co., 247 Dundee Ave., Elgin, Ill. 8 self-propelled models sweep 24-48" swaths. Model 1200 for municipalities.

STREET WASHING DETERGENTS

Colgate-Palmolive Co., 105 Hudson St., Jersey City 2, N.J. Street washing detergents.

Monsanto Chemical Co., St. Louis, Mo. Santomerse No. 1, all purpose detergent and wetting agent.

National Aniline Div., Allied Chemical & Dye Corp., 40 Rector St., New York, N. Y. Nacconol.

The Procter & Gamble Distributing Co., 301 E. Sixth St., Cincinnati 1, Ohio. Detergents for washing streets, municipal vehicles and building maintenance.

Wyandotte Chemicals Corp., Michigan Alkali Div., Wyandotte, Mich. Kreelon for flushing streets. Also Pluronic L62, a colorless liquid street washing detergent, foams very little. Available in 5-gallon drums.

STRUCTURAL MATERIALS

Allied Steel & Tractor Products, Inc., 7835 Broadway, Cleveland 5, Ohio. Tool steel bars, rounds, flats, squares, manganese plate, also fabricate items to specification and print. See page 77.

American Bridge Division, U. S. Steel Corp., 525 William Penn Place, Pittsburgh 30, Pa. Structural steel fabricating and erecting. See page 1101.

Bethlehem Steel Co., Bethlehem, Pa. All sizes of American Standard and Wide Flange sections; also structural steel fabrication and erection. See pages 326, 327; 485.

American Steel & Wire Div., U. S. Steel, 802 Rockefeller Bldg., Cleveland 13, Ohio. Highway guard cable.

Joseph T. Ryerson & Son, Inc., 2558 W. 16th St., Chicago, Ill. Steel bars, structural shapes, plates, sheets, tubing, at warehouses in Boston, Buffalo, Chicago, Charlotte, New York (Jersey City, N. J.), Philadelphia, Pittsburgh, St. Louis, San Francisco, Seattle, Spokane.

Timber Structures, Inc., P. O. Box 3782-X, Portland 8, Oreg. Engineered timber arches, beams, trusses, bridges.

TAILGATES, HYDRAULIC

Gar Wood Industries, 36253 Michigan Ave., Wayne, Mich. Frate-Gate, power end-gate for pickup trucks and for 1½ ton and larger platform, stake and utility body trucks. See pages 242, 243; 532, 533.

Fruehauf Trailer Co., Avon Lake, Ohio. Anthony Lift-Gate, hydraulic power or spring powered closing, with or without permanent ramp.

Hercules Galion Products Inc., Galion, Ohio. Hydraulic lift tailgates.

Marion Metal Products Co., Marion, Ohio. Hydrogate, hydraulic elevator tailgate.

TAMPERS

(See Pavement Breakers, Tampers)

TESTING EQUIPMENT, MATERIALS

Loadometer Corp., P. O. Box 4724, Baltimore 11, Md. Compression Test Loadometers for testing concrete and tile products and soils. Model T-50,000 lb. capacity, manually operated.

C. L. Berger & Sons, Inc., 37 Williams St., Boston 19, Mass. Road building and construction instruments.

Bico, Inc., 3116 Valhalla Dr., Burbank, Calif. The Bico-Braun-Dulin Rotarex for rapid, efficient determination of bitumen in paving mixtures. The portable Bico-Porter Sieve Shaker for use in the laboratory or in the field. Also laboratory sample crushers and pulverizers.

Soiltest Inc., 4711 West North Ave., Chicago 39, Ill. Concrete tester. Also scientific apparatus for soils, concrete and asphalt.

TOOLS FOR MAINTENANCE AND REPAIR

(See page 748)

TRACTORS

Allis-Chalmers Mfg. Co., 886 S. 70th St., Milwaukee 1, Wis. Crawler tractors: HD-21, with hydraulic torque converter drive, 204 net engine hp.; HD-16, 141 Belt hp. with standard transmission, or 150 net engine hp. with hydraulic torque converter drive; HD-11, 94 Belt hp.; HD-6, 63 Belt hp. Wheel-type tractors: Model IB with mounting frame, 18 drawbar hp., gasoline powered; Model B, 20.6 drawbar hp. Attachments available. See pages 285-288.

Deere & Co., Moline, Ill. John Deere crawler and wheel-type municipal tractors. See pages 101-104.

Gravely Tractors, Inc., Box 78, Dunbar, W. Va. 5 hp. tractors with 25 attachments: Reel, sickle and rotary mowers; water ballast rollers, power brushes, snow plows, rotary plows, cultivators. 5' seeder-spreader, lawn aerator, lawn sweeper, planter drill. See page 1001.

The Frank G. Hough Co., 955 Sunnyside Ave., Libertyville, Ill. "Payloader" tractor with torque converter, model TM 16,000# hp. drawbar pull; gas or diesel. Model TU 120. 1200# drawbar pull. Attachments. See pages 113-116.

LeTourneau-Westinghouse Co., 2301 N. Adams St., Peoria, Ill. Tournatractor for use with bulldozer, angledozer or snowplow. Two-wheel tractors for use with scrapers. See pages 58-63.

Work Bulls Div., Massey-Harris-Ferguson, Inc., 1721 Packard Ave., Racine, Wis. 5 models—34 to 52 hp. —with 20 integrated front and rear attachments. See pages 213-216.

American Tractor Corp., 800 Ft. Wayne St., Churubusco, Ind. Terratrac 30 to 75 hp. gasoline crawler and 30 to 75 hp. diesel crawler tractors. Terra-Lift 34 hp. gasoline crawler fork-lift, 3,500 lbs. capacity. Also full line of bulldozers, angledozers and shovel loaders for all models of terratrac crawlers.

J. I. Case Co., 700 State St., Racine, Wis. Tractors, wheel type, gasoline powered; four models can be equipped with front mounted loaders, rotary brooms, snow plows and other equipment.

Caterpillar Tractor Co., Peoria, Ill. Diesel track-type tractors—six sizes from 38 to 260 drawbar hp. diesel wheel-type, two 4-wheel sizes, 186 and 300 hp. for use with scraper, for cutting and leveling. One 2-wheel size, 300 hp. for use with scraper. Rippers, track-type tractor-mounted, 4 sizes, up to 5 tooth.

The Eimco Corp., 654 So. 4th West St., Salt Lake City 10, Utah. Tractor with loading or bulldozing attachment.

International Harvester Co., Chicago 1, Ill. Industrial utility wheel tractors, gasoline, diesel and LP Gas. Six sizes, from 10 to 60 drawbar hp. Crawler type tractors, gasoline or diesel, in seven sizes, ranging from 42 drawbar hp to 200 net engine hp with torque converter. All these tractors can be matched with all attachments.

Minneapolis-Moline Co., Box 1050, Minneapolis 1, Minn. Industrial tractors, wheel-type gasoline, LP gas diesel and distillate models for heavy-duty drawbar jobs.

Monarch Road Machinery Co., 1331 Michigan St., N.E., Grand Rapids 3, Mich. Hydraulic power controls; Hy-Lo-Jack fan-belt driven pump and power control unit, and Dyna-Might storage battery powered electric control unit for operating snow plows, road machinery, agricultural implements, etc.

The Oliver Corp., 400 W. Madison St., Chicago 6, Ill. Crawler, gas or diesel, 22 to 133 hp.; wheel type industrial tractors, 4 sizes; with bulldozers, trail-builders, loaders, snow plows, scrapers, winches, shovel loader attachments.

TRAILERS

M B Corp., Box 260, New Holstein, Wis. Tilt bed trailers, 2 to 5 ton capacity. See pages 246, 247; 560; 967.

Birmingham Manufacturing Co., Inc., P. O. Box 1351, Birmingham, Alabama. Heavy duty low bed trailers, standard models 10-100 tons capacity, special models 40-265 tons capacity.

The Cleveland Trencher Co., 20100 St. Clair Ave., Cleveland, Ohio. Single and 2-axle trailers for machinery and material transportation.

Dorsey Trailers, Elba, Ala. Low bed heavy duty trailers, 10 to 100 tons. Platforms, self-loading floats. Tilt-to-Load trailers.

Fayette Manufacturing Co., 400 First St., Fayette, Ohio. Tractor trailers.

Fruehauf Trailer Co., 15 Hackensack Ave., So., Kearny, N. J. Manufacturer's local factory branch for trailers, including vans, reefers, platforms, dumps and tanks. Maintenance and repair of trailers.

Highway Trailer Co., Edgerton, Wis. Pipe, pole and cable reel trailers.

La Crosse Trailer Corp., 415 Gould St., La Crosse, Wis. Complete line heavy duty trailers 8 to 200 tons.

Martin Machine Co., Kewanee, Ill. Heavy duty low bed trailers, 6 to 100 tons capacities.

Omaha Standard, 2411 W. Broadway, Council Bluffs, Ia. Center dump trailer, built in all yardages, for any material, single or tandem, for on or off highway.

Rogers Brothers Corp., Albion, Pa. Low bed duty trailers, from 5 to 150 tons capacity.

Trailmobile Inc., Robertson & 31st, Cincinnati 9, Ohio.

TRASH CONTAINERS

(See Waste Receptacles)

TRENCHING MACHINES

Arps Corp., New Holstein, Wis. Low-cost trencher that digs up to 800 ft. per hour and up to 7 ft. deep, 20 in. wide; 6 ft. bulldozer for backfilling. See pages 64-67.

Badger Machine Co., 1124 W. Fifth St., Winona, Minn. Badger trencher digs up to 600 ft. per hour. Tracklayer or rubber tire models. Road speeds up to 20 mph; capacity 24" wide, 11' deep. Over 50 digging speeds. See pages 87-90.

Barber-Greene Co., 400 N. Highland Ave., Aurora, Ill. Ditch diggers. See pages 73-76.

The Cleveland Formgrader Co., Mills Road, Avon, Ohio. Cleveland Formgrader leaves trench all cut and rolled, ready for forms. See pages 166, 167.

Gar Wood Industries, Inc., 36253 Michigan Ave., Wayne, Mich. Ditchers for laying pipeline, gas lines, water mains, etc. Complete line for all ditching needs. See pages 242, 243; 532, 533.

Mid-Western Industries, Inc., 1009 S. West St., Wichita, Kans. Model "185" Back-Hoe digs 13' deep, dumping height of 7'6". See pages 133-136.

Shawnee Mfg. Co., Inc., 1947 N. Topeka, Topeka, Kans. Shawnee Scout backhoe, 14' reach, 12' digging depth, 12" to 24" widths. Shawnee Ditcher, 7½' digging depth, chine. Shawnee Chief backhoe, effective digging to 14'. Shawnee Hydro-Clam digs 8½' deep up to 36" wide. See pages 222-225.

Sherman Products, Inc., 3200 W. 14 Mile Rd., Royal Oak, Mich. The Sherman Power Digger, hydraulic back-hoe with variety of interchangeable shovels for digging and loading, mounted on Ford and Fordson Major diesel tractor. Digs 10 and 12' below grade, 180° digging arc. See pages 172ABCD

The Charles Machine Works, 617 B Street, Perry, Okla. Ditch Witch lightweight trenchers, 3 models: 2" to 12" straight and cornered trenches to 36" depth.

The Cleveland Trencher Co., 20100 St. Clair Ave., Cleveland, Ohio. Trenching machines for every application.

Earth Equipment Corp., 2036 Sacramento St., Los Angeles 21, Calif. Everett trenchers—Model S series digs 12"-18" wide, 42" deep at 1½ ft. to 5 ft. per minute; Model 60 series digs 12"-18" wide, 60" deep at 1½ ft. to 5 ft. per minute. Both trenchers mounted on Ferguson, Ford-Ferguson, Ford or Massey-Harris tractors.

Energy Farm Eqpt. Co., Monticello, Ia. Hydraulic truck-mounted backhoe for loading and digging, digs up to 11 ft. deep.

Henry Mfg. Co., Inc., 1700 N. Clay St., Topeka, Kans. Backhoes, tractor shovels, backfill blades.

The Mississippi Engineering Co., Inc., Ground Mound, Iowa. Tractor-mounted trencher, digs up to 5½' deep, 7½" or 10" wide up to 350 ft. per hour.

Ottawa Steel Div., L. A. Young Spring & Wire Corp., Ottawa 60, Kansas. Heavy duty deep digger backhoe—digs 11 ft. deep.

The Parsons Co., Newton, Ia. Trenchliners, both wheel and ladder type, full crawler mounted and pneumatic tire mounted for sewer, water, gas, drainage, conduit installation, and service connections. Five models from 5 to 17 ft. digging depth and from 8 to 72 in. digging widths. Either gasoline or diesel power.

Salem Tool Co., So. Ellsworth Ave., Salem, Ohio. McCarthy rock and earthboring trench machine drills at zero to 6 ft. per minute. Eliminates cutting pavements.

Vermeer Manufacturing Co., Pella, Iowa. Model 4T Pow-R-Ditcher, digs 6" to 14" wide and 4½' deep. Model 524 T Pow-R-Ditcher, digs 6" to 24" wide and 6' deep.

TROWELERS

(See Concrete Finishers, Trowelers, page 734.)

TRUCK AND TRACTOR ACCESSORIES

Allied Steel & Tractor Products Inc., 7835 Broadway Ave., Cleveland 5, Ohio. Alloy wear resisting rail plates to repair worn tractor track links. Also tractor grip-lugs for increased traction efficiency. See page 77.

Exide Automotive Div., 42 S. 15th St., Philadelphia 2, Pa. Exide storage batteries for automobiles, trucks, buses, snow plows, and all other storage battery purposes. See page 987.

Fulton Bag & Cotton Mills, P. O. Box 198, New Orleans 3, La. Covers for sanitation and other municipal vehicles. See page 991.

Gar Wood Industries, Inc., 36253 Michigan Ave., Wayne, Mich. Truck mounted winches, cranes and pole derricks. Frate-Gate, power end-gate for pickup trucks and for 1½ ton and larger platform, stake and utility body trucks. Snowlift, hydraulic snow plow controls. See pages 242, 243, 532, 533.

LoDal Inc., Norway, Mich. Hydraulic truck loader mounts on any 2-ton dump truck. See pages 162-165.

United States Rubber Co., Rockefeller Center, New York 20, N. Y. Complete line of passenger and heavy service tires and tubes. Also tractor and heavy equipment tires and tubes. Industrial pneumatic and solid tires. See page 1121.

Brighton Steel Co., Stormville, N. Y. Cross chains, chain sets and tow chains.

Delco-Remy Div., General Motors Corp., Anderson, Ind. A.C.-D.C. charging systems (alternators) and extra-output D.C. generators for fire, police, and public conveyance vehicles. Maximum output 180 amperes. Delco batteries for above applications.

Detroit Automotive Products Corp., 8701 Grinnell Ave., Detroit 13, Mich. Thornton four-rear-wheel tandem drive; Super Load-Booster dead axle tandem of the "pusher" type; NoSpin differential designed to replace conventional differential in truck axles to prevent "wheel-spin."

Federal Sign and Signal Corp., 8704 S. State St., Chicago 19, Ill. Blue, red, amber lens lights for snow plows, road graders and other maintenance and service equipment including the Beacon Ray and Fire Ball 360° revolving lights.

The Goodyear Tire & Rubber Co., Inc., 1144 E. Market St., Akron 16, Ohio. Batteries for all types of ground vehicles. Also brake lining and tires and tubes.

Highway Safety Appliances, Div. of NAPCO Industries, Inc., 834 N. 7th St., Minneapolis, Minn. Electric sanders for trucks, buses, trailers and cars.

Highway Trailer Co., Edgerton, Wis. Winches, drum type; pole derricks.

Hyster Company, 2902-68 N.E. Clackamas St., Portland 8, Oregon. Towing winches for use with Caterpillar tractors.

Lee Engineering Co., 266 Armistice Blvd., Pawtucket, R. I. Hydraulic tire demounters for all size truck tires, 3 models. Hydraulic service jack, 2-ton capacity. Portable, hydraulic, elevator-type lifts.

Leece-Neville Co., 1374 E. 51 St., Cleveland 5, Ohio. Alternator system for cars, school buses, trucks, police cruisers, 25 to 40 amperes at idle speed of most engines. Available with transformer giving 110 volts A.C. for such accessories as floodlights, small power tools, emergency radios.

The Julian A. McDermott Corp., 40-22 National St., Corona, N. Y. Work-warning and safety lights and flashers, vehicle; and battery operated.

Monarch Road Machinery Company, 1351 Michigan Street, N.E., Grand Rapids 3, Michigan. HY-LO-JACK, HY-LO-JEEP, DYNA-MIGHT hydraulic power controls for municipal trucks, snow plows, brooms. DYNA-CHUTE electric hydraulic power controls for operating discharge chute on ready-mix trucks.

Prehy Company, 420 Lexington Ave., New York 17, N. Y. Machines for sandblasting auto fenders, wheels, rusted steel, deteriorated concrete.

Phoenix Products Co., 4727 N. 27th St., Milwaukee 9, Wis. Sturdilite heavy-duty flood lamps for service on shovels, excavators, drag-lines, road-building equipment, locomotive cranes, tractors; 6-8, 12-16, 24-28, and 110-120 voltages.

Trippe Mfg. Co., 133 N. Jefferson St., Chicago 6, Ill. Red warning lights, flashing, oscillating and still.

Tulsa Winch Div., 815 E. First St., Tulsa 20, Okla. Tulsa winches in 34 models, 6,500 to 80,000 pounds for use on all makes and sizes of trucks and crawler tractors.

Tuthill Spring Co., Chicago 7, Ill. Leaf springs for vehicles.

Ward's Trucksign Transfers, 8504 Lyndon Ave., Detroit 38, Mich. Complete truck and equipment lettering service by transfer. Ward's Trucksign Transfers—multicolored, any shape in sizes to 20 x 30 in. Application kit contains varnish, roller, squeegee, brushes.

TRUCKS, DUMP AND SPECIAL BODIES

Gar Wood Industries, Inc., 36253 Michigan Ave., Wayne, Mich. Dump bodies and hoists of all sizes and types for installation on trucks and trailers. See pages 242, 243; 532, 533.

The Heil Co., 3042 W. Montana, Milwaukee 1, Wis. Bodies and hoists, both light and heavy duty dump bodies, rock bodies, for all makes of trucks and for all purposes, twin-arm single and twin-cylinder, conversion, and telescopic hoists. Colectomatic garbage and refuse collection units; 16 and 20 cu. yd. capacities. See pages 488-491.

Ingersoll Kalamazoo Div., Borg-Warner Corp., 1810 N. Pitcher St., Kalamazoo, Mich. Load Lugger is a one-man operated, self-loading vehicle consisting of truck, hoist and detachable leak-proof containers suited for most types of loading and hauling and does work of several conventional trucks. See pages 497-500.

Sicard Industries, Inc., Waterown 1, N. Y. Heavy-duty trucks, two and four wheel traction models available. Snow removers, refuse collectors, flushers. See pages 110-112; 566.

American-Coleman Co., Littleton, Colo. All wheel drive trucks.

Asplundh Chipper Co., 505 York Rd., Jenkintown, Pa. Asplundh truck body mounted on any 1½ or 2 ton standard chassis. Crew compartment and storage.

Boyertown Auto Body Works, Inc., Boyertown, Pa. Panel police patrol, ambulances, rescue, utility, canteen and service units.

Chevrolet Motor Div., General Motors Corp., 3044 W. Grand Blvd., Detroit 2, Mich. Complete trucks; chassis for special equipment.

Cook Bros. Eqpt. Co., 3334 San Fernando Rd., Los Angeles 65, Calif. Heavy duty trucks. Dump bodies, hoists, truck equipment.

Dempster Brothers, Inc., Knoxville 17, Tenn. Truck mounted DEMPSTER-DUMPSTER Hoisting Unit with detachable containers for all types material.

Dixie Tallyho, Inc., Fairburn, Ga. One piece unit which converts a standard ½-ton pickup truck to a 10-man station wagon. Tirematic tire removal units; tire jacks.

Federal Motor Truck Co., 5780 Federal Ave., Detroit 9, Mich. Conventional and 6-wheeler models.

The Four Wheel Drive Auto Co., Clintonville, Wis. FWD 4 and 6 wheel drive motor trucks, 1½ to 16 tons, normal rating.

GMC Truck & Coach Div., 660 S. Blvd., East, Pontiac, Mich.

Gar-Bro Mfg. Co., 2415 E. Washington Blvd., Los Angeles 21, Calif. 1-ton load, or 11 cu. ft. power cart. Dump Hopper Body for hauling concrete and other materials on ramps, runways, and into other inaccessible places. Gasoline powered.

Hercules Steel Products Co., Galion, Ohio. Low mounted truck body and bulldog hoist for maintenance and refuse removal. Hydraulic hoists and dump bodies.

Highway Trailer Co., Edgerton, Wis. Truck bodies, utility.

International Harvester Co., Chicago 1, Ill. International trucks with bodies and styles for every municipal use.

Mack Trucks, Inc., 1355 W. Front St., Plainfield, N. J. Mack vehicles in such forms as dumpers, flushers, as snow plows, catch-basin cleaners, tower trucks, and wreckers.

The Marion Metal Products Co., Marion, Ohio. Dump truck bodies and hoists.

Marmon-Herrington Co., Inc., 1511 W. Washington St., Indianapolis 7, Ind. All-wheel-drive trucks.

The Prime-Mover Co., Muscatine, Ia. Prime-Mover, wheelbarrow type dump hopper of 10 cu. ft. capacity, interchangeable with platform body in few seconds; 50-inch steel grader blade attachment. Also Model M30, 18 cu. ft., 1½ ton bulk handling truck with hydraulic torque converter drive. Dumping hopper, flatbed or special bodies available.

Walter Motor Truck Co., 1001-19 Irving Ave., Ridgewood 27, L. I., N. Y. Tractor trucks.

The White Motor Co., 842 E. 79th St., Cleveland 1, Ohio. Chassis for sprinklers, fire apparatus, police rescue units.

Willys Motors, Inc., 940 N. Cove Blvd., Toledo 1, Ohio. 4-wheel drive 'Jeep' trucks and 'Jeep' utility vehicles.

TRUCK TAILGATES

(See Tailgates, Hydraulic)

WASTE RECEPTACLES

The Bennett Mfg. Co., Alden, N. Y. Bennett Bilt self-closing waste receptacles. See pages 93-96.

Cyclone Fence Dept., American Steel & Wire Div., U. S. Steel Corporation, Waukegan, Ill. Wire mesh rubbish baskets. See pages 148; 395; 1012, 1013.
W. E. Grace Mfg. Co., 6000 S. Lamar St., Dallas, Texas. Street-cleaners' carts, rubber tired. See page 239.
United Metal Cabinet Corp., 14th & Laurel Sts., Pottsville, Pa. Self-closing receptacles, swing top, removable container. See pages 193-196.
Mills Engr. Co., 2520 W. 8th St., Los Angeles 57, Calif. Mills rust-proof aluminum waste receptacles require no paint, no inner linings.
Norwich Wire Works, Inc., 47 Collins Court, Norwich, N. Y.
Rochester Can Company, Rochester 9, N. Y.
Sydell Manufacturing, Inc., 1211 S. Blvd., Charlotte, N. C. Sydell waste receptacles can be suspended on walls and standards. Holds 23 gals. or 3½ cu. ft.
Tarrant Mfg. Co., 27-29 Jumel St., Saratoga Springs, N. Y. Street refuse cans and can carriers.
Wheeling Corrugating Co., Wheeling, W. Va.
The Witt Cornice Co., 2118 Winchell Ave., Cincinnati, Ohio.

WRECKERS

Ernest Holmes Co., 2505 E. 43rd St., Chattanooga, Tenn. 6, 8, 12, 20, 30 ton wreckers, light pick-up to heavy-duty handling. See pages 142-145.
Weld-Built Body Co., Inc., 5903 Preston Court, Brooklyn 34, N. Y. Wreckers, 12 models ranging from 3 to 20 tons.

Tools for Maintenance and Repair

BUILDINGS, PREFABRICATED

(See page 786)

CONCRETE CUTTERS

Clipper Mfg. Co., 2813 Warwick, Kansas City 8, Mo. Concrete and asphalt saws. Masonry saws. Concrete, asphalt and masonry cutting diamond blades. Wet and dry abrasive blades. See pages 240, 241.
Felker Mfg. Co., Torrance, Calif. Felker Di-Met concrete cutters and segmented diamond blades. Cutters for all types of abrasive materials. See pages 118-121.
Tri-Line Co., 921 Carroll St., Racine, Wis. Tri-Line concrete cutter with diamond cutting blades for fast cut to 13". See pages 252, 253.
Cutcrete Mfg. Corp., 9530 East Rush St., El Monte, Calif. Concrete sawing, breaking and finishing equipment.
Concut Sales, Inc., 331 N. Santa Anita Ave., Arcadia, Calif. "Concut and Jointmaster concrete sawing machines and blades." Precision Bump Cutter and Concut masonry saws; diamond and abrasive blades.
Diamond Tool Associates, P. O. Box 85, 940 E. El Segundo Blvd., Hawthorne, Calif. Boart diamond blades for masonry and concrete cutting.
Joint Saw Co., 30 E. Santa Clara Ave., Arcadia, Calif. Multiple blade saws for sawing weakened plane joints in highways, airport runways and strips.
Rotary Concrete Drill Co., Pasadena, Calif. Rotary drills for cutting through concrete, brick or stone.

CONCRETE GUNS, GROUTERS

Air Placement Equipment Company, 1005A West 24th Street, Kansas City, Mo. Manufacturers of Airplaco concrete gunning equipment, including the Bondactor, Nucretor and Mix-Elvator. See page 68.
Prehy Company, 420 Lexington Ave., New York 17, N. Y. Pneumatic grouting and material placing equipment for arresting ground settlement and sealing leaks and road grouting.
True Gun-All Equipment Corp., Midstate Bldg., Tulsa, Okla. A wet-mix machine for pneumatically applying concrete and cementitious materials.

CUTTERS, BOLT, CHAIN, ETC.

C. H. & E. Manufacturing Co., 3810 N. Palmer St., Milwaukee 12, Wis. Bar cutters and benders up to 1¾" capacity.
H. K. Porter Inc., Somerville 43, Mass. Cutters: bolt, rod, wire, cable, chain.

DRILLS

Greenlee Tool Co., 2136 Twelfth St., Rockford, Ill. Automatic push drills, brace drills, etc. See pages 333-336.
Pippin Construction Eqpt. Co., Inc., White River Jct., Vt. Rock drill attachment carries a 3", 3½" or 4" drifter of the wagon drill type mounted at the end of the dipper stick of the Excavator. See pages 248, 249.
Schramm, Inc., West Chester, Pa. Hand held rock drills, wagon drills, towing type and self-propelled, self-powered. See pages 218-221.
Barco Mfg. Co., 500 Hough St., Barrington, Ill. Portable gasoline drills.
The Black and Decker Mfg. Co., Towson 4, Md. Portable electric drills, drill stands.
Brunner & Lay Rock Bit of Philadelphia, Inc., 2514 E. Cumberland St., Philadelphia, Pa.; Brunner & Lay Rock Bit of Asheville, Inc., Sweeten Creek Rd., Asheville, N. C. Paving breaker: moil points and chisel bits, asphalt cutters and concrete busters, pipe drivers, clay spades, tampers, rock bits.
Chicago Pneumatic Tool Co., 6 East 44th Street, New York 17, N. Y. Portable air and electric.
Cleco Div. of Reed Roller Bit Co., P. O. Box 2119, Houston, Texas. Air operated drills and small rock drills.
Complete Machinery & Equipment Co., Inc., 36-40 11th St., Long Island City 6, N. Y. "Pinazza" flexible shaft driven heavy rock drills, gasoline or electric drive.
Cummins Portable Tool, Div. of John Oster Mfg. Co., 5055 N. Lydell Ave., Milwaukee 17, Wis. Portable electric drills.
Gardner-Denver Co., 100 Williamson St., Quincy, Ill. Drills.
Mall Tool Co., Div. of Remington Arms Co., Inc., 25000 S. Western Ave., Park Forest, Ill. Drills, portable electric and pneumatic for drilling holes in wood or metal, ¼ to 1¼".
McCulloch Motors Corp., 6101 W. Century Blvd., Los Angeles 45, Calif. Earth drills, 9 hp.
Mobile Drilling, Inc., 960 N. Pennsylvania St., Indianapolis 4, Ind. Earth, auger-type and core drills.
Pioneer Gen-E-Motor Corp., 5841 M West Dickens Ave., Chicago 39, Ill. Pincor Blue Diamond portable electric drills, ¼" and ½".
Portable Electric Tools, Inc., 320 W. 83rd St., Chicago 20, Ill. Pet and Shopmate electric drills, ¼ inch. Also ⅜-inch and ½-inch models.
Syntron Co., 431 Lexington Ave., Homer City, Pa. Gasoline rock hammer drill.
Termite Drills, Inc., 99 N. Lotus Ave., Pasadena 8, Calif. Termite rotary masonry drills.
Thor Power Tool Co., 181 N. State St., Aurora, Ill. Portable air and electric drills, heavy or light duty, ¼, 5/16, ⅜, ½, ¾, ⅞, or 1¼". Drill accessories.
Worthington Corp., Harrison N. J. Wagon and rock drills.

EARTHBORING

Tel-E-Lect Products, Inc., 10027 Minnetonka Boulevard, Minneapolis 26, Minn. Earth augers dig holes 8" to 20" in diameter and up to 8' deep. Hydraulic and mechanical digging machines. See page 835.
Allis-Chalmers, Buda Div., Harvey, Ill. Earth boring machines for tree transplanting, fence post holes, wide variety of municipal and other applications.
M. J. Crose Mfg. Co., Inc., 2715 Dawson Rd., Tulsa, Okla. Crose auger-type under-road boring machine for installing and casing pipe up to and including 34" diameters.

Bucyrus-Erie Co., 1046 Monroe Ave., S. Milwaukee, Wis. All-hydraulic Model H-3 and H-5 Hydrocranes with hydraulic earth auger. Available in sizes ranging from 3 to 28" in diameter. Maximum digging depth 40'.
Highway Trailer Co., Edgerton, Wis. Earth boring machines.
Hydrauger Corp., Ltd., 681 Market St., San Francisco 5, Calif. Earth boring machines.
Industrial Supply Co., Irwin, Pa. Earthworm boring machine powered by 6-hp motor drills 1' per minute using 2 or 2½" bit. For drilling for water or gas lines under city sewers.
Ka-Mo Tools, Inc., 1845 S. 55th Ave., Cicero 50, Ill. Earthboring tool for pole and post holes. Also horizontal and angular boring.
Lube Jack Co., P. O. Box 1100, Santa Monica, Calif. Earthworm boring units bore up to 6-in. hole at 1½ ft. per min., 150 ft. in length. Automatic warning of underground hazard. See page 465.
Mall Tool Co., Div. of Remington Arms Co., Inc., 25000 S. Western Ave., Park Forest, Ill. Underwalk and driveway borer.
Mobile Drilling, Inc., 940 N. Pennsylvania St., Indianapolis, Ind. The B-36 combination rotary, auger and percussion drill rig with hydraulic feed of 8,000 lbs. pressure.
Petersen Engineering Co., 460 Kifer Rd., Santa Clara, Calif. Double-helix earth auger fits all makes of earth boring machines. In 25 sizes 6" to 6' in diameter. Shot hole drill heads 2½" to 10" in diameter.
Salem Tool Co., So. Ellsworth Ave., Salem, Ohio. McCarthy rock and earthboring trench machine, and also earth augers of 1¼ to 60" in diameter.

GRINDERS

The Black and Decker Mfg. Co., Towson 4, Md. Bench and portable grinders.
Chicago Pneumatic Tool Co., 6 E. 44th St., N. Y. 17, N. Y. Portable air & electric grinders.
Cleco Div. of Reed Roller Bit Co., P. O. Box 2119, Houston, Texas. Rotary type portable pneumatic grinders, 3,000 to 20,000 rpm; wire brush attachments available.
Portable Electric Tools, Inc., 320 83rd St., Chicago 20, Ill. Bench grinders, ⅓ and ½ hp.
Stow Mfg. Co., Binghamton, N. Y. Concrete grinding machines, portable.
Thor Power Tool Co., 181 N. State St., Aurora, Ill. Portable grinders, 4 to 6" cup; bench grinders 6 to 10" cup. Completely ball bearings.

GROUTERS

(See Concrete Guns, Grouters)

HAMMERS

Arrow Mfg. Co., Box 4120 South Denver Sta., Denver, Colo. Arrow mobile hydraulic hammer for breaking concrete, cutting asphalt, compacting trench backfill, driving posts and piling.
Barco Mfg. Co., 500 Hough St., Barrington, Ill. Portable gasoline hammers.
The Black and Decker Mfg. Co., Towson 4, Md. Portable electric hammers and hammer tools.
Cleco Div. of Reed Roller Bit Co., P. O. Box 2119, Houston, Texas. Cleco chipping hammers in 47 different sizes and styles.
Complete Machinery & Equipment Co., Inc., 36-40 Eleventh St., Long Island City 6, N. Y. "Pinazza" flexible shaft driven demolition hammers, gasoline or electric drive.
Dotmar Industries, 502 Hanselman Bldg., Kalamazoo, Mich. Pneumatic hammers.
Master Vibrator Co., 149 Stanley Ave., Dayton 1, Ohio. Master "Power-Blow" electric hammers.
McKiernan-Terry Corp., 19 Park Row, New York 38, N.Y. Single and double acting pile hammers.
Ottawa Steel Div., L. A. Young Spring & Wire Corp., Ottawa 60, Kans. Hydra-Hammer, self-propelled one man tool, to break concrete, cut asphalt and to tamp backfill in trenches.
Thor Power Tool Co., 181 N. State St., Aurora, Ill. Thor portable electric hammer. Sling shot drive gives 1,600 blows per minute. Hammer accessories.
Vulcan Iron Works, Inc., 327 N. Bell Ave., Chicago 12, Ill. Pile-driving hammers.

LIFTING, HOISTS

Blackhawk Mfg. Co., 5325 W. Rogers St., Milwaukee 46, Wis. Hydraulic jacks, 1½ to 100 tons.
Burtchaell Heating Co., Hoist Div., 2944 S.E. Powell, Portland 2, Oreg. Portable hoists powered by truck battery.
Chicago Pneumatic Tool Co., 6 East 44th St., New York 17, N. Y. Pneumatic chain hoists.
Chisholm-Moore Hoist Div., Columbus McKinnon Chain Corp., Fremont Ave., Tonawanda, N. Y. Pullers; hoists, hand or electric with or without trolleys; overhead cranes.
Coffing Hoist Div. (Duff-Norton Co.), Danville, Ill. Ratchet lever hoists, electric hoists, spur gear hoists.
The Harrington Co., Gravers Rd. at the Turnpike, Plymouth Meetings, Pa. Hand and electric chain hoists.
Hyster Co., 2902-63 N.E. Clackamas St., Portland 8, Oreg. Industrial fork lift trucks, 1,000 lb. to 20,000 lb. capacity, gasoline, LP-Gas or diesel power, complete line of attachments.
Reading Crane and Hoist Corp., 2100 Adams St., Reading, Pa. Traveling cranes, chain and electric hoists.
The Rocklin Mfg. Co., Grand Ave. at Jenning St., Sioux City 2, Iowa. Tractor crane lifts up to 1000 lb. & reaches to 6½ ft.
Sasgen Derrick Co., 3101 W. Grand Ave., Chicago 22, Ill. Hoists, derricks and winches.
Unit Mfg. Co., 69 S. 13th St., Minneapolis 13, Minn. Truck hoist for hydrants. Portable cranes, lift trucks and hydraulic cylinders.
The Yale & Towne Mfg. Co., Roosevelt Blvd., Philadelphia 15, Pa. Industrial hoists, industrial fork lift trucks—hand, electric, gasoline or propane powered.

PIPE BENDING MACHINES

Greenlee Tool Co., 2136 Twelfth St., Rockford, Ill. Hand benders and hydraulic for pipe, tubing, and conduit. See pages 333-336.
American Pipe Bending Machine Co., Inc., Poultney, Vt. Pipe bending machines.
Blackhawk Mfg. Co., 5325 W. Rogers St., Milwaukee 46, Wis. Pipe benders, hydraulic, 10 to 20 tons.

PIPE CUTTING AND TAPPING MACHINES

James B. Clow & Sons, Inc., P. O. Box 6600-A, 201-209 N. Talman Ave., Chicago 80, Ill. Strickler pipe cutter. See pages 270-275.
Hays Mfg. Co., 12th and Liberty Sts., Erie, Pa. Tapping machines. See page 436.
The Toledo Pipe Threading Machine Co., 1425 Summit St., Toledo 4, Ohio. Geared pipe cutters 2½ to 12" pipe. See page 449.
Beaver Pipe Tools, Inc., 349-649 Dana Ave., Warren, Ohio. Beaver thin-wheel pipe cutters for pipe ⅛ to 4". Beaver automatic knife pipe cutters for pipe ⅛ to 2", hand or power use. Also abrasive cut-off machines for the quick cutting of pipe of all kinds.
Ellis & Ford Mfg. Co., 2423 Goodrich, Ferndale 20, Mich. Ellis pipe cutter for cutting large sizes of pipe. Cutters for 4 to 12" pipe available.
Mueller Co., 512 W. Cerro Gordo St., Decatur, Ill. Tapping machines.
The Ridge Tool Co., Elyria, Ohio. Pipe cutters for 1 to 6" pipe. Special 4 wheel cutter for cutting pipe in close quarters up to 4 inches.
The A. P. Smith Mfg. Co., East Orange, N. J. Tapping drilling machines, 2" through 42," pipe cutting machines, 4" through 48".
Spring Load Mfg. Corp., 3610 First Ave., So., Seattle 4, Wash. Pipe cutters for cast iron, steel, vitreous clay and asbestos-cement pipe.
The E. H. Wachs Co., 1525 N. Dayton St., Chicago 22, Ill. Wachs national pipe saw cuts steel or cast iron pipe from 10" to 48" diameter. Also Wachs National pipe tapper. Wachs Guillotine saw cuts cast-iron or steel pipe 2 to 8-inch diameter. Wachs Strickler ratchet type pipe cutters for 2½" to 24" diameter.
The Welsbach Corp., Kitson Valve Div., Westmoreland and Stokley Sts., Philadelphia 29, Pa. Tapping machines for water main insertions of corporation stops under pressure.

PIPE PUSHERS

Greenlee Tool Co., 2136 Twelfth St., Rockford, Ill. Hydraulic pipe pushers, two sizes, for pipe up to 4"; for larger pipe, drainage ducts, concrete sewer pipe, etc. See pages 333-336.
Giant Mfg. Co., Council Bluffs, Ia. Pipe pushers.
Hydrauger Corp., Ltd., 681 Market St., San Francisco 5, Calif. Pipe pushers.

Lube Jack Co., P. O. Box 1100, Santa Monica, Calif. Earthworm boring units, use pipe as drill and leave as permanent installations. Bores 1000' of underground line per gal. of gasoline.

The Trojan Mfg. Co., 1112 Race Dr., P. O. Box 328, Troy, Ohio. Pipe puller and pusher.

PIPE THREADERS

The Toledo Pipe Threading Machine Co., 1425 Summit St., Toledo 4, Ohio. Bolt die stock set for threading bolts ¼ to 1"; ratchet pipe-threading devices ⅛ to 3" pipe; geared threaders 2½ to 12" pipe. See page 449.

Beaver Pipe Tools, Inc., 349-649 Dana Ave., Warren, Ohio. Complete line of hand and electric tools for threading pipe, bolts and conduit.

The Ridge Tool Co., Elyria, Ohio. Pipe threaders for iron, steel, brass or copper pipe of 1 to 2"; handy threaders for ⅛ to 2" pipe.

PIPE TOOLS, MISCELLANEOUS

Aeroil Products Company, Inc., 50 Wesley St., South Hackensack, N. J. Thawing and heating torches. Lead melting and compound pots. See pages 69-72.

Hauck Mfg. Co., 124-136 Tenth St., Brooklyn 15, N. Y. Thawing and melting torches; lead melting furnaces on legs and wheels; compound melting furnaces for melting joint compounds; the new Speed-Master melting kettle; the standard under-fired kettle. For gas and oil. See pages 138-141.

Hays Mfg. Co., 12th and Liberty Streets, Erie, Pa. Tapping and drilling machines. See page 436.

The Toledo Pipe Threading Machine Co., 1425 Summit St., Toledo 4, Ohio. Reamers ⅛ to 3" pipe, and pipe vises ⅛ to 4½" pipe. Power drives for electric operation of threading and cutting devices, and for opening or closing gate valves and sluice gates. See page 449.

Beaver Pipe Tools, Inc., 349-649 Dana Ave., Warren, Ohio. Beaver pipe and bolt machines and pipe reamers.

Henke Mfg. Corp., Janesville, Iowa. Culvert band tool for pulling and spreading.

Hydrauger Corp., Ltd., 681 Market St., San Francisco 5, Calif. Horizontal earth boring tools, 3 models boring from 2 to 14½" in diameter.

Mueller Co., 512 W. Cerro Gordo St., Decatur, Ill. Tapping and drilling machines.

The Ridge Tool Co., Elyria, Ohio. Pipe tools for city maintenance. Pipe wrenches including compound leverage wrench. Pipe vises equipped with pipe rest and benders.

Salem Tool Co., So. Ellsworth Ave., Salem, Ohio. Rock-boring machine for laying conduit, gas, water and small sewer lines.

Spring Load Mfg. Corp., 3610 First Ave., So., Seattle 4, Wash. Model B tenon tool makes all cuts and profiles necessary for asbestos-cement pipe installations. Also gravity grip pipe vises.

Thor Power Tool Co., 181 N. State St., Aurora, Ill. ¼ or ⅜ inch tappers.

SAWS

Gravely Tractors, Inc., Box 78, Dunbar, W. Va. Chain and circular saw. See page 1001.

Homelite, Port Chester, N. Y. High-cycle electric chain saw for limbing, buckling or felling trees, powered by a Homelite generator. Gasoline engine driven chain saw, sizes 12", 14", 17", 18", 20", 21", 23", 25", 28", 30", 33", 38", 44", 50" & 60", one-man models; 14" and 18" bow saws. See pages 263-267.

Asplundh Chipper Co., 505 York Rd., Jenkintown, Pa. Asplundh brush saw 2 HP motor, Model 54N, 36 lb., 70" length.

Atkins Saw Div., Borg-Warner Corp., 402 South Illinois St., Indianapolis 9, Ind. Chamfer chain for all makes of chainsaws.

The Black and Decker Mfg. Co., Towson 4, Md. Portable electric saws.

C. H. & E. Manufacturing Co., 3810 N. Palmer St., Milwaukee 12, Wis. Woodcutting band saws, gasoline and electric, 20" size. Table saws (saw rigs)—capacities to 6"—gasoline or electric.

Chicago Pneumatic Tool Co., 6 East 44th St., New York 17, N. Y. Portable electric saws.

Cummins Portable Tool, Div. of John Oster Mfg. Co., 5055 N. Lydell Ave., Milwaukee 17, Wis. Maxaw portable electric saws with Cummins Magic Pivot for increased power at the cutting edge.

Hoffco, Inc., 411 North 8th St., Richmond, Ind. Sawette fells trees up to 18." Gasoline chain saws, 16" to 36", including direct drive.

Henry Disston Div., H. K. Porter Co., Inc., Unruh & Milnor Sts., Philadelphia 35, Pa. Lawn rakes, pruning saws.

Lombard Governor Corp., Ashland, Mass. Chain saws.

Mall Tool Co., Div. of Remington Arms Co., Inc., 25000 S. Western Ave., Park Forest, Ill. Chainsaws and saws for wood or with abrasive blades for grooving tile, terrazzo, or cutting light gauge metals. 2" to 4¼" capacities. See pages 000-000.

McCulloch Motors Corp., 6101 W. Century Blvd., Los Angeles 45, Calif. Chain saws.

Peerless Machine Co., 1600 Junction Ave., Racine, Wis. Power hack saws.

Pioneer Gen-E-Motor Corp., 5841 M West Dickens Ave., Chicago 39, Ill. Portable power saw; tilt saw attachment for all ¼" electric drills.

Portable Electric Tools, Inc., 320 83rd St., Chicago 20, Ill. Electric saws, 5½", 6¼" and 6½"; jig saw, oscillating sander. Disc sanders ¾ H.P. and 1½ H.P.; impact wrench, ½" sq. drive.

The Porter-Cable Machine Co., 1714 N. Salina St., Syracuse 8, N. Y. Portable, electric hand saws (circular) 4 to 12" blade diameters.

The Rocklin Mfg. Co. Grand Ave. at Jenning St., Sioux City 2, Iowa. Sawmobile with 30" blade, fells trees, trims limbs, clears brush. Also portable power buzz saw.

Thor Power Tool Co., 181 N. State St., Aurora, Ill. Thor portable air and electric saws in blade sizes 6½ to 12".

The E. H. Wachs Co., 1525 N. Dayton St., Chicago 22, Ill. Wachs National Pipe Saw for cutting 10-48" steel and cast-iron pipe at 2½" per minute. Wachs Guillotine saw cuts cast iron or steel pipe—2 to 8" diameter. Also new "Big Guillotine" cuts 10"-12" 14"-16" cast-iron or steel pipe. Wachs Strickler ratchet type pipe cutters for 2½" to 24" diameter.

Wright Power Saw and Tool Corp., A Subsidiary of Thomas Industries, Inc., 1415 Illinois Ave., Sheboygan, Wisconsin. Precision power saw weighs 14 lbs., has twin reciprocating 21" blades.

WELDERS

Allied Steel & Tractor Products, Inc., 7835 Broadway, Cleveland 5, Ohio. Weldments, plate, flats, rounds, squares, also high alloy Grip Lug to relug tractor grouser shoes. See page 77.

Hobart Brothers Co., 1221 Hobart Rd., Troy 1, Ohio. Arc welding machine accessories and supplies. Machines, manual or automatic.

The K-G Equipment Co., Inc., 13-11 44th Ave., Long Island City 1, N. Y. Welding and cutting equipment, accessories, and supplies.

Miller Electric Mfg. Co., 781 Bounds St., Appleton, Wis. Engine-driven DC and AC arc welders. Also AC and DC welders, inert gas welders, spot welders, combination AC/DC welders.

TOOLS AND SPECIAL EQUIPMENT, MISCELLANEOUS

Aeroil Products Company, Inc., 50 Wesley St., South Hackensack, N. J. Tool Master tool trailer keeps tools safe on the job. 6' and 8' lengths, pneumatic tires. See pages 69-72.

Greenlee Tool Co., 2136 Twelfth St., Rockford, Ill. Auger bits, car bits, augers, etc.; carpenters' chisels, spiral screw drivers, screw anchor expanders, and other tools. See pages 333-336.

Barco Mfg. Co. 500 Hough St., Barrington, Ill. Barco rammer for earth compaction.

The Black and Decker Mfg. Co., Towson 4, Md. Heavy-duty portable electric sanders, polishers, vacuum cleaners, valve and valve seat reconditioning equipment and wire wheel brushes.

Chicago Pneumatic Tool Co., 6 East 44th St., New York 17, N. Y. Screwdrivers, nutrunners.

Cleco Div. of Reed Roller Bit Co., P. O. Box 2119, Houston, Texas. Air operated scaling tool with chisel, and star drill attachments for removal of weld splatter, rust and paint scraping. Impact wrenches. Precision built chisels for chippers and scalers.

Gardner-Denver Company, 100 Williamson St., Quincy, Ill. Clay spaders, sheeting drivers, trench diggers, airline oilers.

Homestead Valve Mfg. Co., Hypressure Jenny Div., Coraopolis, Pa. Steam cleaner for trucks and other municipal equipment.

Mall Tool Co., Div. of Remington Arms Co., Inc., 25000 S. Western Ave., Park Forest, Ill. Portable electric and pneumatic screwdrivers. See pages 000-000.

Monarch Road Machinery Co., 1331 Michigan St., N.E., Grand Rapids 3, Mich. Morco culvert cleaning tool for clogged culverts.

Owatonna Tool Co., Owatonna, Minn. Pullers, hydraulic or mechanical, for removing and installing bearings, gears, pinions, pulleys, cylinder liners, etc. Wrenches for crawler and wheel type tractors, road and dirt moving machinery trucks. Hydraulic presses, 17½, 30, 50, 100 ton capacities.

Thor Power Tool Co., 181 N. State St., Aurora, Ill. Up to ½ inch capacity screwdrivers and nut setters.

Vulcan Iron Works, Inc., 327 N. Bell Ave., Chicago 12, Ill. Pile extractors.

Water Supply, Sewage and Refuse Disposal

AERATION EQUIPMENT

In water treatment, aerators are used to remove (1) tastes and odors, (2) carbon dioxide, (3) hydrogen sulfide, (4) methane and (5) to oxidize iron and manganese so that they can be removed by filtration. The air can be administered to the water by letting it flow over shelves, sometimes filled with coke, or over specially designed cones. The water can be sprayed into the air, or through a forced-draft aerator; or it can receive the air while in a tank under pressure. Another method is to introduce air into the water through porous ceramic diffusers.

In sewage treatment, the aerators supply air for any of the various types of activated sludge processes or modified aeration. The air can be administered through fixed or removable porous plates, through fixed or removable air diffuser tubes, or other jet-type diffuser devices. Small plants may use various mechanical devices to bring the sewage in contact with the water.

The aerators may be employed as a pre-aeration step to help remove grease or to stop septic action in the sewage and make it easier to purify in the balance of the plant.

The Carborundum Company, Refractories Div., Perth Amboy, N. J. Porous air diffuser plates and tubes for all types of sewage and water aeration. See page 501.

Chicago Pump Co., 622 Diversey Parkway, Chicago 14 Ill. Chicago aerator-clarifier units for complete treatment for small communities and airports. Wide band air-diffusion system with Swing diffusers affords consistent secondary sewage treatment. See page 523.

Dorr-Oliver Inc., Barry Place, Stamford, Conn. Currie Claraetor for clarification and aeration of sewage in the activated sludge process. See pages 466-469.

General Filter Co., Ames, Ia. See pages 400, 401.

Graver Water Conditioning Co., 216 W. 14th St., N.Y. 11, N. Y. Aerators, degasifiers, diffusers, iron removal systems. See pages 402, 403.

Pacific Flush Tank Company, 4241 Ravenswood Avenue, Chicago 13, Illinois. Air diffusion equipment, Kraus interchange process for control of activated sludge. See pages 519-522.

The Permutit Co., 330 W. 42nd St., New York 36, N. Y. Open Aerator. Degasifier for removal of CO_2 and H_2S. See pages 416, 417.

American Well Works, Aurora, Ill. Aeration equipment.

American Water Softener Co., Inc., S.E. Cor. Lehigh Ave. & Fourth St., Philadelphia 3, Pa. Aeration equipment.

Cochrane Corp., 3122 N. 17th St., Philadelphia 32, Pa. Aeration equipment.

Elgin Softener Corp., Inc., Elgin, Ill. Aerator and degasifier equipment for elimination of dissolved iron and objectionable gases, tastes, and odors from water. Either open or closed types.

Filtros Inc., 3348 Kuppinger St., E. Rochester, N. Y. Porous air diffuser plates and tubes, ceramically fritted or synthetic bond for all types of sewage aeration.

Infilco Inc., Box 5033, Tucson, Ariz. Aerators, degasifiers, COLAFLEX® diffusers for activated sludge treatment. Ion, CO_2 and H_2S removal.

Link-Belt Co., Dept. MI, Prudential Plaza, Chicago 1, Ill. Air diffusers.

Norton Co., Worcester 6, Mass. Porous plates and tubes for activated sludge sewage disposal plants.

Smith & Loveless, Inc., P. O. Box 8172, Kansas City, Mo.

Walker Process Equipment Inc., Box 266, Aurora, Ill. Diffusair and impingement aeration units, mechanical aerators and packaged activated sludge plants.

Yeomans Bros. Co., Melrose Park, Ill. Activated sludge treatment plants, aerators, Cavitator and Hi-Cone electrical and mechanical device.

AIR COMPRESSORS

Invaluable for general maintenance and repair. Almost limitless list of air-actuated tools. Light-weight units (30-1,785 pounds) 1 to 60 cfm at 200 psi maximum pressure will spray paint, make traffic markings, drive plant feeder tubes into the ground, operate light rock drills, tamp earth backfill and do light pavement breaking; 55-60 cfm (1,200-2,000 pounds) will do some heavy pavement breaking; 60 to 105 cfm (1,700-3,100 pounds) will operate 2 heavy breakers, or 4 light breakers, or 4 tampers; 105-125 cfm (2,100-3,000 pounds) for general maintenance and repair work; 160-210 cfm (4,000-4,500 pounds) will operate 4 heavy breakers or 9 to 12 tampers or 7-8 spades, or 3-4 sheeting drivers, at 70 pounds pressure; 315-365 cfm (5,200-6,000 pounds) will operate 7-9 light breakers, 3-7 heavy breakers, one wagon drill; to 600 cfm (8,000-8,500 pounds) will operate 10-15 heavy breakers, 3-7 wagon drills. Trailer and truck-mounted sizes to suit your work. Self-propelled units are also available and popular in sizes around 125 cfm.

De Laval Steam Turbine Co., 863 Nottingham Way, Trenton 2, N. J. Centrifugal compressors. See pages 313-316.

The Jaeger Machine Co., 702 Dublin Ave., Columbus 16, Ohio. "Air Plus" portable compressors, force feed lubricated, automatic drainage, Timken bearing wheels, gas, diesel, electric; sizes 70 to 600 ft.; also Jaeger truck mounted compressors. See pages 158-161.

Schramm, Inc., West Chester, Pa. Portable, self-propelled and stationary; portable in gasoline and diesel engine drive, 20 to 600 cfm actual free air delivery; self-propelled 125 cfm, industrial ½ to 150 hp for V belt or direct built-in motor drive. See pages 218-221.

American Brake Shoe Co., Kellogg Div., 97 Humboldt St., Rochester 9, N. Y. ⅛ to 20 hp. portable and stationary air compressors up to 105.9 displacement.

Brunner Mfg. Co., Gilbert at Broad St., Utica 1, N. Y. ¼ to 100 hp. air compressors.

Champion Pneumatic Machinery Co., 825 N. Pleasant St., Princeton, Ill. Portable and stationary air compressors up to 40 cfm ¼ to 10 hp.

Chicago Pneumatic Tool Co., 6 East 44th St., New York 17, N. Y.

Complete Machinery & Equipment Co., Inc., 36-40 Eleventh St., Long Island City 6, N. Y. Portable or stationary units up to 600 cfm.

Davey Compressor Co., Kent, Ohio. Portable, stationary and truck-mounted (Auto-Airs).

Essick Mfg. Co., 1950 Santa Fe Ave., Los Angeles 21, Calif. Portable and stationary.

Gardner-Denver Co., 100 Williamson St., Quincy, Ill. Gasoline or diesel portable air compressors.

Ingersoll-Rand Co., 11 Broadway, New York 4, N. Y. Portable compressors.

Joy Mfg. Co., Henry W. Oliver Bldg., Pittsburgh 22, Pa. Portable air compressors, 75 to 600 cfm; stationary air compressors with displacements up to 3,896 cfm. at 125 psi.

Keystone Compressor Co., Ashburner and Hegerman Streets, Philadelphia 26, Pa. Air compressors up to 92 cfm ⅛ to 20 hp.

Le Roi Div., Westinghouse Air Brake Co., 1706 S. 68th St., Milwaukee 14, Wis. Airmaster portable compressors, 85 thru 600 cfm. Westinghouse stationary compressors ½ thru 100 hp.

P. K. Lindsay Co., Inc., 97 Tileston St., Everett 49, Mass. Portable; capable of being handled by one man for service trench digging.

Pennsylvania Pump & Compressor Co., Bushkill Blvd., Easton, Pa. Air compressors.

Gordon Smith & Co., 425 College St., Bowling Green, Ky. 45 to 230 cfm—gasoline, diesel and electrically driven.

The Wayne Pump Co., Salisbury, Md. Stationary air compressors up to 46 cfm, ⅓ to 10 hp.

Worthington Corp., Harrison, N. J. Portable and stationary air compressors.

ALLOYS

The American Brass Co., Waterbury 20, Conn. Everdur. See pages 526, 527.

Federated Metals Div. of American Smelting and Refining Co., 120 Broadway, New York 5, N. Y. Tenzaloy special highstrength aluminum alloy. Non-ferrous metals. See page 905.

Revere Copper and Brass, Inc., 230 Park Ave., New York 17, N. Y. Herculoy, copper silicon alloy, corrosion-resistance of copper, strength of mild steel, excellent for sewage-treatment equipment. See page 445.

Bridgeport Brass Co., 30 Grand St., Bridgeport, Conn. Duronze alloys (silicon bronze and aluminum bronzes).

Chase Brass & Copper Co., Inc., 1949 Rodney St., Waterbury 20, Conn. Copper alloys of all types.

Phelps Dodge Copper Products Co., 300 Park Ave., New York 22, N. Y. P M G metal bronzes with castings which are corrision resistant.

BLOWERS

Allis-Chalmers Mfg. Co., 886 S. 70th St., Milwaukee 1, Wis. Centrifugal blowers, multi-stage 1,000 to 100,000 cfm; single stage 1,400 to 60,000 cfm; axial 8,000 to 1,000,000 cfm; rotary to 3,245 cfm. See pages 285-288.

Roots-Connersville Blower Div., Dresser Industries, Inc., Connersville, Ind. Rotary positive and centrifugal blowers for activated sludge-type sewage disposal plants. See page 564.

American Blower Corp., Tireman Ave. at Roselawn, Detroit 32, Mich. Forced and induced draft fans and blowers.

BOXES, METER, SERVICE, VALVE

Alabama Pipe Co., Anniston, Ala. Valve, roadway, service and meter boxes. See pages 277-280.

Buffalo Pipe & Foundry Corp., Box 55, Station B, Buffalo 7, N. Y. Valve and roadway boxes, meter boxes and service boxes for gas or water. See pages 281-284.

Clarksville Foundry and Machine Works, Clarksville, Tenn. Meter boxes, frames and covers. Street and sewer castings. See page 373.

The Ford Meter Box Co., Inc., 1000 Manchester Ave., Wabash, Ind. Meter box covers of several types equipped with Lifter Worm Lock; double lid Wabash meter box covers; monitor covers for large settings, rectangular and round pit covers. Meter boxes: Crescent, Ironcrete, Yokeboxes, Yokes, Copperhorns, Coppersetters, Linesetters, Kornerhorns, Handyhorns, Ring-style valves and couplings. See pages 329-332.

American Foundry & Mfg. Co., 1015 Herbert St., St. Louis 7, Mo. Service boxes, valve boxes, and cast iron frame and grates.

Bingham & Taylor Corp., Culpeper, Va. Cast iron service, valve, roadway and meter boxes.

H. W. Clark Co., 1112-1216 Hayes Ave., Mattoon, Ill. Meter boxes, yokes.

Mueller Co., 512 W. Cerro Gordo St., Decatur, Ill. Meter yokes, angle valves and meter box covers.

Opelika Foundry Co., P. O. Box 326, Opelika, Ala. Service valves and roadway boxes.

CASTINGS

Alabama Pipe Co., Anniston, Ala. Cast-iron boxes for valve, roadway, service and meter covers. Manhole frames, covers. See pages 277-280.

Buffalo Pipe & Foundry Corp., Box 55, Station B, Buffalo 7, N. Y. Manhole frames and covers in several sizes or to meet your specifications. See pages 281-284.

Clarksville Foundry and Machine Works, Clarksville, Tenn. Street and sewer castings. See page 373.

Irving Subway Grating Co., Inc., 5046 27th St., Long Island City 1, N. Y.; P. O. Box 333, Bayshore Sta., Oakland 23, Calif. Catch basin or inlet grating covers, steel grid. See page 257.

Neenah Foundry Co., 505 Winneconne Ave., Neenah, Wis. Construction castings in 15,000 different gray iron patterns used on construction projects. See page 259.

Trinity Valley Iron & Steel Co., P. O. Box 664, Fort Worth, Texas. Cast iron pipe fittings, AWWA Standard in both long and short pattern, also mechanical joint, ring-tite and fluid-tite fittings. Manhole frames and covers and sewer castings. See page 451.

The Vapor Recovery Systems Co., 2820 N. Alameda, Compton, Calif. "Varec" nonsparking, gastight manhole cover installed on digester and gas holder domes. Sizes 18, 20, 24, 30 inches. See page 471.

A. Reed Wilson Co., 1320 McGee St., Kansas City 6, Mo. Manhole adapter for use when resurfacing streets. See page 262.

Bingham & Taylor Corp., Culpeper, Va. Cast iron manhole frames and covers. See page 000.

Klemp Metal Corp., 6601 South Melvina Ave., Chicago 38, Ill. Manhole ventilating covers of open steel grating.

Lynchburg Foundry Co., 58 Courtland Bldg., Lynchburg, Va. Special cast iron fittings and castings of all kinds.

Opelika Foundry Co., P. O. Box 326, Opelika, Ala. Castings for service, valve and roadway boxes.

The E. H. Wachs Co., 1525 N. Dayton St., Chicago 22, Ill. Counterbalanced safety manhole covers for valve, meter and district governor vaults.

CATCH BASIN, CESSPOOL, SEPTIC TANK CLEANERS

The Hayward Co., Dept. G, 50 Church St., New York 7, N. Y. Catch basin buckets. See pages 534, 535.

Pippin Construction Eqpt. Co., Inc., White River Jct., Vt. Catch basin attachment quickly mounts on Excavator. Cleans basins rapidly and loads directly into truck. See pages 248, 249.

Stedt Hydraulic Crane Co., 93 Cordaville Rd., Ashland, Mass. Fully hydraulic Stetco catch basin cleaner and Hiab crane with bucket for truck mounting. See pages 546, 547; 1118, 1119.

Bucyrus-Erie Co., 1046 Monroe Ave., S. Milwaukee, Wis. All-hydraulic Model H-3 Hydrocrane equipped with 1½" cu. ft. capacity catch basin bucket which has 15" diameter when closed.

The Elgin Corp., 231 S. La Salle St., Chicago, Ill. Elgin Eductor, empties contents of basins directly to disposal body by suction system.

The Gorman-Rupp Co., Mansfield, Ohio. Odorless Sanitary septic tank cleaners for cisterns, vaults, septic tanks by agitation and pumping into truck tank.

Netco Div., Clark-Wilcox Co., 118 Western Ave., Boston 34, Mass. Netco catch-basin cleaners with (1) orange peel bucket which operates in 16" opening; (2) clam shell for rectangular frames as small as 13½" x 19".

Silent Hoist & Crane Co., 842 63rd St., Brooklyn 20, N.Y. Power-operated cranes (for motor truck mountings) and equipped with orange peel bucket for catch-basin duty.

CATHODIC PROTECTION

Electro-Rust Proofing Corp., 30 Main St., Belleville, N. J. Cathodic protection: engineering design, equipment, installation, and maintenance for preventing corrosion of steel structures. See page 381.

Pipe Line Anode Corp., Box 996, Tulsa, Okla. An-Spec magnesium anodes for controlling corrosion of tanks and other steel structures. See page 45.

The Dow Chemical Co., Cathodic Protection Sales, Magnesium Dept., Midland, Mich. Dow magnesium anodes eliminate corrosion problems in pipelines and tanks.

The Duriron Co., Inc., Dayton 1, Ohio. Duriron impressed current anodes for the cathodic protection of elevated water towers, storage tanks, accelator basins, pipe lines, sewage disposal systems, and other municipal equipment.

Harco Corp., Cathodic Protection Div., P. O. Box 7026, Cleveland 28, Ohio. Cathodic protection devices to increase the life of water-storage tanks.

CHEMICALS

Activated Carbon

General Filter Co., Ames, Iowa. Powdered or granular activated carbon for removal of taste and odor from water. See pages 400, 401.

Industrial Chemical Sales Div., West Virginia Pulp and Paper Co., 230 Park Ave., New York 17, N. Y. Activated carbon for removal of tastes and odors in water supplies.

Aluminum Sulphate

General Chemical Div., Allied Chemical & Dye Corp., 40 Rector St., New York 6, N. Y. Aluminum sulfate: aqua ammonia; ammonium & potassium sulfate. See pages 234; 430.

American Cyanamid Company, 30 Rockefeller Plaza, New York 20, N. Y. Aluminum sulphate.

Consolidated Chemical Industries, Inc., Houston, Texas. Aluminum sulphate.

Chlorine

Columbia-Southern Chemical Corp., 1 Gateway Center, Pittsburgh 22, Pa. Alkalies, heavy chemicals, caustic soda, soda ash, bicarbonate of soda, calcium chloride, liquid chlorine, and calcium hypochlorite (Pittchlor). See page 382.

Diamond Alkali Co., 300 Union Commerce Bldg., Cleveland 14, Ohio. Liquid chlorine.

Hooker Electrochemical Co., 7 Union St., Niagara Falls, N. Y., and Tacoma, Washington. Liquid chlorine in cylinders of 100 and 150 lbs. net; multi-unit cars of 15 one-ton containers; tank cars of 16, 30 and 55 tons net.

John Wiley Jones Co., Caledonia, N. Y., and 6 branches. Liquid chlorine in 16- to 150-lb. cylinders and ton containers; calcium hypochlorite in 3¾, 5-lb. tins or 100-lb. drums; sodium hypochlorite in gallons or carboys, or by tank truck load.

Pennsylvania Salt Mfg. Co., 3 Penn Center Plaza, Philadelphia 2, Pa. Calcium hypochlorite, liquid chlorine, ferric chloride, acid-proof cements, corrosion-resistant coatings.

Solvay Process Div., Allied Chemical & Dye Corp., 61 Broadway, New York 6, N. Y. Liquid chlorine.

Wyandotte Chemicals Corp., Michigan Alkali Div., Wyandotte, Mich. Chlorine, shipped as liquid in 16- and 30-ton single unit tank cars only.

Copper Sulphate

Tennessee Corp., 617-29 Grant Bldg., Atlanta 1, Ga. Ferri-Floc, a ferric iron sulfate, coagulant for water and sewage treatment; liquid sulphur dioxide for dechlorination; copper sulfate for algae control in water treatment and industrial applications. See pages 276; 304; 325; 567.

Phelps Dodge Refining Corp., 300 Park Ave., New York 22, N. Y. Copper sulphate for destroying and controlling micro-organisms in water and tree roots in sewers, available in 100-pound bags and 400 lb. drums. Crystal and powdered (Instant) grade.

Fluoride

General Chemical Division, Allied Chemical & Dye Corp., 40 Rector St., New York 6, N. Y. Sodium fluoride and sodium silicofluoride. See pages 234; 430.

Lyon Chemicals, Inc., 2305 Hampden Ave., St. Paul 14, Minn. Sodium silicofluoride and sodium fluoride.

Miscellaneous Chemicals

Fine Organics, 211 E. 19th St., New York, N. Y. Cifon, an emulsifiable solution of orthodichlorobenzene used by sewage disposal plants and in landfill operations for control of odor. Foamwilt to control foam in activated sludge plants. Arodon for control of odor by the "spray method" (curtain of mist). See page 553.

General Chemical Div., Allied Chemical & Dye Corp., 40 Rector St., New York 6, N. Y. Sodium silicate, sulfuric acid, hydrochloric acid, the sodium phosphates, anhydrous sodium bisulfite. See pages 234; 430.

Modern Swimming Pool Co., Inc., 1 Holland Ave., White Plains, N. Y. Chemicals for water-treatment and algae control. Filter cleansers, swimming pool stain removers. See page 1035.

Olin Mathieson Chemical Corp., Industrial Chemicals Div., Mathieson Bldg., Baltimore 3, Md. HTH granular and HTH tablets for hypochlorination of water supplies, sewage effluents and swimming pool water; PH-Plus for water softening and pH control; soda ash, caustic soda and chlorine. See pages 410, 411; 1038, 1039.

Reliance Chemicals Corp., P. O. Box 6724, Houston 5, Texas. Bionetic, a dry powder of preserved micro-organisms designed to accelerate biological waste treatment processes. Solids in sludge digesters may be reduced by 50% and sludge dries more rapidly without odor. Grease and solids can be removed from lift stations and collections with odor elimination. Flocculation of sewage may be improved. Aqua-Rx series of 3 products specifically designed for treatment of recirculated waters in open or closed heat exchange systems. Simplifies control of corrosion, bio-fouling and delignification. See page 562.

J. T. Baker Chemical Co., Phillipsburg, N. J. 'Baker Analyzed' Reagents (chemical reagents for the laboratory). Also bulk quantities of fine and industrial chemicals.

Calgon Co., Div. of Hagan Chemicals & Controls, Inc., Box 1346, Pittsburgh 30, Pa. Calgon Threshold Treatment for scale prevention, corrosion control, and stabilization of dissolved iron and manganese in municipal and industrial water. Weltone for water well cleaning and Zeotone for cleaning zeolite type water softeners.

Chemical Insecticide Corp., 129 Montague St., Brooklyn 1, N. Y. Chem-Larv, special compound for control of psychoda flies in trickling filter beds. Tifacide germicide for control of odors around sewage plants and garbage dumps.

Cochrane Corp., 3122 N. 17th St., Philadelphia 32, Pa. Softening chemicals and compounds.

The Dow Chemical Co., Midland, Mich. Ferric chloride solution for sewage and water treatment.

Elgin Softener Corp., Elgin, Ill. Water treating chemicals, for prevention of scale formation and corrosion. Inhibitant treatment for prevention of lime and scale depositions, corrosion and "red water" troubles in hot and cold water lines, engine jackets, condensers, cooling towers, etc.

National Aluminate Corp., 6225 W. 66th Pl., Chicago, Ill. Sodium aluminate, a coagulant for water softening and filtration; cuprose, for algae control; water stabilization chemicals.

Rhodia Inc., 60 E. 56th St., New York 22, N. Y. Alamask® CPM-X and other Alamask chemicals for control of odors around sewage plants, incinerators, garbage dumps.

E. M. Sergeant Pulp and Chemical Co., Inc., 7 Dey St., New York 7, N. Y. Copperas (Sulfate of Iron). Also sodium silico fluoride.

Solvay Process Div., Allied Chemical & Dye Corp., 61 Broadway, New York 6, N. Y. Soda ash, modified soda, caustic soda. Also Solvay Ozene, an emulsifiable orthodichlorobenzene for controlling odors at sewage and garbage disposal plants, in landfill operations.

Stuart Corp. Baltimore 1, Md. Activated alum and black alum.

U. S. Rubber Co., Naugatuck Chemical Div., Naugatuck, Conn. Phygon—XL for control of algae.

Virginia Smelting Co., West Norfolk, Va. Liquid sulphur dioxide (SO_2) for dechlorination.

Wyandotte Chemical Corp., Michigan Alkali Div., Wyandotte, Mich. Bicarbonate of soda, and soda ash in 100 lb. bags and bulk. Chlorine in tank cars, caustic soda.

CHEMICAL FEEDERS

Chemical control equipment used in water treatment systems may be classified as solution feeders, dry feeders, gas feeders, and slurry feeders. In most cases the first two feed coagulating chemicals that help remove suspended matter, or chemicals that soften the water. Sterilizing action and/or taste-and-odor control may be provided by any of the first three types although the first and third types are most frequently used for this purpose.

Solution feeders may be used to feed soluble chemicals such as alum, copperas, soda ash, sodium silicates, phosphates, hypochlorites, and some fluorides. Some designs of solution feeders may also be used to feed insoluble or slightly soluble materials such as hydrated lime and activated carbon in the form of a suspension. These are also known as slurry feeders.

Dry chemical feeders may be used to feed either soluble or insoluble materials and are widely employed where the amounts of chemicals to be fed are large. These feeders also are used to apply some of the fluoride compounds used in water as a dental health measure.

The gas feeders are used for feeding gases such as chlorine, ammonia, sulfur dioxide, and carbon dioxide. Gas feeders meter gaseous chemicals and apply them either directly as a gas or as a solution which is formed within the feeders.

In sewage treatment, solution or dry chemical feeders can be used to induce a coagulation floc in the sewage and increase the effectiveness of primary settling type of treatment. Gas feeders generally apply chlorine for odor control, for final sterilization of the treated effluent, keeping filters clean, and other uses.

Automatic feed of chemicals with all types of feeders is accomplished with auxiliary equipment where it is desired to maintain a given feed rate in proportion to flow. Recording of chemicals fed is also possible.

Fischer & Porter Co., 850 Warminster Road, Hatboro, Pa. Chemical and reagent feeders. Flow rate meters for small, medium and large flow rate measurements. See pages 317-320.

General Filter Co., Ames, Ia. Pressure liquid, gravity, liquid, solution. See pages 400, 401.

Graver Water Conditioning Co., 216 W. 14th St., N. Y. 11, N. Y. Pressure or gravity type chemical feeders, dry or wet, proportioning the flow of chemicals to water flow or on a time cycle basis. See pages 402, 403.

Modern Swimming Pool Co., Inc., 1 Holland Ave., White Plains, N. Y. Robot Mechanical Chlorinator, a chemical feeder for chlorine, alum, soda ash, and others. See page 1035.

Olin Mathieson Chemical Corp., Industrial Chemicals Div., Mathieson Bldg., Baltimore 3, Md. Tablet hypochlorinators, differential pressure type, providing for a reservoir of tableted hypochlorite, dissolved at rates **controlled by metering the dissolving water and applied to the system as hypochlorite solution. See pages** 410, 411; 1038, 1039.

The Permutit Co., 330 W. 42nd St., New York 36, N. Y. Chemical feeders, wet or dry, constant or proportionating; with the exception of orifice or differential pressure types, all are mechanically operated. See pages 416, 417.

Roberts Filter Mfg. Co., 601 Columbia Ave., Darby, Pa. Chemical feeders. See page 1042.

Wallace & Tiernan Incorporated, 25 Main St., Belleville 9, N. J. Dry chemical feeders (volumetric and gravimetric), fluoridators, ammoniators. See pages 378-381.

American Water Softener Co., Inc., S.E. Cor. Lehigh Ave. and Fourth St., Philadelphia 33, Pa. Chemical feeders.

Beaumont Birch Co., Philadelphia 2, Pa. Rotary feeders and gates for handling chlorine and other chemicals for water conditioning.

Chemical Equipment Co., P. O. Box 3098, Los Angeles 54, Calif. Ammoniators.

Cochrane Corp., 3122 N. 17th St., Philadelphia 32, Pa. Constant rate and proportioning feeders for chemicals in solution and dry powders.

Culligan, Inc., S. Shermer Rd., Northbrook, Ill. Chemical feeders.

Elgin Softener Corp., Elgin, Ill. Chemical feeders.

B. F. Gump Co., Inc., 1325 S. Cicero Ave., Chicago 50, Ill. Draver "Micro-Master" wing type feeders and style JJ for handling lime, soda, activated carbon, and other chemicals used in water purification and sewage treatment plants.

Infilco Inc., Box 5033, Tucson, Ariz. Chemical feeders, for constant or variable rate feeding of dry or wet chemicals. Lime slakers and feeders.

Omega Machine Company, Div. of B-I-F Industries, Inc., 351 Harris Ave., Providence 1, R. I. Volumetric and gravimetric type dry-chemical feeders; volumetric gravity-feed-type solution feeders; lime slakers; **fluoride feeders.**

Phipps & Bird, Inc., 303 S. 6th St., Richmond 5, Va. Solution feeders.

Proportioneers, Inc., Div. of B-I-F Industries, Inc., 351 **Harris Ave., Providence 1, R. I. Chemical feeders; diaphragm and plunger pumps for chemical-solution injection into low and high pressures and for main-line and emergency sterilization. Constant-rate, manually-adjustable and automatic flow-proportional models.**

Milton Roy Co., 1300 E. Mermaid Lane, Philadelphia 18, Pa. Controlled volume chemical and high pressure pumps for pumping all water- and sewage-treating chemicals in precisely controlled volume. Completely automatic control systems, pumps. Meters. Boiler water treating systems, complete units motor driven or air powered.

Syntron Co., 420 Lexington Ave., Homer City, Pa. **Gravimetric and dry feeders operated on Vibra-flow principle of flowing material by vibration. Wide range of capacity.**

The Welsbach Corp., Ozone Processes Div., 1500 Walnut St., Philadelphia 2, Pa. Ozonators for water and sewage odor treatment.

CHEMICAL HANDLING

Chain Belt Co., 4640 W. Greenfield Ave., Milwaukee 1, Wis. Conveyors. See page 105.

Dracco Corp., 4063 E. 116th St., Cleveland 5, Ohio. "Air-steam" conveyors for handling bulk, granular or powdered chemicals.

The Jeffrey Mfg. Co., 970 N. 4th St., Columbus 16, Ohio. Elevating and conveying equipment, feeders, crushers. Weigh-feeding devices.

CHLORINATION EQUIPMENT

Fischer & Porter Co., 850 Warminster Rd., Hatboro, Pa. Chlorinators in two types; dry-vacuum solution feed and dry-gas pressure feed. See pages 317-320.

Modern Swimming Pool Co., Inc., 1 Holland Ave., White Plains, N. Y. Mechanical chlorinator for up to 3,000,000 gal. of water a day. See page 1035.

Olin Mathieson Chemical Corp., Industrial Chemicals Div., Mathieson Bldg. Baltimore 3, Md. HTH granular and HTH tablets and the HTH tablet hypochlorinator for hypochlorination of water supplies and pools. See pages 410, 411; 1038, 1039.

Wallace & Tiernan Incorporated, 25 Main St., Belleville 9, N. J. Chlorinators, residual chlorine recorders. See pages 378-381.

The American Water Softener Co., Inc., S.E. Cor. Lehigh **Ave. and Fourth St., Philadelphia 33, Pa. Chemical feeders wet or dry for hypochlorites.**

Builders-Providence, Inc., Div. of B-I-F Industries, Inc., 351 Harris Ave., Providence 1, R.I. Chlorinizer vis**ible-flow, visible-vacuum, gas-feeding chlorinators for** water and sewage treatment with maximum feed rates **up to 8,000 pounds per day.**

Chemical Equipment Co., P. O. Box 3098, Los Angeles 54, Calif. Chlorinators, gas type.
Culligan, Inc., S. Shermer Rd., Northbrook, Ill. Chlorinators.
Elgin Softener Corp., Elgin, Ill. Chlorinators.
Everson Mfg. Corp., 205 W. Huron St., Chicago 10, Ill. Sterelators.
Proportioneers, Inc., Div. of B-I-F Industries, Inc., 351 Harris Ave., Providence 1, R. I. Hypochlorinators.

CLAMPS

(See Pipe Clamps, page 763.)

CLARIFIERS

In water treatment clarifiers or settling basins (1) allow the flocculated suspended matter to settle out of the water (2) permit suspended matter from a softening step to settle out along with the removed chemicals of hardness. They may be of the suspended solids type or a conventional gravity-type settling basin.

Either type may be circular, square or rectangular. If only one basin is needed, the circular is generally the most economical unless it can be combined with some other structure. If several are required, the rectangular or square type may be preferable. To save space with the gravity-type, rectangular tanks are sometimes built with two decks since they can be built with common walls. They can be equipped with mechanical sludge collecting mechanisms with automatic blowoff valves, with hopper bottoms, or they can be cleaned by dewatering them and removing the sludge by shovels and small rubber-tired bulldozers.

Suspended solids contact basins require less space than the gravity type and incorporate the treatment functions of flash mixing and flocculation in the same basin.

Most sewage treatment (settling) tanks are of the gravity type. Like water settling basins they may be circular or rectangular. Since all the solids are not settleable, the basins, particularly the primary type, should be provided with grease skimming devices, either manual or mechanical to remove floating matter from the surface for transfer to the digesters. Since they must handle a large volume of sludge that becomes septic quickly, they almost always have motor-driven removal mechanisms.

Chain Belt Co., 4640 W. Greenfield Ave., Milwaukee, Wis. Conveyor type sludge collectors. Tow Bro clarifiers, Verti Flo clarifiers, Float Treat systems, for water and sewage treatment. See page 105.

Dorr-Oliver Inc., Barry Place, Stamford, Conn. Conventional or high-rate treatment. Continuous mechanically cleaned sedimentation units for round, square or rectangular tanks. See pages 466-469.

General Filter Co., Ames, Ia. Coagulation and clarification. See pages 400, 401.

Graver Water Conditioning Co., 216 W. 14th St., New York 11, N. Y. High-rate upflow clarifiers and cold lime-soda softeners. "Conventional" treatment equipment, Rota-Rake sedimentation unit, compact, self-contained plants. See pages 402, 403.

Hardinge Co., Inc., 240 Arch St., York, Pa. Rectangular and circular. See page 556.

The Permutit Co., 330 W. 42nd St., New York 36, N. Y. Horizontal and vertical precipitators for municipal water treatment. See pages 416, 417.
American Water Softener Co., Inc., S.E. Cor. Lehigh & Fourth St., Philadelphia 33, Pa. Suspended sludge bed reactors.
Ralph B. Carter Co., 196 Atlantic Ave., Hackensack, N. J. Primary and secondary clarifiers for sewage treatment.
Cochrane Corp., 3122 N. 17th St., Philadelphia 32, Pa. water clarifiers and solids contact reactors.
Elgin Softener Corp., Elgin, Ill. Clarifiers of all types. Suspended sludge bed upflow types for round or square tanks.
Infilco Inc., Box 5033, Tucson, Ariz. ACCELATOR® ACCELAPAK®, and CYCLATOR® high-rate clarifiers, SEDIFLOTOR® clarifiers for sewage treatment by flotation.
The Jersey Mfg. Co. 970 N. 4th St., Columbus 13, Ohio. Clarifiers for rectangular tanks, primary and secondary, grease skimming equipment, sludge elevators.
Lakeside Engineering Corp., 222 W. Adams St., Chicago 6, Ill. Spiragesters and spiraflo clarifiers, scum breakers.
Link-Belt Co., Dept. MI, Prudential Plaza, Chicago 1, Ill. Straight-line and Circuline collectors.
Smith & Loveless, Inc., P. O. Box 8172, Kansas City, Mo. Clarifiers.
Walker Process Equipment, Inc., Box 266, Aurora, Ill. Clarifiers for sludge removal for circular, rectangular or square settling basins.
Yeomans Bros. Co., Melrose Park, Ill. "Spiraflo," "Streamline" and Center Drive, automatic skimmer and flusher.

CLEANERS, MISCELLANEOUS

Aeroil Products Company, Inc., 50 Wesley St., South Hackensack, N. J. Steam cleaners for tanks. See pages 69-72.
G. H. Tennant Co., 701 N. Highway 100, Minneapolis, Minn. Semiself-propelled gas-powered reservoir scrapers for removing algae deposits. See pages 130-132; 957.
Brulin & Co., Inc., 2939 Columbia Ave., Indianapolis 7, Ind. Steam cleaning equipment and compounds for garages and shops.
Friend Mfg. Co., Gasport, N. Y. High pressure cleaners for sewage plants.
Monarch Road Machinery Company, 1331 Michigan St., N.E. Grand Rapids 3, Michigan. Culvert cleaner tools.
Newport News Shipbuilding & Drydock Co., Newport News, Va. Power-operated mechanical rake for cleaning trash racks at water intakes.
Wheelabrator Corporation, Byrkit Ave., Mishawaka, Ind. Blast cleaning equipment.

CLEANERS

CATCH BASIN

(See page 733.)

Sewer

(See Sewer Cleaning, page 767)

WATER MAIN

(See Water Main Cleaners, page 771.)

CONTROLLERS

Bailey Meter Co., 1035 Ivanhoe Rd., Cleveland 10, Ohio. Automatic control; flume meters, liquid level recorders. See page 480.
Fischer & Porter Co., 850 Warminster Rd., Hatboro, Pa. Flowrator instruments measure, indicate, record, control, proportion, totalize, transmit the flow of liquids, gases, abrasive fluids, liquid level and specific gravity instruments. See pages 317-320.
General Filter Co., Ames, Ia. Pneumatic-Operated Control (P.O.C.) measures loss of head, indicates, records and totalizes rate of filter flow, backwash, raw water, treated water. It also indicates and records loss of head through filters and any water levels. It controls rate of flow of filter, backwash, raw water rate of flow. See pages 400, 401.
The Hays Corp., Michigan City, Ind. Flow, pressure, liquid level, gas analysis, indicating, recording, controlling; draft gages; combustion control sewage meters; feed water regulators; flow meters. See page 436.

Healy-Ruff Co., Water Level Controls Div., 838 Hampden Ave., St. Paul 14, Minn. Pressure Roto-Trols give independent start and stop for 1-5 pumps automatically compensating for surges. Float Roto-Trols 1 to 10 pumps on either sequence or programming operation. Automatic alternation 1 to 5 pumps. Pressure operated sewage pumping station Roto-Trols. Remote supervisory controls using one pair of wires will start and stop one or multi pump installation. See page 438.

Simplex Valve & Meter Co., 7 East Orange St., Lancaster, Pa. Direct acting rate controllers for gravity or pressure type filters type S or type B units. Controllers also used for control or flow in pipe lines up to 24", special butterfly-valve design in sizes above 24". Electrical, pneumatic or telemetering transmission systems for remote control of filter and sewage treatment plants. See pages 422, 423.

American Meter Co., 60 E. 42 St., New York 17, N. Y. Orifice meters, controllers.

Automatic Control Co., St. Paul 4, Minn. Complete control systems for municipal water or sewage plants.

B/W Controller Corp., 2222 E. Maple Rd., Birmingham, Mich. Liquid level controls, floatless, all electric, no moving parts in liquid; pump controls and special pump control panels.

Black, Sivalls & Bryson, Inc., Climax Controls Div., 15 N. Cincinnati, Tulsa, Okla. A complete line of automatic controls for use in control of temperature, pressure, flow and liquid level.

The Bristol Co., P. O. Box 1790 MI, Waterbury 20, Conn. Recorders, indicators, telemeters, and controllers.

Builders-Providence, Inc., Div. of B-I-F Industries, Inc., 351 Harris Ave., Providence 1, R. I. Direct-acting or Power-operated (electric, hydraulic, pneumatic) tight-closing controllers for filter effluent and wash water. Mechanical and pneumatic filter gauges for indicating, recording loss of head, rate of flow and water level, and sand expansion. Gauges for table, panel or floor mounting. Chronoflo electrical, and pneumatic, remote-operated gauges.

The Foxboro Co., Foxboro, Mass. Altitude control, master meter, rate-of-flow, liquid level, pH, pressure and test gauges.

Hagan Chemicals & Controls, Inc., Box 1346, Pittsburgh, Pa. Control systems for filtration plants.

Infilco Inc., Box 5033, Tucson, Ariz. C-A-P System instruments automatically measure and control rate of flow and loss of head through filters. Backwash rates of flow gauges indicate, record, and totalize operations.

Lumenite Electronic Co., 407 S. Dearborn St., Chicago 5, Ill. Lumenite electronic liquid level controls.

The Mercoid Corp., 4213 Belmont Ave., Chicago 41, Ill. Temperature, liquid-level and pressure controls. Also tank & pump controls, heating and air conditioning controls.

Minneapolis-Honeywell Regulator Co., Industrial Div., Wayne and Windrim Aves., Philadelphia 44, Pa. Instruments and controls.

Pelton Division of Baldwin-Lima-Hamilton Corporation, 2929-19 St., San Francisco 10, Calif. Pelton surge suppressor affords protection against pipeline failures caused by pressure rises from abrupt pump stoppages.

Republic Flow Meter Co., 2240 Diversey Parkway, Chicago 47, Ill. Flow, liquid level and pressure recorders, indicators, controllers.

Smith & Loveless, Inc., P. O. Box 8172 Kansas City, Mo. Complete custom-built electrical control panels, telephone, radio and air bubbler type for pump stations, water and sewage treatment plants.

CORPORATION AND CURB STOPS

The Haydenville Co., Haydenville, Mass. Water works brass goods, corporation and curb stops. See page 434.

Hays Mfg. Co., 12th and Liberty Sts., Erie, Pa. Water works brass goods, corporation stops, curb stops, tapping machine for installing corporation stops, curb boxes, lead goosenecks, couplings, adaptors, as well as extension service boxes; new Hays Duo stop. See page 436.

A. Y. McDonald Mfg. Co., 12th and Pine St., Dubuque, Ia. Corporation and curb stops, lead goosenecks, copper service pipe couplings, adaptors, copper goosenecks, gas service stops, extension service boxes. See pages 352-355.

Crane Co., 836 S. Michigan Ave., Chicago 5, Ill. Cocks: curb, meter, corporation, etc.

The Farnan Brass Works Co., Cleveland 1, Ohio. Corporation and curbstops.

Mueller Co., 512 W. Cerro Gordo St., Decatur, Ill. Curb and corporation stops, meter yokes, goosenecks, copper service equipment, service boxes, drilling and tapping machines, caulking tools.

The Welsbach Corp., Kitson Valve Div., Westmoreland and Stokley Sts., Phila. 29, Pa. Corporation stops and fittings.

DIGESTERS

Digesters receive the sludge from sewage treatment settling tanks, and allow it to decompose under anaerobic conditions. This reduces the volume substantially, and transforms the sludge into an inoffensive peat-like humus that can be used as a soil conditioner in many cases. The gas of digestion is principally methane that is often used as a fuel in internal combustion engines or for heating.

Chicago Pump Co., 622 Diversey Pkwy., Chicago 14, Ill. Chicago-Wiggins digester covers and gas holders for sewage digester; Chicago-Selas heat transfer systems and Chicago-Cyclotherm systems for sludge heating; Catalytic Reduction Process for accelerating biological digestion. See page 523.

Dorr-Oliver Inc., Barry Place, Stamford, Conn. Sludge digestion tanks for single or two-stage digestion. See pages 466-469.

Hardinge Co., Inc., 240 Arch St., York, Pa. Sewage sludge digesters. See page 556.

Pacific Flush-Tank Co., 4241 Ravenswood Ave., Chicago 13, Ill. Sludge digestion tanks; floating covers; digesters, heaters and heat exchangers; selectors and gages; sludge gas control equipment. Pearth gas system for scum control. See pages 519-522.

Ralph B. Carter Co., 196 Atlantic Ave., Hackensack, N. J. Digestion tanks.

Infilco Inc., Box 5036, Tucson, Ariz. Digesters and floating covers.

Lakeside Engineering Corp., 22 W. Adams St., Chicago 6, Ill. Spiragester and digester mechanisms.

Link-Belt Co., Dept. MI, Prudential Plaza, Chicago 1, Ill. Straightline scum breakers.

Walker Process Equipment, Inc., Box 266, Aurora, Ill. Heatx for digester sludge heating, gas holders, floating covers, superdraw for digester supernatant withdrawal and viggers valve for automatic sludge blow-off control.

DRAIN GRATES

Clarksville Foundry and Machine Works, Clarksville, Tenn. Cast iron catch basin, drainage or inlet grates with frames. See page 373.

Irving Subway Grating Co., Inc., 5046 27th St., Long Island City 1, N. Y.; P. O. Box 333 Bayshore Sta., Oakland 23, Calif. Catch basin or inlet grating covers, steel grid. See page 257.

Klemp Metal Corp., 6601 South Melvina Ave., Chicago 38, Ill. Highway and pavement steel drain grating.

EJECTORS

Blackburn-Smith Mfg. Co., Inc., 150 Observer Highway, Hoboken, N. J. Pneumatic sewage ejectors and strainers. See page 496.

Chicago Pump Co., Sewage Equipment Div., 622 Diversey Pkwy., Chicago 14, Ill. Clog-proof Flush-Kleen sewage ejectors for handling raw sewage or liquid containing coarse matter. See page 523.

Buffalo Pumps, Inc., 505 Broadway, Buffalo, N. Y. Duplex sewage ejectors for use in shutdowns; Vertical sewage ejectors; non-clogging sewer ejectors, submerged type.

Ralph B. Carter Co., 196 Atlantic Ave., Hackensack, N. J. Sewage ejectors.

Smith & Loveless, Inc., P. O. Box 8172, Kansas City, Mo.

Weil Pump Co., 1518 A North Fremont St., Chicago, Ill. Non-clog submersible sewage ejectors for underground lift stations and highway underpass drainage.

Worthington Corp., Water Works Eqpt., Harrison, N. J. Steam-jet ejectors, one to four stages.

Yeomans Bros. Co., Melrose Park, Ill. Pneumatic sewage ejectors (Shone, Expelsor, Packex), capacities up to 1000 gpm.

ENGINES

(See Engines-Internal Combustion)
Page 774

FILTERS, OIL

(See Oil Purifiers)

FILTERS, SCREENS

Edward E. Johnson, Inc., 315 N. Pierce St., St. Paul 4, Minn. Johnson screens for diatomite filters, cylindrical filter elements. See page 439.

FILTERS, TRICKLING (SEWAGE)

(See Trickling Filters, page 769)

FILTERS, VACUUM (SEWAGE)

Chicago Bridge & Iron Co., 332 So., Michigan Ave., Chicago 4, Ill. Conkey sludge filter. See pages 297-299; 514.

Dorr-Oliver Inc., Barry Place, Stamford, Conn. Sludge continuous vacuum filters, vacuum drum, pressure. See pages 466-469.

The Eimco Corp., 654 So. 4th West St., Salt Lake City 10, Utah. Continuous vacuum filters (drum, disc, and top feed pan, pressure, plate and frame, clarifying and tray).

Komline-Sanderson Engineering Corp., 100 Holland Ave., **Peapack, N. J. Vacuum filters for sewage.**

FILTERS, WATER

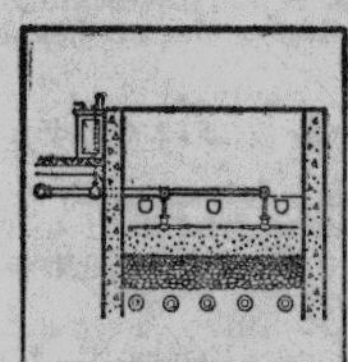

Filters are used for the removal of turbidity, color, iron and manganese. They produce the final polishing action to the water after it has been coagulated and settled. Filters are divided into two classifications: gravity filters and pressure filters. The gravity filters are the type most widely used in municipal water treatment. Pressure filters are commonly used in swimming pools.

Iron and manganese may be removed by aeration, settling and filtration. Another type of equipment sometimes employed to remove small amounts of iron or manganese (not over 1 ppm) from water is the manganese zeolite filter. In some surface waters, iron or manganese occur in the colloidal or organic form and may be removed by coagulation, settling and filtration.

Diatomite pressure filtration for municipal supplies and swimming pool use is gaining wide acceptance. Another class of filter that is rapidly coming into prominence is the filter aid type of filter. Filter aid is a fine powdery type of media usually diatomaceous earth. This material is supported as a coating on a plate or tube surface. The filter aid filter is used with or without pretreatment depending on the condition of the raw water.

Anthracite Eqpt. Corp., Anthracite Institute Bldg., Wilkes-Barre, Pa. Anthrafilt filter medium. See pages 414, 415.

The Carborundum Co., Refractories Div., Perth Amboy, N. J. Porous underdrain plates and discs for direct support of media in pressure and gravity filters and softeners. See page 501.

General Filter Co., Ames, Ia. Pressure, gravity, diatomite. See pages 400, 401.

Graver Water Conditioning Co., 216 W. 14th St., N. Y. 11, N. Y. Water filters, pressure or gravity types; diatomite filters for removal of suspended matter, iron, or objectionable taste and odor. Neutralizing and oil removal—manual or automatic. See pages 402, 403.

Hardinge Co., Inc., 240 Arch St., York, Pa. Automatic back wash sand filters. See page 556.

Modern Swimming Pool Co., Inc., 1 Holland Ave., White Plains, N. Y. Pressure filters. See page 1035.

Northern Gravel Co., Box 307, Muscatine, Ia. Filter sand and gravel. See pages 185-188.

Palmer Filter Equipment Co., P. O. Box 1696, Erie, Pa. Palmer surface wash. Anthrafilt, the hard coal filter medium. See pages 412, 413.

The Permutit Co., 330 W. 42 St., New York 36, N. Y. Filters for iron and manganese removal, neutralizing and oil removal. Automatic or manually controlled pressure or gravity. Carbo-dur filters for removal of bad taste and odor. See pages 416, 417.

Roberts Filter Mfg. Co., 601 Columbia Ave., Darby, Pa. All sizes and types. See page 1042.

Sparkler Mfg. Co., Mundelein, Ill. Jet spray self-cleaning diatomite filters; standard sizes 25 to 1000 sq. ft. area per unit. See pages 424, 425; 1040, 1041.

American Water Softener Co., Inc., S.E. cor. Lehigh & Fourth Sts., Philadelphia 33, Pa.

Builders-Providence, Inc., Div. of B-I-F Industries, Inc., 351 Harris Ave., Providence 1, R. I. Wheeler filter bottoms for gravity-filter underdrain systems give unusually low loss of head and uniform wash-water distribution; precast, formed blocks available, or demountable construction forms available to contractor.

Chemical Equipment Co., P. O. Box 3098, Los Angeles 54, Calif. Filter systems, sand pressure type.

Cochrane Corp., 3122 N. 17th St., Philadelphia 32, Pa. Gravity and pressure sand filters; diatomite filters. Surface wash equipment.

Culligan, Inc., S. Shermer Rd., Northbrook, Ill. Iron removal; rapid sand and anthrafilt.

Elgin Softener Corp., Elgin, Ill. Automatic and manual equipment for removal of suspended impurities, iron, **taste, and odor. Diatomite filters and pressure sand types.**

Everson Mfg. Corp., 205 W. Huron St., Chicago 10, Ill. Domestic and individual filters of various sizes, also complete filtration systems.

Filtros Inc., 3343 Kuppinger St., E. Rochester, N. Y. Porous underdrain plates and discs, ceramically fritted or synthetic bond, for supporting media in pressure and gravity filters and water softeners.

Green Bay Foundry & Machine Works, 401 S. Broadway, Green Bay, Wis. North rotating gravity type water filter units for extremely fine solid screening.

Holyoke Machine Co., 517 Main St., Holyoke, Mass. Pressure and gravity filters.

Hungerford & Terry, Inc., Atlantic Blvd., Clayton, N. J. Iron and manganese removal filters; pressure and gravity type; pressure sand filters; gravity filters.

Infilco Inc., Box 5033, Tucson, Ariz. Gravity and pressure filters. Automatic or manual controls. Hydrodarco purifiers for the removal of odors, taste, residual chlorine.

Lakeside Engineering Corp., 222 W. Adams St., Chicago 6, Ill. Water filters, pressure and gravity, sand, anthrafilt, diatomaceous.

F. B. Leopold Co. Inc., 2275 S. Division St., Zelienople, Pa. Filter bottoms.

Norton Co., Worcester 6, Mass. Porous plates for rapid sand filters.

Proportioneers, Inc., Division of B-I-F Industries, Inc., 351 Harris Ave., Providence 1, R. I. Purecel Diatomaceous-earth filters for swimming pools and small communal water supplies. Can accommodate constant rate or variable supplies and includes slurry and hypochlorite feeders.

Smith & Loveless, Inc., P. O. Box 8172, Kansas City, Mo.

Stuart Corp. Baltimore 1, Md. Main line surface wash for incorporation in new and existing plants to increase filter capacity. Palmer filter bed agitators.

Walker Process Equipment, Inc., Box 266, Aurora, Ill. **Iron and manganese removal from water by contact** aeration and filtration through anthracite media. CO_2 **is removed to irreducible minimum by gravity unit.**

FIRE HYDRANTS

(See page 785)

FLOCCULATING EQUIPMENT

In water supply, flocculation refers to the period in which the coagulating chemicals react to form a floc that traps the suspended matter. This action is speeded by the mechanical flocculation equipment or by air agitation in some cases.

In sewage treatment, flocculation equipment occasionally is included since sewage will form a floc without chemicals. If chemicals are used, as in chemical precipitation, then flocculating equipment aids in making them more effective.

Where chemicals are dosed to form floc, it is usually advantageous to install rapid mixers directly ahead of the flocculators to assure a thorough mixing of the chemicals with the raw sewage or water. Complete treatment plants include chemical mixing, flocculation and settling in a single basin by employing slurry recirculation.

Chain Belt Co., 4640 W. Greenfield Ave., Milwaukee 1, Wis. Float-Treat systems. See page 105.

Dorr-Oliver Inc., Barry Place, Stamford, Conn. Flocculators for both water and sewage treatment. Also flash-mixers. See pages 466-469.

General American Transportation Corp., Field Bldg., Chicago 3, Ill. Turbo-mixers. See page 554.

General Filter Co., Ames, Ia. See pages 400, 401.

Graver Water Conditioning Co., 216 West 14th St., New York 11, N. Y. High-rate, solids—contact Reactivator® for clarification and softening. Spirol-Mix Flocculator for "conventional" treatment. Removal of turbidity, hardness and color. Completely integrated Reactivator® treatment plants for the smaller community. See pages 402, 403.

Hardinge Co., Inc., 240 Arch St., York, Pa. Flocculating equipment. See page 556.

The Permutit Co., 330 W. 42nd St., New York 36, N. Y. Permutit Floc-Formers, remove turbidity and color by forming a tough, easily settleable floc. See pages 416, 417.

Ralph B. Carter Co., 196 Atlantic Ave., Hackensack, N. J. Mechanical mixing equipment.

Cochrane Corp., 3122 N. 17th St., Philadelphia 32, Pa. Solids contact reactors for clarification of water by coagulation and settling.

Infilco Inc., Box 5033, Tucson, Ariz. Vorti®-MIXers and VORTI-FLOC® coagulators for water and sewage treatment.

The Jeffrey Mfg. Co., 970 N. 4th St., Columbus 16, Ohio. Rapid mixers, flocculating equipment; sludge collectors.

Link-Belt Co., Dept. MI, Prudential Plaza, Chicago 1, Ill. Straightline slow mixers and flash mixers.

Smith & Loveless, Inc., P. O. Box 8172, Kansas City, Mo. Flocculators and rapid and slow mixers.

Stuart Corp., Baltimore 1, Md. Kwik-Way mixers and flocculating equipment, walking beam type.

Walker Process Equipment, Inc., Box 266, Aurora, Ill. Mixers for rapid or slow mechanical mixing and flocculation units.

FLUORIDATION

General Chemical Div., Allied Chemical & Dye Corp., 40 Rector St., New York 6, N. Y. Sodium fluoride and sodium silico-fluoride and hydrofluoric acid. See pages 234; 430.

W. A. Taylor & Co., 418 Rodgers Forge Rd., Baltimore 4, Md. Fluoride comparator for control of fluoride dosage. See page 448.

Wallace & Tiernan, Incorporated, 25 Main St., Belleville 9, N. J. Dry chemical and solution feeders, fluoridators. See pages 378-381.

Omega Machine Company, Division of B-I-F Industries, Inc., 351 Harris Ave., Providence 1, R. I. Dry and liquid fluoride feeders.

Proportioneers, Inc., Div. of B-I-F Industries, Inc., 351 Harris Ave., Providence 1, R. I. Complete line of chemical feeders and feeding accessories. Sodium-fluoride hydrofluosilicic acid and sodium-silico-fluoride feeders also available.

Blockson Chemical Co., Div. Olin Mathieson Chemical Corp., P. O. Box 1407, Patterson Rd., Joliet, Ill. Sodium silico fluoride and sodium fluoride. Also sodium hexametaphosphate and hydrofluoric acid.

Hellige, Inc., 877 Stewart Ave., Garden City, N. Y. Aqua Tester and color disc for fluoridation determinations.

FOOD WASTE DISPOSERS, KITCHEN

General Electric Co., Dishwasher and Disposall Dept., Major Appliance Div., Louisville 2, Ky. Disposall. See pages 569-572.

Waste King Corp., 3300 East 50th St., Los Angeles 58, Calif. Waste King Pulverator. See pages 573-576.

Youngstown Kitchens, Warren, Ohio. Youngstown Kitchens Foods Waste Disposer. See pages 577-580.

American Kitchens Div., Avco Mfg. Corp., Connersville, Ind. American Kitchens disposers.

Colerain Metal Products Co., 2021 Eastern Ave., Cincinnati 2, Ohio. Red Goat heavy-duty disposer with high-speed disintegrating action for all types of food waste.

Frigidaire Div. of General Motors Corp., Dayton 1, Ohio. Frigidaire food waste disposer.

Hotpoint Co., 5600 W. Taylor St., Chicago 44, Ill. Hotpoint disposers. Disposall® electric food waste disposers.

In-Sink-Erator Mfg. Co., 1225 14th St., Racine, Wis. Food waste disposer.

National Rubber Mchy. Co., 47 W. Exchange St., Akron 8, Ohio. National Disposer.

Westinghouse Electric Corp., 246 E. 4th St., Mansfield, Ohio. Westinghouse food waste disposer.

FORMS
(See Streets—Forms)

GARBAGE GRINDERS, COMMERCIAL

Gruendler Crusher & Pulverizer Co., 2915 N. Market St., St. Louis 6, Mo. Garbage shredders, sewage screenings, grinders, rubbish and refuse shredders, portable and stationary. See Page 470.

Mitts & Merrill, 1002 S. Water St., Saginaw 8, Mich. Garbage "Hogs" or grinders; compost hogs or grinders. See page 1024.

Waste King Corp., 3300 East 50th St., Los Angeles 58, Calif. Food waste disposers for commercial food handling establishments, the Waste King Commercial Pulverator. See pages 573-576.

Buffalo Hammer Mill Corp., 1239 McKinley Parkway, Buffalo 18, N. Y. Garbage disposal units (Garb-El) for restaurants and super-markets. Waste vegetable disposal units for commercial packers and packagers.

Enterprise Engine and Machinery Co., sub. of General Metals Corp., 622 Florida St., San Francisco 10, Calif. Continuous feeding waste disposer for institutions, hotels, etc.

The Jeffrey Mfg. Co., 970 N. 4th St., Columbus 16, Ohio. Garbage grinders and handling equipment.

Pick-Edmunds & Co., 19755 James Couzens Highway, Detroit 35, Mich. Jeffrey Garbridder.

Williams Patent Crusher and Pulverizer Co., 807 Montgomery St., St. Louis 6, Mo.

GARBAGE TRUCKS
(See Refuse Trucks)

GATES, SLUICE AND SHEAR

The Chapman Valve Mfg. Co., Essex St., Indian Orchard, Mass. Sluice gates and shear gates; floor stands manually or electrically operated. See page 552.

Filer & Stowell Co., 147 E. Becher St., Milwaukee 7, Wis. Sluice gates for every kind and size of service. Floor-stands manually or electrically operated. See page 552.

Iowa Valve Co., Oskaloosa, Iowa. Sub. of James B. Clow & Sons, Inc. Iowa Sluice Gates: Heavy cast iron bronze mounted construction—all styles and types—manual, hydraulic or motor operated, wide range of sizes. See pages 274-275.

Rodney Hunt Machine Co., 112 Lake St., Orange, Mass. Cast iron, bronze-mounted sluice gates 12 to 120," including new HY-Q flush bottom closure gate design. Also fabricated gates of steel, stainless, brass and aluminum, timber gates and gate hoisting equipment.

GRATING, OPEN STEEL, STAIR TREADS

Blaw-Knox Co., 300 Sixth Ave., Pittsburgh, Pa. Electroforged steel stair treads and steel grating for open floor and other requirements. See pages 82-85.

Irving Subway Grating Co., Inc., 5046 27th St., Long Island City 1, N. Y.; P. O. Box 333 Bayshore Sta., Oakland 23, Calif. Gratings—stair treads and open steel and aluminum flooring. See page 257.
Kerrigan Iron Works, Inc., 1033 Herman St., Nashville, Tenn. Weldforged steel gratings and stair treads, 24" and 36" width panels. See pages 258; 807-809.
Neenah Foundry Co., 505 Winneconne Ave., Neenah, Wis. Cast-iron manhole steps and covers, stair treads, grating. See page 259.
Hendrick Mfg. Co., 40 Dundaff St., Carbondale, Pa. Grilles, gratings; open steel flooring.
Klemp Metal Corp., 6601 South Melvina Ave., Chicago 38, Ill. Open steel gratings (structural footwalks) and stair treads.

GRIT CHAMBERS (Sewage)

Grit chambers are used mostly in sewage treatment, but sometimes in waste plants. They are devices that allow the sewage to flow at a velocity that will allow the inorganic matter to settle out and the organic matter to flow on for removal elsewhere. Many have grit washing arrangements, some using compressed air. Most of the larger chambers have mechanical removal mechanisms.

Since variations in flow over a day period are considerable, grit channels having enough capacity to remove objectionable sand at high flows tend also to remove considerable organic material at lesser flows. For this reason it is often advisable to provide some means of grit conditioning to remove and re-introduce organic matter to the flow. This is particularly advisable where the grit disposal area is limited or where cover material is difficult or expensive to obtain.

Chain Belt Co., 4640 W. Greenfield Ave., Milwaukee 1, Wis. Grit collectors, conveyors and washing equipment. See page 105.
Chicago Pump Co., 622 Diversey Pkwy., Chicago 14, Ill. Aer-Degritter systems for grit and odor removal in sewage plants, and in power plant and water-works intakes. See page 523.
Dorr-Oliver Inc., Barry Place, Stamford, Conn. Grit chambers, grit washing equipment. See pages 466-469.
Infilco Inc., Box 5033, Tucson, Ariz. VORTEX® grit removers, grit washers, and conveyors.
The Jeffrey Mfg. Co., 970 N. 4th St., Columbus 16, Ohio. Collector mechanisms for grit chambers and "Jigrit" washers.
Link-Belt Co., Dept. MI, Prudential Plaza, Chicago 1, Ill. Straightline grit collectors and Tritor screens.
Walker Process Equipment, Inc., Box 266, Aurora, Ill. Units for grit separation, grit washing and grit conveyors.

GUNITE

Air Placement Equipment Company, 1005A West 24th Street, Kansas City, Mo. Manufacturers of Airplaco concrete gunning equipment, including the Bondactor, Nucretor, and Mix-Elvator. See page 68.
Pressure Concrete Co., 193 Emmet St., Newark 5, N. J.; 315 S. Court St., Florence, Ala. Gunite for repairing reservoirs, dams, sewage-disposal and water filter plants, lining tunnels, sewers and for constructing prestressed tanks, stacks, side walls and roofs. See pages 420, 421.
Cement Gun Co., Allentown, Pa. Gunite for repairing old, leaky reservoirs.
Gunite Concrete and Construction Co., 1301 Woodswether Rd., Kansas City 5, Mo.; 2016 W. Walnut, Chicago, Ill.; 3206 Houston, Houston, Texas; 3545 Lindell Blvd., St. Louis 3, Mo. Cement gun specialists.
Prehy Company, 420 Lexington Ave., New York 17, N. Y. Concrete gun equipment for spraying concrete coatings, constructing walls, swimming pools, reservoirs, lining tunnels, tanks, repairing deteriorated concrete. Wet or dry sandblasting.

True Gun-All Equipment Corp. Midstate Bldg., Tulsa, Okla. A wet-mix machine for pneumatically applying concrete and cementitious materials.

HYDRANTS

(See page 785.)

INCINERATOR BUCKETS

Blaw-Knox Co., 300 Sixth Ave., Pittsburgh, Pa. Clamshell buckets for incinerator service. See pages 82-85.
The Hayward Co., Dept. S, 50 Church St., New York 7, N. Y. Clamshell buckets for charging incinerators. See pages 534, 535.
Williams Bucket Division, The Wellman Engineering Co., 7004 Central Ave., Cleveland 14, Ohio. Clamshell.

INCINERATOR EQUIPMENT

American Engineering Co., Wheatsheaf Lane & Sepviva St., Philadelphia 37, Pa. Incinerator stoker grates. See page 568.
The Carborundum Co., Refractories Div., Perth Amboy, N. J. Refractories for incinerators, boiler furnaces, etc. See page 501.
M. H. Detrick, 111 W. Washington St., Chicago 2, Ill. Detrick engineered heat enclosures for incinerators. See page 550.
Illinois Stoker Co., 102 W. 7th St., Alton, Ill. Chain grate stokers built to any design. Specially designed for incineration of refuse and garbage. See page 557.
Plibrico Co., 1800 N. Kingsbury St., Chicago 14, Ill. Furnace lining for incinerators and incinerator stacks. See page 561.
Balemaster Div., East Chicago Machine Tool Corp., 4801 Railroad Ave., East Chicago, Ind. Baling presses for paper, cardboard boxes, textiles, scrap metals.
Beaumont Birch Co., Philadelphia 2, Pa. Ash gates and charging gates. Skip hoists for charging; skip hoists, conveyors and bucket elevators for the ashes.
Calcinator Corp., 28 and Water St., Bay City, Mich. Gas, electric and LP gas models for home incineration of all garbage and burnable trash.
Fitch Recuperator Co., 111 E. Front St., Plainfield, N. J. Preheated air for combustion means less auxiliary fuel and more economical furnace operation.
Flynn and Emrich Co., 301 N. Holliday St., Baltimore 2, Md. F & E incinerator stokers.
Laclede Christy Div., H. K. Porter Company, Inc., 2000 Hampton Ave., St. Louis 10, Mo. Laclede H-type refractory wall construction for incinerators and boilers.
Minnich Machine Works, 1607 Ridgely St., Baltimore, Md. Baling presses for salvaging papers and bags.
Norton Co., Worcester 6, Mass. Crystolon silicon carbide cements, brick and special fired shapes for use in municipal incinerators.

INCINERATORS AND SLUDGE DRYERS

American Incinerator Corp., 5710 E. Nevada, Detroit 34, Mich. American custom built or standard incinerators and incinerator equipment. See pages 528-529.
Combustion Engineering, Inc., Raymond Div., 1315 North Branch St., Chicago 22, Ill. C-E Raymond flash drying and incinerations systems. See pages 461-464.
Dravo Corp., Dravo Bldg., Pittsburgh 22, Pa. Package unit incinerator provides continuous, controlled combustion of all burnable refuse regardless of moisture content. See pages 168, 551.
Illinois Stoker Co., 102 W. 7th St., Alton, Ill. Chain grate stokers built to any design. Specially designed for incineration of refuse and garbage. See page 557.
Morse Boulger Destructor Co., 80 Fifth Ave., New York 11, N. Y. Manually or mechanically stoked incinerators for municipal, industrial, institutional or residential wastes including garbage, rubbish, sludge, etc. See pages 502-505.
Nichols Engineering & Research Co., 70 Pine St., New York, N. Y. Multiple hearth sludge furnaces. See pages 510-513.
Pittsburgh-Des Moines Steel Co., 3460 Neville Island, Pittsburgh, Pa. Garbage and rubbish incinerators. See pages 418, 419; 544, 545.
Joseph Goder Incinerators, 4241 N. Honore St., Chicago 13, Ill. Incinerators, destructors, portable incinerators.
International Incinerators, Inc., Walton Bldg., Atlanta 3, Ga. International Incinerators (Volund Patents) designed both with or without heat recovery.

INSTRUMENTS, ENGINEERING

(See page 795.)

INSTRUMENTS AND LABORATORY EQUIPMENT

Bailey Meter Co., 1035 Ivanhoe Rd., Cleveland 10, Ohio. Differential, flow, gas analysis, liquid level, position, pH, pressure, smoke density, specific gravity, specific weight, speed, temperature, vacuum, weight. See page 480.

Fischer & Porter Co., 850 Warminster Rd., Hatboro, Pa. Local and remote indicating, transmitting, and recording and controlling instruments for flow, temperature, pressure, liquid level, humidity, density, viscosity. Also data reduction systems, laboratory and industrial glass products. See pages 317-320.

Industrial Radio Corp., 428 N. Parkside Ave., Chicago 44, Ill. Two-way communications equipment for use in water and sewage plants and in municipally-owned utility companies. See page 992.

Simplex Valve & Meter Co., 7 East Orange St., Lancaster, Pa. Pitot equipment for water waste surveys; WK tap meters for measuring water through hydraulic turbine; manometers. See pages 422, 423.

W. A. Taylor & Co., 418 Rodgers Forge Rd., Baltimore 4, Md. Colorimetric equipment, for control of pH, chlorine, phosphate, and water analysis. See page 448.

W. H. & L. D. Betz, Gillingham & Worth Sts., Philadelphia 24, Pa. Test sets for hardness, alkalinity, chloride, sulfate; colorimetric comparators.

The Bristol Co., P. O. Box 1790 MI, Waterbury 20, Conn. Indicating, telemetering, recording, automatic controlling instruments for temperature, pressure, liquid level, pH, humidity and flow. Also, pump operating controllers and operation recorders.

Burgess-Manning Co., Penn Instruments Div., 4110 Haverford Ave., Philadelphia 4, Pa. Temperature and pressure recorders and controllers.

Fisher Research Laboratory, Inc., Palo Alto, Calif. Well testing equipment.

General Laboratory Supply Co., P. O. Box 2607, Patererson, N. J. Specialists in laboratory and testing equipment for sewage and trade wastes. Battery-operated Ardco Model 535 for D O determination and oxygen utilization rates, measures any reducible ion such as nitrate or copper.

The Goldak Co., Inc., 1542-44 Glenoaks, Glendale 1, Calif. Model G-6 gas appliance tester enables service man to read thermocouple voltages, check gas valves, etc.

W. & L. E. Gurley, 510-514 Fulton St., Troy, N. Y. Current meters and water level recorders for water and sewage plants.

Hellige, Inc., 877 Stewart Ave., Garden City, N. Y. Comparators and Aqua Testers employing non-fading glass color standards for precise pH control, analyses of water sewage and industrial wastes.

Klett Mfg. Co., 179 E. 87th St., New York, N. Y. Klett-Summerson photoelectric colorimeter; laboratory apparatus.

Lakeside Engineering Corp., 222 W. Adams St., Chicago 6, Ill. Sewage samplers (trebler).

La Motte Chemical Co., Towson, Baltimore 4, Md. Control equipment and reagents for pH, chlorine, phosphates, etc.

Pango Manufacturing Co., P. O. Box 104, Yardville Station, Trenton, N. J. Pango Sewage Sampler with 800 cc capacity.

Payne Dean & Co., Madison, Conn. Wind direction and velocity indicators, electric remote gate position indicators, electric remote water level indicators.

Phipps & Bird, Inc., 303 S. 6th St., Richmond 5, Va. Flocculation stirrers, laboratory turbidimeters.

Stuart Corp., Baltimore 1, Md. Automatic samplers. Also jar test machines, laboratory stirrers.

U. S. Gauge, Div. American Machine and Metals, Inc., Sellersville, Pa. Laboratory test gages. Ranges from 15 lb. to 20,000 lb. make gages suitable for replacing or augmenting dead weight testers or manometers.

ION EXCHANGERS
(See Water Softeners)

IRON AND MANGANESE REMOVAL
(See Water Softeners)

LEAK DETECTORS
(See Pipe Finders and Leak Detectors)

LINERS, RESERVOIRS, ETC.

W. R. Meadows, Inc., 4 Kimball St., Elgin, Ill. Hydromat liners are composed of a core of asphalt and fibrous and filler materials for flexibility at all temperatures. It is shipped in sheets 4' x 15'. Installed in reservoirs, sewage lagoons, sludge ponds, ice-skating ponds, swimming pools.

LOCATORS, VALVE, PIPE
(See Pipe Finders and Leak Detectors)

JOINTING COMPOUNDS

Byerlyte Corp., 2302 W. 3rd St., Cleveland 13, Ohio. Sewer joint compound. See pages 146, 147.

The Philip Carey Mfg. Co., Lockland, Cincinnati 15, Ohio. Sewer joint compound with or without tar base. Hot pour asphalt. See page 92.

Presstite-Keystone Engineering Products Co., Div. American Marietta Co., 3772 Chouteau Ave., St. Louis 10, Mo. Kapco rock shield for pipelines. Kapco hot pour and Kapco cold trowel sewer joint compounds. See pages 189-192.

Radiator Specialty Co., 1400 W. Independence Blvd., Charlotte 1, N. C. Titeseal gasket and joint sealing compound for sealing pipe threads, pump gaskets and valves, etc. See pages 959-962.

The Robinson Clay Products Co., 65 W. State St., Akron 9, Ohio. Wedge-Lock sewer pipe joint. See page 563.

The Atlas Mineral Products Co., 135 Walnut St., Mertztown, Pa. For cast-iron bell and spigot water pipe and clay and concrete sewer pipe.

Berry Asphalt Co., of Arkansas, 141 W. Jackson Blvd., Chicago 4, Ill. Permaseal sewer joint compound, waterproof, root resistant, on vitrified clay pipe.

The Bond-O Co., Spring Valley, N. Y. Self-caulking pipe joint compound. Also rubber packing gaskets for Bell and Spigot cast iron pipe.

Crane Co., 836 S. Michigan Ave., Chicago 5, Ill. Jointing compounds.

Michael Hayman & Co., 870 E. Ferry St., Buffalo, N. Y. M. H. Brand soft caulking lead and Haymanite joint compound.

Hydraulic Development Co., 50 Church St., New York 7, N. Y. Fibrex sanitary joint packing. Hydro-tite.

The Leadite Co., Inc., 1400 S. Penn Square, Philadelphia, Pa. Jointing compounds.

W. R. Meadows, Inc., 4 Kimball St., Elgin, Ill. Both hot pouring and cold troweling sewer joint compounds, also joint sealing compounds of plain asphalt and rubber-asphalt types.

X-Pando Corp., 43-12 36th St., Long Island City 1, N. Y. Pipe joint compound for threaded and flanged joints.

MANHOLE ADAPTERS
(See Castings)

MANHOLE COVERS, CASTINGS
(See Castings, page 752)

METER BOXES
(See Boxes)

METERS, FLOW

Bailey Meter Co., 1035 Ivanhoe Rd., Cleveland 10, Ohio. Flow meters. See page 480.

Fischer & Porter Co., 850 Warminster Rd., Hatboro, Pa. Flow and rate of flow indicators, recorders, and controllers. Variable-Area meters, static and kinetic manometers. See pages 317-320.

Simplex Valve & Meter Co., 7 East Orange St., Lancaster, Pa. Flow controllers, recorders, indicators, totalizers. See pages 422, 423.

Sparling Meter Co., 225 N. Temple City Blvd., El Monte, Calif. Open flow meters. See page 447.

The Bristol Co., P. O. Box 1790 MI, Waterbury 20, Conn. Flow, flume, open channel and weir meters.

Builders-Providence, Inc., Div. of B-I-F Industries, Inc., 351 Harris Ave., Providence, 1, R. I. Kennison open-flow nozzles; rate-of-flow controllers; Chronoflo electric telemeters; pneumatic meters; Type M and Flo-Watch mechanical totalizing-indicating-recording instruments; steam, air and gas meters; and multi-function supervisory control system.

Burgess-Manning Co., Penn Instruments Div., 4110 Haverford Ave., Philadelphia 4, Pa. Flow meters. Flume meters.

Foster Engineering Co., 835 Lehigh Ave., Union, N. J. Gentile flow tubes—primary meter (differential producer) for measurement and regulation of fluid flow.

The Foxboro Co., Foxboro, Mass. Flow and rate-of-flow meters, electromagnetic; telemetering systems.

The Hays Corp., Michigan City, Ind. Flow meters.
Infilco Inc., Box 5033, Tucson, Ariz. Rate of flow controllers, manometers, TI meters, and gauges (indicating, recording, totalizing).
Republic Flow Meters Co., 2240 Diversey Parkway, Chicago 47, Ill. Mechanical ring-balance flow meters; open channel flow meters.
Minneapolis-Honeywell Regulator Co., Industrial Div., Wayne and Windrim Aves., Philadelphia 44, Pa. Flow and rate of flow meters. Flume meters.

METERS, GAS, SEWAGE GAS

Bailey Meter Co., 1035 Ivanhoe Rd., Cleveland 10, Ohio. See page 480.
Roots-Connersville Blower Div., Dresser Industries, Inc. Connersville, Ind. Rotary displacement meters for measuring sewage sludge gas. See page 564.
American Meter Co., 60 E. 42 St., New York 17, N. Y. Also pressure regulators.
The Foxboro Co, Foxboro, Mass.
The Sprague Meter Co., Bridgeport, Conn. Cast iron and aluminum case gas meters and regulators for high, medium and low pressure.

METERS, MAIN LINE

Bailey Meter Co., 1035 Ivanhoe Rd., Cleveland 10, Ohio. Flow, pressure, temperature, liquid level, gas analysis, indicating, recording, controlling; mechanical and electronic; open channel and Venturi meters for sewage and water; control systems for steam power stations, water works and sewage treatment plant. See page 480.
Simplex Valve & Meter Co., 7 East Orange St., Lancaster, Pa. Venturi tubes, flow nozzles or orifice type meters, rectangular or circular chart type, high or low head operation. Type S Parabolic Flumes for measurement of liquids under low head conditions or through partially filled pipe lines or sewers. See pages 422, 423.
Sparling Meter Co., 225 N. Temple City Blvd., El Monte, Calif. Totalizing meters for all main lines, 2 inches up. Flow-rate indicators and recorders, installed with the meter or later. Sparling compound meters for lines from 6 to 36", with flanged, bell and spigot ends, widely used for auto-metered chlorination. See page 447.
The Bristol Co., P. O. Box 1790 MI, Waterbury 20, Conn.
Builders-Providence, Inc., Div. of B-I-F Industries, Inc., 851 Harris Ave., Providence 1, R. I. Kennison open-flow nozzles; rate of flow controllers; Chronoflo electric telemeters, pneumatic meters; Type M and Flo-Watch mechanical totalizing-indicating-recording instruments; steam, air, and gas meters; and multi-function supervisory control system.
Burgess-Manning Co., Penn Instruments Div., 4110 Haverford Ave., Philadelphia 4, Pa. Flow; temperature and pressure recorders and controllers.
The Foxboro Co., Foxboro, Mass. Main line.
Minneapolis-Honeywell Regulator Co., Industrial Div., Wayne and Windrim Aves., Philadelphia 44, Pa. Venturi and orifice type meters. Flow, pressure, liquid level, temperature recorders and controllers.
Republic Flow Meters Co., 2240 Diversey Parkway, Chicago 47, Ill. Flow; remote liquid level and pressure recorders and indicators.

METERS, WATER

Badger Meter Mfg. Co., 2371 N. 30th St., Milwaukee 45, Wis. Diversified line of cold water disc, oscillating piston turbine and compound meters with Badger multiple meter testers, portable test meters, meter coupling yokes, etc., adaptable to all metering requirements. See pages 293-296.
Buffalo Meter Co., 2900 Main St., Buffalo 14, N. Y. Meters, water, disc type, bronze or galvanized iron castings, sizes ⅝" to 6". See page 356.
Hersey Mfg. Co., "E" and 2nd Sts., South Boston, Mass. Fire service compound, torrent, disc and proportional water meters. See pages 404, 405.
Neptune Meter Co., 19 W. 50th St., New York 20, N. Y. Full line with interchangeability feature. See page 369-372.
Well Machinery & Supply Co., Inc., Calmet Water Meter Div., 1629 Main St., Fort Worth, Texas. Calmet meter is all bronze split case design, frost proof bolts, ⅝" to 2". See pages 383-386.
Worthington-Gamon Meter Div., Worthington Corp., 296 South St., Newark 5, N. J. Liquid meters cold and hot water, oil, gasoline, other liquids. See pages 391-394.
Magnamatic Corp. of America, 1121 Kinney Ave., Corpus Christi, Texas. Magnetic heads that eliminate stuffing box leaks, corrosion of register, broken or fogged glass, and tampering with dials.
Minneapolis-Honeywell Regulator Co., Industrial Div., Wayne and Windrim Aves., Philadelphia 44, Pa.
Rockwell Mfg. Co., 400 N. Lexington Ave., Pittsburgh 8, Pa. Complete line: disc, oscillating piston, current, compound types.

METER COUPLINGS

Smith-Blair Inc., 535 Railroad Ave., San Francisco, Calif. Smith-Blair flexible meter couplings. Flanged coupling adapters. See pages 374-377.
Jasco Products Co., 8102 Bonner Drive, Houston 17, Texas. Adjustable water meter couplings, for ⅝", ¾", and 1" meters, all brass.

METER SEALS

E. J. Brooks Co., 169 N. 13th St., Newark 7, N. J
Fog-Tite Meter Seal Co, 4609 6th Ave., So., Seattle 8, Wash.
United Seal Co., 450 S. Pearl St., Columbus 15, Ohio. Lead-wire and reusable padlock seals for utility meters; wire on coils, spools or to cut lengths. Metal checks, tags and wires. Renewable cast-iron seals for stopcocks and unions, ½ to 2" pipe sizes.

METER TESTING AND READING EQUIPMENT

Badger Meter Mfg. Co., 2371 N. 30th St., Milwaukee 45, Wis. Multiple meter testers, portable test meters, meter coupling yokes. See pages 293-296.
The Ford Meter Box Co., Inc., 1000 Manchester Ave., Wabash, Ind. Calibrated and portable tanks, test benches. Testerate indicators, tester clamps. See pages 329-332.
Hays Mfg. Co., 12th and Liberty Sts., Erie, Pa. Meter setting equipment: Copper meter setters with couplings for either iron pipe or copper tubing; meter raisers. See page 436.
Neptune Meter Co., 19 W. 50th St., New York 20, N. Y. Test benches. See pages 369-372.
Smith-Blair Inc, 535 Railroad Ave. S., San Francisco, Calif. Smith-Blair flexible meter tee testing couplings. See pages 374-377.
Magnamatic Corp. of America, 1121 Kinney Ave., Corpus Christi, Texas. Magnetic recording devices that give accurate reading either visually or on tape.

PIPE

Cast Iron Pipe

Alabama Pipe Co., Anniston, Ala. Super deLavaud cast-iron pipe in 18-foot length. See pages 277-280.
American Cast Iron Pipe Co., 2930 16th St., N., Birmingham 2, Ala. Cast iron pipe and fittings, supplied with or without tar coating, cement, or Enameline lining, in sizes 2 through 48". See pages 289-292.
James B. Clow & Sons, Inc., P. O. Box 6600-A, 201-299 N. Talman Ave., Chicago 80, Ill Cast-iron pipe, fittings, valves, fire hydrants, and specials for water distribution systems and treatment plants, and for sewage disposal plants. Cast iron mechanical joint pressure pipe & fittings. River crossing cast iron pipe. See pages 270-275.
Lone Star Steel Co., Box 12226, Dallas 25, Tex. Cast-iron pipe. See page 443.
R. D. Wood Co., Philadelphia 5, Pa. Cast-iron pipe, fittings. "Sand spun" pipe, sizes up to 30." See pages 387-390.
Glamorgan Pipe and Foundry Co., 1938 Capren St., Lynchburg, Va. Cast iron bell and spigot pressure pipe and fittings; cast iron mechanical joint pipe and fittings; cast iron flanged pipe and fittings.
Lynchburg Foundry Co., 58 Courtland Bldg., Lynchburg, Va. 4 to 24" Super deLavaud centrifugally cast iron bell and spigot and/or standard mechanical joint pipe in 18' lengths.
McWane Cast Iron Pipe Co., 1201 Vanderbilt Rd., Birmingham 2, Ala. Cast-iron water pipe 2" through 12" sizes. Pipe furnished B&S or with mechanical joints.
Pacific States Cast Iron Pipe Co., Provo, Utah. 4" through 24" cast-iron water and gas pipe, bell and spigot or mechanical joint; cast iron water fittings.

United States Pipe and Foundry Co., 3300 First Ave. N., Birmingham, Ala. Centrifugally cast-pipe, sizes 3 to 24"; pit cast pipe, 3 to 84"; cast iron pipe and fittings.
Warren Foundry & Pipe Div., Shahmoon Industries, Inc., 55 Liberty St., New York 5, N. Y. Cast-iron pipe and fittings from 4" to 84" furnished with bell and spigot, mechanical joint, plain end or flange, for water, gas and sewer service.

Pipe, Concrete Pressure

American Vitrified Products Co., National City Bank Bldg., Cleveland 14, Ohio. Concrete pressure pipe. See page 465.
Lock Joint Pipe Co., P. O. Box 269, East Orange, N. J. Prestressed and reinforced concrete pipes, transmission, distribution and subaqueous lines. See pages 341-343; 558.
American-Marietta Co., Concrete Products Div., 101 East Ontario St., Chicago 11, Ill. Amseal pressure pipe for siphons, intakes, circulating systems and low pressure supply lines.
American Pipe and Construction Co., P. O. Box 3428, Terminal Annex, Los Angeles 54, Calif. Concrete pipe for main water supply lines, storm and sanitary sewers, subaqueous pipe lines and irrigation lines.
Brighton Steel Co., Stormville, N. Y. Reinforced concrete pipe.
No-Joint Concrete Pipe Co., P. O. Box 512, Yuba City, Calif. Cast-on-the-spot no-joint concrete pipe for sewers and irrigation lines.
Price Brothers Company, 1932 E. Monument Ave., Dayton 1, Ohio. Concrete pressure pipe—cylinder and non-cylinder in 16" lengths, 16, 20, 24, 30, 36, 42, 48" diameters and larger.
Universal Concrete Pipe Co., 101 E. Ontario St., Chicago 11, Illinois. Amseal pressure pipe for siphons, intakes, circulating systems and low pressure supply lines.

Copper and Brass Pipe

The American Brass Co., Waterbury 20, Conn. Copper. See pages 526, 527.
Revere Copper and Brass, Inc., 230 Park Ave., New York 17, N. Y. Copper water service pipe and tube for water, oil, or gas for underground systems, and hot and cold water service lines. See page 445.
Bridgeport Brass Co., 30 Grand St., Bridgeport, Conn. Copper water tube.
Chase Brass and Copper Co., 1949 Rodney St., Waterbury 20, Conn. Brass and copper pipe; copper water tube and fittings.
Lewin-Mathes Co., 1111 Chouteau Ave., St. Louis 2, Mo. Brass and copper tube and pipe for general heating and plumbing, gas, steam and oil lines, severe service conditions. Copper drainage tube.
Mueller Brass Co., Port Huron, Mich. Copper tube and solder type fittings. Check, gate, globe, and compression valves for plumbing systems in installations of plumbing, heating, air conditioning, water works, and industrial applications; non-rusting. Polyethylene.
Phelps Dodge Copper Products Corp., 300 Park Ave., New York 22, N. Y. Phelps Dodge copper water tubes ¼" to 6" in 20 foot length; up to 1½" in 60-foot coils.
Wolverine Tube, Division of Calumet & Hecla, Inc., Guardian Towers, Guardian Bldg., Detroit, Mich. Wolverine S.P.S. pipe copper water tube.

Insulated Pipe

Ric-wiL Incorporated, Barberton, Ohio. Insulated pipe units for underground or overhead piping in central heating systems.

Non-Metallic Pipe

Johns-Manville, 22 E. 40th St., New York 16, N. Y. Transite® asbestos-cement pipe in various pressure classes in diameters of 4" through 36". See pages 406, 407; 536, 537.
Keasbey & Mattison Co., Ambler, Pa. Asbestos-cement pipe. See pages 408, 409; 538, 539.
Lock Joint Pipe Co., P. O. Box 269, East Orange, N. J. Prestressed and reinforced concrete pipes; pressure, subaqueous sewer, culvert. See pages 341-343; 558.
Natco Corp., 327 Fifth Ave., Pittsburgh 22, Pa. Natco clay sewer pipe.
Price Brothers Company, 1932 E. Monument Ave., Dayton 1, Ohio. Concrete pressure pipe—cylinder and non-cylinder in 16' lengths, 14, 20, 24, 30, 36, 42, 48" diameters and larger.

Plastic Pipe

Yardley Plastics Co., 142 Parsons Ave., Columbia 15, Ohio. Plastic pipe for water or waste disposal systems, ½-6". See pages 426, 427.
Carlon Products Corp., 10300 Meech Ave., Cleveland 5, Ohio. Carlon plastic pipe for medium-pressure, low-temperature applications.
The Carpenter Steel Co., Alloy Tube Div., Union, N. J. PVC (polyvinyl chloride) plastic pipe. 8 pipe sizes of ½" to 4".
Johnson Plastic Corp., Chagrin Falls 2, Ohio. Johnson plastic pipe.
National Tube Div., U. S. Steel Corp., 525 William Penn Place, Pittsburgh 30, Pa. Normal-impact and high-impact polyvinyl chloride plastic pipe.
Triangle Conduit and Cable Co., New Brunswick, N. J. Plastic pipe.

Sewer Pipe

American Vitrified Products Co., National City Bank Bldg., Cleveland 14, Ohio. Amvit jointed clay sewer pipe, 4" through 24" sizes. See page 465.
Johns-Manville, 22 E. 40th St., New York 16, N. Y. Transite® asbestos-cement pipe, also building sewer pipe for disposal of sewage from buildings to street sewers and septic tanks. Furnished in standard 10" lengths with inside diameter of 4, 5, and 6". See pages 406, 407; 536, 537.
Lock Joint Pipe Co., P. O. Box 269, East Orange, N. J. Reinforced concrete pipe for sewers, culverts, irrigation lines. See pages 341-343; 558.
The Robinson Clay Products Co., 65 W. State St., Akron 9, Ohio. In 16 states east of Wisconsin and Illinois. Vitrified clay for sewers, culverts, drainage, etc. See page 563.
Armco Drainage & Metal Products, Inc., 5896 Curtis St., Middletown, Ohio. Corrugated metal sewer pipe. Asphalt covered sewer pipe; ASBESTOS-BONDED sewer pipe; PAVED-INVERT pipe; SMOOTH-FLO sewer pipe. Pipe-Arch for drainage and sewers under limited headroom.
Brighton Steel Co., Stormville, N. Y. Corrugated metal pipe.
Brown Co., 150 Causeway St., Boston 14, Mass. Bermico® bituminized fibre sewer pipe and complete line of fittings.
Cannelton Sewer Pipe Co., Cannelton, Ind. Vitrified clay sewer pipe, standard and extra strength.
W. S. Dickey Clay Mfg. Co., P. O. Box 2028, Kansas City 42, Mo. Salt glazed clay sewer pipe, flue lining and wall coping.
Laclede-Christy Div., H. K. Porter Co., Inc., 2000 Hampton Ave., St. Louis 10, Mo. Vitrified clay sewer pipe.
Natco Corp., 327 Fifth Ave., Pittsburgh 22, Pa. Natco vitrified salt-glazed clay sewer pipe.
National Clay Pipe Mfg., Inc., 1820 "N" Street, N.W., Washington 6, D. C. Vitrified clay pipe for sewers. Perforated pipe.
No-Joint Concrete Pipe Co., P. O. Box 512, Yuba City, Calif. Cast-on-the-spot no-joint concrete pipe for sewers and irrigation lines.
Price Brothers Company, 1932 E. Monument Ave., Dayton 1, Ohio. Concrete pressure sewer pipe; subaqueous pipe, 16, 20, 24, 30, 36, 42, 48" diameters and larger.
Texas Vitrified Pipe Co., Box 111, Mineral Wells, Texas. Vitrified clay sewer pipe and drain tile.
Universal Concrete Pipe Co., 101 E. Ontario St., Chicago 11, Illinois. Culvert, sewer, flat-base Amseal pressure pipe, hi-hed, and lo-hed pipe.
Universal Sewer Pipe Corp., 1500 Union Commerce Bldg., Cleveland 14, Ohio. Fire brick and fire clay sewer pipe. Vit. sewer pipe with tylox gaskets.

Steel Pipe

Bethlehem Steel Co., Inc., Bethlehem, Pa. Welded steel, tar enameled pipe for water distribution lines and force mains in sewage systems. See pages 326, 327; 485.
R. D. Cole Mfg. Co., Newnan, Ga. Welded steel pipe. See pages 305-308.
Lone Star Steel Co., Box 12226, Dallas 25, Texas. Steel pipe. See page 443.
Alco Products, Inc., Schenectady 5, N. Y. Electric welded steel pipe for water supply systems and distribution lines and sewage systems, to 96".
Armco Drainage & Metal Products, Inc., 5896 Curtis St., Middletown, Ohio. Spiral welded steel pipes, 6-in. to 36-in. for water supply lines.

National Tube Div., United States Steel Corp., 525 William Penn Place, Pittsburgh, Pa. Steel pipe.
Naylor Pipe Co., Chicago 19, Ill. Lockseam spiralweld pipe and fittings.

PIPE CLAMPS, BELL JOINT

James B. Clow & Sons, Inc., P. O. Box 6600-A, 201-299 N. Talman Ave., Chicago 80, Ill. Clow mechanical joint bell split sleeves for making permanent repairs to damaged cast-iron pipe joints 3 to 16". See pages 270-275.
Dresser Mfg. Div., Dresser Industries, Inc., Bradford, Pa. Clamps and sleeves for repairing steel and cast-iron pipe; joints for use in initial installation of cast-iron pipe. See pages 321-324.
M. B. Skinner Co., 3502 W. Sample St., South Bend 21, Ind. Bell joint clamps, split coupling clamps for broken mains, emergency pipe clamps, pipe line clamps, high pressure weld clamps, service saddles. See page 446.
Smith-Blair Inc., 535 Railroad Ave., S. San Francisco. Calif. Smith-Blair repair clamps, split couplings, and special fabrications. See pages 374-377.
H. Y. Carson Co., 1221 Pinson St., Birmingham, Ala. Carson leak clamps 3 to 36", flexibility without leaks. Also charcoal cast-iron bolts. For cast-iron pipe joints.
Mueller Co., 512 W. Cerro Gordo St., Decatur, Ill. Service clamps.

PIPE CLAMPS, PIPE LINE

James B. Clow & Sons, Inc., P. O. Box 6600-A, 201-299 N. Talman Ave., Chicago 80, Ill. Clow mechanical joint split sleeves for making permanent repairs to damaged cast-iron pipe 3 to 16". See pages 270-275.
Dresser Mfg. Div., Dresser Industries, Inc., Bradford, Pa. Clamps and sleeves for repairing steel and cast-iron pipe; joints for use in initial installation of cast-iron pipe. Couplings, etc. See pages 321-324.
M. B. Skinner Co., 3502 W. Sample St., South Bend 21, Ind. Pipe line clamps, emergency pipe clamps, bell joint clamps, split coupling clamps for broken mains, service saddles. See page 446.
Smith-Blair Inc., 535 Railroad Ave., S. San Francisco. Calif. Clamps: full circle, pipe repair, collar, service saddles. See pages 374-377.
Atlas Industries, P. O. Box 8152, Houston, Texas. Water pipe repair clamps; pipe leak repair tools and patches; cold-weld pipe leak repair.
R. H. Baker & Co., Inc., 2244 E. 37th St., Los Angeles 58, Calif. Baker CirclSeal fully cushioned wrap-around clamps for asbestos-cement, cast iron and steel pipe. ShurSeal bronze and cast iron service saddles; HiPressure leak repair clamps.
Mueller Co., 512 W. Cerro Gordo St., Decatur, Ill. Service clamps.

PIPE CLAMPS, SERVICE SADDLES

M. B. Skinner Co., 3502 W. Sample St., South Bend 21, Ind. Service saddles, bell joint clamps, split coupling clamps for repairing broken mains, emergency pipe clamps, pipe line clamps. See page 446.
Smith-Blair, Inc., 535 Railroad Ave., S. San Francisco, Calif. Service saddles. See page 374-377.

PIPE CLEANING

(See Sewer Cleaning)
(See Water Main Cleaners)

PIPE COUPLINGS AND FITTINGS

Dresser Mfg. Div., Dresser Industries, Inc., Bradford, Pa. Couplings, fittings, repair products. Regular couplings to make tight joints in plain-end pipe; boltless fittings to make tight joints in plain-end pipe boltless fittings (male and female) and straight tees. See pages 321-324.
Hamilton Kent Mfg. Co., 218 Gougler Ave., Kent, Ohio. Tylox rubber gaskets, in two types. Also Rexon rubber gaskets. See page 555.
Hays Mfg. Co., 12th and Liberty Sts., Erie Pa. See page 436.
A. Y. McDonald Mfg. Co., 12th and Pine Sts., Dubuque, Ia. Lead goosenecks, copper service pipe couplings, adapters, copper goosenecks, gas service stops, extension service boxes. See pages 352-355.
Trinity Valley Iron & Steel Co., P. O. Box 664, Fort Worth, Texas. Cast iron pipe fittings, AWWA Standard in both long and short pattern, also mechanical joint, ring-tite, and fluid-tite fittings. See page 451.
Smith-Blair Inc., 535 Railroad Ave., S. San Francisco, Calif. Smith-Blair flexible couplings for all types of pipe; transition and reducing couplings; blind, tee, and split couplings; service, insulating and full circle clamp couplings; service clamps; cast iron tees; pressure seal plugs; water lock rings. See pages 374-377.
American Foundry & Mfg. Co., 1015 Hebert St., St. Louis 7, Mo. Cast iron water main fittings.
Alco Products, Inc., Schenectady 5, N. Y. Forged steel pipe flanges, elbows and fittings to 84".
R. H. Baker & Co., Inc., 2244 E. 37th St., Los Angeles 58, Calif. TriplSeal pressed steel flexible pipe couplings; AllSteel couplings; AllCopper fittings for use with asbestos Ring-Tite or Fluid-Tite pipe.
Jasco Products Co., Dept. P, 8102 Bonner Drive, Houston 17, Texas. Couplings, ⅝", ¾" and 1" sizes, all brass. Female, Male and copper tubing connections.
Mueller Co., 512 W. Cerro Gordo St., Decatur, Ill. Couplings for copper service pipe.
National Clay Pipe Mfg., Inc., 1820 "N" Street, N. W., Washington 6, D. C. Vitrified clay pipe fittings.
Nelson Foundry Co., Morton Grove, Ill. Barracuda brass fittings for plastic pipe—non slip.
Victaulic Co. of America, 1100 Morris Ave., Union, N. J. Pipe couplings for steel, cast iron, plastic and other pipe.
The E. H. Wachs Co., 1525 N. Dayton St., Chicago 22, Ill. Weld + Ends coupling in sizes from 2" to 36" and larger. Also special cast iron pipe fittings.

PIPE FINDERS AND LEAK DETECTORS

Computer-Measurements Corp., 5528 Vineland Ave., North Hollywood, Calif. Model 505 pipe locator for pipes and cables. Model 303 box and valve detector; Model 505-C combination pipe-leak detector. See pages 309-312.
Aqua Survey & Instrument Co., 2010 Leslie Ave., Cincinnati 12, Ohio. Aqua water or gas valve box locator.
Fisher Research Laboratory, Inc., Palo Alto, Calif. M-Scope pipe and cable finder; leak detector; box locator.
Globe Phone Mfg. Co., Reading, Mass. Geophone Leak Locator.
The Goldak Co., Inc., 1542-44 Glenoaks, Glendale 1, Calif. Electronic locators for pipe, valve box, and leaks. Dualtronic, combination pipe locator and leak detector.
Joseph G. Pollard Co., Inc., New Hyde Park, N. Y. Eastern distributors of Fisher Research Laboratory, Inc.
Wilkinson Products Co., 3987 Chevy Chase Drive, Pasadena 3, Calif. Wgt. 10 lb., all circuits etched. Built-in battery tester. Designed to reach very deep pipes, cables, etc. Indicates depth of underground structures. Cases of wear resisting phenolic material.

PIPE LINING

Centriline Corp., 140 Cedar St., New York 6, N. Y. Cement mortar lining new or existing pipe in place from 4 to 144" in diameter. See pages 429; 431; 433; 435.
Amercoat Corporation, 4809 Firestone Blvd., South Gate, Calif. T-Lock Amer-Plate sheet sewer lining composed of inert resins and plasticizers.
Pipe Linings, Inc., P. O. Box 457, Wilmington, Calif. Relining of cast iron or steel pipe lines in place with cement mortar—service is not appreciably disturbed.

PIPE MACHINES

(See Listings page 749)

PIPE PLACING

Boyce Co., Clearwater, Fla. Submerged pipe lines placed anywhere in the world.
Caterpillar Tractor Co., Peoria, Ill. Three sizes of pipelayers, from 26,530 to 130,000 lbs. lifting capacity.

PIPE WRAP

The Philip Carey Mfg. Co., Lockland, Cincinnati 15, Ohio. Pipe coverings and insulations for low or high pressure steam lines. See page 92.
Johns-Manville, 22 E. 40th St., New York 16, N. Y. Complete line of pipe insulations for high and low temperatures. Protective tape for pipeline coating. Complete line of pipeline felts. See pages 406, 407; 536, 537.
L-O-F Glass Fibers Co., 1810 Madison Ave., Toledo 1, Ohio. "Blue Flag" reinforcing pipe wrap. See page 441.
M. J. Crose Mfg., 2715 Dawson Rd., Tulsa, Okla. Traveling coating and wrapping machines for pipes of any size.

Hill, Hubbell & Co., Div. of General Paint Corp., 3091 Mayfield Rd., Cleveland, Ohio. Application of coating and wrapping to steel pipe.

Owens-Corning Fiberglas Corp., Nichols Bldg., Toledo 1, Ohio. Coromat inner wrap, pipe line outer wrap.

PROTECTIVE COATINGS
For Concrete and Masonry

Barrett Div., Allied Chemical & Dye Corp., 40 Rector St., New York 6, N. Y. Paints, waterproofing, dampproofing, bituminous paints and cements; pipe line enamel, waterworks enamel, pipe line felts. See page 269.

Byerlyte Corp., 2302 W. 3rd St., Cleveland 13, Ohio. Waterproofing for pools, foundations, bridges. See pages 146, 147.

The Phillip Carey Mfg. Co., Lockland, Cincinnati 15, Ohio. Waterproofing, dampproofing, foundation, patching and resurfacing cements. See page 92.

Hamilton Kent Mfg. Co., 218 Gougler Ave., Kent, Ohio. Rexon coating No. 2 for acid proofing concrete. See page 555.

Inertol Co., Inc., 476A Frelinghuysen Ave., Newark 12, N. J.; Western Division: Suite 24, 27 S. Park, San Francisco 7, Calif. Paints, chemical-resistant enamels and protective coatings; special grades for swimming pools, water works and sewage plants. See page 473.

Johns-Manville, 22 E. 40th St., New York 16, N. Y. Asbestos-cement shingles, asphalt roll and built-up roofings, roof insulation. Also asbestos and asphalt roof coatings, putties, waterproofing cement, sheathing paper. See pages 406, 407; 536, 537.

Amercoat Corp., 4809 Firestone Blvd., South Gate, Calif. Protective coatings for concrete and masonry.

The Atlas Mineral Products Co., 135 Walnut St., Mertztown, Pa. Corrosion-proof protective coatings, cements and linings.

Continental Car-Na-Var Corp., 1765 E. National Ave., Brazil, Ind. Grip-Kote non slippery, waterproof, self-polishing coating for practically all types of floors, especially asphalt. Car-Na-Crete rubber resin enamel for concrete floors.

Dewey & Almy Chemical Co., 62 Whittemore Ave., Cambridge 40, Mass. Daracone, silicone water repellent for above grade masonry.

Koppers Company, Inc., Tar Products Div., 1450 Koppers Bldg., Pittsburgh 19, Pa. Cold-applied coal-tar protective coatings for concrete, and masonry.

Maintenance, Inc., Box 35, Wooster, Ohio. Jennite J-16 surface seal for reservoirs, sewage plants, sludge tanks. water treatment plants, flood gates, drains, water and fuel tanks.

Master-Builders Co., Cleveland 3, Ohio. 21 products for concrete and mortar treatment — including concrete floor hardeners, curing compounds, patching and resurfacing products, protective coatings, and finishers.

W. R. Meadows, Inc., 4 Kimball St., Elgin, Ill. Sealtight premoulded membrane underlayment for vapor pressure and capillary shielding between concrete and grade level.

Protective Products Mfg. Co., 2305 Superior Ave., Kalamazoo, Mich. Raincheck, a water repellent which penetrates masonry and protects against moisture.

Reilly Tar & Chemical Corp., 11 S. Meridan St., Indianapolis 4, Ind. Protective coatings for metal, brick, cement, wood.

Smith & Loveless, Inc., P. O. Box 8172, Kansas City, Mo.

Stonhard Co., Inc., 1306 Spring Garden St., Philadelphia 23, Pa. Stonseal, liquid chemical for waterproofing masonry; Stontite for sealing leaks underground. Also floor patches.

Techkote Co., Inc., 600 Lairport St., El Segundo, Calif. Masonry water repellent.

Tropical Paint Company, 1210-52 W. 70th St., Cleveland 2, Ohio. Cementkote rubber base paint for all masonry surfaces. Floorkote for concrete floors. Tropicalk plastic compound for caulking and glazing.

Truscon Laboratories, Caniff and G.T.R.R., Detroit 11, Mich. Masonry protective coatings; exterior and interior rubber base paints.

Williams Form Engr. Corp., 1051 Madison Ave., S.E., Grand Rapids 7, Mich. Crete-Driseal, a water repellent for all kinds of masonry.

X-Pando Corp., 43-15 36th St., Long Island City 1, N. Y. X-Pandoseal with silicone for brick, masonry.

Coatings for Metals

Barrett Div., Allied Chemical & Dye Corp., 40 Rector St., New York 6, N. Y. Bituminous paints and coatings; pipeline enamel, waterworks enamel, pipeline felts. See page 269.

Byerlyte Corp., 2302 W. 3rd St., Cleveland 13, Ohio. Protective coatings of asphalt and tar for all surfaces. Waterproof, acid-proof, rot-proof, and indestructible. See pages 146, 147.

The Philip Carey Mfg. Co., Lockland, Cincinnati 15, Ohio. Waterproofing materials, roofings. See page 92.

Electro-Rust Proofing Corp., 30 Main St., Belleville, N. J. Cathodic protection; engineering design, equipment, installation, and maintenance for preventing corrosion of steel structures. See page 381.

Inertol Co., Inc. 476A Frelinghuysen Ave., Newark 12, N. J. Western Division: Suite 24, 27 S. Park, San Francisco 7, Calif. Paints, chemical-resistant enamels and protective coatings. See page 473.

Amercoat Corporation, 4809 Firestone Blvd., South Gate, Calif. Protective coatings to prevent the corrosion of metals.

The Atlas Mineral Products Co., 135 Walnut St., Mertztown, Pa. Corrosion-proof protective coatings, cements, and linings.

Calgon Co., Div. of Hagan Chemicals & Controls, Inc., Box 1346, Pittsburgh 30, Pa. Calgon controls corrosion by forming a sub-microscopic protective film over all metal surfaces in a water system.

Continental Car-Na-Var Corp., 1765 E. National Ave., Brazil, Ind. Terra-plate, sealer to prevent corrosion in metals and for terrazzo floors.

Dearborn Chemical Co., Merchandise Mart Plaza, Chicago 54, Ill. No-Ox-Id protective coatings for steel tanks and piping.

Joseph Dixon Crucible Co., Jersey City 3, N. J. Graphite paints for outdoor metals.

Hercules Powder Co., Cellulose Products Dept., 997 Market St., Wilmington 99, Del. Parlon chlorinated rubber paints for storage tanks, sewage and water works structures.

Hill, Hubbell & Co. Div., General Paint Corp., 3091 Mayfield Rd., Cleveland, Ohio.

Koppers Company, Inc., Tar Products Div., 1450 Koppers Bldg., Pittsburgh 19, Pa. Hot and cold-applied coal-tar enamels for water and sewer pipelines, tanks and steel equipment.

Maintenance, Inc., Box 35, Wooster, Ohio. Protective coatings for metals.

The Master Mechanics Co., 2097 Columbus Rd., Cleveland 13, Ohio. Rust finish coat for tanks, machinery and equipment.

Paint Corp. of America, Fidelity Bldg., Cleveland 14, Ohio. Anti-rust paints to apply on virtually every metal surface. In 6 shades—PCA-100, black and PCA-101, clear. PCA-102, aluminum, PCA-103, light gray, PCA-104, oxide red and PCA-105, chrome green.

The Pittsburgh Coke & Chemical Co., Grant Building, Pittsburgh 19, Pa. Pitt Chem tar base protective coatings for application over metal or concrete surfaces in sewage, industrial waste, waterfront construction and water distribution systems.

Reilly Tar & Chemical Corp., 11 S. Meridian St., Indianapolis 4, Ind. Protective coatings for metal, brick, cement, wood pipe. Pipe enamel for water lines; bituminous dip compound for cast-iron pipe; cold application coatings to fight corrosion of tanks and steel work.

Rust-Oleum Corp., 2430 Oakton St., Evanston, Ill. Rust-Oleum for most rustable metal surfaces. Machinery and implement finishes that match original manufacturer's colors.

Smith & Loveless, Inc., P. O. Box 8172, Kansas City, Mo.

Steelcote Mfg. Co., 3418 Gratiot St., St. Louis 3, Mo. Steelcote Epo-lux coatings for severe corrosion problems.

Stonhard Co., Inc., 1306 Spring Garden St., Philadelphia 23, Pa. Stoncote plastic formula for the protection of metals. Also heavy black mastic protective coatings for steel.

Tropical Paint Company, 1210-52 W. 70th St., Cleveland 2, Ohio. Coatings for metals.

Coatings for Roofing

Barrett Div., Allied Chemical & Dye Corp., 40 Rector St., New York 6, N. Y. Asphalt shingles, asphalt roll roofing, asbestos-cement shingles, asphalt felt, asbestos felt, tarred felt, roofing paper, roofing pitch, roofing asphalt, asphalt coatings and cements, asphalt siding, rock wool insulation. Insulation board. See page 269.

Byerlyte Corp., 2302 W. 3rd St., Cleveland 13, Ohio. Protective coatings of asphalt and tar for all surfaces. Waterproof, acid-proof, rot-proof, and indestructible. See pages 146, 147.

The Philip Carey Mfg. Co., Lockland, Cincinnati 15, Ohio. Asphalt and aluminum roof coatings to preserve roofs. Also built-up roofing materials to maintain or replace built-up roofs. See page 92.

Bitucote Products Co., 1337 So. Kings Highway, St. Louis 10, Mo. Protective coatings—roof coatings.

W. R. Meadows, Inc., 4 Kimball St., Elgin, Ill. Asphalt roll roofing and all purpose building paper. Roof coatings.

Rust-Oleum Corp., Inc., 2430 Oakton St., Evanston, Ill. Rust-Oleum for most rustable metal surfaces. Available in many colors, aluminum and white. Applies directly over rust.

Stonhard Co., Inc., 1306 Spring Garden St., Philadelphia 23, Pa. Roof resurfacers, plastic or liquid, for any type roof patching or complete overlay (without heating).

Tropical Paint Company, 1210-52 W. 70th St., Cleveland 2, Ohio. Roofkoter compound forms a continuous rubber-like sheet for protection of roofs.

Coatings for Wood

Barrett Div., Allied Chemical & Dye Corp., 40 Rector St., New York 6, N. Y. Creosote wood preservatives. See page 269.

Byerlyte Corp., 2302 W. 3rd St., Cleveland 13, Ohio. Protective coatings of asphalt and tar for all surfaces. Waterproof, acidproof, rot-proof, and indestructible. See pages 146, 147.

Inertol Co., Inc., 476A Frelinghuysen Ave., Newark 12, N. J. Western Division: Suite 24, 27 S. Park, San Francisco 7, Calif. Paints, chemical-resistant enamels and protective coatings. See page 473.

Carbolineum Wood Preserving Co., 528 W. Highland Blvd., Milwaukee 3, Wis. Carbolineum stops decay and termites.

Joseph Dixon Crucible Co., Jersey City 3, N. J. Graphite paints for wood.

Ebony Paint Mfg. Co., 18th and Agnes Ave., Kansas City 1, Mo. Ebony paint kills rust, prevents termites, waterproofs concrete. Refined coal tar base.

Monsanto Chemical Co., 445 Park Ave., New York, N. Y.

Protection Products Mfg. Co., 2305 Superior Ave., Kalamazoo, Mich. Woodlife water repellent preservative protects wood against warping, swelling, shrinking, checking, grain-raising, fungus decay or rot, staining, termites. P.A.R. water repellent protects and restores the naturalness of unfinished wood. Penta preservative for posts, poles or any lumber in contact with the ground or fresh water.

Reilly Tar & Chemical Corp., 11 S. Meridian St., Indianapolis 4, Ind. Creosote paint for poles and guard rails.

Stonhard Co., Inc., 1306 Spring Garden St., Philadelphia 23, Pa. Wood floor preservative prevents rotting and splintering.

Tropical Paint Company, 1210-52 W. 70th St., Cleveland 2, Ohio. B&P enamel for interior walls, woodwork and ceilings. Elastikote for exterior surfaces. Fume-fite enamel resists acid fumes. Tropelite heavy duty coating. Rhinamel enamel in 14 colors.

X-Pando Corp. 43-15 36th St., Long Island City 1, N. Y. Standard X-Pandoseal, water repellent preservative for wood.

PUMP PRIMERS

Valve and Primer Corp., 341 W. Superior, Chicago 10, Ill. Apco automatic pump primers for suction-lift, unsubmerged centrifugal pumps. The V-Apco primer will operate on any vacuum under which the centrifugal pump will operate. Also air and vapor release valves.

PUMPS

Allis-Chalmers Mfg. Co., Milwaukee 1, Wis. Water supply, boiler feed, booster, centrifugal, fire, sewage, sludge, sump, vacuum. See pages 285-288.

Blackburn-Smith Mfg. Co., Inc., 150 Observer Highway, Hoboken, N. J. Pneumatic sewage ejectors and strainers. See page 496.

Chicago Pump Co., 622 Diversey Pkwy., Chicago 14, Ill. Clog-proof sewage pumps; also Scru-Peller centrifugal. See page 523.

Chain Belt Co., 4640 W. Greenfield Ave., Milwaukee 1, Wis. Portable water pumps. See page 105.

De Laval Steam Turbine Co., 863 Nottingham Way, Trenton 2, N. J. Single and multi-stage centrifugal pumps. See pages 313-316.

Dorr-Oliver Inc., Barry Place, Stamford, Conn. Plunger type sludge pumps and variable stroke diaphragm pumps. See pages 466-469.

Fairbanks Morse & Co., Fairbanks-Morse Bldg., Chicago 5, Ill. Sewage, trash; vertical open impeller centrifugal pumps for sump pumping, underpass and storm water installations; deep well turbine pumps including Pomona pumps. See pages 530, 531.

W. E. Grace Mfg. Co., 6000 S. Lamar St., Dallas, Texas. Asphalt pumps. See page 239.

Homelite, Port Chester, N. Y. Gasoline engine-driven self-priming centrifugal pumps. See pages 263-267.

The Jaeger Machine Co., 702 Dublin Ave., Columbus 16, Ohio. Self-priming, centrifugal pumps 1½ to 10" sizes, diaphragm pumps and pressure pumps. See pages 158-161.

Layne & Bowler, Inc., Box 6697, Hollywood Sta., Memphis 8, Tenn. Vertical turbine, high lift, low lift, centrifugal, close coupled. Fire Underwriters Approved, booster, gasoline and fuel oil transfer, angle flow, propeller, deep well, bilge, mine and sump, also gravel wall wells, shutter screen and complete water treatment. See pages 344-347.

A. Y. McDonald Mfg. Co., 12th and Pine St., Dubuque, Ia. Artesian, deep well, bilge, sump, centrifugal, submersible, direct or fresh water, jet, rotary and tank pumps. See pages 352-355.

Marlow Pumps, Box 200, Midland, N. J. Self-priming centrifugal pumps up to 240,000 gph.; Mud Hog diaphragm pump for heavy, dirty pumping; plunger sludge pumps for sewage. See pages 361-364.

Roots-Connersville Blower Div., Dresser Industries Inc., Connersville, Ind. Rotary positive vacuum pumps for priming large centrifugal waterworks pumps, and water filtration processes, sewage plant filters and dryers. See page 564.

Schramm, Inc., West Chester, Pa. Pneumatic sump pump, maximum capacity 375 g.p.m., will pump water, sludge and raw sewage. See pages 218-221.

American-Marsh Pumps, Inc., 205 Capital Ave., N.E., Battle Creek, Mich. Centrifugal and turbine pumps, sewage and sludge pumps, sump pumps.

American Well Works, Aurora, Ill. Water, sludge and sewage, deep well turbines. Centrifugal, booster, circulation.

Aurora Pump Div., The New York Air Brake Co., 4610 Loucks St., Aurora, Ill. Horizontal centrifugal and vertical deep well turbine types for water supply. Non-clog type, both horizontal and vertical for handling sewage and waste.

Barrett, Haentjens & Co., Hazleton, Pa. Horizontal and vertical pumps.

Buffalo Pumps, Inc., 505 Broadway, Buffalo, N. Y. Sewage pumps, non-clogging centrifugal water pumps.

Byron Jackson Co., Box 2017 Terminal Annex, Los Angeles 54, Calif. Acid boiler feed, booster, centrifugal, condensation, drainage, house, contractors, deep well, fire, gasoline and oil, portable, power, sand, sewage, sludge.

Ralph B. Carter Co., 196 Atlantic Ave., Hackensack, N. J. Plunger sludge pumps.

Chemical Equipment Co., P.O. Box 3098, Los Angeles 54, Calif. "Chemco" pumps for feeding chemicals.

Chicago Pneumatic Tool Co., 6 E. 44th St., New York 17, N. Y. Portable sludge and sump pump.

Cleco Div. of Reed Roller Bit Co., P. O. Box 2119, Houston, Texas. Air operated centrifugal sump pump.

Complete Machinery & Equipment Co., Inc., 36-40 Eleventh St., Long Island City 6, N. Y. Complete wellpoint pumps with 3" to 10" discharge openings: "Complete" wellpoint systems. Jetting pumps up to 300 psi. Trash pumps up to 8". Diaphragm and standard centrifugal pumps of all sizes.

W. S. Darley & Co., 2810 Washington Blvd., Chicago 12, Ill. Portable pumps.

The Deming Co., 15 Broadway, Salem, Ohio. Vertical turbine pumps, centrifugal, triplex, and sump.

The Duriron Co., Inc. Dayton 1, Ohio. Durcopumps for handling severe corrosives.

Frederick Iron & Steel, Inc., Frederick, Md. Single and multi-stage centrifugal pumps for all capacities, electric motor, steam turbine, gasoline or diesel engine drive.

The Gorman-Rupp Co., Mansfield, Ohio. Centrifugal and trash-type sump pumps.

Griffin Wellpoint Corp., 880 E. 141st St., New York 54, N. Y. Wellpoint pumps powered by diesel and gasoline engines, and electric motors. Jetting or pressure pumps, large and small sizes.

Hills-McCanna Co., 2397 Nelson St., Chicago 18, Ill. Chemical proportioning pumps for boiler feed treatment and fluoridization.

Johnson Gear & Mfg. Co., Ltd., 8 and Parker Sts., Berkeley 10, Calif. Right Angle gear drives hollow & solid shaft for continuous water supply or sewerage pumping.

Johnston Pump Co., 3272 E. Foothill Blvd., Pasadena 8, Calif. Johnston vertical turbine and propeller pumps.
Kinney Mfg. Div., The New York Air Brake Co., 3535 Washington Ave., Boston 30, Mass. Rotary pumps.
Komline-Sanderson Engineering Corp., 100 Holland Ave., Peapack, N. J. Diaphragm and plunger sludge pumps.
Lawrence Pumps, Inc., Lawrence, Mass. Centrifugal, for water supply, sewage, drainage and irrigation, acid and chemicals, dredging.
Morris Machine Works, Baldwinsville, N. Y. Pumps for water supply, sewage, storm water, drainage.
Peerless Pump Div., Food Machinery and Chemical Corp., 301 W. Ave. 26, Los Angeles 31, Calif. Sewage, sump, turbine, and water pumps.
Pennsylvania Pump & Compressor Co., Bushkill Blvd., Easton, Pa. Centrifugal pumps.
Proportioneers, Inc., Division of B-I-F Industries, Inc., 351 Harris Ave., Providence 1, R. I. Variable-delivery chemical pumps.
Reda Pump Co., Bartlesville, Okla. Submergible electric pump for water supply.
Red Jacket Mfg. Co., 1055 S. Rolff, Davenport, Ia. Close coupled centrifugal pumps. Complete line of reciprocal, jet, centrifugal, submergible, deep well plungers, and hand windmill pumps.
W. S. Rockwell Co., 200 Eliot St., Fairfield, Conn. Diaphragm pumps.
Milton Roy Co., 1300 E. Mermaid Lane, Philadelphia 18, Pa. Controlled volume chemical pumps from a few cubic centimeters to 2760 gals. per hour. Motor driven and air powered models.
A. O. Smith Corporation, Pacific Coast Works, Los Angeles, Calif. Smithway vertical turbine pumps, 15 to 5,000 gpm.
S. Morgan Smith Co., Lincoln & N. Hartley Sts., York, Pa. Hydraulic turbines and accessories, axial flow pumps.
John W. Stang Corp., 8221 Atlantic Ave., P. O. Box 631, Bell, Calif. Pumps and wellpoints for draining trenches and excavations.
Warren Steam Pump Co., 68 Bridges Ave., Warren, Mass. Complete line centrifugal, reciprocating and rotary pumps, 5 gpm to 50,000 gpm. Pressure range to 1200 psi.
Waterous Company, 82 E. Fillmore Ave., St. Paul 1, Minn. Motor apparatus pumps.
Weinman Pump Mfg. Co. 290 W. Spruce St., Columbus 8, Ohio. Centrifugal pumps, single or multistage, standard or non-clogging belt or motor driven. Also sump pumps and condensate return pumps.
C. H. Wheeler Mfg. Co., Economy Pump Div., 19 and Lehigh, Philadelphia 32, Pa. Both sewage and water pumps, from 10 to 200,000 gpm., horizontal and vertical.
Worthington Corp., Harrison, N. J. Centrifugal, vertical turbine, rotary and reciprocating types, for any condition of head and capacity.
Yeomans Bros. Co., Melrose Park, Ill. Sewage, non-clog, centrifugal, 3 to 24", capacities 50 to 2400 gpm each. Pneumatic sewage ejectors (Shone, Expelsor, Packex) capacities up to 1000 gpm.

RADIO

(See page 786)

REFUSE TRUCKS

Baughman Mfg. Co., Inc., 157 Shipman Rd., Jerseyville, Ill. Garbage disposal body, trailer mounted for hauling refuse from a centrally located collection station to the disposal area. 30' body has a 60 cu. yd. capacity and unloads in 3 to 5 minutes. See page 86.
Gar Wood Industries, Inc., 36253 Michigan Ave., Wayne, Mich. Load-Packer, refuse collection bodies, 10-24 cu. yd. capacities. Speed Packer refuse collection bodies, 16-20 cu. yd. capacities. See pages 242, 243; 532, 533.
The Heil Co., 3042 W. Montana, Milwaukee 1, Wis. Collectomatic enclosed garbage and refuse bodies. See pages 488-491.
Hyde Corp., P. O. Box 1265, Fort Worth, Texas. Hydepack, an hydraulic refuse collection body. See pages 492-495.
Hydro E-Z Pack Div., Hercules Galion Products, Inc., Galion, Ohio. Garbage and refuse bodies. See pages 481-484.
Ingersoll Kalamazoo Div., Borg-Warner Corp., 1810 N. Pitcher St., Kalamazoo, Mich. Load Lugger is a one-man operated, self-loading vehicle consisting of truck, hoist and detachable leak-proof containers suited for the collection and disposal of refuse and garbage. See pages 497-500.
LoDal, Inc., Norway, Mich. Truck self loader system of refuse hauling; mounted on standard truck chassis with bucket capacity of ¾ to 2 cu. yd. See pages 162-165.
M-B Corporation, Box 260, New Holstein, Wis. Packer body; in 12-14-16-20-24 cu. yd. capacities. See pages 246, 247; 560; 967.
Pak-Mor Mfg. Co., Loop 13 & Roosevelt Ave., P. O. Box 6147, San Antonio, Texas. Pak-Mor refuse collection bodies; 13-16-20-24 cu. yd. truck-mounted units and up to 50 cu. yd. trailer units. See pages 474, 475; 486, 487.
City Tank Corp., 53-09 97th Pl., Corona 68, Long Island, N. Y. Roto-Pac truck body.
Dempster Brothers, Inc., Knoxville, Tenn., DEMPSTER-DUMPSTER System of sanitary refuse handling, using detachable containers up to 15 cu. yd., as rubbish depositories placed at strategic points either in the town or within an industrial plant. A truck mounted DEMPSTER-DUMPSTER Hoisting Unit services the containers.
The Elgin Corp., 231 S. LaSalle St., Chicago, Ill. Leach Refuse-Getter and Leach Packmaster.
Hercules Steel Products Co., Galion, Ohio. Low mounted truck body and bulldog hoist for maintenance and refuse removal. Hydraulic hoists and dump bodies.
The Herman Body Co., 4400 Clayton Ave., St. Louis, Mo. Herman "Ram-Pak" automatic pre-pak refuse loader, 16 cu. yd., holds up to 13,000 lb.
Leach Co., Box 200, Oshkosh, Wis. Refuse and garbage collection bodies. Two models; 8½ cu. yd. capacity; hydraulic packing type Packmaster, 10, 13, 16, 17, 20 and 25 cu. yd. capacity.
Mack Trucks, Inc., 1355 W. Front St., Plainfield, N. J.
The Marion Metal Products Co., Marion, Ohio. Dump bodies; hydraulic hoists; special refuse bodies.
The White Motor Co., 842 E. 79th St., Cleveland, Ohio. White "3000" garbage and refuse collection truck with cab room for 3, larger body.

REFUSE TRUCK ACCESSORIES

Allied Steel & Tractor Products, Inc., 7835 Broadway, Cleveland 5, Ohio. Repair materials, corrosive resistant, wear resistant plate, bars, flats, rounds, squares to repair and maintain refuse truck bodies. See page 77.
Fulton Bag & Cotton Mills, P. O. 198, New Orleans 3, La. Covers for sanitation and other municipal vehicles. See page 991.

SCALES

The Conveyor Co., 3260 E. Slauson Ave., Los Angeles 58, Calif. Remote control and automatic weighing scales. See page 255.
Fairbanks, Morse & Co., Fairbanks-Morse Bldg., Chicago 5, Ill. Full line for practically all purposes. See pages 530, 531.
Builders-Providence, Inc., Div. of B-I-F Industries, Inc., 351 Harris Ave., Providence 1, R. I. Conveyflo weighing meter for continuous weighing of sewage sludge filter cake, or coal, being carried on conveyor belt. Totalizing, indicating and recording instruments available for local or remote installation.
Merrick Scale Mfg. Co., Passaic, N. J. Used for weighing filter cake, sludge and grits. Weightomaster is an automatic scale for use with belt conveyors, and can be equipped with a load indicator or chart recorder when rate of flow is desired.
Richardson Scale Co., Clifton, N. J. Automatic dust-tight bulk and bagging scales for weighing dry, ground, granular, dusty, non-free-flowing and small lumpy materials. Models to accommodate screw, belt or vibrating feeders. Also liquid scales and proportioning equipment.

SCREENS, SEWAGE

At sewage plants, bar screens and racks segregate rags, sticks and skins which in most plants are removed by mechanical racks controlled by time clocks or operated by float controls. Subsequent to these screens are fine screens of the rotary type having 1/16 to ¼ inch openings that catch small-sized wastes of canneries, tanneries, meat packing plants, and breweries, and are self-cleaning. These screen units are of the revolving type, cleaned by overhead shower spray pipes or brushes, and are manufactured in various sizes to cope with varying volumes of waste matter. Volumes are handled and determined per the wire mesh around the cylinder. A finer mesh wire will handle a smaller volume of liquid and vice-versa.

Where the screenings are largely organic it is advisable to add screening grinders to macerate the screening to small size and re-introduce it to the flow for collection in the settling basins. Traveling water screens are available for water plants. Sewage and water screens may be pneumatically or electrically controlled by differential pressure controllers as well as by time clocks and floats.

Chain Belt Co., 4640 W. Greenfield Ave., Milwaukee 1, Wis. Mechanically cleaned sewage bar screen with or without grinder; intake screens (traveling). See page 105.

Chicago Pump Co., 622 Diversey Pkwy., Chicago 14, Ill. Barminutors and Comminutors which screen and cut sewage solids under water in the inlet channel. See page 523.

Dorr-Oliver Inc., Barry Place, Stamford, Conn. Bar screens, fine screens, screening, disintegrators. See pages 466-469.

American Well Works, Aurora, Ill. Mechanically cleaned screen and grinder.

Green Bay Foundry & Machine Works, 401 S. Broadway, Green Bay, Wis. North self-cleaning sewage disposal screens in 4, 6, 8, 10′ sizes.

Hendrick Mfg. Co., 40 Dundaff St., Carbondale, Pa. Screens, perforated metal, wedge slot, milled slot, for sizing and dewatering. Also grilles, gratings; open steel flooring.

Infilco Inc., Box 5033, Tucson, Ariz. ROTAGRATOR® screen and comminuter; GRIDUCTOR® comminuter for screening and comminuting sewage without removal from channel.

The Jeffrey Mfg. Co., 9709 N. 4th St., Columbus 16, Ohio. Self-cleaning bar and industrial screens and screenings, grinders. Traveling water screens.

Link-Belt Co., Dept. MI, Prudential Plaza, Chicago 1, Ill. Bar and trash screens, liquid vibrating screens, revolving drum and disc screens, traveling water screens.

Walker Process Equip., Inc., Box 266, Aurora, Ill. Sewage. Mechanical bar screens for solids removal.

SCREENS, WATER WELL

Cook Well Strainer Co., 6330 Glenway Ave., Cincinnati 11, Ohio. Well strainers. See pages 396, 397

Emsco Screen Pipe Co., 2219 Brooks St., Houston, Texas. Slotted and wire wrapped screen pipe. See page 428.

Edward E. Johnson, Inc., 315 N. Pierce St., St. Paul 4, Minn. Johnson well screen, custom built for every requirement. See page 439.

Layne & Bowler, Inc., Box 6697, Hollywood Sta., Memphis 8, Tenn. Shutter type well screens, gravel wall wells, well water supplies and vertical turbine pumps; also complete water treatment. See pages 344-347.

Kelly Well Co., Inc., Grand Island, Nebr. Plain or concrete well screens with centrifugal cast concrete casing.

SEPARATING OIL AND WATER

Hardinge Co., Inc., 240 Arch St., York, Pa. Rectangular separating tanks with skimmers and scrapers. See page 556.

Gale Separator Co., Inc., 2 Broad St., Bloomfield, N. J. Gosco interceptors and separators to conserve water, prevent stream pollution, de-emulsifying and acid treatment systems.

SERVICE BOXES
(See Boxes)

SERVICE SADDLES
(See Pipe Clamps, Service Saddles)

SETTLING BASINS
(See Clarifiers, page 755)

SEWAGE GAS EQUIPMENT

Chicago Bridge & Iron Co., 332 So. Michigan Ave., Chicago 4, Ill. Gas holders. Elevated steel tanks and steel storage tanks. See pages 297-299; 514

R. D. Cole Mfg. Co., Newnan, Ga. Tanks. See pages 305-308.

Dorr-Oliver Inc., Barry Place, Stamford, Conn. Gas collecting digester covers. See pages 466-469

General American Transportation Corp., Field Bldg., Chicago 3, Ill. Gasholders for storing sewage digester gas. See page 554.

Pacific Flush Tank Company, 4241 Ravenswood Ave., Chicago 13, Ill. Gas collecting digester covers and gas safety equipment including waste gas burners, flame traps, drip traps, gas pressure gauges, and other items for control and safe use of digester sludge gas. See pages 519-522.

Pittsburgh-Des Moines Steel Co., 3460 Neville Island, Pittsburgh, Pa. Tanks. See pages 418, 419; 544, 545.

The Vapor Recovery Systems Co., 2820 N. Alameda, Compton, Calif. Pressure relief and vacuum breaker valves; flame traps. Drip traps, automatic and manual; back pressure regulator, single port and double port; back pressure check valve; flame arrester, horizontal type and vertical type; flame checks; flame trap assembly; man-hole or entrance hatch cover. Manometers; sampling hatch or handhole cover, sediment and drip trap assemblies; Waste gas burner. Trade name is "Varec." See page 471.

Connelly, Inc., Elizabeth 1, N. J. Sponge for removal of hydrogen sulfide from natural gas, manufactured gas and sewage gas.

SEWAGE GAS METERS
(See Meters, Gas, Sewage Gas)

SEWAGE LIFT STATIONS, PACKAGE

Chicago Pump Co., 622 Diversey Pkwy., Chicago 14, Ill. "Package" sewage plants. Equipment specifically developed for small communities and industrial plants. See page 523.

Smith & Loveless, Inc., P. O. Box 8172, Kansas City, Mo. Factory-built pumping stations. Six standard size lift stations with capacities from 20 gpm to 3,000 gpm per pump or ejector.

SEWER CLEANING

Ace Pipe Cleaning, Inc., 3513 E. 18th St., Kansas City, Mo. Complete mobilized service for cleaning sewer and water pipes. See pages 524, 525.

American Pipe Cleaning Co., 1819 Nicollet Ave., Minneapolis 3, Minn. Sewers cleaned by contract; labor, trucks and equipment furnished. Distributors for O.K. Champion sewer cleaning equipment in Minnesota, North Dakota, Iowa and western Wisconsin. See pages 453-456.

Champion Corporation, Sheffield at Johnson St., Hammond, Indiana. Eleven models of Power Sewer Cleaners. Motorized units for hand windlasses. Hand operated all purpose windlasses; wood sewer rods; steel sewer rods; steel rod accessories; power drives for steel rods; expanding root cutters; sewer buckets; brushes, cables and pole suspended manhole jacks. See pages 457-460.

Expanding Sewer Machine Co., 108 E. Walnut St., Nappanee, Ind. Sewer cleaners, sewer rods, and accessories; manhole braces, expanding root cutters in three sizes. See page 472

Flexible Inc., 3786 Durango Ave., Los Angeles 34, Calif. For removing roots, rags, and all types of solid stoppages, sewer rodding equipment is offered. Consists of Flexicrome steel sewer rods, cleaning tools such as corkscrews, root saws, augers, porcupines, etc. Rods are turned by hand, small gasoline Power Drive, or SeweRodeR (a rodding robot). Everything is self-contained in the SeweRodeR, but for smaller equipment a Carry-All Trailer tows the outfit to the job. For removal of deposists of sand, ten models of bucket machines. See pages 476-479.

National Power Rodding Corp., 1000 South Western Ave., Chicago 12, Ill. Complete service for cleaning, reboring and bucketing pipes and ducts underground, above ground, anywhere. See pages 540, 541.

O'Brien Mfg. Co., 5662 Northwest Highway, Chicago 30, Ill. Dual-purpose sewer cleaning machines use both flexible steel cable and solid rods. See pages 515-518.

Roto-Rooter Corp., 301 University Ave., Des Moines 14, Ia. Sewer and drain cleaning equipment; Roto-Rod equipped with 1000-ft. solid steel rod. Revolving blades cut roots, grease, scale and other debris. See page 565.

W. H. Stewart, 202 Kratz Ave., Syracuse 9, N. Y. Sewer and pipe cleaning equipment for lines from 4" to the largest. Sewer rods, root cutters, buckets, hand operated and motor driven, cleaning machines. See pages 506-509.

Turbine Sewer Machine Co., 1303 N. Fourth St., Milwaukee 12, Wis. Turco Maxi-Power sewer cleaning units; manually operated drag and bucket type cleaners; sectional steel sewer rods; wooden sewer rods; hydraulic sewer flushing bags; self-propelling ferrets and nozzles; surface hung manhole guide jacks; Turco Hercules brushes; Turco sewer cleaning buckets; adjustable turbine sewer cleaners; Turco Robot portable power drive for all hand winches; sewer suits; dewatering pumps, centrifugal and diaphragm. See pages 548. 549; 1122, 1123.

Fitzgerald Engr. Co., Inc., P. O. Box 289-G, Coral Gables 34, Fla. Sewer Scooter, hydraulically propelled machine, cleans sewers 6 to 96" in diameter. Also contract pipe cleaning of sewer and water mains.

Kollmann Manufacturing Co., 4854 Peach St., Erie, Pa. Power driven sewer and drain cleaning machines. Also hand tools for small drain lines.

Miller Sewer Rods, Dept. MI, 4642 N. Central Ave., Chicago 30, Ill. All types of sewer rod equipment including flushing gun which cleans pipes instantly, sewer rods, Miller's triple action grease and root cutter featuring self-expanding blades for 3" to 12" pipe. Tools for toilets, sinks, sewers, septic tanks.

The Ohio Tool & Engineering Co., 128 N. Spring St., Springfield, Ohio. Gasoline engine-driven Electric Eel with self-feeding flexible cable cleans sewers up to 16".

Pittsburgh Pipe Cleaner Co., 5847 Centre Ave., Pittsburgh 6, Pa. Contract pipe cleaning of water mains and sewers. Gas main cleaning.

Rodding-Cleaning Machines, Inc., 7827 Melrose Ave., Los Angeles 46, Calif. RCM self-contained, mobile, portable plant for cleaning all 2 to 48" sewers and water mains.

The Sidu Co., Box 3537, Long Beach, Calif. Sewer cleaning equipment and manhole cushions, sewer plugs.

Thomas Drain Service, 35 S. College St., Akron 8, Ohio. Will supply equipment to clean your sewers and a man to supervise the operation on a rental basis.

SLUDGE DRYERS

(See Incinerators, page 759)

SLUDGE FILTERS

(See Filters, Vacuum, page 757)

SLUDGE HANDLING

Chain Belt Co., 4640 W. Greenfield Ave., Milwaukee 1, Wis. Sludge collectors. Tow Bro sludge removers. See page 105.

Dorr-Oliver Inc., Barry Place, Stamford, Conn. Sludge thickeners, digesters, sludge heaters, mixers. See pages 466-469.

Hardinge Co., Inc., 240 Arch St., York, Pa. Sludge thickeners See page 556.

Lord & Burnham, Irvington, N. Y. Glass covers for sewage treatment plant sludge beds. See page 559.

Ralph B. Carter Co., 196 Atlantic Ave., Hackensack, N. J. Sludge thickeners, digesters, pumps, clarifiers, mixers.

Infilco Inc., Box 5033, Tucson, Ariz. Sludge thickeners, heaters, digesters.

The Jeffrey Mfg. Co., 970 N. 4th St., Columbus 16, Ohio. Sludge and grit collectors, elevating and conveying equipment.

Link-Belt Co., Dept. MI, Prudential Plaza, Chicago 1, Ill. Straightline sludge collectors for rectangular settling tanks. Circuline collectors for round or square tanks.

Pango Manufacturing Co., P. O. Box 104, Yardville Station, Trenton, N. J. The Pango Sewage Sampler with 800 cc capacity.

Royer Foundry & Machine Company, 166 Pringle St., Kingston, Pa. Sewage sludge disintegrators for converting sewage sludge into useable fertilizer, 12 stationary and portable models, with electric motor, gasoline engine or belt-to-tractor driven, capacities 4 to 15.0

Walker Process Equip., Inc., P. O. Box 266, Aurora, Ill. Sludge thickeners, sludge heaters, mixers, clarifiers.

SLUICE GATES

(See Gates, Sluice and Shear)

SPLIT REPAIR SLEEVES

James B. Clow & Sons, Inc., P. O. Box 6600-A, 201-299 N. Talman Ave., Chicago 80, Ill. Clow mechanical joint split sleeves for making permanent repairs to damaged cast-iron pipe, 3 to 16" See pages 270-275.

Dresser Mfg. Div., Dresser Industries, Inc., Bradford, Pa. Clamps and sleeves for repairing steel and cast-iron pipe; joints for use in initial installation of cast-iron pipe See pages 321-324.

M. B. Skinner Co., 3502 W. Sample St., South Bend 21, Ind. Split coupling clamps for repairing broken mains, bell joint clamps, pipe line clamps, emergency pipe clamps, service saddles. See page 446.

Smith-Blair Inc., 535 Railroad Ave., S. San Francisco, Calif. Smith-Blair full circle clamp couplings, fast action clamps, split couplings, and special fabrications. See pages 374-377.

Traverse City Iron Works, P. O. Box 348, Traverse City, Mich Repair sleeves. See page 450.

Mueller Co., 512 W. Cerro Gordo St., Decatur, Ill. Repair sleeves, service clamps.

The A. P. Smith Mfg. Co., East Orange, N. J. Complete line of mechanical joint repair sleeves in sizes 3 to 24", inclusive. Bell End type split repair sleeves in sizes 3 to 60" inclusive.

SWEEPERS, PLANT FLOOR

G. H. Tennant Co., 701 N. Highway 100, Minneapolis, Minn. Vacuum-equipped power sweepers with 24" to 48" swath. Gas, LP-gas and electric models. Drive like car at speeds 6-8 mph. Heavy duty scarifying machines for removing incrusted grime from floors. Floor machines for polishing, scrubbing, and reconditioning. See pages 130-132; 957.

Wayne Manufacturing Co., 1201 E. Lexington St., Pomona, Calif. Power sweepers, pick-up type for sidewalk, street and garage use, rider operated, vacuum dust control. Models from 24" to 68" in sweeping widths. See pages 226-229.

Continental Car-Na-Var Corp., 1765 E. National Ave., Brazil, Ind. The Bee Hive, portable industrial vacuum cleaner, Silent Chief floor machines for polishing and scrubbing floors. Also Saf-T-Vac vacuum cleaners with by-pass motor.

Ideal Power Mower Co., P. O. Box 629, Springfield, Ohio, Power-driven sweeper for factory floor—steel brush, fibre brush, sprinkler for dust control.

Lambert Incorporated, 519 Hunter Ave., Dayton 4, Ohio. Floor sweepers—gasoline or electric powered.

Modern Power Sweeper Co., 738 N. McKeever Ave., Azusa, Calif. Industrial power sweeper for all type surface, 27", 36" and 48" sweep medium duty models with gutter brush. Also heavy duty riding type 36" and 48" sweep models with self starter engines.

Parker Sweeper Co., 91 Bechtle Ave., Springfield, Ohio. Parker industrial floor sweepers, manually operated, heavy-duty brushes. Also motorized floor sweepers.

Wilshire Power Sweeper Co., 247 Dundee Ave., Elgin, Ill. Industrial model with dust control, 24, 36 and 48" sweep.

TANKS

Bethlehem Steel Co., Bethlehem, Pa. Welded or riveted steel standpipes and reservoirs. See pages 326, 327; 485.

Chicago Bridge & Iron Co., 322 So. Michigan Ave., Chicago 4, Ill. Elevated steel tanks; steel storage tanks, reservoirs and high pressure gas holders. See pages 297-299; 514.

R. D. Cole Mfg. Co., Newnan, Ga. Elevated water tanks and towers. Also flat bottom tanks and standpipes. See pages 305-308.

General American Transportation Corp., Field Bldg., Chicago 3, Ill. Wiggins conservation structures. Dry seal gasholders. Fabricated steel specialties. Storage tanks. See page 554.

Graver Tank & Mfg. Co., Inc., East Chicago, Ind. Engineering, fabrication and field erection of water reservoirs and standpipes of all capacities. See pages 448 AB.

Hammond Iron Works, 630 Fifth Ave., N. Y. 20, N. Y. Elevated water tanks from 25,000 to 3,000,000 gal. capacity. Stand pipes and steel reservoirs. See page 432.

Koven Fabricators, Inc., 90 East Dickerson St., Dover, N. J. Steel reservoirs and standpipes. See page 440.

Nooter Corporation, 1407 South 2nd St., St. Louis 4, Mo. Design, fabrication and field erection of wide variety of elevated water tanks, ground level storage tanks and standpipes. See page 442.

Pittsburgh-Des Moines Steel Co., 3460 Neville Island, Pittsburgh, Pa. Steel tanks, elevated for water storage up to 2,500,000 gals., steel tanks, steel standpipes, pressure tanks and spheres. See pages 418, 419; 544, 545.

Alco Products, Inc., Schenectady 5, N. Y. Steel tanks, welded or riveted construction for storage of oil, gas or water.

The Preload Company, Inc., New York 16, N. Y. Prestressed concrete water supply storage and sewage treatment tanks and reservoirs.

TANK PROTECTION AND MAINTENANCE

(Also see Gunite, page 759)

Air Placement Company, 1005A West 24th Street, Kansas City, Mo., Manufacturers of Airplaco concrete gunning equipment, including the Bondactor, Nucretor and Mix-Elevator. See page 68.

Electro-Rust Proofing Corp., 30 Main St., Belleville, N. J. Cathodic protection: engineering design, equipment, installation, and maintenance for preventing corrosion of steel structures. See page 381.

Inertol Co., Inc., 476A Frelinghuysen Ave., Newark 12, N. J., Western Division: Suite 24, 27 South Park, San Francisco 7, Calif. Specialized paint coatings for interior and exterior of metal tanks, concrete tanks, and reservoirs. See page 473.

Pipe Line Anode Corp., Box 996, Tulsa, Okla. An-Spec magnesium anodes for controlling corrosion of tanks and other steel structures. See page 45

The Atlas Mineral Products Co., 135 Walnut St., Mertztown, Pa., Corrosion-proof bricks, rubber and plastic linings for steel and concrete tanks.

Cement Gun Co., Allentown, Pa. Tank linings for constructing tanks.

Dixie Tank & Bridge Co., P. O. Box 14, Memphis 1, Tenn. Nationwide water tank repair service.

The Dow Chemical Co., Cathodic Protection Sales, Magnesium Dept., Midland, Mich. Dow magnesium anodes eliminate corrosion problems in pipelines and tanks.

The Duriron Co., Inc., Dayton 1, Ohio. Duriron impressed current anodes for the cathodic protection of elevated water towers, storage tanks, accelator basins, pipe lines, sewage disposal systems, and other municipal equipment.

Harco Corp., Cathodic Protection Div., P. O. Box 7026, Cleveland 28, Ohio. Cathodic protection devices to increase the life of water-storage tanks.

Herosite and Chemical Co., 822 South 14th St., Manitowoc, Wis. Sheet rubber linings for tanks.

Water Tank Service Co., 6115 Denton Drive, Dallas 9, Texas. Complete maintenance service for tanks and other steel structures.

TAPPING SLEEVES, TAPPING VALVES

Eddy Valve Co., Waterford, N. Y. Sub. of James B. Clow & Sons, P. O. Box 6600-A, Chicago 80, Ill. Tapping valves, tapping sleeves. See pages 272, 273.

Iowa Valve Co., Oskaloosa, Iowa. Sub. James B. Clow & Sons, Inc. Tapping sleeves and valves. See pages 274-275.

The Ludlow Valve Mfg. Co., Troy, N. Y. Tapping valves and sleeves. See pages 348-351.

M & H Valve and Fittings Co., Anniston, Ala. Tapping valves, tapping sleeves. See pages 357-360.

Traverse City Iron Works, P. O. Box 348, Traverse City, Mich. Tapping valves and sleeves. See page 450

Darling Valve and Mfg. Co., Walnut and Marshall Sts., Williamsport 61, Pa. Tapping valves, tapping sleeves.

Mueller Co., 512 W. Cerro Gordo St., Decatur, Ill. Tapping sleeves, tapping valves.

Rensselaer Valve Co., Div. Ludlow Valve Mfg. Co., Inc., Troy, N. Y. Tapping sleeves, tapping valves.

The A. P. Smith Mfg. Co., East Orange, N. J. Tapping sleeves, tapping valves and 3"x2" through 72"x42" and tapping machines 2" through 42".

Vogt Brothers Mfg. Co., P. O. Box 922, Louisville 1, Ky.

TRICKLING FILTERS

The trickling or sprinkling filter is a bed of stone, gravel, slag, special tile or broken bricks to which the waste is applied continuously or by a dosing tank. The modern version uses a distributor which is a hollow central revolving column through which the waste enters. Hollow arms equipped with spray nozzles extend from it to the periphery of the bed. The reaction of the sewage flowing out of the nozzles turns the machine. The sewage floating over the rocks promotes the growth of slimes that attack the polluting matter in the sewage. The necessity for adequate drainage and ventilation in a trickling filter is becoming more fully appreciated. Use of the recognized underdrainage and ventilation units designed for this purpose is now accepted practice. These units are generally quadrangular prisms made of vitrified clay blocks. Recirculation from affluent to influent improves treatment and reduces overall filter dimensions.

Dorr-Oliver Inc., Barry Place, Stamford, Conn. Trickling filter distributors. Biofiltration systems. See pages 466-649.

General Filter Co., Ames, Iowa. Gard gravity actuated rotary distributor for trickling filters. Also Multi-Plate underdrain system for collection of water from filter bed and for filter backwash. See pages 400, 401.

Pacific Flush-Tank Co., 4241 Ravenswood Ave., Chicago 13, Ill. Sprinkling filters, separate and common field types; rotary distributors; alternating siphons; filter nozzles; twin tank controls. See pages 519-522.

The Bowerston Shale Co., P. O. Box 17, Bowerston, Ohio. Filter bottom block for waste and sewage trickling filters.

Cannelton Sewer Pipe Co., Cannelton, Ind. Translot filter block for underdrains in trickling filters.

Ralph B. Carter Co., 196 Atlantic Ave., Hackensack, N. J. Rotary distributors, alternating siphons.

W. S. Dickey Clay Mfg. Co., P. O. Box 2028, Kansas City 42, Mo. Salt glazed filter bed blocks.

Infilco Inc., Box 5033, Tucson, Ariz. Rotary distributors. ACCELO ® filters.

The Jeffrey Mfg. Co., 970 N. 4th St., Columbus 16, Ohio. Biofiltration systems for secondary treatment.

Lakeside Engineering Corp., 222 W. Adams St., Chicago 6, Ill. Trickling filter distributors—reaction type and disc type.

Link-Belt Co., Dept. MI, Prudential Plaza, Chicago 1, Ill. Biofiltration systems.

The Metropolitan Brick, Inc., Renkert Bldg., Canton 2, Ohio. Sewer brick, acid resisting brick, ceramic glazed tile, shale or fireclay paving brick, building brick, face brick.

Natco Corp., 327 Fifth Ave., Pittsburgh 22, Pa. Natco salt glazed unifilter block underdrains for trickling filter beds.

Smith & Loveless, Inc., P. O. Box 8172, Kansas City, Mo. "Sy-No-Seal" rotary distributors for trickling filter systems, constructed so that no seal is required between the stationary and rotating parts; capacities 120 to 4,000 gpm.

Texas Vitrified Pipe Co., Box 111, Mineral Wells, Texas. Translot filter block for underdrains in trickling filters.

Walker Process Equipment, Inc., Box 266, Aurora, Ill. Rotoseal rotary distributors for sewage plant trickling filters.

Yeomans Brothers Co., Melrose Park, Ill. Both standard rate and high capacity.

TOOLS FOR MAINTENANCE AND REPAIR

(See page 748)

TRENCHING MACHINES

(See page 746)

VALVE BOX LOCATORS

(See Pipe Finders and Leak Detectors)

VALVE, BOXES

(See Boxes)

VALVES, AIR

Simplex Valve & Meter Co., 7 East Orange St., Lancaster, Pa. Air release valves for all pressure conditions and air inlet (vacuum breaking) valves, 4" to 10" inclusive inlet diameters. See pages 422, 423.

Cleco Div. of Reed Roller Bit Co., P. O. Box 2119, Houston, Texas. Pressure-seated air valves of strong construction having only 3 parts. Designed for maximum working pressure of 125 lb. in sizes 1¼" or smaller.

Multiplex Mfg. Co., 3282 Fowler Ave., Berwick, Pa. Crispin air control valves for all types of pipe-line installation.

Rensselaer Valve Co., Div. Ludlow Mfg. Co., Inc., Troy, N. Y. Air valves.
Valve and Primer Corp., 341 W. Superior, Chicago 10, Ill. Air release and air and vacuum valves in sizes and types for every condition.

VALVES, BACKFLOW PREVENTION

Backflow Engineering & Equipment Co., 5725 Alcoa Ave., Los Angeles 58, Calif. Backflow Preventers (¾" to 16") using reduced pressure principle, operate under full line pressure for all cross-connection control purposes.
Josam Mfg. Co., Michigan City, Ind. Backwater and sewer valves to prevent flooded basements caused by water and sewage backing up through floor drains and fixtures.

VALVES, BUTTERFLY

Builders-Providence, Inc., Div. of B-I-F Industries, Inc., 351 Harris Ave., Providence 1, R. I. Tight-closing, rubber-seat butterfly valves; line sizes 4" through 48"; velocities up to 16 fps; pressures up to 50 psi; operators include manual, electric, hydraulic, pneumatic and float type.
Davis Mfg. Co., 321 North Maple Dr., Beverly Hills, Calif. Butterfly valves and rotary plug valves.
Pelton Division of Baldwin-Lima-Hamilton Corp., 2929 19th St., San Francisco, Calif. Butterfly valves 16" to 17'.
Henry Pratt Co., 2222 S. Halsted St., Chicago, Ill. Butterfly valves: 10 through 168" suitable for 50 psi; also, 6 through 72" suitable for 125 psi.
W. S. Rockwell Co., 200 Eliot St., Fairfield, Conn. Rubber seat and metal seat butterfly valves. AWWA butterfly valves.
S. Morgan Smith Co., Lincoln & N. Hartley Sts., York, Pa. Butterfly, ball and cone valves.

VALVES, CHECK

The Chapman Valve Mfg. Co., Essex St., Indian Orchard, Mass. Iron body, bronze mounted and all bronze check valves, bell, hub, flange or screw end, inside or outside screw. Also tilting disc type. See pages 300-303.
Eddy Valve Co., Waterford, N. Y., Sub. James B. Clow & Sons, P. O. Box 6600-A, Chicago 80, Ill. Check valves. See pages 272-273.
Golden-Anderson Valve Specialty Co., 1232 Ridge Ave., Pittsburgh 33, Pa. Cushioned check valves. Sizes range from 2 to 36". See page 437.
Iowa Valve Co., Oskaloosa, Ia., Sub. of James B. Clow & Sons, Inc. P. O. Box 6600-A, Chicago 80, Ill. Check valves. See pages 274-275.
The Kennedy Valve Mfg. Co., 1069 E. Water St., Elmira, N. Y. Check valves. See pages 337-340.
A. Y. McDonald Mfg. Co., 12th and Pine Sts., Dubuque, Ia. Check valves, iron body, swing. See pages 352-355.
M & H Valve & Fittings Co., Anniston, Ala. Check valves—full way. See pages 357-360.
Traverse City Iron Works, P. O. 348, Traverse City, Mich. Check, clearway and Underwriters Approved. See page 450.
Anderson Valve Works, Marion, Ind. Cushioned swing check, hydraulic check, solenoid globe, cone and ball checks, diaphragm globe.
Cla-Val Co., Newport Beach, Calif. Non-slam check valves.
Cochrane Corp., 3122 N. 17th St., Phila. 32, Pa. Check valves.
Darling Valve & Mfg. Co., Walnut and Marshall Sts., Williamsport 61, Pa. Check valves.
The Duriron Co., Inc., Dayton 1, Ohio. Check valves in different alloys for handling corrosives.
Edward Valves, Inc., Sub. Rockwell Mfg. Co., East Chicargo, Ind. Check valves.
Mueller Co., 512 W. Cerro Gordo St., Decatur, Ill. Check valves.
Ohio Brass Co., 380 N. Main St., Mansfield, Ohio. Check valves, sizes ⅛ to 3".
Ohio Injector Co., 101 Pine St., Wadsworth, Ohio. Check valves.
Pennsylvania Pump and Compressor Company, Bushkill Blvd., Easton, Pa. Pennsylvania Airchek and Gaschek line of check valves for reciprocating compressor service prevents the back flow of air or gas through a discharge line.
Rensselaer Valve Co., Div. Ludlow Valve Mfg. Co., Inc., Troy, N. Y. Check valves.
W. S. Rockwell Co., 200 Eliot St., Fairfield, Conn. Check valves.
The Smolensky Valve Co., Inc., Bedford, Ohio. Check valves, for water pumps, sewage pumps. Sizes 1" to 72".
The E. H. Wachs Co., 1525 N. Dayton St., Chicago 22, Ill. Swing check valves, 2 to 48", for gas lines.
The Williams Gauge Co., Inc., 2 Gateway Center, Pittsburgh 22, Pa. The Williams-Hager flanged silent check valve for water hammer.

VALVES, GATE

The Chapman Valve Mfg. Co., Essex St., Indian Orchard, Mass. Iron body, bronze mounted and all bronze gate valves, bell, hub, flange or screw end, inside or outside screw. See pages 300-303.
Eddy Valve Co., Waterford, N. Y., Sub. James B. Clow & Sons, P. O. Box 6600-A, Chicago 80, Ill. Eddy bell end and mechanical joint gate valves. See pages 272, 273.
Filer & Stowell Co., 147 E. Becher St., Milwaukee 7, Wis. Gate valves. See page 552.
Iowa Valve Co., Oskaloosa, Ia. Sub. James B. Clow & Sons, Inc., P. O. Box 6600-A, Chicago 80, Ill. Gate valves. See pages 274-275.
The Kennedy Valve Mfg. Co., 1069 E. Water St., Elmira, N. Y. Water gate valves, 2 to 48", designed for working pressure from 50 to 150 lbs., furnished for manual, gear, electric motor or cylinder control. Gate valves, hose gate, and indicator post gate valves. See pages 337-340.
The Ludlow Valve Mfg. Co., Inc., Troy, N. Y. Gate valves, 2 to 72", 50 to 800 lbs., manually, gear electric motor or hydraulically operated. See pages 348-351.
A. Y. McDonald Mfg. Co., 12th and Pine Sts., Dubuque, Ia. Gate valves. See pages 352-355.
M & H Valve & Fittings Co., Anniston, Ala. AWWA Approved manual, hydraulic, motor or gear operated, sizes 2 to 36". Also, gate valves for 50 and 100 lbs. low pressure services, either double disc or solid wedge. See pages 357-360.
Traverse City Iron Works, P. O. Box 348, Traverse City, Mich. AWWA gate valves, bell, flanged or mech. **jt. valves and indicator posts for automatic sprinkler** installations. See page 450.
R. D. Wood Co., Philadelphia 5, Pa. Gate valves, designed for severe underground service, fully bronze mounted, suitable for pressures up to 175 lbs., tested to 300 lbs. by hydrostatic pressure. Available with bell, flange universal and standardized mechanical joint end connections. See pages 387-390.
American Foundry & Mfg. Co., 1015 Hebert St., St. Louis 7, Mo. Gate valves, American Water Works specifications.
Anderson Valve Works, Marion, Ind. Cone and ball stop valves.
Crane Co., 836 So. Michigan Ave., Chicago 5, Ill. A.W.W.A. double disc gate valves. Light standard and low pressure I.B.B.M. double disc gate valves.
Darling Valve & Mfg. Co., Walnut and Marshall Sts., Williamsport 61, Pa. Iron, bronze, and steel gate valves.
Edward Valves, Inc., Sub. Rockwell Mfg. Co., East Chicago, Ind. Gate valves.
Mueller Co., 512 W. Cerro Gordo St., Decatur, Ill. Mueller A.W.W.A. approved gate valves, parallel seat, double-disc type, fully mounted; 2" through 48".
Ohio Brass Co., 380 N. Main St., Mansfield, Ohio. Gate valves, sizes ⅛ to 3".
Ohio Injector Co., 101 Pine St., Wadsworth, Ohio. Gate valves.
Pacific States Cast Iron Pipe Co., Provo, Utah. Gate valves. Fire hydrants.
Rensselaer Valve Co., Div. Ludlow Valve Mfg. Co., Inc., Troy, N. Y. Gate valves.
W. S. Rockwell Co., 200 Eliot St., Fairfield, Conn. Gate valves.
The A. P. Smith Mfg. Co., East Orange, N. J. Gate valves, 2 through 66". Also inserting valves, 4" to 48", inclusive, and the machines required to insert the valves under pressure in cast iron and steel fluid service piping.
Vogt Brothers Mfg. Co., P. O. Box 922, Louisville 1, Ky. Gate valves.
The E. H. Wachs Co., 1525 N. Dayton St., Chicago 22, Ill. Gate valves, 2 to 60" for gas lines only; no brass trim for water service.

VALVES, GAS AND REGULATING

Bailey Meter Co., 1035 Ivanhoe Rd., Cleveland 10, Ohio. Pneumatically operated control valves. See page 480.
Eddy Valve Co., Waterford, N. Y. Sub. of James B. Clow & Sons, P. O. Box 6600-A, Chicago 80, Ill. Gas valves. See pages 272, 273.
Golden-Anderson Valve Specialty Co., 1232 Ridge Ave., Pittsburgh 33, Pa. Gas valves. See page 437.
The Kenndey Valve Mfg. Co., 1069 E. Water St., Elmira, N. Y. Gas valves. See pages 337-340.
Anderson Valve Works, Marion, Ind. Automatic gas valves.

Fisher Governor Co., 1700 Fisher Building, Marshalltown, Ia. Pressure control valves, gas regulators, liquid level controllers.
Homestead Valve Mfg. Co., Coraopolis, Pa. Lubricated or non-lubricated plug valves for gas lines.
Mueller Co., 512 W. Cerro Gordo St., Decatur, Ill. Valves with iron body, brass key, all brass, plain, lubricated, complete range sizes and types.
Rensselaer Valve Co., Div. Ludlow Valve Mfg. Co., Inc., Troy, N. Y. Gas valves.
The E. H. Wachs Co., 1525 N. Dayton St., Chicago 22, Ill. All for gas lines. Venturi valves 18, 20, and 24 x 16".
The Welsbach Corp., Westmoreland & Stokley Sts., Philadelphia 29, Pa. Curb & Corporation Stops for water service. Gas Stops and High Pressure Service Gas Valves.

VALVES, PLUG

DeZurik Corp., Sartell, Minn. A complete line of plug valves with resilient-faced plugs operating on an eccentric principle. Friction-free operation requires no lubrication. ½" to 20". See page 115.
Iowa Valve Co., Oskaloosa, Ia., Sub. James B. Clow & Sons, Inc., P. O. Box 6600-A, Chicago 80, Ill. Plug and drain valves. See pages 274-275.
A. Y. McDonald Mfg. Co., 12th and Pine Sts., Dubuque, Ia. Plug and relief valves, quick opening and closing. See pages 352-355.
American Car and Foundry Co., New York 8, N. Y. Lubricated plug valves for sewage and water systems, asphalt plants, paving department.
The Duriron Co., Inc., Dayton 1, Ohio. Type F plug valves in different alloys for handling severe corrosives.
Homestead Valve Mfg. Co., Coraopolis, Pa. Lubricated or non-lubricated plug valves for water works and sewage lines.
Ohio Injector Co., 101 Pine St., Wadsworth, Ohio. Lubricated plug valves.
Rockwell Mfg. Co., 400 N. Lexington Ave., Pittsburgh 8, Pa. Nordstrom plug valves and valve lubricants and lubrication equipment.

VALVES, POWER OPERATION

Payne Dean & Co., Clinton, Conn. Portable equipment for power operation of large gate valves.

VALVES, SPECIAL

The Chapman Valve Mfg. Co., Essex St., Indian Orchard, Mass. Cone valves. See pages 300-303.
Eddy Valve Co., Waterford, N. Y., Sub. of James B. Clow & Sons, P. O. Box 6600-A, Chicago 80, Ill. Water, steam, oil. Eddy mechanical joint cutting-in valves and cutting-in sleeves. No lead, no furnace, no jute needed. See pages 272, 273.
The Ford Meter Box Co., Inc., 1000 Manchester Ave., Wabash, Ind. Ringstyle valves and couplings for connecting to both iron and copper pipe. The meter coupling nut is retained behind the flange with a square bronze pin forced into a groove in the nut. See pages 329-332.
The Kennedy Valve Mfg. Co., 1069 E. Water St., Elmira, N. Y. Globe, angle and sprinkler valves. Complete line of standard and extra-heavy cast iron screwed and flanged fittings. See pages 337-340.
The Ludlow Valve Mfg. Co., Inc., Troy, N. Y. Mud, flap, tapping, automatic drip valves. Indicator post valves, floorstands. See pages 348-351.
M & H Valve & Fittings Co., Anniston, Ala. Valves and accessories for use in water distribution systems, pumping stations, filtration plants, sewage disposal plants. See pages 357-360.
Rockwood Sprinkler Co., 38 Harlow St., Worcester 5, Mass. Bronze ball valves ⅜ to 2½" and cast-steel 3 and 4". See pages 984, 985.
Traverse City Iron Works, P. O. Box 348, Traverse City, Michigan. Flap valves, shear gates, mud valves, floor stands for water and sewage treatment plant work. See page 450.
American Water Softener Co., Inc., S. E. Cor. Lehigh Ave. & Fourth St., Philadelphia 33, Pa. Tri-Filter valve for control of a 3-filter battery.
Anderson Valve Works, Marion, Ind. Automatic; surge suppressors.
Birch Mfg. Co., 1523 N. Sedgwick St., Chicago 10, Ill. Pump valves for reciprocating BF and vacuum pumps.
Crane Co., 836 So. Michigan Ave., Chicago 5, Ill. Complete line of brass and iron valves, cocks, fittings, chlorine valves, etc.
Cochrane Corp., 3122 N. 17th St., Philadelphia 32, Pa. Special valves.
Davis Mfg. Co., 321 N. Maple Dr., Beverly Hills, Calif. Ball, cone and control valves for stop and check, pump check.
Edward Valves, Inc., Sub., Rockwell Mfg. Co., East Chicago, Ind. Steel valves; globe and angle stop valves; instrument and gage valves; hydraulic valves.
Hills-McCanna Co., 2397 Nelson St., Chicago 18, Ill. Saunders patent diaphragm valves for water, acid and slurries.
Josam Mfg. Co., Michigan City, Ind. Shock absorbers to eliminate water hammer in pipe lines on mechanical equipment.
Mueller Co., 512 W. Cerro Gordo St., Decatur, Ill. Tapping and inserting valves and machines. Non-rising stem mud valves. Flap valves.
Ohio Brass Co., 380 N. Main St., Mansfield, Ohio. Brass valves, globe, angle, needle, whistle and radiator, and Equatemp sizes ⅛ to 3".
Ohio Injector Co., 101 Pine St., Wadsworth, Ohio. Valves: air, globe; hydraulically operated valves, and indicator posts.
Pelton Division of Baldwin-Lima-Hamilton Corp., 2929 19th St., San Francisco, Calif. Valves; needle; surge suppressor; hollow stream, hollow cone, relief, duplex strainers, air valves spherical, and butterfly.
Ross Valve Mfg. Co., Inc., 1940 William Ave., Troy, N. Y. Automatic valves and specialties for water and fire departments.

VALVES, WATER REGULATING

Eddy Valve Co., Waterford, N. Y., Sub. James B. Clow & Sons, P. O. Box 6600-A, Chicago 80, Ill. Pressure reducing relief valves. See pages 272, 273.
Golden-Anderson Valve Specialty Co., 1232 Ridge Ave., Pittsburgh 33, Pa. Float, solenoid-operated electric water service, water pressure reducing, non-return, altitude control, surge relief, swing check, engine stop and throttle, water level control, flowtrol valves. See page 437.
Iowa Valve Co., Oskaloosa, Ia., Sub. James B. Clow & Sons, Inc., P. O. Box 6600-A, Chicago 80, Ill. Valves: motor operated; pneumatic and hydraulically operated gate valves; square bottom valves. See pages 274, 275.
Kennedy Valve Mfg. Co., Elmira, N. Y. Motor operated water regulating valves. See pages 337-340.
Ludlow Valve Mfg. Co., Inc., Troy, N. Y. Motor operated valves; square bottom valves. See pages 348-351.
Palmer Filter Equipment Co., P. O. Box 1696, Erie, Pa. Hydromatic 4-way control valves. See pages 412, 413.
Philadelphia Gear Works, Erie Ave. & G St., Philadelphia 34, Pa. Automatic valve controls, for operation of globe, gate, butterfly, sluice gates, either manual, push button or automatic control. See page 444.
Anderson Valve Works, Marion, Ind. Water regulating valves; altitude, float, relief, reducing, motor operated, solenoid operated, control valves.
Cla-Val Co., Newport Beach, Calif. Automatic diaphragm types, hydraulically operated; float and altitude valves; pressure relief and reducing valves.
Darling Valve & Mfg. Co., Williamsport 61, Pa. Motor operated valves.
Edward Valves, Inc., Sub. Rockwell Mfg. Co., East Chicago, Ind. Motor operated valves; pressure reducing and relief valves.
Fisher Governor Co., 1700 Fisher Bldg., Marshalltown, Ia. Altitude and float valves; pressure reducing and relief valves.
Foster Engineering Co., 835 Lehigh Ave., Union, N. J. Pressure reducing valves for water service; float valves.
Minneapolis-Honeywell Regulator Co., Industrial Div., Wayne and Windrim Aves., Philadelphia 44, Pa. Water, steam, gas or air control valves; motor operated and solenoid operated valves; relief and pressure reducing valves.
Ross Valve Mfg. Co., Inc., Troy, N. Y. Altitude and float valves; relief and pressure reducing valves; back pressure, surge, pump control, and automatic valve combinations.

WATER MAIN CLEANERS

Ace Pipe Cleaning, Inc., 3513 E. 18th St., Kansas City, Mo. Complete service for cleaning sewer and water pipes. See pages 524, 525.
American Pipe Cleaning Co., 1819 Nicollet Ave., Minneapolis 3, Minn. Water mains cleaned by contract; labor, trucks and equipment furnished. See pages 453-456.
National Power Rodding Corp., 1000 South Western Ave., Chicago 12, Ill. Complete service for cleaning, reboring and bucketing pipes and ducts underground, above ground, anywhere. See pages 540, 541.

National Water Main Cleaning Co., 50 Church St., New York 7, N. Y. Removal of incrustation, tuberculation, and sediment from pipe ranging from 4 to 72" in diameter. See pages 365-368.
Flexible, Inc., 3786 Durango Ave., Los Angeles 34, Calif. Power rodding equipment for removal of hard scale. For softer deposits and long cleaning runs, pressure line scrapers are offered. See pages 476-479.
Pittsburgh Pipe Cleaner Co., 5847 Centre Ave., Pittsburgh 6, Pa. Complete service for restoring efficiency.
Rodding-Cleaning Machines, Inc., 7827 Melrose Ave., Los Angeles 46, Calif. RCM self-contained, mobile, portable plant for cleaning all 2 to 48" sewers and water mains.

WATER SOFTENERS

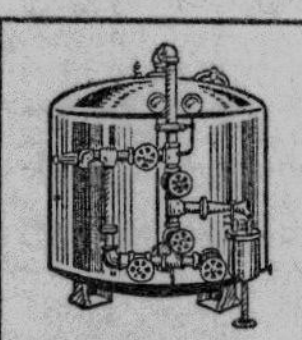

The water softeners used in the municipal field may be of the following types: (1) cold process type, either lime or lime soda, (2) zeolite—(or cation exchanger), (3) combination lime zeolite. The cold lime soda water softener may be either (a) suspended solids contact type or (b) conventional type. The zeolite water softener may be (a) fully automatic or (b) semi-automatic or (c) slurry recirculation type or (d) manually operated type. The combination lime zeolite type consists of (a) a cold or hot process lime type softener followed by (b) a zeolite (or sodium cation exchanger) softener.

Dorr-Oliver Inc., Barry Place, Conn. Water softeners and complete ion-exchange systems for practically any degree of purity and of flow. See pages 466-469.
General Filter Co., Ames, Ia. Zeolite and lime soda water softening units. Monobed demineralization unit for complete ion removal from raw water and removal of mineral acidity from water supply. See pages 400, 401.
Graver Water Conditioning Co., 216 W. 14th St., New York 11, N. Y. Zeolite softeners, manual, semi-automatic, and full automatic operation. Reactivator high-rate water softeners and clarifiers. Conventional plants, hot process softener, hot zeolite softeners, ion exchangers, demineralizers, deaerating heaters. Iron removal filters. See pages 402, 403.
The Permutit Co., 330 W. 42nd St., New York 36, N. Y. All types, all sizes. Zeolite Water Softeners—deliver water of zero hardness, manual or automatic controls. Ion exchange resins: Permutit Q, Zeo-Karb, Decalso, Zeo-Dur—insoluble, granular, bead-like solids used in water softening equipment of the percolation type. Cold lime-soda softeners: Precipitator—range from 500 gal. per hour up, Spiractor — for treatment of clear, hard water. See pages 416, 417.
Roberts Filter Mfg. Co., 601 Columbia Ave., Darby, Pa. Zeolite water softeners. See page 1042.
American Well Works, Aurora, Ill.
American Water Softener Co., Inc., S.E. Cor. Lehigh & Fourth Sts., Philadelphia 33, Pa.
Chemical Equipment Co., P. O. Box 3098, Los Angeles 54, Calif. Zeolite water softeners—Ion exchanger.
Cochrane Corp., 3122 N. 17th St., Philadelphia 32, Pa. Zeolite water softeners, both sodium and hydrogen types; demineralizing equipment; ion exchange equipment; cold lime water softeners; hot process and hot lime zeolite softeners; degasifiers and decarbonators for removing CO_2 from water; deaerating heaters to remove dissolved oxygen from water; process and equipment for removing silica, iron, manganese and fluorides from water; equipment for removing color, taste and odor from water.
Culligan, Inc., S. Shermer Rd., Northbrook, Ill. Zeolite and resin water softeners, bulk zeolite, and soft water service systems.
Elgin Softener Corp., Elgin, Ill. Water softeners, all sizes and types of zeolite softeners—sodium and hydrogen cycle. Deliver up to 44% more soft water and prevent zeolite loss. All types of zeolite. Demineralizers, dealkalizers, lime soda softeners, chemical water treatment. Automatic and manual controls.
Holyoke Machine Co., 517 Main St., Holyoke, Mass.
Hungerford & Terry, Inc., Atlantic Blvd., Clayton, N. J. Zeolite and cold process softeners, manual or automatic.
Infilco Inc., Box 5033, Tucson, Ariz. ACCELATOR® and ACCELAPAK® softeners, zeolite softeners; recarbonators; coagulators; operating and sampling tables; flow controllers; Hydrodarco Purifiers for removing taste, odors, chlorine; Fluorex organic color, fluorine.
International Salt Co., Inc., Scranton Life Bldg., Scranton, Pa. Sterling Salt for regenerating zeolite water softeners.
Lakeside Engineering Corp., 222 W. Adams St., Chicago 6, Ill. Zeolite water softeners. Also Zeolites-resins and greensands-demineralizers (deionizers).
The McKays Co., 473 N. Cleveland Ave., St. Paul 4, Minn. McKays water conditioning equipment, softens, or completely deionizes.
Morton Salt Co., Industrial Div., 120 So. LaSalle St., Chicago 3, Ill. Morton "Purex" salt for water softening.
Smith & Loveless, Inc., P. O. Box 8172, Kansas City, Mo. Recarbonation equipment with and without water cooling, capacities 1,500 to 10,000 pounds CO_2 per day.
Walker Process Equipment, Inc., Box 266, Aurora, Ill. Carball CO_2 producer for carbonation of lime softened water, and clariflow units for line softening process.

WATER WASTE SURVEY

The Pitometer Associates Engineers, 50 Church St., New York 7, N. Y. Engineering services in connection with water waste surveys and engineering studies of municipal water systems.

WATER WELL SYSTEMS

Layne & Bowler, Inc., Box 6697, Hollywood Sta., Memphis 8, Tenn. Gravel wall wells, shutter screen, vertical turbine pumps and complete water treatment. See pages 344-347.
A. Y. McDonald Mfg. Co., 12th and Pine Sts., Dubuque, Ia. Convertible deep and shallow well and deep well water systems. See pages 352-355.
A. W. Williams Co., Inc., 208 Virginia St., Mobile, Ala. Gravel wall wells, straight wells, stainless steel screen, vertical turbine pumps, either electric or engine driven, complete water treatment.

WELLS AND WELLPOINT SYSTEMS

Edward E. Johnson, Inc., 315 N. Pierce St., St. Paul 4, Minn. Drive well points, dewatering points. See page 439.
Complete Machinery & Equipment Co., Inc., 36-40 Eleventh St., Long Island City 6, N. Y. "Complete" wellpoint systems with 3, 6, 8 and 10 in. pumps and featuring the patented fluted type wellpoint, on rental or purchase option. Wellpoint pumps available with gas, electric or diesel drive. Systems usable for water supply, irrigation or dewatering on construction operations.
Fisher Research Laboratory, Inc., Palo Alto, Calif. Well testing equipment.
Griffin Wellpoint Corp., 880 E. 141st St., New York 54, N. Y. Wellpoint systems for dewatering wet excavations and water supply. Wellpoint pumps powered by diesel and gasoline engines, and electric motors. Wellpoints.
Kelly Well Co., Inc. Grand Island, Nebr. Full concrete cased wells including concrete screen.
Moretrench Corp., 90 West St., New York 6, N. Y. Wellpoint systems.
John W. Stang Corporation, 8221 Atlantic Ave., P. O. Box 631, Bell, Calif. Wellpoint systems and centrifugal pumps.

Electrical Generation and Distribution

ASH AND COAL HANDLING

Baugham Mfg. Co., Inc., 157 Shipman Rd., Jerseyville 1, Ill. Baugham model 215 bin-to-stoker screw conveyor, feeds one or more hoppers, moves up to 500 lb. of stoker coal per minute. See page 86.

Gruendler Crusher & Pulverizer Co., 2915 N. Market St. St. Louis, Mo. Coal crushers, portable and stationary cinder crushing plants. See page 470.

Illinois Stoker Co., 102 W. 7th St., Alton, Ill. Chain grate stokers built to any design. Specially designed for incineration. See page 557.

LoDal, Inc., Norway, Mich. Truck self loader for mounting on standard truck chassis. Overhead discharge with straight buckets—capacity of ⅜, ¾ and 1¼ cu. yd. Forward tilting buckets for loading over trucks. For coal handling, ash removal and disposal. See pages 162-165.

Beaumont Birch Co., Philadelphia 2, Pa. Complete coal handling equipment including conveyors, buckets, scrapers, weighing scales, skip hoists. Pneumatic, hydraulic, and mechanical ash handling equipment. Bucket elevators, drag conveyors, ash gates, charging gates, chemical feeders, chain.

Wm. Bros Boiler & Mfg. Co., 1057 Tenth Ave., S.E., Minneapolis 14, Minn. Continuous ash discharge grates. Overfeed stokers.

The Fairfield Engineering Co., 342 Chicago Ave., Marion, Ohio. Fairfield coal-handling systems in silo or cylindrical bunker types; complete ash-handling systems.

A. B. Farquhar Div., The Oliver Corp., 221 Duke St., York, Pa. Conveyors, sand, gravel, stone, coal ashes, etc.

Gifford-Wood Co., 23 Hill St., Hudson, N. Y. Coal handling systems for steam generating plants.

The Jeffrey Mfg. Co., 970 N. 4th St., Columbus 16, Ohio. Crushers, conveyors, track hoppers, bucket elevators, weigh larries, feeders, chutes, bins, valves, etc.

Link-Belt Co., Prudential Plaza, Chicago 1, Ill. Elevating, conveying and power transmission machinery.

United Conveyor Corp., 6505 Ridge Blvd., Chicago 26, Ill. Pneumatic and hydraulic ash conveyors.

HEATING, POWER

Bailey Meter Co., 1035 Ivanhoe Rd., Cleveland 10, Ohio. Automatic control of steam generating and hot water heating boilers. See page 480.

Cleaver-Brooks Co., 326 E. Keefe Ave., Milwaukee 12, Wis. Automatic self-contained steam and hot water boilers, gas, oil, combination gas and oil burners.

Copes-Vulcan Div., Blaw-Knox Co., Erie 4, Pa. Copes fully automatic, continuous boiler feed water regulators, combustion control, desuper-heaters and pressure reducing valves; Vulcan soot blowers.

Enterprise Engine and Machinery Co., sub. of General Metals Corp., 622 Florida St., San Francisco 10, Calif. Enterprise burners provide for either oil or combination oil-gas fuel; V-belt drive utilizes standard motors; latest control and accessory units; eleven models 13 to 666 boiler hp.

Todd Shipyards Corp., Products Div., Columbia & Halleck Sts., Brooklyn 31, N. Y. Oil, gas and combustion burners for firing boilers in power houses, warehouses, garages, sewage disposal plants, and for augmenting combustion in incinerators.

The Will-Burt Co., 12 Ray St., Orrville, Ohio. Will-Burt air controlled stoker for heating.

CONDULETS

Crouse-Hinds Co., Syracuse 1, N. Y. Condulets for ordinary and hazardous locations. Power plugs and receptacles. Vapor-tight, dust-tight and explosion-proof lighting equipment. See pages 878-881.

DUST COLLECTORS (SMOKE CONTROL)

Bailey Meter Co., 1035 Ivanhoe Rd., Cleveland 10, Ohio. Smoke density recorders. Automatic control of smoke correction and/or alarms. See page 480.

American Blower Corp., Tireman Ave. at Roselawn, Detroit 32, Mich. American Blower dust collection.

Wm. Bros. Boiler & Mfg. Co., 1057 Tenth Ave., S. E. Minneapolis 14, Minn. Smoke stacks.

Dracco Corp., 4063 E. 116th St., Cleveland 5, Ohio. Dust control equipment for the collection and removal of dust from municipal plant operations.

Prat-Daniel Corp., So. Main & Meadow St., So. Norwalk, Conn. Dust collectors, stacks, steel. Fans (induced and forced draft).

ELECTRICAL DISTRIBUTION EQUIPMENT

Bethlehem Steel Co., Bethlehem, Pa. Galvanized steel towers and Switchyard structures for electric systems. See pages 326, 327; 485.

Elreco Corp., 2902 Cormany Ave., Cincinnati 25, Ohio. Tubular steel poles and brackets for power distribution, mast arms and brackets for street lighting and floodlighting. See page 828.

General Electric Co., Apparatus Sales Div., Schenectady, N. Y. Cabinetrol®, switchgear, unit substations, etc. See pages 398, 399; 791-794.

Hubbard and Co., 6301 Butler St., Pittsburgh 1, Pa. Pole line hardware complete line. Cable material, insulators, secondary racks, cross-arm brackets, lightning arresters; mast arms and brackets for street lighting; aluminum poles. See pages 799-802.

Line Material Industries, McGraw-Edison Co., 700 W. Michigan St., Milwaukee 1, Wis. Complete pole line hardware pins and pole top fixtures; transmission line hardware; guying material; anchors and tools; grounding equipment; secondary and service racks; clevises, wireholders and brackets; glass and poreclain insulators. See pages 803-806.

W. H. Stewart, Inc., 202 Kratz Ave., Syracuse 9, N. Y. Safety frame that reels and unreels steel snakes for use in conduit work; conduit cleaning equipment. See pages 506-509.

Westinghouse Electric Corp., 3 Gateway Center, P. O. Box 868, Pittsburgh 30, Pa. Capacitors, feeder voltage boosters, instrument transformers, meters, instruments. See pages 821-824.

Copperweld Steel Co., Wire & Cable Div., 1015 Monongahela Ave., Glassport, Pa. Copperweld ground rods.

Electric Service Works, Delta-Star Electric Div., H. K. Porter Co., Inc., 17th and Cambria St., Philadelphia 32, Pa. "Crystal Valve" lightning arresters.

The Joslyn Mfg. and Supply Co., 155 North Wacker Drive, Chicago, Ill. Pole line hardware, insulators, porcelain and glass; anchors; ground rods; street lighting, mast arms, pipe brackets; lightning arresters; poles of cedar, pine, lodgepole, fir, larch; bridge timbers; piling, cedar, pine, fir; timber treating; cross arms; connectors; wood pins and brackets; guying material; secondary racks; wire holders.

Pennsylvania Transformer Co., Box 330, Canonsburg, Pa. Step voltage regulators up to 2500 Kva for plus or minus 10% regulation in 32 steps.

Petersen Engineering Co., 460 Kifer Rd., Santa Clara, Calif. Pengo Tension Wire Stringer and Pulling-in equipment.

ELECTRIC POWER SETS

Homelite, Port Chester, N. Y. Gasoline-driven generators, light-weight carryable units, in sizes from 1,000 to 5,000 watts, AC or DC. See pages 263-267.

D. W. Onan & Sons Inc., University Ave., S.E. at 25th, Minneapolis 14, Minn. Gasoline-driven electric generating plants—AC models from 400 to 50,000 watts. DC models from 750 to 5,000 watts. Battery charging models from 400 to 8,500 watts, 6-12-32 volts. Diesel electric generating plants—AC models from 3,000 to 5,000 watts. Battery charging model rated at 3,000 watts, 32 volts. See pages 845-848.

Allis-Chalmers, Buda Div., Milwaukee 1, Wis. 5 to 30 kw. diesel and gasoline electric sets.

Caterpillar Tractor Co., Peoria, Ill. Diesel electric sets, 12 sizes, 30 to 350 KW rating polyphase, 60 cycle.

Chicago Pneumatic Tool Co., 6 E. 44th St., New York 17, N. Y. Portable diesel generating sets.

Complete Machinery & Equipment Co., Inc., 36-40 Eleventh St., Long Island 6, N. Y. Ratings from 500 watts to 10 kva. capacity.

Consolidated Diesel Electric Corp., Stamford, Conn. Diesel and gasoline electric generator sets.

Detroit Diesel Engine Div., General Motors Corp., 13400 W. Outer Drive, Detroit, Mich. Diesel generator sets, 20 to 200 kw.

Griffin Equipment Corp., 880 E. 141st St., New York 54, N. Y. Portable electric generators from 1,500 watts up. AC or DC for construction, emergency lighting and standby.

International Diesel Electric Co., Inc., Hillburn, N. Y. Diesel electric and gasoline-electric generator sets.

International Harvester Co., Chicago 1, Ill. Electrall portable electrical generator, for three International truck models, to supply on-the-job electric power wherever a truck can go.

Jackson Vibrators, Inc., Ludington, Mich. Portable gas-electric power plants—110-120 volts, 3-phase and single phase, 60 cycle, A.C.

Katolight Corp., First Ave. at Chestnut St., Mankato, Minn. Gasoline, gas, diesel and butane, electric, power plants, 500 watts to 400 KW. Standby generators and rotary converters.

Kohler Co., Kohler, Wis. Kohler electric plants from 500 to 35,000 watts in A.C. or D.C. Available in manual start, push button at plant, remote control, automatic and automatic standby.

Le Roi Division, Westinghouse Air Brake Co., 1706 S. 68th St., Milwaukee 14, Wis. 600 to 300 KW gas engine powered generator sets.

Master Vibrator Co., 149 Stanley Ave., Dayton 1, Ohio. 900 to 3,000 watt D.C. and 5,000 watt A.C. engine driven generators.

Minneapolis-Moline Co., Box 1050, Minneapolis 1, Minn. Power units in 9 sizes 27 to 300 hp for gasoline, distillate, natural gas, LP gas, diesel.

Murphy Diesel Co., 5317 W. Burnham Ave., Milwaukee 14, Wis. In 4 and 6 cylinder models with rated continuous capacities from 67 kw to 165 kw, 60 cycle AC, 50 cycle AC-DC sets are also available.

Nordberg Mfg. Co., 3073 S. Chase Ave., Milwaukee 1, Wis. Diesel engine generator sets for lighting or electric power service, permanent or standby, 5 to 30 kw.

Pioneer Gen-E-Motor Corp., 5841M W. Dickens Ave., Chicago 39, Ill. Portable and standby gasoline electric generating plants, AC or DC, 250 to 12,000 watts, 7.5 to 230 volts, 50 to 60 cycles.

The Ready-Power Co., 11231 Freud Ave., Detroit, Mich. Engine generators for continuous duty or standby electric power.

United States Motors Corp., 420 Nebraska St., Oshkosh, Wis. Gasoline, gas, and diesel engine generator sets. Portable, stationary, standby or regular source of power.

White Diesel Engine Division, The White Motor Company, Springfield, Ohio. 5 to 1,500 kw electric generating sets.

Wincharger Corp., Commerce Bldg., Sioux City, Ia. Portable electric generators.

Witte Engine Works, Oil Well Supply Div., United States Steel Corp., 1601 Oakland Ave., Kansas City 26, Mo. "Dieselectric" plants.

ENGINES—INTERNAL COMBUSTION

Allis-Chalmers Mfg. Co., 886 So. 70th St., Milwaukee 1, Wis. 5 models of diesel power units from 30 to 244 brake hp. 2 models of gasoline power units 50.6 and 24.5 max. brake hp. See pages 285-288.

Climax Engine & Pump Mfg. Co., Room 928, 208 S. LaSalle St., Chicago 4, Ill. A complete line of engines for driving pumps and generators in water works; and pumps, generators and blowers in sewage treatment plants. Engines operate on natural gas, gasoline, sewage gas or butane. Sizes to 600 hp. See page 850.

Continental Motors Corp., Muskegon 82, Mich. Engines driven by gasoline, butane, natural gas, diesel oil, and fuel oil. See pages 841-844.

Fairbanks, Morse & Co., Fairbanks-Morse Bldg., Chicago 5, Ill. Diesel, gas and gasoline: 5 to 3,500 hp. See pages 530, 531.

Allis-Chalmers, Buda Div., Milwaukee 1, Wis. Diesel and gasoline engines, sizes 4 to 510 hp; diesel and gasoline electric sets, 5 to 300 kw; diesel nozzle testers.

Alco Products, Inc., Schenectady 5, N. Y. Diesel engines for power generation; dual fuel, 550 to 2400 hp.

Briggs & Stratton Corp., 2711 N. 13th St., Milwaukee 1, Wis. Four-cycle single cylinder air-cooled gasoline for operating equipment.

Caterpillar Tractor Co., Peoria, Ill. Diesel engines, 9 sizes, from 25 to 650 hp. Spark ignition engines, 2 sizes, 267 & 400 hp.

Chicago Pneumatic Tool Co., 6 E. 44th St., New York 17, N. Y. Diesel, gas, and dual fuel engines.

Clinton Machine Co., Maquoketa, Iowa. Air cooled gasoline engines—1¾ to 9 H.P.

The Cooper-Bessemer Corp., Mt. Vernon, Ohio. Diesel, gas, gas-diesel, spark-ignited gas engines, atmospheric or supercharged, 250-5450 hp.

Cummins Engine Co., Inc., 5th & Wilson, Columbus, Ind. Lightweight high-speed diesel engines, 60-600 hp, for on-highway trucks, off-highway trucks, buses, tractors, earthmovers, shovels, cranes, air compressors, oilwell drilling rigs, centrifugal pumps, generator sets and power units.

Detroit Diesel Engine Div., General Motors Corp., 13400 W. Outer Drive, Detroit, Mich. General Motors diesel engines with unit injector fuel systems, interchangeable parts, uniflow principle. Single and multiple engine units available 30 to 893 bhp.

Enterprise Engine & Machinery Co., 622 Florida St., San Francisco 10, Calif. Stationary and marine engines, for pumping, auxiliary, standby, and direct power generation in normally aspirated and turbo-charged full diesel, dual fuel, tri-fuel, gas-spark type ignition. Heavy duty; medium speed in 12 sizes. 48 models from 73 BHP-7703 BHP. Generator sets from 55 KW to 5502 KW.

Gardner-Denver Co., 100 Williamson St., Quincy, Ill. Geared air motor for starting diesel engines, in place of air injection or electric motor.

Hamilton Div., Baldwin-Lima-Hamilton Corp., Hamilton, Ohio. Diesel and dual fuel engines; 900 to 5450 BHP.

Harnischfeger Corp., P & H Diesel Div., 500 S. Main St., Crystal Lake, Ill. 1, 2, 3, 4 and 6 cylinder, two-cycle, high-speed, light-weight metal-alloy diesel engine 15 to 175 hp.

Hercules Motors Corp., Canton, Ohio. High-Speed, heavy-duty gasoline, kerosene, natural gas, butane-propane and diesel engines, 2, 4, 6 and 8 cylinders, 3 to 500 hp.

International Harvester Co., Chicago, Ill. Diesel, LP Gas, and gasoline engines for self-propelled equipment.

Lauson Engine Div., Tecumseh Products Co., New Holstein, Wis. 2-6.3 hp gasoline air-cooled. 4 cycles.

Le Roi Division, Westinghouse Air Brake Co., 1706 S. 68th St., Milwaukee 14, Wis. Engines, gas, natural gas and LP. 540 through 4,000 cu. in. displacement.

Murphy Diesel Co., 5317 W. Burnham Ave., Milwaukee 14, Wis. Engines 90-268 hp; generators 67 to 125 kw.

Nordberg Mfg. Co., 3073 S. Chase Ave., Milwaukee 1, Wis. Diesel, dual fuel and gas engines, two and four-cycle, 10 to over 12,000 hp. for municipal power plants, auxiliary and standby service for hospitals, airports, etc.

The Oliver Corp., 400 W. Madison St., Chicago 6, Ill. Industrial gasoline and diesel units; 4 sizes 38 to 73 max. BHP.

Waukesha Motor Co., P. O. Box 379, Waukesha, Wis. Internal combustion engines for operation on natural or artificial gas, gasoline, or diesel oil, from 10-1,100 hp, portable and stationary, for use in driving generators, water pumps, and all types of industrial, construction and road building machinery. Complete engine-generator sets, 50-600 KW capacity.

White Diesel Engine Division, The White Motor Company, Springfield, Ohio. Diesel engines, natural gas engines, dual fuel engines, HP range. 11-2150 BHP.

Willys Motors, Inc., Industrial Engine Dept., 1505 N. Cove Blvd., Toledo 1, Ohio. 'Jeep' Power Giant industrial engines and power units.

Witte Engine Works, Oil Well Supply Div., United States Steel Corp., 1601 Oakland Ave., Kansas City 26, Mo. Diesel engines; full diesels. 4 stroke cycle, sizes 4 and 9 hp. vertical, 6 to 18 hp. horizontal models. Diesel engine-driven electric generating sets, direct or belt connected 2.4 kw to 12 kw.

Worthington Corp., Harrison, N. J. Diesel, vertical 4-cycle, direct or air injection; gas engines, 4-cycle, vertical single-acting; dual fuel engines, vertical 4-cycle, convertible from gas to diesel fuel.

METER SEALS

E. J. Brooks Co., 169 N. 13th St., Newark 7, N. J. Amalead wire seals and sealing tools for gas and electric meters. Padlock type seals, self-locking type seals also available.

United Seal Co., 450 S. Pearl St., Columbus 15, Ohio. Lead-wire and reusable padlock seals for utility meters, governors, cash and ballot boxes, lockers. Metal checks, tags and wires. Renewable cast-iron seals for stop cocks and unions, ½ to 2" pipe sizes.

MOTORS, CONTROLS, AND SUBSTATIONS

Allis-Chalmers Mfg. Co., 886 So. 70th St., Milwaukee 1, Wis. Motors from 1 to 100,000 hp and up, switchgear, three types of circuit breakers, magnetic, oil and air, compact unit substations, motor-generator sets, mercury arc rectifiers, switchboards and a wide line of controls. See pages 285-288.

Fairbanks, Morse & Co., Fairbanks-Morse Bldg., Chicago 5, Ill. See pages 530, 531.

General Electric Co., Apparatus Sales Div., Schenectady 5, N. Y. 1. Unit substations for transforming and switching incoming power; protective devices. 2. Motors, induction or synchronous for horizontal or vertical mounting; also gear-motors. 3. Control for these motors in steel cabinets which also contain electric and electronic instruments for recording the plant processes and operating characteristics of the machines. See pages 398, 399; 791-794.

Westinghouse Electric Corp., 3 Gateway Center, P. O. Box 868, Pittsburgh 30, Pa. Fractional and integral AC and DC motors and gearmotors. AC and DC manual and magnetic controls. See pages 821-824.

B/W Controller Corp., 2222 E. Maple Rd., Birmingham, Mich. AC motor starters and contactors.

Electric Machinery Mfg. Co., Minneapolis 13, Minn. Synchronous induction motors and controls; synchronous generators and switchgear.

Eseco Div., H. K. Porter Co., Inc., 11th & Commerce St., Lockport, Ill. Switchgear: Generator controls, distribution boards, voltage regulators, relays and automatic controls for diesel engines.

The Mercoid Corp., 4213 Belmont Ave., Chicago 41, Ill. Mercoid, controls and switches regulate electrically operated equipment in accordance with changes in pressure, temperature, fluid level or mechanical movement. Typical applications are controlling pumps to maintain pressure, and liquid levels in boilers, tanks and reservoirs, and for alarms.

Wagner Electric Corp., 6400 Plymouth Ave., St. Louis 14, Mo. Single phase and direct current motors 1/125 to 5 hp; polyphase squirrel cage 1/6 to 250 hp.

OIL PURIFIERS

Bowser, Inc., 1365 E. Creighton Ave., Fort Wayne 2, Ind. Hydro-Volifier for transformer oils; Reconditioner for turbine oil; Degasifier for oil filled cable. See page 1032.

Briggs Filtration Co., River Road, Washington 16, D. C. Oil filters and oil filter elements.

The De Laval Separator Co., Poughkeepsie, N. Y.

Fram Corp., Providence 16, R. I. Oil, air, fuel and water filters.

The Hilliard Corp., 102 W. 4th St., Elmira, N. Y. Hilco filters, oil lube and fuel for diesel and gas engines. Hilco purifiers, oil for steam turbines, transformer oils.

Indiana Commercial Filters Corp., Lebanon, Indiana. Oil filters-coolant clarifiers, tubular conveyors.

RADIO

(See page 786)

SERVICE TRUCKS AND BODIES

J. H. Holan Corp., 4100 W. 150th St., Cleveland 11, Ohio. Construction and maintenance bodies, general service bodies. Liveboom hydraulic derricks to 12,000 lb. capacity. Mechanical and hydraulic aerial ladders to 40'. Hydraulic towers to 30.' Mechanical and hydraulic earth borers. Hydraulic jacks. Aerial arms to 45'. See page 831.

Tel-E-Lect Products, Inc., 10027 Minnetonka Blvd., Minneapolis 26, Minn. Complete units for 2-man operation, including hydraulic or mechanical derricks, diggers and self-storing derrick kits. See page 835.

Auto Body Works, Inc., Appleton, Wis. Utility bodies: line construction, ladder, aerial tower bodies.

Electric Service Works, Delta-Star Electric Div., H. K. Porter Co., Inc., 17th and Cambria St., Philadelphia 32, Pa. "Sky-Mount" Keystone ladder mounts, sizes: 24, 28, 32'.

International Harvester Co., Chicago 1, Ill. Four International truck models with service-utility bodies.

McCabe-Power Auto Body Company, 5900 North Broadway, St. Louis 15, Mo. Utility bodies — service, line construction, maintenance; winches; derricks; aerial ladders; aerial towers; Sky-Master (hydraulic aerial beam).

Mobile Aerial Towers, Inc., 1730 N. Harrison St., Fort Wayne, Indiana. Hydraulic Hi-Ranger for overhead work; of arc welded steel construction.

Murray Mfg. Co., 1250 Atlantic Ave., Brooklyn 16, N. Y. "Crowsnest" aerial ladder.

Pitman Manufacturing Co., 300 W. 79th Terrace, Kansas City, Mo. Pitman Giraffe, a tower truck for servicing street lights, trimming trees, at heights to 40', 360° rotation.

The Sky-Worker Corp., Milford, Conn. Hydro-Sky-Worker on truck with articulated boom, 42', 360°.

Telsta Corp., 2900 Spring St., Redwood City, Calif. Telsta electric lift for street light maintenance and other overhead service operations.

York-Hoover Corp., York, Pa. Complete line of utility truck bodies for water, electric and gas.

TRANSFORMERS

Allis-Chalmers Mfg. Co., 886 So. 70th St., Milwaukee 1, Wis. Power, distribution instrument and metering. See pages 285-288.

General Electric Co., Apparatus Sales Div., Schenectady 5, N. Y. All types. See pages 398, 399; 791-794.

Line Material Industries, McGraw-Edison Co., 700 W. Michigan St., Milwaukee 1, Wis. Transformers, single phase, conventional, completely self-protected, rural, three phase, subway, booster and dry type. See pages 803-806.

Moloney Electric Company, 5390 Bircher Blvd., St. Louis 20, Mo. Transformers: Power, regulating, load tap changing, network, Class B dry type, Sealed Class H dry type, subway, distribution, constant current street lighting, transformers for electronics, feeder voltage regulators, primary and secondary units substations, and capacitors. See page 852.

Westinghouse Electric Corp., 3 Gateway Center, P. O. Box 868, Pittsburgh 30, Pa. Oil, Inerteen and dry-type transformers, distribution, instrument, power and specialty types, also power centers and substations. Also street lighting transformers and ballasts. See pages 821-824.

Jefferson Electric Co., 910 25th Ave., Bellwood, Ill. A complete line of street lighting transformers for operation of incandescent and mercury vapor lamps. Types available for multiple or series circuits.

Pennsylvania Transformer Co., Box 330, Canonsburg, Pa. Wagner Electric Corp., 6400 Plymouth Ave., St. Louis 14, Mo. Distribution, power, current.

Wagner Electric Corp., 6400 Plymouth Ave., St. Louis 14, Mo. Distribution, power, current.

WIRE AND CABLE

The Anaconda Wire and Cable Co., Hastings-on-Hudson, N. Y. Street-lighting cable for underground installation, direct burial or duct. Pole and bracket cable. Fire alarm, police signal and traffic control cable to IMSA specifications. See page 849.

Collyer Insulated Wire Co., 245 Roosevelt Ave., Pawtucket, R. I. Power and control cables for generating and substations. Power cables for overhead and underground distribution systems. See page 851.

General Electric Co., Construction Materials Div., 1285 Boston Ave., Bridgeport 2, Conn. Wire and Cable Department: aerial cables, appliance lead wires, asbestos- and asbestos-varnished-cambric-insulated cables, boiler-room cables. BX armored cables, control cables, portable cords and cables, fixture wires, Flamenol wires and cables, parkway cables, remote-control wires, rubber power cable, service-entrance cables, switchboard cables, and varnished-cambric-insulated cables. See pages 398, 399; 791-794.

United States Rubber Co., Rockefeller Center, New York 20, N. Y. U. S. pole and bracket cable and neoprene-sheathed for use where voltage between conductors is low but voltage between conductors and ground is relatively high. U. S. low-voltage street-lighting cable, "zip-cord" types. See page 1121.

American Steel & Wire Div., U. S. Steel, 816 Rockefeller Bldg., Cleveland 13, Ohio. Electrical wire and cable for power and light, including parkway and submarine cable.

The Ansonia Wire & Cable Co., 111 Martin St., Ashton, R. I. Cables (all plastic) for street lighting, traffic control and fire alarm.

General Cable Corp., 420 Lexington Ave., New York 17, New York.

The Okonite Co., Passaic, N. J. Okocord. Lead-covered, lead and steel taped parkway cable for airport and street lighting, rubber-covered wires and cables for all types of electrical power. Also single and multi-conductor electrical wires and cables for communications.

John A. Roebling's Sons Corp., 640 S. Broad St., Trenton 2, N. J.

Rome Cable Corp., P. O. Box 71, Rome, N. Y.

Simplex Wire & Cable Co., 79 Sidney St., Cambridge 39, Mass. Power, lighting, fire alarm, police telegraph, traffic.

Triangle Conduit and Cable Co., New Brunswick, N. J. Wire, cable and conduit.

Outdoor Lighting Equipment

AIRPORT LIGHTING

Crouse-Hinds Co., Syracuse 1, N. Y. Complete line of equipment meeting CAA specifications. See pages 878-881.

Elreco Corp., 2902 Cormany Ave., Cincinnati 25, Ohio. Floodlighting standards for hangar and service areas, passenger unloading areas, parking lots and drives. See page 828.

Line Material Industries, McGraw-Edison Co., 700 W. Michigan St., Milwaukee 1, Wis. Complete lighting equipment from Class 1 to 7 airports. See pages 803-806.

Revere Electric Mfg. Co., 6009 Broadway, Chicago 40, Ill. Airport lighting, airway equipment, obstruction lights, code beacons, code flashers. See pages 814-817.

Westinghouse Electric Corp., Lighting Div., 1216 W. 58th St., Cleveland 1, Ohio. See pages 821-824.

AGA Div., Elastic Stop Nut Corp. of America, 1030 Newark Ave., Elizabeth 3, N. J.

Luxor Lighting Products, Inc., Empire State Bldg., New York 1, N. Y. Long life 500 and 620 lamps for radio and aerial towers.

The Julian A. McDermott Corp., 40-22 National St., Corona, N. Y. Battery operated obstruction and contact lights, vehicles and snow plow warning lights.

CONTROL OF OUTDOOR CIRCUITS

The Fisher-Pierce Co., Inc., South Braintree, Boston 85, Mass. Photoelectric street light controls. See page 829.

General Electric Co., Apparatus Sales Div., Schenectady, N. Y. A complete line of street-lighting control equipment for both series and multiple control circuits, including photoelectric control. Controllers are available both aerial and subway for both series and multiple control. See pages 398, 399; 791-794.

South Bend Current Controller Co., 1237 N. Side Blvd., South Bend 15, Ind. Oil switches and relays for remote control of series or multiple distribution circuits energizing street lighting, airport lighting, and floodlighting installations. R-C-O-C Remote Control of Outdoor Circuits. See page 833.

Westinghouse Electric Corp., 3 Gateway Center, P. O. Box 868, Pittsburgh 30, Pa. Controls for lighting of streets, airports, athletic fields. See pages 821-824.

Mercotec Corporation, 24 Stone St., N. Y. Sauter time switches for automatic operation of on-off systems for control of lighting of streets, airports, athletic fields. Can handle more than one circuit.

Micro Balancing Inc., Herricks Rd. & Washington Pl., Garden City Park, L. I., N. Y. Lumatrol photoelectric light switch features plug-in installation into a prespecified receptacle on luminaire or in circuit: 4" diameter, 5" height, ½ lbs. weight; light sensitivity more than 0.5 candlepower.

Ripley Co., Inc., 48 Factory St., Middletown, Conn. Photoelectric controls, electronic relays, lighting controls.

FLOODLIGHTING POLES

Elreco Corp., 2902 Cormany Ave., Cincinnati 25, Ohio. Tubular steel poles with tenon, or bracket, light mountings for general area work such as recreation facilities, parking lots, and industrial uses. Single or multiple platform mountings for large areas such as stadiums, freight yards, utilities. See page 828.

Kerrigan Iron Works Inc., 1033 Herman St., Nashville, Tenn. See pages 258; 807-809.

Millerbernd Mfg. Co., Winsted, Minn. Millerbernd four-post angle, galvanized steel towers. Conventional self-supporting design. For floodlighting, radio, microwave, etc. Also steel floodlighting poles. See pages 810-813.

Pfaff and Kendall, Newark 5, N. J. All aluminum floodlight poles. Custom made towers to 50'. See pages 826, 827.

Revere Electric Mfg. Co., 6009 Broadway, Chicago 40, Ill. Hinged and rigid floodlight poles. See pages 814-817.

The Union Metal Mfg. Co., 1400 Maple Ave., N.E., Canton 5, Ohio. Self-supporting steel flood-lighting poles (Monotubes) for sportsfield and all types of area lighting, in heights 20' to 100'. See pages 818-820; 896.

Hubbard Aluminum Products Co., 6301 Butler St., Pittsburgh 1, Pa. Aluminum flood lighting poles. See pages 799-802.

FLOODLIGHTS

Crouse-Hinds Co., Syracuse 1, N. Y. Floodlights for night sports and general applications, 200 to 2,000 watts. See pages 878-881.

General Electric Co., Apparatus Sales Div., Schenectady 5, N. Y. Floodlights for municipal playgrounds. In the sportlighting field, technical advice and efficient sports lighting equipment for baseball fields, softball fields, football fields, tennis courts, swimming pools or other outdoor recreation facilities. See pages 398, 399; 791-794.

Line Material Industries, McGraw-Edison Co., 700 W. Michigan St., Milwaukee 1, Wis. See pages 803-806.

Revere Electric Mfg. Co., 6009 Broadway, Chicago 40, Ill. Floodlights. See pages 814-817.

Westinghouse Electric Corp., Lighting Div., 1216 W. 58th St., Cleveland 1, Ohio. See pages 821-824.

Benjamin Electric Mfg. Co., Des Plaines, Ill. Floodlights for lighting sub-structures, bridges, sports areas, safety islands, buildings, drives, subways and underpasses.

Luxor Lighting Products, Inc., Empire State Bldg., New York 1, N. Y. 1,000-1,500 watt flood lamps for sports-fields.

The Pyle National Co., 1361 N. Kostner Ave., Chicago 51, Ill. Sirens, floodlights, conduit fittings, subway and tunnel lights.

Steber Mfg. Co., Broadview, Ill. Floodlights for recreational and parking areas.

LAMPS, STREET LIGHTING AND TRAFFIC SIGNAL

General Electric Co., Large Lamp Dept., Nela Park, Cleveland, Ohio. Complete line of filament, fluorescent and mercury lamps available for all outdoor lighting applications. Sodium lamps available from Apparatus Sales Div., Schenectady, N. Y. See pages 398, 399; 791-794.

Westinghouse Electric Corp., Lamp Div., Bloomfield, N. J. Incandescent, mercury vapor and fluorescent lamps for outdoor lighting. See pages 821-824.

Amplex Corp., 111 Water St., Brooklyn 1, N. Y. Street lighting and traffic signal lamps. Incandescent, mercury vapor and fluorescent lamps.

Champion Lamp Works, Lynn, Mass. Series and multiple type street lighting lamps of 2,000 or 3,000 hours rated life, traffic signal lamps and a complete line of general service incandescent and fluorescent lamps.

Duro-Test Corp., North Bergen, N. J. Duro-Test V-Beam traffic lamp produces a symmetrical pattern with higher center-beam intensity for safety. 4,000-6,000 hour life. 40, 60, 67, 100 and 150 watt.

Luxor Lighting Products, Inc., Empire State Bldg., New York 1, N. Y.

LUMINAIRES

General Electric Co., Apparatus Sales Div., Schenectady 5, N. Y. A complete line of luminaires for street and highway lighting; filament, mercury, and fluorescent types. Filament luminaires for multiple and series lighting circuits. See pages 398, 399; 791-794.

Graybar Electric Co., Inc., 1502 Graybar Bldg., New York 17, New York. Electrical equipment for maintenance of lighting facilities; electrical installations; street lighting, flood lighting, interior lighting, traffic signals, communication wiring, portable emergency lighting units. See page 830.

Line Material Industries, McGraw-Edison Co., 700 W. Michigan St., Milwaukee 1, Wis. Incandescent, mercury-vapor and fluorescent luminaires. See pages 803-806.

Pfaff & Kendall, Newark 5, N. J. Outdoor fluorescent luminaire for area and street lighting. Can be equipped with hinged base and rotatable shaft for easy installation and maintenance as well as true alignment. See pages 826, 827.

Revere Electric Mfg. Co., 6009 Broadway, Chicago 40, Ill. White-Way Pylon-Lites, fluorescent columns for all weather: street lighting luminaires, incandescent and mercury for series or multiple circuits. See pages 814-817.

Street Lighting Equipment Corp., 31-23 61st St., Woodside 7, N. Y. Medium-priced incandescent and mercury luminaires for streets and parks, for lamps of 1,500 to 20,000 lumens; another fixture for 1,500 to 2,500 lumens for replacing radial wave reflectors. An ornamental lantern for parks; a large round globe for fire alarm boxes. See page 834.

Westinghouse Electric Corp., Lighting Div., 1216 W. 58th St., Cleveland 1, Ohio. Complete line of incandescent and mercury-vapor luminaires for either series or multiple circuits. Incandescent luminaires meet the EEI-NEMA standards and are available in all ASA-IES light-distribution patterns. Also fluorescent street lighting luminaires. See pages 821-824.

Wheeler Reflector Co., 275 Congress St., Boston 10, Mass. Wheeler street lighting luminaires for incandescent and mercury lamps with or without photo-electric controls. See page 836.

Benjamin Electric Mfg. Co., Des Plaines, Ill. Sign lights for safety island and underpass.

The Joslyn Mfg. and Supply Co., 155 N. Wacker Dr., Chicago, Ill. Complete line of modern enclosed street-lighting luminaires.

Philadelphia Electrical and Mfg. Co., 1200-36 N. 31 St., Philadelphia 21, Pa. Pemco street and highway luminaires and accessories.

Steber Mfg. Co., Broadview, Ill. Steberlites are cast-aluminum lampholders for PAR-38 and R-40 sealed-beam lamps for outdoor areas and pin-point illumination.

LUMINAIRE GLASSWARE

Holophane Company, Inc., 342 Madison Ave., New York 17, N. Y. Refractors for street lighting; outdoor lighting units for parking yards, loading platforms, plant grounds, etc. See pages 795-798.

POLE DIGGING AND SETTING

Gravely Tractors, Inc., Box 78, Dunbar, W. Va. Posthole digger. See page 1001.

Tel-E-Lect Products, Inc., 10027 Minnetonka Blvd., Minneapolis 26, Minn. Hydraulic or mechanical derricks and diggers. Earth augers; complete winch and digger drive systems. Complete installations including bodies and self-storing kits. See page 835.

Batavia Metal Products Corp., 51 Liberty St., Batavia, N. Y. Pole-setting derricks, rear-mounted, all sizes; also front-mounted derrick for Dodge power wagon.

Danuser Machine Co., Fulton, Mo. Danuser post driver, tractor or trailer mounted, strikes 25 blows per min. Danuser Digger, tractor mounted, and earth drill for post holes, seedling settings.

Ottawa Steel, Div. L. A. Young Spring & Wire Corp., Ottawa 60, Kans. Self-propelled Hydra-Hammer breaks concrete pavement, cuts asphalt, sets posts, tamps rock or soil.

Tulsa Winch Div., 815 E. First St., Tulsa 20, Okla. Tulsa winches in 34 models 6,500 to 80,000 lbs. for use on all makes and sizes of trucks and crawler tractors. Furnished with extended drum shaft and removable niggerhead for pole-setting, pulling cables and handling transformers. Also, power takeoffs and transmissions.

POLES AND BRACKETS

American Concrete Corp., 5092 N. Kimberly Ave., Chicago 30, Ill. Water-polished granite-finished lighting standards meeting I.E.S. and E.E.I. recommendations. Mounting heights limited to 21½, 26½ and 31½ ft. Standards are adaptable for fluorescent lighting. See page 825.

Elreco Corp., 2902 Cormany Ave., Cincinnati 25, Ohio. Tubular steel lighting standards and brackets for bridges, streets, highways, parks, shopping centers, industrial roadways and parking lots. See page 828.

General Electric Co., Apparatus Sales Div., Schenectady 5, N. Y. Aluminum and steel straight and upsweep brackets, mast arms and hanging devices for mounting any and all street lighting luminaires. Aluminum poles in all standard sizes and special applications. See pages 398, 399; 791-794.

Hubbard & Co., 6301 Butler St., Pittsburgh 1, Pa. One-piece upsweep brackets in sizes of 3 to 8 ft. extensions. Upsweep mast arms of tie-rod and truss type. One-piece tubular aluminum alloy poles and lighting standards up to 40 ft. See pages 799-802.

Hubbard Aluminum Products Co., 6301 Butler St., Pittsburgh 1, Pa. Complete line of Hapco aluminum alloy lighting standards, lighting brackets, mast arms and accessories. See pages 799-802.

Kerrigan Iron Works, Inc., 1033 Herman St., Nashville, Tenn. Kerrigan weld-forged continuous tapered steel light standards. See pages 258; 807-809.

Line Material Industries, McGraw-Edison Co., 700 W. Michigan St., Milwaukee 1, Wis. Luminaire support designs. See pages 803-806.

Millerbernd Mfg. Co., Winsted, Minn. Octa-Tube high-strength steel standards, continuous-taper octagon. Single and twin arm, all standard heights. Advanced and conventional designs. See pages 810-813.

Pfaff & Kendall, Newark 5, N. J. All-aluminum standards for street, highway lighting and traffic control signals. Also, all aluminum brackets for wood and steel pole mount. See pages 826, 827.

Revere Electric Mfg. Co., 6009 Broadway, Chicago 40, Ill. Single and double arm octagonal standards and hinged street lighting standards. See pages 814-817.

The Ryther-Purdy Lumber Co., 501 Tiffany St., New York 59, N. Y. Lighting standards of Western red cedar that resist decay, need no concrete foundation, require no maintenance. Single and twin-arm, height as desired. See page 832.

The Union Metal Mfg. Co., 1400 Maple Ave., N.E., Canton 5, Ohio. Union Metal Monotube tapered steel or aluminum poles, fluted or plain round, standardized at 20, 25, 30 and 35 ft., with or without transformer bases. Also poles for bridge lighting; floodlighting sports fields, recreational and parking areas; traffic signal standards; pedestals for fire alarm and police call boxes. Also upsweep brackets and mast arms for wood and steel pole mounting. See pages 818-820; 896.

Westinghouse Electric Corp., Lighting Div., 1216 W. 58th St., Cleveland 1, Ohio. Steel aluminum and concrete poles. Also brackets for mounting on metal or steel poles. See pages 821-824.

Wheeler Reflector Co., 275 Congress St., Boston 10, Mass. Complete line of mast arms and brackets including upsweep levalarms for quick positive leveling of bracket after attachment to poles. See page 836.

Koppers Company, Inc., Wood Preserving Div., 1450 Koppers Bldg., Pittsburgh 19, Pa. Wood poles, pressure-creosoted for long life—30 to 40 years.

Pacific Car and Foundry Co., 4th and Factory St., Renton, Wash. Carco steel street & flood light poles, and component parts. Wood pole brackets and pole extensions.

STREET LIGHT SERVICING

The Thompson Electric Co., 1198 Power Ave., Cleveland 14, Ohio. Complete metal pole units, wall and wood pole bracket units with disconnecting "servisafe" lowering-hangers incorporated in them.

STREET LIGHTING REFRACTORS

Holophane Co., Inc., 342 Madison Ave., New York 17, N. Y. Refractors for lighting highways and residential streets; outdoor lighting units for parking lots, loading platforms, plant grounds, etc. See pages 795-798.

Revere Electric Mfg. Co., 6009 Broadway, Chicago 40, Ill. See pages 814-817.

Traffic Control Equipment

ALTERNATORS, GENERATORS, BATTERIES AND TREATMENT
(See Power, Emergency)
(Page 785)

BADGES
(See page 783)

CITY TRANSPORTATION

General Electric Co., Apparatus Sales Div., Schenectady 5, N. Y. A fast modern transit system that effectively co-ordinates all forms of transportation can reduce traffic congestion and help solve parking problems by converting auto drivers into transit riders. See pages 398, 399; 791-794.

Marmon-Herrington Co., Inc., 511 W. Washington St., Indianapolis 7, Ind. Trolley coaches, school buses and motor coaches.

Ohio Brass Co., 380 N. Main St., Mansfield, Ohio. Trolley coach and street railway line materials. Trolley coach information.

Timken-Detroit Axle Division, Rockwell Spring and Axle Co., 100-400 Clark Ave., Detroit, Mich. Axles and brakes for all types of vehicles.

COIN HANDLING
(See page 794)

GATES, CROSSING, BRIDGES

B & B Engineering Corp., B & B Bldg., Norwood, La. Safety gates for the protection of vehicular and pedestrian traffic at railway grade crossings, bridges, plant entrances and schools. Navigation lights for bridges and piers. Approach warning signals for hazardous crossings. See pages 33; 976, 977.

Western Railroad Supply Co., 24 St. & Ashland Ave., Chicago 8, Ill. Gates and lights for bridge and pier approach, flashing lights, bells for railway crossings. See pages 972-975.

HIGHWAY GUARDS

Bethlehem Steel Co., Bethlehem, Pa. Bethlehem Safety-Beam Guard Rail of heavy steel plate in channel type design and posts for bridges and highways. Also cable guard rails. See pages 326, 327; 485

American Steel & Wire Div., U. S. Steel, 970 Rockefeller Bldg., Cleveland 13, Ohio. Highway guard cable.

Armco Drainage & Metal Products Inc., 5896 Curtis St., Middletown, Ohio. Guardrail. Bridge rail.

Tuthill Spring Co., Chicago 7, Ill. Highway guard rail, beam type, non-tension.

United Steel Fabricators, Inc., 333 Gasche St., Wooster, Ohio. Beam type highway and bridge guard rail.

IDENTIFICATION, DETECTION

Dashew Business Machines, Inc., 5886 Smiley Dr., Culver City, Calif. DASHaplate metal tags for positive inventory of all municipal property and material.

Faurot, Inc., 299 Broadway, New York 7, N. Y. Fingerprint kits for all purposes including baby foot printing for identification. Professional investigation kit for making blood tests, narcotic analysis, dental identifications and many other detections.

Norsid Mfg. Co., Inc., 33 Prospect St., Dept. M, Yonkers 1, N. Y. Consecutive number decals available for windshield, inventory-licenses, truck inspection. Civil Defense decals of all types and sizes. CD armbands.

JAIL EQUIPMENT

Decatur Iron & Steel Co., Inc., P. O. Box 72, Decatur, Ala. Complete line of cells for city and county jails, bunks, jail doors and locking devices and detention type aluminum windows.

Pauly Jail Building Co., Inc., St. Louis 4, Mo. Cell equipment, locking devices, seats, tables, benches.

Roanoke Iron & Bridge Works, Inc., Roanoke, Va. Steel equipment for jails and police stations.

Southern Steel Co., P. O. Drawer 2021, San Antonio 6, Texas. Complete line of jail and prison equipment.

The Stewart Iron Works Co., Inc., 1302 Stewart Block, Cincinnati 1, Ohio. Grating and police cells, doors, bunks, tables, seats, locks and locking devices, iron stairways and railings; iron and wire window guards, wire mesh partitions; folding and sliding steel gates.

The Van Dorn Iron Works Co., 2691 E. 79th St., Cleveland 4, Ohio. Cells, locks, doors, window guards, padded cells, bunks.

LOUDSPEAKERS

Municipal Street Sign Co., Inc., 775-7 Meeker Ave., Brooklyn 22, N. Y. ELECTR-O-TALKER for recorded or live microphone messages, announcements, warnings, commands—portable, mobile, or stationary. See page 910.

University Loudspeakers, Inc., 80 S. Kensico Ave., White Plains, N. Y. Horn-type projectors and weatherproof driver units. Speakers for warning and communications, indoor and outdoor.

OUTBOARD MOTORS

Evinrude Motors Div., Outboard Marine Corp., 4143 N. 37th St., Milwaukee 16, Wis. Outboard motors 3 to 30 hp.

Hart-Carter Co., Peoria, Ill. Sports King, 4 cycle air cooled outboard motors, 3-6 hp.

Johnson Motors Div., Outboard Marine Corp., 8000 Pershing Rd., Waukegan, Ill. Sea Horse outboard motors from 3 to 35 hp. for use by police and fire departments.

PARKING GARAGES

Bowser Parking System, Inc., 112 S. W. Second St., Des Moines 9, Ia. Engineers and manufacturers of a mobile mechanical elevator system for parking garages and office buildings, where cars are driven on and off by attendant.

Pigeon Hole Parking, Inc., 716 Peyton Bldg., Spokane 1, Wash. Multi-story structure consisting of stalls or pigeon holes and hydraulic car parkers, where cars are mechanically handled with dollies.

Webb & Knapp Parking Corp., 383 Madison Ave., New York 17, N.Y. "Minit Park" system for multi-story structures of steel or concrete. All-electric mobile elevators and under-wheel pickup automatic dollies.

PARKING LOT EQUIPMENT

Parking Corp. of America, Div. of Johnson Fare Box Co., 4619-25 Ravenswood Ave., Chicago 40, Ill. Parcoa, automatically operated parking lot control system that works either by a card-key, coin, token, tickets or any combination. No attendant needed. See pages 968, 969.

Western Railroad Supply Co., 24 St. & Ashland Ave., Chicago 8, Ill. Electric parking gates with remote controls for operation by coin, key, token or combination for the operation of parking lots without attendants. See pages 972-975.

Automatic Parking Devices, Inc., 10333 Shoemaker, Detroit 13, Mich. Ticket spitters, automatic gates.

Em-Ro Distributors, 120 S. LaSalle St., Chicago 3, Ill. Coin operated parking gates provide self-service parking on municipal lots. No attendant needed.

Fred Ex Enterprises, Inc., 469 E. Ohio St., Chicago 11, Ill. "X" Parking Barrier with all aluminum castings.

Globe Ticket Co., 112 North 12th St., Philadelphia 7, Pa. PARKONTROL systems for self parking, attendant parking, and coin parking, for off street parking, indoor and outdoor. Tickets and ticket issuing equipment for coin operation.

Harris-Barrier, Inc., 2140 Montcalm Ave., Indianapolis, Ind. Har-Bar traffic barriers for off-street parking, used with or without parking meters.

Taller & Cooper, Inc., 75 Front St., Brooklyn 1, N. Y. Parking lot entrance control systems.

PARKING METER ACCESSORIES

The Michaels Art Bronze Co., Inc., Kenton Land Rd., Erlanger, Ky.; P. O. Box 668, Covington, Ky. Device for straightening parking-meter posts. See pages 862-864; 1060.

The Parkit-Lockit Co., 77 N. Church St., Newton, Ohio. Coin changers for installation on streets and parking lots. See pages 872, 873.

E. J. Brooks Co., 169 N. 13th St., Newark 7, N. J. Amalead wire seals for parking meter coin containers.

H. K. Porter, Inc., Somerville 43, Mass. Metal post straightener for parking meter posts, highway signs and metal fence posts.

Traf-O-Teria System, Dept. Y, El Dorado, Kansas. Traf-O-Teria System for easy payment of parking meter fines.

U. S. Porcelain Enamel Co., 4635 E. 52nd Dr., Los Angeles 22, Calif. Parking meter zone marking signs of vitreous porcelain enamel.

United Seal Co., 450 S. Pearl St., Columbus 15, Ohio. Lead-wire and reusable padlock seals for utility meters and ballot boxes. Metal checks, tags and wires. Special parking meter and money bag seals.

PARKING METER CLEANERS

Acoustica Associates, Inc., Glenwood Landing, L. I., N. Y. Ultrasonic cleaner for parking meter mechanisms.

Wheelabrator Corp., Mishawaka, Ind. Blast cleaning equipment.

Zenith Mfg. and Chemical Corp., 82 Beekman St., New York 38, N. Y. "Instro-Met" machine for cleaning all types of parking meters; cleaning and rinsing solutions for parking meters and small parts cleaning.

PARKING METERS

The Dual Parking Meter Co., Sub. Rockwell Manufacturing Co., 400 North Lexington Ave., Pittsburgh 8, Pa. Single Dual and Dubl (2-car) Dual Automatic on and off-street meters; penny-nickel-dime and nickel-dime-quarter coin combinations. Convertible 1-2 hours and 12-24 hours, and any time limit within. Dual manual meters for on-street, convertible 1-2 hours. See page 869.

Duncan Parking Meter Corp., 835 N. Wood St., Chicago 22, Ill. Specializing in traffic control equipment. Line includes Miller and Automaton Parking Meters. Duncan-Fine-O-Meter. New improved Miller manual meter accepts dimes, nickels, pennies and quarters, and is adjustable to a wide range of time limits and coin combinations for street and parking lot use. The Automaton is completely automatic and self-energizing upon insertion of coin. See page 874.

The Karpark Corp., McMillan St. and Dover, Cincinnati 6, Ohio. Two models—Twin-O-Matic, Unimatic; single and two-car parking. Housings of aluminum alloy. Automatic operation, cumulative or non-cumulative time, full flag signals, power actuated coin mechanism, changeable time or coin requirements of any type. See pages 853-856.

Magee-Hale Park-O-Meter Co., Commerce Exchange Bldg., Oklahoma City 2, Okla. Model H-4 Park-O-Meter accepts pennies, nickels, dimes and quarters through the one coin slot—in any combinations or singly, for time limits varying from 6 minutes for one penny up through 24-hour operation. See pages 857-860.

The Michael Art Bronze Co., Inc., Kenton Land Rd., Erlanger, Ky.; P. O. Box 668, Covington, Ky. Parking meters for every street or off-street need. Mi-Co manual parking meter and Mi-Co Twin Automatic; combinations from 12 minutes to 12 hr. See pages 862-864; 1060.

The Parkit-Lockit Co., 77 N. Church St., Newton, Ohio. Meters are clockless, no moving parts to get out of order. Yields up to 60% more revenue by removing free-time from meter. Street-fringe and parking lot meters in nickel, dime and/or quarter combinations in either the single or twin types. See pages 872, 873.

Red Ball Parking Meters, Div. J. W. MenHall Drilling Co., Oil Producers, Benton, Ill. The parking meter with the Red-Ball violation signal visible from all directions, and positive coin control. Parking lot model made to your specifications. Clockless model for fringe areas. See page 876.

M. H. Rhodes, Inc., 30 Bartholomew Ave., Hartford 6, Conn. Mark-Time Hurricane on-street and off-street parking meters, single and twin models; patented Rhodes escapement; self locking sealed coin boxes; factory sealed timing mechanism eliminates need for skilled repairmen. See pages 865-868.

Trafico Parking Meter Company, Div., J. W. MenHall Drilling Co., Oil Producers, Benton, Ill. Manual parking meter for both on and off street parking. Simplicity in design permits quick access to mechanism and disassembly. Anti-ratchet and wipe-off assembly eliminates tampering and cocking of meter. See page 876.

Voglesong Products Corp., Emeryville, Calif. Turret parking meters, manual and automatic, handling pennies, nickels, dimes, quarters and half-dollars; quickly changes to suit time and rate wanted. Easy policing. Red signal shows in turret at expiration of parking time.

PAVEMENT MARKING MATERIALS

Cataphote Corp., 2505 Albion St., Toledo 6, Ohio. Cataline Compound (Premix) or Cataline Combination (Beads-On), the newest, quick-dry, rubber-based pavement striping materials. And Cataphote Thermaline hot-applied extruded plastic marking material. Fully reflectorized. White or yellow. Also Cataphote reflective pavement marking beads, plain or waterproof, drop-on or premix. See pages 911-914.

Flex-O-Lite Mfg. Corp., P. O. Box 3066, Affton Br., St. Louis 23, Mo. Flex-O-Lite reflective glass beads, for centerlines, parking zones, runway markings, for drop on or pre-mix application. See pages 915-918.

M. B. Corporation, Box 260, New Holstein, Wis. Striping paints, superay enamels and reflective beads for line marking and for street signs. Complete kits, including beads, binders. See pages 246, 247; 560; 967.

Minnesota Mining and Mfg. Co., 900 Fauquier Ave., St. Paul 6, Minn. Quick-drying Beeline brand reflective pavement marking materials consist of millions of microscopic glass spheres pre-mixed in a white or yellow compound. Applied with regular spray equipment. See pages 927-930.

J. W. Neff Laboratories, Inc., Stockertown 1, Pa. NEFSLABS, plastic "traffic-tested" markers and strips for traffic markings, letters, numerals and arrows. NEFMATS, brightly colored, reflective plastic one piece traffic letters. See page 970.

Prismo Safety Corp., Huntingdon, Pa. Prismo Life-Line for reflective center-lines and other markings; Prismo Plastix, a reflective pre-fabricated marking material in white or yellow applied in 6" squares or discs for crosswalks, parking zones, pavement legends and other markings. Also reflective paint compounds and premixed paints. All types of glass spheres. Rubber "Zee-Gards" for wet traffic line protection—also mechanical device for picking up line protectors. See pages 944-947.

Radiator Specialty Co., 1400 W. Independence Blvd., Charlotte 1, N. C. Safe-T-Cones, all rubber traffic barricade. Can be placed directly over freshly painted lines to eliminate smearing. See pages 959-962.

Veon Chemical Corp., 22-09 Bridge Plaza North, Long Island City 1, N. Y. PERMA-LINE, a moltenly applied, instant-setting thermoplastic traffic stripe. Permanent-type, non-smudging marking material, guaranteed to outlast paint 6-8 times. Available plain or reflectorized, white or Federal yellow. See page 1120.

Armor-Flex Co., 6969 Amherst Ave., St. Louis 5, Mo. Permanent-type plastic markers.

J. E. Bauer Co., 1021 N. Mission Rd., Los Angeles 33, Calif. Bauer's Zone-Lac traffic paint and Prismo reflective coatings, binder, beads, and bead dispensers.

S. B. Beugler Co., 3667 Tracy St., Los Angeles 39, Calif. Beugler gravity feed Mark-A-Zone applies stripes automatically, 2" to 5".

Hanline Bros., 1400 Warner St., Baltimore 30, Md. Zone-mark quick-drying traffic paint.

Hawkins-Hawkins Co., Inc., 1255 Eastshore Highway, Berkeley 10, Calif. Both trafficones and Safeti-Bars for channelizing vehicular and pedestrian traffic.

Interstate Rubber Products Corp., 908 Avila St., Los Angeles 12, Calif. Trafficone system of traffic control.

Premax Products, Div. Chisholm-Ryder Co., Inc., 5500 Highland Ave., Niagara Falls, N. Y. Signs and marking devices of stamped and embossed metal.

Robbins Tire and Rubber Co., Inc., Tuscumbia, Alabama. Vinyline street markers.

Traffic Safety Supply Co., 2636 N.E. Sandy Blvd., Portland 12, Oreg. Dur-O-Line round, plastic traffic lane markers in red, yellow or white. TEMLINE removable paint for temporary painting.

Tropical Paint Company, 1210-52 W. 70th St., Cleveland 2, Ohio. High visibility yellow, bright medium yellow and white street marking paint.

POLICE AND TRAFFIC EQUIPMENT

B & B Engineering Corp., B & B Bldg., Norwood, La. Police communication systems. Klyo police gongs. See pages 33; 976, 977.

Electronic Protection Inc., 2085 North Hawthorne Ave., Melrose Park, Ill. El-Tec electronic device on city emergency vehicles for control of traffic signals along route. See pages 885-888.

Federal Laboratories, Inc., Saltsburg, Pa. Tear gas equipment, sub-machine guns, ammunition, lights and sirens. See page 998.

The Gamewell Co., Newton Upper Falls 64, Mass. Police signalling systems. See pages 982, 983.

Grimm Stamp & Badge Co., 8105 Rosalie Ave., St. Louis 17, Mo. License plates: auto, bicycle, taxi. See pages 906-909.

Industrial Radio Corp., 428 N. Porkside Ave., Chicago 44, Ill. Police communication systems. Pak-Fone, the 2-way portable radio with 5-way power supply for continuous operation. See page 992.

Loadometer Corp., P. O. Box 4724, Baltimore 11, Md. Hi-Way Loadometer scales quickly weigh vehicles on road to determine overloads. Load capacities of 20,000 lb. See page 958.

Lyle Signs, Inc., 2720 University Ave., S.E., Minneapolis 14, Minn. Saf-T-Pak emergency traffic control kits, temporary barricades, Safe-T-Cones, school and other signs. See pages 923-926.

Municipal Street Sign Co., Inc., 775-7 Meeker Ave., Brooklyn 22, N. Y. Signs and posts. ELECTR-O-TALKER recorded or live public address system with continuous tape recorder for all types of police use. See page 910.

Radiator Specialty Co., 1400 Independence Blvd., Charlotte 1, N. C. Safe-T-Cone, all rubber traffic guide painted or reflectorized, 12, 18 or 28" sizes. Adapter for danger flags and flasher lights on cones. See pages 959-962.

Rolatape Inc., P. O. Box 1190, Santa Monica, Calif. Rolatape, a compact one-hand operation measuring wheel that registers feet and inches as you walk. See page 260.

Black Light Corp. of America, San Gabriel, Calif. Blak-Ray criminology kit.

Cushman Motor Works, Inc., 942 N. 31st St., Lincoln, Neb. Motor vehicles for policing and servicing parking meters.

W. S. Darley & Co., 2810 Washington Blvd., Chicago 12, Ill. Complete line of Police Department equipment.

Faurot, Inc., 299 Broadway, New York 7, N. Y. Fingerprint kits for all purposes including baby foot printing for identification. Professional investigation kit for making blood tests, narcotic analysis, dental identifications and many other detections.

The Gledhill Road Machinery Co., 57 S. Lera Rd., Galion, Ohio. Mobilweigh portable weighing station enforces truck axle load laws.

Harley-Davidson Motor Co., 3700 W. Juneau Ave., Milwaukee 1, Wis. Police motorcycles; sidecars and Servi-Cars.

Hawkins-Hawkins Co., Inc., 1255 Eastshore Highway, Berkeley 10, Calif. Reflectors, street name signs, trafficones, delineators, markers, portable traffic signals, traffic signs, Safeti-Bar for channelizing traffic.

Interstate Rubber Products Corp., 908 Avila St., Los Angeles 12, Calif. Trafficones for barriers and lane channelling.

Monarch Road Machinery Co., 1331 Michigan St., N. E., Grand Rapids 3, Mich. Guard-Gate folding emergency barricade.

Norsid Mfg. Co., Inc., 33 Prospect St., Dept. M, Yonkers 1, N. Y. City department and crest decals, all types and sizes. CD armbands.

Premax Products, Div. Chisholm-Ryder Co., Inc., 5500 Highland Ave., Niagara Falls, N. Y. Mobile radio antennas, mountings and fittings.

Robbins Tire & Rubber Co., Inc., Tuscumbia, Ala. Colored rubber traffic cones.

Stephenson Corp., Red Bank, N. J. "Harger" Drunkometer, Breathalyzer breath test for intoxication. Resuscitators.

PROTECTIVE COATINGS

Byerlyte Corp., 2300 W. 3rd St., Cleveland, Ohio. Paviseal protects asphalt pavements from petroleum solvents, actinic rays of the sun, battery acids, salt and frost action. See pages 146, 147.

RADIO

(See page 786)

ROAD LANTERNS, TORCHES, ETC.

R. E. Dietz Co., 255 Wilkinson St., Syracuse 1, N. Y. Safety lanterns and highway torches.

The Julian A. McDermott Corp., 40-22 National St., Corona, N. Y. Battery and line operated warning lights and flashers.

Neo-Flasher Mfg. Co., Inc., 3210 Valhalla Drive, Burbank, Calif. Neo-Flasher battery-operated warning lights and barricade units; operate up to 1,000 hrs. (30 days and nights); weather-proof, theft-proof, lock type case with lock nut.

Portable Light Co., Inc., 216 William St., New York 38, N. Y. Portable emergency lights, flashing red warning lights and revolving ray lights.

The Toledo Pressed Steel Co., 399 Phillips Ave., Toledo 12, Ohio. Road torches and truck flares for warning traffic of road obstructions, both self-righting and non-self-righting.

Trippe Mfg. Co., 133 N. Jefferson St., Chicago 6, Ill. Red warning lights including flashers.

U-C Lite Mfg. Co., 1063 W. Hubbard St., Chicago 22, Ill. Big Beam portable electric hand lamps, automatic emergency lights, and flashing flares.

SAFETY LANE EQUIPMENT

John Bean Div., Food Machinery and Chemical Corp., Box 840, Lansing 4, Mich. Automotive wheel balancers and aligners; headlight testers and front end correction tools. See pages 971; 1009.

Bear Mfg. Co., Rock Island, Ill. Complete line includes wheel aligners and balancers, frame straighteners, brake testers, wheel alignment testers, headlight testers, front end lift and tire re-truers.

Weaver Mfg. Co., Springfield, Ill. Complete line of safety lane equipment.

SAFETY TREADS

Wooster Products, Inc., Loehr and Wyant Sts., Wooster, Ohio. Wooster safety treads for stairs, ramps, and platforms, can be superimposed on steps, however badly worn.

SIGNS, DIRECTIONAL, TRAFFIC

B & B Engineering Corp., B & B Bldg., Norwood, La. Highway, special warning, railroad crossing signs, reflectorized or plain, brackets and posts. See pages 33; 976, 977.

Cataphote Corp., 2505 Albion St., Toledo 6, Ohio. Standard traffic signs, 6061-T6 aluminum or embossed zinc-coated steel. Plain or reflectorized. Also sign posts, mounting brackets and bolts, reflector signals, reflector buttons, aluminum sign blanks. Cataflex 202 reflective coating kits for reflectorizing signs in your own shop. See pages 911-914.

Eastern Metal of Elmira, Inc., Elmira Heights 1, N. Y. Complete line of directional, warning, parking and school safety traffic signs. Aluminum bolts for all signs installation. Manufacturers of Eastern A-Stand for work areas. Eastern E-Z Barricade. See pages 901-904.

Flex-O-Lite Mfg. Corp., P. O. Box 3066, Affton Br., St. Louis 23, Mo. Flex-O-Lite reflective glass beads for street signs, including complete sign kits and reflective bead binder. See pages 915-918.

The General Tire & Rubber Co., Reinforced Plastics Div., Marion, Ind. SY-LOY plastic-reinforced fiber glass traffic signs. Color, finish and legends are molded in. See pages 950, 951.

Grimm Stamp & Badge Co., 8105 Rosalie Ave., St. Louis 17, Mo. Traffic, parking, directional. See pages 906-909.

The Grote Mfg. Co., Inc., 500 Lafayette Ave., Bellevue, Ky. Complete line of traffic warning, regulatory and guide signs. Reflectorized with "Grotelite Smooth Surface" reflective sheeting or plain enameled. Railroad crossing signs, directional markers, school signs, delineators, barricade strips and plastic reflex reflectors, etc. See pages 919-922.

Lake Shore Markers, Inc., P. O. Box 59, Erie, Pa. Permanent aluminum safety and traffic signs. Also fiberglass traffic signs. See pages 952, 953.

Lyle Signs, Inc., 2720 University Ave., S.E., Minneapolis 14, Minn. Complete line of traffic and highway, warning, regulator, parking, school, railroad, welcome and street name signs to meet latest standards; plain or with any accepted reflecting medium desired; delineators, posts, brackets, temporary barricades and Saf-T-Pak emergency traffic control kits. See pages 923-926.

M. B. Corporation, Box 260, New Holstein, Wis. Reflective street signs. Reflective paints, beads, binder and waterproofer for sign finishing and refinishing. See pages 246, 247; 560; 967.

Minnesota Mining and Mfg. Co., 900 Fauquier Ave., St. Paul 6, Minn. Reflectorized traffic signs of "Scotchlite" reflective sheeting available in all standard traffic colors and shapes. Also reflectorized roadside guide signs, delineators, barricades; and unmounted sign faces. See pages 927-930.

Miro-Flex Co., Inc., 1824 E. Second St., Wichita, Kans. Traffic signs of zinc-coated bonderized steel finished in highest grade enamels. Available either plain or reflectorized, with glass or plastic buttons or reflective coating. See pages 931-934.

Municipal Street Sign Co., Inc., 775-7 Meeker Ave., Brooklyn 22, N. Y. All U. S. standard traffic signs of plastic fiberglass, vitreous porcelain enamel, and embossed baked enamel. Also complete line of posts, brackets and stanchions. See page 910.

National Safety Engineers, Inc., P.O. Box 1069, Birmingham 1, Ala. Highway and Municipal Traffic Signs, steel or aluminum, baked enamel or reflectorized. See pages 935-938.

Prismo Safety Corp., Huntingdon, Pa. Prismo "200" for reflective signs, and reflective sign finishing and refinishing materials. Also the "Monoprinter" for sign, layout and imprinting. The "Automatic Sign Shop Unit" for uniform coating and reflectorization. See pages 944-947.

Radiator Specialty Co., 1400 Independence Blvd., Charlotte 1, N. C. Safe-T-Cones, all rubber traffic guide for traffic channeling, emergency barricades, etc. Flasher-light and flag adaptors that fit into cones. See pages 959-962.

Sargent & Sowell, Inc., 1211 E. Jefferson, Grand Prairie, Texas. Complete line of traffic control signs, safety signs, highway signs, and traffic buttons. See pages 939-942.

Traffic & Street Sign Co., 84 Foundry St., Newark 5, N. J. Tassco traffic signs in all standard traffic color combinations and shapes. Overall or spot reflectorizing. Arrow, guide signs and markers. See pages 954, 955.

AGA Div., Elastic Stop Nut Corp. of America, 1030 Newark Ave., Elizabeth, N. J. Reflectors and traffic signs, markers and highway delineators.

S. G. Adams Co., 960 Olive St., St. Louis 1, Mo. Embossed steel signs, highway markers, traffic signs.

G. D. Bavin Co., 2500 W. Sixth St. Bldg., Los Angeles 57, Calif. Commando sign standard.

Brighton Steel Co., Stormville, N. Y. Traffic signs and sign posts, paint.

Dominion Signal Co., Inc., 1606-10 Magnolia St., Richmond 22, Va. All street and highway signs.

Ferro Enameling Co., 1100 57th Ave., Oakland 21, Calif. Embossed porcelain-enamel highway signs.

A. J. Gerard & Co., 1956 Hawthorne Ave., Melrose Park, Ill. Stainless and galvanized sign brackets and steel straps and strap-banding tools for attaching all types of street, highway and traffic signs.

Grace Sign & Mfg. Co., 210 President St., St. Louis 18, Mo. Ez-On reflectorized sign faces, standard yellow or approved red backgrounds; 24" and 30" square, diamond or octagon. Light gage for easy covering of old faces on location.

Hawkins-Hawkins Co., Inc., 1255 Eastshore Highway, Berkeley 10, Calif. A complete line of traffic signs, markers, reflectors, and delineators.

Nite-Bright Sign Co., 140 James St., Bridgeport 4, Conn. Directional and traffic control signs of heavy gauge aluminum faced with finest reflective material for wide angle day and night visibility.

Ready Made Sign Co., Inc., 117 Worth St., New York 13, N. Y. Street, warning, traffic, directional and general information signs.

Standard Signs, Inc., 3199 E. 65th St., Cleveland 27, Ohio. Safety signs for all purposes. Accident prevention signs and tags.

U. S. Porcelain Enamel Co., 4635 E. 52nd Dr., Los Angeles 22, Calif. Street name, and uniform city and state traffic signs, plain or reflectorized with Scotchlite.

SIGN POSTS

Allied Steel & Tractor Products, Inc., 7835 Broadway, Cleveland 5, Ohio. Bulldog "Easy Set" rail steel sign posts resist severe impact and stress and distortion without snapping, minimize replacement for street highway signs. See page 77.

Cataphote Corp., 2505 Albion St., Toledo 6, Ohio. Sign posts, portable standards. See pages 911-914.

Eastern Metal of Elmira, Inc., Elmira Heights 1, N. Y. Reflectorized or plain U-type steel posts. See pages 901-904.

Lyle Signs, Inc., 2720 University Ave., S. E., Minneapolis 14, Minn. Posts. See pages 923-926.

Municipal Street Sign Co., Inc., 775-7 Meeker Ave., Brooklyn 22, N. Y. Complete line of posts.See page 910.

National Safety Engineers, Inc., P. O. Box 1068, Birmingham 1, Ala. Posts. See pages 935-938.

Traffic & Street Sign Co., 84 Foundry St., Newark 5, N. J. Tassco posts. See pages 954, 955.

The Union Metal Mfg. Co., 1400 Maple Ave., N. E., Canton 5, Ohio. Steel Monotube supports which span the roadway and mount overhead signs and/or traffic signals. Also, single Monotube poles for side-mounted or center mounted signs. See pages 818-820; 896.

Brighton Steel Co., Stormville, N. Y. Sign posts.

Buffalo Steel Corp., Tonawanda, N. Y. "Quick-Set" rail-steel sign posts for route marker and highway sign posts and fence posts.

The Hunt Co., 18308 James Couzens Highway, Detroit 35, Mich. Rail-steel sign posts, and street and highway signs.

Nite-Bright Sign Co., 140 James St., Bridgeport 4, Conn. Steel channel posts.

SIGNS, HOUSE NUMBER

Lake Shore Markers, Inc., P. O. Box 59, Erie, Pa. House numbers. Aluminum homemakers. See pages 952, 953.

Lyle Signs, Inc., 2720 University Ave., S.E., Minneapolis 14, Minn. House numbers. See pages 923-926.

The Cambridge Tile Mfg. Co., Cambrite Div., Caldwell Drive, Cincinnati 15, Ohio. Cambrite tile house numbers installed by sliding individual numbers into aluminum frame. Frames hold one to five numbers.

Curtis Development & Mfg. Co., 3266 N. 33rd St., Milwaukee 16, Wis. Curtis porcelain house numbers, jet black numerals on white background, non-corrosive.

Premax Products, Div. Chisholm-Ryder Co., Inc., 5500 Highland Ave., Niagara Falls, N. Y. House numbers of stamped and embossed brass or aluminum.

Reflecto Letters, 411 E. 101st St., New York 29, N. Y. Specialists in house numbers for housing projects, etc. Numbers of plastic or rust proof "Zamac" metal and reflecting & luminous units. Mail boxes.

SIGNS, STREET NAME

B & B Engineering Corp., B & B Building, Norwood, La. Street-name signs, reflectorized or plain, brackets and posts. See pages 33; 976, 977.

Cataphote Corp., 2505 Albion St., Toledo 6, Ohio. Street name signs, embossed, zinc-coated steel. Various styles and mountings. Plain or reflectorized with Cataflex 202 reflective coating. See pages 911-914.

Eastern Metal of Elmira, Inc., Elmira Heights 1, N. Y. Embossed steel street-name signs, white enamel finish. See pages 901-904.

Grimm Stamp & Badge Co., 8105 Rosalie Ave., St. Louis 17, Mo. Street name signs. See pages 906-909.

Lake Shore Markers, Inc., P. O. Box 59, Erie, Pa. Lifetime aluminum, day and night street name signs. See pages 952, 953.

Lyle Signs, Inc., 2720 University Ave., S.E., Minneapolis 14, Minn. Wide variety of street name sign styles with or without block numbers; plain or reflectorized; several letter sizes and colors; also sign brackets, tubular and channel posts. See pages 923-926.

Minnesota Mining and Mfg. Co., 900 Fauquier Ave., St. Paul 6, Minn. Street-name signs of "Scotchlite" reflective sheeting. See pages 927-930.

Miro-Flex Co., Inc., 1824 E. Second St., Wichita 7, Kans. Street name, brackets, posts. See pages 931-934.

Municipal Street Sign Co., Inc., 775-7 Meeker Ave., Brooklyn 22, N. Y. Flat letter and embossed letter street name signs. Vitreous porcelain on steel or aluminum, cast aluminum and baked enamel, plain or reflectorized. Also complete line of frames, brackets and posts. See page 910.

National Safety Engineers, Inc., P. O. Box 1069, Birmingham 1, Ala. Street Name Signs, steel or aluminum, embossed, baked enamel or "Prismo" reflectorized, brackets and posts. See pages 935-938.

Traffic & Street Sign Co., 84 Foundry St., Newark 5, N. J. Tassco plates in any size or shape in both alodined aluminum or bonderized steel in baked enamel or reflectorized finish. Tassco sign brackets and posts. See pages 954, 955.

Brighton Steel Co., Stormville, N. Y. Street name signs and pipe posts.

Dominion Signal Co., Inc., 1606-10 Magnolia St., Richmond 22, Va.

Ferro Enameling Co., 1100 57th Ave., Oakland 21, Calif. Embossed porcelain-enamel street signs.

Hawkins-Hawkins Co., Inc., 1255 Eastshore Highway, Berkeley 10, Calif. Street name signs of porcelain or baked enamel. Also "Scotchlite" reflective street name signs.

U. S. Porcelain Enamel Co., 4635 E. 52nd Dr., Los Angeles 22, Calif. Street name signs of vitreous porcelain enamel.

SIRENS AND LIGHTS

(See page 786.)

SPEED METERS, VEHICLE COUNTERS

Automatic Signal Division, Eastern Industries, Inc., Regent St., Norwalk, Conn. Radar Speed Meter indicates continuous vehicle speeds in miles per hour. Vehicle counters. See pages 837-840.

The Denominator Company, Inc., 261 Broadway, New York 7, N. Y. "Keep Count" Denominator for manually tabulating and analyzing traffic flow. See page 956.

Muni-Quip Corp., 868 W. Center St., Decatur, Ill. TRAFFIC TIMER.

Streeter-Amet Co., Grayslake, Illinois. Ametron Speed Meter indicates vehicle speed in miles per hr. & the Traficounter built to count 900 or more cars a minute.

TOLL EQUIPMENT

Remington Rand Inc., 315 Fourth Ave., New York 10, N. Y. Punched card equipment for toll collection. See pages 1051-1054.

International Business Machines Corp., 590 Madison Ave., New York 22, N. Y. Toll collection equipment integrated with punched card equipment.

Taller & Cooper, Inc., 75 Front St., Brooklyn 1, N. Y. Toll booths and toll collection equipment.

TRAFFIC LINE MARKING CONTRACTORS

Prismo Safety Corp., Huntingdon, Pa. See pages 944-947.

Bowman Western Stamping Co., Inc., 1420 W. 107th St., Cleveland 2, Ohio.

Townsco Contracting Co., 1115 Cravens Building, Oklahoma City, Okla.

TRAFFIC LINE MARKING MACHINES

Aeroil Products Company, Inc., 50 Wesley St., South Hackensack, N. J. Line markers. See pages 69-72.

Cataphote Corp., 2505 Albion St., Toledo 6, Ohio. Cataphote Thermaline striping machine for application of new, hot-applied, extruded plastic permanent marking material. See pages 911-914.

Flex-O-Lite Mfg. Corp., P. O. Box 3066, Affton Br., St. Louis 23, Mo. Flex-O-Lite bead dispensers. Gravity type FREE FLOW dispenser 4" and 6" attachable any zone marking machine. Automatic dispenser 4" and 6" variable speed controlled flow of reflective beads. Attachable by hinged mounting to Kelly-Creswell zone marking machine. See pages 915-918.

Kelly-Creswell Co., Xenia, Ohio. Zone marking equipment, highway, municipal and industrial, portable and truck mounted, single, double and two-color triple line; air curtain guide plates featured on all models. See pages 963-966.

M. B. Corporation, Box 260, New Holstein, Wis. A complete line of self-propelled, truck mounted and manually operated markers. Lay single, double, triple lines —solid or intermittent and multiple colors. Bead reflectorizing attachment available. Also compact trailer for transporting markers. See pages 246, 247; 560; 967.

G. H. Tennant Co., 701 N. Highway 100, Minneapolis Minn. Traffic line removers (mechanical). Gas powered; semi-propelled. Cylindrical erasing head. See pages 130-132; 957.

Wald Industries, Inc., Montgomery, Pa. Exec. and Sales offices at Huntingdon, Pa. Reflecto-Liner striping equipment for single, double, and triple line operation. Also, the Carry-Liner transport trailer for transporting single line marking machines. See pages 948, 949.

G. D. Bavin Co., 2500 W. Sixth St. Bldg., Los Angeles 57, Calif. Bavin glass bead dispenser for street, highway and airport runway marking. From 1 to 3 dispensers operate from a single power unit attached to any striping machine.

Brighton Steel Co., Stormville, N. Y. Traffic paint machines.

H. C. Sweet Co., 12345 Telegraph Rd., Detroit 39, Mich. Florline hand machine makes traffic lines at walking speed.

Unimasco, Inc., 424 W. Redondo Beach Blvd., Gardena, Calif. Mark-Rite traffic line marking devices; Econo-Liners, gravity and pressure models. Models to paint double lines. All models dispense standard or reflectorized paints.

TRAFFIC SIGNAL POLES

Elreco Corp., 2902 Cormany Ave., Cincinnati 25, Ohio. Standards for traffic signals and combination standards for street lighting, street signs and traffic signals. See page 828.

Kerrigan Iron Works Inc., 1033 Herman St., Nashville, Tenn. Traffic signal standards. See pages 258; 807-809.

Millerbernd Mfg. Co., Winsted, Minn. Traffic signal standards. See pages 810-813.

Pfaff and Kendall, Newark 5, N. J. Standards and brackets for traffic signals. Also traffic and sign spans. See pages 826, 827.

The Union Metal Mfg. Co., 1400 Maple Ave., N.E., Canton 5, Ohio. Poles for mounting pedestal, span wire suspension or mast arm type traffic signals. Also, mast arms for mounting on existing wood or steel poles. See pages 818-820; 896.

TRAFFIC SIGNALS & CONTROLS

Automatic Signal Div., Eastern Industries, Inc., Regent St., Norwalk, Conn. Traffic actuated signal controllers; radar, pressure and magnetic vehicle detectors; master coordinated systems. Vehicle counters. See pages 837-840.

Crouse-Hinds Co., Syracuse 1, N. Y. Complete line of traffic signals and controllers for control of vehicular and pedestrian traffic. See pages 878-881.

Eagle Signal Corp., 202-20th St., Moline, Ill. Isolated and interconnected pre-timed traffic signal controllers, single and multi-dial types; vehicle and pedestrian actuated controllers and associated equipment; Monotrol and radio controlled master systems; traffic signals; beacons and flashers; Natecs emergency radio controlled traffic system. See pages 882-884.

General Electric Co., Apparatus Sales Div., Schenectady 5, N. Y. Traffic signals and controllers, including full and semi-vehicle actuated. See pages 398, 399; 791-794.

Graybar Electric Co., Inc., 1502 Graybar Bldg., New York 17, N. Y. See page 830.

The Marbelite Co., Inc., 27 Warren St., New York 7, N. Y. Adjustable and non-adjustable traffic signals, pre-timed and pedestrian actuated controllers 1, 2 and 3 dial types, beacons, flashers, pedestals and accessories. See page 877.

Municipal Street Sign Co., Inc., 775-7 Meeker Ave., Brooklyn 22, N. Y. ELECTR-O-TALKER audible traffic controller, automatic or supervised direction, portable, mobile or stationary. See page 910.

Portable Traffic Signals, Inc., 146 W. 21st St., Los Angeles 7, Calif. "Traffic Sentry" portable traffic signals, completely automatic, standard, 8⅜-inch lenses. See pages 897-900.

Southern Signals, Inc., 222 Beach St., P. O. Box 1303, Shreveport 91, La. Adjustable and non-adjustable traffic signals and pre-timed and semi-vehicle actuated traffic signal controllers. See pages 889-894.

Time-O-Matic Inc., 1100 Bahls St., Danville, Ill. Flashers for all types flashing signals—stop signs, warning beacons, detours, etc. See page 895.

The Adams & Westlake Co., Elkhart, Ind. Adlake mercury relays for all types of traffic control. Constant timing, compactness, hermetically sealed against dirt and weather. Require no maintenance.

Crown Signal, Inc., 1132 1st St., N.W., Cedar Rapids, Ia. Pedestrian and school crossing signal for traffic control consists of two lighting heads—flashing amber and a red stop light actuated by a push button.

Hawkins-Hawkins Co., Inc., 1255 Eastshore Highway, Berkeley 10, Calif. Hawkins twin flash mobile street signals.

Luxor Lighting Products, Inc., Empire State Bldg., New York 1, N. Y. Luxor traffic-signal lamps for longer light life. Available in 11, 28, 40, 60, 67 and 110 watt sizes with rated life 6500-7500 hrs.

Neo-Flasher Mfg. Co., 3210 Valhalla Drive, Burbank, Calif. Neo-Flasher battery-operated flashing warning lights and barricade units. Battery operates up to 1,000 hrs. (30 days and nights); weather-proof. Also semi-permanent "Stop" and "Caution" battery-operated warning lights.

The Winko-Matic Signal Co., 1854 Elyria Ave., Lorain, Ohio. Winko-Matic alternating flash on and off mechanism adds to the attention value of roadside warning signals. Illuminated plexiglas directional signs. Pedestrian WALK-DON'T WALK Signals, high intensity, two color signals in two different sizes. Automatic school period speed signals.

UNIFORM FABRICS

Franklin Worsted Co., 40 E. 34th St., N. Y. 16, N. Y. Police and fire uniform fabrics. See page 989.

Metcalf Bros. & Co., Inc., 1450 Broadway, N. Y. 18, N. Y. Standard serges, tropicals, and twist gabardines for police, firemen, bus drivers. For uniforms certified by U. S. Testing Co. See page 990.

Charlottesville Woolen Mills, Charlottesville, Va. Woolen uniform fabrics.

Maier-Lavaty Co., 815 So. Peoria, Chicago 7, Ill. Cloths for uniforms.

Reeves Bros., 54 Worth St., New York 13, N. Y. Cotton fabrics for uniforms and work clothes.

Fire Protection Equipment

AIR RAID SIGNALS

B & B Engineering Corp., B & B Bldg., Norwood, La. Kylo air horns, electric sirens, air raid warning systems. See pages 33; 976, 977.

The Gamewell Co., Newton Upper Falls 64, Mass. Warning horns operated by compressed air. See pages 982, 983.

Municipal Street Sign Co., Inc., 775-7 Meeker Ave., Brooklyn 22, N. Y. ELECT-O-TALKER siren redirections interspersed with siren. See page 910.

The Sterling Siren Fire Alarm Co., Inc., 8 Bartlett St., Rochester 8, N. Y. Sterling electric sirens. See page 994.

Benjamin Electric Mfg. Co., Des Plaines, Ill. Sirens, horns and howlers for supplementary interior and exterior warning systems.

Biersach & Niedermeyer Co., 1937 N. Hubbard St., Milwaukee, Wis. Mobil-Directo sirens, rotating directional gasoline and electric driven sirens.

Federal Sign & Signal Corp., 8704 S. State St., Chicago 19, Ill. Federal vertical electric sirens. Also the Thunderbolt for air raid warning purposes.

Foster Engineering Co., 835 Lehigh Ave., Union, N. J. Foster steam siren.

Keystone Signalphone Co., 1908 Law & Finance Bldg., Pittsburgh 19, Pa. Keystone Signalphone air raid horn.

Leslie Co., Lyndhurst, N. J. Leslie-Tyfon air and steam whistles. Leslie-Supertyfon Warbler disaster alarm.

Marine & Industrial Engine Div., Chrysler Corp., Trenton, Mich. Air raid sirens, powered by 180-hp. Chrysler Industrial V-8 engine.

Sireno Co., Inc., 214 William St., New York 38, N. Y. Warning sirens of fractional hp., 3 hp., and 5 hp.

University Loudspeakers, Inc., 80 S. Kensico Ave., White Plains, N. Y. Super power speakers, Model B-12 has 300 watt power, 12 driver units. 2 miles projection.

AMBULANCES

National Body Mfg. Co., Knightstown, Ind. Minute man ambulance on chassis of your choice.

Shop of Siebert Assoc., Inc., 222 Farnsworth Rd., Waterville, Ohio. Siebert Municipal and Industrial Ambulances carry four patients. Also Police Patrol Ambulances, Emergency Ambulances, Leeds Ambulances, Buses & Carry-alls.

Superior Coach Corp., Ambulance Div., Lima, Ohio. Two and four patient ambulances and rescuer models on Cadillac chassis.

BADGES

AGA Div., Elastic Stop Nut Corp. of America, 1030 Newark Ave., Elizabeth 3, N. J. Reflectorized batons.

V. H. Blackinton & Co., Inc., Attleboro Falls, Mass. Badges for police, fire, town, city, county and state officials; also civilian defense.

The C. G. Braxmar Co., Inc., 216 E. 45th St., New York 17, N. Y. Manufacturers of metal badges used by fire and police departments, sheriffs and all city, county, and state officials.

The Dickey-Grabler Co., 10302 Madison Ave., Cleveland 2, Ohio. Service badges for police and fire departments.

C. H. Hanson Co., 303 W. Erie St., Chicago 10, Ill. Police identification badges and cap devices.

Nielsen-Rionda, Inc., 40 John Street, New York 38, N. Y. Badges for police, fire, sheriff, civil defense, etc.

S. H. Reese, 57 Warren St., New York 7, N. Y. Police badges, whistles, police caps, billies, insignia, belts, holsters and dog license checks.

The Robbins Co., Attleboro, Mass. Uniform badges and insignia, service and safety award emblems.

Wentworth-Forman Co., Inc., 21 Edinboro St., Boston 11, Mass. "Head-Master" uniform caps, rubber cap covers; badges; uniform supplies, embroideries, cap straps, buttons, police and sheriff equipment; Civil defense equipment. Plastic helmets.

BREATHING EQUIPMENT

E & J Mfg. Co., 102 E. Graham Pl., Burbank, Calif. Portable Resuscitator-Inhalator-Aspirators; infant incubators and anesthetic gas machines.

J. H. Emerson Co., 22 Cottage Park Ave., Cambridge 40, Mass. Resuscitators, respirators, adult and infant models (iron lungs); hot pack apparatus or polio pack.

Mine Safety Appliances Co., 230 N. Braddock Ave., Pittsburgh 8, Pa. Gas masks, breathing apparatus, hose masks, firemen's helmets and safety clothing; first aid kits, stretchers, inhalators, and resuscitators.

Scott Aviation Corp., 191 Erie St., Lancaster, N. Y. Scott Air-Pak mask. Scott oxygen demand inhalator. Also Hydro-Pak-self-contained underwater breathing equipment.

Stephenson Corp., Red Bank, N. J. Automatic resuscitator, inhalator, aspirator.

EMERGENCY EQUIPMENT

Homelite, Port Chester, N. Y. Gasoline engine-driven blower for ventilating manholes; may be used either as blower or exhaust fan, one size, 1,500 cu. ft. per minute. See pages 963-967.

Atlas Safety Equipment Co., Inc., 27 Warren St., New York 7, N. Y. Atlas life nets. Safety belts of web and leather. Rope nets and emergency axes.

The Goldak Co., Inc., 1542-44 Glenoaks, Glendale 1, Calif. Radiation warning devices and geiger counters.

The K-G Equipment Co., Inc., 13-11 44th Ave., Long Island City 1, N. Y. Welding and cutting equipment, accessories, and supplies.

The Kinnear Mfg. Co., Fields Ave., Columbus 16, Ohio. Underwriters' labeled fire doors and shutters, steel rolling doors.

Herman Nelson Products, American Air Filter Co., Inc., 215 Central Ave., Louisville, Ky. Portable heaters, gasoline or kerosene, for emergency or temporary heating.

Peerless Machine Co., 1600 Junction Ave., Racine, Wis. Power hack saws for cutting off pipe.

Superior Fire Equipment Corp., 198 Broadway, New York 38, N. Y. Fire escape ladders, life saving nets.

Victor Equipment Co., 840-854 Folsom St., San Francisco 7, Calif. Gas welding and flame cutting equipment for use by fire rescue squads.

FIRE ALARM, BUILDING & INDUSTRIAL

B & B Engineering Corp., B & B Bldg., Norwood, La. Auxiliary fire alarm and sprinkler supervisory systems for plants and buildings, including valve supervision in combination with automatic heat detection. See pages 33; 976, 977.

The Gamewell Co., Newton Upper Falls 64, Mass. Alarms for plant and buildings. See pages 982, 983.

Rockwood Sprinkler Co., 38 Harlow St., Worcester 5, Mass. Dualguard fire protection system comprising sprinkler system plus rate-of-rise heat detecting and alarm systems. Also FogFOAM, FOAM and Water-FOG spot protection systems. **See pages 984, 985.**

The Autocall Co., 1960 Warden Ave., Shelby, Ohio. Alarm equipment for plant protection.

Benjamin Electric Mfg. Co., Des Plaines, Ill. Warning and fire alarm devices for industry and commerce.

Central Station Signals, Inc., 53 W. 23rd St., New York 10, N. Y. Automatic protection services, fire and burglar alarm.

Safa Alarm Division of the Fyr-Fyter Co., 243 W. Market St., Orville, Ohio. Public fire alarm equipment.

Sireno Co., Inc., 214 William St., New York 38, N. Y. Industrial and public siren alarms.

Sperti Faraday, Inc., 1322 E. Church St., Adrian, Mich. Fire alarm systems.

FIRE ALARM, MUNICIPAL

B & B Engineering Corp., B & B Bldg., Norwood, La. Municipal fire alarm systems, types A & B. Automatic fire detection systems with features for extending basic municipal systems for the protection of public and private property. See pages 33; 976, 977.

The Gamewell Co., Newton Upper Falls 64, Mass. Municipal fire alarm systems, including the feature of automatic fire detector which extends the basic municipal system to the interiors of public and private properties. See pages 982, 983.

The Sterling Siren Fire Alarm Co., Inc., 8 Bartlett St., Rochester 8, N. Y. Electric siren fire alarm systems. See page 994.

Safa Alarm Division of the Fyr-Fyter Co., 243 W. Market St., Orville, Ohio. Municipal fire alarm and police signal systems and a complete line of central office components.

FIRE APPARATUS

John Bean Div., Food Machinery and Chemical Corp., Box 840, Lansing 4, Mich. Volume pumpers, high pressure fog fire fighting trucks, combined volume and high pressure fog trucks. Brush, grass and forest fire fighters. Stationary and mobile industrial fire fighters. See pages 971; 1009.

Maxim Motor Co., Middleboro, Mass. Fire trucks, pumpers all sizes, 500 to 1500 gals. per minute; ladder trucks; aerial and city service types; airport, crash trucks; fire department supplies. See pages 980, 981.

Peter Pirsch & Sons Co., 1508 35th, Kenosha, Wis. Fire apparatus, triple combination pumpers, 500 to 1,500 gals.; aerial ladder trucks, 50 to 100 ft.; wood or aluminum main ladders; fire department ground ladders of wood or aluminum. **See page 993.**

American Fire Apparatus Co., Golden Ave. at Main St., Battle Creek, Mich.

American La France Corp., 116 E. LaFrance St., Elmira, N. Y. Complete fire-fighting equipment from largest and most powerful apparatus to hand operated portable units.

The Four Wheel Drive Auto Co., Clintonville, Wis. Fire trucks, 500, 750, 1,000, 1,250 gal. triple combination pumpers. Rural fire truck units.

Howe Fire Apparatus Co., Anderson, Ind. Automobile fire trucks; crash trucks for use on airplane land fields.

Mack Trucks, Inc., 1355 W. Front St., Plainfield, N. J. Complete line of **fire engines.**

Oren Roanoke Corp., Roanoke 16, Va. Triple and quadruple combinations, city service, ladder trucks, booster trucks, and rescue squad trucks; pump capacities 200 through 1,500 gals. per minute.

The Seagrave Corp., Columbus 7, Ohio. Complete line of fire-fighting apparatus. Seagrave builds its own motors, pumps, ladders, frames, and bodies.

Sharpsville Steel Fabricators, Inc., Sharpsville, Pa. Builders of service, squad, ladder trucks, pumping engines.

Walter Motor Truck Co., 1001-19 Irving Ave., Ridgewood 27, L. I., N. Y. Crash trucks for airports.

Ward LaFrance Truck Corporation, Grand Central Ave., Elmira, N. Y. Triple combination pumpers, quadruples, ladder trucks, hose wagons.

FIRE FIGHTING APPLIANCES NOZZLES, FOG, ETC.

Rockwood Sprinkler Co., 38 Harlow St., Worcester 5, Mass. WaterFOG, FogFOAM and FOAM, nozzles and Rockwood "Wet" and FOAM Liquid. Applicators and applicator clips. **See pages 984, 985.**

Akron Brass Mfg. Co., Inc., 1450 Spruce St., Wooster, Ohio. Shut-off nozzles, fog nozzles, Multiversals, playpipes.

American Fire Apparatus Co., Golden Ave. at Main St. Battle Creek, Mich. Small line Barton Super-Fog system 250 to 800 lb. pressures.

Buckeye Iron & Brass Works, P. O. Box 883, Dayton 1, Ohio. Shut-off nozzles.

Elkhart Brass Mfg. Co., 1302 W. Beardsley Ave., Elkhart, Ind. Mystery nozzles, couplings, adapters and fittings.

F. N. McIntire Brass Works, Inc., 377 Putnam Ave., Cambridge 39, Mass. Nozzles; deluge and monitor, Invincible nozzle, Morse shutoff nozzle and playpipe. Hydrant gates.

Powhatan Brass & Iron Works, Ranson, W. Va. Nozzles.

Wooster Brass Div., The Fyr-Fyter Co., Index and Bowman St., Wooster, Ohio. Nozzles.

FIRE APPLIANCES, MISCELLANEOUS

Homelite, Port Chester, N. Y. Self-priming centrifugal pumps gasoline-engine-driven units for feeding pumpers or booster tanks from streams, lakes or wells. Carryable gasoline-engine-driven generators for night floodlighting. Light weight aluminum floodlights. See pages 963-967.

Municipal Street Sign Co., Inc., 775-7 Meeker Ave., Brooklyn 22, N. Y. ELECTR-O-TALKER, for fire trucks, command cars, to control crowds, direct firemen—range ½ mile. **See page 910.**

Akron Brass Mfg. Co., Inc., 1450 Spruce St., Wooster, Ohio. Fire department brass goods, including adapters, couplings, shut-off nozzles, fog nozzles, siamese, siphons, etc.

American-Marsh Pumps, Inc., 205 Capital Ave., N.E., Battle Creek, Mich. Fire pumps.

Ansul Chemical Co., Fire Equipment Div., 1 Stanton St., Marinette, Wis. Dry chemical fire extinguishing equipment for all class "B" & "C" and certain class "A" hazards.

E. J. Brooks Co., 169 N. 13th St., Newark 7, N. J. Surelock seals for fire system sprinkler valves.

Buckeye Iron & Brass Works, P. O. Box 883, Dayton 1, Ohio. Valves and fittings for handling petroleum products.

Circul-Air Corp., 575 E. Milwaukee St., Detroit 2, Mich. Electro-mechanical dryer, 500 ft. of fire hose in a few hours. Fire hose washers, hose loading turn tables, hose storage racks.

Duo-Safety Ladder Corp., 9th St. at Soo R R, Oshkosh, Wis. Aluminum and Douglas fir fire ladders; folding and step ladders; scaffolds.

The General Detroit Corp., Detroit 32, Mich. Portable fire extinguishers, safety equipment.

McCulloch Motors Corp., 6101 West Century Blvd., Los Angeles 45, Calif. Self-priming portable pump, rated 15,000 gph. For fire fighting.

F. N. McIntire Brass Works, Inc., 377 Putnam Ave., Cambridge 39, Mass. Sliding poles, automatic siameses, hydrant gates, high-pressure valves.

National Foam System, Inc., Adams & Union Ave., West Chester, Pa. Foam fire protection equipment for fighting fires in petroleum products and organic solvents.

Powhatan Brass & Iron Works, Ranson, W. Va. Valves, nozzles, nipples, couplings, fire protection items.

The Unox Co., Div. of McFarland Mfg. Corp., 1630 Roberts St., Houston 3, Tex. Unox wetting agent for wetter water; wetter water fire wagons of 10 to 100 gals., throwing spray 40′; wetter water emulsion, spray nozzles, & proportioners.

Walter Motor Truck Co., 1001-19 Irving Ave., Ridgewood 27, L. I., N. Y. Crash trucks for airports.

Wooster Brass Div., The Fyr-Fyter Co., Index and Bowman St., Wooster, Ohio. Fire truck accessories, fire hose fittings, valves.

The Zierden Co., 3815 S. Kinnickinnic Ave., Milwaukee 7, Wis. Zierden fire truck hose reel for chemical and booster hose.

FIREMEN'S CLOTHING

Eureka Fire Hose, Div. of U. S. Rubber Co., 1 Market St., Passaic, N. J. Rubber coats, boots and Nor'Easter hats, helmets, featuring strength, protection, comfort and neatness. **See pages 978, 979.**

Franklin Worsted Co., 40 E. 34th St., N. Y. 16, N. Y. Police and fire uniform fabrics. See **page 989.**

Metcalf Bros. & Co., Inc., 1450 Broadway, New York 18, N. Y. Standard serges, tropicals, and twist gabardines. For uniforms certified by U. S. Testing Co. See **page 990.**

United States Rubber Co., Rockefeller Center, New York 20, N. Y. Firemen's coats. See **page 1121.**

Cairns & Bro. Inc., Allwood, Clifton, N. J. Helmets, boots, coats, caps, shirts, life belts, badges, car plates.

Charlottesville Woolen Mills, Charlottesville, Va. Woolen uniform **fabrics.**

Goodall Rubber Co., Whitehead Rd., Trenton, N. J. Rubber clothing and boots for policemen and firemen.

B. F. Goodrich Industrial Products Co., 500 South Main St., Akron, Ohio. Protective clothing.

Industrial Safety Specialties Co., Inc., Sellersville, Pa. ISSCO fire rescue suit weighs 28 lb.

Janesville Apparel Co., Janesville, Wis. Firemen's rubber and duck coats, with or without Scotchlite trim; bunker pants, firemen's boots, etc.

Maier-Lavaty Co., 315 So. Peoria Street, Chicago 7, Ill. Uniforms for firemen, plant guards, and police.

Midwestern Safety Mfg. Co., Mackinaw, Ill. Policemen's and firemen's protective clothing, also used by street and water departments.

Morning Pride Mfg. Co., 1986 Home Ave., Dayton 7, Ohio. Firemen's coats and pants, rubber fleece lined, duck flannel lined; suspenders, gloves, mittens.

S. H. Reese, 57 Warren St., New York 7, N. Y. Fire badges; hand made shields, badges for honorary members, miniature badges, insignia. Firemen's caps, auto plates.

Wentworth-Forman Co., Inc., 21 Edinboro St., Boston 11, Mass. Head-Master uniform caps and badges, rain cap covers. Civil defense auxiliary firemen's equipment—armbands, badges, helmets, decals, auto emblems.

FIRE HYDRANTS

Eddy Valve Co., Waterford, N. Y. **Sub. of James B. Clow & Sons, Inc.**, P. O. Box 6600-A, Chicago 80, Ill. Fire hydrants. See **pages 272, 273.**

Iowa Valve Co., Oskaloosa, Ia., **Sub. James B. Clow & Sons, Inc.**, P. O. Box 6600-A, Chicago 80, Ill. Fire hydrants. See **pages 274, 275.**

The Kennedy Valve Mfg. Co., 1069 E. Water St., Elmira, N. Y. The "Safetop" design provides for a clean break "of safety breakable section" on violent contact in order to prevent extensive injury to hydrants, vehicles, or persons. Repaired quickly at low cost. One-piece hydrants also available. See **pages 337-340.**

The Ludlow Valve Mfg. Co., Inc., Troy, N. Y. Water works valves and hydrants. See **pages 348-351.**

M & H Valve and Fittings Co., Anniston, Ala. Standard and special hydrant. See **pages 357-360.**

Traverse City Iron Works, P. O. Box 348, Traverse City, Mich. Fire hydrants. AWWA and Underwriters' Approved. See **page 450.**

R. D. Wood Co., Philadelphia 5, Pa. Mathews fire hydrants; feature a swivel flange that permits the taking off of the nozzle section before lifting out the barrel. See **pages 387-390.**

American Foundry & Mfg. Co., 1015 Hebert St., St. Louis 7, Mo. Underwriters' and Factory Mutual Approved type fire hydrants and also flush hydrants and 2" National hydrants.

Darling Valve & Mfg. Co., Walnut & Marshall Sts., Williamsport 61, Pa.

The John C. Kupferle Foundry Co., 81 Hempstead, St. Louis, Mo. Fire hydrants with revolving head, yard hydrants.

Mueller Co., 512 W. Cerro Gordo St., Decatur, Ill. Fully bronze mounted Mueller fire hydrants with 4¼, 4½, 5¼, or 6¼" valve opening.

Pacific States Cast Iron Pipe Co., Provo, Utah. Fire hydrants.

Rensselaer Valve Co., Div. of Ludlow Valve Mfg. Co., Inc., Troy, N. Y. Fire hydrants.

The A. P. Smith Mfg. Co., East Orange, N.J. Hydrants for low, intermediate and high pressure service.

Vogt Brothers Mfg. Co., P. O. Box 922, Louisville 1, Ky.

Waterous Company, 82 E. Fillmore Ave., St. Paul 1, Minn. Fire pumps and hydrants, industrial pumps.

FLOODLIGHTS

(See page 776.)

HOSE

Bi-Lateral Fire Hose Company, 20 N. Wacker Dr., Chicago, Ill. Cotton, rubber-lined, high pressure fire hose. Also suction and chemical fire engine hose. See **page 968.**

Eureka Fire Hose Div., U. S. Rubber Co., 1 Market St., Passaic, N. J. Complete line of multiwoven, double jacket and single jacket cotton, rubber lined, fire hose. Also suction and chemical fire engine hose. See **pages 978, 979.**

United States Rubber Co., Rockefeller Center, New York 20, N. Y. Cotton, rubber-lined fire and suction hose and chemical fire engine hose. See **page 1121.**

American LaFrance Corp., 116 E. LaFrance St., Elmira, N. Y. All-Weather, water repellent, mildew resistant white fire hose. Available with synthetic fiber filler.

American Rubber Mfg., 1145 Park Ave., Oakland, Calif. Municipal fire hose; suction hose, both soft and hard; booster hose. Rubber covered hose for street and sewer depts.

Boston Woven Hose and Rubber Co., P. O. Box 1071, Boston, Mass. Fire hose.

Fabric Fire Hose, Sandy Hook, Conn.

The General Detroit Corp., Detroit 32, Mich. Fire hose.

B. F. Goodrich Industrial Products Co., 500 South Main St., Akron, Ohio.

Goodyear Tire & Rubber Co., Inc., 1144 E. Market St., Akron, Ohio.

Quaker Rubber Div., H. K. Porter Co., Inc., Philadelphia 24, Pa.

Republic Rubber Div., Lee Rubber & Tire Corp., Youngstown, Ohio. Complete line of hose including air, chemical, fire.

HOSE CLEANERS, DRYERS

Bi-Lateral Fire Hose Company, 20 N. Wacker Dr., Chicago, Ill. Bi-Kleen fire hose detergent. See **page 968.**

Circul-Air Corp., 575 E. Milwaukee St., Detroit 2, Mich. Electro-mechanical dryer, 500' of fire hose in a few hours. Also fire hose washer. Hose loading turn tables. Hose storage racks.

LIGHTING, BATTERY FOR EMERGENCY

Exide Industrial Div., The Electric Storage Battery Co., 42 South 15th St., Philadelphia 2, Pa. Exide Lightguard operates automatically in case of power outage, 3-8 hours of lighting from 6-volt battery. See **page 987.**

Alpurlite Products, 693 Highland Ave., Needham Hgts. 94, Mass. All glass sealed beam emergency lites. Maximum lite with minimum current consumption from battery. Fully automatic. Double or single unit. U.L. approved.

Dual Lite Co., Inc., 183 Front St., Bridgeport 6, Conn. Emergency lighting systems, all voltages, nickel cadmium battery, battery racks, automatic transfer equipment, battery chargers. 32 & 48 volt cabinet type systems. Portable type units. Recessed and surface mounting fixtures. Combination normal & emergency exit signs.

Light Alarms, Inc., 95 Atlantic Ave., Brooklyn 1, N. Y. "Lamplighter" automatic emergency lights, fire alarms, trouble lights, lanterns.

The Julian A. McDermott Corp., 40-22 National St., Corona, N. Y. Standby lights that automatically come on if line power falls.

Portable Light Co., Inc., 216 William St., New York 38, N. Y. Portable combination search, flood and warning lights battery operated, for emergencies. Also automatic relay lights for buildings for public assembly.

OUTBOARD MOTORS

(See page 778.)

POWER, EMERGENCY

(See Electric Power Sets, page 773.)

Exide Industrial Div., The Electric Storage Battery Co., 42 South 15th St., Philadelphia 2, Pa. Exide batteries, police and fire alarm systems and emergency services. See page 987.

Homelite, Port Chester, N. Y. Gasoline-driven generators, light-weight carryable units, in sizes from 1,000 to 5,000 watts, AC or DC. See **pages 263-267.**

D. W. Onan & Sons, Inc., University Ave., S.E. at 25th, Minneapolis 14, Minn. Emergency power for emergencies in police and fire radio, sewer and water systems. Portable sets 400 to 5,000 watts. Trailer mounted 5,000 watts up. Stationary 1,000 to 50,000 watts. Battery charging models for 6-12-32 volts. See **pages 845-848.**

Delco-Remy Div., General Motors Corp., Anderson, Ind. A.C.-D.C. charging systems (alternators) and extra-output D.C. generators for fire, police, and public conveyance vehicles. Maximum output 180 amperes. Delco batteries for above applications.

Jackson Vibrators, Inc., Ludington, Mich. Portable electric power plants fitted with single and 3-phase outlets.

Katolight Corporation, First Ave. at Chestnut St., Mankato, Minn. Emergency electric power plants and belt-driven generator, 500 watts to 400 kw. Gasoline, gas, butane and diesel fuel.

Leece-Neville Co., 1374 E. 51 St., Cleveland 5, Ohio. Alternator system for cars, school buses, trucks, police cruisers 25 to 40 amperes at idle speed of most engines. Available with transformer giving 110 volts A.C. for such accessories as flood lights, small power tools, emergency radios.

Pioneer Inc., 2411 Grove St., Oakland 12, Calif. Battery AD—X2 battery treatment for longer battery life.

RADIO

General Electric Co., Industrial Electronics Div., Electronics Park, Syracuse, N. Y. G-E 2-way and microwave radio communication equipment, mobile and stator grinders. See page 1024.
tion. Radio traffic control. See pages 398, 399; 791-794.

Industrial Radio Corp., 428 N. Parkside Ave., Chicago 44, Ill. Pak-Fone, the 2-way portable radio with 5-way power supply for continuous operation. Also portable Field-Fone, smaller and lighter weight. See page 992.

Municipal Street Sign Co., Inc., 775-7 Meeker Ave., Brooklyn 22, N. Y. ELECTR-O-TALKER—Range ½ mile, car to car audio communication, mobile and stationary for civil defense, police, fire, etc. See page 910.

Kaar Engineering Corp., 2995 Middlefield Rd., P. O. Box 1320, Palo Alto, Calif. Conalert, Conelrad Radio, Alarm Receiver—for CD agencies, radio control centers, etc.

Monitoradio Division of I.P.E.A., 7900 Pendleton Pike, Indianapolis 26, Ind. FM 2 way radio communication equipment, mobile and stationary, for police, fire, civil defense, transportation. Complete line of crystal controlled or tunable receivers.

Motorola, Inc., 4545 Augusta Blvd., Chicago 51, Ill. FM 2-way radio mobile, portable, fixed station, remote supervisory control equipment, microwave systems.

Radio Corporation of America, Front and Cooper Sts., Camden, N. J.

Sonar Radio Corp., 3050 W. 21st St., Brooklyn 24, N. Y. Two-way v.h.f. radio communications equipment, AM/FM, mobile and stationary, for civil defense, police, fire, hospital, other municipal services. Also marine radio.

SALVAGE COVERS

Fulton Bag & Cotton Mills, P. O. Box 198, New Orleans 3, La. Shuredry Salvage Covers. See page 991.

SIRENS AND LIGHTS

B & B Engineering Corp., B & B Bldg., Norwood, La. Electric and mechanical sirens. See pages 33; 976, 977.

Federal Laboratories, Inc., Saltsburg, Pa. Lights and sirens. See page 988.

Graybar Electric Co., 1502 Graybar Bldg., New York 17, N. Y. Horns and sirens. See page 830.

Municipal Street Sign Co., Inc., 775-7 Meeker Ave., Brooklyn 22, N. Y. ELECTR-O-TALKER tape recorded siren sound heard ½ mile. Also live public address warning system. See page 910.

The Sterling Siren Fire Alarm Co., Inc., 8 Bartlett St., Rochester 8, N. Y. Electric siren fire alarm systems, apparatus sirens for police, fire trucks and sheriffs' cars. See page 994.

Alphurlite Products, 693 Highland Ave., Needham Hgts. 94, Mass. The Beacon Lite visible in 360 degree circle for roof of motor vehicle to aid identification and traffic congestion.

Benjamin Electric Mfg. Co., Des Plaines, Ill. Floodlighting, industrial lighting, commercial lighting, sirens, horns and signals.

Buckeye Iron & Brass Works. P. O. Box 883, Dayton 1, Ohio. Warning lights for all kinds of emergency cars.

R. D. Fageol Co., Kent, Ohio. Battery-operated flasher safety lights.

Federal Sign & Signal Corp., 8704 S. State St., Chicago 19, Ill. Sirens, with or without "Propello-Ray" or flashing light, for fire and police officers. Also the Beacon Ray and Fire Ball, 360 degree revolving lights.

The Julian A. McDermott Corp., 40-22 National St., Corona, N. Y. Emergency vehicle and snow plow work truck lights, flashing road flares, portable spot and flood lights, flashers, battery operated illuminated traffic stanchions for oil lantern elimination.

Portable Light Co., Inc., 216 William St., New York 38, N. Y. Emergency vehicle flashing and revolving warning lights. Portable spot, flood and warning lights, battery operated.

Sireno Co., Inc. 214 William St., New York 38, N. Y. Vehicle roof mounted sirens with flashing warning lights giving 360 degree visibility. All types of sirens and warning lights for police and fire trucks. Also revolving ray warning light.

Trippe Mfg. Co., 133 N. Jefferson St., Chicago 6, Ill. Red warning lights for fire and police flashing and oscillating.

Parks, Playgrounds, Swimming Pools

PARKS

BRUSH REMOVAL AND DISPOSAL

Fitchburg Engineering Corp., Fitchburg, Mass. Portable and stationary model chippers for easy brush disposal. See page 1023.

Gruendler Crusher & Pulverizer Co., 2915 N. Market St., St. Louis 6, Mo. Compost grinders. Chippers, coal and rubbish grinders. See page 470.

Mitts & Merrill, Saginaw 8, Mich. Portable brush hogs or grinder. See page 1024.

Servis Equipment Co., 1000 Singleton Blvd., Dallas, Texas. Servis Gyro 57", 66" and 84" brush cutters and SC-80 rotary mower for cutting weeds on vacant lots, alleys, traffic islands, roadside, pipe line right-of-way, etc. See page 1006.

Wood Bros. Mfg. Co., Box 148F, Oregon, Ill. Tractor-drawn rotary cutters and mowers cut and shred weeds and brush, mulch leaves. See page 1007.

Asplundh Chipper Co., 505 York Road, Jenkintown, Pa. Basic power unit or truck skid mounted or trailer-mounted unit for brush disposal.

Hoffco, Inc., 411 North 8th St., Richmond, Ind. Brushette is capable of cleaning brush up to 6" in diameter, 3 hp. gasoline engine portable.

Kut-Kwick Corp., Brunswick, Ga. Kut-Kwick self-propelled "Professional" combination unit with weed and brush cutting attachments. Also drives 30 in. circular saw-blade for tree and stump clearing.

The Rocklin Mfg. Co., Grand Ave. at Jennings, Sioux City 7, Iowa. Shred-mobile cuts a 48" swath through weeds.

Seaman-Andwall Corp., 305 N. 25th St., Milwaukee 3, Wis. Brush and land clearing equipment.

BUILDINGS, PREFABRICATED

United Steel Fabricators, Inc., 333 Gasche St., Wooster, Ohio. Prefabricated steel buildings of all sizes and types; also handy-huts for supplies and tools.

Stran-Steel Corp., Detroit 29, Mich. Prefabricated steel buildings—truck terminals, warehouses, bus stations, municipal garages.

CHAIN LINK FENCE

Anchor Fence Div., Anchor Post Products, Inc., Baltimore 24, Md. Fourteen types chain link protective fences with or without barbed-wire topping. See page 1019.

The Colorado Fuel & Iron Corp., Continental Oil Bldg., Denver, Colorado. Wickwire Spencer Steel Div., Buffalo 2, N. Y. Pacific Coast Div., Oakland 2, Calif. Realock fence for all municipal property. See page 1018.
Continental Steel Corp., 1150 So. Main St., Kokomo, Ind. Chain link fence, steel wire, welded wire reinforcing fabric, culvert sheets. See page 1020.
Cyclone Fence Dept., American Steel & Wire Div., U. S. Steel Corporation, Waukegan, Ill. Chain link fences and gates. See pages 148; 395; 1012, 1013.
Nichols Wire and Aluminum Co., 1725 Rockingham Rd., Davenport, Iowa. Neverstain aluminum chain link fence. See pages 1014, 1015.
Page Fence Assn., Monessen, Pa. Chain link, with fabric heavily galvanized after weaving, partitions, wire, for interior enclosures. See page 1021.
Atlas Fence Co., 2458 E. Venango St., Philadelphia 34, Pa. Tennis court fence and baseball backstops.
Copperweld Steel Co., Wire & Cable Div., 1015 Monongahela Ave., Glassport, Pa. Copperweld non-rusting chain link fence.
The Robertson Steel & Iron Co., 71 Elm St., Cincinnati 2, Ohio.
The Stewart Iron Works Co., Inc., 1302 Stewart Block, Cincinnati 1, Ohio. Chain link wire fences and gates, plain and ornamental iron fences and gates.

COMPOST SHREDDER

Royer Foundry & Machine Company, 166 Pringle St., Kingston, Pa. Compost Shredder-Mixers for grinding compost, leaf mold, or preparing top dressing and potting soil, for parks, golf courses, cemeteries, and greenhouses, 12 stationary and portable models with electric motor, gasoline engine, or belt-to-tractor driven. Capacities 4 to 150 yds. per hour.

DRINKING FOUNTAINS

American Concrete Corp., 5092 N. Kimberly Ave., Chicago 30, Ill. Drinking fountains, concrete, for parks and playgrounds. See page 825.
Bettis Corp., P. O. Drawer 9365, Houston 11, Texas. Igloo water cooler, a portable drinking container for maintenance trucks and crews and men in the field; crystalined to keep water crystal clear. See page 254.
James B. Clow & Sons, Inc., P. O. Box 6600-A, 201-299 N. Talman Ave., Chicago 80, Ill. Cast-iron pedestal type, porcelain enameled, for in or out door installation. See pages 270-275.
The Halsey W. Taylor Co., 137 North St., N.W., Warren, Ohio. Drinking fountains, electric water coolers, ice water coolers. See pages 1044, 1045.
Century Brass Works, Inc., Belleville, Ill. Drinking fountains, wall and pedestal type. Ice coolers & electric water coolers from 3 to 300 G.P.H. capacity.
The Murdock Mfg. & Supply Co., Cincinnati 2, Ohio. Pedestal drinking fountains (not anti-freezing) for municipal buildings, schools, park shelter houses. Outdoor anti-freezing drinking fountains, for parks, playground, school yards, street and boulevard installation.

EARTHBORING

(See page 748.)

FENCE

(See Chain Link Fence)

FLAGPOLES

American Playground Device Co., Anderson, Ind. Flagpoles and flags. See pages 1026-1029.
Kerrigan Iron Works, Inc., 1033 Herman St., Nashville 2, Tenn. Steel flagpoles, either continuous tapered or sectional steel, to exposed height of 125'. See pages 258; 807-809.
Trojan Playground Eqpt. Mfg. Co., St. Cloud, Minn. Trojan Take-Down poles, pinned between 2 supporting poles, allows pole to be tipped when raised or lowered. Non-collapsible poles, 15 to 70 ft. See page 1030.
The Everwear Mfg. Co., P. O. Box 958, Springfield, Ohio. Flagstaffs.
John E. Lingo & Sons, Inc., Cramer Hill, Camden, N. J. Flagpoles, steel, bronze, stainless steel, aluminum, from 8 to 150 ft.
The Stewart Iron Works Co., Inc., 1302 Stewart Block, Cincinnati 1, Ohio. Flagpoles.

FLOODLIGHTING, RECREATIONAL

American Playground Device Co., Anderson, Ind. Floodlights. See pages 1026-1029.
Crouse-Hinds Co., Syracuse 1, N. Y. Lighting equipment for night sports. 200-2,000 watt; for swimming pools, 500-1,500 watts. See pages 878-881.
Elreco Corp., 2902 Cormany Ave., Cincinnati 25, Ohio. Floodlighting standards and brackets for tennis courts, swimming pools, sports areas, playgrounds. See page 828.
General Electric Co., Apparatus Sales Div., Schenectady 5, N. Y. Floodlights for municipal playgrounds. In the sportlighting field, technical advice and efficient sports lighting equipment for baseball fields, softball fields, football fields, tennis courts, swimming pools or other outdoor recreation facilities. See pages 398, 399; 791-794.
Graybar Electric Co., Inc., 1502 Graybar Bldg., New York 17, N. Y. Floodlighting. See page 830.
Millerbernd Mfg. Co., Winsted, Minn. Millerbernd four-post angle, galvanized steel towers. Conventional self-supporting design. For floodlighting, radio, microwave, etc. Also steel floodlighting poles. See pages 810-813.
Modern Swimming Pool Co., Inc., 1 Holland Ave., White Plains, N. Y. Wet-niche underwater floodlights. U.L. labeled. See page 1035.
Revere Eectric Mfg. Co., 6009 Broadway, Chicago 40, Ill. Floodlights. See pages 814-817.
The Union Metal Mfg. Co., 1400 Maple Ave., N.E., Canton 5, Ohio. Steel or aluminum floodlighting poles from 20' to 40' for all types of recreation areas, parking lots, etc. See pages 818-820; 896.
Westinghouse Electric Corp., 3 Gateway Center, P. O. Box 868, Pittsburgh 30, Pa. Floodlights, also underwater floodlights. See pages 821-824.
Benjamin Electric Mfg. Co., Des Plaines, Ill. Floodlighting for swimming pools and play areas.
Giant Mfg. Co., Council Bluffs, Ia. Recreational sports lighting in open and closed type reflectors.
Luxor Lighting Products, Inc., Empire State Bldg., New York 1, N. Y. 1,000-1,500 watt lamps for sportsfields.
Steber Mfg. Co., Broadview, Ill. Floodlights for recreational and parking areas.

GRANDSTANDS

(See Bleachers and Grandstands)

GRASS SEED

O. M. Scott & Sons Co., Marysville, Ohio. Seed, turf-builder Weed-feed compound, feeds grass slowly while controlling most broad-leaved weeds; Scott spreader, distributes grass seed and grass food. See page 1046.
Albert Dickinson Co., Chicago 32, Ill. Seeds of domestic and imported turf grasses correctly blended and suited to any climate.
F. H. Woodruff & Sons, Inc., Milford, Conn. Lawn seeds and fertilizer.

LAWN AND TREE CULTIVATION

Cyclone Fence Dept., American Steel & Wire Div., U. S. Steel Corporation, Waukegan, Ill. Wire flower bed border; wire trellis and trellis arches. Wire mesh, rubbish baskets. See pages 148; 395; 1012, 1013.
Power Development Co., Inc., Mills Road, Avon, Ohio. Scimitar "Poweroll," self-propelled lawn roller. See page 1005.
Bartlett Mfg. Co., 3003 E. Grand Blvd., Detroit 2, Mich. Tree trimming equipment, long pole trimmers, saws, shears, safety belts and straps, tree paint, earth augers, tree wrap and stump remover. All equipment required by tree surgeon. Also metal cutting shears.
Birch Mfg. Co., 1523 N. Sedgwick St., Chicago 10, Ill. Lawn sprinklers (Rain-mate); quick couplers (Hose-mate); root soakers.
Hellige, Inc., 877 Stewart Ave., Garden City, N. Y. Soil reaction testers for rapid and dependable determination of the acidity and alkalinity (pH) of all types of soils.
Kut-Kwik Corp., Brunswick, Ga. Kut-Kwik self-propelled combination units with attachments for moving, felling trees, clearing stumps, cultivating, cutting weeds, etc. Power range up to 8½ hp.
The Murdock Mfg. & Supply Co., Cincinnati 2, Ohio. Street washers or lawn hose boxes, ¾ to 1½," inclusive, for lawn sprinkling, larger sizes suitable for flooding tennis courts in parks for ice skating.
Musser Forests, Inc., Box 19, Indiana, Pa. Musser forests, 20,000 trees a year. Put them on idle land and transplant them as needed. Seedlings of wide variety.

Ryan Landscaping Equipment Co., 871 Edgerton St., St. Paul 1, Minn. Power sod cutter, lawn edger and trimmer, tree movers and tree slings.

J. S. Sebrell Corp., 300 S. Los Angeles St., Los Angeles 13, Calif. Pruning tools; tree pruners; palm front cutters; limb hookers; light-weight sectional aluminum poles; sectional insulated tree poles for pruning; aluminum ladders, aluminum and steel safety ladders.

Sensation Mower, Inc., Ralston, Neb. Lawn edgers—hand, electric and gasoline.

The Skinner Irrigation Co., 501 E. Canal St., Troy, Ohio. Rain-Wave Sprinkler covers 50 square feet with 5 gals. of water per minute.

United Steel Fabricators, 333 Gasche St., Wooster, Ohio. Galvanized corrugated metal tree wells to protect standing trees in fill areas.

Williams & Harvey Nurseries Co., Box 8822, Kansas City, Mo. Automotive tree moving equipment to fit on any standard truck. Also trees and shrubs.

LAWN MOWERS

(See Mowers, Power)

LAWN MOWER SHARPENERS

The Fate-Root-Heath Co., Grinder Div., 607 Bell St., Plymouth, Ohio. Ideal and Peerless lawnmower sharpeners.

Foley Mfg. Co., 3300 Fifth St., N.E., Minneapolis 18, Minn. Electric or gasoline powered mower sharpeners; power saw filers, retoothers and setters. Gas engine or electric rotary mowers.

Modern Mfg. Co., 160 N. Fair Oaks Ave., Pasadena 1, Calif. Sharpens all reel type mowers.

LAWN ROLLERS

(See Rollers, Road, page 742.)

LAWN SWEEPERS

Lambert Incorporated, 519 Hunter Ave., Dayton 4, Ohio. Hand and power lawn sweepers with 21 or 30" sweep.

Modern Power Sweeper Co., 738 N. McKeever Ave., Azusa, Calif. INDUSTRIAL POWER SWEEPER 27", 36" and 48" sweep. Operates on lawns and paved surface. Riding sulky and gutter brush optional.

Parker Sweeper Co., 91-99 N. Bechtle Ave., Springfield, Ohio. Manually operated lawn sweepers to 28" width; powered to 36".

Savage Arms Corp., Lawn Mower Div., Chicopee Falls, Mass. Lawn sweepers.

Worcester Lawn Mower Co., Div. of Savage Arms Corp., Chicopee Falls, Mass. Lawn sweepers.

LAWN AND HEDGE TRIMMERS

Hal-Gan Products, Inc., 13000 W. Blue Mound Rd., Elm Grove, Wis. Spinaway 10" rotary trimmer. **See page 1002.**

Hoffco, Inc., 411 North 8th St., Richmond, Ind. Trimette power trimmer with 8" rotary blade is capable of trimming and edging around tombstones, walks, buildings, curbings, 2 hp. gasoline engine.

Kaufman Mfg. Co., 547 Meadow Lane, Manitowoc, Wis. Electric hedge trimmer and grass trimmer. Also combination edger or trimmer with interchangeable head and blade.

Modern Mfg. Co., 160 N. Fair Oaks Ave., Pasadena 1, Calif. Power lawn edger and trimmer, cuts at many angles.

H. K. Porter, Inc., Somerville 43, Mass. Brush cutters, pole pruners, pruning & lopping shears.

The Porter-Cable Machine Co., 1714 N. Salina St., Syracuse 8, N. Y. Hedgeshear electric trimmer and electric grass trimmers.

Weed Control Service, Inc., 2605 S.W. First Ave., Portland, Oreg. Ackley portable air pruner.

LEAF LOADER

(See page 738.)

MEMORIALS

Lake Shore Markers, Inc., P. O. Box 59, Erie, Pa. Memorial tablets, honor rolls, grave markers, cemetery lot markers. Cemetery urns and name plates. **See pages 952, 953.**

The Michaels Art Bronze Co., Inc., Kenton Land Rd., Erlanger, Ky.; P. O. Box 668, Covington, Ky. Bronze plaques, signs, memorials and nameplates; building directories; bronze, aluminum and stainless steel doors and entrances, exhibit cases. **See pages 862-864; 1060.**

Chicago Architectural Bronze Co., 17 N. Desplaines St., Chicago 6, Ill. Signs, tablets, name-plates, honor rolls and plaques. Individual letters in all metals; Bas-Reliefs.

Flour City Ornamental Iron Co., 2637 27th Ave., S., Minneapolis 6, Minn. Bronze tablets and historical markers "Statuary."

The Gorham Company, 333 Adelaide Ave., Providence, R. I. Also 6 W. 48th St., New York 19, N. Y. Bronze tablets, plaques, honor rolls.

M. Greenberg's Sons, 765 Folsom St., San Francisco 7, Calif. Bronze or aluminum plaques and letters.

The Robbins Co., Attleboro, Mass. Commemorative plaques, medallions and medals.

The Stewart Iron Works, Inc., 1302 Stewart Block, Cincinnati, Ohio. Bronze tablets.

United States Bronze Sign Co., Inc., New York 12, N. Y. Bronze tablets. Building signs, individual letters, name plates, honor rolls, plaques, aluminum and bronze castings.

MOWERS, POWER

Allis-Chalmers Mfg. Co., 886 70th St., Milwaukee 1, Wis. Wheel tractor power mower, 5- or 6-ft. cutter bar mowing range 85° above or 45° below horizontal, hydraulic lifting mechanism. **See pages 285-288.**

Devere Co., Machine Div., 2000-12 Clark St., Racine, Wis. Rotary-type mowers, 18, 20, 22, 24, and 31"; also 27" and 32" self-contained riding mowers; 1½, 2.5, 3, 5.6, and 8.1 hp. ratings; incorporating original suction-lift cutting principle. Leaf mulchers available for all models. See page 999.

The Eclipse Lawn Mower Co., 428 Railroad St., Prophetstown, Ill. Hand lawn mowers, gasoline powered reel and rotary type mowers, 17" to 32" width; gasoline powered sickle mowers, 36" width. **See page 1000.**

General Playground Equipment, Inc., Kokomo, Ind. Power lawn mowers. **See page 1025.**

Gravely Tractors, Inc., Box 78, Dunbar, W. Va. 30" gear-driven reel mower, 75" gear-driven gang mowers with steering sulky, 42" sickle mowers, 30" rotary mower. Attachments to 5-hp. tractor unit. **See page 1001.**

Hal-Gan Products, Inc., 13000 W. Blue Mound Rd., Elm Grove, Wis. Spinaway rotary suction power mowers, 18-20-26-31" cut. **See page 1002.**

Locke Power Lawn Mowers, 1327 Connecticut Ave., Bridgeport 1, Conn. 4 sizes: single 25" or 30," triplex 70" or 75". Riding sulky attachments. **See page 1003.**

Power Development Co., Inc., Mills Road, Avon, Ohio. "Scimitar" self-propelled lawn mower. Blades adjusted to any cutting height from ½" to 3". **See page 1005.**

Power Implement Div., McDonough Power Equipment, Inc., McDonough, Ga. Snappin' Turtle rotary power mowers, Snappin' Turtle rotary riding mowers, Snapper Twenty rotary power mowers, Snapper Thirty rotary riding mowers, Big Snapper, 36" rotary riding mowers. **See page 1004.**

Wood Bros. Mfg. Co., Box 148F, Oregon, Ill. Tractor-drawn rotary mowers with 42-114" swath. **See page 1007.**

Worthington Mower Co., Worthington Bldg., Stroudsburg, Pa. Tractors, gang mowers, self-propelled Triplex and large capacity rotaries for golf courses, parks, institutions, airfields, highways and other large area mowing. **See pages 995-998.**

Yazoo Mfg. Co., 3607 Livingston Rd., Jackson, Miss. Master mower in 16 models, gasoline engine, takes grades up to 45 degrees. Also pasture and stalk cutters in 2 models—5 and 7 ft. cutting width. **See page 1008.**

J. I. Case Co., 700 State St., Racine, Wis. Mowers, sickle bar, hydraulic lift, 5 or 6' cutter bar for use with Case Model 'VAI' tractor.

Cooper Mfg. Co., Marshalltown, Ia. Gasoline powered, 8 models, reel and rotary, wheel and/or roller driven 18 to 65" cut.

Hoffco, Inc., 411 N. 8th St., Richmond, Ind. Scythette power scythe with 20" cutting head. Will cut under water. 2 hp. gasoline engine, portable.

Jacobsen Mfg. Co., Racine, Wis. Size and type for every lawn and grounds.

Jari Products, Inc., 2938 Pillsbury Ave., Minneapolis 8, Minn. Jari power scythe, 36 and 44" bars, 2¾-hp. engine, 145 lbs. net weight. Snow plow, reel and sprayer. Rotary tiller and cultivator.

Kut-Kwick Corp., Brunswick, Ga. "Kut-Kwick" self-propelled lawn mower cuts up to 30" swath. One or two wheel riding sulky attachments.
The Moto-Mower Division, Detroit Harvester Co., 625 South "G" St., Richmond, Ind. Complete line of power mowers, 15 models, sizes 18 to 70".
Pearce Corp., 146 E. Highland Ave., Milwaukee 2, Wis. Airlift rotary power mower, 25 and 31" cuts, slashes grass clippings into mulch.
Pioneer Gen-E-Motor Corp., 5841 M West Dickens Ave., Chicago 39, Ill. Pincor Blue Diamond gasoline and electric lawn mowers, 17" to 22", both reel and rotary types.
Roseman Mower Corp., 2626 Crawford, Evanston, Ill. 3, 5 and 7 gang rollers and rear wheel drive type for use in mowing parks, parkways, golf courses, cemeteries, institutions, estates and airfields.
Savage Arms Corp., Lawn Mower Div., Chicopee Falls, Mass. Hand and power, reel and rotary lawn-mowers. Lawn sweepers.
Sensation Mower, Inc., Ralston, Neb. Full line gasoline and electric mowers. Grass catcher and leaf grinder attachments.
Sunflower Industries, Inc., 103 S. Kansas Ave., Olathe, Kans. Reel-type gang mowers and rotary cutters.
Toro Mfg. Corp., 3042 Snelling Ave., Minneapolis, Minn. Grass cutting machinery, for airport and highway, park, cemetery and golf course; gang mowers, reel and rotary type power mowers, tractors.
Worcester Lawn Mower Co., Division of Savage Arms Corp., Chicopee Falls, Mass. Hand and power, reel and rotary lawn mowers.

NURSERIES

The Cole Nursery Co., Painesville, Ohio. Pedigreed trees and nursery stock.
Musser Forests, Inc., Box 19, Indiana, Pa. Musser forests, 20,000 trees a year. Put them on idle land and transplant them as needed. Seedlings of wide variety.

PARK BENCHES

American Playground Device Co., Anderson, Ind. Park benches. **See pages 1026-1029.**
Trojan Playground Eqpt. Mfg. Co., St. Cloud, Minn. Park benches. **See page 1030.**
J. E. Burke Co., Fond du Lac, Wis. & New Brunswick, N. J. Park benches.
Concrete Machinery Co., Inc., Drawer 60, Dept. M.I., Hickory, N. C. Molds for concrete park benches.
J. W. Fiske Architectural Metals, Inc., 111-117 Pennsylvania Ave., Paterson 3, N. J. Park settees with galvanized iron legs and ash wood slats.
The Stewart Iron Works Co., Inc., 1302 Stewart Block, Cincinnati 1, Ohio. All-steel settees, steel framework and wood slat settees, pipe railings.

PEST CONTROL CHEMICALS

General Chemical Division, Allied Chemical and Dye Corp., 40 Rector St., New York 6, N. Y. DDT, BHC, lindane. T.D.E. and other insecticides. **See pages 234; 430.**
Modern Swimming Pool Co., Inc., 1 Holland Ave., White Plains, N. Y. Fungicides, algaecides for reservoirs, lakes, ponds. **See page 1035.**
Acme Quality Paints, Inc., 8250 St. Aubin Ave., Detroit 11, Mich. All agricultural insecticides.
Brulin & Co., Inc., 2939 Columbia Ave., Indianapolis 7, Ind. Brulin insecticides and insecticidal fogging units.
Chemical Insecticide Corp., 129 Montague St., Brooklyn 1, N. Y. Pest control chemicals for fog machines, mist blowers, hydraulic sprayers and regular spray equipment. Mist Blo Dutch Elm disease spray; Chem Hex T-fly and mosquito spray.
Chipman Chemical Co., Bound Brook, N. J. Insecticides, fungicides.
Doggett-Pfeil Co., Springfield, N. J. Agricultural and horticultural insecticides and fertilizers.
The C. B. Dolge Co., Westport, Conn.
Dow Chemical Co., Midland, Mich. Insecticides for municipal fly and insect control.
Michigan Chemical Corp., St. Louis, Mich. Insecticides and fumigants.
Miller Products Co., Foot of S.W. Caruthers St., Portland 1, Oreg. Wood preservation. Insecticides and fungicides.
Monsanto Chemical Co., 445 Park Ave., New York, N. Y.
National Bird Control Laboratories, 5315 W. Touhy Ave., Skokie, Ill. "Roost-No-More" bird control spray.
Niagara Chemical Division, Food Machinery and Chemical Corporation, Middleport, N. Y. DDT Spray and dust materials.
U. S. Rubber Co., Naugatuck Chemical Div., Naugatuck, Conn., Fungicides, including seed protectants and spray fungicides. Insecticides, miticides.
Wyco, Inc., 5200 S. Dixie Highway, West Palm Beach, Fla. Tossitts kill mosquito larvae in all breeding places—swamps, canals, catch basins.

PLAQUES (See Memorials)

PLAYGROUND AND SPORTS EQUIPMENT
(See page 791.)

REFUSE CONTAINERS

The Bennett Mfg. Co., Alden, N. Y. Bennett Bilt self-closing waste receptacles. **See pages 93-96.**
Cyclone Fence Dept., American Steel & Wire Div., U. S. Steel Corporation, Waukegan, Ill. Wire mesh rubbish baskets. **See pages 148; 395; 1012, 1013.**
W. E. Grace Mfg. Co., 6000 S. Lamar St., Dallas 1, Texas. Street-cleaners' carts, rubber tired. **See page 239.**
United Metal Cabinet Corp., 14th & Laurel Sts., Pottsville, Pa. Self-closing receptacles, swing top, removable container. **See pages 193-196.**
Mills Engr. Co., 2520 W. 8th St., Los Angeles 57, Calif. Mills rust-proof aluminum waste receptacles, require no paint, no inner linings.
Norwich Wire Works Inc., 47 Collins Court, Norwich, N. Y.
Rochester Can Co., Rochester 9, N. Y. Refuse containers and incinerators.
Tarrant Mfg. Co., 27-29 Jumel St., Saratoga Springs, N. Y. Closed refuse receptacles.
Wheeling Corrugating Co., Wheeling, W. Va. Garbage and ash cans; rubbish burners; waste baskets; litter baskets; metal culverts; expanded metal for reinforcing.
Wirt & Knox Mfg. Co., Sedgley Ave., York & 23rd Sts., Philadelphia 32, Pa. White wing can carrier.
The Witt Cornice Co., 2118 Winchell Ave., Cincinnati, Ohio. Trash can with push-top cover.

SAWS, CHAIN

Gravely Tractors, Inc., Box 78, Dunbar, W. Va. Chain saws. Tractor attachments. **See page 1001.**
Homelite, Port Chester, N. Y. High-cycle electric chain saw for limbing, bucking or felling trees or for cutting heavy timbers, powered by a Homelite generator. Gasoline engine driven chain saw, sizes 12", 14", 17", 18", 20", 21", 23", 25", 28", 30", 33", 38", 44", 50", 60", one-man models; 14" and 18" bow saws. **See pages 263-267.**
Atkins Saw Div., Borg-Warner Corp., 402 South Illinois St., Indianapolis 9, Ind. Chamfer chain and new B-W chain for all makes of chain-saws.
Clinton Chain Saw Div., Clinton, Mich. Clinton chain saws with air-cooled gasoline engine.
Complete Machinery & Equipment Co., Inc., 36-40 Eleventh St., Long Island City 6, N. Y. Gasoline and electric chain saws. Also pneumatic chain saws.
Henry Disston Div., H. K. Porter Company, Inc., Unruh & Milnor Sts., Tacony, Philadelphia 35, Pa. Chain saw parts.
Hoffco, Inc., 411 North 8th St., Richmond, Ind. Gasoline chain saws, 16" to 36", including direct drive.
Lombard Governor Co., Ashland, Mass.
Mall Tool Co., Div. of Remington Arms Co., Inc., 25000 S. Western Ave., Park Forest, Ill. For felling trees or cutting or bucking timbers of any sizes. Available in gasoline engine, electric or pneumatic models. Capacity 12" to 60". **See pages 000-000.**
McCulloch Motors Corp., 6101 W. Century Blvd., Los Angeles 45, Calif. Chain saws.
Sensation Mower, Inc., Ralston, Neb. 8 models of gasoline chain saws.

SEEDERS, SPREADERS

Flink Co., Streator, Ill. Fertilizer spreaders truck type. **See page 217.**

O. M. Scott & Sons Co., Marysville, Ohio. Scott spreader for distributing seed and food and weed controls. See page 1046.
Masters Planter Co., Benton Harbor, Mich. "Commercial Fertilizer & Seed Distributors and heavy duty garden Handi-Carts."
F. H. Woodruff & Sons, Milford, Conn. Fertilizer and seed spreaders.

SPRAYERS

Aeroil Products Company, Inc., 50 Wesley St., South Hackensack, N. J. Hand and power sprayers for dispersing weed killers, kerosene, disinfectants, etc. See pages 69-72.
John Bean Div., Food Machinery and Chemical Corp., Box 840, Lansing 4, Mich. High pressure sprayers for golf courses, fly control, park spraying, weed control, greenhouses, cemeteries, roadways and shade trees. See pages 971; 1009.
Gravely Tractors, Inc., Box 78, Dunbar, W. Va. 50-gal. estate sprayer. Attachment to 5-hp. tractor unit. See page 1001.
Essick Mfg. Co., 1950 Santa Fe Ave., Los Angeles 21, Calif. Air-powered weed and pest control equipment.
Fitzhenry-Guptill Co., 135 First St., Cambridge 41, Mass. Power sprayers on skids for high shade-tree street and park spraying.
Friend Mfg. Co., Gasport, N. Y. Power sprayers, park and golf course sprayers.
The Gledhill Road Machinery Co., 57 S. Lera Rd., Galion, Ohio. Gledhill low pressure roadside sprayer eliminates damage to adjacent crops and gardens. 300 gal. sizes. 20 to 30 lb. pressure.
The Hardie Mfg. Co., Hudson, Mich. Power sprayers for shade trees, mosquito control, Dutch Elm disease, golf courses, orchards, and row crops. High pressure spray pumps. Spraying accessories such as hose fittings, gauges, hose, spray guns, etc.
Unimasco, Inc., 424 W. Redondo Beach Blvd., Gardena, Calif. Model M4-432 portable spray painting rig, four wheel trailer mounted, heavy duty. All sizes of portable painting equipment are available.

FOG MACHINES

Curtis Automotive Devices, Inc., Dyna Products Div., P. O. Box 232-B, Bedford, Ind. Dyna-Fog insecticidal fog generator for insect control.
Todd Shipyards Corp., Products Division, Columbia & Halleck Sts., Brooklyn 31, N. Y. Tifa insecticidal fog applicator for dispensing insecticides, other chemicals, deodorants, repellents, germicides, fungicides, etc.

MIST BLOWERS

John Bean Div., Food Machinery and Chemical Corp., Box 840, Lansing 4, Mich. High pressure and air-blast sprayers for golf courses, insect control, weed control, shade tree spraying, greenhouses, cemeteries and highways. See pages 971; 1009.
Buffalo Turbine Agricultural Equipment Co., Inc., Gowanda, N. Y. Duster (power); combination mist sprayer and duster (power) for fly and mosquito control.
Cooley Spray Equipment Works, Somers, Conn. Cooley-Mist concentrate sprayers (Potts-Spencer model) wheelbarrow and skid styles. Also low pressure nozzles and spray discs and whirls.
A. B. Farquhar Div., The Oliver Corp., 221 Duke St., York, Pa. Oliver Iron Age mist sprayers feature 90-125 mph air blast with jets adjustable to type of job.
Fitzhenry-Guptill Co., 135 First St., Cambridge 41, Mass. Portable, orchard and shade-tree mist blowers; mist gun, for low foliage spraying.
The Hardie Mfg. Co., Hudson, Mich. Power sprayer and mist blowers for shade trees, mosquito control, Dutch Elm disease, golf courses, orchards, and low crops. High pressure spray pumps.
The Oliver Corp., 400 W. Madison St., Chicago 6, Ill. Mist and hydraulic sprayers for shade tree protection, fly and mosquito control.

STUMP CUTTERS

Asplundh Chipper Co., 505 York Rd., Jenkintown, Pa. Basic unit, 8½" and 15" cutter, mounted on any tractor. Cuts out any size stump below ground level.
Metal Parts Machining Corp., Watervliet, N. Y. The O'Brien stump cutter with a two-man crew cuts out 3 to 4, 30" stumps per day.

TOOLS FOR MAINTENANCE AND REPAIR

See page 748.)

WEED KILLERS

Aeroil Products Company, Inc., 50 Wesley St., South Hackensack, N. J. Sprayers. Weed burners. See pages 69-72.
General Chem. Div., Allied Chem. & Dye Corp., 40 Rector Street, New York 6, N. Y. 2, 4-D and 2, 4, 5-T weed and brush killers, "Urox" and other organic weed control materials. See pages 234; 430.
Hauck Mfg. Co., 124-136 Tenth St., Brooklyn 15, N. Y. Hauck flame guns for destroying weeds. See pages 138-141.
O. M. Scott & Sons Co., Marysville, Ohio. 4-XD, applied dry for broad-leaved weeds; weed-feed compound, feeds grass slowly and also controls broad-leaved weeds; spreaders for distributing pest control. Scutl, a dry applied compound for selective control of crabgrass in lawns. See page 1046.
Brulin & Co., Inc., 2939 Columbia Ave., Indianapolis 7, Ind. Brulin selective and non-selective chemical weed killer.
Chemical Insecticide Corp., 129 Montague St., Brooklyn 1, N. Y. Weed control chemicals including 2, 4-D, 2, 4, 5-T, Sodium Arsenite, T.C.A. and Potassium Cyanate.
Chipman Chemical Co., Bound Brook, N. J. Weed killer chemicals.
The C. B. Dolge Co., Westport, Conn. Weed killers, fungicides.
The Dow Chemical Co., Midland, Mich. Weed killers.
Miller Products Co., Foot of S.W. Caruthers St., Portland 1, Oreg. Also wood preservative.
National Aluminate Corp., 6225 W. 66th Pl., Chicago, Ill. Non-selective type weed control chemicals.
U. S. Rubber Co., Naugatuck Chemical Div., Naugatuck, Conn. Weed killer, growth regulators, grass retardant.

MISCELLANEOUS

American Playground Device Co., Anderson, Ind. Park tables and All-American picnic grills. See pages 1026-1029.
Columbia-Southern Chemical Corp., 1 Gateway Center, Pittsburgh 22, Pa. Calcium chloride for dustless surface on playgrounds, tennis courts, athletic fields. See page 382.
Fulton Bag & Cotton Mills, P. O. Box 198, New Orleans 3, La. Tarpaulins for sports fields. See page 991.
Ingersoll Kalamazoo Div., Borg-Warner Corp., 1810 N. Pitcher St., Kalamazoo, Mich. Load Lugger is a one-man operated, self-loading vehicle consisting of truck, hoist and detachable leak-proof containers suited for loading, hauling and depositing. See pages 497-500.
Trojan Playground Eqpt. Mfg. Co., St. Cloud, Minn. Picnic tables. See page 1030.
American Bitumuls & Asphalt Co., Executive Offices, 200 Bush St., San Francisco 4, Calif. Laykold and Grass-tex-all-weather, tennis courts, and playground surfacing.
J. E. Burke Co., Fond du Lac, Wis. & New Brunswick, N. J. Bicycle racks, picnic tables, picnic grilles, all-steel bleachers, portable steel "Form-a-Stage" (bandstand).
Calumet Coach Co., 11575 S. Wabash Ave., Chicago 28, Ill. Custom type trailers for refreshment, concessions, display. Fire-resistant interiors and equipment suiting requirements of the purchasers.
Concrete Machinery Co., Inc., Drawer 60, Dept. MI, Hickory, N. C. Specialty aluminum molds for making concrete park decorations including benches, bird baths, flower pots, statuary items, table sets.
Cushman Motor Works, Inc., 942 N. 21st St., Lincoln, Neb. Motor vehicles for miscellaneous hauling on recreational and play areas.
Foster Oar Co., Conway, Ark. Oars, ash, 5 to 7½', packed 6 pair per carton. Paddles, ash and/or linwood, 2½ to 6.
Metal Parts Machining Corp., Watervliet, N. Y. The O'Brien Stump Cutter with a two-man crew is capable of cutting out 3 to 4, 30" stumps, 8" below ground surface, per day.
The Monroe Co., 53 Church St., Colfax, Ia. Folding tables, benches and chairs. Also steel trucks for folding tables and folding chairs, and portable partitions.

The Nor-way Mfg. Co., Ossineke, Mich. Rustic picnic tables and form fit benches.

Pioneer Gen-E-Motor Corp., 5841 M West Dickens Ave., Chicago 39, Ill. Blue Diamond Sno-mover, gathers, throws and blows snow away. For sidewalks and driveways.

Ravenna Ceramics Corp., 635 S. Prospect, Ravenna, Ohio. A hard burned Stoneware lot marker with natural Terra Cotta finish or with a White Top for easy location.

Sensation Mower, Inc., Ralston, Neb. Sno-Blo with 3½ hp. self propelled engine for paths and crosswalks. Also push type Sno-Blo, 2½ hp.

Willys Motors, Inc., 940 N. Cove Blvd., Toledo 1, Ohio. 4-wheel drive 'Jeep' trucks and 'Jeep' utility vehicles for park maintenance.

PLAYGROUND AND SPORTS EQUIPMENT

BLEACHERS, GRANDSTANDS

American Bridge Div., U. S. Steel Corp., 525 William Penn Place, Pittsburgh 30, Pa. Steel grandstands. **See page 1001.**

Leavitt Products Co., 206-220 Griggs St., Urbana, Ill. Knock Down portable wood bleachers for indoor or outdoor use. Also steel grandstands, stadiums. **See pages 1016, 1017.**

Modern Swimming Pool Co., Inc., 1 Holland Ave., White Plains, N. Y. Bleacher inserts, iron, bronze and bronze-chromed. In stock. **See page 1035.**

Pittsburgh-Des Moines Steel Co., 3460 Neville Island, Pittsburgh, Pa. Steel deck grandstands. **See pages 418, 419; 544, 545.**

Safway Steel Products, Inc., 6228 West State St., Milwaukee 13, Wis. Steel bleachers for permanent or temporary seating applications. **See page 1022.**

Berlin Chapman Co., Berlin, Wis. Berlin portable bleachers with all welded steel construction framework and seats and footboards of structural Douglas Fir.

Hussey Mfg. Co., Inc., 566 R. R. Ave., N. Berwick, Me. Portable steel bleachers and grandstands. Also "Roll Out" gym seats.

Reeves Steel Inc., 205 N. Twelfth Street, Tampa, Fla. Portable bleachers and grandstands, steel construction treated seats and footboards.

Universal Bleacher Co., Champaign, Ill. Bleachers, portable wood or steel, from two to thirty rows high. Also indoor folding bleachers.

Virginia Bridge Co., U. S. Steel Subsidiary, Roanoke 9, Va. Stadium, all-steel construction.

PROTECTIVE COATINGS

Byerlyte Corp., 2300 W. 3rd St., Cleveland, Ohio. Paviseal protects asphalt pavements from petroleum solvents, actinic rays of the sun, battery acids, salt and frost action. **See pages 146, 147.**

MISCELLANEOUS

American Playgrounds Device Co., Anderson, Ind. American approved playground equipment includes basketball and softball backstops, checking and gymnasium baskets, park benches, bicycle racks, Castle Tower climbing structures, outdoor gyms, horizontal bars, merry-go-rounds, ocean wave units, parallel bars, see-saws, slides, swing sets and seats, chain link tennis nets and uniform hangers, paint for playground apparatus. See pages 1026-1029.

Cyclone Fence Dept., American Steel & Wire Div., U. S. Steel Corporation, Waukegan, Ill. Tennis court enclosures; baseball and softball and tennis court backstops. See pages 148; 395; 1012, 10[illegible].

General Playground Equipment, Inc., Kokomo, Ind. Spiral slides, all-metal playground slides, swings, combination sets, see-saws, merry-go-rounds, giant strides, pyramid climbing structures, horizontal ladders and bars, basketball backstops, all-metal tennis sets, other recreation equipment. **See page 1025.**

Page Fence Assn., Monessen, Pa. Stainless steel tennis nets. Fences for swimming pools, playgrounds, tennis courts. **See page 1021.**

Trojan Playground Eqpt. Mfg. Co., St. Cloud, Minn. Playground equipment including merry-go-rounds, whirlers, slides, see-saws, ladders, swings, triple bars, bicycle racks, giant strides. **See page 1030.**

Brunner Mfg. Co., Gilbert at Broad St., Utica 1, N. Y. Refrigeration condensing units, ¼ to 100 hp., for use in skating rinks applications.

J. E. Burke Co., Fond du Lac, Wis. & New Brunswick, N. J. Swings—kindergarten hobby horse and standard slides, seesaws, merry-go-rounds, Climb-A-Rounds, turning bars, horizontal ladders, all-metal sand boxes, outdoor basketball backstops, and other outdoor playground and park equipment.

The Everwear Mfg. Co., P. O. Box 958, Springfield, Ohio. Playground apparatus, basketball backstops. Also bicycle racks.

Giant Mfg. Co., Council Bluffs, Ia. Slides, strides, swings, see-saws, horizontal ladders, turning bars, parallel bars, merry-go-rounds, ocean waves, Giant climbers and replacement parts.

Jamison Mfg. Co., 8782 S. Mettler St., Los Angeles 3, Calif. Merry-go-rounds, slides, swings, combination gyms, basketball equipment, bars, giant strides, etc.

The J. E. Porter Corp., Ottawa, Ill. Merry-go-rounds, ladders and bars, jungle gyms, swing sets, slides and see-saws. Also gymnasium and basketball equipment.

Recreation Equipment Corp., Dept. MI, 724 W. 8th St., Anderson, Ind. Basketball equipment; climbing devices, slides, swings, see-saws, gym combinations, and horizontal ladders; bicycle racks; picnic tables.

The Robertson Steel & Iron Co., 71 Elm St., Cincinnati 2, Ohio. Tennis court enclosures, baseball backstops.

Standard Playground Equipment Co., 1629 W. 18th St., Anderson, Ind. Complete line of swings, see-saws, slides; climbing tower, merry-go-round, gym set, diving-stand, pool ladders, life-guard chair.

SWIMMING POOLS

ACCESSORIES

American Playground Device Co., Anderson, Ind. Checking baskets and steel racks, diving boards and units, footbaths, life-buoys, and official lifelines, diving masks, pool ladders and brackets, springboards, bench umbrellas, thriller slides, lifeguard chairs, water slides, cocoa matting, racing lanes, regulation fulcrums, bicycle racks, locker room seats, etc. **See pages 1026-1029.**

Cardinal Pools, Inc., 11525 North Central Expressway, Dallas, Texas. Swimming pool equipment and lighting. See page 1033.

General Electric Co., Apparatus Sales Div., Schenectady 5, N. Y. Floodlights for municipal playgrounds. In the sportlighting field, technical advice and efficient sports lighting equipment for baseball fields, softball fields, football fields, tennis courts, swimming pools or other outdoor recreation facilities. **See pages 398, 399; 791-794.**

General Playground Equipment, Inc., Kokomo, Ind. All-metal natatorium slides, diving stands, diving boards, life-guard chairs and buoys, pool ladders, water basketball backstops, life lines, other pool equipment. See page 1025.

Modern Swimming Pool Co., Inc., 1 Holland Ave., White Plains, N. Y. Diving boards, ladders, underwater lights, rafts, life lines, life rings, life saving poles (Shepherds' Crooks). **See page 1035.**

National Pool Equipment Co., 2516 Eight Ct. N., Birmingham, Ala. Pool ladders, diving boards, drains, underwater lights, heaters. **See pages 1036, 1037.**

Swimquib, Inc., 3301 Gilman Rd., El Monte, Calif.; 1040 Huff Rd., N. W., Atlanta, Ga. Aluminum diving boards, and towers. **See page 1043.**

Westinghouse Electric Corp., 3 Gateway Center, P. O. Box 868, Pittsburgh 30, Pa. Swimming pool lighting. **See pages 821-824.**

American Pool Co., Fox Island Rd., Port Chester, N. Y. Underwater lighting, pool ladders, diving boards and stands, life guard chair, lane markers.

Norman Buck Mfg. Co., 2332 Eastlake, Seattle 2, Wash. The Multi-Unit "ALUMINUM BUCKBOARD" springboard.

Chemical Equipment Co., Box 3098, Los Angeles 54, Calif. Underwater lights, springboards, ladders, lifeguard chairs, high dives, etc.

Elgin Softener Corp., Elgin, Ill. Drains, diving boards and stands, ladders, guard chairs, buoys, markers, life lines and anchors.

Giant Mfg. Co., Council Bluffs, Ia. Aluminum alloy springboards, diving stands (one and three-meter and pool level), diving tower, pool ladders.

Hussey Mfg. Co., Inc., 566 R. R. Ave., N. Berwick, Me. Watersports equipment—landing piers, floats, diving boards, etc.

Recreation Equipment Corp., Dept. MI, 724 W. 8th St., Anderson, Ind. Diving boards, pool ladders, slides, cleaning equipment, diving masks, lifeguard chairs, life buoys, umbrellas.

Standard Playground Equipment Co., 1629 W. 18th St., Anderson, Ind. One-meter and three-meter diving stands, laminated douglas fir diving boards, pool ladders, lifeguard chairs, and life lines.

CHEMICALS

Columbia Southern Chemical Corp., 1 Gateway Center, Pittsburgh 22, Pa. Chemicals for water treatment, swimming pools, wash rooms, locker rooms, and toilets. See page 382.
General Chemical Div., Allied Chemical & Dye Corp., 40 Rector St., New York 6, N. Y. Crystal alums. See pages 234; 430.
Inertol Co., Inc., 476A Frelinghuysen Ave., Newark 12, N. J., Western Division: Suite 24, 27 South Park, San Francisco 7, Calif. Algaecidal compound for swimming pools. See page 473.
Modern Swimming Pool Co., Inc., 1 Holland Ave., White Plains, N. Y. Chlorine, algaecides, alum, soda ash. See page 1035.
National Pool Equipment Co., 2516 Eight Ct., N., Birmingham, Ala. Algae and fungus killers. See pages 1036, 1037.
Olin Mathieson Chemical Corp., Industrial Chemicals Div., Mathieson Bldg., Baltimore 3, Md. Chemicals for swimming pool sanitation. See pages 410, 411; 1038, 1039.
American Pool Co., Fox Island Rd., Port Chester, N. Y. Chemicals.
Halogen Supply Co., 4653 W. Lawrence Ave., Chicago 30, Ill. Calking compounds and a complete line of chemicals.
U. S. Rubber Co., Naugatuck Chemical Div., Naugatuck, Conn. Phygon-XL for control of algae.

CHEMICAL FEEDERS

Fischer & Porter Co., 850 Warminster Rd., Hatboro, Pa. Chlorinators, solution feed and gas feed. See pages 317-320.
General Filter Co., Ames, Ia. Pool chemical feeders. See pages 400, 401.
Graver Water Conditioning Co., 216 W. 14th St., New York 11, N. Y. Complete sterilization, filtration and recirculation systems. See pages 402, 403.
Modern Swimming Pool Co., Inc., 1 Holland Ave., White Plains, N. Y. Low-cost chemical feeders for chlorine, alum, soda ash. See page 1035.
Olin Mathieson Chemical Corp., Industrial Chemicals Div., Mathieson Bldg., Baltimore 3, Md. Tablet hypochlorinators, differential pressure type, providing for a reservoir of tableted hypochlorite, dissolved at rates controlled by metering the dissolving water and applied to the swimming pool water as hypochlorite solution. See pages 410, 411; 1038, 1039.
The Permutit Co., 330 W. 42nd St., New York 36, N. Y. See pages 416, 417.
Roberts Filter Mfg. Co., 601 Columbia Ave., Darby, Pa. Chemical feeders. See page 1042.
Wallace & Tiernan, Incorporated, 25 Main St., Belleville 9, N. J. Chlorinators. See pages 378-381.
American Pool Co., Fox Island Rd., Port Chester, N. Y. Chlorinators and hypochlorinators, standard and heavy duty models.
American Water Softener Co., Inc., Cor. S. E. Lehigh & Fourth Sts., Philadelphia 33, Pa. Feeders, wet and dry.
Builders-Providence, Inc., Div. of B-I-F Industries, Inc., 351 Harris Ave., Providence 1, R. I. Chlorinizer visible flow, visible-vacuum chlorine gas feeders for swimming-pool disinfection with maximum feed rates up to 8,000 lbs. per day.
Chemical Equipment Co., P. O. Box 3098, Los Angeles 54, Calif. Chlorinators, ammoniators.
Cochrane Corp., 3122 N. 17th St., Philadelphia 32, Pa. Wet and dry.
Elgin Softener Corp., Elgin, Ill.
Everson Mfg. Corp., 205 W. Huron St., Chicago 10, Ill.
Halogen Supply Co., 4653 W. Lawrence Ave., Chicago 30, Ill. Halobrom feeders, chlorinators, hypochlorinators.
Infilco Inc., Box 5033, Tucson, Arizona. Dry chemical feeders, volumetric and gravimetric; solution feeders; lime-slakers; chemical proportioners.
Omega Machine Company, Div. of B-I-F Industries, Inc., 351 Harris Ave., Providence 1, R. I. Complete line of volumetric and gravimetric feeders for dry materials and the feeding of liquids by gravity.
Phipps & Bird, Inc., 303 S. 6th St., Richmond 5, Va.
Proportioneers, Inc., Div. of B-I-F Industries, Inc., 351 Harris Ave., Providence, R. I. Pool chemical feeders and hypochlorinators. Diaphragm and plunger pumps for chemical solution injection into low and high pressures. Constant rate manually adjustable models available.

CLEANERS

Aeroil Products Company, Inc., 50 Wesley St., South Hackensack, N. J. Steam cleaner completely cleans, scours, sterilizes all surfaces. See pages 69-72.
American Playground Device Co., Anderson, Ind. Pool cleaning equipment and diving equipment. See pages 1026-1029.
Cardinal Pools, Inc., 11525 North Central Expressway, Dallas, Texas. See page 1033.
General Playground Equipment, Inc., Kokomo, Ind. See page 1025.
Modern Swimming Pool Co., Inc., 1 Holland Ave., White Plains, N. Y. Pool vacuum cleaners that operate off the filter or portable vacuum pump. All sizes, many models, 13" or 18" head. Also suction cleaners. One-man underwater cleaning equipment for extra-wide pools. See page 1035.
National Pool Equipment Co., 2516 Eight Ct. N., Birmingham, Ala. Pool cleaners 16". See pages 1036, 1037.
American Pool Co., Fox Island Rd., Port Chester, N. Y. Pool vacuum cleaners, 13 or 18" head. Pumps available.
Chemical Equipment Co., P. O. Box 3098, Los Angeles 54, Calif.
Elgin Softener Corp., Elgin, Ill. Vacuum cleaning equipment, wall and floor brushes, diving helmets.
Everson Mfg. Corp., 205 W. Hurson St., Chicago 10, Ill.
Halogen Supply Co., 4653 W. Lawrence Ave., Chicago 30, Ill. Suction cleaners, hose and cleaning tools.
Hygeia Filter Co., 3422 Denton Ave., Detroit, Mich.
Infilco Inc., Box 5033, Tucson, Arizona.
The Recreation Equipment Corp., Dept. MI, 724 W. 8th St., Anderson, Ind.
Spencer Turbine Co., Drawer E, Station A, Hartford 6, Conn. Vacuum cleaners, portable and stationary, commercial and industrial.
Standard Pool Cleaner Co., 1320 Greenfield Ave., Canton 6, Ohio.

ENGINEERS

Wesley Bintz, P. E., Consulting Engr., Civil, 301 S. Washington Ave., Lansing 25, Mich. Swimming pool designs and consultation exclusively. See page 1031.
Cardinal Pools, Inc., 11525 North Central Expressway, Dallas, Texas. Swimming pool design and consultation. See page 1033.
Amcrete Corp., P. O. Box 587, Port Chester, N. Y. Swimming pool design consultants and constructors. Pre-cast, steel-reinforced poured concrete swimming pools.

FILTERS

Bowser, Inc., 1365 E. Creighton Ave., Fort Wayne 2, Ind. Water filters for swimming pools. See page 1032.
Cardinal Pools, Inc., 11525 North Central Expressway, Dallas, Texas. Rapid-sand filter system. See page 1033.
General Filter Co., Ames, Ia. Pressure, gravity, diatomite. See pages 400, 401.
Graver Water Conditioning Co., 216 W. 14th St., New York 11, N. Y. Pressure and gravity filters, sand, Anthrafilt and diatomaceous earth filters. See pages 402, 403.
Modern Swimming Pool Co., Inc., 1 Holland Ave., White Plains, N. Y. Pressure filters, all sizes. See page 1035.
National Pool Equipment Co., 2516 Eight Ct. N., Birmingham, Ala. Rapid sand pressure filters of recirculating type. Also diatomite filters with tank, valves and gauges. See pages 1036, 1037.
Palmer Filter Equipment Co., P. O. Box 1696, Erie, Pa. Palmer filter bed agitator; hydromatic four-way valve; standard bronze strainers. Anthrafilt, the hard coal filter medium. See pages 412, 413.
The Permutit Co., 330 W. 42nd St., New York 36, N. Y. Pressure, gravity and diatomite filters. See pages 416, 417.
Roberts Filter Mfg. Co., 601 Columbia Ave., Darby, Pa. Pressure and gravity filters, filtration plant equipment, zeolite water softeners. See page 1042.
Sparkler Mfg. Co., Mundelein, Ill. Jet spray self-cleaning diatomite filters; standard sizes 25 to 400 sq. ft. area per unit. See pages 424, 425; 1040, 1041.
Swimquip, Inc., 3301 Gilman Rd. El Monte, Calif.; 1040 Huff Rd., N.W., Atlanta, Ga. Centri-Mite filters, diatomaceous earth filters. See page 1043.
R. P. Adams Co., Inc., 232 E. Park Dr., Buffalo 17, N. Y. Adams SPF-Poro-Stone-diatomite swimming pool filters in a range of capacities.
American Pool Co., Fox Island Rd., Port Chester, N. Y. Diatomaceous earth, sand and gravel pressure, anthrafilt filters.

American Water Softener Co., Inc., S.E. Cor. Lehigh & Fourth Sts., Philadelphia 33, Pa. Pressure and gravity filters.

Belco Industrial Equipment Div., Bogue Electric Mfg. Co., 52 Iowa Ave., Paterson 3, N. J. Pressure filter and diatomaceous earth filters; "package" filtration system.

Chemical Equipment Co., P. O. Box 3098, Los Angeles 54, Calif. Pressure and gravity, sand and diatomaceous earth.

Cochrane Corp., 3122 N. 17th St., Philadelphia 32, Pa. Pressure, gravity and diatomaceous earth filters.

Elgin Softener Corp., Elgin, Ill. Diatomite and pressure sand filters, automatic and manual control.

Halogen Supply Co., 4653 W. Lawrence Ave., Chicago 30, Ill. Filters, swimming pool or portable diatomite, sand or anthrafilt.

Hercules Filter Corp., Hawthorne, N. J. Pressure filters for use with diatomaceous earth, loose asbestos filtering material, or both.

Hungerford & Terry, Inc., Atlantic Blvd., Clayton, N. J. Pressure sand filters.

Hygeia Filter Co., 3422 Denton Ave., Detroit, Mich.

Infilco Inc., Box 5033, Tucson, Ariz. Pressure and gravity filters; diatomaceous earth filters.

Proportioneers, Inc., Div. of B-I-F Industries, Inc., 351 Harris Ave., Providence 1, R. I. Purecel diatomaceous earth filters.

MAINTENANCE, MISCELLANEOUS

Air Placement Equipment Company, 1005A West 24th Street, Kansas City, Mo. Manufacturers of Airplaco concrete gunning equipment, including the Bondactor, Nucretor, and Mix Elvator. **See page 68.**

Modern Swimming Pool Co., Inc., 1 Holland Ave., White Plains, N. Y. Filter aids, drains and pool plumbing fittings, water test sets, pool thermometers, foot baths. See page 1035.

Olin Mathieson Chemical Corp., Industrial Chemicals Div., Mathieson Bldg., Baltimore 3, Md. Equipment for swimming pool sanitation. **See pages 410, 411; 1038, 1039.**

Roberts Filter Mfg. Co., 601 Columbia Ave., Darby, Pa. Hair and lint catchers, inlet, outlet, and scum gutter fittings. **See page 1042.**

Swimquip, Inc., 3301 Gilman Rd. El Monte, Calif.; 1040 Huff Rd., N. W., Atlanta, Ga. Vacuum and maintenance equipment, chrome fittings. **See page 1043.**

American Pool Co., Fox Island Rd., Port Chester, N. Y. Expansion joint filler. Fittings.

Berman Chemical Co., Toledo 4, Ohio. Saf-T-Klenz is in dry powder form and is used to remove iron rust, lime deposit, soap oil, body grease and algae.

The Chicago Hardware Foundry Co., 5195 Commonwealth Ave., North Chicago, Ill. Sani-Dri electric hand or hair dryers. "CHF" stools and tables.

Diving Equipment & Supply Co., 212 N. Broadway, Milwaukee 2, Wis. Diving mask units for pool cleaning. Nose clips, ear protectors, swim goggles and masks, lungs for rescue work.

The C. B. Dolge Co., Westport, Conn. Cleaners, soaps, disinfectants, deodorizing-equipment.

Electric-Aire Engineering Corp., 209 W. Jackson Blvd., Chicago 6, Ill. Hair dryers, specially designed for heavy duty institutional and public swimming pool use.

Elgin Softener Corp., Elgin, Ill. Hair and lint catchers, diving helmets, scum gutter and walk drains.

Infilco Inc., Box 5033, Tucson, Arizona.

Josam Mfg. Co., Michigan City, Ind. Inlets, outlets, hair interceptors, vacuum cleaning outlets.

PAINTS

Inertol Co., Inc., 476A Frelinghuysen Ave., Newark 12, N. J., Western Division: Suite 24, 27 S. Park, San Francisco 7, Calif. Swimming pool enamel and mildew resistant enamel for shower and locker rooms. See page 473.

Modern Swimming Pool Co., Inc., 1 Holland Ave., White Plains, N. Y. Chlorinated rubber base paint and paint products for concrete, steel and aluminum swimming pools. Expansion joint compound and primer; steel pool primer and undercoat. **See page 1035.**

National Pool Equipment Co., 2516 Eight Ct. N., Birmingham, Ala. Pool paints. **See pages 1036, 1037.**

American Pool Co., Fox Island Rd., Port Chester, N. Y. Special rubber base chlorinated paint.

The Glidden Company, 11001 Madison Ave., Cleveland 2, Ohio. Vinyl-Cote paints for steel swimming pools.

Halogen Supply Co., 4653 W. Lawrence Ave., Chicago 30, Ill. Paints.

Hercules Powder Co., Cellulose Products Dept., 997 Market St., Wilmington 99, Del. Parlon chlorinated rubber paints for steel or concrete swimming pools.

The Master Mechanics Co., 2097 Columbia Rd., Cleveland 13, Ohio. Rubbertex Sanitile base coat and Masterkote Sanitile vapor-resistant finish coat for shower and swimming pool rooms. For pools—Stein Fest.

Phelan-Faust Paint Mfg. Co., 932 Loughborough Ave., St. Louis 11, Mo. Hydroflex chlorinated rubber base swimming pool paint for beautifying your pool and retarding algae.

RECIRCULATING SYSTEMS

Graver Water Conditioning Co., 216 West 14th St., New York 11, N. Y. Complete recirculation and purification systems with all accessories. **See pages 402, 403.**

Modern Swimming Pool Co., Inc., 1 Holland Ave., White Plains, N. Y. Recirculation and purification systems—all sizes, all accessories. **See page 1035.**

The Permutit Co., 330 W. 42nd St., New York 36, N. Y. Automatic water recirculating systems. **See pages 416, 417.**

Roberts Filter Mfg. Co., 601 Columbia Ave., Darby, Pa. Swimming pool recirculating plants. **See page 1042.**

Elgin Softener Corp., Elgin, Ill. Recirculation system.

STEEL AND CONCRETE POOLS

American Bridge Div., U. S. Steel Corp., 525 William Penn Place, Pittsburgh 30, Pa. All steel swimming pools. **See page 1101.**

Koven Steel Swimming Pools, Inc., A Div. of L. O. Koven & Bro., Inc., 154 Ogden Ave., Jersey City 7, N. J. Koven Steel swimming pools of welded steel construction. **See page 1034.**

National Pool Equipment Co., 2516 8th Ct., N., Birmingham, Ala. Prestressed precast concrete unit packages. **See pages 1036, 1037.**

Tower Iron Works, 60 Borden St., Providence 3, R. I. All steel swimming pools, packaged installations.

WATER TESTING EQUIPMENT

Modern Swimming Pool Co., Inc., 1 Holland Ave., White Plains, N. Y. Water test sets. **See page 1035.**

W. A. Taylor & Co., 418 Rodgers Forge Rd., Baltimore 4, Md. Colorimetric equipment for determination of chlorine and pH of swimming pool water. **See page 448.**

American Pool Co., Fox Island Rd., Port Chester, N. Y. Chlorine testing equipment.

Hellige, Inc., 877 Stewart Ave., Garden City, N. Y. Twin-Kit for precise pH and chlorine or bromine determinations of swimming pool water.

Public Office Equipment

ADDING MACHINES

National Cash Register Co., Main & K Sts., Dayton 9, Ohio. See pages 1047-1050.

Remington Rand, Division of Sperry Rand Corporation, 315 Fourth Ave., New York 10, N. Y. 10 key touch-control adding machines; all-electric and hand models; optional wide carriage for special applications. See pages 1051-1054.

Underwood Corp., One Park Ave., New York 16, N. Y. 10-key adding machines, manual, electric; adding-figuring machines that provide individual, group, and grand totals; adding tabular with carriage. See pages 1055-1058.

Burroughs Corp., 6071 2nd Blvd., Detroit, Mich. Adding machines; full keyboard and ten key.

Friden Calculating Machine Co., Inc., 2350 Washington, San Leandro, Calif. Ten-key electric, 7-8-, 10-column capacities.

Monroe Calculating Machine Co., Inc., 555 Mitchell St., Orange, N. J.

ADDRESSING MACHINES

Addressograph-Multigraph Corp., 1200 Babbitt Rd., Cleveland 17, Ohio. Addressing equipment.

Elliot Addressing Machine Co., Cambridge, Mass. Addressing machines.

AERIAL SURVEYS, TAX REAPPRAISAL & PLANNING

Abrams Aerial Survey Corp., 606 E. Shiwassee St., Lansing 1, Mich. Complete photogrammetric engineering services for municipal agencies by aerial surveys. Atlas sheets, mosaics, planimetric and topographic maps. See pages 34; 54.

Aero Service Corp., 210 E. Courtland St., Philadelphia 20, Pa. Low-cost controlled photo-mosaics for city planning; topographic maps for engineering planning. Complete tax map service. See pages 46; 55.

Jack Ammann Photogrammetric Engineers, Inc., Broadway at Tenth, San Antonio 5, Texas; or P. O. Box 411, Manhasset, N. Y. Write for location of our office nearest you. See page 49.

The J. M. Cleminshaw Co., 1601 Brookpark Rd., Cleveland 9, Ohio. Real estate and personal property appraisals for local tax equalization purposes. See pages 43; 50, 51.

Cole-Layer-Trumble Co., 11 W. Monument Ave., Dayton 2, Ohio. Tax equalization and reassessment service. Also tax mapping. Specialists in the revaluation of real and personal property, including machinery and equipment for local tax equalization purposes. See pages 44; 52, 53.

Fairchild Aerial Surveys, Inc., 224 E. 11th St., Los Angeles 15, Calif. Aerial photographic surveys, controlled photographic mosaics and topographic maps for city planning and engineering study. See page 26.

Lockwood, Kessler & Bartlett, Inc., 1 Aerial Way, Syosset, L. I., N. Y. Aerial and ground surveys, mapping, civil engineering, seismic subsurface investigations. See page 42.

Raynor Aerial Surveys, Georgetown, Conn. Complete photogrammetric services including; aerial photographic surveys, atlas sheets, mosaics, tax maps and low-coast topographic maps for city planning. See page 27.

BLUEPRINTING—WHITEPRINTING

Charles Bruning Co., Inc., 4700 Montrose Ave., Chicago 41, Ill. Whiteprinting. Copyflex reproduction machines and materials.

Ozalid, Division of General Aniline and Film Corp., 14 Ozaway, Johnston City, N. Y. Manufacturers of positive-printing, dry-developing Ozalid machines and sensitized materials.

Paragon-Revolute Corp., 69 South Ave., Rochester 4, N. Y. Printers, developers, dryers for exposing and processing any type of sensitized materials for contact copies.

The C. F. Pease Company, 2631 W. Irving Park Rd., Chicago 18, Ill. Continuous blueprint and whiteprint (dry direct process) machines; cut sheet dryers; blueprint, negative and whiteprint papers; photographic arc lamps and drafting room furniture.

Peck & Harvey Mfg. Corp., 5650 N. Western Ave., Chicago 45, Ill. Blueprinting and direct process dry printing equipment for making ammonia-dry blue line or black line prints. Also photocopy equipment and photographic processing.

BONDING

National Surety Corp., 4 Albany St., New York, N. Y. Performance bonds that guarantee completion of contracts. Bonds for public officials and their employees. Also, burglary and robbery policies.

BOOKKEEPING MACHINES

National Cash Register Co., Main & K Sts., Dayton 9, Ohio. Typewriter bookkeejing machines, check writing machines, cash registers. See pages 1047-1050.

Remington Rand, Division of Sperry Rand Corporation, 315 Fourth Ave., New York 10, N. Y. Both bookkeeping machines and punched-card equipment. See pages 1051-1054.

Underwood Corp., One Park Ave., New York 16, N. Y. Flat-bed Elliott Fisher and 10-key Underwood Sundstrand accounting machines for all municipal accounting operations. Underwood "Simplamatic" accounting machine performs bookkeeping functions from standard electric typewriter keyboard. See pages 1055-1058.

Burroughs Corp., 6071 2nd Blvd., Detroit, Mich. Sensimatic taxbilling, budgetary, typewriter bookkeeping machines.

Monroe Calculating Machine Co., Inc., 555 Mitchell St., Orange, N. J. Bookkeeping, accounting machines.

CALCULATING MACHINES

Remington Rand, Division of Sperry Rand Corporation, 315 Fourth Ave., New York 10, N. Y. 10-key-touch-control printing calculator; automatic division and multiplication, rapid addition and subtraction; printed tape proof of all computations. See pages 1051-1054.

Underwood Corp., One Park Ave., New York 16, N. Y. 10-key printing calculator that adds, subtracts, multiplies, divides, and furnishes a tape record. See pages 1055-1058.

Burroughs Corp., 6071 2nd Blvd., Detroit, Mich. Calculating machines.

Friden Calculating Machine Co., Inc., 2350 Washington, San Leandro, Calif. Fully automatic high speed calculators.

Marchant Calculators, Inc., Oakland 8, Calif.

Monroe Calculating Machine Co., Inc., 555 Mitchell St., Orange, N. J.

CODES, CITY

The Michie City Publications Co., Charlottesville, Va. City codes published, codified, edited and indexed.

COIN HANDLING

Abbott Coin Counter Co., Inc., 411 Wales Ave., New York 54, N. Y. Coin counting machines, coin sorters, coin payers for making up payrolls, cash drawers, coin bags, coin trays and boxes, cashiers' supplies. Coin wrappers and currency straps. All coin and currency handling supplies. See page 875.

Brandt Automatic Cashier Co., 515 First St., Watertown, Wis. Brandt coin sorters, counters and packagers. Brandt automatic cashiers (coin payers and changers), coin wrappers and bill straps, and coin storage trays. See page 861.

Johnson Fare Box Co., 4619 N. Ravenswood Ave., Chicago 40, Ill. Downey-Johnson coin counters, changers, combination sorter-counter, coin wrappers. See page 870, 871.

E. J. Brooks Co., 169 N. 13th St., Newark 7, N. J. Brooks Red Cap coin bag seals for coin and currency shipments. Bag seal presses.

Globe Distributing Co., 1623 N. California Ave., Chicago 47, Ill. Coin counters, sorters, counting sorting combinations, wrappers cartridge and tubular, repairing, parts and supplies.

United Seal Co., 450 S. Pearl St., Columbus 15, Ohio. Metal checks, tags and wires. Special money bag seals.

Universal Business Equipment Co., 533 S. Dearborn St., Chicago 5, Ill. Downey-Johnson coin counter counts, wraps or bags coins of all denominations. Universal coin sorter.

The Vendo Co., 7400 East Twelfth St., Kansas City 26, Mo. The Vendo coin changer provides ready cash. Available as a wall-mounted unit or with a floor stand.

DUPLICATING EQUIPMENT

Addressograph-Multigraph Corp., 1200 Babbitt Rd., Cleveland 17, Ohio. Multigraph and Multilith machines.

A. B. Dick Co., 5700 W. Touhy Ave., Chicago 31, Ill. A. B. Dick Mimeographs, 8 models. Spirit and Azograph (new patented duplicating process) . . . duplicators and supplies, offset duplicating equipment and supplies, impression papers.

Ditto, Inc., 6800 McCormick Rd., Chicago 45, Ill. Direct process, and offset duplicating machines and supplies.

General Binding Corp., 818 W. Belmont Ave., Dept. AC-2, Chicago 14, Ill. Rex-O-Graph spirit duplicator and supplies.

The Haloid Co., 2 Haloid St., Rochester 3, N. Y. Xerox copying equipment for preparing masters by xerography.

F. G. Ludwig Inc., Old Saybrook, Conn. Photo Copier, a portable machine, copies anything printed, written, typed, drawn.

Milo Harding Co., 500 South Monterey Pass Road, Monterey Park, Calif.

Speedliner Co., 4404 Ravenswood, Chicago 40, Ill.; and 629 Ocean Parkway, Apt. D7, Brooklyn 30, N. Y. Spirit-type duplicators and supplies.

ELECTRONIC COMPUTERS

The National Cash Register Co., Main & K Sts., Dayton 9, Ohio. National Post-tronic, the new electronic machine especially designed for use by banks. **See pages 1047-1050.**

Remington Rand, Division of Sperry Rand Corporation, 315 Fourth Ave., New York 10, N. Y. Remington Rand "Univac Systems." See pages 1051-1054.

Underwood Corp., One Park Ave., New York 16, N. Y. Manufactures the "Elecom" computers. Elecom 50 "Business Brain" for payroll and accounting applications. Also "Elecom" 125 computers and file processors. **See pages 1055-1058.**

Burroughs Corp., 6071 2nd Blvd., Detroit, Mich. G101 punched card systems.

International Business Machines Corp., 590 Madison Ave., New York 22, N. Y. Electronic Data Processing and Scientific Computing Systems—IBM 704 and IBM 705. Data Processing Center at New York for special services.

Marchant Calculators, Inc., Oakland 8, Calif.

Radio Corporation of America, Front and Cooper Sts., Camden, N. J. RCA Bizmac.

ENGINEERING AND SURVEYING INSTRUMENTS

Rolatape Inc., P. O. Box 1190, Santa Monica, Calif. A compact one-hand operation measuring wheel that registers feet and inches as you walk. Three models. **See page 260.**

Wild Heerbrugg Instruments, Inc., Main at Covert Sts., Port Washington, N. Y. Levels for setting-out of roads and structures; transits and Theodolites for triangulation, traversing and route surveying. **See page 56.**

American Paulin System, 1524 S. Flower St., Los Angeles 15, Calif. Recording micro barograph. Precision surveying altimeters, precision barometers.

C. L. Berger & Sons, Inc., 37 Williams St., Boston 19, Mass. Surveying, engineering instruments.

Charles Bruning Co., Inc., 4700 Montrose Ave., Chicago, Ill. Transits, levels, tapes, rods. Engineering and drafting equipment and supplies.

Copperweld Steel Co., Wire and Cable Div., 1015 Monongahela Ave., Glassport, Pa. Copperweld non-rusting survey markers.

Eugene Dietzen Co., 2425 Sheffield Ave., Chicago 14, Ill. Surveying, drafting, printmaking.

Henry J. Green Instruments, Inc., 1191 Bedford Ave., Brooklyn 16, N. Y. Meteorological instruments; barometers; thermometers: recording instruments; rain gages and wind instruments.

W. & L. E. Gurley, 510-514 Fulton St., Troy, N. Y. Transits, levels, plane table outfits, rods, meteorological instruments for airports, surveying instruments.

Kern Instruments, Inc., 120 Grand St., White Plains, N. Y. Complete line of theodolites, levels and plane-table equipment for every type of surveying work.

Keuffel & Esser Co., 303 Adams St., Hoboken, N. J.

The Lufkin Rule Co., 1732 Hess Ave., Saginaw, Mich. Chrome Clad steel measuring tapes. Chrome Clad tape-rules and "Red End" folding wood rules.

Umeco Optical Div., 465 California, San Francisco, Calif. Complete line of transits, levels, compasses, planimeters.

Varigraph Co., Inc., 841 W. Lakeside St., Madison 1, Wis. Lettering instrument and templets for producing professional lettering.

Warren-Knight Co., 136 N. 12th St., Philadelphia 7, Pa. Transits; levels; precision clinometers; three-arm protractors; drawing instruments; slide rules; lettering guides. Engineering field equipment; drafting room supplies; surveying instruments repairs.

FOLDING MACHINES

Davidson Corp., 29 Ryerson St., Brooklyn 5, N. Y. (A subsidiary of Mergenthaler Linotype Co.) Folding machines made in three sizes that will handle sheets from 3 x 3" to 14 x 20".

A. B. Dick Co., 5700 W. Touhy Ave., Chicago 31, Ill. A. B. Dick Folder, folding machine.

LOUDSPEAKERS

University Loudspeakers, Inc., 80 S. Kensico Ave., White Plains, N. Y. Complete line of loudspeakers including large trumpets, radial projectors with heavy duty driver units for high power speaker systems and paging and intercom type speakers for low level systems.

MICROFILMING

Remington Rand, Division of Sperry Rand Corporation, 315 Fourth Ave., New York 10, N. Y. Dual Film-a-record copies both sides of records simultaneously. Model 8 Film-a-record, portable with same precision as bigger models. Model 4, flat bed type camera for microfilming bound record. **See pages 1051-1054.**

Burroughs Corp., 6071 2nd Blvd., Detroit, Mich. Microfilm recorders and readers.

Diebold, Inc., 3018 Mulberry Rd., S.E., Canton 2, Ohio.

Recordak Corp., 415 Madison Ave., New York 17, N. Y. Complete line of 16mm and 35mm microfilming equipment and accessories. Sales, service, and film processing.

OFFICE FURNISHINGS, SUPPLIES

Cramer Posture Chair Co., Inc., 1205 Charlotte, Kansas City 6, Mo. Posture chairs, hi-model and production chairs, office machine stands, stools and stop-steps. See page 1059.

The Michaels Art Bronze Co., Inc., Kenton Land Rd., Erlanger, Ky.; P. O. Box 668, Covington, Ky. Bronze plaques, signs, memorials and nameplates; building directories; bronze, aluminum and stainless steel doors and entrances; exhibit cases. **See pages 862-864; 1060.**

Remington Rand, Division of Sperry Rand Corporation, 315 Fourth Ave., N. Y. 10, N. Y. Chairs; desks; vault doors; safes; insulated "Point-of-Use" records storage equipment; steel shelving; steel filing cabinets including conventional and new "Kompakt" models with "extra drawer"; card index and microfilm cabinets, cards, forms, paper, ribbons. **See pages 1051-1054.**

Underwood Corp., One Park Ave., New York 16, N. Y. Underwood Corporation carbon paper, ribbons, desk stabilizers, and other supplies. Also new line of Underwood fanfold writing machine stands. **See pages 1055-1058.**

Acme Visible Records, Inc., Crozet, Va. Cabinets, tubs, safes and rotaries.

Burroughs Corp., 6071 2nd Blvd., Detroit, Mich. Carbon papers, ribbons, other business machine supplies.

Clarin Mfg. Co., 4640 W. Harrison St., Chicago 44, Ill. Steel folding chairs.

Diebold, Inc., 3018 Mulberry Rd., S.E., Canton 2, Ohio. Metal shelving and lockers. Also filing equipment.

The Federal Equipment Co., 370 N. West St., Carlisle, Pa. Bag racks, letter sorting cases, cash and stamp cabinets, bulletin board. Standard U. S. Post Office Department lock type boxes.

General Binding Corp., 818 W. Belmont Ave., Dept. AC-2, Chicago 14, Ill. GBC plastic binding equipment binds pages of all sizes into custom-made booklets.
International Business Machines Corp., 590 Madison Ave., New York 22, N. Y. Electronic and electric clock, time recording and signaling systems.
Wilson Jones Co., 209 S. Jefferson St., Chicago 6, Ill. County record books, public record indexing systems, visible record binders and forms. Filing supplies.
The Monroe Co., 55 Church St., Colfax, Ia. Folding tables and folding benches, folding chairs and steel trucks for folding tables and chairs and portable partitions.
Oxford Filing Supply Co., Inc., Clinton Rd., Garden City, N. Y. Filing systems, folders, index cards and card index guides.

PHOTOPRINTING EQUIPMENT

Remington Rand, Division of Sperry Rand Corporation, 315 Fourth Ave., New York 10, N. Y. Transcopy units in 3 sizes for photo transfer of records. Used with Portagraph for copying from bound records — with Rotoflo contact printer for single sheets. Transcopy Duplex combines negative and positive processes in one unit for single sheet records (two sizes); Dexigraph copies records in actual size, reduces or enlarges, from single sheets to heavy bound volumes. See pages 1051-1054.
American Photocopy Equipment Co. (APECO), 1920 W. Petersen Ave., Chicago 26, Ill. Photocopy equipment and supplies.
The Haloid Co., 2 Haloid St., Rochester 3, N. Y. Foto-Flo machine for copying anything written, printed, typed or drawn in actual, enlarged or reduced size. Maximum size 18" x 24".
Ozalid Div. of General Aniline and Film Corp., 14 Ozaway, Johnson City, N. Y. Positive, sensitized paper and aluminum offset plates.
Paragon-Revolute Corp., 69 South Ave., Rochester 4, N. Y. The Revolute No. 5 Printer for making contact photocopies up to 42" wide by any length.
Recordak Corp., 415 Madison Ave., New York 17, N. Y. Verifax photocopy equipment, supplies and service.

REST ROOM EQUIPMENT

The Bennett Mfg. Co., Alden, N. Y. Bennett Bilt paper towel dispensers, 6 models, double or single sheet dispensers. Also Bennett Bilt Self Closing waste receptacles. See pages 93-96.
The Chicago Hardware Foundry Co., 5195 Commonwealth Ave., North Chicago, Ill. Sani-Dri electric hand or hair dryers. "CHF" stools and tables.
Electric-Aire Engineering Corp., 209 W. Jackson Blvd., Chicago 6, Ill. Hand dryers of new design; provides continuous 24 hr. drying service, specially designed for heavy duty public Rest Room use.

TAGS

Dashew Business Machines, Inc., 5886 Smiley Dr., Culver City, Calif. Metal tags for control of municipal equipment and material.
The Dickey-Grabler Co., 10302 Madison Ave., Cleveland 2, Ohio. Metal tags and plates for identifying poles and municipal equipment of all kinds; numbering machines.
C. H. Hanson Co., 303 W. Erie St., Chicago 10, Ill. Dogtags, metal beach and locker checks, municipal license plates.

TABULATING AND STATISTICAL MACHINES

Remington Rand, Division of Sperry Rand Corporation, 315 Fourth Ave., New York 10, N. Y. Punched-card accounting machines for all phases of county and municipal accounting records and reports. See pages 1051-1054.
Burroughs Corp., 6071 Second Blvd., Detroit, Mich. Statistical machines.
Friden Calculating Machine Co., Inc., 2350 Washington, San Leandro, Calif. Automatic, tape-operated machines for processing integrated data of tax work, payroll, stores, police, costs.
International Business Machines Corp., 590 Madison Ave., New York 22, N. Y. Data Processing—punched card and electronic systems.
Marchant Calculators, Inc., Oakland 8, Calif. Data processing equipment.
Monroe Calculating Machine Co., Inc., 555 Mitchell St., Orange, N. J. Machines for data processing.

TYPEWRITERS

Remington Rand, Division of Sperry Rand Corporation, 315 Fourth Ave., New York 10, N. Y. Electric, standard, and noiseless in office size; standard in portable size; billing and adding; stenographic. See pages 1051-1054.
Underwood Corp., One Park Ave., New York 16, N. Y. Electric and standard typewriters, and portable typewriters. Underwood all electric Fanfold Writing Machine eliminates all non-productive operations in the preparation of forms requiring one or more copies. Also Solenoid electric typewriters for automatic recording of data via electric impulses. See pages 1055-1058.
Addressograph-Multigraph Corp., 1200 Babbitt Rd., Cleveland 17, Ohio. Varityper, typing and composing machine. Also Multigraph Accra-Feed collators.
International Business Machines Corp., 590 Madison Ave., New York 22, New York. Electric typewriters.

VISIBLE RECORDS

Remington Rand, Division of Sperry Rand Corporation, 315 Fourth Ave., New York 10, N. Y. Kardex and other Visible systems for all municipal departments. See pages 1051-1054.
Acme Visible Records, Inc., Crozet, Va. Visible record equipment.
Wheeldex & Simpla Products, Inc., 40 Bank St., White Plains, N. Y. Manual or motorized visible card files in 57 models.

VOTING EQUIPMENT

Automatic Voting Machine Corp., Jamestown, N. Y. Automatic voting machines. See pages 1116, 1117.
Remington Rand, Division of Sperry Rand Corporation (Systems), 315 Fourth Ave., New York 10, N. Y. Index Visible precinct panels easily kept to date; at election time they are photo-offset for accurate, authentic copies. See pages 1051-1054.
The Shoup Voting Machine Corp., 41 East 42nd St., New York 17, N. Y. Voting machines. See pages 1111-1114.
Douglas Mfg. Corp., Crete, Nebr. Steel frame election booths, ballot boxes, collapsible steel tables, jury wheels.
S. G. Adams Metalware Co., 2947 Delmar Blvd., St. Louis 3, Mo. Steel ballot boxes, available in 3 sizes.

THESE POST CARDS ARE FOR YOUR CONVENIENCE IN SECURING CATALOGS OR QUOTATIONS

I should like to receive catalogs and price lists on the following products:

....

....

....

....

....

....

Name ....

Title ....

....

City .... **State** ....

57

I should like to receive catalogs and price lists on the following products:

....

....

....

....

....

....

Name ....

Title ....

....

City .... **State** ....

57

I should like to receive catalogs and price lists as listed below:

Name of **manufacturer** ....

....

.... **Page of ad** .....

Name of **manufacturer** ....

....

.... **Page of ad** .....

I should also like further information on:

....

....

Name ....

Title ....

....

City .... **State** ....

57

I should like to receive catalogs and price lists as listed below:

Name of **manufacturer** ....

....

.... **Page of ad** .....

Name of **manufacturer** ....

....

.... **Page of ad** .....

I should also like further information on:

....

....

Name ....

Title ....

....

City .... **State** ....

57

Postage Will be Paid by Addressee

No Postage Stamp Necessary If mailed in the United States

BUSINESS REPLY CARD

FIRST CLASS PERMIT No. 281, Sec. 34.9, P. L. & R., NEW YORK, N. Y.

The Municipal Index,
470 Fourth Avenue,
New York 16, N. Y.

Postage Will be Paid by Addressee

No Postage Stamp Necessary If mailed in the United States

BUSINESS REPLY CARD

FIRST CLASS PERMIT No. 281, Sec. 34.9, P. L. & R., NEW YORK, N. Y.

The Municipal Index,
470 Fourth Avenue,
New York 16, N. Y.

No Postage Stamp Necessary If mailed in the United States

BUSINESS REPLY CARD

FIRST CLASS PERMIT No. 281, Sec. 34.9, P. L. & R., NEW YORK, N. Y.

The Municipal Index,
470 Fourth Avenue,
New York 16, N. Y.

Postage Will be Paid by Addressee

BUSINESS REPLY CARD

FIRST CLASS PERMIT No. 281, Sec. 34.9, P. L. & R., NEW YORK, N. Y.

The Municipal Index,
470 Fourth Avenue,
New York 16, N. Y.

PLEASE NOTE THAT NO POSTAGE STAMPS ARE NECESSARY FOR MAILING

Public Service and Safety Equipment

Street Lighting

Power and Central Heating

Traffic Control

Fire, Police and Safety Equipment

Parks, Playground and Pools

Public Office Equipment

General Electric FLOODLIGHTS

Stocked By Your Nearest Distributor

General Electric floodlights are designed to solve your floodlighting problems—and your local General Electric distributor can provide off-the-shelf delivery.

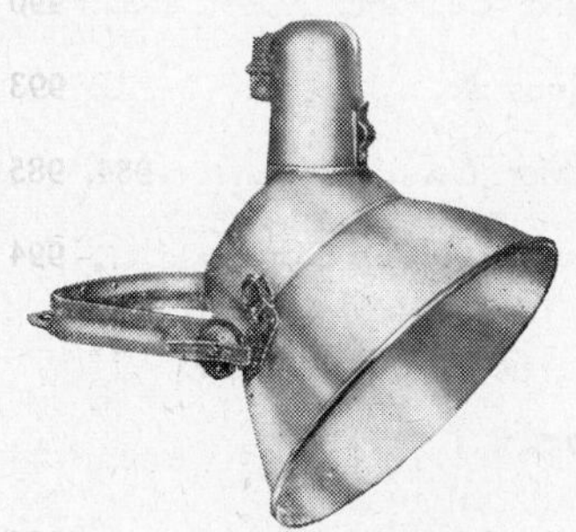

L-69A—A general-purpose floodlight ideally suited for parks, playgrounds, and recreation areas; athletic plants; work, loading, and storage areas; parking lots; etc. Designed to accommodate incandescent lamp sizes up to 1500 watts and mercury-vapor lamp sizes up to 1000 watts, and to provide maximum light output per watt consumed. Noncorrosive parts; aluminum reflectors with faceted rear-reflector design; spun-sealed-gasketless or clamp-band door glass; choice of very narrow, narrow, medium, and wide beam patterns.

L-45A—An inexpensive, rugged, open floodlight with porcelain-enameled steel reflector, for close-range illumination of work, storage, parking, and recreation areas. Wide beam, 300-1500 watts.

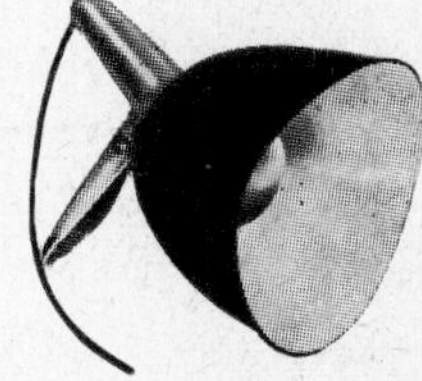

L-82 and L-83—General-purpose floodlights. Extensive use in recreation areas and building illumination. Engineered for long life and easy servicing. 300-1000 watts. Available in either narrow or wide beam.

For other floodlighting installations—or for your specialized applications—General Electric manufactures a complete line of floodlights for outdoor use. All floodlights are engineered specifically for the job and designed for quick installation and easy maintenance. Your General Electric distributor can supply you with all the details, and he has the unit you need for your job, right on his shelf.

Bulletin GEA-6175 contains descriptive information designed to help you select equipment that will properly meet your floodlighting requirements. In addition, experienced application engineering assistance is available on request. Also available, "Chance To Play," a 16-mm documentary film, prepared for General Electric by the March Of Time. This dramatic film will help you sell your community on the need for adequate recreational facilities. Address inquiries to Section 640-461, Apparatus Sales Division, General Electric Company, Schenectady 5, N. Y.

Progress Is Our Most Important Product

GENERAL ELECTRIC

When you plan Street Lighting

Use General Electric service, available to your community

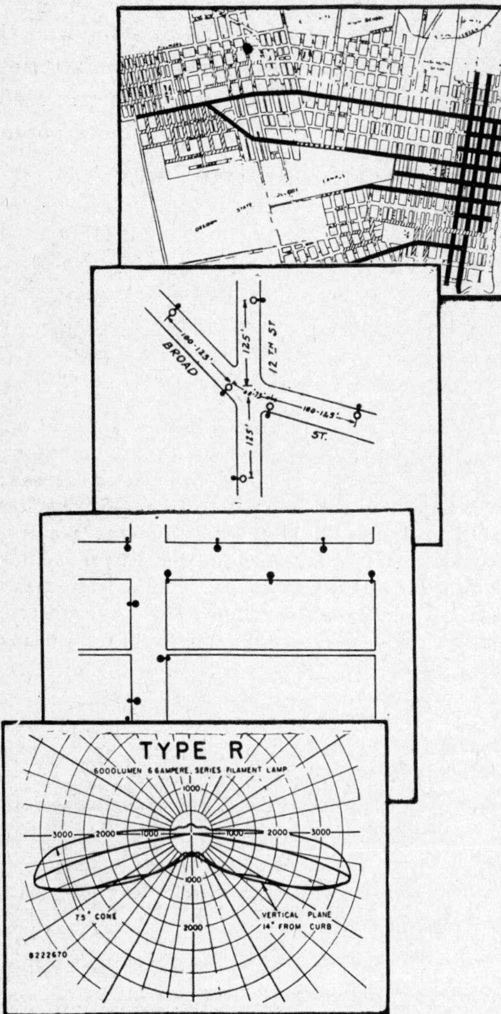

Typical pages from a street-lighting survey, prepared by General Electric, show lighting plans for a downtown street, for a particularly hazardous intersection, and light-distribution characteristics of recommended luminaires.

Whether you are considering replacing a major portion of your street-lighting system—or the lighting of a single street or of an intersection with an accident record—it will pay you to *plan* the installation with the aid of General Electric Lighting Specialists. For, unless your existing equipment is really modern, you will not get either the best in lighting or the most in efficiency by simply extending your present system.

DETAILED PLANS FOR YOUR PROBLEMS

General Electric Lighting Specialists will be glad to assist you in planning any street-lighting installation. These Specialists, located in General Electric offices throughout the country, are ready to help public officials—in collaboration with the electric utility company, if one is involved—to work out requirements for a single corner or for an entire city. They are backed by the General Electric Outdoor Lighting Center at Hendersonville, N. C., and will consult with this organization on any unusual problems.

AVAILABLE WITHOUT COST

This service is available without cost through the nearest General Electric office. It is of top professional quality. It is offered by the company that makes every type of light source and luminaire that is economically feasible for any street-lighting job — a company that is therefore sincerely interested in seeing that users get equipment that best meets their needs. *Section 640-461, Apparatus Sales Division, General Electric Company, Schenectady 5, N. Y.*

Progress Is Our Most Important Product

GENERAL ELECTRIC

Use General Electric Luminaires

For better street lighting at lower cost

Because of their carefully designed optical characteristics, General Electric luminaires provide a high degree of effectively distributed light. Designed for functional simplicity, they promote standardization and lower maintenance costs.

By use of various General Electric luminaires, you can meet I.E.S. standards of distribution for all types of traffic arteries from residential streets to high-speed super highways. A few of the more popular types are illustrated below.

Form 400—Provides flexible, economical pavement illumination. Either Type II or Type III distribution may be obtained by changing snap-in reflectors. Five different mercury lamps may be used, and a choice of sockets for either multiple or ballastless circuits is available. New, easy servicing speeds up maintenance and lowers cost. The glassware may be lifted off the hinge and removed—simplifying relamping and cleaning.

Fluorescent's First Family—A fluorescent luminaire for every street-lighting application, from residential to whiteway, from 2700 lumens to 64,000 lumens. Five handsome units, one of which is shown here, feature aluminum hoods; clear, acrylic, one-piece plastic globes; hinged aluminum reflectors, terminal boards, and integral-mounted ballasts prewired at the factory. Employing standard or new power-groove rapid-start fluorescent lamps, these luminaires mean safer, more comfortable vision. This "seeability," combined with lower maintenance, easier installation, and weatherproof engineering, means economy plus practicality—more value per dollar invested.

Form 79R—Provides the highly efficient, asymmetric light distribution that is ideal for light-to-heavy traffic streets, arteries, and highways. It is designed for filament lamps. The Form 79 hood is also available with other standard General Electric optical assemblies for other light-distribution patterns.

Form 101VR—Designed for use in lighting residential and very light-traffic streets and intersections, the Form 101VR luminaire provides either a two- or four-beam distribution. Economy is achieved by use of 4000- and 6000-lumen filament lamps at long spacing.

Form 110SO—A modern, open-reflector luminaire offering Type II light distribution and specially designed for use with 2500-lumen lamps, at spacings normally used for residential streets. The Form 110SO consists of a die-cast aluminum hood with integrally cast 1¼-inch slip-fitter, internal wiring, a plug-in photoelectric control unit, and an aluminum reflector.

For further information,
contact your nearest General Electric Apparatus Sales Office or Supplier.

THERE'S AN ENTIRE FAMILY OF G-E COMMUNICATIONS EQUIPMENT

G-E Communications Equipment Covers the Range

30 kc to 2,000,000 kc • 1 watt to 3,000 watts

G.E. offers a complete line of communications equipment—from audio to microwave—for police, fire, oil, lumber, industrial and civil defense applications. Typical are:

Tone Equipment—Selective signalling systems up to 900 calls. Telemetering up to 18 quantities on one audio channel. Remote and supervisory control. Powerline protective relaying channel equipment.

Microwave—G-E microwave equipment offers dependable communication over long distances and in difficult terrain areas. Up to 24 channels available for heavy traffic use.

2-Way Radio Communication—G-E 2-way radio steps up production—increases profits. Industrial, public safety, and emergency personnel use it for better co-ordination of activities.

● **For full information on G-E communications equipment call the G-E office near you or write direct: *General Electric Company, Communications Equipment, Section C457, Electronics Park, Syracuse, New York.***

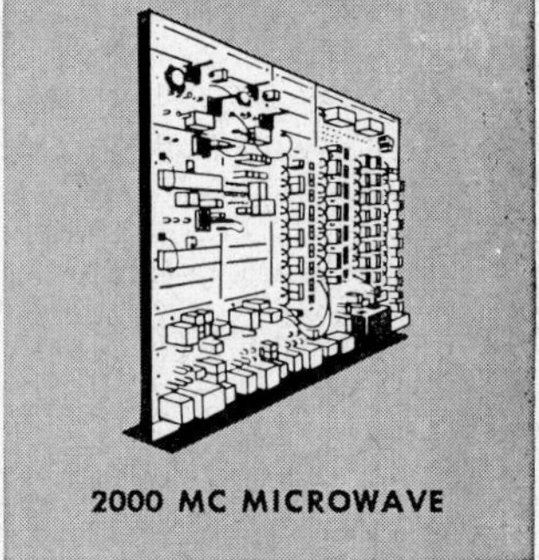

G-E 2-WAY RADIO FEATURES:

- **FREQUENCY STABILITY AND SELECTIVITY** guaranteed for life
- Narrow or wide band operation—6/12 volt operation
- Low battery drain—cooler running equipment
- Quality components—G.E. makes more of its 2-way radio components than any other manufacturer

Progress Is Our Most Important Product

GENERAL ELECTRIC

HOLOPHANE COMPANY, INC.

342 Madison Avenue, New York 17, N.Y.

Street Lighting Dept.: NEWARK, OHIO . . . Canadian Office: Toronto

FOR BETTER, SAFER, MORE ECONOMICAL STREET LIGHTING

specify HOLOPHANE Refractors

•

THE UNIQUE PRISMATIC DESIGN OF HOLOPHANE REFRACTORS MAKES THESE ADVANTAGES POSSIBLE:

HIGHER PAVEMENT BRIGHTNESS—high angle distributions mean brighter roadways, particularly on dark-top pavements . . .

LUMINOUS REFRACTORS—provide improved beacon effect for residential streets . . .

SIDEWISE LIGHT CONTROL—directs stray light away from unwanted areas . . . four different I.E.S. type distributions . . .

MORE ILLUMINATION—on the roadway and sidewalks . . .

BETTER UNIFORMITY of light between luminaires . . .

LONGER SPACINGS—high angle distributions project light farther . . .

LOW SYSTEM COST—fewer units per mile of street required for most effective job . . .

•

Photos: Courtesy of City of Chicago Dept. of Streets and Electricity.

Compare the Brightness of the Road

(Above) Night-time photograph of a residential street in Chicago . . . (Left) Daylight view of same street from same camera location. Note how the brightness of the roadway at night compares favorably with the daylight picture.

HOLOPHANE REFRACTORS offer

PRISMATIC CONTROL OF LIGHT

(1) Concentrate More Light on Roadway
(2) Distribute Light Uniformly

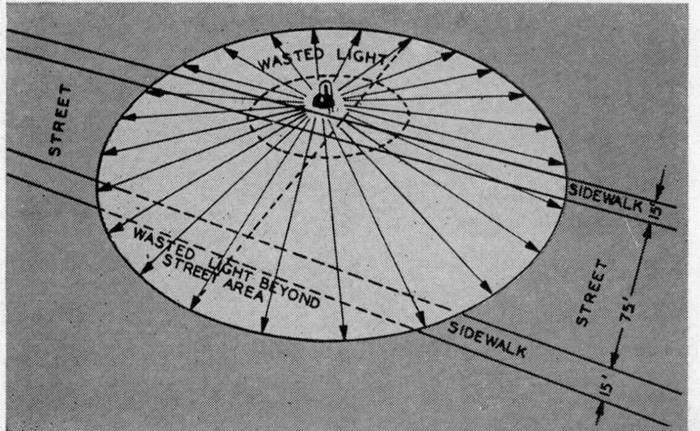

(Left) Typical pattern of light from a luminaire *without* Refractor.

(Below) Typical pattern of light from a luminaire *with* Holophane Refractor.

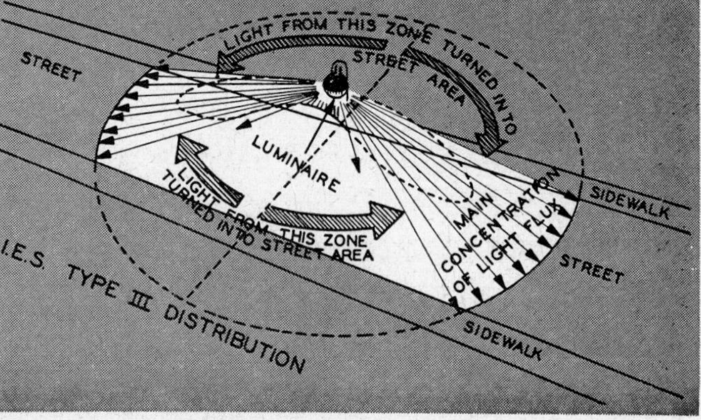

Holophane Refractors Give

GREATER VISIBILITY DISTANCE

More Street Illumination Per Dollar

• To achieve the purposes of modern street lighting installations, motorists and pedestrians must be able to see adequately. Better visibility on streets at night depends on: 1: Greater object illumination; 2: Greater background brightness; 3: Less glare.

Holophane REFRACTORS adequately fulfill these three reqiuirements! Their efficient prismatic design produces correct lateral and vertical distributions of light which put the right amount of illumination in the right places. This not only increases the amount but improves the uniformity of object illumination and background brightness. At the same time the proper balance of light flux at all points in the distribution reduces the glare effect which also improves visibility.

REFRACTORS for thoroughfares and business streets are designed to give adequate light outside the main concentrated beam to properly light sidewalks and building fronts. REFRACTORS are also available foı light traffic and residential streets that provide excellent sidewise shielding to keep light confined to the roadway and away from upper story windows. (See page 798)

HOLOPHANE CO., INC., Street Lighting Dept., Newark, Ohio

American Standard Practice—IES Recommended Lateral Distributions

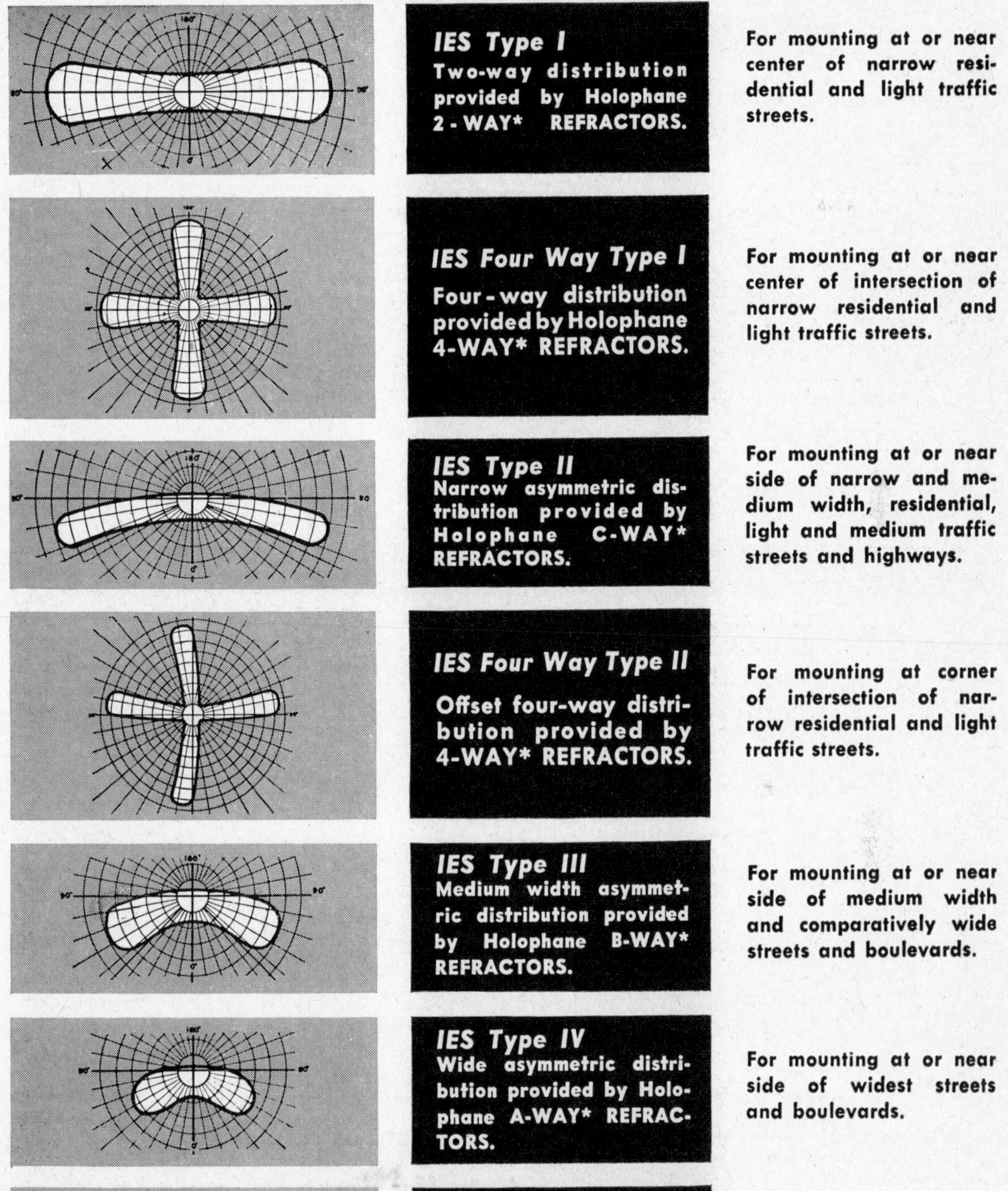

IES Type I
Two-way distribution provided by Holophane 2-WAY* REFRACTORS.

For mounting at or near center of narrow residential and light traffic streets.

IES Four Way Type I
Four-way distribution provided by Holophane 4-WAY* REFRACTORS.

For mounting at or near center of intersection of narrow residential and light traffic streets.

IES Type II
Narrow asymmetric distribution provided by Holophane C-WAY* REFRACTORS.

For mounting at or near side of narrow and medium width, residential, light and medium traffic streets and highways.

IES Four Way Type II
Offset four-way distribution provided by 4-WAY* REFRACTORS.

For mounting at corner of intersection of narrow residential and light traffic streets.

IES Type III
Medium width asymmetric distribution provided by Holophane B-WAY* REFRACTORS.

For mounting at or near side of medium width and comparatively wide streets and boulevards.

IES Type IV
Wide asymmetric distribution provided by Holophane A-WAY* REFRACTORS.

For mounting at or near side of widest streets and boulevards.

IES Type V
Symmetric distribution provided by Holophane symmetric REFRACTORS.

For large area lighting.

These are Candlepower Curves and the area is not in proportion to Light Output. *®

Typical Holophane Refractors for Residential Streets

Typical Holophane Refractors for Business Streets & Highways

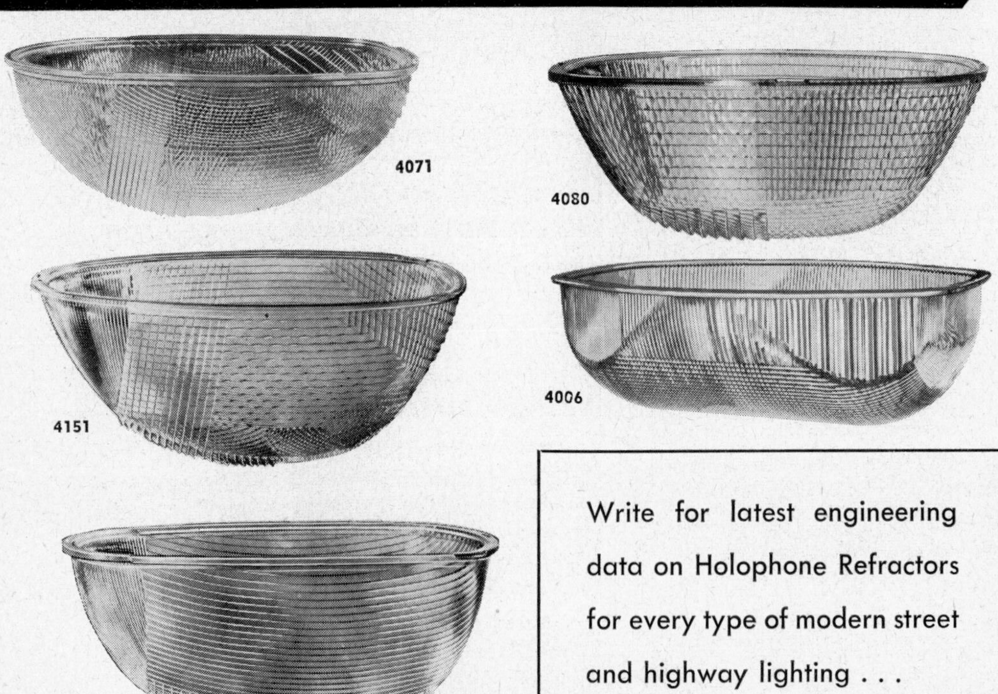

Write for latest engineering data on Holophone Refractors for every type of modern street and highway lighting . . .

HOLOPHANE CO., INC., Street Lighting Dept., Newark, Ohio

HUBBARD ALUMINUM PRODUCTS COMPANY

Division of Hubbard and Company
PITTSBURGH 1, PA.

HAPCO

aluminum outdoor lighting products

street lighting standards
flood lighting standards
traffic signal poles
brackets

SPECIAL FEATURES

ONE PIECE CONSTRUCTION—One piece, seamless shaft construction. Uniform wall thickness in lengths up to forty feet and diameters to ten inches.

EASE OF INSTALLATION—Lightweight HAPCO poles require less manpower, time and equipment to install.

STRENGTH—Specially selected heat treated aluminum alloy provides strength necessary to withstand winds up to 125 miles per hour without taking permanent set.

NO MAINTENANCE—No initial or maintenance painting required even in heavily corrosive industrial and coastal areas.

typical applications

PARKING AREAS—Twin Style "B," transformer base HAPCO standards 25 feet high are used in many parking areas to provide maximum service with no maintenance.

BRIDGE LIGHTING—Where moisture creates a recurring maintenance problem, HAPCO aluminum bridge lighting brackets require no painting maintenance (Style "S").

STREET LIGHTING—HAPCO standards and brackets add to the appearance of a revitalized community street, provide greater night visibility and cut maintenance (Style "S" at left—"W" at right).

TRAFFIC CONTROL STANDARDS—And a wide variety of traffic signal standards, special poles, sign posts and pedestals can be supplied to meet your specific requirements.

PARKWAYS—SUPERHIGHWAYS—THRUWAYS—BRIDGES—The rigorous service conditions in these applications have proven the dollar advantage of HAPCO aluminum alloy standards and brackets (Style "S").

HAPCO

lighting brackets for attachment to wood poles

available in aluminum alloy or galvanized steel

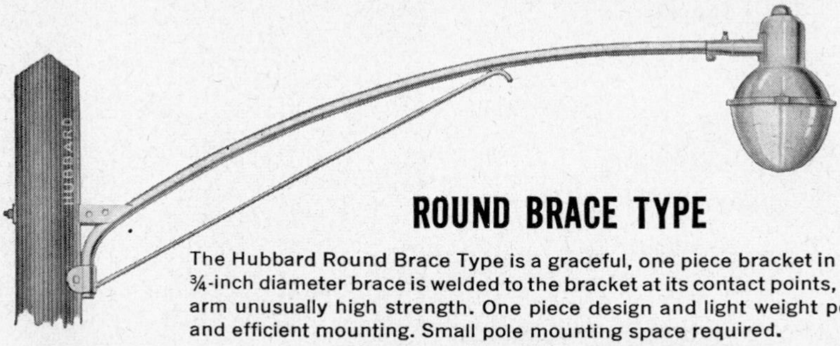

ROUND BRACE TYPE

The Hubbard Round Brace Type is a graceful, one piece bracket in which the ¾-inch diameter brace is welded to the bracket at its contact points, giving the arm unusually high strength. One piece design and light weight permit fast and efficient mounting. Small pole mounting space required.

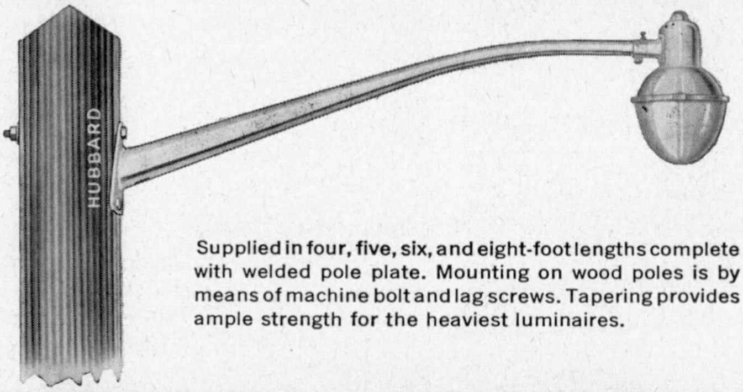

TAPERED TYPE

Supplied in four, five, six, and eight-foot lengths complete with welded pole plate. Mounting on wood poles is by means of machine bolt and lag screws. Tapering provides ample strength for the heaviest luminaires.

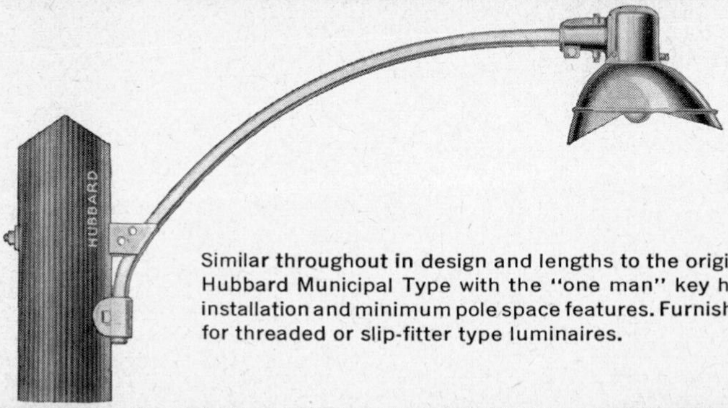

MUNICIPAL TYPE

Similar throughout in design and lengths to the original Hubbard Municipal Type with the "one man" key hole installation and minimum pole space features. Furnished for threaded or slip-fitter type luminaires.

For complete design specifications and installation views write today for Catalog HAL-754.

HUBBARD
ALUMINUM PRODUCTS COMPANY
Division of Hubbard & Company
Pittsburgh 1, Pa.

LINE MATERIAL DIVISION

McGRAW-EDISON CO.

700 W. MICHIGAN STREET • MILWAUKEE 1, WISCONSIN

Manufacturing Plants at: Barton, Wisconsin; Birmingham, Alabama; East Stroudsburg, Penna.; Olean, New York; Sherman, Texas; South Milwaukee, Wisconsin (2); Zanesville, Ohio; Toronto 13, Ontario, Canada.

For over 45 years, Line Material has been producing electrical distribution and transmission equipment which helps bring electricity to the home, the farm, and industry. L-M also produces a complete line of incandescent, mercury vapor and fluorescent lighting for all types of outdoor applications, and a complete line of airport lighting equipment. L-M's line of lighting is the culmination of years of study, and engineering development which today ranks it among the industry's leaders.

Line Material points with pride to its extensive field service organization which consists of more than 150 engineers, who are ever at work servicing customers' needs. Nine factories, plus 70 warehouses and 73 sales offices are further assurance that all needs and requirements can be given immediate attention.

SALES OFFICES

Albany 4, N. Y. .... 966 Broadway
Albuquerque, N. M. .... 324-B Jefferson St., N. E.
Allentown, Pa. .... 2405 Fairview St.
Anchorage, Alaska .... 102 First Ave.
Arlington 6, Va. .... 124 Shirlington Trust Bldg.
Ashland, Ky. .... P. O. Box 268
Atlanta 6, Ga. .... 1107 Glidden St., N. W.
Austin, Texas .... 604 West Ave.
Birmingham, Ala. .... 1700 Vanderbilt Rd.
Bismarck, No. Dakota .... 1213 Prospect Place
Boise, Idaho .... 614½ State St.
Boston, Mass — Revere .... 570 Revere Beach Pkwy.
Buffalo 2, N. Y. .... 443 Delaware Ave.
Butte, Montana .... 743 Wyoming St.
Charlotte, No. Carolina .... 228 W. First St.
Chicago, Ill. — Melrose Park .... 4700 Lake St.
Cincinnati 27, Ohio .... Erie Court & Penn, R. R.
Cleveland 14, Ohio .... 818 Citizens Bldg.
Columbia 4, So. Carolina .... 1824 York Drive
Columbus, Ohio .... 17 S. High Street
Dallas 2, Texas .... 1909 Hi-Line Drive
Denver 2, Colo. .... 5075 Colorado Blvd.
Des Moines, Iowa .... 1116 Paramount Bldg.
Detroit 2, Mich. .... 611 Stephenson Bldg.
Duluth 4, Minn. .... 3331 E. Superior St.
East Stroudsburg, Pa. .... North Burson St.
Fergus Falls, Minn. .... 626 Highland
Fort Worth, Texas .... 1100 E. Presidio
Grand Rapids 5, Mich. .... 668 Rudy St., N. E.
Green Bay, Wis. .... 1119 Spence St.
Harrisburg, Pa. .... 2700 Paxton St.
Hartford, Conn. — Newington .... P. O. Box 9
Houston, Texas .... 5715 Navigation Blvd.
Indianapolis 4, Ind. .... 814 Union Title Bldg.
Jackson 6, Mich. .... 1514 Daniel Road
Jackson, Miss. .... 608 Colonial Circle
Jacksonville, Fla. .... 1620 Holly Oaks Lake Rd.
Los Angeles 22, Calif. .... 6490 E. Fleet St.
Madison, Wis. .... 405 Tompkins Drive
Memphis 7, Tenn. .... 1169 Morehead St.
Miami 38, Florida .... 7240 N. E. 4th Ct.
Milwaukee 1, Wis. .... 700 W. Michigan St.
Minneapolis 20, Minn. .... 500 W. 79th St.
Nashville 4, Tenn. .... 1503 Laurel St.
New Orleans 22, La. .... 2860 Arts St.
New York 6, N. Y. .... 74 Trinity Pl.
No. Kansas City, Mo. .... 10th & Erie Sts.
Oklahoma City 5, Okla. .... 317 N. E. Hill St.
Omaha 3, Neb. .... 3415 Cuming St.
Philadelphia 2, Pa. .... 2416 Girard Trust Co. Bldg.
Phoenix, Ariz. .... 625 W. Madison St.
Pine Bluff, Ark. .... 1904 W. 31st
Pittsburgh 22, Pa. .... 535 Smithfield St., Oliver Bldg.
Portland 9, Ore. .... 1333 N. W. 12th Ave.
Raleigh, No. Carolina .... 216 Russ St.
Richmond 20, Va. .... 1717 Rhoadmiller St.
Roanoke, Va. .... 915 S. Jefferson St.
Sacramento 18, Calif. .... 1123 Teneighth Way
St. Louis 1, Mo. .... 1024 Title Guaranty Bldg.
Salt Lake City 10, Utah .... 980 S. 6th West St.
San Antonio, Texas .... 825 Majestic Bldg.
Seattle 99, Wash. .... 1220 W. Nickerson St.
Sioux City 4, Iowa .... P. O. Box 443
So. Milwaukee, Wis. .... 12th & Madison Aves.
So. San Francisco, Calif. .... 360 Shaw Road
Spokane 24, Wash. .... E. 3303 Ferry St.
Springfield, Ill. .... 504 E. Monroe
Springfield, Mo. .... 961 S. Weller
Syracuse 2, N. Y. .... 221 Erie Blvd. W.
Tampa 2, Florida .... 306 No. Newport Ave.
Union, N. J. .... P. O. Box 306
Wichita 16, Kansas .... 1400 N. Charles
Zanesville, Ohio .... Pershing Road

L-M LUMINAIRES ARE BEST FOR YOUR STREET LIGHTING REQUIREMENTS

Line Material lighting specialists are available to help you plan any type of street lighting installation. L-M's Lighting Department is ever ready to help public officials plan a lighting system whether it be for a single block or for an entire community. The lighting specialists are backed not only by complete experience with L-M lighting equipment, but also a vast knowledge of all IES and NEMA practices and standards.

L-M offers the most advanced equipment and operating systems for incandescent, mercury vapor and fluorescent street lighting, whether it is for application in residential streets, or high-speed super highways. A few of the more popular types of L-M luminaires available are illustrated below.

FLUORESCENT LUMINAIRE — L-M's fluorescent luminaire, the ultimate in modern styling, is available in deep and shallow styles, either four or six feet in length, and is designed to accommodate present and future very high output (VHO) fluorescent lamps. In application, this modern fluorescent luminaire distributes the light over a broad area, giving good balance between buildings and road surfaces, and is intended primarily for street and highway lighting. For other outdoor lighting applications, such as parking lots, store front lighting, etc., other styles are available.

OVALITE® LUMINAIRE — L-M's Ovalite luminaire has been photometrically, electrically, and mechanically designed to meet todays many requirements for good street lighting. It provides IES Types II, III and IV medium, medium-wide and wide light distribution patterns and can accommodate mercury vapor lamps up to 21,000 lumens, and incandescent lamps up to 10,000 lumens. It has an eye-pleasing, modern appearance, and may be used for lighting busy downtown shopping and commercial areas, highways, and interchanges, and store fronts, parking areas, loading docks and railroad yards. This luminaire has many features which bear investigation.

SPHEROLITE® SR. AND JR. LUMINAIRES—The L-M Spherolite Sr., luminaire is designed for use with incandescent lamps up to and including 575 watts on multiple circuits, or 10,000 lumens on series circuits. Its high degree of effectiveness make it especially adaptable for low-cost lighting of business districts and principal routes of traffic. Light distribution patterns are provided in IES Types I, II, III, IV, V and 4-way Types I and II. The Spherolite, Jr., is a small shielded light source type unit, which is intended primarily for residential lighting where narrow streets and wide spacings prevail. It has strong, yet narrow beam characteristics which provide effective lighting for streets with proper cut-off for residential property. It provides IES Types II, V, and 4-way Type II light patterns.

L-M SUBURBANAIRE AND DIRECTOLITE LUMINAIRES — L-M's two open type luminaires place the efficiency of modern and scientifically controlled street lighting within the reach of smaller communities and in outlying areas of larger cities where high intensity is not required and where economy is a consideration. The open refractor Suburbanaire provides for excellent cooling, larger lamps and easy relamping, and has a pleasing daytime appearance. It is available in IES Type I, II, III, V and 4-way Type II light patterns. The Directolite luminaire is available with stainless steel asymmetric and symmetric reflectors which provide IES Type II and V light patterns. The stainless steel reflector has excellent lighting characteristics and produces a high utilization of light on street surfaces. Houses and street side shields are available for the asymmetric reflector.

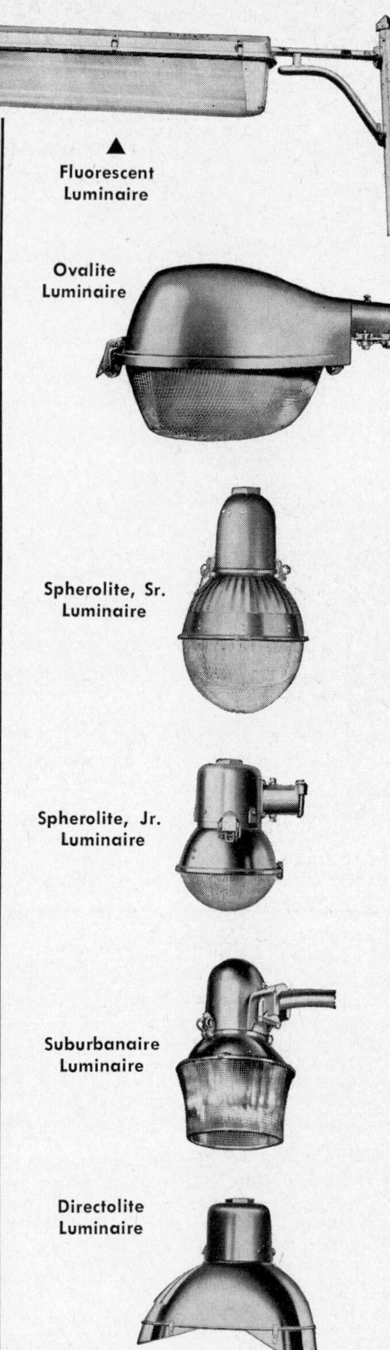

▲ Fluorescent Luminaire

Ovalite Luminaire

Spherolite, Sr. Luminaire

Spherolite, Jr. Luminaire

Suburbanaire Luminaire

Directolite Luminaire

For further information on L-M's complete line of luminaires, contact on L-M field engineer or lighting specialist, or write Line Material Division, Milwaukee 1, Wisconsin.

L-M STREET LIGHTING ACCESSORIES

A full line of accessories to complete your street lighting requirements is available through Line Material Division. A representative group of this class of material is shown here.

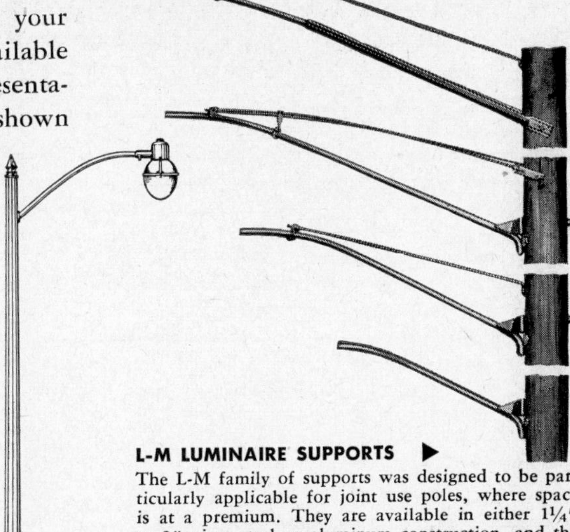

STREET LIGHTING POLES ▶

Line Material furnishes a variety of street lighting poles to meet the requirements of all lighting installations. More complete data on aluminum, steel, and concrete poles, which are available through Line Material Company will be furnished upon request.

L-M LUMINAIRE SUPPORTS ▶

The L-M family of supports was designed to be particularly applicable for joint use poles, where space is at a premium. They are available in either 1¼" or 2" pipe, steel or aluminum construction, and the four harmonizing models available, provide sizes in 2-foot increments from 4 feet through 20 feet which meet proposed EEI-NEMA Standards in both strength and minimum pole space mounting requirements. All threaded parts of each support are protected with a plastic coating, and complete installation instructions are clearly marked on each support. They are all unit-packaged with steel bands to facilitate handling, shipping and warehousing.

L-M'S TYPE CW CONSTANT WATTAGE BALLAST assures more uniform individual light output for mercury vapor street lighting systems. This lightweight, moisture-proof ballast offers an excellent voltage regulation and has outstanding sub-zero starting characteristics. The unit is easy to mount and presents no stocking problem since the same ballast may be used for pole base, pole top, or aerial application. ◀

L-M TABET PHOTOELECTRIC RELAYS are rugged, delayed action units which are designed specifically for street lighting control. They are comprised of a light sensitive photocell, a two-tube amplifier of proven performance and long life, and a power switching relay of high capacity and versatile design. The circuit provides delaying action to prevent false operation due to momentary incidental light changes. These photo-electric relays come in various models for crossarm or pole mounting, or in a weatherproof standard watthour meter case with a socket plug-in base, or directly mounted on one of L-M's Type A metal luminaire heads. ▶

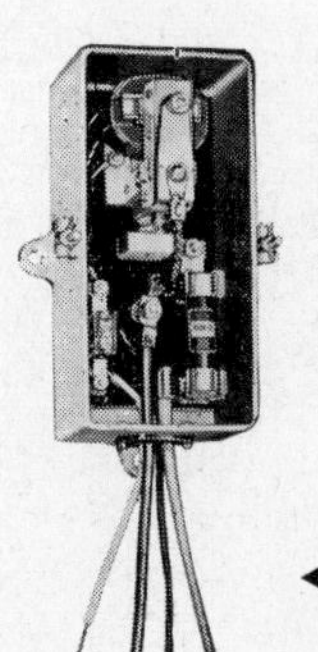

RCOC REMOTE CONTROL RELAYS with 120-volt, 60-cycle operating coils and with load contacts rated for switching the supply to 120-volt AC street lighting circuits are designated as multiple relays. The ◀ Type MR Relay shown here is usually controlled from a pilot circuit which is energized by a reliable automatic control from a central location in a control area. A complete line of multiple relays are available with both load contacts normally closed or normally open. Voltage ratings other than 120-volt AC are available on request.

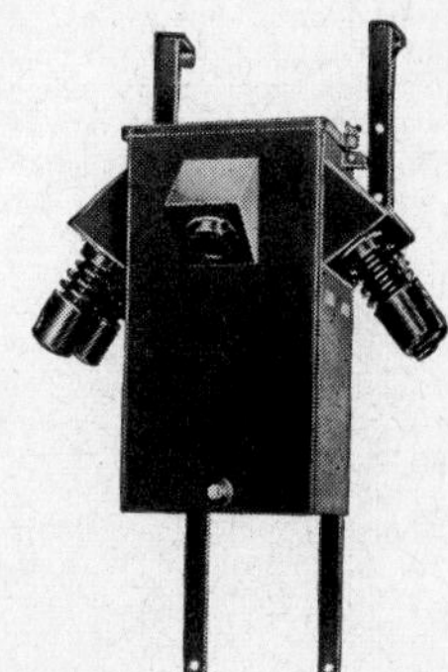

▶

RCOC MANUAL AND REMOTE CONTROL OIL SWITCHES are available for switching of the primary to transformers which energize outdoor lighting circuits. Shown here is the Type AN oil switch which is recommended for this type of application.

LINE MATERIAL AIRPORT LIGHTING EQUIPMENT

L-M leads the field in development and application of airport ramp and runway lighting. Equipment includes high intensity fixed focus, and controllable Thermal Beam® runway lights, and medium intensity runway and taxiway markers, all of which are CAA approved. In addition, a "Flying Farmer" landing strip lighting unit is available in a complete 2000-foot to 3000-foot runway package for as little as $600.

L-M also makes available a fluorescent luminaire for ramp lighting. These luminaires provide a broad light source, with a high level of illumination with a minimum of glare to incoming pilots.

RUNWAY LIGHTS at Birmingham (Ala.) Municipal Airport are L-M's high-intensity units. L-M's units compensate in intensity and beam direction for fog and other low-visibility conditions.

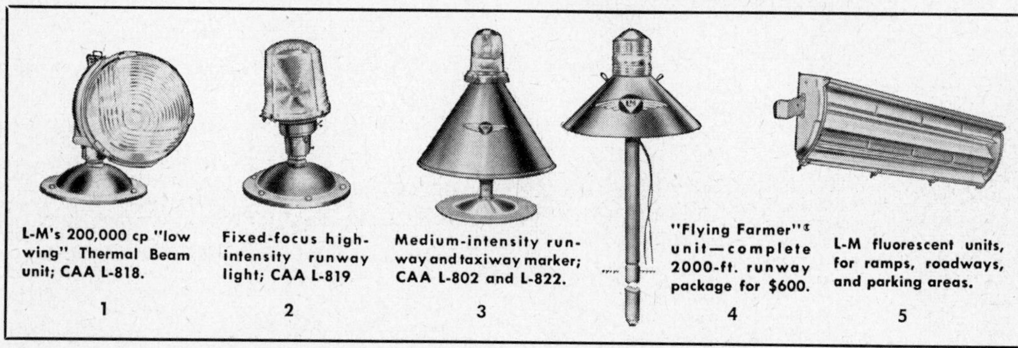

L-M's 200,000 cp "low wing" Thermal Beam unit; CAA L-818. 1

Fixed-focus high-intensity runway light; CAA L-819 2

Medium-intensity runway and taxiway marker; CAA L-802 and L-822. 3

"Flying Farmer"® unit—complete 2000-ft. runway package for $600. 4

L-M fluorescent units, for ramps, roadways, and parking areas. 5

1. L-M 200,000 candlepower "low wing" Thermal-Beam unit is the solution to many of the more serious operating problems in high intensity airport lighting. It provides simplified automatic beam control by the tower operator and eliminates many items to give lower installation and maintenance costs. Made in accordance with CAA Specification L-818.

2. This fixed focus L-M runway and threshold marker light is designed to comply with CAA Specification L-819 for high intensity lighting on instrument runways. The unit is of simple construction requiring a minimum of maintenance and has good operational safety since it is less than 17″ high and weighs only 7 pounds.

3. This elevated runway-taxiway marker light complies with both CAA Specification L-802 (elevated runway light) and CAA Specification L-822 (elevated taxiway marker light). The same fixture is used for both applications, the only exception being that an asymmetrical lens is used on the former and a symmetrical lens on the latter.

4. The L-M "Flying Farmer" runway light is a 15 watt, 25 candlepower unit, designed for operation on ordinary house current, 120-240 a-c or d-c. It is especially adaptable to private air strips and for use in Class I Airports, and is simple enough to be installed by the aircraft operator. The completely self-contained, ready-to-install Flying Farmer package is available for 2000-ft through 3000-ft runways.

5. L-M's 2-lamp fluorescent luminaire is especially adaptable to airport ramp lighting since the soft, non-glare light it provides is conducive to safe aircraft movement as attested to by commercial and private pilots. The unit is light in weight, easy to mount and demands a minimum of maintenance.

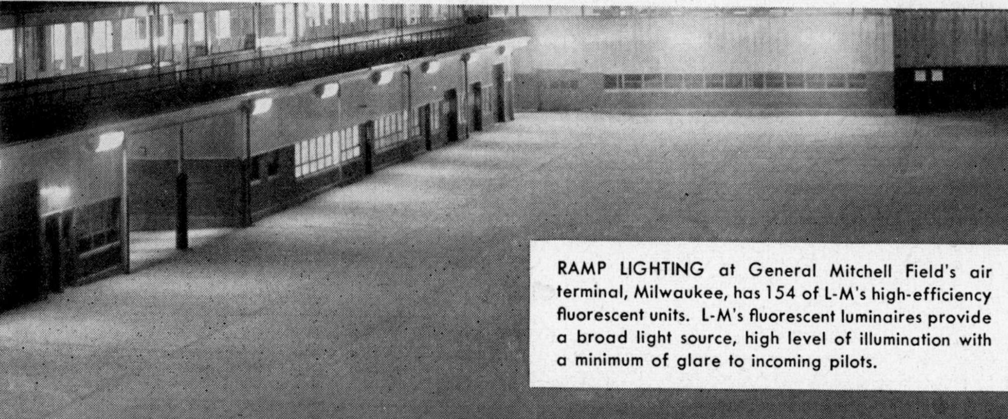

RAMP LIGHTING at General Mitchell Field's air terminal, Milwaukee, has 154 of L-M's high-efficiency fluorescent units. L-M's fluorescent luminaires provide a broad light source, high level of illumination with a minimum of glare to incoming pilots.

KERRIGAN IRON WORKS, Inc., Nashville, Tenn.

THE FORGES OF KERRIGAN

MANUFACTURERS OF *Weldforged* TRADEMARK

STREET LIGHTING STANDARDS

GENERAL SALES OFFICE: 274 MADISON AVE., NEW YORK CITY

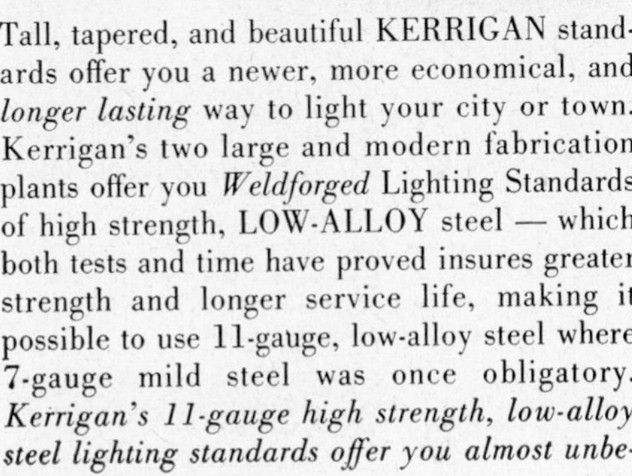

Tall, tapered, and beautiful KERRIGAN standards offer you a newer, more economical, and *longer lasting* way to light your city or town. Kerrigan's two large and modern fabrication plants offer you *Weldforged* Lighting Standards of high strength, LOW-ALLOY steel — which both tests and time have proved insures greater strength and longer service life, making it possible to use 11-gauge, low-alloy steel where 7-gauge mild steel was once obligatory. *Kerrigan's 11-gauge high strength, low-alloy steel lighting standards offer you almost unbelievable resistance to high winds and to chemical and salt-air corrosion.*

Let us prove that KERRIGAN Lighting Standards are your city's best investment. Let us send you our STREET LIGHTING CATALOG with complete information and technical data. Discover for yourself how Kerrigan welds (made by the submerged arc process and rigidly controlled by MAGNA-FLUX Magnetic Particles Test) and improved LOW-ALLOY steels insure greater service. Write for your copy today.

KERRIGAN IRON WORKS, Inc., Nashville, Tenn.

THE FORGES OF KERRIGAN

MANUFACTURERS OF *Weldforged*

STEEL BRACKETS AND MAST ARMS

GENERAL SALES OFFICE: 274 MADISON AVE., NEW YORK CITY

FOR WOOD OR STEEL POLE MOUNTING

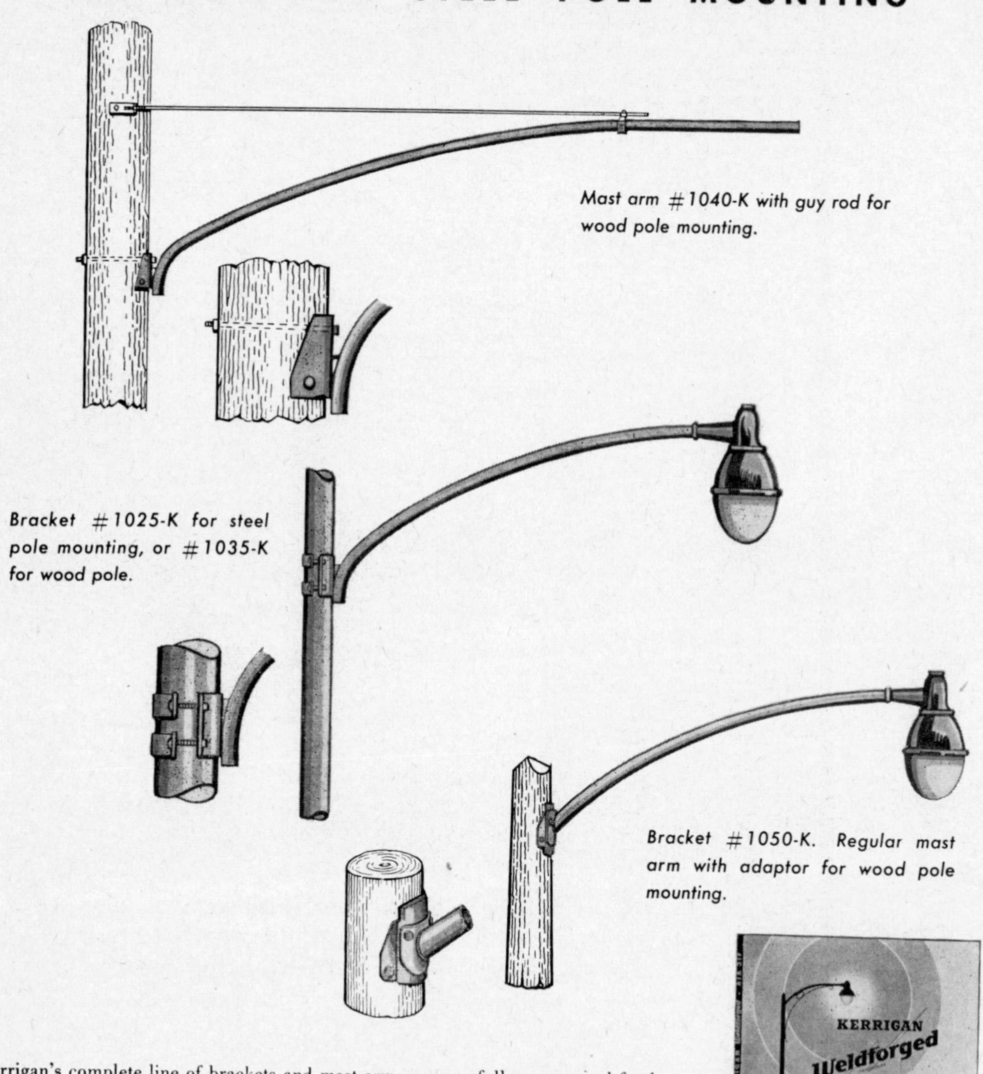

Mast arm #1040-K with guy rod for wood pole mounting.

Bracket #1025-K for steel pole mounting, or #1035-K for wood pole.

Bracket #1050-K. Regular mast arm with adaptor for wood pole mounting.

KERRIGAN
Weldforged
LIGHTING
STANDARDS
KERRIGAN IRON WORKS Inc., NASHVILLE, TENNESSEE

Kerrigan's complete line of brackets and mast arms are carefully engineered for long life, easy installation and wiring. They meet all I. E. S. street lighting recommendations. So, take advantage of your wood poles now in place and brighten up your city or town.

LET US HELP YOU!

solve your city's lighting problems. Send for our FREE catalog containing engineering data and installation views. It shows how simple installation really is.

MILLERBERND MANUFACTURING CO.

WINSTED, MINNESOTA

ELITE Model—Classic beauty with super-strength! No other lighting standard matches its clean, modern design. Its gentle curve forms a natural wireway, free from sharp bends.

1. Continuous taper, cold roll-formed.
2. Wide selection of mastarm types.
3. Choice of simplified base styles.
4. A complete line of accessories.
5. Special designs from stock components.

ADVANCED DESIGN

OCTA·TUBE

LIGHTING STANDARDS

for every thorofare lighting requirement...

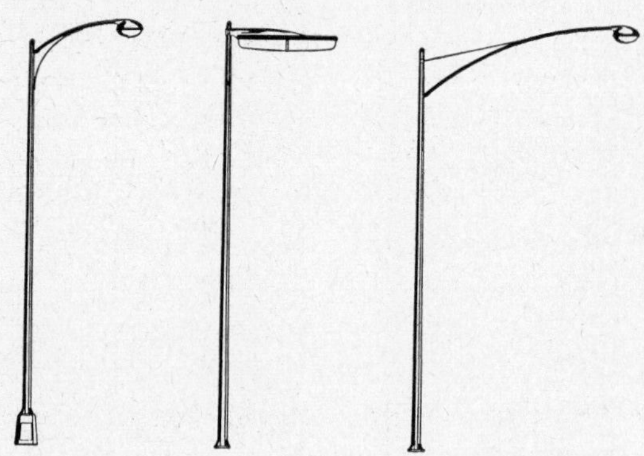

OCTA-TUBES are fabricated of High-Strength steel for extra service life. Advanced designs to meet every need for lighting modernization, as well as styles and types to match existing installations.

Write for Bulletin OTA

MILLERBERND MANUFACTURING CO.

WINSTED, MINNESOTA

TYPICAL LOCATIONS OF MILLERBERND LIGHTING STANDARDS:

Aberdeen, S. D.
Battle Creek, Mich.
Butte, Mont.
Cedar Rapids, Iowa
Cleveland, Ohio
Dallas, Texas
Davenport, Iowa
Denver, Colo.
Des Moines, Iowa
Detroit, Mich.
Dubuque, Iowa
Duluth, Minn.
Elko, Nev.
Fargo, N. D.
Gary, Ind.
Grand Forks, N. D.
Havre, Mont.
Helena, Mont.
Huntington, W. Va.
Kalamazoo, Mich.
La Crosse, Wisc.
La Grande, Ore.
Lafayette, La.
Lake Charles, La.
Lansing, Mich.
Lexington, Ky.
Lincoln, Nebr.
Lincoln Park, Mich.
Madison, Wisc.
Manchester, Conn.
Mankato, Minn.
Milwaukee, Wisc.
Minneapolis, Minn.
Minot, N. D.
Newport News, Va.
Ogden, Utah
Omaha, Nebr.
Paducah, Ky.
Pasadena, Texas
Port Arthur, Texas
Portsmouth, Va.
Pocatello, Idaho
Provo, Utah
Rochester, Minn.
Rock Island, Ill.
Rockford, Ill.
Royal Oak, Mich.
St. Paul, Minn.
Salt Lake City, Utah
Sheridan, Wyo.
Shillington, Pa.
Springfield, Mo.
Tacoma, Wash.
Waco, Texas
Warwick, Va.
Waterloo, Iowa
Watertown, S. D.
Waukegan, Ill.
Wichita, Kans.
Youngstown, Ohio
and hundreds more

FLUORESCENT ELITE Model—The ultimate in graceful beauty for fluorescents . . . this fine standard is of simplified design for reduced costs. Utilizing high-strength steel, it is available in all popular mounting heights.

MILLERBERND MANUFACTURING CO.

WINSTED, MINNESOTA

101 OF THE HUNDREDS OF LOCATIONS OF MILLERBERND TOWERS:

Winsted, Minn.
Sparta, Wisc.
Wagner, S.D.
Carroll, Iowa
Poplar, Mont.
Lorain, Ohio
Menominee, Mich.
Spring Valley, Ill.
Minot, N.D.
Fremont, Nebr.
Denver City, Texas
Lowell, Oregon
Yacolt, Wash.
Demopolis, Ala.
Austin, Minn.
Tomah, Wisc.
Keokuk, Iowa
DeSoto, Wisc.
Williston, N.D.
Alexandria, Minn.
Wisconsin Dells, Wisc.
Chamberlain, S.D.
Ellsworth, Wisc.
Steelton, Minn.
Kermit, Texas
Rice Lake, Wisc.
Huron, S.D.
International Falls, Minn.
La Farge, Wisc.
Brainerd, Minn.
Sisseton, S.D.
Barron, Wisc.
Ames, Iowa
Glenwood, Minn.
Omaha, Nebr.
Wichita Falls, Texas
Bismarck, N.D.
Des Moines, Iowa
University of Minn.
Riverdale, N.D.
Brookings, S.D.
Shakopee, Minn.
Graettinger, Iowa
Marinette, Wisc.
Chaska, Minn.
Winner, S.D.
Soldiers Grove, Wisc.
Britton, S.D.
Thief River Falls, Minn.
Manawa, Wisc.
Bemidji, Minn.
Flandreau, S.D.
Kewaunee, Wisc.
Hopkins, Minn.
Hastings, Nebr.
New York Mills, Minn.
Oelwein, Iowa
Hurley, Wisc.
Sherburn, Minn.
West Salem, Wisc.
St. Charles, Minn.
Arlington, S.D.
Morris, Minn.
Waukesha, Wisc.
Mason City, Iowa
Anoka, Minn.
Cornell, Wisc.
Highmore, S.D.
Stephenson, Mich.
Sidney, Mont.
Canton, Ohio
Wink, Texas
York, Nebr.
Marquette Univ.
Waseca, Minn.
Muscoda, Wisc.
Pickstown, S.D.
La Crosse, Wisc.
Oakes, N.D.
Maple Lake, Minn.
Clinton, Iowa
Franksville, Wisc.
Edina, Minn.
Aberdeen, S.D.
N. St. Paul, Minn.
Marshfield, Wisc.
Perham, Minn.
Cumberland, Wisc.
Valley City, N.D.
New Ulm, Minn.
Park Falls, Wisc.
Excelsior, Minn.
Sioux City, Iowa
Cashton, Wisc.
Bloomington, Minn.
New London, Wisc.
Milbank, S.D.
Jordan, Minn.
Osceola, Wisc.
Enderlin, N.D.
Abbotsford, Wisc.

Write for Bulletin F-102

MILLERBERND FLOODLIGHTING TOWERS in use at Maple Lake, Minn. ball park (above) and at Garrison Dam, N.D. (left).

REVERE ELECTRIC MANUFACTURING CO.

6009-17 Broadway — Chicago 40, Ill.

A Complete Line of Poles and Luminaires for STREET LIGHTING

The ENDOVAL

"2 in 1" LUMINAIRE

Reversible Slip Fitter Provides 10° Tilt and Horizontal Mounting

Designed for all roadways where high levels of glare-free illumination are required. Modern, streamlined, easily serviced, using 11,000 and 21,000 lumen Mercury Lamps. "W" Modified Parabolic Reflector provides sharp, vertical cut-off and proper IES distribution patterns. Reflector design assures positive alignment at all times. Housing is die-cast Aluminum Alloy, light in weight, strong, uniform, attractive in size and shape, finer finish. Ample wiring area, "easy-on and off" glassware holding ring. Many other features combine to make it the most outstanding Unit on the Market.

STREET LIGHTING POLES

Revere ASA-Standard Street Lighting Poles are made of one-piece tapered octagonal 11 gauge steel with cast steel base with covers welded to shaft. Top of Pole adorned with cast steel finial. Mast Arms of 2" Standard Steel Pipe mounted with Revere "Kwiklok" Fittings for fast, easy, secure mounting. Sub-bases with removable doors provided to house Transformers. Nominal mounting heights 20, 25 and 30 foot. Mast arms 4 to 15 foot for single or double lights.

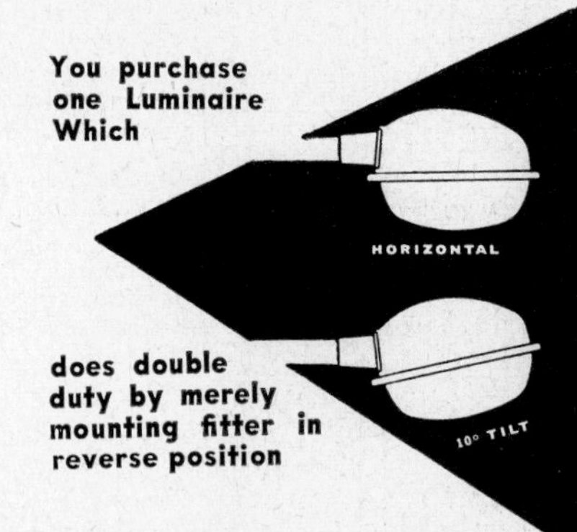

The STAR★LUX

MERCURY or INCANDESCENT LUMINAIRES

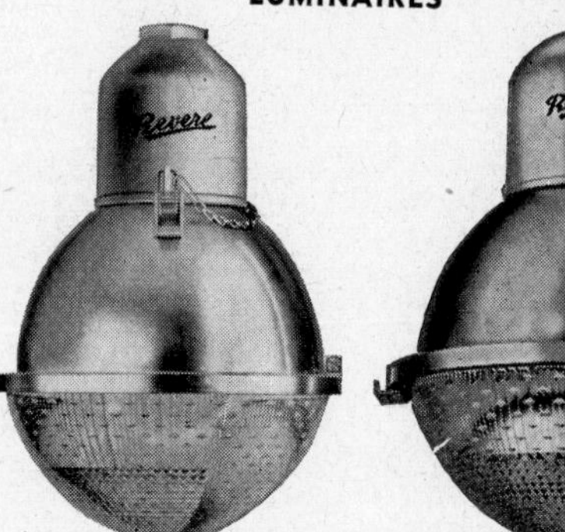

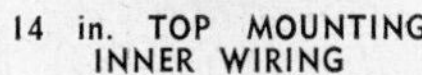

14 in. TOP MOUNTING INNER WIRING

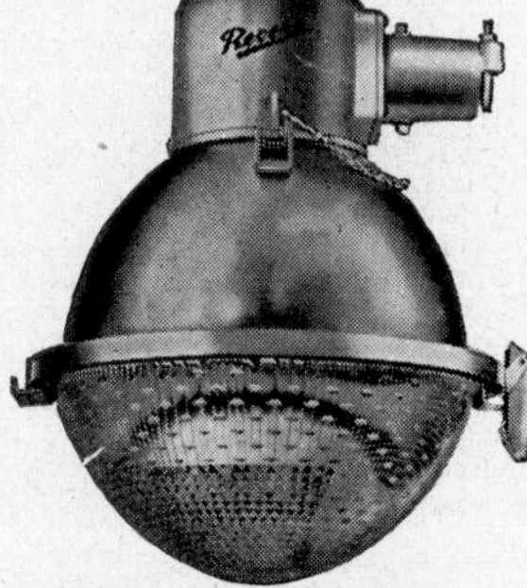

14 in. SLIP FITTER MOUNTING INNER WIRING

Ideal for low cost traffic safety lighting. Have Standard "ASA" metal heads for 2500 to 10,000 lumen incandescent lamps, series or multiple. 14 in. Star-Lux will also accommodate 250 to 400 Watt Mercury Lamps. 10 in. size designed for 1000 or 2500 Lumen incandescent lamps.

All "IES" distribution patterns are provided. Available in clamp band or automatic latch construction, also with top or side mounting latch collar heads for external or internal wiring.

The Urban-lite

END MOUNTING MERCURY LUMINAIRE

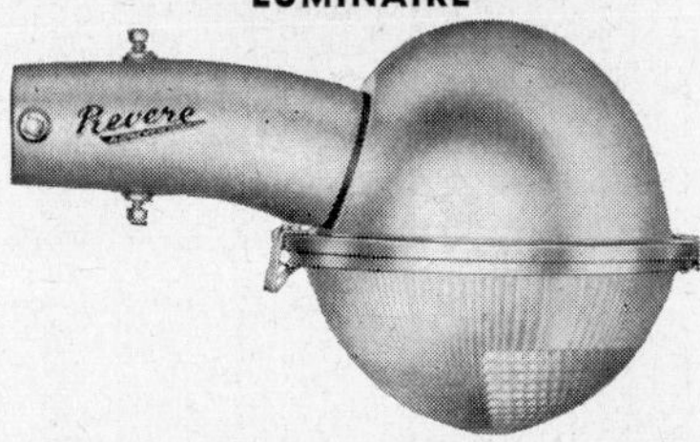

An "economy type" Luminaire for 250W/H5, 175 Watt H22 or 100W/H4 Mercury Lamps or Incandescent Lamps up to 4000 Lumens. Alzak processed aluminum reflector combined with Revere-Corning prismatic glassware produces distribution patterns conforming to ASA-IES Types II or II-A with beams of varying widths.

Write for Literature

REVERE ELECTRIC MANUFACTURING CO.

6009-17 Broadway Chicago 40, Ill.

HINGED AND RIGID POLES
OPEN AND ENCLOSED FLOODLIGHTS
FOR SPORTS AND GENERAL PURPOSE LIGHTING

ALZAK ENCLOSED FLOOD

4210 SERIES

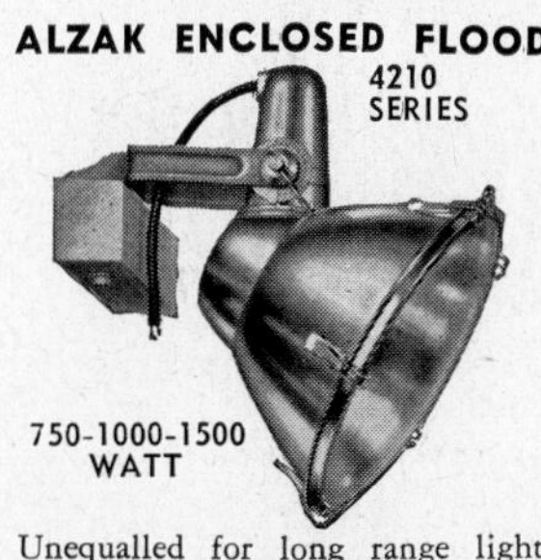

750-1000-1500 WATT

Unequalled for long range lighting. Alzak Aluminum housing. Dust and weather-tite. Provides maximum light output. Wide choice of beam control. Degree marked for easy setting.

OPEN OR ENCLOSED 7100 SERIES 12"-14"-16" LENS SIZES

Very efficient Units embodying many outstanding features. Quality construction throughout. Alzak Aluminum Housings.

REAR SERVICE FLOOD

2000 SERIES

750-1000-1500 WATT

18" and 20" lens sizes. Lens remains stationary when servicing. No breakage of glass—no loose parts to dangle in wind. Alzak Aluminum housing.

FAMOUS ELIPTOR

300 to 1500 WATT general service
400 WATT MERCURY

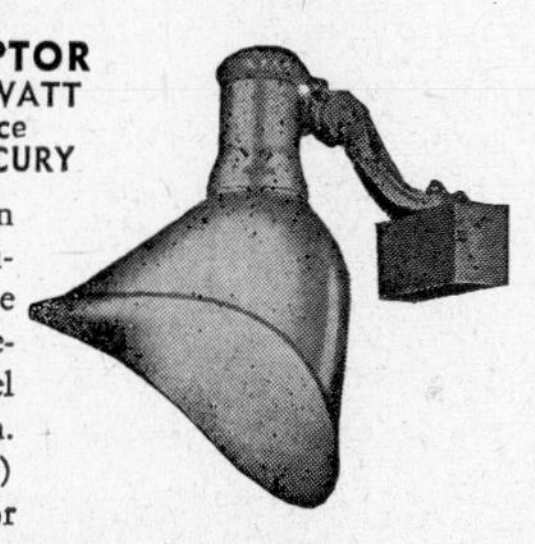

A master-piece in design and efficiency. Available in colored Porcelain enameled steel or all aluminum. (Green standard.) Degree marked for all settings.

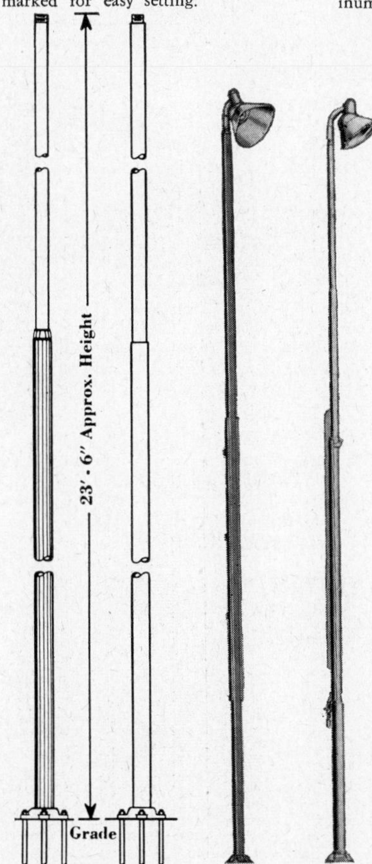

Separable One-Piece CORRUGATED OR ROUND POLES for various types of mounting

199 Series Hinged Pole

300 Series Round Hinged Pole

POLES

Revere is headquarters for Poles of all types and sizes. Whatever the lighting job—there is a Revere Pole to fit requirements from 20 to 60 ft. in height. The Corrugated and Round Series illustrated at left is for 24 ft. mounting height. They are made of separable sections of 3½" O.D. and 2" standard steel pipe.

The one-piece Poles are of welded construction—made of 3½" and 2⅞" dia. corrugated or round pipe. Shafts come with a variety of bases, or poles can be mounted in concrete. Pole tops have 2" threaded pipe stubs.

The Poles at right are fabricated in a range of mounting heights from 20 to 60 ft., for loads up to 10 floodlights. Poles of greater capacity and greater length made special. Our long experience in constructing Poles is your guide to quality and satisfaction.

HINGED TYPES

Revere Hinged Poles were perfected and introduced over 25 years ago and to this day are unequalled in design and efficiency. Made in Square, Square Tapered and Round Types.

Whatever the lighting need we have a pole to fit it!

Write for Literature

3" THREADED PIPE STUB
"C" DIA. AT TOP
"A" MOUNTING HEIGHT
3" x 5" HAND HOLE
2" PIPE COUPLING WELDED TO POLE
"B" DEPTH OF INSERTION

ELEVATION BASE & BOLT MOUNTING

ELEVATION CONCRETE MOUNTING

REVERE ELECTRIC MANUFACTURING CO.

6009-17 Broadway — Chicago 40, Ill.

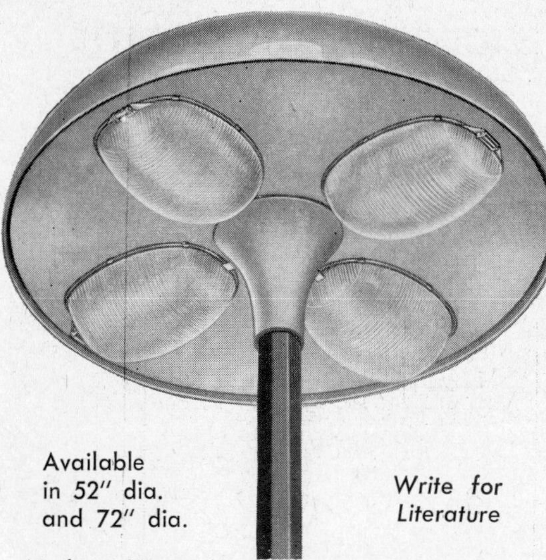

Available in 52" dia. and 72" dia.

Write for Literature

Nothing like it for Parking Areas, Swimming Pools, Playgrounds, etc.

Embodies four Mercury Luminaires scientifically arranged in its spherical dome to produce a more comfortable light that makes seeing easier.
Housing of 52" Unit is made of porcelain enameled steel. Available in colors (green standard). Mounting fitter slips over 4" O.D. shaft.
72" Unit is of spun aluminum. Its larger dome is deeper and more spectacular.

TYPICAL INSTALLATION OF ULTRA-LITES IN LARGE PARKING FACILITY

RIGID POLES USED WITH NO. 3357-NP INCANDESCENT FLOODLIGHTS

Where mounting heights of 20, 25 or 30 foot are desired the "560" series Poles make an ideal installation. Pole has a capacity of five floodlights which can be used in combinations of incandescent and mercury.

New "4 in 1 Spectacular" for large area illumination

The "Ultra-Lite"

TRADE MARK REGISTERED U. S. PAT. OFF.

- ★ *Provides abundant light for both vertical and horizontal surfaces*
- ★ *Achieves more light with fewer poles and fixtures*
- ★ *Gives lighted area greater impetus*
- ★ *Reduces maintenance and repair costs*
- ★ *Produces a square light pattern*

for mounting on COR-TEN HEAVY-DUTY HINGED POLE or OCTAGONAL TAPERED RIGID POLES

COR-TEN Pole is made of a new special low alloy steel of high strength offering weight reduction and increased resistance to atmospheric corrosion.

The RIGID POLE is of octagonal design fabricated of 11 ga. steel—7" wide at bottom tapering to 3¾" at top. Ornamental cast steel base is welded to bottom. Illustration shows pole mounted on transformer Housing.

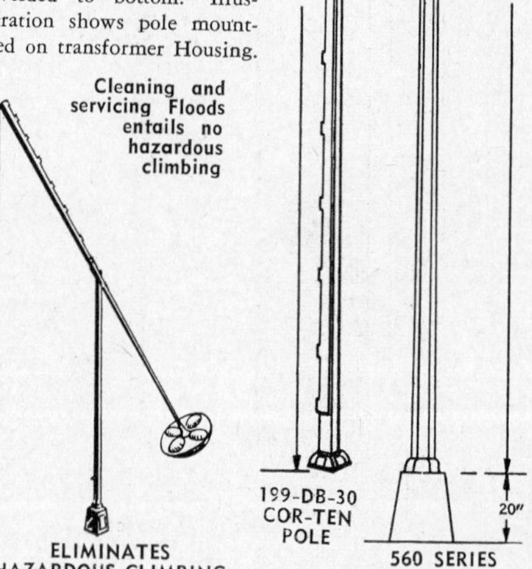

ELIMINATES HAZARDOUS CLIMBING

199-DB-30 COR-TEN POLE

560 SERIES RIGID POLE

REVERE ELECTRIC MANUFACTURING CO.

6009-17 Broadway Chicago 40, Ill.

A COMPLETE LINE OF LIGHTING EQUIPMENT FOR LARGE OR SMALL AIRPORTS

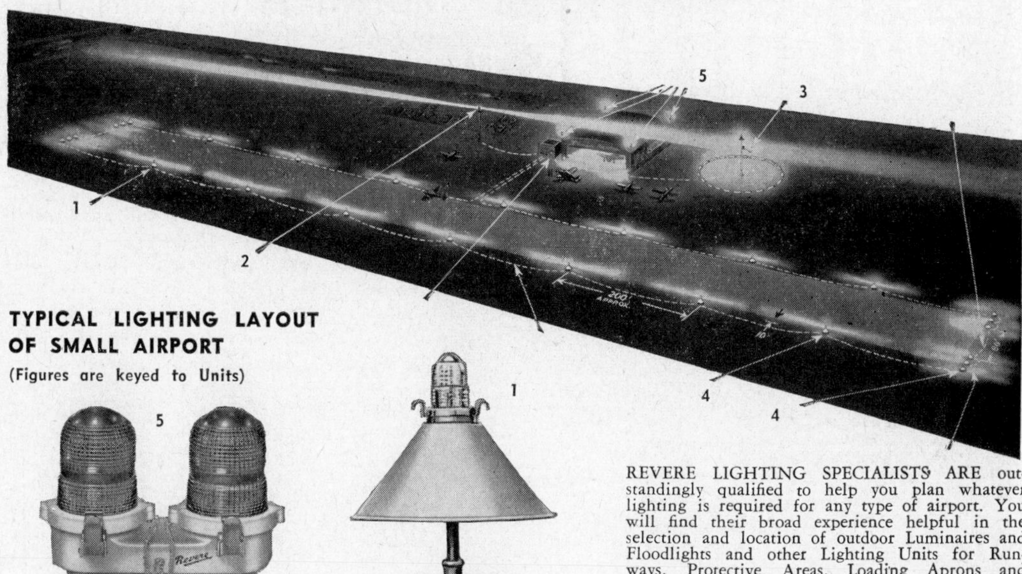

TYPICAL LIGHTING LAYOUT OF SMALL AIRPORT

(Figures are keyed to Units)

5

SINGLE and DOUBLE OBSTRUCTION LIGHTS

1

ELEVATED RUNWAY MARKERS and TAXIWAY LIGHTS

REVERE LIGHTING SPECIALISTS ARE outstandingly qualified to help you plan whatever lighting is required for any type of airport. You will find their broad experience helpful in the selection and location of outdoor Luminaires and Floodlights and other Lighting Units for Runways, Protective Areas, Loading Aprons and Working Areas.

In addition to the approved units shown here we manufacture a wide variety of general purpose floodlights, cluster-lites, Mercury and Incandescent Luminaires, also Hinged and Rigid Poles for Parking Areas, Perimeter Lighting, etc. Do not hesitate to call on us to review your lighting needs with you.

2

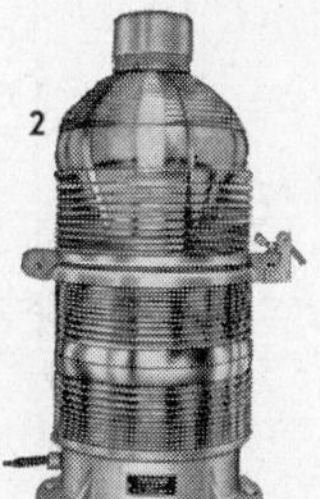

CODE BEACONS and FLASHERS

4

ULTRA-HIGH INTENSITY RUNWAY MARKERS

4

BI-DIRECTIONAL HIGH INTENSITY RUNWAY MARKERS

No. 7031 FLUSH RUNWAY MARKER

Constructed in accordance with Military Spec's. Mil-L-7111-A. A strong, rugged unit that will withstand a minimum dead load of 100,000 lbs. Mounts on Deep Base at right.

4

No. 7017 DEEP BASE for 1 to 3 Transformers

Write for Literature

8 and 12 Foot Windcones

Revere 12 ft. Wind Cones are manufactured to AN-Spec. AN-I-23 for all airports. Basket is 36" in dia. Wind Cone supported on 2" steel shaft. Light assembly consists of 4-Deep Bowl Reflectors (200W/PS-30 Lamps.) An obstruction light is mounted in top center of assembly.

8 ft. Wind Cones are in accordance with C. A. A. Spec. L-807. Sock mounted on 20 ft. Revere Hinged Pole for easy, safe servicing. Pipe extension supports area lighter and obstruction light.

3

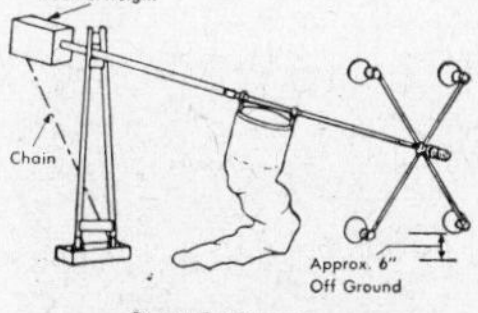

ILLUMINATED WIND CONE FIXTURE

Manufactured in accordance with Aeronautical Spec. No. AN-I-23. Sturdily constructed to withstand wind pressures offering long, dependable service. "A" Frame in accordance with CAA Spec. L-827.

THE UNION METAL MFG. COMPANY

General Offices and Factory: Canton 5, Ohio

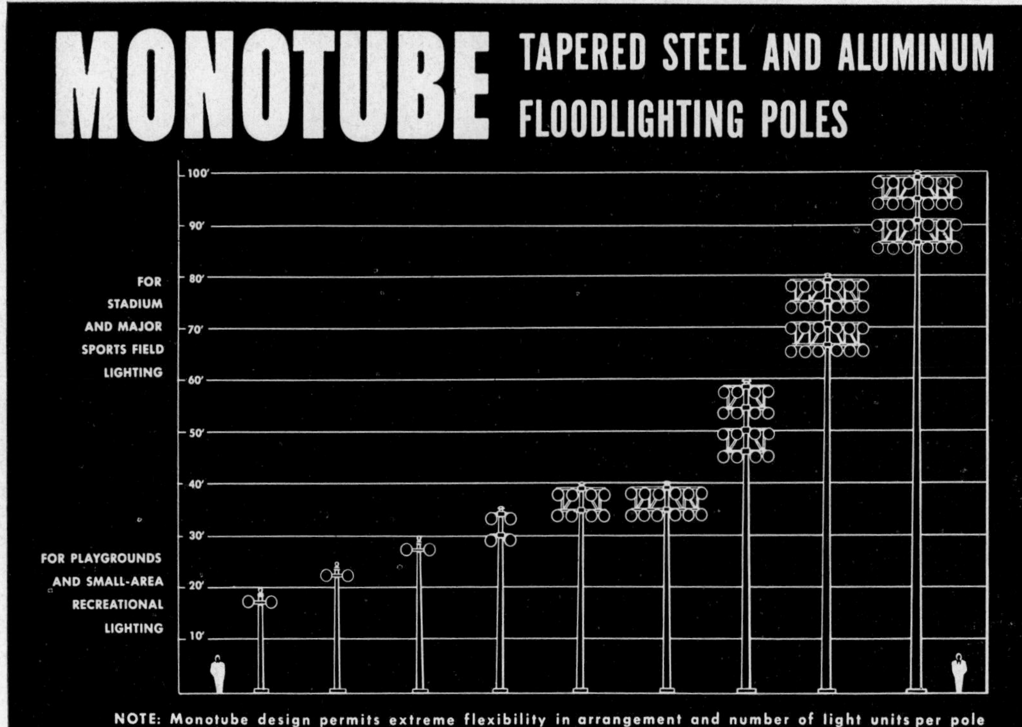

Typical Monotube stadium installation.

Monotubes floodlighting recreational area.

For the smallest recreational areas to the largest stadiums . . . there's a Monotube floodlighting pole designed to give you ideal light distribution, attractive appearance and long-life economy.

Send for a copy of Catalog No. 87, today!

THE UNION METAL MFG. COMPANY
Canton 5, Ohio

THE UNION METAL MFG. COMPANY

General Offices and Factory: Canton, Ohio

Tapered

MONOTUBE POLES

of steel
or aluminum
for every outdoor
lighting service

UNION METAL

THE UNION METAL MFG. COMPANY

Canton 5, Ohio

Monotube design features that will save time and money in your lighting modernization plans. . . .

- One piece pole construction . . . smooth, continuous taper . . . minimum maintenance requirements.
- Modern designs for residential areas, bridges, parks, highways, freeways and business streets.
- Unmatched strength to resist wind loads, icing and other stresses or shocks.
- Available in either fluted or plain round tapered styles.
- Correct heights and designs that meet all recommended good lighting practices.
- Simplified installation and wiring with either transformer or anchor base construction.

More cities use UNION METAL poles than any other type

For half a century Union Metal has been the leading manufacturer of street lighting poles.

This unmatched manufacturing, engineering, research and application experience is your best assurance of complete and lasting satisfaction.

WRITE FOR CATALOGS . . .
containing engineering data and typical installation views.

WESTINGHOUSE ELECTRIC CORPORATION

Lighting Division — Cleveland, Ohio

flood lighting

Westinghouse floodlighting units have been designed for ease of mounting, rigidity of construction, maximum service under both normal and adverse weather conditions and simplicity of maintenance. The list below is a typical sampling of the Westinghouse floodlighting range which covers from 200 to 2000 watts. Write to the Westinghouse District Office nearest you for further information.

	TYPE	DESCRIPTION
C-14	C-14NP	Floodlight Complete—Plain Lens—Specular Alzak
	C-14NS	Floodlight Complete—Stippled Lens—Specular Alzak
	C-14NV	Floodlight Complete—Ver. Spread Lens—Specular Alzak
	C-14NH	Floodlight Complete—Hor. Spread Lens—Specular Alzak
	C-14WP	Floodlight Complete—Plain Lens—Diffuse Alzak
	C-14WS	Floodlight Complete—Stippled Lens—Diffuse Alzak
	C-14WV	Floodlight Complete—Ver. Spread Lens—Diffuse Alzak
	C-14WH	Floodlight Complete—Hor. Spread Lens—Diffuse Alzak
AH 16	AH-16WP	Floodlight Complete—Plain Lens—Specular Alzak
	AH-16WS	Floodlight Complete—Stippled Lens—Specular Alzak
	AH-16WH	Floodlight Complete—Spread Lens—Specular Alzak
	AH-16NP	Floodlight Complete—Plain Lens—Diffuse Alzak
	AH-16NS	Floodlight Complete—Stippled Lens—Diffuse Alzak
	AH-16NH	Floodlight Complete—Spread Lens—Diffuse Alzak
VEK 16	VEK-16EP	Floodlight Complete—Plain Lens—2" Post Top Bracket
	VEK-16P	Floodlight Complete—Stippled Lens—2" Post Top Bracket
	VEK-16S	Floodlight Complete—Spread Lens—2" Post Top Bracket
	VEK-16R	Floodlight Complete—Plain Lens—2" Post Top Bracket for A-H1 Lamp
	VEK-16AP	Floodlight Complete—Plain Lens—2" Post Top Bracket for E-H1 & J-H1 Lamp
AFA 16	AFA-16C	Floodlight Complete with Cross Arm Bracket
	AFA-16P	Floodlight Complete with 2" Post Top Bracket
	AFA-16S	Floodlight Complete with Swingover Bracket
VRC 18	VRC-18NO	Floodlight Complete—No Lens—Specular Alzak
	VRC-18NP	Floodlight Complete—Plain Lens—Specular Alzak
	VRC-18NS	Floodlight Complete—Stippled Lens—Specular Alzak
	VRC-18NR	Floodlight Complete—Spread Lens—Specular Alzak
	VRC-18WO	Floodlight Complete—No Lens—Diffuse Alzak
	VRC-18WP	Floodlight Complete—Plain Lens—Diffuse Alzak
	VRC-18WS	Floodlight Complete—Stippled Lens—Diffuse Alzak
	VRC-18WR	Floodlight Complete—Spread Lens—Diffuse Alzak
	NOTE: All equipped with Swingover Brackets.	
PAL 2	PAL-0	Reflector Assembly Less Spots
	PAL-1	Reflector Assembly and One Spot
	PAL-2	Reflector Assembly and Two Spots
	PAL-3	Reflector Assembly and Three Spots

street lighting

Westinghouse street lighting applies the "science of "seeing" to the roadway lighting problem. The equipment, a minor portion of which is shown below, is designed to promote safety, convenience and increased attractiveness of the streets lighted. Westinghouse Application Engineers are on call to help you classify your needs, prepare a plan and provide a solution to your street lighting problems. Contact the nearest Westinghouse District Office.

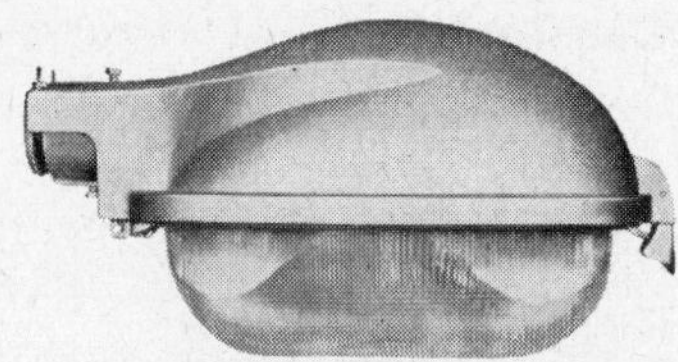
Type OV-20

voltage classifications

HV series heads, 5000 volt class, are for use on straight series circuits, either 6.6 or 20 amperes.

HV series heads can also be used without insulating current transformers on 20 amp series circuits or on 6.6 amp series circuits 25 KW regulators and below.

LV series heads are for use on secondary of insulating current transformers.

LV series heads can also be used without insulating transformers on 20 amp series circuit 7½ kw regulators and below; 6.6 amp straight series circuit 2 kw regulators only.

Multiple heads can be used on any multiple circuit up to 600 volts.

TYPE OV-20 LUMINAIRES

LAMP	LUMENS	WATTS
C-H5	11,000	250
D-H5	9,500	250
E-H1	21,000	400
J-H1	20,000	400
A-H17	21,000	425
B-H17	20,000	425

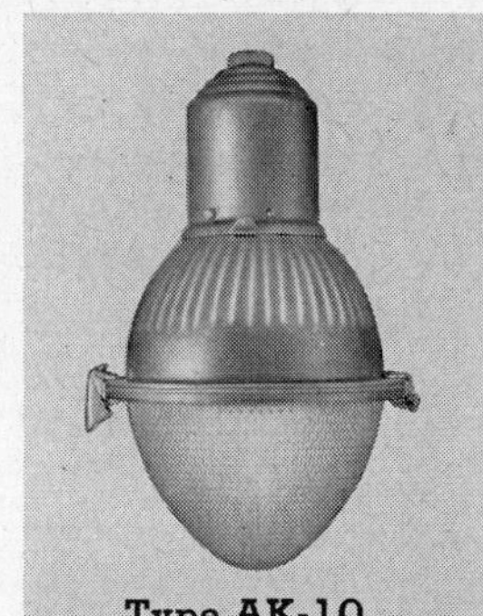
Type AK-10

TYPE AK-10 LUMINAIRES

TYPE	CLASS	LAMPS
HIGH VOLTAGE	5,000 Volts	**Incandescent** 2,500 to 10,000 lumen
LOW VOLTAGE	600 Volts	**Mercury** C-H5, A-H1 or E-H1
MOGUL MULTIPLE	600 Volts	

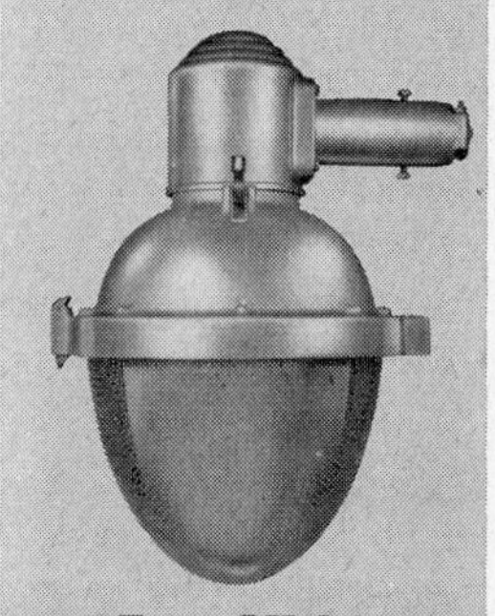
Type AK-14

TYPE AK-14 LUMINAIRES

TYPE	CLASS	LAMPS
HIGH VOLTAGE	5,000 Volts	**Incandescent** 4,000 to 15,000 lumen
LOW VOLTAGE	600 Volts	**Mercury** C-H5 A-H1 E-H1
MOGUL MULTIPLE	600 Volts	

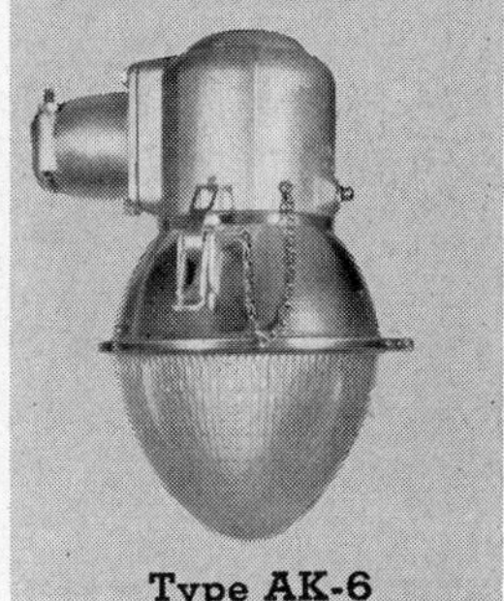
Type AK-6

TYPE AK-6 LUMINAIRES

TYPE	CLASS	LAMPS
HIGH VOLTAGE	5,000 Volts	1,000 and 2,500 lumen incandescent.
LOW VOLTAGE	600 Volts	
MOGUL MULTIPLE	600 Volts	

accessories

In addition to planning new street and highway lighting systems, the Westinghouse Application Engineers are versed in solving the problems presented in expanding and modifying existing lighting systems. With almost every conceivable lighting accessory available and years of "know-how" experience to rely on, Westinghouse can help you modernize your municipality's lighting at reasonable cost and save money on year-to-year maintenance.

Constant Current Transformers

Type CPH

TYPE CPH, 60 CYCLES, PRIMARY 2400 VOLTS 6.6 AMPERE SECONDARY—WITH 2160 VOLT TAP

Rating KW	Secondary Open Circuit Voltage	Normal Secondary Load Voltage	Style Number (Standard)
10	2090	1515	1803 632
15	3090	2270	1803 633
20	4090	3030	1803 634
25	5110	3790	1803 635
30	6130	4550	1803 636

Type CPH Transformer is an oil insulated, self-cooled automatically controlled unit which prevents the current from varying more than one percent from rated values within rated capacities.

Type CSPH transformer is a "package unit" containing Type AN Oil Switch, Type PC Relay, Fusible Protective Links, and De-Ion® Gap Arrestors in addition to complete Core and Coil Assembly.

TYPE CSPH, 60 CYCLES, PRIMARY 2400 VOLTS 6.6 AMPERE SECONDARY—WITH 2160 VOLT TAP

Rating KW	Secondary Open Circuit Voltage	Normal Secondary Load Voltage	Style Number (Standard)
10	2090	1515	1803 703
15	3090	2270	1803 704
20	4090	3030	1803 705
25	5110	3790	1803 706
30	6130	4550	1803 707

Type CSPH

BALLASTS

Pole Top Type 4⅛" Slipfitter

Pole Base Type Wiping Nipples

BALLAST FOR MERCURY VAPOR LAMPS

LAMP RATING		Primary Circuit 60 Cycles Only	POLE BASE	POLE TOP
Lumens	Watts		Style Number	Style Number
20,000	400	120/240 Volts (High P.F.) Mult. Circuit	1760 048 1760 049	1760 341
20,000	400	6.6 Amp. Series	1760 548	1760 553
11,000	250	120/240 Volts (High P.F.) Mult. Circuit	1569 894	1566 039
11,000	250	6.6 Amp. Series	1121 083	1566 034

In addition to constant current transformers, ballasts, and luminaires as covered in these pages, Westinghouse offers a complete line of fittings, attachments, reflectors, holders, poles, glassware, standards and brackets, sockets, relays, switches and photo-electric control. With such a preponderance of interchangeable equipment available, the Westinghouse Application Engineer is able to suggest the best solution to any given lighting problem.

airport lighting

Modern Airport Lighting consists essentially of runway lights of either medium or high intensity with associated auxiliary equipment such as beacons, wind cones, obstruction lights, and the necessary power and control equipment. Westinghouse equipment conforms to CAA requirements and matches ANC color codes. You can be sure if Westinghouse lighting engineers help with your problems.

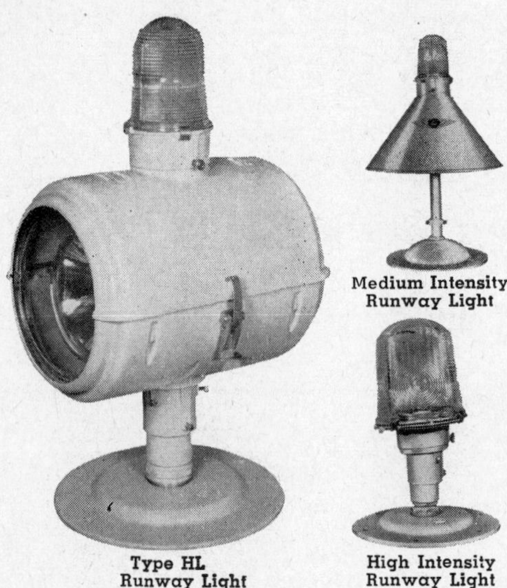

Type HL Runway Light

Medium Intensity Runway Light

High Intensity Runway Light

runway lights

Type LD—Medium Intensity Runway Light for non-instrument runways and taxiways. (CAA Spec. L-802).

Type US—Low Cost High Intensity Runway Light for instrument type runways. (CAA Spec. L-819).

Type HL—Deluxe, economical High intensity runway light for bad weather landings or instrument runways. (CAA Spec. L-820).

auxiliary equipment

Rotating beacons, code and hazard beacons, wind cones, angle-of-approach indicators, and obstruction lights are used on and around airports.

power and control

All airport lighting equipment should use specially designed control equipment to operate correctly. Constant current regulators for supplying series runway circuits, brightness control assemblies, and selector switching assemblies are all available.

underwater floodlighting

Westinghouse Aqualux® swimming pool floodlights are designed to provide all of the advantages of wet niche illumination together with low installation cost and minimum maintenance servicing. Floodlights are easily removed for relamping or servicing without draining the pool. Clear lens units are Underwriters' Lab., Inc. listed.

WS-8

for pools 50 feet or less in width

TYPE NO.	DESCRIPTION
WS-8R5	Floodlight Complete—Spread Lens—500 Watt
WS-8C5	Floodlight Complete—Clear Lens—500 Watt
WS-8S5	Floodlight Complete—Stippled Lens—500 Watt
WS-8C2	Floodlight Complete—Clear Lens—250 Watt
WS-8R2	Floodlight Complete—Spread Lens—250 Watt
WS-8S2	Floodlight Complete—Stippled Lens—250 Watt

CS-14

for pools 50 feet or more in width

TYPE NO.	DESCRIPTION
CS-14CR	Floodlight Complete for Receptacle Mounting—Clear Lens
CS-14RR	Floodlight Complete for Receptacle Mounting—Spread Lens
CS-14SR	Floodlight Complete for Receptacle Mounting—Stippled Lens
CS-14CN	Floodlight Complete for Niche Mounting—Clear Lens
CS-14RN	Floodlight Complete for Niche Mounting—Spread Lens
CS-14SN	Floodlight Complete for Niche Mounting—Stippled Lens

THE MODERN, LOGICAL WAY TO GET THE MOST ADVANCED IDEAS AND DESIGNS INTO YOUR OUTDOOR LIGHTING PLANS

STREET AND HIGHWAY—Illustrates and describes the most up-to-the-minute all aluminum standards and supports for street and highway lighting as well as for special applications. *Write for P & K Catalog "Lighting Standards."*

Arms and Brackets of specially designed, high strength aluminum alloys, for wood, metal or concrete pole mounting. Provides modern, high-efficiency lighting on existing poles at minimum cost. *Write for P & K Catalog BR-10.*

FLUORESCENT—A new, simple, advanced design to provide high level, glarefree light for whiteways, as well as for commercial installation. LUXaire (R) Fluorescent Luminaires are available in single and multiple units with or without companion designed standards and davits. *Write for P & K Catalog "LUXaire."*

AREA LIGHTING—This catalog offers a wealth of ideas in the most modern and practical concepts of area lighting. Shows many unusual and interesting architectural applications of luminaires, standards and davits used in recent installations. *Write for P & K Catalog L-2.*

PFAFF & KENDALL

84 FOUNDRY ST., NEWARK 5, N. J.

THE ELRECO CORPORATION

2917 CORMANY AVE., CINCINNATI 25, OHIO

Standards that really stand up!

Here's proof that Elreco tubular steel standards give you extra strength—for years of service with minimum upkeep and replacement. Write for Catalog SL for complete specifications.

STANDARDS for:

Street Lighting
Flood Lighting
Traffic Signals

News photo of fire engine shortly after it struck Elreco pole. Absolutely no pole repairs were necessary.

Since 1892

THE E LRECO CORPORATION

THE FISHER-PIERCE CO., INC.

79 Pearl Street, So. Braintree • Boston 35, Mass.

FISHER-PIERCE

for every lighting system requirement

PHOTOELECTRIC CONTROLS

The extreme versatility and quality of Fisher-Pierce photoelectric lighting controls are evidenced by their widespread use over the past eight years, in controlling hundreds of street lighting systems . . . aircraft obstruction and beacon lights . . . outdoor signs and store window lights . . . parking, loading and storage area lights . . . poultry house and roadside telephone illumination, etc. All Fisher-Pierce controls employ a basic circuit whose dependability, ruggedness and trouble-free performance have been proven in use.

SERIES 63300C CONTROLS

Rugged, easily installed, accessible units for switching up to 3000 watts of lighting load. For operation at 105-130 or 210-250 V, 50-60 cycles. Standard models come with SPST, SPDT, or DPST power contactors. Special models are available with a switching capacity of 6000 watts. The electronic chassis is enclosed in a weatherproof watt-hour meter case assembly which plugs into a standard meter socket. The new 63300C design represents the results of eight years' extensive, specialized experience in the field.

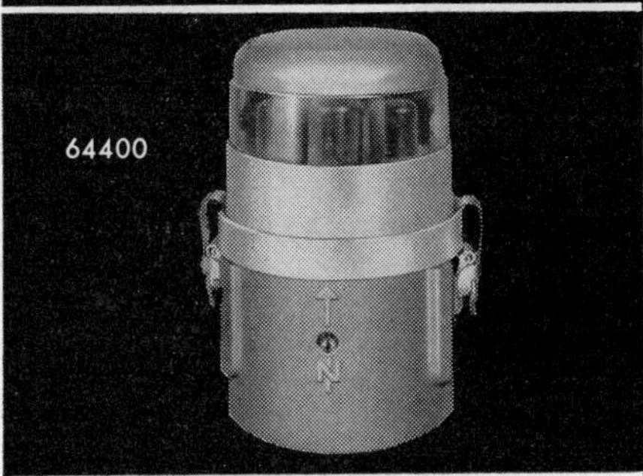

SERIES 64400 CONTROLS

Small, compact, low cost units for switching 1000 watts of incandescent, mercury or sodium vapor lamps at 120 V, 50-60 cycles. Designed for use as an integral part of various manufacturers' luminaires, as well as for ballast, pole top, cross arm, standard and other mountings. Low initial cost and low maintenance make the use of one Series 64400 control per lamp economically practical for new street lighting installations and isolated locations.

THE *nitelighter*

. . . for automatic control of home lights

An inexpensive, compact, automatic control made especially for domestic use. Operates on 110 volts AC, switches up to 300 watts. Plug lamp to be controlled into NITELIGHTER plug, face "eye" toward window; living room, hall, garage lights, etc. go on at dusk, off at dawn automatically and without attention. You'll never come home to darkness. Protects the home when you're away. Get it at your dealer, or if he cannot supply you, send a check or money order for $15.95. A NITELIGHTER will be sent postpaid and insured.

MULTIPLE RELAYS FOR SWITCHING LOW VOLTAGE OUTDOOR LIGHTING CIRCUITS

Fisher-Pierce multiple relays incorporate a maintenance-free mercury plunger relay conservatively rated to switch 30 amps. at 110-115 volts AC. Series 100 relay is housed in a standard meter case and is available with or without line and coil protective equipment. The low cost Series 200 (not shown) is housed in a weatherproof cast aluminum case. Both series are designed for outdoor use as pilot wire control or for cascading street lighting circuits. Available with normally open or normally closed relays.

Complete Specifications and Data Available on Request

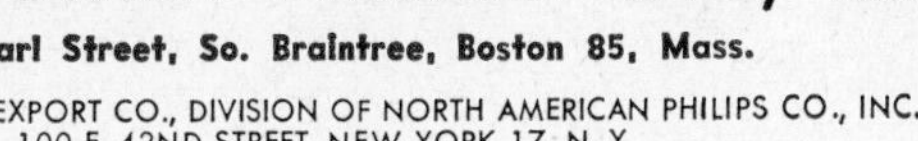

THE FISHER-PIERCE CO., INC.

72 Pearl Street, So. Braintree, Boston 85, Mass.

EXPORT: PHILIPS EXPORT CO., DIVISION OF NORTH AMERICAN PHILIPS CO., INC.
100 E. 42ND STREET, NEW YORK 17, N. Y.

GRAYBAR ELECTRIC COMPANY, INC.

Executive Offices
420 Lexington Avenue
New York 17, N. Y.

ONE CALL SOURCE RESPONSIBILITY

for everything electrical!

STREET LIGHTING · FLOOD LIGHTING · INTERIOR LIGHTING · TRAFFIC SIGNALS HORNS AND SIRENS · COMMUNICATION EQUIPMENT · CIVIL DEFENSE REQUIREMENTS · WIRING SUPPLIES · PORTABLE EMERGENCY LIGHTING UNITS

When municipal plans include an electrical installation, call on your nearby Graybar Representative.

He can supply facts and figures to help you or your electrical contractor make ready for fast action when the time is right. He'll also obtain for you the services of Graybar Specialists to assist in solving out-of-the-ordinary problems in any electrical field.

Check the list below — you're sure to find a Graybar office or warehouse located conveniently close to you. Remember — always call Graybar first! 6001

There's a Graybar Office or warehouse near you!

Abilene, Texas
Akron, Ohio
Albany, N. Y.
Allentown, Pa.
Amarillo, Texas
Arlington, Texas
Asheville, N. C.
Atlanta, Ga.
Austin, Texas
Baltimore, Md.
Baton Rouge, La.
Beaumont, Texas
Binghamton, N. Y.
Birmingham, Ala.
Boise, Idaho
Boston, Mass.
Bristol, Tenn.
Buffalo, N. Y.
Butte, Montana
Charleston, W. Va.
Charlotte, N. C.
Chattanooga, Tenn.
Chicago, Ill.
Cincinnati, Ohio
Cleveland, Ohio
Clifton, N. J.
Columbia, S. C.
Columbus, Ohio
Corpus Christi, Texas
Dallas, Texas
Davenport, Iowa
Dayton, Ohio
Denver, Colo.
Des Moines, Iowa
Detroit, Mich.
Duluth, Minn.
Durham, N. C.
El Paso, Texas
Erie, Pa.
Eugene, Ore.
Evansville, Ind.
Flint, Mich.
Fort Lauderdale, Fla.
Fort Worth, Texas
Fresno, Calif.
Garden City, N. Y.
Grand Rapids, Mich.
Green Bay, Wisc.
Greenville, S. C.
Hammond, Ind.
Harrisburg, Pa.
Houston, Texas
Indianapolis, Ind.
Jackson, Miss.
Jacksonville, Fla.
Kansas City, Mo.
Knoxville, Tenn.
Lake Charles, La.
Lansing, Mich.
Lexington, Ky.
Little Rock, Ark.
Long Beach, Calif.
Los Angeles, Calif.
Louisville, Ky.
Lubbock, Texas
Madison, Wisc.
Manchester, N. H.
Memphis, Tenn.
Miami, Fla.
Milwaukee, Wisc.
Minneapolis, Minn.
Mobile, Ala.
Nashville, Tenn.
Newark, N. J.
New Brunswick, N. J.
New Haven, Conn.
New Orleans, La.
New York, N. Y.
Norfolk, Va.
Oakland, Calif.
Oklahoma City, Okla.
Omaha, Nebr.
Orlando, Fla.
Peoria, Ill.
Philadelphia, Pa.
Phoenix, Ariz.
Pittsburgh, Pa.
Port Arthur, Texas
Portland, Me.
Portland, Ore.
Portsmouth, Ohio
Providence, R. I.
Reading, Pa.
Richmond, Va.
Roanoke, Va.
Rochester, N. Y.
Rocky Mount, N. C.
Sacramento, Calif.
St. Louis, Mo.
St. Paul, Minn.
St. Petersburg, Fla.
Salt Lake City, Utah
San Antonio, Texas
San Bernardino, Calif.
San Diego, Calif.
San Francisco, Calif.
Santa Ana, Calif.
Savannah, Ga.
Seattle, Wash.
Shreveport, La.
Sioux City, Iowa
Sioux Falls, S. D.
Spokane, Wash.
Springfield, Ill.
Springfield, Mass.
Springfield, Mo.
Syracuse, N. Y.
Tacoma, Wash.
Tampa, Fla.
Toledo, Ohio
Tucson, Ariz.
Tulsa, Okla.
Washington, D. C.
West Hartford, Conn.
Wichita, Kan.
Wilmington, Del.
Winston-Salem, N. C.
Worcester, Mass.
Youngstown, Ohio

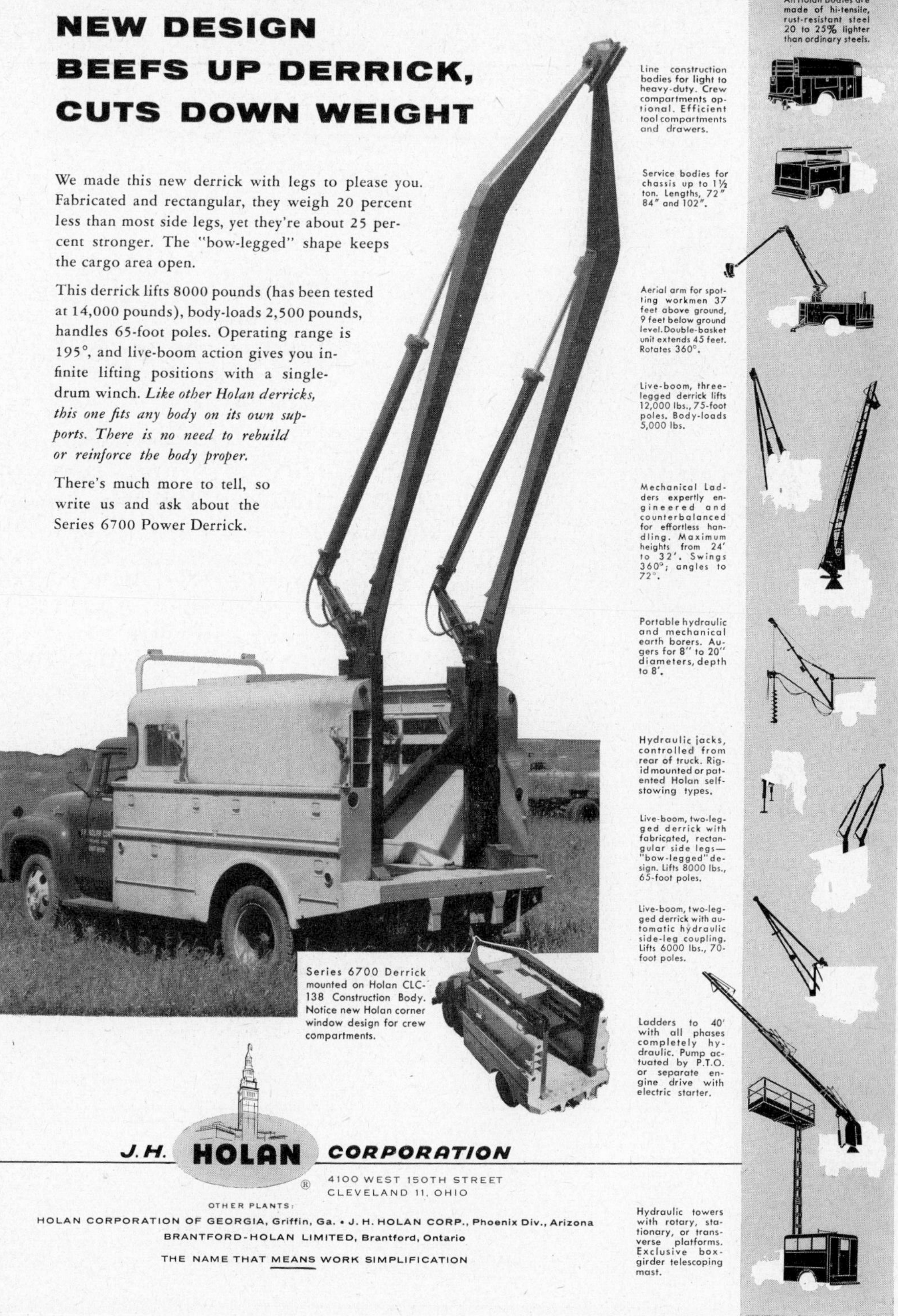
NEW DESIGN
BEEFS UP DERRICK,
CUTS DOWN WEIGHT
We made this new derrick with legs to please you. Fabricated and rectangular, they weigh 20 percent less than most side legs, yet they're about 25 percent stronger. The "bow-legged" shape keeps the cargo area open.
This derrick lifts 8000 pounds (has been tested at 14,000 pounds), body-loads 2,500 pounds, handles 65-foot poles. Operating range is 195°, and live-boom action gives you infinite lifting positions with a single-drum winch. Like other Holan derricks, this one fits any body on its own supports. There is no need to rebuild or reinforce the body proper.
There's much more to tell, so write us and ask about the Series 6700 Power Derrick.
Series 6700 Derrick mounted on Holan CLC-138 Construction Body. Notice new Holan corner window design for crew compartments.
All Holan bodies are made of hi-tensile, rust-resistant steel 20 to 25% lighter than ordinary steels.
Line construction bodies for light to heavy-duty. Crew compartments optional. Efficient tool compartments and drawers.
Service bodies for chassis up to 1½ ton. Lengths, 72" 84" and 102".
Aerial arm for spotting workmen 37 feet above ground, 9 feet below ground level. Double-basket unit extends 45 feet. Rotates 360°.
Live-boom, three-legged derrick lifts 12,000 lbs., 75-foot poles. Body-loads 5,000 lbs.
Mechanical Ladders expertly engineered and counterbalanced for effortless handling. Maximum heights from 24' to 32'. Swings 360°; angles to 72°.
Portable hydraulic and mechanical earth borers. Augers for 8" to 20" diameters, depth to 8'.
Hydraulic jacks, controlled from rear of truck. Rigid mounted or patented Holan self-stowing types.
Live-boom, two-legged derrick with fabricated, rectangular side legs—"bow-legged" design. Lifts 8000 lbs., 65-foot poles.
Live-boom, two-legged derrick with automatic hydraulic side-leg coupling. Lifts 6000 lbs., 70-foot poles.
Ladders to 40' with all phases completely hydraulic. Pump actuated by P.T.O. or separate engine drive with electric starter.
Hydraulic towers with rotary, stationary, or transverse platforms. Exclusive box-girder telescoping mast.
J. H. HOLAN CORPORATION ®
4100 WEST 150TH STREET
CLEVELAND 11, OHIO
OTHER PLANTS:
HOLAN CORPORATION OF GEORGIA, Griffin, Ga. • J. H. HOLAN CORP., Phoenix Div., Arizona
BRANTFORD-HOLAN LIMITED, Brantford, Ontario
THE NAME THAT MEANS WORK SIMPLIFICATION

THE RYTHER-PURDY LUMBER CO.

503 Tiffany Street, New York 59, N. Y.

Western Red Cedar Lighting Standards

DURABILITY Western Red Cedar poles are made of all heart wood and have a natural preservative oil that resists decay and is equal to ten times the toxicity of coal tar creosote. Standards installed on New York parkways 25 years ago are still in good condition.

LOW-COST INSTALLATION No concrete foundations are required. The poles are merely set in a hole in the ground and tamped with soil.

NO MAINTENANCE Painting is not needed when the standards are installed or at any time thereafter.

ATTRACTIVE APPEARANCE Western Red Cedar is brownish red in color and the knots are hard and sound. An adz finish gives a hand-hewn effect. Chamfered corners give a tapered look without sacrificing strength or size of the pole.

LESSENS HAZARDS IN AUTO ACCIDENTS When hit by a car, a Western Red Cedar pole gives with the blow and usually breaks. This stops the car, but lessens the shock and danger to human life.

• SPECIFICATIONS •

Write for Bulletin showing dimensions and details of construction.

SOUTH BEND CURRENT CONTROLLER CO., Inc.

1237 North Side Blvd., South Bend 15, Indiana

Switches and Relays for the Control of Series or Multiple Circuits
For Street Lighting—Athletic Field Lighting—Airport Lighting

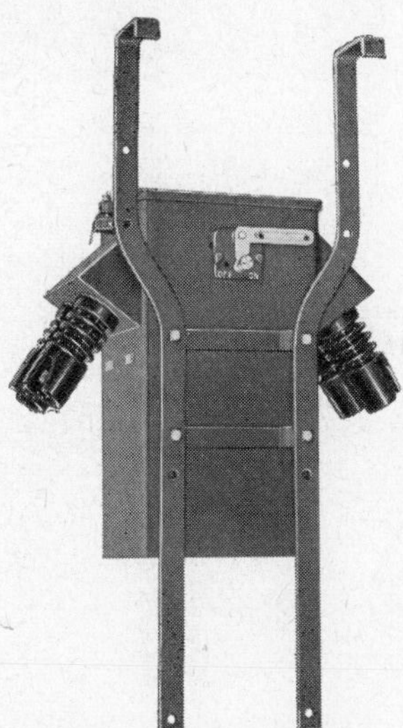

Type AN-2 Pole Remote Control Oil Switch Rated for Use on a 5.0/8.66 KV System in Weatherproof Tank with the Auxiliary Hand Lever on the Pole Side

Remote Control Oil Switches in Weatherproof Tanks for Crossarm Mounting are Recommended for Switching the Primary to Transformers Energizing Lighting Loads. Switches are Available One, Two, or Three Pole for Use on 5.0/8.66 KV or 8.66/15 KV Systems.

Manually Operated Oil Switches in Weatherproof Tanks for Crossarm Mounting with an Attachment for Pole Base Manual Operation are Available Two Pole and Three Pole for Use on 5.0/8.66 KV Systems.

Series Protective Relays Provide an Important Protection Against the High Voltage Hazard which Develops when an Open Circuit Fault Occurs in a Series Lighting Circuit.

Series Multiple Relays have Operating Coils Designed for Connection in a Series Lighting Circuit. Energizing the Series Coil Actuates the Load Contacts to Switch the 120 Volt Supply to a Multiple Lighting Circuit.

Multiple Relays are Standard with 120 Volt 60 Cycle Operating Coils which Actuate the Load Contacts to Switch the 120 Volt Supply to Lighting Loads. The Relays are Available with the Load Contacts Normally Open or Normally Closed with the Coil De-energized and with Single Pole Load Contacts Rated 15, 30, or 60 Amperes at 125 Volts AC.

Type SPR-1 Pole Remote Control Oil Switch in Pole Type Tank with Load contacts N/O with 120 Volt Coil De-energized for Use on 8.66/15 KV system

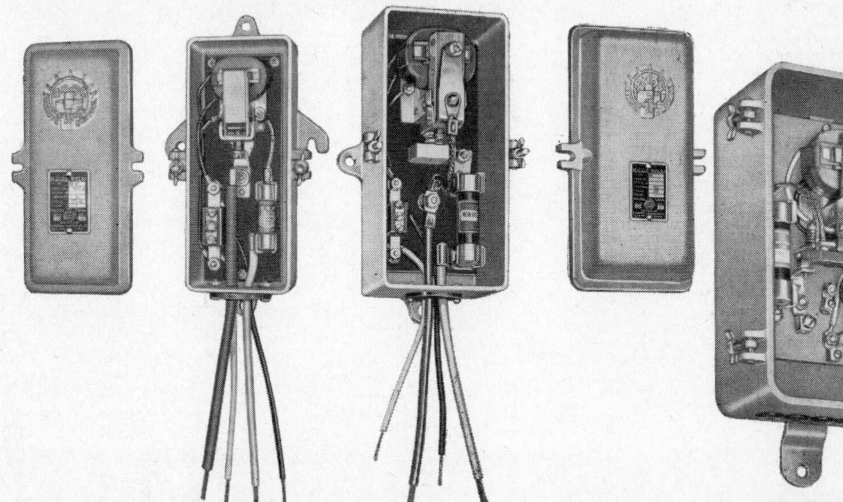

Type MR-AF Single Pole Multiple Relay Rated 30 Amps 125 Volts AC

Type MR-DO Single Pole Multiple Relay with Load Rating 60 Amps 125 Volts AC

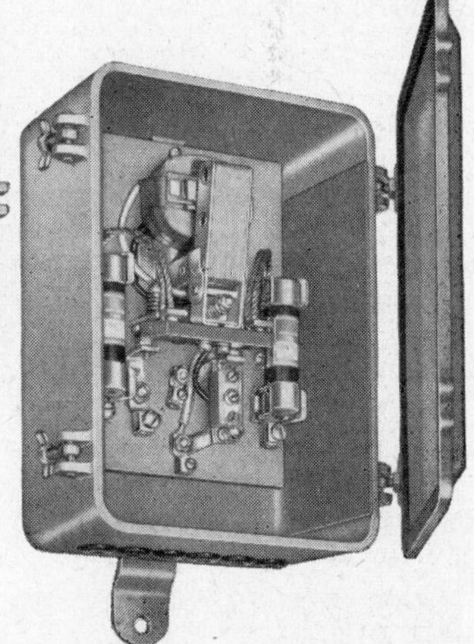

Type MR-OD Two Pole Multiple Relay Rated 40 Amps 250 Volts AC with Control Circuit Lightning Arrester and Load Circuit Fuses

R-C-O-C REMOTE CONTROL FOR OUTDOOR LIGHTING CIRCUITS

Design, Quality, Flexibility, Lightness and Durability of Material Preferred for Service at

Terminals, Parking Areas, Loading Platforms, Airfields, Shipyards, Industrial Plants, Institutions College Campuses, Playgrounds, Parks, Swimming Pools, Ball Parks, Golf Courses, Banks, Office Buildings and Retail Stores.

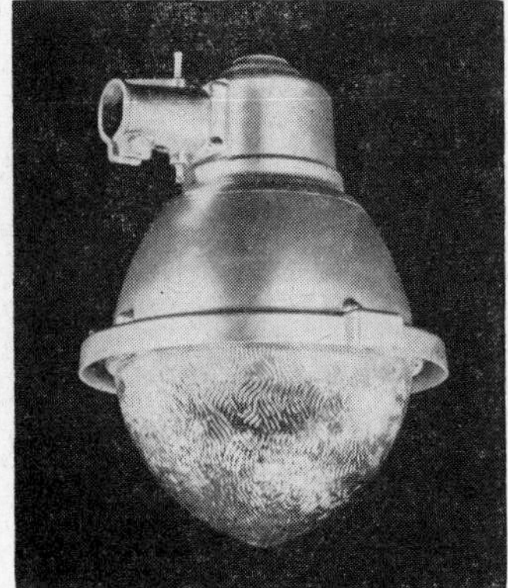

STREET LUMINAIRE

TYPE 3438-2

A highly versatile Luminaire designed by street lighting engineers, with years of experience, to meet the rigid requirements for an efficient unit with the minimum amount of maintenance work and the maximum durability and with full interchangeability of *all* parts.

This unit embodies all the top features of the best known street lighting units in addition to their outstanding flexibility in the range and type of lighting for which they may be adapted by merely a change of reflector or glass globe for a lighting fixture of 1500 to 2500 lumens to a 20,000 lumen incandescent luminaire, or by simply adding a ballast and a lamp to a mercury vapor unit.

Briefly, this unit consists of five major parts: Namely, body and ring (highly corrosive resistant die cast aluminum alloy), reflector (specular Alzak aluminum) glass globe (either asymmetric or symmetric), socket and support.

Modern Lighting Devices for Industrial Engineering and Municipal Projects Services for all kinds of Sports Areas

INCANDESCENT TYPES

	Lumens
3438-1 Open Reflector Type	1500 to 2,500
3438-2 Close Glass Globe Type	6,000 to 10,000
3438-3 Close Glass Globe Type	16,000 to 20,000
Mercury	15,000 to 20,000
3438-2	18,000
3438-3	20,000

All type can be furnished with "top" or "side" mounting, for series or multiple circuits.

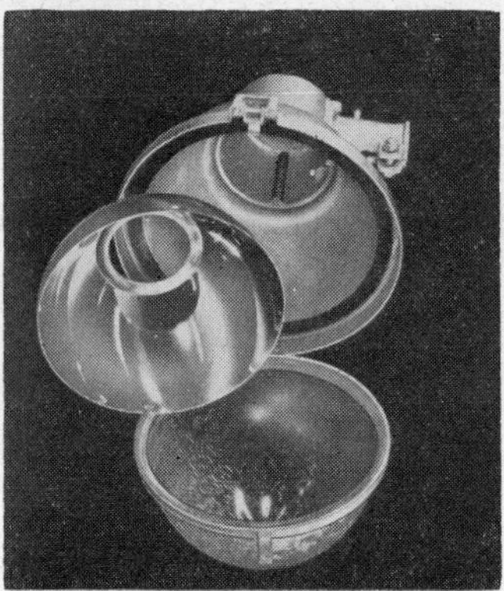

Ease Of Maintenance

TYPE 3438-2-SO

Die cast aluminum body, spun Alzak reflector, removable ring and either symmetric or asymmetric glass globe, 1¼", 1½" and 2" opening in slip fitter for side mounting. Furnished for series or multiple circuit. Equipped with either wet or dry process porcelain receptacle.

E.T.L. Report of Typical 3438-2 Candlepower Distribution, and additional Units upon request.

We will gladly assist you to place and classify your street lighting problems. Consult our dependable Service.

Inquiries concerning specific applications or installations are invited. Our engineers will be pleased to advise you.

STREET LIGHTING EQUIPMENT CORPORATION

Manufacturers of Street Lighting, Park Lighting and Traffic Light Equipment

31-23 Sixty-First Street **Woodside 77, N. Y.**

Telephone: RAvenswood 6-1052

YOUR TRUCK with 2 MEN and *Tel·E·Lect* —a complete pole setting unit!

Specialists in POLE LINE CONSTRUCTION *and* MAINTENANCE EQUIPMENT

- **Easy-to-install kits for front or rear derrick and digger drives . . .**
- **Derricks and pole hole diggers for "hard-to-reach" jobs . . .**
- **Complete utility bodies with derrick and digger . . .**

Line construction and maintenance equipment manufactured and distributed by Tel-E-Lect Products, Inc., is designed in cooperation with the public utility industry. Tel-E-Lect products, tailor-made to fit all trucks, can be quickly and easily installed by your local mechanic. Tel-E-Lect kits contain every needed part and are ready to bolt on to your truck's chassis.

Ready-to-mount Tel-E-Lect products include complete derrick and digger drive kits for front or rear application on all trucks; utility bodies complete with derrick and digger for economical 2-man pole setting; single-lever operated forward and reverse transmissions; power take-offs; "Fold-Over" derrick storage kits; and a complete selection of derricks, augers, pole trailers, ground rod drivers and accessories.

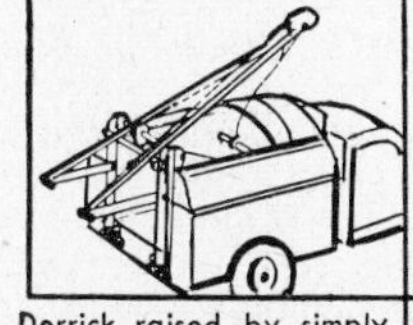

Derrick raised by simply engaging the winch.

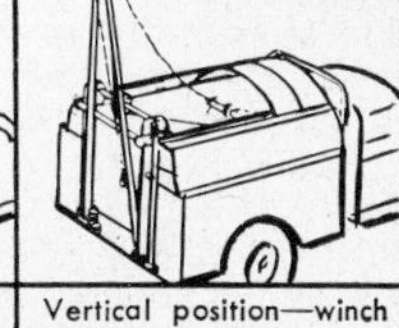

Vertical position—winch rotation reversed.

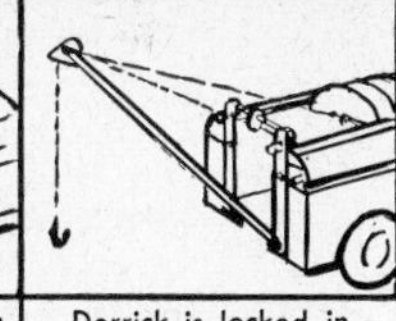

Derrick is locked in operating position.

GIVE YOUR LINE CREW AUTOMATIC DERRICK STORAGE

Tel-E-Lect's Fold-Over Storage Kit Offers:

- **Time and Money Saving Advantages**
- **Increased Truck Flexibility**
- **Crew Safety**

Dangerous, time consuming hand erection and knock-down of "A" frame derricks is eliminated with this Tel-E-Lect kit. The power of your truck's winch is used to raise and lower the derrick in less than one minute. The kit is designed to fit any standard utility truck body and, like all Tel-E-Lect products, can be quickly installed by your local mechanic.

Your trucks become more flexible with the fold-over storage features because the derrick stores horizontally over the cab and body; space formerly used for derrick storage is available for other purposes. Maneuverability and safety is increased too.

New in the line are Tel-E-Lect Hydraulic Derricks and Diggers for either front or rear operation. This portable pressure digging equipment is available in several models to fit your job requirements. If your truck has a double drum winch you'll get live boom operation; with a single drum winch you'll find the easily adjustable derrick elevation a big advantage.

For complete information about your particular utility truck equipment needs call or write:

Tel·E·Lect **PRODUCTS, INC., 10,011 Minnetonka Blvd.**
Minneapolis 26, Minn. • Phone WEst 8-2723

Wheeler STREET LIGHTING

Wheeler Street Lighting Equipment includes a line of products for all common sizes of lamps used on either series or multiple lighting systems. Wheeler Street Lighting Fixtures incorporate exclusive Wheeler features of design and construction, including the widely accepted screw ring reflector attachment for open reflectors pioneered by Wheeler and embody the best practices of street lighting developed and proved by Wheeler ever since the first electric street lighting was introduced.

INTEGRAL PHOTOELECTRIC CONTROL LUMINAIRES

A small multiple head with integrally mounted Fisher-Pierce photoelectric control. Inside or outside wired for Screw Ring or Groove Neck style of reflector attachment. All-aluminum or porcelain enameled steel Crescent Reflector can be used, providing I. E. S. Type I or Type II distribution. Crescent Reflectors available with all EEI-NEMA Standard Type Necks. Other types also available.

STANDARD EEI-NEMA HEAD WITH 4-WAY INTERSECTION REFLECTOR

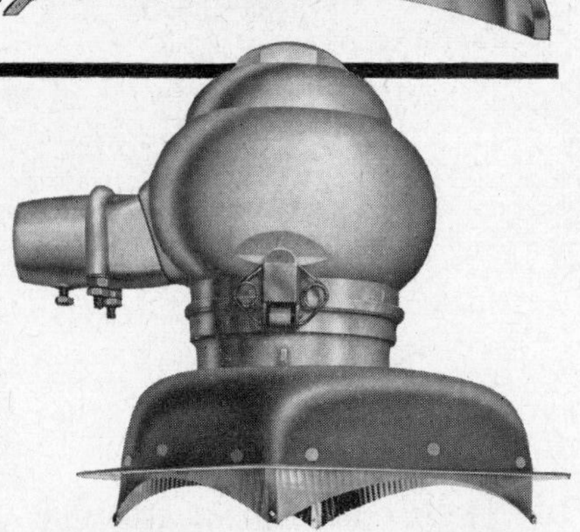

New 4-way intersection reflector available in aluminum or porcelain enameled steel — in types I and II 4-way distribution. When porcelain enameled reflector is used without stainless steel chrome-plated edgeflectors, Type V equivalent distribution is obtained. Available with all standard EEI-NEMA Standard Type Necks. Other types also available. Standard EEI-NEMA large aluminum head is designed for use on multiple circuits or on series circuits up to 10,500 Volts. Self contained ballasts included in multiple heads for 100 watt and 175 watt mercury lamps.

NEW! LLB LUMINAIRES

The first low brightness mercury street and highway luminaire — the first directional luminaire for divided highways and one-way streets. View shown is highway lighting test installation on U. S. Route 1 in Old Lyme, Conn. Units in foreground are Wheeler LLB (Linear Low Brightness) Mercury Vapor Luminaires with 400 Watt EH-1 Lamps. Insert shows detailed view of Luminaire. Available in Standard I.E.S. Patterns (I, II, III, IV), this 4-ft. long unit provides all the advantages of elongated linear fluorescent street lighting *plus* the high efficiency and optical control which present fluorescent cannot give. Available with integrally mounted Fisher-Pierce photoelectric controls.

SMALL HEAD RADIAL WAVE REFLECTOR

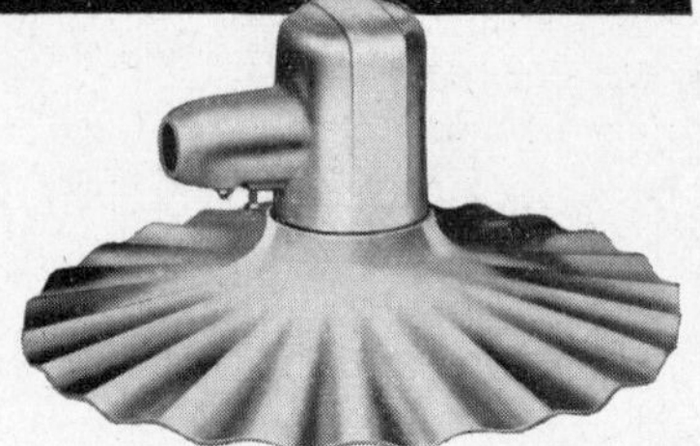

Rugged, side-mounted, one-piece cast aluminum head for low voltage circuits, series to 2,500 volts or multiple. With leveling adjustment for plus or minus 5° and no-slip socket support. Dual purpose reflector attachment for Screw Neck or Groove Neck Radial Reflector. Shallow Neck, Bowl Neck or Deep Dome Reflector available in steel with Lustergray porcelain enamel exterior or in aluminum with synthetic lacquer finish.

WHEELER REFLECTOR COMPANY

275 Congress Street • Boston 10, Mass.

WHEELER Represents the most advanced engineering in Street Lighting

Catalogs with complete specifications and data available on request.

LET YOUR

TRAFFIC

CONTROL ITSELF

. . . WITH ELECTRO-MATIC®

TRAFFIC-ACTUATED CONTROLS

here's how they work . . .

1. DETECTORS. Every vehicle approaching a traffic-actuated signal is registered by a unit sensitive to the movement of vehicles. This information is relayed in the form of an electrical impulse to the . . .

2. CONTROLLER. Depending upon the type of traffic supervision needed in the area, a controller of the correct specifications receives the impulses from the vehicle detectors and transfers them into time intervals based on the demand indicated by the volume of traffic. Since these time intervals are controlled by the traffic itself, it means that a maximum amount of traffic can be handled in a minimum time by following the . . .

3. TRAFFIC-ACTUATED RESPONSE SIGNALS. These signal heads, of conventional design, indicate to drivers and pedestrians the proper signals which will avoid traffic snarls and dangerous "jay-walking" by allocating passage time on a system with superhuman ability.

self-controlled traffic at . . .

COMPLEX URBAN INTERSECTIONS

No urban intersection is too difficult to control. Electro-Matic equipment eliminates human error and moves traffic efficiently and safely.

COORDINATED INTERSECTIONS

Repeated "stops and starts" for successive signals can be minimized by coordinated systems; thereby assuring free movement of traffic.

MAJOR AND MINOR STREET INTERSECTIONS

The green light should never be transferred from a major street unless side street traffic is actually present. Thus, waiting time is held to an absolute minimum.

RURAL INTERSECTIONS

Controlled speed on open stretches of highway plus safety at the crossroads can be achieved with Electro-Matic equipment.

SCHOOL CROSSINGS

School children are safe with controlled traffic speed and walk intervals provided for with many types of traffic-actuated equipment.

PEDESTRIAN CROSSINGS

Pedestrian protection often can best be served by signals called only by push button activities.

SPEED CONTROL AREAS

Any desired speed limit can be actuated and enforced with Electro-Matic Controllers and the Radar Speed Meter.

. . . a complete line of Controllers that "think for themselves" and fit every need of towns, large or small

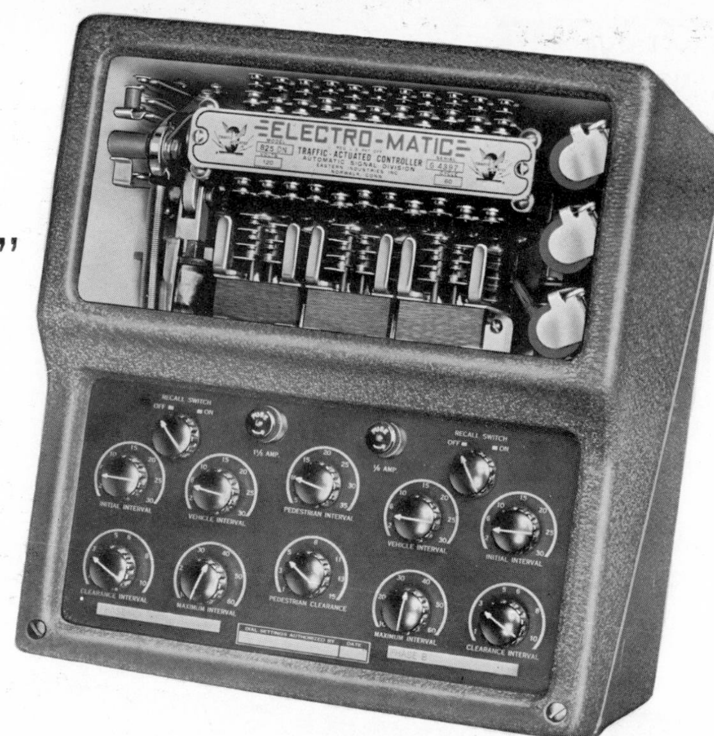

502DA

PX CONTROLLER — pedestrian actuated

Push Button Control • Safe Passage for Pedestrians • Minimum Delay to Vehicles • Ideal for School, Shopping, Bus Stops and Church Crossings

505A

TWO-PHASE SEMI-ACTUATED CONTROLLER

for the Intersection of an Artery and a Side Street

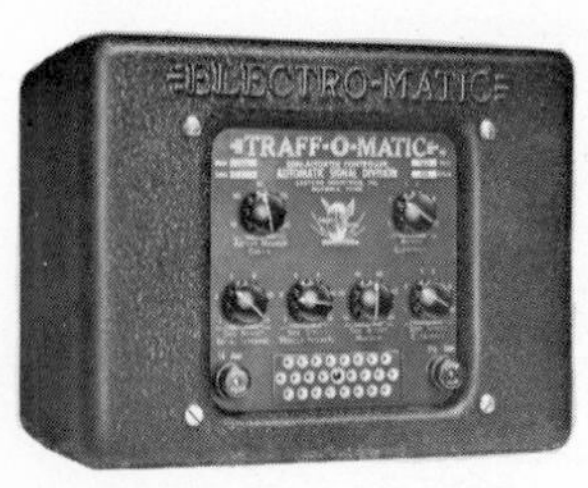

Green light remains on artery except when called by side street detectors or push buttons • Side street right of way proportioned to demand • Accurate, flexible, electronic control of modern proven design • All timing intervals independently knob-adjustable • Coordination with adjacent intersections

804D

TWO-PHASE FULL or SEMI-ACTUATED CONTROLLER

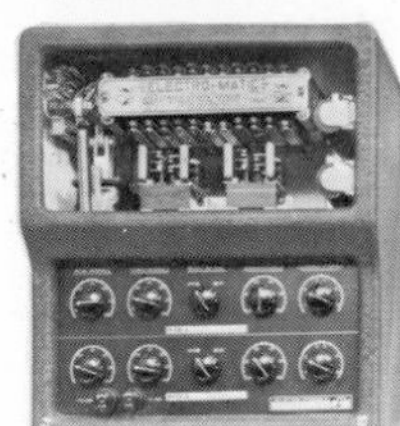

Controls Traffic in Two Actuated Movements • Provides Time Extension and Memory of Actuation on Both Phases • May be Used for Semi-Actuated Control

804T

TWO-PHASE FULL-ACTUATED CONTROLLER

with All Red Clearance Intervals

Time Extension and Memory of Actuation on Both Phases • Particularly Adaptable to Narrow Stretches of Roadway Suitable For One Way Traffic Only

812

TWO-PHASE FULL-ACTUATED CONTROLLER

with Speed Control Features

Controls Two Actuated Phases with Protection Against High Approach Speeds • Double Clearance Intervals — Yellow and All-Red • Time Extension and Memory of Actuation on Both Phases

824DN

TWO-PHASE SEMI-ACTUATED CONTROLLER

with Exclusive Pedestrian-Actuated Phase

Exclusive Pedestrian-Actuated Phase • Two Semi-Actuated Phases • Skipping of Any Actuated Phase Having No Demand • May be Operated in a Coordinated System

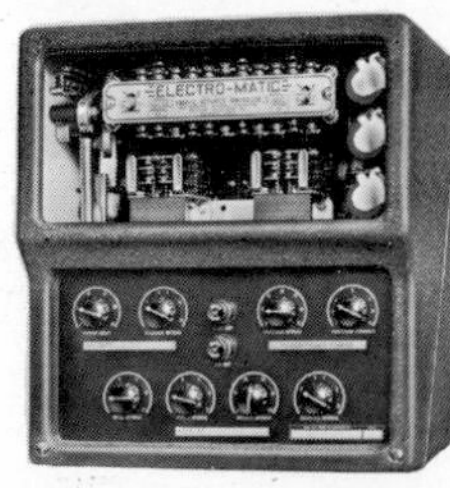

825DN

TWO-PHASE FULL-ACTUATED CONTROLLER

with Exclusive Pedestrian-Actuated Phase

Exclusive Pedestrian Actuated Phase • Two Full Vehicle-Actuated Phases • Skipping of Any Phase Having No Demand • Time Extension and Memory of Actuation

1826D
THREE-PHASE FULL OR SEMI-ACTUATED CONTROLLER

For Full or Semi-Actuated Control of an Intersection where Three Traffic Movements are Required

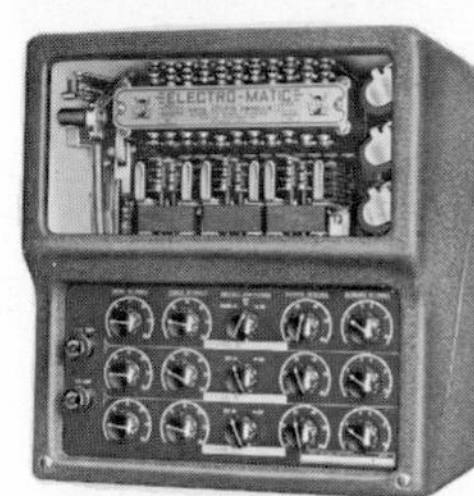

Controls Traffic in Three Actuated Movements • Time Extension and Memory on Each Phase • Omits Phase Having No Demand • May Be Operated in Coordinated System

922
MULTI-PHASE FULL-ACTUATED CONTROLLER

Provides:

Four Phase Full Actuated Control • Two Overlap Phases • Time Extension and Memory on Each Phase • Skipping of Phases Having No Demand • Ability to Assign One Phase to Pedestrians

1022
TWO-PHASE VOLUME-DENSITY CONTROLLER

Two Phase Control of an Intersection on the Volume-Density Principle • Movement of Maximum Traffic Volumes • Delay Reduced to Absolute Minimum • Self Coordinating without Interconnection

1033
THREE-PHASE VOLUME-DENSITY CONTROLLER

Three Phase Voulume-Density Control • Moves Maximum Traffic Volumes with Minimum Delay • Omits Phases Having No Traffic Demand • Time Extension and Memory on Each Phase

S-30 & S-35
SPEED CONTROLLERS

Limits Speed at Non-Intersection Locations • Timing intervals adjustable to meet all conditions • Protects curves, school zones, town approaches, and other hazardous locations

CABINETS

Type D

Type G

Type M

Weather-proof cabinets to house control equipment safely from corrosion and tampering. Three sizes available to accommodate everything from the simplest to the most complex installations.

HR & HRD
PRESSURE SENSITIVE VEHICLE DETECTORS

NON-DIRECTIONAL, MODEL HR and DIRECTIONAL, MODEL HRD

Strength and simplicity of design • Long life under all operating conditions • Maximum accuracy of count • Replaceable contact unit • Many applications, including traffic control, highway counting, toll collection, door opening, and others

MCH
MAGNETIC VEHICLE DETECTOR

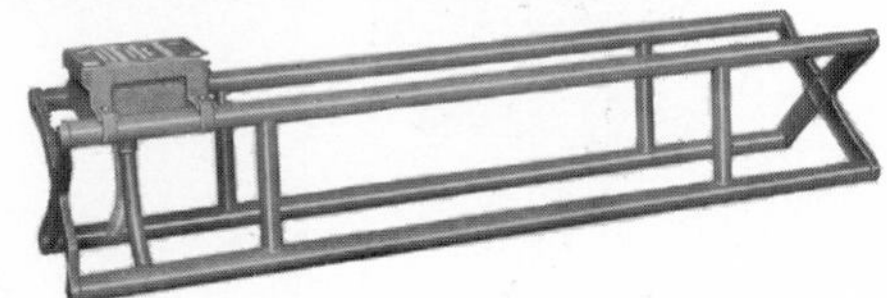

Economical • Easily Installed • Efficient • Adjustable range

MK
MAGNETIC VEHICLE DETECTOR

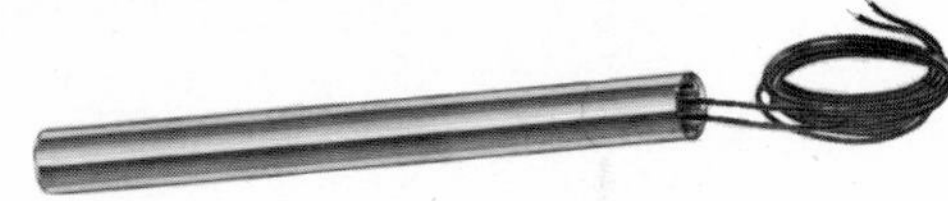

Compensated • Highly Directional • Sharp Cutoff

RD-1
RADAR VEHICLE DETECTOR

Economical overhead installation • Adjustable coverage • No amplifying unit required • Dependable operation under all conditions

"PR" SYSTEM OF COORDINATED TRAFFIC CONTROL...

- Utilizes all of the traffic analyzing abilities of the Electro-Matic Master as well as the all-new, all-electronic PR local controllers.
- The Master selects cycles and offsets best suited to prevailing traffic conditions and feeds this information to the PR's at each intersection.
- Completely electronic
- Controls downtown grids or arteries
- Six cycle lengths—4 offsets—3 cycle splits—all determined by traffic volume and direction
- Offsets shifted smoothly by increasing or decreasing green intervals — eliminating long dwell periods
- Simple dial settings for Offsets and Cycle Splits
- Green intervals are traffic-adjusted while clearance and special intervals are constant at each intersection
- Maintenance-minded design includes printed timing circuit and accessible chassis construction

For details, write for Bulletin E-224

RADAR SPEED METER

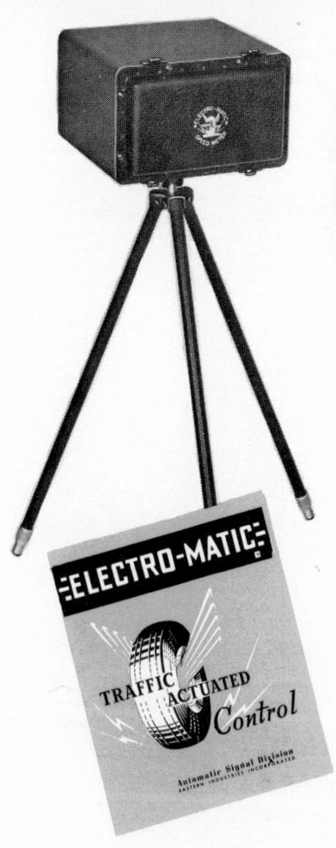

Radar works magic in detecting and controlling speeders. The Electro-Matic Model S-2A Radar Speed Meter operated by law enforcement officers provides a safe, positive means of detecting and controlling speeders. Violators soon discover the magic of radar equipment accurately indicates their excessive speed to the police-operator. Enforcement officials find many advantages in using the Speed Meter: Checks far more vehicles than a cruiser car • Eliminates hazards to pursuing officers and to motorists • Effective day and night in all weather • Psychological deterrent to would-be speeders • Portable for spot checking • Ideal for investigating complaints of neighborhood speeding • Either one-man or two-man usage of the Speed Meter can be employed.

ENGINEERING ANALYSIS

A brief outline of your problem in the hands of our engineering staff will aid us in making suggestions based on years of experience in working out similar installations. We will also be pleased to send a copy of our complete catalog, on request.

Electro-Matic . . . the most accepted name in traffic control

AUTOMATIC SIGNAL DIVISION

EASTERN INDUSTRIES, INCORPORATED

NORWALK • CONNECTICUT

CONTINENTAL MOTORS CORPORATION

Muskegon, Michigan

DISTRIBUTORS AND DEALERS FROM COAST TO COAST

CONTINENTAL MOTORS · Powerful as the Nation · AMERICA'S STANDARD ®

CHOOSE THE EQUIPMENT WHOSE BUILDER THINKS ENOUGH OF HIS GOOD NAME TO STANDARDIZE ON

RED SEAL POWER

•

92 BASIC ENGINES IN THE 14 TO 280 H.P. RANGE— TRANSPORTATION—INDUSTRIAL—OIL FIELD—IRRIGATION AND AGRICULTURAL APPLICATIONS — STANDARDIZED ENGINES

GASOLINE—NATURAL GAS—LPG—FUEL OIL—DIESEL FUEL

•

TRANSPORTATION (GASOLINE) MODELS

Model	Cyl.	Bore	Str.	800	1200	1600	2000	2200	2400	2600	2800	3000	3200	3400	3500	TORQUE lbs. ft. @ R.P.M.
N-4062	4	2 3/8	3 1/2	5.2	8.8	12.2	15.6	17.2	18.9	20.4	22.0	23.4	24.7	25.8	26.3	39.5 @ 1200
Y-4069	4	2 1/2	3 1/2	7.0	11.2	15.2	19.4	21.0	22.7	24.2	25.5	26.7	27.5	28.0	....	51.0 @ 2000
4091	4	2 7/8	3 1/2	9.5	15.7	21.2	26.2	28.5	30.5	32.0	33.5	34.7	35.5	36.0	....	70.0 @ 1500
F-4124	4	3	4 3/8	13.2	21.2	28.7	35.0	37.8	40.4	42.7	44.7	46.4	47.0	....	....	94.8 @ 1500
4140	4	3 3/16	4 3/8	15.0	24.1	32.5	40.2	43.3	46.2	48.5	51.2	51.7	52.0	....	....	107.8 @ 1500
4162	4	3 7/16	4 3/8	17.0	27.6	37.3	45.6	49.1	52.2	54.7	56.5	57.9	58.0	....	....	122.8 @ 1500
F-6186	6	3	4 3/8	19.2	31.7	43.5	53.9	58.5	62.8	66.7	70.0	72.9	75.2	76.6	77.0	141.5 @ 1500
6209	6	3 3/16	4 3/8	21.8	35.8	48.7	60.8	66.3	71.4	76.0	80.3	83.8	87.5	89.3	90.0	160.3 @ 1500
6226	6	3 5/16	4 3/8	25.5	41.0	55.0	67.3	72.7	77.7	82.5	87.0	91.2	95.0	98.0	98.8	180.0 @ 1500
M-6271	6	3 5/8	4 3/8	31.0	48.0	63.5	77.0	83.0	88.0	92.5	95.5	96.5	.....	....	....	209.2 @ 1400
6290	6	3 3/4	4 3/8	33.5	52.0	69.0	84.0	90.5	97.0	102.0	106.0	108.0	.....	....	....	226.0 @ 1400
6330	6	4	4 3/8	37.5	58.5	78.0	95.5	103.5	111.0	117.0	121.5	125.0	.....	....	....	257.8 @ 1400
M-6363	6	4	4 13/16	42.5	69.0	93.0	113.5	122.5	130.0	136.5	142.0	146.0	.....	....	....	305.0 @ 1600
B-6371	6	4 1/8	4 5/8	42.0	64.5	85.0	102.0	109.0	115.0	120.0	123.0	123.5	.....	....	....	285.0 @ 1200
6427	6	4 5/16	4 7/8	48.0	74.0	97.5	117.5	125.5	132.5	137.5	141.0	142.0	.....	....	....	327.0 @ 1200
K-6271	6	3 5/8	4 3/8	31.5	49.5	66.0	81.5	89.0	95.5	102.0	107.5	111.5	114.5	....	....	216.0 @ 1400
6290	6	3 3/4	4 3/8	34.5	53.0	70.5	87.5	95.0	102.5	109.0	115.0	119.5	123.0	....	....	232.0 @ 1400
K-6330	6	4	4 3/8	32.5	58.0	82.0	104.5	115.0	124.0	132.0	139.0	145.0	147.0	....	....	274.0 @ 2000
T-6371	6	4 1/8	4 5/8	43.5	67.5	90.0	111.5	121.0	129.5	136.5	141.5	143.8	.....	....	....	297.0 @ 1400
T-6427	6	4 5/16	4 7/8	51.0	79.5	107.0	131.5	142.5	153.5	161.5	167.0	170.0	.....	....	....	350.0 @ 1300
U-6501	6	4 1/2	5 1/4	62.0	94.8	125.5	151.0	162.5	171.5	178.0	.....	.....	.....	....	....	414.0 @ 1200
R-6513	6	4 1/2	5 3/8	62.0	96.0	128.8	157.8	171.0	181.0	189.0	192.2	.....	.....	....	....	410.0 @ 1200
6572	6	4 3/4	5 3/8	70.0	106.0	140.8	172.5	187.0	199.0	210.0	220.0	.....	.....	....	....	463.8 @ 1200
6602	6	4 7/8	5 3/8	73.0	110.8	146.7	181.0	196.0	210.0	222.0	232.0	.....	.....	....	....	482.7 @ 1200
S-6749	6	5 3/8	5 1/2	85.0	131.0	174.0	211.0	226.0	238.0	247.0	250.0	.....	.....	....	....	575.0 @ 1300
6820	6	5 5/8	5 1/2	92.5	143.0	193.0	231.0	247.0	260.0	271.0	275.0	.....	.....	....	....	629.0 @ 1300
V-8603	8	4 3/4	4 1/4	70.0	112.0	150.5	184.0	199.8	212.0	222.0	230.0	236.0	240.0	....	....	500.0 @ 1400

(CONTINUED)

POWER SPECIALISTS FOR MORE THAN FIFTY YEARS

INDUSTRIAL (GASOLINE) MODELS

Model	Cyl.	Bore	Str.	800	1000	1200	1400	1600	1800	2000	2200	2400	2600	2800	TORQUE lbs. ft. @ R.P.M.
N-56	4	2¼	3½	5.7	7.4	9	10.5	11.8	12.9	13.8	14.2	....	....	....	39.5 @ 1200
N-62	4	2⅜	3½	6.0	7.8	9.6	11.1	12.5	13.7	14.5	15.0	....	....	....	41.8 @ 1200
Y-69	4	2½	3½	6.4	8.4	10.4	12.5	14.4	16.4	18.2	20.0	21.4	....	....	48.0 @ 2000
Y-91	4	2⅞	3½	9.8	12.4	15.0	17.8	20.4	22.8	25.0	27.0	28.5	....	....	67.0 @ 1600
Y-112	4	3 3/16	3½	11.6	15.4	18.6	21.9	24.6	27.0	29.0	30.8	32.0	....	....	82.0 @ 1200
F-124	4	3	4⅜	13.2	17.0	20.8	24.2	27.3	30.2	32.6	34.7	36.5	....	....	91.1 @ 1200
F-140	4	3 3/16	4⅜	15.8	20.2	24.2	28.2	31.8	35.0	37.8	40.0	42.0	....	....	106.4 @ 1200
F-162	4	3 7/16	4⅜	18.5	23.6	28.4	33.0	37.0	40.8	44.0	46.8	49.0	....	....	124.0 @ 1200
F-186	6	3	4⅜	21.7	27.8	33.5	38.8	44.0	48.8	53.2	57.1	60.5	....	....	146.5 @ 1200
F-209	6	3 3/16	4⅜	24.4	31.3	37.6	43.7	49.3	54.7	59.7	64.2	68.0	....	....	164.6 @ 1200
F-226	6	3 5/16	4⅜	26.3	33.8	40.7	47.3	53.7	59.4	64.7	69.3	73.0	....	....	178.0 @ 1200
F-244	6	3 7/16	4⅜	28.5	36.5	44.0	51.0	58.0	64.5	70.0	75.0	79.0	....	....	192.0 @ 1200
M-271	6	3⅝	4⅜	31.0	39.0	46.8	54.5	61.8	68.7	75.1	81.0	86.2	....	....	206.0 @ 1000
M-290	6	4¾	4⅜	33.3	42.0	50.4	58.4	66.0	73.2	80.0	86.3	92.2	....	....	220.8 @ 1000
M-330	6	4	4⅜	37.8	47.5	57.0	66.5	75.0	83.5	91.1	98.2	104.4	....	....	250.5 @ 1000
M-363	6	4	4 13/16	42.0	54.5	67.0	79.0	90.0	100.0	109.0	116.6	122.2	126.5	129.0	294.0 @ 1400
B-371	6	4⅛	4⅝	42.0	54.0	63.0	74.0	83.0	92.0	99.0	106.0	110.0	....	....	280.0 @ 1000
B-427	6	4 5/16	4⅞	49.0	61.0	73.0	84.0	96.0	106.0	110.0	122.0	127.0	....	....	322.0 @ 1000
G-134	4	3⅛	4⅜	16.0	20.5	24.5	27.9	30.2	32.4	34.2	....	....	....	....	106.5 @ 1100
G-157	4	3⅜	4⅜	18.5	23.8	28.3	32.4	35.5	38.0	40.0	....	....	....	....	124.0 @ 1100
****E-201	4	3⅝	4⅞	25.0	32.5	38.0	45.0	50.0	55.0	59.0	62.5	65.9	....	....	171.0 @ 1200
H-227	4	3⅝	5½	29.5	37.8	44.9	49.7	53.0	54.0	....	....	....	....	....	198.0 @ 1000
H-243	4	3¾	5½	31.9	40.4	47.8	53.0	56.7	57.9	....	....	....	....	....	213.0 @ 1000
****H-260	4	3⅞	5½	34.0	43.0	51.0	56.9	60.9	62.0	....	....	....	....	....	226.5 @ 1100
****H-277	4	4	5½	36.2	46.0	54.0	60.3	64.5	66.1	....	....	....	....	....	242.0 @ 1000
****J-382	4	4½	6	42.8	54.0	64.7	74.2	....	....	....	....	....	....	....	283.0 @ 1000
T-371	6	4⅛	4⅝	42.7	54.3	65.5	76.3	86.4	96.0	104.5	112.5	119.0	....	....	286.0 @ 1200
T-427	6	4 5/16	4⅞	50.4	63.7	76.7	89.4	101.5	113.2	123.5	132.5	140.0	....	....	335.3 @ 1000
U-501	6	4½	5¼	58.0	73.2	88.0	102.3	116.5	129.0	141.0	151.5	160.0	....	....	384.0 @ 1200
R-513	6	4½	5⅜	59.0	74.8	89.7	104.5	118.5	131.8	144.4	155.0	164.3	....	....	392.0 @ 1400
R-572	6	4¾	5⅜	65.8	83.0	100.0	116.5	132.2	147.0	161.0	172.8	182.4	....	....	437.0 @ 1400
R-602	6	4⅞	5⅜	69.5	87.5	105.4	123.0	139.5	155.0	169.6	182.2	191.7	....	....	460.0 @ 1200
V-603	8	4¾	4¼	73.0	94.0	114.0	133.0	151.8	168.0	183.0	195.0	206.0	214.0	220.0	500.0 @ 1400
S-749	6	5⅜	5½	87.0	109.5	131.0	152.0	171.0	188.5	204.8	217.0	....	....	....	572.0 @ 1000
S-820	6	5⅝	5½	95.0	119.5	143.5	166.0	187.0	205.5	223.0	237.0	....	....	....	625.0 @ 1000

TRANSPORTATION (DIESEL) MODELS

Model	Cyl.	Bore	Stroke	800	1200	1600	2000	2200	2400	2600	2800			TORQUE lbs. ft. @ R.P.M.
TD-6427	6	4 5/16	4⅞	43.2	69.5	91.8	107.8	113.2	116.0	.....	.....	....	....	307.0 @ 1200
RD-6572	6	4¾	5⅜	59.5	97.8	128.7	153.8	163.7	172.0	.....	.....	....	....	428.0 @ 1300
VD-8603	8	4¾	4¼	65.0	109.0	138.6	161.0	169.0	175.5	180.0	182.0	....	....	469.0 @ 1300
SD-6802	6	5 9/16	5½	86.0	142.0	185.0	214.5	225.0	.....	.....	.....	....	....	620.0 @ 1300

INDUSTRIAL (DIESEL) MODELS

Model	Cyl.	Bore	Stroke	800	1000	1200	1400	1600	1800	2000	2200	2400	MAX. TORQUE lbs. ft. @ R.P.M.
ZD-129	4	3¼	3⅞	13.5	17.5	21.4	25.1	28.5	31.3	34.0	....	....	94.9 @ 1200
GD-157	4	3⅜	4⅜	15.9	21.1	26.0	30.2	33.8	36.7	39.0	....	....	113.3 @ 1200
****ED-201	4	3⅝	4⅞	22.0	27.8	33.3	37.8	41.7	44.4	45.8	....	....	145.2 @ 1100
HD-243	4	3¾	5½	24.5	33.2	40.5	46.6	50.9	53.5	54.7	....	....	178.2 @ 1200
****HD-260	4	3⅞	5½	28.2	35.8	42.9	49.1	54.0	57.4	59.3	....	....	188.0 @ 1100
****HD-277	4	4	5½	30.0	38.0	45.5	52.0	57.5	61.0	62.8	63.2	....	202.0 @ 1100
****JD-382	4	4½	6	41.7	52.5	61.9	68.5	72.5	....	....	....	....	276.0 @ 1000
TD-427	6	4 5/16	4⅞	43.0	57.5	70.3	81.7	91.7	100.0	106.5	....	....	310.0 @ 1200
RD-572	6	4¾	5⅜	60.0	80.0	97.5	113.5	128.5	142.0	154.0	....	....	428.0 @ 1300
VD-603	8	4¾	4¼	65.0	88.0	107.5	124.0	138.5	150.3	160.0	167.0	***172.3	469.0 @ 1300
SD-802	6	5 9/16	5½	86.0	115.0	142.0	165.8	185.5	202.0	....	....	....	620.0 @ 1200

***175 @ 2600

FUEL OIL

Model	Cyl.	Bore	Str.	800	1000	1200	1400	1600	1800	2000	2200	2400		TORQUE lbs. ft @ R.P.M.
N-62	4	2⅜	3½	4.5	6.5	8.4	10.0	11.0	11.5	....	....	....	....	37 @ 1400
Y-112	4	3³⁄₁₆	3½	9.8	12.7	15.6	18.3	20.6	22.6	24.0	....	....	....	68 @ 1400
F-124	4	3	4⅜	10.9	14.2	17.3	20.2	22.8	24.9	....	....	....	....	76 @ 1400
F-140	4	3³⁄₁₆	4⅜	13.2	17.0	20.3	23.2	25.5	27.3	28.6	....	....	....	88 @ 1200
F-162	4	3⁷⁄₁₆	4⅜	15.7	20.1	24.3	28.0	31.3	33.8	....	....	....	....	105 @ 1200
F-226	6	3⁵⁄₁₆	4⅜	21.0	26.3	31.3	35.9	40.0	43.2	....	....	....	....	138 @ 1000
F-244	6	3⁷⁄₁₆	4⅜	23.0	28.8	34.0	38.8	43.0	47.0	50.6	54.0	57.2	....	150 @ 1000
M-330	6	4	4⅜	30.5	38.0	45.3	52.5	58.7	64.5	....	....	....	....	199 @ 800
B-427	6	4⁵⁄₁₆	4⅞	40.0	51.0	61.5	71.2	79.5	85.0	....	....	....	....	270 @ 1200
G-134	4	3⅛	4⅜	12.7	15.8	18.4	20.6	22.0	22.8	23.2	....	....	....	84 @ 800
G-157	4	3⅜	4⅜	15.7	19.9	23.8	27.2	29.6	30.4	....	....	....	....	105 @ 1000
H-227	4	3⅝	5½	23.2	29.2	34.0	37.4	38.4 @ 1500		....	....	....	....	154 @ 1000
H-243	4	3¾	5½	24.8	31.4	36.5	39.8	41 @ 1500						164 @ 1000
****H-260	4	3⅞	5½	26.5	33.5	39.0	42.7	44 @ 1500						176 @ 1000
****J-382	4	4½	6	37.8	47.8	55.5	60.8	62.5 @ 1500						250 @ 1000

TRANSPORTATION (LPG) MODELS

Model	Cyl.	Bore	Str.	800	1200	1600	2000	2200	2400	2600	2800	3000	3200	TORQUE lbs. ft. @ R.P.M.
K-6271	6	3⅝	4⅜	30.7	48.5	65.5	81.5	88.5	95.3	101.5	107.0	111.3	115.0	217.0 @ 1400
K-6330	6	4	4⅜	39.2	60.5	81.4	102.0	111.5	120.5	128.3	135.0	140.8	145.2	266.2 @ 1600
T-6427	6	4⁵⁄₁₆	4⅞	50.0	79.0	105.5	129.0	139.0	148.3	156.5	162.4	166.0	....	342.0 @ 1400
U-6501	6	4½	5¼	63.5	95.0	123.5	148.3	159.0	168.5	176.5	....	....	....	410 @ 1200
R-6513	6	4½	5⅜	60.5	93.2	122.2	146.5	156.4	164.3	170.0	....	....	....	405.0 @ 1200
R-6572	6	4¾	5⅜	70.0	107.0	141.0	169.8	182.0	192.0	200.0	....	....	....	467.0 @ 1200
R-6602	6	4⅞	5⅜	73.5	112.5	148.5	178.5	191.3	201.7	210.0	....	....	....	492.0 @ 1200
S-6749	6	5⅜	5½	83.0	131.0	173.0	211.0	226.0	237.5	246.0	....	....	....	576.0 @ 1200

Bare engine horsepower is according to ICEI and SAE test codes and is based on our standard curves. For specific applications contact our engineering dept.
Power rating derived with bare engine, including flywheel, water pump, carburetor and ignition system. For accessory deductions, see individual bulletins.

Deduct 1% for each 10° above 60°F. carburetor air.
Deduct 3½% for each 1000 ft. above Sea Level (on diesel engines, deduct 2%)

Deduct 15% for max. Shaft H. P. for INTERMITTENT duty.
Deduct 25% for max. Shaft H. P. for CONTINUOUS duty.

$$\text{TORQUE in Lbs. Ft.} = \frac{5252 \times \text{H.P.}}{\text{RPM}}$$

****For Industrial Application Only.

IRRIGATION (LPG) MODELS

Model	Cyl.	Bore	Str.	800	1000	1200	1400	1600	1800	2000	2200	2400	2600	TORQUE lbs. ft. @ R.P.M.
F-162	4	3⁷⁄₁₆	4⅜	17.5	23.5	28.8	34.0	38.6	42.8	46.2	49.0	51.5	53.0	127.0 @ 1400
F-226	6	3⁵⁄₁₆	4⅜	26.5	33.5	40.5	47.1	53.5	59.3	64.5	69.1	72.9	76.0	178.0 @ 1200
M-330	6	4	4⅜	37.5	48.5	58.5	69.0	78.5	87.5	96.4	104.0	111.3	117.3	260.0 @ 1400
B-427	6	4⁵⁄₁₆	4⅞	49.5	62.3	74.2	86.0	96.5	106.1	114.2	121.3	126.5	131.0	327.0 @ 1000
H-260	4	3⅞	5½	21.6	37.8	45.5	52.4	58.3	63.0	.....	.....	.....	.....	200 @ 1100
J-382	4	4½	6	43.2	55.2	66.5	76.2	84.2	90.0	.....	.....	.....	.....	295 @ 1200
U-501	6	4½	5¼	60.5	76.0	92.5	117.5	122.0	135.0	147.4	158.2	168.0	176.0	407.0 @ 1200
R-602	6	4⅞	5⅜	75.0	94.8	114.0	133.0	151.8	170.0	187.0	202.8	216.5	....	500.0 @ 1200
S-820	6	5⅝	5½	97.0	122.0	148.0	173.0	196.0	216.8	236.0	252.0	267.0	280.0	651.0 @ 1200

(CONTINUED)

NATURAL GAS

Model	Cyl.	Bore	Str.	800	1000	1200	1400	1600	1800	2000	2200	2400	2600	TORQUE lbs. ft. @ R.P.M.
Y-112	4	3³⁄₁₆	3½	11.0	14.8	18.0	20.8	23.5	25.7	27.5	28.7	29.2	....	80.0 @ 1200
F-162	4	3⁷⁄₁₆	4⅜	17.8	23.5	28.7	33.5	38.0	41.7	45.0	47.8	49.8	51.2	126.0 @ 1400
F-226	6	3⁵⁄₁₆	4⅜	24.0	30.2	36.5	42.5	48.0	53.5	58.0	62.0	66.0	69.0	162.0 @ 1200
M-330	6	4	4⅜	37.0	47.2	57.0	66.5	75.0	82.5	89.5	95.4	100.0	104.0	250.0 @ 1200
B-427	6	4⁵⁄₁₆	4⅞	46.0	58.0	70.0	81.0	92.0	102.0	110.5	119.0	119.0	....	306.0 @ 1200
U-501	6	4½	5¼	60.0	75.0	90.0	105.0	118.5	132.0	143.5	154.0	163.0	170.5	397.0 @ 1200
R-602	6	4⅞	5⅜	73.0	91.0	110.0	128.0	145.0	160.0	174.0	187.0	197.0	205.0	485.0 @ 1200
S-749	6	5⅜	5½	82.5	107.0	128.2	147.4	165.0	179.8	190.5	....	....	....	564.0 @ 1200
S-820	6	5⅝	5½	95.0	120.0	145.0	170.0	192.0	212.0	230.0	240.6	260.0	271.0	638.0 @ 1400

POWER TAKE OFF VARIATIONS AVAILABLE

ENGINE SERIES		N-400	Y-400	F-400	E-400	F-600	M-600	B-600	G-400	H-400	J-400	T-600	U-600	R-600	S-600	GD-157	ED-201	HD-260	JD-382	TD-427	RD-572	SD-802
1 Stubshaft		X	X	X	X	X	X	X	X	X	X	X	X	X	X	X	X	X	X	X	X	X
2 Clutch Power Take Off	Direct	X	X	X	X	X	X	X	X	X	X	X	X	X	X	X	X	X	X	X	X	X
	Belt	X	X	X	X	X	X	X	X	X	X	X	X	X	X	X	X	X	X	X	X	X
3 Clutch Power Take Off with gear Reduction unit		X	X	X	X	X	X	X	X	X	X	X	X	X	X	X	X	X	X	X	X	X
4 Torque Convertor		—	—	X		X	X	X		X	X	X	X	X				X	X	X	X	X
5 Clutch Power Take Off with extended shaft & outboard bearing							X	X				X	X	X	X					X	X	X

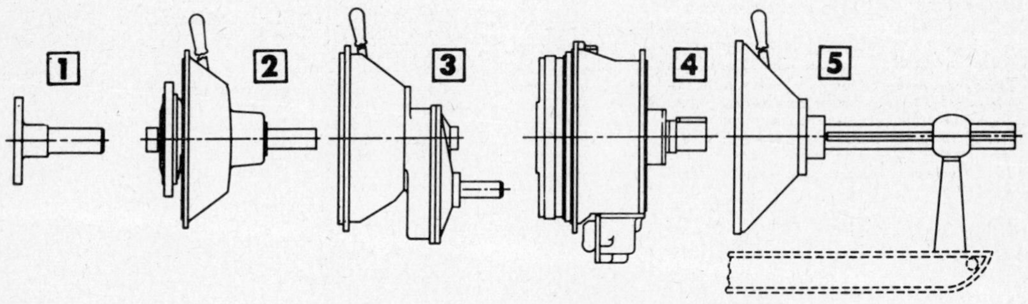

4-CYCLE AIR-COOLED MODELS

In addition to its large engines, Continental builds an outstanding line of heavy-duty air-cooled four-cycle models for industrial applications requiring 2 to 3 h.p. Advanced engineering gives them easy starting, high dependability, and unusual lugging capacity at low speeds . . . Options: patented and exclusive Contex® external ignition system, built-in electric generator for operating lights or charging battery, low-level ignition cut-off, 6-1 reduction gear, and other features. Available also for use on kerosene . . . For information on these models, address Air-Cooled Industrial Engine Division, 12800 Kercheval Ave., Detroit 15, Mich.

D. W. ONAN & SONS INC.

3603 University Ave. S.E., Minneapolis 14, Minnesota

ONAN Electric Plants — 500 to 75,000 watts

The range of the Onan line covers every requirement for electrical generating equipment up to 75,000 watts. Lightweight, air-cooled plants from 500 to 10,000 watts provide portable and mobile sources of electricity. Heavy-duty air-cooled plants and high-capacity water-cooled units from 10,000 to 75,000 watts fill any need for standby power. For auxiliary use or where heavy-duty continuous service is called for, Onan builds Air-Cooled Diesel Electric Plants in 3,000 and 5,000 watts.

A wide variety of accessories adds versatility to many models enabling you to choose generating equipment which fits your job exactly.

Onan Electric Plants combine many advantages. Every plant is Unit-built with engine and generator direct-connected for permanent alignment. They are compact for easier installation. Ratings are conservative and performance is fully warranted. The widespread Onan sales organization has distributors and dealers in every state. Repair parts and service are available regardless of your location.

This trailer-mounted, high-capacity, water-cooled Onan Electric Plant is towed behind a Civil Defense emergency comunications truck. It supplies current for loudspeakers, radio transmitter, lights and other equipment.

With this dolly-mounted, 1,500-watt Onan model, two men can clip hedges and trim grass with electric tools, in a fraction of the time that hand tools would require. Easily wheeled from place to place, it provides plug-in power anywhere.

Mounted on the fire rig, this 2,500-watt Onan air-cooled model operates searchlights and electric tools of all kinds. The Onan 4-cycle engine is direct-connected to an Onan all-climate generator in a compact, permanently-aligned, long-life unit.

Hundreds of traveling libraries are equipped with Onan Electric Plants for light and power. The 10KW Onan CW model shown here has the capacity to operate lights, fans, air-conditioners and all other equipment necessary. Quiet-running.

D. W. ONAN & SONS INC.

3603 University Ave. S.E., Minneapolis 14, Minnesota

500 to 2,500 watts A.C.

Onan 2,500-watt model. Lightweight. 4-cycle engine.

Portable, single-cylinder, air-cooled, gasoline driven models. Carry, wheel or truck one of these Onan Electric Plants to any spot for a dependable source of plug-in A.C. electricity. Supply power for floodlights, A.C. or A.C.-D.C. electric tools and other motor-driven equipment. Extremely compact, light in weight and ruggedly constructed. Can be equipped with carrying frame or 2-wheel dolly at added cost. Easily moved, quick to start, simple to service.

TYPICAL APPLICATIONS: On fire-fighting rigs, emergency trucks, park and boulevard maintenance, utility service.

Model	*Watts*	*Volts*	*Starting Method**	*R.P.M.*	*Lgth.*	*Width*	*Ht.*	*Weight (lbs.)*
05AK-1M	500	115 AC	Manual	1800	18¾"	19⅛"	21⅝"	122
07AK-1M	750	115 AC	Manual	1800	22"	19⅛"	22½"	152
1AJ-1M	1000	115 AC	Manual	1800	22"	13⅞"	19½"	159
105AK-1M	1500	115 AC	Manual	3600	20½"	19⅛"	21⅝"	130
105AK-1P (2)	1500	115 AC	Manual	3600	26¾"	18¼"	20⅝"	125
2LK	2000	115 AC	Manual	1800	28"	16"	20⅜"	235
205AJ-1M (1)	2500	115 AC	Manual	3600	23"	13⅞"	19½"	154
205AJ-1P (2)	2500	115 AC	Manual	3600	26¾"	14"	17⅛"	139

* Remote starting models can be supplied in most sizes.
(1) Equipped with Readi-Pull recoil rope starter.
(2) Completely self-contained with carrying frame and Readi-Pull recoil rope starter.

3,500 watts and 5,000 watts A.C.

Designed to produce unusually large output for their size and weight, these heavy-duty plants make ample power available for lighting, for operating a wide range of electric tools and other motor-driven equipment.

Powered by economical-to-operate Onan 2-cylinder gasoline engines. Give outstanding service on every job . . . portable or stationary. Portable models are equipped with carrying frame, engine hood, 6-receptacle outlet box, muffler and ready-mounted fuel tank. Shipped complete.

Model 5CCK-1P 5,000 watts A.C.

Model	*Watts*	*Volts**	*Starting Method*	*Lgth.*	*Width*	*Ht.*	*Weight (lbs.)*
305CCK-1P (1)	3,500	115 AC	Manual	38"	27⅛"	22¼"	330
305CCK-1M	3,500	115 AC	Manual	28⅜"	21⅛"	19½"	285
5CCK-1P (1)	5,000	115 AC	Manual	38"	27⅛"	22¼"	390
5CCK-1M	5,000	115 AC	Manual	31⅞"	21⅛"	19½"	350

(1) Portable models with carrying frame. Completely self-contained.
All models equipped with Readi-Pull recoil starter.
Standard voltage combinations available on all models.

D. W. ONAN & SONS INC.

3603 University Ave. S.E., Minneapolis 14, Minnesota

7,500 and 10,000 watts A.C.

Extremely compact units require less than one cubic yard of space, making them adaptable to many types of portable and stationary jobs requiring 7½ or 10 KW.

Powered by heavy-duty 2-cylinder, air-cooled engines designed specifically for electric plant service. Exclusive suction-air-cooling maintains proper operating temperatures for both engine and generator and ventilates installation compartment as well. Heated air and exhaust gases can be ejected from a single vent. Smooth-running and quiet.

Model 10CW 10,000 watts A.C.

Model	*Watts*	*Volts*	*Method Starting*	*Dimensions* Lgth.	Wdth.	Ht.	*Wt. (lbs.)*
705CW-4R (1)	7,500	120/208 A.C.	Remote	37"	25¼"	28"	710
705CW-3R (2)	7,500	115/230 A.C.	Remote	37"	25¼"	28"	750
10CW-4R (1)	10,000	120/208 A.C.	Remote	39½"	25¼"	31½"	760
10CW-3R (2)	10,000	115/230 A.C.	Remote	39½"	25¼"	31½"	775

(1) 3 phase (2) single-phase

10KW to 75KW

Series 25EC. 25KW. 6-cylinder, water-cooled industrial engine.

Prime movers are 4, 6 and 8-cylinder, water-cooled gasoline engine which operate at moderate speed (1800 rpm.) for longer engine life.

Built for heavy-duty stationary or portable operation, unhoused Onan Electric Plants supply dependable A.C. power for large scale projects. These compact, easy-to-install units provide current for area lighting, for tools and other motor-driven equipment, and for emergency service.

All engine and electric controls essential for plant operation are standard equipment; and ample space is available on the generator-mounted control box for addition of optional electric instruments.

All unhoused models are remote starting with controls located at the plant. (Fully housed electric plants can be supplied in capacities of 10, 15, 25 and 35KW.)

Model (unhoused)	*Watts (KW)*	*Volts**	*Phase*	*Wire*	*Weight (lbs.)*
25EC-3R8	25	115/230 A.C.	1	3	1585
35ED-3R8	35	115/230 A.C.	1	3	1765
10HQ-3R8	10	115/230 A.C.	1	3	1265
15HQ-3R8	15	115/230 A.C.	1	3	1270
75HR-4R8	75,000	120/208 A.C.	3	4	2850
50KA-4R8	50,000	120/208 A.C.	3	4	4200

* All standard voltages and 3-phase available. All models voltage regulated.

D. W. ONAN & SONS INC.

3603 University Ave. S.E., Minneapolis 14, Minnesota

ONAN DIESEL ELECTRIC PLANTS

3 and 5KW, Air-cooled

Designed and built for continuous, heavy-duty operation. Deliver low-cost electricity for auxiliary use or on construction jobs.

With Onan Diesel Electric Plants, you get real operating economy . . . approximately one pint of inexpensive Diesel fuel is required per kilowatt hour. Running costs are about 50 per cent less than for gasoline-powered models of equal capacity.

Recommended wherever dependable day-in and day-out electric service is required.

3DSP Series—One-cylinder, electric starting, 3,000 watts.

5DRP Series—Two-cylinder, electric starting, 5,000 watts.

Available with all standard voltages.

Model 5DRP-3R 5,000 watts A.C.

ACCESSORIES

AUTOMATIC LINE TRANSFER CONTROLS

Line transfer controls, designed for use with Onan A.C. Standby Plants, make transfer of the load and standby plant operation completely automatic. When the normal electric power supply fails, these controls shift the load from the mainline to the emergency standby plant; and, simultaneously, control the electric cranking. When normal service is restored, the controls stop the standby plant and re-transfer the load to the regular mainlines.

TRAILERS AND DOLLIES

Many models of Onan Electric Plants can be equipped for mobile operation. Rubber-tired, two-wheeled dollies with handles for smaller plants permit moving them easily around on the job. Two-wheel dollies and four-wheel trailers for larger plants give them a wide range of mobility.

High speed trailers are available for most Onan Electric Plants.

Underground fuel tanks
Starting batteries
Gas carburetors
Plant exercisers
Signal lights and alarms

Manual transfer switches
Instrument panels
Running-time meters
Heat exchangers
Fuel lines and fittings

ANACONDA WIRE & CABLE COMPANY

25 Broadway, New York 4, N. Y.

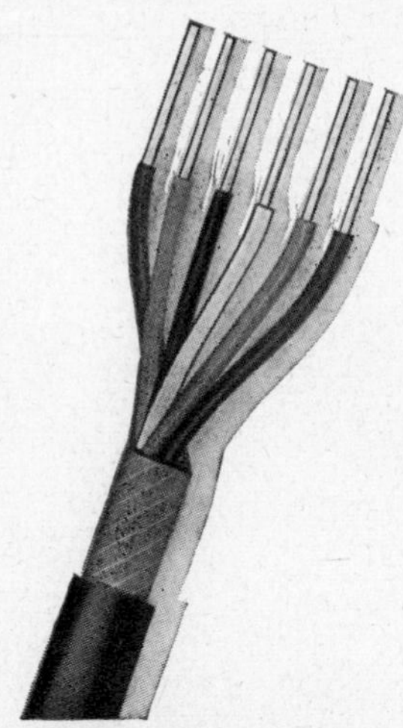

MULTI-CONDUCTOR, #12 AWG SOLID, 30 MILS POLYETHYLENE INSULATION

DENSHEATH JACKET—IMSA CABLE SPEC. 19

MUNICIPAL SIGNAL CABLE

MULTI-CONDUCTOR, #12 AWG SOLID, 30 MILS POLYETHYLENE INSULATION DENSHEATH JACKET—IMSA CABLE SPEC. 19

No. of Conductors	Jacket Thickness 64ths	Approx. Diameter inch	Net Weight lbs/M ft.	Shipping Weight lbs/M ft.
2	5	.47	139	210
3	5	.49	160	231
4	5	.54	193	284
6	6	.65	262	353
7	6	.65	280	371
10	6	.80	390	486
12	6	.82	437	533
16	7	.92	582	755
19	7	.96	662	835
27	7	1.13	903	1183
30	7	1.17	986	1266
37	7	1.25	1179	1459

MULTI-CONDUCTOR, #14 AWG SOLID, 25 MILS POLYETHYLENE INSULATION

DENSHEATH JACKET—IMSA CABLE SPEC. 19

MULTI-CONDUCTOR, #14 AWG SOLID, 25 MILS POLYETHYLENE INSULATION DENSHEATH JACKET—IMSA CABLE SPEC. 19

No. of Conductors	Jacket Thickness 64ths	Approx. Diameter inch	Net Weight lbs/M ft.	Shipping Weight lbs/M ft
2	5	.42	112	183
3	5	.43	124	195
4	5	.46	147	218
6	5	.54	173	264
7	5	.54	185	276
10	6	.69	276	367
12	6	.70	307	398
16	6	.77	385	481
19	6	.80	437	533
27	7	.96	618	791
30	7	.99	672	845
37	7	1.07	803	1083

MULTI-CONDUCTOR, #16 AWG SOLID, 25 MILS POLYETHYLENE INSULATION

DENSHEATH JACKET—IMSA CABLE SPEC. 19

MULTI-CONDUCTOR, #16 AWG SOLID, 25 MILS POLYETHYLENE INSULATION DENSHEATH JACKET—IMSA CABLE SPEC. 19

No. of Conductors	Jacket Thickness 64ths	Approx. Diameter inch	Net Weight lbs/M ft.	Shipping Weight lbs/M ft.
2	5	.39	97	147
3	5	.41	103	153
4	5	.43	121	192
6	5	.49	135	206
7	5	.49	141	212
10	6	.63	213	304
12	6	.65	223	324
16	6	.70	289	380
19	6	.73	324	420
27	6	.85	433	529
30	6	.88	470	566
37	7	.97	583	756

Evansville, Indiana
Sewage Treatment Plant – five Climax V-8 gas engines driving vertical sewage pumps through right angle gears.

V-122—12 cyl. - 7" bore x 7" stroke.
V-125—12 cyl. - 7½" bore x 7" stroke.

V-80 — 8 cyl. - 7" bore x 7" stroke.
V-85 — 8 cyl. - 7½" bore x 7" stroke.

K-67 — 6 cyl. - 7" bore x 7" stroke.
K-75 — 6 cyl. - 7½" bore x 7" stroke.

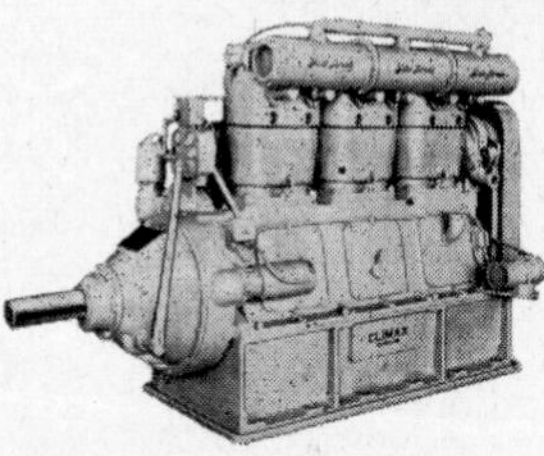

R-4I — 4 cyl. - 6" bore x 7" stroke.
R-6I — 6 cyl. - 6" bore x 7" stroke.

MUNICIPAL POWER!

IN SEWAGE TREATMENT PLANTS from coast to coast, Climax engines can be found on the job every day of the year — powering sewage pumps, blowers and generators. Tremendous savings are being realized by using readily available **sludge gas** for fuel and also by utilizing heat from the jacket water and exhaust gas of the engines to heat digesters and buildings. When a shortage of sludge gas is encountered these engines operate on an auxiliary fuel — either gasoline, butane or natural gas, or a combination thereof. Climax offers eight rugged engines for continuous duty service in Sewage Plants — in a range of sizes from 50 to 300 H.P.

IN WATER WORKS, in over 100 cities throughout the country, Climax engines can be depended upon to take over when the normal source of power is interrupted by storms or mechanical failures. In addition to powering pumps and generators during emergencies, these engines drive pumps when peak load periods are encountered — to supplement regular pumping equipment. Climax Water Works engines operate on natural gas, butane or gasoline and are available in a range of sizes up to 600 H.P.

WRITE TODAY for complete information, bulletins or engineering consultation.

climax

ENGINE AND PUMP MANUFACTURING CO.
208 S. LA SALLE ST. • CHICAGO 4, ILLINOIS
FACTORY • CLINTON, IOWA
DISTRICT OFFICE • DALLAS, TEXAS

Collyer

MUNICIPAL SIGNAL AND LIGHTING CABLES

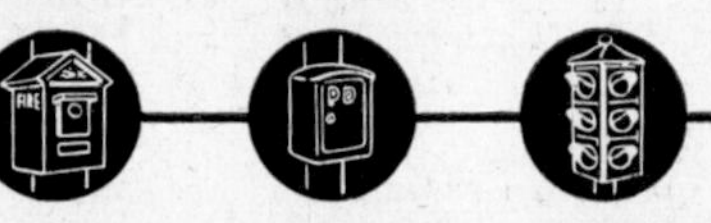

SIGNAL AND CONTROL CABLES

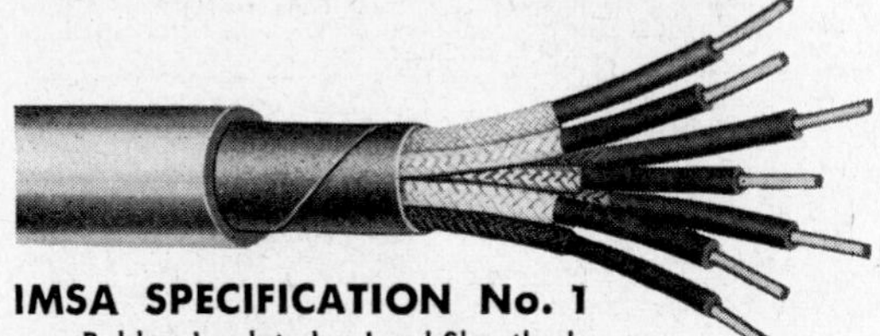

IMSA SPECIFICATION No. 1
Rubber Insulated — Lead Sheathed

IMSA SPECIFICATION No. 5
Rubber Insulated — Suprene Sheathed

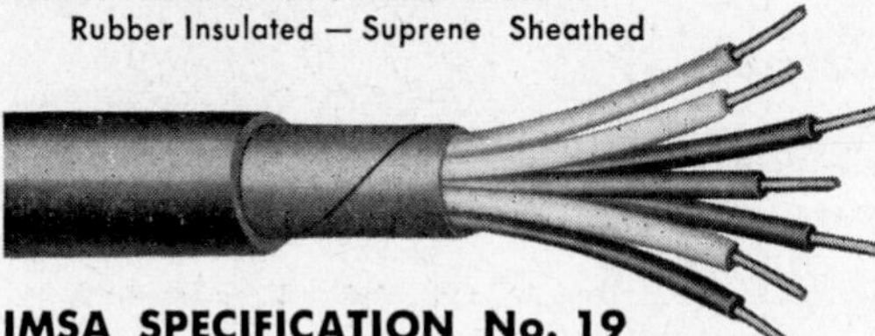

IMSA SPECIFICATION No. 19
Polyethylene Insulated — Resistol Sheathed

IMSA SPECIFICATION No. 20
Resistol Insulated — Resistol Sheathed

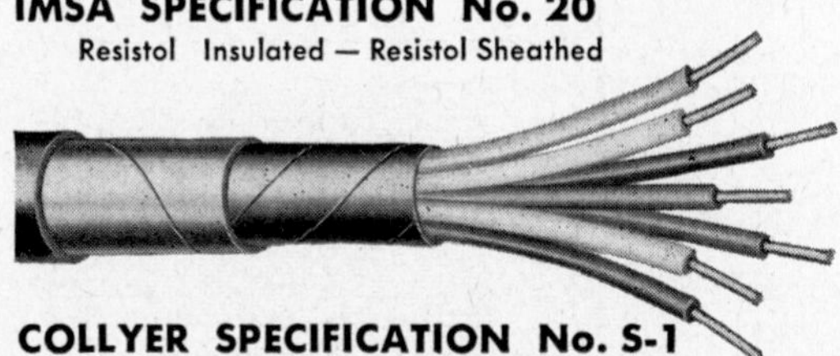

COLLYER SPECIFICATION No. S-1
Polyethylene Insulated and Belted — Shielded — Resistol Sheathed

COLLYER SPECIFICATION No. S-2
Rubber Insulated — Neoprene Sheathed

SERIES LIGHTING CABLES

IMSA SPECIFICATON No. 9
Rubber Insulated — Suprene Sheathed

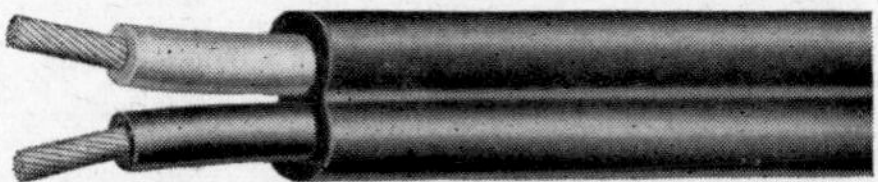

COLLYER SPECIFICATION SL-No. 10
Resistol Insulated and Polyethylene Sheathed

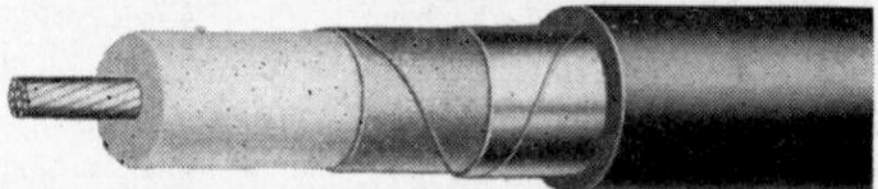

COLLYER SPECIFICATION SL-No. 20
Polyethylene Insulated — Shielded
Resistol Sheathed

COLLYER SPECIFICATION SL-No. 30
Neoprene Insulated Figure 8

LINE WIRE

Neoprene Covered
Polyethylene Covered

INSULATED WIRE COMPANY
245 Roosevelt Ave.
Pawtucket, R. I.

MOLONEY ELECTRIC COMPANY

General Offices: St. Louis 20, Mo.

FACTORIES AT: St. Louis, Mo., and Toronto, Ont., Canada

SALES OFFICES

Alexandria, Va. .... 401 Doniphan Bldg.
Amarillo, Tex. .... 428 Amarillo Bldg.
Atlanta 18, Ga. 1537 Howell Mill Rd., N.W.
Birmingham 9, Ala. ...... 3128 Roxbury Road
Bluefield, W. Va. .... P. O. Box 33
Boston 16, Mass. .... Statler Office Bldg., 20 Providence St.
Buffalo 3, N. Y. .... 564 Ellicott Square Bldg.
Butte, Montana .... 829 Maryland Ave.
Charlotte, N. C. .... 109 W. Griffith St.
Chicago 3, Illinois .... 100 West Monroe St.
Dallas 1, Tex. .... 1205 Fidelity Union Life Bldg.
Denver 4, Colo. .... 1236 Elati St.
Detroit 2, Mich. .... 744 New Center Bldg.
Houston 1, Tex. .... 4411 Navigation Blvd.
Indianapolis 2, Ind. .... 2011 N. Meridian
Jacksonville, Fla. .... 4157 Timuquana Rd.
Los Angeles 13, Calif. .... Subway Terminal Bldg., 417 So. Hill
Kansas City 12, Mo. .... Suite 219, Plaza Theatre Bldg.
Knoxville 17, Tenn. .... 1243 N. Broadway
Memphis, Tenn. .... 1352 Madison Ave.
Minneapolis 1, Minn. .... 632 Midland Bank Bldg.
New Orleans 15, La. .... 4018 Thalia St.
New York 5, N. Y. .... 55 Liberty St.
San Francisco 4, Calif. .... 407 Holbrook Bldg., 58 Sutter St.
Omaha 2, Nebr. .... 524 WOW Bldg.
Philadelphia, Pa. (Narberth) .... 105 Forest Ave., Rm. 5, Commerce Bldg.
Phoenix, Ariz. .... 1825 E. Jefferson St.
Pittsburgh 22, Pa. .... 1337 Oliver Bldg.
Portland, Ore. .... 1233 N. W. Twelfth Ave.
Salt Lake City, Utah ...... 422 Kearns Bldg.
Toronto, Ont., Canada, Moloney Electric Co. of Canada, Ltd., 213-219 Sterling Rd.
St. Petersburg 6, Fla. 1763 Ninth Ave., N.
Syracuse 2, New York .... Syracuse Kemper Bldg., 218 Harrison St.
Seattle 1, Wash. .... 2603 Western Ave.
Shreveport, La. .... 630 Spring Ave.
Wheeling, W. Va. .... 22nd & Market Sts.
Montreal 2, Que., Canada, Moloney Electric Co. of Canada, Ltd., Birks Bldg., Phillips Square

Power Transformers—Both standard design and Load Tap Changing Power Transformers.

Moloney HyperCore Dry Type Transformers—For general purpose power and lighting service. 1½ through 15 Kva are totally enclosed for outdoor installation and are suitable for wall mounting. 25 through 50 Kva available in both indoor and outdoor types.

MOLONEY PRODUCTS

POWER TRANSFORMERS
•
UNIT SUBSTATIONS
•
LOAD TAP CHANGING TRANSFORMERS
•
FEEDER VOLTAGE REGULATORS
•
REGULATING TRANSFORMERS
•
HYPERCORE DISTRIBUTION TRANSFORMERS (Conventional and CSP Types)
•
LOAD CENTER TRANSFORMERS
•
ASKAREL (Non-inflammable Liquid) COOLED TRANSFORMERS
•
AIR-COOLED (Group 2 and Group 3 Insulated) TRANSFORMERS
•
CONSTANT CURRENT STREET LIGHTING TRANSFORMERS
•
SUBMERSIBLE TYPE TRANSFORMERS
•
NETWORK TRANSFORMERS
•
MAGNETIC COMPONENTS FOR ELECTRONICS

Write for Catalog

Oil and Askarel-Immersed Load Center Transformers for Secondary Unit Substations. Available in Kva and voltage ratings to meet your specifications.

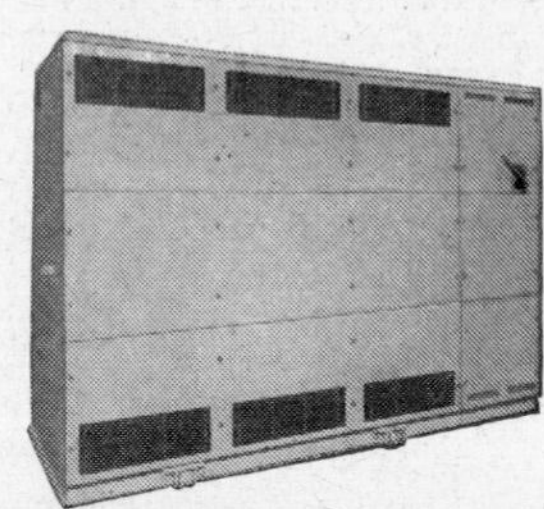

Ventilated Dry-Type Load Center Transformers (Group 2 Insulation). For Secondary Unit Substations. Available in Kva and voltage ratings to your specifications for indoor installations.

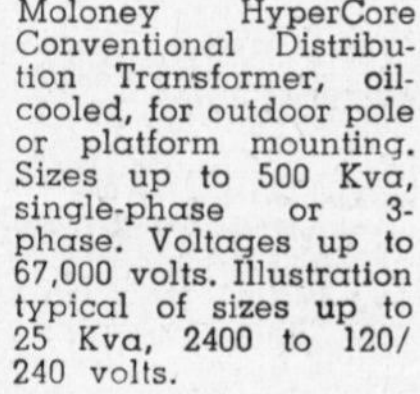

Moloney HyperCore Conventional Distribution Transformer, oil-cooled, for outdoor pole or platform mounting. Sizes up to 500 Kva, single-phase or 3-phase. Voltages up to 67,000 volts. Illustration typical of sizes up to 25 Kva, 2400 to 120/240 volts.

Moloney HyperCore Completely Self-Protected Transformer, oil cooled, equipped with built-in lightning and secondary overload protection. Sizes up to 100 Kva single-phase and 150 Kva 3-phase. Voltages up to 14,400 volts. Illustration typical of sizes up to 25 Kva, 2400 to 120/240 volts.

THE KARPARK CORPORATION

McMillan Street & Essex Place, Cincinnati 6, Ohio

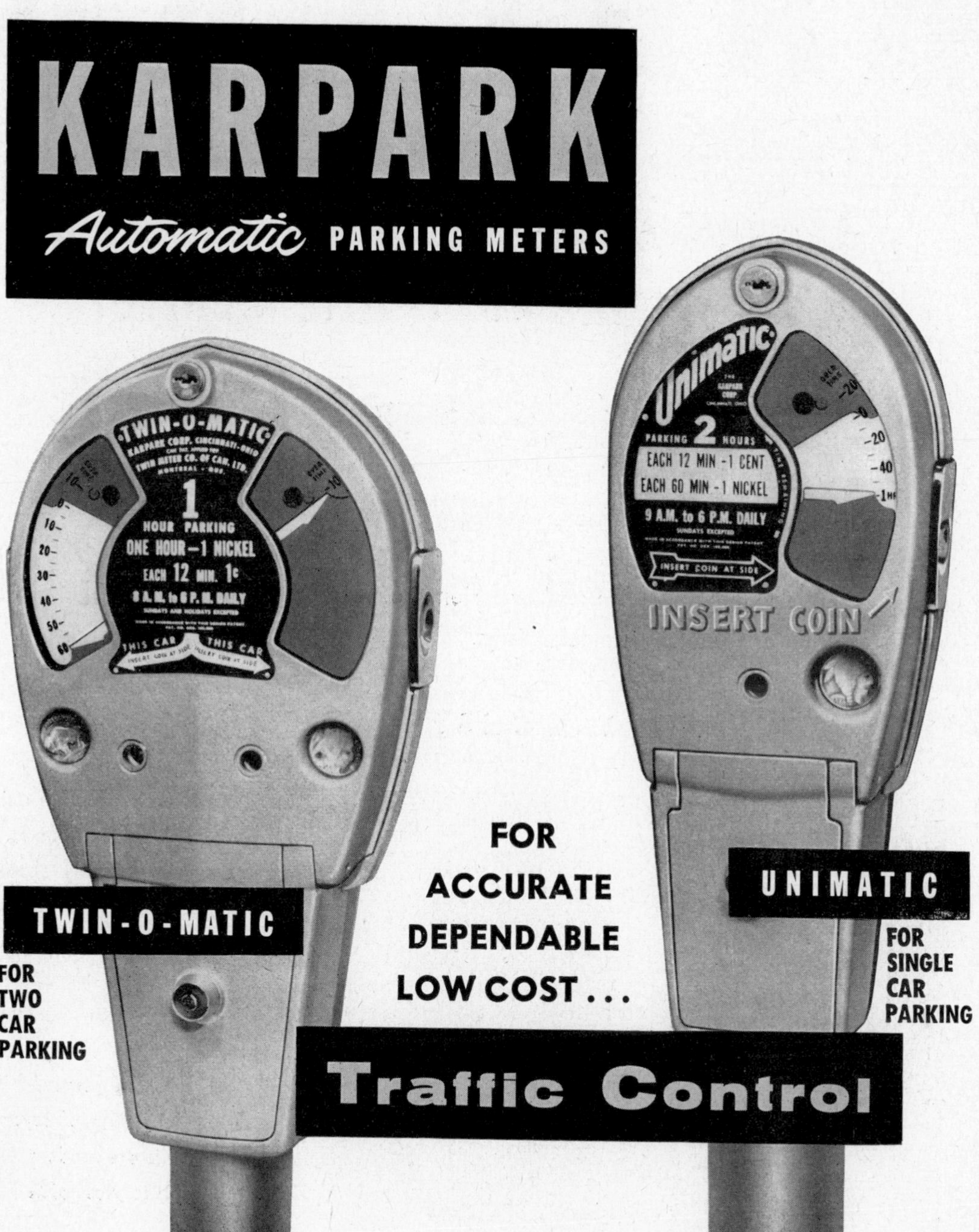

KARPARK

As replacements or as new installations, KARPARK Meters meet every requirement for low-cost, efficient Traffic Control

Karpark meters are made by the same master craftsmen who, for three generations, have produced the famous Herschede Hall Clocks. Every feature of design and construction reflects the knowledge and experience of men who have devoted their lives to the creation of fine timing mechanisms.

UNIT CONSTRUCTION

Exclusive interchangeable units keep Karpark service time to a minimum. If difficulty should develop, a Karpark is "down" only while a replacement unit is installed—a matter of minutes. Service costs are low, as clock mechanisms, main springs and coin slot units are removed by the simple loosening of several screws. Repairs are made quickly without the services of skilled technicians.

AUTOMATIC OPERATION

The simple, easy insertion of a coin is all that is required to operate a Karpark meter. No handles to turn, no plungers to push, no levers to move—there is nothing to forget. Saves motorist time and trouble, eliminates disputes, permits 100% enforcement, increases use of meters and produces greater revenue.

INTERCHANGEABLE MECHANISMS

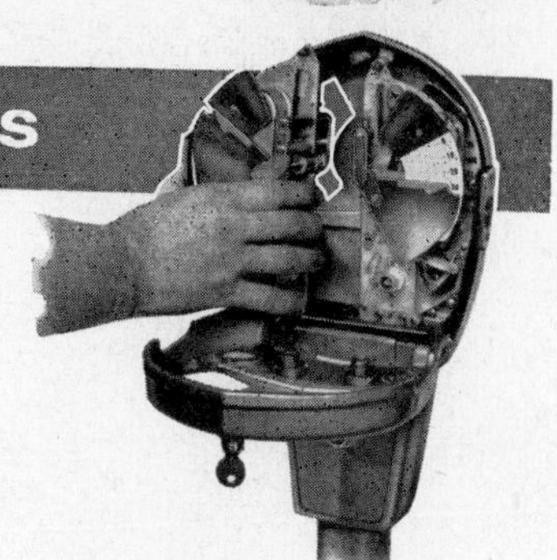

Each Karpark mechanism, in either the Twin-O-Matic or Unimatic, is a complete unit interchangeable from one meter to another. Fewer replacement units are required and substantial savings are speedily effected in both service and maintenance.

HEAVY DUTY HOUSING

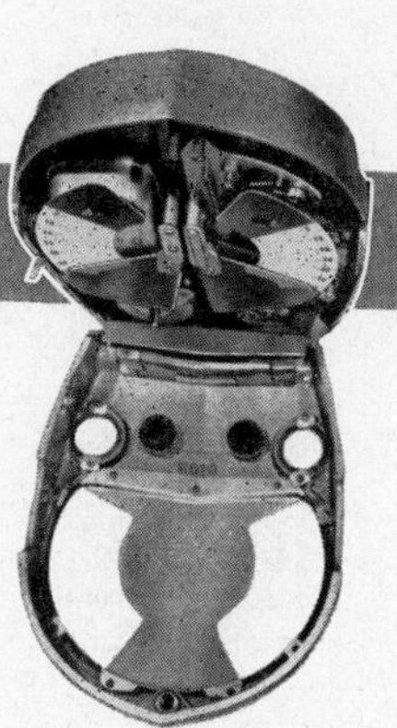

Karparks are constructed to give maximum resistance to damage from vandalism, collision and the elements. The housing is cast of a tremendously strong aluminum alloy (Federated No. F-480), finished in standard gray baked enamel or in any color specified. The dial windows are of heavy shock proof Lucite with waterproof seals. Units fit either 2′ or 2½″ standards.

PRECISION CONSTRUCTION

Karpark meters are precision-made to assure unfailing accuracy under the most adverse conditions. Gears and pinions are machine cut and polished, main spring is sealed with "lifetime" lubrication, rugged lever escapement has jewelled balance staff and entire unit is constructed of clock brass, stainless steel and aluminum for rustproof operation.

MAGEE-HALE PARK-O-METER COMPANY

Oklahoma City, Oklahoma

FACTORIES IN U.S.A., CANADA, ENGLAND

Model H Automatic

PARK-O-METER

is a good investment

Park-O-Meter is a long-term investment which pays continuing dividends in increased revenues, minimum service and maintenance, and resolved parking problems for many years.

- **Buy Quality**
- **Buy Good Design**
- **Buy Equipment** engineered to be adjustable to meet every requirement for any location under today's or tomorrow's changing needs.

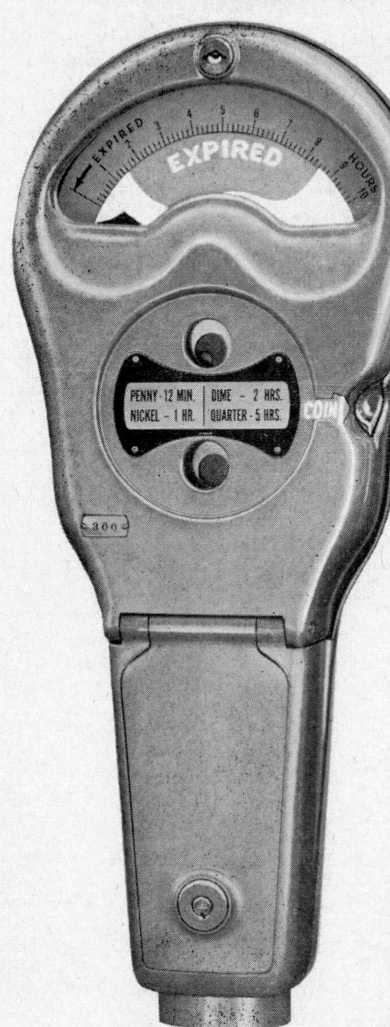

simple . . . positive . . . dependable

uses all four common coins through a single coin slot

Pennies, nickels, dimes, quarters . . . any one or all . . . in any combination, activate the mechanism by simple finger pressure when inserted in the coin slot.

- **Convenient**
- **Trouble-Free**
- **Versatile**

No handle to turn or fail to turn
No exposed working parts

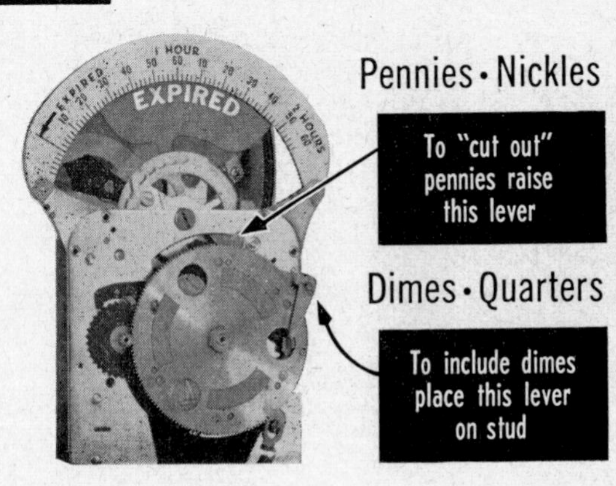

Adjustable • Adaptable

A new, important Development Specified by Traffic Consultants

RATES and SPLIT RATES

A simple setting of the Rate Adjustment Ring predetermines the amount of time allowed for each coin according to the requirements of each location.

Split rates permit setting a certain rate for a portion of the time limit with a different rate for the extended time. This is ideal for parking lot applications by either: (1) Encouraging long-time parking at a reduced rate after the initial period, or (2) to encourage short-time parking by charging a premium rate for extra time.

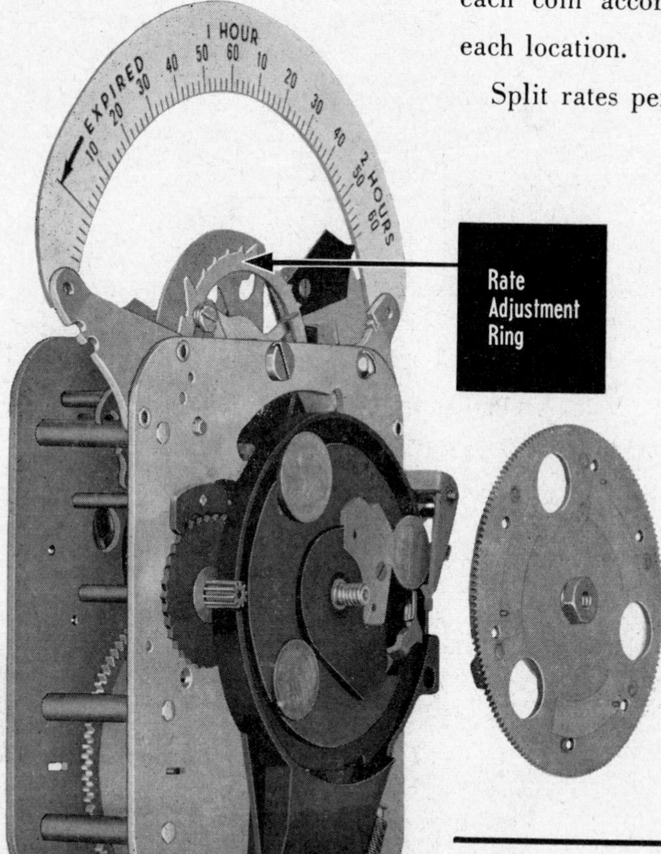

BRANDT AUTOMATIC CASHIER CO.

Watertown • Wisconsin

WHY SORT AND COUNT COLLECTIONS FROM PARKING METERS BY HAND?

Use

BRANDT

COIN HANDLING PRODUCTS

Many cities throughout the land are saving time and money by sorting, counting, bagging and packaging coins collected from parking meters with speedy Brandt machines.

A Brandt machine can be depended upon for absolute accuracy.

We shall gladly arrange for a demonstration of Brandt equipment right in your office — without cost or obligation.

COUNTING DIALS KEEP AN ACCURATE COUNT

SIMPLY DUMP COINS INTO HOPPER

COINS SORTED BY DENOMINATION INTO DRAWERS OR COIN BAGS

MODEL SL BRANDT COIN SORTER AND COUNTER

(Motor Driven)

Sorts and counts mixed coins— pennies to half dollars inclusive — in one quick, easy operation. Long life and absolute accuracy assured by exclusive features.

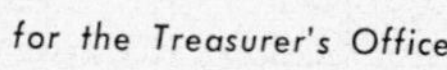

MODEL CHM BRANDT COIN COUNTER AND PACKAGER

(Motor Driven)

Counts and packages coins from pennies through silver dollars. Mechanical improvements make for speedy counting and packaging of coins with less effort. Hand operated machine is also available.

for the Treasurer's Office

MODEL 251 BRANDT AUTOMATIC CASHIER

Change delivered to customers upon depression of a single key.

BRANDT AUTOMATIC CASHIER CO.

WATERTOWN *Established 1890* WISCONSIN

MI-CO PARKING METERS

Manufactured by The Michaels Art Bronze Co., Inc.

P. O. Box 668-MI, Covington, Kentucky

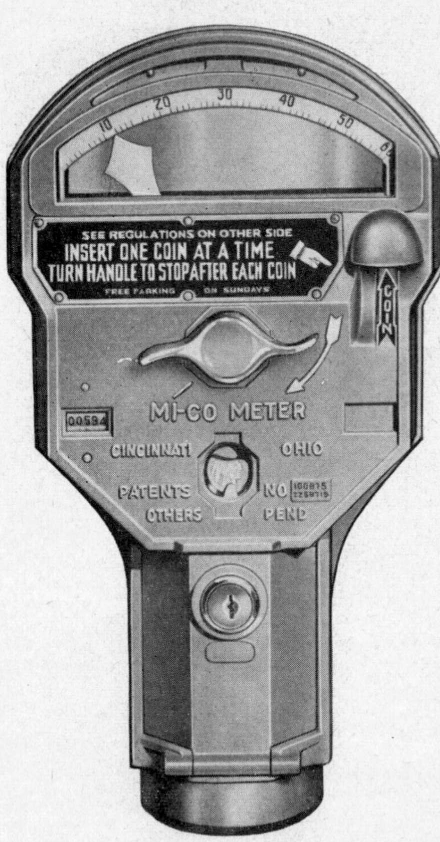

When motorist inserts a coin he gives the handle a one-third turn to the right. This action winds the spring which sets the mechanism in motion to deliver the exact amount of parking time purchased.

MI-CO MANUAL
PARKING METER

TIME DIAL—visible from both sides
INDICATOR HAND—visible from both sides
INSTRUCTION PLATE—aluminum, flush mounted, alumilite finish
HANDLE—nonslip
COUNTER—automatic nonreversible
COIN OBSERVATION WINDOW—Plexiglas
VIOLATION SIGNAL WINDOWS—1/8" Plexiglas
COIN SLOT—weather protection cover
CASE—die cast. Tensile strength 45,000 pounds
LOCKS—cylinder. Super pick-resisting mechanism with non-duplicable type key
COIN COMPARTMENT DOOR—reinforced, interlocked and securely hinged to case
SPECIAL LOCKING SCREWS—removal releases entire mechanism
FINISH—case Bonderized inside and out. Color optional—standard color is aluminum with instruction plate in green
STANDARD—2 3/8" O.D. hot galvanized steel pipe. Meter is attached by special locking bolt accessible only through coin compartment

LOW MAINTENANCE • DEPENDABLE SERVICE
STURDY CONSTRUCTION • FEWER MOVING PARTS

Large Red Violation Signal is clearly visible 200 feet away. Patrolmen supervise both sides of the street at the same time. Coin Counter registers actual amount of money passing through the meter. Nickel registers five—penny registers one. All coins are deposited in the same slot. By a simple mechanical adjustment, the MI-CO Meter may be adjusted to exact parking time for a one-cent or a five-cent deposit. MI-CO Parking Meters were designed, and are manufactured in our own plant. All materials are noncorrosive and will withstand the most severe weather conditions.

HERE'S WHY YOU CAN DEPEND ON MI-CO METERS:

1) MI-CO Meters have fewer moving parts to get out of order and cause trouble; 2) Correct engineering and structural ruggedness assure many extra years of dependable, trouble-free service; 3) Interior parts are made of stainless steel, clock brass and brass forgings, or die castings; 4) Simplicity of construction—no winding by maintenance men. Motorist gives handle one-third of a turn when coin is deposited; 5) MI-CO Meters are built to operate in all kinds of weather—hot or cold, wet or dry.

Illustration below shows the parking method for the MI-CO Manual Meter.

Manufactured by The Michaels Art Bronze Co., Inc., P.O. Box 668-MI, Covington, Kentucky

MI-CO TWIN

AUTOMATIC PARKING METER . . .

is the best Twin Parking Meter on the market. It is the original, time-tested twin automatic parking meter . . . the only meter actually designed as a twin. The engineers who developed the MI-CO Twin were not satisfied to do what so many other manufacturers have since done—fasten two single meters together and call the result a twin. They designed a meter with only one mechanism to function as a twin . . . one meter to service two cars. There are many advantages to this type of construction:

- Only one meter of service instead of two
- One clock to wind
- One coin box
- Fewer moving parts
- Half the number of posts to install
- Only half the number of meters to police
- Maintenance costs reduced about one-half
- Mechanism quickly accessible (this may be removed without touching a bolt, nut or screw).

By a simple mechanical adjustment the MI-CO Twin Automatic may be set for any number of hours on various coin combinations.

The red violation signals on both sides of the meter are visible from a considerable distance. This makes policing the meters a simple matter for the patrolman on foot, or the motorcycle officer.

The excellent performance record of the MI-CO Twin is the result of more than six years of on-the-street service in many cities. We'll be glad to furnish you with the names of these cities and suggest you communicate with the officials of any or all as to their experience with the MI-CO Twin Automatic Parking Meter. Also available on request is fully illustrated literature giving complete details about the MI-CO Twin.

MI-CO TWIN AUTOMATIC

Motorist inserts the correct coin for the amount of time he wishes to purchase, and the meter goes into operation automatically.

Illustration below shows the MI-CO Twin Automatic method of parking two cars at one meter.

MI-CO PARKING METERS

Manufactured by The Michaels Art Bronze Co., Inc.

P. O. Box 668-MI, Covington, Kentucky

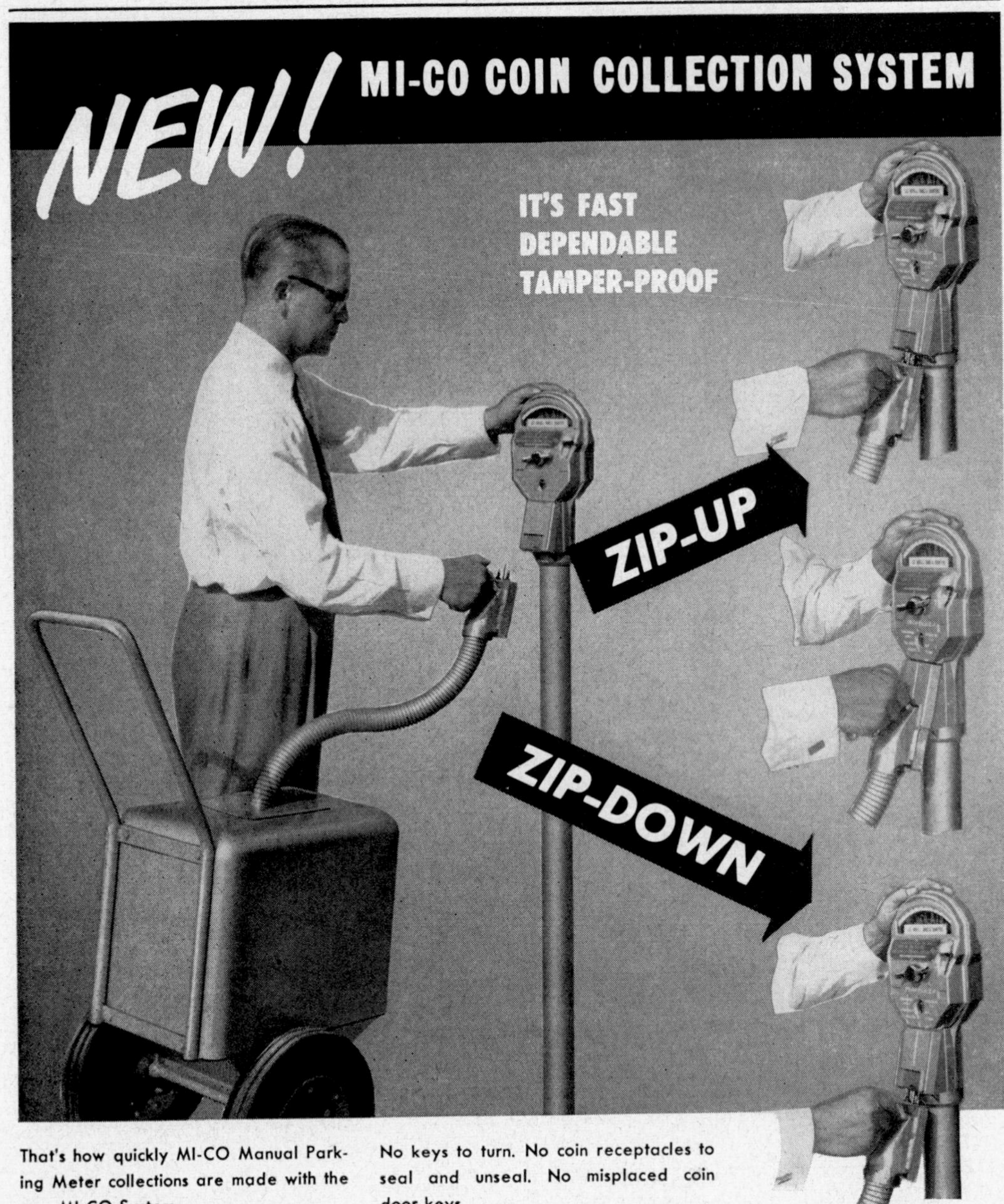

That's how quickly MI-CO Manual Parking Meter collections are made with the new MI-CO System.

Coins drop through collector unit into locked coin cart.

Coins do not drop into a funnel which could be blocked, but are guided into cart unseen and untouched by collector.

No keys to turn. No coin receptacles to seal and unseal. No misplaced coin door keys.

Sliding coin door double locked and protected by stainless steel sheathing.

Registered keyway — your guarantee that key blanks cannot be obtained from local locksmiths.

And . . . the new MI-CO Coin Collection System is adaptable to MI-CO Manual Parking Meters already installed.

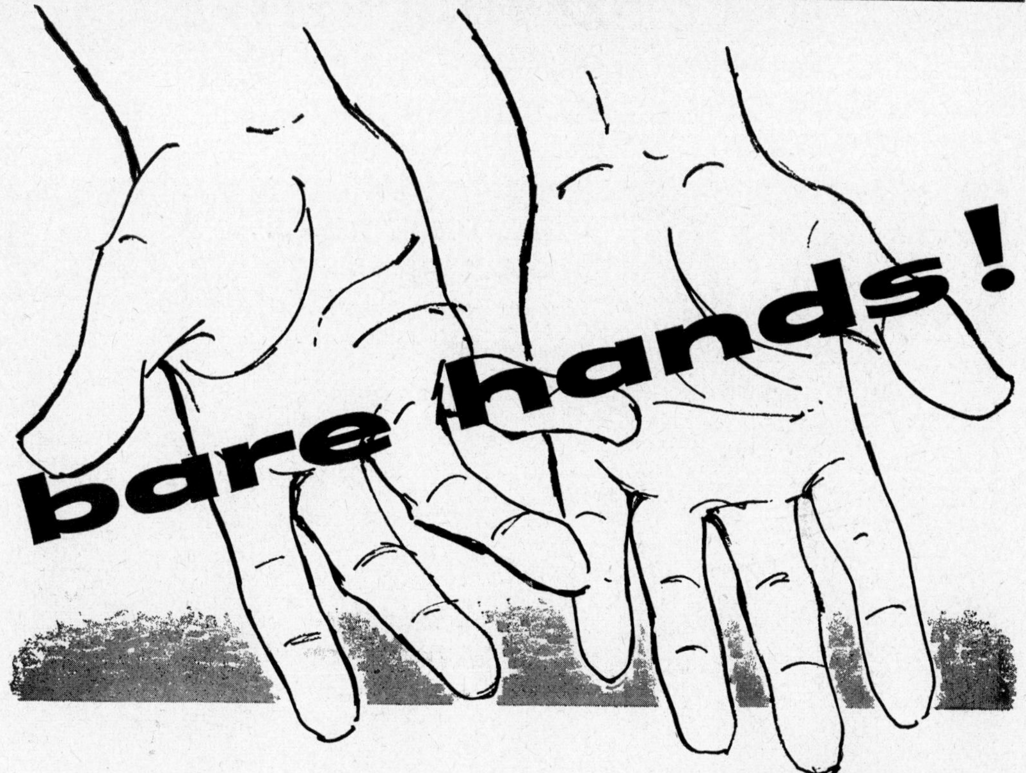

. . . That's all you need to assemble and disassemble a MARK-TIME Parking Meter.

Five expertly engineered units fit together *like a glove* for fast, easy assembly and "take-apart" of this manually operated meter . . . another exclusive "MARK-TIME" feature.

Because of the MARK-TIME design with its sealed timing mechanism and "no clockwork," on-the-job maintenance is greatly minimized . . . saving time, upping meter-income for the city.

MARK-TIME PARKING METER
No. 1 choice for modern parking control

FEATURES: Low maintenance cost, long-view time and violation dials, sealed self-locking coin box collection system, magnifying coin window, simple, trouble-free movement, magic link protection, factory repair and service.

Modernized, clean-cut, attractive design . . . adds progressive appearance to parking areas.

M. H. RHODES, INC., 30 BARTHOLOMEW AVE., HARTFORD, CONN.

Manufactured and Sold in Canada by: SPERRY GYROSCOPE OTTAWA Ltd., Ottawa, Ontario, Canada

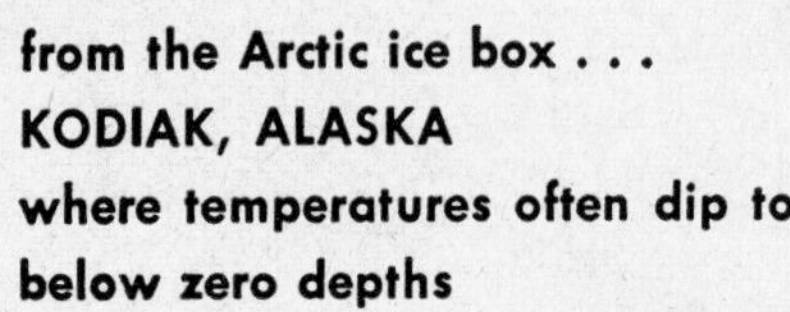

from the Arctic ice box . . .
KODIAK, ALASKA
where temperatures often dip to below zero depths

. . . to the heart of the broiling tropics in VENEZUELA where temperatures soar

despite temperature variations

MARK-TIME PARKING METERS

are dependable

High Revenue . . . Low Maintenance. The rugged simplicity of Mark-Time design and construction cuts maintenance costs to the bone . . . saving maintenance time, earning steady profits for the city.

Magic Link is the key to low cost. Protects mechanism from serious damage by insertion of bent coins or foreign matter. Link replaceable in seconds, cost nil!

Sealed Timing Mechanism . . . sealed at the plant; for dust, dirt, moisture protection. Removed from housing with a twist of the wrist. Serviced at our factory if needed; no "clockmakers" on your payroll.

Oilite Bushing . . . in handle permits complete freedom of movement, always . . . no lubrication needed, no grease or oil to collect dirt or dust.

Sealed Coin Box. Coins fall into a lock-box, with tamper-proof seal. Coin slot automatically closed and locked when box is "collected."

Distant, Clear, Visibility. Big, red violation dials readable from almost a block away, enabling one policeman to check a long row of meters at a glance.

M. H. RHODES, INC., 30 BARTHOLOMEW AVE., HARTFORD, CONN.

Manufactured and Sold in Canada by: SPERRY GYROSCOPE OTTAWA Ltd., Ottawa, Ontario, Canada

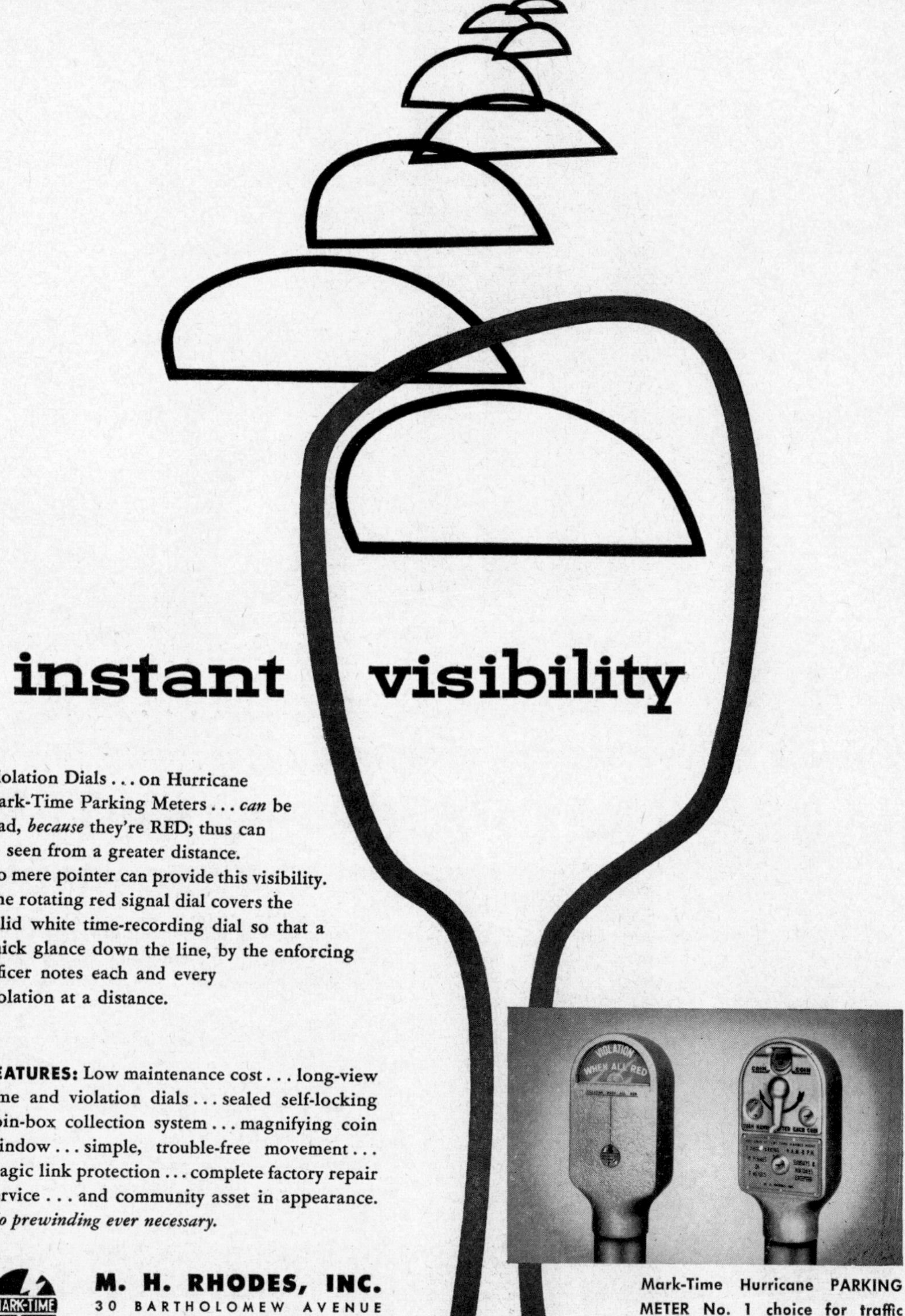

Manufactured and Sold in Canada by: SPERRY GYROSCOPE OTTAWA Ltd., Ottawa, Ontario, Canada

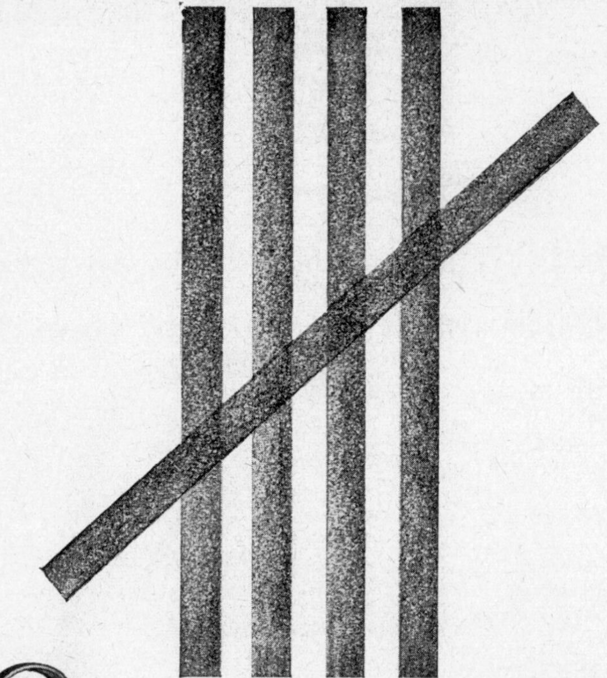

CASE ASSEMBLY

SEALED MOVEMENT ASSEMBLY

HEAD ASSEMBLY

DOOR ASSEMBLY

COIN BOX ASSEMBLY

FIVE expertly engineered units fit together *like a glove* . . . to form the most universally approved manually-operated parking meter.

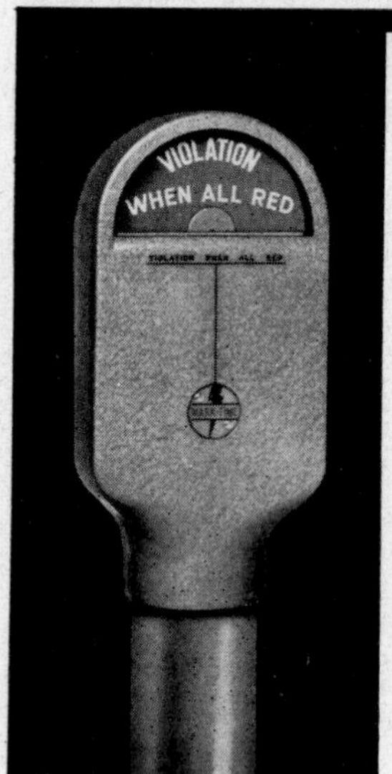

MARK-TIME

hurricane model

Parking Meter

M. H. RHODES, INC.

30 BARTHOLOMEW AVENUE
HARTFORD, CONNECTICUT

Manufactured and Sold in Canada by: SPERRY GYROSCOPE OTTAWA Ltd., Ottawa, Ontario, Canada

THE DUAL PARKING METER COMPANY

A subsidiary of Rockwell Manufacturing Company

Pittsburgh 8, Pa.

CHECK DUALS . . . for every on-street and off-street parking control need!

DUAL PARKING meters, with their unmatched on-the-spot time-and-coin conversion flexibility, are helping solve the growing traffic problems in city after city . . . in the most effective, most economical way!

Whether it is the popular single head Dual . . . or new "Dubl" Dual . . . for either street or lot use, you get the highest quality and efficiency built into any meter today . . . your best assurance of long-range, low-cost performance.

Traffic experts everywhere, after careful studies, choose these Dual "gearshift" meters because their quality and unique features insure efficient operation far beyond the normal amortization period.

ASK FOR FREE BULLETINS

DU-521 DUAL AUTOMATIC ON-STREET PARKING
DU-522 DUAL AUTOMATIC OFF-STREET PARKING

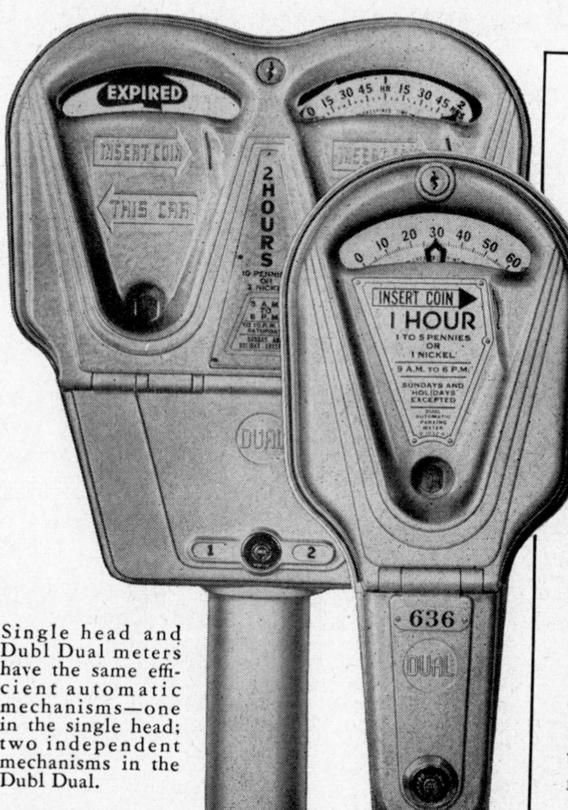

Single head and Dubl Dual meters have the same efficient automatic mechanisms—one in the single head; two independent mechanisms in the Dubl Dual.

6 Reasons Why

DUALS STAND THE "GAFF" AND GIVE BETTER SERVICE LONGER!

1. **Precision-Built Clock Movement** . . . Quality where it counts—in the "heart" of the meter.
2. **Stainless Steel Coin Mechanism** . . . Smoother running in all weather conditions.
3. **Weatherproof Head** . . . With handy work-shelf door.
4. **Superior Design** . . . Discourages cruising; time indicator visible only from sidewalk side.
5. **On-The-Street Time-And-Coin Conversion** . . . To meet changing traffic conditions.
6. **Easy To Patrol And Operate** . . . Observation window shows slug or tampering at a glance. No levers to move.

JOHNSON FARE BOX COMPANY

Subsidiary of BOWSER, Inc.

4619 North Ravenswood Avenue, Chicago 40, Illinois

NEW YORK OFFICE: 420 Lexington Ave., New York 17, N. Y.
BOSTON OFFICE: 35 Leon Street, Boston, Mass.

END COIN-HANDLING WORRIES FROM PARKING METERS

Let these dependable JOHNSON *Products help you make more money*

DOWNEY-JOHNSON COIN COUNTERS

Available either manual or motorized, Johnson portable coin counters are priced for outstanding value. Wrap or bag. Features include quick-setting lock for package count; double-check for package count; feed roller adjustable for long wear; quick removal of hopper ring and other parts for easy cleaning.

DOWNEY-JOHNSON Model 40-SC Combination Sorter-Counter

Sorts and counts mixed coins from 1 cent to 50 cents inclusive. Gives you running total of all coins handled on **one** totalizing cyclometer, so you always know the total in dollars and cents.

Write for Full Details Today

DOWNEY-JOHNSON Universal Crimper

Takes headaches out of coin-wrapper crimping. Operates from sitting or standing position. Equipped with 5 interchangeable crimper heads —pennies, nickels, dimes, quarters and halves. Assures trouble-free operation—nothing to get out of order.

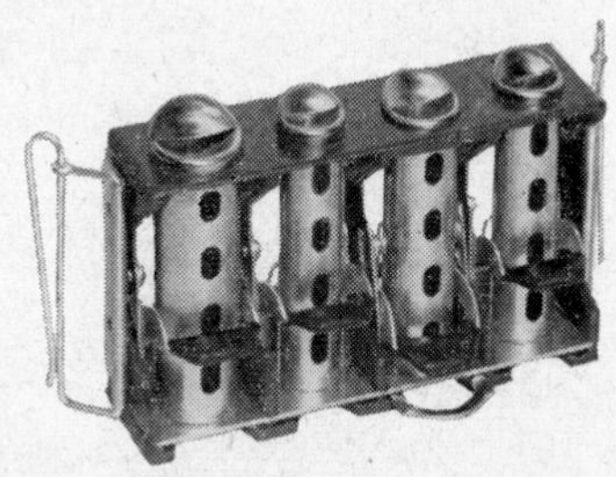

JOHNSON UNIVERSAL CHANGER

The most **rugged** changer available today. It's **flexible**—you can add as many standard or extra-long barrels as you need. It's **adjustable**—each barrel can be adjusted to eject as many coins as desired. It's **universal**—handles all coins, including half dollars.

LIGHTNING CHANGE MAKER

Makes change fast and accurately, stops short-change and over-change. Reinforced construction for long, trouble-free service. Bank or swivel chute delivery attachment (either right or left-hand delivery).

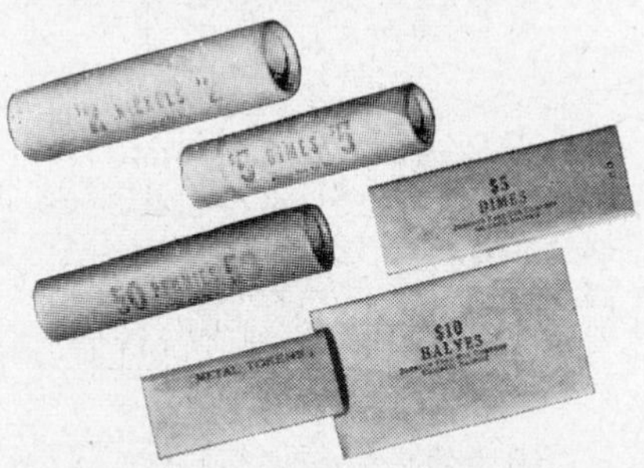

JOHNSON COIN WRAPPERS

Available in cartridge type and flat tubular. Cartridge type ideal for use with automatic coin-counting and packaging machines. Where smaller quantities of coins are to be packaged, Johnson flat tubular wrappers are recommended. They are packed slightly oval to pop open instantly when pressed between thumb and finger.

Prices on tubular wrappers as low as .60 per M, f.o.b. Chicago, in lots of 250,000. Smaller quantities proportionately higher.

JOHNSON

COIN CHANGERS

STURDILY BUILT

The changer is encased in a 3/16″ thick all steel housing welded to two-2″ I.D. supporting pipe standards. Entrance to the changer is protected by two extra heavy padlocks made to government specifications.

TROUBLE FREE

The changers are manufactured by Standard Change-Makers, Inc. Embodied in the mechanism is the famous National Rejector which insures coin return when empty. The simplicity of the mechanically operated changer mechanism accounts for its superior performance.

EASILY MAINTAINED

The changer has a very large coin capacity and a minimum of working parts. The selector-rejector assembly is a compact unit which can be replaced on the spot in less than one minute without the use of tools. The cost of overhauling or replacing this unit is only $5.00.

THREE MODELS TO FIT ALL NEEDS

MODEL 21—Dispenses 2 dimes, 1 nickel for quarer. Changes 128 quarters

MODEL 55—Dispenses 5 nickels for quarter. Changes 175 quarters

MODEL 25—Dispenses 2 nickles for dime. Changes 175 dimes

Why not give both the motorist and the merchant a break. Install PARKIT-LOCKIT coin changers at convenient locations on both streets and parking lots. Make it easy for parking meter users to make change.

It will increase revenue and be appreciated by the motorist. The merchant will also appreciate relief from the constant nuisance of making change.

DUNCAN PARKING METER CORPORATION

835 North Wood Street, Chicago 22, Illinois

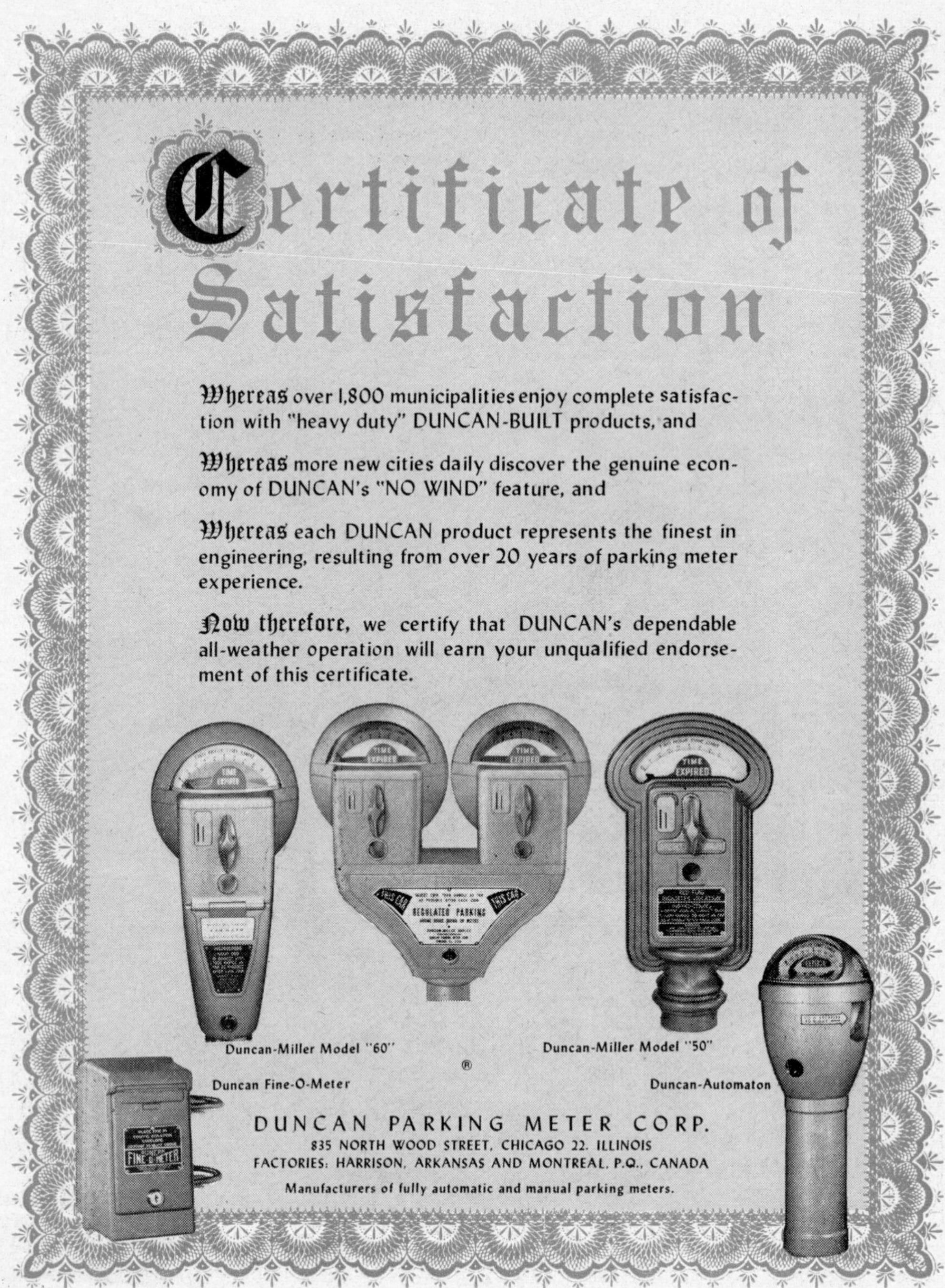

ABBOTT COIN COUNTER COMPANY, INC.

Manufacturers of Coin Handling Equipment Since 1911

143rd to 144th Streets and Wales Avenue New York 54

COIN COUNTING—PACKAGING AND SORTING MACHINES FOR EVERY PURPOSE

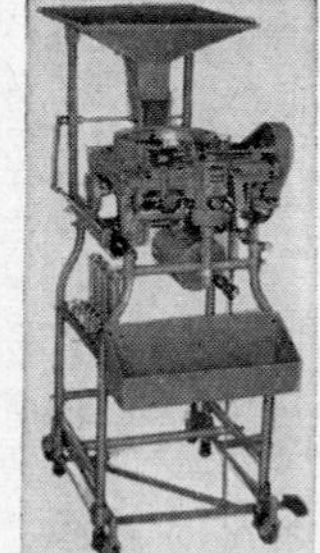

EXTRA HEAVY DUTY 75 ELEC. COUNTER-PACKAGER

Extra fast, Counter-Packager with stand, feed hopper, foot control and crimper-packager VERY FAST

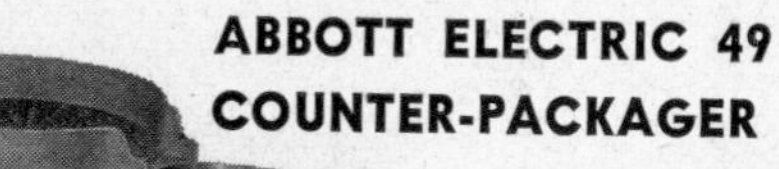

ABBOTT ELECTRIC 49 COUNTER-PACKAGER

Heavy duty, fast, rugged. Easy to clean, easy to service. Long lived, modestly priced.

COIN WRAPPERS

Abbott originated colored flat tubular coin wrappers and today manufactures top quality wrappers from the highest quality materials.

Write for quotation.

RAPID COIN ASSORTER

Electric table model—separates 1200 mixed coins per minute. $265 plus tax.

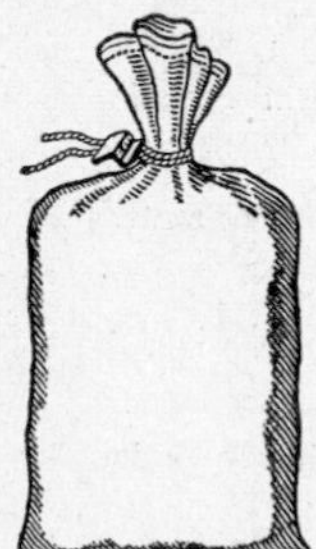

COTTON COIN BAGS

Thirteen sizes, heavy weight "X" grade.

Regular weight "B" Grade.

LEAD SEAL PRESSES

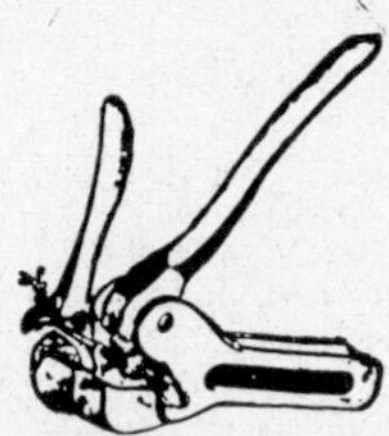

Two dies can be engraved with 2 lines each . . . 8 letters to line.

All types of Lead Bag Seals are available.

Let us help you with any coin or currency handling problem. Write today for our complete catalog of money handling supplies.

RED BALL PARKING METERS
TRAFICO PARKING METER CO.

Division of J. W. MenHall Drilling Company, Oil Producers

Benton, Illinois

RED BALL PARKING METERS

DIV. OF J. W. MENHALL DRILLING CO. - OIL PRODUCERS
BENTON, ILLINOIS

- Red Ball violation signal is visible from all directions. (Reduces policing costs.)
- Force Feed Coin Receiver will not jam or clog easily when foreign objects are inserted. (Less than 1% maintenance per day.)
- Enclosed coin slot provides protection against all elements. Will not freeze.
- Simple mechanical meter—only 5 major moving parts all made of stainless steel.
- Flexible coin and time combinations.
- Parking Lot and Fringe Area models available.

Backed by $2,000,000.00

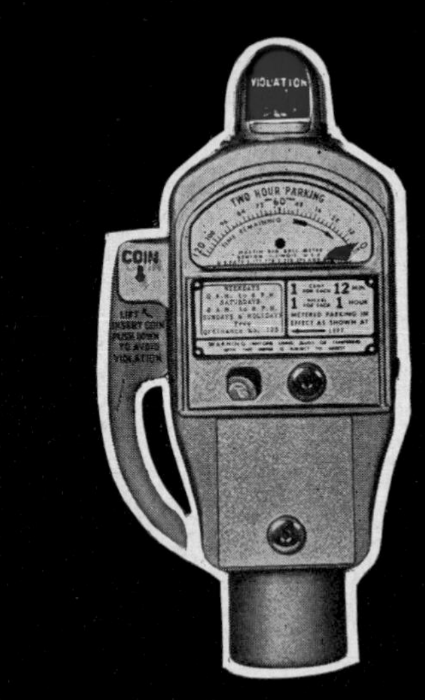

The All Weather Meters

THAT DEFY ICE, SLEET, SNOW, RAIN, SALT WATER

TRAFICO PARKING METER CO.

DIV. OF J. W. MENHALL DRILLING CO. - OIL PRODUCERS
BENTON, ILLINOIS

- 15 years continuous operation in Miami, Fla. Of original purchase of 1300, there are still 1020 in daily service.
- 70% less parts than any manual or automatic meter with clocks.
- Registers all overtime parking up to 30 minutes or more.
- Multiple coin and time combinations with one coin slot.
- Completely enclosed case with Air Tight Clock.
- A model for every parking need and climate.
- Complete mechanism can be changed in less than 30 seconds.

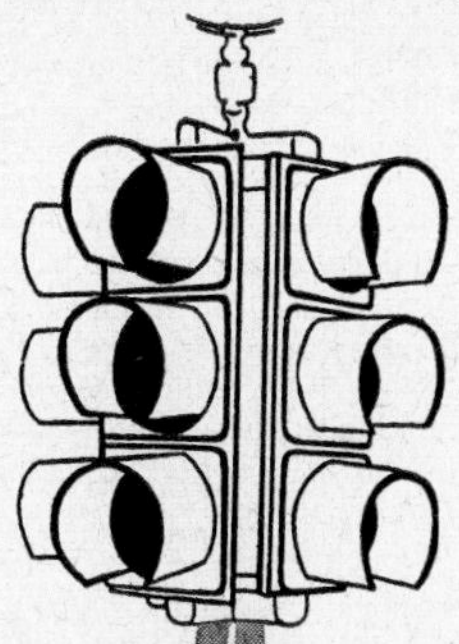

CROUSE-HINDS COMPANY

Syracuse 1, N.Y., U.S.A.

OFFICES: Baton Rouge — Birmingham — Boston — Buffalo — Chicago — Cincinnati — Cleveland — Corpus Christi — Dallas Denver — Detroit — Houston — Indianapolis — Kansas City — Los Angeles — Milwaukee — New Orleans — New York Philadelphia — Pittsburgh — Portland, Ore. — St. Louis — St. Paul — San Francisco — Seattle — Tulsa — Washington.
RESIDENT REPRESENTATIVES: Albany — Atlanta — Baltimore — Charlotte — Chattanooga — Jacksonville — Reading, Pa. Richmond, Va. — Shreveport

Crouse-Hinds Municipal Services

CONDULETS®

FLOODLIGHTING

AIRPORT LIGHTING

TRAFFIC SIGNALS

Crouse-Hinds Company: Suppliers of an important share of electrical equipment to progressive municipalities throughout the world. Crouse-Hinds has become synonymous with safety, durability and unfailing reliability. The wide scope of equipment produced includes high-quality Condulets (conduit fittings), plugs, receptacles and switches for large buildings, floodlights for athletic fields, swimming pools, and playgrounds; all types of modern airport illumination and the universally accepted Trafflex® traffic control system.

Crouse-Hinds CONDULETS

The complete line of Crouse-Hinds Condulets includes over 15,000 items in standard, explosion-proof, dust ignition proof, weather resistant, rain-tight and vapor-tight types. "Condulet" is a coined word registered in the U.S. Patent Office, and designates a product made only by Crouse-Hinds. Condulets provide safe, convenient, durable electrical installations, indoors or outdoors, for all municipally-owned structures, such as those listed at the right:

- Auditoriums and community buildings
- Bulk coal handling plants
- City Hospitals
- Garbage disposal operations
- Gas storage tanks
- Municipal pumping stations
- Schools and universities
- Service and maintenance buildings
- Sewage disposal operations
- Steam stations

TYPE ARE

Arktite Plug and Receptacle with Spring Door. Snuffs electrical arcs occurring when opening or closing circuit. 20-400 amps 600 V., A.C.

TYPE LBD

For making 90° bend in conduit system

TYPE RS JUNCTION

Condulet with Hub Plates

TYPE FS

Watertight Pushbutton and Pilot Light Condulet

Crouse-Hinds FLOODLIGHTING

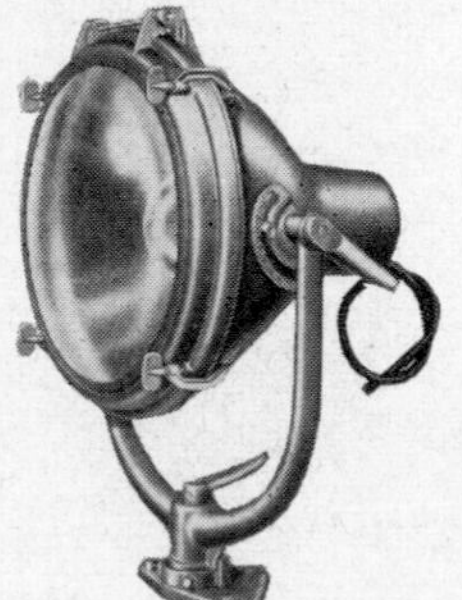

TYPE ADR HEAVY DUTY PORTABLE FLOODLIGHT
250-1000 Watts

Crouse-Hinds Floodlights are practical indoors and out. They provide property protection; enhance building appearance; are ideal for many indoor locations. All lamps, including those in swimming pool lights, are easily and safely replaced. Crouse-Hinds floodlights may be used for indoor and outdoor sports events of all kinds, as well as emergency lighting of fires, riots, rescue attempts . . . providing more-than-adequate light wherever needed.

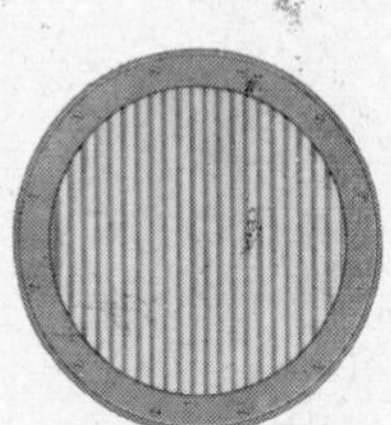

TYPE SPS
Underwater Floodlight for Swimming Pools.
500-1500 Watts

TYPE ADE HEAVY DUTY
200-1000 Watts

Lighting Little League Baseball parks such as the one pictured above, is but one manner in which Crouse-Hinds floodlighting is helping up-to-date municipalities everywhere.

TYPE MDB GENERAL PURPOSE
200-1000 Watts

TYPE RPS 500-1000 Watts
Underwater Floodlight for Swimming Pools

TYPE LCE
1500-2000 Watts

TYPE FLA SPORTSLIGHT
750-1500 Watts

Crouse-Hinds SIGNALS *speed traffic.. save lives*

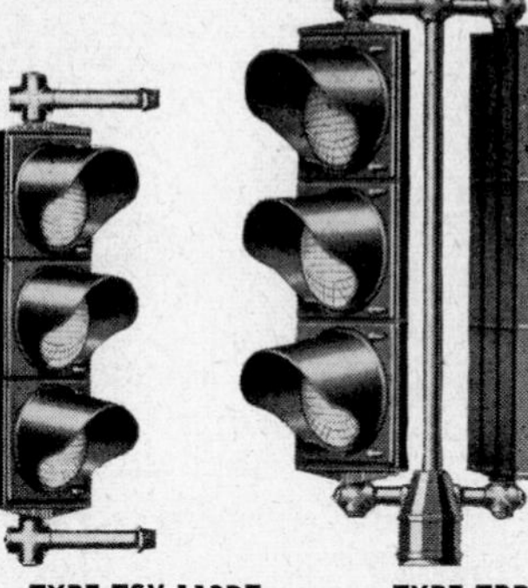

TYPE TSV-113DT ONE-WAY SIGNAL VERTICAL BRACKET-ARM MOUNTING

TYPE TRP-223DT. TWO-WAY SIGNAL POST MOUNTING

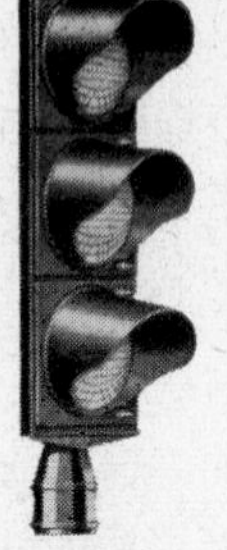

TYPE TSP-113DT ONE-WAY SIGNAL POST MOUNTING

At right: Type TSW-443DT Four-Way Signal for Span-Wire Mounting

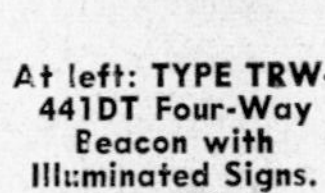

At left: TYPE TRW-441DT Four-Way Beacon with Illuminated Signs. Span-Wire Mounting.

All Crouse-Hinds traffic signals feature a dust-tight optical system: twin-ring dust seal on reflector ring, reflector gasket, and receptacle gasket insure positively dust-free performance throughout.

Street and highway traffic-flow as well as heavily saturated intersections such as the one pictured at right, are smoothly controlled by Crouse-Hinds automatic traffic signals.

Crouse-Hinds TRAFFIC *Controllers*

Above: Type LF Expansible Controller. Can be used with any existing *Trafflex* system.

Left: Type LS synchronous expansible controller. For 1, 2, or 3 dial units. Can be used isolated or as part of synchronous system.

At right is dial unit which can be set for a different time-cycle, different timing-split and a different offset. All dial-units may be quickly and readily removed or mounted.

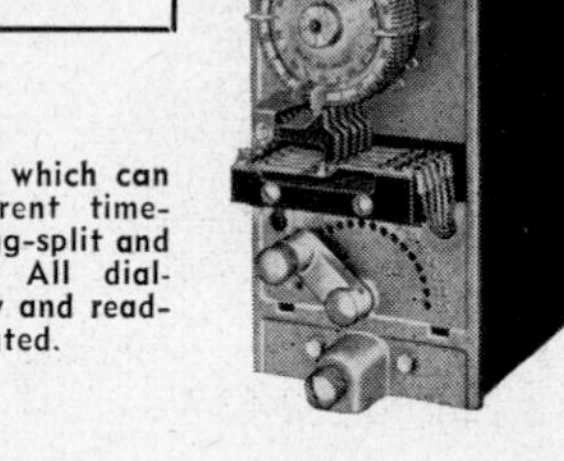

Type KS Synchronous Controller for simple, isolated intersections.

The Crouse-Hinds **Trafflex system**, employing the use of devices shown here and other Crouse-Hinds products, regulates traffic speed in relation to block length, pavement condition, traffic density, etc. It provides for a full flexible progressive traffic movement with remote control of time cycle from the Master Controller to obtain varying traffic speeds. Simple to install, it is easy to maintain, inexpensive to operate and may be readily expanded as traffic conditions warrant.

Crouse-Hinds TRAFFIC Signals — NEON ILLUMINATION

ONE-LINE SIGNAL TYPE TNO-1 NEON SIGNALS. 4-INCH POST MOUNTING

Large, brilliant letters assure positive information to motorist and pedestrian 24 hours a day. Rigid, lightweight cast aluminum housing lasts indefinitely. Dust-proof, weather-proof. Easily serviced.

TYPE TNO-2 NEON PEDESTRIANS SIGNAL OR TRAFFIC SIGN

Crouse-Hinds AIRPORT LIGHTING

The Crouse-Hinds line includes the development and manufacture of lighting and control equipment for the requirements of every airport: from small field for private flying to large commercial air terminal. The usual Crouse-Hinds dependability and safety factors are found in its aviation lighting equipment.

Airport tower control desks and panels, runway and marker lights, beacons, weather equipment . . . all are high-quality Crouse-Hinds products.

AIRPORT LIGHTING CONTROL PANEL

TYPE HRC MOVABLE BEAM INTENSITY RUNWAY MARKER LIGHT

TYPE DCB 36 ROTATING AIRPORT BEACON

TYPE EOL DOUBLE OBSTRUCTION MARKER LIGHT

TYPE TGS TAXIWAY GUIDANCE SIGN

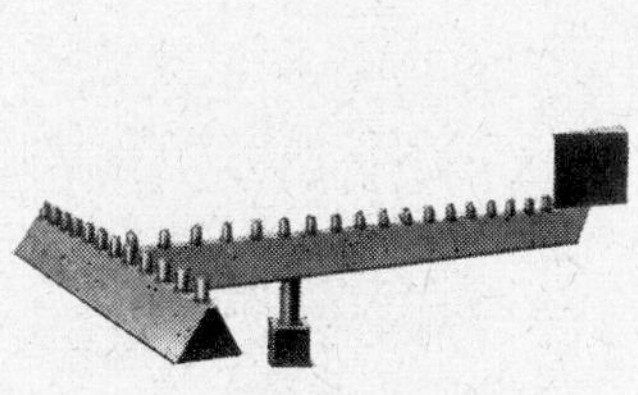

TYPE WT AUTOMATIC WIND TEE

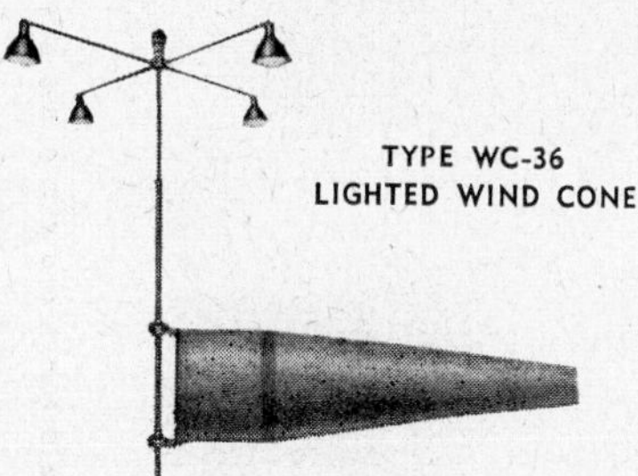

TYPE WC-36 LIGHTED WIND CONE

TYPE ERL ELEVATED RUNWAY AND TAXI LIGHT WITH TRANSFORMER HOUSING

S23CTCH Two-way, 3-section, adjustable type signal for post top mounting.

STANDARD EAGLE TRAFFIC SIGNALS

Standard Eagle Traffic Signals, like those illustrated are made of lightweight, die-cast aluminum. All sections are interchangeable. Signals are also available in two or four section. Optical unit includes Eagle's exclusive "Anti-Sun" Phantom feature which eliminates false indication caused by sun's rays or other external source of light. Write for Bulletin A 10 for complete information.

43E Four-way, 3-section, non-adjustable type signal for span-wire suspension.

KBS79 type signal with 12" lens. Originally designed as a "Lane" Signal, it is equally effective as a pedestrian signal. It's square shape sets it apart from vehicle signals and the large 4½" letters of the message are easy to read.

KBS83 Signal illustrated shows KB355 signal with 12" lens mounted on standard 2-section signal. Extra large lens make signal ideal for high speed highways.

KB312 type exclusive pedestrian signal. Has large 3" letters in each section. Uses standard traffic signal lamp. Mounts on standard signal brackets.

BEACONS AND FLASHERS

Beacons and flashers are used to advantage to mark dangerous intersections, dead end streets, divided pavements, etc. For complete details write for Bulletin B 10.

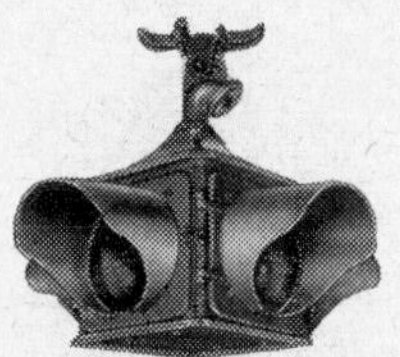

41E Four-way, non-adjustable type beacon for span-wire suspension.

S41EE Four-way, adjustable type beacon for span-wire suspension.

EP9 Flasher Unit illustrated consists of the Eagle HT80 jack-mounted flasher, jack panel and fuse clips, enclosed in glass-covered meter housing with terminal facilities in base. Also available in cabinet style, Eagle No. EP10.

PUSH BUTTON SCHOOL SIGNAL SYSTEM

Eliminates Patrol Boy in the street. Consists of 8 ft. signal posts and 2-way, 2-section traffic signals with push buttons that operate on 12 volts —no shock hazard. School Crossing Signs yellow with black letters. Complete with controller which is operated by pre-setting of time clock for periods of push-button operation. Write for Bulletin A10-A.

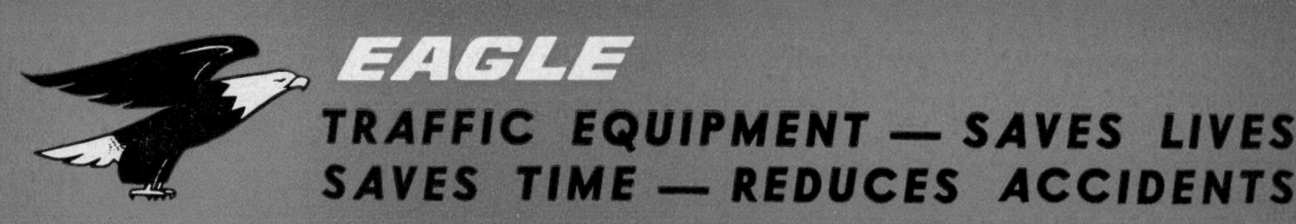

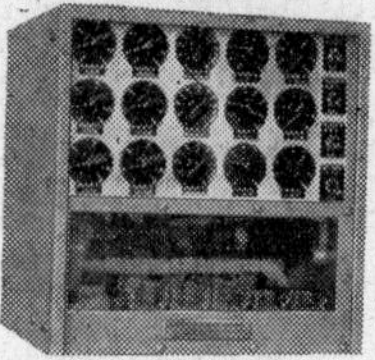
Eagle 3-Phase Vehicle Actuated Controller

VEHICLE AND PEDESTRIAN ACTUATED CONTROLLERS

Eagle Signal Corporation offers a complete line of Vehicle and Pedestrian Actuated equipment. Eagle Actuated Controllers are extremely simple to maintain. Whether your application is for a simple semi-actuated controller on a heavily traveled street or a 3-phase controller for a five or six way intersection Eagle has the right controller for you. Pressure or magnetic vehicle detectors as well as all accessories are available. Write for Bulletin F 10 for more information.

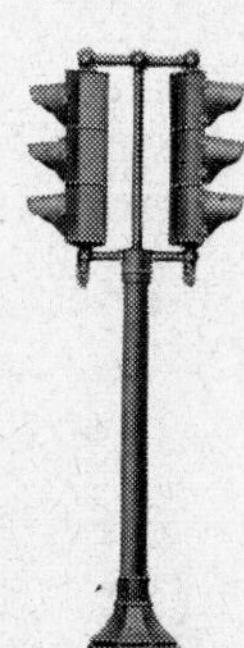

CABINETS — Eagle Signal Corporation offers a complete line of weatherproof cabinets for all equipment associated with street lighting, traffic control, and other outdoor equipment. All cabinets are of aluminum body or heavy sheet aluminum welded to cast aluminum top and bottom. Cabinets have heavy duty gasket around door openings making a weather-tight seal for protection of enclosed equipment. Send for Bulletin L 10 for more information.

PEDESTALS — Eagle pedestals are constructed with a high grade cast iron base into which the tubular shaft is set and leaded or threaded. The shaft is 4½" outside diameter seamless steel pipe. For more information, send for Bulletin N 10.

SALES REPRESENTATIVES OF EAGLE SIGNAL CORPORATION

ARKANSAS, Pine Bluff
S. J. Lavender, Jr.
903 West 34th Street

CALIFORNIA, Los Angeles (65)
Hundley Company
3282 Fletcher Drive
P.O. Box 65916
Glassel Station

CALIFORNIA, San Francisco (10)
Campbell & George Co.
1601 Cortland Avenue

FLORIDA, Jacksonville
Ward Engineering Co., Inc.
2727 Phyliss Street

FLORIDA, Orlando
Ward Engineering Co., Inc.
P.O. Box 5545
1015 West Central Avenue

GEORGIA, Atlanta
Thomas B. Combs Co.
1823 Gordon Road S.W.

IDAHO, Boise
Starline Equipment Co.
503 South 16th Street
P.O. Box 2571

ILLINOIS, Chicago (41)
Bell & Gustus, Inc.
4328 North Elston Ave.

INDIANA, Indianapolis (4)
James H. Drew Corp.
Architects & Builders Bldg.

IOWA, Des Moines (9)
H. B. Allen, Inc.
1204 Grand Ave.

KANSAS, Topeka
Fred H. Gades Sales Co.
P.O. Box 262
511 West 10th Street

MASSACHUSETTS, Arlington
R. W. LeBaron, Inc.
9 Swan Place

MICHIGAN, Detroit (26)
Carrier & Gable, Inc.
Office 414 — Murphy Bldg
155 West Congress St.

MINNESOTA, Minneapolis (11)
Griswold Signal Company
700 Plymouth Avenue

MISSISSIPPI, Jackson
Harry Corneil Company
Robert E. Lee Hotel

MISSOURI, St. Louis (10)
P. A. Rafferty
7031 Manchester Ave.

NEW YORK, Buffalo (2)
Munhall Company
170 Franklin Street

NEW YORK, Hicksville
Varrelman-Gorman Co.
P.O. Box 503

OHIO, Cincinnati (2)
Johnson Electric Supply Co.
317-321 Sycamore Street

OHIO, Columbus (15)
Baldwin & Sours
83 South High St.

OKLAHOMA, Oklahoma City
C. B. Anderson Electric Co.
P.O. Box 761

OKLAHOMA, Tulsa (3)
C. B. Anderson Electric Co.
712 Oil Capital Bldg.

PENNSYLVANIA, Emsworth (PGH 2)
Koontz Equipment Corp.
325 Ohio River Blvd.

PENNSYLVANIA, Upper Darby
W. F. Keegan & Co.
P.O. Box 146
771 Shelbourne Road

TEXAS, Amarillo
C. B. Anderson Electric Co.
P.O. Box 1836
111 East 1st Street

TEXAS, Dallas
Maxson Company
703 Valencia Street

TEXAS, Lubbock
C. B. Anderson Electric Co.
P.O. Box 1385

UTAH, Salt Lake City (9)
Richards G. Smith
2160 So. 21st East

WASHINGTON, Seattle (4)
Leo J. Proby
422 Smith Tower

WISCONSIN, Milwaukee (10)
Harry G. Bevin
2757 North 40th Street

CANADIAN REPRESENTATIVE
Northern Electric Co., Ltd.
P.O. Box 400
250 Sidney Street
Belleville, Ontario, Canada

SIGNAL CORPORATION
MOLINE, ILLINOIS

ELECTRONIC PROTECTION INC.

2085 North Hawthorne Avenue • Melrose Park, Illinois

What is EL-TEC?

EL-TEC is an electronic system for controlling traffic lights at any signalized intersection from an emergency vehicle employing UHF-radio equipment to initiate the desired lighting sequence to permit the vehicle's safe and unimpeded passage.

This is an engineer's definition—but in layman's language, here is how EL-TEC works . . . how the driver automatically controls the traffic ahead of him.

There are SEVEN basic pieces of equipment in the EL-TEC system.

Installed in each emergency vehicle:
- Control Box
- UHF Radio Transmitter
- Transmitting Antenna

Installed at each traffic light:
- Receiving Antenna
- UHF Radio Receiver
- Relay Control Unit
- Rotary Warning Beacon

CONTROL BOX

This Control Box is mounted in each EL-TEC-equipped vehicle within easy reach of the driver. As soon as the driver starts the engine's motor, he turns "ON" the EL-TEC equipment by throwing the right hand switch to the upward position.

If the emergency vehicle is to travel North or South, the driver throws the left hand switch to the upward position.

If the route is East or West, the left hand switch is thrown to the downward position.

If the emergency vehicle changes direction while enroute to its destination, the appropriate switch change is made by the driver corresponding to the direction the vehicle has turned.

Only these simple functions are manual, everything else is automatic.

MOBILE UHF RADIO TRANSMITTER IN WEATHERPROOF HOUSING

This UHF Radio Transmitter is installed in each EL-TEC-equipped emergency vehicle where it can be reached for servicing and testing. It is a multiple-frequency (carrier and tone) transmitter. It automatically transmits interference-free coded signals—one combination when the vehicle is traveling East or West, a different combination when the vehicle is traveling North or South. This is determined by the lefthand switch position on the Control Box. The coded signals are carried to the transmitting antenna by an interconnecting cable.

TRANSMITTING ANTENNA

The Transmitting Antenna is mounted on the hood of the emergency vehicle, as illustrated. Alternate transmitter antenna is available for open-cab or cab-over-engine types of apparatus.

RECEIVING ANTENNA

A Receiving Antenna is installed at each EL-TEC-equipped intersection, usually on the signal light standard nearest to the traffic sig-

ELECTRONIC PROTECTION INC.

2085 North Hawthorne Avenue • Melrose Park, Illinois

nal control box. The receiving antenna picks up the coded signal sent out by the transmitter and feeds it (via an interconnecting cable) to the UHF radio receiver, which is usually mounted on the traffic signal control box, as shown in the following illustration.

UHF RADIO RECEIVER

RELAY CONTROL UNIT

IN WEATHERPROOF HOUSING

The UHF Radio Receiver interprets the coded signals which in turn tells the Relay Control Unit exactly what lighting sequence should be put into effect. The Relay Control Unit is properly inter-wired into the traffic signal controller (regardless of type or manufacture) so that it can assume immediate and positive control of the traffic signals at any time and dictate what lighting sequence is to be put into effect. Municipal Officials (Police Chiefs, Fire Chiefs, Traffic Engineers, Civilian Defense Directors, etc.) make the policy decisions regarding the system of lighting sequences to be followed. The lighting sequences can be set up to follow any one of several patterns. Standard relay units are available to provide signal functions as follows:

1. **Flashing yellow for pre-determined period, followed by four-way red.**
2. **Flashing yellow for pre-determined period, followed by leading green and side street red.**
3. **Selective yellow, followed by leading green and side street red.**
4. **Selective yellow, followed by leading green and side street red with control of pedestrian signals and turn indication.**

The foregoing functions are entirely flexible and adaptable to whatever sequence Municipal Officials want to install.

ROTARY WARNING BEACON

The Rotary Warning Beacon is that extra measure of safety usually installed on the same standard with the receiving antenna. As the relay control unit automatically sets up the signals in favor of the EL-Tec-equipped emergency vehicle, the rotary warning beacon operates as an indication that the intersection is being controlled by an emergency vehicle and also serves as warning to other motorists that the intersection is under emergency control.

MORE IMPORTANT INFORMATION ON THE FOLLOWING PAGE

F14SW—one-section, four-way beacon, span wire mounted.

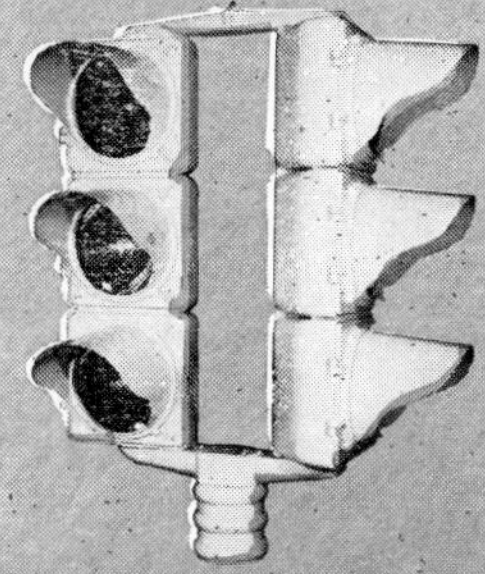
A32PM—three-section, two-way, adjustable face, pedestal mounting.

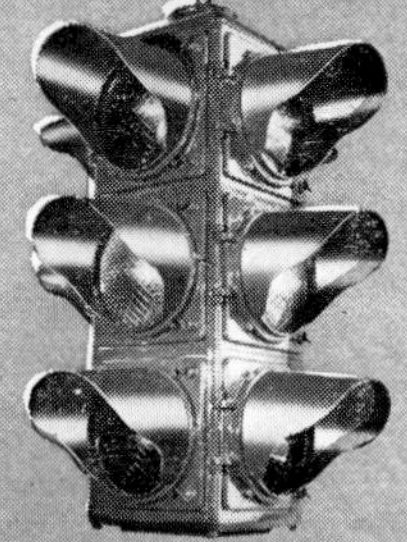
F34SW—three-section, four-way, span wire mounted.

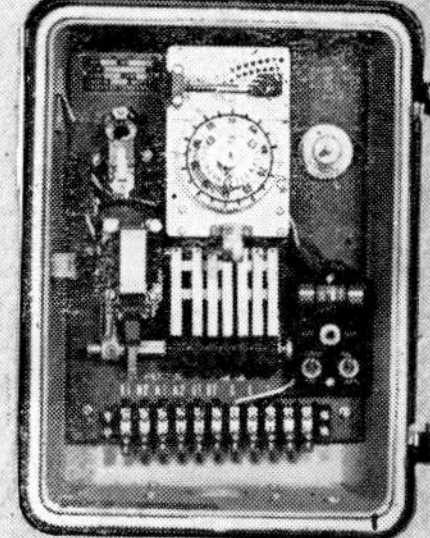
Model 102S Non-expansible. Single timer, six circuits.

AUTOFLOW

WPCF1S — single-circuit flasher control with radio suppressor.

dependable equipment

simple, low-cost maintenance

versatile operation

Model 102L expansible control. 3 programs, 3 resets, 18 circuits.

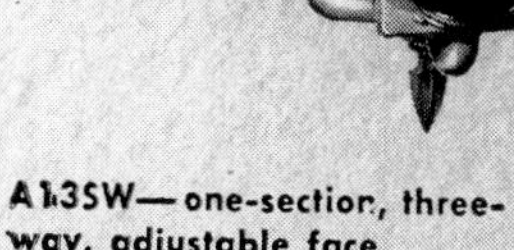
A13SW—one-section, three-way, adjustable face.

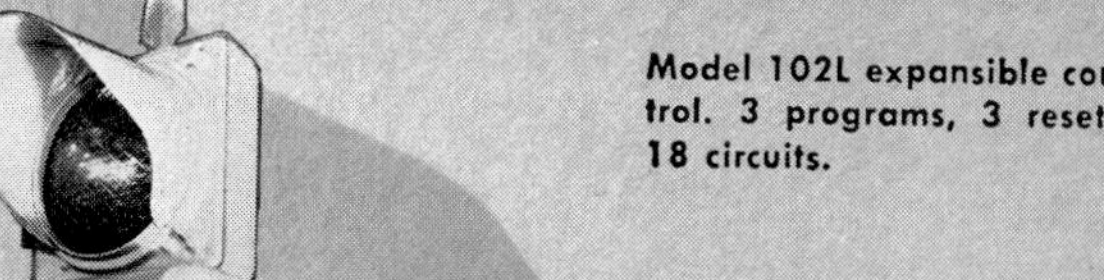
A11DL-U2—flashing beacon with down-light. 2" post mounting.

BULLETIN 5603

SOUTHERN SIGNALS
shreveport, louisiana

AUTOFLOW

FIXED-FA

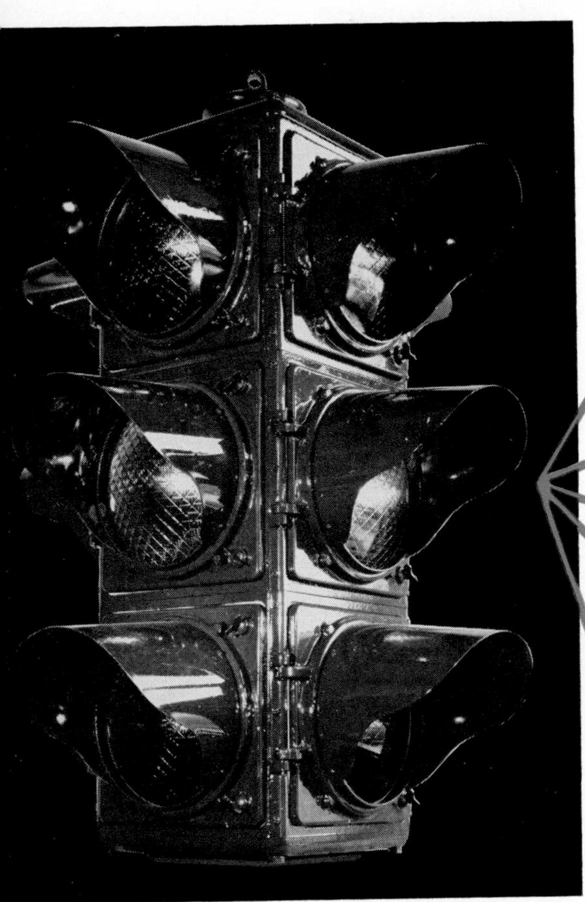

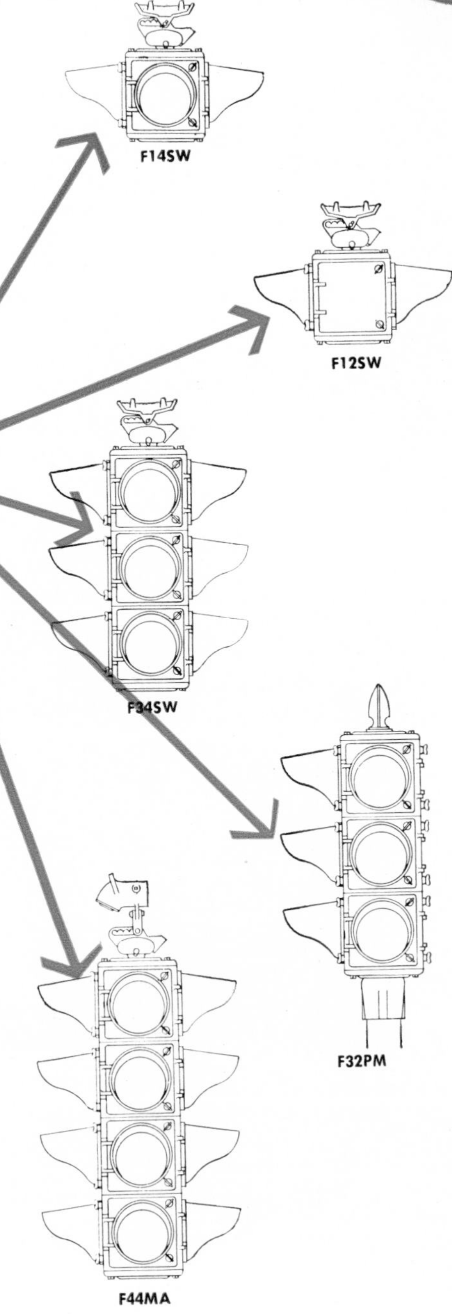

specifications

One simple, compact, well-constructed unit is the basis for all AUTOFLOW fixed-face traffic signals. AUTOFLOW simplicity and versatility are still your keys to adequate traffic control without extravagance in either initial cost or maintenance.

AUTOFLOU CONT

MODEL 102 S

MODEL 102S fixed time, synchronous, single timer control for non-interconnected or interconnected operation — basically a two phase control with a maximum of six circuits. Extra features available — flashing, All Red, multiple program, multiple reset, etc.

MODEL 102 L-NON-EXPANSIBLE

MODEL 102L NON-EXPANSIBLE, synchronous, single timer control for isolated or interconnected operation. A single timer control for two phase or multi-phase operation with 6 to 18 circuits and 18 intervals. Extra features available.

MODEL 102 L-EXPANSIBLE

MODEL 102L EXPANSIBLE, synchronous control with one, two, or three jack-mounted timers. For isolated or interconnected operation where a selection of total cycles and program splits are required. For two phase or multi-phase operation, 6 to 15 circuits and 18 intervals. Extra features available.

AUTOFLOW

ADJUSTABLE

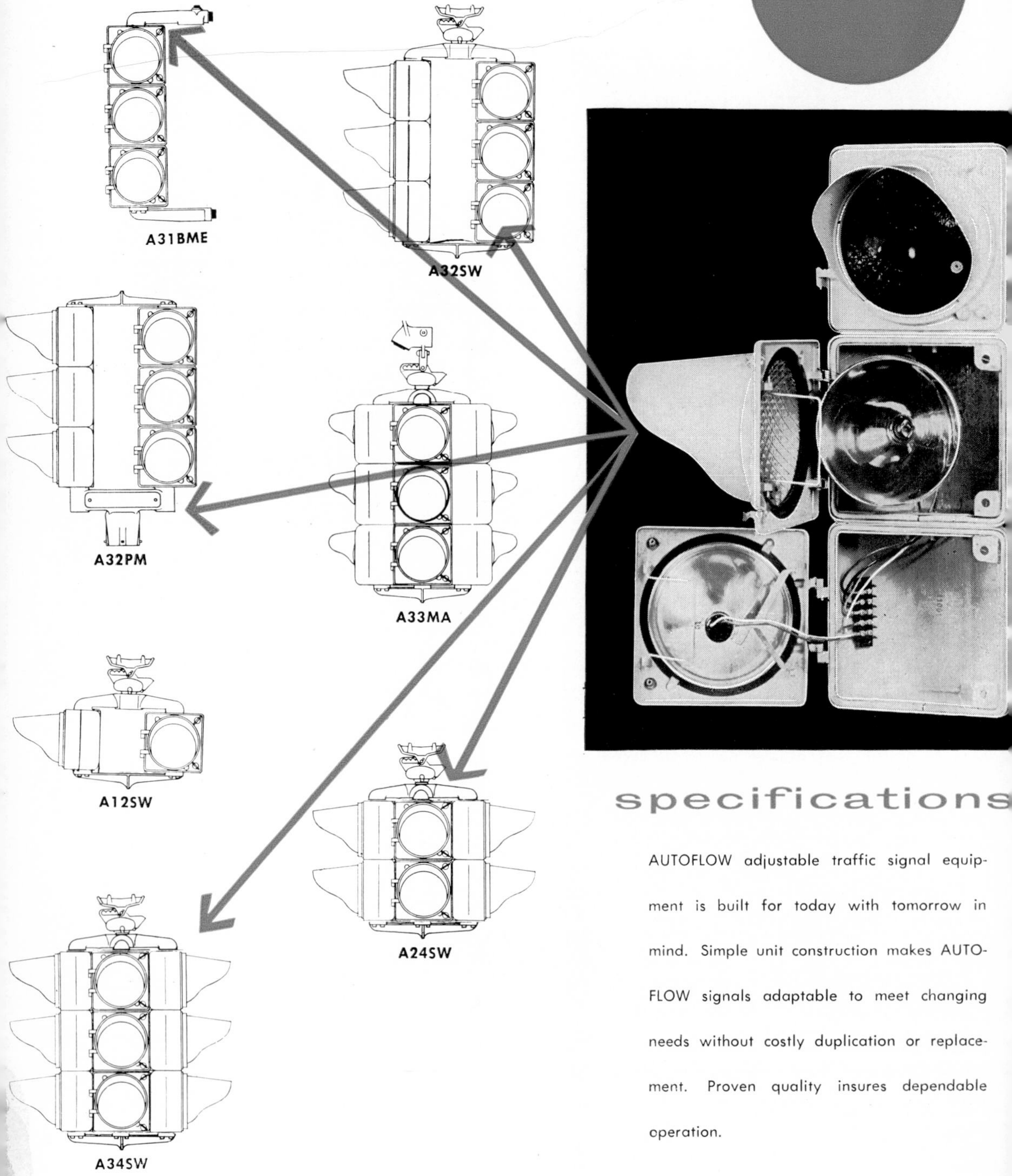

A31BME

A32SW

A32PM

A33MA

A12SW

A24SW

A34SW

specifications

AUTOFLOW adjustable traffic signal equipment is built for today with tomorrow in mind. Simple unit construction makes AUTOFLOW signals adaptable to meet changing needs without costly duplication or replacement. Proven quality insures dependable operation.

TRAFFIC SIGNALS

AUTOFLOW FIXED FACE TRAFFIC SIGNALS are designed to provide a complete selection for lividual traffic needs. These designs include all types of mounting arrangements and feature simplicity of design to assure low-cost, efficient operation.

Constructed of precision sand-cast aluminum, AUTOFLOW signals resist wear and weather conditions under any circumstances. Individually mounted doors have internal locking latches that are unaffected by ice accumulation or repainting and will not jar open by vibration or severe impact.

Over the edge of the lens is fitted a one piece olded neoprene gasket which presses firmly into the signal door and clamps into position. his gasket effectively seals the front, the edge and the back of the lens against dust or moisture entering around the lens or through the door opening.

These and many other features included in the JTOFLOW fixed face traffic signals design are your assurance of dependable, efficient operation. And, because all common parts are interchangeable and easily accessible with simple tools, will result in the minimum of maintenance expense, an important factor in determining the ultimate cost of your equipment.

AUTOFLOW ADJUSTABLE TRAFFIC SIGNALS are designed for multiple section signal face assembly by fastening individual housings together with three-stud fittings, thus combining housings to compose multiple signal units for specific signal face requirements.

AUTOFLOW ADJUSTABLE TRAFFIC SIGNALS are designed to insure maximum resistance to shock and impact and for simple maintenance with a minimum of tools which combine to assure low-cost, dependable operation.

AUTOFLOW signal reflectors are precision spun, "Alzak" finished aluminum, for accuracy of contour and reflective efficiency. The reflector is polished to a high lustre providing a surface free of distortion, with superior resistance to corrosion and tarnish.

The AUTOFLOW ADJUSTABLE signal line includes a complete assortment of cast aluminum mounting brackets for all types of mounting arrangements. Accessories include balance adjustors, open bottom and full circle tunnel visors, special lens, etc.

ROLS

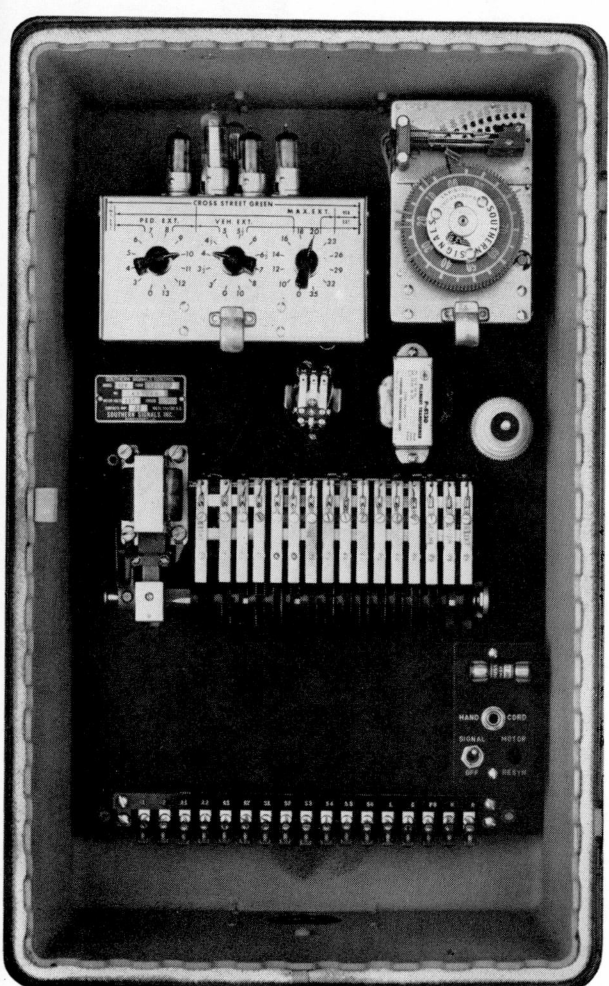

specifications

The Model 102V semi-actuated traffic signal controller is designed to provide all of the normal functions required of this type of control. It responds to impulses received from either pressure sensitive, magnetic or electronic vehicle detectors as well as impulses received from pedestrian push buttons. The design includes components of a standard pre-timed synchronous controller operating in conjunction with an electronic extension timer.

. . . also

Downlight BEACC

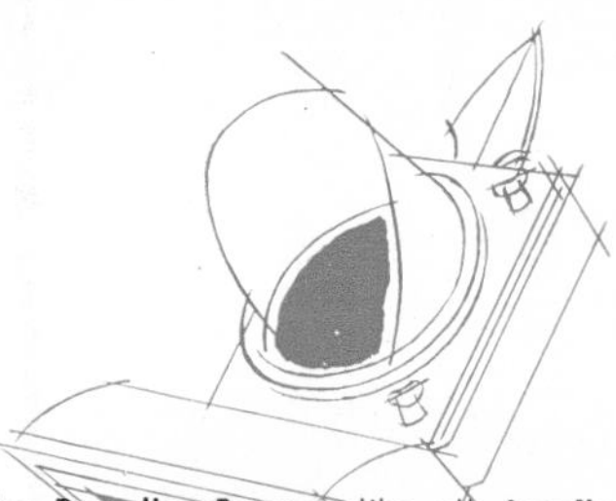

The **Downlite Beacon,** like all **Autoflow** traffi signal equipment, is built to provide maximun operational efficiency through simplicity. De signed and constructed so that all parts ar readily accessible for maintenance. The beaco is complete, including the Flasher control.

Neon Signals

AUTOFLOW **Neon Signals** are engineered fo application to standard AUTOFLOW adjustabl signals without modification. Designed for a conventional mounting arrangements with stand ard brackets. Letters are 4'' high and signa face is 10'' x 15''.

Pulsating Red

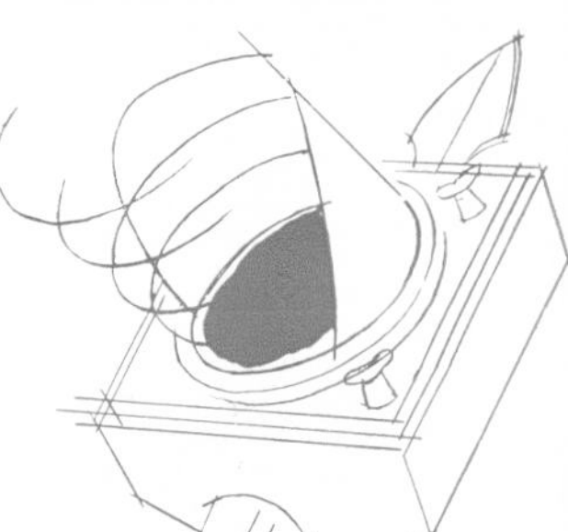

PULSATING RED commands attention from greate distances . . . instantly identifies traffic signals . . . prevents washout from sun phantom and backlighting . . . increases safety for both driver and pedestrian and operates efficiently at 340-420 pulses per minute—never goes out.

SOUTHERN *Signals* INC.

PHONE 2-5121

222 BEACH STREET P. O. BOX 1303 SHREVEPORT, LOUISIAN

TIME-O-MATIC FLASHERS

2 Types for Every Flashing Signal Need

Jack Mounted Flasher in Standard Meter Case

INCLUDING:

- FLASHING STOP SIGNS
- LOADING ZONES
- WARNING BEACONS
- TRAFFIC ISLANDS
- SAFETY ZONES
- BRIDGE ABUTMENTS
- CAUTION SIGNALS
- DETOURS
- DEAD ENDS

. . . AND MANY OTHERS

1. The New JACK MOUNTED Flasher

Here's the latest flasher development: sturdy, durable and so easy to install. In single or two circuit models, you get dependable operation in *any* weather. In the standard meter case (above) or as a separate unit with handy Jack Panel, you can mount it anywhere. It's the safe, sure answer to all flashing signal needs.

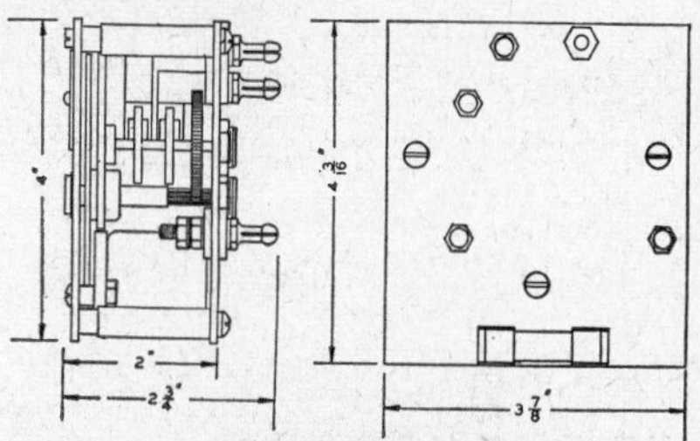

Jack Mounted Flasher and Jack Connecting Panel

2. Front Mounted Flasher

Proved dependable for more than 20 years, in single or two circuit models with or without radio interference eliminator. Flashing speed is 50-60 F.P.M., adjusted easily on the job by convenient lever. Works well in any position, any weather.

Front Mounted Flasher

Front Mounted Flasher Dimensions:

1 circ.—4⅝" x 4⅜" x 2⅜"
2 circ.—4⅝" x 5¾" x 2⅜"

A Sign of Good Control

Write us for full details on both flashers: 1102 Bahls St., Danville, Ill.

TIME-O-MATIC Inc.

P. O. BOX 850 DANVILLE, ILLINOIS

THE UNION METAL MFG. COMPANY

Canton 5, Ohio

UNION METAL TRAFFIC SIGNAL POLES

FOR: **LONG LIFE**
HIGH STRENGTH
LOW MAINTENANCE
ATTRACTIVE APPEARANCE
EASY INSTALLATION

Union Metal tapered steel poles, plain round or fluted . . . the most practical, economical solution to your traffic signal support problems. Available for either mast arm, suspension or pedestal type signals. For catalog information write to The Union Metal Manufacturing Company, Canton 5, Ohio.

MONOTUBE OVERHEAD SIGN SUPPORTS

for modern traffic control

On today's high-speed highways, signs that can be read at a glance are essential. To provide a simple, lasting means for mounting such signs, Union Metal developed Monotube Overhead Sign Supports, which have already proved their effectiveness and economy in numerous installations.

These steel supports offer the same outstanding design, strength and construction features for which Monotube street lighting, floodlighting and strain poles have long been noted. The exclusive cold-rolling process, for example, increases the yield strength of the metal by more than 50% of its original value.

Send for catalog data on this modern approach to effective highway marking. Address The Union Metal Manufacturing Company, Canton 5, Ohio.

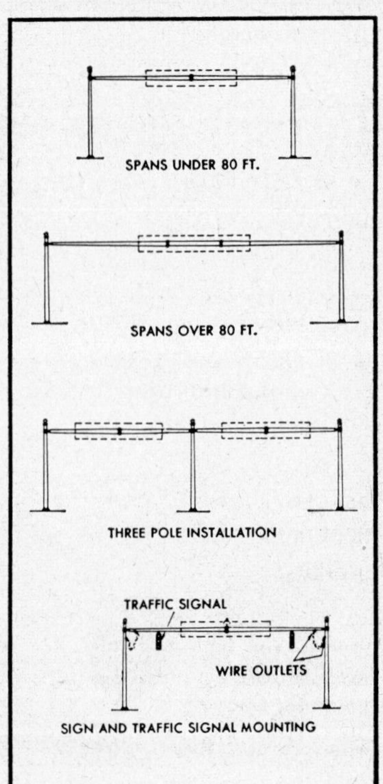

7 ADVANCED ENGINEERING IMPROVEMENTS

MAKE THE *NEW*

"TRAFFIC SENTRY"

A Sensation For Emergency Traffic Control

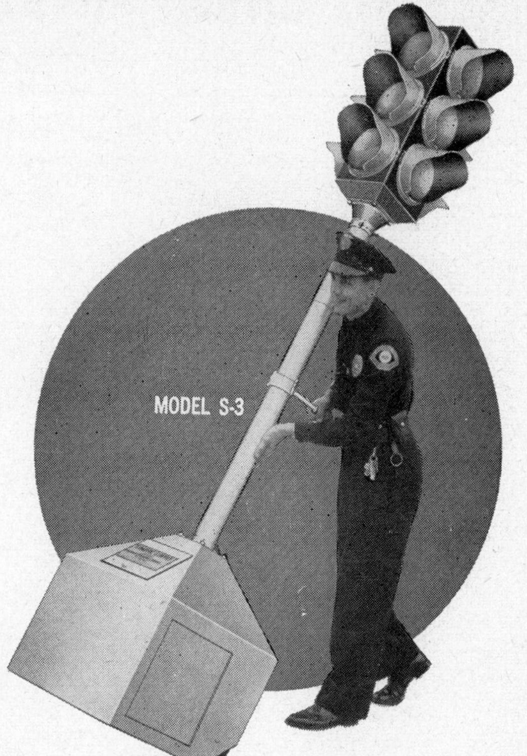

The "TRAFFIC SENTRY" Portable Traffic Signal has been completely re-engineered to bring you 7 big improvements that completely revolutionize its use, service and versatility.

- *1. All aluminum light-weight head with each lens opening individually.*
- *2. New specular aluminum, highly polished reflectors, alzac process.*
- *3. Improved design aluminum visors greatly increase visibility.*
- *4. New 12-volt electrical system.*
- *5. New, stronger, one-piece welded, reinforced heavy-gauge steel pedestal-based smaller size.*
- *6. Improved, fully automatic, flotation equalizer, heavy duty charger, mounted in pedestal base.*
- *7. NEW, more positive, greater cycling range controller mounted in pedestal base for easy access.*

DEALER INQUIRIES INVITED

Write or wire today for fully illustrated brochure.

Rugged, lightweight construction. Can be easily handled by one man or quickly moved to widely separated localities on dolly trailers by auto or motorcycle.

PORTABLE TRAFFIC SIGNALS, INC.
146 West 21st Street
Los Angeles 7, Calif.

The following three pages tell more . . .

The New, Improved "TRAFFIC SENTRY"

MODEL S-3

Provides Traffic Safety and Control at Any Location or Emergencies

The new "TRAFFIC SENTRY" Model S-3 has been engineered to conform to the design standards for permanent signals as set forth in the Manual on Uniform Traffic Control Devices for Streets and Highways. During peak traffic loads or in emergencies you can control traffic swiftly and safely with the "TRAFFIC SENTRY".

Cities and counties everywhere are using the "TRAFFIC SENTRY" to control traffic in many ways. Your city too will find many uses for this new, improved PORTABLE TRAFFIC SIGNAL.

Standard 4-Way Portable Traffic Signal—Equipped with I.T.E. Standard Lenses

Regular 8⅜" diameter prismatic diffusing lenses are used in the new, improved "TRAFFIC SENTRY". This and other design features make it a standard 4-way signal that is acceptable for every emergency use. The fact that it is fully portable makes it easy to move quickly, from one location to another.

Easily Handled By One Man

Two 8" wheels with air-cushion tires make the mobile "TRAFFIC SENTRY" Portable Signal easy to move. Rugged, lightweight construction is counterbalanced for ease of handling. Signals can be quickly moved to widely separated localities on dolly trailers, by auto or motorcycle, increasing their usefulness.

On its way to Third and Walnut

Perhaps your city doesn't have a Third and Walnut intersection, but one thing is sure and that is that nearly every city has many intersections and traffic spots where the Portable "TRAFFIC SENTRY" will relieve traffic worries.

A Score of NEW Improvements that Win the Approval of Everyone

The new "TRAFFIC SENTRY", Model S-3 incorporates a large number of improvements that are winning wide approval from city officials, traffic engineers, police officers and others. Check for yourself all of the features shown in the signal at the right. You will quickly realize that the new, improved "TRAFFIC SENTRY" provides all the safety and convenience features that a portable signal should have.

Self-Contained—Automatic Charger

"TRAFFIC SENTRY" is self-contained, battery operated. It can be kept in service 15 hours continuously without recharging. The charger, which is completely automatic, is housed in the base assembly. Once it is plugged into a 110-115 volt outlet, it needs no further attention. It is easy to keep battery charged and signal in good operating condition at all times.

"TRAFFIC SENTRY" is designed for fully automatic operation without any attention whatever. However, it may also be operated manually by any authorized person. Regardless of the type of operation you use, you may be sure of its dependable ability and protection.

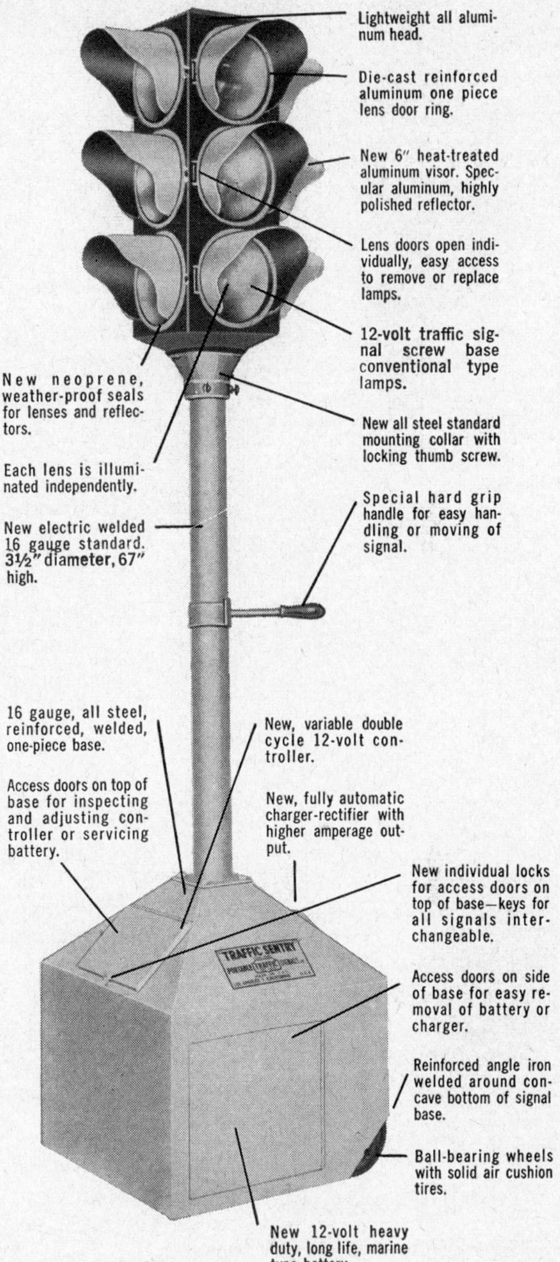

AUTOMATIC TIMING provides Finger Tip Control. The flow of traffic in both directions is regulated by the automatic controller which is pre-set to meet your requirements. Timing condition continues automatically until knob settings are changed.

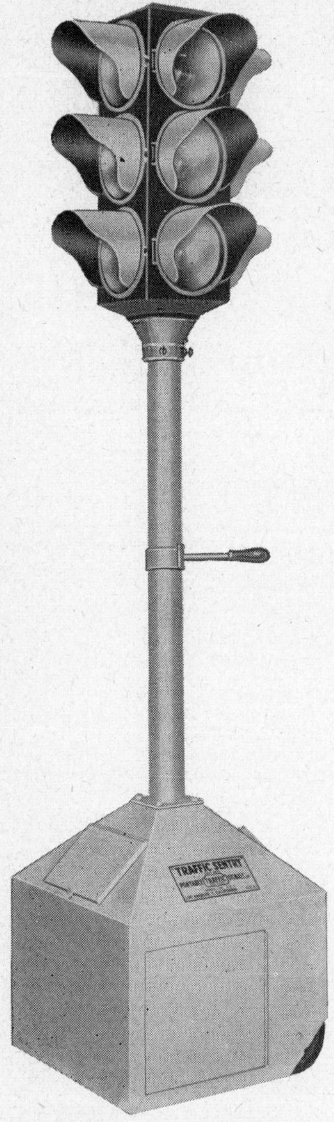

The New, Improved

"TRAFFIC SENTRY"

MODEL S-3

Provides the Same Control and Safety In Emergencies as Permanent Signal Installations

✓ CHECK THESE SPECIFICATIONS

Base: Constructed entirely of heavy 16 gauge sheet steel and equipped with two 8-inch diameter, ball-bearing wheels with solid rubber air cushioned tires, 600 lbs. static test. Equipped with access doors on top and side. Overall height of base 26″ width and depth 23″.

Height: 8′0″ to bottom of green lens. 10′3″ overall height. Additional height available upon request.

Head Assembly: Made of .051 heat treated sheet aluminum. ⅛″ x ½″ reinforcing struts for extra rigidity. 8⅜″ diameter prismatic diffusing lenses, I.T.E. Standard. Dimensions, 31½″ high, 10″ square.

Lamp Assemblies: 12 reflectors of highly spun specular aluminum, alzak process. Equipped with 12-volt conventional traffic signal bulbs.

Battery: 153 ampere hour 12-volt, slow discharge, heavy duty, long-life. 3 year guarantee.

Battery Charger: Self-contained, 110-volt AC, 50-60 cycle. Also available 220-volt AC or DC, on request.

Write for our new Colorful Brochure on "TRAFFIC SENTRY" The Portable Signal.

PORTABLE TRAFFIC SIGNALS, INC.

Manufacturers of the "TRAFFIC SENTRY"

146 WEST 21st STREET **LOS ANGELES 7, CALIF.**

EASTERN "A" STANDS

"Standard of the Industry"

—Won't Blow Over

—Speed-E-Lok

—Folds and Locks in Place

—Most Effective Warning

These are America's most popular warning "A" stands for slowing down motorists, marking work areas, and protecting emergency repair operations. Widely used by municipal traffic, street, and public works departments.

Unit is lightweight, compact, easy to store, and quickly set up and taken down. Free-swinging sign—won't blow over.

Specifications	Sign size	Total weight	Distance across Flags	Distance across Frame	Sign Ga.	Size angle	Height open
Eastern "A" Senior	24x24"	20 lbs.	56"	25"	18	1x1x⅛"	36"
Eastern "A" Heavy-duty	18x18"	18 "	46"	19¼"	19	1x1x⅛"	27½"
Eastern "A" Standard	18x18"	13 "	46"	19"	19	¾x¾x⅛"	27"

MEN WORKING — STOP — SLOW — ROAD REPAIR AHEAD

MEN WORKING IN TREES — STOP FRESH OIL DO NOT ENTER — STREET CLOSED — MEN WORKING OVERHEAD

For severe conditions and rough handling, we recommend the **SENIOR "A" STAND** with almost double the sign face area and the **HEAVY DUTY "A" STAND** with the heavier angle frame construction. All Eastern Metal "A" Stand models fold completely flat for convenient carrying or storage.

Illustrated at left are eight legends regularly stocked for Eastern "A" Standards. These are free swinging signs that contribute to the stability of the "A" Stand. Lettered both sides. Reflectorized if desired.

WRITE FOR ILLUSTRATED FOLDER AND PRICE LIST

EASTERN METAL OF ELMIRA, INC. Elmira Hts., N. Y.

EASTERN "IRON COP"

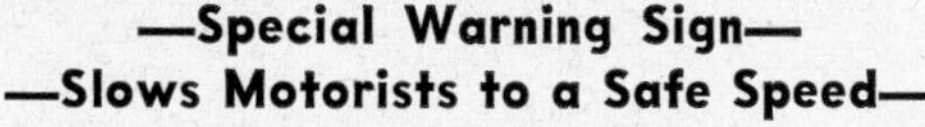

—Special Warning Sign—
—Slows Motorists to a Safe Speed—

The Eastern "Iron Cop" is an effective guardian for school zones, playgrounds, and dangerous crosswalks and will release your police force for other duties. Policeman figure has official blue uniform in baked enamel finish, stands 6′4″ high, and is easily rolled into position on stable iron base. Available with single or double facing figure.

TRAFFIC STANCHION

Eastern Metal's Traffic Stanchion is supplied in Model TS-30—30# base—1″ pipe with pipe cap. Total height of unit 46″; Base 20″ diameter. This unit is designed to hold 12″ x 18″; 18″ x 24″; or 24″ x 24″ signs. Eastern Metal Stanchions are durable, well built and supplied in yellow color.

DRIVE SLOW
15 M.P.H.

WRITE FOR ILLUSTRATED FOLDERS AND PRICE LISTS

EASTERN E-Z BARRICADE

The first major advance in barricade construction in many years. More lightweight, portable, and easy to assemble than ordinary bulky wooden barricades.

All-steel welded construction, baked enamel chrome yellow finish, 36″ high in 4′ or 8′ lengths. 4′ model weighs only 13 lbs. Free swinging warning signs for a variety of conditions available.

EASTERN HI-LITE

Red Flasher Warning Light

for street repair, public work construction, and emergencies. Blinks a brilliant red warning light every half second. Shielded, directional beam operates under all weather conditions with wet or dry cell battery. Battery *not* provided. Extends to 8′ 8″ on steady leg support.

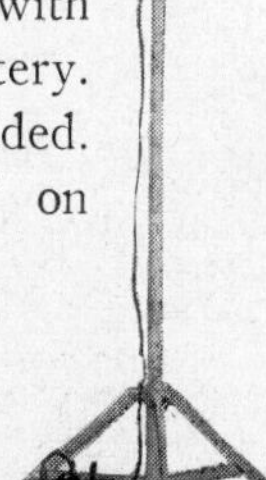

EASTERN METAL OF ELMIRA, INC. Elmira Hts., N. Y.

EASTERN METAL TRAFFIC SIGNS

Your One Source For ALL METAL SIGNS

We stock over 1200 standard legend signs ready for immediate shipment and have facilities for creating special signs for your particular requirements. Your request for information and prices will be given our prompt attention.

Check these EASTERN METAL Safety and Traffic Sign features against your specifications.

- **U.S. Dept. of Commerce and States' Official Uniform Designs**
- **Heavy Gauge Bonderized Steel**
- **Weather Resistant Flexible Enamels—heavy coats applied by hot spray method for enduring good appearance**
- **Embossed Borders — to give additional strength**
- **Silk Screened Legends — for the sharpest, clearest lettering of any signs on the highway today.**

RED STOP SIGNS

Up to three times more effective in stopping cars than standard yellow signs. They meet specifications and recommendations of the Joint Committee on Uniform Traffic devices.

ALUMINUM SIGN BOLTS

Adds life and good appearance to signs. Includes aluminum bolt, nut, and lock washer, plus fiber washer. 2—5/16″ long.

WRITE TODAY FOR ILLUSTRATED FOLDERS AND PRICE LISTS ON ALL EASTERN METAL SIGNS AND EQUIPMENT.

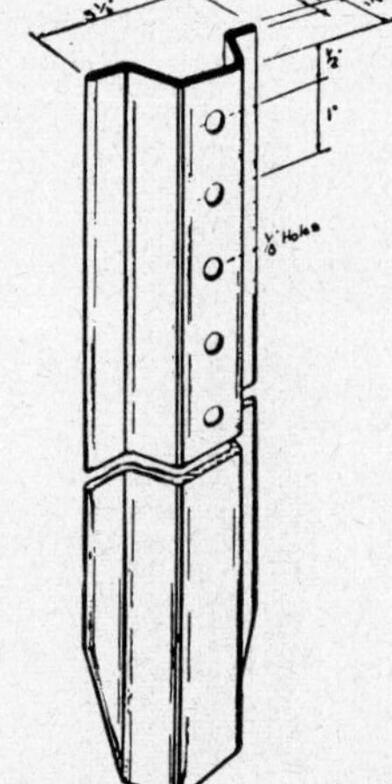

U-TYPE STEEL HIGHWAY POSTS

Weatherproof Enamel Finish
3/8″ holes, 1″ centers
6′ to 12′ lengths.

EMBOSSED STREET SIGNS

Baked white enamel finish for lasting weatherproof service. 20 Gauge bonderized steel. 2-way, 4-way, and 6-way assemblies.

WRITE TODAY FOR ILLUSTRATED FOLDERS AND PRICE LISTS ON ALL EASTERN METAL SIGNS AND EQUIPMENT.

EASTERN METAL OF ELMIRA, INC. Elmira Hts., N. Y.

GRIMM STAMP & BADGE CO.

8105 ROSALIE AVE.
ST. LOUIS 17, MO.

STOP
STOP
STOP
STOP

SLOW
NARROW BRIDGE

SPEED LIMIT 50
SPEED LIMIT 30
NO U TURN
ONE WAY DO NOT ENTER
ONE WAY

SLOW SCHOOL
SLOW PLAYGROUND
SLOW CHILDREN
KEEP TO RIGHT
NO LEFT TURN

A brand new, block-long plant, specially designed for high quality workmanship, also helps make GRIMM Stamp and Badge Co. a pleasant place to work.

Just inside receiving doors is steel storage, cutting and shearing departments. A continual flow of zinc coated and bonderized steel is cut to sign sizes.

GRIMM STAMP & BADGE CO.

8105 ROSALIE AVE.
ST. LOUIS 17, MO.

NO PARKING ANY TIME

NO PARKING IN THIS BLOCK

NO PARKING ⟷

NO PARKING BETWEEN SIGNS

NO STOPPING OR STANDING

NO PARKING LOADING ZONE

NO PARKING BUS STOP

NO PARKING HERE TO CORNER

NO PARKING TAXI STAND

NO PARKING — AM TO — PM

NO PARKING THIS SIDE

NO PARKING FIRE LANE

NO PARKING SCHOOL DAYS

NO PARKING IN ALLEY

DO NOT ENTER

SCHOOL ZONE

HOSPITAL ZONE

NO DUMPING

BRIDGE OUT

ONE WAY

IOWA U.S. 50

BUSINESS DISTRICT

DETOUR

After rounding corners, trimming to exact size and punching holes, this large press sharply embosses letters and borders in one operation.

Dog licenses, vendors tags and numbered plates are produced on presses in the foreground. Larger presses emboss traffic and street name signs.

CONTINUED

GRIMM STAMP & BADGE CO.

8105 ROSALIE AVE.
ST. LOUIS 17, MO.

000-000
19 OREGON 57

MIAMI 2 BEACH
1956-1957

GUATEMALA-57
15-001

SALINA
19 20 57
DOG TAX

SAGINAW
8000
EXP. 4-30-57
BICYCLE

U.S. COAST GUARD
101
C.G. BASE BOSTON, MASS.

MOTOS 407
PANAMA 1957

SPEED
ELECTRICALLY
TIMED

SPRINGFIELD	233
JOPLIN	307
TULSA	430

KEEP YOUR
PARK
BEAUTIFUL

STATE
HIGHWAY
DEPT.
UNIT

PROPERTY OF
MADISON
COUNTY

PROPERTY OF
CITY OF ALTON

Primer coat and background colors are sprayed on both sides of all GRIMCO signs. Only the best grades of enamels are used, insuring maximum protection and life.

In and out of the baking ovens 2 — 3 and 4 times as successive coats of enamel are baked on, gives GRIMCO signs a harder, more durable finish than automobiles. GRIMCO makes signs that last!

MORE

GRIMM STAMP & BADGE CO.

8105 ROSALIE AVE.
ST. LOUIS 17, MO.

GRIMCO Signs

Thousands of standard worded signs are stored ready to ship the day your order is received. No finer signs are made anywhere, yet GRIMCO prices are competitively low.

Grimco manufactures first quality **die embossed** Street and Highway traffic signs and licenses. Quick quotations at any time . . . or we can fill and ship from stock to meet your immediate needs.

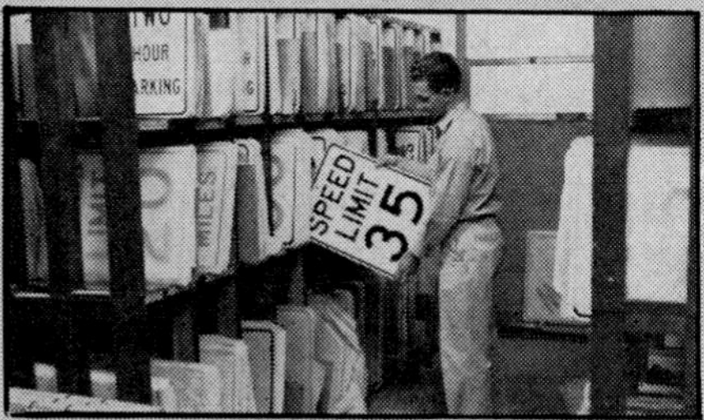

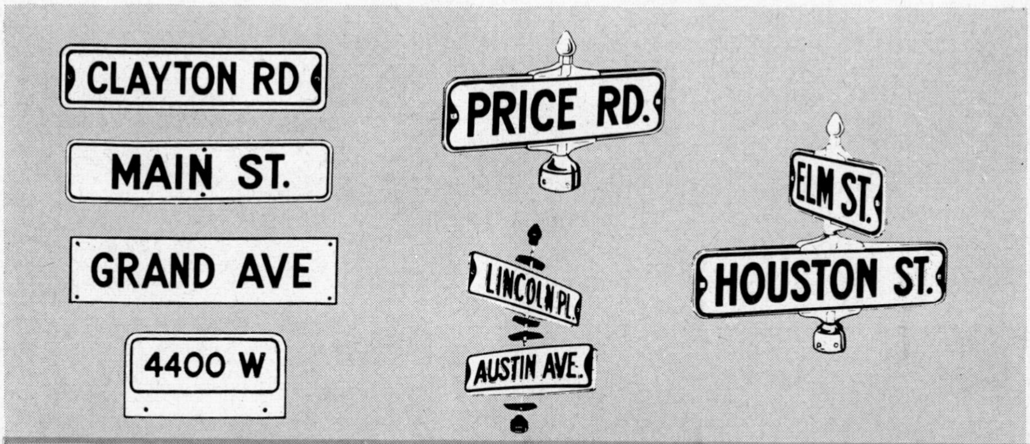

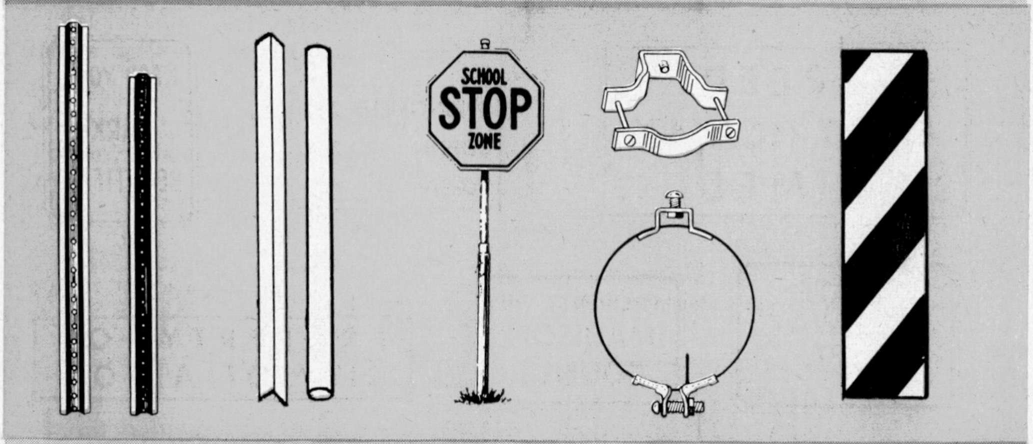

BLACK ON YELLOW 24" x 24" — 30" x 30" | WHITE ON RED 24" x 24" — 30" x 30" | BLACK ON YELLOW 24" x 24" — 30" x 30"

R-51 12" x 18" | R-18 12" x 18" | R-40 12" x 18" | R-41 12" x 18" | R-46 12" x 18" | R-43 12" x 18"

NO PARKING LOADING ZONE | NO PARKING BUS STOP | NO PARKING 8:30 A.M. TO 5:30 P.M. | NO TRUCK PARKING | ONE HOUR PARKING | ONE HOUR PARKING 9 A.M.-7 P.M.

R-25 12" x 18" | R-26 12" x 18" | R-19 12" x 18" | R-44 12" x 18" | GREEN ON WHITE R-56 12" x 18" | R-22 12" x 18"

W-40 18" x 24" | W-31 24" x 24" | W-42 24" x 24" | W-401 18" x 24"

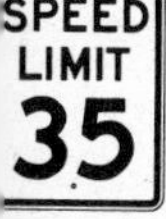

R-2 18" x 24" | R-2 18" x 24" | R-66 18" x 24" | R-65 18" x 24" | R-14 18" x 24"

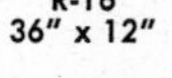
R-16 36" x 12"

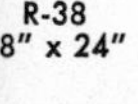
R-38 18" x 24" | R-15 24" x 24"

W-51 24" x 24" | W-13 24" x 24" | W-55 24" x 24" | W-22 24" x 24"

W-26 24" x 24" (with easel) | W-2 24" x 24" | W-9 24" x 24" | W-30 24" x 24"

ORDER POSTS AND BRACKETS WITH SIGNS

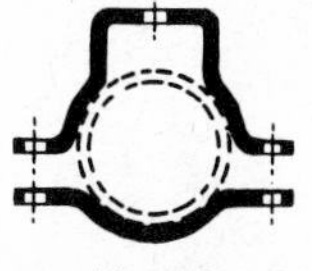
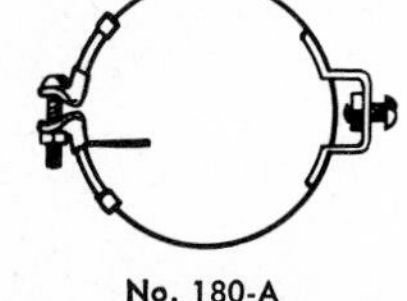

No. 200B U-POST | No. 170 PIPE POST BRACKET | No. 180-A ADJUSTABLE BAND BRACKET

CATAPHOTE TRAFFIC SIGNS

- **STEEL or ALUMINUM**
- **REFLECTORIZED or PLAIN**
- **MEET U. S. STANDARD SPECIFICATIONS**

Cataphote is your sign of quality, based on over 25 years experience working with municipalities in development and manufacture of long lasting street and highway traffic markers.

All standard wordings are available covering Stop, Parking, School, Speed, Movement, Warning and Railroad. You can get Cataphote signs plain or reflectorized by three different methods—buttons, sheeting (over-all and panel), or Cataflex Reflective Coating over-all. All regular types of danger signs are also available.

Enamel finishes of the highest quality are baked at over 300° on heavy gauge, zinc-coated, bonderized steel. All signs have embossed borders.

Posts, easels, standards, brackets, bolts and other accessories are carried in stock for your convenience.

The complete Cataphote line is manufactured to State and Federal standards and provides effective and economical traffic control under all conditions with long life and minimum upkeep. Write for more information and Catalog 65.

TOLEDO 10, OHIO
AND
JACKSON, MISSISSIPPI
U. S. A.

CATAPHOTE

STREET NAME SIGNS

Reflectorized

or Plain

GUARANTEED FOR 3 YEARS

Reflectorized

Name plates are made of long lasting, 18 gauge embossed zinc-coated bonderized steel, measuring 6" x 18" to 32" long with 4" letters. Cataflex "202" Reflective Coating overall assures excellent nighttime visibility and legibility from long distances, (black on white). Economy reflectorization is also available at nominal cost, with letters and border only coated with Cataflex "202" reflectorization (white on black). The exceptional visibility of reflectorized street name signs at night contributes to faster, easier identification of streets, and greater safety.

Plain

Plates are of 18 gauge zinc-coated, bonderized steel—6" high by 18" to 32" long with 4" letters. Three coats of baked, high gloss enamel assure long life. Embossing is 1/10" deep, which insures sturdy, rigid signs with wide angle visibility, lasting beauty and durability. Any two-color combination is available.

Brackets for Cataphote street name signs are high quality, zinc-coated, bonderized steel with cadmium plated bolts and nuts. Steel parts are rust-proofed and finished with baked enamel.

Cataphote *quality* has made these street name signs a choice of municipalities for over a quarter century. Let Cataphote help you with your Street Marker engineering problems. No obligation.

TOLEDO 10, OHIO

AND

JACKSON, MISSISSIPPI

U. S. A.

GN 1-2A

(Half Box)
GN 1-2B

CATAPHOTE REFLECTIVE MARKING MATERIALS

PREMIXED CATALINE

Reflective Striping Compound

(Special binder with reflective glass beads premixed)

:ataline Reflective Striping Compound consists of eflective beads PREMIXED into traffic binder. The inder is a super-tough, plastic, latex rubber mateial of special Cataphote composition that firmly rips the millions of tiny optical-crown-glass beads o produce unusually brilliant reflection.

he compound is extra fast drying—will not track fter six minutes. Cataline Compound eliminates he necessity for glass bead dispenser. Applied asily and rapidly with standard line marking quipment of any type or make.

***olors:* White and Federal Yellow. Furnished in 5-allon non-returnable steel containers. Prices and orm No. P-2 furnished upon request.**

.ONGER EFFECTIVE LIFE AT LESS COST PER MONTH/MILE

Drop-On Combination ***Premixed Compound***

th Cataline Combination (Drop-On) and Cataline mpound (Premixed) have been "mileage proved" r wear in actual street and highway use, averag-g 50% longer life than ordinary traffic paints. th are "weather-proofed" with pure latex to ithstand severe climatic and surface conditions.

—CATAPHOTE—
your assurance of quality for over 25 years.

DROP-ON CATALINE

Reflective Striping Combination

(Special binder accompanied by moisture-proof reflective glass beads)

Cataline Reflective Striping Combination consists of a super-tough plastic, latex rubber binder of special Cataphote composition onto which the accompanying moisture-proof, optical-crown-glass beads are dropped by a bead dispenser attachment, as the binder is applied with standard marking equipment to streets or highways.

The combination is super-fast drying and will not track after six minutes. Moisture-proof in all weather conditions, both in application and in performance.

***Colors:* White and Federal Yellow. Binder is furnished in 5-gallon non-returnable steel containers—beads in 30-pound moisture-proof bags (6 pounds per gallon). Send for prices and Form P-1.**

TOLEDO 10, OHIO
AND
JACKSON, MISSISSIPPI
U. S. A.

Cataflex 202

REFLECTIVE COATING

NEWEST . . . BRIGHTEST CHEAPEST METHOD

FOR REFLECTORIZING TRAFFIC SIGNS

Cataflex Reflective Coating Kits include a special Cataphote binder; high intensity, waterproof Cataphote "202" glass spheres; and self-cleaning, waterproofing, weather-resisting SMOOTHKOTE. Cataflex "202" Reflective Coating is the "easiest-to-use", least expensive method of reflectorizing traffic signs and markers for night and day brilliance. Any warning design or lettering may be reflectorized on signs, barricades or even irregular surfaces.

Reflectorizing with Cataflex "202" costs one-tenth that of sheeting methods, requires no special equipment, no special training of sign shop personnel. Complete instructions are furnished with every kit. Binder comes in red, white, yellow and clear (transparent). Specify drying method (air or bake) used.

Cataflex "202" Kit Sizes

INTRODUCTORY	........Covers	100 Square Feet
STANDARD	................Covers	600 Square Feet
ECONOMY	..................Covers	3000 Square Feet
SUPER	........................Covers	6000 Square Feet

See your nearest Cataphote Distributor or send $25.00 for INTRODUCTORY KIT (100 square feet) and free catalog P-3.

TOLEDO 10, OHIO
AND
JACKSON, MISSISSIPPI
U. S. A.

Form ML-2 Printed in U.S.A. GBC-125620

New or old signs can be reflectorized in your own shop without special training and special equipment.

For a cost of 1/10th other methods Cataflex "202" reflectorizing can be done in your own shop.

Signs of all kinds can be reflectorized at surprisingly low cost with Cataflex "202" Reflective Coating.

"202" Reflective Coating does not reduce daytime brilliance, but actually improves daytime appearance.

FLEX-O-LITE MANUFACTURING CORP.

P. O. Box No. 3066, (Affton Branch) St. Louis 23, Missouri

REFLECTIVE GLASS BEADS

Flex-O-Lite Products Offer You Top Eye-Catching Brilliance and Dependable Reflectorization. Satisfied Users All Over The World.

SIGN REFLECTORIZING KITS:

Obtain uniformity and bright signs with Flex-O-Lite special bead binder and closely graded brilliant glass beads.

Uses: Traffic Signs, Commerical Signs, Street Signs, House Numbers, etc.

BEAD DISPENSERS:

Solve your highway reflectorizing problems with the Flex-O-Lite Bead Dispenser. Saves time . . . money . . . labor. New, simplified operation. Thoroughly tested and approved. Write for full details.

AIRPORT RUNWAY BEADS:

Meeting Corps of Engineers Specification T-1290A, or any other airport specification.

Uses: Warning Messages on Runways, Apron Zone Lines.

FLEX-O-LITE HIGHWAY CENTERLINE BEADS:

Manufactured to provide the maximum amount of reflectivity when applied with traffic paint. Any specification can be formulated.

Uses: Centerlines, Letters, Cross Walks, Parking Lots and Zone Lanes.

Write for literature, name of nearest dealer and particulars regarding export shipments.

FLEX-O-LITE MANUFACTURING CORP.

Post Office Box 3066 (Affton Branch)
St. Louis 23, Missouri

GROTE SIGNS

Insure Maximum Warning!

Reflectorized warning signs have Grotelite SS reflective sheeting on aluminum or steel. Yellow reflective background with black screen processed message and border. Enameled warning signs also available, heavy gauge rust resisting steel, baked on primer and enamel finish, black screen processed message and border.

Directional Symbols

24" x 24"
W-1-R—Turn Right
W-1-L—Turn Left
W-2-R—Curve Right
W-2-L—Curve Left
W-3-R—Reverse Turn Right
W-3-L—Reverse Turn Left
W-4-R—Reverse Curve Right
W-4-L—Reverse Curve Left
W-5-R—Winding Road Right
W-5-L—Winding Road Left
W-6—Cross Road
W-7-R—Side Road Right—90°
W-7-L—Side Road Left—90°
W-8-R—Side Road Right—45°
W-8-L—Side Road Left—45°
W-9—T Symbol
W-10—Y Symbol
W-30—Double Arrow

40" x 20"
W-11-R—Large Arrow Right
W-11-L—Large Arrow Left
W-12—Large Double Arrow

Advance Warnings

24" x 24"
W-13—Stop Ahead
W-14—Signals Ahead
W-15—Hill
W-16—Bump
W-17—Dip
W-18—Narrow Road
W-22—Narrow Bridge
W-23—One Lane Bridge
W-25—Pavement Ends
W-26—Men Working
W-27—Fresh Oil
W-28—Soft Shoulders
W-29—Slippery When Wet
W-31—School
W-34—Truck Crossing
W-34-S—School Crossing
W-34-C—Cattle Crossing
W-37—Children
W-38—Dead End
W-39—Dead End Street
W-40—Hospital
W-101—Slow
W-102—Road Closed
W-103—Winding Road

30" x 30"
W-19—Pavement Narrows
W-20—Divided Highway Ahead
W-21—Divided Highway Ends
W-24—Low Clearance 12 ft. 6 in.

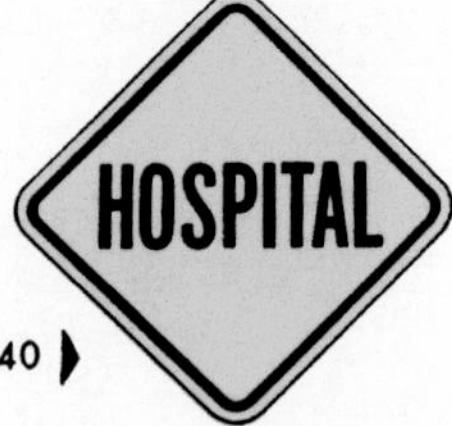

GROTE REGULATORY SIGNS

Get Quick Attention

Grote Regulatory Signs—enameled or reflectorized—are extremely easy to read. Screen processed in fade-resisting colors of red, green and black. Enameled signs are rust resisting steel, finished in baked enamel—reduces maintenance and replacement to a minimum. Reflectorized signs on either aluminum or steel.

Signs with special messages can be furnished promptly.

Parking Signs.

12" x 18"

R-18—No Parking Anytime
R-18-D—No Parking Anytime—Double Arrow
R-18-R—No Parking Anytime—Arrow Right
R-18-L—No Parking Anytime—Arrow Left
R-20—No Parking Except Sundays and Holidays
R-21—No Stopping or Standing
R-25—No Parking Loading Zone
R-26—No Parking Bus Stop
R-26-R—No Parking Bus Stop—Arrow Right
R-26-L—No Parking Bus Stop—Arrow Left
R-41—No Parking Here To Corner
R-41-R—No Parking Here To Corner—Arrow Right
R-41-L—No Parking Here To Corner—Arrow Left
R-42—No Parking Taxi Stand
R-43—No Parking Between Signs
R-43-D—No Parking Between Signs—Double Arrow
R-43-R—No Parking Between Signs—Arrow Right
R-43-L—No Parking Between Signs—Arrow Left
R-44—No Parking This Side
R-44-D—No Parking This Side—Double Arrow
R-45—Parallel Parking
R-46—No Parking
R-46-D—No Parking—Double Arrow
R-46-R—No Parking—Arrow Right
R-46-L—No Parking—Arrow Left
R-47—No Parking Driveway
R-48—No Parking In Driveway
R-49—No Parking Theater Exit
R-50—No Truck Parking
R-54—No Parking Official Cars Only
R-55—No Parking School Days
R-56—No Parking In This Block
R-57—No Parking Fire House
R-58—No Parking Doctors Office
R-59—No Parking Fire Lane
R-60—No Outlet
R-61—One Hour Parking
R-62—Two Hour Parking
R-63—Parking 15 Minutes

Regulatory Signs

All Standard Sizes
R-2 —Speed Limit ( )
R-40—Speed Limit ( ) Miles
R-6 —No Right Turn
R-7 —No Left Turn
R-8 —No U Turn
R-14—Keep (arrow) Right
R-51—Keep To Right
R-52—No Dumping Allowed
R-53—One Way Do Not Enter
R-64—One Way Arrow
R-64-L—One Way—Arrow Left

Grote Special Signs

Reflectorized or Enameled
W-32—Railroad Warning, 30" dia.
W-3350—50°, 6 ft. blades—Railroad Crossbuck *Reflectorized Only
W-3390—90°, 4 ft. blades—Railroad Crossbuck *Reflectorized Only
C-151—Slow School
C-155—Slow Children
R-16—One Way (arrow) 24" x 18" or 36" x 12"
R-16-L—One Way (arrow) 24" x 18" or 36" x 12"

Directional Markers

M-9—Horizontal Arrow—Right
M-10-R—Diagonal Arrow Upward—Right
M-10-L—Diagonal Arrow Upward—Left
M-11—Vertical Arrow Upward
M-12—Horizontal Double Arrow

Cardinal Direction Markers

M-21-N—North
M-21-S—South
M-21-E—East
M-21-W—West
M-21-A—Alternate

NO PARKING ANY TIME

R-18

NO PARKING THEATER EXIT

R-49

NO PARKING OFFICIAL CARS ONLY

R-54

NO PARKING FIRE LANE

R-59

SPEED LIMIT 50

R-2

NO U TURN

R-8

W-32

W-3390

C-151

R-16

M-12

M-21-N

Important!

When ordering Grote Signs, please specify: catalog number, size, complete message, and reflectorized or enameled type. Color of message and border on all Grote Signs adheres to standards of "Manual on Uniform Traffic Devices for Streets and Highways." Standard signs supplied with two ⅜" holes, punched and ready for mounting. For signs with special messages, consult our company.

ALL GROTE SIGNS ADHERE STRICTLY TO U. S. STANDARD SPECIFICATIONS.

So Much Safety...

So Quickly!

with the

LYLE

PORTABLE MERGENCY TRAFFIC CONTROL KIT

You'll wonder how you ever got along without them after the new LYLE SAF-T-PAK portable emergency traffic control kits go to work for you.

They are quickly set up to block approaches to fires, accidents and emergency situations of all kinds. They fold open in less than a minute's time; large size and clarity plus flags, blinker lights and reflective sheeting provide dominant authority respected on sight – day or night.

Extra sign wordings available for every possible emergency. Blinker lights and extra signs are easily stored right *inside* the unit.

Compact and rugged, SAF-T-PAK Sign Kits are engineered and built of heavy gauge metal to provide long, useful service.

Wordings available include:

TRAFFIC CHECK	DO NOT ENTER
ROAD BLOCK	ROAD CLOSED
WATER OVER ROAD	DETOUR
HIGH VOLTAGE	KEEP LEFT
FIRE	ACCIDENT AHEAD
MEN WORKING	ONE WAY TRAFFIC

Many other options, also.

Tested and proved effective for many uses, SAF-T-PAK Sign Kits are like extra manpower in emergencies. You'll welcome the added safety and control they provide. So write today for LYLE's new illustrated SAF-T-PAK brochure, No. S-P 10; no obligation, of course.

LYLE SIGN CO.

2722 UNIVERSITY AVE. S.E.
MINNEAPOLIS, MINN.

DANGER

ROAD CLOSED

POLICE DEPT.

MODERN LYLE

MO

NIGHT VIEW DAY VIEW

Above Sign with Reflecting Background Coating

SPEED LIMIT 35

NO PARKING BETWEEN SIGNS

SIGNS PROTECT

ORISTS AND PEDESTRIANS

DO
NOT
PASS

PASS
WITH
CARE

Signs you can always see bring safety to your city

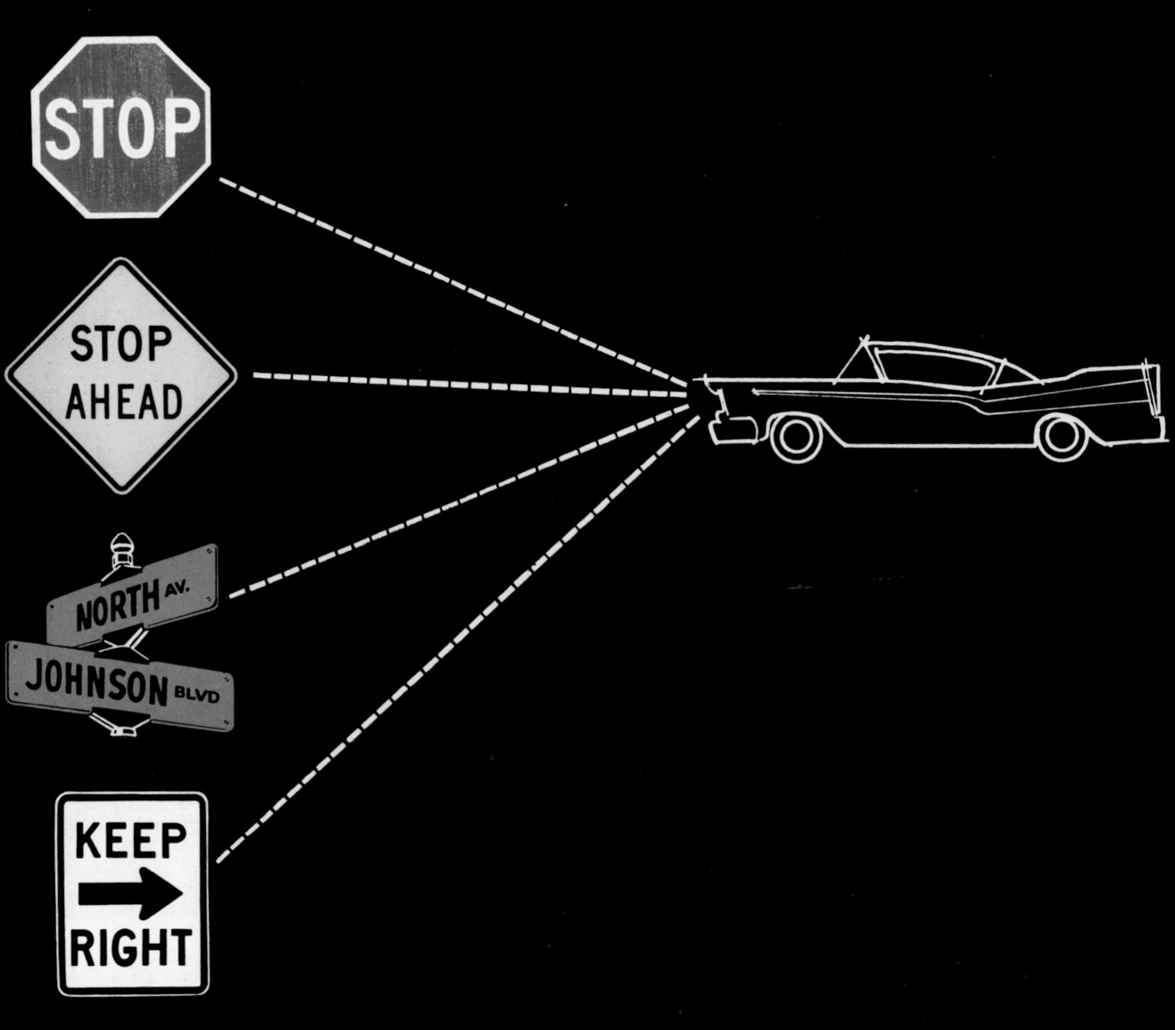

. . . and now, there is a full line of reflective, 24 hour-a-day traffic control devices available from the "3M" Company . . . your *specialists in nighttime safety.*

PRODUCTS OF 3M COMPANY RESEARCH

Whatever you need in r
always specify pro

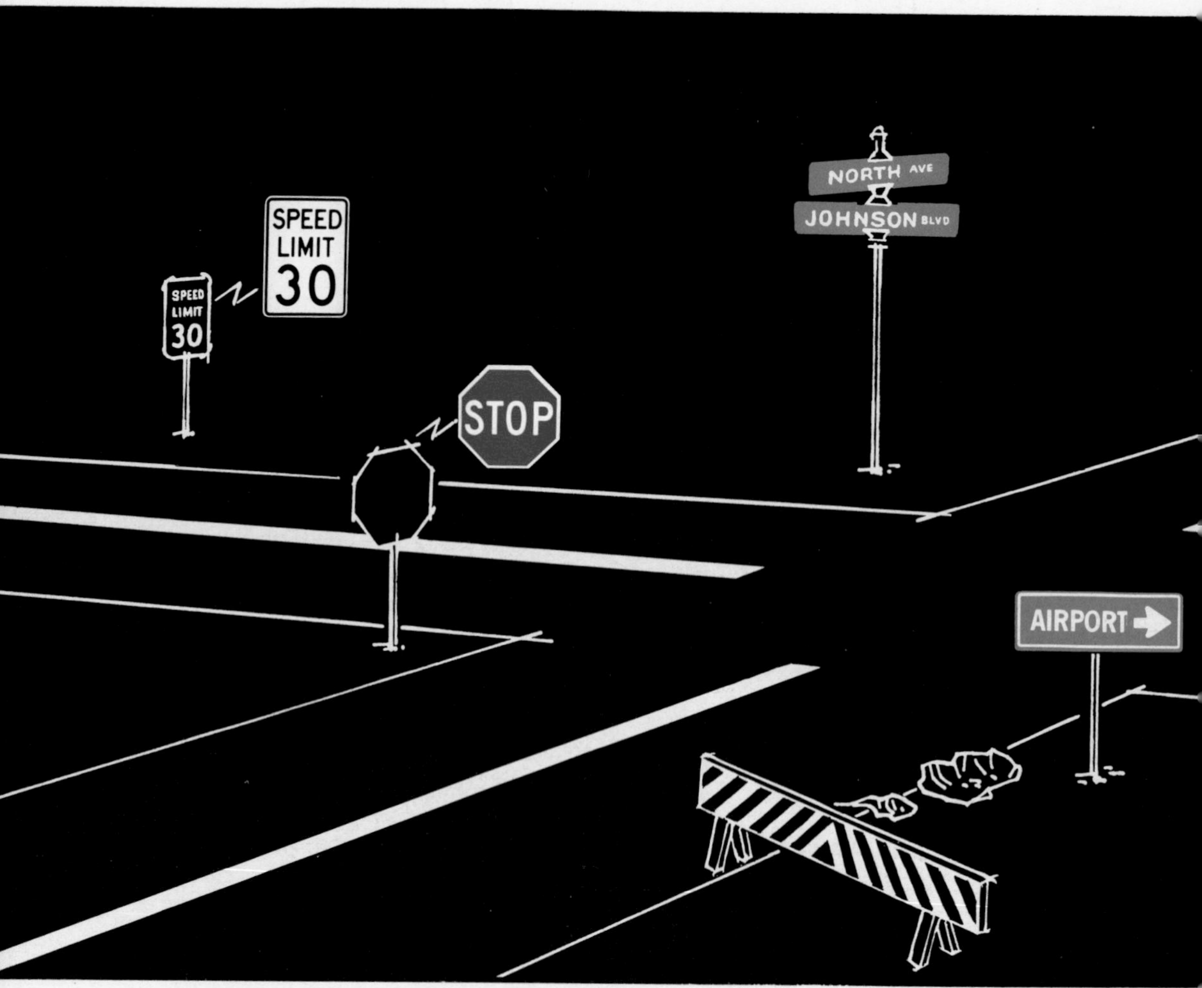

Now available from the manufacture

FINISHED SIGNS

Mounted on 6061-T6., 081 aluminum blanks, these signs reflectorized with Wide Angle Flat-Top SCOTCHLITE Sheeting come ready to use. Screened legends and symbols meet Bureau of Public Roads standards. Non-exposed lens surface never blacks-out in rain. Reflects at any angle.

PREPARED SIGN FACES

These are Wide Angle Flat-Top SCOTCHLITE Sheeting screened with standard Bureau of Public Roads legends and symbols. Ready-to-mount in an automatic applicator to new or reclaimed sign blanks. Self-cleaning smooth surface cuts maintenance costs. Performs at all angles, in any weather.

SIGN APPLICATORS

These machines automatically bond SCOTCHLITE Sheeting to sign blanks. They give you professional sign results with lower production costs. Now available: new 3′ x 4′ heat lamp vacuum applicator. Other size units can be ordered to fit your requirements. Operation is simple, easily learned.

Write for additional illustrated literat

ctive traffic controls . . .
ts of 3M Research

SCOTCHLITE, CENTERLITE and CODIT

REFLECTIVE SHEETING · REFLECTIVE COMPOUND · REFLECTIVE LIQUID

STREET SIGN FACES

Reflectorized street name signs never hide in the dark. Your city can have easy-to-follow street name signs made in your own shop. Faces of Wide Angle Flat-Top SCOTCHLITE Sheeting, screened with legends to order, easily applied to old or new flat backings. Applicator cuts costs.

PAVEMENT STRIPING

New CENTERLITE Reflective Compound is now *extra fast drying*. Beads-in-paint suspension means reflectivity lasts the life of the stripe. Apply with standard equipment—no clogging, no gun wear. Gives lower cost per mile per month of useful life. Easy, fast, one-operation application.

HAZARD MARKINGS

For barricades, new construction, curbing, posts, etc., that need nighttime visibility, use CODIT Reflective Liquid. Either paint it on, or spray it on. Use on concrete, metal, wood or other rough surfaces. Dries in minutes. Available in bulk or 6 oz. spray cans or complete marking kit.

these reflectorized signs and markings.

NIGHT DAY

DAY NIGHT

Miro-Flex Stop signs are available white on red or black on yellow in 18", 24", 30" or 36" sizes; plain or reflectorized. Use following code in sequence to order proper sign:

- R-1 Octagonal stop sign
- 18-24-30-36—size
- P- Plain (no reflectorization)
- B- Beaded reflectorization
- S- Reflective Sheeting
- SL Reflective Sheeting Panel
- X- Button reflectorization
- Y- Black on yellow
- R- White on red
- A- Aluminium

R-95

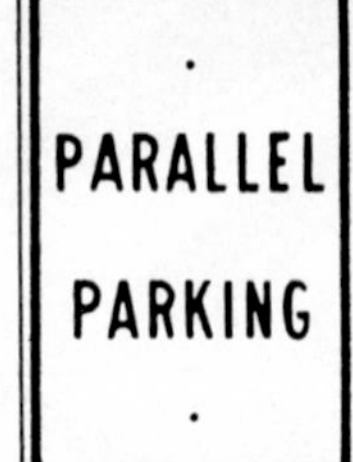

R-28A

R-7 or R-7A

DAY R-2DN or R-102DN

NIGHT

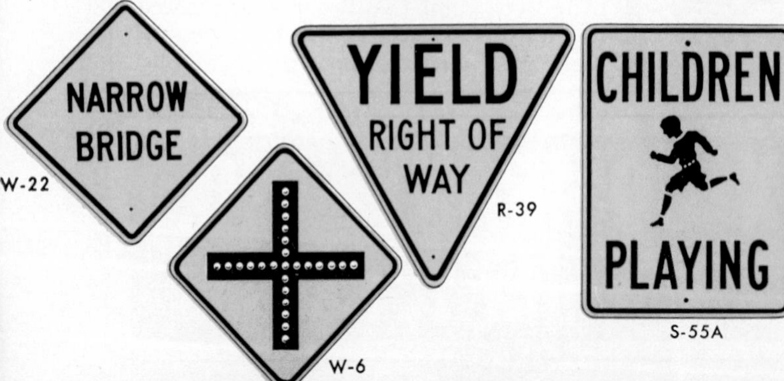

W-22 W-6 R-39 S-55A

REGULATORY STOP SIGNS BLACK ON YELLOW

Plain (no reflectorization)

R-1-18PY R-1-24PY R-1-30PY R-1-3

Beaded Reflectorization Background

R-1-18BY R-1-24BY R-1-30BY R-1-36B
R-1-18BY-A R-1-24-BY-A R-1-30BY-A R-1-36B

Reflective Sheeting Background

R-1-18SY R-1-24SY R-1-30SY R-1-3

Reflective Sheeting Panel

R-1-18SLY R-1-24SLY R-1-30SLY R-1-3

Button Reflectorized

R-1-18XY R-1-24XY R-1-30XY R-1-3

WHITE OR SILVER ON RED

Plain

R-1-18PR R-1-24PR R-1-30PR R-1-3

Beaded Reflectorization

R-1-18BR R-1-24BR R-1-30BR R-1-36B
R-1-18BR-A R-1-24BR-A R-1-30BR-A R-1-36B

Reflective Sheeting

R-1-24SR (24" size only)
R-1-18SR-A R-1-24SR-A R-1-30SR-A R-1-36S

Button Reflectorized

R-1-18XR R-1-24XR R-1-30XR R-1-3

REGULATORY SIGNS

Complete Line of Regulatory Signs

Parking Prohibition, 12" x 18", red copy white.

Parking Restrictions, 12" x 18", green c on white.

Turning Regulations, 18" x 24", 12" x 1 14" x 9", black copy on white.

WARNING SIGNS

Miro-Flex has a complete line of warn signs, 24" x 24" diamond shaped with st dard messages or symbols. Reflectoriza can be had with choice of beaded bc ground, yellow reflective sheeting or pla reflectors.

ALIGNMENT AND EXCLUSION SIGNS

Complete line conforming to recommendati of the Bureau of Public Roads, in 18" x and 24" x 30" sizes as specified. Bl copy on white background.

SPEED REGULATORY SIGNS

Miro-Flex has complete speed limit si with choice of reflectorization of bea background, reflective sheeting backgro or panel, or reflector buttons in numer The NEW MIRO-FLEX DA-NITE signs (R-2 or R-102DN) shows daylight speed limit a different reflectorized speed limit at nig

YIELD SIGNS

Standard 30" equilateral triangular s black copy on yellow, plain or reflectoriz Also available in 24" x 24" x 12" keyst shape.

CHILDREN PLAYING

18" x 24" black on yellow with optio copy changes.

OTHER MIRO-FLEX SIGNS INCLUDE

Railroad Crossing Signs—Advance Warni cross bucks, track number indicator railroad name signs.

Guide and Route Markers—A complete as specified in *Manual on Uniform Tra Control Devices.*

SCHOOL SIGNS

S-56

S-54R

S-53

20 MPH SCHOOL ZONE

S-99

S-60

W-231s SCHOOL LANE AHEAD, 36″ x 36″ diamond.
S-50 ____*MPH SCHOOL ZONE, 24″ x 24″ square.
S-51 NO PARKING SCHOOL DAYS, 12″ x 18″.
S-53 SCHOOL SLOW ZONE, 24″ x 24″ diamond.
S-54 SCHOOL STOP LANE, black on yellow, 24″ x 24″ octagonal.
W-31 SCHOOL, 24″ x 24″ diamond
S-54R SCHOOL STOP LANE, white on red, 24″ x 24″ octagonal.
S-56 Safety Sue and 30″ x 20″ SCHOOL ____MPH.
S-60 STOP School Boy Patrol.
S-99 ____*MPH SCHOOL ZONE, 18″ x 24″ for mounting on portable base.
Plus Other School Signs.

ROAD CONSTRUCTION SIGNS

CAUTION
PROJECT BEGINS
BRODERICK & GIBBONS INC.

HS-1

Miro-Flex manufactures all types of Road Construction signs to the exact specifications of the purchaser, and because of the company's vast experience in this field, can aid in the designing of special signs for specific circumstances. The Portable sign illustrated here has a tripod easily adaptable for 24″ x 24″, 30″ x 30″, or 36″ x 36″ signs, rectangular or diamond shaped. Double-faced hand-warning sign, HS-1, is 16″ in diameter on aluminum.

ELINEATORS AND AZARD MARKERS

-1K

Various sizes of hazard markers and delineators with either red or silver reflective sheeting are available. L-1K with post is 6″ x 30″ double-faced; mounted on 9′ channel steel post.

MW-1

MEN WORKING SIGN is double-faced, 18″ x 18″ processed sign mounted in sturdy steel frame. Available with or without warning flag. Optional copy such as ROAD CLOSED is available.

CIVIL DEFENSE SIGNS

Civil Defense Evacuation signs follow specifications of the Federal Civil Defense administration. They are white letters on blue background; 18″ diameter. Area civil defense signs can be furnished to your specifications.

CD-2

MODEL 18BF MIRO-FLARE

Miro-Flare is the original and still America's most prominent reflecting flare. Model 18BF has set of three economy Model 18 Miro-Flares, flexible staff and flag for each in a compact, sturdy metal box. Ideal for temporary road repair warnings or for vehicle warning flares.

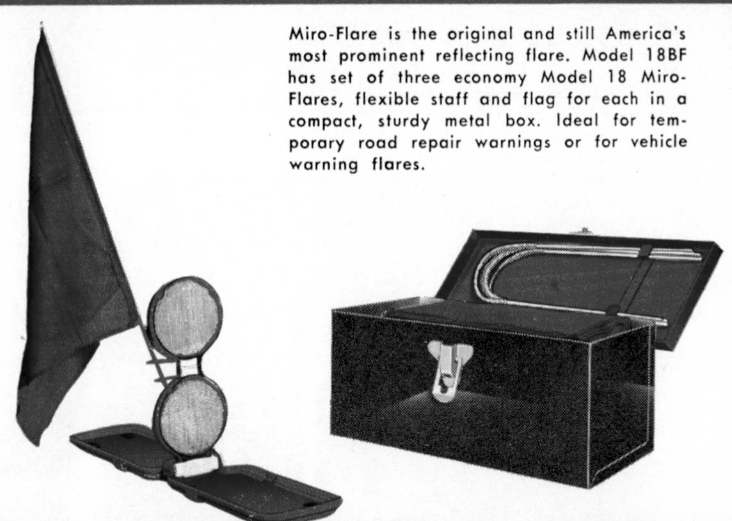

MIRO-FLEX STREET NAME ASSEMBLIES

W-2P

W-4P

B-4P

B-4PBN

B-4PB

B-4PU

B-4B or B-2B

B-2RB or B-4RB

BN-1

Block Number Plate

W-4B or W-2B

B-3L

PEDESTAL ASSEMBLIES

(Designated by part number ending in P)
Available with caps to fit 1½", 2", or 3" ID pipe, or 2½" and 3" OD pipe.

- W-2P Two-way Pedestal Assembly, debossed flange
- W-4P Four-way Pedestal Assembly, debossed flange
- B-4PBN DeLuxe Four-way Pedestal Assembly with block numbers, embossed border
- B-4PB Four-way bracket pedestal assembly for whiteway or utility poles, embossed border
- B-2P Two-way Pedestal Assembly, embossed border
- B-4P Four-way Pedestal Assembly, embossed border

BRACKET ASSEMBLIES

For mounting on utility or whiteway poles with 4" or larger diameter.

- W-4B Four-Way Bracket Assembly, debossed flange
- W-2B Two-Way Bracket Assembly, debossed flange
- B-4B Four-Way Bracket Assembly, embossed border
- B-2B Two-Way Bracket Assembly, embossed border

CHANNEL IRON POST PEDESTAL ASSEMBLY

- B-4PU Four-way Channel Iron Pedestal Assembly, embossed border

ECONOMY RING BRACKET ASSEMBLIES

For mounting on pipe with 2⅜" or 3½" OD pipe.

- B-2RB Two-Way Ring Bracket Assembly, embossed border
- B-4RB Four-Way Ring Bracket Assembly, embossed border

Many communities with limited funds purchase the B-2RB assembly containing two plates, one for each intersecting street, and later add the additional plates, converting it to a B-4RB to provide four-way readability.

MISCELLANEOUS STREET SIGNS

- BN-1 12" x 6" block name plate
- B-3L 6" Plate, 3" Letters, embossed border
- B-4L 6" Plate, 4" Letters, embossed border

ABBREVIATIONS: Compass and street abbreviations will be furnished in 2" copy unless otherwise specified.

Miro-Flex Street Name Assemblies are embossed on 18-gauge, zinc-coated, Bonderized steel. There are assemblies, either two-way or four-way, which will fit every desired application. The B-4PU unit, for instance, was designed to fill a need for an economy street marker. Plates have 4" embossed letter on a 6" background. Three and one-half inch letters are available when desired. All are finished in best enamel and baked in thermostatically controlled ovens. Plates are available with embossed borders (B series) or debossed flange (W series).

WRITE FOR COMPLETE CATALOG

Miro-Flex's complete catalog will aid you in ordering specific signs. However, for your convenience, most Miro-Flex catalog numbers adhere to those set forth in the *Manual on Uniform Traffic Control Devices.*

THE **MIRO-FLEX** CO., INC.

1824 EAST SECOND ST. WICHITA, KANSAS

"GUARDING the CROSSROADS of AMERICA"

WITH

STEEL AND ALUMINUM

TRAFFIC CONTROL SIGNS

ONE WAY

ONE WAY

YIELD RIGHT OF WAY

SCHOOL 10 MILES PER HOUR

SLOW

TWO HOUR PARKING 9A.M.-6P.M.

NO PARKING BETWEEN SIGNS

LOAD LIMIT 10 TONS

R R

NO PARKING LOADING ZONE

STOP

SLOW CHILDREN PLAYING

EVACUATION ROUTE

SPEED LIMIT 25

STOP AHEAD

KEEP RIGHT

NATIONAL *Safety* ENGINEERS

Manufacturers of TRAFFIC CONTROL SIGNS for STREETS and HIGHWAYS

Illustrated are most of the signs classified as standard in accordance with the Manual on Uniform Traffic Control Devices for Streets and Highways, as recommended by the U. S. Bureau of Public Roads.

Non-standard or custom-worded signs can be furnished upon inquiry, based on size, legend, quantity and other essential specifications. We welcome the opportunity to offer quotations on any "special" sign requirement. You are urged to call or write today.

All signs in this brochure are available on choice of one or more of the following metal bases, reflectors or finishes described on next page.

NATIONAL *Safety* ENGINEERS

Manufacturers of TRAFFIC CONTROL SIGNS for STREETS and HIGHWAYS

BIRMINGHAM, ALA.

METAL BASE— Prime, U. S. Steel or 6061-T6 Alcoa Aluminum.
TREATMENT— Steel—degreased and bonderized; Aluminum—degreased, etched or alodized.
PRIMER— Zinc chromate, oven baked.
FINISH— Highest quality alkyd baked enamel. Reflectorized: 3-M "Scotchlite" Sheeting or Prismo "200".
FINISH CODE
ALUMINUM
-- BEA— Baked Enamel
-- SLA— "Scotchlite" reflectorized
STEEL
-- BES— Baked Enamel
-- SLS— "Scotchlite" reflectorized
-- PRS— Prismo "200" reflectorized
NO PARKING THIS SIDE
PH-3
NO PARKING DRIVEWAY
PH-11A
ONE WAY
RE-15 (L)
KEEP RIGHT
RE-5
ONE WAY DO NOT ENTER
RE-10
ONE WAY
RE-9
SPEED LIMIT 50
RE-1
NO PARKING ANY TIME
PH-2
NO LEFT TURN
RE-8
NO PARKING LOADING ZONE
PH-9
KEEP TO RIGHT
RE-5A
NO PARKING BETWEEN SIGNS
PH-12
NO U TURN
RE-6
15 MINUTE PARKING
RS-6
SLOW SCHOOL
SCH-8
2 TRACKS
RRT-2
STOP ON RED SIGNAL
RRS-1
NO PARKING TAXI STAND
PH-5
R R
RRW-32
RAIL ROAD CROSSING
90°
EXW-34
ONE WAY
RE-15 (R)
NATIONAL Safety ENGINEERS
Manufacturers of
TRAFFIC CONTROL SIGNS for STREETS and HIGHWAYS

95% of orders for standard signs are shipped within days.

Sargent-Sowell carries in stock the greatest selection of copy of any municipal sign manufacturer.

Steel or aluminum, embossed or flat plain or reflectorized, baked enamel or porcelain, beaded or Scotchlite —Whatever combination you want!

In addition to the largest selection of signs, we carry the most widely used municipal supply items.

'ONOMY—with all necessary features for effective, safe traffic control.

E-ENGINEERED — self-contained, complete traffic signal and controller or beacon and controller.

:ADY-TO-INSTALL—just hang it up, span wire or mast arm, and complete connections.

Police Plasticals
Smith & Wesson Guns
Badges
Sirens
Warning Lights
Flares
Hand Cuffs
Measuring Wheel

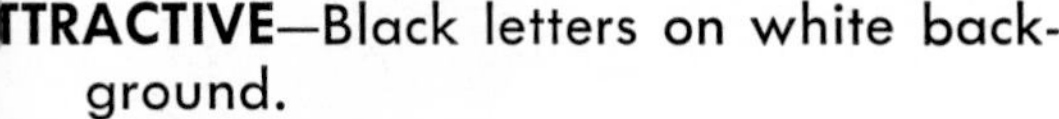

TTRACTIVE—Black letters on white background.

:ONOMICAL—Low original cost.

DNG-LASTING — embossed for extra strength, baked enamel finish.

HEFT-PROOF—brass theft proof hardware.

.ountings Available: Pedestal, Ring racket, Utility Pole.

ırnished—plain or reflectorized.

Write for our catalogue giving complete details of our signs and municipal supplies

ARGENT-SOWELL, INC. P. O. BOX 1176 GRAND PRAIRIE, TEXAS

HEAT-TREATED ALUMINUM STENCILS

Stencils made of lifetime, heat-treated aluminum to be used for stenciling SLOW, SCHOOL, STOP, 20, etc. on city streets and highways.

INDIVIDUAL CHARACTERS

Letters A thru Z, 24″, 36″ or 72″
Figures 1 thru 0, 24″, 36″ or 72″
Arrows, straight, curved in 72″

ALSO available 4″ and 2¼″ one-piece stencils, i.e.: NO PARKING, LOADING ZONE, etc.

The Labor Saving MARK-RITE Paint Marker

For painting centerlines, cross walks, parking lines, parking lots, factory areas, warehouses, etc. with regular traffic paint or reflective compounds.

For larger mechanized line-marking equipment see our catalogue.

TRAFFIC PAINT AND STRIPING BEADS

SAFE-T-CONE RUBBER TRAFFIC GUIDES

Wherever traffic control is needed the Safe-T-Cone is in demand for channeling traffic, utility repairs, line painting and emergency blockades.

Available in sizes :
12″, 18″ or 28″
plain or reflectorized

SARGENT-SOWELL, INC. P. O. BOX 1176 GRAND PRAIRIE, TEXAS

G. D. BAVIN CO.

Manufacturers of Traffic Safety Equipment and Bavin Fully Automatic Glass Bead Dispensers

2500 West Sixth Street Building, Los Angeles 57, California

The safe way to display temporary signs on busy thoroughfares . . .
Hold signs firmly in place and readable position with a . . .

COMMANDO multi-purpose SIGN STANDARD

Patent No. 2,718,080—Other Patents Pending

Used by States, Cities, Counties, Contractors, Public Utility Companies, Industry

ADAPTABLE. Supports signs of various sizes and shapes—not limited to one-size sign. Flag holders provided for use in spread position.

STURDY. Sturdy yet light weight (10 lbs.). Made of high tensile strength steel.

SERVICEABLE. Will not blow down in high winds or gusts of wind created by fast moving traffic.

CONVENIENT TO USE. Ready for use. No time waste in assembly. Sign held between frames in upright position. Locking device holds sign firm between hinges in spread position.

EASY TO STORE. Minimum space required for storage in truck or warehouse.

FINISH: Black Enamel.

ONE STANDARD DOES THE WORK OF TWO . . .

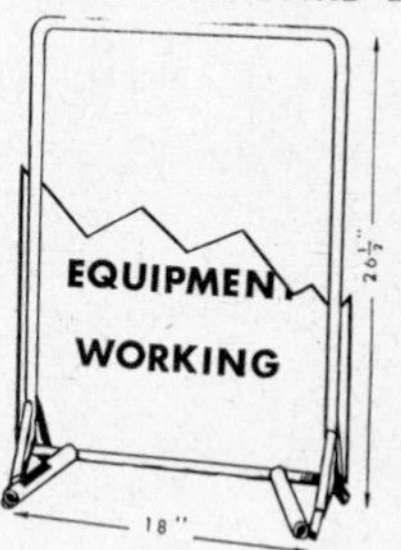

↑ THIS STANDARD

OPENS INTO THIS ↑

COMMANDO Sign Standard in upright position is always ready for use. Holds signs firmly.

COMMANDO

Supports signs of various sizes and shapes . . . light weight, sturdy, ready for use!

Write for complete information on the
COMMANDO Multi-Purpose SIGN STANDARD TODAY!

Also ask for information on the BAVIN Fully Automatic Glass Bead Dispenser for Street, Highway and Airport Marking. For greater Traffic Safety . . . Beaded lines are better! The Bavin Glass-Bead Dispenser does the job efficiently and economically. It can be attached to any striping machine. Only one Bavin Glass-Bead Dispenser is needed to meter beads on any width up to 6"—solid or skip line.

PRISMO SAFETY CORPORATION

HUNTINGDON • PENNSYLVANIA

PRISMO PLASTIX®

Permanent-Type Reflective Pavement Markings—

For crosswalks, safety zones and other municipal pavement markings, Prismo Plastix reflective markers command the attention of drivers and pedestrians alike. Its sure-fire brilliance has unvarying intensity—provides outstanding visibility around the clock in all weathers.

What's more, Prismo Plastix is absolutely moisture proof. And it has extraordinary long-life wear under today's rigorous traffic conditions—often remains effective even after four—or more—years service in dense traffic locations, according to actual road-test data.

Prismo Plastix can be applied in a jiffy, thereby minimizing both traffic interruptions and labor costs.

Low initial cost, long-life service and star-bright brilliance make Prismo Plastix the logical choice for your reflective marking requirements.

Write today for complete information about Prismo Plastix, and we'll send our Catalog PX-56 immediately.

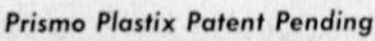
Prismo Plastix Patent Pending

PRISMO SAFETY CORPORATION

HUNTINGDON • PENNSYLVANIA

A new, revolutionary hi-target sign finish with the highest reflective index ever attained . . . Prismo '200' Hi-Reflective Finish has complete angularity, assuring full-vision legibility at maximum distance by day or night.

It is equally adaptable to all types of regulatory, warning and guide signs, and is surprisingly easy and economical to use.

Can be applied to metal, hardboard, wood, rubber, plastic or polyester resin board.

Can be applied by any type spray, brayer, roller coater, brush or silk screen to any place that can be painted. It won't peel, and gives years of service in all kinds of weather.

Prismo Bulletin P-256 gives full details about this advance in reflectory sign finish that gives greater effectiveness at much lower cost. Your copy will be sent to you by return mail. Just write:

PRISMO

The SPHERE of SAFETY

Safety Corporation, HUNTINGDON • PENNSYLVANIA

WALD INDUSTRIES, INCORPORATED

HUNTINGDON, PENNSYLVANIA

WALD

the finest in striping equipment . . .

The Wald people specialize in one thing—pavement striping equipment. Each Wald Reflecto-Liner is designed for a specific range of duties required by municipalities of various sizes, from small towns to big cities. There is a Wald striper that's just right for your particular traffic marking problems, one that will give you the best performance at minimum cost for operation and maintenance.

All Wald Reflecto-Liners have well-balanced construction for easy handling . . . are designed with operator comfort in mind for greater efficiency . . . built to withstand hard use . . . can apply all types of paint and reflective materials . . . have many exclusive features, including the patented Wald Shroud for clean-cut stripe definition. A complete line of Wald matched accessories convert striping machines to all-purpose air plants.

WALD INDUSTRIES, INCORPORATED
HUNTINGDON, PENNSYLVANIA

REFLECTO-LINERS

a special model for every marking requirement

Wald Reflecto-Liners and Truck-O-Liners are respected all over the world as the finest in striping equipment.

TRAFFIC SIGNS BY AUTOMATION

A continuous, conveyorized assembly line system for painting, reflectorizing and baking traffic signs with standardized high-quality finish automatically at high speed. A two-man operation, the Wald Automatic Sign Shop is the most economical method of producing reflective and non-reflective signs in quantity lots. Complete information sent on request.

Why not find out how Wald Reflecto-Liners or Truck-O-Liners can solve your pavement marking problems . . . send for the fully-illustrated Wald Reflecto-Liner Catalog W-56.

Wald Industries Inc.

"There's nothing finer than the Reflecto-Liner"

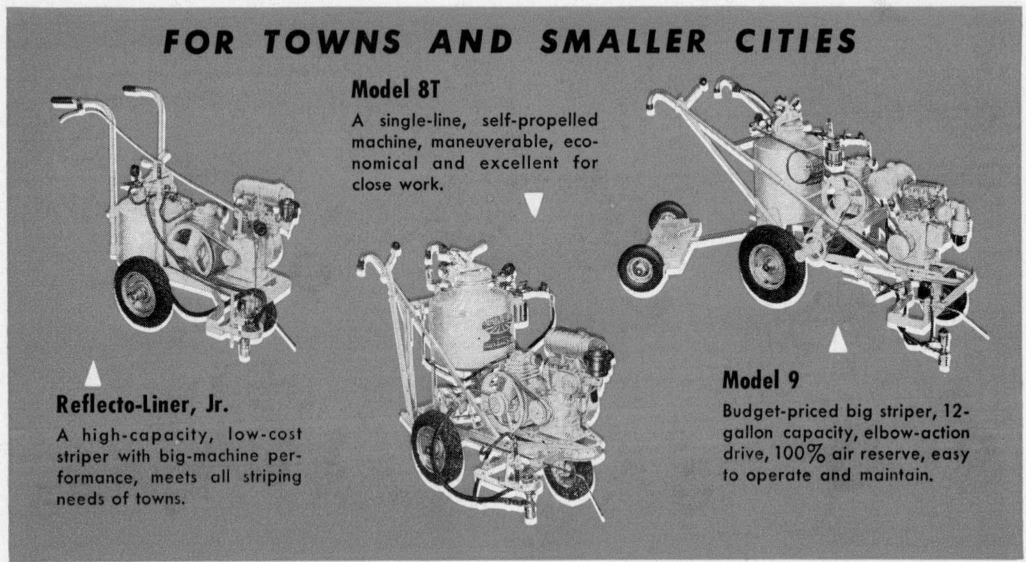

SY-LOY FIBER GLASS TRAFFIC SIGNS

Here, at last, is a really permanent traffic sign . . . requires no painting, no budget-wrecking maintenance. Made of plastic-reinforced fiber glass, SY-LOY signs are virtually impervious to destructive forces normally encountered in traffic control operations.

Color, finish and legends are molded right in, and snow and ice will not stick to SY-LOY. These signs will always have excellent readability in any weather. Vandalism ceases to be a threat, too. SY-LOY bounces back every time . . . without chipping, cracking, or denting.

We'll send you literature and a full-size SY-LOY sign for testing . . . write today, on your company letterhead, to The General Tire & Rubber Company, Reinforced Plastics Division, Marion, Indiana.

LAKE SHORE MARKERS, Inc.

P. O. Box 59 ERIE, PENNSYLVANIA

CUSTOM LIFETIME ALUMINUM SIGNS AND BUILDING LETTERS

Followng distributors offer personal service in widespread areas surrounding the territory in which their offices are located

Belding Highway Equipment Co., No. Canton, Ohio
Wm. Eyermann, 9122 Pueblo Dr., St. Louis 23, Missouri Phone Flanders 29-467
Frieshon & Belsom, P. O. Box 7044, New Orleans 19, Louisiana Phone Raymond 6763
Arthur G. Huson Co., 18 Lindsley Avenue, West Orange, N. J. Phone Orange 5-1460
Russell K. Homer Co., P. O. Box 1693, Honolulu 6, Hawaii Phone Cable Homco 8-8300
Nevelow Bros., 105-107 Convent St., San Antonio, Texas
A. C. Nichols, Rt. 3, P. O. Box 314, Wilmington, North Carolina Phone Wrightsville Beach 2530
Frank Rullan & Associates, Inc., P. O. Box 4665, San Juan, Puerto Rico Phone 2-2918
Miami Fire Equipment Co., 2260 W. Flagler St., Miami, Fla.
T. O. Tompkins, 1094 Laurel Ave., Bridgeport, Conn.
T. E. Potts Equipment Co., 2260 Sheridan Ave., Buffalo, N. Y.
Koontz Equipment Co., 325 Ohio River Blvd., Emsworth, Penna.
Capitol Highway Materials, Inc., Route 6 Putnam Co., Baldwin Place, N. Y.

For further information: Phone collect Erie 4-0189, or write, sending us rough sketch, or pertinent information, and we will respond promptly with our drawing and quotations. Full cooperation assured.

GREENE TOWNSHIP SCHOOL
ERECTED BY
GREENE TOWNSHIP SCHOOL BUILDING AUTHORITY
1954
AUTHORITY MEMBERS
JOHN MAJERIK - CHAIRMAN
ROBERT J. DUMARS - VICE-CHAIRMAN
RUSSELL K. RAYBUCK - SECRETARY
ERNEST H. HINKLER - TREASURER
RAY W. CHAPMAN
SCHOOL DIRECTORS
ROBERT A. ROSENBERG - PRESIDENT
GEORGE S. TURNER - VICE-PRESIDENT
SMITH E. MAY - TREASURER
FRANK WHEELER
JAMES M. MALONEY
MARJORIE WHEELER - NON-MEMBER SECRETARY
HOLMES CROSBY - ARCHITECT
HENRY SHENK COMPANY - CONTRACTORS

24-36—24" x 36" School Dedication plaque in two tone aluminum finish showing gray metallic background, satin finish aluminum letters and border.

Stock and Custom BUILDING LETTERS LIFETIME ALUMINUM —11 STYLES TO CHOOSE. We invite your inquiries on any permanent sign requirements. Weatherproof. Permanently attractive.

historical markers

Lake Shore Markers, Inc. have been furnishing many State and local government agencies, and many private groups across the nation, permanent Historical Markers designed to preserve the memory of our "American Heritage." Lake Shore Markers, Inc. are fully equipped to serve the most discriminating requirements.

Markers offer solution to problems in Historical Marking where interesting highlights may be told publicly in a manner befitting the excellence of many of the Historical Sites. A few representative styles in both post type and plaque type, typical of thousands in service in continental North America, Alaska, Puerto Rico and Hawaii are shown. A broad selection of stock patterns are available.

Special design for Anthony Wayne Parkway, Columbus, Ohio, approximately 43" x 39" in letter panel. Note intricate map design.

Write for Free sign and letter catalog!!

LAKE SHORE MARKERS, Inc.

P. O. Box 59 ERIE, PENNSYLVANIA

Lifetime ALUMINUM SIGNS

BRILLIANT DAY AND NIGHT!

21-4—21" x 4" carrying 3" U.S. P.W.A. Series A, B, or C letters, as required by length of name, with cap to fit from 1½" to 4" pipe. Four-way unit composed of one T21-4 and one B21-4 designed to be attached in one, two or more sign units, with aluminum screws. Post cap is also detachable. No center rod required! Signs are shock proof and widely used from coast to coast in all climates. Write for complete catalog.

NO. 24-6 Same as above except 24" x 6"—4"

SP21-4—21" x 4" above shows name of sponsoring organization in special name panel. U. S. Standard Series C letters shown. All street signs shown are reflectorized with genuine rainproof process. Street name signs custom made to your specifications and requirements. Write or phone for prompt quotation.

NY24-10—24" x 10" sign carrying 4" approved Series A, B and C, P.W.A. letters. As illustrated, designed for mounting on utility poles for banding with ¾" stainless steel bands applied quickly with special banding tools and cutter. Variety of uses for top panel include block numbers, intersecting street, sponsoring agency, etc. Above sign is also available with center post mounting same as Style #21-4.

#43-36 Doublefaced, fitted for 4" tapered octagonal post, reflectorized background with green letters.

Lifetime Aluminum, single-face, institutional identification sign shown above, furnished in special logotype and made to Government Specifications. Lettering approximately ½" raised above background, and border approximately ¾" raised above background. Background web ¼". Illustration shows custom extruded aluminum channel stakes and special ½" round head SAE thread aluminum bolts.

P20-40—20" x 40" Double-face cast aluminum sign finished in weatherproof vinyl bronze and 23 carat gold letters and border. Illustration shows 2' galvanized pipe and cast aluminum bracket.

S-60—48" x 60" standard Colonial Type yard sign, with heavy galvanized steel bracket and 3" galvanized steel pipe, ornamental aluminum ball cap.

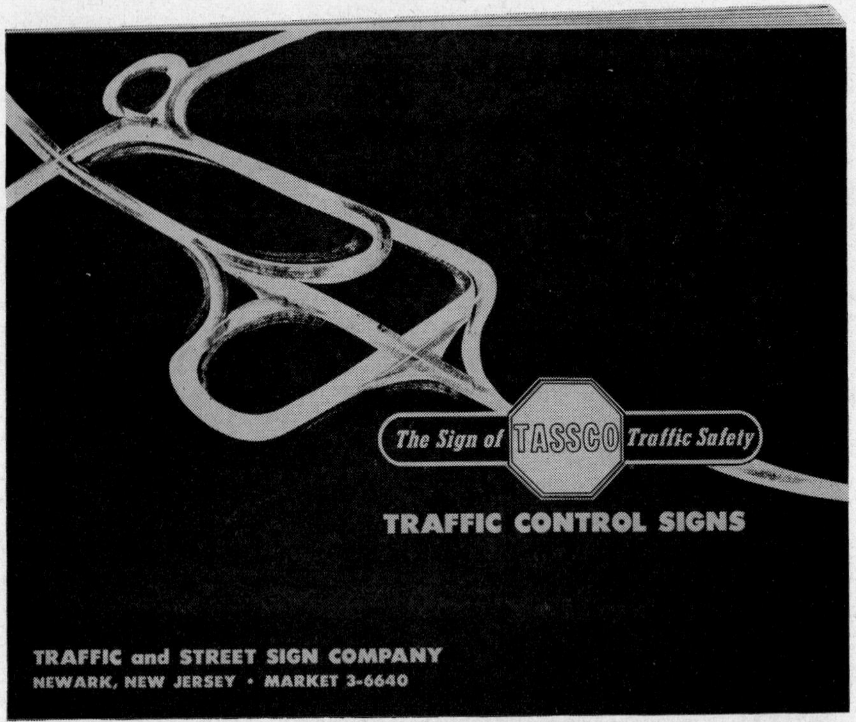

YOU'LL WANT A PERSONAL COPY

Here's the big, new, comprehensive catalog from the nation's leading specialist manufacturer of traffic and street signs in every category.

The Tassco catalog is illustrated in full color, showing hundreds of signs now in use by many of the most modern, economy-minded municipalities in America.

For your copy of the new Tassco Catalog, write for Catalog TSM.

TRAFFIC & STREET SIGN COMPANY, 84 FOUNDRY ST., NEWARK 5, N. J.

DENOMINATOR CO., INC.

261 Broadway, New York 7, N. Y.

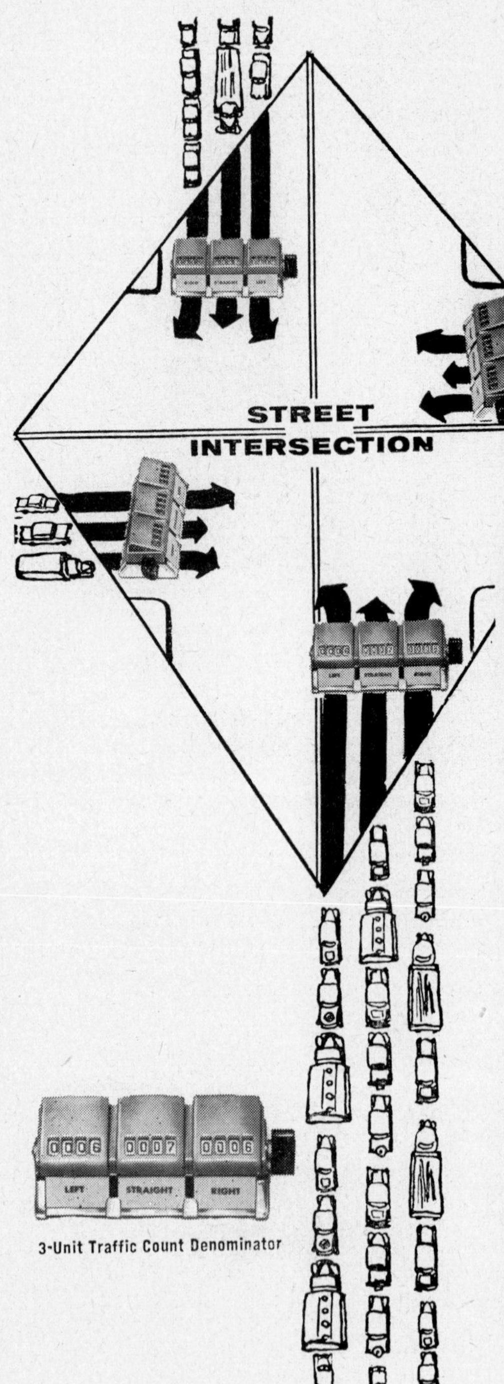

3-Unit Traffic Count Denominator

Get Traffic Facts Fast... Use DENOMINATOR Traffic Counters!

Observe • Record Volume Count and Directional Flow • Take Periodic Readings • Preserve Records to note Trend and Corrective Measures Needed.

Sturdy, light-weight, metal-cased counters can be carried in hand or easily mounted on your own clipboard.

All counting units have capacity of 9999 (4 digits).

Broad cover, used to activate mechanism, gives largest possible striking surface.

Easy to read. Easy to clean. No lubrication needed. Fully guaranteed for 1 year.

In 30 seconds any unit can be removed and a spare unit inserted. Even with unit out remaining units can still be operated and reset.

Designation strips provided for TURNING-MOVEMENT STUDIES, reading:

"LEFT • STRAIGHT • RIGHT"
or
"RIGHT • STRAIGHT • LEFT"

For other types of studies as Destination — Parking — or Vehicle-type — any desired number of counting units can be assembled into rows or "steps"—as 2 rows of 12.

In use today by over 1,000 communities, counties and state-road depts. 43 years of experience built into this aid to traffic surveys.

For special bulletin on compilation of traffic statistics, write Dept. MI-71.

G. H. TENNANT COMPANY

765 North Lilac Drive · Minneapolis 22, Minnesota

Model "CR"

TRAFFIC LINE ERASER

- **Removes lines permanently at low cost. Usually does job for about 1¢ to 3¢ per ft.**
- **Works extra fast . . . operates in traffic. Removes 4 to 10 ft. of markings per minute.**
- **Easy to use. Has self-propelling action.**

OPERATOR GUIDES MACHINE over painted line at a slow walk. Permanently removes lines in 1 operation without damaging pavement surface.

WORKS IN TRAFFIC. No need to block off streets or tie up traffic with bulky equipment. Safety guard deflects flying particles.

Here's a new machine that removes traffic lines faster, easier, and at lower cost than any method we know of. Already widely used by highway departments, cities and airports throughout the country – the Tennant "CR" mechanizes an almost impossible job.

It shears off 4 to 10 ft. of obsolete traffic markings per minute – without damaging the surface. Lets one man remove traffic lines for about 1¢ to 3¢ per foot. Works on concrete or asphalt; needs no chemicals or solvents.

Cleans traffic markings for repainting. Removes surface scale (oxidized concrete) to insure a firm bond for new paint. Tests show that cleaning the surface in this manner helps make new markings *last up to 4 times longer.* The Model "CR" is ideal for this new technique. It's safe . . . economical . . . works fast . . . completely removes flaking surface scale that causes paint to deteriorate. *Write for details.*

Machine features include: self-propelling action; heavy-duty 6 hp Wisconsin engine; triple v-belt drive; compact design (only 18½ in. wide . . . weighs only 254 lbs.); has sturdy hoisting frame; large capacity air cleaner.

MACHINE'S 1,450 RPM REVO-TOOL has extra-fast scraping action. Scores of steel cutters rapidly shave off paint.

LOADOMETER CORPORATION

P.O. Box 4724
Baltimore 11, Maryland, U.S.A

"WEIGH THE LOADS
and
SAVE THE ROADS"

The
"HI-WAY"
LOADOMETER*
SCALE

Furnished in load capacities of 20,000 lbs., with 10-lb. graduations; and 10,000 kgs., with 10-kgs. graduations.

Complete information and catalogs upon request

End View of new "HI-WAY" LOADOMETER and Ramps

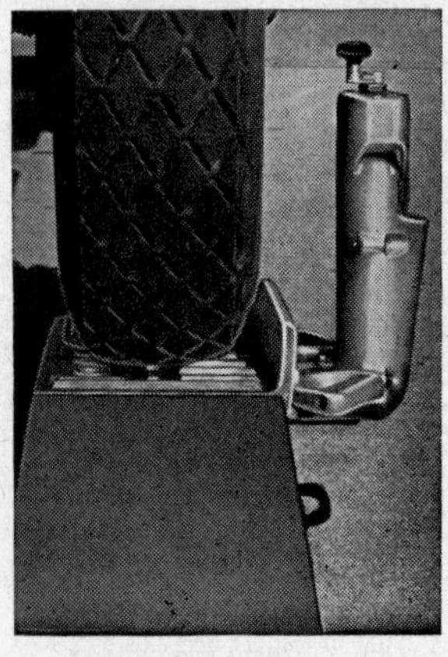

OVERLOADED trucks and buses quickly pound costly roads to pieces. Traffic officials everywhere prevent violation of weight laws with LOADOMETERS, which quickly weigh vehicles to determine overloads, **at the point at which they are stopped.**

Now it is easy for traffic officials to prevent overloading of trucks or buses. With the "HI-WAY" Portable Loadometer Scales, they can enforce the law in all sections and are not confined to easily-avoided weighing stations. Loadometers are so light and easy to operate that their location can be changed at will, making it almost impossible for violators to continue breaking the law.

"HI-WAY" LOADOMETER SCALES are used in pairs, thus weighing a truck axle in one easy operation. The sum of the two readings equals the axle load. By weighing each axle of the truck, the total weight and load can be determined. These data can be submitted to the court when prosecuting violators.

The "HI-WAY" LOADOMETER SCALES are greatly improved. The platform completely covers the mechanism. No dust, moisture, water, tar, mud or other foreign substance can reach the operating parts. Accuracy comparable to platform scales is assured by the use of a calibrated spring, micrometer screw and automatic recorder.

Complete Information and Catalog Upon Request

*Trade Mark Reg. U.S. Pat. Off.

SAFE-T-CONE
ALL RUBBER TRAFFIC GUIDE
SAFE-T-CONE RUBBER TRAFFIC Guides are used by traffic engineers from coast to coast . . . in all major cities. SAFE-T-CONES guide heavy traffic safely, efficiently. They are used for channeling traffic, for emergency "Road-Blocks" and barricades.
SLOW
SCHOOL
28" REFLECTORIZED

For MODERN, EFFIC

SAFE-T-CONES are proven and accepted by Federal, State and Municipal Traffic Authorities in hundreds of major cities . . . for traffic channeling, utility repairs, line painting and emergency blockades. Their special construction allows them to be "stacked" together in small space. They are lightweight and easily handled, yet made for lasting durability even under the most difficult conditions. An emergency barricade can be installed in minutes.

NOTE THE SPECIAL FEATURES

Reinforced top SAFE-T-SIGNS, adaptors and la adaptors firmly safely.

SAFE-T-CONES ar inforced on the i for additional str and longer wear.

Outsides of SA CONES are painted special rubber pain lasting durability.

Square base cones from rolling knocked over. F each corner cones to set d over painted lines out smearing.

NOW AVAILABLE IN

3-SIZES

12" - 18" and 28"

Now, a SAFE-T-CONE for every use! All 3 sizes made of best quality natural rubber, with a durometer of 72-80 and tensile strength of 1,200 lbs. Oxidizing agent prevents deterioration, insures longer life.

The 28-inch SAFE-T-CONE weighs 8 and has a 14½" square base. Suppo by feet ½" in height on each corner. base is a weighted platform type 1⅝" h and is reinforced by ribbing; can be m extra heavy on special order. The body the cone is reinforced on interior wit molded vertical ribs, 24" long, ¾" w The apex of the cone is reinforced b molded 1" shoulder formed inside, to h SAFE-T-SIGNS, FLAG, and FLASHER-LIG ADAPTORS firmly.

The 18-inch SAFE-T-CONE weighs 2¾ lbs. and has a 10¾" square base, supported by feet ½" in height, on each corner. The base is a weighted platform type 1" high and is reinforced with ribbing.

The 12-inch SAFE-T-CONE weighs 15-oz., and has 8¼" square base, supported by feet ⅜" high, ½" in diameter. Available only with painted yellow top and black base. Hundreds of uses wherever size is not important.

IT TRAFFIC CONTROL

SAFE-T-CONES are the answer to the traffic engineers problems. Their low original cost, their long life, their light-weight and ease in handling make them ideal for every traffic control requirement. SAFE-T-CONES eliminate the necessity of using old-fashioned, costly wood barriers. Even when knocked over by careless motorists, the all-rubber SAFE-T-CONE is unharmed. Its paint and special construction gives it extremely long life even with the most abusive handling.

SPECIAL ADAPTORS INCREASE VALUE OF SAFE-T-CONES

Because of their unique design, SAFE-T-CONES allow the application of various adaptors, directly in to the top of the cone . . . for every requirement.

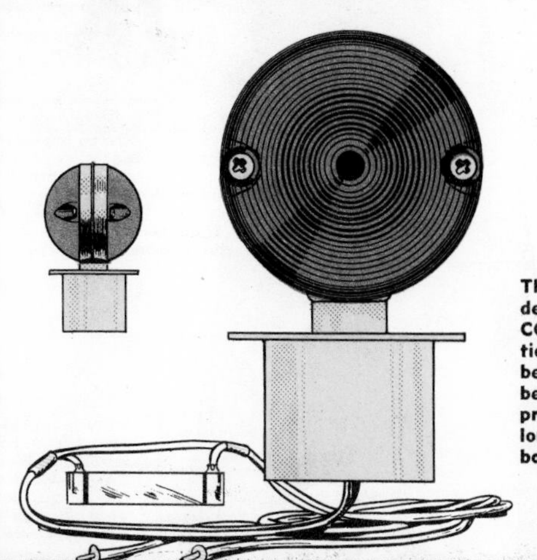

SAFE-T-CONE FLASHER-LIGHT ADAPTOR

The SAFE-T-CONE Flasher-Light has been developed to fit into the top of all SAFE-T-CONE Rubber Traffic Guides to offer additional safety at night. Flashing light can be seen a long distance by motorists, even beyond car's headlights. Completely waterproof, unbreakable plastic lens, fluted for long-range visibility. Uses standard 6-volt battery.

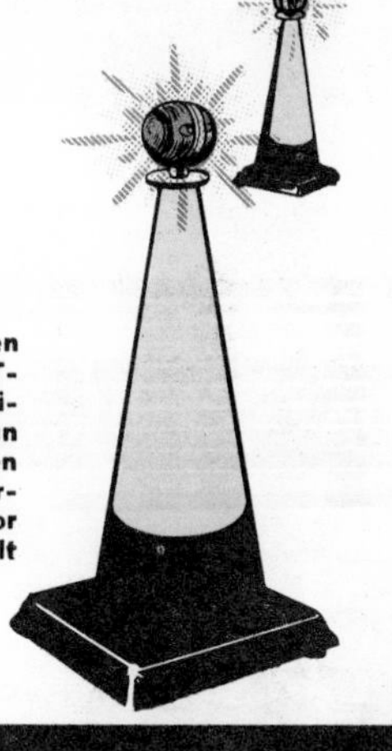

SAFE-T-CONE FLAG ADAPTORS

The "flag-apaptor" is a special molded rubber unit that fits into the top of either the 18" or 28" SAFE-T-CONE and holds either flags or reflectorized tape for positive barricade protection.

Here is a typical SAFE-T-CONE barricade using flag adaptors, SAFE-T-SIGNS and reflectorized tape . . . warning motorists of danger and giving added protection to workmen.

SAFE-T-SIGNS

The "SAFE-T-SIGN" is a special molded rubber adaptor-sign that fits into the top of the 28" cone . . . giving additional information to motorists at once. It is 12" wide, 11¾" high and weighs 1 lb. 5½ oz. Available with stock lettering or any special lettering desired.

SAFE-T-CONES MAY BE PAINTED OR REFLECTORIZED

The 12" SAFE-T-CONE is available painted all yellow on black base only. Either the 18" or 28" SAFE-T-CONE can be obtained in standard tri-color, yellow with red tip and black base or REFLECTORIZED all-yellow on black base, which can be seen clearly at a distance of 450 feet at night.

SAFE-T-CONES ARE MANUFACTURED ONLY BY RADIATOR SPECIALTY COMPANY, CHARLOTTE, N. C.

- ★ LINE PAINTING
- ★ CHANNELING
- ★ TOLL BRIDGES
- ★ DETOURS
- ★ SCHOOL ZONES
- ★ DANGER AREAS
- ★ INDUSTRIAL SAFETY AND PARKING AREAS

Because of their big "steel-like" appearance, commanding motorists respect, SAFE-T-CONES are readily adaptable for setting up any type of emergency barricades . . . in a matter of minutes. They are especially valuable during rush hours, through toll gates, during road construction and repair or other hazardous conditions.

SAFE-T-CONES are indispensable for immediate protection during line painting. The four feet on each corner allows them to set directly over the painted line without smearing.

For DAY *or* NIGHT-TIME VISIBILITY

Brightly painted in red and yellow, standard SAFE-T-CONES demand motorists respect during day time use. SAFE-T-SIGNS give increased value by "guiding" motorists, without confusion. The SAFE-T-SIGN fits directly into the 28" SAFE-T-CONE.

Because of the ease in handling and installation of SAFE-T-CONES, they are especially valuable for use at any emergency barricade. Fast . . . Effective!

18" and 28" SAFE-T-CONES can be reflectorized . . . and with the addition of the SAFE-T-CONE Flasher light, they become glowing semaphores at night-time, warning motorists of dangerous road conditions ahead. SAFE-T-SIGNS may also be reflectorized.

DANGER

Rush-hour traffic channeling at intersections or on narrow streets is simple with the use of SAFE-T-CONES because they can be set up so quickly and easily . . . day or night.

RADIATOR SPECIALTY COMPANY

CHARLOTTE, NORTH CAROLINA

RADIATOR SPECIALTY COMPANY OF CANADA, LTD

PRINTED IN U.S.A.

THE KELLY-CRESWELL COMPANY

Manufacturers of Centerlining and Safety Lane Equipment

Xenia, Ohio

FAST, ACCURATE, LOW COST TRAFFIC ZONE MARKING

...a striper for every municipal and highway need

Kelly-Creswell Company . . . the leader in the field . . . is a pioneer manufacturer of a complete line of road-marking equipment. From the beginning, the company has specialized in striping equipment ranging from small, hand-operated models to big, truck-mounted units used extensively by larger municipalities as well as counties and State Highway Departments. Kelly-Creswell's dominance in the field is indicated by the fact that K-C *equipment is used by more than 31 State Highway Departments and 7 Provinces in Canada.*

Kelly-Creswell construction features speed the job, reduce maintenance

Exclusive K-C Air Curtains, a patented feature, are specially engineered to direct a flow of exhaust gas (or compressed air) against the spray pattern, assuring sharp, uniform lines without contacting the surface. Guide marks and heavily built-up edges are eliminated, with savings of up to 20% in striping material. Material can be accurately applied over any type of surface, smooth or rough, at any desired speed.

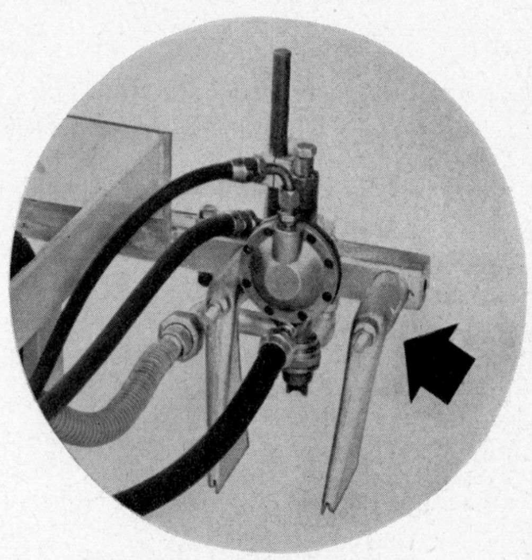

Exclusive K-C Striping Guns, (Patented) diaphragm-operated, produce a completely atomized, fan-shaped pattern with uniform cross distribution. Positive control of film thickness, produces square-cut beginnings and endings. Stripe width adjustable from 3″ to 6″.

Exclusive K-C Pressure Cleaner forces atomized cleaner fluid through fluid line as well as atomizing line to spray gun. Minimizes time of cleaning, does a thorough job. Standard equipment on all K-C models.

Exclusive K-C Air Traction assures uniform film distribution, makes it easy to apply a straight line. Drive rolls, actuated by air pressure, provide constant traction. Sensitive governor on engine maintains constant speed up hill and down. Wobbling is reduced to a minimum. Wide range of traction speed is provided.

Automatic Intermittent Line Mechanism produces broken lines and spaces of uniform length. Can be instantly engaged or disengaged so either broken or continuous lines can be applied. Beginnings and endings of new lines can be advanced or retarded at will to register with old lines.

KELLY-CRESWELL ALL-PURPOSE STRIPER, MODEL B-3-P

A completely self-contained striper, with spray gun and air curtain assembly mounted just inside the left rear wheel. Designed to meet the requirements of municipalities, State and County Highway Departments and airports for a high-speed, portable zone marking machine.

FEATURES: Length 72″, width 32″, height 42″. Welded heavy-duty tubular construction. Roller bearing wheels, pneumatic tires. 12-gal. material container, tested to 150 lbs. 6 hp air-cooled engine with governor for constant speeds, variable from 2½ to 5 mph. K-C air-actuated traction.

Twin-cylinder compressor. Special K-C diaphragm-operated striping gun, with adjustable volume and Y type strainer. K-C AIR CURTAINS, using exhaust gas for pressure. Instant and positive spray gun control. Adjustable and removable 60″ guide arm, suitable for chalk line or retracing. One quart pressure cleaner. Manually operated brakes. Sturdy riding trailer.

REFLECTORIZED LINE APPLICATION

Manually and air-controlled types of sphere dispensing units, specially designed for Kelly-Creswell stripers, are available for efficient and accurate application of reflectorized material, including pre-mixed types. Buying data supplied on request.

ATTACHMENTS

A full line of hand spray equipment is available for attachment to all Kelly-Creswell models . . . for painting guard rails, bridges, garages, etc. Side-delivery attachment for application of airport runway numerals and rotatable side delivery attachments for painting curbs, both vertically and horizontally.

KELLY-CRESWELL HIGHWAY STRIPER, MODEL D

For applying one, two or three stripes simultaneously. Offers a big saving in initial cost over truck-mounted units, yet it is capable of performing much the same type and volume of work. The material containers and compressor are mounted on a trailing service truck. The Model D increases visibility and ease of accurate striping. Any service truck can be used. When painting season is over, material containers and compressor can be removed so truck can resume its regular duties.

FEATURES: Length 72″, width 32″, height 45″. Heavy-duty tubular construction. Roller bearing wheels, pneumatic tires. 6 hp air-cooled engine, with governor for constant speeds from 2½ to 5 mph. Twin-cylinder compressor. K-C air-actuated traction. Special K-C diaphragm-operated striping guns, with Y type strainer. K-C AIR CURTAINS, using exhaust gas for pressure. Adjustable and removable 60″ guide arm. Manually operated brake. Sturdy riding trailer. Special blow-back valves to avoid loss of material when disconnecting hose line from spray gun. Equipment includes standard material containers and engine-driven compressor to be carried on service truck, and 35 ft. of flexible supply hose lines.

KELLY-CRESWELL TRUCK-MOUNTED STRIPERS

Complete truck-mounted units utilizing compressed air for air curtain pressure offer a modern, efficient and economical method of high speed zone marking. Designed for single, double or two-color triple line application. Information and detailed specifications supplied on request. More than 180 in service.

KELLY-CRESWELL MUNICIPAL STRIPER, MODEL B-3

Designed especially for municipal operation. Completely self-contained, with spray gun and air curtain assembly mounted just inside the left rear wheel. Light in weight . . . easily transported from place to place.

FEATURES: Length 72", width 32", height 42". Rigid tubular construction. Roller bearing wheels, pneumatic tires. 7-gal. material container, tested to 150 lbs., with clamp-on lid. 4 hp air-cooled engine with governor for constant speeds to 3¼ mph. K-C air-actuated traction. Special K-C diaphragm operating striping gun with adjustable volume and Y type strainer. K-C AIR CURTAINS, using exhaust gas for pressure. Instant and positive spray gun control. Adjustable and removable 60" guide arm. One quart pressure cleaner.

KELLY-CRESWELL HEAVY-DUTY MODEL C FOR CLOSE QUARTERS

Municipalities are finding extensive use for this manually-propelled model for the many jobs too small for self-propelled units. Especially adapted for cross-walk markings, parking lanes, meter limits and other applications involving maneuvering back and forth in close quarters. Both straight lines and sweeping curves can easily be applied. Air curtain and spray gun assembly is mounted outside the line of wheels, making possible application close to curbs, walls, posts, and in corners. Unit is light and easy to maneuver over rough or smooth pavement.

FEATURES: Length 58¼", width 37", height 42½". Rigid tubular construction. Roller bearing wheels, rear tires 4.00 x 8 pneumatic, front tire 3.00 x 5 pneumatic. 7-gal. material container, tested to 150 lbs. 3 hp air-cooled engine. Twin-cylinder compressor. Special K-C diaphragm-operated striping gun, with Y type strainer. K-C curtains, using exhaust gas for pressure. 18" adjustable guide. One quart pressure cleaner.

M. B. CORPORATION

FORMERLY MEILI-BLUMBERG CORP.

New Holstein, Wisc.

FAST • VERSATILE • ECONOMICAL

LINE MARKERS

A complete line of self-propelled, truck-mounted and manually operated markers for streets, highways, parking zones, and in plant use!

FOR EVERY MARKING JOB

Single Lines	**Intermittent Lines**	**Enamels, Beads In or**
Multiple Lines	**Multiple Colors**	**Beads on Paint**

ALL SIZES—TYPES

MODEL	TYPE	CAPACITY
Model 1-10	Hand Propelled	10 gal.
Model 6-18	Self Propelled	18 gal.
LineMaster	Self Propelled	18 gal.
Model E 3	Hand Propelled	10 gal.
Model E 4	Self Propelled	10 gal.
Model 8	Truck mounted	Any paint volumn to truck capacity
Super 10	Self Propelled	30 to 120 gal.
Super 16	Self Propelled	18 to 36 gal.

(Specials—self-propelled and truck mounted built to your specifications)

SUPER 10—The big marker for all highway marking jobs. Lays one, two or three lines, 2 colors, solid or intermittent. Bead reflectorizing attachment available.

SUPER 16—One-man operated all-around utility marker. Lays double solid lines 3" to 6" wide. Bead dispenser and intermittent attachments available.

6-18—Low-priced striper for regular or reflective painting. Feature packed. Built-in riding trailer with foot and parking brake, easy steering, lays solid or intermittent lines with any kind of paint or reflective compounds! Travels 3 to 5 MPH.

LINEMASTER—Big machine performance with low original cost. Double line marking—regular or reflective. Effortless, automotive-type steering; built-in riding platform; 18 gal. paint tank—50% greater capacity over machines of comparable price; self-propelled—one-man operated; speed of 3 to 5 miles per hour.

PARKING CORPORATION OF AMERICA

Subsidiary of Johnson Fare Box Company

4619 North Ravenswood, Chicago 40, Illinois

SALES AND SERVICE OFFICES IN PRINCIPAL CITIES LISTED UNDER BOWSER, INC.

End Parking Headaches!

Operate Your Parking Lots

AUTOMATICALLY... 24 Hours a Day

WITHOUT ATTENDANTS

with PARCOA

the NEW Automatic Card-Key Control*

Here's the answer to parking problems in congested areas! This new PARCOA System does the job for you safely, selectively . . . cuts costs, protects profits. Now in use from coast to coast at hospitals, universities, and in public and private parking operations.

Low in first cost and amazingly easy to operate and maintain, PARCOA eliminates the need for attendants. The heart of this self-service system is a simple electrical mechanism that automatically controls the entrance and exit gates. A card-key actuates the mechanism, serves as a "key" to admit only legal parkers. The system works for you day and night dependably, safely and economically to eliminate losses and protect profits.

Only PARCOA gives you *all* these advantages: Complete safety. Low first cost. Minimum maintenance. Easy to install. No attendants needed. 100% collection of fees. Reduced operating costs. Controlled capacity. Smooth efficiency with coded-card control that can be changed as desired. Pays for itself. Backed by Johnson Fare Box Company, leaders in dependable revenue collection systems since 1909.

**Your choice of controls (coin, card, token or any combination) makes this system readily adaptable to individual requirements.*

Write for illustrated brochure and name of nearest distributor.

PARCOA . . . Proved in service in 40 cities

from coast to coast

TYPICAL INSTALLATIONS
Now in Operation

CHICAGO TRANSIT AUTHORITY, Chicago

CITY OF PETERSBURG, Virginia

NEW YORK PORT OF AUTHORITY, Newark

CITY OF COLUMBUS, Ohio

INTERNATIONAL AIRPORT, New York City

SEATTLE-TACOMA AIRPORT, Seattle

ST. LOUIS PUBLIC SERVICE CO., St. Louis

READING RAILROAD, Lansdale and Langhorn, Pa.

ROLLING HILLS COMMUNITY ASS'N., Palos Verdes, Cal.

COLUMBIA BROADCASTING CO., Los Angeles

JOHN HANCOCK MUTUAL LIFE INSURANCE CO., Boston

GEORGE WASHINGTON UNIVERSITY, Washington, D. C.

UNIVERSITY OF ILLINOIS, Chicago

UNIVERSITY OF MICHIGAN, Ann Arbor

UNIVERSITY OF MINNESOTA, Minneapolis

NORTHWESTERN UNIVERSITY, Chicago

WAYNE UNIVERSITY, Detroit

METROPOLITAN JUNIOR COLLEGE, Los Angeles

CLEVELAND CLINIC FOUNDATION, Cleveland

SETON GENERAL HOSPITAL, Austin, Tex.

ST. LUKE'S HOSPITAL, Denver

ST. ANTHONY'S HOSPITAL, Oklahoma City

ST. JOSEPH'S HOSPITAL, Providence, R. I.

JOHNS HOPKINS HOSPITAL, Baltimore

HERMAN KIEFER HOSPITAL, Detroit

For SAFETY, DIRECTION and PARKING
Your Check Sheet for AIDS to BEST TRAFFIC CONTROL
NEFSLABS®
TRAFFIC MARKERS STRIPS ARROWS
☐ Toughest, flexible plastic. ☐ Reflective and non-reflective.
☐ Resist abrasion and tearing. ☐ Repel water, oils, salt.
☐ 5 brilliant, durable colors. ☐ 4 different shapes - also strip.
☐ 15 sizes and 2 thicknesses. ☐ Bevelled edges.
NEFMATS*
NEW DELUXE TRAFFIC LETTERS
*TRADE MARK APPLIED FOR
☐ One piece, roll-down letter mats. ☐ Same "Traffic-Tested" plastic as NEFSLABS. ☐ 6 high contrast color-code combinations. ☐ Letters 1 to 10 feet high. ☐ No cutting, piecing or fitting.
STOP
★NEFSLABS and NEFMATS give you the most complete line of plastic markings, letters, numerals and arrows. ★The very highest quality and longest life of any traffic marking materials mean year-after-year safety and savings for all uses. ★These aids to modern traffic control go down in minutes and stay down for years with special formula NEFGLU. ★Proven best by traffic test!
Write now for colorful NEFSLABS and NEFMATS literature
NEFGLU®
ADHESIVE
NEFGLU
☐ Cold, quick drying. ☐ Strongest all - weather bonding. ☐ Light, neutral color. ☐ Easily applied by brush or pressure spray. ☐ No pegging or grouting.
New Sales Territories are Open for Capable Representatives.
J. W. NEFF
LABORATORIES, INC.
TRAFFIC MARKINGS DIVISION
STOCKERTOWN 13, PA.

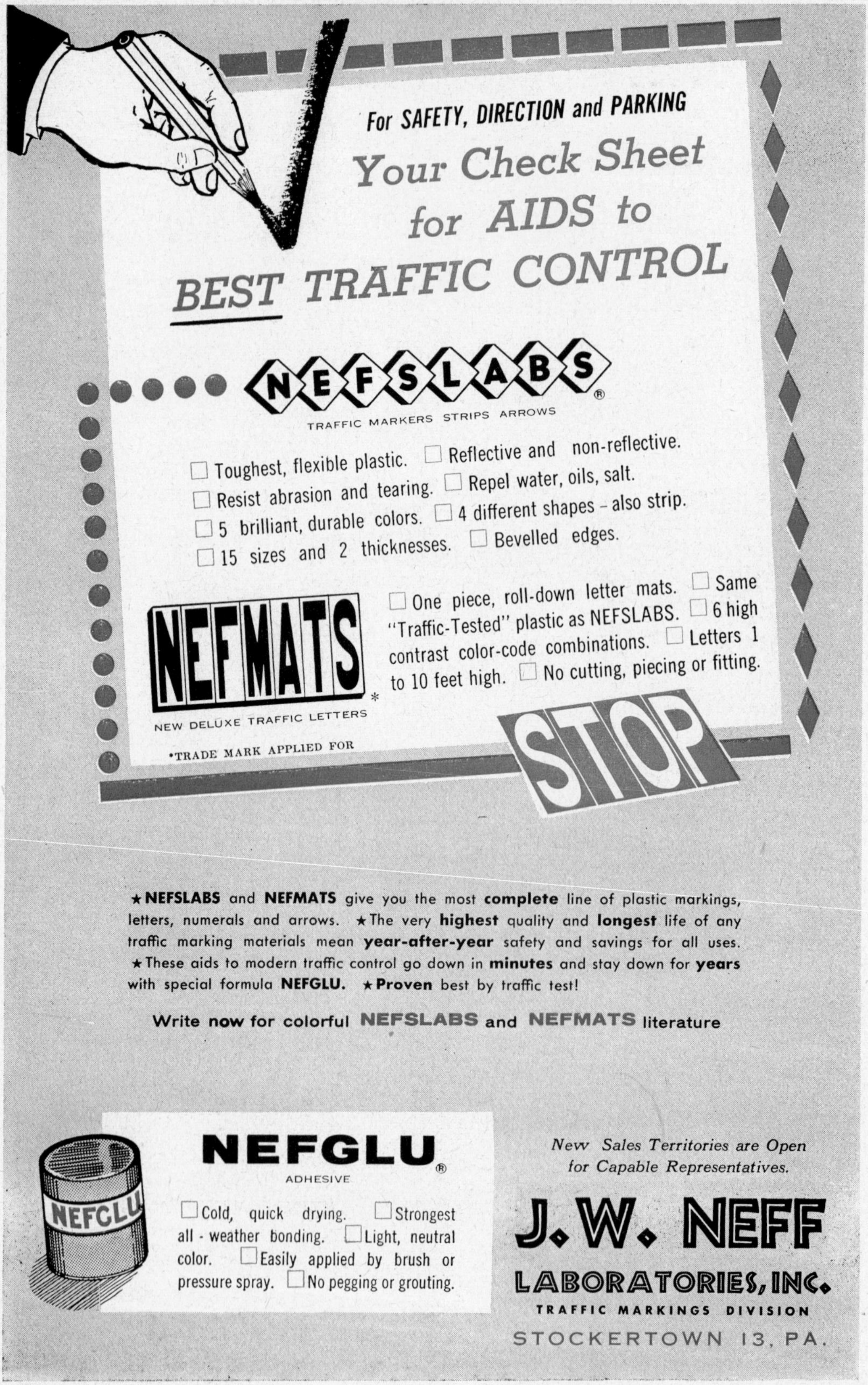

WESTERN RAILROAD SUPPLY COMPANY

General Offices and Factory

2410 South Ashland Avenue, Chicago 8, Illinois

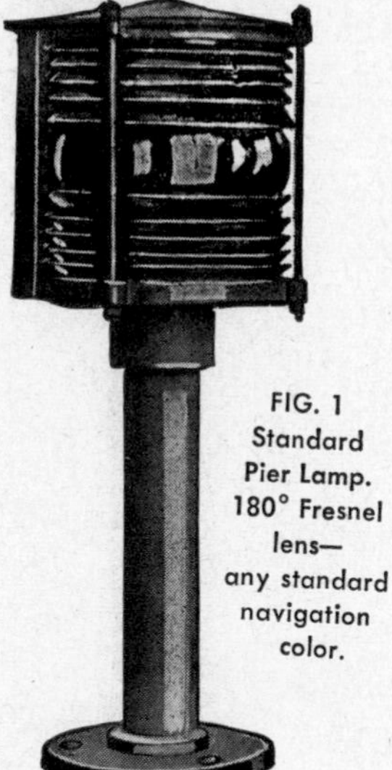

FIG. 1 Standard Pier Lamp. 180° Fresnel lens—any standard navigation color.

ELECTRIC BRIDGE AND PIER LAMPS

WRRS offers a complete line of electric pier and channel navigation lamps for both movable and fixed bridges. In addition, we design and manufacture lamps for special navigation requirements.

The quality and performance of WRRS bridge accessories are the results of more than forty years of experience in this specialized field. Long, trouble-free service is built into these products.

Our full line of electric bridge and pier lamps and WRRS signal lights for bridge approaches are pictured in color in the new 16-page WRRS Bulletin 954. Write for your free copy today.

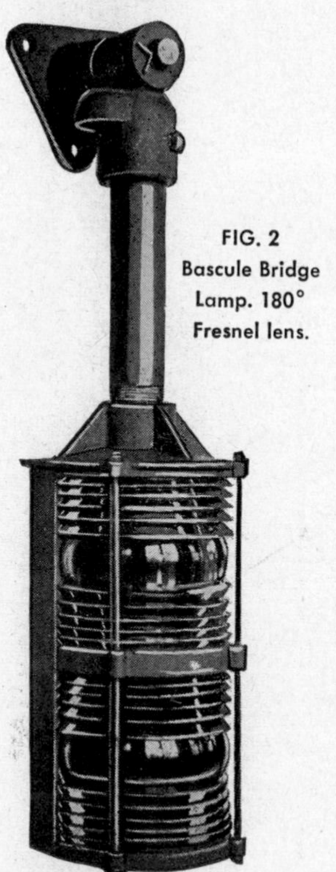

FIG. 2 Bascule Bridge Lamp. 180° Fresnel lens.

FIG. 3 Spring mounted vertical lift or bascule bridge lamp.

WESTERN RAILROAD SUPPLY COMPANY

General Offices and Factory

2410 South Ashland Avenue, Chicago 8, Illinois

ELECTRIC TRAFFIC GATES FOR BRIDGE APPROACHES

Fast, reliable operation and dependable performance have made the Model N-N Gate preferred protection at bridge approaches everywhere. They are also widely used at busy railroad-highway grade crossings as well as industrial plant entrances.

Model N-N gates are usually controlled by manual or magnetic reversing switches, and can be furnished for operation from any standard commercial power source—direct or alternating.

Four models of the N-N gate are available, with gear ratios varying in accordance with the length of gate arm used and speed of operation required (7, 9, 11, or 13 seconds clearing time). Furnished with steady burning or flashing lights; with or without sidewalk arm. Folding metal fence also optional. A twelve-inch traffic bell, motor or magnetically operated, can be mounted on the cover of the gate mechanism.

WRRS is also the sole source of supply for Buda or Elliott Gate Parts. Fast express service on all parts orders.

When writing for prices, give requirements as follows:

A. Electric power available for motor.

B. Length of roadway arm to be used.

C. Length of sidewalk arm, if any.

D. Angle of travel desired—75° or 90°.

E. Are we to furnish wooden arms?

F. Is bell to be mounted on cover?

G. Special circuits required through limit switch: Interlocking — Gate lighting — Indicator lights, etc.

H. Are gate arm lights required?

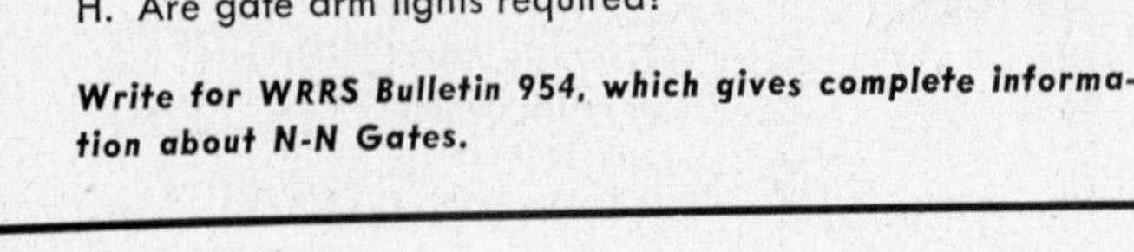

Write for WRRS Bulletin 954, which gives complete information about N-N Gates.

WESTERN RAILROAD SUPPLY COMPANY

General Offices and Factory

2410 South Ashland Avenue • Chicago 8, Illinois

IN CANADA: Cameron, Grant Inc., 465 St. John St., Montreal 1, Quebec

Automation Parking Pays Big Revenues In Over 300 Installations in 55 Cities

WRRS ELECTRIC PARKING GATES

Public auditorium parking lot equipped with coin operated parking gates.

Eliminate Labor Costs — Easy to Operate

Municipalities and parking operators find that Automation Parking with WRRS Gates pays big revenues. It results from low installation costs, practically no maintenance costs, and no labor costs—the largest expense of parking lot operation. And it's a simple matter to make periodic collections at one or two coin boxes.

This is the answer to the off-the-street parking problems. WRRS Gates operate with Remote Controls, using coins, tokens, keys, or any combination of these methods. WRRS Gates are safe, function in all types of weather, and are built to last 20 to 30 years.

Send us a diagram of your lot, and you will receive, without obligation, a parking plan and cost estimate.

Special gate for collecting service charge from taxi cabs using Municipal Airport—untapped income source.

Typical key operated electric parking gate in large city where elimination of labor costs assures large profits.

AMERICA'S FINEST FIRE ALARM SYSTEMS

OPERATORS CONSOLE, WITH "PENTEFOLD" 5-DIGIT TRANSMITTER, 10-CIRCUIT "FIREPHONE" AND AUTOMATIC DOOR CONTROL.

FOUR-CIRCUIT R-A-X, Type "B" SWITCHBOARD. INSTALLED BY CITY FORCES.

BELOW:
TWO 10-CIRCUIT R-A-X, TYPE "B" SWITCHBOARDS. INSTALLATION TIME 6 HOURS 15 MINUTES BY CITY CREW.

"FIREPHONE" TRANSMITTER AND RECEIVER. INSTALLED AT RIVERSIDE, CALIFORNIA.

THE SWING IS TO – – –

YOU CAN PAY MORE—BUT WHAT FOR?

SIX-CIRCUIT R-A-X SWITCHBOARD. INSTALLATION COST $35.60.

SIX-CIRCUIT, R-A-X, TYPE B" SWITCHBOARD. INSTALLATION TIME 3 HOURS 20 MINUTES WITH CITY CREW.

BELOW:
TWO 10-CIRCUIT R-A-X, TYPE "A" AND "B" SWITCHBOARDS.

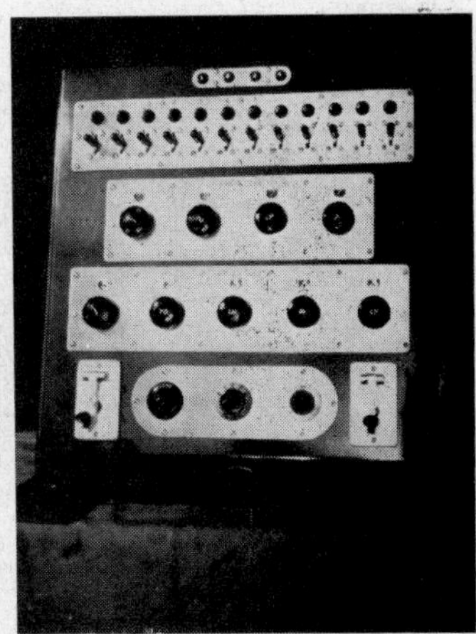

FAMOUS "PENTEFOLD" 9-DIGIT, 12-CIRCUIT, PRE-CODE, TRANSMITTER. INSTALLED AT STOCKTON, CALIFORNIA.

B & B ENGINEERING CORPORATION

NORWOOD, LOUISIANA

Let's talk DOLLARS and SENSE

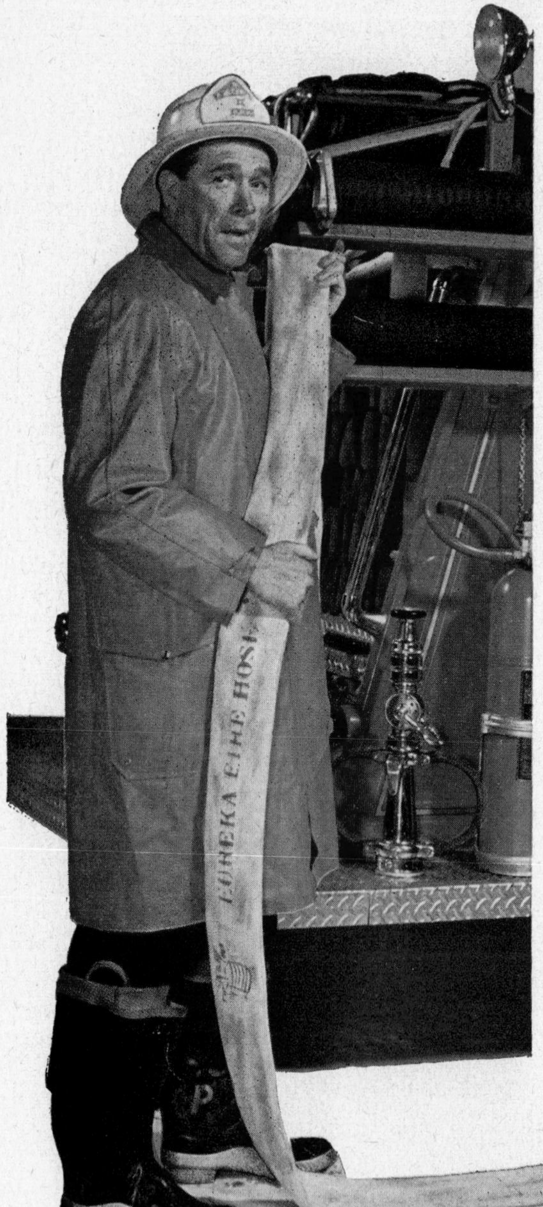

The best is usually *least expensive in the long run*. And that goes double for fire hose! Here's why:

Your dollar spent for the lowest-priced approved hose can be divided over an average service life of about 4 years . . . or 25 cents per year. Suppose, however, you invest *not one* dollar but *two dollars* in the same footage of premium quality Eureka MULTIPLE-WOVEN Hose. According to the experience of users, your two-dollar investment in this uniquely constructed hose may well be spread over a useful service life of 16, 20 or even 24 years . . . or 8 to 12 cents per year!

In the long run, then, Eureka MULTIPLE-WOVEN may easily cut your hose expenditures *by more than half!* At the same time you'll have a hose you know won't let you down . . . won't warp or writhe excessively . . . and *will* deliver maximum pressure to the nozzle! *There's no other hose like it.* Specify it on your next order! You'll have the added satisfaction of dealing with a *specialist* in fire hose!

The Multiple-Woven construction of Eureka Fire Hose makes the hose stronger, safer to handle, more dependable in action.

"For greater protection to life and property"

Since 1875, Manufacturers of a Complete Line of Multiple-Woven, Rubber-Lined Fire Hose.

about EUREKA Multiple-Woven

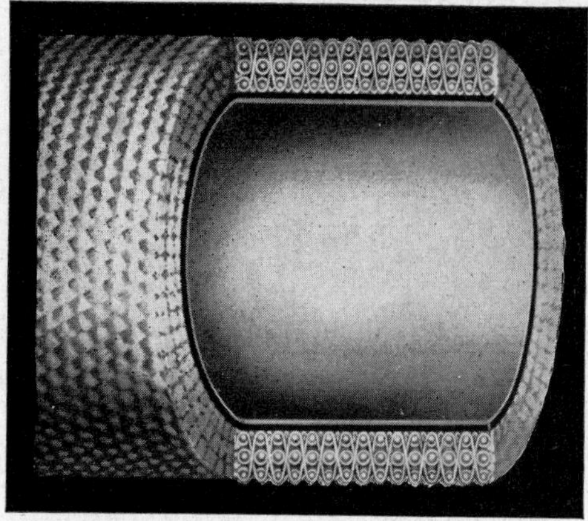

All plies of Eureka Multiple-Woven Hose are woven *and interwoven* simultaneously, leaving no space between plies for collection of water, dirt or mildew.

Instead of being separate, as in loose-jacketed hose, the plies of Eureka Multiple-Woven Fire Hose are circular-woven and bound together by one operation of the loom into one homogeneous unit. All cords in the fabric are woven under uniform tension, thus eliminating dangerous writhing, wriggling or serpentining of the hose when under hydraulic pressure.

Eureka Multiple-Woven Fire Hose is safer for firemen to handle on ladders—safer on the ground, too, because it will not "run amuck." This type of hose is available in two-, three- or four-ply construction, all embodying these three additional features:

NO WASHBOARDING—Eureka Smooth-Interior Filler Ply is an individual set of warp and weft cords filling the valleys in the weave of the inner ply, making this surface perfectly smooth and level. There are no valleys into which the rubber lining can recede when the hose is under hydraulic pressure. Consequently, there is maximum pressure at the nozzle.

IMPROVED RUBBER LININGS—Eureka Fire Hose Linings consist of four plies of heat-resisting, long-lived rubber calendered into one homogeneous body and formed into a tube in such a manner as to eliminate the old-fashioned lap seam bump. By means of a severe laboratory test in an oxygen bomb, the superior aging qualities of Eureka improved linings are scientifically proved.

MILDEW PROOFING — Fabrics used in all brands of Eureka Fire Hose are antiseptically treated to retard the formation of mildew and rot. The exclusive mildew-repellent solution used does not add to the weight of the hose, discolor it, nor make it greasy and hard to handle.

EUREKA FIRE HOSE

Division of United States Rubber

1 Market Street, Passaic, N. J.

SALES AGENTS IN THE FOLLOWING CITIES

Alexandria, La.
Atlanta, Ga.
Baltimore, Md.
Billings, Mont.
Dallas, Tex.
Denver, Colo.
Des Moines, Ia.
Framingham, Mass.
Great Falls, Mont.
Harper Woods, Mich.
Hutchinson, Kans.
Lansdowne, Pa.
Nashville, Tenn.
Milwaukee, Wisc.
Oklahoma City, Okla.
Pataskala, Ohio
Philadelphia, Pa.
Phoenix, Ariz.
Pittsburgh, Pa.
Portland, Ore.
Rivera, Calif.
Southern Pines, N. C.
St. Paul, Minn.
Syracuse, N. Y.
Thetford Hill, Vt.
Unionville, Mo.
Yonkers, N. Y.

Simplicity of operation with positive control makes tight situations less hazardous.

MAXIM MOTOR COMPANY MAXIM MIDDLEBORO, MASS.

65'-75'-85'-100' AERIAL LADDERS

The MAXIM All-Steel Aerial Ladder Truck is 100% hydraulically operated —raised, rotated and extended hydraulically. This new principle of ladder extension by hydraulic cylinder adds speed, efficiency and safety. The hydraulic system is entirely above the turntable. Four sizes: 65′, 75′, 85′ and 100′. MAXIM Tractor-Drawn Aerials available with all sizes of MAXIM hydraulic aerial ladders and with either hydraulic or air brakes.

The NEW 100′ aerial features high strength to weight ladder design.

THE GAMEWELL COMPANY

Newton Upper Falls 64, Massachusetts

CODED TELEGRAPH FIRE ALARM SYSTEMS

The Gamewell Telegraph Fire Alarm System offers three special advantages to Municipalities:

1. It is specifically designed and engineered for fire service.

2. It is automatic, and complete, from fire box to central office to engine house.

3. It is a direct, independent system which is easy to operate, precise in its information and never misunderstood.

In addition, a correctly engineered Gamewell system offers these important benefits: lowest possible yearly cost; contributes to improvement of communities' fire insurance ratings; and provides the fire chief a completely independent, separately controlled system to provide dependable fire protection on a round-the-clock basis.

Gamewell offers a complete line of equipment which allows a system to be tailored exactly to the fire chief's needs and the city's fire defense plan.

POLICE and EMERGENCY SIGNALLING SYSTEMS

Gamewell Police Signalling Systems provide communities and police chiefs with a means for adequate police supervision and a communications network for emergency and civil defense use.

The Gamewell system consists of:

1. Signalling and telephone stations — police patrol boxes — including code devices and standard telephone hand set;

2. Police recall signal to notify patrolmen;

3. A central or precinct station operator's desk for the receipt and dispatch of calls and signals;

4. Wire circuits for electrically connecting the various components of the system and a common power supply.

Gamewell Police Signalling Systems are designed to order. They can be engineered to meet the particular requirements of any city, industrial plant or institution.

NEW FLEXALARM SYSTEM

. . . *for Commercial Buildings, Institutions, Schools and Public Buildings*

Flexalarm is a new line of fire alarm signal systems designed by Gamewell for general industrial, commercial and institutional applications. The new system takes advantage of Gamewell experience in signalling and communications, allowing the user to tailor a fire alarm system exactly to his needs. Flexalarm is designed to provide maximum protection at minimum cost.

In addition, Flexalarm, coupled with the Gamewell *Master Box*, extends municipal fire protection *automatically* to every area where there is a place of public assembly.

Flexalarm is covered in Bulletin F249 which outlines the basic plan and describes the major components which make up the various types of alarm systems.

Send for FIRE ALARM "FACTS KIT"

A special kit provides information and data to help in evaluating and selecting fire alarm systems. "Conversation or Organization" answers operational questions about the modern coded fire alarm systems. "The Economics of a Fire Alarm System" provides valuable cost data and important facts to be weighed when considering the purchase of any type of fire signalling system.

This material is available without cost or obligation to assist communities and municipal officials in the selection and application of fire alarm systems.

FIRE ALARM COST ANALYSIS

Ask for a FREE SURVEY

A *free* Gamewell survey will provide you with the necessary facts and figures to make a sound, honest analysis of your fire alarm requirements and the equipment which will give you the greatest amount of protection at the lowest possible cost. Requests for a free survey should be addressed to: The Gamewell Company, Department RA, Newton Upper Falls 64, Massachusetts. Remember — a Gamewell system is FIRST when seconds count!

Remember-a Gamewell System is FIRST when seconds count!

THE GAMEWELL COMPANY
Newton Upper Falls 64, Massachusetts

FOR FIRE
OPEN
THEN PULL DOWN HOOK
32
FIRE

THE BOX IS POSITIVE

ROCKWOOD SPRINKLER COMPANY

3002 Harlow Street, Worcester 5, Massachusetts

PROVEN FIRE-STOPPERS — EVERY ONE!

These are not just fire fighters — they're fire-stoppers.

The Rockwood portable units shown here have been proved in action, and with a collective versatility that covers every type of fire.

Rockwood Portable Fire Fighting Equipment offers you invaluable protection for your property and personnel. Yet this security is yours at very low cost, and backed by Rockwood's long experience and constant research. It will pay you to learn more about these Rockwood-engineered developments that have brought new efficiency and economy to fire fighting throughout the country. Write today for your copy of the Rockwood catalog.

FOAM Eductor with FW Metering-Check Valve. Incorporates both the Metering Valve and Ball Check Valve in one unit. Meters FOAM liquid or "Wet" into the hose line in any proportion from 1% through 6%. Eductors also designed to introduce wetting agents.

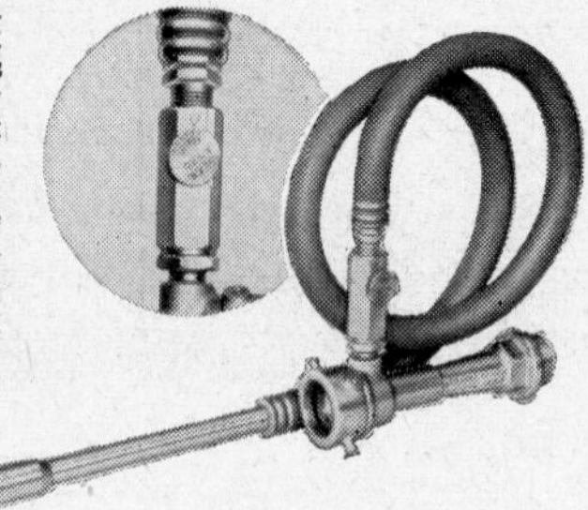

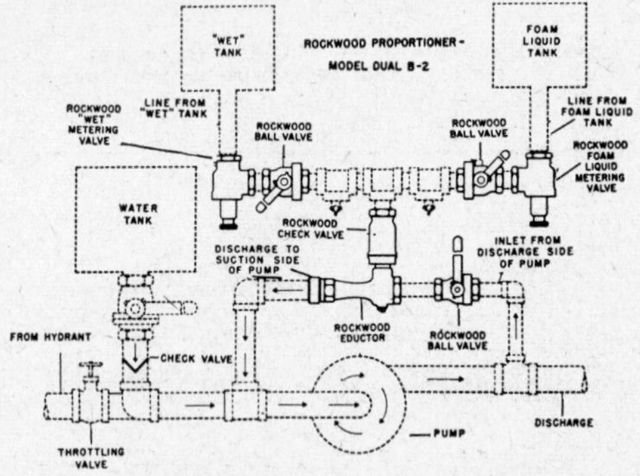

Automatic Proportioning Systems. For fire truck applications. Automatically proportions proper amounts of Rockwood FOAM or Rockwood "Wet" with water. Custom-engineered systems also available.

Type FFF FogFOAM Nozzle. Discharges Fog-FOAM, solid FOAM stream and high velocity WaterFOG.

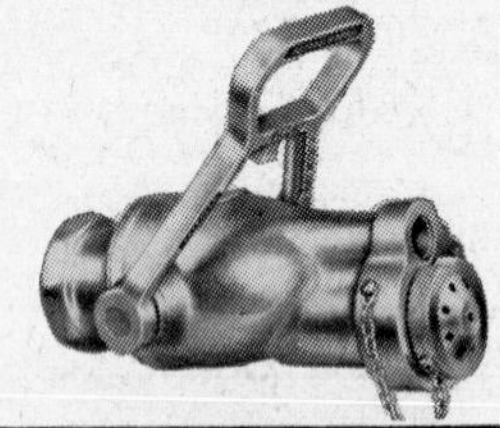

Type SG-48 Water-FOG Nozzle. Easy to handle. Discharges high or low velocity Water-FOG or straight water stream.

Rockwood FOAM Maker and Chamber. Used for fighting flammable liquid tank fires.

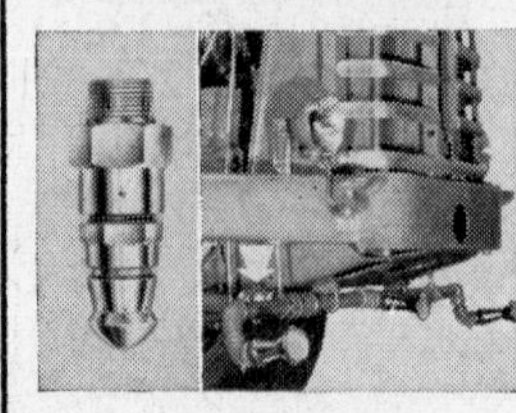

Under Truck and Ground Sweep Nozzles. Used to protect front of fire trucks and parts under trucks.

Type FFF FogFOAM Turret Nozzles. Two control types: (A) Remote control, hydraulic or manual and (B) Direct manual control. For airport crash fire fighting trucks and special fire fighting trucks for municipalities. Also available in portable form for direct connection to hose lines.

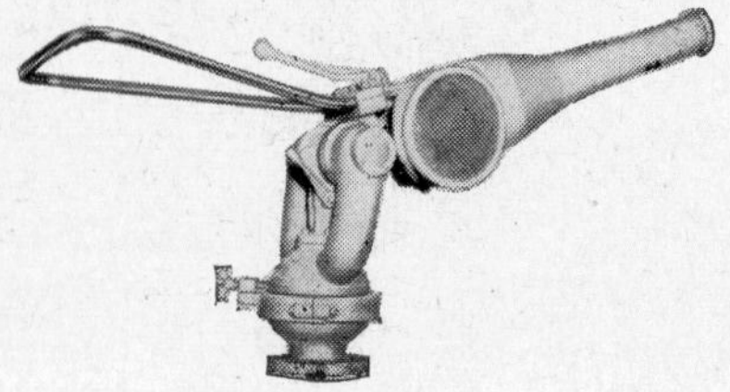

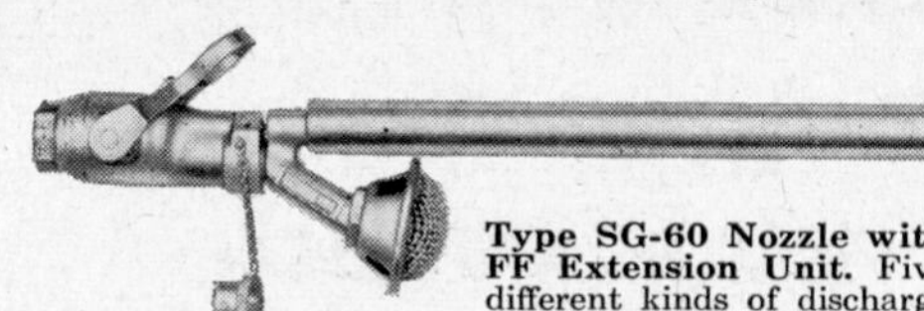

Type SG-60 Nozzle with FF Extension Unit. Five different kinds of discharge from only one nozzle.

Extension Applicator with Type SG-48 WaterFOG Nozzle. Discharges low velocity WaterFOG. Standard applicator with ball type shut-off also available.

Type N22 WaterFOG Nozzle. Discharges high velocity WaterFOG. For general use around live electrical equipment.

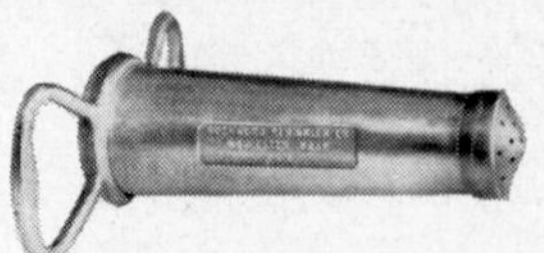

Type N23 WaterFOG Nozzle with Swivel Handles. Discharges high velocity WaterFOG with higher volume and greater range than Type N22 Nozzle.

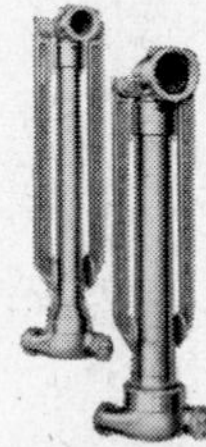

Lightweight Rotating Cellar and Attic Pipe. Fights fires in cellars, attics, under piers, bridges, etc.

Rockwood Ball Type Shut-Off. Gives operator complete control of water flow from nozzles.

All-Purpose FOAM Liquid. For use against fires in alcohols, ketones, ethers, acetones and similar water soluble materials — as well as petroleum derivatives.

Rockwood "Wet" Wetting Agent. Increases fire extinguishing action of water, making a little water go a long way. Excellent for use on fires of wood, paper, cloth, rubbish, etc.

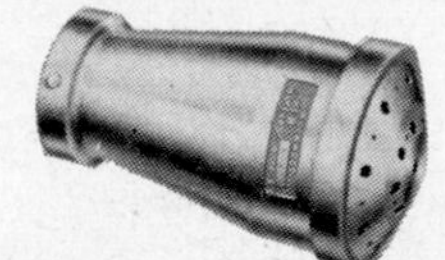

High Capacity WaterFOG Nozzle. Quickly controls and extinguishes large fires in buildings and flammable liquids.

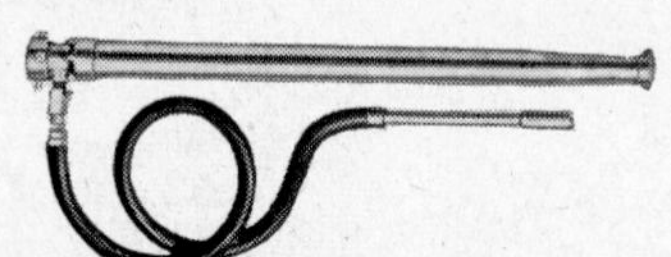

Standard Straight FOAM Play Pipe and FOAM Pick-Up Tube. Discharges 60 gpm at 100 psi. Range: approximately 55 feet.

Double Strength FOAM Liquid. Can be automatically proportioned into fire hose lines. Fights fires in gasoline and other petroleum type liquids.

ROCKWOOD SPRINKLER COMPANY

Engineers Water . . . to Cut Fire Losses

PORTABLE FIRE PROTECTION DIVISION

3002 Harlow Street, Worcester 5, Massachusetts

DISTRIBUTORS IN ALL PRINCIPAL CITIES

BI-LATERAL FIRE HOSE CO.

20 N. Wacker Drive • Chicago 6, Ill.

when you buy with your conscience you'll BI-LATERAL

Manufacturers of Cotton Rubber Lined Fire Hose and all other types of Fire Department Hose . . .

BI-LATERAL constructed hose leaves the rubber free and unattached from the jacket at both points of fold, for the space that is affected by flattening. This permits the rubber lining to protect itself from creasing or compression and prevents it from cracking, leaking, "pin-holes," or "seepers."

THIS IS HOW IT FLATTENS . . .

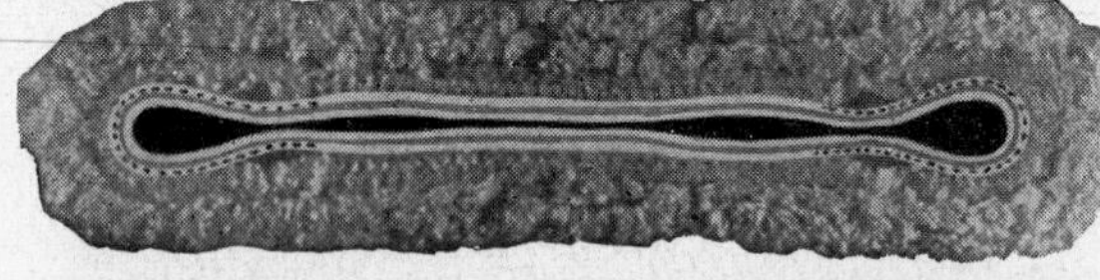

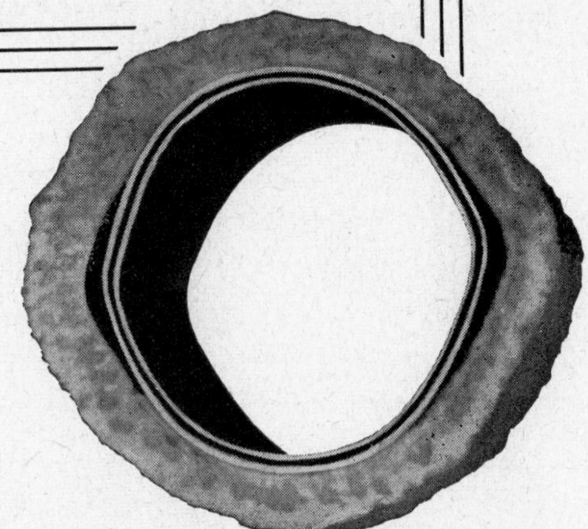

THIS IS BI-LATERAL FIRE HOSE

DISTRIBUTORS IN THE FOLLOWING CITIES

ALABAMA, TUSCALOOSA
Sam Davis
1300 10th St.
Tel. Plaza 4-9495

CALIFORNIA, ENCINO
Dick Cornell
5126 Encino Ave.
Tel. State 9-1335

COLORADO, DENVER
Paul Nelson
Nelson Fire Equip. Co.
920 Inca St.
Tel Cherry 4-6548

CONNECTICUT, OLD GREENWICH
Orville A. Sawyer
P.O. Box 73
Tel. Old Gr. 7-0450

FLORIDA, JACKSONVILLE
W. Q. Dowling
P.O. Box 6338
Tel. Evergreen 9-8255

ILLINOIS, BARRINGTON
Great Lakes Fire Equipment Co.
Mike Dalton

INDIANA, INDIANAPOLIS
Midwest Fire & Safety
Equipment Company
1605 Prospect St.
Tel. Melrose 2-9338

IOWA, BELLE PLAINE
Earl Byers
710 17th St.
Tel. 220

KENTUCKY
James Gore
Box 335
Collinsville, Ill.
Tel. Dickens 4-5229

MAINE, WINTHROP
Don Blanchard
Blanchard Associates, Inc.
Tel. 304

MASSACHUSETTS, MEDFIELD
Charles H. Clougherty Co.
39 Miller St.
Tel. Fleetwood 9-6232

MICHIGAN, BENTON HARBOR
Joseph Platte
1461 Ogden Ave.
Tel. Walnut 6-2317

MINNESOTA, MINNEAPOLIS 4
C. F. Coyer
2426 Clinton Ave. South
Tel. Federal 9-5410

MISSOURI, VERSAILLES
L. W. Graves
Interstate Fire Equipment Co.
Rockledge—Lake Road #16
Tel. Frontier 4-5261
(Sunrise Beach, Mo.)

NEW JERSEY, LAUREL SPRINGS
Nat Alexander Company, Inc.
White Horse Pike (U.S. Rt. 30)
Tel. 4-0720

NEW JERSEY, KEARNY
Bi-Lateral Fire Hose Company
T. F. Murphy
9 Livingston
Tel. 2-9374

NEW YORK, ELMIRA
W. J. Lawless
207 West Third Street
Tel. 3-9392

NORTH CAROLINA, RALEIGH
Otto C. Wipper
P.O. Box 1704

OHIO, COLUMBUS
Birch Fire Equipment Co.
W. L. Birch
2148 E. Livingston Ave.
Tel. Douglas 7842

OREGON, PORTLAND
Wilco Fire Equipment Co.
1123 S. E. Market St.
Tel. Belmont 4-8476

TEXAS, DALLAS
Jno. T. Hanway
6403 Goliad
Tel. Tremont 7-0713

UTAH, SALT LAKE CITY
Universal Safety & Fire Equip.
727 S.W. Temple St.
Tel. Empire 3-5901

WISCONSIN, MADISON 5
James Fenton
114 Merlham Drive
Tel. Cedar 3-4633

EXIDE® INDUSTRIAL DIVISION

The Electric Storage Battery Company, Philadelphia 2, Pa.

Atlanta 10, Ga. .... 1246 Allene Ave., S.W.
Boston 34, Mass. .... 100 Ashford Street
Chicago 9, Ill. .... 5335 S. Western Blvd.
Cleveland 14, Ohio .... 1014 Engineers Bldg.
Dallas 1, Texas .... 2133 McKinney Avenue
Detroit 4, Mich. .... 8051 W. Chicago Blvd.
Kansas City 23, Mo. .... 129 Belmont Blvd.
Los Angeles 15, Calif. .... 1043 S. Grand Avenue
Minneapolis 3, Minn. .... 1750 Hennepin Avenue
New Orleans 12, La. .... 406 Civic Center Bldg.
New York 36, N. Y. .... 25 West 43rd Street
Philadelphia 4, Pa. .... 101 N. 33rd Street
Pittsburgh 16, Pa. .... 1608 Potomac Avenue
St. Louis 8, Mo. .... 3928 Lindell Blvd.
San Francisco 24, Calif. ...... 6150 Third Street
Seattle 4, Wash. .... 1919 Smith Tower Bldg.
Washington 6, D. C. .... 1819 "L" Street, N.W.

There's an Exide Battery for every municipal use!

Fire alarm and police telegraph systems

Police cars, fire engines and other vehicles

Pavers, tractors and similar equipment

Harbor and river patrol vessels

Electric lift trucks and pallet movers

Emergency lighting systems and packaged units

In use everywhere. And giving greater value for every dollar of cost. Higher quality construction insures longer life and consistent dependability. Exide Batteries feature Silvium, a patented grid alloy that resists corrosion—sometimes up to 100% longer than alloys used in other batteries. Get complete information. Call your nearby Exide office.

THE ELECTRIC STORAGE BATTERY COMPANY

FEDERAL LABORATORIES, INC.

Specialists in Law Enforcement and Protective Equipment

Saltsburg, Pa.

FEDERAL Tear Gas Equipment

Federal
Spedeheat Grenade

Federal 1½" Caliber
Gas Gun

Spedeheat and Flite-Rite
Projectiles

Short Range Gas Shell
or Parachute Flare

Federal Laboratories, Inc., with over 35 years of Chemical Research and experience recommends its products to Law Enforcement Agencies for emergency assignments. Use of the Federal Gas Gun and Flite-Rite Projectiles is the practical method for dislodging barricaded criminals and insane persons with minimum risk. Federal Grenades can also be used for this purpose under favorable conditions.

Federal Spedeheat and Triple-Chaser Grenades, Spedeheat Projectiles and Short Range Shells deliver heavy gas concentrations and are most effective in dispersing unruly and riotous groups.

Federal Spedeheat Grenades forcefully discharge gas through openings in the top, sides and bottom, delivering heavy gas concentrations. Federal Triple-Chaser Grenades, after being thrown, separate into three sections, each traveling in a different direction and functioning as individual Grenades. Federal Gas Products are loaded with Solid Crystalline VISIBLE Gas. Most Nationally known Law Enforcement Agencies rely upon Federal Gas Products.

FEDERAL ELECTRIC MEGAPHONE

OTHER FEDERAL PRODUCTS:—Gas Masks, Liquid Gas Projectors, Sirens, Armored Vests and Shields, Fingerprint Supplies, Handcuffs, Leg Irons, Billies, Badges, Police Lights, Leather Goods, Sub-Machine Guns, Ammunition, and many other items used by Law Enforcement Agencies.

Now available a new type bullet stopping vest front, weight medium size only five pounds, which will protect wearer against .38 Cal. lead ammunition with muzzle velocities up to 1115 ft. per sec.

Write for Literature and Prices on Your Requirements
FEDERAL LABORATORIES, INC., SALTSBURG, PA.

FRANKLIN WORSTED COMPANY

G and Venango Streets, Philadelphia 34, Pa.

INDUSTRIAL RADIO CORP.

428 N. Parkside Ave., Chicago 44, Ill.

PAK-FONE PORTABLE 2-WAY RADIO

Industrial Radio PAK-FONES are the newest, most efficient types available for portable services. They are widely used in police and fire departments, water and sanitary departments, utilities and many other municipal operations requiring completely flexible 2-way communications. Wherever competitive field tests of performance are conducted, PAK-FONES usually have at least *twice* the operating range of the next best available units. All PAK-FONES have built-in loud speakers.

PAK-FONE Model AU

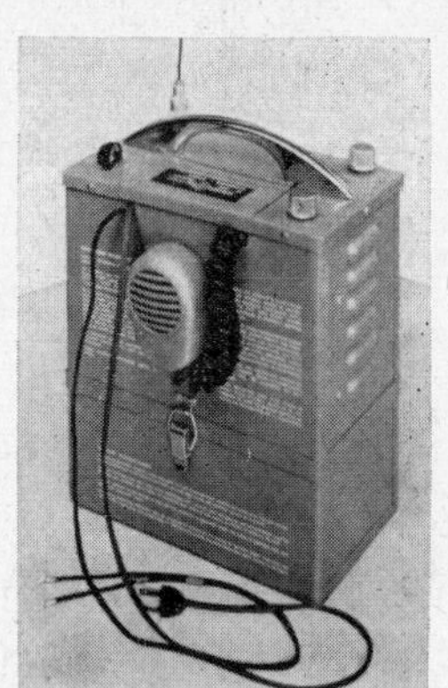

The famous 2-way portable that has the most power and exclusive features of any unit in its classification. It operates on long-life self-contained batteries and on 117 V.A.C., 6, 12 and 24 V.D.C. without an external power supply. Many other features.

The VOLUNTEER FM-VHF

Radio Communications Receiver

Models for auto or home use employ newest, top performing circuits. Crystal controlled for utmost stability. Most sensitive monitoring equipment at any price. The outstanding value in all communications at $99.00 (less crystal).

PAK-FONE Model H/M

The smallest hand-carried 2-way portable with built-in loud speaker, relay operated squelch and other big portable features. Connector provided for power supply UPC-100. Because of its light weight and convenient small size, the H/M is one of the most popular portables on the market.

FIELD-FONE Model FF-D

Camera-size portable is an exclusive Industrial Radio design. As powerful as many cumbersome portables. Ideal for the chief, patrolmen, guards and construction workers.

UPC-100 POWER CONVERTER

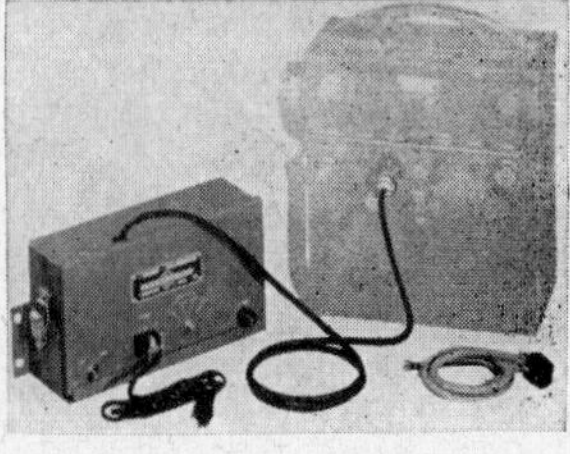

External power supply operates from 117 V.A.C. and from 6, 12 and 24 volt storage batteries to supply power for any 2-way portables using 1¼ volt filament tubes.

Write for complete information and specifications. Sales and service facilities in all principal cities.

PETER PIRSCH & SONS CO.

Kenosha, Wisconsin

THE LATEST AND BEST IN HYDRAULIC AERIAL HOISTS

The new Pirsch Full-Hydraulic Aerial Ladder Hoisting and Operating Mechanism offers the last word in modern design and incorporates the latest and best in the way of hydraulic application to the operation of aerial ladders.

Either the Pirsch Hydro-Mechanical Aerial Ladder Hoisting Mechanism (America's first all-powered aerial hoist) or the new Pirsch Full-Hydraulic Hoisting Mechanism are offered as optional equipment on Pirsch Aerial Ladder Trucks.

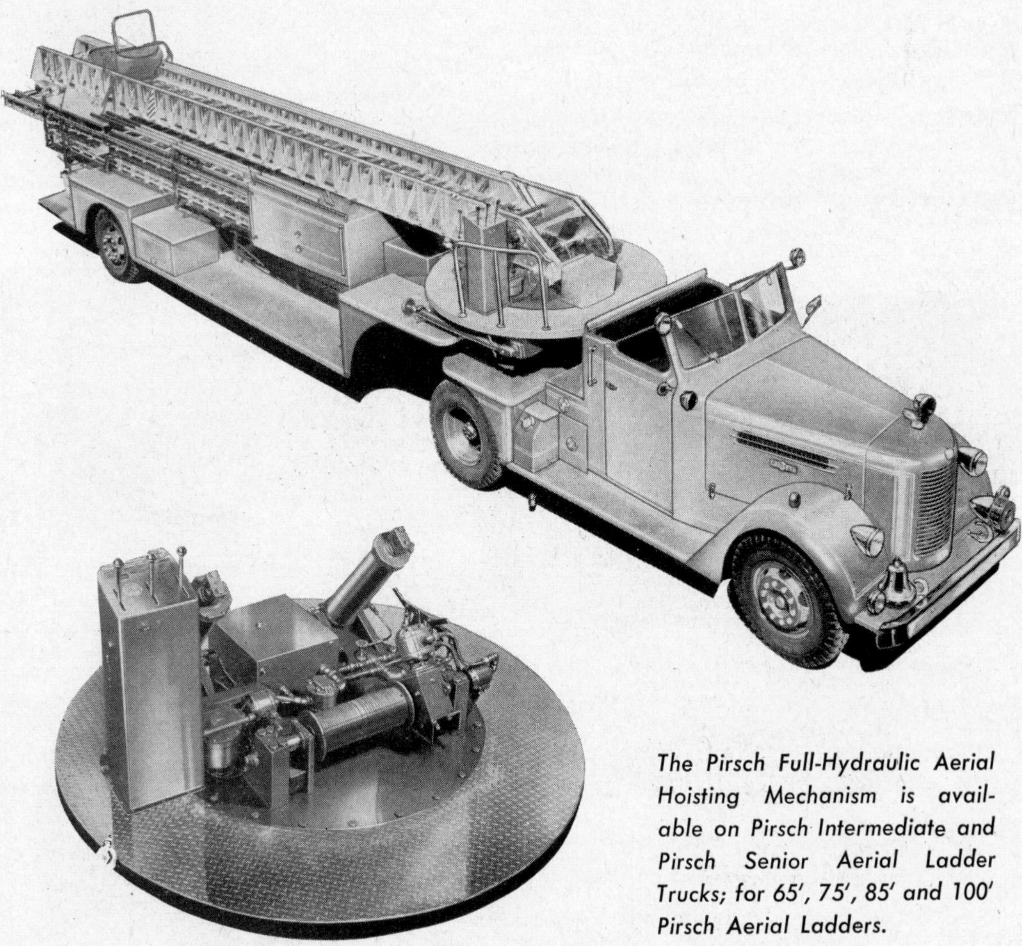

The Pirsch Full-Hydraulic Aerial Hoisting Mechanism is available on Pirsch Intermediate and Pirsch Senior Aerial Ladder Trucks; for 65', 75', 85' and 100' Pirsch Aerial Ladders.

STERLING SIREN FIRE ALARM CO., INC.

8 BARTLETT STREET, ROCHESTER 8, N. Y.

For more than 40 years, Sterling has maintained its leadership in the design and production of efficient and practical alarm equipment. Sterling Sirens are powerful, compact, handsome in appearance and built throughout to assure extra years of wear under the most grueling service requirements.

IMPROVED MODEL "M" FOR GENERAL FIRE ALARM SYSTEMS

We recommend this model (illustrated below) as the most effective, most enduring non-coded public fire alarm. It is large, powerful, fully weatherproof, made of the best materials available (parts exposed to the weather are of the most indestructible metals). Write for Bulletin.

MOTORS: Built according to our own specifications and subjected to rigid tests before acceptance. Standard makes or stock motors are never used. Quicker acceleration, provisions for heat radiation, larger shafts and oversize bearings are a few of the features found only in Sterling Siren motors.

STERLING Model "M," the most efficient sound distributor made. A powerful alarm that carries a great distance.

COMPLETE LINE AVAILABLE, INCLUDING TWINLITES & CODE SYSTEMS.

WRITE, MENTIONING YOUR SPECIAL INTERESTS.

MODELS FOR FIRE, POLICE, AND OTHER EMERGENCY SERVICE

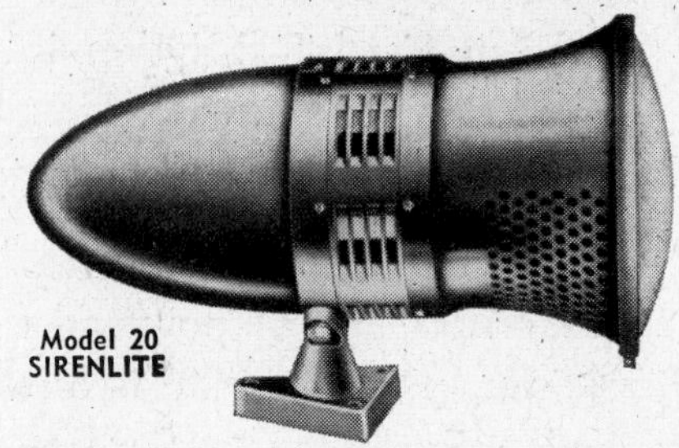

Model 20
SIRENLITE

SIRENLITE: Powerful, authoritative siren combined with automatically flashing red beacon—doubly efficient—quickly clears your path for blocks ahead. LIGHT or SIREN may be used alone. Large, specially designed lens, light bulb and optically correct reflector compactly built into projector. High grade ball bearing motor, dynamically balanced rotor machined to micrometer accuracy. FREE ROLLING. Entire unit built for long life and heavy duty in one of the world's largest factories devoted exclusively to siren manufacture. Both the Model 20 and the Model 30 are large, powerful sirens, but the Model 30 is really a super-siren with a tremendous sound volume. Write for Sirenlite Bulletins.

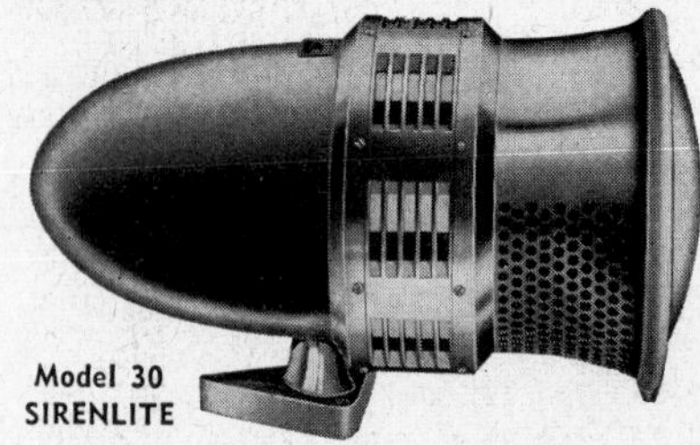

Model 30
SIRENLITE

The "Sentinels" illustrated below (Twinlite styles of vehicle siren models 20 and 30) flash a bright, penetrating light BOTH FRONT AND REAR—turn ALL traffic away and serve as an "extra man" to keep the danger area clear.

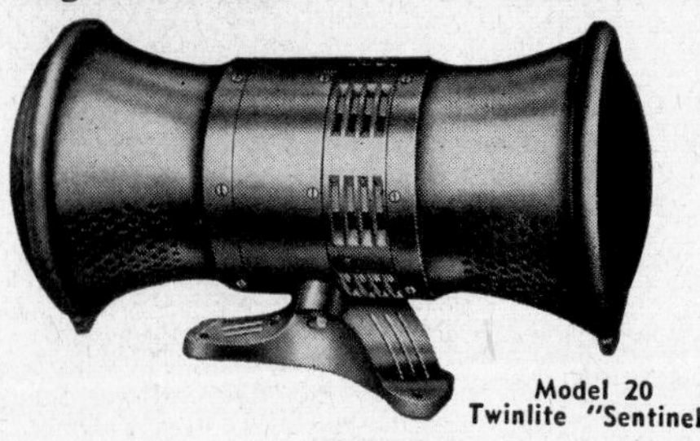

Model 20
Twinlite "Sentinel"

WORTHINGTON
MOWER COMPANY

NGINE: Heavy-duty industrial, 4-cylinder.
UEL: Gasoline—11 gallons, total capacity.
GNITION: Weather-proofed. Distributor tightly ealed.
RANSMISSION: Heavy-Duty. 4 Speeds forward, reverse. Speed range from 2 to 25 mph.
RIVING AXLE: Timken-Detroit one-ton truck type.
TEERING AXLE: Heavy-duty, pivotally mounted.
TEERING: Automotive type with adjustable olumn. Turning radius, 7 ft.
RAKES: Foot hydraulic and parking mechanical n drive wheels.
RAWBAR: Ball coupler type, convertible to pin ype.
CCESSORIES AVAILABLE: Snow Plow, Front End oader, Cab.

Model "F" Tractor

The Model "F" Tractor, a new concept in design with front-wheel drive and rear-wheel steering, is a great gang-mower power unit. Articulated mowers are mounted ahead of all tractor wheels, allowing operators to see where they're cutting. Grass is cut before the wheels mat it down without streaking or "over again" mowing. Fairway and Blitzer units with convertible frames are available in 3-, 5-, and 7-gang.

ENERAL: Available for use with either Fairway r Grass Blitzer mowers. Specifications are the ame as for Model "F" Tractor as shown above, ut with the addition of the following equipment.

YDRO-TRAVEL LIFT: Rugged, engine-driven ydraulic pump raises and lowers mowers moothly and easily. Action is controlled from an asy to reach lever located at the operator's seat. nit is designed to lift and transport 3- or 5- ang mowers. When in raised position, mowers re held securely in place. Safety chains prevent ccidental lowering when traveling at road peeds. When lifted, mowers afford ample ground learance to cross over curbs or obstacles.

Model "F" Tractor
with Hydro-Travel Lift.

Speed mowing and cut travel time between jobs with Model "F" Tractors equipped with Hydro-Travel Gang Mower Control. This method raises and lowers mowers smoothly through a positive hydraulic system controlled from the driver's seat. During travel, mowers are held securely for safety at road speeds. Climbs curbs easily with mowers raised. Unit can be stored without dismantling. Available for 3- and 5-gang mowers.

GENERAL: Attachments and accessories for both the Model "F" and Model "G" tractors can be nstalled either at the factory or in the field. Further information and complete sepcifications can be obtained from your Worthington franchised dealer.

Tractor Attachments

The use of attachments with both the Model "F" and Model "G" Tractors makes these units versatile, all-season workhorses. When equipped with front-end loaders, the tractors can handle sand, coal, gravel, and loose dirt. The bucket can be replaced with a plow blade for snow removal. A cab is also available for foul weather work. Other accessories include power-take-offs light graders, and utility carts.

ENGINE: Heavy-duty industrial, 4-cylinder.
FUEL: Gasoline—11 gallons total capacity.
IGNITION: Weather-proofed. Distributor tightly sealed.
TRANSMISSION: Heavy-duty. 4 Speeds forward, 1 reverse. Speeds from 3 to 40 mph.
DRIVING AXLE: Timken-Detroit one-ton truck type.
STEERING AXLE: Heavy-duty, pivotally mounted.
STEERING: Automotive-type, adjustable steering column. Turning radius, 5½ ft.
BRAKES: Foot hydraulic and parking mechanical on drive wheels.
DRAWBAR: Ball type coupler, convertible to pin type.
ACCESSORIES AVAILABLE: Snow Plow, Front End Loader, Cab, Mechanical Sickle Bar, Hydraulic Sickle Bar.

Model "G" Tractor

The exceptionally low-center of gravity found in this tractor gives it the ability to cut side hills and slopes as steep as 36° without danger of upset. A rugged, dependable, heavy-duty industrial engine provides the Model "G" with power to spare on mowing and power-take-off work. Fast 40 mph. road speed reduces travel time betwen jobs. Short 5½-foot turning radius means greater maneuverability in close quarter work. The Model "G" combines utility with low-cost performance.

Mowing Equipment for Large Area Grass Maintenance

WORTHINGTON

CUTTER BAR: Heavy-duty Highway Detroit Harvester. 5 ft. (3" knife sections).

DRIVE: From rear power-take-off through V-belts.

CUTTING ANGLE: 90° above horizontal, 45° below.

LIFT & CONTROLS: Power, Hydraulic. Levers easily accessible.

SAFETY DEVICES: V-belt drive and spring tension swing back.

TILT: Hand lever and notched quadrant permit blade tilt.

SPEED: First and second gear transmission offer wide range of cutting speeds to meet varying cutting conditions. Cutting speeds range from 1.5 to 6.5 mph.

INNER SHOE REGULATION: From ground to 8".

Model "G" Tractor

with Mechanical Sickle Bar.

When the Sickle Bar Attachment is used with the dual wheel Model "G" Tractor, irregular terrain and slopes as steep as 36° can be mowed with complete safety. Extreme low center-of-gravity of the "G," plus extra-big, dual, low-pressure tires for maximum flotation makes this possible. Sickle Bar is mounted ahead of driver, making it possible to avoid obstructions. Special safety features minimize Bar damage.

CUTTER BAR: Heavy-duty, Hydro-Clipper, full-floating type, 5 ft. bar (3" knife sections).

DRIVE: Fully hydraulic.

CUTTING ANGLE: 90° above horizontal, 45° below.

LIFT & CONTROL: Hydraulic. 3 control levers within easy reach of operator.

TILT: Made quickly and positively with single lock nut.

SAFETY DEVICES: Self-returning 90° breakaway. Positive transport locks. Pressure relief valve unloads the instant the knife is stopped, relieving all pressure from the knife.

SPEED: Hydraulic pump operates in direct ratio to engine speed. Cutting speeds range from 1.5 to 9 mph.

INNER SHOE REGULATION: From ground to over 12".

Model "G" Tractor

with Hydraulic Sickle Bar.

The Model "G" Tractor with Hydraulic Sickle Bar meets every highway cutting requirement. Extremely low tractor center-of-gravity permits cutting of slopes up to 36° without danger of upset. The Hydraulic Sickle Bar cuts at much higher speeds than average highway sickle bars. Safety features reduce maintenance costs between 50% to 75%, giving more cutting mileage between knife sharpenings.

MAIN DRIVE: From heavy-duty Detroit Harvester Power-Take-Off at tractor transmission through 1" shaft to driving sheaves.

DRIVE SHAFT: 6 spline, S.A.E., regulation size. Guarded for safety.

BEARINGS: Heavy-duty, pre-lubricated, sealed ball type.

SHEAVES: Two 4-groove. Keyed to shaft.

V-BELTS: Four B-section, nylon cord, matched belts.

FINGER TOUCH CONTROL: Easy-to-reach lever engages and disengages power-take-off.

Model "G" Tractor

with S.A.E. Power-Take-Off.

The S.A.E. Rear Power-Take-Off Drive Assembly was specially engineered for operating Worthington Power-Take-Off Rotaries, sprayers, shredders, and other types of equipment. The unit was designed so that the Model "G" Tractor can be operated in second gear at speeds up to 10 miles per hour and still transmit adequate power to the rotary mower blades. This means double cutting capacity.

CUTTING WIDTH: 30 inches (each unit).

OVERALL CUTTING SWATH: 3-gang, 6' 10"; 5-gang, 11' 2"; 7-gang, 15' 6".

WHEELS: Pressed steel discs with demountable rims. Pneumatic-tired wheel optional.

GEARS: Machine-cut, heat-treated.

REVOLVING KNIVES: 8" diameter reel, 6-blade standard, 5-blade optional. Blades of specially heat-treated alloy attached to shaft by five steel discs.

BED KNIFE: Oil-hardened, special alloy steel.

DRIVE: Separate gear train for each ground wheel.

BEARINGS: Roller for ground wheel and intermediate gear. Shielded ball for fly-knife reel and rear roller.

HEIGHT OF CUT: Steel wheels, 11/32" to 2¾".

ADJUSTMENTS: Done entirely by hand.

Fairway Gang Mowers

A broad expanse of carpet-smooth turf is the trade mark of Worthington Fairway Gang Mowers. Articulated frame design permits mowers to follow ground contours. Units can be telescoped in width for passing through narrow openings. A patented spring supplies a 50 pound downward pressure on the roller, preventing skipping and bouncing. Lever regulates pressure to suit cutting conditions. Available in 3-, 5-, and 7-gang units.

WORTHINGTON MOWER COMPANY

STROUDSBURG, PENNSYLVANIA

The Big Name in Big Area Grass Maintenance

Blitzer Gang Mowers

Blitzer Gang Mowers are built to take abuse and mow rough grass areas with increased speed and decreased cost per acre. Blitzer gangs are capable of cutting rough areas at speeds up to 20 mph. Articulated frame design permits each unit to conform to ground contours. Large diameter reel with extra space between knives allows Blitzers to gather in and clip tall grass. Available in 3-, 5-, 7-, and 9-gang units.

CUTTING WIDTH: 30 inches (each unit).

OVERALL CUTTING SWATH: 3-gang, 7′ 2″; 5-gang, 11′ 10″; 7-gang, 16′ 6″; 9-gang, 21′ 2″.

WHEELS: 4.00 x 12 pneumatic tires (4.00 x 18 optional) mounted on drop center rims.

GEARS: Machine-cut, heat-treated.

REVOLVING KNIVES: 10″ diameter reels, 4-blade standard, 5-blade optional. Blades of specially heat-treated alloy attached to shaft by 5 steel discs.

BED KNIFE: Oil-hardened special alloy steel.

BED KNIFE PROTECTIVE SKID: 1/4″ steel.

DRIVE: Separate gear train for each ground wheel.

BEARINGS: Roller for ground wheel and intermediate gear. Shielded ball for fly-knife reel.

HEIGHT OF CUT: 4.00 x 12 tires, 1 1/2″ to 3 1/2″.

ADJUSTMENTS: Done entirely by hand.

Model "G" Tractor

with Self-Lift Ranger.

The Self-Lift Ranger when used with any tractor, is unexcelled for maintaining fast cutting schedules on widely separated areas. It's faster on the grass . . . faster on the highway, too, when used with the 40-mile-per-hour Model "G" Tractor. The Ranger's cutting units are famous Grass Blitzers which are noted for smooth cutting at high speeds. Travel wheels raised or lowered hydraulically from driver's seat.

GENERAL: Available with either three Blitzer or three Fairway units. Specifications of cutting units are the same as listed on page 2 and 3, but with the addition of the following:

LIFTING MECHANISM: Hydraulic ram raises or lowers travel wheels. Pressure is supplied by automotive starting motor, hydraulic pump, reservoir and valves. Electric cable connects starting motor and push button switch on tractor. Release valve is controlled from tractor seat.

FRAMES: Fully articulated. In transport position, mowers and frames become rigid, eliminating bobbing and swaying.

CUTTING SWATH: 7′.

Ranger Assembly

for Farm Tractors.

The Ranger Assembly, combined with either a Ford, John Deere "40," International "300," Oliver "55," "Massey-Harris "50" or Ferguson Tractor, makes a low-cost mowing unit that's ideal for cutting widely-separated turf areas. This easy-to-install Ranger utilizes the three-point hydraulic lift system of the tractors to raise or lower the mowers. The assembly incorporates three standard 30-inch Blitzer mowers that produce a 7-foot cutting swath.

GENERAL: Available with either three Blitzer or three Fairway units. Specifications of cutting units are the same as listed on page 2 and 3, but with the addition of the following:

LIFTING MECHANISM: The three-point hydraulic lift system of the tractor is utilized to raise or lower the mowers. Units are raised high enough to permit tractor to climb curbs with ease.

FRAMES: Fully articulated. In transport position, mowers and frames become rigid, eliminating bobbing and swaying.

Ranger Attachment

for Farmall Cub Tractors.

The Three-Gang Ranger Attachment for Farmall Cub Tractors combines fast cutting with easy between-job travel. With two cutting units mounted directly in front of the drive wheels, and a third located behind the wheels, the Ranger trims right up to obstructions. Mowers are raised hydraulically and locked in position for safe highway travel and curb climbing. Cutting units are standard Fairway mowers.

GENERAL: The Ranger has been approved by the International Harvester Company for use on the Farmall Cub and its use will in no way affect the warranty of the tractor.

CUTTING WIDTH: 30 inches (each unit).

OVERALL CUTTING SWATH: 80 inches.

WHEELS: Pressed steel discs with demountable rims. Pneumatic-tired wheel optional.

GEARS: Machine-cut, heat-treated.

REVOLVING KNIVES: 8″ diameter reel. 5-blade standard, 6-blade optional. Blades of specially heat-treated alloy attached to shaft by 5 steel discs. All parts electrically welded.

OTHER SPECIFICATIONS: Same as listed under Fairway Gang Mowers on page 2.

WORTHINGTON MOWER COMPANY

STROUDSBURG, PENNSYLVANIA

Worthington Mows it... Better... Faster... Cheaper

Ranger Attachment

for Massey-Harris Pony Tractor.

The Ranger Attachment combines speedy mowing with fast between-job travel. The unit's mobility and ease of operation, makes it suited for maintaining widely separated grass areas. Cutting units mount directly on the tractor in full view of the operator. They are raised hydraulically and locked rigidly in position for highway travel and curb climbing. Fairway mowers are standard cutting units.

CUTTING WIDTH: 30 inches (each unit).
OVERALL CUTTING SWATH: 80 inches.
WHEELS: Pressed steel disc with demountable rims. Pneumatic-tired wheel optional.
GEARS: Machine cut, heat-treated.
REVOLVING KNIVES: 8″ diameter reel. 5-blade standard, 6-blade optional. Blades of specially heat-treated alloy, attached to shaft by 5 steel discs. All parts electrically welded.
BED KNIFE: Oil-hardened special alloy steel.
BEARINGS: Roller on ground wheels and intermediate gears. Shielded ball on fly knife reel and rear roller.
HEIGHT OF CUT: Steel wheels, 11/32″ to 2¾″.
ADJUSTMENTS: Done entirely by hand.

Model "72P" Rotary

The Model "72P" Rotary is a heavy-duty mowing unit for use with an existing tractor. This Rotary can be used with a Ford, Feguson, Massey Harris 22, John Deere 40, or any similar tractor with a three-point hitch. In dense brush or light grass, when you have a Model "72P" behind your tractor your mowing problems are solved. You get a smooth, clean mowing job with this easy-to-maneuver unit.

WIDTH OF CUT: 72″.
POWER REQUIRED: Standard two-plow tractor.
FRAME: Welded steel construction.
MAIN DRIVE: Power-take-off shaft equipped wi 2 Blood Brothers needle bearing universals—50 hp. rated.
GEAR BOX: Special heavy-duty—60 hp. rated Timken roller bearing equipped. Oil flood lubricated.
GEARS: Forged steel, machined and heat-treate
CUTTER SPINDLES: Timken roller bearing equippe
CUTTER BLADES: Twin arms, suction-lift type, staggered. Precision ground knives made of speci alloy, oil-hardened steel for long cutting life.
HEIGHT OF CUT: Fully adjustable from ground level up to 24 inches.
LEAF MULCHING ATTACHMENT: Sold separatel

Triplex Mower

The Triplex Mower with its 85″ swath can easily mow up to 30 acres per day. The Triplex has three 30″ Fairway type mowers that cut the grass ahead of the wheels and prevent streaking. The unit, with automotive type steering is powered by an 8.4 hp. 4-cycle air-cooled engine. Mower has cutting speeds up to 6 mph. and can climb grades up to 36%.

ENGINE: 8.4 hp.
SPEEDS: 3—Forward; 1—Reverse.
MOWING SPEEDS: Up to 8 mph.
STEERING: Automotive wheel.
TURNING RADIUS: Approximately 18″
LENGTH OVERALL: 72″.
HEIGHT OVERALL: 42¼″.
WIDTH OVERALL: 46½″ Wing units raised. 89-5/16″ Wing units lowered.
HEIGHT OF CUT: ⅜″ to 2⅜″.
CUTTING SWATH: 85″.
REEL: 8″ diameter, 5-blade.
CUTTING ANGLE OF SIDE UNITS: 45° Above o below horizontal.
BRAKES: Automotive type.

Triplex Mower

with Snow Plow.

The Worthington Triplex, when equipped with a snow plow, gives the mower all-season utility at golf courses, parks, cemeteries, highways, estates, etc. The rugged, 8.4 hp. air-cooled engine has power to spare for plowing snow on sidewalks, driveways and parking areas at clubs, institutions or estates. It can be used effectively to plow around toll booths on turnpikes and to clear service areas.

GENERAL: The snow plow attachment for the Worthington Triplex mower can be installed at the factory or in the field. Further information an complete specifications can be obtained from your Worthington franchised dealer.

WORTHINGTON
MOWER COMPANY
STROUDSBURG, PENNSYLVANIA

Litho in U.S.A.

Model 31R, 31-inch cut, self-propelled powered by 8 hp heavy-duty air cooled engine.

. . . all easy for you with DEVERE Rotary POWER MOWERS

Heavy duty performance . . . at LOW COST!

These mowers can take it! You can run them by the hour . . . up hill and down . . . over any kind of terrain . . . cut high, thick grass that would stall other mowers. You can trim neatly, cut backward as well as forward, edge close to trees and shrubs, do a fast, smooth job in less time.

Unique "suction-lift" holds grass in position for the high-speed cutters, giving you uniform results on all kinds of grass or weed growth.

Powerful, easy-starting motors, rugged transmissions and chassis and positive controls insure dependability and low maintenance. There's a Devere mower to fit every mowing requirement . . . 12 models from rider-type 32″ unit to handy, hand-pushed 18″ . . . the most comprehensive line of rotary mowers in the industry. Thousands of Devere mowers are in daily operation at parks, institutions and schools . . . your assurance of performance and satisfaction. Write for literature.

12 Different Models

Model 18—18″ hand-propelled trimmer
Model 18HD—18″ heavy duty, hand-propelled trimmer
Model 20—20″ heavy duty, hand-propelled
Model 420—20″ heavy duty, self-propelled
Model 22—22″ 3 H.P., self-propelled
Model 22V—Model 22 with variable speed
Model 24—24″ heavy duty, self-propelled
Model 24R—24″ with reverse
Model 31—31″ heavy duty, self-propelled
Model 31R—31″ with reverse
Model 27R—27″ self-propelled rider, reverse
Model 32R—32″ self-propelled rider, reverse

The Original Rotary Scythe Suction-Lift Mower With a Reverse

DEVERE COMPANY, RACINE WISCONSIN, U.S.A.

Quality Products Only—Since 1922

A 8630-1P

Ask The City That Owns One!

YOU CAN EXPECT YOUR *Eclipse*® LAWN MOWER TO LAST YEARS LONGER!

32" SPEEDWAY with riding sulky

● It's a proven fact that an Eclipse Lawn Mower can be expected to give you more years of low cost operation. Reports covering mowers in use 5, 10, 25 or even 50 years show how inexpensive it is to own an Eclipse. They're made to cut efficiently, last longer. Check the specifications below and you'll understand why those extra, exclusive features found in an Eclipse mower make it a top value . . . assure consistent mowing satisfaction for years to come. No mowing job is too big or too tough for an Eclipse—and there's a model for every need. Leaf mulchers are available for all rotaries.

MODEL "L" HAND MOWER — TORNADO SICKLE BAR MOWER — 21" PARKHOUND

Reel, Rotary, Sickle Bar Types—19 Power and 5 Hand Models

ECLIPSE REEL TYPE AND SICKLE BAR POWER MOWERS

MODEL	TYPE	WIDTH OF CUT	HEIGHT OF CUT	ENGINE 4 CYCLE—B&S H.P.	RATED R.P.M.	STARTER	DRIVE	LUBRICATION	DAILY ACREAGE CAPACITY	RIDING SULKY
Lark	Reel	18"	½"-1½"*	1.75	3200	Reccil	Diamond Roller Chain	Oil cups	....	No
Bel Mar	Reel	18"	½"-1½"	1.75	3200	Rope	Diamond Roller Chain	Oil cups	....	No
Rocket Deluxe	Reel	20"	¾"-1½"*	1.75	3200	Recoil or 110V. elect.	¼" Diamond Roller Chain	Oil cups	....	Optional Extra
Parkhound	Reel	21"	¾"-1½"	2.25	3600	Recoil or 110V. elect.	5/16" Diamond Roller Chain	Zerk fittings	2-4	Optional Extra
Rolloway	Reel	25"	¾"-2½"	2.5	3600	Rope	5/16" Diamond Roller Chain	Zerk fittings	3-5	Optional Extra
Speedway	Reel	32"	1"-2½"	5.1	3200	Crank	⅜" Diamond Roller Chain	Zerk fittings	7-15	Optional Extra
Tornado	Sickle Bar	36"	¾" or 2"	2	3600	Rope	5/16" Diamond Roller Chain	Zerk fittings	....	No

*Also available in Hi-Cut Model to cut from 1½" to 2½".
Only Eclipse mowers have fatigue-free, natural-grip handles.
All reel type mowers have adjustable reel bearings and are available with automatic sharpeners (optional extra).

ECLIPSE ROTARY POWER MOWERS

MODEL	TYPE	WIDTH OF CUT	HEIGHT OF CUT	ENGINE 4 CYCLE—B&S H.P.	RATED R.P.M.	STARTER	DRIVE	WHEEL BEARINGS	HOUSING	SULKY
Pal	Rotary	17"	1"-2" & 2⅞"	Power Products 2 cycle Develops 2 H.P. at 3400 R.P.M.		Rope	Vertical shaft	Steel Roller Bearings Through-out	One piece pressed Steel Housing	No
Duo-Master	Rotary	17"	1"-1½" 2¼"-3"	1.75	3600	Rope or Recoil	Direct connected (Special safety slip coupling)			No
Duo-Master	Rotary	19"	1"-1½" 2¼"-3"	2.25	3600	Recoil or 110V. elect.	Direct connected (Special safety slip coupling)			No
Century	Rotary	20"	1"-3"	2.25	3600	Recoil	Direct connected (Special safety slip coupling)			No
Duo-Master	Rotary	21"	1"-1½" 2¼"-3"	2.75	3600	Recoil or 110V. elect.	Direct connected (Special safety slip coupling)		Aluminum Housing	No

ECLIPSE HAND MOWERS

MODEL	WIDTH OF CUT	HEIGHT OF CUT	REEL	CUTTER BLADE ADJUSTMENT	WHEELS	ROLLER	HANDLE
*Eclipse "L" (Std.)	16" or 18"	½"-1½"	5 blade, 4 spider reel, cylindrically ground	Single thumb screw	Rubber-tired	Rubber-covered	All steel natural grip
*Eclipse "L" (Hi-Cut)	16"	1"-2"	5 blade, 4 spider reel, cylindrically ground	Single thumb screw	Rubber-tired	Rubber-covered	All steel natural grip
Arlington	16" or 18"	½"-1½"	5 blade, 4 spider reel, cylindrically ground	4 Micro-adjusting screw	Rubber-tired	Seasoned maple	Seasoned maple

*Models equipped with automatic self-sharpeners.

THE ECLIPSE LAWN MOWER CO. Div. of Buffalo-Eclipse Corporation **728 Railroad St. • Prophetstown, Ill.**

GRAVELY TRACTORS, INC.

Box 78, Dunbar, W. Va.

SWEEP WALKS—DRIVES WINTER OR SUMMER

BLOW SNOW AWAY

MOW LAWN AREAS

MOW GRASS OR WEEDS MULCH LEAVES

NEW STEERING SULKY for Fast Mowing . . . Accurate Control

The NEW Steering Sulky makes handling the big Gravely 75-Inch Gang Mowers as easy as driving your car—with power steering!
One finger on sharp turns . . instant, *accurate* mowing and trimming. Mows a circle 14″ in diameter . . . makes extreme right and left maneuvers with one full turn of the steering wheel!

30 ATTACHMENTS

Steering sulky and Gangs are only TWO of the 30 attachments for the Gravely Tractor that will save time, work and costs on your maintenance jobs. . . . On special order there are available such attachments as Lawn Aerator, Lawn Sweeper, 5′ Seeder-Spreader, Drill for making holes for planting shrubbery, etc. . . . In fact, from large-area mowing to sidewalk snow removal, the powerful 5-HP Gravely will do your maintenance jobs faster, easier, better—all year long!

THREE MODELS . . . To Fit YOUR Work

Gravely now offers three models, with ground speeds to fit your particular jobs. The LS Model is geared to a ground speed maximum of 2 MPH; the LI to a maximum speed of 3 MPH; the L to a maximum speed of 4 MPH. Write for Free Catalog—or FREE DEMONSTRATION at absolutely no obligation.

FREE
Write for 24-Page Illustrated Booklet today.

POWER vs. Drudgery

HAUL HALF-TON LOADS

GRAVELY

NEW SELF STARTER OPTIONAL EQUIPMENT

GRAVELY TRACTORS, INC.

BOX 78 **DUNBAR, W. VA.**

HAL-GAN PRODUCTS, INC.

13000 W. Blue Mound Road, Elm Grove, Wisconsin
Phone Milwaukee, SUnset 2-8500

The powerful suction-action of the Spinaway blades lift matted and flat-lying grasses into the cutting zone where they are slashed into a fine mulch. Spinaway Mowers easily handle weeds, undergrowth, seedlings, etc., even large pine cones or small tree branches will not clog mower or injure the Spinaway blades.

• SPINAWAY FEATURES •

- Spinaway Mowers are the product of many years of experience in the design and manufacture of heavy-duty rotary mowers. They are exceptionally well-balanced which makes them easier to handle and maneuver and much easier on the operator.
- Spinaway Mowers are safer to use, they have a ***completely enclosed cutter unit*** with adjustable front and free-swinging, hinged, rear guards which ***prevent throwing.*** They will cut close to trees, shrubs, walks, walls and other objects. Height of cut is quickly adjustable. Blades are easily sharpened by filing.
- Spinaway Mowers are equipped with ball, roller or needle bearing wheels. Self-propelled models 26 and 31 have pneumatic rear tires and semi-pneumatic front tires. Smaller models have semi-pneumatic tires.
- ***Spinaway Mowers are noted for their sturdy construction, efficient operation and long trouble-free performance.***

New
HAND-PROPELLED
★ MODEL 18

Powerful • Light-weight TRIMMER-MOWER

Trims close and clean from either side and also mows a full 18 inches. 2½ hp. 4 cycle engine.

Spinaway

ROTARY SUCTION MOWERS

SELF-PROPELLED
★ MODEL 31

8 hp. 4 cycle ENGINE

•

Twin disc clutch

•

2 speeds forward

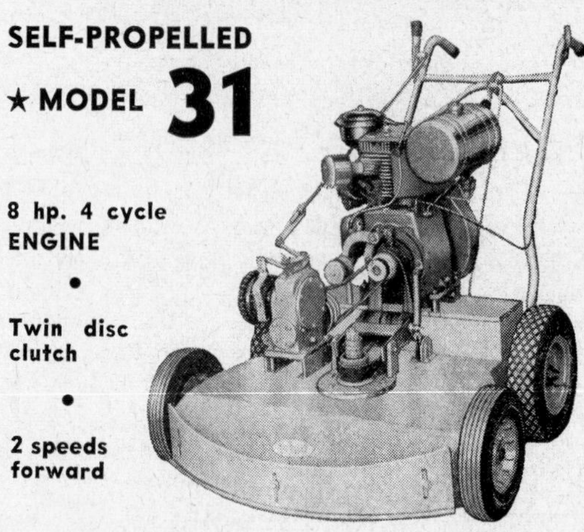

Full 31 inch cut. Easily mows up to eight acres a day at normal operating speeds. Reverse Gear running in oil and Riding Sulky optional.

★ MODEL 20. Hand propelled; full 20 inch cut. A favorite for mowing smaller areas and working around flower beds and shrubbery.

★ MODEL 26. Self propelled; full 26 inch cut. 6 hp. 4 cycle engine. Twin disc clutch. Reverse Gear running in oil and Riding Sulky optional.

Leaf Mulching attachments available for all models.

★ MODEL 10. ROTARY TRIMMER: Hand propelled; Economical close trimming and edging. Full 10 inch cut. 1.6 hp. engine.

Write for descriptive folder and prices

POWER IMPLEMENT DIVISION
McDONOUGH POWER EQUIPMENT, INC.

formerly Southern Saw Works
Established 1890
McDonough, Georgia

SNAPPIN' TURTLE MOWERS

The 3 models of Snappin' Turtle, one 19" and two 25" . . . are all self-propelled, power reverse rotaries . . . the safest on the market, with heavy 12 gauge steel decks. No Wheels; they glide on Skid Pan and Roller (See underside cut). Powered with 2¾ to 6 HP, heavy duty 4 cycle engines, they climb steep banks, cut clean, trim close. Handle tenderest grass or tough weeds. Riding Sulkies available. Leaf mulchers available. A dream to handle . . . truly America's finest mower.

SNAPPER THIRTY

An easy handling, rugged piece of equipment that gives a perfect 30" cut. Powered with 6½ HP, 4 cycle heavy duty engine, the Snapper Thirty climbs steep banks under its own power. Features the sensational Channel Spray Grass Chute that sprays the grass clippings out in a fine even pattern. Eliminates clumps and windrows.

BIG SNAPPER 36

Big Snapper is a rugged, heavy duty mower with a full 36" cut. 8 hp. 4 cycle engines. Also features the Channel Spray Grass Chute. Cut clean on the finest lawns or the most rugged terrain, up to 15 acres a day with ease. Easy to maneuver. Model with electric self starter also available.

The Snapper Line also includes 19" and 25" Snappin' Turtle Riding Mowers and 18 and 20" Rotary mowers, both self-propelled and push-type. All are expertly designed, ruggedly built for long continuous use.

THE PROVEN MOWERS FOR MUNICIPAL WORK!
WRITE FOR FREE LITERATURE

POWER DEVELOPMENT COMPANY, INC.

MILLS ROAD DEPT. M AVON, OHIO

THE *SCIMITAR* MULTI-PURPOSE POWEROLL

An all purpose lawn roller for park, municipal and school maintenance crews.

Equipped with a 3 HP, 4 cycle air cooled gas engine, roller chain, forward and reverse drives, a 10 gauge x 24″ OD x 35″ wide electric welded drum, steering roller is 10 ga. x 14″ OD x 20″ wide.

Weight approximately ½ ton when filled with water.

THE SCIMITAR, JR. *SELF-PROPELLED* LAWN ROLLER

A practical lightweight roller that when filled with water weighs 525 lbs.

A well constructed roller powered with a 1½ HP, 4 cycle air cooled gas engine.

Moving parts are shielded—yet simple and easy to get at for adjusting purposes.

Will not tip—has safety bars back and front.

So well balanced that you get maximum weight at the point roller meets the ground.

THE SCIMITAR SELF-PROPELLED ROTARY MOWER

Cuts extremely heavy weed growth as easily as it mows finely kept lawns.

A daily eight hour cutting capacity of six acres has been proved in actual test.

The whirling action of the Scimitar blade eliminates windrows of cut grass as the mower scatters the cuttings evenly as it cuts a 24″ swath. The cuttings also act as a beneficial mulch.

Platform Construction allows flush cutting.

Powered by a 4 cycle air cooled 3 HP engine.

An automatic governor maintains an even walking speed through light and heavy grass and weed growth.

A Scimitar Sulky is also available to reduce operator fatigue. The Sulky is a rubber tired all welded piece of equipment with a comfortable saddle seat.

WOOD BROTHERS MANUFACTURING COMPANY

27700 South 4th Street • Oregon, Illinois

WOOD'S TRACTOR ROTARIES

For Economical Lawn Mowing, Weed Control and Leaf Disposal

- 42 to 114-inch cutting width
- Less expensive to maintain
- Staggered blades for cleanest cut
- Heavy duty construction—long life

These high speed Wood's Tractor Mowers clip fine grass, shred and mulch leaves or cut brush. Easy to maneuver close to buildings. Cutting height adjustable from 1 inch to 14 inches (most models). Equipped with V-belt drive to absorb sudden shock; 3/16" boiler plate housing; 15" dropcenter wheels or 8" non-pneumatic tires. All working parts enclosed.

MODEL 42C
Mounts quickly on Farmall Cub

MODEL 80
Operates off 2-3 plow tractors

12 MODELS FOR EVERY TRACTOR · TRAILER OR MOUNTED

CUTTING WIDTH AND TRACTOR NEEDED	NO. OF CUTTER BLADES	LEAF MULCHER AVAILABLE (YES OR NO)	V-BELTS IN DRIVE (NUMBER)
114" pull-type for 3-4 Plow	3	No	6
80" pull-type for 2-3 Plow	2	Yes	3
80" offset pull-type for 2-3 Plow	2	Yes	4
80" rear-mounted for 2-3 Plow with 3 point hitch and Fast-Hitch Farmall 300 or 400	2	Yes	3
61" pull-type for 2-Plow	2	Yes	3
61" rear-mounted for 2-Plow with 3 point hitch and Fast-Hitch Farmall 300 or 400	2	Yes	3
42" under-mounted for Farmall Super A or 100	1	Yes	1
42" under-mounted for Farmall Cub	1	Yes	1
42" under-mounted for Farmall Lo-Boy	1	Yes	1
42" rear-mounted for Farmall Cub and Lo-Boy with fast-hitch	1	Yes	1
42" under-mounted for M-H Pony and Pacer	1	Yes	1
42" under-mounted for AC-Model G	1	Yes	1

WHY THE BIG WHEELS HAVE IT . . . FOR MUNICIPAL USERS ALL OVER AMERICA!

- Outstanding Performance!
- Simplicity of Repair!
- Low Upkeep!
- Easy Maneuverability!

Model 7C-66-27-SP

HERE ARE THE UNBEATABLE FEATURES OF AMERICA'S FINEST POWER MOWER

ENGINE—Clinton 6.0 hp 4-cycle air-cooled.

DRIVE—Double V-Belt to furnish maximum horse power.

CUTTING HEIGHT—1" to 3½".

CUTTING WIDTH—27".

WHEELS—Rear, 20" Disc heavy duty with adjustable cone type ball bearings and semi-pneumatic tires. Front, 6 x 1.75 with ½" ball bearings, semi-pneumatic tires.

BLADE—One-piece tempered spring steel with full cutting edge for maximum mulching effect. Easily removed to resharpen.

BLADE SHAFT ASSEMBLY — Equipped with factory-sealed ball bearings and case-hardened shaft.

MOTOR MOUNT—¾" Exterior plywood.

FRAME—Heavy duty tubular and sheet steel construction. Mower is self-propelled through gear reduction unit and over-running ratchets to both rear wheels with hand mechanism for disengaging clutch.

SHIPPING WT.—Approx. 242 lbs.

Equipped for riding sulky. Two forwara speeds. Adjustable handles. Both Front and Side trim feature.

COLOR—Red.

See How Yazoo Master Mowers Out-Perform All Others!

WRITE, WIRE OR CALL TODAY FOR CATALOG, PRICES, COMPLETE INFORMATION!

YAZOO MANUFACTURING COMPANY

3607 Livingston Road • Phone 6-6421 • Jackson, Mississippi

John BEAN

DIVISION OF FOOD MACHINERY AND CHEMICAL CORP.

Lansing 4, Mich. San Jose 1, California

PROTECT YOUR TREES with a John BEAN 100-ROTOMIST

You'll spray more per day with a 100-Rotomist because of these exclusive features:

GREATEST "RATE OF WORK" CAPACITY OF ANY MIST SPRAYER—STRAIGHT-THOUGH AIR DISCHARGE WITH AXIAL FLOW FAN—HYDRAULIC TURN-TABLE AND AIRPLANE TYPE CONTROLS—HIGH PRESSURE PUMP WITH "SAPPHITE" LIFE-TIME CYLINDERS

Providing the greatest "rate of work" capacity on the market, the John Bean 100-Rotomist gives you 28,000 cubic feet per minute of air volume, spray delivery to the micro-mist nozzle at 400 pounds pressure and 100-gallon tank capacity. In a day's time, you spray more trees and larger areas more effectively. A Rotomist works fast, yet assures thorough coverage and penetration with minimum use of spray materials.

Operators like the Rotomist's effortless hydrualic 360° rotation and full 110° vertical pivoting . . . its spring-filled seat and back rest. Budget-wise owners like its fully enclosed transmission and plunger-type pump, both with positive lubrication . . . among the many outstanding features that mean trouble-free operation.

You'll get MULTIPLE COST-SAVING USE from your Rotomist on these additional jobs:

LEAF WINDROWING (proven labor savings on big grounds)
FLY AND MOSQUITO CONTROL—SANITATION

Model 100-TE

THE 75-ROTOMIST—BIG CAPACITY MIST SPRAYING *plus* ECONOMY

Model 100-E, truck-mounted.

Straight-through air delivery from the axial-flow fan puts 19,000 cubic feet of air at your command. High-Pressure spray is delivered from the 75-gal. tank at 400 PSI. Fan assembly counterbalanced for easy, manual, 360° rotation and tilting through 110° arc. Automatic centrifugal clutch. Oil-bath pump with life-time cylinders.

Both the 100 and the medium capacity 75-Rotomist (shown above) come in trailer-mounted models as well as for truck mounting.

NEW PESTAIRE SANITATION SPRAYER

. . . the mist sprayer specially designed for fly & mosquito control in recreation areas. Saves time, labor and spray materials.

COMPACT—LIGHT IN WEIGHT—EASY TO OPERATE—
Manual 360° Rotation—Large Air Volume for Rapid Coverage

WRITE FOR DETAILS TODAY!

CONTROL DUST...

Quickly, Effectively, Economically with Gulf Sani-Soil-Set

GULF SANI-SOIL-SET is the practical answer to *your* dust annoyance problems. Here are a few of the many good reasons why it will pay you to investigate this efficient dust-control medium now:

HIGHLY EFFECTIVE—Gulf Sani-Soil-Set eliminates dust annoyance completely immediately after application.

LONG LASTING—Remains effective for long periods because of its extremely low volatility and insolubility in water. One application per season or year is usually sufficient.

EASILY APPLIED—Free-flowing, can be applied by hand-sprinkling or by sprinkling truck, and spreads quickly.

SAVES MAINTENANCE EXPENSE—Gulf Sani-Soil-Set minimizes dust annoyance and cleaning expense.

Contact your nearest Gulf office today and ask for a demonstration of the advantages of this modern proven dust allayer. Or write to the address below for a copy of the pamphlet which gives complete details.

GULF OIL CORPORATION • GULF REFINING COMPANY

1822 Gulf Building, Pittsburgh 30, Pa.

AMERICAN BRIDGE

DIVISION OF UNITED STATES STEEL CORPORATION

GENERAL OFFICES: 525 WILLIAM PENN PLACE, PITTSBURGH, PA.

Contracting Offices in: AMBRIDGE · ATLANTA · BALTIMORE · BIRMINGHAM · BOSTON · CHICAGO · CINCINNATI CLEVELAND · DALLAS · DENVER · DETROIT · ELMIRA · GARY · HOUSTON · LOS ANGELES · MEMPHIS · MINNEAPOLIS · NEW YORK ORANGE, TEXAS · PHILADELPHIA · PITTSBURGH · PORTLAND, ORE. · ROANOKE · ST. LOUIS · SAN FRANCISCO · TRENTON

UNITED STATES STEEL EXPORT COMPANY, NEW YORK

UNITED STATES STEEL

STEEL-DECK STADIUMS AND GRANDSTANDS

Sugar Bowl Stadium
Tulane University
New Orleans, La.
Largest steel-deck stadium in the world.

Combining the inherent qualities of strength, safety and durability, steel-deck stadiums and grandstands cost less to build and less to maintain than other types of permanent construction.

They are easily adapted to any local requirements as to size and design . . . and to ground contour without extensive grading. They are easy to extend by adding standard sections at the ends, or by double-decking. The watertight steel plates form a perfect roof for room facilities beneath the stadium for lockers, showers, classrooms, concession booths, etc.

Our more than 30 years of technical and practical experience in this specialized field assures you of the finest steel-deck construction obtainable anywhere. We scientifically plot and design every job for maximum spectator comfort and convenience. Cost estimates furnished without obligation for definite projects. For free consultation, please address your inquiry to our nearest office.

USS AMBRIDGE STEEL SWIMMING POOLS

Available in standard "Pleasure and Regulation Pool" sizes: Pleasure Pools of 20′ x 40′, 50′ and 60′; Regulation Pools of 42′ x 82′6″, 35′ x 75′, and 35′ x 105′. We welcome an opportunity to help you select and install the pool best suited to your needs, including "T" or "L" shaped pools.

The revolutionary, new USS AMBRIDGE *Steel* Swimming Pool, because of its all-steel construction, is the most durable type on the market. It is the result of more than a decade of research, experimentation, and testing by the world's largest fabricator and erector of structural steelwork. The copper-bearing, rust-resistive steel sections fit snugly and easily together. Prefabricated sections are permanently welded watertight. *It will never crack* or be troubled by freezing or frost action. And, except for an occasional coat of paint, it requires no maintenance. Write or phone our nearest office for more information.

CYCLONE FENCE DEPARTMENT

AMERICAN STEEL AND WIRE DIVISION
UNITED STATES STEEL CORPORATION

General Offices: Waukegan, Illinois

FACTORIES—Waukegan, Ill.; Newark, N. J.; Fort Worth, Texas; Greensburg, Ind.; DeKalb, Ill.; Oakland, Calif.

UNITED STATES STEEL

CYCLONE NON-CLIMBABLE CHAIN LINK FENCE

U•S•S Cyclone Non-Climbable Fence is the same as Cyclone Invincible Fence except that the barbed wire arms at the top extend out on both sides of the fence instead of only one. The barbed wire may be set in an A-shape as shown in the illustration, or inverted into a V-shape atop the chain link fence. Non-climbable comes in either No. 6 or No. 9 gauge wire woven in a two-inch chain link mesh.

Cyclone Non-Climbable Fence stands at the very top of the list of fences which are designed to keep outsiders out. When you consider the tremendous damage that can be perpetrated by a single marauder of criminal intent or by a mentally-deficient person around a water reservoir or power plant, the outlay for fence affording such positive protection seems small indeed.

CYCLONE STEEL PICKET FENCE

This is a dignified and beautiful fence ideally suited for schools, cemeteries and similar municipal property. It affords a high degree of protection from trespassers and marauders.

Like other types of Cyclone Fence, it can be built to desired height and with various combinations of posts, gates, rails and the like. Gates and posts often are specially made in accordance with architect's specifications for individual designs.

U•S•S Cyclone Picket Fence is ordinarily finished in the standard black paint.

CYCLONE'S 4 POPULAR STYLES OF CHAIN-LINK FENCE

"SAFEGUARD"

This fence is ideal for schools, suburban homes, estates — effectively guards your grounds from trespassers. A good-looking fence that blends well into landscaping plans.

"INVINCIBLE"

Gives positive protection at comparatively low cost. Three strands of barbed wire strung on extension arms above fabric. Extension arms can be set vertically or at a 45° angle either inside or outside fence line.

"NON-CLIMBABLE"

This top construction is positively discouraging to thieves and marauders. "A"-shaped extension arms hold five strands of four-pronged aluminum barbed wire extended over both sides of the vertical fence line.

"VICTORY"

If preferred, Cyclone "Victory" extension arms can be furnished. "V"-shaped with six strands of barbed wire. Topmost strands are 12 inches above fabric. This type of construction is the ultimate in Property Protection Fence.

CYCLONE FENCE DEPARTMENT

AMERICAN STEEL AND WIRE DIVISION
UNITED STATES STEEL CORPORATION

General Offices: Waukegan, Illinois

FACTORIES—Waukegan, Ill.; Newark, N. J.; Fort Worth, Texas; Greensburg, Ind.; DeKalb, Ill.; Oakland, Calif.

UNITED STATES STEEL

CYCLONE TENNIS ENCLOSURES AND BACKSTOPS

The same qualities which make Cyclone a fine fence make it equally good for tennis court enclosures and backstops. In fact, Cyclone is standard specification in many of the finest tennis clubs in the country.

The sturdy H-column posts, firmly set in concrete, will stand much more use and abuse than ordinary posts. The fence fabric, itself, is the same high standard chain link that goes into all Cyclone fences. The mesh, however, is 1¾-inch and the wire is No. 11 gauge, hot-dip galvanized after weaving.

Baseball backstops for either soft or hard ball are offered with overhang at the top or straight up. Baseball backstops may be constructed according to your design or from those in our files.

CYCLONE WIRE MESH WINDOW GUARDS

FRAMES: Either 1" channel, ¾" channel or ⅜" round iron.

FABRIC: No. 10 gauge wire, woven in 1½" diamond mesh is standard. Always furnish exact opening sizes for estimates and quotations. All guards given heavy coat of special black metal paint.

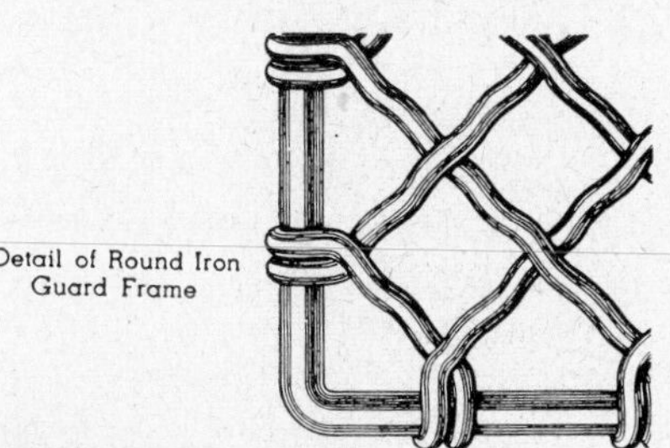

Detail of Round Iron Guard Frame

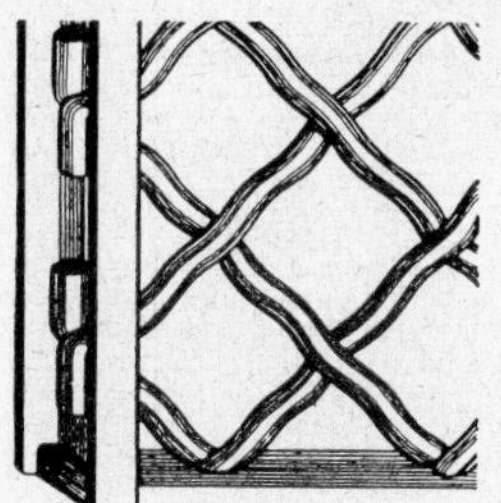

Detail of Channel Iron Frame

COMPLETE RESPONSIBILITY—NATIONWIDE SERVICE

Cyclone engineers will make a complete study of your fencing requirements and submit recommendations, layouts and estimates of cost; then carry out the erection of the fence if you desire. For more complete information write for our book, "Your Fence—How to Choose It—How to Use It." Also for our folder giving detailed specifications for Cyclone Fence and other wire products used for municipal properties. And remember—NO JOB IS TOO LARGE—NO JOB IS TOO SMALL FOR CYCLONE.

MAINTENANCE FREE

NEVER REQUIRES PAINTING

WHY COATED WIRE FENCES RUST

The mesh joint of coated ferrous metal fencing is the most vulnerable point of wear. At this junction of wires, constant abrasion occurs which eventually wears through the coating and exposes the raw metal to the elements. This is where ordinary fence fails.

NICHOLS "Solid" ALUMINUM FENCING has no coating to chip, crack or wear through.

IT'S RUSTPROOF!

- IT IS VIRTUALLY MAINTENANCE FREE
- IT BLENDS BEAUTIFULLY WITH ANY ARCHITECTURAL STYLE AND LANDSCAPE DESIGN
- IT ELIMINATES PAINTING EXPENSE
- Write for informative 16-page catalog giving full details.

QUALIFIED FENCE ERECTORS

From coast-to-coast are NICHOLS franchised dealers who have qualified to display the certificate of merit shown at right as certified NICHOLS "Never-Stain" Aluminum Chain Link Fence erectors, a protection to you that assures a professional installation at the right price.

Authorized Distributor

NEVER-STAIN Aluminum Chain Link Fencing

This is to Certify that John Doe Fence Co. is an Authorized Distributor of and is duly qualified to sell and erect Never-Stain Aluminum Chain Link Fencing, a product of Nichols Wire & Aluminum Company, Davenport, Iowa.

NICHOLS WIRE & ALUMINUM COMPANY
Davenport, Iowa

Dated Feb. 1st 1956

nichols NEVER-STAIN ®

NICHOLS

Chain Link Fencing

LONG LASTING

RUSTPROOF

SPECIFICATIONS		
GAUGE	HEIGHT — INCHES	WEIGHT PER 100 FT. — POUNDS
9* (.148") dia.	36	77
	42	90
	48	102
	60	128
	72	154
	84	179
	96	205
	108	230
	120	255
6** (.192") dia.	36	130
	42	152
	48	172
	60	216
	72	258
	84	300
	96	344
	108	388
	120	432

*9 gauge — 100 feet per roll
**6 gauge — 50 feet per roll

Also available in 132" and 144" heights. Heights 36", 42" and 48" — selvages knuckled and barbed. Heights 60" and over, selvages barbed and barbed. 2" Mesh.

Aluminum barbed wire

SPECIFICATIONS				
DIAMETER	DIAMETER	NO. OF POINTS	LENGTH PER SPOOL FEET	WGT. PER SPOOL POUNDS
.110"	.080"	4	132	40

WIRE & ALUMINUM CO.

DAVENPORT, IOWA

LEAVITT PRODUCTS COMPANY

218 Griggs Street, Urbana, Illinois

Leavitt Bleachers have seated millions wherever crowds assemble, since 1895.

LEAVITT

STANDS ... ANY CROWD... ANY LOCATION

Leavitt Company began making bleachers in 1895 and, in 1911, helped pioneer the first portable wood bleachers. Leavitt understructure is all-steel, shop-welded . . . seat and foot boards carry weight only—are not used for bracing. Seat boards tilted for comfort, drainage in wet weather . . . backrail offset for comfort. Leavitt stands are recognized as the world's best.

KNOCKDOWN WOOD BLEACHERS

KNOCKDOWN's are a completely portable bleacher. Years of comfort and service have made the name *KNOCKDOWN* a famous one; many of these bleachers are still in use after more than 30 years dependable service, season after season. Available in any lengths, and heights from 2 to 20 tiers. Load capacities greatly exceed legal requirements. Only a minimum space is required for storage when dismantled. Cast connectors keep seat boards straight and tight fitting. Patented stringer tie safety-locks unit. Many other features.

"FAST-LOCK" STEEL BLEACHERS

"FAST-LOCK" Portable Steel Stands, a completely portable bleacher of all-steel understructure. Spring-loaded pins enable all-steel factory-welded panels to be fastened quickly together *without tools* of any kind! Rapidly and easily dismantled or erected by only two men. Extra cross-braced . . . engineered for maximum loads . . . all members interchangeable . . . completely safe . . . indoor or outdoor use. Sloping seat boards for extra comfort, quick drainage in wet weather. Minimum storage space required. Budget priced.

ELEVATED GRANDSTAND

Constructed to permit easy expansion, either in height or length, to accommodate growing crowds. Eye level of front row occupants 7 feet above ground—permits standing room or box seat construction in front. Entrance gained by sloping ramp or steps; 10" wide seat boards tilted slightly to rear for maximum comfort; seat connections lapless; all-steel stands erected in 42 to 306 feet lengths, 6 to 25 tiers, 4 feet wide aisles, seats 186 to 5725 people.

NON-ELEVATED GRANDSTAND (PORTABLE)

All-steel understructure; each tower is a self-sustained supporting structure; seat connections lapless; stands erected in 42 to 306 feet lengths, 6 to 25 tiers, 4 feet wide aisles, seats 186 to 5725 people. Portable nature permits seasonal use indoors or out. Seat boards tilted slightly to rear give maximum comfort; extra wide (16") footboards for extra comfort and safety. As in all Leavitt stands, all steel members are ¼ inch thick; all shop connections are welded (riveting not permitted).

PERMANENT STEEL STADIUM

Leavitt ADD-A-SEAT Stadium is unsurpassed in appearance, comfort, safety, and economy. As the crowds grow, so can the stadium. All-steel understructure easily enclosed for dressing rooms, rest rooms, concession stands, etc. Aisles, ramps, other extras can be furnished and installed where desired. Erected on concrete piers; 12" seat boards tilted for comfort; 16" wide footboards; 4' wide aisles and walkways; unobstructed 6' wide exit ramps; completely enclosed by railing. ADD-A-SEAT can be moved if necessary!

HILLSIDE INSTALLATION

Note how easily Leavitt stands can take advantage of hillsides. Shown is an Elevated grandstand erected on concrete piers and installed on a hillside. Entrance to seating has been easily adapted to the top of each aisle, as well as the front walkway. The radio booth can be furnished and erected wherever the buyer desires, in this case just off the center of the stands.

Specifications for this installation are the same as Elevated grandstand described elsewhere on this page.

Write for Leavitt catalog giving full details about all Leavitt bleachers and grandstands.

LEAVITT PRODUCTS COMPANY, 218 GRIGGS STREET, URBANA, ILLINOIS

Leavitt Bleachers have seated millions wherever crowds assemble, since 1895.

ANCHOR FENCE

Division of ANCHOR POST PRODUCTS, INC.

6677 Eastern Avenue, Baltimore 24, Md. Sales Offices in Principal Cities

Where could you use Anchor Fence to protect people and property?

Municipal Authorities find Anchor Fence ideal for parks, public building grounds, school yards . . . in fact for countless municipal installations.

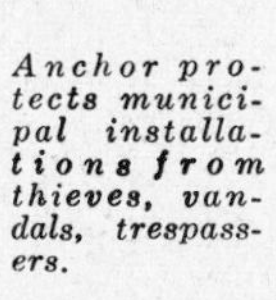

Anchor protects municipal installations from thieves, vandals, trespassers.

Anchor is used extensively around recreational areas. Assures complete privacy.

For over half a century Anchor Chain Link Fences and Gates have been erected to suit many varied requirements:

To protect municipal installations from thieves, vandals, trespassers.

To prevent malicious vandalism or desecration.

To prohibit illegal entrance, petty pilfering.

About Anchor's Nation-Wide Fencing Service. Reaching from coast to coast, it consists of more than two hundred sales offices backed up by our manufacturing plants in Baltimore, Houston and Los Angeles. Fully qualified representatives will advise you and relieve you of all measuring and erecting details. Trained crews of men are maintained at many of our sales offices, to insure you a well-done, economical job.

About the Anchor Chain Link Fence itself. Made by makers of America's first chain link fence, the Anchor Post Fence combines 4 outstanding construction features. First, is the Anchor Gate. This is built with a square tubular steel frame, arc-welded at the corners. The square shape of the heavy steel tubing plus corner welding result in exceptional strength . . . eliminates diagonal bracing or reinforcing . . . makes this gate outstanding for durability and beauty.

Second is the Square Anchor Terminal posts. They have no fabric holding bands, they provide no hand or footholds for climbing . . . increase protection. And they are handsome looking because of their trim lines.

Third is the Line Post structure. "H" shaped in cross section, it insures maximum strength and efficient drainage. Galvanized for long life, it will *Keep* it's attractive appearance.

Fourth is Drive Anchors. Anchor's method of drive anchor postsetting gives a ground grip like a tree. Engineered to imitate nature's firm hold, this method provides line posts with a broad foundation to defy frost, thaws and the many other strains to which fence is subjected.

Note: While drive-anchor method is recommended, post can also be set in concrete footings when desired.

For Anchor-Chain Link Fence Catalog containing full information about the four exclusive Anchor features that make an Anchor Chain Link Fence exceptionally attractive and durable. *Write for Anchor Chain Link Catalog.*

CONTINENTAL STEEL CORPORATION

General Offices: Kokomo, Indiana

DEPT. 19-C

Manufacturers of Chain Link Fence for All Purposes

STYLE 3B-R

STYLE NB-R

STYLE 5B-R

COMPLETE CHAIN LINK FENCE

To meet the fencing requirements of municipalities, Continental has developed a wide range of structural variations in its Chain Link fence. The selection in styles, heights, types of top construction, gates and accessories make it possible to select fence for any installtion.

10 STYLES

Continental offers 10 styles of top construrtion. The illustrations above show three popular styles of Continental fence protecting municipal property. It is engineered for each specific job.

GATES

Strong, easily operated gates and locks. Single and double types with improved pivot type hinges. Manually or mechanically operated.

POSTS AND FITTINGS

Continental fence has heavier, sturdier posts with improved brace construction. Top rails are joined by a special Inside-Outside coupling. Post caps and barbed wire arms are sturdy, heavier. Self-locking slots hold barb wire. New type lock pin eliminates bolts and nuts for fastening fabric to tension bands.

TAILORED TO FIT YOUR PROPERTY

No matter what your property protection problem, Continental engineers will work with you in laying out the most effective and economical installation—planned to harmonize with the character of municipal property, and provide the type of protection you want.

ENGINEERING AND ERECTION SERVICE

Our engineers are prepared to assist you in laying out the best installation for your purposes. Trained erection crews are available for correct and economical construction. When local labor is used Continental will supply competent foreman and inspection service.

*Trademark Reg. U. S. Pat. Off.

FABRIC OF KONIK STEEL

The wire fabric in Continental fence is made of KONIK for greater strength and rust resistance "clear through." KONIK* has high tensile strength and is tougher. This fabric carries a zinc coating applied by special process to insure uniformity and adhesion to the base steel. A uniform, bright finish enhances the appearance of Continental fence fabric. Wire is full gauge and woven in exact mesh.

Continental Sales Representatives are located in Principal Cities. Check with your nearest Representative, and he'll show you a Continental Installation . . . so you can see for yourself the added protection features Continental Fence offers.

SEND FOR FREE COPY

"PLANNED PROTECTION"

Get a copy of "Planned Protection" complete manual on modern protection and control of property. Write or phone the Continental Steel Corporation, or nearest sales office.

***CONTINENTAL *Chain Link* FENCE**

PAGE FENCE ASSOCIATION

Headquarters: Monessen, Pa.

Atlanta, Bridgeport, Chicago, Denver, Detroit
Los Angeles, New York, Philadelphia, San Francisco

America's First Wire Fence—Since 1883

WHAT MAKES A PAGE FENCE THE RIGHT FENCE FOR YOU?

Page Provides a Choice of Units that Best Meet Your Needs

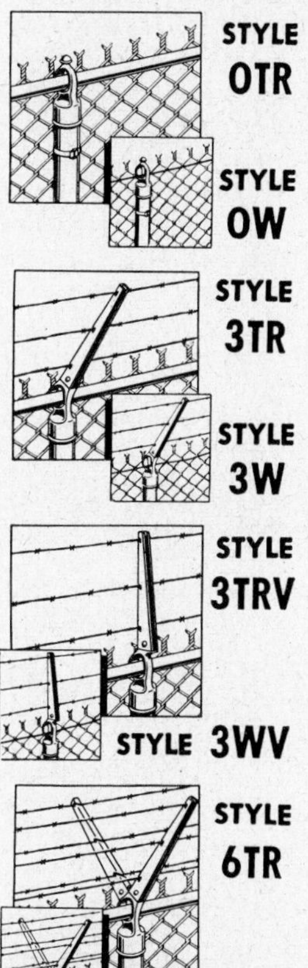

CHOOSE FROM:

- —8 Basic Fence Styles
- —8 Fence Heights
- —4 Fabric Metals
- —2 Types Metal Posts
- —6 Gate Styles
- —Single or Double Extension Arms
- —Barbed or Knuckled Fabric Edges
- —Top Rail or Top Wire

EIGHT STYLES — EIGHT HEIGHTS • **PAGE CHAIN LINK FENCE** is made in a variety of styles and heights from 5' to 12', both with and without barbed wire on Single or Double **EXTENSION ARMS. (See illustration at left.)** Because of added structural strength and fabric safeguarding, the use of **GALVANIZED PIPE TOP RAIL** is preferred, but when first cost must be kept at minimum, **PAGE ALUMINIZED STEEL WIRE** may be used.

FOUR SUPERIOR FABRIC METALS • 1. **ALUMINIZED STEEL WIRE,** developed and patented by **PAGE,** provides far longer corrosion resistance than zinc coating, yet its cost is comparable with fabric having shorter life expectancy. 2. **OPEN HEARTH STEEL WIRE,** galvanized after weaving in conformity with A.S.T.M. and Federal Specifications. 3. **STAINLESS STEEL,** immune to practically all corrosive elements and particularly advantageous near salt water, factory smoke, sulphur and other erodents. 4. **ALL-ALUMINUM,** another long-lasting, non-corrosive metal. It will not rust or discolor materially, and because of **PAGE** semi-flat weaving it has exceptional strength and endurance.

SIX GATE STYLES • **PAGE** supplies single or double **SWINGING, OVERHEAD SLIDING** and **CANTILEVER GATES** to match the type and height of fence you select. All are rigidly braced and welded at all joints.

TWO TYPES METAL LINE POSTS • First, standard **TUBULAR POST** of 2½" OD hot galvanized steel. Second, **H-BEAM POST** 2¼" x 1⅞" heavily galvanized high carbon steel. Both to be deep set in bell-shaped concrete footings.

EXPERT ERECTING SERVICE • Your **PAGE** Fence will be expertly erected by a nearby Page Fence Association member firm which is technically trained, long experienced and thoroughly reliable. It knows regional conditions affecting fence and can render expert service.

Write to Headquarters for Informative File-Size Folder

PAGE-fenced swimming pools enable proper control of crowds and make possible the collecting of revenue.

PAGE provides a choice of 6 styles of gates to match the type and height of fence you select.

PAGE backstops for baseball, and PAGE-fenced tennis courts and playgrounds, control & protect users.

SAFWAY STEEL PRODUCTS, INC.

6210 W. State St. • Milwaukee 13, Wis.

Portable and Permanent Steel Bleachers and Grandstands; Telescoping Gym Seats; Sectional Steel Chair Risers; Ski and Toboggan Slides

REPRESENTATIVES IN PRINCIPAL CITIES

'Budget Master' Portable Steel Bleachers Can Be Assembled in 5, 10 or 15 Rows

ECONOMICAL FOR 20 PERSONS TO 10,000 OR MORE; SECTIONS MOVE WITHOUT DISASSEMBLY

AT LOW COST, you can handle many different seating needs—outdoors or inside—with versatile Safway "Budget Master" portable steel bleachers, assembled in 5, 10 or 15 rows. Your own personnel easily erect bleachers or change set-ups without tools.

Placed all around a football field, 15 rows will seat over 10,000 persons. Main bleachers are quickly broken down into smaller sections for any number of persons from 20 up. Complete sections to 18 ft. long can be re-located without disassembly.

Top photo shows 5-row bleachers as erected along both sides of a football field. **Bottom photo** shows same equipment combined into one 10-row bleacher, with the addition of a few simple box frames and guard rails.

COMPLETE SAFETY

Budget Master bleachers are engineered to provide unobstructed vision, ample legroom, easy climbing and complete spectator safety. Cross braces tie supporting frames into a unified steel structure that evenly distributes strains and shock loads.

Tubular steel guard rails (2 rails high) provided at sides and rear wherever required. Elevated front cross aisles available. Budget Master bleachers furnished with or without seat and floor boards.

Submit details of your seating needs for recommendations (no obligation). And write for........... **FREE BULLETIN 4A.**

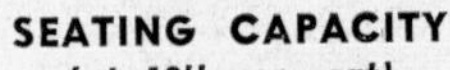

SEATING CAPACITY

(at 18" per seat)

Bleacher Length	First 18 ft.	Each 6 ft. Additional
5 rows	70	20
10 rows	120	40
15 rows	180	60

'DE LUXE' STEEL BLEACHERS FOR PORTABLE OR PERMANENT SEATING

Can be used for a complete stadium seating many thousands—additions to existing facilities—or temporary set-ups, outdoors or inside. Provide de luxe seating with excellent vision, comfort and unexcelled safety. Easily demountable tubular steel parts can be assembled without tools by your personnel.

Other Safway Products

TELESCOPING GYM SEATS—To fit every requirement. 3 types—wall-attached, recessed and movable. Automatic safety latches; handsome enclosure. Full comfort and safety.

SKI AND TOBOGGAN SLIDES—Long-life sectional steel construction. Easy to erect—can be stored compactly.

FITCHBURG *SAFETY SPRING*. Fitchburg Chippers are designed by engineers for busy, trouble-free service. Every model, regardless of capacity, has the patented *Fitchburg Safety Spring*—an effective built-in feature which permits chipping of larger size wood without extra power, assures smooth, efficient operation.

A WORD ABOUT SEALED BIDS. Know what you are buying! Bids on Fitchburg Chippers are made on a complete machine ready to operate—NOT a stripped-down model with extra costs to come later. Price alone, is often misleading under the sealed bid system.

FOR FURTHER INFORMATION or the name of the dealer nearest to you, write FITCHBURG ENGINEERING CORPORATION, Dept. CT, Fitchburg, Mass.

SPECIFICATIONS: FITCHBURG CHIPPER *(unit guaranteed for workmanship and material for one year.)*

CHIPPING UNIT — MODEL (Trailer Type)	TWC-6	TWC-612	TWC-9	TWC-915
Diameter of cutter head	9½″	9½″	11½″	11½″
Length of cutter head body	6″	12″	9″	15″
Number and length of cutter blades	4—6⅜″	4—12⅜″	4—9″	4—15″
Type of blade	Special High-Chrome, High-Carbon Tempered Steel			
Cutter head shaft size, (diameter)	1¾″	1¾″	2½″	2½″
Shaft keyway size	⅜″ x 3/16″	⅜″ x 3/16″	⅝″ x 5/16″	⅝″ x 5/16″
Approximate weight of chipper only	415#	650#	630#	1,000#
Maximum knife setting	¼″	¼″	⅜″	⅜″
Capacity—maximum size round (limbs, etc.)	4½″	4½″	8″	8″
maximum size width (slabs, etc.)	6″	12″	8½″	14½″

All units equipped with exclusive *Fitchburg Safety Spring*-activated feed plates (U.S. Patent No. 2634062)

POWER UNIT — Gasoline fuel.	TWC-6	TWC-612	TWC-9	TWC-915
Number of cylinders	4	6	6	6
Cu. In. Piston Displacement	162	226	226	251, 330, or 427
Water Cooled	Yes	Yes	Yes	Yes
Electric starter and generator	Yes	Yes	Yes	Yes
Clutch Power Take-Off	Disc Clutch	Disc Clutch	Disc Clutch	Disc Clutch
Battery	6-volt	6-volt	6-volt	6-volt
Governor	Yes	Yes	Yes	Yes
Oil level and pressure gauge	Yes	Yes	Yes	Yes
Water temperature gauge	Yes	Yes	Yes	Yes
Ammeter	Yes	Yes	Yes	Yes
Key ignition switch	Yes	Yes	Yes	Yes

Power Units are the enclosed type, with industrial engines of proper horsepower and torque ratings.

TRAILER UNIT. All welded steel construction. Steel I-Beam axle. Steel hubs with roller bearings. Drop forged ring-type tow bar to fit Army-type pintle hook. Safety chains. Front and rear legs, front retractable jack-type with steel caster, rear adjustable for height. Automotive drop-center type wheels. 6-ply Commercial pneumatic tires, ranging from 6.00 to 7.50. 6-leaf springs of 3,500# capacity. Trailer equipped with combination tail light and number plate bracket, with tail light operated by toggle-switch on motor panel (stop light furnished when required.) Tire tread widths range from 63″ on TWC-6 to 72½″ on TWC-915. Fenders and tool boxes are standard equipment. **EQUIPMENT.** Proper sheaves and high-capacity v-belts. Feed apron, chip spout, side delivery chute, 2-piece truck loading chute with chip deflector. Belt guard. Extra set of cutter blades with each unit. Tools furnished consist of necessary Allen wrenches, handle, 3 gauges, honing stone, can of grease, grease gun adapter. Operating and parts manuals. Fitchburg Chippers supplied with standard gray paint unless otherwise requested.

Specifications subject to change without notice

Some of the many uses for your Fitchburg Chipper: **STORM DAMAGE • PARKS • ROADSIDE CLEARANCE • CHRISTMAS TREE DISPOSAL • DUTCH ELM DISPOSAL • SHADE TREES TRIMMINGS • HIGHWAY CONSTRUCTION**

MITTS AND MERRILL

1022 South Water Street — Saginaw, Michigan

MANUFACTURERS OF INDUSTRIAL AND MUNICIPAL WASTE REDUCTION MACHINERY FOR GRINDING WOOD, MEAT, BONES, GARBAGE, ETC. LEADERS IN THIS FIELD SINCE 1854.

New M & M PORTABLE BRUSH GRINDER

. . . reduces brush haulaway costs up to 85%

The new Mitts & Merrill Brush Grinder is an ideal machine for anyone concerned with brush disposal. It is a portable unit with its own power plant for grinding up branches, tree trimmings and brush into small wood chips. Grinding branches up to 6" in diameter with a speed heretofore unknown for a portable machine the M & M Brush Grinder soon pays for itself with labor and haulaway cost savings.

GARBAGE REDUCTION MACHINES

M & M reduction machines similar to the one illustrated are now in use in hundreds of American and Foreign cities. Over 100 years of leadership in this field have made the Mitts and Merrill name famous. M & M Hogs are available in standard and special models for virtually every materials reduction operation. M & M Flat Face One-piece Cylinder Hogs are available in six sizes with capacities from 1½ tons to 18 tons per hour. Safety device protects machine from tramp metal.

AIR-FLUFF PAPER SHREDDERS

M & M Paper Shredders will shred newspapers, magazines, correspondence, cartons and practically any other waste paper into uniform strips for excelsior or easy disposal. Operation is swift and economical. Models available to handle up to 18 inch widths and capacities to 1800 lbs. per hour. All models are equipped with automatic feed, enclosed knives and protected belts for complete safety so that they can be operated by inexperienced workers.

Write and send us your problem.

GENERAL PLAYGROUND EQUIPMENT, INC.

Kokomo, Indiana

FUN-FUL

PLAYGROUND AND SWIMMING POOL EQUIPMENT

- Swings
- Seesaws
- Slides
- Climbing Structures
- Merry-Go-Rounds
- Gymnasium Equipment
- Bike Racks

- Ladders
- Diving Towers
- Diving Stands
- Diving Boards
- Water Slides
- Life Guard Chairs
- Pool Cleaning Equipment
- Life Savers
- Rotary Power Lawn Mowers

Slides

To get the peak of performance and satisfaction buy our Fun-Ful Fiberglas boards.

FUN-FUL FIBERGLAS DIVING BOARDS

No. FG-16—16 ft. Fiberglas Board........ **$180.00**
No. FG-14—14 ft. Fiberglas Board........ **160.00**
No. FG-12—12 ft. Fiberglas Board........ **140.00**

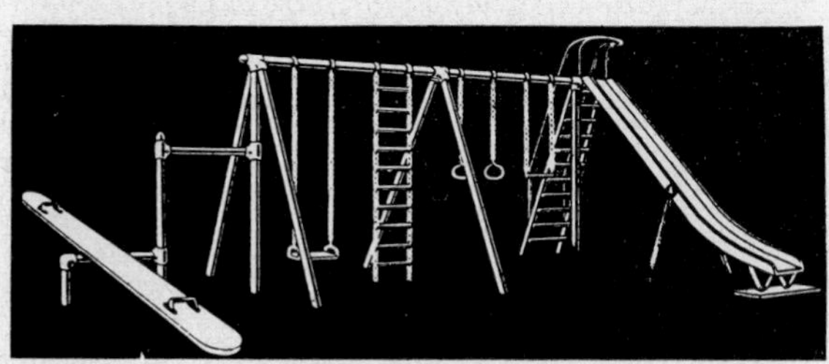

School Combination No. 670

These super quality boards are made from the finest Douglas Fir to be had. They are then covered with layers of Fiberglas cloth impregnated with plastic resin. Boards have a special non-skid surface to prevent slipping.

Our Fiberglas boards give the extra spring that makes the difficult dives easy.

WRITE FOR CATALOG NOW

AMERICAN APPROVED Playground Equipment

FOR GREATER STRENGTH, MAXIMUM SAFETY AND UNEQUALLED PERFORMANCE

American Approved SCT Senior Castle Tower

American Approved DeLuxe Combination Unit

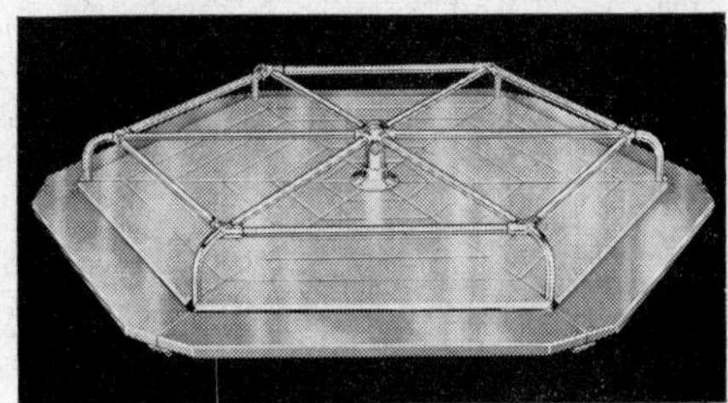

American Approved Heavy Duty Merry-Go-Round With Enclosed Safety Platform

Why American Excels

- All frames and members of new, Tested Hot-Dip Galvanized Pipe
- No unsightly, imperfect welded joints or fittings in American, but, Certified Malleable Frame Fittings which can never break
- No metalizing, zinc spraying, which merely films the surface, but, Hot-Dip Galvanizing which alloys the Zinc with the Steel and rustproofs for a *Lifetime*
- Only the finest, well seasoned select Hardwood and Oregon Fir
- Hand brushed finishes to assure enduring wear, weather proofing
- Higher construction standards, American's Lifetime Guarantee, Products *Liability Insurance*

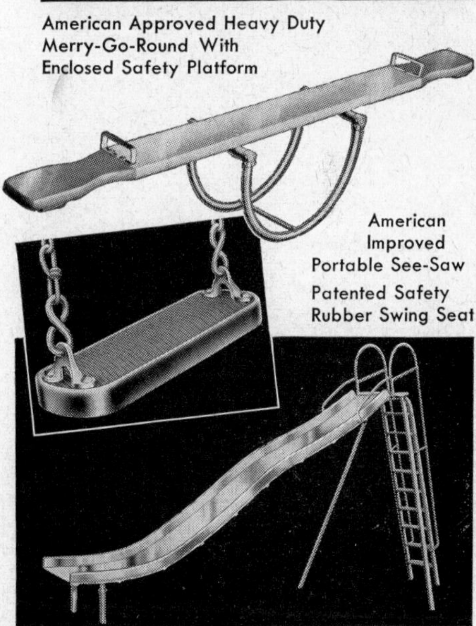

American Improved Portable See-Saw

Patented Safety Rubber Swing Seat

American Approved All-Steel Slide

AMERICAN PLAYGROUND DEVICE COMPANY • ANDERSON, INDIANA

AMERICAN APPROVED
Park, Picnic, and Dressing Room Equipment, made for LIFETIME DURABILITY

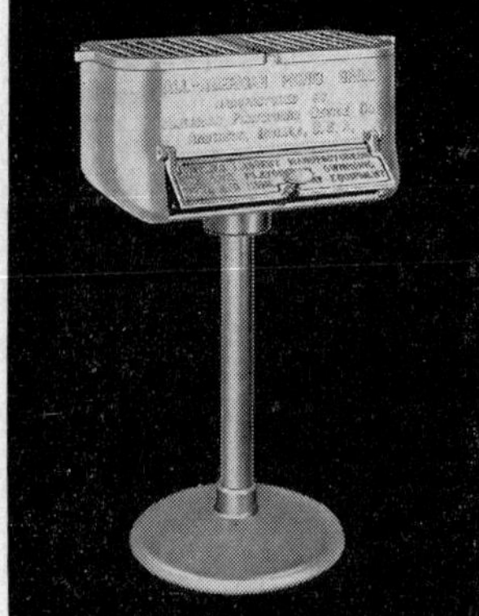

All American Approved No. AG-P Heavy Duty Picnic Grill

American Approved Heavy Duty Streamlined Picnic Table

American Approved APB-4 Heavy Duty Streamlined Park Bench

American Approved Chain Link Steel Fabric Tennis Net

American Approved Heavy Duty Steel Basket Rack

American Approved Heavy Duty All Steel Bicycle Rack

American Approved No. 80 Heavy Duty Checking Basket With Large Metal Number Plate

AMERICAN PLAYGROUND DEVICE COMPANY • ANDERSON, INDIANA

TROJAN PLAYGROUND EQUIP. MFG. CO.

11 Second Ave., N.E., St. Cloud, Minnesota

FOR 60 YEARS...

MANUFACTURING AMERICA'S FINEST PLAYGROUND EQUIPMENT!

STEEL SLIDES, WHIRLERS, SEE-SAWS, MERRY-GO-ROUNDS, HORIZONTAL LADDERS & BARS, SWINGS & COMBINATIONS, GIANT STRIDES, BIKE RACKS, LOOP-O-BALL, FLAG POLES, PARK BENCHES & PICNIC TABLES

NATIONALLY DISTRIBUTED; WRITE FOR CATALOG AND NAME OF NEAREST DISTRIBUTOR

FOR MAXIMUM SAFETY — FOR HIGH YOUTH-APPEAL, FOR SUPERIOR DURABILITY

PLAYGROUND EQUIPMENT

*

Scout Camp to Get New Pool

Camp Madron Site Of Modern Structure

"It's the first one of its kind anywhere in the country," asserted Scout Executive Clifford A. Klapp proudly.

Klapp was referring to the combination indoor-outdoor swimming pool, a new concept in pool construction, to be built at Camp Madron by the Southwestern Michigan Council, Boy Scouts of America.

Bids for the estimated $65,000 project will be advertised Aug. 1, according to Klapp, and all bids should be in by Oct. 1. He said the council expects the pool to be completed by May 1, 1957, in time for next year's camping season.

The pool, designed by consulting engineer Wesley Bintz, of Lansing, will actually have two separate sections. The outdoor section will be a 40 by 60 foot ovoid pool with depths ranging from three to five feet.

The indoor pool, housed in an overall 50 sq foot structure, will be 30 by 40 feet and rectangular in shape. It will have depths ranging from three to nine feet.

"There will be separate dressing rooms so that mixed groups can use the pool, which will be helpful for our older scouts who have many mixed social events," Klapp said.

Camp Madron, located about five miles from Buchanan, now has swimming facilities in a lake with a peat bottom.

"The water is the color of light coffee in spite of our efforts to cover the bottom with sand," Klapp said.

He pointed out that the new pool will be a boon to younger scouts who are beginning swimmers, giving them a place where they can learn and practice swimming throughout the year.

"It'll promote advancement of Scouts held up by swimming requirements, keep boys in Scouting longer, and will definitely increase weekend camping," according to Klapp.

He explained that the older boy program will be helped because the more advanced Scouts will have facilities to practice lifesaving and other activities formerly limited to the summer months with occasional winter classes in civic indoor pools throughout the council.

Construction cost of the new pool will be financed from funds collected in the camp expansion fund campaign.

*

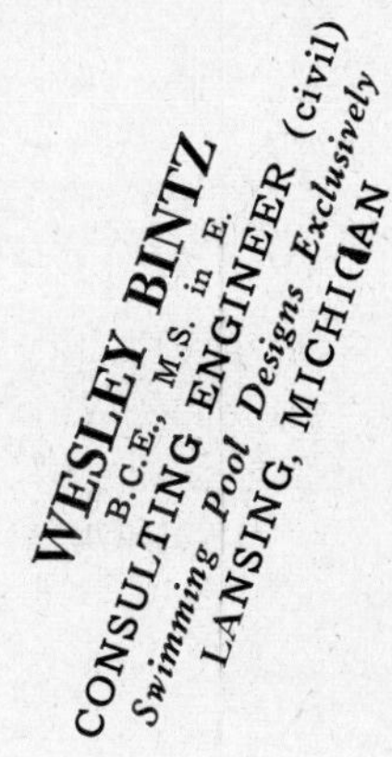

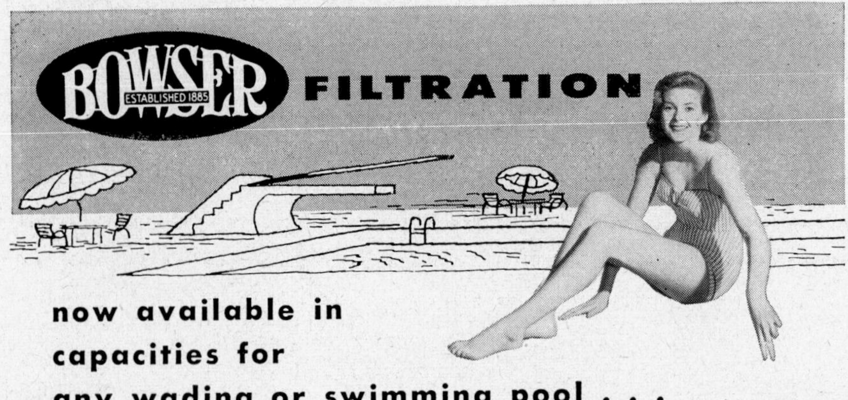

now available in capacities for any wading or swimming pool . . .

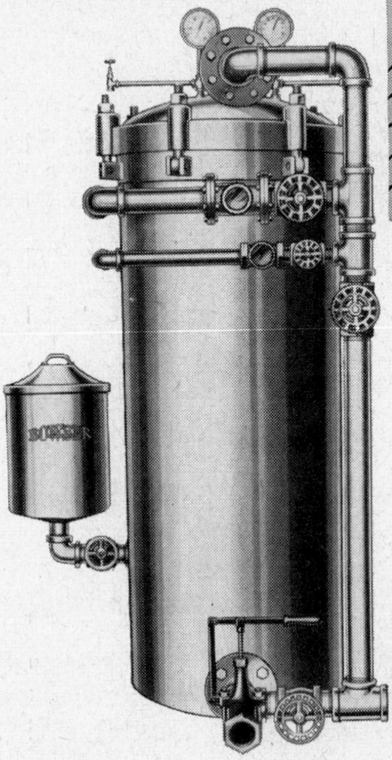

PURE, CLEAR WATER

Every swimming or wading pool needs a dependable water-filtering system. Bowser engineers will provide reliable data for specifying the correct filter for your pool. Bowser Filters are completely dependable — backed by Bowser, Inc., specialists in liquid control equipment since 1885.

GET THE FACTS . . .

Write for helpful Bulletins 816 and 614 containing filter facts.

Commercial, Civic or Residential

BOWSER
NATIONWIDE SALES AND SERVICE

REGIONAL OFFICES: ATLANTA · BOSTON · CHICAGO · CLEVELAND · DALLAS · KANSAS CITY · LOS ANGELES · NEW YORK

BOWSER, INC. 1302 E. Creighton, Fort Wayne, Ind.

11525 NORTH CENTRAL EXPRESSWAY
DALLAS TEXAS

DESIGNERS ENGINEERS
BUILDERS

• HOTELS
• SCHOOLS
• RESIDENCES
• COMMUNITIES
• COUNTRY CLUBS
• MUNICIPAL POOLS

CARDINAL

Swimming Pools and Filter Equipment

CARDINAL POOLS ARE KNOWN THROUGHOUT THE NATION FOR THEIR MATCHLESS BEAUTY, SUPERIOR QUALITY, FINEST WORKMANSHIP, AND COMPLETE CUSTOMER SATISFACTION.

EACH CARDINAL POOL AND FILTER SYSTEM IS CUSTOM DESIGNED TO MEET YOUR INDIVIDUAL REQUIREMENTS BY AMERICA'S FOREMOST SWIMMING POOL DESIGNERS, ENGINEERS AND BUILDERS.

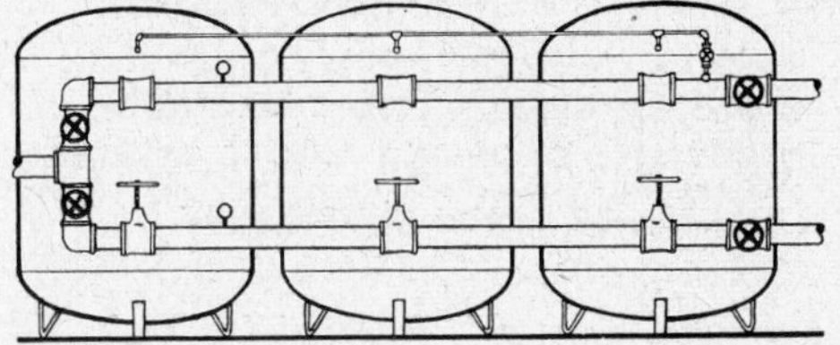

Modernize Your Pool with a

CARDINAL

RAPID — SAND FILTER SYSTEM

WRITE FOR BROCHURE OR ENGINEERING CONSULTATION

KOVEN STEEL SWIMMING POOLS, INC.

A DIVISION OF

L. O. KOVEN & BRO., INC.

90 East Dickerson St., Dover, N. J.

KOVEN ALL STEEL swimming pools... for outstanding community service...

the pool with the

It's a rare community that doesn't enjoy a swimming pool. And it's a rare administration that doesn't enjoy one that's especially satisfactory from every point of view: economy, durability, maintenance.

KOVEN pools are carefully designed and built of leak-proof heavy welded steel to provide perfect year 'round performance even in severe climates. That's why they carry their famous 10-year guarantee—last a long time—yet cost little to maintain. Upkeep? Just an occasional coat of paint.

Inquire now about KOVEN pools. Call or write for a free colorfully illustrated booklet or a consultation with a trained representative. There's no obligation.

THE POOL WITH THE LOWEST MAINTENANCE

- INDOOR AND OUTDOOR MODELS
- 10-YEAR GUARANTEE ON ALL POOLS
- ANY SIZE OR DESIGN CAN BE ORDERED

STANDARD SIZES FROM 16' x 30' STOCKED FOR IMMEDIATE DELIVERY

Koven STEEL SWIMMING POOLS, Inc. a division of L. O. KOVEN & BRO., Inc.
90 EAST DICKERSON ST., DOVER, N. J. PLANTS: JERSEY CITY, N. J. • DOVER, N. J. • TRENTON, N. J.

modern

SWIMMING POOL CO., INC.

One Holland Avenue
White Plains, N. Y.
Phone: WHite Plains 8-3932

—your most reliable source for all

SWIMMING POOL
lake and reservoir **SUPPLIES**

Manufacturers since 1935 of the most complete line of quality equipment and chemicals for municipal and public pools, lakes and reservoirs. Over 100 different products including filters, drains, chlorinators, diving boards, pool paint, algaecides, chemicals—everything to build or maintain any type of pool.

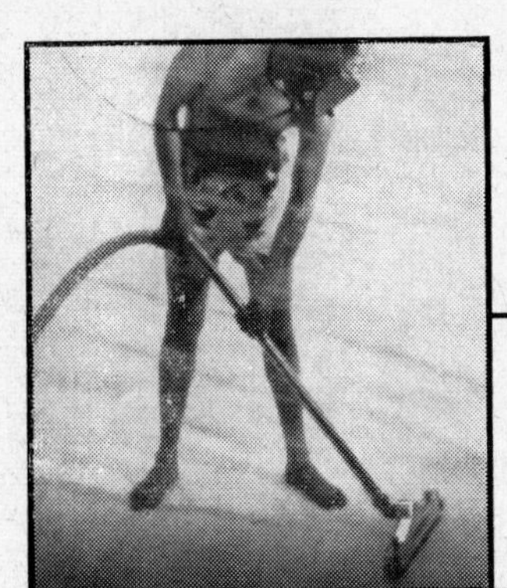

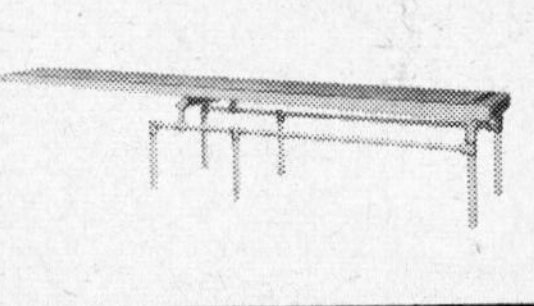

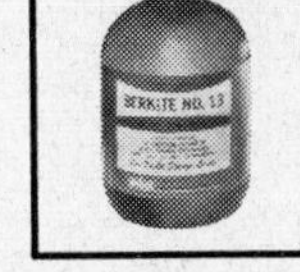

LOW PRICES! • FAST SHIPMENT!

Send today for 52-page Catalog & Data Book No. 24B

See *Modern* exhibit at Architects Samples Corp., 101 Park Ave., New York City. Complete displays in our White Plains showroom and at your nearest *Modern* distributor . . . see classified telephone directory under "*Swimming Pool Equipment*" or *write us . . .*

SWIMMING POOL CO., INC. • ONE HOLLAND AVENUE, WHITE PLAINS, N. Y.
Manufacturers of Swimming Pool Supplies Since 1935

THE BEST *equipment and supplies for your pool by*

NATIONAL

National Pool Equipment Co. has a complete line of the highest quality swimming pool equipment and supplies at the lowest possible prices. From the largest complete filter system to the smallest pool fitting available for fast shipment.

EVERYTHING YOU NEED FOR SWIMMING POOLS

Filtration Systems	Heaters
Filter accessories	Lighting equipment
Deck fittings	Chemicals
Paints of all kinds	Vacuum cleaners
Chlorinating equipment	Water test sets
Pool fittings	Safety equipment

Write today for our full color catalog of pool equipment and supplies.

NATIONAL

pool equipment co.

Dept. MI, Lee Highway

Tel. AT-2-1620

Florence, Alabama

OLIN MATHIESON CHEMICAL CORPORATION

INDUSTRIAL CHEMICALS DIVISION

Baltimore 3, Md.

BRANCH OFFICES

Atlanta 2, Georgia • Buffalo 3, N. Y. • Charlotte 2, N. C. • Chicago 11, Ill. • Cincinnati 2, Ohio Houston 2, Tex. • Montreal, Can. • New Orleans 12, La. • New York 22, N. Y. • Pasadena 8, Calif. Philadelphia 7, Pa. • Providence 3, R. I. • St. Louis 2, Mo.

HTH GRANULAR

For continuous or periodic chlorination of swimming pools HTH offers the advantages of simplicity, dependability and low first cost of chlorinating equipment. For fill-and-draw pools, irregularly shaped pools, and semi-artificial pools constructed at ponds, streams, etc., the flexibility of HTH makes it possible to chlorinate where and when required without equipment other than an ordinary watering can.

HTH Granular is a dry, readily soluble powder containing 70% available chlorine. Retains its full strength even after months of storage. Packed in cases of nine 5-lb. cans and in drums of 100 lbs., net. Available throughout the United States and Canada.

Equipment is available for continuous chlorination of pools of every size with HTH solutions, offering accurate dosage and economies in operation. Thousands of swimming pools throughout the country also keep a supply of HTH constantly on hand for emergency and peak-load use.

In addition to its use in the pool water, HTH is now being widely used in a co-ordinated entrance-to-exit sanitation routine to keep dressing rooms, toilets, runways and other pool surroundings safe and sanitary.

HTH solutions meet health department requirements for fungicidal use in foot-baths to prevent transmission of Athlete's Foot. A valuable 48-page manual, "Keeping the Pool Safe and Sanitary", is available free upon request.

PH-PLUS (FUSED ALKALI)

PH-Plus restores alkalinity which pool water often loses during treatment — eliminates acidity that makes eyes smart —makes purification more effective and residual chlorine less noticeable. Comes in convenient fused ½-lb. cakes packed in 100-lb. bags.

HTH TABLETS

For convenient handling in swimming pool water treatment as well as in many water treatment applications, HTH is also available as HTH Tablets. This product is simply HTH in the form of compressed, easy-to-handle tablets which dissolve slowly and provide a continuous source of available chlorine over an extended period of time.

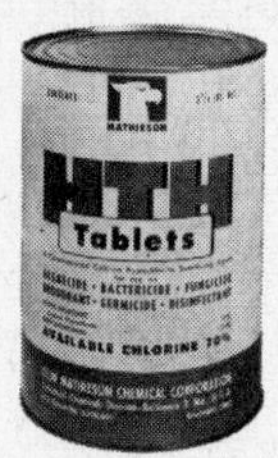

HTH Tablets, in cases of 12 3¾-lb. cans, are available throughout the United States and Canada.

HTH Tablets are made wholly of dependable HTH and contain 70% available chlorine the same as the time-tested HTH Granular. The tablets are stable and dust-free and thus offer an exceptionally safe and convenient means of handling, measuring and storing available chlorine.

HTH TABLET HYPOCHLORINATOR

By use of the HTH Tablet Hypochlorinator the convenience offered by HTH in tablet form can be combined with accurate metering and feeding of hypochlorite solutions. This equipment, specifically designed by Mathieson to dissolve HTH Tablets and to meter the resultant hypochlorite solutions, provides a convenient and efficient method of feeding available chlorine at rates which can be accurately controlled and quickly varied to cover a wide range of operating demands.

The HTH Tablet Hypochlorinator is of practical design, compact construction, and attractive appearance; it is easy to install and very simple to operate. Moreover, HTH Tablet Hypochlorination eliminates all measuring and weighing operations, and requires no preparation of stock solutions. The HTH Tablet Hypochlorinator is engineered to give long-time reliable service. First cost is low, and since the unit operates with no moving parts, maintenance and upkeep expenses are negligible.

The HTH Tablet Hypochlorinator (1) stores a supply of HTH Tablets, (2) dissolves the tablets, (3) measures and controls the rate of feeding of available chlorine, and (4) feeds the hypochlorite solution to the point of application. The tablet charge (approximately 8½ pounds of HTH Tablets, equivalent to about 6 pounds of chlorine) is contained in the transparent plastic body of the unit, thus enabling the operator to tell at a glance when refilling becomes necessary. The water comes in contact only with the bottom portion of the tablet bed so that the bulk of the tablet charge serves solely as a gravity-fed supply.

Full information on HTH Tablets and the HTH Tablet Hypochlorinator may be obtained from Olin Mathieson or from HTH supply houses.

SULPHATE OF ALUMINA

Activated Alum Brand sulphate of alumina—the only alum designed exclusively for use in the field of water and sewage treatment—contains finely ground natural silicates, providing a free-flowing, less hygroscopic product of porous structure and higher alumina content.

SPARKLER MANUFACTURING CO.

Mundelein, Ill.

Service Representatives in principal cities

SWIMMING POOL FILTERS

The highest quality pure crystal clear water is maintained constantly in the pool with the Sparkler Model SCJ diatomite filter. The water is introduced into the filter tank through a baffle covered opening and flows through a filter cake built up on the surface of the plates which are covered with orlon cloth, and out through openings in a center shaft. The construction of the filter is very simple. The filter discs are located on a center shaft with spacers and sealed against by-passing. The discharge shaft has ample flow space so that friction is reduced to a negligible factor.

The first cost of a Sparkler SCJ filter is about ½ that of a sand filter and the floor space required is only 1/6 to 1/10 depending on size:

The high quality of filtering is constant in the SCJ filter right up to the cleaning period which is indicated by an increased pressure drop rather than a deterioration in quality.

In a 400 sq. ft. SCJ filter the plates can be cleaned with the built-in jet spray and the filter flushed out with only 1000 gallons. Only 5 minutes time is required for this operation and the plates can be precoated and the filter back in service in a 15 minute cleaning cycle.

The Sparkler automatic continuous overflow closed system, an exclusive Sparkler development, is completely automatic in operation and adds greatly to the successful operation of a pool, particularly where raw water is highly contaminated and where considerable debris is blown into the pool.

Sparkler filtration engineers will help plan your installation and personally supervise its initial operation.

Write for swimming pool bulletin which gives detailed information about SCJ filter.

SPARKLER MODEL SCJ available in capacities up to 5,000,000 gallons per 24 hour operation.

SPARKLER SCJ FILTER CAPACITIES

Based on rate of 3 GPM Per Sq Ft.*

Model	Filter Area Sq. Ft.	Pipe Conn. Inches	Approx. Floor Area (Feet)	Pool Size 6 Hr. Turnover	Pool Size 8 Hr. Turnover
Model SCJ-24-9	50	4	5 x 3	54,000	72,000
Model SCJ-24-13	75	4	5½ x 3	81,000	108,000
Model SCJ-24-17	100	4	6½ x 3	108,000	144,000
Model SCJ-33-13	150	6	7½ x 5	162,000	216,000
Model SCJ-33-18	200	6	8½ x 5	216,000	288,000
Model SCJ-40-16	250	8	8½ x 6	270,000	360,000
Model SCJ-40-19	300	8	9 x 6	324,000	432,000
Model SCJ-40-22	350	8	9 x 6	378,000	503,000
Model SCJ-40-25	400	8	9 x 6	432,000	575,000

Larger models up to 2000 sq. ft. can be built on order.
*Lower flow rates are used when required by state regulations.

Pool owners and operators who have had experience with the Sparkler SCJ filter have nothing but praise for the efficiency and performance of this filter.

*One pool operator says: "Our Sparkler filter is performing satisfactorily in every way. The quality of the water in our 65,000 gallon pool is excellent. It is crystal clear, and always tests 'A.' The coliform MPN count is always less than 3, as is the Entercocci MPN count. The pool carries a very large load of students during eleven months of the year. Water turnover rate is 3½ hours. The total cost of water purification for this pool is $27.50 per week. This includes bromine, diatomaceous earth, wash water, electric power and operator's time.

A FEW SPARKLER FILTERED POOLS

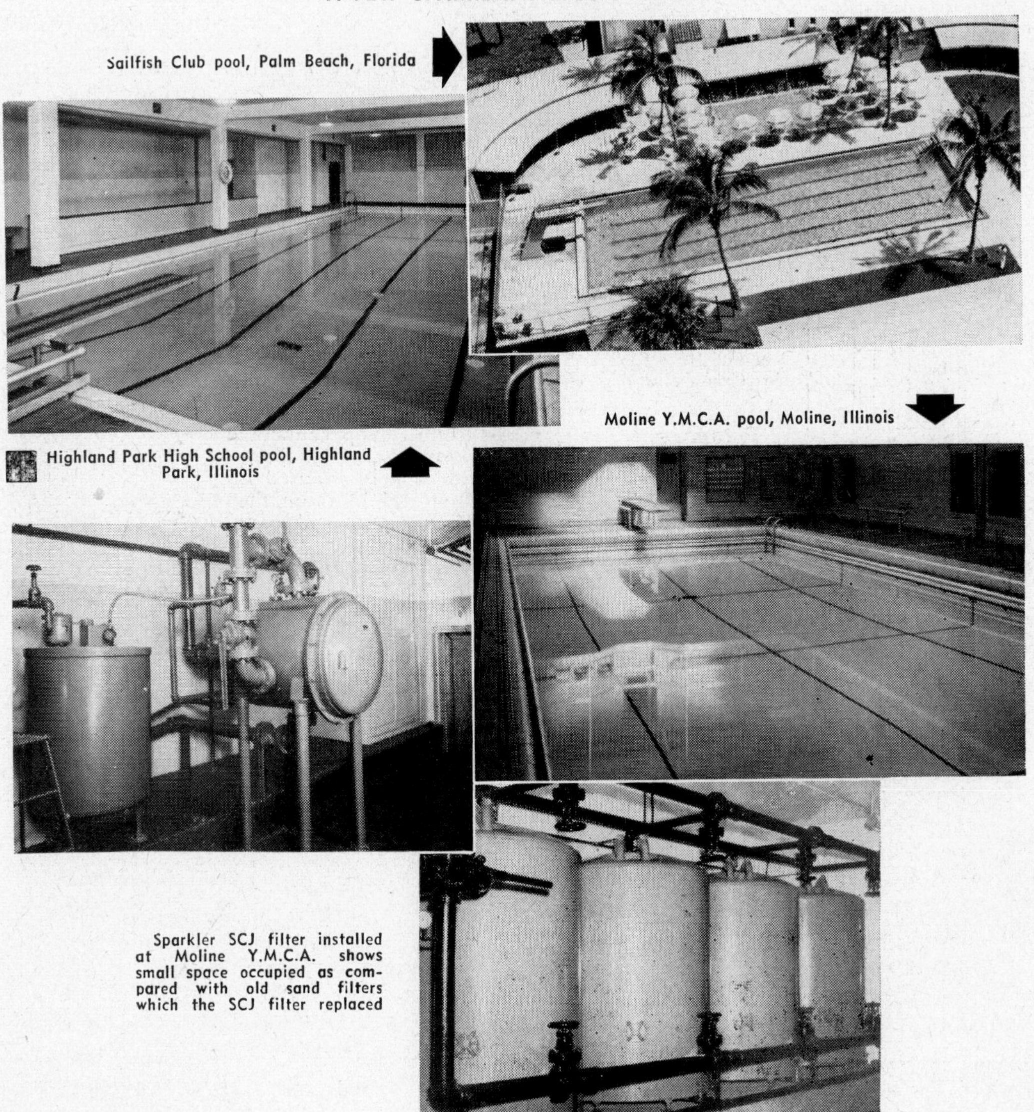

Sailfish Club pool, Palm Beach, Florida

Highland Park High School pool, Highland Park, Illinois

Moline Y.M.C.A. pool, Moline, Illinois

Sparkler SCJ filter installed at Moline Y.M.C.A. shows small space occupied as compared with old sand filters which the SCJ filter replaced

ROBERTS FILTER MANUFACTURING CO.

601 Columbia Avenue, Darby, Penna.

"INSTALL A ROBERTS RECIRCULATING PLANT AND SWIM IN SPARKLING WATER"

"ROBERTS FILTERS — STANDARD OF QUALITY FOR MORE THAN 40 YEARS"

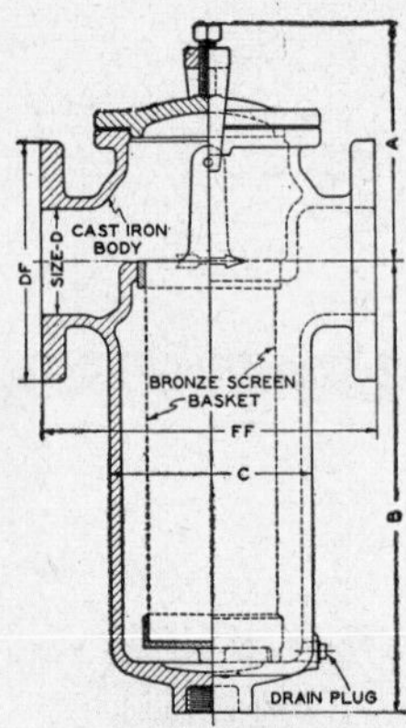

HAIR CATCHER

SCHEDULE OF DIMENSIONS

SIZE-D	DF	FF	A	B	C
2½"	7"	10"	7½"	13"	5¾"
4"	9"	13"	6½"	17"	8"
6"	11"	17"	9½"	23"	10"
8"	13½"	20"	9½"	23"	10"

PRODUCTS

Complete Swimming Pool Recirculating Plants
Filters—all sizes and types
Hair and Lint Catchers
Inlet, Outlet and Scum Gutter Fittings
Chemical Feeding Devices

EXPERIENCE

More than 40 years devoted exclusively to the art of water purification. Over 1000 Swimming Pool installations in service throughout the United States and in Canada and Latin America

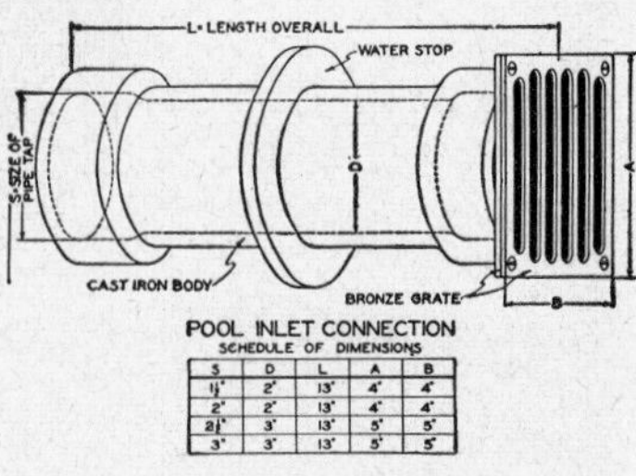

POOL INLET CONNECTION

SCHEDULE OF DIMENSIONS

S	D	L	A	B
1½"	2"	13"	4"	4"
2"	2"	13"	4"	4"
2½"	3"	13"	5"	5"
3"	3"	13"	5"	5"

DESIGN

We recommend recirculation of all pools containing 100,000 gallons or less in not more than eight hours. The same period of recirculation should be used for large pools where the congestion will be more than average. In no case, regardless of size of pool or anticipated number of bathers, should the period for recirculation exceed twelve hours. Many States have adopted regulations, mandatory or otherwise, requiring or recommending certain standards with regard to the "Period of Recirculation" and "Rate of Filtration." Architects and Engineers planning the design and construction of a Swimming Pool should consult the State Board of Health, having jurisdiction, before establishing these important design factors.

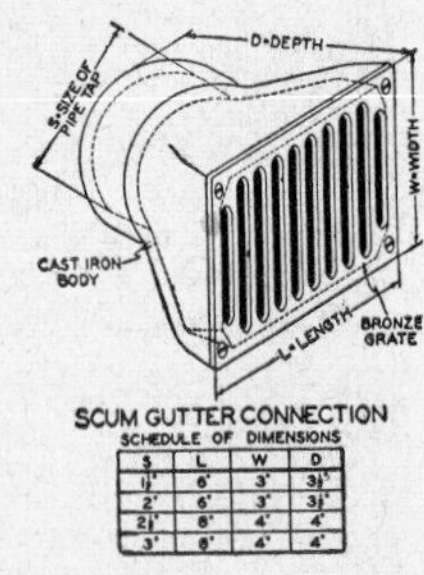

SCUM GUTTER CONNECTION

SCHEDULE OF DIMENSIONS

S	L	W	D
1½"	6"	3"	3½"
2"	6"	3"	3½"
2½"	8"	4"	4"
3"	8"	4"	4"

COOPERATION

We welcome every opportunity of cooperation with those interested in matters of Swimming Pool Sanitation and Economy. Architects and Engineers are invited to submit their problems to our Engineering Department, who will gladly check and criticize layout drawings and submit recommendations, estimates, typical specification data, etc. Write for our bulletins pertaining to Swimming Pool Recirculation.

Roberts Style L Vertical Pressure Filter

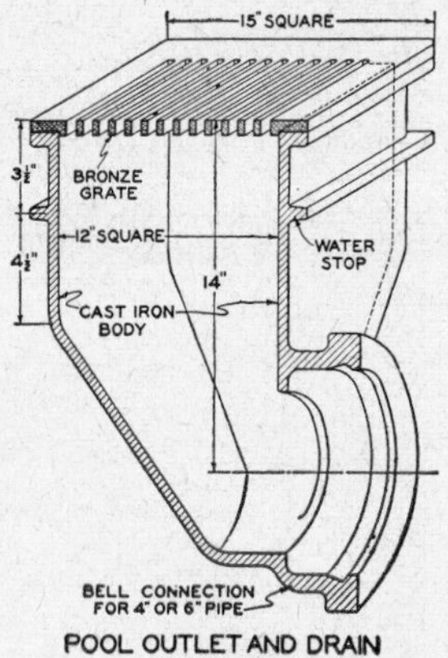

POOL OUTLET AND DRAIN CONNECTION

SWIMQUIP, INC.

3301 Gilman Rd., El Monte, Calif. 1040 Huff Rd., N.W., Atlanta, Ga.

THE HALSEY W. TAYLOR CO.

Main Office and Factory: 137 North Street, N. W., Warren, Ohio

OFFICES IN THE FOLLOWING CITIES

BRANCH OFFICES

Albany, New York
Atlanta, Georgia
Baltimore, Maryland
Birmingham, Alabama
Boston, Massachusetts
Chicago, Illinois
Cincinnati, Ohio
Cleveland, Ohio
Dallas, Texas
Denver, Colorado
Des Moines, Iowa
Detroit, Michigan
Greensboro, N. C.
Hartford, Connecticut
Houston, Texas
Kansas City, Missouri
Los Angeles, California
Memphis, Tennessee
Miami, Florida
Middleport, New York
Milwaukee, Wisconsin
Minneapolis, Minnesota
Nashville, Tennessee
Newark, New Jersey
New Orleans, Louisiana
New York, New York
Philadelphia, Pennsylvania
Pittsburgh, Pennsylvania
Rochester, New York
San Francisco, California
Seattle, Washington
St. Louis, Missouri
Toronto, Canada
Washington, D. C.

Halsey Taylor Drinking Fountains

also Combination Cooler and Drinking Fountains

To Municipal Officials:

You buy more than a mere fountain when you buy Halsey Taylor Drinking Fountains. . . . You buy definite assurance of trouble-free service, positive health-safety, maximum convenience, built-in patented features exclusive with Halsey Taylor!

Halsey Taylor Drinking Fountains have a record of years of specialized manufacture behind them. Since 1912 Halsey Taylor has been the last word in sanitation in fountain installations, in public buildings, in schools and hospitals, in churches, and wherever people gather . . . gymnasiums, auditoriums, stadiums, playgrounds, parks, etc.

They embody every desirable feature of hygiene and convenience, with advantages that promote the utmost in health-safe drinking.

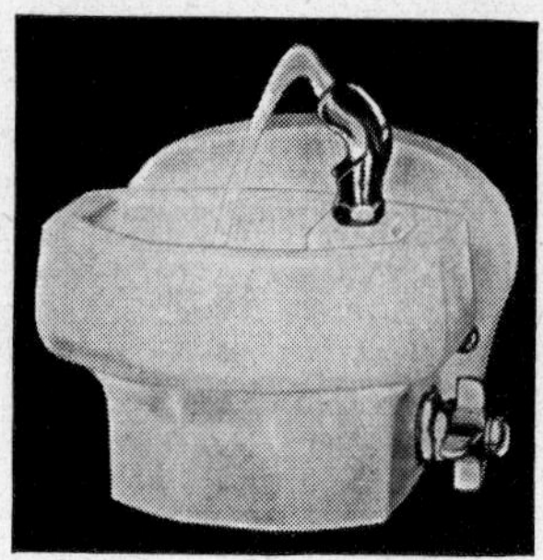

No. 4903

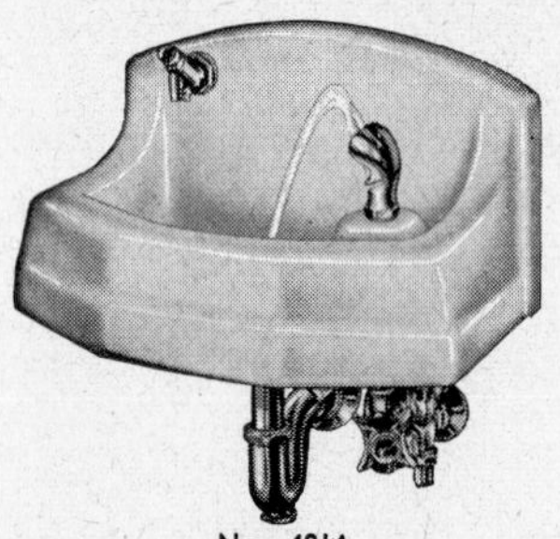

No. 4914

Distinctive Features:

1. **Practical Automatic Stream Control:** An automatic device maintains constant height in drinking stream regardless of line pressure variation. Stream never too high, never too low.
2. **Ideal Drinking Mound:** The two-stream projector with latest type guard makes the side-stream both practical and health-safe, removing objections found with ordinary side-streams.
3. **Positive Sanitation:** The drinking mound is formed by the convergence of two streams of water, setting up a localized drinking mound which makes it impractical to drink from any other point but the ideal height of the mound. Fingers or lips cannot come in contact with or contaminate the water source. It is impossible to squirt the water, doing away with the mess and annoyance of playful children.

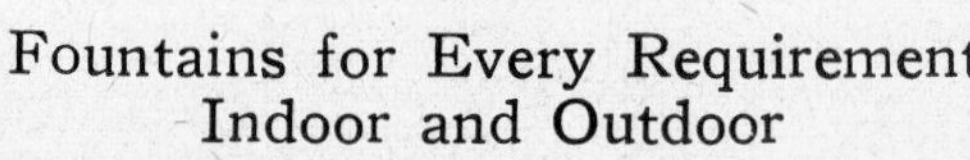

Fountains for Every Requirement Indoor and Outdoor

This page shows only a few types . . . there are many models to select from, all with the fundamental Halsey Taylor features. Send for catalog illustrating and describing complete line.

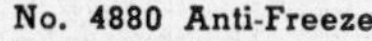

No. 4880 Anti-Freeze

This Halsey Taylor Pedestal Fountain has special anti-freeze feature. Heavy cast iron top and base. Foot operated anti-freeze self-closing stop for various lengths of bury. All exposed fittings chromium plate. Height of base cover, 10½ inches. Finished in gray.

No. 4615
Pedestal Type

Heavy Vitreous China Construction. Available in 30" & 36" Heights.

Halsey Taylor Electric Coolers

in Models to Meet Every Need

The Halsey Taylor line comprises both air-cooled and water-cooled models. When operating temperature is not too high, air-cooled models will serve most requirements. Where air temperatures exceed 110° F and where lint, dirt or dust laden atmospheres are encountered, such as in mills, foundries, factories and textile mills, and especially where climate is decidedly warmer throughout the year, water-cooled models will prove ideal.

The projector used on all Halsey Taylor Coolers provides the utmost in sanitation and meets all health requirements.

No. HT 1015—LO-LEVEL
Convenient for Children

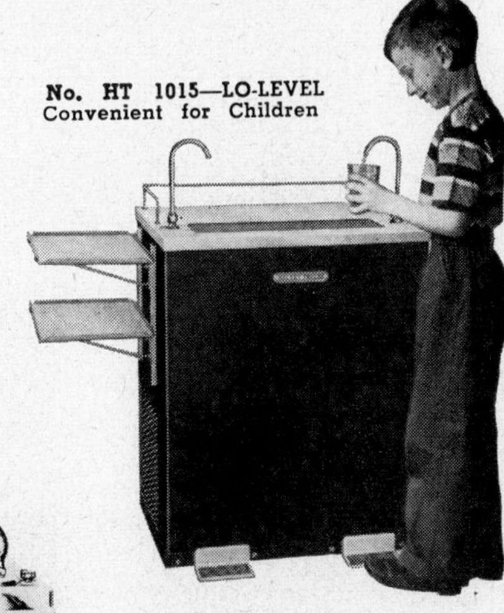

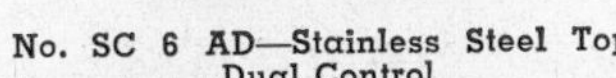

No. SC 6 AD—Stainless Steel Top Dual Control

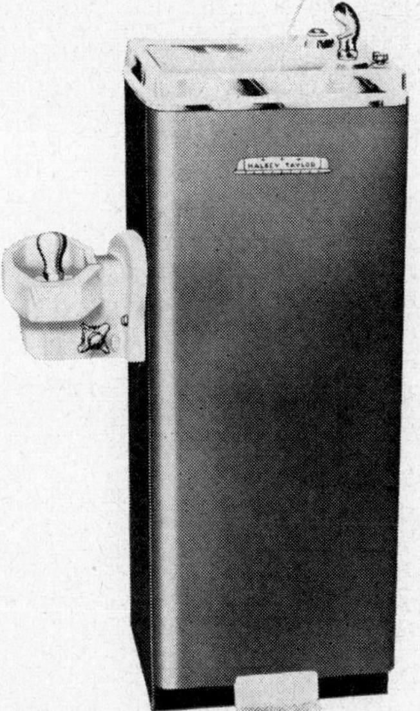

No. SC 11 F Side-Mounted Fountain Dual Control

In addition to types illustrated, many other models are available, some in plain top for remote installations, and still others for cafeteria use. On all pressure-type coolers, glass filler connection and remote fountain outlets are provided. Hermetically sealed condenser units are standard.

No. HB 3—Bottle Cooler

WRITE FOR COMPLETE CATALOG.

BEAUTIFUL *Scotts*® TURF ADDS COMMUNITY DISTINCTION

Schools, municipal buildings, parks and recreational areas look their best with the sparkling green of well kept lawns. And the beautiful weed-free *Scotts* kind are unmistakable symbols of civic pride and good service management.

Regardless of your turf problems or climate area, *Scotts* is your dependable source for securing outstanding turf perfection. You'll discover, too, the cost for *Scotts* is actually no more than for ordinary lawns. Write for recommendations and estimates on your requirements.

FREE *Lawn Care*® PLANNING SERVICE tells how to get and maintain outstanding lawn perfection.

36 years of intensive lawn research are assembled in this edition of over 100 *Lawn Care* bulletins. This helpful lawn encyclopedia plus a free subscription to future *Lawn Care* issues are yours for the asking on official or business stationery. No obligation, of course.

O M *Scott* & SONS CO

Seedsmen since 1870 — Marysville, Ohio — *Palo Alto, Calif.* — *Salem, Oregon* — *Cranbury, N. J.*

THE NATIONAL CASH REGISTER COMPANY

DAYTON 9, OHIO

Makes Copies without Carbon!

National has important news for business everywhere! The duplicate copies you see above were made without carbon paper! This is made possible by use of a special paper developed by the research laboratories of The National Cash Register Company. It is called "NCR Paper" (No Carbon Required). NCR Paper puts an end to irksome handling of carbon paper — inserting, removing, storing. It may be used for almost all types of business forms.

Saves Time, Avoids Smudges. Faster, can't smudge copies or fingers. Making multiple records is now as easy as picking up 3, 4, (or more) forms from a stack and inserting them in a typewriter or business machine. And NCR Paper provides exactly the same advantages when making copies by hand (receipts, sales slips, guest checks, etc.).

Better Copies. When forms are placed together and written on — by typewriter, business machine, or by hand — clear, clean copies are made without carbon paper.

Ends Carbon Paper Disposal. With NCR Paper, removal and disposal of used carbon sheets are avoided.

Try the new NCR Paper and be amazed at the new ease, simplicity, cleanliness and time-saving it brings to multiple copying.

Contact your local business forms printer for NCR Paper — or your nearby National representative — or write to The National Cash Register Co., Dayton 9, Ohio.

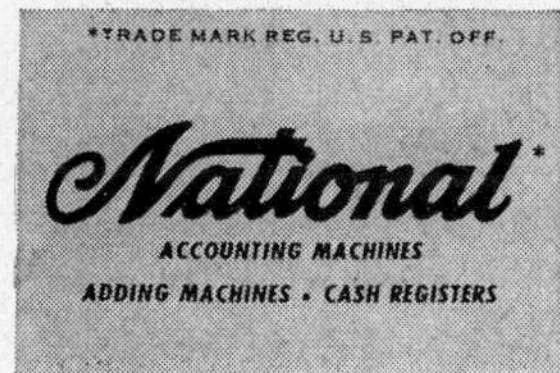

***THE NATIONAL CASH REGISTER COMPANY,* DAYTON 9, OHIO**

989 OFFICES IN 94 COUNTRIES

THE NATIONAL CASH REGISTER COMPANY

DAYTON 9, OHIO

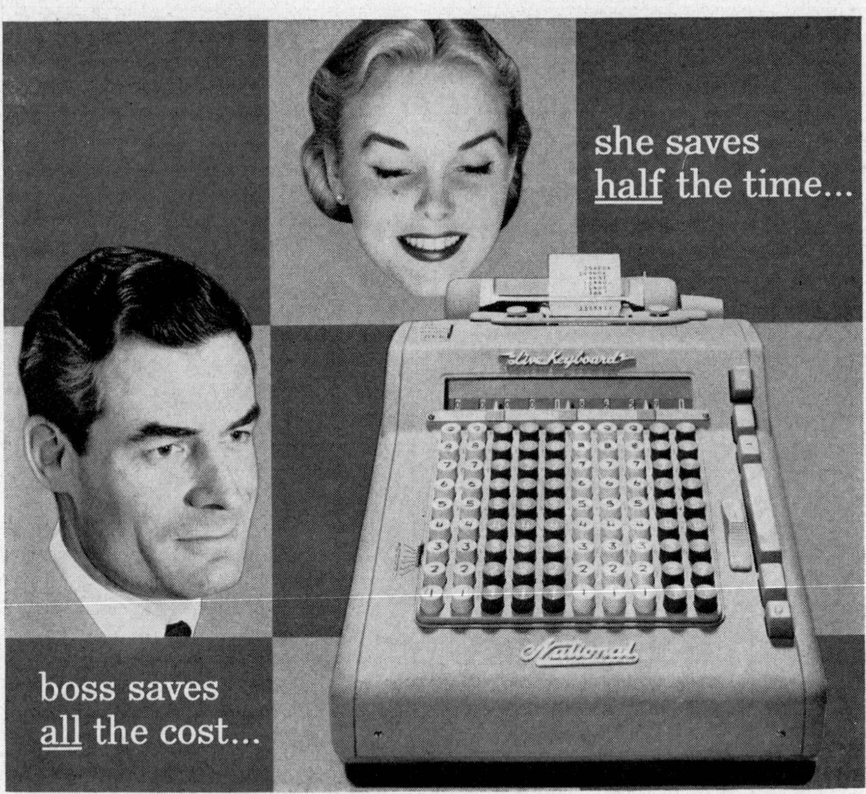

National's adding machine . . .

Live Keyboard* with keytouch adjustable to each operator!

Saves up to 50% hand motion—and effort! Never before have so many time-and-effort-saving features been placed on one adding machine.

Every key operates the motor—so you can now *forget the motor bar*. No more of those back-and-forth hand motions!

Keys are instantly adjustable to *each* operator's touch! No wonder operators are so enthusiastic about it. They do their work faster with up to 50% *less effort!*

"Live" Keyboard with Adjustable Keytouch *plus* 8 other time-saving features are combined only on the amazing National Adding Machine!

THE NATIONAL CASH REGISTER COMPANY, DAYTON 9, OHIO
989 OFFICES IN 94 COUNTRIES

A National Adding Machine pays for itself with the time-and-effort it saves, continues savings as yearly profit. See a demonstration, today, on your own work. Call the nearest National branch office or dealer.

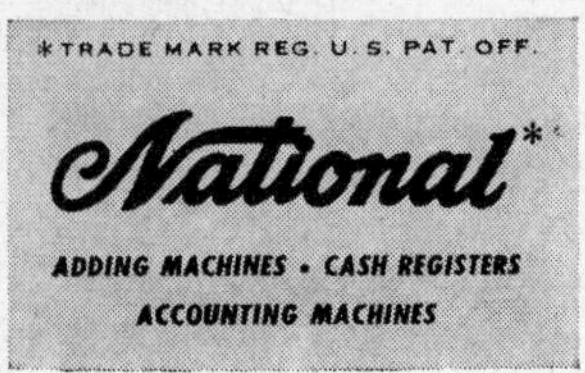

RAND® SYSTEMS AND MACHINES GOVERNMENTS ARE...

photo processing for public records

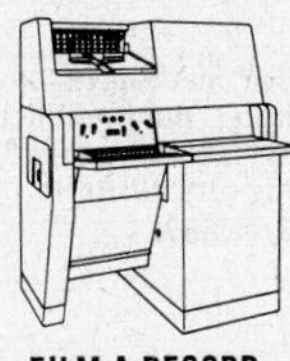

FILM-A-RECORD

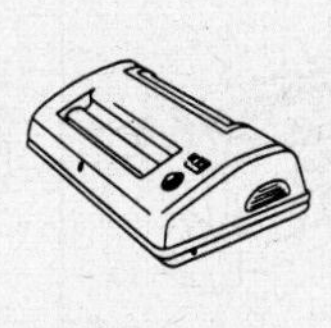
TRANSCOPY® Duplex

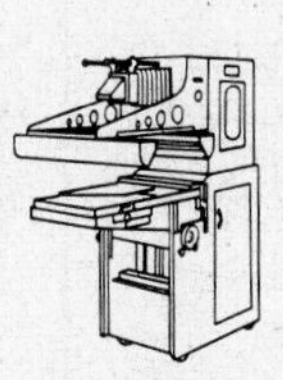
DEXIGRAPH®

Save 99% of filing space with **Film-a-record** microfilming; newest type machines for photocopying written, printed or drawn documents. Write for F405, P401, D399.

filing systems and equipment

FLEXOPRINT

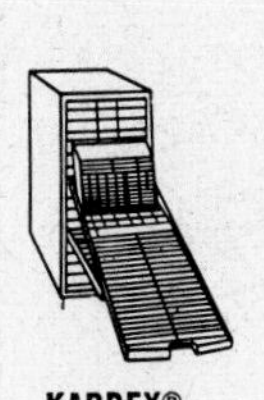
KARDEX®

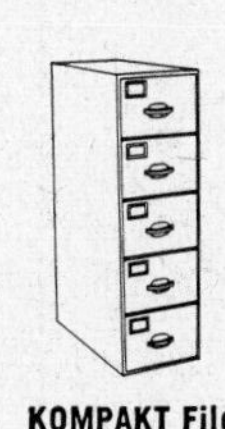
KOMPAKT File

Flexoprint for Voters' Lists and Stock Catalogs; **Kardex** for Voters' Permanent Registration records; **Kompakt** Files for space-saving active record storage. Write for KD610, KD614, LBV676.

At your disposal, without obligation, are many years of experience in providing the "Tools of Government Administration." We are government record specialists!

For efficient service to your taxpayers . . . in the production, handling and protection of vital records and statistics . . . consult . . .

YOUR BUSINESS EQUIPMENT CENTER — a source of ideas:

In your own city—or a city nearby—is a Remington Rand Business Equipment Center. This is a clearing house for the newest, most ingenious ideas to keep you abreast of current business practice.

Here you can find authoritative answers to your problems of administrative control.

You can see demonstrations of the best in machines, methods and equipment for getting office work done efficiently and economically.

HELP FROM MANAGEMENT CONTROLS REFERENCE LIBRARY

For your needs we have no reason to recommend anything but the right machines and systems.

We make them all

Hundreds of factual booklets are available . . . many outlining proved methods and procedures of specific systems for government offices. Make use of Remington Rand Management Controls Reference Library at your Business Equipment Center . . . also without obligation.

Some describe simplified methods . . . ways to cut out needless paperwork and at the same time supply complete facts and figures for effective management. Others show how to get greater clerical output from office machines and equipment which facilitates meeting legal deadlines. And many show the profitable results obtained by private firms and governmental departments whose problems are like yours.

Remington Rand

DIVISION OF SPERRY RAND CORPORATION

ROOM 2956A, 315 FOURTH AVENUE, NEW YORK 10, NEW YORK

Simple ten-key operation speeds posting output

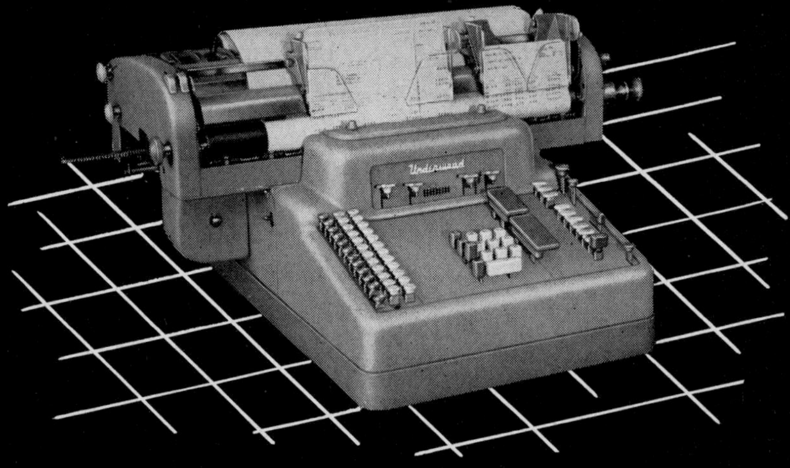

Flat writing-surface saves form-handling time

THE MICHAELS ART BRONZE CO., INC.

P. O. Box 668-MI

COVINGTON, KENTUCKY

MICHAELS BRONZE AND ALUMINUM PLAQUES

Because of their natural beauty and workability, bronze and aluminum are ideally suited to the production of memorials, name plates, honor rolls, historical tablets, intaglio and bas-relief portraits, directories, commemorative plaques, entrance signs, waterworks and sewage disposal plants, fire and police stations, city halls, municipal buildings, parks and playgrounds, and other purposes. In addition to its beauty, bronze possesses enduring qualities—in fact, it is virtually indestructible, defying the ravages of time and the elements. Aluminum is equally durable and used extensively for matching the exteriors and interiors of buildings.

TOWN OF FRONT ROYAL, VIRGINIA.
·SEWAGE TREATMENT PLANT·
·CONSTRUCTED 1950·
RUFUS E. PURDUM MAYOR
·COUNCILMEN·
FLOYD J. BOARD JOHNNIE MARCHI
HOWARD A. DUNCAN FRANK A. STOUTAMYER
L. B. DUTROW TOWN MANAGER
JOHN D. RIVES TOWN ENGINEER
CASTLE CONSTRUCTION COMPANY CONTRACTOR
R. STUART ROYER AND ASSOCIATES
·ENGINEERS·

Plaques are made of genuine bronze or aluminum with lettering, borders and ornamentation hand chased and burnished for contrast. They are available in a wide range of styles—any shape, any size, any design. A few examples are illustrated here. Tell us what you need, and we'll be glad to furnish sketches and quotations without cost or obligation. Write for illustrated literature.

DIRECTORIES OF MUNICIPAL OFFICIALS

Page numbers in parenthesis ( )

Council-Manager Municipalities and Their City Managers

1,399 Municipalities; 15 Counties (listed on page 1066)

Compiled by Orin F. Nolting, Executive Director, International City Managers' Association, 1313 East 60th Street, Chicago, Ill.

List Revised to January 1, 1957

Municipalities appearing in this directory have chief administrative officers who are appointed by the governing body and who in turn appoint and remove department heads and other administrative personnel; keep the council informed of the financial conditions and future needs of the city; prepare the budget for submission to the council; attend council meetings; make recommendations to the council on municipal affairs; and direct, supervise and coordinate the activities of city departments.

State and City	Name of Manager
Alabama	
Clanton	David Wale
Fairhope	Vacancy
Jackson	Vacancy
Jasper	H. O. Barton
Mountain Brook (Birmingham)	Jos. J. Swenson
Prattville	John F. Watkins
Arizona	
Casa Grande	E. M. Pederson
Chandler	James E. Johnson
Coolidge	R. L. Briscoe
Eloy	H. C. Jones
Gilbert	R. R. Beard, Jr.
Glendale	W. A. Gilchrist
Globe	Murray D. Snyder
Mesa	J. A. Petrie
Miami	Jack Phillips
Peoria	Vacancy
Phoenix	Ray W. Wilson
Prescott	Raymond T. Olsen
Tempe	John R. Ellingson
Tucson	Porter W. Homer
Wickenburg	Reuben Stifel
Arkansas	
Little Rock	Vacancy
California	
Alameda	Carl Froerer
Alhambra	A. E. Stockburger
Anaheim	Keith Murdoch
Antioch	Phil Minner
Arcadia	Neil F. Anderson
Avalon	Vacancy
Bakersfield	C. Leland Gunn
Banning	Bernard Owen
Belmont	Fred J. Nelson
Belvedere	Britton Rey
Berkeley	John D. Phillips
Beverly Hills	John B. Wentz
Brawley	W. O. Cuthbertson
Buena Park	Philip W. Storm
Burbank	H. R. Bennett
Carlsbad	Herbert E. Nelson
Chico	Robert O. Bailey
Chula Vista	Glenn Wade
California (cont.)	
Claremont	Wm. H. Parness
Colton	Lyman H. Cozad
Compton	Harry S. Scott
Concord	Ray Doran
Corona	Ralph D. Pfiffner
Coronado	Earl F. Ketcham
Costa Mesa	Robert L. Unger
Covina	Neil Goedhard
Culver City	Deane Seeger
Dairyland	B. B. Wesenberg
Daly City	Howard I. Stites
Davis	Frank Fargo
Delano	G. Walker Burgess
Downey	Arthur W. Brewer
El Cajon	Bernard J. Noden
El Centro	Leonard McClintock
El Cerrito	Kenneth H. Smith
El Segundo	John J. Sailors
Escondido	Lloyd M. Mitchell
Fairfield	Byron Gale Wilson
Fillmore	Leon Harthorn
Fontana	Doyle Miller
Fort Bragg	Vacancy
Fremont	F. R. Coop
Fullerton	H. A. Hiltscher
Glendale	C. E. Perkins
Glendora	Craig McMicken
Hanford	George M. Minturn
Hawthorne	Meno L. Wilhelms
Hayward	S. Douglas Smith
Hemet	Paul E. Wilcox
Hermosa Beach	Chapman L. Bone
Hillsborough	Norman Stiene
Indio	James O. Tennant
Inglewood	Walter Hahn, Jr.
Laguna Beach	C. J. Mercer, Jr.
La Habra	H. C. Billings
Lakewood	Robert T. Andersen
La Mesa	Lester Halcomb
Larkspur	Vacancy
LaVerne	W. F. Cornett, Jr.
Lincoln	L. F. Kengle
Lodi	H. D. Weller
Long Beach	Samuel E. Vickers
Los Banos	M. Dambrosio
Los Gatos	Karl Baldwin
Lynwood	A. J. Bateman
California (cont.)	
Madera	J. F. Frymire
Manhattan Beach	Gale T. Martin
Martinez	Gerald F. McMahon
Menlo Park	C. L. Longson
Merced	Russell J. Cooney
Mill Valley	A. E. Almcrants
Milpitas	Vacancy
Modesto	Ross Miller
Monrovia	Lloyd E. Brady
Monterey	Alfred D. Coons
Monterey Park	E. Frederick Bien
Mountain View	Phil Lawlor
Napa	Lee M. Roberts
National City	James A. Bird
Needles	Harry Hardinge
Nevada City	H. James Ray
Newark	John H. Nail
Newport Beach	Robert H. Shelton
No. Sacramento	Earnest D. Lindsay
Oakdale	John T. Schulte
Oakland	Wayne Thompson
Oceanside	F. W. Lilley
Ontario	Harold J. Martin
Oxnard	Paul E. Wolven
Pacific Grove	Vacancy
Palm Springs	Robt. W. Peterson
Palo Alto	Jerome Keithley
Pasadena	Don C. McMillan
Paso Robles	S. S. Tucker
Petaluma	Ed. Frank
Pittsburg	Ernest C. Marriner
Placentia	Denis M. Kelleher
Pomona	F. W. Sharp
Porterville	Chas. J. Cummings
Redding	Robert W. Cowden
Redlands	Fred H. Workman
Redondo Beach	F. E. Hopkins
Redwood City	E. A. Rolison
Rialto	W. H. Cunningham
Richmond	Edwin S. Howell
Ripon	Lanien S. Brady
Riverside	Oren L. King
Roseville	David C. Koester
Sacramento	B. W. Cavanaugh
Salinas	Ted B. Adsit
San Bruno	John C. Keefe
San Buenaventura	Lawrence E. Olson

State and City	Name of Manager
Calif. (cont.)	
San Carlos	Vacancy
San Clemente	D. L. Evans
San Diego	O. W. Campbell
San Fernando	Ray A. Woods
San Gabriel	Wm. J. Probert
Sanger	Douglas J. Flautt
San Jose	A. P. Hamann
San Leandro	Wesley McClure
San Luis Obispo	Richard D. Miller
San Marino	Charles Martin
San Mateo	Arthur B. Sullivan
San Pablo	K. B. Williams
San Rafael	Wilber Smith
Santa Ana	Carl J. Thornton
Santa Barbara	Perry W. Scott
Santa Clara	Loyd E. Brady
Santa Cruz	R. N. Klein
Santa Maria	Robert H. Oldland
Santa Monica	Randall M. Dorton
Santa Paula	Vacancy
Santa Rosa	Samuel B. Hood
Sausalito	D. A. Duerr
Sierra Madre	L. Bevington
South Pasadena	Frank M. Clough
S. San Francisco	Eugene Aiello
Stockton	John C. Lilly
Sunnyvale	H. K. Hunter
Tehachapi	Vacancy
Torrance	George W. Stevens
Tracy	Robert L. Williams
Tulare	George Aiassa
Ukiah	Lyell C. Cash
Upland	Elwin Alder
Vacaville	Robert Meyer
Vallejo	John R. Ficklin
Visalia	E. A. Dunn
Walnut Creek	Ira E. Gunn
West Covina	C. G. Petrie
Whittier	K. B. Douglas
Woodland	John H. Ferns
Yuba City	Edw. E. McCombs
Colorado	
Alamosa	Glynn Mills
Arvada	Karl G. Williams
Aurora	Earl P. Sandquist
Boulder	M. Don Harmon
Canon City	Allen Cuthbertson
Colorado Springs	John M. Biery
Delta	Riney F. Wilbert
Durango	M. W. Thomas
Englewood	Leslie R. Rudd
Florence	J. Joe Cox
Fort Collins	G. H. Palmes
Glenwood Springs	Albert E. Axtell
Golden	Arthur Lowther
Grand Junction	Robert E. Cheever
Greeley	B. H. Cruce
La Junta	Tom Russell
Monte Vista	Ronald Iske
Montrose	John R. McGinn
Pueblo	Vacancy
Sterling	Thos. W. Thorson
Trinidad	W. B. Cunningham
Wray	Harold B. Whyte
Connecticut	
Bloomfield	Preston C. King
Farmington	Stephen A. Flis
Hartford	C. F. Sharpe
Killingly (Danielson)	Owen Bell
Manchester	Richard Martin
Milford	John J. Desmond
New London	Edward R. Henkle
Norwich	Jay M. Etlinger
Stratford	Harry B. Flood
West Hartford	Donald H. Blatt
Wethersfield	Albert Gray, Jr.
Windsor	Robert B. Weiss
Delaware	
Dover	G. P. Ward
Milford	Vacancy
Newark	Orville F. Over
Rehoboth Beach	Lawrence I. Turner
Smyrna	Rex D. Gilmore
Florida	
Alachua	J. O. Langford
Apalachicola	W. N. Creekmore
Auburndale	Bruce Canova
Bal Harbour	Wilbur H. Webb
Bar Harbor Is.	J. M. Lulchuk
Bartow	Charles R. Odom
Belle Glade	C. E. Robinson
Clearwater	Vacancy
Florida (cont.)	
Cocoa	Vacancy
Coral Gables	Ira F. Willard
Dade City	Oscar Hettema
Dania	C. R. Chevalier, Jr.
Daytona Beach	Cletus R. Allen
Deerfield Beach	Vacancy
Deland	H. W. Johnson
Delray Beach	William E. Lawson
Dunedin	T. M. Wardwell
Eau Gallie	Vacancy
Eustis	Ernest P. Kidd
Fernandina Beach	Evett N. Allen
Fort Lauderdale	William J. Veeder
Fort Meade	John L. Green
Fort Pierce	Walter F. Johnson
Fort Walton	O. M. Early
Gainesville	Vacancy
Green Cove Spgs.	C. B. Bowles
Gulfport	Vacancy
Haines City	R. G. Simmons
Hallandale	Ralph L. Smith
Hollywood	Jos. W. Watson
Homestead	Vacancy
Jacksonville Bch.	J. Floyd Glisson
Jasper	James V. Doyle
Jupiter Island	Richard Tuggle
Key West	Fred R. Lane
Kissimmee	B. Harold Farmer
Lake Alfred	Geo. G. Costello
Lake Wales	Howard F. Burns
Lake Worth	H. F. Snuggs
Lakeland	David O. Payne
Largo	C. F. Fussell
Leesburg	J. Keener Mizell
Lynn Haven	Lee Curtis
Madeira Beach	Vacancy
Madison	Jesse Hughey
Marianna	Vacancy
Melbourne	Tevis Hugely
Miami	Edw. A. Evans
Miami Beach	Claude A. Renshaw
Miami Shores	C. Lawton McCall
Miami Springs	J. D. Ryan
Naples	F. M. Lowdermilk
New Smyrna Bch.	L. A. Weston
Niceville	Vacancy
North Bay Vil. (Miami)	David R. Walker
North Miami	Robt. V. Youkey
Ocala	John M. Baldwin
Opa-Locka	Wilbur R. Dale
Palatka	J. H. Bryan
Palm Beach	Jacob M. Boyd
Panama City	G. Courtney
Pensacola	O. J. Semmes, Jr.
Plant City	T. J. McCall
Polk City	Charles G. Smith
Pompano Beach	James S. Hughes
Quincy	Herbert C. Gregory
Riviera Beach	W. J. Johnstone
Safety Harbor	Mrs. Ida Samuelson
St. Augustine	G. Marvin Grier
St. Petersburg	Ross E. Windom
Sanford	Warren Knowles
Sarasota	Kenneth Thompson
South Miami	L. M. McConnell
Stuart	Joe N. Crowder
Surfside (Miami Beach)	F. M. Bowen, Jr.
Tallahassee	A. B. Hopkins
Tarpon Springs	Vacancy
Temple Terrace	H. P. Wardwell
Titusville	James Stewart
Vero Beach	Charles C. Jewett
West Palm Beach	Keith R. Chinn
Winter Haven	J. H. Fuller
Winter Park	Clark Maxwell
Georgia	
Albany	Carey Burnett
Avondale Estates	Dewey C. Brown
Brunswick	H. B. Lovvorn
Buford	J. C. Dover
Cartersville	Ernest E. Watkins
Cedartown	Robert L. Veal
Columbus	J. A. William
Coredele	S. E. Cox
Cornelia	Pope Ellard
Decatur	John D. Powell
Douglas	Glenn Tanner
Eastman	John J. Thomas
Elberton	Charles M. Dixon
Gainesville	Riley Milam
Griffin	W. E. George
Hawkinsville	G. L. Simpson
Jesup	Edwin O. Martin
LaGrange	H. M. Crane
Georgia (cont.)	
Manchester	Ellis McCurdy
Moultrie	Lloyd Baxter
Quitman	R. E. Dorough
Rome	S. S. King
Savannah	F. A. Jacocks
Sylvania	Vacancy
Thomasville	Vacancy
Tifton	Shell Hartley
Toccoa	W. S. Sharman
Waycross	Vacancy
Idaho	
Pocatello	William B. Webb
Twin Falls	Jos. H. Latimore
Illinois	
Arlington Height	F. R. Buechner
Bloomington	Eugene G. Moody
Brookfield	C. Harold Eash
Champaign	Vacancy
Deerfield	Harwood F. Rupp
East Moline	Chas. H. Buettner
Elgin	Raymond P. Botch
Elmhurst	Robert T. Palmer
Elmwood Park	Howard A. Olson
Evanston	Bert W. Johnson
Galena	Orville E. Meyer
Galesburg	Vacancy
Glencoe	Robert B. Morris
Glenview	Walter J. Hoffman
Greenville	Vacancy
Highland Park	Vacancy
Hinsdale	Vacancy
Homewood	E. Alan Webster
Joliet	Chester B. Lewis
Kenilworth	W. C. Drager
LaGrange	Robert A. Finley
Lake Forest	William B. Douglas
Lombard	Hugh T. Henry
Mascoutah	Chester F. Williams
Maywood	Vacancy
Mount Prospect	H. G. Appleby
Mt. Vernon	H. R. Richardson
Northbrook	Troy Miller, Jr.
Oak Lawn	Camille D. Andre
Oak Park	Mark E. Keane
Park Forest	John L. Scott
Park Ridge	James L. Galloway
Peoria	Geo. E. Bean
Princeton	Vacancy
Riverside	G. L. Opper
Rochelle	Vacancy
Rock Island	C. Bodine, Jr.
Savanna	D. A. Longmire
Villa Park	Vacancy
Westchester	Arthur S. Johnson
Western Springs	Richard Brown
Wilmette	William A. Wolff
Winnetka	C. R. Miller
Wood River	Ray E. Harbaugh
Woodstock	William H. Day
Iowa	
Ames	John M. Carpenter
Clarinda	R. H. van Deusen
Coon Rapids	Lyle Knight
Council Bluffs	Vacancy
Des Moines	George Forster
Dubuque	Laverne J. Schiltz
Grinnell	M. B. Starr
Iowa City	Peter F. Roan
Iowa Falls	Angus Crawford
Manchester	Francis M. Hoag
Mapleton	William Jensen
Maquoketa	Vacancy
Mt. Pleasant	Ed. Lampe
Ottumwa	Robt. L. Price
Shenandoah	Paul G. Osterholm
Sioux City	R. M. Hoisington
Villisca	Henry C. Fastenau
Webster City	C. C. McCarthy
West Liberty	Waldo C. Myers
Kansas	
Abilene	Carl L. Nicolay
Arkansas City	Wayne B. Lambert
Atchison	Wm. R. Yerkes
Augusta	R. J. Hayes
Belleville	Earl Whitney
Chanute	Ross Cooper
Colby	Thomas C. Browne
Concordia	Harold E. Horn
El Dorado	Stanley H. Dial
Emporia	R. W. Cunningham
Garden City	Dean P. Wiley
Great Bend	Vacancy
Hays	Harley E. Lucas

State and City	Name of Manager
Kans. (cont.)	
Hoisington	Jack Branum
Holton	Stanley D. Fisher
Hutchinson	Hal L. Everett
Independence	Glen Hackmaster
Junction City	Virgil Basgall
Kinsley	Albert E. Wilson
La Crosse	Leroy Trafton
Larned	Wayne N. Baxter
Lawrence	J. H. Wigglesworth
Liberal	W. D. Pittser
Manhattan	D. C. Wesche
McCracken	J. I. Edwards
Newton	Chester E. Petersen
Parsons	Bernard P. Budd
Pittsburg	Albert W. Noland
Russell	John B. LaDuex
St. Marys	M. E. Coleman
Salina	Leland M. Srack
Sterling	Ray A. Hanfeld
Stockton	C. N. Harper
Wamego	K. F. Sanborn
Wichita	F. H. Backstrom
Winfield	Kenneth F. Watts
Kentucky	
Ashland	Vacancy
Corbin	W. L. Walker
Covington	Oscar Hesch
Frankfort	Vacancy
Hazard	Hobart Wootan
Lexington	Herbert D. Fritz
Maysville	Miss H. Larkin (Temp.)
Morehead	Felix Wellman
Newport	Vacancy
Owensboro	John A. Hettler
Paducah	Lloyd C. Emery
Pikeville	Hugh B. Hall
Maine	
Amity	Fred C. Greaves
Ashland	Kermit Crandall
Auburn	B. B. Allen
Baileyville (Woodland)	Frank Foggia
Bangor	Jos. R. Coupal, Jr.
Bar Harbor	Ralph F. W. Eye
Bath	Stanley W. Judkins
Belfast	Lawrance E. Dow
Benedicta	Theo. R. Bartlett
Berwick	Sidney O. Young
Bethel	O. T. Rozelle
Blaine	Beulah Vinsonhaler
Boothbay	R. P. McLaughlin
Boothbay Harbor	Chester A. Swett
Bowdoinham	Bert D. Merrill
Brewer	Donald J. Waring
Bridgewater	Vacancy
Bridgton	H. Dayton Benway
Brownville	Lyle C. Towne
Brunswick	Thomas M. Libby
Bucksport	L. W. O'Connor
Calais	E. H. Higgins
Camden	Sterling G. Morris
Caribou	Charles D. Hatch
Carmel	Clyde Hewes
Castle Hill	Melvin Higgins
Chelsea	J. Merton Wyman
Clinton	Harold L. Bean
Corinna	John Bird
Corinth	Vacancy
Crystal	Basil Campbell
Danforth	Rollin Thurlow
Dexter	Vance E. Dearborn
Dover-Foxcroft	L. A. Peabody
Dyer Brook	V. W. McLaughlin
Eagle Lake	Leo Martin
Eastport	Walter R. Benson
Ellsworth	Elton M. Rich
Fairfield	Vacancy
Farmington	Millard S. Quimby
Fort Fairfield	Leonard H. Kyle
Fort Kent	Elbridge Gagnon
Freeport	Osmond C. Bonsey
Frenchville	John C. Michaud
Gardiner	Jules Deshaies
Garland	Harry A. Roach
Greenville	Archie D. Sanborn
Guilford	Charles A. Haynes
Hartland	Claude E. Fisher
Haynesville	John H. Hatch
Hermon	John S. Taylor
Hodgdon	Fred C. Greaves
Houlton	J. Maynard Austin
Island Falls	Edward Quinlan
Islesboro	Vacancy
Jackman	Leon W. Smiley
Maine (cont.)	
Kennebunk	John N. Balch
Levant	Walter Whitney
Limestone	Bernard Cameron
Lincoln	Vacancy
Linneus	Fred C. Greaves
Lisbon	Elton O. Feeney
Litchfield	H. R. Johnson
Littleton	Anna Schools
Lubec	Harold Thurlow
Machias	Charles A. Ross
Madawaska	Adrian O. Jacques
Madison	Mrs. M. Huggins
Mapleton	Melvin Higgins
Mars Hill	Stanley Lavery
Massardis	Charles Sylvester
Mechanic Falls	Edward Sawyer
Merrill	Leland G. Adams
Mexico	Ronald W. Clifford
Millbridge	Clarence J. Buckley
Milo	Bion F. Jose
Millinocket	Vacancy
Monmouth	Robert Hanson
Monroe	Frank E. Riley
Monson	Wilbur Kronholm
Monticello	Arnot Archibald
Mount Desert (Northeast Harbor)	F. T. Staples
New Canada (Soldier Pond)	Claude Dumond
New Gloucester	Conrad L. Drapeau
New Portland	M. D. Davis
Norridgewock	Chester Carson
Norway	H. B. Carsley
Oakfield	V. W. McLaughlin
Oakland	Leigh Webber
Ogunquit	Harold W. Putnam
Old Orchard Bch.	Vacancy
Old Town	John P. Bibber
Orono	Seth P. Jackson
Orrington	Roland J. Dubay
Oxford	Mrs. B. Staples
Patten	Robt. L. Anderson
Phillips	Chas. E. Toothaker
Pittsfield	O. Lionel Pomroy
Portage Lake	Donald Abbott
Portland	Julian H. Orr
Presque Isle	N. W. McDonald
Rangeley	O. R. Rowe
Reed	Fred C. Greaves
Richmond	Chas. E. Danforth
Rockland	Lloyd K. Allen
Rockport	Archie A. Stevens
Rumford	Leo J. Morency
St. Agatha	Sylvio Michaud
St. Francis	Geo. M. Jones
Sangerville	Orville D. Carr
Scarborough	Earle D. Stevens
Searsport	Dudley E. Foley
Sherman	Theo. R. Bartlett
Skowhegan	Elbert M. Prince
Smyrna	Leland G. Adams
South Berwick	J. H. Thompson
South Portland	J. Harold Webster
Stacyville	Theo. R. Bartlett
Stockholm	Mrs. Agnes Baxter
Stonington	A. C. Brown
Thomaston	Leon E. Fitts
Van Buren	Albert G. Cyr
Vassalboro	Francis E. Munsey
Waldoboro	E. H. Shute
Wallagrass (Soldier Pond)	Emery Labbe
Warren	Vacancy
Washburn	M. H. Blackstone
Wells	Richard J. Bowen
Wilton	Jas. M. Ordway
Maryland	
Greenbelt	Chas. T. McDonald
Princess Anne	R. S. Cox, Jr.
Rockville	John H. Markland
Massachusetts	
Amherst	Allen L. Torrey
Arlington	Edw. C. Monahan
Brockton	Vacancy
Cambridge	John J. Curry
Concord	Theo. M. Nelson
Danvers	D. J. McFadden
Gloucester	Richard W. Mayo
Haverhill	G. D. Chavenelle
Holden	Earle D. Hardy
Ipswich	N. W. Stilphen
Lowell	Frank E. Barrett
Mansfield	Cecil O. Lancaster
Medford	John B. Kennedy
Mass. (cont.)	
Middleboro	Edwin O. Wilson
North Adams	Vacancy
Norwood	Vacancy
Provincetown	James V. Coyne
Quincy	Edward T. Lewis
Randolph	Charles R. Iovino
Revere	Edw. O. O'Toole
Saugus	Daniel E. McLean
Shrewsbury	Allen L. Wilcox
Williamstown	Vacancy
Wilmington	Jos. F. Courtney
Worcester	F. J. McGrath
Michigan	
Allegan	P. H. Beauvais
Alma	J. D. McNaughton
Alpena	F. N. Jackson
Bay City	C. F. Jablonski
Benton Harbor	H. H. Crow
Berkley	John W. Short
Big Rapids	Geo. Granger
Birmingham	Harold K. Schone
Bloomfield Hills	Elmer Kephart
Brighton	John F. Quigley
Buchanan	John H. Kennaugh
Cadillac	L. A. Hanson
Caspian	Joseph F. Doyle
Cheboygan	Vacancy
Clare	H. W. Wedge
Clawson	Robt. O. Wright
Crystal Falls	W. F. Jacka
Davison	Donald R. Smith
Durand	Boyd K. Benedict
East Detroit	Charles Beaubien
E. Grand Rapids	L. Henry Gork
East Lansing	J. M. Patriarche
Escanaba	A. V. Aronson
Farmington	E. F. Scherffius
Ferndale	Wilfred A. Laking
Flint	Harold C. Chirgwin
Flushing	Vacancy
Fremont	Jacob J. Goll
Gaastra	Walter Johnson
Garden City	Douglas F. Waddell
Gaylord	Walter E. Looney
Gladstone	H. J. Henrikson
Grand Haven	R. V. Terrill
Grand Rapids	Donald M. Oakes
Grayling	Russell Carlson
Greenville	Alan G. Davis
Grosse Pte. Farms	Sidney de Boer
Grosse Pte. Park	Everitt B. Lane
Grosse Pte. Shores	T. K. Jefferis
Grosse Pte. Woods	William H. Lange
Harbor Springs	Aldwyn C. Wager
Harper Woods	Robert J. McNutt
Hart	Howard Gwinnup
Hazel Park	Calvin C. Henry
Holland	Herb H. Holt
Holly	Norman E. Tufford
Howell	Fred H. Tholen
Hudson	Wm. E. Besuden
Huntington Woods	Fred L. Yockey
Imlay City	D. E. Firestone
Inkster	W. E. Meadowcroft
Iron River	Julius S. Metros
Ironwood	Lloyd Waterstraut
Ishpeming	Olaf E. Stolen
Jackson	Jos. A. Warren
Kalamazoo	C. H. Elliott
Kingsford	Jas. J. Cummings
Lapeer	Howard R. Gohlke
Lathrup	L. Watchowski
Ludington	Jas. F. Cartier
Madison Heights	Donald B. Smith
Manistee	James R. Burch
Manistique	O. E. Livermore
Marine City	A. J. Westrick
Marquette	Geo. Meholick, Jr.
Marysville	H. M. Davenport
Mason	Vacancy
Midland	Ray Fry
Mount Clemens	R. D. Heitsch, Jr.
Mount Pleasant	Allan J. Kronbach
Muskegon	Geo. F. Liddle
Muskegon Hgts.	Roy J. Miles
Negaunee	Earl P. Wagner
Northville	John Robertson
Norway	Paul Trione
Oak Park	Virgil C. Knowles
Otsego	James R. Schubert
Oxford	Ralph W. Precious
Petoskey	E. L. Neumann

State and City	Name of Manager
Mich. **(cont.)**	
Pleasant Ridge	Paul D. Foxworthy
Plymouth	A. F. Glassford
Pontiac	W. K. Willman
Port Huron	J. F. Gibbs
Portland	Bernard C. Morse
Rochester	Robert A. Slone
Rockford	Paul A. York
Rogers City	Charles R. McKee
Roseville	O. R. Pearson
Royal Oak	E. M. Shafter
Saginaw	C. A. Miller
St. Clair Shores	A. A. Lingemann
St. Johns	K. W. Anderson
St. Joseph	Leland L. Hill
St. Louis	Donald P. Ziemke
Sault Ste. Marie	R. E. Speer
Springfield (Battle Creek)	Paul Garvin
Stambaugh	Geo. Hammar
Sturgis	Worth N. Yoder
Sylvan Lake (Pontiac)	Ernest Ethier
Tecumseh	Ernest J. Nelson
Three Rivers	Clifford R. Miles
Traverse City	N. G. Damoose
Troy	Vacancy
Vassar	William F. Wilson
Wakefield	Leonard J. Harris
Walled Lake	George A. Shaw
Wayne	W. G. Arrowsmith
Whitehall	John E. Kane
Ypsilanti	Sinclair Powell
Minnesota	
Albert Lea	Barkley G. Omans
Anoka	C. R. Johnson
Bemidji	James Deneen
Bloomington	Frank H. Lawler
Columbia Heights	Ray L. Ernest
Edina	Warren C. Hyde
Fridley	Ernest Madsen
Granite Falls	Orvil J. Johnson
Hopkins	Sidney S. Frissell
Mankato	Harold B. Vasey
Montevideo	Roy Rodeberg
Morris	Vacancy
Mound	Vernon Boxell
New Ulm	Philip L. White
North St. Paul	Gordon E. Olson
Richfield	O. Van Krevelen
St. Louis Park	T. E. Chenoweth
Wayzata	Donald E. Pipes
White Bear Lake	Edward G. Bayuk
Mississippi	
Grenada	John E. McEachin
Meridian	L. B. Cresswell
Moorhead	W. L. Jackson, Jr.
Picayune	A. J. Read
Missouri	
Brookfield	Robert L. Hegel
Cameron	Glen Woods
Charleston	Clyde E. Swank
Columbia	W. Leo Hill
DeSoto	A. J. O'Rourke
Excelsior Springs	David H. Pence
Ferguson	Robert C. Storey
Joplin	J. D. Baughman
Kansas City	L. P. Cookingham
Lebanon	Stanley Brooks
Marceline	Lawrence Gish
Maryville	Robert G. Pierce
Mexico	Calvin M. Lakin
Moberly	Kenneth L. Bolin
Neosho	Homer B. Ball, Jr.
Nevada	Thos. B. Herring
Slater	A. J. Mulvihill
Springfield	W. B. Avery
University City	Elder Gunter
Webster Groves	H. C. McClintock
Montana	
Bozeman	M. E. Henderson
Helena	Henry Rolfes
Missoula	Vacancy
Nebraska	
Alliance	R. W. Laing
Chadron	F. Kenneth Kyle
Gordon	A. H. Britton
Kearney	Ray E. Lundy
Lexington	Maurice E. Cole
McCook	Leland Nelson
Scottsbluff	C. D. Leikvold
Sidney	Murrey W. Fuller
Nevada	
Elko	Henry Etchemendy
Las Vegas	A. H. Kennedy
Nevada (cont.)	
Reno	C. B. Kinnison
Sparks	Vacancy
New Hampshire	
Ashland	Robert W. Rhodes
Claremont	Gordon Dillon
Concord	Woodbury Brackett
Conway	P. H. Wardwell
Exeter	Allen M. Marks
Goffstown	Vacancy
Hampton	John W. True
Keene	Donald E. Chick
Lancaster	Donald E. Crane
Meredith	David Sullivan
Newport	Harry B. Ripley
Northumberland	K. D. Boehner
Portsmouth	Robt. C. Violette
New Jersey	
Asbury Park	J. O. Armstrong
Cedar Grove	R. M. Urquhart
Clifton	William Holster
Fair Lawn	W. T. Williamson
Hackensack	Harold V. Reilly
Keansburg	Vacancy
Livingston	Robert H. Harp
Lodi	Albert H. Branea
Medford Lakes	J. A. Weaver, Jr.
Mount Holly	William P. Hatch
Newton Twp.	Dana T. Whitman
Parsippany-Troy Hills	Vacancy
Pequannock Twp.	Vacancy
Ridgewood	Wayne P. Mitchell
Teaneck	Jas. T. Welsh
Teterboro	Frank A. Battell
New Mexico	
Alamagordo	H. H. Holcomb
Albuquerque	Edmund L. Engel
Clayton	Manson Edmondson
Clovis	Marion S. Hass
Farmington	A. J. Vasilakis
Hobbs	Neil Harr
Las Cruces	Patrick McClernon
Lovington	James W. Harrison
Roswell	C. M. Woodbury
Santa Fe	C. O. Erwin
Truth or Consequences	Robert B. Laursen
Tucumcari	J. A. Fleming
New York	
Ardsley	Vacancy
Auburn	George F. Train
Elmira	Thos. A. Banfield
Hastings-on-Hudson	Alfred S. Harding
Long Beach	M. J. Fleischman
Mamaroneck	Wm. H. Johnson
Monticello	Thomas S. Belmont
Newburgh	Wm. H. Kennedy
New Rochelle	Edward G. Conroy
Niagara Falls	Vacancy
Patchogue	Wm. W. Parrott
Pleasantville	Frederick Tubman
Poughkeepsie	Vacancy
Rochester	Robert P. Aex
Rome	Robt. H. McManus
Saranac Lake	Frank G. Buck, Sr.
Scarsdale	Reeves Newsom
Schenectady	Arthur Blessing
Sherrill	Clarence Garner
Watertown	Arnold G. Forbes
Watervliet	N. J. Normile
Yonkers	Charles L. Curran
North Carolina	
Asheboro	Clifford Pace
Asheville	J. Weldon Weir
Black Mountain	R. T. Greene
Burlington	J. Mackintosh, Jr.
Carolina Beach	Vacancy
Chapel Hill	Thos. D. Rose
Charlotte	Henry A. Yansey
Dunn	A. B. Uzzle, Jr.
Durham	Robt. W. Flack
Elizabeth City	E. T. Hyman
Fayetteville	Gilbert W. Ray
Fuquay Springs	W. O. Council
Gastonia	Jas. S. Carter
Goldsboro	Zeno G. Hollowell
Graham	Vacancy
Greensboro	Jas. R. Townsend
Greenville	Leonard P. Bloxam
Hamilton Lakes (Guilford)	W. McCormick, Jr.
Hickory	H. L. Burdette
High Point	T. E. Hinson
N. Car. (cont.)	
Jacksonville	H. B. Hines, Jr.
Kinston	Roy R. Robinson
Laurinburg	J. Guy Smith, Jr.
Lexington	George H. Aull, Jr.
Louisburg	Vacancy
Lumberton	A. B. Sansbury
Marion	Reece C. Snyder
Monroe	Lott T. Rogers
Mooresville	Ridley T. Nichol
Morganton	Robert Carr
New Bern	C. L. Barnhardt
Newton	Bruce Turney
Oxford	W. F. Parham
Raleigh	Wm. H. Carper
Reidsville	J. L. Womach
Rocky Mount	S. C. MacIntire, Jr.
Roxboro	W. F. Timberlake
Salisbury	C. L. Lineback
Sanford	Robert H. Peck
Selma	A. C. Turnage, Jr.
Southern Pines	L. E. Scheipers, Jr.
Southport	Vacancy
Statesville	Vacancy
Tarboro	W. B. Howard
Thomasville	W. T. Green, Jr.
Tryon	Claude Smith
Valdese	Lee Ribet
Washington	J. A. Rickards
Whiteville	W. S. Huggins
Wilmington	James R. Benson
Wilson	Jack Maynard
Winston-Salem	John M. Gold
North Dakota	
Grand Forks	Vacancy
Minot	R. B. Riddle
Ohio	
Amberly	Oscar T. Egolf
Bedford	O. E. Hutchinson
Carey	George Dunn
Cincinnati	C. A. Harrell
Cleveland Hgts.	Ray P. Martin
Dayton	H. W. Starick
Delaware	Roger W. Stilwell
East Cleveland	Charles A. Carran
Fairborn	C. R. Lukens
Gallipolis	Austin O. Cotton
Hamilton	Vacancy
Indian Hill (Cincinnati)	Warren W. Parks
Ironton	O. M. Wiseman
Kettering (Dayton)	Ervin L. Welch
Middletown	C. W. Thompson
Oakwood (Dayton)	A. C. Bergman
Oberlin	Fred E. Weisbrod
Painesville	Paul D. Cook
Piqua	R. M. Hance, Jr.
Portsmouth	Robert E. Layton
Sandusky	Karl H. Kugel
Sidney	Glenn Lovern
South Charleston	Elton Tindall
Springfield	Harold R. Cheek
Toledo	Russell W. Rink
Upper Arlington	C. C. Ryan
Washington Court House	J. F. Parkinson
Westerville	John P. Willison
Worthington	Vacancy
Wyoming	R. A. Anderegg
Xenia	J. J. Salovaara
Yellow Springs	W. Howard Kahoe
Zanesville	Vacancy
Oklahoma	
Ada	John R. Hamman
Altus	Leon Carver
Anadarko	A. E. Ash
Ardmore	Emmett Brown
Atoka	Vacancy
Bartlesville	Erbin E. Jones
Bethany	Harry B. Macrory
Broken Arrow	Morgan Hays
Chandler	C. L. Kessler
Cherokee	Glenn D. Garner
Chickasha	H. B. McDowell
Claremore	Lee E. Fettig
Cleveland	J. D. Cheek
Coalgate	R. M. Lacy
Crescent	John Paris
Cushing	L. L. Houston
Davis	Vacancy
Dewey	Huey Long
Drumright	W. B. Browning
Duncan	John B. Davidson
Edmond	J. B. Marshall
Elk City	Ray Damron

State and City	Name of Manager
Okla. (cont.)	
El Reno	C. A. Bentley
Enid	Gerald D. Wilkins
Fairview	E. M. Evans
Grandfield	W. G. Medlock
Guthrie	R. O. Whitechurch
Hartshorne	John E. White
Heavener	J. Ray Farley
Henryetta	H. R. Youngmeyer
Konawa	Roy E. Adair
Lindsay	Archie High
McAlester	C. Harold Tippit
Madill	J. H. Kirley
Mangum	Edward W. Day
Midwest City	Robt. W. Quinlan
Muskogee	C. Clay Harrell
Norman	Vacancy
Nowata	G. F. Hill
Oklahoma City	William Gill, Jr.
Okmulgee	R. M. Bingham
Pauls Valley	E. T. Barber
Pawhuska	W. T. Loman
Ponca City	Frank A. Winsted
Purcell	Leon Williams
Sallisaw	Leon W. Black
Sapulpa	Add Allyson
Shawnee	Willard B. Moran
Stigler	John A. Wells
Tecumseh	G. E. Horne
Tonkawa	Hal H. Hunt
Walters	Robert Wilson
Waurika	T. R. McCasling
Woodward	Thos. W. Keltch
Yale	C. W. Stepp
Oregon	
Albany	Wm. D. Bollman
Astoria	Brewer A. Billie
Baker	Robert Applegate
Bend	Walter Thompson
Coos Bay	Robt. G. Kyle
Cornelius	J. D. Harleman
Corvallis	John F. Porter
Eugene	R. A. Finlayson
Forest Grove	M. O. Gardner
Grants Pass	Hugh McKinley
Hillsboro	J. W. Barney
LaGrande	Fred J. Young
Medford	Robert H. Duff
Milton-Freewater	J. R. Castner
Milwaukie	Earl S. Burdick
North Bend	R. J. Herrington
Nyssa	A. R. Middaugh
Oregon City	Robert Clute
Pendleton	Leland M. Swanson
Roseburg	George W. Farrell
Salem	Kent Mathewson
Silverton	R. E. Borland
Springfield	E. Robert Turner
Sutherlin	C. Dean Smith
Sweet Home	Roy Eames
The Dalles	Gifford W. Miller
Tillamook	H. S. Paulson
Toledo	Archie French
Warrenton	E. R. Baldwin
Pennsylvania	
Ashland	Franklin L. Lane
Aspinwall	Winfield S. Lea
Avalon	Jos. Arthur
Beaver Borough	Lyle C. Kimple
Bellefonte	Dale F. Helsel
Bethel	Chas. A. Geisler
Blairsville	John A. Fatora
Boyertown	Rowland A. Read
Bristol	Vacancy
Bristol Twp.	Vacancy
Camp Hill	R. J. Rountree, Jr.
Carlisle	Paul L. White
Cheltenham Twp. (Elkins Park)	Harold C. Pike
Clarks Summit	Vacancy
Dormont	William H. Struwe
Downingtown	Walter I. Leland
Edgewood	N. Michael Markl
Edgeworth (Sewickley)	Robert E. Lunn
Ellwood City	Arthur Emmerson
Ephrata	Carl W. Fuehrer
Fox Chapel (Pittsburgh)	Richard R. Moore
Grove City	W. A. Scheiber
Hampton Twp. (Allison Park)	John H. Eisenman
Hanover	Vacancy
Hollidaysburg	Robt. R. Mitchell
Homer City	Andrew W. Mock
Indiana	George H. Shea
Lansdowne	Fred Roberts
Penna. (cont.)	
Lehighton	W. H. Niehoff
Lewistown	Bernard F. Smith
Lititz	David J. Bauer
L. Merion Twp. (Ardmore)	Evan L. James
Lower Southampton Twp.	Vacancy
McCandless Twp. (Pittsburgh)	S. V. Erdelyi
Marple Twp. (Broomall)	Chas. M. Melchior
Martinsburg	F. B. Higgins
Mechanicsburg	Samuel H. Pressley
Middletown Twp. (Langhorne)	Angus Johnson
Mifflinburg	Guy L. Krapp
Milton	Wm. J. Ganster
Monaca	Vacancy
Mt. Lebanon Tp. (Pittsburgh)	John A. Paulus
Narberth	John L. Taylor
New Brighton	W. S. McDanel
Newton (Newton Square)	D. W. Llewellyn
Northampton	Hale A. Guss
Oakmont	Robert T. Roche
Penn. Twp. (Allegheny Co.)	John H. Immel
Phoenixville	John T. Bush
Pottstown	R. H. McKinney
Quakertown	Ralph L. Yanish
Ross (Pittsburgh)	Wade Winner
St. Marys	D. S. Harding
Schuylkill Haven	Richard Davis, Jr.
Scottdale	W. H. Steelsmith
Sewickley	Raymond L. Howe
Sewickley Hgts.	Frank C. Sturm
Shaler Twp. (Pittsburgh)	J. Wynn Thompson
Sharpsville	Vacancy
Shillington	H. L. Burmeister
Snowden Twp. (Library)	Jas. A. Ross
Springdale	Vacancy
State College	Robt. Y. Edwards
Warren	George Geracimos
Warrington Twp.	L. H. Point
Watsontown	J. G. Joseph
Waynesboro	Roy N. Hawbaker
Wellsboro	John Daugherty
West Reading	H. F. Rickenback
West View	Clarence F. Deem
Whitehall	C. Heckerman, Jr.
Wilkinsburg	John C. Deal
Rhode Island	
Newport	Irving H. Beck
North Kingstown	Roderic A. Gardner
South Carolina	
Aiken	R. Powell Black
Beaufort	J. McDonald Wray
Camden	Max Holland
Chester	Hood C. Worthy
Columbia	Irving G. McNayr
Florence	Aaron Marsh
Greenville	Gerald W. Shaw
Greenwood	A. L. Atkinson
Lake City	V. L. Lyerly
Lancaster	Ivey Poovey (Act.)
Newberry	E. L. Blackwell
Orangeburg	A. T. Brown
Rock Hill	W. M. Kennedy
Spartanburg	R. E. Froneberger
Sumter	Wade S. Kolb
Winnsboro	Hugh N. Thompson
South Dakota	
Hot Springs	James L. Kay, Jr.
Madison	Ralph R. Johnson
Rapid City	H. S. Thorgrimson
Yankton	James L. Jensen
Tennessee	
Adair	Vanden Griffin
Alcoa	Ross F. Walker
Athens	John B. Elliott
Atwood	W. G. Belew
Beersheba Spgs.	Vacancy
Bell Meade (Nashville)	W. T. Mallinson
Berry Hill (Nashville)	Bryan H. Alsup
Clifton	J. James Dowdy
Collinwood	Thornton L. Ryan
Columbia	Lowell Long
Dayton	Jesse Clarke
Elizabethton	Paul W. Crumley
Gatlinburg	Walter W. Mynatt
Tenn. (cont.)	
Johnson City	D. A. Burkhalter
Kingsport	Denzil W. Moulton
Murfreesboro	H. L. McCullough
Oak Hill (Nashville)	W. Fletcher Hardy
Paris	Philip B. Watson
Red Bank (White Oak)	Cliff Greenwood
Rutledge	W. E. Holt
Savannah	Dennie R. Tyler
Shelbyville	Jos. D. Brown
Spring City	V. Z. Cline
Texas	
Abilene	Vacancy
Alice	E. C. Drumb
Amarillo	N. V. Moss
Andrews	J. L. Horner
Aransas Pass	Howard L. McCalla
Arlington	Wm. J. Pitstick
Austin	W. T. Williams
Baytown	C. D. Middleton
Beaumont	Mrs. W. Brockman
Beeville	Douglas Henslee
Bellaire	Gary O. Summers
Belton	J. G. Nash
Big Springs	H. W. Whitney
Bonham	R. G. Fisher
Borger	A. C. Spears
Breckenridge	Glen A. Doty
Brownfield	E. D. Jones
Brownsville	E. W. Watts
Brownwood	Jack Broad
Bryan	Casey C. Fannin
Burkburnett	A. W. Newman
Burnet	Fred Garrison
Carrizo Springs	E. W. Marlowe
Carthage	T. A. Grissom
Center	Price Ramsey, Jr.
Childress	Vacancy
Clarksville	C. R. Dinwiddie
Cleburne	Floyd J. Carroll
Coleman	Albert J. Pope
College Station	Ran Boswell
Colorado City	R. K. Snethen
Commerce	M. B. Messler
Corpus Christi	R. E. McClure
Corsicana	Morgan W. Works
Crystal City	L. L. Williams
Dalhart	A. J. Browning
Dallas	Elgin E. Crull
Denison	David A. Harner
Eastland	James W. Young
Edinburg	C. W. Vetters
El Campo	R. A. Baca
Farmers Branch	John J. Gray
Fort Stockton	E. B. Ligon
Fort Worth	J. F. Davis
Gainesville	Homer B. Bly
Garland	Jack Shelley
Georgetown	Lee C. Black
Giddings	R. A. Toler
Gilmer	James Croley
Gladewater	Lee S. Vickers
Graham	J. P. Tackett
Grand Prairie	Dean I. Dauley
Greenville	Henry B. Nabers
Haltom City	Vacancy
Harlingen	L. M. Crow, Jr.
Hearne	N. L. McCarver
Hereford	C. Dudley Bayne
Hubbard	J. C. Boone
Irving	John S. Stiff
Jacksonville	Walter E. Cook
Jasper	P. V. Werner
Kermit	Jas. C. Hill
Kerrville	Rudolph H. Weiss
Killeen	John G. Sarris
Kingsville	G. G. Medders
Lake Jackson	A. A. MacLean
Lamesa	C. A. Taylor
Levelland	Kenneth Harper
Livingston	W. C. de Cordova
Lockhart	Howard Grantham
Longview	Harry G. Mosley
Lubbock	H. P. Clifton
Lufkin	Harold Schmitzer
McAllen	Wm. L. Schupp
Marshall	Ivan P. Oliver
Mesquite	C. J. Griggs
Mexia	Howard F. Mace
Midland	J. M. Orman
Mission	G. A. Scrimshire
Monahans	Morris M. Howard
Mount Pleasant	A. E. Taylor
Nacogdoches	H. G. Stallings
Navasota	M. B. Thomas

State and City	Name of Manager
Texas (cont.)	
Nederland	G. H. Petkousek
Odessa	R. G. Pepin
Orange	Gene Gatlin
Pampa	F. W. Brook
Panhandle	Frank Vice
Paris	A. K. Steinheimer
Perryton	J. B. Whigham, Jr.
Pittsburg	C. E. Wynne
Port Arthur	Charles Brazil
Port Lavaca	Morgan White
Ranger	L. Crossley
Richardson	R. B. Sherrill
Rosebud	Louis J. Smitzes
San Angelo	Del Green
San Antonio	Steve Matthews
San Benito	Francis A. Vaughn
Santa Anna	Vacancy
Sherman	Robert L. Brown
Snyder	Roy L. Dunlap
Spur	Vacancy
Stamford	Harry D. Steenson
Sulphur Springs	J. B. Henderson
Sweetwater	Garland P. Franks
Taylor	F. R. Cromwell
Temple	W. E. Routh
Terrell	R. H. Hayes, Jr.
Tulia	H. Fritz Lanham
Tyler	C. P. Stewart
Uvalde	R. R. Evans
Victoria	Vacancy
Waco	J. W. Jeffrey
Waxahachie	J. H. Greenwell
Weslaco	V. C. Thompson
West Columbia	Ernest F. Lee
W. Univ. Place	W. F. Johnson
Wichita Falls	F. A. Thomason
Yoakum	R. H. Koether
Utah	
Bountiful	Alvin Sessions
Cedar City	Vacancy
Clearfield	R. Clay Allred
Monticello	Byron M. Oberg
Nephi	L. E. Wiscombe
Ogden	E. J. Allison
Orem	O. V. Farnsworth
Provo	E. Earl Udall
Richfield	Guy Baker
South Salt Lake	H. C. Chandler
Tooele	Dale Wm. James
Vernal	Vacancy
Vermont	
Barre	Paul H. Hermann
Barretown (Websterville)	Arthur H. Curtis
Bellows Falls	C. A. Bissonnette
Bethel	Roy A. Kane
Brattleboro	Geo. F. Miller
Castleton	Vacancy
Cavendish	Vacancy
Chester	A. F. Hawkes
Chester Village	A. F. Hawkes
Essex Junction	Corwin S. Elwell
Hardwick	H. E. Rowell
Hartford (White River Junction)	Roland F. Burke
Hartland	L. E. L. O'Rourke
Manchester	Oakley K. Porter
Middlebury	Thos. E. Duff
Middlebury Vil.	Thos. E. Duff
Montpelier	Ralph Irving
North Troy	Ernest Westberg
Vermont (cont.)	
Northfield	Richard F. Cahill
Northfield Vil.	Richard F. Cahill
Poultney	Earl Hubbard
Randolph	Jos. C. Babineau
Randolph Vil.	Jos. C. Babineau
Rockingham	C. A. Bissonnette
St. Johnsbury	Chas. S. Sumner
St. Johnsbury Vil.	Chas. S. Sumner
South Burlington	W. O. Anderson
Springfield	J. Leslie Giddings
Troy	Ernest Westberg
Windsor	William Blaisdell
Windsor Vil.	William Blaisdell
Virginia	
Abingdon	David Goodman
Alexandria	Edw. G. Heatwole
Altavista	R. C. Klepper
Appalachia	J. H. Fletcher
Ashland	W. C. Blanton
Bedford	Philip W. Ancell
Big Stone Gap	Wilson D. Coleman
Blacksburg	Wm. F. LaVecchia
Blackstone	R. D. Maben, Jr.
Bluefield	W. N. Lambert
Bristol	R. L. Morrison
Buena Vista	R. H. Beach
Charlottesville	Jas. E. Bowen, Jr.
Christiansburg	John E. Lemley
Clifton Forge	William S. Coburn
Covington	J. G. Kyle
Crewe	H. B. Prichard
Culpeper	R. W. Huffman
Danville	T. Edward Temple
Emporia	Geo. R. House, Jr.
Fairfax	Glenn Saunders
Falls Church	Wm. R. Woodbury
Farmville	L. Z. Johnston, Jr.
Franklin	Harold S. Atkinson
Fredericksburg	F. Freeman Funk
Front Royal	Harold D. Hamner
Galax	W. G. Andrews
Hampton	C. E. Johnson
Harrisonburg	Arthur L. Dow
Hopewell	Levin D. James
Lexington	J. V. Berberich, III
Luray	T. F. Ewers
Lynchburg	Robt. D. Morrison
Manassas	G. Carpenter, Jr.
Marion	J. W. Ritter, Jr.
Martinsville	Julian F. Hirst
Narrows	Wm. P. Larew
Newport News	J. C. Biggins
Norfolk	Thomas F. Maxwell
Norton	Philip Davis
Orange	H. F. Knoell
Pearisburg	E. L. Quisenberry
Petersburg	Roy F. Ash
Portsmouth	I. G. Vass
Pulaski	Thomas B. Noland
Radford	W. A. Woodward
Richlands	J. E. Cranwell, Jr.
Richmond	Horace H. Edwards
Roanoke	Arthur S. Owens
Salem	W. F. Chapman
South Boston	J. A. Houghton
South Norfolk	Vacancy
Staunton	Seth Burnley
Suffolk	Jas. C. Causey, Jr.
Tappanhannock	R. H. Burton, Jr.
Vinton	Guy L. Gearhart
Virginia (cont.)	
Virginia Beach	W. R. Hatchett
Warrenton	Sidney Shumate
Warwick	J. C. Morris
Waynesboro	Charles T. Yancey
Williamsburg	Hugh B. Rice
Winchester	S. Lee Grant
Wytheville	Carter W. Beamer
Washington	
Bellevue	W. W. Kennedy
East Redmond	Earl Diller
Ellensburg	B. H. Mead, Jr.
Kennewick	Wm. E. Hansen
Medina	Edwin C. Baum
Mountlake Terrace	Evan E. Peterson
Normandy Park	John Nicholson
Port Angeles	Gerard S. Vergeer
Puyallup	Vacancy
Sunnyside	E. G. Hubbert
Tacoma	David D. Rowlands
Vancouver	Jas. E. Neal
Yakima	Vacancy
West Virginia	
Bluefield	William L. Kell
Clarksburg	Walter Neeley
Fayetteville	J. H. Allen
Grafton	Harry Batson
Morgantown	Elmer W. Prince
Oak Hill	W. R. Bennett
Princeton	A. R. England, Jr.
St. Marys	J. Bernard Riggs
Salem	W. Farson (Act.)
Weirton	Vacancy
Wheeling	Robert L. Plummer
Wisconsin	
Beloit	A. D. Telfer
Eau Claire	Douglas G. Weiford
Elm Grove	Vacancy
Fort Atkinson	Elmore F. Klement
Fox Point (Milwaukee)	E. G. Teschan
Greendale	J. M. Kuglitsch
Janesville	Vacancy
Kenosha	Richard H. Custer
Lake Geneva	Dean Van Ness
Lake Mills	William Hanson
Marinette	K. W. Gardiner
Oshkosh	Vacancy
River Hills (Milwaukee)	J. M. Frederickson
Shorewood	Charles T. Henry
Superior	W. R. L. Taylor
Two Rivers	Vacancy
Watertown	Claire C. Congdon
Whitefish Bay (Milwaukee)	John Katzban
Whitewater	C. F. Trinkle
Wyoming	
Laramie	A. J. Hull, Jr.
Alaska	
Anchorage	Geo. C. Shannon
Cordova	Edward B. Millett
Fairbanks	W. W. Slankard
Ketchikan	Robert E. Sharp
Kodiak	Charles A. Truitt
Seward	Vacancy
Puerto Rico	
San Juan	Mrs. F. Ricon de Gautier

County Managers

State and County	Name of Manager
California	
Sacramento County	M. D. Tarshes
San Mateo County (Redwood City)	E. R. Stallings
Santa Clara County (San Jose)	Frank H. Thill
Georgia	
Fulton County (Atlanta)	A. E. Fuller
Maryland	
Anne Arundel Co. (Annapolis)	Edw. R. Lonergan
Maryland (cont.)	
Montgomery County (Rockville)	Melvin L. Reese
Montana	
Petroleum County (Winnett)	Carl Yerrington
New York	
Monroe County (Rochester)	Clarence A. Smith
North Carolina	
Durham County	E. S. Swindell, Jr.
N. Car. (cont.)	
Guilford County (Greensboro)	J. H. Weatherly
Tennessee	
McMinn County (Athens)	Eugene B. Torbett
Virginia	
Albemarle County (Charlottesville)	M. M. Pence
Arlington County	A. T. Lundberg
Fairfax County	C. C. Massey
Henrico County (Richmond)	Edward A. Beck

City and Town Purchasing Agents In Places of 10,000 Population

List revised to January 1, 1957

If the Purchasing Agent has more than one title and is listed elsewhere in this book, his name is not duplicated below.

State and City	Purchasing Agent
Alabama	
Anniston	Claude F. Dear, Jr.
Birmingham	C. E. Wiberg
Homewood	Col. M. R. Rice
Mobile	A. J. Siegelman
Montgomery	J. Percy Spruell
Arizona	
Phoenix	Bert Gragg
Tucson	Carl Walker (Act.)
Arkansas	
Little Rock	Floyd Peek
California	
Albany	Robert G. Olson
Alhambra	Chas. R. Prawitz
Anaheim	Harold W. Daoust
Arcadia	L. W. Larson
Bakersfield	K. P. Graham
Bell	Harold W. Attlesey
Berkeley	John A. Mattis
Chula Vista	Fred Ross
Colton	George Dismukes
Culver City	Charles Gartman
El Cajon	T. R. Parks
El Centro	George Lechner
Fresno	Jess Laughlin
Fullerton	Robert Kidwell
Gardena	P. A. Rowley
Glendale	R. A. Lillyman
Hawthorne	Alonzo C. Gabriel
Huntington	Thomas N. Lord
Lodi	Fred Wilson
Long Beach	Edwin W. Hyka
Los Angeles	Alvin J. Holm
Lynwood	Mrs. G. R. Francis
Maywood	Milton Strauss
Merced	Ted Hand, Jr.
Monterey Park	Glen Witham
Mountain View	Mary Harris
Newport Beach	Donald W. Means
Oakland	Thomas C. Russell
Oceanside	Phil B. Rowley
Ontario	David L. Weil
Oxnard	Jerry Ritch
Palm Springs	Shelby V. Langford
Palo Alto	J. D. Brodie
Pasadena	Edgar C. Outten
Redding	Charles E. Barry
Redlands	John F. Nies
Richmond	W. T. Mayfield
Riverside	Don E. Vanderzyl
Sacramento	William J. Roberts
Salinas	Elton Tavernetti
San Bruno	Robert Bodeman
San Diego	J. H. Shaw
San Francisco	Ben G. Kline
San Leandro	E. Rawlinson
San Mateo	Arthur Smith
San Rafael	John H. Shelly
Santa Ana	C. S. Markee
Santa Barbara	William C. Baise
Santa Cruz	George D. Knapp
Santa Monica	A. D. Shaw
Santa Rosa	M. J. Bankhead
South Pasadena	Robert Hoback
Stockton	George Poehner
Torrance	D. W. Mansfield
Colorado	
Aurora	Mrs. Irene Carney
Colorado Springs	Wayne Jackson
Denver	L. S. Middlemist
Englewood	Joe M. Lacy
Grand Junction	Thomas C. Charles
Pueblo	K. L. Tharp
Connecticut	
Bridgeport	R. Donald Meath
Bristol	Henry A. Corden

State and City	Purchasing Agent
Conn. (cont.)	
Fairfield	D. W. Sullivan
Greenwich	Roger E. Anderson
Hartford	N. B. Henson
New Britain	Otto Winter
New Haven	G. F. Robinson
New London	William J. Ruddy
Norwich	Edward Frechette
Plainville	R. B. Kincaid
Stamford	Frank Bennevelli
Stratford	Dorothy Brown
Torrington	Robert McLaughlin
Waterbury	Henry J. Dowling
Dist. of Columbia	
Washington	Roland M. Brennan
Florida	
Bradenton	Melvin F. Clapper
Coral Gables	C. H. Wiggins
Daytona Beach	G. D. Porter
Fort Lauderdale	R. K. Lowry
Gainesville	I. X. Cheves
Hollywood	Arthur Dobay
Jacksonville	Henry Schneitman
Key West	Myrtland Cates, Jr.
Lakeland	F. A. Sheridan
Melbourne	G. B. Adams
Miami	L. E. Tuttle
North Miami	Wm. B. Henderson
Ocala	R. R. Wynn
Orlando	I. Y. Suggs
St. Petersburg	John T. Andrews
Sarasota	C. E. McEachern
Tampa	W. P. McLeran
West Palm Beach	Gordon Wheaton
Georgia	
Atlanta	Ernest J. Brewer
Brunswick	Mrs. Wm. Miller
East Point	D. H. Montgomery
Macon	A. McAfee
Savannah	Sidney Wortsman
Idaho	
Idaho Falls	T. R. Peters
Moscow	Dan S. Crimmins
Pocatello	B. B. Reese
Illinois	
Bloomington	Alvin J. Keller
Chicago	John Ward
Elgin	Marvin Andrews
Granite City	John Dooher
Harvey	A. E. Christian
Kankakee	J. Wm. Spillane
Kewanee	Robert C. Richards
Lombard	Arthur Spellenberg
Maywood	James Kay, Jr.
Moline	Gertrude Rosene
Peoria	P. G. BardezBanian
Springfield	J. F. Gerzin
Sterling	John F. DeWind
Waukegan	John E. Bower
Wilmette	Ralph Clay
Winnetka	Robert A. Weidaw
Indiana	
Anderson	Louis Madden
Baltimore	J. Albert Gaston
Evansville	Paul Padgett
Fort Wayne	Arthur F. Lenz
Gary	John Visclosky
Indianapolis	Albert Loesche
Mishawaka	Joseph W. Snyder
Muncie	E. Peckenpaugh
Iowa	
Ames	A. A. Magill
Council Bluffs	Charles Jackson
Davenport	H. P. Nelson
Des Moines	H. W. Odendahl

State and City	Purchasing Agent
Iowa (cont.)	
Ottumwa	Francis Phillips
Sioux City	James W. Law
Kansas	
El Dorado	R. G. Newcomer
Hutchinson	Milton N. Martin
Junction City	C. W. Moss
Kansas City	Walter J. Willard
Pittsburg	Neil J. Vest
Wichita	John M. Pierce
Winfield	H. A. Hetherington
Kentucky	
Ashland	Margaret Wheeler
Henderson	Ernest Gregory
Lexington	James L. Wilder
Louisville	Wm. Johnson
Owensboro	Max N. Rhoads
Louisiana	
Abbeville	Evence Hebert
Alexandria	Joe Dear
Baton Rouge	Gordon L. Lenoir
Bogalusa	Royal Timberlake
Gretna	Henry F. Bender
Lafayette	Mack L. Dupuis
New Orleans	Geo. R. Bosworth
Shreveport	L. T. Baker
Maine	
Bangor	Virgie Kane
Lewiston	L. T. Raymond
Portland	Lester F. Wallace
Maryland	
Annapolis	G. T. Quaid (Act.)
Baltimore	J. Albert Gaston
Hagerstown	E. G. Mogensen
Mt. Rainier	W. B. Brown
Massachusetts	
Boston	John V. Moran
Brookline	H. G. Saumsiegle
Cambridge	John H. Corcoran
Chelsea	Frank Milley
Greenfield	Harold B. Roche
Haverhill	W. M. Walker
Lawrence	Thomas A. Barry
Lowell	Emile H. Daigle
Medford	Cyril N. Buckley
New Bedford	A. E. Catterall
Newton Centre	Thomas J. Forde
Peabody	Thomas Karolides
Quincy	Joseph Erickson
Revere	Raymond Dahl
Salem	William H. Webb
Springfield	Charles Healey
Waltham	W. A. Shaughnessy
Watertown	Wm. F. Oates
Woburn	John R. Reddy
Worcester	G. A. Herpich
Michigan	
Battle Creek	Allan Manby
Bay City	C. W. Kindermann
Dearborn	Harold deWyk
Detroit	Hazen L. Funk
East Lansing	Arthur T. Carney
Ecorse	Walter Chase
Escanaba	E. A. Olson
Flint	Albert Hull
Grand Rapids	James E. Baker
Hamtramck	Marie Respondek
Highland Park	Clark P. Smith
Jackson	Lloyd M. Head
Muskegon	G. W. Trap
Pontiac	Frank Reed
Port Huron	Wm. McCloy
Roseville	James Bottomley
Royal Oak	Bruce W. Love
Saginaw	Roy A. Benway
Wyandotte	Wilfred Kane

State and City	Purchasing Agent
Minnesota	
Duluth	Raleigh Gottschald
Minneapolis	George R. Arneson
Richfield	Roy E. Swenson
St. Cloud	C. J. Hollenhorst
St. Paul	Lyle E. Kinvig
Mississippi	
Biloxi	Stuart Evans
Jackson	W. F. Powell
Missouri	
Columbia	Wm. Estel Palmer
Joplin	Rosella Trudell
Kansas City	Wm. I. Hornbuckle
Kirkwood	Lurton Akard
Richmond Heights	Robert E. Ries
St. Joseph	B. T. Andrews
St. Louis	Edw. J. Sweeney
Springfield	Russell Ferguson
University City	V. A. Ellman
Webster Groves	N. E. Blaske
Montana	
Billings	L. W. Townsend
Great Falls	Fred T. Brown
Helena	George Felsch
Nebraska	
Fremont	F. L. Hintz
Lincoln	Wayne Harvey
Omaha	Ivan Swanson
Nevada	
Henderson	Donald M. Dawson
Reno	Harold Curran
New Jersey	
Asbury Park	Walter P. Haight
Atlantic City	Florence Clark
Bayonne	Clarence J. Wall
Belleville	T. J. McLaughlin
Dover	H. A. Armitage
Garfield	Joseph Russinko
Irvington	D. Clyde Goode
Jersey City	C. F. Hayes
Linden	Harold Powers
Maywood	Louis M. Caras
Montclair	G. E. McMillen
Newark	H. J. Aston
New Brunswick	Chas. F. Horrocks
North Bergen	Robert J. Drew
Nutley	M. F. Johnson
Orange	Alfred A. Monica
Passaic	Aaron J. Troast
Paterson	Alfred Kane
Perth Amboy	J. P. Sieber
Plainfield	R. J. Myzie
Rahway	Charles Vaughn
Ridgewood	John Flaker
South Orange	Donald E. Platner
South Plainfield	Chas. A. Mobus
Teaneck	J. W. Stucke
Trenton	H. Carl Schlicher
Wayne	John J. Crowley
Westfield	Dennis N. Lever
West New York	Charles Boniface
West Orange	Victor Fischer
New Mexico	
Albuquerque	George Lowe
New York	
Albany	Francis W. Grady
Amsterdam	John Cline (Act.)
Binghamton	Lawrence A. Mucci
Buffalo	J. R. Stiglmeier
Floral Park	Jordan L. Klahn
Freeport	R. T. Keirnan
Glen Cove	John G. Slater
Harrison	Wm. A. Bauer, Jr.
Lackawanna	Geo. Kustrich
Long Beach	Mrs. A. Rosenberg
New Rochelle	Betty A. Meagher
New York	Joseph V. Spagna
Niagara Falls	E. T. Arnold
Poughkeepsie	Aubrey B. Coons
Rensselaer	Chas. G. Maloy
Rochester	Fred Ereth
Rome	Edward M. Glavin
Schenectady	Ward Alexander
Syracuse	George F. Waite
Utica	Chas. Merlini
N. Y. (cont.)	
Watertown	Floyd Bresnehan
White Plains	Harry A. Brocking
Yonkers	Mrs. A. L. Mahoney
North Carolina	
Asheville	J. T. Hocking
Charlotte	C. E. Beatty
Durham	A. T. Crutchfield
Greensboro	H. Winston, Jr.
High Point	A. R. McMullan
Raleigh	S. F. Taylor
Rocky Mount	A. C. Dozier
Wilmington	L. C. LeGwin
Wilson	T. Bruce Boyette
Winston-Salem	A. C. Shepherd
North Dakota	
Minot	Alton Long
Ohio	
Akron	G. McQuiggan
Canton	H. B. Ritz
Cincinnati	John G. Krieg
Cleveland	Leo Weil
Columbus	C. J. Nogawick
Dayton	R. Herman (Act.)
East Cleveland	W. B. Boise
Hamilton	R. B. Garrett
Lakewood	P. F. Adsit
Middletown	Harlan D. Helsel
Norwood	Clarence Hornbach
Painesville	C. J. Gray
Parma	K. F. Stoessner
Shaker Heights	Robert C. Beth
South Euclid	M. Waldschmidt
Springfield	E. R. Swackhamer
Struthers	Frank J. Unick
Toledo	Howard Rebensal
Oklahoma	
Bartlesville	Paul Allee
Duncan	A. I. Ray
Muskogee	Arch Sheets
Seminole	Glenn Wilson
Tulsa	J. D. Rush
Oregon	
Eugene	Jack Merritt
Portland	L. W. Rayner
Salem	H. D. Brandvold
Pennsylvania	
Allentown	....
Lower Merion Twp. (Ardmore)	Richard Allen
Bethlehem	James Kernan
Chester	Clarence Smedley
Clairton	S. Honeygosky
Connellsville	Ira D. Younkin
Farrell	Roy DeBrakeleer
Mt. Lebanon Tp. (Pittsburgh)	Joseph A. James
New Castle	Edwin McBride
Philadelphia	Michael Sura
Pittsburgh	Chas. D. McCarthy
Reading	Ignatius Spurio
Scranton	John Graham
Springfield Twp. (Springfield)	Chas. W. Haslett
Uniontown	B. R. Williams
Washington	Herbert Riser
Wilkes Barre	David Thomas
Rhode Island	
Cranston	Viola B. Dawson
Newport	J. A. Murray, Jr.
North Kingstown (Wickford)	Edwin T. Chase
Pawtucket	Edwin J. Carty
Providence	Joseph H. Healey
Woonsocket	A. B. Jolicoeur
South Carolina	
Charleston	T. L. Weeks
Columbia	G. C. Robinette, Jr.
Tennessee	
Chattanooga	Gradey Jacoway
Knoxville	C. C. Currier
Memphis	Walter Joyce
Nashville	E. B. Smith
Texas	
Abilene	Bernard Huett
Amarillo	J. L. Pate
Austin	O. G. Brush
Baytown	A. V. Barber
Beaumont	Robert L. Harris
Bellaire	Burgess Pool
Big Springs	Roy C. Anderson
Borger	J. W. Harrison
Brownwood	Mayfield Gibbs
Bryan	J. E. Tatum
Corpus Christi	Thomas B. Murphy
Dallas	G. L. Dorff (Act.)
Denton	Chas. C. Orr, Jr.
El Paso	Ben Luhm
Fort Worth	G. L. Cline
Galveston	John Lolosevich
Garland	Leslie Gouge
Harlingen	A. W. Groce
Houston	Lewis James
Jacksonville	Dan Mize
Lubbock	Roy Grimes
Marshall	R. H. Hightower
Midland	Jay Jorden
Pampa	John S. Koontz
Paris	R. A. Harvey
Port Arthur	Kirby Lilljedall
San Angelo	Jack Morrison
San Antonio	A. L. Tripp
University Park (Dallas)	Wm. E. West
Vernon	R. B. Smith
Victoria	Al. Heibner
Waco	Elmer A. Roberts
Wichita Falls	Geo. A. Mobley
Utah	
Ogden	James R. Eide
Provo	J. W. Prothero
Salt Lake City	L. P. Broberg
Virginia	
Alexandria	Catherine Hoover
Lynchburg	Richard A. Berry
Newport News	Roy T. Scott
Norfolk	L. O. Branch
Petersburg	I. C. Chandler
Portsmouth	J. A. Borum
Richmond	J. W. Huffman
Roanoke	R. B. Moss
Washington	
Olympia	Ralph Hallgren
Pasco	S. A. Connell
Renton	Vernal Church
Seattle	Paul R. Hendricks
Spokane	I. S. Fetterman
Tacoma	Oscar Carlson
Vancouver	Robert E. Moisant
Wenatchee	D. C. King (Act.)
Yakima	Philip H. Parker
West Virginia	
Huntington	J. C. Shelor
Wheeling	Jean de France
Wisconsin	
Eau Claire	Raymond W. Beede
Kenosha	Joseph V. Duffy
La Crosse	M. R. Birnbaum
Madison	B. L. Gill
Milwaukee	J. W. Nicholson
Oshkosh	Orville Gartman
Racine	George S. Quinn
Stevens Point	Norman J. Meshak
Wauwatosa	Edgar R. Boeck
West Allis	Carl E. Peters
Wyoming	
Casper	E. A. Grant
Cheyenne	Vivian S. Rodin
Alaska	
Anchorage	C. A. Hostetler
Fairbanks	Mrs. E. R. Finden
Hawaii	
Hilo City	Masuo Masutani
Honolulu	Robert Smythe
Puerto Rico	
San Juan	Mrs. A. Christensen
Virgin Islands	
Charlotte Amalie	Mario Lewis

City Engineers and Superintendents of Water Works, Streets, Sewage Treatment

In Cities of More Than 10,000 Population

List revised to January 1, 1957

Practically every city has a City Engineer, Water Superintendent, Street Superintendent and if its sewage is treated, a Superintendent of Sewage Treatment. In many cities these departments are made into a group called the department or division of public works. The official in charge may be one of the regular department or bureau chiefs or a different official. His name and title code (explained on page 1087) are given in the second column, below.

The letter "p" in small type in the Water-Works column means "Private Water Company." The letter "s" in small type in the Sewage Treatment column means the sewage works are managed by a Sanitary District or its equivalent. The figures in small type refer to footnotes at the end of the lists, on page 1087.

State and City	Public Works **Head**	City Engineer	Water-Works Superintendent	Street Superintendent	Superintendent of Sewage Treatment
Alabama					
Anniston	....	J. G. Grumm	E. C. Knowlton	W. E. Johnson	....
Auburn	W. Wilson Hill	W. C. Wood	L. S. Cato, Jr.	J. A. Baker	....
Bessemer	Raymond Parsons	F. D. Kuzmicki	D. J. O'Gara	W. V. Hallmark[1]	....
Birmingham	J. T. Waggoner[2]	A. L. McWhorter	H. L. Shiflett	Neal McRae	....
Decatur	Chas. N. Harvey	Carol C. Smith	George Goodwin	Joe S. Elliott	J. W. Pettey
Dothan	R. C. McClintock[3]	Floyd Clayton[1]	H M. Holloway	John H. Davis	Floyd Clayton
Fairfield	J. T. Duncan	J. T. Duncan	J. T. Duncan	J. T. Duncan	....
Florence	R. G. Hibbett[3]	Wm. A. White	Robt. McKinney	C. L. Liles	Herman Staggs
Gadsden	S. Lasseter, Jr.[3]	W. R. Hooks	A. F. Lankford	George Sizemore	E. M. Pledger
Homewood	....	Hendon & Assoc.	....	Roscoe C. Payne	....
Huntsville	....	G. W. Jones & Sons	James S. Wall	R. L. Mann	R. L. Mann
Mobile	....	H. L. Fisher	E. M. Stickney	L. H. Meyers	E. M. Stickney
Montgomery	Frank W. Parks[3]	O. L. Skinner	C. T. Perry	Oliver Wright	M. B. Mathews
Mountain Brook	G. A. Eddins[4, 5]	....	....	Gordon A. Eddins	....
Opelika	N. L. McCrory	G. E. Culp	K. P. Lynch	Clyde Jennings	Owen Waldrep
Phenix City	Byron Preer[6]	....	....	Byron Preer	....
Prichard	....	....	C. D. Lamon	F. L. Sanders	C. D. Lamon
Selma	....	....	J. S. Lamar	F. H. Terry[7]	....
Sheffield	B. T. Gardner[3]	Paxton-Alexander Engrs.	W. F. McCormack	Raleigh McIntire	....
Sylacauga	....	Troy Smithwick	Earl Hamm	J. T. Bryant	Earl Hamm
Talladega	....	....	W. F. Tucker	M. F. Beverly	....
Tuscaloosa	R. V. Hawkins	R. V. Hawkins	....	John McKinley	....
Arizona					
Douglas	Wm. E. Wood	....	Walter Spence	Wm. E. Wood	Walter Spence
Glendale	W. A. Gilchrist[5]	....	O. T. Ramsey[8]	Elton A. Kirby	Earl Rosengren[9]
Mesa	....	David B. Harmon	Lorin Hostetter[10]	Otis E. Redd[10]	David B. Harmon
Phoenix	K. K. King[11]	Gail Baker	Dario Traviani	James Stokley	Merle V. Ellis
Tucson	G. G. Sykes[1, 11]	G. G. Sykes	P. J. Martin, Jr.[5]	Clinton L. Helbig	E. O'Neal Dye
Arkansas					
Blytheville	....	....	C. W. Kapp[5]..[p]	J. R. Gunter	Murl Bratton
Camden	Frank M. Bray[6]	....	Frank M. Bray	Harry Gammill	Harry Gammill
Eldorado	....	E. K. Williamson	....	A. W. Littlejohn	Edward E. Shaw
Fayetteville	W. C. Smith	W. C. Smith	W. C. Smith	Roy A. Scott[12]	W. C. Smith
Fort Smtih	H. H. Brewer[3]	Roy Williamson	John Luce	Cecil Atchison	Cecil Atchison
Helena	....	L. R. Parmelee	C. J. Burns	....	L. R. Parmelee[3]
Hot Springs	T. C. Witt	John Faye	....	Tom C. Witt	Buck Alford
Jonesboro	Neal Thayer[5]	H. Sanderson[12]	Dan Millender	R. L. Petillo	....
Little Rock	Jack L. Taylor	Jack L. Taylor	L. A. Jackson	Eddie Davis	T. W. Clapman[7]
No. Little Rock	Shelby Smith[13]	Glen Douglas	J. Montgomery[p]	....	....
Pine Bluff	Creed Caldwell[11]	Creed Caldwell	J. R. Pierce[5]..[p]	John Pitts	John F. Gillespie
Texarkana	....	Richard V. Hall	Wm. J. Weems	Vernon M. Glover	....
California					
Alameda	Mark J. Hanna	Mark J. Hanna	....	Mark J. Hanna	....
Albany	W. M. McAuley	W. M. McAuley	....	W. M. McAuley	....
Alhambra	Charles E. Lortz	Charles E. Lortz	John W. Clay	Charles E. Lortz	A. M. Rawn[15, 16] [s]
Anaheim	W. F. Priday[11]	Geo. E. Holyoke	Geo. F. Oelkers[17]	W. F. Priday	W. F. Priday
Antioch	B. M. Maynard	B. M. Maynard	Martin Tillman	P. K. Biglow	Martin Tillman
Arcadia	M. J. Carozza[11]	M. J. Carozza	John C. Hays	M. J. Carozza	John C. Hays
Azusa	Jas. Brusnahan[6]	Wm. Kirkgaard	Virgil Smith[14]	....	....
Bakersfield	J. B. Holfelder[11]	J. B. Holfelder	....	J. B. Holfelder	J. B. Holfelder
Bell	John M. Manok	....	A. Crichton[5]..[p]	John M. Manok	....
Berkeley	S. C. Jacka[11]	....	....	....	....
Beverly Hills	David Speer[11]	David Speer	John Perhab	David Speer	..........[s]
Brawley	Jeff Kissee	H. E. Hough[1]	Jeff Kissee	Jeff Kissee	Jeff Kissee
Burbank	C. W. Paige	C. W. Paige	Ralph Foy[5]	C. W. Paige	....
Burlingame	George J. Marr	George J. Marr	George J. Marr	George J. Marr	George J. Marr

State and City	Public Works Head	City Engineer	Water-Works Superintendent	Street Superintendent	Superintendent of Sewage Treatment
Calif. (cont.)					
Chico	Fred Davis[11]	....	Aymer Stolp[5]..[p]	Glenn Hardesty	Fred Davis ..
Chula Vista	Richard A. Floyd	R. A. Floyd	A. F. Poulter[5]..[p]	....	Wm. Harshman
Colton	Norman A. Neste	Norman A. Neste	Norman A. Neste	Norman A. Neste	Norman A. Neste
Compton	....	Don W. Robins	....	Don W. Robins	....
Concord	F. A. Stewart[11]	F. A. Stewart	C. C. Nutting[5]..[p]	F. A. Stewart	G. J. Coppa ..
Corona	....	David Smith	M. Brewer[5]..[p]	L. G. Young	Gilbert Cleveland
Coronado	E. F. Ketcham[5]	....	..........[p]	R. B. Livengood	....
Costa Mesa	....	Don Southworth	A. C. Swartz	Don Southworth	....
Covina	Edw. E. Tufte	....	....	C. E. Freeman	....
Culver City	Louis A. Molnar	Louis A. Molnar	F. Cleveland[5]..[p]	Philip C. Angel	....
Daly City	O. T. Calhoun[11]	O. T. Calhoun	Chas. A. Ford	O. T. Calhoun	..........[s]
Delano	R. K. Russell	G. W. Burgess	Louie McDaniel	Geo. Hardesty	....
El Cajon	John T. Hart	Robt. C. Howes	....	John T. Hart	R. J. Pallette[18]
El Centro	L. McClintock[11]	L. E. McClintock	C. K. Patton[19]	L. E. McClintock	....
El Cerrito	Marvin Anaya[11]	Marvin Anaya	....	....	....
El Segundo	R. L. Webb, Jr.[11]	R. L. Webb, Jr.	....	R. L. Webb, Jr.	....
Eureka	J. F. Lockhart[6]	S. B. Roscoe	Jos. F. Lockhart	N. Underwood	Berle Helderman
Fairfield	C. V. Carlson[11]	C. V. Carlson	Charles Crane	Ed. Stanton	....
Fontana	V. J. Van Lint	Johnson & Lockwood	..........[p]	F. Barnes	....
Fresno	A. Segel[3]	Donald Baird	George Bowman[5]	John Mahon	Louis Fogal
Fullerton	G. L. Walters	W. S. Stookey	W. Otto Blume	John W. King	....
Gardena	C. G. Borgen	H. A. Barnett	D. Ammons[5]..[p]	C. G. Borgen	....
Glendale	C. E. Perkins	W. L. O. Martini	Lauren Grayson	W. L. O. Martini	W. L. O. Martini
Glendora	D. Atkinson[11]	Paul E. Kressly	R. J. Moore	R. R. Baiotto	D. Atkinson[5]..[s]
Hanford	....	....	..........[p]	Arie Scheeringa	Glen Blaylock
Hawthorne	Charles Handy	Charles Handy	Melvin G. Lloyd	T. B. McDermott	....
Hayward	E. E. Phillips[11]	D. Cruickshank	Edw. E. Phillips	Harry Brandt	John Hay
Hermosa Beach	J. P. Reynolds	Martin M. Denn	L. E. Carlson[5]..[p]	J. P. Reynolds	....
Huntington Park	....	H. E. Robinson	H. E. Robinson	Wm. A. Lough	....
Inglewood	Wade E. Peebles	Wade E. Peedles	W. H. Stokes	Wade E. Peebles	....
La Habra	....	Geo. D. Stringer	Raymond Evans	H. R. Roberts	A. C. Earley[5]..[s]
La Mesa	Albert Smelko[6]	Lane F. Cole	....	....	....
Livermore	Alfred Winter	....	H. Emmerick[5]..[p]	....	Alfred Winter
Lodi	....	Art Heckenlaible	Tom Killelea	Art Heckenlaible	Art Heckenlaible
Long Beach	Jas. P. Kincaid[11]	J. D. Gilkerson	B. S. Thomas	Daniel T. Dean	Sydney Preen
Los Altos	....	P. I. Baker	....	....	....
Los Angeles	C. Phillips[29]	L. A. Pardee	W. S. Peterson[16]	Ben R. Paris[11]	G. A. Parkes
Lynwood	....	A. J. Bateman	H. R. Rutter	Bert McIntyre	....
Madera	....	A. C. Norton	Loy E. Cook	J. E. Haynes	Russell Murray
Manhattan Bch.	....	F. C. Butcher	O. A. Gierlich	F. C. Butcher	....
Maywood	L. U. Young[20]	F. E. Alderman	....	Robt. H. Nieweg	....
Menlo Park	C. L. Longson[6]	Edwin H. Smith	C. L. Longson	....	C. Webster..[s]
Merced	Wm. Presslerr[11]	George Mimmack	Sam Cornell	George Mimmack	Wm. Presslerr
Millbrae	A. F. Pacheco	Lee Ham	....	Lee Ham	James Kennefick
Modesto	Marvin Ray[11]	Roy Fredricksen	Marvin Ray	Marvin Ray	Marvin Ray
Monrovia	....	Fritz Zapf	A. Jorgensen	A. Stenman	..........[s]
Montebello	P. R. Warwick	P. R. Warwick	....	C. W. Hale	....
Monterey	....	M. R. Pearce	Mr. Goldsworthy[5]..[p]	M. R. Pearce	T. P. McCormack
Monterey Park	Wm. Jensen	Wm. Jensen	Harold Gould	Chet Cathers	....
Mountain View	A. M. McKinnon[11]	A. M. McKinnon	....	John C. Purser	H. P. Anderson[10]
Napa	H. C. McDonald[11]	H. C. McDonald	H. C. McDonald	Wm. Van Wood	A. T. Merritt[5]..[s]
National City	....	Wayne P. Lill	....	James A. Bird	....
Newport Beach	J. B. Webb[11]	J. B. Webb	....	L. W. Covert	J. B. Webb
Oakland	....	J. A. Morin	....	J. A. Morin	....
Oceanside	....	Alton L. Ruden	Robt. A. Weese	Ernest A. Taylor	Edward Sampson
Ontario	Harold J. Martin	H. A. Halldin	W. A. Ross	H. G. Taylor	W. A. Ross
Orange	J. C. Harper[11]	B. H. Dyson[1]	C. E. Sturdevant	Harold A. Casteel	....
Oxnard	Hugh Clark, Jr.[11]	E. O. Imus	O. L. Isham	W. R. Eastwood	O. L. Isham
Palm Springs	F. Hamerschlag[11]	F. Hamerschlag	....	F. Hamerschlag	Alva Anderson
Palo Alto	H. M. Witbeck	H. M. Witbeck	H. L. May[15]	H. M. Witbeck	H. L. May
Pasadena	D. C. Mackenzie	D. C. Mackenzie	D. A. Blackburn	D. C. Mackenzie	....
Petaluma	R. W. Ingram[11]	R. W. Ingram	....	R. W. Ingram	R. W. Ingram
Piedmont	Arthur Boscow	Larry Taylor	....	Arthur Boscow	....
Pittsburg	Chas. Ferreira[6]	E. L. O'Hara	Robert L. Heck	Chas. Ferreira	Lloyd Bright
Pomona	Arthur H. Cox	Glen Crawford	Everett Phillips	Glen Crawford	A. M. Rawn[6]..[s]
Redding	Hal E. Marron[11]	Hal E. Marron	Elbert E. Dick	Hal E. Marron	Herbert Olson
Redlands	....	P. E. Johnson	John Jones	P. E. Johnson	....
Redondo Beach	R. L. Smith[11]	Franz C. Nybve	L. E. Carlson..[p]	F. E. Hopkins	....
Redwood City	Glenn M. Jain	Glenn M. Jain	H. L. Winter	Glenn M. Jain	Chas. Crummey
Rialto	....	C. E. Johnson	Leo Smith	Leslie J. Lindner	Leo Smith
Richmond	R. F. Lovejoy	R. F. Lovejoy	....	R. F. Lovejoy	....
Riverside	J. F. Martinek[11]	J. F. Martinek	A. J. Kennedy[16]	O. R. Addington	Homer Parker
Roseville	N. J. Bartolome[6]	K. Thompson	J. E. Riley	N. J. Bartolome	N. J. Bartolome
Sacramento	E. A. Fairbairn	E. A. Fairbairn	Ray Jones	E. A. Fairbairn	Ray Jones
Salinas	H. Munger, Jr.[11]	H. Munger, Jr.	....	Thos. G. Dunne	Thos. G. Dunne
San Bernardino	....	R. E. Wolford	L. A. Hosegood	John G. Center	....
San Bruno	Dana Russell[11]	Dana Russell	Dana Russell	Dana Russell	....
San Buenaventura (See Ventura)					
San Carlos	R. T. Penney	E. H. Smith	....	E. H. Smith	Roy Collins
San Diego	R. Gallagher[11]	A. K. Fogg	Paul Beermann	R. A. Hall	Eric Quartley
San Fernando	Raymond Walker	Robt. E. James	Raymond Walker	Robert E. James	....
San Francisco	S. P. Duckel[11]	Reuben H. Owens	....	F. D. Brown	Ben Benas
San Gabriel	....	H. B. Keebaugh	W. Forrester[5]..[p]	R. B. McClelland	....
San Jose	Harold Flannery	Harold Flannery	C. Parberry[5]..[p]	Harold Flannery	Frank Belick
San Leandro	G. H. Hamlin[11]	G. H. Hamlin	....	G. H. Hamliln	G. H. Hamliln
San Luis Obispo	D. F. Romero[11]	D. F. Romero	E. P. Thompson	Millo Tappa	Frank Reed
San Marino	Paul F. Barton[11]	H. A. Barnett	D. Fiscus[5]..[p]	Paul F. Barton	Paul F. Barton
San Mateo	N. B. Smith	N. B. Smith	A. L. Stulp[5]..[p]	N. B. Smith	N. B. Smith
San Pablo	....	Phil R. Jones	....	Phil R. Jones	....

State and City	Public Works Head	City Engineer	Water-Works Superintendent	Street Superintendent	Superintendent of Sewage Treatment
Calif. (cont.)					
San Rafael	....	W. C. Gonnason	....	Norris N. Rawles	....
Santa Ana	H. H. Forman[11]	H. H. Forman[11]	H. H. Forman[11]	H. H. Forman[11]	....
Santa Barbara	R. G. Martin[11]	R. G. Martin	C. E. Richardson	R. G. Martin	Russell Keeler
Santa Clara	....	Edgar C. Schott	Ben J. Tamone	Ernest Oliver[22]	....
Santa Cruz	A. D. Russell	A. D. Russell	W. L. Webber	Donald A. Bruce	Donald A. Bruce
Santa Maria	W. S. Litzenberg	....	John Weldon	Harold Turner	Tom Mays
Santa Monica	M. M. King[11]	M. M. King	J. R. Patten	F. A. Goodbody	....
Santa Paula	W. B. Godfrey[11]	W. B. Godfrey	M. Teague[5]..p	Roy Moore	Byron Cox
Santa Rosa	Mervyn Daw[23]	R. VanGuelpen	Frank Poulsen	William White	M. B. McKinnie
South Gate	Carl E. Berry[11]	Carl E. Berry	Carl E. Berry	Carl E. Berry	....
South Pasadena	....	Charles H. Lane	Don H. Dollison	G. W. Garwood	....
South San Francisco	Louis H. Goss[11]	Louis H. Goss	Sam Volonte[5]..p	....	H. Schweining
Stockton	....	Marshall Dunlap	E. Anderson[5]..p	Frank Wallace	W. Jones
Torrance	Ralph S. Perkins	R. W. Bishop	A. E. McVicar	Ralph S. Perkins	Ralph S. Perkins
Tulare	B. Westkamper	B. Westkamper	Herbert Glover	Ralph Sisson	Herbert Glover
Upland	....	Harold Wilder	E. Alder	E. Alder	....
Vallejo	Glenn A. Harris	Glenn A. Harris	Robert Hunter	Glenn A. Harris	Fred A. Lange
Ventura	J. Edward Sheehy	J. Edward Sheehy	Hugh M. Wood	Jack Dugan	Walter L. Witz[18]
Visalia	H. A. Tow	H. A. Tow	D. A. Hendrix[5]..p	L. A. Kirby	Maxey Harrell
Watsonville	....	Royal E. Fowle	Jack L. Kistler	Royal E. Fowle	I. B. Andersen
West Covina	Harold Johnson[11]	R. E. Pontow	..........p	James Heath	W. Nollac..s
Whittier	Jack W. Sheetz	Jack W. Sheetz[4]	K. R. Warren	K. R. Warren[27]	..........s
Woodland	Alvin Hiatt[11]	Alvin Hiatt	H. E. Martin	George Hazeman	H. E. Martin
Yuba City	W. R. Jennings[11]	W. R. Jennings	....	W. R. Jennings	W. R. Jennings
Colorado					
Aurora	Leonard Kuiper[24]	Leonard Kuiper	....	T. T. Brewer	....
Boulder	W. C. Light[11, 24]	R. J. Gallagher	C. M. Dixon	D. C. Barton	E. M. Hamilton
Colorado Sprgs.	James J. Murray	W. H. Kuenning	J. S. Nichols	Don Lawrie	John Fredericks
Denver	R. Y. Batterton[5]	Dewey S. Wright	Robert Millar[26]	....	Cecil Gunson
Englewood	Neil J. Barde	Neil J. Barde	H. H. Babcock	F. A. Lidolph	H. H. Babcock
Fort Collins	Howard E. Evans	Howard E. Evans	Howard E. Evans	Howard E. Evans	R. M. Schultz
Grand Junction	John A. Burton[11]	Carl A. Alstatt	A. L. Wing	Paul Savoya	Art. Traynor
Greeley	George Fellows	George Fellows	A. H. Bolenbaugh	Vern Schaffer	A. H. Bolenbaugh
Longmont	....	Kenneth Bruns	Clarence Lee	Glen Overturf	Clarence Lee
Pueblo	Glen S. Turner[11]	Glen S. Turner	J. Jones, Dist. 1 F. Dunlap, Dist. 2	Harry Innman	Nels P Nielsen
Trinidad	....	H. H. Kellum	W. Cunningham	Pete Ruscetti	W. Cunningham
Connecticut					
Ansonia	....	Vincent B. Clark	L. Shull[5]..p	....	....
Branford	....	....	L. H. Warner	....	....
Bridgeport	Peter Brewster[11]	Charles Smith	..........p	Peter Brewster	Peter Brewster
Bristol	T. H. Donovan	Clair M. Pfennig	....	T. H. Donovan	John D. Miller
Danbury	Sydney A. Rapp	Sydney A. Rapp	Sydney A. Rapp	Sydney A. Rapp	Joseph LaCava
Darien	W. A. Bates[6]	....	S. J. Gannon[5]..p	A. L. Brunner	William W. Pratt
Derby	....	G. E. Thompson	J. B. Atwater[29] p	John Benanto	John Benanto
East Hartford	Geo. J. Penney[11]	Fred Wheeler	....	Geo. J. Penney	....
East Haven	....	C. H. Miller[61]	Robert E. Decker	....	....
Fairfield	Frank E. Daniels	Frank E. Daniels	S. P. Senior[5]..p	S. E. Butzko	Stephen Stankey
Glastonbury	Angelo Malespina	Clarence Welti	....	Angelo Malespina	....
Greenwich	W. F. Johnson[3]	....	....	Harold T. Close[27]	Roscoe J. Kent
Hamden	Richard Vining[11]	Valentine Dyer	....	Thomas Callahan	....
Hartford	L. C. Lovell[11]	W. W. DeMay	W. A. D. Wurts[5]	....	W. A. D. Wurts[5]
Killingly (Danielson)	....	....	John Marland..p	Owen Bell[62]	....
Manchester	Richard Martin[16]	J. H. Sheekey	Fred E. Thrall	J. H. Sheekey	Fred E. Thrall
Mansfield	....	....	....	....	....
Meriden	....	C. P. Prann	Paul Cook	F. H. Edwards	Lawrence Daniels
Middletown	Samuel Cannon	Samuel Cannon	Samuel Cannon	Samuel Cannon & J. C. O'Brien	Samuel Cannon
Milford	Lloyd Kniffen[11]	Theodore Risberg	H. Ritchie[5]..p	....	John Rogers
Naugatuck	Leo J. Brophy	Charles A. Nott	Wm. Moody[5]..p	....	Michael Segetti
New Britain	H. J. Crowley[29]	Geo. J. Molleur	....	L. F. Majewicz	A. L. Stowell[3]
New Haven	A. T. Barbieri[11]	Wm. M. Bolton	A. L. Corbin[5]..p	Anthony Carbone	John Eichler
New London	C. P. DeBiasi[11]	Chas. P. DeBiasi	G. A. Beckwith	Wm. M. Baker	G. A. Beckwith
Newington	E. J. Keleher[30]	E. C. Fresen	....	....	....
Norwalk (So. Norwalk)	Paul J. James[3]	Charles P. Rumpf	E. F. Bracken	William E. Silk	Joseph A. Perry
Norwich	Harold M. Walz[11]	....	J. F. Kane	August Hoelck	....
Plainville	Joseph Edward	R. E. Beveridge	E. L. Minor[5]..p	Jos. R. Eddman	H. P. Palmer
Shelton	....	....	....	E. Bienkowski	....
Southington	....	....	S. W. Bowers	Frank J. Hurley	Frank J. Hurley
Stamford	P. J. Scarella[3]	Charles White	H. C. Veit[6]..p	Aaron Chase	P. J. Scarella
Stonington	....	....	Edwin Jett[5]..p	Walter Seigal	....
Stratford	R. E. Blake[11]	Wesley C. Cronk	..........p	Richard E. Blake	W. E. Thompson
Thompsonville	Edward Piepul	....	....	....	George Howard
Torrington	A. Gelormino	Jules Bresson	M. Lawton[5]..p	A. Gelormino	W. T. McMahon
Wallingford	John Nolan	Boyce Engr. Asso.	Vincent Mascia	John Nolan	....
Waterbury	T. B. Sullivan[23]	Henry Whitlock	Michael J. Rossi	Wm. J. Barton	W. M. Kunsch
Watertown	G. Hungerford[30]	....	B. E. Lockwood	George Williams	....
West Hartford	....	P. Martelli[61]	....	Raymond M. Fish	....
West Haven	C. E. Miller[11]	John F. Lynch[61]	A. L. Corbin, Jr.[29]..p	Harold A. Allen	Robert Burrell
Westport	W. C. Grossman[30]	....	....	Anthony Manere	....
Wethersfield	A. Gray, Jr.[5]	C. F. Langtry	....	Albert Gray, Jr.	....
Willimantic	Alexis Caisse, Jr.	J. Nelson Harger	L. J. Paradis	Alexis Caisse, Jr.	Alexis Caisse, Jr.
Windsor	James J. Lee[11]	Alphonse Boczar	....	James J. Lee	....
Winchester (Winsted City)	Joseph E. Carey[6]	Joseph E. Carey[61]	....	Joseph E. Carey	Joseph E. Carey
Delaware					
Wilmington	....	Edwin F. Koester	W. C. Wills	Charles Hynson	William Henry
District of Col.					
Washington	David V. Auld[11]	Brig.Gen.T.Lane[3]	David V. Auld[11]	J. Robertson[11, 28]	H. A. Schrieber

State and City	Public Works Head	City Engineer	Water-Works Superintendent	Street Superintendent	Superintendent of Sewage Treatment
Florida					
Bradenton	R. B. Culler[3]	....	R. B. Culler	R. B. Culler	Perry A. Cessna
Clearwater	Paul Kane[6]	Sidney Lickton	G. B. Weimer[2]	Paul Kane	D. J. Raye
Coral Gables ..	E. A. Smith[11]	E. A. Smith	H. E. Keating[29] . p	Harley Pittman	Wm. C. Tims
Daytona Beach.	R. L. Lafferty[11]	Russell C. Smith	R. F. Brennan	R. L. Lafferty	R. F. Brennan
Fort Lauderdale	G. B. Bennett[11]	E. L. Patterson	Walter Peele	G. B. Bennett	Lee Gentry
Fort Myers ...	W. A. Grimes	....	Lamar Bomar	W. A. Grimes	Julian Hudson
Fort Pierce	....	....	H. A. Gahn	Milton Davis	....
Gainesville	John R. Kelly[17]	R. B. Sensabaugh	R. P. Vogh	R. B. Sensabaugh	R. P. Vogh
Hialeah	Earl C. Crooks[11]	Earl C. Crooks	C. Coensparger	George Wheeler	....
Hollywood	H. A. Pickle[11]	Jarrett C. White	Seth Hulmes	H. A. Pickle	William Wright
Jacksonville ...	....	W. G. Daniel	C. H. Helwick	R. E. Parrish	....
Key West	Fred R. Lane		E. A. Ramsey[5] . . p	Fred R. Lane	Fred R. Lane
Lakeland	John Stokes	F. E. Wilson	Charles Larson	John Stokes	F. E. Wilson
Lake Worth ...	Ralph C. Howard	C. F. Wright	Robt. Burkitt[14]	Ralph C. Howard	Ralph C. Howard
Melbourne	....	Robert Legner	F. U. Bennett	Wm. C. Ewing	J. W. Mathews
Miami	E. A. Fort[11, 25]	A. E. Darlow	C. F. Wertz[11]	H. J. Mangum	D. P. Backmeyer
Miami Beach ..	Morris N. Lipp	Morris N. Lipp	Jay D. Roth	Frank E. Hoban	....
Miami Springs.	Lee A. Tyler[6]	M. H. Connell & Assoc.	Lee A. Tyler	Lee A. Tyler	....
North Miami .	Benjamin Vitale[25]	Stanley Goldberg	D. W. Jones	Benjamin Vitale[25]	D. W. Jones
Ocala	Ralph Serven	Van Walker	B. C. Oliver	Ralph Serven	Charlie Shreve
Orlando	A. B. Herndon	A. B. Herndon	L. L. Garrett	A. W. Crosby	Jessie Burkett
Panama City ..	C. C. Spivey	C. E. Peterson	H. Berkstressor	C. C. Price	H. Berkstressor
Pensacola	J. P. Jennings[6]	Paul T. Matthes	Stanley Sweeney	Jos. P. Jennings	Jos. P. Jennings
St. Augustine..	G. Marvin Grier	J. H. Lauper	A. C. Pomar	V. J. Usina, Jr.	....
St. Petersburg	A. K. Henry[11, 25]	P. J. Jorgensen	Harry Oberly	H. H. Girard	Timothy Goodrow
Sanford	S. M. Richard	....	R. L. Dallas	Ed. Griffith	....
Sarasota	Max Sturm	Max Sturm	E. T. Carlson	Max Sturm	E. T. Carlson
Tallahassee ...	....	Miller Walston	George Brand	N D. Rowell	Ed. Krause
Tampa	Roy Van Camp	Roy Van Camp	L. C. Cobb	Jeff Lovell	B. M. Duncan
W. Palm Beach	D. A. Hanlon[6]	John Klinck	John Simmons	D. A. Hanlon	....
Georgia					
Albany	E. J. Ford[11]	....	E. B. Adams	E. J. Ford	L. N. Hall[7]
Americus	....	G. E. Ansley	....	Dan Avery	F. S. Broadhurst
Athens	J. G. Beacham	J. G. Beacham	J. G. Beacham	J. G. Beacham	....
Atlanta	Clark Donaldson[31]	Clark Donaldson	....	Ray Nixon	M. B. Nixon
Augusta	W. R. Barnes[10]	M. P. Phillips	M. B. Cooper	W. R. Barnes	....
Brunswick	Amos Williams[6]	Carl Leavy	Paul Killian	I. J. Nettles	
Cedartown ...	....	Robert L. Veal	L. W. Wally	Jeff T. Price	L. W. Wally
College Park .	T. H. McLendon	Harry F. Wiley	T. H. McLendon	W. F. Dilbeck	T. H. McLendon
Columbus	D. T. Grider[6]	Paul S. Grimes	G. R. Lowe, Jr.	J. S. Schrimshire	....
Dalton	Paul Mitchell	....	V. D. Parrott	Paul Mitchell	V. D. Parrott
Decatur	S. A. Ross	S. A. Ross	....	S. A. Ross	....
Dublin	E. F. Moxley	....	Z. H. Perry	B. H. Martin	....
East Point ...	W. Moore, Jr.	W. Moore, Jr.	George Sparks	W. Moore, Jr.	W. Moore, Jr.
Gainsville	....	H. L. Pittard	H. L. Dooley	H. L. Pittard	H. L. Dooley
Griffin	....	J. T. Bearden	C. I. Smith, Jr.	John K. Avery	L. R. Simonton
Hapeville	....	W. B. Adams	Paul Eskew	....	....
La Grange	R. E. Hadley[6]	Fred Lamb	R. M. Haliburton	R. E. Hadley	Hollis Flournoy
Macon	J. C. Hardy[6]	J. Witherington	Emory Matthews	J. C. Hardy	J. C. Hardy
Marietta	T. E. Williams	T. E. Williams	Claude Bishop	Harold Landers	Wilburt Lambert
Moultrie		W. R. Robinson	H. J. Collins	Roy Folsom	John Bragg
Rome	Bruce Hamler[6]	W. C. Hall	Bruce Hamler	A. B. Brock	....
Savannah	Norris Sherry[2]	Wm. H. Reed[4, 2]	Bruce J. Sams	Louis F. Cornell	Paul K. Helmly
Thomasville ...	Sollie Allen	C. H. Jones, Jr.	Roland Clayton	Von Hurst	R. B. VanDame
Valdosta	....	E. F. Ledford	M. B. Price	C. A. Dunbar	J. W. Force
Waycross	....	T. L. Watts	Earl Hiott	Marvin L. Rouse	H. O. Dees
Idaho					
Boise	J. L. Morris	J. L. Morris	....	James White	A. J. Wahl
Caldwell	....	Melvin Lewis	....	Melvin Lewis	....
Coeur D'Alene	....	E. E. Soniville	Oscar Hill[5] . . p	....	James L. Ingalls
Idaho Falls ...	....	Claud R. Black	William Rushton	Chet G. Taylor[3]	....
Lewiston	R. P. Kerns	R. P. Kerns	R. P. Kerns	R. P. Kerns	....
Moscow	Harvey J. Smith	Harvey J. Smith	Mart Early	Geo. Torgerson	Mart Early
Nampa	....	Clark Murphy	Lawrence Good	Ellis Newman	Alfred Strate
Pocatello	....	W. W. Wilson	J. E. Fuger	Ralph Bair	W. W. Wilson
Twin Falls ...	....	N. S. Crossley	H. H. Ballenger	H. H. Ballenger	....
Illinois					
Alton	....	Guy M. Fairfield	F. H. King[5] . . p	Lucian Harris	....
Aurora	R. J. Weiland[3]	Harold B. Greene	James E. Barry	Leo Stratton	Walter Sperry . . s
Belleville	....	John Thompson	.... p	Thos. Schnipper	Irvin Knoebel
Berwyn	Anton Pav[6]	Edwin Hancock	Frank Broucek	James Dubek	....
Bloomington ..	H. R. Greene	Don Ferguson	M. L. Burgin[17]	H. R. Greene	G. L. Hall . . s
Blue Island ...	Charles A. Dewar	....	Charles A. Dewar	Charles A. Dewar	....
Brookfield	Peter Natale	....	....	....	....
Cairo	C. H. Simmons[3]	Donald E. Ball	H. L. Hileman	Dee Dorsett	....
Calumet City ..	....	Consoer, Townsend & Assoc.	S. J. Maciejewski	J. Radziewicki	J. Radziewicki
Canton	....	Howard Gibbons	Orval Kuhn	Robert Jennings	Eugene Waddell
Carbondale	....	Paul O. Hall	Jack Tripp	Ray Clutts	John Wooten
Centralia	....	H. B. Stover	Rex Gaston	Oliver Ferguson	Rex Gaston
Champaign ..	....	J. T. Kerns, Jr.	E. R. Healy[5] . . p	Leo J. Ducey	E. J. Beatty . . s
Chicago	George DeMent[3]	Dick Van Gorp	James Jardine	L. M. Johnson[3] . .	.... s
Chicago Hgts..	Geo. R. Brooke[3]	Mulford Eng. Ser.	A. H. Bonvouloir	James Shelley	Edward Meers . . s
Cicero	Frank Masa	Louis Mongreig	George Diamond	Frank Masa	George Diamond
Collinsville ...	J. Brancaglione[3]	Paul Johns	H. B. Wiese	H. B. Wiese	Wm. McMullen
Danville	Robert Elliott	Ferman O. Gunn	A. F. Ell[5] . . p	Robert Elliott	W. Glavey . . s
Decatur	H. L. Chastain[3]	P. J. Stephens	Gerald L. Davis	F. L. Kirby[3]	Dr. W. Hatfield s
Dekalb	....	R. S. Haldeman	....	Joe O'Brien	....
Des Plaines ...	Earl Warnicke[6]	E. N. Fletcher			
Dixon	O. Gearhart, Jr.[3]	....	G. F. Coe[5] . . p	O. Gearhart, Jr.[3]	Clarence Hill

State and City	Public Works Head	City Engineer	Water-Works Superintendent	Street Superintendent	Superintendent of Sewage Treatment
Ill. (cont.)					
Downers Grove	....	C. L. Baylor[63]	Wm. J. Duever	Edwin J. Dewey	Ben McEwan..[s]
East Moline ...	C. H. Buettner[11]	....	....	C. H. Buettner	....
East Peoria ...	....	J. W. Crenshaw	Charles Baylor	Clinton Dale	Fred Hosbrough
East St. Louis	....	David Johnston	..........[p]	J. M. Broderick	....
Elgin	A. J. Kuecker[11]	C. G. Brown	S. A. Jepson[11]	Godfred Kern	F. E. Johnson..[s]
Elmhurst	....	A. H. Nelson	....	Thos. Mansell	Fred Toppel
Elmwood Park.	....	....	J. Dal Cerro	Walter Lorence	....
Evanston	Joseph L. Rose[11]	James F. Moring	Horace R. Frye	E. W. Smedberg	E. W. Smedberg
Evergreen Park	E. J. Polzin[6]	....	Edw. J. Polzin	....	....
Forest Park ...	Henry C. Meyer[3]	Glenn Sunde	A. J. Klenske	H. A. Petersohn	....
Freeport	....	Edward O'Malley	W. A. Hutchins	Ray Staas	....
Galesburg	....	Floyd Burrell	Geo. Lofgren	Geo. McElwain	....
Glen Ellyn	....	W. Deuschler	Albert Ludeke	George Miller	James Brody
Granite City ..	....	D. J. Johnston	Mr. Casteel[5]..[s]	Wm. Warfield	Jack Fricker
Harrisburg	....	R. R. Brown	Amos Doom	D. S. Jordan	Harrison Kibler
Harvey	W. A. McLaren[3]	A. J. Hamilton	C. J. O'Connor	Clifton Campbell	....
Highland Park	Edw. P. Hart[11]	Philip E. Cole	Russell Poulson	Andrew C. Beck	....
Homewood	....	Donald Wikan	Henry Utermark	Donald Wikan	Henry Utermark
Jacksonville ..	....	Casler & Stapleton[23]	L. Quinlan	S. Pevey	....
Joliet	....	H. R. Goodspeed	Robt. J. Murphy	Elmer Latz	....
Kankakee	Leo Tetrault	Chas. F. Gregg	L. O. Minor[5]..[p]	Leo Tetrault	P. J. Schriner
Kewanee	C. Andrews	Wm. Pharmer	R. C. Richards	George Bennett[1]	Walter Buswell
La Grange	R. A. Finley[6]	Edwin Hancock[63]	John W. Krause	W. M. Fowler	....
Lansing	....	Ray Robinson	H. R. Wishart	H. R. Wishart	H. R. Wishart
La Salle	L. J. McGonigal	L. J. McGonigal	L. J. McGonigal	L. J. McGonigal	....
Lincoln	....	....	..........[p]	A. Kavelman	Lawrence Arthur
Lombard	H. T. Henry	Consoer Townsend Assoc.[33]	Harold Schneider	R. Goldbach	Fred Laske
Macomb	....	....	Wm. Newell	Charles Stover	Roy White
Marion	....	W. W. Miller	Ernest Brown	W. Feurer, Sr.	Albert Anderson
Mattoon	....	....	Karl J. Fuss	John Fryman	Karl J. Fuss
Maywood	Bazel Crowe[6]	Mr. Creelman	Bazel Crowe	Bazel Crowe	..........[s]
Melrose Park..	....	Edwin Hancock	F. Schulewitz	Peter Tassi	....
Moline	....	Lloyd Johnson	A. E. Anderson	Clark Hartzell	Arno Paulsen
Monmouth	....	....	J. E. Jessen	Clyde Bebok	W. P. Merwin
Mt. Vernon ...	D. A. Whitlock[6]	K. Setzekorn	Clifford Fore[5]..[p]	Emmit Lemay	D. A. Whitlock
Niles	Edward Bacher[6]	Arthur Consoer	Edward Bacher	Edward Bacher	....
North Chicago	....	W. Hooper, Jr.	Michael Opeka	Leo Walczak	..........[s]
Oak Lawn	....	E. Hancock Engrg.[33]	Charles Reich	J. J. Philbin, Jr.	Charles Reich
Oak Park	Wm. F. Bartels	Glenn Sunde	Harris Stevens	Warren McFeely	....
Ottawa	O. P. Walker[3]	Fred N. Spurgin	Harvey Cheatham	Robert Hilliard[3]	....
Park Forest ...	A. L. Heitmann	A. L. Heitmann[63]	R. Enzweiler[5]..[p]	A. L. Heitmann	Edward Meers[5]..[s]
Park Ridge ...	E. Knowles[1, 11]	Edward Knowles	Marvin Bublitz	....	....
Pekin	....	Jack Crenshaw	B. G. Hecker[5]..[p]	Henry Pfanz	Wm. Maurer
Peoria	....	Arno J. Pfeiler	....	Anthony Trunk	J. R. Longley[5]..[s]
Quincy	Donald Lenane[6]	C. A. Bunting	R. W. Gelston	Donald Lenane	Roy E. Higgins
River Forest ..	H. Demney[6]	Merrill Knox	D. Peterson[22]	H. Demney	H. Demney
Rockford	H. L. Danforth[3]	Ted Johnson	H. S. Merz	J. P. Bruno	Chas. Larson
Rock Island ...	Earl T. Miller	Pete A. Pakey	N. J. Hoeltzner	M. Kettering	G. Moellering
Skokie	Henry Weber[6]	U. F. Turpin	Henry Weber	Henry Weber	..........[s]
Springfield	O. J. Darling[3]	Chas. A. Nelson	S. T. Anderson	D. Shymansky	C. C. Larsen[5]..[s]
Sterling	J. Leander Hess	W. H. Haefliger	J. C. Moomau[5]..[p]	Fred O. Johnson	Leo L. Seidel
Streator	....	Fred Renz	C. F. Hord[5]..[p]	George Micklos	George Nichols
Urbana	Jay B. Boyd[3]	Max Kinch	..........[p]	Jay B. Boyd	....
Villa Park	....	W. D. Wilson	Charles Wawak	Al White	Al White
Waukegan	....	R. G. Kramer	L. C. Domke	G. T. Teeling	....
West Frankfort	....	P. O. Hall	Alex Smothers	Ira Flood	....
Wheaton	E. G. Phillips	....	....	E. G. Phillips[3]	O. Gettinger[5]..[s]
Wilmette	Armon Lund	John Scapin	Armon Lund	Armon Lund	....
Winnetka	R. L. Anderson[6]	R. L. Anderson	A. G. Olson	R. L. Anderson	R. L. Anderson
Wood River ...	F. F. Penning[11]	Walter Johansen	Fred F. Penning	Steve Pavelek	....
Indiana					
Anderson	Louis Eggman[29]	Donald Gwinnup	Sig. Jones	Earl Toombs	A. E. Holenbach
Bedford	....	John G. Owens	Desha Gipson	A. C. McPheeters	Desha Gipson
Bloomington ..	Thos. L. Lemon	M. B. Doyle	Lester Thornton	R. Richardson	Joseph E. Ellis
Columbus	Fred C. Owens	Ross J. Buck	Ed. Christopher	Jesse Butler	James Dickey[18]
Connersville ...	....	William Little	R. Leonard	R. Thomas	G. Dickerson
Crawfordsville .	....	Mark Gray	....	S. Switzer	Mark Gray
East Chicago ..	....	Chas. Sandor	John Moldovan	John Brozovic	John Suty
Elkhart	R. E. Long[29]	F. B. Rupe[1]	C. K. Parkhurst	James C. Hiatt	F. B. Rupe
Elwood	R. Fortson[29]	J. Seright	Jesse Miller	Luther Stockdale	H. Hershey
Evansville	J. W. Davidson[29]	Delbert Gunder	L. Killian	Eugene Nelligan	Louie Duncan
Fort Wayne ...	B. Swanson, Jr.[23]	D. C. Morin	Leo R. Mathews	A. Gladieux	Paul Brunner
Frankfort	K. S. Power	L. L. Fisher	Doyal Adkins	Fred Ticen	L. L. Fisher
Gary	Geo. Chacharis	Harold Zweig	....	Michael Puskar	....
Goshen	R. B. Messick[29]	Merle J. Miller	Merle J. Miller	H. D. Thomas	Merle J. Miller
Hammond	J. Wysong	J. Wysong	A. G. Gianinni	Irvin Venzke	Wm. Kolas
Hobart	Fred Rose	G. P. Huntington	....	Harry Young	C. R. Boutilier
Huntington ...	Roy Howell[12]	Eldon J. Rogers	Eugene Ehinger	Roman Schenkel	E. J. Rogers
Indianapolis ..	R. J. Dean[29]	Wm. H. Hunt	....	R. Bredell	D. Bender
Jeffersonville ..	C. W. Hoodenpyl	Wm. Goyne	....	Chas. Gannon	Wm. Goyne
Kokomo	Emerson Martin[34]	H. Coblentz	Max Stearn[5]..[p]	Harry Hart	H. Coblentz
Lafayette	Don McClurg[29]	Don McClurg	....	Jan Ludwig	....
La Porte	E. A. Koomler[29]	D. C. Ford	Wm. Carey	Grant Hunsley	Jackson Miller
Lebanon	....	....	Thos. J. Burrin	Russell Jackson	Thos. J. Burrin
Logansport ...	Robt. E. Price[14]	Wayne D. Doran	Robert E. Price	Wm. A. Rush	....
Madison	....	....	Arthur Wakefield	....	Fred Clements
Marion	Edward Wert	Howard Chestnut	Gordon Watson	Clark Wert	Gordon Watson
Michigan City..	....	John A. Kelley	Harry J. Draves	O. Sassaman	J. B. Gifford
Mishawaka	....	....	A. R. Klein	Fred Beehler	R. Kronewitter
Muncie	S. Terhune[34]	Horace Weber	R. Bartholemew	Herbert Bishop	Horace Weber

State and City	Public Works Head	City Engineer	Water-Works Superintendent	Street Superintendent	Superintendent of Sewage Treatment
Indiana (cont.)					
New Albany	C. Pralle Erni[29]	A. E. Graybrook	..........[p]	Frank Hartman	Frank Hartman
New Castle	Sidney E. Baker[29]	Ernest L. Guyer	Marvin Brown	James Clinton	Luther Withers
Peru	Ward Roberts[6]	Levi Wilson	Ralph L. Kerns	Ward Roberts	Ralph L. Kerns
Richmond	Wm. E. Wilson[34]	Ben H. Deuker	W. Shoemaker[5].[p]	Chas. Darr	Edwin Ross[5]..[s]
Seymour	....	George Crowder	G. R. Hamlin[5].[p]	William Edwards	....
Shelbyville	....	Kenny Bowman	..........[p]	Kenny Bowman	....
South Bend	Anthony Sabo	R. S. Andrysiak	Fred Wagner	D. Richardson	Louis Bourdon
Terre Haute	R. F. Thomas[29]	Albert Ellis	Arthur Blood	Timothy O'Leary	....
Valparaiso	....	Chas. G. Peller	William Peters	Harry Gustafson	James W. Sipe
Vincennes	L. T. Wampler[12]	Noble Spiker	M. H. Schwartz	Isaac Crawford	Wm. D. Frisz[35]
Wabash	....	L. O. Yarian	....	Bruce V. Worth	....
Washington	Othmar C. Frye[29]	....	Lawrence Gutsch	Peter Turk	Orville Chambers
West Lafayette	Fred L. Willis[29]	A. D. Ruth, Jr.	....	Otto A. Bossune	....
Iowa					
Ames	....	Lloyd Dove	Harris Seidel	Harold Tice	Harris Seidel
Boone	Fred J. Sandell[6]	D. R. Eschliman	....	....	....
Burlington	....	Roy Ellerhof	Mark Driftmier	Harry Staff	Harry Staff
Cedar Falls	H. F. Beisner[11]	H. F. Beisner	E. L. Cummins	....	O. K. Jensen
Cedar Rapids	....	F. E. Young	George S. Lee	John Storey[3]	W. Meaney, Jr.
Charles City	....	Ralph D. Briggs	Adolph Brumund	Harry O'Harrow	James Beard
Clinton	....	Benton Anderson	Don Bragg	Harold P. Ytzen	....
Council Bluffs	F. E. Grover[11]	F. E. Grover	M. E. Rew	Art Sarratt	....
Davenport	R. C. Graham[31]	R. D. Matthews	....	E. Kistenmacher	John Strelow
Des Moines	John Tippee[11]	John Tippee	M. K. Tenny	L. J. Formaro	John L. Dailey
Dubuque	....	Ken Cullen	Jos. J. Hail	Cletus Allen	....
Fort Dodge	....	John E. Wright	John W. Pray	John E. Wright	D. D. Douglas
Fort Madison	....	A. E. J. Johnson	Frank Freitag	K. E. Hancock	K. E. Hancock
Iowa City	....	Fred E. Gartzke	D. Edwards[5]..[p]	Willard Irvin	M. F. Neuzil
Keokuk	....	Chas. J. Nelson	Walter Garrison	R. O. Bramhall	....
Marshalltown	....	C. John Anderson	Kenneth Mains	Ervine Harland	L. Skorczeski
Mason City	C. W. Hamblin	C. W. Hamblin	C. W. Hamblin	W. Fitzgerald	L. W. Helbling
Muscatine	....	Ed. Knott[4]	Walter Molis	Ed. Knott	....
Newton	....	J. G. McFadden	D. Y. Caldwell	Clarence Bisom	F. Jungwirth
Oskaloosa	....	Wayne E. Foster	Roy O. Ellis	Ralph Clough	C. Bergstresser
Ottumwa	Wm. Packard[6]	Howard Adams	Geo. Ahrens	....	....
Sioux City	P. V. Roberts[11]	C. VanderWicken	William Murphy	Jay Elliot	....
Waterloo	....	D. Larrabee	Walter Lang	Carl Fagerlind	Fred Tiesinger
Kansas					
Arkansas City	W. E. Lambert[5]	R. E. Bridges	W. E. Lambert	Ralph E. Bridges	....
Atchison	....	J. Broder Frans	L. Weatherford[5] [p]	J. Broder Frans	....
Chanute	....	Paschal Grimes	....	Emile Betost	W. K. Moffatt
Coffeyville	....	F. L. Kramer	F. L. Kramer	Grover Jackson	Wm. O'Connell
Dodge City	....	Fred Kirkpatrick	Rex Reynolds	R. O. Bailey	M. O. Wolf
El Dorado	R. A. Shook[6]	L. A. Martindale	C. R. McGahan	R. A. Shook	W. A. Blake
Emporia	R. Cunningham[5]	Lee R. Stolfus	....	M. B. Bowers	M. B. Bowers
Fort Scott	Albert Price[3]	....	Jesse Mabery	Albert Price	....
Garden City	....	Karl Svaty	Walter Baker	Bill Wagner	....
Great Bend	....	Herbert Callon	....	Sam Radke	Herbert Callon
Hays	H. E. Lucas[5]	....	Norman Bissing[36]	Joe A. Koerner	Roy Binder
Hutchinson	....	R. W. Bruggeman	D. McCammot[5] [p]	Floyd Terrill	Chet Goble
Independence	G. Hackmaster[5]	G. Hackmaster	R. F. Bluejacket	Joe Allen	Loile Corle
Junction City	Jake Moyer	Robert B. Clary	Nelson Connlly	Edwin Albright	Roy Ellis
Kansas City	J. P. Regan[3]	F. B. McKinnell	Elmer Chapman	Joe Dressler	E. Edwards
Lawrence	A. T. Hodges	E. J. Allison	R. M. Mounsey	A. T. Hodges	Charles Winters
Leavenworth	Henry Johnson	W. B. Jennings	H. H. Kansteiner	George Bollin	....
Manhattan	D. C. Wesche	....	B. Van Blarcum	Herbert Knox	Virgil Spain
Newton	L. Armstrong	L. Armstrong	C. C. Thompson	Milo Carter	C. C. Thompson
Ottawa	....	A J. Jefferis	O. L. E. Haff	Hiram Browning	R. E. Honn
Parsons	Bernard T. Budd	Bernard T Budd	Bernard T. Budd	Earl Blackburn	L. Cunningham
Pittsburg	....	C. M. Cooper	O R. Green	Francis M. Lee	D. Boisdrenghien
Salina	....	H. F. Harper	R. S. Fassnacht	....	....
Topeka	....	Abram Pratt	G. Dorr Pelton	Frank Magnuson	D. B. Kissinger
Wichita	Geo. J. Fisher[11]	Bill E. Smith	Robert H. Hess	John L. Allen	Robert H. Hess
Winfield	....	Gerard W. Finuf	James D. Barker	Roy Cromley	Lloyd Hankins
Kentucky					
Ashland	J. P. Brownstead	June Pope	J. P. Brownstead	Geo. Brammer	Geo. Brammer
Bowling Green	R. D. Graham	D. A. Lawson	F. R. Gonce	C. B. Deweese	F. R. Gonce
Covington	Robert Davis[6]	Gordon Willis	Robert Fischer	Larry Gronefeld	....
Fort Thomas	Chas. H. Kuhn	Chas. H. Kuhn	L. Dodson[16]..[p]	Chas. H. Kuhn	W. Anderson[5]..[s]
Frankfort	Earl Harrod	Russell Marshall	....	Jessie Louden	Forrest Hoover
Henderson	Chas. T. Raber[3]	....	....	Richard Branson	....
Hopkinsville	....	....	Jack Boxley	Chas. Vaughn	Jack Boxley
Lexington	George W. Gard[11]	George W. Gard	E. Jacobson[5]..[p]	George W. Gard	H. D. Regan
Louisville	H. T. Meiners[11]	W. W. Sanders	Henry M. Gerber	Tom Kohler	John Leake[37]
Madisonville	....	Thomas O. Long	W. R. Holland	G. C. Cardwell	Harold Berry
Mayfield	....	....	W. L. Harrington	C. R. Adams	....
Middlesborough	Luther Meyers[23]	G. F. Justice	Mr. Hupp[5]..[p]	R. McGlamery[22]	D. Williams
Newport	T. R. Williams[11]	Albert Root	John Nesto	Edw. Stertmeyer	W. Anderson[5]..[s]
Owensboro	Earl Patton[11]	Earl Patton	Elmer Smith	Russell Shifley	....
Paducah	Ray Kayse[11]	Thos. A. Bradley	William Decker	....	....
Richmond	....	H. deB. Forbes	A. D. Burns	Austin Whitaker	Dan Burns
Louisiana					
Abbeville	P. D. Dauterive	V. A. Pendleton	O. J. Broussard	Lawrence Landry	Zenon Conner
Alexandria	....	Chas. W. Cook	R. L. Lawrence	....	Wm. J. Semple
Bastrop	....	Ray Day	H. Porter[5]..[p]	Curtis Bridges	....
Baton Rouge	Ray Burgess[11]	L. J. Muse	D. R. Taylor[5]..[p]	....	....
Bogalusa	Archie Pounds[8]	B. C. Sones[10]	Archie Pounds	W. Golloway[22]	....
Bossier City	C. W. Fowler[8]	....	J. A. Phillips	J. C. Waldrop[8]	....
Crowley	....	L. Mouton	Coley Prudhomme	John Gautreaux	Clint Carlin
Gretna	....	Alvin E. Hotard	Joseph L. Bishop	....	....

State and City	Public Works Head	City Engineer	Water-Works Superintendent	Street Superintendent	Superintendent of Sewage Treatment
La. (cont.)					
Houma	A. L. Badeaux	R. J. Yakupsak	R. J. Yakupsak	A. L. Badeaux	Frank Shain
Lafayette	....	Dalten Reid	J. L. Love	Oniel Mouton	J. L. Love
Lake Charles	....	D. W. Jessen	F. Gibson[29]..p	Walter J. Goos[3]	S. S. Crawford
Monroe	....	Luther T. Harper	J. K. Brothers	Fred Hill	....
Morgan City	....	L. H. Roes	Joseph Cefalu	T. E. Davis	....
New Iberia	W. Jefferson[3]	John M. Rochel	Geo. Gwrlach[5]..p	Cleo Hebert	D. Delahoussaye
New Orleans	A. G. Wyler[38]	Louis M. Buja	E. F. Hughes[6]	T. B. Becnel	....
Opelousas	James Prados[6]	M. Goudeau, Jr.	James Prados	Raleigh Vige	James Prados
Ruston	....	....	P. Grambling, Jr.	O. W. Hogan	Clyde Gilmore
Shreveport	H. Lane Mitchell	Robert L. Horton	Thomas L. Amiss	L. Middlebrooks	....
West Monroe	....	....	J. O. Fleming	W. R. Townsend	....
Maine					
Auburn	R. W. Merrill[28]	R. L. Clifford	L. K. Parker[5]..p	R. W. Merrill	L. K. Parker
Augusta	....	Waldo W. Hill	S. S. Anthony	Waldo W. Hill	Waldo W. Hill
Bangor	C. Wiswell[11]	J. L. MacLeod	D. P. Johnston	Carlton Wiswell	Carlton Wiswell
Bath	Arthur Avery	....	M. Libby[5]..p	Arthur Avery	....
Biddeford	S. Duquette	....	..........p	S. Duquette[3]	....
Brunswick	F. W. Landers	F. W. Landers	E. Boyd Livesay	....	T. M. Libby[5]..s
Lewiston	George Maher[11]	F. Cunningham	Adelard Gauthier	George Maher	Adelard Gauthier
Portland	B. O. Whitney[3]	P. M. Burnham	....	Frank W. Bryant	....
Saco	Carl Carter	....	..........p	Carl Carter	Walter White
Sanford	George Fortier[3]	E. E. Gallant	S. Littlefield	Charles A. Day	Edwin Thayer..s
So. Portland	A. W. Waterman[3]	A. W. Waterman	....	....	Herman Kendall
Waterville	R. Knowlton[11]	R. Knowlton[11]	J. E. Hale..p	R. Knowlton	S. K. Smith..s
Westbrook	P. D. Spiller[6]	....	....	....	A. Bragdon..s
Maryland					
Annapolis	J. M. Axelrod	J. M. Axelrod	Francis Leitch	Loree Basil	August Damps
Baltimore	G. A. Carter[11]	....	B. L. Werner	James H. McKay	John J. Hunt
Cambridge	....	John H. Cosby	....	....	Clayton Bramble
College Park	H. E. Hughes[6]	M. F. Greenhorne	..........p	H. E. Hughes	....
Cumberland	....	C. R. Nuzum	G. M. Hitchcock	A. W. Heller	....
Frederick	W. R. Walter	W. R. Walter	Wm. J. Davis	Roger A. Cook	R. H. Hartman
Hagerstown	E. S. Guth[29]	C. D. Williams	R. C. Willson	William Henson	L. G. Eyerly
Havre de Grace	....	Leo C. Davis	W. Curtis Perry	J. L. Walker	....
Hyattsville	....	W. S. Machen	....	T. E. Arnold[20]	..........s
Mt. Rainier	....	Roy T. Fowkes	....	L. Soper	..........s
Salisbury	P. C. Cooper[11]	Philip C. Cooper	C. O. Wooten	C. O. Wooten[19]	Wm. Esham
Takoma Park	Peter Remsen[11]	....	..........p	....	..........s
Massachusetts					
Adams	....	....	R. E. Griswold	John Miles	....
Agawan	....	P. W. Schubach	Louis Mercadante	P. W. Schubach	....
Amesbury	Albert J. Roy	....	Albert J. Roy	Albert J. Roy	....
Amherst	....	....	John A. White	....	Nelson Damon
Andover	Allen M. Flye[23]	R. Preble, Jr.[61]	R. E. Preble, Jr.	E. R. Lawson	....
Arlington	F. N. O'Hara[6]	Wilbur H. Roby[61]	....	F. N. O'Hara	....
Athol	H. J. Brovillet[40]	....	R. W. Glasheen	H. J. Brovillet	....
Attleboro	Russell Tennant	Russell Tennant	Russell Tennant	....	....
Auburn	....	....	S. Satcher	R. E. Witcher	....
Barnstable	....	L. F. Rogers[61]	..........p	S. R. Doane	K. S. Bearse
Belmont	Geo. B. Olsen[6]	J. W. Kales[61]	E. P. Looney	....	....
Beverly	R. F. Duwart[3]	....	Roger F. Duwart	Roger F. Duwart	Roger F. Duwart
Billerica	Vernon Packard[21]	....	F. O'Hara	Jacob Elmer	....
Boston	Geo. G. Hyland[3]	....	D. M. Sullivan[39]	R. J. Kelley[39]	Robert P. Shea[39]
Braintree	J. Wentworth[28, 6]	Harold C. Pearl	Geo. N. Watson	J. Q. Wentworth	G. N. Brousseau
Brockton	....	Wm. T. Boyle	Paul F. Kingman	Henry W. Hall	....
Brookline	....	W. A. Devine	K. W. Robie	Walter A. Devine	Walter A. Devine
Cambridge	R. J. Dunphy[3]	Edward Smith	W. H. McGinness	....	....
Canton	J. E. Bamber[6]	....	....	....	....
Chelmsford	....	....	....	F. R. Greenwood[28]	....
Chelsea	John Marion	John Marion	Thomas Quigley	John Marion	John Marion
Chicopee	....	T. F. Robinson	F. J. Driscoll[6]	Thos. A. Laramee	Thos. A. Laramee
Clinton	....	....	John A. Hastings	Patrick Ball	Patrick Ball
Concord	Thomas Flint[23]	....	J. H. Robinson	David Nelson	J. H. Robinson
Danvers	....	C. R. Grinnell	C. Vernon Russell	Walter J. Ennis	....
Dartmouth	....	R. Viereck[40]	John Whitehead	M. Burghardt[28, 6]	John Whitehead
Dedham	John J. Shea[3]	John Tullock	W. Newman[5]..p	....	....
Dracut	....	....	H. Garland[6]..p	Armand Beaudry	....
Easthampton	Walter Szary[23]	W. P. Lawler[61]	Victor Arrighi[1]	George Lapan	Edward McGrath
Everett	J. F. McPhee[23]	Joseph F. Kelly	B. W. Vaughan	Wm. E. Driscoll	B. W. Vaughan
Fairhaven	....	....	....	Henry T. Howard	....
Fall River	T. J. Logan[3]	T. J. Logan	M. Sullivan	Thos. J. Logan	Arthur Slater
Fitchburg	J. M. Peirce[3]	J. M. Peirce	T. E. Kennedy	Robt. T. Barnicle	Wilfred Lamothe
Framingham	John T. Dias[23]	Richard Mackey	Harry Brillhart	F. D. Williams	Harold D. Flood
Gardner	Eugene J. Teir	Eugene J. Teir	E. V. O'Donnell	Wm. E. Gouslin	....
Gloucester	Henry Lasley[11]	....	....	H. P. Sawyer	Jos. A. Peters
Greenfield	Eugene L. Bond[6]	Eugene L. Bond	John F. Collins	Eugene L. Bond	Eugene L. Bond
Haverhill	H. W. Bailey[1]	Harry W. Bailey	F. E. Driscoll	....	....
Hingham	....	....	R. Bartlett[5]..p	H. A. Cole, 3rd.	....
Holyoke	Wm. G. Cowie[19]	Edward A. Maher	T. Shaughnessy	William G. Cowie	William G. Cowie
Lawrence	N. J. Callahan	S. S. Nicolosi	Joseph L. Dunlap	N. J. Callahan	....
Leominster	George Damon	....	Wayne F. Damon	Geo. W. Damon	....
Lexington	R. J. Gayer[6]	Richard J. Gayer	Richard J. Gayer	Richard J. Gayer	....
Lowell	F. P. Cogger[3]	Stephen Kearney	Wm. H. Molloy	P. Joseph Garrity	P. Joseph Garrity
Ludlow	....	....	....	....	Stanley Sepiol[3]
Lynn	T. Costin, Jr.[23]	Frank E. Gowdy	J. C. Callahan	Fred L. Kennedy	Edw. F. Carroll
Malden	D. J. Brandano[6]	T. W. Sheehan	....	D. J. Brandano	D. J. Brandano
Marblehead	....	R. O. Burlingham	J. Willard Harris	W. B. Powers[40]	Irving Bridges
Marlborough	....	John A. Bigelow	Harry P. Loftus	J. F. Granger	Harry P. Loftus
Medford	H. Nicholson[1, 11]	H. J. Nicholson	John J. Murphy	H. J. Nicholson	..........s
Melrose	Glen S. Weeks[6]	Glen S. Weeks	....	Glen S Weeks	....
Methuen	....	A. Nicholson	T. H. Mahoney	Carl W. Woekel	Carl W. Woekel

State and City	Public Works Head	City Engineer	Water-Works Superintendent	Street Superintendent	Superintendent of Sewage Treatment
Mass. (cont.)					
Middleboro	....	....	E. E. Gardiner	Louis Forney	....
Milford	....	....	..........[p]	E. C. Carroll[40]	..........[3]
Milton	....	A. E. Manning[61]	M. J. Hannigan	J. Maloney, Jr.	Fred E. Joy
Natick	Thos. E. Huddy[3]	B. G. Sargent	B. G. Sargent	B. G. Sargent	B. G. Sargent
Needham	L. C. Hollis[6]	H. G. Martin[61]	Roger G. Oakman	Louis W. Wise	E. A. Symonds[s]
New Bedford	Nathan S. Ellis[3]	....	H. C. Mandell	....	Nathan S. Ellis[3]
Newburyport	....	....	Clark T. Lunt[15]	James H. Ronan	....
Newton Centre	W. S. Pratt[11]	U. M. Schiavone	M. F. Croker[3]	F. K. Perkins[3]	E. F. Cannon
North Adams	H. A. Galipeau[3]	T. H. Milette	H. A. Galipeau	H. A. Galipeau	H. A. Galipeau
Northampton	W. A. Howes	Francis P. Ryan	F. M. Hennessy	W. A. Howes	O. E. Brainerd[35]
No. Attleboro	....	Herman C. Razee	Ernest H. Ebert	James J. McKeon	F. B. Clavette
Northbridge	....	....	D. K. Barnes[5]..[p]	W. M. Williams	Nicholas DeHaas
Norwood	A. E. Casey[6]	A. W. Thompson	....	....	....
Palmer	....	T. D. Crimmins[61]	William Ammann	Stanley G. Wilk	....
Peabody	F. J. McCarthy[3]	F. J. McCarthy	F. J. McCarthy	F. J. McCarthy	F. J. McCarthy
Pittsfield	J. F. Daniels[3]	J. F. Daniels	C. S. Dickie	J. F. Gilligan	Charles H. Benz
Plymouth	....	Edward Chase	Theodore Brink	E. C. Chandler	E. C. Chandler
Quincy	C. R. Herbert[3]	Henry Nilsen	Charles Carey	C. R. Herbert	Patrick Tyman
Randolph	....	Eugene Mulligan	William Almond	Eugene Mulligan	....
Reading	J. T. Putnam[6]	....	James T. Putnam	J. T. Putnam	J. T. Putnam
Revere	....	G. S. Burnett	G. S. Burnett	G. S. Burnett	G. S. Burnett
Rockland	E. J. Wallace[40]	....	J. B. Studley	Earl J. Wallace	....
Salem	Thomas L. Hever	E. W. Nickerson	....	Thomas L. Hever	....
Saugus	E. F. Pesce[1, 6]	E. F. Pesce	....	....	....
Shrewsbury	....	J. J. McKinnon[61]	....	Lyle F. Casten	....
Somerville	W. J. Manning[3]	W. J. Manning	J. J. Corbett	A. N. Tantasia	....
Southbridge	....	Henry Raciot[61]	C. Spielvogel[5]..[p]	Joseph Benoit	....
South Hadley	Chas. E. Barney	Chas. E. Barney	Robert Moos	Chas. E. Barney	C. E. Barney
Springfield	J. J. Sullivan	J. J. Sullivan	M. Shaughnessy[1]	J. J. Sullivan	R. Greaney[18]
Stoneham	E. D. Callahan[6]	M. J. Markham[61]	E. D. Callahan	E. D. Callahan	E. D. Callahan
Stoughton	J. W. Williams[6]	L. C. Morrill	J. W. Williams	J. W. Williams	....
Swampscott	P. A. Polisson[6]	H. L. Hamill		T. J. Ryan	
Taunton	....	W. F. O'Donnell	T. Williams, Jr.	John E. Sousa	Frank L. Smith
Tewksbury	....	....	Charles Kent	R. J. O'Neill	....
Wakefield	George Winters	....	M. P. Curran	Carl Chelman	M. P. Curran
Waltham	H. F. Howe[11]	H. F. Howe	Herbert F. Howe	Herbert F. Howe	Herbert F. Howe
Watertown	....	J. H. Sullivan	Michael B. Oates	T. V. Dwyer	
Webster	....	J. R. Kleindienst	S. G. Wylie	J. W. Dziedzic	J. R. Kleindienst
Wellesley	H. S. Estey[6]	Philip Plaisted[61]	T. F. Coughlin	William Oakes	T. F. Coughln
Westfield	R. E. Sanville[23]	A. E. Reynolds	G. C. Brew[1]	F. J. Martin	....
W. Springfield	....	W. W. Wyman	C. M. Jacobson	T. F. Roche	....
Weymouth (E. Weymouth)	....	A. J. Bilodeau	Sidney C. Beane	D. J. Slattery	Norman M. Smth
Winchester	J. Wakefield, Jr.	J. Wakefield, Jr.	J. H. Halwartz	J. Wakefield, Jr.	....
Winthrop	....	....	E. T. Roach	Fritz Westlin	John J. Kennedy
Woburn	A. J. Wall[6]	George W. Olson	A. J. Wall	A. J. Wall	A. J. Wall
Worcester	Earl R. Perry[3]	V. M. Hynes	Chas. B. Hardy	J. F. Donahue	G. E MacDowell
Michigan					
Adrian	Nick Miller[3]	Walter E. Frazier	H. E. Smith	....	Vern Snedeker
Albion	....	....	Herman Beilfuss	L. McAuliffe	Jake Craaybeek
Allen Park	Edward Himick[22]	L. N. Hayden	Edward Aniol	....	....
Alpena	M. A. Olsen[11]	F. N. Jackson	M. A. Olsen	M. A. Olsen	M. A. Olsen
Ann Arbor	G. Sandenburgh[6]	G. Sandenburgh	H. H. Caswell	G. Sandenburgh	C. P. Witcher
Battle Creek	R. R. McIntosh[11]	R. R. McIntosh	Kenneth Garvey	Nels Skulstad	Kenneth Garvey
Bay City	R. McGillivray[11]	R. K. McGillivray	Alex Krzyminski	Otis Nelson	Louis Harrison
Benton Harbor	C. C. Smith[6]	Samuel Wells	Wm. J. Russell	C. C. Smith	C. W. Thompson[5]
Berkley	E. C. Carlson[6]	Pate & Hirn[33]	E. C. Carlson	E. C. Carlson	E. C. Carlson
Birmingham	Thomas Brien[1]	G. Serenbetz	H. K. Schone	Thomas Brien[1]	R. Grinnell
Cadillac	L. A. Hanson[5]	....	George Penney	Carl Tyler	T. Haner
Clawson	Chas. Nugent[6]	L. G. Hendricks	Chas. Nugent	Chas. Nugent	Chas. Nugent
Dearborn	James M. Dick[11]	H. L. Lilley	S. A. Wagerson	....	Michael Groen
Detroit	G. C. Richards[3]	M. F. Wagnitz	G. J. Remus[3, 5]	Jan Schmedding[41]	F. E. Weber[35]
East Detroit	C. Paternoster[6]	H. J. Fuller[33]	Owen Arnold	C. Paternoster	....
East Lansing	J. John Wibert[6]	Robert M. Bruce	Marvin Garrison	J. John Wibert	Edgar Sneiders
Ecorse	Lester Vida	M. L. Brown & Son[33]	C. J. Livernois	....	....
Escanaba	Ken Touschak[6]	Ken Buckland	A. Christiansen	Ken Touschak	A. Christiansen
Farmington Tp. (Farmington)	....	....	....	....	....
Ferndale	R. F. Goodspeed[11]	James Taylor	E. Strohpagel	Norris Arnold	....
Flint	T. D. Moss[17]	Tolan Hammond	Herschel Self	T. D. Moss	T. D. Moss
Grand Rapids	G. G. Schmidt[11, 25]	R. Bruggink	Spencer Ferris	Leo TePaske	Huntley DeLano
Grosse Pte. Farms	....	Murray M. Smith	Murray M. Smith	Peter Allard	....
Grosse Pte. Pk.	Herbert Heger[11]	Everitt B. Lane	....	Victor Huvaere	....
Grosse Pte. Woods	J. Fred Hansen[6]	Pate & Hirn[33]	A. Guaresimo	....	....
Hamtramck	A. J. Celmer[6]	I. M. Kopkowski	A. Smolenski	....	....
Hazel Park	Oliver Godsey[6]	....	Mr. Neusius	Oliver Godsey	....
Highland Park (Detroit)	D. E. Drummond[6]	Geo. Dunkirk	V. Hinebrook	D. E. Drummond	....
Holland	Guy Bell[14]	Laverne Serne	Guy Bell	Louis B. Dalman	Guy Bell
Inkster	W. Meadowcroft	....		C. Bauer	..........[s]
Ironwood	Edmund Pickard	Kenneth E. Long	Patrick Sullivan	Edmund Pickard[22]	
Jackson	Frank Smoyer[6]	Wm. D. Monroe	Jos. M. Rogeven	Frank Smoyer	R. Alton Greene
Kalamazoo	H. L. Andrus[11]	Harold L. Andrus	Albert Sabo	Melvin Hatfield	Donald H. Swets
Lansing	C. E. Thornton[11]	C. E. Thornton	Otto E. Eckert	C. E. Thornton	Geo. F. Wyllie
Lincoln Park	C. F. Mozena[6]	Edwin H. Pate	L. M. Bailey	C. F. Mozena	....
Livonia	D. Meinzinger[11]	W. R. McCary	Jesse Ziegler[3]	W. R. McCary	....
Marquette	V. E. Swan[6]	Geo. T. Meholick	Howard Greene	V. E. Swan	Howard Greene
Melvindale	Geo. Slepsky[1, 3]	George Jerome	Geo. Slepsky	Geo. Slepsky	..........[s]
Menominee	C. Arvid Lundin	George Byrnes	C. E. Young	C. Arvid Lundin	C. E. Young
Midland	Chas. A. Johnson	Chas. A. Johnson	Paul Stegeman	Chas. A. Johnson	Paul Stegeman

State and City	Public Works Head	City Engineer	Water-Works Superintendent	Street Superintendent	Superintendent of Sewage Treatment
Mich. (cont.)					
Monroe	J. I. Godfroy	Mark G. Dance	C. L. Reighard	James I. Godfroy	C. C. Gessner
Mt. Clemens	E. E. Whedon[11]	E. E. Whedon	Robert E. Hansen	J. F. Gardner	H. E. McEntee
Mt. Pleasant	....	A. J. Kronbach	Wyman Paullin	Spencer Strouse	....
Muskegon	Geo. Clark, Jr.	Geo. Clark, Jr.	R. L. Sensabaugh	Elwyn Langmo	C. T. Mudgett
Muskegon Hgts.	....	....	Sherman Carrier	Chas. Swenor	C. Harrison
Niles	N. Koerwitz[5]	Clifford Eden	Roy Edwards	Frank Seals	Charles Clem
Oak Park	W. E. Chlopan[6]	R. L. Castle	J. B. Thompson	....	....
Owosso	W. H. Stickel[2]	S. E. Harrington	W. H. Bennett	W. H. Stickel	La Ville Jennings
Pontiac	J. W. Jewell[6]	Lewis M. Wrenn	Joseph Gable	J. W. Jewell	W. Dubay[1]
Port Huron	A. T. Carlisle	A. T. Carlisle	John McPhee	Earl Metzger	Lester Working
River Rouge	A Greig, Jr.[6]	M. L. Brown & Son[33]	Richard Crosson	A. Greig, Jr.	....
Roseville	Frederick Kaiser	Roy Carter	August H. Peters	Frederick Kaiser	Arthur Perreault
Royal Oak	M. W. Harrs[6]	G. L. Nampa	G. L. Nampa	M. W. Harris	....
Saginaw	Hugh A. Benner[11]	Carl T. Dust	J. C. Richardson	Bernard Tunney	Fred. Galarno
St. Clair Shores	E. Kurtzhals	Fred Cheek	C. Vernier[1]	E. Kurtzhals	Harry Cook[42]
St. Joseph	D. E. Bicknell[6]	Neil Berndt	Frank Dansfield	Martin Schultz	Wm. Russell[6]..s
Sault Ste. Marie	A. J. Lipsett, Jr.	A. J. Lipsett, Jr.	Ralph E. Speer	Hector MacInnis	....
Traverse City	Anthony Eikey	J. A. Rowley	Anthony Eikey	Anthony Eikey	R. Gerald Forton
Trenton	C. H. Knopes[6]	Geo. H. Cully	A. L. Mulheisen	Riley Cohoon	....
Warren Twp. (Van Dyke)	N. J. Eckstein[6]	C. P McGrath	Thomas Butcher	N. J. Eckstein	Floyd Vermette
Wayne	Ray Wardell[6]	Richard Gillespie	Patrick Cullen	Ray Wardell	....
Wyandotte	....	Louis H. Moehr	Carl Bufe	....	W. Assenmacher[5]s
Ypsilanti	John Larsen[11]	....	John Max	William Hughes	John Max
Minnesota					
Albert Lea	R. O. Folland[11]	R. O. Folland	Marinus Jensen	Lawrence Parks	Leonard Zuehl
Austin	....	Roger Nelson	Harold Lamon	Martin Hanson	Leon Johnson
Bemidji	....	....	Archie Bowers	Wm. Olson	Roy Green[7]
Bloomington	Frank Laska	Frank Laska	....	Stanley Kelley	....
Brainerd	....	C. O. Markson	Evolt Kukko	Len Adair	K. St. Marie, Sr.
Brooklyn Ctr. (Minneapolis)	....	A. J. Lee	Frank Smith	Henry Davis	....
Crystal (Robbinsdale)	....	J. Klememhagen	....	Robert Fishbach	Jack Irving
Duluth	Olaf E. Berg[6]	John Fredin	M. Lubratovich	Olaf E. Berg	Carl Lund
Faribault	P. Theo. Olsson	P. Theo. Olsson	George LaRoche	Francis Ford	Melvin Koch
Fergus Falls	....	E. F. Hensch	H. J. Sowden	Thore Glende	H. J. Sowden
Hibbing	J. H. Rough	J. H. Rough	Roy Ingels	J. H. Rough	Charles Rolando
Mankato	E. G. Hill	E. G. Hill	L. G. Lloyd	Mel Sheehan	....
Minneapolis	....	H. G. Erickson	Leslie Halladay	Elmer Lund	K. L. Mick[5]..s
Moorhead	....	Geo. T. Anderson	Joseph E. Young	William Arndt	Joseph E. Young
Owatonna	....	R. R. Fleming	Frank Harlicker	Lowell King	Anton Pirkl
Red Wing	Chas. Claydon[29]	James F. Enz	Leo H. Pieper	F. K. Johnson	....
Richfield	Leo J. Jolly	Leo J. Jolly	..........p	Robert Long	....
Robbinsdale	....	Graydon Boeck	Glenn Cass	Arvil Olson	....
Rochester	....	C. A. Armstrong	G. E. Marek	....	W. C. Hogenson
Roseville (St. Paul)	....	Charles Soutter	....	E. C. Bather	Charles Soutter
St. Cloud	Richard Teague	Richard Teague	Fred Thielman	Harry Beumer	L. S. Craig[18]
St. Louis Park	Phil. W. Smith[11]	Phil. W. Smith	Ira Vraalstad	Kenneth Johnson	....
St. Paul	F. D. Marzitelli[3]	Geo. M. Shepard	L. N. Thompson	John Gleason	K. L. Mick[5]..s
So. St. Paul	....	John Badalich	John Badalich	James Kennedy	W. H. Cropsey
Virginia	Mike Woods[13]	Paul Lagerstedt	Carol Elliott	Mike Woods	Clyde Semon
Willmar	Neil Erickson	Neil Erickson	A. S. Heiberg	Frank Rahn	Carl Bakken
Winona	....	J. Kleinschmidt	Gerald Harvey	Thomas J. Gile	James Puck
Mississippi					
Biloxi	J. A. Tony Creel[3]	....	Albert Jacquet	J. A. Tony Creel	R. E. Smith
Clarksdale	....	R. A. Miller	Jess L. Haley	B. J. Jennings	....
Columbus	....	....	W. P. Gearhiser	Louis Shull, Sr.	....
Corinth	....	J. F. Morgan	G. G. Howell	W. E. Carter	W. E. Carter
Greenville	J. Teunisson, Jr.	J. Teunisson, Jr.	D. H. Wicker	....	....
Greenwood	Roy Stott[5, 43]	C. G. Abbott	A. D. Spengler	C. G. Abbott	A. D. Spengler
Gulfport	H. E. Blakeslee[3]	W. L. Coon	H. E. Blakeslee	H. E. Blakeslee	H. E. Blakeslee
Hattiesburg	Hugh Batson	J. R. Estes	John Nelson	Hugh Batson	....
Jackson	J. J. Halbert[11]	J. J. Halbert	R. M. Coker[44]	C. E. McMillin[45] F. Stewart[46]	....
Laurel	W. P. Smyly[3]	T. I. Carter	W. I. Glenn	W. P. Smyly[3]	....
McComb	....	....	W. H. Green	H. S. Harrison	W. H. Green
Meridian	J. Slaughter, Jr.	J. Slaughter, Jr.	L. M. Howell	Ronald Gough	....
Natchez	Ed. Stiles	Ed. Stiles	Marion Stewart	Alfred Karie	....
Pascagoula	H. C. Ezell[6]	D. J. Simmons	H. C. Ezell	H. C. Ezell	H. C. Ezell
Tupelo	....	....	Ray Aycock	A. E. Bratton	Edsel Posey
Vicksburg	F. M. Garvey[47]	John L. Hyland	A. H. Douat	F. M. Garvey[47]	F. M. Garvey[47]
Missouri					
Berkeley	L. E. Spotswood	L. E. Spotswood	....	Earl Lewis	....
Brentwood	Chas. B. Paige[47]	J. L. Willingham	....	A. C. Watters	....
Cape Girardeau	Max Stovall[3]	John R. Walther	..........p	John Eldridge	....
Carthage	Howard Berry[6]	E. S. Glenn	Howard Berry	....	Howard Berry
Clayton	....	E. Petersen, Jr.	....	Nelson Alexander	....
Columbia	F. E. Grundler[11]	F. E. Grundler	Fred F. Williams	F. E. Grundler	B. Breedlove
Ferguson	A. H. Beck[11]	A. H. Beck	....	G. J. Schulte, Jr.	....
Florissant	F. Laramie	H. Shifrin	H. F. Koch	F. Laramie	Mr. Kerr[11]..s
Fulton	....	J. Russel Calder	D. Elrow Crane[14]	Ray Mirts	Paul Worsham
Hannibal	Alvin Seckman[6]	Warren Barrett	Alvin Seckman	Fred K. Lock	Fred K. Lock
Independence	....	....	G. H. Dyer[5]..p	L. J. Campbell	Dan Thurman
Jefferson City	....	R. D. Fowler	W. Helmrich[5]..p	W. A. Curtis	....
Jennings	....	J. Ray Graham	....	J. Ray Graham	Mr. Kerr[5]..s
Joplin	U. W. Johnston[11]	U. W. Johnston	C. E. Schanze[5]..p	C. E. Musgrave	Sidney C. Smith
Kansas City	Reed McKinley[11]	S. C. Palmer	M. P. Hatcher[11]	Ray Blessing	....
Kirksville	....	Emil Lehr	Leo Tart	....	....

State and City	Public Works Head	City Engineer	Water-Works Superintendent	Street Superintendent	Superintendent of Sewage Treatment
Missouri (cont.)					
Kirkwood	....	Clarence Temme	Walter Theiss	Clarence Temme	..........[s]
Maplewood	....	T. S. Richardson	....	T. S. Richardson	..........[s]
Mexico	....	James R. Huff	..........[p]	John Cline	
Moberly	W. R. Barclay	W. R. Barclay	Wayne Switzer	Dow Ratliff	Weldon Elsberry
Overland	W. G. Temme[11]	Wilbur G. Temme	..........[p]	Wilbur G. Temme	..........[s]
Poplar Bluff	J. C. Berryman	F. Scarborough	J. C. Berryman	Ralph Sullivan	
Richmond Hgts.	F. D. Debolt[48]	Frank R. Nohl	Victor Weir[29]..[p]	E. A. Tonella, Jr.	W. H. Kehr[11]..[s]
Rolla	H. Castleman[29]	J. Kilpatrick	J. B. Bronson	J. F. Kilpatrick	J. F. Kilpatrick
St. Charles	M. F. Walendy[29]	Edgar Rapp, Jr.	W. G. Oelklaus	L. Hachtmeyer	L. Hachtmeyer
St. Joseph	H. W. Kurtz[29]	Glen B. Riddle	F. McAndrew[5]..[p]	Carl Wray	....
St. Louis	F. J. McDevitt[29]	W. R. Crecelius	T. J. Skinker	Frank Kriz	..........[s]
Sedalia	E. V. Bishop	E. V. Bishop	I. H. Reed[5]..[p]	Harry Meyers	....
Sikeston	Chas. Moose[6]	Alex C. Waters	Dan Delplane	L. W. Ables	Joseph Bishop
Springfield	W. E. Hedges[11]	James Davis[4]	....	Everett Kelly	Allen Mayfield
University City	W. Heimbuecher[11]	W. Heimbuecher	W. V. Weir[29]..[p]	James J. Leahy	Wm. Q. Kehr[5]..[s]
Webster Groves	J. Clayton, Jr.[11]	J. Clayton, Jr.	W. T. Valentine	W. Winning, Jr.	....
Montana					
Anaconda	....	....	....	John L. O'Leary	....
Billings	....	Samuel B. Ward	E. R. Waldo	....	John C. Voelker
Bozeman	M. E. Henderson[5]	S. D. Waldorf	W. R. Border	Willis Springer	R. Batchelder
Butte	James P. Egan	James P. Egan	J. B. Hazen[5]..[p]	Les Boyer	James P. Egan
Great Falls	A. J. Richardson	A. J. Richardson	Ben Chestnut	Jack Wiprud	Harold Funk
Helena	W. J. Leary	W. J. Leary	George Malben	J. C. Jackson	....
Kalispell	....	L. B. McClintick	A. L. Johnson	Dick Barnum	E. Billsborough
Missoula	Sam Marek	Pat Whelan	H. McCann[5]..[p]	Sam Marek	....
Nebraska					
Beatrice	Geo. R. Miller[49]	....	George R. Miller	R. Smith	....
Fremont	Wm. J. Sommers[6]	Duane E. Funk	Hugh Seagle	Ed. Ranslem	....
Grand Island	C. W. Burdick	E. H. Cordes	C. W. Burdick	Leo McCann	Alex Kehm
Hastings	David R. Hill[5]	T. R. Stewart	....	....	....
Kearney	....	....	R. H. Lancaster	C. L. Sear	....
Lincoln	D. L. Erickson[11]	Carl L. Fisher	F. L. Blumer	A. Lynn Meyers	..........[s]
Norfolk	....	Z. N. Dewey	R. D. Carrick	Jos. L. Luikens	....
North Platte	M. L. Sievers[5]	R. F. Nosky	M. L Sievers	C. B. Farrell	M. L. Sievers
Omaha	W. E. Milner[6, 50]	E. Woodbridge	L. Tester[5]..[p]	A. J. Hanson	Wm. E. Milner
Scottsbluff	....	K. G. Roberts	F. E. Hagmeister	Lester Mortensen	....
Nevada					
Henderson	H. Muehleisen[11]	L. R. Douglass	James H. Keller	H. Muehleisen	James H. Keller[17]
Las Vegas	George E. Wade[11]	George E. Wade	W. Renshaw[16]..[p]	Kenneth Smith	Louis Anton
Reno	....	Elliott Cann	..........[p]	Robert Callahan	L. Bernasconi
New Hampshire					
Berlin	C. Brungot	C. Brungot	Ernest Tankard	C. Brungot	C. Brungot
Claremont	Haakon Pederson	E. S. Pegram, Jr.	Haakon Pederson	J. Gennessey	L. Easter
Concord	H. Raymond[1]	H. Raymond[1]	G. Arthur Faneuf	....	W. H. Murphy[35]
Dover	E. C. Smith[11]	G. Crawford	P. F. Hanratty	E. C. Smith	E. C. Smith
Keene	G. E. Hawkins	G. E. Hawkins	G. E. Hawkins	G. E. Hawkins	G. E. Hawkins
Laconia	W. McLaughlin[23]	A. O'Mara	T. Cate	A. O'Mara	A. O'Mara
Manchester	R. F. Dusseault	E. W. Graupner	J. A. Sweeney	R. F. Dusseault[40]	....
Nashua	....	Joel B. Hill	....	Romeo Anger	....
Portsmouth	Nat Stevens[6]	Nat Stevens	Nat Stevens	Nat Stevens	....
Rochester	Geo. C. Nadeau[3]	Joe Morrison	Geo. C. Nadeau	Geo. C. Nadeau	Geo. C. Nadeau
New Jersey					
Asbury Park	A. E. Lawrence[11]	Wm. M. Birtwell	J. L. Mauro, Jr.	Felix Petillo	J. L. Mauro, Jr.
Atlantic City	Wm. F. Casey[11]	Geo. R. Swinton	M. Brunstein	Fred M. Herrick	....
Bayonne	G. T. DiDomenico	A. Drogin	J. L. Lindner	Louis Giordano	J. L. Lindner
Belleville	K. D. Smith[3]	R. Daly	Ralph Vara	Ralph Vara	....
Bergenfield	D. H. Townsend[3]	Fraleigh & Schwanewede[33]	..........[p]	J. Kostelecky	John Feeley
Bloomfield	M. B. Huber	M. B. Huber[61]	....	....	....
Bridgeton	V. E. Edwards[3]	Wm. A. Kirby	....	Colin G. Irving	....
Burlington	A. Hoffman[6]	Sherman, Taylor & Sleeper[33]	Earl H. Naylor	....	S. A. Probasco
Camden	F. A. Abbott[11]	Geo. C. Rogers	E. Sheehan	James P. Carr	F. Gondolf
Carteret	John Nemish[6]	Fred Simons[64]	....	Paul Bagala	Steven Kovacs
Cliffside Park	J. W. Mahoney[6]	McClave & McClave	....	J. W. Mahoney	J. W. Mahoney
Clifton	Wm. Holster[11]	Wm. A. Miller	....	....	....
Collingswood	A. E. Armitage[11]	John H. Osler	Wm. E. Collings	Wm. E. Collings	Wm. E. Collings
Cranford	....	P. J. Grall	Geo. Haskew[6]..[p]		L. Fontenelli[6]..[s]
Dover	....	R. Shark	J. J. Richards	E. M. Francis	....
Dumont	A. J. Schafer[6]	H. L. Boswell	E. Fricker, V.P.[p]	A. J. Schafer	C. E. Feeley, Jr.
E. Brunswick Twp.	J. H. Godwin	Wm. H. Baker	V. L. Appleby	J. H. Godwin[23]	....
East Orange	A. T. Brokaw	A. T. Brokaw	C. G. Bourgin[51]	Carl Vogt	....
East Paterson	Joseph M. Fox[4]	Florio C. Job	Joseph M. Fox..[p]	Joseph M. Fox	....
Elizabeth	C. G. Forman[29]	J. D. McLevey	....	J. L. Sullivan[1]	Leslie E. West[15]
Englewood	T. V. Frank[6]	E. A. Blackwell	....	T. V. Frank	J. J. O'Brien
Ewing Twp. (Trenton)	Frank Moody[12]	W. E. Rochford[62]	....	M. J. Phillips	W. Higgins..[s]
Fair Lawn	Sam Greydanus[6]	Frank Peruggi	A. Ryan	S. Greydanus	Leonard Knapp
Fort Lee	W S. Corker[1]	McClave & McClave		....	F. Cavaliere..[s]
Garfield	John Kimack[23]	David Cascino	Joseph Benigno	Geo. Kovalyscik	....
Glen Rock	Jacobus Jacobs[6]	Frank M. Evans	....	Jacobus Jacobs	....
Gloucester	....	Wm. Andrews	Joseph Keown	Ed. McGuire	Wm. Hoyle
Hackensack	L. K. Fishbough[6]	L. K. Fishbough	..........[p]	....	John May
Haddon Twp. (Westmont)	....	John Osler	Warren Wood	Warren Wood	Warren Wood
Haddonfield	F. Westermaier[11]	W. Macnamara	M. W. Pharo[1]	Martin Start	T. Whitehead

State and City	Public Works Head	City Engineer	Water-Works Superintendent	Street Superintendent	Superintendent of Sewage Treatment
N. J. (cont.)					
Hamilton Sq. (Trenton)	....	M. X. Feld[62]	L. Klockner[5]..[p]	E. Stilwell	R. Klockner
Harrison	....	Jos. A. Cundari	..........[p]	C. J. Villanova[3]	....
Hawthorne	John G. Rozema[3]	P. Schilling[64]	R. Snyder	Louis C. Bay	Louis C. Bay
Hillside	....	J. S. Fuhrmann[62]	....	Arthur L. Ritche	R. K. Bloy, Jr.
Hoboken	Hugh McGuire[11]	Patrick Caulfield	....	A. Romano	....
Irvington	H. Kruttschnitt[11]	H. F. Fredericks	..........[p]	Cyrus England	....
Jersey City	J. A. Soriero[11]	F. Manning[15]	H. Ohland[15]	James Cassell	F. Manning[15]
Kearny	F. Vincent	G. A. Joa	H. Kenworthy	Carl Sax	M. Andolino
Linden	John Mesler[6]	J. F. Davison	....	John Mesler	..........[s]
Livingston	N. N. Papandrea	N. N. Papandrea	E. J. Bear	N. N. Papandrea	N. N. Papandrea
Lodi	....	John A. Sepede	Joseph De Boise	Anthony Roma	Joseph Messino
Long Branch	G. R. Woolley[11, 3]	O. W. Morris	A. Newquist[5]..[p]	G. R. Woolley[11, 3]	M. A. Potter[29]..[s]
Lyndhurst	J. C. Garde[3]	M. Neglia	F. Muhleisen	Harry Gutheil	Harry Gutheil
Madison	J. H. Ziegler	John P. Sliwa	Oscar Van Auken	J. J. Artiglere[10]	....
Manville	M. S. Kachorsky[6]	M. S. Kachorsky	E. J. Purzycki	Edward Braun	M. S. Kachorsky
Maplewood	E. Barbehenn[11]	E. W. Barbehenn	T J. Coleman[5]..[p]	Geo. M. Rogers	....
Maywood	George Gerdes[6]	W. Schwanewede	....	....	H. Van Der Vliet
Metuchen	S. P. Owen[23]	W. F. Buchanan	A. Mundy[5]..[p]	Thomas Eosso	Samuel Reid
Millburn	H. J. Curran[10]	Levi Price	..........[p]	....	....
Millville	Wm. L. Ewan[11]	M. C. Barber	....	....	....
Monroe (Williamstown)	....	John Reutter[62]	J. M. Conover	Jos. M. Conover	....
Montclair	F. M. Galloway[19]	J. D. Groff[61]	A. S. Giannetti	Walter F. Harder	W. F. Harder[35]
Morristown	G. E. Burke[6]	V. L. Woodhull	S. Taylor	A. Cutter	Geo. Burke
Mt. Holly	Wm. P. Hatch[5]	A. C. Jones	A. Cross, Sr.[5]..[p]	Wm. P. Hatch	J. W. Goodfellow
Neptune	J. Wardell	C. W. Birdsall	..........[p]	L. Herbert	W. S. Applegate
Newark	G. W. Andress[11]	A E. Zentgraf	A. J. Simpson	W. L. Roder	W. S. Bauer
New Brunswick	H. D. Dailey[11]	M. W. Taylor	T. F. Boylan	Thomas Sebolt	Sol. Seid
New Milford	J. Entwistle[6]	Fraleigh & Schwanewede	..........[p]	J. Entwistle	J. Entwistle
No. Arlington	....	Gerhardt A. Joa	Wm. A. Coupe	Joseph Luty	....
North Bergen	A. J. Sarubbi[11]	Joshua Muss	..........[p]	T. J. Smith, Jr.	J. J. Latchford
No. Plainfield	R. Snyder, Jr.[20]	F. S. Blifford[64]	..........[p]	J. DeNise	A. Palmer
Nutley	D. R. Shepard[6]	D. R. Shepard	Jos. Van Treek	Otto Fouser	J. Scaperatto[22]
Orange	W. B. Savage[11]	F. Caspar	Fred Luthy	D. Liguori[22]	....
Palisades	W. Todd[6]	J. A. Boyle	..........[p]	....	..........[s]
Paramus	N. F. Robertson[20]	D. Boswell, P.E.	..........[p]	James Tedesco	....
Parsippany Tp. (Troy Hills)	Anthony Mara	H. J. Ahlers[62]	Anthony J. Mara	....	R. J. Budrick..[s]
Passaic	Paul G. DeMuro[11]	John Schneider	....	William Godla	....
Paterson	M. Della Torre[23]	V. J. Scanlon	R. Bonyon	Wm. S. Turner	....
Pennsauken	E. Raymond, III	James J. Boyd	Harry Wirth[5]..[p]	H. Z. Matthews	R. V. Case
Perth Amboy	S. P. Mihalko[11]	Louis P. Booz	J. J. Reager	James Harding	Patrick Duffy
Phillipsburg	Edward Korp[13, 50]	S. R. Pursel	J. A. Exley[5]..[p]	John Roth	Eugene Peterson
Plainfield	J. Fleming, Jr.	J. Fleming, Jr.	W. Spears[29]..[p]	John E. Zaremba	Andrew Palmer .[s]
Pleasantville	....	L. H. Lake	E. Feldman[5]..[p]	J. R. VanSant[20]	Frank Bruce
Princeton	I. Russell Riker	I. R. Riker[64]	..........[p]	I. Russell Riker	I. Russell Riker
Rahway	C. W. O'Key	Kenneth Richie	Herman Klenner	James Scarpitto	....
Red Bank	Ensley M. White[6]	H. La Brecque	E. M. White	....	Ensley M. White
Ridgefield	J. N. Marshall	....	....	....	J. N. Marshall
Ridgefield Park	Ross S. Vogt[11]	D. C. Boswell	....	Anthony Zoda	....
Ridgewood	B. Reinauer, II[3]	R. P. Raymond	H. Florence, Sr.	R. P. Raymond	John Hood
Roselle	J. J. Gambone[6]	M. A. Leber[64]	....	J. J. Gambone	J. J. Gambone
Roselle Park	V. Scopelleti[6, 28]	J. S. Fuhrman	....	....	....
Rutherford	John A. Ordway[6]	R. B. Brown	..........[p]	....	....
Sayreville	....	K. H. Wilber[64]	....	George Boyler	K. H. Wilber
Somerville	E. S. VanFleet[6]	E. S. VanFleet	J. J. Mann[5]..[p]	....	I. P. Zugermayer
South Orange	W. Kruse, Jr.[23]	A. L. Demarest[63]	Lemuel Eldridge	T. F. Tracey, Jr.	..........[s]
South Plainfield	P. A. Schkeeper[23]	Chas. A. Beagle	....	Julius Celentano	....
South River	Frank E. Navin[6]	....	Frank E. Navin	....	Frank E. Navin
Summit	Hugo Riemer[23]	J. Henry Negus	....	Frank Pryce	Vincent Vitale
Teaneck	M. Kilmurray	Hermann Meyer	..........[p]	M. Kilmurray	M. Kilmurray
Tenafly	A. F. Marquez[6]	E. A. Blackwell	E. J. Fricker[5]..[p]	A. F. Marquez	....
Trenton	D. J. Connolly[11]	J. R. Walsh	L. W. Klockner	J. S. Petrino	Lester Sodan[51]
Union	....	H. Kreh, Jr.[62]	....	George Kling	....
Union City	Wm. V. Musto[11]	Peter LaMort	..........[p]	Bernard Reichert	F. Oleri, Jr.[6]..[s]
Verona	D. Carmichael[64]	D. Carmichael[64]	D. Carmichmael [p]	D. W. Carmichael	D. W. Carmichael
Vineland	....	R. Bartholomew	Elbert Basolis	A. Castellini	....
Wall Twp. (Belmar)	LeRoy Querns	C. W. Birdsall	Robert Crowther	James R. Ely	....
Wayne	H. R. Campbell	H. R. Campbell	H. R. Campbell	Joseph Daly	H. R. Campbell
Weehawken	J. F. Maher, Jr.[3]	....	..........[p]	T. Hanuszek	....
Westfield	John T. Hopkins	John T. Hopkins	Geo. Haskew[5]..[p]	W. T. Vanderbilt	....
West New York	J. C. Cendo[11]	Frank J. Oleri[61]	..........[p]	Fred Loehr	Frank Oleri, Jr.
West Orange	L. P. Falcone[11]	H. C. Warnick	T. J. Coleman[5]..[p]	R. E. Werner	....
Woodbridge	L. Clement[22]	H. Madison[62]	..........[p]	L. Clement	H. A. Anderson
Woodbury	....	Earl R. Davis	S. J. Scott	Samuel Scott	Samuel Scott
New Mexico					
Albuquerque	E. O. Betts[11]	W. Stevens	Conrad Gonzales	Manuel Gonzales	John Beehler
Artesia	W. D. Fowler[10]	W. D. Fowler	L. M. Vaughn	Alvin Payne	....
Carlsbad	H. E. McMinn	Duce D. Bivins	Ferrell McLean	H. G. May	Ferrell McLean
Clovis	....	Clinton Craig	..........[p]	Clay Thomas	R. L. Leach
Gallup	....	G. Petranovich	J. Petranovich[6]	Transito Lopez	Chas. Kettel, Sr.
Hobbs	Don L. Benge	Don L. Benge	M. H. Alexander	A. B. Chastain	Charlie Gregory
Las Cruces	H. Gaines, Jr.[14]	P. L. McClernon	H. U. Gaines, Jr.	Cruz Nevarez	R. A. Smith
Roswell	C. M. Woodbury	C. M. Woodbury	Asa M. Guffey	Ira Meredith	C. T. Robertson
Santa Fe	....	J. H. Ashbaugh	..........[p]	Henry Montoyo	R. H. Siler
New York					
Albany	K. W. Marsh[3]	J. A. Kaestner	Wm. F. Devane[3]	Jesse Parker	William King
Amsterdam	A. H. McCaffrey[3]	A. H. McCaffrey	A H. McCaffrey	A. H. McCaffrey	....
Auburn	A. J. Adams	A. J. Adams	H. J. McNaney	Jay Cunningham	James T. Lynch

State and City	Public Works Head	City Engineer	Water-Works Superintendent	Street Superintendent	Superintendent of Sewage Treatment
N. Y. (cont.)					
Batavia	Harry S. Boyd	Norman H. Hall	Nelson Fuller	Harry S. Boyd	Nelson Fuller
Beacon	W. W. Tompkins[3]	A. T. Rowan	Edmund Murphy	Harold Brewer[1]	Armand Rival
Bedford (Bedford Hills)	....	....	D. V. Matteson	Arthur S. Bailie	....
Binghamton	W. J. Spellicy[3]	R. C. McNamara	G. E. Rickard	....	....
Buffalo	Geo. J. Goetz[3]	Chas. T. Love	F.Szuniewicz,Jr.[11]	Frank J. Stahl[11]	David J. Laub[35]
Camillus	....	....	J. B. Strait, Sr.	C. E. Peterson[28]	....
Cohoes	J. Archambeault	Frank Hines	Walter Raleigh	....	....
Corning	Philip Grannan[6]	Philip Grannan	Philip Grannan	Philip Grannan	Philip Grannan
Cortland	A. R. Reilly[6]	A. R. Reilly	D. J. Houlihan	A. R. Reilly	H. B. Holcomb
Dunkirk	Harold T. Stumpf	Harold T. Stumpf	G. W. Yeomans	C. Zientowski	....
Eastchester	Harry L. Grant	Mont M. Mathes	E. C. Stinnett[5]..p	Harry L. Grant	Harry L. Grant
Elmira	W. B. Smith[11]	A. L. Oppenheim	John G. Copley	Thomas J. Cerio	G. J. McInerney
Endicott	N. F. English[6]	....	Earl Grippen[5]..p	Nick F. English	....
Floral Park	F. C. Boes[6]	....	..........p	....	..........s
Freeport	....	Baldwin & Cornelius[63]	Wm. Crevoiserat	H. J. Chuisano	E. C. McKeeman
Fulton	Roy Van Alstine[3]	H. S. Andrews	H. S. Andrews	Roy Van Alstine	....
Garden City	Allan H. Rogers[6]	Allan H. Rogers	....	....	....
Geneva	Harry M. Bolton[6]	C. F. Hartman	Harry M. Bolton	Harry M. Bolton	Harry M. Bolton
Glen Cove	Robert H. Danis[3]	Sidney B. Bowne	..........p	Harland Phillips	Harland Phillips
Glens Falls	E. J. Anderson[6]	Earl C. Reardon	G. C. Tripp, Jr.	E. J. Anderson	J. F. Lapham
Gloversville	....	Geo. M. Naginey	W. Van Brocklin	Milton R. Wandel	W. R. Smith
Greenburgh (Tarrytown)	Louis M. Russo[3]	....	Louis Russo	....	....
Harrison	B. E. Bradner[6, 28]	N. C. Penna	George Straub	Basil E. Bradner	....
Hempstead	F. R. Rundle[6]	L. S. Marshall[63]	Adam H. Ziegler	Fred Esterbrook[22]	H. Sherman[s]
Hornell	G. E. Clancy[6]	....	Clayton Roe[1]	G. E. Clancy	....
Hudson	Edwin J. Folz[3]	H. V. Harding	H. V. Harding	H. V. Harding	H. V. Harding
Huntington	....	....	....	James A. Pryce	Gilbert Scudder
Irondequoit (Rochester)	J. Bevacqua[3]	....	..........p	J. Bevacqua	Carl A. Harvey
Islip	....	J. M. Lednum[61]	Edw. Sonderling	Charles Maier[28]	....
Ithaca	F. J. Laverty[6]	Leon H. Cass	Chas. W. Rich	Paul Fidler	Chas. W. Rich
Jamestown	L. A. Bergman[11]	L. A. Bergman	M. W. Smedberg	L. A. Bergman	L. A. Bergman
Johnson City	W. G. Sleeper[6]	W. G. Sleeper	Edward Griffin	W. G. Sleeper	W. G. Sleeper
Johnstown	C. W. Knowles	C. W. Knowles	C. W. Knowles	C. W. Knowles	....
Kenmore	F. S. Creamer[6]	F. S. Creamer	F. S. Creamer	F. S. Creamer	....
Kingston	Ernest Steuding[6]	Arthur Hallinan	Edmund Cloonan	Ernest Steuding	Ernest Steuding
Lackawanna	Chas. Delmont	T. McCormick	....	Chas. Delmont[3]	....
Lockport	H. W. Treadwell[3]	Albert G. Ward	....	Ralph C. Loomis	J. F. Ruppert
Long Beach	M. J. Fleischman	S. Schiffman[53, 3]	S. Schiffman[53, 3]	S. Herschkowitz[28]	S. Schiffman[53, 3]
Lynbrook	Floyd F. Wilcox[6]	C. Dunne Inc.	..........p	....	....
Mamaroneck	G. D. Perschke[22]	....	George Straub	....	....
Massena	R. D. Cross[6]	R. D. Cross	Joseph Oliveria	....	....
Middletown	G. W. Chumard[3]	G. W. Chumard[3]	Kenneth B. Abt	Ellis Bright	Kenneth B. Abt
Mineola	S. W. Downs[22]	Sidney B. Bowne & Son	Charles F. Smith	....	....
Mt. Vernon	A. Annunziata[3]	Paul Brienza	Arthur Jewell	....	....
Newark	LeRoy H. Wright	LeRoy H. Wright	LeRoy H. Wright	E. J. Kennedy	Wm. H. VerDow
Newburgh	Rudolph Todd[6]	E. D. Kennedy	J. F. Kingsley	Rudolph Todd	....
New Rochelle	E. H. Feldmann[11]	Arthur Jonas	J. Albertson[5]..p	William Kennedy	Charles Keyser..s
New York	F. H. Zurmuhlen[3]	R. McCullough[15]	Arthur C. Ford[3]	5 Comrs.—Boro Works	Wm. A. O'Leary
Niagara Falls	David Mann[11]	H. J. Curts	J. J. Burnett[53, 11]	V. Chiarenza	Edward Smith
No. Tonawanda	T. H. Werth[6]	W. R. Hardleben	W. R. Hardleben	T. H. Werth	W. R. Hardleben
Ogdensburg	Ross R. Jermano	Ross R. Jermano	Ross R. Jermano	Ross R. Jermano	Ross R. Jermano
Olean	C. Weatherell, Jr.[11]	Francis Flinn	Edward Catlin	Leo J. Dumboski	Alfred Mann
Oneida	A. T. Ernenwein[3]	....	Seymour Clark	....	....
Oneonta	Clarence Taylor[11]	William Filkin	Clarence Taylor	Clarence Taylor	Clarence Taylor
Ossining	H. Victor Cordy	....	....	Frank W. Becker	....
Oswego	R. H. Turner[3]	G. W. Allen	K. D. Jensen	....	....
Peekskill	Franklin Couch[3]	Wilbur J. Irish	William Foster	Franklin Couch	Franklin Couch
Pelham	....	John C. Peck[61]	....	....	....
Plattsburg	J. J. Martina[6]	Jos. J. Martina	Frank D. Behan	Jos. J. Martina	Frank D. Behan
Port Chester	Felix Fidelibus[6]	F. I. McGrath	....	Felix Fidelibus	George Mowbray
Poughkeepsie	Harold R. Dean[6]	Harold R. Dean	Harold R. Dean	Fred J. Healy	J. B. Hackett
Rensselaer	M. Barnard[3]	A. J. Kaufman[33]	Sprague Claflin[3]	James DeJuilo	....
Riverhead	....	Alden W. Young[61]	Roselle Banjamin	M. C. Young[28, c]	....
Rochester	F. Dow Hamblin[3]	Kenneth Knapp	Lewis Smith	F. Dow Hamblin	....
Rockville Centre	F. J. Klaess[6]	E. S. Voorhis & Son[63]	Frank Picucci	Francis J. Klaess	Chas. P. Ketler
Rome	S. H. Zingerline	S. H. Zingerline	Louis Zellwager	Fred Tavntor	Jesse Cole[6]
Rye	Edw. Dempsey[27]	R. W. Murphy	A. Cronkright[5]..p	Edward Dempsey	..........s
Saratoga Sprgs.	C. A. McTygue[3]	John Sheehan	Frank Cherry	John Cassidy	Frank Cherry
Scarsdale	....	P. M. Ferraro[59]	Reeves Newson	John J. Doyle[3]	....
Schenectady	John F. Lucey	John F. Lucey	John J. Meehan[51]	John Szumilowski	Clifford Irving
Smithtown	M. Kondenar	Harry Spitzer	..........p	M. Kondenar[28, 6]	Harry Spitzer
Syracuse	C. F. Stanton[3]	Potter W. Kelly	Elon P. Stewart	E. L. Sanborn	Wm. P. Gyatt
Tonawanda	Frank Keller[6]	Perry A. Wilson	Oscar Schulte	Frank Keller	James Kampas
Troy	J. F. Hayden[3]	Oley S. Cutler	Jos. F. Hayden	James F. Carroll	....
Utica	George G. Moore[3]	Frank Romano	D. P. O'Dowd	....	....
Valley Stream	P. B. Sprague[6]	Justin T. Flick[63]	....	....	....
Watertown	Roy Howard[6]	H. R. Dwyer	T. B. Tyldesley	....	....
Watervliet	N. J. Normile[49]	Frank J. Keis[1]	N. J. Normile	Joseph H. Early	Edw. J. Graham
West Seneca	T. E. Glynn[35, 28]	Jesse E. Aber	....	T. E. Glynn[28]	Robert Dobstaff
White Plains	Eric A. Andrews[3]	....	John H. Friese	T. W. Orth[28]	....
Yonkers	T. J. Cooney[3]	Earle F. Griffen	J. M. Fitzgibbons	Thos. J. Cooney	....
Yorktown	L. C. Johnson[6, 28]	Wm. A. Marcon	Geo. D. Hancock	L. C. Johnson[28]	....
North Carolina					
Albemarle	George S. Moore[14]	Dale Mills	George S. Moore	Ralph P. Smith	George S. Moore
Asheville	J. Weldon Weir[11]	John C. Walker	Floyd J. Padgett	Greer Johnson	....
Burlington	....	W. M. Garrison	D. Y. Brannock	Bryce Moore	D. Y. Brannock[35]

State and City	Public Works Head	City Engineer	Water-Works Superintendent	Street Superintendent	Superintendent of Sewage Treatment
N. Car. (cont.)					
Charlotte	....	R. T. James[1]	W. M. Franklin	R. T. James	W. M. Franklin
Concord	....	S. Hawfield, Jr.	Donald T. Howell	James Trull	....
Durham	H. W. Kueffner[11]	H. W. Kueffner	D. M. Williams	H. W. Cristie	W. G. Brown
Elizabeth City	E. T. Hyman[5]	....	R. W. Luther	A. E. Perry	....
Fayetteville	D. J. Gore[5]	W. W. Baker	J. E. Freeman	Fleet Hall	....
Gastonia	R. Van Sleen[11]	W. T. Cox	D. W. Yoder[14]	F. P. Barnhill	W. A. Gardner
Goldsboro	E. L. Simmons[6]	E. G. Porter, Sr.	K. N. Massey	E. L. Simmons	....
Greensboro	H. L. Medford[11]	K. L. Ponzer	N. L. Mitchell	W. C. Medlin	D. O. Holder
Greenville	C. K. Beatty	C. A. Holliday	L. P. Bloxam	Gentry N. Mills	L. P. Bloxam
Henderson	J. E. Hamlett[11]	....	J. T. Powell	J. E. Hamlett	J. E. Hamlett
Hickory	C. G. Sigmon[6]	T. R. Morris, Jr.	C. Glenn Sigmon	C. Glenn Sigmon	C. Glenn Sigmon
High Point	G. B. Dean[11]	....	R. E. Hutchinson	E. J. Sharpe	Earl Kearns
Jacksonville	John Arthur	Jos. E. Simpson	A. V. Crouch	John Arthur	A. V. Crouch
Kinston	W. G. McAdams[14]	W. G. McAdams	W. G. McAdams	M. C. Croom	....
Lenoir	....	R. C. Wallace	L. G. Huffstetler	J. B. Winkler	L. G. Huffstetler
Lexington	W. Mont Beck[17]	A. B. Cole	Claude Brockett	Grady Wilson	Joe R. Leonard
Monroe	....	T. C. Dove	J. E. Hinkel	T. C. Dove	Wade Broome
New Bern	W. B. Bartling[14]	J. E. Blue	W. B. Bartling	Cedric Boyd	....
Raleigh	W. J. Mann[11]	V. C. Peebles	E. M. Johnson[17]	....	Troy Doby
Reidsville	Wm. E. Edens[11]	W. E. Edens	W. E. McAlister	R. L. Goolsby	W. E. McAlister
Rocky Mount	Dr. A. Whitaker	F. H. Cothran	Allan DeRatt	F. H. Cothran	Allan DeRatt
Salisbury	J. A. English[11]	J. A. English	J. A. English	L. R. Alexander	J. N. Lesslie, Jr.
Sanford	T. Paul Watson[11]	....	L. P. Gunter, Jr.	A. C. Thomas	L. P. Gunter, Jr.
Shelby	....	W. Andrews, Jr.	....	R. A. Spangler	....
Statesville	E. B. Stafford	E. B. Stafford	Ed. Holcomb	E. B. Stafford	G. E. Hughey, Jr.
Thomasville	L. E. Honeycutt[11]	L. E. Honeycutt	H. E. Tysinger	Joe F. Mitchell	H. E. Tysinger
Wilmington	R. F. Coleman[11]	Robt. F. Coleman	Colin Churchill	R. A. Chadwick	Colin Churchill
Wilson	J. Goodman, Jr.[11]	....	Jas. Ray Barnes	Hardy Skinner	George L. Meeks
Winston-Salem	R. W. Neilson[11]	Fred Fansler	S. E. Harris	D. O. Coggins	R. M. Rodgers
North Dakota					
Bismarck	E. J. Booth	E. J. Booth	E. J. Booth	E. J. Booth	....
Fargo	....	W. P. Tarbell	H. H. Behlmer	Jorgen Miller	F. W. Pinney
Grand Forks	John B. Kleven	A. F. Hulteng	R. M. Jenson	John B. Kleven	R. M. Jenson
Jamestown	....	Erik D. Peterson	Benjamin Darby	R. Hausauer	Herbert Prince
Minot	W. V. Fahy[11]	Paul J. Hays	S. K. Svenkeson	Vernon Rossow	S. K. Svenkeson
Williston	....	Herbert Arnold	Herbert Arnold	Herbert Arnold	....
Ohio					
Akron	Leo Walter[25]	....	Wendell LaDue	Iver Schmidt	Ralph Bushee
Alliance	D. Mainwaring	W. D. Sponseller	D. Heffelfinger	C. L. McDonald	D. Heffelfinger
Ashland	....	H. Maxheimer	E. F. Petzke	C. E. Iceman	Don Copeland
Ashtabula	R. W. B. Logan[6]	F. A. Collins	C. Arbogast[5]..p	R. W. B. Logan	F. A. Collins
Athens	F. Woodworth[25]	....	F. Woodworth	Clyde Beasley	Earl Beeman
Barberton	Samuel Bonner[25]	Harry D. Bushey	Charles Petit	D. Stevenson	....
Bedford	O. Hutchinson[5]	O. Hutchinson[5]	G. E. Martin	J. J. Squire	M. W. Ake
Bellaire	Warner J. Belt[25]	James P. Dean	John J. Pyles	Warner J. Belt	Warner J. Belt
Bellefontaine	F. M. Baxley[54]	Foster F. Wright	....	James Ricks	....
Berea	Joseph Skodis[25]	Warren Root	Philip Kobie	Ben Woidke	Harry Winters
Bexley	....	Jennings Lawrence Co.	Ted Petzinger	W. Montgomery	....
Bowling Green	....	....	Harry Instone	Cloyce Schall	L. B. Barnes
Bucyrus	C. G. Richard[25]	....	Eugene Rockwell	V. Fawley	....
Cambridge	Fred L. Boyd[25]	P. P. Sheehan	Willard Smith[14]	....	Willard Smith[14]
Campbell	John V. DeMart[25]	Theodore Dastoli	John V. Demart	Ben Oles	Theodore Dastoli
Canton	H. Y. McCool[25]	LeRoy L. Luke	A. E. Ransom	D. D. DeMeo	L. C. Yohe
Chillicothe	W. Howson, Jr.[25]	H. M. Alexander	R. R. Deem[5]	W. Howson, Jr.	....
Cincinnati	W. C. Wichman[11]	T. J. Montgomery	Chas. H. Bolton	C. Heidschuch	A. D. Caster[28]
Cleveland	L. L. Drasler[25]	Jay R. Katz[3]	Emil J. Crown[11]	A. J. Preusser[3]	G. E. Flower[3]
Cleveland Hgts.	Ray Martin	H. C. Gallimore	Wiley C. Davis[3]	Gorman Lamont	....
Columbus	F. C. Redick[25]	Robt. F. Werner	Paul C. Laux	Heinie Butler	J. H. Blodgett
Conneaut	Leo S. Eaton[25]	Wm. V. Kantola	Wm. V. Kantola	Edward Kent	Wm. V. Kantola
Coshocton	Max Rusk[25]	Aston Stewart	Karl West	Clyde Johnston	....
Cuyahoga Falls	W. W. Gibson[25]	Geo. F. Johnston	Louis F. Cook	Mathew Boyd	Louis F. Cook
Dayton	Karl Woditsch[25]	John F. Hale	....	William Price	Lloyd Hagerty
Defiance	A. A. Nickels[25]	Theodore Blue	Mrs. F. Slocum[5]	Bernard Gutman	....
Delaware	Don Mackley[25]	Don Mackley	Frank Lanning	Nick Nutt	Ray Mantor
East Cleveland	....	M. S. Douglas	J. E. Barnes	J. V. Henry	....
East Liverpool	....	G. S. Bloomgren[33]	F. K. Robinson	Floyd Tice[22]	....
Elyria	M. J. Lotko[25]	R. E. Kleinoeder	N. E. Humason	George Carrick	Charles Coen
Euclid	Walter Nason[25]	LeRoy Williams	....	Walter Nason	Robert Henn
Findlay	Chas. W. Cain[25]	Otto C. Gohlke	Otto C. Gohlke	L. B. Hagerman	Otto C. Gohlke
Fostoria	H. R. Bradner[25]	James C. Leahy	Herbert Lord	Merrill Ward	Harrison Fling
Fremont	J. H. Weigman[25]	Dean Morgan	John Hess	Walter Roser	John Hess
Garfield Hgts.	....	Ralph Kelsey[63]	....	Robert W. King	....
Girard	T. R. Rees, Jr.[25]	Brooks Church	T. R. Rees, Jr.	Eugene Rochette[3]	....
Hamilton	R. J. Fiemeyer[25]	Fred E. Hardy	H. Augenstein	Walter J. Pabst	....
Ironton	....	Karl Wentz	H. J. Walser	Henry C. Stapf	W. D. Herrell
Kent	Louis Hansen[25]	L. R. Satrom	Louis Hansen[25]	....	K. Singleton
Kettering	....	George V. Clow	....	Robert Higgens	....
Lakewood	....	H. F. Bartels	Loren W. Morlan	Edw. C. Sargent	Edw. C. Sargent
Lancaster	W. Russel Evans[25]	Walter W. Graf	Earnest Deeds	Cliff Lantz	Russell Swisher
Lima	....	H. C. Hollinger	S. A. Bresler	Earl M. Kimpel	Wm. Jacobs
Lorain	Pete Goohs[25]	Lewis Goodell	A. V. Agnew	Robert Francis	A. V. Agnew
Mansfield	Jesse J. Schwab[25]	George R. Cunitz	Chas. O. Anglin	Jacob Thomas	Chas. Gandert
Maple Heights	H. Trefsger[25]	H. C. Gallimore	....	....	....
Marietta	H. L. Miller[25]	P. S. Rovegno	Gilbert Shears	Sheldon B. Pitts	Edwin Kahrig
Marion	R. Guy Bigelow[25]	John V. Ruth	L. O. Porter[5]..p	Wesley Honaker	Merle Burnett
Martins Ferry	L. McGlumphy[25]	Ray McFarland	Alfred Kelly	Harold Beazle	Harold Beazle
Massillon	Karl Gise[25]	Harry Piper	A. A. Ulrich[5]..p	Leo H. Helline	Theodore Jikutz
Middletown	C. A. Boeke[25]	R. K. Clark[15]	D. W. Kothe[17]	Robert Holida	Robert Holida[35]
Mt. Vernon	S. Bumpus[25]	R. L. Moffitt	....	Clarence Hissong	....
Newark	G. A. Kappler[25]	Edw. F. Roubal	Harvey Loy	Rudy Schenk	Harvey Loy

State and City	Public Works Head	City Engineer	Water-Works Superintendent	Street Superintendent	Superintendent of Sewage Treatment
Ohio (cont.)					
New Philadelphia	Michael Franz[25]	Albert Rosch	Noble Sherrard	James Rankin	....
Niles	Calvin Dix[25]	G. P. Fisher	Chas. W. Burgess	Samuel Lapolla	....
No. College Hill	H. M. Joesting[25]	Joseph Allen	....	....	....
Norwood	Edwin J. Tepe[11]	Charles Harmon	Richard Green	....	....
Painesville	Paul D. Cook[5]	W. C. Anderson	Earl W. Russell	K. R. Waterman	....
Parma	F. W. Newcomb[25]	....	....	Albert Connors	....
Piqua	....	Plez Gastineau	Fred Hickey	L. D. Minnich	Lawrence Hufford
Portsmouth	C. S. Stevenson	C. S. Stevenson	Howard Growden	....	Howard Growden
Rocky River	L. D. Andrus[25]	John R. Cloyd	....	Earl Martin	....
Salem	....	F. S. Barckhoff	Aubrey Hayes	James E. Feiler	Aubrey Hayes
Sandusky	....	Edw. E. Hartung	A. W. Grathwol	Ward Kline	....
Shaker Heights	R. Rife[25]	C. W. Courtney Engr. Co.	....	....	....
Sidney	W. G. Fultz[25]	W. G. Fultz	Harold Parke	Wilfred Simon	John Woodell
South Euclid	....	....	....	M. Montagano	....
Springfield	Fred Hughes[6]	Harold Lorton	Robert Holt	Fred Hughes	Chas. T. Bryant
Steubenville	J. Williamson[25]	Paul Jenkins	Clarence Rest	J. F. Lopresto	Chas. Sackett
Struthers	....	Theodore Dastoli	Taylor Evans[5]..p	Emil Elias	....
Tiffin	Carl Hunker[25]	Herman G. Kunn	....	Willard Griffin	....
Toledo	Wm. J. Gross[25]	John H. Davis	Ralph E. Reed	Harry Loucke[3]	Arthur Niles
Troy	H. E. Anderson[25]	G. McConnell, Jr.	Franklin Ruck	Arthur Anderson	Franklin Ruck
University Hts.	H. P. Peterson	H. P. Peterson	....	H. P. Peterson	H. P. Peterson
Van Wert	....	....	C. E. Young	F. J. Buechner	True Felger
Wadsworth	....	F. G. Randall	F. G. Randall	J. B. Edmonds	Wm. R. Hill
Warren	....	Reed Stump	Paul Price	Andrew Pearle	....
Washington C.H.	....	J. F. Parkinson	....	Clyde Smith	George R. Hall
Whitehall	....	Harley B. Watts	....	H. E. Worley	....
Wooster	W. Brenneman[25]	Harold H. Slater	W. Brenneman	W. Brenneman	Harold H. Slater
Xenia	J. J. Salovaara[5]	G. D. Ackerman	G. D. Ackerman	R. T. Bales	C. M. Robertson
Youngstown	J. C. Ryan[53, 11]	James C. Ryan[3]	D. Gambrell[3]	Joseph Booth	....
Zanesville	....	Leon Reed	Carlos Allman	Ernest E. Davis	....
Oklahoma					
Ada	J. R. Hamman[5]	....	Joe Thompson	C. B. Oliver	Homer Reed
Altus	....	R. H. Fox, Jr.	Wesley Bryant	Cato McGee	....
Ardmore	Ancel Love[6]	L. T. McKee	Ancel Love	Ernest Jackson	Ancel Love
Bartlesville	....	J. E. McMormick	W. J. Robertson	Bob L. Campbell	J. E. McCormick
Chichasha	....	Woodrow Bowers	Wes Venable	Dan M. Allen	Wes Venable
Duncan	....	Wm. Trotter	L. A. Wheeler	R. C. Coburn	C. C. Roberson
Durant	H. C. Fortenberry	....	H. Fortenberry	Beal Nix	H. Fortenberry
El Reno	John Roblyer	....	H. O. Harrell	John W. Roblyer	N. E. Stansbury
Enid	Waldo M. Porr	Waldo M. Porr	L. M. Wells	Ben Mathers	M. A. Wortz
Guthrie	R. Whitchurch	....	Bill Lowe	Ernest Latchaw	Marvin Grindle
Lawton	....	Douglas L. Smith	W. M. McMillan	Earl Christmas[3]	R. J. Schram
McAlester	Wm. T. Reed	....	Clayton Burns	Wm. T. Reed	Clayton Burns
Miami	....	J. T. Sprague	H. G. Freehauf	G. W. Cornog	J. T. Sprague
Midwest City	....	Joseph M. Plank	Roscoe Flinchum	Clifford Ensley	B. J. Bourlon
Muskogee	Earl Brewer	J. R. Keeth	W. T. Smith	Earl Brewer	....
Norman	....	Jack Kalman	R. G. Wampler	Frank Bernard	Toney Morrow
Oklahoma City	M. Cunningham[11]	W. W. Baker	M. Cunningham	W. W. Baker	W. W. Baker
Okmulgee	....	....	Ernest Skinner	Joe Morrow	Ernest Skinner
Ponca City	....	Carl T. Norris	Pat Schlesinger	O. L. Vannest	Pat Schlesinger
Sapulpa	A. F. Ellyson[1]	A. F. Ellyson[1]	Aaron H. Hughes	George Belk	A. F. Ellyson[1]
Seminole	H. Montgomery[6]	....	C. Robertson	C. Blaylock	....
Shawnee	....	Col. J. B. Bennett	G. A. Jones	E. W. Bell	G. A. Jones
Stillwater	E. E. McDaniel	E. E. McDaniel	Troy Davis	John Caldwell	Fred Lewis
Tulsa	....	Wm. R. Wooten	W. F. McMurry	F. M. Anderson	W. F. McMurry
Oregon					
Albany	....	Daniel J. Lee	R. McFarland[5]..p	F. Uhrhammer	Paul L. Page
Astoria	H. M. Olsvick[6]	H. M. Olsvick	H. M. Olsvick	H. M. Olsvick	....
Bend	....	John H. Eaton	W. Percy Drost	W. Percy Drost	....
Corvallis	V. L. Goodnight	V. L. Goodnight	Wm. Troxel	Lester Thompson	Ray Borrall
Eugene	Wm. C. Clubb[6]	Wm. C. Clubb	Ray Boals	Wm. Mullins	Wm. Newell
Klamath Falls	E. A. Thomas	E. A. Thomas	Glenn Bowen	Paul Hamblin	Thomas Barnes
Medford	Vernon Thorpe[11]	E. N. McKinstry	Robert L. Lee	Lester Anderson	R. S. Fish
Pendleton	....	Gerald Ulett	Ray Struthers	Ray Corwin	Sam Krause
Portland	Wm. A. Bowes[3]	L. G. Apperson	Geo. A. Marshall	....	David R. Westby
Roseburg	Kenneth Meng	Kenneth Meng	A. Andrews[5]..p	Guy Meigs	E. W. Naas
Salem	J. H. Davis	J. H. Davis	John Geren	J. H. Davis	Clifford Reed
Springfield	....	E. L. Williams[1]	A. J. Moore[5]..p	C. E. Libby	Frank Brown[5]..s
Pennsylvania					
Abington Twp.	C. W. Fowler[11]	E. A. Bitting	....	....	Robt. M. Bolenius
Aliquippa	....	Edw. F. Twomey	E. Grimshaw[5]..p	Wm. Colonna[3]	....
Allentown	....	E. W. Meckley	Harry J. Krum	Jos. Anderson	Ambrose Metzger
Altoona	Harry H. Penny[20]	C. L. Fields, Jr.	Haven S. Ale	Geo. A. Sessler	Edwin W. Kuhn
Ambridge	....	M. Baker Engrs.	J. Z. Columbia	Alex Firich	....
Arnold	....	P. J. Malick	....	Carl Martz[20]	....
Beaver Falls	E. P. Kline[20]	I. P. Lindeman	E. Goehring[5]..p	George Yoho	K. Hendrickson
Bellevue	Dr. J. C. Pillow[23]	Braun & Fulton	....	James Greenough	....
Berwick	....	James Timbrell	E. Westbrook[5]..p	George Lowery	....
Bethel (Pittsburgh)	Chas. A. Geisler[5]	Lorenzi, Dodds & Gunill	..........p	Thomas Campbell	Chas. A. Geisler
Bethlehem	A. N. Wiegner	A. N. Wiegner[48]	John G. Soltis	Robt. R. Gross[50]	R. W. Woodring
Bloomsburg	....	Harold Shulde	..........p	C. Dison White	....
Braddock	S. A. Lipovsky[3]	....	Henry J. Frain[51]	S. A. Lipovsky[3]	....
Bradford	....	J. Henry Quirk	S. F. Heffner	J. Henry Quirk	....
Brentwood	....	R. A. Schneider	..........p	L. F. Uecker	....

State and City	Public Works Head	City Engineer	Water-Works Superintendent	Street Superintendent	Superintendent of Sewage Treatment
Penna. (cont.)					
Bristol Boro...	....	Livingston Joyce	Livingston Joyce	Livingston Joyce	Livingston Joyce
Bristol Twp. (Bristol P.O.)	Elbert A. Kohli[3]	William S. Erwin	Paul Blattler	William McCool	Robert Stutzman
Butler Twp. (Butler P.O.)	....	L. C. Greenough	....	....	....
Butler	....	Leon Hoffman	....	O. J. Keck	Ben S. Johns
Cannonsburg ..	....	H. M. Day[64]	Geo. K. Leary[5]..[p]	Charles Taylor	....
Carbondale	Thomas F. Moran	....	..........[p]	Thomas F. Moran	....
Carlisle	Paul L. White[5]	Paul L. White	Paul L. White	Floyd Fuls[22]	Paul L. White
Carnegie	Fred Mathias[20]	P. C. Swiech	..........[p]	J. Coyle	....
Chambersburg .	....	J. Gordon Cree	Robert Monn	....	Robert Monn
Cheltenham Tp. (Elkins Park)	....	G. Hesselbacher[62]	Fred Neef[5]..[p]	Chalmer Hare[55]	Nicholas Melair[56]
Chester	L. Comisiak	Norman Young	..........[p]	J. Killgallen	John Ross
Clairton	Robt. D. Baird[38]	George Margetto	..........[p]	R. Medvidovich	....
Coal Twp. (Shamokin) ..	....	Robert Weary[62]	..........[p]	Harry Kline, Edw. Sadoski[10]	....
Coatesville	Geo. L. Gordon[12]	Roger Haydock	Roger Haydock	F. C. Gray, Sr.	Roger Haydock
Columbia	....	J. H. Shertzer	....	J. E. Ellwein	B. Mimnall
Connellsville .	Clyde Rude[11]	J. E. Hoenshel	E. Wagner[5]..[p]	Chas. B. Raygor	....
Conshohocken .	....	Lawrence Myers	....	John Audrey	....
Coraopolis	....	C. A. Cooper	H. B. Harriger	Frank Stemmler	....
Darby	Harold Finigan	Damon & Foster	....	Manuel Oliver	Jos. Dollymore..[s]
Donara	W. W. Dennis	A. A. McDonald	W. T. Darby[5]..[p]	W. W. Dennis[3]	....
Dormont (Pittsburgh)	Thomas Maddor[6]	Vegler & Ramsey	Mr. Eynon[5]..[p]	Thomas Madden	....
Du Bois	....	E. P. Baum	R. A. Marsh	H. D. Wilson	....
Dunmore	A. Gatto[13]	....	..........[p]	Ralph Colo	....
Duquesne	J. W. Bires[20]	Frank Everett	Stephen Denne	R. Aston	....
Easton	E. S. Correll[38]	Roy E. Zellers	W. B. Johnson	Ernest J. May	Harold L. Rogers
Ellwood City..	....	....	....	E. S. Bleakney	....
Erie	....	Robert Steytler	John D. Johnson	J. A. Walczak[11]	Paul Cygan
Farrell	....	Anton Bauer	....	....	Anton Bauer
Franklin	R. Bleakley, Jr.[12]	K. H. Yarnell	K. H. Yarnell	Fred A. Alex	V. S. Varner
Greensburg	....	Robt. A. Ramsay	J. Matthews[5]..[p]	Samuel Lopes	....
Hanover	....	....	E. J. Masemer	....	....
Hanover Twp. (Wilkes-Barre)	....	Robt. N. Bierly[62]	....	James Scanlon[42]	....
Harrisburg ...	R. H. Lyon, Jr.[11]	R. M. Andrews	George D. Hocker	W. H. Barnes	....
Harrison Twp. (Natrona) ..	Harold Caugherty	D. E. Taylor	J. Henschel[5]..[p]	John Adrian[22]	....
Haverford Twp. (Havertown)	....	Gus Houtman	....	Frank Ryan	Paul N. Langley
Hazleton	....	Paul Lamont	D. E. Keller	Thomas Walker	....
Homestead	....	Kurch-Housley Assoc. Inc.		John Macko	....
Indiana	George H. Shea	George H. Shea	Ernest Shaw[5]..[p]	George H. Shea	George H. Shea
Jeannette	Andrew Kendi	L. Schnupp	Chas. E. Murray	....	Sam Casino
Johnstown	D. Comiskey[38, 50]	H. Lee Wilson	C. W. Kunkle[16]	....	....
Kingston	F. C. Kachensky[23]	R. L. Williams	....	Henry Avery	....
Lancaster	....	J. H. Shertzer	C. V. Abraham	Harry Schweers	Joseph McDonald
Lansdowne ...	....	N. P. Foster	..........[p]	Fred K. Roberts	..........[s]
Latrobe	....	Gibson-Thomas Engrg. Co.	Robt. Kremer[5]..[p]	John Husch	....
Lebanon	Grant Feeser[20]	F. L. Gardner	Kermit K. Kohr	R. L. Heverling	J. Beamesderfer
Lewistown	M. E. Johnson	B. F. Smith	George E. Ross	M. E. Johnson[8]	Guy E. Croyle
Lock Haven ..	W. C. Cowher[20]	Warren H. Ohl	Boyd R. Keller	Harry Shuey	George Myers
Lower Merion Twp. (Ardmore)	C. E. Stone	C. E. Stone	..........[p]	....	G. M. Olewiler
McKeesport ...	....	Jas. S. Fiedler	H. Helmstadter	D. Baldridge	....
McKees Rocks Boro.	....	J. W. Edmundson	..........[p]	John Rehtorik	John Rehtorik
Mahanoy City..	E. M. Dougherty	....	W. R. Miller[5]..[p]	George Hettner	....
Meadville	....	....	Dewayne Day	Minor Layton	R. L. Phillips
Monessen	D. R. Victoria[20]	John E. Kotch	Chas. Darby[5]..[p]	Charles Richie	....
Mount Carmel	....	Harry W. Jones		C. Rettinger	....
Mt. Lebanon Twp. (Pittsburgh)	W. C. Peternel[6]	Wm. F. Vegeler	G. F. Eynon[5]..[p]	....	J. F. Laboon[5]..[s]
Munhall	Earl Nau	Kurch-Housley & Assoc. Inc.	....	....	....
Nanticoke	....		....	Jos. Rapudowski	....
Natrona	Harold Caugherty	D. E. Taylor	....	John Adrian[22]	....
New Castle ...	....	D. A. Woolcock	Vincent Corle[5]..[p]	Joe O'Leary	Roy McMillen
New Kensington	J. B. Bordonaro[20]	F. M. Carothers	S. Davis[5]..[p]	J. B. Bordonaro	....
Norristown ..	Charles E. Deem[23]	H. C. Rothrock	W. Zimmerman[5p]	H. C. Rothrock	George H. Boone
North Braddock (Braddock) .	R. J. Petrusky	J. W. Edmundson	..........[p]	R. J. Petrusky[3]	R. J. Petrusky
N. Huntingdon Twp. (Irwin)	....	....		....	....
Oil City	....	B. B. Weber	Harry Dalrymple	A. E. Stanton	Lee Kaster
Penn Twp. (Pittsburgh)	....	A. Hutchinson & Son	....	Harry E. Brown[22]	James V. Volk
Philadelphia ..	D. Smallwood[3]	F. T. Thorp, Jr.	Samuel S. Baxter[3]	D. Smallwood[3]	Samuel S. Baxter
Phoenixville ..	John T. Bush[5]		Harold K. Malin	George C. Natter	Harold K. Malin
Pittsburgh	J. S. Devlin[11]	C. H. Barrett	John A. Murphy	John G. Cornman	J. F. Laboon..[s]
Pittston	G. Bonchonsky[11]	R. N. Myers	....	Carmen Marranca	....
Plains Twp. (Plains)	....	Robt. McCaffrey	....	Joseph Guerra	....
Plymouth	....	Elmer B. Jones	....	Herbert Shaw	....

State and City	Public Works Head	City Engineer	Water-Works Superintendent	Street Superintendent	Superintendent of Sewage Treatment
Penna. (cont.)					
Pottstown	....	R. McKinney, Jr.	E. B. Swinehart	S. H. Reider	E. B. Swinehart
Pottsville	D. H. Reeves[11, 50]	Geo. H. Steidel	C. E. Gliem[5]..[p]	D. M. Wilson	....
Punxsutawney	....	W. Zimmerman	Lloyd Payne[5]..[p]	Walter G. Means	....
Radnor Twp. (Wayne)	F. Weightman[23]	John W. Leidy[62]	....	Ernest Marmer	Paul J. Longley
Reading	....	Robert S. Chubb	F. A. Heine	C. Castner	Leon Karnat
Ridley Twp. (Folsom)	....	Damon & Foster	....	A. F. Damon, 3rd	....
Ross Twp. (Pittsburgh)	J. H. Fairley[3]	Webster Hinneu	..........[p]	Christ Meyer	....
Scranton	John Washa[11]	Thos. F. Kennedy	R. Evans[5]..[p]	James D. Lydon	....
Shamokin	....	Webster Yocum	D. McWilliams[5].[p]	C. Readley, Jr.	....
Sharon	....	Merle Patten	..........[p]	Joseph Fragle[38]	Joseph Norman
Shenandoah	....	....	Jos. Matlavage	Joseph Zagorski	....
Springfield Tp. (Philadelphia)	E. C. Perry[11, 28]	D. W. Bainbridge	..........[p]	Wm. MacFarland	....
Springfield Tp. (Springfield)	....	J. Robert Stiller	..........[p]	R. J. Kershaw	..........[s]
State College	....	Donald Dorneman	C. Jackson..[p]	Otis Pheasant	Howard Gilligan
Steelton	C. P. Belmont	Wm. A. Sees, Jr.	C. W. Baskin	D. J. Crowley[3]	C. W. Baskin
Stowe Twp. (McKees Rocks)	A. G. Trombetta[23]	G. McGinness[61]	Mr. Weidemeyer[5p]	Albert Ciccone[10]	Mr. Laboon[5]..[s]
Sunbury	....	Mark E. Starr	..........[p]	Fred T. Grant	....
Susquehanna Twp. (Harrisburg)	....	Wm. E. Sees, Jr.	....	Chas. W. Christ	....
Swissvale	Joseph Morgan[6]	J. W. Edmundson	....	....	....
Tamaqua	Geo. E. Willing[6]	Robt. F. Miller	Geo. E. Willing	John Clemson	....
Turtle Creek	J. B. Cummings	F. W. Stotler	....	J. B. Cummings[3]	....
Uniontown	T. B. Jaquette	Geo. P. McCombs	E. C. Schalm[5]..[p]	Percy D. Coates[3]	Sol B. Litman
Upper Darby Twp. (Upper Darby)	J. Earl Kirk[54]	....	..........[p]	G. E. Hill, Jr.[3, 28]	Edward Heller
Warren	....	R. I. DeBell[64]	D. E. Troxell	L. A. Webster	....
Washington	....	Donald Morrow	..........[p]	Allan Shultz	....
Waynesboro	....	A. D. Keagy	C. O. Robinson	C. O. Robinson	John H. Shank
West Chester	....	E. B. Bayliss	....	....	....
West Mifflin	....	A. Hutchinson & Son	....	A. E. Haupt	W. R. Irwin
Wilkes Barre	....	Guy B. Walker	R. Evans[5]..[p]	Mrs. E. A. Price	....
Wilkinsburg	John C. Deal[5]	Geo. F. Siefers	Carl Davis[5]..[p]	John C. Deal	....
Williamsport	W. Dale Sholder[11]	H. F. Thompson	....	K. C. Smith	F. E. Heller..[s]
Whitehall Twp. (Hokendaqua)	....	A. Weisenberger[62]	J. De Groot[5]..[p]	....	....
Yeadon	....	H. Gilroy Damon	..........[p]	....	..........[s]
York	R. M. Schaffner	Wm. E. Weigle	Chas. Kerr[29]..[p]	Ralph Schaffner	W. E. Sacra, Jr.
Rhode Island					
Bristol	R. G. Northup[40]	....	..........[p]	....	....
Central Falls	L. Bessette[11]	R. Z Macomber	....	Lorenzo Bessette	....
Cranston	E. F. Durfee[3]	E. F. Durfee	....	E. F. Durfee	W. C. Anderson
Cumberland (Valley Falls)	....	Edw. J. Hayden	A. W. Costigan	....	....
East Providence	Frank S. Lewis[40]	....	James V. Turner	Frank S. Lewis[40]	Theose L. Smith
Johnston	Salvatore Butera[3]	....	P. J. Holton..[p]	Salvatore Butera	A. F. Lusi[23]..[s]
Lincoln	A. Beauregard	A. Beauregard	Wm. Spaulding	....	....
Newport	R. P. Garcia[11]	John Howieson	H. D. Watson	George H. Behan	John Hammond
No. Kingstown (Wickford P. O.)	R. A. Gardner[11]	E. E. Newman	C. A. Parker	C. A. Northrup[10]	....
No. Providence	Philip Russo[1]	....	..........[p]	Philip Russo	....
Pawtucket	Jos. A. Keith[11]	W. J. Pulawski	R. W. Anderson	Joseph A. Keith	....
Providence	C. F. McElroy[11]	....	P. Holton, Jr.[15]	William V. Lee	Robert B. Strong
So. Kingstown	....	Jerry J. Gentile	Earl L. Pike	E. R. McNulty	....
Warwick	....	Albert Johnson	John H. Miller	....	....
Westerly	....	....	Clarence Dion	James Naccarato	Clarence K. Dion
West Warwick	H. Petsarca	....	..........[p]	H. Petsarca	P. Harpin
Woonsocket	C. H. Hammann[11]	W. T. Daigneault	Frank W. Pooley	R. Ferrelli[28, 6]	Edwin K. Marrah
South Carolina					
Aiken	C. Muckenfuss[11]	C. Muckenfuss	C. Muckenfuss	Odell Gregory	Perry Helms
Anderson	....	C. C. Andrews	W. G. Wiatt[5]..[p]	V. B. Mullikin	T. H. Busha
Charleston	Joseph Needle	Joseph Needle	John R. Bettis	Joseph Needle	....
Columbia	H. Bellinger[11]	H. O. B. Bellinger	Dr. P. J. Philson	M. W. Roper	....
Florence	H. J. Dickman[11]	L. P. Hamilton	Thos. Boatwright	D. C. Moody	Ralph Sebrell
Greenville	....	R. H. Cureton	John L. Hawkins	M. A. Poole	E. D. Fry..[s]
Greenwood	W. R. Wise	G. Marshall, Jr.		Sloan Hodges	....
North Augusta	Dean Tannehill	Dean Tannehill	A. L. Metz	L. L. Bell	....
Orangeburg	J. C. Kizer[6]	J. C. Langford	O. T. Miller	Jack Sanford	J. C. Kizer
Rock Hill	J. F. Abernathy[6]	J. Y. Scruggs	J. F. Thomasson	John D. Hoke	
Spartanburg	R. B. Simms[6]	R. C. Williams	R. B. Simms	D. Zimmerman	R. B. Simms
Sumter	R. B. Dixon	R. B. Dixon	F. K. Ellis	L. C. Disher	Ray Dagley
Union	O. M. Fuller[5]	O. M. Fuller	....	Lewis Gault	....
South Dakota					
Aberdeen	....	Ronald Rosenberg	Andrew Kraft	Fred W. Gerdes	Siger Bies
Huron	....	Harlan W. Meyer	Wally Johnson	Walt Brodersen	Alfred Ross
Mitchell	....	Marvin R. Heck	Chas. E. Clark	Marshall Adams	John M. Endres
Rapid City	V. C. Francis	V. C. Francis	L. Steiling	Julius Hurley	Chas. R. Price
Sioux Falls	....	R. E. Bragstad	H. O. Hanson	Forrest Williams	Leland Bradney
Watertown	C. Sonnenberg[14]	J. O. Babcock	Lyle Meadows	M. J. Hoy	Arne Vallard
Yankton	....	....	Erwin Hirschman	Joe Brewer	....

State and City	Public Works Head	City Engineer	Water-Works Superintendent	Street Superintendent	Superintendent of Sewage Treatment
Tennessee					
Bristol	Maurice Conn	....	Odell W. Gray	Maurice Conn[3]	W. J. Bricker
Chattanooga	P. Wilcox[3]	B. F. Barnes	W. S. Teppenpaw	L. H. Templeton	W. S. Teppenpaw
Clarksville	....	J. Cunningham, Jr.	R. C. Cowan	Garfield Manning	....
Cleveland	O. L. Giles	....	E. D. Gilliland	Oscar L. Giles	E. D. Gilliland
Columbia	G. M. Jacobs	G. M. Jacobs	R. Williamson[5]..p	R. U. Swann	....
Dyersburg	R. B. Stevenson	R. B. Stevenson	J. P. Crawford	....	A. L. Klutts
East Ridge (Chattanooga)	....	R. L. Proctor	....	M. L. Smith	....
Elizabethton	J. A. Clear, Jr.[11]	....	C. B. Allen	J. A. Grindstaff	....
Jackson	W. F. Voss[3]	D. W. Allen	J. L. Danuiels	W. F. Voss[3]	....
Johnson City	W. V. Ricker[4, 5]	Geo. A. Hardin	P. B. Therrell	Robert L. Jobe	P. B. Therrell
Kingsport	M. L. West[11]	S. K. Addington	R. L. Collins	....	....
Knoxville	Roy I. Gentry[25]	H. R. Neal	C. E. Eubanks	J. L. Vesser	J. W. Whisman
Memphis	H. Loeb, 3rd[3]	Wm. B. Fowler	J. J. Davis	A. C. Holbrook	W. T. Mattox
Morristown	R. W. Pritchard[6]	Allen J. Davis	R. W. Pritchard	Allen J. Davis	....
Murfreesboro	H. McCullough[5]	H. L. McCullough	Joe W. Lovell	Fred Arnette	W. T. Blackman
Nashville	K. B. Stallings[11]	K. B. Stallings	H. Lawrence, Jr.	Joe Harris	....
Shelbyville	Jack Taylor[6]	V. A. Cline	P. J. Scudder	Jack Taylor	P. J. Scudder
Tullahoma	Chas. A. Osborne[6]	Chas. A. Osborne	Chas. A. Osborne	Chas. A. Osborne	Chas. A. Osborne
Texas					
Abilene	....	M. M. Anderson	....	Fred Bell	....
Alice	W. L. Burton[6]	....	W. H. Smith[14]	W. L. Burton	W. H. Smith
Amarillo	H. R. Smith	S. M. Field	H. R. Smith	H. R. Smith	Clarence Shearer
Austin	S. Rountree, Jr.[11]	....	A. R. Davis	E. I. Purser	A. H. Ullrich
Baytown	C. W. Grantham[11]	C. J. Bush, Jr.	Barnev E. Berry	J. D. Adcox	F. G. Adcox
Beaumont	....	J. D. Martin	Jas. T. Garrard	H. Trahan	Joe Dust
Bellaire	L. M. Rice[11]	J. E. Noser	Emmett B. Cox	L. M. Rice	D. Jeter
Big Springs	R. V. Foresyth	C. N. Bellamy	Lee Nuckels[57]	R. V. Foresyth	Jones Lamar
Borger	Ned V. Brookes[11]	Ned V. Brookes	Curtis Lamar	J. A. Collins	Curtis Lamar
Brownsville	F. L. Rockwell	F. L. Rockwell	....	Jim Byrn	James Wilson
Brownwood	P. T. Martin[14]	J. S. Palmer	N. E. Trostle[5]..p	R. D. Edwards	P. T. Martin
Bryan	G. Barton Adams	Fred C. Sandlin	Chas. N. Ramsey	E. M. Bryant	E. J. Fuchs
Cleburne	Leo Hearne[11]	Pete Styner	F. Stephens	Leo Hearne	....
Corpus Christi	Drahn Jones[11]	J. E. Johnson	A. Cunningham	Henry Lewis	S. L. Ellison
Corsicana	Raymond Henry	Raymond Henry	I. Estelle (Lines) G. Buck (Supply)	Charles Price	Bacil Herod
Dallas	H. H. Stirman[11]	Hampton Couch	H. J. Graeser	G. C. Brinkley	R. R. Cooke
Del Rio	A. C. Kennedy	Conger Jones	Jim Meadows	T. Contreras	J. Meadows
Denison	....	....	C. L. May	J. V. Manor	Jack M. Calhoun
Denton	....	R. D. Courtney	R. D. Courtney	R. D. Courtney	R. D. Courtney
Edinburg	P. Wisenbaker, Jr.[6]	Chas. L. Melden	B. Jack Owen	P. Wisenbaker, Jr.	B. Jack Owen
El Paso	....	Gerald L. Turner	Harlan H. Hugg	J. D. Lamontine	C. Hendrickson
Fort Worth	C. M. Thelin[11]	C. M. Thelin	Uel Stephens	H. H. Hester	W. S. Mahlie[60]
Gainesville	....	....	F. L. Eikman	W. O. Springfield	Lee H. Barton
Galveston	T. F. Juneman[3]	Owen Holzheuser	Lind B. Nelson	Edgar C. Dawson	Lind B. Nelson
Garland	Lloyd Ross[11]	Cayton Knox	L. E. Stark[17]	Lloyd Ross	....
Grand Prairie	R. A. Burleson	R. A. Burleson	J. D. Steadman	R. D. Walker	J. D. Steadman
Greenville	T. A. Smithey	T. A. Smithey	J. F. Monroe	Mark A. Woodard	T. A. Smithey
Harlingen	K. R. Caldwell	K. R. Caldwell	M. F. Runnion	C. M. Meador	L. N. Rice, Jr.
Highland Park (Dallas)	R. B. Allen	R. B. Allen[61]	....	R. B. Allen	....
Houston	J. M. Nagle[11]	J. M. Nagle	F. N. Baldwin[17]	Harry Hord	F. N. Baldwin
Jacksonville	Dan Mize	Dan Mize	D. E. Spivey	C. W. Johnston	D. E. Spivey
Killeen	M. A. Moss	M. A. Moss	D. C. Glazener	B. M. McBride	D. C. Glazener
Kingsville	W. P. Skipper	M. M. Truitt	W. P. Skipper	H. I. Smith	W. P. Skipper
Lamesa	C. A. Taylor[5]	L. E. Petty	W. E. Sealy	W. R. Chilton	W. E. Sealy
Laredo	....	G. F. Farias	H. T. Elsworth	J. R. Rodriquez	....
Longview	B. A. Crocker	B. A. Crocker	R. C. Burnett	J. R. Murray	W. B. Jones
Lubbock	N. McCullough[11]	John Hickerson	R. Campbell	R. Campbell	John Hickerson
Lufkin	....	Bob Henson	M. Flournoy	R. Bargainer	M. Flournoy
McAllen	....	C. L. Fabian[1]	G. C. Moseley	G. C. Moseley	G. C. Moseley
McKinney	J. R. Bryan	....	....	R. A. McPeak	....
Marshall	J. E. Albright	J. E. Albright	J. W. Schonhardt	Lonnie Coleman	J. W. Schonhardt
Mercedes	H. L. German	A. E. Beil	....	A. E. Beil	H. L. German
Midland	K. McFarland[11]	T. G. Jenkins	H. E. Nunn	Geo. L. Williams	H. E. Nunn
Mineral Wells	Homer Carriker	A. E. Price	John McCuan	E. O. Moore[3]	John McCuan
Mission	C. E. Langston[11]	C. L. Fabian	C. E. Langston	C. E. Langston	C. E. Langston
Nacogdoches	H. G. Stallings[5]	Lee H. Powell	S. F. Collins	J. L. Clevenger	J. L. Clevenger
New Braunfels	....	R. S. Jahn	A. Gerog	Max C. Schwab	Paul Scheibe
Odessa	G. T. Morris[11]	Paul West	A. L. Wright	G. T. Morris	A. L. Wright
Orange	....	Joe Jenkins	Ruby Brooms	G. H. Hoffpauir	G. Robinson
Palestine	O. J. Wagner[11]	O. J. Wagner	O. J. Wagner	O. J. Wagner	O. J. Wagner
Pampa	Jas. H. Cowan[11]	James H. Cowan	E. S. Lowery	J. W. Myatt	E. S. Lowery
Paris	R. B. Hayter[11]	R. B. Havter	W. T. Heuberger	Clyde Ray	Ed. Gillespie
Pasadena	....	Geo. A. Smith	Hoyal Sanford	Charles Little	Hoyal Sanford
Pharr	....	M. B. Gore	Val Rindfuss	H. K. West	Val Rindfuss
Plainview	....	W. R. Hogge	S. E. Bolles	H. U. Spain	L. D. Fitch
Port Arthur	M. C. Creswell[6]	H. H. Poole	J. L. Swanson	M. C. Creswell	J. L. Swanson[35]
River Oaks (Fort Worth)	W. F. Harrison[11]	Paul Reaves	W. F. Harrison	W. F. Harrison	....
Robstown	....	....	E. W. Wasson	R. P. Carroll	G. W. Wilson
San Angelo	J. P. Burden	J. P. Burden	J. E. Williams	J. P. Burden	J. P. Burden
San Antonio	S. Granata, Jr.[11]	V. P. Newman[58]	R. A. Thompson	E. L. Hansen	W. N. Wells
San Benito	M. I. Crow[6]	E. Woodson, Jr.	H. J. Harvill	M. I. Crow	H. J. Harvill
Sherman	Tom Dennis	....	R. S. Russell	C. L. Stewart	R. S. Russell
Snyder	....	Doyle Henricks	Geo. J. Lee	Geo. J. Lee	Doyle Henricks
Sweetwater	Roy Duckett[11]	M. D. Shipley	Roy Duckett	M. D. Shipley	Roy Duckett
Temple	....	Joe Gilbreth	L. W. Smith	Ray D. Morgan	C. W. Stephenson
Terrell	....	....	Dick Grier	Marrie Burns	F. A. Moore
Texarkana	....	....	W. J. Weems	Roy Bitner	W. J. Weems
Texas City	R. M. Jennings[11]	....	Grady Alston	....	W. Gundermann

State and City	Public Works Head	City Engineer	Water-Works Superintendent	Street Superintendent	Superintendent of Sewage Treatment
Texas (cont.)					
Tyler	J. P. Ferrill[11]	J. P. Ferrill	Buck Campbell	Ernest Dunn	Buck Campbell
University Park (Dallas)	L. H. Sullivan[6]	J. B. Kirven	J. B. Kirven	Joe Ueckert	....
Vernon	....	R. B. Smith	C. K. Robinson	Tom Turkett	C. K. Robinson
Victoria	....	D. R. Voekel	V. A. Atkinson	A. M. Salziger	Wm. Wolff
Waco	P. G. Dieter, Jr.	P. G. Dieter, Jr.	Curtis Harlin	C. N. Murphy	W. Biederman
Waxahachie	....	....	H. R. Moses	R. G. Helms	H. R. Moses
W. University Pl. (Houston)	J. I. Cornelison	J. I. Cornelison	E. J. Hood	A. L. Bearden	C. E. Posey
White Settlement (Fort Worth)	Clifford Johnson	....	J. M. Waggoman	....	....
Wichita Falls	F. M. Rugeley[11]	W. L. Baugh. Jr.	J. P. Ruhmann	M. F. Feltman	F. M. Rugeley
Utah					
Logan	....	Ray C. Hugie	Alton Eames	Leo Kimball	....
Ogden	E. J. Allison[5]	C. R. Kimball	W. F. Richards	Wm. D. Core	....
Provo	Clark Newell	Earl Conder	Clark Newell	W. O. Facer	Earl Conder
Salt Lake City	....	Roy W. McLeese	Chas. W. Wilson	J. L. Christensen[3]	....
Vermont					
Barre	T. W. Dix[6]	T. W. Dix	....	T. W. Dix	T. W. Dix
Burlington	....	Ed. J. Crowley	Joseph E. Moore	Ed. J. Crowley	John T. Vincent
Rutland	P. C. Wagner[3]	P. C. Wagner	P. C. Wagner	P. C. Wagner	....
Virginia					
Alexandria	P. B. Hall[11]	P. B. Hall	C. Richards[5]..p	Kenneth Smith	Robert Mangum
Bristol	....	L. R. Warriner	Earl C. Coalson	W. A. Stephenson	Earl C. Coalson
Charlottesville	R. E. Hall, Jr.[66]	T. W. Edwards	C. G. Haney	R. E. Hall, Jr.[66]	R. E. Hall, Jr.[66]
Covington	....	E. L. Huffman	C. L. Overholt	H. F. Kohne	Virgil L. Keyser
Danville	H. D. Bowling	H. D. Bowling	Howard Johnson	William Bradley	....
Fredericksburg	....	C. H. Pierson	W. Sykes	R. McCarty	W. Sykes
Hampton	Clem Snyder[11]	....	W. Harmon[5]..p	W. H. Huneycutt	Col. C. Borland[5].s
Harrisonburg	A. T. Wilcox	A. T. Wilcox	Earl R. Smith	A. T. Wilcox	Earl R. Smith
Hopewell	W. P. Cleveland[6]	W. Altman, Jr.	Elmer F. Eld[5]..p	W. P. Cleveland	W. P. Cleveland
Lynchburg	J. D. Wright[11]	J. D. Wright	R. D. Wright	J. E. McCarrow	R. D. Wright
Martinsville	G. W. Brown[11]	....	W. H. Graves	B. D. Pinkard	....
Newport News	Wol Ellenson[11]	Wm. Lyons	W. B. Harman[49]	J. E. Boyd	....
Norfolk	S. C. Morrisette[11]	G. W. Shoemaker	R. W. Fitzgerald	Chas. H. Hughes	Col. C. Borland[5].s
Petersburg	W. W. Cotton	W. W. Cotton	R. H. Harrison	J. E. Brockwell	T. Musgrove, Jr.
Portsmouth	F. J. Bergeron[11]	E. B. Hilton	X. D. Murden	....	S. E. Liljegren
Richmond	Robt. S. Hopson[11]	....	J. E. Metzger[17]	....	....
Roanoke	J. Wentworth[11]	H. C. Broyles	G. N. Ruston[5]	M. A. McGuire	F. C. Funnell
Salem	....	F. A. Spiggle	C. A. Johnston	J. C. Yates	C. A. Johnston
South Norfolk	C. W. Holdskom[11]	....	G. W. Shoemaker	....	Col. C. Borland[5] s
Staunton	....	C. M. Moyer, Jr.	A. O. Dunn	H. A. Larner, Sr.	O. R. Holtz
Suffolk	J. C. Causey, Jr.[5]	K. R. McGahee	F. E. Howell, Jr.	C. H. Holland	....
Waynesboro	E. A. Via[6]	J. H. Harman	Chas. E. Fielder	S. E. Brooks	R. N. Fountaine
Winchester	S. L. Grant[5]	J. R. Brandon	S. H. Reaves	J. R. Brandon	S. H. Reaves
Washington					
Aberdeen	....	C. C. Kirkwood	N. J. Salmon	George Salmi	....
Bellingham	James C. Thiel	T. P. Scholz	H. Donnelly	J. C. Thiel	H. J. Donnelly
Bremerton	D. B. Wheaton[3]	E. S. Severance	C. C. Casad	J. L. Hatfield	C. C. Casad
Everett	Geo. Gebert[3]	Rodney Colvin	S. Paine	P. Gallaspy	....
Hoquiam	....	Anton Paulson[1]	Allen Boyer	R. Sandstrom	J. A. Tannahill s
Kennewick	Harry Ray	M. B. Winegar	Harry Ray	C. W. Coates	Harry Ray
Longview	Jack Jones	Jack Jones	Lloyd Inman	Jack Jones	Lloyd Inman
Moses Lake	....	Gray & Osborne	Jim Baun	Jim Pippins	Jim Pippins
Olympia	....	Earl W. Elton	Guy Myatt	Robert G. Wood	Robert G. Wood
Pasco	....	Geo. R. Fisher	George R. Fisher	I. N. Brickey	A. J. Reisdorph
Port Angeles	....	Herman Ahlvers	H. E. Dodge	A. A. Donahue	
Pullman	Ben. O. Nelson	C. L. Waggener	Ben. O. Nelson	Ben. O. Nelson	Fred H. Cooper
Puyallup	....	....	....	Rue Thomas	Chas. Rohlman
Renton	James Dunstan[14]	James Highton	James Dunstan	James Highton	James Dunstan
Seattle	Wm. E. Parker[23]	Wm. E. Parker	J. Ray Heath, Sr.	Wm. E. Parker	Wm. E. Parker
Spokane	A. R. Meehan[3]	P. G. Holgren	Glenn A. Yake	L. W. Espey	....
Tacoma	L. P. Staman[11]	Myron Calkins	J. A. Kuehl	C. E. Henriot	L. Ketchum
Vancouver	B. G. Smith[11]	Herbert Nunn	Marvin Schroeder	Bruce Roberts	A. S. Wood
Walla Walla	W. J. Russell[3]	C. W. Cote	P. H. Meyer	Roy Davis	Chas. Zickfoose
Wenatchee	Geo. S. McLean[3]	C. E. Murray	Marion Sterling	W. Cunningham	....
Yakima	L. C. Mathews[3]	Sam H. Hobbs	Harper Grimes	Geo. Timpke	Harper Grimes
West Virginia					
Beckley	....	....	W. A. Stanley[5]..p	A. K. Minter S. Horwath	F. E. Wilder
Bluefield	....	E. C. Barton	D. H. Clark..p	C. W. Houseman	Thomas Bruce
Charleston	....	J. Lewis Hark	T. Blair, Jr.[29]..p	Walter E. Moore	D. C. Shonk
Clarksburg	....	E. V. Selby	Ben Stout[5]..p	J. Romano	Frank Patsy
Fairmont	....	J. Nichols	A. F. Robinson	C. A. Jenkins	....
Huntington	....	F. S. Whitney	M. K. Jones	Oney Dunfee	Oney Dunfee
Martinsburg	....	John C. Potts	Guy A. Saine	Luther W. Grimm	....
Morgantown	....	J. E. Snyder	G. B. Flegal, Jr.	D. C. Rexroad	....
Moundsville	....	Gordon Sammons	Ralph Berry	A. C. Thompson	....
Parkersburg	....	L. G. Merrill	C. C. Coffield	J. M. Beckett, Jr.	Harry Pitts
St. Albans	....	J. H. Milam	J. L. Martin[57]	Rufus Dunlap	....
So. Charleston	....	J. A. Holsclaw	E. E. Vader[5]..p	Roy Smith	O. P. Frame
Weirton	Chas. McCall	....	Melvin Boyd	Guy Little	....
Wheeling	J. C. Boyd[6]	J. C. Boyd	A. R. Todd	R. G. McCollam	....
Wisconsin					
Appleton	E. J. Duszynski[11]	E. J. Duszynski	Wm. U. Gallaher	R. F. Schulze	E. J. Duszynski
Ashland	R. Wheeler	R. Wheeler	James Snow	W. MacDonald	Paul Solberg

State and City	Public Works Head	City Engineer	Water-Works Superintendent	Street Superintendent	Superintendent of Sewage Treatment
Wisc. (cont.)					
Beaver Dam ..	J. R. Birch	J. R. Birch	Oscar Bedker	E. F. Roedl	Oscar Bedker
Beloit	E. C. Bennett	E. C. Bennett	....	....	....
Chippewa Falls	....	Seymour R. Cray	A. E. Nelson	Oscar Bjork	Clyde Lehman
Cudahy	R. Palkowitz[23]	James Tiry	James Tiry	John Havlik	John Havlik
Eau Claire	N. Bartholomew[11]	Wm. Wolf	C. Barney	R. C. Bates	L. V. Owens
Fond du Lac...	....	Elmer Bray	Fred Whitely	J. E. Murray[20]	C. Bogenhagen
Green Bay	F. J. Euclide[6]	F. J. Euclide[6]	Harold Londo	C. Cohen	Geo. F. Martin
Janesville	J. Lustig	J. Lustig	R. Krempel	A. Badger	O. Rimmele
Kenosha	C. R. Nicolazzo[11]	B. Seal	C. R. Nicolazzo	K. Norcross	F. I. Vilen
La Crosse	C. Wahlstrom[11]	Z. A. Gorder	C. A. Allen	A. C. Hahn	C. A. Wahlstrom
Madison	J. G. Thompson	J. G. Thompson	E. L. Nordness	J. A. Brophy	....
Manitowoc	....	E. F. Walter	R. E. Cannard[5]	E. Karl[22]	Wm. Reardon
Marinette	J. E. Brickert[6]	R. J. Poss	E. N. Hansen	J. E. Brickert	A. Trepanier
Marshfield	H. H. Atwood[23]	R. H. Schneider	E. F. Kipp	M. Jirschele	O. Ward
Menasha	....	M. J. Noth	T. McGuire	E. Baldwin	A. Sorensen
Milwaukee	L. D. Knapp[3]	E. A. Schmidt	A. Rynders	C. Distelhorst	R. D. Leary
Neenah	W. G. Bryan[11]	....	E. C. Westfahl	....	A. Sorensen
Oshkosh	....	Ivar VanAkkeren	A. C. Hintz	Wm. Hubbard	R. W. Frazier
Racine	H. A. Nelson[3]	Wm. J. Chadwick	W. A. Peirce	H. A. Nelson	T. T. Hay
Sheboygan	R. E. Fleischer[11]	R. F. Ottensmann	J. Zufelt	W. Muehlenburg	Jake Klein
Shorewood	R. D. Sullivan[3]	....	D. E. McGee	H. F. Albrecht	..........[s]
So. Milwaukee..	W. G. Nienow	W. G. Nienow	J. Skorupski, Jr.	O. McCann	Vern Zingsheim
Stevens Point..	H. L. Krebs[11]	H. L. Krebs	Verne Somers	Ernest G. Bruske	Verne Somers
Superior	E. W. Berg[11]	E. W. Berg	....	Ray Lozon	....
Two Rivers ...	J. D. Markham[11]	Jack D. Markham	D. Laubenstein	Leonard Birr	D. Laubenstein
Watertown ...	F. W. Usher	F. W. Usher	H. G. Reichardt	L. T. Strunz	W. H. Schlueter
Waukesha	W. E. Dick[29]	W. E. Dick	A. P. Kuranz	A. Kutschenreuter	R. Vanden Noven
Wausau	L. A. Manteufel[11]	H. J. Erickson	W. F. Leistikow	W. Kluever	L. A. Manteufel
Wauwatosa ..	F. D. Kuckuck[11]	F. D. Kuckuck	Jack Nash	E. Baumann[8]	....
West Allis ...	A. L. Wichner[6]	P. H. Burbach	A. L. Wichner	A. L. Wichner	..........[s]
Whitefish Bay (Milwaukee)	H. T. Rapp[6]	J. M. Katzban	A. Hansen	H. T. Rapp	....
Wisconsin Rapids	....	A. R. Engler	V. W. Baker	E. Brandt	L. O'Dell
Wyoming					
Casper	Joe Bartu[6]	Ben B. Lummis	Roel K. Stratton	Art Gronning	....
Cheyenne	Worth Story[3]	R. C. Kay	Ray Sherard	A. W. Trout, Sr.	
Laramie	....	W. J. Nelson	W. Cheesbrough	F. J. Treinen	W. Cheesbrough
Rock Springs .	....	Ellis Hudman	K. Darling[5]..p	A. Angelovic	C. Sandstrom
Sheridan	....	E. J. Johnson	T. J. Pelesky	T. J. Pelesky[3]	Glenn Jenks
Alaska					
Anchorage	B. L. Anderson[6]	Geo. O. Matkin	B. L. Anderson	B. L. Anderson	....
Fairbanks	E. LeRoy Smith[6]	Robert Crow	....	E. LeRoy Smith	....
Hawaii					
Hilo	Yoshio Inaba	Yoshio Inaba[54]	Wm. H. Chun[5]	Wm. Upchurch	....
Honolulu	Yoshio Kunimoto	Yoshio Kunimoto[54]	A. R. Tyler[6]..p	Hamilton Rodrigues	L. H. L. Hart
Puerto Rico					
Aguadilla	R. Guntin-Lopez[11]	Cosme A. Banks	....	....	Ing. Lionel Motta
Arecibo	....	J. Negron Crespo	....	E. C. Fernandez	....
Bayamon	Adolfo Torrech	Adolfo Torrech	P. J. Gonzalos	Adolfo Torrech	P. J. Gonzalos
Cagus	....	....	....	....	....
Caomo	....	....	....	....	....
Cavey	....	R. A. Orraca	Jorge Melendez	....	....
Guayama	Obdulia Lorenzo	L. R. Madera	F. Santiago	R. Roca	E. Damondt
Humacao	Jose H. Mendez[65]	....	T. G. Millan	....	....
Manati	....	....	....	....	R. R. Marrero
Mayaguez	H. E. Quintero	H. E. Quintero	M. Bev Sanchez	L. R. Torres	F. F. Montalvo
Ponce	Andres Ortis	Andres Ortis	Luis Villamarzo	Dionisio Rivera	....
San Juan	Juan J. Sandin[11]	....	Rafael Vrrutia[11]	....	Rafael Vrrutia[35]
Virgin Islands					
Charlotte Amalie	R. B. Galiber[3]	R. B. Galiber	R. B. Galiber	R. B. Galiber	R. B. Galiber

1 Acting
2 Commissioner of Public Improvements
3 Commissioner
4 Assistant
5 Manager
6 Superintendent
7 Sanitary Superintendent
8 Foreman
9 Sewer Operator
10 Supervisor
11 Director
12 Mayor
13 Street Commissioner
14 Superintendent Utilities
15 Chief Engineer
16 General Manager
17 Director of Utilities
18 Chief Operator
19 General Superintendent
20 Councilman
21 Administrator
22 Foreman
23 Chairman
24 Co-ordinator
25 Service Director
26 Secretary-Treasurer
27 Maintenance Superintendent
28 Highways
29 President
30 Selectman
31 Chief of Construction
32 Street Warden
33 Consulting Engineers
34 Controller
35 Sewers
36 Production Superintendent
37 Director of Sanitation
38 Director of Streets
39 Division Engineer—Construction
40 Highway Surveyors
41 Maintenance and Construction
42 Inspector
43 Utilities Commissioner
44 Plant Superintendent
45 Construction Engineer
46 Maintenance Engineer
47 Alderman
48 Director of Parks
49 General Manager
50 Public Improvement
51 Engineer
52 Sanitation Commissioner
53 Deputy
54 Chief
55 Highway Engineers
56 Sewer Engineer
57 Supt. of Water Distribution
58 Street Engineer
59 Principal Engineer
60 City Chemist
61 Town Engineer
62 Township Engineer
63 Village Engineer
64 Borough Engineer
65 District Engineer
66 Supt. of Public Service

"p"—Private Water Company *"s"—Sanitary District*

Mayors, Police Chiefs, Fire Chiefs, Park Superintendents and City Clerks

In Places of Over 10,000 Population

List Revised to January 1, 1957

In a number of instances small figures will be found to the right of the names listed in this tabulation. For the actual title of such officials, turn to the footnotes on page 1106.

State and City	Mayor	Police Chief	Fire Chief	Park Superintendent	City Clerk
Alabama					
Anniston	Geo. T. Morris	J. L. Peek	E. E. White	W. G. Boyd	L. O. Treadway
Auburn	G. H. Wright	C. B. Ellis	C. B. Ellis	R. G. Pitts[1]	W. Wilson Hill
Bessemer	Jess Lanier	Geo. W. Barron	C. O. Davis	G. S. Godwin	Frances C. Jones
Birmingham	James W. Morgan	Jamie Moore	Hoyt M. Ayers	King Sparks, Jr.	Eunice S. Hewes
Decatur	Knox L. McRae	....	L. Floyd Elkins	....	Joe Pettey
Dothan	R. C. McClintock	Herbert Deal	Floyd Harris	W. D. Hewes	L. R. Driggers
Fairfield	C. J. Smithson	Wilson E. Moore	Wilson E. Moore	....	Mamie R. Byrne[2]
Florence	W. N. Harrison	Noah H. Danley	L. D. Lovelace	J. M. Spain[3]	S. B. Howard
Gadsden	Hugh S. Patterson	C. Fay Boman	Clyde Landers	Burney Smith	P. M. McCall
Homewood	E. G. Walker	Edwin H. Wood	E. H. Knox	Jas. Willis Nealy	Cassie L. Miller
Huntsville	R. B. Searcy	Grover A. Pylant		W. E. McBride	N. M. Payne
Mobile	Henry R. Luscher	D. E. McFadyen	C. D. Sirmon	J. W. Matthews	S. H. Hendrix
Montgomery	W. A. Gayle	G. J. Ruppenthal	R. L. Lampley	T. A. Belser	Silas D. Cater
Mountain Brook	D. W. Hamilton	R. W. Tibbett	R. W. Tibbett	....	Grady M. Ellison
Opelika	Ealon M. Lambert	Floyd H. Mann	G. A. Mitchell	W. J. Calhoun	W. F. Pearson
Phenix City	C. M. Knowles, Jr.	P. H. Mihelic	John L. Newsome	Jack Chapman	W. P. Farrar
Prichard	G. V. Dismukes	E. C. Anderson	G. E. Dixon	T. W. West	....
Selma	Chris B. Heinz	E. W. Mullen	H. H. Berry	W. C. Sims[4]	C. C. Ward
Sheffield	C. L. Beard	Bob Price	James S. Tirey	Russell Appleton	E. S. Enoch
Sylacauga	Ed. J. Howard	W. D. Ashcraft	E. L. Blankenship	....	C. J. Johnson, Jr.
Talladega	Dr. J. Hardwick	Leon Curlee	W. C. Holmes	....	Joe L. Grambrell
Tuscaloosa	G. M. Van Tassel	W. C. Tompkins	E. L. Mathews	John McKinley	W. F. DaLee
Arizona					
Douglas	H. W. Beumler	Peecy Bowden	Paul Taylor	Wm. E. Wood	Oakley Lucas
Glendale	R. D. Lundberg	S. Van de Putte	Don Heatwold	....	Elton A. Kirby
Mesa	R. G. Johnson	Gail K. Brimhall	H. D. Hutchinson	Maurice Bateman[3]	Marston Richards
Phoenix	Jack Williams	....	Harold Dean	....	John E. Burke
Tucson	Don Hummel	Paul Bohardt[2]	John H. Freeman	Gene C. Reid	Mary Fields
Arkansas					
Blytheville	T. B. Buchanan	Chas. W. Short	Roy Head	....	W. I. Malin
Camden	James M. Rowan	C. B. Cole	....		F. P. Benson
Eldorado	Asa C. Neel	W. E. Hickman	Frank H. Smith	James Bozman	Geo. W. Jackson
Fayetteville	Roy A. Scott	Pearl Watts	....	Elza Starelton	George Davis
Fort Smith	H. R. Hestand	Jones Floyd	R. L. Rudd	E. W. Eadie	Carl R. Atkins
Helena	Jas. T. Hornor	W. T. Phillips	J. A. Beveliaque	....	Clare M. Tappan
Hot Springs	Floyd A. Housley	John H. Ermey	Alfred Nichols	Tom Dunnivant	Emmett Jackson
Jonesboro	H. Sanderson	Wes Mooneyham	Jas. M. Coleman	....	Mrs. P. Stringer
Little Rock	W. W. Mann	Marvin H. Potts	Gann L. Nalley	William K. Amo	W. C. Ware
No. Little Rock	A. C. Perry	Bert Campbell	J. P. Caldwell	....	Percy H. Machin
Pine Bluff	Offie Lites	Norman Young	George Alford	....	F. O. Rice
Texarkana	Haskell C. Hay	Max A. Tackett	S. F. Walsh	....	Leslie V. Young
California					
Alameda	R. P. Kranelly	George R. Doran	Thomas M. Lane	Mark J. Hanna	S. H. Tennier
Albany	Lewis M. Howell	Ralph M. Jensen	Fred Pimental	Emmett Devine	Myrtle J. McLean
Alhambra	T. D'Arcy Quinn	R. J. Buhman	Cecil M. Lochard	Fred C. Cope	Lora M. Williams
Anaheim	Chas. A. Pearson	M. A. Stephenson	Edw. J. Stringer	Donald K. Derr[4]	Mrs. D. Williams
Antioch	Ruben R. Reimche	Harry H. Boyer	J. J. Grangnelli	P. K. Biglow	Jean Fashbaugh
Arcadia	D. S. Camphouse	Wm. S. Orr	James Nellis	John Panatier[4]	C. Van Maanen
Azusa	L. Memmesheimer	Albert Kendrick	Marlowe Madison	Jas. Brusnahan[6]	James Miller[5]
Bakersfield	M. J. Carnakis	H. V. Grayson	P. C. Pifer	J. B. Holfelder	Marian S. Irvin
Bell	L. F. Brown	R. H. Sparks	Adolph Treder	John M. Manok	William H. Poole
Berkeley	C. B. Hutchison	John D. Holstrom	R. T. Paine[2]	A. Gustavson[2, 3]	Ruth C. Kemp
Beverly Hills	D. Tannenbaum	C. H. Anderson	Lloyd B. Canfield	John Marasco	C. R. Wood[3]
Brawley	W. L. Powell	Joe Gabard	Leroy Jones	Jeff Kissee	Chas. A. Warren
Burbank	H. B. Bank	Rex Andrews	William J. Taylor	D. R. Kruckeberg	Naomi Putnam
Burlingame	Charles W. Rooth	R. C. Theuer	R. E. Moorby	Jules Francard	Herbert K. White
Chico	Theodore Meriam	James Evans	Elmer Brouillard	Ord Canfield	Deming Hobart
Chula Vista	Peter DeGraaf	Eugene Roberts	George Lee	Chester Norman	K. P. Campbell
Colton	Woodrow Miller	Frank LeVezu	L. E. Temby	Noel Crabtree	Elizabeth Davis
Compton	Frank G. Bussing	Wm. K. Ingram	Lewis Parsons	Harland D. King	Mrs. C. J. Harlan
Concord	Geo. H. Krueger	R. W. Orin	Ray Mangini	Robert Leedy	Anna M. Brown
Corona	F. A. Stearns	J. S. Lowery	Glen Hart	Chester Boland	R. N. Annis
Coronado	Coleman M. Gray	R. H. Manchester	C. N. Damren	J. Keane	A. A. Mathewson
Costa Mesa	Claire M. Nelson	A. R. McKenzie	Ralph Lee	L. E. Shotwell	A. C. Swartz
Covina	Paul Welsch	Allen Sill	Barney Dial	Robert Boyles[8]	Clarke Chapman
Culver City	Harold J. Shields	E. L. Mueller	John A. Kearney	Roy O. Wells	Theo. R. Owings
Daly City	Jos. J. Verducci	R. A. Petrocchi	J. E. Kennedy	Otis T. Calhoun	Evelyn Mosman

State and City	Mayor	Police Chief	Fire Chief	Park Superintendent	City Clerk
Calif. (cont.)					
Delano	Clifford F. Loader	Wm. C. Coleman	Ray Pratt	....	Fay C. Short
El Cajon	C. H. Judy	J. C. O'Connor	R. M. Halgren	....	Delight V. Swain
El Centro	J. P. Morgan	Wyatt Briggs	R. R. Birchfield	Marshall King	Celia Sweeden
El Cerrito	Robt. J. Cooney	H. A. Thulin	Edw. P. Herman	....	Maryellen Foley
El Segundo	K. R. Benfield	T. B. DeBerry	Leo B. Freedman	Keith Kelly	Neva M. Elsey
Eureka	Geo. J. Cole[2]	C. E. Emahiser	Allan Pettingill	Roland Desrosiers	Ruby C. Shanahan
Fairfield	Allan Witt	Rex O. Clift	W. R. Glusen	Frank Z. Perez	C. C. Hutcheon
Fontana	M. W. Leetzow	Henry J. Younge	Guy Kuykendall	Bart McDermott	Geo. W. Vierra
Fresno	Gordon G. Dunn	H. R. Morton	Gayle V. Coger	....	D. E. Roughton
Fullerton	William Kroeger	E. E. Garner	Lloyd Eckels	Francis Lemon	Mrs. Fitzsimmons
Gardena	Thomas K. Ware	Elmo W. Field	G. C. Springstead	C. G. Borgen	Mrs. L. Randolph
Glendale	John Lawson	C. R. Eggers	E. H. Aiman	William A. Burr	G. E. Chapman
Glendora	J. L. Crumpler	Day Fay, Jr.	Claud Midkiff	Larry McClay[8]	R. R. Baiotto
Hanford	Joseph Longfield	R. O. Stanley	Ernest Filippi	Wm. H. Wallace	Arthur E. Hird
Hawthorne	Victor Zaccaglin	Harry Severns	Joy M. West	Marvin Arnold	Kenneth L. Keel
Hayward	Art C Phillips	George Forth	Matthew Jiminez	Frank Hall	Irene T. Jamieson
Hermosa Beach.	Wm. D. Sachau	Frank C. Harlow	Fred B. Kelterer	....	Mrs. B. Bright
Huntington Pk.	Kermit M. Bill	M. H. Armstrong	John M. Slocum	Wm. A. Lough	Agnes R. Platt
Inglewood	Geo. C. England	C. C. Cupp	Bacil Roberts	....	Leonard C. Fox
La Habra	Winfred A. Lee	A. G. Johnson	L. C. McDonald	Charles Parga	Thad Wilson
La Mesa	Glenn G. Crosbie	Glenn Adams	Raymond Lyles	Thomas Lean, Jr.	L. L. Freeman
Livermore	Bernard O. Burch	John R. Michelis	Al Bonne	....	Dorothy Hock
Lodi	Boyd B. Mitchell	Fred R. Hunt	Geo. D. Polenske	Ed. DeBenedetti	H. A. Glaves, Jr.
Long Beach	G. M. Vermillion	William H. Dovey	F. S. Sandeman	Donald D. Obert	M. L. Heartwell
Los Altos	I. L. Atkinson	J. H. McCelland	Richard Bassett	....	J. M. R. Hope[5]
Los Angeles	Norris Poulson	W. H. Parker	Wm. L. Miller[9]	G. Hjelte[11]	W. C. Peterson
Lynwood	Robt. B. Compton	Ralph E. Darton	Earl Gallaher	Clifford Wallace	H. M. Campbell
Madera	Albert Barasotti	Walter E. Thomas	A. T. Potter	W. Bryce Smith	Betty A. Forte
Manhattan Bch.	Thomas P. Foye	H. J. Withers	R. H. Swain	Clarence G. Koon	H. R. Brandt
Maywood	Verne K. Tennis	Edward E. Bray	C. M. Coon	Robert H. Nieweg	Isabel Dedmore
Menlo Park	George S. Ford	George Potter	George Carter	....	Margaret Becker
Merced	Reno Ferrero	Ralph Bond	George Coolures	Wm. Robinson	A. H. Groesel
Millbrae	Geo. T. Warman	Larry Picket	Lester Pallas	....	Isobel Smart
Modesto	Harry Marks	James C. Neel	Jack Wemyss	....	Rex E. Gailfus
Monrovia	J. H. Walker	Grant Petersen	Fritjof Becker	Virgil Stevens	W. C. Gerfen
Montebello	Elmo Vickers	M. L. Peek	Loren R. Beech	Frank Loftis	Mrs. C. Bott
Monterey	Dan H. Searle	Chas. E. Simpson	C. H. Hebrard	Harry W. Shaw	George W. Smith
Monterey Park.	Rod Irvine	John Y. Cordell	Harry Moore	James Swendig	Mrs. M. Alstrom
Mountain View	L. E. Anderson	A. C. Nielsen	Frank Tripiano	....	H. R. Duarte[4, 6]
Napa	Joe Creco	Sherwood Munk	John E. Stone	Ben Adan	Allen R. Thorpe
National City	Walter F. Hodge	Harry D. Smith	James Bailey	B. J. Gautereaux	Irene M. Alston
Newport Beach	Dora O. Hill	John L. Upson	J. S. Briscoe	Robert Gingrich[4]	M. Schrouder
Oakland	C. E. Rishell	W. W. Vernon	J. J. Sweeney, Jr.	W. Penn Mott, Jr.	Gladys Murphy
Oceanside	Vince E. Lewis	Wm. H. Wingard	Walter Johnson	Jos. G. Renaud	Tom Lapham
Ontario	C. E. Petersen	H. W. Swinney	L. H. Hopkins	John V. Cooley	Anna E. Topliff
Orange	L. K. Housley	Earl E. Pursell	Geo. W. Horton	Leo Mathis	T. H. Elijah
Oxnard	Carl E. Ward	Carl Hartmeyer	F. O. Witt	R. H. Abernethy	Mrs. Ethel Dale
Palm Springs.	Florian G. Boyd	A. C. Kettmann	Wm. P. Leonesio	....	Mrs. L. McCarn
Palo Alto	Noel E. Porter	Wm. A. Hydie	Louis F. Ledford	Robert Lahn[8]	Winifred Kidd
Pasadena	Seth Miller[10, 3]	C. H. Morris	S. H. Edmondson	R. B. Townsend	C. B. MacLellan
Petaluma	V. J. Scheningh	M. Del Maestro	James M. Eaglin	Clifford Knott	Mrs. G. Wallin
Piedmont	Roy S. Milligan	Wm. V. Pflaum	Frank J. Sandy	Leonard Ferreira	Julien Dodelin[7]
Pittsburg	Vincent A. Davi	Sal P. Jimno	V. J. Scudero	John Crivello	Mary Erbez
Pomona	Arthur H. Cox	Ralph Parker	Robert Crawford	Clyde Edmundson	L. B. Thomas
Redding	Geo. C. Fleharty	Scott Lincecum	Henry Klaukens	Merritt Nelson	Mrs. D. Blood
Redlands	Ray J. Lamm	Glen Solberg[2]	Carl M. Rundberg	Chas. E. Dawson	H. R. Whaley
Redondo Beach.	J. Russell Shea	C. R. Richardson[2]	C. E. Sneary	George B. Wells	Fred M. Arnold
Redwood City	Wm. H. Royer	Wm. Faulstich	Jos. L. Lodi	Pasco Balzarini	R. S. Dodge
Rialto	G. R. Johnston	Sidney A. Jones	Lorne Eastwood	Leslie J. Lindner	Merritt Cornell
Richmond	W. A. Cannon	Charles E. Brown	H. J. Schmidt	Thomas Wilson	John DeRoy
Riverside	E. V. Dales	J. A. Bennett	Ray E. Allen	E. L. Kindig[3]	W. G. Waiet
Roseville	Geo. A. Campbell	Emmet McCrary	Pete Badovinac	W. Dieterick	R. W. Terry
Sacramento	C. L. Azevedo	James V. Hicks	Thomas A. Deise	R. G. Renfree	Paul H. Manby
Salinas	Alva D. Andrus	R. J. McIntyre	E. B. Anderson	B. V. Amyx	F. E. Heple
San Bernardino	R. H. Gregory	James W. Ellis[2]	D. E. Littleton	Joseph L. Myers	Jack T. Felton
San Bruno	J. Fitzgerald, Jr.	Wm. L. Maher	Herbert Freitas	Robert Meloling	R. E. Woodman
San Buenaventura (See Ventura)	....	....	....	....	....
San Carlos	J. C. Williams	Geo. P. Seely	Lyle G. Clark	R. J. Penney	K. M. Grant
San Diego	Charles C. Dail	A. E. Jansen	Geo. E. Courser	Leo Calland	Fred W. Sick
San Fernando	Dan G. Spencer	W. E. Slaughter	H. R. VanBebber	James Donohue	Ray A. Woods
San Francisco	Geo. Christopher	Francis J. Ahern	Frank P. Kelly	Louis Sutter	John R. McGrath
San Gabriel	George H. Smith	F. L. Carpenter	George Duguid	F. H. Carpenter	W. A. Wolford
San Jose	Robert C. Doerr	J. R. Blackmore	Arthur J. Gilbert	Harold Flannery	F. L. Greiner
San Leandro	Thomas O. Knick	Artel Lamoureux	Manuel Rodriquez	....	H. H. Burbank
San Luis Obispo	F. H. Lucksinger	Wm. Schofield	....	....	J. H. Fitzpatrick
San Marino	Corson W. Ide	Robert S. Seares	A. P. Hughes	Armin Thurnher	E. R. Kerr
San Mateo	Edw. J. Reilly	M. C. McDonnell	Hugh Morris	Stanley Pitcher	Wm. J. O'Farrell
San Pablo	Wm. E. Zachary	W. A. Pedretti	Manuel Mello	S. J. Ross	Gertrude Yurko
San Rafael	Edw. W. Culver	Frank Kelly	C. M. Johansen	....	W. L. Morgan
Santa Ana	Milford W. Dahl	Edw. J. Allen	John Garthe	Dale Griggs	Erma Hunter[12]
Santa Barbara	John T. Rickard	R. W. Cooley	C. L. Tenney	Finlay MacKenzie	Wm. S. Wagner
Santa Clara	Frank J. Bucher	Frank Sapena	L. J. George	Bryce Bailey	A. S. Belick
Santa Cruz	Paul E. Forgey	Geno J. Pini	John T. Sinnott	H. C. Winterburn	A. J. Miller
Santa Maria	Curtis Tunnell	Harold English	....	Joseph White	C. E. Winter
Santa Monica	Ben A. Barnard	O. Faulkner	C. N. Carrell	Irwin Troeger	K. O. Grubb
Santa Paula	E. G. Morrison	George Weiner	George Harding	....	Ruth L. Tudor
Santa Rosa	H. A. Jensen	Melvin Flohr	George Magee	Joe Juliana	John Hawkes
South Gate	Russell L. Hardy	John C. Gutting	Guy E. Peterson	Burt L. Anderson	Dorothy McGaffey
South Pasadena	Roy L. Anderson	Clifton J. Brown	Victor Ross[2]	G. W. Garwood	Marjorie Merritt

State and City	Mayor	Police Chief	Fire Chief	Park Superintendent	City Clerk
Calif. (cont.)					
So. San Francisco	G. J. Rozzi	Louis Belloni	Alex J. Welte	Duane Mattison	A. A. Rodondi
Stockton	F. L. Bitterman	Jack O'Keefe	J. Lyle Stevenson	Emil Seifert	B. L. Trahern
Torrance	Albert Isen	W. H. Haslam	J. J. Benner	Casper Clemmer	A. H. Bartlett
Tulare	Carl D. Miller	Edw. D. Houk	Benj. I. Jones	K. R. Raper	Hazel Hoyt
Upland	E. Tweed Stone	Ralph Palmer	Howard Paulin	....	Mrs. H. Cassell
Vallejo	G. W. Hewitt	Jack Stiltz	John McCormack	William Murphy	Melvin F. Brooks
Ventura	Chas. W. Petit	S. G. Taylor	A. J. Comstock	Austin B. Perley	Chas. W. Reiman
Visalia	John H. Copley	Frank Bentzen	Walter A. Wood	Earl McPheeters	Jean S. Banks
Watsonville	W. J. C. Ramsay	Frank E. Osmer	J. C. Hagerty	J. L. Allegretti	Thos. J. Rowan
West Covina	Jay D. Brown	T. J. Stanford	Ralph E. Hardin	Lee Hamby	Robert Flotten
Whittier	A. C. Newsom	Arthur I. Mallory	Arch B. Alford	W. J. Barrows	Guy N. Dixon
Woodland	Frank E. Heard	Frank Elston	E. H. Runkle	R. G. Harris	S. R. Fairlee
Yuba City	J. F. Henderson	George Garcia	Harold Rudge	W. R. Jennings[6]	Lewis A. Duncan
Colorado					
Aurora	Allen C. Bradley	Spencer Garrett	Wm. H. Hawkins	R. Armstrong	R. J. Goodman
Boulder	Dr. L. Riethmayer	Myron Teegarden	Frank Johnson	Harold Guy	Leonard R. Jones
Colorado Sprgs.	C. Harry Blunt	I. B. Bruce	Fred Lausch	James Taylor	R. F. Sonnekson
Denver	W. F. Nicholson	W. F. Johnson	Allie A. Feldman	James A. Bible	Geo. Manerbino
Englewood	R. J. Purcell	B. B. Tillman	R. George Woods	E. P. Romans	J. Leo Barron
Fort Collins	Wm. H. Allen	Orville P. Kelly	C. R. Carpenter	Richard S. Baker	Miles F. House
Grand Junction	W. D. Lowe[13]	Karl M. Johnson	Frank E. Kreps	Ralph Stocker	H. C. Tomlinson
Greeley	Oscar Beck	C. C. Hunter	E. A. Brumley	Vern Schaffer	Mort Balch
Longmont	Otto F. Vliet	H. Cunningham	Joe Greeno	E. J. Shrauger	P. K. Spangler
Pueblo	C. J. Burress, Jr.	Roy F. Harper	E. G. Colglazier	George Williams	Mary E. Weaver
Trinidad	Jas. E. Donnelly	Charles Garlutzo	C. W. Nolan	Nicholas Swetky	Frank Hoch
Connecticut					
Ansonia	Joseph A. Doyle	William O'Brien	Charles W. Dick	....	P. E. Schumacher
Branford	D. J. Bontatibus[14]	Leo. V. Morawski	John Zvonkovie	....	D. H. Holabird[31]
Bridgeport	Jasper McLevy	John A. Lyddy	S. E. Jennings	George Mallett	John Shenton
Bristol	James P. Casey	T. V. McCarthy	Geo. C. Graham	Joseph J. Riley	Rolfe E. Rowe
Danbury	J. A. Define, Jr.	Favorino Mazzia	George C. Hanna	James Albano	John A. Brennan
Darien	T. F. Kerrigan[14]	P. D. Brencher	....	....	A. L. Brunner
Derby	Anthony Direnzo	F. J. Manion	Anthony Rizzo	....	J. S. Donahue[31]
East Hartford	John W. Torpey[13]	Veto A. Bushnell	Francis Dagon	Edw. E. Busiere	Wm. E. Hines
East Haven	D. H. Ferrara[14]	Edwin B. Priest	Thomas Hayes	A. Ferraiolo	M. Tucker[31]
Fairfield	Dimil L. Kinnie[14]	James Kranyik	Thos. J. Carroll	Geo. A. Drew, Jr.	Samuel Glover
Glastonbury	Wm. F. Connery	T. McKaig	Albert W. Dickau	....	John A. Miller
Greenwich	W. A. Hayes[14]	David W. Robbins	Stuart M. Potter	Jos. A. Dietrich	F. D. Barrett
Hamden	H. C. Hume[14]	H. H. Barrows	R. C. Spencer	Aldo Verneris	Walter D. Connor
Hartford	Joseph V. Cronin	M. J. Godfrey	Henry C. Thomas	E. A. Piester[4]	Wm. A. Linnane
Killingly (Danielson)	Owen Bell[15]	George Gardner	Harold Burgess	....	Louisa B. Viens
Manchester	H. A. Turkington	H. O. Schendel	Wm. C. Mason	H. F. Murphey	Edward Tomkiel
Mansfield	Daniel A. Graf[14]	Daniel A. Graf	Howard Reynolds	....	R. E. Anthony[31]
Meriden	H. J. Altobello	M. B. Carroll	L. A. Petrucelli	James Barry	Ruth E. Payne
Middletown	Harry T. Clew	John J. Pomfret	J. F. Dunn	John W. English	F. J. Roccapriore
Milford	J. J. Desmond[15]	Arthur Harris	Richard Coley	....	George F. Weed
Naugatuck	Charles F. Clark	A. A. Malone	Edward Galvin	John H. Breen	Charles F. Daly
New Britain	Joseph F. Morelli	Daniel J. Cosgove	Geo. W. Scarlett	Geo. J. Chesley	Harry E. Scheuy
New Haven	Richard C. Lee	F. V. McManus	Thos. J. Collins	Jas. E. Coogan[3]	Milton Rice
New London	Moses A. Savin	John J. Courtney	Frank Sullivan	Wm. M. Baker	Eliz. T. Roath
Newington	E. J. Keleher[14]	Wm. E. Halleran	Gustave Bochman	Clem Lemire	Edw. S. Seremet
Norwalk (S. Norwalk)	Geo. R. Brunjes	Max Orlins	Charles A. Volk	Charles DiSanza	William H. Flynn
Norwich	Chas. A. Adams[13]	Jos. L. Gendron	Wm. B. Confrey	Gustave Dick	J. Dyer Potter
Plainville	Joseph Edward[14]	Arthur Datoli	William Foran	Robert Cassidy	James J. Graham
Shelton	Frank E. Cicia	B. Flaherty	Roger Bodyk	....	Harry A. Kelly
Southington	Joseph A. Luty[14]	G. Robert Triano	Charles Linke	....	Robert E. Foley
Stamford	T. F. J. Quigley	Jos. J. Kinsella	T. F. Richardson	Edw. A. Connell	Jos. V. Toner[31]
Stonington	N. F. Culver[14]	Charles Murphy	....	....	John J. Donahue
Stratford	Harry B. Flood[15]	P. J. Flanagan	Theo. Lockwood	....	W. H. Wilcoxson
Thompsonville	Robt. D. Senio[14]	Earl Reynolds	....	Angelo Lamagna	Lodovico Magrini
Torrington	Wm. T. Carroll	Hugh E. Meade	....	John Milewski	A. G. Constable
Wallingford	John A. Buza[16]	Edward Loughlin	John Czine	George Lacoske	David Ferguson
Waterbury	Edw. D. Bergin	William J. Roach	F. T. Scully	James J. Curtin	Armand Fiorelli
Watertown	G. Hungerford[14]	Frank Minucci	M. H. McCleery	Joseph Gallagher	Mabel B. Hannon
West Hartford	Harold F. Keith	W. A. Sandstrom	J. T. O'Loughlin	....	Everett D. Dow
West Haven	M. J. Coyle[14]	John F. Monahan	William Johnson	F. J. Fitzgerald	A. A. MacLeod
Westport	W. C. Crossman[14]	John A. Dolan	H. A. Shippey	....	Mrs. L. R. Clark
Wethersfield	Wm. A. Elrick[13]	Thos. J. Sullivan	John F. McCue	Albert Gray, Jr.	W. Birmingham
Willimantic	F. J. Bergeron	F. R. Laramie	J. Leo Rivard	Alexis Caisse, Jr.	Roger F. Paulhus
Windsor	Jas. J. Hartnett	Arthur G. Wall	George Patterson	Carl Engelmann	George J. Tudan
Winchester (Winsted City)	P. Francis Hicks	Waldo S. Heath	L. W. Scanlon	....	C. W. Winslow[31]
Delaware					
Wilmington	August F. Walz	Arthur B. Wilson	Maurice K. Clark	John B. Quinn	David Sklut
District of Columbia					
Washington	R. McLaughlin	Robt. V. Murray	Millard H. Sutton	Edward J. Kelly	G. M. Thornett[18]
Florida					
Bradenton	A. Sterling Hall	Mack G. Britt	A. W. Harris	D. H. Tallant	Harold F. Siver
Clearwater	Lewis Homer	Willis Booth[2]	R. C. Dobson[2]	Virgil Dobson	R. G. Whitehead
Coral Gables	Fred B. Hartnett	W. G. Kimbrough	P. T. Matheson	Harley Pittman	L. Robinson, Jr.
Daytona Beach	James H. Long	H. LeRoy Allen	R. M. Chapman	Beverly Brown	Rhea B. Mordt
Fort Lauderdale	P. G. Reynolds	Lester Holt	J. R. Carter	A. A. Colquitt	S. H. Marshall
Fort Myers	H. M. Edwards	Burl Underhill	R. S. Bass	W. A. Grimes	Mrs. S. N. Grans
Fort Pierce	Bernard Rubin	R. F. Cassens	R. M. Register	....	G. M. Mitchell
Gainesville	R. Chamberlin[11]	W. D. Joiner	H. J. Richardson	C. E. Nelson	A. C. O'Neill

State and City	Mayor	Police Chief	Fire Chief	Park Superintendent	City Clerk
Florida (cont.)					
Hialeah	H. A. Milander	H. U. Warner	....	D. H. Hambleton	Jas. H. Goodlet
Hollywood	W. G. Zinkil, Sr.	P. A. Thompson	H. L. Cook	Taft Green	Blanche E. Mann
Jacksonville	Haydon Burns	L. A. Reynolds	Frank C. Kelly	C. E. Carlton	W. C. Almand
Key West	C. B. Harvey	B. G. Perez	Charles Cremata	Paul G. Albury	Victor Lowe
Lakeland	M. Cunningham	Leo Brooker	C. M. Deal	John Stokes	L. R. Shuman
Lake Worth	Ralph K. Dupee	G. S. Sanders	S. D. McMillan	R. C. Howard[6]	Mrs. R. U. Fales[2]
Melbourne	Rudi Oudshoff	John D. Thomas	Roy Gilbreath	Rex Riley	M. L. Knecht
Miami	R. N. Christmas	W. Headley, Jr.	N. Wheeler, Sr.	P. R. Plumer	F. L. Correll
Miami Beach	D. Lee Powell	R. J. Shepard	D. C. Kennett	John P. Poulos	R. W. L Johnson
Miami Springs	F. J. Black, Jr.	H. V. Yocum	G. A. Krous-kroup, Jr.	Lee A Tyler	J. D. Ryan
North Miami	C. B. Hamilton	Karl E. Engel	Herbert Goyer	Benjamin Vitale[3]	E. May Avil
Ocala	Dr. R. Cumming	K. C. Alvarez	Thomas Sexton	H. A. Davies	H. C. Sistrunk
Orlando	Robert S. Carr	V. L. Rogers[2]	Paul Pennington	A. T. Coith	Ed. McDowell[2]
Panama City	F. M. Nelson, Jr.	Geo. W. McCall	A. T. Revell	Willie Brookins	Leon E. Mathis
Pensacola	C. P. Mason	Crosby Hall	Claude Wright	J. P. Jennings[6]	J. E. Frenkel[19]
St. Augustine	Hubert P. Hahn	William Lindsey	E. W. Hartley	John F. Masters	Pauline Boyt
St. Petersburg	S. G. Johnson	J. R. Reichert	S. O. Griffith	Boyd Hill	Jannie Cook
Sanford	F. D. Scott	R. G. Williams	M. N. Cleveland	James L. Dunn	H. N. Sayer
Sarasota	J. D. Kicklighter	R. N. Wilson	James Cowsert	T. F. Wilson	L. B. Ashby
Tallahassee	J. Y. Humphress	F. Stoutamire	Earl Levy	Ralph Taylor	George C. White
Tampa	Nick Nuccio	J. D. Latture	C. F. Dreves	B. B. Bradley	W. L. Stark
W. Palm Beach	M. E. Holley	R. W. Milburn	J. Witherspoon	Paul Dreher	J. R. Gardner
Georgia					
Albany	W. F. McAfee	W. S. Lee	J. J. Romeo	R. B. Wills	Mrs. S. Dillingham
Americus	F. P. Bowen	V. L. Autry	H. K. Henderson	....	A. Gaterwood, Jr.
Athens	Jack R. Wells	C. O. Roberts	W. C. Thompson	D. D. Quillian	A. G. Smith
Atlanta	W. B. Hartsfield	H. T. Jenkins	C. C. Styron	George Simons	J. L. Richardson
Augusta	H. L. Hamilton	F. B. Green	J. C Wilkerson	F. B. Thomas	T. D. Beckum
Brunswick	W. H. Sigman	J. H. Bisson	J. W. Greenfield	J. F. Sumner	Mrs. R. Jennings
Cedartown	Albert F. Moore	W. M. Moss	D. K. Russell	Mrs. M. Russell	....
College Park	J. Stephenson, Jr.	T. O. Smith	J. B. Eley	G. Morris	Mrs. M. A. Hunt
Columbus	B. F. Register	E. F. Moncrieff	T. C. Turner	P. B. Austin	H. G. Brannon
Dalton	Clarence Green	L. L. Vining	Luther Broome	....	Albert Rollins
Decatur	A. Mell Turner	Luther Spinks	....	Mrs. R. Magargee[3]	Mrs M. Christian
Dublin	J. Felton Pierce	....	....	....	A. F. Geesiln
East Point	J. G. Stith	W. H. Tyler	Max Wiggins	Roy Grayson	W. P. Kidd
Gainesville	P. H. Chapman	Hoyt H. Henry	R. E. Spence	Clayton Deavers	Geo. A. Whiten
Griffin	H. S. Mashburn	Leo D. Blackwell	S. E. Simonton	H. S. Struble	Mrs. A. W. Cook
Hapeville	E. E. Dixon, Jr.	Geo. B. Pearson	J. P. Nunn	Robt. Shellnutt	Barbara Lee
La Grange	Frank Tigner	T. E. McClung	R. L. Dorman	....	C. H. Day
Macon	B. F. Merritt, Jr.	Ben T. Watkins	B. H. Brown	Cleveland James	Alex B. Cameron
Marietta	C. W. Bramlett	E. R. Sanders	H. A. Schaffer	Albert H. Bishop	A. L. Bagley, Jr.
Moultrie	W. B. Withers	C. R. Ranew	Lawrence Rhodes	James Goff	Jas. Humphreys
Rome	J. E. Yarbrough	Smith Horton	W. T. McKinney	W. Montgomery	Mrs. R. Beard
Savannah	W. Mingledorff, Jr.	S. B. Barnes, Jr.	J. L. Evans	S. E. Monk	Mrs. K. Redmond
Thomasville	Heeth Varnedoe	N. A. Stegall	C. A. Smith	Sollie Allen	Julius F. Ariail
Valdosta	Emory P. Bass	Wilbur Perkerson	T. M. Cook	R. J. Drexel	A. S. Myddleton
Waycross	John Harrison	A. L. Ball	R. L. Carpenter	Henry Thomas	C. O. Parker
Idaho					
Boise	R. E. Edlefsen	F. T. Damarest	Steve Taylor	Gordon S. Bowen	Fred R. Bagley
Caldwell	Jason C. Smith	Keith Judd	Waldo Paddock	George Hammar	Mrs. Hartenbower
Coeur D'Alene	P. Christianson	Arnold E. Engen	W. W. Swafford	Avery Shadduck	D. E. Nedry
Idaho Falls	John B. Rogers	F. G. Perrin	Bert O. Brown	....	Sam R. Rostad
Lewiston	Dr. D. K. Worden	Frank F. Hunt	D. R. Gill	Gregory Eaves	A. M. Quane
Moscow	Everett Will	H. B. Thoreson	Carl Smith	K. D. Lyons	R. G. Fredekind
Nampa	Preston Capell	Nick Collear	L. T. Lessinger	W. Christensen	G. Shellaberger
Pocatello	W. B. Webb[15]	A. L. Oliver	A. A. Girard	Pete Hiskey	Mrs. J. Ball
Twin Falls	R. Lyons Smith	H. W. Gillette	L. Z. Bartlett	E. C. Craner	Constance Leiser
Illinois					
Alton	Leo J. Struif	John M. Heaffner	James Lewis	Erwin Dormann	Paul A. Price
Aurora	Paul Egan	Francis Tighe	Walter Hannon	Ray Moses	John P. Thill
Belleville	H. V. Calhoun	Reese G. Dobson	John Wade	....	Vic Geolat, Jr.
Berwyn	Wm. J. Kriz	Joseph Pilot	Robert Kafka	John Jindrich	Ann D. Langner
Bloomington	O. Lloyd Welsh	Fred Giermann	Roland Behrend	Richard Greene	M. L. Zook
Blue Island	John M. Hart	Edward W. Boyd	William Barzycki	S. Biedenkopf[23]	John C. Joens
Brookfield	Dan Kulie[20]	W. T. Griffin	Fred McDowell	William Radtke[4]	C. E. Slack, Jr.
Cairo	Dr. Paul S. Baur	F. T. Clifford	Wm. N. Brooks	Dee Dorsett	C. F. Walker
Calumet City	S. E. Bejger	H. A. Wleklinski	Charles Sikorski	Joseph Wilhelm	S. J. Maciejewski
Canton	W. Paul Woods	Kenneth Lindzey	Julian Coultas	H. J. Kramer	Katherine Sporer
Carbondale	John I. Wright	Roy Bain	U. Crawshaw	....	Elisabeth Leighty
Centralia	H. B. Blanchard	L. C. Peters	R. E. Goin	D. L. Auberry	James Maxfield
Champaign	V. F. Lafferty	....	Hobart Kruse	Clyde R. Davis	Walter F. Bailey
Chicago	Richard J. Daley	T. O'Connor	A. J. Mullaney	Walter Wright	John C. Marcin
Chicago Hgts.	Carl W. McGehee	Ralph Howard	Ira George	Melvin Schramm	A. P. Soderman
Cicero	H. J. Sandusky[20]	E. Konovsky[21]	T. Wesolowski[22]	George Nesladek	Jerry F. Justin
Collinsville	A. R. Delbartes	Paul Cigliana	Harold Meier	....	Vernon Lucas
Danville	Girth N. Hicks	Robert Christy	Howard Rindt	Howard Cutler	Mrs. Betty Oakes
Decatur	C. A. Sablotny	W. Glenn Kerwin	Lynn P. Martin	Lacy Chandler[23]	C. Eugene Fluss
Dekalb	J. Clayton Pooler	John Remsey	Clayton Kennedy	....	Bertha Schropell
Des Plaines	K. G. Meyer	John Wigham	Raymond Kolze	Clarence Leis	O. W. J. Henrich
Dixon	Wm. Slothower	Earl L. Kelchner	Wm. G. Keyser	A. H. Nichols[20]	Irene E. Hamill
Downers Grove	Ben H. Groves	O. A. Springborn	Grant Dicke	Otto Hummer[10]	Mrs. L. S. Geffert
East Moline	Chas. A. Olson	A. Van Quathem	George Le Rette	Carl Mitchell	Arnold Niehaus
East Peoria	John W. Keayes	Vernie Roberson	Charles Cusac	....	W. Mauschbaugh
East St. Louis	Alvin G. Fields	George Dowling	Gerald M. Fallan	....	John Tierney
Elgin	Orlo E. Salisbury	H. W. Lange	Chas. E. Bickler	Louis F. Puffpaff	Myrtle Spiegler

State and City	Mayor	Police Chief	Fire Chief	Park Superintendent	City Clerk
Illinois (cont.)					
Elmhurst	Earl W. Ogden	Wilbert Rusteberg	Wilbert Hayman	....	Barthel Nelson
Elmwood Park	Elmer W. Conti[20]	Chas. E. Woods	Henry Sells, Sr.	....	G. M. Dietzel
Evanston	B. W. Johnson[15]	Hubert G. Kelsh	H. A. Dorband[22]	Chas. T. Byrnes	Edward W. Bell
Evergreen Park	Jos. H. Tanner[20]	Louis Riddering	....	....	A. E. Maday
Forest Park	Wm. H. Meyer	Jos. L. Cortino	Henry H. Lange	Earl Whelpley	Chas. W. Meseke
Freeport	Glen F. Kunkle	Walter Marsh	Ray Pontius	Theodore Gunkle	Mrs. L. McHugh
Galesburg	Leo W. Morrison	Geo. Fuller	W. T. Ekwall	Russell Johnson	Alfred Nystrom
Glen Ellyn	Dwight S. Reed[20]	Lee W. Brierton	James Brody	....	Wm. D. Galligan
Granite City	Leonard R. Davis	Ed. F. Holmes	Elijah King	....	A. L. Stevens
Harrisburg	Claud Gibbons	....	L. G. Martin	....	O. Patterson
Harvey	A. E. Turngren	Matt Romer	Edward Mulder	....	R. K. Bentley
Highland Park	Robt. S. Cushman	Anthony Schmieg	William Hennig	....	Roy Millen
Homewood	T. G. Bernhardi	Melvin Meyer	Tom White	....	Robert Anderson
Jacksonville	E. L. Hoagland	Ike Flynn	H. Reynolds, Sr.	John W. McGee	John R. Phillips
Joliet	Jas. P. Hennessy	Jos. R. Trizna	H. R. Rasmussen	....	Ann Ulrich
Kankakee	Ed. P. Madison	Wallace Flannery	Jas. P. Marnell[2]	....	Patrick J. Cleary
Kewanee	C. Andrews	Clyde Rorah	Albert J. Lyons	Paul West	Mrs. N. E. Hall
La Grange	John G. Birks[20]	John G. Walker	John R. Weber	A. R. Groeser	R. A. Ryder, Jr.
Lansing	E. C. Schultz[20]	E. V. Laningham	Elmer Schultz	John Koenes	D. Wernicke
La Salle	B. D. Bruno	Walter Nijak	Joseph Ficek	W. J. Farnam	Genevieve Kudla
Lincoln	A. M. Feldman	Earl F. Minder	Edgar Smith	....	P. O. Williamson
Lombard	G. S. Schroedter	John Biell	William Fleege	Richard Moulds	Francis Mitchell
Macomb	R. C. Houtchens	Lawrence Brown	Fred D. Wilson	....	Mrs. M. Ruth
Marion	Robt. L. Cooksey	Chas. E. Edwards	Herman May	R. McCormick	I. C. Nelson
Mattoon	H. B. Ewing	Marion A. Joseph	L. E. Weaver	Vernie Carman	Jas. L. Warren
Maywood	Earle K. Broberg	Donald Nolen	David Smith	Bazel Crowe	Jos. M. Kearns
Melrose Park	Andy H. Frenzel	Chas. J. Caliendo	A. Prignano	....	Michael J. Laraia
Moline	Paul C. Johnson	H. S. M. Nelson	John Polchow	Ralph Birks	Mrs. L. Carlson
Monmouth	Don M. Vance	Vincent Romano	Robert Watson	....	Mildred Wilford
Mt. Vernon	O. R. Buford	Verner L. Pigg	Paul Partridge	Erwin McKay	H. A. DeWitt
Niles	F. J. Stankowicz	Robert A. Romey	George B. Pasek	....	James G. Kozak
North Chicago	A. Macrowski, Jr.	Jacob J. Novak	William Brewer	....	John Darrow
Oak Lawn	Harvey N. Wick[20]	Gerhard Hein	Elmore Harker	....	Robert G. Parke
Oak Park	J. Christianson[20]	Thos. Kearin	Wm. Watters	Karl Johnson	C. W. Schilke[2]
Ottawa	F. W. Eichelkraut	Walter M. Kein	William Warren	....	A. A. Lausch
Park Forest	R. A. Dinerstein[20]	M. N. Plavsic[24]	Olaf S. Sorenson	Gregory Sloan[4]	M. S. Paterson
Park Ridge	Fred Haack, Jr.	Willis F. Jones	N. A. Brown	Ed. Vaughn	C. W. Richards
Pekin	N. E. Wolfer	Roy Brees	Fred Nolte	Ben Dirksen	W. D. Jansen
Peoria	Robt. D. Morgan	Bernard Kennedy	Ray W. Miller	R. E. Owens[3]	Francis D. Nash
Quincy	Leo W. Lenane	Ray A. Welsh	John Heelon	Bernard Vest	L. Kuhlman
River Forest	I. P. Rieger[20]	Bernard Gerard	Herman Flohr	Clayton Youkes	P. W. Hazelton
Rockford	M. Lundstrom	T. E. Boustead	W. E. Swanson	....	William E. White
Rock Island	Carl F. Bauer	Claus C. Miller	Chas. Wahlheim	Louis F. Barth	Emil A. Johnson
Skokie	George D. Wilson	Wm. C. Griffin	Edward Steek	....	John E. Seeley
Springfield	N. O. Howarth	Silver Suarez	F. M. Durkin	Roy Kilgore	O. Mack Wagner
Sterling	F. D. Higby, Sr.	Edward E. Ohda	Richard Nicol	....	Myrtle Bucher
Streator	Ray Eutsey	John Gaydos	William Uebler	Martin Blasco	Roy Rathbun
Urbana	Glen E. Chapman	Wilbur R. Jones	V. C. Wimmer	....	Bess M. Holmes
Villa Park	P. H. Engweiler	William Holler	Geo. T. Williams	....	Mrs. M. Noble[37]
Waukegan	Robt. E. Coulson	John Brake	Norman Litz	....	E. R. Holmberg
West Frankfort	John Heaton	John Karnes	Fred Harkins	George Willard	Alex Smothers
Wheaton	Edwin R. Farrar	....	E. H. Holstein	....	C. O. Freedlund
Wilmette	W. M. McKnight	E. F. Whiteside	R. K. Reardon	Gordon Wallace	M. E. Brush
Winnetka	K. Henderson[20]	Don R. Derning	Rod A. Porter	George B. Caskey	Chas. R. Miller
Wood River	Ivan Kramer	Roy Coutre	Russell Pinkerton	Leroy Emerick	E. J. Clabaugh
Indiana					
Anderson	R. E. Ferguson	Robert Morgan	Herbert Johnson	George Slimkard	E. W. Coburn
Bedford	Ivan H. Brinegar	L. P. Simmons	R. C. Williams	Russell D. Baker	Kathleen Edgell
Bloomington	Thos. L. Lemon	G. Huntington, Jr.	Bernard Glover	Gilbert Knight	Mary A. Dunlap
Columbus	Fred C. Owens	Richard C. Welsh	Donald Owens	Paul Stacker	Lynn Barkhimer
Connersville	Roy L. Haley, Jr.	Talcott Keller	Calvin Porter	William Davis	Carolyn Deeds
Crawfordsville	Paul Stump	Paul Branagin	Merle Patton	R. E. Gaughn	Esther Hawkins
East Chicago	W. M. Jeorse	Michael Vinovich	Nick Palla	Dan Medrea	James F. Ginther
Elkhart	E. L. Danielson	Ivan E. Carlson	M. B. Houghton	K. Mark Cowan	Ralph H. Schafer
Elwood	Robert Fortson	Joseph Hickey	Harold Thomas	Oscar Van Meter	Gladys Land
Evansville	R. Vance Hartke	Charles M. Gash	C. J. Bassemier	Pete Harms	C. R. McCoy
Fort Wayne	Robert E. Meyers	M. D. Cleveland	Clinton J. Baals	F. B. Shoaff[20, 30]	Walter C. Meyers
Frankfort	K. S. Power	Gilbert Clidence	Raye Power	A. H. Sawalish	R. E. Kirkwood
Gary	Peter Mandich	John Foley	Joseph Zale	Griffith Rees	Betty Malinka
Goshen	Ray B. Messick	Edgar J. Smith	C. Copenhaver	P. B. Underwood	C. R. Landaw
Hammond	Edw. C. Dowling	....	....		Stanley Kulik
Hobart	Fred Rose	William McGinn	Richard Harrigan	Frank Kurth	Mrs. L. Bracken
Huntington	Roy Howell	Wallace P. Smith	Archie Slater	Santford Minch	Jesse A. Barrick
Indianapolis	Phillip L. Bayt	Henry L. Mueller	A. L. Phillips	A. J. Thatcher	Mrs. T. F. Laffey
Jeffersonville	C. W. Hoodenpyl	William Ell	William Cox	Richard Colston	Carl Braun
Kokomo	Raymon Golbert	Don Scott	F. X. Mannion	W. E. Weller	Mrs. E. Bender
Lafayette	K. R. Snyder	J. V. Weinhardt	Peter Kuipers	....	E. V. McQueen
La Porte	E. A. Koomler	Leo Kramer	Lloyd Hutton	Carl Nowak	C. E. Anderson
Lebanon	Max Edwards	James Stout	Chester Spurr	Archie Rose	R. H. Kinkaid
Logansport	Ralph T. Eberts	Lee Morris	....	J. Ridleberger	Ralph C. Smith
Madison	Charles Vaughn	Ralph Bruther	Harold Lohig	....	Mrs. C. Wildman
Marion	Edward Wert	Charles Rodgers	Arthur Plank	George Smith	Mrs. Verna Hays
Michigan City	F. G. Fedder	Edwin H. Fedder	C. J. Noveroske	Gerald Olvaney	F. A. Wentland
Mishawaka	Albert L. Doyle	H. D. Bolerjack	Thomas Pressler	R. De Cook	O. Van De Putte
Muncie	H. Arthur Tuhey	Jack Young	Orville O. Falls	Harold Collins	James D. DeVoe
New Albany	C. Pralle Erni	Asa E. Wilson	Thos. A. Daniel	Sam Pedan	I. L. Hammond
New Castle	Sidney E. Baker	F. Breckenridge	Thomas Nipp	Roscoe Arnold	Percy Scott
Peru	John P. Devine	M. Groeschel	Walter Burrous	Earl Glassburn	Mrs. L. C. Bonx
Richmond	Roland H. Cutter	Dan Mitrione	L. E. Williams	Don McBride	David O. Keyser
Seymour	John C. Isaacs	Walter LaMaster	Tom Bryant	Chas. W. Burkart	Gaynelle Moritz
Shelbyville	John S. Anderson	Gene Junken	William Branson	James Reeves	E. T. Vatchett

State and City	Mayor	Police Chief	Fire Chief	Park Superintendent	City Clerk
Illinois (cont.)					
South Bend ..	Edw. F. Voorde	J. Chas. Dutrieux	A. Andrzejewski	Ralph Newman	Freda G. Noble
Terre Haute ..	Ralph Tucker	Frank Riddle	Zenis Nicoson	L. V. Letzkus	Joseph P. Pipp
Valparaiso	John E. Wiggins	Dale W. Gott, Sr.	Stanley Conner	H. L. Rogers	Hallie B. Edge
Vincennes	L. T. Wampler	Carl Woodall	Dewey Shepherd	Isaac Crawford	Floyd G. Combs
Wabash	J. Robert Mitten	Robert Marks	Robert V. Iden	Bruce V. Worth	Mrs. L. Usher
Washington ..	Othmar C. Frye	Harry Burkhardt	Joseph Daily	Jeff Abbott	Geraldine V. Day
West Lafayette	Fred L. Willis	Jay F. Watson	....	....	R. Harshbarger
Iowa					
Ames	Joseph P. Lawlor	O. J. Erickson	K. E. Taylor	....	John W. Prather
Boone	Earl R. Senholz	E. L. Peterson	Robert Robertson	....	Galen M. Wiley
Burlington ...	A. A. Drebenstedt	R. J. Wiesel	H. M. Duke	Harry Hatt	Robert Schlampp
Cedar Falls ..	J. E. Cundy	Earl Immer	Dale Holmes	....	Kenneth TeWalt
Cedar Rapids	Jas. J. Meaghan	Wm. J. Kudrna	Jesse G. Hunter	....	Maude M. Krebs
Charles City ..	Michael Micich	Kermit Binger	M. D. Carbiener	Niels Kristiansen	Helen B. Webster
Clinton	Andrew H. Dall	Robert LaZonby	Harold Nelson	Fred Grumstrup	Frank J. Voda
Council Bluffs..	C. Woodward, Jr.	Earl E. Miller	Waldo Merrill	Earl Parchert	R. G. Bunten
Davenport	Walter H. Beuse	Harvey Smith	Lester Schick	Emil Plambeck	F. A. Hass
Des Moines ...	Ray Mills	Howard R. Eide	Wayne Ulm	Paul Sandahl	Walter Brick
Dubuque	C. P. Welu	Hugh Callahan	Thos. H. Hickson	James Kaesbauer	Leo F. Frommelt
Fort Dodge ..	M. B. Vedvig	W. Fred Etzel	E. W. Park	R. D. Mitchell	R. H. Celland
Fort Madison .	W. J. Guenther	E. R. Rainey	A. W. Huffaker	J. C. Brockman[25]	Doyle C. Huett
Iowa City	Leroy S. Mercer	Oliver A. White	Al. Dolezal	Geo. J. Turecek	W. D. Shellady
Keokuk	J. F. O'Brien	E. C. Alberts	John Breheny	Louis Betts	Clarita Langston
Marshalltown .	L. G. Grimes	Delos Dooley	Richard F. Ellis	E. C. Porter	Rena Van Orman
Mason City ...	Geo. E. Mendon	Leo Risacher	A. Boyd Arnold	Floyd W. Kinnan	Metta Hugi
Muscatine	W. I. Conway	Joseph G. Maher	Alex Bender	Ollie Bentley	Mrs. F. Mason
Newton	C. C. Harp	N. C. Shaver	John W. Weldon	....	Dale Andrews
Oskaloosa	Chas. G. Brown	L. K. Winn	M. C. Whitmore	Glen Upton[1]	Laura H. Spooner
Ottumwa	O. W. Stoltz	Lester Canney	Harley McClure	C. Radoscevich	D. E. Shepard
Sioux City	Geo. W. Young	James O'Keefe	John Hill	Robert Eldridge	C. A. Norrbom
Waterloo	Glenn S. Stech	Harry Krieg	Ray Tiller	....	A. C. Schmanski
Kansas					
Arkansas City.	R. P. Guyot	Paul E. Lesh	Joe Hutchinson	J. W. Bricker	James F. Clough
Atchison	A. C. Ferrell	M. A. Wood	Harley Yocum	....	Robert L. Noble
Chanute	Chas. W. Rice	Tom Morehead	C. W. Brennan	Kenneth Dillon	Howard Parsons
Coffeyville ...	Denver D. Hargis	Arthur Gamble	Cal Durand	Harry Meginn	Jos. F. Walter
Dodge City ...	G. R. Morgan	Ramon K. House	G. G. Daeschner	Farrow F. Ford	Merle E. Smith
El Dorado	C. G. Wilke	A. L. Pasquan	D. J. Rayburn	R. A. Shook	F. E. Brooks
Emporia	E. E. Fanestil	A. L. Bates	C. C. Johnson	W. E. Kircher	Mrs. P. Archer
Fort Scott ...	William Rardin	Claude O. Emrick	S. E. Ayers	....	Vera Schweppe
Garden City ..	G. P. Powers	Mitchel F. Geisler	Jim Fare	Claude Owens	Chas. R. Peebles
Great Bend	J. E. McMullen	James H. May	Clarence Meyer	Britt Spaugh	K. W. Hoar
Hays	Henry J. Drees	L. Younger	Louis Berens	....	Mrs. D. Soderblom
Hutchinson ...	Joe E. Bennett	Carl Spriggs	Fred Dimond	Paul Neff	C. H. Ash
Independence	Archie E. Doss	V. C. Palmer	Roy Pitts	C. I. Frye	G. H. Krienhagen
Junction City.	C. A. Mohn	B. M. Wolf	Dan Baker	Orville Britt	Wayne L. George
Kansas City ...	Paul F. Mitchum	John Theroff	Francis Doherty	Leo Barnes	Howard Payne
Lawrence	John P. Crown	William Cox	John W. Miller	Vernon Cooper	Harold C. Fisher
Leavenworth ..	Ed. Reilly	Alois C. Mistler	R. C. Schroeder	Carl Behrle	John C. Walker
Manhattan	Charles Arthur	Leo Osbourn	Paul Bostick	Ellis Beardsley	Mrs. O. Stewart
Newton	B. F. Sanford	C. E. Patterson	Elvin Warhurst	R. L. Funk	Allison Schroeder
Ottawa	K. E. Andrews	C. L. Hough	H. W. Gilliland	Jas. Woodworth	Donald R. Capper
Parsons	W. N. Taylor	H. L. Cohoon	J. E. Dodson	F. O. Nibarger	Dale M. Raymond
Pittsburg	Lynn McCool	Ralph M. Beard	Elmer Fields	Francis M. Lee	Agnes M. Young
Salina	A. W. Hawkes	....	J. E. Travis	....	H. E. Peterson
Topeka	G. Schnellbacher	S. R. Purdue	Wm. J. Cawker	E. S. McCarthy	Edwin R. Jones
Wichita	A. E. Howse	R. L. Anderson	F. E. Wood	Emory L. Cox	C. C. Ellis
Winfield	W. E. Sheneman	A. V. Froemming	Charles A. Ford	W. J. Winn	H. H. Hanlen
Kentucky					
Ashland	Wilburn Caskey	Chas. F. Howard	Borris Hensley	R. D. Davis	Clem S. Howard
Bowling Green	C. W. Lampkin	Murrell Waddell	Bret Basham	....	Louise B. Bilyeu
Covington	H. W. Schneider	John Bornhorn	Walter Salyers	Vince Keller	Frank Gillespie
Fort Thomas ..	F. B. Stegeman	Richard H. Quehl	....	Chas. H. Kuhn[9]	Mrs. A. B. King
Frankfort	Robert C. Yount	W. C. Wash	Bernard Carter	Humzey Yessin[3]	Carl B. Morris
Henderson ...	Hecht S. Lackey	Fred J. Hallf	Ben Clark	Louis Denton	Phil J. Thomy
Hopkinsville ..	Chester A. Porta	Russell Greenwell	Doris E. James	....	Hattie C. Wood
Lexington ...	S. C. Kinkead	E. C. Hale	Earl R. McDaniel	John Gettler[4]	Florence C. Todd
Louisville	Andrew Broaddus	Carl Heustis	John Krusenklaus	William Moore[2]	L. Ogburn[26]
Madisonville ..	David Parish	W. H. Collins	Frank McKinsey	H. Welborn, Sr.	Lamoine Barton
Mayfield	J. Clifton Boyd	Lloyd Clark	Carey Pritchard	....	Cleo N. Apperson
Middlesborough	F. R. Whalin	George Ridings	R. M. Knipp	....	Mrs. K. E. Dance
Newport	A. G. Maybury	George Gugel	Edward Miles	Ralph Mussman	R. G. Schomaker
Owensboro	C. S. Gardner	Vernie Bidwell	Starling Lambert	Dan Beam[4]	Adelle Shelton
Paducah	George G. Jacobs	Rulie Elliott	Ed. Turner	F. Brandstetter	Sarah Thurman
Richmond	J. P. Reichspfarr	Carl T. Newland	R. Montgomery	Joe Reeves	W. V. Jackson
Louisiana					
Abbeville	Roy R. Theriot	Nelson P. Hollier	A. L. Lene	Mrs. J. McClellan	Jo Ann Russo
Alexandria	W. Bowdon, Jr.	Stafford J. Riche	R. A. Neff	W. L. Lambdin[11]	Hal T. Dulany[25]
Bastrop	A. P. Carter	Ray J. Sibley	Maurice Grimes	C. W. Traylor	Mrs. D. Mallory
Baton Rouge ..	Jack Christian	Shirley S. Arright	Robert A. Bogan	....	Elwood Sartain[27]
Bogalusa	Chas. J. Cassidy	W. E. Boyd	Mack Hughes	....	Bertha Pierce
Bossier City ..	B. E. McCranie	J. L. Cathey, Jr.	F. M. Smith	....	Jas. A. Barksdale
Crowley	Arnold J. Gielen	Maxwell Barousse	J. W. Andrus	....	I. B. Broussard
Gretna	William J. White	Beauregard Miller	Leo Rose	....	Julius F. Hotard
Houma	Leon Gary	G. L. Broussard	Leonce A. Doiron	A. L. Badeaux	Robt. F. Bourg
Lafayette	J. E. Donengeaux	Carlos Listi	A. Broussard	Micky Domingue	C. Rodemacher
Lake Charles ..	Sidney L. Gray	Harry Hebert	G. H. Stitzlein	Walter J. Goos[11]	F. N. Moore
Monroe	W. L. Howard	J. C. Kelly	H. L. Hales	H. W. McSherry	P. A. Poag[25]

State and City	Mayor	Police Chief	Fire Chief	Park Superintendent	City Clerk
La. (cont.)					
Morgan City ..	Dr. C. Brownell	A. A. Deslatte	J. C. Price	G. H. Buckley	R. M. Williams
New Iberia ..	P. A. Viator	Andrew Viator	Stanley Vitter	J. H. Ledbetter	Edw. J. LeBlanc
New Orleans ..	deL. S. Morrison	Col. P. Dayries	Howard L. Dey	Felix Seeger	Michel H. Foto[12]
Opelousas	Percy Ledoux	Roland Chachere	Leo Lafleur	Percy Durio	Louis A. Darby
Ruston	T. C. Beasley	R. P. Whitman	J. T. Mabry	O. W. Hogan	J. L. Perry
Shreveport	James C. Gardner	Harvey Teasley	W. J. Cook	Clyde Stallcup	J. Tom Tanner
West Monroe ..	J. A. Norris	J. W. Caldwell	Earl C. Taylor	W. Townsend[21]	L. L. Wood
Maine					
Auburn	H. E. Callahan	Alton Savage	J. Coleman Miller	Theo. Fournier	Leon H. Cole
Augusta	H. Lloyd Carey	V. W. Dudley	....	W. Garside	Paul G. Poulin
Bangor	F. A. Finnegan	John B. Toole	John J. Nelligan	Harold Hodgkins	Jay E. Alley
Bath	S. W. Judkins[15]	E. L. Gaudreau	Richard J. Frates	Walter Millett	Harry E. Ring
Biddeford	A. C. Lambert	Edgar Sevigny	Arthur King	....	Armand Duquette
Brunswick	T. M. Libby[15]	Joel P. LeBel	G. E. Sylvester	....	Fern O. Duquette
Lewiston	George Rancourt	R. C. Amnott	Z. F. Drouin	....	Lucien Lebel
Portland	Julian Orr[15]	Leon T. Webber	Carl Johnson	Karl F. Switzer	A. H. Duffett
Saco	Peter A. Garland	Raymond Kerry	Arthur Emmons	Everett Spaulding	Albert A. Cabana
Sanford	M. J. Maurice[28]	Ralph Rodgers	Fredk. Hammond	Roland Langlais	Leo C. Pelletier
South Portland	J. H. Webster[15]	F. R. Whitten	Horace S. Jose	Lee Shaw	J. H. Webster[15]
Waterville	C. A. Clauson	J. D. MacIntyre	Ralph E. Gilman	Ralph Knowlton[35]	F. P. Sheerin
Westbrook	Elmer Currier	B. A. Bittner	W. H. Rochleau	F. Allen Small	Wm. L. Clarke
Maryland					
Annapolis	A. G. Ellington	G. W. Rawlings[11]	R. L. Lacey, Sr.	Earl F. Lawson	K. S. Russell
Baltimore	T. D'Alesandro, Jr.	Jas. M. Hepbron[11]	Michael H. Lotz	R. B. Maxwell	E. P. O'Malley[12]
Cambridge	R. P. Smith, Jr.	B. G. Kinnamon	B. G. Kinnamon[2]	Riley Hurley	Carroll L. Dail
College Park ..	Chas. R. Davis	D. R. Thompson	....	....	Mary E. Cherry
Cumberland ...	Roy W. Eves	R. Emmett Flynn	Virgil A. Parker	....	W. G. Ullery
Frederick	John A. Derr	Chas. V. Main	....	C. Cyril Klein	J. Eisenhauer[25]
Hagerstown ...	W. F. Burhans	Jesse B. Brown	John W. Hall	Harold Morris	Elden L. Kerney
Havre de Grace	W. McLhinney	Wm. A. Bullock	G. R. Pennington	Robt. K. Whitney	Edward U. Way
Hyattsville	George J. O'Hare	S. E. Dennis, Jr. (Major)	Chas. DeVincenzo	J. F. Lilly[29]	Ellery W. Baker
Mt. Rainier ...	F. J. Richardson	Edward Franer	George M. Hutton	....	John E. Parsell
Salisbury	R. W. Hastings	Wm. J. Chatham	W. A. Moore, Sr.	....	J. M. Troublefield
Takoma Park..	George M. Miller	Samuel A. Foster	R. E. Carter	....	H. M. Pridgen
Massachusetts					
Adams	Clayton Couture[28]	Edward W. Reid	Arthur Hathaway	H. J. Brosseau	I. A. Scully[31]
Agawam	A. C. Gallano[28]	Roland C. Reed	John W. Parent	....	B. N. Letellier
Amesbury	W. M. Hellen[28]	E. J. McLaughlin	Louis J. Bartley	Albert J. Roy[10]	J. H. Gillespie
Amherst	Robt. D. Hawley[28]	W. Engelmann	G. A. Cavanaugh	H. G. Wentworth	G. L. Fitzgerald
Andover	Sidney P. White[28]	David L. Nicoll	Henry L. Hilton	Edw. R. Lawson	Geo. H. Winslow
Arlington	Jos. P. Greeley[28]	Albert E. Ryan	Thomas H. Egan	Wm. F. Canty	James J. Golden
Athol	E. L. Bruno[28]	W. J. Callahan	Mervin Perley	A. M. Warren	W. E. Farnum[31]
Attleboro	Cyril K. Brennan	Peter J. Marron	H. R. Packard	Bull Sharkey	K. F. Blandin
Auburn	G. Henry Ulter[28]	Wm. P. Cronin	Ralph H. White	H. R. Anderson	John E. Riley
Barnstable	V. F. Adams[28]	H. W. Lawes, Jr.	....	C. N. Savery[10]	Howard W. Sears
Belmont	J. Watson Flett[28]	Wm. G. Heyd	Edw. F. Crowley	Michael J. Egan[3]	Chas. B. Wiggin
Beverly	C. S. Wilkinson	Edward Aucone	John E. Callely	R. F. Duwart	B. E. Merry
Billerica	....	Joseph L. Ryan	Paul H. Roper	George Williams	M. A. Westhaver
Boston	John B. Hynes	T. F. Sullivan[11]	F. X. Cotter[11]	F. R. Kelley[11]	W. J. Malloy
Braintree	H. B. Hollis[28]	Edward D. Cahill	Harry T. Sears	George Abell	C. Johnson, Jr.
Brockton	H. R. Peterson	Joseph C. Wright	L. F. Lynch	John J. Dorgan	M. B. Clifford
Brookline	Edward Dane[28]	James W. Tonra	Geo. L. Gettings	D. Warren, Jr.	A. J Shinners
Cambridge	Edw. J. Sullivan	P. F. Ready	H. E. Kilfoyle	Wm. J. Cleary[2]	F. H. Burke
Canton	L. P. Graham[28]	T. J. Galligan	Wm. F. Curtis	....	M. Ronayne, Jr.
Chelmsford ...	....	R. J. Hulslander	Allan Kidder	....	C. P. Dewolf[2]
Chelsea	H. J. McLaughlin	John J. Kirby	Charles G. Voke	A. J. Carolan	Jos. A. Tyrrell
Chicopee	Walter M. Grocki	T. A. Fisher	C. L. Rivest	Joseph Preston	Arthur Balthazar
Clinton	R. P. Naughton[28]	Michael E. Kelly	Thos. F. Moore	Robt. J. McCarty	Mrs. M. Fallon[31]
Concord	H. W. Brown[28]	Robt. E. Kelley	H. E. Patterson	....	Mrs. C. Lawrence
Danvers	D. J. McFadden[15]	R. F. Kirwin	Joseph E. Kelley	T. Curtis King	Arthur W. Gay
Dartmouth	M. V. Medeiros	James Hervey	3 Fire Districts	James Ogden	Thos. B. Hawes
Dedham	Wm. P. Browne[28]	W. H. Carroll	J. B. Hartnett	....	John T. Carey
Dracut	Wm. Bromley[28]	Wilfred Paquette	E. Gunther, Jr.	Elie Daigle	H. H. Berube
Easthampton ..	K. M. Root[28]	F. C. Skrsyniarz	Robert F. Ulm	Walter Fink[30]	F. J. Janik[31]
Everett	Philip J. Crowley	B. V. Elliott	R. J. Kirby[2]	Edw. M. Hogan	John M. Carroll
Fairhaven	A. E. Stanton[28]	N. C. Shurtleff	Frank Rogers	E. Tripanier[30]	M. J. O'Leary[31]
Fall River	John F. Kane	C. A. McDonald	F. J. McDonald	Henry Boulds	James T. Carey
Fitchburg	Hedley Bray	C. F. Taylor	N. M. Fletchner	A. Membrino	D. H. McLean
Framingham ..	John C. Acton[28]	E. T. McCarthy	Leroy Trevitt	J. Cunningham	Wm. S. Walsh[1]
Gardner	U. O. Fredette	Joseph J. Renes	Jas. F. Casavant	John Juslin[2]	S. E. Bourgeois
Gloucester	B. K. Corliss	John J. Coyle	L. A. Blatchford	....	Allen F. Grant
Greenfield	J. F. Donovan[28]	Wm. J. O'Connell	S. R. Zanieski	C. Cunningham	W. Cunningham[31]
Haverhill	Joseph Willett	Wm. J. Collins	Wm. B. Hunt	Fred C. Basile	B. H. Donahue
Hingham	H. L. Downing[28]	Oscar P. Beck	A. W. Kimball	John W. Fee	Wm. L. Howard
Holyoke	Edwin A. Seibel	Wm. H. McGarry	John H. Roham	Henry McNulty	J. Jubinville, Jr.
Lawrence	N. J. Callahan	D. P. Kiley	Joseph Baggett	A. E. Donahue	J. R. Smith
Leominster	Lauri J. Cormier	George H. Smith	F. W. Johnson	Otto Erdmann	A. G. Kennard
Lexington	Hakell W. Reed[28]	John W. Rycroft	Roy A. Cook	R. J. Gayer[6]	James J. Carroll
Lowell	S. S. Pollard	F. M. O'Laughlin	F. P. Kelleher	F. P. Cogger[30]	Wm. H. Sullivan
Ludlow	A. Letourneau[28]	A. Thompson	Rene Dubois	S. Gosciminski	Albert Dias
Lynn	T. P. Costin, Jr.	John F. Healey	Jos. E. Scanlon	Francis McDonald	Albert L. Flynn
Malden	Fred Lamson	Jos. B. Henry[33]	Arthur C. Green	J. H. Brandano[6]	R. F. Mooney
Marblehead ...	J. N. Skinner[28]	S. H. Bradish	John S. Adams	Joseph Barry	W. F. Bragdon[31]
Marlborough ..	R. J. Gadbois	J. J. Stattery[2]	John W. Brecken	Louis F. Ghiloni	R. D. Lavallee
Medford	A. P. Pompeo	Thomas Kirwan	J. E. P. Plante[2]	John F. Howard	G. P. Hassett
Melrose	L. W. Lloyd	G. MacWilliams[33]	Sidney C. Field	F. J. Meehan	R. H. Greenlaw
Methuen	....	Cyril Feugill	B. M. Bean	George DeGasoe	E. V. Sanborn
Middleboro ...	E. O. Wilson[15]	Wm. E. Gardiner	Bertram Tripp	Joseph Masi	Waldo S. Thomas

State and City	Mayor	Police Chief	Fire Chief	Park Superintendent	City Clerk
Mass. (cont.)					
Milford	M. P. Visconti[28]	W. F. Fitzpatrick	John F. Adams	A. P. Ferrario[1]	C. L. Coyne[31]
Milton	D. E. Duggan[28]	John E. Whearty	Fred E. Whalen	John L. Kelly	T. Shaughnessy[31]
Natick	Wm. F. Wells[28]	W. Joseph Shea	Lyman L. Brown	....	Jas. H. Fleming
Needham	E. C. Cross[28]	Thomas H. Welch	R. N. Salamone	....	Mrs. M. S. Peterson[31]
New Bedford	F. J. Lawler	Thomas E. Carr	M. C. Andrews	Ed. W. Barrett	Charles W. Deasy
Newburyport	Henry Graf, Jr.	Jas. E. Sullivan	H. H. C. Bryant	Walter O. Noyes	Vera M. Kelly
Newton Centre	H. Whitmore, Jr.	Philip Purcell	F. A. Perkins, Jr.	C. E. Johnson[11]	Monte G. Basbas
North Adams	J. M. Calvi	John F. Flaherty	Arthur A. Girard	H. A. Galipeau[11]	Albert L. Fuller
Northampton	James Cahillane	George J. Bernier	Chas. E. Martin	....	John P. Foley
No. Attleboro	L. J. Quinn	Carl MacDonald	R. C. Robertson	William E. Young	E. R. Sherman
Northbridge	George L. Searles	T. J. Fitzgerald	Philip B. Walker	K. D. Anderson	Mrs. R. Keeler[31]
Norwood	C. L. Rich[28]	Mark Folan	Harry J. Butler	....	W. A. Blasenak[31]
Palmer	G. B. Cheney	J. F. Donahue	Victor M. French	....	John T. Brown[31]
Peabody	P. C. O'Donnell	John J. Purcell	Arthur Flynn	H. J. Turgeon	J. F. O'Meara
Pittsfield	Harvey E. Lake	Thos. H. Calnan	Ward G. Whalen	V. J. Bebert	J. J. Fitzgerald
Plymouth	J. T. Frazier[28]	R. P. Dearborn	Everett Wood	Arthur Sirrico	H. K. Bartlett[31]
Quincy	A. D. Chiesa	Wm. Ferrazzi	Thomas Gorman	J. E. Collins	D. P. Crane
Randolph	Jos. J. Semonsi[28]	P. T. McDonnell	C. P. Harris	....	Edw. T. Clark[31]
Reading	K. C. Latham[28]	Roland E. Ellis	Hugh L. Eames	....	B. H. Stewart[31]
Revere	H. D. Russo	William Gillis	T. J. McCarrick	Geo. S. Burnett	J. F. McChristal
Rockland	A. H. Marks[28]	A. L. Johnson	Clyson P. Inkley	....	R. L. Belcher[31]
Salem	F. X. Collins	J. McDonough[22]	Arthur L. Flynn	Frank P. Ryan[2]	A. J. Toomey
Saugus	D. E. McLean[15]	R. E. Mansfield	Jos. L. Maguire	....	Mrs. R. Stevens[31]
Shrewsbury	I. Donohue, Jr.[28]	K. F. Burns	Jas. W. Parsons	Walter Harvey	Ernest A. Tosi[31]
Somerville	Wm. J. Donovan	A. F. Sharry	James H. O'Hara	W. J. Manning[39]	N. E. Corwin
Southbridge	A. O. DeGrenier	Ovide Desrosiers	O. Meunier	Jos. G. Gendreu	Care P. Boyer[31]
South Hadley	H. E. Ballard[28]	John J. Sullivan	#1, #2 Fire Dist.	Robert Hunter	A. E. Savacheck[31]
Springfield	D. B. Brunton	R. P. Gallagher	Rene J. Patingre	T. R. Geisel	Clifford F. Smith
Stoneham	F. A. Schneider	J. C. Nelson[33]	Wm. E. Crosby	Fred J. Porter	W. A. McCarthy[31]
Stoughton	R. J. M. O'Hare[15]	P. J. McGarvey	Fredk. H. Pye	Jas. W. Williams	M. E. Fitzpatrick
Swampscott	G. B. Thomson[28]	Francis P. Wall	W. M. Champion	Frederick Burk	M. MacLean, Jr.
Taunton	J. C. Chamberlain	T. J. Galligan	Wm. F. Hanna	Wm. Chamberlain	H. L. Galipeau
Tewksbury	V. N. Cluff[28]	J. F. Sullivan	Anthony Obdens	....	Alice A. Pike[31]
Wakefield	C. Simpson[28]	John G. Gates	Wm. Hurton	J. Henry Vik	Chas. F. Young[31]
Waltham	P. Shaughnessy	Wm. F. Carmody	John F. Steede	John Ford	Wm. J. Lanagan
Watertown	T. J. Galligan[28]	James M. Igoe	Wm. C. McElroy	Joseph Dwyer	Geo. B. Wellman
Webster	C. Sczepanski[28]	D. J. Nadeau	Edward Poblicki	A. A. Starzec	Pearl C. Mahon
Wellesley	E. T. Kilmain[28]	Robt. P. MacBey	Thos. H. Slaman	Wm. O'Donaghue	Mrs. M. Ditano
Westfield	L. J. Warner	Malcolm Donald	John F. Clark	L. B. Needham[1]	H. Whittemore
W. Springfield	R. J. Rosa[28]	John B. O'Brien	Fred. H. Sibley	R. H. Brassard[1]	J. F. Crean, Jr.
Weymouth (E. Weymouth)	Joseph Crehan[28]	J. B. O'Kane	Walter R. Murray	E. J. McIntosh[11]	H. Christensen
Winchester	Geo. B. Redding[28]	Chas. J. Harrold	Jas. E. Callahan	Herbert S. Mullen	H. E. Stinson[31]
Winthrop	Harold Katz[28]	W. F. Pumphret	Wm. A. Floyd	Manuel Costa	....
Woburn	W. Shaughnessy	Thos. J. Maguire	Michael J. Kane[9]	Albert J. Wall	M. G. Kane
Worcester	J. D. O'Brien	Wm. P. Finneran	H. F. Travers	John J. Nugent	Robt. J. O'Keefe
Michigan					
Adrian	E. Ballenberger	T. VanOrden[11]	John H. Hawley	....	C. A. Landel
Albion	Hugo A. Riegar	George E. Lewis	Samuel O'Dell	Russell Day	John P. Bentley
Allen Park	G. G. Schafer[20]	Marvin D. Driver	Chas. V. Julian	Wilford Riley	R. Don Pretty[37]
Alpena	Harlo Herron	L. D. Walker	F. C. McKim	Morris A. Olsen[35]	Edw. E. Seguin
Ann Arbor	W. E. Brown, Jr.	C. M. Enkemann	Ernest Heller	Elis A. Gallup	Fred J. Looker
Battle Creek	Frank C. Wagner	George W. Cheek	Charles Crosier	Arch Flannery	Joseph M. Boos
Bay City	James L. Tanner	Frank Anderson	Jos. L. Truedell	Louis Eichhorn	Jas. H. Gates
Benton Harbor	A. Hinkelman	E. Lindemann	M. Shepherdson	Wayne Willment	Earl L. Tidey
Berkley	Wm. R. Judy	Peter P. Sykes	Peter P. Sykes	....	E. J. Johnston
Birmingham	James C. Allen	Ralph Moxley	Park Smith	Charles W. Gale	Irene E Hanley
Cadillac	Sol H. Young	Fred Weber	Robert Gilchrist	....	Emil F. Meyer
Clawson	John Darbee	Frank Cribb	J. Albert Thomas	Charles Nugent	Gertrude Cadger
Dearborn	O. L. Hubbard	....	F. J. Gilligan	H. Manchester[3]	Myron A. Stevens
Detroit	Albert E. Cobo	E. S. Piggins[11]	Edward J. Blohm	J. J. Considine	T. D. Leadbetter
East Detroit	A. Kapelczak	Lyman Eckhardt	August Zado	Chas. Paternoster	C. H. Beaubien
East Lansing	Max R. Strother	Chas. F. Pegg	Murle V. Croy	J. John Wibert[6]	T. G. McDougall
Ecorse	Wm. W. Voisine	Alvin T. Royal	Fred A. Pudvan	....	P. B. Trondle
Escanaba	Wesley Hansen	Harold Finman	Nels Bergeon	Robert Clayton	Geo. M. Harvey
Farmington Tp. (Farmington)	Albert Gain[36]	Irving Yakes	Roy Bell	John Spicer	Floyd A. Cairns[31]
Ferndale	Bruce D. Garbutt	Reginald Lemkie	Ray Wixson	Lester Van Order	L. P. Kress
Flint	George M. Algoe	George B. Paul	Calvin Johnson	Donald Sinn	Harry Cull
Grand Rapids	Paul G. Goebel	Dewey Beaver	Frank H. Burns	Fred C. See	R. S. Kilpatrick
Grosse Pte. Farms	W. Connolley, Jr.	Walter R. Hoyt	M. Wm. Mason	Edward Goodsen	D. F. Nacy
Grosse Pte. Park	Homer Fritsch	Arthur Louwers	George deCaussin	Herbert Heger	Charles Heise
Grosse Pte. Woods	Kenneth Koppin	V. C. Bailey	V. C. Bailey	D. J. Hallmann	H. L. Brauns
Hamtramck	Albert J. Zak	Walter Jaros	George Schultz	....	W. J. Gajewski
Hazel Park	Louis Elias	Paul Marvin	Frank S. Durbin	....	Mrs. L. Armour
Highland Park (Detroit)	P. V. Winkler	Dewey T. Schultz	Frank A. Ford	Cecil Moore	T. E. Shawcross
Holland	Robert Visscher	Jacob Van Hoff	A. Klomparens	Dick Smallenburg	C. Grevengoed
Inkster	D. E. Olson[20]	C. L. DePlanche	K. L. Roberts	....	Mrs. F. DePlanche
Ironwood	Eugene B. Velin	John L. Sullivan	Edward Laitala	....	Leo Adriansen
Jackson	Harold D. Miller	Roscoe V. Gray	H. E. Crawford	Lyle Ambs	E. D. Cattell
Kalamazoo	G. S. Allen, Jr.	Sherwin Hayward	Lloyd J. Curry	N. Kik, Jr.	Mrs. M. Filarski
Lansing	Ralph W. Crego	Paul R. Taylor	Chas. H. Decker	H. Lee Bancroft	Millie M. Brown
Lincoln Park	George A. Barber	F. M. Crichton	Thomas Dickson	C. F. Mozena	Wm. G. Suzore
Livonia	W. W. Brashear	Dallas E. Hay[11]	Calvin Roberts	D. Meinzinger[35]	Mrs. M. W. Clark
Marquette	R. C. Hammerschmidt	Don McCormick	....	Leonard McKie	Everett H. Kent

State and City	Mayor	Police Chief	Fire Chief	Park Superintendent	City Clerk
Mich. (cont.)					
Melvindale	William P. Radak	George Dragos	George Dragos	George Slepsky	Irene Coogan
Menominee	James A. Spies	H. W. Peterson	Wm. L. Sporrer	....	B. W. Delgoffe
Midland	Glenn W. Warren	D. F. Craig	Earl Engwis	C. James Reid	K. W. Lybolt
Monroe	M. J. Knabusch	Harris W. Lapp	Russell Emerson	....	D. A. Soleau
Mt. Clemens	Harold Lindsey	Philip H. Oakey	Clayton E. DuBay	Jos. R. Gardner	John H. Hahn
Mt. Pleasant	G. R. Denison	Vernell Davis	Lawrence Tanner	....	A. J. Kronbach
Muskegon	Wm. E. Steiner	F. E. Castenholz	Leonard Bailke	Chase Hammond	A. J. Leutscher
Muskegon Hgts.	B. P. O'Grady	Alex J. Bell	....	Frank Siplon	R. J. Miles
Niles	Mowitt S. Drew	Arthur Pears	Harold Lowe	....	Burt C. Luth
Oak Park	R. W. Marshall	G. S. Leonard	E. C. Nowak[22]	George Hamilton	Mrs. Louise Shaw
Owosso	G. E. Rubelman	T. A. Rice	Roy Coakes	Floyd Carmody	G. A. Van Epps
Pontiac	W. W. Donaldson	H. W. Straley	John Schroeder	David Ewalt	Mrs. Ada Evans
Port Huron	Etta Reid	Daniel O'Leary	George Hisscock	Floyd Myron	Robert E. Krenke
River Rouge	M. W. Duncan	Ralph Phillips	A. J. Sassack	Joseph Ferstle	D. R. Nettlow
Roseville	Glen Alsip	Michael A. Miller	Harold Flechsig	Fred O. Fischer	Robert J. Nunn
Royal Oak	H. K. Kelley	Ray C. Hayward	Clyde Wray	L. Westfall	Mrs. G. Holmes
Saginaw	M. E. Brown	William A. Yule	R. G. Braman	Edward Tabaka	F. B. Niederstadt
St. Clair Shores	Thos. S. Welsh	H. E. Champine	Earl Dildine	....	D. J. Harm
St. Joseph	Tom H. Sparks	Thomas Gillespie	W. M. Mitchell	J. B. Schwerdt	Ira D. Wagner
Sault Ste. Marie	James Robertson	J. Willard Welsh	E. B. Peterson	A. J. Lipsett, Jr.	D. K. Strickland
Traverse City	Dr. F. H. Power	Charles Woodrow	John W. Cooper	G. M. Williams	F. A. McCall
Trenton	K. J. Dahlka	Guy Shepard	Cam T. Walldorf	....	F. E. Pomeraning
Warren Twp. (Van Dyke)	Arthur J. Miller	S. Hamacher	Wm. Van Hulle	....	H. M. Lowe
Wayne	Duncan R. Miller	L. C. Knox	Henry Goudy	Angelo DeMario	Clarence H. Ladd
Wyandotte	Wm. E. Kreger	Edward E. Path	Floyd C. Scharf	Howard Solo	Ford Wagar
Ypsilanti	R. E. Hutchinson	Emil Susterka	Gerald Kelly	Rex Shively	Betty E. Fenker
Minnesota					
Albert Lea	K. C. Jordahl	Chas. Heilman	Joseph Spark	Herbert Schlagel	Ila Dudley
Austin	Chas. R. Hansen	George Roope	John Tobar	Harry Strong	J. H. Weiland
Bemidji	Virgil Heathman	James McDowell	C. O. Johnson	Peter Cameron	Mrs. R. Hunter
Bloomington	Gordon Miklethun	Clay Nord	A. Friendshuh	....	Milo Hull[37]
Brainerd	Levi Johnson	Louis Rofidal	George W. Lucas	Lester Ahlgrim	Walter Fall
Brooklyn Center (Minneapolis)	William Soper	Robert Cahlander	....	....	H. R. Jones
Crystal (Robbinsdale)	R. O. Overlie	Lester Albrecht	Arnold Sibet	....	Ken Evans
Duluth	E. R. Lambert	Oscar Brewer	Edward Blaski	....	Bert H. Parson
Faribault	Frank H. Duncan	Edw. D. O'Brien	Marvin Morgan	Vernon Meder	Roland Kruger
Fergus Falls	H. A. Winther	Coleman Slatten	Harvey Glorvigen	A. T. Van Dyk	Harold H. Drews
Hibbing	G. M. Thomas	Powell Majerle	Hugh Riley	Joe Krak[8]	R. E. Mickelson
Mankato	Rex H. Hill	S. W. Christ	Ben Bangerter	Oliver Moyer	H. J. Matson
Minneapolis	Eric G. Hoyer	E. I. Walling	R. C. Malmquist	Charles E. Doell	L. A. Johnson
Moorhead	T. F. Wells	L. H. Bielfeldt	F. I. Remley	J. Hannsman[10]	Paul A. Cook
Owatonna	Glen M. Myers	Julius Stark	Edwin Slezak	....	L. R. Haberman
Red Wing	Harry E. Rardin	Eric Carlson	Steve Rosener	Wm. Sauer	H. E. Nordholm
Richfield	Fred O. Kittell	Cyril Johnson	R. W. Meeker	....	Paul H. Haugen
Robbinsdale	Robt. A. Merwin	....	Adolph Tulie	....	Roger K. Ulstad
Rochester	C. H. McQuillan	J. J. Macken, Jr.	F. W. Everett	Wm. Van Hook	Elfreda L. Reiter
Roseville (St. Paul)	Harry W. Kitts	Raymond Goneau	Herbert Lynch	....	B. Hammersten
St. Cloud	George Byers	Joseph Ebnet[2]	Ray Harry	P. Nierengarten	A. J. Haberkorn
St. Louis Park	R. C. Fernstrom	Andy Nelson	C. M. Williams	Dorthea Nelson	Joseph Justad
St. Paul	Joseph E. Dillon	Wm. F. Proetz	William Mattocks	W. L. Kaufman	Jos. R. Okoneski
So. St. Paul	David Hardman	Louis Fuller	H. E. Rund	....	J. F. O'Donnell
Virginia	John Vukelich	George Forte	Oscar Poirieo	W. W. Nelson	J. G. Milroy, Jr.
Willmar	S. Grossman	Robt. N. McLane	Harold Anderson	Gene Kelly	E. H. Brogren
Winona	L. E. Pfeiffer	A. J. Bingold	Frank P. Witt	Bruce Reed	R. G. Wildgrube
Mississippi					
Biloxi	Laz Quave	H. McDonnell	Walter Clark	Albert Bosarge	Carl Short
Clarksdale	John C. Newman	J. A. Herring	H. H. Moore	Bob Haux	T. C. Fox
Columbus	Wm. J. Propst	Mahlon Vickery	O. B. Spruill	....	M. Youngblood
Corinth	Leslie T. Horn	E. D. Allen	C. A. Forsyth	....	Gerald Harrison
Greenville	George F. Archer	C. Hollingsworth	A. Z. Lokey	E. M. Ward	C. L. Lancaster
Greenwood	A. D. Saffold	R. R. Shurden	J. C. Evans	Alfred Elliott	Bonner Duggan
Gulfport	R. Meadows, Jr.	E. E. Klein	H. H. Lacy	J. H. McMannis	R. Washington, Jr.
Hattiesburg	D. G. Sutherland	H. W. Herring	E. J. Barksdale	Jos. F. Delia	Fewell Thompson
Jackson	A. C. Thompson	W. D. Rayfield	L. F. McDonald	W. D. Windham	Mrs. J. Skinner
Laurel	A. S. Scott	Wayne Valentine	Hardy Temple	W. P. Smyly	John D. Robinson
McComb	C. H. Douglas	George H. Guy	J. Bellipanni	....	John B. Ewing
Meridian	W. S. Smylie	O. A. Booker	W. G. Bishop	Frank Cochran	Joel Forrester
Natchez	T. B. Watkins	S. C. Croft	P. Guido	Bill McKinney	S. J. Junkin
Pascagoula	W. Ed. Wiggins	J. J. Sullivan	A. N. Ferrer	A. E. Rolls[4]	R. C. Abbey
Tupelo	James L. Ballard	Robert Monaghan	A. Hutcheson	....	W. T. Franks
Vicksburg	Pat Kelly	Otto Finane	J. F. Hosemann	M. A. Peyton	Marie Pantoliano
Missouri					
Berkeley	Bill Bangert	Robert J. Stark	H. Brandriff, Jr.	Virgil Ousley	K. P. Lloyd
Brentwood	A. Ray Parker	Fred O. Lain	Arthur R. Noss	....	C. C. Crosswhite
Cape Girardeau	Walter H. Ford	Percy R. Little	Carl Lewis	J. W. McBride[11]	Verna L. Landis
Carthage	C. Glenn Joyce	Bill Loyd	John Brydges	Mike Forlow	Mrs. M. E. White
Clayton	Jule A. Schweig	Chas. J. Tacke	Otto G. Brexler	Arthur J. Bange	C. W. Niedner
Columbia	H. B. Lang, Jr.	Paul B. Cheavens	Max Woods	W. C. Harris	F. L. Boggs
Ferguson	C. E. Helmsing	Wm. L. Mathews	D. N. Bindbeutel	M. S. Blavatt	Mrs. R. Becker
Florissant	Jules M. O'Neil	Chas. E. Ewald	Harry Nemnich	Felix Laramie	Henry F. Koch
Fulton	Edward H. Estes	W. W. Lewis	Clinton Harris	....	Byron Dysart
Hannibal	John R. Schroder	John B. Lawson	Milton Finks	....	W. C. Fisher
Independence	R. P. Weatherford, Jr.	Louis Howell	Thos. J. Pollard	J. A. Van Hook	James S. Craig
Jefferson City	Arthur W. Ellis	Louis Rackers	John Sullivan	Ben Porter[35]	Henry W. Ells

State and City	Mayor	Police Chief	Fire Chief	Park Superintendent	City Clerk
Mo. (cont.)					
Jennings	O. R. Koeneman	John Obertz	Al Wiese	....	O. J. Galbraith
Joplin	F. R. Johnson	Roy E. Isgrigg	D. W. Abernathy	Kit Vickrey	Maude E. Fones
Kansas City	H. Roe Bartle	B. C. Brannon	Edgar M. Grass	J. V. Lewis	Margaret Strahm
Kirksville	Tom A. Eichorn	Harley Gill	....	....	Park Jones
Kirkwood	Wm. L. Berthold	Kenneth Peek	John Bryce	R. Englehardt	Wm. C. Mason
Maplewood	S. Davidson, Jr.	Leo F. Buck	....	Patrick Norton	John P. Usher
Mexico	F. B. Edwards	Earl Jones	Thomas Merritt	....	Mrs. Fae Lowry
Moberly	Earl B. Noel	....	S. R. Stinebaker	....	R. W. Daly
Overland	Mort Jacobs	Brown Hairgrove	Community Fire Dept.	....	D. L. Miller
Poplar Bluff	Harold Gamblin	L. Massingham	Johnny Ryan	Ronald Perry	Donald R. Jones
Richmond Hgts.	Lee M. Duggan	O. Brueggeman	Geo. M. Hawkins	....	A. Benoist Riley
Rolla	Curtis W. Logan	Rowe Fort	....	....	W. L. Bradford
St. Charles	Henry C. Vogt	E. W. Humphrey	Earl Bricker	N. Wapelhorst	F. Brockgreitens
St. Joseph	Stanley I. Dale	H. W. Crowell	R. K. McLaury	M. N. Thomas	Walter T. Welsh
St. Louis	R. R. Tucker	Jeremiah Casey	Hugh F. Lyon	P. B. Baumes	Lucille Darst[53]
Sedalia	Julian H. Bagby	Edgar Neighbors	John G. Lueck	L. W. Black	W. C. Ream
Sikeston	Chas. H. Butler	Arthur Bruce	L. D. Ramsey	Eugene Prayor	John W. Vaughn
Springfield	W. M. Turner	W. M. Norman	Ray Fraker	James Ewing	Donald H. Kelley
University City	H. C. Ackert[38]	Peter Gaffney	Ernest Byrne	C. I. Linhart[4]	Francis C. Flynn
Webster Groves	Wm. F. Guffey	Ovid Yadon	James P. Yadon	Harry Cordell	E. H. Healey
Montana					
Anaconda	John L. O'Leary	Michael T. Morris	W. N. Riley	Pat J. Connors	Regina Connor
Billings	Earle Knight	C. E. Maness	....	Vern F. Prill	Wm. J. Fry, Jr.
Bozeman	A. M. Swanson	A. N. Haas	....	T. Cloninger	L. G. Shadoan
Butte	Tim J. Sullivan	Bart J. Riley	John McCarthy	Robert Sparks	Beryl Wilson
Great Falls	Russel Conklin	Harold M. Mady	Chas. Carrico	C. Gonser, Jr.	Fred L. Hill
Helena	O. L. Brackman	John Fred	Joseph Munger	H. M. Garrity	Nina M. Settles
Kalispell	Claude Walter	Meade James	W. J. Price	A. L. Johnson	H. J. Hunt
Missoula	James A. Hart	Dan L. Rice	Clare Kern	Frank Reich	Mrs. A. Jaqueth
Nebraska					
Beatrice	Allen Davison	Gene H. Burton	Cecil Hess	Adolph Gerdes	A. G. Kleman
Fremont	F. A. Johnson	Robt. F. Millard	J. H. Mordhorst	R. B. English	L. L. Larsen
Grand Island	E. M. McDermott	Joe M. Bosler	Richard Evans	John Paustian	F. S. White
Hastings	Wendell Foote	George Maul	R. J. Van Fleet	Jacob Trupp	Edward L. Dier
Kearney	E. G. Tunks	R. T. Nelson	Bernard Harden	James Harvey	Mrs. H. J. Nelson
Lincoln	B. S. Martin	Jos. T. Carroll	E. P. Feaster	James H. Ager	Theo. H. Berg
Norfolk	B. A. McCreary	Irvin F. Ferris	R. H. Wolff	C. F. Cochran	Alvin S. Ahlman
North Platte	C. J. Frazier	Dorrall Young	L. E. Mills	W. L. Wood	L. E. Mehlmann
Omaha	J. Rosenblatt	Harry Green	....	R. McClintock	M. J. Dineen, Jr.
Scottsbluff	C. N. Williams	Cecil Rhoads	Jim Bramwell	Arnold Gesterfield	C. D. Schwaner
Nevada					
Henderson	James B. French	George Grisler	Donald Richards	H. Muehleisen[35]	H. E. Parsons
Las Vegas	C. D. Baker	Ray Sheffer	Elmer Gates	Kenneth Hadland	Shirley Ballinger
Reno	Len Harris	T. R. Berrum	Karl Evans	Bruce Clogston	E. E. Gill
New Hampshire					
Berlin	Aime Tondreau	Herman Oleson	O. B. Burquist	Robert Lowe	James E. Cryans
Claremont	Mrs. M. Phillips	William C. Hobbs	E. J. Dansereau	Wilfred Picard	Mrs. R. Haugsrud
Concord	Howe Anderson	Walter Carlson	C. H. Green	....	Arthur E. Roby
Dover	Thos. H. Keenan	John Murphy	Carroll M. Nash	Larry Myers	A. J. Guilmette
Keene	J. Alfred Dennis	W. T. Bridgham	W. R. Messer	P. A. Hanley	Mrs. L. Warren
Laconia	Bernard Boutin	Charles Dunleavy	Merle Sargent	....	K. R. Dunlap
Manchester	J. T. Benoit	F. McGranaghan	G. N. Guevin	T. E. McIntyre	M. J. Quinn
Nashua	L. H. Burnham	Joseph L. Regan	A. J. Molloy	Raymond Lee	Edw. S. LeBlanc
Portsmouth	John J. Leary	Martin O. Betz	F. R. Crompton	Nat O. Stevens	T. J. McDonough
Rochester	Robt. W. Watson	J. E. J. Levesque	R. G. Seavey	Geo. C. Nadeau[39]	D. Arlene Baker
New Jersey					
Asbury Park	Roland J. Hines	Fred Lembke	E. C. Hutchinson	....	Mrs. M. Martin
Atlantic City	Joseph Altman	J. J. Sullivan	Zenus Mathis	Isaac Pincus	B. E. Whitman
Bayonne	G. Di Domenico	Robert O'Connor	P. Kenny, Sr.	D. J. Hennessey	John F. Lee
Belleville	I. J. Padula	George R. Spatz	Harry White	Elmer S. Hyde[11]	Mrs. F. R. Morey
Bergenfield	Edward C. Meyer	K. Vehrkens	John Maddocks	Walter Foley[8]	E. L. Willis[32]
Bloomfield	Donald H. Scott	Fred Hess	Thos. F. Gussner	....	J. Cory Johnson[31]
Bridgeton	Thomas A. Dailey	J. F. Semple	John Peguesse	Howard L. Gandy	J. W. Chinnici
Burlington	A. T. Greski	P. J. Yurngling	Franklin Janson	....	Elmer S. Gares
Camden	Geo. E. Brunner	Gustav Koerner	....	C. M. Harris	J. T. Odorisio
Carteret	Frank Bareford	George Sheridan	Stanley Macioch	Michael Breza	G. J. Brechka[32]
Cliffside Park	F. J. Murphy	John J. McEvoy	James McGrath	J. W. Mahoney	John J. Bird
Clifton	Dr. J. Surgent	Paul Dittrich	John Zanet	Edward de Vido	Edith M. Marrion
Collingswood	A. E. Armitage	Frank J. McCart	C. B. Rudderow	Wm. E. Collings	R. S. Wigfield
Cranford	....	Lester W. Powell	H. G. Schindler	....	J. Walter Coffee
Dover	John Roach, Jr.	John J. Valley	Chas. A. Gustin	K. A. Heaton	Earl C. Nelson
Dumont	Joseph J. Hishon	H. Allmers, Sr.	....	A. J. Schafer	J. R. Zellweger
East Brunswick Twp.	Louis F. May, Jr.	J. W. Maslanka	3 Volunteer Cos.	....	Frank H. Smith
East Orange	W. M. McConnell	John F. McGinty	Geo. J. Rebhan	Graham Skea[40]	Alice I. Webster
East Paterson	Louis Dodero	Ralph Bloor	Geo. Geissler, Jr.	....	W. A. Bredder
Elizabeth	Steven J. Bercik	Edw. E. Flaherty	Edw. F. Deignan	J. L. Sullivan	T. P. Luchio
Englewood	Albert Moskin	Jack Abrams	Edw. T. Truslowe	E. Brarmann, Jr.	J. T. Carney
Ewing Twp. (Trenton)	Peter J. de Flesco	W. C. Forst, Jr.	Vol. Fire Dept.	Edw. J. Leadem	W. L. Nason
Fair Lawn	Frank Sogorka	Louis Risacher	H. Fensterer	Rolf Hempel	Donald DeBruin
Fort Lee	J. H. Kerwien	Theo. D. Grieco	D. Bridenberg	....	W. S. Corker
Garfield	Emil J. Sadloch	N. L. Perrapato	Gasmer Rembish	....	Joseph J. Novack
Glen Rock	F. A. Demarest	John J. Mulqueen	Raymond Struck	Jacobus Jacobs[6]	Ruth G. Sterger
Gloucester	F. W. Floyd	T. Winkelspecht	Walter Klaus	....	Edward J. Ronan
Hackensack	Edgar P. Deuell	W. Demarest	W. C. Frodsham	Carl Blume	Ethel M. Hoyt

State and City	Mayor	Police Chief	Fire Chief	Park Superintendent	City Clerk
N. J. (cont.)					
Haddon Twp. (Westmont)	W. G. Rohrer, Jr.	William Snyder	Edward Turner	....	Ethel Atkinson
Haddonfield	E. A. Farrington	William Padgett	Russell M. Hunt	....	J. Ross Logan[32]
Hamilton Sq. (Trenton)	Jos. A. Jansen	Philip Booz	....	....	Frank A. Priest[31]
Harrison	F. E. Rodgers	Martin A. Flynn	Walter B. Tuite	....	Chas. A. Farley[31]
Hawthorne	Louis Bay, 2nd.	Ryan Vandervalk	Dominic Mele	....	George V. Grillo[32]
Hillside	V. Wm. DiBuono	Paul F. Korlesky	A. H. Daviet, Sr.	Peter Humanik	Howard J. Bloy[31]
Hoboken	John J. Grogan	John Reynolds	George F. Bonin	....	Arthur C. Malone
Irvington	Edw. J. McKenna	August Hock	Wm. S. Holleran	Harry Schipper	T. M. Maloney[31]
Jersey City	Bernard J. Berry	M. J. Cusack	Thos. J. Maloney	David Post	J. F. Fitzpatrick[2]
Kearny	Joseph M. Healey	James Hanna	Wm. Wandras	Philip Alden	Donald Allan
Linden	William J. Hurst	Chas. H. Bettle	Frank T. Miller	F. M. Krysiak	Thos. J. Wieser
Livingston	Arthur N. Skeels	Richard D. Swain	Charles Schilling	Robert D. Sisco	W. P. Schilling[31]
Lodi	Joseph F. Cuccia	Paul A. Trocola	John Gutches	....	J. D. Pacella
Long Branch	Daniel J. Maher	Thomas J. Marks	Arthur T. Green	Paul Kiernan[11]	S. J. Camassa
Lyndhurst	W. F. Gallagher	Otto Bayer	Edw. L. Barbieri	Patsy De Loy	Fred O. Taub
Madison	Thomas T. Taber	Edward W. Hinch	R. L. Chambers	Carl J. Granese	Mrs. E. Garrett[32]
Manville	Frank W. Baron	John J. Jasinski	John Lisay	Joseph Halar[10]	F. A. Peltack[32]
Maplewood	T. W. Sweeney	Harold R. Dowd	Louis Zimmer	Richard Walter	S. Y. Ronnie[31]
Maywood	W. C. Layton, Jr.	H. A. Herzog	John Stedtler	George Gerdes	Catherine Odgen[32]
Metuchen	Karl E. Metzger	Enos J. Fouratt	Walter DuDasko	....	R. D. Renninger[32]
Millburn	William B. Gero	F. J. Stoeckle	F. David Hayes	George H. Bauer	T. L. Widmayer[31]
Millville	B. H. Corson	S. G. Fithian	J. F. Wettstein	....	C. A. Waltman
Monroe (Williamstown)	Louis J. Pace	Joseph Burger	Roy Agresta	....	H. B. Horn[31]
Montclair	Wm. L. Dill, Jr.	Harry Knowles	Arthur W. Bilby	Alan L. Heil	Mrs. R. E. Ives[31]
Morristown	J. R. Manahan	Eugene B. Bauer	Elliott Lindquist	Paul Abato	Edw. V. Ehlers[31]
Mt. Holly	Wm. S. Vaughan	Earl J. Donnelly	Clifford Boxer	Wm. J. Gordon	Wm. P. Hatch[31]
Neptune	Jos. A. Shafto	S. Wm. Maas	....	....	John Knox[31]
Newark	Leo P. Carlin	F. R. Lacey	H. J. Sommers	M. E. Petrone	H. Reichenstein
New Brunswick	C. W. Paulus	George F. Kane	Arthur C. Jaques	Thomas Baker	H. W. Dwyer
New Milford	M. R. LaBarbera	Harry L. Jordan	Henry Ventor	....	F. J. J. Kehoe
No. Arlington	Peter R. Tonner	John F. Eagan	Ed. J. Kelly	....	Miss C. Shavinsky[32]
North Bergen	Angelo J. Sarubbi	John Schlicht	Warren Andes	....	Joseph Kelly[31]
No. Plainfield	H. R. McCusker	Ralph C Farmer	F. S. Reynolds	....	Mrs. L. Borman[32]
Nutley	H. W. Chenoweth	Charles Rummel	Andrew Hutch	F. H. Young[21, 41]	Miss F. Rutan[31]
Orange	Russell A. Riley	Edward Burke	Edward Burke	R. E. Giordano[3]	M. J. Donlon
Palisades	Edw. J. Reisch	Leonard Cottrell	Joseph Benedetto	William Todd	Mary E. McGee
Paramus	Fred C. Galda	Carl W. Jockish	Chas. W. Ehret	....	H. W. Hebberd
Parsippany Twp. (Troy Hills)	F. E. Walter, Jr.	Leo D'Orsi	....	....	Mrs. B. Spitzel[31]
Passaic	Paul G. Demuro	Edward Boyko	John Boyko	Benj. Turner, Jr.	A. C. Martini
Paterson	Edw. J. O'Byrne	James Walker	H. Strathearn	Fred Heuser	Frank J. Sciro
Pennsauken	W. B. Hutchinson, Jr.	R. C. Walton	W. R. Clements	E. Raymond III	G. E. Ruddick
Perth Amboy	J. J. Flynn, Jr.	John Swallick	Arthur Brown	Andrew Dillman	P. P. Costello
Phillipsburg	Francis B. Moule	John W. Budd	B. G. Hughes	Gabriel Dobos	H. R. Carhart
Plainfield	A. D. Tompkins	P. J. Murray	F. F. Donovan	....	Fred Toegel
Pleasantville	W. Scott Ireland	W. H. Atkinson	Clarence Johnson	Geo. B. Martin[29]	N. Andrews
Princeton	P. MacK. Sturges	John H. Smith	George Cahill	I. Russell Riker	R. F. Mooney[32]
Rahway	James G. Egolf	L. E. Coman	James R. Stevens	....	Robt. W. Schrof
Red Bank	George A. Gray	Frank Reuther	Everett Brower	....	Mrs. A. E. Shinn
Ridgefield	Howard Mayer	Walter Gallagher	Theodore Berger	....	Otto Ehrlich[32]
Ridgefield Park	Ross S. Vogt	Jos. E. Gorman	Emil Schmidt	Anthony Zoda	H. J. Jones[37]
Ridgewood	Robert L. Olson	Stephen Janas	Wm. Haldane	Henry Leuning	W. P. Mitchell
Roselle	James G. Argyros	W. M. Personette	E. M. Johns	....	Mrs. J. Krulish[32]
Roselle Park	A. M. Dorfner	Edward Stevens	Stephen Mangan[2]	....	Chas. E. Renton[32]
Rutherford	R. Van Winkle	E. E. Bigelman	Chas. Divona	V. Brydon	H. J. Landshof
Sayreville	A. J. Popowski	Harry Olson	Julius Szkodny	Joseph Ziemba[29]	Mary Guilfoyle[32]
Somerville	Walter F. Scott	Fredk. Eckhoff[2]	Luther B. Speer	....	Edith A. Varley
South Orange	J. Augenblick[20]	T. Fitzsimmons	John J. Reynolds	T. F. Tracey, Jr.	M. S. Jenkins[37]
South Plainfield	Robt. M. Baldwin	A. A. Phillips	Joseph Delaney	....	Charles Carone
South River	W. W. Schack	M. Zaleski	Geza Kish	Geza Kish	W. A. Reichenhach, Jr.
Summit	C. Philip Dean	Edward K. Egan	Thos. J. Murray	....	Harry C. Kates
Teaneck	C. J. Harte	C. J. Harte	Wm. Lindsay[2]	Maurice S. Bowen	C. A. Christensen
Tenafly	Clifton S. Fleet	C. B. Campbell	Edmund A. Hoag	A. F. Marquez	E. B. Phillips[32]
Trenton	D. J. Cnonolly	James A. DiLouie	Thos. J. Phelan	Dennis Kuhn	S. H. Maziarz
Union	F. Biertuempfel	Jacob F. Denk	Harold H. Denk	Mrs. E. Egbert	W. Friberger[31]
Union City	Harry J. Thourot	Edw. J. Mescall	C. Friedel, Jr.	V. Nagele	W. G. Turner
Verona	Willard E. Dodd	Edgar D. Coffin	Alex Owens	....	C. C. Krouder
Vineland	Frank J. Testa	A. L. Joseph[24]	Thomas Dell[3]	Jack Claes[4]	John J. Daneri
Wall Twp. (Belmar)	B. H. Danskin	Vernon Shibla	3 Fire Dist.	Earl W. Stines	Boris S. Blum
Wayne	Robt. A. Roe, Jr.	Frank C. Harris	J. Spencer Smith	....	Peter MacDonald
Weehawken	C. F. Krause, Jr.	Edward J. Kirk	Isreal Reeves	Theo. Hanuszek	J. S. Mirabelli[31]
Westfield	H. E. Thomas	A. Pfirrmann	William Linden	W. T. Vanderbilt	Mrs. J. F. Jones[31]
West New York	J. R. Armellino	Fred Roos	Albert Schneider	Dominick Strada	R. F. Gabriel[31]
West Orange	Walter A. Quinn	Harry H. Hain	G. Leo Coleman	Wm. E. Boland	T. J. Williams[31]
Woodbridge	H. B. Quigley	John R. Egan	....	Edward Kath	B. J. Dunigan[31]
Woodbury	H. W. Peterson	R. Braithwood	Albert R. Lutz	Samuel Scott	Wm. A. Costello[7]
New Mexico					
Albuquerque	M. Sanchez[42]	Paul Shaver	A. Westerfeld	Robert Burgan[4]	Ida V. Malone
Artesia	W. H. Yeager	....	....	....	T. H. Ragsdale
Carlsbad	Elmer L. Skinner	Rex Morris	Ira J. Stockwell	Ed. Daniel	H. E. McMinn
Clovis	O. G. Potter	C. Witherspoon	George Maddox	Ellis Green	Mabel Pate
Gallup	D. F. Mollica	Manuel Gonzales	R. Kauzlaric		Dean Middleton
Hobbs	J. T. Sayers	Earl D. Westfall	Archie Conner	J. H. Siler	Mrs. H. Anderson
Las Cruces	James E. Neleigh	Santos Ramirez	P. O. Maese	C. N. Vlachakis	R. E. Howell
Roswell	Ernest C. Tucker	L. Thompson, Jr.	Geo. Daniels	A. B. Gwinn	L. G. Lint
Santa Fe	Leo T. Murphy	Ben A. Martinez	Ellis Bauer	Henry Montoya	M. T. Sebastian

State and City	Mayor	Police Chief	Fire Chief	Park Superintendent	City Clerk
New York					
Albany	E. Corning, 2nd	John P. Tuffey	M. J. Fleming	M. Leisenfelder	J. E. Gilmartin
Amsterdam	F. J. Martuscello	Andrew Celmer	Samuel Palombo	Charles J. Piltz	Anthony Sandy
Auburn	H. T. Anderson	John F. Tenity	Luke J. Bergan	Patsy DeLuca[2]	Wm. H. McKeon
Batavia	H. D. Gabriel	Stanley N. Smith	Harold Case[2]	Harry S. Boyd	Frank Corti
Beacon	H. A. Kennelly	Jesse B. Dingee	Joseph Catalano	John L. Roberts	George Mordas
Bedford (Bedford Hills)	D. L. Barrett[36]	F. R. Mallette	3 Fire Dists.	John Kinkel	Wm. J. Millmore
Binghamton	D. W. Kramer	M. J. Hanifin	F. J. Buckman	M. J. Bednar[3]	George R. Beers
Buffalo	Steven Pankow	J. A. DeCillis[11]	Wm. H. Daly[11]	J. A. Ulinski	A. J. Partyka
Camillus	W. H. Forward[21]	Frank Pugh	....	....	Lloyd O'Hara[31]
Cohoes	R. I. Roulier	Jos. R. Garrett	Harold Grogan	William Harris	George O. Boivin
Corning	Daniel Stimson	R. J. Laurence	J. A. Doolittle	Philip Grannan	Charles E. Hause
Cortland	Robert C. Keeney	M. Canestaro	Leland Foster	Alfred R. Reilly	Chas. G. Houser
Dunkirk	Geo. T. Wheeler	Richard M. Kinn[2]	William Cybulski	....	J. J. Ricotta
Eastchester	F. X. O'Rourke[36]	V. D. Fisher	Robert J. White	V. D. Bellew	A. N. Ferris[31]
Elmira	Edw. A. Mooers	Eugene F. Golden	Louis J. Mosher	James McGovern	Edward L. Kelly
Endicott	C. B. Parkhurst	Leon F. Coleman	Paul L. Brown	....	R. A. Jackson[37]
Floral Park	Wm. N. Lewis	P. V. Maickel	Robert Channing	Arthur J. Ennis	C. J. Hartman[37]
Freeport	Wm. F. Glacken	Peter Elar	D. Mauersberger	Theodore Combs	M. F. VanRiper[37]
Fulton	J. S. Johnson, Jr.	Karl Stewart	George Allen	Roy Van Alstine	F. A. Campbell
Garden City	W. J. Caye, Jr.	S. J. Vandewater	R. F. Rowden	....	E. R. Courtney[37]
Geneva	W. Erle Rogers	J. E. McDonough	L. L. McGuigan	....	Mrs. L. Wright
Glen Cove	J. A. Snozzi	Frank V. McCue	Rocco Genova	John Callahan	M. Capobianco
Glen Falls	M. G. Tibbitts	F. D. Sullivan[2]	F. M. Preston	E. J. Anderson	Basil J. Durkee
Gloversville	R. B. Haviland	John G. Farrell	H. C. Maxson	T. R. Dukelow	Donald W. Fox
Greenburgh (Tarrytown)	E. H. Innet[36]	J. F. Sheridan	C. B. Nichols	....	Eliz. Smith[31]
Harrison	J. M. Landis[36]	Wm. W. Donovan	Ludwig Okon	A. J. Valentino	Joseph F. Fiore
Hempstead	Wm. O. Gulde	John L. Feeley	Jos. Nadolony	Arthur Seigmann	Lael Von Elm[37]
Hornell	Lloyd R. Burdett	Harold P. Lewis	F. V. Kinnerney	G. E. Clancy[6]	Jas. O. Stephens
Hudson	John L. Kelly	John J. Sullivan	T. L. Montana	H. V. Harding	H. R. Deacon
Huntington	Jos. W. Ceremak	Ray Leighton	....	Gilbert Scudder	R. J. McNulty[31]
Irondequoit (Rochester)	W. G. Lauterbach	H. R. McFarlin	5 Volunteer	....	Fred E. Hussey
Islip	Thos. J. Harwood	B. W. Gaiser	....	....	T. J. Harwood[31]
Ithaca	John F. Ryan	Wm. C. Simmers	Frank C. Stamp[2]	Richard S. Baker	George A. Blean
Jamestown	Carl F. Sanford	John Paladino	Chas. R. Dorman	....	C. H. Watson
Johnson City	D. E. Stocum	Floyd L. Allen	George Hannon	Arthur Hibler	Herbert Schaefer
Johnstown	Harvey Mansfield	J. P. Cerrone	John H. Walker	C. W. Knowles	Archibald Wands
Kenmore	Geo. D. Toomey	Elmer A. Arnet	R. J. Kirsch	R. J. Kirsch	C. F. Lane[37]
Kingston	F. H. Stang	R. Van Buren	James Brett	A. Murphy, 3rd	B. S. Kramer
Lackawanna	W. J. Paryz, Jr.	Walter Woyshner	George Yovienne	....	Andrew Eszak
Lockport	F. J. Moyer, Jr	F. J. Tracy	Daniel N. Haley	Nelson C. Goehle	K. F. Anderson
Long Beach	M. J. Fleischman	Philip B. Kohut	Nicholas Green	Michael McNulty	A. De Paola
Lynbrook	Fred A. Greis	Walter Waring	Albert J. Hart	....	H. E. Dana[37]
Mamaroneck	Edwin B. Dooley	J. P. Geary	John Grainger	....	F. H. Bull, Jr.
Massena	Ralph M. Johns	Thomas O'Neil	Joseph King	....	Wm. B. McMillan
Middletown	R. E. Swalm	Russell Adgate	G. R. Truex	....	N. F. Vuolo
Mineola	C. N. Williams	Nassau County	H. P. Cornwell	....	D. G. Hunt[37]
Mt. Vernon	J. P. Vaccarella	Eugene Bradford	Edward V. Gall	....	Walter Meyer
Newark	M. H. Elzufon	Edwin J. Lawton	Karl E. West	T. S. Knight	C. A. Hausman, Jr.[37]
Newburgh	Wm. D. Ryan	J. J. Mullarkey	G. W. M. Brown	William Cooney	L. B. Crabtree
New Rochelle	George Vergara	Alfred Breuckner	Raymond Rumery	Anthony J. Drew	Chas. U. Combes
New York	Robert F. Wagner	S. P. Kennedy[11]	E. Cavanagh, Jr.[11]	Robert Moses[11]	Thos. A. Lenane[2]
Niagara Falls	Calvin L. Keller	Charles Gorman	Leo F. Heck	Thos. DeFranco	James E. Collins
No. Tonawanda	F. B. Durkee	P. F. Grimaldi	R. J. Kropp	Wm. L. Ramsay	Edw. L. Bothwell
Ogdensburg	Lee W. Keyes	Leo P. LeBeau	Francis Cadieux	Ross R. Jermano	Simon S. Sargent
Olean	Ivers J. Norton	George Finger	Frank W. Savage	James Driscoll	F. L. Kelly
Oneida	Robert D. Kruger	James A. Murphy	E. H. McCulley	....	M. A. Whitcombe
Oneonta	Roger G. Hughes	Robert Simmons	Joseph Scanlon	Clarence Taylor	Olof N. Nelson
Ossining	J. A. Collyer, Jr.	Arthur W. Mead	Duane C. Byble	....	John E. Susse
Oswego	Robert G. Iles	John J. Reed	Monte R. Lass	....	Frank D. Dowdle
Peekskill	John E. Hayes	Peter King	Charles Olah	Larry Gallo	D. J. Schneider
Pelham	Gordon Miller[36]	Westchester Co.	Westchester Co.	....	Geo. O'Sullivan[31]
Plattsburg	John J. Tyrell	C. J. Young	J. K. Gervais	M. W. Walker	George E. Miller
Port Chester	A. J. Zaccagnino	Fred C. Ponty	W. E. Studwell	George Craig	F. S. Tarascio
Poughkeepsie	J. Thomas Dietz	J. L. Martin, Jr.	I. D. Merrick	John Miller	H. D. Matteson[43]
Rensselaer	C. A. McNally	Charles Stewart	Louis Dombrosch	....	H. C. Younghans
Riverhead	Wm. J. Leonard[36]	S. J. Grodski	Edw. Gadzinski	....	A. F. Gadzinski[31]
Rochester	Peter Barry	William Winfield	W. J. Adams	Wilbur Wright[3]	Thos. P. O'Leary
Rockville Ctr.	W. Harry Lister	Thomas A. Eibler	John J. Murray	Joseph Deziadus	Frank A. Ernst[37]
Rome	Joseph G. Herbst	James C. Dunn	Wm. M. Campbell	....	Joseph E. Lolo
Rye	Robert P. Hughes	Robt. A. Warren	Emil Palombo	....	R. Fred Talento
Saratoga Sprgs.	Addison Mallery	Robert Flanagan	Robert Carroll	John Comiskey	Jerome V. Pitney
Scarsdale	Willard P. Scott	James M. Lyons	Wm. J. Duhigg	....	Ethel M. Hyde
Schenectady	S. S. Stratton	Wm. F. Brandt	Edw. M. Moffett	....	F. K. Keller
Smithtown	H. F. Potter[36]	Cyril Donnelly	....	Thos. E. Heasley	Victor T. Liss[31]
Syracuse	Donald H. Mead	Harry F. Kelly	F. J. Ferren	Wm. A. Barry[11]	Edward R. Apps
Tonawanda	Eugene H. Duffy	C. O. Luther	Wm. Schreiber	Frank Keller	Mrs. I. Rogalsky
Troy	John J. Purcell	J. W. Dougherty	Carl A. Smith		T. Monahan, Jr.
Utica	J. T. McKennan	....	Leo Wheeler	Joseph Arcuri	A. DeGironomo
Valley Stream	Henry Waldinger	....	Daniel Coakley	....	F. G. Chalmers
Watertown	W. G. Lachenauer	Edward G. Curtin	Joseph Dibble	Kenneth Osborne	E. D. Brior
Watervliet	H. F. Donnelly	M. J. Kennan	Edw. G. Hughes	Frank Blair	Robt. L. Diamond
West Seneca	C. G. Germain[36]	C. J. Kauderer[2]	Volunteer	Joseph Pfeulb	J. S. Lehmann[31]
White Plains	E. G. Michaelian	Wm. A. Sullivan	E. J. MacDonald	....	M. W. Kane
Yonkers	K. Kristensen	James McCue	William Garvin	L. Tartaglione	Wm. Gray, Jr.
Yorktown	J. H. Downing[36]	Earl Hawk	Charles DeMilo	....	K. K. Wyand[31]
North Carolina					
Albemarle	D. A. Moose	C. C. Tarleton	C. E. Morris	Wm. T. Robinette	Henry T. Deane
Asheville	Earl W. Eller	A. R. Sluder	J. C. Fitzgerald	Augusta Barnett	M. Simmons

State and City	Mayor	Police Chief	Fire Chief	Park Superintendent	City Clerk
N. C. (cont.)					
Burlington	Paul J. Craig	Jesse R. James	Roma C. Fortune	J. C. Davidson	R. P. Pope[44]
Charlotte	P. L. Van Every	F. N. Littlejohn	Donald S. Charles	Marion Dhiel	L. R. Hoffman
Concord	Zack L. Roberts	A. L. Murr	Charles L. Miller	....	C. S. Morgan, Jr.
Durham	E. J. Evans	W. W. Pleasants	C. L. Cox	C. R. Wood	Mrs. E. N. Jones
Elizabeth City	L. S. Blades, Jr.	W. C. Owens	W. K. Davis	....	H. K. Houtz
Fayetteville	Geo. B. Herndon	L. F. Worrell	C. A. Cain	Selwyn Orcutt	Mrs. L. Talbot
Gastonia	Leon I. Schneider	G. F. Peninger	John Farris	J. W. Emmett	John T. Beam
Goldsboro	Scott B. Berkeley	H. A. Lane	C. Wesley Howell	E. L. Simmons	Ralph G. Jones
Greensboro	J. A. Cannon, Jr.	Paul Calhoun	C. W. Wyrick	Oka T. Hester	Mrs. H. N. Burch
Greenville	W. L. Whedbee	S. G. Gibbs	Geo. W. Gardner	J. Goodman, Jr.	H. H. Duncan
Henderson	Henry T. Powell	J. E. Parks	C. G. Ellis	J. E. Hamlett	W. G. Royster
Hickory	D. S. Menzies	M. L. Little	E. G. Moser	R. C. Carlton	H. L. Burdette[15]
High Point	G. A. Covington	C. C. Stoker	C. S. Canady	W. B. Stronach[3]	Mrs. L. W. Smith
Jacksonville	A. J. Lewis	Clyde R. Cook	Edward Riddle	J. E. Amyette	W. D. Starling
Kinston	Guy Elliott	Marion Haskins	J. S. Gray	....	T. W. Heath
Lenoir	Earl H. Tate	Stanley E. Crisp	A. Y. Cottrell	....	E. A. Poe, Jr.
Lexington	Dr. E. J. Catheli	V. G. Price	Norman Owen	....	P. Yarborough
Monroe	M. W. Williams	A. A. Mauney	J. A. Helms	....	Mrs. Clara Smith
New Bern	Mack L. Lupton	Ed. Belangia	R. M. Whitley	....	H. E. Russell
Raleigh	Fred B. Wheeler	Tom Davis	J. B. Keeter	E. J. Anderson	C. H. Pritchard
Reidsville	George Hunt	M. F. Loftis	H. W. White	W. L. Harrelson	N. R. Baker, Jr.
Rocky Mount	Page K. Gravely	J. I. Nichols	W. B. Parrish	H. G. Bolick	L. B. Aycock
Salisbury	E. Linwood Foil	D. L. Shuler	Chas. L. Burkett	C. W. Kesler	J. W. Ellis
Sanford	H. Makepeace	Joe B. Watson	J. O. Bridges	....	A. B. Harrington
Shelby	H. S. Woodson	W. K. Hardin	James Reid	Robert Hartley	Reeves Forney
Statesville	J. Garner Bagnal	Frank Hartness	L. M. Gaither, Sr.	E. B. Stafford	A. E. Guy
Thomasville	Carl C. Wilson	Paul M. Shore	Lindsay Loftin	J. D. Foust	Mrs. Eva Jones
Wilmington	Dan D. Cameron	J. J. Padrick	J. A. West	Arnold Peterson	Mrs. M. Southerland
Wilson	John D. Wilson	A. A. Privette	Tyrus R. Bissett	J. B. Gillette	Troy T. Lynn
Winston-Salem	M. C. Kurfees	James I. Waller	E. M. Dixon	C. R. Faust[45]	Ralph L. Dixon
North Dakota					
Bismarck	Evan E. Lips	D. Schoeneman	Harry Homan	Geo. Schaumberg	Tom Baker[46]
Fargo	H. Lashkowitz[17]	J. Walter Olson	Fred E. Saefke	C. P. Reed	W. G. Johnson[46]
Grand Forks	Oscar Lunseth	R. H. Jagd	J. P. Newark	Homer A. Abbott	R. S. Niles[46]
Jamestown	W. F. Sharp	Wm. M. Bennett	Percy Wellman	....	F. P. Gilronan[46]
Minot	W. M. Harrington	W. L. Trout	Gilbert C. Malek	D. T. Ritchey	R. E. Barcus[46]
Williston	W. O. Burk[17]	Donald Hewson	D. L. McCrory	C. W. Halphide	H. Grimstvedt[46]
Ohio					
Akron	Leo Berg	Harry Whiddon	Gerald Vernotzy	R. Barnhardt	C. M. Butler
Alliance	Harley R. Ewing	A. O. Lower	Milo Sights	E. E. Kidwell	C. D. Steffy[12]
Ashland	Paul Chorpening	Harry Smith	Paul Soles	F. Brownson	R. H. Moore
Ashtabula	C. R. Kadon	Leo J. Kane	A. T. Rohl	Arthur Venditti	Nelmo Rinto
Athens	P. B. Seel	J. B. Grogan	Charles Dalton	....	O. G. Houck[12]
Barberton	C. R. Dobbs	Martin Seryak	Luther Culbertson	Chas. McCafferty	R. E. Flickinger[46]
Bedford	Robert J. Krauss	Jas. F. Gresham	E. R. Smith	....	F. B. Morris
Bellaire	A. G. DeMarco	Edward Good	Chas. Jewell, Sr.	Raymond Potter	Mrs. B. Bennett
Bellefontaine	G. Louie Wren	A. D. Paden	George Young	Homer Arnett	Mrs. C. Kerns[46]
Berea	Edw. T. Manning	Augustine Yanke	Ronald Garlick	....	P. O. Miller
Bexley	W. A. Schneider	R. E. McNamee	....	W. Montgomery	R. C. Linscott[46]
Bowling Green	Lorin H. Janzer	Guy Spitler	Morris Instone	C. C. Foster	Jane Coller
Bucyrus	J. L. Sullivan	A. L. Stuckert	Ralph L. Mead	....	Anita Deisler
Cambridge	Russell B. Diehl	H. W. Watkins	H. C. Callihan	Wynn Clipner	P. L. Phillips[12]
Campbell	M. J. Kovach	John Putko	Julius Torok	....	John Sambolec[46]
Canton	Carl F. Wise	J. B. Quilligan	W. H. Rosche	Carl O. Weis	M. Kouskouris[12]
Chillicothe	F. D. Harper	A. Russell Poole	Floyd J. Irwin	....	J. K. Rudell[46]
Cincinnati	Charles P. Taft	S. J. Schrotel	B. J. Houston	....	R. A. MacDonald
Cleveland	A. J. Celebrezze	Frank W. Story	Elmer M. Cain	....	Thad Fusco[12]
Cleveland Hgts.	Karl J. Ertle	Edward Gaffney	Frank Veasley	Ray Martin	Edward Schuele
Columbus	M. Sensenbrenner	George Scholer	W. Strickfaden	Ray Dietz	A. Brown Cain
Conneaut	Ralph S. Wright	John W. Sanford	Louis F. Stevens	....	Geo. Kitinoja
Coshocton	F. E. Wisenburg	R. Schumaker	Walter Weaver	....	N. H. Lewis
Cuyahoga Falls	Elmer Wolf	Menzo Preston	Louis P. Seiler	Carl F. Fuerst	A. McKinnon[47]
Dayton	Henry S. Stout	Paul J. Price	Forrest B. Lucas	Robert S. Miller[48]	Oscar F. Mauch
Defiance	Elmer C. Rost	C. D. Nestleroad	Harvey Hughes	Ezra Whitney	R. A. Crossland
Delaware	Edw. A. Flahive	D. M. Morris	Carl Zimmerman[2]	John Woodworth	R. E. Bayliff
East Cleveland	Chas. A. Carran[15]	H. S. Weaver	F. W. Lange	W. L. Robertson	G. T. Apthorp[49]
East Liverpool	Arnold W. Devon	Robert Pyle	Charles Bryan	Wm. Bell	H. J. Gallimore[46]
Elyria	J. Grant Keys	Maurice C. Flood	W. E. Bates	John Machock	Carol Cerlan
Euclid	Kenneth J. Sims	Ernest Peters	Robert Gill	Robert Henn	Wm. Johnson[44]
Findlay	Wm. J. Carlin	Wayne F. Ethell	Homer Johnson	....	Reva E. Schimmel
Fostoria	Ray R. Coburn	E. A. Richard	T. E. Walsh	Park Munger	L. C. Huth[12]
Fremont	John M. Collins	Myron Bork	Urban Myers	Walter Roser	P. P. Leite[12]
Garfield Hghts.	Neil E. Bowler	William Schiederl	A. Provenzano	....	E. Szymkowski[37]
Girard	Joseph Catone	W. R. Flory	Nathan Walker	....	D. V. Gorenc[46]
Hamilton	Edward Beckett	John A. Bippus	G. Schlotterbeck	Virgil M. Ellis	Adele Edmonds
Ironton	O. M. Wiseman[15]	Harold F. Haas	John McGerty	Donald R. Malone	Don Hopkins[12]
Kent	R. E. Manchester	F. R. Grubb	Fred Miller	A. H. Dessum[1]	Mrs. E. Kline[12]
Kettering	R. Stanley Dybvig	John Shryock	William Melke	....	Martha G. Wood
Lakewood	Frank P. Celeste	F. E. Stephens	J. V. Redmond	Russell Southack	Henry A. Rees
Lancaster	J. Harvey Weis	Sam H. Hutsler	Walter O. Myers	Donald Bainter	J. W. Brocker[12]
Lima	Clyde Welty	Donald F. Miller	W. L. Hydaker	Rex Settlemire	E. T. Anderson[12]
Lorain	John C. Jaworski	Frank Pawlak	Elmer Stough	John Lisisky	John J. Slivka
Mansfield	Robert S. Lemley	Paul Martin	L. J. Steele	Frank Burton	D. Ray Fields
Maple Heights	Walter K. Maser	Edw. J. Prasek	Edw. J. Prasek	....	John J. Wetzel[46]
Marietta	Forester Farley	T. B. Sprague	D. E. Drennen	....	C. K. Smith Kitts
Marion	Gale D. Ireland	Justin Cornely	Owen A. Sifritt	George Hanley	Irene Addison
Martins Ferry	Dale Fulton	J. W. Muhleman	Wayne Troy	Frank Ellis	Maud Griffiths
Massillon	Edgar L. Lash	S. W. Switter	Donald E. Simon	C. W. Bullach	Thos. J. Coleman

State and City	Mayor	Police Chief	Fire Chief	Park Superintendent	City Clerk
Ohio (cont.)					
Middletown	F. Carmody[42]	Joseph Blackmore	Wm. Fishbaugh	Thos. R. Carlson[4]	D. E. Kronborg[49]
Mt. Vernon	P. G. Mauger	W. M. Kelly	Carrol L. White	....	Elaine Swigeart[12]
Newark	Clint E. Comer	L. L. Hall	H. C. Hannum	....	R. K. Neff[12]
New Philadelphia	Fred Schneider	Louis Clark	....	Harold Meese	Robert Stemple[46]
Niles	Edw. P. Lenney	M. McGowan	George Neiss	George Hayman	P. J. Sullivan[46]
No. College Hill	Robert V. Reuss	F. X. Niehaus	Henry Meyer	....	Rose Miller
Norwood	R. Edward Tepe	Charles W. Fritz	Thomas S. Fisher	....	Walter Pfeifer[12]
Painesville	Paul D. Cook[15]	A. E. Ivary	C. Gordon Smith	G. F. Sweet	C. V. Boudreaux
Parma	Stephen A. Zona	Lester A. Roeper	Clyde G. Jones	....	T. A. Smith[12]
Piqua	R. A. Geater	Earl McClannan	Arthur Russell	Richard Hair	William Fox[49]
Portsmouth	J. Harold Frecka	Albert Bailey[2]	Howard Kiebler	Lloyd Henderson	E. Justice
Rocky River	J. Frank Gibson	Robert Kelley	Chas. R. Duggan	Albert Scherer	C. W. Brown[46]
Salem	Dean B. Cranmer	George T. Earley	C. W. Wright	Lee A. Burton	W. C. Adams[12]
Sandusky	R. B. Fuller	Victor Adcock	W. McLaughlin	Christ Goltz & E. E. Erdman	Carl F. Breining
Shaker Heights	W. G. Stapleton	H. M. Benethum	Merle M. Hand	....	T. E. Cook[12]
Sidney	Urban H. Doorley	John Warner	Don M. Kies	Roy Detrick	Mrs. A. J. Wells[12]
South Euclid	George J. Urban	M. F. Schmies	William Fibich	M. Montagano	Lester L. Askue[46]
Springfield	Harry Strachan	Lawrence Abbott	W. G. Compton	Henry S. Cooke	W. O. Stewart[49]
Steubenville	S. S. McCormick	Ross Cunningham	Michael Cody	Frank Linton	F. A. Januszkiewicz[12]
Struthers	H. L. Milligan	G. W. Sickafuse	Sam Richards	Charles F. Mohr	M. G. Orenic, Jr.
Tiffin	Robert L. Booth	Harold J. Fraley	R. R. McElheny	Willard Griffin	M. Beidleman[46]
Toledo	Ollie Czelusta	Anthony Bosch	A. Papenhagen	Ralph C. Girkins	C. F. Diefenbach
Troy	O. S. Metcalf	J. C. Hennessey	John Kessler	Vernon Leethy	H. H. Tamplin[46]
University Heights	Earl W. Aurelius	R. Bucklin, Jr.	R. J. Benjamin	....	Jean L. Keller
Van Wert	Clark E. Spitler	M. L. Kennedy	R. G. Cryer	....	J. A. Jones[46]
Wadsworth	Don Merriman	Roderick Lonier	Charles Albers	Martin Setko	Dixie Witschey[46]
Warren	W. C. Burbank	Manley English	George Mock	Gould Stewart	A. R. Larmi[12]
Washington C. H.	B. F. Norris[20]	D. Vaiden Long	George R. Hall	R. Waters[10]	Marie Melvin
Whitehall	W. B. Moling	Ralph K. Walker	Arthur T. Reddy	....	Walter Helber[37]
Wooster	J. Edwin Johnson	Kenneth Walters	Lloyd Eberhart	Louis Cramer	M. Zimmerman
Xenia	C. M. Harner	Robert Killeen	W. T. Buffington	....	A. V. Perrill[46]
Youngstown	F. X. Kayzan	Paul H. Cress	John R. Lynch	Edward Finamore	John H. Lemon
Zanesville	S. J. Johnson	Geo. L. Hodgson	Kenneth Kerner	Harold Dillion	G. Rex Noble
Oklahoma					
Ada	A. L. Fentem	Cecil Smith	J. R. Ellis	M. L. Condren	Jas. N. King
Altus	Ben Claiborne	C. C. Brake	Charles T. White	Nollie D. Barnes	Roy Giles
Ardmore	Ab Jolly	W. O. Welch	Ed. Jennings	J. N. Pack	Tom H. Hefley
Bartlesville	W. A. Hensley	W. J. Jarvis	Walter Crowder	W. E. Young	Oleta Martin
Chickasha	Jack Linn	Roy Carman	L. J. Suddarth	Edgar Beaty	Mrs. D. Holder
Duncan	Wayne M. Holden	Jack Culberson	C. C. Lawson	Luther Prater	C. H. Smith
Durant	Charles F. Fuller	Neel Bolin	Preston Greeson	R. L. Sherrer	Mrs. J. Duncan
El Reno	Paul G. Liebmann	Lee Harvey	H. LeRoy Searcy	Arthur Mitchell	Ethel Dowell
Enid	George J. Emrick	Dale P. Moxley	A. W. Lang	Clyde A. Rowley	Clint O. Thrasher
Guthrie	R. M. Patterson	Virgil Fisher	Melvin Daniels	Wm. Thorn	H. A. Braun
Lawton	C. R. Ellsworth	Ronald Wheatley	H. V. Hancock	Jess Percival	R. M. Dodson
McAlester	Fritz Neill	Roy Anders	Ernest Rager	Wm. T. Reed	Celest O'Bannon
Miami	Roy Green	A. C. Masterson	J. R. Huxall	George Francis	E. C. Wright
Midwest City	R. D. Bamford	O. P. Bawcum	M. W. Johnson	Clifford Ensley	F. B. Foster
Muskogee	Lyman B. Beard	R. M. Pickens	Ray Jordan	Art Johnson	R. L. Davis
Norman	Paul V. Keen	J. W. Wheeler	T. Townley, Jr.	M. Clinkenbeard	D. K. Wilcox
Oklahoma City	Allen Street	Roy J. Bergman	Geo. R. McAlpine	R. R. Murphy	Earle M. Simon
Okmulgee	Dr. J. Vanderpool	Clyde Murrell	Toy McGowin	J. O. Miles	Chas. R. Poulton
Ponca City	I. H. Needham	D. F. B. Harsh	Kenneth A. Long	Wayne I. Moler	C. P. Pitts
Sapulpa	C. M. Gibson	R. C. Bradford[2]	W. M. Collier	Geo. W. Gleason	John S. Egan
Seminole	R. T. Harber	Lester Bush	John Thomas	J. W. Scruggs	H. C. Sullivan
Shawnee	A. F. Hornbeck	J. W. Holt	R. Whitecotton	R. E. Stearns	R. Hathcock
Stillwater	A. B. Alcott	Homer Boughton	Max Peery	A. E. Jantz	L. E. Goble
Tulsa	George E. Norvell	P. J. Livingston	G. R. Sartain	O. A. Zeigler	A. J. Lawrence[46]
Oregon					
Albany	W. L. Fitzpatrick	Ray H. Maddy	Don Hayne	R. O. Robertson[4]	A. R. Johnson[50]
Astoria	P. G. Cosovich	A. J. Ellsworth	Wayne Osterby	H. M. Olsvick	E. M. Opdycke[46]
Bend	H. Taylor	John T. Truett	Vernon Carlon	....	Julia S. Johnson
Corvallis	Carl Williams	C. W. Fruitt	Percy Tallman	Olin Phipps	Geo. Simerville[50]
Eugene	John J. McGinty	Vern Hill	E. L. Smith	W. Riley Matsler	D. O. Potter[50]
Klamath Falls	Lawrence Slater	O. H. Hamilton	LeRoy Rowe	Robert Bonney	F. A. Glackmer
Medford	John W. Snider	Charles Champlin	Gordon Barker	D. F. Huson	D. F. Huson
Pendleton	Norman Gorfkle	James Ness	Wm. Batchelor	....	D. L. Hitchman
Portland	T. D. Schrunk	....	Edward Grenfell	H. B. Buckley	Will Gibson[46]
Roseburg	Arlo Jacklin	Carl Rumpf	W. E. Mills	H. Isbell	Mrs. C. Farrell
Salem	Robert White	Clyde A. Warren	Robert Mills	Walter Wirth	Alfred Mundt[50]
Springfield	E. C. Harms, Jr.	Floyd L. Clower	Harry R. Krieger	Clayton Anderson	W. E. Mansell[50]
Pennsylvania					
Abington	E. U. Smiley[20]	A. G. Streeper	John Manzinger[22]	....	F. H. Schaefer[31]
Aliquippa	James Bruno[51]	Chas. J. Sorok	Ernest Kleber	....	John Mihalic[32]
Allentown	Donald V. Hock	J. L. Christine	John Butz	J. J. Gackenbach	Geo. W. Kistler
Altoona	R. W. Anthony	Vaul E. Rouzer	Samuel M. Ake	Haven S. Ale	Fred R. Walker
Ambridge	Walter Panek[51]	Andrews Bires	Wm. Rittleman	....	Joseph Rodio[32]
Arnold	M. F. Horne	George Seigart	Michael Frank	Louis Bruncsak[29]	Tom Tannas
Beaver Falls	Edw. C. Corcoran	Theodore Smith	E. H. Phillips	....	Gene B. George
Bellevue	J. H. Bragdon[51]	R. A. Morcroft	Geo. T. Kimberlin	....	Geo. R. Landers[32]
Berwick	R. C. Culp[51]	H. C. Peterson	Howard Shotwell	W. O. Hicks	D. Wm. Arndt
Bethel (Pittsburgh)	Chas. A. Geisler[15]	John Maskunas	Edward Tomsik	....	Mrs. H. Carter[32]

State and City	Mayor	Police Chief	Fire Chief	Park Superintendent	City Clerk
Penna. (cont.)					
Bethlehem	Earl E. Schaffer	R. R. Rueter	J. L. Schweder	Thomas F. Joyce	Bertram L. Nagle
Bloomsburg ...	C. Martin Lutz	Clair Collins	C. H. Learn, Jr.	....	Paul D. Jacobs
Braddock	James J. Butler[51]	Edward Goldstein	John Morenzi	....	J. J. O'Hara[32]
Bradford	Hugh J. Ryan	Edward Edmonds	Edw. F. Brophy	Edw. Sutherland	L. Schoolmaster
Brentwood	A. G. Kaufmann	A. Otto Jordan	R. P. Bauman	W. A. Colteryahn	F. E. Yeager[32]
Bristol Boro....	Anthony Niccol	Linford J. Jones	C. Haggerman	....	S. B. Rafferty[32]
Bristol Twp. (Bristol P.O.)	E. A. Wiler, Jr.[17]	John R. Stewart	Fredrick Hibbs[22]	....	T. P. Coman[31]
Butler Twp. (Butler P.O.)	L. E. Singer[20]	....	....	....	....
Butler	Walter Schweppe	J. W. Harmon	Joseph Langland	L. Loutzenhiser	Philip O. Miller
Cannonsburg ..	Fred A. Caruso[51]	N. Lesniakowski	Edward Briceland	....	Ann Bushta[32]
Carbondale	Frank P. Kelly	Francis P. Judge	Joseph Healy	Santo A. Pascoe	Thos. A. Boles
Carlisle	Harry P. Breen[51]	Charles E. Strock	Ray Kelly	I. L. Carter, Jr.	Sarah E. Coover
Carnegie	T. T. Coyne[51]	....	M. F. Schulte	J. Coyle	A. B. Lafferty
Chambersburg	H. Kottcamp	H. S. Byers	J. L. Shatzer	D. Niemond	G. B. Jacobs
Cheltenham Twp. (Elkins Park)	H. C. Pike[15]	S. C. Johnston	Owen Adams[22]	Winfred Smith	H. C. Pike[25]
Chester	J. L. Eyre	Howard Winfree	Harry Bomberger	W. Clark	R. J. Larkin, Sr.
Clairton	K. L. Stilley	Peter P. Orsini	Thomas Gregg	B. J. Watko	Wm. R. Miller
Coal Twp. (Shamokin)	Torrence Spotts[17]	William Shuey	Ed. Kropinski	....	Mrs. M. Evans[31]
Coatesville	George L. Gordon	J. D. Dougherty	J. D. Dougherty	Edw. Hause, Jr.	F. P. Pennegar
Columbia	Walter Roye[51]	E. H. McManus	Larry Smith	....	Edw. J. Dinkel[32]
Connellsville ..	Abe I. Daniels	Geo. C. Johnson	Wm. E. DeBolt	C. A. Deiter	Ralph Falco[25]
Conshohocken .	E. K. Williams	W. Phipps, Sr.	Jos. P. Thomas	Joseph Burns	Jos. J. Quinn[32]
Coraopolis	C. L. Isenberg[51]	John J. Brush	Harry G. Barker	....	Edw. N. Weaver
Darby	Alex Abbot[51]	John Buley	Russell Dodge	....	W. L. Purfield[32]
Donora	A. Z. Chambon[51]	John Pykosh	John Volk	....	T. E. Petrus[32]
Dormont (Pittsburgh).	J. K. K. Smith[51]	Ralph Miller	John Sentz	Oliver Dogleman	....
Du Bois	Wm. H. Shaw	Bert Hetrick	Homer Moncks	....	Edna Jones
Dunmore	M. F. Monahan[51]	Edw. J. Conway	M. E. Fitzpatrick	....	Jas. E. Hennigan
Duquesne	F. Kopriver, Jr.	Walter Weir	Lawrence Trainor	....	Geo. L. Vesonder
Easton	O. H. Reeves	John I. Schwarz	George T. Keller	R. R. Schooley	C. E. Rogers
Ellwood City...	J. A. McCandless	C. W. Ricer	C. V. Rodgers	....	Ethel F. Nagel
Erie	A. J. Gardner	Edw. V. Williams	Peter J. Kuhn	C. G. Downing[3]	Eugene Graney
Farrell	John E. Giroski	Albert Timparo	James C. Davis	....	John Pandza
Franklin	R. Bleakley, Jr.	R. J. Brown	A. W. Hanna	F. W. Fry, Sr.	L. A. Arnold
Greensburg ...	Robert L. Potts	Wm. Wolinsky	Ed. Hutchinson	A. A. Wesbecher[28]	F. M. Newcomer
Hanover	Wm. H. Menges[51]	J. S. Berkheimer	V. W. Kroh	....	S. D. Michael[32]
Hanover Twp. (Wilkes-Barre)	Wm. A. Ruddy[20]	H. Woodeshick	F. Cunningham	....	Andrew Garber[31]
Harrisburg ..	N. F. Ziegler	Russell R. Shot	Wm. C. McBride[2]	Clarence Beck	L. T. Burns
Harrison Twp. (Natrona) ..	H. Lamparski[17]	Alex Sosinski	Frank Brucker	....	C. A. Grove[31]
Haverford Twp. (Havertown)	O. T. Higgins[20]	Jas. F. Hartness	J. F. Hartness[22]	....	H. A. Fritschman
Hazleton	S. T. Capparell	Steve Havrilla	Paul Ziegler	Thomas Powell	F. M. West
Homestead	D. J. Lapp, Jr.	J. E. Armstrong	Geo. Bayuzick	....	Alex E. Ackley
Indiana	Wm. J. Hoey[51]	H. T. Sanford	Wm. Simpson	....	A. B. Ansley[32]
Jeannette	Frank Binda	Chas. E. Walter	Othmar Seiler	D. D. Gillespie	J. Claire Manson
Johnstown	Walter E. Rose	Chas. R. Griffith	Carl W. Espey	Louis Saylor[3]	John J. Cullen
Kingston	Wm. I. Martin	E. G. Williams	Ralph Schmoll	Henry Avery	Thos. J. Reese[32]
Lancaster	Kendig C. Bare	F. G. McCartney	Harry E. Miller	Mylin Micken	Mrs. J. B. Pontz
Lansdowne	A. S. Beers, Jr.[51]	Fred K. Roberts	R. P. Wentzel	....	Clarence H. Fox[32]
Latrobe	V. B. Stader, Jr.	C. A. College	R. P. Wible	Harold Deichert[4]	V. E. Lynch[32]
Lebanon	F. D. Miller	Lloyd E. Wolfe	Alfred Schroff	Geo. F. Paine	Mervin P. Light
Lewistown	John J. Lawler	H. O. Landis	H. E. Sheaffer	....	E. A. Stimely[32]
Lock Haven ...	D. H. Peddie	R. Merritts	Joseph Montevino	Walter Lebo	William Hollis
Lower Merion Twp. (Ardmore) ..	Evan L. James[15]	G. A. McLaughlin	Harvey Benson	C. K. Beatty	Evan L. James[31]
McKeesport ...	A. J. Jakomas	James Loizes	J. S. McDermott	....	T. C. Stashko
McKees Rocks Boro	D. Hershman[51]	David Hershman	Thomas Cairns	....	Fred Kwiatek[25]
Mahanoy	Patrick J. Foley	A. P. McLaughlin	John Wertz, Sr.	....	H. S. Williams[32]
Meadville	A. T. Honeycutt	E. C. Gibson	Fred Carman	Otto Schweitzer	G. S. Maxwell
Monessen	Hugo J. Parente	Michael Kuvinka	Roy McShaffrey	James Shawley	Francis H. Crum
Mount Carmel..	Jos. P. Bradley	Tony Trefsgar	Donald Williams	....	E. J. Fincato[32]
Mt. Lebanon Twp. (Pittsburgh)	Wm. B. Davison	W. B. Kunkle	R. D. Goettel	A. F. Meneilly	John A. Paulus[31]
Munhall	Thomas Laird[51]	B. H. Roberts	Wm. Freshwater	Earl Nau	F. V. Lancas[32]
Nanticoke	Frank E. Keiler	S. Kupinewicz	Wm. Davis	Wm. Dudeck	Sam Ziontz
Natrona	H. Lamparski[52]	Alex Sosinski	Frank Brucker	....	C. A. Grove[31]
New Castle ..	Edw. A. DeCarbo	Geo. Rigby	Clyde R. Rohrer	Pat Kearns	Jack H. Fritz
New Kensington	R. E. Gardlock	Dan J. Zeloyle	Edward Clawson	Arthur Mildren	Jack H. Crumley
Norristown ..	Wm. A. March	Robert E. Reilly	Jos. H. Hartman	L. F. Whitehead	J. Chamberlin[32]
North Braddock (Braddock)	Michael Pendro	John J. Duhon	Frank Sprute	....	P. C. Cicco[32]
N. Huntingdon Twp. (Irwin)	Albert R. Cervi[20]	....	....	....	Mrs. K. Walker
Oil City	R. R. Van Kirk	Philip Cheles	Frank M. Riddle	John E. Ruth	C. S. Hetrick
Penn Twp. (Pittsburgh)	John H. Immel	P. F. Moran	....	....	J. W. Wason[31]
Philadelphia ..	R. Dilworth	Thomas Gibbons[11]	F. McNamee[11]	F. C. Deegan	N. Wolfman[12]
Phoenixville ..	A. R. Hoffman	F. K. MacInnis	Leo J. Cosgrove	....	M. W. Friday[32]
Pittsburgh	D. L. Lawrence	Jas. W. Slusser	Stephen P. Adley	R. J. Templeton	Geo. Boxheimer
Pittston	J. F. Saporito	P. J. O'Brien	Robert Mitchell	....	Edwin A. Sites

State and City	Mayor	Police Chief	Fire Chief	Park Superintendent	City Clerk
Penna. (cont.)					
Plains Twp. (Plains)	Albert Janerich[20]	J. F. Chehutski	Chas. Fillippini	....	V. Gudaitis
Plymouth	H. C. Cooper[51]	L. L. Kendig	M. Kalafut	....	S. D. Bird, Jr.[32]
Pottstown	J. Hartenstine, Jr.[51]	J. A. Laughead	R. E. Lindauer	....	Wm. Shaeffer[32]
Pottsville	Geo. S. Heffner	A. J. Downey	George A. Smith	John Farber	F. A. Matthews
Punxsutawney	H. B. Hilton[51]	Joseph S. Volpe	F. R. Chambers	....	Mary L. Means[32]
Radnor Twp. (Wayne)	F. Weightman[20]	James H. Bones	Edwin J. Clark	John W. Foster[10]	R. W. Barringer[31]
Reading	D. F. McDevitt	B. F. Richards	Russell C. Bowers	Harold Lebo	S. H. Rothermel
Ridley Twp. (Folsom)	T. F. Beck[20]	V. P. Kuberski[21]	....	....	Roy W. Hocker[31]
Ross Twp. (Pittsburgh)	H. E. McDonald[20]	....	....	....	Wade Winner[25]
Scranton	James T. Hanlon	Leo Ruddy	Wm. L. Morgan	H. M. Kerber	Sam Druck
Shamokin	Lester W. Weller	George Haddock	Wm. Bashore	Amos G. Miller	John C. Wary
Sharon	Michael J. Dunn	Wm. E. Stuart	John R. Davies	Thos. Bailey[8]	F. Llandsdowne
Shenandoah	A. Balkiewicz, Jr.[51]	Frank Alinsky	Joseph Zarcufsky	....	Leona Cubinsky[32]
Springfield Twp. (Philadelphia)	G. A. Schwab[17]	J. C. Jellison, Jr.	3 Fire Cos.	....	J. R. Fulginiti[31]
Springfield Twp. (Springfield)	Louis Wagner[20]	C. L. Forrester	William Reeps	Betram Schilder	H. A. Bornman[31]
State College	David R. Mackey	John R. Juba	Thos. Sauers, Jr.	John Dittmar	Sara A. Dunlap
Steelton	Wm. P. Dailey[51]	Joseph N. Sostar	Chas. F. Kramer	....	M. S. Zerance[32]
Stowe Twp. (McKees Rocks)	L. J. Buchek[20]	Max Homer	John Kocak	....	R. L. Heinauer[31]
Sunbury	Allen M. Wolfe	H. C. F. Gass	W. J. Hassinger	Geo. W. Schubert	H. T. Metzger
Susquehanna Twp. (Harrisburg)	H. C. Sheets[20]	G. A. Riley[11]	G. A. Riley[11]	....	D. O. Smeltz
Swissvale	Christy Cariher[51]	J. M. Harrington	L. Mulkerin	....	Ruth Greeley[32]
Tamaqua	S. N. Johns[51]	H. Lester Baer	Charles Schlorf	....	S. Radcliffe[32]
Turtle Creek	Mrs. A. E. Fresch	Wm. J. Whalen	Fred Schmidt	....	P. Kingston, Jr.
Uniontown	J. W. Sembower[3]	A. W. Davis	John A. Matheny	H. W. Little[29]	E. H. Baker
Upper Darby Twp. (Upper Darby)	W. Merner, Jr.[20]	Wm. H. Merner, Jr.[20, 11]	R. G. Kelly[11]	Frank Harrison	J. E. Malone[25]
Warren	W. E. Rice	Michael Evan	James Tridico	G. H. Reier	C. W. Barwis[25]
Washington	T. S. Fitch	Ray Spragg	L. A. Loar	Victor G. Ross	Leroy W. Porter
Waynesboro	Dr. R. Brown[51]	D. R. Pryor	O. E. Helm, Jr.	....	Roy N. Hawbaker
West Chester	H. V. DeHaven[51]	George R. Guss	H. T. Ammon	E. B. Ritter	John S. Groff[32]
West Mifflin	Geo. W. Lynn	S. B. Hampton	Cyril Starr	....	Mrs. I. L. Trautman[32]
Wilkes Barre	L. M. Kniffen	J. Russell Taylor	Ambrose Saricks	Frank A. Goeckel	Robert S. Foote
Wilkinsburg	T. W. Stephens[51]	James Harris	Wm. Thomson	....	John C. Deal
Williamsport	T. H. Levering	John G. Good	H. E. Kinley	Clifford Markle	T. F. Meconi
Whitehall Twp. (Hokendauqua)	Nevin A. Fritzinger[20]	Luther A. Kline	Terry T. Kuntz	....	Saxon A. A. Scheirer[25]
Yeadon	F. K. Hartley[51]	C. S. Robinson	James J. Donnon	....	Frank R. Culp[32]
York	Fred A. Schiding	R. K. Johnson	L. Ellis Wagner	Jack H. Barton[3]	Irma C. Ziegler
Rhode Island					
Bristol	Jos. A. Murgo[13]	A. J. Ferrara	Oscar A. Rishe	....	A. Dennis, Jr.[31]
Central Falls	R. J. Garvey	J. P. Stetkiewicz	G. F. Salisbury	....	Peter B. Clare
Cranston	Earl A. Colvin	L. B. Fouchecourt	N. D. Broden	James M. Cornell	E. L. Johnson
Cumberland (Valley Falls)	Robt. B. Butler[20]	Wm. J. Boyle	....	....	J. J. Conway[31]
East Providence	D. E. Marso[13]	H. W. Lester	E. C. Griffith	F. Delle Femine	C. C. Viall[31]
Johnston	A. Cappelli[20]	C. B. Colwell	Volunteer	....	M. F. McGuire[31]
Lincoln	R. H. Graham[20]	William Wright	Volunteer	....	G. A. Oster[31]
Newport	John J. Sullivan	Samuel H. Dugan	W. H. Connerton	George Donnelly	J. F. Fitzgerald
No. Kingstown (Wickford P.O.)	L. M. Lucas[20]	Burton W. Moon	Arthur Selley	C. A. Northup	H. L. Corey[31]
No. Providence	Michael Costello[20]	Wm. J. Donovan	Volunteer	Anthony Messore	B. M. Bernard[31]
Pawtucket	L. A. McCarthy	Edw. F. Parker	Romeo D. Monast	H. Williamson	Howard H. Rex
Providence	W. H. Reynolds	John A. Murphy	L. A. Marshall	M. F. Noonan	D. E. Whelan
So. Kingstown	J. O. Stitely[13]	Jos. B. Congdon	Donald E. Dobson	Wm. E. Arnold	F. R. Sheldon
Warwick	Joseph Mills	F. R. Sprague	R. C. Barker	G. J. Nardone	F. E. McVay
Westerly	Edwin Kenyon[20]	Edw. P. Lallo	Columbus Passetti	James Brown	A. B. Gervasini
West Warwick	Francis Fozzano[20]	Arthur Groleau	Lionel Gareau	....	Susan V. Lamb[31]
Woonsocket	K. K. Coleman	E. C. Turcotte	Leo J. Roy	Wm. E. Renaud	W. Chester Rose
South Carolina					
Aiken	H. Odell Weeks	E. M. Hanna	Frank Harley	Odell Gregory	Lee D. Ellis
Anderson	Wm. C. Johnston	W. J. Burden	W. B. Maddox	Dan Coleman[4]	H. M. Wilson
Charleston	W. McG. Morrison	William F. Kelly	N. G. Olsen	J. Coleman, Jr.	A. J. Tamsberg[12]
Columbia	J. C. Dreher, Jr.	L. J. Campbell	A. McC. Marsh	Wm. B. Moore	Guy A. Pitts
Florence	D. H. McLeod	M. D. Adams	Ben Dosier	G. A. Benton	S. H. McCall
Greenville	J. Kenneth Cass	P. P. Oakes	J. E. Poole	H. F. A. Lange	B. F. Dillard
Greenwood	R. E. McCaslan	R. P. McCellan	W. W. Wash	....	S. L. Colvert, Jr.
North Augusta	R. A. Toole, Jr.	R. T. Weeks	H. E. Barber	....	A. E. Graybill[31]
Orangeburg	R. Jennings, Jr.	C. H. Hall	C. A. Fischer	A. C. Dibble	L. F. Theiling
Rock Hill	J. E. Jerome	W. S. Rhodes	E. W. Cole	F. C. Hill	Ben R. Neely
Spartanburg	Neville Holcombe	Ralph D. Prince	W. O. Blackwell	Joe Helms	I. T. Williams
Sumter	S. A. Harvin	E. E. McIntosh	C. C. Wilder	S. P. Wright	R. H. Windham
Union	J. T. Gregory	W. S. Harris	J. W. Sullivan	....	Jean Arthur

State and City	Mayor	Police Chief	Fire Chief	Park Superintendent	City Clerk
South Dakota					
Aberdeen	J. C. Hurlbert	S. N. Swenson	Chas. Myers	Erwin Kuhnert	M. J. Connell
Huron	E. F. Karstens	Leslie C. Sawyer	H. Contowine[41]	Jack Kunhart	R. E. Peterson[46]
Mitchell	Robt. N. Graham	Donald G. Licht	A. D. Claussen	Herbert Munroe	Margaret Gales[46]
Rapid City	H. J. Baker	Lewis Nordbye	Glen Burdine	Merle Gunderson	R. R. Lang[46]
Sioux Falls	Fay Wheeldon	K. Chamberlain	V. Crusinberry	George Pardoe	G. L. Sutton[46]
Watertown	E. E. Creaser	C. C. Paterson	Ray DeVetter	Edward Linderer	O. J. Fromke[46]
Yankton	D. H. Stuelpnagel	Edward Sampson	Howard Frick	A. N. Appletoft	Anna M. Goetz[46]
Tennessee					
Bristol	Thomas S. Curtin	W. J. Rogers	W. A. Buckles	....	Albert W. Stone
Chattanooga	P. R. Olgiati	E. S. Brown	R. R. Gouldy	W. S. Teppenpaw	W. H. Zachry
Clarksville	William Kleeman	John P. Balthrop	Thomas Seay	W. E. King	J. H. Marable
Cleveland	James F. Corn	L. E. Goodwin	L. F. McDaris	C. F. Kelly	C. L. Wilson
Columbia	Tom F. Williams	Emmett P. Fox	J. Polk White	....	H. F. Roach[46]
Dyersburg	Page V. Hart	N. A. Bond	C. C. Rogers	....	R. Sellers
East Ridge (Chattanooga)	J. W. Anderson	....	....	Lucian D. Smith	James E. Smith
Elizabethton	W. G. Frost	W. C. Glover	Dana H. Reynolds	....	G. J. Holly[50]
Jackson	George Smith	Robt. A. Mainord	Jen L. Warlick	....	B. F. Graves[46]
Johnson City	Guy W. Blackwell	C. W. Wilkinson	L. L. Geisler	H. A. Johnson	Calvin Guthrie
Kingsport	Milton DeVault	G. W. Fletcher	C. M. Kenner	....	J. R. Pecktal[46]
Knoxville	J. W. Dance	Joe Kimsey	Roy Conner	H. Mack Franse	Mrs. N. Beeler[46]
Memphis	Edmund Orquill	J. C. Macdonald	John C. Klinck	H. S. Lewis	C. W. Crutchfield
Morristown	C. Frank Davis	E. H. Winstead	James E. Burke	W. R. Hayter	Chas. E. Smith
Murfreesboro	A. L. Todd, Jr.	N. W. Powers	B. B. Qualls	....	Albert Williams
Nashville	Ben West	D. E. Hosse	H. Demonbreun	F. W. Pickens	W. M. Carr, Jr.
Shelbyville	J. D. Templeton	B. Richardson	J. W. Foster	....	Stanley Sissom[46]
Tullahoma	Jack T. Farrar	T. F. McEwen	M. R. Ragan	C. A. Osborne[6]	Alice Berry
Texas					
Abilene	C. E. Gatlin	W. B. McDonald	D. C. Musick	Scott Fikes	L. Fern Martin[25]
Alice	Mrs. B. J. Harper	C. K. Rowland	Jack Linder	Joe Brookshire	Mrs. L. Hobbs
Amarillo	R. C. Jordan	W. C. Alexander	Roy P. Hill	Mark T. Miles	K. Burwell[25]
Austin	Tom Miller	R. D. Thorp	John E. Woody	Walter Hill	Elsie Woosley
Baytown	R. H. Pruett	W. Montgomery	A. H. Lintelman	....	Mrs. Edna Oliver
Beaumont	J. P. Cokinos	J. H. Mulligan	S. D. O'Conor	Reese Martin	Jas. T. Garrard
Bellaire	Harry L. Reed	Jack O'Brien	G. O. Hutchens	Robert Smith[4]	Verena Engstrom
Big Springs	G. W. Dabney	C. L. Rogers	....	J. O. Johansen	C. R. McClenny
Borger	L. D. Patton	J. B. Wilkinson	N. G. Leonard	James B. Lair	Mrs. Carpenter
Brownsville	M. M. Vicars	Gus O. Krausse	Fred Lerma	Jim Byrne	J. W. Sloss
Brownwood	Murray Milner	W. A. Middleton	C. M. Alford	Roger Sweeney	Jas. B. Embrey[25]
Bryan	H. C. Dishman	H. W. Collins	Sam Noto	Jack Ashworth	Noah W. Dansby
Cleburne	Walter Holliday	Carroll Cook	T. Wigginton	Brooks Conover	Johnnie Gordon[25]
Corpus Christi	Farrell D. Smith	R. T. Runyan	John Carlisle	Kenneth Krenec	T. Ray Kring[25]
Corsicana	Walter Erwin	C. A. Patterson	H. P. Bivins	F. A. Bunch	W. M. Elliott[25, 44]
Dallas	R. Thornton, Sr.	Carl F. Hansson	C. N. Penn	L. B. Houston[3]	H. G. Shank[25]
Del Rio	A. C. Kennedy	C. W. McBee	W. E. Zorn	Felix Hernandez	Fred Underwood[25]
Denison	E. J. Lilley	Paul S. Borum	Geo. L. Cravens	J. C. Hock	Alice Crabtree
Denton	Jack Bryson	Glen Lanford	Thos. Robinson	D. W. Shoulders	W. D. Buttrill[25]
Edinburg	Nix Harrington	Leroy V. Eastin	A. E. Sanders	Phil Jordan	P. W. Henderson
El Paso	Tom E. Rogers	J. C. Risinger	H. A. Davis	Bryce Lammert	J. M. Herrera
Fort Worth	F. E. Garrison	C. Hightower, Sr.	P. C. Fontaine	H. H. Hittson	R. A. Bateman[25]
Gainesville	F. Aldridge, Sr.	L. T. Theobold	Wm. Lewie	B. C. Morris	Mrs L. Owen[25]
Galveston	George R. Clough	Wm. J. Burns	W. Henderson,	Bernard Davis	Mrs. M. Quiroga[25]
Garland	W. Bradfield, Sr.	H. Y. Grantham	....	Cecil Winters	D. M. Holmes[25]
Grand Prairie	C. R. Sargent	B. W. Adams	J. C. Swadly	Loyd Rigby	Becky Ellis
Greenville	E. B. Sorrells	LeRoy Brigman	Harvey F. Peyton	T. A. Smithey[9]	Mrs. K. Blalack
Harlingen	F. G. Parker	John Guseman	W. T. Hamilton	Eugene Hill	F. R. Lucas[25]
Highland Park (Dallas)	C. C. English	W H. Naylor	W. H. Naylor	R. B. Allen	E. E. Crowell[25]
Houston	O. F. Holcombe	Carl Shuptrine	Joe Lobue	Gus H. Haycock	M. Westerman[25]
Jacksonville	R. C. Buckner	Sam Bollinger	Charlie Williams	....	G. L. Crawford[25]
Killeen	Samuel G Wood	J. J. Heaton	V. B. Rucker	Bill Allbright	Ernest L. Brown
Kingsville	E. R. Cauley	D. D. Condron	Paul E. Dacke	Eugene Corbin	F. D. Johnson
Lamesa	W. B. Crawley	....	J. D. McAmis	....	Jack N. Goodloe
Laredo	J. C. Martin, Jr.	D. O. Gallagher	Geo. E. Renkin	....	James Haynes[25]
Longview	J. C. Tomlinson	Roy Stone	E. S. Scott	Paul Stamper	L. W. Summers[25]
Lubbock	S. S. Forrest, Jr.	Bill Lamb	Glen Smith	A. C. Hamilton	Mrs. L. Lowe[25]
Lufkin	W. W. Scott	Willie T. Ricks	D. McPherson	Paul McWilliams	Lynn Durham[25]
McAllen	Phillip Boeye	Clint C. Mussey	Alfred S. Myers	....	H. H. Hensley
McKinney	W. R. West	Euel Ford	Walter Cockrell	Geo. Wells	G. F. Welford[25]
Marshall	Charles Spangler	C. M. Ezell	Carl L. Bechtold	Leo Hightower	Clark Ross[25]
Mercedes	E. K. O'Shea	C. Castaneda	Garland Leavell	....	A. J. Hagan[25]
Midland	E. Sidwell	H. S. Wallace	Jas. M. Little	C. Campbell, Jr.	J. C. Hudman[25]
Mineral Wells	C. K. Davis	Frank Granbury	....	....	Mrs. S. F. Scott
Mission	O. V. Bridges	Truett Jordan	Ben Brandt	C. E. Langston	Alma Bishop[41, 25]
Nacogdoches	A. J. Streit	Tom Drewry	D. A. Teutsch	Harold Rucker	J. T. Alders
New Braunfels	Joseph Faust	W. Davidson	W. A. Staats	....	E. O. Haas
Odessa	Harold R. Downs	Jess L. Cariker	Chas. Meadows	....	R. H. Alvey[25]
Orange	C. H. Meeks	Raymond Sanders	Vertis Sands	R. L. York	Charles Cottle[25]
Palestine	R. H. Pickel, Jr.	H. D. Barton	Milton Turner	....	J. C. Hardgrave[25]
Pampa	Lynn Boyd	J. B. Conner	J. E. Winborne	Lee Roberts	Edwin S. Vicars
Paris	James R. Gill	H. R. Marks	Miller Steed	R. B. Hayter	M. F. Shelton
Pasadena	Clyde T. Gary	A. Schammerhorn	Frank E. Smith	Ed. Wilcox	M. F. Jackson[25]
Pharr	R. S. Bowe	John Payton	A. L. Wood	H. K. West	L. B. Phillips[25]
Plainview	M. B. Hood	H. Pelphrey	Leedy Maxey	....	P. H. Bryan[25]
Port Arthur	C. R. Eisler	G. B. Douglas	Eugene Ray	M. C. Creswell	Ernest W. Meyer
River Oaks (Fort Worth)	R. R. Blevins	L. B. Dorris	A. T. Huffhines	....	Jack Joyner[25]
Robstown	H. G. Balzer	Lester C. Newell	Leo J. Schannen	....	Belo Kellam[25]
San Angelo	H. E. McCulloch	Leo Braziel	Tom Biggs	James M. Rogers	Mamie Barfield[25]
San Antonio	J. E. Kuykendall	Geo. W. Bichsel	M. L. Butler	Robt. A. Frazer	J. F. Gallagher

State and City	Mayor	Police Chief	Fire Chief	Park Superintendent	City Clerk
Texas (cont.)					
San Benito	W. T. Ballenger	W. F. Gilbert	Lee Roy Dillard	M. I. Crow	L. Kendrick[25]
Sherman	Melvin Dunham	Les Tribble	A. C. Jones	J. E. Stephenson	R. L. Brooks
Snyder	T. H. Bennett	Travis L. Steele	D. A. Porter	Wm. J. Ramsey	K. O. Pitner
Sweetwater	S. J. May	A. B. McGuire	A. C. Forgay	D. M. Teel	W. H. Whaley[25]
Temple	C. A. Wheeler, Jr.	Thomas B. Ellis	A. J. Giesbers	Jay Williams	C. H. Thompson
Terrell	E. A. Wolcott	F. W. Richie	J. P. Barnett	....	H. W. Hindman
Texarkana	A. P. Miller, Jr.	Leon Arhold	C. Birmingham	G. R. Felton, Jr.	M. E. Young[25]
Texas City	W. J. Godard	R. L. DeWalt	Jim Collin	....	K. T. Nunn[25]
Tyler	Dave Talley	D. C. Butler	W. G. Heath	R. L. Shelton, Jr.	G. V. McNallie
University Park (Dallas)	Roy C. Coffee	Forrest E. Keene	Forrest E. Keene	I. I. Chambers	R. E. Hamman
Vernon	W. D. Curtis	J. T. Looper	L. L. Howell	D. D. Hollars[11]	T. W. Daniels[25]
Victoria	Cliff Berkman	Elmo Anderson	A. M. Shaw	G. Frank Pena	J. P. Daly
Waco	D. T. Hicks, Jr.	J. V. Gunterman	L. P. Harrington	Alva Stem	Otis W. DeHay[25]
Waxahachie	Osce Miller	Willis Cox	J. W. Parrish	Roscoe Jenkins	P. A. Russell[25]
W. University Pl. (Houston)	J. W. Hammond	H. E. Shipp	C. E. Duffin	Joe W. Clarke	Mrs. Verna Mills
White Settlement (Fort Worth)	V. O. Cammel	A. D. Stephens	C. W. Flowers	....	Mrs. Franklin[25]
Wichita Falls	K. C. Spell	C. C. Daniel	E. C. White	Spencer Ellis	G. T. Henderson
Utah					
Logan	Wm. W. Owens	Eli Drakulich	Ivo Borg	Leo Kimball	H. R. Pedersen
Ogden	R. S. Wright	M. J. Schoof	Clyde Peterson	W. F. Richards	E. M. Tillotson[50]
Provo	H. Van Wagenen	Jesse Evans	Dean Muhlestein	William Andrews	Irene G. Bench
Salt Lake City	Adiel F. Stewart	W. C. Skousen	J. K. Piercey	Warren L. White	H. J. Hogensen[50]
Vermont					
Barre	C. O. Granai	Floyd D. Chandler	Roy Macdonald	Archie Buttura	Ralph Olliver
Burlington	J. E. Moran	Donald P. Russell	Daniel Richards	W. L. Hammond	Wesley T. Abell
Rutland	Dan J. Healy	John F. Dinn	A. H. Koltonski	Joe Colodonato	H. P. Battles
Virginia					
Alexandria	L. S. Bendheim	Major R. Hawes	Bernard Padgett	Grover Fones	Mrs. P. Altizer
Bristol	M. A. Hassinger	John W. Stover	Hugh Warley	....	Hugh Adair
Charlottesville	R. Marshall Davis	J. E. Adams	L. S. Key	....	C. E. Moran
Covington	H. W. Robertson	George E. Arritt	L. A. Wolfe	B. Albert	J. G. Kyle
Danville	Dr. C. V. Bishop	J. C. Garrett	J. C. Long	T. E. Davis	T. F. Tucker
Fredericksburg	C. M. Cowan	A. G. Kendall	George D. Smith	....	B. S. Roberts
Hampton	George C. Bentley	L. H. Nicholson	F. F. Hopkins	J. M. Eason	C. E. Johnson
Harrisonburg	F. C. Switzer	J. F. Ritchie	L. J. Painter	....	E. R. Heneberger
Hopewell	J. W. Enochs, Jr.	F. C. Gwalmey	Wm. Ray Taylor	Raymond Mathis	Mrs. L. S. Belch
Lynchburg	Rev. J. Suttenfield	Robt. O. Brooks	Marvin K. Evans	F. K. McKenna	O. L. Bradford[12]
Martinsville	F. V. Woodson	Floyd M. Bowman	C. A. Easterly[2]	....	W. H. Yeaman[12]
Newport News	Robert B. Smith	W. F. Peach	T. C. Sparkman	C. C. Nixon	C. L. Williams
Norfolk	W. F. Duckworth	Harold Anderson	W. J. Lewis	Frederic Heutte	John D. Corbell
Petersburg	C. G. Dunn	W. E. Traylor	J. N. Farmer	W. G. Bulifant	W. F. Spotswood
Portsmouth	A. C. Bartlett	L. C. Warren	B. O. Benton	....	A. P. Johnson
Richmond	F. Henry Garber	O. D. Garton	J. F. Finnegan	Jesse Reynolds[4]	Wm. T. Wells
Roanoke	Walter L. Young	Frank H. Webb	J. B. Brown	R. P. Hunter	J. Robt. Thomas
Salem	James I. Moyer	George T. Eades	L. A. Ballard	C. F. Turner	Wm. Paxton, Jr.
South Norfolk	N. J. Babb	D. J. Leet[2]	J. B. Gibson, Sr.	....	R. L. Spence
Staunton	Dr. S. S. Loewner	B. A. Gill	W. J. Rohr	E. L. Bragg	C. J. Musser
Suffolk	W. P. Griffin	L. B. Butler	Rufus A. Baines	Frank S. Burns	Wm. S. Holland
Waynesboro	W. C. Caldwell	C. H. Benson	J. G. Rusmiselle	O. K. Cook	John W. Jones[12]
Winchester	C. B. Smaltz, Jr	J. Thomas Boyd	Taylor Barr	Charles L. Aikin	P. J. Marshall
Washington					
Aberdeen	Ed. Lundgren	A. M. Gallagher	C. L. Kromm	Hugo Larson	Victor Lindberg
Bellingham	J. E. Westford	E. H. Hartleson	Wilton Jepperson	Herbert J. Olson	Alfred B. Loop
Bremerton	H. O. Domstad	....	T. R. Tillett	A. Pendergast	E. H. McGowan
Everett	George Culmback	George Nelson	F. F. Schroeder	John Hall	John L. Sugars
Hoquiam	F. W. McGuire	Norman C. Foote	Fred Gibcke	Richard Barnes	Ola E. Hall
Kennewick	B. B. Smith	O. C. Lincoln	H. O. Malchow	Cameron Haslam	M. A. Miller
Longview	H. R. Nichols	Ralph Benefiel	J. R. Holwege	Frank Willis	D. W. Carpenter
Moses Lake	Marshall Burress	Wm. E. Bjork	Leonard Cook	Ozie Walker	M. J. Waterman
Olympia	Amanda B. Smith	Roy L. Kelly	Harry A. Lynch	W. R. Turner	G. E. Marshall
Pasco	Harry V. Custer	A. L. McKibbin	Lyle Cooney	H. A. Wyman	Adah M. Perry
Port Angeles	Paul M. Neer	Harry Kochanek	C. A. Wolverton	Wm. C. Adams	J. E. Law
Pullman	Kester B. Grimes	Arch Campbell	C. Fredrickson	Boyd Lebold	Frankie Allen
Puyallup	Charles Bond	Cecil Archer	Paul Parkhurst	....	Harris F. Green[15]
Renton	Joe R. Baxter	Angelo Busato	Floyd Lawrence	Gene Coulon	E. L. Alexander
Seattle	G. S. Clinton	H. J. Lawrence	Wm. Fitzgerald	Paul V. Brown	W. C. Thomas
Spokane	Willard Taft	Clyde Phelps	W. A. Dunham	Harold Abbott	A. A. Brown
Tacoma	J. H. Anderson	Roy H. Kerr	Harold H. Fisk	Tom Lantz	J. Melton
Vancouver	H. L. Schumacher	H. C. Diamond	P. E. DuPaul	....	R. G. Lovette
Walla Walla	Harold Buerstatte	A. L. Watts	Leonard Adams	Earl Haney	Kenneth B. Moss
Wenatchee	E. Simenson	Gleo E. Allen	T. A. Weaver	George J. Knauss	H. F. Rumohr[2]
Yakima	J. K. Alderson	Oscar Soderstrom	W. K. Moore	Ed. Putnam	J. A. Smith
West Virginia					
Beckley	A. K. Minter	M. E. Tyree[2]	Bernard Martin	Jas. Kessinger[10]	E. J. Smith
Bluefield	W. L. Thornton	Wm. E. DeMoss	E. L. McClure	....	Janet R. Calfee
Charleston	J. T. Copenhaver	Dallas Bias[2]	O. E. Boggess	Robert E. Kresge	J. A. Hudson
Clarksburg	W. W. Neeley[15]	E. F. Amsler[2]	J. J. Martin	....	A. R. Marshall
Fairmont	W. G. Meyer	H. R. Arnette	Ralph L. Gump	....	Neil H. Shreve
Huntington	Eugene Willis	C. Jarrell	John Gallagher	Russell Ward	Chas. F. Albright
Martinsburg	Wm. H. Peery	H. K. Cushwa[33]	Bruce Martin	....	Mrs. M. Wright[50]
Morgantown	Earl L. Core	....	J. P. Samsel	James Shepherd	F. R. Reppert
Moundsville	J. R. Austin	R. C. Gillespie	Edgar Boso	....	Novella Y. Henry
Parkersburg	F. W. Gove, Jr.	Bruce E. Parsons	H. O. Neal	J. Beckett, Jr.	Grace V. Haskins

State and City	Mayor	Police Chief	Fire Chief	Park Superintendent	City Clerk
W. Va. (cont.)					
St. Albans	Gregory L. Funk	Evan Hall	Fred E. Short	A. L. Ramsey[1]	Mrs. VandeLinde
So. Charleston	Jos. W. Londeree	Earl E. Kidd	Chas. J. Schmidt	W. W. Edge	H. S. Shumate
Weirton	Samuel Kusio	Dave Reese	John Fergerson	Vincent Cooper[4]	Ralph Cottilli
Wheeling	Jack R. Adams	Wm. J. Thomas	W. S. McFadden	....	A. L. Dailer
Wisconsin					
Appleton	Robert L. Roemer	Herbert W. Kapp	Paul Neuman	Harold Jerke	Elden J. Broehm
Ashland	Mark F. Movrich	E. F. Hennell	William Griffith	F. Lewandowski	Mrs. V. Burns
Beaver Dam	Alvin J. Beers	Louis W. Zwieg	Clair R. Knoll	Rudolf Bock	W. A. Tomashek
Beloit	A. D. Telfer[15]	George E. Griffin	Glen J. Davis	....	R. H. Callan
Chippewa Falls	A. J. Webb	F. J. Maloney	E. H. Kalk, Sr.	C. J. Ermatinger	Lee C. Millard
Cudahy	Vincent Totka	Anthony Wise	S. Bukowski	....	James F. Keller
Eau Claire	L. C. Haas[13]	B. L. Garmire	Ernest E. Moss	Paul Braun	G. D. Campbell
Fond du Lac	Edwin F. Weis	James D. Cahill	Howard Munson	P. J. Bunker[2]	G. J. Ondrasek
Green Bay	Otto Rachals	H. J. Bero	D. Zuidmulder	Marshall Simonds	C. A. Centen
Janesville	George Forster[15]	Jasper Webb	Alex Andreski	James Harvey	H. C. Bradford
Kenosha	E. C. Fechner[13]	S. G. Haukedahl	Wm. C. Brady	L. G. Gallagher	Jos. R. Sawicki
La Crosse	Milo G. Knutson	George C. Long	Adolph Kessel	Wm. F. Kruger	Alice A. Dickson
Madison	I. A. Nestingen	Bruce Weatherly	Edward J. Page	J. G. Marshall	A. W. Bareis
Manitowoc	Walter Koepke	J. J. Kuplic	James Danielson	Louis Norteman	Arthur Post
Marinette	K. W. Gardiner[15]	Fred A. Schultz	Peter Berg	....	Robert B. Zill
Marshfield	Glen Madison	W. H. Wohlfahrt	Verlyn Ziegahn	M. Jirschele	E. H. Olson
Menasha	R. G. DuCharme	Peter J. Clark	Edward Heim	Harry Kargus	Ira H. Clough
Milwaukee	F. P. Zeidler	John W. Polcyn	Edw. E. Wischer	Howard Gregg	S. J. Witkowski
Neenah	George E. Sande	Irving H. Stilp	John Zick	Edgar Patterson	R. V. Hauser
Oshkosh	E. R. Siewert	William A. Golz	Bernard Geffers	Nick Jasperson	Roger Kliss
Racine	Jack H. Humble	LeRoy Jenkins	R. Anderson	F. A. Carlson	Frank J. Becker
Sheboygan	R. J. Ploetz	Steen W. Heimke	August Sokoll	G. Z. Rayner	Jos. E. Leberman
Shorewood	N. A. Lemke	E. F. Bartels	E. F. Bartels	....	John L. Jones[37]
So. Milwaukee	W. P. Atkinson	Henry Tylicki	Raymond Gee	....	L. J. Mosakowski
Stevens Point	L. L. Sorenson	Elmer L. Zeaman	C. E. Maslowski	Harry Groshek	Clara Trierweiler
Superior	W. R. L. Taylor[15]	A. E. Buchanan	Albert Gee	J. T. Leszcynski	R. E. McKeague
Two Rivers	John E. Dever[15]	Edward Pazdera	Henry Willert	Leonard Birr	H. J. Rath
Watertown	Chas. E. Kading[15]	Herbert Vehlow	Alfred Linde	Ewald E. Brumm	E. Kuckkahn[7]
Waukesha	P. Steinert, Jr.	James Hannon	Emery P. Downie	Chuck Heyer	Esther Winn
Wausau	Arthur M. Smith	Everett Gleason	Wilbur Petzold	I. S. Horgen	Jay L. Brown
Wauwatosa	Wm. B. Knuese	Louis R. Wrasse	D. J. Dunlop	Robert Mews	P. H. Riemer
West Allis	A. H. Klentz	T. H. Kastello	Henry C. Nelson	Rudy Lohmann	Phil Elliott
Whitefish Bay (Milwaukee)	T. E. Hayes[20]	Orval H. Meister	Joseph P. Kasal	....	L. R. Eichfeld[37]
Wisconsin Rapids	Nels M. Justeson	Rudolph J. Exner	Cloyd Vallin	Clarence Spaid	R. O. Boyarski
Wyoming					
Casper	Tom Nicholas	Paul V. Danigan	A. L. Piper	Ray Robey	Lois E. Culver
Cheyenne	V. S. Christensen	F. M. Schmoker	R. E. Garnett	A. E. Steinke	M. D. O'Connell
Laramie	Josephine Fay	B. A. Deti	Blake Fanning	Arlie Hammons	Lois J. Holmes
Rock Springs	Edwin E. James	John Zakovich	Pete J. Tronquet	John Skubic	Carl F. Asiala
Sheridan	C. L. Crawford	W. W. Morrow	A. E. Powers	Elgin Ekis	C. H. Campbell
Alaska					
Anchorage	Anton Anderson	J. C. Flanigan	George Burns	Alice Moffat	Ben W. Boeke
Fairbanks	D. G. Preston	Stanley J. Zaverl	E. B. Woodcox	....	E. A. Tonseth
Hawaii					
Hilo	James Kealoha[10]	Anthony Paul	R. H. Kahakua	R. Carvalho	Edwin M. Desna
Honolulu	N. S. Blaisdell	Daniel Liu	H. C. Pate	J. Edward Lyons	Paul Chung
Puerto Rico					
Aguadilla	....	....	....	....	....
Arecibo	....	....	....	....	....
Bayamon	R. Torrech, Jr.	Lt. Galo Segarra	....	....	E. Medina Cruz
Cagus	A. R. Rodriguez	M. Martinez[33]	Manuel Bernardo	....	Santos J. Sola
Caomo	....	....	....	....	....
Cavey	F. Colon Juila	....	....	....	Virginia Aponte
Guayama	....	....	....	....	....
Humacao	....	....	....	....	....
Manati	....	....	....	....	....
Mayaguez	....	....	....	....	....
Ponce	....	....	....	....	....
San Juan	Felisa deGautier	....	Raul Gandara	....	J. R. Marreko[25]
Virgin Islands					
Charlotte Amalie	....	Otis L. Felix	Omar Brown	R. B. Galiber[39]	C. K. Claunch[25]

1 Chairman of Park Commission
2 Acting
3 Director
4 Recreation Director
5 Administrative Officer
6 Superintendent Public Works
7 Deputy
8 Foreman
9 Engineer
10 Chairman
11 Commissioner
12 Clerk of Council
13 President of Council
14 First Selectman
15 Manager
16 Warden
17 President Board of Commission
18 Secy.—Bd. of Commissioners
19 Comptroller
20 President
21 Superintendent
22 Marshal
23 Park District
24 Director Public Safety
25 Secretary
26 Clerk—Board of Aldermen
27 Parish Clerk
28 Chairman—Board of Selectmen
29 Councilman
30 Commissioner of Parks
31 Town Clerk
32 Borough Clerk
33 Captain
34 Commissioner of Public Safety
35 Director of Public Works
36 Township Supervisor
37 Village Clerk
38 Councilman at Large
39 Commissioner of Public Works
40 Superintendent of Recreation
41 Assistant
42 Chairman of City Commission
43 Chamberlain
44 Director of Finance
45 Superintendent Buildings and Grounds
46 Auditor
47 Assistant Service Director
48 Park Supervisor
49 Clerk of Commission
50 Recorder
51 Burgess
52 Assistant
53 Registrar
54 President of Township Commission

State Highway Department Officials

List Revised to January 1, 1957

ALABAMA
State Highway Department, Montgomery 4
Highway Director, H. L. Nelson
Construction Engineer, Marvin Taylor
Maintenance Engineer, G. W. Philips
Superintendent of Equipment, J. B. Tucker

ARIZONA
State Highway Department, Phoenix
Chairman of Commission, Grover J. Duff
State Highway Engineer, Wm. E. Wiley
Superintendent of Equipment, Brice Covington
Director of Purchases, W. F. Frerichs

ARKANSAS
State Highway Commission, Little Rock
Chairman, Cecil S. Lynch
Director of Highways, Herbert Eldridge
Chief Engineer, Wm. Ward Goodman
Supervisor of Maintenance, A. G. Rives
Construction Engineer, E. E. Mashburn
Director of Equipment & Procurement, C. Don Hayes

CALIFORNIA
State Highway Commission, Sacramento 5
Chairman, Frank B. Durkee
State Highway Engineer, G. T. McCoy
Maintenance Engineer, F. E. Baxter
Prin. Equipment Engineer, E. E. Sorenson
Construction Engineer, Milton Harris
Traffic Engineer, G. M. Webb

COLORADO
State Department of Highways, Denver 22
Chairman, Ben Jorgensen
Chief Engineer, Mark U. Watrous
Administrative Engineer, Chas. E. Shumate

CONNECTICUT
State Highway Department, Hartford 15
State Highway Commissioner, Newman E. Argraves
Deputy Highway Commissioner, Roland A. Bennett
Chief Engineer, Warren M. Creamer
Assistant Chief Engineer (Office) E. T. Perkins
Assistant Chief Engineer (Field) Walter T. Schuler

DELAWARE
State Highway Department, Dover
Chairman, J. Gordon Smith
Chief Engineer, R. A. Haber
Secretary, J. J. Deputy

FLORIDA
State Highway Department, Tallahassee
Chairman, Wilbur Jones
State Highway Engineer, H. E. Lewis
Executive Director, Ralph Davis

GEORGIA
State Highway Department, Atlanta
Chairman of Board, Roger A. Lawson
State Highway Engineer, M. L. Shadburn
Construction Engineer, C. W. Leftwich
Maintenance Engineer, J. O. Bacon
Materials Engineer, W. F. Abercrombie

IDAHO
State Department of Highways, Boise
State Highway Engineer, G. Bryce Bennett
Maintenance Engineer, Norman L. McCrea
Equipment Supervisor, Tom C. Pethick
Construction Engineer, A. F. Rath
Chief Accountant, M. C. Whaley

ILLINOIS
State Department of Public Roads & Buildings
Director, E. A. Rosenstone
Division of Highways, Springfield
Chief Highway Engineer, R. R. Bartelsmeyer
Engineer of Construction, R. H. Tittle
Engineer of Maintenance, H. E. Diers
Engineer of Traffic, H. H. Harrison
Engineer of Design, E. L. Sherertz
Engineer of Local Roads & Streets, Wm. M. Dutelle

INDIANA
State Highway Commission, Indianapolis 9
Chairman, Virgil W. Smith
Chief Engineer, Carl Vogelgesang
Superintendent of Maintenance, L. L. Poindexter
Purchasing Agent, C. P. McDonough

IOWA
State Highway Commission, Ames
Chairman, Robert K. Beck (Centerville)
Chief Engineer, John G. Butter
Maintenance Engineer, R. C. Boyd
Supt. of Property & Equipment, George Dunlap
Construction Engineer, C. L. Gleason

KANSAS
State Highway Commission, Topeka
Director, Frank Harwi
State Highway Engineer, Walter Johnson
Engineer of Traffic Services, Claud R. McCamment
Engineer of Maintenance, L. J. Siler

KENTUCKY
State Highway Department, Frankfort
Commissioner of Highways, Robert Humphreys
State Highway Engineer, D. H. Bray
Director, Division of Construction, T. H. Baker
Director, Division of Equipment, W. A. Tincher
Director, Division of Maintenance, J. A. Spears

LOUISIANA
State Department of Highways, Baton Rouge 4
Director, R. B. Richardson
Chief Engineer, E. J. James
Construction & Maintenance Engineer, R. H. Vaughan
Asst. Const. & Maintenance Engineers, E. A. Landry & T. W. Parish, Jr.
Purchasing Agent, A. J. Berey

MAINE
State Highway Commission, Augusta
Chairman, David H. Stevens
Chief Engineer, Vaughan M. Daggett
Superintendent of Maintenance, John B. Church

MARYLAND
State Roads Commission, Baltimore 3
Chairman, Robert O. Bonnell
Chief Engineer, Norman M. Pritchett
Maintenance Engineer, Frank P. Scrivener
Construction Engineer, T. M. Linthicum
Equipment Engineer, J. C. Grannan

MASSACHUSETTS
State Department of Public Works, Boston 14
Commissioner, Carl A. Sheridan
Chief Engineer, H. Gordon Gray
Maintenance Engineer, G. Gordon Love
Asst. Chief Engineer for Maintenance & Equipment, John F. McGovern
Supt. of Equipment & Repairs, Earle P. Herrick, (Wellesley)

MICHIGAN
State Highway Department, Lansing 13
State Highway Commissioner, Charles M. Ziegler
Chief Deputy Commissioner, George M. Foster
Deputy Commissioner-Chief Engineer, Carlos A. Weber
Maintenance Engineer, E. D. Suino
Construction Engineer, H. J. Rathfoot
Road Engineer, C. Homer Cash

MINNESOTA
State Highway Department, St. Paul 4
Commissioner of Highways, M. J. Hoffman
Assistant Commissioner, A. O. Torgerson
Chief Engineer, L. P. Zimmerman
Construction Engineer, C. C. Colwell
Maintenance Engineer, G. A. Meskel

MISSISSIPPI
State Highway Department, Jackson 114
Chairman of Commission, John D. Smith (Mendenhall)
Commissioner, Roy C. Adams (Tupelo)
Commissioner, Felder W. Dearman (Jackson)
Director, T. C. Robbins
Chief Engineer, Eugene M. Johnson

MISSOURI
State Highway Commission, Jefferson City
Chairman of Commission, Harris D. Rodgers (Benton)
Chief Engineer, Rex M. Whitton
Engineer of Construction, J. J. Corbett
Engineer of Maintenance, Dean Wilson
Superintendent of Equipment, O. L. Steele

MONTANA
State Highway Commission, Helena
Chairman, Frank G. Connelly (Billings)
State Highway Engineer, Scott P. Hart
State Highway Comm. Secy., C. E. Cunningham
Construction Engineer, S. B. Sanders
Maintenance Engineer, W. E. Bawden

NEBRASKA
State Department of Roads and Irrigation, Lincoln
State Engineer, L. N. Ress
Maintenance Engineer, John McMeekin
Equipment Engineer, J. H. MacDonald
Construction Engineer, L. O. Graham
Purchasing Agent, Tom Coffey

NEVADA
State Department of Highways, Carson City
Chairman Board of Directors, Hon. Charles Russell, Governor
State Highway Engineer, H. D. Mills
Construction, Maintenance & Secondary Roads Engineer, J. D. Meacham
Equipment Engineer, Charles C. Blaker

NEW HAMPSHIRE
State Department of Public Works & Highways, Concord
Commissioner, J. O. Morton
Deputy Commissioner & Chief Engineer, R. H. Whitaker
Maintenance Engineer, L. F. Johnson
Construction Engineer, C. J. Downing
Superintendent of Equipment, E. M. Sawyer
Bridge Engineer, H. E. Langley

NEW JERSEY
State Highway Department, Trenton
State Highway Commissioner, Dwight R. G. Palmer
State Highway Engineer, O. H. Fritzsche
Acting Director, Division of Administrative Services, Kenneth D. Rice
Supervising Engineer, Construction, Neil MacDougall
Supervising Engineer, Division of State-Aid Projects, John H. Hulse
Director and Chief Bridge Engineer, L. C. Petersen

NEW MEXICO
State Highway Commission, Santa Fe
Chairman of Commission, T. J. Helmann, (Mosquero)
Chief Highway Engineer, L. D. Wilson
Pre-Construction Engineer, T. B. White
Construction Engineer, H. F. Leslie
Operations Engineer, L. B. Miller
Equipment Superintendent, J. W. Whittington

NEW YORK
State Department of Public Works, Albany 1
Superintendent of Public Works, John W. Johnson
Administrative Deputy, Raymond M. Fisher
Chief Engineer, Thomas F. FitzGerald

NORTH CAROLINA
State Highway & Public Works Commission, Raleigh
Chairman, A. H. Graham
State Highway Engineer, W. H. Rogers, Jr.
State Equipment Engineer, Ivan Hardesty
State Construction Engineer, H. D. Irving
Purchasing Agent, J. M. Potter

NORTH DAKOTA
State Highway Department, Bismarck
Highway Commissioner, S. W. Thompson
Chief Engineer, Mark P. Wynkoop
Maintenance Engineer, Ray Robinson
Construction Engineer, F. H. Brasie
Materials Engineer, W. A. Wise, (Mandan)

OHIO
State Department of Highways, Columbus 15
Director of Highways, S. O. Linzell
Assistant Director, L. F. Schaeublin
Deputy Director of Operations, C. W. McCaughey
Deputy Director Design and Construction, H. F. Gerold
Deputy Director Planning and Programming, J. Heier
Deputy Director Administration, C. K. Bradley
Acting Purchasing Agent, L. C. Masters

OKLAHOMA
State Highway Department, Oklahoma City 5
Chairman, H. Tom Kight, Jr.
Director, C. A. Stoldt
Chief Engineer, G. H. Bittle
Construction Engineer, J. J. Stobaugh, Jr.
Maintenance Engineer, R. B. Winfrey
Purchasing Agent, G. C. Smith

OREGON
State Highway Commission, Salem
Chairman, Ben R Chandler (Coos Bay)
State Highway Engineer, W. C. Williams
Deputy State Highway Engineer, Forrest Cooper
Construction Engineer, Tom Edwards
Maintenance & Equipment Engineer, E. A. Collier

PENNSYLVANIA
State Department of Highways, Harrisburg
Secretary of Highways, Joseph J. Lawler
Chief Engineer, Robert A. Farley
Chief Construction Engineer, William J. Raves
Chief Maintenance Engineer, Edwin H. Jones

RHODE ISLAND
State Department of Public Works, Providence
Director, Joseph M. Vallone
Deputy Director, Thomas E. Harding
Principal Highway Engineer, George H. Henderson
Road Construction Engineer, L. V. Spencer
Road Maintenance Engineer, Edgar E. Maynard
Secondary Road Engineer, R. W. Bowden
Traffic & Highway Planning Engineer, P. S. Mancini

SOUTH CAROLINA
State Highway Department, Columbia 191
Chief Highway Commissioner, C. R. McMillan
State Highway Engineer, S. N. Pearman
Assistant State Highway Engineer, W. K. Beckham
Construction Engineer, J. D. McMahan, Jr.
Maintenance Engineer, H. L. Sligh
Supply & Equipment Engineer, T. H. Hewitt
Purchasing Agent, C. R. Sanders

SOUTH DAKOTA
State Highway Commission, Pierre
Chairman, Hon. Joseph Foss, Governor
Director, C. J. Dalthorp
State Highway Engineer, H. C. Rempfer
Construction Engineer, R. K. Morrell

TENNESSEE
State Department of Highways & Public Works, Nashville 3
Commissioner, W. M. Leech
State Highway Engineer, H. M. Bates
State Construction Engineer, H. D. Long
State Maintenance Engineer, F. P. Swaim

TEXAS
State Highway Department, Austin 14
Chairman of Commission, E. H. Thornton, Jr. (Houston)
State Highway Engineer, D. C. Greer
Chief Engineer of Maintenance Operations, J. A. Waller
Construction Engineer, Jed N. Robinson

UTAH
State Road Commission, Salt Lake City 14
Chairman, C. Taylor Burton
Acting Chief Engineer, R. W. Griffin
Chief Construction Engineer Dist 1, 4 and 6-J. B. Skewes
Chief Construction Engineer Dist 2, 3, and 5-Sheridan Flack

VERMONT
State Department of Highways, Montpelier
Chairman, State Highway Board, Cleon A. Perkins (Rutland)
Commissioner of Highways, William Poeter (Montpelier)
Chief Engineer, Hubert E. Sargent
Highway Engineer, Harold W. Marsett
Construction Engineer, F. Carlisle Coates
Maintenance Engineer, Loyd W. Brownell
Equipment Engineer, Earl W. Carley
Procurement Agent, L. W. Pierce

VIRGINIA
State Department of Highways, Richmond 19
Chairman State Highway Commission, J. A. Anderson
Deputy Commissioner and Chief Engineer, F. A. Davis
Construction Engineer, J. E. Johnson
Equipment Engineer, Charles B. Leech, Jr.
Maintenance Engineer, S. V. Munsey
Purchasing Agent, G. L. Nunnally

WASHINGTON
State Department of Highways, Olympia
Chairman of Comm. E. C. Huntley (Colfax)
Director of Highways, W. A. Bugge
Construction Engineer, E. C. Simpson
Maintenance Engineer, J. L. Stackhouse

WEST VIRGINIA
State Road Commission, Charleston 5
Commissioner, Burl A. Sawyers
Chief Engineer, M. L. O'Neale
State Construction Engineer, Wilson H. Ward
State Maintenance Engineer, A. L. McMillion
State Equipment Engineer, Kenneth M. Dunn

WISCONSIN
State Highway Commission, Madison 2
Chairman, Harold L. Plumber
State Highway Engineer, E. L. Roettiger
Construction Engineer, S. E. Hicks

WYOMING
State Highway Department, Cheyenne
Chairman of Commission, Homer Oxley (Lingle)
Superintendent & Chief Engineer, J. R. Bromley
Construction Engineer, R. G. Stapp
Maintenance Engineer, William Sutton
Chief Materials Engineer, I. E. Russell

State Health Department Officials

List Revised to January 1, 1957

ALABAMA

State Department of Health, State Office Building, Montgomery 4
State Health Officer, D. G. Gill, M.D., D.P.H.
Director of Sanitation, Arthur N. Beck, M.S.

ARIZONA

State Department of Health, Phoenix
Commissioner, C. G. Salsbury, M.D.
Director & Chief Engineer, Bureau of Sanitation, George W. Marx, M.P.H.

ARKANSAS

State Board of Health, Little Rock
State Health Officer, J. T. Herron, M.D., M.P.H.
Director of Sanitary Engineering, Glen T. Kellogg, B. S. Chem., M.S.S.E.

CALIFORNIA

State Department of Public Health, Berkeley 4
Director of Public Health, Malcolm H. Merrill, M.D., M.P.H.
Chief Division of Environmental Sanitation, Frank M. Stead
Chief, Bureau of Sanitary Engineering, Edward A. Reinke

COLORADO

State Department of Public Health, Denver 2
Executive Director, R. L. Cleere, M.D., M.P.H.
Director, Div. of Sanitation & Chief Engineer, William N. Gahr, C.E., M.S., San. Engineer

CONNECTICUT

State Department of Health, Hartford 15
Commissioner of Health, Stanley H. Osborn, M.D., Dr. P.H.
Director, Bureau of Sanitary Engineering, Warren J. Scott
Director, State Water Commission, William S. Wise

DELAWARE

State Board of Health, Dover
Executive Secretary, Floyd I. Hudson, M.D., M.P.H.
Dir. of Sanitary Engineering & Chief Engineer, Donald K. Harmeson, M.S., M.P.H.

FLORIDA

State Board of Health, Jacksonville 1
State Health Officer, Wilson T. Sowder, M.D., M.P.H.
Director of Sanitary Engineering & Chief Engineer, David B. Lee, M.S.

GEORGIA

State Department of Public Health, Atlanta 3
Director, T. F. Sellers, M.D.
Director, Sanitary Engineering, Louva G. Lenert
Director, Water Pollution Control, W. H. Weir

IDAHO

State Board of Health, Boise
Director of Health, L. J. Peterson, M.S.P.H.
Director of Engineering and Sanitation, & Chief Engineer, Vaughn Anderson, B.S. (Chem. E.)

ILLINOIS

State Department of Public Health, Springfield
Director of Public Health, Roland R. Cross, M.D.
Deputy Director for Sanitary Engineering & Chief Engineer, Clarence W. Klassen

INDIANA

State Board of Health, Indianapolis 7
State Health Commissioner, A. C. Offutt, M.D.
Director of Environmental Sanitation, B. A. Poole

IOWA

State Department of Health, Des Moines 19
State Commissioner of Health, Edmund G. Zimmerer, M.D.
Director of Public Health Engineering, Paul J. Houser, M.S.

KANSAS

State Board of Health, Topeka
Executive Secretary, Thomas R. Hood, M.D., M.P.H.
Chief Engineer & Director, Division of Sanitation, Dwight F. Metzler (Lawrence)

KENTUCKY

State Department of Health, Louisville 2
State Health Commissioner, Russell E. Teague, M.D.
Director of Public Health & Chief Engineer, Ralph C. Pickard, B.S.C.E.

LOUISIANA

State Department of Health, New Orleans 7
President, State Board of Health and State Health Officer, W. J. Rein, M.D.
Director of Public Health Engineering, John E. Trygg, B.S., C.E., M.P.H.

MAINE

State Department of Health & Welfare, Augusta
Commissioner, Dean Fisher, M.D.
Director, Bureau of Health, Dean Fisher, M.D.
Director of Sanitary Engineering, & Chief Engineer, Elmer W. Campbell, D.P.H.

MARYLAND

State Department of Health, Baltimore 18
Director of Public Health, Perry F. Prather, M.D.
Chief Div. of Sanitary Engineering & Chief Engineer, George L. Hall
Chief, Bureau of Environmental Hygiene, Robert M. Brown, M.P.H.

MASSACHUSETTS

State Department of Public Health, Boston 33
Commissioner of Public Health, Samuel B. Kirkwood, M.D.
Director of Environmental Sanitation & Chief Sanitary Engineer, Clarence I. Sterling, Jr.

MICHIGAN

State Department of Health, Lansing 4
State Health Commissioner, Albert E. Heustis, M.D., M.P.H.
Division of Engineering, W. F. Shephard, Director
Water Resources Comm.-Exec. Secretary, Milton P. Adams

MINNESOTA

State Department of Health
Campus, University of Minnesota, Minneapolis 14
Secretary and Executive Officer, R. N. Barr, M.D., M.P.H.
Director of Environmental Sanitation, Frank L. Woodward, M.P.H.

MISSISSIPPI

State Board of Health, Jackson 5
Secretary and Executive Officer, Felix J. Underwood, M.D.
Director of Sanitary Engineering & Chief Engineer, J. E. Johnston

MISSOURI

State Dept. of Public Health and Welfare, Jefferson City
Director of Division of Health, James R. Amos, M.D.
Director of Bureau of Public Health Engineering, A. W. Happy, Jr., M.P.H.

MONTANA

State Board of Health, Helena
Executive Officer and Secretary, G. D. Carlyle Thompson, M.D., M.P.H.
Director of Environmental Sanitation & Chief Engineer, C W. Brinck, M.S.

NEBRASKA

State Department of Health, Lincoln 9
Director of Health, E. A. Rogers, M.D., M.P.H.
Director, Division of Sanitation, T. A. Filipi, B.Sc., M.Sc.

NEVADA

State Department of Health, Carson City
Acting State Health Officer, Daniel J. Hurley, M.D., M.P.H.
Director of Public Health Engineering & Chief Engineer, W. W. White

NEW HAMPSHIRE

State Health Department, Concord
Acting State Health Officer, Mary Atchison, M.D., M.P.H.
Director of Sanitary Engineering, William A. Healy

NEW JERSEY

State Department of Health, Trenton 7
State Commissioner of Health, Daniel Bergsma, M.D., M.P.H.
Director of Environmental Sanitation & Chief Engineer, Alfred H. Fletcher, M.S.

NEW MEXICO

Department of Public Health, Santa Fe
Director of Public Health, Stanley J. Leland, M.D., M.P.H.
Director of Environmental Services & Chief Engineer, Charles G. Caldwell, M.S.

NEW YORK

State Department of Health, Albany 1
Commissioner of Health, Herman E. Hilleboe, M.D., M.P.H.
Director of Environmental Sanitation & Chief Engineer, Earl Devendorf

NORTH CAROLINA

State Board of Health, Raleigh
State Health Officer, J. W. R. Norton, M.D., M.P.H
Director of Sanitary Engineering & Chief Engineer, J. M. Jarrett

NORTH DAKOTA

State Department of Health, Bismarck
Director of Public Health and Chief Sanitary Engineer, Jerome H. Svore

OHIO

State Department of Health, Columbus 15
Director of Health, Ralph E. Dwork, M.D., M.P.H.
Chief of Sanitary Engineering, Fred Holman Waring, C.E.

OKLAHOMA

State Department of Health, Oklahoma City 5
Commissioner of Health, G. F. Mathews, M.D.
Chief, Sanitary Engineering, Harold L. Malone

ORFGON

State Board of Health, Portland
State Health Officer, Harold M. Erickson, M.D., M.P.H.
Director of Sanitation & Chief Engineer, Curtiss M. Everts, Jr., M.S.

PENNSYLVANIA

State Department of Health, Harrisburg
Secretary of Health, Berwyn F. Mattison, M.D.
Director, Bureau of Environmental Health & Chief Engineer, Karl M. Mason
Director, Division of Sanitary Engineering, H. E. Moses
Director, Bureau of Preventable Disease, J. Thomas Millington, M.D.
Director, Bureau of Local Health, Carl C. Kuehn, M.D.

RHODE ISLAND

State Department of Health, Providence 2
Director of Health, Edward A. McLaughlin, M.D.
Public Health Engineer, Division of Sanitary Engineering, Walter J. Shea, M.S.

SOUTH CAROLINA

State Board of Health, Columbia 1
State Health Officer, G. S. T. Peeples, M.D., M.P.H
Director of Sanitary Engineering and Chief Engineer, W. T. Linton, M.S.P.H.

SOUTH DAKOTA

State Department of Health, Pierre
State Health Officer, G. J. Van Heuvelen, M.D., M.P.H.
Director of Sanitary Engineering, Charles E. Carl, M.S.

TENNESSEE

State Department of Public Health, Nashville 3
Commissioner of Public Health, R. H. Hutcheson, M.D., M.P.H.
Director of Sanitary Engineering and Chief Engineer, J. R. Fleming, M.S.

TEXAS

State Department of Health, Austin 1
Commissioner of Health, Henry A. Holle, M.D.
Director of Sanitary Engineering, V. M. Ehlers

UTAH

State Department of Health, Salt Lake City 1
Acting Director of Public Health, Joseph P. Kesler, M.D.
Director of Sanitary Engineering, C. N. Stutz
Chief, Bureau of Sanitation, Lynn M. Thatcher

VERMONT

State Department of Health, Burlington
State Health Commissioner, R. B. Aiken, M.D., M.P.H.
Chief of Environmental Sanitation, Edward L. Tracy
Commissioner, State Water Conservation Board, Philip Shutler

VIRGINIA

State Department of Health, Richmond 19
State Health Commissioner, Mack I. Shanholtz, M.D., M.P.H.
Director of Engineering, E. C. Meredith

WASHINGTON

State Department of Health, Seattle 4
Director, Bernard Bucove, M.D., D.P.H.
Chief of Engineering and Sanitation, Emil C. Jensen, M.S.

WEST VIRGINIA

State Department of Health, Charleston 5
State Director of Health, N. H. Dyer, M.D., M.P.H.
Director of Sanitary Engineering, Vacant
Acting Directors:
Environmental Sanitation—J. B. Baker
Sanitary Engineer—John Millar
Executive Secretary, State Water Commission, John Lester

WISCONSIN

State Board of Health, Madison 2
State Health Officer, Carl N. Neupert, M.D., M.S.P.H.
State Sanitary Engineer, O. J. Muegge, M.S.
Director, Committee on Water Pollution, Theodore F. Wisniewski, B.S.

WYOMING

State Department of Health, Cheyenne
Director of Public Health, Franklin D Yoder, M.D., M.P.H.
Dir. of Environmental Sanitation & Chief Engineer, Arthur E. Williamson, M.S.

HERE'S WHY THE *Shoup* VOTING MACHINE MAKES OTHERS AS OLD-FASHIONED AS THE PAPER BALLOT

HERE'S WHAT IMPARTIAL EXPERTS SAY ABOUT *Shoup* VOTING MACHINES

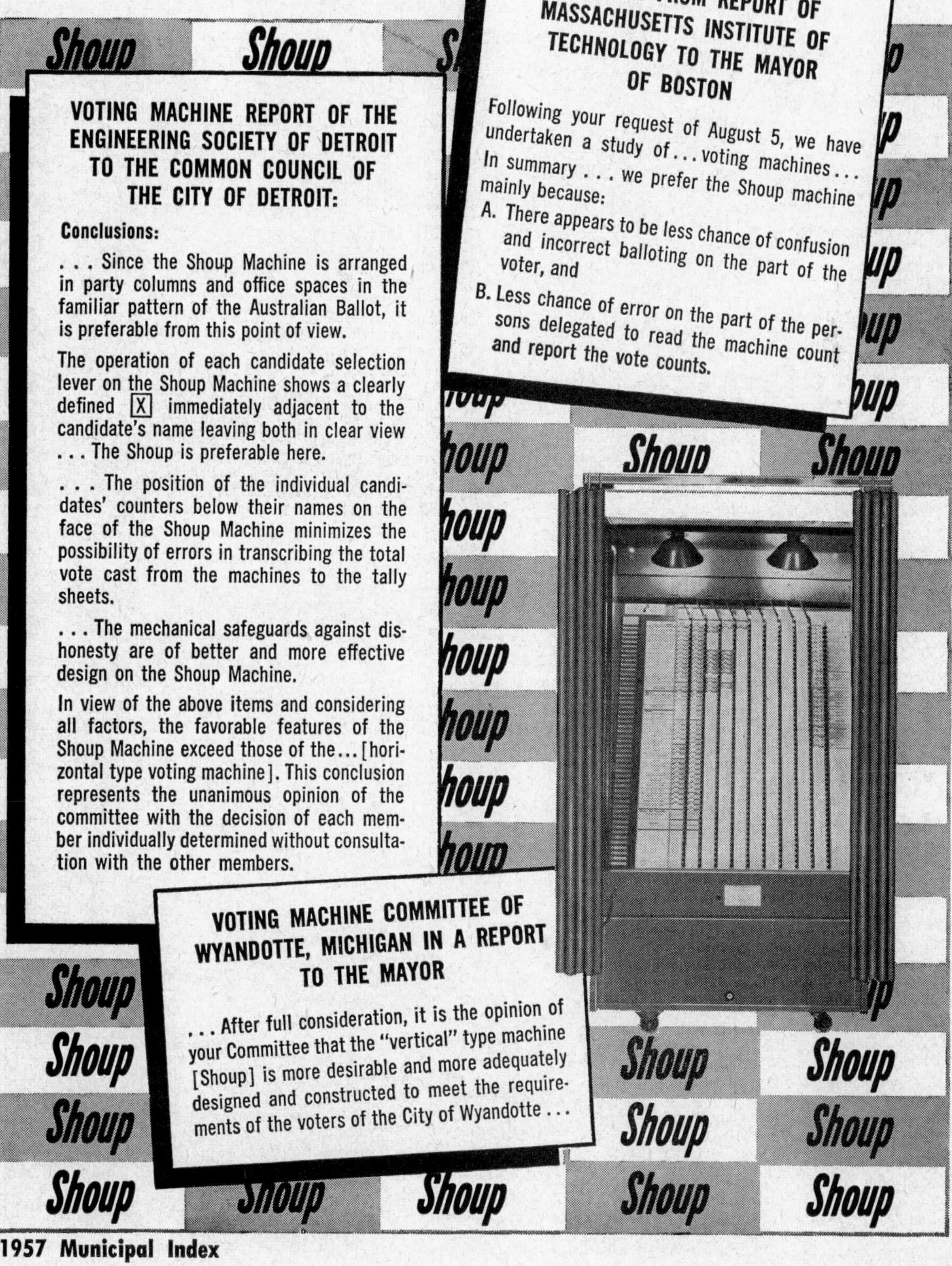

25 Reasons Why ...

1. **FACE OF MACHINE LOOKS LIKE BALLOT**
   Candidates listed in vertical columns.
2. **☒ MARK APPEARS DIRECTLY ALONGSIDE CANDIDATE'S NAME**
   Moves into position as voter indicates choice, guarding against error.
3. **INSTANTANEOUS TABULATION**
   Total count appears on face of machine under each candidate's name when machine is unlocked at close of polls. No decoding necessary.
4. **ELECTRICALLY OR MANUALLY OPERATED**
   Instantly convertible. Tested and proved by years of use.
5. **EASIEST AND SIMPLEST MACHINE TO OPERATE**
   Average voter learns to operate it in few seconds.
6. **FRAUD-PROOF DEVICE FOR RESETTING COUNTERS**
   Counters cannot be reset without machine recording fact.
7. **FRAUD-PROOF DEVICE FOR PROTECTING FINAL COUNT**
   Once keys used to obtain results have been turned, machine will not operate and keys cannot be removed.
8. **TAMPER-PROOF COUNTERS**
   Cannot be illegally operated or changed. Ballots must be removed before counters can be reset.
9. **TAMPER-PROOF OFFICER'S CONTROL LATCH**
   Designed to be mechanically tamper-proof, preventing abuse. Latch cannot be made inoperative. Adheres to the law.
10. **VOTER CAN EASILY CORRECT OWN MISTAKE**
    Can change selections up to time he turns switch lever to register vote.
11. **SPACE FOR GREATER NUMBER OF CANDIDATES**
    All columns can be used.
12. **EXTRA LARGE PRINTING AREA FOR OFFICES, CANDIDATES, QUESTIONS OR REFERENDA**
    Permits use of large, legible type.
13. **NO BLANK BALLOTS**
    Automatically protects voter from losing vote in error.
14. **RESULTS QUICKLY AND PERMANENTLY DOCUMENTED**
    For permanent record, photograph can be taken showing all final tabulations on face of machine.
15. **LOCKING DEVICE FOR VOTING SPACES AND DEVICES NOT NEEDED**
    Lockout arrangement is simple, practical, tamper-proof.
16. **TRANSPARENT COVERING FULLY PROTECTS BALLOT LABELS**
    Guards against mutilation, disfigurement, shifting.
17. **FACE OF MACHINE EASILY READ**
    Scientifically tilted for best reading angle.
18. **LARGE PERSONAL CHOICE WRITE-IN SPACE ARRANGED IN VERTICAL ROW**
    Conveniently located at left of machine.
19. **PERSONAL CHOICE WRITE-IN PAPER ROLL SPACED AND NUMBERED**
    No portion can be destroyed without fact being known.
20. **FACE OF MACHINE ALWAYS HAS SAME APPEARANCE**
    No cover plates or loose parts used, or changes ever made. Eliminates voter confusion.
21. **ABSOLUTELY SECRET VOTE**
    Doors form steel sided booth almost instantly. No cranking necessary.
22. **COMPLETELY SELF CONTAINED IN STEEL CABINET**
    No removable parts to take off at polling place.
23. **STRONG AND RIGID CURTAIN RAIL**
    Curtain forms rear of booth, making complete enclosure.
24. **PORTABLE LIGHTS NOT NEEDED**
    Permanent light fixture illuminates both ballots and results.
25. **VISIBLE COUNT OF VOTERS**
    Shows voter how many other voters have preceded him.

23 States Use Shoup!

- Alabama
- Arizona
- Delaware
- Florida
- Georgia
- Illinois
- Kentucky
- Louisiana
- Maryland
- Massachusetts
- Michigan
- Minnesota
- Missouri
- Montana
- New Jersey
- North Carolina
- Ohio
- Pennsylvania
- Rhode Island
- Tennessee
- Texas
- Washington
- West Virginia

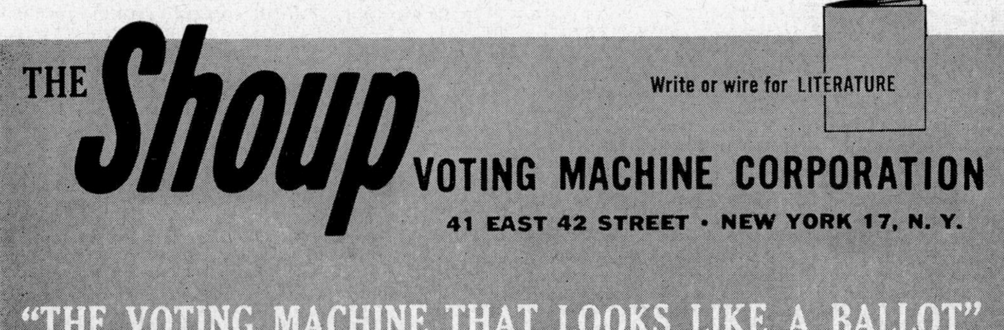

DeZURIK CORPORATION

57 Riverview Road Sartell, Minnesota

REPRESENTATIVES IN PRINCIPAL CITIES

ONLY *DeZurik* MAKES THE NON-LUBRICATED EASY-OPERATING PLUG VALVE *with* ECCENTRIC ACTION!

And they're finding wider and wider acceptance in so many municipal fields. Sewage plants and water works are discovering that whenever dead-tight shut-off is required, DeZurik Plug Valves consistently out-perform and out-last ordinary valves.

EXCLUSIVE ECCENTRIC ACTION accounts for some of the many advantages of DeZurik Valves. It guarantees easy operation—every time—without lubrication! The resilient-faced plug is pivoted eccentrically and contacts the body ONLY IN THE CLOSED POSITION! When the valve is opened, the first fractional movement of the plug swings the face *back* and away from the seat; throughout the rest of the quarter-turn there is no contact between the plug face and the valve body.

And the resilient plug facing of the metal-cored plug provides drip-free, dead-tight shut-off—despite solids in the flow! Why not specify DeZurik the next time you need new or replacement valves?

DeZurik Valves are manufactured in sizes from ½" thru 20", with screwed, flanged, mechanical joint or bell and spigot ends, and for manual, hydraulic, pneumatic or automatic operation. Write for details.

AUTOMATIC VOTING MACHINES

Jamestown, New York

Nearly 30,000,000 Voters Used Automatic Voting Machines At The 1956 Presidential Election.

Voting Is Easy . . . !

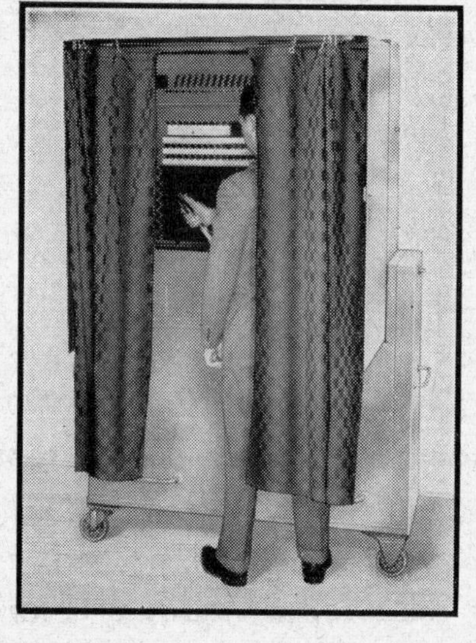

Advantages of Automatic Voting Machines

•

Absolute Secrecy

An Accurate Election Count

Speedy Election Returns

No Spoiled Ballots

Prevents Expensive Recounts

Safeguards and Preserves Final Tabulations For All Candidates

---

SINCE 1898 WE HAVE BUILT AND INSTALLED 60,000 MACHINES IN 7,000 COMMUNITIES

AUTOMATIC VOTING MACHINE CORPORATION

Jamestown, New York

AUTOMATIC VOTING MACHINES

Jamestown, New York

Automatic Voting Machines
ASSURE
Quick, Mechanically Accurate Returns

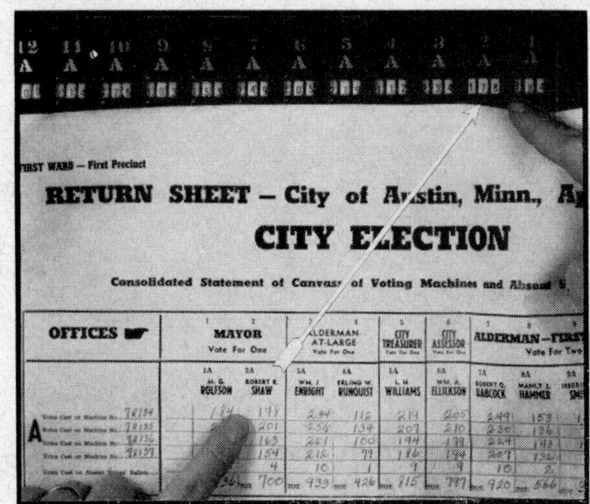

The long, laborious counting of paper ballots, the inaccuracies of the count, the demands for recounts are all eliminated through the use of AUTOMATIC VOTING MACHINES.

With more than a half century's experience, today's Automatic Voting Machine is the finest voting machine manufactured. It has an indisputable reputation for accuracy and dependability and honesty of computation.

For Information and Literature write—

AUTOMATIC VOTING MACHINE CORPORATION

Jamestown, New York

STEDT HYDRAULIC CRANE CO.

Originators and Manufacturers of Stetco Catch Basin Cleaner

93 Cordaville Road, Ashland, Mass.

The Versatile HIAB

FULLY HYDRAULIC

TRUCK CRANE

EASILY INSTALLED ON YOUR TRUCK

WORLD'S GREATEST LABOR SAVER

FOR

MATERIAL HANDLING

Also see pages 546, 547

TRADE MARK

*HIAB CRANES HAVE GREATER FLEXIBILITY

TRUCK ENGINE Supplies The Power Through A Single Speed Power Take-Off Unit Which Drives The Hydraulic Pump Through Connecting Drive Shaft And Universal Joints.

SILENT • FAST • EASY IN OPERATION — No Chains, Sprockets, Drums, Ratchets, Brakes, Etc. ONE MAN Can Load Or Unload His Own Or Other Trucks: Control Lever can be set in any position and left unattended, which enables operator to be his own helper.

OPERATION — From Either Side Of Cab By Driver.

ONLY 10"-14" SPACE Required For Installation On Any Type Truck.

TELESCOPIC BOOM Easily Adjustable From 3'-10" to 11'-8" Length.

HIAB CRANES Are Made From HIGH QUALITY STEEL By EXPERT WORKMEN And Are GUARANTEED Against Faulty Material Or Workmanship.

For Emergency and Disaster Uses: During the recent hurricane disasters, the Town of Bridgewater, Mass., as well as many others, helped to clear their blocked streets of trees and branches by the use of the versatile STETCO Catch Basin Cleaner. By simply removing two blades, the bucket became a powerful Hydraulic tong. Trucks were loaded with small branches in three minutes. No time was needed for making hitches. The emergency was solved.

HIAB CRANES ARE EASILY MOUNTED AND SIMPLE TO OPERATE

Hiab Cranes are made to clear 56 inches from top of truck frame to top of cab on regular trucks and 66 inches on cab-over-engine trucks. Oil Container is an integral part of base for added strength. Gear pump has through-shaft and adjustable mounting bracket for easy installation.

HIAB CRANES will handle loads of every description:

BARRELS — CASES — CRATES — DRUMS — HYDRANTS — WATER and GAS PIPES — STEEL — TIMBER — LOGS — CURBINGS — BALES — UTILITY POLES — CASTINGS — MACHINERY — ELECTRIC MOTORS — SHRUBBERY — SAND — GRAVEL — LOAM — CINDERS and SNOW — as typical examples.

HIAB TRUCK CRANES ARE FULLY HYDRAULIC FOR LIFTING AND SWINGING

The HIAB CRANE will lift and swing from 1125-2200 lbs. according to the length of the arm. It will lift 1125 lbs. with boom fully extended. For loads greater than 1125-lbs., the boom length should be shortened. If necessary, the wire cable can be doubled and a loose pulley (Snatch block) used.

A Snatch Block is Supplied With Every Unit.

ACCESSORIES

Grabucket—1/3 Cu. yd.—fully automatic
Dragscoop
Boom Extension
Timber Tongs
Pulp Wood Loader
Board Lumber Loader
Metal Chip & Manure Loader
Stone Loader — Four Prongs
Case Claws
Barrel Claws
Barrel Tongs
Case Tongs
Sling Bag Loader — Sling Hook
Concrete Pipe Hook
Diverter Valves, Wire Rope, Safety Hooks, etc.
Dual and Single Hose Reels and Swivel Joints

SPECIFICATIONS FOR HIAB CRANE

Space Required Between Cab and Body—10"-14" Approx.
Height Above Frame (Driving Position)—71½" Approx.
Max. Lifting and Swinging Height—20'-22' Approx.
Size of Crane Base Frame—25" x 34" Approx.
Weight—900 lbs. Approx.
Pump (Gear) 6-8 G.P.M.—750—850 P.S.I.—300-500 R.P.M.

***Write for details on the Hiab crane and we will send you also the facts about the NEW Model 170 that weighs 1400 pounds and lifts three tons.**

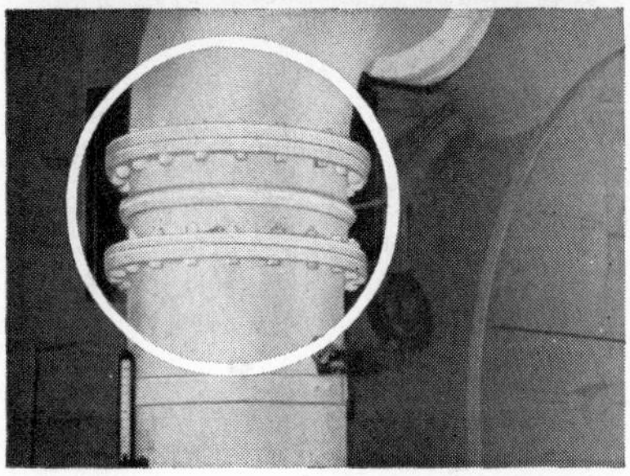

TURBINE SEWER MACHINE CO.

DIVISION OF CHAS. H. STEHLING CO.

1303 North 4th STREET Milwaukee 12, Wis., U. S. A.

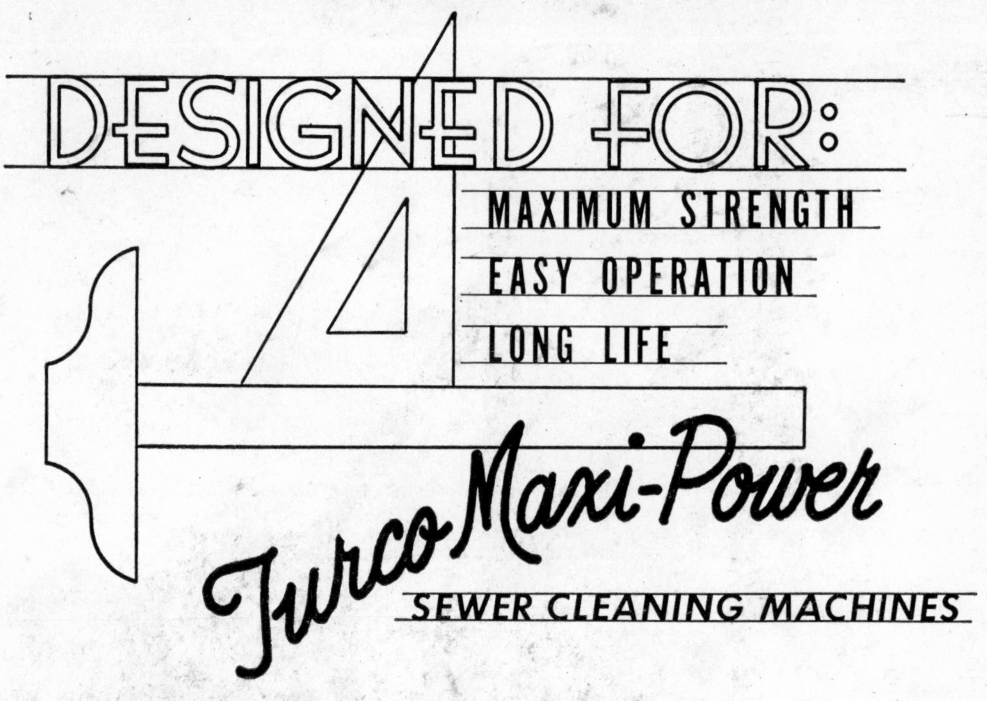

HYDRAULIC STIFF LEGS

Here are machines in a class all by themselves when it comes to modern design — ruggedness — power units with entirely new and exclusive features, pioneered and developed by Turbine to handle every sewer cleaning job faster with greater efficiency.

WRITE for our big FREE New Catalog on complete Sewer Cleaning Equipment.

Engineered for Peak Efficiency